American Casebook Series
Hornbook Series and Basic Legal Texts
Black Letter Series and Nutshell Series

of

WEST PUBLISHING COMPANY
P.O. Box 64526
St. Paul, Minnesota 55164–0526

Accounting

FARIS' ACCOUNTING AND LAW IN A NUT-SHELL, 377 pages, 1984. Softcover. (Text)

FIFLIS, KRIPKE AND FOSTER'S TEACHING MATERIALS ON ACCOUNTING FOR BUSINESS LAWYERS, Third Edition, 838 pages, 1984. (Casebook)

SIEGEL AND SIEGEL'S ACCOUNTING AND FINANCIAL DISCLOSURE: A GUIDE TO BASIC CONCEPTS, 259 pages, 1983. Softcover. (Text)

Administrative Law

BONFIELD AND ASIMOW'S STATE AND FEDERAL ADMINISTRATIVE LAW, 826 pages, 1989. Teacher's Manual available. (Casebook)

GELLHORN AND LEVIN'S ADMINISTRATIVE LAW AND PROCESS IN A NUTSHELL, Third Edition, approximately 420 pages, 1990. Softcover. (Text)

MASHAW AND MERRILL'S CASES AND MATERIALS ON ADMINISTRATIVE LAW—THE AMERICAN PUBLIC LAW SYSTEM, Second Edition, 976 pages, 1985. (Casebook) 1989 Supplement.

ROBINSON, GELLHORN AND BRUFF'S THE ADMINISTRATIVE PROCESS, Third Edition, 978 pages, 1986. (Casebook)

Admiralty

HEALY AND SHARPE'S CASES AND MATERIALS ON ADMIRALTY, Second Edition, 876 pages, 1986. (Casebook)

MARAIST'S ADMIRALTY IN A NUTSHELL, Second Edition, 379 pages, 1988. Softcover.

(Text)

SCHOENBAUM'S HORNBOOK ON ADMIRALTY AND MARITIME LAW, Student Edition, 692 pages, 1987 with 1989 pocket part. (Text)

Agency—Partnership

FESSLER'S ALTERNATIVES TO INCORPORATION FOR PERSONS IN QUEST OF PROFIT, Second Edition, 326 pages, 1986. Softcover. Teacher's Manual available. (Casebook)

HENN'S CASES AND MATERIALS ON AGENCY, PARTNERSHIP AND OTHER UNINCORPORATED BUSINESS ENTERPRISES, Second Edition, 733 pages, 1985. Teacher's Manual available. (Casebook)

REUSCHLEIN AND GREGORY'S HORNBOOK ON THE LAW OF AGENCY AND PARTNERSHIP, Second Edition, 683 pages, 1990. (Text)

SELECTED CORPORATION AND PARTNERSHIP STATUTES, RULES AND FORMS. Softcover. 727 pages, 1989.

STEFFEN AND KERR'S CASES ON AGENCY-PARTNERSHIP, Fourth Edition, 859 pages, 1980. (Casebook)

STEFFEN'S AGENCY-PARTNERSHIP IN A NUTSHELL, 364 pages, 1977. Softcover. (Text)

Agricultural Law

MEYER, PEDERSEN, THORSON AND DAVIDSON'S AGRICULTURAL LAW: CASES AND MATERIALS, 931 pages, 1985. Teacher's Manual available. (Casebook)

Alternative Dispute Resolution

KANOWITZ' CASES AND MATERIALS ON ALTERNATIVE DISPUTE RESOLUTION, 1024 pages,

Alternative Dispute Resolution—Cont'd

1986. Teacher's Manual available. (Casebook) 1990 Supplement.

RISKIN AND WESTBROOK'S DISPUTE RESOLUTION AND LAWYERS, 468 pages, 1987. Teacher's Manual available. (Casebook)

RISKIN AND WESTBROOK'S DISPUTE RESOLUTION AND LAWYERS, Abridged Edition, 223 pages, 1987. Softcover. Teacher's Manual available. (Casebook)

American Indian Law

CANBY'S AMERICAN INDIAN LAW IN A NUTSHELL, Second Edition, 336 pages, 1988. Softcover. (Text)

GETCHES AND WILKINSON'S CASES AND MATERIALS ON FEDERAL INDIAN LAW, Second Edition, 880 pages, 1986. (Casebook)

Antitrust—see also Regulated Industries, Trade Regulation

FOX AND SULLIVAN'S CASES AND MATERIALS ON ANTITRUST, 935 pages, 1989. Teacher's Manual available. (Casebook)

GELLHORN'S ANTITRUST LAW AND ECONOMICS IN A NUTSHELL, Third Edition, 472 pages, 1986. Softcover. (Text)

HOVENKAMP'S BLACK LETTER ON ANTITRUST, 323 pages, 1986. Softcover. (Review)

HOVENKAMP'S HORNBOOK ON ECONOMICS AND FEDERAL ANTITRUST LAW, Student Edition, 414 pages, 1985. (Text)

OPPENHEIM, WESTON AND McCARTHY'S CASES AND COMMENTS ON FEDERAL ANTITRUST LAWS, Fourth Edition, 1168 pages, 1981. (Casebook) 1985 Supplement.

POSNER AND EASTERBROOK'S CASES AND ECONOMIC NOTES ON ANTITRUST, Second Edition, 1077 pages, 1981. (Casebook) 1984–85 Supplement.

SULLIVAN'S HORNBOOK OF THE LAW OF ANTITRUST, 886 pages, 1977. (Text)

Appellate Advocacy—see Trial and Appellate Advocacy

Architecture and Engineering Law

SWEET'S LEGAL ASPECTS OF ARCHITECTURE, ENGINEERING AND THE CONSTRUCTION PROCESS, Fourth Edition, 889 pages, 1989. Teacher's Manual available. (Casebook)

Art Law

DUBOFF'S ART LAW IN A NUTSHELL, 335 pages, 1984. Softcover. (Text)

Banking Law

LOVETT'S BANKING AND FINANCIAL INSTITUTIONS LAW IN A NUTSHELL, Second Edition, 464 pages, 1988. Softcover. (Text)

SYMONS AND WHITE'S TEACHING MATERIALS ON BANKING LAW, Second Edition, 993 pages, 1984. Teacher's Manual available. (Casebook) 1987 Supplement.

Business Planning—see also Corporate Finance

PAINTER'S PROBLEMS AND MATERIALS IN BUSINESS PLANNING, Second Edition, 1008 pages, 1984. (Casebook) 1990 Supplement.

Statutory Supplement. *See Selected Corporation and Partnership*

SELECTED CORPORATION AND PARTNERSHIP STATUTES, RULES AND FORMS. 727 pages, 1989. Softcover.

Civil Procedure—see also Federal Jurisdiction and Procedure

AMERICAN BAR ASSOCIATION SECTION OF LITIGATION—READINGS ON ADVERSARIAL JUSTICE: THE AMERICAN APPROACH TO ADJUDICATION, 217 pages, 1988. Softcover. (Coursebook)

CLERMONT'S BLACK LETTER ON CIVIL PROCEDURE, Second Edition, 332 pages, 1988. Softcover. (Review)

COUND, FRIEDENTHAL, MILLER AND SEXTON'S CASES AND MATERIALS ON CIVIL PROCEDURE, Fifth Edition, 1284 pages, 1989. Teacher's Manual available. (Casebook)

COUND, FRIEDENTHAL, MILLER AND SEXTON'S CIVIL PROCEDURE SUPPLEMENT. Approximately 450 pages, 1990. Softcover. (Casebook Supplement)

FEDERAL RULES OF CIVIL PROCEDURE—EDUCATIONAL EDITION. Softcover. Approximately 635 pages, 1990.

FRIEDENTHAL, KANE AND MILLER'S HORNBOOK ON CIVIL PROCEDURE, 876 pages, 1985. (Text)

KANE AND LEVINE'S CIVIL PROCEDURE IN CALIFORNIA: STATE AND FEDERAL 498 pages, 1989. Softcover. (Casebook Supplement)

Civil Procedure—Cont'd

KANE'S CIVIL PROCEDURE IN A NUTSHELL, Second Edition, 306 pages, 1986. Softcover. (Text)

KOFFLER AND REPPY'S HORNBOOK ON COMMON LAW PLEADING, 663 pages, 1969. (Text)

MARCUS, REDISH AND SHERMAN'S CIVIL PROCEDURE: A MODERN APPROACH, 1027 pages, 1989. Teacher's Manual available. (Casebook)

MARCUS AND SHERMAN'S COMPLEX LITIGATION–CASES AND MATERIALS ON ADVANCED CIVIL PROCEDURE, 846 pages, 1985. Teacher's Manual available. (Casebook) 1989 Supplement.

PARK'S COMPUTER-AIDED EXERCISES ON CIVIL PROCEDURE, Second Edition, 167 pages, 1983. Softcover. (Coursebook)

SIEGEL'S HORNBOOK ON NEW YORK PRACTICE, 1011 pages, 1978, with 1987 pocket part. (Text)

Commercial Law

BAILEY AND HAGEDORN'S SECURED TRANSACTIONS IN A NUTSHELL, Third Edition, 390 pages, 1988. Softcover. (Text)

EPSTEIN, MARTIN, HENNING AND NICKLES' BASIC UNIFORM COMMERCIAL CODE TEACHING MATERIALS, Third Edition, 704 pages, 1988. Teacher's Manual available. (Casebook)

HENSON'S HORNBOOK ON SECURED TRANSACTIONS UNDER THE U.C.C., Second Edition, 504 pages, 1979, with 1979 pocket part. (Text)

MURRAY'S COMMERCIAL LAW, PROBLEMS AND MATERIALS, 366 pages, 1975. Teacher's Manual available. Softcover. (Coursebook)

NICKLES' BLACK LETTER ON COMMERCIAL PAPER, 450 pages, 1988. Softcover. (Review)

NICKLES, MATHESON AND DOLAN'S MATERIALS FOR UNDERSTANDING CREDIT AND PAYMENT SYSTEMS, 923 pages, 1987. Teacher's Manual available. (Casebook)

NORDSTROM, MURRAY AND CLOVIS' PROBLEMS AND MATERIALS ON SALES, 515 pages, 1982. (Casebook)

NORDSTROM, MURRAY AND CLOVIS' PROBLEMS

AND MATERIALS ON SECURED TRANSACTIONS, 594 pages, 1987. (Casebook)

RUBIN AND COOTER'S THE PAYMENT SYSTEM: CASES, MATERIALS AND ISSUES, 885 pages, 1989. (Casebook)

SELECTED COMMERCIAL STATUTES. Softcover. Approximately 1650 pages, 1990.

SPEIDEL'S BLACK LETTER ON SALES AND SALES FINANCING, 363 pages, 1984. Softcover. (Review)

SPEIDEL, SUMMERS AND WHITE'S COMMERCIAL LAW: TEACHING MATERIALS, Fourth Edition, 1448 pages, 1987. Teacher's Manual available. (Casebook)

SPEIDEL, SUMMERS AND WHITE'S COMMERCIAL PAPER: TEACHING MATERIALS, Fourth Edition, 578 pages, 1987. Reprint from Speidel et al., Commercial Law, Fourth Edition. Teacher's Manual available. (Casebook)

SPEIDEL, SUMMERS AND WHITE'S SALES: TEACHING MATERIALS, Fourth Edition, 804 pages, 1987. Reprint from Speidel et al., Commercial Law, Fourth Edition. Teacher's Manual available. (Casebook)

SPEIDEL, SUMMERS AND WHITE'S SECURED TRANSACTIONS: TEACHING MATERIALS, Fourth Edition, 485 pages, 1987. Reprint from Speidel et al., Commercial Law, Fourth Edition. Teacher's Manual available. (Casebook)

STOCKTON'S SALES IN A NUTSHELL, Second Edition, 370 pages, 1981. Softcover. (Text)

STONE'S UNIFORM COMMERCIAL CODE IN A NUTSHELL, Third Edition, 580 pages, 1989. Softcover. (Text)

WEBER AND SPEIDEL'S COMMERCIAL PAPER IN A NUTSHELL, Third Edition, 404 pages, 1982. Softcover. (Text)

WHITE AND SUMMERS' HORNBOOK ON THE UNIFORM COMMERCIAL CODE, Third Edition, Student Edition, 1386 pages, 1988. (Text)

Community Property

MENNELL AND BOYKOFF'S COMMUNITY PROPERTY IN A NUTSHELL, Second Edition, 432 pages, 1988. Softcover. (Text)

VERRALL AND BIRD'S CASES AND MATERIALS

Community Property—Cont'd

ON CALIFORNIA COMMUNITY PROPERTY, Fifth Edition, 604 pages, 1988. (Casebook)

Comparative Law

BARTON, GIBBS, LI AND MERRYMAN'S LAW IN RADICALLY DIFFERENT CULTURES, 960 pages, 1983. (Casebook)

GLENDON, GORDON AND OSAKWE'S COMPARATIVE LEGAL TRADITIONS: TEXT, MATERIALS AND CASES ON THE CIVIL LAW, COMMON LAW AND SOCIALIST LAW TRADITIONS, 1091 pages, 1985. (Casebook)

GLENDON, GORDON AND OSAKWE'S COMPARATIVE LEGAL TRADITIONS IN A NUTSHELL. 402 pages, 1982. Softcover. (Text)

LANGBEIN'S COMPARATIVE CRIMINAL PROCEDURE: GERMANY, 172 pages, 1977. Softcover. (Casebook)

Computers and Law

MAGGS AND SPROWL'S COMPUTER APPLICATIONS IN THE LAW, 316 pages, 1987. (Coursebook)

MASON'S USING COMPUTERS IN THE LAW: AN INTRODUCTION AND PRACTICAL GUIDE, Second Edition, 288 pages, 1988. Softcover. (Coursebook)

Conflict of Laws

CRAMTON, CURRIE AND KAY'S CASES–COMMENTS–QUESTIONS ON CONFLICT OF LAWS, Fourth Edition, 876 pages, 1987. (Casebook)

HAY'S BLACK LETTER ON CONFLICT OF LAWS, 330 pages, 1989. Softcover. (Review)

SCOLES AND HAY'S HORNBOOK ON CONFLICT OF LAWS, Student Edition, 1085 pages, 1982, with 1988–89 pocket part. (Text)

SEIGEL'S CONFLICTS IN A NUTSHELL, 470 pages, 1982. Softcover. (Text)

Constitutional Law—Civil Rights—see also Foreign Relations and National Security Law

ABERNATHY'S CASES AND MATERIALS ON CIVIL RIGHTS, 660 pages, 1980. (Casebook)

BARRON AND DIENES' BLACK LETTER ON CONSTITUTIONAL LAW, Second Edition, 310 pages, 1987. Softcover. (Review)

BARRON AND DIENES' CONSTITUTIONAL LAW IN A NUTSHELL, 389 pages, 1986. Softcover. (Text)

ENGDAHL'S CONSTITUTIONAL FEDERALISM IN A NUTSHELL, Second Edition, 411 pages, 1987. Softcover. (Text)

FARBER AND SHERRY'S HISTORY OF THE AMERICAN CONSTITUTION, 458 pages, 1990. Softcover. Teacher's Manual available. (Text)

GARVEY AND ALEINIKOFF'S MODERN CONSTITUTIONAL THEORY: A READER, 494 pages, 1989. Softcover. (Reader)

LOCKHART, KAMISAR, CHOPER AND SHIFFRIN'S CONSTITUTIONAL LAW: CASES–COMMENTS–QUESTIONS, Sixth Edition, 1601 pages, 1986. (Casebook) 1990 Supplement.

LOCKHART, KAMISAR, CHOPER AND SHIFFRIN'S THE AMERICAN CONSTITUTION: CASES AND MATERIALS, Sixth Edition, 1260 pages, 1986. Abridged version of Lockhart, et al., Constitutional Law: Cases–Comments–Questions, Sixth Edition. (Casebook) 1990 Supplement.

LOCKHART, KAMISAR, CHOPER AND SHIFFRIN'S CONSTITUTIONAL RIGHTS AND LIBERTIES: CASES AND MATERIALS, Sixth Edition, 1266 pages, 1986. Reprint from Lockhart, et al., Constitutional Law: Cases–Comments–Questions, Sixth Edition. (Casebook) 1990 Supplement.

MARKS AND COOPER'S STATE CONSTITUTIONAL LAW IN A NUTSHELL, 329 pages, 1988. Softcover. (Text)

NOWAK, ROTUNDA AND YOUNG'S HORNBOOK ON CONSTITUTIONAL LAW, Third Edition, 1191 pages, 1986 with 1988 pocket part. (Text)

ROTUNDA'S MODERN CONSTITUTIONAL LAW: CASES AND NOTES, Third Edition, 1085 pages, 1989. (Casebook) 1990 Supplement.

VIEIRA'S CONSTITUTIONAL CIVIL RIGHTS IN A NUTSHELL, Second Edition, 322 pages, 1990. Softcover. (Text)

WILLIAMS' CONSTITUTIONAL ANALYSIS IN A NUTSHELL, 388 pages, 1979. Softcover. (Text)

Consumer Law—see also Commercial Law

EPSTEIN AND NICKLES' CONSUMER LAW IN A NUTSHELL, Second Edition, 418 pages,

Consumer Law—Cont'd

1981. Softcover. (Text)

SELECTED COMMERCIAL STATUTES. Softcover. Approximately 1650 pages, 1990.

SPANOGLE AND ROHNER'S CASES AND MATERIALS ON CONSUMER LAW, 693 pages, 1979. Teacher's Manual available. (Casebook) 1982 Supplement.

Contracts

CALAMARI AND PERILLO'S BLACK LETTER ON CONTRACTS, Second Edition, approximately 450 pages, 1990. Softcover. (Review)

CALAMARI AND PERILLO'S HORNBOOK ON CONTRACTS, Third Edition, 1049 pages, 1987. (Text)

CALAMARI, PERILLO AND BENDER'S CASES AND PROBLEMS ON CONTRACTS, Second Edition, 905 pages, 1989. Teacher's Manual Available. (Casebook)

CORBIN'S TEXT ON CONTRACTS, One Volume Student Edition, 1224 pages, 1952. (Text)

FESSLER AND LOISEAUX'S CASES AND MATERIALS ON CONTRACTS—MORALITY, ECONOMICS AND THE MARKET PLACE, 837 pages, 1982. Teacher's Manual available. (Casebook)

FRIEDMAN'S CONTRACT REMEDIES IN A NUTSHELL, 323 pages, 1981. Softcover. (Text)

FULLER AND EISENBERG'S CASES ON BASIC CONTRACT LAW, Fifth Edition, approximately 1100 pages, 1990. (Casebook)

HAMILTON, RAU AND WEINTRAUB'S CASES AND MATERIALS ON CONTRACTS, 830 pages, 1984. (Casebook)

JACKSON AND BOLLINGER'S CASES ON CONTRACT LAW IN MODERN SOCIETY, Second Edition, 1329 pages, 1980. Teacher's Manual available. (Casebook)

KEYES' GOVERNMENT CONTRACTS IN A NUTSHELL, Second Edition, approximately 530 pages, 1990. Softcover. (Text)

SCHABER AND ROHWER'S CONTRACTS IN A NUTSHELL, Third Edition, approximately 438 pages, 1990. Softcover. (Text)

SUMMERS AND HILLMAN'S CONTRACT AND RELATED OBLIGATION: THEORY, DOCTRINE AND PRACTICE, 1074 pages, 1987. Teacher's Manual available. (Casebook)

Copyright—see Patent and Copyright Law

Corporate Finance

HAMILTON'S CASES AND MATERIALS ON CORPORATION FINANCE, Second Edition, 1221 pages, 1989. (Casebook)

Corporations

HAMILTON'S BLACK LETTER ON CORPORATIONS, Second Edition, 513 pages, 1986. Softcover. (Review)

HAMILTON'S CASES AND MATERIALS ON CORPORATIONS—INCLUDING PARTNERSHIPS AND LIMITED PARTNERSHIPS, Fourth Edition, approximately 1250 pages, 1990. (Casebook) 1990 Statutory Supplement.

HAMILTON'S THE LAW OF CORPORATIONS IN A NUTSHELL, Second Edition, 515 pages, 1987. Softcover. (Text)

HENN'S TEACHING MATERIALS ON THE LAW OF CORPORATIONS, Second Edition, 1204 pages, 1986. Teacher's Manual available. (Casebook)

Statutory Supplement. *See Selected Corporation and Partnership*

HENN AND ALEXANDER'S HORNBOOK ON LAWS OF CORPORATIONS, Third Edition, Student Edition, 1371 pages, 1983, with 1986 pocket part. (Text)

SELECTED CORPORATION AND PARTNERSHIP STATUTES, RULES AND FORMS. Softcover. 727 pages, 1989.

SOLOMON, SCHWARTZ AND BAUMAN'S MATERIALS AND PROBLEMS ON CORPORATIONS: LAW AND POLICY, Second Edition, 1391 pages, 1988. Teacher's Manual available. (Casebook) 1990 Supplement.

Statutory Supplement. *See Selected Corporation and Partnership*

Corrections

KRANTZ' CASES AND MATERIALS ON THE LAW OF CORRECTIONS AND PRISONERS' RIGHTS, Third Edition, 855 pages, 1986. (Casebook) 1988 Supplement.

KRANTZ' THE LAW OF CORRECTIONS AND PRISONERS' RIGHTS IN A NUTSHELL, Third Edition, 407 pages, 1988. Softcover. (Text)

ROBBINS' CASES AND MATERIALS ON POST-CONVICTION REMEDIES, 506 pages, 1982. (Casebook)

Creditors' Rights

BANKRUPTCY CODE, RULES AND OFFICIAL FORMS, LAW SCHOOL EDITION. Approximately 875 pages, 1990. Softcover.

EPSTEIN'S DEBTOR-CREDITOR RELATIONS IN A NUTSHELL, Third Edition, 383 pages, 1986. Softcover. (Text)

EPSTEIN, LANDERS AND NICKLES' CASES AND MATERIALS ON DEBTORS AND CREDITORS, Third Edition, 1059 pages, 1987. Teacher's Manual available. (Casebook)

LOPUCKI'S PLAYER'S MANUAL FOR THE DEBTOR-CREDITOR GAME, 123 pages, 1985. Softcover. (Coursebook)

NICKLES AND EPSTEIN'S BLACK LETTER ON CREDITORS' RIGHTS AND BANKRUPTCY, 576 pages, 1989. (Review)

RIESENFELD'S CASES AND MATERIALS ON CREDITORS' REMEDIES AND DEBTORS' PROTECTION, Fourth Edition, 914 pages, 1987. (Casebook) 1990 Supplement.

WHITE'S CASES AND MATERIALS ON BANKRUPTCY AND CREDITORS' RIGHTS, 812 pages, 1985. Teacher's Manual available. (Casebook) 1987 Supplement.

Criminal Law and Criminal Procedure—see also Corrections, Juvenile Justice

ABRAMS' FEDERAL CRIMINAL LAW AND ITS ENFORCEMENT, 866 pages, 1986. (Casebook) 1988 Supplement.

AMERICAN CRIMINAL JUSTICE PROCESS: SELECTED RULES, STATUTES AND GUIDELINES. 723 pages, 1989. Softcover.

CARLSON'S ADJUDICATION OF CRIMINAL JUSTICE: PROBLEMS AND REFERENCES, 130 pages, 1986. Softcover. (Casebook)

DIX AND SHARLOT'S CASES AND MATERIALS ON CRIMINAL LAW, Third Edition, 846 pages, 1987. (Casebook)

GRANO'S PROBLEMS IN CRIMINAL PROCEDURE, Second Edition, 176 pages, 1981. Teacher's Manual available. Softcover. (Coursebook)

HEYMANN AND KENETY'S THE MURDER TRIAL OF WILBUR JACKSON: A HOMICIDE IN THE FAMILY, Second Edition, 347 pages, 1985. (Coursebook)

ISRAEL, KAMISAR AND LAFAVE'S CRIMINAL

PROCEDURE AND THE CONSTITUTION: LEADING SUPREME COURT CASES AND INTRODUCTORY TEXT. Approximately 725 pages, 1990 Edition. Softcover. (Casebook)

ISRAEL AND LAFAVE'S CRIMINAL PROCEDURE—CONSTITUTIONAL LIMITATIONS IN A NUTSHELL, Fourth Edition, 461 pages, 1988. Softcover. (Text)

JOHNSON'S CASES, MATERIALS AND TEXT ON CRIMINAL LAW, Fourth Edition, approximately 790 pages, 1990. Teacher's Manual available. (Casebook)

JOHNSON'S CASES AND MATERIALS ON CRIMINAL PROCEDURE, 859 pages, 1988. (Casebook) 1990 Supplement.

KAMISAR, LAFAVE AND ISRAEL'S MODERN CRIMINAL PROCEDURE: CASES, COMMENTS AND QUESTIONS, Seventh Edition, 1593 pages, 1990. (Casebook) 1990 Supplement.

KAMISAR, LAFAVE AND ISRAEL'S BASIC CRIMINAL PROCEDURE: CASES, COMMENTS AND QUESTIONS, Seventh Edition, 792 pages, 1990. Softcover reprint from Kamisar, et al., Modern Criminal Procedure: Cases, Comments and Questions, Seventh Edition. (Casebook) 1990 Supplement.

LAFAVE'S MODERN CRIMINAL LAW: CASES, COMMENTS AND QUESTIONS, Second Edition, 903 pages, 1988. (Casebook)

LAFAVE AND ISRAEL'S HORNBOOK ON CRIMINAL PROCEDURE, Student Edition, 1142 pages, 1985, with 1989 pocket part. (Text)

LAFAVE AND SCOTT'S HORNBOOK ON CRIMINAL LAW, Second Edition, 918 pages, 1986. (Text)

LANGBEIN'S COMPARATIVE CRIMINAL PROCEDURE: GERMANY, 172 pages, 1977. Softcover. (Casebook)

LOEWY'S CRIMINAL LAW IN A NUTSHELL, Second Edition, 321 pages, 1987. Softcover. (Text)

LOW'S BLACK LETTER ON CRIMINAL LAW, Revised First Edition, approximately 430 pages, 1990. Softcover. (Review)

SALTZBURG'S CASES AND COMMENTARY ON AMERICAN CRIMINAL PROCEDURE, Third Edition, 1302 pages, 1988. Teacher's Manual available. (Casebook) 1990 Supplement.

Criminal Law and Criminal Procedure—Cont'd

UVILLER'S THE PROCESSES OF CRIMINAL JUSTICE: INVESTIGATION AND ADJUDICATION, Second Edition, 1384 pages, 1979. (Casebook) 1979 Statutory Supplement. 1986 Update.

VORENBERG'S CASES ON CRIMINAL LAW AND PROCEDURE, Second Edition, 1088 pages, 1981. Teacher's Manual available. (Casebook) 1990 Supplement.

Decedents' Estates—see Trusts and Estates

Domestic Relations

CLARK'S HORNBOOK ON DOMESTIC RELATIONS, Second Edition, Student Edition, 1050 pages, 1988. (Text)

CLARK AND GLOWINSKY'S CASES AND PROBLEMS ON DOMESTIC RELATIONS, Fourth Edition. Approximately 1125 pages, 1990. Teacher's Manual available. (Casebook)

KRAUSE'S BLACK LETTER ON FAMILY LAW, 314 pages, 1988. Softcover. (Review)

KRAUSE'S CASES, COMMENTS AND QUESTIONS ON FAMILY LAW, Third Edition, 1433 pages, 1990. (Casebook)

KRAUSE'S FAMILY LAW IN A NUTSHELL, Second Edition, 444 pages, 1986. Softcover. (Text)

KRAUSKOPF'S CASES ON PROPERTY DIVISION AT MARRIAGE DISSOLUTION, 250 pages, 1984. Softcover. (Casebook)

Economics, Law and—see also Antitrust, Regulated Industries

GOETZ' CASES AND MATERIALS ON LAW AND ECONOMICS, 547 pages, 1984. (Casebook)

MALLOY'S LAW AND ECONOMICS: A COMPARATIVE APPROACH TO THEORY AND PRACTICE, Approximately 152 pages, 1990. Softcover. (Text)

Education Law

ALEXANDER AND ALEXANDER'S THE LAW OF SCHOOLS, STUDENTS AND TEACHERS IN A NUTSHELL, 409 pages, 1984. Softcover. (Text)

Employment Discrimination—see also Women and the Law

ESTREICHER AND HARPER'S CASES AND

MATERIALS ON THE LAW GOVERNING THE EMPLOYMENT RELATIONSHIP, 962 pages, 1990. Teacher's Manual available. (Casebook) Statutory Supplement.

JONES, MURPHY AND BELTON'S CASES AND MATERIALS ON DISCRIMINATION IN EMPLOYMENT, (The Labor Law Group). Fifth Edition, 1116 pages, 1987. (Casebook) 1990 Supplement.

PLAYER'S FEDERAL LAW OF EMPLOYMENT DISCRIMINATION IN A NUTSHELL, Second Edition, 402 pages, 1981. Softcover. (Text)

PLAYER'S HORNBOOK ON EMPLOYMENT DISCRIMINATION LAW, Student Edition, 708 pages, 1988. (Text)

PLAYER, SHOBEN AND LIEBERWITZ' CASES AND MATERIALS ON EMPLOYMENT DISCRIMINATION LAW, Approximately 810 pages, 1990. (Casebook)

Energy and Natural Resources Law—see also Oil and Gas

LAITOS' CASES AND MATERIALS ON NATURAL RESOURCES LAW, 938 pages, 1985. Teacher's Manual available. (Casebook)

SELECTED ENVIRONMENTAL LAW STATUTES—EDUCATIONAL EDITION. Softcover. Approximately 1040 pages, 1990.

Environmental Law—see also Energy and Natural Resources Law; Sea, Law of

BONINE AND MCGARITY'S THE LAW OF ENVIRONMENTAL PROTECTION: CASES—LEGISLATION—POLICIES, 1076 pages, 1984. Teacher's Manual available. (Casebook)

FINDLEY AND FARBER'S CASES AND MATERIALS ON ENVIRONMENTAL LAW, Second Edition, 813 pages, 1985. (Casebook) 1988 Supplement.

FINDLEY AND FARBER'S ENVIRONMENTAL LAW IN A NUTSHELL, Second Edition, 367 pages, 1988. Softcover. (Text)

RODGERS' HORNBOOK ON ENVIRONMENTAL LAW, 956 pages, 1977, with 1984 pocket part. (Text)

SELECTED ENVIRONMENTAL LAW STATUTES—EDUCATIONAL EDITION. Softcover. Approximately 1040 pages, 1990.

Equity—see Remedies

Estate Planning—see also Trusts and Estates; Taxation—Estate and Gift

LYNN'S AN INTRODUCTION TO ESTATE PLANNING IN A NUTSHELL, Third Edition, 370 pages, 1983. Softcover. (Text)

Evidence

BROUN AND BLAKEY'S BLACK LETTER ON EVIDENCE, 269 pages, 1984. Softcover. (Review)

BROUN, MEISENHOLDER, STRONG AND MOSTELLER'S PROBLEMS IN EVIDENCE, Third Edition, 238 pages, 1988. Teacher's Manual available. Softcover. (Coursebook)

CLEARY, STRONG, BROUN AND MOSTELLER'S CASES AND MATERIALS ON EVIDENCE, Fourth Edition, 1060 pages, 1988. (Casebook)

FEDERAL RULES OF EVIDENCE FOR UNITED STATES COURTS AND MAGISTRATES. Softcover. Approximately 380 pages, 1990.

GRAHAM'S FEDERAL RULES OF EVIDENCE IN A NUTSHELL, Second Edition, 473 pages, 1987. Softcover. (Text)

LEMPERT AND SALTZBURG'S A MODERN APPROACH TO EVIDENCE: TEXT, PROBLEMS, TRANSCRIPTS AND CASES, Second Edition, 1232 pages, 1983. Teacher's Manual available. (Casebook)

LILLY'S AN INTRODUCTION TO THE LAW OF EVIDENCE, Second Edition, 585 pages, 1987. (Text)

MCCORMICK, SUTTON AND WELLBORN'S CASES AND MATERIALS ON EVIDENCE, Sixth Edition, 1067 pages, 1987. (Casebook)

MCCORMICK'S HORNBOOK ON EVIDENCE, Third Edition, Student Edition, 1156 pages, 1984, with 1987 pocket part. (Text)

ROTHSTEIN'S EVIDENCE IN A NUTSHELL: STATE AND FEDERAL RULES, Second Edition, 514 pages, 1981. Softcover. (Text)

Federal Jurisdiction and Procedure

CURRIE'S CASES AND MATERIALS ON FEDERAL COURTS, Fourth Edition, approximately 1125 pages, 1990. (Casebook)

CURRIE'S FEDERAL JURISDICTION IN A NUTSHELL, Third Edition, approximately 260 pages, 1990. Softcover. (Text)

FEDERAL RULES OF CIVIL PROCEDURE—EDUCATIONAL EDITION. Softcover. Approxi-

mately 635 pages, 1990.

REDISH'S BLACK LETTER ON FEDERAL JURISDICTION, 219 pages, 1985. Softcover. (Review)

REDISH'S CASES, COMMENTS AND QUESTIONS ON FEDERAL COURTS, Second Edition, 1122 pages, 1989. (Casebook) 1990 Supplement.

VETRI AND MERRILL'S FEDERAL COURTS PROBLEMS AND MATERIALS, Second Edition, 232 pages, 1984. Softcover. (Coursebook)

WRIGHT'S HORNBOOK ON FEDERAL COURTS, Fourth Edition, Student Edition, 870 pages, 1983. (Text)

Foreign Relations and National Security Law

FRANCK AND GLENNON'S FOREIGN RELATIONS AND NATIONAL SECURITY LAW, 941 pages, 1987. (Casebook)

Future Interests—see Trusts and Estates

Health Law—see Medicine, Law and

Human Rights—see International Law

Immigration Law

ALEINIKOFF AND MARTIN'S IMMIGRATION PROCESS AND POLICY, Second Edition, approximately 1100 pages, October, 1990 (Casebook)

Statutory Supplement. *See Immigration and Nationality Laws*

IMMIGRATION AND NATIONALITY LAWS OF THE UNITED STATES: SELECTED STATUTES, REGULATIONS AND FORMS. Softcover. Approximately 400 pages, 1990.

WEISSBRODT'S IMMIGRATION LAW AND PROCEDURE IN A NUTSHELL, Second Edition, 438 pages, 1989, Softcover. (Text)

Indian Law—see American Indian Law

Insurance Law

DEVINE AND TERRY'S PROBLEMS IN INSURANCE LAW, 240 pages, 1989. Softcover. Teacher's Manual available. (Coursebook)

DOBBYN'S INSURANCE LAW IN A NUTSHELL, Second Edition, 316 pages, 1989. Softcover. (Text)

KEETON'S CASES ON BASIC INSURANCE LAW,

Insurance Law—Cont'd

Second Edition, 1086 pages, 1977. Teacher's Manual available. (Casebook)

KEETON'S COMPUTER-AIDED AND WORKBOOK EXERCISES ON INSURANCE LAW, 255 pages, 1990. Softcover. (Coursebook)

KEETON AND WIDISS' INSURANCE LAW, Student Edition, 1359 pages, 1988. (Text)

WIDISS AND KEETON'S COURSE SUPPLEMENT TO KEETON AND WIDISS' INSURANCE LAW, 502 pages, 1988. Softcover. (Casebook)

WIDISS' INSURANCE: MATERIALS ON FUNDAMENTAL PRINCIPLES, LEGAL DOCTRINES AND REGULATORY ACTS, 1186 pages, 1989. (Casebook)

YORK AND WHELAN'S CASES, MATERIALS AND PROBLEMS ON GENERAL PRACTICE INSURANCE LAW, Second Edition, 787 pages, 1988. Teacher's Manual available. (Casebook)

International Law—see also Sea, Law of

BUERGENTHAL'S INTERNATIONAL HUMAN RIGHTS IN A NUTSHELL, 283 pages, 1988. Softcover. (Text)

BUERGENTHAL AND MAIER'S PUBLIC INTERNATIONAL LAW IN A NUTSHELL, Second Edition, 275 pages, 1990. Softcover. (Text)

FOLSOM, GORDON AND SPANOGLE'S INTERNATIONAL BUSINESS TRANSACTIONS—A PROBLEM-ORIENTED COURSEBOOK, 1160 pages, 1986. Teacher's Manual available. (Casebook) 1989 Documents Supplement.

FOLSOM, GORDON AND SPANOGLE'S INTERNATIONAL BUSINESS TRANSACTIONS IN A NUTSHELL, Third Edition, 509 pages, 1988. Softcover. (Text)

HENKIN, PUGH, SCHACHTER AND SMIT'S CASES AND MATERIALS ON INTERNATIONAL LAW, Second Edition, 1517 pages, 1987. (Casebook) Documents Supplement.

JACKSON AND DAVEY'S CASES, MATERIALS AND TEXT ON LEGAL PROBLEMS OF INTERNATIONAL ECONOMIC RELATIONS, Second Edition, 1269 pages, 1986. (Casebook) 1989 Documents Supplement.

KIRGIS' INTERNATIONAL ORGANIZATIONS IN THEIR LEGAL SETTING, 1016 pages, 1977. Teacher's Manual available. (Casebook) 1981 Supplement.

WESTON, FALK AND D'AMATO'S INTERNATIONAL LAW AND WORLD ORDER—A PROBLEM-ORIENTED COURSEBOOK, Second Edition, approximately 1305 pages, 1990. Teacher's Manual available. (Casebook) Documents Supplement.

Interviewing and Counseling

BINDER AND PRICE'S LEGAL INTERVIEWING AND COUNSELING, 232 pages, 1977. Teacher's Manual available. Softcover. (Coursebook)

BINDER, BERGMAN AND PRICE'S LAWYERS AS COUNSELORS: A CLIENT CENTERED APPROACH, Approximately 400 pages, October, 1990 Pub. Softcover. (Coursebook)

SHAFFER AND ELKINS' LEGAL INTERVIEWING AND COUNSELING IN A NUTSHELL, Second Edition, 487 pages, 1987. Softcover. (Text)

Introduction to Law—see Legal Method and Legal System

Introduction to Law Study

HEGLAND'S INTRODUCTION TO THE STUDY AND PRACTICE OF LAW IN A NUTSHELL, 418 pages, 1983. Softcover. (Text)

KINYON'S INTRODUCTION TO LAW STUDY AND LAW EXAMINATIONS IN A NUTSHELL, 389 pages, 1971. Softcover. (Text)

Judicial Process—see Legal Method and Legal System

Jurisprudence

CHRISTIE'S JURISPRUDENCE—TEXT AND READINGS ON THE PHILOSOPHY OF LAW, 1056 pages, 1973. (Casebook)

Juvenile Justice

FOX'S CASES AND MATERIALS ON MODERN JUVENILE JUSTICE, Second Edition, 960 pages, 1981. (Casebook)

FOX'S JUVENILE COURTS IN A NUTSHELL, Third Edition, 291 pages, 1984. Softcover. (Text)

Labor and Employment Law—see also Employment Discrimination, Social Legislation

FINKIN, GOLDMAN AND SUMMERS' LEGAL PROTECTION OF INDIVIDUAL EMPLOYEES, (The La-

Labor and Employment Law—Cont'd

bor Law Group). 1164 pages, 1989. (Casebook)

GORMAN'S BASIC TEXT ON LABOR LAW— UNIONIZATION AND COLLECTIVE BARGAINING, 914 pages, 1976. (Text)

LESLIE'S LABOR LAW IN A NUTSHELL, Second Edition, 397 pages, 1986. Softcover. (Text)

NOLAN'S LABOR ARBITRATION LAW AND PRACTICE IN A NUTSHELL, 358 pages, 1979. Softcover. (Text)

OBERER, HANSLOWE, ANDERSEN AND HEINSZ' CASES AND MATERIALS ON LABOR LAW—COLLECTIVE BARGAINING IN A FREE SOCIETY, Third Edition, 1163 pages, 1986. (Casebook) Statutory Supplement.

RABIN, SILVERSTEIN AND SCHATZKI'S LABOR AND EMPLOYMENT LAW: PROBLEMS, CASES AND MATERIALS IN THE LAW OF WORK, (The Labor Law Group). 1014 pages, 1988. Teacher's Manual available. (Casebook) 1988 Statutory Supplement.

Land Finance—Property Security—see Real Estate Transactions

Land Use

CALLIES AND FREILICH'S CASES AND MATERIALS ON LAND USE, 1233 pages, 1986. (Casebook) 1988 Supplement.

HAGMAN AND JUERGENSMEYER'S HORNBOOK ON URBAN PLANNING AND LAND DEVELOPMENT CONTROL LAW, Second Edition, Student Edition, 680 pages, 1986. (Text)

WRIGHT AND GITELMAN'S CASES AND MATERIALS ON LAND USE, Third Edition, 1300 pages, 1982. Teacher's Manual available. (Casebook) 1987 Supplement.

WRIGHT AND WRIGHT'S LAND USE IN A NUTSHELL, Second Edition, 356 pages, 1985. Softcover. (Text)

Legal History—see also Legal Method and Legal System

PRESSER AND ZAINALDIN'S CASES AND MATERIALS ON LAW AND JURISPRUDENCE IN AMERICAN HISTORY, Second Edition, 1092 pages, 1989. Teacher's Manual available. (Casebook)

Legal Method and Legal System—see also Legal Research, Legal Writing

ALDISERT'S READINGS, MATERIALS AND CASES IN THE JUDICIAL PROCESS, 948 pages, 1976. (Casebook)

BERCH AND BERCH'S INTRODUCTION TO LEGAL METHOD AND PROCESS, 550 pages, 1985. Teacher's Manual available. (Casebook)

BODENHEIMER, OAKLEY AND LOVE'S READINGS AND CASES ON AN INTRODUCTION TO THE ANGLO-AMERICAN LEGAL SYSTEM, Second Edition, 166 pages, 1988. Softcover. (Casebook)

DAVIES AND LAWRY'S INSTITUTIONS AND METHODS OF THE LAW—INTRODUCTORY TEACHING MATERIALS, 547 pages, 1982. Teacher's Manual available. (Casebook)

DVORKIN, HIMMELSTEIN AND LESNICK'S BECOMING A LAWYER: A HUMANISTIC PERSPECTIVE ON LEGAL EDUCATION AND PROFESSIONALISM, 211 pages, 1981. Softcover. (Text)

KEETON'S JUDGING, 842 pages, 1990. Softcover. (Coursebook)

KELSO AND KELSO'S STUDYING LAW: AN INTRODUCTION, 587 pages, 1984. (Coursebook)

KEMPIN'S HISTORICAL INTRODUCTION TO ANGLO-AMERICAN LAW IN A NUTSHELL, Third Edition, approximately 302 pages, 1990. Softcover. (Text)

REYNOLDS' JUDICIAL PROCESS IN A NUTSHELL, 292 pages, 1980. Softcover. (Text)

Legal Research

COHEN'S LEGAL RESEARCH IN A NUTSHELL, Fourth Edition, 452 pages, 1985. Softcover. (Text)

COHEN, BERRING AND OLSON'S HOW TO FIND THE LAW, Ninth Edition, 716 pages, 1989. (Text)

COHEN, BERRING AND OLSON'S FINDING THE LAW, 570 pages, 1989. Softcover reprint from Cohen, Berring and Olson's How to Find the Law, Ninth Edition. (Coursebook)

Legal Research Exercises, 3rd Ed., for use with Cohen, Berring and Olson, 229 pages, 1989. Teacher's Manual available.

ROMBAUER'S LEGAL PROBLEM SOLVING—

Legal Research—Cont'd

ANALYSIS, RESEARCH AND WRITING, Fourth Edition, 424 pages, 1983. Teacher's Manual with problems available. (Coursebook)

STATSKY'S LEGAL RESEARCH AND WRITING, Third Edition, 257 pages, 1986. Softcover. (Coursebook)

TEPLY'S LEGAL RESEARCH AND CITATION, Third Edition, 472 pages, 1989. Softcover. (Coursebook)

Student Library Exercises, 3rd ed., 391 pages, 1989. Answer Key available.

Legal Writing

CHILD'S DRAFTING LEGAL DOCUMENTS: MATERIALS AND PROBLEMS, 286 pages, 1988. Softcover. Teacher's Manual available. (Coursebook)

DICKERSON'S MATERIALS ON LEGAL DRAFTING, 425 pages, 1981. Teacher's Manual available. (Coursebook)

FELSENFELD AND SIEGEL'S WRITING CONTRACTS IN PLAIN ENGLISH, 290 pages, 1981. Softcover. (Text)

GOPEN'S WRITING FROM A LEGAL PERSPECTIVE, 225 pages, 1981. (Text)

MELLINKOFF'S LEGAL WRITING—SENSE AND NONSENSE, 242 pages, 1982. Softcover. Teacher's Manual available. (Text)

PRATT'S LEGAL WRITING: A SYSTEMATIC APPROACH, 422 pages, 1989. Teacher's Manual available. (Coursebook)

RAY AND RAMSFIELD'S LEGAL WRITING: GETTING IT RIGHT AND GETTING IT WRITTEN, 250 pages, 1987. Softcover. (Text)

SQUIRES AND ROMBAUER'S LEGAL WRITING IN A NUTSHELL, 294 pages, 1982. Softcover. (Text)

STATSKY AND WERNET'S CASE ANALYSIS AND FUNDAMENTALS OF LEGAL WRITING, Third Edition, 424 pages, 1989. Teacher's Manual available. (Text)

TEPLY'S LEGAL WRITING, ANALYSIS AND ORAL ARGUMENT, 576 pages, 1990. Softcover. Teacher's Manual available. (Coursebook)

WEIHOFEN'S LEGAL WRITING STYLE, Second Edition, 332 pages, 1980. (Text)

Legislation

DAVIES' LEGISLATIVE LAW AND PROCESS IN A NUTSHELL, Second Edition, 346 pages, 1986. Softcover. (Text)

ESKRIDGE AND FRICKEY'S CASES AND MATERIALS ON LEGISLATION: STATUTES AND THE CREATION OF PUBLIC POLICY, 937 pages, 1988. Teacher's Manual available. (Casebook) 1990 Supplement.

NUTTING AND DICKERSON'S CASES AND MATERIALS ON LEGISLATION, Fifth Edition, 744 pages, 1978. (Casebook)

STATSKY'S LEGISLATIVE ANALYSIS AND DRAFTING, Second Edition, 217 pages, 1984. Teacher's Manual available. (Text)

Local Government

FRUG'S CASES AND MATERIALS ON LOCAL GOVERNMENT LAW, 1005 pages, 1988. (Casebook)

MCCARTHY'S LOCAL GOVERNMENT LAW IN A NUTSHELL, Third Edition, approximately 400 pages, 1990. Softcover. (Text)

REYNOLDS' HORNBOOK ON LOCAL GOVERNMENT LAW, 860 pages, 1982, with 1990 pocket part. (Text)

VALENTE'S CASES AND MATERIALS ON LOCAL GOVERNMENT LAW, Third Edition, 1010 pages, 1987. Teacher's Manual available. (Casebook) 1989 Supplement.

Mass Communication Law

GILLMOR, BARRON, SIMON AND TERRY'S CASES AND COMMENT ON MASS COMMUNICATION LAW, Fifth Edition, 947 pages, 1990. (Casebook)

GINSBURG'S REGULATION OF BROADCASTING: LAW AND POLICY TOWARDS RADIO, TELEVISION AND CABLE COMMUNICATIONS, 741 pages, 1979 (Casebook) 1983 Supplement.

ZUCKMAN, GAYNES, CARTER AND DEE'S MASS COMMUNICATIONS LAW IN A NUTSHELL, Third Edition, 538 pages, 1988. Softcover. (Text)

Medicine, Law and

FURROW, JOHNSON, JOST AND SCHWARTZ' HEALTH LAW: CASES, MATERIALS AND PROBLEMS, 1005 pages, 1987. Teacher's Manual available. (Casebook) 1989 Supplement.

HALL AND ELLMAN'S HEALTH CARE LAW AND

Medicine, Law and—Cont'd

ETHICS IN A NUTSHELL, 401 pages, 1990. Softcover (Text)

KING'S THE LAW OF MEDICAL MALPRACTICE IN A NUTSHELL, Second Edition, 342 pages, 1986. Softcover. (Text)

SHAPIRO AND SPECE'S CASES, MATERIALS AND PROBLEMS ON BIOETHICS AND LAW, 892 pages, 1981. (Casebook)

SHARPE, BOUMIL, FISCINA AND HEAD'S CASES AND MATERIALS ON MEDICAL LIABILITY, Approximately 500 pages, September, 1990 Pub. (Casebook)

Military Law

SHANOR AND TERRELL'S MILITARY LAW IN A NUTSHELL, 378 pages, 1980. Softcover. (Text)

Mortgages—see Real Estate Transactions

Natural Resources Law—see Energy and Natural Resources Law, Environmental Law

Negotiation

GIFFORD'S LEGAL NEGOTIATION: THEORY AND APPLICATIONS, 225 pages, 1989. Softcover. (Text)

WILLIAMS' LEGAL NEGOTIATION AND SETTLEMENT, 207 pages, 1983. Softcover. Teacher's Manual available. (Coursebook)

Office Practice—see also Computers and Law, Interviewing and Counseling, Negotiation

HEGLAND'S TRIAL AND PRACTICE SKILLS IN A NUTSHELL, 346 pages, 1978. Softcover (Text)

STRONG AND CLARK'S LAW OFFICE MANAGEMENT, 424 pages, 1974. (Casebook)

Oil and Gas—see also Energy and Natural Resources Law

HEMINGWAY'S HORNBOOK ON OIL AND GAS, Second Edition, Student Edition, 543 pages, 1983, with 1989 pocket part. (Text)

KUNTZ, LOWE, ANDERSON AND SMITH'S CASES AND MATERIALS ON OIL AND GAS LAW, 857 pages, 1986. Teacher's Manual available. (Casebook) Forms Manual. Revised.

LOWE'S OIL AND GAS LAW IN A NUTSHELL,

Second Edition, 465 pages, 1988. Softcover. (Text)

Partnership—see Agency—Partnership

Patent and Copyright Law

CHOATE, FRANCIS AND COLLINS' CASES AND MATERIALS ON PATENT LAW, INCLUDING TRADE SECRETS, COPYRIGHTS, TRADEMARKS, Third Edition, 1009 pages, 1987. (Casebook)

MILLER AND DAVIS' INTELLECTUAL PROPERTY—PATENTS, TRADEMARKS AND COPYRIGHT IN A NUTSHELL, Second Edition, approximately 440 pages, 1990. Softcover. (Text)

NIMMER'S CASES AND MATERIALS ON COPYRIGHT AND OTHER ASPECTS OF ENTERTAINMENT LITIGATION ILLUSTRATED—INCLUDING UNFAIR COMPETITION, DEFAMATION AND PRIVACY, Third Edition, 1025 pages, 1985. (Casebook) 1989 Supplement.

Products Liability

FISCHER AND POWERS' CASES AND MATERIALS ON PRODUCTS LIABILITY, 685 pages, 1988. Teacher's Manual available. (Casebook)

NOEL AND PHILLIPS' CASES ON PRODUCTS LIABILITY, Second Edition, 821 pages, 1982. (Casebook)

PHILLIPS' PRODUCTS LIABILITY IN A NUTSHELL, Third Edition, 307 pages, 1988. Softcover. (Text)

Professional Responsibility

ARONSON, DEVINE AND FISCH'S PROBLEMS, CASES AND MATERIALS IN PROFESSIONAL RESPONSIBILITY, 745 pages, 1985. Teacher's Manual available. (Casebook)

ARONSON AND WECKSTEIN'S PROFESSIONAL RESPONSIBILITY IN A NUTSHELL, 399 pages, 1980. Softcover. (Text)

MELLINKOFF'S THE CONSCIENCE OF A LAWYER, 304 pages, 1973. (Text)

PIRSIG AND KIRWIN'S CASES AND MATERIALS ON PROFESSIONAL RESPONSIBILITY, Fourth Edition, 603 pages, 1984. Teacher's Manual available. (Casebook)

ROTUNDA'S BLACK LETTER ON PROFESSIONAL RESPONSIBILITY, Second Edition, 414 pages, 1988. Softcover. (Review)

SCHWARTZ AND WYDICK'S PROBLEMS IN LE-

Professional Responsibility—Cont'd

GAL ETHICS, Second Edition, 341 pages, 1988. (Coursebook)

SELECTED STATUTES, RULES AND STANDARDS ON THE LEGAL PROFESSION. Softcover. Approximately 600 pages, 1990.

SMITH AND MALLEN'S PREVENTING LEGAL MALPRACTICE, 264 pages, 1989. Reprint from Mallen and Smith's Legal Malpractice, Third Edition. (Text)

SUTTON AND DZIENKOWSKI'S CASES AND MATERIALS ON THE PROFESSIONAL RESPONSIBILITY FOR LAWYERS, 839 pages, 1989. Teacher's Manual available. (Casebook)

WOLFRAM'S HORNBOOK ON MODERN LEGAL ETHICS, Student Edition, 1120 pages, 1986. (Text)

Property—see also Real Estate Transactions, Land Use, Trusts and Estates

BERNHARDT'S BLACK LETTER ON PROPERTY, 318 pages, 1983. Softcover. (Review)

BERNHARDT'S REAL PROPERTY IN A NUTSHELL, Second Edition, 448 pages, 1981. Softcover. (Text)

BOYER'S SURVEY OF THE LAW OF PROPERTY, Third Edition, 766 pages, 1981. (Text)

BROWDER, CUNNINGHAM, NELSON, STOEBUCK AND WHITMAN'S CASES ON BASIC PROPERTY LAW, Fifth Edition, 1386 pages, 1989. Teacher's Manual available. (Casebook)

BRUCE, ELY AND BOSTICK'S CASES AND MATERIALS ON MODERN PROPERTY LAW, Second Edition, 953 pages, 1989. Teacher's Manual available. (Casebook)

BURKE'S PERSONAL PROPERTY IN A NUTSHELL, 322 pages, 1983. Softcover. (Text)

CUNNINGHAM, STOEBUCK AND WHITMAN'S HORNBOOK ON THE LAW OF PROPERTY, Student Edition, 916 pages, 1984, with 1987 pocket part. (Text)

DONAHUE, KAUPER AND MARTIN'S CASES ON PROPERTY, Second Edition, 1362 pages, 1983. Teacher's Manual available. (Casebook)

HILL'S LANDLORD AND TENANT LAW IN A NUTSHELL, Second Edition, 311 pages, 1986. Softcover. (Text)

KURTZ AND HOVENKAMP'S CASES AND

MATERIALS ON AMERICAN PROPERTY LAW, 1296 pages, 1987. Teacher's Manual available. (Casebook) 1988 Supplement.

MOYNIHAN'S INTRODUCTION TO REAL PROPERTY, Second Edition, 239 pages, 1988. (Text)

Psychiatry, Law and

REISNER AND SLOBOGIN'S LAW AND THE MENTAL HEALTH SYSTEM, CIVIL AND CRIMINAL ASPECTS, Second Edition, approximately 1127 pages, 1990. (Casebook)

Real Estate Transactions

BRUCE'S REAL ESTATE FINANCE IN A NUTSHELL, Second Edition, 262 pages, 1985. Softcover. (Text)

MAXWELL, RIESENFELD, HETLAND AND WARREN'S CASES ON CALIFORNIA SECURITY TRANSACTIONS IN LAND, Third Edition, 728 pages, 1984. (Casebook)

NELSON AND WHITMAN'S BLACK LETTER ON LAND TRANSACTIONS AND FINANCE, Second Edition, 466 pages, 1988. Softcover. (Review)

NELSON AND WHITMAN'S CASES ON REAL ESTATE TRANSFER, FINANCE AND DEVELOPMENT, Third Edition, 1184 pages, 1987. (Casebook)

NELSON AND WHITMAN'S HORNBOOK ON REAL ESTATE FINANCE LAW, Second Edition, 941 pages, 1985 with 1989 pocket part. (Text)

Regulated Industries—see also Mass Communication Law, Banking Law

GELLHORN AND PIERCE'S REGULATED INDUSTRIES IN A NUTSHELL, Second Edition, 389 pages, 1987. Softcover. (Text)

MORGAN, HARRISON AND VERKUIL'S CASES AND MATERIALS ON ECONOMIC REGULATION OF BUSINESS, Second Edition, 666 pages, 1985. (Casebook)

Remedies

DOBBS' HORNBOOK ON REMEDIES, 1067 pages, 1973. (Text)

DOBBS' PROBLEMS IN REMEDIES. 137 pages, 1974. Teacher's Manual available. Softcover. (Coursebook)

DOBBYN'S INJUNCTIONS IN A NUTSHELL, 264 pages, 1974. Softcover. (Text)

Remedies—Cont'd

FRIEDMAN'S CONTRACT REMEDIES IN A NUT-SHELL, 323 pages, 1981. Softcover. (Text)

LEAVELL, LOVE AND NELSON'S CASES AND MATERIALS ON EQUITABLE REMEDIES, RESTITUTION AND DAMAGES, Fourth Edition, 1111 pages, 1986. Teacher's Manual available. (Casebook)

McCORMICK'S HORNBOOK ON DAMAGES, 811 pages, 1935. (Text)

O'CONNELL'S REMEDIES IN A NUTSHELL, Second Edition, 320 pages, 1985. Softcover. (Text)

SCHOENBROD, MACBETH, LEVINE AND JUNG'S CASES AND MATERIALS ON REMEDIES: PUBLIC AND PRIVATE, Approximately 807 pages, 1990. Teacher's Manual available. (Casebook)

YORK, BAUMAN AND RENDLEMAN'S CASES AND MATERIALS ON REMEDIES, Fourth Edition, 1029 pages, 1985. Teacher's Manual available. (Casebook)

Sea, Law of

SOHN AND GUSTAFSON'S THE LAW OF THE SEA IN A NUTSHELL, 264 pages, 1984. Softcover. (Text)

Securities Regulation

HAZEN'S HORNBOOK ON THE LAW OF SECURITIES REGULATION, Second Edition, Student Edition, approximately 1000 pages, 1990. (Text)

RATNER'S MATERIALS ON SECURITIES REGULATION, Third Edition, 1000 pages, 1986. Teacher's Manual available. (Casebook) 1989 Supplement.

Statutory Supplement. *See Selected Securities Regulation*

RATNER'S SECURITIES REGULATION IN A NUTSHELL, Third Edition, 316 pages, 1988. Softcover. (Text)

SELECTED STATUTES, REGULATIONS, RULES, DOCUMENTS AND FORMS ON SECURITIES REGULATION. Softcover. 1272 pages, 1990.

Social Legislation

HOOD, HARDY AND LEWIS' WORKERS' COMPENSATION AND EMPLOYEE PROTECTION LAWS IN A NUTSHELL, Second Edition, 361 pages, 1990. Softcover. (Text)

LAFRANCE'S WELFARE LAW: STRUCTURE AND ENTITLEMENT IN A NUTSHELL, 455 pages, 1979. Softcover. (Text)

MALONE, PLANT AND LITTLE'S CASES ON WORKERS' COMPENSATION AND EMPLOYMENT RIGHTS, Second Edition, 951 pages, 1980. Teacher's Manual available. (Casebook)

Sports Law

SCHUBERT, SMITH AND TRENTADUE'S SPORTS LAW, 395 pages, 1986. (Text)

Tax Practice and Procedure

GARBIS, STRUNTZ AND RUBIN'S CASES AND MATERIALS ON TAX PROCEDURE AND TAX FRAUD, Second Edition, 687 pages, 1987. (Casebook)

MORGAN'S TAX PROCEDURE AND TAX FRAUD IN A NUTSHELL, Approximately 382 pages, 1990. Softcover. (Text)

Taxation—Corporate

KAHN AND GANN'S CORPORATE TAXATION, Third Edition, 980 pages, 1989. Teacher's Manual available. (Casebook)

WEIDENBRUCH AND BURKE'S FEDERAL INCOME TAXATION OF CORPORATIONS AND STOCKHOLDERS IN A NUTSHELL, Third Edition, 309 pages, 1989. Softcover. (Text)

Taxation—Estate & Gift—see also Estate Planning, Trusts and Estates

McNULTY'S FEDERAL ESTATE AND GIFT TAXATION IN A NUTSHELL, Fourth Edition, 496 pages, 1989. Softcover. (Text)

PENNELL'S CASES AND MATERIALS ON INCOME TAXATION OF TRUSTS, ESTATES, GRANTORS AND BENEFICIARIES, 460 pages, 1987. Teacher's Manual available. (Casebook)

Taxation—Individual

DODGE'S THE LOGIC OF TAX, 343 pages, 1989. Softcover. (Text)

GUNN AND WARD'S CASES, TEXT AND PROBLEMS ON FEDERAL INCOME TAXATION, Second Edition, 835 pages, 1988. Teacher's Manual available. (Casebook) 1990 Supplement.

HUDSON AND LIND'S BLACK LETTER ON FEDERAL INCOME TAXATION, Third Edition, approximately 390 pages, 1990. Softcover. (Review)

Taxation—Individual—Cont'd

KRAGEN AND MCNULTY'S CASES AND MATERIALS ON FEDERAL INCOME TAXATION—INDIVIDUALS, CORPORATIONS, PARTNERSHIPS, Fourth Edition, 1287 pages, 1985. (Casebook)

MCNULTY'S FEDERAL INCOME TAXATION OF INDIVIDUALS IN A NUTSHELL, Fourth Edition, 503 pages, 1988. Softcover. (Text)

POSIN'S HORNBOOK ON FEDERAL INCOME TAXATION, Student Edition, 491 pages, 1983, with 1989 pocket part. (Text)

ROSE AND CHOMMIE'S HORNBOOK ON FEDERAL INCOME TAXATION, Third Edition, 923 pages, 1988, with 1989 pocket part. (Text)

SELECTED FEDERAL TAXATION STATUTES AND REGULATIONS. Softcover. Approximately 1650 pages, 1991.

SOLOMON AND HESCH'S PROBLEMS, CASES AND MATERIALS ON FEDERAL INCOME TAXATION OF INDIVIDUALS, 1068 pages, 1987. Teacher's Manual available. (Casebook)

Taxation—International

DOERNBERG'S INTERNATIONAL TAXATION IN A NUTSHELL, 325 pages, 1989. Softcover. (Text)

KAPLAN'S FEDERAL TAXATION OF INTERNATIONAL TRANSACTIONS: PRINCIPLES, PLANNING AND POLICY, 635 pages, 1988. (Casebook)

Taxation—Partnership

BERGER AND WIEDENBECK'S CASES AND MATERIALS ON PARTNERSHIP TAXATION, 788 pages, 1989. Teacher's Manual available. (Casebook)

Taxation—State & Local

GELFAND AND SALSICH'S STATE AND LOCAL TAXATION AND FINANCE IN A NUTSHELL, 309 pages, 1986. Softcover. (Text)

HELLERSTEIN AND HELLERSTEIN'S CASES AND MATERIALS ON STATE AND LOCAL TAXATION, Fifth Edition, 1071 pages, 1988. (Casebook)

Torts—see also Products Liability

CHRISTIE AND MEEKS' CASES AND MATERIALS ON THE LAW OF TORTS, Second Edition, 1264 pages, 1990. (Casebook)

DOBBS' TORTS AND COMPENSATION—PERSONAL ACCOUNTABILITY AND SOCIAL RESPONSIBILITY FOR INJURY, 955 pages, 1985. Teacher's Manual available. (Casebook) 1990 Supplement.

KEETON, KEETON, SARGENTICH AND STEINER'S CASES AND MATERIALS ON TORT AND ACCIDENT LAW, Second Edition, 1318 pages, 1989. (Casebook)

KIONKA'S BLACK LETTER ON TORTS, 339 pages, 1988. Softcover. (Review)

KIONKA'S TORTS IN A NUTSHELL: INJURIES TO PERSONS AND PROPERTY, 434 pages, 1977. Softcover. (Text)

MALONE'S TORTS IN A NUTSHELL: INJURIES TO FAMILY, SOCIAL AND TRADE RELATIONS, 358 pages, 1979. Softcover. (Text)

PROSSER AND KEETON'S HORNBOOK ON TORTS, Fifth Edition, Student Edition, 1286 pages, 1984 with 1988 pocket part. (Text)

ROBERTSON, POWERS AND ANDERSON'S CASES AND MATERIALS ON TORTS, 932 pages, 1989. Teacher's Manual available. (Casebook)

Trade Regulation—see also Antitrust, Regulated Industries

MCMANIS' UNFAIR TRADE PRACTICES IN A NUTSHELL, Second Edition, 464 pages, 1988. Softcover. (Text)

OPPENHEIM, WESTON, MAGGS AND SCHECHTER'S CASES AND MATERIALS ON UNFAIR TRADE PRACTICES AND CONSUMER PROTECTION, Fourth Edition, 1038 pages, 1983. Teacher's Manual available. (Casebook) 1986 Supplement.

SCHECHTER'S BLACK LETTER ON UNFAIR TRADE PRACTICES, 272 pages, 1986. Softcover. (Review)

Trial and Appellate Advocacy—see also Civil Procedure

APPELLATE ADVOCACY, HANDBOOK OF, Second Edition, 182 pages, 1986. Softcover. (Text)

BERGMAN'S TRIAL ADVOCACY IN A NUTSHELL, Second Edition, 354 pages, 1989. Softcover. (Text)

BINDER AND BERGMAN'S FACT INVESTIGATION: FROM HYPOTHESIS TO PROOF, 354 pages, 1984. Teacher's Manual available. (Coursebook)

Trial and Appellate Advocacy—Cont'd

CARLSON AND IMWINKELRIED'S DYNAMICS OF TRIAL PRACTICE: PROBLEMS AND MATERIALS, 414 pages, 1989. Teacher's Manual available. (Coursebook)

GOLDBERG'S THE FIRST TRIAL (WHERE DO I SIT? WHAT DO I SAY?) IN A NUTSHELL, 396 pages, 1982. Softcover. (Text)

HAYDOCK, HERR, AND STEMPEL'S FUNDAMENTALS OF PRE-TRIAL LITIGATION, 768 pages, 1985. Softcover. Teacher's Manual available. (Coursebook)

HEGLAND'S TRIAL AND PRACTICE SKILLS IN A NUTSHELL, 346 pages, 1978. Softcover. (Text)

HORNSTEIN'S APPELLATE ADVOCACY IN A NUTSHELL, 325 pages, 1984. Softcover. (Text)

JEANS' HANDBOOK ON TRIAL ADVOCACY, Student Edition, 473 pages, 1975. Softcover. (Text)

LISNEK AND KAUFMAN'S DEPOSITIONS: PROCEDURE, STRATEGY AND TECHNIQUE, Law School and CLE Edition. 250 pages, 1990. Softcover. (Text)

MARTINEAU'S CASES AND MATERIALS ON APPELLATE PRACTICE AND PROCEDURE, 565 pages, 1987. (Casebook)

NOLAN'S CASES AND MATERIALS ON TRIAL PRACTICE, 518 pages, 1981. (Casebook)

SONSTENG AND HAYDOCK'S TRIAL: THEORIES, TACTICS, TECHNIQUE, Approximately 650 pages, 1990. Softcover. (Text)

SONSTENG, HAYDOCK AND BOYD'S THE TRIALBOOK: A TOTAL SYSTEM FOR PREPARATION AND PRESENTATION OF A CASE, 404 pages, 1984. Softcover. (Coursebook)

WHARTON, HAYDOCK AND SONSTENG'S CALIFORNIA CIVIL TRIALBOOK, Law School and CLE Edition. Approximately 300 pages, 1990. Softcover. (Text)

Trusts and Estates

ATKINSON'S HORNBOOK ON WILLS, Second Edition, 975 pages, 1953. (Text)

AVERILL'S UNIFORM PROBATE CODE IN A NUTSHELL, Second Edition, 454 pages, 1987. Softcover. (Text)

BOGERT'S HORNBOOK ON TRUSTS, Sixth Edition, Student Edition, 794 pages, 1987. (Text)

CLARK, LUSKY AND MURPHY'S CASES AND MATERIALS ON GRATUITOUS TRANSFERS, Third Edition, 970 pages, 1985. (Casebook)

DODGE'S WILLS, TRUSTS AND ESTATE PLANNING—LAW AND TAXATION, CASES AND MATERIALS, 665 pages, 1988. (Casebook)

KURTZ' PROBLEMS, CASES AND OTHER MATERIALS ON FAMILY ESTATE PLANNING, 853 pages, 1983. Teacher's Manual available. (Casebook)

MCGOVERN'S CASES AND MATERIALS ON WILLS, TRUSTS AND FUTURE INTERESTS: AN INTRODUCTION TO ESTATE PLANNING, 750 pages, 1983. (Casebook)

MCGOVERN, KURTZ AND REIN'S HORNBOOK ON WILLS, TRUSTS AND ESTATES—INCLUDING TAXATION AND FUTURE INTERESTS, 996 pages, 1988. (Text)

MENNELL'S WILLS AND TRUSTS IN A NUTSHELL, 392 pages, 1979. Softcover. (Text)

SIMES' HORNBOOK ON FUTURE INTERESTS, Second Edition, 355 pages, 1966. (Text)

TURANO AND RADIGAN'S HORNBOOK ON NEW YORK ESTATE ADMINISTRATION, 676 pages, 1986. (Text)

UNIFORM PROBATE CODE, OFFICIAL TEXT WITH COMMENTS. 615 pages, 1989. Softcover.

WAGGONER'S FUTURE INTERESTS IN A NUTSHELL, 361 pages, 1981. Softcover. (Text)

WATERBURY'S MATERIALS ON TRUSTS AND ESTATES, 1039 pages, 1986. Teacher's Manual available. (Casebook)

Water Law—see also Energy and Natural Resources Law, Environmental Law

GETCHES' WATER LAW IN A NUTSHELL, Second Edition, approximately 441 pages, 1990. Softcover. (Text)

SAX AND ABRAMS' LEGAL CONTROL OF WATER RESOURCES: CASES AND MATERIALS, 941 pages, 1986. (Casebook)

TRELEASE AND GOULD'S CASES AND MATERIALS ON WATER LAW, Fourth Edition, 816 pages, 1986. (Casebook)

THE AMERICAN CONSTITUTION

CASES—COMMENTS—QUESTIONS

Sixth Edition

By

William B. Lockhart

Professor of Law, University of California, Hastings
Dean and Professor of Law Emeritus, University of Minnesota

Yale Kamisar

Henry K. Ransom Professor of Law, University of Michigan

Jesse H. Choper

Dean and Professor of Law, University of California, Berkeley

Steven H. Shiffrin

Professor of Law, University of California, Los Angeles

AMERICAN CASEBOOK SERIES

WEST PUBLISHING CO.
ST. PAUL, MINN., 1986

American Casebook Series, the key number appearing on the front cover
and the WP symbol are registered trademarks of West Publishing Co.
Registered in U.S. Patent and Trademark Office.

Library of Congress Cataloging in Publication Data

The American Constitution.

    (American casebook series)
    Includes index.
    1. United States—Constitutional law—Cases.
I. Lockhart, William B. II. Series.

KF4549.A48 1986   342.73'029   86–13145
                  347.30229
ISBN 0–314–96669–2

L.K.C. & S.Amer.Const. 6th Ed. ACB
1st Reprint—1990

For Bill Lockhart, who pulls as heavy an oar as ever, on his 80th birthday.

J.C.
Y.K.
S.S.

*

Preface

This book continues to be designed as a teaching tool. We have sought both to inform students as to existing law and current trends and to stimulate critical examination of present and potential future developments. To fulfill this second aim, we have reproduced many selections from the literature or woven them into the notes and questions.

In the six years since the fifth edition of this book was published, an imposing number of significant decisions have been handed down. These, in turn, have generated a wealth of scholarly commentary. Thus, this new edition represents a thorough revision of its predecessor and a fresh reevaluation, for purposes of re-editing and reorganizing, of all existing materials. It also constitutes the product of an extensive examination of the recent literature—in an effort to further enrich the notes, comments and questions.

The addition of a new co-author—a first amendment specialist—has led to a complete restructuring and reconceptualization of the free speech materials. Older material has been significantly pruned to make room for the new. The overall strategy has been to pick the great teaching cases and to give them detailed treatment. Material, for example, has been added to principal cases throughout, even to such old standbys as *Beauharnais*, *Chaplinsky*, and *Gitlow*.

The new organization downplays the issues current in the 1950's (e.g., loyalty oaths) and instead requires the student to consider the speech that is *not* protected before moving on to the difficult questions associated with regulating "protected" speech. Freedom of association has risen from an important theme to a major organizational category. The public forum materials have been reduced to teachable proportions, and the movement of some "public forum" materials to an important new section on government support of speech significantly tightens the organization. Finally, new sections have been added on a range of topics, including material addressing government subsidies of speech, the relationship between feminism and pornography, and public and private speech.

The addition of a new co-author has allowed the original authors to devote more attention to their areas of special interest. For example, *Roe v. Wade*, and the debate it stirred over "interpretivist"/"noninterpretivist" constitutional decisionmaking have been the subject of intensive treatment; the chapter on State Power to Tax has been pruned considerably and completely reorganized and reoriented in the light of recent developments; and the sections on Procedural Due Process and The Death Penalty and Related Problems have been greatly enriched. (We are all well aware that many other constitutional law casebooks completely exclude the "death penalty" cases, but we are convinced that they belong in a constitutional law casebook. Although nominally "cruel and unusual punishment" material, the "death penalty" cases are striking illustrations of standards and methodology in due process adjudication).

We have been unable to include developments during the 1985–86 Supreme Court Term. These materials will appear in a supplement that will be published in the summer of 1986. Important developments thereafter will appear in annual supplements.

Case and statute citations, as well as footnotes, of the Court and commentators have been omitted without so specifying; other omissions are indicated by asterisks or by brackets. Numbered footnotes are from the original materials; lettered footnotes are ours. The composition of the Court on any date may be obtained by consulting the Table of Justices in the Appendix, prepared by Professor John J. Cound, who has also compiled basic biographical data on all members of the Court.

Over the years of these six editions, we have become indebted to many teachers (and students) of constitutional law for their valuable suggestions and insights. The contributions to the first edition by Carl A. Auerbach, John J. Cound and Terrance Sandalow persist to date. The book reviews of Robert B. McKay, Lester J. Mazor, Charles W. Quick, Norman Redlich, Christopher D. Stone, William W. Van Alstyne and Lawrence G. Wallace have all been very helpful, as have the criticisms and suggestions of Vincent A. Blasi, Arthur E. Bonfield, William B. Cohen, Samuel D. Estep, Frank I. Goodman, Lino A. Graglia, Jerold H. Israel, Kenneth Karst, Michael E. Smith, Laurence H. Tribe, and Jonathan Varat. Our thanks go also to the able and dedicated student research assistants who contributed so much to this book: Donn Meindertsma and Sandra Seville-Jones. And we are most appreciative of the excellent secretarial assistance provided, too often under great stress, by Vera G. Masur, Margaret McIvor and Faye Smoller.

> WILLIAM B. LOCKHART
> YALE KAMISAR
> JESSE CHOPER
> STEVEN SHIFFRIN

June, 1986

Summary of Contents

*

Table of Contents

Table of Cases

The principal cases are in bold type. Cases cited or discussed are in roman type. References are to Pages.

li

*

Table of Authorities

For authorities from which extracts have been taken, page numbers appear in bold; for others, page numbers appear in roman.

THE AMERICAN CONSTITUTION

CASES—COMMENTS—QUESTIONS

Sixth Edition

*

Chapter 1

NATURE AND SCOPE OF
JUDICIAL REVIEW

SECTION 1. ORIGINS, EARLY CHALLENGES,
AND CONTINUING CONTROVERSY

"Whoever hath an absolute authority to interpret any written or spoken laws, it is he who is truly the lawgiver, to all intents and purposes, and not the person who first spoke or wrote them."

—Bishop Hoadly's Sermon,
preached before the King,
1717.

MARBURY v. MADISON
1 Cranch 137, 2 L.Ed. 60 (1803).

[Thomas Jefferson, an Anti-Federalist (or Republican), who defeated John Adams, a Federalist, in the presidential election of 1800, was to take office on March 4, 1801. On January 20, 1801, Adams, the defeated incumbent, nominated John Marshall, Adams' Secretary of State, as fourth Chief Justice of the United States. Marshall assumed office on February 4 but continued to serve as Secretary of State until the end of the Adams administration. During February, the Federalist Congress passed (1) the Circuit Court Act, which, inter alia, doubled the number of federal judges and (2) the Organic Act which authorized appointment of 42 justices-of-the-peace in the District of Columbia. Senate confirmation of Adams' "midnight" appointees, virtually all Federalists, was completed on March 3. Their commissions were signed by Adams and sealed by Acting Secretary of State Marshall, but due to time pressures, several for the justices-of-the-peace (including that of William Marbury) remained undelivered when Jefferson assumed the presidency the next day. Jefferson ordered his new Secretary of State, James Madison, to withhold delivery.

[Late in 1801, Marbury and several others sought a writ of mandamus in the Supreme Court to compel Madison to deliver the commissions. The Court ordered Madison "to show cause why a mandamus should not issue" and the case was set for argument in the 1802 Term.

[While the case was pending, the new Republican Congress—incensed at Adams' efforts to entrench a Federalist judiciary and at the "Federalist" Court's order against a Republican cabinet officer—moved to repeal the Circuit Court Act. Federalist congressmen argued that repeal would be unconstitutional as

1

violative of Art. III's assurance of judicial tenure "during good behavior" and of the Constitution's plan for separation of powers assuring the independence of the Judiciary. It "was in this debate that for the first time since the initiation of the new Government under the Constitution there occurred a serious challenge of the power of the Judiciary to pass upon the constitutionality of Acts of Congress. Hitherto, [it had been the Republicans] who had sustained this power as a desirable curb on Congressional aggression and encroachment on the rights of the States, and they had been loud in their complaints at the failure of the Court to hold the Alien and Sedition laws unconstitutional. Now, however, in 1802, in order to counteract the Federalist argument that the Repeal Bill was unconstitutional and would be so held by the Court, [Republicans] advanced the proposition that the Court did not possess the power." [a]

[The Repeal Law passed early in 1802. To forestall its constitutional challenge in the Supreme Court until the political power of the new administration had been strengthened, Congress also eliminated the 1802 Supreme Court Term. Thus, the Court did not meet between December, 1801 and February, 1803.]

[On] 24th February, the following opinion of the court was delivered by MR. CHIEF JUSTICE MARSHALL: * * *

No cause has been shown, and the present motion is for a mandamus. The peculiar delicacy of this case, the novelty of some of its circumstances, and the real difficulty attending the points which occur in it require a complete exposition of the principles on which the opinion to be given by the court is founded.
* * *

1st. Has the applicant a right to the commission he demands? * * *

Mr. Marbury, [since] his commission was signed by the President and sealed by the Secretary of State, was appointed; and as the law creating the office gave the officer a right to hold for five years, independent of the executive, the appointment was not revocable, but vested in the officer legal rights, which are protected by the laws of his country.

To withhold his commission, therefore, is an act deemed by the court not warranted by law, but violative of a vested legal right.[b] * * *

2dly. If he has a right, and that right has been violated, do the laws of his country afford him a remedy?

The very essence of civil liberty certainly consists in the right of every individual to claim the protection of the laws, whenever he receives an injury. One of the first duties of government is to afford that protection. * * *

The government of the United States has been emphatically termed a government of laws, and not of men. It will certainly cease to deserve this high appellation, if the laws furnish no remedy for the violation of a vested legal right. * * *

[W]here the heads of departments are the political or confidential agents of the executive, merely to execute the will of the president, or rather to act in

a. 1 Warren, *The Supreme Court in United States History* 215 (1922).

b. Consider Van Alstyne, *A Critical Guide to Marbury v. Madison,* 1969 Duke L.J. 1, 8: "[T]here is clearly an 'issue' of sorts which preceded any of those touched upon in the opinion. Specifically, it would appear that Marshall should have recused himself in view of his substantial involvement in the background of this controversy. * * * Proof of the status of Marbury's commission not only involved circumstances within the Chief Justice's personal knowledge, it was furnished in the Supreme Court by Marshall's own younger brother who had been with him in his office when, as Secretary of State, he had made out the commissions."

cases in which the executive possesses a constitutional or legal discretion, nothing can be more perfectly clear than that their acts are only politically examinable. But where a specific duty is assigned by law, and individual rights depend upon the performance of that duty, it seems equally clear that the individual who considers himself injured, has a right to resort to the laws of his country for a remedy.[c] * * *

It remains to be inquired whether,

3dly. He is entitled to the remedy for which he applies? This depends on,

1st. The nature of the writ applied for; and,

2dly. The power of this court.

1st. The nature of the writ. * * *

This writ, if awarded, would be directed to an officer of government, and its mandate to him would be, to use the words of Blackstone, "to do a particular thing therein specified, which appertains to his office and duty, and which the court has previously determined, or at least supposes, to be consonant to right and justice." Or, in the words of Lord Mansfield, the applicant, in this case, has a right to execute an office of public concern, and is kept out of possession of that right.

These circumstances certainly concur in this case.

Still, to render the mandamus a proper remedy, the officer to whom it is to be directed, must be one to whom, on legal principles, such writ may be directed; and the person applying for it must be without any other specific and legal remedy.

1st. With respect to the officer to whom it would be directed. The intimate political relation subsisting between the President of the United States and the heads of departments, necessarily renders any legal investigation of the acts of one of those high officers peculiarly irksome, as well as delicate; and excites some hesitation with respect to the propriety of entering into such investigation. Impressions are often received without much reflection or examination, and it is not wonderful that in such a case as this the assertion, by an individual, of his legal claims in a court of justice, to which claims it is the duty of that court to attend, should at first view be considered by some, as an attempt to intrude into the cabinet, and to intermeddle with the prerogatives of the executive.

It is scarcely necessary for the court to disclaim all pretensions to such a jurisdiction. An extravagance, so absurd and excessive, could not have been entertained for a moment. The province of the court is, solely, to decide on the rights of individuals, not to inquire how the executive, or executive officers, perform duties in which they have a discretion. Questions in their nature political, or which are, by the constitution and laws, submitted to the executive, can never be made in this court.

But [what] is there in the exalted station of the officer, which shall bar a citizen from asserting, in a court of justice, his legal rights, or shall forbid a court to listen to the claim, or to issue a mandamus, directing the performance of a duty, not depending on executive discretion, but on particular acts of congress, and the general principles of law? * * *

---

c. Consider Redlich, *The Supreme Court—1833 Term,* 40 N.Y.U.L.Rev. 1, 4 (1965): "[T]he Court could have ruled that, since the President had the power to appoint the judges, he also had the power to deliver the commissions which was in a sense the final act of appointment. Viewed as a component of the act of appointment, the delivery of the commissions could have simply been considered as lying within the discretion of the President."

This, then, is a plain case for a mandamus, either to deliver the commission, or a copy of it from the record; and it only remains to be inquired,

Whether it can issue from this court.

The act to establish the judicial courts of the United States authorizes the supreme court "to issue writs of mandamus, in cases warranted by the principles and usages of law, to any courts appointed, or persons holding office, under the authority of the United States." [d]

The secretary of state, being a person holding an office under the authority of the United States, is precisely within the letter of the description; and if this court is not authorized to issue a writ of mandamus to such an officer, it must be because the law is unconstitutional, and therefore absolutely incapable of conferring the authority, and assigning the duties which its words purport to confer and assign. * * *

In the distribution of [the judicial power of the United States] it is declared that "the supreme court shall have original jurisdiction in all cases affecting ambassadors, other public ministers and consuls, and those in which a state shall be a party. In all other cases, the supreme court shall have appellate jurisdiction."

It has been insisted, at the bar, that as the original grant of jurisdiction, to the supreme and inferior courts, is general, and the clause, assigning original jurisdiction to the supreme court, contains no negative or restrictive words, the power remains to the legislature, to assign original jurisdiction to that court in other cases than those specified in the article which has been recited; provided those cases belong to the judicial power of the United States.

If it had been intended to leave it in the discretion of the legislature to apportion the judicial power between the supreme and inferior courts according to the will of that body, it would certainly have been useless to have proceeded further than to have defined the judicial power, and the tribunals in which it should be vested. The subsequent part of the section is mere surplusage, is

---

d. § 13 of the Judiciary Act of 1789 provided: "That the Supreme Court shall have exclusive jurisdiction of all controversies of a civil nature, where a state is a party, except between a state and its citizens; and except also between a state and citizens of other states, or aliens, in which latter case it shall have original but not exclusive jurisdiction. And shall have exclusively all such jurisdiction of suits or proceedings against ambassadors or other public ministers, or their domestics, or domestic servants, as a court of law can have or exercise consistently with the law of nations; and original, but not exclusive jurisdiction of all suits brought by ambassadors or other public ministers, or in which a consul, or vice consul, shall be a party. And the trial of issues of fact in the Supreme Court in all actions at law against citizens of the United States shall be by jury. The Supreme Court shall also have appellate jurisdiction from the circuit courts and courts of the several states, in the cases hereinafter specially provided for; and shall have power to issue writs of prohibition to the district courts, when proceeding as courts of admiralty and maritime jurisdiction, and writs of mandamus, in cases warranted by the principles and usages of law, to any courts appointed, or persons holding office under the authority of the United States."

Consider Van Alstyne, supra, at 15: "Textually, the provision regarding mandamus says nothing expressly as to whether it is part of original or appellate jurisdiction or both, and the clause itself does not speak at all of 'conferring jurisdiction' on the court. The grant of 'power' to issue the writ, however, is juxtaposed with the section of appellate jurisdiction and, in fact, follows the general description of appellate jurisdiction in the same sentence, being separated only by a semicolon. No textual mangling is required to confine it to appellate jurisdiction. Moreover, no mangling is required even if it attaches both to original and to appellate jurisdiction, not as an enlargement of either, but simply as a specification of power which the Court is authorized to use in cases which are *otherwise* appropriately under consideration. Since this case is not otherwise within the specified type of original jurisdiction (e.g., it is not a case in which a state is a party or a case against an ambassador), it should be dismissed."

entirely without meaning, if such is to be the construction. If congress remains at liberty to give this court appellate jurisdiction, where the constitution has declared their jurisdiction shall be original; and original jurisdiction where the constitution has declared it shall be appellate; the distribution of jurisdiction, made in the constitution, is form without substance.

Affirmative words are often, in their operation, negative of other objects than those affirmed; and in this case, a negative or exclusive sense must be given to them, or they have no operation at all.

It cannot be presumed that any clause in the constitution is intended to be without effect; and, therefore, such a construction is inadmissible, unless the words require it. * * *

The authority, therefore, given to the Supreme Court, by the Act establishing the judicial courts of the United States, to issue writs of mandamus to public officers, appears not to be warranted by the Constitution;[e] and it becomes necessary to inquire whether a jurisdiction so conferred can be exercised.

The question whether an Act repugnant to the Constitution can become the law of the land, is a question deeply interesting to the United States; but, happily, not of an intricacy proportioned to its interest. It seems only necessary to recognize certain principles, supposed to have been long and well established, to decide it.

That the people have an original right to establish, for their future government, such principles as, in their opinion, shall most conduce to their own happiness, is the basis on which the whole American fabric has been erected. The exercise of this original right is a very great exertion; nor can it nor ought it to be frequently repeated. The principles, therefore, so established, are deemed fundamental. And as the authority from which they proceed is supreme, and can seldom act, they are designed to be permanent.

This original and supreme will organizes the government, and assigns to different departments their respective powers. It may either stop here, or establish certain limits not to be transcended by those departments.

The government of the United States is of the latter description. The powers of the legislature are defined and limited; and that those limits may not be mistaken, or forgotten, the constitution is written. To what purpose are powers limited, and to what purpose is that limitation committed to writing, if these limits may, at any time, be passed by those intended to be restrained? The distinction between a government with limited and unlimited powers is abolished, if those limits do not confine the persons on whom they are imposed, and if acts prohibited and acts allowed, are of equal obligation. It is a proposition too plain to be contested, that the constitution controls any legislative act repugnant to it; or, that the legislature may alter the constitution by an ordinary act.

Between these alternatives there is no middle ground. The constitution is either a superior paramount law, unchangeable by ordinary means, or it is on a level with ordinary legislative acts, and, like other acts, is alterable when the legislature shall please to alter it.

If the former part of the alternative be true, then a legislative act contrary to the constitution is not law: if the latter part be true, then written constitutions are absurd attempts, on the part of the people, to limit a power in its own nature illimitable.

---

e. By Marshall's interpretation of Art. III, may Congress authorize the Court to exercise appellate jurisdiction in cases involving foreign consuls? See *Bors v. Preston,* 111 U.S. 252, 4 S.Ct. 407, 28 L.Ed. 419 (1884).

Certainly all those who have framed written constitutions contemplate them as forming the fundamental and paramount law of the nation, and consequently, the theory of every such government must be, that an act of the legislature, repugnant to the constitution, is void.

This theory is essentially attached to a written constitution, and is, consequently, to be considered, by this court, as one of the fundamental principles of our society. It is not therefore to be lost sight of in the further consideration of this subject.

If an act of the legislature, repugnant to the Constitution, is void, does it, notwithstanding its invalidity, bind the courts, and oblige them to give it effect? Or, in other words, though it be not law, does it constitute a rule as operative as if it was a law? This would be to overthrow in fact what was established in theory; and would seem, at first view, an absurdity too gross to be insisted on. It shall, however, receive a more attentive consideration.

It is emphatically the province and duty of the judicial department to say what the law is. Those who apply the rule to particular cases, must of necessity expound and interpret that rule. If two laws conflict with each other, the courts must decide on the operation of each.

So if a law be in opposition to the constitution; if both the law and the constitution apply to a particular case, so that the court must either decide that case conformably to the law, disregarding the constitution; or conformably to the constitution, disregarding the law; the court must determine which of these conflicting rules governs the case. This is of the very essence of judicial duty.

If, then, the courts are to regard the constitution, and the constitution is superior to any ordinary act of the legislature, the constitution, and not such ordinary act, must govern the case to which they both apply.

Those then who controvert the principle that the constitution is to be considered in court, as a paramount law, are reduced to the necessity of maintaining that courts must close their eyes on the constitution, and see only the law.

This doctrine would subvert the very foundation of all written constitutions. It would declare that an Act which, according to the principles and theory of our government, is entirely void, is yet, in practice, completely obligatory. It would declare that if the legislature shall do what is expressly forbidden, such Act, notwithstanding the express prohibition, is in reality effectual. It would be giving to the legislature a practical and real omnipotence, with the same breath which professes to restrict their powers within narrow limits. It is prescribing limits, and declaring that those limits may be passed at pleasure.

That it thus reduces to nothing what we have deemed the greatest improvement on political institutions, a written constitution, would of itself be sufficient, in America, where written constitutions have been viewed with so much reverence, for rejecting the construction. But the peculiar expressions of the Constitution of the United States furnish additional arguments in favor of its rejection.

The judicial power of the United States is extended to all cases arising under the Constitution.

Could it be the intention of those who gave this power, to say that in using it the Constitution should not be looked into? That a case arising under the Constitution should be decided without examining the instrument under which it arises?

This is too extravagant to be maintained.

In some cases, then, the Constitution must be looked into by the judges. And if they can open it at all, what part of it are they forbidden to read or to obey?

There are many other parts of the Constitution which serve to illustrate this subject.

It is declared that "no tax or duty shall be laid on articles exported from any State." Suppose a duty on the export of cotton, of tobacco, or of flour; and a suit instituted to recover it. Ought judgment to be rendered in such a case? Ought the judges to close their eyes on the Constitution, and only see the law?

The Constitution declares "that no bill of attainder or ex post facto law shall be passed."

If, however, such a bill should be passed, and a person should be prosecuted under it, must the court condemn to death those victims whom the Constitution endeavors to preserve?

"No person," says the Constitution, "shall be convicted of treason unless on the testimony of two witnesses to the same overt act, or on confession in open court."

Here the language of the Constitution is addressed especially to the courts. It prescribes, directly for them, a rule of evidence not to be departed from. If the legislature should change that rule, and declare one witness, or a confession out of court, sufficient for conviction, must the constitutional principle yield to the legislative act?

From these, and many other selections which might be made, it is apparent, that the framers of the constitution contemplated that instrument as a rule for the government of courts, as well as of the legislature.

Why otherwise does it direct the judges to take an oath to support it? This oath certainly applies in an especial manner, to their conduct in their official character. How immoral to impose it on them, if they were to be used as the instruments, and the knowing instruments, for violating what they swear to support!

The oath of office, too, imposed by the legislature, is completely demonstrative of the legislative opinion on this subject. It is in these words: "I do solemnly swear that I will administer justice without respect to persons, and do equal right to the poor and to the rich; and that I will faithfully and impartially discharge all the duties incumbent on me as _____, according to the best of my abilities and understanding agreeably to the constitution and laws of the United States."

Why does a judge swear to discharge his duties agreeably to the constitution of the United States, if that constitution forms no rule for his government? If it is closed upon him, and cannot be inspected by him?

If such be the real state of things, this is worse than solemn mockery. To prescribe, or to take this oath, becomes equally a crime.

It is also not entirely unworthy of observation, that in declaring what shall be the supreme law of the land, the constitution itself is first mentioned; and not the laws of the United States generally, but those only which shall be made in pursuance of the constitution, have that rank.

Thus, the particular phraseology of the Constitution of the United States confirms and strengthens the principle, supposed to be essential to all written constitutions, that a law repugnant to the constitution is void; and that courts, as well as other departments, are bound by that instrument.

The rule must be discharged.[f]

"We are under a Constitution, but the Constitution is what the judges say it is."

—Charles Evans Hughes,
Speech, 1907.

Comments and Questions

Further Historical Context

CHARLES WARREN, 1 *The Supreme Court in United States History,* 232, 242–43 (1922): "Contemporary writings make it very clear that the Republicans attacked the decision, not so much because it sustained the power of the Court to determine the validity of Congressional legislation, as because it enounced the doctrine that the Court might issue mandamus to a Cabinet official who was acting by direction of the President. In other words, Jefferson's antagonism to Marshall and the Court at that time was due more to his resentment at the alleged invasion of his Executive prerogative than to any so-called 'judicial usurpation' of the field of Congressional authority. [It] seems plain [that Marshall might] have construed the language of the section of the Judiciary Act [to escape the necessity] to pass upon its constitutionality. Marshall naturally felt that in view of the recent attacks on judicial power it was important to have the great principle firmly established, and undoubtedly he welcomed the opportunity of fixing the precedent in a case in which his action would necessitate a decision in favor of his political opponents."

MORRIS COHEN, *The Faith of a Liberal* 178–80 (1946) (written in 1938): "The section of [the] Act of 1789 which Marshall declared unconstitutional had been drawn up by Ellsworth, his predecessor as Chief Justice, and by others who a short time before had been the very members of the constitutional convention that had drafted its judicial provisions. It was signed by George Washington who had presided over the deliberations of that Convention. Fourteen years later, John Marshall by implication accused his predecessor on the bench, the members of Congress such as James Madison, the Father of the Constitution, and President Washington, of either not understanding the Constitution (which some of them had drawn up), or else wilfully disregarding it. [To] a secular historian, it is obvious that John Marshall was motivated by the fear of impeachment if he granted the mandamus or dared to declare the Republican Judiciary Repeal Act of 1802 unconstitutional. Having thus refused aid to his fellow Federalists ousted from offices created for them by a 'lame duck' congress, he resorted to a line of sophistical dicta to get even with his political enemy, as indeed he did also in the *Aaron Burr* case. In his letter to his colleague Chase, Marshall offered to abandon judicial supremacy in the interpretation of the Constitution in return for security against impeachment." [g]

f. Six days later, the Circuit Court Act Repeal Law was held to be constitutional. *Stuart v. Laird,* 5 U.S. (1 Cranch) 299, 2 L.Ed. 115 (1803). After *Marbury,* the Court did not hold an act of Congress unconstitutional until *Dred Scott v. Sandford,* 60 U.S. (19 How.) 393, 15 L.Ed. 691 (1857).

g. In 1804, the House impeached Justice Chase due, inter alia, to what the Republicans believed to be Chase's partisan Federalist ac-

Text of the Constitution

Is the doctrine of "judicial review," which gives the Court power to declare an act of a coordinate branch of the government unconstitutional, compelled because a contrary rule "would subvert the very foundation of all written constitutions"?

WILLIAM VAN ALSTYNE, *A Critical Guide to Marbury v. Madison,* 1969 Duke L.J. 1, 17: "[E]ven in Marshall's time (and to a great extent today), a number of nations maintained written constitutions and yet gave national legislative acts the full force of positive law without providing any constitutional check to guarantee the compatibility of those acts with their constitutions [e.g.,] France, Switzerland, and Belgium (and to some extent Great Britain where Magna Carta and other written instruments are roughly described as the constitution but where acts of Parliament are not reviewable)." [h]

Does the "judges' oath" provision (Art. VI, cl. 3) furnish the necessary textual support for the doctrine of judicial review?

JUSTICE GIBSON, dissenting in *Eakin v. Raub,* 12 S. & R. 330 (Pa.1825): [i] "The oath to support the Constitution is not peculiar to the judges, but is taken indiscriminately by every officer of the government, and is designed rather as a test of the political principles of the man, than to bind the officer in the discharge of his duty: otherwise, it were difficult to determine, what operation it is to have in the case of a recorder of deeds, for instance, who, in execution of his office, has nothing to do with the Constitution. But granting it to relate to the official conduct of the judge, as well as every other officer, and not to his political principles, still, it must be understood in reference to supporting the Constitution, only as far as that may be involved in his official duty; and consequently, if his official duty does not comprehend an inquiry into the authority of the legislature, neither does his oath. * * *

"But do not the judges do a positive act in violation of the Constitution, when they give effect to an unconstitutional law? Not if the law has been passed according to the forms established in the Constitution. The fallacy of the question is, in supposing that the judiciary adopts the acts of the legislature as its own; whereas, the enactment of a law and the interpretation of it are not concurrent acts, and as the judiciary is not required to concur in the enactment, neither is it in the breach of the constitution which may be the consequence of the enactment; the fault is imputable to the legislature, and on it the responsibility exclusively rests."

tivities and statements both on and off the Bench. After a lengthy trial in the Senate, the constitutional majority to convict was not obtained. It was generally assumed that, if the effort had been successful, Marshall and other Federalist judges would suffer the same fate. See generally 1 Warren, supra, ch. 6. For a further account of *Marbury,* see 3 Beveridge, *The Life of John Marshall* 105–156 (1919).

h. Consider Cohen, supra, at 185: "Nor is it necessary to consider in detail the argument that this power is necessary for a federal system. The Swiss constitution is a perfect example of a federal system without the judiciary having such power. The late Justice Holmes said, 'I do not think the United States would come to an end if we lost our power to declare an Act of Congress void. I do think the Union would be imperiled if we could not make that declaration as to the laws of the several states.'"

For discussion of the modern growth of various forms of judicial review in other countries—Australia, Austria, Canada, Cyprus, Denmark, Germany, India, Italy, Japan, Norway, Sweden, Turkey, Yugoslavia—see Cappelletti, *Judicial Review in Comparative Perspective,* 58 Calif.L.Rev. 1017 (1970).

i. This opinion is widely regarded as the most effective answer of the era to Marshall's reasoning supporting judicial review.

What of Art. III, § 2, cl. 1, extending "the judicial Power" "to *all* cases * * * arising under this Constitution"? See Bickel, *The Least Dangerous Branch* 5–6 (1962).

What of the supremacy clause (Art. VI, cl. 2)? Compare Wechsler, *Toward Neutral Principles of Constitutional Law,* 73 Harv.L.Rev. 1, 3–5 (1959), with Van Alstyne, supra, at 20–22.[l]

The Court as "Final" Arbiter

THOMAS JEFFERSON, writing in 1804, 8 *The Writings of Thomas Jefferson* 310 (1897): "The Judges, believing the [Sedition Law] constitutional, had a right to pass a sentence of fine and imprisonment; because that power was placed in their hands by the Constitution. But the Executive, believing the law to be unconstitutional, was bound to remit the execution of it; because that power has been confided to him by the Constitution. The instrument meant that its co-ordinate branches should be checks on each other. But the opinion which gives to the Judges the right to decide what laws are constitutional, and what not, not only for themselves in their own sphere of action, but for the Legislative and Executive also in their spheres, would make the Judiciary a despotic branch."

———

ANDREW JACKSON, veto message in 1832 on act to recharter Bank of United States (the constitutionality of which had earlier been upheld by the Court), 2 Richardson, *Messages and Papers of the Presidents* 576, 581–82 (1900): "It is as much the duty of the House of Representatives, of the Senate, and of the President to decide upon the constitutionality of any bill or resolution which may be presented to them for passage or approval as it is of the supreme judges when it may be brought before them for judicial decision. The opinion of the judges has no more authority over Congress than the opinion of Congress has over the judges, and on that point the President is independent of both. The authority of the Supreme Court must not, therefore, be permitted to control the Congress or the Executive when acting in their legislative capacities, but to have only such influence as the force of their reasoning may deserve."

———

l. Much has been written on the matter of "historical original intent" in respect to judicial review—generally examining pre-Convention judicial precedents in England and the colonies, statements of the framers both within and outside the Constitutional Convention (see especially Alexander Hamilton in Nos. 78 and 80 of *The Federalist* (1788)), and debate during the ratification period—arriving at conflicting conclusions. See, e.g., Beard, *The Supreme Court and the Constitution* (1912); Berger, *Congress v. The Supreme Court* (1969); Boudin, *Government by Judiciary* (1932); Corwin, *The Doctrine of Judicial Review* (1914); Crosskey, *Politics and the Constitution in the History of the United States* (1953); Goebel, *History of the Supreme Court of the United States: Antecedents and Beginnings to 1801* (1971); Haines, *The American Doctrine of Judicial Supremacy* (2d ed. 1932); Nelson, *Changing Conceptions of Judicial Review: The* *Evolution of Constitutional Theory in the States, 1790–1860,* 120 U.Pa.L.Rev. 1166 (1972). Warren, *Congress, the Constitution, and the Supreme Court* (1925). For brief discussion see Levy, *Judicial Review, History, and Democracy: An Introduction,* in Judicial Review and the Supreme Court 1–12 (1967); Kernochan, *On Constitutionalism and the Antecedents of Judicial Review,* in Dowling & Gunther, Constitutional Law 19–31 (7th ed. 1965). For the view that "strict intentionalism" is not a "tenable approach to constitutional decisionmaking," see Brest, *The Misconceived Quest for the Original Understanding,* 60 B.U.L.Rev. 204 (1980).

For review of the broader historical setting, see Bailyn, *The Ideological Origins of the American Revolution* (1967); Wood, *The Creation of the American Republic, 1776–1787* (1969).

ABRAHAM LINCOLN, inaugural address in 1861, 2 Richardson, supra, at 5, 9–10: "I do not forget the position assumed by some that constitutional questions are to be decided by the Supreme Court, nor do I deny that such decisions must be binding in any case upon the parties to a suit as to the object of that suit, while they are also entitled to very high respect and consideration in all parallel cases by all other departments of the Government. And while it is obviously possible that such decision may be erroneous in any given case, still the evil effect following it, being limited to that particular case, with the chance that it may be overruled and never become a precedent for other cases, can better be borne than could the evils of a different practice. At the same time, the candid citizen must confess that if the policy of the Government upon vital questions affecting the whole people is to be irrevocably fixed by decisions of the Supreme Court, the instant they are made in ordinary litigation between parties in personal actions the people will have ceased to be their own rulers, having to that extent practically resigned their Government into the hands of that eminent tribunal. Nor is there in this view any assault upon the court or the judges. It is a duty from which they may not shrink to decide cases properly brought before them, and it is no fault of theirs if others seek to turn their decisions to political purposes."

Are these views inconsistent with *Marbury?* Does *Marbury* decide anything more than that *"the Court may refuse to give effect to an act of Congress where the act pertains to the judicial power itself"?* Van Alstyne, supra, at 34. Than that the Court claimed the power of judicial review "only in the defensive sense of safeguarding the Court's original jurisdiction from congressional enlargement"? Strong, *Judicial Review: A Tri-Dimensional Concept of Administrative-Constitutional Law,* 69 W.Va.L.Rev. 111, 249 (1967).

LEARNED HAND, *The Bill of Rights* 11–15 (1958): "[L]et us try to imagine what would have been the result if the power [of judicial review] did not exist. There were two alternatives, each prohibitive, I submit. One was that the decision of the first 'Department' before which an issue arose should be conclusive whenever it arose later. That doctrine, coupled with its conceded power over the purse, would have made Congress substantially omnipotent, for by far the greater number of issues that could arise would depend upon its prior action.

* * *

"As Hamilton intimated, every legislator is under constant pressure from groups of constituents whom it does not satisfy to say, 'Although I think what you want is right and that you ought to have it, I cannot bring myself to believe that it is within my constitutional powers.' Such scruples are not convincing to those whose interests are at stake; and the voters at large will not usually care enough about preserving 'the balance of the Constitution' to offset the votes of those whose interests will be disappointed. [But] the second alternative would have been even worse, for under it each 'Department' would have been free to decide constitutional issues as it thought right, regardless of any earlier decision of the others. Thus it would have been the President's privilege, and indeed his duty, to execute only those statutes that seemed to him to be constitutional, regardless even of a decision of the Supreme Court. The courts would have entered such judgments as seemed to them consonant with the Constitution; but neither the President, nor Congress, would have been bound to enforce them if he or it disagreed, and without their help the judgments would have been waste paper.

"For centuries it has been an accepted canon in interpretation of documents to interpolate into the text such provisions, though not expressed, as are essential to prevent the defeat of the venture at hand; and this applies with especial force to the interpretation of constitutions, which, since they are designed to cover a great multitude of necessarily unforeseen occasions, must be cast in general language, unless they are constantly amended. If so, it was altogether in keeping with established practice for the Supreme Court to assume an authority to keep the states, Congress, and the President within their prescribed powers. Otherwise the government could not proceed as planned; and indeed would almost certainly have foundered, as in fact it almost did over that very issue.

"However, since this power is not a logical deduction from the structure of the Constitution but only a practical condition upon its successful operation, it need not be exercised whenever a court sees, or thinks that it sees, an invasion of the Constitution."

May a Congressman vote against a bill because he believes it to be unconstitutional even though the Court has held to the contrary? May the President veto such a bill on this ground? If the Court has upheld the constitutionality of a federal criminal statute, may a subsequent President grant pardons to all persons convicted under it (see Art. II, § 2, cl. 1)?

COOPER v. AARON (1958), set forth more fully, Ch. 10, Sec. 2, IV: "Article VI of the Constitution makes the Constitution the 'supreme Law of the Land.' In 1803, [*Marbury*] declared the basic principle that the federal judiciary is supreme in the exposition of the law of the Constitution, and that principle has ever since been respected by this Court and the Country as a permanent and indispensable feature of our constitutional system. [Every] state legislator and executive and judicial officer is solemnly committed by oath taken pursuant to Art. VI, ¶ 3 'to support this Constitution.' * * * Chief Justice Marshall spoke for a unanimous Court in saying that: 'if the legislatures of the several states may, at will, annul the judgments of the courts of the United States, and destroy the rights acquired under those judgments, the constitution itself becomes a solemn mockery * * *.' *United States v. Peters,* 5 Cranch 115, 136. A Governor who asserts a power to nullify a federal court order is similarly restrained." [m]

Cooper involved the refusal of Arkansas officials to abide by federal court decrees requiring school desegregation. In contrast, if the Court *upholds* the constitutionality of a state law, may that state's supreme court subsequently rule that the state law violates the Constitution? Would the state court's ruling "annul the judgment" of the Supreme Court? See Tribe, *American Constitutional Law* 27–33 (1978).

Comparative Competence and "Expertise"

HART & WECHSLER'S *The Federal Courts and the Federal System* 82 (2d ed. 1973): "Congress and the President can obviously contribute to the sound interpretation of the Constitution. But are they, or can they be, so organized [as] to be able, without aid from the courts, to build up a body of coherent and intelligible constitutional principle, and to carry public conviction that these

---

m. For criticism and defense of this "judicial supremacy" analysis, see Farber, *The Supreme Court and the Rule of Law: Cooper v. Aaron Revisited,* 1982 U.Ill.L.Rev. 387.

principles are being observed? In respect of experience and temperament of personnel? Of procedure for decision? Of means of recording grounds of decision? Of opportunity for close examination of particular questions?"

CLIFTON McCLESKEY, *Judicial Review in a Democracy: A Dissenting Opinion,* 3 Hous.L.Rev. 354, 360–61 (1966): "Can we really be sure that it was Marshall or Taney rather than Clay or Webster who did the better job of articulating values? Which of the Civil War Justices excelled Lincoln in voicing the hopes and goals of the republic? Are we to believe that Woodrow Wilson had a poorer grasp of the principles of American government than the Supreme Court Justices of his era? Which Justice in the 1920's gave better tongue than Norris or LaFollette to the American dream? Which Justice before or after the shift of 1937 was better than Franklin Roosevelt at communicating our ideals? [Further,] it appears reasonably clear that a background of political experience for Supreme Court Justices is the prevalent pattern. This not only casts doubt on the thesis that there is something peculiar to the judicial process that brings out these noble traits, but also suggests that even without judicial review the nation would have had the benefit of the wisdom and insights of these persons."

MARTIN SHAPIRO, *Freedom of Speech: The Supreme Court and Judicial Review* 29–30 (1966): "Congressional statutes [are] the product of a series of marginal adjustments and compromises among various semi-independent groups. It is nearly impossible to interject black and white questions like constitutionality into the early stages of such a process. And when the process has been so nearly completed that a bill reaches the final debate and voting stage, so many commitments have already been made that the interjection of a constitutional issue would not only be futile but in many instances appear to be a traitorous repudiation of pre-established agreements. It is, therefore, highly probable that considerations of constitutionality could only take their place among the multitude of other considerations which acquire various weights at various stages of the negotiations depending on how important they appear to any given legislative power holder."

The Standard of Review

JAMES THAYER, *The Origin and Scope of the American Doctrine of Constitutional Law,* 7 Harv.L.Rev. 129, 143–44 (1893): "[The Court] can only disregard the Act [of the legislature] when those who have the right to make laws have not merely made a mistake, but have made a very clear one,—so clear that it is not open to rational question. That is the standard of duty to which the courts bring legislative Acts; that is the test which they apply,—not merely their own judgment as to constitutionality, but their conclusion as to what judgment is permissible to another department which the constitution has charged with the duty of making it. This rule recognizes that, having regard to the great, complex, ever-unfolding exigencies of government, much which will seem unconstitutional to one man, or body of men, may reasonably not seem so to another; that the constitution often admits of different interpretations; that there is often a range of choice and judgment; that in such cases the constitution does not impose upon the legislature any one specific opinion, but leaves open this range of choice; and that whatever choice is rational is constitutional."

ALEXANDER BICKEL, supra, at 37–41: " 'Taken seriously,' Felix S. Cohen wrote in a later day, 'this conception makes of our courts lunacy commissions sitting in judgment upon the mental capacity of legislators and, occasionally, of judicial brethren.' That is cleverly put, but the principle of the constitutional rationality of legislation is nevertheless meaningful [in respect to certain types of issues]. The rule of the clear mistake aims at accommodation with the theory of representative democracy. It proceeds from the realization, in the words of Mr. Justice Frankfurter, that courts 'are not representative bodies. They are not designed to be a good reflex of a democratic society.' Therefore the rule is meant to limit the area of judicial policymaking, keeping the judicial function distinct from the legislative and thus capable of being justified. It is a conceptual tool for distilling out of a typical public issue one element of principle, as distinguished from a number of allowable choices that may be made on grounds of expediency. But the rule does not lead by indirection to a total abdication of the power of judicial review. ＊ ＊ ＊

"The relevant distinction [on certain types of questions] is not between rationality and lunacy but between rationality and will, or, perhaps it is meaningful to say, between rationality and uncontrolled emotion. It is not lunatic to take the position that the public service must be kept clear of any taint of disloyalty, and that to exclude from it even possibly innocent persons is to take absolutely no chances. That is a sane and a zealous attitude. But it is not rational; it is not even thoughtful. It is governed by a heightened emotion—anxiety, in this case—and it will not pass the test of a calm judgment resting on allowable inferences drawn from common human experience. Such a judgment will vary with what is known of relevant human experience. It must be an informed judgment, and it may change as it becomes better informed. But it will discriminate between arbitrary guesses and calculations of probability. In any event, this is the Court's independent judgment to make, and unless one takes a cynical view of the human capacity to reason, it is a possible judgment and one that will answer to descriptions of 'correct' or 'erroneous.' "

Whatever the deference owed by the Court to Congress (or the President), is the same deference due federal administrative officials? State legislatures? City councils? Local police officers?

Judicial Review and Democracy

ALEXANDER BICKEL, supra, at 16–20: "The root difficulty is that judicial review is a counter-majoritarian force in our system. [W]hen the Supreme Court declares unconstitutional a legislative act or the action of an elected executive, it thwarts the will of representatives of the actual people of the here and now; it exercises control, not in behalf of the prevailing majority, but against it. That [is] the reason the charge can be made that judicial review is undemocratic.

"Most assuredly, no democracy operates by taking continuous nose counts on the broad range of daily governmental activities. ＊ ＊ ＊ Nevertheless, although democracy does not mean constant reconsideration of decisions once made, it does mean that a representative majority has the power to accomplish a reversal. This power is of the essence, and no less so because it is often merely held in reserve.

"It is true, of course, that the process of reflecting the will of a popular majority in the legislature is deflected by various inequalities of representation and by all sorts of institutional habits and characteristics, which perhaps tend most often in favor of inertia.[p]   Yet, impurities and imperfections, if such they be, in one part of the system are no argument for total departure from the desired norm in another part.   *   *   *

"No doubt ['interest' or 'pressure groups'] operate forcefully on the electoral process, and no doubt they seek and gain access to and an effective share in the legislative and executive decisional process.   Perhaps they constitute also, in some measure, an impurity or imperfection.   But no one has claimed that they have been able to capture the governmental process except by combining in some fashion, and thus capturing or constituting (are not the two verbs synonymous?) a majority.   They often tend themselves to be majoritarian in composition and to be subject to broader majoritarian influences.   And the price of what they sell or buy in the legislature is determined in the biennial or quadrennial electoral marketplace.   *   *   * Judicial review works counter to this characteristic.

"It therefore does not follow from the complex nature of a democratic system that, because admirals and generals and the members, say, of the Federal Reserve Board or of this or that administrative agency are not electorally responsible, judges who exercise the power of judicial review need not be responsible either, and in neither case is there a serious conflict with democratic theory.   For admirals and generals and the like are most often responsible to officials who are themselves elected and through whom the line runs directly to a majority.   What is more significant, the policies they make are or should be interstitial or technical only and are reversible by legislative majorities *   *   *—a fact of great consequence.   Nor will it do to liken judicial review to the general lawmaking function of judges.   In the latter aspect, judges are indeed something like administrative officials, for their decisions are also reversible by any legislative majority—and not infrequently they are reversed.[q]   Judicial review, however, is the power to apply and construe the Constitution in matters of the greatest moment, against the wishes of a legislative majority, which is, in turn, powerless to affect the judicial decision."

JESSE CHOPER, *The Supreme Court and the Political Branches: Democratic Theory and Practice,* 122 U.Pa.L.Rev. 810, 830–32 (1974): "In the main, the effect of judicial review in ruling legislation unconstitutional is to nullify the finished product of the lawmaking process.   It is the very rare Supreme Court decision on constitutionality that affirmatively mandates the undertaking of government action.   To make the point in another way, when the Supreme

p. For a forceful position "that there can be no automatic and blanket equation of Congress or the Executive branch with the voice of the people," see Shapiro, supra, at 17–25. Consider Krislov, *The Supreme Court and Political Freedom* 20 (1968): "If one analyzes the actual rules of behavior in the so-called democratic units of government, we find that they also have mixed aspects, with the possibility— sometimes the actuality—of minority control. The power of the Rules Committee, the filibuster, and the Senate are obvious shortcomings; [the] operational consequences of seniority, and the population base of districts likely to maintain continuity in representation are more veiled aspects."   See also Kommers, *Professor Kurland, The Supreme Court, and Political Science,* 15 J.Pub.L. 230 (1966).

q. Compare Bishin, *Judicial Review in Democratic Theory,* 50 So.Cal.L.Rev. 1099, 1110 (1977): "Closer examination suggests [that] not all of the decisions that such office-holders make can, in fact or theory, be reversed by majoritarian action.   [It] must be remembered [that] Congress—especially the Senate—is so structured that representatives of only a minority of the people can prevent the passage of legislation which would overturn prior decisions *   *   *.   Wherever the position of such a minority coincides with the [judge's or administrative officer's] position, therefore, the Constitution gives the principle of reversibility no effect at all."

Court finds legislative acts unconstitutional it holds invalid only those enactments that have survived the many hurdles fixed between incipient proposals and standing law.

"The significance of this [is] that most of the antimajoritarian elements that have been found in the American legislative process [are] negative ones. They work to *prevent* the translation of popular wishes into governing rules rather than to *produce* laws that are contrary to majority sentiment. [S]enators representing only fifteen percent of the population may hold sway in the upper house; but their real impact (as is obviously the case with the filibuster as well) is to halt ultimate action rather than facilitate it. For the enactment of law also requires the concurrence of the lower [house]. Furthermore, within each legislative chamber, the ability of the committees and their chairmen and minority members—and frequently of the lobbies and other interest groups as well—to circumvent the majority will of the assembly is most saliently manifested in obstructing the process rather than in making laws. The more formidable task usually is not to stall or defeat a proposal but to organize the requisite support among the dispersed powers so as to form a coalition for its passage. * * *

"Thus, although exceptions exist, '[a] distinguishing feature of our system, perhaps impelled by heritage of sectional division and heterogeneity, is that our governmental structure, institutional habits, and political parties with their internal factional divisions, have combined to produce a system in which major programs and major new directions cannot be undertaken unless supported by a fairly broad popular consensus. This normally has been far broader than 51 percent and often bipartisan as well.' [Consequently,] when the Supreme Court, itself without conventional political responsibility, says 'thou shalt not' to acts of Congress, it usually cuts sharply against the grain of majority rule. The relatively few laws that finally overcome the congressional obstacle course generally illustrate the national political branches operating at their majoritarian best while the process of judicial review depicts that element of the Court's work and that exertion of federal authority with the most brittle democratic roots.[59] "

J. SKELLY WRIGHT, *The Role of the Supreme Court in a Democratic Society,* 54 Corn.L.Rev. 1, 11 (1968): "This argument for judicial restraint not only overplays the Court's deviancy but also overstresses its immunity from democratic processes. To begin with, the Justices are appointed by the President, the one elected official whose constituency is the nation as a whole. On the average a new appointment is made every twenty-two months.[40] And, as Justice Frankfurter reminds us, 'Judges are men, not disembodied spirits' who are blind to the political reality among them. Moreover, if the Justices are not themselves sufficiently attuned to the times, Congress can bring reality home to them through its power over the Court's appellate jurisdiction. Indeed, if the Court is too far out of touch with the people, the Congress and the executive can annul its directives simply by refusing to execute them, or the people can do so

---

59. Although no detailed examination of the legislative systems in the states and their political subdivisions has been ventured here, the same conclusion appears to have substantially similar merit in respect to the Court's overturning the laws they produce.

40. See Dahl, *Decision-Making in a Democracy: The Supreme Court as a National Policy Maker,* 6 J.Pub.L. 279, 284–86 (1957).

by constitutional amendment. In sum, although the Court is not politically responsible, it is likely to be politically responsive."[r]

LEONARD LEVY, *Judicial Review, History, and Democracy: An Introduction*, in Judicial Review and the Supreme Court 1, 12 (1967): "Judicial review would never have flourished had the people been opposed to it. They have opposed only its exercise in particular cases, but not the power itself. They have the sovereign power to abolish it outright or hamstring it by constitutional amendment. The President and Congress could bring the Court to heel even by ordinary legislation. The Court's membership, size, funds, staff, rules of procedure, and enforcement agencies are subject to the control of the 'political' branches. Judicial review, in fact, exists by the tacit consent of the governed."

EUGENE ROSTOW, *The Democratic Character of Judicial Review*, 66 Harv. L.Rev. 193, 199–209 (1963): "It is error to insist that no society is democratic unless it has a government of unlimited powers, and that no government is democratic unless its legislature has unlimited powers. Constitutional review by an independent judiciary is a tool of proven use in the American quest for an open society of widely dispersed powers. In a vast country, of mixed population, with widely different regional problems, such an organization of society is the surest base for the hopes of democracy.

"[The] price of judicial independence, [Judge Hand] concludes, is that the judges 'should not have the last word in those basic conflicts of "right and wrong—between whose endless jar justice resides." You may ask what then will become of the fundamental principles of equity and fair play which our constitutions enshrine; and whether I seriously believe that unsupported they will serve merely as counsels of moderation. I do not [know]; but this much I think I do know—that a society so riven that the spirit of moderation is gone, no court *can* save; that a society where that spirit flourishes no court *need* save; that in a society which evades its responsibility by thrusting upon the courts the nurture of that spirit, that spirit in the end will perish.'[s]

"This gloomy and apocalyptic view is a triumph of logic over life. It reflects the dark shadows thrown upon the judiciary by the Court-packing fight of 1937. Judge Hand is preoccupied with a syllogism. The people and the Congress have the naked power to destroy the independence of the courts. Therefore the courts

---

r. See also Deutsch, *Neutrality, Legitimacy, and the Supreme Court: Some Intersections Between Law and Political Science*, 20 Stan.L. Rev. 169 (1968).

s. Hand, *The Contribution of an Independent Judiciary to Civilization*, in The Spirit of Liberty 164 (Dilliard 3d ed. 1960); this chapter originally published in 1942.

Further, consider Thayer, *John Marshall* 106 (1904): "[T]he exercise of [judicial review], even when unavoidable, is always attended with a serious evil, namely, that the correction of legislative mistakes comes from the outside, and the people thus lose the political experience, and the moral education and stimulus that come from fighting the question out in the ordinary way, and correcting their own errors. [The] tendency of a common and easy resort to this great function now lamentably too common, is to dwarf the political capacity of the people, and to deaden its sense of moral responsibility." Compare Franklin Roosevelt, message to Congress in 1935, 4 *The Public Papers and Addresses of Franklin D. Roosevelt* 297–98 (1938): "Manifestly, no one is in a position to give assurance that the proposed act will withstand constitutional tests. [But] the situation is so urgent and the benefits of the legislation so evident that all doubts should be resolved in favor of the bill, leaving to the courts, in an orderly fashion, the ultimate question of constitutionality. * * * I hope your committee will not permit doubts as to constitutionality, however reasonable, to block the suggested legislation."

must avoid arousing the sleeping lion by venturing to construe the broad and sweeping clauses of the Constitution which would 'demand the appraisal and balancing of human values which there are no scales to weigh.' Presumably he would include in this catalogue of forbidden issues problems of freedom of speech, the separation of church and state, and the limits, if any, to which 'the capable, the shrewd or the strong' should 'be allowed to exploit their powers.' Are we to read the last phrase as encompassing the right of habeas corpus, the central civil liberty and the most basic of all protections against the authority of the state? Would it deny the possibility of constitutional review by the courts for laws denying the vote to Negroes, for searches and seizures without warrant, for bills of attainder or test oaths?

"In the first place, the judicial decisions which brought on the storm in 1937 were not in this area at all. They concerned the division of power between the states and the nation,[21] and between Congress and the President [22]—issues which Judge Hand regards as inescapably within the province of the courts and not likely in any event to have 'seismic consequences.' Further, it is important to reiterate the obvious but sometimes forgotten fact that the historic conception of the Supreme Court's duties, however challenged in 1937, prevailed in that struggle. * * *

"The possibility of judicial emasculation by way of popular reaction against constitutional review by the courts has not in fact materialized in more than a century and a half of American experience. When the Court has differed from the Congress and the President in its notions of constitutional [law] time has unfailingly cured the conflicts, such as they were. * * *

"It may of course be true that no court can save a society bent on ruin. But American society is not bent on ruin. It is a body deeply committed in its majorities to the principles of the Constitution and both willing and anxious to form its policy and programs in a constitutional way. Americans are, however, profoundly troubled by fears—intense and real fears, raised by unprecedented dangers and by the conduct of perilous tasks unprecedented in the history of the government. It is difficult for legislators confronting the menace of the world communist movement to reject any proposals which purport to attack communism or to protect the community from it. This does not mean, however, that the President and the Congress would refuse to obey the Supreme Court's rulings on the constitutionality of some of the means with which they have [chosen]. Ruin can come to a society not only from the furious resentments of a crisis. It can be brought about in imperceptible stages by gradually accepting, one after another, immoral solutions for particular problems. The 'relocation camps' conducted during World War II [for] Americans of Japanese descent[t] are the precedent for the proposal that concentration camps be established for citizens suspected of believing in revolutionary ideas. * * *

"Nor, more broadly, is it true as a matter of experience that a vigorous lead from the Supreme Court inhibits or weakens popular responsibility in the same area. The process of forming public opinion in the United States is a continuous one with many participants—Congress, the President, the press, political parties, scholars, pressure groups, and so on. The discussion of problems and the declaration of broad principles by the courts is a vital element in the community

---

21. See, e.g., *United States v. Butler* [set forth, p. 112 infra.].

22. See, e.g., *Schechter Poultry Corp. v. United States* [discussed, p. 81 infra]. See also

Youngstown Sheet & Tube Co. v. Sawyer [set forth, p. 148 infra].

t. See *Korematsu v. United States,* set forth Ch. 10, Sec. 2, I.

experience through which American policy is made. The Supreme Court is, among other things, an educational body, and the Justices are inevitably teachers in a vital national seminar."[u]

ALEXANDER BICKEL, supra, at 24–26, 258: "It is a premise we deduce not merely from the fact of a written constitution but from the history of the race, and ultimately as a moral judgment of the good society, that government should serve not only what we conceive from time to time to be our immediate material needs but also certain enduring values. This in part is what is meant by government under law. * * *

"Men in all walks of public life are able occasionally to perceive this second aspect of public questions. Sometimes they are also able to base their decisions on it; that is one of the things we like to call acting on principle. Often they do not do so, however, particularly when they sit in legislative assemblies. There, when the pressure for immediate results is strong enough and emotions ride high enough, men will ordinarily prefer to act on expediency rather than take the long view. * * * Judges have, or should have, the leisure, the training, and the insulation to follow the ways of the scholar in pursuing the ends of government. This is crucial in sorting out the enduring values of a society * * *. Another advantage that courts have is that questions of principle never carry the same aspect for them as they did for the legislature or the executive. Statutes, after all, deal typically with abstract or dimly foreseen problems. The courts are concerned with the flesh and blood of an actual case. This tends to modify, perhaps to lengthen, everyone's view.[v] * * *

---

u. See also Bishin, supra, at 1136: "Of course, the courts will often be wrong. But their decisions are not irrevocable; in the meantime, their errors nevertheless contribute to understanding. In a sense, the courts become the focus of the trial and error by which the society determines what balance of individual and majority rule it desires. If judicial review did not exist, perhaps a relatively small number of academicians and moralists would involve themselves in the problem of freedom. But it is unlikely that the society generally would engage itself in the process of solving that problem. If this is so, then it is quite arguable that the trial and error process which detractors of judicial review invoke against the institution is one of the strongest arguments for giving courts the power to adjudicate the constitutionality of majority action."

Compare Levy, supra, at 33–34, 36: "[O]ne may say, paraphrasing Rostow in reverse, that it is true as a matter of experience that a vigorous lead from the Supreme Court inhibits or weakens popular responsibility in the areas of liberty, equality, and justice. Bearing in mind that the Court is an institution of enormous prestige whose declaration of principles teaches and leads the nation in the making of public policy, one cannot doubt the pernicious, highly undemocratic influence of the series of decisions in which the Court crippled and voided most of the comprehensive program for protecting the civil rights of Negroes after the Civil War. These decisions paralyzed or supplanted legislative and community action, created bigotry, and played a crucial role in destroying public opinion that favored meeting the challenge of the Negro problem * * *.

"The historian must take the long view of the matter, recalling that the justices on circuit duty enforced the Sedition Act of 1798; that the Fugitive Slave Acts were sustained but the Missouri Compromise and Personal Liberty Laws were invalidated; that the Fourteenth Amendment was turned into a nightmare of injustice for all but corporations; that Congressional statutes to combat the evils of yellow-dog contracts, child labor, and subliminal wages were held unconstitutional; [that] Debs' conviction was sustained under the Espionage Act of 1917 by a unanimous Court in an opinion by Holmes and that President Harding, of all people, pardoned Debs; and so on, ad nauseum."

v. [But, "in dealing with problems of great magnitude and pervasive ramifications, problems with complex roots and unpredictably multiplying complex offshoots," "the judicial process is"] "too remote from conditions, and deals, case by case, with too narrow a slice of reality. It is not accessible to all the varied interests that are in play in any decision of great consequence. It is, very properly, independent. It is passive. It has difficulty controlling the stages by which it approaches a problem. It rushes forward too fast, or it lags;

"Their insulation and the marvelous mystery of time give courts the capacity to appeal to men's better natures, to call forth their aspirations, which may have been forgotten in the moment's hue and cry. This is what Justice Stone called the opportunity for 'the sober second thought.' * * *

"[After the school desegregation decisions, the] southern leaders understood and acted upon an essential truth, which we do not often have occasion to observe * * *. The Supreme Court's law, the southern leaders realized, could not in our system prevail—not merely in the very long run, but within the decade—if it ran counter to deeply felt popular needs or convictions, or even if it was opposed by a determined and substantial minority and received with indifference by the rest of the country. This, in the end, is how and why judicial review is consistent with the theory and practice of political democracy. This is why the Supreme Court is a court of last resort presumptively only."

CLIFTON McCLESKEY, supra, at 357–59, 365: "It is sometimes said that judicial review is compatible with democracy because it cannot really block popular action. [I]t is argued that eventually the will of the people always prevails in spite of any resistance by the judiciary. * * * We have known at least since David Hume that all governments—even the dictatorial ones—rest 'ultimately' on the consent of the governed, but the democratic theory [denies] the propriety of resorting to such a subterfuge—democracy is an attempt to provide popular control here and now, not ultimately. We must therefore reject this justification of judicial review for the same reasons that we would condemn a proposal to schedule national elections only once every quarter century.

"Some proponents of this view, recognizing that judicially-imposed delay is a fact that cannot be denied, have attempted to convert that liability into an asset. Such frustration of popular will, they argue, is itself advantageous to a democracy, for it allows an appeal to be taken from the people drunk to the people sober. [The] most intriguing implication, however, is that someone somewhere must oversee and protect the people from themselves. Is this not the classic line of anti-democrats from time immemorial? [w] * * *

"Now, it may be entirely proper for the Supreme Court to lecture us on the principles of American government, and to have them make whatever use they can of the 'marvelous mystery of time' to formulate appeals to our better nature, for such is the privilege of college professors and of clergymen as well. There is, however, this crucial difference: The strictures emanating from the lectern are not legally enforceable, whereas judges do have the power to compel that 'sober

---

its pace hardly ever seems just right. For all these reasons, it is, in a vast, complex, changeable society, a most unsuitable instrument for the formation of policy." Bickel, *The Supreme Court and the Idea of Progress* 175 (1970).

Compare Barron, *The Ambiguity of Judicial Review: A Response to Professor Bickel,* 1970 Duke L.J. 591, 595, 604: "The difficulty with this approach is that it enormously decreases the role of the Supreme Court in American life. Bickel is really making a radical request: if the great political cases are incapable of principled resolution, then the Court ought to decline decision of such cases. But it is the great political cases which have made the Supreme Court, historically and now, a branch of government. [The] judiciary is designed to have occasional political uses. [The] enormous resiliency, the constant possibilities for modest advance and subtle retreat, makes the Court one of the most sensitive sources for social change in the United States."

w. Consider Cohen, supra, at 192: "[I]t is curious to note that it is those Americans who are at heart distrustful of democracy who speak of the courts as standing between us and dictatorship and yet their arguments are precisely those which the adherents of Hitler and Mussolini use against the frailty of democratically representative or elective government."

second thought.' No matter how desirable that may be, it still is not democratic."

————

JESSE CHOPER, supra, at 848–58: "The most encompassing argument to 'democratize' the Court's power as ultimate constitutional arbiter has been that judicial review [has] been institutionally adopted by a continuing consensus of American society as an integral rule of the system; that, thus, judicial review operates by majority will, with the consent of the governed.

"Proper evaluation of [this] contention necessitates review of the efficacy and legitimacy of both the general force of public reaction and the particular controls available to elected and appointed officials in responding to the Court's constitutional pronouncements. * * *

"*Constitutional Amendment*—[This] has been employed but four times in our history to overcome the Court's decisions; [120] such meager utilization evidences the difficulty involved. More importantly, there is no more plainly designated antimajoritarian obstacle in our governmental system [than] the constitutionally prescribed amendment procedures. * * *

"*Political Control Over Composition*—[The] authority to impeach sitting Justices, the gravest aspect of this power, may be readily discredited as a factor that enhances the Court's democratic image. [Because] of its severe consequences, prodigious energy is needed to put the impeachment machinery in motion. And the critical fact [is] that the two-thirds Senate vote required for conviction strips it of any majoritarian pretenses.

"The authority to appoint new Justices [depends] upon natural fortuities beyond the reach of even the most indomitable President. It may well take several successive presidential terms—[and] cooperative Senates—to change the judicial philosophy of a majority of the bench. Moreover, it requires a keen executive prediction of appointees' present and future views on known and unknown issues, a clairvoyance that our history, even the most recent, has proven to fall far short of being wholly reliable. * * * Manipulation through use of the appointment power further requires the assumption that the new appointees will disregard precedent, [a] quantity that no President can buy with real assurance. * * *

"[Reversing particular constitutional paths the Court has taken has] often been sought by the political departments through use of the power of increasing the number of Justices, coupled with the making of new appointments. [The] most dramatic example concerned the *Legal Tender Cases*. President Grant, on the day that *Hepburn v. Griswold* [124] was decided, nominated two new Justices following a resignation and an increase in the Court's membership from eight to nine; in just a little more than a year, the *Hepburn* decision was overruled [125] because of the votes of the new appointees.

"This last occasion, over a century ago, appears, however, to be the only clear victory achieved by the political branches in exercising the authority to enlarge. [The technique's] most celebrated day occurred when President Frank-

120. U.S.Const. amend. XI, adopted 1795—overruling *Chisholm v. Georgia*, [Ch. 13, Sec. 2, I]; U.S.Const. amend. XIV, § 1, adopted 1868—overruling *Scott v. Sandford;* U.S. Const. amend. XVI, adopted 1913—overruling *Pollock v. Farmers' Loan & Trust Co.*, 157 U.S. 429, 15 S.Ct. 673, 39 L.Ed. 759 (1895); U.S.

Const. amend. XXVI, adopted 1971—overruling *Oregon v. Mitchell*, [Ch. 12, Sec. 2].

124. 75 U.S. (8 Wall.) 603 (1870) (5–3 decision).

125. *Legal Tender Cases*, 79 U.S. (12 Wall.) 457 (1871) (5–4 decision).

lin Roosevelt, just elected by an overwhelming popular majority and possessed of legendary influence over Congress, nonetheless saw his Court-packing plan defeated, despite the extremely disreputable position of the Court for having thwarted both executive *and* legislative efforts to combat a great national crisis. [T]he facts are that, even under this extraordinary combination of auspicious circumstances, the Court's traditional independence of the political will survived, and that during subsequent periods of momentous judicial impact and unpopularity the political departments' power over the Court's composition, far from being seriously considered a consequential weapon, has been effectively discredited.

"Political Curtailment of Appellate Jurisdiction—In the past quarter century, the device most frequently threatened by the political branches for use against the Court has been Congress' power, specified in article three, to make 'Exceptions' to and 'Regulations' of the Court's appellate jurisdiction. [But] the theoretical underpinnings for a wide legislative power [are] hardly as firm as the literal phrasing of article three [suggests.] A variety of interpretations of the delegated authority have been offered by prominent constitutional scholars, none of which results in any consequential political check on judicial review.[x] * * *

"But even if this legislative ability to retaliate against the judiciary rested on a firm theoretical foundation, its pragmatic potential as a majoritarian restraint on judicial review would be severely limited. As Herbert Wechsler has lucidly revealed, since the political branches realize that the use of federal courts is essential to administer federal [law,] Congress cannot, as a practical matter, withdraw all federal jurisdiction, even if it were authorized to do so constitutionally. If Congress instead were to choose only to curtail the Supreme Court's appellate jurisdiction, it could attempt to rest final resolution of all constitutional questions with the eleven federal courts of appeals. Although this may be preferable to leaving it to the highest courts of the fifty states—the result of abolishing *all* federal jurisdiction or of restricting the adjudication of some or all constitutional questions to the state courts—the potential for national inconsistency in constitutional interpretation would still be unbearable. Alternatively, the tradition of stare decisis could lead these other courts to follow the very Supreme Court decisions that sparked the congressional counteraction. The jurisdictional withdrawal thus might work to freeze the very doctrines that had prompted its enactment, placing an intolerable moral burden on the lower courts. [The] federal system needs federal courts and the judicial institution needs an organ of supreme authority'.[136]

"This convincing line of argument helps explain why on only one occasion in American history—and that one of questionable significance in effect, and ultimately determined to be incomplete in scope [137]—has hostility prompted the political branches (Congress overriding a presidential veto) to utilize article three to diminish the Court's jurisdiction, though many such efforts have been made.

* * *

"Conclusion—[The] most entrenched popular barriers to the rule of the Court are both more discrete and less formalized than those already mentioned. [If] either of the political branches opposes a judicial doctrine that requires

x. But see Black, *Decision According to Law* 17–19, 37–39 (1981); Perry, *The Constitution, the Courts and Human Rights* 128–38 (1982). For full discussion, see Sec. 3 infra.

136. Wechsler, *The Courts and the Constitution,* 65 Colum.L.Rev. 1001, 1006–07 (1965).

137. See *Ex parte Yerger,* 75 U.S. (8 Wall.) 85 (1869) (demonstrating that the act of Congress upheld in *Ex parte McCardle,* 74 U.S. (7 Wall.) 506 (1869), closed only one of the existing avenues of appeal to the Supreme Court) [discussed in Sec. 3 infra].

support for its effectuation—and many do, in varying degrees—the legislative or executive opportunity is clear. The presidential response may range from Abraham Lincoln's outright refusal to obey Chief Justice Taney's order in *Ex parte Merryman*,[141] to Andrew Jackson's alleged edict that he would leave John Marshall to enforce his own decision in the *Cherokee Indian Cases*,[142] to Dwight Eisenhower's seeming ambivalence immediately following *Brown v. Board of Education*. The congressional power of the purse may also be employed to enfeeble the Court's will, as is illustrated by the recent repeated efforts to deny funds for school busing to achieve racial desegregation. [Furthermore], lesser officials (including the judges) at all levels of government, and, ultimately, the people themselves, may move grudgingly and hesitatingly in adhering to the Court's mandate, or they may simply refuse to obey, with varying degrees of blatancy.[y] * * *

"Neither this reasoning nor its supporting data, however, lead to the conclusion that judicial review is compatible with majoritarian democracy as traditionally conceived or practiced. Many eventful and controversial constitutional decisions—especially those involving use of the judicial system itself (as in the field of criminal procedure)—although subject to being undercut by resentful administrative officials and lower courts, do not depend for their complete effectiveness on the cooperation of other public agencies or of the people in general. Further, it must be conceded that it is only those Supreme Court mandates perceived as exceedingly flagrant that are capable of generating the intensity of opposition necessary to prevent enforcement. Nor is popular resistance universal in impact, either geographically or temporally; even if certain rulings eventually fall into disuse because of opposition by the requisite majority will, their force will be felt by a segment of the people for some time and often by many of the people for a long time. And impelling the Court to bend or draw up in developing doctrine falls far short of causing the Court to break or retreat.

"At the surface, the antimajoritarian features of all three federal departments bear a certain similarity. The leeway afforded the political branches by the people and the tenacity of popular feeling needed for radical change through election revolt are not absolutely different from the independence granted the judiciary by the Constitution and the assiduous efforts required to affect the Court and its decisions through the restraints ultimately retained by the citizenry and their elected representatives. But in both democratic theory and practice, the distinction between control of the legislature and executive on one side and control of the judiciary on the other, if not one of kind, is one of substantial degree."

Varying Standards of Review

UNITED STATES v. CAROLENE PRODUCTS CO., 304 U.S. 144, 152, n. 4, 58 S.Ct. 778, 783, 82 L.Ed. 1234, 1241 (1938): "There may be narrower scope for operation of the presumption of constitutionality when legislation appears on its face to be within a specific prohibition of the Constitution, such as those of the first ten amendments, which are deemed equally specific when held to be embraced within the Fourteenth.

---

141. 17 F.Cas. 144 (C.C.D.Md.1861).

142. President Jackson's exact words in response to the decision [were] said to be: "John Marshall has made his decision. Now let him enforce it."

y. For elaboration, see Choper, *Judicial Review and the National Political Process* ch. 3—"The Fragile Character of Judicial Review: The Problems of Popular Noncompliance and Exhaustible Institutional Capital"—(1980).

"It is unnecessary to consider now whether legislation which restricts those political processes which can ordinarily be expected to bring about repeal of undesirable legislation, is to be subjected to more exacting judicial scrutiny under the general prohibitions of the Fourteenth Amendment than are most other types of legislation. ＊ ＊ ＊

"Nor need we enquire whether similar considerations enter into the review of statutes directed at particular religious, or national, or racial minorities: whether prejudice against discrete and insular minorities may be a special condition, which tends seriously to curtail the operation of those political processes ordinarily to be relied upon to protect minorities, and which may call for a correspondingly more searching judicial inquiry." [z]

JESSE CHOPER, *On the Warren Court and Judicial Review,* 17 Cath.U.L. Rev. 20, 38–41 (1967): "Granting that the Supreme Court is a 'deviant institution in the American democracy,' it must also be recognized that [the] Constitution itself is similarly antimajoritarian or, if you will, antidemocratic, at least in a limited fashion. Its provisions set the boundaries of each federal department's power vis-à-vis that of the others, of federal power vis-à-vis that of the states, of governmental power vis-à-vis that of the individual. The Constitution commands that these powers may not be exceeded by simple majority will. ＊ ＊ ＊

"The perplexing questions here are: *When* is the Constitution violated? *What body* of government should decide? *Marbury* assigned the task to the Court. [But] by what standard should the Court decide?

"In exploring this ultimately crucial problem, it seems to me that we must distinguish between two different types of constitutional issues. One is whether authority over the subject matter of federal action has been 'delegated' by the Constitution to the national government or whether it has been 'reserved to the States.' ＊ ＊ ＊

"The other general issue that arises [a] is whether a particular exercise of governmental power, national or state, infringes individual rights guaranteed by the Constitution. [O]ne need only refer, as examples, to the original Constitution's prohibitions of bills of attainder and ex post facto laws, to the first eight amendments (popularly known as the Bill of Rights), to the fourteenth amendment's guarantees of due process and equal protection.

"It seems to me that if the constitutional issue is one only of states' rights, the role of the Supreme Court [should] be severely limited. The justification for *judicial* review in this instance, for the final constitutional word to be spoken by a 'deviant institution' in a democracy, is weak. The states, whose constitutional rights are allegedly being assaulted, are well represented in the councils of national government [and] the political process may generally be depended upon to produce a fair judgment. If a majority of the states' representatives (and I believe this is a wholly accurate description of members of Congress) determine that federal power has not been exceeded, then the Court should overturn the

---

z. The impact of this footnote is further discussed at many points in the materials, especially Chs. 7, 8 and 10.

a. The matter of division of power among the federal departments is considered in Ch. 3.

decision, if at all, only if it is so clearly in error as not to be 'open to rational question.'[158]

"But if the issue is one of alleged governmental infringement of individual rights protected by the Constitution, it seems to me that the Court's role should be quite different. These constitutional guarantees—such as the freedoms of speech and religion, the constitutional rights of those accused of crime, the right to be free from certain racial discrimination—are generally rights of 'politically impotent minorities.' By definition, the processes of democracy bode poorly for the security of such rights. [Thus], the task of guarding these constitutionally prescribed liberties sensibly falls upon a body that is not politically responsible, that is not beholden to the grace of excited majoritarianism—[the] Supreme Court. Herein lies the great justification for the power of judicial review, the wisdom of *Marbury*. In this area, the Court, if it is properly to fulfill its place in American democratic society, must act more forcefully—perhaps 'by creating a presumption against the validity of the contested action,' perhaps 'by more closely scrutinizing the methods employed and the objectives to which they lead.' "

J. SKELLY WRIGHT, *Professor Bickel, The Scholarly Tradition, and the Supreme Court,* 84 Harv.L.Rev. 769, 787–89 (1971): "Professor Bickel [*The Supreme Court and the Idea of Progress* 37 (1970)] appears to believe that reliance on the political process for protection of most fundamental rights and liberties is somehow inherent in democratic theory. [He contends] that in fact minorities play an important though indirect role in most governmental decisions, may be presumed to consent to them, and have substantial opportunity to defend their interests without the help of the courts. No minority willing to wheel and deal with other minorities, he says, need despair of eventually vindicating its rights. [But his "empirical assertion" is] highly doubtful. Perhaps its basic defect is the fact that power is not distributed equally among the various groups in our society. Bickel explicitly recognizes that the formation of majorities at election time is but one part of our political system. At least equally important is the trading and pressuring that goes on all the rest of the time. The Professor would have us believe that this is just fine: those groups with the most 'intense' interests will be the most active in the process, and it is proper that the more 'intense' interests be more richly rewarded. This is nonsense. The big winners in the pluralistic system are the highly organized, wealthy, and motivated groups skilled in the art of insider politics. They have the resources to trade for other benefits, and the resources that it takes to press their claims successfully. Perhaps the interest of a great corporation in a tax break is more 'intense' than that of a political minority in its first amendment rights—that is, if intensity is defined by how conscious of their interests they are, how articulate and persistent they are in presenting them, and how much

---

158. Some limited degree of judicial supervision in this area may be justified if the confinement of federal power to that specified in the Constitution is seen as having a purpose beyond the protection of "states' rights" * * *.

[Consider Henkin, *Voice of a Modern Federalism,* in Felix Frankfurter the Judge 68, 71 (Mendelson ed. 1964): "To Justice Frankfurter, in fact, federalism in the United States has been a guarantee of freedom. Like the horizontal separation of powers, the vertical distribution between state and nation was designed, and has served, to frustrate possible tyrannies of centralization. 'Time has not lessened the concern of the Founders in devising a federal system which would likewise be a safeguard against arbitrary government.' He invokes 'the principle of diffusion of power not as a matter of doctrinaire localism but as a promoter of democracy.' "]

political muscle they bring to bear. Intensity, so defined, however, is largely an attribute of the already powerful elite. Unorganized, poor, unskilled minorities simply do not have the sort of 'intense' interests in their rights which the pluralistic system regularly rewards."

ROBERT BORK, *Neutral Principles and Some First Amendment Problems,* 47 Ind.L.J. 1, 2–3 (1971): "[T]he model of government embodied in the structure of the Constitution [may] for convenience, though perhaps not with total accuracy, [be called] 'Madisonian.'

"A Madisonian system is not completedly democratic, if by 'democratic' we mean completely majoritarian. It assumes that in wide areas of life majorities are entitled to rule for no better reason than that they are majorities. [The] model has also a counter-majoritarian premise, however, for it assumes there are some areas of life a majority should not control. [These] are areas properly left to individual freedom, and coercion by the majority in these aspects of life is tyranny.

" * * * Minority tyranny occurs if the majority is prevented from ruling where its power is legitimate. Yet, quite obviously, neither the majority nor the minority can be trusted to define the freedom of the other. This dilemma is resolved in constitutional theory, and in popular understanding, by the Supreme Court's power to define both majority and minority freedom through the interpretation of the Constitution. Society consents to be ruled undemocratically within defined areas by certain enduring principles believed to be stated in, and placed beyond the reach of majorities by, the Constitution.

"But this resolution of the dilemma imposes severe requirements upon the Court. For it follows that the Court's power is legitimate only if it has, and can demonstrate in reasoned opinions that it has, a valid theory, derived from the Constitution, of the respective spheres of majority and minority freedom. If it does not have such a theory but merely imposes its own value choices, or worse if it pretends to have a theory but actually follows its own predilections, the Court violates the postulates of the Madisonian model that alone justifies its power. It then necessarily abets the tyranny either of the majority or of the minority."

Some Further Observations

LOUIS JAFFE, *Impromptu Remarks,* 76 Harv.L.Rev. 1111–12 (1963): "There is no area in which criticism at its most intense is more appropriate [than] the area of constitutional adjudication. There will be and there should be popular response to the Supreme Court's decision; not just the 'informed' criticism of law professors but the deep-felt, emotion-laden, unsophisticated reaction of the laity. This is so because more than any court in the modern world the Supreme Court 'makes policy,' and is at the same time so little subject to formal democratic control. * * * Violently expressed hostility to a decision may indeed increase the difficulty of enforcing it, [but once] granting that public opinion is intrinsic to a democratic system its operation cannot be cabined, cribbed, and confined to formal legal paths. We are, of course, deeply shocked where it is not the private citizen but the public official under oath to uphold the law who leads in flouting it. But great political decisions such as desegregation and reapportionment *do* involve major confrontations of political power and the form in which such decisions become viable is inevitably a consequence of the whole political process, a process which involves a great variety and gradation of lawmaking phenomena. It is precisely to conserve its power and prestige in those cases in which it cannot do otherwise that the Supreme Court should be made aware that each and every bold policy decision will bring it into the political arena." [c]

CHARLES BLACK, *Structure and Relationship in Constitutional Law* 74–76 (1969): "[T]here is nothing in our entire governmental structure which has a more leak-proof claim to legitimacy than the function of the courts in reviewing state acts for federal constitutionality. [I]t seems to me Congress could have provided for this even without an Article III, simply by creating a court and endowing it with the power to perform this necessary and proper function. Insofar, then, as legitimacy in origin is relevant to judicial or public attitude toward the judicial work, the Court ought to feel no slightest embarrassment about its work of reviewing state acts for their federal constitutionality. It seems very clear, moreover, that all present-day political considerations strongly impel toward the same conclusion. In policing the actions of the states for their conformity to federal constitutional guarantees, the Court represents the whole nation, and therefore the whole nation's interest in seeing those guarantees prevail, in their spirit and in their entirety. The Court is in all practical effect the delegate of Congress to do this work.

"[V]irtually all intense political trouble about the Court's role in the last three decades concerns its functioning in the [role] whose legitimacy is not so much as fairly debatable. [T]he Supreme Court in our times is a dangerously controversial institution charged with the duty of bringing the states into line with national law, and [is] it not plain that what is chiefly objected to is not the Court as such, but the fact of being brought into line?"

MARTIN v. HUNTER'S LESSEE, 14 U.S. (1 Wheat.) 304, 4 L.Ed. 97 (1816), came from the Court of Appeals of Virginia, which had refused to obey the mandate of the U.S. Supreme Court, "requiring the judgment rendered in this very cause [at an earlier term] to be carried into due execution." The Court, per STORY, J. (Marshall, C.J., not sitting), held that the federal appellate power "does extend to cases pending in the state courts; and that the 25th section of the judiciary act, which authorizes the exercise of [the instant] jurisdiction is supported by the letter and spirit of the constitution":

"The third article of the constitution is that which must principally attract our attention. [A]ppellate jurisdiction is given by the constitution to the supreme court, in all cases [within 'the judicial power of the United States'] where it has not original [jurisdiction. What] is there to restrain its exercise over state tribunals, in the enumerated cases? [If] the judicial power extends to the case, it will be in vain to search in the letter of the constitution for any qualification as to the tribunal where it depends. [Suppose,] an indictment for a crime, in a state court, and the defendant should allege in his defence, that the crime was created by an ex post facto act of the state, must not the state court [have] a right to pronounce on the validity and sufficiency of the defence? [It] was foreseen, that in the exercise of their ordinary jurisdiction, state courts would incidentally take cognisance of cases arising under the constitution, the laws and

---

c. See also Wellington, *The Nature of Judicial Review,* 91 Yale L.J. 486, 519 (1982): "[I]ncreased political activity over Supreme Court decisions does not constitute disrespect for law. Our law must be based on consent. It is everyone's obligation to insist that all branches of government, including the courts, remain true to this central understanding. Peaceful resistance is part of the minorities' arsenal of weapons against the majority. It is a standard political weapon of minorities and the majority against the Court."

treaties of the United States. Yet, to all these cases, the judicial power, by the very terms of the constitution, is to extend. It cannot extend, by original jurisdiction, if that was already rightfully and exclusively attached in the state courts, which (as has been already shown) may occur; it must, therefore, extend by appellate jurisdiction, or not at all. It would seem to follow, that the appellate power of the United States must, in such cases, extend to state [tribunals].

"It has been argued, that such an appellate jurisdiction over state courts is inconsistent with the genius of our governments, and the spirit of the constitution. That the latter was never designed to act upon state sovereignties, but only upon the people, and that if the power exists it will materially impair the sovereignty of the states, and the independence of their courts. [But the Constitution] is crowded with provisions which restrain or annul the sovereignty of the states, in some of the highest branches of their prerogatives. The tenth section of the first article contains a long list of disabilities and prohibitions imposed upon the states. ⁎ ⁎ ⁎

"Nor can such a right be deemed to impair the independence of state judges. It is assuming the very ground in controversy, to assert that they possess an absolute independence of the United States. In respect to the powers granted to the United States, they are not independent; they are expressly bound to obedience, by the letter of the constitution ⁎ ⁎ ⁎. [A]dmitting that the judges of the state courts are, and always will be, of as much learning, integrity and wisdom, as those of the courts of the United States (which we very cheerfully admit), it does not aid the argument. It is manifest, that the constitution has proceeded upon a theory of its own, and given or withheld powers according to the judgment of the American people, by whom it was adopted. We can only construe its powers, and cannot inquire into the policy or principles which induced the grant of them. The constitution has presumed (whether rightly or wrongly, we do not inquire), that state attachments, state prejudices, state jealousies, and state interests, might sometimes obstruct, or control, or be supposed to obstruct or control, the regular administration of justice. ⁎ ⁎ ⁎

"This is not all. A motive of another kind, perfectly compatible with the most sincere respect for state tribunals, might induce the grant of appellate power over their decisions. ⁎ ⁎ ⁎ Judges of equal learning and integrity, in different states, might differently interpret the statute, or a treaty of the United States, or even the constitution itself: if there were no revising authority to control these jarring and discordant judgments, and harmonize them into uniformity, the laws, the treaties and the constitution of the United States would be different, in different states, and might, perhaps, never have precisely the same construction, obligation or efficiency, in any two states. The public mischiefs that would attend such a state of things would be truly deplorable."

JOHNSON, J., concurred, observing "that the court disavows all intention to decide on the right to issue compulsory process to the state courts; thus leaving us, in my opinion, where the constitution and laws place us—supreme over persons and cases, so far as our judicial powers extend, but not asserting any compulsory control over the state tribunals. In this view, I acquiesce in their opinion, but not altogether in the reasoning ⁎ ⁎ ⁎."

Notes and Questions

1. *Was the judgment executed?* Charles Warren reports that the Court "decided to avoid the chance of further friction" with the Virginia Court of

Appeals "and accordingly, instead of issuing a second mandate to that Court, it issued its process directly to the District Court [in] which the suit had been originally instituted," 1 Warren, supra, at 450. See also Dodd, *Chief Justice Marshall and Virginia 1813–21*, 12 Am.Hist.Rev. 776, 779 (1907), claiming that the United States marshal was eventually ordered to execute the judgment of the Supreme Court. But William Crosskey insists that execution of judgment was neither issued nor required. Under the Virginia practice, he contends, the proceeding under which the case was brought "served much the same purpose in settling points of law in dispute in land-title controversies, as does a modern action for a declaratory judgment," 2 Crosskey, supra, at 786. Moreover, he adds, "upon the peculiar facts of the case, execution of the judgment would have been a completely vain proceeding; for Hunter could at once have brought a successful action to recover possession again, based on the compromise. There was not a word in the Supreme Court's decision that forbade it." Id. at 806 n.[d]

2. COHENS v. VIRGINIA, 19 U.S. (6 Wheat.) 264, 5 L.Ed. 257 (1821)— which sustained the Court's appellate jurisdiction under § 25 of the Judiciary Act to review state criminal proceedings, and is generally viewed as reaffirming and "supplementing" *Martin*, see 2 Warren, supra, at 10—has stronger historical links with *McCulloch v. Maryland* (set forth, p. 60 infra), see 4 Beveridge, *The Life of John Marshall* 343 (1919).

Appellants were found guilty in a Virginia court of selling lottery tickets in violation of state law. Their defense was that the lottery was organized by the City of Washington, under a congressional statute authorizing the lottery. On appeal to the Supreme Court, they were met with the contentions that the Court had no jurisdiction to review a state criminal case and, in any event, Congress had no power to permit the sale of lottery tickets in a state which prohibited such sale. On the jurisdictional point, Virginia argued that (1) if when the state is a party the Supreme Court has original jurisdiction, this grant excludes appellate jurisdiction; (2) federal courts cannot take original jurisdiction over criminal cases, since that rightfully belongs to the courts of the state whose laws have been violated; (3) consequently, the Supreme Court has no jurisdiction at all. As in *Marbury*, MARSHALL, C.J., used the occasion to express a broad view of the Court's powers, but decided the case on a narrow ground in favor of the Jeffersonians—the federal statute authorizing a lottery had no effect outside the City of Washington.

The case was decided at a time when the state autonomy and states' rights generally were being boldly proclaimed. Two years earlier, most southern and western states had vehemently denounced the decision in *McCulloch v. Maryland*, invalidating a state tax on the Bank of the United States. Indeed, in disregard of *McCulloch* and in defiance of a federal circuit court injunction, the state auditor of Ohio had enforced his state's tax on the Bank by entering its vaults, seizing whatever specie and notes he could find, and conveying them to the state treasurer. See 1 Warren, supra, at 514–30. And only a year before *Cohens*, in the hot debate which finally resulted in the Missouri Compromise, "constant fears were expressed by Southern statesmen lest Marshall's broad

d. For post-*Martin* instances of state court resistance to Supreme Court orders and various efforts to secure compliance see Murphy, *Lower Court Checks on Supreme Court Power*, 53 Am.Pol.Sci.Rev. 1017 (1959); Warren, *Federal and State Court Interference*, 43 Harv.L. Rev. 345 (1930); Beatty, *State Court Evasion of United States Supreme Court Mandates During the Last Decade of the Warren Court*, 6 Val.L.Rev. 260 (1972); Notes, 67 Harv.L.Rev. 1251 (1954), 56 Yale L.J. 574 (1947). On the theory of "interposition," see Note, *Interposition vs. Judicial Power—A Study of Ultimate Authority in Constitutional Questions*, 1 Race Rel.L.Rep. 465 (1956).

views of the 'necessary and proper' clause of the Constitution might support Congressional interference with the States on the subject of slavery," 2 Warren, supra, at 2–3. "The final settlement" of the existence and powers of the Bank of the United States and the extension of slavery in the new states "were felt to depend largely upon the future trend of the Supreme Court," id. at 4.

In the course of his "immortal Nationalist address," 4 Beveridge, supra, at 343, Marshall said: "When we consider [the] nature of our constitution; the subordination of the state governments to that constitution; the great purpose for which jurisdiction over all cases arising under the constitution and laws of the United States, is confided to the judicial department; are we at liberty to insert in this general grant, an exception of those cases in which a state may be a party? Will the spirit of the constitution justify this attempt to control its words? We think it will not. We think a case arising under the constitution or laws of the United States, is cognizable in the Courts of the Union, whoever may be the parties to that case. * * *

"In many states, the judges are dependent for office and for salary on the will of the legislature. [When] we observe the importance which that constitution attaches to the independence of judges, we are the less inclined to suppose, that it can have intended to leave these constitutional questions to tribunals where this independence may not exist * * *.

"[A] constitution is framed for ages to come, and is designed to approach immortality, as nearly as human institutions can approach it. Its course cannot always be tranquil. It is exposed to storms and tempests, and its framers must be unwise statesmen indeed, if they have not provided it, so far as its nature will permit, with the means of self-preservation from the perils it may be destined to encounter. No government ought to be so defective in its organization, as not to contain within itself, the means of securing the execution of its own laws against other dangers than those which occur every day. Courts of justice are the means most usually employed; and it is reasonable to expect, that a government should repose on its own courts, rather than on others."

SECTION 2. POLITICAL QUESTIONS

Does the principle of judicial review comprehend the Court's acting as "final arbiter" on *all* constitutional questions presented by a case properly within its jurisdiction? Or are some constitutional issues inappropriate for judicial resolution and thus "nonjusticiable"?

BAKER v. CARR

369 U.S. 186, 82 S.Ct. 691, 7 L.Ed.2d 663 (1962).

MR. JUSTICE BRENNAN delivered the opinion of the Court.

[Appellants sought a federal declaratory judgment that the apportionment of the Tennessee General Assembly violated fourteenth amendment equal protection "by virtue of the debasement of their votes." They alleged that, although the state constitution allocated representation on a population basis, no reapportionment law had passed since 1901. They further sought an injunction against any further elections under the 1901 scheme and] until the General Assembly enacts a valid reapportionment, the District Court should either decree a reapportionment by mathematical application of the Tennessee constitutional formulae to the most recent Federal Census figures, or direct the appellees to conduct legislative elections, primary and general, at large. * * *

[W]e hold today only (a) that the court possessed jurisdiction of the subject matter; (b) that a justiciable cause of action is stated upon which appellants would be entitled to appropriate relief; and (c) [that] the appellants have standing to challenge the Tennessee apportionment statutes. Beyond noting that we have no cause at this stage to doubt the District Court will be able to fashion relief if violations of constitutional rights are found, it is improper now to consider what remedy would be most appropriate if appellants prevail at the trial.

JURISDICTION OF THE SUBJECT MATTER

The District Court was uncertain whether our cases withholding federal judicial relief rested upon a lack of federal jurisdiction or upon the inappropriateness of the subject matter for judicial consideration—what we have designated "nonjusticiability." The distinction between the two grounds is significant. In the instance of nonjusticiability, consideration of the cause is not wholly and immediately foreclosed; rather, the Court's inquiry necessarily proceeds to the point of deciding whether the duty asserted can be judicially identified and its breach judicially determined, and whether protection for the right asserted can be judicially molded. In the instance of lack of jurisdiction the cause either does not "arise under" the Federal Constitution, laws or treaties (or fall within one of the other enumerated categories of Art. III, § 2), or is not a "case or controversy" within the meaning of that section; [a] or the cause is not one described by any jurisdictional statute. Our conclusion that this cause presents no nonjusticiable "political question" settles the only possible doubt that it is a case or controversy. Under the present heading of "Jurisdiction of the Subject Matter" we hold only that the matter set forth in the complaint does arise under the Constitution and is within [a statute conferring federal court jurisdiction].

An unbroken line of our precedents sustains the federal courts' jurisdiction of the subject matter of federal constitutional claims of this nature. [Unlike] many other cases in this field which have assumed without discussion that there was jurisdiction, all three opinions filed in *Colegrove v. Green*, 328 U.S. 549, 66 S.Ct. 1198, 90 L.Ed. 1432 (1946), discussed the question. Two of the opinions expressing the views of four of the Justices, a majority, flatly held that there was jurisdiction of that subject matter.[b] * * *

---

a. This topic is considered in Ch. 13, Sec. 1.

b. *Colegrove* affirmed dismissal of a suit by voters in Illinois congressional districts, that had much larger populations than others, to enjoin the forthcoming election on federal constitutional and statutory grounds. Frankfurter, J., joined by Reed and Burton, JJ., held that the applicable congressional apportionment statute did not require equality of population in districts. He also felt that the case should be "dismissed for want of equity" because the issue was "of a peculiarly political nature and therefore not meet for judicial determination." The result of judicial interference might be elections-at-large—"a mode that defies the direction of Congress for selection by districts * * *. In the exercise of its power to judge the qualifications of its own members, the House may reject a delegation of Representatives-at-large. Article I, § 5, Cl. 1." "[T]his controversy concerns matters that bring courts into immediate and active rela-tions with party contests. * * * Courts ought not to enter this political thicket." Art. I, § 4 of the Constitution confers "upon Congress exclusive authority to secure fair representation by the States in the popular House." If Congress fails, "the remedy ultimately lies with the people."

Rutledge, J., concurred in the result, believing the issues to be "justiciable" but that the case should be dismissed for want of equity due to "the gravity of the constitutional questions" and "the possibilities for collision [with] the political departments of the Government."

Black, J., joined by Douglas and Murphy, JJ., dissented, believing the apportionment to be unconstitutional: "[I]t is a mere 'play on words' to refer to a controversy such as this as 'political' in the sense that courts have nothing to do with protecting and vindicating the right of a voter to cast an effective ballot."

JUSTICIABILITY

[I]t is argued that apportionment cases, whatever the actual wording of the complaint, can involve no federal constitutional right except one resting on the guaranty of a republican form of government, [Art. IV, § 4,] and that complaints based on that clause have been held to present political questions which are nonjusticiable. [But appellants'] claim that they are being denied equal protection is justiciable, and if "discrimination is sufficiently shown, the right to relief under the equal protection clause is not diminished by the fact that the discrimination relates to political rights." *Snowden v. Hughes,* 321 U.S. 1, 11, 64 S.Ct. 397, 402, 88 L.Ed. 497. [B]ecause there appears to be some uncertainty as to why [Guaranty Clause] cases did present political questions, and specifically as to whether this apportionment case is like those cases, we deem it necessary first to consider the contours of the "political question" doctrine.

[I]n the Guaranty Clause cases and in the other "political question" cases, it is the relationship between the judiciary and the coordinate branches of the Federal Government, and not the federal judiciary's relationship to the States, which gives rise to the "political question."

We have said that "In determining whether a question falls within [the political question] category, the appropriateness under our system of government of attributing finality to the action of the political departments and also the lack of satisfactory criteria for a judicial determination are dominant considerations." *Coleman v. Miller,* 307 U.S. 433, 454–455, 59 S.Ct. 972, 982, 83 L.Ed. 1385. The nonjusticiability of a political question is primarily a function of the separation of powers. Much confusion results from the capacity of the "political question" label to obscure the need for case-by-case inquiry. Deciding whether a matter has in any measure been committed by the Constitution to another branch of government, or whether the action of that branch exceeds whatever authority has been committed, is itself a delicate exercise in constitutional interpretation, and is a responsibility of this Court as ultimate interpreter of the Constitution. To demonstrate this requires no less than to analyze representative cases and to infer from them the analytical threads that make up the political question doctrine. We shall then show that none of those threads catches this case.

Foreign relations: There are sweeping statements to the effect that all questions touching foreign relations are political questions. Not only does resolution of such issues frequently turn on standards that defy judicial application, or involve the exercise of a discretion demonstrably committed to the executive or legislature; but many such questions uniquely demand single-voiced statement of the Government's views. Yet it is error to suppose that every case or controversy which touches foreign relations lies beyond judicial cognizance. Our cases in this field seem invariably to show a discriminating analysis of the particular question posed, in terms of the history of its management by the political branches, of its susceptibility to judicial handling in the light of its nature and posture in the specific case, and of the possible consequences of judicial action.[c] For example, though a court will not ordinarily inquire whether a treaty has been terminated, since on that question "governmental action [must] be regarded as of controlling importance," if there has been no conclusive

---

For *Colegrove's* formal demise, see *Wesberry v. Sanders,* p. 1022 infra.

c. See generally Henkin, *Viet-Nam in the Courts of the United States: "Political Questions,"* 63 Am.J.Int'l L. 284 (1969).

"governmental action" then a court can construe a treaty and may find it provides the answer. * * *

Dates of duration of hostilities: [H]ere too analysis reveals isolable reasons for the presence of political questions, underlying this Court's refusal to review the political departments' determination of when or whether a war has ended. Dominant is the need for finality in the political determination, for emergency's nature demands "A prompt and unhesitating obedience," *Martin v. Mott*, 12 Wheat. 19, 30, 6 L.Ed. 537 (calling up of militia). [But] deference rests on reason, not habit. The question in a particular case may not seriously implicate considerations of finality—e.g., a public program of importance (rent control) yet not central to the emergency effort. Further, clearly definable criteria for decision may be available. In such case the political question barrier falls away * * *.

Validity of enactments: [*Coleman*] held that the questions of how long a proposed amendment to the Federal Constitution remained open to ratification, and what effect a prior rejection had on a subsequent ratification, were committed to congressional resolution and involved criteria of decision that necessarily escaped the judicial grasp. Similar considerations apply to the enacting process: "The respect due to coequal and independent departments," and the need for finality and certainty about the status of a statute contribute to judicial reluctance to inquire whether, as passed, it complied with all requisite formalities. *Field v. Clark*, 143 U.S. 649, 672, 676–677, 12 S.Ct. 495, 497, 499, 36 L.Ed. 294. But it is not true that courts will never delve into a legislature's records upon such a quest: If the enrolled statute lacks an effective date, a court will not hesitate to seek it in the legislative journals in order to preserve the enactment. The political question doctrine, a tool for maintenance of governmental order, will not be so applied as to promote only disorder. * * *

It is apparent that several formulations which vary slightly according to the settings in which the questions arise may describe a political question, although each has one or more elements which identify it as essentially a function of the separation of powers. Prominent [is] found a textually demonstrable constitutional commitment of the issue to a coordinate political department; or a lack of judicially discoverable and manageable standards for resolving it; or the impossibility of deciding without an initial policy determination of a kind clearly for nonjudicial discretion; or the impossibility of a court's undertaking independent resolution without expressing lack of the respect due coordinate branches of government; or an unusual need for unquestioning adherence to a political decision already made; or the potentiality of embarrassment from multifarious pronouncements by various departments on one question.

Unless one of these formulations is inextricable from the case at bar, there should be no dismissal for non-justiciability on the ground of a political question's presence. The doctrine of which we treat is one of "political questions," not one of "political cases." The courts cannot reject as "no law suit" a bona fide controversy as to whether some action denominated "political" exceeds constitutional authority. * * *

But it is argued that this case shares the characteristics of decisions that constitute a category not yet considered, cases concerning [Art. IV, § 4]. We shall discover that Guaranty Clause claims involve those elements which define a "political question," and for that reason and no other, they are nonjusticiable. In particular, we shall discover that the nonjusticiability of such claims has nothing to do with their touching upon matters of state governmental organization.

Republican form of government: Luther v. Borden, 7 How. 1, 12 L.Ed. 581, though in form simply an action for damages for trespass was, as Daniel Webster said in opening the argument for the defense, "an unusual case." The defendants, admitting an otherwise tortious breaking and entering, sought to justify their action on the ground that they were agents of the established lawful government of Rhode Island, which State was then under martial law to defend itself from active insurrection; that the plaintiff was engaged in that insurrection; and that they entered under orders to arrest the plaintiff. The case arose "out of the unfortunate political differences which agitated the people of Rhode Island in 1841 and 1842," and which had resulted in a situation wherein two groups laid competing claims to recognition as the lawful government. * * *

Clearly, several factors were thought by the Court in *Luther* to make the question there "political": the commitment to the other branches of the decision as to which is the lawful state government; the unambiguous action by the President, in recognizing the charter government as the lawful authority; the need for finality in the executive's decision; and the lack of criteria by which a court could determine which form of government was republican.

But the only significance that *Luther* could have for our immediate purposes is in its holding that the Guaranty Clause is not a repository of judicially manageable standards which a court could utilize independently in order to identify a State's lawful government. The Court has since refused to resort to the Guaranty Clause—which alone had been invoked for the purpose—as the source of a constitutional standard for invalidating state [or congressional] action. [See] *Pacific States Tel. & T. Co. v. Oregon,* 223 U.S. 118, 32 S.Ct. 224, 56 L.Ed. 377 (claim that initiative and referendum negated republican government held nonjusticiable); *Highland Farms Dairy v. Agnew,* 300 U.S. 608, 57 S.Ct. 549, 81 L.Ed. 835 (claim that delegation to agency of power to control milk prices violated republican government, rejected).

[In] *Georgia v. Stanton,* 6 Wall. 50, 18 L.Ed. 721, the State sought by an original bill to enjoin execution of the Reconstruction Acts, claiming that [the] Acts "Instead of keeping the guaranty against a forcible overthrow of its government by foreign invaders or domestic insurgents [are] destroying that very government by force." Congress had clearly refused to recognize the republican character of the government of the suing State. It seemed to the Court that the only constitutional claim that could be presented was under the Guaranty Clause, and Congress having determined that the effects of the recent hostilities required extraordinary measures to restore governments of a republican form, this Court refused to interfere with Congress' action at the behest of a claimant relying on that very guaranty. * * *

We come, finally, to the ultimate inquiry whether our precedents as to what constitutes a nonjusticiable "political question" bring the case before us under the umbrella of that doctrine. [We find none] of the common characteristics which we have been able to identify * * *. The question here is the consistency of state action with the Federal Constitution. We have no question decided, or to be decided, by a political branch of government coequal with this Court. Nor do we risk embarrassment of our government abroad, or grave disturbance at home if we take issue with Tennessee as to the constitutionality of her action here challenged. Nor need the appellants, in order to succeed in this action, ask the Court to enter upon policy determinations for which judicially manageable standards are lacking. Judicial standards under the Equal Protection Clause are well developed [to determine] that a discrimination reflects *no* policy, but simply arbitrary and capricious action.

This case does, in one sense, involve the allocation of political power within a State, and the appellants might conceivably have added a claim under the Guaranty Clause. [Although it] could not have succeeded it does not follow that appellants may not be heard on the equal protection claim which in fact they tender. * * *

Reversed and remanded. * * *

MR. JUSTICE WHITTAKER did not participate in the decision of this case.

MR. JUSTICE DOUGLAS [who joined the Court's opinion], concurring. * * *

So far as voting rights are concerned, there are large gaps in the Constitution. Yet the right to vote is inherent in the republican form of government * * *.[2] That the States may specify the qualifications for voters is implicit in Article I, Section 2, Clause 1 * * *. It is, however, clear that by reason of the commands of the Constitution there are several qualifications that a State may not require [referring to the fifteenth and nineteenth amendments, as well as equal protection].

It is said that any decision in cases of this kind is beyond the competence of courts. Some make the same point as regards the problem of equal protection in cases involving racial segregation. [The] constitutional guide is often vague, as the decisions under the Due Process and Commerce Clauses show. The problem under the Equal Protection Clause is no more intricate.

There are, of course, some questions beyond judicial competence. Where the performance of a "duty" is left to the discretion and good judgment of an executive officer, the judiciary will not compel the exercise of his discretion one way or the other (*Kentucky v. Dennison,* 24 How. 66, 109, 16 L.Ed. 717), for to do so would be to take over the office.

Where the Constitution assigns a particular function wholly and indivisibly[3] to another department, the federal judiciary does not intervene. None of those cases is relevant here. * * *

MR. JUSTICE CLARK, concurring.

[An] examination of Table I accompanying this opinion conclusively reveals that the apportionment picture in Tennessee is a topsy-turvical of gigantic proportions. This is not to say that some of the disparity cannot be explained,

2. The statements in *Luther* that this guaranty is enforceable only by Congress or the Chief Executive is not maintainable [and are] contrary to [the] modern decisions of the Court that give the full panoply of judicial protection to voting rights. * * *

Moreover, the Court's refusal to examine the legality of the regime of martial law which had been laid upon Rhode Island is indefensible, as Mr. Justice Woodbury maintained in his dissent. * * *

What he wrote was later to become the tradition, as expressed by Chief Justice Hughes in *Sterling v. Constantin,* 287 U.S. 378, 401, 53 S.Ct. 190, 196, 77 L.Ed. 375: "What are the allowable limits of military discretion, and whether or not they have been overstepped in a particular case, are judicial questions."

3. The category of the "political" question is, in my view, narrower than the decided cases indicate. * * *

Georgia v. Stanton involved the application of the Reconstruction Acts to Georgia—laws which destroyed by force the internal regime of that State. [The] question was no more "political" than a host of others we have entertained. See, e.g., *Pennsylvania v. West Virginia,* 262 U.S. 553, 43 S.Ct. 658, 67 L.Ed. 1117; *Youngstown Sheet & Tube Co. v. Sawyer,* [p. 148 infra]; *Alabama v. Texas,* 347 U.S. 272, 74 S.Ct. 481, 98 L.Ed. 689.

Today would this Court hold nonjusticiable or "political" a suit to enjoin a Governor who, like Fidel Castro, takes everything into his own hands and suspends all election laws? * * *

but when the entire table is examined—comparing the voting strength of counties of like population as well as contrasting that of the smaller with the larger counties—it leaves but one conclusion, namely that Tennessee's apportionment is a crazy quilt without rational basis. * * *

Although I find the Tennessee apportionment statute offends the Equal Protection Clause,[d] I would not consider intervention by this Court into so delicate a field if there were any other relief available to the people of Tennessee. But the majority of the people of Tennessee have no "practical opportunities for exerting their political weight at the polls" to correct the existing "invidious discrimination." Tennessee has no initiative and referendum. [T]he legislative policy has riveted the present seats in the Assembly to their respective constituencies, and by the votes of their incumbents a reapportionment of any kind is prevented. The people have been rebuffed at the hands of the Assembly; they have tried the constitutional convention route, but since the call must originate in the Assembly, it, too, has been fruitless. They have tried Tennessee courts with the same result,[9] and Governors have fought the tide only to flounder. It is said that there is recourse in Congress and perhaps that may be, but from a practical standpoint this is without substance. To date Congress has never undertaken such a task in any State. * * *

Finally, we must consider if there are any appropriate modes of effective judicial relief. [One] plan might be to start with the existing assembly districts, consolidate some of them, and award the seats thus released to those counties suffering the most egregious discrimination. Other possibilities are present and might be more effective. But the plan here suggested would at least release the stranglehold now on the Assembly and permit it to redistrict itself. * * *

[It] is well for this Court to practice self-restraint and discipline in constitutional adjudication, but never in its history have those principles received sanction where the national rights of so many have been so clearly infringed for so long a time. National respect for the courts is more enhanced through the forthright enforcement of those rights rather than by rendering them nugatory through the interposition of subterfuges. * * *

MR. JUSTICE STEWART, concurring.

The separate writings of my dissenting and concurring Brothers stray so far from the subject of today's decision as to convey, I think, a distressingly inaccurate impression of what the Court decides. * * * Contrary to the suggestion of my Brother Harlan, the Court does not say or imply that "state legislatures must be so structured as to reflect with approximate equality the voice of every voter" [or] that there is anything in the Federal Constitution "to prevent a State, acting not irrationally, from choosing any electoral legislative structure it thinks best suited to the interests, temper, and customs of its people." * * * My Brother Clark has made a convincing prima facie showing that Tennessee's system of apportionment is in fact utterly arbitrary—without any possible justification in rationality. My Brother Harlan has, with imagination and ingenuity, hypothesized possibly rational bases for Tennessee's system. But the merits of this case are not before us now. * * *

MR. JUSTICE FRANKFURTER, whom MR. JUSTICE HARLAN joins, dissenting.

---

d. Clark, J., "not being able to muster a court to dispose of the case on the merits," joined the Court's opinion. this Court has precluded adjudication of the federal claim.

9. It is interesting to note that state judges often rest their decisions on the ground that

The Court today reverses a uniform course of decision established by a dozen cases [which] reflected the equally uniform course of our political history regarding the relationship between population and legislative representation—a wholly different matter from denial of the franchise to individuals because of race, color, religion or sex. Such a massive repudiation of the experience of our whole past in asserting destructively novel judicial power demands a detailed analysis of the role of this Court in our constitutional scheme. Disregard of inherent limits in the effective exercise of the Court's "judicial Power" not only presages the futility of judicial intervention in the essentially political conflict of forces by which the relation between population and representation has time out of mind been and now is determined. It may well impair the Court's position as the ultimate organ of "the supreme Law of the Land" in that vast range of legal problems, often strongly entangled in popular feeling, on which this Court must pronounce. The Court's authority—possessed of neither the purse nor the sword—ultimately rests on sustained public confidence in its moral sanction. Such feeling must be nourished by the Court's complete detachment, in fact and in appearance, from political entanglements and by abstention from injecting itself into the clash of political forces in political settlements.

[The claim in this case] is hypothetical and the assumptions [on which it rests] are abstract because the Court does not vouchsafe the lower courts—state and federal—guidelines for formulating specific, definite, wholly unprecedented remedies for the inevitable litigations that today's umbrageous disposition is bound to stimulate in connection with politically motivated reapportionments in so many States. In such a setting, to promulgate jurisdiction in the abstract is meaningless. It is as devoid of reality as "a brooding omnipresence in the sky" for it conveys no intimation what relief, if any, a District Court is capable of affording that would not invite legislatures to play ducks and drakes with the judiciary. [One] of the Court's supporting opinions, as elucidated by commentary, unwittingly affords a disheartening preview of the mathematical quagmire (apart from divers judicially inappropriate and elusive determinants) into which this Court today catapults the lower courts of the country without so much as adumbrating the basis for a legal calculus as a means of extrication. Even assuming the indispensable intellectual disinterestedness on the part of judges in such matters, [t]o charge courts with the task of accommodating the incommensurable factors of policy that underlie these mathematical puzzles is to attribute, however flatteringly, omnicompetence to judges. * * * Considering the gross inequality among legislative electoral units within almost every State, the Court naturally shrinks from asserting that in districting at least substantial equality is a constitutional requirement enforceable by courts [and] implies that geography, economics, urban-rural conflict, and all the other non-legal factors which have throughout our history entered into political districting are to some extent not to be ruled [out]. To some extent—aye, there's the rub. In effect, today's decision empowers the courts of the country to devise what should constitute the proper composition of the legislatures of the fifty States. * * *

We were soothingly told at the bar of this Court that we need not worry about the kind of remedy a court could effectively fashion once the abstract constitutional right to have courts pass on a statewide system of electoral districting is recognized as a matter of judicial rhetoric, because legislatures would heed the Court's admonition. This is not only a euphoric hope. It implies a sorry confession of judicial impotence in place of a frank acknowledgment that there is not under our Constitution a judicial remedy for every political mischief, for every undesirable exercise of legislative power. The Framers carefully and with deliberate forethought refused so to enthrone the judiciary. In this situation, as in others of like nature, appeal for relief does not belong here. Appeal must be to an informed, civically militant electorate. In a democratic society like ours, relief must come through an aroused popular conscience that sears the conscience of the people's representatives. [From] its earliest opinions this Court has consistently recognized a class of controversies which do not lend themselves to judicial standards and judicial remedies. To classify the various instances as "political questions" is rather a form of stating this conclusion * * *.

The Court has been particularly unwilling to intervene in matters concerning the structure and organization of the political institutions of the States. * * *

The cases involving Negro disfranchisement are no exception to the principle of avoiding federal intervention into matters of state government in the absence of an explicit and clear constitutional imperative. For here the controlling command of Supreme Law is plain and unequivocal. * * *

The present case [is], in effect, a Guarantee Clause claim masquerading under a different label. But it cannot make the case more fit for judicial action that appellants invoke the Fourteenth Amendment rather than Art. IV, § 4, where, in fact, the gist of their complaint is the same. * * *

At first blush, this charge of discrimination based on legislative underrepresentation is given the appearance of a more private, less impersonal claim, than the assertion that the frame of government is askew. Appellants appear as representatives of a class that is prejudiced as a class, in contradistinction to the polity in its entirety. However, the discrimination relied on is the deprivation of what appellants conceive to be their proportionate share of political influence. * * * Hardly any distribution of political authority that could be assailed as rendering government nonrepublican would fail similarly to operate to the prejudice of some groups, and to the advantage of others, within the body politic. [T]he real battle over the initiative and referendum, or over a delegation of power to local rather than statewide authority, is the battle between forces whose influence is disparate among the various organs of government to whom power may be given. [What] Tennessee illustrates is an old and still widespread method of representation—representation by local geographical division, only in part respective of population—in preference to others, others, forsooth, more appealing. Appellants contest this choice and seek to make this Court the arbiter of the disagreement. * * * Certainly, "equal protection" is no more secure a foundation for judicial judgment of the permissibility of varying forms of representative government than is "Republican Form." * * *

The notion that representation proportioned to the geographic spread of population is so universally accepted as a necessary element of equality between man and man that it must be taken to be the standard of a political equality preserved by the Fourteenth Amendment—that it is, in appellants' words "the basic principle of representative government"—is, to put it bluntly, not true. However desirable and however desired by some among the great political thinkers and framers of our government, it has never been generally practiced, today or in the past. It was not the English system, it was not the colonial system, it was not the system chosen for the national government by the Constitution, it was not the system exclusively or even predominantly practiced by the States at the time of adoption of the Fourteenth Amendment, it is not predominantly practiced by the States today. Unless judges, the judges of this Court, are to make their private views of political wisdom the measure of the

Constitution—views which in all honesty cannot but give the appearance, if not reflect the reality, of involvement with the business of partisan politics so inescapably a part of apportionment controversies—the Fourteenth Amendment [provides] no guide for judicial oversight of the representation problem. * * *

[In] all of the apportionment cases which have come before the Court, a consideration which has been weighty in determining their nonjusticiability has been the difficulty or impossibility of devising effective judicial remedies in this class of case. An injunction restraining a general election unless the legislature reapportions would paralyze the critical centers of a State's political system * * *. A declaration devoid of implied compulsion of injunctive or other relief would be an idle threat. Surely a Federal District Court could not itself remap the State [and] the choice of elections at large as opposed to elections by district, however unequal the districts, is a matter of sweeping political judgment having enormous political implications, the nature and reach of which are certainly beyond the informed understanding of, and capacity for appraisal by, courts.

In Tennessee, moreover, the *McCanless* [case] said, "There is no provision of law for election of our General Assembly by an election at large over the State." 200 Tenn., at 277, 292 S.W.2d, at 42. Thus, a legislature elected at large would not be the legally constituted legislative authority of the State. [A] federal court cannot provide the authority requisite to make a legislature the proper governing body of the State of Tennessee. * * *

Dissenting opinion of MR. JUSTICE HARLAN, whom MR. JUSTICE FRANKFURTER joins.

[I]n my opinion, appellants' allegations [do not] show an infringement by Tennessee of any rights assured by the Fourteenth Amendment. Accordingly, I believe the complaint should have been dismissed for "failure to state a claim upon which relief can be granted." [Thus], we need not reach the issues of "justiciability" or "political question" * * *.

In the last analysis, what lies at the core of this controversy is a difference of opinion as to the function of representative government. It is surely beyond argument that those who have the responsibility for devising a system of representation may permissibly consider that factors other than bare numbers should be taken into account. The existence of the United States Senate is proof enough of that. To consider that we may ignore the Tennessee Legislature's judgment in this instance because that body was the product of an asymmetrical electoral apportionment would in effect be to assume the very conclusion here disputed. Hence we must accept the present form of the Tennessee Legislature as the embodiment of the State's choice, or, more realistically, its compromise, between competing political philosophies. The federal courts have not been empowered by the Equal Protection Clause to judge whether this resolution of the State's internal political conflict is desirable or undesirable, wise or unwise.

* * *

The claim that Tennessee's system of apportionment is so unreasonable as to amount to a capricious classification of voting strength stands up no better under dispassionate analysis.[e] * * *

e. In his opinion and in an appendix to it, Harlan, J., challenged Clark, J.'s original formula for determining how many representatives each county presently had. He then demonstrated that no feasible formula "could provide proportionately equal 'total representation' for each of Tennessee's 95 counties," and argued the relevancy and legitimacy of factors other than numbers, e.g., "a proper balance between urban and rural interest," "the size of a county in terms of its total area," "the location within a county of some major industry," "various economic, political, and geographical considerations," and defer-

The suggestion of my Brother Frankfurter that courts lack standards by which to decide such cases as this, is relevant not only to the question of "justiciability," but also, and perhaps more fundamentally, to the determination whether any cognizable constitutional claim has been asserted in this case. [Those] observers of the Court who see it primarily as the last refuge for the correction of all inequality or injustice, no matter what its nature or source, will no doubt applaud this decision and its break with the past. Those who consider that continuing national respect for the Court's authority depends in large measure upon its wise exercise of self-restraint and discipline in constitutional adjudication, will view the decision with deep concern. * * *[f]

POWELL v. McCORMACK, 395 U.S. 486, 89 S.Ct. 1944, 23 L.Ed.2d 491 (1969): Petitioner was elected to the House of Representatives for the 90th Congress. Although he met the age, citizenship and residence requirements of Art. I, § 2, cl. 2, he was not permitted to take his seat pursuant to a House resolution after a Select Committee "reported that Powell had asserted an unwarranted privilege and immunity from the processes of the courts of New York; that he had wrongfully diverted House funds for the use of others and himself; and that he had made false reports on expenditures of foreign currency to the Committee on House Administration." Powell sought, inter alia, a federal declaration that his exclusion was unconstitutional and that his salary be paid by the Sergeant-at-Arms. The lower courts dismissed the complaint.

The Court, per WARREN, C.J., reversed, (Stewart, J., dissenting on the ground that the case was moot) holding that the claim did not present a political question. It rejected the contention—after lengthy examination of the pre-Constitutional Convention precedents of the English Parliament and American colonial assemblies, the debates at the Constitutional Convention and state conventions, and the early and more recent congressional precedents—that Art. I, § 5, cl. 1 ("Each House shall be the Judge of the * * * Qualifications of its own Members") contained a "textually demonstrable constitutional commitment" to the House of "judicially unreviewable power to set qualifications for membership and to judge whether prospective members meet those qualifications." "In order to determine whether there has been a textual commitment to a co-ordinate department of the Government, we must interpret the Constitution. [Our] examination of the relevant historical materials leads us to the conclusion [that] the Constitution leaves the House without authority to *exclude* any person, duly elected by his constituents, who meets all the requirements for membership expressly prescribed in" Art. I, § 2.[g]

ring reapportionment "in the interest of stability of government."

f. For detailed consideration of the reapportionment problem, see Ch. 10, Sec. 4, I, A.

g. For a contrary conclusion, see Dionisopoulous, *A Commentary on the Constitutional Issues in the Powell and Related Cases,* 17 J.Pub.L. 103 (1968). Consider Sandalow, in *Symposium,* 17 U.C.L.A.L.Rev. 164, 172–73 (1969): "The most striking feature of the Court's review of history [is] that not until the *Powell* case can one find any suggestion that courts are empowered to sit in judgment on the question whether the House or Senate exceeded their authority in excluding a person

elected to membership. [Having] begun by asking the right question, whether there was a 'constitutional commitment of the issue' to the House, the Court proceeded to answer a quite different one, whether the 'qualifications' which Article I, Section 5 authorized the House to 'judge' were only those specified in Article I, Section 2 (and perhaps elsewhere in the Constitution). The opinion reflects, in short, a classic instance of confusion between 'jurisdiction'—the power to decide—and 'the merits'—the correctness of decisions."

Query: Could Congress enact a mandatory retirement age for its members?

"Had the intent of the Framers emerged from these materials with less clarity, we would nevertheless have been compelled to resolve any ambiguity in favor of a narrow construction of the scope of Congress' power to exclude members-elect. A fundamental principle of our representative democracy is, in Hamilton's words, 'that the people should choose whom they please to govern them.' As Madison pointed out at the Convention, this principle is undermined as much by limiting whom the people can select as by limiting the franchise itself. * * * Unquestionably, Congress has an interest in preserving its institutional integrity, but in most cases that interest can be sufficiently safe-guarded by the exercise of its power to punish its members for disorderly behavior and, in extreme cases, to expel a member with the concurrence of two-thirds." The Court expressed no view on what limitations may exist on Congress' power to "expel or otherwise punish" a member, under Art. I, § 5, cl. 2 once he has been seated.

"Respondents' alternate contention is that the case presents a political question because judicial resolution of petitioners' claim would produce a 'potentially embarrassing confrontation between coordinate branches' of the Federal Government. But, [our interpretation of Art. I, § 5] falls within the traditional role accorded courts to interpret the law, and does not involve a 'lack of respect due [a] coordinate branch of government,' nor does it involve an 'initial policy determination of a kind clearly for nonjudicial discretion.' *Baker.* Our system of government requires that federal courts on occasion interpret the Constitution in a manner at variance with the construction given the document by another branch. The alleged conflict that such an adjudication may cause cannot justify the courts' avoiding their constitutional responsibility. * * *

"Nor are any of the other formulations of a political question 'inextricable from the case at bar.' *Baker.* Petitioners seek a determination [for] which clearly there are 'judicially manageable standards.' Finally, a judicial resolution of petitioners' claim will not result in 'multifarious pronouncements by various departments on one question.' For, as we noted in *Baker,* it is the responsibility of this Court to act as the ultimate interpreter of the Constitution. * * *

"Petitioners seek additional forms of equitable relief, including mandamus for the release of Petitioner Powell's back pay. The propriety of such remedies, however, is more appropriately considered in the first instance by the courts below." [i]

Notes and Questions

1. *"Judicially manageable standards."* COLEMAN v. MILLER stated: "[T]he question of a reasonable time [for the pendency of a constitutional amendment before the states involves] an appraisal of a great variety of relevant conditions, political, social and economic, which can hardly be said to be within the appropriate range of evidence receivable in a court of justice and as to which it would be an extravagant extension of judicial authority to assert judicial notice. [T]hese conditions are appropriate for the consideration of the political

i. Powell was re-elected to the 91st Congress. Pursuant to a House resolution, he was seated but fined $25,000 and denied all prior seniority. Would a suit challenging this action present a "political question"?

Suppose a defeated House candidate brings an action challenging the House's seating of his opponent—who is a 23 year-old alien who has never resided outside of the District of Columbia since coming to the United States?

See generally *Symposium,* 17 U.C.L.A.L.Rev. 1 (1969).

departments of the Government. The questions they involve are essentially political and not justiciable." If the *Coleman* question was "political" for this reason, what of the questions in *Baker* and *Powell?* What of the questions in the *School Segregation Cases,* p. 892 infra? Is this a helpful test by which to determine justiciability?

2. *Foreign relations.* GOLDWATER v. CARTER, 444 U.S. 996, 100 S.Ct. 533, 62 L.Ed.2d 428 (1979), summarily reversed a court of appeals decision that the President had power to terminate a treaty with Taiwan without congressional approval. REHNQUIST, J., joined by Burger, C.J., and Stewart and Stevens, JJ., believed "that the controversy [is] a nonjusticiable political dispute [because] it involves foreign relations—specifically a treaty commitment to use military force in the defense of a foreign government if attacked. [W]e are asked to settle a dispute between coequal branches of our government, each of which has resources available to protect and assert its interests, resources not available to private litigants outside the judicial forum."

POWELL, J., concurred because of "prudential considerations": "[A] dispute between Congress and the President is not ready for judicial review unless and until each branch has taken action asserting its constitutional authority. [Since] Congress has taken no official [action], we do not know whether there ever will be an actual confrontation between the Legislative and Executive Branches."

But "reliance upon the political-question doctrine is inconsistent with our precedents. [First,] the text of the Constitution does not unquestionably commit the power to terminate treaties to the President alone. Second, there is no 'lack of judicially discoverable and manageable [standards.]' Resolution of the question may not be easy, but it only requires us to apply normal principles of interpretation to the constitutional provisions at issue. [This] case 'touches' foreign relations, but the question presented to us concerns only the constitutional division of power between Congress and the President. [Finally,] [i]nterpretation of the Constitution does not imply lack of respect for a coordinate branch. *Powell.* * * *" [a]

BRENNAN, J., who would have affirmed on the merits, dissented: "[T]he political question doctrine restrains courts from reviewing an exercise of foreign policy judgment by the coordinate political branch [but] the doctrine does not pertain when a court is faced with the *antecedent* question whether a particular branch has been constitutionally designated as the repository of political decisionmaking power. Cf. *Powell.* The issue of decisionmaking authority must be resolved as a matter of constitutional law, not political discretion; accordingly, it falls within the competence of the courts." [b]

3. *Controversial nature of subject matter.* Should this be an important criterion for determining "political questions"? If so, was it omitted from the *Baker* "checklist"? Consider Finkelstein, *Judicial Self-Limitation,* 37 Harv.L. Rev. 338, 344 (1924): "There are certain cases which are completely without the sphere of judicial interference. They are called, for historical reasons, 'political questions'. [The term] applies to all those matters of which the court, at a given time, will be of the opinion that it is impolitic or inexpedient to take jurisdiction. Sometimes this idea of expediency will result from the fear of the vastness of the consequences that a decision on the merits might entail." See generally Bickel, *The Least Dangerous Branch* 183–98 (1962). Compare Weston, *Political Ques-*

---

a. Marshall, J., concurred in the result.

b. Blackmun, J., joined by White, J., dissented. They "would set the case for oral argument and give it the plenary consideration it so obviously deserves."

tions, 38 Harv.L.Rev. 296, 298–99 (1925): "[T]he courts in the obligatory exercise of unquestioned jurisdiction walk every day upon ground still shaken by the conflict of public opinion."

4. *"Textually demonstrable constitutional commitment."* (a) *Amending process.* (i) Concurring in *Coleman v. Miller,* Black, J., joined by Roberts, Frankfurter and Douglas, JJ., stated that Art. V "grants Congress exclusive power [over] the amending process" and that Congress "is under no duty to accept the pronouncements upon that exclusive power by this Court." Does this distinguish *Coleman* from *Baker?* From *Colegrove* (see *Wesberry v. Sanders,* p. 1022 infra)? From *Powell?* Does the language of Art. V support Black, J.? Suppose Congress submitted a proposed constitutional amendment to the states and provided that no black could participate in the state ratification process? See generally Tribe, *A Constitution We Are Amending: In Defense of a Restrained Judicial Role,* 97 Harv.L.Rev. 433 (1983); Dellinger, *The Legitimacy of Constitutional Change: Rethinking the Amendment Process,* 97 Harv. L.Rev. 386 (1983).

(ii) In *Coleman,* the Court held that "the question of the efficacy of ratifications by state legislatures, in the light of previous rejection or attempted withdrawal, should be regarded as a political question pertaining to the political departments, with the ultimate authority in the Congress in the exercise of its control over the promulgation of the adoption of the Amendment." Does this also apply to the question of whether a state legislature, which has already ratified a proposed amendment, may subsequently rescind that ratification? [c]

(iii) If, pursuant to Art. V, "the legislatures of two-thirds of the several states" apply to Congress to "call a convention for proposing amendments" and Congress ignores the application, is an action for a mandatory injunction "nonjusticiable"? See Bonfield, *The Dirksen Amendment and the Article V Convention Process,* 66 Mich.L.Rev. 949, 976–85 (1968).

(b) *Impeachment.* Does Art. I, § 3, cl. 6—"The Senate shall have the sole power to try all impeachments"—"demonstrably commit" final constitutional decision "to a coordinate political department"? Consider Berger, *Impeachment: The Constitutional Problems* 105–06, 117–18, 120 (1973): "Like the three qualifications of Art. I, § 2(2) [in *Powell*], impeachment, by Art. II, § 4, is limited to three grounds, 'treason, bribery, or other high crimes and misdemeanors,' * * *. Although impeachment was chiefly designed to check Executive abuses and oppressions, there was no thought of delivering either the President or the Judiciary to the unbounded discretion of Congress. This is attested by the Framers' rejection of the unfettered removal by Address [formal request of Congress], by their rejection of 'maladministration' because that was 'so vague' as to leave tenure, 'at the pleasure' of the Senate, and by the substitution of 'high crimes and misdemeanors' with knowledge that it had a 'limited' and 'technical meaning.' * * * 'Limits' on Congress determined by Congress itself would be no limits at all. [I]f it be assumed that the 'sole power to try' conferred insulation from review, it must yield to the subsequent Fifth Amendment ['due process' provision]." See also Rezneck, *Is Judicial Review of Impeachment Coming?* 60 A.B.A.J. 681, 682–83 (1974): "Nothing in the text of the Constitution expressly bars judicial review of an impeachment conviction. On the

c. For varying views on this issue, both as to justiciability and the merits, see Kanowitz & Klinger, *Can a State Rescind Its Equal Rights Amendment Ratification: Who Decides and How?* 28 Hast.L.J. 979 (1977); Comment, *The Equal Rights Amendment and Article V: A Framework for Analysis of the Extension and Rescission Issues,* 127 U.Pa.L.Rev. 494 (1978); Note, *The Process of Constitutional Amendment,* 79 Colum.L.Rev. 109 (1979).

contrary, Art. III provides that the 'judicial Power' of the [federal courts] 'shall extend to all cases, in Law and Equity, arising under this Constitution.' [If, in *Powell*], the constitutional provision that 'Each House shall be the Judge of the Elections, Returns and Qualifications of its own Members' did not commit the final determination of Powell's exclusion to the House of Representatives, why should the language on impeachment be read to commit final decision of all impeachment questions to the Senate? The grant of power to 'judge' is at least as comprehensive as a power to 'try,' but it did not prevent judicial review in *Powell.* [Moreover, the] use of the word 'try' suggests a limited, not absolute, measure of finality for decisions of the Senate in an impeachment proceeding. [The] 'trial,' in which the facts are determined, is different from an 'appeal' or other mode of review in which questions of law are resolved in an appellate court."

Compare Black, *Impeachment: A Handbook* 54–55, 61–62 (1974): "If the Supreme Court [were] to order reinstatement of an impeached and convicted president, there would be, to say the least, a very grave and quite legitimate doubt whether that decree had any title to being obeyed, or whether it was [as] widely outside judicial jurisdiction as would be a judicial order to Congress to increase the penalty for counterfeiting. To cite the most frightening consequence, our military commanders would have to decide for themselves which president they were bound to obey, the reinstated one or his successor. [It] would be most unfortunate if the notion got about that the Senate's verdict were somewhat tentative. [No] senator should be encouraged to think he can shift to any court responsibility for an unpalatable or unpopular decision. [Further,] if a removed president tried [judicial review], and had his case (as would almost surely happen) dismissed for want of jurisdiction, he might be able, though quite wrongly, to persuade a part of the people that he had been denied his rightful day in court."

(c) *Regulating the militia.* In GILLIGAN v. MORGAN, 413 U.S. 1, 93 S.Ct. 2440, 37 L.Ed.2d 407 (1973), students at Kent State University sought various relief against government officials to prevent repetition of events that had occurred on that campus in May 1970. The court of appeals instructed the federal district court to evaluate the "pattern of training, weaponry and orders in the Ohio National Guard" so as to determine whether it made "inevitable the use of fatal force in suppressing civilian disorders." The Court, per BURGER, C.J., reversed, relying heavily on Art. I, § 8, cl. 16—which grants to Congress "the responsibility for organizing, arming and disciplining the Militia (now the National Guard), with certain responsibilities being reserved to the respective States"—and on federal legislation enacted pursuant thereto: "[T]he nature of the questions to be resolved on remand are subjects committed expressly to the political branches of government. [It] would be difficult to think of a clearer example of the type of governmental action that was intended by the Constitution to be left to the political branches [or] of an area of governmental activity in which the courts have less competence. The complex, subtle, and professional decisions as to the composition, training, equipping, and control of a military force are essentially professional military judgments, subject *always* to civilian control of the Legislative and Executive Branches [which] are periodically subject to electoral accountability." [e]

---

e. Douglas, Brennan, Stewart and Marshall, JJ., dissented because "this case is now moot."

(d) Do *Baker, Powell, Coleman* and *Gilligan* establish that the "political question" doctrine is "a function of the separation of powers"—presently confined exclusively to "the relationship between the judiciary and the coordinate branches of the Federal Government"? That the other *Baker* criteria—including "judicially manageable standards" (note 1 supra) and "effective judicial remedies" (note 5 infra)—are all subsumed within this specific principle? See Jackson, *The Political Question Doctrine: Where Does It Stand After Powell v. McCormack, O'Brien v. Brown and Gilligan v. Morgan,* 44 U.Colo.L.Rev. 477 (1973). If so, and if the political branches specifically authorize the Court to decide the question, may (should) the Court do so? See Choper, *Judicial Review and the National Political Process* 405–15 (1980). See also note 3, after *Poe v. Ullman,* p. 1220 infra.

For the view that the leading political question cases have *not* "involved abstention from judicial review, or other extraordinary deference" to the political branches—i.e., that the Court has *not* held that the other branches' "determinations were binding on the courts 'right or wrong,' constitutional or unconstitutional"—but rather involved the Court's either "accept[ing] decisions by the political branches [as being] within their constitutional authority," or "refus[ing] some (or all) remedies for want of equity," see Henkin, *Is There a Political Question Doctrine?* 85 Yale L.J. 597 (1976). See also Note, *A Dialogue on the Political Question Doctrine,* 1978 Utah L.Rev. 523.

(e) O'BRIEN v. BROWN, 409 U.S. 1, 92 S.Ct. 2718, 34 L.Ed.2d 1 (1972), per curiam, stayed judgments which had adjudicated the merits of challenges to "recommendations of the Credentials Committee of the 1972 Democratic National Convention regarding the seating of certain delegates to the convention that will meet three days hence": "[N]o holding of this Court up to now gives support for judicial intervention in the circumstances presented here, involving as they do, relationships of great delicacy and essentially political in nature. [It] has been understood since our national political parties first came into being as voluntary associations of individuals that the convention itself is the proper forum for determining intra-party disputes as to which delegates shall be seated. [While] the Court is unwilling to undertake final resolution of the important constitutional questions presented without full briefing and argument and adequate opportunity for deliberation, we entertain grave doubts as to the action taken by the Court of Appeals." [f]

Douglas, White and Marshall, JJ., would have denied the stays, Marshall, J., joined by Douglas, J., believing that "the doctrine of 'political questions' was fashioned to deal with a very different problem, which has nothing to do with this case. [T]he full convention of the National Democratic Party [is] most assuredly not a coordinate branch of government to which the federal courts owe deference within the meaning of the separation of powers or the political question doctrine." [g]

5. *Effective judicial remedies.* To what extent should "the difficulty or impossibility of devising effective judicial remedies" influence "justiciability"? [h] How effective (seemly?) were the possible remedies available in *Baker*? What remedies could (should) a court afford in the various situations discussed in the above notes?

---

f. Brennan, J., concurred in the result.

g. Does *O'Brien* suggest a revival of Frankfurter, J.'s view in *Colegrove* and *Baker*?

h. For detail, see p. 1025 infra.

6. *"Judicial restraint" and the political process.* Consider Frank, *Political Questions,* in Supreme Court & Supreme Law 36, 46 (Cahn ed. 1954): "[T]he basic objective of a plan of government ought to be to put the responsibility for the decision of questions some place, and [the] political question doctrine is useful when it operates to put responsibility at the best place, and is harmful when it puts the decision no place. [W]hat happens in the redistricting cases is that the responsibility, if not taken by the court, is transferred to a body which has a completely vested interest in the maldistricting." Does this adequately respond to Frankfurter, J.'s "appeal must be to an informed, civically militant electorate" argument? Compare Auerbach, *The Reapportionment Cases: One Person, One Vote—One Vote, One Value,* 1964 Sup.Ct.Rev. 1, 2: "It is paradoxical [for] the advocates of judicial self-limitation to criticize the Court for helping to make majority rule effective, because the case for self-restraint rests on the assumption that the Court is reviewing the legislative acts of representatives who are put in office and can be turned out of office by a majority of the people. Since malapportionment destroys this assumption, judicial intervention to remove this obstacle to majority rule may be less intolerable than the self-perpetuation of minority rule."

7. *Republican form of government.* (a) Do you agree with *Baker* "that Guaranty Clause claims involve those elements which define a 'political question' and for that reason are nonjusticiable"? Consider Emerson, *Malapportionment and Judicial Power,* 72 Yale L.J. 64, 67–68 (1962): "[S]ince Brennan, J., repudiates the notion that 'political questions' are to be determined by blanket categories and makes clear that each case must be determined on its own facts, it would seem that the issue of justiciability under the guaranty clause would likewise turn on whether the essential elements of a 'political question' are present in any particular case." See McCloskey, *The Reapportionment Case,* 76 Harv.L.Rev. 54, 63 (1962): "[I]f the guaranty clause intrinsically raises political questions, this cannot be because it 'is not a repository of judicially manageable standards.' Its standards are not any more nebulous than those of the equal protection clause in this context." See also Bonfield, *Baker v. Carr: New Light on the Constitutional Guarantee of Republican Government,* 50 Calif.L.Rev. 245, 250 (1962): "The clause is neither textually committed to the exclusive enforcement of another department, nor bare of judicially discoverable or manageable standards for resolving questions dependent for their resolution upon it. It is therefore the 'political question' aspects of the issue raised under the guarantee and not the mere invocation of that provision that should determine justiciability." For an attempt to demonstrate the existence of satisfactorily ascertainable standards under the guaranty clause, see Bonfield, *The Guarantee Clause of Article IV, Section 4: A Study in Constitutional Desuetude,* 46 Minn.L.Rev. 513 (1962). See also Scharpf, *Judicial Review and the Political Question: A Functional Analysis,* 75 Yale L.J. 517, 589–96 (1966).

(b) If Congress, legislating under the guaranty clause, permitted a state to establish its government as a monarchy, would a dissenting citizen be barred from Supreme Court review on the ground that this was a "political question"? Is this what Douglas, J., had in mind in his fn. 3? How would Brennan, J., decide this? Frankfurter and Harlan, JJ.? Consider Bonfield, supra, at 564–65: "[J]udicial abstinence would give Congress unlimited power to impose on the states whatever government it deemed republican. Not only would such authority spell the complete end of our federal system, but it would also create an unchecked power capable of destroying rather than guaranteeing republican government."

SECTION 3. CONGRESSIONAL REGULATION OF JUDICIAL POWER

Beginning with the Judiciary Act of 1789, Congress has enacted various statutes defining the Supreme Court's jurisdiction. For example, it was not until 1914 that the Court was authorized to review state court decisions holding state laws violative of the Constitution. The Court's original jurisdiction, which typically comprises only a handful of cases each year (mainly concerning "controversies between two or more states"), is presently governed by 28 U.S.C. § 1251. The most important current provisions respecting the Court's appellate jurisdiction are 28 U.S.C. §§ 1254 (federal courts of appeals) and 1257 (state courts).

———

§ 1254. Cases in the courts of appeals may be reviewed by the Supreme Court by the following methods:

(1) By writ of certiorari granted upon the petition of any party to any civil or criminal case, before or after rendition of judgment or decree;

(2) By appeal by a party relying on a State statute held by a court of appeals to be invalid as repugnant to the Constitution, treaties or laws of the United States, but such appeal shall preclude review by writ of certiorari at the instance of such appellant, and the review on appeal shall be restricted to the Federal questions presented;

(3) By certification at any time by a court of appeals of any question of law in any civil or criminal case as to which instructions are desired, and upon such certification the Supreme Court may give binding instructions or require the entire record to be sent up for decision of the entire matter in controversy.

§ 1257. Final judgments or decrees rendered by the highest court of a State in which a decision could be had, may be reviewed by the Supreme Court as follows:

(1) By appeal, where is drawn in question the validity of a treaty or statute of the United States and the decision is against its validity.

(2) By appeal, where is drawn in question the validity of a statute of any state on the ground of its being repugnant to the Constitution, treaties or laws of the United States, and the decision is in favor of its validity.

(3) By writ of certiorari, where the validity of a treaty or statute of the United States is drawn in question or where the validity of a State statute is drawn in question on the ground of its being repugnant to the Constitution, treaties or laws of the United States, or where any title, right, privilege or immunity is specially set up or claimed under the Constitution, treaties or statutes of, or commission held or authority exercised under, the United States.

*   *   *

EX PARTE McCARDLE
74 U.S. (7 Wall.) 506, 19 L.Ed. 264 (1869).

[On February 5, 1867, Congress empowered federal courts to grant habeas corpus to persons restrained in violation of the Constitution, treaty, or federal law. Appeal could be to the Supreme Court. McCardle—imprisoned by the military government of Mississippi pursuant to the Reconstruction Acts for publishing "incendiary and libelous" articles—"alleging unlawful restraint by military force," sought habeas corpus which was denied by the Circuit Court. He appealed to the Supreme Court, apparently presenting it with the opportunity finally to reach the merits of the Reconstruction laws' constitutionality. However, in 1868, after argument but before decision, Congress (over President Johnson's veto) passed the following act:] "That so much of the act approved February 5, 1867 [as] authorized an appeal from the judgment of the Circuit Court to the Supreme Court of the United States, or the exercise of any such jurisdiction by said Supreme Court, on appeals which have been, or may hereafter be taken, [is] hereby repealed."

* * * Argument was now heard upon the effect of the repealing act.

The CHIEF JUSTICE [CHASE] delivered the opinion of the Court.

[T]he appellate jurisdiction of this Court is not derived from acts of Congress. It is, strictly speaking, conferred by the Constitution. But it is conferred "with such exceptions and under such regulations as Congress shall make."

It is unnecessary to consider whether, if Congress had made no exceptions and no regulations, this court might not have exercised general appellate jurisdiction under rules prescribed by itself. From among the earliest acts of the first Congress [was the Judiciary Act of 1789 which] provided for the organization of this court, and prescribed regulations for the exercise of its jurisdiction.

[In] *Durousseau v. United States* [6 Cranch, 307 (1810)], particularly, the whole matter was carefully examined, and the court held, that [the] judicial act was an exercise of the power given by the Constitution to Congress "of making exceptions to the appellate jurisdiction of the Supreme Court." "They have described affirmatively," said the court, "its jurisdiction, and this affirmative description has been understood to imply a negation of the exercise of such appellate power as is not comprehended within it."

The principle [thus] established, it was an almost necessary consequence that acts of Congress, providing for the exercise of jurisdiction, should come to be spoken of as acts granting jurisdiction and not as acts making exceptions to the constitutional grant of it.

The exception to appellate jurisdiction in the case before us, however, is not an inference from the affirmation of other appellate jurisdiction. It is made in terms. * * *

We are not at liberty to inquire into the motives of the legislature. We can only examine into its power under the Constitution * * *.

What, then, is the effect of the repealing act upon the case before us? * * * Jurisdiction is power to declare the law, and when it ceases to exist the only function remaining to the court is that of announcing the fact and dismissing the cause. And this is not less clear upon authority than upon principle. [J]udicial duty is not less fitly performed by declining ungranted jurisdiction than in exercising firmly that which the Constitution and the laws confer.

Counsel seem to have supposed, if effect be given to the repealing act in question, that the whole appellate power of the court, in cases of habeas corpus, is denied. But this is an error. The act of 1868 does not except from that jurisdiction any cases but appeals from Circuit Courts under the act of 1867. It does not affect the jurisdiction which was previously exercised.

The appeal [must] be dismissed for want of jurisdiction.[a]

Notes and Questions

1. *Extent of the decision.* (a) In *Ex Parte Yerger,* 75 U.S. (8 Wall.) 85, 19 L.Ed. 332 (1869), also challenging the Reconstruction Acts, the Court, upholding its appellate jurisdiction by writ of certiorari in a habeas corpus proceeding based on pre-1867 legislation, said of *McCardle*: "The effect of the Act was to oust the court of its jurisdiction of the particular case then before it on appeal, and it is not to be doubted that such was the effect intended. Nor will it be questioned that legislation of this character is unusual and hardly to be justified except upon some imperious public exigency." More recently, Douglas, J., joined by Black, J., stated: "There is a serious question whether [*McCardle*] could command a majority view today." *Glidden Co. v. Zdanok,* 370 U.S. 530, 605 n. 11, 82 S.Ct. 1459, 1501–02, 8 L.Ed.2d 671, 718–19 (1962).

(b) How great an incursion into the Court's jurisdiction did *McCardle* really permit? Consider Ratner, *Congressional Power Over the Appellate Jurisdiction of the Supreme Court,* 109 U.Pa.L.Rev. 157, 180 (1960): "The statute [did] not deprive the Court of jurisdiction to decide McCardle's case; he could still petition the Supreme Court for [an original] writ of habeas corpus * * *. The legislation did no more than eliminate one procedure for Supreme Court review of decisions denying habeas corpus while leaving another equally efficacious one available."

(c) Does *McCardle* stand for the proposition that Congress may *completely* deprive the Court of power to review certain federal questions? Apart from *McCardle,* does Congress have this power? The power to deprive the Court of *all* appellate jurisdiction? If not, what is the meaning of the "Exceptions" language in Art. III? Is it "that Congress may except certain cases otherwise subject only to the Court's appellate jurisdiction *by adding them to the Court's original jurisdiction*"? Van Alstyne, *A Critical Guide to Marbury v. Madison,* 1969 Duke L.J. 1, 32. It is that the Constitution *itself* only grants appellate jurisdiction in "all the other cases before mentioned" and that Congress may make "Exceptions" to this by adding to the appellate jurisdiction cases that Art. III has assigned to the original jurisdiction? For the position that this clause was intended to permit congressional control of the Court's appellate jurisdiction only as to questions of fact, not questions of law, see Merry, *Scope of the Supreme Court's Appellate Jurisdiction: Historical Basis,* 47 Minn.L.Rev. 53 (1962); Berger, *Congress v. The Supreme Court* 285–86 (1969).[c]

Consider Ratner, supra at 171–72: "It is reasonable to conclude [that the Constitutional] Convention gave Congress authority to specify * * * orderly procedures and to modify the jurisdiction from time to time in response to prevailing social and political requirements, within the limits imposed by the Court's essential constitutional role. It is not reasonable to conclude that the Convention gave Congress the power to destroy that role. Reasonably interpreted the clause means 'With such exceptions and under such regulations as

---

a. For an historical account, see Fairman, *Reconstruction and Reunion, 1864–88, Part One,* c. X (1971).

c. See also *Luckenbach S.S. Co. v. United States,* 272 U.S. 533, 47 S.Ct. 186, 71 L.Ed. 394 (1926) (upholding statute limiting Supreme Court review of Court of Claims decisions to

questions of law); *Barry v. Mercein,* 46 U.S. (5 How.) 103, 12 L.Ed. 70 (1847) (Supreme Court review of action based on diversity of citizenship unavailable because action did not involve minimum monetary value required by statute).

Congress may make, not inconsistent with the essential functions of the Supreme Court under this Constitution.' "

What is the Court's "essential constitutional role"? Consider Ratner, *Majoritarian Constraints on Judicial Review: Congressional Control of Supreme Court Jurisdiction,* 27 Vill.L.Rev. 929, 935, 956 (1982): "The supremacy clause of article VI mandates one supreme federal law throughout the land, and article III establishes the Supreme Court as the constitutional instrument for implementing that clause. [As] such, its essential functions under the Constitution are: 1) ultimately to resolve inconsistent or conflicting interpretations of federal law, and particularly of the Constitution, by state and federal courts; 2) to maintain the supremacy of federal law, and particularly the Constitution, when it conflicts with state law or is challenged by state authority." Compare Redish, *Congressional Power to Regulate Supreme Court Appellate Jurisdiction Under the Exceptions Clause: An Internal and External Examination,* 27 Vill.L.Rev. 900, 907 (1982): "I might well agree, as a policy matter, that Congress should not possess the power to tamper with performance of the Supreme Court's role, [but] I can find no constitutional basis for erecting such a limitation." See also Rice, *Congress and the Supreme Court's Jurisdiction,* 27 Vill.L.Rev. 959, 962–81 (1982). Contrast Sager, *Constitutional Limitations on Congress' Authority to Regulate the Jurisdiction of the Federal Courts,* 95 Harv.L.Rev. 17, 57 (1981): "The Court must be available to superintend *state compliance* with federal law unless Congress provides effective review elsewhere within the *federal* judiciary." [d]

2. *Legislative proposals.* From the early nineteenth century, there have been numerous congressional attempts to limit the Supreme Court's appellate jurisdiction over various issues.[e] Since the late 1970s, the most prominent have concerned abortion, school prayer, and busing for school integration. See Baucus & Kay, *The Court Stripping Bills,* 27 Vill.L.Rev. 988 (1982).

Suppose Congress sought to deny Supreme Court appellate jurisdiction in any case brought by a black? Is this distinguishable from the recent proposals? What role do other constitutional provisions play in respect to the "Exceptions and Regulations" clause? See Tribe, *Jurisdictional Gerrymandering: Zoning Disfavored Rights Out of the Federal Courts,* 16 Harv.Civ.Rts.-Civ.Lib.L.Rev. 129, 141–46 (1981); Sager, note 1(c) supra, at 78–80. Compare Bator, *Congressional Power Over the Jurisdiction of the Federal Courts,* 27 Vill.L.Rev. 1030, 1034–37 (1982).

3. *Proposal for a National Court of Appeals.* In 1972, a committee chaired by Professor Paul Freund, appointed by Chief Justice Burger "to study the case load of the Supreme Court," proposed, inter alia: "The establishment [of] a National Court of Appeals, [with] seven judges drawn on a rotating basis from the federal courts of appeals and serving staggered three-year terms. This Court would have the two-fold function of (1) screening all petitions for certiorari and appeals that would at present be filed in the Supreme Court, referring the most review-worthy [to] the Supreme Court [and] denying the rest; and (2) retaining for decision on the merits cases of genuine conflict between circuits (except those of special moment, which would be certified to the Supreme Court)." Federal

---

d. For a detailed study of the background and debates in the Constitutional Convention and during the ratification process, reaching a similar conclusion, see Clinton, *A Mandatory View of Federal Court Jurisdiction: A Guided Quest for the Original Understanding of Article III,* 132 U.Pa.L.Rev. 741 (1984).

e. See Elliott, *Court-Curbing Proposals in Congress,* 33 Not.D.Law. 597 (1958); Nagel, *Court-Curbing Periods in American History,* 18 Vand.L.Rev. 925 (1965).

Judicial Center Study Group, *Report on the Case Load of the Supreme Court* (1972).

Does this recommendation of the "Freund Report" comport with Art. III? Consider Black, *The National Court of Appeals: An Unwise Proposal*, 83 Yale L.J. 883, 885–86 (1974): "A court that can finally determine, *for the whole nation*, questions over the whole range of federal law, without the possibility of further review, is a 'Supreme Court' in everything but name, and the Constitution provides for *one* Supreme Court, quite as clearly as it provides for one President. This National Court of Appeals * * * would (in its own unreviewable discretion) be a 'Supreme Court,' for the entire nation, *on the full and final merits* of all questions where, in its own view, an intercircuit conflict happened to have arisen." [f] Compare Freund, *Why We Need the National Court of Appeals*, 59 A.B.A.J. 247, 251 (1973): "[T]he appellate jurisdiction of the Supreme Court, from 1789 to the present day, has never extended by law over the full range of cases to which it might extend under Article III. [F]or a long time there was a special jurisdictional amount requirement for review of circuit court decisions, [and] for a century criminal cases could reach the Supreme Court from the circuit courts only on a certificate of division in the circuit court. Review of state court decisions depended on how the state court decided a federal question; thus for a time, when workmen's compensation was held unconstitutional in a state court, there was no possible review in the Supreme Court. Were all these tribunals—the circuit courts and the state courts—the Supreme Court, in violation of Article III?" Contrast Black, supra, at 886: "[These] examples [are] one and all broadly and crucially distinguishable for they excepted from or regulated the exercise of the uniquely 'supreme' appellate review rather than providing an alternative supreme appellate review—just what we cannot do if we are to have 'one Supreme Court.'" [g]

SECTION 4. DISCRETIONARY REVIEW

If review in the Supreme Court is authorized by "appeal," the Court is obligated to decide the case; but if it is authorized by "writ of certiorari," the Court has discretion whether to grant the petition for review. Because of the Court's increasing difficulty in managing its docket, Congress, as early as 1891, authorized the Court to exercise some discretion in selecting cases to hear and decide. This discretion was greatly enlarged at the behest of the Court itself in the so-called Judges' Bill of 1925, as presently reflected in the statutory provisions set forth in Sec. 3 supra. Prior to 1925, the appellate docket contained about 80% obligatory and 20% discretionary cases. As a result of the Judges' Bill, less than 10% of the present docket consists of appeals. In the words of Vinson, C.J., 69 S.Ct. vi (1949), the Supreme Court is not "primarily concerned with the correction of errors in lower court decisions. In almost all cases within the Court's appellate jurisdiction, the petitioner has already received one appellate review of his [case]. If we took every case in which an interesting legal question is raised, or our prima facie impression is that the decision below is

f. See also Gressman, *The Constitution v. The Freund Report*, 41 Geo.Wash.L.Rev. 951 (1973); Note, *The National Court of Appeals: A Constitutional "inferior Court"?* 72 Mich.L. Rev. 290 (1973).

g. For a proposal "to leave with the present Court final jurisdiction for review of constitutionality, transferring finality [for non-

constitutional] judicial review to one or more separate judicial bodies," see Strong, *The Time Has Come to Talk of Major Curtailment in the Supreme Court's Jurisdiction*, 48 N.C.L. Rev. 1 (1969).

Other proposals of the Freund Report (and others) to reduce the Court's workload are considered in Sec. 4 infra.

erroneous, we could not fulfill the Constitutional and statutory responsibilities placed upon the Court. To remain effective, the Supreme Court must continue to decide only those cases which present questions whose resolution will have immediate importance far beyond the particular facts and parties involved."

UNITED STATES SUPREME COURT RULES

Rule 17. Considerations Governing Review on Certiorari

1. A review on writ of certiorari is not a matter of right, but of judicial discretion, and will be granted only when there are special and important reasons therefor. The following, while neither controlling nor fully measuring the Court's discretion, indicate the character of reasons that will be considered:

(a) When a federal court of appeals has rendered a decision in conflict with the decision of another federal court of appeals on the same matter; or has decided a federal question in a way in conflict with a state court of last resort; or has so far departed from the accepted and usual course of judicial proceedings, or so far sanctioned such a departure by a lower court, as to call for an exercise of this Court's power of supervision.

(b) When a state court of last resort has decided a federal question in a way in conflict with the decision of another state court of last resort or of a federal court of appeals.

(c) When a state court or a federal court of appeals has decided an important question of federal law which has not been, but should be, settled by this Court, or has decided a federal question in a way in conflict with applicable decisions of this Court. * * *

Notes and Questions

1. *Proper judicial discretion.* What considerations beyond those outlined in Rule 17 should be pertinent ("proper," "principled") to the granting of certiorari? Consider Harper & Rosenthal, *What The Supreme Court Did Not Do In The 1949 Term—An Appraisal of Certiorari,* 99 U.Pa.L.Rev. 293, 299, 300 (1950): "[T]he Court, in determining whether the issue involved is of the required importance, may, and indeed perhaps should in some instances, consider whether the time is one for decision of the particular question. [Further], a justice [might] very properly vote for denial because persuaded that if the writ were granted, five or more justices might decide the issue wrongly. It is altogether understandable that a justice who has strong convictions about a case of public importance might prefer to have the decision of an inferior court stand rather than to have it authenticated in affirmance by the highest Court." [b]

b. Compare Henkin *On Drawing Lines,* 82 Harv.L.Rev. 63, 90–91 (1968): "Surely the Court did not consider the question [in *Mora v. McNamara,* 389 U.S. 934, 88 S.Ct. 282, 19 L.Ed.2d 287 (1967), of the constitutionality of United States military activity in Vietnam,] 'unimportant.' Rather, [one] is tempted to guess that the Court recognized that if it heard the case it could not give the relief requested. Even if the Justices privately thought that the President exceeded his constitutional authority in sending Mr. Mora to fight in Vietnam, it would not so declare and presume to restrain the President. Nor would the Court adjudicate claims that acts of the political branches violate international law. If it heard the case, the Court would have to decide that the issues are 'political questions' and not justiciable; or, that even if the war is illegal, Mora is not justified thereby in refusing to serve and therefore the legality of the war is not properly in issue; or that the war is not in fact illegal. Any of these judgments might be less politic than a decision not to hear the case at all, might give the impression that the Court supports the political branches in the Vietnam war, and might make the Court itself a target of the national malaise. Denying certiorari may well have been the better part of valor. [Or the] Justices might

2. *The Court's increased workload.* The past decade and a half has produced a flurry of proposals to reduce the Court's workload.

(a) The "FREUND REPORT" (note 3, Sec. 3 supra), justified its recommending creation of a National Court of Appeals to relieve the Supreme Court of some of its present duties, because "the statistics of the Court's current workload, both in absolute terms and in the mounting trend, are impressive evidence that the conditions essential for the performance of the Court's mission do not exist." The figures revealed that "approximately three times as many cases were filed in the 1971 Term as in the 1951 Term"—"by 1971, 3,643 new cases were filed, an increase of 1,458 in ten years.[f] [The] most dramatic growth has been in the number of cases filed in forma pauperis (ifp) by persons unable to pay the cost of litigation,[g] mostly defendants in criminal cases [resulting] both from a substantive enlargement of defendants' rights in the field of criminal justice and from the greater availability [of] counsel to indigent criminal defendants. [The] regular appellate filings (the non-ifp cases) have also steadily increased" due to the general population growth and because "more subjects are committed to the courts as the fields covered by legislation expand. Civil rights, environmental, safety, consumer, and other social and economic legislation are recent illustrations. And lawyers are now provided to a markedly increasing extent for persons who cannot afford litigation. Changes in constitutional doctrines have also contributed, as the reapportionment and school desegregation cases, as well as the criminal cases, attest." Further, "the percentage of petitions for certiorari granted has sharply dropped as the filings have [increased]. In 1971, 5.8% were granted[h] in contrast to 17.5%, 11.1% and 7.4% in 1941, 1951 and 1961, respectively." Similarly, "the number of cases argued and decided by opinion has not changed significantly despite the rising flood of petitions and appeals. [At] the 1971 Term 143 cases were so disposed of, with 129 opinions of the Court;[i] during the preceding 15 years the average was 120 cases, with 100 opinions."

The report suggested that the decline in the percentage of petitions granted "would seem to reflect, not a lessening of the proportion of cases worthy of

at least like to keep open the possibility of intervention rather than read themselves out 'forever.'" Contrast Hughes, *Civil Disobedience and the Political Question Doctrine,* 43 N.Y.U.L.Rev. 1, 15 (1968): "Those who advocate civil disobedience have, I think, some warrant for saying that a dearth of reasoned opinions on the political question doctrine in its application to issues that surround the war in Vietnam leaves them without a satisfactory response to their challenge. And by a satisfactory response I do not of course mean one that agrees with the petitioner nor one that will enable neat predictions to be made in the future, but only one which presents a reasoned justification for the denial of his claim." See also Rehnquist, J., dissenting from denial of certiorari in *Ratchford v. Gay Lib,* 434 U.S. 1080, 98 S.Ct. 1276, 55 L.Ed.2d 789 (1978): "[T]he existence [of] discretion does not imply that it should be used as a sort of judicial storm cellar to which we may flee to escape from controversial or sensitive cases."

f. In the 1973 to 1978 Terms, the number of new cases filed averaged about 3900. See

Casper & Posner, *The Caseload of The Supreme Court: 1975 and 1976 Terms,* 1977 Sup. Ct. 87. For the 1979 to 1984 Terms, the average increased to almost 4200.

g. For a description of in forma pauperis proceedings, see Stern & Gressman, *Supreme Court Practice* ch. 8 (5th ed. 1978).

h. The percentage granted continued to be "around 6%" into the late 1970s, Stern & Gressman, supra, at 260, but fell to an average of below 4.5% in the 1979 to 1984 Terms.

i. These figures remained substantially constant through the late 1970s. See Hellman, *The Business of the Supreme Court Under the Judiciary Act of 1925: The Plenary Docket in the 1970's,* 91 Harv.L.Rev. 1711, 1728 (1978), who also shows a significant increase in the number of opinions by the Burger Court as compared to the Warren and Vinson Courts, id. at 1730–34. In the 1980 to 1984 Terms, the Court disposed of an average of 164 cases by signed opinion.

review, but rather the need to keep the number of cases argued and decided on the merits within manageable limits as the docket increases." Thus, "two consequences can be inferred. Issues that would have been decided on the merits a generation ago are passed over by the Court today; and second, the consideration given to the cases actually decided on the merits is compromised by the pressures of 'processing' the inflated docket of petitions and appeals."

See also Griswold, *Rationing Justice—The Supreme Court's Caseload and What the Court Does Not Do,* 60 Corn.L.Rev. 335, 341–43 (1975): "It is a rather astonishing fact that less than 1% of the cases decided by our courts of appeals are reviewed on the merits by the Supreme Court [and] this had led, I think, to a considerable lack of what I would call institutional responsibility on the part of many court of appeals judges. [In consequence], it is hard to say that there is any national law on many subjects. [If] 10% of the court of appeals cases were reviewed by a court with national authority, the law would soon be clarified and stabilized, and the amount of litigation could be markedly reduced. [Further], I do not think that the public or the bar is fully aware of the extent to which the Supreme Court of the United States has become a civil rights court.[j] [If] all our Court can do is to handle the most important civil rights cases, and a few others, then we are rationing justice, and should be prepared to do something about it."

(b) Apart from the constitutionality of the Freund Report's National Court of Appeals proposal (see note 3, Sec. 3 supra), is it necessary? Desirable? BICKEL, THE CASELOAD OF THE SUPREME COURT 15–19 (1973) fairly summarizes the "main grounds of objection":[l] "(1) Contrary to the study group's conclusion, no need for relief has been shown, certainly no imperative need. 'The case for our "overwork" is a myth,' Mr. Justice Douglas [remarked]. The increase in the caseload, he continued, had been largely [filed] by prisoners free of cost and often without benefit of counsel. Most such cases are wholly frivolous and extraordinarily few of them are ever accepted for review. They burden no one. 'We are' said the justice, 'if anything, underworked, not overworked.' The Court disposes of 'vast leisure time.'[19]

"Former Chief Justice Warren declared that the study group's 'facile and unevaluated use of numbers [leaves] the public with a false impression as to the workload of the Court and the ability of the justices to manage that workload.' He also emphasized the large number of in forma pauperis cases and added that more than half of the rest of the docket consisted of cases that 'were equally without certiorari merit and were doubtless denied with a minimum expenditure of the justices' time and effort.'[20] Mr. Justice Brennan stated categorically 'that I spent no more time screening the 3,643 cases of the 1971 term than I did screening half as many in my first term in 1956.'[21] * * *

"(2) Even critics who did not subscribe to Justice Douglas's view that the Court commands 'vast leisure time' doubted that the justices are or need to be very heavily occupied in the task of screening cases. [Judge Friendly suggested] that the justices might find it possible to dispose of petitions for certiorari more speedily, on the basis of one-sentence memoranda from their law clerks or just a

---

j. In support, see Casper & Posner, *The Workload of the Supreme Court* (1976); Hellman, supra, at 1737–46.

l. Professor Bickel was a member of the Freund committee and supported its report.

19. *Tidewater Oil Co. v. United States,* 409 U.S. 151, 174, 93 S.Ct. 408, 421, 34 L.Ed.2d 375 (1972) (dissenting opinion).

20. Warren, *Attacks Freund Study Group's Composition and Proposal,* 59 A.B.A.J. 721, 724, 726 (1973).

21. Brennan, [*The National Court of Appeals: Another Dissent,* 40 U.Chi.L.Rev. 473, 479 (1973)].

few minutes' talk with them. Or else, he wrote, the justices could pool their clerks, which [a] few of them are [doing], instead of each getting a memorandum on each case from one of his own clerks. Then again, the justices could have more clerks or a small senior staff.[23] * * *

"(3) A common theme among the critics is that the study group's proposal would entail a loss of control, as Chief Justice Warren put it, over 'national priorities in constitutional and legal matters.' [The] flow of petitions for review, it has been argued, enables the Court to keep its finger on the pulse of the legal order. 'Across the screen each Term' wrote Mr. Justice Douglas, 'come the worries and concerns of the American people—high and low—presented in concrete, tangible form.' Chief Justice Warren observed: 'The very flow of those cases through the chambers of the Court serves to inform the justices of what is happening to the system of justice.'

"Occasional dissents by one or more justices from a denial of review, Justice Brennan pointed out, 'often herald the appearance on the horizon of a possible reexamination' of previously settled law. The judges of the new National Court would have and could acquire no sense of such impending changes. Only the justices of the Supreme Court in their own assessment of their own collective thinking can know what changes may be trembling on the brink. [The] judges of the new court, wrote Chief Justice Warren, being necessarily 'trained to follow precedent,' would 'deny review of those decisions that fall into the traditional molds and that seem correctly decided in terms of precedent and settled law.' Former Justice Goldberg thought [m] it doubtful that many of the cases in which the Court in the 1960s reformed various aspects of criminal procedure, [or] even the first legislative apportionment case (*Baker v. Carr*), or indeed *Brown v. Board of Education* would ever have reached the Supreme Court from a new National Court of Appeals. * * *

"(4) The other side of the coin of loss of control by the Court is loss of access to [it]. Chief Justice Warren [said] the Court 'would lose its symbolic but vitally important status as the ultimate tribunal to which all citizens, poor or rich, may submit their claims.' " [n]

(c) Several other plans for relieving the Supreme Court's workload by creating a new federal appellate court inferior to it—but one that would not interfere with the Supreme Court's power to control its own docket—have been proposed. An ABA-developed suggestion would have Congress authorize "the Supreme Court [to] refer classes of cases or individual cases for initial recommendations or initial decision by the new court. The Supreme Court retains its power to accept or to reject any case for hearing," and the final authority to review decisions. Hufstedler, *Courtship and Other Legal Arts*, 60 A.B.A.J. 545, 548 (1974). In 1975, the congressionally established Commission on Revision of the Federal Appellate Court System (chaired by Sen. Roman Hruska) made a similar proposal (see 67 F.R.D. 195).[o]

---

23. Friendly, *Federal Jurisdiction: A General View* 48–51 (1973).

m. Goldberg, *One Supreme Court*, New Republic, Feb. 10, 1973, p. 14.

n. In contrast, several justices, although "not giving immediate and unqualified endorsement of the study group's principal recommendation" solicited its "open-minded consideration." Bickel, supra, at 14. See Burger, *Defends Freund Study Group's Composition and Proposal*, 59 A.B.A.J. 721 (1973); Rehn-

quist, *The Supreme Court: Past and Present*, 59 A.B.A.J. 361 (1973). Compare Black, note 3, Sec. 3 supra; Gressman, fn. e, Sec. 3 supra and authorities cited therein.

o. "Of the active members of the Court (all of whom were polled by the Commission), Justice Rehnquist was perhaps the most emphatic in joining the Commission's criticism of the present system. The Justice stated flatly that the Supreme Court can no longer meet the country's need for thorough and deliberative

(d) One of the Freund Report's recommendations was "the substitution of certiorari for appeal in all cases where appeal is now the prescribed procedure for review in the Supreme Court." In 1979, the Senate passed a bill to eliminate the Court's obligatory appellate jurisdiction in almost all cases. The proposal was drafted by the Justice Department and endorsed by the ABA and all witnesses at the Senate hearings. It was also unanimously supported by the Court which pointed out that "during the 1976 term almost half of the cases decided by this Court on the merits were cases brought here as of right under the Court's mandatory jurisdiction [and] unduly expended the Court's resources on cases better left to other courts." Enactment by the House of Representatives was stalled by an unrelated amendment. See generally Gressman, *Requiem for the Supreme Court's Obligatory Jurisdiction,* 65 A.B.A.J. 1325 (1979). In 1982, a similar bill passed the House (H.R. 6872, 97th Cong. 2d Sess.), but not the Senate.

MARYLAND v. BALTIMORE RADIO SHOW, INC.

338 U.S. 912, 70 S.Ct. 252, 94 L.Ed. 562 (1950).

Opinion of MR. JUSTICE FRANKFURTER respecting the denial of the petition for writ of certiorari. * * *

A variety of considerations underlie denials of the writ, and as to the same petition different reasons may lead different Justices to the same result. This is especially true of petitions for review on writ of certiorari to a State court. Narrowly technical reasons may lead to denials. [For detail, see Sec. 5 infra.] A

decision making on important issues of federal constitutional and statutory law. The Chief Justice and Justices White, Blackmun, and Powell were somewhat more guarded, but they plainly agreed with Justice Rehnquist. [On] the other hand, Justices Douglas, Brennan, Stewart, and Marshall see no present need for the creation of a new court [and former] Justices Fortas and Goldberg are also opposed." Owens, *The Hruska Commission's Proposed National Court of Appeals,* 23 U.C. L.A.L.Rev. 580, 591 & n. 53 (1976). For criticism of the proposal, see id.; Casper & Posner, fn. j supra.

More recently, see the dissenting opinions of Stevens, J., in *Michigan v. Long,* 463 U.S. 1032, 103 S.Ct. 3469, 77 L.Ed.2d 1201 (1983), and *Florida v. Meyers,* 466 U.S. 380, 104 S.Ct. 1852, 80 L.Ed.2d 381 (1984) (joined by Brennan and Marshall, JJ.), complaining of "error" in the Court's "allocation of resources": "I believe that in reviewing the decisions of state courts, the primary role of the Court is to make sure that persons who seek to *vindicate* federal rights have been fairly heard. [Since] the beginning of the 1981 term, the Court has decided in summary fashion 19 [cases] concerning the constitutional rights of persons accused or convicted of crimes. All 19 were decided on the petition of the warden or prosecutor, and in all he was successful in obtaining reversal of a decision upholding a claim of constitutional right. [The] result is a docket swollen with requests by states to reverse judgments that their courts have rendered in favor of their citizens."

See also Choper, in Choper, Kamisar & Tribe, *The Supreme Court: Trends and Developments 1981–82* 260–61 (1983): "[O]f the 24 criminal law-criminal procedure cases [that] the Court has already taken for review for the next Term, 22 involve petitions or appeals either by the state or by the United States. That means that the court below held the challenged criminal procedure rule or criminal law rule unconstitutional. I think at least four members of the Court feel a compulsion to correct that lower Court decision. As I looked over the other constitutional decisions, there were 17 cases involving the constitutionality of federal, state, or local actions. Thirteen involved rulings of unconstitutionality by the courts below. Now, I do not want to take the view that none of these cases is important. But if one perceives the role of the United States Supreme Court (as I do) [as] dominantly concerned with protecting the interests of minorities against the majoritarian political process, it does seem to me [a] somewhat wasteful expenditure of judicial resources to simply take up a large number of cases in which the courts below may have given, in the opinion of four Justices, undue protection to minorities. One way of curing the work load is to let what may be perhaps an overly expansive interpretation of constitutional rights stand for at least awhile."

Legislation to implement the approach of the Hruska Commission continues to be introduced in Congress. See Hellman, *Caseload, Conflicts and Decisional Capacity: Does the Supreme Court Need Help?,* 67 Judic. 28 (1983).

decision may satisfy all these technical requirements and yet may commend itself for review to fewer than four members of the Court. Pertinent considerations of judicial policy here come into play. A case may raise an important question but the record may be cloudy. It may be desirable to have different aspects of an issue further illumined by the lower courts. Wise adjudication has its own time for ripening.

Since there are these conflicting and, to the uninformed, even confusing reasons for denying petitions for certiorari, it has been suggested from time to time that the Court indicate its reasons for denial. Practical considerations preclude. [The] time that would be required is prohibitive, apart from the fact as already indicated that different reasons not infrequently move different members of the Court * * *. It becomes relevant here to note that failure to record a dissent from a denial of a petition for writ of certiorari in nowise implies that only the member of the Court who notes his dissent thought the petition should be granted. * * *

SECTION 5. PREREQUISITES TO FEDERAL JURISDICTION AND JUDICIAL REVIEW: AN INTRODUCTION

Under Art. III, federal judicial power extends only to resolving "cases" and "controversies." Thus, federal courts are precluded from giving "advisory opinions" or deciding "moot" cases. In determining whether there is a "case or controversy" capable of and suitable for resolution by federal courts, parties asserting particular contentions must have "standing"; at a minimum, they must allege "such a personal stake in the outcome of the controversy as to assure that concrete adverseness which sharpens the presentation of issues." [a] Further, claims must be asserted at a time when they are "ripe" for adjudication: "a hypothetical threat is not enough"; [b] "determination of [the] constitutionality of legislation in advance of its immediate adverse effect in the context of a concrete case involves too remote and abstract an inquiry for the proper exercise of the judicial function." [c]

Because all these matters must be resolved before a federal court may consider the merits of a constitutional contention, they could profitably be explored in detail here. But their consideration is often intertwined with and requires understanding of the substantive constitutional provision in issue. Thus, their presentation is deferred to Ch. 13 when students will be better equipped to comprehend and evaluate them.

a. *Baker v. Carr*, Sec. 2 supra.

b. *United Public Workers v. Mitchell*, p. 1209 infra.

c. *International Longshoremen's and Warehousemen's Union v. Boyd*, 347 U.S. 222, 74 S.Ct. 447, 98 L.Ed. 650 (1954).

Chapter 2

NATIONAL LEGISLATIVE POWER

SECTION 1. SOURCES AND NATURE OF
NATIONAL LEGISLATIVE POWER

INTRODUCTION

From the outset the Constitution has been viewed as creating a national government of vast, but nonetheless limited, legislative powers that must find their source in the Constitution itself. This stems in part from listing the powers of Congress in 18 "enumerated" clauses in Art. 1, § 8, and then providing in the tenth amendment that "powers not delegated to the United States by the Constitution * * * are reserved to the States respectively, or to the people." This listing of national legislative powers takes on added significance when contrasted with vastly different proposals advanced, but not adopted, at the Constitutional Convention. The Convention spurned Hamilton's proposal that the national legislature should have "power to pass all laws which they shall judge necessary to the common defense and general welfare of the Union," [a] but tentatively approved a proposal that the national legislature should have power "to legislate in all cases for the general interests of the Union, and also in those to which the States are separately incompetent." [b] In the end, however, what emerged was a list of specified or "enumerated," broadly-stated legislative powers.

To these specified powers was added at the end of § 8 the "necessary and proper clause," which gave Congress power "To make all Laws which shall be necessary and proper for carrying into Execution the foregoing Powers, and all other Powers vested by this Constitution in the Government of the United States, or in any Department or Officer thereof."

This clause gave rise to much controversy in the debates revolving around the state conventions called to take action on the proposed Constitution. Once the Constitution was ratified and the new government launched, the necessary and proper clause and the issue of implied powers were again the subject of much dispute in the early years between those who favored and those who opposed a strong national government.

---

a. 3 Farrand, *Records of the Federal Convention* 617, 627 (1911).

b. 2 Farrand, supra, 26–27. For more detail, see, Sec. 2, I infra.

THE FEDERALIST NO. 33

[Alexander Hamilton] [c]

These two clauses [the necessary and proper clause and the supremacy clause] are only declaratory of a truth, which would have resulted by necessary and unavoidable implication from the very act of constituting a Federal Government, and vesting it with certain specified [powers].

What is a power, but the ability or faculty of doing a thing? What is the ability to do a thing but the power of employing the *means* necessary to its execution? What is LEGISLATIVE power but a power of making Laws? [What] are the proper means of executing such a power but *necessary* and *proper* laws?

CHARLES WARREN—THE SUPREME COURT IN UNITED STATES HISTORY

Vol. I, Chapter Twelve, The Bank of the United States 499, 500–503 (1922).

Reprinted with the permission of the publisher,
copyright © 1922, Little, Brown & Co.

While the fears of the opponents of a consolidated form of government had been somewhat allayed by the adoption of the Constitution in its final form, specifically and expressly delegating the powers of Congress in definite terms, there still remained a grave anxiety over the indeterminate language contained in [the necessary and proper clause]. With the initiation of the new Government in 1789, the broad or narrow interpretation of this clause marked a line of division between schools of political thought and action; and it has been truly said that "the history of the United States is in a large measure a history of the arguments which sought to enlarge or restrict its import." As early as 1791, those who feared lest the powers of the Federal Government should be expanded, at the expense of the States, by legislative practice or by judicial interpretation, saw their fears confirmed, when Congress, without any express power vested by the Constitution, chartered a National bank. * * *

In 1811, 1814 and 1816, the debates on the incorporation of the Bank of the United States developed the line of cleavage on this primary constitutional issue. "Little did the framers of the Constitution imagine," said the strict constructionists, "that there lay concealed under its provision a secret and sleeping power which could in a moment prostrate all their labors with the dust. [Let] the principle of constructive or implied powers be once established and you will have planted in the bosom of the Constitution a viper which, one day or another, will sting the liberties of this country to the heart." It is a "monstrous", "alarming" doctrine converting us into "one entire consolidated Government of general, undefined powers." [On] the other hand, those who upheld the maintenance of an adequately strong Federal Government joined with Henry Clay in eloquent defense and protest against "construing the Constitution as one would a bill of indictment [reducing] it to an inanimate skeleton," its "atrophy" by "water gruel regimen."

c. *The Federalist* 203, 204–05 (Cooke ed. 1961)—was a series of essays published in New York newspapers in late 1787 and early 1788 to defend the proposed Constitution against attacks aimed at defeating its ratification in New York. The essays were republished in book form as "The Federalist" in the Spring of 1788. The principal authors, anonymous at the time of publication, were Alexander Hamilton, James Madison, and John Jay. See id., xi–xxx.

BACKGROUND OF McCULLOCH v. MARYLAND

The Bank of the United States was first incorporated by Congress in 1791, only two years after the new government was launched. The Bank engaged in a private banking business, acting as a depository for private funds, making private loans, and issuing bank notes. It also acted as a depository for United States funds wherever it established branches. The preamble of the Act incorporating the Bank stated that its establishment "will be very conducive to the successful conducting of the national finances; will tend to give facility to the obtaining of loans, for the use of the government, in sudden emergencies; and will be productive of considerable advantages to trade and industry in general." [d]

The Bank charter was allowed to expire in 1811 due to a variety of political considerations, but a second Bank of the United States was incorporated in 1816 over strenuous political opposition. One-fifth of its stock was owned by the United States, the rest privately. Five of its 25 directors were appointed by the President of the United States, the rest elected by the private stockholders. The Bank made itself extremely unpopular, particularly in the West and South, when it made the mistake of over-expanding credits and then drastically curtailed them, contributing in part to the failure of many state-incorporated banks. As a result a number of states sought to exclude the Bank from operating branches within the state, either by state constitutional prohibitions against operating any bank not chartered by the state or by imposing heavy discriminatory taxes against such banks. The tax in *McCulloch* was one of the milder taxes aimed at the Bank; three states imposed on it annual taxes of $50,000 to $60,000.

McCULLOCH v. MARYLAND

17 U.S. (4 Wheat.) 316, 4 L.Ed. 579 (1819).

MR. CHIEF JUSTICE MARSHALL delivered the opinion of the Court.

[A Maryland statute made it unlawful for the branch of any bank established in Maryland without state authority to issue bank notes without payment of an annual tax of $15,000 or 2% of the face value of the notes. The Maryland Court of Appeals upheld a judgment for the statutory penalty against the cashier of the Baltimore branch of the Bank of United States for issuing bank notes without payment of the required tax. The Supreme Court reversed in an opinion handed down only three days after completion of nine days of oral argument.] [e]

The first question [is], has Congress power to incorporate a bank? * * *

This government is acknowledged by all to be one of enumerated powers. [Among] the enumerated powers, we do not find that of establishing a bank or creating a corporation. But there is no phrase in the instrument which, like the Articles of Confederation [Article II: "Each state retains [every] power [not] expressly delegated."] excludes incidental or implied powers; and which requires

d. Extended opinions in which Jefferson and Hamilton disagreed in advising President Washington on the power of Congress to create this first Bank anticipated by 28 years the principal arguments of counsel in *McCulloch*. See 8 *Papers of Alexander Hamilton* 97 (1965); Padover, *The Complete Jefferson* 342 (1943).

e. But see White, *The Working Life of the Marshall Court,* 1815–1835, 70 Va.L.Rev. 1,

30–33 (1984), commenting on the frequent short intervals between arguments and decisions during the Marshall period of unlimited oral arguments, unanimous opinions, light appellate calendars, short sojourns in Washington, and heavy circuit-riding duties.

that everything granted shall be expressly and minutely described. Even the tenth amendment, which was framed for the purpose of quieting the excessive jealousies which had been excited, omits the word "expressly," and declares only that the powers "not delegated to the United States, nor prohibited to the states, are reserved to the states or to the people"; thus leaving the question, whether the particular power which may become the subject of contest has been delegated to the one government, or prohibited to the other, to depend on a fair construction of the whole instrument. The men who drew and adopted this amendment had experienced the embarrassments resulting from the insertion of this word in the Articles of Confederation, and probably omitted it to avoid those embarrassments. A constitution, to contain an accurate detail of all the subdivisions of which its great powers will admit, and of all the means by which they may be carried into execution, would partake of the prolixity of a legal code, and could scarcely be embraced by the human mind. It would probably never be understood by the public. Its nature, therefore, requires, that only its great outlines should be marked, its important objects designated, and the minor ingredients which composed those objects be deduced from the nature of the objects themselves. [In] considering this question, then, we must never forget, that it is *a constitution* we are expounding.

Although, among the enumerated powers of government, we do not find the word "bank," or "incorporation," we find the great powers to lay and collect taxes; to borrow money; to regulate commerce; to declare and conduct a war; and to raise and support armies and navies. The sword and the purse, all the external relations, and no inconsiderable portion of the industry of the nation, are intrusted to its government. It can never be pretended that these vast powers draw after them others of inferior importance, merely because they are inferior. [But] it may, with great reason be contended that a government, intrusted with such ample powers, on the due execution of which the happiness and prosperity of the nation so vitally depends, must also be intrusted with ample means for their execution. The power being given, it is the interest of the nation to facilitate its execution. It can never be their interest, and cannot be presumed to have been their intention, to clog and embarrass its execution by withholding the most appropriate means. Throughout this vast republic * * * revenue is to be collected and expended, armies are to be marched and supported. The exigencies of the nation may require, that the treasure raised in the North should be transported to the South, that raised in the East conveyed to the West, or that this order should be reversed. Is that construction of the Constitution to be preferred which would render these operations difficult, hazardous, and expensive? Can we adopt that construction (unless the words imperiously require it) which would impute to the framers of that instrument, when granting these powers for the public good, the intention of impeding their exercise by withholding a choice of means? * * *

But the Constitution of the United States has not left the right of Congress to employ the necessary means, for the execution of the powers conferred on the government, to general reasoning. To its enumeration of powers is added that of making "all laws which shall be necessary and proper, for carrying into execution the foregoing powers, and all other powers vested by this Constitution, in the government of the United States, or in any department thereof."

The counsel for the state of Maryland have urged [that] this clause, though in terms a grant of power, is not so in effect; but is really restrictive of the general right, which might otherwise be implied, of selecting means for executing the enumerated powers. The word *"necessary"* is considered as controlling the whole sentence, and as limiting the right to pass laws for the execution of the granted powers, to such as are indispensable, and without which the power would be nugatory. That it excludes the choice of means, and leaves to Congress in each case, that only which is most direct and simple.

Is it true, that this is the sense in which the word "necessary" is always used? [If] reference be had to its use, in the common affairs of the world, or in approved authors, we find that it frequently imports no more than that one thing is convenient, or useful, or essential to another. To employ the means necessary to an end, is generally understood as employing any means calculated to produce the end, and not as being confined to those single means, without which the end would be entirely unattainable. [It] is essential to just construction, that many words which import something excessive, should be understood in a more mitigated sense—in that sense which common usage justifies. The word "necessary" is of this description. [A] thing may be necessary, very necessary, absolutely or indispensably necessary. To no mind would the same idea be conveyed, by these several phrases. This comment on the word is well illustrated, by the passage cited at the bar, from the tenth section of the first article of the Constitution. It is, we think, impossible to compare the sentence which prohibits a state from laying "imposts, or duties on imports or exports, except what may be *absolutely* necessary for executing its inspection laws," with that which authorizes Congress "to make all laws which shall be necessary and proper for carrying into execution" the powers of the general government, without feeling a conviction that the convention understood itself to change materially the meaning of the word "necessary" by prefixing the word "absolutely." This word, then like others, is used in various senses; and in its construction, the subject, the context, the intention of the person using them, are all to be taken into view.

Let this be done in the case under consideration. The subject is the execution of those great powers on which the welfare of a nation essentially depends. It must have been the intention of those who gave these powers, to insure, as far as human prudence could insure, their beneficial execution. [This] provision is made in a constitution intended to endure for ages to come, and, consequently, to be adapted to the various crises of human affairs. To have prescribed the means by which government should, in all future time, execute its powers, would have been to change, entirely, the character of the instrument, and give it the properties of a legal code. It would have been an unwise attempt to provide, by immutable rules, for exigencies which, if foreseen at all must have been seen dimly, and which can be best provided for as they occur. To have declared that the best means shall not be used, but those alone without which the power given would be nugatory, would have been to deprive the legislature of the capacity to avail itself of experience, to exercise its reason, and to accommodate its legislation to circumstances. If we apply this principle of construction to any of the powers of the government, we shall find it so pernicious in its operation that we shall be compelled to discard it. * * *

But the argument which most conclusively demonstrates the error of the construction contended for by the counsel for the state of Maryland, is founded on the intention of the convention, as manifested in the whole clause: * * *

1st. The clause is placed among the powers of Congress, not among the limitations on those powers.

2nd. Its terms purport to enlarge, not to diminish the powers vested in the government. It purports to be an additional power, not a restriction on those already granted. No reason has been or can be assigned, for thus concealing an intention to narrow the discretion of the national legislature, under words which purport to enlarge it. * * *

We admit, as all must admit, that the powers of the government are limited, and that its limits are not to be transcended. But we think the sound construction of the Constitution must allow to the national legislature that discretion, with respect to the means by which the powers it confers are to be carried into execution, which will enable that body to perform the high duties assigned to it, in the manner most beneficial to the people. Let the end be legitimate, let it be within the scope of the Constitution, and all means which are appropriate, which are plainly adapted to that end, which are not prohibited, but consist (sic) with the letter and spirit of the Constitution, are constitutional. * * *

If a corporation may be employed indiscriminately with other means to carry into execution the powers of the government, no particular reason can be assigned for excluding the use of a bank, if required for its fiscal operations. [That] it is a convenient, a useful, and essential instrument in the prosecution of its fiscal operations, is not now a subject of controversy. * * *

But were its necessity less apparent, none can deny its being an appropriate measure; and if it is, the degree of its necessity, as has been very justly observed, is to be discussed in another place. [S]hould Congress, under the pretext of executing its powers, pass laws for the accomplishment of objects not entrusted to the government; it would become the painful duty of this tribunal, should a case requiring such a decision come before it, to say that such an act was not the law of the land. But where the law is not prohibited, and is really calculated to effect any of the objects entrusted to the government, to undertake here to inquire into the degree of its necessity, would be to pass the line which circumscribes the judicial department, and to tread on legislative ground. This court disclaims all pretensions to such a power. * * *

2. [The Court invalidated Maryland's tax on the United States Bank, invoking the supremacy clause (Art. VI, Par 2). This ruling and its progeny are considered in Sec. 5 infra.]

Notes and Questions

1. *Function of necessary and proper clause.* Judging from this opinion, would the Court have reached the same result had the Constitution contained no necessary and proper clause? Whether needed or not, the necessary and proper clause has long been a useful tool in sustaining congressional legislation. See, e.g., *Legal Tender Cases,* 110 U.S. 421, 4 S.Ct. 122, 28 L.Ed. 204 (1884) (making United States circulating notes legal tender in payment of private debts is necessary and proper exercise of power to create a national currency arising out of the express power to borrow on the credit of the United States and to coin money and regulate its value); *Lichter v. United States,* 334 U.S. 742, 68 S.Ct. 1294, 92 L.Ed. 1694 (1948) (determination and recovery of excess profits is necessary and proper for execution of war powers); *Adams v. Maryland,* 347 U.S. 179, 74 S.Ct. 442, 98 L.Ed. 608 (1954) (barring use in state prosecution of evidence given before congressional committee is necessary and proper to effectuate power to get testimony); *United States v. Oregon,* 366 U.S. 643, 81 S.Ct. 1278, 6 L.Ed.2d 575 (1961) (statutory escheat to United States of property of veteran who dies in veterans hospital without will or heirs, superceding state escheat law, is necessary and proper exercise of war powers, which include power to build hospitals for veterans).

2. *Applicability outside § 8 powers.* Should the necessary and proper clause, and Marshall's broad standard for implying powers appropriate in carrying out specified powers, apply to grants of legislative power found elsewhere in the Constitution? To grants of legislative power in constitutional amendments, e.g., the enforcement clauses of the Civil War amendments? See Ch. 12, Sec. 2.

SPECIFIED POWERS AS THE ONLY SOURCES OF FEDERAL LEGISLATIVE POWER

1. *The traditional concept.* With one debatable exception (note 4 below), the Court has consistently ruled that federal legislative powers must be based on powers granted to the federal government in the Constitution. This chapter illustrates how flexibly the Court has applied this concept, although KANSAS v. COLORADO, 206 U.S. 46, 27 S.Ct. 655, 51 L.Ed. 956 (1907), per BREWER, J., applied it unbendingly in ruling that no federal legislative power over reclamation of non-federal arid lands within a state could be implied from the Constitution: "Turning to the enumeration of the powers granted to Congress by the 8th section of the 1st article of the Constitution, it is enough to say that no one of them, by any implication, refers to the reclamation of arid lands. The [necessary and proper clause] is not the delegation of a new and independent power, but simply provision for making effective the powers theretofore mentioned.

"[The] proposition that there are legislative powers [not] expressed in the grant of powers, is in direct conflict with the doctrine that this is a government of enumerated powers. That this is such a government clearly appears from the Constitution, independently of the Amendments. [This] natural construction of the original body of the Constitution is made absolutely certain by the 10th Amendment."

Since there were no tracts of arid land in the United States when the Constitution was adopted, it "makes no provision for a national control of the arid regions or their reclamation. But, as our national territory has been enlarged, we have within our borders extensive tracts of arid lands which ought to be reclaimed, and it may well be that no power is adequate for their reclamation other than that of the national government. But, if no such power has been granted, none can be exercised.

"It does not follow from this that the national government is entirely powerless in respect to this matter. [As] to those lands within the limits of the states, at least of the Western states, the national government is the most considerable owner and has power to dispose of and make all needful rules and regulations respecting its property. [Art. 4, § 3] We do not mean that its legislation can override state laws in respect to the general subject of reclamation."

2. *An exercise in implying powers.* Was this rigid view of the granted powers necessary? Which of the granted powers might reasonably be interpreted as the source of implied power to reclaim arid land and by what rationale? By what reasoning could Congress authorize federal construction of the Boulder Dam in the Colorado River, and creation of a great reservoir, to be used: "First, for river regulation, improvement of navigation, and flood control; second, for irrigation and domestic uses and satisfaction of present perfected [rights]; and third, for power." If Congress did not provide for improvement of navigation, by what reasoning might the creation of such a dam and reservoir for irrigation, power, and flood control be justified? Cf. *Arizona v. California,*

283 U.S. 423, 51 S.Ct. 522, 75 L.Ed. 1154 (1931); *Ashwander v. TVA,* 297 U.S. 288, 56 S.Ct. 466, 80 L.Ed. 688 (1936); *Oklahoma v. Atkinson Co.,* 313 U.S. 508, 61 S.Ct. 1050, 85 L.Ed. 1487 (1941).

3. *Must the source be a regulatory power?* Should it be necessary to rely on a *regulatory* power to sustain federal creation and operation of a dam and reservoir designed for irrigation of privately owned lands? Where else might this power be found without disregarding the necessity to base federal action on some specified power in the Constitution? See *United States v. Gerlach Live Stock Co.,* 339 U.S. 725, 738, 70 S.Ct. 955, 962, 94 L.Ed. 1231 (1950); *Ivanhoe Irrig. Dist. v. McCracken,* 357 U.S. 275, 294, 78 S.Ct. 1174, 1185, 2 L.Ed.2d 1313, 1327 (1958).

4. *An exception for foreign affairs?* A possible foreign affairs exception is considered in Sec. 4 infra.

5. *Continued vitality of specified powers concept.* As you study the legislative powers decisions, infra, consider whether, except for foreign affairs, the Court continues to look to the Constitution as the ultimate and exclusive source of congressional legislative powers.

SECTION 2. THE NATIONAL COMMERCE POWER

I. ORIGINS OF THE COMMERCE POWER

CARL BRENT SWISHER—AMERICAN CONSTITUTIONAL DEVELOPMENT

25–27 (2d Ed.1954).
Reprinted with permission of the publisher,
copyright © 1954, Little, Brown & Co.

Merchants engaging in foreign trade, who had resented bitterly the efforts of Great Britain to prevent them from trading with other countries, now paid for their nominal freedom the price of exclusion from the ports of the British West Indies and of costly discrimination in ports across the sea. Other nations likewise refused to trade with American merchants on satisfactory terms. Congress had the theoretical power to make treaties, but it lacked effective power to enforce obedience to them, since it was authorized neither to exclude nor to tax commerce coming into the ports of any state. The infant industries built up in some of the states during the war operated at the mercy of established industries abroad, for Congress had no power to levy protective tariffs and the states could not be expected to act unanimously in such a cause.

The import duties levied by the states created conflicts between the states. Some states—New York particularly—greatly lightened the burden of internal taxation by collecting substantial levies from foreign commerce. New Jersey was embittered by the fact that both New York and Pennsylvania collected import duties on goods intended for sale in New Jersey, duties which were eventually paid by the residents of New Jersey. North Carolina suffered similarly from action taken by Virginia and South Carolina. The states collected duties, not merely on goods from abroad, but on those brought in from other states as well. Virginia, with an eye particularly to the commerce of Pennsylvania and Maryland, provided for the confiscation of vessels which failed to pay duties. Restrictive laws applied to importations by land as well as by sea. Pennsylvania collected toll on large numbers of items imported from other states. Some states enacted similar tariff measures for the combined purpose of raising revenue and giving protection to home products. If the legislation achieved these ends to some extent, it achieved also the undesirable results of interfering with the development of interstate business and of creating antagonism among the states. * * *

Experience with government under the Articles of Confederation demonstrated the need for certain fundamental changes if order was to be maintained and business and commercial relationships preserved and promoted. The federal government needed the power to raise revenue without the intervention of the states. In order to maintain satisfactory relations with foreign countries, it needed the power to regulate foreign commerce. In order to promote industry and commerce at home, it needed the power to levy import duties and to take over from the states the regulation of interstate commerce. It needed the power to break down and prohibit commercial barriers among the states, to deal with the national and state debts, and to prevent the forcible satisfaction of debts by depreciated paper money or by the tender of other property less acceptable to creditors than coin. It was believed that these and related measures would restore order, promote industry and commerce, and redound to the benefit of all classes of people. These considerations provide the background for the story of the adoption of the new Constitution.

ROBERT L. STERN—THAT COMMERCE WHICH CONCERNS MORE STATES THAN ONE

47 Harv.L.Rev. 1335, 1337–41 (1934).
Reprinted with permission of the publisher, copyright © 1934, Harvard Law Review Association.

The Constitutional Convention was called because the Articles of Confederation had not given the Federal Government any power to regulate commerce. This defect proved to be so serious that the Virginia General Assembly appointed commissioners to meet with commissioners of other states to "take into consideration the trade of the United States; to examine the relative situation and trade of the said states; to consider how far the uniform system in their commercial regulations may be necessary to their common interest and their permanent harmony; and to report to the several states such an act relative to this great [object]." Representatives of but five states met at Annapolis in September, 1786. They determined that they could do nothing by themselves, and that the adequate protection of commerce required a complete revision of the structure of government. Accordingly, they recommended that a convention be called for the purpose of revising the Articles of Confederation, and Congress thereupon asked the various states to send delegates to Philadelphia in May, 1787.

The Virginia delegation, led by Washington, Madison, and Randolph, feeling largely responsible for the calling of the Convention, had prepared a series of resolutions as a basis for discussion. The sixth of these resolutions, proposed by Governor Randolph four days after the Convention assembled, read in part as follows:

"[That] the National Legislature ought to be impowered to enjoy the legislative Rights vested in Congress by the Confederation & moreover to legislate in all cases to which the separate States are incompetent, or in which the Harmony of the United States may be interrupted by the exercise of individual Legislation."

The broad standard thus proposed for the division of power between state and nation was criticized by some of the delegates as being too indefinite, but was approved by the Convention on May 31st by a vote of nine states in favor, none against, one divided. The language of the resolution and the vote upon it indicated clearly that the Convention intended to grant the national government power over those matters which could not effectively be regulated by the states.

[Later, an eight to two vote clarified and approved the Randolph resolution] as follows:

"Resolved, that the national legislature ought

"1. to possess the legislative rights vested in Congress by the confederation; and

"2. moreover, to legislate in all cases for the general interests of the Union, and

"3. also in those to which the states are separately incompetent, or

"4. in which the harmony of the United States may be interrupted by the exercise of individual legislation."

With the other resolutions approved by the Convention, this resolution was then sent to the "Com. of detail [to] report the Constitution." This committee [changed] the indefinite language of Resolution VI into an enumeration of the powers of Congress closely resembling Article I, Section 8 of the Constitution as it was finally adopted. The commerce clause, which was passed unanimously, read: "The Legislature of the United States shall have the power * * * to regulate commerce with foreign nations, and among the several States."

Significantly, the Convention did not at any time challenge the radical change made by the committee in the form of the provision for the division of powers between state and nation. It accepted *without discussion* the enumeration of powers made by a committee which had been directed to prepare a constitution based upon the general propositions that the Federal Government was "to legislate in all cases for the general interests of the Union [and] in those to which the states are separately incompetent." With a few changes and additions, the enumeration by the committee became the present Section 8 of Article I of the Constitution. This absence of objection to or comment upon the change is susceptible of only one explanation—that the Convention believed that the enumeration conformed to the standard previously approved, and that the powers enumerated comprehended those matters as to which the states were separately incompetent and in which national legislation was essential. If the Convention had thought that the committee's enumeration was a departure from the general standard for the division of powers to which it had thrice agreed, there can be little doubt that the subject would have been thoroughly debated on the Convention floor.

The commerce clause was the only one of the enumerated powers in which Congress was given any broad power to regulate trade or business. The Convention must, therefore, have understood that in that clause it was granting to Congress all the power over trade or business which the national government would need to possess to provide for situations which the states separately would be unable to meet. In view of the fact that the need for centralized commercial regulation was universally recognized as the primary reason for preparing a new constitution, the Convention would not have been likely to have meant the commerce clause to have a narrow or restrictive meaning.

II. DEVELOPMENT OF BASIC COMMERCE
CLAUSE CONCEPTS

GIBBONS v. OGDEN

22 U.S. (9 Wheat.) 1, 6 L.Ed.2d 23 (1824).

MR. CHIEF JUSTICE MARSHALL delivered the opinion of the Court.

[A New York statute granted Livingston and Fulton the exclusive right to navigate steamboats in state waters; by assignment Ogden secured the right to navigate between New York City and New Jersey. Ogden secured an injunction in the state courts against the violation of this right by Gibbons, who was navigating between New York and New Jersey two steamboats enrolled and licensed in the coasting trade under an act of Congress. The Supreme Court reversed.]

The appellant contends that this decree is erroneous, because the laws which purport to give the exclusive privilege it sustains, are repugnant [to] that clause in the constitution which authorizes Congress to [regulate] "commerce with foreign nations, and among the several states, and with the Indian tribes."

The subject to be regulated is commerce [and to] ascertain the extent of the power, it becomes necessary to settle the meaning of the word. The counsel for the appellee would limit it to traffic, to buying and selling, or the interchange of commodities, and do not admit that it comprehends navigation. This would restrict a general term, applicable to many objects, to one of its significations. Commerce, undoubtedly, is traffic, but it is something more,—it is intercourse. It describes the commercial intercourse between nations, and parts of nations in all its branches, and is regulated by prescribing rules for carrying on that intercourse. [All] America understands, and has uniformly understood the word "commerce" to comprehend navigation. It was so understood, and must have been so understood, when the Constitution was framed. The power over commerce, including navigation, was one of the primary objects for which the people of America adopted their government, and must have been contemplated in forming [it].

To what commerce does this power extend? The Constitution informs us, to commerce "with foreign nations, and among the several states, and with the Indian tribes." It has, we believe, been universally admitted that these words comprehend every species of commercial intercourse between the United States and foreign nations. No sort of trade can be carried on between this country and any other to which this power does not extend. ＊ ＊ ＊

The subject to which the power is next applied is to commerce "among the several States." The word "among" means intermingled with. A thing which is among others is intermingled with them. Commerce among the states cannot stop at the external boundary-line of each state, but may be introduced into the interior. ＊ ＊ ＊

Comprehensive as the word "among" is, it may very properly be restricted to that commerce which concerns more states than one. [The] enumeration of the particular classes of commerce to which the power was to be extended [presupposes] something not enumerated; and that something, if we regard the language or the subject of the sentence, must be the exclusively internal commerce of a state. The genius and character of the whole government seem to be, that its action is to be applied to all the external concerns of the nation, and to those internal concerns which affect the states generally; but not to those which are completely within a particular state, which do not affect other states, and with which it is not necessary to interfere for the purpose of executing some of the general powers of the government. The completely internal commerce of a state, then, may be considered as reserved for the state itself.

But, in regulating commerce with foreign nations, the power of Congress does not stop at the jurisdictional lines of the several states. It would be a very useless power if it could not pass those lines. The commerce of the United States with foreign nations is that of the whole United States. Every district has a right to participate in it. The deep streams which penetrate our country in every direction pass through the interior of almost every state in the Union, and furnish the means of exercising this right. If Congress has the power to regulate it, that power must be exercised whenever the subject exists. If it exists within the states, if a foreign voyage may commence or terminate at a port within a state, then the power of Congress may be exercised within a state.

This principle is, if possible, still more clear when applied to commerce "among the several states." They either join each other, in which case they are separated by a mathematical line, or they are remote from each other, in which case other states lie between them. What is commerce "among" them; and how is it to be conducted? Can a trading expedition between two adjoining states commence and terminate outside of each? And if the trading intercourse be between two states remote from each other, must it not commence in one, terminate in the other, and probably pass through a third? Commerce among the states must, of necessity, be commerce with the states. * * *

We are now arrived at the inquiry, What is this power? It is the power to regulate; that is, to prescribe the rule by which commerce is to be governed. This power, like all others vested in Congress, is complete in itself, may be exercised to its utmost extent, and acknowledges no limitations other than are prescribed in the Constitution. These are expressed in plain terms, and do not affect the questions which arise in this case, or which have been discussed at the bar. If, as has always been understood, the sovereignty of Congress, though limited to specified objects, is plenary as to those objects, the power over commerce with foreign nations, and among the several states, is vested in Congress as absolutely as it would be in a single government, having in its constitution the same restrictions on the exercise of the power as are found in the Constitution of the United States. * * *[a]

[We consider infra, Ch. 4, Sec. 1, Marshall, C.J.'s inconclusive discussion in *Gibbons* of the challenge to the New York law as inconsistent with Congress' power to regulate commerce, viewed as exclusive. The Court left that issue unresolved when it found New York's grant of exclusive rights to use New York waters inconsistent with the federal licenses to engage in the coastal trade authorized by Congress under its commerce power.]

Notes and Questions

1. *Impact of Gibbons.* 2 WARREN, THE SUPREME COURT IN UNITED STATES HISTORY, c. 15 (1922), pointed out the almost immediate and dramatic effect of *Gibbons* in opening up greater freedom in interstate transportation (pp. 75–76): "The effects of the decision were at once felt in the waters of New York and the other States. Shortly after the fourteenth of March, the newspapers of

---

a. Johnson, J., concurred on the ground that the power of Congress to regulate commerce was exclusive.

the North carried this item: 'Yesterday the Steamboat *United States,* Capt. Bunker, from New Haven, entered New York in triumph, with streamers flying, and a large company of passengers exulting in the decision of the United States Supreme Court against the New York monopoly. She fired a salute which was loudly returned by huzzas from the wharves.' A representative Southern paper spoke of 'the immense public advantages that flow from the decision. The fare in the steamboats that ply between New York and New Haven has been reduced from five to three dollars. The boats that heretofore went from Charleston to Hamburg now touch at Savannah and come directly to the wharves of Augusta. On Monday, the 29th, two steamboats from Charleston arrived at Augusta. Their arrival was greated by the citizens who fired a *feu de joie,* accompanied by a band of music, which was returned by one of the boats, amidst repeated huzzas and cries of "down with all monopolies of commerce and manufactories—one is as great an evil as the other. Give us free trade and sailor's rights!"' Shortly over a year after the decision, *Niles Register* reported that the number of steamboats plying from New York had increased from six to forty-three.

"As revealed in the above comments, the chief importance of the case in the eyes of the public that day was its effect in shattering the great monopoly against which they had been struggling for fifteen years. It was the first great 'trust' decision in this country, and quite naturally met with popular approval on this account. But economic results of more far-reaching importance than the mere demolition of the monopoly were involved, which were not appreciated until later years. The opening of the Hudson River and Long Island Sound to the free passage of steamboats was the most potent factor in the building up of New York as a commercial center. The removal of danger of similar grants of railroad monopolies in other States promoted immensely the development of interstate communication by steam throughout the country; for the first railroad was built only five years later. The coal industry, then but an experiment, was developed through the growth of New England's manufacturing industries, made possible by cheap transportation of coal by water. In short, Marshall's opinion was the emancipation proclamation of American commerce."

2. *Meaning of "commerce."* (a) Should "commerce" be held to include, not only exchange of commodities and transportation, as ruled in *Gibbons,* but also business transactions in financial obligations, such as insurance policies and securities? How about the communications business, manufacturing, and publishing?

(b) The Court's commerce clause concepts were first developed largely in cases challenging state regulatory laws and taxes as regulations of "commerce" exclusively within the power of Congress. At the time, Congress had left business regulation to the states,[b] and made little use of its power to regulate commerce until adoption of the Interstate Commerce Act in 1887 and the Sherman Act in 1890. Were concepts so developed likely to prove viable when Congress finally enacted substantial business regulation and the true issue became the extent of congressional, not state, power? See Myers, *Interstate Commerce—The Constitutional Interpretation of a Non-Constitutional Term,* 17 U.Pitt.L.Rev. 329, 331 (1956); *Polish Nat'l Alliance v. NLRB,* 322 U.S. 643, 649, 64 S.Ct. 1196, 1199, 88 L.Ed. 1509, 1515 (1944).

---

b. Chs. 4 and 5 are concerned with the Court's efforts to protect interstate commerce against harmful state regulation and taxation without thwarting state efforts to protect legitimate state interests.

(c) *Paul v. Virginia,* 75 U.S. (8 Wall.) 168, 19 L.Ed. 357 (1869), upheld state regulation of interstate insurance business on the ground that "issuing a policy of insurance is not a transaction of commerce" and insurance contracts "are not articles of commerce." Would *Paul* be a persuasive precedent for insurance companies contending that the Sherman Act's bar on restraints of trade in interstate commerce may not apply to an interstate insurance rate fixing arrangement? See *United States v. South-Eastern Underwriters Ass'n,* 322 U.S. 533, 64 S.Ct. 1162, 88 L.Ed. 1440 (1944) (prosecution upheld), considered Part III, B infra.

(d) KIDD v. PEARSON, 128 U.S. 1, 9 S.Ct. 6, 32 L.Ed. 346 (1888), upheld Iowa's ban on manufacture of liquor as applied to an Iowa distillery that sold its entire output in other states. It rejected the contention that manufacture for exclusively out-of-state sales was interstate commerce subject only to congressional regulation: "No distinction is more popular to the common mind, or more clearly expressed in economic and political literature, than that between manufacturing and commerce. Manufacturing is transformation—the fashioning of raw materials into a change of form for use. The functions of commerce are different. The buying and selling and the transportation incident thereto constitute commerce. [If] it be held that the term includes the regulation of all such manufactures as are intended to be the subject of commercial transactions in the future, it is impossible to deny that it would also include all productive industries that contemplate the same thing. The result would be that Congress would be invested, to the exclusion of the States, with the power to regulate, not only manufactures, but also agriculture, horticulture, stock raising, domestic fisheries, mining—in short, every branch of human industry. For is there one of them that does not contemplate, more or less clearly, an interstate or foreign market? [The] power being vested in Congress and denied to the States, it would follow as an inevitable result that the duty would devolve on Congress to regulate all these delicate, multiform and vital interests—interests which in their nature are and must be, local in all details of their successful management."

The Court has consistently adhered to the *Pearson* ruling that manufacture and production are not "commerce." See the cases in Part III infra. Accepting that conclusion, on what bases might Congress be found to have power under the commerce clause to regulate manufacturing?

3. *Meaning of "among the several states."* (a) THE DANIEL BALL, 77 U.S. (10 Wall.) 557, 19 L.Ed. 999 (1871) sustained a federal safety regulation as applied to a small ship navigating in shallow water on the Grand River exclusively within the State of Michigan: "So far as she was employed in transporting goods destined for other States, or goods brought from without the limits of Michigan and destined to places within that State, she was engaged in commerce between the States. [She] was employed as an instrumentality of that commerce; for whenever a commodity has begun to move as an article of trade from one State to another, commerce in that commodity between the States has commenced. The fact that several different and independent agencies are employed in transporting the commodity, some acting entirely in one State, and some acting through two or more States does in no respect affect the character of the transaction.

"[W]e are unable to draw any clear and distinct line between the authority of Congress to regulate an agency employed in commerce between the States, when that agency extends through two or more States and when it is confined in its action entirely within the limits of a single State. If its authority does not extend to an agency in such commerce, when that agency is confined within the limits of a State, its entire authority over interstate commerce may be defeated."

(b) *Application.* Assume the following: Company operates a mine and coarse crushing plant for taconite rock at Babbitt, Minn., a processing plant at Mile Post, Minn., where by fine crushing and a magnetic process iron ore is removed from the taconite rock received from Babbitt and converted into iron ore pellets; and a docking facility at Silver Bay, Minn., where all iron ore pellets created at Mile Post are loaded onto ships on Lake Superior for shipment to Great Lakes ports in other states. Railroad operates only between Babbitt, Mile Post, and Silver Bay. Which of the following activities should be classified as *intrastate* (Marshall's "completely internal commerce") and which *interstate* (Marshall's "commerce that concerns more states than one")? (1) Through its Cleveland, Ohio, sales office Company contracts to sell to Bell Foundry of Cleveland, a specified quantity of iron ore pellets to be shipped from Silver Bay. (2) The Cleveland office unsuccessfully negotiates for a similar contract with Ohio Foundry of Cleveland.[c] (3) Railroad hauls used crushing equipment from Babbitt to Mile Post for use there. (4) Railroad hauls iron ore pellets from Mile Post to Silver Bay for loading onto a ship to fulfill the contract with Bell Foundry of Cleveland. (5) Railroad hauls coarsely crushed rock from Babbitt to Mile Post where the fine particles of iron ore are to be separated from the much greater volume of rock waste and converted into pellets to fulfil out-of-state sales contracts.[d]

(c) *"Between the states" or "among the people"?* *The Daniel Ball* referred three times to commerce "between the states." Arguably "among" could be given a broader meaning than "between". 1 Crosskey, *Politics and the Constitution in the History of the United States,* c. 3 (1953), contended that the framers of the Constitution intended to give Congress power to regulate all commercial and business activities, irrespective of state lines or interstate movement. Crosskey's view of the 1787 usage and understanding of *among* and *the several states* led him to conclude that "commerce among the several states" really meant "commerce among the people of the several states," with no territorial connotation at all.[e]

4. *Business purpose.* Is a business or "commercial" purpose necessary before Congress can exercise its commerce power to control interstate movement or transportation? For example, should the commerce power include power in Congress to forbid a fundamentalist Mormon from driving his two wives in a car from Utah to Nevada to set up housekeeping? Forbid carrying liquor for one's own use across state lines? Forbid fleeing from one state to another to avoid state criminal prosecution? Forbid a parent from "kidnapping" its child from the other parent's custody and taking it into another state? Under our federal system are there good reasons for making the commerce power applicable to such non-commercial actions? See *Caminetti v. United States,* 242 U.S. 470, 37

---

c. Cf. *Robbins v. Shelby Cty. Tax. Dist.,* 120 U.S. 489, 7 S.Ct. 592, 30 L.Ed. 694 (1887).

d. Cf. *Bacon v. Illinois,* 227 U.S. 504, 33 S.Ct. 299, 57 L.Ed. 615 (1913) (interstate commerce ceased, subjecting grain to state taxation, when grain consigned from State *A* to State *C* temporarily stopped in elevator in State *B* for weighing, grading and mixing, purposes unrelated to transportation and for the owner's benefit).

e. The reception of Crosskey's views on this and other constitutional issues was varied and intense. In addition to many single book reviews, two law reviews published symposia of several articles or reviews from differing viewpoints. See 21 U.Chi.L.Rev. 1–92 (1953): 54 Colum.L.Rev. 438–83 (1954). His book appears to have had little influence on constitutional developments.

S.Ct. 192, 61 L.Ed. 442 (1917) (transportation of mistress for non-commercial but immoral purposes); *Cleveland v. United States,* 329 U.S. 14, 67 S.Ct. 13, 91 L.Ed. 12 (1946) (Mormon and his plural wives); *United States v. Hill,* 248 U.S. 420, 39 S.Ct. 143, 63 L.Ed. 337 (1919) (transporting liquor for personal use); *Gooch v. United States,* 297 U.S. 124, 56 S.Ct. 395, 80 L.Ed. 522 (1936) (taking kidnapped person across state lines); *Hemans v. United States,* 163 F.2d 228 (6th Cir.1947), cert. denied 332 U.S. 801, 68 S.Ct. 100, 92 L.Ed. 380 (1947) (fleeing across state lines to escape giving testimony in a criminal case).

FOUNDATIONS FOR EXTENDING REACH OF CONGRESSIONAL POWER

There have been no serious challenges to the power of Congress to regulate interstate trade, transportation or communication, so long as the activity regulated is clearly "commerce" and "among the several states." The more significant problems relate to Congress using its commerce power to deal with (1) national economic problems by regulating local aspects that may be neither "commerce" nor "among the several states," such as labor relations in a local factory or the quantity of a crop produced and used on a farm, (2) disfavored local police-type problems, such as gambling, prostitution, distribution of unhealthful foods or harmful or improperly labeled drugs, and local loan shark enterprises, (3) other socially undesirable activities, particularly discrimination based on race, sex, or age, and (4) activities harmful to the environment.

The next two cases reveal the origins of two quite different methods of dealing with such problems under the commerce clause, even when this extends the reach of congressional power to activities that are neither "commerce" nor "interstate." The rest of Section 2 then deals with the evolution of these methods in the four areas noted above.

LOTTERY CASE (CHAMPION v. AMES)
188 U.S. 321, 23 S.Ct. 321, 47 L.Ed. 492 (1903).

MR. JUSTICE HARLAN delivered the opinion of the Court.

[After twice ordering the case reargued, the Court upheld the Federal Lottery Act, which prohibited causing interstate carriage of lottery tickets, as applied to shipping a box of lottery tickets from Texas to California.]

[We] are of opinion that lottery tickets are subjects of traffic, and therefore are subjects of commerce, and the regulation of the carriage of such tickets from state to state, at least by independent carriers, is a regulation of commerce among the several states. * * *

If lottery traffic, *carried on through interstate commerce,* is a matter of which Congress may take cognizance and over which its power may be exerted, can it be possible that it must tolerate the traffic, and simply regulate the manner in which it may be carried on? Or may not Congress, for the protection of the people of all the states, and under the power to regulate interstate commerce, devise such means, within the scope of the Constitution, and not prohibited by it, as will drive that traffic out of commerce among the states?

* * * When enacting [the Lottery Act] Congress no doubt shared the views upon the subject of lotteries heretofore expressed by this court. In *Phalen v. Virginia,* 8 How. 163, 168, 12 L.Ed. 1030, after observing that the suppression of nuisances injurious to public health or morality is among the most important duties of government, this court said: "Experience has shown that the common forms of gambling are comparatively innocuous when placed in contrast with the widespread pestilence of lotteries. The former are confined to a few persons and places, but the latter infests the whole community; it enters every dwelling; it reaches every class; it preys upon the hard earnings of the poor; it plunders the ignorant and simple."

[If] a state, when considering legislation for the suppression of lotteries within its own limits, may properly take into view the evils, that inhere in the raising of money, in that mode, why may not Congress, invested with the power to regulate commerce among the several states, provide that such commerce shall not be polluted by the carrying of lottery tickets from one state to another? In this connection it must not be forgotten that the power of Congress to regulate commerce among the states is plenary, is complete in itself, and is subject to no limitations except such as may be found in the Constitution. [What] clause can be cited which, in any degree, countenances the suggestion that one may, of right, carry or cause to be carried from one state to another that which will harm the public morals? * * *

Congress [does] not assume to interfere with traffic or commerce in lottery tickets carried on exclusively within the limits of any state, but has in view only commerce of that kind among the several states. It has not assumed to interfere with the completely internal affairs of any state, and has only legislated in respect of a matter which concerns the people of the United States. As a state may, for the purpose of guarding the morals of its own people, forbid all sales of lottery tickets within its limits, so Congress, for the purpose of guarding the people of the United States against the "widespread pestilence of lotteries" and to protect the commerce which concerns all the states, may prohibit the carrying of lottery tickets from one state to another. In legislating upon the subject of the traffic in lottery tickets, as carried on through interstate commerce, Congress only supplemented the action of those states—perhaps all of them—which, for the protection of the public morals, prohibit the drawing of lotteries, as well as the sale or circulation of lottery tickets, within their respective limits. It said, in effect, that it would not permit the declared policy of the states, which sought to protect their people against the mischiefs of the lottery business, to be overthrown or disregarded by the agency of interstate commerce. We should hesitate long before adjudging that an evil of such appalling character, carried on through interstate commerce, cannot be met and crushed by the only power competent to that end. We say competent to that end, because Congress alone has the power to occupy, by legislation the whole field of interstate commerce. * * *

MR. CHIEF JUSTICE FULLER, with whom concur MR. JUSTICE BREWER, MR. JUSTICE SHIRAS, and MR. JUSTICE PECKHAM, dissenting:

[D]oubtless an act prohibiting the carriage of lottery matter would be necessary and proper to the execution of a power to suppress lotteries; but that power belongs to the states and not to Congress. To hold that Congress has general police power would be to hold that it may accomplish objects not intrusted to the general government, and to defeat the operation of the 10th Amendment. * * *

Notes and Questions

1. *Commerce clause as source of national police power.* Despite the close division of the Court, *Lottery* firmly established the power of Congress to exclude from the channels of interstate commerce commodities and activities found by

Congress to be harmful to the national interest. For a thorough analysis of the legislation and decisions to 1919, see Cushman, *The National Police Power Under the Commerce Clause of the Constitution,* 3 Minn.L.Rev. 289, 381–412 (1919). Exclusions from interstate commerce to that date included: (1) Lottery tickets. (2) Obscene material. *United States v. Popper,* 98 F. 423 (N.D.Cal.1899), cited with approval in *Hoke v. United States,* 227 U.S. 308, 33 S.Ct. 281, 57 L.Ed. 523 (1913). (3) White slave traffic. *Hoke v. United States.* (4) Impure, unwholesome or adulterated food or drugs. *Hipolite Egg Co. v. United States,* 220 U.S. 45, 31 S.Ct. 364, 55 L.Ed. 364 (1911). (5) Misbranded products. (6) Diseased plants and animals. For later developments, see Parts III–V infra.

2. *The Lottery policy.* Professor Cushman, note 1 supra, stated the underlying policy in 1919: "One of the most interesting and important steps in the development of a national police power under the commerce clause has been the enactment of a group of laws by which the channels of interstate commerce have been closed to commodities or transactions which are injurious, not to that commerce or to any of the agencies or facilities thereof, but to the health, morals, safety, and general welfare of the nation. When Congress punishes the man who ships across a state line bottles of colored water declared by their labels to be a cure for cancer, it does so not because those bottles are a whit more dangerous to commerce than would be a consignment of shoes, but because it desires to prevent the facilities of commerce from being used as a means of distributing goods which are a fraud upon the people who buy and use them.

* * *

"There ought to be no difficulty in concluding that the authority to pass such laws is reasonably implied from the plenary power of Congress to regulate commerce. * * * Whatever controversy may arise as to the power of Congress to prohibit or restrict under certain circumstances the shipment in interstate commerce of commodities which are legitimate and wholesome and are destined for legitimate and wholesome uses, there ought to be no serious doubt about the congressional authority to keep the arteries of interstate commerce from being employed as conduits for articles hurtful to the public health, safety, or morals."

HOUSTON, EAST & WEST RY. v. UNITED STATES (SHREVEPORT CASE)

234 U.S. 342, 34 S.Ct. 833, 58 L.Ed. 1341 (1914).

MR. JUSTICE HUGHES delivered the opinion of the Court.

[The Court upheld an Interstate Commerce Commission order fixing interstate railroad rates westward from Shreveport, La., to Texas points and finding that the railroad's lower rates, prescribed by the Texas Railroad Commission, for comparable traffic eastward from Dallas and Houston to the same Texas points resulted in "unlawful and undue preference" and "discrimination" in violation of the Interstate Commerce Act.[a] The court below held] that the order relieved the appellants from further obligation to observe the intrastate rates, and that they were at liberty to comply with the ICC's requirements by increasing these rates sufficiently to remove the forbidden discrimination. The invalidity of the order in this aspect is challenged upon [the ground that] Congress is impotent to

---

a. For example "a rate of 60 cents carried first-class traffic [160 miles] eastward from Dallas, while the same rate [carried] the same class of traffic only 55 miles into Texas from Shreveport. [The] rate on wagons from Dallas to Marshall, Texas, 147.7 miles, was 36.8 cents, and from Shreveport to Marshall, 42 miles, 56 [cents]."

control the intrastate charges of an interstate carrier even to the extent necessary to prevent injurious discrimination against interstate traffic. * * *

[Where the power of Congress] to regulate [commerce] exists, it dominates. Interstate trade was not left to be destroyed or impeded by the rivalries of local government. The purpose was to make impossible the recurrence of the evils which had overwhelmed the Confederation, and to provide the necessary basis of national unity by insuring "uniformity of regulation against conflicting and discriminating state legislation." By virtue of the comprehensive terms of the grant, the authority of Congress is at all times adequate to meet the varying exigencies that arise, and to protect the national interest by securing the freedom of interstate commercial intercourse from local [control].

Its authority, extending to these interstate carriers as instruments of interstate commerce, necessarily embraces the right to control their operations in all matters having such a close and substantial relation to interstate traffic that the control is essential or appropriate to the security of that traffic, to the efficiency of the interstate service, and to the maintenance of conditions under which interstate commerce may be conducted upon fair terms and without molestation or [hindrance].

While *Baltimore & O.R. Co. v. ICC* [b] and *Southern R. Co. v. United States* [c] relate to measures adopted in the interest of the safety of persons and property, they illustrate the principle that Congress, in the exercise of its paramount power, may prevent the common instrumentalities of interstate and intrastate commercial intercourse from being used in their intrastate operations to the injury of interstate commerce. This is not to say that Congress possesses the authority to regulate the internal commerce of a state, as such, but that it does possess the power to foster and protect interstate commerce, and to take all measures necessary or appropriate to that end, although intrastate transactions of interstate carriers may thereby be controlled.

This principle is applicable here. We find no reason to doubt that Congress is entitled to keep the highways of interstate communication open to interstate traffic upon fair and equal terms. That an unjust discrimination in the rates of a common carrier, by which one person or locality is unduly favored as against another under substantially similar conditions of traffic, constitutes an evil, is undeniable; and where this evil consists in the action of an interstate carrier in unreasonably discriminating against interstate traffic over its line, the authority of Congress to prevent it is equally clear. It is immaterial, so far as the protecting power of Congress is concerned, that the discrimination arises from intrastate rates as compared with interstate rates. The use of the instrument of interstate commerce in a discriminatory manner so as to inflict injury upon that commerce, or some part thereof, furnishes abundant ground for Federal intervention. * * *

It is for Congress to supply the needed correction where the relation between intrastate and interstate rates presents the evil to be corrected. [In] removing the injurious discriminations against interstate traffic arising from the relation

---

b. 221 U.S. 612, 31 S.Ct. 621, 55 L.Ed. 878 (1911). *Baltimore & O.R.* upheld federal regulation of hours of service of employees working on interstate railroad service, even though the effect was to control their hours on intrastate service as well, because of the impracticality of limiting their work to one or the other.

c. 222 U.S. 20, 32 S.Ct. 2, 56 L.Ed. 72 (1911). *Southern R.* upheld the federal safety appliance act's application to vehicles used by an interstate railroad only in intrastate traffic, as well as those used interstate, in order to assure the safety of interstate traffic moving over the same railroad as the intrastate.

of intrastate to interstate rates, Congress is not bound to reduce the latter below what it may deem to be a proper standard, fair to the carrier and to the public. Otherwise, it could prevent the injury to interstate commerce only by the sacrifice of its judgment as to interstate rates. Congress is entitled to maintain its own standard as to these rates, and to forbid any discriminatory action by interstate carriers which will obstruct the freedom of movement of interstate traffic over their lines in accordance with the terms it establishes.[d] * * *

Notes and Questions

1. *Relation of local activities to interstate commerce.* How does the relation of the regulated local activity to interstate commerce differ in *Shreveport* from that in *Baltimore & Ohio* and *Southern R. Co.?* Which regulation more closely advances the historic commerce clause objectives?

2. *Shreveport contrasted with Lottery.* Contrast the *Shreveport* and *Lottery* methods of achieving a regulation of local activities in terms of the regulatory point of impact, professed objective, and rationale. Each method has a long line of progeny, considered in Parts III to VI.

III. REGULATION OF NATIONAL ECONOMIC PROBLEMS THROUGH THE COMMERCE POWER

A. LIMITATIONS ON COMMERCE POWER THROUGH 1936

HAMMER v. DAGENHART

247 U.S. 251, 38 S.Ct. 529, 62 L.Ed. 1101 (1918).

MR. JUSTICE DAY delivered the opinion of the Court.

[Is] it within the authority of Congress in regulating commerce among the states to prohibit the transportation in interstate commerce of manufactured goods, the product of a factory in which, within thirty days prior to their removal therefrom, children under the age of fourteen have been employed or permitted to work, or children between the ages of fourteen and sixteen years have been employed or permitted to work more than eight hours in any day, or more than six days in any week, or after the hour of 7 o'clock p.m., or before the hour of 6 o'clock a.m.?

[The commerce] power is one to control the means by which commerce is carried on, which is directly the contrary of the assumed right to forbid commerce from moving and thus destroying it as to particular commodities. But it is insisted that adjudged cases in this court establish the doctrine that the power to regulate given to Congress incidentally includes the authority to prohibit the movement of ordinary commodities. [The] cases demonstrate the contrary. They rest upon the character of the particular subjects dealt with and the fact that the scope of governmental authority, state or national, possessed over them is such that the authority to prohibit is as to them but the exertion of the power to regulate.

[The opinion summarized the *Lottery Case* and others which followed it, quoting from the *Hoke* emphasis on taking "the facility of interstate commerce [away] from the demoralization of lotteries, the debasement of obscene literature, the contagion of diseased cattle and persons, the impurity of drugs, [the] enslavement in prostitution and debauchery."]

---

d. Lurton and Pitney, JJ., dissented.

In each of these instances the use of interstate transportation was necessary to the accomplishment of harmful results. In other words, although the power over interstate transportation was to regulate, that could only be accomplished by prohibiting the use of the facilities of interstate commerce to effect the evil intended.

This element is wanting in the present case. The thing intended to be accomplished by this statute is the denial of the facilities of interstate commerce to those manufacturers in the states who employ children within the prohibited ages. The act in its effect does not regulate transportation among the states, but aims to standardize the ages at which children may be employed in mining and manufacturing within the states. The goods shipped are of themselves harmless. The act permits them to be freely shipped after thirty days from the time of their removal from the factory. When offered for shipment, and before transportation begins, the labor of their production is over, and the mere fact that they were intended for interstate commerce transportation does not make their production subject to federal control under the commerce power. * * *

Over interstate transportation, or its incidents, the regulatory power of Congress is ample, but the production of articles, intended for interstate commerce, is a matter of local regulation. [If] it were otherwise, all manufacture intended for interstate shipment would be brought under federal control to the practical exclusion of the authority of the states, a result certainly not contemplated by the framers of the Constitution when they vested in Congress the authority to regulate commerce among the States. *Kidd v. Pearson.*

It is further contended that the authority of Congress may be exerted to control interstate commerce in the shipment of child-made goods because of the effect of the circulation of such goods in other states where the evil of this class of labor has been recognized by local legislation, and the right to thus employ child labor has been more rigorously restrained than in the state of production. In other words, that the unfair competition, thus engendered, may be controlled by closing the channels of interstate commerce to manufacturers in those states where the local laws do not meet what Congress deems to be the more just standard of other states.

There is no power vested in Congress to require the states to exercise their police power so as to prevent possible unfair competition. Many causes may cooperate to give one state, by reason of local laws or conditions, an economic advantage over others. The commerce clause was not intended to give to Congress a general authority to equalize such conditions. In some of the states laws have been passed fixing minimum wages for women, in others the local law regulates the hours of labor of women in various employments. Business done in such states may be at an economic disadvantage when compared with states which have no such regulations; surely, this fact does not give Congress the power to deny transportation in interstate commerce to those who carry on business where the hours of labor and the rate of compensation for women have not been fixed by a standard in use in other states and approved by Congress. * * *

The grant of power to Congress over the subject of interstate commerce was to enable it to regulate such commerce, and not to give it authority to control the states in their exercise of the police power over local trade and manufacture. * * *

In interpreting the Constitution it must never be forgotten that the nation is made up of states to which are entrusted the powers of local government. And to them and to the people the powers not expressly delegated to the national government are reserved. [To] sustain this statute [would] sanction an invasion by the federal power of the control of a matter purely local in its character, and over which no authority has been delegated to Congress in conferring the power to regulate commerce among the states. * * *

MR. JUSTICE HOLMES, dissenting.[a]

[T]he statute in question is within the power expressly given to Congress if considered only as to its immediate effects. [The] statute confines itself to prohibiting the carriage of certain goods in interstate or foreign commerce. [Regulation] means the prohibition of something, and when interstate commerce is the matter to be regulated I cannot doubt that the regulation may prohibit any part of such commerce that Congress sees fit to [forbid].

The question then is narrowed to whether the exercise of its otherwise constitutional power by Congress can be pronounced unconstitutional because of its possible reaction upon the conduct of the States in a matter upon which [they] are free from direct control. [I] should have thought that the most conspicuous decisions of this Court had made it clear that the power to regulate commerce and other constitutional powers could not be cut down or qualified by the fact that it might interfere with the carrying out of the domestic policy of any [State.]

It does not matter whether the supposed evil precedes or follows the transportation. It is enough that in the opinion of Congress the transportation encourages the evil. [The] notion that prohibition is any less prohibition when applied to things now thought evil I do not understand. But if there is any matter upon which civilized countries have agreed—far more unanimously than they have with regard to intoxicants and some other matters over which this country is now emotionally aroused—it is the evil of premature and excessive child labor. I should have thought that if we were to introduce our own moral conceptions where in my opinion they do not belong, this was preeminently a case for upholding the exercise of all its powers by the United States.

But I had thought that the propriety of the exercise of a power admitted to exist in some cases was for the consideration of Congress alone and that this Court always had disavowed the right to intrude its judgment upon questions of policy or morals. * * *

The Act does not meddle with anything belonging to the States. They may regulate their internal affairs and their domestic commerce as they like. But when they seek to send their products across the State line they are no longer within their rights. If there were no Constitution and no Congress their power to cross the line would depend upon their neighbors. Under the Constitution such commerce belongs not to the States but to Congress to regulate. It may carry out its views of public policy whatever indirect effect they may have upon the activities of the States. Instead of being encountered by a prohibitive tariff at her boundaries the State encounters the public policy of the United States which it is for Congress to express. The public policy of the United States is shaped with a view to the benefit of the nation as a whole. [The] national welfare as understood by Congress may require a different attitude within its sphere from that of some self-seeking State.[b] * * *

a. McKenna, Brandeis, and Clarke, JJ., joined this dissent.

b. For excellent discussions of the issues in *Dagenhart*, see Powell, *The Child Labor Law,* *The Tenth Amendment, and the Commerce Clause,* 3 So.L.Q. (now Tul.L.Rev.) 175 (1918); Corwin, *The Power of Congress to Prohibit Commerce,* 18 Corn.L.Q. 477 (1933).

Notes and Questions

1. *Harmful effects from child labor products in interstate commerce.* (a) Can harm extending beyond the state of origin be found to result from interstate shipment of the products of child labor? Does the harm have any relationship to interstate commerce? See Grant, *Commerce, Production, and the Fiscal Powers of Congress*, 45 Yale L.J. 751, 754 (1936).

(b) Which "harmful results" were more of a threat to the interests the commerce clause was intended to protect—those guarded against by the laws sustained in the *Lottery, Hoke* and similar cases or those guarded against by the federal child labor law held invalid in *Dagenhart?*

(c) Do you agree that "the commerce clause was not intended to give Congress the general authority to [equalize] conditions" that give one state, "by reason of local laws or conditions, an economic advantage over others"? What if the local laws authorize harmful hours of labor or labor conditions that give the state's industry an economic advantage over competitors in other states imposing more stringent standards?

2. *Tenth Amendment.* Did *Dagenhart* accurately paraphrase the tenth amendment as reserving to the states and the people "the powers not expressly delegated"? Compare Marshall, C.J.'s discussion of the tenth amendment in *McCulloch.*

3. *The need for national power.* (a) The *Dagenhart* majority sought to preserve "the authority of the states over matters purely local." But did *Dagenhart's* invalidation of federal control advance or impede the states' ability to make effective their own child labor laws? Without the support of federal laws could New York or Massachusetts protect their textile industries from the competition of child labor mills in North Carolina? Could New York protect its home market by forbidding the sale in New York of the products of child labor? Cf. *Leisy v. Hardin* (1890), p. 194 infra (prohibition state cannot forbid sale in original package of liquor shipped in from another state); *Baldwin v. Seelig* (1935), p. 207 infra (state cannot forbid sale within state of milk bought outside of state at price lower than minimum price established by state for its own milk producers).

(b) The need for federal control over child labor was reflected in Congress' enactment within nine months after *Dagenhart* of a law seeking to control child labor through use of the taxing power. See *Child Labor Tax Case*, Sec. 3 infra.

BACKGROUND FOR CONSTITUTIONAL STRUGGLE: THE NEW DEAL vs. THE GREAT DEPRESSION

The great depression of the 1930's gave rise to a pressing need for national regulatory legislation to deal with national economic problems. Unprecedented unemployment, drastic cutbacks in production, 60% declines in farm and labor income, widespread business and bank failures, devastating home and farm mortgage foreclosures, all reacted on each other in a downward spiral that required immediate and widescale action by the national government. The resulting flood of New Deal legislation between 1933 and 1938 is well summarized in Swisher, *American Constitutional Development*, 875–919 (2d ed. 1954).

A participant in the successful struggle to find constitutional bases for national regulatory power competent to deal adequately with the national economic problems wrote a classic analysis of the constitutional litigation. STERN, THE COMMERCE CLAUSE AND THE NATIONAL ECONOMY, 1933–

1946, 59 Harv.L.Rev. 645, 883 (1946). In his article Stern summarized the problem as it looked to a government lawyer at the outset: "The problems were economic, and the Commerce Clause was the enumerated power most directly concerned with business and economic, or commercial, matters. Consequently, although other powers, particularly the fiscal and appropriative, were brought into play, it was upon the Commerce Clause that the legislation directed at controlling many aspects of the national economic system was principally predicated.

"The commerce power had previously been exerted mainly in connection with interstate transportation, although the Sherman Act was exceptional in this respect. The conditions responsible for the business depression, although they had affected the railroads as much as any other industry, were considerably more deepseated. Unemployment, the purchasing power of workers and farmers, prices in business and agriculture, unsellable surpluses which overhung the markets and the quantity of goods produced and grown—these were the elements with which it was necessary to deal. Could the Commerce Clause bear the load?

"Although these ingredients of the economic crises often preceded the movement of goods across state lines and occurred during the course of manufacture and production, they were of national consequence because the products of the national economy were distributed throughout a national market. The channels of interstate commerce were the arteries through which the impact of these forces affected the nation. Because of the nation-wide market, and the constitutional impediment placed by the Commerce Clause itself in the way of regulation by the states, the state governments were unable to cope with economic problems affecting the nation as a whole. The depressed state of business activity obviously affected interstate commerce in the most elementary sense, since it greatly reduced the quantity of products to be transported across state lines.

"Nevertheless there could be no assurance that federal legislation directed at the economic causes of the depression would be constitutional. For that depended on what the Supreme Court thought. And there was ample authority in the Supreme Court opinions looking both ways."

CARTER v. CARTER COAL CO., 298 U.S. 238, 56 S.Ct. 855, 80 L.Ed. 1160 (1936), per SUTHERLAND, J., ruled that the commerce clause did not give Congress power to require Bituminous Coal Code members to observe the hours and wages agreed upon between producers of two-thirds of the bituminous coal volume and one-half of the employed bituminous mine workers: [a]

"[T]he effect of the labor provisions of the [act] primarily falls upon production and not upon commerce; [production] is a purely local activity. It follows that none of these essential antecedents of production constitutes a transaction in or forms any part of interstate commerce. [T]he local character of mining, of manufacturing, and of crop growing is a fact, and remains a fact, whatever may be done with the [products].

"That the production of every commodity intended for interstate sale and transportation has some effect upon interstate commerce may be, if it has not already been, freely granted; and we are brought to the final and decisive inquiry, whether here that effect is direct [or] indirect. The distinction is not formal, but substantial in the highest degree, as we pointed out in [*Schechter*]. [b]

---

a. Hours negotiated on a national level and wages on a district level.

b. *Schechter Poultry Corp. v. United States*, 295 U.S. 495, 55 S.Ct. 837, 79 L.Ed. 1570 (1953)

'If the commerce clause were construed,' we there said, 'to reach all enterprises and transactions which could be said to have an indirect effect upon interstate commerce, the federal authority would embrace practically all the activities of the people, and the authority of the state over its domestic concerns would exist only by sufferance of the federal [government].'

"Whether the effect of a given activity or condition is direct or indirect is not always easy to determine. The word 'direct' implies that the activity or condition invoked or blamed shall operate proximately—not mediately, remotely, or collaterally—to produce the effect. It connotes the absence of an efficient intervening agency or condition. And the extent of the effect bears no logical relation to its character. The distinction between a direct and an indirect effect turns, not upon the magnitude of either the cause or the effect, but entirely upon the manner in which the effect has been brought about. If the production by one man of a single ton of coal intended for interstate sale and shipment, and actually so sold and shipped, affects interstate commerce indirectly, the effect does not become direct by multiplying the tonnage, or increasing the number of men employed, or adding to the expense or complexities of the business, or by all combined. It is quite true that rules of law are sometimes qualified by considerations of degree, as the government argues. But the matter of degree has no bearing upon the question here, since that question is not—What is the extent of the local activity or condition, or the extent of the effect produced upon interstate commerce? but—What is the relation between the activity or condition and the effect?

"Much stress is put upon the evils which come from the struggle between employers and employees over the matter of wages, working conditions, the right of collective bargaining, etc., and the resulting strikes, curtailment, and irregularity of production and effect on prices; and it is insisted that interstate commerce is greatly affected thereby. But, in addition to what has just been said, the conclusive answer is that the evils are all local evils over which the federal government has no legislative control. The relation of employer and employee is a local relation. At common law, it is one of the domestic relations. The wages are paid for the doing of local work. Working conditions are obviously local conditions. The employees are not engaged in or about commerce, but exclusively in producing a commodity. And the controversies and evils, which it is the object of the act to regulate and minimize, are local controversies and evils affecting local work undertaken to accomplish that local result. Such effect as they may have upon commerce, however extensive it may be, is secondary and indirect. An increase in the greatness of the effect adds to its importance. It does not alter its character. [The] only perceptible difference between [*Schechter*] and this is that in the *Schechter Case* the federal power was asserted with respect to commodities which had come to rest after their interstate transportation; while here, the case deals with commodities at rest before interstate commerce has begun. That difference is without significance. The federal regulatory power ceases when interstate commercial intercourse ends; and, correlatively, the power does not attach until interstate commercial intercourse begins. * * *"c

(federal regulation of wages, hours, labor relations and trade practices in local processing and distribution held beyond commerce power).

c. Concurring in the result, Hughes, C.J., withheld approval of the Sutherland opinion, stating only that "Congress may not use this protective authority [over commerce] as a pretext [to] regulate activities and relations within the states which affect interstate commerce only indirectly." He gave no indication as to how he would determine directness.

CARDOZO, J., joined by Brandeis and Stone, JJ., argued that the suits were premature for a ruling on the labor provisions, but his comments on the commerce issue as it related to the regulation of intrastate coal prices should be contrasted with the majority's: [d]

"Mining and agriculture and manufacture are not interstate commerce considered by themselves, yet their relation to that commerce may be such that for the protection of the one there is need to regulate the [other]. Sometimes it is said that the relation must be 'direct' to bring that power into play. In many circumstances such a description will be sufficiently precise to meet the needs of the occasion. But a great principle of constitutional law is not susceptible of comprehensive statement in an adjective. The underlying thought is merely this, that 'the law is not indifferent to considerations of degree.' [It] cannot be indifferent to them without an expansion of the commerce clause that would absorb or imperil the reserved powers of the states. At times, as in [Schechter] the waves of causation will have radiated so far that their undulatory motion, if discernible at all, will be too faint or obscure, too broken by cross-currents, to be heeded by the [law]. Perhaps, if one group of adjectives is to be chosen in preference to another, 'intimate' and 'remote' will be found to be as good as any. At all events, 'direct' and 'indirect,' even if accepted as sufficient, must not be read too narrowly. Cf. Stone, J. in *Di Santo v. Pennsylvania* [p. 254 infra]. A survey of the cases shows that the words have been interpreted with suppleness of adaptation and flexibility of meaning. The power is as broad as the need that evokes it.

"One of the most common and typical instances of a relation characterized as direct has been that between interstate and intrastate rates for carriers by rail where the local rates are so low as to divert business unreasonably from interstate competitors. In such circumstances Congress has the power to protect the business of its carriers against disintegrating encroachments. To be sure, the relation even then may be characterized as indirect if one is nice or overliteral in the choice of words. Strictly speaking, the intrastate rates have a primary effect upon the intrastate traffic and not upon any other, though the repercussions of the competitive system may lead to secondary consequences affecting interstate traffic also. What the cases really mean is that the causal relation in such circumstances is so close and intimate and obvious as to permit it to be called direct without subjecting the word to an unfair or excessive strain."

Notes and Questions

1. *"Direct" or "indirect" effect on interstate commerce.* For a study of the origins and "questionable legitimacy" of the direct-indirect test as a requisite for federal power, see Farage, *That Which "Directly" Affects Interstate Commerce,* 42 Dick.L.Rev. 1 (1937).

2. *The "manner" of affecting commerce.* (a) Does *Carter's* emphasis upon the *"manner* in which the effect has been brought about" focus on the appropriate considerations for deciding what "local evils" Congress may control because of their effect on interstate commerce? See, Farage, supra, at 5. If not, what are the appropriate considerations?

(b) Despite the vulnerability of the tort-law-proximate-cause terminology as a test of the constitutional power of Congress, does this language in *Carter*

---

d. Cardozo, J., would have sustained the Code's price provisions, while the majority ruled them inseparable from the invalid labor provisions.

suggest considerations that ought to be weighed in deciding whether the activities regulated have a sufficient relationship to interstate commerce?

B. EXPANSION OF COMMERCE POWER AFTER 1936

BACKGROUND FOR A JUDICIAL REVERSAL OF POSITION

At the time of the 1936 Presidential election the Court had dealt devastating blows to President Franklin D. Roosevelt's New Deal program for economic recovery. It had invalidated six federal laws designed to advance that program, four of major importance: the National Industrial Recovery Act and the Bituminous Coal Act, both considered supra, the Agricultural Adjustment Act, *United States v. Butler,* considered Sec. 3 infra, and the Railway Pension Act, *Railroad Retirement Bd. v. Alton R.R.,* 295 U.S. 330, 55 S.Ct. 758, 79 L.Ed. 1468 (1935).[a]

Only one New Deal measure aimed at the economic crisis had been sustained, and by the narrowest margin—the Gold Clause legislation. *Norman v. Baltimore & O.R. Co.,* 294 U.S. 240, 55 S.Ct. 407, 79 L.Ed. 885 (1935) (5–4). Some of the more vital Acts of the New Deal legislative program still awaited the Court's scrutiny. These included the National Labor Relations Act, the Social Security Act (both old age pensions and unemployment compensation), and the Public Utility Holding Company Act. In addition, new legislation was needed to replace the minimum labor standards lost in *Schechter* and *Carter* and the control over agricultural surpluses lost in *Butler.*[b]

Viewing his overwhelming victory in the 1936 elections as "an endorsement of his legislative program [despite] the recent Supreme Court opinions which seemingly blocked his path," President Roosevelt "determined not to permit the Court to flout the popular will by what he, as well as Justices Brandeis, Stone and Cardozo, felt to be a reactionary interpretation of the Constitution."[c] Flooded with proposals for dealing with such judicial roadblocks, Roosevelt sought Congressional approval for what became known popularly as the "court packing" plan. Recommended by Attorney General Cummings,[d] this plan would have authorized appointment of "as many as six new justices to the Supreme [Court], one to sit in addition to each justice over seventy years of age."[e]

Responding to criticisms of the plan, the President described and defended it in a radio address on March 9, 1937:

"What is my proposal? It is simply this: whenever a Judge or Justice of any Federal Court has reached the age of seventy and does not avail himself of the opportunity to retire on a pension [at full pay for life], a new member shall be appointed by the President then in office, with the approval, as required by the Constitution, of the Senate of the United States.

"That plan has two chief purposes. By bringing into the Judicial system a steady and continuing stream of new and younger blood, I hope, first, to make the administration of all Federal justice speedier and, therefore, less costly; secondly, to bring to the decision of social and economic problems younger men who have had personal experience and contact with modern facts and circum-

---

a. The other two were the Farm Mortgage Act and the Municipal Bankruptcy Act. *Louisville Joint Stock Land Bank v. Radford,* 295 U.S. 555, 55 S.Ct. 854, 79 L.Ed. 1593 (1935); *Ashton v. Cameron County Dist.,* 298 U.S. 513, 56 S.Ct. 892, 80 L.Ed. 1309 (1936).

b. *United States v. Butler* (1936), Sec. 3, II infra.

c. Stern, *The Commerce Clause and the National Economy,* 1933–46, 59 Harv.L.Rev. 645, 677 (1946).

d. Leuchtenburg, *The Origins of Franklin D. Roosevelt's "Court Packing" Plan,* 1966 Sup.Ct.Rev. 347–394.

e. Stern, fn. c supra.

stances under which average men have to live and work. This plan will save our national Constitution from hardening of the judicial arteries.

"The number of Judges to be appointed would depend wholly on the decision of present Judges now over seventy, or those who would subsequently reach the age of seventy.

"If, for instance, any one of the six Justices of the Supreme Court now over the age of seventy should retire [no] additional place would be created. Consequently, although there never can be more than fifteen, there may be only fourteen, or thirteen, or twelve. And there may be only nine." f

The story of the battle over the Roosevelt Court Packing plan has been told elsewhere. See Alsop & Catledge, *168 Days* (1938); Jackson, *The Struggle for Judicial Supremacy* (1941); 2 Pusey, *Charles Evans Hughes* 759–65 (1951); Mason, *Harlan Fiske Stone and FDR's Court Plan*, 61 Yale L.J. 791 (1952).

NLRB v. JONES & LAUGHLIN STEEL CORP.

301 U.S. 1, 57 S.Ct. 615, 81 L.Ed. 893 (1937).

MR. CHIEF JUSTICE HUGHES delivered the opinion of the Court.

[The NLRB found that Jones & Laughlin had engaged in unfair labor practices in violation of the National Labor Relations Act by discharging employees at its Aliquippa, Pa., plant for union activity. It ordered reinstatement and other relief. The court of appeals refused to enforce the order on the ground that it lay beyond the reach of federal power. The Supreme Court reversed.]

[The] Labor Board has found: The corporation [is] engaged in the business of manufacturing iron and steel in plants situated in Pittsburgh and nearby Aliquippa, Pa. It manufactures and distributes a widely diversified line of steel and pig iron, being the fourth largest producer of steel in the United States. With its subsidiaries—nineteen in number—it is a completely integrated enterprise, owning and operating ore, coal and limestone properties, lake and river transportation facilities and terminal railroads located at its manufacturing plants. * * *

Summarizing these operations, the Labor Board concluded that the works in Pittsburgh and Aliquippa "might be likened to the heart of a self-contained, highly integrated body. They draw in the raw materials from Michigan, Minnesota, West Virginia, Pennsylvania in part through arteries and by means controlled by the respondent; they transform the materials and then pump them out to all parts of the nation through the vast mechanism which the respondent has [elaborated]." * * *

First. [The] act is challenged in its entirety as an attempt to regulate all industry, thus invading the reserved powers of the States over their local concerns. * * *

We think it clear that the National Labor Relations Act may be construed so as to operate within the sphere of constitutional authority. The jurisdiction conferred upon the Board, and invoked in this instance, is found in [the Act], which provides: "[The] Board is empowered, as hereinafter provided, to prevent any person from engaging in any unfair labor practice (listed in section 8) affecting commerce. [The] term 'affecting commerce' means in commerce, or burdening or obstructing commerce or the free flow of commerce, or having led

f. Jackson, *The Struggle for Judicial Supremacy* 340, 346 (1941).

or tending to lead to a labor dispute burdening or obstructing commerce or the free flow of commerce."

[Third]. Respondent says that, whatever may be said of employees engaged in interstate commerce, the industrial relations and activities in the manufacturing department of respondent's enterprise are not subject to federal regulation. The argument rests upon the proposition that manufacturing in itself is not [commerce].

The fundamental principle is that the power to regulate commerce is the power to enact "all appropriate legislation" for its "protection or advancement"; to adopt measures "to promote its growth and insure its safety"; "to foster, protect, control, and restrain." That power is plenary and may be exerted to protect interstate commerce "no matter what the source of the dangers which threaten it." Although activities may be intrastate in character when separately considered, if they have such a close and substantial relation to interstate commerce that their control is essential or appropriate to protect that commerce from burdens and obstructions, Congress cannot be denied the power to exercise that control. Undoubtedly the scope of this power must be considered in the light of our dual system of government and may not be extended so as to embrace effects upon interstate commerce so indirect and remote that to embrace them, in view of our complex society, would effectually obliterate the distinction between what is national and what is local and create a completely centralized government. The question is necessarily one of degree. * * *

The close and intimate effect which brings the subject within the reach of federal power may be due to activities in relation to productive industry although the industry when separately viewed is local. [T]hat the employees here concerned were engaged in production is not determinative. The question remains as to the effect upon interstate commerce of the labor practice involved. In *Schechter,* we found that the effect there was so remote as to be beyond the federal power. To find "immediacy or directness" there was to find it "almost everywhere," a result inconsistent with the maintenance of our federal system. In *Carter,* the Court was of the opinion that the provisions of the statute relating to production were invalid upon several grounds,—that there was improper delegation of legislative power, and that the requirements not only went beyond any sustainable measure of protection of interstate commerce but were also inconsistent with due process. These cases are not controlling here.

[Fourth]. Giving full weight to respondent's contention with respect to a break in the complete continuity of the "stream of commerce" by reason of respondent's manufacturing operations, the fact remains that the stoppage of those operations by industrial strife would have a most serious effect upon interstate commerce. In view of respondent's far-flung activities, it is idle to say that the effect would be indirect or remote. It is obvious that it would be immediate and might be catastrophic. We are asked to shut our eyes to the plainest facts of our national life and to deal with the question of direct and indirect effects in an intellectual vacuum. Because there may be but indirect and remote effects upon interstate commerce in connection with a host of local enterprises throughout the country, it does not follow that other industrial activities do not have such a close and intimate relation to interstate commerce as to make the presence of industrial strife a matter of the most urgent national concern. When industries organize themselves on a national scale, making their relation to interstate commerce the dominant factor in their activities, how can it be maintained that their industrial labor relations constitute a forbidden field into which Congress may not enter when it is necessary to protect interstate commerce from the paralyzing consequences of industrial war? We have often said that interstate commerce itself is a practical conception. It is equally true that interferences with that commerce must be appraised by a judgment that does not ignore actual experience.

Experience has abundantly demonstrated that the recognition of the right of employees to self-organization and to have representatives of their own choosing for the purpose of collective bargaining is often an essential condition of industrial peace. Refusal to confer and negotiate has been one of the most prolific causes of strife. This is such an outstanding fact in the history of labor disturbances that it is a proper subject of judicial notice and requires no citation of instances. * * *

These questions have frequently engaged the attention of Congress and have been the subject of many inquiries. The steel industry is one of the great basic industries of the United States, with ramifying activities affecting interstate commerce at every point. The Government aptly refers to the steel strike of 1919–1920 with its far-reaching consequences. The fact that there appears to have been no major disturbance in that industry in the more recent period did not dispose of the possibilities of future and like dangers to interstate commerce which Congress was entitled to foresee and to exercise its protective power to forestall. It is not necessary again to detail the facts as to respondent's enterprise. Instead of being beyond the pale, we think that it presents in a most striking way the close and intimate relation which a manufacturing industry may have to interstate commerce and we have no doubt that Congress had constitutional authority to safeguard the right of respondent's employees to self-organization and freedom in the choice of representatives for collective [bargaining].

Mr. Justice McReynolds delivered the following dissenting opinion, [joined by Van Devanter, Sutherland, and Butler, JJ.]

Any effect on interstate commerce by the discharge of employees shown here would be indirect and remote in the highest degree, as consideration of the facts will show. In No. 419 ten men out of ten thousand were discharged; in the other cases only a few. The immediate effect in the factory may be to create discontent among all those employed and a strike may follow, which, in turn, may result in reducing production, which ultimately may reduce the volume of goods moving in interstate commerce. By this chain of indirect and progressively remote events we finally reach the evil with which it is said the legislation under consideration undertakes to deal. A more remote and indirect interference with interstate commerce or a more definite invasion of the powers reserved to the states is difficult, if not impossible, to [imagine].

It is gravely stated that experience teaches that if an employer discourages membership in "any organization of any kind" "in which employees participate, and which exists for the purpose in whole or in part of dealing with employers concerning grievances, labor disputes, wages, rates of pay, hours of employment or conditions of work," discontent may follow and this in turn may lead to a strike, and as the outcome of the strike there may be a block in the stream of interstate commerce. Therefore Congress may inhibit the discharge! Whatever effect any cause of discontent may ultimately have upon commerce is far too indirect to justify congressional regulation. Almost anything—marriage, birth, death—may in some fashion affect commerce.

Notes and Questions

1. *Impact of Jones & Laughlin.* STERN—THE COMMERCE CLAUSE AND THE NATIONAL ECONOMY, 1933–46, 59 Harv.L.Rev. 645, 681–82 (1946): "No other opinions were rendered that day, and the courtroom rapidly cleared. The corridors and the cafeteria buzzed with excited conversation. For the second time in two weeks the Court had in substance overruled cases decided less than one year before on major constitutional issues.[a] No serious effort had been made to distinguish the *Carter* case; the connection between interstate commerce and labor relations in the coal mines shown in the *Carter* record far exceeded in quantity and effect anything appearing in the *Labor Board* cases. There had been no change in the membership of the Court. What had induced Mr. Justice Roberts to switch his vote, after his opinion in the *Butler* case emphasizing the limitations imposed by the Tenth Amendment upon control of production and his full concurrence in *Carter?* What of the Chief Justice, who had joined in the *Butler* decision and approved of *Carter* insofar as it nullified the labor relations provisions of the Coal Act?

"No one who did not participate in the conferences of the Court will know the answers to those questions. But few attributed the difference in results between the decisions in 1936 and those in 1937 to anything inherent in the cases themselves—their facts, the arguments presented, or the authorities cited. Perhaps the series of violent strikes had educated Mr. Justice Roberts as to the close relationship between labor relations and interstate commerce. But the consensus among the lawyers speculating on the Court's sudden reversal was that the Chief Justice and Mr. Justice Roberts believed that the continued nullification of the legislative program demanded by the people and their representatives—as manifested in the 1936 election—would lead to acceptance of the President's Court plan, and that this would seriously undermine the independence and prestige of the federal judiciary, and particularly of the Supreme Court, without preventing the President from attaining his objective. Chief Justice Hughes was subsequently cited for his 'statesmanship' in using the cases as potent weapons in a successful campaign, in which he was somewhat inhibited by his judicial position, to combat the plan. Whether or not there was any basis for these conjectures, Government counsel, or most of them, accredited their victory more to the President than to anything they had said or done."

2. *A new standard for local activities affecting commerce?* (a) In contrast with *Carter* and *Schechter,* what kind of a guide, if any, does *Jones & Laughlin* provide for determining the relationship to interstate commerce required to support federal regulation of local industrial activities? What were the significant factors that appeared to influence the Court to find that the labor relations activities of Jones & Laughlin were subject to federal control?

(b) After *Jones & Laughlin,* was the *Carter* ruling on hours and wages in local production still "good law"? In answering such a question, consider whether (1) the results are consistent, (2) the reasoning is consistent, and (3) what the later case says about the earlier one. Is there any significance in the statement that in *Carter,* "the Court was of the opinion" etc. See Lockhart,

---

a. The first was *West Coast Hotel Co. v. Parrish* (1937), p. 262 infra, holding that a state minimum wage law did not violate the fourteenth amendment due process clause, and overruling *Morehead v. New York ex rel.* *Tipaldo,* 298 U.S. 587, 56 S.Ct. 918, 80 L.Ed. 1347 (1936) and *Adkins v. Children's Hosp.,* 261 U.S. 525, 43 S.Ct. 394, 67 L.Ed. 785 (1923). See p. 260 infra.

Gross Receipts Taxes on Interstate Transportation and Communication, 57 Harv. L.Rev. 40, 77 n. 160 (1943).

3. *Aftermath of Jones & Laughlin.* The following illustrative cases, show the subsequent impact of *Jones & Laughlin:*

NLRB v. FRIEDMAN–HARRY MARKS CLOTHING CO., 301 U.S. 58, 57 S.Ct. 642, 81 L.Ed. 893 (1937), decided with *Jones & Laughlin,* ruled that the National Labor Relations Act was properly applied to a small clothing manufacturer, employing only 800 of the 150,000 engaged in manufacturing men's clothing, and producing less than ½ of 1% of the men's clothing manufactured in this country. In stating the facts the Court mentioned (1) shipment of most of the Company's raw materials into the state and shipment out of the state of most of its finished products, (2) size and importance of the clothing industry generally and its general interstate character, and (3) disastrous effects of one general strike in the industry in New York in 1924. It sustained the Labor Board's jurisdiction on authority of *Jones & Laughlin* without further reasoning.

NLRB v. FAINBLATT, 306 U.S. 601, 59 S.Ct. 668, 83 L.Ed. 1014 (1939), held the Labor Act applicable to a small New Jersey shop employing 60 women doing piece work for a New York company, which delivered the cloth to the New Jersey shop and picked it up. The Court ruled that the small volume of business was immaterial: "Given the other needful conditions, commerce may be affected in the same manner and to the same extent in proportion to its volume, whether it be great or small. [There] are not a few industries in the United States which, though conducted in relatively small units, contribute in the aggregate a vast volume of interstate commerce."

NLRB v. RELIANCE FUEL OIL CORP., 371 U.S. 224, 83 S.Ct. 312, 9 L.Ed.2d 279 (1963), held the NLRA applicable to a New York distributor of fuel oil, whose customers were all home owners in New York, and who secured its fuel oil ($650,000 worth in 1959) from New York tanks of Gulf Oil Corporation, which shipped most of the oil into New York from other states. Noting that the evidence relating to the effect on commerce showed only the source and volume of oil sold by Reliance, the Court of Appeals remanded the case to the Board "to take further evidence and make further findings on the manner in which a labor dispute at Reliance would affect or tend to affect commerce." It suggested that the number and availability of alternate distributors, and Gulf's proportion of the relevant market, might be important. 297 F.2d 94 (2d Cir.1961). The Supreme Court reversed, simply stating that "the Board properly found that by virtue of Reliance's purchases from Gulf, Reliance's operations and the related unfair practices 'affected' commerce, within the meaning of the Act." What significance?

4. Note that under the NLRA "Congress intended to and did vest in the Board the fullest *jurisdictional* breadth constitutionally permissible under the Commerce Clause." See *NLRB v. Reliance Fuel Oil Corp.,* supra. This conclusion is based upon the incorporation in the Act of the Court's own broad constitutional terms: "affecting commerce", "burdening or obstructing commerce." See *Guss v. Utah Labor Board,* 353 U.S. 1, 3, 1 L.Ed.2d 601, 77 S.Ct. 598 (1957).

This broad statutory jurisdiction should be contrasted with the narrower jurisdiction specified in the Fair Labor Standards Act. See *United States v. Darby,* infra, and note 4 thereafter.

UNITED STATES v. DARBY

312 U.S. 100, 61 S.Ct. 451, 85 L.Ed. 609 (1941).

MR. JUSTICE STONE delivered the opinion of the Court. * * *

The two principal questions raised by the record in this case are, first, whether Congress has constitutional power to prohibit the shipment in interstate commerce of lumber manufactured by employees whose wages are less than a prescribed minimum or whose weekly hours of labor at that wage are greater than a prescribed maximum, and, second, whether it has power to prohibit the employment of workmen in the production of goods "for interstate commerce" at other than prescribed wages and hours. * * *

The indictment charges that appellee is engaged, in the state of Georgia, in the business of acquiring raw materials, which he manufactures into finished lumber with the intent when manufactured, to ship it in interstate commerce to customers outside the state, and that he does in fact so ship a large part of the lumber so produced. * * *

The prohibition of shipment of the proscribed goods in interstate commerce. Section 15(a)(1) prohibits, and the indictment charges, the shipment in interstate commerce, of goods produced for interstate commerce by employees whose wages and hours of employment do not conform to the requirements of the Act. [T]he only question arising under the commerce clause with respect to such shipments is whether Congress has the constitutional power to prohibit them.

While manufacture is not of itself interstate commerce the shipment of manufactured goods interstate is such commerce and the prohibition of such shipment by Congress is indubitably a regulation of the commerce. The power to regulate commerce is the power "to prescribe the rule by which commerce is to be governed". It extends not only to those regulations which aid, foster and protect the commerce, but embraces those which prohibit it. It is conceded that the power of Congress to prohibit transportation in interstate commerce includes noxious articles, stolen articles, [and] articles such as intoxicating liquor or convict made goods, traffic in which is forbidden or restricted by the laws of the state of destination. *Kentucky Whip & Collar Co. v. Illinois Central R. Co.,* [note 3 infra].

But it is said that the present prohibition falls within the scope of none of these categories; that while the prohibition is nominally a regulation of the commerce its motive or purpose is regulation of wages and hours of persons engaged in manufacture, the control of which has been reserved to the states and upon which Georgia and some of the states of destination have placed no restriction. * * *

Congress, following its own conception of public policy concerning the restrictions which may appropriately be imposed on interstate commerce, is free to exclude from the commerce articles whose use in the states for which they are destined it may conceive to be injurious to the public health, morals or welfare even though the state has not sought to regulate their [use].

The motive and purpose of the present regulation are plainly to make effective the Congressional conception of public policy that interstate commerce should not be made the instrument of competition in the distribution of goods produced under substandard labor conditions, which competition is injurious to the commerce and to the states from and to which the commerce flows. The motive and purpose of a regulation of interstate commerce are matters for the legislative judgment upon the exercise of which the Constitution places no restriction and over which the courts are given no control. * * * [Whatever] their motive and purpose, regulations of commerce which do not infringe some constitutional prohibition are within the plenary power conferred on Congress by the Commerce Clause. Subject only to that limitation, presently to be considered, we conclude that the prohibition of the shipment interstate of goods produced under the forbidden substandard labor conditions is within the constitutional authority of Congress.

[T]hese principles of constitutional interpretation have been so long and repeatedly recognized by this Court as applicable to the Commerce Clause, that there would be little occasion for repeating them now were it not for the decision of this Court twenty-two years ago in *Dagenhart*. In that case it was held by a bare majority of the Court over the powerful and now classic dissent of Mr. Justice Holmes setting forth the fundamental issues involved, that Congress was without power to exclude the products of child labor from interstate commerce. The reasoning and conclusion of the Court's opinion there cannot be reconciled with the conclusion which we have reached, that the power of Congress under the Commerce Clause is plenary to exclude any article from interstate commerce subject only to the specific prohibitions of the Constitution.

Dagenhart has not been followed. The distinction on which the decision was rested that Congressional power to prohibit interstate commerce is limited to articles which in themselves have some harmful or deleterious property—a distinction which was novel when made and unsupported by any provision of the Constitution—has long since been abandoned. [See note 2 infra.] The thesis of the opinion that the motive of the prohibition or its effect to control in some measure the use or production within the states of the article thus excluded from the commerce can operate to deprive the regulation of its constitutional authority has long since ceased to have [force].

The conclusion is inescapable that *Dagenhart* was a departure from the principles which have prevailed in the interpretation of the commerce clause both before and since the decision and that such vitality, as a precedent, as it then had has long since been exhausted. It should be and now is overruled.

Validity of the wage and hour requirements. Section 15(a)(2) and §§ 6 and 7 require employers to conform to the wage and hour provisions with respect to all employees engaged in the production of goods for interstate commerce. As appellee's employees are not alleged to be "engaged in interstate commerce" the validity of the prohibition turns on the question whether the employment, under other than the prescribed labor standards, of employees engaged in the production of goods for interstate commerce is so related to the commerce and so affects it as to be within the reach of the power of Congress to regulate [it]. [The] purpose of the Act was [to] stop the initial step toward transportation, production with the purpose [of] transporting it. [T]he power of Congress to regulate interstate commerce extends to the regulation [of] activities intrastate which have a substantial effect on the commerce or the exercise of the Congressional power over it. In such legislation Congress has sometimes left it to the courts to determine whether the intrastate activities have the prohibited effect on the commerce, as in the Sherman Act. It has sometimes left it to an administrative board or agency to determine whether the activities sought to be regulated or prohibited have such effect, as in the case [of] the National Labor Relations Act. [And] sometimes Congress itself has said that a particular activity affects the commerce, as it did in the present Act, the Safety Appliance Act and the

Railway Labor Act. In passing on the validity of legislation of the class last mentioned the only function of courts is to determine whether the particular activity regulated or prohibited is within the reach of the federal power.

Congress, having by the present Act adopted the policy of excluding from interstate commerce all goods produced for the commerce which do not conform to the specified labor standards, it may choose the means reasonably adapted to the attainment of the permitted end, even though they involve control of intrastate activities. Such legislation has often been sustained with respect to powers, other than the commerce power granted to the national government, when the means chosen, although not themselves within the granted power, were nevertheless deemed appropriate aids to the accomplishment of some purpose within an admitted power of the national government. [A] familiar like exercise of power is the regulation of intrastate transactions which are so commingled with or related to interstate commerce that all must be regulated if the interstate commerce is to be effectively controlled. *Shreveport Case; Wisconsin Railroad Comm.* [Similarly] Congress may require inspection and preventive treatment of all cattle in a disease infected area in order to prevent shipment in interstate commerce of some of the cattle without the treatment. *Thornton v. United States,* 271 U.S. 414, 46 S.Ct. 585, 70 L.Ed. 1013. [And] we have recently held that Congress in the exercise of its power to require inspection and grading of tobacco shipped in interstate commerce may compel such inspection and grading of all tobacco sold at local auction rooms from which a substantial part but not all of the tobacco sold is shipped in interstate commerce. *Currin v. Wallace,* 306 U.S. 11, 59 S.Ct. 385, 83 L.Ed. 441. * * *

We think also that § 15(a)(2), now under consideration, is sustainable independently of § 15(a)(1), which prohibits shipment or transportation of the proscribed goods. As we have said the evils aimed at by the Act are the spread of substandard labor conditions through the use of the facilities of interstate commerce for competition by the goods so produced with those produced under the prescribed or better labor conditions; and the consequent dislocation of the commerce itself caused by the impairment or destruction of local businesses by competition made effective through interstate commerce. The Act is thus directed at the suppression of a method or kind of competition in interstate commerce which it has in effect condemned as "unfair", as the Clayton Act, 38 Stat. 730, has condemned other "unfair methods of competition" made effective through interstate commerce. * * *

The means adopted by § 15(a)(2) for the protection of interstate commerce by the suppression of the production of the condemned goods for interstate commerce is so related to the commerce and so affects it as to be within the reach of the commerce power. Congress, to attain its objective in the suppression of nationwide competition in interstate commerce by goods produced under substandard labor conditions, has made no distinction as to the volume or amount of shipments in the commerce or of production for commerce by any particular shipper or producer. * * *

So far as *Carter Coal Co.* is inconsistent with this conclusion, its doctrine is limited in principle by the decisions under the Sherman Act and the National Labor Relations Act, which we have cited and which we follow.

Our conclusion is unaffected by the Tenth Amendment [which] states but a truism that all is retained which has not been surrendered. There is nothing in the history of its adoption to suggest that it was more than declaratory of the relationship between the national and state governments as it had been established by the Constitution before the amendment or that its purpose was other than to allay fears that the new national government might seek to exercise powers not granted, and that the states might not be able to exercise fully their reserved powers.[b]

Reversed.

Notes and Questions

1. *Unanimity.* The unanimity in *Darby* can be attributed to the departure of the four justices who dissented in *Jones & Laughlin,* Butler, J., by death in 1938, and the other three by retirement: Van Devanter, J., in 1937, Sutherland, J., in 1938 and McReynolds, J., in 1940, just two days before the announcement of *Darby.* Of the five who joined the majority opinion in *Carter,* only Roberts, J., remained, and his views had undergone much change since 1936.

2. *Exclusion from commerce as basis for economic controls—a lesson in judicial attrition of a doctrine.* In support of the statement that the *Dagenhart* "harmful and deleterious property" distinction had "long since been abandoned," the Court cited the cases summarized below. Should those cases have forewarned lawyers who advised clients that they need not comply with the "unconstitutional" Fair Labor Standards Act, and thus caused heavy financial loss for retroactive premium overtime pay?

(a) *Forbidden commerce in stolen vehicles and convict-made goods. Brooks v. United States,* 267 U.S. 432, 45 S.Ct. 345, 69 L.Ed. 699 (1925), sustained a ban on transporting stolen vehicles in interstate commerce, and *Kentucky Whip & Collar Co. v. Illinois Central R.R.,* 299 U.S. 334, 57 S.Ct. 277, 81 L.Ed. 270 (1937) upheld a ban on interstate transportation of convict-made goods into states forbidding their sale. In both cases the Court distinguished *Dagenhart* on the ground that there the purpose was to regulate labor at the local production level, whereas in *Brooks* and *Kentucky Whip* it was to prevent use of interstate channels to cause "harmful results." What "harmful results" in *Kentucky Whip?*

(b) *Forbidding marketing of farm production in excess of quota.* MULFORD v. SMITH, 307 U.S. 38, 59 S.Ct. 648, 83 L.Ed. 1092 (1939), per ROBERTS, J., sustained a federal act that authorized assigning a marketing quota to each tobacco farm to avoid depressed prices, enforced by penalties on tobacco auction warehousemen who marketed tobacco in excess of the quota assigned to each farm. "[In] markets where tobacco is sold to both interstate and intrastate purchasers it is not known, when the grower places his tobacco on the warehouse floor for sale, whether it is destined for interstate or intrastate commerce. Regulation, to be effective, must, and therefore may constitutionally, apply to all sales. [Any] rule, such as that embodied in the Act, which is intended [to] prevent the flow of commerce from working harm to the people of the nation, is within the competence of Congress."[a]

3. *Scope of Fair Labor Standards Act.* The narrower scope of the jurisdictional provisions in the Fair Labor Standards Act should be compared with the broad constitution-wide terms of the National Labor Relations Act. See *Warren-*

b. For authority supporting this view, see Choper, *The Scope of National Power Vis-à-Vis the States: The Dispensability of Judicial Review,* 86 Yale L.J. 1552, 1612–13 (1977).

The Court also held that the minimum wage and maximum hours provisions did not violate the due process clause of the fifth amendment, citing *West Coast Hotel Co. v. Parrish,* p. 261 infra.

a. Butler and McReynolds, JJ., dissented.

Bradshaw Drilling Co. v. Hall, 317 U.S. 88, 89–90, 63 S.Ct. 125, 126, 87 L.Ed. 83, 84 (1942), noting that "Congress did not exercise in this Act the full scope of the commerce power." See *Walling v. Jacksonville Paper Co.,* 317 U.S. 564, 570, 63 S.Ct. 332, 336, 87 L.Ed. 460, 467 (1943).

In 1961 Congress extended coverage of the Fair Labor Standards Act from employees "engaged in commerce or in the production of goods for commerce" to *all* employees of any *"enterprise"* so engaged. In 1966 it extended coverage further to include hospitals, nursing homes, and educational institutions— elementary, secondary or higher education—whether private or public.[b] MARY-LAND v. WIRTZ, 392 U.S. 183, 88 S.Ct. 2017, 20 L.Ed.2d 1020 (1968) sustained these extensions through an elaboration of the *Darby* and *Jones & Laughlin* rationale. The "enterprise" extension was justified on two grounds: (1) the competitive position of an interstate enterprise is affected by *all* its labor costs, not simply the costs of employees producing goods for commerce; and (2) a labor dispute caused by substandard labor conditions "among any group of employees, whether or not they are personally engaged in commerce or production, may lead to strife disrupting an entire enterprise." Extension of coverage to schools and hospitals was sustained under the commerce power on the ground that these institutions are major users of goods imported from other states, and work stoppages involving their employees would interrupt this flow of goods across state lines.

WICKARD v. FILBURN, 317 U.S. 111, 63 S.Ct. 82, 87 L.Ed. 122 (1942), per JACKSON, J., upheld a marketing penalty imposed under the Agricultural Adjust-ment Act of 1938 on 239 bushels of wheat raised by Filburn in excess of his marketing allotment of 11.1 acres at a normal yield of 20.1 bushels per acre. Filburn's normal practice was to plant a small acreage of wheat, to sell a portion of the crop, feed a part to livestock, use some to make flour for home consump-tion, and keep some for seed:

"The general scheme of the Agricultural Adjustment Act of 1938 as related to wheat is to control the volume moving in interstate and foreign commerce in order to avoid surpluses and shortages and the consequent abnormally low or high wheat prices and obstructions to [commerce].

"It is urged that under the Commerce [Clause] Congress does not possess the power it has in this instance sought to exercise. The question would merit little consideration since our decision in [*Darby*], except for the fact that this Act extends federal regulation to production not intended in any part for commerce but wholly for consumption on the farm. [The] Federal Government fixes a quota including all that the farmer may harvest for sale or for his own farm needs, and declares that wheat produced on excess acreage may neither be disposed of nor used except upon payment of the penalty or except it is stored as required by the [Act.]

"Appellee says that this is a regulation of production and consumption of wheat. Such activities are, he urges, beyond the reach of Congressional power under the Commerce Clause, since they are local in character, and their effects upon interstate commerce are at most 'indirect.' In answer the Government argues that the statute regulates neither production nor consumption, but only

b. For problems of the Act's application to state activities, see Sec. 5 infra.

marketing; and, in the alternative, [is] sustainable as a 'necessary and proper' implementation of the power of Congress over interstate commerce.

"The Government's concern lest the Act be held to be a regulation of production or consumption rather than of marketing is attributable to a few dicta and decisions of this Court which might be understood to lay it down that activities such as 'production,' 'manufacturing,' and 'mining' are strictly 'local' and, except in special circumstances which are not present here, cannot be regulated under the commerce power because their effects upon interstate commerce are, as matter of law, only 'indirect.' [We] believe that a review of the course of decision under the Commerce Clause will make plain, however, that questions of the power of Congress are not to be decided by reference to any formula which would give controlling force to nomenclature such as 'production' and 'indirect' and foreclose consideration of the actual effects of the activity in question upon interstate commerce. * * *

"The Court's recognition of the relevance of the economic effects in the application of the Commerce Clause has made the mechanical application of legal formulas no longer feasible. Once an economic measure of the reach of the power granted to Congress in the Commerce Clause is accepted, questions of federal power cannot be decided simply by finding the activity in question to be 'production' nor can consideration of its economic effects be foreclosed by calling them 'indirect.' * * *

"Whether the subject of the regulation in question was 'production,' 'consumption,' or 'marketing' is, therefore, not material for purposes of deciding the question of federal power before us. That an activity is of local character may help in a doubtful case to determine whether Congress intended to reach it. [But] even if appellee's activity be local and though it may not be regarded as commerce, it may still, whatever its nature, be reached by Congress if it exerts a substantial economic effect on interstate commerce and this irrespective of whether such effect is what might at some earlier time have been defined as 'direct' or 'indirect.' * * *

"In the absence of regulation the price of wheat in the United States would be much affected by world conditions. During 1941 producers who cooperated with the Agricultural Adjustment program received an average price on the farm of about $1.16 a bushel as compared with the world market price of 40 cents a bushel. * * *

"The effect of consumption of home-grown wheat on interstate commerce is due to the fact that it constitutes the most variable factor in the disappearance of the wheat crop. Consumption on the farm where grown appears to vary in an amount greater than 20 per cent of average production. The total amount of wheat consumed as food varies but relatively little, and use as seed is relatively constant.

"The maintenance by government regulation of a price for wheat undoubtedly can be accomplished as effectively by sustaining or increasing the demand as by limiting the supply. The effect of the statute before us is to restrict the amount which may be produced for market and the extent as well to which one may forestall resort to the market by producing to meet his own needs. That appellee's own contribution to the demand for wheat may be trivial by itself is not enough to remove him from the scope of federal regulation where, as here, his contribution, taken together with that of many others similarly situated, is far from trivial. [*Fainblatt; Darby*]."

"It is well established by decisions of this Court that the power to regulate commerce includes the power to regulate the prices at which commodities in that commerce are dealt in and practices affecting such prices. One of the primary purposes of the Act in question was to increase the market price of wheat and to that end to limit the volume thereof that could affect the market. It can hardly be denied that a factor of such volume and variability as home-consumed wheat would have a substantial influence on price and market conditions. This may arise because being in marketable condition such wheat overhangs the market and if induced by rising prices tends to flow into the market and check price increases. But if we assume that it is never marketed, it supplies a need of the man who grew it which would otherwise be reflected by purchases in the open market. Home-grown wheat in this sense competes with wheat in commerce. The stimulation of commerce is a use of the regulatory function quite as definitely as prohibitions or restrictions thereon. This record leaves us in no doubt that Congress may properly have considered that wheat consumed on the farm where grown if wholly outside the scheme of regulation would have a substantial effect in defeating and obstructing its purpose to stimulate trade therein at increased prices." [a]

Notes and Questions

1. *National market concept.* Assuming that federal power does not depend on whether control is asserted over "marketing" or "production," how important in *Wickard* was the concept of a national market affected by local activities? For analogous uses of a national or regional market concept, see *Mulford v. Smith,* supra; *United States v. Wrightwood Dairy,* supra; *United States v. Rock Royal Coop.,* 307 U.S. 533, 59 S.Ct. 993, 83 L.Ed. 1446 (1939); *Sunshine Coal Co. v. Adkins,* 310 U.S. 381, 60 S.Ct. 907, 84 L.Ed. 1263 (1940).

2. *Standard for determining required effect on commerce.* How would you state the *Wickard* standard for determining whether a local activity has the required effect on interstate commerce to support regulations by Congress?

CONTROL OVER TRANSACTIONS RELATING TO INTANGIBLES

1. *Insurance.* UNITED STATES v. SOUTH–EASTERN UNDERWRITERS ASS'N, 322 U.S. 533, 64 S.Ct. 1162, 88 L.Ed. 1440 (1944) held that the Sherman Antitrust Act applied to the fixing of non-competitive rates by 200 fire insurance companies and their trade association. The 6 to 3 division in the Court related primarily to whether the act should be applied to insurance when at the time of its enactment in 1890, and for roughly 50 years thereafter, it had been established doctrine that insurance was not commerce. See *Paul v. Virginia* (1868), note 2(c) after *Gibbons v. Ogden.* But the Court, per BLACK, J., affirmatively ruled that Congress had authority over interstate insurance business.[b]

"We may grant that a contract of insurance, considered as a thing apart from negotiation and execution, does not itself constitute interstate commerce. [But] it does not follow from this that the Court is powerless to examine the

---

a. The Court also held that application of the Act to Filburn did not violate the due process clause of the fifth amendment.

b. In 1945 Congress responded to *South Eastern Underwriters* with the McCarran Act which (1) left insurance subject to state regu-

lation and taxation, and (2) made federal antitrust laws applicable to insurance only "to the extent that such business is not regulated by state law." 15 U.S.C.A. §§ 1011–1015, considered in *Prudential Insurance Co. v. Benjamin,* p. 195 infra.

entire transaction, of which that contract is but a part, in order to determine whether there may be a chain of events which becomes interstate commerce. [In] short, a nationwide business is not deprived of its interstate character merely because it is built upon sales contracts which are local in nature. Were the rule otherwise, few businesses could be said to be engaged in interstate commerce." In a dissent contending that the Act did not cover the insurance business, Stone, C.J., argued that the local formation of an insurance contract is not interstate commerce and that the power of Congress "is derived, not from its authority to regulate the business of insurance, but from its power to regulate interstate communication and transportation." He was joined by Frankfurter, J., who added his own comments to make clear he was concerned only with the statutory question.[c]

2. *Public utility holding companies.* Under an Act requiring that public utility holding companies using channels of interstate commerce limit their operations to a single integrated system, NORTH AMERICAN CO. v. SEC, 327 U.S. 686, 66 S.Ct. 785, 90 L.Ed. 945 (1946), per MURPHY, J., unanimously upheld an SEC order that North American divest itself of security holdings of geographically or economically unrelated properties. After pointing out the abuses and practices that led to the Act, the opinion related the divestiture remedy to interstate commerce:

"The ownership of securities of operating companies [has] a real and intimate relation to the interstate activities of holding companies and cannot be effectively divorced therefrom. That ownership is the generating force of the constant interstate flow of reports, letters, equipment, securities, accounts, instructions and money—all of which constitute the life blood of holding companies and allow the numerous abuses to be effectuated. [Without] the factor of stock ownership the very foundation and framework of holding company systems would be gone and the amount of their interstate activity would be at a minimum; centralized management and control of widely scattered utility properties would be difficult if not impossible.

"We may assume without deciding that the ownership of securities, considered separately and abstractly, is not commerce. But when it is considered in the context of public utility holding companies and their subsidiaries, its relationship to interstate commerce is so clear and definite as to make any other conclusion [unreasonable].

"[Congress] may impose relevant conditions and requirements on those who use the channels of interstate commerce in order that those channels will not become the means of promoting or spreading evil, whether of a physical, moral or economic nature. This power permits Congress to attack an evil directly at its source, provided that the evil bears a substantial relationship to interstate commerce. [The] fact that an evil may involve a corporation's financial practices, its business structure or its security portfolio does not detract from the power of Congress under the commerce clause to promulgate rules in order to destroy that evil. Once it is established that the evil concerns or affects commerce in more states than one, Congress may act."

c. *Polish Nat'l Alliance v. NLRB,* 322 U.S. 643, 64 S.Ct. 1196, 88 L.Ed. 1509 (1944), per Frankfurter, J., decided the same day, reflected a similar difference in analysis in unanimously holding that an insurance company's unfair labor practices were subject to the National Labor Relations Act. The opinion relied upon the disruptive effect of a strike on interstate transmission of funds, policies, and communications. But Black, J., joined by Douglas and Murphy, JJ., concurred to state explicitly that "the business of insurance is commerce, subject to federal regulation as such when conducted across state lines."

For a brief treatment of the background of the Public Utility Holding Company Act, and the tactical litigation maneuvers that culminated in *North American*, see Stern, *The Commerce Clause and the National Economy, 1933–1946*, 59 Harv.L.Rev. 645, 883, 925 (1946).

3. *Scope of commerce power.* For an excellent summation and analysis of the scope of the commerce power see Stern, *The Scope of the Phrase Interstate Commerce*, 41 A.B.A.J. 823, 871–72 (1955). The thesis is that despite the Court's departure from the broad Marshall view expressed in *Gibbons v. Ogden* that the commerce clause covers all "commerce that concerns more states than one" to the narrower territorial concept of "interstate commerce" as commerce "between the states," the Court has now arrived at the point that "almost every aspect of a business or industry which has interstate ramifications may be subjected to the federal commerce power. [The] Court is now unwilling to sever for legal purposes what Congress has determined to be economically united."

4. *Analogous rationale for war powers.* Invoking the war powers, WOODS v. CLOYD W. MILLER CO., 333 U.S. 138, 68 S.Ct. 421, 92 L.Ed. 596 (1948), per DOUGLAS, J., upheld continuation of federal rent control long after hostilities had ceased, using effect-type reasoning analogous to the foregoing commerce clause opinions:

"The legislative history of the present Act makes abundantly clear that there has not yet been eliminated the deficit in housing which in considerable measure was caused by the heavy demobilization of veterans and by the cessation or reduction in residential construction during the period of hostilities due to the allocation of building materials to military projects. Since the war effort contributed heavily to that deficit, Congress has the power even after the cessation of hostilities to act to control the forces that a short supply of the needed article created. If that were not true, the Necessary and Proper Clause would be drastically limited in its application to the several war [powers.]

"We recognize the force of the argument that the effects of war under modern conditions may be felt in the economy for years and years, and that if the war power can be used in days of peace to treat all the wounds which war inflicts on our society, it may not only swallow up all other powers of Congress but largely obliterate the Ninth and the Tenth Amendments as well. There are no such implications in today's decision. [W]e cannot assume that Congress is not alert to its constitutional responsibilities. And the question whether the war power has been properly employed in cases such as this is open to judicial inquiry." [a]

5. *Political limits on undue expansion of federal power.* Considering the dependence of Congress and the President on political support at the local level, are there sufficient practical restraints against undue encroachment on local interests and power to make relatively unimportant the Court's role in determining whether an Act of Congress can fairly find its source in the granted powers? Does the President's dependency on Congress for any new program, and Congress' "intrinsic sensitivity" to "any insular opinion that is dominant in a substantial number of states," create an "inherent tendency" for our system to require "the widest support before intrusive measures of importance can receive significant consideration?" See Wechsler, *The Political Safeguards of Federalism* in his *Principles, Politics and Fundamental Law* 49–82 (1961). Does this

---

a. For other economic regulations based on the war powers see *Yakus v. United States*, 321 U.S. 414, 64 S.Ct. 660, 88 L.Ed. 834 (1944); *Bowles v. Willingham*, 321 U.S. 503, 64 S.Ct. 641, 88 L.Ed. 892 (1944).

mean that the specification of federal legislative powers in the Constitution has little importance? On the contrary, Professor Wechsler suggests:

"It is in the light of this inherent tendency, reflected most importantly in Congress, that the governmental power distribution clauses of the Constitution gain their largest meaning as an instrument for the protection of the states. Those clauses, as is well known, have served far more to qualify or stop intrusive measures in Congress than to invalidate enacted legislation in the Supreme Court.

"This does not differ from the expectation of the framers quite as markedly as might be thought. For the containment of national authority Madison did not emphasize the function of the Court; he pointed to the composition of the Congress and the political [processes].

"The prime function envisaged for judicial review—in relation to federalism—was the maintenance of national supremacy against nullification or usurpation by the individual [states]. [E]xcept for the brief interlude that ended with the crisis of the thirties, it is mainly in the realm of policing of the states that the Supreme Court has in fact participated in determining the balances of federalism. This is not to say that the Court can decline to measure national enactments by the Constitution when it is called upon to face the question in the course of ordinary litigation [but] to say that the Court is on weakest ground when it opposes its interpretation of the Constitution to that of Congress in the interest of the states, whose representatives control the legislative process and, by hypothesis, have broadly acquiesced in sanctioning the challenged Act of Congress."

Similar considerations led Professor Choper to recommend that the Court now abandon altogether, as nonjusticiable, judicial review over whether federal action is beyond the powers of the federal government and thus violates states' rights. Choper, *The Scope of National Power Vis-à-Vis the States: The Dispensability of Judicial Review,* 86 Yale L.J. 1552 (1977), considered Sec. 6 infra.

IV. REGULATION OF POLICE PROBLEMS THROUGH COMMERCE POWER

A. EXCLUSION FROM COMMERCE

The *Lottery Case* and the notes that follow it direct attention to the pre-1918 development of the power of Congress to exercise a "national police power" to close the channels of interstate commerce to commodities and transactions thought harmful to the health, morals, safety or welfare of the nation, even though the harm itself occurred only at the local level. In those cases the harm to be prevented occurred in the state of destination, but this need not be so.[a]

Since 1918, this use of the commerce power has been expanded to meet evils as they developed from time to time when Congress considered them important enough, and the evils were amenable to control through exclusion from interstate commerce. Some of the more important uses of this power since 1918 include prohibitions on interstate transportation of stolen vehicles[b] or other

---

a. See, e.g., *Brooks v. United States,* 267 U.S. 432, 45 S.Ct. 345, 69 L.Ed. 699 (1925) (interstate transportation of stolen motor vehicle, which causes loss in state of origin, as well as bad title in state of destination); *Gooch v. United States,* 297 U.S. 124, 56 S.Ct. 395, 80 L.Ed. 522 (1936) (interstate transportation of kidnapped persons); *Hemans v. United States,* 163 F.2d 228 (6th Cir.1947) (interstate flight to avoid testifying).

b. *Brooks v. United States,* fn. a supra.

stolen goods,[c] interstate transportation of kidnapped persons,[d] interstate flight to avoid prosecution or to avoid testifying in a criminal case,[e] interstate shipment of gambling devices [f] and wagering materials,[g] causing persons to be transported in furtherance of a scheme to defraud,[h] interstate shipment of firearms to or by persons under indictment or convicted of a serious crime,[i] and interstate travel to incite, encourage or participate in a riot.[j]

Forbidding interstate travel in aid of "racketeering enterprises." The *Travel Act* [k] provides:

"Whoever travels in interstate or foreign commerce or uses any facility in interstate or foreign commerce, including the mail, with intent to—

(1) distribute the proceeds of any unlawful activity [l]; or

(2) commit any crime of violence to further any unlawful activity; or

(3) otherwise promote, manage, establish, carry on, or facilitate the promotion, management, establishment, or carrying on, of any unlawful activity, and thereafter performs or attempts to perform any of the acts specified in subparagraphs (1), (2), and (3), shall be fined not more than $10,000 or imprisoned for not more than five years, or both."

B. LOCAL ACTIVITIES AFFECTING INTERSTATE COMMERCE

1. In addition to regulating interstate movement of persons or commodities to achieve police-type objectives, Congress has increasingly resorted to direct regulation of the undesired local activity when it "in any way or degree obstructs, delays or adversely affects [interstate] commerce," [a] or in some cases, Congress has simply concluded that the controlled local activity adversely affects interstate commerce.[b]

For example, Title VIII of the *Organized Crime Control Act* of 1970 made it a federal offense for five or more persons to engage in a "gambling business" illegal under state law.[c] And Title IX, the now widely used RICO ("Racketeer Influenced and Corrupt Organizations") statute, made it a federal offense for "any person employed by or associated with any enterprise engaged in, or the activities of which affect, interstate or foreign commerce, to * * * participate in the conduct" of its affairs through a "pattern of racketeering activity," defined to embrace two or more of a wide range of acts made criminal by state or federal law.[d] To support these and other provisions of the 1970 Act, Congress found that "organized crime * * * drains billions of dollars from America's economy by unlawful conduct, * * * derives a major portion of its power

---

c. 18 U.S.C.A. § 2314.

d. *Gooch v. United States,* fn. a supra.

e. *Hemans v. United States,* fn. a supra.

f. 15 U.S.C.A. §§ 1171–78.

g. 18 U.S.C.A. § 1953.

h. 18 U.S.C.A. § 2314.

i. 18 U.S.C.A. § 922(d)(1) (1968).

j. 18 U.S.C.A. § 2101 (1968).

k. 18 U.S.C.A. § 1952 (1961). For a summary of 1961 legislation aimed at organized crime see Pollner, *Attorney General Robert F. Kennedy's Legislative Program to Curb Organized Crime and Racketeering,* 28 Brooklyn L.Rev. 37 (1961).

l. "Unlawful activity" was defined to include prostitution, extortion, bribery, or arson

under state or federal laws and gambling, liquor and narcotics offenses under federal laws.

a. See, e.g., 18 U.S.C.A. § 231 (teaching another to use a firearm or explosive for use in a civil disorder, or interference with fireman or police carrying out duties during civil disorder, where commerce is adversely affected).

b. For details on this trend see Note, 1972 U.Ill.L.F. 805 (1972).

c. 18 U.S.C.A. § 1955, 84 Stat. 937 (1970).

d. 18 U.S.C.A. §§ 1961–1962, 84 Stat. 941–943 (1970).

through money obtained from such illegal endeavors as syndicated gambling, [and] loan sharking * * *," uses "this money and power to infiltrate and corrupt legitimate business and labor unions * * *, weaken[s] the stability of the Nation's economic system * * *, interfere[s] with free competition, [and] seriously burden[s] interstate and foreign commerce." [e]

Do these 1970 statutes raise debatable constitutional issues when applied to instances of local gambling [f] or local racketeering [g] not shown to be related to organized crime or to have any discernable impact on interstate commerce? The following case raised a similar issue under a 1968 statute.

2. (a) PEREZ v. UNITED STATES, 402 U.S. 146, 91 S.Ct. 1357, 28 L.Ed.2d 686 (1971), per DOUGLAS, J., upheld the federal Consumer Credit Protection Act's ban on "extortionate extension of credit" in strictly local activities because of the dependence of nationally organized crime on revenue from this loan shark racket: "Extortionate credit transactions, though purely intrastate, may in the judgment of Congress affect interstate commerce. [R]eports and hearings [supplied] Congress with the knowledge that the loan shark racket provides organized crime with its second most lucrative source of revenue, exacts millions from the pockets of people, coerces its victims into the commission of crimes against property, and causes the takeover by racketeers of legitimate businesses.

"We have mentioned in detail the economic, financial, and social setting of the problem as revealed to Congress [to] answer the impassioned plea of petitioner that all that is involved in loan sharking is a traditionally local activity. It appears, instead, that loan sharking in its national setting is one way organized interstate crime holds its guns to the heads of the poor and the rich alike and syphons funds from numerous localities to finance its national operations."

The Court rejected the contention that the extortionate activities of Perez were not shown to have any effect on commerce. "Where the *class of activities* is regulated and that *class* is within the reach of federal power, the courts have no power 'to excise, as trivial, individual instances' of the class. *Maryland v. Wirtz*." STEWART, J., dissented.

(b) Would the Court have reached the same result if Perez had clearly established that he had no connections whatever with organized crime? Does the principle emerge in *Perez* "that Congress may regulate local acts which in themselves have no interstate nexus or effect if as a practical matter it is difficult to distinguish such transactions from others which may have some relation to interstate commerce"? Stern, *The Commerce Clause Revisited—The Federalization of Intrastate Crime*, 15 Ariz.L.Rev. 271, 280 (1973). Are *Thornton v. United States* and *Currin v. Wallace*, stated in *Darby*, sound analogies? Cf. *Katzenbach v. McClung*, Part V infra.

C. LOCAL ACTIVITIES AFTER INTERSTATE COMMERCE ENDS

1. McDERMOTT v. WISCONSIN, 228 U.S. 115, 33 S.Ct. 431, 57 L.Ed. 754 (1913), per DAY, J., upheld the federal Pure Food and Drug Act's requirement

e. 84 Stat. 922 (1970), also quoted in notes to 18 U.S.C.A. § 1961. For reference to RICO's rapidly increasing use see Tarlow, *RICO: New Darling of the Prosecutor's Nursery*, 49 Fordham L.Rev. 167, 169 (1980).

f. Cf. *United States v. Harris*, 460 F.2d 1041 (5th Cir.1972), cert. denied 409 U.S. 877, 93 S.Ct. 128, 34 L.Ed.2d 130 (1972); *United States v. Sacco*, 491 F.2d 995, 999 (9th Cir.

1974, en banc); *United States v. Farris*, 624 F.2d 890, 892 (9th Cir.1980), cert. denied 449 U.S. 1111, 101 S.Ct. 919, 66 L.Ed.2d 839 (1981).

g. Cf. *United States v. Vignola*, 464 F.Supp. 1091, 1098 (E.D.Pa.1979), affirmed without opinion 605 F.2d 1199 (3d Cir.1979), cert. denied 444 U.S. 1072, 100 S.Ct. 1015, 62 L.Ed.2d 753 (1980).

that prescribed labels for goods shipped in interstate commerce must remain on the goods until sold, as when displayed on the dealer's shelves:

"To make the provisions of the act effectual, Congress has provided not only for the seizure of the goods while being actually transported in interstate commerce, but has also provided for such seizure after such transportation and while the goods remain 'unloaded, unsold, or in original unbroken packages.' The opportunity for inspection en route may be very inadequate. The real opportunity of Government inspection may only arise when, as in the present case, the goods as packed have been removed from the outside box in which they were shipped and remain, as the act provides, 'unsold.' "

2. UNITED STATES v. SULLIVAN, 332 U.S. 689, 68 S.Ct. 331, 92 L.Ed. 297 (1948), affirmed the conviction of a retail druggist under the federal Food, Drug and Cosmetic Act for "misbranding" two pills boxes, in which he had placed 12 sulphathiazole tablets, by failing to affix to the boxes the required warning label that was printed on the large bottle of pills bought from an instate wholesaler, who had secured them through interstate commerce. The Court, per BLACK, J., interpreted the Act to cover any holding for sale without the required label and held it constitutional as applied to Sullivan:

"[The] Act as a whole was designed primarily to protect consumers from dangerous products. [Its] purpose was to safeguard the consumer by applying the Act to articles from the moment of their introduction into interstate commerce all the way to the moment of their delivery to the ultimate consumer. [Doubtless] it was this purpose to insure federal protection until the very moment the articles passed into the hands of the consumer by way of an intrastate transaction that moved the House Committee [to] report on this section of the Act as follows: 'In order to extend the protection of consumers contemplated by the law to the full extent constitutionally possible, paragraph (k) has been inserted prohibiting the changing of labels so as to misbrand articles held for sale after interstate shipment.' We hold that § 301(k) prohibits the misbranding charged in the information.

"Fifth. It is contended that the Act as we have construed it is beyond any authority granted Congress by the Constitution and that it invades the powers reserved to the States. A similar challenge was made against the Pure Food and Drug Act of 1906 and rejected, in *McDermott*. [There] are two variants between the circumstances of that case and this one. In *McDermott* the labels involved were on the original containers; here the labels are required to be put on other than the original containers—the boxes to which the tablets were transferred. Also, in *McDermott* the possessor of the labeled cans held for sale had himself received them by way of an interstate sale and shipment; here, while the petitioner had received the sulphathiazole by way of an intrastate sale and shipment, he bought it from a wholesaler who had received it as the direct consignee of an interstate shipment. These variants are not sufficient we think to detract from the applicability of the *McDermott* holding to the present decision. In both cases alike the question relates to the constitutional power of Congress under the commerce clause to regulate the branding of articles that have completed an interstate shipment and are being held for future sales in purely local or intrastate commerce. The reasons given for the *McDermott* holding therefore are equally applicable and persuasive here. And many cases decided since *McDermott* lend support to the validity of § 301(k). See, e.g.,

enforce and protect civil rights? For lengthy discussions of this and related issues see *Hearings, Senate Committee on Commerce*, 88th Cong., 1st Sess., on S. 1732, pt. 1 & 2 (1963).

(b) Should the Court have ruled on whether Section 5 authorized the Civil Rights Act of 1964? On this issue, what was the relevance of (1) the Court's unanimity on the commerce clause ground, and (2) its inability a few months earlier to reach a majority position on whether state trespass convictions of "sit-in" demonstrators protesting a restaurant's racial discrimination violated the fourteenth amendment? See *Bell v. Maryland*, 378 U.S. 226, 84 S.Ct. 1814, 12 L.Ed.2d 822 (1964).

(c) Would basing *Heart of Atlanta* and *McClung* on the fourteenth amendment have had "the more settling effect" urged by Douglas, J., lessening "unnecessary litigation" in enforcing the Civil Rights Act? Which basis has more potential issues for litigation in future applications of the Act? Under the commerce clause basis were any substantial factual issues left to litigate? Cf. 79 Harv.L.Rev. 130–31 (1965).

3. *Discrimination in employment.* (a) Title VII of the Civil Rights Act of 1964 prohibits discrimination in employment practices based on "race, color, religion, sex, or national origin" when an employer with 25 or more employees is "engaged in an industry affecting commerce," [f] defined as one "in commerce or in which a labor dispute would hinder or obstruct commerce or the free flow of commerce." 21 U.S.C.A. §§ 2000–2000e–2 (1964). Congress has also prohibited discrimination in employment because of an individual's age between 40 and 70 in "industries affecting commerce" as defined above for the Civil Rights Act. See 29 U.S.C.A. §§ 621–631. On what commerce clause reasoning can such national regulation best be sustained?

VI. PROTECTION OF THE ENVIRONMENT THROUGH THE COMMERCE POWER

HODEL v. VIRGINIA SURFACE MINING AND RECLAMATION ASS'N, 452 U.S. 264, 101 S.Ct. 2352, 69 L.Ed.2d 1 (1981), per MARSHALL, J., unanimously invoked the principles emphasized in *Heart of Atlanta* and *McClung* to uphold in general the constitutionality of the Surface Mining Control and Reclamation Act of 1977 [a] against a pre-enforcement challenge: "The court must defer to a congressional finding that a regulated activity affects interstate commerce, if there is any rational basis for such a finding. *Heart of Atlanta; McClung.* This established, the only remaining question for judicial inquiry is whether 'the means chosen by [Congress] is reasonably adapted to the end permitted by the Constitution.' The judicial task is at an end once the court determines that Congress acted rationally in adopting a particular regulatory scheme.

"[Here] the District Court properly deferred to Congress' express findings [about] the effects of surface coal mining on interstate commerce." [b] The Court

f. See *Phillips v. Martin Marietta Corp.*, 400 U.S. 542, 91 S.Ct. 496, 27 L.Ed.2d 613 (1971) (sex discrimination).

a. 30 U.S.C.A. § 1201ff, 91 Stat. 447.

b. The opinion recited the following findings of Congress: "[M]any surface mining operations result in disturbances of surface areas that burden and adversely affect commerce and the public welfare by destroying or diminishing the utility of land for commercial, industrial, residential, recreational, agricultural, and forestry purposes, by causing erosion and landslides, by contributing to floods, by polluting the water, by destroying fish and wildlife habitats, by impairing natural beauty, by damaging the property of citizens, by creating hazards dangerous to life and property by degrading the quality of life in local communities, and by counteracting governmental programs and efforts to conserve soil, water, and other natural resources."

saw in the legislative record "ample support for these statutory findings," based on six years of "the most thorough legislative consideration" with extended hearings and detailed findings by committees from both Houses of Congress. After noting that Congress had concluded that "additional measures were necessary to deal with the interstate commerce effects of surface coal mining, the Court ruled that "the Act's regulatory scheme is reasonably related to the goal Congress sought to accomplish. The Act's restrictions [all] serve to control the environmental and other adverse effects of surface coal mining."

The Court also relied on a "congressional finding that nationwide 'surface mining and reclamation standards are essential in order to insure that competition in interstate commerce among sellers of coal produced in different States will not be used to undermine the ability of the several States to improve and maintain adequate standards on coal mining operations within their borders.' The prevention of this sort of destructive interstate competition is a traditional role for congressional action under the Commerce Clause." [c]

A companion case, HODEL v. INDIANA, 452 U.S. 314, 101 S.Ct. 2376, 69 L.Ed.2d 40 (1981), per MARSHALL, J., gave similar reasons for upholding the Act's "prime farmland" provisions, which required for a permit to operate a surface mine on "prime farmland" historically used as "cropland" that the mine operator demonstrate its "technological capability to restore such mined area, within a reasonable time, to equivalent or higher levels of yield as nonmined prime farmland in the surrounding area under equivalent levels of management" and that it can "meet the soil reconstruction standards" of the statute. These require the distinct soil layers to be separately removed, segregated, stockpiled, and then properly replaced and regraded to the approximate original contour. To secure a permit an operator must also submit proposed reclamation plans specifying the proposed post-mining use of the land and the method by which that use will be achieved and must post a performance bond to be released only on a showing that soil productivity has returned to the required equivalent yields of nonmined soil.

Apart from applying its rational-basis analysis, the Court found "questionable" the District Court's conclusion that since surface mining disturbed annually only 21,800 acres, or .006% of the nation's prime farmland, it had only an "infinitessimal," not a "substantial," effect on interstate commerce. After noting that the acreage removed from production yearly by surface mining would produce $5 million worth of corn—"surely [not] an insignificant amount of commerce"—the Court added, "[The] court below incorrectly assumed that the relevant inquiry under the rational basis test is the volume of commerce actually affected by the regulated activity. This Court held in *NLRB v. Fainblatt* that '[t]he power of Congress to regulate interstate commerce is plenary and extends to all such commerce be it great or small.' The pertinent inquiry therefore is not how much commerce is involved but whether Congress could rationally conclude that the regulated activity affects interstate commerce." [d]

c. The opinion expressly rejected the claim that "land as such" is not subject to regulation under the commerce clause.

d. Rehnquist, J., separately concurring in the judgment in both *Hodel* cases, expressed concern that the opinions did not always state the qualification that the regulated activity must have a "substantial effect upon interstate commerce." In a separate statement applicable to both cases, Burger, C.J., agreed with the necessity for a substantial effect but added: "I join the Court's opinion because in it the Court * * * reaffirms that doctrine."

Notes and Questions

1. *Substantial effect.* Was *Fainblatt,* note 3 after *Jones & Laughlin,* supra, good authority for the substantial effect issue in *Hodel?* After *Hodel,* must the effect of the regulated local activity on interstate commerce still be substantial? If so, and if the "volume of commerce actually affected" is not relevant, as the Court says, what does "substantial effect" in this context appear to mean?

2. *Any limit?* Based on the constitutional distribution of powers, is there now any real limit on Congress' power to regulate local, non-governmental activities if Congress makes supportive findings based on information embodied in a record of hearings and committee staff research? Is there any need for judicial review of such a limit? This last question is considered briefly at p. 145 infra.

SECTION 3. THE NATIONAL TAXING AND SPENDING POWERS

INTRODUCTION

The first grant of power to Congress in Art. I, § 8, is "to lay and collect taxes, duties, imposts and excises, to pay the debts and provide for the common defense and general welfare of the United States." Note that by its terms this grant includes both the power to tax and the power to spend. This section is concerned primarily with the use of these two related powers to achieve regulatory ends.

The Court has long recognized that Congress may use its taxing power both to enforce its regulatory powers and to produce "incidental" regulatory effects outside those powers. The issues raised by such use of the taxing power, and analogous use of the spending power, have declined in importance as the expanding view of Congress' regulatory powers has left few occasions for Congress to resort to taxing or spending for regulatory purposes. Still, use of these fiscal powers to regulate is a sufficiently important aspect of the evolution of national powers to require brief consideration.

I. REGULATION THROUGH TAXING

Between 1922 and 1935, the Court thwarted the efforts of Congress to bypass the Court's narrow interpretation of the commerce clause by imposing burdensome taxes for deviation from a specified course of conduct beyond the congressional power to regulate.[a] Because Congress has had little occasion to resort to the taxing power for regulatory purposes after *Darby* and *Wickard* approved a greatly expanded commerce power, the Court has not found it necessary to review critically the distinction it drew in the *Child Labor Tax Case* (1922) between (a) taxes it condemned as a "penalty" for departure from a detailed and

---

a. *Bailey v. Drexel Furniture Co. (Child Labor Tax Case),* 259 U.S. 20, 42 S.Ct. 449, 66 L.Ed. 817 (1922) (struck down 10% net profit tax on manufacturers who employed children deviating from standards like those in *Dagenhart*); *Hill v. Wallace,* 259 U.S. 44, 42 S.Ct. 453, 66 L.Ed. 822 (1922) (struck down tax on futures contracts in grain unless made through a board of trade meeting federal requirements); *United States v. Constantine,* 296 U.S. 287, 56 S.Ct. 223, 80 L.Ed. 233 (1935) (struck down tax on liquor manufacturers and dealers operating in violation of state law 10 to 40 times greater than tax on those operating lawfully).

specified course of conduct" and (b) those typical excise taxes it sustained on sales or businesses set at a burdensome amount designed to discourage the taxed activity.[b] For a thoughtful discussion of that distinction when the *Child Labor Tax Case* was the latest word, see Cushman, *Social and Economic Control Through Federal Taxation*, 18 Minn.L.Rev. 759 (1934).

II. REGULATION THROUGH SPENDING

UNITED STATES v. BUTLER, 297 U.S. 1, 56 S.Ct. 312, 80 L.Ed. 477 (1936), per ROBERTS, J., held invalid the Agricultural Adjustment Act of 1933. To raise farm prices by reducing production, the Act authorized the government to contract with farmers to reduce their acreage planted to particular commodities in exchange for benefit payments derived from a tax on processors of that commodity. In the majority's view, the tax and benefits payments were beyond the powers of Congress:

"When an act of Congress is appropriately challenged in the courts as not conforming to the constitutional mandate the judicial branch of the Government has only one duty,—to lay the article of the Constitution which is invoked beside the statute which is challenged and to decide whether the latter squares with the former. All the court does, or can do, is to announce its considered judgment upon the question. * * *

"The clause thought to authorize the legislation [confers] upon the Congress power 'to lay and collect Taxes, Duties, Imposts and Excises, to pay the Debts and provide for the common Defence and general Welfare of the United States.' [It] is not contended that this provision grants power to regulate agricultural production upon the theory that such legislation would promote the general welfare. The government concedes that the phrase 'to provide for the general welfare' qualifies the power 'to lay and collect taxes.' The view that the clause grants power to provide for the general welfare, independently of the taxing power, has never been authoritatively accepted. Mr. Justice Story points out that, if it were adopted, 'it is obvious that under color of the generality of the words, to "provide for the common defence and general welfare", the government of the United States is, in reality, a government of general and unlimited powers, notwithstanding the subsequent enumeration of specific powers.' The true construction undoubtedly is that the only thing granted is the power to tax for the purpose of providing funds for payment of the nation's debts and making provision for the general welfare. * * *

"Since the foundation of the nation, sharp differences of opinion have persisted as to the true interpretation of the phrase. Madison asserted [that], as the United States is a government of limited and enumerated powers, the grant of power to tax and spend for the general national welfare must be confined to the enumerated legislative fields committed to the Congress. [Hamilton], on the other hand, maintained the clause confers a power separate and distinct from those later enumerated, is not restricted in meaning by the grant of them, and

---

b. *McCray v. United States*, 195 U.S. 27, 24 S.Ct. 769, 49 L.Ed. 78 (1904) (upheld 10¢ federal tax on yellow margarine when the tax on white was ¼¢); *Sonzinsky v. United States*, 300 U.S. 506, 57 S.Ct. 554, 81 L.Ed. 772 (1937) (upheld $200 annual federal tax on dealers in short-barrel shotguns and rifles in a statute also taxing each transfer $200); *United States v. Kahriger*, 345 U.S. 22, 73 S.Ct. 510, 97 L.Ed. 754 (1953) (upheld 10% federal tax on amount of all wagers accepted); cf. *United States v. Doremus*, 249 U.S. 86, 39 S.Ct. 214, 63 L.Ed. 493 (1919) (upheld federal requirement that narcotics be dispensed under prescription with detailed records as reasonably related to enforcement of $1 yearly tax on manufacturers, importers and sellers).

Congress consequently has a substantive power to tax and to appropriate, limited only by the requirement that it shall be exercised to provide for the general welfare of the United States. [Mr. Justice Story], in his *Commentaries,* espouses the Hamiltonian position. We shall not review the writings of public men and commentators or discuss the legislative practice. Study of all these leads us to conclude that the reading advocated by Mr. Justice Story is the correct one. While, therefore, the power to tax is not unlimited, its confines are set in the clause which confers it, and not in those of section 8 which bestow and define the legislative powers of the Congress. It results that the power of Congress to authorize expenditure of public moneys for public purposes is not limited by the direct grants of legislative power found in the Constitution. * * *

"We are not now required to ascertain the scope of the phrase 'general welfare of the United States' or to determine whether an appropriation in aid of agriculture falls within it. Wholly apart from that question, another principle embedded in our Constitution prohibits the enforcement of the Agricultural Adjustment Act. The act invades the reserved rights of the states. It is a statutory plan to regulate and control agricultural production, a matter beyond the powers delegated to the federal [government].

"If the taxing power may not be used as the instrument to enforce a regulation of matters of state concern with respect to which the Congress has no authority to interfere, may it, as in the present case, be employed to raise the money necessary to purchase a compliance which the Congress is powerless to command? The government asserts that whatever might be said against the validity of the plan, if compulsory, it is constitutionally sound because the end is accomplished by voluntary co-operation. There are two sufficient answers to the contention. The regulation is not in fact voluntary. The farmer, of course, may refuse to comply, but the price of such refusal is the loss of benefits. The amount offered is intended to be sufficient to exert pressure on him to agree to the proposed regulation. The power to confer or withhold unlimited benefits is the power to coerce or destroy. If the cotton grower elects not to accept the benefits, he will receive less for his crops; those who receive payments will be able to undersell him. The result may well be financial ruin. [This] is coercion by economic pressure. The asserted power of choice is illusory.

"[But] if the plan were one for purely voluntary co-operation it would stand no better so far as federal power is concerned. At best, it is a scheme for purchasing with federal funds submission to federal regulation of a subject reserved to the states. [Congress] cannot invade state jurisdiction to compel individual action; no more can it purchase such action. * * *

"[It] does not help to declare that local conditions throughout the nation have created a situation of national concern; for this is but to say that whenever there is a widespread similarity of local conditions, Congress may ignore constitutional limitations upon its own powers and usurp those reserved to the states. If, in lieu of compulsory regulation of subjects within the states' reserved jurisdiction, which is prohibited, the Congress could invoke the taxing and spending power as a means to accomplish the same end, clause 1 of section 8 of article 1 would become the instrument for total subversion of the governmental powers reserved to the individual states. * * *"

STONE, J, dissented, joined by Brandeis and Cardozo, JJ.: "As the present depressed state of agriculture is nation wide in its extent and effects, there is no basis for saying that the expenditure of public money in aid of farmers is not within the specifically granted power of Congress to levy taxes to 'provide for [the] general welfare.'

"[The] suggestion of coercion finds no support in the record or in any data showing the actual operation of the act. Threat of loss, not hope of gain, is the essence of economic coercion. Members of a long-depressed industry have undoubtedly been tempted to curtail acreage by the hope of resulting better prices and by the proffered opportunity to obtain needed ready money. But there is nothing to indicate that those who accepted benefits were impelled by fear of lower prices if they did not accept, or that at any stage in the operation of the plan a farmer could say whether, apart from the certainty of cash payments at specified times, the advantage would lie with curtailment of production plus compensation, rather than with the same or increased acreage plus the expected rise in prices which actually occurred. [Of] the total number of farms growing cotton, estimated at 1,500,000, 33 per cent. in 1934 and 13 per cent. in 1935 did not participate. * * *

"The Constitution requires that public funds shall be spent for a defined purpose, the promotion of the general welfare. Their expenditure usually involves payment on terms which will insure use by the selected recipients within the limits of the constitutional purpose. [The] power of Congress to spend is inseparable from persuasion to action over which Congress has no legislative control. Congress may not command that the science of agriculture be taught in state universities. But if it would aid the teaching of that science by grants to state institutions, it is appropriate, if not necessary, that the grant be on the condition, incorporated in the Morrill Act, that it be used for the intended purpose. * * *

"The spending power of Congress is in addition to the legislative power and not subordinate to it. This independent grant of the power of the purse, and its very nature, involving in its exercise the duty to insure expenditure within the granted power, presuppose freedom of selection among divers ends and aims, and the capacity to impose such conditions as will render the choice effective. It is a contradiction in terms to say that there is power to spend for the national welfare, while rejecting any power to impose conditions reasonably adapted to the attainment of the ends which alone would justify the expenditure.

"[If] the expenditure is for a national public purpose, that purpose will not be thwarted because payment is on condition which will advance that purpose. [If] appropriation in aid of a program of curtailment of agricultural production is constitutional, and it is not denied that it is, payment to farmers on condition that they reduce their crop acreage is constitutional."[a]

Notes and Questions

1. *Spending or regulation?* Can *Butler's* ruling that Congress' spending power is not limited by its other powers be soundly reconciled with its ruling on spending to relieve the national agricultural crisis by paying farmers to reduce production? Consider Grant, fn. a supra, at 1012–13; Note, 20 Minn.L.Rev. 413, 418 (1936)

2. *Conditional grants in aid distinguishable?* Both opinions assumed the validity of the long-standing practice of making federal grants-in-aid, conditioned

---

a. For critical studies of *Butler,* see Collier, *Judicial Bootstraps and the General Welfare Clause,* 4 Geo.Wash.L.Rev. 211 (1936); Grant, *Commerce, Production, and the Fiscal Powers* of *Congress,* 45 Yale L.J. 751, 991, at 1009 (1936); Hart, *Processing Taxes and Protective Tariffs,* 49 Harv.L.Rev. 610 (1936); Note, 20 Minn.L.Rev. 413 (1936).

upon the recipient spending the funds for the stated purpose and pursuant to federally prescribed standards, though beyond the scope of federal regulatory power. Later decisions confirmed that validity. See *Steward Machine Co. v. Davis* (1937), *Oklahoma v. Civil Service Commission* (1947), and *Lau v. Nichols* (1974), considered Sec. 5, IV, infra. Is there a difference of constitutional dimension between educational grants conditioned on the education meeting federal standards beyond the federal power to command and financial grants to farmers conditioned on their reduction of planted acreage?

STEWARD MACHINE CO. v. DAVIS

301 U.S. 548, 57 S.Ct. 883, 81 L.Ed. 1279 (1937).

MR. JUSTICE CARDOZO delivered the opinion of the Court.

[The Court upheld Title IX of the Social Security Act relating to unemployment compensation under which the proceeds of a federal payroll tax on employers went into the general funds, not earmarked. Taxpayers were entitled to 90% credit on their federal tax for payments to a state unemployment compensation fund under a state law that met federal requirements, some designed to assure a genuine unemployment compensation program and others to protect the state fund against loss. One of the latter required that payments to state funds be paid over to the Secretary of the Treasury to the credit of the "Unemployment Trust Fund," subject to repayment under state requisitions. Appropriations from the general funds were authorized to assist states in the administration of their unemployment compensation laws.]

The excise is not void as involving the coercion of the states in contravention of the Tenth Amendment or of restrictions implicit in our federal form of government.

[To] draw the line intelligently between duress and inducement, there is need to remind ourselves of facts as to the problem of unemployment. [During] the years 1929 to 1936, when the country was passing through a cyclical depression, the number of the unemployed mounted to unprecedented heights. Often the average was more than 10 million; at times a peak was attained of 16 million or more. Disaster to the breadwinner meant disaster to dependents. Accordingly the roll of the unemployed, itself formidable enough, was only a partial roll of the destitute or needy. * * * [The] states were unable to give the requisite relief. The problem had become national in area and dimensions. There was need of help from the nation if the people were not to starve. It is too late today for the argument to be heard with tolerance that in a crisis so extreme the use of the moneys of the nation to relieve the unemployed and their dependents is a use for any purpose narrower than the promotion of the general welfare. Cf. *United States v. Butler; Helvering v. Davis* [Part III infra], decided herewith. The nation responded to the call of the distressed. Between January 1, 1933, and July 1, 1936, [the] obligations for emergency relief incurred by the national government were $2,929,307,125, or twice the obligations of states and local agencies combined. [The] parens patriae has many reasons—fiscal and economic as well as social and moral—for planning to mitigate disasters that bring these burdens in their train.

In the presence of this urgent need for some remedial expedient, the question is to be answered whether the expedient adopted has overleapt the bounds of power. The assailants of the statute say that its dominant end and aim is to drive the state Legislatures under the whip of economic pressure into the enactment of unemployment compensation laws at the bidding of the central government. Supporters of the statute say that its operation is not constraint, but the creation of a larger freedom, the states and the nation joining in a co-operative endeavor to avert a common evil. Before Congress acted, unemployment compensation insurance was still, for the most part, a project and no more. Wisconsin was the pioneer. Her statute was adopted in 1931. At times bills for such insurance were introduced elsewhere, but they did not reach the stage of law. In 1935, four states (California, Massachusetts, New Hampshire, and New York) passed unemployment laws on the eve of the adoption of the Social Security Act, and two others did likewise after the federal act and later in the year. The statutes differed to some extent in type, but were directed to a common end. In 1936, twenty-eight other states fell in line, and eight more the present year. But if states had been holding back before the passage of the federal law, inaction was not owing, for the most part, to the lack of sympathetic interest. Many held back through alarm lest in laying such a toll upon their industries, they would place themselves in a position of economic disadvantage as compared with neighbors or competitors. [Two] consequences ensued. One was that the freedom of a state to contribute its fair share to the solution of a national problem was paralyzed by fear. The other was that in so far as there was failure by the states to contribute relief according to the measure of their capacity, a disproportionate burden, and a mountainous one, was laid upon the resources of the government of the nation.

The Social Security Act is an attempt to find a method by which all these public agencies may work together to a common end. Every dollar of the new taxes will continue in all likelihood to be used and needed by the nation as long as states are unwilling, whether through timidity or for other motives, to do what can be done at home. [On] the other hand, fulfillment of the home duty will be lightened and encouraged by crediting the taxpayer upon his account with the Treasury of the nation to the extent that his contributions under the laws of the locality have simplified or diminished the problem of relief and the probable demand upon the resources of the fisc. * * *

Who then is coerced through the operation of this statute? Not the taxpayer. He pays in fulfillment of the mandate of the local legislature. Not the state. Even now she does not offer a suggestion that in passing the unemployment law she was affected by duress. For all that appears, she is satisfied with her choice, and would be sorely disappointed if it were now to be annulled. The difficulty with the petitioner's contention is that it confuses motive with coercion. [E]very rebate from a tax when conditioned upon conduct is in some measure a temptation. But to hold that motive or temptation is equivalent to coercion is to plunge the law in endless difficulties. The outcome of such a doctrine is the acceptance of a philosophical determinism by which choice becomes impossible. Till now the law has been guided by a robust common sense which assumes the freedom of the will as a working hypothesis in the solution of its problems. The wisdom of the hypothesis has illustration in this case. [We] cannot say that [Alabama] was acting, not of her unfettered will, but under the strain of a persuasion equivalent to undue influence, when she chose to have relief administered under laws of her own making, by agents of her own selection, instead of under federal laws, administered by federal officers, with all the ensuing evils, at least to many minds, of federal patronage and power. There would be a strange irony, indeed, if her choice were now to be annulled on the basis of an assumed duress in the enactment of a statute which her courts have accepted as a true expression of her [will].

In ruling as we do, we leave many questions open. We do not say that a tax is valid, when imposed by act of Congress, if it is laid upon the condition that a state may escape its operation through the adoption of a statute unrelated in subject-matter to activities fairly within the scope of national policy and power. No such question is before us. In the tender of this credit Congress does not intrude upon fields foreign to its function. The purpose of its intervention, as we have shown, is to safeguard its own treasury and as an incident to that protection to place the states upon a footing of equal opportunity. [It] is one thing to impose a tax dependent upon the conduct of the taxpayers, or of the state in which they live, where the conduct to be stimulated or discouraged is unrelated to the fiscal need subserved by the tax in its formal operation, or to any other end legitimately national. The *Child Labor Tax Case* [was] decided in the belief that the statute there condemned [was] exposed to that reproach. It is quite another thing to say that a tax will be abated upon the doing of an act that will satisfy the fiscal need, the tax and the alternative being approximate equivalents. In such circumstances, if in no others, inducement or persuasion does not go beyond the bounds of power. We do not fix the outermost line. Enough for present purposes that wherever the line may be, this statute is within it. Definition more precise must abide the wisdom of the future.

[The] statute does not call for a surrender by the states of powers essential to their quasi sovereign existence. [Section 903] defines the minimum criteria to which a state compensation system is required to conform if it is to be accepted by the Board as the basis for a [credit].

A credit to taxpayers for payments made to a state under a state unemployment law will be manifestly futile in the absence of some assurance that the law leading to the credit is in truth what it professes to be. [What] is basic and essential may be assured by suitable conditions. The terms embodied in these sections are directed to that end. A wide range of judgment is given to the several states as to the particular type of statute to be spread upon their books. [What] they may not do, if they would earn the credit, is to depart from those standards which in the judgment of Congress are to be ranked as fundamental.

* * *[a]

Notes and Questions

1. *Spending to induce action Congress cannot command.* (a) Compare the economic pressure on the farmers in *Butler* and on the states in *Steward Machine.* Which comes closer to "coercion" or "the strain of persuasion equivalent to undue influence"? Who was more free to resist the federal "inducement" or "coercion" or "temptation"—the farmers in *Butler* or the states in *Steward?* Are the cases consistent?

(b) *Steward* concludes that when Congress used the tax and credit device to induce states to adopt unemployment compensation laws it did not "intrude upon fields foreign to its function" in view of the national fiscal responsibility for relief of the unemployed. Can spending to "purchase" compliance by the farmers with a reduced acreage program in order to provide relief for a depressed national agriculture be fairly distinguished?

a. McReynolds and Butler, JJ., dissented in separate opinions. Sutherland, J., joined by Van Devanter, J., agreed that the act did not coerce the states into adopting unemployment legislation. But, dissenting in part, they contended that the administrative provisions of the act unconstitutionally encroached on state powers. The latter issue is considered in Sec. 5 infra.

(c) Assuming no power under the commerce clause to regulate agricultural production, was *Butler* a dependable precedent after *Steward?*

2. *Limitation on such use of spending power.* Did the Court intimate any constitutional limitation on use of the spending power to induce action that Congress cannot command? Should it have done so? How might it be formulated?

III. SPENDING FOR GENERAL WELFARE

HELVERING v. DAVIS, 301 U.S. 619, 57 S.Ct. 904, 81 L.Ed. 1307 (1937), per CARDOZO, J., decided with *Steward Machine,* sustained the exclusively-federal old age pension program embodied in Titles II and VIII of the Social Security Act, ruling that this taxing and spending program was authorized by the general welfare clause: "The line must still be drawn between one welfare and another, between the particular and the general. [The] discretion [belongs] to Congress, unless the choice is clearly wrong, a display of arbitrary power, not an exercise of judgment. [Nor] is the concept of the general welfare static. Needs that were narrow or parochial a century ago may be interwoven in our day with the well-being of the [nation].

"The problem is plainly national in area and dimensions. Moreover, laws of the separate states cannot deal with it effectively. Congress, at least, had a basis for that belief. States and local governments are often lacking in the resources that are necessary to finance an adequate program of security for the aged. This is brought out with a wealth of illustration in recent studies of the problem. Apart from the failure of resources, states and local governments are at times reluctant to increase so heavily the burden of taxation to be borne by their residents for fear of placing themselves in a position of economic disadvantage as compared with neighbors or competitors. We have seen this in our study of the problem of unemployment compensation. *Steward.* A system of old age pensions has special dangers of its own, if put in force in one state and rejected in another. The existence of such a system is a bait to the needy and dependent elsewhere, encouraging them to migrate and seek a haven of repose. Only a power that is national can serve the interests of all." [a]

Notes and Questions

1. *Land reclamation. United States v. Gerlach Live Stock Co.,* 339 U.S. 725, 70 S.Ct. 955, 94 L.Ed. 1231 (1950), relying on *Butler,* found in the power to spend for the general welfare an appropriate basis for federal land reclamation projects: "Congress has a substantive power to tax and appropriate for the general welfare, limited only by the requirement that it shall be exercised for the common benefit as distinguished from some mere local purpose. If any doubt of this power remained, it was laid to rest the following year in *Helvering.* Thus the power of Congress to promote the general welfare through large-scale projects for reclamation, irrigation, or other internal improvement, is now as clear and ample as its power to accomplish the same results indirectly through resort to strained interpretation of the power over navigation." See also *Ivanhoe Irrig. Dist. v. McCracken,* 357 U.S. 275, 78 S.Ct. 1174, 2 L.Ed.2d 1313 (1958).

2. *National as distinct from local welfare? Helvering* made a point of the "national dimensions" of the old age support problem, and *Gerlach* spoke of "the

---

a. Butler and McReynolds, JJ., dissented.

requirement that [the power to tax and spend for the general welfare] be exercised for the common benefit as distinguished from some mere local purpose." [b] Is some nationwide need or some common benefit, widely shared, a requisite for federal spending? Should it be? Would an appropriation for an irrigation project that would only benefit land within a 50 mile radius be valid? An appropriation to prevent the bankruptcy of Detroit?

SECTION 4. FOREIGN AFFAIRS POWER

INTRODUCTION

The foregoing consideration of the commerce, taxing, and spending powers should provide adequate background for professional treatment of issues relating to the many other Congressional powers. See, e.g., the reliance on the war powers as the source for Congressional regulation to cope with economic problems arising out of war-related activities.[a] We add here consideration of one other source of Congressional power because it is atypical.

I. TREATIES AS A SOURCE OF LEGISLATIVE POWER

MISSOURI v. HOLLAND, 252 U.S. 416, 40 S.Ct. 382, 64 L.Ed. 641 (1920), per HOLMES, J., upheld the Migratory Bird Treaty Act that regulated the taking of migratory birds in the United States in fulfillment of a treaty with Canada. The treaty obligated both countries to seek legislation protecting migratory birds that traversed both countries and were valued highly, both for food and as destroyers of insects harmful to vegetation:

"[It] is not enough to refer to the Tenth Amendment [because] by Article 2, Section 2, the power to make treaties is delegated expressly, and by Article 6 treaties made under the authority of the United States, along with the Constitution and laws of the United States made in pursuance thereof, are declared the supreme law of the land. If the treaty is valid there can be no dispute about the validity of the statute under Article 1, Section 8, as a necessary and proper means to execute the powers of the Government. * * *

"It is said [that] there are [constitutional limits] to the treaty-making power, and that one such limit is that what an act of Congress could not do unaided, in derogation of the powers reserved to the States, a treaty cannot do. [What Congress can enact] 'by itself and not in pursuance of a treaty' cannot be accepted as a test of the treaty power. [Acts] of Congress are the supreme law of the land only when made in pursuance of the Constitution, while treaties are declared to be so when made under the authority of the United States. It is open to question whether the authority of the United States means more than the formal acts prescribed to make the convention. We do not mean to imply that there are no qualifications to the treaty-making power; but they must be ascertained in a different way. It is obvious that there may be matters of the sharpest exigency for the national well being that an act of Congress could not

b. See also the dictum in *Cincinnati Soap Co. v. United States,* 301 U.S. 308, 317, 57 S.Ct. 764, 768, 81 L.Ed. 1122, 1130 (1937), that "a federal tax levied for the express purpose of paying the debts or providing for the welfare of a state might be invalid."

a. *Woods v. Miller Co.,* 333 U.S. 138, 68 S.Ct. 421, 92 L.Ed. 596 (1948) (post-war rent control); *Yakus v. United States,* 321 U.S. 414, 64 S.Ct. 660, 88 L.Ed. 834 (1944) (price control); *United States v. Central Eureka Mining Co.,* 357 U.S. 155, 78 S.Ct. 1097, 2 L.Ed.2d 1228 (1958) (controls on use of economic resources).

deal with but that a treaty followed by such an act could, and it is not lightly to be assumed that, in matters requiring national action, 'a power which must belong to and somewhere reside in every civilized government' is not to be found. [We] are not yet discussing the particular case before us but only are considering the validity of the test proposed. With regard to that we may add that when we are dealing with words that also are a constituent act, like the Constitution of the United States, we must realize that they have called into life a being the development of which could not have been foreseen completely by the most gifted of its begetters. It was enough for them to realize or to hope that they had created an organism; it has taken a century and has cost their successors much sweat and blood to prove that they created a nation. The case before us must be considered in the light of our whole experience and not merely in that of what was said a hundred years ago. The treaty in question does not contravene any prohibitory words to be found in the Constitution. The only question is whether it is forbidden by some invisible radiation from the general terms of the Tenth Amendment. We must consider what this country has become in deciding what that amendment has reserved.

"[No] doubt it is true that as between a State and its inhabitants the State may regulate the killing and sale of [migratory] birds, but it does not follow that its authority is exclusive of paramount powers. [The] whole foundation of the State's rights is the presence within their jurisdiction of birds that yesterday had not arrived, tomorrow may be in another State and in a week a thousand miles away. If we are to be accurate we cannot put the case of the State upon higher ground than that the treaty deals with creatures that for the moment are within the state borders, that it must be carried out by officers of the United States within the same territory, and that but for the treaty the State would be free to regulate this subject itself.

"As most of the laws of the United States are carried out within the States and as many of them deal with matters which in the silence of such laws the State might regulate, such general grounds are not enough to support Missouri's claim. 'Valid treaties of course are as binding within the territorial limits of the States as they are elsewhere throughout the dominion of the United States.' No doubt the great body of private relations usually fall within the control of the State, but a treaty may override its power. * * *

"Here a national interest of very nearly the first magnitude is involved. It can be protected only by national action in concert with that of another power. The subject matter is only transitorily within the State and has no permanent habitat therein. But for the treaty and the statute there soon might be no birds for any powers to deal with. We see nothing in the Constitution that compels the Government to sit by while a food supply is cut off and the protectors of our forests and our crops are destroyed. It is not sufficient to rely upon the States. The reliance is vain, and were it otherwise, the question is whether the United States is forbidden to act. We are of opinion that the treaty and statute must be upheld." [a]

Notes and Questions

Extent of treaty power as source of legislative power. (a) Are there judicially manageable limits on the federal government's power to expand its regulatory power through treaties by which each signatory obligates itself to take regulato-

---

a. Van Devanter and Pitney, JJ., dissented without opinion.

ry action within its boundaries? Field, J., in *Geofrey v. Riggs*, 133 U.S. 258, 10 S.Ct. 295, 33 L.Ed. 642 (1890), wrote that the treaty power "extends to all proper subjects of negotiation between our government and the government of other nations." On what basis could a court decide whether a treaty requiring federal legislation is "proper subject" for international negotiations? See generally Henkin, *The Constitution, Treaties, and International Human Rights*, 116 U.Pa. L.Rev. 1012 (1968).

(b) Where does the final authority lie to determine whether a treaty deals with a "proper subject of negotiation" with foreign nations? Should this be viewed as a nonjusticiable political question, absent invasion of constitutionally-protected freedoms?

II. OTHER BASES FOR LEGISLATIVE POWER OVER FOREIGN AFFAIRS

Is congressional power to legislate on foreign affairs limited to laws implementing treaties and to such sources as are found in Article I, Section 8, the Civil War Amendments, and similar grants of power? Is a broader source of legislative power needed? May the absence of any general grant of power to legislate on foreign affairs, as distinct from the limited subject-matter powers like treaties, foreign commerce, declaration of war, piracy, and offenses against the law of nations, justify resort to a broader basis for attributing such power to Congress? Consider the following opinions.

PEREZ v. BROWNELL, 356 U.S. 44, 78 S.Ct. 568, 2 L.Ed.2d 603 (1958), per FRANKFURTER, J., upheld a federal statute mandating loss of U.S. citizenship for "voting in a political election in a foreign state." The Court viewed this drastic sanction to prevent the international tensions risked by a citizen's "participat[ing] in the political or governmental affairs of another country" as based upon Congress' "power to regulate foreign affairs:" "Although there is in the Constitution no specific grant to Congress of power to enact legislation for the effective regulation of foreign affairs, there can be no doubt of the existence of this power in the law-making organ of the Nation. See *United States v. Curtiss-Wright Export Corp.* 299 U.S. 304, 318, 57 S.Ct. 216, 81 L.Ed. 255, 261 (1936); *Mackenzie v. Hare*, 239 U.S. 299, 311, 312, 36 S.Ct. 106, 60 L.Ed. 297, 301. The States that joined together to form a single Nation and to create, through the Constitution, a Federal Government to conduct the affairs of that Nation must be held to have granted that Government the powers indispensable to its functioning effectively in the company of sovereign nations. The Government must be able not only to deal affirmatively with foreign nations, as it does through the maintenance of diplomatic relations with them and the protection of American citizens sojourning within their territories. It must also be able to reduce to a minimum the frictions that are unavoidable in a world of sovereigns sensitive in matters touching their dignity and interests." [b]

---

b. In three opinions Warren, C.J., and Black, Douglas and Whittaker, JJ., dissented from the ruling that Congress could impose involuntary expatriation, but did not question the *Perez* comments on Congress' power to legislate on foreign affairs. Nor did *Afroyim v. Rusk*, 387 U.S. 253, 87 S.Ct. 1660, 18 L.Ed. 2d 757 (1967), which overruled the *Perez* expatriation ruling as inconsistent with § 1 of the fourteenth amendment.

Notes and Questions

1. *"Springing" sovereignty?* (a) In the CURTISS–WRIGHT passage cited in *Perez,* SUTHERLAND, J., gave judicial endorsement to views he had advanced earlier in another capacity [a]—that in the international area federal power is not dependent upon those specified in the constitution:

"The broad statement that the federal government can exercise no powers except those specifically enumerated in the Constitution, and such implied powers as are necessary and proper to carry into effect the enumerated powers, is categorically true only in respect of our internal affairs. In that field, the primary purpose of the Constitution was to carve from the general mass of legislative powers *then possessed by the states* such portions as it was thought desirable to vest in the federal government, leaving those not included in the enumeration still in the states. That this doctrine applies only to powers which the states had is self-evident. And since the states severally never possessed international powers, such powers could not have been carved from the mass of state powers but obviously were transmitted to the United States from some other source. During the Colonial period, those powers were possessed exclusively by and were entirely under the control of the Crown. ＊ ＊ ＊

"As a result of the separation from Great Britain by the colonies, acting as a unit, the powers of external sovereignty passed from the Crown not to the colonies severally, but to the colonies in their collective and corporate capacity as the United States of America. [Rulers] come and go; governments end and forms of government change; but sovereignty survives. A political society cannot endure without a supreme will somewhere. Sovereignty is never held in suspense. When, therefore, the external sovereignty of Great Britain in respect of the colonies ceased, it immediately passed to the Union. ＊ ＊ ＊

"The Union existed before the Constitution. [Prior] to that event, [the] Union, declared by the Articles of Confederation to be 'perpetual,' was the sole possessor of external sovereignty, and in the Union it remained without change save in so far as the Constitution in express terms qualified its exercise. ＊ ＊ ＊

"It results that the investment of the federal government with the powers of external sovereignty did not depend upon the affirmative grants of the Constitution. The powers to declare and wage war, to conclude peace, to make treaties, to maintain diplomatic relations with other sovereignties, if they had never been mentioned in the Constitution, would have vested in the federal government as necessary concomitants of nationality. [As] a member of the family of nations, the right and power of the United States in that field are equal to the right and power of the other members of the international family. Otherwise, the United States is not completely sovereign."

2. *Sutherland's doctrine without his history.* Scholars have challenged the historical accuracy of Sutherland, J.'s view that sovereignty with all foreign affairs power was vested in the Continental Congress, and none in state governments, between the peace treaty (1783) and the adoption of the Constitution (1789).[b] Would error in this history fatally flaw the Sutherland doctrine

---

a. See Sutherland, *The Internal and External Powers of the National Government,* Sen. Doc. No. 417, 61st Cong. 2nd Sess. (1910); Sutherland, *Constitutional Power and World Affairs* 25–47, 116–26 (1919).

b. Levitan, *The Foreign Relations Power: An Analysis of Mr. Justice Sutherland's Theo-* ry, 55 Yale L.J. 467 (1946); Lofgren, *United States v. Curtiss-Wright Export Corporation: An Historical Reassessment,* 83 Yale L.J. 1 (1973).

concerning federal power over foreign affairs? Or do *Perez* and *Curtiss-Wright* both reflect a common, solid basis for finding a general power in Congress to legislate on foreign affairs regardless of whether the states had some foreign affairs power before 1789? See Professor Henkin's thoughtful analysis, *Foreign Affairs and the Constitution* 24 (1972).

3. *Limits on Congress' foreign affairs power?* Are there manageable standards by which to limit the Congressional power over foreign affairs? Would it be appropriate to follow the commerce clause example and uphold foreign affairs legislation to the extent the Court concludes that Congress had a rational basis for viewing the legislation as an appropriate solution to a foreign affairs problem? [c] That was the Court's view in *Perez.*[d] See Henkin, supra 74–76, for a comprehensive view of Congress' "foreign affairs power" under the *Curtiss-Wright-Perez* rationale, coupled with a recognition of the breadth of Congress' power over foreign affairs derived from the specified powers of Congress. Id. at 69–74, 79–85.

SECTION 5. LIMITATIONS ON APPLYING NATIONAL POWERS TO STATE GOVERNMENTS: INTERGOVERNMENTAL IMMUNITIES

I. ORIGINS OF IMMUNITIES

Intergovernmental immunity as a constitutional limit on state and federal power started with immunity of the federal government from state taxation under the supremacy clause. McCULLOCH v. MARYLAND, Sec. 1 supra, held invalid Maryland's $15,000 tax [a] on the Bank of United States, imposed on any bank in Maryland issuing bank notes without state authority: "[The] great principle [that sustains the bank's] claim to be exempted from the power of the state to tax its operations [is] that the Constitution and the laws made in pursuance thereof are supreme; that they control the Constitution and laws of the respective states, and cannot be controlled by them. From this, which may be almost termed an axiom, other propositions are deduced as corollaries. [These] are, 1st. That a power to create implies a power to preserve. 2d. That a power to destroy, if wielded by a different hand, is hostile to, and incompatible with, these powers to create and to preserve. 3d. That where this repugnancy exists, that authority which is supreme must control, not yield to that over which it is supreme. * * *

"That the power of taxing [the bank] by the states may be exercised so as to destroy it, is too obvious to be denied. [It] is of the very essence of supremacy to remove all obstacles to its action within its own sphere, and so to modify every power vested in subordinate governments, as to exempt its own operations from their own influence. This effect need not be stated in terms. It is so involved in the declaration of supremacy, so necessarily implied in it, that the expression of it could not make it more certain. We must, therefore, keep it in view while construing the Constitution. * * *

c. Cf. *Heart of Atlanta*, p. 103 supra, 379 U.S. at 258, 85 S.Ct. at 358, 13 L.Ed.2d at 269.

d. "[A] rational nexus must exist between the content of a specific power in Congress and the action of Congress. [In this case,] withdrawal of citizenship [must] be reasonably related to the end—here, regulation of foreign affairs."

a. Or an alternative 2% tax on the face value of all bank notes issued.

"Would the people of any one state trust those of another with a power to control the most insignificant operations of their state government? We know they would not. Why, then, should we suppose that the people of any one state should be willing to trust those of another with a power to control the operations of a government to which they have confided their most important and most valuable interests? In the legislature of the Union alone, are all represented. The legislature of the Union alone, therefore, can be trusted by the people with the power of controlling measures which concern all, in the confidence that it will not be abused. * * *

"If the states may tax one instrument, employed by the government in the execution of its powers, they may tax any and every other instrument. They may tax the mail; they may tax the mint; they may tax patent rights; they may tax the papers of the customhouse; they may tax judicial process; they may tax all the means employed by the government, to an excess which would defeat all the ends of government.

"[If] the controlling power of the states be established; if their supremacy as to taxation be acknowledged; what is to restrain their exercising this control in any shape they may please to give it? Their sovereignty is not confined to taxation. That is not the only mode in which it might be displayed. The question is, in truth, a question of supremacy; and if the right of the states to tax the means employed by the general government be conceded, the declaration that the Constitution, and the laws made in pursuance thereof, shall be the supreme law of the land, is empty and unmeaning declamation. * * *"

Notes and Questions

1. *Basis for decision.* Could the Court have invalidated the Maryland tax on narrower grounds, such as its discriminatory or burdensome nature? What considerations may have influenced the decision's broader basis?

2. *Birth of state immunity from federal taxes.* Just as *Dobbins v. Comm'rs of Erie Co.* (1942) [b] invoked *McCulloch* to strike down a state tax on the salary of a federal officer, COLLECTOR v. DAY (1871) [c] invoked *McCulloch* and its reasoning to invalidate a federal income tax on the salary of a state judge as an "instrumentality" of state government. It viewed the independent, "sovereign powers" "reserved" to the states by the tenth amendment as the foundation for state immunity from federal taxes, analogous to the role of the supremacy clause as the foundation for federal immunity from state taxes:

"[If] the means and instrumentalities employed by [the General Government] to carry into operation the powers granted to it are, necessarily, and, for the sake of self-preservation, exempt from taxation by the States, why are not those of the States depending upon their reserved powers, for like reasons, equally exempt from federal taxation? Their unimpaired existence in the one case is as essential as in the other. It is admitted that there is no express provision in the Constitution that prohibits the General Government from taxing the means and instrumentalities of the States, nor is there any prohibiting the States from taxing the means and instrumentalities of that government. In both cases the exemption rests upon necessary implication, and is upheld by the great law of self-preservation; as any government, whose means employed in conducting its operations, if subject to the control of another and distinct govern-

b. 41 U.S. (16 Pet.) 435, 10 L.Ed. 1022 (1842).

c. 78 U.S. (11 Wall.) 113, 20 L.Ed. 122 (1871).

ment, can exist only at the mercy of that government. Of what avail are these means if another power may tax them at discretion?"

II. STATE IMMUNITY FROM FEDERAL TAXES

Since its renunciation of tax immunity benefits for private taxpayers in 1938, the Court has invalidated no federal tax on a state, its activities, agencies or property, but has not questioned a state's right to immunity in appropriate cases. During that period the issue of state tax immunity, independent of private taxpayers' interests, has reached the Court only twice, due, presumably, to congressional restraint. Both cases upheld the federal tax, but neither produced a majority statement of the controlling considerations.

The latest of these,[a] MASSACHUSETTS v. UNITED STATES, 435 U.S. 444, 98 S.Ct. 1153, 55 L.Ed.2d 403 (1978), per BRENNAN, J., upheld 6 to 2, as applied to state police planes, a federal registration tax on all civil aircraft imposed to pay part of the cost of federal air navigational facilities and services. Three other justices [b] joined BRENNAN, J.'s, discussion of the state immunity policy:

"As the contours of the principle evolved in later decisions, 'cogent reasons' were recognized for narrowly limiting the immunity of the States from federal imposts. The first is that any immunity for the protection of state sovereignty is at the expense of the sovereign power of the National Government to tax. Therefore, when the scope of the States' constitutional immunity is enlarged beyond that necessary to protect the continued ability of the States to deliver traditional governmental services, the burden of the immunity is thrown upon the National Government without any corresponding promotion of the constitutionally protected values. The second is that the political process is uniquely adapted to accommodating the competing demands 'for national revenue, on the one hand, and for reasonable scope for the independence of state action, on the other' * * * *Helvering v. Gerhardt* [fn. h supra.]

"[In] recognition of these considerations, decisions of the Court either have declined to enlarge the scope of state immunity or have in fact restricted its reach. Typical of this trend are decisions holding that the National Government may tax revenue-generating activities of the States that are of the same nature as those traditionally engaged in by private persons. See, e.g., *New York v. United States*, (1946) [infra note 1] (tax on water bottled and sold by State upheld); *Allen v. Regents*, 304 U.S. 439, 58 S.Ct. 980, 82 L.Ed. 1448 (1938) (tax on admissions to state athletic events approved notwithstanding use of proceeds for essential state functions); *Helvering v. Powers*, 293 U.S. 214, 55 S.Ct. 171, 79 L.Ed. 291 (1934) (tax on operations of railroad by State); *Ohio v. Helvering*, 292 U.S. 360, 54 S.Ct. 292, 78 L.Ed. 1307 (1934) (tax on state liquor operation); *South Carolina v. United States*, 199 U.S. 437, 26 S.Ct. 110, 50 L.Ed. 261 (1905) (tax on state-run liquor business). It is true that some of the opinions speak of the state activity taxed as 'proprietary' and thus not an immune essential *governmental* activity, but the opinions of the Members of the Court in *New York v. United States*, supra, the most recent decision, rejected the governmental-proprietary distinction as untenable. Rather the majority [15] reasoned that a nondiscrimina-

---

a. The first was *New York v. United States* (1946), note 1 infra.

b. White, Marshall, and Stevens, JJ., joined in that part of the opinion considered below. Stewart and Powell, JJ., saw "no need to discuss the general contours of state immunity from federal taxation," but concurred in

the ruling that the registration tax was valid as a "user fee."

15. In *New York v. United States*, Mr. Justice Frankfurter announced the judgment of the Court and an opinion joined by only one of the eight Justices participating in the case. That opinion upheld the tax on a broader

tory tax may be applied to a state business activity where, as was the case there, the recognition of immunity would accomplish a withdrawal from the taxing power of the nation a subject of taxation of a nature which has been traditionally within that power from the beginning. Its exercise by a nondiscriminatory tax, does not curtail the business of the state government more than it does the like business of the citizen.

"[Where] the subject of tax is a natural and traditional source of federal revenue and where it is inconceivable that such a revenue measure could ever operate to preclude traditional state activities, the tax is valid. While the Court has by no means abandoned its doubts concerning its ability to make particularized assessments of the impact of revenue measures on essential state operations, it has recognized that some generic types of revenue measures could never seriously threaten the continued functioning of the States and hence are outside the scope of the implied tax immunity.

"A nondiscriminatory taxing measure that operates to defray the cost of a federal program by recovering a fair approximation of each beneficiary's share of the cost is surely no more offensive to the constitutional scheme than is either a tax on the income earned by state employees or a tax on a State's sale of bottled water. [There] is no danger that such measures will not be based on benefits conferred or that they will function as regulatory devices unduly burdening essential state activities. It is, of course, the case that a revenue provision that forces a State to pay its own way when performing an essential function will increase the cost of the state activity. But [an] economic burden on traditional state functions without more is not a sufficient basis for sustaining a claim of immunity." [c]

Notes and Questions

1. NEW YORK v. UNITED STATES, 326 U.S. 572, 66 S.Ct. 310, 90 L.Ed. 326 (1946) upheld application of a federal excise tax to New York's sale of mineral waters bottled and sold by the state to provide funds for a state health resort. FRANKFURTER, J., assigned to write the opinion, was joined only by Rutledge, J., because his opinion limited state immunity from nondiscriminatory federal taxes to those on "State activities and State-owned property that partake of uniqueness from the point of view of intergovernmental relations. These inherently constitute a class by themselves. Only a State can own a Statehouse; only a State can get income by taxing. These could not be included for purposes of federal taxation in any abstract category of taxpayers without taxing the State as a State. But so long as Congress generally taps a source of revenue by whomsoever earned and not uniquely capable of being earned only by a State, the Constitution of the United States does not forbid it merely because its incidence falls also on a State."

STONE, C.J.'s plurality opinion [d] rejected so narrow a concept of state immunity: "[W]e are not prepared to say that the national government may constitutionally lay a nondiscriminatory tax on every class of property and activities of States and individuals alike. [It] is plain that there may be non-discriminatory

ground than the concurring opinion of Mr. Chief Justice Stone, joined by three Justices. We therefore conclude that a majority supported the Chief Justice's rationale.

c. Rehnquist, J., joined by Burger, C.J., dissented on the user fee issue, which they viewed as the "only issue before" the Court.

d. Only Justices Reed, Murphy and Burton joined the opinion. But see in fn. 15, *Massachusetts v. United States*, Justice Brennan's view that Chief Justice Stone's basis for upholding the tax represented a majority of the Court.

taxes which, when laid on a State, would nevertheless impair the sovereign status of the State quite as much as a like tax imposed by a State on property or activities of the national government. *Mayo v. United States,* 319 U.S. 441, 447, 448, 63 S.Ct. 1137, 1140, 1141, 87 L.Ed. 1504 (1943).[e] This is not because the tax can be regarded as discriminatory but because a sovereign government is the taxpayer, and the tax, even though non-discriminatory, may be regarded as infringing its sovereignty. * * *

"[To] say that the tax fails because the State happens to be the taxpayer is only to say that the State, to some extent undefined, is constitutionally immune from federal taxation. Only when and because the subject of taxation is State property or a State activity must we consider whether such a non-discriminatory tax unduly interferes with the performance of the State's functions of government. If it does, then the fact that the tax is non-discriminatory does not save it. If we are to treat as invalid, because discriminatory, a tax on State activities and State-owned property that partake of uniqueness from the point of view of intergovernmental relations, it is plain that the invalidity is due wholly to the fact that it is a State which is being taxed so as unduly to infringe, in some manner, the performance of its functions as a government which the Constitution recognizes as sovereign."

Douglas, J., joined by Black, J., dissented: "A tax is a powerful, regulatory instrument. Local government in this free land does not exist for itself. The fact that local government may enter the domain of private enterprise and operate a project for profit does not put it in the class of private business enterprise for tax purposes. Local government exists to provide for the welfare of its people, not for a limited group of stockholders. If the federal government can place the local governments on its tax collector's list, their capacity to serve the needs of their citizens is at once hampered or curtailed. The field of federal excise taxation alone is practically without limits. Many state activities are in marginal enterprises where private capital refuses to venture. Add to the cost of these projects a federal tax and the social program may be destroyed before it can be launched. In any case, the repercussions of such a fundamental change on the credit of the States and on their programs to take care of the needy and to build for the future would be considerable."

2. *Major considerations.* What appear to be the major considerations affecting state tax immunity decisions? Is one dominant? Where both state and federal interests are weighty, as when a federal tax on an important, "natural and traditional source of federal revenue" "seriously threatens the continued functioning" of a traditional state function, which interest prevails? Are such cases likely to arise if the Court views "an economic burden on traditional state functions" as "not a sufficient basis for sustaining a claim of immunity"? (*Massachusetts v. United States*).

3. *The role of the "traditional."* Was the rejection of the distinction between state governmental and proprietary functions consistent with retention of a "traditional governmental activities" limit on state immunity? Would that limited scope for state tax immunity adequately protect the state interests underlying such immunity?

Would the interest in avoiding "withdrawal" of federal taxing power be adequately protected if limited to "natural and traditional" sources of federal

---

e. *Mayo* held a state may not impose inspection fees on fertilizer distributed to farmers by the United States.

revenue? Would the same concern cause the Court to look askance at state immunity from a nontraditional federal value-added tax?

III. FEDERAL IMMUNITY FROM STATE TAXES

Federal immunity from state taxes has not undergone the same attrition as state immunity from federal taxes. Indeed, since *McCulloch* "the Court has never questioned the propriety of absolute federal immunity from state taxation." [a] Nor has it upheld a single state tax laid "directly upon the United States" [b] without the consent of Congress,[c] despite its wholesale erasure of immunity for private taxpayers, starting in 1938.[d] But the Court has carefully restricted such immunity to state taxes imposed "on the United States itself, or an agency or instrumentality so closely connected to the Government that the two cannot realistically be viewed as separate entities, at least insofar as the activity being taxed is concerned." [e]

Is such sweeping federal immunity justified in view of the much more limited state immunity from federal taxes? To what may the difference be attributable? A view that all federal activities are "governmental"? [f] The supremacy clause? Judicial deference to the power of Congress to permit or not permit state taxes on federal activities, depending on Congress' view of the need to protect the federal activity? [g] The differing weight and respect due the action of a national legislature, and that due a single state legislature whose action has adverse impact on a national interest? [h]

Federal immunity from state regulation. For consideration of analogous federal immunity from state *regulatory* power, and the extent of immunity for individuals acting on behalf of the government, see Tribe, *American Constitutional Law* 391–394 (1978).

IV. STATE IMMUNITY FROM FEDERAL REGULATION

MARYLAND v. WIRTZ (1968), Sec. 2, III, B supra, per HARLAN, J., upheld 7 to 2 the 1966 extension of the Fair Labor Standards Act to state schools and hospitals. Noting that the Act excluded professional personnel and regulated only minimum wages and maximum hours without premium overtime pay, the opinion stressed that "Congress has 'interfered with' these state functions only to the extent of providing that when the State employs people in performing such functions it is subject to the same restrictions as a wide range of other employers whose activities affect commerce, including privately operated schools and hospitals." It found "not tenable" the argument that the commerce power "must

---

a. See *United States v. New Mexico,* 455 U.S. 720, 733, 102 S.Ct. 1373, 1382, 71 L.Ed.2d 580, 591 (1982). (government contractors whose tax costs are passed on to the federal government are not to that extent "government instrumentalities" immune from state taxation.)

b. Ibid.

c. See e.g., *Federal Land Bank v. Bismarck Lumber Co.,* 314 U.S. 95, 62 S.Ct. 1, 86 L.Ed. 65 (1941) (lending functions); *New York ex rel. Rogers v. Graves,* 299 U.S. 401, 57 S.Ct. 269, 81 L.Ed. 306 (1937) (operation of Panama railroad); *Mayo v. United States,* 319 U.S. 441, 63 S.Ct. 1137, 87 L.Ed. 1504 (1943) (distribution of fertilizer); *Dep't of Employ. v. United States,*

385 U.S. 355, 87 S.Ct. 464, 17 L.Ed.2d 414 (1966) (American Red Cross); *United States v. Mississippi Tax Comm'n,* 421 U.S. 599, 95 S.Ct. 1872, 44 L.Ed.2d 104 (1975) (sale of liquor at post exchange on military installation).

d. See note 3, Part I supra.

e. *United States v. New Mexico,* supra.

f. Cf., e.g., *Graves v. New York, ex rel. O'Keefe,* 306 U.S. 466, 478, 59 S.Ct. 595, 597, 83 L.Ed. 927, 932 (1939).

g. Cf. id., at 306 U.S. 479–80, 59 S.Ct. 598, 83 L.Ed. 932–33.

h. Cf. *McCulloch v. Maryland,* Part I; *Helvering v. Gerhardt,* Part I supra, 304 U.S. at 412, 58 S.Ct. at 971–72, 82 L.Ed. at 1433.

yield to state sovereignty in the performance of governmental functions." In exercising a "delegated power" the federal government "may override countervailing state interests whether these be described as 'governmental' or 'proprietary' in character." The argument that *United States v. California* [a] was not "controlling" because the "state activity involved there was less central to state sovereignty misses the mark. This Court [will] not carve up the commerce power to protect enterprises indistinguishable in their effect on commerce from private businesses, simply because those enterprises happen to be run by the States for the benefit of their citizens." [b]

NATIONAL LEAGUE OF CITIES v. USERY

426 U.S. 833, 96 S.Ct. 2465, 49 L.Ed.2d 245 (1976).

MR. JUSTICE REHNQUIST delivered the opinion of the Court.

[In actions by states, cities, the National League of Cities, and the National Governors Council, the D.C. District Court invoked *Wirtz* to uphold the 1974 extension of the Fair Labor Standards Act to all employees of states and their subdivisions.[c] The Court reversed, 5 to 4.]

[Appellants] asserted in effect that when Congress sought to apply the Fair Labor Standards Act provisions virtually across the board to employees of state and municipal governments it "infringed a constitutional prohibition" running in favor of the States *as States*. The gist of their complaint was [that] the established constitutional doctrine of intergovernmental immunity consistently recognized in a long series of our cases affirmatively prevented the exercise of [the commerce power] in the manner which Congress chose in [1974].

[Congressional] enactments which may be fully within the grant of legislative authority contained in the Commerce Clause may nonetheless be invalid because found to offend against the right to trial by jury contained in the Sixth Amendment, or the Due Process Clause of the Fifth Amendment. Appellants' essential contention is that the 1974 amendments to the Act, while undoubtedly within the scope of the Commerce Clause, encounter a similar constitutional barrier because they are to be applied directly to the States and subdivisions of States as employers.

This Court has never doubted that there are limits upon the power of Congress to override state sovereignty, even when exercising its otherwise plenary powers to tax or to regulate commerce. [In] *Wirtz*, for example, the Court took care to assure the appellants that it had "ample power to [prevent] 'the utter destruction of the State as a sovereign political entity,'" which they feared. [In] *Fry*,[d] the Court recognized that an express declaration of this

a. 297 U.S. 175, 56 S.Ct. 421, 80 L.Ed. 567 (1936) (unanimously upholding application of the federal Safety Appliance Act to a state-owned and operated railroad, which served San Francisco wharves and industrial plants:

"The sovereign power of the states is necessarily diminished to the extent of the grants of power to the federal government in the Constitution. * * * [Unlike limitations on federal taxing power] there is no such limitation upon the plenary power to regulate commerce.")

b. Douglas, J., joined by Stewart, J., dissented, expressing concerns related to those underlying his *New York v. United States* dis-

sent: "In none of [the earlier cases] did the federal regulation overwhelm state fiscal policy. It is one thing to force a State to purchase safety equipment for its railroad and another to force it either to spend several million more dollars on hospitals and schools or substantially reduce services in these areas. [In] this case the State as a sovereign power is being seriously tampered with, potentially crippled."

c. The Act exempted executive, administrative, and professional personnel.

d. *Fry v. United States*, 421 U.S. 542, 95 S.Ct. 1792, 44 L.Ed.2d 363 (1975) upheld Congress' power under the commerce clause to combat inflation by limiting wage increases

limitation is found in the Tenth Amendment: "While the Tenth Amendment has been characterized as a 'truism,' stating merely that 'all is retained which has not been surrendered,' it is not without significance. The Amendment expressly declares the constitutional policy that Congress may not exercise power in a fashion that impairs the States' integrity or their ability to function effectively in a federal system."

In *New York v. United States,* Mr. Chief Justice Stone, speaking for four Members of an eight-Member Court in rejecting the proposition that Congress could impose taxes on the States so long as it did so in a non-discriminatory manner, observed: "[W]e could hardly say that a general nondiscriminatory real estate tax (apportioned), or an income tax laid upon citizens and States alike could be constitutionally applied to the State's capitol, its State-house, its public school houses, public parks, or its revenues from taxes, or school lands, even though all real property and all income of the citizen is taxed." [14]   *   *   *

Appellee Secretary argues that the cases in which this Court has upheld sweeping exercises of authority by Congress, even though those exercises pre-empted state regulation of the private sector, have already curtailed the sovereignty of the States quite as much as the 1974 amendments to the Fair Labor Standards Act. We do not agree. It is one thing to recognize the authority of Congress to enact laws regulating individual businesses necessarily subject to the dual sovereignty of the government of the Nation and of the State in which they reside. It is quite another to uphold a similar exercise of congressional authority directed not to private citizens, but to the States as States. We have repeatedly recognized that there are attributes of sovereignty attaching to every state government which may not be impaired by Congress, not because Congress may lack an affirmative grant of legislative authority to reach the matter, but because the Constitution prohibits it from exercising the authority in that manner. In *Coyle v. Smith,* 221 U.S. 559, 31 S.Ct. 688, 55 L.Ed. 853 (1911), the Court gave this example of such an attribute: "The power to locate its own seat of government and to determine when and how it shall be changed from one place to another, and to appropriate its own public funds for that purpose, are essentially and peculiarly state powers.   *   *   *"

One undoubted attribute of state sovereignty is the States' power to determine the wages which shall be paid to those whom they employ in order to carry out their governmental functions, what hours those persons will work, and what compensation will be provided where these employees may be called upon to work overtime. The question we must resolve in this case, then, is whether these determinations are "functions essential to separate and independent existence," *Coyle,* so that Congress may not abrogate the States' otherwise plenary authority to make them.   *   *   *

for state and local government employees, along with all others in the economy, citing *Wirtz:* "It seems inescapable that the effectiveness of federal action would have been drastically impaired if wage increases to this sizeable group of employees (14% of the Nation's work force) were left outside the reach of these emergency federal wage controls." Rehnquist, J., dissented, urging the overruling of *Wirtz.* Douglas, J., would have dismissed the writ as improvidently granted.

14. Mr. Justice Brennan suggests that "the Chief Justice was addressing not the question of a state sovereignty restraint upon the exercise of the commerce power, but rather the principle of implied immunity of the States and Federal Government from taxation by the other." The asserted distinction, however, escapes us. Surely the federal power to tax is no less a delegated power than is the commerce power: both find their genesis in Art. I, § 8. Nor can characterizing the limitation recognized upon the federal taxing power as an "implied immunity" obscure the fact that this "immunity" is derived from the sovereignty of the States and the concomitant barriers which such sovereignty presents to otherwise plenary federal authority.

Increased costs are not, of course, the only adverse effects which compliance with the Act will visit upon state and local governments, and in turn upon the citizens who depend upon those governments. In its complaint in intervention, for example, California asserted that it could not comply with the overtime costs (approximately $750,000 per year) which the Act required to be paid to California Highway Patrol cadets during their academy training program. California reported that it had thus been forced to reduce its academy training program from 2,080 hours to only 960 hours, a compromise undoubtedly of substantial importance to those whose safety and welfare may depend upon the preparedness of the California Highway Patrol. * * *

Quite apart from the substantial costs imposed upon the States and their political subdivisions, the Act displaces state policies regarding the manner in which they will structure delivery of those governmental services which their citizens require. [The] State might wish to employ persons with little or no training or those who wish to work on a casual basis, or those who for some other reason do not possess minimum employment requirements, and pay them less than the federally prescribed minimum wage. It may wish to offer part time or summer employment to teenagers at a figure less than the minimum wage, and if unable to do so may decline to offer such employment at all. But the Act would forbid such choices by the States. The only "discretion" left to them under the Act is either to attempt to increase their revenue to meet the additional financial burden imposed upon them by paying congressionally prescribed wages to their existing complement of employees, or to reduce that complement to a number which can be paid the federal minimum wage without increasing revenue. * * *

This dilemma [differs] from that faced by private employers [in that] a State is not merely a factor in the "shifting economic arrangements" of the private sector [but] is itself a coordinate element in the system established by the Framers for governing our Federal Union. * * *

This congressionally imposed displacement of state decisions may substantially restructure traditional ways in which the local governments have arranged their affairs. [The] requirement imposing premium rates upon any employment in excess of what Congress has decided is appropriate for a governmental employee's workweek, for example, appears likely to have the effect of coercing the States to structure work periods in some employment areas, such as police and fire protection, in a manner substantially different from practices which have long been commonly accepted among local governments of this Nation. In addition, appellee represents that the Act will require that the premium compensation for overtime worked must be paid in cash rather than with compensatory time off, unless such compensatory time is taken in the same pay period. This too appears likely to be highly disruptive of accepted employment practices in many governmental areas where the demand for a number of employees to perform important jobs for extended periods on short notice can be both unpredictable and critical. * * *

* * * Application [of the 1974 amendments will] significantly alter or displace the States' abilities to structure employer-employee relationships in such areas as fire prevention, police protection, sanitation, public health, and parks and recreation. These activities are typical of those performed by state and local governments in discharging their dual functions of administering the public law and furnishing public services. [If] Congress may withdraw from the States the authority to make those fundamental employment decisions upon

which their systems for performance of these functions must rest, we think there would be little left of the States' "separate and independent existence." *Coyle.* Thus, [the] dispositive factor is that Congress has attempted to exercise its Commerce Clause authority to prescribe minimum wages and maximum hours to be paid by the States in their capacities as sovereign governments. In so doing, Congress has sought to wield its power in a fashion that would impair the States' "ability to function effectively within a federal system," *Fry.* This exercise of congressional authority does not comport with the federal system of government embodied in the Constitution. We hold that insofar as the challenged amendments operate to directly displace the States' freedom to structure integral operations in areas of traditional governmental functions, they are not within the authority granted Congress by Art. I, § 8, cl. 3.[17]

[We] think our holding today quite consistent with *Fry.* The enactment at issue there was occasioned by an extremely serious problem which endangered the well-being of all the component parts of our federal system and which only collective action by the National Government might forestall. The means selected were carefully drafted so as not to interfere with the States' freedom beyond a very limited, specific period of time. The effect of the across-the-board freeze authorized by that Act, moreover, displaced no state choices as to how governmental operations should be structured nor did it force the States to remake such choices themselves. Instead, it merely required that the wage scales and employment relationships which the States themselves had chosen be maintained during the period of the emergency. * * *

[We] have reaffirmed today that the States as States stand on a quite different footing than an individual or a corporation when challenging the exercise of Congress' power to regulate commerce. * * * [Congress] may not exercise that power so as to force directly upon the States its choices as to how essential decisions regarding the conduct of integral governmental functions are to be made. [While] there are obvious differences between the schools and hospitals involved in *Wirtz,* and the fire and police departments affected here, each provides an integral portion of those governmental services which the States and their political subdivisions have traditionally afforded their citizens. We are therefore persuaded that *Wirtz* must be overruled. * * *

MR. JUSTICE BLACKMUN, concurring.

* * * Although I am not untroubled by certain possible implications of the Court's opinion—some of them suggested by the dissents—I do not read the opinion so despairingly as does my Brother Brennan. In my view, the result with respect to the statute under challenge here is necessarily correct. I may misinterpret the Court's opinion, but it seems to me that it adopts a balancing approach, and does not outlaw federal power in areas such as environmental protection, where the federal interest is demonstrably greater and where state facility compliance with imposed federal standards would be essential. With this understanding on my part of the Court's opinion, I join it.

MR. JUSTICE BRENNAN, with whom MR. JUSTICE WHITE and MR. JUSTICE MARSHALL join, dissenting.

[My] Brethren do not successfully obscure today's patent usurpation of the role reserved for the political process by their purported discovery in the

---

17. We express no view as to whether different results might obtain if Congress seeks to affect integral operations of state governments by exercising authority granted it under other sections of the Constitution such as the Spending Power, Art. I, § 8, cl. 1, or § 5 of the Fourteenth Amendment [considered in note 6 infra].

Constitution of a restraint derived from sovereignty of the States on Congress' exercise of the commerce power. Chief Justice Marshall recognized that limitations "prescribed in the constitution," *Gibbons,* restrain Congress' exercise of the power. Thus laws within the commerce power may not infringe individual liberties protected by the First Amendment, the Fifth Amendment, or the Sixth Amendment. But there is no restraint based on state sovereignty requiring or permitting judicial enforcement anywhere expressed in the Constitution; our decisions over the last century and a half have explicitly rejected the existence of any such restraint on the commerce power. * * *

The reliance of my Brethren upon the Tenth Amendment as "an express declaration of [a state sovereignty] limitation" not only suggests that they overrule governing decisions of this Court that address this question but must astound scholars of the Constitution. For not only early decisions, *Gibbons; McCulloch,* hold that nothing in the Tenth Amendment constitutes a limitation on congressional exercise of powers delegated by the Constitution to Congress. See Frankfurter, *The Commerce Power Under Marshall, Taney, and Waite* 39–40 (1937). Rather, as the Tenth Amendment's significance was more recently summarized: "The amendment states but a truism that all is retained which has not been surrendered. [From] the beginning and for many years the amendment has been construed as not depriving the national government of authority to resort to all means for the exercise of a granted power which are appropriate and plainly adapted to the permitted end." *Darby.*

My Brethren purport to find support for their novel state-sovereignty doctrine in the concurring opinion of Mr. Chief Justice Stone in *New York v. United States.* That reliance is plainly misplaced. * * * [Mr.] Chief Justice Stone observed in his concurring opinion that "a federal tax which is not discriminatory as to the subject matter may nevertheless so affect the State, merely because it is a State that is being taxed, as to interfere unduly with the State's performance of its sovereign functions of government." But the Chief Justice was addressing not the question of a state sovereignty restraint upon the exercise of the commerce power, but rather the principle of implied immunity of the States and Federal Government from taxation by the other. * * *

My Brother Blackmun suggests that controlling judicial supervision of the relationship between the States and our National Government by use of a balancing approach diminishes the ominous implications of today's decision. Such an approach, however, is a thinly veiled rationalization for judicial supervision of a policy judgment that our system of government reserves to Congress.

Judicial restraint in this area merely recognizes that the political branches of our Government are structured to protect the interests of the States, as well as the Nation as a whole, and that the States are fully able to protect their own interests in the premises. Congress is constituted of representatives in both Senate and House *elected from the States.* Decisions upon the extent of federal intervention under the Commerce Clause into the affairs of the States are in that sense decisions of the States themselves. [See] Wechsler, *The Political Safeguards of Federalism: The Role of the States in the Composition and Selection of the National Government,* 54 Col.L.Rev. 543 (1954). [Any] realistic assessment of our federal political system, dominated as it is by representatives of the people *elected from the States,* yields the conclusion that it is highly unlikely that those representatives will ever be motivated to disregard totally the concerns of these [States].

We are left then with a catastrophic judicial body blow at Congress' power under the Commerce Clause. Even if Congress may nevertheless accomplish its objectives—for example, by conditioning grants of federal funds upon compliance with federal minimum wage and overtime standards, cf., *Oklahoma v. CSC,* [Sec. III infra]—there is an ominous portent of disruption of our constitutional structure implicit in today's mischievous decision. * * * [e]

Notes

1. *The short life of National League of Cities.* In the first four Supreme Court cases in which counsel invoked the *National League of Cities* principle the Court found it not applicable and sustained:

   a. Federal regulation of privately operated surface mining, displacing state regulation unless the states opted to regulate under federal standards to avoid total preemption.[a]

   b. Federal regulation of labor-management relations on the state-owned and operated Long Island Railroad, found not to be a "traditional" state governmental function.[b]

   c. Federal legislation that required state agencies regulating gas and electrical utilities to "consider" federally proposed rate designs and standards under federally prescribed notice and comment procedures, and to give reasons for their decisions on the federal proposals.[c]

   d. Application of the federal Age Discrimination in Employment Act to bar mandatory retirement of state game and fish wardens at age 55.[d]

   The first two decisions were without dissent.[e] The third and fourth were 5 to 4 decisions in which Blackmun, J. joined the National League of Cities dissenters.

2. *The dissenters prevail.* When the issue arose in a fifth case Justice Blackmun joined the dissenters to overrule *National League of Cities.*[f]

GARCIA v. SAN ANTONIO METRO. TRANSIT AUTHORITY [SAMTA]
__ U.S. __, 105 S.Ct. 1005, 83 L.Ed.2d 1016 (1985).

MR. JUSTICE BLACKMUN delivered the opinion of the Court.

[*Garcia* upheld application of the Fair Labor Standards Act to a municipally-owned and operated mass transit system and expressly overruled *National*

---

e. Stevens, J., also filed a dissenting opinion.

a. *Hodel v. Virginia Surface Mining & Reclamation Ass'n* (1981), Sec. 2, VI, supra. The opinion drew a "sharp distinction between congressional regulation of private persons [and] federal regulation 'directed [to] States as States'".

b. *United Transp. Union v. Long Island R. Co.,* 455 U.S. 678, 102 S.Ct. 1349, 71 L.Ed.2d 547 (1982). The unanimous Burger opinion noted that the regulatory scheme for railroad collective bargaining provided by the Railway Labor Act "for the past 56 years" was thought essential by Congress "to prevent disruptions in vital rail service." See the opinions in *Garcia,* infra, for discussion of the *Long Island*

consideration of the "traditional governmental function" standard.

c. *Federal Energy Regulatory Commission v. Mississippi,* 456 U.S. 742, 102 S.Ct. 2126, 72 L.Ed.2d 532 (1982). See note 5 after Garcia for brief consideration of this case.

d. *Equal Employment Opportunities Comm'n v. Wyoming,* 460 U.S. 226, 103 S.Ct. 1054, 75 L.Ed.2d 18 (1983).

e. In *Hodel* Rehnquist, J., concurred in the result but confined his separate opinion to the commerce clause issue, not commenting on the *National League of Cities* issue.

f. See *Garcia v. San Antonio Metro. Transit Auth.,* this page.

League of Cities. The four dissenters in *National League* joined in the Blackmun opinion.]

In [*National League of Cities*] this Court, by a sharply divided vote, ruled that the Commerce Clause does not empower Congress to enforce the minimum-wage and overtime provisions of the Fair Labor Standards Act (FLSA) against the States "in areas of traditional governmental functions." [Since] then, federal and state courts have struggled with the task, thus imposed, of identifying a traditional function for purposes of state immunity under the Commerce Clause.

[Our] examination of this "function" standard applied in these and other cases over the last eight years now persuades us that the attempt to draw the boundaries of state regulatory immunity in terms of "traditional governmental function" is not only unworkable but is inconsistent with established principles of federalism and, indeed, with those very federalism principles on which *National League of Cities* purported to rest. That case, accordingly, is overruled.

* * *

II

The prerequisites for governmental immunity under *National League of Cities* were summarized by this Court in *Hodel.* Under that summary, four conditions must be satisfied before a state activity may be deemed immune from a particular federal regulation under the Commerce Clause. First, it is said that the federal statute at issue must regulate "the 'States as States.' " Second, the statute must "address matters that are indisputably 'attribute[s] of state sovereignty.' " Third, state compliance with the federal obligation must "directly impair [the States'] ability 'to structure integral operations in areas of traditional governmental functions.' " Finally, the relation of state and federal interests must not be such that "the nature of the federal interest * * * justifies state submission."

The controversy in the present cases has focused on the third *Hodel* requirement—that the challenged federal statute trench on "traditional governmental functions." The District Court voiced a common concern: "Despite the abundance of adjectives, identifying which particular state functions are immune remains difficult." Just how troublesome the task has been is revealed by the results reached in other federal cases. Thus, courts have held that regulating ambulance services, * * * licensing automobile drivers, operating a municipal airport, performing solid waste disposal, and operating a highway authority, are functions *protected* under *National League of Cities.* At the same time, courts have held that issuance of industrial development bonds, regulation of intrastate natural gas sales, regulation of traffic on public roads, regulation of air transportation, operation of a telephone system, leasing and sale of natural gas, operation of a mental health facility, and provision of in-house domestic services for the aged and handicapped, are *not* entitled to immunity. We find it difficult, if not impossible, to identify an organizing principle that places each of the cases in the first group on one side of a line and each of the cases in the second group on the other side. * * *

Thus far, this Court itself has made little headway in defining the scope of the governmental functions deemed protected under *National League of Cities.* In that case the Court set forth examples of protected and unprotected functions, but provided no explanation of how those examples were identified. The only other case in which the Court has had occasion to address the problem is *Long*

Island. We there observed: "The determination of whether a federal law impairs a state's authority with respect to 'areas of traditional [state] functions' may at times be a difficult one." The accuracy of that statement is demonstrated by this Court's own difficulties in *Long Island* in developing a workable standard for "traditional governmental functions." We relied in large part there on "the *historical reality* that the operation of railroads is not among the functions *traditionally* performed by state and local governments," but we simultaneously disavowed "a static historical view of state functions generally immune from federal regulation." (first emphasis added; second emphasis in original). We held that the inquiry into a particular function's "traditional" nature was merely a means of determining whether the federal statute at issue unduly handicaps "basic state prerogatives," but we did not offer an explanation of what makes one state function a "basic prerogative" and another function not basic. Finally, having disclaimed a rigid reliance on the historical pedigree of state involvement in a particular area, we nonetheless found it appropriate to emphasize the extended historical record of *federal* involvement in the field of rail transportation. * * *

The distinction [between governmental and proprietary functions that] the Court discarded as unworkable in the field of tax immunity has proved no more fruitful in the field of regulatory immunity under the Commerce Clause. Neither do any of the alternative standards that might be employed to distinguish between protected and unprotected governmental functions appear manageable. We rejected the possibility of making immunity turn on a purely historical standard of "tradition" in *Long Island,* and properly so. The most obvious defect of a historical approach to state immunity is that it prevents a court from accommodating changes in the historical functions of States, changes that have resulted in a number of once-private functions like education being assumed by the States and their subdivisions. At the same time, the only apparent virtue of a rigorous historical standard, namely, its promise of a reasonably objective measure for state immunity, is illusory. Reliance on history as an organizing principle results in linedrawing of the most arbitrary sort; the genesis of state governmental functions stretches over a historical continuum from before the Revolution to the present, and courts would have to decide by fiat precisely how longstanding a pattern of state involvement had to be for federal regulatory authority to be defeated.

A nonhistorical standard for selecting immune governmental functions is likely to be just as unworkable as is a historical standard. The goal of identifying "uniquely" governmental functions, for example, has been rejected by the Court in the field of government tort liability in part because the notion of a "uniquely" governmental function is unmanageable. * * *

We believe, however, that there is a more fundamental problem at work here, a problem that explains why the Court was never able to provide a basis for the governmental/proprietary distinction in the intergovernmental tax immunity cases and why an attempt to draw similar distinctions with respect to federal regulatory authority under *National League of Cities* is unlikely to succeed regardless of how the distinctions are phrased. The problem is that neither the governmental/proprietary distinction nor any other that purports to separate out important governmental functions can be faithful to the role of federalism in a democratic society. The essence of our federal system is that within the realm of authority left open to them under the Constitution, the States must be equally free to engage in any activity that their citizens choose for the common weal, no matter how unorthodox or unnecessary anyone else—

including the judiciary—deems state involvement to be. Any rule of state immunity that looks to the "traditional," "integral," or "necessary" nature of governmental functions inevitably invites an unelected federal judiciary to make decisions about which state policies it favors and which ones it dislikes. * * *

We therefore now reject, as unsound in principle and unworkable in practice, a rule of state immunity from federal regulation that turns on a judicial appraisal of whether a particular governmental function is "integral" or "traditional." Any such rule leads to inconsistent results at the same time that it disserves principles of democratic self-governance, and it breeds inconsistency precisely because it is divorced from those principles. If there are to be limits on the Federal Government's power to interfere with state functions—as undoubtedly there are—we must look elsewhere to find them. We accordingly return to the underlying issue that confronted this Court in *National League of Cities*—the manner in which the Constitution insulates States from the reach of Congress' power under the Commerce Clause.

III

The central theme of *National League of Cities* was that the States occupy a special position in our constitutional system and that the scope of Congress' authority under the Commerce Clause must reflect that position. * * * *National League of Cities* reflected the general conviction that the Constitution precludes "the National Government [from] devour[ing] the essentials of state sovereignty." *Maryland v. Wirtz*, 392 U.S., at 205 (dissenting opinion). In order to be faithful to the underlying federal premises of the Constitution, courts must look for the "postulates which limit and control."

[We] doubt that courts ultimately can identify principled constitutional limitations on the scope of Congress' Commerce Clause powers over the States merely by relying on a priori definitions of state sovereignty. In part, this is because of the elusiveness of objective criteria for "fundamental" elements of state sovereignty, a problem we have witnessed in the search for "traditional governmental functions." There is, however, a more fundamental reason: the sovereignty of the States is limited by the Constitution itself. A variety of sovereign powers, for example, are withdrawn from the States by Article I, § 10. Section 8 of the same Article works an equally sharp contraction of state sovereignty by authorizing Congress to exercise a wide range of legislative powers and (in conjunction with the Supremacy Clause of Article VI) to displace contrary state legislation. See *Hodel*. By providing for final review of questions of federal law in this Court, Article III curtails the sovereign power of the States' judiciaries to make authoritative determinations of law. Finally, the developed application, through the Fourteenth Amendment, of the greater part of the Bill of Rights to the States limits the sovereign authority that States otherwise would possess to legislate with respect to their citizens and to conduct their own affairs.

The States unquestionably do "retai[n] a significant measure of sovereign authority." *EEOC v. Wyoming* (Powell, J., dissenting). They do so, however, only to the extent that the Constitution has not divested them of their original powers and transferred those powers to the Federal Government. [The] fact that the States remain sovereign as to all powers not vested in Congress or denied them by the Constitution offers no guidance about where the frontier between state and federal power lies. In short, we have no license to employ freestanding conceptions of state sovereignty when measuring congressional authority under the Commerce Clause.

When we look for the States' "residuary and inviolable sovereignty," *The Federalist* No. 39, p. 285 (B. Wright ed. 1961) (J. Madison), in the shape of the constitutional scheme rather than in predetermined notions of sovereign power, a different measure of state sovereignty emerges. Apart from the limitation on federal authority inherent in the delegated nature of Congress' Article I powers, the principal means chosen by the Framers to ensure the role of the States in the federal system lies in the structure of the Federal Government itself. It is no novelty to observe that the composition of the Federal Government was designed in large part to protect the States from overreaching by Congress.[11] The Framers thus gave the States a role in the selection both of the Executive and the Legislative Branches of the Federal Government. The States were vested with indirect influence over the House of Representatives and the Presidency by their control of electoral qualifications and their role in presidential elections. They were given more direct influence in the Senate, where each State received equal representation and each Senator was to be selected by the legislature of his State. The significance attached to the States' equal representation in the Senate is underscored by the prohibition of any constitutional amendment divesting a State of equal representation without the State's consent. Art. V.

The extent to which the structure of the Federal Government itself was relied on to insulate the interests of the States is evident in the views of the Framers. James Madison explained that the Federal Government "will partake sufficiently of the spirit [of the States], to be disinclined to invade the rights of the individual States, or the prerogatives of their governments." *The Federalist* No. 46, p. 332 (B. Wright ed. 1961). [In] short, the Framers chose to rely on a federal system in which special restraints on federal power over the States inhered principally in the workings of the National Government itself, rather than in discrete limitations on the objects of federal authority. State sovereign interests, then, are more properly protected by procedural safeguards inherent in the structure of the federal system than by judicially created limitations on federal power.

The effectiveness of the federal political process in preserving the States' interests is apparent even today in the course of federal legislation. On the one hand, the States have been able to direct a substantial proportion of federal revenues into their own treasuries in the form of general and program-specific grants in aid. [At] the same time that the States have exercised their influence to obtain federal support, they have been able to exempt themselves from a wide variety of obligations imposed by Congress under the Commerce Clause. For example, the Federal Power Act, the National Labor Relations Act, the Labor-Management Reporting and Disclosure Act, the Occupational Safety and Health Act, the Employee Retirement Insurance Security Act, and the Sherman Act all contain express or implied exemptions for States and their subdivisions. The fact that some federal statutes such as the FLSA extend general obligations to the States cannot obscure the extent to which the political position of the States in the federal system has served to minimize the burdens that the States bear under the Commerce Clause.

---

11. See, e.g., J. Choper, *Judicial Review and the National Political Process* 175–184 (1980); Wechsler, *The Political Safeguards of Federalism: The Role of the States in the Composition and Selection of the National* Government, 54 Colum.L.Rev. 543 (1954); La Pierre, *The Political Safeguards of Federalism, Redux: Intergovernmental Immunity and the States as Agents of the Nation*, 60 Wash. U.L.Q. 779 (1982).

[Against] this background, we are convinced that the fundamental limitation that the constitutional scheme imposes on the Commerce Clause to protect the "States as States" is one of process rather than one of result. Any substantive restraint on the exercise of Commerce Clause powers must find its justification in the procedural nature of this basic limitation, and it must be tailored to compensate for possible failings in the national political process rather than to dictate a "sacred province of state autonomy." *EEOC.*

Insofar as the present cases are concerned, then, we need go no further than to state that we perceive nothing in the overtime and minimum-wage requirements of the FLSA, as applied to SAMTA, that is destructive of state sovereignty or violative of any constitutional provision. SAMTA faces nothing more than the same minimum-wage and overtime obligations that hundreds of thousands of other employers, public as well as private, have to meet.

In these cases, the status of public mass transit simply underscores the extent to which the structural protections of the Constitution insulate the States from federally imposed burdens. When Congress first subjected state mass-transit systems to FLSA obligations in 1966, and when it expanded those obligations in 1974, it simultaneously provided extensive funding for state and local mass transit. [In] short, Congress has not simply placed a financial burden on the shoulders of States and localities that operate mass-transit systems, but has provided substantial countervailing financial assistance as well, assistance that may leave individual mass transit systems better off than they would have been had Congress never intervened at all in the area. Congress' treatment of public mass transit reinforces our conviction that the national political process systematically protects States from the risk of having their functions in that area handicapped by Commerce Clause regulation.

IV

This analysis makes clear that Congress' action in affording SAMTA employees the protections of the wage and hour provisions of the FLSA contravened no affirmative limit on Congress' power under the Commerce Clause. * * *

Of course, we continue to recognize that the States occupy a special and specific position in our constitutional system and that the scope of Congress' authority under the Commerce Clause must reflect that position. But the principal and basic limit on the federal commerce power is that inherent in all congressional action—the built-in restraints that our system provides through state participation in federal governmental action. The political process ensures that laws that unduly burden the States will not be promulgated. In the factual setting of these cases the internal safeguards of the political process have performed as intended. * * *

We do not lightly overrule recent precedent. We have not hesitated, however, when it has become apparent that a prior decision has departed from a proper understanding of congressional power under the Commerce Clause. *Darby.* Due respect for the reach of congressional power within the federal system mandates that we do so now. *National League of Cities* is overruled. * * *

JUSTICE POWELL, with whom THE CHIEF JUSTICE, JUSTICE REHNQUIST, and JUSTICE O'CONNOR join, dissenting.

I

[A] unique feature of the United States is the *federal* system of government guaranteed by the Constitution and implicit in the very name of our country. Despite some genuflecting in the Court's opinion to the concept of federalism, today's decision effectively reduces the Tenth Amendment to meaningless rhetoric when Congress acts pursuant to the Commerce Clause. * * *

To leave no doubt about its intention, the Court renounces its decision in *National League of Cities* because it "inevitably invites an unelected federal judiciary to make decisions about which state policies it favors and which ones it dislikes." In other words, the extent to which the States may exercise their authority, when Congress purports to act under the Commerce Clause, henceforth is to be determined from time to time by political decisions made by members of the federal government, decisions the Court says will not be subject to judicial review. * * *

II

A. Much of the Court's opinion is devoted to arguing that it is difficult to define *a priori* "traditional governmental functions." *National League of Cities* neither engaged in, nor required, such a task.[4] The Court discusses and condemns as standards "traditional governmental function[s]," "purely historical" functions, " 'uniquely' governmental functions," and " 'necessary' governmental services." But nowhere does it mention that *National League of Cities* adopted a familiar type of balancing test for determining whether Commerce Clause enactments transgress constitutional limitations imposed by the federal nature of our system of government. [The] Court's analysis reaffirming *Fry* explicitly weighed the seriousness of the problem addressed by the federal legislation at issue in that case, against the effects of compliance on State sovereignty. Our subsequent decisions also adopted this approach of weighing the respective interests of the States and federal government.[5] [In] overruling *National League of Cities,* the Court incorrectly characterizes the mode of analysis established therein and developed in subsequent cases.

B. Today's opinion does not explain how the States' role in the electoral process guarantees that particular exercises of the Commerce Clause power will not infringe on residual State sovereignty. Members of Congress are elected from the various States, but once in office they are members of the federal government. Although the States participate in the Electoral College, this is hardly a reason to view the President as a representative of the States' interest against federal encroachment. We noted recently "the hydraulic pressure

---

4. [Rather] than carefully analyzing the case law, the Court simply lists various functions thought to be protected or unprotected by courts interpreting *National League of Cities*. In the cited cases, however, the courts considered the issue of State immunity on the specific facts at issue; they did not make blanket pronouncements that particular things inherently qualified as traditional governmental functions or did not. Having thus considered the cases out of context, it was not difficult for the Court to conclude that there is no "organizing principle" among them.

5. In undertaking such balancing, we have considered, on the one hand, the strength of the federal interest in the challenged legislation and the impact of exempting the States from its reach. Central to our inquiry into the federal interest is how closely the challenged action implicates the central concerns of the Commerce Clause, viz., the promotion of a national economy and free trade among the states. [Similarly,] we have considered whether exempting States from federal regulation would undermine the goals of the federal program. [On] the other hand, we have also assessed the injury done to the States if forced to comply with federal Commerce Clause enactments.

inherent within each of the separate Branches to exceed the outer limits of its power * * *." *Immigration and Naturalization Service v. Chadha,* [p. 161 infra.] The Court offers no reason to think that this pressure will not operate when Congress seeks to invoke its powers under the Commerce Clause, notwithstanding the electoral role of the States.[9]

[The] States' success at obtaining federal funds for various projects and exemptions from the obligations of some federal statutes [is] not relevant to the question whether the political *processes* are the proper means of enforcing constitutional limitations. The fact that Congress generally does not transgress constitutional limits on its power to reach State activities does not make judicial review any less necessary to rectify the cases in which it does do so. The States' role in our system of government is a matter of constitutional law, not of legislative grace. * * *

III

A. In our federal system, the States have a major role that cannot be preempted by the national government. [Much] of the initial opposition to the Constitution was rooted in the fear that the national government would be too powerful and eventually would eliminate the States as viable political entities. This concern was voiced repeatedly until proponents of the Constitution made assurances that a bill of rights, including a provision explicitly reserving powers in the States, would be among the first business of the new Congress. * * *

This history, which the Court simply ignores, [exposes] the fundamental character of the Court's error today. Far from being "unsound in principle," judicial enforcement of the Tenth Amendment is essential to maintaining the federal system so carefully designed by the Framers and adopted in the Constitution. * * *

B. [The] Framers believed that the separate sphere of sovereignty reserved to the States would ensure that the States would serve as an effective "counterpoise" to the power of the federal government. The States would serve this essential role because they would attract and retain the loyalty of their citizens. [Hamilton] argued that the States "regulat[e] all those personal interests and familiar concerns to which the sensibility of individuals is more immediately awake * * *." *The Federalist* No. 17, p. 107. Thus, he maintained that the people would perceive the States as "the immediate and most visible guardian of life and property," a fact which "contributes more than any other circumstance to impressing upon the minds of the people affection, esteem and reverence

---

9. [Professor] Wechsler, whose seminal article in 1954 proposed the view adopted by the Court today, predicated his argument on assumptions that simply do not accord with current reality. Professor Wechsler wrote: "National action has * * * always been regarded as exceptional in our polity, an intrusion to be justified by some necessity, the special rather than the ordinary case." Wechsler [supra, n. 11, at 544.] Not only is the premise of this view clearly at odds with the proliferation of national legislation over the past 30 years, but "a variety of structural and political changes in this century have combined to make Congress particularly *insensitive* to state and local values." Advisory Comm'n on Intergovernmental Relations [ACIR], Regulatory Federalism: Policy, Process, Impact and Reform 50 (1984). The adoption of the Seventeenth Amendment (providing for direct election of senators), the weakening of political parties on the local level, and the rise of national media, among other things, have made Congress increasingly less representative of State and local interests, and more likely to be responsive to the demands of various national constituencies. Id., at 50–51. * * *

See also Kaden, *Politics, Money, and State Sovereignty: The Judicial Role,* 79 Colum.L. Rev. 847 (1979) * * *

towards the government." Ibid. [Like] Hamilton, Madison saw the States' involvement in the everyday concerns of the people as the source of their citizens' loyalty. [The Federalist No. 46, p. 316.] See also Nagel, *Federalism as a Fundamental Value: National League of Cities in Perspective,* 1981 Sup.Ct.Rev. 81 (1981).

Thus, the harm to the States that results from federal overreaching under the Commerce Clause is not simply a matter of dollars and cents. Nor is it a matter of the wisdom or folly of certain policy choices. Rather, by usurping functions traditionally performed by the States, federal overreaching under the Commerce Clause undermines the constitutionally mandated balance of power between the States and the federal government, a balance designed to protect our fundamental liberties. * * *

D. [The] Court recasts [the Tenth Amendment] to say that the States retain their sovereign powers "only to the extent that the Constitution has not divested them of their original powers and transferred those powers to the Federal Government." This rephrasing is not a distinction without a difference; rather, it reflects the Court's unprecedented view that Congress is free under the Commerce Clause to assume a State's traditional sovereign power, and to do so without judicial review of its action. Indeed, the Court's view of federalism appears to relegate the States to precisely the trivial role that opponents of the Constitution feared they would occupy.

In *National League of Cities,* we spoke of fire prevention, police protection, sanitation, and public health as "typical of [the services] performed by state and local governments in discharging their dual functions of administering the public law and furnishing public services." Not only are these activities remote from any normal concept of interstate commerce, they are also activities that epitomize the concerns of local, democratic self-government. In emphasizing the need to protect traditional governmental functions, we identified the kinds of activities engaged in by state and local governments that affect the everyday lives of citizens. These are services that people are in a position to understand and evaluate, and in a democracy, have the right to oversee. We recognized that "it is functions such as these which governments are created to provide * * *" and that the states and local governments are better able than the national government to perform them.

The Court maintains that the standard approved in *National League of Cities* "disserves principles of democratic self government." In reaching this conclusion, the Court looks myopically only to persons elected to positions in the federal government. It disregards entirely the far more effective role of democratic self-government at the state and local levels. [Federal] legislation is drafted primarily by the staffs of the congressional committees. [Federal] departments and agencies customarily are authorized to write regulations. [The] administration and enforcement of federal laws and regulations necessarily are largely in the hands of staff and civil service employees. [Members] of the immense federal bureaucracy are not elected, know less about the services traditionally rendered by States and localities, and are inevitably less responsive to recipients of such services, than are state legislatures, city councils, boards of supervisors, and state and local commissions, boards and agencies. It is at these state and local levels—not in Washington as the Court so mistakenly thinks— that "democratic self-government" is best exemplified. * * *

JUSTICE O'CONNOR, with whom JUSTICE POWELL and JUSTICE REHNQUIST join, dissenting. * * *

Due to the emergence of an integrated and industrialized national economy, this Court has been required to examine and review a breathtaking expansion of the powers of Congress. In doing so the Court correctly perceived that the Framers of our Constitution intended Congress to have sufficient power to address national problems. But the Framers were not single-minded. [They] also envisioned a republic whose vitality was assured by the diffusion of power not only among the branches of the Federal Government, but also between the Federal Government and the States. In the 18th century these intentions did not conflict because technology had not yet converted every local problem into a national one. A conflict has now emerged, and the Court today retreats rather than reconcile the Constitution's dual concerns for federalism and an effective commerce power. * * *

It is not enough that the "end be legitimate"; the means to that end chosen by Congress must not contravene the spirit of the Constitution. Thus many of this Court's decisions acknowledge that the means by which national power is exercised must take into account concerns for state autonomy. [The] operative language of these cases varies, but the underlying principle is consistent: state autonomy is a relevant factor in assessing the means by which Congress exercises its powers. This principle requires the Court to enforce affirmative limits on federal regulation of the States to complement the judicially crafted expansion of the interstate commerce power. * * *

The problems of federalism in an integrated national economy are capable of more responsible resolution than holding that the States as States retain no status apart from that which Congress chooses to let them retain. The proper resolution, I suggest, lies in weighing state autonomy as a factor in the balance when interpreting the means by which Congress can exercise its authority on the States as States. * * *

It has been difficult for this Court to craft bright lines defining the scope of the state autonomy protected by *National League of Cities*. Such difficulty is to be expected whenever constitutional concerns as important as federalism and the effectiveness of the commerce power come into conflict. Regardless of the difficulty, it is and will remain the duty of this Court to reconcile these concerns in the final instance. That the Court shuns the task today by appealing to the "essence of federalism" can provide scant comfort to those who believe our federal system requires something more than a unitary, centralized government. I would not shirk the duty acknowledged by *National League of Cities* and its progeny, and I share Justice Rehnquist's belief that this Court will in time again assume its constitutional responsibility.[a]

Notes and Questions

1. *Constitutional basis?* Were there defensible constitutional bases for the state immunity asserted in *National League of Cities?* Consider Barber, *National League of Cities v. Usery: New Meaning for the Tenth Amendment?* 1976 Sup.

---

a. While joining the Powell and O'Connor dissents, Rehnquist, J., withheld full acceptance of their "balancing" approaches and concluded: "[U]nder any one of these approaches the judgment in this case should be affirmed, and I do not think it incumbent on those of us in dissent to spell out further the fine points of a principle that will, I am confident, in time again command the support of a majority of this Court."

Ct.Rev. 161, 165–173, 176–177, 181; Nagel, *Federalism as a Fundamental Value: National League of Cities in Perspective,* 1981 Sup.Ct.Rev. 81, 98–101.

2. *Values underlying state sovereignty?* What values critical to our federal system would be advanced or threatened by the resuscitation of *National League of Cities?* Cf. Barber, supra at 179; Tribe, *American Constitutional Law* 310–312 (1978); Nagel, supra at 108–109 (value of maintaining federalism "to sustain [the] understandings, the attitudes, the emotional ties that underlie the system of power allocation" in which states serve "partly as a tool for assuring adequate levels of political responsiveness, competition and participation.")

3. *Balancing federal and state interests?* Would it be an appropriate judicial function to "balance" the federal and state interests at stake as the standard for deciding whether federal regulation of state functions affecting interstate commerce invalidly infringe state "sovereignty"? Are judges likely to be equipped by training and experience to make the judgment that a federal interest rationally advanced by a commerce clause regulation of a state function is not sufficiently weighty to justify the resulting impingement on "state autonomy"[a]? Or is such a judgment political in nature, more appropriately left with Congress, subject to the political restraints of the electoral process?

4. *The political process as the insurer of state "sovereignty."* Are you persuaded by Blackmun, J., that "the built-in restraints that our system provides through state participation in federal governmental action" "ensures that laws that unduly burden the States' [special and specific position in our constitutional system] will not be promulgated?" Is the "significant measure of sovereignty" that the majority recognizes the States "unquestionably do retain" under the Constitution unduly placed at risk by *Garcia?* On the broader question of whether the Court should judicially review *any* congressional legislation challenged as violating states' rights, see Choper, *The Scope of National Power Vis-A-Vis the States: The Dispensability of Judicial Review,* 86 Yale L.J. 1552, 1556–57, 1621 (1977), considered Sec. 6 infra.

5. *Potential exceptions to National League of Cities—if revived.* In footnote 17 *National League of Cities* expressly left open whether its policy applied also to laws enforcing the fourteenth amendment or to controls imposed on the states pursuant to the congressional spending power. Since appointment of one new justice *could* result in a revival of *National League* principles, brief consideration of these open issues seems appropriate.

(a) *Fourteenth amendment.* Should state sovereignty concepts limit Congress' power under Section 5 of the fourteenth amendment to enforce its limitations on state action? *Rome v. United States,* 446 U.S. 156, 100 S.Ct. 1548, 64 L.Ed.2d 119 (1980), ruled that the *National League* principle did not limit Congress' power to regulate state voting procedures under the fifteenth amendment's identical enforcement section: "[P]rinciples of federalism that might otherwise be an obstacle to congressional authority are necessarily overridden by the power to enforce the Civil War Amendments 'by appropriate legislation.' Those Amendments were specifically designed as an expansion of federal power and an intrusion on state sovereignty." Later, both the majority and dissenting opinions in *EEOC v. Wyoming* (1983), this Part supra, restated this position in

---

a. Would such a judicial balancing judgment be fairly analogous to, or distinguishable in nature from, those in the commerce clause "negative implication" cases, such as *Southern Pacific* and *Bruce Church,* Ch. 4 infra, in which the Court balanced federal and state interests in deciding the validity of state regulations of commerce when Congress had not acted?

recognizing that the fourteenth amendment Section 5 enforcement laws are not subject to "Tenth Amendment constraints."

(b) *Spending power.* Before *National League of Cities,* the Court recognized that Congress could validly condition grants-in-aid to states on their compliance with related requirements beyond Congress' power to command. *Oklahoma v. Civil Service Comm'n,* 330 U.S. 127, 67 S.Ct. 544, 91 L.Ed. 794 (1947), had upheld the Hatch Act requirement that highway officers of states receiving federal highway funds forego political activities: "[While the United States] has no power to regulate local political activities as such of state officials, it does have power to fix the terms upon which its money allotments to states shall be disbursed." *Lau v. Nichols,* 414 U.S. 563, 94 S.Ct. 786, 39 L.Ed.2d 1 (1974), had upheld the Civil Rights Act requirement that state schools receiving federal aid "take affirmative steps to rectify [English language deficiency that excludes national origin-minority group children from effective participation in the educational program:" "The Federal Government has power to fix the terms on which its money allotments to the States shall be disbursed."

If *National League of Cities* were to become the law again, could Congress "condition federal law enforcement assistance grants to States on their payment of designated minimum wages to state police, [or] stipulate that state recipients of federal air pollution funds adopt specific auto or industrial emission rules, [or] require that local governments provide property tax relief in order to participate in federal revenue sharing" ? See Choper, *The Scope of National Power Vis-a-Vis the States: The Dispensability of Judicial Review,* 86 Yale L.J. 1552, 1598–99 (1977). Should the Court uphold conditions on federal grants-in-aid to states when the condition would be invalid under the *National League* rule were it a commerce clause regulation? When should the interest in state sovereignty receive the greater protection—when it collides with federal spending power or with federal commerce power? Or should there be no difference? Which federal interest should receive the greater weight when confronting a state sovereignty interest—the power to control expenditure of federal funds or the power to exercise fully the commerce power? Or should there be no difference? Should the answer vary with the particular interests at stake? What other considerations may be important in deciding the impact of the *National League* principle on spending conditions? Might the validity of conditions on grants depend upon how they are enforced?

SECTION 6. RECONSIDERATION OF JUDICIAL REVIEW OF STATES' RIGHTS ISSUES

Based on the history to date of judicial review of congressional legislation challenged as violating states' rights, should the Court continue to decide such issues?

JESSE CHOPER—THE SCOPE OF NATIONAL POWER VIS-A-VIS THE STATES: THE DISPENSABILITY OF JUDICIAL REVIEW

86 Yale L.J. 1552, 1556–57, 1621 (1977).

[T]he Federalism Proposal [is that] the federal judiciary should not decide constitutional questions respecting the ultimate power of the national government vis-a-vis the states; the constitutional issue whether federal action is beyond the authority of the central government and thus violates "states' rights" should be treated as nonjusticiable, with final resolution left to the political branches.[a] * * *

The functional, borderline question posed by federalism disputes is one of comparative skill and effectiveness of governmental levels: in a word, an issue of practicability.[b] Whatever the [judiciary's] special competence in adjudicating disputes over individual rights, when the fundamental constitutional issue turns on the relative competence of different levels of government to deal with societal problems, the courts are no more inherently capable of correct judgment than are the companion federal branches. Indeed, the judiciary may well be less capable than the national legislature or executive in such inquiries, given both the highly pragmatic nature of federal-state questions and the forceful representation of the states in the national process of political decisionmaking. Thus for Madison, we are told, "[t]he roles of the [state and national] governments would not depend upon legal line-drawing but upon the political process by which they were constituted."

The contention here is not that the political branches should make constitutional decisions of federalism because they are better equipped to gather the underlying factual data necessary for intelligent judgment or because they are more adept at fashioning the broad evaluations required for making wise public policy. A great many personal rights questions passed upon by the Court—such as the nature of the threat posed by political "subversives," the ability of the accused criminal to defend without the assistance of counsel, the requirement that an abortion be performed in a licensed hospital—similarly subsume large policy issues with complex and debatable factual considerations. Rather, the point is that constitutional questions of federalism differ from those of individual liberty both in their distinctive, pragmatic quality and in the likelihood of their fair resolution within the national political chambers.

This article will argue that state representation in the national executive and legislature places the President and Congress in a trustworthy position to view the issues involved in federalism disputes. In contrast, beneficiaries of individual rights, such as members of minority groups, are often not adequately represented in the deliberations of the political branches. A more active judicial role in personal rights cases is thus necessitated. But when democratic processes may be trusted to produce a fair constitutional judgment, as in cases involving the allocation of power between the states and the national government, it advances the democratic tradition to vest that judgment with popularly responsible institutions.

[N]o suggestion is put forward that the Federalism Proposal was originally ordained. But neither is it contradicted by the historical record or by the basic themes and values then expressed. Indeed, the Proposal is consistent with and furthers the overriding concern for the rights of the individual.

As a bald statement, the Federalism Proposal takes a radical tone by urging the Court to reject the long-established system of judicial review over questions of states' rights. But because the Court has generally left decisions on federal-

---

a. "[T]he Proposal would not affect the Court's jurisdiction over challenges to state encroachments on national power, since the rationale for its adoption does not apply to that aspect of federalism adjudication." 86 Yale L.J. at 1577. See generally id. at 1583–87.

b. The preceding paragraph notes that "one of the principal purposes behind the abandonment of the Articles of Confederation and the adoption of the Constitution, if not *the* major purpose, was to establish a workable central government." Id. at 1555.

ism to the national political branches, the Proposal [would] change few results in concrete cases. This is not to say, however, that the Proposal would be of no real consequence. That the Court now rarely exercises its power of review to invalidate national action is no guarantee that it will not revert to a mistaken policy. A turnabout has already been accomplished in the *National League of Cities* decision, and further shifts may be on the horizon, especially on the presently unsettled question of the reach of federal legislative power under § 5 of the Fourteenth Amendment. On the other hand, if continuing judicial review in this field would produce only the most infrequent invalidations, then there is little justification for the Court to stamp its imprimatur on so many exercises of national power to protect against so few violations of the federalism precept. For the Court to continue to review such federalism cases, moreover, would sap the Court's strength to act on behalf of individual rights. Finally, in the face of extreme national abridgments of federalism, the Court's pronouncements would most likely be futile, symbolic rulings.

Chapter 3

DISTRIBUTION OF FEDERAL POWERS: SEPARATION OF POWERS

INTRODUCTION

In contrast with last chapter's consideration of the allocation of legislative powers to the national government, and their expanding scope, this chapter is concerned with the distribution within the federal government of the broad range of national governmental powers—legislative, executive and judicial. A principal concern is the extent to which the separation of powers and checks and balances concepts embodied in the constitutional structure, and express grants of power in the Constitution, limit the branch or agency that may perform particular governmental functions. A related concern is the extent to which a granted power must be exercised with a view to avoiding interference with the effective exercise of powers granted to another branch of government.

Illustrative of these concerns are the issues raised in this chapter's three sections: (1) Presidential action affecting "congressional powers." (2) Congressional action affecting "presidential powers." (3) Executive privilege and congressional and executive immunity.

SECTION 1. PRESIDENTIAL ACTION AFFECTING "CONGRESSIONAL" POWERS

YOUNGSTOWN SHEET & TUBE CO. v. SAWYER [THE STEEL SEIZURE CASE]
343 U.S. 579, 72 S.Ct. 863, 96 L.Ed. 1153 (1952).

MR. JUSTICE BLACK delivered the opinion of the Court. * * *

In [late] 1951, a dispute arose between the steel companies and their employees over terms and conditions [for] new collective bargaining agreements. [T]he President [referred] the dispute to the Federal Wage Stabilization Board to [recommend fair] terms of settlement. [Its] report resulted in no settlement. On April 4, 1952, the Union gave notice of a nation-wide strike called to begin [April 9]. The indispensability of steel as a component of substantially all weapons and other war materials led the President to believe that the proposed work stoppage would immediately jeopardize our national defense and that governmental seizure of the steel mills was necessary in order to assure the continued availability of steel. Reciting these considerations for his action, the President, a few hours before the strike was to begin, issued Executive Order 10340 [directing] the Secretary of Commerce to take possession of most of the steel mills and keep them running. The Secretary immediately issued his own possessory orders, calling upon the presidents of the various seized companies to serve as operating managers for the United States. [The] next morning the President sent a message to Congress reporting his [action]. Congress has taken no action.

[On April 30 the U.S. District Court enjoined the Secretary of Commerce from "continuing the seizure and possession" of the mills.] On the same day the Court of Appeals stayed the District Court's injunction. [Deeming] it best that the issues raised be promptly decided by this court, we granted certiorari on May 3 and set the cause for argument on May 12.[b] * * *

The President's power, if any, to issue the order must stem either from an act of Congress or from the Constitution itself.

[T]he use of the seizure technique [to] prevent work stoppage was not only unauthorized by any congressional enactment; prior to this controversy, Congress had refused to adopt that method of settling labor disputes. When the Taft-Hartley Act [Labor Management Relations Act of 1947] was under [consideration], Congress rejected an amendment which would have authorized such governmental seizures in cases of emergency. [Instead], the plan sought to bring about settlements by use of the customary devices of mediation, conciliation, investigation by boards of inquiry, and public reports. In some instances temporary injunctions were authorized to provide cooling-off periods. All this failing, unions were left free to strike after a secret vote by employees as to whether they wished to accept their employers' final settlement offer.[c]

It is clear that if the President had authority to issue the order he did, it must be found in some provision of the Constitution. And it is not claimed that express constitutional language grants this power to the President. The contention is that presidential power should be implied from the aggregate of his powers under the Constitution. * * *

The order cannot properly be sustained as an exercise of the President's military power as Commander in Chief of the Armed Forces. [We] cannot with faithfulness to our constitutional system hold that the Commander in Chief of the Armed Forces has the ultimate power as such to take possession of private property in order to keep labor disputes from stopping production. This is a job for the Nation's lawmakers, not for its military authorities.

Nor can the seizure order be sustained because of the several constitutional provisions that grant executive power to the President. In the framework of our Constitution, the President's power to see that the laws are faithfully executed refutes the idea that he is to be a lawmaker. The Constitution limits his functions in the lawmaking process to the recommending of laws he thinks wise and the vetoing of laws he thinks bad. And the Constitution is neither silent

---

b. The Court's announced its decision on June 2.

c. Sections 206–210 of the Act, 29 U.S.C. §§ 176–180, provide that "whenever in the opinion of the President [a] threatened or actual strike [will], if permitted to occur or to continue, imperil the national health or safety," on the President's initiative, the strike

may be enjoined while a board of inquiry studies the dispute, but that the strike may continue after 80 days if the employees reject the employer's last offer of settlement. The President is then obligated under the Act to report on the emergency to Congress, which presumably could then take action if warranted.

nor equivocal about who shall make laws which the President is to execute. The first section of the first article says that "All legislative Powers herein granted shall be vested in a Congress of the United States." After granting many powers to the Congress, Article I goes on to provide that Congress may "make all Laws which shall be necessary and proper for carrying into Execution the foregoing Powers and all other Powers vested by this Constitution in the Government of the [United States]".

[The] preamble of the order itself, like that of many statutes, sets out reasons why the President believes certain policies should be adopted, proclaims these policies as rules of conduct to be followed, and again, like a statute, authorizes a government official to promulgate additional rules and regulations consistent with the policy proclaimed and needed to carry that policy into execution. The power of Congress to adopt such public policies as those proclaimed by the order is beyond question. It can authorize the taking of private property for public use. It can make laws regulating the relationships between employers and employees, prescribing rules designed to settle labor disputes, and fixing wages and working conditions in certain fields of our economy. The Constitution did not subject this lawmaking power of Congress to presidential or military supervision or control.

It is said that other Presidents without congressional authority have taken possession of private business enterprises in order to settle labor disputes. But even if this be true, Congress has not thereby lost its exclusive constitutional authority to make laws necessary and proper to carry out the powers vested by the Constitution "in the Government of the [United States]."

The Founders of this Nation entrusted the lawmaking power to the Congress alone in both good and bad times. It would do no good to recall the historical events, the fears of power and the hopes for freedom that lay behind their choice. Such a review would but confirm our holding that this seizure order cannot stand. * * *

Affirmed.

MR. JUSTICE FRANKFURTER, [joining the Court's opinion and] concurring.

[C]ongress has frequently—at least 16 times since 1916—specifically provided for executive seizure of production, transportation, communications, or storage facilities. In every case it has qualified this grant of power with limitations and safeguards. [This] demonstrates that Congress deemed seizure so drastic a power as to require that it be carefully circumscribed whenever the President was vested with this extraordinary authority. * * *

In adopting the provisions which it did, by the Labor Management Relations Act of 1947, for dealing with a "national emergency" arising out of a breakdown in peaceful industrial relations, Congress was very familiar with Government seizure as a protective measure. On a balance of considerations Congress chose not to lodge this power in the President. [In] deciding that authority to seize should be given to the President only after full consideration of the particular situation should show such legislation to be necessary, Congress [evidently] assumed that industrial shutdowns in basic industries are not instances of spontaneous generation, and that danger warnings are sufficiently plain before the event to give ample opportunity to start the legislative process into action. In any event, nothing can be plainer than that Congress made a conscious choice of policy in a field full of perplexity and peculiarly within legislative responsibility for [choice].

[By the Labor Management Relations Act of 1947] Congress has expressed its will to withhold this power from the President as though it had said so in so many words. [It has] said to the President, "You may not seize. Please report to us and ask for seizure power if you think it is needed in a specific situation."

* * *

MR. JUSTICE JACKSON, concurring in the judgment and opinion of the Court.

That comprehensive and undefined presidential powers hold both practical advantages and grave dangers for the country will impress anyone who has served as legal adviser to a President in time of transition and public anxiety. [A] judge, like an executive adviser, may be surprised at the poverty of really useful and unambiguous authority applicable to concrete problems of executive power as they actually present themselves. * * *

The actual art of governing under our Constitution does not and cannot conform to judicial definitions of the power of any of its branches based on isolated clauses or even single Articles torn from context. While the Constitution diffuses power the better to secure liberty, it also contemplates that practice will integrate the dispersed powers into a workable government. It enjoins upon its branches separateness but interdependence, autonomy but reciprocity. Presidential powers are not fixed but fluctuate, depending upon their disjunction or conjunction with those of Congress. We may well begin by a somewhat over-simplified grouping of practical situations in which a President may doubt, or others may challenge, his powers, and by distinguishing roughly the legal consequences of this factor of relativity.

1. When the President acts pursuant to an express or implied authorization of Congress, his authority is at its maximum, for it includes all that he possesses in his own right plus all that Congress can delegate. * * *

2. When the President acts in absence of either a congressional grant or denial of authority, he can only rely upon his own independent powers, but there is a zone of twilight in which he and Congress may have concurrent authority, or in which its distribution is uncertain. Therefore, congressional inertia, indifference or quiescence may sometimes, at least as a practical matter, enable, if not invite, measures on independent presidential responsibility. In this area, any actual test of power is likely to depend on the imperatives of events and contemporary imponderables rather than on abstract theories of law.

3. When the President takes measures incompatible with the expressed or implied will of Congress, his power is at its lowest ebb, for then he can rely only upon his own constitutional powers minus any constitutional powers of Congress over the matter. Courts can sustain exclusive Presidential control in such a case only by disabling the Congress from acting upon the subject. Presidential claim to a power at once so conclusive and preclusive must be scrutinized with caution, for what is at stake is the equilibrium established by our constitutional system.

Into which of these classifications does this executive seizure of the steel industry fit? It is eliminated from the first by admission, for it is conceded that no congressional authorization exists for this seizure. * * *

[It] seems clearly eliminated from [the "second category"] because Congress has not left seizure of private property an open field but has covered it by three statutory policies inconsistent with this seizure [none of which] were [invoked].

This leaves the current seizure to be justified only by the severe tests under the third grouping, where [we] can sustain the President only by holding that seizure of such strike-bound industries is within his domain and beyond control by Congress. * * *

[I] cannot accept the view that [Art. II, § 1, cl. 1, vesting "the executive power" in the President] is a grant in bulk of all conceivable executive power but regard it as an allocation to the presidential office of the generic powers thereafter stated.

The [Commander in Chief] appellation is sometimes advanced as support for any Presidential action, internal or external, involving use of force, the idea being that it vests power to do anything, anywhere, that can be done with an army or navy. [However, the] Constitution expressly places in Congress power "to raise and *support* Armies" and "to *provide* and *maintain* a Navy." (Emphasis supplied.) This certainly lays upon Congress primary responsibility for supplying the armed forces. Congress alone controls the raising of revenues and their appropriation and may determine in what manner and by what means they shall be spent for military and naval procurement. I suppose no one would doubt that Congress can take over war supply as a Government enterprise.

* * *

The third clause in which the Solicitor General finds seizure powers is that "he shall take Care that the Laws be faithfully executed." That authority must be matched against [the due process clause of the fifth amendment]. One [clause] gives a governmental authority that reaches so far as there is law, the other gives a private right that authority shall go no farther. * * *

The Solicitor General lastly grounds support of the seizure upon nebulous, inherent powers never expressly granted but said to have accrued to the office from the customs and claims of preceding administrations. The plea is for a resulting power to deal with a crisis or an emergency according to the necessities of the case, the unarticulated assumption being that necessity knows no law. Loose and irresponsible use of adjectives colors all non-legal and much legal discussion of presidential powers. "Inherent" powers, "implied" powers, "incidental" powers, "plenary" powers, "war" powers and "emergency" powers are used, often interchangeably and without fixed or ascertainable meanings.

* * *

In view of the ease, expedition and safety with which Congress can grant and has granted large emergency powers, certainly ample to embrace this crisis, I am quite unimpressed with the argument that we should affirm possession of them without statute. Such power either has no beginning or it has no end. If it exists, it need submit to no legal restraint. I am not alarmed that it would plunge us straightway into dictatorship, but it is at least a step in that wrong direction.

[The] Executive, except for recommendation and veto, has no legislative power. The executive action we have here originates in the individual will of the President and represents an exercise of authority without law. [We] do not know today what powers over labor or property would be claimed to flow from Government possession if we should legalize it, what rights to compensation would be claimed or recognized, or on what contingency it would end. With all its defects, delays, and inconveniences, men have discovered no technique for long preserving free government except that the Executive be under the law, and that the law be made by parliamentary deliberations.[e]

e. Douglas and Burton, JJ., each concurred in Black, J.'s opinion but also wrote separate concurrences. Douglas, J., contended that the fifth amendment required compensation for even temporary seizure, and that since only Congress can raise revenues, "the branch of government that has the power to pay compensation for a seizure is the only one able to authorize a seizure." Burton, J.'s opinion was similar in thrust to those of Frankfurter and Jackson, JJ., stressing that "the President's [order] invaded the jurisdiction of Congress,"

*   *   *

Mr. Justice Clark, concurring in the judgment of the Court.

[T]he Constitution does grant to the President extensive authority in times of grave and imperative national emergency. [Such] a grant may well be necessary to the very existence of the Constitution itself. * * * I care not whether one calls [this authority] "residual," "inherent," "moral," "implied," "aggregate," "emergency," or otherwise. * * *

[I] conclude that where Congress has laid down specific procedures to deal with the type of crisis confronting the President, he must follow those procedures in meeting the crisis; but that in the absence of such action by Congress, the President's independent power to act depends upon the gravity of the situation confronting the nation. I cannot sustain the seizure in question because [here] Congress had prescribed methods to be followed by the President in meeting the emergency at hand. * * *

Mr. Chief Justice Vinson, with whom Mr. Justice Reed and Mr. Justice Minton join, dissenting.

[Our] Presidents have on many occasions exhibited the leadership contemplated by the Framers when they made the President Commander in Chief, and imposed upon him the trust to "take Care that the Laws be faithfully executed." With or without explicit statutory authorization, Presidents have [dealt] with national emergencies by acting promptly [to] enforce legislative programs, at least to save those programs until Congress could act. Congress and the courts have responded to such executive initiative with consistent approval. [Historic episodes from Washington to Franklin D. Roosevelt were summarized in 17 pages. One follows:]

Some six months before Pearl Harbor, a dispute at a single aviation [plant] interrupted a segment of the production of military aircraft. In spite of the comparative insignificance of this work stoppage to total defense production as contrasted with the complete paralysis now threatened by a shutdown of the entire basic steel industry, and even though our armed forces were not then engaged in combat, President Roosevelt ordered the seizure of the plant "pursuant to the powers vested in [him] by the Constitution and laws of the United States, as President of the United States of America and Commander in Chief of the Army and Navy of the United States." The Attorney General (Jackson) vigorously proclaimed that the President had the moral duty to keep this Nation's defense effort a "going concern." [A]lso prior to Pearl Harbor, the President ordered the seizure of a ship-building company and an aircraft parts plant. Following the declaration of war, but prior to the Smith-Connally Act of 1943, five additional industrial concerns were seized to avert interruption of needed production. During the same period, the President directed seizure of the Nation's coal mines to remove an obstruction to the effective prosecution of the war. * * *

At the time of the seizure of the coal mines, Senator Connally's bill to provide a statutory basis for seizures [was] again before Congress. As stated by its sponsor, the purpose of the bill was not to augment Presidential power, but to "let the country know that the Congress is squarely behind the President." [Congress] again recognized that the President already had the necessary power, for there was no intention to "ratify" past actions of doubtful [validity].

which "reserved to itself" the remedy of
seizure.

At the minimum, the executive actions reviewed herein sustain the action of the President in this case. And many of the cited examples of Presidential practice go far beyond the extent of power necessary to sustain the President's order to seize the steel mills. [T]hat temporary executive seizures of industrial plants to meet an emergency have not been directly tested in this Court furnishes not the slightest suggestion that such actions have been illegal. Rather, the fact that Congress and the courts have consistently recognized and given their support to such executive action indicates that such a power of seizure has been accepted throughout our history. * * *

The President reported to Congress the morning after the seizure that he acted because a work stoppage in steel production would immediately imperil the safety of the Nation by preventing execution of the legislative programs for procurement of military equipment. And, while a shutdown could be averted by granting the price concessions requested by plaintiffs, granting such concessions would disrupt the price stabilization program also enacted by Congress. Rather than fail to execute either legislative program, the President acted to execute both.

[We] do not now have before us the case of a President acting solely on the basis of his own notions of the public welfare. Nor is there any question of unlimited executive power in this case. The President himself closed the door to any such claim when he sent his Message to Congress stating his purpose to abide by any action of Congress, whether approving or disapproving his seizure action. [There] is no question that the possession was other than temporary in character and subject to congressional direction—either approving, disapproving or regulating the manner in which the mills were to be administered and returned to the owners. The President [clearly] stated his intention to abide by the legislative will. [Judicial,] legislative and executive precedents throughout our history demonstrate that in this case the President acted in full conformity with his duties under the Constitution. * * *

DAMES & MOORE v. REGAN, 453 U.S. 654, 101 S.Ct. 2972, 69 L.Ed.2d 918 (1981), per REHNQUIST, J., unanimously upheld the following 1981 Presidential Executive Orders to implement the January 19, 1981 Executive Agreement between Iran and the United States, which called for release of the American hostages held in Iran from November 4, 1979 until January 20, 1981 and for the termination of "all litigation between the Government of each party and the nationals of the other, and to bring about the settlement [of] all such claims through binding arbitration" before a Claims Tribunal established under the Agreement. The Executive Orders (1) suspended all claims within the jurisdiction of the Claims Tribunal pending in American courts, (2) nullified all prejudgment attachments against Iran's assets in actions against Iran, which had been authorized by earlier executive action that had blocked removal or transfer of Iran's assets and had permitted judicial proceedings against Iran with prejudgment attachment of its assets without entry of judgment, and (3) ordered transfer to Iran of all Iranian assets held in U.S. banks, except for one billion dollars ordered transferred to the Bank of England to cover awards against Iran by the Claims Tribunal.

Dames & Moore had properly obtained in federal district court a prejudgment attachment of Iranian bank assets to secure its large claim for services rendered Iran, only to have the attachment vacated pursuant to the Executive Orders. In a declaratory judgment action, Dames & Moore unsuccessfully challenged the President's power to take the foregoing actions. Reviewing on certiorari after an expedited hearing, the Supreme Court affirmed:

"Because the President's action in nullifying the attachments and ordering the transfer of the assets was taken pursuant to specific congressional authorization [under the International Emergency Economic Powers Act (IEEPA)][a] it is 'supported by the strongest of presumptions and the widest latitude of judicial interpretation, and the burden of persuasion would rest heavily upon any who might attack it.' [*Steel Seizure* case] (Jackson, J., concurring). Under the circumstances of this case, we cannot say that petitioner has sustained that heavy burden. A contrary ruling would mean that the Federal Government as a whole lacked the power exercised by the President, and that we are not prepared to say."

The Court concluded, however, [that] "neither the IEEPA nor the Hostage Act constitutes specific authorization of the President's action suspending claims. [But this is] not to say that these statutory provisions are entirely irrelevant to the question of the validity of the President's action. We think both statutes highly relevant in the looser sense of indicating congressional acceptance of a broad scope for executive action in circumstances such as those presented in this case.

"[W]e cannot ignore the general tenor of Congress' legislation in this area in trying to determine whether the President is acting alone or at least with the acceptance of Congress. * * * Congress cannot anticipate and legislate with regard to every possible action the President may find it necessary to take or every possible situation in which he might act. [T]he enactment of legislation closely related to the question of the President's authority in a particular case which evinces legislative intent to accord the President broad discretion may be considered to 'invite' 'measures on independent presidential responsibility.' *Steel Seizure* case (Jackson, J., concurring). At least this is so where there is no contrary indication of legislative intent and when, as here, there is a history of congressional acquiescence in conduct of the sort engaged in by the [President.]

"Not infrequently in affairs between nations, outstanding claims by nationals of one country against the government of another country are 'sources of friction' between the two sovereigns. To resolve these difficulties, nations have often entered into agreements settling the claims of their respective nationals. As one treatise writer puts it, international agreements settling claims by nationals of one state against the government of another 'are established international practice reflecting traditional international theory.' Henkin, *Foreign Affairs and the Constitution* 262 (1972). Consistent with that principle, the United States has repeatedly exercised its sovereign authority to settle the claims of its nationals against foreign countries. Though those settlements have sometimes been made by treaty, there has also been a longstanding practice of settling such claims by executive agreement without the advice and consent of the Senate. Under such agreements, the President has agreed to renounce or extinguish claims of United States nationals against foreign governments in return for lump sum payments or the establishment of arbitration procedures. [T]he 'United States has sometimes disposed of the claims of citizens without their consent, or even without consultation with them, usually without exclusive regard for their interests, as distinguished from those of the nation as a whole.'

---

a. Section 1702(a)(1)(B) of IEEPA empowered the President to "compel," "nullify" or "prohibit" any "transfer" with respect to, or transactions involving, any property subject to the jurisdiction of the United States in which any foreign country has any interest.

Henkin at 263. Accord, *The Restatement (Second) of the Foreign Relations Law of the United States* § 213 (1965). [T]he practice of settling claims continues today. Since 1952, the President has entered into at least 10 binding settlements with foreign nations, including an $80 million settlement with the People's Republic of China.

"Crucial to our decision today is the conclusion that Congress has implicitly approved the practice of claim settlement by executive agreement. This is best demonstrated by Congress' enactment of the International Claims Settlement Act of 1949. The Act had two purposes: (1) to allocate to United States nationals funds received in the course of an executive claims settlement with Yugoslavia, and (2) to provide a procedure whereby funds resulting from future settlements could be distributed. To achieve these ends Congress created the International Claims Commission, now the Foreign Claims Settlement Commission, and gave it jurisdiction to make final and binding decisions with respect to claims by United States nationals against settlement funds. By creating a procedure to implement future settlement agreements, Congress placed its stamp of approval on such agreements. Indeed, the legislative history of the Act observed that the United States was seeking settlements with countries other than Yugoslavia and stated that the bill 'contemplates that settlements of a similar nature are to be made in the future.'

"Over the years Congress has frequently amended the International Claims Settlement Act to provide for particular problems arising out of settlement agreements, thus demonstrating Congress' continuing acceptance of the President's claim settlement authority. [Finally,] the legislative history of the IEEPA further reveals that Congress has accepted the authority of the Executive to enter into settlement agreements. Though the IEEPA was enacted to provide for some limitation on the President's emergency powers, Congress stressed that 'nothing in this Act is intended to interfere with the authority of the President to [block assets], or to impede the settlement of claims of United States citizens against foreign countries.' [1977 Senate Report.]

"In addition to congressional acquiescence in the President's power to settle claims, prior cases of this Court have also recognized that the President does have some measure of power to enter into executive agreements without obtaining the advice and consent of the Senate. In *United States v. Pink*, 315 U.S. 203, 62 S.Ct. 552, 86 L.Ed. 796 (1942), for example, the Court upheld the validity of the Litvinov Assignment, which was part of an Executive Agreement whereby the Soviet Union assigned to the United States amounts owed to it by American nationals so that outstanding claims of other American nationals could be paid. The Court explained that the resolution of such claims was integrally connected with normalizing United States' relations with a foreign state. * * *[b]

---

b. *Pink* also ruled, as did an earlier case, *United States v. Belmont*, 301 U.S. 324, 57 S.Ct. 758, 81 L.Ed. 1134 (1937), that without approval or implementation by Congress or the Senate the executive agreement became the "supreme Law of the Land," overriding New York's court-made policy not to recognize government appropriation of property. Both asserted the President's power to negotiate claims settlement agreements to remove obstacles to full recognition of each nation, stating in *Pink*: "The powers of the President in the conduct of foreign relations included the power, without consent of the Senate, to determine the public policy of the United States with respect to the Russian nationalization [decrees]. Power to remove such obstacles to full recognition as [claims settlement] certainly is a modest implied power of the President who is the sole organ of the federal government in the field of international relations.' *Curtiss-Wright*. Effectiveness in handling the delicate problems of foreign relations requires no [less]."

"In light of all of the foregoing—the inferences to be drawn from the character of the legislation Congress has enacted in the area, such as the IEEPA and the Hostage Act, and from the history of acquiescence in executive claims settlement—we conclude that the President was authorized to suspend pending claims pursuant to Executive Order * * *. As Justice Frankfurter pointed out in the *Youngstown* case, 'a systematic, unbroken executive practice, long pursued to the knowledge of Congress and never before questioned [may] be treated as a gloss on "Executive Power" vested in the President by § 1 of Art. II.' * * *

"Our conclusion is buttressed by the fact that the means chosen by the President to settle the claims of American nationals provided an alternate forum, the Claims Tribunal, which is capable of providing meaningful relief. [Moreover,] it is important to remember that we have already held that the President has the *statutory* authority to nullify attachments and to transfer the assets out of the country. The President's power to do so does not depend on his provision of a forum whereby claimants can recover on those claims. The fact that the President has provided such a forum here means that the claimants are receiving something in return for the suspension of their claims, namely, access to an international tribunal before which they may well recover something on their claims. Because there does appear to be a real 'settlement' here, this case is more easily analogized to the more traditional claim settlement cases of the past.

"Just as importantly, Congress has not disapproved of the action taken [here.] We are thus clearly not confronted with a situation in which Congress has in some way resisted the exercise of presidential authority.

"Finally, we re-emphasize the narrowness of our decision. We do not decide that the President possesses plenary power to settle claims, even as against foreign governmental entities. [But] where, as here, the settlement of claims has been determined to be a necessary incident to the resolution of a major foreign policy dispute between our country and another, and where, as here, we can conclude that Congress acquiesced in the President's action, we are not prepared to say that the President lacks the power to settle such claims."

Notes and Questions

1. *Role of "separation of powers."* (a) Does the Constitution's allocation of government powers among Congress, the President and the Judiciary mandate Black, J.'s "uncompromising line between legislative power and executive authority" in *Youngstown?*[a] See Kauper, *The Steel Seizure Case: Congress, the President and the Supreme Court,* 51 Mich.L.Rev. 141, 180 (1951). Was Black, J.'s view, "purporting to stem from the principle of the separation of powers"— that the President's steel seizure order was "law making" that invaded Congress' "exclusive constitutional authority to make laws"—a "purely arbitrary construct [devoid] of historical verification?" See Corwin, *The Steel Seizure Case: A Judicial Brick Without Straw,* 53 Col.L.Rev. 53, 64 (1953). Can or should classification of a governmental function as "legislative" or "executive" categorically determine what department or agency of government may perform that function?[b] Or do "[p]ractical considerations require a recognition that [the

a. For other analyses of *Youngstown* see Freund, *The Year of the Steel Case,* 66 Harv.L. Rev. 89 (1952); Lea, *The Steel Case,* 47 Nw. U.L.Rev. 289 (1952); 2 Schwartz, *Commentary on the Constitution of the United States* 65–83 (1963).

b. Consider Ratner, *Executive Privilege, Self Incrimination, and the Separation of Powers Illusion,* 22 U.C.L.A. L.Rev. 92, 93 (1974) ("no matter how solemnly reiterated, the phrase provides no talismanic precept.")

legislative and executive] authorities may overlap or merge in limited areas?" Kauper, supra at 180–81.

(b) "Below the very apex of governmental structure, [should] the rigid separation-of-powers compartmentalization of governmental functions [be] abandoned in favor of analysis in terms of separation of functions [to assure individual fairness and objectivity] and checks and balances [to protect against emergence of tyrannical government]?" See Strauss, *The Place of Agencies in Government: Separation of Powers and the Fourth Branch,* 84 Col.L.Rev. 573, 578 (1984). At the apex, where action by the President or Congress is challenged, can a good case be made for greater rigidity? For a thoughtful analysis of the varying concerns relating to separation of powers, see id. at 573–80.

2. *Dominance in the "zone of twilight."* (a) In Jackson, J.'s "zone of twilight" where both Congress and the President may reasonably claim independent sources of authority, which should be recognized as the paramount power? Commenting on the "importance" of Frankfurter, J.'s concurring "suggestion * * * that the President should have heeded the intention of the Taft-Hartley Act," Professor Corwin noted that "[o]nly Justice Clark [had] the courage to draw the appropriate conclusion: Congress having entered the field, its ascertainable intention supplied the law of the case." Corwin, supra at 65. In Corwin's view, "The Court would unquestionably have assented to the proposition that in all emergency situations the last word lies with Congress when it chooses to speak such last word." Id. at 66.

(b) Does *Dames & Moore* indicate whether the Court would still recognize Congress as the paramount power in case of conflict in the twilight zones, in foreign as well as domestic affairs?

3. *Impoundment of appropriated funds.* (a) May the President withhold (impounded) expenditures authorized and appropriated by Acts of Congress [a] when neither the Acts nor other legislation can be found to authorize [b] or to forbid such impoundment? E.g., may the "harsh reality [that] time and time again Congress has passed swollen appropriation acts and failed to levy the taxes necessary to avoid inflation" justify the conclusion that, absent a congressional mandate to the contrary, the President's executive authority includes power to

a. Conflicts over Presidential impoundment of appropriated funds reached their peak in the Nixon administration. See Choper, *Judicial Review and the National Political Process* 370–71 (1980). The constitutionality of impoundment has been considered in non-judicial studies and in a few federal court cases, but it has not yet been addressed by the Supreme Court. See, e.g., Statement of Joseph T. Sneed, *Joint Hearings before Subcommittee on Impoundment of Funds of Senate Committee on Government Operations and Subcommittee on Separation of Powers of Senate Committee on Judiciary on S. 373,* 93d Cong., 1st Sess. 364–70 (1973); Mikva & Hertz, *Impoundment of Funds—The Courts, the Congress and the President: A Constitutional Triangle,* 69 Nw.U.L.Rev. 335 (1974); Levinson & Mills, *Impoundment: A Search for Legal Principles,* 26 U.Fla.L.Rev. 191 (1973); Note, 59 Iowa L.Rev. 50 (1973); *Louisiana ex rel. Guste v. Brinegar,* 388 F.Supp. 1319, 1324–25, (D.D.C.1975) (impoundment unconstitutional); *Guadamuz v. Ash,* 368 F.Supp. 1233, 1241

(D.D.C.1973) (same) *Community Action Programs v. Ash,* 365 F.Supp. 1355 (D.N.J.1973) (same).

Before President Nixon resigned, Congress enacted over his veto the Congressional Budget and Impoundment Control Act of 1974, by which Congress sought to give itself the last word on impoundments. 2 U.S.C. §§ 682–88. While his successor sought many impoundments, when Congress withheld approval of most of them he acquiesced. See Fisher, *Congressional Budget Reform: The First Two Years,* 14 Harv.J.Leg. 413, 450–54 (1977). Since Nixon, no President appears to have challenged Congress' assertion of paramount power over impoundment.

b. E.g., the Executive was authorized to set up reserves from appropriated funds "to effect savings whenever [possible by] changes in requirements or greater efficiency of operations." P.L. 93–344, Sec. 1002, 88 Stat. 332 (1974), amending the Anti-Deficiency Act.

withhold authorized expenditures in order to "protect purchasing power to avoid intolerable inflation?" [c] Or could the President, as chief Executive and Commander in Chief, refrain from expending funds appropriated over his veto for "Star Wars" space weapons that he has rationally concluded would endanger national security and intensify a global nuclear arms race? [d]

Does the President's duty "to take Care that the Laws be faithfully executed" obligate the President to expend the full amount authorized and appropriated to the extent needed for the specified purpose? [e] Does impoundment of appropriated funds without statutory authority encroach upon Congress' legislative power? Would recognition of a presidential power to impound a portion of an appropriation act without congressional authorization in effect confer on the President "not only an item veto, but also what amounts to an absolute veto" that would preclude Congress' right to override the veto? [f]

(b) How should the analysis differ when Congress mandates a particular expenditure that the President impounds? [g] Are *Youngstown* and *Dames & Moore* useful guides? Persuasive precedents? Would a congressional mandate to expend funds authorized and appropriated to build "Star Wars" disapproved by the President, who impounded the funds, "intrude impermissibly" into the President's "substantial authority to control spending in the areas of national defense and foreign affairs?" [h] The Impoundment Control Act, supra, 2 U.S.C. § 683, requires that an appropriation be "available for obligation" unless Congress completes action on a bill to rescind the appropriation within 45 days after a required notice to Congress that the President "has determined" that the appropriation should be rescinded or reserved. [i]

SECTION 2. CONGRESSIONAL ACTION AFFECTING PRESIDENTIAL POWERS

I. APPOINTMENTS POWER

BUCKLEY v. VALEO, 424 U.S. 1, 96 S.Ct. 612, 46 L.Ed.2d 659 (1976), per curiam, held that the Federal Election Campaign Act's provision—that two of the six members of the Federal Election Commission be appointed by the President pro tempore of the Senate and two by the Speaker of the House of Representatives (the remaining two to be appointed by the President)—violated the Appointments Clause of Art. II, § 2, cl. 2: "We think [that] any appointee exercising significant authority pursuant to the laws of the United States is an Officer of the United States, and must, therefore, be appointed in the manner prescribed by [the Appointments Clause]. While the second part of the Clause authorizes Congress to vest the appointment of the officers described in that part in 'the Courts of Law, or in the Heads of Departments,' neither the Speaker of

c. Sneed statement, supra n. a, at 367.

d. Cf. Harner, *Presidential Power to Impound Appropriations for Defense and Foreign Relations*, 5 Harv.J.L. & Pub. Pol'y 131 (1982).

e. Cf. Mikva & Hertz, supra at 378–80; 59 Iowa L.Rev. 50, 71–72.

f. Id. at 382; 59 Iowa L.Rev. 50, 72.

g. The Court has not decided this issue. *Train v. New York*, 420 U.S. 35, 95 S.Ct. 839, 43 L.Ed.2d 1 (1975) interpreted the Federal Water Pollution Control Act to require the full allotment of funds on the statutory time-

table, but did not consider whether the President had unreviewable discretion to impound. The Government raised that issue in the court below, but not in the Supreme Court.

h. See Sneed statement, supra at 368.

i. The Impoundment Control Act, § 684, also foreclosed *temporary deferrals* (those ending within the fiscal year when Congress was notified) in case "either House of Congress" passed a disapproving resolution. But note the invalidity of an analogous legislative veto in *Chadha*, infra Sec. 2.

the House nor the President pro tempore of the Senate comes within this language. ＊ ＊ ＊

"[W]e see no reason to believe that the authority of Congress over federal election practices is of such a wholly different nature from the other grants of authority to Congress that it may be employed in such a manner as to offend well established constitutional restrictions stemming from the separation of powers. The position that because Congress has been given explicit and plenary authority to regulate a field of activity, it must therefore have the power to appoint those who are to administer the regulatory statute is both novel and contrary to the language of the Appointments Clause. Unless their selection is elsewhere provided for, *all* Officers of the United States are to be appointed in accordance with the Clause. [Neither] has it been disputed [that] the Clause controls the appointment of the members of a typical administrative agency even though its functions, as this Court recognized in *Humphrey's Executor* [note 1 infra], may be 'predominantly quasi-judicial and quasi-legislative' rather than executive. The Court in that case carefully emphasized that although the members of such agencies were to be independent of the executive in their day-to-day operations, the executive was not excluded from selecting them. ＊ ＊ ＊

"Insofar as the powers confided in the Commission are essentially of an investigative and informative nature, falling in the same general category as those powers which Congress might delegate to one of its own committees, there can be no question that the Commission as presently constituted may exercise them. [But] when we go beyond this type of authority to the more substantial powers exercised by the Commission, we reach a different result. The Commission's enforcement power, exemplified by its discretionary power to seek judicial relief, is authority that cannot possibly be regarded as merely in aid of the legislative function of Congress. ＊ ＊ ＊

"Congress may undoubtedly under the Necessary and Proper Clause create 'offices' in the generic sense and provide such method of appointment to those 'offices' as it chooses. But Congress' power under that Clause is inevitably bounded by the express language of Art. II, § 2, cl. 2, and unless the method it provides comports with the latter, the holders of those offices will not be 'Officers of the United States.' They may, therefore, properly perform duties only in aid of those functions that Congress may carry out by itself, or in an area sufficiently removed from the administration and enforcement of the public law as to permit them being performed by persons not 'Officers of the United States.' ＊ ＊ ＊

"All aspects of the Act are brought within the Commission's broad administrative powers: rule-making, advisory opinions, and determinations of eligibility for funds and even for federal elective office itself. These functions, exercised free from day-to-day supervision of either Congress or the Executive Branch, are more legislative and judicial in nature than are the Commission's enforcement powers, and are of kinds usually performed by independent regulatory agencies or by some department in the Executive Branch under the direction of an Act of Congress. [Yet] each of these functions also represents the performance of a significant governmental duty exercised pursuant to a public law. While the President may not insist that such functions be delegated to an appointee of his removable at will, *Humphrey's Executor,* none of them operates merely in aid of congressional authority to legislate or is sufficiently removed from the administration and enforcement of public law to allow it to be performed by the present

Commission. These administrative functions may therefore be exercised only by persons who are 'Officers of the United States.' "

Notes and Questions

1. *The removal power.* (a) In a sweeping opinion that went well beyond the issues raised, *Myers v. United States,* 272 U.S. 52, 47 S.Ct. 21, 71 L.Ed. 160 (1926), ruled that the President's Sec. II executive power included the power to remove executive officers of the United States, even when their appointment was subject to the advice and consent of the Senate. *Myers* ruled unconstitutional a statute establishing a four year term for first-class postmasters, subject to removal for cause "by the President [with] the advice and consent of the Senate."

Nine years later HUMPHREY'S EXECUTOR v. UNITED STATES, 295 U.S. 602, 55 S.Ct. 869, 79 L.Ed. 1611 (1935), per SUTHERLAND, J., unanimously [a] cut back on *Myers,* limiting it to an "executive officer [performing] executive functions." It ruled that Congress could limit the grounds for removal of a Commissioner of the Federal Trade Commission in order to effectuate "the Congressional intent to create a body of experts * * * independent of Executive authority, except in its selection, and free to exercise its judgment without leave or hindrance of any other official or department of the government.

"[The] authority of Congress, in creating quasi-legislative or quasi-judicial agencies, to require them to act in discharge of their duties independently of executive control, cannot well be doubted; and that authority includes, as an appropriate incident, power to fix the period during which they shall continue, and to forbid their removal except for cause in the meantime. For it is quite evident that one who holds his office only during the pleasure of another cannot be depended upon to maintain an attitude of independence against the latter's will."

2. For consideration of limits on Congressional power over appointments and removal in the light of *Buckley* and earlier cases, see Tribe, *American Constitutional Law* 184–91 (1978); Burkoff, *Appointment and Removal under the Federal Constitution: The Impact of Buckley and Valeo,* 22 Wayne L.Rev. 1335 (1976).

II. LEGISLATIVE VETOES

IMMIGRATION AND NATURALIZATION SERV. v. CHADHA, 462 U.S. 919, 103 S.Ct. 2764, 77 L.Ed.2d 317 (1983): The Immigration and Nationality Act of 1952 authorized the Attorney General to suspend deportation of a deportable alien if he met specified conditions and would suffer "extreme hardship" if deported. It required a report to Congress on each such suspension. Sec. 244(c)(2) provided that if, within a specified period thereafter, either house of Congress "passes a resolution stating [that] it does not favor the suspension the Attorney General shall thereupon deport such alien." Chadha was an East India deportable alien, who remained in the United States after his student visa expired. The Attorney General suspended his deportation pursuant to § 244 and so notified Congress. After the House committee chairman stated that the committee felt that Chadha and five others "did not meet these statutory requirements, particularly as it relates to hardship," the House of Representatives passed a resolution that the "deportation[s] should not be suspended." It was not submitted to the Senate or presented to the President. The court of appeals held

a. McReynolds, J., concurred in the result, noting that his views on the President's removal power were stated in his separate opinion in *Myers.*

§ 244(c)(2) unconstitutional and ordered Chadha not deported. The Court, per BURGER, C.J., affirmed, holding § 244(c)(2)—"the Congressional veto provision"— unconstitutional, but severable from the Act:

"Although not 'hermetically' sealed from one another, *Buckley*, the powers delegated to the three Branches are functionally identifiable. When any Branch acts, it is presumptively exercising the power the Constitution has delegated to it. See *Hampton & Co. v. United States*, 276 U.S. 394, 406, 48 S.Ct. 348, 351, 72 L.Ed. 624 (1928). When the Executive acts, it presumptively acts in an executive or administrative capacity as defined in Art. II. And when, as here, one House of Congress purports to act, it is presumptively acting within its assigned sphere.

"Beginning with this presumption, we must nevertheless establish that the challenged action under § 244(c)(2) is of the kind to which the procedural requirements of Art. I, § 7 apply. Not every action taken by either House is subject to the bicameralism and presentment requirements of Art. I. Whether actions taken by either House are, in law and fact, an exercise of legislative power depends not on their form but upon 'whether they contain matter which is properly to be regarded as legislative in its character and effect.'

"Examination of the action taken here by one House pursuant to § 244(c)(2) reveals that it was essentially legislative in purpose and effect. In purporting to exercise power defined in Art. I, § 8, cl. 4 to 'establish an uniform Rule of Naturalization,' the House took action that had the purpose and effect of altering the legal rights, duties and relations of persons, including the Attorney General, Executive Branch officials and Chadha, all outside the legislative branch. Section 244(c)(2) purports to authorize one House of Congress to require the Attorney General to deport an individual alien whose deportation otherwise would be cancelled under § 244. The one-House veto operated in this case to overrule the Attorney General and mandate Chadha's deportation; absent the House action, Chadha would remain in the United States. Congress has *acted* and its action has altered Chadha's status.

"The legislative character of the one-House veto in this case is confirmed by the character of the Congressional action it supplants. Neither the House of Representatives nor the Senate contends that, absent the veto provision in § 244(c)(2), either of them, or both of them acting together, could effectively require the Attorney General to deport an alien once the Attorney General, in the exercise of legislatively delegated authority,[16] had determined the alien should remain in the United States. Without the challenged provision in § 244(c)(2), this could have been achieved, if at all, only by legislation requiring deportation. Similarly, a veto by one House of Congress under § 244(c)(2) cannot be justified as an attempt at amending the standards set out in § 244(a)(1), or as a repeal of § 244 as applied to Chadha. Amendment and repeal of statutes, no less than enactment, must conform with Art. I.

---

16. Congress protests that affirming the Court of Appeals in this case will sanction "lawmaking by the Attorney General." [The] Attorney General acts in his presumptively Art. II capacity when he administers the Immigration and Nationality Act. Executive action under legislatively delegated authority that might resemble "legislative" action in some respects is not subject to the approval of both Houses of Congress and the President for the reason that the Constitution does not so require. That kind of Executive action is always subject to check by the terms of the legislation that authorized it; and if that authority is exceeded it is open to judicial review as well as the power of Congress to modify or revoke the authority entirely. A one-House veto is clearly legislative in both character and effect and is not so checked; the need for the check provided by Art. I, §§ 1, 7 is therefore clear. Congress' authority to delegate portions of its power to administrative agencies provides no support for the argument that Congress can constitutionally control administration of the laws by way of a Congressional veto.

"The nature of the decision implemented by the one-House veto in this case further manifests its legislative character. After long experience with the clumsy, time consuming private bill procedure, Congress made a deliberate choice to delegate to the Executive Branch, and specifically to the Attorney General, the authority to allow deportable aliens to remain in this country in certain specified circumstances. * * * Disagreement with the Attorney General's decision on Chadha's deportation—that is, Congress' decision to deport Chadha—no less than Congress' original choice to delegate to the Attorney General the authority to make that decision, involves determinations of policy that Congress can implement in only one way: bicameral passage followed by presentment to the President. Congress must abide by its delegation of authority until that delegation is legislatively altered or revoked.[19]

"Finally, we see that when the Framers intended to authorize either House of Congress to act alone and outside of its prescribed bicameral legislative role, they narrowly and precisely defined the procedure for such action. There are but four provisions in the Constitution, explicit and unambiguous, by which one House may act alone with the unreviewable force of law, not subject to the President's veto: [The House of Representative's power to initiate impeachment proceedings, and the Senate's powers to try and convict on impeachment charges, to approve or disapprove Presidential appointments, and to ratify treaties.]

"Clearly, when the Draftsmen sought to confer special powers on one House, independent of the other House, or of the President, they did so in explicit, unambiguous terms.

"[The] bicameral requirement, the Presentment Clauses, the President's veto, and Congress' power to override a veto were intended to erect enduring checks on each Branch and to protect the people from the improvident exercise of power by mandating certain prescribed steps. To preserve those checks, and maintain the separation of powers, the carefully defined limits on the power of each Branch must not be eroded. To accomplish what has been attempted by one House of Congress in this case requires action in conformity with the express procedures of the Constitution's prescription for legislative action: passage by a majority of both Houses and presentment to the President.

"The veto authorized by § 244(c)(2) doubtless has been in many respects a convenient shortcut; the 'sharing' with the Executive by Congress of its authori-

---

19. This does not mean that Congress is required to capitulate to "the accretion of policy control by forces outside its chambers." Javits and Klein, *Congressional Oversight and the Legislative Veto: A Constitutional Analysis,* 52 N.Y.U.L.Rev. 455, 462 (1977). The Constitution provides Congress with abundant means to oversee and control its administrative creatures. Beyond the obvious fact that Congress ultimately controls administrative agencies in the legislation that creates them, other means of control, such as durational limits on authorizations and formal reporting requirements, lie well within Congress' constitutional power. See also note 9, supra.

[Fn. 9, *Chadha* stated: "Without the one-House veto, § 244 resembles the 'report and wait' provision approved by the Court in *Sibbach v. Wilson,* 312 U.S. 1, 61 S.Ct. 422, 85 L.Ed. 479 (1941). The statute examined in Sibbach provided that the newly promulgated Federal Rules of Civil Procedure 'shall not take effect until they shall have been reported to Congress by the Attorney General at the beginning of a regular session thereof and until after the close of such session.' Act of June 19, 1934, ch. 651, § 2, 48 Stat. 1064. This statute did *not* provide that Congress could unilaterally veto the Federal Rules. Rather, it gave Congress the opportunity to review the Rules before they became effective and to pass legislation barring their effectiveness if the Rules were found objectionable. This technique was used by Congress when it acted in 1973 to stay, and ultimately to revise, the proposed Rules of Evidence. Compare Act of March 30, 1973, Pub.L. No. 93–12, 87 Stat. 9, with Act of Jan. 2, 1975, Pub.L. 93–595, 88 Stat. 1926."]

ty over aliens in this manner is, on its face, an appealing compromise. In purely practical terms, it is obviously easier for action to be taken by one House without submission to the President; but it is crystal clear from the records of the Convention, contemporaneous writings and debates, that the Framers ranked other values higher than efficiency. * * *

"The choices we discern as having been made in the Constitutional Convention impose burdens on governmental processes that often seem clumsy, inefficient, even unworkable, but those hard choices were consciously made by men who had lived under a form of government that permitted arbitrary governmental acts to go unchecked. There is no support in the Constitution or decisions of this Court for the proposition that the cumbersomeness and delays often encountered in complying with explicit Constitutional standards may be avoided, either by the Congress or by the President." [a]

Noting that the "Court's decision * * * apparently will invalidate every use of the legislative veto," Powell, J., concurred in the judgment on the "narrower ground" that the House finding that a "particular person does not satisfy the statutory criteria for permanent residence * * * assumed a judicial function in violation of [the] separation of powers."

WHITE, J., dissented: "The prominence of the legislative veto mechanism in our contemporary political system and its importance to Congress can hardly be overstated. It has become a central means by which Congress secures the accountability of executive and independent agencies. Without the legislative veto, Congress is faced with a Hobson's choice: either to refrain from delegating the necessary authority, leaving itself with a hopeless task of writing laws with the requisite specificity to cover endless special circumstances across the entire policy landscape, or in the alternative, to abdicate its lawmaking function to the executive branch and independent agencies. To choose the former leaves major national problems unresolved; to opt for the latter risks unaccountable policymaking by those not elected to fill that role. Accordingly, over the past five decades, the legislative veto has been placed in nearly 200 statutes. The device is known in every field of governmental concern: reorganization, budgets, foreign affairs, war powers, and regulation of trade, safety, energy, the environment and the economy.

"[T]he legislative veto is more than 'efficient, convenient, and useful.' It is an important if not indispensable political invention that allows the President and Congress to resolve major constitutional and policy differences, assures the accountability of independent regulatory agencies, and preserves Congress' control over lawmaking. Perhaps there are other means of accommodation and accountability, but the increasing reliance of Congress upon the legislative veto suggests that the alternatives to which Congress must now turn are not entirely satisfactory.[10]

a. In finding § 244(c)(2) severable from § 244, which authorized the Attorney General to suspend the deportation of a particular deportable alien, the Court relied heavily on § 406 of the Act, which provides: "If *any* particular provision of this Act, or the application thereof to *any* person or circumstance, is held invalid, *the remainder of the Act and the application of such provision to other persons or circumstances shall not be affected thereby.*" (Emphasis by the Court). The Court also found support for the severability of § 244(c)(2) in the legislative history of § 244. For

consideration of the severability issue see Tribe, *The Legislative Veto Decision: A Law by Any Other Name,* 21 Harv.J. on Leg. 1, 21–27 (1984); 97 Harv.L.Rev. 1182 (1984).

10. While Congress could write certain statutes with greater specificity, it is unlikely that this is a realistic or even desirable substitute for the legislative veto. "Political volatility and the controversy of many issues would prevent Congress from reaching agreement on many major problems if specificity were required in their enactments." Fuchs, *Adminis-*

"The history of the legislative veto also makes clear that it has not been a sword with which Congress has struck out to aggrandize itself at the expense of the other branches—the concerns of Madison and Hamilton. Rather, the veto has been a means of defense, a reservation of ultimate authority necessary if Congress is to fulfill its designated role under Article I as the nation's lawmaker. While the President has often objected to particular legislative vetoes, generally those left in the hands of congressional committees, the Executive has more often agreed to legislative review as the price for a broad delegation of authority. To be sure, the President may have preferred unrestricted power, but that could be precisely why Congress thought it essential to retain a check on the exercise of delegated authority.

" [The] Court's Article I analysis appears to invalidate all legislative vetoes irrespective of form or subject. Because the legislative veto is commonly found as a check upon rulemaking by administrative agencies and upon broad-based policy decisions of the Executive Branch, it is particularly unfortunate that the Court reaches its decision in a case involving the exercise of a veto over deportation decisions regarding particular individuals. Courts should always be wary of striking statutes as unconstitutional; to strike an entire class of statutes based on consideration of a somewhat atypical and more-readily indictable exemplar of the class is irresponsible. * * *.[11]

"[T]he constitutional question posed today is one of immense difficulty over which the executive and legislative branches—as well as scholars and judges— have understandably disagreed. That disagreement stems from the silence of the Constitution on the precise question: The Constitution does not directly authorize or prohibit the legislative veto. Thus, our task should be to determine whether the legislative veto is consistent with the purposes of Art. I and the principles of Separation of Powers which are reflected in that Article and throughout the Constitution. We should not find the lack of a specific constitutional authorization for the legislative veto surprising, and I would not infer disapproval of the mechanism from its absence. * * *

"I do not dispute the Court's truismatic exposition of [the prerequisites for lawmaking set forth in Art. I of the Constitution.[16]] All of this [part of the Court's opinion] is entirely unexceptionable.

trative Agencies and the Energy Problem, 47 Ind.L.J. 606, 608 (1972); Stewart, *Reformation of American Administrative Law,* 88 Harv.L. Rev. 1667, 1695–1696 (1975). * * *

11. Perhaps I am wrong and the Court remains open to consider whether certain forms of the legislative veto are reconcilable with the Article I requirements. One possibility for the Court and Congress is to accept that a resolution of disapproval cannot be given legal effect in its own right, but may serve as a guide in the interpretation of a delegation of lawmaking authority. The exercise of the veto could be read as a manifestation of legislative intent, which, unless itself contrary to the authorizing statute, serves as the definitive construction of the statute. Therefore, an agency rule vetoed by Congress would not be enforced in the courts because the veto indicates that the agency action departs from the Congressional intent.

This limited role for a redefined legislative veto follows in the steps of the longstanding practice of giving some weight to subsequent legislative reaction to administrative rulemaking. The silence of Congress after consideration of a practice by the Executive may be equivalent to acquiescence and consent that the practice be continued until the power exercised be revoked. * * *

16. I agree with Justice Rehnquist [who dissented on the severability issue] that Congress did not intend the one-House veto provision of § 244(c)(2) to be severable.

[F]or forty years Congress has insisted on retaining a voice on individual suspension cases—it has frequently rejected bills which would place final authority in the Executive branch. It is clear that Congress believed its retention crucial. Given this history, the Court's rewriting of the Act flouts the will of Congress.

"It does not, however, answer the constitutional question before us. The power to exercise a legislative veto is not the power to write new law without bicameral approval or presidential consideration. The veto must be authorized by statute and may only negative what an Executive department or independent agency has proposed. On its face, the legislative veto no more allows one House of Congress to make law than does the presidential veto confer such power upon the President. * * *

"The Court's holding today that all legislative-type action must be enacted through the lawmaking process ignores that legislative authority is routinely delegated to the Executive branch, to the independent regulatory agencies, and to private individuals and groups. [For] some time, the sheer amount of law—the substantive rules that regulate private conduct and direct the operation of government—made by the agencies has far outnumbered the lawmaking engaged in by Congress through the traditional process. There is no question but that agency rulemaking is lawmaking in any functional or realistic sense of the term. [These] regulations bind courts and officers of the federal government, may pre-empt state law, and grant rights to and impose obligations on the public. In sum, they have the force of law.

"If Congress may delegate lawmaking power to independent and executive agencies, it is most difficult to understand Article I as forbidding Congress from also reserving a check on legislative power for itself. Absent the veto, the agencies receiving delegations of legislative or quasi-legislative power may issue regulations having the force of law without bicameral approval and without the President's signature. It is thus not apparent why the reservation of a veto over the exercise of that legislative power must be subject to a more exacting test. In both cases, it is enough that the initial statutory authorizations comply with the Article I requirements.

"[Under] the Court's analysis, the Executive Branch and the independent agencies may make rules with the effect of law while Congress, in whom the Framers confided the legislative power, Art. I, § 1, may not exercise a veto which precludes such rules from having operative force. If the effective functioning of a complex modern government requires the delegation of vast authority which, by virtue of its breadth, is legislative or 'quasi-legislative' in character, I cannot accept that Article I—which is, after all, the source of the nondelegation doctrine—should forbid Congress from qualifying that grant with a legislative veto.[21]

"The Court also takes no account of perhaps the most relevant consideration: However resolutions of disapproval under § 244(c)(2) are formally characterized, in reality, a departure from the status quo occurs only upon the concurrence of opinion among the House, Senate, and President. * * *

"The central concern of the presentation and bicameralism requirements of Article I is that when a departure from the legal status quo is undertaken, it is

---

21. [The] Court also argues that "the legislative character of the challenged action of one House is confirmed by the fact that when the Framers intended to authorize either House of Congress to act alone and outside of its prescribed bicameral legislative role, they narrowly and precisely defined the procedure for such action." [T]he short answer is that all of these carefully defined exceptions to the presentment and bicameralism strictures do not involve action of the Congress pursuant to a duly-enacted statute. Indeed, for the most part these powers—those of impeachment, review of appointments, and treaty ratification—are not legislative powers at all. The fact that it was essential for the Constitution to stipulate that Congress has the power to impeach and try the President hardly demonstrates a limit upon Congress' authority to reserve itself a legislative veto, through statutes, over subjects within its lawmaking authority.

done with the approval of the President and both Houses of Congress—or, in the event of a presidential veto, a two-thirds majority in both Houses. This interest is fully satisfied by the operation of § 244(c)(2). The President's approval is found in the Attorney General's action in recommending to Congress that the deportation order for a given alien be suspended. The House and the Senate indicate their approval of the Executive's action by not passing a resolution of disapproval within the statutory period. Thus, a change in the legal status quo—the deportability of the alien—is consummated only with the approval of each of the three relevant actors. The disagreement of any one of the three maintains the alien's pre-existing status: the Executive may choose not to recommend suspension; the House and Senate may each veto the recommendation. The effect on the rights and obligations of the affected individuals and upon the legislative system is precisely the same as if a private bill were introduced but failed to receive the necessary approval. 'The President and the two Houses enjoy exactly the same say in what the law is to be as would have been true for each without the presence of the one-House veto, and nothing in the law is changed absent the concurrence of the President and a majority in each House.' "

Notes and Questions

1. *Extension of Chadha to regulatory agency rulemaking.* Two weeks after *Chadha,* with no explanation, citation, or oral argument, PROCESS GAS CONSUMERS GROUP v. FERC[a] affirmed per curiam Court of Appeals decisions invalidating one-house legislative vetoes of regulatory rulemaking by the Federal Energy Regulatory Commission and two-house vetoes of such rulemaking by the Federal Trade Commission. Rehnquist, J., would have noted probable jurisdiction and set the cases for oral argument. Powell, J., took no part. WHITE, J., dissented:

"[The] National Gas Policy Act was a compromise, reached only after months of impasse between the two Houses over the optimal means of deregulating natural gas prices while preventing excessive fuel bills for consumers and industry. [The] compromise [provided] for an initial experiment with incremental pricing for a small class of industrial users, while authorizing FERC to propose expansion of incremental pricing to other industrial users [that] would be submitted to Congress and would become effective unless disapproved by either House. The veto provision was central to this accommodation, because it allowed the Congress to observe the effects of the initial phase of incremental pricing without committing the nation to a broader program which, it was feared, would [raise] the cost of gas for residential consumers.

"[For] three years, Congress debated the breadth of the [Federal Trade] Commission's rulemaking authority, noting that the FTC could, pursuant to the Act, 'regulate virtually every aspect of America's commercial life.' 124 Cong. Rec. 5012 (1978) (Rep. Broyhill). The two-House veto provision was settled upon as a means of allowing Congress to study and review the broad and important policy pronouncements of the Commission.

"I cannot agree that the legislative vetoes in these cases violate the requirements of Article I of the Constitution. Where the veto is placed as a check upon the actions of the independent regulatory agencies, the Article I analysis relied

---

a.   463 U.S. 1216, 103 S.Ct. 3556, 77 L.Ed. 2d 1413 (1983), affirming *Consumer Energy Council v. FERC,* 673 F.2d 425 (D.C.Cir.1982), and *Consumers Union v. FTC,* 691 F.2d 575 (D.C.Cir.1982).

upon in *Chadha* has a particularly hollow ring. [These] regulations have the force of law without the President's concurrence; nor can he veto them if he disagrees with the law that they make. [To] invalidate the [legislative veto,] which allows Congress to maintain some control over the law-making process, merely guarantees that the independent agencies, once created, for all practical purposes are a fourth branch of the government not subject to the direct control of either Congress or the executive branch. I cannot believe that the Constitution commands such a result."

2. Commentaries on legislative vetoes are cited below.[b]

3. *Variant uses of legislative vetoes.* First used in 1932 when Congress authorized the President to reorganize the executive departments subject to a one-House veto, legislative vetoes in various forms have had a divergent range of applications. They are loosely classifiable [a] into four categories:

(1) *Those that "allowed the President and Congress to resolve directly constitutional and policy differences on issues of high political and small legal moment."* See Strauss supra at 791. For example, Section 5(c) of the 1973 War Powers Resolution, enacted over the President's veto, requires that U.S. armed forces engaged in hostilities outside United States "shall be removed by the President if Congress so directs by concurrent resolution." 50 U.S.C. § 1544(c).[b] And the 1977 IEEPA delegated broad economic powers to the President to "deal with any unusual or extraordinary threat" to United States national security, foreign policy or economy, "having its sources" outside the United States, "if the President declares a national emergency with respect to such threat," subject to the emergency being "terminated by the Congress by concurrent resolution." 50 U.S.C. §§ 1701, 1706(b).

(2) *Those legislative vetoes that "accommodate a necessarily continuing dialogue between Congress and the President on matters internal to government."* [c] Typical are those that retain in Congress power to override the President's decisions on reorganizing the structure of the government [d] and on impoundment of funds appropriated by Congress.[e]

b. Before *Chadha*: Bruff & Gellhorn, *Congressional Control of Administrative Regulation*, 90 Harv.L.Rev. 1369 (1977); Javits & Klein, *Congressional Oversight and the Legislative Veto: A Constitutional Analysis*, 52 N.Y.U.L.Rev. 455 (1977); Miller & Knapp, *The Constitutional Veto: Preserving the Constitutional Framework*, 52 Ind.L.J. 367 (1977); Dixon, *The Congressional Veto and Separation of Powers: The Executive on a Leash?* 56 N.C.L. Rev. 423 (1978); Schwartz, *The Legislative Veto and the Constitution—A Reexamination*, 46 Geo.Wash.L.Rev. 351 (1978); Tribe, *American Constitutional Law* 161–63 (1978).

After *Chadha*: Breyer, *The Legislative Veto After Chadha*, 72 Geo.L.J. 785 (1984); Elliott, *INS v. Chadha: The Administrative Constitution, the Constitution, and the Legislative Veto*, 1983 Sup.Ct.Rev. 125; Strauss, *Was There A Baby in the Bathwater? A Comment on the Supreme Court's Legislative Veto Decision*, 1983 Duke L.J. 789; Tribe, *The Legislative Veto Decision: A Law by Any Other Name?* 21 Harv.J. on Leg. 1 (1984).

a. Professor Strauss noted these four types of use for legislative vetoes in discussing the Court's failure to take their differences into consideration in the *Chadha* opinion. See Strauss, supra at 791.

b. The War Powers Resolution also seeks to trigger a Presidential duty to withdraw troops from hostilities upon *nonaction* by Congress. For consideration of the Resolution, see Part III, infra.

c. See Strauss, supra at 791.

d. From 1932 to 1982, 24 of the 230 legislative vetoes actually exercised related to government reorganization. See Smith & Struve, *Aftershocks of the Fall of the Legislative Veto*, 69 A.B.A.J. 1258, 1258 (1983).

e. See Sec. 1, supra: Congressional Impoundment and Budget Control Act of 1974, 31 U.S.C. § 1403(a)–(c). Of the 230 legislative vetoes, 65 involved impoundment. See Smith & Struve, supra.

(3) *Those in which Congress sheds the historic legislative burden of private bills on "highly individual matters" by delegating the decision-making to the executive, subject to legislative veto in individual cases, as in Chadha.*[f]

(4) *Those in which the legislative veto is used for "oversight of agency conduct such as public rulemaking directly affecting obligations of the public."*[g]

4. *Chadha's broad sweep.* (a) The *Chadha* Supplemental Brief on Reargument for the Senate urged the Court to avoid a "sweeping approach" that "would deny to the Court an understanding of the actual roles of legislative review provisions with their varying histories, constitutional contexts and justifications." The Brief pointed out that "in cases currently pending [a] the Court will have the opportunity to examine legislative review in two of its uses." From the extensive White dissent it is fair to infer that in considering *Chadha* substantial discussion occurred among the Justices over many facets of the legislative veto issue—including use of the veto in regulatory rulemaking situations—far removed from the *Chadha* setting.

(b) Should the Court have limited its *Chadha* opinion to the validity of legislative vetoes of individual deportation decisions, like *Chadha*, perhaps recognized as representative of a potentially broader class of decisions on "highly individual matters" (i.e. status)? Are the considerations that should affect the validity of legislative vetoes under differing uses likely to be so similar in nature and weight as to foreclose the need to appraise the particular use at issue, analyzing in that setting the veto's functions, values, and potential threats to the constitutional structure? Cf. Strauss, supra at 791–92, 812–19; Breyer, supra at 796–98; Tribe, supra at 2, 7. See, e.g., discussions of the pro and con considerations applicable to legislative vetoes of regulatory rulemaking. See, Elliott, supra at 150–156; Strauss, supra at 807–811.

5. *Alternatives to legislative veto.* Since *Chadha*, considerable attention has been given to possible alternatives to legislative vetoes.[b] Consider e.g., the following alternatives: their validity, practicality and whether they would satisfy the congressional interest in effective review and control over the exercise of delegated power:

(a) In delegating power, provide that its exercise *shall* be effective 60 days after being laid before Congress unless disapproved by legislation enacted within the 60 days. Cf. *Chadha*, n. 19 and n. 9, supra; Levitas & Brand, supra fn. b, at 804–05.

(b) In delegating power, provide that its exercise shall *not* be effective unless a confirmatory statute is enacted within 60 days after the action is laid before Congress. Id. at 805–806.

(c) Couple alternative (b) with "fast track" rules changes in each house, requiring a vote within 60 days without reference to committee, and not subject

---

f. See Breyer, *The Legislative Veto After Chadha,* supra at 787, cf. Strauss, supra at 791 ("questions of individual status such as deportability"). Suspension of deportation issues accounted for 111 of the 230 legislative vetoes between 1932 and 1982. See Smith & Struve, supra. Judge Breyer suggested that but for *Chadha* similar procedures might have developed for private claims on the legislature for money.

g. Strauss, supra at 791.

a. The "currently pending" cases were those involving legislative vetoes over regulatory rulemaking by FERC and FTC decided per curiam two weeks after *Chadha*. See note 1, supra.

b. Breyer, supra at 792–96; Tribe, supra at 18–21, Strauss, supra at 811–12; Levitas & Brand, *Congressional Review of Executive and Agency Actions after Chadha: "The Son of Legislative Veto" Lives On,* 72 Geo.L.J. 801 (1984).

to debate, amendment, filibuster or motion to table, but subject to being derailed by a majority vote of either house. Breyer, supra at 793.

III. THE WAR POWERS

THE "YALE PAPER"—INDOCHINA: THE CONSTITUTIONAL CRISIS

Part One appears in 116 Cong.Rec. S 7117–S 7123 (daily ed. May 13, 1970);
Part Two in 116 Cong.Rec. S 7591–S 7593 (May 21, 1970).

Part One [a]

IV. The Theoretical Bases for Unilateral Presidential Action. [b] The theories on which various Presidents have relied for the use of military force abroad without congressional approval may be divided into three general categories * * *.

(1) *The Sudden Attack Theory.*—The President as the Chief Executive has the inherent power to defend the sovereignty and integrity of the nation itself and to respond to an armed attack on the territory of the United States without requesting congressional approval. [But in] the absence of an armed attack on American territory proper, the power of the President is more closely circumscribed.[40]

a. According to Senator McGovern, who had Part One printed in the Congressional Record, "the basic research and drafting" for this Part was done by 12 Yale law students and authored by Professors Alexander Bickel, Elias Clark and Burke Marshall of Yale Law School; former Attorney General Ramsey Clark; former Assistant Attorneys General John Doar, John Douglas, Louis Oberdorfer, Stephen Pollak and Edwin Zimmerman; former Assistant Secretary of Defense Paul Warnke; former Judge Bruce Bromley; and attorneys William Coleman, George Lindsay and Robert Pennoyer.

b. Part One also dealt with the historical development of the division of power between the President and Congress over the use of military force. For a thorough study of the first thirty years under the Constitution, see Sofaer, *War, Foreign Affairs and Constitutional Power: The Origins* (1976) and Judge Sofaer's briefer study, *The Presidency, War, and Foreign Affairs: Practice under the Framers,* 40 Law & Contemp.Prob. 12 (Spring 1976). Part One noted that most of the military action ordered by the President alone in the nineteenth century did not involve "conflicts with foreign states [but] the protection of individuals, police action against pirates, or actions against primitive peoples." But in the early twentieth century the Executive "began to exercise greater discretion in the use [of] armed forces abroad," starting with President Theodore Roosevelt sending troops into Panama in 1903 without specific congressional approval.

"Since 1945, the executive has regularly used military force abroad as a tool of diplomacy. Aside from Indochina [and Korea], American forces were sent in the Formosan Strait in 1955, into Lebanon in 1958, and into the Dominican Republic in 1965. The Navy was used to blockade Cuba during the missile crisis in 1962. And most recently, naval vessels were dispatched to the vicinity of Haiti and Trinidad in response to internal conflicts in those countries. Prior congressional resolutions were obtained by the President for the Formosan and Lebanese actions, but both the validity of those resolutions and the degree to which President Eisenhower relied on them has been questioned."

40. [In] the event of an armed attack on the territory of the United States proper, there is little question that the executive possesses the power to respond with all means at his disposal. Congressional approval of such action would probably be immediate. When, on the other hand, an attack is made on American persons or property abroad, then the response should generally be proportional to the attack. [N]ot every use of force against the United States is an act which places the country at [war].

There is also the danger of provocation, either planned or accidental. The mere presence of American forces near a hostile nation may provoke a "sudden attack." [If] the response to such an attack is not limited, then the country may become involved in a much larger conflict with little or no executive-legislative collaboration. [See also Note, 81 Harv. L.Rev. 1771, 1783–84 (1968)].

(2) *The Neutrality Theory.*—Also known as "interposition," the neutrality theory was developed during the nineteenth century as a justification for American military involvement abroad to protect American citizens and property. When American armed forces were sent into a foreign nation, their presence was supposed to be "neutral" with respect to any conflicts there. *The executive, in taking such action, [was] merely dispatching troops to act as security guards for American citizens and their property. The real difficulty, clearly, was in remaining neutral and avoiding conflict.*[41]

(3) *The Collective Security Theory.*—Since 1945, the United States has entered into many security treaties with foreign nations [with] clauses which indicate that the security of each signatory is vital to the security of each other signatory. Unilateral presidential action under these agreements may be justified as necessary for the protection of American security even though the conflict may arise thousands of miles from American shores, but, *carried to its extreme, the collective security theory would justify almost any unilateral presidential use of armed force abroad, a result contrary to Constitutional standards.*

* * *

Part Two [c]

I. The Congressional and Executive Roles in War-Making: An Analytical Framework. In [the *Steel Seizure* case], Justice Jackson developed a theory of the power relationship between Congress and the President which is useful in analyzing the current constitutional crisis over the Indochina War. *Justice Jackson posited that a large measure of power to make national policy is fixed in neither the Presidency nor the Congress, but rather fluctuates with the initiatives and actions of each branch.* [T]he implications [are] that: 1) In the zone of exclusive executive power, any legislation attempting to restrict presidential action is void and can be ignored by the President, even if it is "passed" over his veto. 2) In the zone of exclusive congressional power, any presidential action is illegal and can be prevented or ended by action of Congress. 3) In the twilight zone of concurrent power, either the President or Congress can act in the absence of initiative by the other. If both attempt to act in ways that bring their wills into conflict, the deadlock must be resolved in favor of congressional action through valid legislation, which includes legislation passed over a presidential veto. * * *

The federal government [possesses] all the "necessary concomitants of nationality" [*Curtiss-Wright*]—all those powers necessary to enable the United States to act in the international arena on an equal footing with other nations. It is doubtful whether [such powers] could be enumerated in any constitution: they are too much dependent on an evolving historical context, and too little susceptible of definition. In any case, our constitution did not attempt to enumerate them. The sum of the war and foreign policy powers specifically

---

41. * * * "Interposition" may easily lead to "intervention" and the Congress may be faced with a fait accompli. President Roosevelt accomplished an actual "intervention" in Panama in 1903 by "interposing" American troops there under an executive order, ostensibly to protect American property and citizens, but actually to support a friendly government.

However, American citizens who live or own property abroad probably should be able to expect some degree of aid from their government in time of conflict. But [in] many cases, the risks of deployment may be greater than the risks of restraint. [See also Note, 81 Harv.L.Rev. 1771, 1790, 1796–98 (1968)].

* * *

c. This part of the memorandum was signed by Dean Louis Pollak and Professors Alexander Bickel and Charles Black, Jr., of the Yale Law School.

granted to the legislative and executive branches is less than the totality of power inherent in the concept of sovereignty. And it is precisely because there exists an amorphous residuum of national power above and beyond the sum of enumerated powers that Jackson's twilight zone *must* exist, despite its apparent incongruity with traditional separation of powers and checks and balances notions. Those powers must vest somewhere, and there is *nothing*—nothing in the Constitution, nothing in history, nothing in the case law,[13] and nothing in common sense—to suggest that the entire residuum vests exclusively in one or the other branch.

[T]he best approach is to attempt to reach a general understanding of the nature of the power appropriate to each branch, based on (1) the special competences of each, and (2) the probable internal consequences of external [actions].

The foregoing considerations support two conclusions: (1) When a decision in foreign or military affairs demands speed and decisiveness, there is a presumption that it is within the exclusive power of the President. (2) *All other decisions* are within the power of Congress. Some of that congressional power is in the twilight zone and held concurrently with the President. But when the decision entails a significant commitment of the nation's human, physical, and moral resources, there is a presumption of congressional exclusivity. The presumption can be rebutted: The President can unilaterally commit a significant amount of the nation's human, physical, and moral resources; but he can do so *only if* there is a *clear need* for speed and decisiveness.

There are, of course, no clear lines of division. It is impossible to define "a significant amount" of resources; and certainly the President has twilight zone power to commit less than "a significant amount" to foreign and military actions (but only in the absence of a prior expression of conflicting congressional will). [But] *there is a point at which decisions become so momentous—in human, physical, and moral terms—that power passes from the twilight zone into the exclusively legislative zone.*

II. The Indochina War in Context: Institutional Responsibility. [The] thrust of Justice Jackson's analysis and the thrust of history support strongly one basic conclusion: *Within the twilight zone of shared power, if members of Congress have views on the conduct of foreign and military affairs which differ from those of the President, there is no reason—in the Constitution, in theory, or in precedent—why they should hesitate to write their policy preferences into [law].*

In our opinion, the major questions [in] Indochina approach the zone of authority which belongs exclusively to the Congress. Thousands of our young men are killing and being killed; billions of dollars of resources are being expended; and the moral strength of the nation is being undermined. Indochina *does* go further toward the legislative pole than any President has gone unilaterally in the [past]. Whenever Congress acquiesces in the actions of a President, it admits that the power to act was not exclusively legislative—that the President had at least concurrent authority. In short, *Congress as an institution must realize that its action or inaction in the current situation will define for the future the boundary between the twilight and exclusively legislative zones.*

---

13. The statement in *Curtiss-Wright* that the President is "the sole organ of the federal government in the field of international relations" is not to the contrary. It asserts that the President is the sole executor of American international policy, but does not deal with the question of which branch is to make that policy.

WAR POWERS RESOLUTION

The War Powers Resolution, 87 Stat. 555, 50 U.S.C. §§ 1541–48 (1982 ed.), was passed over presidential veto, Nov. 7, 1973:

PURPOSE AND POLICY

Sec. 2.   (a) It is the purpose of this joint resolution to fulfill the intent of the framers of the Constitution of the United States and insure that the collective judgment of both the Congress and the President will apply to the introduction of United States Armed Forces into hostilities, or into situations where imminent involvement in hostilities is clearly indicated by the circumstances, and to the continued use of such forces in hostilities or in such situations.

* * *

CONSULTATION

Sec. 3.   The President in every possible instance shall consult with Congress before introducing United States Armed Forces into hostilities or into situations where imminent involvement in hostilities is clearly indicated by the circumstances, and after every such introduction shall consult regularly with the Congress until United States Armed Forces are no longer engaged in hostilities or have been removed from such situations.

REPORTING

Sec. 4.   (a) In the absence of a declaration of war, in any case in which United States Armed Forces are introduced—

(1) into hostilities or into situations where imminent involvement in hostilities is clearly indicated by the circumstances;

(2) into the territory, airspace or waters of a foreign nation, while equipped for combat, except for deployments which relate solely to supply, replacement, repair, or training of such forces; or

(3) in numbers which substantially enlarge United States Armed Forces equipped for combat already located in a foreign nation;

the President shall submit within 48 hours to the Speaker of the House of Representatives and to the President pro tempore of the Senate a report, in writing [setting forth "the circumstances necessitating the introduction of armed forces," "the constitutional and legislative authority" under which it occurred, "the estimated scope and duration of the hostilities," and "such other information as the Congress may request."]

CONGRESSIONAL ACTION * * *

Sec. 5.   * * * (b) Within sixty calendar days after a report is submitted or is required to be submitted pursuant to section 4(a)(1), whichever is earlier, the President shall terminate any use of United States Armed Forces with respect to which such report was submitted (or required to be submitted), unless the Congress (1) has declared war or has enacted a specific authorization for such use of United States Armed Forces, (2) has extended by law such sixty-day period, or (3) is physically unable to meet as a result of an armed attack upon the United States. Such sixty-day period shall be extended for not more than an additional thirty days if the President determines and certifies to the Congress in writing that unavoidable military necessity respecting the safety of United States Armed

Forces requires the continued use of such armed forces in the course of bringing about a prompt removal of such forces.

(c) Notwithstanding subsection (b), at any time that United States Armed Forces are engaged in hostilities outside the territory of the United States, its possessions and territories without a declaration of war or specific statutory authorization, such forces shall be removed by the President if the Congress so directs by concurrent resolution. * * *

Notes and Questions

1. *Commentaries.* For a wide range of views on legal issues raised by the War Powers Resolution see the commentaries cited below.[a]

2. *When Congress and the President disagree.* An internal revolt against the government of Grenada led to the death of its Prime Minister and to chaotic conditions with "shoot to kill" curfews and no government protection of life or property. On October 25, 1983, President Reagan, "consistent with the War Powers Resolution", reported to Congress that early that day 1900 U.S. Army and Marine Corps troops, joined by 300 from Caribbean States, landed in Grenada supported by the U.S. Navy and Air Force. The stated objective was to restore "conditions of law and order and of governmental institutions to Grenada and to facilitate protection and evacuation of [up to 1,000] U.S. citizens. 129 Cong.Rec. S14725. With order restored and a temporary government set up, the combat troops were withdrawn in mid-December.

(a) Had hostilities continued in Grenada in early December, could Congress by a joint resolution passed over the President's veto have created a legal obligation on the President to withdraw from hostilities and remove the troops from Grenada as speedily as safety permitted? Would this have been a usurpation of the President's powers? Or an exercise of Congress' powers to declare—and not to declare—war? Or to "decide when the President's actions slide down the scale from use of troops in time of peace to use of troops in time of war?" See Carter, fn. a at 112. Or a withdrawal in this situation of congressional acquiescence in the President's temporary use of troops in hostilities abroad? Cf. Carter, supra at 123–26.

(b) Assuming no congressional action respecting Grenada, had troops not been withdrawn within the 60 to 90 days prescribed by the War Powers Resolution, could Sec. 5(b) of the Resolution have created a legal obligation on the President to remove the troops? Is Sec. 5(b) invalid as the equivalent of a one-house legislative veto on executive action? See Lundgren, *The War Powers Resolution after the Chadha Decision,* 17 Loy.L. Rev. 767, 782–86 (1984). Or is Sec. 5(b) the "functional equivalent of a statute reading, 'The President may not commit troops to combat for longer than sixty days.'" See Carter, supra at 133.

(c) If standing is satisfied, should the issues raised by (a) and (b) above be found justiciable? Consider Carter, supra at 107 n. 32, 115; Choper, *Judicial Review and the National Political Process* 263 (1980); Firmage, *The War Powers and the Political Question Doctrine,* 49 U.Colo.L.Rev. 65 (1977). If "[u]ltimately, the real check upon executive abuse of the war [powers] must come from

a. Carter, *The Constitutionality of the War Powers Resolution,* 70 Va.L.Rev. 101 (1984); Turner, *The War Powers Resolution: Unconstitutional, Unnecessary, and Unhelpful,* 17 Loy.L.A.L.Rev. 683 (1984); Frank, *After the Fall: The New Procedural Framework for Congressional Control over the War Powers,* 71 Am.J.Int'l.L. 605 (1977); Emerson, *The War Powers Resolution Tested: The President's Independent Defense Power,* 51 Notre Dame Law. 187 (1975); Rostow, *Great Cases Make Bad Law: The War Powers Act,* 50 Tex.L.Rev. 833 (1972); Berger, *War-Making by the President,* 121 U.Pa.L.Rev. 29 (1972).

congressional action," should the Court feel "substantially free from the limitations of the doctrine of political questions" when "Congress expresses its view of the war powers as it did in the War Powers Resolution"? See Firmage, supra, at 101.

SECTION 3. EXECUTIVE PRIVILEGE AND IMMUNITY

I. EXECUTIVE PRIVILEGE

UNITED STATES v. NIXON

418 U.S. 683, 94 S.Ct. 3090, 41 L.Ed.2d 1039 (1974).

MR. CHIEF JUSTICE BURGER delivered the opinion of the Court.

[In the wake of Watergate the Attorney General appointed a special prosecutor authorized to control the course of investigations and litigation relating to "all offenses arising out of the 1972 Presidential Election," and "to contest the assertion of 'Executive Privilege.' " [a] After securing an indictment against seven staff members and political associates of President Nixon for conspiracy to obstruct justice and other Watergate-related offenses, naming the President an unindicted coconspirator, the Special Prosecutor caused the district court on April 18, 1974, to issue a subpoena to the President to produce certain precisely identified tapes and documents. The President moved to quash the subpoena, asserting executive privilege. The court denied the motion and ordered the material delivered for *in camera* inspection. When the President appealed, the Supreme Court granted the Special Prosecutor's petition for a writ of certiorari, bypassing the court of appeals. After a hearing on July 8, the decision was announced on July 24 upholding the subpoena.]

* * *

IV. *The Claim of Privilege.* [W]e turn to the claim that the subpoena should be quashed because it demands "confidential conversations between a President and his close advisors that it would be inconsistent with the public interest to produce." * * *

In the performance of assigned constitutional duties each branch of the Government must initially interpret the Constitution, and the interpretation of its powers by any branch is due great respect from the others. The President's counsel [reads] the Constitution as providing an absolute privilege of confidentiality for all presidential communications. Many decisions of this Court, however, have unequivocally reaffirmed the holding of *Marbury v. Madison* that "it is emphatically the province and duty of the judicial department to say what the law is." [b]

a. Fn. 8 of the full opinion provides details on the Special Prosecutor's independence.

b. Does the use of the *Marbury* statement "convey a misleadingly broad view of judicial competence, exclusivity and supremacy"? Did the Court intend to announce that "every constitutional issue requires final adjudication on the merits by the judiciary"? See Gunther, note 1 following this case, at 33–34. Did anything in *Marbury* prevent the Court from "declar[ing] 'the law' to be that the President is the sole determiner of the need for protect-

ing the confidentiality of particular communications, just as 'the law' grants him sole authority over recognition of the legal government of a foreign state"? See Freund, note 4 following this case, at 21–22. Cf. Karst & Horowitz, *Presidential Prerogative and Judicial Review,* 22 U.C.L.A.L.Rev. 47, 55 (1974): "[T]he very question at issue is whether the assertion of executive privilege lies within the sphere of *law* (so that courts can legitimately review the assertion) or within the sphere of *discretion* (so that the executive's determina-

* * * Notwithstanding the deference each branch must accord the others, the "judicial power of the United States" vested in the federal courts by Art. III, § 1 [can] no more be shared with the Executive Branch than the Chief Executive, for example, can share with the Judiciary the veto power, or the Congress share with the Judiciary the power to override a presidential veto. Any other conclusion would be contrary to the basic concept of separation of powers and the checks and balances that flow from the scheme of a tripartite [government].

In support of his claim of absolute privilege, the President's counsel urges two [grounds]. The first [is] the valid need for protection of communications between high government officials and those who advise and assist them in the performance of their manifold duties; the importance of this confidentiality is too plain to require further discussion. Human experience teaches that those who expect public dissemination of their remarks may well temper candor with a concern for appearances and for their own interests to the detriment of the decisionmaking process. Whatever the nature of the privilege of confidentiality of presidential communications in the exercise of Art. II powers, the privilege can be said to derive from the supremacy of each branch within its own assigned area of constitutional duties. Certain powers and privileges flow from the nature of enumerated powers; [16] the protection of the confidentiality of presidential communications has similar constitutional underpinnings.

The second ground asserted [for] the claim of absolute privilege rests on the doctrine of separation of powers. Here it is argued that the independence of the Executive Branch within its own sphere insulates a president from a judicial subpoena in an ongoing criminal prosecution, and thereby protects confidential presidential communications.

However, neither the doctrine of separation of powers, nor the need for confidentiality of high level communications, without more, can sustain an absolute, unqualified presidential privilege of immunity from judicial process under all circumstances. The President's need for complete candor and objectivity from advisers calls for great deference from the courts. However, when the privilege depends solely on the broad, undifferentiated claim of public interest in the confidentiality of such conversations, a confrontation with other values arises. Absent a claim of need to protect military, diplomatic or sensitive national security secrets, we find it difficult to accept the argument that even the very important interest in confidentiality of presidential communications is significantly diminished by production of such material for in camera inspection with all the protection that a district court will be obliged to provide.

The impediment that an absolute, unqualified privilege would place in the way of the primary constitutional duty of the Judicial Branch to do justice in criminal prosecutions would plainly conflict with the function of the courts under Art. III. In designing the structure of our Government and dividing and allocating the sovereign power among three coequal branches, the Framers [sought] to provide a comprehensive system, but the separate powers were not

---

tion is final). The boundary between those spheres defines the limits of the judicial function." See also Ratner, note 2 following this case, at 100.

16. The Special Prosecutor argues that there is no provision in the Constitution for a presidential privilege as to the President's communications corresponding to the privilege of Members of Congress under the Speech or Debate Clause. But the silence of the Con-

stitution on this score is not dispositive. "The rule of constitutional interpretation announced in *McCulloch v. Maryland*, [Ch. 2, Sec. 1], that that which was reasonably appropriate and relevant to the exercise of a granted power was to be considered as accompanying the grant, has been so universally applied that it suffices merely to state it." *Marshall v. Gordon*, 243 U.S. 521, 537, 37 S.Ct. 448, 451, 61 L.Ed. 881 (1917).

intended to operate with absolute independence. [To] read the Art. II powers of the President as providing an absolute privilege as against a subpoena essential to enforcement of criminal statutes on no more than a generalized claim of the public interest in confidentiality of nonmilitary and nondiplomatic discussions would upset the constitutional balance of "a workable government" and gravely impair the role of the courts under Art. III.

Since we conclude that the legitimate needs of the judicial process may outweigh presidential privilege, it is necessary to resolve those competing interests in a manner that preserves the essential functions of each branch. The right and indeed the duty to resolve that question does not free the judiciary from according high respect to the representations made [by] the President. *United States v. Burr,* 25 Fed.Cas. 187 (No. 14,694) (1807).

The expectation of a President to the confidentiality of his conversations and correspondence, like the claim of confidentiality of judicial deliberations, for example, has all the values to which we accord deference for the privacy of all citizens and added to those values the necessity for protection of the public interest in candid, objective, and even blunt or harsh opinions in presidential decision-making. A President and those who assist him must be free to explore alternatives in the process of shaping policies and making decisions and to do so in a way many would be unwilling to express except privately. These are the considerations justifying a presumptive privilege for presidential communications. The privilege is fundamental to the operation of government and inextricably rooted in the separation of powers under the Constitution. * * *

But this presumptive privilege must be considered in light of our historic commitment to the rule of law. This is nowhere more profoundly manifest than in our view that "the twofold aim [of criminal justice] is that guilt shall not escape or innocence suffer." We have elected to employ an adversary system of criminal justice in which the parties contest all issues before a court of law. The need to develop all relevant facts in the adversary system is both fundamental and comprehensive. The ends of criminal justice would be defeated if judgments were to be founded on a partial or speculative presentation of the facts. The very integrity of the judicial system and public confidence in the system depend on full disclosure of all the facts, within the framework of the rules of evidence. To ensure that justice is done, it is imperative to the function of courts that compulsory process be available for the production of evidence needed either by the prosecution or by the defense. * * *

In this case the President [does] not place his claim of privilege on the ground [of] military or diplomatic secrets [where courts] have traditionally shown the utmost deference to presidential responsibilities. * * * No case of the Court, however, has extended this high degree of deference to a President's generalized interest in confidentiality. [Y]et to the extent this interest relates to the effective discharge of a President's powers, it is constitutionally based.

The right to the production of all evidence at a criminal trial similarly has constitutional dimensions. [In] this case we must weigh the importance of the general privilege of confidentiality of presidential communications in performance of his responsibilities against the inroads of such a privilege on the fair administration of criminal justice.[19] The interest in preserving confidentiality is

---

19. We are not here concerned with the balance between the President's generalized interest in confidentiality and the need for relevant evidence in civil litigation, nor with that between the confidentiality interest and congressional demands for information, nor with the President's interest in preserving state secrets.

weighty indeed and entitled to great respect. However we cannot conclude that advisers will be moved to temper the candor of their remarks by the infrequent occasions of disclosure because of the possibility that such conversations will be called for in the context of a criminal prosecution.

On the other hand, the allowance of the privilege to withhold evidence that is demonstrably relevant in a criminal trial would cut deeply into the guarantee of due process of law and gravely impair the basic function of the courts. A President's acknowledged need for confidentiality in the communications of his office is general in nature, whereas the constitutional need for production of relevant evidence in a criminal proceeding is specific and central to the fair adjudication of a particular criminal case in the administration of justice. Without access to specific facts a criminal prosecution may be totally frustrated. [The] generalized assertion of privilege must yield to the demonstrated, specific need for evidence in a pending criminal trial.

[If] a president concludes that compliance with a subpoena would be injurious to the public interest he may properly, as was done here, invoke a claim of privilege on the return of the subpoena. Upon receiving a claim of privilege from the Chief Executive, it became the further duty of the District Court to treat the subpoenaed material as presumptively privileged and to require the Special Prosecutor to demonstrate that the presidential material was "essential to the justice of the [pending criminal] case." *Burr.* Here the District Court treated the material as presumptively privileged, proceeded to find that the Special Prosecutor had made a sufficient showing to rebut the presumption and ordered an *in camera* examination of the subpoenaed material. [W]e affirm the order of the District Court that subpoenaed materials be transmitted to that court. We now turn to the important question of the District Court's responsibilities in conducting the in camera examination of presidential materials or communications delivered under the compulsion of the subpoena duces tecum.

* * * Statements that meet the test of admissibility and relevance must be isolated; all other material must be excised. [T]he District Court has a very heavy responsibility to see to it that presidential conversations, which are either not relevant or not admissible, are accorded that high degree of respect due the President of the United States. [A] President's communications and activities encompass a vastly wider range of sensitive material than would be true of any "ordinary individual." It is therefore necessary in the public interest to afford presidential confidentiality the greatest protection consistent with the fair administration of justice. The need for confidentiality even as to idle conversations with associates in which casual reference might be made concerning political leaders within the country or foreign statesman is too obvious to call for further treatment. * * *[c]

Notes and Questions [a]

1. *Impact of United States v. Nixon on impeachment.* For consideration of the impact and appropriateness of expediting the Supreme Court's consideration and decision of *U.S. v. Nixon* at a time when the House Judiciary Committee had

c. Rehnquist, J., did not participate.

a. The extracts from the U.C.L.A.L.Rev. symposium on the *Nixon* case are reprinted with permission of the publisher; copyright © 1974 by the Regents of the University of California. The extracts from Cox, *Executive Privilege,* 122 U.Pa.L.Rev. 1383 (1974), are re-printed with permission of the publisher; copyright © 1974 by the University of Pennsylvania. The extracts from Freund, *On Presidential Privilege,* 88 Harv.L.Rev. 13 (1974), are reprinted with permission of the publisher; copyright © 1974 by the Harvard Law Review Association.

before it the proposed articles of impeachment against President Nixon, see Gunther, *Judicial Hegemony and Legislative Autonomy: The Nixon Case and the Impeachment Process*, 22 U.C.L.A.L.Rev. 30, 31–33, 35–39 (1974); Mishkin, *Great Cases and Soft Law: A Comment on United States v. Nixon*, 22 U.C.L.A.L.Rev. 76, 76–80, 90–91 (1974); Van Alstyne, *A Political Constitutional Review of United States v. Nixon*, 22 U.C.L.A.L.Rev. 116, 124, 127 (1974).

2. *Executive privilege.* Consider Mishkin, supra, at 83–85, 89: "[*Nixon*] firmly pronounces [the] existence of a presidential executive privilege [that] rests on a constitutional base. [But the] substantial body of scholarly learning on the subject [e.g., Berger, *Executive Privilege: A Constitutional Myth* (1974); Dorsen & Shattuck, *Executive Privilege, the Congress and the Courts*, 35 Ohio State L.J. 1 (1974)], which includes historical and analytical treatments, is not considered or refuted, but simply ignored. [The] conclusion carried no real consequences in the case—at least as compared to recognition of a simple common-law privilege— for the Court proceeds to hold that the constitutionally-based privilege must nevertheless yield to the need for complete evidence in [federal] criminal prosecutions [on] a showing by the Prosecutor that the material involved is specific, relevant and admissible ∗ ∗ ∗."

See also LEONARD RATNER, *Executive Privilege, Self Incrimination, and the Separation of Powers Illusion*, 22 U.C.L.A.L.Rev. 92, 97–100 (1974): "[In *Nixon*] the trial court [is] not instructed to determine whether the need for the evidence 'outweighs' the need for confidentiality in the particular case. [Unless] 'presumptive privilege' and [the Court's admonishment to accord presidential records 'that high degree of deference suggested in *Burr*'] imply, without explication, that the court may sometimes exclude relevant and admissible presidential communications, executive privilege, except for national secrets, is almost eliminated. It is to be upheld only when the evidence is irrelevant or inadmissible. A constitutional privilege is scarcely needed to exclude such evidence. That solution suggests subordination of the executive to the judicial function rather than accommodation.

"[The] Court is confident that candid executive communication is not significantly inhibited by the possibility of infrequent disclosure but that due process and the judicial function are seriously impaired by infrequent nondisclosure of demonstrably relevant criminal evidence. [The frequent] exclusion of traditionally privileged communications between husband and wife, doctor and patient, priest and penitent, attorney and client has not heretofore been viewed as destructive of the judicial function nor a violation of procedural due process, though truth ascertainment is manifestly hampered. And can it be said with confidence that candid executive communication will not be inhibited by the possibility of unpredictable, though infrequent, disclosure?"

3. *Executive Privilege in Congress: Role of the Courts.* Executive privilege has rarely been used to deny information in court; but since 1952, the privilege has been asserted more than fifty times to deny documents or testimony to Congress, at least twenty times by the Nixon administration alone. See Dorsen & Shattuck, *Executive Privilege, The Congress and the Courts*, 35 Ohio St.L.J. 1, 2–3 (1974). This long struggle between President and Congress over executive privilege so far has eluded resolution by the Court.[a] Consider Dorsen & Shattuck, supra, at 23, 40: "[I]f an issue concerning [executive privilege in Congress] cannot be negotiated, it should be resolved by the Supreme Court.

---

a. Cf. *Senate Select Committee v. Nixon,* 498 F.2d 725 (1974).

Neither the President nor the Congress should be the judge in its own cause. [All] unlimited power is inherently dangerous, and it is the salutary function of the courts to circumscribe the boundaries of the executive and legislative powers so that neither branch is exalted at the expense of the other." See also Berger, *Executive Privilege: A Constitutional Myth* 340 (1974): "[T]he political question doctrine [presents] no obstacle to judicial determination of the rival legislative-executive claims to receive or withhold information. The power to decide these claims plainly has not been lodged in either the legislative or executive branch; equally plainly, the jurisdiction to demark constitutional boundaries between the rival claimants has been given to the courts. The criteria for judgment whether a claim of 'executive privilege' is maintainable can be found in parliamentary practice, and, if need be, in the private litigation cases. [J]udicial arbitrament [is] the rational substitute for eyeball to eyeball confrontation, such as was narrowly averted with respect to the continued bombing of Cambodia. It is functioning admirably in the controversy over presidential 'impounding' of funds appropriated for specific purposes, and there is no reason to believe that it would be less effective were Congress to assert its rights directly." But see Choper, *Judicial Review and the National Political Process,* 334–49 (1980).

Compare Freund, *On Presidential Privilege,* 88 Harv.L.Rev. 13, 37–38 (1974): "The tapes case arose in the setting of a criminal proceeding. That factor gives rise to three distinctive characteristics that bear on the appropriateness of judicial [settlement of direct "congressional-presidential disputes"]. In the first place, there was a conventional case already lodged in the court, not a plenary proceeding between two branches of government. Second, [is] the fact that private interests of the most acute kind—the potential loss of liberty of the defendants—were at stake. Third, the weighing of the need for disclosure is more congruent with the judicial function, and more comfortably performed, in a criminal case than in a legislative investigation: relevance and materiality are more focused in the search for defined facts than in a wide-ranging inquiry either to furnish a basis for legislation or to probe into maladministration."

See also Cox, *Executive Privilege,* 122 U.Pa.L.Rev. 1383, 1425–26, 1431–32 (1974): "Courts are accustomed to weighing the need for specific pieces of evidence in a judicial proceeding against the public interest in preserving the confidentiality of particular relationships, but they have no experience in weighing the legislative needs of Congress against other public interests. The need for access to executive papers and communications arises too seldom in traditional forms of civil or criminal proceedings for the judicial rulings to have much impact upon the effectiveness of the Presidency, but the occasions upon which Congress may demand information are virtually unlimited. Any binding definition of the power of [Congress] to obtain the internal communications of the Executive Branch and of the President to withhold them might greatly affect the relative political power and effectiveness of the Executive and Legislative Branches. [History] contains little evidence that the nation has suffered from the want of legal power to compel the President to satisfy the demands of Congress to information in the Executive Branch. Congress has powerful political weapons. * * * The question again boils down to whether the risks and costs of enmeshing the courts in contests for political advantage are outweighed by the benefits of providing a method of final resolution of the merits of claims of executive privilege that would, in at least some cases, strengthen the power of Congress. Judging solely from the past, I would be content to see the Judicial Branch deny its constitutional power and leave questions of executive privilege vis-à-vis Congress to the ebb and flow of political power." See also

Henkin, *Executive Privilege: Mr. Nixon Loses but the Presidency Largely Prevails*, 22 U.C.L.A.L.Rev. 40, 43 (1974). Nathanson, *From Watergate to Marbury v. Madison: Some Reflections on Presidential Privilege in Current Historical Perspectives*, 16 Ariz.L.Rev. 59, 76–77 (1974).

4. *Congressionally-mandated control over former President's papers.* On the day former President Nixon was pardoned he and the Administrator of General Services (GSA) signed an agreement that neither could gain access to Presidential materials (42 million documents and 880 tape recordings) without the other's consent but that after three years Nixon could withdraw any materials he wished except tape recordings, any of which he could direct GSA to destroy after five years. When Congress and the public learned of this arrangement, Congress enacted The Presidential Recordings and Materials Preservation Act, which required GSA to take "possession and control" of all such Presidential materials. It was to screen them and return to Nixon those that are private and not of "general historical interest," and to promulgate regulations to protect the materials from loss and to govern eventual access to them. NIXON v. ADMINISTRATOR OF GENERAL SERVICES, 433 U.S. 425, 97 S.Ct. 2777, 53 L.Ed.2d 867 (1977), per BRENNAN, J., upheld the "facial validity" of the Act's requirement that the GSA take the materials "into the Government's custody, subject to screening by Government archivists:"

"[I]n determining whether the Act disrupts the proper balance between the coordinate branches, the proper inquiry focuses on the extent to which it prevents the Executive Branch from accomplishing its constitutionally assigned functions. *United States v. Nixon* [*Nixon I*]. Only where the potential for disruption is present must we then determine whether that impact is justified by an overriding need to promote objectives within the constitutional authority of Congress.

"[I]t is clearly less intrusive to place custody and screening of the materials within the Executive Branch itself than to have Congress or some outside agency perform the screening function. While the materials may also be made available for use in judicial proceedings, this provision is expressly qualified by any rights, defense, or privileges that any person may invoke including, of course, a valid claim of executive privilege. Similarly, although some of the materials may eventually be made available for public access, the Act expressly recognizes the need both 'to protect any party's opportunity to assert any legally or constitutionally based right or privilege,' and to return purely private materials to appellant. * * *

"Thus, whatever are the future possibilities for constitutional conflict in the promulgation of regulations respecting public access to particular documents, nothing contained in the Act renders it unduly disruptive of the Executive Branch and, therefore, unconstitutional on its face. * * *

"The appellant bases his claim of Presidential privilege in this case on the assertion that the potential disclosure of communications given to the appellant in confidence would adversely affect the ability of future Presidents to obtain the candid advice necessary for effective decisionmaking. We are called upon to adjudicate that claim, however, only with respect to the process by which the materials will be screened and catalogued by professional archivists. [T]hus framed, the question is readily resolved. The screening constitutes a very limited intrusion by personnel in the Executive Branch sensitive to executive concerns. These very personnel have performed the identical task in each of the Presidential libraries without any suggestion that such activity has in any way interfered with executive confidentiality. Indeed, in light of this consistent historical practice, past and present executive officials must be well aware of the possibility that, at some time in the future, their communications may be reviewed on a confidential basis by professional archivists. Appellant has suggested no reason why review under the instant Act, rather than the Presidential Libraries Act, is significantly more likely to impair confidentiality, nor has he called into question the District Court's finding that the archivists' 'record for discretion in handling confidential material is unblemished.'

"Moreover, adequate justifications are shown for this limited intrusion into executive confidentiality comparable to those held to justify the in camera inspection [in *Nixon I.*] Congress acted to establish regular procedures to deal with the perceived need to preserve the materials for legitimate historical and governmental purposes. ＊ ＊ ＊

"Other substantial public interests [influencing Congress] were the desire to restore public confidence in our political processes by preserving the materials as a source for facilitating a full airing of the events leading to appellant's resignation, and Congress' need to understand how those political processes had in fact operated in order to gauge the necessity for remedial legislation. [And], of course, the Congress repeatedly referred to the importance of the materials to the Judiciary in the event that they shed light upon issues in civil or criminal litigation, a social interest that cannot be doubted.

"[G]iven the safeguards built into the Act to prevent disclosure of [personal and private] materials and the minimal nature of the intrusion into the confidentiality of the Presidency, we believe that the claims of Presidential privilege clearly must yield to the important congressional purposes of preserving the materials and maintaining access to them for lawful government and historical purposes.

"In short, [the] Act on its face does not violate the Presidential privilege." [a]

BURGER, C.J., dissented: "[Recasting], for the immediate purposes of this case, our narrow holding in *Nixon I,* the Court distills separation-of-powers principles into a simplistic rule which requires a 'potential for disruption' or an 'unduly disruptive' intrusion, before a measure will be held to trench on Presidential powers. ＊ ＊ ＊ But even taking the 'undue disruption' test as postulated, the Court engages in a facile analysis, as Mr. Justice Rehnquist so well demonstrates. ＊ ＊ ＊ Separation-of-powers principles are no less eroded simply because *Congress* goes through a 'minuet' of directing Executive Department employees, rather than the Secretary of the Senate or the Doorkeeper of the House, to possess and control Presidential papers. Whether there has been a violation of separation-of-powers principles depends not on the identity of the custodians, but upon which Branch has commanded the custodians to [act]. Congress has previously legislated with respect to Presidential papers, by providing for Presidential Libraries *at the option* of every former President. Title I, however, breaches the nonmandatory tradition that has long been a vital incident of separation of powers. ＊ ＊ ＊

"[T]here can be no room for doubt that, up to now, it has been the implied prerogative of the President—as of Members of Congress and of judges—to memorialize matters, establish filing systems, and to provide unilaterally for

---

a. The Court also rejected the claim that the Act constituted a bill of attainder in violation of Art. I, Sec. 9[3], and that it abridged first amendment rights. White and Stevens, JJ., each concurred in the opinion, except for the discussion of the bill of attainder issue. Powell and Blackmun, JJ., each concurred separately.

disposition of his work papers. Control of Presidential papers is, obviously, a natural and necessary incident of the broad discretion vested in the President in order for him to discharge his duties. * * *

"Finally, [the] Act violates principles of separation of powers by intruding into the confidentiality of Presidential communications protected by the constitutionally based doctrine of Presidential privilege. [T]he President, if he is to have autonomy while in office, needs the assurance that Congress will not immediately be free to coerce him to open all his files and records and give an account of Presidential actions at the instant his successor is sworn in. Absent the validity of the expectation of privacy of such papers (save for a subpoena under *Nixon I*), future Presidents and those they consult will be well advised to take into account the possibility that their most confidential correspondence, work papers, and diaries may well be open to congressionally mandated review, with no time limit, should some political issue give rise to an inter-branch conflict.

"[Here], nothing remotely like the *particularized need* we found in *Nixon I* has been shown with respect to these Presidential papers. No one has suggested that Congress will find its own 'core' functioning impaired by lack of the impounded papers, as we expressly found the judicial function would be impaired by lack of the material subpoenaed in *Nixon I*." [b]

II. EXECUTIVE IMMUNITY

NIXON v. FITZGERALD, 457 U.S. 731, 102 S.Ct. 2690, 73 L.Ed.2d 349 (1982), per POWELL, J., ruled that "absolute immunity" of the President from "damages liability predicated on his official acts" entitled former President Nixon to summary dismissal of a damages action for statutory and constitutional violations in terminating a Department of Defense employee who had embarrassed his superiors by testifying on cost overruns to a congressional committee shortly prior to losing his job in a departmental "reorganization":

"This [case] presents the claim that the President of the United States is shielded by absolute immunity from civil damages liability. [Because] the Presidency did not exist through most of the development of common law, any historical analysis must draw its evidence primarily from our constitutional heritage and structure. [This] inquiry involves policies and principles that may be considered implicit in the nature of the President's office in a system structured to achieve effective government under a constitutionally mandated separation of powers.

"Here a former President [stands] named as a defendant in a direct action under the Constitution and in two statutory actions under federal laws of general applicability. In neither case has Congress taken express legislative action to subject the President to civil liability for his official acts.[27]

---

b. Rehnquist, J., also dissenting, "fully subscribe[d] to most of what is said respecting the separation of powers" in Burger, C.J.'s dissent, and took issue with those claiming that lack of support for the Nixon claim by President Ford and President Carter weakened the case for concluding that the Act had a disruptive effect on the President's communications: "[R]equiring an ex-President to depend upon his successor, blinks at political and historical reality. The tripartite system of government established by the Constitution has on more than one occasion bred political hostility not merely between Congress and a lame duck President, but between the latter and his successor."

27. Our holding today need only be that the President is absolutely immune from civil damages liability for his official acts in the absence of explicit affirmative action by Congress. We decide only this constitutional issue, which is necessary to disposition of the case before us.

"Applying the principles of our cases to claims of this kind, we hold that petitioner, as a former President of the United States, is entitled to absolute immunity from damages liability predicated on his official acts. We consider this immunity a functionally mandated incident of the President's unique office, rooted in the constitutional tradition of the separation of powers and supported by our history. * * *

"In arguing that the President is entitled only to qualified immunity, the respondent relies on cases in which we have recognized immunity of this scope for governors and cabinet officers. E.g., *Butz v. Economou,* 438 U.S. 478, 98 S.Ct. 2894, 57 L.Ed.2d 895 (1978); *Scheuer v. Rhodes,* 416 U.S. 232, 94 S.Ct. 1683, 40 L.Ed.2d 90 (1967). We find these cases to be inapposite. The President's unique status under the Constitution distinguishes him from other executive officials.[31]

"Because of the singular importance of the President's duties, diversion of his energies by concern with private lawsuits would raise unique risks to the effective functioning of government. As is the case with prosecutors and judges—for whom absolute immunity now is established—a President must concern himself with matters likely to 'arouse the most intense feelings.' Yet, as our decisions have recognized, it is in precisely such cases that there exists the greatest public interest in providing an official 'the maximum ability to deal fearlessly and impartially with' the duties of his office. This concern is compelling where the officeholder must make the most sensitive and far-reaching decisions entrusted to any official under our constitutional system. Nor can the sheer prominence of the President's office be ignored. In view of the visibility of his office and the effect of his actions on countless people, the President would be an easily identifiable target for suits for civil damages. Cognizance of this personal vulnerability frequently could distract a President from his public duties, to the detriment not only of the President and his office but also the Nation that the Presidency was designed to serve.

"Courts traditionally have recognized the President's constitutional responsibilities and status as factors counselling judicial deference and restraint. For example, while courts generally have looked to the common law to determine the scope of an official's evidentiary privilege, we have recognized that the Presidential privilege is 'rooted in the separation of powers under the Constitution.' *Nixon.* [When] judicial action is needed to serve broad public interests—as when the Court acts, not in derogation of the separation of powers, but to maintain their proper balance, cf. *Steel Seizure Case,* or to vindicate the public interest in an ongoing criminal prosecution, see *Nixon*—the exercise of jurisdiction has been held warranted. In the case of this merely private suit for damages based on a President's official acts, we hold it is not.[37]

"In defining the scope of an official's absolute privilege, this Court has recognized that the sphere of protected action must be related closely to the immunity's justifying purposes. Frequently our decisions have held that an

---

31. Noting that the "Speech and Debate Clause" provides a textual basis for congressional immunity, respondent argues that the Framers must be assumed to have rejected any similar grant of Executive immunity. This argument is unpersuasive. First, a specific textual basis has not been considered a prerequisite to the recognition of immunity. No provision expressly confers judicial immunity. Yet the immunity of judges is well settled. Second, this Court already has established that absolute immunity may be extended to certain officials of the Executive Branch. *Butz.* * * *

37. The Court has recognized before that there is a lesser public interest in actions for civil damages than, for example, in criminal prosecutions. It never has been denied that absolute immunity may impose a regrettable cost on individuals whose rights have been violated. * * *

official's absolute immunity should extend only to acts in performance of particular functions of his office. See *Butz*. But the Court also has refused to draw functional lines finer than history and reason would support. [In] view of the special nature of the President's constitutional office and functions, we think it appropriate to recognize absolute Presidential immunity from damages liability for acts within the 'outer perimeter' of his official responsibility.

"Under the Constitution and laws of the United States the President has discretionary responsibilities in a broad variety of areas, many of them highly sensitive. In many cases it would be difficult to determine which of the President's innumerable 'functions' encompassed a particular action. In this case, for example, respondent argues that he was dismissed in retaliation for his testimony to Congress—a violation of [federal law, but the Air Force] has claimed that the underlying reorganization was undertaken to promote efficiency. Assuming that the petitioner Nixon ordered the reorganization in which respondent lost his job, an inquiry into the President's motives could not be avoided under the kind of 'functional' theory asserted both by respondent and the dissent. Inquiries of this kind could be highly intrusive.

"Here respondent argues that petitioner Nixon would have acted outside the outer perimeter of his duties by ordering the discharge of an employee who was lawfully entitled to retain his job in the absence of 'such cause as will promote the efficiency of the service.' Because Congress has granted this legislative protection, respondent argues, no federal official could, within the outer perimeter of his duties of office, cause Fitzgerald to be dismissed without satisfying this standard in prescribed statutory proceedings.

"This construction would subject the President to trial on virtually every allegation that an action was unlawful, or was taken for a forbidden purpose. Adoption of this construction thus would deprive absolute immunity of its intended effect. It clearly is within the President's constitutional and statutory authority to prescribe the manner in which the Secretary will conduct the business of the Air Force. Because this mandate of office must include the authority to prescribe reorganizations and reductions in force, we conclude that petitioner's alleged wrongful acts lay well within the outer perimeter of his authority.

"A rule of absolute immunity for the President will not leave the Nation without sufficient protection against misconduct on the part of the chief executive. There remains the constitutional remedy of impeachment. In addition, there are formal and informal checks on Presidential action that do not apply with equal force to other executive officials. The President is subjected to constant scrutiny by the press. Vigilant oversight by Congress also may serve to deter Presidential abuses of office, as well as to make credible the threat of impeachment. Other incentives to avoid misconduct may include a desire to earn re-election, the need to maintain prestige as an element of Presidential influence, and a President's traditional concern for his historical stature." [a]

WHITE, J., joined by Brennan, Marshall and Blackmun, JJ., dissented: "The four dissenting members of the Court in *Butz* argued that all federal officials are entitled to absolute immunity from suit for any action they take in connection with their official duties. * * * Fortunately, the majority of the Court

---

a. Burger, C.J., joined the Court's opinion and added a short concurrence to "underscore [that] presidential immunity derives from and is mandated by the constitutional doctrine of separation of powers." It does not put the President "above the law" but "on essentially the same footing as judges."

rejected that approach: We held that although public officials perform certain functions that entitle them to absolute immunity, the immunity attaches to particular functions—not to particular offices. ＊ ＊ ＊

"The Court now applies the dissenting view in *Butz* to the office of the President: A President acting within the outer boundaries of what Presidents normally do may, without liability, deliberately cause serious injury to any number of citizens even though he knows his conduct violates a statute or tramples on the constitutional rights of those who are injured. [He] would be immune regardless of the damage he inflicts, regardless of how violative of the statute and of the Constitution he knew his conduct to be, and regardless of his purpose. ＊ ＊ ＊

"Attaching absolute immunity to the office of the President, rather than to particular activities that the President might perform, places the President above the law. It is a reversion to the old notion that the King can do no wrong. Until now, this concept had survived in this country only in the form of sovereign immunity. That doctrine forecloses suit against the government itself and against government officials, but only when the suit against the latter actually seeks relief against the sovereign. Suit against an officer, however, may be maintained where it seeks specific relief against him for conduct contrary to his statutory authority or to the Constitution. Now, however, the Court clothes the office of the President with sovereign immunity, placing it beyond the law.[2]

"The possibility of liability may, in some circumstances, distract officials from the performance of their duties and influence the performance of those duties in ways adverse to the public interest. But when this 'public policy' argument in favor of absolute immunity is cast in these broad terms, it applies to all officers, both state and federal: All officers should perform their responsibilities without regard to those personal interests threatened by the possibility of a lawsuit. Inevitably, this reduces the public policy argument to nothing more than an expression of judicial inclination as to which officers should be encouraged to perform their functions with 'vigor,' although with less care.

"The Court's response, until today, to this problem has been to apply the argument to individual functions, not offices, and to evaluate the effect of liability on governmental decision-making within that function, in light of the substantive ends that are to be encouraged or discouraged. In this case, therefore, the Court should examine the functions implicated by the causes of action at issue here and the effect of potential liability on the performance of those functions.

"The functional approach to the separation of powers doctrine and the Court's more recent immunity decisions converge on the following principle: The scope of immunity is determined by function, not office. The wholesale claim that the President is entitled to absolute immunity in all of his actions stands on no firmer ground than did the claim that all presidential communications are

2. [T]he Chief Justice, like the majority, misses the point in his wholly unconvincing contentions that the Court today does no more than extend to the President the same sort of immunity that we have recognized with respect to Members of Congress, judges, prosecutors, and legislative aides. In none of our previous cases have we extended absolute immunity to all actions "within the scope of the official's constitutional and statutory duties." Indeed, under the immunity doctrine as it existed prior to today's decision, each of these officials could have been held liable for the kind of claim put forward by Fitzgerald—a personnel decision allegedly made for unlawful reasons. Although such a decision falls within the scope of an official's duties, it does not fall within the judicial, legislative, or prosecutorial functions to which absolute immunity attaches. ＊ ＊ ＊

entitled to an absolute privilege, which was rejected in favor of a functional analysis, by a unanimous Court in *Nixon*. Therefore, whatever may be true of the necessity of such a broad immunity in certain areas of executive responsibility,[30] the only question that must be answered here is whether the dismissal of employees falls within a constitutionally assigned executive function, the performance of which would be substantially impaired by the possibility of a private action for damages. I believe it does not. * * *

"The majority may be correct in its conclusion that 'a rule of absolute immunity will not leave the Nation without sufficient remedies for misconduct on the part of the chief executive.' Such a rule will, however, leave Mr. Fitzgerald without an adequate remedy for the harms that he may have suffered. More importantly, it will leave future plaintiffs without a remedy, regardless of the substantiality of their claims. The remedies in which the Court finds comfort were never designed to afford relief for individual harms. Rather, they were designed as political safety-valves. Politics and history, however, are not the domain of the courts; the courts exist to assure each individual that he, as an individual, has enforceable rights that he may pursue to achieve a peaceful redress of his legitimate grievances.

"I find it ironic, as well as tragic, that the Court would so casually discard its own role of assuring 'the right of every individual to claim the protection of the laws,' *Marbury*, in the name of protecting the principle of separation of powers." [b]

HARLOW v. FITZGERALD, 457 U.S. 800, 102 S.Ct. 2727, 73 L.Ed.2d 396 (1982), per POWELL, J. (a companion case to *Nixon v. Fitzgerald*), held that two White House aides of former President Nixon, codefendants with him in the damages action for alleged conspiracy to violate Fitzgerald's rights, were entitled only to qualified immunity, except when performing a "function so sensitive as to require" absolute immunity:

"For executive officials in general, [our] cases make plain that qualified immunity represents the norm. In *Scheuer* we acknowledged that high officials require greater protection than those with less complex discretionary responsibilities. Nonetheless, we held that a governor and his aides could receive the requisite protection from qualified or good-faith immunity. In *Butz* we extended the approach of *Scheuer* to high federal officials of the Executive Branch [explaining that the recognition] of a qualified immunity defense for [such officials] reflected an attempt to balance competing values: not only the importance of a damages remedy to protect the rights of citizens, but also 'the need to protect officials who are required to exercise their discretion and the related public interest in encouraging the vigorous exercise of official authority.' * * *

"Having decided in *Butz* that members of the Cabinet ordinarily enjoy only qualified immunity from suit, we conclude today that it would be equally untenable to hold absolute immunity an incident of the office of every Presidential subordinate based in the White House. Members of the Cabinet are direct subordinates of the President, frequently with greater responsibilities, both to

---

30. I will not speculate on the presidential functions which may require absolute immunity, but a clear example would be instances in which the President participates in prosecutorial decisions.

b. Blackmun, J., joined by Brennan and Marshall, JJ., also dissented.

the President and to the Nation, than White House staff. The considerations that supported our decision in *Butz* apply with equal force to this case. ＊ ＊ ＊

"We have recognized that the judicial, prosecutorial and legislative functions require absolute immunity. But this protection has extended no further than its justification would warrant. In *Gravel*,[a] for example, we emphasized that Senators and their aides were absolutely immune only when performing 'acts legislative in nature,' and not when taking other acts even 'in their official capacity.' Our cases involving judges and prosecutors have followed a similar line. The undifferentiated extension of absolute 'derivative' immunity to the President's aides therefore could not be reconciled with the 'functional' approach that has characterized the immunity decisions of this Court, indeed including *Gravel* itself.[17]

"Petitioners also assert an entitlement to immunity based on the 'special functions' of White House aides. This form of argument accords with the analytical approach of our cases. For aides entrusted with discretionary authority in such sensitive areas as national security or foreign policy, absolute immunity might well be justified to protect the unhesitating performance of functions vital to the national interest. But a 'special functions' rationale does not warrant a blanket recognition of absolute immunity for all Presidential aides in the performance of all their duties. This conclusion too follows from our decision in *Butz*, which establishes that an executive official's claim to absolute immunity must be justified by reference to the public interest in the special functions of his office, not the mere fact of high station.

"[In] order to establish entitlement to absolute immunity a Presidential aide first must show that the responsibilities of his office embraced a function so sensitive as to require a total shield from liability. He then must demonstrate that he was discharging the protected function when performing the act for which liability is asserted.

"Applying these standards to the claims advanced by [petitioners], we cannot conclude on the record before us that either has shown that 'public policy requires [for any of the functions of his office] an exemption of [absolute] scope.' *Butz* [or] that the acts charged in this lawsuit—if taken at all—would lie within the protected area. We do not, however, foreclose the possibility that petitioners, on remand, could satisfy the standards properly applicable to their claims. ＊ ＊ ＊ [34]" [b]

BURGER, C.J., dissenting, was "at a loss" to reconcile the Court's decision with *Gravel*: "[In *Gravel*,] going far beyond any words found in the Constitution itself, we held that [aides of Members of Congress] who implement policies and decisions of the Member are entitled to the same absolute immunity as a Member. [Like] a Member of Congress, but on a vastly greater scale, the

---

a. *Gravel v. United States*, 408 U.S. 606, 92 S.Ct. 2614, 33 L.Ed.2d 583 (1972).

17. Our decision today in *Nixon v. Fitzgerald* in no way abrogates this general rule. As we explained in that opinion, the recognition of absolute immunity for all of a President's acts in office derives in principal part from factors unique to his constitutional responsibilities and station. Suits against other officials—including Presidential aides—generally do not invoke separation-of-powers considerations to the same extent as suits against the President himself.

34. We emphasize that our decision applies only to suits for civil *damages* arising from actions within the scope of an official's duties and in "objective" good faith. We express no view as to the conditions in which injunctive or declaratory relief might be available.

b. Brennan, J., joined by Marshall and Blackmun, JJ., who joined the Court's opinion, also filed a separate concurrence, as did Rehnquist, J.

President cannot personally implement a fraction of his own policies and day to day decisions.

"For some inexplicable reason the Court declines to recognize the realities in the workings of the Office of a President, despite the Court's cogent recognition in *Gravel* concerning the realities of the workings of 20th-century Members of Congress. Absent equal protection for a President's aides, how will Presidents be free from the risks of 'intimidation [by Congress] and accountability before a possibly hostile judiciary?' *Gravel.* Under today's holding in this case the functioning of the Presidency will inevitably be 'diminished and frustrated.'

* * *

"By ignoring *Gravel* and engaging in a wooden application of *Butz,* the Court significantly undermines the functioning of the Office of the President."

Notes and Questions

1. *Basis for presidential immunity.* After *Nixon v. Fitzgerald,* could Congress by legislation replace the President's absolute immunity with a well-defined qualified immunity? Is the *Nixon v. Fitzgerald* presidential immunity a constitution-based bar to civil damages or a policy-based, court-created limit on liability for damages for alleged federal statutory and constitutional violations, influenced by separation-of-powers considerations? Cf. Carter, *The Political Aspects of Judicial Power: Some Notes on the Presidential Immunity Decision,* 131 U.Pa.L.Rev. 1341, 1345–57 (1983). For a stimulating analysis of historical, structural, and policy reasons for Constitution-based presidential immunity in order to preserve the "delicate construct" of the constitutional balance of powers, see *Carter,* supra at 1353–67. But cf. Note, 96 Harv.L.Rev. 226, 230–32 (1982).

2. *Immunity for White House aides, cabinet officers, and other high officials.* (a) What may explain the refusal in *Harlow* to extend to White House aides and cabinet officers engaged in official action fulfilling the President's duties the same absolute immunity recognized for the President? Were such officers any less likely than the President "to be distract[ed from] public duties, to the detriment of [the] Nation" by "cognizance of [their] personal vulnerability" to civil damages without the protection of absolute immunity?[c] Under qualified immunity who was more exposed to the risk of civil damages actions— the President or the White House assistant, cabinet officer, or executive who gave the order that led to the challenged action? Could the Court have believed there was greater need to retain a potential civil damages sanction to discourage official misconduct by such officials than by the President?[d] Or did the Court's declared apprehension that "personal vulnerability" to civil damages would "distract the President from his public duties" "mask a more fundamental fear for the stature and reputation of the Presidency" unshielded by absolute immunity, akin to sovereign immunity?[e]

(b) To what extent, if at all, would you view the immunity of White House aides, cabinet officers and the like, recognized in *Harlow,* as constitution-based?

---

c. Indeed, was "the President, who must confront issues with global ramifications, * * * least likely to be swayed by the possibility of civil suit?" 68 Corn.L.Rev. 236, 250 (1983).

d. Carter, supra at 1398–99.

e. Cf. 68 Cornell L.Rev. at 251.

Chapter 4

STATE POWER TO REGULATE

INTRODUCTION

This chapter explores the impact of a national regulatory power upon state power to regulate. Its focus is on the commerce power, though similar problems arise under other grants of power.[a] Some powers of Congress are exclusive because the Constitution expressly withholds the power from states,[b] but when the Constitution gave Congress the power to regulate commerce it did not expressly negate state power.[c] Did this leave the states with concurrent power to regulate those aspects of interstate and foreign commerce within their jurisdiction that Congress does not regulate? Or did the broad grant to Congress create a negative implication against state power, making the congressional power over commerce exclusive? If the answer is sometimes concurrent, sometimes not, what considerations determine whether the states may regulate commerce, absent relevant federal legislation? Further, what effect does congressional legislation relating to commerce have on state regulations on the same subject: To the extent that state power is concurrent and Congress has legislated on an aspect of commerce, may states enforce additional non-conflicting regulations on that same aspect of commerce? And may Congress authorize state legislation that would be found to impinge on the grant of power to Congress but for such authorization?

SECTION 1. IN THE ABSENCE OF FEDERAL REGULATION

I. EVOLUTION OF STANDARDS

In GIBBONS v. OGDEN (1824), Ch. 2, Sec. 2, CHIEF JUSTICE MARSHALL discussed but did not decide whether the grant of commerce power to Congress excluded all state regulation of interstate and foreign commerce: "In support of [the argument for concurrent power] it is said that [the states] possessed it as an inseparable attribute of sovereignty before the formation of the Constitution, and still retain it, except so far as they have surrendered it by that instrument; that this principle results from the nature of the government, and is secured by the

---

a. See, e.g., *Hines v. Davidowitz* and *Zschernig v. Miller,* Sec. 2 infra.

b. E.g., Art. I, § 8 authorizes Congress to "coin money" while Art. 1, § 10 expressly denies such power to states.

c. Except for the special, express limits on tonnage duties and duties on imports and exports. Art. I, Sec. 10.

tenth amendment; that an affirmative grant of power is not exclusive, unless in its own nature it be such that the continued exercise of it by the former possessor is inconsistent with the grant, and that this is not of that description.

"[It] has been contended by the counsel for the appellant that, as the word to 'regulate' implies in its nature full power over the thing to be regulated, it excludes, necessarily, the action of all others that would perform the same operation on the same thing. That regulation is designed for the entire result, applying to those parts which remain as they were, as well as to those which are altered. It produces a uniform whole, which is as much disturbed and deranged by changing what the regulating power designs to leave untouched, as that on which it has operated.

"There is great force in this argument, and the court is not satisfied that it has been refuted."

Notes

Until *Cooley,* infra, in 1851 the Court was divided on whether the commerce power was exclusively in Congress or shared concurrently with the states subject to federal supremacy.[e] Finally, 27 years after Daniel Webster pointed the way in the lengthy *Gibbons v. Ogden* arguments the Court unanimously embraced the basic element in his argument that some "commercial powers [are] exclusive in their nature" and others are not.[f]

COOLEY v. BOARD OF WARDENS
OF PHILADELPHIA
53 U.S. (12 How.) 299, 13 L.Ed. 996 (1851).

MR. JUSTICE CURTIS delivered the opinion of the Court.

[The Court upheld Pennsylvania's 1803 law that required ships using the Philadelphia port to receive a local pilot, considered in the light of a 1789 Act of Congress providing that harbors and ports of the United States shall "continue to be regulated in conformity with the existing laws of the states [or] with such laws as the states [may] hereafter enact."]

If the states were divested of the power to legislate on this subject by the grant of the commercial power to Congress, it is plain this act could not confer upon them power thus to legislate. If the Constitution excluded the states from making any law regulating commerce, certainly Congress cannot regrant, or in any manner reconvey to the states that power. And yet this act of 1789 gives its sanction only to laws enacted by the states. * * * Entertaining these views, we are brought [to the] question, whether the grant of the commercial power to Congress did per se deprive the states of all power to regulate [pilots].

The grant of commercial power to Congress does not contain any terms which expressly exclude the states from exercising an authority over its subject-matter. If they are excluded, it must be because the nature of the power thus granted to Congress requires that a similar authority should not exist in the states. If [the] nature of this power, like that to legislate for the District of Columbia, is absolutely and totally repugnant to the existence of similar power in the states, probably no one would deny that the grant of the power to Congress, as effectually and perfectly excludes the states from all future legislation on the subject, as if express words had been used to exclude them. And on

---

e. See *The License Cases,* 46 U.S. (5 How.) 504, 12 L.Ed. 256 (1847); *The Passenger Cases,* 48 (7 How.) 282, 12 L.Ed. 702 (1849).

f. See argument of William Wirt, Webster's colleague, 22 U.S. (9 Wheat.) 180, 6 L.Ed. 178.

the other hand, if [the] existence of this power in Congress, like the power of taxation, is compatible with the existence of a similar power in the states, then it would be in conformity with the contemporary exposition of the Constitution ("*Federalist*," No. 32), and with the judicial construction given from time to time by this court [to] hold that the mere grant of such a power to Congress, did not imply a prohibition on the states to exercise the same power.

[W]hen it is said that the nature of the power requires that it should be exercised exclusively by Congress, it must be intended to refer to the subjects of that power, and to say they are of such a nature as to require exclusive legislation by Congress. Now, the power to regulate commerce, embraces a vast field, containing not only many, but exceedingly various subjects, quite unlike in their nature; some imperatively demanding a single uniform rule, operating equally on the commerce of the United States in every port; and some, like the subject now in question, as imperatively demanding that diversity, which alone can meet the local necessities of navigation.

Either absolutely to affirm, or deny that the nature of this power requires exclusive legislation by Congress, is to lose sight of the nature of the subjects of this power, and to assert concerning all of them, what is really applicable but to a part. Whatever subjects of this power are in their nature national, or admit only of one uniform system, or plan of regulation, may justly be said to be of such a nature as to require exclusive legislation by Congress. That this cannot be affirmed of laws for the regulation of pilots and pilotage, is plain. The act of 1789 contains a clear and authoritative declaration by the first Congress, that the nature of this subject is such that until Congress should find it necessary to exert its power, it should be left to the legislation of the states; that it is local and not national; that it is likely to be the best provided for, not by one system, or plan of regulations, but by as many as the legislative discretion of the several states should deem applicable to the local peculiarities of the ports within their limits.

[The] practice of the states, and of the national government, has been in conformity with this declaration, from the origin of the national government to this time; and the nature of the subject when examined, is such as to leave no doubt of the superior fitness and propriety, not to say the absolute necessity, of different systems of regulation, drawn from local knowledge and experience, and conformed to local wants. How, then, can we say that, by the mere grant of power to regulate commerce, the states are deprived of all the power to legislate on this subject, because from the nature of the power the legislation of Congress must be exclusive? * * *

It is the opinion of a majority of the court that the mere grant to Congress of the power to regulate commerce, did not deprive the states of power to regulate pilots, and that although Congress has legislated on this subject, its legislation manifests an intention, with a single exception, not to regulate this subject, but to leave its regulation to the several states. To these precise questions, which are all we are called on to decide, this opinion must be understood to be confined. It does not extend to the question what other subjects, under the commercial power, are within the exclusive control of Congress, or may be regulated by the states in absence of all congressional legislation; nor to the general question, how far any regulation on a subject by Congress, may be deemed to operate as an exclusion of all legislation by the states upon the same subject. * * * *[a]

a. Daniel, J., concurred on other grounds.
McLean and Wayne, JJ., dissented.

Notes and Questions

1. *Need for uniform regulation.* (a) Is the need for uniform regulation a defensible, manageable standard for deciding what regulations of commerce are exclusively for Congress and what are within concurrent state power? Can it be justified as based on the constitution?

(b) Is need for uniform regulation a good reason to invalidate state legislation when Congress has not acted and "the only uniformity [the Court can] furnish is uniform lack of regulation?" [b] When regulation is needed, and needs to be uniform, which is preferable—diverse state regulation or no regulation unless Congress acts?[c]

(c) Are considerations relevant to the need for uniformity the only appropriate ones to weigh in deciding whether states have concurrent power to enact particular regulations? Does *Cooley* appear to so limit the judicial inquiry? On what basis could *Cooley* be viewed as leaving room for "some weighing of the advancement of local interests as against interference with national interests?" See Dowling, *Interstate Commerce and State Power,* 27 Va.L.Rev. 1, 5 (1940).

2. *Discrimination against interstate commerce.* (a) An early application of the *Cooley* formula struck down a state statute that required only peddlers of out-of-state merchandise to secure a license and pay a tax. WELTON v. MISSOURI, 91 U.S. (1 Otto) 275, 23 L.Ed. 347 (1876), per FIELD, J.: "[T]ransportation and exchange of commodities is of national importance, and admits and requires uniformity of regulation. The very object of investing this power in the General Government was to insure this uniformity against discriminating State legislation. [If state power to exact such a license tax were admitted,] all the evils of discriminating State legislation, favorable to the interests of one State and injurious to the interests of other states and countries, which existed previous to the adoption of the Constitution, might follow, and the experience of the last fifteen years shows would follow, from the action of some of the States. [It] is sufficient to hold now that the commercial power continues until the commodity has ceased to be the subject of discriminating legislation by reason of its foreign character. That power protects it, even after it has entered the State, from any burdens imposed by reason of its foreign origin."

(b) Since *Welton,* the Court has consistently invalidated state taxes and regulations found to discriminate against interstate or foreign commerce, absent approval by Congress.

NEGATIVE IMPLICATIONS OF THE COMMERCE CLAUSE 1876–1945

After *Cooley* and *Welton* the Court regularly acknowledged and exercised the power to invalidate state legislation found to violate "negative implications"

b. See Shenton, *Interstate Commerce During the Silence of Congress,* 23 Dick.L.Rev. 78, 118–19 (1919).

c. Cf. *Wabash, St. L. & P. Ry. v. Illinois,* 118 U.S. 557, 7 S.Ct. 4, 30 L.Ed. 244 (1886), which invalidated state regulation of interstate railroad rates on the need-for-uniformity ground just three months before Congress enacted the Interstate Commerce Act. It is probably erroneous to infer that the absence of railroad rate regulation resulting from *Wabash* influenced enactment of the Interstate Commerce Act. Three months before *Wabash* was decided on October 25, 1886, both the Senate and House versions of the bill had been approved and referred to a conference committee on July 31. 17 Cong.Rec. 4423, 7756, 7818, 7832. The conference committee reported on December 15, and the Act was finally passed by the Senate and House on January 14 and 21, 1887. 18 Cong.Rec. 169, 633, 695, 881.

derived from the commerce clause, but until 1945 its opinions did little to develop meaningful standards to guide lawyers and courts faced with such issues. Contrast, for example, LEISY v. HARDIN, 135 U.S. 100, 10 S.Ct. 681, 34 L.Ed. 128 (1890) with PLUMLEY v. MASSACHUSETTS, 155 U.S. 461, 15 S.Ct. 154, 39 L.Ed. 223 (1894).

Leisy held invalid an Iowa law forbidding sale of intoxicating liquor, as applied to a sale in Iowa of liquor from another state, while still in the original shipping package.[a] But *Plumley* upheld a Massachusetts law forbidding sale of oleomargarine colored like butter, as applied to a sale in Massachusetts of such oleomargarine from another state, while still in the original package. *Leisy* invoked *Welton's* sweeping need-for-uniformity rationale, concluding that, "whatever our individual views [as to] the deleterious" qualities of the articles, the required uniformity of regulation for commodities in commerce bars the state from "power to exclude, directly or indirectly," from commerce, without congressional permission, articles that "Congress recognizes as subjects of commerce." But four years later *Plumley* gave controlling weight to the state power to protect its residents from fraud and deception in the sale of commodities, despite harmful impact on interstate commerce. *Plumley* expressly limited to *Leisy* the broad sweep of the *Leisy* reasoning, and reasserted in the *Plumley* context the broad power of the states to make "ordinary regulations of police" to promote "public health, good order, and prosperity."[b] *Plumley* did little to clarify the standard by which to decide concurrent state power issues. But it did make clear that a weighty factor in such decisions is the importance of the state interest protected by the challenged regulation.[c]

THE ROLE OF CONGRESS IN NEGATIVE IMPLICATION DECISIONS

Notes and Questions

1. *Silence of Congress.* (a) Marshall, C.J.'s, "great force" endorsement in *Gibbons* of counsel's argument that "the uniform whole * * * is as much disturbed and deranged by changing what the regulatory power designs to leave untouched, as that on which it has operated" became Court-approved legal doctrine to support the ruling in *Leisy*: "[Whenever a] power of the general government [must] be exercised by it, and Congress remains silent, [the] only legitimate conclusion is that the general government intended that power should not be affirmatively exercised, and the action of the states cannot be permitted to effect that which would be incompatible with such intention."

(b) What inferences, if any, may reasonably be drawn from "silence of Congress" on a subject of commerce not regulated by Congress? For commentaries and a spoof, see Powell, *The Still Small Voice of the Commerce Clause*, Proceedings National Tax Association 337, 338–39 (1938); Bikle, *The Silence of*

---

a. The Court here adapted to the implied limit on state power to regulate interstate commerce the original package line it had drawn much earlier in *Brown v. Maryland*, 25 U.S. (12 Wheat.) 419, 6 L.Ed. 678 (1827) to decide when imported goods were so "mingled in the common mass of property in the state" as to escape the ban on duties on imports.

b. The Court here quoted from *In re Rahrer*, infra, which, one year after *Leisy*, upheld the Wilson Act restoring state power over liquor.

c. In the *Plumley* majority were three new justices (Jackson, Shira, and White, JJ.) who had replaced three in the *Leisy* majority (Blatchford, Bradley and Lamar, JJ.), two who had dissented in *Leisy* (Harlan and Gray, JJ.) and one who had joined the *Leisy* majority (Brown, J.). Might the increased weight given in *Plumley* to state interests also be attributable in part to Congress' quick enactment of the Wilson Act disapproving and nullifying *Leisy's* limitation on state liquor laws? See *In re Rahrer*, infra.

Congress, 41 Harv.L.Rev. 200 (1927). Did the fiction serve any useful purpose in *Leisy?*

2. *Approval by Congress.* Should the Court give controlling effect to the expressed will of Congress when deciding the validity of state regulation (and taxation) of commerce? In upholding state power, *Cooley* gave weight to Congress' expressed "intention * * * to leave [pilotage] regulation to the several states." And in striking down state power *Leisy* limited its sweeping foreclosure of state power to exclude articles of commerce with the careful qualification, "without congressional permission."

This qualification was put to the test one year later. IN RE RAHRER, 140 U.S. 545, 11 S.Ct. 865, 35 L.Ed. 572 (1891), per FULLER, C.J. sustained the Wilson Act, which sought to nullify the effect of *Leisy* by making liquor transported into a state subject to its prohibition laws, even though sold in the original package. The Court rejected the "position that congress could not, in the exercise of the discretion reposed in it, concluding that the common interests did not require entire freedom in the traffic in ardent spirits, enact the law in question. In so doing, congress has not attempted to delegate the power to regulate commerce, or to exercise any power reserved to the states, or to grant a power not possessed by the [states].

"The power to regulate is solely in the general government, and it is an essential part of that regulation to prescribe the regular means for accomplishing the introduction and incorporation of articles into and with the mass of property in the country or state. [No] reason is perceived why, if congress chooses to provide that certain designated subjects of interstate commerce shall be governed by a rule which divests them of that character at an earlier period of time than would otherwise be the case, it is not within its competency to do so.

"[Congress] did not use terms of permission to the state to act, but simply removed an impediment to the enforcement of the state laws in respect to imported packages in their original condition, created by the absence of a specific utterance on its part. It imparted no power to the state not then possessed, but allowed imported property to fall at once upon arrival within the local jurisdiction."

(b) Do more fundamental considerations underlie *Rahrer* than whether Congress may redefine the point at which goods from other states become subject to state regulatory power? If the Court concludes that a particular state regulation is unconstitutional because unduly harmful to interstate commerce may Congress override that judgment and authorize such state regulation? By what rationale?

3. *Congressionally authorized discrimination.* After *South-Eastern Underwriters,* considered p. 124 supra, upheld the power of Congress to regulate interstate insurance business, the McCarran Act subjected all insurance business "to the laws of the several states which relate to the regulation or taxation of such business." Thereafter PRUDENTIAL INS. CO. v. BENJAMIN, 328 U.S. 408, 66 S.Ct. 1142, 90 L.Ed. 1342 (1946), per RUTLEDGE, J., interpreted the McCarran Act to authorize state taxes that discriminate against interstate insurance business. It upheld a South Carolina tax on insurance companies that exempted South Carolina insurance companies from the tax measured by gross premiums on South Carolina business:

"Prudential chiefly relies [on] the cases which from *Welton* until now have outlawed state taxes found to discriminate against interstate commerce. [Those cases] presented no question of the validity of such a tax where Congress had taken affirmative action consenting to it or purporting to give it validity.

"[I]n all the variations of commerce clause theory it has never been the law that what the states may do in the regulation of commerce, Congress being silent, is the full measure of its power. Much less has this boundary been thought to confine what Congress and the states acting together may accomplish. So to regard the matter would invert the constitutional grant into a limitation upon the very power it confers.

"[T]he cases most important for the decision in this cause [are] the ones involving situations where the silence of Congress or the dormancy of its power has been taken judicially, on one view or another of its constitutional effects, as forbidding state action, only to have Congress later disclaim the prohibition or undertake to nullify it. Not yet has this Court held such a disclaimer invalid or that state action supported by it could not stand. On the contrary in each instance it has given effect to the Congressional judgment contradicting its own previous one.

"It is true that rationalizations have differed concerning those decisions. [But] the results have been lasting and are at least as important, for the direction given to the process of accommodating federal and state authority, as the reasons stated for reaching [them].

"Some part of this readjustment may be explained in ways acceptable on any theory of the commerce clause and the relations of Congress and the Courts toward its functioning.[32] Such explanations, however, hardly go to the root of the matter. For the fact remains that, in these instances, the sustaining of Congress' overriding action has involved something beyond correction of erroneous factual judgment in deference to Congress' presumably better-informed view of the facts.

"[The McCarran Act] was a determination by Congress that state taxes, which in its silence might be held invalid as discriminatory, do not place on interstate insurance business a burden which it is unable generally to bear or should not bear in the competition with local business. Such taxes were not uncommon among the states, and the statute clearly included South Carolina's tax now in issue.

"That judgment was one of policy and reflected long and clear experience. For, notwithstanding the long incidence of the tax and its payment by Prudential without question prior to the *South-Eastern* decision, the record of Prudential's continuous success in South Carolina over decades refutes any idea that payment of the tax handicapped it in any way tending to exclude it from competition with local business or with domestic insurance companies.

"[This] broad authority [over commerce] Congress may exercise alone [or] in conjunction with coordinated action by the states, in which case limitations imposed for the preservation of their powers become inoperative and only those designed to forbid action altogether by any power or combination of powers in

---

32. Thus, in some instances conceivably the reversal might be rationalized as only one of factual judgment, made in deference to the contrary finding of like character made by a body better able to make such a determination. Moreover, Congress' supporting action deprives the Court's adverse view concerning state legislation of any strength which may have been derived from the inference that Congress, by its silence, had impliedly forbidden it. Hence insofar as its judgment may be taken, not as conclusive, but as being entitled to deference here on questions relating to its [power], Congress' explicit repudiation of the attitude inferentially attributed to it from its silence, compels reversal of the Court's earlier pronounced view.

our governmental system remain effective. Here both Congress and South Carolina have acted, and in complete coordination, to sustain the tax. It is therefore reinforced by the exercise of all the power of government residing in our scheme.[a] [Congress and the states] were not forbidden to cooperate or by doing so to achieve legislative consequences, particularly in the great fields of regulating commerce and taxation, which, to some extent at least, neither could accomplish in isolated exertion." [b]

4. *Historical perspective.* (a) Based on its terms and historical origins, does the constitution place prime responsibility on Congress or on the judiciary to protect the national interest in freedom of interstate and foreign commerce from harmful state legislation? What light is shed on this question by the absence from 1789 to 1824 (*Gibbons*) of any court challenge to the large volume of contemporaneous state legislation that restricted and burdened such commerce? [c]

(b) After enacting the Interstate Commerce Act in 1887 and the Sherman Antitrust Act in 1890, Congress made extensive use of its commerce power, as reflected in chapter 2, but it made little use of that power to protect interstate and foreign commerce from harmful state regulations and taxes. Instead, Congress appeared content to leave that task largely to the judiciary's extensive case-by-case adjudications aimed at effectuating commerce clause objectives.[d] On only a few occasions [e] did Congress disagree with these judicial judgments; when it did so, the Court acquiesced. And Congress never took steps to negate or countermand this broad judicial power to invoke the commerce clause to restrict state regulations of commerce.

(c) What does this history suggest concerning the respective roles of the Court and Congress in controlling state regulation inimical to commerce clause objectives? Might the Court's role in applying commerce clause policies to state regulation fairly be characterized as making tentative or provisional decisions? Cf. Hartman, *State Taxation of Interstate Commerce* 247–53 (1953); Dowling, *Interstate Commerce and State Power—Revised Version*, 47 Col.L.Rev. 547, 558–60 (1947); Dimond, *Provisional Review: An Exploratory Essay on an Alternative Form of Judicial Review*, 12 Hastings Const.L.Q. 201 (1985).

THE ORIGINS OF A MORE ADEQUATE STANDARD

From *Cooley* to 1945 the Court did not articulate any really adequate standards to guide its decisions—or counsel. "[W]ithout ever openly abandoning the *Cooley* test, [it] used many other expressions—such as whether the state law was a 'burden,' or a 'substantial' or 'undue' burden, on commerce, whether the

---

a. Cf. Powell, *The Validity of State Regulation under the Webb-Kenyon Law,* 2 S.L.Q. (now Tul. L.Rev.) 112 (1917); *Clark Distilling Co. v. Western Maryland R. Co.,* 242 U.S. 311, 331, 37 S.Ct. 180, 187, 61 L.Ed. 326, 341 (1917).

b. Black, J., concurred in the result. Jackson, J., took no part.

c. See Able, *Commerce Regulation Before Gibbons v. Ogden: Interstate Transportation Enterprise,* 18 Miss.L.J. 335 (1947); Able, *Commerce Regulation Before Gibbons v. Ogden: Interstate Transportation Facilities,* 25 N.C.L. Rev. 121 (1947); Able, *Commerce Regulation Before Gibbons v. Ogden: Trade and Traffic,* 14 Brooklyn L.Rev. 38, 215 (1947–48).

d. The shaping of the law in this area by judicial decision is apparent from the 571 Supreme Court rulings on the validity of state regulations of interstate commerce between 1824 and 1932. Of these, 325 upheld the regulation and 246 invalidated it. Of those invalidated, 181 were state regulations on matters involving no relevant federal legislation. For individual listing of the cases see Gavit, *The Commerce Clause* 541–56 (1932). Since 1932 the volume of such litigation has continued at a high rate.

e. See *Prudential Ins. Co.,* supra, and cases there cited.

effect on commerce was 'direct' or 'indirect,' whether the regulation was or was not imposed 'on' interstate commerce itself. It was difficult, if not impossible, to tell—at least with any certainty—whether these expressions merely constituted different methods of stating the *Cooley* doctrine, or whether the court was applying different tests." [a]

NOEL T. DOWLING—INTERSTATE COMMERCE AND STATE POWER

27 Va.L.Rev. 1 (1940).
Reprinted with permission of the publisher; copyright © 1940,
Virginia Law Review Ass'n.

From what has gone before, a doctrine can be drawn which offers, I believe, desirable and helpful guidance for the Court in the future. It is, that in the absence of affirmative consent a Congressional negative will be presumed in the courts against state action which in its effect upon interstate commerce constitutes an unreasonable interference with national interests, the presumption being rebuttable at the pleasure of Congress. Such a doctrine would free the states from any constitutional disability but at the same time would not give them license to take such action as they see fit irrespective of its effect upon interstate commerce. With respect to such commerce, the question whether the states may act upon it would depend upon the will of Congress expressed in such form as it may choose. State action falling short of such interference would prevail unless and until superseded or otherwise nullified by Congressional action.

Five principal reasons support the foregoing:

1. The congressional consent aspect of the doctrine would entail no sharp break with the past, and its adoption would constitute the acceptance of some of the best efforts of the Court. Indeed, except for explicitness and generalization, it is the position to which the Court itself had come by a process of trial and error over nearly a hundred years. * * *

2. The substantive standard embodied in the doctrine, "unreasonable interference with national interests," would commit the Court to no new or untried principle. It would, to be sure, involve an avowal that the Court is deliberately balancing national and local interests and making a choice as to which of the two *should* prevail.[c] That, as I see the matter, is a policy judgment. But the test of reasonableness in interstate commerce cases is not the same as, for example, in due process cases. Additional factors are involved. In a sense, a state law must take the hurdle of due process before it comes to the interstate barrier. * * *

As already indicated, *Cooley* comprehended a certain balancing of state and national interests, though the Court did not go into the subject in detail. And it was just there, in an effort to discover the relevant considerations for answering

a. Stern, *The Problems of Yesteryear— Commerce and Due Process,* 4 Vand.L.Rev. 446, 451–52 (1951).

c. But compare the views of recent commentators questioning both the soundness and the actuality of such balancing, despite the Court's consistent and repeated embracing of the Dowling rationale. See Regan, The Supreme Court and State Protectionism: Making Sense of the Dormant Commerce Clause, 84 Mich.L.Rev. ___ (1986); Sedler, *The Negative Commerce Clause As a Restriction on State Regulation and Taxation: An Analysis in Terms of Constitutional Structure,* 31 Wayne L.Rev. 885 (1985). In studying the remaining cases in this Section, consider the extent to which a policy against discrimination favoring in-state interests may explain the results. Cf. Regan, supra; Sedler, supra.

the question whether the "national interest in maintaining freedom of commerce across state lines" has been infringed, that Mr. Justice Stone tackled the problem in his *Di Santo* dissent. His approach in that opinion appears to be well calculated to produce a "realistic" judgment whether any given state action constitutes an unreasonable interference with national interests. The several considerations to which he referred have been noted and discussed above. He essayed no exhaustive list, nor would he exclude such factors as the desirability of uniform regulation (the principal point of *Cooley*); or the consequences to the state if its action were disallowed—how serious and widespread the evil and what the prospect for national action; or the intangible but nevertheless real benefits to be had from giving the people of the states the satisfaction of, and stimulus to responsibility from, home government as against distant government. And in order to bring all such considerations into the judicial forum, could not the rules of evidence be made more generous and elastic? It is true that the litigation is between private parties, but the issue touches the relative jurisdictions of nation and state. After all, this is statecraft in which the courts are engaged.

3. This doctrine would provide flexibility in the adjustment and accommodation of national and state interests, at the same time preserving the judicial and amplifying the legislative function. From the judicial point of view it would preserve a role which the Court, beginning with the leadership of Marshall, has worked out for itself and which has conspicuously contributed to the functioning of the federal system. That role brings to constitutional cases the best of the common law methods in the building up of principles from specific decisions. The trial courts would operate out on the front line, where the impact of state action on interstate commerce is first felt, and they could appraise at close range the conflicting state and national interests. Furthermore, the judicial sifting of the facts would have the manifest merit of sharpening the issues and facilitating legislative efforts in the event that Congress, dissatisfied with the judicial results, should desire to take corrective action of its own.

From the legislative standpoint, the fullest power of Congress would be guaranteed. In no event could the courts forestall or impede Congressional action. If the state law complained of were sustained in the courts, Congress could step in and occupy the field if in its judgment the state action went too far. On the other hand, if the state law were disallowed in the courts, Congress could obviate the results by giving its consent for the operation of the law. In this respect the doctrine would amplify the power of Congress, for no longer would congressional consent be thought of as somehow dependent upon the nature of the subject matter involved. And such consent would be given (the point is worth repeating) in the light of the issues developed in the litigation. It can hardly be doubted, for instance, that the liquor cases gave Congress a clear lead for its own part in establishing the disputed power of the states.

There is no assurance that the commerce problem would be as well handled by Congress alone as where both Congress and the courts participate in its solution. I say "would", drawing a distinction between what seems likely and what is theoretically possible. Congress is a big and heavy machine to set in motion, and its progress is sometimes impeded even when national interests of the highest order are at stake. Meanwhile much damage to interstate commerce, to say nothing of the otherwise amicable relationships among the states, might be caused by unrestrained state [action].

To aid analysis the following opinions are organized by related problems, not time of decision. But they are grouped to minimize departure from chronological order and to respect chronology within each group.

II. REGULATION OF TRANSPORTATION

SOUTHERN PACIFIC CO. v. ARIZONA

325 U.S. 761, 65 S.Ct. 1515, 89 L.Ed. 1915 (1945).

MR. CHIEF JUSTICE STONE delivered the opinion of the Court.

[The Court reversed an Arizona Supreme Court decision upholding an Arizona law limiting the length of trains in Arizona to 70 freight cars.]

[E]ver since *Gibbons,* the states have not been deemed to have authority to impede substantially the free flow of commerce from state to state, or to regulate those phases of the national commerce which, because of the need of national uniformity, demand that their regulation, if any, be prescribed by a single authority.[2] Whether or not this long recognized distribution of power between the national and the state governments is predicated upon the implications of the commerce clause itself, or upon the presumed intention of Congress, where Congress has not spoken, Dowling, *Interstate Commerce and State Power,* the result is the same.

[S]ome enactments may be found to be plainly within and others plainly without state power. But between these extremes lies the infinite variety of cases in which regulation of local matters may also operate as a regulation of commerce, in which reconciliation of the conflicting claims of state and national power is to be attained only by some appraisal and accommodation of the competing demands of the state and national interests involved.

For a hundred years it has been accepted constitutional doctrine that the commerce clause, without the aid of Congressional legislation, thus affords some protection from state legislation inimical to the national commerce, and that in such cases, where Congress has not acted, this Court, and not the state legislature, is under the commerce clause the final arbiter of the competing demands of state and national interests.

Congress has undoubted power to redefine the distribution of power over interstate commerce. It may either permit the states to regulate the commerce in a manner which would otherwise not be permissible, or exclude state regulation even of matters of peculiarly local concern which nevertheless affect interstate commerce.

But in general Congress has left it to the courts to formulate the rules thus interpreting the commerce clause in its application, doubtless because it has appreciated the destructive consequences to the commerce of the nation if their protection were withdrawn. [Meanwhile], Congress has accommodated its legislation, as have the states, to these rules as an established feature of our constitutional system. There has thus been left to the states wide scope for the regulation of matters of local state concern, even though it in some measure affects the commerce, provided it does not materially restrict the free flow of commerce across state lines, or interfere with it in matters with respect to which uniformity of regulation is of predominant national concern.

2. In applying this rule the Court has often recognized that to the extent that the burden of state regulation falls on interests outside the state, it is unlikely to be alleviated by the operation of those political restraints normally exerted when interests within the state are affected. * * *

Hence the matters for ultimate determination here are the nature and extent of the burden which the state regulation of interstate trains, adopted as a safety measure, imposes on interstate commerce, and whether the relative weights of the state and national interests involved are such as to make inapplicable the rule, generally observed, that the free flow of interstate commerce and its freedom from local restraints in matters requiring uniformity of regulation are interests safeguarded by the commerce clause from state [interference].

The findings show that the operation [of trains of] more than seventy freight cars is standard practice over the main lines of the railroads of the United States, and that, if the length of trains is to be regulated at all, national uniformity [is] practically indispensable to the operation of an efficient and economical national railway system. [Compliance with the Arizona law increases the costs of operation by $1,000,000 annually for the two railroads in Arizona, and impedes efficient operation by delays in breaking up and remaking long trains.]

The unchallenged findings leave no doubt that the Arizona [law] imposes a serious burden on the interstate commerce conducted by appellant. It materially impedes the movement of appellant's interstate [trains]. Enforcement of the law in Arizona, while train lengths remain unregulated or are regulated by varying standards in other states, must inevitably result in an impairment of uniformity of efficient railroad operation because the railroads are subjected to regulation which is not uniform in its application. Compliance with a state statute limiting train lengths requires interstate trains of a length lawful in other states to be broken up and reconstituted as they enter each state according as it may impose varying limitations upon train lengths. The alternative is for the carrier to conform to the lowest train limit restriction of any of the states through which its trains pass, whose laws thus control the carriers' operations both within and without the regulating state.

[The] trial court found that the Arizona law had no reasonable relation to safety, and made train operation more dangerous. [T]his conclusion was rested on facts found which indicate that such increased danger of accident and personal injury as may result from the greater length of trains [through increase in slack action] is more than offset by the increase in the number of accidents, [generally more severe] resulting from the larger number of trains when train lengths are reduced. In considering the effect of the statute as a safety measure, [the] decisive question is whether in the circumstances the total effect of the law as a safety measure in reducing accidents and casualties is so slight or problematical as not to outweigh the national interest in keeping interstate commerce free from interferences which seriously impede it and subject it to local regulation which does not have a uniform effect on the interstate train journey which it interrupts. * * *

We think, as the trial court found, that the Arizona [law,] viewed as a safety measure, affords at most slight and dubious advantage, if any, over unregulated train lengths. [The state's] regulation of train lengths, admittedly obstructive to interstate train operation, and having a seriously adverse effect on transportation efficiency and economy, passes beyond what is plainly essential for safety since it does not appear that it will lessen rather than increase the danger of accident. Its attempted regulation of the operation of interstate trains cannot establish nationwide control such as is essential to the maintenance of an efficient transportation system, which Congress alone can prescribe. The state interest cannot be preserved at the expense of the national interest by an enactment which regulates interstate train lengths without securing such control, which is a matter of national concern. To this the interest of the state here asserted is subordinate.

Appellees especially rely on the full train crew cases [b] and also on *South Carolina State Highway Dep't v. Barnwell Bros.*, [note 2 infra]. While the full train crew laws undoubtedly placed an added financial burden on the railroads in order to serve a local interest, they did not obstruct interstate transportation or seriously impede it. They had no effects outside the state beyond those of picking up and setting down the extra employees at the state boundaries; they involved no wasted use of facilities or serious impairment of transportation efficiency, which are among the factors of controlling weight here.

[*Barnwell*] was concerned with the power of the state to regulate the weight and width of motor cars passing interstate over its highways. [In] that case, we were at pains to point out that there are few subjects of state regulation affecting interstate commerce which are so peculiarly of local concern as is the use of the state's highways. Unlike the railroads local highways are built, owned and maintained by the state or its municipal subdivisions. The state is responsible for their safe and economical administration. Regulations affecting the safety of their use must be applied alike to intrastate and interstate traffic. The fact that they affect alike shippers in interstate and intrastate commerce in great numbers, within as well as without the state, is a safeguard against regulatory abuses. Their regulation is akin to quarantine measures, game laws, and like local regulations of rivers, harbors, piers, and docks, with respect to which the state has exceptional scope for the exercise of its regulatory power, and which, Congress not acting, have been sustained even though they materially interfere with interstate commerce.

* * * Here examination of all the relevant factors makes it plain that the state interest is outweighed by the interest of the nation in an adequate economical and efficient railway transportation service, which must prevail.[c]

MR. JUSTICE BLACK, dissenting.

[In] the state court a rather extraordinary "trial" took place. [Before] the state trial judge finally determined that the dangers found by the legislature in 1912 no longer existed, he heard evidence over a period of $5\frac{1}{2}$ months which appears in about 3000 pages of the printed record. [This] new pattern of trial procedure makes it necessary for a judge to hear all the evidence offered as to why a legislature passed a law and to make findings of fact as to the validity of those reasons. If under today's ruling a court does make findings, as to a danger contrary to the findings of legislature, and the evidence heard "lends support" to those findings, a court can then invalidate the law. In this respect, the Arizona County Court acted, and this Court today is acting, as a "super-legislature."

Even if this method of invalidating legislative acts is a correct one, I still think that the "findings" of the state court do not authorize today's decision. [Everyday] knowledge as well as direct evidence presented at the various hearings, substantiates the report of the Senate Committee that the danger from slack movement is greater in long trains than in short trains. It may be that offsetting dangers are possible in the operation of short trains. The balancing of

---

b. For the latest decision upholding a "full crew" law, and for citations to the earlier cases, see *Brotherhood v. Chicago, R.I. & P.R.*, 393 U.S. 129, 89 S.Ct. 323, 21 L.Ed.2d 289 (1968).

c. Rutledge, J., concurred only in the result.

these probabilities, however, is not in my judgment a matter for judicial determination, but one which calls for legislative consideration. * * *[d]

Notes and Questions

1. *Earlier rulings.* Prior decisions on regulations aimed at railroad and highway safety and local train service are summarized and contrasted in *Morgan v. Virginia*, 328 U.S. 373, 378–80, fn. 16 & 17, 66 S.Ct. 1050, 1054–55, 90 L.Ed. 1317, 1323–24 (1946).

2. *Highway regulations.* (a) SOUTH CAROLINA STATE HIGHWAY DEP'T v. BARNWELL BROS., 303 U.S. 177, 58 S.Ct. 510, 82 L.Ed. 734 (1938), per STONE, J., upheld width and gross weight limits that excluded from South Carolina highways 85–90% of all vehicles used in interstate motor freight traffic in the country:

"In resolving [under the commerce clause the validity of such highway regulations courts] cannot act as Congress does when, after weighing all the conflicting interests, state and national, it determines when and how much the state regulatory power shall yield to the larger interests of a national commerce, [or as] state Legislatures, to determine what, in its judgment is the most suitable restriction to be applied of those that are possible. [When] the action of a Legislature is within the scope of its power, fairly debatable questions as to its reasonableness, wisdom, and propriety are not for the determination of courts, but for the legislative body, on which rests the duty and responsibility of decision. [In] reviewing the present determination, we examine the record, not to see whether the findings of the court below are supported by evidence, but to ascertain upon the whole record whether it is possible to say that the legislative choice is without rational basis. [Citing fourteenth amendment due process and equal protection cases.]"

(b) Can you reconcile Stone, J., on the Court's role in such cases in 1938 with Stone, C.J., in 1945? What might explain this shift in viewpoint? Can you reconcile the *result* in *Barnwell* with the *rationale* in *Southern Pacific?*

3. *Determination of facts relevant to constitutional issue.* Do you share Black, J.'s concern over the appropriateness of basing the constitutionality of a state statute regulating commerce upon factual evidence developed at the trial level concerning the need and effect of the statute? What are the alternatives for informing courts faced with applying the *Southern Pacific* standard? Cf. Karst, *Legislature Facts in Constitutional Litigation*, 1960 Sup.Ct.Rev. 75; Auerbach, Garrison, Hurst & Mermin, *The Legal Process* 90–137 (1961).

SPECIAL DEFERENCE FOR HIGHWAY SAFETY REGULATIONS?

Southern Pacific's distinguishing of *Barnwell* on the basis of the states' special concern with highway safety and maintenance left open which approach the Court would apply to highway safety regulations—*Southern Pacific* balancing or *Barnwell* rational basis—or something in between. The following three cases dealt with this issue. What appears to be the Court's answer?

d. Douglas, J., dissenting, agreed with Black, J.'s, views. He also expressed doubts that the judiciary should interfere with state commerce legislation, absent discrimination against interstate commerce. Later he abandoned this position. See *Bibb v. Navaho* *Freight Lines, Inc.*, infra. Black, J., explained a similar change of position in *Morgan v. Virginia*, note 1 infra: "So long as the Court remains committed to the 'undue burden on commerce formula,' I must make decisions under it."

BIBB v. NAVAJO FREIGHT LINES, 359 U.S. 520, 79 S.Ct. 962, 3 L.Ed.2d
1003 (1959), per DOUGLAS, J., held invalid an Illinois law that required contour
rear fender mudguards on all trucks and trailers on Illinois highways in place of
the straight mudflaps that were legal in "at least" 45 states: "[Highway] safety
measures carry a strong presumption of validity when challenged in court. If
there are alternative ways of solving a problem, we do not sit to determine which
of them is best suited to achieve a valid state objective. Policy decisions are for
the state legislature, absent federal entry into the field. Unless we can conclude
on the whole record that 'the total effect of the law as a safety measure in
reducing accidents and casualties is so slight or problematical as not to outweigh
the national interest in keeping interstate commerce free from interferences
which seriously impede it' (*Southern Pacific*) we must uphold the statute.

"[Arkansas requires] that trailers operating in that State be equipped with
straight or conventional mud flaps. Vehicles equipped to meet the standards of
the Illinois statute would not comply with Arkansas standards, and vice versa.
Thus if a trailer is to be operated in both States, mudguards would have to be
interchanged, causing a significant delay in an operation where prompt movement may be of the essence. * * *

"It was also found that the Illinois statute seriously interferes with the
'interline' operations of motor carriers—that is to say, with the interchanging of
trailers between an originating carrier and another carrier when the latter
serves an area not served by the former. These 'interline' operations provide a
speedy through-service for the shipper. Interlining contemplates the physical
transfer of the entire trailer; there is no unloading and reloading of the cargo.
The interlining process is particularly vital in connection with shipment of
perishables, [or] with the movement of explosives carried under seal. * * *

"Appellants did not attempt to rebut the appellees' showing that the statute
in question severely burdens interstate commerce. Appellants' showing was
aimed at establishing that contour mudguards prevented the throwing of debris
into the faces of drivers of passing cars and into the windshields of a following
vehicle. They concluded that, because the Illinois statute is a reasonable
exercise of the police power, a federal court is precluded from weighing the
relative merits of the contour mudguard against any other kind of mudguard
and must sustain the validity of the statute notwithstanding the extent of the
burden it imposes on interstate commerce. They rely in the main on *Barnwell*.
There is language in that opinion which, read in isolation from such later
decisions as *Southern Pacific* and *Morgan*, would suggest that no showing of
burden on interstate commerce is sufficient to invalidate local safety regulations
in absence of some element of discrimination against interstate commerce.
* * *

"Local regulations which would pass muster under the Due Process Clause
might nonetheless fail to survive other challenges to constitutionality that bring
the Supremacy Clause into play. Like any local law that conflicts with federal
regulatory measures state regulations that run afoul of the policy of free trade
reflected in the Commerce Clause must also bow.

"This is one of those cases—few in number—where local safety measures
that are nondiscriminatory place an unconstitutional burden on interstate
commerce. This conclusion is especially underlined by the deleterious effect
which the Illinois law will have on the 'interline' operation of interstate motor
carriers. The conflict between the Arkansas regulation and the Illinois regulation also suggests that this regulation of mudguards is not one of those matters

'admitting of diversity of treatment, according to the special requirements of local conditions.' [A] State which insists on a design out of line with the requirements of almost all the other States may sometimes place a great burden of delay and inconvenience on those interstate motor carriers entering or crossing its territory. Such a new safety device—out of line with the requirements of the other States—may be so compelling that the innovating State need not be the one to give-way. But the present showing—balanced against the clear burden on commerce—is far too inconclusive to make this mudguard meet that test.[a]

"We deal not with absolutes but with questions of degree. The state legislatures plainly have great leeway in providing safety regulations for all vehicles—interstate as well as local. Our decisions so hold. Yet the heavy burden which the Illinois mudguard law places on the interstate movement of trucks and trailers seems to us to pass the permissible limits even for safety regulations."[b]

In KASSEL v. CONSOLIDATED FREIGHTWAYS, 450 U.S. 662, 101 S.Ct. 1309, 67 L.Ed.2d 580 (1981), after a 14-day trial on safety and burden on commerce issues, a divided Court invalidated Iowa's 65-foot double trailer ban. Both the District Court and the Court of Appeals held the ban invalid as applied to interstate highways, concluding that the 65-foot "twin" was as safe as the 60-foot twin or 55-foot trailer permitted by Iowa. The Court affirmed. POWELL, J., announced the judgment, and delivered an opinion joined by White, Blackmun and Stevens, JJ.: " '[If] safety justifications are not illusory, the court will not second guess legislative judgment about their importance in comparison with related burdens on interstate commerce.' *Raymond Motor Transport, Inc. v. Rice*, 434 U.S. 429, 98 S.Ct. 787, 54 L.Ed.2d 664 (1978), (Blackmun, J., concurring [joined by BURGER, C.J., and BRENNAN and REHNQUIST, JJ.]). Those who would challenge such bona fide safety regulations must overcome a 'strong presumption of validity.'

"[But regulations] to promote the public health or safety [may] further the purpose so marginally, and interfere with commerce so substantially, as to be invalid under the Commerce Clause. In the Court's recent unanimous decision in *Raymond*, we declined to 'accept the State's contention that the inquiry under the Commerce Clause is ended without a weighing of the asserted safety purpose against the degree of interference with interstate commerce.' This 'weighing' by a court requires—and indeed the constitutionality of the state regulation depends on—'a sensitive consideration of the weight and nature of the state regulatory concern in light of the extent of the burden imposed on the course of interstate commerce.'

"Applying these general principles, we conclude that the Iowa truck-length limitations unconstitutionally burden interstate commerce.

"Here, as in *Raymond*, the State failed to present any persuasive evidence that 65-foot doubles are less safe than 55-foot singles. Moreover, Iowa's law is now out of step with the laws of all other midwestern and western States. Iowa thus substantially burdens the interstate flow of goods by truck. In the absence of congressional action to set uniform standards, some burdens associated with

---

a. Earlier in the opinion the Court mentioned but gave no weight to the three-judge District Court finding that contour mudguards increased the safety hazards by decreasing brake effectiveness through accumulating heat in the brake drums.

b. Harlan, J., joined by Stewart, J., concurred.

state safety regulations must be tolerated. But where, as here, the State's safety interest has been found to be illusory, and its regulations impair significantly the federal interest in efficient and safe interstate transportation, the state law cannot be harmonized with the Commerce Clause."

The plurality declined Iowa's request to "defer to the safety judgment of the State." The "deference traditionally accorded a State's safety judgment is not warranted" because the "disproportionate burden" on "out-of-state residents and businesses" by several exemptions for Iowans made it less likely that the usual political processes served as a "check on unduly burdensome regulations." [c]

BRENNAN, J., joined by Marshall, J., concurred in the judgment but not the Powell opinion. He viewed the Iowa law as "protectionist legislation" subject to a "virtual per se rule of illegality," because aimed at deflecting traffic around Iowa. While he viewed balancing highway safety and burden on commerce as irrelevant because of protectionism, he restated in a footnote his position on balancing safety considerations.[1]

REHNQUIST, J., joined by Burger, C.J. and Stewart, J., dissented: "A determination that a state law is a rational safety measure does not end the Commerce Clause inquiry. A 'sensitive consideration' of the safety purpose in relation to the burden on commerce is required. *Raymond.* When engaging in such a consideration the Court does not directly compare safety benefits to commerce costs and strike down the legislation if the latter can be said in some vague sense to 'outweigh' the former. Such an approach would make an empty gesture of the strong presumption of validity accorded state safety measures, particularly those governing highways. It would also arrogate to this Court functions of forming public policy, functions which, in the absence of congressional action, were left by the Framers of the Constitution to state legislatures.[4] * * *

"The purpose of the 'sensitive consideration' referred to above [is] to determine if the asserted safety justification, although rational, is merely a pretext for discrimination against interstate commerce. We will conclude that it is if the safety benefits from the regulation are demonstrably trivial while the burden on commerce is great. Thus the Court in *Bibb* stated that the 'strong presumption of validity' accorded highway safety measures could be overcome only when the safety benefits were 'slight or problematical.' See *Raymond,* (Blackmun, J., concurring) ('If safety justifications are not illusory, the Court will not second-guess legislative judgment about their importance in comparison with related burdens on interstate commerce'). The nature of the inquiry is perhaps best illustrated by examining those cases in which state safety laws have been

---

c. For references to similar considerations in earlier cases see note 3 after *Southern Pacific* and the full opinion in *Raymond.*

1. Moreover, I would emphasize that in the field of safety—and perhaps in other fields where the decisions of State lawmakers are deserving of a heightened degree of deference—the role of the courts is not to balance asserted burdens against intended benefits as it is in other fields. [In] the field of safety, once the court has established that the intended safety benefit is not illusory, insubstantial, or nonexistent, it must defer to the State's lawmakers on the appropriate balance to be struck against other interests. I therefore disagree with my Brother Powell when he asserts that the degree of interference with

interstate commerce may in the first instance be "weighed" against the State's safety interests: "Regulations designed [to promote the public health or safety] nevertheless may further the purpose so marginally, *and interfere with commerce so substantially,* as to be invalid under the Commerce Clause." *Pike* (emphasis added).

4. It should not escape notice that a majority of the Court goes on record today as agreeing that courts in Commerce Clause cases do not sit to weigh safety benefits against burdens on commerce when the safety benefits are not illusory. See concurring opinion, n. 1. Even the plurality gives lip service to this principle. * * *

struck down on Commerce Clause grounds. [Citing *Southern Pacific's* finding of 'slight and dubious advantage' in the train length law and *Bibb's* finding of 'no safety advantage over conventional mudguards.'] The cases thus demonstrate that the safety benefits of a state law must be slight indeed before it will be struck down under the dormant Commerce Clause."

Reviewing the evidence, the dissenters concluded that Iowa had demonstrated that the safety benefits of the law were "not illusory." In doing so, they considered "the overall safety benefits *from the regulation,* [not] any marginal benefit" between the regulation and the previous 60-foot length limit. (emphasis in original.)

Notes and Questions

1. *Nonillusory highway safety regulations.* (a) What now appears to be "the law" on whether the Court will balance the importance of the justifications for nonillusory state highway safety regulations against their burden on interstate commerce? What *should* it be?

(b) Do Powell and Rehnquist, JJ., disagree in *Kassell* only on whether the claimed benefits were illusory or on the standard by which to judge highway safety regulations' burdens on commerce?

2. *Aim of "sensitive consideration."* Was the *Kassell* dissent's limited view of the "purpose" for the "sensitive consideration" consistent with the use of that phrase in *Raymond?* Should it be so limited?

3. *Nonhighway safety regulations.* Based on these opinions would you expect the same judicial deference for other safety and health regulations as for highway safety regulations? Are they soundly distinguishable?

III. REGULATION OF TRADE

A. INCOMING COMMERCE

BALDWIN v. G.A.F. SEELIG INC.
294 U.S. 511, 55 S.Ct. 497, 79 L.Ed. 1032 (1935).

MR. JUSTICE CARDOZO delivered the opinion of the Court.

[New York regulated minimum milk prices for sales by producers to dealers, and prohibited the sale in New York of milk bought outside the state at lower prices. The Court held the prohibition invalid.]

New York has no power to project its legislation into Vermont by regulating the price to be paid in that state for milk acquired there. [It] is equally without power to prohibit the introduction within her territory of milk of wholesome quality acquired in Vermont, whether at high prices or [low]. Accepting those postulates, New York asserts her power to outlaw milk so introduced by prohibiting its sale thereafter if the price that has been paid for it to the farmers of Vermont is less than would be owing in like circumstances to farmers in New York. The importer in that view may keep his milk or drink it, but sell it he may not.

Such a power, if exerted, will set a barrier to traffic between one state and another as effective as if customs duties, equal to the price differential, had been laid upon the thing transported.

[Nice] distinctions * * * between direct and indirect burdens [are] irrelevant when the avowed purpose of the obstruction, as well as its necessary tendency, is to suppress or mitigate the consequences of competition between the states. [If] New York, in order to promote the economic welfare of her farmers, may guard them against competition with the cheaper prices of Vermont, the door has been opened to rivalries and reprisals that were meant to be averted by subjecting commerce between the states to the power of the nation.

The argument is pressed upon us, however, that the end to be served by the Milk Control Act is something more than the economic welfare of the farmers. [The] end to be served is the maintenance of a regular and adequate supply of pure and wholesome milk; the supply being put in jeopardy when the farmers of the state are unable to earn a living income. On that assumption we are asked to say that intervention will be upheld as a valid exercise by the state of its internal police power, though there is an incidental obstruction to commerce between one state and another. Let such an exception be admitted, and all that a state will have to do in times of stress and strain is to say that its farmers and merchants and workmen must be protected against competition from without, lest they go upon the poor relief lists or perish altogether. To give entrance to that excuse would be to invite a speedy end of our national solidarity. The Constitution was framed under the dominion of a political philosophy less parochial in range. It was framed upon the theory that the peoples of the several states must sink or swim together, and that in the long run prosperity and salvation are in union and not division.

[T]he evils springing from uncared for cattle must be remedied by measures of repression more direct and certain than the creation of a parity of prices between New York and other states. Appropriate certificates may be exacted from farmers in Vermont and elsewhere (*Mintz v. Baldwin,* 289 U.S. 346, 53 S.Ct. 611, 77 L.Ed. 1245; *Reid v. Colorado,* 187 U.S. 137, 23 S.Ct. 92, 47 L.Ed. 108); milk may be excluded if necessary safeguards have been omitted; but commerce between the states is burdened unduly when one state regulates by indirection the prices to be paid to producers in another, in the faith that augmentation of prices will lift up the level of economic welfare, and that this will stimulate the observance of sanitary requirements in the preparation of the [product.] Whatever relation there may be between earnings and sanitation is too remote and indirect to justify obstructions to the normal flow of commerce in its movement between states. * * *

Notes and Questions

1. *Barriers to competition.* Was the New York law distinguishable in principle from an embargo on competing milk from out of state? From a tax imposed only on competing goods from out of state? In what way was the New York law "an economic barrier against competition?" Does *Baldwin* foreclose state legislative cures for local evils by remedies that increase the cost of local products that compete with unregulated production from other states? Are federal controls[a] the only solution in such situations? Cf. 10 Wis.L.Rev. 388, 392–93 (1935).

2. *Continued authority of Baldwin.* Though decided before the emergence of the open balancing process in state commerce regulation cases, the Court has widely cited *Baldwin* as a basic authority and has never questioned it. See, e.g.,

a. See *United States v. Rock Royal Coop.,* 307 U.S. 533, 59 S.Ct. 993, 83 L.Ed. 1446 (1939); *United States v. Wrightwood Dairy Co.,* 315 U.S. 110, 62 S.Ct. 523, 86 L.Ed. 726 (1942).

Hood & Sons v. Du Mond (1949), Part III, B infra; *Philadelphia v. New Jersey* (1978), Part V infra.

DEAN MILK CO. v. MADISON

340 U.S. 349, 71 S.Ct. 295, 95 L.Ed. 329 (1951).

MR. JUSTICE CLARK delivered the opinion of the Court.

[A Madison, Wis., ordinance prohibited sale of milk unless processed and bottled at an approved pasteurization plant within five miles of the central square of Madison. Every 30 days Madison officials inspected the five processing plants within the five-mile area and the 5600 dairy farms in the county. Dean Milk, based in Illinois, bought milk from Illinois and Wisconsin farms and pasteurized it at its two Illinois plants 65 and 85 miles from Madison. These farms and plants were licensed and inspected by Chicago public health authorities under the Chicago ordinance, which adopted the U.S. Public Health Service rating standards. Both the Chicago and Madison ordinances were patterned after the Public Health Service's Model Milk Ordinance, though the Court noted that "Madison contends and we assume that in some particulars its ordinance is more rigorous than that of Chicago."]

[W]e agree with appellant that the ordinance imposes an undue burden on interstate commerce. [T]his regulation, like the provision invalidated in *Baldwin,* in practical effect excludes from distribution in Madison wholesale milk produced and pasteurized in Illinois. [In] thus erecting an economic barrier protecting a major local industry against competition from without the State, Madison plainly discriminates against interstate commerce.[4] This it cannot do, even in the exercise of its unquestioned power to protect the health and safety of its people, if reasonable nondiscriminatory alternatives, adequate to conserve legitimate local interests, are available. Cf. *Baldwin; Minnesota v. Barber,* 136 U.S. 313, 10 S.Ct. 862, 34 L.Ed. 455 (1890). A different view, that the ordinance is valid simply because it professes to be a health measure, would mean that the Commerce Clause of itself imposes no limitations on state action other than those laid down by the Due Process Clause, save for the rare instance where a state artlessly discloses an avowed purpose to discriminate against interstate goods. Our issue then is whether the discrimination inherent in the Madison ordinance can be justified in view of the character of the local interests and the available methods of protecting them.

It appears that reasonable and adequate alternatives are available. If Madison prefers to rely upon its own officials for inspection of distant milk sources, such inspection is readily open to it without hardship for it could charge the actual and reasonable cost of such inspection to the importing producers and processors. Cf. *Sprout v. South Bend,* 1928, 277 U.S. 163, 169, 48 S.Ct. 502, 504, 72 L.Ed. 833 (1928). Moreover, appellee Health Commissioner of Madison testified that as proponent of the local milk ordinance he had submitted the provisions here in controversy and an alternative proposal based on § 11 of the Model Milk Ordinance recommended by the United States Public Health Service. The model provision imposes no geographical limitation on location of milk sources and processing plants but excludes from the municipality milk not produced and pasteurized conformably to standards as high as those enforced by the receiving city, [subject to verification of ratings through the P.H.S.] The

---

4. It is immaterial that Wisconsin milk from outside the Madison area is subjected to the same proscription as that moving in interstate commerce. Cf. *Brimmer v. Rebman,* 1891, 138 U.S. 78, 82–83, 11 S.Ct. 213, 214, 34 L.Ed. 862.

Commissioner testified that Madison consumers "would be safeguarded adequately" under either proposal and that he had expressed no preference. The milk sanitarian of the Wisconsin State Board of Health testified that the State Health Department recommends the adoption of a provision based on the Model Ordinance. Both officials agreed that a local health officer would be justified in relying upon the evaluation by the P.H.S. of enforcement conditions in remote producing areas.

To permit Madison to adopt a regulation not essential for the protection of local health interests and placing a discriminatory burden on interstate commerce would invite a multiplication of preferential trade areas destructive of the very purpose of the Commerce Clause. Under the circumstances here presented, the regulation must yield to the principle that "one state in its dealings with another may not place itself in a position of economic isolation." [*Baldwin*].

Mr. Justice Black, with whom Mr. Justice Douglas, and Mr. Justice Minton concur, dissenting. * * *

(2) Characterization of § 7.21 as a "discriminatory burden" on interstate commerce is merely a statement of the Court's result, which I think incorrect. [B]oth state courts below found that § 7.21 represents a good-faith attempt to safe-guard public health by making adequate sanitation inspection possible. While we are not bound by these findings, I do not understand the Court to overturn them. Therefore, the fact that § 7.21, like all health regulations, imposes some burden on trade, does not mean that it "discriminates" against interstate commerce.

(3) This health regulation should not be invalidated merely because the Court believes that alternative milk-inspection methods might insure the cleanliness and healthfulness of Dean's Illinois milk. [W]hile the "reasonable alternative" concept has been invoked to protect First Amendment rights, [see Ch. 8, Sec. 3] it has not heretofore been considered an appropriate weapon for striking down local health laws. [In] my view, to use this ground now elevates the right to traffic in commerce for profit above the power of the people to guard the purity of their daily diet of milk. * * *

From what this record shows, and from what it fails to show, I do not think that either of the alternatives suggested by the Court would assure the people of Madison as pure a supply of milk as they receive under their own ordinance. On this record I would uphold the Madison law. At the very least, however, I would not invalidate it without giving the parties a chance to present evidence and get findings on the ultimate issues the Court thinks crucial—namely, the relative merits of the Madison ordinance and the alternatives suggested by the Court today.

Notes and Questions

1. *What did "discrimination" mean*, as used here? How do discriminatory burdens differ, if at all, from other unconstitutional burdens on commerce? Was the Court concerned with *purpose or effect*?

2. *Effect of intrastate discrimination.* Since the decision was based on "discrimination", why was it "immaterial" that the regulation also excluded *Wisconsin* milk not pasteurized in Madison?

3. *Adequate alternatives.* Was the weight given in *Dean Milk* to the availability of "reasonable and adequate alternatives" soundly related to the underlying standard for judgment? Is basing a decision on the adequacy of less burdensome alternatives an appropriate judicial function?

4. *Actually based on preventing protectionism?* In studying *Dean Milk* and the cases that follow consider Professor Robert Sedler's view that outside the transportation area it is consistent with the cases and with their "conceptual justification" to hold regulations that burden interstate commerce invalid only where their "essential *effect* is to discriminate against or disadvantage interstate commerce or out-of-state interests in favor of local commerce or in-state interests because of the interstate nature of that commerce or the out-of-state nature of those interests." Sedler, p. 255 fn. c supra, at 895–912. Compare Professor Donald Regan's thesis that in cases involving interstate movement of goods the Court has been and should be concerned exclusively with preventing *purposeful* economic protectionism, and that the Court should not otherwise try to "balance" local interests against the national commerce interests. See Regan, p. 255 fn. c supra.

BREARD v. ALEXANDRIA, 341 U.S. 622, 71 S.Ct. 920, 95 L.Ed. 1233 (1951), per REED, J., upheld, over a commerce clause claim, an ordinance forbidding door-to-door soliciting of orders for the sale of merchandise, as applied to Breard and his crew of sales persons seeking subscriptions to out-of-state magazines.[a] The Court viewed the ordinance as protecting an important social interest: "[O]pportunists, for private gain, cannot be permitted to arm themselves with an acceptable principle, such as that of a right to work, a privilege to engage in interstate commerce, or a free press, and proceed to use it as an iron standard to smooth their path by crushing the living rights of others to privacy and repose.

"[Door-to-door] canvassing has flourished increasingly in recent years with the ready market furnished by the rapid concentration of housing. The infrequent and still welcome solicitor to the rural home became to some a recurring nuisance in towns when the visits were multiplied. Unwanted knocks on the door by day or night are a nuisance, or worse, to peace and quiet.[b] The local retail merchant, too, has not been unmindful of the effective competition furnished by house-to-house selling in many lines. As a matter of business fairness, it may be thought not really sporting to corner the quarry in his home and through his open door put pressure on the prospect to purchase. As the exigencies of trade are not ordinarily expected to have a higher rating constitutionally than the tranquillity of the fireside, responsible municipal officers have sought a way to curb the annoyances while preserving complete freedom for desirable visitors to the homes. The idea of barring classified salesmen from homes by means of notices posted by individual householders was rejected early as less practical than an ordinance regulating solicitors.[4]

"Appellant argues that the ordinance violates the Commerce Clause 'because the practical operation of the ordinance, as applied to appellant and others similarly situated, imposes an undue and discriminatory burden upon interstate commerce and in effect is tantamount to a prohibition of such commerce.' The attempt to secure the householder's consent is said to be too costly and the results negligible. The extent of this interstate business, as stipulated, is large.[18]

---

a. The Court also denied a freedom of the press claim.

b. Later in the opinion the Court quoted Professor Chafee's stress on the problems of door-to-door canvassing, and the need for protection of the privacy of the home. See Chafee, *Free Speech in the United States* (1941) 406.

4. *Green River v. Bunger,* 50 Wyo. 52, 70, 58 P.2d 456, 462.

18. "The solicitation of subscriptions in the field regularly accounts for from 50% to 60% of the total annual subscription circulation of nationally-distributed magazines."

[It] is urged [that] *Dean Milk* demonstrate[s] that this Court will not permit local interests to protect themselves against out-of-state competition by curtailing interstate business.

"It was partly because the regulation in *Dean Milk* discriminated against interstate commerce that it was struck down. [Nor] does the clause as to alternatives [in *Dean Milk*] apply to the Alexandria ordinance. Interstate commerce itself knocks on the local door. It is only by regulating that knock that the interests of the home may be protected by public as distinct from private [action].

"We recognize the importance to publishers of our many periodicals of the house-to-house method of selling by solicitation. As a matter of constitutional law, however, they in their business operations are in no different position so far as the Commerce Clause is concerned than the sellers of other wares. Appellant, as their representative or in his own right as a door-to-door canvasser, is no more free to violate local regulations to protect privacy than are other solicitors. As we said above, the usual methods of seeking business are left open by the ordinance.[c] That such methods do not produce as much business as house-to-house canvassing is, constitutionally, immaterial and a matter for adjustment at the local level in the absence of federal legislation. Taxation that threatens interstate commerce with prohibition or discrimination is bad, but regulation that leaves out-of-state sellers on the same basis as local sellers cannot be invalid for that reason. * * *

"The general use of the Green River type of ordinance shows its adaptation to the needs of the many communities that have enacted it. We are not willing even to appraise the suggestion, unsupported in the record, that such wide use springs predominantly from the selfish influence of local merchants. * * *

"When there is a reasonable basis for legislation to protect the social, as distinguished from the economic, welfare of a community, it is not for this Court because of the Commerce Clause to deny the exercise locally of the sovereign power of Louisiana. Changing living conditions or variations in the experiences or habits of different communities may well call for different legislative regulations as to methods and manners of doing business. Powers of municipalities are subject to control by the states. Their judgment of local needs is made from a more intimate knowledge of local conditions than that of any other legislative body. We cannot say that this ordinance of Alexandria so burdens or impedes interstate commerce as to exceed the regulatory powers of that city. * * *"

VINSON, C.J., joined by Douglas, J., dissented: "I think it plain that a 'blanket prohibition' upon appellant's solicitation discriminates against and unduly burdens interstate commerce in favoring local retail merchants. 'Whether or not it was so intended, those are its necessary effects.' The fact that this ordinance exempts solicitation by the essentially local purveyors of farm products shows that local economic interests are relieved of the burdensome effects of the ordinance. No one doubts that protection of the home is a proper subject of legislation, but that end can be served without prohibiting interstate commerce. [I] cannot agree that this Court should defer to the City Council of Alexandria as though we had before us an act of Congress regulating commerce. '[T]his Court, and not the state legislature [or the city council], is under the commerce clause the final arbiter of the competing demands of state [or local] and national interests.' [*Southern Pacific.*]"

c. In rejecting a due process argument, the opinion had referred to the availability of the "usual methods of soliciting—radio, periodicals, mail, local agencies."

Notes and Questions

1. *A different standard for social interests?* Did *Breard* call for a *Barnwell*-type acceptance of the legislative judgment in the case of regulations that protect "social, as distinguished from economic" interests? Would that be consistent with *Southern Pacific?* With *Dean Milk?* How else might *Breard* be interpreted?

2. *Discrimination?* Did *Breard* soundly conclude there was no discrimination in the *Dean Milk* sense? Should such discrimination be required to invalidate a regulation that seriously burdens commerce while advancing a social interest?

3. *Alternative methods.* Were there adequate alternative methods for protecting privacy in the home? For advancing the commerce clause interest? Are both uses of such reasoning relevant to the balancing approach? In the same case?

4. *Diminution of interstate business.* By what reasoning could *Breard* conclude that it is "constitutionally immaterial" that the other "usual methods of seeking business" "do not produce as much business as house-to-house canvassing." Is that conclusion sound?

HUNT v. WASHINGTON STATE APPLE ADVERTISING COMM'N, 432 U.S. 333, 97 S.Ct. 2434, 53 L.Ed.2d 383 (1977), per BURGER, C.J., unanimously [a] held invalid a North Carolina statute requiring that closed apple containers bear only the applicable U.S.D.A. grade or be marked "not graded." Half of the fresh apples sold in United States were from Washington, which shipped nearly 40 million closed apple containers in interstate commerce yearly, with half a million going to North Carolina. North Carolina refused to permit Washington apple containers to show both the U.S.D.A., and the Washington grades. The latter were widely accepted in the trade as equivalent or superior to the U.S.D.A. grades as a result of 60 years of strict Washington state inspection and grading, coupled with advertising. Choosing not to rely on an "economic protection motive" despite "suspect indications," the Court ruled the statute invalid "even if enacted for the declared purpose of protecting consumers from deception and fraud in the market place," where divergent apple grading standards from seven states competed with North Carolina apples that used only USDA grades:

"[T]hat state legislation furthers matters of legitimate local concern, even in the health and consumer protection areas, does not end the inquiry. [Rather], when such state legislation comes into conflict with the Commerce Clause's overriding requirement of a national 'common market', we are confronted with the task of effecting an accommodation of the competing national and local interests. *Pike v. Bruce Church, Inc.,* [Sec. III, B infra].

"[T]he challenged statute has the practical effect of not only burdening interstate sales of Washington apples, but also discriminating against them. This discrimination takes various forms. [First], the statute [raises] the costs of doing business in the North Carolina market for Washington apple growers and dealers, while leaving those of their North Carolina counterparts unaffected. [T]his disparate effect results from the fact that North Carolina apple producers, unlike their Washington competitors, were not forced to alter their marketing

---

a. Rehnquist, J., did not participate.

practices in order to comply with the statute.[d] [The] increased costs imposed by the statute would tend to shield the local apple industry from the competition of Washington apple growers and dealers * * *.

"Second, the statute [stripped] away from the Washington apple industry the competitive and economic advantages it has earned for itself through its expensive inspection and grading system. * * *

"Third, by prohibiting Washington growers and dealers from marketing apples under their State's grades, the statute has a leveling effect which insidiously operates to the advantage of local apple producers. [Washington] apples which would otherwise qualify for, and be sold under the superior Washington grades will now have to be marketed under their inferior U.S.D.A. counterparts. Such 'down grading' offers the North Carolina apple industry the very sort of protection against competing out-of-state products that the Commerce Clause was designed to prohibit. * * *

["When] discrimination against commerce of the type we have found is demonstrated, the burden falls on the State to justify it both in terms of the local benefits flowing from the statute and the unavailability of nondiscriminatory alternatives, adequate to preserve the local interests at stake. North Carolina has failed to sustain that burden on both scores.

"The several States unquestionably possess a substantial interest in protecting their citizens from confusion and deception in the marketing of foodstuffs, but the challenged statute does remarkably little to further that laudable goal at least with respect to Washington apples and grades. The statute [permits] the marketing of closed containers of apples under *no* grades at all. Such a result can hardly be thought to eliminate the problems of deception and confusion created by the multiplicity of differing state grades; indeed, it magnifies them by depriving purchasers of all information concerning the quality of the contents of closed apple containers."

EXXON CORP. v. MARYLAND, 437 U.S. 117, 98 S.Ct. 2207, 57 L.Ed.2d 91 (1978), per STEVENS, J., upheld 7 to 1 [a] a Maryland statute forbidding producers or refiners of petroleum products from operating retail service stations in the state. Its objective was to foreclose suspected favoritism by producers for their own outlets in times of short supply: "Plainly, the Maryland statute does not discriminate against interstate goods, nor does it favor local producers and refiners. Since Maryland's entire gasoline supply flows in interstate commerce and since there are no local producers or refiners, such claims of disparate treatment between interstate and local commerce would be meritless. Appellants, however, focus on the retail market arguing that the effect of the statute is to protect in-state independent dealers from out-of-state competition. [T]hey rely on the fact that the burden of the divestiture requirements falls solely on interstate companies. But this fact does not lead, either logically or as a practical matter, to a conclusion that the State is discriminating against interstate commerce at the retail level.

---

d. The Court had noted that for North Carolina shipments the statute would require Washington growers to (a) obliterate Washington grades imprinted on their standard containers, or (b) repack specially all shipments to North Carolina, or (c) pack and store in specially marked containers apples sufficient to meet the estimated demand from North Carolina.

a. Powell, J., did not participate.

"As the record shows, there are several major interstate marketers of petroleum that own and operate their own retail gasoline stations [but] are not affected by the Act because they do not refine or produce gasoline. [While] the refiners will no longer enjoy their same status in the Maryland market, in-state independent dealers will have no competitive advantage over out-of-state dealers. The fact that the burden of a state regulation falls on some interstate companies does not, by itself, establish a claim of discrimination against interstate commerce.[16]

"[The] source of the consumers' supply may switch from company-operated stations to independent dealers, but interstate commerce is not subjected to an impermissible burden simply because an otherwise valid regulation causes some business to shift from one interstate supplier to another.

"The crux of appellants' claim is that, regardless of whether the State has interfered with the movement of goods in interstate commerce, it has interfered 'with the natural functioning of the interstate market.' [Appellants] claim that the statute 'will surely change the market structure by weakening the independent refiners.' We cannot, however, accept appellants' underlying notion that the Commerce Clause protects the particular structure or methods of operation in a retail market. See *Breard*. [The] Clause protects the interstate market, not particular interstate firms, from prohibitive or burdensome regulations."

BLACKMUN, J., dissenting, saw in the statute "discrimination against interstate commerce in retail gasoline marketing," because its effect was to exclude from the Maryland retail market "a class of predominantly out-of-state gasoline retailers while providing protection from competition to a class of nonintegrated retailers that is overwhelmingly composed of local businessmen."[b]

"[It] is true that merely demonstrating a burden on some out-of-state actors does not prove unconstitutional discrimination. But when the burden is significant, when it falls on the most numerous and effective group of out-of-state competitors, when a similar burden does not fall on the class of protected in-state businessmen, and when the State cannot justify the resulting disparity by showing that its legislative interests cannot be vindicated by more evenhanded regulation, unconstitutional discrimination exists."

Maryland has not shown why its "vague interest in preserving competition in its retail gasoline market" could not be "vindicated by legislation less discriminatory toward out-of-state retailers."

Notes and Questions

Discrimination. Should the policy against discrimination apply only when the "favored and disfavored interests are similarly situated *except for* the interstate or out-of-state nature of the disfavored interests," as urged by Professor Sedler's comments on *Exxon*, not when the regulation favors "one kind of

---

16. If the effect of a state regulation is to cause local goods to comprise a larger share, and goods with an out-of-state source to comprise a smaller share, of the total sales in the market—as in *Hunt* and *Dean Milk*—the regulation may have a discriminatory effect on interstate commerce. But the Maryland statute has no impact on the relative proportions of local and out-of-state goods sold in Maryland and, indeed, no demonstrable effect whatsoever on the interstate flow of goods. The sales by independent retailers are just as much a part of the flow of interstate commerce as the sales made by the refiner-operated stations.

b. 98% of the integrated dealers were from out of state while 99% of the nonintegrated dealers were local.

[local] economic interest over a different kind of [out-of-state] economic interest?" c

B. OUTGOING COMMERCE

H.P. HOOD & SONS v. DU MOND
336 U.S. 525, 69 S.Ct. 657, 93 L.Ed. 865 (1949).

MR. JUSTICE JACKSON delivered the opinion of the Court.

[Hood operated three licensed milk-receiving depots in New York for milk to be distributed in Boston. New York denied Hood a license for a fourth depot for the same purpose in the same general area under a law requiring that the Commissioner find that "issuance of the license will not tend to a destructive competition in a market already adequately served, and ∗ ∗ ∗ is in the public interest." The Commissioner concluded that a fourth depot would (1) divert milk from other distributors' depots and thus tend to reduce their volume and increase their milk-handling costs, and (2) would tend to deprive local markets, like Troy, of a milk supply needed during the short season. The Court held that the law as applied violated the commerce clause.]

The present controversy begins where *Eisenberg* a left off. [It] is only additional restrictions, imposed for the avowed purpose and with the practical effect of curtailing the volume of interstate commerce to aid local economic interests, that are in question here, and no such measures were attempted or such ends sought to be achieved in the *Eisenberg* Case. [The opinion quotes at length from *Baldwin v. Seelig.*]

This distinction between the power of the State to shelter its people from menaces to their health or safety and from fraud, even when those dangers emanate from interstate commerce, and its lack of power to retard, burden or constrict the flow of such commerce for their economic advantage, is one deeply rooted in both our history and our law.b ∗ ∗ ∗

Baldwin is an explicit, impressive, recent and unanimous condemnation by this Court of economic restraints on interstate commerce for local economic advantage, but it does not stand alone. This Court consistently has rebuffed attempts of states to advance their own commercial interests by curtailing the movement of articles of commerce, either into or out of the state, while generally supporting their right to impose even burdensome regulations in the interest of local health and safety. As most states serve their own interests best by sending their produce to market, the cases in which this Court has been obliged to deal with prohibitions or limitations by states upon exports of articles of commerce are not numerous. However, [in] *West v. Kansas Natural Gas Co.*, 221 U.S. 229, 31 S.Ct. 564, 55 L.Ed. 716 (1911), the Court denied constitutional validity to a statute by which Oklahoma [sought] to restrict the export of natural gas.c

c. Sedler, supra Part I, 31 Wayne L.Rev. at 996.

a. *Milk Control Bd. v. Eisenberg Co.*, 306 U.S. 346, 59 S.Ct. 528, 83 L.Ed. 752 (1939), upheld a Pennsylvania law that required licenses for milk receiving depots, bonds to protect producers, and payment of prescribed prices, as applied to a New York milk distributor operating a receiving depot in Pennsylvania for milk to be shipped to New York.

b. The Court found "In neither *Baldwin* nor *Hood* is the measure supported by health or safety considerations but solely by protection of local economic interests, such as supply for local consumption and limitation of competition."

c. Accord, *Pennsylvania v. West Virginia*, 262 U.S. 553, 43 S.Ct. 658, 67 L.Ed. 1117 (1923).

[This] principle that our economic unit is the Nation, which alone has the gamut of powers necessary to control of the economy, including the vital power of erecting customs barriers against foreign competition, has as its corollary that the states are not separable economic units. As the Court said in *Baldwin,* "What is ultimate is the principle that one state in its dealings with another may not place itself in a position of economic isolation." In so speaking it but followed the principle that the state may not use its admitted powers to protect the health and safety of its people as a basis for suppressing competition.

The material success that has come to inhabitants of the states which make up this federal free trade unit has been the most impressive in the history of commerce, but the established interdependence of the states only emphasizes the necessity of protecting interstate movement of goods against local burdens and repressions. We need only consider the consequences if each of the few states that produce copper, lead, high-grade iron ore, timber, cotton, oil or gas should decree that industries located in that state shall have priority. What fantastic rivalries and dislocations and reprisals would ensue if such practices were begun! Or suppose that the field of discrimination and retaliation be industry. May Michigan provide that automobiles cannot be taken out of that State until local dealers' demands are fully met? Would she not have every argument in the favor of such a statute that can be offered in support of New York's limiting sales of milk for out-of-state shipment to protect the economic interests of her competing dealers and local consumers? Could Ohio then pounce upon the rubber-tire industry, on which she has a substantial grip, to retaliate for Michigan's auto monopoly?

Our system, fostered by the Commerce Clause, is that every farmer and every craftsman shall be encouraged to produce by the certainty that he will have free access to every market in the Nation, that no home embargoes will withhold his export, and no foreign state will by customs duties or regulations exclude them. Likewise, every consumer may look to the free competition from every producing area in the Nation to protect him from exploitation by any. Such was the vision of the Founders; such has been the doctrine of this Court which has given it reality. * * *

MR. JUSTICE FRANKFURTER, with whom MR. JUSTICE RUTLEDGE joins, dissenting.

If the Court's opinion has meaning beyond deciding this case in isolation, its effect is to hold that no matter how important to the internal economy of a State may be the prevention of destructive competition, and no matter how unimportant the interstate commerce affected, a State cannot as a means of preventing such competition deny an applicant access to a market within the State if that applicant happens to intend the out-of-state shipment of the product that he buys. I feel constrained to dissent because I cannot agree in treating what is essentially a problem of striking a balance between competing interests as an exercise in absolutes. Nor does it seem to me that such a problem should be disposed of on a record from which we cannot tell what weights to put in which side of the scales.

[G]uarding against out-of-state competition is a very different thing from curbing competition from whatever source. [In] the determination that an extension of petitioner's license would tend to destructive competition, the fact that petitioner intended the out-of-state shipment of what it bought was so far as the record tells us, wholly irrelevant; under the circumstances, any other applicant, no matter where he meant to send his milk, would presumably also have been refused a [license]. [a]

[The opinion called attention to several questions relevant to a balancing analysis.] We should, I submit, have answers at least to some of these questions before we can say either how seriously interstate commerce is burdened by New York's licensing power or how necessary to New York is that power. [I] believe we should seek further light by remanding the case to the courts of the State.

* * *

Notes and Questions

1. *Purpose of the restriction.* Was the restriction in *Hood* "imposed for the avowed purpose and with the practical effect of curtailing the volume of interstate commerce to aid local economic interests"? Can this statement be reconciled with the Black dissent? Should the quotation have been recast for accuracy?

2. *Hood and balancing.* Did *Hood* mean that the Court would not use a balancing analysis when the state law protected local economic interests? Or only that it would not do so when a state law shielding established businesses from new competitors, whether local or not, was applied to out-of-state newcomers? Might *Hood* be interpreted as an implicit balancing judgment that in such circumstances the state interest was outweighed by the actual or potential harm to commerce?

3. *Local economic interests.* (a) *Hood's* disapproval of protecting local economic interests at the expense of commerce should be considered in the light of two earlier cases. *Eisenberg,* supra note a, upheld substantial regulations that burdened interstate commerce in outgoing milk but did not necessarily "curtail the volume." The opinion recognized that the purpose was to advance the "welfare of the producers and consumers of milk" in the regulating state. *Parker v. Brown*, 317 U.S. 341, 63 S.Ct. 307, 87 L.Ed. 315 (1943), per Stone, C.J., upheld a California statute that, to increase the price of raisins, required each producer to give a marketing committee control over the sale of $2/3$ of his raisins, 95% of which were shipped in commerce: "The evils attending the production and marketing of raisins in that state present a problem local in character and urgently demanding state action for the economic protection of those engaged in one of its important industries."

(b) Were *Eisenberg* and *Parker* still dependable law after *Hood?* Should the *Hood* dicta be restrictively interpreted in view of the actual issues and *Hood's* distinction of *Eisenberg?*

(c) In interpreting *Hood* what is the significance of CITIES SERVICES GAS CO. v. PEERLESS OIL & GAS CO., 340 U.S. 179, 71 S.Ct. 215, 95 L.Ed. 190 (1950), per CLARK, J. which upheld state minimum price regulation of natural gas leaving the state and distinguished *Hood* thus: "The vice in the regulation invalidated by *Hood* was solely that it denied facilities to a company in interstate commerce on the articulated ground that such facilities would divert milk supplies needed by local consumers; in other words, the regulation discriminated against interstate commerce. There is no such problem here." Did Jackson, J., who authored *Hood* and joined the Clark opinion in *Cities Service,* overlook the word *solely?*

---

a. Accord, Black, J., joined by Murphy, J., dissenting.

4. *Retention for local needs.* Could a good case be made for limiting sale for distant markets of milk needed for local consumption? Are the natural gas decisions and other industrial examples used in *Hood* distinguishable?

PIKE v. BRUCE CHURCH, INC.
397 U.S. 137, 90 S.Ct. 844, 25 L.Ed.2d 174 (1970).

MR. JUSTICE STEWART delivered the opinion of the Court.

[An Arizona statute required all cantaloupes grown in Arizona and offered for sale to be packed in closed containers bearing on the outside the name and address of the packer. Bruce Church grew cantaloupes of exceptionally high quality at its Parker, Ariz. ranch, where it had no packing shed. It transported them in bulk 31 miles to its Blythe, Cal. packing shed, where it packed them in compliance with the Arizona and California standards, but the containers bore only the California name and address and did not identify them as Arizona cantaloupes. The Court unanimously struck down an Arizona order prohibiting Bruce Church from shipping its cantaloupes out of Arizona unless packed in containers as required by the statute.]

[The] general rule [can] be phrased as follows: Where the statute regulates evenhandedly to effectuate a legitimate local public interest, and its effects on interstate commerce are only incidental, it will be upheld unless the burden imposed on such commerce is clearly excessive in relation to the putative local benefits. If a legitimate local purpose is found, then the question becomes one of degree. And the extent of the burden that will be tolerated will of course depend on the nature of the local interest involved, and on whether it could be promoted as well with a lesser impact on interstate activities.

[Arizona's order] would forbid the company to pack its cantaloupes outside Arizona, not for the purpose of keeping the reputation of its growers unsullied, but to enhance their reputation through the reflected good will of the company's superior produce. The appellant, in other words, is not complaining because the company is putting the good name of Arizona on an inferior or deceptively packaged product, but because it is not putting that name on a product that is superior and well packaged. As the appellant's brief puts the matter, "It is within Arizona's legitimate interest to require that interstate cantaloupe purchasers be informed that this high quality Parker fruit was grown in Arizona."

[T]he State's tenuous interest in having the company's cantaloupes identified as originating in Arizona cannot constitutionally justify the requirement that the company build and operate an unneeded $200,000 packing plant in the State. The nature of that burden is, constitutionally, more significant than its extent. For the Court has viewed with particular suspicion state statutes requiring business operations to be performed in the home State that could more efficiently be performed elsewhere. Even where the State is pursuing a clearly legitimate local interest, this particular burden on commerce has been declared to be virtually per se illegal. *Foster-Fountain Packing Co. v. Haydel,* 278 U.S. 1, 49 S.Ct. 1, 73 L.Ed. 147 (1928); [b] *Toomer v. Witsell,* 334 U.S. 385, 68 S.Ct. 1156, 92 L.Ed. 1460 (1948).

The appellant argues that the above cases are different because they involved statutes whose express or concealed purpose was to preserve or secure

---

b. *Foster-Fountain* struck down Louisiana's ban on shipment of shrimp from the state until removal of the hulls and heads, which were useful for fertilizer. The Court found that the purpose was "to bring about the removal of the packing and canning industry from Mississippi to Louisiana."

employment for the home State, while here the statute is a regulatory one and there is no hint of such a purpose. But in *Toomer*, the Court indicated that such a burden upon interstate commerce is unconstitutional even in the absence of such a purpose. In *Toomer* the Court held invalid a South Carolina statute requiring that owners of shrimp boats licensed by the State to fish in the maritime belt off South Carolina must unload and pack their catch in that State before "shipping or transporting it to another State." What we said there applies to this case as well:

"There was also uncontradicted evidence that appellants' costs would be materially increased by the necessity of having their shrimp unloaded and packed in South Carolina ports rather than at their home bases in Georgia where they maintain their own docking, warehousing, refrigeration and packing facilities. In addition, an inevitable concomitant of a statute requiring that work be done in South Carolina, even though that be economically disadvantageous to the fishermen, is to divert to South Carolina employment and business which might otherwise go to Georgia; the necessary tendency of the statute is to impose an artificial rigidity on the economic pattern of the industry."

While the order issued under the Arizona statute does not impose such rigidity on an entire industry, it does impose just such a strait-jacket on the appellee company with respect to the allocation of its interstate resources. Such an incidental consequence of a regulatory scheme could perhaps be tolerated if a more compelling state interest were involved. But here the State's interest is minimal at best—certainly less substantial than a State's interest in securing employment for its people. If the Commerce Clause forbids a State to require work to be done within its jurisdiction to promote local employment, then surely it cannot permit a State to require a person to go into a local packing business solely for the sake of enhancing the reputation of other producers within its borders.

Notes and Questions

1. *Authoritative version.* Since 1970 the first paragraph of *Pike* has been the authoritative version of the balancing standard, repeatedly restated and applied in a wide variety of state regulation situations. But it omitted some considerations. Note the refinement of *Pike* in the second paragraph of *Hughes*, Part V infra.

2. *"Virtually per se illegal."* Should statutes like those in *Toomer* and *Foster-Fountain* be viewed as "virtually per se illegal?" Does this mean an "on its face" commerce clause violation, or something less than this? Watch for this concept in later cases.

IV. REGULATION OF INTERSTATE MIGRATION

EDWARDS v. CALIFORNIA, 314 U.S. 160, 62 S.Ct. 164, 86 L.Ed. 119 (1941), per BYRNES, J., invalidated a California statute that made it unlawful knowingly to bring into the state any indigent person. Despite California's "huge influx of migrants," causing staggering "problems of health, morals and especially finance," no single state may "isolate itself from difficulties common to all of them by restraining the transportation of persons and property across its borders. It is frequently the case that a State might gain a momentary respite from the pressure of events by the simple expedient of shutting its gates to the outside world. But in the words of Mr. Justice Cardozo: 'The Constitution was framed [upon] the theory that the peoples of the several States must sink or swim together, and that in the long run prosperity and salvation are in union and not division.' *Baldwin.*

"It is difficult to conceive of a statute more squarely in conflict with this theory than the [one] challenged here. Its express purpose and inevitable effect is to prohibit the transportation of indigent persons across the California border. The burden upon interstate commerce is intended and immediate.

"[The] social phenomenon of large-scale interstate migration is as certainly a matter of national concern as the provision of assistance to those who have found a permanent or temporary abode.[a] Moreover, and unlike the relief problem, this phenomenon does not admit of diverse treatment by the several States. The prohibition against transporting indigent non-residents into one State is an open invitation to retaliatory measures, and the burdens upon the transportation of such persons become cumulative. Moreover, it would be a virtual impossibility for migrants and those who transport them to acquaint themselves with the peculiar rules of admission of many States."

DOUGLAS, J., joined by Black and Murphy, JJ., concurred:[b] "I express no view on whether or not the statute here in question runs afoul of [the commerce clause]. But I am of the opinion that the right of persons to move freely from State to State occupies a more protected position in our constitutional system than does the movement of cattle, fruit, steel and coal across state lines.

"[The] right to move freely from State to State is an incident of *national* citizenship protected by the privileges and immunities clause of the Fourteenth Amendment against state interference. [*Twining v. New Jersey,* 211 U.S. 78, 97, 29 S.Ct. 14, 18, 53 L.Ed. 97.] Now it is apparent that this right is not specifically granted by the Constitution. Yet before the Fourteenth Amendment it was recognized as a right fundamental to the national character of our Federal government. [*Crandall v. Nevada,* 6 Wall. 35, 18 L.Ed. 745 (1867)] struck down a Nevada tax 'upon every person leaving the State' by common carrier. Mr. Justice Miller writing for the Court held that the right to move freely throughout the nation was a right of *national* citizenship. That the right was implied did not make it any the less 'guaranteed' by the Constitution.

"[So] when the Fourteenth Amendment was adopted in 1868, it had been squarely and authoritatively settled that the right to move freely from State to State was a right of *national* citizenship. As such it was protected by the privileges and immunities clause of the Fourteenth Amendment against state interference. *Slaughter House Cases* [p. 250 infra]. [And] Chief Justice Fuller in *Williams v. Fears,* 179 U.S. 270, 274, 21 S.Ct. 128, 129, 45 L.Ed. 186 stated: 'Undoubtedly the right of locomotion, the right to remove from one place to another according to inclination, is an attribute of personal liberty, and the right, ordinarily, of free transit from or through the territory of any State is a right secured by the Fourteenth Amendment and by other provisions of the Constitution.'"

---

a. The opinion had noted that the federal government had shared with the states the "common responsibility" and heavy burden of financial assistance to indigents.

b. Jackson, J., concurring, agreed that the commerce ground was a "permissible" one, but preferred to base his decision on the privileges and immunities clause of the fourteenth amendment.

Notes and Questions

1. *The privileges and immunities clauses.* (a) The reluctance of the *Edwards* majority to base the decision on the privileges and immunities clause of the fourteenth amendment reflects the Court's historic narrow treatment of that clause. See note 3 after *Slaughterhouse Cases,* p. 254 infra.

2. *Sources of right to travel.* For discussion of the right to travel and its varied sources, see Ch. 7, Sec. 3.

V. PROTECTING THE ENVIRONMENT AND NATURAL RESOURCES

PHILADELPHIA v. NEW JERSEY

437 U.S. 617, 98 S.Ct. 2531, 57 L.Ed.2d 475 (1978).

MR. JUSTICE STEWART delivered the opinion of the Court.

[Operators of New Jersey landfills, and out-of-state cities that had agreements with them for waste disposal, challenged under the commerce clause Ch. 363, N.J.Laws, 1973, which provided: "No person shall bring into this State any solid or liquid waste which originated or was collected outside [the] state." The New Jersey Supreme Court upheld the statute, ruling that it advanced vital health and environmental objectives with no economic discrimination against interstate commerce and that its substantial benefits outweighed its "slight" burden on interstate commerce. The Supreme Court reversed.]

[All] objects of interstate trade merit Commerce Clause protection; none is excluded by definition at the outset. [Just] as Congress has power to regulate the interstate movement of these wastes, States are not free from constitutional scrutiny when they restrict that movement.

[The] opinions of the Court through the years have reflected an alertness to the evils of "economic isolation" and protectionism, while at the same time recognizing that incidental burdens on interstate commerce may be unavoidable when a State legislates to safeguard the health and safety of its people. Thus, where simple economic protectionism is effected by state legislation, a virtually per se rule of invalidity has been erected. See, e.g., *Hood; Toomer.* [But] where other legislative objectives are credibly advanced and there is no patent discrimination against interstate trade, the Court has adopted a much more flexible approach, the general contours of which were outlined in [*Pike*]. [The] crucial inquiry, therefore, must be directed to determining whether ch. 363 is basically a protectionist measure, or whether it can fairly be viewed as a law directed to legitimate local concerns, with effects upon interstate commerce that are only incidental.

The purpose of ch. 363 is set out in the [statute]: "The Legislature finds and determines that [the] volume of solid and liquid waste continues to rapidly increase, that the treatment and disposal of these wastes continues to pose an even greater threat to the quality of the environment of New Jersey, that the available and appropriate landfill sites within the State are being diminished, that the environment continues to be threatened by the treatment and disposal of waste which originated or was collected outside the State." [The] state court additionally found that New Jersey's existing landfill sites will be exhausted within a few years; that to go on using these sites or to develop new ones will take a heavy environmental toll, both from pollution and from loss of scarce open lands; that new techniques to divert waste from landfills to other methods of disposal and resource recovery processes are under development, but that these changes will require time; and finally, that "the extension of the lifespan of existing landfills, resulting from the exclusion of out-of-state waste, may be of crucial importance in preventing further virgin wetlands or other undeveloped lands from being devoted to landfill purposes."

[The] evil of protectionism can reside in legislative means as well as legislative ends. Thus, it does not matter whether the ultimate aim of ch. 363 is to reduce the waste disposal costs of New Jersey residents or to save remaining open lands from pollution, for we assume New Jersey has every right to protect its residents' pocketbooks as well as their environment. And it may be assumed as well that New Jersey may pursue those ends by slowing the flow of *all* waste into the State's remaining landfills, even though interstate commerce may incidentally be affected. But whatever New Jersey's ultimate purpose, it may not be accomplished by discriminating against articles of commerce coming from outside the State unless there is some reason, apart from their origin, to treat them differently. Both on its face and in its plain effect, ch. 363 violates this principle of nondiscrimination.

The Court has consistently found parochial legislation of this kind to be constitutionally invalid, whether the ultimate aim of the legislation was to assure a steady supply of milk by erecting barriers to allegedly ruinous outside competition, *Baldwin;* or to create jobs by keeping industry within the State, *Foster-Fountain; Toomer;* or to preserve the State's financial resources from depletion by fencing out indigent immigrants, *Edwards.* In each of these cases, a presumably legitimate goal was sought to be achieved by the illegitimate means of isolating the State from the national economy.

Also relevant here are the Court's decisions holding that a State may not accord its own inhabitants a preferred right of access over consumers in other States to natural resources located within its borders. *West v. Kansas Natural Gas Co.; Pennsylvania v. West Virginia.*

[The] New Jersey law at issue in this case falls squarely within the area that the Commerce Clause puts off-limits to state regulation. On its face, it imposes on out-of-state commercial interests the full burden of conserving the State's remaining landfill space. It is true that in our previous cases the scarce natural resource was itself the article of commerce, whereas here the scarce resource and the article of commerce are distinct. But that difference is without consequence. In both instances, the State has overtly moved to slow or freeze the flow of commerce for protectionist reasons. It does not matter that the State has shut the article of commerce inside the State in one case and outside the State in the other. What is crucial is the attempt by one State to isolate itself from a problem common to many by erecting a barrier against the movement of interstate trade. * * *

The New Jersey statute is not such a quarantine law. There has been no claim here that the very movement of waste into or through New Jersey endangers health, or that waste must be disposed of as soon and as close to its point of generation as possible. The harms caused by waste are said to arise after its disposal in landfill sites, and at that point, as New Jersey concedes, there is no basis to distinguish out-of-state waste from domestic waste. If one is inherently harmful, so is the other. Yet New Jersey has banned the former while leaving its landfill sites open to the latter. The New Jersey law blocks the importation of waste in an obvious effort to saddle those outside the State with the entire burden of slowing the flow of refuse into New Jersey's remaining landfill sites. That legislative effort is clearly impermissible under the Commerce Clause of the Constitution.

Today, cities in Pennsylvania and New York find it expedient or necessary to send their waste into New Jersey for disposal, and New Jersey claims the right to close its borders to such traffic. Tomorrow, cities in New Jersey may find it expedient or necessary to send their waste into Pennsylvania or New York for disposal, and those States might then claim the right to close their borders. The Commerce Clause will protect New Jersey in the future, just as it protects her neighbors now, from efforts by one State to isolate itself in the stream of interstate commerce from a problem shared by all.

MR. JUSTICE REHNQUIST, with whom The Chief Justice joins, dissenting.

* * * New Jersey should be free under our past precedents to prohibit the importation of solid waste because of the health and safety problems that such waste poses to its citizens. The fact that New Jersey continues to, and indeed must continue to, dispose of its own solid waste does not mean that New Jersey may not prohibit the importation of even more solid waste into the State.

[I] do not see why a State may ban the importation of items whose movement risks contagion, but cannot ban the importation of items which, although they may be transported into the State without undue hazard, will then simply pile up in an ever increasing danger to the public's health and safety. The Commerce Clause was not drawn with a view to having the validity of state laws turn on such pointless distinctions.

[The] fact that New Jersey has left its landfill sites open for domestic waste does not, of course, mean that solid waste is not innately harmful. Nor does it mean that New Jersey prohibits importation of solid waste for reasons other than the health and safety of its population. New Jersey must out of sheer necessity treat and dispose of its solid waste in some fashion, just as it must treat New Jersey cattle suffering from hoof-and-mouth disease. It does not follow that New Jersey must, under the Commerce Clause, accept solid waste or diseased cattle from outside its borders and thereby exacerbate its problems. * * *

Notes and Questions

1. *Governmental "out-of-state commercial interests."* The only out-of-state litigants were cities claiming the right to continue to "send their waste into New Jersey for disposal"—a governmental function. Was it appropriate to invoke commerce clause concerns to protect such interests? Were they "out-of-state commercial interests?" Has the Court used the commerce clause in analogous situations, either as a limit on state regulation or as a source of congressional power? [a]

2. *"Protectionism" against non-economic problems.* Are the commerce clause considerations underlying the "principle of nondiscrimination" soundly applicable to the conflict between New Jersey's interest in prolonging the life of its limited landfills and the interest of other states' cities in using New Jersey's convenient landfills? Is the policy against "protectionism" soundly applicable to a state's efforts to isolate itself from commerce-spread national social problems as well as economic problems? Is the "virtually per se rule of invalidity" against "simple economic protectionism" transferable to New Jersey's effort? What of

a. Cf. e.g., *Edwards,* supra, Part IV, supra; *Heart of Atlanta Motel,* Ch. 2, Sec. V; note 4 after *Gibbons,* Ch. 2, Sec. 2, II.

the *Pike* "flexible" approach that weighs the state interest against the national interest?

3. *Natural gas cases distinguishable?* Is *Philadelphia* soundly distinguishable from the natural gas cases there cited, which hold that a state may not require suppliers of natural gas from in-state wells to give priority to in-state domestic and industrial consumers?

4. *Adequate alternatives.* Does *Philadelphia's* emphasis on the protectionist means without exploring the availability and adequacy of alternative means to protect New Jersey's interest, as in *Dean Milk* and *Hunt,* suggest abandonment of the adequate alternatives approach in cases of discriminatory effect? Or possibly only its irrelevance to legislatively explicit discriminatory means toward a legitimate end? Cf. 92 Harv.L.Rev. 61–66 (1978).

HUGHES v. OKLAHOMA, 441 U.S. 322, 99 S.Ct. 1727, 60 L.Ed.2d 250 (1979), per BRENNAN, J., held invalid under the commerce clause an Oklahoma statute forbidding any person to "transport or ship minnows for sale outside the state which were seined or procured within the waters of this state," as applied to a Texas minnow dealer who transported to Texas a load of minnows bought from an Oklahoma minnow dealer, who took them in Oklahoma waters:

"We now conclude that challenges under the Commerce Clause to state regulations of wild animals should be considered according to the same general rule applied to state regulations of other natural resources, and therefore expressly overrule *Geer.*[b] [T]he general rule we adopt in this case makes ample allowance for preserving, in ways not inconsistent with the Commerce Clause, the legitimate state concerns for conservation and protection of wild animals underlying the 19th century legal fiction of state ownership.

"We turn then to the question whether the burden imposed on interstate commerce in wild game by § 4–115(B) is permissible under the general rule articulated in our precedents governing other types of commerce. See, e.g., *Pike.* Under that general rule that we must inquire (1) whether the challenged statute regulates evenhandedly with only 'incidental' effects on interstate commerce, or discriminates against interstate commerce either on its face or in practical effect; (2) whether the statute serves a legitimate local purpose; and, if so, (3) whether alternative means could promote this local purpose as well without discriminating against interstate commerce. '[When] discrimination against commerce [is] demonstrated, the burden falls on the State to justify it both in terms of the local benefits flowing from the statute and the unavailability of nondiscriminatory alternatives adequate to preserve the local interests at stake.' [*Hunt*].

"[Section 4–115(b)] on its face discriminates against interstate commerce. It forbids the transportation of natural minnows out of the State for purposes of sale, and thus 'overtly blocks the flow of interstate commerce at [the] State's border.' *Philadelphia.* Such facial discrimination by itself may be a fatal defect, regardless of the State's purpose, because 'the evil of protectionism can reside in legislative means as well as legislative ends.' Ibid. At a minimum such facial discrimination invokes the strictest scrutiny of any purported legitimate local purpose and of the absence of nondiscriminatory alternatives.

---

b. *Geer v. Connecticut,* 161 U.S. 519, 16 S.Ct. 600, 40 L.Ed. 793 (1896), had held that a state ban on exporting wild game from the state was not subject to the commerce clause, because of a theory of state ownership of the game, later recognized as a fiction facilitating conservation.

"[The] State's interest in maintaining the ecological balance in state waters by avoiding the removal of inordinate numbers of minnows may well qualify as a legitimate local purpose. *   *   *

"Far from choosing the least discriminatory alternative, Oklahoma has chosen to 'conserve' its minnows in the way that most overtly discriminates against interstate commerce. The State places no limits on the numbers of minnows that can be taken by licensed minnow dealers; nor does it limit in any way how these minnows may be disposed of within the State. Yet it forbids the transportation of any commercially significant number of natural minnows out of the State for sale. Section 4–115(B) is certainly not a 'last ditch' attempt at conservation after nondiscriminatory alternatives have proven unfeasible. It is rather a choice of the most discriminatory means even though nondiscriminatory alternatives would seem likely to fulfill the State's purported legitimate local purpose more effectively.

"[The] overruling of *Geer* does not leave the States powerless to protect and conserve wild animal life within their borders. Today's decision makes clear, however, that States may promote this legitimate purpose only in ways consistent with the basic principle that 'our economic unit is the Nation,' *Hood,* and that when a wild animal 'becomes an article of commerce [its] use cannot be limited to the citizens of one State to the exclusion of citizens of another State.' *Geer* (Field, J., dissenting)."

REHNQUIST, J., joined by Burger, C.J., dissented, concluding that Oklahoma's "substantial interest in conserving and regulating exploitation of its natural minnow population" "outweighed" the "minimal burden" on commerce of requiring all who export minnows from the state, residents as well as nonresidents, to secure them from hatcheries.

Notes and Questions

1. *Explicit discrimination and adequate alternatives.* What light does *Hughes* shed on the issues raised in note 4 after *Philadelphia?* Should a statute that expressly discriminates against interstate commerce be valid if no adequate alternative means is available to protect an important state interest that outweighs the harm to interstate commerce? Would a per se rule of invalidity for explicit discrimination give excessive weight to form over substance? To draftsmanship over practical realities? Cf. 92 Harv.L.Rev. 62 (1978). Is explicit discrimination a greater threat to interstate commerce than "incidental" discriminatory effect? Are regulations that explicitly discriminate more likely to burden interstate commerce unduly than those with incidental discriminatory effects?

2. *Environmental regulation "incidentally" favoring local products.* MINNESOTA v. CLOVER LEAF CREAMERY CO., 449 U.S. 456, 101 S.Ct. 715, 66 L.Ed.2d 659 (1981), per BRENNAN, J., upheld a state law that banned nonreturnable containers made of plastic but permitted other nonreturnable milk containers, largely cartons made of pulpwood, though the plastic originated out of state and the pulpwood instate. In enacting the law, the legislature found that the use of nonreturnable milk containers "presents a solid waste management problem for the state, promotes energy waste, and depletes natural resources" in violation of a legislative policy to encourage "the reduction of the amount and type of material entering the solid waste stream."

"[Minnesota's statute] does not effect 'simple protectionism,' but 'regulates even-handedly' by prohibiting all milk retailers from selling their products in plastic, nonreturnable milk containers, without regard to whether the milk, the containers, or the sellers are from outside the State.

"Since the statute does not discriminate between interstate and intrastate commerce, the controlling question is whether the incidental burden imposed on interstate commerce by the Minnesota Act is 'clearly excessive in relation to the putative local benefits.' *Pike.* We conclude that it is not. * * *

"Pulpwood producers are the only Minnesota industry likely to benefit significantly from the Act at the expense of out-of-state firms. Respondents point out that plastic resin, the raw material used for making plastic nonreturnable milk jugs, is produced entirely by non-Minnesota firms, while pulpwood, used for making paperboard, is a major Minnesota product. Nevertheless, it is clear that respondents exaggerate the degree of burden on out-of-state interests, both because plastics will continue to be used in the production of plastic pouches, plastic returnable bottles, and paperboard itself, and because out-of-state pulpwood producers will presumably absorb some of the business generated by the Act.

"Even granting that the out-of-state plastics industry is burdened relatively more heavily than the Minnesota pulpwood industry, we find that this burden is not 'clearly excessive' in light of the substantial state interest in promoting conservation of energy and other natural resources and easing solid waste disposal problems, which we have already reviewed in the context of equal protection analysis. We find these local benefits ample to support Minnesota's decision under the Commerce Clause. Moreover, we find that no approach with 'a lesser impact on interstate activities,' *Bruce Church,* is available. Respondents have suggested several alternative statutory schemes, but these alternatives are either more burdensome on commerce than the Act (as, for example, banning all nonreturnables) or less likely to be effective (as, for example, providing incentives for recycling).

"In *Exxon,* we upheld a Maryland statute barring producers and refiners of petroleum products—all of which were out-of-state businesses—from retailing gasoline in the State. We stressed that the Commerce Clause 'protects the interstate market, not particular interstate firms, from prohibitive or burdensome regulations.' A nondiscriminatory regulation serving substantial state purposes is not invalid simply because it causes some business to shift from a predominantly out-of-state industry to a predominantly in-state industry. Only if the burden on interstate commerce clearly outweighs the State's legitimate purposes does such a regulation violate the Commerce Clause." [a]

VI. THE STATE AS A MARKET PARTICIPANT

REEVES, INC. v. STAKE

447 U.S. 429, 100 S.Ct. 2271, 65 L.Ed.2d 244 (1980).

Mr. Justice Blackmun delivered the opinion of the Court.

[Responding to a 1919 cement shortage, South Dakota built and operated a cement plant, which sold to both in-state and out-of-state buyers. The latter bought 40% of the plant's production in the mid-70's. When booming construc-

---

a. Powell and Stevens, JJ., dissenting separately, would have referred the commerce clause issue back to the Minnesota Supreme Court. Rehnquist, J., took no part.

tion caused a cement shortage in 1978, Reeves, an out-of-state buyer for 20 years, challenged as a commerce clause violation South Dakota's policy of giving preference to South Dakota buyers.

[The Court upheld the policy, invoking *Hughes v. Alexandria Scrap Corp.*, 426 U.S. 794, 96 S.Ct. 2488, 49 L.Ed.2d 220 (1976). That case had upheld a Maryland bounty program to encourage recycling of junk autos, which had caused autos qualifying for the state bounty to be supplied largely to in-state processors, due to the Maryland law requiring out-of-state processors to provide more demanding title documentation. The *Reeves* court explained *Alexandria Scrap:*]

In the Court's view, however, *Alexandria Scrap* did not involve "the kind of action with which the Commerce Clause is concerned." Unlike prior cases voiding state laws inhibiting interstate trade, "Maryland has not sought to prohibit the flow of hulks, or to regulate the conditions under which it may occur. Instead, it has entered into the market itself to bid up their price as a purchaser, in effect, of a potential article of interstate commerce," and has restricted "its trade to its own citizens or businesses within the State."

Having characterized Maryland as a market participant, rather than as a market regulator, the Court found no reason to "believe the Commerce Clause was intended to require independent justification for [the State's] action." The Court couched its holding in unmistakably broad terms. "Nothing in the purposes animating the Commerce Clause prohibits a State, in the absence of congressional action, from participating in the market and exercising the right to favor its own citizens over others." [8]

The basic distinction drawn in *Alexandria Scrap* between States as market participants and States as market regulators makes good sense and sound law. As that case explains, the Commerce Clause responds principally to state taxes and regulatory measures impeding free private trade in the national marketplace. [There] is no indication of a constitutional plan to limit the ability of the States themselves to operate freely in the free market. See L. Tribe, American Constitutional Law 336 (1978) ("the commerce clause was directed, as an historical matter, only at regulatory and taxing actions taken by states in their sovereign capacity"). The precedents comport with this distinction. [9]

Restraint in this area is also counseled by considerations of state sovereignty, [10] the role of each State " 'as guardian and trustee for its people,' " and "the

---

8. The dissent's central criticisms of the result reached here seem to be that the South Dakota policy does not emanate from " 'the power of governments to supply their own needs,' " and that it threatens "the natural functioning of the interstate market." The same observations, however, apply with equal force to the subsidy program challenged in *Alexandria Scrap.*

9. *Alexandria Scrap* does not stand alone. In *American Yearbook Co. v. Askew,* 339 F.Supp. 719 (N.D.Fla.1972), a three-judge District Court upheld a Florida statute requiring the State to obtain needed printing services from in-state shops. It reasoned that "state proprietary functions" are exempt from Commerce Clause scrutiny. This Court affirmed summarily. 409 U.S. 904, (1972). Numerous courts have rebuffed Commerce Clause challenges directed at similar preferences that ex-

ist in "a substantial majority of the states." Note, 58 Iowa L.Rev. 576 (1973). [The opinion cites state court decisions from 8 states.]

10. See *American Yearbook Co. v. Askew,* 339 F.Supp., at 725 ("ad hoc" inquiry into burdening of interstate commerce "would unduly interfere with state proprietary functions if not bring them to a standstill"). Considerations of sovereignty independently dictate that marketplace actions involving "integral operations in areas of traditional governmental functions"—such as the employment of certain state workers—may not be subject even to congressional regulation pursuant to the commerce power. *National League of Cities.* It follows easily that the intrinsic limits of the Commerce Clause do not prohibit state marketplace conduct that falls within this sphere. Even where "integral operations" are not implicated, States may fairly claim some mea-

long recognized right of trader or manufacturer, engaged in an entirely private business, freely to exercise his own independent discretion as to parties with whom he will deal." *United States v. Colgate & Co.*, 250 U.S. 300, 307, 39 S.Ct. 465, 63 L.Ed. 992 (1919). Moreover, state proprietary activities may be, and often are, burdened with the same restrictions imposed on private market participants. Evenhandedness suggests that, when acting as proprietors, States should similarly share existing freedoms from federal constraints, including the inherent limits of the Commerce Clause. Finally, as this case illustrates, the competing considerations in cases involving state proprietary action often will be subtle, complex, politically charged, and difficult to assess under traditional Commerce Clause analysis. Given these factors, *Alexandria Scrap* wisely recognizes that, as a rule, the adjustment of interests in this context is a task better suited for Congress than this Court.

South Dakota, as a seller of cement, unquestionably fits the "market participant" label more comfortably than a State acting to subsidize local scrap processors. Thus, the general rule of *Alexandria Scrap* plainly applies here.[14] Petitioner argues, however, that the exemption for marketplace participation necessarily admits of exceptions. While conceding that possibility, we perceive in this case no sufficient reason to depart from the general rule. * * *

We find the label "protectionism" of little help in this context. The State's refusal to sell to buyers other than South Dakotans is "protectionist" only in the sense that it limits benefits generated by a state program to those who fund the state treasury and whom the State was created to serve. Petitioner's argument apparently also would characterize as "protectionist" rules restricting to state residents the enjoyment of state educational institutions, energy generated by a state-run plant, police and fire protection, and agricultural improvement and business development programs. Such policies, while perhaps "protectionist" in a loose sense, reflect the essential and patently unobjectionable purpose of state government—to serve the citizens of the State.

[Cement] is not a natural resource, like coal, timber, wild game, or minerals. Cf. *Hughes v. Oklahoma* (minnows); *Philadelphia v. New Jersey* (landfill sites); *Pennsylvania v. West Virginia,* (natural gas); Note, 32 Rutg.L.Rev. 741 (1979). It is the end-product of a complex process whereby a costly physical plant and human labor act on raw materials. South Dakota has not sought to limit access to the State's limestone or other materials used to make cement. Nor has it restricted the ability of private firms or sister States to set up plants within its borders.

MR. JUSTICE POWELL, with whom [Brennan, White, and Stevens, JJ.,] join, dissenting.

[In] procuring goods and services for the operation of government, a State may act without regard to the private marketplace and remove itself from the reach of the Commerce Clause. See *American Yearbook Co.* But when a State itself becomes a participant in the private market for other purposes, the Constitution forbids actions that would impede the flow of interstate commerce.

sure of a sovereign interest in retaining freedom to decide how, with whom, and for whose benefit to deal. *The Supreme Court,* 1975 Term, 90 Harv.L.Rev. 1, 56, 63 (1976).

14. The criticism received by *Alexandria Scrap* in part has been directed at its application of the proprietary immunity to state subsidy programs. See Note, 18 BC.Ind. & Com. L.Rev. 893, 924–925 (1977). But see *The Supreme Court,* 1975 Term, 90 Harv.L.Rev. 1, 60–61 (1976). We have no occasion here to inquire whether subsidy programs unlike that involved in *Alexandria Scrap* warrant characterization as proprietary, rather than regulatory, activity. Cf. 18 BC.Ind. & Com.L.Rev., at 913–915.

These categories recognize no more than the "constitutional line between the State as Government and the State as trader." *New York v. United States,* [p. 126 supra]; see *United States v. California,* [p. 129 supra].

The Court holds that South Dakota, like a private business, should not be governed by the Commerce Clause when it enters the private market. But precisely because South Dakota is a State, it cannot be presumed to behave like an enterprise "engaged in an entirely private business." A State frequently will respond to market conditions on the basis of political rather than economic concerns. To use the Court's terms, a State may attempt to act as a "market regulator" rather than a "market participant." In that situation, it is a pretense to equate the State with a private economic actor. State action burdening interstate trade is no less state action because it is accomplished by a public agency authorized to participate in the private market. * * *

Unlike the market subsidies at issue in *Alexandria Scrap,* the marketing policy of the South Dakota Cement Commission has cut off interstate trade.[3] The State can raise such a bar when it enters the market to supply its own needs. In order to ensure an adequate supply of cement for public uses, the State can withhold from interstate commerce the cement needed for public projects. Cf. *National League of Cities.*

The State, however, has no parallel justification for favoring private, in-state customers over out-of-state customers.[4] In response to political concerns that likely would be inconsequential to a private cement producer, South Dakota has shut off its cement sales to customers beyond its borders. That discrimination constitutes a direct barrier to trade "of the type forbidden by the Commerce Clause, and involved in previous cases." *Alexandria Scrap.* The effect on interstate trade is the same as if the state legislature had imposed the policy on private cement producers. The Commerce Clause prohibits this severe restraint on commerce.

Notes and Questions

1. *Distinctions between state as buyer, seller, and producer?* Could a good case be made for applying commerce clause concerns to the state as seller, as urged by the dissent, while not applying them to the state as buyer on which the Court appears unanimous in *Reeves?* Are the "government function" considerations advanced by the dissent to distinguish the state as buyer always inapplicable to the state as seller? Always applicable to the state as buyer? Should it make a difference if the state is both producer and seller, serving its residents' needs? Cf. Varat, *State Citizenship and Interstate Equality,* 48 U.Chi.L.Rev. 487, 548–52 (1981).

3. One distinction between a private and a governmental function is whether the activity is supported with general tax funds, as was the case for the reprocessing program in *Alexandria Scrap,* or whether it is financed by the revenues it generates. In this case, South Dakota's cement plant has supported itself for many years. There is thus no need to consider the question whether a state-subsidized business could confine its sales to local residents.

4. The consequences of South Dakota's "residents-first" policy were devastating to petitioner Reeves, Inc., a Wyoming firm. For 20 years, Reeves had purchased about 95% of its cement from the South Dakota plant. When the State imposed its preference for South Dakota residents in 1978, Reeves had to reduce its production by over 75%. As a result, its South Dakota competitors were in a vastly superior position to compete for work in the region.

2. *State subsidies.* (a) *Reeves,* fn. 14, left undecided the validity of a subsidy program that, unlike *Alexandria Scrap,*[a] aims at aiding local business in competition with outsiders. Should state subsidies to in-state producers or distributors, designed to enable them to compete more favorably against out-of-staters, be subject to commerce clause analysis and constraints similar to those applied to state regulation? Are the reasons for not applying commerce clause restraints to the state as trader applicable to the state as subsidizer?

(b) In *Alexandria Scrap,* Stevens, J., joined the Court's opinion "without reservations" but added that the commerce clause does not "inhibit a State's power to experiment with different methods of encouraging local industry," such as "a cash subsidy, a tax credit, or a special privilege to attract investment capital," which "should not be characterized as a burden on commerce."

(c) Are state subsidies limited to in-state producers consistent with the policy of invalidating taxes that favor in-state over out-of-state producers? On subsidies and the commerce clause, consider *Varat,* supra at 540–46 (1981).

3. *Scope of market participant concept.* (a) WHITE v. MASSACHUSETTS COUNCIL OF CONST. EMPLOYERS, 460 U.S. 204, 103 S.Ct. 1042, 75 L.Ed.2d 1 (1983), per REHNQUIST, J., "reaffirmed" the *Alexandria Scrap* and *Reeves* "proposition that when a state or local government enters the market as a participant it is not subject to the restraints of the Commerce Clause." It sustained a Boston requirement that 50% of the work force on city-funded construction projects must be Boston residents, even though the work force was employed by a private contractor paid by the city: "If the city is a market participant, then the Commerce Clause establishes no barrier to conditions such as these which the city demands for its participation. * * * Insofar as the city expended its own funds in entering into construction contracts for public projects, it was a market participant [7] and entitled to be treated as such under the rule of *Alexandria Scrap.*"[a]

BLACKMUN, J., joined by White, J., dissented in part:[b] "Neither *Reeves* nor *Alexandria Scrap* [went] beyond ensuring that the States enjoy ' "the long recognized right of trader or manufacturer, engaged in an entirely private business, freely to exercise his own independent discretion as to parties with whom he will deal." ' *Reeves.*

"Boston's executive order goes much further. The city has not attempted merely to choose the 'parties with whom [it] will deal.' Instead, it has imposed as a condition of obtaining a public construction contract the requirement that *private firms* hire only Boston residents for 50% of specified jobs. Thus, the

---

a. There the objective was to rid the state's environment of junk cars.

7. Justice Blackmun's opinion dissenting in part argues that the mayor's order goes beyond market participation because it regulates employment contracts between public contractors and their employees. We agree with Justice Blackmun that there are some limits on a state or local government's ability to impose restrictions that reach beyond the immediate parties with which the government transacts business. We find it unnecessary in this case to define those limits with precision, except to say that we think the Commerce Clause does not require the city to stop at the boundary of formal privity of contract. In this case, the mayor's executive order covers a discrete, identifiable class of economic activity in which the city is a major participant. Everyone affected by the order is, in a substantial if informal sense, "working for the city." Wherever the limits of the market participation exception may lie, we conclude that the executive order in this case falls well within the scope of *Alexandria Scrap* and *Reeves.*

a. In addition, the Court ruled without dissent that to the extent projects were funded in part with federal funds the 50% preference was valid because "affirmatively sanctioned" by federal regulations.

b. The dissenters concurred in the ruling noted in fn. a, supra.

order directly restricts the ability of private employers to hire nonresidents, and thereby curtails nonresidents' access to jobs with private employers. * * *

"The line between regulation and market participation, for purposes of the Commerce Clause, should be drawn with reference to the constitutional values giving rise to the market participant exemption itself. As the Court recognized in *Reeves,* the most important of these is that historically the 'Commerce Clause responds principally to state taxes and regulatory measures impeding private trade in the national marketplace'; it was not designed 'to limit the ability of the States themselves to operate freely in the free market.' *Reeves.* [The] legitimacy of a claim to the market participant exemption thus should turn primarily on whether a particular state action more closely resembles an attempt to impede trade among private parties, or an attempt, analogous to the accustomed right of merchants in the private sector, to govern the State's own economic conduct and to determine the parties with whom it will deal.

"The simple unilateral refusals to deal the Court encountered in *Reeves* and *Alexandria Scrap* were relatively pure examples of a seller's or purchaser's simply choosing its bargaining partners, 'long recognized' as the right of traders in our free enterprise system. The executive order in this case, in notable contrast, by its terms is a direct attempt to govern private economic relationships. The power to dictate to another those with whom *he* may deal is viewed with suspicion and closely limited in the context of purely private economic relations. When exercised by government, such a power is the essence of regulation.

"[The] 'sense' in which those affected by the mayor's order 'work for the city' [c] is so 'informal,' in my view, as to lack substance altogether. The city does not hire them, fire them, negotiate with them or their representative about the terms of their employment, or pay their wages."

(b) Should the reasons underlying *Reeves* and *Alexandria Scrap* apply to a city giving priority to city residents in hiring city employees? Should they apply when the city, expending city funds, requires a private contractor engaged in construction for the city to give hiring priority to city residents? Cf. *Varat,* supra at 546–48.

(c) SOUTH–CENTRAL TIMBER DEVELOPMENT, INC. v. WUNNICKE, 467 U.S. 82, 104 S.Ct. 2237, 81 L.Ed.2d 71 (1984), held that the market participant concept did not free Alaska from commerce clause invalidation of Alaska's contractual requirement that purchasers of state-owned standing timber must saw it into "cants" ("primary manufacture")[a] before shipping it out of state. WHITE, J.'s, plurality opinion, joined by Brennan, Blackmun and Stevens, JJ., stressed the requirement's reach beyond the market transaction in which the state participated:

"The limit of the market-participant doctrine must be that it allows a State to impose burdens on commerce within the market in which it is a participant, but allows it to go no further. The State may not impose conditions, whether by statute, regulation, or contract, that have a substantial regulatory effect outside of that particular market.[10] Unless the 'market' is relatively narrowly defined, the doctrine has the potential of swallowing up the rule that States may not impose substantial burdens on interstate commerce even if they act with the permissible state purpose of fostering local industry.

c. See n. 7 supra.

a. "Primary manufacture" required all logs to be slabbed on one side into *cants,* "no thicker than 8¾ inches unless slabs are taken from all four sides."

"[Alaska] contends that it is participating in the processed timber market, although it acknowledges that it participates in no way in the actual processing. South-Central argues, on the other hand, that although the State may be a participant in the timber market, it is using its leverage in that market to exert a regulatory effect in the processing market, in which it is not a participant. We agree with the latter position.

"[We] reject the contention that a State's action as a market regulator may be upheld against Commerce Clause challenge on the ground that the State could achieve the same end as a market participant. We therefore find it unimportant for present purposes that the State could support its processing industry by selling only to Alaska processors, by vertical integration, or by direct subsidy."

Having found the commerce clause applicable, the opinion concluded that Alaska's log processing requirement fell within the *Pike* and *Philadelphia* "rule of virtual *per se* invalidity" because of its "protectionist nature." [b]

VII. INTERSTATE PRIVILEGES AND IMMUNITIES CLAUSE

BALDWIN v. MONTANA FISH & GAME COMM'N, 436 U.S. 371, 98 S.Ct. 1852, 56 L.Ed.2d 354 (1978), per BLACKMUN, J., upheld Montana's non-resident license fee of $225 for hunting elk, compared to $30 for residents. It ruled the interstate privileges and immunities clause (Art. IV § 2) not applicable because elk hunting was not a "basic" right:

"[T]he contours of Art. IV, § 2, cl. 1, are not well developed, and [the] relationship if any, between the Privileges and Immunities Clause and the 'privileges or immunities' language of the Fourteenth Amendment is less than clear. We are, nevertheless, not without some pronouncements by this Court as to the Clause's significance and reach. [Field, J.,] writing for a unanimous Court in *Paul v. Virginia*, 8 Wall. 168, 180, 19 L.Ed. 357 (1869), [emphasized] nationalism, the proscription of discrimination, and the assurance of equality of all citizens within any State: 'It was undoubtedly the object of the clause in question to place the citizens of each State upon the same footing with citizens of other States, so far as the advantages resulting from citizenship in those States are concerned. It relieves them from the disabilities of alienage in other States; it inhibits discriminating legislation against them by other States; it gives them the right of free ingress into other States, and egress from them; it insures to them in other States the same freedom possessed by the citizens of those States in the acquisition and enjoyment of property and in the pursuit of happiness; and it secures to them in other States the equal protection of their laws. It has been justly said that no provision in the Constitution has tended so strongly to constitute the citizens of the United States one people as this.'

" * * * Mr. Justice Roberts, writing for himself and Mr. Justice Black in *Hague v. CIO*, 307 U.S. 496, 511, 59 S.Ct. 954, 83 L.Ed. 1423 (1939), [pointed out], 'It has come to be the settled view that Article IV, § 2, does not import that a citizen of one State carries with him into another fundamental privileges and immunities [based on] his citizenship in [his] State, but, on the contrary, that in any State every citizen of any other State is to have the same privileges and immunities which the citizens of that State enjoy.'

---

b. Powell, J., joined by Burger, C.J., would have remanded the foregoing issues for consideration by the court of appeals. Rehnquist, J., joined by O'Connor, J., dissented. Marshall, J. took no part.

"[T]he Privileges and Immunities Clause [has] been interpreted to prevent a State from imposing unreasonable burdens on citizens of other States in their pursuit of common callings within the State, *Ward v. Maryland,* 12 Wall. 418, 20 L.Ed. 449 (1871); in the ownership and disposition of privately held property within the State, *Blake v. McClung,* 172 U.S. 239, 19 S.Ct. 165, 43 L.Ed. 432, (1898); and in access to the courts of the State, *Canadian Northern R. Co. v. Eggen,* 252 U.S. 553, 40 S.Ct. 402, 64 L.Ed. 713 (1920). [But the clause permits a state to limit to its citizens the right to vote [a] and hold elective office.[b]]

"Some distinctions between residents and nonresidents merely reflect the fact that this is a Nation composed of individual States, and are permitted; other distinctions are prohibited because they hinder the formation, the purpose, or the development of a single Union of those States. Only with respect to those 'privileges' and 'immunities' bearing upon the vitality of the Nation as a single entity must the State treat all citizens, resident and nonresident, equally. Here we must decide into which category falls a distinction with respect to access to recreational big-game hunting.

"[A] State's interest in its wildlife and other resources must yield when, without reason, it interferes with a nonresident's right to pursue a livelihood in a State other than his own, a right that is protected by the Privileges and Immunities Clause. *Toomer.* * * * [With] respect to such basic and essential activities, interference with which would frustrate the purposes of the formation of the Union, the States must treat residents and nonresidents without unnecessary distinctions.

"Does the distinction made by Montana between residents and nonresidents in establishing access to elk hunting threaten a basic right in a way that offends the Privileges and Immunities Clause? Merely to ask the question seems to provide the answer. [Elk] hunting by nonresidents in Montana is a recreation and a sport. In itself—wholly apart from license fees—it is costly and obviously available only to the wealthy nonresident. [It] is not a means to the nonresident's livelihood. The mastery of the animal and the trophy are the ends that are sought; appellants are not totally excluded from these. The elk supply, which has been entrusted to the care of the State by the people of Montana, is finite and must be carefully tended in order to be preserved.

"Appellants' interest in sharing this limited resource on more equal terms with Montana residents simply does not fall within the purview of the Privileges and Immunities Clause. Equality in access to Montana elk is not basic to the maintenance or well-being of the Union. [We] do not decide the full range of activities that are sufficiently basic to the livelihood of the Nation that the States may not interfere with a nonresident's participation therein without similarly interfering with a resident's participation. Whatever rights or activities may be 'fundamental' under the Privileges and Immunities Clause, we are persuaded, and hold, that elk hunting by nonresidents in Montana is not one of them."

BRENNAN, J., joined by White and Marshall, JJ., dissented:

"I think the time has come to confirm explicitly that which has been implicit in our modern privileges and immunities decisions, namely that an

a. *Dunn v. Blumstein,* 1058 infra.

b. *Kanapaux v. Ellisor,* 419 U.S. 891, 95 S.Ct. 169, 42 L.Ed.2d 136 (1974).

inquiry into whether a given right is 'fundamental' has no place in our analysis of whether a State's discrimination against nonresidents [violates] the Clause. Rather, our primary concern is the State's justification for its discrimination. Drawing from the principles announced in *Toomer* * * *, a State's discrimination against nonresidents is permissible where (1) the presence or activity of nonresidents is the source or cause of the problem or effect with which the State seeks to deal, and (2) the discrimination practiced against nonresidents bears a substantial relation to the problem they present. [This] requirement that a State's unequal treatment of nonresidents be reasoned and suitably tailored furthers the federal interest in ensuring that 'a norm of comity,' prevails throughout the Nation while simultaneously guaranteeing to the States the needed leeway to draw viable distinctions between their citizens and those of other States."

Notes and Questions

1. *The Baldwin standard.* Is *Baldwin*'s limitation of the privileges and immunities clause protection to "fundamental" rights "basic to the maintenance and well-being of the nation" or "basic to the livelihood of the nation," "bearing on the vitality of the Nation as a single entity" or "Union" made up of "one people," a defensible and manageable standard? Does it include protection of non-business activities from discrimination that would threaten the unity of "the citizens of the United States [as] one people?" Suppose, e.g., California were to confine to Californians the use of its state-owned parks, campgrounds and beaches? Cf. Varat, *State Citizenship and Interstate Equality,* 48 U.Chi.L.Rev. 487, 509–516 (1981).

2. *Employment preference for state residents.* HICKLIN v. ORBECK, 437 U.S. 518, 98 S.Ct. 2482, 57 L.Ed.2d 397 (1978), per BRENNAN, J., unanimously held invalid an Alaska statute, dubbed "Alaska Hire," that required employers in wide-ranging oil and gas operations to give employment preference to qualified residents over nonresidents: "[No] showing was made on this record that nonresidents were 'a peculiar source of the evil' Alaska Hire was enacted to remedy, namely Alaska's 'uniquely high unemployment.' What evidence the record does contain indicates that the major cause of Alaska's high unemployment was not the influx of nonresidents seeking employment, but rather the fact that a substantial number of Alaska's jobless residents—especially the unemployed Eskimo and Indian residents—were unable to secure employment either because of their lack of education and job training or because of their geographical remoteness from job opportunities; and that the employment of nonresidents threatened to deny jobs to Alaska residents only to the extent that jobs for which untrained residents were being prepared might be filled by nonresidents before the residents' training was completed.

"Moreover, even if the State's showing is accepted as sufficient to indicate that nonresidents were 'a peculiar source of evil,' [the] discrimination the Act works against nonresidents does not bear a substantial relationship to the particular 'evil' they are said to present. Alaska Hire simply grants all Alaskans, regardless of their employment status, education, or training, a flat employment preference for all jobs covered by the Act. A highly skilled and educated resident who has never been unemployed is entitled to precisely the same preferential treatment as the unskilled, habitually unemployed Arctic Eskimo enrolled in a job training program. If Alaska is to attempt to ease her unemployment problem by forcing employers within the State to discriminate against nonresidents—again, a policy which may present serious constitutional questions—the means by which she does so must be more closely tailored to aid the unemployed the Act is intended to benefit. ＊ ＊ ＊

"Relying on *McCready v. Virginia,* 94 U.S. 391, 24 L.Ed. 248 (1877), however, Alaska contends that because the oil and gas that are the subject of Alaska Hire is *owned* by the State, this ownership, of itself, is sufficient justification for the Act's discrimination against nonresidents, and takes the Act totally without the scope of the Privileges and Immunities Clause. [Rather] than placing a statute completely beyond the Clause, a State's ownership of the property with which the statute is concerned is a factor—although often the crucial factor—to be considered in evaluating whether the statute's discrimination against noncitizens violates the Clause. Dispositive though this factor may be in many cases in which a State discriminates against nonresidents, it is not dispositive here.

"The reason is that Alaska has little or no proprietary interest in much of the activity swept within the ambit of Alaska Hire; and the connection of the State's oil and gas with much of the covered activity is sufficiently attenuated so that it cannot justifiably be the basis for requiring private employers to discriminate against nonresidents. [The] Act goes so far as to reach suppliers who provide goods or services to subcontractors who, in turn, perform work for contractors despite the fact that none of these employers may themselves have direct dealings with the State's oil and gas or ever set foot on state land."

3. *Employment preference for city residents.* UNITED BUILDING TRADES COUNCIL v. CAMDEN, 465 U.S. 208, 104 S.Ct. 1020, 79 L.Ed.2d 249 (1984) per REHNQUIST, J., held the interstate privileges and immunities clause applicable to a Camden, N.J., ordinance that required at least 40% of contractors' employees on city-funded construction projects to be Camden residents. The Court ruled that out-of-staters' "opportunity to seek employment" from contractors on city-funded projects was " 'sufficiently basic to the livelihood of the Nation,' *Baldwin,* to fall within the purview of the Privileges and Immunities Clause." [7] It remanded to the state courts for findings relevant to the *Toomer-Hicklin* standard for determining whether there was a sufficiently " 'substantial reason' for the difference in treatment."

United Building Trades Council ruled that the state-as-trader concept did not free the state from the privileges and immunities clause as it had from the commerce clause in *Alexandria Scrap, Reeves,* and *White v. Massachusetts Council.*

4. *State ownership or funding.* By what reasoning might state ownership of natural resources justify state-required preference for employment of state residents to extract such resources, as suggested in *Hicklin?* How could state ownership of extracted resources be relevant to the *Toomer-Baldwin* standard at issue in *Hicklin?* How could state funding of projects requiring employment preference for state residents be relevant to that standard? The *United Building Trades* opinion said it was: Citing the *Hicklin* dicta that state property ownership may often be a "crucial factor" in privilege and immunities issues involving employment discrimination against noncitizens, the Court added: "Much the same analysis, we think, is appropriate to a city's efforts to bias private employment decisions in favor of its residents on construction projects funded with public monies. The fact that Camden is expending its own funds [is]

7. In *White,* 103 S.Ct., at 1048, n. 12, we specifically declined to pass on the merits of a privileges and immunities challenge to the mayor's executive order because the court below did not reach the issue.

certainly a factor—perhaps the crucial factor—to be considered in evaluating whether the statute's discrimination violates the Privileges and Immunities Clause. But it does not remove the Camden ordinance completely from the purview of the Clause." But the Court did not analyze the role this factor should play in applying the *Toomer-Baldwin* standard on remand. Consider Sedler, p. 198 fn. c supra, at 1020–23.[b]

SECTION 2. THE EFFECT OF FEDERAL REGULATION: PREEMPTION

INTRODUCTION

One issue considered in Section 1 was the *expansion* of state regulatory power by federal legislation. Here we consider the *restriction* of state regulatory power by federal legislation. When Congress, acting within its granted powers, expressly preempts state regulatory power, the supremacy clause controls. Only the scope of the Congressional power, interpretation of the federal legislation, and its application to the challenged state regulation are potential issues. Preemption issues may arise from the exercise of any federal legislative power concurrently shared by the states but they most commonly arise from exercises of the commerce power.

Most preemption problems arise when a state regulation is challenged as precluded by specified congressional acts in which Congress has not dealt explicitly with their effect on state regulation. Such issues present sui generis problems whose resolution depends on widely variant considerations, including, of course, the unique terms, history, and objectives of the relevant federal legislation. For an excellent, comprehensive commentary see Tribe, *American Constitutional Law* (1978) 376–390.

PACIFIC GAS & ELEC. CO. v. STATE ENERGY COMM'N

461 U.S. 190, 103 S.Ct. 1713, 75 L.Ed.2d 752 (1983).

MR. JUSTICE WHITE delivered the opinion of the Court.

[For construction of an electric power plant California required prior certification by the State Energy Commission (SEC). Calif.Pub.Res.Code § 25524.2 prohibited certification of nuclear-powered plants until SEC "finds that * * * the United States through its authorized agency has approved and there exists a demonstrated * * * method for the permanent and terminal disposition of high level nuclear waste." In a declaratory judgment action the Court affirmed unanimously a 9th Circuit Court of Appeals holding that the federal Atomic Energy Act did not preempt § 25524.2.]

[It] is well-established that within Constitutional limits Congress may preempt state authority by so stating in express terms. *Jones v. Rath Packing Co.*, 430 U.S. 519, 525, 97 S.Ct. 1305, 1309, 51 L.Ed.2d 604 (1977). Absent explicit preemptive language, Congress' intent to supercede state law altogether may be found from a "scheme of federal regulation so pervasive as to make reasonable

---

b. *United Building Trades* ruled that the state as trader concept did not free the state from privileges and immunities clause restrictions as it had from the commerce clause restrictions, contrasting the "implied restraint" of the commerce clause with the "direct restraint" of the privileges and immunities clause "in the interests of interstate harmony." But cf. id. at 1018–23.

the inference that Congress left no room to supplement it," [a] "because the Act of Congress may touch a field in which the federal interest is so dominant that the federal system will be assumed to preclude enforcement of state laws on the same subject," [b] or because "the object sought to be obtained by the federal law and the character of obligations imposed by it may reveal the same purpose." *Fidelity Federal Savings & Loan Ass'n v. de la Cuesta,* 458 U.S. 141, 153, 102 S.Ct. 3014, 3022, 73 L.Ed.2d 664 (1982); *Rice v. Santa Fe Elevator Corp.,* 331 U.S. 218, 230, 67 S.Ct. 1146, 1152, 91 L.Ed. 1447 (1947). Even where Congress has not entirely displaced state regulation in a specific area, state law is preempted to the extent that it actually conflicts with federal law. Such a conflict arises when "compliance with both federal and state regulations is a physical impossibility," *Florida Lime & Avocado Growers, Inc. v. Paul,* 373 U.S. 132, 142–143, 83 S.Ct. 1210, 1217–1218, 10 L.Ed.2d 248 (1963), or where state law "stands as an obstacle to the accomplishment and execution of the full purposes and objectives of Congress." *Hines v. Davidowitz,* 312 U.S. 52, 67, 61 S.Ct. 399, 404, 85 L.Ed. 581 (1941). * * *

A. [The Atomic Energy Act] despite its comprehensiveness, [does] not at any point expressly require the States to construct or authorize nuclear power plants or prohibit the States from deciding [not] to permit the construction of any further reactors. Instead, petitioners argue that the Act is intended to preserve the federal government as the sole regulator of all matters nuclear, and that § 25524.2 falls within the scope of this impliedly preempted field. But as we view the issue, Congress, in passing the 1954 Act and in subsequently amending it, intended that the federal government should regulate the radiological safety aspects involved in the construction and operation of a nuclear plant, but that the States retain their traditional responsibility in the field of regulating electrical utilities for determining questions of need, reliability, cost and other related state concerns.

Need for new power facilities, their economic feasibility, and rates and services, are areas that have been characteristically governed by the States. [These] economic aspects of electrical generation have been regulated for many years and in great detail by the states. [Thus,] "Congress legislated here in a field which the States have traditionally occupied . . . so we start with the assumption that the historic police powers of the States were not to be superseded by the Federal Act unless that was the clear and manifest purpose of Congress." *Rice.*

[The] Atomic Energy Act of 1954 * * * grew out of Congress' determination that the national interest would be best served if the Government encouraged the private sector to become involved in the development of atomic energy for peaceful purposes under a program of federal regulation and licensing. See H.R.Rep. No. 2181, 83d Cong., 2d Sess., 1–11 (1954). The Act implemented this policy decision by providing for licensing of private construction, ownership, and operation of commercial nuclear power reactors. The AEC [was] given exclusive jurisdiction to license the transfer, delivery, receipt, acquisition, possession and use of nuclear materials. Upon these subjects, no role was left for the states.

The Commission, however, was not given authority over the generation of electricity itself, or over the economic question whether a particular plant should

---

a. *Pennsylvania v. Nelson,* note 4 infra, illustrates preemption by "pervasive" federal regulation.

b. The "dominant" federal interest reasoning is based on *Hines v. Davidowitz,* note 3 infra. See *Rice,* 331 U.S. at 230.

be built. [The] Nuclear Regulatory Commission (NRC), which now exercises the AEC's regulatory authority, does not purport to exercise its authority based on economic considerations * * *. [Utility] financial qualifications are only of concern to the NRC if related to the public health and safety. It is almost inconceivable that Congress would have left a regulatory vacuum; the only reasonable inference is that Congress intended the states to continue to make these judgments. Any doubt that ratemaking and plant-need questions were to remain in state hands was removed by § 271 which provided: "Nothing in this chapter shall be construed to affect the authority or regulations of any Federal, State or local agency with respect to the generation, sale, or transmission of electric power produced through the use of nuclear facilities licensed by the Commission * * *."

This account indicates that from the passage of the Atomic Energy Act in 1954, through several revisions, and to the present day, Congress has preserved the dual regulation of nuclear-powered electricity generation: the federal government maintains complete control of the safety and "nuclear" aspects of energy generation; the states exercise their traditional authority over the need for additional generating capacity, the type of generating facilities to be licensed, land use, ratemaking, and the like.

[Respondents] broadly argue, [that] although safety regulation of nuclear plants by states is forbidden, a state may completely prohibit new construction until its safety concerns are satisfied by the federal government. We reject this line of reasoning. State safety regulation is not preempted only when it conflicts with federal law. Rather, the federal government has occupied the entire field of nuclear safety concerns, except the limited powers expressly ceded to the states. When the federal government completely occupies a given field or an identifiable portion of it, as it has done here, the test of preemption is whether "the matter on which the state asserts the right to act is in any way regulated by the federal government." *Rice.* A state moratorium on nuclear construction grounded in safety concerns falls squarely within the prohibited field. Moreover, a state judgment that nuclear power is not safe enough to be further developed would conflict directly with the countervailing judgment of the NRC that nuclear construction may proceed notwithstanding extant uncertainties as to waste disposal. A state prohibition on nuclear construction for safety reasons would also be in the teeth of the Atomic Energy Act's objective to insure that nuclear technology be safe enough for widespread development and use—and would be preempted for that reason.

That being the case, it is necessary to determine whether there is a non-safety rationale for § 25524.2. California has maintained, and the Court of Appeals agreed, that § 25524.2 was aimed at economic problems, not radiation hazards. The California Assembly Committee On Resources, Land Use, and Energy, which proposed a package of bills including § 25524.2, reported that the waste disposal problem was "largely economic or the result of poor planning, *not* safety related." [c] [The] Committee explained that the lack of a federally approved method of waste disposal created a "clog" in the nuclear fuel cycle. Storage space was limited while more nuclear wastes were continuously produced. Without a permanent means of disposal, the nuclear waste problem could become critical leading to unpredictably high costs to contain the problem or, worse, shutdowns in reactors. "Waste disposal *safety*," the [committee] notes,

---

c. Reassessment of Nuclear Energy in California: A Policy Analysis of Proposition 15 and its Alternatives (1976) (Reassessment Report) at 18 (emphasis in original).

"is not directly addressed by the bills, which ask only that a method [of waste disposal] be chosen and accepted by the federal government." (emphasis in original).

[We] accept California's avowed economic purpose as the rationale for enacting § 25524.2. Accordingly, the statute lies outside the occupied field of nuclear safety regulation.

B.   Petitioners [contend] that § 25524.2 conflicts with federal regulation of nuclear waste disposal, with the NRC's decision that it is permissible to continue to license reactors, notwithstanding uncertainty surrounding the waste disposal problem, and with Congress' recent passage of legislation directed at that problem.

[The federal Nuclear Regulatory Commission (NRC) regulations specify design and control requirements for handling and storing radioactive wastes, both at the reactor site and away from the reactor, but the NRC has not licensed any permanent disposal methods or facilities for high level waste.   In 1977 the NRC declined to halt reactor licensing until a method of permanent disposal was determined.]   The NRC concluded that, given the progress toward the development of disposal facilities and the availability of interim storage, it could continue to license new reactors.

The NRC's imprimatur, however, indicates only that it is safe to proceed with such plants, not that it is economically wise to do so.   Because the NRC order does not and could not compel a utility to develop a nuclear plant, compliance with both it and § 25524.2 are possible.   Moreover, because the NRC's regulations are aimed at insuring that plants are safe, not necessarily that they are economical, § 25524.2 does not interfere with the objective of the federal regulation.

C.   Finally, it is strongly contended that § 25524.2 frustrates the Atomic Energy Act's purpose to develop the commercial use of nuclear power.   It is well established that state law is preempted if it "stands as an obstacle to the accomplishment of the full purposes and objectives of Congress."

There is little doubt that a primary purpose of the Atomic Energy Act was, and continues to be, the promotion of nuclear power.   The Act itself states that it is a program "to encourage widespread participation in the development and utilization of atomic energy for peaceful purposes to the maximum extent consistent with the common defense and security and with the health and safety of the public."   *   *   *

The Court of Appeals is right, however, that the promotion of nuclear power is not to be accomplished "at all costs."   The elaborate licensing and safety provisions and the continued preservation of state regulation in traditional areas belie that.   Moreover, Congress has allowed the States to determine—as a matter of economics—whether a nuclear plant vis-a-vis a fossil fuel plant should be built.   The decision of California to exercise that authority does not, in itself, constitute a basis for preemption.   Therefore, while the argument of petitioners and the United States has considerable force, the legal reality remains that Congress has left sufficient authority in the states to allow the development of nuclear power to be slowed or even stopped for economic reasons.   Given this statutory scheme, it is for Congress to rethink the division of regulatory authority in light of its possible exercise by the states to undercut a federal objective. The courts should not assume the role which our system assigns to Congress.

*   *   *

JUSTICE BLACKMUN, with whom Justice Stevens joins, concurring in part and concurring in the judgment.

I join the Court's opinion, except to the extent it suggests that a State may not prohibit the construction of nuclear power plants if the State is motivated by concerns about the safety of such plants. Since the Court finds that California was not so motivated, this suggestion is unnecessary to the Court's holding. More important, I believe the Court's dictum is wrong in several respects.

* * *

Notes and Questions

1. *Relevant factors.* In ruling that Congress "occupied" the "field of nuclear safety" but not the field of economic decision on whether to authorize additional nuclear power plants until a permanent disposal method is in existence, what factor or factors appeared important other than the statutory terms and legislative history? Does the application of the *Rice* quotation, requiring a "clear and manifest purpose" to supersede state power "in a field [the] states have traditionally occupied," "look to the nature of the subject regulated rather than the character of the federal regulatory scheme?" See Tribe, *American Constitutional Law* 385 (1978). Is this relevant or appropriate when the issue is whether in view of the supremacy clause a particular state regulation may stand in the face of specified federal legislation?

2. *Strong state interest.* (a) Compare MAURER v. HAMILTON, 309 U.S. 598, 60 S.Ct. 726, 84 L.Ed. 969 (1940), where by a strained interpretation of the federal Motor Carrier Act (MCA) the Court, per STONE, J., avoided preemption of a Pennsylvania ban on carrying cars over the cab of auto transport trucks. It interpreted ICC's power to issue regulations relating to "safety of operations and equipment," (under which ICC had found cars over cabs to be safe), not to include power to forbid cars over cabs because the MCA withheld from ICC power over "size and weight" of motor vehicles.[d] Prior to its analysis of the MCA, the Court stressed the states' interest in safety and maintenance on the highways, their capacity to consider variations in "grades, curves, * * * and overhead obstructions" (invoking the *Barnwell* opinion), and emphasized that assumption of national control over highway safety involved "problems of peculiar difficulty and delicacy." Which was likely more influential in *Maurer*— the terms of the federal statute or the nature of the subject regulated?

(b) Consider SILKWOOD v. KERR–McGEE CORP., 464 U.S. 238, 104 S.Ct. 615, 78 L.Ed.2d 443 (1984), per WHITE, J., for a puzzling sequel to *Pacific Gas and Elec.* *Silkwood* continued to proclaim total federal preemption of the field of regulating nuclear energy safety while upholding 5 to 4 state tort remedies for punitive damages for harm caused by the escape of hazardous nuclear energy materials. Since Congress provided no tort remedy for such cases, the dissenters did not question the majority view that state law properly applied to compensatory damages.[a] But they viewed the award of punitive damages,[b] here not even based on violation of federal safety requirements, as state-law invasion of exclusively-established federal power and responsibility for nuclear energy safety

---

d. In the Court's view cars over cabs related to distribution of "weight" and to "dimensions,", hence "size."

a. The judgment for $500,000 compensatory damages, in favor of the estate of the victim who died in an unrelated car accident shortly after exposure to the materials, was

not before the Court. It was set aside earlier because workmen's compensation law controlled.

b. The Court left open for review on remand the amount of the punitive damages judgment, set at $10,000,000 by the jury.

through federally-adopted and enforced regulations.[c] The majority responded: "Punitive damages have long been a part of traditional state tort law. As noted above, Congress assumed that traditional principles of state tort law would apply with full force [unless] expressly supplanted."

What may explain *Silkwood?* Were there here strong state concerns analogous to those underlying *Maurer?*

3. *Dominant federal interest.* HINES v. DAVIDOWITZ, 312 U.S. 52, 61 S.Ct. 399, 85 L.Ed. 581 (1941), per BLACK, J., held a Pennsylvania requirement that aliens register yearly, and carry an alien identification card to be shown to police and other named officers, preempted by the federal Alien Registration Act that required registration only once and did not require a card to be carried. The Court noted that "international controversies of the gravest moment ＊ ＊ ＊ may arise from real or imagined wrongs to [another country's] subjects. ＊ ＊ ＊ Our primary function is to determine whether, under the circumstances of this particular case, Pennsylvania's law stands as an obstacle to the accomplishment and execution of the full purposes and objectives of Congress. And in that determination, it is of importance that this legislation is in a field which affects international relations, the one aspect of our government that from the first has been most generally conceded imperatively to demand broad national authority. Any concurrent state power that may exist is restricted to the narrowest of limits. ＊ ＊ ＊"

After noting the opposition in Congress to proposals for alien identification cards, the Court concluded: "[Congress] has provided a standard for alien registration in a single integrated and all-embracing system in order to obtain the information deemed to be desirable in connection with aliens. When it made this addition to its uniform naturalization and immigration laws, it plainly manifested a purpose to do so in such a way as to protect the personal liberties of law-abiding aliens through one uniform national registration system, and to leave them free from the possibility of inquisitorial practices and police surveillance that might not only affect our international relations but might also generate the very disloyalty which the law has intended guarding against. Under these circumstances, the Pennsylvania Act cannot be enforced."

STONE, J., joined by Hughes and McReynolds, JJ., dissented: "[N]o words of the statute or of any committee report, or any Congressional debate indicate that Congress intended to withdraw from the states any part of their constitutional power over aliens within their borders. We must take it that Congress was not

c. Powell, J., joined by Burger, C.J. and Blackmun and Marshall, JJ., summed up the dissent:

"The Court's decision, in effect, authorizes lay juries and judges in each of the states to make regulatory judgments as to whether a federally licensed nuclear facility is being operated safely. Such judgments then become the predicate to imposing heavy punitive damages. This authority is approved in this case even though the Nuclear Regulatory Commission (NRC)—the agency authorized by Congress to assure the safety of nuclear facilities—found no relevant violation of its stringent safety requirements worthy of punishment.

"[The] effectiveness of the overall program requires that nuclear policy and regulation be insulated from *ad hoc,* uninformed and perhaps biased decision-making. It is reasonable for a nuclear facility to be held liable, even without fault on its part, to compensate for injury or loss occasioned by the operation of the facility. It is not reasonable to infer that Congress intended to allow juries of lay persons, selected essentially at random, to impose unfocused penalties solely for the purpose of punishment and some undefined deterrence. These purposes wisely have been left within the regulatory authority and discretion of the NRC."

Blackmun, J., joined by Marshall, J., also filed a separate dissent.

unaware that some nineteen states have statutes or ordinances requiring some form of registration for aliens, seven of them dating from the last war. The repeal of this legislation is not to be inferred from the silence of Congress in enacting a law which at no point conflicts with the state legislation and is harmonious with it."

4. *Pervasive federal regulation.* PENNSYLVANIA v. NELSON, 350 U.S. 497, 76 S.Ct. 477, 100 L.Ed. 640 (1956), per WARREN, C.J., held that extensive federal anti-communist legislation (the 1940 Smith Act, the 1950 Internal Security Act, and the 1954 Communist Control Act), preempted the Pennsylvania Sedition Act on the same subject: [d] " '[T]he scheme of federal regulation [is] so pervasive as to make reasonable the inference that Congress left no room for the States to supplement it.' * * * Looking to all of [these Acts] in the aggregate, the conclusion is inescapable that Congress has intended to occupy the field of sedition. Taken as a whole, they evince a congressional plan which makes it reasonable to determine that no room has been left for the States to supplement [it]." [e] Who made the judgment that the federal legislation "left no room for state regulation—Congress or the Court?

d. Reed, J., joined by Minton and Burton, JJ., dissented.

e. *Nelson* gave as additional grounds for preemption the "dominant" federal interest and the risk of conflict between state enforcement and administration of the federal program. Note that *Burbank*, supra, also illustrates the Court's use of pervasiveness of federal legislation.

Chapter 5

STATE POWER TO TAX

This book, designed for somewhat shortened courses, does not treat the impact of the commerce clause and other national regulatory powers on state power to tax. This is a challenging topic, but its practical value is primarily for those representing business interests or the state. The subject is considered in Lockhart, Kamisar, Choper & Shiffrin, *Constitutional Law: Cases—Comments—Questions* ch. 5 (6th ed. 1986).

Chapter 6

SUBSTANTIVE PROTECTION OF ECONOMIC INTERESTS

PREFATORY NOTE

Most of the remaining chapters are concerned with constitutional limitations on governmental power, independent of limitations arising out of the distribution of powers within the federal system. Some of the limitations are identical, or nearly so, whether applied to the state or federal governments, but are based on different sources. The major limitations on the federal government are found in the Bill of Rights and in Art. I, § 9, while those on state government are based largely on the thirteenth, fourteenth, and fifteenth amendments and on Art. I, § 10. But the fourteenth amendment has now been held to impose on the states most of the limitations the Bill of Rights imposes on the federal government.

These materials do not deal with all limitations based on the federal Constitution but only those of major significance and difficulty. State constitutions include additional limitations on state government, some similar to federal limitations though occasionally interpreted differently, and some quite dissimilar in terms and purposes. Study of the federal limitations should provide adequate training and background for handling the state-imposed limitations with professional skill.

SECTION 1. ORIGINS OF SUBSTANTIVE DUE PROCESS AS A LIMITATION ON GOVERNMENTAL POWER

INTRODUCTION

One important concern of this and later chapters is the extent to which the due process clauses of the fifth and fourteenth amendments may be invoked to impose limits on the *substance* of governmental regulations and other activities, as well as to govern the *procedures*—the due process—by which government affects "life, liberty and property." That the due process clauses could be thought to embody any limitation on the substance of state legislation requires some initial explanation, since the clauses appear to related only to "due process."

Professor Edward S. Corwin traced the origin and evolution of due process as a substantive limitation on governmental power in a series of articles[a], later revised in his *Liberty Against Government* (1948). This book, concerned primarily with judicial evolution of concepts designed to limit government regulation of property and economic interests, provides a valuable background for understanding, as well, some of the underpinnings for the later use of the due process clause and first amendment to limit governmental interference with the more basic personal liberties.

Space limits preclude detailed study here of the judicial search for tools by which to limit governmental power, culminating in the "substantive due process" concept. Here we only sketch, by suggestive excerpts, some of the more significant steps.

I. JUDICIAL RESPONSE TO PHILOSOPHICAL LIMITATIONS ON GOVERNMENTAL POWER

CALDER v. BULL, 3 U.S. (3 Dall.) 386, 1 L.Ed. 648 (1798), is not remembered for its ruling, declining to interfere with the state legislature's setting aside a probate court ruling, but for two opinions expressing diametrically opposed views on the nature and source of limitations on governmental power:

"CHASE, JUSTICE. [I] cannot subscribe to the omnipotence of a State legislature, or that it is absolute and without control; although its authority should not be expressly restrained by the constitution, or fundamental law of the state. The people of the United States erected their constitutions, or forms of government, to establish justice, to promote the general welfare, to secure the blessings of liberty, and to protect their persons and property from violence. The purposes for which men enter into society will determine the nature and terms of the social compact; and as they are the foundation of the legislative power, they will decide what are the proper objects of it. The nature and ends of legislative power will limit the exercise of it. This fundamental principle flows from the very nature of our free republican governments, that no man should be compelled to do what the laws do not require; nor to refrain from acts which the laws permit. There are acts which the federal, or state, legislature cannot do, without exceeding their authority. There are certain vital principles in our free republican governments, which will determine and overrule an apparent and flagrant abuse of legislative power; as to authorize manifest injustice by positive law; to take away that security for personal liberty, or private property, for the protection whereof the government was established. An act of the legislature (for I cannot call it a law), contrary to the great first principles of the social compact, cannot be considered a rightful exercise of legislative authority. The obligation of a law in governments established on express compact, and on republican principles, must be determined by the nature of the power on which it is founded. A few instances will suffice to explain what I mean. A law that punished a citizen for an innocent action or, in other words, for an act, which, when done, was in violation of no existing law; a law that destroys, or impairs, the lawful private contracts of citizens; a law that makes a man a judge in his own cause; or a law that takes property from A and gives it to B: It is against all reason and justice, for a people to intrust a legislature with SUCH powers; and therefore, it cannot be presumed that they have done it. The genius, the

---

a. Corwin, *The Doctrine of Due Process of Law Before the Civil War*, 24 Harv.L.Rev. 366, 460 (1911); Corwin, *The Basic Doctrine of American Constitutional Law*, 12 Mich.L.Rev. 247 (1914); Corwin, *The "Higher Law" Background of American Constitutional Law*, 42 Harv.L.Rev. 149, 365 (1928–1929).

nature, and the spirit, of our State governments, amount to a prohibition of such acts of legislation; and the general principles of law and reason forbid them.[a]

"IREDELL, JUSTICE. "[I]t has been the policy of all the American states, which have, individually, framed their state constitutions, since the revolution, and of the people of the United States, when they framed the federal constitution, to define with precision the objects of the legislative power, and to restrain its exercise within marked and settled boundaries. If any act of Congress, or of the legislature of a state, violates those constitutional provisions, it is unquestionably void. [If], on the other hand, the legislature of the Union, or the legislature of any member of the Union, shall pass a law, within the general scope of their constitutional power, the court cannot pronounce it to be void, merely because it is, in their judgment, contrary to the principles of natural justice. The ideals of natural justice are regulated by no fixed standard: the ablest and the purest men have differed upon the subject; and all that the court could properly say, in such an event, would be that the legislature (possessed of an equal right of opinion) had passed an act which, in the opinion of the judges, was inconsistent with the abstract principles of natural justice. * * *""

Notes and Questions

1. Compare the following by Lord Coke in *Dr. Bonham's Case*, 8 Co. 113b, 118a, 77 Eng.Rep. 646, 652 (1610): "And it appears in our books, that in many cases, the common law will controul Acts of Parliament, and sometimes adjudge them to be utterly void: for when an Act of Parliament is against common right and reason, or repugnant, or impossible to be performed, the common law will controul it, and adjudge such Act to be void." For commentary on the influence of the Coke dictum, see Corwin, *Liberty Against Government* 34–40 (1948).

2. For philosophical origins of the Chase viewpoint, see Corwin, *Liberty Against Government* 10–57 (1948); Corwin, *The "Higher Law" Background of American Constitutional Law*, 42 Harv.L.Rev. 149, 365 (1928–1929). For the extent to which similar viewpoints crept into judicial opinions and decisions between the revolution and 1830, see Corwin, *Liberty Against Government* 58–67 (1948): "The truth is that Iredell's tenet that courts were not to appeal to natural rights and the social compact as furnishing a basis for constitutional decisions was disregarded at one time or another by all of the leading judges and advocates of the initial period of our constitutional history, an era which closes about 1830."

3. *Other early reflections of natural law.* Some early decisions combined the Chase philosophy in *Calder* with broad interpretations of the contract clause, forbidding state legislative impairment of the obligation of contracts, as a means of protecting property rights against state legislative encroachments. Note, e.g., MARSHALL, J.'s, conclusion in FLETCHER v. PECK, 10 U.S. (6 Cranch.) 87, 3 L.Ed. 162 (1810) (contract clause barred law annulling land title bought in good faith from grantee of corruptly secured legislative grant): "It is, then, the unanimous opinion of the court, that, in this case, the estate having passed into the hands of a purchaser for a valuable consideration, without notice, the state of Georgia was restrained, either by general principles which are common to our free institutions, or by the particular provisions of the Constitution of the United States, from passing a law whereby the estate of the plaintiff in the premises so

---

a. Dean Ely interprets Chase, J.'s, opinion as a philosophical, not a constitutional, argument. See Ely, *On Discovering Fundamental Values*, 92 Harv.L.Rev. 5, 26–27 n. 95 (1978).

purchased could be constitutionally and legally impaired and rendered null and void."

JOHNSON, J., concurred in the result: "I do not hesitate to declare that a state does not possess the power of revoking its own grants. But I do it on a general principle, on the reason and nature of things: a principle which will impose laws even on the deity."

Note also STORY, J.'s, similar reasoning in TERRETT v. TAYLOR, 13 U.S. (9 Cranch.) 43, 3 L.Ed. 650 (1815) (barring Virginia from claiming title to church property under a statute authorizing its sale and the use of the proceeds for the poor of the parish: "[We] think ourselves standing upon the principles of natural justice, upon the fundamental laws of every free government, upon the spirit and the letter of the constitution of the United States, and upon the decisions of most respectable judicial tribunals in resisting such a doctrine."

During this same period the state courts were protecting vested property rights against legislative interference through a variety of rationales similar to that in *Calder*. See Corwin, *Liberty Against Government* 65–82 (1948).

II. NARROWING OF FEDERAL CONSTITUTIONAL LIMITS ON STATES

Bill of Rights applicable to states. BARRON v. MAYOR AND CITY COUNCIL, 32 U.S. (7 Pet.) 243, 8 L.Ed. 672 (1833), per MARSHALL, C. J., ruled that the fifth amendment prohibition on taking private property for a public use without compensation applied only to action by the federal government, not to the states or their subdivisions: "Each state established a constitution for itself, and in that constitution, provided such limitations and restrictions on the powers of its particular government as its judgment dictated. The people of the United States framed such a government for the United States as they supposed best adapted to their situation, and best calculated to promote their interests. The powers they conferred on this government were to be exercised by itself; and the limitations on power, if expressed in general terms are naturally, and, we think, necessarily applicable to the government created by the instrument. They are limitations of power granted in the instrument itself; not of distinct governments framed by different persons and for different [purposes].

"[The] great revolution which established the constitution of the United States was not effected without immense opposition. Serious fears were extensively entertained that those powers which the patriot statesmen, who then watched over the interests of our country, deemed essential to union, and to the attainment of those invaluable objects for which union was sought, might be exercised in a manner dangerous to liberty. In almost every convention by which the constitution was adopted, amendments to guard against the abuse of power were recommended. These amendments demanded security against the apprehended encroachments of the general government, not against those of the local governments.

"In compliance with a sentiment thus generally expressed, to quiet fears thus extensively entertained, amendments were proposed by the required majority in Congress, and adopted by the states. These amendments contain no expression indicating an intention to apply them to the state governments. This court cannot so apply them."

Formally the Court has consistently adhered to the *Barron* ruling that the Bill of Rights applies only to the federal government, but during the twentieth century most of its limitations have gradually been made applicable to the states through the fourteenth amendment. See Ch. 7–9 infra.

Shrinking contract clause protection. Four years after *Barron,* the Court also began to narrow the protective scope of the contract clause. *Charles River Bridge v. Warren Bridge* (1837)[a] refused to view a state grant of the right to operate a toll bridge as implying an obligation not to authorize a competing bridge. This was only step one in the Court's growing unwillingness to use the contract clause to block state action needed to protect vital public interests,[b] but the opinion seemed designed to discourage resort to the federal constitution to escape regulation of economic interests: "It is well settled by the decisions of this court, that a state law may be retrospective in its character, and may divest vested rights; and yet not violate the constitution of the United States, unless it also impairs the obligation of a contract." "Thus it *became more and more evident that the doctrine of vested rights must, to survive, find anchorage in some clause or other of the various State constitutions."* Corwin, *Liberty Against Government* 89 (1948).

III. DEVELOPMENT OF STATE CONSTITUTIONAL BASIS

With federal constitutional grounds not available to protect against most encroachments on economic interests, lawyers and state judges resorted to the "due process" and "law of the land" clauses of state constitutions. These provisions originally referred to proceeding in accordance with the law and accepted legal procedure. Professor Corwin pointed out how the state courts began to evolve out of these clauses a substantive limitation on legislative power, aimed first at special legislation designed to affect the rights of specific individuals, and then applied to general legislation interfering with vested rights. See Corwin, *Liberty Against Government* 89–115 (1948); Corwin, *The Doctrine of Due Process of Law Before the Civil War,* 24 Harv.L.Rev. 366, 460 (1911). He summarized in *Liberty Against Government* 173–74:

"Most State constitutions contained from the outset a paraphrase of chapter 29 of Magna Carta, which declared that no person should be deprived of his 'estate' 'except by the law of the land or a judgment of his peers'; and following the usage of the Fifth Amendment of the United States Constitution, more and more State constitutions came after 1791 to contain a clause which, paraphrasing a statute of Plantagenet times, declared that 'no person shall be deprived of life, liberty or property without due process of law.' By the outbreak of the Civil War a more or less complete transference of the doctrine of vested rights and most of its Kentian corollaries had been effected in the vast majority of the State jurisdictions. One exception was Kent's distinction between the power of 'regulation,' which he conceded the State, and that of 'destruction,' which he denied it unless it was prepared to compensate disadvantaged owners. The division of judicial opinion on this point was signalized in the middle fifties, when the New York Court of Appeals, in the great *Wynehamer* case, stigmatized a State-wide prohibition statute as an act of destruction, in its application to existing stocks of liquor, which was beyond the power of the State legislature to authorize *even by*

a. 36 U.S. (11 Pet.) 420, 9 L.Ed. 773, 9 L.Ed. 938 (1837).

b. A few years later *West River Bridge Co. v. Dix,* 47 U.S. (6 How.) 507, 12 L.Ed. 535 (1848) ruled that a state grant of the exclusive privilege to operate a toll bridge did not prevent the state from acquiring it by eminent domain. *Stone v. Mississippi,* 101 U.S. (11 Otto) 814, 25 L.Ed. 1079 (1879) held that for the legislature to ban a lottery business 3 years after giving it a 25 year charter did not violate the contract clause in view of the vital public interest at stake. For more current cases see those discussed in Sec. 5 infra.

the procedures of due process of law. In several other States similar statutes were sustained in the name of the 'police power.' " [a]

WYNEHAMER v. PEOPLE, 13 N.Y. 378 (1856) held by a divided court that a New York prohibition statute violated the state due process clause as applied to the sale of liquor owned at the time of the enactment of the statute. Professor Corwin commented on *Wynehamer* in *Liberty Against Government* 103, 114–15:

"In *Wynehamer,* [the] court was confronted with a frankly penal statute which provided a procedure, for the most part unexceptionable, for its enforcement. That statute was nonetheless overturned under the due 'process of law' clause, which was hereby plainly made to prohibit, regardless of the matter of procedure, a certain kind or degree of exertion of legislative power altogether. The result serves to throw into strong light once more the dependence of the derived notion of due process of law on extra constitutional principles; for it is nothing less *than the elimination of the very phrase under construction from the constitutional clause in which it occurs.* The main proposition of [*Wynehamer*] is that the legislature cannot destroy by any method whatever what by previous law was property. But why not? To all intents and purposes the answer of the court is simply that 'no person shall be *deprived* of life, liberty or *property.*'

* * *

"In less than twenty years from the time of its rendition the crucial ruling in *Wynehamer* was far on the way to being assimilated into the accepted constitutional law of the country.[b] The 'due process' clause, which had been intended originally to consecrate a *mode of procedure,* had become a constitutional test of ever increasing reach of *the substantive content of legislation.* Thus was the doctrine of vested rights brought within the constitutional fold, although without dominating it. For confronting it was the still-expanding concept of the police power."

IV. FOURTEENTH AMENDMENT

Historical background. The history of the Civil War amendments, particularly the fourteenth, insofar as that history relates to the problems considered in this and later chapters, is thoroughly treated elsewhere. See, e.g., Fairman, *Does the Fourteenth Amendment Incorporate the Bill of Rights? The Original Understanding,* 2 Stan.L.Rev. 5 (1949); Bickel, *The Original Understanding and the Segregation Decision,* 69 Harv.L.Rev. 1 (1955); Frank & Munro, *The Original Understanding of "Equal Protection of the Laws"* 1972 Wash.U.L.Q. 421 (where other historical studies are cited).

SLAUGHTER–HOUSE CASES, 83 U.S. (16 Wall.) 36, 21 L.Ed. 394 (1873), per MILLER, J., upheld a legislatively-granted monopoly to operate slaughterhouses in the New Orleans area, subject to letting others use the facilities at state-regulated fees. The Court viewed this as an "appropriate, stringent, and effectual" means to "remove from the more densely populated part of the city, the noxious slaughterhouses and large and offensive collections of animals, [and]

---

a. Extracts from this book reprinted with permission of the publisher, copyright © 1948 Louisiana State University Press.

b. Corwin was referring here to the broad principle exemplified by *Wynehamer*; its actu-

al ruling on state liquor prohibition was rejected by all states but one. See id. at 107.

to locate them where the convenience, health and comfort of the people require," [a] but that was not the basis for its rejection of the challenge to the monopoly under the privileges and immunities clause of the fourteenth amendment:

"The first section of the fourteenth article, to which our attention is more specially invited, opens with a definition of citizenship—not only citizenship of the United States, but citizenship of the states. * * * 'All persons born or naturalized in the United States, and subject to the jurisdiction thereof, are citizens of the United States and of the state wherein they reside.' [T]he distinction between citizenship of the United States and citizenship of a state is clearly recognized and established. Not only may a man be a citizen of the United States without being a citizen of a state, but an important element is necessary to convert the former into the latter. He must reside within the state to make him a citizen of it, but it is only necessary that he should be born or naturalized in the United States to be a citizen of the Union. * * *

"The language is, 'No state shall make or enforce any law which shall abridge the privileges or immunities of citizens of the United States.' It is a little remarkable, if this clause was intended as a protection to the citizen of a state against the legislative power of his own state, that the word citizen of the state should be left out when it is so carefully used, and used in contradistinction to citizens of the United States, in the very sentence which precedes it. It is too clear for argument that the change in phraseology was adopted understandingly and with a purpose.

"Of the privileges and immunities of the citizen of the United States, and, of the privileges and immunities of the citizen of the state, and what they respectively are, we will presently consider; but we wish to state here that it is only the former which are placed by this clause under the protection of the federal Constitution, and that the latter, whatever they may be, are not intended to have any additional protection by this paragraph of the amendment."

The opinion distinguished Article IV "privileges and immunities" for which states must give equal treatment to the citizens of other states: "[U]p to the adoption of the recent amendments, no claim or pretence was set up that those rights depended on the federal government for their existence or protection, beyond the very few express limitations which the federal Constitution imposed upon the states—such, for instance, as the prohibition against ex post facto laws, bills of attainder, and laws impairing the obligation of contracts. But with the exception of these and a few other restrictions, the entire domain of the privileges and immunities of citizens of the states [lay] within the constitutional and legislative power of the states, and without that of the federal government. Was it the purpose of the Fourteenth Amendment by the simple declaration that no state should make or enforce any law which shall abridge the privileges and immunities of *Citizens of the United States,* to transfer the security and protection of all the civil rights which we have mentioned, from the states to the federal government? And where it is declared that Congress shall have the power to enforce that article, was it was intended to bring within the power of

a. See Hovenkamp, *Technology, Politics and Regulated Monopoly: An American Historical Perspective,* 62 Tex.L.Rev. 1263, 1295–1308 (1984), for a dramatic historical account of the legislative conversion of the fragmented, unhealthful, mislocated New Orleans slaughtering industry into a well-placed, price-regulated public utility monopoly open to every butcher to use, which solved the health problem and drastically reduced the price of beef.

Congress the entire domain of civil rights heretofore belonging exclusively to the states?

"All this and more must follow, if the proposition of the plaintiffs in error be sound. [F]urther, such a construction [would] constitute this court a perpetual censor upon all legislation of the states, on the civil rights of their own citizens, with authority to nullify such as it did not approve as consistent with those rights as they existed at the time of the adoption of this amendment. [When] these consequences are [so] great a departure from the structure and spirit of our institutions; [when] in fact it radically changes the whole theory of the relations of the state and federal governments to each other and of both these governments to the people; the argument has a force that is irresistible, in the absence of language which expresses such a purpose too clearly to admit of doubt.

"We are convinced that no such results were intended by the Congress which proposed these amendments, nor by the legislatures of the states which ratified them.[b]

"The argument has not been much pressed in these cases that the defendant's charter deprives the plaintiffs of their property without due process of law, or that it denies to them the equal protection of the law. The first of these paragraphs has been in the Constitution since the adoption of the Fifth Amendment, as a restraint upon the federal power. It is also to be found in some form of expression in the constitutions of nearly all the states, as a restraint upon the power of the States.

"[U]nder no construction of that provision that we have ever seen, or any that we deem admissible, can the restraint imposed by the state of Louisiana upon the exercise of their trade by the butchers of New Orleans be held to be a deprivation of property within the meaning of that provision.

"[In] the light of the history of these amendments, and the pervading purpose of them, which we have already discussed, it is not difficult to give a meaning to [the equal protection] clause. [We] doubt very much whether any action of a state not directed by way of discrimination against the negroes as a class, or on account of their race, will ever be held to come within the purview of this provision. It is so clearly a provision for that race and that emergency, that a strong case would be necessary for its application to any other."

FIELD, J., dissented.[c] "If this [clause] only refers, as held by the majority of the court in their opinion, to such privileges and immunities as were before its

---

b. Here the opinion added:

"[L]est it should be said that no such privileges and immunities are to be found if those we have been considering are excluded, we venture to suggest some which owe their existence to the federal government, its national character, its Constitution, or its laws.

"One of these is well described in *Crandall v. Nevada,* 73 U.S. (6 Wall.) 35, 18 L.Ed. 745. It is said to be the right of the citizen of this great country, protected by implied guarantees of its Constitution, 'to come to the seat of government to assert any claim he may have upon that government, to transact any business he may have with it, to seek its protection, to share its offices, to engage in administering its functions.' * * *

"The right to peaceably assemble and petition for redress of grievances, the privilege of

the writ of habeas corpus, are rights of the citizen guaranteed by the federal Constitution. The right to use the navigable waters of the United States, however they may penetrate the territory of the several states, all rights secured to our citizens by treaties with foreign nations, are dependent upon citizenship of the United States, and not citizenship of a state. [To] these may be added the rights secured by the thirteenth and fifteenth articles of amendment, and by the other clause of the fourteenth."

c. Chase, C.J., and Swayne and Bradley, J., joined this dissent. Bradley, J., joined by Swayne, J., also dissented, asserting that the statute also violated due process and equal protection.

adoption specially designated in the Constitution or necessarily implied as belonging to citizens of the United States, it was a vain and idle enactment, which accomplished nothing, and most unnecessarily excited Congress and the people on its passage. With privileges and immunities thus designated or implied no State could ever have interfered by its laws, and no new constitutional provision was required to inhibit such interference. The supremacy of the Constitution and the laws of the United States always controlled any State legislation of that character. But if the amendment refers to the natural and inalienable rights which belong to all citizens, the inhibition has a profound significance and consequence. ∗ ∗ ∗

"The terms, privileges and immunities, are not new in the amendment; they were in the Constitution before the amendment was adopted. They are found in [Art. IV, § 2.] The privileges and immunities designated are those which of right belong to the citizens of all free governments. Clearly among these must be placed the right to pursue a lawful employment in a lawful manner, without other restraint than such as equally affects all persons. In the discussions in Congress upon the passage of the Civil Rights Act repeated reference was made to this language of Mr. Justice Washington. It was cited by Senator Trumbull with the observation that it enumerated the very rights belonging to a citizen of the United States set forth in the first section of the [act].

"The privileges and immunities designated in [Art. IV, § 2] are, then, according to the decision cited, those which of right belong to the citizens of all free governments. [What] the clause in question did for the protection of the citizens of one State against hostile and discriminating legislation of other States, the fourteenth amendment does for the protection of every citizen of the United States against hostile and discriminating legislation against him in favor of others, whether they reside in the same or in different [States].

"This equality of right, with exemption from all disparaging and partial enactments, in the lawful pursuits of life, throughout the whole country, is the distinguishing privilege of citizens of the United States. To them, everywhere, all pursuits, all professions, all avocations are open without other restrictions than such as are imposed equally upon all others of the same age, sex, and condition. The State may prescribe such regulations for every pursuit and calling of life as will promote the public health, secure the good order and advance the general prosperity of society, but when once prescribed, the pursuit or calling must be free to be followed by every citizen who is within the conditions designated, and will conform to the regulations. This is the fundamental idea upon which our institutions rest, and unless adhered to in the legislation of the country our government will be a republic only in name."

Notes and Questions

1. *Objectives of privileges and immunities and citizenship provisions.* An historical study protests that the *Slaughter-House* opinion flies in the face of the congressional purpose for inserting the citizenship sentence. Graham, supra, at 23–26: "Significantly, no one observed that while citizenship was made dual in this first sentence, only the privileges or immunities of 'citizens of the United States' were specifically protected in the second sentence against abridgment by the states. The reason for this apparent oversight is that ever since Birney's day, opponents of slavery had regarded all important 'natural' and constitutional rights as being privileges and immunities of *citizens of the United States.* This had been the cardinal premise of antislavery theory from the beginning, and this

had been the underlying theory and purpose of Section One from the beginning. The real purpose of adding this citizenship definition was to remove any possible or lingering doubt about the freedman's citizenship."

2. *Resulting scope of privileges and immunities.* Professor McGovney paraphrased the clause as interpreted: "No State shall make or enforce any law which shall abridge any privilege or immunity conferred *by this Constitution, the statutes or treaties of the United States* upon any person who is a citizen of the United States." He then commented, "This narrower construction [renders] it an idle provision, in that it only declares a principle already more amply and more simply expressed in the constitution." McGovney, *Privileges or Immunities Clause, Fourteenth Amendment,* 4 Iowa Law Bull. (now Ia.L.Rev.) 219, 220, 221 (1918).

3. *The "idle provision."* The restrictive interpretation given the privileges and immunities clause in *Slaughter-House* has been consistently followed. Except for one quickly-overruled case,[d] the Court has never invalidated state legislation under the fourteenth amendment privileges and immunities clause. On a few occasions a minority of the Court invoked the clause. For details and analysis see Tribe, *American Constitutional Law* 418–26 (1978).

4. *Creative dicta.* Two closely related factors played important roles in the emergence of substantive due process. (1) Lawyers in speeches, treatises, articles and briefs strongly advanced the *laissez faire* concept of government, often urging the due process clause as a constitutional limitation on governmental regulation of business. See the remarkable study of the influence of lawyers in this respect in Twiss, *Lawyers and the Constitution* 18–173 (1942). (2) Supreme Court justices in dissenting opinions, and state courts, strongly reflected these views, until majority opinions sustaining state regulation began also to recognize that the due process clause imposes some limits on the regulatory power of government. See Corwin, *Liberty Against Government* 129–152 (1948).

LOCHNER v. NEW YORK
198 U.S. 45, 25 S.Ct. 539, 49 L.Ed. 937 (1905).

MR. JUSTICE PECKHAM delivered the opinion of the Court.

[The Court held invalid a New York statute forbidding employment in a bakery for more than 60 hours a week or 10 hours a day.]

[It] must, of course, be conceded that there is a limit to the valid exercise of the police power by the state. [Otherwise] the 14th Amendment would have no efficacy and the legislatures of the states would have unbounded power. [In] every case that comes before this court, therefore, where legislation of this character is concerned, and where the protection of the Federal Constitution is sought, the question necessarily arises: Is this a fair, reasonable, and appropriate exercise of the police power of the state, or is it an unreasonable, unnecessary, and arbitrary interference with the right of the individual to his personal liberty, or to enter into those contracts in relation to labor which may seem to him appropriate or necessary for the support of himself and his family? Of course the liberty of contract relating to labor includes both parties to it. The one has as much right to purchase as the other to sell labor.

---

d. *Colgate v. Harvey,* 296 U.S. 404, 56 S.Ct. 252, 80 L.Ed. 299 (1935), overruled by *Madden* v. *Kentucky,* 309 U.S. 83, 60 S.Ct. 406, 84 L.Ed. 590 (1940).

This is not a question of substituting the judgment of the court for that of the legislature. If the act be within the power of the state it is valid, although the judgment of the court might be totally opposed to the enactment of such a law. But the question would still remain: Is it within the police power of the state? and that question must be answered by the court.

The question whether this act is valid as a labor law, pure and simple, may be dismissed in a few words. There is no reasonable ground for interfering with the liberty of person or the right of free contract, by determining the hours of labor, in the occupation of a baker. There is no contention that bakers as a class are not equal in intelligence and capacity to men in other trades or manual occupations, or that they are not able to assert their rights and care for themselves without the protecting arm of the state. [They] are in no sense wards of the state. Viewed in the light of a purely labor law, with no reference whatever to the question of health, we think that a law like the one before us involves neither the safety, the morals, nor the welfare, of the public, and that the interest of the public is not in the slightest degree affected by such an act. The law must be upheld, if at all, as a law pertaining to the health of the individual engaged in the occupation of a baker. It does not affect any other portion of the public than those who are engaged in that occupation. Clean and wholesome bread does not depend upon whether the baker works but ten hours per day or only sixty hours a week. [There] is, in our judgment, no reasonable foundation for holding this to be necessary or appropriate as a health law to safeguard the public health, or the health of the individuals who are following the trade of a baker. * * *

We think that there can be no fair doubt that the trade of a baker, in and of itself, is not an unhealthy one to that degree which would authorize the legislature to interfere with the right to labor, and with the right of free contract on the part of the individual, either as employer or employee. In looking through statistics regarding all trades and occupations, it may be true that the trade of a baker does not appear to be as healthy as some other trades, and is also vastly more healthy than still others. To the common understanding the trade of a baker has never been regarded as an unhealthy one. [Some] occupations are more healthy than others, but we think there are none which might not come under the power of the legislature to supervise and control the hours of working therein, if the mere fact that the occupation is not absolutely and perfectly healthy is to confer that right upon the legislative department of the government. [It] is unfortunately true that labor, even in any department, may possibly carry with it the seeds of unhealthiness. But are we all, on that account, at the mercy of legislative majorities? A printer, a tinsmith, a locksmith, a carpenter, a cabinet maker, a dry goods clerk, a bank's, a lawyer's, or a physician's clerk, or a clerk in almost any kind of business, would all come under the power of the legislature, on this assumption. No trade, no occupation, no mode of earning one's living, could escape this all-pervading power, and the acts of the legislature in limiting the hours of labor in all employments would be valid, although such limitation might seriously cripple the ability of the laborer to support himself and his family. In our large cities there are many buildings into which the sun penetrates for but a short time in each day, and these buildings are occupied by people carrying on the business of bankers, brokers, lawyers, real estate, and many other kinds of business, aided by many clerks, messengers, and other employees. Upon the assumption of the validity of this act under review, it is not possible to say that an act, prohibiting lawyers' or bank clerks, or others, from contracting to labor for their employers more than eight hours a day would be invalid. * * *

It is also urged, pursuing the same line of argument, that it is to the interest of the state that its population should be strong and robust, and therefore any legislation which may be said to tend to make people healthy must be valid as health laws, enacted under the police power. If this be a valid argument and a justification for this kind of legislation, it follows that the protection of the Federal Constitution from undue interference with liberty of person and freedom of contract is visionary, wherever the law is sought to be justified as a valid exercise of the police power. Scarcely any law but might find shelter under such assumptions. [Not] only the hours of employees, but the hours of employers, could be regulated, and doctors, lawyers, scientists, all professional men, as well as athletes and artisans, could be forbidden to fatigue their brains and bodies by prolonged hours of exercise, lest the fighting strength of the state be impaired. We mention these extreme cases because the contention is extreme. We do not believe in the soundness of the views which uphold this law. [The] act is not, within any fair meaning of the term, a health law, but is an illegal interference with the rights of individuals, both employers and employees, to make contracts regarding labor upon such terms as they may think best, or which they may agree upon with the other parties to such contracts. Statutes of the nature of that under review, limiting the hours in which grown and intelligent men may labor to earn their living, are mere meddlesome interferences with the rights of the individual. * * *

This interference on the part of the legislatures of the several states with the ordinary trades and occupations of the people seems to be on the increase. [It] is impossible for us to shut our eyes to the fact that many of the laws of this character, while passed under what is claimed to be the police power for the purpose of protecting the public health or welfare, are, in reality, passed from other motives. We are justified in saying so when, from the character of the law and the subject upon which it legislates, it is apparent that the public health or welfare bears but the most remote relation to the [law].

It seems to us that the real object and purpose were simply to regulate the hours of labor between the master and his employees (all being men, sui juris), in a private business, not dangerous in any degree to morals, or in any real and substantial degree to the health of the employees. Under such circumstances the freedom of master and employee to contract with each other in relation to their employment [cannot] be prohibited or interfered with, without violating the Federal Constitution. * * *

Mr. Justice Holmes dissenting: * * *

This case is decided upon an economic theory which a large part of the country does not entertain. If it were a question whether I agree with that theory, I should desire to study it further and long before making up my mind. But I do not conceive that to be my duty, because I strongly believe that my agreement or disagreement has nothing to do with the right of a majority to embody their opinions in law. It is settled by various decisions of this court that state constitutions and state laws may regulate life in many ways which we as legislators might think as injudicious, or if you like as tyrannical, as this, and which, equally with this, interfere with the liberty to contract. Sunday laws and usury laws are ancient examples. A more modern one is the prohibition of lotteries. The liberty of the citizen to do as he likes so long as he does not interfere with the liberty of others to do the same, which has been a shibboleth for some well-known writers, is interfered with by school laws, by the Postoffice, by every state or municipal institution which takes his money for purposes thought desirable, whether he likes it or not. The 14th Amendment does not enact Mr. Herbert Spencer's *Social Statics*. [Some] of these laws embody convictions or prejudices which judges are likely to share. Some may not. But a Constitution is not intended to embody a particular economic theory, whether of paternalism and the organic relation of the citizen to the state or of laissez faire. It is made for people of fundamentally differing views, and the accident of our finding certain opinions natural and familiar, or novel, and even shocking, ought not to conclude our judgment upon the question whether statutes embodying them conflict with the Constitution of the United States.

[I] think that the word "liberty," in the 14th Amendment, is perverted when it is held to prevent the natural outcome of a dominant opinion, unless it can be said that a rational and fair man necessarily would admit that the statute proposed would infringe fundamental principles as they have been understood by the traditions of our people and our law. It does not need research to show that no such sweeping condemnation can be passed upon the statute before us. A reasonable man might think it a proper measure on the score of health. Men whom I certainly could not pronounce unreasonable would uphold it as a first instalment of a general regulation of the hours of work. * * *

MR. JUSTICE HARLAN (with whom MR. JUSTICE WHITE and MR. JUSTICE DAY concurred) dissenting:

[Whether] or not this be wise legislation it is not the province of the court to inquire. Under our systems of government the courts are not concerned with the wisdom or policy of legislation.

[The opinion quoted from writers on health problems of workers, pointing out that long hours, night hours, and difficult working conditions, such as excessive heat and exposure to flour dust, were injurious to the health of bakers, who "seldom live over their fiftieth year."]

We judicially know that the question of the number of hours during which a workman should continuously labor has been, for a long period, and is yet, a subject of serious consideration among civilized peoples, and by those having special knowledge of the laws of health. * * *

I do not stop to consider whether any particular view of this economic question presents the sounder theory. [It] is enough for the determination of this case, and it is enough for this court to know, that the question is one about which there is room for debate and for an honest difference of opinion. There are many reasons of a weighty, substantial character, based upon the experience of mankind, in support of the theory that, all things considered, more than ten hours' steady work each day, from week to week, in a bakery or confectionery establishment, may endanger the health and shorten the lives of the workmen, thereby diminishing their physical and mental capacity to serve the state and to provide for those dependent upon them.

If such reasons exist that ought to be the end of this case, for the state is not amenable to the judiciary, in respect of its legislative enactments, unless such enactments are plainly, palpably, beyond all question, inconsistent with the Constitution of the United States. * * *

SECTION 2. THREE DECADES OF CONTROL OVER LEGISLATIVE POLICY

From *Lochner* in 1905 to *Nebbia* in 1934, infra, the Court frequently substituted its judgment for that of Congress and state legislatures on the wisdom of economic regulation interfering with contract and property interests.[a] It relied mainly upon the due process clauses of the fifth and fourteenth amendments, with occasional resort to the equal protection clause. Between 1899 and 1937, after excluding the civil rights cases, 159 Supreme Court decisions held state statutes unconstitutional under the due process and equal protection clauses and 25 more statutes were struck down under the due process clause coupled with some other provision of the Constitution. Wright, *The Growth of American Constitutional Law* 154 (1942).

The Court most freely substituted its judgment for that of the legislature in labor legislation, regulation of prices, and limitations on entry into business. It was most tolerant in the regulation of trade and business practices, such as insurance, financial institutions and competitive practices.[b] A few examples will suffice to show the extent to which the Court interfered with legislative policymaking in economic regulation. With regularity Holmes, J., dissented from this use of the due process clause, joined later by Brandeis and Stone, JJ., and Hughes, C.J.

1. *Control over hours of labor.* We have already seen how the Court barred control over the hours of labor, even in an industry where long hours threatened health. *Lochner* (1905). But in 1908 the Court sustained regulation of work hours for women in *Muller v. Oregon,* 208 U.S. 412, 28 S.Ct. 324, 52 L.Ed. 551 (1908), basing the decision on special considerations relating to women, and in 1917 the Court overruled *Lochner* 5 to 3 in sustaining a regulation of work hours for men in manufacturing establishments. *Bunting v. Oregon,* 243 U.S. 426, 37 S.Ct. 435, 61 L.Ed. 830 (1917). In *Muller* the majority was influenced by the so-called "Brandeis brief," which furnished the Court with overwhelming documentation justifying regulation of hours of labor for women. Felix Frankfurter, Esq., successfully followed the same technique in *Bunting.* See 208 U.S. at 419–20, and 243 U.S. at 433; Bikle, *Judicial Determination of Questions of Fact Affecting the Constitutional Validity of Legislative Action,* 38 Harv.L.Rev. 6, 13 (1924).

2. *Control over anti-union discrimination.* At an early date the Court struck down labor legislation forbidding discrimination by employers for union activity and requiring employees to sign "yellow dog" agreements not to join a union. *Adair v. United States,* 208 U.S. 161, 28 S.Ct. 277, 52 L.Ed. 436 (1908) (5th amendment); *Coppage v. Kansas,* 236 U.S. 1, 35 S.Ct. 240, 59 L.Ed. 441 (1915) (14th amendment).

Adair held that for Congress to forbid an interstate railroad to discharge an employee for union membership denied due process. For the Court, Harlan, J., who had dissented in *Lochner,* relied upon the liberty of contract approach in *Lochner* and equated the right of an employee to quit his employment with "the right of the employer, for whatever reason, to dispense with the services of the employee." McKenna and Holmes, JJ., dissented. *Coppage,* per Pitney, J., rejected the claim that the legislature could protect employees from being required to sign yellow dog contracts to obtain or keep needed employment.

These restrictive decisions were distinguished away in *Texas & N.O.R.R. v. Brotherhood of Ry. & S.S. Clerks,* 281 U.S. 548, 50 S.Ct. 427, 74 L.Ed. 1034 (1930) and *NLRB v. Jones & Laughlin Steel Corp.* (1937). They were finally expressly overruled in *Phelps Dodge Corp. v. NLRB,* 313 U.S. 177, 61 S.Ct. 845, 85 L.Ed.

---

a. See Pound, *Liberty of Contract,* 18 Yale L.J. 454 (1909); Brown, *Due Process of Law, Police Power, and the Supreme Court,* 40 Harv. L.Rev. 943 (1927).

b. See summary of such cases in *Nebbia v. New York,* 291 U.S. 502, 527–529, 54 S.Ct. 505, 511–13, 78 L.Ed. 940, 950–53 (1934), infra.

1271 (1941) and *Lincoln Fed. Labor Union v. Northwestern Iron & Met. Co.* (1949), Sec. 3 infra.

3. *Regulation of wages.* Six years after the Court had upheld regulation of hours of labor, it held 5 to 3 that regulation of wages violated due process. *Adkins v. Children's Hosp.,* 261 U.S. 525, 43 S.Ct. 394, 67 L.Ed. 785 (1923) (fifth amendment); *Murphy v. Sardell,* 269 U.S. 530, 46 S.Ct. 22, 70 L.Ed. 396 (1925) (14th amendment); *Morehead v. New York ex rel. Tipaldo,* 298 U.S. 587, 56 S.Ct. 918, 80 L.Ed. 1347 (1936) (same). Not until 1937 were these decisions overruled in *West Coast Hotel Co. v. Parrish,* Sec. 3 infra, where the Court expressly recognized the unequal bargaining position of workers, and that the wisdom of debatable policy is for the legislature.

4. *Regulation of prices.* The Court also held that regulation of prices for commodities and services violated due process except for a limited class labeled "business affected with a public interest." [c] *Tyson & Bro. v. Banton,* 273 U.S. 418, 47 S.Ct. 426, 71 L.Ed. 718 (1927) (theatre tickets); *Ribnik v. McBride,* 277 U.S. 350, 48 S.Ct. 545, 72 L.Ed. 913 (1928) (fees of employment agency); *Williams v. Standard Oil Co.,* 278 U.S. 235, 49 S.Ct. 115, 73 L.Ed. 287 (1929) (gasoline prices); cf. *Wolff Packing Co. v. Industrial Court,* 262 U.S. 522, 43 S.Ct. 630, 67 L.Ed. 1103 (1923) (compulsory arbitration of wages). *Nebbia v. New York* (1934) severely limited these rulings and they were expressly overruled in *Olsen v. Nebraska ex rel. Western Ref. & Bond Ass'n* (1941), both in Sec. 3 infra.

5. *Limitations on entry into business.* The Court also relied on the "liberty of contract" concept to strike down legislation limiting entry into a business, despite strong demonstrations of need for such limitations. *New State Ice Co. v. Liebmann,* 285 U.S. 262, 52 S.Ct. 371, 76 L.Ed. 747 (1932) (invalid to deny entry into ice business without a finding of "necessity" and that existing facilities are not "sufficient to meet the public needs"); *Louis K. Liggett Co. v. Baldridge,* 278 U.S. 105, 49 S.Ct. 57, 73 L.Ed. 204 (1928) (invalid to limit new entrants into pharmacy business to pharmacists; *Adams v. Tanner,* 244 U.S. 590, 37 S.Ct. 662, 61 L.Ed. 1336 (1917) (invalid to ban private employment agencies that charge fees paid by employees).

In 1973, *North Dakota State Board v. Snyder's Drug Stores,* Sec. 3 infra, overruled *Liggett.* While no cases precisely like *Adams* or *New State Ice* have arisen, the Court in 1963 asserted in effect that *Adams* had been overruled when it unanimously sustained a state prohibition on engaging in the debt adjusting business. See *Ferguson v. Skrupa,* Sec. 3 infra.

SECTION 3. DECLINE OF CONTROL OVER LEGISLATIVE POLICY

NEBBIA v. NEW YORK

291 U.S. 502, 54 S.Ct. 505, 78 L.Ed. 940 (1934).

MR. JUSTICE ROBERTS delivered the opinion of the Court.

[The Court upheld New York's regulation of minimum milk prices, aimed at assuring a "reasonable return" to producers and milk dealers, which was adopted after extensive legislative study.]

---

c. See McAllister, *Lord Hale and Business Affected with a Public Interest,* 43 Harv.L.Rev. 759 (1930); Hamilton, *Affectation with Public Interest,* 39 Yale L.J. 1089 (1930); Finkelstein,

From Munn v. Illinois to Tyson v. Banton: A Study in the Judicial Process, 27 Colum.L.Rev. 769 (1927).

[T]he guaranty of due process, as has often been held, demands only that the law shall not be unreasonable, arbitrary, or capricious, and that the means selected shall have a real and substantial relation to the object sought to be attained. [A] regulation valid for one sort of business, or in given circumstances, may be invalid for another sort, or for the same business under other circumstances, because the reasonableness of each regulation depends upon the relevant facts.

[The opinion here summarized many different kinds of business and property regulations and controls previously sustained against due process attacks.]

The legislative investigation of 1932 was persuasive of the fact [that] unrestricted competition aggravated existing evils and the normal law of supply and demand was insufficient to correct maladjustments detrimental to the community. The inquiry disclosed destructive and demoralizing competitive conditions and unfair trade practices which resulted in retail price cutting and reduced the income of the farmer below the cost of production. [The Legislature] believed conditions could be improved by preventing destructive price-cutting by stores which, due to the flood of surplus milk, were able to buy at much lower prices than the larger distributors and to sell without incurring the delivery costs of the latter. In the order of which complaint is made the Milk Control Board fixed a price of 10 cents per quart for sales by a distributor to a consumer, and 9 cents by a store to a consumer, thus recognizing the lower costs of the store, and endeavoring to establish a differential which would be just to both. In the light of the facts the order appears not to be unreasonable or arbitrary, or without relation to the purpose to prevent ruthless competition from destroying the wholesale price structure on which the farmer depends for his livelihood, and the community for an assured supply of milk.

But we are told that because the law essays to control prices it denies due process. Notwithstanding the admitted power to correct existing economic ills by appropriate regulation of business, [the] appellant urges that direct fixation of prices is a type of regulation absolutely forbidden. [The] argument runs that the public control of rates or prices is per se unreasonable and unconstitutional, save as applied to businesses affected with a public interest; that a business so affected is one in which property is devoted to an enterprise of a sort which the public itself might appropriately undertake, or one whose owner relies on a public grant or franchise for the right to conduct the business, or in which he is bound to serve all who apply; in short, such as is commonly called a public utility; or a business in its nature a monopoly. The milk industry, it is said, possesses none of these characteristics.

[T]here is no closed class or category of businesses affected with a public interest, and the function of courts in the application of the Fifth and Fourteenth Amendments is to determine in each case whether circumstances vindicate the challenged regulation as a reasonable exertion of governmental authority or condemn it as arbitrary or discriminatory. The phrase "affected with a public interest" can, in the nature of things, mean no more than that an industry, for adequate reason, is subject to control for the public good. [There] can be no doubt that upon proper occasion and by appropriate measures the state may regulate a business in any of its aspects, including the prices to be charged for the products or commodities it sells.

So far as the requirement of due process is concerned, and in the absence of other constitutional restriction, a state is free to adopt whatever economic policy may reasonably be deemed to promote public welfare, and to enforce that policy by legislation adapted to its purpose. The courts are without authority either to declare such policy, or, when it is declared by the legislature, to override it. If the laws passed are seen to have a reasonable relation to a proper legislative purpose, and are neither arbitrary nor discriminatory, the requirements of due process are satisfied. [If] the legislative policy be to curb unrestrained and harmful competition by measures which are not arbitrary or discriminatory it does not lie with the courts to determine that the rule is unwise. With the wisdom of the policy adopted, with the adequacy or practicability of the law enacted to forward it, the courts are both incompetent and unauthorized to deal.

* * *

Separate opinion of MR. JUSTICE MCREYNOLDS.

[P]lainly, I think, this Court must have regard to the wisdom of the enactment. At least, we must inquire concerning its purpose and decide whether the means proposed have reasonable relation to something within legislative power—whether the end is legitimate, and the means appropriate. * * *

The court below [has] not attempted to indicate how higher charges at stores to impoverished customers when the output is excessive and sale prices by producers are unrestrained, can possibly increase receipts at the farm. * * *

Not only does the statute interfere arbitrarily with the rights of the little grocer to conduct his business according to standards long accepted—complete destruction may follow; but it takes away the liberty of 12,000,000 consumers to buy a necessity of life in an open market. It imposes direct and arbitrary burdens upon those already seriously impoverished with the alleged immediate design of affording special benefits to others. * * *[b]

Notes and Questions

1. *The Nebbia rationale.* (a) Did *Nebbia* appear to retain any degree of judicial review over legislative policy in state economic regulation? What standards of judgment did *Nebbia* suggest the Court would apply? May the makeup of the majority explain the standards advanced in the opinion?

(b) *Interests justifying price controls; sources of information.* Do you see any significance in the type of interests the Court found sufficient to justify price controls in *Nebbia*? In the sources relied upon by the Court to establish the factual basis for justifying price regulation?

2. *Control over wages.* WEST COAST HOTEL CO. v. PARRISH, 300 U.S. 379, 57 S.Ct. 578, 81 L.Ed. 703 (1937), sustained 5 to 4 a state regulation of women's wages, overruling earlier decisions. The opinion, per HUGHES, C. J., devoted substantial space to the reasons for regulation of women's wages, stressing the special problems of protecting women from "unscrupulous and overreaching employers," and to the need for protecting "workers who are in an unequal position with respect to bargaining power and are thus relatively defenseless against the denial of a living wage." The Court found that the legislative conclusion "cannot be regarded as arbitrary or capricious and that is all we have to decide. Even if the wisdom of the policy be regarded as debatable and its effects uncertain, still the Legislature is entitled to its judgment." Four years later, the Court sustained federal regulation of men's wages over due process objection, citing *Parrish* as authority. *United States v. Darby*, 312 U.S. 100, 125, 61 S.Ct. 451, 462–63, 85 L.Ed. 609, 623 (1941).

b. Van Devanter, Sutherland and Butler, JJ., concurred in the dissent.

3. *Does the Court still review economic policy?* UNITED STATES v. CAROLENE PRODUCTS CO., 304 U.S. 144, 58 S.Ct. 778, 82 L.Ed. 1234 (1938), per STONE, J., sustained against due process challenge a federal statute excluding "filled milk" (non-milk fats added) from interstate commerce: "[R]egulatory legislation affecting ordinary commercial transactions is not to be pronounced unconstitutional unless in the light of the facts made known or generally assumed it is of such a character as to preclude the assumption that it rests upon some rational basis within the knowledge and experience of the legislators."

4. *Renunciation of former due process philosophy.* (a) OLSEN v. NEBRASKA, 313 U.S. 236, 61 S.Ct. 862, 85 L.Ed. 1305 (1941), upheld a Nebraska statute fixing maximum fees for employment agencies. DOUGLAS, J.'s, unanimous opinion[a] bluntly rejected the state court's reliance on *Ribnik v. McBride,* 277 U.S. 350, 48 S.Ct. 545, 72 L.Ed. 913 (1928), which had held a similar statute violated due process: "The drift away from *Ribnik* has been so great that it can no longer be deemed a controlling authority. [The Court summarized several cases overruling earlier due process rulings.] These cases represent more than scattered examples of constitutionally permissible price-fixing schemes. They represent in large measure a basic departure from the philosophy and approach of the majority in *Ribnik.* The standard there employed [was] that the constitutional validity of price-fixing legislation, at least in absence of a so-called emergency, was dependent on whether or not the business in question was 'affected with a public interest'. [That] test, labelled by Mr. Justice Holmes in his dissent in [*Tyson*] as 'little more than a fiction', was discarded in *Nebbia.*

"The *Ribnik* case, freed from the test which it employed, can no longer survive. But respondents maintain that the statute here in question is invalid for other reasons. They insist that special circumstances must be shown to support the validity of such drastic legislation as price-fixing, that the executive technical and professional workers which respondents serve have not been shown to be in need of special protection from exploitation, that legislative limitation of maximum fees for employment agencies is certain to react unfavorably upon those members of the community for whom it is most difficult to obtain jobs, that the increasing competition of public employment agencies and of charitable, labor union and employer association employment agencies have curbed excessive fees by private agencies, and [that] there are no conditions which the legislature might reasonably believe would redound to the public injury unless corrected by such legislation.

"We are not concerned, however, with the wisdom, need, or appropriateness of the legislation. Differences of opinion on that score suggest a choice which 'should be left where [it] was left by the Constitution—to the states and to Congress.' *Ribnik,* dissenting opinion. There is no necessity for the state to demonstrate before us that evils persist despite the competition which attends the bargaining in this field. In final analysis, the only constitutional prohibitions or restraints which respondents have suggested for the invalidation of this legislation are those notions of public policy embedded in earlier decisions of this Court but which, as Mr. Justice Holmes long ago admonished, should not be read into the Constitution. [Since] they do not find expression in the Constitution, we cannot give them continuing vitality as standards by which the constitutionality of the economic and social programs of the states is to be determined."

---

a. McReynolds, J., the last of the four *Nebbia* and *West Coast Hotel* dissenters, re-tired two days before *Darby* and two months before *Olsen.*

Is the absence in *Olsen* of any judicial explanation of the need to regulate employment agency rates significant? Were there reasons in 1941 to be less skeptical of the *Olsen* expression of no concern over "the wisdom, the need, or appropriateness of the legislation" than of the similar statement in *Nebbia* in 1934?

(b) After *Olsen* the Court consistently repudiated *Lochner*-type reasoning in rejecting substantive due process challenges to economic regulation.[b]

5. *Social, as distinct from economic, regulation.* WHALEN v. ROE, 429 U.S. 589, 97 S.Ct. 869, 51 L.Ed.2d 64 (1977), per STEVENS, J., upheld a New York law requiring those who fill prescriptions for specified harmful drugs to send copies to the New York Department of Health, where the information, including the patient's name, was to be retained on computers for five years under strict non-disclosure regulations: "There was a time when [the state's inability to demonstrate the need for patient identification] would have provided a basis for invalidating the statute. *Lochner.* [The] holding in *Lochner* has been implicitly rejected many times. State legislation which has some effect on individual liberty or privacy may not be held unconstitutional simply because a court finds it unnecessary, in whole or in part. For we have frequently recognized that individual States have broad latitude in experimenting with possible solutions to problems of vital local concern.

"The New York statute challenged in this case represents a considered attempt to deal with such a problem. It is manifestly the product of an orderly and rational legislative decision. It was recommended by a specially appointed commission which held extensive hearings on the proposed legislation, and drew on experience with similar programs in other States. There surely was nothing unreasonable in the assumption that the patient identification requirement might aid in the enforcement of laws designed to minimize the misuse of

b. *Lincoln Fed. Labor Union v. Northwestern Iron & Met. Co.*, 335 U.S. 525, 69 S.Ct. 251, 93 L.Ed. 212 (1949), per Black, J., sustained a state right-to-work law that barred employers' pro-union discrimination: "This Court beginning at least as early as 1934, when [*Nebbia*] was decided, has steadily rejected the due process philosophy enunciated in the *Adair-Coppage* line of cases. [Just] as we have held that the due process clause erects no obstacle to block legislative protection of union members [see Sec. 2, note 2, par. 3 supra], we now hold that legislative protection can be afforded non-union workers.

Day-Brite Lighting, Inc. v. Missouri, 342 U.S. 421, 72 S.Ct. 405, 96 L.Ed. 469 (1952), per Douglas, J., sustained a requirement that employees have four hours off work with full pay in order to vote: "The liberty of contract argument pressed on us is reminiscent of the philosophy of [*Lochner, Coppage, Adkins v. Children's Hospital*] and others of that vintage. Our recent decisions make plain that we do not sit as a super-legislature to weigh the wisdom of legislation nor to decide whether the policy it expresses offends the public welfare. * * * The judgment of the legislature that time out for voting should cost the employee nothing may be a debatable one. [But] if our recent cases mean anything, they leave debatable issues as respects business,

economic and social affairs to legislative decisions." Jackson, J., dissented and Frankfurter, J., concurred in the result without opinion.

Similarly, *Ferguson v. Skrupa*, 372 U.S. 726, 83 S.Ct. 1028, 10 L.Ed.2d 93 (1963), per Black, J., unanimously spurned a due process challenge to a state law that barred all but lawyers from the business of debt adjusting: "Under the system of government created by our Constitution, it is up to the legislatures, not the courts, to decide on the wisdom and utility of legislation. [The] doctrine that prevailed in *Lochner, Coppage, Adkins* and like cases [has] long since been discarded. We have returned to the original constitutional proposition that courts do not substitute their social and economic beliefs for the judgment of legislative bodies, who are elected to pass [laws]. [Arguments that] the business of debt adjusting has social utility [are] properly addressed to the legislature, not to us." Harlan, J., concurred in the judgment on the ground that "[this] measure bears a rational relation to a constitutionally permissible objective."

For similar rulings and opinions see *Williamson v. Lee Optical of Okla.*, 348 U.S. 483, 75 S.Ct. 461, 99 L.Ed. 563 (1955); *North Dakota State Bd. v. Snyders' Store*, 414 U.S. 156, 94 S.Ct. 407, 38 L.Ed.2d 379 (1973).

dangerous drugs. For the requirement could reasonably be expected to have a deterrent effect on potential violators as well as to aid in the detection or investigation of specific instances of apparent abuse. At the very least, it would seem clear that the State's vital interest in controlling the distribution of dangerous drugs would support a decision to experiment with new techniques for control. For if an experiment fails—if in this case experience teaches that the patient identification requirement results in the foolish expenditure of funds to acquire a mountain of useless information—the legislative process remains available to terminate the unwise experiment." [c]

ABSTENTION FOR FIVE DECADES

When faced with substantive due process challenges to economic legislation after 1940, the Court's actual decisions gave full effect to its strong opinions repeatedly asserting that on such matters legislative policy is for the legislature, not the courts. Not since 1937 has the Court struck down economic legislation as violating substantive due process;[a] and only in rare instances have individual justices withheld their approval of opinions renouncing power under the due process clause to review the wisdom, need, or soundness of such legislation.[b]

Referring to the foregoing due process decisions, and to a similar line of equal protection decisions,[c] Professor McCloskey concluded in 1962: "[T]here could be little doubt as to the practical result: no claim of substantive economic rights would now be sustained by the Supreme Court. The judiciary has abdicated the field." [d]

Has the Court "abdicated?" Has it renounced all substantive due process review power over economic legislation? Or has the Court hedged its opinions sufficiently to enable it, without recanting, to reassert substantive due process if it ever concludes that a legislative economic enactment is devoid of any arguable justification? [e]

With such questions in mind, consider DUKE POWER CO. v. CAROLINA ENV. STUDY GROUP, INC., 438 U.S. 59, 98 S.Ct. 2620, 57 L.Ed.2d 595 (1978). *Duke Power,* per BURGER, C.J., upheld the Price-Anderson Act's limit on the aggregate liability for a single nuclear incident in the atomic energy industry to the amount available through private insurance ($60 million) plus the $500 million indemnification undertaken by the federal government:[f] "[I]t is clear that Congress' purpose was to remove the economic impediments in order to stimulate the private development of electric energy by nuclear power while simultaneously providing the public compensation in the event of a catastrophic nuclear incident. The liability limitation provision thus emerges as a classic

c. For cases applying stricter scrutiny to legislation impinging on a limited category of "fundamental" personal rights. See Ch. 7, Sec. 2. However, *Whalen* ruled that the New York law did not unduly impinge on the right to privacy. Ch. 7, Sec. 2.

a. The last substantive due process decision invalidating economic legislation was *Thompson v. Consolidated Gas Co.,* 300 U.S. 55, 57 S.Ct. 364, 81 L.Ed. 510 (1937), where the regulation was viewed as taking property for a private purpose.

b. See the Harlan concurrence in *Ferguson v. Skrupa,* and the Jackson dissent and Frankfurter concurrence "in the result" in *Day-Brite Lighting.*

c. For the equal protection cases relating to economic regulation see Ch. 10, Sec. 1.

d. McClosky, *Economic Due Process and the Supreme Court,* 1962 Sup.Ct.Rev. 34, 38.

e. Cf. Wonnell, *Economic Due Process and the Preservation of Competition,* 11 Hast. Const.L.Q. 91 (1983) (a strongly reasoned argument that substantive due process should be extended to protect "free and open competition for society's lawful occupations [as] a constitutional value" that could invalidate legislation enforcing monopoly conditions, absent a sufficiently strong state interest).

f. Stewart, Rehnquist and Stevens, JJ., concurred in the result without reaching the merits.

example of an economic regulation—a legislative effort to structure and accommodate 'the burdens and benefits of economic life.' *Usery v. Turner Elkhorn Mining Co.*, 428 U.S. 1, 96 S.Ct. 2882, 49 L.Ed.2d 752 (1976). 'It is by now well established that [such] legislative Acts [come] to the Court with a presumption of constitutionality, and that the burden is on one complaining of a due process violation to establish that the legislature has acted in an arbitrary and irrational way.' Ibid. That the accommodation struck may have profound and far-reaching consequences, contrary to appellees' suggestion, provides all the more reason for this Court to defer to the congressional judgment unless it is demonstrably arbitrary or irrational.

"When examined in light of this standard of review, the Price-Anderson Act, in our view, passes constitutional muster. The record before us fully supports the need for the imposition of a statutory limit on liability to encourage private industry participation and hence bears a rational relationship to Congress' concern for stimulating the involvement of private enterprise in the production of electric energy through the use of atomic power; nor do we understand appellees or the District Court to be of a different view. Rather, their challenge is to the alleged arbitrariness of the *particular figure* of $560 million, which is the statutory ceiling on liability. The District Court aptly summarized its position: 'The amount of recovery is not rationally related to the potential losses, [which] could well be many, many times [that] limit.'

"Assuming, arguendo, that the $560 million fund would not insure full recovery in all conceivable circumstances,—and the hard truth is that no one can ever know—it does not by any means follow that the liability limitation is therefore irrational and violative of due process. The legislative history clearly indicates that the $560 million figure was not arrived at on the supposition that it alone would necessarily be sufficient to guarantee full compensation in the event of a nuclear incident. Instead, it was conceived of as a 'starting point' or a working hypothesis. The reasonableness of the statute's assumed ceiling on liability was predicated on two corollary considerations—expert appraisals of the exceedingly small risk of a nuclear incident involving claims in excess of $560 million, and the recognition that in the event of such an incident, Congress would likely enact extraordinary relief provisions to provide additional relief, in accord with prior practice. * * *

"Given our conclusion that in general limiting liability is an acceptable method for Congress to utilize in encouraging the private development of electric energy by atomic power, candor requires acknowledgment that whatever ceiling figure is selected will, of necessity, be arbitrary in the sense that any choice of a figure based on imponderables like those at issue here can always be so characterized. This is not, however, the kind of arbitrariness which flaws otherwise constitutional action. When appraised in terms of both the extremely remote possibility of an accident where liability would exceed the limitation and Congress' now statutory commitment to 'take whatever action is deemed necessary and appropriate to protect the public from the consequences of' any such disaster, 42 U.S.C. § 2210(e) (1970 ed. Supp. V), we hold the congressional decision to fix a $560 million ceiling, at this stage in the private development and production of electric energy by nuclear power, to be within permissible limits and not violative of due process."

Notes and Questions

1. *The standard of review.* Was the standard of review that *Turner Elkhorn* and *Duke Power* asserted with no dissenting voices—"demonstrably

arbitrary or irrational"—consistent with the opinions from *Olsen* (1941) to *Snyder* (1973)? In forecasting future decisions on such issues, is it significant that *Duke Power* used four pages to explain why Price-Anderson was not "arbitrary or irrational" and hence "passes constitutional muster?"

(b) Did "arbitrary or irrational" mean something different in 1978 than from 1905 (*Lochner*) to 1934 (*Nebbia*)? *North Dakota State Board v. Snyder's Store* (1973), supra, per Douglas, J., in overruling *Liggett Co. v. Baldridge* (1928) [Sec. 2, note 5 supra] to uphold a requirement that pharmacies be owned by pharmacists noted that "'a pronounced shift in emphasis since [*Liggett*]' had deprived the words 'unreasonable' and 'arbitrary' of the meaning which *Liggett* ascribed to them." Realistically, what appears to be the standard after *Duke Power?*

2. *Substance or style?* Does *Duke Power* portend a difference in the results of due process challenges to economic regulation, or does it reflect only a different pattern of opinion writing?

3. *Protection of "personal" rights.* The Court gives far stricter scrutiny and greater constitutional protection to some *personal* rights, often viewed as "fundamental," than to *economic* or *social welfare* interests. This development is considered primarily in Ch. 7, Sec. 2, and Ch. 10, Sec. 4.

4. *Equal protection.* The rise and fall of judicial protection of economic and social welfare interests under the equal protection clause is similar to that under due process, though equal protection issues involve somewhat different concerns and values. See Ch. 10, Sec. 1.

5. *Substantive due process under state constitutions.* Most state constitutions contain due process clauses identical or similar to that in the fourteenth amendment. Not all state courts, whose interpretations and applications of their own state constitutions are not ordinarily subject to Supreme Court review,[f] have followed the Court's lead in leaving economic policy decisions to the legislature. Several have continued to follow the Court's 1905–1934 approach, invalidating under state due process clauses economic legislation that the Supreme Court would have upheld.[g]

SECTION 4. "TAKING" OF PROPERTY INTERESTS

INTRODUCTION

The fifth amendment limits the federal government's power of eminent domain: "nor shall private property be taken for a public use without just compensation." Similarly the due process clause has long been held to require a state to compensate the owner when it takes property for a public use,[a] and to forbid taking property for a private use, even with compensation.[b] Space limits do not permit consideration of the extensive body of law relating to eminent domain. Two aspects only are considered here: (1) What are the limits, if any,

---

f. See Ch. 1, Sec. 5.

g. The cases to 1958 are found in Paulsen, *The Persistence of Substantive Due Process in the States,* 34 Minn.L.Rev. 91 (1950); Hetherington, *State Economic Regulation and Substantive Due Process of Law,* 53 Nw.U.L.Rev. 13, 226 (1958). A few such decisions continue. See e.g. *Gillette Dairy, Inc. v. Nebraska Dairy*

Products Bd., 192 Neb. 89, 219 N.W.2d 214 (1974) (milk price control).

a. See *Chicago, B. & Q.R.R. v. Chicago,* 166 U.S. 226, 241, 17 S.Ct. 581, 586, 41 L.Ed. 979, 986 (1897).

b. *Missouri Pac. Ry. v. Nebraska,* 164 U.S. 403, 17 S.Ct. 130, 41 L.Ed. 489 (1896).

on the purposes for which property may be taken, even with compensation? (2) Under what circumstances may, or should, a regulation be considered a "taking" that requires compensation?

I. PURPOSE OF "TAKING"

BERMAN v. PARKER, 348 U.S. 26, 75 S.Ct. 98, 99 L.Ed. 27 (1954), per DOUGLAS, J., unanimously upheld the District of Columbia Redevelopment Act, which authorized the Redevelopment Agency to acquire and assemble, by eminent domain or otherwise, real property "for the redevelopment of blighted territory (and) the prevention, reduction, or elimination of blighting factors." The Agency was empowered to transfer such property to public agencies for streets, utilities, recreational facilities and schools; and to lease or sell the remainder, preferably to a private redevelopment company, under terms that required the lessee or purchaser to conform to the redevelopment plan adopted by the National Capital Planning Commission. The Court found no fifth amendment violation in the Agency's taking by eminent domain a well-maintained department store posing no blight or health problem itself, located in a redevelopment area where roughly two-thirds of the dwellings were beyond repair or otherwise blighted:

"The power of Congress over the District of Columbia includes all the legislative powers which a state may exercise over its affairs. We deal, in other words, with what traditionally has been known as the police power. [Subject] to specific constitutional limitations, when the legislature has spoken, the public interest has been declared in terms well-nigh conclusive. In such cases the legislature, not the judiciary, is the main guardian of the public needs to be served by social legislation. [This] principle admits of no exception merely because the power of eminent domain is involved. The role of the judiciary in determining whether that power is being exercised for a public purpose is an extremely narrow one.

"Public safety, public health, morality, peace and quiet, law and order— these are some of the more conspicuous examples of the traditional application of the police power to municipal affairs. Yet they merely illustrate the scope of the power and do not delimit it. Miserable and disreputable housing conditions may do more than spread disease and crime and immorality. They may also suffocate the spirit * * *; make living an almost insufferable burden. They may [be] a blight on the community which robs it of charm, which makes it a place from which men turn. * * *

"We do not sit to determine whether a particular housing project is or is not desirable. The concept of the public welfare is broad and inclusive. The values it represents are spiritual as well as physical, aesthetic as well as monetary. It is within the power of the legislature to determine that the community should be beautiful as well as healthy, spacious as well as clean, well-balanced as well as carefully patrolled. In the present case, the Congress and its authorized agencies have made determinations that take into account a wide variety of values. It is not for us to reappraise them. If those who govern the District of Columbia decide that the Nation's Capital should be beautiful as well as sanitary, there is nothing in the Fifth Amendment that stands in the way.

"Once the object is within the authority of Congress, the right to realize it through the exercise of eminent domain is clear. For the power of eminent domain is merely the means to the end. [Here] one of the means chosen is the use of private enterprise for redevelopment of the area. Appellants argue that this makes the project a taking from one businessman for the benefit of another businessman. But the means of executing the project are for Congress and Congress alone to determine, once the public purpose has been established. [We] cannot say that public ownership is the sole method of promoting the public purposes of community redevelopment projects. * * *

"In the present case, Congress and its authorized agencies attack the problem of the blighted parts of the community on an area rather than on a structure-by-structure basis. [It] was not enough, they believed, to remove existing buildings that were insanitary or unsightly. It was important to redesign the whole area so as to eliminate the conditions that cause slums—the overcrowding of dwellings, the lack of parks, the lack of adequate streets and alleys, the absence of recreational areas, the lack of light and air, the presence of outmoded street patterns. [The] entire area needed redesigning so that a balanced, integrated plan could be developed for the region, including not only new homes but also schools, churches, parks, streets, and shopping centers. [Such] diversification in future use is plainly relevant to the maintenance of the desired housing standards and therefore within congressional power."

Notes and Questions

1. *Historical development.* For a study of the rise and fall of limitations on the exercise of the power of eminent domain see Note, *The Public Use Limitation on Eminent Domain: An Advance Requiem,* 58 Yale L.J. 599 (1949); Dunham, *Griggs v. Allegheny County in Perspective: Thirty Years of Supreme Court Expropriation Law,* 1962 Sup.Ct.Rev. 63, 65.

2. *"Taking" to lessen concentrated land ownership.* HAWAII HOUSING AUTHORITY v. MIDKIFF, 467 U.S. 229, 104 S.Ct. 2321, 81 L.Ed.2d 186 (1984), per O'CONNOR, J., upheld the use of eminent domain to lessen the concentration of fee simple land ownership, inherited from Hawaii's early feudal land tenure system. In the 1960's the Hawaii legislature found that 72 private owners owned 47% of Hawaiian land, and the state and federal government 49%, leaving only 4% for all other private owners. On Oahu, the most urbanized island, 22 landowners owned 72.5% of the fee simple titles. The legislature found, as summarized by the Court, that such concentrated land ownership was "responsible for skewing the State's residential fee simple market, inflating land prices, and injuring public tranquillity and welfare." The resulting Land Reform Act authorized "eligible tenants" from residential tracts of at least five acres to invoke the Hawaii Housing Authority's (HHA) power to acquire the fee owners "right, title and interest" at a "fair market value" set by negotiation between the lessee and the lessor or by condemnation trial, and then to sell that fee title interest to the tenant-lessee.[a]

[The] Court relied heavily on *Berman* from which it concluded, "The 'public use' requirement is thus coterminus with the scope of a sovereign's police powers. [Where] the exercise of the eminent domain power is rationally related to a conceivable public purpose, the Court has never held a compensated taking to be proscribed by the Public Use Clause.

a. In fn. 1 the opinion listed the requisites for an "eligible tenant" as one who "owns a house on the lot, has a bona fide intent to live on the lot or be a resident of the State, shows proof of ability to pay for a fee interest in it, and does not own residential land elsewhere nearby." The HHA was authorized to proceed under the Act only when 25 such eligible tenants from the tract, or those from half the lots in the tract, whichever is less, filed applications with HHA for the remedy provided by the Act.

[The] land oligopoly has, according to the Hawaii Legislature, created artificial deterrents to the normal functioning of the State's residential land market and forced thousands of individual homeowners to lease, rather than buy, the land underneath their homes. Regulating oligopoly and the evils associated with it is a classic exercise of a State's police powers. We cannot disapprove of Hawaii's exercise of this power.

"[When] the legislature's purpose is legitimate and its means are not irrational, our cases make clear that empirical debates over the wisdom of takings—no less than debates over the wisdom of other kinds of socioeconomic legislation—are not to be carried out in the federal courts. Redistribution of fees simple to correct deficiencies in the market determined by the state legislature to be attributable to land oligopoly is a rational exercise of the eminent domain power. Therefore, the Hawaii statute must pass the scrutiny of the Public Use Clause:" [b]

II. "TAKING" THROUGH REGULATION

PENN CENTRAL TRANSP. CO. v. NEW YORK CITY

438 U.S. 104, 98 S.Ct. 2646, 57 L.Ed.2d 631 (1978).

MR. JUSTICE BRENNAN delivered the opinion of the Court.

[Pursuant to New York City's Landmarks Preservation Law, the Preservation Commission designated Grand Central Terminal, owned by Penn Central, as a "landmark." [a] It denied Penn Central a certificate of "appropriateness" to construct a 55 story office building resting on the roof of the Terminal, cantilevered to preserve the existing Terminal facade. The Commission emphasized the harmful effect of the proposed construction on the dramatic view of the Terminal from Park Avenue South.[b] Choosing not to modify its proposal, or to use its right under New York laws to transfer its unused landmark site development rights to one or more of its eight nearby lots, Penn Central unsuccessfully challenged in the New York courts the constitutionality of this application of the Landmarks Law. The Court upheld the Law as applied.]

Over the past 50 years, all 50 States and over 500 municipalities have enacted laws to encourage or require the preservation of buildings and areas with historic or aesthetic importance.

[The issue is] whether the restrictions [upon] appellants' exploitation of the Terminal site effect a "taking" of appellants' property for a public use within the

b. Marshall, J., did not participate.

a. The Commission's report stated:

"Grand Central Station, one of the great buildings of America, evokes a spirit that is unique in this City. It combines distinguished architecture with a brilliant engineering solution, wedded to one of the most fabulous railroad terminals of our time. Monumental in scale, this great building functions as well today as it did when built. In style, it represents the best of the French Beaux Arts."

b. "[To] balance a 55-story office tower above a flamboyant Beaux-Arts facade seems nothing more than an aesthetic joke. Quite simply, the tower would overwhelm the Terminal by its sheer mass. The 'addition' would

be four times as high as the existing structure and would reduce the Landmark itself to the status of a curiosity.

"Landmarks cannot be divorced from their settings—particularly when the setting is a dramatic and integral part of the original concept. The Terminal, in its setting, is a great example of urban design. Such examples are not so plentiful in New York City that we can afford to lose any of the few we have. And we must preserve them in a meaningful way—with alterations and additions of such character, scale, materials and mass as will protect, enhance and perpetuate the original design rather than overwhelm it."

meaning of the Fifth Amendment, [made] applicable to the States through the Fourteenth.[25]

A. [W]hat constitutes a "taking" for purposes of the Fifth Amendment has proved to be a problem of considerable difficulty. While this Court has recognized that the "Fifth Amendment's guarantee [is] designed to bar Government from forcing some people alone to bear public burdens which, in all fairness and justice, should be borne by the public as a whole," *Armstrong v. United States,*[c] this Court, quite simply, has been unable to develop any "set formula" for determining when "justice and fairness" require that economic injuries caused by public action be compensated by the government, rather than remain disproportionately concentrated on a few persons. See *Goldblatt v. Hempstead,* 369 U.S. 590, 594, 82 S.Ct. 987, 8 L.Ed.2d 130 (1962). Indeed, we have frequently observed that whether a particular restriction will be rendered invalid by the government's failure to pay for any losses proximately caused by it depends largely "upon the particular circumstances [in that] case." *United States v. Central Eureka Mining Co.,* 357 U.S. 155, 168, 78 S.Ct. 1097, 2 L.Ed.2d 1228 (1958), see *United States v. Caltex, Inc.,* 344 U.S. 149, 156, 73 S.Ct. 200, 97 L.Ed. 157 (1952).

In engaging in these essentially ad hoc, factual inquiries, the Court's decisions have identified several factors that have particular significance. The economic impact of the regulation on the claimant and, particularly, the extent to which the regulation has interfered with distinct investment-backed expectations are, of course, relevant considerations. See *Goldblatt.* So, too, is the character of the governmental action. A "taking" may more readily be found when the interference with property can be characterized as a physical invasion by government, see, e.g., *United States v. Causby,* 328 U.S. 256, 66 S.Ct. 1062, 90 L.Ed. 1206 (1946), than when interference arises from some public program adjusting the benefits and burdens of economic life to promote the common good.

"Government hardly could go on if to some extent values incident to property could not be diminished without paying for every such change in the general law,"[d] *Pennsylvania Coal Co. v. Mahon,* 260 U.S. 393, 413, 43 S.Ct. 158, 67 L.Ed. 322 (1922), and this Court has accordingly recognized, in a wide variety of contexts, that government may execute laws or programs that adversely affect recognized economic values. * * *

[I]n instances in which a state tribunal reasonably concluded that "the health, safety, morals, or general welfare" would be promoted by prohibiting particular contemplated uses of land, this Court has upheld land-use regulations that destroyed or adversely affected recognized real property interests. See *Nectow v. Cambridge,* 277 U.S. 183, 188, 48 S.Ct. 447, 72 L.Ed. 842 (1928). Zoning laws are, of course, the classic example, see *Euclid v. Ambler Realty Co.,* 272 U.S. 365, 47 S.Ct. 114, 71 L.Ed. 303 (1926) (prohibition of industrial use); *Gorieb v. Fox,* 274 U.S. 603, 608, 47 S.Ct. 675, 71 L.Ed. 1228 (1927) (requirement

---

25. As is implicit in our opinion, we do not embrace the proposition that a "taking" can never occur unless government has transferred physical control over a portion of a parcel.

c. 364 U.S. 40, 49, 80 S.Ct. 1563, 4 L.Ed.2d 1554 (1960). *Armstrong* found a "taking" in the destruction of a materialman's lien when, on default of the builder, the government took possession of boats he was building for the United States.

d. When writing this sentence, Holmes, J., was probably tempted to refer to "the petty larceny of the police power," a phrase he had used about six weeks earlier in the original draft of his opinion in *Jackman v. Rosenbaum Co.,* 260 U.S. 22, 43 S.Ct. 9, 67 L.Ed. 107 (1922), but deleted at the urging of "my brethren, as usual and as I expected." See 1 *Holmes-Laski Letters* 456–57 (Howe ed. 1953).

that portions of parcels be left unbuilt); *Welch v. Swasey,* 214 U.S. 91, 29 S.Ct. 567, 53 L.Ed. 923 (1909) (height restriction), which have been viewed as permissible governmental action even when prohibiting the most beneficial use of the property. See *Goldblatt.*

Zoning laws generally do not affect existing uses of real property, but "taking" challenges have also been held to be without merit in a wide variety of situations when the challenged governmental actions prohibited a beneficial use to which individual parcels had previously been devoted and thus caused substantial individualized harm. *Miller v. Schoene,* 276 U.S. 272, 48 S.Ct. 246, 72 L.Ed. 568 (1928), is illustrative. In that case, a state entomologist, acting pursuant to a state statute, ordered the claimants to cut down a large number of ornamental red cedar trees because they produced cedar rust fatal to apple trees cultivated nearby. Although the statute provided for recovery of any expense incurred in removing the cedars, and permitted claimants to use the felled trees, it did not provide compensation for the value of the standing trees or for the resulting decrease in market value of the properties as a whole. A unanimous Court held that this latter omission did not render the statute invalid. The Court held that the State might properly make "a choice between the preservation of one class of property and that of the other" and since the apple industry was important in the State involved, concluded that the State had not exceeded "its constitutional powers by deciding upon the destruction of one class of property [without compensation] in order to save another which, in the judgment of the legislature, is of greater value to the public."

Again, *Hadacheck v. Sebastian,* 239 U.S. 394, 36 S.Ct. 143, 60 L.Ed. 348 (1915), upheld a law prohibiting the claimant from continuing his otherwise lawful business of operating a brickyard in a particular physical community on the ground that the legislature had reasonably concluded that the presence of the brickyard was inconsistent with neighboring uses. * * *

Goldblatt is a recent example. There, a 1958 city safety ordinance banned any excavations below the water table and effectively prohibited the claimant from continuing a sand and gravel mining business that had been operated on the particular parcel since 1927. The Court upheld the ordinance against a "taking" challenge, although the ordinance prohibited the present and presumably most beneficial use of the property and had, like the regulations in *Miller* and *Hadacheck,* severely affected a particular owner. The Court assumed that the ordinance did not prevent the owner's reasonable use of the property since the owner made no showing of an adverse effect on the value of the land. Because the restriction served a substantial public purpose, the Court thus held no taking had occurred. It is, of course, implicit in *Goldblatt* that a use restriction on real property may constitute a "taking" if not reasonably necessary to the effectuation of a substantial public purpose, see *Nectow;* or perhaps if it has an unduly harsh impact upon the owner's use of the property.

Pennsylvania Coal is the leading case for the proposition that a state statute that substantially furthers important public policies may so frustrate distinct investment-backed expectations as to amount to a "taking." There the claimant had sold the surface rights to particular parcels of property, but expressly reserved the right to remove the coal thereunder. A Pennsylvania statute, enacted after the transactions, forbade any mining of coal that caused the subsidence of any house, unless the house was the property of the owner of the underlying coal and was more than 150 feet from the improved property of another. Because the statute made it commercially impracticable to mine the coal, and thus had nearly the same effect as the complete destruction of rights claimant had reserved from the owners of the surface land, the Court held that the statute was invalid as effecting a "taking" without just compensation. See also *Armstrong*. (Government's complete destruction of a materialman's lien in certain property held a "taking"). [See] generally Michelman, *Property, Utility, and Fairness: Comments on the Ethical Foundations of "Just Compensation" Law,* 80 Harv.L.Rev. 1165, 1229–1234 (1967).

Finally, government actions that may be characterized as acquisitions of resources to permit or facilitate uniquely public functions have often been held to constitute "takings." *Causby* is illustrative. In holding that direct overflights above the claimant's land, that destroyed the present use of the land as a chicken farm, constituted a "taking," *Causby* emphasized that Government had not "merely destroyed property [but was] using a part of it for the flight of its planes." See also *Griggs v. Allegheny County,* 369 U.S. 84, 82 S.Ct. 531, 7 L.Ed. 2d 585 (1962) (overflights held a taking); *United States v. Cress,* 243 U.S. 316, 37 S.Ct. 380, 61 L.Ed. 746 (1917) (repeated floodings of land caused by water project is taking). See generally Michelman, supra, at 1226–29; Sax, *Takings and the Police Power,* 74 Yale L.J. 36 (1964).

B. [A]ppellants do not contest that New York City's objective of preserving structures and areas with special historic, architectural, or cultural significance is an entirely permissible governmental goal. [They] do not challenge any of the specific factual premises of the decision below. They accept for present purposes both that the parcel of land occupied by Grand Central Terminal must, in its present state, be regarded as capable of earning a reasonable return, and that the transferable development rights afforded appellants by virtue of the Terminal's designation as a landmark are valuable, even if not as valuable as the rights to construct above the Terminal. In appellants' view none of these factors derogate from their claim that New York City's law has effected a "taking."

[First, they] urge that the Landmarks Law has deprived them of any gainful use of their "air rights" above the Terminal, [entitling] them to "just compensation" measured by the fair market value of these air rights.

[T]he submission that appellants may establish a "taking" simply by showing that they have been denied the ability to exploit a property interest that they heretofore had believed was available for development is quite simply untenable. Were this the rule, this Court would have erred not only in upholding laws restricting the development of air rights, see *Welch,* but also in approving those prohibiting both the subjacent, see *Goldblatt,* and the lateral, see *Gorieb,* development of particular parcels. "Taking" jurisprudence does not divide a single parcel into discrete segments and attempt to determine whether rights in a particular segment have been entirely abrogated. In deciding whether a particular governmental action has effected a taking, this Court focuses rather both on the character of the action and on the nature and extent of the interference with rights in the parcel as a whole—here, the city tax block designated as the "landmark site."

Secondly, appellants [argue that the New York law] effects a "taking" because its operation has significantly diminished the value of the Terminal site. Appellants concede that the decisions sustaining other land use-regulations, which, like the New York City law, are reasonably related to the promotion of the general welfare, uniformly reject the proposition that diminution in property value, standing alone, can establish a "taking," see *Euclid* (75% diminution in value caused by zoning law); *Hadacheck* (87½% diminution in value). [But] appellants argue that New York City's regulation of individual landmarks is fundamentally different from zoning or from historic-district legislation because the controls imposed by New York City's law apply only to individuals who own selected properties.

Stated baldly, appellants' position appears to be that the only means of ensuring that selected owners are not singled out to endure financial hardship for no reason is to hold that any restriction imposed on individual landmarks pursuant to the New York City scheme is a "taking" requiring the payment of "just compensation." Agreement with this argument would, of course, invalidate not just New York City's law, but all comparable landmark legislation in the Nation. We find no merit in it.

It is true [that] both historic-district legislation and zoning laws regulate all properties within given physical communities whereas landmark laws apply only to selected parcels. But, contrary to appellants' suggestions, landmark laws are not like discriminatory, or "reverse spot," zoning: that is, a land-use decision which arbitrarily singles out a particular parcel for different, less favorable treatment than the neighboring ones. See 2 Rathkopf, *The Law of Zoning and Planning* 26–4 and 26–4–26–5, n. 6 (4th ed. 1978). In contrast to discriminatory zoning, which is the antithesis of land-use control as part of some comprehensive plan, the New York City law embodies a comprehensive plan to preserve structures of historic or aesthetic interest wherever they might be found in the city, and as noted, over 400 landmarks and 31 historic districts have been designated pursuant to this plan. * * *

Next, appellants observe that New York City's law differs from zoning laws and historic-district ordinances in that the Landmarks Law does not impose identical or similar restrictions on all structures located in particular physical communities. It follows, they argue, that New York City's law is inherently incapable of producing the fair and equitable distribution of benefits and burdens of governmental action which is characteristic of zoning laws and historic-district legislation and which they maintain is a constitutional requirement if "just compensation" is not to be afforded. It is, of course, true that the Landmarks Law has a more severe impact on some landowners than on others, but that in itself does not mean that the law effects a "taking." Legislation designed to promote the general welfare commonly burdens some more than others. The owners of the brickyard in *Hadacheck,* of the cedar trees in *Miller,* and of the gravel and sand mine in *Goldblatt,* were uniquely burdened by the legislation sustained in those cases.[30] Similarly, zoning laws often affect some property owners more severely than others but have not been held to be invalid on that account. * * *

[T]he New York City law applies to vast numbers of structures in the city in addition to the Terminal—all the structures contained in the 31 historic districts and over 400 individual landmarks, many of which are close to the Terminal.

---

30. Appellants attempt to distinguish these cases on the ground that, in each, government was prohibiting a "noxious" use of land and that in the present case, in contrast, appellants' proposed construction above the Terminal would be beneficial. We observe that the uses in issue in *Hadacheck, Miller,* and *Goldblatt* were perfectly lawful in themselves. They involve no "blameworthiness, [moral] wrongdoing or conscious act of dangerous risk-taking which induce[d society] to shift the cost to a pa[rt]icular individual." Sax, *Takings and the Police Power,* 74 Yale L.J. 36, 50 (1964). These cases are better understood as resting not on any supposed "noxious" quality of the prohibited uses but rather on the ground that the restrictions were reasonably related to the implementation of a policy—not unlike historic preservation—expected to produce a widespread public benefit and applicable to all similarly situated property.

Unless we are to reject the judgment of the New York City Council that the preservation of landmarks benefits all New York citizens and all structures, both economically and by improving the quality of life in the city as a whole—which we are unwilling to do—we cannot conclude that the owners of the Terminal have in no sense been benefited by the Landmarks Law. Doubtless appellants believe they are more burdened than benefited by the law, but that must have been true, too, of the property owners in *Miller, Hadacheck, Euclid,* and *Goldblatt.* * * *

C. [A]ll we thus far have established is that the [law] is not rendered invalid by its failure to provide "just compensation" whenever a landmark owner is restricted in the exploitation of property interests, such as air rights, to a greater extent than provided for under applicable zoning laws. We now must consider whether the interference with appellants' property is of such a magnitude that "there must be an exercise of eminent domain and compensation to sustain [it]." *Pennsylvania Coal.* That inquiry may be narrowed to the question of the severity of the impact of the law on appellants' parcel, and its resolution in turn requires a careful assessment of the impact of the regulation on the Terminal site.

Unlike the governmental acts in *Goldblatt, Miller, Causby, Griggs,* and *Hadacheck,* the [law] does not interfere in any way with the present uses of the Terminal. Its designation as a landmark not only permits but contemplates that appellants may continue to use the property precisely as it has been used for the past 65 years: as a railroad terminal containing office space and concessions. So the law does not interfere with what must be regarded as Penn Central's primary expectation concerning the use of the parcel. More importantly, on this record, we must regard the [law] as permitting Penn Central not only to profit from the Terminal but also to obtain a "reasonable return" on its investment.

Appellants, moreover, exaggerate the effect of the law on their ability to make use of the air rights above the Terminal in two respects. First, it simply cannot be maintained, on this record, that appellants have been prohibited from occupying *any* portion of the airspace above the Terminal. While the Commission's actions in denying applications to construct an office building in excess of 50 stories above the Terminal may indicate that it will refuse to issue a certificate of appropriateness for any comparably sized structure, nothing the Commission has said or done suggests an intention to prohibit *any* construction above the Terminal. The Commission's report emphasized that whether any construction would be allowed depended upon whether the proposed addition "would harmonize in scale, material and character with [the Terminal]." Since appellants have not sought approval for the construction of a smaller structure, we do not know that appellants will be denied any use of any portion of the airspace above the Terminal.[34] * * *

On this record we conclude that the application of New York City's [law] has not effected a "taking" of appellants' property. The restrictions imposed are substantially related to the promotion of the general welfare and not only permit reasonable beneficial use of the landmark site but afford appellants opportunities further to enhance not only the Terminal site proper but also other properties.[36] * * *

---

34. Counsel for appellants admitted at oral argument that the Commission has not suggested that it would not, for example, approve a 20-story office tower along the lines of that which was part of the original plan for the Terminal.

36. We emphasize that our holding today is on the present record which in turn is based

MR. JUSTICE REHNQUIST, with whom The Chief Justice and Mr. Justice Stevens join, dissenting.

[The] question in this case is whether the cost associated with the city of New York's desire to preserve a limited number of "landmarks" within its borders must be borne by all of its taxpayers or whether it can instead be imposed entirely on the owners of the individual properties. * * *

Appellees have thus destroyed—in a literal sense, "taken"—substantial property rights of Penn Central. [Because] "not every destruction or injury to property by governmental action has been held to be a 'taking' in the constitutional sense," however, this does not end our inquiry. But an examination of the two exceptions where the destruction of property does *not* constitute a taking demonstrates that a compensable taking has occurred here.

1. As early as 1887, the Court recognized that the government can prevent a property owner from using his property to injure others without having to compensate the owner for the value of the forbidden use. [Thus], there is no "taking" where a city prohibits the operation of a brickyard within a residential city, see *Hadacheck,* or forbids excavation for sand and gravel below the water line, see *Goldblatt.* Nor is it relevant, where the government is merely prohibiting a noxious use of property, that the government would seem to be singling out a particular property owner. *Hadacheck.*[8] * * * Appellees are not prohibiting a nuisance. [Instead], Penn Central is prevented from further developing its property basically because *too good* a job was done in designing and building [it].

2. Even where the government prohibits a noninjurious use, the Court has ruled that a taking does not take place if the prohibition applies over a broad cross section of land and thereby "secure[s] an average reciprocity of advantage." *Pennsylvania Coal.* It is for this reason that zoning does not constitute a "taking." While zoning at times reduces *individual* property values, the burden is shared relatively evenly and it is reasonable to conclude that on the whole an individual who is harmed by one aspect of the zoning will be benefited by another.

Here, however, a multimillion dollar loss has been imposed on appellants; it is uniquely felt and is not offset by any benefits flowing from the preservation of some 400 other "landmarks" in New York City. Appellees have imposed a substantial cost on less than one one-tenth of one percent of the buildings in New York City for the general benefit of all its people. It is exactly this imposition of general costs on a few individuals at which the "taking" protection is [directed.] *Armstrong.*

As Mr. Justice Holmes pointed out in *Pennsylvania Coal,* "the question at bottom" in an eminent domain case "is upon whom the loss of the changes desired should fall." The benefits that appellees believe will flow from preservation of the Grand Central Terminal will accrue to all the citizens of New York City. There is no reason to believe that appellants will enjoy a substantially greater share of these benefits. If the cost of preserving Grand Central Terminal were spread evenly across the entire population of the city of New York, the

on Penn Central's present ability to use the Terminal for its intended purposes and in a gainful fashion. The city conceded at oral argument that if appellants can demonstrate at some point in the future that circumstances have changed such that the Terminal ceases to be, in the city's counsel's words, "economically viable," appellants may obtain relief.

8. Each of the cases cited by the Court for the proposition that legislation which severely affects some landowners but not others does not effect a "taking" involved noxious uses of property. See *Hadacheck; Miller; Goldblatt.*

burden per person would be in cents per year—a minor cost appellees would surely concede for the benefit accrued. Instead, however, appellees would impose the entire cost of several million dollars per year on Penn Central. But it is precisely this sort of discrimination that the Fifth Amendment prohibits.

Appellees in response would argue that a taking only occurs where a property owner is denied *all* reasonable value of his property. The Court has frequently held that, even where a destruction of property rights would not *otherwise* constitute a taking, the inability of the owner to make a reasonable return on his property requires compensation under the Fifth Amendment. But the converse is not true. A taking does not become a noncompensable exercise of police power simply because the government in its grace allows the owner to make some "reasonable" use of his property. "[I]t is the character of the invasion, not the amount of damage resulting from it, so long as the damage is substantial, that determines the question whether it is a taking." *Cress,*[e] 243 U.S. 316, 328, 37 S.Ct. 380, 61 L.Ed. 746 (1917). *Causby.*[f] * * *[g]

Notes and Questions

1. *The "character of the governmental action."* Penn Central recognizes that uncompensated banning of noxious or harmful uses of property, or uncompensated land use zoning that secures an "average reciprocal advantage to all affected land," are not "takings," while government actions that amount to appropriation of private property for "uniquely public functions" or "strictly governmental purposes" are "takings." Absent such "clear cases," does "the character of the governmental action" appear from *Penn Central* to have any relevance to "taking" issues other than its bearing on whether the challenged action advances a "permissible governmental goal"?

2. *Balancing judgments?* (a) Earlier decisions led thoughtful commentators to conclude that in determining whether a regulation constituted a "taking" the "extent of the diminution of the owner's rights must be weighed against the importance of that diminution to the public,"[a] and that "[c]ourts have never been able to develop [a] standard more meaningful than balancing the public need against the private cost."[b] For a helpful critique of such a balancing

---

e. Compensation required for damage to property when a federal dam raised water level in tributary stream, causing frequent overflows in one case and loss of water power for mill in the other.

f. The dissenters doubted that the transfer development rights available to Penn Central constituted "just compensation" within the "strict meaning" of the fifth amendment, but would have remanded that issue to the Court of Appeals for determination. At that point the dissent suggested in its fn. 14 other ways to preserve landmarks: "The Court suggests that if appellees are held to have 'taken' property rights of landmark owners, not only the New York City Landmarks Preservation Law, but 'all comparable landmark legislation in the Nation,' must fall. [This] ignores the fact that many States and cities in the Nation have chosen to preserve landmarks by purchasing or condemning restrictive easements over the facades of the landmarks and

are apparently quite satisfied with the results. The British National Trust has effectively used restrictive easements to preserve landmarks since 1937. Other States and cities have found that tax incentives are also an effective means of encouraging the private preservation of landmark sites."

g. On the "taking" issue, see generally—in addition to articles cited in *Penn Central*— Kratovil & Harrison, *Eminent Domain—Policy and Concept,* 42 Calif.L.Rev. 596 (1954); Dunham, *Griggs v. Allegheny County in Perspective: Thirty Years of Supreme Court Expropriation Law,* 1962 Sup.Ct.Rev. 63; Sax, *Takings, Private Property and Public Right,* 81 Yale L.J. 149 (1971); Note, *Zoning,* 91 Harv.L. Rev. 1427, 1462–86 (1978); 92 Harv.L.Rev. 222–32 (1977).

a. Kratovil & Harrison, fn. g supra, at 609.

b. Dunham, fn. g supra, at 76.

approach, see Michelman, *Property, Utility, Fairness,* 80 Harv.L.Rev. at 1193–96, 1234–35.

(b) Is such balancing consistent with *Penn Central?* Did *Penn Central* "demonstrat[e] a method by which competing social and individual interests might be weighed"? Did it "balance public necessity and legitimacy of the regulation against the degree of physical invasion and economic harm"? See Note, 11 Conn.L.Rev. 273, 290 (1979). Or did *Penn Central* reflect "a belief that given the validity of the governmental interest asserted, the nature of the interest plays no further role in determining whether a taking has occurred," and that "[a]ny nondiscriminatory enactment reasonably related to a goal within the police power will be subjected only to a test of economic impact"? See 92 Harv.L.Rev. at 229.

(c) What *ought* the standard to be? *Should* the extent of economic harm that can be imposed without compensation depend on the degree of importance of an admittedly valid governmental interest?

3. *Economic impact on claimant.* What factors appear relevant to deciding whether the "economic impact of the regulation on the claimant" suffices to support a judgment of "taking?" Does *Penn Central* mean that, absent the "clear cases" stated in note 1, an economic impact will not suffice if the regulation permits continuation of the property's pre-regulation uses and a "reasonable return" on the investment? What kinds of problems are likely to arise from basing such decisions on factors like "reasonable return on investment, "investment-backed expectations," and "primary expectation concerning use?" Cf. 92 Harv.L.Rev. at 231.

4. *Permanent physical occupation.* LORETTO v. TELEPROMPTER MANHATTAN CATV CORP., 458 U.S. 419, 102 S.Ct. 3164, 73 L.Ed.2d 868 (1982), per MARSHALL, J., found a "taking" in a New York law that, as applied, authorized cable TV installations for tenants of privately-owned apartment houses. The cables, permanently attached to the roofs and outside walls by bolts, screws and other means, were subject to a one-time $1 payment to the landlord:

"[We] have long considered a physical intrusion by government to be a property restriction of an unusually serious character for purposes of the Takings Clause. Our cases further establish that when the physical intrusion reaches the extreme form of a permanent physical occupation, a taking has occurred. In such a case, 'the character of the government action' not only is an important factor in resolving whether the action works a taking but is determinative.

"When faced with a constitutional challenge to a permanent physical occupation of real property, this Court has invariably found a taking.[5] * * *

"To the extent that the government permanently occupies physical property it effectively destroys" the rights to possess, use and dispose of it. 'The owner has no right to possess the occupied space himself [or] to exclude the occupier.'

---

5. Professor Michelman has accurately summarized the case [law]: "[The] modern significance of physical occupation is that courts, while they sometimes do hold non-trespassory injuries compensable, *never* deny compensation for a physical takeover. The one incontestable case for compensation (short of formal expropriation) seems to occur when the government [or] the public at large, 'regu-larly' use, or 'permanently' occupy, space or a thing [theretofore] under private ownership." Michelman, *Property, Utility, and Fairness: Comments on the Ethical Foundations of "Just Compensation" Law,* 80 Harv.L.Rev. 1165, 1184 (1967) (emphasis original). See also 2 Sackman, *Nichols' Law of Eminent Domain* 6–50—6–51 (rev. 3d ed. 1980); Tribe, *American Constitutional Law* 460 (1978).

It 'denies the owner any power to control the use of the property [or] to dispose of [it] by sale, [since] the purchaser will be unable to make any use of' it.

"Our holding today is very narrow. We affirm the traditional rule that a permanent physical occupation of property is a taking. In such a case, the property owner entertains an historically-rooted expectation of compensation, and the character of the invasion is qualitatively more intrusive than perhaps any other category of property regulation. We do not, however, question the equally substantial authority upholding a State's broad power to impose appropriate restrictions upon an owner's *use* of his property."

BLACKMUN, J., joined by Brennan and White, JJ., dissented: "In a curiously anachronistic decision, the Court today acknowledges its historical disavowal of set formulae in almost the same breath as it constructs a rigid *per se* takings rule. * * *

"The Court's recent Takings Clause decisions teach that *nonphysical* government intrusions on private property, such as zoning ordinances and other land-use restrictions, have become the rule rather than the exception. Modern government regulation exudes intangible 'externalities' that may diminish the value of private property far more than minor physical touchings. * * *

"Precisely because the extent to which the government may injure private interests now depends so little on whether or not it has authorized a 'physical contact,' the Court has avoided per se takings rules resting on outmoded distinctions between physical and nonphysical intrusions. As one commentator has observed, a takings rule based on such a distinction is inherently suspect because 'its capacity to distinguish, even crudely, between significant and insignificant losses is too puny to be taken seriously.' Michelman.

"In sum, history, teaches that takings claims are properly evaluated under a multifactor balancing test. By directing that all 'permanent physical occupations' automatically are compensable, 'without regard to whether the action achieves an important public benefit or has only minimal economic impact on the owner,' the Court does not further equity so much as it encourages litigants to manipulate their factual allegations to gain the benefit of its per se rule. I do not relish the prospect of distinguishing the inevitable flow of certiorari petitions attempting to shoehorn insubstantial takings claims into today's 'set formula.' "

SECTION 5. CONTRACT CLAUSE

ALLIED STRUCTURAL STEEL CO. v. SPANNAUS
438 U.S. 234, 98 S.Ct. 2716, 57 L.Ed.2d 727 (1978).

MR. JUSTICE STEWART delivered the opinion of the Court.

[In 1963, Allied adopted an employer-funded pension plan that provided monthly pensions based on earnings and length of employment. Under the plan, rights to the pension vested, regardless of later termination of employment, when an employee worked to age 65, or worked for 15 years to age 60 or for 20 years to age 55. Those who quit or were terminated before the pension vested acquired no rights. Allied made yearly contributions to the pension trust fund based on actuarial predictions. It retained the right to terminate the plan at any time for any reason, subject to use of the fund's assets to meet its obligations under vested pensions in a specified order of priorities. Pension benefits were payable only from fund assets. Allied informed its employees that the plan implied no assurance against dismissal from employment at any time.

[A 1974 Minnesota Act required Minnesota employers with an employee pension plan, who terminated the plan or went out of business in Minnesota, to provide full pensions for all Minnesota employees who had worked for 10 years, and, if the pension fund was insufficient, to pay a "pension funding charge" in an amount that would purchase deferred annuities that would make up the deficiency. In July 1974, as the first step in closing its 30-employee Minnesota activity, Allied, based in Illinois, terminated 11 Minnesota employees, 9 of whom had worked for Allied more than 10 years but not long enough to acquire vested pension rights under the plan. Under the Minnesota Act, Allied's "pension funding charge" was $185,000. The Court held 5 to 3 that this application of the Act violated the contract clause.]

The Act substantially altered [the company's contractual relationships with its employees] by superimposing pension obligations upon the company conspicuously beyond those that it had voluntarily agreed to undertake. But it does not inexorably follow that the Act, as applied to the company, violates the Contract Clause. * * *

Although it was perhaps the strongest single constitutional check on state legislation during our early years as a Nation, the Contract Clause receded into comparative desuetude [with] the development of the large body of jurisprudence under the Due Process Clause.[12] Nonetheless, the Contract Clause remains part of the Constitution. It is not a dead [letter.]

First of all, [the] Contract Clause does not operate to obliterate the police power of the States. "[It] does not prevent the State from exercising such powers as are vested in it for the promotion of the common weal, or are necessary for the general good of the public, though contracts previously entered into between individuals may thereby be affected. This power, which in its various ramifications is known as the police power, is an exercise of the sovereign right of the Government to protect the lives, health, morals, comfort and general welfare of the people, and is paramount to any rights under contracts between individuals." *Manigault v. Springs,* 199 U.S. 473, 480, 26 S.Ct. 127, 50 L.Ed. 274.[a] As Mr. Justice Holmes succinctly put the matter [in] *Hudson Water Co. v. McCarter,* 209 U.S. 349, 357, 28 S.Ct. 529, 52 L.Ed. 828: "One whose rights, such as they are, are subject to state restriction, cannot remove them from the power of the State by making a contract about them. The contract will carry with it the infirmity of the subject matter."

If the Contract Clause is to retain any meaning at all, however, it must be understood to impose *some* limits upon the power of a State to abridge existing contractual relationships, even in the exercise of its otherwise legitimate police power. The existence and nature of those limits were clearly indicated in a series of cases in this Court arising from the efforts of the States to deal with the unprecedented emergencies brought on by the severe economic depression of the early 1930's.

---

12. Indeed, at least one commentator has suggested that "the results might be the same if the contract clause were dropped out of the Constitution, and the challenged statutes all judged as reasonable or unreasonable deprivations of property." Hale, *The Supreme Court and the Contract Clause,* 57 Harv.L.Rev. 852, 890–91 (1944).

a. *Manigault* held the contract clause did not bar legislation that authorized a riparian owner to dam a creek to facilitate reclamation of lowlands, in violation of his contract with another riparian owner. Cf. *Union Dry Goods Co. v. Georgia Pub. Service Corp.,* 248 U.S. 372, 39 S.Ct. 117, 63 L.Ed. 309 (1919) (contract clause not violated by statute authorizing utility to charge rates fixed by commission higher than pre-existing contract rate).

In *Home Building & Loan Assn. v. Blaisdell,* 290 U.S. 398, 54 S.Ct. 231, 78 L.Ed. 413 (1934), the Court upheld [a] mortgage moratorium law that Minnesota had enacted to provide relief for homeowners threatened with foreclosure. Although the legislation conflicted directly with lenders' contractual foreclosure rights, the Court there acknowledged that, despite the Contract Clause, the States retain residual authority to enact laws "to safeguard the vital interests of [their] people." In upholding the state mortgage moratorium law, the Court found five factors significant. First, the state legislature had declared in the Act itself that an emergency need for the protection of homeowners existed. Second, the state law was enacted to protect a basic societal interest, not a favored group. Third, the relief was appropriately tailored to the emergency that it was designed to meet. Fourth, the imposed conditions were reasonable.[b] And, finally, the legislation was limited to the duration of the emergency.

The *Blaisdell* opinion thus clearly implied that if the Minnesota moratorium legislation had not possessed the characteristics attributed to it by the Court, it would have been invalid under the Contract Clause of the Constitution. These implications were given concrete force in [cases] that followed closely in *Blaisdell's* wake.[c] * * *

The most recent Contract Clause case in this Court was *United States Trust Co. v. New Jersey.*[d] In that case the Court again recognized that although the absolute language of the Clause must leave room for "the 'essential attributes of sovereign power,' necessarily reserved by the States to safeguard the welfare of their citizens," that power has limits when its exercise effects substantial modifications of private contracts. Despite the customary deference courts give to state laws directed to social and economic problems, "[l]egislation adjusting the rights and responsibilities of contracting parties must be upon reasonable conditions and of a character appropriate to the public purpose justifying its adoption." Evaluating with particular scrutiny a modification of a contract to which the State itself was a party, the Court in that case held that legislative alteration of the rights and remedies of Port Authority bondholders violated the Contract Clause because the legislation was neither necessary nor reasonable.

In applying these principles to the present case, the first inquiry must be whether the state law has, in fact, operated as a substantial impairment of a contractual relationship.[16] The severity of the impairment measures the height of the hurdle the state legislation must clear. Minimal alteration of contractual obligations may end the inquiry at its first stage. Severe impairment, on the

---

b. *Blaisdell* stressed that the law did not impair the mortgage indebtedness, that the ultimate right to foreclosure and a deficiency judgment remained, that interest continued to accrue, and that the mortgagor must pay the rental value to be applied to taxes, insurance, and interest.

c. The Court briefly stated the rulings in three cases of contract clause violations: *W.B. Worthen v. Thomas,* 292 U.S. 426, 54 S.Ct. 816, 78 L.Ed. 1344 (1934); *W.B. Worthen v. Kavanaugh,* 295 U.S. 56, 55 S.Ct. 555, 79 L.Ed. 1298 (1935); *Treigie v. Acme Homestead Assn.,* 297 U.S. 189, 56 S.Ct. 408, 80 L.Ed. 575 (1936).

d. 431 U.S. 1, 97 S.Ct. 1505, 52 L.Ed.2d 92 (1977).

16. [The] narrow view that the Clause forbids only state laws that diminish the duties

of a contractual obligor and not laws that increase them, a view arguably suggested by *Satterlee v. Matthewson,* 2 Pet. 380, 7 L.Ed. 458, has since been expressly repudiated. *Detroit United Ry. v. Michigan,* 242 U.S. 238, 37 S.Ct. 87, 61 L.Ed. 268; *Georgia Ry. & Power Co. v. Decatur,* 262 U.S. 432, 43 S.Ct. 613, 67 L.Ed. 1065. Moreover, in any bilateral contract the diminution of duties on one side effectively increases the duties on the other.

The even narrower view that the Clause is limited in its application to state laws relieving debtors of obligations to their creditors is, as the dissent recognizes, completely at odds with this Court's decisions. See generally Hale, 57 Harv.L.Rev. 512, 514–16 (1944).

other hand, will push the inquiry to a careful examination of the nature and purpose of the state legislation.

The severity of an impairment of contractual obligations can be measured by the factors that reflect the high value the Framers placed on the protection of private contracts. Contracts enable individuals to order their personal and business affairs according to their particular needs and interests. Once arranged, those rights and obligations are binding under the law, and the parties are entitled to rely on them.

Here, the company's contracts of employment with its employees included as a fringe benefit or additional form of compensation, the pension plan. The company's maximum obligation was to set aside each year an amount based on the plan's requirements for vesting. The plan satisfied the current federal income tax code and was subject to no other legislative requirements. [The] company [had] no reason to anticipate that its employees' pension rights could become vested except in accordance with the terms of the plan. It relied heavily, and reasonably, on this legitimate contractual expectation in calculating its annual contributions to the pension fund.

The effect of Minnesota's [Act] on this contractual obligation was severe. The company was required in 1974 to have made its contributions throughout the pre-1974 life of its plan as if employees' pension rights had vested after 10 years, instead of vesting in accord with the terms of the plan. Thus a basic term of the pension contract—one on which the company had relied for 10 years—was substantially modified. The result was that although the company's past contributions were adequate when made, they were not adequate when computed under the 10-year statutory vesting requirement. The Act thus forced a current recalculation of the past 10 years' contributions based on the new, unanticipated 10-year vesting requirement.

Not only did the state law thus retroactively modify the compensation that the company had agreed to pay its employees from 1963 to 1974, but it did so by changing the company's obligations in an area where the element of reliance was vital—the funding of a pension plan.[18] * * *

[The company was] forced to make all the retroactive changes in its contractual obligations at one time. By simply proceeding to close its office in Minnesota, a move that had been planned before the passage of the Act, the company was assessed an immediate pension funding charge of approximately $185,000.

Thus, the [statute] nullifies express terms of the company's contractual obligations and imposes a completely unexpected liability in potentially disabling amounts. [Yet] there is no showing in the record before us that this severe disruption of contractual expectations was necessary to meet an important general social problem. The presumption favoring "legislative judgment as to the necessity and reasonableness of a particular measure," *United States Trust Co.*, simply cannot stand in this case.

[Whether] or not the legislation was aimed largely at a single employer, [which closed one of its Minnesota plants and attempted to terminate its pension plan][20] it clearly has an extremely narrow focus. It applies only to private

18. In some situations the element of reliance may cut both ways. Here, the company had relied upon the funding obligation of the pension plan for more than a decade. There was no showing of reliance to the contrary by its employees. Indeed, Minnesota did not act to protect any employee reliance interest demonstrated on the record. Instead, it compelled the employer to exceed bargained-for expectations and nullified an express term of the pension plan.

20. In *Malone v. White Motor Corp.*, 435 U.S. at 501 n. 5, 98 S.Ct. 1185, 55 L.Ed.2d 443,

employers [who] have established voluntary private pension plans, [and] only when such an employer closes his Minnesota office or terminates his pension plan. Thus, this law can hardly be characterized, like the law at issue in the *Blaisdell* case, as one enacted to protect a broad societal interest rather than a narrow class.[22]

[This] legislation, imposing a sudden, totally unanticipated, and substantial retroactive obligation upon the company to its employees, was not enacted to deal with a situation remotely approaching the broad and desperate emergency economic conditions of the early 1930's—conditions of which the Court in *Blaisdell* took judicial notice.[24] * * *

This Minnesota law simply does not possess the attributes of those state laws that in the past have survived challenge under the Contract Clause of the Constitution. The law was not even purportedly enacted to deal with a broad, generalized economic or social problem. Cf. *Blaisdell*. It did not operate in an area already subject to state regulation at the time the company's contractual obligations were originally undertaken, but invaded an area never before subject to regulation by the State. It did not effect simply a temporary alteration of the contractual relationships of those within its coverage, but worked a severe, permanent, and immediate change in those relationships—irrevocably and retroactively. And its narrow aim was leveled, not at every Minnesota employer, not even at every Minnesota employer who left the State, but only at those who had in the past been sufficiently enlightened as voluntarily to agree to establish pension plans for their employees. * * *

MR. JUSTICE BRENNAN, with whom Mr. Justice White and Mr. Justice Marshall join, dissenting.[e] * * *

[The Minnesota Act] does not abrogate or dilute any obligation due a party to a private contract; rather, like all positive social legislation, the Act imposes new, additional obligations on a particular class of persons. In my view, any constitutional infirmity in the law must therefore derive, not from the Contract Clause, but from the Due Process Clause of the Fourteenth Amendment.

[The Act was] designed to remedy a serious social problem arising from the operation of private pension plans. [Not] only would employers often neglect to furnish their employees with adequate information concerning their rights under the plans, leading to erroneous expectations, but because employers often failed to make contributions to the pension funds large enough adequately to fund their plans, employees often ultimately received only a small amount of those benefits they reasonably anticipated. [Denial] of all pension benefits not because of job related failings but only because the employees are unfortunate

the Court noted that the White Motor Corp., an employer of more than 1,000 Minnesota employees, had been prohibited from terminating its pension plan until the expiration date of its collective-bargaining agreement, May 1, 1974. On April 9, 1974, the Minnesota Act was passed, to become effective the following day. When White Motor proceeded to terminate its collectively bargained pension plan at the earliest possible date, May 1, 1974, the State assessed a deficiency of more than $19 million, based upon the Act's 10-year vesting requirement. [*Malone* decided only that the Minnesota Act was not preempted by federal legislation until 1975. It left the contract clause issue to the District Court.]

22. In upholding the constitutionality of the Act, the District Court referred to Minnesota's interest in protecting the economic welfare of its older citizens, as well as their surrounding economic communities.

24. This is not to suggest that only an emergency of great magnitude can constitutionally justify a state law impairing the obligations of contracts. See, e.g., *Veix v. Sixth Ward Building & Loan Assn.*, 310 U.S. at 39–40, 60 S.Ct. 792, 84 L.Ed. 1061; *East New York Savings Bank v. Hahn*, 326 U.S. 230, 66 S.Ct. 69, 90 L.Ed. 34; *El Paso v. Simmons*.

e. Blackmun, J., did not participate.

enough to be employed at a plant that closes for purely economic reasons is harsh indeed. [The] closing of a plant is a contingency outside the range of normal expectations of both the employer and the employee. [Although] the Court glides over this fact, it should be apparent that the Act will impose only minor economic burdens on employers whose pension plans have been adequately funded. [An] adequate pension plan fund would include contributions on behalf of terminated employees of 10 or more years service whose rights had not vested. Indeed, without the Act, the closing of the plant would create a windfall for the employer, because, due to the resulting surplus in the fund, his future contributions would be reduced. * * *

[The] Act does not relieve either the employer or his employees of any existing contract obligation. Rather, the Act simply creates an additional, supplemental duty of the employer, no different in kind from myriad duties created by a wide variety of legislative measures which defeat settled expectations but which have nonetheless been sustained by this Court. For this reason, the Minnesota Act, in my view, does not implicate the Contract Clause in any way. The basic fallacy of today's decision is its mistaken view that the Contract Clause protects all contract-based expectations, including that of an employer that his obligations to his employees will not be legislatively enlarged beyond those explicitly provided in his pension plan.

A. Historically, [the] Contract Clause was not intended to embody a broad constitutional policy of protecting all reliance interests grounded in private contracts. It was made part of the Constitution to remedy a particular social evil—the state legislative practice of enacting laws to relieve individuals of their obligations under certain contracts—and thus was intended to prohibit States from adopting "as [their] policy the repudiation of debts or the destruction of contracts or the denial of means to enforce them," *Blaisdell*. But the Framers never contemplated that the Clause would limit the legislative power of States to enact laws creating duties that might burden some individuals in order to benefit others.

B. [It] is nothing less than an abuse of the English language to interpret, as does the Court, the term "impairing" as including laws which create new duties. While such laws may be conceptualized as "enlarging" the obligation of a contract when they add to the burdens that had previously been imposed by a private agreement, such laws cannot be prohibited by the Clause because they do not dilute or nullify a duty a person had previously obligated himself to perform.[7] * * *

C. [More] fundamentally, the Court's distortion of the meaning of the Contract Clause [threatens] to undermine the jurisprudence of property rights developed over the last 40 years. The Contract Clause, of course, is but one of several clauses in the Constitution that protect existing economic values from governmental interference. The Fifth Amendment's command that "private property [shall not] be taken for public use, without just compensation" is such a clause. A second is the Due Process Clause, which during the heyday of substantive due process, see *Lochner*, largely supplanted the Contract Clause in

---

7. In *Georgia Ry. & Power Co. v. Decatur, Detroit United Ry. v. Michigan*, [fn. 16 supra], and in dictum in other cases, this Court embraced, without any careful analysis and without giving any consideration to *Satterlee v. Matthewson*, the contrary view that the impairment of a contract may consist in "adding to its burdens" as well as in diminishing its efficacy. These opinions reflect the then-prevailing philosophy of economic due process which has since been repudiated. See *Ferguson v. Skrupa*. In my view, the reasoning of *Georgia Ry.* and *Detroit United Ry.* is simply wrong.

importance and operated as a potent limitation on Government's ability to interfere with economic expectations. Decisions over the past 50 years have developed a coherent, unified interpretation of all the constitutional provisions that may protect economic expectations and these decisions have recognized a broad latitude in States to effect even severe interference with existing economic values when reasonably necessary to promote the general welfare. See, *Penn Central; Goldblatt*. At the same time the prohibition of the Contract Clause, consistently with its wording and historic purposes, has been limited in application to state laws that diluted, with utter indifference to the legitimate interests of the beneficiary of a contract duty, the existing contract obligation, *W.B. Worthen Co. v. Kavanaugh*; see *United States Trust Co.*; cf. *El Paso; Blaisdell*.

[There] is nothing sancrosanct about expectations rooted in contract that justify according them a constitutional immunity denied other property rights. Laws that interfere with settled expectations created by state property law (and which impose severe economic burdens) are uniformly held constitutional where reasonably related to the promotion of the general welfare. * * *

There is no logical or rational basis for sustaining the duties created by the laws in *Miller* and *Hadacheck*, but invalidating the duty created by the Minnesota Act. Surely, the Act effects no greater interference with reasonable reliance interests than did these other laws. Moreover, the laws operate identically: they all create duties that burden one class of persons and benefit another. The only difference between the present case and *Hadacheck* or *Miller* is that here there was a prior contractual relationship between the members of the benefited and burdened classes. I simply cannot accept that this difference should possess constitutional significance. The only means of avoiding this anomaly is to construe the Contract Clause consistently with its terms [and] hold it is inapplicable to laws which create new duties. * * *

Notes and Questions

1. *Contract vs. other property rights.* (a) In what respects, if any, is there a significant difference in the Court's review of economic legislation when challenged under the contract clause as compared to due process? Consider particularly (1) the professed standard of review, (2) the degree of deference to the legislature or strictness of judicial scrutiny, (3) the Court's willingness to hypothesize state purposes to justify the legislation. Cf. 92 Harv.L.Rev. 94–99 (1978).

(b) Ought the degree of judicial protection from legislative interference differ under the constitution as between preexisting contract interests and preexisting noncontractual property interests?

2. *Legislatively-added burdens.* Did *Allied Steel* soundly interpret the contract clause to protect against "impairment" by legislatively-added burdens that increase those stated in the contract? Would it have made a difference in the law's validity if it added a burden of sounder *funding* of the contractual pension benefits without adding to the *benefits?*

3. *"Incidental effect" of regulation.* EXXON CORP. v. EAGERTON, 462 U.S. 176, 103 S.Ct. 2296, 76 L.Ed.2d 497 (1983), per MARSHALL, J., unanimously held that a ban on oil and gas producers passing a severance tax increase on to consumers did not violate the contract clause even though pre-existing contracts required consumers to reimburse producers for all severance taxes:

"[T]he pass-through prohibition did not prescribe a rule limited in effect to contractual obligations or remedies, but instead imposed a generally applicable rule of conduct designed to advance 'a broad societal interest,' *Allied Steel*, protecting consumers from excessive prices. The prohibition applied to all oil and gas producers, regardless of whether they happened to be parties to sale contracts that contained a provision permitting them to pass tax increases through to their purchasers. The effect of the pass-through prohibition on existing contracts that did contain such a provision was incidental to its main effect of shielding consumers from the burden of the tax increase.

"Because the pass-through prohibition imposed a generally applicable rule of conduct, it is sharply distinguishable from the measures struck down in *United States Trust* and *Allied Steel*. *United States Trust* involved New York and New Jersey statutes whose sole effect was to repeal a covenant that the two States had entered into with the holders of bonds issued by The Port Authority of New York and New Jersey. Similarly, the statute at issue in *Allied Steel* directly 'adjust[ed] the rights and responsibilities of contracting parties,' quoting *United States Trust*. * * *

"Alabama's power to prohibit oil and gas producers from passing the increase in the severance tax on to their purchasers is confirmed by several decisions of this Court rejecting Contract Clause challenges to state rate-setting schemes that displaced any rates previously established by contract. * * * And if the Contract Clause does not prevent a State from dictating the price that sellers may charge their customers, plainly it does not prevent a State from requiring that sellers absorb a tax increase themselves rather than pass it through to their customers."

4. *The law summarized.* For a unanimous summary of the controlling considerations in modern contract clause cases see Blackmun, J.'s, opinion in *Energy Reserves Group, Inc. v. Kansas Power and Light Co.,* 459 U.S. 400, 103 S.Ct. 697, 74 L.Ed.2d 569 (1983).

Chapter 7

PROTECTION OF INDIVIDUAL RIGHTS: DUE PROCESS, THE BILL OF RIGHTS, AND NONTEXTUAL CONSTITUTIONAL RIGHTS

SECTION 1. NATURE AND SCOPE OF FOURTEENTH AMENDMENT DUE PROCESS; APPLICABILITY OF THE BILL OF RIGHTS TO THE STATES

I. THE "ORDERED LIBERTY—FUNDAMENTAL FAIRNESS," "TOTAL INCORPORATION" AND "SELECTIVE INCORPORATION" THEORIES

Twining v. New Jersey, 211 U.S. 78, 29 S.Ct. 14, 53 L.Ed. 97 (1908); *Palko v. Connecticut*, 302 U.S. 319, 58 S.Ct. 149, 82 L.Ed. 2888 (1937); and *Adamson v. California*, 332 U.S. 46, 67 S.Ct. 1672, 91 L.Ed. 1903 (1947), rejected the "total incorporation" view of the history of the fourteenth amendment, the view—which has never commanded a majority—that the fourteenth amendment made all of the provisions of the Bill of Rights fully applicable to the states.[a] But *Twining* recognized that "it is possible that some of the personal rights safeguarded by the first eight Amendments against National action may also be safeguarded against state action, because a denial of them would be a denial of due process" or because "the specific pledge of particular amendments have been found to be implicit in the concept of ordered liberty and thus through the Fourteenth Amendment, become valid as against the states" (*Palko*). And the Court early found among the procedural requirements of fourteenth amendment due process certain rules paralleling provisions of the first eight amendments. For example, *Powell v. Alabama*, 287 U.S. 45, 53 S.Ct. 55, 77 L.Ed. 158 (1932), held that defendants in a capital case were denied due process when a state

---

a. *Palko,* which held that the fourteenth amendment did not encompass at least certain aspects of the double jeopardy prohibition of the fifth amendment, was overruled in *Benton v. Maryland* (1969), discussed below. The *Twining-Adamson* view that the fifth amendment privilege against self-incrimination is not incorporated in the fourteenth was rejected in *Malloy v. Hogan* (1964), discussed below. *Griffin v. California* (1965), Part IV infra, subsequently applied *Malloy* to overrule the specific holdings of *Twining* and *Adamson,* which had permitted comment on a defendant's failure to take the stand at his criminal trial. These later decisions, however, were still consistent with the rejection of the "total incorporation" interpretation.

refused them the aid of counsel. "The logically critical thing, however," pointed out Harlan, J., years later, "was not that the rights had been found in the Bill of Rights, but that they were deemed * * * fundamental." [b]

Under the "ordered liberty"—"fundamental fairness" test, which procedural safeguards included in the Bill of Rights were applicable to the states and which were not? Consider CARDOZO, J., speaking for the *Palko* Court: "[On reflection and analysis there] emerges the perception of a rationalizing principle which gives to discrete instances a proper order and coherence. The right to trial by jury and the immunity from prosecution except as the result of an indictment [are] not of the very essence of a scheme of ordered liberty. To abolish them is not to violate a 'principle of justice so rooted in the traditions and conscience of our people as to be ranked as fundamental.' [What] is true of jury trials and indictments is true also, as the cases show, of the immunity from compulsory self-incrimination. This too might be lost, and justice still be [done.] [c]

"We reach a different plane of social and moral values when we pass [to those provisions of the Bill of Rights] brought within the Fourteenth Amendment by a process of absorption. These in their origin were effective against the federal government alone. If the Fourteenth Amendment has absorbed them, the process of absorption has had its course in the belief that neither liberty nor justice would exist if they were sacrificed. This is true, for illustration, of freedom of thought and speech. Of that freedom one may say that it is the

---

b. *Duncan v. Louisiana* (dissent joined by Stewart, J.), discussed below.

c. As pointed out in fn. a supra, the fifth amendment privilege against self-incrimination was subsequently held to be fully applicable to the states via the fourteenth amendment. So was the sixth amendment right to jury trial in criminal cases. *Duncan v. Louisiana* (1968), discussed below.

The above language in *Palko* and language in *Adamson,* infra, and other cases are susceptible of the interpretation that when the Court held that a particular Bill of Rights guarantee was not "incorporated into," or implicit in, fourteenth amendment due process it was *completely* "out." But such a reading of these cases seems unsound. Typically the Court dealt with state procedures transgressing the "outer edges," rather than the basic concept, of a particular Bill of Rights guarantee. It seems most doubtful that in sustaining such challenged procedures the Court was authorizing the states to abolish completely—or to violate the "hardcore" of— e.g., the protection against double jeopardy, or the privilege against self-incrimination, or the right to trial by jury in criminal cases. Rather the Court probably meant that the state rules did not violate the fourteenth amendment because the Bill of Rights guarantee invoked by defendant did not apply to the states *to the full extent* it applied to the federal government. To hold that a particular provision of the Bill of Rights is not *totally* "incorporated," i.e., not binding on the states *in its entirety,* is not to say it is *completely* "out" of the fourteenth amendment. See generally Henkin, *"Selective Incorporation" in the*

Fourteenth Amendment, 73 Yale L.J. 74, 79 & n. 18, 80–81 (1963).

At issue in *Palko* was not whether a state could completely disregard the basic notion against twice putting a person in jeopardy for the same offense, but a Connecticut statute permitting prosecution appeals "upon all questions of law arising [in criminal trials] with the permission of the presiding judge." Thus, elsewhere in the opinion the Court asked: "Is *that kind of double jeopardy* to which the [Connecticut] statute has subjected [appellant] *a hardship so acute and shocking* that our polity will not endure it? [What] the answer would have to be if the state were permitted *after a trial free from error* to try the accused over again or to bring another case against him, we have no occasion to consider." (Emphasis added).

Nor should *Adamson* be read for the proposition that a state could make it a felony for a person to "plead the fifth" or for a defendant to refuse to take the stand. Rather the Court merely sustained a California provision infringing upon the *periphery* of the guarantee by allowing comment upon a defendant's failure to explain or to deny evidence against him.

Nor, as the Court later emphasized in *Duncan,* discussed below, did *Maxwell v. Dow* (1900), discussed below, hold that a state could abolish trial by jury *altogether* in criminal cases; only that fourteenth amendment due process did not prevent a state from trying a noncapital defendant before a jury with fewer than 12 persons.

matrix, the indispensable condition, of nearly every other form of freedom. * * * Fundamental too in the concept of due process, and so in that of liberty, is the thought that condemnation shall be rendered only after trial. The hearing, moreover, must be a real one, not a sham or pretense [discussing *Powell* which] did not turn upon the fact that the benefit of counsel would have been guaranteed to the defendants by [the] Sixth Amendment if they had been prosecuted in a federal court [but on] the fact that in the particular situation laid before us [the aid of counsel] was essential to the substance of a hearing."

The "total incorporation" position received its strongest support in the *Adamson* dissents. In the principal dissent, BLACK, J., joined by Douglas, J., observed: "I cannot consider the Bill of Rights to be an outworn 18th Century 'strait jacket' as the *Twining* opinion did. Its provisions may be thought outdated abstractions by some. And it is true that they were designed to meet ancient evils. But they are the same kind of human evils that have emerged from century to century wherever excessive power is sought by the few at the expense of the many. In my judgment the people of no nation can lose their liberty so long as a Bill of Rights like ours survives and its basic purposes are conscientiously interpreted, enforced and respected so as to afford continuous protection against old, as well as new, devices and practices which might thwart those purposes. I fear to see the consequences of the Court's practice of substituting its own concepts of decency and fundamental justice for the language of the Bill of Rights as its point of departure in interpreting and enforcing that Bill of Rights. If the choice must be between the selective process of the *Palko* decision applying some of the Bill of Rights to the States, or the *Twining* rule applying none of them, I would choose the *Palko* selective process. But rather than accept either of these choices, I would follow what I believe was the original purpose of the Fourteenth Amendment—to extend to all the people of the nation the complete protection of the Bill of Rights. To hold that this Court can determine what, if any, provisions of the Bill of Rights will be enforced, and if so to what degree, is to frustrate the great design of a written Constitution.

"Conceding the possibility that this Court is now wise enough to improve on the Bill of Rights by substituting natural law concepts for the Bill of Rights, I think the possibility is entirely too speculative to agree to take that course. I would therefore hold in this case that the full protection of the Fifth Amendment's proscription against compelled testimony must be afforded by California. This I would do because of reliance upon the original purpose of the Fourteenth Amendment.

"[T]o pass upon the constitutionality of statutes by looking to the particular standards enumerated in the Bill of Rights and other parts of the Constitution is one thing; to invalidate statutes because of application of 'natural law' deemed to be above and undefined by the Constitution is another. 'In the one instance, courts proceeding within clearly marked constitutional boundaries seek to execute policies written into the Constitution; in the other they roam at will in the limitless area of their own beliefs as to reasonableness and actually select policies, a responsibility which the Constitution entrusts to the legislative representatives of the people.' " [d]

d. Dissenting separately in *Adamson*, Murphy, J., joined by Rutledge, J., "agree[d] that the specific guarantees of the Bill of Rights should be carried over intact into [the fourteenth amendment but was] not prepared to say that the latter is entirely and necessarily limited by the Bill of Rights. Occasions may arise where a proceeding falls so far short of conforming to fundamental standards of procedure as to warrant constitutional condemnation in terms of a lack of due process despite the absence of a specific provision of the Bill

Responding, FRANKFURTER, J.'s concurrence in *Adamson* stressed the "independent potency" of the fourteenth amendment due process clause, maintaining that it "neither comprehends the specific provisions by which the founders deemed it appropriate to restrict the federal government nor is confined to them": [e] "Between the incorporation of the Fourteenth Amendment into the Constitution and the beginning of the present membership of the Court—a period of 70 years—the scope of that Amendment was passed upon by 43 judges. Of all these judges only one, who may respectfully be called an eccentric exception, ever indicated the belief that the Fourteenth Amendment was a shorthand summary of the first eight Amendments theretofore limiting only the Federal Government, and that due process incorporated those eight Amendments as restrictions upon the powers of the States. [To] suggest that it is inconsistent with a truly free society to begin prosecutions without an indictment, to try petty civil cases without the paraphernalia of a common law jury, to take into consideration that one who has full opportunity to make a defense remains silent is, in de Tocqueville's phrase, to confound the familiar with the necessary.

"[Those] reading the English language with the meaning which it ordinarily conveys, those conversant with the political and legal history of the concept of due process, those sensitive to the relations of the States to the central government as well as the relation of some of the provisions of the Bill of Rights to the process of justice, would hardly recognize the Fourteenth Amendment as a cover for the various explicit provisions of the first eight Amendments. Some of these are enduring reflections of experience with human nature, while some express the restricted views of Eighteenth-Century England regarding the best methods for the ascertainment of facts. The notion that the Fourteenth Amendment was a covert way of imposing upon the States all the rules which it seemed important to Eighteenth Century statesmen to write into the Federal Amendments, was rejected by judges who were themselves witnesses of the process by which the Fourteenth Amendment became part of the Constitution. [A]t the time of the ratification of the Fourteenth Amendment the constitutions of nearly half of the ratifying States did not have the rigorous requirements of the Fifth Amendment for instituting criminal proceedings through a grand jury. It could hardly have occurred to these States that by ratifying the Amendment they uprooted their established methods for prosecuting crime and fastened upon themselves a new prosecutorial system.

"Indeed, the suggestion that the Fourteenth Amendment incorporates the first eight Amendments as such is not unambiguously urged. [There] is suggested merely a selective incorporation of the first eight Amendments into the Fourteenth Amendment. Some are in and some are out, but we are left in the dark as to which are in and which are out. Nor are we given the calculus for determining which go in and which stay out. If the basis of selection is merely that those provisions of the first eight Amendments are incorporated which

of Rights." In this connection, consider fn. e infra.

e. See also Friendly, *The Bill of Rights as a Code of Criminal Procedure,* 53 Calif.L.Rev. 929, 937 (1965): "[N]o facile formula will enable the Court to escape its assigned task of deciding just what the Constitution protects from state action, as *Estes v. Texas,* 381 U.S. 532, 85 S.Ct. 1628, 14 L.Ed.2d 543 (1965), where no 'specific' could be invoked, showed

[for] procedural due process, and *Griswold v. Connecticut* [Sec. 2 infra] demonstrated for substantive due process." Consider, too, *In re Winship,* Part IV infra, holding that "proof beyond a reasonable doubt is among the essentials of due process" over the protest of dissenting Justice Black that nowhere in the Bill of Rights could he find any command that conviction of crime or adjudication of delinquency requires such a high standard of proof.

commend themselves to individual justices as indispensable to the dignity and happiness of a free man, we are thrown back to a merely subjective test. [In] the history of thought 'natural law' has a much longer and much better founded meaning and justification than such subjective selection of the first eight Amendments for incorporation into the Fourteenth. If all that is meant is that due process contains within itself certain minimal standards which are 'of the very essence of a scheme of ordered liberty,' *Palko,* putting upon this Court the duty of applying these standards from time to time, then we have merely arrived at the insight which our predecessors long ago expressed. * * *

"A construction which gives to due process no independent function but turns it into a summary of the specific provisions of the Bill of Rights [would] deprive the States of opportunity for reforms in legal process designed for extending the area of freedom. It would assume that no other abuses would reveal themselves in the course of time than those which had become manifest in 1791. Such a view not only disregards the historic meaning of 'due process.' It leads inevitably to a warped construction of specific provisions of the Bill of Rights to bring within their scope conduct clearly condemned by due process but not easily fitting into the pigeonholes of the specific provisions.

" * * * Judicial review of [the Due Process Clause] of the Fourteenth Amendment inescapably imposes upon this Court an exercise of judgment upon the whole course of the proceedings in order to ascertain whether they offend those canons of decency and fairness which express the notions of justice of English-speaking peoples even toward those charged with the most heinous offenses. These standards of justice are not authoritatively formulated anywhere as though they were prescriptions in a pharmacopoeia. But neither does the application of the Due Process Clause imply that judges are wholly at large. The judicial judgment in applying the Due Process Clause must move within the limits of accepted notions of justice and is not to be based upon the idiosyncracies of a merely personal judgment."

Notes and Questions

1. Are Frankfurter and Black, JJ., each more persuasive in demonstrating why the *other's* test is subjective, ill-defined and unilluminating than in explaining why his own is *not?*

2. *Escape from the "idiosyncrasy of a personal judgment".* If, as Frankfurter, J., insists, the *Palko-Adamson* test is not based upon "the idiosyncrasies of a merely personal judgment," *whose* moral judgments furnish the answer? And *where* and *how* are they discoverable? The opinions of the progenitors and architects of our institutions? The opinions of the policy-making organs of state governments? Of state courts? The opinions of other countries? Of other countries in the Anglo-Saxon tradition? See Kadish, *Methodology and Criteria in Due Process Adjudication—A Survey and Criticism,* 66 Yale L.J. 319, 328–333 (1957). What judgments were relied on in *Palko* and *Adamson?* In *Rochin v. California,* Part III infra?

3. *History.* Historical research has produced ample support—and ample skepticism—for the "incorporation" theory. Compare 2 Crosskey, *Politics and the Constitution,* chs. XXXI, at 1083, XXXII, at 1119 (1953); Flack, *The Adoption of the Fourteenth Amendment* (1908); and Guthrie, *The Fourteenth Article of Amendment to the Constitution of the United States* (1898) with tenBroek, *The Antislavery Origins of the Fourteenth Amendment* (1951); Fairman, *Does the Fourteenth Amendment Incorporate the Bill of Rights? The Original Under-*

standing, 2 Stan.L.Rev. 5 (1949); Graham, *The "Conspiracy Theory" of the Fourteenth Amendment,* 47 Yale L.J. 371 (1938). For brief but incisive criticism of both Black, J.'s position and Professor Fairman's attack, see Kelly, *Clio and the Court: An Illicit Love Affair,* 1965 Sup.Ct.Rev. 119, 132–34.

Is further historical search likely to do more than "further obscure the judicial value-choosing inherent in due process adjudication which can proceed with greater expectation of success if pursued openly and deliberately rather than under disguise"? Is due process more a moral command than a jural or historical concept? Ought it be? See Kadish, supra, at 340–41.

––––––––––

Although the Court continued to apply the *"Palko* selective process" approach to the Bill of Rights, DUNCAN v. LOUISIANA, 391 U.S. 145, 88 S.Ct. 1444, 20 L.Ed.2d 491 (1968) (holding the sixth amendment right to jury trial applicable to the states via the fourteenth amendment), no longer employed the Cardozo-Frankfurter terminology (e.g., whether a particular guarantee was "implicit in the concept of ordered liberty" or required by "the 'immutable principles of justice' as conceived by a civilized society") but instead inquired whether the procedural safeguard included in the Bill of Rights was "fundamental to the *American scheme of justice*" (emphasis added) or "fundamental *in the context of the criminal processes maintained by the American states*" (emphasis added). As WHITE, J., noted for the *Duncan* majority (fn. 14), the different phraseology is significant:

"Earlier the Court can be seen as having asked, when inquiring into whether some particular procedural safeguard was required of a State, if a civilized system could be imagined that would not accord the particular protection [quoting from *Palko*]. The recent cases, on the other hand, have proceeded upon the valid assumption that state criminal processes are not imaginary and theoretical schemes but actual systems bearing virtually every characteristic of the common-law system that has been developing contemporaneously in England and this country. The question thus is whether given this kind of system a particular procedure is fundamental—whether, that is, a procedure is necessary to an Anglo-American regime of ordered liberty. It is this sort of inquiry that can justify the conclusions that state courts must exclude evidence seized in violation of the Fourth Amendment, *Mapp v. Ohio* [Part IV infra] [and] that state prosecutors may not comment on a defendant's failure to testify, *Griffin v. California* [fn. a supra]. [Of] each of these determinations that a constitutional provision originally written to bind the Federal Government should bind the States as well it might be said that the limitation in question is not necessarily fundamental to fairness in every criminal system that might be imagined but is fundamental in the context of the criminal processes maintained by the American States.

"When the inquiry is approached in this way the question whether the States can impose criminal punishment without granting a jury trial appears quite different from the way it appeared in the older cases opining that States might abolish jury trial. A criminal process which was fair and equitable but used no juries is easy to imagine. It would make use of alternative guarantees and protections which would serve the purposes that the jury serves in the English and American systems. Yet no American State has undertaken to construct such a system. Instead, every American State, including Louisiana, uses the jury extensively, and imposes very serious punishments only after a trial at which the defendant has a right to a jury's verdict. In every State, including Louisiana, the structure and style of the criminal process—the supporting framework and the subsidiary procedures—are of the sort that naturally complement jury trial, and have developed in connection with and in reliance upon jury trial." *f*

Because the *Duncan* Court believed that "trial by jury in criminal cases is fundamental to the American scheme of justice," it held that it was guaranteed by the fourteenth amendment: "The guarantees of jury trial in the Federal and State Constitutions reflect a profound judgment about the way in which law should be enforced and justice administered. A right to jury trial is granted to criminal defendants in order to prevent oppression by the Government. Those who wrote our constitutions knew from history and experience that it was necessary to protect against unfounded criminal charges brought to eliminate enemies and against judges too responsive to the voice of higher authority. The framers of the constitutions strove to create an independent judiciary but insisted upon further protection against arbitrary action. Providing an accused with the right to be tried by a jury of his peers gave him an inestimable safeguard against the corrupt or overzealous prosecutor and against the compliant, biased, or eccentric judge. If the defendant preferred the common-sense judgment of a jury to the more tutored but perhaps less sympathetic reaction of the single judge, he was to have it. Beyond this, the jury trial provisions in the Federal and State Constitutions reflect a fundamental decision about the exercise of official power—a reluctance to entrust plenary powers over the life and liberty of the citizen to one judge or to a group of judges. Fear of unchecked power, so typical of our State and Federal Governments in other respects, found expression in the criminal law in this insistence upon community participation in the determination of guilt or innocence. The deep commitment of the Nation to the right of jury trial in serious criminal cases as a defense against arbitrary law enforcement qualifies for protection under the Due Process Clause of the Fourteenth Amendment, and must therefore be respected by the States."

HARLAN, J., joined by Stewart, J., dissented: "Even if I could agree that the question before us is whether Sixth Amendment jury trial is totally ['incorporated into' the fourteenth amendment] or totally 'out' [see Sec. II infra], I can find in the Court's opinion no real reasons for concluding that it should be 'in.' The basis for distinguishing among clauses in the Bill of Rights cannot be that [only] some are old and much praised, or that only some have played an important role in the development of federal law. These things are true of all. The Court says that some clauses are more 'fundamental' than others, but [uses] this word in a sense that would have astonished Mr. Justice Cardozo and which, in addition, is of no help. The word does not mean 'analytically critical to procedural fairness' for no real analysis of the role of the jury in making procedures fair is even attempted. Instead, the word turns out to mean 'old,' 'much praised,' and 'found in the Bill of Rights.' The definition of 'fundamental' thus turns out to be circular.

f. See also Powell, J., concurring in the companion 1972 "jury unanimity" cases of *Johnson v. Louisiana* and *Apodaca v. Oregon,* discussed below: "I agree with Mr. Justice White's analysis in *Duncan* that the departure from earlier decisions was, in large measure, a product of a change in focus in the Court's approach to due process. No longer are questions regarding the constitutionality of particular criminal procedures resolved by focusing alone on the element in question and ascer-taining whether a system of criminal justice might be imagined in which a fair trial could be afforded in the absence of that particular element. Rather, the focus is, as it should be, on the fundamentality of that element viewed in the context of the basic Anglo-American jurisprudential system common to the States. That approach to due process readily accounts both for the conclusion that jury trial *is* fundamental and that unanimity *is not.*"

"[Jury trial] is of course not without virtues [but its] principal original virtue—[the limitations it] imposes on a tyrannous judiciary—has largely disappeared. [The] jury system can also be said to have some inherent defects, which are multiplied by the emergence of the criminal law from the relative simplicity that existed when the jury system was devised. It is a cumbersome process, not only imposing great cost in time and money on both the State and the jurors themselves, but also contributing to delay in the machinery of justice. [That] trial by jury is not the only fair way of adjudicating criminal guilt is well attested by the fact that it is not the prevailing way, either in England or in this country.

"[The majority recognizes that not every, or any particular, criminal trial before a judge alone is unfair, or less fair than one held before a jury.] I agree. I therefore see no reason why this Court should reverse the conviction of appellant absent any suggestion that his particular trial was in fact unfair, or compel the State of Louisiana to afford jury trial in an as yet unbounded category of cases that can, without unfairness, be tried to a court.

"[In] sum, there is a wide range of views on the desirability of trial by jury, and on the ways to make it most effective when it is used; there is also considerable variation from State to State in local conditions such as the size of the criminal caseload, the ease or difficulty of summoning jurors, and other trial conditions bearing on fairness. We have before us, therefore, an almost perfect example of a situation in which [the states should serve as laboratories.] [Instead,] the Court has chosen to impose upon every State one means of trying criminal cases; it is a good means, but it is not the only fair means, and it is not demonstrably better than the alternatives States might devise." [g]

Although the Court has remained unwilling to accept the total incorporationists' reading of the fourteenth amendment, in the 1960s it "selectively" "incorporated" or "absorbed" more and more of the specifics of the Bill of Rights into the fourteenth amendment. As WHITE, J., observed in *Duncan*:

"In resolving conflicting claims concerning the meaning of this spacious [fourteenth amendment] language, the Court has looked increasingly to the Bill of Rights for guidance; many of the rights guaranteed by the first eight Amendments to the Constitution have been held to be protected against state action by the Due Process Clause of the Fourteenth Amendment.[h] That clause now protects [the] Fourth Amendment rights to be free from unreasonable searches and seizures and to have excluded from criminal trials any evidence illegally seized; the right guaranteed by the Fifth Amendment to be free of compelled self-incrimination; and the Sixth Amendment rights to counsel, to a

g. Cf. *McKeiver v. Pennsylvania*, 403 U.S. 528, 91 S.Ct. 1976, 29 L.Ed.2d 647 (1971), holding that a state may use its juvenile court proceedings to prosecute a juvenile for a criminal act without providing trial by jury because, inter alia, the jury is not "a necessary component of accurate fact-finding" and its "inject[ion] into the juvenile court system as a matter of right" might bring with it "the traditional delay, the formality and the clamor of the adversary system, and, possibly, the public trial."

h. See also Black, J., joined by Douglas, J., concurring in *Duncan*: "[I] believe as strongly as ever that the Fourteenth Amendment was intended to make the Bill of Rights applicable to the States. I have been willing to support the selective incorporation doctrine, however, as an alternative, although perhaps less historically supportable than complete incorporation [because it] keeps judges from roaming at will in their own notions of what policies outside the Bill of Rights are desirable and what are not. And, most importantly for me, the selective incorporation process has the virtue of having already worked to make most of the Bill of Rights' protections applicable to the States."

speedy and public trial [*Klopfer v. North Carolina*, 386 U.S. 213, 87 S.Ct. 988, 18 L.Ed.2d 1 (1967); *In re Oliver*, 330 U.S. 257, 68 S.Ct. 499, 92 L.Ed. 682 (1942)], to confrontation of opposing witnesses [*Pointer v. Texas*, 380 U.S. 400, 85 S.Ct. 1065, 13 L.Ed.2d 923 (1965)] and to compulsory process for obtaining witnesses [*Washington v. Texas*, 388 U.S. 14, 87 S.Ct. 1920, 18 L.Ed.2d 1019 (1967)]." [i]

II. SHOULD THE "SELECTED" PROVISION APPLY TO THE STATES "JOT–FOR–JOT"? "BAG AND BAGGAGE"?

In the 1960s, the Court seemed to be "incorporating" not only the basic notion or general concept of the "selected" provision of the Bill of Rights, but applying the provision to the states *to the same extent* it applied to the federal government. As some justices, especially Harlan, protested, the federal guarantees were being incorporated into the fourteenth "freighted with their entire accompanying body of federal doctrine" (Harlan, J., joined by Clark, J., dissenting in *Malloy v. Hogan*, discussed below); "jot-for-jot and case-for-case" (Harlan, J., joined by Stewart, J., dissenting in *Duncan*); "bag and baggage, however securely or insecurely affixed they may be by law and precedent to federal proceedings" (Fortas, J., concurring in *Duncan*).

Thus, Brennan, J., observed for a majority in *Malloy v. Hogan*, 378 U.S. 1, 84 S.Ct. 1489, 12 L.Ed.2d 653 (1964): "We have held that the guarantees of the First Amendment, the prohibition of unreasonable searches and seizures of the Fourth Amendment, *Ker v. California*, 374 U.S. 23, 83 S.Ct. 1623, 10 L.Ed.2d 726 (1965), and the right to counsel guaranteed by the Sixth Amendment, *Gideon v. Wainwright* [Sec. IV infra], are all to be enforced against the States under the Fourteenth Amendment *according to the same standards that protect those personal rights against federal encroachment.* [The] Court thus has rejected the notion that the Fourteenth Amendment applies to the States only a 'watered-down, subjective version of the individual guarantees of the Bill of Rights.' " (Emphasis added.)

And White, J., put it for a majority in *Duncan:* "Because we believe that trial by jury in criminal cases is fundamental to the American scheme of justice, we hold that the Fourteenth Amendment guarantees a right of jury trial in all criminal cases which—*were they to be tried in a federal court*—would come within the Sixth Amendment's guarantee." (Emphasis added.)

Similarly, Marshall, J., observed for a majority in *Benton v. Maryland*, 395 U.S. 784, 89 S.Ct. 2056, 23 L.Ed.2d 707 (1969): "Once it is decided that a particular Bill of Rights guarantee is 'fundamental to the American scheme of justice,' the same constitutional standards apply against both the State and Federal Governments. [Like] the right to trial by jury, [the guarantee against double jeopardy] is clearly 'fundamental to the American scheme of justice.' The validity of [the conviction] must be judged, not by the watered-down standard enunciated in *Palko*, but *under this Court's interpretations of the Fifth Amendment double jeopardy provision.*" (Emphasis added.)

Harlan, J., repeatedly voiced his opposition to the *Malloy-Duncan-Benton* approach to fourteenth amendment due process. "The ultimate result," he protested in his *Malloy* dissent, "is compelled uniformity, which is inconsistent

---

i. In the area of criminal procedure, the Court has come very close to incorporating all of the relevant Bill of Rights guarantees. But still on the books, is a lonely exception. *Hurtado v. California*, 110 U.S. 516, 4 S.Ct. 111, 28 L.Ed. 232 (1884), refusing to apply to the states the fifth amendment requirement that prosecution be initiated by grand jury indictment.

with the purpose of our federal system and which is achieved either by encroachment on the State's sovereign powers or by dilution in federal law enforcement of the specific protections found in the Bill of Rights."

Dissenting in *Duncan,* HARLAN, J., joined by Stewart, J., protested: "Today's Court still remains unwilling to accept the total incorporationists' view of the history of the Fourteenth Amendment. This, if accepted, would afford a cogent reason for applying the Sixth Amendment to the States. The Court is also, apparently, unwilling to face the task of determining whether denial of trial by jury in the situation before us, or in other situations, is fundamentally unfair. Consequently, the Court has compromised on the ease of the incorporationist position, without its internal logic. It has simply assumed that the question before us is whether the Jury Trial Clause of the Sixth Amendment should be incorporated into the Fourteenth, jot-for-jot and case-for-case, or ignored. Then the Court merely declares that the clause in question is 'in' rather than 'out.'

"The Court has justified neither its starting place nor its conclusion. If the problem is to discover and articulate the rules of fundamental fairness in criminal proceedings, there is no reason to assume that the whole body of rules developed in this Court constituting Sixth Amendment jury trial must be regarded as a unit. The requirement of trial by jury in federal criminal cases has given rise to numerous subsidiary questions respecting the exact scope and content of the right. It surely cannot be that every answer the Court has given, or will give, to such a question is attributable to the Founders; or even that every rule announced carries equal conviction of this Court; still less can it be that every such subprinciple is equally fundamental to ordered liberty.

"Examples abound. I should suppose it obviously fundamental to fairness that a 'jury' means an 'impartial jury.' I should think it equally obvious that the rule, imposed long ago in the federal courts, that 'jury' means 'jury of exactly twelve,' is not fundamental to anything: there is no significance except to mystics in the number 12. Again, trial by jury has been held to require a unanimous verdict of jurors in the federal courts, although unanimity has not been found essential to liberty in Britain, where the requirement has been abandoned."

Concurring in *Duncan,* FORTAS, J., too, balked: "Neither logic nor history nor the intent of the draftsmen of the Fourteenth Amendment can possibly be said to require that the Sixth Amendment or its jury trial provision be applied to the States together with the total gloss that this Court's decisions have supplied. The draftsmen of the Fourteenth Amendment intended what they said, not more or less: that no State shall deprive any person of life, liberty, or property without due process of law. It is ultimately the duty of this Court to interpret, to ascribe specific meaning to this phrase. There is no reason whatever for us to conclude that, in so doing, we are bound slavishly to follow not only the Sixth Amendment but all of its bag and baggage, however securely or insecurely affixed they may be by law and precedent to federal proceedings. To take this course, in my judgment, would be not only unnecessary but mischievous because it would inflict a serious blow upon the principle of federalism. The Due Process Clause commands us to apply its great standard to state court proceedings to assure basic fairness. It does not command us rigidly and arbitrarily to impose the exact pattern of federal proceedings upon the 50 States. [Our] Constitution sets up a federal union, not a monolith."

Concurring in *Pointer,* GOLDBERG, J., responded to Justice Harlan's repeated criticism of the "selective" incorporation approach as follows: "[My Brother

Harlan] would have the Fourteenth Amendment apply to the States 'only a "watered-down, subjective version of the individual guarantees of the Bill of Rights." ' It would allow the States greater latitude than the Federal Government to abridge concededly fundamental liberties protected by the Constitution. While I quite agree with Mr. Justice Brandeis that '[i]t is one of the happy incidents of the federal system that [a State may] serve as a laboratory; and try novel social economic experiments,' I do not believe that this includes the power to experiment with the fundamental liberties of citizens safeguarded by the Bill of Rights. My Brother Harlan's view would also require this Court to make the extremely subjective and excessively discretionary determination as to whether a practice, forbidden the Federal Government by a fundamental constitutional guarantee, is, as viewed in the factual circumstances surrounding each individual case, sufficiently repugnant to the notion of due process as to be forbidden the States.

"Finally, I do not see that my Brother Harlan's view would further any legitimate interests of federalism. It would require this Court to intervene in the state judicial process with considerable lack of predictability and with a consequent likelihood of considerable friction. [T]o deny to the States the power to impair a fundamental constitutional right is not to increase federal power, but, rather, to limit the power of both federal and state governments in favor of safe-guarding the fundamental rights and liberties of the individual. In my view this promotes rather than undermines the basic policy of avoiding excess concentration of power in government, federal or state, which underlies our concepts of federalism." [a]

In the 1970s matters were brought to a head by the "right to jury trial" cases: *Baldwin v. New York,* 399 U.S. 66, 90 S.Ct. 1914, 26 L.Ed.2d 437 (1970) (no offense can be deemed "petty," thus dispensing with the fourteenth and sixth amendment rights to jury trial, where more than six months incarceration is authorized); *Williams v. Florida,* 399 U.S. 78, 90 S.Ct. 1893, 26 L.Ed.2d 446 (1970) ("that jury at common law was composed of precisely 12 is an historical accident, unnecessary to effect the purposes of the jury system"; thus 6-person jury in criminal cases does not violate sixth amendment, as applied to the states via fourteenth); [b] and the 1972 *Apodaca* and *Johnson* cases, discussed below, dealing with whether unanimous jury verdicts are required in criminal cases.

Dissenting in *Baldwin* and concurring in *Williams,* HARLAN, J., maintained: "[*Williams*] evinces [a] recognition that the 'incorporationist' view of the Due Process Clause of the Fourteenth Amendment, which underlay *Duncan* and is now carried forward into *Baldwin,* must be tempered to allow the States more elbow room in ordering their own criminal systems. With that much I agree. But to accomplish this by diluting constitutional protections within the federal system itself is something to which I cannot possibly subscribe. Tempering the rigor of *Duncan* should be done forthrightly, by facing up to the fact that at least in this area the 'incorporation' doctrine does not fit well with our federal structure, and by the same token that *Duncan* was wrongly decided.

a. To the same effect is the opinion of Black, J., joined by Douglas, J., concurring in *Duncan* and responding to the views of Harlan, J., dissenting and Fortas, J., concurring.

b. But *Ballew v. Georgia,* 435 U.S. 223, 98 S.Ct. 1029, 55 L.Ed.2d 234 (1978), subsequently held that a state trial in a non-petty criminal case to a jury of only five persons did deprive a defendant of the right to trial by jury guaranteed by the sixth and fourteenth amendments.

"[Rather] than bind the States by the hitherto undeviating and unquestioned federal practice of 12-member juries, the Court holds, based on a poll of state practice, that a six-man jury satisfies the guarantee of a trial by jury in a federal criminal system and consequently carries over to the States. This is a constitutional *renvoi*. With all respect, I consider that before today it would have been unthinkable to suggest that the Sixth Amendment's right to a trial by jury is satisfied by a jury of six, or less, as is left open by the Court's opinion in *Williams,* or by less than a unanimous verdict, a question also reserved in today's decision.[c]

"[These decisions] demonstrate that the difference between a 'due process' approach, that considers each particular case on its own bottom to see whether the right alleged is one 'implicit in the concept of ordered liberty,' and 'selective incorporation' is not an abstract one whereby different verbal formulae achieve the same results. The internal logic of the selective incorporation doctrine cannot be respected if the Court is both committed to interpreting faithfully the meaning of the federal Bill of Rights and recognizing the governmental diversity that exists in this country. The 'backlash' in *Williams* exposes the malaise, for there the Court dilutes a federal guarantee in order to reconcile the logic of 'incorporation,' the 'jot-for-jot and case-for-case' application of the federal right to the States, with the reality of federalism. Can one doubt that had Congress tried to undermine the common law right to trial by jury before *Duncan* came on the books the history today recited would have barred such action? Can we expect repeated performances when this Court is called upon to give definition and meaning to other federal guarantees that have been 'incorporated'?

"[I]t is time [for] for this Court to face up to the reality implicit in today's holdings and reconsider the 'incorporation' doctrine before its leveling tendencies further retard development in the field of criminal procedure by stifling flexibility in the States and by discarding the possibility of federal leadership by example."

In the companion cases of *Apodaca v. Oregon,* 406 U.S. 404, 92 S.Ct. 1628, 32 L.Ed.2d 184 (1972) and *Johnson v. Louisiana,* 406 U.S. 356, 92 S.Ct. 1620, 32 L.Ed.2d 152 (1972), upholding the constitutionality of less-than-unanimous jury verdicts in state criminal cases, eight justices adhered to the *Duncan* position that each element of the sixth amendment right to jury trial applies to the states to the same extent it applies to the federal government, but split 4–4 over whether the federal guarantee *did require* jury unanimity in criminal cases. State convictions by less than unanimous votes were sustained only because the ninth member of the Court, newly appointed POWELL, J., read the sixth amendment as requiring jury unanimity, but—taking a Harlan-type approach—concluded that *this feature* of the federal right is not "so fundamental to the essentials of jury trial" as to require unanimity in state criminal cases as a matter of fourteenth amendment due process: [d]

c. Cf. Frankfurter, J., for the Court in *Rochin v. California* (1952) (discussed in Part III infra): "Words being symbols do not speak without a gloss. [T]he gloss may be the deposit of history, whereby a term gains technical content. Thus the requirements of the Sixth and Seventh Amendments for trial by jury in the federal courts have a rigid meaning. No changes or chances can alter the content of the verbal symbol of 'jury'—a body of twelve men who must reach a unanimous conclusion if the verdict is to go against the defendant."

d. But *Burch v. Louisiana,* 441 U.S. 130, 99 S.Ct. 1623, 60 L.Ed.2d 96 (1979), subsequently held, without a dissent on this issue, that conviction by a nonunanimous *six-person* jury in a state criminal trial for a nonpetty offense did violate the sixth and fourteenth amendment rights to trial by jury.

"[I]n holding that the Fourteenth Amendment has incorporated 'jot-for-jot and case-for-case' every element of the Sixth Amendment, the Court derogates principles of federalism that are basic to our system. In the name of uniform application of high standards of due process, the Court has embarked upon a course of constitutional interpretation that deprives the States of freedom to experiment with adjudicatory processes different from the federal model. At the same time, the Court's understandable unwillingness to impose requirements that it finds unnecessarily rigid (e.g., *Williams*), has culminated in the dilution of federal rights that were, until these decisions, never seriously questioned. The doubly undesirable consequence of this reasoning process, labeled by Mr. Justice Harlan as 'constitutional schizophrenia,' may well be detrimental both to the state and federal criminal justice systems. Although it is perhaps late in the day for an expression of my views, I [believe] that, at least in defining the elements of the right to jury trial, there is no sound basis for interpreting the Fourteenth Amendment to require blind adherence by the States to all details of the federal Sixth Amendment standards." [e]

BRENNAN, J., joined by Marshall, J., dissented: "Readers of today's opinions may be understandably puzzled why convictions by 11–1 and 10–2 jury votes are affirmed [when] a majority of the Court agrees that the Sixth Amendment requires a unanimous verdict in federal criminal jury trials, and a majority also agrees that the right to jury trial guaranteed by the Sixth Amendment is to be enforced against the States according to the same standards that protect that right against federal encroachment. The reason is that while my Brother Powell agrees that a unanimous verdict is required in federal criminal trials, he does not agree that the Sixth Amendment right to a jury trial is to be applied in the same way to State and Federal Governments. In that circumstance, it is arguable that the affirmance of the convictions [is] not inconsistent with a view that today's decision is a holding that only a unanimous verdict will afford the accused in a state criminal prosecution the jury trial guaranteed him by the Sixth Amendment. In any event, the affirmance must not obscure that the majority of the Court remains of the view that, as in the case of every specific of the Bill of Rights that extends to the States, the Sixth Amendment's jury trial guarantee, however it is to be construed, has identical application against both State and Federal Governments." [f]

e. In his continued resistance to "jot-for-jot" or "bag and baggage" incorporation of a "selected" provision of the Bill of Rights, Powell, J., has gained two allies. See Powell, J., joined by Burger, C.J., and Rehnquist, J., dissenting in *Crist v. Bretz*, 437 U.S. 28, 98 S.Ct. 2156, 57 L.Ed.2d 24 (1978) (holding that federal rule as to when jeopardy "attaches" in jury trials applies to state cases). In *Ballew*, fn. b supra, although he concurred in the judgment, Powell, J., again joined by Burger, C.J., and Rehnquist, J., did not join Blackmun, J.'s opinion because it "assumes full incorporation of the Sixth Amendment, contrary to my view in *Apodaca*."

See also Burger, C.J.'s separate opinion in *Crist v. Bretz* and Rehnquist, J.'s separate opinion in *Buckley v. Valeo,* p. 1007 infra, maintaining that "not all of the strictures which the First Amendment imposes upon Congress are carried over against the States by the Fourteenth Amendment, [but] only the 'general principle' of free speech."

f. In a separate dissent, Stewart, J., joined by Brennan and Marshall, JJ., protested that "unless *Duncan* is to be overruled," "the only relevant question here is whether the Sixth Amendment's guarantee of trial by jury embraces a guarantee that the verdict of the jury must be unanimous. The answer to that question is clearly 'yes,' as my Brother Powell has cogently demonstrated."

III. BODILY EXTRACTIONS: ANOTHER LOOK AT THE "DUE PROCESS" AND "SELECTIVE INCORPORATION" APPROACHES

As noted earlier, dissenting in *Baldwin* and concurring in *Williams,* Harlan, J., maintained that "the difference between a 'due process' approach [and] 'selective incorporation' is not an abstract one whereby different formulae achieve the same results." But he made this observation in the context of the applicability to the states of the sixth amendment right to trial by jury, which had, or was thought to have, a relatively rigid meaning. Most language in the Bill of Rights, however, is rather vague and general, at least when specific problems arise under a particular phrase. In such cases, does dwelling on the literal language simply *shift the focus of broad judicial inquiry* from "due process" to e.g., "freedom of speech," "establishment of religion," "unreasonable searches and seizures," "excessive bail," "cruel and unusual punishments," and "the assistance of counsel"? See Friendly, *The Bill of Rights as a Code of Criminal Procedure,* 53 Calif.L.Rev. 929, 937 (1965); Kadish, *Methodology and Criteria in Due Process Adjudication—A Survey and Criticism,* 66 Yale L.J. 319, 337–39 (1957); Wechsler, *Toward Neutral Principles of Constitutional Law,* 73 Harv.L.Rev. 1, 17–18 (1959).

In considering whether the right to counsel "begins" at the time of arrest, preliminary hearing, arraignment, or not until the trial itself, or includes probation and parole revocation hearings or applies to juvenile delinquency proceedings, deportation hearings or civil commitments, or, where the defendant is indigent, includes the right to *assigned* counsel or an assigned psychiatrist at state expense, how helpful is the sixth amendment language entitling an accused to "the assistance of counsel for his defense"? Is the specificity or direction of this language significantly greater than the "due process" clause?

To turn to another cluster of problems—which form the basis for this section—in considering whether, and under what conditions, the police may direct the "pumping" of a person's stomach to uncover incriminating evidence, or the taking of a blood sample from him, without his consent, do the "specific guarantees" in the Bill of Rights against "unreasonable searches and seizures" and against compelling a person to be "a witness against himself" free the Court from the demands of appraising and judging involved in answering these questions by interpreting the "due process" clause?

ROCHIN v. CALIFORNIA, 342 U.S. 165, 72 S.Ct. 205, 96 L.Ed. 183 (1952) arose as follows: Having "some information" that Rochin was selling narcotics, three deputy sheriffs "forced upon the door of [his] room and found him sitting partly dressed on the side of the bed, upon which his wife was lying. On a 'night stand' beside the bed the deputies spied two capsules. When asked 'Whose stuff is this?' Rochin seized the capsules and put them in his mouth. A struggle ensued, in the course of which the three officers 'jumped upon him' and [unsuccessfully] attempted to extract the capsules. [Rochin] was handcuffed and taken to a hospital. At the direction of one of the officers a doctor forced an emetic solution through a tube into Rochin's stomach against his will. This 'stomach pumping' produced vomiting. In the vomited matter were found two capsules which proved to contain morphine. [Rochin was convicted of possessing morphine] and sentenced to sixty days' imprisonment. The chief evidence against him was the two capsules."

The Court, per FRANKFURTER, J., concluded that the officers' conduct violated fourteenth amendment due process: "This is conduct that shocks the conscience. Illegally breaking into the privacy of the petitioner, the struggle to open his mouth and remove what was there, the forcible extraction of his stomach's contents—this course of proceeding by agents of government to obtain evidence is bound to offend even hardened sensibilities. They are methods too close to the rack and the screw to permit of constitutional differentiation.

"It has long since ceased to be true that due process of law is heedless of the means by which otherwise relevant and credible evidence is obtained. [The confession cases are] only instances of the general requirement that States in their prosecutions respect certain decencies of civilized conduct. Due process of law, as a historic and generative principle, precludes defining, and thereby confining, these standards of conduct more precisely than to say that convictions cannot be brought about by methods that offend 'a sense of justice.' It would be a stultification of the responsibility which the course of constitutional history has cast upon this Court to hold that in order to convict a man the police cannot extract by force what is in his mind but can extract what is in his stomach.

"[E]ven though statements contained in them may be independently established as true[,] [c]oerced confessions offend the community's sense of fair play and decency. So here, to sanction the brutal conduct which naturally enough was condemned by the court whose judgment is before us, would be to afford brutality the cloak of law. Nothing would be more calculated to discredit law and thereby to brutalize the temper of a society."

Concurring, BLACK, J., reasoned that the fifth amendment's protection against compelled self-incrimination applied to the states and that "a person is compelled to be a witness against himself not only when he is compelled to testify, but also when as here, incriminating evidence is forcibly taken from him by a contrivance of modern science." He maintained that "faithful adherence to the specific guarantees in the Bill of Rights insures a more permanent protection of individual liberty than that which can be afforded by the nebulous [fourteenth amendment due process] standards stated by the majority."

DOUGLAS, J., concurring, also criticized the majority's approach. He contended that the privilege against self-incrimination applied to the states as well as the federal government and because of the privilege "words taken from [an accused's] lips, capsules taken from his stomach, blood taken from his veins are all inadmissible provided they are taken from him without his consent. [This] is an unequivocal, definite and workable rule of evidence for state and federal courts. But we cannot in fairness free the state courts from the [restraints of the fifth amendment privilege against self-incrimination] and yet excoriate them for flouting the 'decencies of civilized conduct' when they admit the evidence. This is to make the rule turn not on the Constitution but on the idiosyncrasies of the judges who sit here." [a]

----

a. *Irvine v. California,* 347 U.S. 128, 74 S.Ct. 381, 98 L.Ed. 561 (1954), limited *Rochin* to situations involving coercion, violence or brutality to the person. In *Irvine* the police made repeated illegal entries into petitioner's home, first to install a secret microphone and then to move it to the bedroom, in order to listen to the conversations of the occupants— for over a month. Jackson, J., who announced the judgment of the Court and wrote the principal opinion, recognized that "few police measures have come to our attention that more flagrantly, deliberately, and persistently violated the fundamental principle declared by the Fourth Amendment as a restriction on the Federal Government," but adhered to the holding in *Wolf v. Colorado* (1949) (Part IV infra) that the exclusionary rule in federal search and seizure cases is not binding on the states. (*Wolf* was overruled in *Mapp v. Ohio*

BREITHAUPT v. ABRAM, 352 U.S. 432, 77 S.Ct. 408, 1 L.Ed.2d 448 (1957), illustrated that under the *Rochin* test state police had considerable leeway even when the body of the accused was "invaded." In *Breithaupt*, the police took a blood sample from an unconscious person who had been involved in a fatal automobile collision. A majority, per CLARK, J., affirmed a manslaughter conviction based on the blood sample (which showed intoxication), stressing that the sample was "taken under the protective eye of a physician" and that "the blood test procedure has become routine in our everyday life." The "interests of society in the scientific determination of intoxication, one of the great causes of the mortal hazards of the road," outweighed "so slight an intrusion" of a person's body.

Dissenting, WARREN, C.J., joined by Black and Douglas, JJ., deemed *Rochin* controlling and argued that police efforts to curb the narcotics traffic, involved in *Rochin*, "is surely a state interest of at least as great magnitude as the interest in highway law enforcement. [Only] personal reaction to the stomach pump and the blood test can distinguish the [two cases]."

DOUGLAS, J., joined by Black, J., dissented, maintaining that "if the decencies of a civilized state are the test, it is repulsive to me for the police to insert needles into an unconscious person in order to get the evidence necessary to convict him, whether they find the person unconscious, give him a pill which puts him to sleep, or use force to subdue him."

Nine years later, even though in the meantime the Court had held in *Mapp v. Ohio*, Part IV infra, that the federal exclusionary rule in search and seizure cases was binding on the states and in *Malloy v. Hogan*, supra, that the fifth amendment's protection against compelled self-incrimination was likewise applicable to the states, the Court still upheld the taking by a physician, at police direction, of a blood sample from an injured person, over his objection. SCHMERBER v. CALIFORNIA, 384 U.S. 757, 86 S.Ct. 1826, 16 L.Ed.2d 908 (1966). In affirming the conviction for operating a vehicle while under the influence of intoxicating liquor, a 5–4 majority, per BRENNAN, J., ruled: (1) that the extraction of blood from petitioner under the aforementioned circumstances "did not offend 'that "sense of justice"' of which we spoke in *Rochin*," thus reaffirming *Breithaupt*; (2) that the privilege against self-incrimination, now binding on the states, "protects an accused only from being compelled to testify against himself, or otherwise provide the State with evidence of a testimonial or communicative nature and that the withdrawal of blood and use of the analysis in question did not involve compulsion to these ends"; and (3) that the protection against unreasonable search and seizure, now binding on the states, was satisfied because (a) "there was plainly probable cause" to arrest and charge petitioner and to suggest "the required relevance and likely success of a test of petitioner's blood for alcohol"; (b) the officer "might reasonably have believed that he was confronted with an emergency, in which the delay necessary to obtain a warrant, under the circumstances, threatened 'the destruction of evidence'"; and (c) "the

(1961) (Part IV infra)). Nor did Jackson, J., deem *Rochin* applicable: "However obnoxious are the facts in the case before us, they do not involve coercion, violence or brutality to the person [as did *Rochin*], but rather a trespass to property, plus eavesdropping."

Because of the "aggravating" and "repulsive" police misconduct in *Irvine*, Frankfurter, J., joined by Burton, J., dissenting, maintained that *Rochin* was controlling, not *Wolf*. (He

had written the majority opinions in both cases.) Black, J., joined by Douglas, J., dissented separately, arguing that petitioner had been convicted on the basis of evidence "extorted" from him in violation of the self-incrimination clause, which he considered applicable to the states. Douglas, J., dissenting separately, protested against the use in state prosecutions of evidence seized in violation of the fourth amendment.

test chosen to measure petitioner's blood-alcohol level was [reasonable and] performed in a reasonable manner."

Dissenting, BLACK, J., joined by Douglas, J., expressed amazement at the majority's "conclusion that compelling a person to give his blood to help the State to convict him is not equivalent to compelling him to be a witness against himself." "It is a strange hierarchy of values that allows the State to extract a human being's blood to convict him of a crime because of the blood's content but proscribes compelled production of his lifeless papers." [a]

Notes and Questions

1. In light of *Rochin, Breithaupt* and *Schmerber,* when courts decide constitutional questions by "looking to" the Bill of Rights, to what extent do they proceed, as Black, J., said in *Adamson,* "within clearly marked constitutional boundaries"? To what extent does resort to these "particular standards" enable courts to avoid substituting their "own concepts of decency and fundamental justice" for the language of the Constitution?

2. Did *Mapp* and *Malloy,* decided in the interim between *Breithaupt* and *Schmerber,* affect any justice's vote? Did the applicability of the "particular standards" of the fourth and fifth amendments inhibit Black, Douglas or Brennan, JJ., from employing their own concepts of "decency" and "justice" in *Schmerber?* After *Schmerber,* how much force is there in Black, J.'s view, concurring in *Rochin,* that "faithful adherence to the specific guarantees in the Bill of Rights assures a more permanent protection of individual liberty than that which can be afforded by the nebulous standards stated by the majority"?

3. For other recent illustrations of standards and methodology in due process adjudication, see the "death penalty" cases (although nominally "cruel and unusual punishment" cases), Sec. 3 infra. See also the "right of privacy" cases, Sec. 2 infra.

IV. LEADING CRIMINAL PROCEDURE DECISIONS AND THE RETROACTIVE EFFECT OF A HOLDING OF UNCONSTITUTIONALITY

In recent years, the Court has considered the retroactive effect of a holding that a law or practice is unconstitutional primarily in the context of criminal procedure decisions.[a] *Linkletter v. Walker,* 381 U.S. 618, 85 S.Ct. 1731, 14 L.Ed. 2d 601 (1965), took the position that "the Constitution neither prohibits nor requires retrospective effect," [b] and that a determination of the effect of a

---

a. Warren, C.J., and Douglas, J., dissented in separate opinions, each adhering to his dissenting views in *Breithaupt.* In a third dissent, Fortas, J., maintained that "petitioner's privilege against self-incrimination applies" and, moreover, "under the Due Process Clause, the State, in its role as prosecutor, has no right to extract blood from [anyone] over his protest."

a. In none of these cases, apparently, did the Court seriously consider applying the new constitutional ruling "purely prospectively," i.e., not even giving the litigant in the very case the benefit of the decision. "Pure prospectivity" raises "difficult problems concerning the nature of a court's functions; persuasive arguments can be made that courts are

badly suited for the general determination and proclamation of future rules and, indeed, that for them to do so violates the Constitution's grant to the judiciary only of power over 'cases' and 'controversies.' " 80 Harv.L.Rev. 140 (1966). Another frequently made point, although it may carry less weight in the criminal procedure area, is that "if the Supreme Court begins regularly to announce new rules prospectively only, petitioners, knowing they will be unlikely to benefit personally, will be deterred from pressing for the new rules." Id.

b. "If an unconstitutional statute or practice effectively never existed as a lawful justification for state action [perhaps the dominant view in the era between the Civil War and the Depression—compare *Norton v. Shelby Coun-*

judgment of unconstitutionality would turn on "the prior history of the rule in question, its purpose and effect," "whether retrospective operation of the rule will further or retard its operation" and what adverse impact on the administration of justice retroactivity would be likely to have. Two years later, the Court articulated "the criteria guiding resolution of the [retroactivity] question": "(a) the purpose to be served by the new standards"—e.g., protecting the reliability of the fact-finding process (such as the right to counsel at trial or the ban against coerced confessions) or furthering some other, independent interest, such as individual privacy—"(b) the extent of the reliance by law enforcement authorities on the old standards, and (c) the effect on the administration of justice of a retroactive application of the new standards." [c]

Consider the retroactivity problem in the context of the leading criminal procedure cases of the past two decades:

GIDEON v. WAINWRIGHT, 372 U.S. 335, 83 S.Ct. 792, 9 L.Ed.2d 799 (1963), held that, at least in all felony prosecutions,[d] an indigent defendant must be appointed counsel. Because, as Black, J., maintained, dissenting in the case *Gideon* was to overrule 20 years later,[e] "whether [one] is innocent cannot be determined from a trial [in which] denial of counsel has made it impossible to [tell] that the defendant's case was adequately represented," and because, as Black, J., pointed out for the Court in *Gideon,* "any person haled into court, who is too poor to hire a lawyer, cannot be assured a fair trial unless counsel is provided for him," *Gideon* was given complete retroactive effect.[f]

---

ty, 118 U.S. 425, 6 S.Ct. 1121, 30 L.Ed. 178 (1886) with *Chicot County Drainage Dist. v. Baxter State Bank,* 308 U.S. 371, 60 S.Ct. 317, 84 L.Ed. 329 (1940)], individuals convicted under the statute or in trials which tolerated the practice were convicted unlawfully even if their trials took place before the declaration of unconstitutionality; such a declaration should have a fully retroactive effect, and previously convicted individuals should be able to win their freedom through the writ of habeas corpus. Alternatively, if a judgment of unconstitutionality affects only the case at hand [a view which also had support], the legality of the convictions of individuals previously tried is not affected. In *Linkletter,* the Court rejected both extremes." Tribe, *American Constitutional Law* 25 (1978).

c. *Stovall v. Denno,* 388 U.S. 293, 87 S.Ct. 1967, 18 L.Ed.2d 1199 (1967), concerning the retroactive effect of the lineup decisions, infra.

d. A decade and a half later, *Scott v. Illinois,* 440 U.S. 367, 99 S.Ct. 1158, 59 L.Ed.2d 383 (1979) (per Rehnquist, J.), held that the sixth and fourteenth amendments require that, regardless of whether the offense be classified as a "misdemeanor" or "felony," "no indigent criminal defendant be sentenced to a term of imprisonment unless the State has afforded him the right to assistance of appointed counsel in his defense." But the Court declined to apply the *Gideon* principle to a case where one is charged with an offense for which imprisonment is *authorized,* but *not*

actually imposed. See also *Argersinger v. Hamlin,* 407 U.S. 25, 92 S.Ct. 2006, 32 L.Ed.2d 530 (1972).

e. *Betts v. Brady,* 316 U.S. 455, 62 S.Ct. 1252, 86 L.Ed. 1595 (1942).

f. Other decisions given retroactive effect: *Ivan v. New York,* 407 U.S. 203, 92 S.Ct. 1951, 32 L.Ed.2d 659 (1972) (per curiam), held that "the major purpose" of the constitutional requirement of "proof beyond a reasonable doubt" announced in *In re Winship,* 397 U.S. 358, 90 S.Ct. 1068, 25 L.Ed.2d 368 (1970) "was to overcome an aspect of a criminal trial that substantially impairs the truth-finding function" and thus *Winship* should be given "complete retroactive effect." In *Robinson v. Neil,* 409 U.S. 505, 93 S.Ct. 876, 35 L.Ed.2d 29 (1973), the Court ruled that because *Waller v. Florida,* 397 U.S. 387, 90 S.Ct. 1184, 25 L.Ed. 2d 435 (1970), holding that the double jeopardy clause barred two prosecutions, state and municipal, based on the same act or offense, was "squarely directed to the prevention of the second trial's taking place at all, even though it might have been conducted with a scrupulous regard for [all] constitutional procedural rights," *Waller* "is to be accorded full retroactive effect." In *Brown v. Louisiana,* 447 U.S. 323, 100 S.Ct. 2214, 65 L.Ed.2d 159 (1980), because he viewed *Burch v. Louisiana,* 441 U.S. 130, 99 S.Ct. 1623, 60 L.Ed.2d 96 (1979), holding that conviction of a nonpetty offense by a nonunanimous *six-person* jury violates a defendant's right to trial by jury, as

MAPP v. OHIO, 367 U.S. 643, 81 S.Ct. 1684, 6 L.Ed.2d 1081 (1961), overruling *Wolf v. Colorado*, 338 U.S. 25, 69 S.Ct. 1359, 93 L.Ed. 1782 (1949), held that the federal "exclusionary rule" in search and seizure cases[g] was binding on the

establishing that "the concurrence of six jurors was constitutionally required to preserve the substance of the jury trial and assure the reliability of its verdict," Brennan, J., joined by Stewart, Marshall and Blackmun, JJ., would give *Burch* full retroactive effect. Since Powell, J., joined by Stevens, J., believed that new constitutional rules should apply retroactively in cases still pending on direct review—and Burch's case was pending on direct appeal—they concurred in the reversal of Burch's conviction on this ground.

g. As noted in Oaks, *Studying the Exclusionary Rule in Search and Seizure*, 37 U.Chi. L.Rev. 665–66 (1970), the Court "currently enforces an exclusionary rule in state and federal criminal proceedings as to four major types of violations: searches and seizures that violate the fourth amendment [and wiretapping and electronic eavesdropping that violate the fourth amendment or federal statutory law], confessions obtained in violation of the fifth and sixth amendments, identification testimony obtained in violation of these amendments [see the landmark lineup cases, *United States v. Wade* and *Gilbert v. California*, both briefly discussed infra], and evidence obtained by methods so shocking that its use would violate the due process clause [see *Rochin*, supra]. The exclusionary rule is the Supreme Court's sole technique for enforcing these vital constitutional rights." In addition to being the most frequent occasion for application of the exclusionary rule, one quality that sets search and seizure apart from other areas is that evidence obtained by an illegal search and seizure "is just as reliable as evidence obtained by legal means. This cannot always be said of evidence obtained by improper methods of lineup identification or interrogation." Id. at 666.

The search and seizure exclusionary rule has been subjected to persistent, heavy attack in recent years. Perhaps the most significant post-*Mapp* decision on the scope of the exclusionary rule is *United States v. Calandra*, 414 U.S. 338, 94 S.Ct. 613, 38 L.Ed.2d 561 (1974). In ruling that a grand jury witness may not refuse to answer questions on the ground that they are based on the fruits of an unlawful search, the *Calandra* Court, per Powell, J., called the exclusionary rule "a judicially created remedy designed to safeguard Fourth Amendment rights generally through its deterrent effect, rather than a personal constitutional right of the party aggrieved." Thus, whether grand jury questions based on evidence seized in violation of the Fourth Amendment should be prohibited "present[ed] a question, not of rights, but of remedies"—a question to be answered by weighing the "potential inquiry" to the functions of the grand

jury against the "potential benefits" of the exclusionary rule in this context; or more generally, by weighing the "likely 'costs' " of the rule against its "likely 'benefits' " in the particular context.

The exclusionary rule "lost" in *Calandra*—as it usually does when the question is presented this way. See *Stone v. Powell*, 428 U.S. 465, 96 S.Ct. 3037, 49 L.Ed.2d 1067 (1976) (state prisoner may not be granted federal habeas corpus relief on search-and-seizure grounds unless denied opportunity for "full and fair litigation" of claim in state courts); *United States v. Janis*, 428 U.S. 433, 96 S.Ct. 3021, 49 L.Ed.2d 1046 (1976) (rule's deterrent purpose would not be served by excluding from federal civil tax proceedings evidence that was obtained illegally by state police); *United States v. Ceccolini*, 435 U.S. 268, 98 S.Ct. 1054, 55 L.Ed.2d 268 (1978) (exclusionary rule "should be invoked with much greater reluctance" where defense seeks to suppress live-witness testimony rather than an inanimate object); *United States v. Havens*, 446 U.S. 620, 100 S.Ct. 1912, 64 L.Ed.2d 559 (1980) (illegally obtained evidence may impeach not only direct testimony of defendant but also statements first elicited from him on cross-examination, if prosecutor's questions were "reasonably suggested" by the direct testimony); *INS v. Lopez-Mendoza*, 468 U.S. 1032, 104 S.Ct. 3479, 82 L.Ed.2d 778 (1984) (because high costs of applying the rule in this setting outweigh the marginal benefits, exclusionary rule inapplicable in a civil deportation hearing).

The most dramatic application to date of the "deterrence" rationale, and its concomitant cost-benefit analysis, is *United States v. Leon*, ___ U.S. ___, 104 S.Ct. 3405, 82 L.Ed.2d 677 (1984), per White, J., where the Court's "evaluation of the costs and benefits of suppressing reliable physical evidence" led it to establish a "good faith" or "reasonable mistake" exception to the fourth amendment exclusionary rule, at least in search warrant cases, so that evidence obtained by police officers pursuant to an invalid search warrant is admissible so long as the police acted in the "reasonable, good-faith belief" that the challenged search or seizure was in accord with the fourth amendment:

Until *Leon*, one could still say that the Court's "deconstitutionalization" of the exclusionary rule—its view that the rule is only a "judicially created" "remedial device" whose application turns on a "pragmatic analysis of [its] usefulness in a particular context" (*Stone v. Powell*, supra)—had only narrowed the thrust of the exclusionary rule in "peripheral" or "collateral" settings, but had not affected the rule in its central application: the prose-

states—"all evidence obtained by searches and seizures in violation of the [fourth and fourteenth amendments] is, by the same authority, inadmissible in a state court." *Linkletter v. Walker,* supra, however, declined to apply *Mapp* to state convictions which had become final prior to the overruling of *Wolf:* [h] The "prime purpose" of the "exclusionary rule"—deterring lawless police action—reasoned

cutor's case-in-chief against the direct victim of a fourth amendment violation. Indeed, *Stone* and other cases had suggested that at least in its central application the exclusionary rule would be spared the ordeal of being subjected to "interest-balancing" or "cost-benefit" analysis—that at least in these circumstances it would not have to demonstrate that it can "pay its way." As *Leon* makes plain, however, this is not the case.

Although the "deterrence" rationale has been in the ascendency ever since *Calandra,* it has not escaped forceful criticism on and off the Court. In *Calandra* itself, dissenting Justice Brennan, joined by Douglas and Marshall, JJ., maintained that curtailment of fourth amendment violations was not (nor should it be) the exclusionary rule's *raison d'etre:* the goals "uppermost in the minds of the framers of the rule" were "enabling the judiciary to avoid the taint of partnership in official lawlessness" and "assuring the people [that] the government would not profit from its lawless behavior, thus minimizing the risk of seriously undermining popular trust in government." A decade later, dissenting in *Leon,* Brennan, J., joined by Marshall, J., observed:

"[T]he question whether the exclusion of evidence would deter future police misconduct was never considered a relevant concern in the early [federal search and seizure cases]. In these formative decisions, the Court plainly understood that the exclusion of illegally obtained evidence was compelled not by judicially fashioned remedial purposes, but rather by a direct constitutional command. [The Fourth Amendment] directly contemplates that some reliable and incriminating evidence will be lost to the government; therefore, it is not the exclusionary rule, but the Amendment itself that has imposed this cost.

"In addition, the Court's decisions over the past decade have made plain that the entire enterprise of attempting to assess the benefits and costs of the exclusionary rule in various contexts is a virtually impossible task for the judiciary to perform honestly or accurately. Although the Court's language in those cases suggests that some specific empirical basis may support its analyses, the reality is that the Court's opinions represent inherently unstable compounds of intuition, hunches, and occasional pieces of partial and often inconclusive data. [By] remaining within its redoubt of empiricism and by basing the rule solely on the deterrence rationale, the Court has robbed the rule of legitimacy. A doctrine that is explained as if it were an empirical proposition but for which there is only limited empir-

ical support is both inherently unstable and an easy mark for critics."

There is a vast literature on the "exclusionary rule." The various arguments are analyzed in 1 LaFave, *Search and Seizure: A Treatise on the Fourth Amendment* 3–39 (1978). See also the Kamisar-Wilkey debate, 62 Judic. 66, 214, 337, 351 (1978–79). For criticism of the *Calandra-Stone-Leon* line of cases, see, e.g., Kamisar, *Does (Did) (Should) The Exclusionary Rule Rest on a "Principled Basis" Rather than an "Empirical Proposition"?,* 16 Creighton L.Rev. 565 (1983); LaFave, *"The Seductive Call of Expediency": U.S. v. Leon, Its Rationale and Ramifications,* 1984 U.Ill.L.Rev. 895 (1984); Schrock & Welsh, *Up from Calandra: The Exclusionary Rule as a Constitutional Requirement,* 59 Minn.L.Rev. 251 (1974); Wasserstrom & Mertens, *The Exclusionary Rule on the Scaffold: But Was It A Fair Trial?,* 22 Am.Crim.L.Rev. 85 (1984). For criticism of the Burger Court's cost-benefit approach to judicial decisionmaking generally, see Tribe, *Constitutional Calculus: Equal Justice or Economic Efficiency?,* 98 Harv.L.Rev. 592 (1985).

h. *Mapp,* however, had been applied to state cases still pending on direct appeal at the time it was handed down. But four years later, *Desist v. United States,* 394 U.S. 244, 89 S.Ct. 1030, 22 L.Ed.2d 248 (1969), concluded that another new fourth amendment decision, *Katz v. United States,* 389 U.S. 347, 88 S.Ct. 507, 19 L.Ed.2d 576 (1967), should only be given what the Court called "wholly prospective application," i.e., applied only to *police activity* occurring after the date of the decision. See also the Court's treatment of the 1967 line up decisions, infra.

Katz held that the reach of the fourth amendment "cannot turn upon the presence or absence of a physical intrusion into any given enclosure" and that electronic eavesdropping upon private conversations constituted a search and seizure which must meet fourth amendment requirements. All of the reasons for applying *Katz* prospectively only, observed *Desist,* per Stewart, J., author of the *Katz* opinion, "also undercut any distinction between final convictions and those still pending on review. Both the deterrent purpose of the exclusionary rule and the reliance of law enforcement officers focus upon the time of the search, not any subsequent point in the prosecution as the relevant date." In a long, powerful dissent, Harlan, J., concluded, inter alia, that "*Linkletter* was right in insisting that all 'new' rules of constitutional law must, at minimum, be applied to all those cases

the Court, per Clark, J., author of the *Mapp* opinion, would not be furthered by making the rule retroactive. "The misconduct of the police prior to *Mapp* has already occurred and will not be corrected by releasing the prisoners involved. [T]he ruptured privacy of the victim's home and effects cannot be restored. Reparation comes too late."

Moreover, retroactive application of *Mapp* to "finalized" cases "would tax the administration of justice to the utmost. Hearings would have to be held on the excludability of evidence long since destroyed, misplaced or deteriorated. [To] thus legitimate such an extraordinary procedural weapon *that has no bearing on guilt* would seriously disrupt the administration of justice." (Emphasis added.)

The Court recognized that it had given full retroactive effect to cases developing a sophisticated and sensitive approach to the admissibility of "coerced" confessions and to cases establishing an indigent's right to assigned counsel at trial, and his right to be furnished a trial transcript on appeal,[i] but those principles "went to the fairness of the trial—the very integrity of the fact-finding process. Here the fairness of the trial is not under attack."

BLACK, J., joined by Douglas, J., dissented: "Despite the Court's resounding promises throughout the *Mapp* opinion that convictions based on such 'unconstitutional evidence' would 'find no sanction in the judgments of the courts,' Linkletter, convicted in the state court by use of 'unconstitutional evidence,' is today denied relief by the judgment of this Court because his conviction became 'final' before *Mapp* was decided. Linkletter must stay in jail; Miss Mapp, whose offense was committed before Linkletter's, is free. This different treatment of Miss Mapp and Linkletter points up at once the arbitrary and discriminatory nature of the judicial contrivance utilized here to break the promise of *Mapp* by keeping all people in jail who are unfortunate enough to have had their unconstitutional convictions affirmed before [the date of the *Mapp* decision]."

GRIFFIN v. CALIFORNIA, 380 U.S. 609, 85 S.Ct. 1229, 14 L.Ed.2d 106 (1965), held that the fifth amendment privilege against self-incrimination, binding on the states via the fourteenth amendment, prohibits adverse comment by prosecutor or judge on a defendant's failure to take the stand in a criminal case. But a 5–2 majority, per Stewart, J., declined to apply the rule to state cases "finalized" before *Griffin* was decided,[j] observing that "the basic purposes that lie behind the privilege against self-incrimination do not relate to protecting the innocent from conviction, but rather to [effectuating] values reflecting the concern of our society for the right of each individual to be let alone." More-

which are still subject to direct review by this Court at the time the 'new' decision is handed down." Douglas and Fortas, JJ., also filed separate dissents.

More than a decade later, however, relying heavily on Harlan, J.'s dissent in *Desist, United States v. Johnson,* 457 U.S. 537, 102 S.Ct. 2579, 73 L.Ed.2d 202 (1982), per Blackmun, J., applied *Payton v. New York,* 445 U.S. 573, 100 S.Ct. 1371, 63 L.Ed.2d 639 (1980) (holding that police must obtain an arrest warrant when entering a suspect's home to make a routine felony arrest) to cases still pending on direct

appeal at the time *Payton* was decided. The Court pointed out that "*Payton* overturned no long-standing practice approved by a near-unanimous body of lower court authority [and thus] does not fall into that narrow class of decisions whose nonretroactivity is effectively preordained because they unmistakably signal 'a clear break with the past.' "

i. *Griffin v. Illinois,* 351 U.S. 12, 76 S.Ct. 585, 100 L.Ed. 891 (1956).

j. *Tehan v. United States ex rel. Shott,* 382 U.S. 406, 86 S.Ct. 459, 15 L.Ed.2d 453 (1966).

over, "for more than half a century" the states had relied, in good faith on the *Twining* rule [fn. a, Sec. I supra].[k]

MIRANDA v. ARIZONA, 384 U.S. 436, 86 S.Ct. 1602, 16 L.Ed.2d 694 (1966), probably the most famous and controversial Warren Court criminal procedure case, applied the privilege against self-incrimination to the stationhouse and other "custodial surroundings" and required the police to give a suspect the familiar "*Miranda* warnings" and to obtain a waiver of his rights before subjecting him to "custodial interrogation." But a week later, the Court, per WARREN, C.J., author of the *Miranda* opinion, held that the new ruling affected only those cases in which *the trial began* after the date of the landmark decision: [1]

While *Miranda* "guard[s] against the possibility of unreliable statements in every instance of in-custody interrogation, [it] encompass[es] situations in which the danger is not necessarily as great as when the accused is subjected to overt and obvious coercion. At the same time, our case law is available for persons whose trials have already been completed. [They] may invoke [the 'voluntariness' or 'coerced confession' test, based on the 'totality of circumstances' in each case, which] has become increasingly meticulous throughout the years [and] now takes specific account of [although it does not give decisive weight to] the failure to advise the accused of his privilege against self-incrimination or to allow him access to outside assistance. [Thus], although *Miranda* provides important new safeguards against the use of unreliable statements at trial, [its nonretroactivity] will not preclude persons whose trials have already been completed from invoking the same safeguards as part of an involuntariness claim." [m]

Black and Douglas, JJ., dissented, again for substantially the same reasons stated in their *Linkletter* dissent.[n] Three years later, dissenting in another case applying a new decision prospectively only,[o] Douglas, J., called the Court's treatment of *Miranda* "the most notorious example" of its unsatisfactory approach in this area. On the eve of *Miranda,* he recalled, the Court had some 80

k. Warren, C.J., and Fortas, J., took no part. Black, J., joined by Douglas, J., dissented for essentially the same reasons in their *Linkletter* dissent.

l. *Johnson v. New Jersey,* 384 U.S. 719, 86 S.Ct. 1772, 16 L.Ed.2d 882 (1966).

A decade and a half later, however, relying heavily on *United States v. Johnson* and Harlan, J.'s reasoning in *Desist,* fn. h, supra, that principled decisionmaking and fairness to similarly situated petitioners requires application of a new rule to all cases pending on direct review, *Shea v. Louisiana,* __ U.S. __, 105 S.Ct. 1065, 84 L.Ed.2d 38 (1985), per Blackmun, J., applied *Edwards v. Arizona,* 451 U.S. 477, 101 S.Ct. 1880, 68 L.Ed.2d 378 (1981) (restricting ability of police to obtain waiver of rights when suspect specifically asserts right to counsel) retroactively to all cases in which the process of appeal had not yet been completed when *Edwards* was decided. White, J., joined by Burger, C.J., and Rehnquist and O'Connor, JJ., dissenting, deemed "hollow" the claim that the majority's rule serves fairness:

"[T]he attempt to distinguish between direct and collateral challenges for purposes of retroactivity is misguided. Under the majority's rule, otherwise identically situated defendants may be subject to different constitutional rules, depending on just how long ago now-unconstitutional conduct occurred and how quickly cases proceed through the criminal justice system. The disparity is no different in kind from that which occurs when the benefit of a new constitutional rule is retroactively afforded to the defendant in whose case it is announced but to no others; the Court's new approach equalizes nothing except the numbers of defendants within the disparately treated classes."

m. But see note 2 infra.

n. The four *Miranda* dissenters (Clark, Harlan, Stewart and White, JJ.,) concurred in the opinion of the Court applying *Miranda* prospectively, but noted continued adherence to their dissent in *Miranda.*

o. *Desist v. United States,* fn. h supra.

cases before it raising the question decided in *Miranda*. "We took [and disposed of four of them], applying the rule retroactively [in those four cases]. But [we denied relief in the rest]. Yet it was sheer coincidence that those precise four were chosen. Any other single case in the group or any other four would have been sufficient for our purposes."

UNITED STATES v. WADE, 388 U.S. 218, 87 S.Ct. 1926, 18 L.Ed.2d 1149 (1967) and GILBERT v. CALIFORNIA, 388 U.S. 263, 87 S.Ct. 1951, 18 L.Ed.2d 1178 (1967) established the right to counsel at certain pre-trial lineups and other identification proceedings.[p] Unlike *Mapp*, which applied to police searches and seizures conducted *before* the date of this decision—so long as the case was still pending on appeal—and unlike *Miranda*, which applied to police questioning conducted *before* the date of this decision—so long as *the trial* began after the date—*Stovall v. Denno*, supra, held that *Wade* and *Gilbert* "affect only those cases [involving] *confrontations for identification purposes* conducted in the absence of counsel *after* [the date of these decisions]" (emphasis added). Thus, the landmark lineup decisions were completely prospective, except that they overturned the convictions of Wade and Gilbert themselves. Selection of *the date of the police* conduct, rather than the date of the trial or some other point in the criminal process indicated that *police reliance* is a major factor in retroactivity disputes.[q]

Notes and Questions

1. Consider Haddad, *"Retroactivity Should Be Rethought": A Call for the End of the Linkletter Doctrine*, 60 J.Crim.L.C. & P. 417, 439 (1969): "The alternative to the prospective-only technique is a more conservative approach to constitutional criminal procedure. Deference to varying state practices would be required. Detailed federal standards such as those laid down in *Miranda* would no longer be possible. Adoption of safeguards, such as the right to counsel at lineups, which not a single state anticipated, would also be impossible. For liberals, the choice is clear." See also F. Allen, *The Judicial Quest for Penal Justice: The Warren Court and the Criminal Cases*, 1975 U.Ill.L.F. 518, 530 (although "at first glance the prospectivity rule appears to be an act of judicial self-abnegation," "in reality [it] encourages the making of new law by reducing some of the social costs").

2. *Miranda. Johnson v. New Jersey*, supra, reasoned that "while [*Miranda*] provide[s] *important new safeguards* against the use of *unreliable* statements" (emphasis added), its nonretroactivity will not prevent defendants "from invoking *the same safeguards* as part of an involuntariness claim." (Emphasis added.) Did *Miranda* indicate dissatisfaction with—and lack of confidence in— the actual operation of the "voluntariness" test, just as *Gideon* manifested dissatisfaction with the overruled *Betts v. Brady* approach? See, e.g., Kamisar, *A Dissent from the Miranda Dissents*, 65 Mich.L.Rev. 59 (1966). If past defen-

---

p. The Court subsequently held that the *Wade-Gilbert* rule did not apply to identification proceedings that took place before the defendant was indicted or otherwise formally charged with a crime, *Kirby v. Illinois*, 406 U.S. 682, 92 S.Ct. 1877, 32 L.Ed.2d 411 (1972), nor to photographic identifications, whether conducted before or after the defendant had been formally charged, *United States v. Ash*, 413 U.S. 300, 93 S.Ct. 2568, 37 L.Ed.2d 619 (1973).

q. Similarly, as discussed in fn. h supra, *Desist* applied *Katz* only to *police conduct* violating reasonable expectations of privacy under the new *Katz* doctrine which occurred after the date of that decision.

dants could be adequately protected by a judicial examination into whether their confessions were "voluntary," then was *Miranda* wrongly decided? See Johnson, *Retroactivity in Retrospect,* 56 Calif.L.Rev. 1612, 1617 (1968); 80 Harv.L.Rev. 138–39 (1966).

3. To a considerable extent the "retroactivity" cases adopt the analysis of Mishkin, *The High Court, the Great Writ, and the Due Process of Time and Law,* 79 Harv.L.Rev. 56 (1965). But consider H. Schwartz, *Retroactivity, Reliability, and Due Process: A Reply to Professor Mishkin,* 33 U.Chi.L.Rev. 719, 748–49 (1966): "Since newly declared constitutional criminal procedure rights 'are of the very essence [of] "ordered liberty,"' states should not be allowed to continue to deprive persons of their freedom on the basis of proceedings now considered contrary to 'the kind of fair trial which is this country's constitutional goal.' [I]f the accusatorial system and the privilege against self-incrimination are indeed of the essence of our system of criminal justice, was a trial which [violated that system any less a violation] merely because it happened five or even twenty-five years ago? [Has] it not always been wrong to compel a man to incriminate himself, or to allow him, because of ignorance, to waive his rights either in the police station or in court?

"[The truth is] that recent decisions have not discovered or created new rights; rather, they have only granted new federal remedies for old wrongs. These remedies have been granted only recently not because the rights they protect are newly conceived or newly relevant, but rather because concern for considerations of federalism has lessened and perhaps because sensitivity to due process problems has increased. But the newness of the remedy does not eliminate the faults of the condemned proceeding, for just as we cannot tolerate the continued imprisonment of a man whose conviction was based on unreliable evidence, so we cannot tolerate the continued imprisonment of a man whose conviction failed in other respects to meet the fundamental legal standards of the community."

SECTION 2. THE RIGHT OF "PRIVACY" (OR "AUTONOMY" OR "PERSONHOOD")

Introductory Note

"Whether as substantive due process or as Privacy, 'fundamentality' needs elaboration, especially with respect to the weight particular rights are to enjoy in the balance against public good. Justices Stone and Cardozo suggested that the freedoms of speech, press and religion required extraordinary judicial protection against invasions even for the public good, because of their place at the foundations of democracy and because of the unreliability of the political process in regard to them. If other rights—those to be described as within the Rights of Privacy—are also to be specially guarded against the democratic political process, similar or other justifications must be found—if there are any. Perhaps unusual respect for autonomy and idiosyncrasy as regards some 'personal' matters is intuitively felt by all of us, including Justices; that such deference is 'self-evident' is not self-evident."

—Henkin, *Privacy and Autonomy,* 74 Colum.L.Rev. 1410, 1428–29 (1974).

———

As noted in Lupu, *Untangling the Strands of the Fourteenth Amendment,* 77 Mich.L.Rev. 981, 1029–30 (1979), "unlike the all-inclusive theory of the *Lochner* era that held all liberties equally inviolable, and unlike the procedural due process theory that assesses the weight of any protected interest in a refined way for purposes of 'balancing' [Sec. 5 infra], [what might be called] modern substantive due process theory has a distinct all-or-nothing quality to it. Most liberties lacking textual support are of the garden variety—like liberty of contract—and thus their deprivation is constitutional if rationally necessary to the achievement of a public good. [See, e.g., *Williamson v. Lee Optical Co.,* p. 263 supra]. Several select liberties, on the other hand, have attained the status of 'fundamental' or 'preferred,' with the consequence that the Constitution permits a state to abridge them only if it can demonstrate an extraordinary justification." A notable example is *Roe v. Wade,* infra, where the Court held that the "right of privacy" encompassed "a woman's decision whether or not to terminate her pregnancy" and thus certain restrictions on abortion could be justified "only by a 'compelling state interest.' " See also *Shapiro v. Thompson,* p. 1053 infra, which can be viewed as a "right to travel" case, which, in the course of invalidating a one-year durational residence requirement for welfare, rejected the argument that "a mere showing of a rational relationship between the waiting period and [administrative governmental] objectives will suffice [for] in moving from state to state [appellees] were exercising a constitutional right, and any classification which serves to penalize the exercise of that right, unless shown to be necessary to promote a *compelling* governmental interest, is unconstitutional." As Lupu observes, ibid., "[b]ecause the review standard for ordinary liberties is so deferential, and the standard for preferred liberties so rigid, outcomes are ordained by the designation of 'preferred' [or 'fundamental'] or not."

Regulations dealing with "fundamental rights" call for "strict scrutiny" review just as government classifications based upon what have come to be known as "suspect" criteria trigger "strict" equal protection review. "[T]here is a case to be made for a significant degree of judicial deference to legislative and administrative choices in some spheres. Yet the idea of strict scrutiny acknowledges that other political choices—those burdening fundamental rights, or suggesting prejudice against racial or other minorities—must be subjected to close analysis in order to preserve substantive values of equality and liberty. Although strict scrutiny in this form ordinarily appears as a standard for judicial review, it may also be understood as admonishing lawmakers and regulators as well to be particularly cautious of their *own* purposes and premises and of the effects of their choices." Tribe, *American Constitutional Law* 1000 (1978).

Not infrequently, as in *Skinner v. Oklahoma* (discussed immediately below), which is an "equal protection" case in form, and which never mentioned any "right of privacy," but to which "the development of a constitutionally protected 'right of privacy' in sexual matters can be traced," Nowak, Rotunda & Young, *Constitutional Law* 736 (2d ed. 1983), a decision can be viewed as either an "equal protection" or a "fundamental rights" (or "substantive due process") case.

Indeed, observes Lupu, at 983–84, "the tangling [of 'liberty' and 'equality'] is most apparent and most serious when viewed in its relationship to the so-called 'fundamental rights' developments in both equal protection and due process clause interpretation. In the sense used here, fundamental rights include all the claims of individual rights, drawn from sources outside of the first eight amendments, that the Supreme Court has elevated to preferred status (that is, rights which the government may infringe only when it demonstrates extraordinary justification). [Which] new rights properly derive from the liberty strand, and which from the equality strand?[6] Sometimes the Court tells us; other times it does not. Often, members of the Court agree upon the preferred status of an interest but disagree about its textual source.[7] On occasion, members of the Court concede that an interest has no textual source, yet battle still over which strand of the fourteenth amendment protects it from state interference."[8]

SKINNER v. OKLAHOMA, 316 U.S. 535, 62 S.Ct. 1110, 86 L.Ed. 1655 (1942), per DOUGLAS, J., held violative of equal protection Oklahoma's Habitual Criminal Sterilization Act, which authorized the sterilization of persons previously convicted and imprisoned two or more times of crimes "amounting to felonies involving moral turpitude" and thereafter convicted of such a felony and sentenced to prison. (Petitioner, previously convicted of "chicken-stealing" and robbery, had again been convicted of robbery.) Expressly exempted were embezzlement, political offenses and revenue act violations. Thus a person convicted three times of larceny could be subjected to sterilization, but the embezzler could not—although "the nature of the two crimes is intrinsically the same" and they are otherwise punishable in the same manner. The Court recognized that "if we had here only a question as to a State's classification of crimes, such as embezzlement or larceny," no substantial federal question would be presented. "But the instant legislation runs afoul of the equal protection clause" because—

"We are dealing here with legislation which involves one of the basic civil rights of man. Marriage and procreation are fundamental to the very existence and survival of the race. [In] evil or reckless hands [the power to sterilize] can cause races or types which are inimical to the dominant group to wither and disappear. There is no redemption for the individual whom the law touches. [He] is forever deprived of a basic liberty.[a] We mention these matters [in] emphasis of our view that strict scrutiny of the classification which a State makes in a sterilization law is essential, lest unwittingly, or otherwise, invidious discriminations are made against groups or types of individuals in violation of the constitutional guaranty of just and equal laws. [When] the law lays an unequal hand on those who have committed intrinsically the same quality of offense and sterilizes one and not the other, it has made as invidious a discrimination, as if it had selected a particular race or nationality for oppressive treatment."[b]

---

6. Compare *Roe v. Wade* [infra] (due process) with *Eisenstadt v. Baird* [infra] (analogous interests protected by the equal protection clause), and *Loving v. Virginia* [p. 900 infra] (analogous interests protected by the due process clause) (alternative ground).

7. The reference is to *Griswold v. Connecticut* [infra], in which Bill of Rights' penumbras, the ninth amendment, and "pure" substantive due process compete for attention.

8. In *Shapiro v. Thompson,* the majority held that the equal protection clause protected the right to travel, while Justice Harlan in dissent believed that the due process clause was the relevant shield. A similar doctrinal dispute split the Court in *Zablocki v. Redhail* [infra], where the majority held that the equal protection clause protected the right to marry. Justice Powell, in a concurring opinion, felt

the right found its source in the due process clause.

a. The Court began its opinion by observing: "This case touches a sensitive and important area of human rights. Oklahoma deprives certain individuals of a right which is basic to the perpetuation of a race—the right to have offspring."

b. As for *Buck v. Bell,* 274 U.S. 200, 47 S.Ct. 584, 71 L.Ed. 1000 (1927), upholding a sterilization law applicable only to mental defectives in state institutions, "it was pointed out that 'so far as the operations enable those who otherwise must be kept confined to be returned to the world, and thus open the asylum to others, the equality aimed at will be more nearly reached.' Here there is no such saving feature."

STONE, C.J., concurred in the result: "[I]f we must presume that the legislature knows—what science has been unable to ascertain—that the criminal tendencies of any class of habitual offenders are transmissible regardless of the varying mental characteristics of its individuals, I should suppose that we must likewise presume that the legislature, in its wisdom, knows that the criminal tendencies of some classes of offenders are more likely to be transmitted than those of others. And so I think the real question [is] not one of equal protection, but whether the wholesale condemnation of a class to such an invasion of personal liberty, without opportunity to any individual to show that his is not the type of case which would justify resort to it, satisfies the demands of due process.

"There are limits to the extent to which the presumption of constitutionality can be pressed, especially where the liberty of the person is concerned [referring to his famous *Carolene Products* footnote, Ch. 1, Sec. 1] and where the presumption is resorted to only to dispense with a procedure which the ordinary dictates of prudence would seem to demand for the protection of the individual from arbitrary action. Although petitioner here was given a hearing to ascertain whether sterilization would be detrimental to his health, he was given none to discover whether his criminal tendencies are of an inheritable type. * * *

"Science has found and the law has recognized that there are certain types of mental deficiency associated with delinquency which are inheritable. But the State does not contend—nor can there be any pretense—that either common knowledge or experience, or scientific investigation, has given assurance that the criminal tendencies of any class of habitual offenders are universally or even generally inheritable. In such circumstances, inquiry whether such is the fact in the case of any particular individual cannot rightly be dispensed with. [A] law which condemns, without hearing, all the individuals of a class to so harsh a measure as the present because some or even many merit condemnation, is lacking in the first principles of due process." [c]

"[In *Griswold*, Douglas, J.,] skipped through the Bill of Rights like a cheerleader—'Give me a P . . . give me an R . . . an I . . . ,' and so on, and found P–R–I–V–A–C–Y as a derivative or penumbral right."

—Dixon, *The "New" Substantive Due Process and the Democratic Ethic: A Prolegomenon,* 1976 B.Y.U.L.Rev. 43, 84.

GRISWOLD v. CONNECTICUT

381 U.S. 479, 85 S.Ct. 1678, 14 L.Ed.2d 510 (1965).

MR. JUSTICE DOUGLAS delivered the opinion of the Court.

Appellant Griswold is Executive Director of the Planned Parenthood League of Connecticut. Appellant Buxton [is] Medical Director for the League at its Center in New Haven—a center open [from] November 1 to November 10, 1961, when appellants were arrested.

They gave information, instruction, and medical advice to *married persons* as to the means of preventing conception. * * * Fees were usually charged, although some couples were serviced free.

---

c. In a separate concurrence, Jackson, J., agreed that the hearings provided are "too limited [to] afford due process" and also agreed with the Court that the classification denies equal protection.

The statutes whose constitutionality is involved [are] §§ 53–32 and 54–196 of the General Statutes of Connecticut (1958 rev.). The former provides: "Any person who uses any drug, medicinal article or instrument for the purpose of preventing conception shall be fined not less than fifty dollars or imprisoned not less than sixty days nor more than one year or be both fined and imprisoned." Section 54–196 provides: "Any person who assists, abets, counsels, causes, hires or commands another to commit any offense may be prosecuted and punished as if he were the principal offender."

The appellants were found guilty as accessories and fined $100 [each].

Coming to the merits,[a] we are met with a wide range of questions that implicate the Due Process Clause of the Fourteenth Amendment. Overtones of some arguments suggest that *Lochner* should be our guide. But we decline that invitation * * *. We do not sit as a super-legislature to determine the wisdom, need, and propriety of laws that touch economic problems, business affairs, or social conditions. This law, however, operates directly on an intimate relation of husband and wife and their physician's role in one aspect of that relation.

The association of people is not mentioned in the Constitution nor in the Bill of Rights. The right to educate a child in a school of the parents' choice— whether public or private or parochial—is also not mentioned. Nor is the right to study any particular subject or any foreign language. Yet the First Amendment has been construed to include certain of those rights. [See] *Pierce v. Society of Sisters*, 268 U.S. 510, 45 S.Ct. 571, 69 L.Ed. 1070 (1925) [and] *Meyer v. Nebraska*, 262 U.S. 390, 43 S.Ct. 625, 67 L.Ed. 1042 (1923).[b] [T]he State may not,

---

a. For resolution of the issue of standing, see p. 1207 infra.

b. Consider Nowak, Rotunda and Young, *Constitutional Law* 735 (2d ed. 1983): In both *Meyer*, invalidating a state law forbidding all grade schools from teaching subjects in any language other than English, and in *Pierce*, holding a state law requiring students to attend public schools violative of due process, "the majority [per McReynolds, J.] found that the law restricted individual freedom without any relation to a valid public interest. Freedom of choice regarding an individual's personal life was recognized as constitutionally protected. These decisions may only have reflected the attitude of the Court towards government regulation during the apex of 'substantive due process.' While these decisions might today be grounded on the First Amendment, their existence is important to the growth of the right to privacy. If nothing else, they show a historical recognition of a right to private decision making regarding family matters as inherent in the concept of liberty."

Consider, too, Lupu, supra, at 988–89, commenting that although *Meyer* and *Pierce* "can be, and at times have been, rerationalized, as attempts to protect values derived from the first amendment," the most recent reliance on these cases, citing e.g., *Moore v. East Cleveland*, infra, and *Roe v. Wade*, infra, "have stressed their nontextual underpinnings of protected interests in family autonomy. The

survival of those two cases in that form suggests that the only durable objection to the *Lochner* era's handiwork is that it generally selected the 'wrong' values for protection." See also Hutchinson, *Unanimity and Desegregation: Decisionmaking in the Supreme Court, 1948–58*, 68 Geo.L.J. 1, 49–51 (1979) (Frankfurter, J., long an outspoken critic of the McReynolds opinions in *Meyer* and *Pierce*, warned that the method used in these cases could just as easily produce "another *Lochner*"); Posner, *The Uncertain Protection of Privacy by the Supreme Court*, 1979 Sup.Ct. Rev. 173, 195–96 ("under ostensible modern test of substantive due process," *Meyer* was "incorrectly decided"; its citation in "privacy" cases shows "survival of substantive due process despite frequent disclaimers.")

Cf. *Runyon v. McCrary* (1976), p. 1172 infra, per Stewart, J., holding (unanimously on this issue) that a federal statute that "prohibits private schools from excluding qualified children solely because they are Negroes" violates neither "parental rights" nor the "right of privacy": "No challenge is made to the petitioners' right to operate their private schools or the right of parents to send their children to a particular private school rather than a public school. Nor do these cases involve a challenge to the subject matter which is taught at any private school. Thus, the [private schools] remain presumptively free to inculcate whatever values and standards they deem desirable. *Meyer* and its progeny entitle

consistently with the spirit of the First Amendment, contract the spectrum of available knowledge. The right of freedom of speech and press includes not only the right to utter or to print, but the right to distribute, the right to receive, the right to read and freedom of inquiry, freedom of thought, and freedom to teach—indeed the freedom of the entire university community. Without those peripheral rights the specific rights would be less secure. And so we reaffirm the principle of the *Pierce* and the *Meyer* cases.

In *NAACP v. Alabama* [p. 726 infra], we protected the "freedom to associate and privacy in one's associations," noting that freedom of association was a peripheral First Amendment right. [In] other words, the First Amendment has a penumbra where privacy is protected from governmental intrusion. In like context, we have protected forms of "association" that are not political in the customary sense but pertain to the social, legal, and economic benefit of the members. *NAACP v. Button*, 371 U.S. 415, 83 S.Ct. 328, 9 L.Ed.2d 405 (1963). [W]hile [association] is not expressly included in the First Amendment its existence is necessary in making the express guarantees fully meaningful.

The foregoing cases suggest that specific guarantees in the Bill of Rights have penumbras, formed by emanations from those guarantees that help give them life and substance. See *Poe v. Ullman*, 367 U.S. 497, 516–522, 81 S.Ct. 1752, 6 L.Ed.2d 989 (1961) [Douglas, J., dissenting]. Various guarantees create zones of privacy. The right of association contained in the penumbra of the First Amendment is one, as we have seen. The Third Amendment in its prohibition against the quartering of soldiers "in any house" in time of peace without the consent of the owner is another facet of that privacy. The Fourth Amendment [is another]. The Fifth Amendment in its Self-Incrimination Clause enables the citizen to create a zone of privacy which government may not force him to surrender to his detriment. The Ninth Amendment provides: "The enumeration in the Constitution, of certain rights, shall not be construed to deny or disparage others retained by the people."

The Fourth and Fifth Amendments were described in *Boyd v. United States,* 116 U.S. 616, 630, 6 S.Ct. 524, 532, 29 L.Ed. 746 (1886), as protection against all governmental invasions "of the sanctity of a man's home and the privacies of life." We recently referred in *Mapp v. Ohio* to the Fourth Amendment as creating a "right to privacy, no less important than any other right carefully and particularly reserved to the people." See Beaney, *The Constitutional Right to Privacy,* 1962 Sup.Ct.Rev. 212; Griswold, *The Right to be Let Alone,* 55 Nw.U.L. Rev. 216 (1960).

We have had many controversies over these penumbral rights of "privacy and repose." [*Skinner* and other cases] bear witness that the right of privacy which presses for recognition here is a legitimate one.

The present case, then, concerns a relationship lying within the zone of privacy created by several fundamental constitutional guarantees.[c] And it

---

them to no more." Further, "it does not follow that because government is largely or even entirely precluded from regulating the child-bearing decision, it is similarly restricted by the Constitution from regulating the implementation of parental decisions concerning a child's education. [See] *Pierce; Meyer.*"

c. Did the Court omit the free exercise clause of the first amendment? Like religious beliefs, are beliefs in the areas of marriage, procreation and child rearing "often deeply

held, involving loyalties fully as powerful as those that bind the citizen to the state"? Will the choice of whom to marry or whether or not to have a child, once taken, "have as strong an impact on the life patterns of the individuals involved [as] any adoption of a religious belief or viewpoint"? See Heymann & Barzelay, *The Forest and the Trees: Roe v. Wade and Its Critics,* 53 B.U.L.Rev. 765, 773–74 (1973).

concerns a law which, in forbidding the *use* of contraceptives rather than regulating their manufacture or sale, seeks to achieve its goals by means having a maximum destructive impact upon that relationship. Such a law cannot stand in light of the familiar principle [that] a "governmental purpose to control or prevent activities constitutionally subject to state regulation may not be achieved by means which sweep unnecessarily broadly and thereby invade the area of protected freedoms." *NAACP v. Alabama.* Would we allow the police to search the sacred precincts of marital bedrooms for telltale signs of the use of contraceptives? The very idea is repulsive to the notions of privacy surrounding the marriage relationship.[d]

We deal with a right of privacy older than the Bill of Rights * * *. Marriage is a coming together for better or for worse, hopefully enduring, and intimate to the degree of being sacred. It is an association that promotes a way of life, not causes; a harmony in living, not political faiths; a bilateral loyalty, not commercial or social projects. Yet it is an association for as noble a purpose as any involved in our prior decisions.

Reversed.

MR. JUSTICE GOLDBERG, whom THE CHIEF JUSTICE and MR. JUSTICE BRENNAN join, concurring.

I [join the Court's opinion]. Although I have not accepted the view that "due process" as used in the Fourteenth Amendment includes all of the first eight Amendments, I do agree that the concept of liberty protects those personal rights that are fundamental, and is not confined to the specific terms of the Bill of Rights. My conclusion [that] it embraces the right of marital privacy though that right is not mentioned explicitly in the Constitution [1] is supported both by numerous decisions [and] by the language and history of the Ninth Amendment [which] reveal that the Framers of the Constitution believed that there are additional fundamental rights, protected from governmental infringement.

[The] Ninth Amendment [was] proffered to quiet expressed fears that a bill of specifically enumerated rights could not be sufficiently broad to cover all essential rights and that the specific mention of certain rights would be interpreted as a denial that others were protected.

[While] this Court has had little occasion to interpret the Ninth Amendment,[6] "[i]t cannot be presumed that any clause in the constitution is intended to be without effect." [To] hold that a right so basic and fundamental and so deep-rooted in our society as the right of privacy in marriage may be infringed

---

d. But consider *Posner,* fn. b supra, at 194: "Such a search would indeed be an invasion of privacy in a conventional sense. But it would be a justifiable invasion if the statute were not otherwise constitutionally objectionable. This case can be seen by imagining that the statute in question forbade not contraception but murder and that the police had probable cause to believe that the suspected murderer had secreted the weapon to his mattress. Furthermore, even if some methods of enforcing the Connecticut statute [violated the Fourth Amendment], that would mean only that the statute was difficult to enforce. [As] the facts of *Griswold* show, the State could enforce the statute without invading anyone's privacy, simply by prosecuting, as accessories, the employees of birth-control clinics."

1. [This Court] has never held that the Bill of Rights or the Fourteenth Amendment protects only those rights that the Constitution specifically mentions by name. See, e.g., *Bolling v. Sharpe* [p. 896 infra]; * * * *Carrington v. Rash* [p. 1045 infra]; *NAACP v. Alabama;* * * *.

6. [It] has been referred to as "*The Forgotten Ninth Amendment,*" in a book with that title by Bennett B. Patterson (1955). Other commentary [includes] Redlich, *Are There "Certain Rights * * * Retained by the People"?* 37 N.Y.U.L.Rev. 787 (1962), and Kelsey, *The Ninth Amendment of the Federal Constitution,* 11 Ind.L.J. 309 (1936). * * *

because that right is not guaranteed in so many words by the first eight amendments to the Constitution is to ignore the Ninth Amendment and to give it no effect whatsoever. ＊ ＊ ＊ I do not mean to imply that the Ninth Amendment is applied against the States by the Fourteenth [nor] to state that the Ninth Amendment constitutes an independent source of rights protected from infringement by either the States or the Federal Government. Rather, the Ninth Amendment shows a belief of the Constitution's authors that fundamental rights exist that are not expressly enumerated in the first eight amendments and an intent that the list of rights included there not be deemed exhaustive.[d] [T]his Court has held, often unanimously, that the Fifth and Fourteenth Amendments protect certain fundamental personal liberties from abridgment by the Federal Government or the States. [I] do not see how this [interpretation of the Ninth Amendment] broadens the authority of the Court; rather it serves to support what this Court has been doing in protecting fundamental rights.

[While] the Ninth Amendment—and indeed the entire Bill of Rights—originally concerned restrictions upon *federal* power, the subsequently enacted Fourteenth Amendment prohibits the States as well from abridging fundamental personal liberties. [In] sum, the Ninth Amendment simply lends strong support to the view that the "liberty" protected by the Fifth and Fourteenth Amendments from infringement by the Federal Government or the States is not restricted to rights specifically mentioned in the first eight amendments.

In determining which rights are fundamental, judges are not left at large to decide cases in light of their personal and private notions. Rather, they must look to the "traditions and [collective] conscience of our people" to determine whether a principle is "so rooted [there] [as] to be ranked as fundamental." ＊ ＊ ＊ "Liberty" also "gains content from the emanations [of] specific [constitutional] guarantees" and "from experience with the requirements of a free society." *Poe* (dissenting opinion of Douglas, J.).

[The] entire fabric of the Constitution and the purposes that clearly underlie its specific guarantees demonstrate that the rights to marital privacy and to marry and raise a family are of similar order and magnitude as the fundamental rights specifically protected.

[Surely] the Government, absent a showing of a compelling subordinating state interest, could not decree that all husbands and wives must be sterilized after two children have been born to them.[e] Yet by [the dissenters'] reasoning such an invasion of marital privacy would not be subject to constitutional challenge because, while it might be "silly," no provision of the Constitution specifically prevents the Government from curtailing the marital right to bear children and raise a family. [I]f upon a showing of a slender basis of rationality, a law outlawing voluntary birth control by married persons is valid, then, by the same reasoning, a law requiring compulsory birth control also would seem to be

d. See generally Note, *The Uncertain Renaissance of the Ninth Amendment,* 33 U.Chi.L.Rev. 814 (1966); Paust, *Human Rights and the Ninth Amendment; A New Form of Guarantee,* 60 Corn.L.Rev. 231 (1975).

e. Compare Comment, *Population Control—The Legal Approach to a Biological Imperative,* 1 Ecol.L.Q. 143, 167 (1971): "It is not completely clear [whether] Justice Goldberg's vaguely defined marital and family rights include the right to unlimited procreation.

Clearly, one family right which is not protected against legislative control is the right to decide how many spouses to have. By custom Americans have one spouse and many children but there would seem to be little difference between legislative control of the number of spouses and the number of children." See also Note, *Legal Analysis and Population Control: The Problem of Coercion,* 84 Harv.L.Rev. 1856 (1971).

valid. In my view, however, both types of law would unjustifiably intrude upon rights of marital privacy which are constitutionally protected.

In a long series of cases this Court has held that where fundamental personal liberties are involved, they may not be abridged by the States simply on a showing that a regulatory statute has some rational relationship to the effectuation of a proper state purpose. "Where there is a significant encroachment upon personal liberty, the State may prevail only upon showing a subordinating interest which is compelling," *Bates v. Little Rock*, 361 U.S. 516, 80 S.Ct. 412, 4 L.Ed.2d 480 [(1960)]. [The] State, at most, argues that there is some rational relation between this statute and what is admittedly a legitimate subject of state concern—the discouraging of extra-marital relations. It says that preventing the use of birth-control devices by married persons helps prevent the indulgence by some in such extra-marital relations. The rationality of this justification is dubious, particularly in light of the admitted widespread availability to all persons [in] Connecticut, unmarried as well as married, of birth-control devices for the prevention of disease, as distinguished from the prevention of conception. But in any event, it is clear that the state interest in safeguarding marital fidelity can be served by a more discriminately tailored statute, which does not, like the present one, sweep unnecessarily broadly, reaching far beyond the evil sought to be dealt with and intruding upon the privacy of all married couples. * * *

Finally, it should be said of the Court's holding today that it in no way interferes with a State's proper regulation of sexual promiscuity or misconduct. As my Brother Harlan so well stated in his dissenting opinion in *Poe:* "Adultery, homosexuality and the like are sexual intimacies which the State forbids [but] the intimacy of husband and wife is necessarily an essential and accepted feature of the institution of marriage, an institution which the State not only must allow, but which always and in every age it has fostered and protected.
* * *

MR. JUSTICE HARLAN, concurring in the judgment.

I [cannot] join the Court's opinion [as] it seems to me to evince an approach [that] the Due Process Clause of the Fourteenth Amendment does not touch this Connecticut statute unless the enactment is found to violate some right assured by the letter or penumbra of the Bill of Rights. [W]hat I find implicit in the Court's opinion is that the "incorporation" doctrine may be used to *restrict* the reach of Fourteenth Amendment Due Process. For me this is just as unacceptable constitutional doctrine as is the use of the "incorporation" approach to *impose* upon the States all the requirements of the Bill of Rights. * * *

[T]he proper constitutional inquiry in this case is whether this Connecticut statute infringes the Due Process Clause of the Fourteenth Amendment because the enactment violates basic values "implicit in the concept of ordered liberty." For reasons stated at length in my dissenting opinion in *Poe v. Ullman* [discussed below], I believe that it does. While the relevant inquiry may be aided by resort to one or more of the provisions of the Bill of Rights, it is not dependent on them or any of their radiations. The Due Process Clause of the Fourteenth Amendment stands, in my opinion, on its own bottom.

[While] I could not more heartily agree that judicial "self restraint" is an indispensable ingredient of sound constitutional adjudication, I do submit that the formula suggested [by the dissenters] for achieving it is more hollow than real. "Specific" provisions of the Constitution, no less than "due process," lend themselves as readily to "personal" interpretations by judges whose constitutional outlook is simply to keep the Constitution in supposed "tune with the times".

[Judicial self-restraint will] be achieved in this area, as in other[s], only by continual insistence upon respect for the teachings of history, solid recognition of the basic values that underlie our society, and wise appreciation of the great roles that the doctrines of federalism and separation of powers have played in establishing and preserving American freedoms. Adherence to these principles will not, of course, obviate all constitutional differences of opinion among judges, nor should it. Their continued recognition will, however, go farther toward keeping most judges from roaming at large in the constitutional field than will the interpolation into the Constitution of an artificial and largely illusory restriction on the content of the Due Process Clause.

[Dissenting in POE v. ULLMAN, 367 U.S. 497, 523, 81 S.Ct. 1752, 6 L.Ed.2d 989 (1961), which failed to reach the merits of the constitutional challenge to the Connecticut anti-birth control statute, Harlan, J., had maintained that the statute, "as construed to apply to these appellants, violates the Fourteenth Amendment" because "a statute making it a criminal offense for *married couples* to use contraceptives is an intolerable and unjustifiable invasion of privacy in the conduct of the most intimate concerns of an individual's personal life." Harlan, J., "would not suggest that adultery, homosexuality, fornication and incest are immune from criminal enquiry, however privately practiced," but "the intimacy of husband and wife is necessarily an essential and accepted feature of the institution of marriage, an institution which the State not only must allow, but which always and every age it has fostered and protected. It is one thing when the State exerts its power either to forbid extra-marital sexuality altogether, or to say who may marry, but it is quite another when, having acknowledged a marriage and the intimacies inherent in it, it undertakes to regulate by means of the criminal law the details of that intimacy."

[Although the state had argued the constitutional permissibility of the moral judgment underlying the challenged statute, Harlan, J., could not find anything that "even remotely suggests a justification for the obnoxiously intrusive means it has chosen to effectuate that policy." He deemed "the utter novelty" of the statute "conclusive." "Although the Federal Government and many States have at one time or another [prohibited or regulated] the distribution of contraceptives, none [has] made the *use* of contraceptives a crime. Indeed, a diligent search has revealed that no nation, including several which quite evidently share Connecticut's moral policy, had seen fit to effectuate that policy by the means presented here." He had to agree with Jackson, J., concurring in *Skinner,* that "there are limits to the extent to which a legislatively represented majority may [experiment] at the expense of the dignity and personality" of the individual and, in this instance, found these limits "reached and passed."

[Because the constitutional challenges to the Connecticut statute "draw their basis from no explicit language of the Constitution, and have yet to find expression in any decision of this Court," Harlan, J., deemed it "desirable at the outset to state the framework of Constitutional principles in which I think the issue must be judged":

["[Were] due process merely a procedural safeguard it would fail to reach those situations where the deprivation of life, liberty or property was accomplished by legislation which by operating in the future could, given even the fairest possible procedure in application to individuals, nevertheless destroy the enjoyment of all three. [I]t is not the particular enumeration of rights in the first eight Amendments which spells out the reach of Fourteenth Amendment due process, but rather [those concepts embracing] rights 'which [are] *fundamental;* which belong [to] the citizens of all free governments.'

["[T]hrough the course of this Court's decisions [due process] has represented the balance which our Nation, built upon postulates of respect for the liberty of the individual, has struck between that liberty and the demands of organized society. [The] balance of which I speak is the balance struck by this country, having regard to what history teaches are the traditions from which it developed as well as the traditions from which it broke. That tradition is a living thing. A decision of this Court which radically departs from it could not long survive, while a decision which builds on what has survived is likely to be sound. No formula could serve as a substitute, in this area, for judgment and restraint.

["It is this outlook which has led the Court continuingly to perceive distinctions in the imperative character of Constitutional provisions, since that character must be discerned from a particular provision's larger context. And inasmuch as this context is one not of words, but of history and purposes, the full scope of the liberty guaranteed by the Due Process Clause cannot be found in or limited by the precise terms of the specific guarantees elsewhere provided in the Constitution. This 'liberty' is not a series of isolated points pricked out in terms of [the] freedom of speech, press, and religion; [the] freedom from unreasonable searches and seizures; and so on. It is a rational continuum which, broadly speaking, includes a freedom from all substantial arbitrary impositions and purposeless restraints [and] which also recognizes, what a reasonable and sensitive judgment must, that certain interests require particularly careful scrutiny of the state needs asserted to justify their abridgment. Cf. *Skinner.*]

MR. JUSTICE WHITE, concurring in the judgment.

In my view this Connecticut law as applied to married couples deprives them of "liberty" without [due process] guaranteed by the Fourteenth Amendment against arbitrary or capricious [denials]. Surely the right [to] be free of regulation of the intimacies of the marriage relationship, "come[s] to this Court with a momentum for respect lacking when appeal is made to liberties which derive merely from shifting economic arrangements." *Kovacs v. Cooper* [p. 690 infra] (opinion of Frankfurter, J.).

The Connecticut anti-contraceptive statute deals rather substantially with this relationship. [And] the clear effect of these statutes, as enforced, is to deny disadvantaged citizens of Connecticut, those without either adequate knowledge or resources to obtain private counseling, access to medical assistance and up-to-date information in respect to proper methods of birth control. In my view, a statute with these effects bears a substantial burden of justification when attacked under the Fourteenth Amendment.

An examination of the justification offered, however, cannot be avoided by saying that the Connecticut anti-use statute invades a protected area of privacy and association or that it demeans the marriage relationship. The nature of the right invaded is pertinent, to be sure, for statutes regulating sensitive areas of liberty do, under the cases of this Court, require "strict scrutiny," *Skinner,* and "must be viewed in the light of less drastic means for achieving the same basic purpose." *Shelton v. Tucker*, 364 U.S. 479, 81 S.Ct. 247, 5 L.Ed.2d 231 [(1960)]. But such statutes, if reasonably necessary for the effectuation of a legitimate and substantial state interest, and not arbitrary or capricious in application, are not invalid under the Due Process Clause. [There] is no serious contention that Connecticut thinks the use of artificial or external methods of contraception immoral or unwise in itself, or that the anti-use statute is founded upon any policy of promoting population expansion. Rather, the statute is said to serve the State's policy against all forms of promiscuous or illicit sexual relationships, be they premarital or extramarital, concededly a permissible and legitimate legislative goal.

Without taking issue with the premise that the fear of conception operates as a deterrent to such relationships in addition to the criminal proscriptions Connecticut has against such conduct, I wholly fail to see how the ban on the use of contraceptives by married couples in any way reinforces the State's ban on illicit sexual relationships. [It] is purely fanciful to believe that the broad proscription on use facilitates discovery of use by persons engaging in a prohibited relationship or for some other reason makes such use more unlikely and thus can be supported by any sort of administrative consideration. Perhaps the theory is that the flat ban on use prevents married people from possessing contraceptives and without the ready availability of such devices for use in the marital relationship, there will be no or less temptation to use them in extramarital ones. This reasoning rests on the premise that married people will comply with the ban in regard to their marital relationship, notwithstanding total nonenforcement in this context and apparent nonenforcibility, but will not comply with criminal statutes prohibiting extramarital affairs and the anti-use statute in respect to illicit sexual relationships, a premise whose validity has not been demonstrated and whose intrinsic validity is not very evident. At most the broad ban is of marginal utility to the declared objective. A statute limiting its prohibition on use to persons engaging in the prohibited relationship would serve the end posited by Connecticut in the same way, and with the same effectiveness, or ineffectiveness, as the broad anti-use statute under attack in this case. I find nothing in this record justifying the sweeping scope of this [statute].

MR. JUSTICE BLACK, with whom MR. JUSTICE STEWART joins, dissenting.

[There are] guarantees in certain specific constitutional provisions which are designed in part to protect privacy at certain times and places with respect to certain activities. [But] I think it belittles [the Fourth] Amendment to talk about it as though it protects nothing but "privacy." [The] average man would very likely not have his feelings soothed any more by having his property seized openly than by having it seized privately and by stealth. [And] a person can be just as much, if not more, irritated, annoyed and injured by an unceremonious public arrest by a policeman as he is by a seizure in the privacy of his office or home.

One of the most effective ways of diluting or expanding a constitutionally guaranteed right is to substitute for the crucial word or words of a constitutional guarantee another word or words, more or less flexible and more or less restricted in meaning. This fact is well illustrated by the use of the term "right of privacy" as a comprehensive substitute for the Fourth Amendment's guarantee against "unreasonable searches and seizures." * * * [1] I like my privacy as well as the next one, but I am nevertheless compelled to admit that government

---

1. The phrase "right to privacy" appears first to have gained currency from an article written by Messrs. Warren and (later Mr. Justice) Brandeis in 1890 which urged that States should give some form of tort relief to persons whose private affairs were exploited by others. *The Right to Privacy,* 4 Harv.L. Rev. 193. * * * Observing that "the right of privacy presses for recognition here," today this Court, which I did not understand to have power to sit as a court of common law, now appears to be exalting a phrase which Warren and Brandeis use in discussing grounds for tort relief, to the level of a constitutional [rule].

has a right to invade it unless prohibited by some specific constitutional provision.

[This] brings me to the arguments made by my Brothers Harlan, White and Goldberg * * *. I discuss the due process and Ninth Amendment arguments together because on analysis they turn out to be the same thing—merely using different words to claim for this Court and the federal judiciary power to invalidate any legislative act [that] it considers to be arbitrary, capricious, unreasonable, or oppressive, or this Court's belief that a particular state law under scrutiny has no "rational or justifying" purpose, or is offensive to a "sense of fairness and justice." If these formulas based on "natural justice," or others which mean the same thing, are to prevail, they require judges to determine what is or is not constitutional on the basis of their own appraisal of what laws are unwise or unnecessary. [I] readily admit that no legislative body, state or national, should pass laws that can justly be given any of the invidious labels invoked as constitutional excuses to strike down state laws. But perhaps it is not too much to say that no legislative body ever does pass laws without believing that they will accomplish a sane, rational, wise and justifiable purpose. [I] do not believe that we are granted power by the Due Process Clause or any [other] provisions to measure constitutionality by our belief that legislation is arbitrary, capricious or unreasonable, or accomplishes no justifiable purpose, or is offensive to our own notions of "civilized standards of conduct." Such an appraisal of the wisdom of legislation is an attribute of the power to make laws, [a] power which was specifically denied to federal courts by the [Framers].

Of the cases on which my Brothers White and Goldberg rely so heavily, undoubtedly the reasoning of two of them supports their result here—[*Meyer* and *Pierce*]. *Meyer* [relying on *Lochner,*] held unconstitutional, as an "arbitrary" and unreasonable interference with the right of a teacher to carry on his occupation and of parents to hire him, a state law forbidding the teaching of modern foreign languages to young children in the schools.[7] [*Pierce,* per McReynolds, J.] said that a state law requiring that all children attend public schools interfered unconstitutionally with the property rights of private school corporations because it was an "arbitrary, unreasonable, and unlawful interference" which threatened "destruction of their business and property." Without expressing an opinion as to whether either of those cases reached a correct result in light of our later decisions applying the First Amendment to the States through the Fourteenth, I merely point out that the reasoning stated in *Meyer* and *Pierce* was the same natural law due process philosophy which many later opinions repudiated, and which I cannot accept. Brothers White and Goldberg also cite other cases, such as *NAACP v. Button; Shelton v. Tucker;* which held that States [could not] pass unnecessarily broad laws which might indirectly infringe on First Amendment [freedoms.] Brothers White and Goldberg now apparently would start from this requirement [and] extend it limitlessly to require States to justify any law restricting "liberty" as my Brethren define "liberty." This would mean at the very least, I suppose, that every state criminal statute—since it must inevitably curtail "liberty" to some extent—would be suspect, and would have to be justified to this Court.

---

7. In *Meyer,* in the very same sentence quoted in part by my Brethren in which he asserted that the Due Process Clause gave an abstract and inviolable right "to marry, establish a home and bring up children," Mr. Justice McReynolds asserted also that the Due Process Clause prevented States from interfering with "the right of the individual to contract."

My Brother Goldberg has adopted the recent discovery [12] that the Ninth Amendment as well as the Due Process Clause can be used by this Court as authority to strike down all state legislation which this Court thinks violates "fundamental principles of liberty and justice," or is contrary to the "traditions and collective conscience of our people." [One] would certainly have to look far beyond the language of the Ninth Amendment to find that the Framers vested in this Court any such awesome veto powers over lawmaking. [The Ninth] Amendment was passed [to] limit the Federal Government to the powers granted expressly or by necessary implication. [This] fact is perhaps responsible for the peculiar phenomenon that for a period of a century and a half no serious suggestion was ever made that [that] Amendment, enacted to protect state powers against federal invasion, could be used as a weapon of federal power to prevent state legislatures from passing laws they consider appropriate to govern local affairs. * * *

I realize that many good and able men have eloquently spoken and written [of] the duty of this Court to keep the Constitution in tune with the times [but I] reject that philosophy. The Constitution makers knew the need for change and provided for it. [The] Due Process Clause with an "arbitrary and capricious" or "shocking to the conscience" formula was liberally used by this Court to strike down economic legislation in the early decades of this century, threatening, many people thought, the tranquility and stability of the Nation. See, e.g., *Lochner.* That formula, based on subjective considerations of "natural justice," is no less dangerous when used to enforce this Court's views about personal rights than those about economic rights. I had thought that we had laid that formula, as a means for striking down state legislation, to [rest]. So far as I am concerned, Connecticut's law as applied here is not forbidden by any provision of the Federal Constitution as that Constitution was written, and I would therefore affirm.

Mr. Justice Stewart, whom Mr. Justice Black joins, dissenting.

[I] think this is an uncommonly silly law. As a practical matter, the law is obviously unenforceable, except in the oblique context of the present case. As a philosophical matter, I believe the use of contraceptives in the relationship of marriage should be left to personal and private [choice]. As a matter of social policy, I think professional counsel about methods of birth control should be available to all, so that each individual's choice can be meaningfully made. But we are not [asked] whether we think this law is unwise, or even asinine. We are asked to hold that it violates the United States Constitution. And that I cannot do.

In the course of its opinion the Court refers to no less than six Amendments [but] does not say which of these Amendments, if any, it thinks is infringed by this Connecticut law. [As] to the First, Third, Fourth, and Fifth Amendments, I can find nothing in any of them to invalidate this Connecticut law, even

---

12. See Patterson, *The Forgotten Ninth Amendment* (1955). Mr. Patterson urges that the Ninth Amendment be used to protect unspecified "natural and inalienable rights." The Introduction by Roscoe Pound states that "there is a marked revival of natural law ideas throughout the world. Interest in the Ninth Amendment is a symptom of that revival."

In Redlich, *Are There "Certain Rights * * * Retained by the People"?,* 37 N.Y.U.L. Rev. 787, Professor Redlich, in advocating reliance on the Ninth and Tenth Amendments to invalidate the Connecticut law before us, frankly states: "[There] are two possible [paths]. One is to revert to a frankly flexible due process concept even on matters that do not involve specific constitutional prohibitions. The other is to attempt to evolve a new constitutional framework within which to meet this and similar problems which are likely to arise."

assuming that all those amendments are fully applicable against the States. [The] Ninth Amendment, like its companion the Tenth [was] simply to make clear that the adoption of the Bill of Rights did not alter the plan that the *Federal* Government was to be a government of express and limited powers, and that all rights and powers not delegated to it were retained by the people and the individual States. Until today no member of this Court has ever suggested that the Ninth Amendment meant anything [else].

What provision of the Constitution, then, does make this state law invalid? The Court says it is the right of privacy "created by several fundamental constitutional guarantees." [I] can find no such general right of privacy in the Bill of Rights, in any other part of the Constitution, or in any case ever before decided by this Court.[7]

At the oral argument [we] were told that the Connecticut law does not "conform to current community standards." But it is not the function of this Court to decide cases on the basis of community standards. [If], as I should surely hope, the law before us does not reflect the standards of the people of Connecticut, the people of Connecticut can freely exercise their true Ninth and Tenth Amendment rights to persuade their elected representatives to repeal it. That is the constitutional way to take this law off the books.

Notes and Questions

1. *Is Douglas, J.'s argument logical?* Consider Henkin, *Privacy and Autonomy,* 74 Colum.L.Rev. 1410, 1421–22 (1974): "Although it is not wholly clear, Justice Douglas's argument seems to go something like this: since the Constitution, in various 'specifics' of the Bill of Rights and in their penumbra, protects rights which partake of privacy, it protects other aspects of privacy as well, indeed it recognizes a general, complete right of privacy. And since the right emanates from specific fundamental rights, it too is 'fundamental,' its infringement is suspect and calls for strict scrutiny, and it can be justified only by a high level of public good. A logician, I suppose, might have trouble with that argument. A legal draftsman, indeed, might suggest the opposite: when the Constitution sought to protect private rights it specified them; that it explicitly protects some elements of privacy, but not others, suggests that it did not mean to protect those not mentioned."

2. *Did Griswold successfully avoid "renewing the romance" with "substantive due process"?* *Griswold,* observes Lupu, at 994, "provided the severest test for a Court determined to advance chosen values [without] renewing the romance with the dreaded demon of substantive due process. [Douglas, J.,] drew upon the incorporation legacy, rather than a doctrine of 'naked' substantive due process, and tortured the Bill of Rights into yielding a protected zone of privacy that would not tolerate a law banning contraceptive use by married couples. Justice Goldberg's reliance upon the ninth amendment [was] equally disingenuous in its attempt to avoid the jaws of substantive due process. Only Justices White and Harlan were willing to grapple directly with the fearful creature, and concluded that a law invading marital choice about contraception violated the due process clause itself, independent of links with the Bill of Rights. Shocking though that analysis may have been at the time, subsequent developments seem to have confirmed the White-Harlan view, and not the magical mystery tour of

---

7. [The] Court does not say how far the new constitutional right of privacy announced today extends. I suppose, however, that even after today a State can constitutionally still punish at least some offenses which are not committed in public.

the zones of privacy, as the prevailing doctrine of *Griswold* [referring to *Moore v. East Cleveland* (1977), infra]."

3. *Emanations-and-penumbras theory and "economic" vs. "personal" rights.* Do any of the Justices analytically distinguish between "economic" and "personal" rights? Or is the distinction "only self-imposed"? Consider Kauper, *Penumbras, Peripheries, Emanations, Things Fundamental and Things Forgotten: The Griswold Case,* 64 Mich.L.Rev. 235, 253 (1965).

4. *"Privacy" or "equality"?* "Seen in the context of the Warren Court's general jurisprudence," observes M. Shapiro, *Fathers and Sons: The Court, the Commentators, and the Search for Values,* in The Burger Court 218, 228 (V. Blasi ed. 1983), "the fact situation in [*Griswold*] was crucial. The living law of Connecticut was that middle-class women received birth control information and purchased birth control supplies, and the Connecticut statute was enforced only to block the operation of birth control clinics that would bring these services to the poor. *Griswold* was an equality not a privacy decision * * *."

5. *Skinner and Griswold taken together.* Consider Tribe, *American Constitutional Law* 923 (1978): "Taken together with *Griswold,* which recognized as equally protected the individual's decision *not* to bear a child, the meaning of *Skinner* is that *whether one person's body shall be the source of another's life must be left to that person and that person alone to decide.* That principle collides in the abortion cases [infra] with a command that seems no less fundamental: *an innocent life may not be taken except to save the life of another.*"

Griswold invalidated a ban on the *use* of contraceptives by *married* couples. EISENSTADT v. BAIRD, 405 U.S. 438, 92 S.Ct. 1029, 31 L.Ed.2d 349 (1972), overturned a conviction for violating a Massachusetts law making it a felony to *distribute* contraceptive materials, *except* in the case of registered physicians and pharmacists furnishing the materials to married persons. Baird had given a woman a package of vaginal foam at the end of her lecture on contraception. He was not charged with distributing to an unmarried person. No proof was offered as to the recipient's marital status. The crime charged was that Baird had no license, and thus no authority, to distribute to anyone. The Court, per BRENNAN, J., concluded that, since the statute is riddled with exceptions making contraceptives freely available and since, if protection of health were the rationale, the statute would be both discriminatory and overbroad, "the goals of deterring premarital sex and regulating the distribution of potentially harmful articles cannot reasonably be regarded as legislative aims." "[V]iewed as a prohibition on contraception per se" the statute "violates the rights of single persons under the Equal Protection Clause." For, "whatever the rights of the individual to access to contraceptives may be, the rights must be the same for the married and the unmarried alike":

"If under *Griswold* the distribution of contraceptives to married persons cannot be prohibited, a ban on distribution to unmarried persons would be equally impermissible. It is true that in *Griswold* the right of privacy in question inhered in the marital relationship. Yet the marital couple is not an independent entity with a mind and heart of its own, but an association of two individuals each with a separate intellectual and emotional make-up. If the right of privacy means anything, it is the right of the *individual,* married or single, to be free from unwarranted governmental intrusion into matters so fundamentally affecting a person as the decision whether to bear or beget a child. On the other hand, if *Griswold* is no bar to a prohibition on the distribution of contraceptives, the State could not, consistently with [equal protection,] outlaw distribution to unmarried but not to married persons. In each case the evil, as perceived by the State, would be identical, and the underinclusion would be invidious."

WHITE, J., joined by Blackmun, J., concurred, emphasizing that "the State did [not] convict Baird for distributing to an unmarried person [but because] Baird had no license and therefore no authority to distribute to anyone." "Given *Griswold,* and absent proof of the possible hazards of using vaginal foam, we could not sustain [Baird's] conviction had it been for selling or giving away foam to a married person. Just as in *Griswold,* where the right of married persons to use contraceptives was 'diluted or adversely affected' by permitting a conviction for giving advice as to its exercise, so here to sanction a medical restriction upon distribution of a contraceptive not proved hazardous to health would impair the exercise of the constitutional right. That Baird could not be convicted for distributing [foam] to a married person disposes of this case. Assuming arguendo that the result would be otherwise had the recipient been unmarried, nothing has been placed in the record to indicate her marital status." [a]

BURGER, C.J., dissented, "see[ing] nothing in the Fourteenth Amendment or any other part of the Constitution that even vaguely suggests that these medicinal forms of contraceptives must be available in the open market. [By] relying on *Griswold* in the present context, the Court has passed beyond the penumbras of the specific guarantees into the uncircumscribed area of personal predilections."

Notes and Questions

1. *Does Eisenstadt offer a new rationale for Griswold?* Did *Eisenstadt* decide one of *Griswold* 's open issues—the constitutionality of a ban on the use or distribution of contraceptive devices that excluded from its reach the married couple—"by assertion, without a pretext of reasoning"? Wellington, *Common Law Rules and Constitutional Double Standards,* 83 Yale L.J. 221, 296 (1973), so charges: "[W]hether the 'different classes' (married, not married) are [as *Eisenstadt* states] 'wholly unrelated to the objective of the statute,' depends on whether, as *Griswold* insists, the marriage relationship is important to that aspect of liberty that the Court calls privacy. How, then, [could the Court write *Eisenstadt* the way it did] without offering a new rationale for *Griswold*[?]" *Cf.* Gerety, *Doing Without Privacy,* 42 Ohio St.L.J. 143–44 (1981).

2. *Griswold "unmasked"?* Consider Posner, *The Uncertain Protection of Privacy by the Supreme Court,* 1979 Sup.Ct.Rev. 173, 198: "*Griswold* had at least attempted to relate the right to use contraceptives to familiar notions of privacy by speculating on the intrusive methods by which a statute banning the use of contraceptives might be enforced. This ground was unavailable in [*Eisenstadt*] because the statute there forbade not the use, but only the distribution, of contraceptives. [*Eisenstadt*] is thus a pure essay in substantive due process. It unmasks *Griswold* as based on the idea of sexual liberty rather than privacy." *Cf.* Perry, *Abortion, the Public Morals, and the Police Power,* 23 U.C.L.A.L.Rev. 689, 705–06 (1976).

a. Douglas, J., who joined the Court's opinion, also concurred on free speech grounds. Powell and Rehnquist, JJ., did not participate.

3. *Griswold and Eisenstadt extended.* As pointed out in Tribe 922, "the effect of *Eisenstadt v. Baird* was to single out as decisive in *Griswold* the element of reproductive autonomy, something the Court made clear in 1977, when it extended *Griswold* and *Baird* " in CAREY v. POPULATION SERVICES INT'L, 431 U.S. 678, 97 S.Ct. 2010, 52 L.Ed.2d 675 (1977), to invalidate a New York law which allowed only pharmacists to sell non-medical contraceptive devices to persons over 16 and prohibited the sale of such items to those under 16. (The Court relied in part on the 1973 *Abortion Cases,* infra.) In striking down the restriction on sales to adults, BRENNAN, J., spoke for six justices; in invalidating the ban on sales to those under 16, he spoke for a four-justice plurality.

As for the restriction on distribution to adults, "where a decision as fundamental as that whether to bear or beget a child is involved, regulations imposing a burden on it may be justified only by compelling interests, and must be narrowly drawn to express only those interests"—and the Court found none of the state interests advanced (e.g., protecting health, facilitating enforcement of other laws) to be "compelling." [a] The state argued that *Griswold* dealt only with the *use* of contraceptives, not their manufacture or sale, but read "in light of its progeny, the teaching of *Griswold* is that the Constitution protects individual decisions in matters of childbearing from unjustified intrusion by the State."

As for the ban on sales to those under 16, Brennan, J., joined by Stewart, Marshall, and Blackmun, JJ., applied a test "apparently less rigorous than the 'compelling state interest' test applied to restrictions on the privacy rights of adults"—restrictions inhibiting privacy rights of minors are valid "only if they serve 'any significant state interest [that] is not present in the case of an adult.' *Planned Parenthood v. Danforth,* infra]." The plurality then rejected what it called "the argument [that] minors' sexual activity may be deterred by increasing the hazards attendant on it," pointing out that that argument had already been rejected by the Court in related areas.[b]

POWELL, J., concurred in the judgment, observing that by restricting not only the kinds of retail outlets that may distribute contraceptives, "but even prohibit[ing] distribution by mail to adults"—"thus requiring individuals to buy contraceptives over the counter"—the New York provision "heavily burdens constitutionally protected freedom." He saw "no justification for subjecting restrictions on the sexual activity of the young to heightened judicial review"—"a standard that for all practical purposes approaches the 'compelling interest' standard"—but concurred in the invalidation of the "distribution to minors" restriction on narrow grounds.[c]

---

a. The Court recognized, however, that "other restrictions may well be reasonably related to the objective of quality control," and thus "express[ed] no opinion on, for example, restrictions on the distribution of contraceptives through vending machines."

b. Nor was the restriction on the privacy rights of minors "saved" by another provision authorizing physicians to supply minors with contraceptives. As with limitations on distribution to adults, "less than total restrictions on access to contraceptives that significantly burden the right to decide whether to bear children must also pass constitutional muster. [This provision] delegates the State's authority to disapprove of minors' sexual behavior to physicians, who may exercise it arbitrarily * * *."

c. White, J., concurred in the invalidation of the restriction on minors "primarily because the State has not demonstrated that [the restriction] measurably contributes to the deterrent purposes which the State advances as justification for the restriction."

Stevens, J., too, concurred only in the judgment with respect to the restriction on minors: "[The State's] central argument is that the statute has the important *symbolic* effect of communicating disapproval of sexual activity by minors. In essence, therefore, the statute is defended as a form of propaganda, rather than a regulation of behavior. Although

ORAL ARGUMENTS IN THE ABORTION CASES *

* * *

THE COURT: [I]s it critical to your case that the fetus not be a person under the due process clause? [W]ould you lose your case if the fetus was a person?

SARAH WEDDINGTON [on behalf of appellant Roe]: Then you would have a balancing of interests.

THE COURT: Well you say you have [that] anyway, don't you? * * *

THE COURT: [If] it were established that an unborn fetus is a person, [protected by] the Fourteenth Amendment, you would have almost an impossible case here, would you not?

WEDDINGTON: I would have a very difficult case. * * *

THE COURT: Could Texas constitutionally, in your view, declare [by] statute [that] the fetus is a person, for all constitutional purposes, after the third month of gestation?

WEDDINGTON: I do not believe that the State legislature can determine the meaning of the Federal Constitution. It is up to this Court to make that determination. * * *

ROBERT FLOWERS [on behalf of appellee]: [I]t is the position of the State of Texas that, upon conception, we have a human being; a person, within the concept of the Constitution of the United States, and that of Texas, also.

THE COURT: Now how should that question be decided? Is it a legal question? A constitutional question? A medical question? A philosophical question? Or, a religious question? Or what is it?

FLOWERS: [W]e feel that it could be best decided by a legislature, in view of the fact that they can bring before it the medical testimony * * *.

THE COURT: So then it's basically a medical question?

FLOWERS: From a constitutional standpoint, no, sir. * * *

THE COURT: Of course, if you're right about [the fetus being a person within the meaning of the Constitution], you can sit down, you've won your case. * * * Except insofar as, maybe, the Texas abortion law presently goes too far in allowing abortions.

FLOWERS: Yes, sir. That's exactly right. * * *

THE COURT: Do you think [you have] lost your case, then, if the fetus or the embryo is not a person? Is that it?

FLOWERS: Yes sir, I would say so. * * *

THE COURT: Under State law [there] are some rights given to the fetus?

the State may properly perform a teaching function, [an] attempt to persuade by inflicting harm on the listener is an unacceptable means of conveying a message that is otherwise legitimate. The propaganda technique used in this case significantly increases the risk of unwanted pregnancy and venereal disease. It is as though a State decided to dramatize its disapproval of motorcycles by forbidding the use of safety helmets. One need not posit a constitutional right to ride a motorcycle to characterize such a restriction as irrational and perverse."

Rehnquist, J., dissented, observing that if those responsible for the Bill of Rights and Civil War Amendments could have lived to know what their efforts had wrought "it is not difficult to imagine their reaction." Burger, C.J., dissented without opinion.

* These extracts are taken from 75 *Landmark Briefs and Arguments of the Supreme Court of the United States: Constitutional Law* 807–33 (Kurland & Casper ed.).

FLOWERS: Yes, sir.

THE COURT: And you are asserting these rights against the right of the mother. [And] that's wholly aside from whether the fetus is a person under the Federal Constitution. * * *

FLOWERS: Yes, sir. * * *

THE COURT: I want you to give me [a] medical writing of any kind that says that at the time of conception the fetus is a person. * * *

FLOWERS: [I] find no way [that] any court or any legislature or any doctor anywhere can say that here is the dividing line. Here is not a life; and here is a life, after conception. Perhaps it would be better left to that legislature. * * *

THE COURT: Well, if you're right that an unborn fetus is a person, then you can't leave it to the legislature to play fast and loose dealing with that person. [I]f you're correct, in your basic submission that an unborn fetus is a person, then abortion laws such as that which New York has are grossly unconstitutional, isn't it?

FLOWERS: That's right, yes.

THE COURT: Allowing the killing of people.

FLOWERS: Yes, sir. * * *

[Rebuttal argument of Weddington]

THE COURT: [I] gather your argument is that a state may not protect the life of the fetus or prevent an abortion [at] any time during pregnancy? Right up until the moment of birth? * * *

WEDDINGTON: [T]here is no indication [that] the Constitution would give any protection prior to birth. That is not before the Court. * * *

THE COURT: Well, I don't know whether it is or isn't. * * *

ROE v. WADE

410 U.S. 113, 93 S.Ct. 705, 35 L.Ed.2d 147 (1973).

MR. JUSTICE BLACKMUN delivered the opinion of the Court.

This Texas federal appeal and its Georgia companion, *Doe v. Bolton*, [infra,] present constitutional challenges to state criminal abortion legislation. The Texas statutes [are] typical of those that have been in effect in many States for approximately a century. The Georgia statutes, in contrast, have a modern cast and are a legislative product that, to an extent at least, obviously reflects the influences of recent attitudinal change, of advancing medical knowledge and techniques, and of new [thinking].

The Texas statutes [make procuring an abortion a crime except] "by medical advice for the purpose of saving the life of the mother."

[Jane] Roe alleged that she was unmarried and pregnant [and] that she was unable to get a "legal" abortion in Texas because her life did not appear to be threatened by the continuation of her pregnancy.[a] [The district court held the

---

a. Who was "Jane Roe"? Her real name was Norma McCorvey. According to Friendly & Elliott, *The Constitution: That Delicate Balance* 202–04 (1984), she had become pregnant through rape, had tried to get an abortion, but had been unable to pay the price ($650) demanded by a doctor she finally found who was willing to perform an abortion. Bobbitt, *Constitutional Fate* 165 (1982), describes "Jane Roe" as follows: "[She] was an unskilled, young white woman. She was also a lesbian."

Texas abortion statutes unconstitutional, but denied the injunctive relief requested. Roe appealed.]

[R]estrictive criminal abortion laws [like Texas'] in effect in a majority of States [today] derive from statutory changes effected, for the most part, in the latter half of the 19th century. [The Court then reviewed, in some detail, "ancient attitudes," "the Hippocratic Oath" which forbids abortion, "the common law," "the English statutory law," and "the American law." Subsequently, it described the positions of the American Medical Association, the American Public Health Association, and the American Bar Association. Thus,] at common law, at the time of the adoption of our Constitution, and throughout the major portion of the 19th century, [a] woman enjoyed a substantially broader right to terminate a pregnancy than she does in most States today. * * *

Three reasons have been advanced to explain historically the enactment of criminal abortion laws in the 19th century and to justify their [continuance].

It has been argued occasionally that these laws were the product of a Victorian social concern to discourage illicit sexual conduct. Texas, however, does not advance this justification [and] it appears that no court or commentator has taken the argument seriously.

[A] second reason is [that when] most criminal abortion laws were first enacted, the procedure was a hazardous one for the woman. [But] medical data indicat[es] that abortion in early pregnancy, that is, prior to the end of first trimester, although not without its risk, is now relatively safe.

[The] third reason is the State's interest—some phrase it in terms of duty—in protecting prenatal life. Some of the argument for this justification rests on the theory that a new human life is present from the moment of conception. * * * Only when the life of the pregnant mother herself is at stake, balanced against the life she carries within her, should the interest of the embryo or fetus not prevail. [In] assessing the State's interest, recognition may be given to the less rigid claim that as long as at least *potential* life is involved, the State may assert interests beyond the protection of the pregnant woman alone.

[It] is with these interests, and the weight to be attached to them, that this case is concerned.

The Constitution does not explicitly mention any right of privacy. [But] the Court has recognized that a right of personal privacy, or a guarantee of certain areas or zones of privacy, does exist under the Constitution. In varying contexts the Court or individual Justices have indeed found at least the roots of that right in the First Amendment, *Stanley v. Georgia* [p. 500 infra]; in the Fourth and Fifth Amendments; in the penumbras of the Bill of Rights, *Griswold;* in the Ninth Amendment, id. (Goldberg, J., concurring); or in the concept of liberty guaranteed by the first section of the Fourteenth Amendment, see *Meyer.* These decisions make it clear that only personal rights that can be deemed "fundamental" or "implicit in the concept of ordered liberty," are included in this guarantee of personal privacy. They also make it clear that the right has some extension to activities relating to marriage, *Loving;* procreation, *Skinner;* con-

---

When pressed by the lawyer who would eventually argue her case in the U.S. Supreme Court, Ms. McCorvey assured her that she would fight the Texas abortion law "all the way." But because she had a young child from a previous marriage and did not want the child subjected to "public ridicule," Ms. McCorvey had one stipulation: she wanted to be anonymous. In June of 1970, a year and a half before her case was first argued in the U.S. Supreme Court, Ms. McCorvey gave birth to a daughter. She never saw the child again after she left the hospital. See Friendly & Elliott, supra.

traception, *Eisenstadt;* family relationships, *Prince v. Massachusetts* [p. 843 infra]; and child rearing and education, *Pierce.*[b]

This right of privacy, whether it be founded in the Fourteenth Amendment's concept of personal liberty [as] we feel it is, [or] in the [Ninth Amendment], is broad enough to encompass a woman's decision whether or not to terminate her pregnancy. The detriment that the State would impose upon the pregnant woman by denying this choice altogether is apparent. Specific and direct harm medically diagnosable even in early pregnancy may be [involved]. Psychological harm may be imminent. Mental and physical health may be taxed by child care. There is also the distress, for all concerned, associated with the unwanted child, and there is the problem of bringing a child into a family already unable, psychologically and otherwise, to care for it. In other cases, as in this one, the additional difficulties and continuing stigma of unwed motherhood may be involved. All these are factors the woman and her responsible physician necessarily will consider in consultation.

On the basis of elements such as these, appellants and some amici argue that the woman's right is absolute and that she is entitled to terminate her pregnancy at whatever time, in whatever way, and for whatever reason she alone chooses. With this we do not agree. [The] Court's decisions recognizing a right of privacy also acknowledge that some state regulation in areas protected by that right is appropriate. [A] state may properly assert important interests in safeguarding health, in maintaining medical standards, and in protecting potential life. At some point in pregnancy, these respective interests become sufficiently compelling to sustain regulation of the factors that govern the abortion decision. [In] fact, it is not clear to us that the claim [that] one has an unlimited right to do with one's body as one pleases bears a close relationship to the right of privacy previously articulated in the Court's decisions. The Court has refused to recognize an unlimited right of this kind in the past. *Jacobson v. Massachusetts,* 197 U.S. 11, 25 S.Ct. 358, 49 L.Ed. 643 (1905), (vaccination); *Buck v. Bell* (sterilization).

[Where] certain "fundamental rights" are involved, the Court has held that regulation limiting these rights may be justified only by a "compelling state interest," and that legislative enactments must be narrowly drawn to express only the legitimate state interests at stake.

[The] appellee and certain amici argue that the fetus is a "person" within the language and meaning of the Fourteenth Amendment. [If so,] appellant's case, of course, collapses, for the fetus' right to life is then guaranteed specifically by the Amendment.

[The] Constitution does not define "person" in so many words. [The Court then listed each provision in which the word appears.] But in nearly all these instances, the use of the word is such that it has application only postnatally. None indicates, with any assurance, that it has any possible pre-natal application. All this, together with our observation that throughout the major portion of the 19th century prevailing legal abortion practices were far freer [than] today, persuades us that the word "person," as used in the Fourteenth Amendment, does not include the unborn. [Thus,] we pass on to other considerations.

The pregnant woman cannot be isolated in her privacy. She carries an embryo and, later, a fetus. [The] situation therefore is inherently different from marital intimacy, or bedroom possession of obscene material, or marriage, or

---

b. Do these parental rights permit parents to forbid public school teachers from imposing corporal punishment on their children? See *Ingraham v. Wright* (1977), Sec. 5, II infra.

procreation, or education, with which *Eisenstadt, Griswold, Stanley, Loving, Skinner, Pierce,* and *Meyer* [were] concerned.

[Texas] urges that, apart from the Fourteenth Amendment, life begins at conception and is present throughout pregnancy, and that, therefore, the State has a compelling interest in protecting that life from and after conception. We need not resolve the difficult question of when life begins. When those trained [in] medicine, philosophy, and theology are unable to arrive at any consensus, the judiciary, at this point in the development of man's knowledge, is not in a position to speculate as to the answer.

[W]e do not agree that, by adopting one theory of life, Texas may override the rights of the pregnant woman that are at stake. We repeat, however, that the State does have an important and legitimate interest in preserving and protecting the health of the pregnant woman [and] that it has still *another* important and legitimate interest in protecting the potentiality of human life. These interests are separate and distinct. Each grows in substantiality as the woman approaches term and, at a point during pregnancy, each becomes "compelling."

With respect to [the] interest in the health of the mother, the "compelling" point, in the light of present medical knowledge, is at approximately the end of the first trimester. This is so because of the now established medical fact that until the end of the first trimester mortality in abortion is less than mortality in normal childbirth. It follows that, from and after this point, a State may regulate the abortion procedure to the extent that the regulation reasonably relates to the preservation and protection of maternal health. Examples of permissible state regulation in this area are requirements as to the qualifications of the person who is to perform the abortion; [as] to the facility in which the procedure is to be performed, [and] the like. This means, on the other hand, that, for the period of pregnancy prior to this "compelling" point, the attending physician, in consultation with his patient, is free to determine, without regulation by the State, that in his medical judgment the patient's pregnancy should be terminated. If that decision is reached, the judgment may be effectuated by an abortion free of interference by the State.

With respect to [the] interest in potential life, the "compelling" point is at viability [which "is usually placed at about seven months (28 weeks) but may occur earlier, even at 24 weeks."] This is so because the fetus then presumably has the capability of meaningful life outside the mother's womb.[c] State regula-

---

c. Earlier in its opinion, 410 U.S. at 160, the Court described the point "at which the fetus becomes 'viable' " as the point that the fetus is "potentially able to live outside the mother's womb, albeit with artificial aid." *Planned Parenthood v. Danforth* (1976) (other aspects of which are discussed infra), per Blackmun, J., upheld a Missouri abortion statute defining "viability" as "that stage of fetal development when the life of the unborn child may be continued indefinitely outside the womb by natural or artificial life-supportive systems." In rejecting contentions that the Missouri statute unduly expanded the *Roe* Court's definition of "viability," failed to contain any reference to a gestational time period, and failed to incorporate and reflect the three stages of pregnancy, the Court observed: "[W]e recognized in *Roe* that viability was a

matter of medical judgment, skill, and technical ability, and we preserved the flexibility of the term. [The Missouri statute] does the same. [I]t is not the proper function of the legislature or the courts to place viability, which essentially is a medical concept, at a specific point in the gestation period. The time when viability is achieved may vary with each pregnancy, and the determination of whether a particular fetus is viable is, and must be, a matter for the judgment of the responsible attending physician. [The statutory definition] merely reflects this fact."

Consider, too, *Colautti v. Franklin*, 439 U.S. 379, 99 S.Ct. 675, 58 L.Ed.2d 596 (1979), per Blackmun, J., striking down on "void for vagueness" grounds a Pennsylvania provision requiring use of a statutorily prescribed tech-

tion protective of fetal life after viability thus has both logical and biological justifications. If the State is interested in protecting fetal life after viability, it may go as far as to proscribe abortion during that period except when it is necessary to preserve the life or health of the mother.

Measured against these standards, [the Texas statute] sweeps too broadly [and] therefore, cannot survive the constitutional attack made upon it here.

[In] *Doe* [infra], procedural requirements contained in one of the modern abortion statutes are considered. That opinion and this one [are] to be read together.[67]

This holding, we feel, is consistent with the relative weights of the respective interests involved, with the lessons and examples of medical and legal history, with the lenity of the common law, and with the demands of the profound problems of the present day. The decision leaves the State free to place increasing restrictions on abortion as the period of pregnancy lengthens, so long as those restrictions are tailored to the recognized state interests. The decision vindicates the right of the physician to administer medical treatment according to his professional judgment up to the points where important state interests provide compelling justifications for intervention. Up to those points, the abortion decision in all its aspects is inherently, and primarily, a medical

nique when the fetus is "viable" or when there is "sufficient reason to believe that the fetus may be viable": "[The provision] subjects the physician to potential criminal liability without regard to fault. [I]t is not unlikely that experts will disagree over whether a particular fetus in the second trimester has advanced to the stage of viability. The prospect of such disagreement, in conjunction with a statute imposing liability for an erroneous determination of viability, could have a profound chilling effect on the willingness of physicians to perform abortions near the point of viability in the manner indicated by their best medical judgment." (White, J., joined by Burger, C.J. and Rehnquist, J., dissented, disagreeing with the Court's interpretation of the statute).

On similar analysis, the *Colautti* majority held "void for vagueness" a provision requiring that "the abortion technique employed shall be that which would provide the best opportunity for the fetus to be aborted alive so long as a different technique would not be necessary to preserve the life or health of the mother."

Colautti reaffirmed that the determination of "viability" is "a matter for medical judgment" and that that point is reached "when, in the judgment of the attending physician on the particular facts of the case before him, there is a reasonable likelihood of the fetus' sustained survival outside the womb, with or without artificial support. Because this point may differ with each pregnancy, neither the legislature nor the courts may proclaim one of the elements entering into the ascertainment of viability—be it weeks of gestation or fetal weight or any other single factor—as the determinant of when the State has a compelling interest in the life or health of the fetus."

Does the *Roe-Danforth-Colautti* approach to viability focus more on the physician's right to practice medicine than on the patient's right of privacy? Do medical advances in extra-uterine gestation threaten the *practicability* of the woman's right to choose abortion? May the state assert its interest in potential life to whatever extent biotechnological advances enable a fetus to survive outside the womb, *no matter how early in its development*? Should the Court limit the definition of viability to the reasonable likelihood of survival outside the womb *without* technological support, thus designating a period in which a woman's decision to abort would be immune from state intervention? But where would we draw the line? Is an incubator a form of technological support? Should the focus of the abortion inquiry be not on the existing state of medical technology, but on the state of fetal development—the point at which a fetus becomes a "thinking, conscious being" (said to be between 19 and 30 weeks after conception)? See generally Notes, 27 U.C.L.A.L.Rev. 1340 (1980), 29 U.C.L.A.L.Rev. 1194 (1982). See also notes 12 & 13 following *Roe*; Justice O'Connor's dissent in *Akron v. Akron Center for Reproductive Health*, infra; and the notes following *Akron*.

67. Neither in this opinion nor in *Doe* do we discuss the father's rights, if any exist in the constitutional context, in the abortion decision. No paternal right has been asserted in either of the [cases]. North Carolina, for example, requires written permission for the abortion from the husband when the woman is a married minor [and] if the woman is an unmarried minor, written permission from the parents is required. * * *

decision, and basic responsibility for it must rest with the physician. If an individual practitioner abuses the privilege of exercising proper medical judgment, the usual remedies, judicial and intra-professional, are available. * * *

MR. JUSTICE STEWART, concurring.

In 1963, this Court, in *Ferguson v. Skrupa* [p. 263 fn. b supra], purported to sound the death knell for the doctrine of substantive due process, [but] [b]arely two years later, in *Griswold,* the Court held a Connecticut birth control law unconstitutional. In view of what had been so recently said in *Skrupa,* the Court's opinion in *Griswold* understandably did its best to avoid reliance on the Due Process Clause of the Fourteenth Amendment as the ground for decision, [but] it was clear to me then, and it is equally clear to me now, that the *Griswold* decision can be rationally understood only as a holding that the Connecticut statute substantively invaded the "liberty" that is protected by the Due Process Clause of the Fourteenth Amendment. As so understood, *Griswold* stands as one in a long line of pre-*Skrupa* cases decided under the doctrine of substantive due process, and I now accept it as such.

[The] Constitution nowhere mentions a specific right of personal choice in matters of marriage and family life, but the "liberty" protected by the Due Process Clause of the Fourteenth Amendment covers more than those freedoms explicitly named in the Bill of Rights. [As] recently as last Term, in *Eisenstadt,* we recognized "the right of the *individual,* married or single, to be free from unwarranted governmental intrusion into matters so fundamentally affecting a person as the decision whether to bear or beget a child." That right necessarily includes the right of a woman to decide whether or not to terminate her pregnancy. [It] is evident that the Texas abortion statute infringes that right directly. [The] question then becomes whether the state interests advanced to justify this abridgment can survive the "particularly careful scrutiny" that the Fourteenth Amendment here requires.

The asserted state interests are protection of the health and safety of the pregnant woman, and protection of the potential future human life within her. These are legitimate objectives, amply sufficient to permit a State to regulate abortions as it does other surgical procedures, and perhaps sufficient to permit a State to regulate abortions more stringently or even to prohibit them in the late stages of pregnancy. But such legislation is not before us, and I think the Court today has thoroughly demonstrated that these state interests cannot constitutionally support the broad abridgment of personal liberty worked by the existing Texas law. Accordingly, I join the Court's opinion holding that the law is invalid under the Due Process Clause of the Fourteenth Amendment.

MR. JUSTICE DOUGLAS, concurring [in *Doe* as well as in *Roe*].

While I join the opinion of the Court, I add a few words.

The questions presented [involve] the right of privacy. [The] Ninth Amendment obviously does not create federally enforceable rights. [But] a catalogue of [the rights "retained by the people"] includes customary, traditional, and time-honored rights, amenities, privileges, and immunities that come within the sweep of "the Blessings of Liberty" mentioned in the preamble to the Constitution. Many of them in my view come within the meaning of the term "liberty" as used in the Fourteenth Amendment.

First is the autonomous control over the development and expression of one's intellect, interests, tastes, and personality. These are rights protected by the First Amendment and in my view they are absolute * * *.

Second is freedom of choice in the basic decisions of one's life respecting marriage, divorce, procreation, contraception, and the education and upbringing of children. These rights, unlike those protected by the First Amendment, are subject to some control by the police power. [They] are "fundamental" and we have held that in order to support legislative action the statute must be narrowly and precisely drawn and that a "compelling state interest" must be shown in support of the limitation. * * *[4]

[Third] is the freedom to care for one's health and person, freedom from bodily restraint or compulsion, freedom to walk, stroll, or loaf. These rights, though fundamental, are likewise subject to regulation on a showing of "compelling state interest." * * * Elaborate argument is hardly necessary to demonstrate that childbirth may deprive a woman of her preferred life style and force upon her a radically different and undesired future.

[Such reasoning] is, however, only the beginning of the problem. [V]oluntary abortion at any time and place regardless of medical standards would impinge on a rightful concern of society. The woman's health is part of that concern; as is the life of the fetus after quickening. These concerns justify the State in treating the procedure as a medical one.

[T]he Georgia statute outlaws virtually all such operations—even in the earliest stages of pregnancy. In light of modern medical evidence [it] cannot be seriously urged that so comprehensive a ban is aimed at protecting the woman's health. Rather, [this ban] can rest only on a public goal of preserving both embryonic and fetal life.

The present statute has struck the balance between the woman and the State's interests wholly in favor of the latter. [We] held in *Griswold* that the States may not preclude spouses from attempting to avoid the joinder of sperm and egg. [I]t is difficult to perceive any overriding public necessity which might attach precisely at the moment of conception.

* * *

[The] protection of the fetus when it has acquired life is a legitimate concern of the State. Georgia's law makes no rational, discernible decision on that score. For under the Act the developmental stage of the fetus is irrelevant when pregnancy is the result of rape or when the fetus will very likely be born with a permanent defect or when a continuation of the pregnancy will endanger the life of the mother or permanently injure her health. When life is present is a question we do not try to resolve. While basically a question for medical experts, [it is], of course, caught up in matters of religion and morality. * * *

Mr. Justice White, with whom Mr. Justice Rehnquist joins, dissenting [in *Doe* as well as in *Roe*].

At the heart of the controversy in these cases are those recurring pregnancies that pose no danger whatsoever to the life or health of the mother but are nevertheless unwanted for any one or more of a variety of reasons—convenience, family planning, economics, dislike of children, the embarrassment

---

4. My Brother Stewart, writing in the present cases, says that our decision in *Griswold* reintroduced substantive due process that had been rejected in [*Skrupa*]. There is nothing specific in the Bill of Rights that covers [the marital relation]. Nor is there anything in the Bill of Rights that in terms protects the right of association or the privacy in one's association. [Other] peripheral rights are the right to educate one's children as one chooses, and the right to study the German language. These decisions with all respect, have nothing to do with substantive due process. One may think they are not peripheral rights to other rights that are expressed in the Bill of Rights. But that is not enough to bring into play the protection of substantive due process. * * *

of illegitimacy, etc. The common claim before us is that for any one of such reasons, or for no reason at all, and without asserting or claiming any threat to life or health, any woman is entitled to an abortion at her request if she is able to find a medical advisor willing to [perform it].

The Court for the most part sustains this position [and] simply fashions and announces a new constitutional right [and], with scarcely any reason or authority for its action, invests that right with sufficient substance to override most existing state abortion statutes. The upshot is that the people and the legislatures of the 50 States are constitutionally disentitled to weigh the relative importance of the continued existence and development of the fetus on the one hand against a spectrum of possible impacts on the mother on the other hand. As an exercise of raw judicial power, the Court perhaps has authority [but] in my view its judgment is an improvident and extravagant exercise of the power of judicial review * * *.

MR. JUSTICE REHNQUIST, dissenting. * * *

I have difficulty in concluding [that] the right of "privacy" is involved in this case. [Texas] bars the performance of a medical abortion by a licensed physician on a plaintiff such as Roe. A transaction resulting in an operation such as this is not "private" in the ordinary usage of that word. Nor is the "privacy" which the Court finds here even a distant relative of the freedom from searches and seizures protected by the Fourth Amendment.

[If] the Court means by the term "privacy" no more than that the claim of a person to be free from unwanted state regulation of consensual transactions may be a form of "liberty" * * * I agree [with] Mr. Justice Stewart [that that "liberty"] embraces more than the rights found in the Bill of Rights. But that liberty is not guaranteed absolutely against deprivation, but only against deprivation without due process of law. The test traditionally applied in the area of social and economic legislation is whether or not a law such as that challenged has a rational relation to a valid state objective. [If] the Texas statute were to prohibit an abortion even where the mother's life is in jeopardy, I have little doubt that such a statute would lack a rational relation to a valid state [objective].[d] But the Court's sweeping invalidation of any restrictions on abortion during the first trimester is impossible to justify under that [standard]. As in *Lochner* and similar cases applying substantive due process standards to economic and social welfare legislation, the adoption of the compelling state interest standard will inevitably require this Court to examine the legislative policies and pass on the wisdom of these policies in the very process of deciding whether a particular state interest put forward may or may not be "compelling." The decision here to break the term of pregnancy into three distinct terms and to outline the permissible restrictions the State may impose in each one, for example, partakes more of judicial legislation than it does of a determination of the intent of the drafters of the Fourteenth Amendment.

The fact that a majority of the States, reflecting after all the majority sentiment in those States, have had restrictions on abortions for at least a century seems to me as strong an indication there is that the asserted right to an abortion is not "so rooted in the traditions and conscience of our people as to be ranked as fundamental." Even today, when society's views on abortion are

---

d. Is it "irrational" or "invalid" for a state to weigh the *possibility* (or even *probability*) that the mother will die without an abortion against the *certainty* that the fetus will not survive with one and then to legislate against abortions in such situations?

changing, the very existence of the debate is evidence that the "right" to an abortion is not so universally accepted as the appellants would have us believe.

[By] the time of the adoption of the Fourteenth Amendment in 1868 there were at least 36 laws enacted by state or territorial legislatures limiting abortion. [The] only conclusion possible from this history is that the drafters did not intend to have the Fourteenth Amendment withdraw from the States the power to legislate with respect to this matter. * * *

DOE v. BOLTON, 410 U.S. 179, 93 S.Ct. 739, 35 L.Ed.2d 201 (1973), the companion case to *Roe v. Wade,* sustained, against the contention that it had been rendered unconstitutionally vague by a three-judge district court's interpretation, a Georgia provision that permitted a physician to perform an abortion when "based upon his best clinical judgment that an abortion is necessary." (The district court had struck down the statutorily specified reasons: because continued pregnancy would endanger a pregnant woman's life or injure her health; the fetus would likely be born with a serious defect; or the pregnancy resulted from rape.) "The net result of the District Court's decision," observed the Court, "is that the abortion determination, so far as the physician is concerned, is made in the exercise of his professional, that is, his 'best clinical,' judgment in the light of all the attendant circumstances. He is not now restricted to the three situations originally specified. Instead, [the] medical judgment may be exercised in light of all factors—physical, emotional, psychological, familial, and the woman's age—relevant to the well-being of the patient. All these factors may relate to health. This allows the attending physician the room he needs to make his best medical judgment. And it is room that operates for the benefit, not the disadvantage, of the pregnant woman."

However, despite the fact that the Georgia statute was patterned after the American Law Institute's Model Penal Code (1962), which had served as the model for recent legislation in about one-fourth of the states, the Court, per BLACKMUN, J., invalidated substantial portions of the statute. Struck down were requirements (1) that the abortion be performed in a hospital accredited by the Joint Commission on Accreditation of Hospitals (JCAH); (2) that the procedure be approved by a hospital staff abortion committee; and (3) that the performing physician's judgment be confirmed by independent examinations of the patient by two other physicians.

As for (1): There is no restriction of the performance of nonabortion surgery in a hospital not accredited by the JCAH. "[T]he State must show more than it has in order to prove that only the full resources of a licensed hospital, rather than those of some other appropriately licensed institution, satisfy [appropriate] health interests. [This requirement], because it fails to exclude the first trimester of pregnancy, see *Roe,* is also invalid." As for (2), [we] see no constitutionally justifiable pertinence [for] the advance approval by the abortion committee. With regard to the protection of potential life, the medical judgment is already completed prior to the committee stage, and review by a committee once removed from diagnosis is basically redundant. We are not cited to any other surgical procedure made subject to committee approval as a matter of state criminal law. The woman's right to receive medical care in accordance with the licensed physician's best judgment and the physician's right to administer it are substantially limited by this statutorily imposed overview." As for (3), the two-doctor concurrence, "the statute's emphasis [is] on the attending physician's 'best clinical judgment that an abortion is necessary.' That should be sufficient. [No] other voluntary medical or surgical procedure for which Georgia requires confirmation by two other physicians has been cited to us."

COMMENTARY ON THE *ABORTION CASES*

1. *Does Roe reflect the same circular reasoning of the earlier substantive due process cases?* Consider JOSEPH GRANO, *Judicial Review and a Written Constitution in a Democratic Society,* 28 Wayne L.Rev. 1, 24 (1981): "*Roe* reflects the same circular reasoning and the same subjectivity that plagued the Court's earlier noninterpretivist efforts [referring to *Allgeyer* and *Lochner*].[a] The right to terminate a pregnancy can be deemed fundamental only if the fetus is not regarded as a form of life entitled to protection. No *a priori* moral principle can resolve the question of the fetus' status. By declaring the woman's right 'fundamental,' however, the Court necessarily rejected the legislative judgment that fetal life deserves protection. At this point, some might object that the Court merely concluded that public opinion was too divided to justify such a restraint on the woman's choice, but this conclusion went to the weight of the state's interest. The Court's test required that it first decide whether a fundamental right was implicated, and it could not do this, any more than it could in *Allgeyer* or *Lochner,* or any more than Justice Harlan could in *Poe v. Ullman,* without making its own moral assessment of the activity in question, an assessment not subject to demonstration by analytic reasoning."

2. *Constitutional values prohibiting abortion: a defense of Roe even assuming that the fetus is a person.* Agreeing with Professor Ely (see p. 343 infra) that "constitutional argument ought to be based on values that can be inferred from the text of the Constitution, the thinking of the Framers, or the structure of our national government," DONALD REGAN, *Rewriting Roe v. Wade,* 77 Mich.L.Rev. 1569, 1618–42 (1977), maintains that such constitutional argument against laws prohibiting abortion may be made, based on three constitutional values: "non-subordination, freedom from physical invasion, and equal protection":[b]

"The non-subordination value that is implicit in the bad-samaritan principle of the common law[c] is at the core of the thirteenth amendment [which] speaks not merely of slavery, but of 'involuntary servitude.' * * * Unwilling pregnancy is not slavery in its fullest sense, [but] it certainly involves the disposition and coercion of the (intensely) personal service of one 'man' for another's benefit. The second value, freedom from physical invasion or imposed physical pain or

a. For commentary on the "interpretivist"/"noninterpretivist" debate generated by *Roe,* see p. 341 infra.

b. As Professor Regan acknowledges, his article builds on an argument made in Thomson, *A Defense of Abortion,* 1 Phil. & Pub.Aff. 47 (1971). Space limitations only permit use of a few passages from Professor Regan's 77-page article to sketch the main thrusts of his thesis.

c. At the outset of his article, id. at 1569, Professor Regan contends that "abortion should be viewed as presenting a problem in what we might call 'the law of samaritanism,' that is, the law concerning obligations imposed on certain individuals to give aid to

others. It is a deeply rooted principle of American law that an individual is ordinarily not required to volunteer aid to another individual who is in danger or in need of assistance. [I]f we require a pregnant woman to carry the fetus to term and deliver it—if we forbid abortion, in other words—we are compelling her to be a Good Samaritan. [I]f we consider the special nature of the burdens imposed on pregnant women by laws forbidding abortion, we must eventually conclude that the equal protection clause forbids imposition of these burdens on pregnant women." Regan refers to "the established principle that one does not have to volunteer aid" as the "bad-samaritan principle," id. at 1572.

hardship, is embodied in the eighth amendment and also plainly counts among those fundamental values of our society which are traditionally subsumed under fifth and fourteenth amendment due process. [There] is no other case, I believe, in which the law imposes comparable physical invasion and hardship as an obligation of samaritanism. * * *

"[E]ven if those parts of our tradition which forbid subordination or physical invasion have historically included an exception for abortion laws, the exception is impermissible. It creates an inequality that is inconsistent with an even more fundamental part of our tradition, reflected in the equal protection clause and the due process clause of the fifth amendment.

"[To] see the equal protection problem, we must look at abortion in a broader context. Life in society [provides] many opportunities to be a good or bad samaritan. The objection to an anti-abortion statute is that it picks out certain potential samaritans, namely women who want abortions, and treats them in a way that is at odds with the law's treatment of other potential samaritans. Women who want abortions are required to give aid in circumstances where closely analogous potential samaritans are not. And they are required to give aid of a *kind* and an *extent* that is required of no other potential samaritan.

"[I]t is important that the inequality of treatment between pregnant women and other potential samaritans touches on the constitutional values of non-subordination and freedom from physical invasion. A woman who is denied an abortion is compelled to serve the fetus and to suffer physical invasion, pain, and hardship. [That it can plausibly] be argued that the Constitution prohibits this imposition outright, [surely] means that any inequality of treatment we can point to becomes harder to justify. * * *

"Other reasons for the Court to give the abortion problem special attention are related to the suspect classification idea. Only women need abortions. [T]he one potential samaritan who is singled out for specially burdensome treatment is a potential samaritan who must, given human physiology, be female. Why is this important?

"First, any inequality that flows from an unchosen and unalterable characteristic is likely to be specially resented. It also works against the idea, deeply rooted in our culture, that people ought to be masters of their own destinies, at least within the limits of legally acceptable behavior that apply to everyone. Since pregnancy happens only to women, and since no one has any choice about whether to be a woman, susceptibility to pregnancy (and to being in the position of wanting an abortion) is a nonchosen characteristic. (It is not an unalterable characteristic, since a woman might have herself sterilized, but this method of altering the characteristic itself involves a significant physical invasion.)

"It might be objected that even if susceptibility to pregnancy is an unchosen characteristic, pregnancy itself is not, and that laws attaching unpleasant consequences to pregnancy therefore do not interfere with women's controlling their own destinies. [But] the only method of avoiding pregnancy with certainty requires, for many people, extraordinary self-denial [and] does not, to my mind, eliminate the force of the suggestion that pregnancy is often sufficiently 'unchosen' so that laws specially disadvantaging pregnant women limit women's control of their lives, are justifiably resented, and deserve more-than-minimal judicial attention.[d]

d. Consider MacKinnon, *Roe v. Wade: A Study in Male Ideology*, in *Abortion: Moral* *and Legal Perspectives* 45, 46–48 (Garfield & Hennessey eds. 1984): "Feminist investiga-

"[M]ost legislatures would defend laws against abortion on the ground that they protect human life (or potential life). [But the] inequality between the treatment of pregnant women and the treatment of other potential samaritans who are not required to undertake burdens (often very much smaller burdens) in order to save life is too great. The inequality trenches on two distinct constitutionally protected interests—the interest in non-subordination and the interest in freedom from serious physical invasion. In addition, the inequality disadvantages a class that is defined by a non-chosen characteristic (whether sex or unwanted pregnancy) and that has suffered from a history of discrimination. This is more than any reasonable American legislature would tolerate. * * *

"Perhaps the greatest advantage of my argument is that it makes it possible to avoid the question of whether the fetus is, or may be treated by the state as, a person. Justice Blackmun claims at one point that the Court need not decide 'when life begins'. But his general argument [seems] plainly to assume that the fetus is *not* a person until the point of viability (at the earliest). Indeed, Blackmun elsewhere suggests that if the fetus were a person within the meaning of the fourteenth amendment, the woman's claim to an abortion would be foreclosed by the Constitution itself.

"On the last point, I think Blackmun is mistaken. [The] people who need the assistance of potential samaritans in ordinary samaritan cases are persons under the fourteenth amendment, and yet the general common law bad-samaritan principle is not unconstitutional. (Similarly, the fact that fourteenth amendment persons are killed does not vitiate the ordinary law of self-defense.)

"[My] argument, unlike Blackmun's, does not depend on refusing to allow the state to regard the fetus as a person. Everything I have said is consistent with the assumption that the fetus is a person. Other persons are allowed to die when potential samaritans are authorized by the bad-samaritan principle to deny aid. The personhood of the fetus, even if it be conceded, is not an adequate reason (indeed it is no reason at all) for treating the pregnant woman differently from other potential samaritans.

"[M]y argument justifies more clearly than the Court's argument the Court's conclusion that abortion may not be forbidden even in the third trimester when the life or health of the mother is at stake. If the problem is ultimately one of balancing, as the Court's opinion suggests, it is not clear why the state's

tions suggest [that women do not significantly control sex]. * * * Feminism has found that women feel compelled to preserve the appearance—which, acted upon, becomes the reality—of male direction of sexual expression, as if it is male initiative itself that we want: it is that which turns us on. Men enforce this. It is much of what men want in a woman. * * *

"Under these conditions, women often do not use birth control because of its social meaning, a meaning we did not create. Using contraception means acknowledging and planning and taking direction of intercourse, accepting one's sexual availability, and appearing nonspontaneous. It means appearing available to male incursions. A good user of contraception is a bad girl. She can be presumed sexually available and, among other consequences, raped with relative impunity. (If you think this isn't true, you should consider rape cases in which the fact that a woman had a diaphragm in is taken as an indication that what happened to her was intercourse, not rape. 'Why did you have your diaphragm in?') * * * I wonder if a woman can be presumed to control access to her sexuality if she feels unable to interrupt intercourse to insert a diaphragm; or worse, cannot even want to, aware that she risks a pregnancy she knows she does not want. * * * Sex doesn't look a whole lot like freedom when it appears normatively less costly for women to risk an undesired, often painful, traumatic, dangerous, sometimes illegal, and potentially life-threatening procedure, than it is to protect oneself in advance. Yet abortion policy has never been explicitly approached in the context of how women get pregnant; that is, as a consequence of intercourse under conditions of gender inequality; that is, as an issue of forced sex."

compelling interest (as the Court describes it) in protecting the potential life of a fetus already capable of 'meaningful life outside the mother's womb' (in the Court's phrase) is outweighed even by the woman's life, much less by her health. On my approach, however, the matter is clear. Even the reader who rejects my general conclusions must admit that there is no other case in which we would even consider requiring one individual to sacrifice his life or health to rescue another." [e]

3. *Prohibiting the government from "coercing intimate acts."* The argument that a state may not compel a pregnant woman to be "a Good Samaritan" is questioned by PHILIP BOBBITT, *Constitutional Fate* 163 (1982): "This argument seems to treat the embryonic child as a stranger who merely happens to be inconveniently placed proximate to the mother. There is much law, however, for the proposition that one owes a duty of care to one's child. This puts us back in the position of deciding when a child's life begins, a position the *Roe* Court was doctrinally forced to take in its argument despite its disclaimers and one which sound constitutional decision ought to avoid completely." Professor Bobbitt proposes a somewhat different "ethical argument [that] avoids the necessity for this determination" and one that "would decide *Roe*" (id. at 160–65):

"Government may not coerce intimate acts. Stated generally, does anyone really doubt this? * * * Whatever else may be an intimate act, carrying a child within one's body and giving birth must be a profoundly intimate act. * * * Who was Jane Roe? Perhaps a fuller record would have strengthened the case for the ethical approach I have advocated and would have made the ethical aspects of coercion and intimacy all the more forceful. [She] was an unskilled, young white woman. She was also a lesbian. She had become pregnant through rape. By the time of the [Supreme Court] argument, she had already terminated her pregnancy. [N]o fetus was left to protect. It is an extreme claim to hold that the state should have prosecuted her and sent her to prison because she had refused to wholly and forever choose the most intimate of human experiences."

4. *"Privacy" or "sex equality"? The "sex-specific impact" of laws restricting abortion.* "Nothing the Supreme Court has ever done," observes SYLVIA LAW, *Rethinking Sex and the Constitution*, 132 U.Pa.L.Rev. 955, 981 (1984), "has been more concretely important for women [than the decision in *Roe*]. Laws denying access to abortion have a sex-specific impact. Although both men and women seek to control reproduction, only women become pregnant. Only women have abortions. Laws restricting access to abortion have a devastating sex-specific impact. Despite the decision's overwhelming importance to women, it was not grounded on the principle of sex equality. The plaintiffs [in *Roe* and *Doe*] had not challenged the abortion restrictions as sex discriminatory." Continues Professor Law (id. at 1020, 1028):

"The rhetoric of privacy, as opposed to equality, blunts our ability to focus on the fact that it is *women* who are oppressed when abortion is denied. [The] rhetoric of privacy also reinforces a public/private dichotomy that is at the heart of the structures that perpetuate the powerlessness of women. [T]he drive to

e. For criticism of Regan's argument, see Alexander, *Modern Equal Protection Theories: A Metatheoretical Taxonomy and Critique,* 42 Ohio St.L.J. 3, 40–42 n. 114 (1981). See also Bobbitt, note 3 infra; Davis, *Abortion and Self-Defense,* in *Abortion: Moral and Legal* *Perspectives* 186 (Garfield & Hennessey eds. 1984) (hereinafter referred to as "*Abortion* "); P. Foot, *Killing and Letting Die,* in *Abortion* 175, 184–85; Michaels, *Abortion and the Claims of Samaritanism,* in *Abortion* 213.

criminalize abortion is animated by an affirmation of the value of a patriarchal society. [But] application of the constitutional ideal of equality to men and women prohibits the state from using its coercive power to enforce patriarchal relations. [The] high place of equality in our constellation of democratic and constitutional values demands that something more compelling than traditionalist moral conviction justify state actions denying women that which is indispensably necessary to their ability to act as moral beings and to participate in civil society. If and when it becomes technologically possible to grow children outside of a woman's body, the moral and constitutional issues we confront in relation to abortion will be categorically different than they are today. But for today, reproductive freedom is, inescapably, the core issue of women's equality and liberty."

5. *In Roe did the woman patient take a back seat to the male physician?* In *Roe,* maintains ANDREA ASARO, *The Judicial Portrayal of the Physician in Abortion and Sterilization Decisions,* 6 Harv. Women's L.J. 51, 53–55 (1983), Justice Blackmun "subsumed the woman's right to privacy within the ambit of the doctor-patient relationship, and ultimately subordinated her interest to the physician's. [For] Blackmun, the key issue was quite simply one of medical discretion, in other words: '[F]or the period of pregnancy prior to the "compelling" point, the attending physician, in consultation with his patient, is free to determine [that], in his medical judgment, the patient's pregnancy should be terminated.' Interestingly, the abortion decision is characterized here neither as primarily the woman's nor as fundamentally or initially a moral or personal one. Blackmun's perspective is clinical, and the woman patient has taken a back seat to the male physician-protagonist. [Concluding] his *Roe* opinion by summarizing the impact of the decision on the state and on the physician [Justice Blackmun states]: '[The] decision vindicates the right of the physician to administer medical treatment according to his professional judgment up to the points where important state interests provide compelling justifications for intervention. Up to these points, *the abortion decision in all its aspects is inherently, and primarily, a medical decision, and basic responsibility for it must rest with the physician.* * * * ' [f] Blackmun has neglected even to mention the pregnant woman as party to the abortion decision! The state, the physician, and the court have displaced Ms. Roe altogether." [g]

ROE v. WADE AND THE DEBATE IT STIRRED OVER "INTERPRETIVIST"/"NONINTERPRETIVIST" CONSTITUTIONAL DECISIONMAKING [a]

1. Consider Lupu, *Constitutional Theory and the Search for the Workable Premise,* 8 Dayton L.Rev. 579, 583 (1983): "*Roe* clarified, as had no other case

f. Emphasis added by Ms. Asaro.

g. See also Law, note 4 supra, at 1020.

a. Although the materials in this section inevitably overlap to some extent with the preceding set of Notes & Questions, it seems useful to focus separately on the general constitutional debate generated by the 1973 *Abortion Cases.*

"Interpretivism" indicates that "judges deciding constitutional issues should confine themselves to enforcing norms that are stated

or clearly implicit in the written Constitution"; "noninterpretivism" indicates that "courts should go beyond that set of references and enforce norms that cannot be discovered within the four corners of the document." Ely, *Democracy and Distrust* 1 (1980). "What distinguishes interpretivism from its opposite is its insistence that the work of the political branches is to be invalidated only in accord with an inference whose starting point, whose underlying premise, is fairly discovera-

since World War II, the Supreme Court's willingness to reach results which no defensible interpretivist position could support. Although rhetorically tied to the meaning of 'liberty' in the fourteenth amendment due process clause, and loosely aligned with the penumbral analysis developed in *Griswold, Roe* cut

ble in the Constitution. That the complete inference will not be found there—because the situation is not likely to have been foreseen—is general common ground." Id. at 1–2.

"Noninterpretivism," comments Van Alstyne, *Interpretations of the First Amendment* 94 n. 27 (1984), "signals a frank resolve to detach judicial review from the Constitution itself by stipulating it purports not to be interpreting the Constitution. It may say too much about the current condition of constitutional scholarship that 'noninterpretivism' is willingly adopted as a mode of describing one's own work in constitutional law. If there were not writers who evidently welcome its fit, e.g., Perry, *Noninterpretive Review in Human Rights Cases: A Functional Justification,* 56 N.Y.U.L.Rev. 278 (1981), one might have supposed that its use was limited and purely pejorative * * *." But compare Professor Perry's early writings with his most recent article, *The Authority of Text, Tradition, and Reason: A Theory of Constitutional "Interpretation,"* 58 S.Cal.L.Rev. 551 (1985).

As might be expected, there is disagreement over the appropriate terminology. Dean Bennett prefers the term "originalists" to describe those who "argue that constitutional language, understood in light of the substantive intentions or values behind its enactment, is the sole proper source for constitutional interpretation," because this term "better captures the static pretense of the approach that seems to me to be its principal flaw." Bennett, *Objectivity in Constitutional Law,* 132 U.Pa.L. Rev. 445, 446 & n. 3 (1984). "On the other side of the debate are 'noninterpretivists' or 'nonoriginalists' who believe it is legitimate for judges to look beyond text and original intention in interpreting constitutional language," but they "are divided on what particular sources should replace or supplement originalist sources and on how to justify their use." Id. at 446.

"There are some legal theorists," observes Fiss, *Objectivity and Interpretation,* 34 Stan.L. Rev. 739, 743 (1982), "who would limit legal interpretation to highly specific constitutional clauses. This school, misleadingly called 'interpretivism,' [should] more properly [be] called 'textual determinism' * * *. For an interpretivist only a specific text can be interpreted. Interpretation is thus confused with execution—the application of a determinate meaning to a situation—and is unproblematic only with regard to clauses like that requiring the president to be at least 35 years old. Most interpretivists, including Justice Black, would recognize the narrowness of such a perspective and want to acknowledge a role for less

specific clauses, like freedom of speech; but in truth such provisions are hardly obvious in their meaning and require substantial judicial interpretation to be given their proper effect."

Grey, *Do We Have an Unwritten Constitution?,* 27 Stan.L.Rev. 703 (1975), probably originated the use of the "interpretivist-noninterpretivist" terminology, but he now thinks these labels "distort the debate": "If the current interest in interpretive theory [does] nothing else, at least it shows that the concept of interpretation is broad enough to encompass any plausible mode of constitutional adjudication. We are all interpretivists; the real arguments are not over whether judges should stick to interpreting, but over what they should interpret and what interpretive attitudes they should adopt. Repenting past errors, I will therefore use the less misleading labels 'textualists' and 'supplementers' for, respectively, those who consider the text the sole legitimate source of operative norms in constitutional adjudication, and those who accept supplementary sources of constitutional law [such as 'conventional morality']." Grey, *The Constitution as Scripture,* 37 Stan.L.Rev. 1 (1984).

Professor Grey notes the emergence in recent years of a third group of constitutional theorists, id. at 1–2, those "who reject the very question ('text alone, or text plus supplement?') to which textualists and supplementers propose different answers. According to these 'rejectionists,' judges are always interpreting the constitutional text, but this is not the kind of significant constraint on judicial activism that textualists think it is—the text, if read with an appropriately generous notion of context, provides as lively a Constitution as the most activist judge might need."

See also Sandalow, *Constitutional Interpretation,* 79 Mich.L.Rev. 1033, 1045–46 (1981): "[A]ll the decisions shaping constitutional law to contemporary values [can] be understood as coming within the general intentions of the framers. All that is necessary is to state those intentions at a sufficiently high level of abstraction. [By] wrenching the framers' 'larger purposes' from the particular judgments that revealed them, we incur a loss of perspective, a perspective that might better enable us to see that the particular judgments they made were not imperfect expressions of a larger purpose but a particular accommodation of competing purposes. In freeing ourselves from those judgments we are not serving larger ends determined by the framers but making room for the introduction of contemporary values."

fundamental rights adjudication loose from the constitutional text. [There followed] a vast array of doctrinal, methodological, and theoretical inquiries into the outcome in *Roe*. More or less detached from the case itself, these scholarly efforts offered a variety of justifications for noninterpretive review—natural law underpinings of the 1787 Constitution,[25] transplantation of common law method into constitutional adjudication,[26] the search for enduring or traditional unwritten norms,[27] [and] judicial manifestation of consensus morality." [28]

2. Ely, *Democracy and Distrust* 2–3 (1980), suggests why "interpretivism may be entering a period of comparative popularity": The first is that *Roe*, "the clearest example of noninterpretivist 'reasoning' [in] four decades," "forced all of us who work in the area to think about which camp we fall into, with the result that a number of persons would today label themselves interpretivists who had not previously given the choice much notice. The second may be that, *Roe* notwithstanding, the Burger Court is by and large a politically conservative Court—or at least more conservative than its predecessor. This means that observers who might earlier have been content to let the justices enforce their own values (or their rendition of society's values) are now somewhat uneasy about doing so and are more likely to pursue an interpretivist line, casting their lot with the values of the framers."

3. *Are the Abortion Cases "bad constitutional law" or "not constitutional law"?* Consider JOHN ELY, *The Wages of Crying Wolf: A Comment on Roe v. Wade,* 82 Yale L.J. 920, 935–37, 939, 943, 947–49 (1973): "What is unusual about *Roe* is that the liberty involved is accorded [a] protection more stringent [than] that the present Court accords the freedom of the press explicitly guaranteed by the First Amendment. What is frightening about *Roe* is that this super-protected right is not inferable from the language of the Constitution, the framers' thinking respecting the specific problem in issue, any general value derivable from the provisions they included, or the nation's governmental structure. Nor is it explainable in terms of the unusual political impotence of the group judicially protected vis-á-vis the interest that legislatively prevailed over it.[b] And [that] is a charge that can responsibly be leveled at no other

25. See Grey, *Do We Have Unwritten Constitution?*, 27 Stan.L.Rev. 703 (1975).

26. See, e.g., Brest, *The Misconceived Quest for the Original Understanding,* 60 B.U.L.Rev. 204 (1980); Michelman, *Constancy to an Ideal Object,* 56 N.Y.U.L.Rev. 406 (1981); Wellington, *Common Law Rules and Constitutional Double Standards,* 83 Yale L.J. 221 (1973).

27. See, e.g., Lupu, *Untangling the Strands of the Fourteenth Amendment,* 77 Mich.L.Rev. 981 (1979).

28. See, e.g., Perry, *Abortion, the Public Morals, and the Police Power,* 23 U.C.L.A.L. Rev. 689 (1976). [But cf. Perry, *The Authority of Text, Tradition, and Reason: A Theory of Constitutional "Interpretation,"* 58 S.Cal.L. Rev. 551 (1985).]

b. Elsewhere in his article, id. at 933–35, Professor Ely argues that Justice Stone's suggestion in his famous *Carolene Products* footnote that the Court provide extraordinary constitutional protection for " 'discrete and insulate minorities' unable to form effective political alliances" does not apply to *Roe*: "Compared with men, very few women sit in our legislatures, [but] *no* fetuses sit [there]. Of course they have their champions, but so have women. The two interests have clashed repeatedly in the political arena, and had continued to do so up to the date of [*Roe*], generating quite a wide variety of accommodations. [Justice Stone's suggestion] was clearly intended and should be reserved for those interests which, as compared with the interests to which they have been subordinated, constitute minorities usually incapable of protecting themselves. Compared with men, women may constitute such a 'minority'; compared with the unborn, they do not."

Professor Ely's challenge of the appropriateness of judicial intervention in *Roe* "is misguided, however," maintains Bennett, *Abortion and Judicial Review,* 75 Nw.U.L.Rev. 978, 995–96 n. 71 (1981), "because it assumes that fetuses are political actors—indeed a political minority—whose 'powerlessness' is relevant to assessing the Court's appropriate role in the abortion controversy. Each political system must define, explicitly or implicitly, the universe of relevant political actors. [But]

decision of the past twenty years. At times the inferences the Court has drawn from the values the Constitution marks for special protection have been controversial, even shaky, but never before has its sense of an obligation to draw one been so obviously lacking.

"[The] problem with *Roe* is not so much that it bungles the question it sets itself, but rather that it sets itself a question the Constitution has not made the Court's business. It *looks* different from *Lochner*—it has the shape if not the substance of a judgment that is very much the Court's business, one vindicating an interest the Constitution marks as special—and it is for that reason perhaps more dangerous. Of course in a sense it is more candid than *Lochner*. But the employment of a higher standard of judicial review, no matter how candid the recognition that it is indeed higher, loses some of its admirability when it is accompanied by neither a coherent account of why such a standard is appropriate nor any indication of why it has not been satisfied.

"[*Roe* is] a very bad decision. Not because it will perceptibly weaken the Court—it won't; and not because it conflicts with either my idea of progress or what the evidence suggests is society's—it doesn't. It is bad because it is bad constitutional law, or rather because it is *not* constitutional law and gives almost no sense of an obligation to try to be. [The] point that often gets lost in the commentary, and obviously got lost in *Roe*, is that *before* the Court can get to the 'balancing' stage, *before* it can worry about the next case and the case after that (or even about its institutional position) it is under an obligation to trace its premises to the charter from which it derives its authority. A neutral and durable principal may be a thing of beauty and joy forever. But if it lacks connection with any value the Constitution marks as special, it is not a constitutional principle and the Court has no business imposing it."[c]

4. *Is it a question of "inventing" a new right, or of the state having to justify an invasion of liberty?* Consider the remarks of Professor Tribe in Choper, Kamisar & Tribe, *The Supreme Court: Trends and Developments 1982–83* (1984) at 215: "[The *Roe* Court] is said to have invented the right to abortion. [To quote Professor Ely], *Roe* was not just *bad* constitutional law, it was not constitutional law at all. I have never found it easy to understand what that criticism means in this context. Once one concedes that the word 'liberty' has substantive content in its application against the states through the Fourteenth Amendment—and it must, if any substantive provisions of the Bill of Rights are to be enforced against the states through the Fourteenth Amendment—it becomes not a question of inventing a new right, but of asking what the justification is for a state intrusion into what is indisputably an aspect of someone's personal liberty."

5. *"The Constitution" vs. "the original Constitution."* "[H]ow," asks Michelman, *Commentary* (panel discussion), 56 N.Y.U.L.Rev. 525, 532 (1981), "is

outside the abortion context there are no indications that fetuses are considered relevant political actors. [E]ven within the context of abortion-related issues, the suggestion that fetuses are a part of the larger political community appears, as in Ely's formulation, only incidentally and as part of the abortion discussion. It is, of course, possible for a legislature to take into account interests outside its own political community. [But] with fetuses, as with other interests outside the relevant universe of political actors, the legislative process can only take them into account insofar as relevant political actors subsume those interests into their own."

c. See also Forrester, *Are We Ready for Truth in Judging?*, 63 A.B.A.J. 1212 (1977); Lusky, *By What Right?* 14, 16–17, 20 (1975); Monaghan, *The Constitution Goes to Harvard*, 13 Harv.Civ.Rts.-Civ.Lib.L.Rev. 116, 131 (1978); Posner, *The Uncertain Protection of Privacy in the Supreme Court*, 1979 Sup.Ct. Rev. 173, 199–200.

it arguably an offense or violation of the Constitution for the New York legislature to do what it did in *Lochner* or for a state legislature to criminalize abortion? [M]y answer to that question is: There is no argument that I can see to the effect that those statutes violate the original Constitution. The argument has to be that they violate the Constitution—meaning the original Constitution with all the interpretive precedents that have arisen in the course of the judicial attempt to carry out the office of the Court, which is to decide hard cases under the Constitution when they arise."

6. *Should the legitimacy of Roe be debated in terms of "institutional continuity"?* "It is plausible," maintains ROBERT BENNETT, *Objectivity in Constitutional Law,* 132 U.Pa.L.Rev. 445, 486 (1984), to see prior decisions protecting the interests of adults with regard to procreation and those of parents with regard to children "as opening a future that could accommodate *Roe.* To be sure *Roe* did require a value judgment beyond those captured by prior decisions. In that respect the case was no more unusual than *Yick Wo v. Hopkins* (1886) [p. 1169 infra] [applicability of fourteenth amendment equal protection to discriminatory administration of ordinance against resident Chinese aliens] or hundreds of other constitutional cases, except perhaps that the judgment required was a particularly wrenching one.

"My point is not that *Roe* was rightly decided, but that the debate about whether the Supreme Court could legitimately invalidate laws prohibiting abortion is often misconceived. Viewed as a question of judicial objectivity, the legitimacy of *Roe* turns not on whether there is some authoritative basis on which the Court can substitute its value judgment for that of the legislature but on whether the Court can successfully define its opinion as a natural outgrowth of what it has received. [The legitimacy of *Roe*] should be debated in terms of institutional continuity and of its substantive merits and not by reference to one or another dubious and inevitably incomplete standard of authoritativeness. In contrast to *Roe,* the state legislative apportionment cases, favorites of Ely, seem much less justifiable in terms of institutional continuity."

POST-*ROE* ABORTION AND BIRTH CONTROL REGULATION

1. *Spousal and parental consent.* PLANNED PARENTHOOD v. DANFORTH, 428 U.S. 52, 96 S.Ct. 2831, 49 L.Ed.2d 788 (1976), per BLACKMUN, J., struck down, inter alia, provisions of a post-*Roe* Missouri abortion statute requiring the spouse's consent to abortion and, in the case of an unmarried woman under 18, parental consent. (These consents were required when a woman sought an abortion during the first trimester unless a physician certified that the abortion was "necessary [to] preserve the life of the mother.")

As for "spousal consent," "the State cannot 'delegate to a spouse a veto power which the state itself is absolutely and totally prohibited from exercising during the first trimester of pregnancy.' [Even] if the State had the ability to delegate to the husband a power it itself could not exercise, [the] obvious fact is that when the wife and the husband disagree on this decision, the view of only one of the two marriage partners can prevail. Since it is the woman who physically bears the child and who is the more directly and immediately affected by the pregnancy, as between the two, the balance weighs in her favor." As for "parental consent," here, too, "the State does not have the constitutional authority to give a third party an absolute, and possibly arbitrary, veto over the decision of the physician and his patient to terminate the patient's pregnancy, regardless of the reason for withholding the consent." The Court emphasized, however, that its holding "does not suggest that every minor, regardless of age or maturity, may give effective consent for termination of her pregnancy."

WHITE, J., joined by Burger, C.J., and Rehnquist, J., dissented, baffled how the Court could find anything in the Constitution or in the 1973 *Abortion Cases* *requiring* a state to "assign a greater value to a mother's decision to cut off a potential human life by abortion than to a father's decision to let it mature into a live child." Nor did he see how it followed from the fact that the mother's interest in seeking an abortion "outweighs the *State's* interest in the potential life of the fetus, that the husband's interest is also outweighed and may not be protected by the State." As for parental consent, a state "is entitled to protect the minor unmarried woman from making the decision [whether or not to obtain an abortion] in a way which is not in her own best interests, and it seeks to achieve this goal by requiring consultation and consent. This is the traditional way by which States have sought to protect children from their own immature and improvident decisions; there is absolutely no reason expressed by the majority why the State may not utilize that method here."

STEVENS, J., joined the Court's invalidation of other provisions, but dissented on parental consent: "[The] Court seems to assume that the capacity to conceive a child and the judgment of the physician are the only constitutionally permissible yardsticks for determining whether a young woman can independently make the abortion decision. I doubt the accuracy of the Court's empirical judgment. Even if it were correct, however, as a matter of constitutional law I think a State has power to conclude otherwise and to select a chronological age as its standard." [a]

Notes and Questions

(a) *If the issue is balancing.* Consider Regan, *Rewriting Roe v. Wade,* 77 Mich.L.Rev. 1569, 1644 (1979): "[I]f the whole issue is one of balancing [as the *Roe* opinion suggests], might it not be that the state's interest, which is less than the interest of the woman or of the woman and her husband together when they are aligned, is greater than the *difference* between the interests of the woman and her husband when they are opposed? Indeed, given the weightiness of the state's interest and the similarity of the woman's interests to her husband's (especially while the Court emphasizes the 'family-planning' aspect rather than the physical burdens of pregnancy), is it not quite likely?" On Regan's approach, however, "the state can no more make the unwilling woman serve the fetus and her husband than it can make her serve the fetus alone."

(b) *Sex discrimination.* Consider Burt, *The Constitution of the Family,* 1979 Sup.Ct.Rev. 329, 394: "[T]he Court's explicit assumption that the father of the fetus is as much a stranger to it as any other community member is not plausible. The Court's apparent position that the mother always has the superior claim and interest, no matter how much the father might show that her burden in childbearing would be less than his burden in losing his child, appears

---

a. Cf. *Parham v. J.R.,* 442 U.S. 584, 99 S.Ct. 2493, 61 L.Ed.2d 101 (1979), rejecting the contention that *Danforth* and other cases require that the parents' decision to commit a child to a mental hospital must be subjected to exacting constitutional scrutiny, including a preadmission adversary hearing: "[*Danforth*] involved an absolute parental veto over the child's ability to obtain an abortion," but Georgia parents have no "absolute right to commit their children to state mental hospitals; the statute requires [each regional hospital superintendent] to exercise independent judgment as to the child's need for confinement."

to me an invidious sex discrimination. Whether or not the Court should forbid all other institutions from engaging in such discrimination, it should not indulge in its own."

2. *Parental or judicial consent.* BELLOTTI v. BAIRD (*Bellotti II*), 443 U.S. 622, 99 S.Ct. 3035, 61 L.Ed.2d 797 (1979), struck down a Massachusetts law which (unlike the statute in *Danforth*) required an unmarried pregnant minor to obtain the consent of both parents for an abortion or, if parental consent was not obtained, authorization from a state judge if he concluded that abortion was in her best interest. POWELL, J., joined by Burger, C.J., and Stewart and Rehnquist, JJ.,[a] announced the judgment of the Court, concluding that if the state requires a pregnant minor to obtain one or both parents' consent to an abortion, it also must provide an "alternative procedure" (which need not be a judicial proceeding) for obtaining authorization for the abortion "ensur[ing] that [the parental consent requirement] does not in fact amount to the 'absolute, and possibly arbitrary, veto' that was found impermissible in *Danforth.*" In such a proceeding a pregnant minor is entitled to show either: (1) that she is able "to make her abortion decision, in consultation with her physician, independently of her parents' wishes"; or (2) that, even if she is not, "the desired abortion would be in her best interests." Such a proceeding must also be conducted "with anonymity and sufficient expedition to provide an effective opportunity for an abortion to be obtained."

The statute fell short "in two respects: First, it permits judicial authorization for an abortion to be withheld from a minor [the court finds] to be mature and fully competent to make this decision independently. Second, it requires parental consultation or notification in every instance, without affording the pregnant minor an opportunity to receive an independent judicial determination that she is mature enough to consent or that an abortion would be in her best interests." [b]

STEVENS, J., joined by Brennan, Marshall and Blackmun, JJ., concurred in the judgment, deeming *Danforth* controlling: "It is inherent in the right to make the abortion decision that the right may be exercised without public scrutiny and in defiance of the contrary opinion of the sovereign or other third parties. In Massachusetts, however, every minor who cannot secure the consent of both her parents—which under *Danforth* cannot be an absolute prerequisite to an abortion—is required to secure the consent of the sovereign." Moreover, "the best interest of the minor" standard "provides little real guidance to the judge, and his decision must necessarily reflect personal and societal values and mores whose enforcement upon the minor [is] fundamentally at odds with privacy interests underlying the constitutional protection afforded to her decision." [c]

A Note on Bellotti II and its Aftermath

For an illuminating and extremely readable case study of *Bellotti II,* see Mnookin, *In the Interest of Children* 150–264 (1985). "The result in *Bellotti,*"

a. Rehnquist, J., joined only until "this Court is willing to reconsider" *Danforth.*

b. Powell, J., explicated: "If, all things considered, the court determines that an abortion is in the minor's best interests, she is entitled to court authorization without any parental involvement. On the other hand, the court may deny the abortion request of an immature minor in the absence of parental consultation if it concludes that her best interests would be served thereby, or the court may in such a case defer decision until there is parental consultation in which the court may participate. But this is the full extent to which parental involvement may be required."

c. Only White, J., dissented.

observes Professor Mnookin, "can perhaps be best understood as a judicially imposed compromise—a compromise of difficult philosophical, political, and policy issues. Nobody won, but nobody quite lost either. [In] essence, Justice Powell rejected the moral claims of both those who argued that a pregnant minor should have the *same* abortion rights as an adult woman and those who argued that parental involvement should be required. On the level of principle, neither parents nor kids get to decide alone. The result can certainly be seen as a political compromise." Id. at 260. Continues Mnookin, id. at 262–63:

"[F]or me, [Justice Powell's plurality opinion] reflects an unwarranted confidence in the ability of judges to make sound decisions on behalf of individual pregnant minors, and to make sound policy for our society as a whole. [I]n essence, it seemed the judge was to act like a parent, with broad discretion to use his personal values to make a decision on behalf of a pregnant woman. Powell's opinion seemed a high water mark of judicial arrogance. Neither legislatures nor families are to be trusted; nor are pregnant minors and their doctors. Only the modern-day secular priest, a judge, is to be trusted with the abortion decision for young women.

"My recent examination of the actual operation of the [post-*Bellotti II* Massachusetts statute] revealed that the new judicial process does not in fact involve a careful individualized assessment, but is instead a rubber-stamp, administrative operation. [Between April 1981, when the statute first went into effect, and February 1983], [n]one of the 1,300 young women who have gone to court have been successfully refused an abortion.[a] [This finding] is perhaps not so surprising. After all, the proceedings before the judges are not contested, and the judge has no independent source of information. More fundamentally, even if the judge decides that the young woman before him is not mature, on what basis (other than moral revulsion to abortion) could he possibly decide that it is not in the best interests of an immature minor to have a first-trimester abortion? [H]ow could the judge determine that it is in the interest of a minor to give birth to a child if she is too immature even to decide to have an abortion? Indeed, if one looks only at the result for pregnant minors who go to court, the process seems an unnecessary and expensive waste of time."

3. *Parental notice.* Distinguishing *Danforth* and *Bellotti v. Baird* (1979) (*Bellotti II*), H.L. v. MATHESON, 450 U.S. 398, 101 S.Ct. 1164, 67 L.Ed.2d 388 (1981), per BURGER, C.J., upheld a Utah statute, as applied to an unemancipated minor living with and dependent upon her parents, that required a physician to "notify, if possible" the parents of a minor upon whom an abortion is to be performed. Although appellant challenged the statute as unconstitutional on its face, contending that it was "overbroad in that it can be construed to apply to all unmarried minor girls, including those who are mature and emancipated," the Court held that since appellant, a 15-year-old living with, and dependent on, her parents, had not shown that she was "mature or emancipated," she lacked

a. Under the new statute, the judge's discretion to deny an abortion is limited. If he decides the young woman is "mature," he allows her to decide for herself. If the judge does not find the minor to be "mature," he gets to decide according to her "best interest." In about 90 percent of the cases the Supreme Court simply found the minor to be "mature." In the remaining cases the court found the abortion to be in the minor's best interest in virtually all instances. See id. at 239, 261–62.

Although the requirement of judicial authorization is not leading to the denial of abortion *for those who go to court,* "the business of Massachusetts abortion clinics has significantly declined. It would appear that many girls who formerly would have secured abortions in Massachusetts are now going to other states, particularly New Hampshire." Id. at 242.

standing to bring such a challenge. In a narrow ruling, the Court sustained the law as applied to appellant and members of her class:

"The Utah statute gives neither parents nor judges a veto power over the minor's abortion decision.[17] [As] applied to immature and dependent minors, the statute plainly serves the important considerations of family integrity and protected adolescents [identified] in *Bellotti II.* [Moreover], the statute serves a significant state interest by providing an opportunity for parents to supply essential medical and other information to a physician." The notice requirement may inhibit some minors from seeking abortions, but "the Constitution does not compel a state to fine-tune its statutes so as to encourage or facilitate abortions. To the contrary, state action 'encouraging child-birth except for the most urgent circumstances' is 'rationally related to the legitimate governmental objective of protecting potential life.' *Harris v. McRae* [infra]." [a]

Dissenting JUSTICE MARSHALL, joined by Brennan and Blackmun, JJ., contended that appellant had standing to challenge the statute in its application to all minors. He then found the statute unconstitutional: "Many minor women will encounter interference from their parents after the state-imposed notification. In addition to parental disappointment and disapproval, the minor may confront physical or emotional abuse, withdrawal of financial support, or actual obstruction of the abortion decision. Furthermore, the threat of parental notice may cause some minor women to delay past the first trimester of pregnancy, after which the health risks increase significantly. [Others] may attempt to self-abort or to obtain an illegal abortion rather than risk parental notification. Still others may foresake an abortion and bear an unwanted [child]. And that hardship is not a mere disincentive created by the State [referring to the abortion funding case of *Harris v. McRae,* infra], but is instead an actual state-imposed obstacle to the exercise of the minor woman's free choice. * * * Significantly, the interference sanctioned by the statute does not operate in a neutral fashion. No notice is required for other pregnancy-related medical care, so only the minor women who wish to abort encounter the burden imposed by the notification statute. * * *

"None of the reasons offered by the State justifies [the infringement upon a minor woman's constitutional right to privacy], for the statute is not tailored to serve them. Rather than serving to enhance the physician's judgment, in cases such as appellant's, the statute prevents implementation of the physician's medical recommendation. Rather than promoting the transfer of information held by parents to the minor's physician, the statute neglects to require anything more than a communication from the physician moments before the abortion. Rather than respecting the private realm of family life, the statute invokes the

---

17. The main premise of the dissent seems to be that a requirement of notice to the parents is the equivalent of a requirement of parental consent. In *Bellotti II,* however, we expressly declined to equate notice requirements with consent requirements.

a. Powell, J., joined by Stewart, J., concurred, emphasizing that they joined the Court's opinion "on the understanding that it leaves open the question whether [the Utah statute] unconstitutionally burdens the right of a mature minor or a minor whose best interests would not be served by parental notification." For the reasons set forth in his plurality opinion in *Bellotti II* (dealing with

parental *consent*), Powell maintained that "a state may not validly require notice to parents in all cases, without providing an independent decisionmaker to whom a pregnant minor can have recourse if she believes that she is mature enough to make the abortion decision independently or that notification otherwise would not be in her best interests."

Stevens, J., concurring only in the judgment, would reach the question reserved by the Court and uphold the statute as applied to *all* unmarried women who are suffering unwanted pregnancies and desire to terminate them, but may not do so because their physicians insist on complying with state law.

criminal machinery of the State in an attempt to influence the interactions within the family."

4. *Abortion funding.* MAHER v. ROE, 432 U.S. 464, 97 S.Ct. 2376, 53 L.Ed. 2d 484 (1977) (also discussed at p. 1079 infra), per POWELL, J., sustained Connecticut's use of Medicaid funds to reimburse women for the costs of childbirth and "medically necessary" first trimester abortions (defined to include "psychiatric necessity"), but not for the costs of elective or nontherapeutic first trimester abortions.[a]

On "the central question"—"whether the regulation 'impinges upon a fundamental right explicitly or implicitly protected by the Constitution' "—the Court held that *Roe* did not establish "an unqualified 'constitutional right to an abortion,' " but only a "right protect[ing] the woman from unduly burdensome interference with her freedom to decide whether to terminate her pregnancy. It implies no limitation on the authority of a State to make a value judgment favoring childbirth over abortion, and to implement that judgment by the allocation of public funds. [The] State may have made childbirth a more attractive alternative, thereby influencing the woman's decision, but it has imposed no restriction on access to abortions that was not already there. The indigency that may make it difficult—and in some cases, perhaps, impossible— for some women to have abortions is neither created nor in any way affected by the [regulation.]

"Our conclusion signals no retreat from *Roe* or the cases applying it. There is a basic difference between direct state interference with a protected activity and state encouragement of an alternative activity consonant with legislative policy. [This] distinction is implicit in [*Meyer* and *Pierce*, fn. b in *Griswold*]. Both cases invalidated substantial restrictions on constitutionally protected liberty interests [but] neither case denied to a State the policy choice of encouraging the preferred course of action. Indeed, in *Meyer* the Court was careful to state that the power of the State 'to prescribe a curriculum' that included English and excluded German in its free public schools 'is not questioned.' Similarly, *Pierce* casts no shadow over a State's power to favor public education by funding [it]. We think it abundantly clear that a State is not required to show a compelling interest for its policy choice to favor normal childbirth any more than a State must so justify its election to fund public but not private education."

The Court then sustained the regulation "under the less demanding test of rationality that applies in the absence of a suspect classification or the impingement of a fundamental right." It had little difficulty finding the distinction drawn between childbirth and nontherapeutic abortion " 'rationally related' to a 'constitutionally permissible' purpose." "*Roe* itself explicitly acknowledged the State's strong interest in protecting the potential life of the fetus. [The] State unquestionably has a 'strong and legitimate interest in encouraging normal childbirth' " and subsidizing the substantial and significantly increasing costs incident to childbirth is "a rational means of encouraging childbirth." [13]

---

a. In a companion case, *Beal v. Doe,* 432 U.S. 438, 97 S.Ct. 2366, 53 L.Ed.2d 464 (1977), per Powell, J., held that the Medicaid Act does not require state funding of nontherapeutic first trimester abortions as a condition of participation in the joint federal-state program.

In another companion case, *Poelker v. Doe,* 432 U.S. 519, 97 S.Ct. 2391, 53 L.Ed.2d 528 (1977), per curiam, for the reasons set forth in

Maher, found "no constitutional violation by the city of St. Louis in electing, as a policy choice, to provide publicly financed hospital services for childbirth without providing corresponding services for nontherapeutic abortions."

13. Much of the rhetoric of the three dissenting opinions would be equally applicable if Connecticut had elected not to fund either

BRENNAN, J., joined by Marshall and Blackmun, JJ., dissented, accusing the majority of "a distressing insensitivity to the plight of impoverished pregnant women." The "disparity in funding [clearly] operates to coerce indigent pregnant women to bear children they would not otherwise choose to have, and just as clearly, this coercion can only operate upon the poor, who are uniquely the victims of this form of financial pressure." *Roe* and its progeny held that "an area of privacy invulnerable to the State's intrusion surrounds the decision of a pregnant woman whether or not to carry her pregnancy to term. The Connecticut scheme clearly infringes upon that area of privacy."

The dissenters maintained that in other abortion cases the Court had rejected the notion that there is a basic difference between direct state interference with a fundamental right and state encouragement of an alternative activity: The spousal consent requirement struck down in *Danforth* was an "absolute obstacle" to abortion "only in the limited sense that a woman who was unable to persuade her spouse to [consent] was prevented from obtaining one. Any woman whose husband [did agree with her] was free to obtain an abortion, and the State never imposed directly any burden of its own." As for the majority's conclusion that the state's interest "in protecting the potential life of the fetus" is sufficient, "[s]ince only the first trimester of pregnancy is involved in this case, that justification is totally foreclosed if the Court is not overruling the holding of *Roe* that '[w]ith respect to the State's important and legitimate interest in potential life, the "compelling" point is at viability,' occurring at about the end of the second trimester."

As for *Poelker,* "the fundamental right of a woman freely to choose to terminate her pregnancy has been infringed by the city of St. Louis through a deliberate policy based on opposition to elective abortions on moral grounds by city officials. [The] city policy is a significant, and in some cases insurmountable, obstacle to indigent pregnant women who cannot pay for abortions in [clinics or private hospitals].

In a second dissent, MARSHALL, J., thought it "all too obvious that the governmental actions in these cases, ostensibly taken to 'encourage' women to carry pregnancies to term, are in reality intended to impose a moral viewpoint that no State may constitutionally enforce. Since efforts to overturn [*Roe* and *Doe*] have been unsuccessful, the opponents of abortion have attempted every imaginable means to circumvent the commands of the Constitution and impose their moral choices upon the rest of society. The present cases involve the most vicious attacks yet devised. The impact of the regulations here fall tragically upon those among us least able to help or defend themselves."

In a third dissent, BLACKMUN, J., joined by Brennan and Marshall, JJ., charged that "the Court concedes the existence of a constitutional right but denies the realization and enjoyment of that right on the ground that existence and realization are separate and distinct. [Implicit in today's holdings] is the condescension that [the indigent woman] may go elsewhere for her abortion. I find that disingenuous and alarming, almost reminiscent of: 'Let them eat cake.' "

abortions or childbirth. Yet none of the dissents goes so far as to argue that the Constitution *requires* such assistance for all indigent pregnant women.

[Compare Simson, *Abortion, Poverty and the Equal Protection of the Laws,* 13 Ga.L.Rev. 505, 508 (1979): "[I]f Connecticut funded neither childbirth nor abortion, poverty would not lead indigent women to prefer childbirth to abortion. Rather, since a safe abortion in the early months of pregnancy is materially cheaper than a safe childbirth, financial considerations probably would militate strongly *in favor of* abortion."]

5. *More on abortion funding; The Hyde Amendment.* Title XIX of the Social Security Act established the Medicaid program to provide federal financial assistance to states choosing to reimburse certain costs of medical treatment for needy persons. Since 1976, various versions of the so-called Hyde Amendment have limited federal funding of abortions under the Medicaid program to those necessary to save the life of the mother and certain other exceptional circumstances.[a] HARRIS v. McRAE, 448 U.S. 297, 100 S.Ct. 2671, 65 L.Ed.2d 784 (1980), per STEWART, J., determined that Title XIX does not obligate a participating state to pay for those medically necessary abortions for which Congress has withheld federal funding and then held—relying heavily on *Maher*—that the Hyde Amendment is constitutionally valid:

"The Hyde Amendment, like [the regulation upheld] in *Maher,* places no governmental obstacle in the path of a woman who chooses to terminate her pregnancy, but rather, by means of unequal subsidization of abortion and other medical services, encourages alternative activity deemed in the public interest. The present case does differ factually from *Maher* insofar as that case involved a failure to fund nontherapeutic abortions, whereas the Hyde Amendment withholds funding of certain medically necessary abortions. [But] regardless of [how] the freedom of a woman to choose to terminate her pregnancy for health reasons [is characterized], it simply does not follow that [this freedom] carries with it a constitutional entitlement to the financial resources to avail herself of the full range of protected choices. The reason why was explained in *Maher:* although government may not place obstacles in the path of a woman's exercise of her freedom of choice, it need not remove those not of its own creation. [T]he Hyde Amendment leaves an indigent woman with at least the same range of choice in deciding whether to obtain a medically necessary abortion as she would have had if Congress had chosen to subsidize no health costs at all.

"[Acceptance of appellees' argument] would mark a drastic change in our understanding of the Constitution. It cannot be that because government may not prohibit the use of contraceptives, *Griswold,* or prevent parents from sending their child to a private school, *Pierce,* government, therefore, has an affirmative constitutional obligation to assure that all persons have the financial resources to obtain contraceptives or send their children to private [schools.][b]

---

a. The version of the Hyde Amendment applicable for fiscal year 1980 prohibited federal funding of abortions "except where the life of the mother would be endangered if the fetus were carried to term" or except for cases of rape or incest "when such rape or incest has been reported promptly to a law enforcement agency or public health service." But the initial version of the Hyde Amendment, which triggered the instant case, did not include the "rape or incest" exception.

b. The Court then rejected the contention that the Hyde Amendment violates the Establishment Clause because, as the argument ran, "it incorporates into law the doctrines of the Roman Catholic Church": A statute does not run afoul of the Establishment Clause "because it 'happens to coincide or harmonize with the tenets of some or all religions,' *McGowan v. Maryland* [p. 808 infra]"; the Hyde Amendment "is as much a reflection of 'traditionalist' values toward abortion, as it is an embodiment of the views of any particular religion."

"Again draw[ing] guidance from" *Maher,* the Court also rejected the argument that the Hyde Amendment "violates the equal protection component of the Fifth Amendment": The Hyde Amendment "is not predicated on a constitutionally suspect classification. [Here,] as in *Maher,* the principal impact of [the] Amendment falls on the indigent. But that fact alone does not itself render the funding restriction constitutionally invalid, for this Court has held repeatedly that poverty, standing alone, is not a suspect classification." See generally Ch. 10, Sec. 3, I and Sec. 4, IV. Thus, the Hyde Amendment need only satisfy the rational-basis standard of review and it does—"by encouraging childbirth except in the most urgent circumstances, [it] is rationally related to the legitimate governmental objective of protecting potential life."

Responding to the arguments of the dissents—especially Stevens, J.'s—WHITE, J. concurring, characterized the constitutional right recognized in *Roe* as "the right to choose to undergo an abortion without coercive interference by the government. [*Roe*] dealt with the circumstances in which the governmental interest in potential life would justify official interference with the abortion choices of pregnant women. There is no such calculus involved here. [The pregnant] woman's choice remains unfettered, the government is not attempting to use its interest in life to justify a coercive restraint, and hence in disbursing its Medicaid funds it is free to implement rationally what *Roe* recognized to be its legitimate interest in a potential life by covering the medical costs of childbirth but denying funds for abortions. Neither *Roe* [nor its progeny] invalidates this legislative preference. We decided as much in *Maher* * * *."

Four justices dissented—Brennan, Marshall and Blackmun, JJ. (the three *Maher* dissenters), and Stevens, J. who had joined the opinion of the Court in *Maher*.

STEVENS, J., maintained that the instant case presented "[a] fundamentally different question" than the one decided in *Maher:* "This case involves the pool of benefits that Congress created by enacting [Title XIX]. Individuals who satisfy two neutral criteria—financial need and medical need—are entitled to equal access to that pool. The question is whether certain persons who satisfy those criteria may be denied access to benefits solely because they must exercise the constitutional right to have an abortion in order to obtain the medical care they need. Our prior cases plainly dictate [the answer].

"Unlike these plaintiffs, [those] in *Maher* did not satisfy the neutral criterion of medical need; they sought a subsidy for nontherapeutic abortions—medical procedures which by definition they did not need. [This case] involves a special exclusion of women who, by definition, are confronted with a choice between two serious harms: serious health damage to themselves on the one hand and abortion on the other. The competing interests are the interest in maternal health and the interest in protecting potential human life. It is now part of our law that the pregnant woman's decision as to which of these conflicting interests shall prevail is entitled to constitutional protection.

"[If] a woman has a constitutional right to place a higher value on avoiding either serious harm to her own health or perhaps an abnormal childbirth [3] than on protecting potential life, the exercise of that right cannot provide the basis for the denial of a benefit to which she would otherwise be entitled. The Court's sterile equal protection analysis evades this critical though simple point. The Court focuses exclusively on the 'legitimate interest in protecting the potential life of the fetus.' [*Roe*] squarely held that the States may not protect that interest when a conflict with the interest in a pregnant woman's health exists. It is thus perfectly clear that neither the Federal Government nor the States may exclude a woman from medical benefits to which she would otherwise be entitled solely to further an interest in potential life when a physician, 'in appropriate medical judgment,' certifies that an abortion is necessary 'for the

---

3. The Court relies heavily on the premise [that] the State's legitimate interest in preserving potential life provides a sufficient justification for funding medical services that are necessarily associated with normal childbirth without also funding abortions that are not medically necessary. The *Maher* opinion repeatedly referred to the policy of favoring "normal childbirth." But this case involves a refusal to fund abortions which are medically necessary to avoid abnormal childbirth.

preservation of the life or health of the mother.' *Roe*. The Court totally fails to explain why this reasoning is not dispositive here.[4]

"[Nor] can it be argued that the exclusion of this type of medically necessary treatment of the indigent can be justified on fiscal grounds. [For] the cost of an abortion is only a small fraction of the costs associated with childbirth.[9] Thus, the decision to tolerate harm to indigent persons who need an abortion in order to avoid 'serious and long lasting health damage' is one that is financed by draining money out of the pool that is used to fund all other necessary medical procedures. Unlike most invidious classifications, this discrimination harms not only its direct victims but also the remainder of the class of needy persons that the pool was designed to benefit. * * *

"Having decided to alleviate some of the hardships of poverty by providing necessary medical care, the Government must use neutral criteria in distributing benefits. It may not deny benefits to a financially and medically needy person simply because he is a Republican, a Catholic, or an Oriental—or because he has spoken against a program the Government has a legitimate interest in furthering. In sum, it may not create exceptions for the sole purpose of furthering a governmental interest that is constitutionally subordinate to the individual interest that the entire program was designed to protect. The Hyde amendments not only exclude financially and medically needy persons from the pool of benefits for a constitutionally insufficient reason; they also require the expenditure of millions of dollars in order to thwart the exercise of a constitutional right, thereby effectively inflicting serious and long lasting harm on impoverished women who want and need abortions for valid medical reasons. [Thus,] these amendments constitute an unjustifiable, and indeed blatant, violation of the sovereign's duty to govern impartially."

The other three dissenters wrote separately, each voicing agreement with Stevens, J.'s analysis. BRENNAN, J., joined by Marshall and Blackmun, JJ., expressed his "continuing disagreement with the Court's mischaracterization of the nature of the fundamental right recognized in *Roe* and its misconception of the manner in which that right is infringed [by] legislation withdrawing all funding for medically necessary abortions":

"The proposition for which [*Roe* and its progeny stand] is not that the State is under an affirmative obligation to ensure access to abortions for all who may desire them; it is that the State must refrain from wielding its enormous power and influence in a manner that might burden the pregnant woman's freedom to choose whether to have an abortion. [By] injecting coercive financial incentives

---

4. [In] responding to my analysis of this case, Mr. Justice White has described the constitutional right recognized in *Roe* as "the right to choose to undergo an abortion without coercive interference by the Government" or a right "only to be free from unreasonable official interference with private choice." No such language is found in the *Roe* opinion itself. Rather, that case squarely held that State interference is unreasonable if it attaches a greater importance to the interest in potential life than to the interest in protecting the mother's health. One could with equal justification describe the right protected by the First Amendment as the right to make speeches without coercive interference by the Government and then sustain a Government subsidy for all medically needy persons except

those who publicly advocate a change of administration.

9. [*Williams v. Zbaraz*, 448 U.S. 358, 100 S.Ct. 2694, 65 L.Ed.2d 831 (1980), a companion case], found that the average cost to the State of Illinois of an abortion was less than $150 as compared with the cost of a childbirth which exceeded $1,350. Indeed, based on an estimated cost of providing support to children of indigent parents together with their estimate of the number of medically necessary abortions that would be funded but for the Hyde Amendment, appellees in *Zbaraz* contend that [in] Illinois alone the effect of the Hyde Amendment is to impose a cost of about $20,000,000 per year on the public fisc.
* * *

favoring childbirth into a decision that is constitutionally guaranteed to be free from governmental intrusion, the Hyde Amendment deprives the indigent woman of her freedom to choose abortion over maternity, thereby impinging on the due process liberty recognized in *Roe*. [W]hat the Court fails to appreciate is that it is not simply the woman's indigency that interferes with her freedom of choice, but the combination of her own poverty and the government's unequal subsidization of abortion and childbirth."

Although he called this case "perhaps the most dramatic illustration to date of the deficiencies in the Court's obsolete 'two-tiered' approach to the Equal Protection Clause" [see generally Ch. 10, Sec. 3, I], Marshall, J. was "unable to see how even a minimally rational legislature could conclude that the interest in fetal life outweighs the brutal effect of the Hyde Amendment on indigent women."

JUSTICE O'CONNOR'S BROAD ATTACK ON, BUT THE COURT'S REAFFIRMATION OF, *ROE*'S ANALYSIS

In AKRON v. AKRON CENTER FOR REPRODUCTIVE HEALTH, 462 U.S. 416, 103 S.Ct. 2481, 76 L.Ed.2d 687 (1983), a 6–3 majority, per POWELL, J., struck down five provisions of an ordinance regulating abortions: (1) a requirement that after the first trimester all abortions be "performed in a hospital," thus preventing abortions in outpatient clinics that are not part of an acute-care, full-service hospital; (2) a prohibition of abortions on unmarried minors under 15 without consent of one of her parents or a court order; (3) a "truly informed" consent provision requiring the "attending physician" to inform his patient, inter alia, of the physical and emotional complications that may result from an abortion and the particular risks associated with her pregnancy and the abortion technique to be utilized; (4) a mandatory 24-hour waiting period after the pregnant woman signs a consent form; and (5) a requirement that physicians performing abortions "insure that the remains of the unborn child are disposed of in a humane and sanitary manner."

The Court reaffirmed that "a state's interest in health regulation becomes compelling at approximately the end of the first trimester,[a] but [the] state's regulation may be upheld only if it is reasonably designed to further that state interest." As for (1) the second-trimester requirement, Akron's defense of it "as a reasonable health regulation [had] strong support at the time of *Roe*, [but since then] the safety of second-trimester abortions has increased dramatically. The

---

a. The Court noted (fn. 11) that "*Roe* identified the end of the first trimester as the compelling point because until that time—according to the medical literature available in 1973—'mortality in abortion may be less than mortality in normal childbirth.'" The Court recognized that "[t]here is substantial evidence that developments in the past decade, particularly the development of a much safer method for performing second-trimester abortions, have extended the period in which abortions are safer than childbirth." But it deemed it "prudent [to] retain *Roe's* identification of the beginning of the second trimester as the approximate time at which the State's interest in maternal health becomes sufficiently compelling to justify significant regulation of abortion. We note that the medical evidence suggests that until approximately the end of the first trimester, the State's interest in maternal health would not be served by regulations that restrict the manner in which abortions are performed by a licensed physician. [The] *Roe* trimester standard thus continues to provide a reasonable legal framework for limiting a State's authority to regulate abortions. Where the State adopts a health regulation governing the performance of abortions during the second trimester, the determinative question should be whether there is a reasonable medical basis for the regulation. The comparison between abortion and childbirth mortality rates may be relevant only where the State employs a health rationale as a justification for a complete prohibition on abortions in certain circumstances."

principal reason is that the [dilation and evacuation] D & E procedure is now widely and successfully used for the second-trimester abortions.

"[A]n even more significant factor is that experience indicates that D & E may be performed safely on an outpatient basis in appropriate nonhospital facilities. The evidence is strong enough to have convinced the American Public Health Association (APHA) to abandon its prior recommendation of hospitalization for all second-trimester [abortions]. Similarly, the American College of Obstetricians and Gynecologists (ACOG) no longer suggests that all second-trimester abortions be performed in a hospital.

"[These] developments, and the professional commentary supporting them, constitute impressive evidence that—at least during the early weeks of the second trimester—D & E abortions may be performed as safely in an outpatient clinic as in a full-service hospital. [Thus,] 'present medical knowledge' convincingly undercuts Akron's justification for requiring that *all* second-trimester abortions be performed in a hospital.

"[Although] a state abortion regulation is not unconstitutional simply because it does not correspond perfectly in all cases to the asserted state interest, [the] lines drawn in a state regulation must be reasonable, and this cannot be said of [the hospitalization requirement]. By preventing the performance of D & E abortions in an appropriate nonhospital setting, Akron has imposed a heavy, and unnecessary, burden on women's access to a relatively inexpensive, otherwise accessible, and safe abortion procedure. [The hospitalization requirement] unreasonably infringes upon a woman's constitutional right to obtain an abortion."

As for (2) the parental consent requirement, "we do not think the Akron ordinance, as applied to Ohio juvenile proceedings, is reasonably susceptible of being construed to create an 'opportunity for case-by-case evaluations of the maturity of pregnant minors.' *Bellotti II.*"

As for (3) the "informed consent" provision, much of the information required, such as the provisions that the physician inform his patient of the numerous possible physical and psychological complications of abortions and inform her that "the unborn child is a human life from the moment of conception," "is designed not to inform the woman's consent but rather to persuade her to withhold it altogether. [A]n additional, and equally decisive, objection to [this provision] is its intrusion upon the discretion of the pregnant woman's physician. This provision specifies a litany of information that the physician must recite to each woman regardless of whether in his judgment the information is relevant to her personal decision. [By] insisting upon recitation of a lengthy and inflexible list of information, Akron unreasonably has placed 'obstacles in the path of the doctor upon whom [the woman is] entitled to rely for advice in connection with her decision.' *Whalen v. Roe.*"

As for (4) the mandatory 24-hour waiting provision, which increases the cost of obtaining an abortion by requiring the woman to make two separate trips to the abortion facility, "Akron has failed to demonstrate that any legitimate state interest is furthered by an arbitrary and inflexible waiting period. [I]f a woman, after appropriate counseling, is prepared to give her written informed consent and proceed with the abortion, a State may not demand that she delay the effectuation of that decision."

As for (5), the provision dealing with the disposal of fetal remains, the phrase "humane and sanitary" suggests, as the court below noted, "a possible intent to 'manifest some sort of "decent burial" of an embryo at the earliest stage of formation.' This level of uncertainty is fatal where criminal liability is imposed."

In the face of a dissenting opinion which, said the Court, "rejects the basic premise of *Roe* and its progeny," the Court stated at the outset: "[A]rguments continue to be made, [that in *Roe*] we erred in interpreting the Constitution. Nonetheless, the doctrine of stare decisis, while perhaps never entirely persuasive on a constitutional question, is a doctrine that demands respect in a society governed by the rule of law.[1] We respect it today, and reaffirm *Roe*."

Before specifically addressing the regulations at issue, O'CONNOR, J., joined by White and Rehnquist, JJ., dissenting, launched a broad attack on the Court's approach and the "trimester framework adopted in *Roe*.": "It is apparent from the Court's opinion that neither sound constitutional theory nor our need to decide cases based on the application of neutral principles can accommodate an analytical framework that varies according to the 'stages' of pregnancy, where those stages, and their concomitant standards of review, differ according to the level of medical technology available when a particular challenge to state regulation occurs. The Court's analysis of the Akron regulations is inconsistent both with the methods of analysis employed in previous cases dealing with abortion, and with the Court's approach to fundamental rights in other areas.

"Our recent cases indicate that a regulation imposed on 'a lawful abortion "is not unconstitutional unless it unduly burdens the right to seek an abortion."'" *Maher v. Roe* (quoting *Bellotti I*). In my view, this 'unduly burdensome' standard should be applied to the challenged regulations throughout the entire pregnancy without reference to the particular 'stage' of pregnancy involved. If the particular regulation does not 'unduly burden[ ]' the fundamental right, then our evaluation of that regulation is limited to our determination that the regulation rationally relates to a legitimate state purpose.

"[D]espite the Court's purported adherence to the trimester approach adopted in *Roe*, the lines drawn in that decision have now been 'blurred' because of what the Court accepts as technological advancement in the safety of abortion procedure. The State may no longer rely on a 'bright line' that separates permissible from impermissible regulation, and it is no longer free to consider the second trimester as a unit and weigh the risks posed by all abortion procedures throughout that trimester. Rather, the State must continuously and conscientiously study contemporary medical and scientific literature in order to determine whether the effect of a particular regulation is to 'depart from

---

1. There are especially compelling reasons for adhering to stare decisis in applying the principles of *Roe*. That case was considered with special care. [Since then] the Court repeatedly and consistently has accepted and applied the basic principle that a woman has a fundamental right to make the highly personal choice whether or not to terminate her pregnancy.

Today, however, the dissenting opinion rejects the basic premise of *Roe* and its progeny. The dissent stops short of arguing flatly that *Roe* should be overruled. Rather, it adopts reasoning that, for all practical purposes, would accomplish precisely that result. The dissent states that "[e]ven assuming that there is a fundamental right to terminate pregnancy in some situations," the State's compelling interests in maternal health and potential human life "are present *throughout* pregnancy" (emphasis in original). The existence of these compelling interests turns out to be largely unnecessary, however, for the dissent does not think that even one of the numerous abortion regulations at issue imposes a sufficient burden on the "limited" fundamental right, to require heightened scrutiny.

[I]t appears that the dissent would uphold virtually any abortion regulation under a rational-basis test. It also appears that even where heightened scrutiny is deemed appropriate, the dissent would uphold virtually any abortion-inhibiting regulation because of the State's interest in preserving potential human life. [This] analysis is wholly incompatible with the existence of the fundamental right recognized in *Roe*.

accepted medical practice' insofar as particular procedures and particular periods within the trimester are concerned. Assuming that legislative bodies are able to engage in this exacting task, it is difficult to believe that our Constitution *requires* that they do it as a prelude to protecting the health of their citizens. It is even more difficult to believe that this Court, without the resources available to those bodies entrusted with making legislative choices, believes itself competent to make these inquires and to revise these standards every time the ACOG or similar group revises its views about what is and what is not appropriate medical procedure in this area. [As] today's decision indicates, medical technology is changing, and this change will necessitate our continued functioning as the nation's 'ex officio medical board with powers to approve or disapprove medical and operative practices and standards throughout the United States.' *Danforth* (White, J., concurring in part and dissenting in part).

"Just as improvements in medical technology inevitably will move *forward* the point at which the State may regulate for reasons for maternal health, different technological improvements will move *backward* the point of viability at which the State may proscribe abortions except when necessary to preserve the life and health of the mother. * * *

"The *Roe* framework, then, is clearly on a collision course with itself. As the medical risks of various abortion procedures decrease, the point at which the State may regulate for reasons of maternal health is moved further forward to actual childbirth. As medical science becomes better able to provide for the separate existence of the fetus, the point of viability is moved further back toward conception. Moreover, it is clear that the trimester approach violates the fundamental aspiration of judicial decision making through the application of neutral principles 'sufficiently absolute to give them roots throughout the community and continuity over significant periods of time.' Cox, *The Role of the Supreme Court in American Government* 114 (1976). The *Roe* framework is inherently tied to the state of medical technology that exists whenever particular litigation ensues. Although legislatures are better suited to make the necessary factual judgments in this area, the Court's framework forces legislatures, as a matter of constitutional law, to speculate about what constitutes 'accepted medical practice' at any given time. Without the necessary expertise or ability, courts must then pretend to act as science review boards and examine those legislative judgments. [Even] assuming that there is a fundamental right to terminate pregnancy in some situations, there is no justification in law or logic for the trimester framework adopted in *Roe* and employed by the Court today on the basis of stare decisis.

"[I agree with *Roe* that the state has legitimate and important interests in seeing that abortion is 'performed under circumstances that insure maximum safety for the patient' and in 'protecting the potentiability of life'], but in my view, the point at which these interests become compelling does not depend on the trimester of pregnancy. Rather, these interests are present *throughout* pregnancy. [The] fallacy inherent in the *Roe* framework is apparent: just because the State has a compelling interest in ensuring maternal safety once an abortion may be more dangerous [than] childbirth, it simply does not follow that the State has *no* interest before that point that justifies state regulation to ensure that first-trimester abortions are performed as safely as possible.

"The state interest in potential human life is likewise extant throughout pregnancy. In *Roe*, the Court held [that] that interest could not become compelling until the point at which the fetus was viable. The difficulty with this analysis is clear: *potential* life is no less potential in the first weeks of pregnancy than it is at viability or afterward. At any stage in pregnancy, there is the *potential* for human life. Although the Court refused to 'resolve the difficult question of when life begins,' [it] chose the point of viability—when the fetus is *capable* of life independent of its mother—to permit the complete proscription of abortion. The choice of viability as the point at which the state interest in *potential* life becomes compelling is no less arbitrary than choosing any point before viability or any point afterward. Accordingly, I believe that the State's interest in protecting potential human life exists throughout the pregnancy.

"' * * * *Roe* did not declare an unqualified "constitutional right to an abortion," [but] protects the woman from unduly burdensome interference with her freedom to decide whether to terminate her pregnancy.' *Maher*. The Court and its individual Justices have repeatedly utilized the 'unduly burdensome' standard in abortion cases.

"[The] 'undue burden' required in the abortion cases represents the required threshold inquiry that must be conducted before this Court can require a State to justify its legislative actions under the exacting 'compelling state interest' standard. [In] determining whether the State imposes an 'undue burden,' we must keep in mind that when we are concerned with extremely sensitive issues, such as the one involved here, 'the appropriate forum for their resolution in a democracy is the legislature. * * * ' '"

Justice O'Connor then concluded that neither (1) the second-trimester hospitalization requirement nor (2) the parental consent provision nor (3) the "informed consent" provision nor (4) the mandatory 24-hour waiting period "unduly burdened" the abortion decision. As for (5) the disposal of fetal remains, since there is no indication that physicians are required to provide " 'decent burials' for fetuses" and since " 'humane' is no more vague than the term 'sanitary,' the vagueness of which Akron Center does not question," the provision could not be deemed void for vagueness.

A companion case to *Akron*, PLANNED PARENTHOOD v. ASHCROFT, 462 U.S. 476, 103 S.Ct. 2517, 76 L.Ed.2d 733 (1983), invalidated a Missouri second-trimester hospitalization requirement under the *Akron* analysis, but upheld other statutory provisions requiring the presence of a second physician during abortions performed after viability; a pathology report for each abortion performed in clinics as well as in hospitals; and that minors seeking abortion secure parental or judicial consent.

As for the second-physician requirement, POWELL, J., joined by Burger, C.J., reasoned that "[b]y giving medical attention to a fetus that is delivered alive, the second physician will assure that the State's interests are protected more fully than the first physician alone would be able to do. And given the compelling interest that the State has in preserving life, we cannot say that [the second-physician requirement] in those unusual circumstances where Missouri permits a third-trimester abortion is unconstitutional." O'CONNOR, J., joined by White and Rehnquist, JJ., concurred in the result "because the State possesses a compelling interest in protecting and preserving fetal life," but maintained that "this state interest is extant throughout pregnancy."

As for the requirement that minors secure parental consent or consent from the juvenile court for an abortion, POWELL, J., joined by Burger, C.J., concluded that, as interpreted by the Court of Appeals to mean that the juvenile court could not deny a petition "for good cause" unless it first found that the minor was not mature enough to make her own decision, the provision avoided any constitutional infirmities. "Assuming arguendo that the State cannot impose a parental veto on the decision of a minor to undergo an abortion," O'CONNOR, J., joined by White and Rehnquist, JJ., agreed that the parental consent provision was constitutional. "However, I believe that the provision is valid because it imposes no undue burden on any right that a minor may have to undergo an abortion."

BLACKMUN, J., joined by Brennan, Marshall and Stevens, JJ., would strike down all the challenged provisions. As for the second-physician requirement, it imposes an unjustified burden on women because "when a D & E abortion is performed, the second physician can do nothing to further the State's compelling interest in protecting life." As for the pathology-report requirement, it "is not in accord with 'generally accepted medical standards'" and "the State has not 'met its burden of demonstrating that [it] furthers important health-related concerns.' *Akron.*" As for the provision prohibiting the performance of an abortion on an unemancipated minor absent parental consent or a court order, "[u]ntil today, the Court has never upheld 'a requirement of a consent substitute, either parental or judicial.'" Justice Blackmun continued to adhere to the views expressed by four Justices in *Bellotti II* that "any judicial-consent statute would suffer from the same flaw identified in *Danforth:* it would give a third party an absolute veto over the decision of the physician and his patient (opinion of Stevens, J.).[a]

Notes and Questions

1. *Should the focus of the abortion inquiry be on the state of fetal development rather than on the existing state of medical technology?* "If the legal system adheres to the reasoning of *Roe,*" warns Comment, 29 U.C.L.A.L.Rev. 1194, 1204–05 (1982), "there is no limit to the extent to which advances in technology may diminish a woman's right to an abortion. [I]f, however, the focus is placed upon the degree of fetal development [rather than on viability], the courts can avoid the problems resulting from technological advances. The ultimate question should be at what point does the fetus become a human being." Continues the UCLA Comment (at 1207–11, 1215):

"An appropriate standard for determining the beginning of human life is when the fetal brain is developed to the point where the fetus is a thinking, conscious being. A survey of existing scientific research indicates that a fetus

---

a. Another companion case to *Akron, Simopoulos v. Virginia,* 462 U.S. 506, 103 S.Ct. 2532, 76 L.Ed.2d 755 (1983), per Powell, J., upheld the conviction of a physician for performing an abortion during the second trimester of pregnancy outside of a licensed "hospital." Unlike the hospitalization requirements invalidated in *Akron* and *Ashcroft,* "the Virginia Statute and regulations do not require that second-trimester abortions be performed exclusively in full-service hospitals. [O]utpatient surgical hospitals may qualify for licensing as 'hospitals' [for this purpose]." As the Court interpreted the Virginia regulations, it saw "no reason to doubt that an adequately equipped clinic could, upon proper application, obtain an outpatient hospital license permitting the performance of second-trimester abortions. [The State's] require-

ment that second-trimester abortions be performed in licensed clinics is not an unreasonable means of furthering the State's compelling interest in 'protecting the woman's own health and safety.' *Roe.* [The requirement] appears to comport with accepted medical practice, and leaves the method and timing of the abortion precisely where they belong— with the physician and the patient." O'Connor, J., joined by White and Rehnquist, JJ., concurred in the judgment, but did "not agree that the constitutional validity of the Virginia mandatory hospitalization requirement is contingent in any way on the trimester in which it is imposed. Rather, I believe that the requirement in this case is not an undue burden on the decision to undergo an abortion."

[reaches this stage] between twelve and thirty-two weeks [and primarily between 19 and 30 weeks] after conception.

"[If] the competing interests of the woman and society are balanced by asking at what point the fetus becomes a human being, then advances in technology will not erode the balance that is struck. In fact, [such advances will enable us] to more accurately determine when the fetus becomes a human being.

"[A] standard for determining when human life begins based on brain function [would] provide a workable and religiously neutral resolution of the competing interests of the woman and the fetus [and] also create a symmetry between the legal definitions for the beginning and end of life, thereby giving us a unified legal theory of what constitutes a human being."

2. *Is the "Roe framework," as Justice O'Connor maintains, "on a collision course with itself"?* Consider the remarks of LAURENCE TRIBE in Choper, Kamisar & Tribe, *The Supreme Court: Trends and Developments, 1982–83* (1984) at 257–58: "I think that [Justice O'Connor is] simply confused about one important aspect of the abortion decision. There are two different rationales on which the states purport to regulate abortion. One is to protect the health of the mother. As to that, it's true that medical advances make later and later abortions safe and, thereby, make it more and more difficult for the government to justify regulating even very late abortions. The other and wholly independent rationale, having absolutely nothing to do with a woman's safety or her health, is the protection of the life of the fetus. As to that, the Supreme Court [concluded] that the power of the state to coerce a woman to remain pregnant is inherently linked to the viability of the fetus. That is, it is when the fetus is not yet viable that saving its life requires coercing continued pregnancy.

"Once, of course, the fetus is viable, then a desire to protect it is no longer necessarily coincident with forcing a woman to remain, as it were, an involuntary incubator. If fetal viability is possible earlier in pregnancy as a result of medical advances, it is possible simultaneously to respect the woman's right not to be pregnant involuntarily, and the fetus' right to survive.

"The fact that medical advances may bring about a kind of brave new world of artificial placenta and artificial uteri earlier and earlier in the pregnancy simply means that regulation on the rationale of protecting the fetus, as opposed to the rationale of protecting the woman's health, may justify governmental intervention even in the first trimester to say, 'If you don't want to remain pregnant, fine. Give us the fetus, and we'll take care of it in the hospital.' Some would find that a nightmarish prospect because it would substitute technology for what ought to be a human undertaking. But that really raises an issue of a very different kind from those in the abortion case itself, and I think that Justice O'Connor is simply wrong in assuming that the two kinds of regulations are on a collision course."

WHAT IF *ROE* WERE OVERRULED AND THE ABORTION CONTROVERSY MOVED TO THE LEGISLATIVE ARENA?

"Should the abortion controversy ever move from the judicial to the legislative chambers," observes Collins, *Is There "Life" (or "Choice") After Roe?*, 3 Const.Comm. —— (1985), "the probable scenarios could bring unexpected victories and losses for both sides." Recalling that prior to *Roe* more than a third of the states permitted abortions under circumstances objectionable to the "pro-life" advocates of the 1980s, Collins predicts that "once the abortion right is stripped of its federal constitutional cloak, 'pro-choice' defenders will apply pressure on legislators with all the fervor of a martyr's cause. Just as *Roe* opened the horizon to a 'pro-life' movement, so too could its demise carry the opposition to the zenith of its political power. In such an atmosphere, how likely would it be for lawmakers to ban abortions, say, within the first twelve weeks of pregnancy?"

Lamana, *Social Science and Ethical Issues,* in *Abortion: Understanding Differences,* 1, 4–7 (Callahan & Callahan eds. 1984), points out that, according to the poll data; only 25% support abortion as defined in *Roe,* but even fewer—almost 20%—support the pro-life position. About 55% are in between, approving abortion in some circumstances, but not in others. Similarly, Luker, *Abortion and the Politics of Motherhood* 224 (1984), emphasizes that all the available data indicates that *neither* the pro-life *nor* the pro-choice movement "has ever been 'representative' of how most Americans feel about abortion."

All but a tiny minority of Americans support abortion for "hard" reasons (e.g., when the woman's health is at risk, the pregnancy is the result of rape or incest, or there is a likelihood that the child will be born with substantial handicaps), yet many Americans feel a deep uneasiness about abortions and balk at abortions for "soft" reasons (e.g., the woman is unmarried or a teenager or simply does not want a child). See Lamana, supra, at 4–7; Luker, supra, at 226–30. "If the pro-life movement were able to 'sell' the American public an anti-abortion law that protected abortions for the 'hard' reasons, it is possible that under certain conditions much of the present support for abortion could evaporate," comments Luker (at 234, 239), but if the pro-life movement were to accept a law permitting abortion in e.g., cases of rape or incest, "it would be conceding a great deal of ideological ground."

If the abortion controversy were to move to the legislative chambers, "the best the pro-life movement could hope for," according to Luker (at 242–43), would be "a modern form of the Prohibition experience"—a "situation in which abortions become harder and more expensive to get but still continue to exist in almost the same numbers as before. * * * Pro-choice people, however, can take little comfort from this prospect. Prohibition, after all, was the law of the land for many years, and it took considerable political resources to overturn it."

FAMILY LIVING ARRANGEMENTS

Relying on earlier decisions sustaining local zoning regulations, BELLE TERRE v. BORAAS, 416 U.S. 1, 94 S.Ct. 1536, 39 L.Ed.2d 797 (1974), per DOUGLAS, J., upheld a village ordinance restricting land use to one-family dwellings (defining "family" to mean not more than two unrelated persons living together as a single housekeeping unit, and expressly excluding from the term lodging, boarding, fraternity or multiple-dwelling houses). Appellees, who had leased their houses to six unrelated college students, challenged the ordinance, inter alia, on the ground that it "trenches on the newcomers' rights of privacy." The Court disagreed: "We deal with economic and social legislation where legislatures have historically drawn lines which we respect [if the law] bears 'a rational relationship to a [permissible] state objective.'" "[B]oarding houses, fraternity houses, and the like present urban problems. [The] police power is not confined to elimination of filth, stench, and unhealthy places."

MARSHALL, J., dissented: The ordinance burdened "fundamental rights of association and privacy," and thus required extraordinary justification, not a mere showing that the ordinance "bears a rational relationship to the accomplishment of legitimate governmental objectives." He viewed "the right to 'establish a home' " as an "essential part" of fourteenth amendment liberty and maintained that "the choice of household companions"—which "involves deeply personal considerations as to the kind and quality of intimate relationships within the home"—"surely falls within the right to privacy protected by the Constitution." The state's purposes "could be as effectively achieved by means of an ordinance that did not discriminate on the basis of constitutionally protected choices of life style." [b]

Distinguishing *Belle Terre* as involving an ordinance "affect[ing] only *unrelated* individuals," MOORE v. EAST CLEVELAND, 431 U.S. 494, 97 S.Ct. 1932, 52 L.Ed.2d 531 (1977), invalidated a housing ordinance that limited occupancy to single families, but defined "family" so as to forbid appellant from having her two grandsons live with her. (It did not permit living arrangements if, as in this case, the grandchildren were cousins rather than brothers.) [a] POWELL, J., announcing the Court's judgment and joined by Brennan, Marshall, and Blackmun, JJ., struck down the ordinance on substantive due process grounds:

"[O]n its face [the ordinance] selects certain categories of relatives who may live together and declares that others may not. [When] a city undertakes such intrusive regulation of the family [the] usual judicial deference to the legislature is inappropriate. 'This Court has long recognized that freedom of personal choice in matters of marriage and family life is one of the liberties protected by [due process].' Of course the family is not beyond regulation. But when the government intrudes on choices concerning family living arrangements, this Court must examine carefully the importance of the governmental interests advanced and the extent to which they are served by the challenged regulation [referring to Harlan, J.'s dissent in *Poe v. Ullman*]." "[T]hus examined, this ordinance cannot survive." [3] Although the city's goals—preventing overcrowding, minimizing congestion and avoiding financial strain on its school system— were "legitimate," the ordinance served them "marginally at best."

"[T]he history of the *Lochner* [era] counsels caution and restraint [but] it does [not] require what the city urges here: cutting off any family rights at the first convenient, if arbitrary boundary—the boundary of the nuclear family. * * * Appropriate limits on substantive due process come not from drawing arbitrary lines but rather from careful 'respect for the teachings of history [and] solid recognition of the basic values that underlie our society.' *Griswold* (Harlan, J., concurring). Our decisions teach that the Constitution protects the sanctity of the family precisely because the institution of the family is deeply rooted in this Nation's history and tradition. [Ours] is by no means a tradition limited to respect for [the] nuclear family. The tradition of uncles, aunts, cousins, and especially grandparents sharing a household along with parents and children [especially in times of adversity] has roots equally venerable and equally deserving of constitutional recognition. [In *Pierce*, the Constitution prevented a state from] 'standardiz[ing] its children by forcing them to accept instruction from public teachers only.' By the same token the Constitution prevents East Cleveland from standardizing its children—and its adults—by forcing all to live in certain narrowly defined family patterns." [b]

b. Compare Marshall, J.'s views in *Belle Terre* with the Court's discussion of "freedom of intimate association" in *Roberts v. United States Jaycees,* p. 741, infra.

a. The second grandson came to live with his grandmother after the death of his mother.

3. Appellant also claims that the ordinance contravenes the Equal Protection Clause, but it is not necessary for us to reach that contention.

b. Brennan, J., joined by Marshall, J., concurred, characterizing the ordinance as "senseless," "arbitrary" and "eccentric" and

STEWART, J., joined by Rehnquist, J., dissented, rejecting the argument that "the importance of the 'extended family' in American society" renders appellant's "decision to share her residence with her grandsons," like the decisions involved in bearing and raising children, "an aspect of 'family life'" entitled to substantive constitutional protection. To equate appellant's interest in sharing her residence with some of her relatives "with the fundamental decisions to marry and to bear children," he maintained, "is to extend the limited substantive contours of the Due Process Clause beyond recognition." He thought the challenged "family" definition "rationally designed to carry out the legitimate governmental purposes identified in *Belle Terre*." A different line "could hardly be drawn that would not sooner or later become the target of a challenge like the appellant's," such as "the hard case of an orphaned niece or nephew."

Nor could he understand "why it follows that the residents of East Cleveland are constitutionally prevented from following what Justice Brennan calls the 'pattern' of 'white suburbia,' even though that choice may reflect 'cultural myopia.' In point of fact, East Cleveland is a predominantly Negro community, with a Negro City Manager and City Commission." [c]

WHITE, J., dissenting, voiced disbelief "that the interest in residing with more than one set of grandchildren is one that calls for any kind of heightened protection under the Due Process Clause. [The] present claim is hardly one of which it could be said that 'neither liberty nor justice would exist if [it] were sacrificed.' *Palko*."

He maintained that Powell, J.'s approach—construing the Due Process Clause to protect from all but "quite important" state interests any right "that in his estimate is deeply rooted in the country's traditions"—"suggests a far too expansive charter for this Court. [What] the deeply rooted traditions of the country are is arguable; which of them deserve [due process protection] is even more debatable. The suggested view would broaden enormously the horizons of the Clause." [d]

as reflecting "cultural myopia" and "a distressing insensitivity toward the economic and emotional needs of a very large part of our society." He called the "extended family" "virtually a means of survival" for many poor and black families. [The] 'nuclear family' is the pattern so often found in much of white suburbia," but "the Constitution cannot * * * tolerate the imposition by government upon the rest of us of white suburbia's preference in patterns of family living." But see dissenting Justice Stewart's response, infra.

Stevens, J., concurring, thought this "unprecedented ordinance" unconstitutional even under the "limited standard of review of zoning decisions": "The city has failed totally to explain the need for a rule which would allow a homeowner to have two grandchildren live with her if they are brothers, but not if they are cousins. Since the ordinance has not been shown to have any 'substantial relation to [East Cleveland's] public health, safety, morals or general welfare' [and] since it cuts so deeply into a fundamental right normally associated with the ownership of residential property—that of an owner to decide who may

reside on his or her property—it must fall [as] a taking of property without due process and without just compensation."

c. "[I]n assessing [appellant's] claim that the ordinance is 'arbitrary' and 'irrational,'" Stewart, J., considered a provision permitting her to request a variance "particularly persuasive evidence to the contrary. [The] variance procedure, a traditional part of American land-use law, bends the straight lines of East Cleveland's ordinance, shaping their contours to respond more flexibly to the hard cases that are the inevitable byproduct of legislative linedrawing."

Burger, C.J., dissented on the ground that appellant should have pursued the "plainly adequate administrative remedy" of seeking a variance, thus finding it "unnecessary to reach the difficult constitutional issue."

d. "[A]n approach grounded in history," replied Justice Powell [fn. 12], "imposes limits on the judiciary that are more meaningful than any based on [White, J.'s] abstract formula taken from *Palko*."

SEXUAL CONDUCT, "LIFESTYLES", THE RIGHTS OF THE IN-VOLUNTARILY COMMITTED MENTALLY RETARDED, AND THE "RIGHT TO DIE"

1. *Consensual adult homosexual conduct.* DOE v. COMMONWEALTH'S ATTORNEY, 425 U.S. 901, 96 S.Ct. 1489, 47 L.Ed.2d 751 (1976), summarily aff'g 403 F.Supp. 1199 (E.D.Va.1975) (three-judge court): Homosexual males unsuccessfully sought federal declaratory relief, contending that Virginia's sodomy statute, as applied to consensual homosexual acts performed in private by adults, violated the right of privacy. A 2–1 majority of the district court quoted dicta in Harlan, J.'s dissent in *Poe v. Ullman* (see *Griswold* and fn. g after *Roe*) that homosexuality could be criminally prohibited even if privately practiced, and maintained that regulation of personal sexual conduct is constitutionally suspect only when it "trespasses upon the privacy of the incidents of marriage [or] the sanctity of the home [or] the nurture of family life." Dissenting, Merhige, J., maintained that *Roe* and *Eisenstadt* (neither of which had been mentioned by the majority) demonstrated that "intimate personal decisions or private matters of substantial importance to the well-being of the individuals involved are protected by [due process and that the] right to select consenting adult sexual partners must be considered within this category." The Supreme Court's summary affirmance (Brennan, Marshall and Stevens, JJ., voting to note probable jurisdiction), however, may have "relatively limited precedential value"; [a] indeed, a year later, in *Carey v. Population Services Int'l*, supra, the Court itself viewed the issue as unsettled.[b]

Notes and Questions

(a) Professor Gerald Gunther has called the Court's summary affirmance in *Doe* "irresponsible" and "lawless." See N.Y. Times, April 8, 1976, p. 37. Under the circumstances, was the summary affirmance also "cynical"? Is the most plausible explanation for the Court's action that while six justices "sympathized with the result reached below, they would have been hard-pressed to compose a palatable opinion justifying their position"? See Perry, *Substantive Due Process Revisited: Reflections on (and Beyond) Recent Cases*, 71 Nw.U.L.Rev. 417, 443 (1976).

(b) Plaintiffs' contention in *Doe*, observes *Tribe*, supra, at 943–44, "should ultimately prevail in light of [the] crucial fact that the conduct proscribed is central to the personal identities of those singled out by the state's law. [A]lthough it is probably the case that the protection provided by *Griswold* was

---

a. Tribe, *American Constitutional Law* 943 (1978). "There appears to have been no evidence that any of the parties was threatened with prosecution," notes Tribe; "arguably the case thus was no more ripe for adjudication than *Poe v. Ullman* [p. 1215 infra], had been. [The summary affirmance] demonstrates nothing, since the doctrine of *Poe* is discretionary in character rather than jurisdictional, and an affirmance would have been entirely consistent with the view that the district court reached the right result—denying relief—for the wrong reason." See also Wilkinson & White, *Constitutional Protection for Personal Lifestyles*, 62 Corn.L.Rev. 562, 593 (1977); Note, 1979 U.Ill.L.F. 469, 506.

b. *Carey*, per Brennan, J., noted that "the Court has not definitively answered the difficult question whether and to what extent the Constitution prohibits state statutes regulating [private consensual sexual] behavior among adults" and that "we do not purport to answer that question now," an observation that Rehnquist, J., dissenting, could not "let pass without comment": "While we have not ruled on every conceivable regulation affecting such conduct the facial constitutional validity of criminal statutes prohibiting certain consensual acts, [citing *Doe*], has been 'definitively' established."

initially limited to acts occurring within a traditional, state-sanctioned relationship, [it] seems clear that 'the liberties of adult intimacy in our society are [too] fundamental' to be indefinitely limited to conduct implicitly sanctioned by the state's compact with the partners to a marriage. 'Equal protection alone requires a more even-handed dispensation.' " [a]

(c) Wilkinson & White, *Constitutional Protection for Personal Lifestyles,* 62 Corn.L.Rev. 562, 596 (1977), not only describe the question raised by *Doe* as "difficult" but provide concrete evidence of the difficulty—their inability to agree on the answer: "The question [is]: Should the State be constitutionally required to abandon an ancient sanction, when abandonment might in time lead to increasing, although statistically unpredictable, defections from heterosexual behavior and traditional family life? On the answer to this last question the authors have been unable to agree. Mr. Wilkinson would uphold the state's interest in the preservation of the traditional family; Mr. White would desire stronger empirical proof that the state interest is truly put in jeopardy by homosexual practices among consenting adults. Both authors acknowledge the intuitive elements in their judgments."

(d) But Richards, *Homosexuality and the Constitutional Right to Privacy,* 8 N.Y.U.Rev.L. & Soc.Change 311, 314 (1979), does not consider the question raised by *Doe* at all difficult: "There is no principled way to defend the earlier right to privacy cases and not extend the right to homosexuality, other than the circular and question-begging assumption that homosexuality, as such, is intrinsically immoral and unnatural, when, in fact, it is a form of non-procreational sexual conduct, not in principle different from other forms of non-procreational sex, which must be liberated from the indefensible procreational model of sexual conduct. The difference between homosexuality and contraception, pornography in the home, and abortion is not constitutional or moral principle, but *popularity:* namely, that the non-procreational model in the other areas is supported by substantial popular sentiment, whereas homosexuality is still the settled object of widespread social hostility and opprobrium. It is the supreme paradox that the constitutional right to privacy has been applied to areas where there is either majoritarian consensus (contraception) or at least substantial popular support (abortion) and not applied to the protection of an oppressed minority, the settled object of unjustified social hate, that is paramountly entitled to the protection of the countermajoritarian rights of the constitutional design." [b]

(e) Consider, however, Grey, *Eros, Civilization and the Burger Court,* Law & Contemp.Probs., Summer 1980, at 83, 86–87, 90: "[T]he Court has given no support to the notion that the right of privacy protects sexual freedom. Not only has the homosexuals' challenge been summarily rejected, but in addition the Court has bypassed a number of chances to make a first incursion into the fantastic array of American laws that have traditionally forbidden virtually all

---

a. Both quotations are from Gerety, *Redefining Privacy,* 12 Harv.C.R.–C.L.L.Rev. 233, 279–80 (1979).

For the view that neither the right of privacy nor the first amendment is broad enough in its conception of sexual orientation nor wide-ranging enough in its remedies to offer an adequate legal response to "the problem of gay inequality," but that the courts "should recognize homosexuality as a suspect classification [and] therefore subject laws that discriminate on the basis of sexual preference to

heightened scrutiny, beyond the 'rational basis' test currently applied," see Note, 98 Harv. L.Rev. 1285, 1287–88, 1309 (1985). See generally Note, 57 S.Cal.L.Rev. 797 (1984).

b. See also Perry, supra, at 437–38; Regan, *Rewriting Roe v. Wade,* 77 Mich.L.Rev. 1569, 1645 (1979); Richards, *Sexual Autonomy and the Constitutional Right of Privacy,* 30 Hast.L.J. 957 (1979); Rivera, *Our Straight-Laced Judges: The Legal Position of Homosexuality in the United States,* 30 Hast.L.J. 799, 944–47 (1979).

sexual expression except wedded missionary-position intercourse. For example, the Court has [recently twice upheld] two of the ludicrous 'crime against nature' sodomy statutes against void-for-vagueness attacks.[c]

"[In] another recent case, the Court declined to review a decision upholding the sodomy conviction *of a husband and wife for an act of fellatio with each other.* The charge was evidently brought because photographs of the act taken by a third party had fallen into the hands of the couple's children, and a conviction for the appropriate offense—child abuse—had been reversed on appeal by the state courts.[28] In [still another case] the Court denied certiorari from a decision upholding the discharge of two public library employees for adulterous cohabitation, where the woman had become pregnant and the man had moved in with her before obtaining a divorce from his wife.[29]

"These cases strongly suggest that the Court meant what it said in *Griswold:* that the right of privacy protects only the historically sanctified institutions of marriage and the family, and has no implication for laws regulating sexual expression outside of traditional marriage.

"[Although some commentators thought that *Griswold* marked the first step in the constitutionalization of some contemporary version of John Stuart Mill's principle that the only legitimate reason for state coercion is to prevent harm to others, the failure to carry the principle through] must represent a prudential guess that to place the protection of the Constitution behind what most people still reject as unnatural sexual practices would too much strain the Court's limited stock of public good will. Such a theory might indeed explain *Doe v. Commonwealth's Attorney.* Perhaps the Court has been surprised by the depth and persistence of the opposition to the abortion decisions, and the swing justices were not ready to risk a foray into the explosive issue of gay rights. But if Mill's principle is in the wings, why have no hints of it appeared in opinions? At least why has the Court not taken some first step, perhaps striking down one of the absurd 'crime against nature' statutes on vagueness grounds—a decision that would invite little public wrath outside the lunatic fringe?"

Relying in part on *Doe v. Commonwealth's Attorney*—noting that "the Supreme Court's summary disposition of a case constitutes a vote on the merits; as such, it is binding on lower federal courts"—DRONENBURG v. ZECH, 741 F.2d 1388 (D.C.Cir.1984), per BORK, J., rejected the argument that the U.S. Navy's policy of mandatory discharge for homosexual conduct violated appellant's constitutional rights to privacy and equal protection. Even assuming that *Doe* is a "somewhat ambiguous precedent," the court could "find no constitutional right to engage in homosexual conduct [and], as judges, we have no warrant to create one":

"[T]he suggestion that we apply [the *Griswold-Roe* line of cases] to protect homosexual conduct in the Navy [presents] a peculiar jurisprudential problem. When the Supreme Court decides cases under a specific provision [of] the Constitution it explicates the meaning and suggests the contours of a value

c. *Rose v. Locke,* 423 U.S. 48, 96 S.Ct. 243, 46 L.Ed.2d 185 (1975) (per curiam) (Brennan, Stewart and Marshall, JJ., dissenting); *Wainwright v. Stone,* 414 U.S. 21, 94 S.Ct. 190, 38 L.Ed.2d 179 (1973) (per curiam).

28. *Lovisi v. Slayton,* 363 F.Supp. 620 (E.D. Va.1973), affirmed 539 F.2d 349 (4th Cir.1976)

(en banc), cert. denied 429 U.S. 977, 97 S.Ct. 485, 50 L.Ed.2d 585 (1976).

29. *Hollenbaugh v. Carnegie Free Library,* 439 U.S. 1052, 99 S.Ct. 734, 58 L.Ed. 713 (1979) (Marshall, J., dissenting from denial of certiorari).

already stated in the document or implied by the Constitution's structure and history. The lower court judge finds in the Supreme Court's reasoning about these legal materials, as well as in the materials themselves, guidance for applying the provision [to] a new situation. But when the Court creates new rights [the] lower courts have none of these materials available and can look only to what the Supreme Court has stated to be the principle involved. [In the 'privacy' cases] we do not find any principle articulated even approaching in breadth that which appellant seeks to have us adopt. The Court has listed as illustrative of the right of privacy such matters as activities relating to marriage, procreation, contraception, family relationships, and child rearing and education. It need hardly be said that none of these covers a right to homosexual conduct.

"[In] dealing with a topic like this, in which we are asked to protect from regulation a form of behavior never before protected, and indeed traditionally condemned, we do well to bear in mind the concerns expressed by Justice White, dissenting in *Moore v. East Cleveland* that '[the Judiciary] is the most vulnerable and comes nearest to illegitimacy when it deals with judge-made constitutional law having little or no cognizable roots in the language or even the design of the Constitution. * * *' [If] the revolution in sexual mores that appellant proclaims is in fact ever to arrive, we think it must arrive through the moral choices of the people and their elected representatives, not through the ukase of this court.

"[Appellant] contends that the existence of moral disapproval for certain types of behavior is the very fact that disables government from regulating it. He says [the fact that] the particular choice of partner may be repugnant to the majority argues for its vigilant protection—not its vulnerability to sanction. This theory that majority morality and majority choice is always made presumptively invalid by the Constitution attacks the very predicate of democratic government. When the Constitution does not speak to the contrary, the choices of those put in authority by the electoral process, or those who are accountable to such persons, come before us not as suspect because majoritarian but as conclusively valid for that very reason. We stress [that] this deference to democratic choice does not apply where the Constitution removes the choice from majorities. [It] is to be doubted that very many laws exist whose ultimate justification does not rest upon the society's morality. For these reasons, appellant's arguments will not withstand examination.

"[Thus, we need ask] only whether the Navy's policy is rationally related to a permissible end. We have said that legislation may implement morality. So viewed, this regulation bears a rational relationship to a permissible end. [Assuming that] a naval regulation, unlike the act of a legislature, must be rationally related not to morality for its own sake but to some further end which the Navy is entitled to pursue because of the Navy's assigned function, [the] effects of homosexual conduct within a naval or military unit are almost certain to be harmful to morale and discipline. The Navy is not required to produce social science data or the results of controlled experiments to prove what common sense and common experience demonstrate." [a]

a. Dissenting from a denial of rehearing en banc in *Dronenburg*, 746 F.2d 1579 (D.C. Cir.1984), Robinson, C.J., joined by Wald, Mikva and Edwards, JJ., found "completely unconvincing the suggestion that *Doe v. Commonwealth's Attorney* controls this case" and maintained that "the dangers hypothesized by [the three-judge panel] provide patently inadequate justification for a ban on homosexuality in a Navy that includes personnel of both sexes and places no parolled ban on all types of heterosexual conduct."

2. *Fornication, cohabitation and adultery.* (a) After examining the state interests which laws forbidding fornication and cohabitation might serve and suggesting that several of these interests are "compelling"—deterring illegitimacy, preventing disease, and preserving the family—Note, *Fornication, Cohabitation, and the Constitution,* 77 Mich.L.Rev. 252, 257, 301–05 (1978), concludes that the laws do not actually serve these interests. "[T]he best evidence—the behavior of the states which have enacted but rarely enforced these laws—shows that [they] are hardly necessary to achieve these [governmental] interests."

Can a "right of sexual expression outside marriage" be reconciled with *Doe v. Commonwealth's Attorney,* assuming that that case approves laws prohibiting sodomy? Consider id. at 292–93: "[H]omosexuality can be distinguished from heterosexuality in terms of the very societal traditions which necessitate a right to sexual freedom. [H]omosexuality may fail the 'traditions and collective conscience' test, since, however wrongly, Americans have long regarded (and still do regard) homosexuality with special reprobation. [T]here is a tension between, on one hand, establishing a right to full sexual expression for most members of society on the grounds that they need it to fulfill their individuality, and, on the other hand, barring the rest from any kind of sexual expression which appeals to them [but,] however unjustifiably, homosexuality is still widely regarded as a threat to social stability and to psychological health in a way that every heterosexual conduct is not." See also Note, 1979 U.Ill.L.F. 469, 508–09.

(b) If not sufficient to justify laws against fornication, are state interests strong enough to justify laws against adultery? Consider Tribe, supra, at 946: "Adultery is often not a 'victimless crime'. [When] there is truly a victimized spouse, it would seem that the state may choose to use the sanctions of law to punish the wrong to the marriage partner—and the marriage—inflicted by

In a separate statement, Bork, J., joined by Scalia, J., could not "take seriously the dissent's suggestion that the Navy may be constitutionally required to treat heterosexual conduct and homosexual conduct as either morally equivalent or as posing equal dangers to the Navy's mission. Relativism in these matters may or may not be an arguable moral stance, [but] moral relativism is hardly a constitutional command, nor is it, we are certain, the moral stance of a large majority of naval personnel."

Did the *Dronenburg* court fail to follow its own warning on judicial restraint? Consider Note, 63 N.C.L.Rev. 749, 764–66 (1985): "[T]he military setting of [the] case provided the court with an obvious analytic framework that the court relegated to minor importance. [The doctrine that the armed services constitute a 'separate community'] allows lower courts to give greater deference to military restrictions on individual rights. [By] expanding the analysis beyond the military context, the *Dronenburg* decision broadly affects all cases seeking right-of-privacy protection for homosexual persons. The court failed to follow its own warning on judicial restraint and decided larger issues [that] should have remained separate from the military setting of [the case]. Besides posing a challenge to military regulations, [*Dronenburg* is hardly the best case for determining whether the right of

privacy protects consensual homosexual behavior between adults because] the case involves activities occurring on military premises and a relationship between a petty officer [appellant] and a lower ranked enlisted man."

For a broad attack on *Dronenburg,* see Note, 3 Yale L. & Pol.Rev. 245 (1984), concluding, id. at 261–62, that the case "offers a significant example of how some judges rely on traditional misconceptions about homosexuality to justify repression of nonconformist behavior. Also, the manner in which [Judge] Bork's decision confines doctrinally important Supreme Court cases to their facts allows courts, when faced with issues involving unconventional activity, to abandon their obligation to protect fundamental rights against infringement."

For a defense of the result reached in *Dronenburg,* see Note, 26 Wm. & Mary L.Rev. 645 (1985), concluding, id. at 681 that the right to privacy "never was intended to protect sodomy. Because the Supreme Court created the right to privacy by judicial Lochnerization, the right must be defined narrowly. The equal protection attacks on sodomy statutes are inapposite because homosexuals are not a suspect class, because no fundamental right to sodomy exists, and because the sodomy statutes rationally support a legitimate state purpose."

adultery. It is less clear whether the social interest in protecting and strengthening marriages generally—through deterrence, or through a symbolic expression of social condemnation which may enter into the solemnity with which people view marriage as an institution—can sustain a per se criminal prohibition on extramarital sexual contacts by married persons. Such an outcome seems to assign too much weight to sex acts themselves as a cause of marital disintegration, and to accord too little weight to the importance of other intimacies in the definition of individual human beings." Compare Wilkinson & White, supra, at 599–600.

3. *Personal appearance and lifestyles.* KELLEY v. JOHNSON, 425 U.S. 238, 96 S.Ct. 1440, 47 L.Ed.2d 708 (1976), per REHNQUIST, J., held that regulations directed at the style and length of male police officers' hair, sideburns and mustaches, and prohibiting beards and goatees except for medical reasons, violated no " 'liberty' interest protected by the Fourteenth Amendment": "The 'liberty' interest claimed [here] is distinguishable from [those] protected in *Roe, Eisenstadt* [and] *Griswold,* [which] involved a substantial claim of infringement on the individual's freedom of choice with respect to certain basic matters of procreation, marriage, and family life."

Assuming that "the citizenry at large has some sort of 'liberty' interest within the Fourteenth Amendment in matters of personal appearance," this assumption is insufficient to topple the regulation, for respondent has sought constitutional protection "as an employee of the county and, more particularly, as a policeman. [T]he county has chosen a mode of organization which it undoubtedly deems the most efficient in enabling its police to carry out the duties assigned to them under state and local law. Such a choice necessarily gives weight to the overall need for discipline, esprit de corps, and uniformity.

"The promotion of safety of persons and property is unquestionably at the core of the State's police [power]. Choice of organization, dress and equipment for law enforcement personnel is a decision entitled to the same sort of presumption of legislative validity as are state choices designed to promote other aims within the cognizance of the State's police power. [Thus] the question is not [whether] the State can 'establish' a 'genuine public need' for the specific regulation [but] whether respondent can demonstrate that there is no rational connection between the regulation, based as it is on petitioner's method of organizing its police force, and the promotion of safety of persons and property.

"[The courts are not] in a position to weigh the policy arguments in favor of and against a rule regulating hairstyles as a part of regulations governing a uniformed civilian service. The constitutional issue [is whether the] determination that such regulations should be enacted is so irrational that it may be branded 'arbitrary,' and therefore a deprivation of respondent's 'liberty' interest in freedom to choose his own hairstyle. *Williamson v. Lee Optical Co.* [p. 263 infra]. The overwhelming majority of state and local police of the present day are uniformed. This fact itself testifies to the recognition by those who direct those operations, and by the people of the States and localities who directly or indirectly choose such persons, that similarity in appearance of police officers is desirable. This choice may be based on a desire to make police officers readily recognizable to the members of the public, or a desire for the esprit de corps which such similarity is felt to inculcate within the police force itself. Either one is a sufficiently rational justification for" the regulations.[a]

---

a. Powell, J., joined the Court's opinion, but underscored that, unlike the dissenters, he found "no negative implications in the opinion with respect to a liberty interest within the

MARSHALL, J., joined by Brennan, J., dissented: "An individual's personal appearance may reflect, sustain, and nourish his personality and may well be used as a means of expressing his attitude and lifestyle.[2] In taking control over a citizen's personal appearance, the Government forces him to sacrifice substantial elements of his integrity and identity as well. To say that the liberty guarantee of the Fourteenth Amendment does not encompass matters of personal appearance would be fundamentally inconsistent with the values of privacy, self-identity, autonomy, and personal integrity that I have always assumed the Constitution was designed to protect [referring, e.g., to *Roe* and *Griswold*].[b]

"[While] fully accepting the aims of 'identifiability' and maintenance of esprit de corps, I find no rational relationship between the challenged regulation and these goals. As for the first justification offered by the Court, I simply do not see how requiring policemen to maintain hair of under a certain length could rationally be argued to contribute to making them identifiable to the public as policemen. [As] for the Court's second justification, the fact that it is the President of the Patrolmen's Benevolent Association, in his official capacity, who has challenged the regulation here would seem to indicate that the regulation would if anything, decrease rather than increase the police force's esprit de corps.[6] And even if one accepted the argument that substantial similarity in appearance would increase a force's esprit de corps, I simply do not understand how implementation of this regulation could be expected to create any increment in similarity of appearance among members of a uniformed police force. While the regulation prohibits hair below the ears or the collar and limits the length of sideburns, it allows the maintenance of any type of hair style, other than a pony tail. Thus, as long as their hair does not go below their collars, two police officers, with an 'Afro' hair style and the other with a crew cut could both be in full compliance with the regulation.[7] * * *[8]"

Fourteenth Amendment as to matters of personal appearance." See also Tribe, supra, at 964: "[R]egulations which exclude someone from a single public position are far less intrusive, and hence less likely to be invalidated, than those which work an exclusion from an entire profession, or from any public employment [or] from all public education."

2. While the parties did not address any First Amendment issues in any detail in this Court, governmental regulation of a citizen's personal appearance may in some circumstances not only deprive him of liberty under the Fourteenth Amendment but violate his First Amendment rights as well. *Tinker v. Des Moines School District* [p. 629 infra].

b. See also Wilkinson & White, supra, at 605: "Appearance, like speech, is a chief medium of self-expression that involves important choices about how we wish to project ourselves and be perceived by others. To link appearance with privacy and speech values is not, of course, to require similar constitutional treatment. It does imply, however, that we deal with a substantive constitutional liberty."

6. Nor, to say the least, is the esprit de corps argument bolstered by the fact that the International Brotherhood of Police Officers, a 25,000 member union representing uniformed police officers, has filed a brief as amicus curiae arguing that the challenged regulation is unconstitutional.

7. The regulation itself eschews what would appear to be a less intrusive means of achieving similarity in the hair length of on-duty officers. According to the regulation, a policeman cannot comply with the hair length requirements by wearing a wig with hair of the proper length while on duty. The regulation prohibits the wearing of wigs or hair pieces "on duty in uniform except for cosmetic reasons to cover natural baldness or physical disfiguration." Thus, while the regulation in terms applies to grooming standards of policemen while on duty, the hair length provision effectively controls both on-duty and off-duty appearance.

[Why did the *Kelley* majority see no need to respond to the dissent's point that simply requiring a police officer to wear an appropriate wig while on duty would serve all of the county's articulated interests? See Tribe, supra, at 962.]

8. Because, to my mind, the challenged regulation fails to pass even a minimal degree of scrutiny, there is no need to determine whether, given the nature of the interests involved and the degree to which they are affected, the application of a more heightened scrutiny would be appropriate.

(b) *Student "long hair" cases.* Apart from *Kelley*, what of such cases as KARR v. SCHMIDT, 460 F.2d 609 (5th Cir.1972), (holding that a school board's regulation restricting the length of male students' hair violated no constitutionally protected right)? The board had argued that the regulation served the goals of inhibiting "classroom distraction" and disruption and eliminating potential health and safety hazards and *Karr* had called these "legitimate objectives." Consider Wilkinson & White, supra, at 606: "Long hair on males is intrinsically no less healthy and no more distracting and disruptive of classroom work than long hair on females. Any difference is the result of custom alone; [and] conformity to custom [seems] insufficient to justify the limitation on individual choice. The rationale suggests the untenable: that mere unconventionality of appearance is enough to bring the state's regulatory apparatus into play."

4. *The substantive due process rights of involuntarily-committed mentally retarded persons.* In YOUNGBERG v. ROMEO, 457 U.S. 307, 102 S.Ct. 2452, 73 L.Ed.2d 28 (1982), the Court considered for the first time the substantive due process rights of involuntarily-committed mentally retarded persons. On his mother's petition, Romeo, a profoundly retarded 33-year-old was involuntarily committed to a Pennsylvania state institution (Pennhurst). Subsequently, concerned about injuries Romeo had suffered at Pennhurst, his mother filed a federal action against institution officials claiming that her son had constitutional rights to (1) safe conditions of confinement, (2) freedom from bodily restraint, and (3) "a constitutional right to minimally adequate habilitation," i.e., minimal training and development of needed skills. (In light of his severe retardation, however, respondent conceded that no amount of training would make his release possible.) The Court, per POWELL, J., pointed out that respondent's first two claims "involve liberty interests recognized by prior decisions of this Court, interests that involuntary commitment proceedings do not extinguish," but found respondent's remaining claim "more troubling":

"On the basis of the record before us, it is quite uncertain whether respondent seeks any 'habilitation' or training unrelated to [his constitutionally protected liberty interest in] safety and freedom from bodily restraints. [If,] as seems the case, respondent seeks only training related to safety and freedom from restraints, this case does not present the difficult question whether a mentally retarded person, involuntarily committed to a state institution, has some general constitutional right to training per se, even when no type or amount of training would lead to freedom. [On the basis of the record], we conclude that respondent's liberty interests require the State to provide minimally adequate or reasonable training to ensure safety and freedom from undue restraint. [W]e need go no further in this case.

"[But the question] is not simply whether a liberty interest has been infringed but whether the extent or nature of the restraint or lack of absolute safety is such as to violate due process. In determining whether a substantive right protected by the Due Process Clause has been violated, it is necessary to balance 'the liberty of the individual' and 'the demands of an organized society.'"

The Court then considered "the proper standard for determining whether a State adequately has protected the rights of the involuntarily-committed mentally retarded." It agreed with the concurring judge below "that 'the Constitution only requires that the courts make certain that professional judgment was in fact exercised. It is not appropriate for the courts to specify which of several professionally acceptable choices should have been made.' Persons who have been involuntarily committed are entitled to more considerate treatment [than] criminals whose conditions of confinement are designed to punish. At the same time, the standard is lower than [a] 'compelling' or 'substantial' necessity [test for justifying restraints] that would place an undue burden on the administration of [state institutions] and also would restrict unnecessarily the exercise of professional judgment as to the needs of residents.

"[In] determining what is 'reasonable'—in this and in any case presenting a claim for training by a state—we emphasize that courts must show deference to the judgment exercised by a qualified professional. [The] decision, if made by a professional, is presumptively valid; liability may be imposed only when the decision by the professional is such a substantial departure from accepted professional judgment, practice or standards as to demonstrate that the person responsible actually did not base the decision on such a judgment.[a] In an action for damages against a professional in his individual capacity, however, the professional will not be liable if he was unable to satisfy his normal professional standards because of budgetary constraints; in such a situation, good-faith immunity would bar liability."

BLACKMUN, J., joined by Brennan and O'Connor, JJ., joined the Court's opinion, but concurred separately to clarify why, because of the uncertainty in the record, "that opinion properly leaves open two difficult and important questions." Unlike Burger, C.J., who considered the issue "frivolous," Blackmun, J., believed that whether Pennsylvania could accept respondent for "care and treatment" and then constitutionally refuse to provide him any "treatment," as that term is defined by state law, would, if properly before the Court, present "a serious issue." As for the second difficult question left open— whether respondent had an "independent constitutional claim [to] that 'habilitation' or training necessary to *preserve* those basic self-care skills he possessed when he first entered Pennhurst"—he believed that "it would be consistent with the Court's reasoning today to include within the 'minimally adequate training required by the Constitution' such training as is reasonably necessary to prevent a person's pre-existing self-care skills from *deteriorating* because of his commitment" and he viewed such deterioration "because of the State's unreasonable refusal to provide him training [a] loss of liberty quite distinct from—and as serious as—the loss of safety and freedom from unreasonable restraints."

BURGER, C.J., concurring, agreed with much of the Court's opinion, but "would hold flatly that respondent has no constitutional right to training, or 'habilitation,' per se." He agreed that "some amount of self-care instruction may be necessary to avoid unreasonable infringement of a mentally-retarded person's interests in safety and freedom from restraint"; but he thought it "clear" that "the Constitution does not otherwise place an affirmative duty on the State to provide any particular kind of training or habilitation—even such as might be encompassed under the essentially standardless rubric 'minimally adequate training,' to which the Court refers." Since respondent had asserted "a right to 'minimally adequate' habilitation '[q]uite apart from its relationship to decent care,'" unlike the Court he saw "no way to avoid the issue."

5. *The "right to die."* Although the Supreme Court is yet to decide the question, the highly publicized case of IN RE QUINLAN, 70 N.J. 10, 355 A.2d 647 (1976), assumed that the right of privacy enumerated by the Supreme Court "is broad enough to encompass a patient's decision to decline medical treatment

---

a. Does this place "a seemingly insurmountable burden" on plaintiff mental patients? See Note, 96 Harv.L.Rev. 77, 85 (1982).

under certain circumstances [even if the decision might lead to the patient's death], in much the same way as it is broad enough to encompass a woman's decision to terminate pregnancy under certain conditions." More recently, the President's Commission for the Study of Ethical Problems in Medicine and Biomedical and Behavioral Research, *Deciding to Forego Life-Sustaining Treatment* 32 (1983) (President's Commission Report) stated that "[r]egardless of how interests are weighed in specific cases, a decision to forego life-sustaining treatment has been firmly established as a constitutionally protected right that can be overcome only by marshalling countervailing considerations of substantial weight."

Assuming this is so, the *Quinlan* case dealt with a person who obviously lacked the capacity to make or express a decision on the subject (she was in a "chronic persistent vegetative state"), and the court dismissed Ms. Quinlan's previous views on the subject as so casual and equivocal as to lack the requisite probative value. The court ruled, nevertheless, that Ms. Quinlan could be taken off her respirator (it was assumed that such removal would cause her death, but it did not) on the approval of her family, subject to agreement by an "ethics committee" that "there is no reasonable possibility of [her] ever emerging from her present comatose condition to a cognitive, sapient state":

"[The] only practical way to prevent destruction of the right [of privacy] is to permit the guardian and family of Karen to render their best judgment [subject to certain safeguards] as to whether she would exercise it in these circumstances. If their conclusion is in the affirmative, this decision should be accepted by a society the overwhelming majority of whose members would, we think, in similar circumstances, exercise such a choice in the same way for themselves or for those closest to them. [Thus,] Karen's right of privacy may be asserted in her behalf, in this respect, by her guardian and family."

Notes and Questions

(a) For the view that *Quinlan* was not a "right of privacy" or "right-to-die" case, although it was almost universally reported and discussed as such, but a "quality of life" case that badly smudged the distinction between the right to choose one's own death and the right to choose someone else's, see Kamisar, *Karen Ann Quinlan and the "Right-to-Die,"* 29 Law Quad Notes 3–4 (Summer, 1985). See also Nowak, Rotunda & Young, *Constitutional Law* 764–65 (2d ed. 1983); Note, 1979 U.Ill.L.F. 469, 517–18.

For close analyses of *Quinlan*, see, e.g., Burt, *Taking Care of Strangers* 144–73 (1979); Grisez & Boyle, *Life and Death with Liberty and Justice* 83–84, 96–98, 283–88 (1979); Ramsey, *Ethics at the Edges of Life* 268–99 (1978); Veatch, *Death, Dying, and the Biological Revolution* 137–44, 152–53, 174–76 (1976); Cantor, *Quinlan, Privacy, and the Handling of Incompetent Patients,* 30 Rutg.L.Rev. 243 (1977). For commentary on *Quinlan* in the context of a general discussion of the "surrogate-choice" approach to constitutional freedoms, see Garvey, *Freedom and Choice in Constitutional Law,* 94 Harv.L.Rev. 1756, 1778–85 (1981). For discussion of euthanasia generally, see President's Commission Report, supra; *Privacy and the Family in Medical Decisions: A Symposium,* 23 J. Family Law 173 (1984–85); Capron, *Euthanasia,* 2 Ency.Crime & Justice 709 (S. Kadish ed. 1983).

(b) Consider Tribe, supra, at 936–37: "The court's belief that Karen's rights were more jeopardized on the facts before it than in a situation where she wished to terminate a still conscious life seems perplexing. Given the supposedly vegetative state that alone justified the court's holding, attributing 'rights' to Karen at all was problematic; more realistically at stake were the desire of her anguished parents to be rid of their torment and the interest of society in freeing medical decision makers from blind adherence to a practice of keeping vegetative persons 'alive' simply out of a fear of prosecution. But to give *those* interests constitutional status even where the state interposes an objection in the interest of the child's life seems most troubling. If, on the other hand, Karen were fully conscious and chose after careful reflection to end her life, the proposition that the state should be empowered to prevent her from carrying out that design, and even to punish her for the attempt, seems hard to square with her dignity and integrity as a person."

(c) *Post-Quinlan cases.* See *Superintendent v. Saikewicz,* 373 Mass. 728, 370 N.E.2d 417 (1977), where physicians obtained judicial authorization to withhold an apparently painful course of chemotherapy for a mentally retarded and institutionalized 67-year-old suffering from leukemia. The case is discussed in Annas, *The Incompetent's Right to Die,* Hastings Center Report 8 (Feb. 1978); Annas, *After Saikewicz: No Fault Death,* Hastings Center Report 8 (June 1978); Burt, supra, at 144–58; Ramsey, supra, at 300–17.

But compare *Quinlan* and *Saikewicz* with *In re Storar,* 52 N.Y.2d 363, 438 N.Y.S.2d 266, 420 N.E.2d 64 (1981): Storar, a profoundly retarded 52-year-old man, suffering from incurable cancer of the bladder, received blood transfusions for several weeks. Then the patient's mother, who was also his legal guardian, refused consent on the ground that the transfusions would only prolong her son's discomfort and would be against his wishes if he were competent. But the court ruled that a state official's request to continue the transfusions should have been granted. Storar "was never competent at any time in his life. [Thus,] it is unrealistic to attempt to determine whether he would want to continue [the] treatment if he were competent. [Even] when the parents' decision to decline necessary treatment is based on constitutional grounds, such as religious beliefs, it must yield to the State's interests [in] protecting the health and welfare of the child. [The] transfusions were analogous to food—they would not cure the cancer, but they could eliminate the risk of death from another treatable cause. [A] court should not in the circumstances of this case allow an incompetent patient to bleed to death because [his family or guardian] feels this is best for one with an incurable disease."

Nine years after its historic decision in the *Quinlan* case, the Supreme Court of New Jersey modified its earlier views, *In re Conroy,* 98 N.J. 321, 486 A.2d 1209 (1985), observing, inter alia: (1) life-sustaining treatment, even artificial feeding, may be withheld or withdrawn from an incompetent person "when it is clear that the particular patient would have refused the treatment under the circumstances involved," because the patient had, e.g., executed a "living will"; (2) absent adequate proof of the incompetent patient's previous wishes, "it is naive to pretend that the right to self-determination serves as the basis for substituted decision-making"; and (3) in the absence of trustworthy evidence that the patient would have declined life-saving treatment, such treatment may still be withheld or withdrawn from a formerly competent person if, but only if, "the net burdens of the patient's life with the treatment should clearly and markedly outweigh the benefits that the patient derives from life," but "[the] unavoidable and severe pain of the patient's life with the treatment should be such that the effect of administering life-sustaining treatment would be inhumane." According to Curran, *Defining Appropriate Medical Care: Providing Nutrients and Hydration for the Dying,* 313 New Eng.J.Med. 940, 942 (1985), "the [*Conroy*] court's position in allowing removal of nutrition and hydration as well as other forms of life support is without precedent in the American courts."

SECTION 3. THE DEATH PENALTY AND RELATED PROBLEMS: CRUEL AND UNUSUAL PUNISHMENT

Introduction

"The question of capital punishment has been the subject of endless discussion and will probably never be settled so long as men believe in punishment. [The] reasons why it cannot be settled are plain. There is first of all no agreement as to the objects of punishment. Next there is no way to determine the results of punishment. [Moreover,] questions of this sort, or perhaps of any sort, are not settled by reason; they are settled by prejudices and sentiments or by emotion. When they are settled they do not stay settled, for the emotions change as new stimuli are applied to the machine."

—Clarence Darrow, *Crime, Its Cause and Treatment* 166 (1922).

———

At the time he made it, Darrow's prediction that the question of capital punishment "will probably never be settled" appeared well-founded. That the issue might ever be settled as a matter of constitutional law seemed almost inconceivable. The Court had already specifically sanctioned death by firing squad and by electrocution. Indeed, 25 years after Darrow's remarks, *Louisiana ex rel. Francis v. Resweber*, 329 U.S. 459, 67 S.Ct. 374, 91 L.Ed. 422 (1947), sustained what the dissenters called the horror of "death by installments." (After a first attempt to electrocute petitioner had failed because of mechanical difficulties, the state strapped him in the electric chair a second time and threw the switch again.) And in the 1950s the Court twice upheld the execution of men whose sanity was in doubt, leaving the question to the judgment of a governor and a warden. See Kamisar, *The Reincarnation of the Death Penalty: Is it Possible?* Student Lawyer, May 1973, pp. 22–23.

In *Trop v. Dulles*, 356 U.S. 86, 78 S.Ct. 590, 2 L.Ed.2d 630 (1958), speaking for four justices, (Brennan, J., had found the "expatriation" provision invalid on other grounds), Warren, C.J., deemed deprivation of a native-born American's citizenship because of wartime desertion from the army—leaving him "stateless"—a "fate forbidden by the principle of civilized treatment guaranteed by the Eighth Amendment," but was quick to add: "[W]hatever the arguments may be against the [death penalty, it] has been employed throughout our history, and, in a day when it is still widely accepted, it cannot be said to violate the constitutional concept of cruelty." As late as 1968, a close student of the problem, observed: "[N]ot a single death penalty statute, not a single statutorily imposed mode of execution, not a single attempted execution has ever been held by any court to be 'cruel and unusual punishment' under any state or federal constitution. Nothing less than a mighty counterthrust would appear to be required to alter the direction of these decisions." Bedau, *The Courts, the Constitution, and Capital Punishment*, 1968 Utah L.Rev. 201.

In the 1960s the NAACP Legal Defense and Educational Fund, Inc. (LDF), led by Professor Anthony Amsterdam, did launch a major constitutional assault on the death penalty. Convinced that "each year the United States went without executions, the more hollow would ring claims that the American people could not do without them" and that "the longer death-row inmates waited, the greater their numbers, the more difficult it would be for the courts to permit the first execution," the LDF developed a "moratorium strategy," creating "a death-row logjam." Meltsner, *Cruel and Unusual: The Supreme Court and Capital Punishment* 107 (1973).

Largely as a result of LDF efforts in blocking all executions on every conceivable legal ground, when the Court handed down *Furman,* infra, in 1972, there had not been a single execution in five years.

Actually, the number of executions had started to decline as early as the 1940s and had dropped dramatically in the 1960s, several years before the LDF had successfully developed its moratorium strategy. After peaking in the 1930s (152 per year during this decade, and reaching an all-time high of 199 executions in 1935), the annual rate of executions averaged 128 in the 1940s and 72 in the 1950s. There were only 21 executions in 1963, 15 in 1964 and a mere seven in 1965. (In the 1930–50 period, executions had averaged more than ten *a month*). See Greenberg, *Capital Punishment as a System,* 91 Yale L.J. 908, 924–25 (1982); Kamisar, supra.

If, as appeared to be the case, the Court was reluctant to enter into the hotly contested capital punishment debate, yet equally hesitant to "legitimate" the punishment, the preferable way to proceed would seem to have been to continue to chip away at the procedural administration of the death penalty rather than launch a more frontal assault as the Court did (or most thought it did at the time) in *Furman.* Thus, LDF lawyers suffered a serious set-back in 1971 when the Court "refused an invitation to abolish capital punishment piecemeal." Meltsner, supra, at 244–45. *McGautha v. California* and *Crampton v. Ohio,* 402 U.S. 183, 91 S.Ct. 1454, 28 L.Ed.2d 711 (1971), rejected (1) petitioners' common claim that permitting the jury to impose the death penalty without any governing standards violated due process and (2) the Ohio petitioner's contention that allowing the jury to impose the death penalty in the same proceeding and verdict which determines the issue of guilt "creates an intolerable tension" between one's constitutional right not to be compelled to be a witness against himself on the issue of guilt and his constitutional right to be heard on the issue of punishment, a tension which can be avoided by a bifurcated trial, such as that required by California and five other states.[a]

In rejecting the contention that the states had to develop and articulate criteria under which convicted felons should be chosen to live and die, a 6–3 majority (including Stewart and White, JJ., whose votes would be pivotal in *Furman*) observed, per Harlan, J.:

"To identify before the fact those characteristics of criminal homicides and their perpetrators which call for the death penalty, and to express those characteristics in language which can be fairly understood and applied by the sentencing authority, appear to be tasks which are beyond present human ability. * * * In light of history, experience, and the present limitations of human knowledge, we find it quite impossible to say that committing to the untrammeled discretion of the jury the power to pronounce life or death in capital cases is offensive to anything in the Constitution. The States are entitled to assume that jurors confronted with the truly awesome responsibility of decreeing death for a fellow human will act with due regard for the conse-

---

a. To what extent did the Court reject *Mc-Gautha* and *Crampton* in subsequent decisions?

quences of their decision and will consider a variety of factors * * *. For a court to attempt to catalog the appropriate factors in this elusive area could inhibit rather than expand the scope of consideration, for no list of circumstances would ever be really complete." [b]

Consider Weisberg, *Deregulating Death*, 1983 Sup.Ct.Rev. 305, 313: "In the end, Harlan concludes [in *McGautha*] that, morally and intellectually, the Court has nothing to teach the states about capital punishment. One can of course dispute the truth of Harlan's central insight—that we cannot write a law of capital punishment in conventional legal language. Even if one accepts that truth, one can reject Harlan's inference from it—that the Court must leave the issue to the states. Indeed what follows *McGautha* is a struggle over both the truth and the significance of Harlan's assertion."

I. IS THE DEATH PENALTY ALWAYS—OR EVER—"CRUEL AND UNUSUAL"?

FURMAN v. GEORGIA, 408 U.S. 238, 92 S.Ct. 2726, 33 L.Ed.2d 346 (1972), considered the death sentence in three cases (all involving black defendants), two dealing with a murderer and rapist in Georgia, the third a rapist in Texas.[c] (Each had been sentenced to death after trial by jury. Under the applicable state statutes, the judge or jury had discretion to impose the death penalty.) Also at stake, however, were the lives of almost 600 condemned persons who had "piled up" in "death rows" throughout the land in recent years. Striking down the laws of 39 states [d] and various federal statutory provisions, a 5–4 majority, per curiam, held that "the imposition and carrying out" of the death penalty under the current arbitrarily and randomly administered system constitutes "cruel and unusual" punishment in violation of the eighth and fourteenth amendments. Each of the justices wrote a separate concurring or dissenting opinion explaining his reasons for invalidating or upholding the death penalty. (The nine opinions totalled 230 pages in the official reports.) *Furman* has been called "not so much a case as a badly orchestrated opera, with nine characters taking turns to offer their own arias." Weisberg, *Deregulating Death*, 1983 Sup. Ct.Rev. 305, 315.

The pivotal opinions of Stewart and White, JJ., left open the question whether *any* system of capital punishment, as opposed to the presently capriciously administered one, would be unconstitutional. A third member of the majority, Douglas, J., also reserved for another day whether a nondiscriminatorily operated mandatory death penalty would be constitutional.

STEWART, J.: "If we were reviewing death sentences imposed under [laws making death the mandatory punishment for every person convicted of engaging in certain designated criminal conduct] we would be faced with the need to

---

b. Brennan, J., joined by Douglas and Marshall, JJ., dissenting, refused to "believe that the legislatures of the 50 states are so devoid of wisdom and the power of rational thought that they are unable to face the problem of capital punishment directly, and to determine for themselves the criteria under which convicted felons should be chosen to live or die." He maintained that such procedures may take a variety of forms, e.g., requiring the decision to rest upon the presence or absence of specific factors, or directing the decision-maker's attention to the basic policy determinations underlying the death penalty statute.

c. Since 1930, murder and rape had accounted for nearly 99% of total executions and murder alone for about 87%. But various jurisdictions also permitted capital punishment for other crimes, e.g., kidnapping, treason, espionage, aircraft piracy.

d. Forty states authorized capital punishment for a variety of crimes, but since Rhode Island's only capital statute, murder by a life term prisoner, carried a mandatory death sentence, it was not invalidated by the instant case.

decide whether capital punishment is unconstitutional for all crimes and under all circumstances. We would need to decide whether a legislature—state or federal—could constitutionally determine that certain criminal conduct is so atrocious that society's interest in deterrence and retribution wholly outweighs any considerations of reform or rehabilitation of the perpetrator, and that, despite the inconclusive empirical evidence, only the automatic penalty of death will provide maximum deterrence.

"On that score I would say only that I cannot agree that retribution is a constitutionally impermissible ingredient in the imposition of punishment. The instinct for retribution is part of the nature of man, and channeling that instinct in the administration of criminal justice serves an important purpose in promoting the stability of a society governed by law. When people begin to believe that organized society is unwilling or unable to impose upon criminal offenders the punishment they 'deserve,' then there are sown the seeds of anarchy—of self-help, vigilante justice, and lynch law.

"The constitutionality of capital punishment in the abstract is not, however, before us in these cases. For the Georgia and Texas legislatures have not provided that the death penalty shall be imposed upon all those who are found guilty of forcible rape [or] murder. In a word, neither State has made a legislative determination that forcible rape and murder can be deterred only by imposing the penalty of death upon all who perpetrate those offenses. As [concurring] Justice White so tellingly puts it, the 'legislative will is not frustrated if the penalty is never imposed.'

"Instead, the death sentences now before us are the product of a legal system that brings them, I believe, within the very core of the Eighth Amendment's guarantee against cruel and unusual punishments, a guarantee applicable against the States through the Fourteenth Amendment. In the first place, it is clear that these sentences are 'cruel' in the sense that they excessively go beyond, not in degree but in kind, the punishments that the state legislatures have determined to be necessary. In the second place, it is equally clear that these sentences are 'unusual' in the sense that the penalty of death is infrequently imposed for murder, and that its imposition for rape is extraordinarily rare. But I do not rest my conclusion upon these two propositions alone.

"These death sentences are cruel and unusual in the same way that being struck by lightning is cruel and unusual. For, of all the people convicted of rapes and murders in 1967 and 1968, many just as reprehensible as these, the petitioners are among a capriciously selected random handful upon whom the sentence of death has in fact been imposed. My concurring Brothers have demonstrated that, if any basis can be discerned for the selection of these few to be sentenced to die, it is the constitutionally impermissible basis of race. But racial discrimination has not been proved, and I put it to one side. I simply conclude that the Eighth and Fourteenth Amendments cannot tolerate the inflicting of a sentence of death under legal systems that permit this unique penalty to be so wantonly and so freakishly imposed."

WHITE, J.: "The imposition and execution of the death penalty are obviously cruel in the dictionary sense. But the penalty has not been considered cruel and unusual punishment in the constitutional sense because it was thought justified by the social ends it was deemed to serve. At the moment that it ceases realistically to further these purposes, however, the emerging question is whether its imposition in such circumstances would violate the Eighth Amendment. It is my view that it would, for its imposition would then be the pointless and needless extinction of life with only marginal contributions to any discernible social or public purposes. A penalty with such negligible returns to the State would be patently excessive and cruel and unusual punishment violative of the Eighth Amendment.

"It is also my judgment that this point has been reached with respect to capital punishment as it is presently administered under the statutes involved in these cases. [A]s the statutes before us are now administered, the penalty is so infrequently imposed that the threat of execution is too attenuated to be of substantial service to criminal justice.

" * * * I must arrive at judgment; and I can do no more than state a conclusion based on 10 years of almost daily exposure to the facts and circumstances of hundreds and hundreds of federal and state criminal cases involving crimes for which death is the authorized penalty. [T]he death penalty is exacted with great infrequency even for the most atrocious crimes [and] there is no meaningful basis for distinguishing the few cases in which it is imposed from the many cases in which it is not.[e] The short of it is that the policy of vesting sentencing authority primarily in juries—a decision largely motivated by the desire to mitigate the harshness of the law and to bring community judgment to bear on the sentence as well as guilt or innocence—has so effectively achieved its aims that capital punishment within the confines of the statutes now before us has for all practical purposes run its course.

"[P]ast and present legislative judgment with respect to the death penalty loses much of its force when viewed in light of the recurring practice of delegating sentencing authority to the jury and the fact that a jury, in its own discretion and without violating its trust or any statutory policy, may refuse to impose the death penalty no matter what the circumstances of the crime. Legislative 'policy' is thus necessarily defined not by what is legislatively authorized but by what juries and judges do in exercising the discretion so regularly conferred upon them. In my judgment what was done in these cases violated the Eighth Amendment."

DOUGLAS, J.: "The words 'cruel and unusual' certainly include penalties that are barbaric. But the words, at least when read in light of the English proscription against selective and irregular use of penalties, suggest that it is 'cruel and unusual' to apply the death penalty—or any other penalty—selectively to minorities whose numbers are few, who are outcasts of society, and who are unpopular, but whom society is willing to see suffer though it would not countenance general application of the same penalty across the boards. * * *

"A law that stated that anyone making more than $50,000 would be exempt from the death penalty would plainly fall, as would a law that in terms said that Blacks, those who never went beyond the fifth grade in school, or those who made less than $3,000 a year, or those who were unpopular or unstable should be

---

e. But consider Vance, *The Death Penalty after Furman,* 48 Notre Dame Law. 850, 858 (1973): "Actually there is a fairly universal consensus on which cases should receive the harshest penalties. [It] is only in the bizarre murder, the killing for hire or during another serious crime, and a few other isolated instances that the people of this country want to see the death penalty applied. [Any prosecutor] (as well as any judge or defense attorney) can listen to a set of facts and tell you whether it is a death penalty case. [T]here *should* be very few death penalty sentences. Only a very few cases warrant this extreme measure. It takes two essential [ingredients]: (1) overwhelming proof [of] guilt and (2) an extremely aggravated fact situation. What is so surprising is Justice White's and Justice Stewart's conclusion that there is something highly improper in so few people receiving the death penalty."

the only people executed. A law which in the overall view reaches that result in practice has no more sanctity than a law which in terms provides the same.

"[T]hese discretionary statutes are unconstitutional in their operation. They are pregnant with discrimination and discrimination is an ingredient not compatible with the idea of equal protection of the laws that is implicit in the ban on 'cruel and unusual' punishments."

Although Stewart and White, JJ., concurring, and the four dissenters all asserted that the remaining members of the majority—Brennan and Marshall, JJ.—had concluded that the eighth amendment prohibits capital punishment for all crimes and under all circumstances, this is not clear from their opinions.

As BRENNAN, J., perceived the question, there are four principles "recognized in our cases and inherent in" the eighth amendment prohibition "sufficient to permit a judicial determination whether a challenged punishment" "does not comport with human dignity" and therefore is "cruel and unusual": (1) "a punishment must not be so severe as to be degrading to the dignity of human beings"; (2) the government "must not arbitrarily inflict a severe punishment"; (3) "a severe punishment must not be unacceptable to contemporary society"; and (4) "a severe punishment must not be excessive," i.e., "unnecessary." Applying the first and "primary" principle, Brennan, J., concluded that capital punishment "involves by its very nature a denial of the executed person's humanity" and, in comparison to all other punishments today, "is uniquely degrading to human dignity." He "would not hesitate to hold, on that ground alone, that death is today a 'cruel and unusual punishment,' *were it not that death is a punishment of longstanding usage and acceptance in this country.*" [Emphasis added.] He then turned to a discussion of the other three principles, in each instance relying heavily upon the fact that today the death sentence is inflicted very rarely and most arbitrarily:

"When the punishment of death is inflicted in a trivial number of the cases in which it is legally available, the conclusion is virtually inescapable that it is being inflicted arbitrarily. Indeed, it smacks of little more than a lottery system. * * *

"When there is a strong probability that an unusually severe and degrading punishment is being inflicted arbitrarily, we may well expect that society will disapprove of its infliction. I turn, therefore, to the third principle. An examination of the history and present operation of the American practice of punishing criminals by death reveals that this punishment has been almost totally rejected by contemporary society.

"* * * When an unusually severe punishment is authorized for wide-scale application but not, because of society's refusal, inflicted save in a few instances, the inference is compelling that there is a deep-seated reluctance to inflict it. Indeed, the likelihood is great that the punishment is tolerated only because of its disuse. The objective indicator of society's view of an unusually severe punishment is what society does with it. And today society will inflict death upon only a small sample of the eligible criminals. Rejection could hardly be more complete without becoming absolute.[f] At the very least, I must conclude that contemporary society views this punishment with substantial doubt.

---

f. But consider Polsby, *The Death of Capital Punishment?*, 1972 Sup.Ct.Rev. 1, 20: "An entirely valid inference [from the infrequent imposition of the death penalty] would be, not that the society has repudiated the penalty, but that it wishes to reserve its use to a small number of cases. A reluctance to impose a penalty is not necessarily the same as its repudiation. Reluctance may spring from moral revulsion; but it may just as commonly proceed from a human and heartfelt sorrow."

"[As for the final principle], whatever the speculative validity of the assumption that the threat of death is a superior deterrent, there is no reason to believe that as currently administered the punishment of death is necessary to deter the commission of capital crimes. * * *

"In sum, the punishment of death is inconsistent with all four principles: Death is an unusually severe and degrading punishment; there is a strong probability that it is inflicted arbitrarily; its rejection by contemporary society is virtually total; and there is no reason to believe that it serves any penal purpose more effectively than the less severe punishment of imprisonment. The function of these principles is to enable a court to determine whether a punishment comports with human dignity. Death, quite simply, does not."

MARSHALL, J.'s "historical foray" led to the question "whether American society has reached a point where abolition is not dependent on a successful grass roots movement in particular jurisdictions, but is demanded by the Eighth Amendment." [g] He concluded that the death penalty constitutes "cruel and unusual" punishment on two independent grounds: (1) "it is excessive and serves no valid legislative purpose," i.e., it is not a more effective deterrent than life imprisonment; (2) "it is abhorrent to currently existing moral values."

As for the first ground: "Punishment for the sake of retribution" is "not permissible under the Eighth Amendment. [At] times a cry is heard that morality requires vengeance to evidence society's abhorrence of the act. But the Eighth Amendment is our insulation from our baser selves. The cruel and unusual language limits the avenues through which vengeance can be channeled.[h] Were this not so, the language would be empty and a return to the rack and other tortures would be possible in a given case." Nor, "in light of the massive amount of evidence before us, [showing no correlation between the rate of murder or other capital crimes and the presence or absence of the death penalty, can capital punishment] be justified on the basis of its deterrent effect. [The] statistical evidence is not convincing beyond all doubt, but, it is persuasive. [The] point has now been reached at which deference to the legislatures is

g. Consider Levy, *Against the Law* 401 (1974): "In effect, the question [Marshall, J.,] asked was this: In view of the fact that the democratic process had failed to achieve abolition, should the Court impose a new public policy upon the country by a novel construction of the cruel-and-unusual punishments clause?" But cf. Kamisar, supra, at 24: "Because a decision 'legitimating' capital punishment would be interpreted by many as 'approving' it, the result would undoubtedly have been a stifling of the current movement for reform in nonjudicial forums and the lending of the Court's prestige to those forces favoring the continuation of the death penalty. [T]o give the imprimatur of legitimacy to the now broadly challenged death penalty 'would defeat the very reason behind judicial restraint—encouragement of decision by the other branches of government' [Goldberg & Dershowitz, *Declaring the Death Penalty Unconstitutional*, 83 Harv.L.Rev. 1773, 1805 (1970)]."

h. But consider Polsby, fn. f supra, at 37, 39–40: "The confusion between the proposition that the death penalty deters and the proposition that it is appropriate is a fairly stable feature of retentionist argument. [I submit] that the declaration that the death penalty is a superior deterrent to serious crime, in spite of evidence to the contrary, amounts to nothing more than the expression of a value preference that, whether the penalty is a superior deterrent or not, it ought to be used. A priori, I can find nothing wrong with this value preference. It may be flinty and stern, but it does not seem to me necessarily barbaric, that someone might believe that certain criminals ought to be put to death, the inhuman brutality of their crimes being so great as to outrun all possibility of forgiveness or amends. But if the argument is to rest upon straight moralistic dogma [why] should it dress itself up in the guise of a utilitarian argument instead? [One] answer may be that retentionists would be ashamed to admit to having such values. If so, surely it is relevant to a judgment whether death is a cruel and unusual punishment." Cf. Black, *Capital Punishment: The Inevitability of Caprice and Mistake* 23–28 (1974).

tantamount to abdication of our judicial roles as factfinders, judges and ultimate arbiters of the Constitution. [There] is no rational basis for concluding that capital punishment is not excessive. It therefore violates the Eighth Amendment."

As for the second independent ground: Although recent opinion polls indicate that Americans are about equally divided on the question of capital punishment, "whether or not a punishment is cruel or unusual depends, not on whether its mere mention 'shocks the conscience and sense of justice of the people,' but on whether people who were fully informed as to the purposes of the penalty and its liabilities would find the penalty shocking, unjust and unacceptable." Marshall, J., then concluded that *if* the average citizen possessed "knowledge of all the facts presently available" (for example, that death is no more effective a deterrent than life imprisonment; "convicted murderers are rarely executed"; "no attempt is made in the sentencing process to ferret out likely recidivists for execution"; the punishment "is imposed discriminatorily against certain identifiable classes of people"; "innocent people have been executed";) "the average citizen *would,* in my opinion, find [capital punishment] shocking to his conscience and sense of justice. [Emphasis added.]" [i] For this reason alone capital punishment cannot stand."

There were four separate dissenting opinions. BURGER, C.J., warned that "it is essential to our role as a court that we not seize upon the enigmatic character of the [eighth amendment] guarantee as an invitation to enact our personal predilictions into law." As for the argument that the death penalty was "excessive" or "unnecessary," he found "no authority suggesting that the Eighth Amendment was intended to purge the law of its retributive elements" nor any basis for prohibiting "all punishments the States are unable to prove necessary to deter crime."

"Real change," maintained the Chief Justice, "could clearly be brought about [by legislatures responding to today's ruling if they] provided mandatory death sentences in such a way as to deny juries the opportunity to bring in a verdict on a lesser charge; under such a system, the death sentence could only be avoided by a verdict of acquittal. If this is the only alternative that the legislatures can safely pursue under today's ruling, I would have preferred that the Court opt for total abolition.

"It seems remarkable to me that with our basic trust in lay jurors as the keystone in our system of criminal justice, it should now be suggested that we take the most sensitive and important of all decisions away from them. I could more easily be persuaded that mandatory sentences of death, without the intervening and ameliorating impact of lay jurors, are so arbitrary and doctrinaire that they violate the Constitution. The very infrequency of death penalties imposed by jurors attests their cautious and discriminating reservation of that penalty for the most extreme [cases.] I do not see how [the history of American abhorrence of the mandatory death sentence] can be ignored and how it can be suggested that the Eighth Amendment demands the elimination of the most sensitive feature of the sentencing system. * * *

"Quite apart from the limitations of the Eighth Amendment itself, the preference for legislative action is justified by the inability of the courts to

i. Is this a valid means of ascertaining whether "popular sentiment" or "the average citizen" abhors capital punishment? Or does Marshall, J.'s approach represent excessive speculation or inappropriate "elitism" about moral judgment? Compare Kamisar, supra, at 48, and Polsby, supra, at 23–24 with Radin, *The Jurisprudence of Death,* 126 U.Pa.L.Rev. 989, 1040–42 (1978).

participate in the debate at the level where the controversy is focused. The case against capital punishment is not the product of legal dialectic but rests primarily on factual claims, the truth of which cannot be tested by conventional judicial processes."

BLACKMUN, J., filed a separate dissent, "personally rejoicing" at the Court's result, but unable to accept it "as a matter of history, of law, or of constitutional pronouncement."

In a third dissent, POWELL, J., called the Court's ruling "the very sort of judgment that the legislative branch is competent to make and for which the judiciary is ill-equipped." He maintained that "the sweeping judicial action undertaken today reflects a basic lack of faith and confidence in the democratic process."

"[T]he weight of the evidence," he observed, "indicates that the public generally has not accepted either the morality or the social merit of [the abolitionists' views]. But however one may assess the amorphous ebb and flow of public opinion generally on this volatile issue,[j] this type of inquiry lies at the periphery—not the core—of the judicial process in constitutional cases. The assessment of public opinion is essentially a legislative, not a judicial function."

In a fourth dissent, REHNQUIST, J., concluded that the majority's ruling "significantly lack[ed]" the "humility" and "deference to legislative judgment" with which the task of judging constitutional cases must be approached; indeed, "it is not an act of judgment, but rather an act of will."

GREGG v. GEORGIA, 428 U.S. 153, 96 S.Ct. 2909, 49 L.Ed.2d 859 (1976), upheld the constitutionality of Georgia's post-*Furman* capital-sentencing procedures, rejecting the basic contention that "the punishment of death always, regardless of the enormity of the offense or the procedure followed in imposing the sentence, is cruel and unusual punishment in violation of the Constitution." STEWART, J., who announced the judgment of the Court and an opinion joined by Powell and Stevens, JJ., concluded that "the concerns expressed in *Furman* that the penalty of death not be imposed in an arbitrary or capricious manner can be met by a carefully drafted statute that ensures that the sentencing authority is given adequate information and guidance. As a general proposition these concerns are best met by a system [such as Georgia's] that provides for a bifurcated proceeding at which the sentencing authority is apprised of the information relevant to the imposition of sentence and provided with standards to guide its use of the information."[a]

By contrast with the procedures before the Court in *Furman*, the new Georgia sentencing procedures "focus the jury's attention on the particularized nature of the crime and the particularized characteristics of the individual

j. "The unpopularity of [*Furman*] is attested by the fact that several months later, according to a Gallup Poll, 57 percent of the Nation favored capital punishment, [a 20-year high and] an increase of 7 percent from the figure at about the time of the decision." Levy, fn. g supra, at 419. Since then, support for the death penalty has risen significantly. A decade after *Furman,* more than 70 percent of the general public and almost the same percentage of college freshmen and ABA member lawyers favored continuation of the death penalty. See Streib, *Executions under*

the Post-Furman Capital Punishment Statutes, 15 Rutgers L.J. 443, 483–84 n. 413 (1984); *Special Project: Capital Punishment in 1984,* 69 Corn.L.Rev. 1129, 1131–32 n. 8 (1984).

a. "We do not intend to suggest," added Stewart, J., "that only the above-described procedures would be permissible under *Furman* or that any sentencing system constructed along these general lines would inevitably satisfy the concerns of *Furman,* for each distinct system must be examined on a individual basis."

defendant. While the jury is permitted to consider any aggravating or mitigating circumstances,[b] it must find and identify at least one [of 10 statutory aggravating circumstances [c] beyond a reasonable doubt] before it may impose a penalty of death. In this way the jury's discretion is channelled. No longer can a jury wantonly and freakishly impose the death sentence; it is always circumscribed by the legislative guidelines. In addition, the review function of the Supreme Court of Georgia [which is required to review every death sentence to determine, inter alia, whether it was imposed under the influence of passion or prejudice and whether it is 'excessive or disproportionate to the penalty imposed in similar cases, considering both the crime and the defendant'] affords additional assurance that the concerns that prompted our decision in *Furman* are not present to any significant degree in the Georgia procedure applied here."

At the guilt stage (or guilt trial) of Georgia's bifurcated procedure, the jury found petitioner guilty of two counts of armed robbery and two counts of murder. At the sentencing stage, which took place before the same jury, the judge instructed the jury that it would not be authorized to consider the death penalty unless it first found beyond a reasonable doubt one of these statutorily defined "aggravating circumstances": (1) that murder was committed while the offender was engaged in the commission of "another capital felony," to-wit armed robbery; (2) the offender committed murder "for the purpose of receiving money"; (3) the murder was "outrageously or wantonly vile [in] that it [involved] depravity of the mind." Finding the first two "aggravating circumstances," the jury returned verdicts of death on each count. The Georgia Supreme Court affirmed the convictions. After reviewing the record and comparing the evidence and sentences in similar cases, the court upheld the death sentences for the murders, but vacated the armed robbery sentences on the ground, inter alia, that the death penalty had rarely been imposed in Georgia for that crime. In rejecting petitioner's claim that his death sentence under the Georgia statute constituted "cruel and unusual" punishment, the plurality observed:

"[A]n assessment of contemporary values concerning the infliction of a challenged sanction is relevant to the application of the Eighth Amendment, [but] our cases also make clear that public perceptions of standards of decency with respect to criminal sanctions are not conclusive. A penalty also must accord with 'the dignity of man,' which is the 'basic concept underlying the Eighth Amendment.' *Trop* (plurality opinion). This means, at least, that the punishment not be 'excessive.' When a form of punishment in the abstract [is challenged], the inquiry into 'excessiveness' has two aspects. First, the punishment must not involve the unnecessary and wanton infliction of pain. Second, the punishment must not be grossly out of proportion to the severity of the crime.

b. The plurality pointed out that the jury is not *required* to find any mitigating circumstance in order to make a recommendation of mercy that is binding on the court, "but it must find a *statutory* aggravating circumstance before recommending a sentence of death."

c. Georgia authorized the death penalty for six categories of crime: murder, kidnapping under certain circumstances, rape, treason and aircraft hijacking. The statutory aggravating circumstances for murder include "a prior record of conviction for a capital offense" or "a substantial history of serious assaultive criminal convictions"; commission of the crime against a police officer or fireman while performing his official duties; commission of the crime while engaged in certain other felonies; or commission of an "outrageously or wantonly vile, horrible or inhuman" murder (§ (b)(7)). *Godfrey v. Georgia*, 446 U.S. 420, 100 S.Ct. 1759, 64 L.Ed.2d 398 (1980), held that the Georgia courts had "adopted such a broad and vague construction" of the § (b)(7) aggravating circumstance as to violate the eighth and fourteenth amendments.

"[I]n assessing a punishment selected by a democratically elected legislature against the constitutional measure, we presume its validity. We may not require the legislature to select the least severe penalty possible so long as the penalty selected is not cruelly inhumane or disproportionate to the crime involved. And a heavy burden rests on those who would attack the judgment of the representatives of the people.

"This is true in part because the constitutional test is intertwined with an assessment of contemporary standards and the legislative judgment weighs heavily in ascertaining such standards. [The] deference we owe to the decisions of the state legislatures under our federal system is enhanced where the specification of punishments is concerned, for 'these are peculiarly questions of legislative policy.'

"[Petitioners renew the argument made in *Furman* that 'standards of decency' have evolved to the point where capital punishment no longer can be tolerated, a view accepted only by Justices Brennan and Marshall four years ago], but developments [since] *Furman* have undercut substantially the assumptions upon which [this] argument rested. [It] is now evident that a large proportion of American society continues to regard [capital punishment] as an appropriate and necessary criminal sanction.

"The most marked indication of society's endorsement of the death penalty for murder is the legislative response to *Furman*. The legislatures of at least 35 States have enacted new statutes that provide for the death penalty for at least some crimes that result in the death of another person.[d] And the Congress of the United States, in 1974, enacted a statute providing the death penalty for aircraft piracy that results in death.

"[The] jury also is a significant and reliable objective index of contemporary values because it is so directly involved. [It] may be true that evolving standards have influenced juries in recent decades to be more discriminating in imposing the sentence of death. But the relative infrequency of jury verdicts imposing the death sentence does not indicate rejection of capital punishment per se. Rather, [it] may well reflect the humane feeling that this most irrevocable of sanctions should be reserved for a small number of extreme cases.

"[H]owever, the Eighth Amendment demands more than that a challenged punishment be acceptable to contemporary society. The Court also must ask whether is comports with the basic concept of human dignity at the core of the Amendment. *Trop* (plurality opinion). * * *

"The death penalty is said to serve two principal social purposes: retribution and deterrence of capital crimes by prospective offenders.

"In part, capital punishment is an expression of society's moral outrage at particularly offensive conduct. This function [is] essential in an ordered society that asks its citizens to rely on legal processes rather than self-help to vindicate their wrongs. 'The instinct for retribution is part of the nature of man, and

---

d. But consider Zimring & Hawkins, *Capital Punishment and the Eighth Amendment: Furman and Gregg in Retrospect*, 18 U.C.Davis L.Rev., 927, 950 (1985): The "legislative extravaganza" of post-*Furman* death penalty statutes "is reminiscent of the 'pouring panic of capital statutes' which was a feature of the history of the criminal law in eighteenth-century England. Whatever the social psychology of that development may have been, the post-*Furman* reaction in America would prob-ably be best characterized as a typical frustration-aggression response. Like parallel incidents in school prayer and pornography, legislative backlash was entirely to be expected by anyone familiar with the history of judicial invalidation in this country."

For a useful summary of the post-*Furman* statutes, see Gillers, *Deciding Who Dies*, 129 U.Pa.L.Rev. 1, 13, 101–10 (1980).

channeling that instinct in the administration of criminal justice serves an important purpose in promoting the stability of a society governed by law. When people begin to believe that organized society is unwilling or unable to impose upon criminal offenders the punishment they "deserve," then there are sown the seeds of anarchy—of self-help, vigilante justice, and lynch law.' *Furman* (Stewart, J., concurring). 'Retribution is no longer the dominant objective of the criminal law,' but neither is it a forbidden objective nor one inconsistent with our respect for the dignity of men. * * *

"Statistical attempts to evaluate the death penalty as a deterrent [have] occasioned a great deal of debate. The results simply have been inconclusive.

"[The] value of capital punishment as a deterrent of crime is a complex factual issue the resolution of which properly rests with the legislatures, which can evaluate the results of statistical studies in terms of their own local conditions and with a flexibility of approach that is not available to the courts.[e] Indeed, many of the post-*Furman* statutes reflect just such a responsible effort to define those crimes and those criminals for which capital punishment is most probably an effective deterrent.

"In sum, we cannot say that the judgment of the Georgia legislature that capital punishment may be necessary in some cases is clearly wrong. Considerations of federalism, as well as respect for the ability of a legislature to evaluate, in terms of its particular state the moral consensus concerning the death penalty and its social utility as a sanction, require us to conclude, in the absence of more convincing evidence, that the infliction of death as a punishment for murder is not without justification and thus is not unconstitutionally severe.

"[Georgia's] procedures require the jury to consider the circumstances of the crime and the criminal before it recommends sentence. No longer can a Georgia jury do as Furman's jury did: reach a finding of the defendant's guilt and then, without guidance or direction, decide whether he should live or die. Instead, the jury's attention is directed to the specific circumstances of the crime [and its] attention is focused on the characteristics of the person who committed the crime. [Thus], 'the discretion to be exercised is controlled by clear and objective standards so as to produce non-discriminatory application.'

"[Moreover] to guard further against a situation comparable to that presented in *Furman,* the Supreme Court of Georgia compares each death sentence with the sentences imposed on similarly situated defendants to ensure that the sentence of death in a particular case is not disproportionate. On their face these procedures seem to satisfy the concerns of *Furman.*

"[Petitioner] contends, however, that the changes in the Georgia sentencing procedures are only cosmetic, [focusing] on the opportunities for discretionary action that are inherent in the processing of any murder case under Georgia law. He notes that the state prosecutor has unfettered authority to select those persons whom he wishes to prosecute for a capital offense and to plea bargain with them. Further, at the trial the jury may choose to convict a defendant of a lesser included offense rather than find him guilty of a crime punishable by death, even if the evidence would support a capital verdict. And finally, a defendant who is convicted and sentenced to die may have his sentence commuted by the Governor of the State and the Georgia Board of Pardons and Paroles.[f]

e. But see Black, *Due Process for Death,* 26 Cath.U.L.Rev. 1, 14 (1976): "Now that is nothing but sheer fiction. * * * The law, to be sure, is full of fictions, but a fiction known to go in the face of fact ought to play no part, not the slightest, in deciding whether the state may rightly take a life."

f. For a forceful statement of the view that the post-*Furman* statutes do not effectively

"The existence of these discretionary stages is not determinative of the issues before us. [*Furman*] dealt with the decision to impose the death sentence on a specific individual who had been convicted of a capital offense. Nothing in any of our cases suggests that the decision to afford an individual defendant mercy violates the Constitution. *Furman* held only that, in order to minimize the risk that the death penalty would be imposed on a capriciously selected group of offenders, the decision to impose it had to be guided by standards so that the sentencing authority would focus on the particularized circumstances of the crime and the defendant.[50] "

WHITE, J., joined by Burger, C.J., and Rehnquist, J., concurred in the judgment: "Petitioner's argument that there is an unconstitutional amount of discretion in the system which separates those suspects who receive the death penalty from those who receive life imprisonment, a lesser penalty, or are acquitted or never charged, seems to be in final analysis an indictment of our entire system of justice. Petitioner has argued, in effect, that no matter how effective the death penalty may be as a punishment, government, created and run as it must be by humans, is inevitably incompetent to administer it. This cannot be accepted as a proposition of constitutional law. [I] decline to interfere with the manner in which Georgia has chosen to enforce [the death penalty] on what is simply an assertion of lack of faith in the ability of the system of justice to operate in a fundamentally fair manner." [g]

BRENNAN, J., dissented: "In *Furman,* I read 'evolving standards of decency' as requiring focus upon the essence of the death penalty itself and not primarily or solely upon the procedures under which the determination to inflict the penalty upon a particular person was made. [That] continues to be my view."

MARSHALL, J., also dissented: "Since the decision in *Furman,* the legislatures of 35 States have enacted new statutes authorizing the imposition of the death sentence for certain crimes, and Congress has enacted a law providing the death penalty for air piracy resulting in death. I would be less than candid if I did not acknowledge that these developments have a significant bearing on a realistic assessment of the moral acceptability of the death penalty to the American people. But if the constitutionality of the death penalty turns, as I have urged, on the opinion of an *informed* citizenry, then even the enactment of new death statutes cannot be viewed as conclusive. * * *

restrict jury discretion by any real standards and that capital sentencing statutes "never will"—"no society is going to kill everybody who meets certain present verbal requirements"—see Black, *Capital Punishment: The Inevitability of Caprice and Mistake* 67–68 (1974).

50. The petitioner's argument is nothing more than a veiled contention that *Furman* indirectly outlawed capital punishment by placing totally unrealistic conditions on its use. In order to repair the alleged defects pointed to by the petitioner, it would be necessary to require that prosecuting authorities charge a capital offense whenever arguably there had been a capital murder and that they refuse to plea bargain with the defendant. If a jury refused to convict even though the evidence supported the charge, its verdict would have to be reversed and a verdict of guilty entered or a new trial ordered, since

the discretionary act of jury nullification would not be permitted. Finally, acts of executive clemency would have to be prohibited. Such a system, of course, would be totally alien to our notions of criminal justice.

Moreover, it would be unconstitutional. Such a system in many respects would have the vices of the mandatory death penalty statutes we hold unconstitutional today in *Woodson* and *Stanislaus Roberts* [infra].

g. For the reasons stated in dissent in *Stanislaus Roberts,* infra, White, J., also disagreed with petitioner's "other basic argument that the death penalty, however imposed and for whatever crime, is cruel and unusual punishment."

Blackmun, J., concurred in the judgment, referring solely to his dissenting opinion in *Furman.*

"Even assuming however, that the post-*Furman* enactment of statutes authorizing the death penalty renders the prediction of the views of an informed citizenry an uncertain basis for a constitutional decision, the enactment of those statutes has no bearing whatsoever on the conclusion that the death penalty is unconstitutional because it is excessive. An excessive penalty is invalid under the Cruel and Unusual Punishments Clause 'even though popular sentiment may favor' [it.]

"The two purposes that sustain the death penalty as nonexcessive in the Court's view are general deterrence and retribution. [The] evidence I reviewed in *Furman* remains convincing, in my view, that 'capital punishment is not necessary as a deterrent to crime in our society.' The justification for the death penalty must be found elsewhere.

"[The plurality's view of the important purpose served by 'channeling' 'the instinct for retribution' in the administration of criminal justice] is wholly inadequate to justify the death penalty. [It] simply defies belief to suggest that the death penalty is necessary to prevent the American people from taking the law into their own hands.

"[The contention] that the expression of moral outrage through the imposition of the death penalty serves to reinforce basic moral values [also] provides no support for the death penalty. It is inconceivable that any individual concerned about conforming his conduct to what society says is 'right' would fail to realize that murder is 'wrong' if the penalty were simply life imprisonment. * * *

"There remains for consideration, however, what might be termed the purely retributive justification for the death penalty—that the death penalty is appropriate, not because of its beneficial effect on society, but because the taking of the murderer's life is itself morally good. Some of the language of the plurality's opinion appears positively to embrace this notion of retribution for its own sake as a justification for capital punishment.

"[T]hat society's judgment that the murderer 'deserves' death must be respected not simply because the preservation of order requires it, but because it is appropriate that society make the judgment and carry it out [is a notion] fundamentally at odds with the Eighth Amendment. The mere fact that the community demands the murderer's life in return for the evil he has done cannot sustain the death penalty, for as the plurality reminds us, 'the Eighth Amendment demands more than that a challenged punishment be acceptable to contemporary society.' [Under appropriate Eighth Amendment] standards, the taking of life 'because the wrong-doer deserves it' surely must fall, for such a punishment has as its very basis the total denial of the wrong-doer's dignity and worth."

Notes and Questions

1. *The Texas statute upheld in Jurek: predictions of future violence.* In companion cases to *Gregg*, dividing the same way, the Court upheld the constitutionality of two other state capital-sentencing procedures which, it concluded, essentially resembled the Georgia system. *Proffitt v. Florida*, 428 U.S. 242, 96 S.Ct. 2960, 49 L.Ed.2d 913 (1976); *Jurek v. Texas*, 428 U.S. 262, 96 S.Ct. 2950, 49 L.Ed.2d 929 (1976). For forceful criticism of *Jurek* and for the view that the Texas statute is "much worse than either the Georgia or the Florida statutes, bad as they are," see Black, *Due Process for Death*, 26 Cath.U.L.Rev. 1, 2 (1976). See also 90 Harv.L.Rev. 71–75 (1976).

Under the Texas capital sentencing procedure, the key question a jury must answer in the affirmative for the death penalty to be imposed is "whether there is a probability that the defendant would commit criminal acts of violence that would constitute a continuing threat to society." This, maintains Black, supra, at 4–6, "is a phrase composed of hopelessly vague terms. 'Criminal' as a blow with the fist is criminal? 'Violent' as such a blow is violent? A 'threat' of what? 'To society' in what sense, since the person is to be in prison, under whatever restraints the state finds necessary, and need not be released until the state is satisfied [that] he is not a threat to society?"

Consider Gillers, *The Quality of Mercy: Constitutional Accuracy at the Selection Stage of Capital Sentencing*, 18 U.C.Davis 1037, 1099–1100 (1985): "Surely, our faith in predictive accuracy is not strong enough to rest a death sentence on the anticipated inadequacy of solitary confinement for particular defendants or on conjecture about their powers of escape, at least not without some proof. Yet if social or medical scientists believe that this projection can be made with confidence, they have so far chosen to remain silent. Does the availability of the less harsh, apparently adequate response of solitary confinement exclude incapacitation as a justification for execution? * * * Assuming [that] the answer is no, *Jurek* also failed to discuss whether a death penalty statute must offer the sentencer the less extreme option of greatly restrictive confinement before the sentencer may conclude that incapacitation demands nothing less than execution."

2. *Gregg, Jurek* and *Proffitt* reached the question reserved in *Furman* — "the constitutionality of capital punishment in the abstract"—and upheld it. But consider Black, *Reflections on Opposing the Penalty of Death*, 10 St. Mary's L.J. 1, 7 (1978): "[T]he *only* question that actually confronts us [is] whether it is right to kill such people as are chosen by our system as it stands. [I]t doesn't really make any difference at all what I think about the abstract rightness of capital punishment. There exists no abstract capital punishment." See also Amsterdam, *Capital Punishment*, in Bedau, *The Death Penalty in America* 346, 349–51 (3rd ed. 1982); Black, *The Death Penalty Now*, 51 Tul.L.Rev. 429, 445 (1977).

II. MANDATORY DEATH SENTENCES

Unlike Georgia, Florida and Texas, whose new capital-sentencing procedures were designed to guide and to channel sentencing authority, 10 states responded to *Furman* by replacing discretionary jury sentencing in capital cases with *mandatory death penalties.* North Carolina did so for a broad range of murders; Louisiana did so for five categories of murder. These mandatory death statutes were invalidated in WOODSON v. NORTH CAROLINA, 428 U.S. 280, 96 S.Ct. 2978, 49 L.Ed.2d 944 (1976) and STANISLAUS ROBERTS v. LOUISIANA,[a] 429 U.S. 325, 96 S.Ct. 3001, 49 L.Ed.2d 974 (1976), both decided the same day as *Gregg.*

STEWART, J., announced the judgment in *Woodson* and an opinion joined by Powell and Stevens, JJ. The history of mandatory death penalty statutes in this country, he observed, reveals that the practice "has been rejected as unduly harsh and unworkably rigid. The two crucial indicators of evolving standards of

a. The plurality, per Stewart, J., noted in *Woodson* that "[t]his case does not involve a mandatory death penalty statute limited to an extremely narrow category of murder, such as murder by a prisoner serving a life sentence, defined in large part in terms of the character or record of the offender. We thus express no opinion regarding the constitutionality of such a statute."

decency respecting the imposition of punishment in our society—jury determination and legislative enactments—both point conclusively to the repudiation of automatic death sentences." He dismissed the post-*Furman* enactments as merely "attempts [to] retain the death penalty in a form consistent with the Constitution, rather than a renewed social acceptance of mandatory death sentencing."

"A separate deficiency" of the North Carolina statute was its failure to respond adequately to "*Furman's* rejection of unbridled jury discretion in the imposition of capital sentences." In light of the widespread and persistent jury resistance to mandatory death penalties—and the high probability that many juries, despite their oaths, would exercise discretion in deciding which murderers "shall live and which shall die" under these "mandatory" statutes—North Carolina had not remedied "the problem of unguided and unchecked jury discretion" that was "central to the limited holding in *Furman,*" but "simply papered over" it. Not only does North Carolina's mandatory death penalty statute provide "no standards to guide the jury in its inevitable exercise" of discretion, but "there is no way under [state law] for the judiciary to check arbitrary and capricious exercise of that power through a review of death sentences. Instead of rationalizing the sentencing process, a mandatory scheme may well exacerbate the problem identified in *Furman* by resting the penalty determination on the particular jury's willingness to act lawlessly."

"A third constitutional shortcoming of the North Carolina statute is its failure to allow the particularized consideration of relevant aspects of the character and record of each convicted defendant before the imposition upon him of a sentence of death. [D]eath is a punishment different from all other sanctions in kind rather than degree. A process that accords no significance to relevant facets of the character and record of the individual offender or the circumstances of the particular offense excludes from consideration in fixing the ultimate punishment of death the possibility of compassionate or mitigating factors stemming from the diverse frailties of humankind. It treats all persons convicted of a designated offense not as uniquely individual human beings, but as members of a faceless, undifferentiated mass to be subjected to the blind infliction of the penalty of death." [b]

Dissenting, REHNQUIST, J., rejected the view that the 10 post-*Furman* mandatory death statutes merely represented "a wrong-headed reading [of] *Furman*. While those States may be presumed to have preferred their prior systems reposing sentencing discretion in juries or judges, they indisputably preferred mandatory capital punishment to no capital punishment at all. Their willingness to enact statutes providing that penalty is utterly inconsistent with the notion that they regarded mandatory capital sentencing as beyond 'evolving standards of decency.' "

"The Court's insistence on 'standards' to 'guide the jury in its inevitable exercise of the power to decide which murderer shall live and which shall die,' is squarely contrary [to the *McGautha* opinion], authorized by Justice Harlan and subscribed to by five other [justices] only five years ago. So is [the Court's claim] that *Furman* requires 'objective standards to guide, regularize, and make rationally reviewable the process for imposing a sentence of death.' "

"[What] the plurality opinion has actually done is to import into the Due Process Clause [what] it conceives to be desirable procedural guarantees where

---

b. For the reasons stated in their *Gregg* dissents, Brennan and Marshall, JJ., concurred in both *Woodson* and *Stanislaus Roberts,* infra.

the punishment of death, concededly not cruel and unusual for the crime of which the defendant was convicted, is to be imposed. This is squarely contrary to *McGautha,* and unsupported by any other decision of this Court." [c]

Dissenting in *Stanislaus Roberts* (which invalidated a Louisiana mandatory death sentence statute the *Woodson* plurality deemed fatally similar to North Carolina's), WHITE, J., joined by Burger, C.J., and Blackmun and Rehnquist, JJ., maintained: "As the plurality now interprets the Eighth Amendment, the Louisiana and North Carolina statutes are infirm because the jury is deprived of all discretion once it finds the defendant guilty. Yet in the next breath it invalidates these statutes because they are said to invite or allow too much discretion: despite their instructions, when they feel that defendants do not deserve to die, juries will so often and systematically disobey their instructions and find the defendant not guilty or guilty of a noncapital offense that the statute fails to satisfy the standards of *Furman.* If it is truly the case that Louisiana juries will exercise *too much* discretion—and I do not agree that it is— then it seems strange indeed that the statute is also invalidated because it purports to give the jury *too little* discretion by making the death penalty mandatory. Furthermore, if there is danger of freakish and too infrequent imposition of capital punishment under a mandatory system such as Louisiana's, there is very little ground for believing that juries will be any more faithful to their instructions under the Georgia and Florida systems where the opportunity is much, much greater for juries to practice their own brand of unbridled discretion.

"[The Louisiana and North Carolina] legislatures have not deemed mandatory punishment, once the crime is proven, to be unacceptable; nor have their juries rejected it, for the death penalty has been imposed with some regularity. Perhaps we would prefer that these States had adopted a different system, but the issue is not our individual preferences but the constitutionality of the mandatory systems chosen by these two States. I see no warrant under the Eighth Amendment for refusing to uphold these statutes.

"[I]n *Gregg,* [the plurality] lectures us at length about the role and place of the judiciary and then proceeds to ignore its own advice, the net effect being to suggest that observers of this institution should pay more attention to what we do than what we say. The plurality claims that it has not forgotten what the past has taught about the limits of judicial review; but I fear that it has again surrendered to the temptation to make policy for and to attempt to govern the country through a misuse of the powers given this Court under the Constitution." [d]

Notes and Questions

1. *Gregg and the "mandatory death" cases.* Are *Gregg* and *Woodson* and *Roberts,* handed down the same day, reconcilable? The *Woodson* plurality points out that "instead of rationalizing the sentencing process, a mandatory scheme may well exacerbate the problem identified in *Furman* by resting the penalty determination on the particular jury's willingness to act lawlessly." But are not "these lawless juries, whose lawlessness will taint and bend a mandatory

---

c. White, J., joined by Burger, C.J., and Rehnquist, J., also dissented, rejecting the Court's analysis for the reasons stated in his dissent in *Stanislaus Roberts,* infra. Blackmun, J., also dissented in *Woodson* for the reasons stated in his *Furman* dissent. All four *Woodson* dissenters also dissented in *Roberts.*

d. Burger, C.J., and Blackmun, J., also dissented separately for the reasons set forth in their *Furman* dissents.

system," the very same juries who are supposed "to follow with patient care the intricacies of the Georgia and Florida statutes [upheld the same day in *Gregg* and *Proffitt*], and the unfathomed mysteries of the Texas statute [upheld the same day in *Jurek*], and base these answers on nothing but sound discretion guided by law"? What reason is there to think that juries "will manipulate frankly mandatory statutes, in order to produce a result seen as equitable," but "not manipulate, to the same ends, a scheme relatively sophisticated—but far from being beyond easy comprehension by people fitted to be on juries at all—such as the scheme in [Texas or Georgia] or many other states"? See Black, *Due Process for Death*, 26 Cath.U.L.Rev. 1, 10 (1976); Black, *The Death Penalty Now*, 51 Tul.L.Rev. 429, 441 (1977). See also Bedau, *Are Mandatory Capital Statutes Unconstitutional?*, in *The Courts, the Constitution, and Capital Punishment* 106 (1977).

2. HARRY ROBERTS v. LOUISIANA, 431 U.S. 633, 97 S.Ct. 1993, 52 L.Ed. 2d 637 (1977) (per curiam) held that the imposition of a mandatory death penalty for the intentional killing of a police officer "engaged in the performance of his lawful duties" constitutes cruel and unusual punishment. Although "the fact that the murder victim was a peace officer may be regarded as an aggravating circumstance," "it is incorrect to suppose that no mitigating circumstances can exist [in such a case]. [T]he youth of the offender, the absence of any prior conviction, [and] the influence of drugs, alcohol or extreme emotional disturbance [are] examples of mitigating facts which might attend the killing of a peace officer and which are considered relevant in other jurisdictions. As we emphasized repeatedly in *Stanislaus Roberts,* [it] is essential that the capital sentencing decision allow for consideration of whatever mitigating circumstances may be relevant to either the particular offender or the particular offense."

REHNQUIST, J., joined by White, J., dissenting, protested that the Court's holding "would have shocked those who drafted the Bill of Rights" and "would commend itself only to the most imaginative observer as being required by today's 'evolving standards of decency' ": "I [remain unpersuaded] that a mandatory death sentence for all, let alone for a limited class of persons, who commit premeditated murder constitutes 'cruel and unusual punishment.' [But] even were I now persuaded otherwise [I would still] disagree with today's decision.[1]

"[The Court] has asked the wrong question. The question is not whether mitigating factors might *exist* [in the case of an intentional murder of an officer], but, rather, whether whatever 'mitigating' factors that might exist are of sufficient *force* so as to constitutionally require their consideration as counterweights to the admitted aggravating circumstance. Like Mr. Justice White [dissenting in *Stanislaus Roberts*], I am unable to believe that a State is not entitled to determine that the premeditated murder of a peace officer is so heinous and intolerable a crime that no combination of mitigating factors can

---

1. In *Woodson,* the plurality noted that a public opinion poll "revealed that a 'substantial majority' of persons opposed mandatory capital punishment." It does not follow, even accepting that poll, that a "substantial majority" oppose mandatory capital punishment for the murderers of police officers. What meager statistics there are indicate that public opinion is at best pretty evenly divided on the subject [referring to various polls and surveys]. With such substantial public support [for mandatory capital punishment for murderers of officers], one would have thought that the determination as to whether a mandatory death penalty should exist was for the legislature, not for the judiciary through some newfound construction of the term "cruel and unusual punishment."
* * *

overcome the demonstration 'that the criminal's character is such that he deserves death.' "

III. OTHER CONSTITUTIONAL CHALLENGES

COKER v. GEORGIA, 433 U.S. 584, 97 S.Ct. 2861, 53 L.Ed.2d 982 (1977): While serving life terms for murder, rape and kidnapping (all capital felonies) and another sentence for aggravated assault, petitioner escaped and raped and abducted an adult woman (after robbing and tying up her husband). After his conviction for rape and other offenses, petitioner was sentenced to death when the jury found two of the statutory aggravating circumstances present: the rape was (i) by a person with a prior capital felony conviction and (ii) in the course of another capital felony, armed robbery of the husband. (The jury was instructed that even if aggravating circumstances were present, the death penalty need not be imposed if it found they were outweighed by mitigating circumstances.) The Court invalidated the death sentence. The principal opinion was written by WHITE, J., joined by Stewart, Blackmun and Stevens, JJ.,[a] who concluded that death is a "grossly disproportionate and excessive punishment" for raping an adult woman and therefore forbidden by the Eighth Amendment:

"At no time in the last 50 years has a majority of the States authorized death as a punishment for rape [and] none of the [34] States that had not previously authorized death for rape [changed its position after *Furman*]. Of the 16 States in which rape had been a capital offense only three provided for rape of an adult woman in their [post-*Furman*] statutes—Georgia, North Carolina, and Louisiana. In the latter two States, the death penalty was mandatory and those laws were invalidated by *Woodson* and *Stanislaus Roberts*. [Louisiana and North Carolina then] reenacted the death penalty for murder but not for rape. [Thus,] Georgia is the sole [American] jurisdiction [that presently] authorizes a sentence of death when the rape victim is an adult woman.[b] [Moreover, in] the vast majority of [rape] cases, at least nine out of 10, [Georgia juries] have not imposed the death sentence. * * *

"Rape is without doubt deserving of serious punishment; but in terms of moral depravity and of the injury to the person and to the public, it does not compare with murder, which does involve the unjustified taking of human life. [Rape] does not include the death or even the serious injury to [another]. Life is over for the [murder victim]; for the rape victim, life may not be nearly so happy as it was, but it is not over and normally is not beyond repair. We have the abiding conviction that the death penalty, which 'is unique in its severity and revocability,' is an excessive penalty for the rapist who, as such, does not take human life.

a. Brennan and Marshall, JJ., concurred in the judgment, adhering to their view that the death penalty is in all circumstances cruel and unusual punishment. Powell, J., concurred in the judgment "on the facts of this case, and also in its reasoning supporting the view that ordinarily death is a disproportionate punishment for the crime of raping an adult woman, [i.e., when, as here,] there is no indication that petitioner's offense was committed with excessive brutality or that the victim sustained serious or lasting injury." But he dissented from what he regarded as the plurality's unnecessarily broad holding

that "capital punishment *always*—regardless of the circumstances—is a disproportionate penalty for the crime of rape. [I]t may be that the death penalty is not disproportionate punishment for the crime of aggravated rape."

b. The Court noted that two other jurisdictions, Florida and Mississippi, provide capital punishment when the rape victim is a child. Tennessee had also authorized the death penalty in some circumstances when the victim was a child, but its statute had been invalidated because the death penalty was mandatory.

"This does not end the matter; for under Georgia law, death may not be imposed [unless] the jury finds one of the statutory aggravating circumstances and then elects to impose that sentence. [But neither of the aggravating circumstances found in the present case], nor both of them together, change our conclusion that [Coker's sentence] is a disproportionate punishment for rape. [Coker's prior capital felony convictions] do not change the fact that the instant crime being punished is a rape not involving the taking of life."

BURGER, C.J., joined by Rehnquist, J., dissenting, protested that the Court's holding prevents the imposition of "any effective punishment upon Coker for his latest rape" and "bars Georgia from guaranteeing its citizens that they will suffer no further attacks from this habitual rapist.[c]   *   *   *

"Unlike the Court, I would narrow the inquiry in this case to the question actually presented: Does the Eighth Amendment's ban against cruel and unusual punishment prohibit [a state] from executing a person who has, within the space of three years, raped three separate women, killing one and attempting to kill another, who is serving prison terms exceeding his probable lifetime and who has not hesitated to escape confinement at the first available opportunity? Whatever one's view may be as to the State's constitutional power to impose the death penalty upon a rapist who stands before a court convicted for the first time, this case reveals a chronic rapist whose continuing danger to the community is abundantly clear. [T]he Eighth Amendment does not prevent the State from taking an individual's 'well-demonstrated propensity for life-endangering behavior'[d] into account in devising punitive measures which will prevent inflicting further harm upon innocent victims.

"[I]t is myopic to base sweeping constitutional principles upon the narrow experience of the past five years. [L]egislatures were left in serious doubt [by *Furman*] as to whether this Court would sustain *any* statute imposing death as a criminal sanction. Failure of more States to enact statutes imposing death for rape of an adult woman may thus reflect hasty legislative compromise occasioned by time pressures following *Furman,* a desire to wait on the experience of those States which did enact such statutes, or simply an accurate forecast of today's holding.[e] "

Notes and Questions

1. Was the question raised by *Coker* whether the eighth amendment prohibits the death penalty for rape or whether the death penalty is "so irrational as to offend due process, an issue that exists quite independently [of] the eighth amendment"? See Packer, fn. d supra at 1074.

2. Coker's prior convictions for capital felonies, stated the *Coker* plurality, "do not change the fact that the instant crime being punished is a rape not involving the taking of life." Why not? Realistically, when a prior capital felony conviction is made an aggravating circumstance in the punishment for

---

c. In 1971 Coker raped and murdered a young woman. Less than 8 months later, he kidnapped, raped and severely beat a 16-year-old woman, leaving her for dead in a wooded area. In 1974, he escaped from the state prison and promptly raped another 16-year-old, for which the death sentence under review was imposed.

d. At this point, the dissent is quoting from Packer, *Making the Punishment Fit the*

Crime, 77 Harv.L.Rev. 1071, 1080 (1964): "A well-demonstrated propensity for life-endangering behavior is thought to provide a more solid basis for infliction of the most severe measures of incapacitation than does the fortuity of a single homicidal incident."

e. See also Note, 78 Colum.L.Rev. 1714, 1718 (1979).

rape, isn't the offender being punished *in part* for rape and *in part* for the earlier capital felony? If, as a number of states provide, capital punishment may be based on a murder committed *after* a conviction for rape and a murder *in the course of* committing a rape, does barring capital punishment for a rape committed after a conviction for murder "make the acceptable level of punishment turn on fortuities of timing in the commission of offenses"? See Note, 78 Colum.L. Rev. 1714, 1724–25 (1978).

3.   After *Coker,* would the Court sustain the death penalty for treason? Would the absence of a death "directly traceable" to the treasonous activity render the death penalty disproportionate to the crime or would treason be viewed as "a crime against masses of people [causing] more aggregate harm than a single murder"? See 91 Harv.L.Rev. 124, 128 (1977). See also Note, 78 Colum. L.Rev. 1714, 1729 (1979) (discussion of death penalty for hijacking).

4.   Was it (should it have been) crucial that only three post-*Furman* statutes made rape a capital offense? The Court gave little weight to legislative enactments in *Roe v. Wade,* which invalidated a Texas abortion statute despite the fact that most states had enacted similar laws. Isn't "[a] defendant's right to life [at] least as fundamental as the mother's right of privacy"? See 91 Harv.L.Rev. 124 n. 127 (1977).

5.   None of the opinions in *Coker* makes any mention of the "racial factor" in the administration of the death penalty for rape. Should the Court have explicitly discussed this factor? Despite the Court's silence on this matter, to what extent was it nevertheless influenced by it? Bedau, *The Death Penalty in America* 188 (3d ed. 1982), calls rape "the most dramatic type of case in which we can see how the racist heritage of our society made the death penalty fall with disproportionate and unfair frequency on nonwhite offenders. [T]he best explanation for the pattern of death sentences for rape in the South [a] is the race of the (black) offender and of the (white) victim." The mid-1960's constitutional assault on the death penalty "began with a campaign to eliminate the discriminatory application of the death penalty for rape. Between 1930 and the present, of the 455 persons executed for rape, 405 were black and two were members of other minorities. Almost 90% of those executed were black men convicted for the rape of white women." Greenberg, *Capital Punishment as a System,* 91 Yale L.J. 908, 912 (1982). See also Meltsner, *Cruel and Unusual* 75–77 (1973).

SECTION 4.   PROCEDURAL DUE PROCESS IN NON–CRIMINAL CASES

I.   DEPRIVATION OF "LIBERTY" AND "PROPERTY" INTERESTS

"When a litigant is adversely affected entirely as a predictable consequence of procedural grossness and not as a consequence of ulterior design by government (or by its agents) to utilize constitutionally impermissible substantive standards, he is in serious difficulty. The essence of his complaint is to the felt unfairness of procedural grossness itself—that it builds in such a large margin of probable mistake as itself to be intolerable in a humane society. [But] *unlike* his freedom [of expression and religion] (sheltered by the first amendment), and

---

a. Since 1930, all of the executions for rape were in southern or border states or the District of Columbia. In ten of these states and the District of Columbia, 137 blacks were executed for rape since 1930, but only five whites. See Wolfgang & Riedel, *Race, Judicial Discretion, and the Death Penalty,* 407 Annals 119 (1973).

unlike his entitlement to privacy (sheltered by the fourth and fifth amendments), [the litigant] cannot anchor a claim to freedom from procedural grossness per se in any clause of the Constitution.

"He cannot rely upon the equal protection clause, for we are here dealing with situations in which all similarly situated persons are uniformly subject to the same degree of procedural grossness * * *. Nor can one say (as doubtless is one's first impulse) that the individual's entitlement to 'due' process is obviously anchored in the very clauses sheltering due process. The difficulty is that such reasoning (ironically akin to the reasoning that created the right-privilege distinction) must imagine a clause *which in fact is not there*. It imagines that the fourteenth amendment (or the same phrase in the fifth amendment) provides something like this: 'No State [shall] deprive any person of life, liberty, property, or of due process of law, without due process of law * * *.' Alternatively, it imagines that the next clause of the fourteenth amendment provides something like this '[Nor shall any State] deny to any person [either] due process of law or the equal protection of the laws.'

"[But as the amendments] read in fact, due process is not itself a protected entitlement. [It] stands in relation to ['life, liberty, [and] property'] not as an equivalent constitutionally established entitlement, but only as a condition to be observed insofar as the state may move to imperil one of the named [interests]. [P]rocedural due process appears never to be anything more than a kind of 'constitutional condition.' It is evidently not a free standing human interest."

—Van Alstyne, *Cracks in "The New Property": Adjudicative Due Process in the Administrative State,* 62 Corn.L.Rev. 445, 450–52 (1977).[a]

---

a. But Professor Van Alstyne goes on to say, id. at 487, that "it is plausible [to] treat *freedom from arbitrary adjudicative procedures* as a substantive element of one's liberty"—"a freedom whose abridgement government must sustain the burden of justifying, even as it must do when it seeks to subordinate other freedoms, such as those of speech and privacy"—"that the protected essences of personal freedom include a freedom from fundamentally unfair modes of governmental action, an immunity (if you will) from procedural arbitrariness." Simon, *Liberty and Property in the Supreme Court: A Defense of Roth and Perry,* 71 Calif.L.Rev. 146, 186 (1983) is not persuaded: "At bottom, Van Alstyne's position seems to be that procedural protection, like Beauty, 'is its own excuse for being.' * * * Procedures are important, not for themselves and not as symbols of the perfect society, but only as a means of protecting matters of value. These matters of value are not the procedures themselves, but the interests which they protect. If there is no sufficiently valuable right at stake, as the Court determined there was not in [*Board of Regents v. Roth,* infra], procedures by themselves are not valuable." See also Smolla, *The Reemergency of the Right-Privilege Distinction in Constitutional Law,* 35 Stan.L.Rev. 69, 85–86 (1982); Williams, *Liberty and Property: The Problem of Government Benefit,* 12 J.Legal Stud. 3, 17–19 (1983).

Compare Van Alstyne, supra, with Ely, *Democracy and Distrust* 19 (1980), maintaining that the phrase "life, liberty or property" used to be, and ought to be, "read as a unit and given an open-ended, functional interpretation," meaning that the government cannot *"seriously hurt* you without due process of law" (emphasis added). But consider Terrell, *"Property," "Due Process," and the Distinction Between Definition and Theory in Legal Analysis,* 70 Geo.L.J. 861, 899–900 (1982): "[I]f the phrase seriously hurt [has] discoverable substance, then its content necessarily would develop [judicially] in the same manner that the substance of 'life, liberty, or property' has developed. [The] analysis would raise the same sort of questions previously raised about property: what is the definition of 'seriously hurt'? [And] why do we use this phrase rather than one which is more restrictive, such as 'extremely seriously hurt,' or less restrictive, such as 'slightly hurt'? That is, what is the justificatory theory for Ely's substitute phrase?

"This analysis indicates that Ely's objection to the Court's treatment of 'life, liberty, or property' is based on an apparent belief that the Court should not engage in a definitional exercise at all. In effect, he argues that the purpose of the due process clause is to protect citizens from government arbitrariness, and, therefore, that these terms should relate solely to that justification. [Ely] recognizes by his

1. According to most commentators, the "procedural due process revolution" began with GOLDBERG v. KELLY, 397 U.S. 254, 90 S.Ct. 1011, 25 L.Ed.2d 287 (1970), holding that due process requires that welfare recipients be afforded an evidentiary hearing *prior* to the termination of benefits. As pointed out in Simon, fn. a supra, at 150, *Goldberg* "did not in fact present the issue of whether welfare benefits were within the 'life, liberty or property' protected by the due process clauses, because [the Social Services Commissioner] conceded that 'the protections of the due process clause apply.' [b] Nevertheless, [the Court] addressed this issue [suggesting] that whether the right to continue receiving a government benefit was within the protection of the due process clause turned upon the importance of the benefit to the individual." Thus, the Court, per BRENNAN, J., observed:

"[Welfare] benefits are a matter of statutory entitlement for persons qualified to receive them.[c] Their termination involves state action that adjudicates important rights. The constitutional challenge cannot be answered by an argument that public assistance benefits are 'a "privilege" and not a "right." ' Relevant constitutional restraints apply as much to the withdrawal of public assistance benefits as to disqualification for unemployment compensation or to denial of a tax exemption or to discharge from public employment. The extent to which procedural due process must be afforded the recipient is influenced by the extent to which he may be 'condemned to suffer grievous loss,' and depends upon whether the recipient's interest in avoiding the loss outweighs the governmental interest in summary adjudication."

2. As observed in Monaghan, *Of "Liberty" and "Property,"* 62 Corn.L.Rev. 401, 407 (1977), BELL v. BURSON, 402 U.S. 535, 91 S.Ct. 1586, 29 L.Ed.2d 90 (1971), "represented the high-water mark of [the] approach [that] whether an interest deserved due process clause process protection involved a simple pragmatic assessment of its 'importance' to the individual." The Court, per BRENNAN, J., invalidated a Georgia statute providing that the vehicle registration and driver's license of an uninsured motorist involved in an accident shall be suspended unless he posts security to cover the damages claimed by agreed parties in accident reports: "[Although a state could bar] the issuance of licenses to all motorists who did not carry liability insurance [or] post security, [o]nce licenses are issued, as in petitioner's case [a clergyman whose ministry requires him to cover three rural communities by car], their continued possession may become *essential* in the pursuit of a livelihood. Suspension of issued licenses thus involves state action that adjudicates *important interests* of the licensees. In such cases the licenses are not to be taken away without that procedural due process required by the Fourteenth Amendment." (Emphasis added.)

use of the phrase seriously hurt the need for a trigger mechanism that must precede any due process inquiry. Yet if arbitrariness is the evil to avoid, why have any preliminary obstacle to judicial scrutiny, much less the one he has rather casually identified?"

b. "[W]hile there were three dissents in *Goldberg* respecting the *fullness* of the procedure that government would be required to observe before terminating an allegedly ineligible welfare recipient, no one (not even the government itself, as Justice Brennan observed) dissented from the proposition that the due process clause was applicable to the case." Van Alstyne 456.

c. At this point, the Court noted [fn. 8] that "[i]t may be more realistic today to regard welfare entitlements as more like 'property' than a 'gratuity,' " citing Reich, *The New Property*, 73 Yale L.J. 733 (1964), and quoting extensively from Reich, *Individual Rights and Social Welfare: The Emerging Social Issues*, 74 Yale L.J. 1245 (1965). In these articles Professor Reich maintained that public employment, welfare assistance, franchises, licenses and other forms of governmental largess should be given the kind of protection afforded traditional property rights.

Bell "eschewed a tight, textually-oriented examination of the interests secured by the due process clause. [It] could have said that the license was sufficient to qualify as 'property,' or that a suspension of an individual's freedom to drive was a restriction on his 'liberty.' The Court said neither; the importance of the interest alone sufficed, and 'importance' was determined as a matter of federal, not state, law." Monaghan 407–08.

3. But "*Bell's* latitudinarian approach to 'liberty' and 'property,'" Monaghan 408, did not prevail. Stressing that before deciding what form of hearing is required by procedural due process the Court must "determine whether due process requirements apply in the first place," i.e., whether one has been deprived of "liberty" or "property"—and in doing so "we must look not to the 'weight' but to the nature of the interest at stake"—BOARD OF REGENTS v. ROTH, 408 U.S. 564, 92 S.Ct. 2701, 33 L.Ed.2d 548 (1972), per STEWART, J., for the first time, rejected a procedural due process claim because it implicated neither "liberty" nor "property." Hired by Wisconsin State University for a fixed term of one year, and given no tenure rights to continued employment, Roth had been informed that he would not be rehired for the next academic year. The Court rejected his contention that the University's failure to give him any reason for its decision or any opportunity to challenge it at any sort of hearing violated procedural due process: "The requirements of procedural due process apply only to the deprivation of interests encompassed within the Fourteenth Amendment's protection of liberty and property. When protected interests are implicated, the right to some kind of prior hearing is paramount. But the range of interests protected by procedural due process is not infinite.

"[The] State, in declining to rehire [Roth], did not make any charge against him that might seriously damage his standing and associations in his community [e.g., accuse him of dishonesty or immorality,] [a] [nor] impose on him a stigma or other disability that foreclosed his freedom to take advantage of other employment opportunities. [It did not, for example, bar him] from all other public employment in State universities.[b] [O]n the record before us,[c] all that clearly appears is that [Roth] was not rehired for one year at one University. It stretches the concept too far to suggest that [one] is deprived of 'liberty' when he simply is not rehired in one job but remains as free as before to seek another.

"[As for 'property' interests protected by procedural due process, to] have a property interest in a benefit, [one] must have more than a unilateral expecta-

---

a. "Had it done so," noted the Court, "this would be a different case. For '[w]here a person's good name, reputation, honor, or integrity is at stake because of what the government is doing to him, notice and an opportunity to be heard are essential.' *Wisconsin v. Constantineau,* 400 U.S. 433, 91 S.Ct. 507, 27 L.Ed.2d 515 (1971)." *Constantineau* (Burger, C.J., and Black and Blackmun, JJ., dissenting on procedural grounds), invalidated on due process grounds a state law providing that when, by "excessive drinking," one produces certain conditions or exhibits certain traits (e.g., exposing himself or family "to want" or becoming "dangerous to the peace"), designated officials may—without notice or hearing to the person involved—post a notice in all retail liquor stores that sales or gifts of liquor to him are forbidden for one year. But cf. *Paul v. Davis* (1976), infra.

b. "Had it done so," noted the Court, "this, again, would be a different case."

c. Roth had also alleged that non-renewal of his contract was based on his exercise of his right to freedom of speech, but this allegation was not before the Court. *Perry v. Sindermann,* 408 U.S. 593, 92 S.Ct. 2694, 33 L.Ed.2d 570 (1972), a companion case, made clear that the lack of a public employee's "right" to reemployment "is immaterial to his free speech claim." For "even though a person has no 'right' to a valuable governmental benefit and even though the government may deny him the benefit for any number of reasons, there are some reasons upon which the government may not act. It may not deny a benefit to a person on a basis that infringes his constitutionally protected interests—especially, his interest in freedom of speech."

tion of it. He must, instead, have a legitimate claim of entitlement to [it]. Property interests, of course, are not created by the Constitution, [but by, and] defined by existing rules or understandings that stem from an independent source such as state law—rules or understandings that secure certain benefits and that support claims of entitlement to those benefits. Thus the welfare recipients in *Goldberg* had a claim of entitlement to [payments] grounded in the statute defining eligibility for them. [So, too, Roth's] 'property' interest in employment at the [University] was created and defined by the terms of his employment. [But these terms] specifically provided that [his] employment was to terminate on June 30. They did not provide for contract renewal absent 'sufficient cause.' Indeed, they made no provision for renewal whatsoever.[d] [Thus, although Roth] surely had an abstract concern in being rehired, [he lacked] a *property* interest sufficient to require the University [to] give him a hearing when [declining] to renew his contract of employment." [e]

4. *"The bitter with the sweet."* ARNETT v. KENNEDY, 416 U.S. 134, 94 S.Ct. 1633, 40 L.Ed.2d 15 (1974): Kennedy, a nonprobationary federal civil service employee in a regional OEO office, was removed by the Regional Director for allegedly publicly accusing the Director of bribery "in reckless disregard" of the facts. The relevant statutes provided, inter alia, that, prior to removal the employee had a right to reply to the charges orally and in writing and to submit affidavits to the official authorized to remove him (the Regional Director).[a] Instead of responding to the charges against him in a proceeding to be conducted and decided by the very person he had allegedly slandered, and who had filed the complaint against him, Kennedy instituted a federal suit, asserting that the discharge procedures denied him procedural due process because they failed to provide for a trial-type hearing before an impartial agency official prior to removal. The Court, with no majority opinion, held that the procedures satisfied due process.

The plurality opinion was by REHNQUIST, J., joined by Burger, C.J., and Stewart, J., but (as pointed out by White, J. joined by three other justices, dissenting in *Bishop v. Wood,* infra) the two justices who concurred in *Arnett,* as well as the four who dissented on this issue, rejected the plurality's analysis. As described by Van Alstyne, supra, at 462, according to Rehnquist, J., it was unnecessary to reach step two and "decide whether submitting Mr. Kennedy's

---

d. But *Sindermann,* fn. c supra, involving another state college teacher serving on a year-to-year basis whose appointment had not been renewed and who had not received a hearing, per Stewart, J., held that a "lack of a contractual or tenure right to re-employment, taken alone," does not defeat one's claim that nonrenewal of his contract violated procedural due process. Sindermann had ten years service and had alleged, but not been permitted to prove, that the college had a de facto tenure program and that he had tenure under that program. He must, ruled the Court, be given an opportunity to prove the legitimacy of his claim of entitlement to continued employment absent "sufficient cause" "in light of 'the policies and practices of the institution.'" (Roth, on the other hand, had failed to establish "anything approaching a 'common law' of re-employment.")

e. Dissenting, Marshall, J., maintained that "every citizen who applies for a govern-

ment job is entitled to it unless the government can establish some reason for denying the employment. This is the 'property' right [that] is protected by the Fourteenth Amendment and that cannot be denied 'without due process of law.' And it is also liberty—liberty to work—which is the 'very essence of the personal freedom and opportunity' secured by the Fourteenth Amendment."

Dissenting, Brennan, J., joined by Douglas, J., agreed with Marshall, J., that Roth had been denied due process when his contract had not been renewed without being informed of the reasons or given a chance to respond. Powell, J., did not participate.

a. The employee may also appeal an adverse decision to a reviewing authority within the agency. Only on appeal is he entitled to an evidentiary trial-type hearing, but if reinstated on appeal he receives full back pay.

fate to the judgment of his accuser was incompatible with [due process] because a close examination of Mr. Kennedy's property interest made it clear that *nothing* was in fact being taken from him to which he had *any* legally recognizable entitlement. In short, he failed at step one." Observed Rehnquist, J.:

"[A]ppellee did have a statutory expectancy that he not be removed other than for 'such cause as will promote the efficiency of the service.' But the very section of the statute [granting him that right] expressly provided also for the procedure by which 'cause' was to be determined, and expressly omitted the procedural guarantees [appellee claims]. Only by bifurcating the very sentence of the [statute conferring] the right not to be removed save for cause could it be said that he had an expectancy of that substantive right without the procedural limitations which Congress attached to it. [An] employee's statutorily defined right is not a guarantee against removal without cause in the abstract, but such a guarantee as enforced by the procedures which Congress has designated for the determination of cause. [W]here the grant of a substantive right is inextricably intertwined with the limitations on the procedures which are to be employed in determining that right, a litigant in the position of appellee must take the bitter with the sweet. [Here] the property interest [in] employment was itself conditioned by procedural limitations [accompanying] the grant of that interest."

As for appellee's contention that the charges on which his dismissal was based "in effect accused [him] of dishonesty, and that therefore a hearing was required before he could be deprived of this element of his 'liberty' ": "Since the purpose of [such a hearing] is to provide the person 'an opportunity to clear his name,' a hearing afforded by administrative appeal procedures after the actual dismissal is a sufficient compliance with [due process requirements]."

POWELL, J., joined by Blackmun, J., concurred in the result, but criticized the plurality's approach: "[The Rehnquist analysis] would lead directly to the conclusion that whatever the nature of [one's] statutorily created property interest, deprivation of that interest could be accomplished without notice or a hearing at any time. This view misconceives the origin of the right to procedural due process. That right is conferred not by legislative grace, but by constitutional guarantee. While the legislature may elect not to confer a property interest in federal employment, it may not constitutionally authorize the deprivation of such an interest, once conferred, without appropriate procedural safeguards." [b]

But after "weighing" the government's interest against the affected employee's,[c] Powell concluded that "a prior evidentiary hearing" was not required before removal. "The Government's interest in being able to act expeditiously to remove an unsatisfactory employee is substantial" and, since he would be reinstated and awarded back pay if he prevailed on the merits, Kennedy's "actual injury" would consist only of "a temporary interruption of his income during the interim." Thus, the challenged statutes and regulations "comport with due process by providing a reasonable accommodation of the competing interests." [d]

---

b. This passage was quoted with approval by the Court in *Logan v. Zimmerman Brush Co.* (1982), and *Cleveland Board of Education v. Loudermill* (1985), both discussed infra.

c. For a more extensive articulation of Powell, J.'s "balancing process," see his opinion for the Court in *Mathews v. Eldridge*, Part II infra.

d. White, J., concurring in part and dissenting in part, rejected the Rehnquist plurality's analysis and largely agreed with Powell, J.'s constitutional analysis. Although he found the pretermination procedures involved in *Arnett* generally adequate, White, J., would affirm the lower court's judgment, ordering reinstatement and backpay, "due to the fail-

5. BISHOP v. WOOD, 426 U.S. 341, 96 S.Ct. 2074, 48 L.Ed.2d 684 (1976), per STEVENS, J., held—over the protest of the dissenters that the majority was adopting an analysis rejected by six members of the Court in *Arnett*—that the dismissal of a city policeman implicated neither the "property" or "liberty" interests protected by due process. The City Manager of Marion, North Carolina, terminated petitioner's employment as a policeman without affording him a hearing to determine the sufficiency of the cause for his dismissal. Petitioner brought suit, contending that since he was classified as a "permanent employee" he had a constitutional right to a pretermination hearing.[a] During pretrial discovery he was informed that he had been discharged for insubordination, "causing low morale," and "conduct unsuited to an officer." The Court reasoned: "A property interest in employment can, of course, be created by ordinance, or by an implied contract. In either case, however, the sufficiency of the claim of entitlement must be decided by reference to state law. The [state supreme court] has held that an enforceable expectation of continued [state employment] can exist only if the employer, by statute or contract, has actually granted some form of guarantee. Whether [this is so] can be determined only by an examination of the particular statute or ordinance in question. * * *

"Based on his understanding of state law, [the federal district court] concluded that petitioner 'held his position at the will and pleasure of the city.' [As the ordinance was thus construed], the City Manager's determination of the adequacy of the grounds for discharge is not subject to judicial review; the employee is merely given certain procedural rights which the District Court found not to have been violated in this case. The District Court's reading of the ordinance is tenable; it derives some support from a [state supreme court decision]; and it was accepted by [the] Fourth Circuit. These reasons are sufficient to foreclose our independent examination of the state law issue. Under [this view], petitioner's discharge did not deprive him of a property interest protected by the Fourteenth Amendment.[b]

"Petitioner's claim that he has been deprived of liberty has two components. He contends that the reasons given for his discharge are so serious as to constitute a stigma that may severely damage his reputation in the community; in addition, he claims that those reasons were false.[c] * * *

---

ure to provide an impartial hearing officer at the preterminiation hearing"—a right he maintained that the challenged statute, although silent on the matter, should be construed as requiring in this case.

Dissenting, Marshall, J., joined by Douglas and Brennan, JJ., rejected the plurality's analysis on grounds similar to Powell's, but as Marshall "balanced" the interests involved (stressing the long delay in the processing of adverse personnel actions), Kennedy was entitled to "an evidentiary hearing before an impartial decision-maker prior to dismissal."

a. The relevant provision of the city ordinance provided:

"*Dismissal.* A permanent employee whose work is not satisfactory over a period of time shall be notified in what way his work is deficient and what he must do if his work is to be satisfactory. If a permanent employee fails to perform work up to the standard of the classification held, or continues to be negligent, inefficient, or unfit to perform his duties, he may be dismissed by the City Manager. Any discharged employee shall be given written notice of his discharge setting forth the effective date and reasons for his discharge if he shall request such a notice."

b. In *Arnett*, noted Stevens, J., "the Court concluded that because the employee could only be discharged for cause, he had a property interest which was entitled to constitutional protection. In this case, a holding that as a matter of state law the employee 'held his position at the will and pleasure of the city' necessarily establishes that he had *no* property interest."

c. Since the District Court granted summary judgment against petitioner, noted the Court, "we [must] assume that his discharge was a mistake and based on incorrect information."

"In *Roth,* we recognized that the nonretention of an untenured college teacher might make him somewhat less attractive to other employers, but nevertheless concluded that it would stretch the concept too far 'to suggest that a person is deprived of "liberty" when he simply is not retained in one position but remains as free as before to seek another.' This same conclusion applies to the discharge of a public employee whose position is terminable at the will of the employer when [prior to his instituting a law suit] there is no public disclosure of the reasons for the discharge.

"[Even if the reasons given for petitioner's discharge were false], the reasons stated to him in private had no different impact on his reputation than if they had been true. And the answers to his interrogatories, whether true or false, did not cause the discharge. The truth or falsity of the City Manager's statement determines whether or not his decision to discharge the petitioner was correct or prudent, but neither enhances nor diminishes petitioner's claim that his constitutionally protected interest in liberty has been impaired.[13] A contrary evaluation of his contention would enable every discharged employee to assert a constitutional claim merely by alleging that his former supervisor made a mistake.

"The federal court is not the appropriate forum in which to review the multitude of personnel decisions that are made daily by public agencies.[14] We must accept the harsh fact that numerous individual mistakes are inevitable in the day-to-day administration of our affairs. The United States Constitution cannot feasibly be construed to require federal judicial review for every such error. In the absence of any claim that the public employer was motivated by a desire to curtail or to penalize the exercise of an employee's constitutionally protected rights, we must presume that official action was regular and, if erroneous, can best be corrected in other ways. The Due Process Clause of the Fourteenth Amendment is not a guarantee against incorrect or ill-advised personnel decisions." [d]

BRENNAN, J., joined by Marshall, J., dissented: "Petitioner was discharged as a policeman on the grounds of insubordination, 'causing low morale,' and 'conduct unsuited to an officer.' It is difficult to imagine a greater 'badge of infamy' that could be imposed on one following petitioner's calling; in a profession in which prospective employees are invariably investigated, petition-

13. Indeed, the impact on petitioner's constitutionally protected interest in liberty is no greater even if we assume that the City Manager deliberately lied. Such fact might conceivably provide the basis for a state law claim, the validity of which would be entirely unaffected by our analysis of the federal constitutional question.

14. [U]nless we were to adopt Mr. Justice Brennan's remarkably innovative suggestion that we develop a federal common law of property rights, or his equally far reaching view that almost every discharge implicates a constitutionally protected liberty interest, the ultimate control of state personnel relationships is, and will remain, with the States; they may grant or withhold tenure at their unfettered discretion. In this case, whether we accept or reject the construction of the ordinance adopted by the two lower courts, the power to change or clarify that ordinance

will remain in the hands of the City Council of the city of Marion.

[But see Rabin, *Job Security and Due Process: Monitoring Discretion Through a Reasons Requirement,* 44 U.Chi.L.Rev. 60, 72 (1976) "[*Bishop's* reference to] 'Justice Brennan's remarkably innovative suggestion that we develop a federal common law of property' [goes] to the heart of the matter. For if the cases beginning with *Goldberg* were not developing 'a federal common law of property rights' it is impossible to comprehend the decisions. One would have thought that the dialogue sparked by Justice Rehnquist in *Arnett* made that clear."]

d. Smolla, first fn. a supra, 88–89, points to this "profoundly honest passage" as providing "the best insights into the motivations that underlie the Court's adoption of the entitlement doctrine."

er's job prospects will be severely constricted by the governmental action in this case. Although our case law would appear to require that petitioner thus be accorded an opportunity 'to clear his name' of this calumny, the Court [holds he] was deprived of no liberty interest thereby. [It holds] that a State may tell an employee that he is being fired for some nonderogatory reason, and then turn around and inform prospective employers that [he] was in fact discharged for a stigmatizing reason that will effectively preclude future employment.

"The Court purports to limit its holding to situations in which there is 'no public disclosure of the reasons for the discharge,' but in this case the stigmatizing reasons have been disclosed, and there is no reason to believe that respondents will not convey these actual reasons to petitioner's prospective employers. [The stigma was not imposed until after petitioner brought suit, but] the 'claim' does not arise until the State has officially branded petitioner in some way, and the purpose of the due process hearing is to accord him an opportunity to clear his [name].

"[T]he strained reading of the local ordinance, which the Court deems to be 'tenable,' cannot be dispositive of the existence vel non of petitioner's 'property' interest. There is certainly a federal dimension to the definition of 'property' in the Federal Constitution [and] at least before a state law is definitively construed as not securing a 'property' interest, the relevant inquiry is whether it was objectively reasonable for the employee to believe he could rely on continued employment.[4] [At] a minimum, this would require in this case an analysis of the common practices utilized and the expectations generated by respondents, and the manner in which the local ordinance would reasonably be read by respondents' employees.[5] "

WHITE, J., joined by Brennan, Marshall and Blackmun, JJ., also dissented: "The majority's holding that petitioner had no property interest in his job in spite of the unequivocal language in the city ordinance that he may be dismissed only for certain kinds of cause rests, then, on the fact that state law provides no *procedures* for assuring that the City Manager dismiss him only for cause. The right to his job apparently given by the first two sentences of the ordinance is thus redefined, according to the majority, by the procedures provided for in the third sentence and as redefined is infringed only if the procedures are not followed.

"This is precisely the reasoning which was embraced by only three and expressly rejected by six Members of this Court in *Arnett*. [The] ordinance plainly grants petitioner a right to his job unless there is cause to fire him. Having granted him such a right it is the Federal Constitution,[3] not state law,

---

4. By holding that States have "unfettered discretion" in defining "property" for purposes of the Due Process Clause, [the] Court is, as my Brother White argues, effectively adopting the analysis rejected by a majority of the Court in *Arnett*. More basically, the Court's approach is a resurrection of the discredited rights/privileges distinction, for a State may now avoid all due process safeguards attendant upon the loss of even the necessities of life, cf. *Goldberg,* merely by labeling them as not constituting "property."

5. For example, petitioner was hired for a "probationary" period of six months, after which he became a "permanent" employee. No reason appears on the record for this dis-

tinction, other than the logical assumption, confirmed by a reasonable reading of the local ordinance, that after completion of the former period, an employee may only be discharged for "cause." As to respondents' personnel practices, it is important to note that in a department which currently employs 17 persons, petitioner's was the only discharge, for cause or otherwise, during the period of over three years from the time of his hiring until the time of pretrial discovery.

3. The majority intimates in [fn. b] that the views of the three plurality Justices in *Arnett* were rejected because the other six Justices disagreed on the question of how the federal *statute* involved in that case should be

which determines the process to be applied in connection with any state decision to deprive him of it." [e]

6. *Reading "liberty" narrowly.* PAUL v. DAVIS, 424 U.S. 693, 96 S.Ct. 1155, 47 L.Ed.2d 405 (1976), arose as follows: After respondent Davis had been arrested on a shoplifting charge, petitioner police officials circulated a "flyer" to 800 merchants in the Louisville, Ky. area designating him an "active shoplifter." When the shoplifting charge was dismissed, Davis brought a § 1983 action alleging that the police officials' action under color of law had deprived him of his constitutional rights, by inhibiting him from entering business establishments and by impairing his employment opportunities. A 5–3 majority, per REHNQUIST, J., was unimpressed:

"[R]espondent's complaint would appear to state a classical claim for defamation actionable in the courts of virtually every State, [but he] brought his action [not] in the state courts of Kentucky, but in a [federal court]. [He contends that since petitioners are government officials] his action is thereby transmuted into one for deprivation by the State of rights secured under the Fourteenth Amendment. [It] is hard to perceive any logical stopping place to [respondent's] line of reasoning. [His] construction would seem almost necessarily to result in every legally cognizable injury which may have been inflicted by a state official acting under 'color of law' establishing a violation of the Fourteenth Amendment. [While we have] pointed out the frequently drastic effect of the 'stigma' which may result from defamation by the government in a variety of contexts, this line of cases does not establish the proposition that reputation alone, apart from some more tangible interests such as employment, is either 'liberty' or 'property' by itself sufficient to invoke the procedural protection of the Due Process Clause." Thus, no inquiry had to be made as to whether the police officials had followed adequate procedures before issuing the flyers.

The Court distinguished *Constantineau,* fn. a in *Roth,* supra, as dependent on the fact that posting the person's name in liquor stores as a chronic drinker "deprived [him] of a right previously held under state law—the right [to] obtain liquor in common with the rest of the citizenry"—and thus "significantly altered his status as a matter of state law. [I]t was that alteration of legal status which, combined with the injury resulting from the defamation, justified the invocation of procedural safeguards." Interests "comprehended within the meaning of either 'liberty' or 'property' as meant in the Due Process Clause attain this constitutional status by virtue of the fact that they have been initially recog-

construed. This is incorrect. All Justices agreed on the meaning of the statute. [I]t was the constitutional significance of the statute on which the six disagreed with the plurality.

Similarly, here, I do not disagree with the majority or the courts below on the meaning of the state law. If I did, I might be inclined to defer to the judgments of the two lower courts. The state law says that petitioner may be dismissed by the City Manager only for certain kinds of cause and then provides that he will receive notice and an explanation, but no hearing and no review. I agree that as a matter of state law petitioner has no remedy no matter how arbitrarily or erroneously the City Manager has acted. This is what the lower courts say the statute means. I differ

with those courts and the majority only with respect to the constitutional significance of an unambiguous state law. A majority of the Justices in *Arnett* stood on the proposition that the Constitution requires procedures *not* required by state law when the state conditions dismissal on "cause."

e. In a third dissent, Blackmun, J., joined by Brennan, J., maintained that the Marion ordinance "contains a 'for cause' standard for dismissal and [thus] creates a proper expectation of privacy of continued employment so long as [the employee] performs his work satisfactorily. At this point, the Federal Constitution steps in and requires that appropriate procedures be followed before the employee may be deprived of his property interest."

nized and protected by state law,[5] and we have repeatedly ruled that the procedural guarantees of the Fourteenth Amendment apply whenever the State seeks to remove or significantly alter that status. [But] the interest in reputation alone which respondent seeks to vindicate [is] quite different from the 'liberty' or 'property' recognized in [such decisions as *Bell v. Burson*]. Kentucky law does not extend to respondent any legal guarantee of present enjoyment of reputation which has been altered as a result of petitioners' actions. [Although the interest in reputation is protected by the state by virtue of its tort law], any harm or injury to that interest, even where as here inflicted by an officer of the State, does not result in a deprivation of any 'liberty' or 'property' recognized by state or federal law, nor has it worked any change of respondent's status as theretofore recognized under the State's laws."

BRENNAN, J., joined by White and Marshall, JJ., dissented: "The Court today holds that public officials, acting in their official capacities as law enforcers, may on their own initiative and without trial constitutionally condemn innocent individuals as criminals and thereby brand them with one of the most stigmatizing and debilitating labels in our society. If there are no constitutional restraints on such oppressive behavior, the safeguards constitutionally accorded an accused in a criminal trial are rendered a sham, and no individual can feel secure that he will not be arbitrarily singled out for similar *ex parte* punishment by those primarily charged with fair enforcement of the law.

"[There] is no attempt by the Court to analyze the question as one of reconciliation of constitutionally protected personal rights and the exigencies of law enforcement. No effort is made to distinguish the 'defamation' that occurs when executive officials arbitrarily and without trial declare a person an 'active criminal.' Rather, the Court by mere fiat and with no analysis wholly excludes personal interest in reputation from the ambit of 'life, liberty, or property' under the Fifth and Fourteenth Amendments, thus rendering due process concerns *never* applicable to the official stigmatization, however arbitrary, of an individual. The logical and disturbing corollary of this holding is that no due process infirmities would inhere in a statute constituting a commission to conduct *ex parte* trials of individuals, so long as the only official judgment pronounced was limited to the public condemnation and branding of a person as a Communist, a traitor, an 'active murderer,' a homosexual, or any other mark that 'merely' carries social approbrium. The potential of today's decision is frightening for a free people."

Despite the majority's efforts to distinguish them, cases such as *Roth, Constantineau* [a] and *Goss v. Lopez,* [b] maintained Brennan, J., "are cogent authori-

---

5. There are other interests, of course, protected not by virtue of their recognition by the law of a particular State, but because they are guaranteed in one of the provisions of the Bill of Rights which has been "incorporated" into the Fourteenth Amendment. Section 1983 makes a deprivation of such rights actionable independently of state law.

a. For the view that "the heart of the complaint" in *Constantineau* was "defamation, not restriction of access to liquor," see Monaghan at 431. See also id. at 423–24; Mashaw, *Due Process in the Administrative State* 95 (1985); D. Shapiro, *Mr. Justice Rehnquist: A Preliminary View,* 90 Harv.L.Rev. 293, 326 (1976); Smolla, *The Displacement of*

Federal Due Process Claims by State Tort Remedies, 1982 U.Ill.L.F. 831, 839–40, 845.

b. GOSS v. LOPEZ, 419 U.S. 565, 95 S.Ct. 729, 42 L.Ed.2d 725 (1975) (also discussed in Part II infra), held that students suspended from public high schools for up to ten days were entitled to procedural protections against unfair suspensions. The *Goss* Court, per WHITE, J., pointed out that state law had established a "property interest" in educational benefits, but also recognized "the liberty interest in reputation" implicated by suspensions: "The Due Process Clause also forbids arbitrary deprivations of liberty. 'Where a person's good name, reputation, honor, or integrity is at stake because of what the govern-

ty that a person's interest in his good name and reputation falls within the broad term 'liberty' and clearly require that the government afford procedural protections before infringing that name and reputation by branding a person as a criminal. [It] is inexplicable how the Court can say that a person's status is 'altered' when the State suspends him from school, revokes his driver's license, fires him from a job, or denies him the right to purchase a drink of alcohol, but is in no way 'altered' when it officially pins upon him the brand of a criminal." [c]

7. (a) *A state is not free to employ such procedures as it pleases for adjudicating a claim it need not have created.* In LOGAN v. ZIMMERMAN BRUSH CO., 455 U.S. 422, 102 S.Ct. 1148, 71 L.Ed.2d 265 (1982), appellant filed a charge with the Illinois Employment Practices Commission, alleging that his employment had been lawfully terminated because of his physical handicap. This triggered the Commission's statutory obligation to convene a fact-finding conference within 120 days, but, apparently through inadvertence, the conference was scheduled five days *after* expiration of the statutory period. The state court held that the failure to convene a conference within 120 days deprived the Commission of jurisdiction to consider appellant's claim under the Illinois Fair Employment Practices Act (FEPA). The Court, per BLACKMUN, J., reversed, deeming appellant's FEPA claim "a species of property" protected by fourteenth amendment due process and holding that the state scheme had deprived appellant of his property right.

The Court pointed out that its recent cases had emphasized that "[t]he hallmark of property [is] an individual entitlement grounded in state law, which cannot be removed except 'for cause.' [And] an FEPA claim, which presumably can be surrendered for value, is at least as substantial as the right to an education labeled as property in *Goss v. Lopez*. Certainly, it would require a remarkable reading of a 'broad and majestic term' to conclude that a horse trainer's license is a protected property interest under the Fourteenth Amendment, while a state-created right to redress discrimination is not."

"Because the entitlement arises from statute, the [state supreme court] reasoned, it was the legislature's prerogative to establish the 'procedures to be followed upon a charge.' [This analysis] misunderstands the nature of the Constitution's due process guarantee. [B]ecause 'minimum [procedural] requirements [are] a matter of federal law, they are not diminished by the fact that the State may have specified its own procedures that it may deem adequate for determining the preconditions to adverse official action.' *Vitek v. Jones*, 445 U.S. 480, 100 S.Ct. 1254, 63 L.Ed.2d 552 (1980). Indeed, any other conclusion would allow the State to destroy at will virtually any state-created property interest. The Court has considered and rejected such an approach [quoting from that portion of the *Vitek* opinion quoting with approval from Powell, J.'s concurring opinion in *Arnett*].

"Of course, the State remains free to create substantive defenses or immunities for use in adjudication—or to eliminate its statutorily created causes of action altogether—just as it can amend or terminate its welfare or employment programs [or adjust benefit levels]. [But the 120-day limitation] is a procedural

ment is doing to him,' the minimal requirements of the Clause must be satisfied. *Constantineau.* [If] sustained and recorded, [the charges of misconduct] could seriously damage the students' standing with their fellow pupils and their teachers as well as interfere with later opportunities for higher education and employment. * * * Neither the

property interest in educational benefits temporarily denied nor the liberty interest in reputation, which is also implicated, is so insubstantial that suspensions may constitutionally be imposed by any procedure the school chooses, no matter how arbitrary."

c. Stevens, J., did not participate.

limitation on the claimant's ability to assert his rights, not a substantive element of the FEPA claim."

(b) *Why can't a state "enfeeble" any entitlement it creates?* Consider Easterbrook, *Substance and Due Process,* 1982 Sup.Ct.Rev. 85–86, 109–110, 120: "The process a legislature describes for vindicating the entitlements that it creates is a way of indicating how effective its plan should be. The more process it affords, the more the legislature values the entitlements and thus is willing to sacrifice to avoid mistakes. A court that protects the legislative power to define substantive entitlements ought to give it control of process as well.

"[The] Court's justification for specifying process once the statute has specified substance is that 'any other conclusion would allow the State to destroy at will virtually any state-created property interest.' This would be a good argument if the Court could explain why a state may not destroy the interest it creates, at least prospectively. But the Court has never so argued. Under the Court's decisions legislatures are free to enact precatory statutes, statutes that contain no rules of decision, retroactive statutes, statutes that lack any methods of enforcement, statutes creating absolute immunities, and otherwise to have vacuous 'entitlements.' To use some invented numbers, if states may elect ten percent reliability in enforcement (the amount of adherence to a precatory statute), why can they not elect ninety percent (the amount obtained from rudimentary procedures)? Why, in other words, is the expedient of enfeebling a statutory entitlement by providing 'deficient' procedures out of bounds? The Court's cases contain no answers to this question because they are not consistent. There is no single view that could be respected in the name of stare decisis.

"[Illinois] need not have created any right to be free of discrimination because of handicap or given the right of any particular dimensions. That being so, [Illinois] also should have been allowed to employ such procedure as it pleased for adjudicating (or not adjudicating) Logan's claim.[105] "

(c) *Why wasn't Logan's right to sue the Commission in tort for its negligence in losing his claim sufficient to satisfy due process?* The Zimmerman Brush Company had another argument in support of the Illinois Supreme Court's decision. As described in Smolla, p. 406 fn. a supra, at 860, the Company argued that even if Logan possessed an "entitlement" under Illinois law "no federal due process violation existed, because Logan could sue the Commission for damages under the Illinois Court of Claims Act for having negligently destroyed his 'property'—his [FEPA cause of action]. Logan in effect had an action for 'malpractice' against the Commission, just as he would have had an action against his own attorney if the attorney had negligently caused Logan's claim to lapse. Under the reasoning in *Parratt v. Taylor,* 451 U.S. 527, 101 S.Ct. 1908, 68 L.Ed.2d 420 (1981), the Company argued, the state had not deprived Logan of property without due process since the state's own tort remedies were adequate to make Logan whole." This argument, responded the Court, "misses *Parratt's* point":

"In *Parratt,* the Court emphasized that it was dealing with 'a tortious loss [of] property as a result of a random and unauthorized act by a state employee [rather than] some established procedure.' Here, in contrast, it is the state system itself that destroys a complainant's property interest, by operation of law,

---

105. [As] the Supreme Court of Illinois saw things, the statute (effectively) allowed Logan's claim to be distinguished for no reason at all. Thus the statute gave Logan no property right. *Bishop.* The Court never told us why it was disregarding the state court's construction of the state's statute.

whenever the Commission fails to convene a timely conference—whether the Commission's action is taken through negligence, maliciousness, or otherwise. *Parratt* was not designed to reach such a situation. Unlike the complainant in *Parratt*, Logan is challenging not the Commission's error, but the 'established state procedure' that destroys his entitlement without according him proper procedural safeguards.

"In any event, the Court's decisions suggest that, absent 'the necessity of quick action by the State or the impracticality of providing any predeprivation process,' a post-deprivation hearing here would be constitutionally inadequate. *Parratt*. [That] is particularly true where, as here, the State's only post-termination process comes in the form of an independent tort action.[10] Seeking redress through a tort suit is apt to be a lengthy and speculative process, which in a situation such as this one will never make the complainant entirely whole: the Illinois Court of Claims Act does not provide for reinstatement [and] even a successful suit will not vindicate entirely Logan's right to be free from discriminatory treatment."

(d) *The post-deprivation due process doctrine: reconciling Zimmerman Brush and Parratt.* The relationship between *Zimmerman Brush* and *Parratt*, observes Smolla at 861–62, "parallels the relationship that arguably existed between *Constantineau* and *Paul.* Random and unauthorized harm caused by the state, for which the state itself provides a remedy, does not implicate the Constitution. But when the state consciously enacts a system that places its imprimatur on arbitrary conduct, whether it be through a bizarre posting statute or a capricious administrative structure for handling handicap discrimination, federal court intervention under the due process clause is warranted."

8. "*[I]t is settled that the 'bitter with the sweet' approach misconceives the [due process] guarantee."* CLEVELAND BOARD OF EDUCATION v. LOUDERMILL, ___ U.S. ___, 105 S.Ct. 1487, 84 L.Ed.2d 494 (1985): Under Ohio law, respondents Loudermill and Donnelly were "classified civil servants" who could be discharged only for cause. Loudermill, a security guard, was dismissed because of dishonesty in filling out his employment application. He was not afforded an opportunity to respond to the dishonesty charge or to challenge the dismissal.[a] Donnelly was fired as a bus mechanic because he had failed an eye examination. He appealed to the Civil Service Commission, which ordered him reinstated without pay. "The statute plainly supports the conclusion [that] respondents possessed property rights in continued employment," but petitioners contended that "the property right is defined by, and conditioned on, the legislature's choice of procedures for its deprivation. [Petitioners stress] that in addition to specifying the grounds for termination, the statute sets out procedures by which termination may take place [and that these procedures were followed]. [Therefore,] '[t]o require additional procedures would in effect expand

---

10. In *Ingraham v. Wright*, 430 U.S. 651, 97 S.Ct. 1401, 51 L.Ed.2d 711 (1977), the Court concluded that state tort remedies provided adequate process for students subjected to corporal punishment in school, [but it] emphasized that the state scheme "preserved what 'has always been the law of the land,' " [and] that adding additional safeguards would be unduly burdensome. Here neither of those rationales is available. Terminating potentially meritorious claims in a random manner is hardly a practice in line with our common-law traditions. And the State's abandonment of the challenged practice [after the inception of the present litigation] makes it difficult to argue that requiring a determination on the merits will impose undue burdens on the state administrative process.

a. On his 1979 job application, Loudermill stated that he had never been convicted of a felony. Eleven months later it was discovered that he had been convicted of grand larceny in 1968. Loudermill maintained that he had thought his larceny conviction was for a misdemeanor rather than a felony.

the scope of the property interest itself.'" The Court, per WHITE, J., rejected this approach:

"[Petitioners' argument] has its genesis in the plurality opinion in *Arnett.* [This approach] garnered three votes in *Arnett,* but was specifically rejected by the other six Justices. [I]n light of [*Zimmerman Brush*], it is settled that the 'bitter with the sweet' approach misconceives the [due process] guarantee. If a clearer holding is needed, we provide it today. The point is straight-forward: the Due Process Clause provides that certain substantive rights—life, liberty, and property—cannot be deprived except pursuant to constitutionally adequate procedures. The categories of substance and procedure are distinct. Were the rule otherwise, the Clause would be reduced to a mere tautology. 'Property' cannot be defined by the procedures provided for its deprivation any more than can life or liberty. The right to due process 'is conferred, not by legislative grace, but by constitutional guarantee. While the legislature may elect not to confer a property interest in [public] employment, it may not constitutionally authorize the deprivation of such an interest, once conferred, without appropriate procedural safeguards.' *Arnett* (Powell, J., [concurring opinion]); see id. (White, J., [concurring in part]). [O]nce it is determined that the Due Process Clause applies, 'the question remains what process is due.' The answer is not to be found in the Ohio statute." [b]

REHNQUIST, J., the sole Justice to dissent on this issue, maintained that the Fourteenth Amendment "does not support the conclusion that Ohio's effort to confer a limited form of tenure upon respondents resulted in the creation of a 'property right' in their employment":

"Here, as in *Arnett,* '[t]he employee's statutorily defined right is not a guarantee against removal without cause in the abstract, but such a guarantee as enforced by the procedures which [the Ohio legislature] has designated for the determination of cause' (opinion of Rehnquist, J.). [We] ought to recognize the totality of the State's definition of the property right in question, and not merely seize upon one of several paragraphs in a unitary statute to proclaim that in that paragraph the State has inexorably conferred upon a civil service employee something which it is powerless to qualify in the next paragraph of the statute. [While] it does not impose a federal definition of property, the Court departs from the full breadth of the holding in *Roth* by its selective choice from among the sentences the Ohio legislature chooses to use in establishing and qualifying a right."

II. WHAT KIND OF HEARING—AND WHEN?

GOLDBERG v. KELLY, 397 U.S. 254, 90 S.Ct. 1011, 25 L.Ed.2d 287 (1970), per BRENNAN, J. (Burger, C.J., and Black and Stewart, JJ., dissenting) held that due process requires an evidentiary hearing prior to termination of welfare benefits, stressing the "crucial factor [that] termination of aid pending resolution of a controversy over eligibility may deprive an *eligible* recipient of the very means by which to live while he waits. Since he lacks independent resources, his situation becomes immediately desperate. His need to concentrate upon [survival], in turn, adversely affects his ability to seek redress from the welfare bureaucracy." The hearing "need not take the form of a judicial or quasi-

---

b. The Court then held that respondents were not entitled to a "full adversarial hearing prior to adverse governmental action. [A]ll the process that is due is provided by a pretermination opportunity to respond, coupled with [a full post-termination hearing] as provided by the Ohio statute."

judicial trial," but a recipient must have "timely and adequate notice detailing the reasons for a proposed termination, and an effective opportunity to defend by confronting any adverse witnesses and by presenting his own arguments and evidence orally." The Court declined to "say that counsel must be provided" but the recipient must be allowed to retain counsel.

Consider JERRY MASHAW, *Due Process in the Administrative State* 35–36 (1985): "[T]he underprotectionist critic may claim that the due process revolution has stopped short of its essential goals: building legal security and democratic control into the administrative state. Legal security for the welfare claimant, for example, would at a minimum require that the hearing right be oriented to the issues that produce erroneous deprivations and that the recipient class has the necessary resources to make use of hearings to protect its interests. Yet neither condition seems to obtain. A careful study of errors suggests that they occur at least as often through misinterpretation of policy as through mistakes on questions of fact. The *Goldberg* decision limits due process hearings to facts. Moreover, welfare recipients generally lack the human or material resources to make use of the hearings *Goldberg* provided. Except for an occasional flurry of political activism expressed through appeals requests, hearings have been utilized about as infrequently after *Goldberg* as before.

"This sort of criticism may be pressed further to suggest that the hearing technique—the demand for individualized and detailed attention through quasi-judicial process—simply misses the point of the welfare state. The problem has become one of mass, not individual, justice. Legal security for the class of welfare claimants lies, not in hearings, but in good management. Unless due process, therefore, comes to terms with administration, becomes systems—rather than case-oriented, it will be irrelevant.

"The underprotectionist case goes further. *Goldberg*'s hearing rights extend only to the protection of what can be termed 'positive entitlements,' substantive interests already enjoying common law or statutory legal significance. Due process hearings are thus only an addition to the legal security of existing rights. They provide no access to the administrative forums in which rights are being created and no opportunity to avoid the application of general rules on the basis of individual circumstances. *Goldberg*'s hearing rights thus leave untouched the contemporary concern with (1) the remoteness of administrative policy making from immediate participation by affected interests and (2) the unfairness and irrationality that seem to attend bureaucratic implementation of general rules." [a]

---

a. At this point, Professor Mashaw turns to O'BANNON V. TOWN COURT NURSING CENTER, 447 U.S. 773, 100 S.Ct. 2467, 65 L.Ed.2d 506 (1980), per STEVENS, J., holding that, because nursing home residents had no government-established entitlement to continued residence at a particular home, they had no right to a hearing before the government decertified the home as provider of services at government expenses under Medicare and Medicaid agreements. Decertification would force the patients to seek care elsewhere and would probably mean that they would be separated from each and might mean that they would have to relocate away from their friends and families. But, responded the Court, Medicaid provisions only give recipi-

ents "the right to choose among a range of *qualified* providers, without government interference, [not the right] to enter an unqualified home and demand a hearing to certify it, nor [the right] to continue to receive benefits for care in a home that has been decertified. [A]lthough the regulations do protect patients by limiting the circumstances under which a *home* may transfer or discharge a Medicaid recipient, they do not purport to limit the Government's right to make a transfer necessary by decertifying a facility. [Whatever rights the patients may have against the nursing home] for failing to maintain its status[,] enforcement by [state and federal agencies] of their valid regulations did not directly affect their legal rights or deprive them of any con-

MATHEWS v. ELDRIDGE, 424 U.S. 319, 96 S.Ct. 893, 47 L.Ed.2d 18 (1976), per POWELL, J., held that although Social Security disability benefits constitute "a statutorily created 'property' interest protected by the Fifth Amendment," due process does not require a *Goldberg*-type hearing prior to their termination on the ground that "the worker is no longer disabled": "In recent years this Court increasingly has had occasion to consider the extent to which due process requires an evidentiary hearing prior to the deprivation of some type of property interest even if such a hearing is provided thereafter. In only one case, *Goldberg*, has the Court held that a hearing closely approximating a judicial trial is necessary. [For example,] *Bell v. Burson* [held] that due process required only that the prerevocation hearing involve a probable-cause determination as to the fault of the licensee, noting that the hearing 'need not take the form of a full adjudication of the question of liability.' [O]ur prior decisions indicate that identification of the specific dictates of due process generally requires consideration of three distinct factors: First, the private interest that will be affected by the official action; second, the risk of an erroneous deprivation of such interest through the procedures used, and the probable value, if any, of additional or substitute procedural safeguards; and finally, the government's interest, including the function involved and the fiscal and administrative burdens that the additional or substitute procedural requirement would entail." [a]

First, in contrast to *Goldberg*, "eligibility for disability benefits [is] not based upon financial need." Rather, such benefits are "wholly unrelated to the worker's income or support from many other sources, such as earnings of other family members, workmen's compensation awards, tort claims awards, savings, [insurance, pensions and public assistance.]" Thus, "there is less reason here than in *Goldberg* to depart from the ordinary principle, established by our decisions, that something less than an evidentiary hearing is sufficient prior to adverse administrative action."

stitutionally protected interest in life, liberty or property."

Blackmun, J., concurred, but found the Court's analysis "simplistic and unsatisfactory." He did not find the distinction between "direct" and "indirect" losses helpful and, in any event, had "great difficulty concluding that the patients' loss of their home should be characterized as 'indirect and incidental.' " For extensive criticism of *O'Bannon,* see Mashaw, supra, at 36–41; Terrell, supra, at 927–35.

a. The Court subsequently utilized the factors set forth in *Eldridge* in analyzing *Ingraham v. Wright* (p. 409 fn. 10 supra) (corporal punishment in public schools) and *Parham v. J.R.* (p. 346 fn. a supra) (parents' commitment of minor children). The *Eldridge* "balancing approach" was also utilized in, e.g., *Dixon v. Love,* 431 U.S. 105, 97 S.Ct. 1723, 52 L.Ed.2d 172 (1977) (Blackmun, J.) (no prior evidentiary hearing required for driver license revocation pursuant to regulation mandating such revocation if license had been suspended three times within 10 years for conviction of traffic violations); *Memphis Light, Gas & Water Division v. Craft,* 436 U.S. 1, 98 S.Ct. 1554, 56 L.Ed.2d 30 (1978) (Powell, J.) (municipal utility must provide its customers with some administrative procedure for entertaining com-

plaints before cutting off services); *Mackey v. Montrym,* 443 U.S. 1, 99 S.Ct. 2612, 61 L.Ed.2d 321 (1979) (Burger, C.J.) (license of driver lawfully arrested for drunk driving may be suspended for 90 days without prior hearing for refusing to take breath-analysis test so long as immediate post-suspension hearing is available; *Little v. Streater,* 452 U.S. 1, 101 S.Ct. 2202, 68 L.Ed.2d 627 (1981) (Burger, C.J.) (state's refusal to pay cost of blood grouping test for indigent defendant in paternity action, a proceeding with " 'quasi-criminal' overtones," denies him "meaningful opportunity to be heard" and thus violates procedural due process); *Walters v. National Association of Radiation Survivors,* __ U.S. __, 105 S.Ct. 3180, 87 L.Ed.2d 220 (1985) (Rehnquist, J.) (federal statute limiting to $10 the fee that may be paid an attorney or agent representing one seeking benefits from Veterans Administration (VA) for service-connected death or disability does not violate procedural due process; since benefits are not granted on basis of need, they are more like social security benefits involved in *Eldridge* than welfare benefits involved in *Goldberg*; elimination of fee limitation "would bid fair to complicate a proceeding which Congress wished to keep as simple as possible").

Second, "the potential value of an evidentiary hearing, or even oral presentation to the decisionmaker, is substantially less in this context than in *Goldberg*." Here, "a medical assessment of the worker's physical or mental condition is required. This is a more sharply focused and easily documented decision than the typical determination of welfare entitlement [where] a wide variety of information may be deemed relevant, and issues of witness credibility and veracity often are critical to the decision-making process." Further, "the information critical [in the disability case] usually is derived from medical sources, [which are likely] to communicate more effectively through written documents than are welfare recipients or the lay witnesses supporting their cause."

Third, as to the "additional cost in terms of money and administrative burden" if pretermination hearings were required, "at some point the benefit of an additional safeguard to the individual affected by the administrative action and to society in terms of increased assurance that the action is just, may be outweighed by the cost. Significantly, the cost of protecting those whom the preliminary administrative process has identified as likely to be found undeserving may in the end come out of the pockets of the deserving since resources available for any particular program of social welfare are not unlimited."

Finally, "in assessing what process is due in this case, substantial weight must be given to the good-faith judgments of the individuals charged by Congress with the administration of the social welfare system that the procedures they have provided assure fair consideration of the entitlement claims of individuals." [b]

The *Eldridge* approach, observes Mashaw, *The Supreme Court's Due Process Calculus for Administrative Adjudication in Mathews v. Eldridge*, 44 U.Chi.L. Rev. 28, 39 (1976), "is subjective and impressionistic. [The Court] assumes that disability recipients are less dependent on income support than welfare recipients. This assumption is buttressed only by the notion that welfare is for the needy and disability insurance is for prior taxpayers. [But], any number of circumstances might make a terminated welfare recipient's plight less desperate than that of his disabled SSA counterpart,[42] or vice versa." Mashaw finds several of the *Eldridge* conclusions questionable, especially that it was dealing with an essentially medical determination. Id. at 40. "The *Goldberg* decision's approach to prescribing due process—specification of the attributes of adjudicatory hearings by analogy to judicial trial—makes the Court resemble an administrative engineer with an outdated professional education. It is at once intrusive and ineffectual. Retreating from this stance, [*Eldridge*] relies on the administrator's good faith—an equally troublesome posture in a political system thatdepends heavily on judicial review for the protection of countermajoritarian values." Id. at 58.

b. Brennan, J., joined by Marshall, J., dissented: "[I]n the present case, it is indicated that because disability benefits were terminated there was a foreclosure upon the Eldridge home and the family's furniture was repossessed, forcing Eldridge, his wife and children to sleep in one bed. [It] is also no argument that a worker, who has been placed in the untenable position of having been denied disability benefits, may still seek other forms of public assistance." Stevens, J., did not participate.

42. The terminated [welfare] recipient may have access to home or general relief depending upon his residence, whereas the disability claimant in a different state or locality may not. The disability claimant may be totally dependent for his livelihood on the disability payments, whereas the welfare recipient who is terminated may have been receiving a small AFDC payment to supplement inadequate family earnings.

Chapter 8

FREEDOM OF EXPRESSION AND ASSOCIATION

SECTION 1. WHAT SPEECH SHOULD BE PROTECTED AND HOW MUCH PROTECTION SHOULD IT GET?

The first amendment provides that "Congress shall make no law * * * abridging the freedom of speech, or of the press." Some have stressed that no law means NO LAW. For example, Black, J., dissenting in *Konigsberg v. State Bar,* 366 U.S. 36, 81 S.Ct. 997, 6 L.Ed.2d 105 (1961) argued that the "First Amendment's unequivocal command * * * shows that the men who drafted our Bill of Rights did all the 'balancing' that was to be done in this field."

Laws forbidding speech, however, are commonplace. Laws against perjury, blackmail, and fraud prohibit speech.[a] So does much of the law of contracts. Black, J., himself conceded that speech pursued as an integral part of criminal conduct was beyond first amendment protection. Indeed no one contends that citizens are free to say anything, anywhere, at any time. As Holmes, J., observed, citizens are not free to yell "fire" falsely in a crowded theater.

The spectre of a man crying fire falsely in the theater, however, has plagued first amendment theory. The task is to formulate principles that separate the protected from the unprotected. But speech interacts with too many other values in too many complicated ways to expect that a single formula will prove productive.

Are advocates of illegal action, pornographers selling magazines, or publishers of defamation like that person in the theater or are they engaged in freedom of speech? Do citizens have a right to speak on government property? Which property? Is there a right of access to the print or broadcast media? Can government force private owners to grant access for speakers? Does the first amendment offer protection for the wealthy, powerful corporations, and media conglomerates against government attempts to assure greater equality in the intellectual marketplace? Can government demand information about private political associations or reporters' confidential sources without first amendment limits? Does the first amendment require government to produce information it might otherwise withhold?

a. But see fn. b in *Roth v. United States,* p. 488 infra.

The Court has approached questions such as these without much attention to the language or history [b] of the first amendment and without a commitment to any general theory.[c] Rather it has sought to develop principles on a case-by-case basis and has produced a complex and conflicting body of constitutional precedent. Many of the basic principles were developed in a line of cases involving the advocacy of illegal action.[d]

I. ADVOCACY OF ILLEGAL ACTION

A. EMERGING PRINCIPLES

SCHENCK v. UNITED STATES, 249 U.S. 47, 39 S.Ct. 247, 63 L.Ed. 470 (1919): Defendants were convicted of a conspiracy to violate the 1917 Espionage Act by causing and attempting to cause insubordination in the armed forces of the United States, and obstruction of the recruiting and enlistment service of the United States, when at war with Germany, by printing and circulating to men accepted for military service approximately fifteen thousand copies of the document described in the opinion. In affirming, HOLMES, J., said for a unanimous Court:

"The document in question upon its first printed side recited the first section of the Thirteenth Amendment, said that the idea embodied in it was violated by the conscription act and that a conscript is little better than a convict. In impassioned language it intimated that conscription was despotism in its worst form and a monstrous wrong against humanity in the interest of Wall Street's chosen few. It said, 'Do not submit to intimidation,' but in form at least confined itself to peaceful measures such as a petition for the repeal of the act. The other and later printed side of the sheet was headed 'Assert Your Rights.' It stated reasons for alleging that any one violated the Constitution when he refused to recognize 'your right to assert your opposition to the draft,' and went on, 'If you do not assert and support your rights, you are helping to deny or disparage rights which it is the solemn duty of all citizens and residents of the United States to retain.' It described the arguments on the other side as coming from cunning politicians and a mercenary capitalist press, and even silent consent to the conscription law as helping to support an infamous conspiracy. It denied the power to send our citizens away to foreign shores to shoot up the people of other lands, and added that words could not express the condemnation such coldblooded ruthlessness deserves, &c., &c., winding up, 'You must do your

---

b. See, e.g., Perry, *The Constitution, The Courts, and Human Rights,* 63–64 (1982). For a variety of views about the history surrounding the adoption of the first amendment, compare Levy, *Legacy of Suppression* (1960) with Levy, *Emergence of a Free Press* (1985); Levy, *The Legacy Reexamined,* 37 Stan.L.Rev. 767 (1985); Levy, *On the Origins of the Free Press Clause,* 32 U.C.L.A.L.Rev. 177 (1984) and Anastaplo, *Book Review,* 39 N.Y.U.L.Rev. 735 (1964); Anderson, *The Origins of the Press Clause,* 30 U.C.L.A.L.Rev. 455 (1983); Hamburger, *The Development of the Law of Seditious Libel and the Control of the Press,* 37 Stan.L.Rev. 661 (1985); Mayton, *Seditious Libel and the Lost Guarantee of a Freedom of Expression,* 84 Colum.L.Rev. 91 (1984); Rabban, *The Ahistorical Historian: Leonard Levy on Freedom of Expression in Early American History,* 37 Stan.L.Rev. 795 (1985).

c. On the difficulties involved in developing general theory, see Alexander & Horton, *The Impossibility of a Free Speech Principle,* 78 Nw.U.L.Rev. 1319 (1983); Shiffrin, *The First Amendment and Economic Regulation: Away From a General Theory of the First Amendment,* 78 Nw.U.L.Rev. 1212 (1983); Tribe, *Toward A Metatheory of Free Speech,* 10 Sw.U.L.Rev. 237 (1978).

d. For discussion of the case law preceding *Schenck v. United States,* infra, see Rabban, *The First Amendment in Its Forgotten Years,* 90 Yale L.J. 514 (1981). A general history of free speech and suppression is much needed. For useful commentary see Chafee, *Free Speech in the United States* (1941); Whipple, *The Story of Civil Liberty in the United States* (1927); Kairys, *Freedom of Speech* in The Politics of Law 160 (Kairys ed. 1982).

share to maintain, support and uphold the rights of the people of this country.' Of course the document would not have been sent unless it had been intended to have some effect, and we do not see what effect it could be expected to have upon persons subject to the draft except to influence them to obstruct the carrying of it out. The defendants do not deny that the jury might find against them on this point.

"But it is said, suppose that that was the tendency of this circular, it is protected by the First Amendment to the Constitution. [We] admit that in many places and in ordinary times the defendants in saying all that was said in the circular would have been within their constitutional rights. But the character of every act depends upon the circumstances in which it is done. The most stringent protection of free speech would not protect a man in falsely shouting fire in a theatre and causing a panic. [The] question in every case is whether the words used are used in such circumstances and are of such a nature as to create a clear and present danger that they will bring about the substantive evils that Congress has a right to prevent. It is a question of proximity and degree.[a] When a nation is at war many things that might be said in time of peace are such a hindrance to its effort that their utterance will not be endured so long as men fight and that no Court could regard them as protected by any constitutional right. It seems to be admitted that if an actual obstruction of the recruiting service were proved, liability for words that produced that effect might be enforced. The statute of 1917 punishes conspiracies to obstruct as well as actual obstruction. If the act, (speaking, or circulating a paper), its tendency and the intent with which it is done are the same, we perceive no ground for saying that success alone warrants making the act a crime."[b]

DEBS v. UNITED STATES, 249 U.S. 211, 39 S.Ct. 252, 63 L.Ed. 566 (1919): Defendant was convicted of violating the Espionage Act for obstructing and attempting to obstruct the recruiting service and for causing and attempting to cause insubordination and disloyalty in the armed services. He was given a ten-year prison sentence on each count, to run concurrently. His criminal conduct consisted of giving the anti-war speech described in the opinion at the state convention of the Socialist Party of Ohio, held at a park in Canton, Ohio, on a

---

a. Although Schenck was convicted for violating a conspiracy statute, Holmes appears to have used the occasion to import the law of criminal attempts into the freedom of expression area. "In *Schenck,* 'clear and present danger,' 'a question of proximity and degree' bridged the gap between the defendant's acts of publication and the [prohibited interferences with the war.] This connection was strikingly similar to the Holmesian analysis of the requirement of 'dangerous proximity to success' [quoting from an earlier Holmes opinion] that, in the law of attempts, bridges the gap between the defendant's acts and the completed crime. In either context, innocuous efforts are to be ignored." Rogat, *Mr. Justice Holmes: Some Modern Views—The Judge as Spectator,* 31 U.Chi.L.Rev. 213, 215 (1964). See also Chafee, *Free Speech in the United States* 81–82 (1941); Shapiro, *Freedom of Speech* 55–58 (1966). But see Holmes, J., dissenting in *Abrams* infra, and fn. b below.

b. See also *Frohwerk v. United States,* 249 U.S. 204, 39 S.Ct. 249, 63 L.Ed. 561 (1919), where a unanimous Court, per Holmes, J., sustained a conviction for conspiracy to obstruct recruiting in violation of the Espionage Act, by means of a dozen newspaper articles praising the spirit and strength of the German nation, criticizing the decision to send American troops to France, maintaining that the government was giving false and hypocritical reasons for its course of action and implying that "the guilt of those who voted the unnatural sacrifice" is greater than the wrong of those who seek to escape by resistance: "[*Schenck* decided] that a person may be convicted of a conspiracy to obstruct recruiting by words of persuasion. [S]o far as the language of the articles goes there is not much to choose between expressions to be found in them and those before us in *Schenck.*"

June 16, 1918 Sunday afternoon before a general audience of 1,200 persons. At the time of the speech, defendant was a national political figure.[a] In affirming, HOLMES, J., observed for a unanimous Court:

"The main theme of the speech was socialism, its growth, and a prophecy of its ultimate success. With that we have nothing to do, but if a part or the manifest intent of the more general utterances was to encourage those present to obstruct the recruiting service and if in passages such encouragement was directly given, the immunity of the general theme may not be enough to protect the speech. [Defendant had come to the park directly from a nearby jail, where he had visited three socialists imprisoned for obstructing the recruiting service. He expressed sympathy and admiration for these persons and others convicted of similar offenses, and then] said that the master class has always declared the war and the subject class has always fought the battles—that the subject class has had nothing to gain and all to lose, including their lives; [and that] 'You have your lives to lose; you certainly ought to have the right to declare war if you consider a war necessary.' [He next said of a woman serving a ten-year sentence for obstructing the recruiting service] that she had said no more than the speaker had said that afternoon; that if she was guilty so was [he].

"There followed personal experiences and illustrations of the growth of socialism, a glorification of minorities, and a prophecy of the success of [socialism], with the interjection that 'you need to know that you are fit for something better than slavery and cannon fodder.' [Defendant's] final exhortation [was] 'Don't worry about the charge of treason to your masters; but be concerned about the treason that involves yourselves.' The defendant addressed the jury himself, and while contending that his speech did not warrant the charges said 'I have been accused of obstructing the war. I admit it. Gentlemen, I abhor war. I would oppose the war if I stood alone.' The statement was not necessary to warrant the jury in finding that one purpose of the speech, whether incidental or not does not matter, was to oppose not only war in general but this war, and that the opposition was so expressed that its natural and intended effect would be to obstruct recruiting. If that was intended and if, in all the circumstances, that would be its probable effect, it would not be protected by reason of its being part of a general program and expressions of a general and conscientious belief.

"[Defendant's constitutional objections] based upon the First Amendment [were] disposed of in *Schenck.*

"[T]he admission in evidence of the record of the conviction [of various persons he mentioned in his speech was proper] to show what he was talking about, to explain the true import of his expression of sympathy and to throw light on the intent of the address. [Properly admitted, too, was an 'Anti-war Proclamation and Program' adopted the previous year, coupled with testimony that shortly before his speech defendant had stated that he approved it]. Its first recommendation was, 'continuous, active, and public opposition to the war, through demonstrations, mass petitions, and all other means within our power.' Evidence that the defendant accepted this view and this declaration of his duties at the time that he made his speech is evidence that if in that speech he used words tending to obstruct the recruiting service he meant that they should have

---

a. Debs had run for the Presidency on the Socialist ticket for the fourth time in 1912. At the 1920 election, while in prison, Debs ran again and received over 900,000 votes as the Socialist candidate, a significant portion of all votes cast in that election. Consider Kalven, *Ernst Freund and the First Amendment Tradition,* 40 U.Chi.L.Rev. 235, 237 (1973): "To put the case in modern context, it is somewhat as though George McGovern had been sent to prison for his criticism of the [Vietnam] war."

that effect. [T]he jury were most carefully instructed that they could not find the defendant guilty for advocacy of any of his opinions unless the words used had as their natural tendency and reasonably probable effect to obstruct the recruiting service [and] unless the defendant had the specific intent to do so in his mind."

Notes and Questions

1. *Reflections.* (a) Consider Kalven, *Ernst Freund and the First Amendment Tradition,* 40 U.Chi.L.Rev. 235, 236–38 (1973): "It has been customary to lavish care and attention on the *Schenck* case, [but *Debs,* argued well before *Schenck* was handed down and decided just one week later,] represented the first effort by Justice Holmes to apply what he had worked out about freedom of speech in *Schenck.* The start of the law of the first amendment is not *Schenck;* it is *Schenck* and *Debs* read together. [Deb's speech] fell into the genre of bitter criticism of government and government policy, sometimes called seditious libel; freedom of such criticism from government marks, we have come to understand, 'the central meaning of the First Amendment' [*New York Times v. Sullivan,* p. 464 infra]. During the Vietnam War thousands of utterances strictly comparable in bitterness and sharpness of criticism, if not in literacy, were made; it was pretty much taken for granted they were beyond the reach of government.[b] [*Debs*] raises serious questions as to what the first amendment, and more especially, what the clear and present danger formula can possibly have meant at the time. [Holmes] does not comment on the fact difference between [*Schenck* and *Debs*]: the defendant in *Schenck* had sent his leaflets directly to men who awaited draft call whereas [Debs] was addressing a general audience at a public meeting. Holmes offers no discussion of the sense in which Debs's speech presented a clear and present danger. [In fact, *Debs*] did not move [Holmes] to discuss free speech at all; his brief opinion is occupied with two points about admissibility of [evidence]. It was for Holmes a routine criminal appeal."

(b) Chafee, *Free Speech in the United States* 85 (1941), observes: "Debs was convicted of an attempt to cause insubordination in the army and obstruct recruiting, yet no provocation to any such definite and particular acts was proved. [Not one word uttered by Debs] was designed for soldiers, not one word urged his hearers to resist the draft, objectionable as he considered it. Undoubtedly he admitted at his trial that he had obstructed the war, [but] the only question before the jury was whether he had tried to obstruct it in the ways made unlawful in the statute. If all verbal or written opposition to the war furnishes a basis for conviction, because it is dangerous under the circumstances and indicates a criminal mind, then none but the most courageous will dare speak out against a future war."

(c) Consider Freund, *The Debs Case and Freedom of Speech,* The New Republic, May 3, 1919, p. 13, reprinted in 40 U.Chi.L.Rev. 239, 240–41 (1973): "[*Debs*] illustrates most clearly the arbitrariness of the whole idea of implied provocation. A violent, if you please, a seditious speech is made; a docile jury finds a design to obstruct recruiting, and the finding is conclusive because the court does not consider it inconsistent with possibility. What are the intrinsic probabilities? An experienced speaker like Debs knows the effect of words. He must have known that while he might keep alive and even create disaffection, his power to create actual obstruction to a compulsory draft was practically nil,

b. Compare *Debs* with *Bond v. Floyd,* p. 455 infra.

and he could hardly have intended what he could not hope to achieve; in fact it is difficult to conceive of a form of obstruction that can be opposed to a compulsory draft.[c] [Yet] Holmes would make us believe that the relation of the speech to obstruction is like that of the shout of Fire! in a crowded theatre to the resulting panic! Surely implied provocation in connection with political offenses is an unsafe doctrine if it has to be made plausible by a parallel so manifestly inappropriate."

2. *"Breathing space" for free speech under the Espionage Act.* Consider Chafee, supra, at 50–51: "[With a few exceptions, notably Judge Learned Hand's opinion in *Masses*, infra, the lower federal courts] allowed conviction [under the Espionage Act] for any words which had an indirect effect to discourage recruiting and the war spirit [so long as] the intention to discourage existed. [Moreover, the] requirement of intention became a mere form since it could be inferred from the existence of the indirect injurious effect. [T]he words of the Espionage Act of 1917 bear slight resemblance to the Sedition Law of 1798, but the judicial construction is much the same, except that under the Sedition Law truth was a defense."

Consider Ernst Freund's criticism of *Debs*, supra at 240–41: "To know what you may do and what you may not do, and how far you may go in criticism, is the first condition of political liberty; to be permitted to agitate at your own peril, subject to a jury's guessing at motive, tendency and possible effect, makes the right of free speech a precarious gift. [For] arbitrary executive, [the Espionage Act] practically substitutes arbitrary, judicial power; since a jury's findings, within the limits of a conceivable psychological nexus between words and deeds, are beyond scrutiny and control; and while the jury may have been a protection against governmental power when the government was a thing apart from the people, its checking function fails where government policies are supported by majority opinion." See also Chafee, supra, at 70: "[As a federal judge] said after much experience in Espionage Act cases: '[I] tried war cases before jurymen [who] under ordinary circumstances would have had the highest respect for my declarations of law, but during that period they looked back into my eyes with the savagery of wild animals, saying by their manner, "Away with the twiddling, let us get at him." Men believed during that period that the only verdict in a war case, which could show loyalty, was a verdict of guilty.'"

Holmes, J.'s response, in private correspondence, see Ginsburg, *Afterword*, 40 U.Chi.L.Rev. 243, 245 (1973), to Professor Freund's objection, in his article on *Debs*, to a jury "guessing at motive, tendency and possible effect" was that this could be said about "pretty much the whole body of the law, which for thirty years I have made my brethren smile by insisting to be everywhere a matter of degree." Holmes recalled the comment he made in a case involving a criminal prosecution under the Sherman Act that "the law is full of instances where a man's fate depends on his estimating rightly, that is, as the jury subsequently estimates it, some matter of degree. If his judgment is wrong, not only may he incur a fine or [prison term, but] the penalty of death."

3. Would a construction of the Espionage Act which punished "direct advocacy" of violations of existing laws or "direct counselling" of others to do so, but protected other antiwar discussion or agitation, be more "workable" than the clear and present danger test of *Schenck* and *Debs*? More consistent with the first amendment? Preferable to the clear and present danger test reiterated

c. See also Nelles, *Espionage Act Cases* 77–80 (1918).

(clarified, revised) in the *Abrams* dissent, infra? Could a jury pass on the *actual nature of the words used* by a speaker much better than it could the "tendency" and "effects" of his words? Moreover, would a standard which focused on the nature of the words not only give the jury something definite to consider but be more easily understood by the opponents of the war? See Chafee, supra, at 42–45, 63, praising the approach taken by "that judge who during the war gave the fullest attention to the meaning of free speech," Learned Hand in *Masses,* set forth below—two years before the Espionage Act reached the Supreme Court. To what extent is Hand's test, which avoids the clear and present danger formula, reflected decades later in *Yates, Scales* and *Noto,* p. 447 infra? In *Brandenburg,* p. 455 infra? In *Bond v. Floyd,* p. 455 infra? In the First Circuit's opinion in the *Spock* case, p. 454 infra?

4. MASSES PUBLISHING CO. v. PATTEN, 244 F. 535 (S.D.N.Y.1917): The Postmaster of New York advised plaintiff that an issue of his monthly revolutionary journal, *The Masses,* would be denied the mails under the Espionage Act since it tended to encourage the enemies of the United States and to hamper the government in its conduct of the war. The Postmaster subsequently specified as objectionable several cartoons entitled, e.g., "Conscription," "Making the World Safe for Capitalism"; several articles admiring the "sacrifice" of conscientious objectors and a poem praising two persons imprisoned for conspiracy to resist the draft. Plaintiff sought a preliminary injunction against the postmaster from excluding its magazine from the mails. LEARNED HAND, D.J., granted relief:

"[The postmaster maintains] that to arouse discontent and disaffection among the people with the prosecution of the war and with the draft tends to promote a mutinous and insubordinate temper among the troops. This [is] true; men who become satisfied that they are engaged in an enterprise dictated by the unconscionable selfishness of the rich, and effectuated by a tyrannous disregard for the will of those who must suffer and die, will be more prone to insubordination than those who have faith in the cause and acquiesce in the means. Yet to interpret the word 'cause' [in the statutory language forbidding one to 'willfully cause' insubordination in the armed forces] so broadly would [necessarily involve] the suppression of all hostile criticism, and of all opinion except what encouraged and supported the existing policies, or which fell within the range of temperate argument. It would contradict the normal assumption of democratic government that the suppression of hostile criticism does not turn upon the justice of its substance or the decency and propriety of its temper. Assuming that the power to repress such opinion may rest in Congress in the throes of a struggle for the very existence of the state, its exercise is so contrary to the use and wont of our people that only the clearest expression of such a power justifies the conclusion that it was intended.

"The defendant's position, therefore, in so far as it involves the suppression of the free utterance of abuse and criticism of the existing law, or of the policies of the war, is not, in my judgment, supported by the language of the statute. Yet there has always been a recognized limit to such expressions, incident indeed to the existence of any compulsive power of the state itself. One may not counsel or advise others to violate the law as it stands. Words are not only the keys of persuasion, but the triggers of action, and those which have no purport but to counsel the violation of law cannot by any latitude of interpretation be a part of that public opinion which is the final source of government in a democratic state. [To] counsel or advise a man to an act is to urge upon him either that it is his interest or his duty to do it. While, of course, this may be accomplished as well by indirection as expressly, since words carry the meaning that they impart, the definition is exhaustive, I think, and I shall use it. Political agitation, by the passions it arouses or the convictions it engenders, may in fact stimulate men to the violation of law. Detestation of existing policies is easily transformed into forcible resistance of the authority which puts them in execution, and it would be folly to disregard the causal relation between the two. Yet to assimilate agitation, legitimate as such, with direct incitement to violent resistance, is to disregard the tolerance of all methods of political agitation which in normal times is a safeguard of free government. The distinction is not a scholastic subterfuge, but a hard-bought acquisition in the fight for freedom, and the purpose to disregard it must be evident when the power exists. If one stops short of urging upon others that it is their duty or their interest to resist the law, it seems to me one should not be held to have attempted to cause its violation. If that be not the test, I can see no escape from the conclusion that under this section every political agitation which can be shown to be apt to create a seditious temper is illegal. I am confident that by such language Congress had no such revolutionary purpose in view.

"It seems to me, however, quite plain that none of the language and none of the cartoons in this paper can be thought directly to counsel or advise insubordination or mutiny, without a violation of their meaning quite beyond any tolerable understanding. I come, therefore to the [provision of the Act forbidding] any one from willfully obstructing [recruiting or enlistment]. I am not prepared to assent to the plaintiff's position that this only refers to acts other than words, nor that the act thus defined must be shown to have been successful. One may obstruct without preventing, and the mere obstruction is an injury to the service; for it throws impediments in its way. Here again, however, since the question is of the expression of opinion, I construe the sentence, so far as it restrains public utterance, [as] limited to the direct advocacy of resistance to the recruiting and enlistment service. If so, the inquiry is narrowed to the question whether any of the challenged matter may be said to advocate resistance to the draft, taking the meaning of the words with the utmost latitude which they can bear.

"As to the cartoons it seems to me quite clear that they do not fall within such a test. [T]he most that can be said [is that they] may breed such animosity to the draft as will promote resistance and strengthen the determination of those disposed to be recalcitrant. There is no intimation that, however, hateful the draft may be, one is in duty bound to resist it, certainly none that such resistance is to one's interest. I cannot, therefore, even with the limitations which surround the power of the court, assent to the assertion that any of the cartoons violate the act.

"[As for the text], it is plain enough that the [magazine] has the fullest sympathy for [those who resist the draft or obstruct recruiting], that it admires their courage, and that it presumptively approves their conduct. [Moreover,] these passages, it must be remembered, occur in a magazine which attacks with the utmost violence the draft and the war. That such comments have a tendency to arouse emulation in others is clear enough, but that they counsel others to follow these examples is not so plain. Literally at least they do not, and while, as I have said, the words are to be taken, not literally, but according to their full import, the literal meaning is the starting point for interpretation. One may admire and approve the course of a hero without feeling any duty to follow him. There is not the least implied intimation in these words that others are under a duty to follow. The most that can be said is that, if others do follow, they will get the same admiration and the same approval. Now, there is surely an appreciable distance between esteem and emulation; and unless there is here some advocacy of such emulation, I cannot see how the passages can be said to fall within the [law.] Surely, if the draft had not excepted Quakers, it would be too strong a doctrine to say that any who openly admire their fortitude or even approved their conduct was willfully obstructing the draft.

"When the question is of a statute constituting a crime, it seems to me that there should be more definite evidence of the act. The question before me is quite the same as what would arise upon a motion to dismiss an indictment at the close of the proof: Could any reasonable man say, not that the indirect result of the language might be to arouse a seditious disposition, for that would not be enough, but that the language directly advocated resistance to the draft? I cannot think that upon such language any verdict would stand." [d]

What result if the Court had applied the *Masses* test in *Schenck* or *Debs*? In *Abrams* or *Gitlow,* infra?

JUSTICE HOLMES—DISSENTING IN
ABRAMS v. UNITED STATES

250 U.S. 616, 624, 40 S.Ct. 17, 20, 63 L.Ed. 1173, 1178 (1919).

[In the summer of 1918, the United States sent a small body of marines to Siberia. Although the defendants maintained a strong socialist opposition to "German militarism," they opposed the "capitalist" invasion of Russia, and characterized it as an attempt to crush the Russian Revolution. Shortly thereafter, they printed two leaflets and distributed several thousand copies in New York City. Many of the copies were thrown from a window where one defendant was employed; others were passed around at radical meetings. Both leaflets supported Russia against the United States; one called upon workers to unite in a general strike. There was no evidence that workers responded to the call.

[The Court upheld the defendants' convictions for conspiring to violate two provisions of the 1918 amendments to the Espionage Act. One count prohibited language intended to "incite, provoke and encourage resistance to the United States"; the other punished those who urged curtailment of war production. As the Court interpreted the statute, an intent to interfere with efforts against a *declared* war was a necessary element of both offenses. Since the United States had not declared war upon Russia, "the main task of the government was to establish an [*intention*] to interfere with the war with Germany." Chafee, supra, at 115. The Court found intent on the principle that "Men must be held to have intended, and to be accountable for, the effects which their acts were likely to produce. Even if their primary purpose and intent was to aid the cause of the Russian Revolution, the plan of action which they adopted necessarily involved, before it could be realized, defeat of the war program of the United States * * *."

[HOLMES, J., dissented in an opinion with which Brandeis, J., concurred:]

[I] am aware of course that the word "intent" as vaguely used in ordinary legal discussion means no more than knowledge at the time of the act that the

---

d. In reversing, 246 Fed. 24 (1917), the Second Circuit observed: "If the natural and probable effect of what is said is to encourage resistance to a law, and the words are used in an endeavor to persuade to resistance, it is immaterial that the duty to resist is not mentioned, or the interest of the person addressed in resistance is not suggested. That one may willfully obstruct the enlistment service, without advising in direct language against enlistments, and without stating that to refrain from enlistment is a duty or in one's interest, seems to us too plain for controversy."

consequences said to be intended will ensue. [But,] when words are used exactly, a deed is not done with intent to produce a consequence unless that consequence is the aim of the deed. It may be obvious, and obvious to the actor, that the consequence will follow, and he may be liable for it even if he regrets it, but he does not do the act with intent to produce it unless the aim to produce it is the proximate motive of the specific act although there may be some deeper motive behind.

It seems to me that this statute must be taken to use its words in a strict and accurate sense. They would be absurd in any other. A patriot might think that we were wasting money on aeroplanes, or making more cannon of a certain kind than we needed, and might advocate curtailment with success, yet even if it turned out that the curtailment hindered and was thought by other minds to have been obviously likely to hinder the United States in the prosecution of the war, no one would hold such conduct a crime. * * *

I never have seen any reason to doubt that the questions of law that alone were before this Court in the cases of *Schenck, Frohwerk* and *Debs* were rightly decided. I do not doubt for a moment that by the same reasoning that would justify punishing persuasion to murder, the United States constitutionally may punish speech that produces or is intended to produce a clear and imminent danger that it will bring about forthwith certain substantive evils that the United States constitutionally may seek to prevent. The power undoubtedly is greater in time of war than in time of peace because war opens dangers that do not exist at other times.

But as against dangers peculiar to war, as against others, the principle of the right to free speech is always the same. It is only the present danger of immediate evil or an intent to bring it about that warrants Congress in setting a limit to the expression of opinion where private rights are not concerned. Congress certainly cannot forbid all effort to change the mind of the country. Now nobody can suppose that the surreptitious publishing of a silly leaflet by an unknown man, without more, would present any immediate danger that its opinions would hinder the success of the government arms or have any appreciable tendency to do so.[a] Publishing those opinions for the very purpose of obstructing, however, might indicate a greater danger and at any rate would have the quality of an attempt.[b] * * *

a. See also Chafee, supra, at 140: "The maximum sentence available against a formidable pro-German plot [20 years] was meted out [for] the silly, futile circulars of five obscure and isolated young aliens, misguided by their loyalty to their endangered country and ideals, who hatched their wild scheme in a garret, and carried it out in a cellar." But cf. Wigmore, *Abrams v. U.S.: Freedom of Speech and Freedom of Thuggery in War-Time and Peace-Time*, 14 Ill.L.Rev. 539, 549–50 (1920): "[The *Abrams* dissent] is dallying with the facts and the law. None know better than judges that what is lawful for one is lawful for a thousand others. If these five men could, without the law's restraint, urge munition workers to a general strike and armed violences then others could lawfully do so; and a thousand disaffected undesirables, aliens and natives alike, were ready and waiting to do so. Though this circular was 'surreptitious,' the next ones need not be so. If such urgings were lawful, every munitions factory in the country could be stopped by them. The relative amount of harm that one criminal act can effect is no measure of its criminality, and no measure of the danger of its criminality. To put forward such a palliation is merely to reveal more clearly the indifference to the whole crisis. [At a time] when the fate of the civilized world hung in the balance, how could the Minority Opinion interpret law and conduct in such a way as to let loose men who were doing their hardest to paralyze the supreme war efforts of our country?"

b. Would it, if, under the circumstances, the defendant had no reasonable prospect of success? If his efforts were utterly ineffectual? Is bad intention or purpose, without more, an attempt? Or even everything done in furtherance of that bad intention? Or is unlawful "intention" or "purpose" merely one factor in determining whether defendant's

I do not see how anyone can find the intent required by the statute in any of the defendants' words. The leaflet advocating a general strike is the only one that affords even a foundation for the charge, and [its only object] is to help Russia and stop American intervention there against the popular government—not to impede the United States in the war that it was carrying on. * * *

In this case sentences of twenty years imprisonment have been imposed for the publishing of two leaflets that I believe the defendants had as much right to publish as the Government has to publish the Constitution of the United States now vainly invoked by them. [E]ven if what I think the necessary intent were shown; the most nominal punishment seems to me all that possibly could be inflicted, unless the defendants are to be made to suffer not for what the indictment alleges but for the creed that they avow—[which,] although made the subject of examination at the trial, no one has a right even to consider in dealing with the charges before the Court.

Persecution for the expression of opinions seems to me perfectly logical. If you have no doubt of your premises or your power and want a certain result with all your heart you naturally express your wishes in law and sweep away all opposition. To allow opposition by speech seems to indicate that you think the speech impotent, as when a man says that he has squared the circle, or that you do not care whole-heartedly for the result, or that you doubt either your power or your premises. But when men have realized that time has upset many fighting faiths, they may come to believe even more than they believe the very foundations of their own conduct that the ultimate good desired is better reached by free trade in ideas—that the best test of truth is the power of the thought to get itself accepted in the competition of the market, and that truth is the only ground upon which their wishes safely can be carried out.[c] That at any rate is the theory of our Constitution. It is an experiment, as all life is an experiment. Every year if not every day we have to wager our salvation upon some prophecy based upon imperfect knowledge. While that experiment is part of our system I

---

conduct comes dangerously near success or stamps the actor as sufficiently dangerous? Cf. Holmes, *The Common Law* 65–66, 68–69 (1881): "Intent to commit a crime is not itself criminal. [Moreover], the law does not punish every act which is done with the intent to bring about a crime. [We] have seen what amounts to an attempt to burn a haystack [lighting a match with intent to start fire to a haystack]; but it was said in the same case, that, if the defendant had gone no further than to buy a box of matches for the purpose, he would not have been liable. [Relevant considerations are] the nearness of the danger, the greatness of the harm and the degree of apprehension felt." See also Holmes, C.J., in *Commonwealth v. Peaslee,* 177 Mass. 267, 59 N.E. 55 (1901) ("if the preparation comes very near to the accomplishment of the act, the intent to complete it renders the crime so probable" that the conduct will constitute an attempt); Holmes, J., dissenting in *Hyde v. United States,* 255 U.S. 347, 387, 32 S.Ct. 793, 56 L.Ed. 1114 (1912) (preliminary acts become an attempt when "so near to the result [completed crime] that if coupled with an intent to produce that result, the danger is very great"). See generally Chafee, supra, at 46–47; Linde,

"Clear and Present Danger" Reexamined, 22 Stan.L.Rev. 1163, 1168–69, 1183–86 (1970); Shapiro, *Freedom of Speech* 55–58 (1966).

c. But see Wigmore, fn. a supra, at 550–51: "This apotheosis of Truth, however, shows a blindness to the deadly fact that meantime the 'power of the thought' of these circulars might 'get itself accepted in the competition of the market,' by munitions workers, so as to lose the war; in which case, the academic victory which Truth, 'the ultimate good,' might later secure in the market, would be too 'ultimate' to have any practical value for a defeated America. [To] weigh in juxtaposition the dastardly sentiments of these circulars and the great theme of world-justice for which [we were fighting], and then to assume the sacred cause of Truth as equally involved in both, is to misuse high ideals. This [dissenting opinion, if it had commanded a majority], would have ended by our letting soldiers die helpless in France, through our anxiety to protect the distribution of a leaflet whose sole purpose was to cut off the soldiers' munitions and supplies. How would this have advanced the cause of Truth?"

think that we should be eternally vigilant against attempts to check the expression of opinions that we loathe and believe to be fraught with death, unless they so imminently threaten immediate interference with the lawful and pressing purposes of the law that an immediate check is required to save the country. [Only] the emergency that makes it immediately dangerous to leave the correction of evil counsels to time warrants making any exception to the sweeping command, "Congress shall make no law * * * abridging the freedom of speech." Of course I am speaking only of expressions of opinion and exhortations, which were all that were uttered [here].

Notes and Questions

1. *"Marketplace of ideas."* (a) Contrast Holmes' statement of the "marketplace of ideas" argument with John Milton's statement in *Areopagitica:* "And though all the winds of doctrine were let loose to play upon the earth, so Truth be in the field, we do injuriously by licensing and prohibiting to misdoubt her strength. Let her and Falsehood grapple; who ever knew Truth put to the worse, in a free and open encounter?" Holmes claims that the competition of the market is the best test of truth; Milton maintains that truth will emerge in a free and open encounter. How would one verify either hypothesis?

Is the "marketplace of ideas" a "free and open encounter"? Consider Lindblom, *Politics and Markets* 207 (1977): "Early, persuasive, unconscious conditioning—[to] believe in the fundamental politico-economic institutions of one's society is ubiquitous in every society. These institutions come to be taken for granted. Many people grow up to regard them not as institutions to be tested but as standards against which the correctness of new policies and institutions can be tested. When that happens, as is common, processes of critical judgment are short-circuited." Consider also Tribe, *American Constitutional Law* 577 (1978): "Especially when the wealthy have more access to the most potent media of communication than the poor, how sure can we be that 'free trade in ideas' is likely to generate truth?"

For a specific example, see Shiffrin, *The First Amendment and Economic Regulation: Away From A General Theory of the First Amendment,* 78 Nw.U.L. Rev. 1212, 1281 (1983): "Living in a society in which children and adults are daily confronted with multiple communications that ask them to purchase products inevitably places emphasis on materialistic values. The authors of the individual messages may not intend that general emphasis, but the whole is greater than the sum of the parts. [Advertisers] spend some sixty billion dollars per year. [Those] who would oppose the materialist message must combat forces that have a massive economic advantage. Any confidence that we will know what is truth by seeing what emerges from such combat is ill placed."

Do the different market failure considerations offered by Lindblom, Tribe, and Shiffrin add up to a rebuttal of the marketplace argument? Consider *Nimmer on Freedom of Speech* 1–12 (1984): "If acceptance of an idea in the competition of the market is not the 'best test' [what] is the alternative? It can only be acceptance of an idea by some individual or group narrower than that of the public at large. Thus, the alternative to competition in the market must be some form of elitism. It seems hardly necessary to enlarge on the dangers of that path." Is elitism the only alternative to the marketplace perspective? Is elitism always wrong?

(b) Evaluate the following hypothetical commentary: "Liberals have favored government intervention in the economic marketplace but pressed for laissez-faire in the intellectual marketplace. Conservatives have done the reverse. Liberals and conservatives have one thing in common: inconsistent positions."

(c) Does the marketplace argument overvalue truth? Consider Schauer, *Free Speech: A Philosophical Enquiry* 23 (1982). Government may seek to suppress opinions "because their expression is thought to impair the authority of a lawful and effective government, interfere with the administration of justice (such as publication of a defendant's criminal record in advance of a jury trial), cause offence, invade someone's privacy, or cause a decrease in public order. When these are the motives for suppression, the possibility of losing some truth is relevant but hardly dispositive. [In such circumstances] the argument from truth [is] not wholly to the point." Is Holmes persuasive when he maintains that before we can suppress opinion we must wait until "an immediate check is required to save the country"?

(d) Does the marketplace argument threaten first amendment values? Consider Ingber, *The Marketplace of Ideas: A Legitimizing Myth*, 1984 Duke L.J. 1, 4–5 "[C]ourts that invoke the marketplace model of the first amendment justify free expression because of the aggregate benefits to society, and not because an individual speaker receives a particular benefit. Courts that focus their concern on the audience rather than the speaker relegate free expression to an instrumental value, a means toward some other goal, rather than a value unto itself. Once free expression is viewed solely as an instrumental value, however, it is easier to allow government regulation of speech if society as a whole 'benefits' from a regulated system of expression."

(e) Does the marketplace argument slight other important free speech values? Consider Wolff, *The Poverty of Liberalism* 18 (1968) "[I]t is not to assist the advance of knowledge that free debate is needed. Rather, it is in order to guarantee that every legitimate interest shall make itself known and felt in the political [process]. Justice, not truth, is the ideal served by liberty of speech." Compare Chevigny, *Philosophy of Language and Free Expression*, 55 N.Y.U.L. Rev. 157 (1980); Leitner, *Liberalism, Separation and Speech*, 1985 Wis.L.Rev. 79, 89–90 & 103–04. See also Shiffrin, *Liberalism, Radicalism, and Legal Scholarship*, 30 U.C.L.A.L.Rev. 1103, 1197–98 (1983): "Freedom of speech [is] associated with a multiplicity of more general moral rights and interests that are valuable, including, but not limited to, individual self-expression, social communion, political participation, the search for truth and for informed choice, social catharsis, the social affirmation of the rights of equality, dignity, and respect, and the freedom from arbitrary, official aggrandizing or excessively intrusive government regulation." The standard starting place for discussion of free speech values continues to be Emerson, *The System of Freedom of Expression* 6–9 (1970).

(f) For a powerful critique of marketplace models, see Baker, *Scope of the First Amendment Freedom of Speech*, 25 U.C.L.A.L.Rev. 964 (1978). For an analytical defense, albeit heavily qualified, see Schauer, *Language, Truth, and the First Amendment*, 64 Va.L.Rev. 263 (1978).

2. In *Schenck,* did the Court ask whether the particular speech interfered with some specific phase of the war effort or whether a *category* of speech *could* interfere with the war effort? In *Abrams,* what did Holmes, J., dissenting, ask? In *Schenck,* did the Court seek to ascertain the speaker's actual intent as one of the factors surrounding the speech which bear on whether a clear and present danger exists or did it simply infer the intent from the general tendency of the speech? In *Abrams,* what did Holmes, J., dissenting, try to do? See Shapiro, *Freedom of Speech* 48–49 (1966).

3. Why did *Abrams*, but not *Debs*, stir Holmes to speak seriously and eloquently about freedom of speech? One suggestion is that "Holmes was biding his time until the Court should have before it a conviction so clearly wrong as to let him speak out his deepest thoughts about the First Amendment" and that "the opportunity [came] eight months after Debs went to prison, in *Abrams*," Chafee, supra, at 86. For the view that the criticism of *Debs* in both the Ernst Freund article and in Learned Hand's correspondence with Holmes may have contributed to a marked change in Holmes' thinking about the first amendment between *Debs* and *Abrams*, see Ginsburg, *Afterword*, 40 U.Chi.L.Rev. 243 (1973). The literature on Holmes' first amendment views and their connection to his larger world view is substantial. See, e.g., Rogat & O'Fallon, *Mr. Justice Holmes: A Dissenting Opinion—The Speech Cases*, 36 Stan.L.Rev. 1349 (1984); Rabban, *The Emergence of Modern First Amendment Doctrine*, 50 U.Chi.L.Rev. 1205 (1983). For further analysis of the Holmes-Hand correspondence, see Gunther, *Learned Hand and the Origins of Modern First Amendment Doctrine: Some Fragments of History*, 27 Stan.L.Rev. 719 (1975).

B. STATE SEDITION LAWS

The second main group of cases in the initial development of first amendment doctrine involved state "sedition laws" of two basic types: criminal anarchy laws, typified by the New York statute in *Gitlow*, infra, and criminal syndicalism laws similar to the California statute in *Whitney*, infra. Most states enacted anarchy and syndicalism statutes between 1917 and 1921, in response to World War I and the fear of Bolshevism that developed in its wake, but the first modern sedition law was passed by New York in 1902, soon after the assassination of President McKinley. The law, which prohibited not only actual or attempted assassinations or conspiracies to assassinate, but advocacy of anarchy as well, lay idle for nearly twenty years, until the *Gitlow* prosecution.

GITLOW v. NEW YORK, 268 U.S. 652, 45 S.Ct. 625, 69 L.Ed. 1138 (1925): Defendant was a member of the Left Wing Section of the Socialist Party and a member of its National Council, which adopted a "Left Wing Manifesto," condemning the dominant "moderate Socialism" for its recognition of the necessity of the democratic parliamentary state; advocating the necessity of accomplishing the "Communist Revolution" by a militant and "revolutionary Socialism" based on "the class struggle"; and urging the development of mass political strikes for the destruction of the parliamentary state. Defendant arranged for printing and distributing, through the mails and otherwise, 16,000 copies of the Manifesto in the Left Wing's official organ, The Revolutionary Age. There was no evidence of any effect from the publication and circulation of the Manifesto.

In sustaining a conviction under the New York "criminal anarchy" statutes, prohibiting the "advocacy, advising or teaching the duty, necessity or propriety of overthrowing or overturning organized government by force or violence" and the publication or distribution of such matter, the majority, per SANFORD, J., stated that for present purposes we may and do assume [a] that first amendment freedoms of expression "are among the fundamental personal rights and 'liber-

---

a. Although *Gitlow* is often cited for the proposition that first amendment freedoms apply to restrict state conduct, its language is dictum. Some would say the first case so holding is *Fiske v. Kansas*, 274 U.S. 380, 47 S.Ct. 655, 71 L.Ed. 1108 (1927) (no evidence to support criminal syndicalism conviction) even though no reference to the first amendment appears in the opinion. See Chafee at 352. Perhaps the honor belongs to *Near v. Minnesota* (1931), p. 584 infra.

ties' protected by the due process clause of the Fourteenth Amendment from impairment by the States," but ruled:

"By enacting the present statute the State has determined, through its legislative body, that utterances advocating the overthrow of organized government by force, violence and unlawful means, are so inimical to the general welfare and involve such danger of substantive evil that they may be penalized in the exercise of its police power. That determination must be given great weight. Every presumption is to be indulged in favor of the validity of the statute. And the case is to be considered 'in the light of the principle that the State is primarily the judge of regulations required in the interest of public safety and welfare'; and that its police 'statutes may only be declared unconstitutional where they are arbitrary or unreasonable attempts to exercise authority vested in the State in the public interest.' That utterances inciting to the overthrow of organized government by unlawful means, present a sufficient danger of substantive evil to bring their punishment within the range of legislative discretion, is clear. Such utterances, by their very nature, involve danger to the public peace and to the security of the State. They threaten breaches of the peace and ultimate revolution. And the immediate danger is none the less real and substantial, because the effect of a given utterance cannot be accurately foreseen. The State cannot reasonably be required to measure the danger from every such utterance in the nice balance of a jeweler's scale. A single revolutionary spark may kindle a fire that, smoldering for a time, may burst into a sweeping and destructive conflagration. It cannot be said that the State is acting arbitrarily or unreasonably when in the exercise of its judgment as to the measures necessary to protect the public peace and safety, it seeks to extinguish the spark without waiting until it has enkindled the flame or blazed into the conflagration. It cannot reasonably be required to defer the adoption of measures for its own peace and safety until the revolutionary utterances lead to actual disturbances of the public peace or imminent and immediate danger of its own destruction; but it may, in the exercise of its judgment, suppress the threatened danger in its incipiency.[b]

"[It] is clear that the question in [this case] is entirely different from that involved in those cases where the statute merely prohibits certain acts involving the danger of substantive evil, without any reference to language itself, and it is sought to apply its provisions to language used by the defendant for the purpose of bringing about the prohibited results. There, if it be contended that the statute cannot be applied to the language used by the defendant because of its protection by the freedom of speech or press, it must necessarily be found, as an original question, without any previous determination by the legislative body, whether the specific language used involved such likelihood of bringing about

---

b. See also Bork, *Neutral Principles and Some First Amendment Problems,* 47 Ind.L.J. 1, 33 (1971): "To his point that proof of the effect of speech is inherently unavailable and yet its impact may be real and dangerous, Sanford might have added that the legislature is not confined to consideration of a single instance of speech or a single speaker. It fashions a rule to dampen thousands of instances of forcible overthrow advocacy. Cumulatively these may have enormous influence, and yet it may well be impossible to show any effect from any single example. The 'clear and present danger' requirement [is improper] because it erects a barrier to legislative rule where none should exist. The speech concerned has no political value within a republican system of government. Whether or not it is prudent to ban advocacy of forcible overthrow and law violation is a different [question]. Because the judgment is tactical, implicating the safety of the nation, it resembles very closely the judgment that Congress and the President must make about the expediency of waging war, an issue that the Court has wisely thought not fit for judicial determination."

the substantive evil as to deprive it of the constitutional protection. In such cases it has been held that the general provisions of the statute may be constitutionally applied to the specific utterance of the defendant if its natural tendency and probable effect was to bring about the substantive evil which the legislative body might prevent. *Schenck; Debs.* And the general statement in the *Schenck* case that the 'question in every case is whether the words are used in such circumstances and are of such a nature as to create a clear and present danger that they will bring about the substantive evils,' [was] manifestly intended, as shown by the context, to apply only in cases of this class, and has no application to those like the present, where the legislative body itself has previously determined the danger of substantive evil arising from utterances of a specified character."

HOLMES, J., joined by Brandeis, J., dissented: "The general principle of free speech, it seems to me, must be taken to be included in the Fourteenth Amendment, in view of the scope that has been given to the word 'liberty' as there used, although perhaps it may be accepted with a somewhat larger latitude of interpretation than is allowed to Congress by the sweeping language that governs or ought to govern the laws of the United States. If I am right then I think that the criterion sanctioned by the full Court in *Schenck* applies. [It] is true that in my opinion this criterion was departed from in *Abrams,* but the convictions that I expressed in that case are too deep for it to be possible for me as yet to believe that it [has] settled the law. If what I think the correct test is applied it is manifest that there was no present danger of an attempt to overthrow the government by force on the part of the admittedly small minority who shared the defendant's views. It is said that this manifesto was more than a theory, that it was an incitement. Every idea is an incitement. It offers itself for belief and if believed it is acted on unless some other belief outweighs it or some failure of energy stifles the movement at its birth. The only difference between the expression of an opinion and an incitement in the narrower sense is the speaker's enthusiasm for the result. Eloquence may set fire to reason. But whatever may be thought of the redundant discourse before us it had no chance of starting a present conflagration. If in the long run the beliefs expressed in proletarian dictatorship are destined to be accepted by the dominant forces of the community, the only meaning of free speech is that they should be given their chance and have their way.

"If the publication of this document had been laid as an attempt to induce an uprising against government at once and not at some indefinite time in the future it would have presented a different question. The object would have been one with which the law might deal, subject to the doubt whether there was any danger that the publication could produce any result, or in other words, whether it was not futile and too remote from possible consequences. But the indictment alleges the publication and nothing more."

Notes and Questions

1. *What if in the long run the belief in genocide is destined to be accepted?* Consider Bickel, *The Morality of Consent* 72 (1975): "[Although, in *Gitlow,* he saw no clear and present danger, Holmes] did admit that all ideas carried the seed of future dangers as well as benefits. His answer was this: 'If in the long run the beliefs expressed in proletarian dictatorships are destined to be accepted [, the] only meaning of free speech [—*the only*—] is that they should be given their chance and have their way.' If in the long run the belief, let us say, in

genocide is destined to be accepted [, the] only meaning of free speech is that it should be given its chance and have its way. Do we believe that? Do we accept it?" But consider Wellington, *On Freedom of Expression*, 88 Yale L.J. 1105, 1142 (1979): "The state cannot prevent advocacy [of genocide] on the ground that individuals will come to believe this false doctrine. But when there is a clear and present danger of action, the state must have the power to stop advocacy. [It] remains unfortunately imaginable that genocide could be implemented in a secular democracy: the state—including the courts—could be captured by a coalition of sick and evil minorities. But I do not believe that more restrictive control of expression would prevent such a catastrophe: unlike his cruelty, man's laws do have effective limits."

2. The statute in *Schenck* was not aimed directly at expression, but at conduct, i.e., certain actual or attempted interferences with the war effort. Thus, an analysis in terms of proximity between the words and the conduct prohibited (by a concededly valid law) seemed useful. But in *Gitlow* (and in *Dennis*, p. 436 infra) the statute was directed expressly against *advocacy* of a certain doctrine. Once the legislature *designates the point at which words became unlawful*, how helpful is the clear and present danger test? Is the question still how close words come to achieving certain consequences? In *Gitlow*, did Holmes "evade" the difficulty of applying an unmodified *Schenck* test to a different kind of problem? See Rogat, *Mr. Justice Holmes: Some Modern Views—The Judge as Spectator*, 31 U.Chi.L.Rev. 213, 217 (1964). See also Berns, *Freedom, Virtue and the First Amendment* 63 (Gateway ed. 1965); Linde, *"Clear and Present Danger" Reexamined*, 22 Stan.L.Rev. 1163, 1169–79 (1970).

3. Evaluate the following hypothetical commentary: "*Gitlow*'s abandonment of clear and present danger was insignificant because *Schenck*'s reference to clear and present danger was toothless. *Schenck* made no effort to prove that the defendant's communication presented a genuine danger. Rather the assumption (followed in *Debs* and *Abrams*) was that any communication intended to encourage resistance to a war was unprotected speech. *Gitlow*'s real significance was that it applied a war policy during a time of peace."

4. Consider Linde, supra, at 1171: "Since New York's law itself defined the prohibited speech, the [*Gitlow*] Court could choose among three positions. It could (1) accept this legislative judgment of the harmful potential of the proscribed words, subject to conventional judicial review; (2) independently scrutinize the facts to see whether a 'danger,' as stated in *Schenck*, justified suppression of the particular expression; or (3) hold that by legislating directly against the words rather than the effects, the lawmaker had gone beyond the leeway left to trial and proof by the holding in *Schenck* and had made a law forbidden by the first amendment." Which course did the *Gitlow* majority choose? The dissenters? Which position should the Court have chosen?

Cases such as *Whitney*, infra, raise questions not only about freedom of speech, but also about the right of assembly. In turn, *Whitney* raises the issue of the existence and scope of a right not mentioned in the first amendment: freedom of association. Freedom of association, together with its connections to speech and assembly is explored in Sec. 9 infra. Several of the cases which follow are primarily characterized as speech cases because the assemblies or associations at issue were designed for the purpose of organizing future speech activity.

WHITNEY v. CALIFORNIA

274 U.S. 357, 47 S.Ct. 641, 71 L.Ed. 1095 (1927).

MR. JUSTICE SANFORD delivered the opinion of the Court.

[Charlotte Anita Whitney was convicted of violating the 1919 Criminal Syndicalism Act of California whose pertinent provisions were]:

"Section 1. The term 'criminal syndicalism' as used in this act is hereby defined as any doctrine or precept advocating, teaching or aiding and abetting the commission of crime, sabotage (which word is hereby defined as meaning willful and malicious physical damage or injury to physical property), or unlawful acts of force and violence or unlawful methods of terrorism as a means of accomplishing a change in industrial ownership or control, or effecting any political change.

"Sec. 2. Any person who: * * * 4. Organizes or assists in organizing, or is or knowingly becomes a member of, any organization, society, group or assemblage of persons organized or assembled to advocate, teach or aid and abet criminal syndicalism; * * *

"Is guilty of a felony and punishable by imprisonment."

The first count of the information, on which the conviction was had, charged that on or about November 28, 1919, in Alameda County, the defendant, in violation of the Criminal Syndicalism Act, "did then and there unlawfully, willfully, wrongfully, deliberately and feloniously organize and assist in organizing, and was, is, and knowingly became a member of [a group] organized and assembled to advocate, teach, aid and abet criminal syndicalism." * * *

1. While it is not denied that the evidence warranted the jury in finding that the defendant became a member of and assisted in organizing the Communist Labor Party of California, and that this was organized to advocate, teach, aid or abet criminal syndicalism as defined by the Act, it is urged that the Act, as here construed and applied, deprived the defendant of her liberty without due process of law. [Defendant's] argument is, in effect, that the character of the state organization could not be forecast when she attended the convention; that she had no purpose of helping to create an instrument of terrorism and violence; that she "took part in formulating and presenting to the convention a resolution which, if adopted, would have committed the new organization to a legitimate policy of political reform by the use of the ballot"; that it was not until after the majority of the convention turned out to be "contrary minded, and other less temperate policies prevailed" that the convention could have taken on the character of criminal syndicalism; and that as this was done over her protest, her mere presence in the convention, however violent the opinions expressed therein, could not thereby become a crime. This contention [is in effect] an effort to review the weight of the evidence for the purpose of showing that the defendant did not join and assist in organizing the Communist Labor Party of California with a knowledge of its unlawful character and purpose. This question, which is foreclosed by the verdict of the jury, [is] one of fact merely which is not open to review in this Court, involving as it does no constitutional question whatever. * * *

[That a state] may punish those who abuse [freedom of speech] by utterances inimical to the public welfare, tending to incite to crime, disturb the public peace, or endanger the foundations of organized government and threaten its overthrow by unlawful means, is not open to question. [*Gitlow*].

The essence of the offense denounced by the Act is the combining with others in an association for the accomplishment of the desired ends through the advocacy and use of criminal and unlawful methods. It partakes of the nature of a criminal conspiracy. That such united and joint action involves even greater danger to the public peace and security than the isolated utterances and acts of individuals is clear. We cannot hold that, as here applied, the Act is an unreasonable or arbitrary exercise of the police power of the State, unwarrantably infringing any right of free speech, assembly or association, or that those persons are protected from punishment by the due process clause who abuse such rights by joining and furthering an organization thus menacing the peace and welfare of the State. ＊ ＊ ＊

Affirmed.

MR. JUSTICE BRANDEIS (concurring.) ＊ ＊ ＊

The felony which the statute created is a crime very unlike the old felony of conspiracy or the old misdemeanor of unlawful assembly. The mere act of assisting in forming a society for teaching syndicalism, of becoming a member of it, or assembling with others for that purpose is given the dynamic quality of crime. There is guilt although the society may not contemplate immediate promulgation of the doctrine. Thus the accused is to be punished, not for attempt, incitement or conspiracy, but for a step in preparation, which, if it threatens the public order at all, does so only remotely. The novelty in the prohibition introduced is that the statute aims, not at the practice of criminal syndicalism, nor even directly at the preaching of it, but at association with those who propose to preach it.

Despite arguments to the contrary which had seemed to me persuasive, it is settled that the due process clause of the Fourteenth Amendment applies to matters of substantive law as well as to matters of procedure. Thus all fundamental rights comprised within the term liberty are protected by the federal Constitution from invasion by the states. The right of free speech, the right to teach and the right of assembly are, of course, fundamental rights. These may not be denied or abridged. But, although the rights of free speech and assembly are fundamental, they are not in their nature absolute. Their exercise is subject to restriction, if the particular restriction proposed is required in order to protect the state from destruction or from serious injury, political, economic or moral. That the necessity which is essential to a valid restriction does not exist unless speech would produce, or is intended to produce,[a] a clear and imminent danger of some substantive evil which the state constitutionally may seek to prevent has been settled. See *Schenck.*

[The] Legislature must obviously decide, in the first instance, whether a danger exists which calls for a particular protective measure. But where a statute is valid only in case certain conditions exist, the enactment of the statute cannot alone establish the facts which are essential to its validity. Prohibitory legislation has repeatedly been held invalid, because unnecessary, where the denial of liberty involved was that of engaging in a particular business. The powers of the courts to strike down an offending law are no less when the interests involved are not property rights, but the fundamental personal rights of free speech and assembly.

a. Unless speech would produce, *or* is intended to produce? Unless speech *would produce* a clear and imminent danger, although the harm produced was neither advocated nor intended by the speaker? Unless the speaker *intended* to produce a clear and imminent danger, even under extrinsic conditions of actual harmlessness? Compare *Brandenburg v. Ohio*, p. 455 infra. See generally Linde, supra, at 1168–69, 1181, 1185.

This Court has not yet fixed the standard by which to determine when a danger shall be deemed clear; how remote the danger may be and yet be deemed present; and what degree of evil shall be deemed sufficiently substantial to justify resort to abridgment of free speech and assembly as the means of protection. To reach sound conclusions on these matters, we must bear in mind why a state is, ordinarily, denied the power to prohibit dissemination of social, economic and political doctrine which a vast majority of its citizens believes to be false and fraught with evil consequence.

Those who won our independence believed that the final end of the state was to make men free to develop their faculties, and that in its government the deliberative forces should prevail over the arbitrary. They valued liberty both as an end and as a means. They believed liberty to be the secret of happiness and courage to be the secret of liberty. They believed that freedom to think as you will and to speak as you think are means indispensable to the discovery and spread of political truth; that without free speech and assembly discussion would be futile; that with them, discussion affords ordinarily adequate protection against the dissemination of noxious doctrine; that the greatest menace to freedom is an inert people; that public discussion is a political duty; and that this should be a fundamental principle of the American government. They recognized the risks to which all human institutions are subject. But they knew that order cannot be secured merely through fear of punishment for its infraction; that it is hazardous to discourage thought, hope and imagination; that fear breeds repression; that repression breeds hate; that hate menaces stable government; that the path of safety lies in the opportunity to discuss freely supposed grievances and proposed remedies; and that the fitting remedy for evil counsels is good ones. Believing in the power of reason as applied through public discussion, they eschewed silence coerced by law—the argument of force in its worst form. Recognizing the occasional tyrannies of governing majorities, they amended the Constitution so that free speech and assembly should be guaranteed.

Fear of serious injury cannot alone justify suppression of free speech and assembly. Men feared witches and burnt women. It is the function of speech to free men from the bondage of irrational fears. To justify suppression of free speech there must be reasonable ground to fear that serious evil will result if free speech is practiced. There must be reasonable ground to believe that the danger apprehended is imminent. There must be reasonable ground to believe that the evil to be prevented is a serious one.[b] Every denunciation of existing law tends in some measure to increase the probability that there will be violation of it. Condonation of a breach enhances the probability. Expressions of approval add to the probability. Propagation of the criminal state of mind by teaching syndicalism increases it. Advocacy of lawbreaking heightens it still further. But even advocacy of violation, however reprehensible morally, is not a justification for denying free speech where the advocacy falls short of incitement and there is nothing to indicate that the advocacy would be immediately acted on. The wide difference between advocacy and incitement, between preparation and attempt, between assembling and conspiracy, must be borne in mind. In order to support a finding of clear and present danger it must be shown either that immediate serious violence was to be expected or was advocated,[c] or that

---

b. Does this suffice, regardless of the intent of the speaker? Regardless of the nature of the words he uses?

c. What if violence is advocated, but the advocacy is utterly ineffectual? What if the speaker neither desires nor advocates vio-

the past conduct furnished reason to believe that such advocacy was then contemplated.

Those who won our independence by revolution were not cowards. They did not fear political change. They did not exalt order at the cost of liberty. To courageous, self-reliant men, with confidence in the power of free and fearless reasoning applied through the processes of popular government, no danger flowing from speech can be deemed clear and present, unless the incidence of the evil apprehended is so imminent that it may befall before there is opportunity for full discussion. If there be time to expose through discussion the falsehood and fallacies, to avert the evil by the processes of education, the remedy to be applied is more speech, not enforced silence. Only an emergency can justify repression. Such must be the rule if authority is to be reconciled with freedom. Such, in my opinion, is the command of the Constitution. It is therefore always open to Americans to challenge a law abridging free speech and assembly by showing that there was no emergency justifying it.

Moreover, even imminent danger cannot justify resort to prohibition of these functions essential to effective democracy, unless the evil apprehended is relatively serious. Prohibition of free speech and assembly is a measure so stringent that it would be inappropriate as the means for averting a relatively trivial harm to society. A police measure may be unconstitutional merely because the remedy, although effective as means of protection, is unduly harsh or oppressive. Thus, a state might, in the exercise of its police power, make any trespass upon the land of another a crime, regardless of the results or of the intent or purpose of the trespasser. It might, also, punish an attempt, a conspiracy, or an incitement to commit the trespass. But it is hardly conceivable that this court would hold constitutional a statute which punished as a felony the mere voluntary assembly with a society formed to teach that pedestrians had the moral right to cross uninclosed, unposted, waste lands and to advocate their doing so, even if there was imminent danger that advocacy would lead to a trespass. The fact that speech is likely to result in some violence or in destruction of property is not enough to justify its suppression. There must be the probability of serious injury to the State.[d] Among free men, the deterrents ordinarily to be applied to prevent crime are education and punishment for violations of the law, not abridgement of the rights of free speech and assembly.

* * * Whenever the fundamental rights of free speech and assembly are alleged to have been invaded, it must remain open to a defendant to present the issue whether there actually did exist at the time a clear danger, whether the danger, if any, was imminent, and whether the evil apprehended was one so substantial as to justify the stringent restriction interposed by the Legislature. The legislative declaration, like the fact that the statute was passed and was sustained by the highest court of the State, creates merely a rebuttable presumption that these conditions have been satisfied.

Whether in 1919, when Miss Whitney did the things complained of, there was in California such clear and present danger of serious evil, might have been made the important issue in the case. She might have required that the issue be

lence, but, under the circumstances the speech nevertheless is "expected" to produce violence?

d. But see Bork, *Neutral Principles and Some First Amendment Problems,* 47 Ind.L.J. 1, 34 (1971): "It is difficult to see how a constitutional court could properly draw the distinction proposed. Brandeis offered no analysis to show that advocacy of law violation merited protection by the Court. Worse, the criterion he advanced is the importance, in the judge's eye, of the law whose violation is urged."

determined either by the court or the jury. She claimed below that the statute as applied to her violated the federal Constitution; but she did not claim that it was void because there was no clear and present danger of serious evil, nor did she request that the existence of these conditions of a valid measure thus restricting the rights of free speech and assembly be passed upon by the court or a jury. On the other hand, there was evidence on which the court or jury might have found that such danger existed. I am unable to assent to the suggestion in the opinion of the court that assembling with a political party, formed to advocate the desirability of a proletarian revolution by mass action at some date necessarily far in the future, is not a right within the protection of the Fourteenth Amendment. In the present case, however, there was other testimony which tended to establish the existence of a conspiracy, on the part of members of the International Workers of the World, to commit present serious crimes, and likewise to show that such a conspiracy would be furthered by the activity of the society of which Miss Whitney was a member. Under these circumstances the judgment of the State court cannot be disturbed. * * *

MR. JUSTICE HOLMES joins in this opinion.[e]

Notes and Questions

1. *"They valued liberty both as an end and as a means."* Should recognition of the value of liberty[f] as an end augment the marketplace perspective or replace it? Compare Baker, *Scope of the First Amendment Freedom of Speech*, 25 U.C.L.A.L.Rev. 964 (1978) (liberty theory should replace marketplace theory) with Redish, *The Value of Free Speech*, 130 U.Pa.L.Rev. 591 (1982) (self-realization should be regarded as the first amendment's exclusive value) and Shiffrin, *The First Amendment and Economic Regulation: Away From a General Theory of the First Amendment*, 78 Nw.U.L.Rev. 1212 (1983) (many values including liberty and self-realization underpin the first amendment; single valued orientations are reductionist). But see Schauer, *Must Speech Be Special?* 78 Nw.U.L. Rev. 1284 (1983) (neither liberty nor self-realization should play *any* role in first amendment theory).

2. *Scope of the opinions.* Did Brandeis, J., simply reaffirm the clear and present danger test? Significantly clarify it? Significantly change it? Did Sanford, J., modify the position he had taken in *Gitlow*? Did he at least make it plain in *Whitney* that some state sedition convictions may be set aside under the first and fourteenth amendments? See Chafee, supra, at 351.

3. Ten years after *Whitney, DeJonge v. Oregon*, 299 U.S. 353, 57 S.Ct. 255, 81 L.Ed. 278 (1937) held that mere participation in a meeting called by the Communist party could not be made a crime. The right of peaceable assembly was declared to be "cognate to those of free speech and free press and is equally fundamental."

e. For background concerning the views of Brandeis and Holmes, JJ., and the relationship between those views and democratic theory generally, see Cover, *The Left, The Right and the First Amendment: 1919–28*, 40 Md.L. Rev. 349 (1981).

f. For discussion of the value of autonomy and its connection to the problem of advocacy of illegal action, compare Scanlon, *A Theory of Freedom of Expression*, 1 Philosophy & Pub. Aff. 204 (1972) with Scanlon, *Freedom of Expression and Categories of Expression*, 40 U.Pitt.L.Rev. 519 (1979).

C. COMMUNISM AND ILLEGAL ADVOCACY

Kent Greenawalt has well described the pattern of decisions for much of the period between *Whitney* and *Dennis* infra: "[T]he clear and present danger formula emerged as the applicable standard not only for the kinds of issues with respect to which it originated but also for a wide variety of other First Amendment problems. If the Court was not always very clear about the relevance of that formula to those different problems, its use of the test, and its employment of ancillary doctrines, did evince a growing disposition to protect expression." *Speech and Crime,* 1980 Am.B.Found.Res.J. 645, 706. By 1951, however, anticommunist sentiment was a powerful theme in American politics. The Soviet Union had detonated a nuclear weapon; communists had firm control of the Chinese mainland; the Korean War had reached a stalemate; Alger Hiss had been convicted of perjury in congressional testimony concerning alleged spying activities for the Soviet Union while he was a State Department official; and Senator Joseph McCarthy of Wisconsin had created a national sensation by accusations that many "card carrying Communists" held important State Department jobs. In this context, the top leaders of the American Communist Party asked the Court to reverse their criminal conspiracy convictions.

DENNIS v. UNITED STATES
341 U.S. 494, 71 S.Ct. 857, 95 L.Ed. 1137 (1951).

MR. CHIEF JUSTICE VINSON announced the judgment of the Court and an opinion in which MR. JUSTICE REED, MR. JUSTICE BURTON and MR. JUSTICE MINTON join.

Petitioners were indicted in July, 1948, for violation of the conspiracy provisions of the Smith Act during the period of April, 1945, to July, 1948. * * * A verdict of guilty as to all the petitioners was [affirmed by the Second Circuit]. We granted certiorari, limited to the following two questions: (1) Whether either § 2 or § 3 of the Smith Act, inherently or as construed and applied in the instant case, violates the First Amendment and other provisions of the Bill of Rights; (2) whether either § 2 or § 3 of the Act, inherently or as construed and applied in the instant case, violates the First and Fifth Amendments, because of indefiniteness.

Sections 2 and 3 of the Smith Act provide as follows:

"Sec. 2.

"(a) It shall be unlawful for any person—

"(1) to knowingly or willfully advocate, abet, advise, or teach the duty, necessity, desirability, or propriety of overthrowing or destroying any government in the United States by force or violence, or by the assassination of any officer of any such government; * * *

"Sec. 3. It shall be unlawful for any person to attempt to commit, or to conspire to commit, any of the acts prohibited by the provisions [of] this title."

The indictment charged the petitioners with wilfully and knowingly conspiring (1) to organize as the Communist Party of the United States of America a society, group and assembly of persons who teach and advocate the overthrow and destruction of the Government of the United States by force and violence, and (2) knowingly and wilfully to advocate and teach the duty and necessity of overthrowing and destroying the Government of the United States by force and violence. The indictment further alleged that § 2 of the Smith Act proscribes these acts and that any conspiracy to take such action is a violation of § 3 of the Act.

The trial of the case extended over nine months, six of which were devoted to the taking of evidence, resulting in a record of 16,000 pages. Our limited grant of the writ of certiorari has removed from our consideration any question as to the sufficiency of the evidence to support the jury's determination that petitioners are guilty of the offense charged. Whether on this record petitioners did in fact advocate the overthrow of the Government by force and violence is not before us, and we must base any discussion of this point upon the conclusions stated in the opinion of the Court of Appeals, which treated the issue in great detail [and] held that the record supports the following broad conclusions: [that] the Communist Party is a highly disciplined organization, adept at infiltration into strategic positions, use of aliases, and double-meaning language; that the Party is rigidly controlled; that Communists, unlike other political parties, tolerate no dissension from the policy laid down by the guiding [forces]; that the literature of the Party and the statements and activities of its leaders, petitioners here, advocate, and the general goal of the Party was, during the period in question, to achieve a successful overthrow of the existing order by force and violence. * * *

The obvious purpose of the statute is to protect existing Government, not from change by peaceable, lawful and constitutional means, but from change by violence, revolution and terrorism. That it is within the *power* of the Congress to protect the Government of the United States from armed rebellion is a proposition which requires little discussion. Whatever theoretical merit there may be to the argument that there is a "right" to rebellion against dictatorial governments is without force where the existing structure of the government provides for peaceful and orderly change. We reject any principle of governmental helplessness in the face of preparation for revolution, which principle, carried to its logical conclusion, must lead to anarchy. No one could conceive that it is not within the power of Congress to prohibit acts intended to overthrow the Government by force and violence. The question with which we are concerned here is not whether Congress has such *power*, but whether the *means* which it has employed conflict with the First and Fifth Amendments to the Constitution.

One of the bases for the contention that the means which Congress has employed are invalid takes the form of an attack on the face of the statute on the grounds that by its terms it prohibits academic discussion of the merits of Marxism-Leninism, that it stifles ideas and is contrary to all concepts of a free speech and a free press. [This] is a federal statute which we must interpret as well as judge. Herein lies the fallacy of reliance upon the manner in which this Court has treated judgments of state courts. Where the statute as construed by the state court transgressed the First Amendment, we could not but invalidate the judgments of conviction.

The very language of the Smith Act negates the interpretation which petitioners would have us impose on that Act. It is directed at advocacy, not discussion. Thus, the trial judge properly charged the jury that they could not convict if they found that petitioners did "no more than pursue peaceful studies and discussions or teaching and advocacy in the realm of ideas." * * * Congress did not intend to eradicate the free discussion of political theories, to destroy the traditional rights of Americans to discuss and evaluate ideas without fear of governmental sanction. * * *

But although the statute is not directed at the hypothetical cases which petitioners have conjured, its application in this case has resulted in convictions for the teaching and advocacy of the overthrow of the Government by force and violence, which, even though coupled with the intent to accomplish that overthrow, contains an element of speech. For this reason, we must pay special heed to the demands of the First Amendment marking out the boundaries of speech.

[T]he basis of the First Amendment is the hypothesis that speech can rebut speech, propaganda will answer propaganda, free debate of ideas will result in the wisest governmental policies. [An] analysis of the leading cases in this Court which have involved direct limitations on speech, however, will demonstrate that both the majority of the Court and the dissenters in particular cases have recognized that this is not an unlimited, unqualified right, but that the societal value of speech must, on occasion, be subordinated to other values and considerations. * * *

Although no case subsequent to *Whitney* and *Gitlow* has expressly overruled the majority opinions in those cases, there is little doubt that subsequent opinions have inclined toward the Holmes-Brandeis rationale. * * *

In this case we are squarely presented with the application of the "clear and present danger" test, and must decide what that phrase imports. We first note that many of the cases in which this Court has reversed convictions by use of this or similar tests have been based on the fact that the interest which the State was attempting to protect was itself too insubstantial to warrant restriction of speech. * * * Overthrow of the Government by force and violence is certainly a substantial enough interest for the Government to limit speech. Indeed, this is the ultimate value of any society, for if a society cannot protect its very structure from armed internal attack, it must follow that no subordinate value can be protected. If, then, this interest may be protected, the literal problem which is presented is what has been meant by the use of the phrase "clear and present danger" of the utterances bringing about the evil within the power of Congress to punish.

Obviously, the words cannot mean that before the Government may act, it must wait until the putsch is about to be executed, the plans have been laid and the signal is awaited. If Government is aware that a group aiming at its overthrow is attempting to indoctrinate its members and to commit them to a course whereby they will strike when the leaders feel the circumstances permit, action by the Government is required. The argument that there is no need for Government to concern itself, for Government is strong, it possesses ample powers to put down a rebellion, it may defeat the revolution with ease needs no answer. For that is not the question. Certainly an attempt to overthrow the Government by force, even though doomed from the outset because of inadequate numbers or power of the revolutionists, is a sufficient evil for Congress to prevent. The damage which such attempts create both physically and politically to a nation makes it impossible to measure the validity in terms of the probability of success, or the immediacy of a successful attempt. In the instant case the trial judge charged the jury that they could not convict unless they found that petitioners intended to overthrow the Government "as speedily as circumstances would permit." This does not mean, and could not properly mean, that they would not strike until there was certainty of success. What was meant was that the revolutionists would strike when they thought the time was ripe. We must therefore reject the contention that success or probability of success is the criterion.

The situation with which Justices Holmes and Brandeis were concerned in *Gitlow* was a comparatively isolated event, bearing little relation in their minds to any substantial threat to the safety of the community. [They] were not confronted with any situation comparable to the instant one—the development of an apparatus designed and dedicated to the overthrow of the Government, in the context of world crisis after crisis.

Chief Judge Learned Hand, writing for the majority below, interpreted the phrase as follows: "In each case [courts] must ask whether the gravity of the 'evil,' discounted by its improbability, justifies such invasion of free speech as is necessary to avoid the danger." We adopt this statement of the rule. As articulated by Chief Judge Hand, it is as succinct and inclusive as any other we might devise at this time. * * *

Likewise, we are in accord with the court below, which affirmed the trial court's finding that the requisite danger existed. The mere fact that from the period 1945 to 1948 petitioners' activities did not result in an attempt to overthrow the Government by force and violence is of course no answer to the fact that there was a group that was ready to make the attempt. The formation by petitioners of such a highly organized conspiracy, with rigidly disciplined members subject to call when the leaders, these petitioners, felt that the time had come for action, coupled with the inflammable nature of world conditions, similar uprisings in other countries, and the touch-and-go nature of our relations with countries with whom petitioners were in the very least ideologically attuned, convince us that their convictions were justified on this score. And this analysis disposes of the contention that a conspiracy to advocate, as distinguished from the advocacy itself, cannot be constitutionally restrained, because it comprises only the preparation. It is the existence of the conspiracy which creates the danger. * * *

Although we have concluded that the finding that there was a sufficient danger to warrant the application of the statute was justified on the merits, there remains the problem of whether the trial judge's treatment of the issue was correct. He charged the jury, in relevant part, as follows:

"In further construction and interpretation of the statute I charge you that it is not the abstract doctrine of overthrowing or destroying organized government by unlawful means which is denounced by this law, but the teaching and advocacy of action for the accomplishment of that purpose, by language reasonably and ordinarily calculated to incite persons to such action. Accordingly, you cannot find the defendants or any of them guilty of the crime charged unless you are satisfied beyond a reasonable doubt that they conspired to organize a society, group and assembly of persons who teach and advocate the overthrow or destruction of the Government of the United States by force and violence and to advocate and teach the duty and necessity of overthrowing or destroying the Government of the United States by force and violence, with the intent that such teaching and advocacy be of a rule or principle of action and by language reasonably and ordinarily calculated to incite persons to such action, all with the intent to cause the overthrow or destruction of the Government of the United States by force and violence as speedily as circumstances would permit. * * *

"If you are satisfied that the evidence establishes beyond a reasonable doubt that the defendants, or any of them, are guilty of a violation of the statute, as I have interpreted it to you, I find as matter of law that there is sufficient danger of a substantive evil that the Congress has a right to prevent to justify the application of the statute under the First Amendment of the Constitution. This is matter of law about which you have no concern. * * *"

It is thus clear that he reserved the question of the existence of the danger for his own determination, and the question becomes whether the issue is of such a nature that it should have been submitted to the jury.

[When] facts are found that establish the violation of a statute, the protection against conviction afforded by the First Amendment is a matter of law. The doctrine that there must be a clear and present danger of a substantive evil that Congress has a right to prevent is a judicial rule to be applied as a matter of law by the courts. The guilt is established by proof of facts. Whether the First Amendment protects the activity which constitutes the violation of the statute must depend upon a judicial determination of the scope of the First Amendment applied to the circumstances of the case.

[In] *Schenck* this Court itself examined the record to find whether the requisite danger appeared, and the issue was not submitted to a jury. And in every later case in which the Court has measured the validity of a statute by the "clear and present danger" test, that determination has been by the court, the question of the danger not being submitted to the jury. * * * Petitioners intended to overthrow the Government of the United States as speedily as the circumstances would permit. Their conspiracy to organize the Communist Party and to teach and advocate the overthrow of the Government of the United States by force and violence created a "clear and present danger" of an attempt to overthrow the Government by force and violence. They were properly and constitutionally convicted * * *.

Affirmed.

MR. JUSTICE CLARK took no part in the consideration or decision of this case.

MR. JUSTICE FRANKFURTER, concurring in affirmance of the judgment.

[The] demands of free speech in a democratic society as well as the interest in national security are better served by candid and informed weighing of the competing interests, within the confines of the judicial process, than by announcing dogmas too inflexible for the non-Euclidian problems to be solved.

But how are competing interests to be assessed? Since they are not subject to quantitative ascertainment, the issue necessarily resolves itself into asking, who is to make the adjustment?—who is to balance the relevant factors and ascertain which interest is in the circumstances to prevail? Full responsibility for the choice cannot be given to the courts. Courts are not representative bodies. They are not designed to be a good reflex of a democratic society. Their judgment is best informed, and therefore most dependable, within narrow limits. Their essential quality is detachment, founded on independence. History teaches that the independence of the judiciary is jeopardized when courts become embroiled in the passions of the day and assume primary responsibility in choosing between competing political, economic and social pressures.

Primary responsibility for adjusting the interests which compete in the situation before us of necessity belongs to the Congress. [We] are to set aside the judgment of those whose duty it is to legislate only if there is no reasonable basis for [it]. Free-speech cases are not an exception to the principle that we are not legislators, that direct policy-making is not our province. How best to reconcile competing interests is the business of legislatures, and the balance they strike is a judgment not to be displaced by ours, but to be respected unless outside the pale of fair judgment. [A] survey of the relevant decisions indicates that the results which we have reached are on the whole those that would ensue from careful weighing of conflicting interests. The complex issues presented by regulation of speech in public places by picketing, and by legislation prohibiting advocacy of crime have been resolved by scrutiny of many factors besides the imminence and gravity of the evil threatened. The matter has been well summarized by a reflective student of the Court's work. "The truth is that the clear-and-present-danger test is an oversimplified judgment unless it takes account also of a number of other factors: the relative seriousness of the danger in comparison with the value of the occasion for speech or political activity; the availability of more moderate controls than those which the state has imposed; and perhaps the specific intent with which the speech or activity is launched. No matter how rapidly we utter the phrase 'clear and present danger,' or how closely we hyphenate the words, they are not a substitute for the weighing of values. They tend to convey a delusion of certitude when what is most certain is the complexity of the strands in the web of freedoms which the judge must disentangle." Freund, *On Understanding the Supreme Court* 27–28 [1949].

* * *

To make validity of legislation depend on judicial reading of events still in the womb of time—a forecast, that is, of the outcome of forces at best appreciated only with knowledge of the topmost secrets of nations—is to charge the judiciary with duties beyond its equipment. * * *

Even when moving strictly within the limits of constitutional adjudication, judges are concerned with issues that may be said to involve vital finalities. The too easy transition from disapproval of what is undesirable to condemnation as unconstitutional, has led some of the wisest judges to question the wisdom of our scheme in lodging such authority in courts. But it is relevant to remind that in sustaining the power of Congress in a case like this nothing irrevocable is done. The democratic process at all events is not impaired or restricted. Power and responsibility remain with the people and immediately with their representation. All the Court says is that Congress was not forbidden by the Constitution to pass this enactment and that a prosecution under it may be brought against a conspiracy such as the one before us. * * *

Mr. Justice Jackson, concurring.

[E]ither by accident or design, the Communist strategem outwits the antianarchist pattern of statute aimed against "overthrow by force and violence" if qualified by the doctrine that only "clear and present danger" of accomplishing that result will sustain the prosecution.

The "clear and present danger" test was an innovation by Mr. Justice Holmes in the *Schenck* case, reiterated and refined by him and Mr. Justice Brandeis in later cases, all arising before the era of World War II revealed the subtlety and efficacy of modernized revolutionary techniques used by totalitarian parties. In those cases, they were faced with convictions under so-called criminal syndicalism statutes aimed at anarchists but which, loosely construed, had been applied to punish socialism, pacifism, and left-wing ideologies, the charges often resting on farfetched inferences which, if true, would establish only technical or trivial violations. They proposed "clear and present danger" as a test for the sufficiency of evidence in particular cases.

I would save it, unmodified, for application as a "rule of reason" in the kind of case for which it was devised. When the issue is criminality of a hotheaded speech on a street corner, or circulation of a few incendiary pamphlets, or parading by some zealots behind a red flag, or refusal of a handful of school children to salute our flag, it is not beyond the capacity of the judicial process to gather, comprehend, and weigh the necessary materials for decision whether it is a clear and present danger of substantive evil or a harmless letting off of steam. It is not a prophecy, for the danger in such cases has matured by the time of trial or it was never present. The test applies and has meaning where a conviction is sought to be based on a speech or writing which does not directly or explicitly advocate a crime but to which such tendency is sought to be attributed by construction or by implication from external circumstances. The formula in such cases favors freedoms that are vital to our society, and, even if sometimes applied too generously, the consequences cannot be grave. But its recent expansion has extended, in particular to Communists, unprecedented immunities. Unless we are to hold our Government captive in a judge-made verbal trap, we must approach the problem of a well-organized, nation-wide conspiracy, such as I have described, as realistically as our predecessors faced the trivialities that were being prosecuted until they were checked with a rule of reason.

I think reason is lacking for applying that test to this case.

If we must decide that this Act and its application are constitutional only if we are convinced that petitioner's conduct creates a "clear and present danger" of violent overthrow, we must appraise imponderables, including international and national phenomena which baffle the best informed foreign offices and our most experienced politicians. We would have to foresee and predict the effectiveness of Communist propaganda, opportunities for infiltration, whether, and when, a time will come that they consider propitious for action, and whether and how fast our existing government will deteriorate. And we would have to speculate as to whether an approaching Communist coup would not be anticipated by a nationalistic fascist movement. No doctrine can be sound whose application requires us to make a prophecy of that sort in the guise of a legal decision. The judicial process simply is not adequate to a trial of such far-flung issues. The answers given would reflect our own political predilections and nothing more.

The authors of the clear and present danger test never applied it to a case like this, nor would I. If applied as it is proposed here, it means that the Communist plotting is protected during its period of incubation; its preliminary stages of organization and preparation are immune from the law; the Government can move only after imminent action is manifest, when it would, of course, be too late.

The highest degree of constitutional protection is due to the individual acting without conspiracy. But even an individual cannot claim that the Constitution protects him in advocating or teaching overthrow of government by force or violence. I should suppose no one would doubt that Congress has power to make such attempted overthrow a crime. But the contention is that one has the constitutional right to work up a public desire and will to do what it is a crime to attempt. I think direct incitement by speech or writing can be made a crime, and I think there can be a conviction without also proving that the odds favored its success by 99 to 1, or some other extremely high ratio. * * *

What really is under review here is a conviction of conspiracy, after a trial for conspiracy, on an indictment charging conspiracy, brought under a statute outlawing conspiracy. With due respect to my colleagues, they seem to me to discuss anything under the sun except the law of conspiracy. * * *

The Constitution does not make conspiracy a civil right. [Although] I consider criminal conspiracy a dragnet device capable of perversion into an instrument of injustice in the hands of a partisan or complacent judiciary, it has an established place in our system of law, and no reason appears for applying it only to concerted action claimed to disturb interstate commerce and withholding it from those claimed to undermine our whole Government. * * *

I do not suggest that Congress could punish conspiracy to advocate something, the doing of which it may not punish. Advocacy or exposition of the doctrine of communal property ownership, or any political philosophy unassociated with advocacy of its imposition by force or seizure of government by unlawful means could not be reached through conspiracy prosecution. But it is not forbidden to put down force or violence, it is not forbidden to punish its teaching or advocacy, and the end being punishable, there is no doubt of the power to punish conspiracy for the purpose. * * *

MR. JUSTICE BLACK, dissenting. * * *

So long as this Court exercises the power of judicial review of legislation, I cannot agree that the First Amendment permits us to sustain laws suppressing freedom of speech and press on the basis of Congress' or our own notions of mere "reasonableness." Such a doctrine waters down the First Amendment so that it amounts to little more than an admonition to Congress. The Amendment as so construed is not likely to protect any but those "safe" or orthodox views which rarely need its protection. I must also express my objection to the holding because, as Mr. Justice Douglas' dissent shows, it sanctions the determination of a crucial issue of fact by the judge rather than by the jury. * * *

Public opinion being what it now is, few will protest the conviction of these Communist petitioners. There is hope, however, that in calmer times, when present pressures, passions and fears subside, this or some later Court will restore the First Amendment liberties to the high preferred place where they belong in a free society.

MR. JUSTICE DOUGLAS, dissenting.

If this were a case where those who claimed protection under the First Amendment were teaching the techniques of sabotage, the assassination of the President, the filching of documents from public files, the planting of bombs, the art of street warfare, and the like, I would have no doubts. The freedom to speak is not absolute; the teaching of methods of terror and other seditious conduct should be beyond the pale along with obscenity and immorality. This case was argued as if those were the facts. The argument imported much seditious conduct into the record. That is easy and it has popular appeal, for the activities of Communists in plotting and scheming against the free world are common knowledge. But the fact is that no such evidence was introduced at the trial. There is a statute which makes a seditious conspiracy unlawful. Petitioners, however, were not charged with a "conspiracy to overthrow" the Government. They were charged with a conspiracy to form a party and groups and assemblies of people who teach and advocate the overthrow of our Government by force or violence and with a conspiracy to advocate and teach its overthrow by force and violence. It may well be that indoctrination in the techniques of terror to destroy the Government would be indictable under either statute. But the teaching which is condemned here is of a different character.

So far as the present record is concerned, what petitioners did was to organize people to teach and themselves teach the Marxist-Leninist doctrine contained chiefly in four books: *Foundations of Leninism* by Stalin (1924); *The Communist Manifesto* by Marx and Engels (1848); *State and Revolution* by Lenin (1917); *History of the Communist Party of the Soviet Union* (B.) (1939).

Those books are to Soviet Communism what *Mein Kampf* was to Nazism. If they are understood, the ugliness of Communism is revealed, its deceit and cunning are exposed, the nature of its activities becomes apparent, and the chances of its success less likely. That is not, of course, the reason why petitioners chose these books for their classrooms. They are fervent Communists to whom these volumes are gospel. They preached the creed with the hope that some day it would be acted upon.

The opinion of the Court does not outlaw these texts nor condemn them to the fire, as the Communists do literature offensive to their creed. But if the books themselves are not outlawed, if they can lawfully remain on library shelves, by what reasoning does their use in a classroom become a crime? It would not be a crime under the Act to introduce these books to a class, though that would be teaching what the creed of violent overthrow of the Government is. The Act, as construed, requires the element of intent—that those who teach the creed believe in it. The crime then depends not on what is taught but on who the teacher is. That is to make freedom of speech turn not on *what is said*, but on the *intent* with which it is said. Once we start down that road we enter territory dangerous to the liberties of every citizen. * * *

The vice of treating speech as the equivalent of overt acts of a treasonable or seditious character is emphasized by a concurring opinion, which by invoking the law of conspiracy makes speech do service for deeds which are dangerous to society. [N]ever until today has anyone seriously thought that the ancient law of conspiracy could constitutionally be used to turn speech into seditious conduct. Yet that is precisely what is suggested. I repeat that we deal here with speech alone, not with speech *plus* acts of sabotage or unlawful conduct. Not a single seditious act is charged in the indictment. To make a lawful speech unlawful because two men conceive it is to raise the law of conspiracy to appalling proportions. * * *

There comes a time when even speech loses its constitutional immunity. Speech innocuous one year may at another time fan such destructive flames that it must be halted in the interests of the safety of the Republic. That is the meaning of the clear and present danger test. When conditions are so critical that there will be no time to avoid the evil that the speech threatens, it is time to call a halt. Otherwise, free speech which is the strength of the Nation will be the cause of its destruction.

Yet free speech is the rule, not the exception. The restraint to be constitutional must be based on more than fear, on more than passionate opposition against the speech, on more than a revolted dislike for its contents. There must be some immediate injury to society that is likely if speech is allowed. * * *

I had assumed that the question of the clear and present danger, being so critical an issue in the case, would be a matter for submission to the jury. [The] Court, I think, errs when it treats the question as one of law.

Yet, whether the question is one for the Court or the jury, there should be evidence of record on the issue. This record, however, contains no evidence whatsoever showing that the acts charged viz., the teaching of the Soviet theory of revolution with the hope that it will be realized, have created any clear and present danger to the Nation. The Court, however, rules to the contrary. [The majority] might as well say that the speech of petitioners is outlawed because Soviet Russia and her Red Army are a threat to world peace.

The nature of Communism as a force on the world scene would, of course, be relevant to the issue of clear and present danger of petitioners' advocacy within the United States. But the primary consideration is the strength and tactical position of petitioners and their converts in this country. On that there is no evidence in the record. If we are to take judicial notice of the threat of Communists within the nation, it should not be difficult to conclude that *as a political party* they are of little consequence. Communists in this country have never made a respectable or serious showing in any election. I would doubt that there is a village, let alone a city or county or state, which the Communists could carry. Communism in the world scene is no bogeyman; but Communism as a political faction or party in this country plainly is. Communism has been so thoroughly exposed in this country that it has been crippled as a political force. Free speech has destroyed it as an effective political party. It is inconceivable that those who went up and down this country preaching the doctrine of revolution which petitioners espouse would have any success. In days of trouble and confusion, when bread lines were long, when the unemployed walked the streets, when people were starving, the advocates of a short-cut by revolution might have a chance to gain adherents. But today there are no such conditions. The country is not in despair; the people know Soviet Communism; the doctrine of Soviet revolution is exposed in all of its ugliness and the American people want none of it.

[Unless] and until extreme and necessitous circumstances are shown our aim should be to keep speech unfettered and to allow the processes of law to be invoked only when the provocateurs among us move from speech to action.

* * *[a]

Notes and Questions

1. What was the "substantive evil" in the *Dennis* case, the danger of which was sufficiently "clear and present" to warrant the application of the rule as originally formulated by Holmes and Brandeis? A *successful* revolution? An *attempted* revolution, however futile such an attempt might be? A *conspiracy* to plan the overthrow of the government by force and violence? A "conspiracy *to advocate* " such overthrow? See Gorfinkel & Mack, *Dennis v. United States and the Clear and Present Danger Rule*, 39 Calif.L.Rev. 475, 496–501 (1951); Nathanson, *The Communist Trial and the Clear-and-Present-Danger Test*, 63 Harv.L. Rev. 1167, 1168, 1173–75 (1950). Suppose it were established in *Dennis* that the odds were 99–1 against the Communists attempting an overthrow of the Government until 1961? 1971? Same result?

2. *Suppression of "totalitarian movements"*. Consider Auerbach, *The Communist Control Act of 1954*, 23 U.Chi.L.Rev. 173, 188–89 (1956): "[I]n suppressing totalitarian movements a democratic society is not acting to protect the status quo, but the very same interests which freedom of speech itself seeks to secure— the possibility of peaceful progress under freedom. That suppression may sometimes have to be the means of securing and enlarging freedom is a paradox which is not unknown in other areas of the law of modern democratic states.

a. Eighteen years later, concurring in *Brandenburg*, p. 455 infra, Douglas, J., declared: "I see no place in the regime of the First Amendment for any 'clear and present danger' test whether strict and tight as some would make it or free-wheeling as the Court in *Dennis* rephrased it. When one reads the opinions closely and sees when and how the 'clear and present danger' test has been applied, great misgivings are aroused. First, the threats were often loud but always puny and made serious only by judges so wedded to the status quo that critical analysis made them nervous. Second, the test was so twisted and perverted in *Dennis* as to make the trial of those teachers of Marxism an all-out political trial which was part and parcel of the cold war that has eroded substantial parts of the First Amendment."

The basic 'postulate,' therefore, which should 'limit and control' the First Amendment is that it is part of the framework for a constitutional democracy and should, therefore, not be used to curb the power of Congress to exclude from the political struggle those groups which, if victorious, would crush democracy and impose totalitarianism. Whether in any particular case and at any particular time, Congress should suppress a totalitarian movement should be regarded as a matter of wisdom for its sole determination. But a democracy should claim the moral and constitutional right to suppress these movements whenever it deems it advisable to do so." See also Bork, *Neutral Principles and Some First Amendment Problems,* 47 Ind.L.J. 1, 30–33 (1971).

3. *Seditious conspiracy.* Consider Jaffe, *Foreword,* 65 Harv.L.Rev. 107, 111 (1951): "[Douglas, J., views the *Dennis* case] as one in which men are being held guilty for teaching the contents of four books. [Vinson, C.J.'s opinion] plays into the hand of such obfuscation by refusing to face the fact that the statute and the indictment indeed do little more than allege mere advocacy, be it in classroom or elsewhere. But the great questions were first whether it had been proved that the defendants were maintaining an organization thoroughly drilled, alert and ready to convert advocacy into sabotage, espionage and subversion at the first propitious moment; second, whether the proof of such organization could avail to define and limit the fatally wide scope of the pleading and the statute; and finally, whether the statute so defined was constitutional. These questions were neither clearly asked nor answered."

See also Shapiro, *Freedom of Speech* 63–64 (1966): "Brandeis had demanded no restriction while there was still time to call the police. The trouble in [*Dennis*] was that the police had been called but hadn't found any evidence of wrong-doing. The prosecution was instituted under the advocacy provisions because there was not sufficient evidence to meet the normal requirements of the criminal law of sedition. Thus, paradoxically, the defendants were convicted in an area where they were protected by the supposedly rigorous demands of the First Amendment *precisely because* they could not be convicted in an area under the routine protections of criminal law."

4. *Deference to legislative judgment.* Consider Linde, *"Clear and Present Danger" Reexamined,* 22 Stan.L.Rev. 1163, 1176–78 (1970): "The Smith Act in 1940 wrote into federal law almost the exact terms of the New York Criminal Anarchy Act sustained in *Gitlow.* New York had enacted that law in 1902, soon after the assassination of [President McKinley]. Between the occupation of Czechoslovakia and the Ribbentrap-Molotov pact of 1939, the House of Representatives was working on a bill [H.R. 5138] whose provenance was the fear of anarchist agitation in 1900 and the hatred of alien radicalism in 1919. It became law in 1940. * * *

"What was the legislative judgment that would deserve deference for its assessment of the danger from revolutionary speech? [A] member of the 76th Congress presumably might stand up in 1940 and demand to know whether H.R. 5138 [violated the first amendment]. Constitutional law, in its original function antecedent to judicial review, owes him an answer. The Congressman's decision must be constitutionally right or wrong, in that place and at that time—not only a prosecutor's, a jury's, or a judge's decisions at the time of a later trial.

"The answer the Congressman would get in 1940, of course, would be that in 1925 the Supreme Court had held that the New York legislature could reasonably have believed in 1902 that advocacy of violent overthrow of government was too dangerous to be permitted. [That theory] simply accepts a lawmaker's judgment of danger intrinsic in the content of such advocacy, quite independent of any extrinsic conditions. This answer would not pretend to anticipate in 1940 the external dangers in an atomic age that were invoked to sustain the act in 1951, nor would it need to. [I]s the answer Holmes and Brandeis would give the member of the 76th Congress more satisfactory—that it all depended on the circumstances; that the constitutionality of H.R. 5138 could be determined only in the context of future eventualities of clear and present danger which he might now be unable to foresee; that the danger which would justify his law to suppress revolutionary speech and organization might shift from indigenous rampages to foreign military menaces and back again so that the bill presently before him for enactment might well be unconstitutional now but might be constitutional in the light of diverse events in 1945, in 1948, in 1951, in 1957, and in 1961, perhaps not in 1966, but again in 1968?"

In 1954, Senator McCarthy was condemned by the United States Senate for acting contrary to its ethics and impairing its dignity. In 1957, when the convictions of the "second string" communist leaders reached the Supreme Court in *Yates*, McCarthy had died, and so had McCarthyism. Although strong anti-communist sentiment persisted, the political atmosphere in *Yates'* 1957 was profoundly different from that of *Dennis'* 1951.

YATES v. UNITED STATES, 354 U.S. 298, 77 S.Ct. 1064, 1 L.Ed.2d 1356 (1957), reversed the convictions of 14 "second-string" Communist Party officials for conspiring, in violation of §§ 2(a)(1) and (3) of the Smith Act, (1) to advocate and teach the duty and necessity of overthrowing the federal government by force and violence, and (2) to organize, as the Communist Party of the United States, a group who so advocate and teach, all with the intent of causing the overthrow of the government by force and violence as speedily as circumstances would permit.

The trial judge, as the Court described it, "regarded as immaterial, and intended to withdraw from the jury's consideration, any issue as to the character of the advocacy in terms of its capacity to stir listeners to forcible action," by instructing the jury: "The kind of advocacy and teaching which is charged and upon which your verdict must be reached is not merely a desirability but a necessity that the Government of the United States be overthrown and destroyed by force and violence and not merely a propriety but a duty to overthrow [by] force and violence." Both the petitioners and the Government had submitted proposed instructions "which would have required the jury to find that the proscribed advocacy was not of a mere abstract doctrine of forcible overthrow, but of action to that end, by the use of language reasonably and ordinarily calculated to incite persons to such action," but the trial court had rejected these instructions on the basis of *Dennis*.

The Court was "thus faced with the question whether the Smith Act prohibits advocacy and teaching of forcible overthrow, as an abstract principle, divorced from any effort to instigate action to that end, so long as such advocacy or teaching is engaged in with evil intent." In holding that it did not, the Court, per HARLAN, J., avoided resolution of the issue "in terms of constitutional compulsion" [a] and construed the Smith Act—in light of the legislative history showing "beyond all question that Congress was aware of the distinction between the advocacy or teaching of abstract doctrine and the advocacy or teaching of

---

a. But see *Brandenburg*, Part D infra.

action, and that it did not intend to disregard it"—as "aimed at the advocacy and teaching of concrete action for the forcible overthrow of the Government, and not of principles divorced from action":

"The Government's reliance on this Court's decision in *Dennis* is misplaced. The jury instructions which were refused here were given there, and were referred to by this Court as requiring 'the jury to find the facts *essential* to establish the substantive crime.' (Emphasis added). It is true that at one point in the late Chief Justice's opinion it is stated that the Smith Act 'is directed at advocacy, not discussion,' but it is clear that the reference was to advocacy of action, not ideas, for in the very next sentence the opinion emphasizes that the jury was properly instructed that there could be no conviction for 'advocacy in the realm of ideas.' * * *

"In failing to distinguish between advocacy of forcible overthrow as an abstract doctrine and advocacy of action to that end, the District Court appears to have been led astray by the holding in *Dennis* that advocacy of violent action to be taken at some future time was enough. [T]he District Court apparently thought that *Dennis* obliterated the traditional dividing line between advocacy of abstract doctrine and advocacy of action.

"This misconceives the situation confronting the Court in *Dennis* and what was held there. Although the jury's verdict, interpreted in light of the trial court's instructions, did not justify the conclusion that the defendants' advocacy was directed at, or created any danger of, immediate overthrow, it did establish that the advocacy was aimed at building up a seditious group and maintaining it in readiness for action at a propitious time. [The] essence of the *Dennis* holding was that indoctrination of a group in preparation for future violent action, as well as exhortation to immediate action, by advocacy found to be directed to 'action for the accomplishment' of forcible overthrow, to violence as 'a rule or principle of action,' and employing 'language of incitement,' is not constitutionally protected when the group is of sufficient size and cohesiveness, is sufficiently oriented towards action, and other circumstances are such as reasonably to justify apprehension that action will occur. This is quite a different thing from the view of the District Court here that mere doctrinal justification of forcible overthrow, if engaged in with the intent to accomplish overthrow, is punishable per se under the Smith Act. That sort of advocacy, even though uttered with the hope that it may ultimately lead to violent revolution, is too remote from concrete action to be regarded as the kind of indoctrination preparatory to action which was condemned in *Dennis*.

"[*Dennis* was] not concerned with a conspiracy to engage at some future time in seditious advocacy, but rather with a conspiracy to advocate presently the taking of forcible action in the future. It was action, not advocacy, that was to be postponed until 'circumstances' would 'permit.' * * *

"In light of the foregoing we are unable to regard the District Court's charge upon this aspect of the case as adequate. [T]he trial court's statement that the proscribed advocacy must include the 'urging,' 'necessity,' and 'duty' of forcible overthrow, and not merely its 'desirability' and 'propriety,' may not be regarded as a sufficient substitute for charging that the Smith Act reaches only advocacy of action for the overthrow of government by force and violence. The essential distinction is that those to whom the advocacy is addressed must be urged to *do* something, now or in the future, rather than merely to *believe* in something.

* * *

"We recognize that distinctions between advocacy or teaching of abstract doctrines, with evil intent, and that which is directed to stirring people to action, are often subtle and difficult to grasp, for in a broad sense, as Mr. Justice Holmes said in his dissenting opinion in *Gitlow*: 'Every idea is an incitement.' But the very subtlety of these distinctions required the most clear and explicit instructions with reference to them, for they concerned an issue which went to the very heart of the charges against these petitioners. The need for precise and understandable instructions on this issue is further emphasized by the equivocal character of the evidence in this [record]. Instances of speech that could be considered to amount to 'advocacy of action' are so few and far between as to be almost completely overshadowed by the hundreds of instances in the record in which overthrow, if mentioned at all, occurs in the course of doctrinal disputation so remote from action as to be almost wholly lacking in probative value. Vague references to 'revolutionary' or 'militant' action of an unspecified character, which are found in the evidence, might in addition be given too great weight by the jury in the absence of more precise instructions. Particularly in light of this record, we must regard the trial court's charge in this respect as furnishing wholly inadequate guidance to the jury on this central point in the case."

On the basis of its interpretation of the Smith Act, the Court ordered an acquittal of five of the 14 petitioners,[b] finding "no adequate evidence in the record" to sustain their convictions on retrial.[c]

BLACK, J., joined by Douglas, J., dissented in part, maintaining, as they had in *Dennis*, that the Smith Act provisions on which the prosecutions were based violated the first amendment and that therefore acquittal should have been directed for all 14 petitioners.

CLARK, J., dissented: "*Dennis* merely held that a charge was sufficient where it requires a finding that 'the Party advocates the theory that there is a duty and necessity to overthrow the Government by force and violence [as] a program for winning adherents and as a policy to be translated into action' as soon as the circumstances permit [concurring opinion of Frankfurter, J.]." Thus, "the trial judge charged in essence all that was required under the *Dennis* opinion." He also maintained that instead of freeing five of the petitioners "solely on the *facts*"—which he regarded an unprecedented usurpation of the jury's function— the Court should have afforded the Government an opportunity, on remand, to present its evidence against petitioners "under the new theories announced by the Court for Smith Act prosecutions."[d]

Notes and Questions

1. *Dennis and Yates compared.* (a) On what did *Yates* focus: whether a *conspiracy* itself presents a "clear and present" danger or whether the *speech* of the conspirators does? On what did *Dennis* focus? Did *Yates* attach the same significance as did *Dennis* to membership in the Communist Party, as either an indication of intent or proof of membership in a conspiracy? To what extent does the fact that the *Yates* petitioners were not first-string leaders of the Party account for the result?

b. None of the remaining nine petitioners were ever tried again. Upon remand, the government requested dismissal of the indictments, explaining that a "comprehensive review [establishes] that we cannot satisfy the evidentiary requirements laid down by" the Court in *Yates*. See Mollan, *Smith Act Prosecutions: The Effect of the Dennis and Yates Decisions*, 26 U.Pitt.L.Rev. 705, 732 (1965).

c. The type of evidence which led the Court to order the acquittal of the five petitioners and the kind of evidence which caused it to deny directed acquittals as to the nine others are summarized in *Scales* infra.

d. Brennan and Whittaker, JJ., took no part. Burton, J.'s concurrence is omitted.

(b) Is it understandable that the *Yates* trial judge was "misled" by language in Vinson, C.J.'s *Dennis* opinion into thinking that punishment of the advocacy of abstract doctrine was permissible under the first amendment? Consider Greenawalt, *Speech and Crime*, 1980 Am.B.Found.Res.J. 645, 720 n. 279: "In defense of the trial court's instruction, it might be said that if someone is told he has a duty to participate in the forcible overthrow of the government, that signifies that he should perform illegal actions when the time arises. If all the Supreme Court opinion demanded is an explicit urging that listeners perform illegal actions at some future time, it is hard to distinguish that from what is clearly implied in advocacy of the ' "duty" of forcible overthrow.' But Justice Harlan may have meant that the advocacy must be more closely linked with action, either in the sense of recommending specific action or in the sense of being more positively directed to producing action among listeners." See generally Gellhorn, *American Rights* 79–80 (1960); Pritchett, *Congress vs. The Supreme Court, 1957–1960,* at 63–66 (1961); 71 Harv.L.Rev. 123–25 (1957).

2. *Advocating "doctrine" and advocating "action."* Consider Gellhorn, supra, at 80–81: "[O]ne can recognize a qualitative distinction between a speaker who expresses the opinion before a student audience that all law professors are scoundrels whose students should band together to beat them within an inch of their lives, and a second speaker who, taking up that theme, urges the audience to obtain baseball bats, meet behind the law faculty building at three o'clock next Thursday afternoon, and join him in attacking any professor who can then be found. The first speaker, in [the *Yates*] view, should not be prosecuted; the second has stepped over the line between advocating a belief and advocating an illegal action." Cf. Hand, *The Bill of Rights* 59–60 (1958).

3. *Clear and present danger test.* After *Yates,* was a call for concrete, forcible action even in the unspecified future still "unprotected speech" and participation in a group calling for such action still "unprotected association"? Did the constitutional criteria developed by Harlan, J.'s majority opinions in *Yates* and *Scales* and *Noto,* infra, concern the advocate's intent and the content of his advocacy or the probability of its success? See Linde, *"Clear and Present Danger" Reexamined,* 22 Stan.L.Rev. 1163, 1166 (1970). To what extent is Harlan, J.'s analysis similar to Judge Hand's in *Masses,* p. 420 supra?

Does *Yates* scrap the clear-and-present standard or establish a special category within that standard? When a subversive group is involved, may evidence of the "presentness of its organizational effectiveness" be substituted for the presentness of the danger? See Shapiro, *Freedom of Speech* 66, 71 (1966).

In an effort to avoid the demanding evidentiary requirements of *Yates,* the government began prosecuting communists under the "membership clause" of the Smith Act, 18 U.S.C. § 2385. After *Scales* and *Noto,* infra, the government abandoned Smith Act prosecutions altogether.

SCALES v. UNITED STATES, 367 U.S. 203, 81 S.Ct. 1469, 6 L.Ed.2d 782 (1961) affirmed the conviction of the Chairman of the North and South Carolina Districts of the Communist Party under the "membership clause" of the Smith Act, 18 U.S.C. § 2385, described by the Court, per HARLAN, J., as making a felony "the acquisition or holding of knowing membership in any organization which advocates the overthrow of the [federal] Government by force or violence." [1] The

---

1. Section 2385 (whose membership clause we place in italics) reads: "Whoever organizes or helps or attempts to organize any society, group, or assembly of persons who teach, advocate, or encourage the overthrow or destruction of any such government by force or vio-

trial judge had instructed the jury that, as the Supreme Court described it, "in order to convict it must find [that] (1) the Communist Party advocated the violent overthrow of the Government, in the sense of 'present advocacy of action' to accomplish that end as soon as circumstances were propitious; and (2) petitioner was an 'active' member of the Party, and not merely 'a nominal, passive * * *' member, with knowledge of the Party's illegal advocacy and a specific intent to bring about violent overthrow 'as speedily as circumstances would permit.'"

The Court held that "the membership clause permissibly bears the construction put upon it below" and as thus construed neither "imputes guilt to an individual merely on the basis of his associations and sympathies" in violation of due process nor infringes First Amendment freedoms:

"It was settled in *Dennis* that the advocacy with which we are here concerned is not constitutionally protected speech, and it was further established that a combination to promote such advocacy, albeit under the aegis of what purports to be a political party, is not such association as is protected by the First Amendment. We can discern no reason why membership, when it constitutes a purposeful form of complicity in a group engaging in this same forbidden advocacy, should receive any greater degree of protection from the guarantees of that Amendment.

"The [membership] clause does not make criminal all association with an organization, which has been shown to engage in illegal advocacy. There must be clear proof that a defendant 'specifically intend[s] to accomplish [the aims of the organization] by resort to violence.' *Noto* [this Part infra]. Thus the member for whom the organization is a vehicle for the advancement of legitimate aims and policies does not fall within the ban of the statute: he lacks the requisite specific intent 'to bring about the overthrow of the government as speedily as circumstances would permit.' Such a person may be foolish, deluded, or perhaps merely optimistic, but he is not by this statute made a criminal."

The Court also rejected the contention "that the evidence was insufficient to establish that the Communist Party was engaged in present advocacy of violent overthrow of the Government in the sense required by the Smith Act": "[T]he evidentiary question here is controlled in large part by *Yates* [which] rested on the view (not articulated in the opinion, though perhaps it should have been) that the Smith Act offenses, involving as they do subtler elements than are present in most other crimes, call for strict standards in assessing the adequacy of the proof needed to make out a case of illegal advocacy. This premise is as applicable to prosecutions under the membership clause of the Smith Act as it is to conspiracy prosecutions under that statute as we had in *Yates*. [*Yates*] indicates what type of evidence is needed to permit a jury to find that (a) there was 'advocacy of action' and (b) the Party was responsible for such advocacy.

"First, *Yates* makes clear what type of evidence is not *in itself* sufficient to show illegal advocacy. This category includes evidence of the following: the teaching of Marxism-Leninism and the connected use of Marxist 'classics' as textbooks; the official general resolutions and pronouncements of the Party at past conventions; dissemination of the Party's general literature, including the

lence; *or becomes or is a member of,* or affiliates with, *any such society, group, or assembly of persons, knowing the purposes thereof—*

"Shall be fined not more than $20,000 or imprisoned not more than twenty years, or both, and shall be ineligible for employment by the United States or any department or agency thereof, for the five years next following his conviction. * * *"

standard outlines on Marxism; the Party's history and organizational structure; the secrecy of meetings and the clandestine nature of the Party generally; statements by officials evidencing sympathy for and alliance with the U.S.S.R. It was the predominance of evidence of this type which led the Court to order the acquittal of several *Yates* [defendants].

"Second, *Yates* also indicates what kind of evidence is sufficient. There the Court pointed to two series of events which justified the denial of directed acquittals as to nine of the *Yates* defendants. The Court noted that with respect to seven of the defendants, meetings in San Francisco might be considered to be 'the systematic teaching and advocacy of illegal action which is condemned by the statute.' In those meetings, a small group of members were not only taught that violent revolution was inevitable, but they were also taught techniques for achieving that end. [T]he Court [also] referred to certain activities in the Los Angeles area 'which might be considered to amount to "advocacy of action"' and with which two *Yates* defendants were linked. Here again, the participants did not stop with teaching of the inevitability of eventual revolution, but went on to explain techniques, both legal and illegal, to be employed in preparation for or in connection with the revolution. [Viewed] together, these events described in *Yates* indicate at least two patterns of evidence sufficient to show illegal advocacy: (a) the teaching of forceful overthrow, accompanied by directions as to the type of illegal action which must be taken when the time for the revolution is reached; and (b) the teaching of forceful overthrow, accompanied by a contemporary, though legal, course of conduct clearly undertaken for the specific purpose of rendering effective the later illegal activity which is advocated."

After examining the *Scales* record, the Court concluded "this evidence sufficed to make a case for the jury on the issue of illegal Party advocacy. *Dennis* and *Yates* have definitely laid at rest any doubt that present advocacy of *future* action for violent overthrow satisfies statutory and constitutional requirements equally with advocacy of *immediate* action to that end. Hence this record cannot be considered deficient because it contains no evidence of advocacy for immediate overthrow. [T]he evidence amply showed that Party leaders were continuously preaching during the indictment period the inevitability of eventual forcible overthrow [and] the jury, under instructions which fully satisfied the requirements of *Yates*,[27] was entitled to infer from this systematic preaching

---

27. The trial court charged: "Moreover, the teaching in the abstract or teaching objectively, that is, teaching, discussing, explaining, or expounding what is meant by the aim or purpose of any author, group, or society of overthrowing the Government by force and violence is not criminal. * * *

"However, if the Party went further, and with the intention of overthrowing the Government by force and violence, it taught, or advocated a rule or principle of action which both, one, called on its members to take forcible and concrete action at some advantageous time thereafter to overthrow the Government by force and violence, and, two, expressed that call in such written or oral words as would reasonably and ordinarily be calculated to incite its members to take concrete and forcible action for such overthrow; then, if the Communist Party did that, the Party became such a society or group, as was outlawed by the Smith Act.

"To be criminal the teaching or advocacy, or the call to action just described need not be for immediate action, that is, for action today, tomorrow, next month, or next year. It is criminal, nonetheless, if the action is to be at an unnamed time in the future, to be fixed by the circumstances or on signal from the Party.

"It is criminal if it is a call upon the members to be ready, or to stand in readiness for action, or for a summons to action at a favorable, or opportune time in the future, or as speedily as circumstances will permit, provided always that the urging of such readiness be by words which would reasonably and ordinarily be calculated to spur a person to ready himself for, and to take action towards, the overthrow of the Government. But those to whom the advocacy or urging is addressed must be urged to do something now or in the future, rather than merely to believe in something. In other words, the advocacy must be of concrete action, and not merely a belief in

[that] the doctrine of violent revolution [was] put forward as a guide to future action * * *; in short that 'advocacy of action' was engaged in." And "such advocacy was sufficiently broadly based to permit its attribution to the Party."

DOUGLAS, J., dissented: "When we allow petitioner to be sentenced to prison for six years for being a 'member' of the Communist Party, we make a sharp break with traditional concepts of First Amendment [rights]. Even the Alien and Sedition Laws—shameful reminders of an early chapter in intolerance— never went so far as we go today. They were aimed at conspiracy and advocacy of insurrection and at the publication of 'false, scandalous and malicious' writing against the Government. [There] is here no charge of conspiracy, no charge of any overt act to overthrow the Government by force and violence, no charge of any other criminal act. The charge is being a 'member' of the Communist Party, 'well-knowing' that it advocated the overthrow of the Government by force and violence, 'said defendant intending to bring about such overthrow by force and violence as speedily as circumstances would permit.' That falls far short of a charge of conspiracy. Conspiracy rests not in intention alone but in an agreement with one or more others to promote an unlawful project. * * *

"The case is not saved by showing that petitioner was an active member. None of the activity constitutes a crime. [Scales] recruited new members into the Party, and promoted the advanced education of selected young Party members in the theory of communism to be undertaken at secret schools. He was a director of one such school [at which] students were told (by someone else) that one of the Party's weaknesses was in failing to place people in key industrial positions. One witness told of a meeting arranged by Scales at which the staff of the school urged him to remain in his position in an industrial plant rather than return to college. In Scales' presence, students at the school were once shown how to kill a person with a pencil, a device which, it was said, might come in handy on a picket line. Other evidence showed Scales [at different times to have said or distributed literature which said] that the Party line was that the Negroes in the South and the working classes should be used to foment a violent revolution; that a Communist government could not be voted into power in this country because the Government controlled communication media, newspapers, the military, and the educational system, and that force was the only way to achieve the revolution; [that] the revolution would come within a generation; that it would be easier in the United States than in Russia to effectuate the revolution because of assistance and advice from Russian Communists. * * *

"Not one single illegal act is charged to petitioner. That is why the essence of the crime covered by the indictment is merely belief—belief in the proletarian revolution, belief in Communist creed."

BLACK, J., dissented primarily for the reasons of Douglas and Brennan, JJ. He also maintained that although the Court had suggested in other cases in which it had applied the "balancing test," that it was justified "because no direct abridgment of First Amendment freedoms was involved," in the instant case "petitioner is being sent to jail for the express reason that he has associated with people who have entertained unlawful ideas and said unlawful things, and that of course is a *direct* abridgment of his freedoms of speech and assembly * * *. Nevertheless, [the] Court relies upon its prior decisions to the effect that the Government has power to abridge speech and assembly if its interest in doing so

abstract doctrine. However, the immediate concrete action urged should be intended to lead towards the forcible overthrow, and be so understood by those to whom the advocacy is addressed."

is sufficient to outweigh the interest in protecting these First Amendment freedoms. This, I think, demonstrates the unlimited breadth and danger of the 'balancing test' as it is currently being employed by a majority of this Court." [a]

In another Smith Act "membership clause" case, the same day as *Scales*, NOTO v. UNITED STATES, 367 U.S. 290, 81 S.Ct. 1517, 6 L.Ed.2d 836 (1961), per HARLAN, J., reversed the conviction of a communist worker in upstate New York, finding that the record "bears much of the infirmity that we found in the *Yates* record, and requires us to conclude that the evidence of illegal Party advocacy was insufficient to support this conviction." There was much evidence of "the Party's teaching of abstract doctrine that revolution is an inevitable product of the 'proletarian' effort to achieve communism in a capitalistic society," but testimony of evidence which supported an inference of " 'advocacy of action' to accomplish that end" was "sparse indeed" and "lacked the compelling quality which in *Scales* was supplied by the petitioner's utterances and systematic course of conduct as a high Party official."

Notes and Questions

1. See Shapiro, *Freedom of Speech* 119 (1966) for the view that when Congress had prohibited "membership" in organizations advocating the forcible overthrow of the government, it plainly had *not* meant "active" membership with "specific intent" and "the acrobatic display of statutory interpretation necessary to have made it mean all that simply demonstrated again the paradox of modest Justices who cannot bring themselves to challenge Congress, but yet cannot completely escape the feeling that they owe some independent duty to the Constitution."

2. Could Scales have been convicted under the advocacy or conspiracy to advocate clauses of the Smith Act? Could any really "active" Party member probably be? Without sufficient proof to satisfy *Yates*, can the government prove "membership" of the sort required for conviction in *Scales* and *Noto*? As a practical matter, did the Court eliminate the membership clause of the Smith Act as a separate means of prosecuting Communist Party members? See Shapiro, supra, at 120; 75 Harv.L.Rev. 116–17 (1961).

3. *Spock.* Dr. Spock, Rev. Coffin and others were convicted of conspiring to counsel and abet Selective Service registrants to refuse to have their draft cards in their possession and to disobey other duties imposed by the Selective Service Act of 1967. Spock signed a document entitled "A Call to Resist Illegitimate Authority," which "had 'a double aspect: in part it was a denunciation of governmental policy [in Vietnam] and, in part, it involved a public call to resist the duties imposed by the [Selective Service] Act.' " Several weeks later, Spock attended a demonstration in Washington, D.C., where an unsuccessful attempt was made to present collected draft cards to the Attorney General. *United States v. Spock,* 416 F.2d 165 (1st Cir.1969), per Aldrich, J., ruled that Spock should have been acquitted:

"[Spock] was one of the drafters of the Call, but this does not evidence the necessary intent to adhere to its illegal aspects. [H]is speech was limited to condemnation of the war and the draft, and lacked any words or content of counselling. The jury could not find proscribed advocacy from the mere fact

a. Brennan, J., joined by Warren, C.J., and Douglas, J., dissented on the ground that subsequent legislation had superseded the membership provision of the Smith Act.

[that] he hoped the frequent stating of his views might give young men 'courage to take active steps in draft resistance.' This is a natural consequence of vigorous speech. Similarly, Spock's actions lacked the clear character necessary to imply specific intent under the First Amendment standard. [H]e was at the Washington demonstration, [but took] no part in its planning. [His statements at this demonstration did not extend] beyond the general anti-war, anti-draft remarks he had made before. His attendance is as consistent with a desire to repeat this speech as it is to aid a violation of the law. The dissent would fault us for drawing such distinctions, but it forgets the teaching of [*Bond v. Floyd* [b]] that expressing one's views in broad areas is not foreclosed by knowledge of the consequences, and the important lesson of *Noto, Scales* and *Yates* that one may belong to a group, knowing of its illegal aspects, and still not be found to adhere thereto."

D. A MODERN "RESTATEMENT"

BRANDENBURG v. OHIO

395 U.S. 444, 89 S.Ct. 1827, 23 L.Ed.2d 430 (1969).

PER CURIAM.

The appellant, a leader of a Ku Klux Klan group, was convicted under [a 1919] Ohio Criminal Syndicalism statute of "advocat[ing] the duty, necessity, or propriety of crime, sabotage, violence, or unlawful methods of terrorism as a means of accomplishing industrial or political reform" and of "voluntarily assembl[ing] with any society, group or assemblage of persons formed to teach or advocate the doctrines of criminal syndicalism." He was fined $1,000 and sentenced to one to 10 years' imprisonment. * * *

The record shows that a man, identified at trial as the appellant, telephoned an announcer-reporter on the staff of a Cincinnati television station and invited him to come to a Ku Klux Klan "rally" to be held at a farm in Hamilton County. With the cooperation of the organizers, the reporter and a cameraman attended the meeting and filmed the events. Portions of the films were later broadcast on the local station and on a national network.

The prosecution's case rested on the films and on testimony identifying the appellant as the person who communicated with the reporter and who spoke at the rally. The State also introduced into evidence several articles appearing in the film, including a pistol, a rifle, a shotgun, ammunition, a Bible, and a red hood worn by the speaker in the films.

One film showed 12 hooded figures, some of whom carried firearms. They were gathered around a large wooden cross, which they burned. No one was present other than the participants and the newsmen who made the film. Most of the words uttered during the scene were incomprehensible when the film was projected, but scattered phrases could be understood that were derogatory of Negroes and, in one instance, of Jews. Another scene on the same film showed the appellant, in Klan regalia, making a speech. The speech, in full, was as follows:

---

b. *Bond v. Floyd*, 385 U.S. 116, 87 S.Ct. 339, 17 L.Ed.2d 235 (1966) found ambiguity in expressions of support for those unwilling to respond to the draft that earlier opinions would have characterized as clear advocacy of illegal action. As Thomas Emerson puts it "the distance traversed [from *Schenck* and *Debs* to *Bond*] is quite apparent." *Freedom of Expression in Wartime*, 116 U.Pa.L.Rev. 975, 988 (1968).

"This is an organizers' meeting. We have had quite a few members here today which are—we have hundreds, hundreds of members throughout the State of Ohio. I can quote from a newspaper clipping from the Columbus Ohio Dispatch, five weeks ago Sunday morning. The Klan has more members in the State of Ohio than does any other organization. We're not a revengent organization, but if our President, our Congress, our Supreme Court, continues to suppress the white, Caucasian race, it's possible that there might have to be some revengence taken.

"We are marching on Congress July the Fourth, four hundred thousand strong. From there we are dividing into two groups, one group to march on St. Augustine, Florida, the other group to march into Mississippi. Thank you."

The second film showed six hooded figures one of whom, later identified as the appellant, repeated a speech very similar to that recorded on the first film. The reference to the possibility of "revengence" was omitted, and one sentence was added: "Personally, I believe the nigger should be returned to Africa, the Jew returned to Israel." Though some of the figures in the films carried weapons, the speaker did not.

[*Whitney*] sustained the constitutionality of California's Criminal Syndicalism Act, the text of which is quite similar to that of the laws of Ohio. The Court upheld the statute on the ground that, without more, "advocating" violent means to effect political and economic change involves such danger to the security of the State that the State may outlaw it. But *Whitney* has been thoroughly discredited by later decisions [such as *Dennis* which] have fashioned the principle that the constitutional guarantees of free speech and free press do not permit a State to forbid or proscribe advocacy of the use of force or of law violation except where such advocacy is directed to inciting or producing imminent lawless action and is likely to incite or produce such action.[2] As we said in *Noto*, "the mere abstract teaching [of] the moral propriety or even moral necessity for a resort to force and violence, is not the same as preparing a group for violent action and steeling it to such action." See also *Bond v. Floyd*. A statute which fails to draw this distinction impermissibly intrudes upon the freedoms guaranteed by the First and Fourteenth Amendments. It sweeps within its condemnation speech which our Constitution has immunized from governmental control. Cf. *Yates* * * *.

Measured by this test, Ohio's Criminal Syndicalism Act cannot be sustained. The Act punishes persons who "advocate or teach the duty, necessity, or propriety" of violence "as a means of accomplishing industrial or political reform"; or who publish or circulate or display any book or paper containing such advocacy; or who "justify" the commission of violent acts "with intent to exemplify, spread or advocate the propriety of the doctrines of criminal syndicalism"; or [who] "voluntarily assemble" with a group formed "to teach or advocate the doctrines of criminal syndicalism." Neither the indictment nor the trial judge's instructions to the jury in any way refined the statute's bald definition of the crime in terms of mere advocacy not distinguished from incitement to imminent lawless action.[3]

2. It was on the theory that the Smith Act embodied such a principle and that it had been applied only in conformity with it that this Court sustained the Act's constitutionality. That this was the basis for *Dennis* was emphasized in *Yates*, in which the Court overturned convictions for advocacy of the forcible overthrow of the Government under the Smith Act, because the trial judge's instructions had allowed conviction for mere advocacy, unrelated to its tendency to produce forcible action.

3. The first count of the indictment charged that appellant "did unlawfully by word of mouth advocate the necessity, or pro-

Accordingly, we are here confronted with a statute which, by its own words and as applied, purports to punish mere advocacy and to forbid, on pain of criminal punishment, assembly with others merely to advocate the described type of action.[4] Such a statute falls within the condemnation of the First and Fourteenth Amendments. The contrary teaching of *Whitney* cannot be supported, and that decision is therefore overruled.

Reversed.

MR. JUSTICE BLACK, concurring.

I agree with the views expressed by Mr. Justice Douglas in his concurring opinion in this case that the "clear and present danger" doctrine should have no place in the interpretation of the First Amendment. I join the Court's opinion, which, as I understand it, simply cites *Dennis*, but does not indicate any agreement on the Court's part with the "clear and present danger" doctrine on which *Dennis* purported to rely.

MR. JUSTICE DOUGLAS, concurring.

While I join the opinion of the Court, I desire to enter a caveat.

[Whether] the war power—the greatest leveler of them all—is adequate to sustain [the "clear and present danger"] doctrine is debatable. The dissents in *Abrams* [and other cases] show how easily "clear and present danger" is manipulated to crush what Brandeis called "the fundamental right of free men to strive for better conditions through new legislation and new institutions" by argument and discourse even in time of war. Though I doubt if the "clear and present danger" test is congenial to the First Amendment in time of a declared war, I am certain it is not reconcilable with the First Amendment in days of peace.

* * *

Mr. Justice Holmes, though never formally abandoning the "clear and present danger" test, moved closer to the First Amendment ideal when he said in dissent in *Gitlow* [quoting the passage beginning, "Every idea is an incitement."] We have never been faithful to the philosophy of that dissent.

"[In *Dennis*, we distorted] the "clear and present danger" test beyond recognition. [I] see no place in the regime of the First Amendment for any "clear and present danger" test whether strict and tight as some would make it or free-wheeling as the Court in *Dennis* rephrased it.

Notes and Questions

1. What pre-*Brandenburg* decisions, if any, "have fashioned the principle" that advocacy may not be prohibited "except [where] directed to inciting or producing *imminent* lawless action *and* * * * *likely* to incite or produce such action"? (Emphasis added.) Did *Dennis, Yates* and *Scales* take pains to *deny* that the unlawful action advocated need be "imminent" or that the advocacy must be "likely" to produce the forbidden action? See Linde, *"Clear and Present Danger" Reexamined,* 22 Stan.L.Rev. 1163, 1166–67, 1183–86 (1970).

2. Is "the *Brandenburg* version of the clear and present danger test"—as Professor Emerson calls it (is this a misnomer?)—subject to criticism on the

priety of crime, violence, or unlawful methods of terrorism as a means of accomplishing political reform * * *." The second count charged that appellant "did unlawfully voluntarily assemble with a group or assemblage of persons formed to advocate the doctrines of criminal syndicalism * * *." The trial judge's charge merely followed the language of the indictment. * * *

4. Statutes affecting the right of assembly, like those touching on freedom of speech, must observe the established distinctions between mere advocacy and incitement to lawless action * * *.

ground that "it permits government interference with expression at too early a stage, allowing officials to cut speech off as soon as it shows signs of being effective"? That it is "an ad hoc test" that does not enable the speaker to "know in advance what the limits will be found to be"? That the test is "excessively vague"? See Emerson, *First Amendment Doctrine and the Burger Court*, 68 Calif.L.Rev. 422, 437–38 (1980).

3. Does *Brandenburg* adopt the *Masses* incitement test as a major part of the required showing? Consider Gunther, *Learned Hand and the Origins of Modern First Amendment Doctrine: Some Fragments of History*, 27 Stan.L.Rev. 719, 754–55 (1975): "An incitement-nonincitement distinction had only fragmentary and ambiguous antecedents in the pre-*Brandenburg* era; it was *Brandenburg* that really 'established' it; and, it was essentially an establishment of the legacy of Learned Hand. [Under] *Brandenburg*, probability of harm is no longer the central criterion for speech limitations. The inciting language of the speaker—the Hand focus on 'objective' words—is the major consideration. And punishment of the harmless inciter is prevented by the *Schenck*–derived requirement of a likelihood of dangerous consequences." (citing *Brandenburg*'s note 4.) But see Shiffrin, *Defamatory Non-Media Speech and First Amendment Methodology*, 25 U.C.L.A.L.Rev. 915, 947 n. 206 (1978): "Several leading commentators assume that *Brandenburg* adopts an incitement requirement. [The] conclusion is apparently based on this line from *Brandenburg*: 'Neither the indictment nor the trial judge's instructions to the jury in any way refined the statute's bald definition of the crime in terms of mere advocacy, not distinguished from incitement to imminent lawless action' [also citing note 4]. The difficulty with attaching significance to this ambiguous statement is that the term 'incitement' is used in the alternative in the Court's statement of its test. Thus, advocacy of imminent lawless action is protected unless it is directed to inciting *or* producing imminent lawless action and is likely to incite *or* produce imminent lawless action. Thus, even assuming that the use of the word incitement refers to express use of language, as opposed to the nature of results (an interpretation which is strained in light of the Court's wording of the test), incitement is not necessary to divorce the speech from first amendment protection. It is enough that the speech is directed to producing imminent lawless action and is likely to produce such action."

If one wants to argue that *Brandenburg* adopted *Masses*, is there anything to be made of the phrase "directed to" in the *Brandenburg* test? Alternatively, did *Yates* adopt the *Masses* test? If so, does its favorable citation in *Brandenburg* constitute an adoption of the *Masses* test?

4. The *Brandenburg* "inciting or producing imminent lawless action" standard was the basis for reversal of a disorderly conduct conviction in HESS v. INDIANA, 414 U.S. 105, 94 S.Ct. 326, 38 L.Ed.2d 303 (1973) (per curiam). After antiwar demonstrators on the Indiana University campus had blocked a public street, police moved them to the curbs on either side. As an officer passed him, appellant stated loudly, "We'll take the fucking street later (or again)," which led to his disorderly conduct conviction. His statement, observed the Court, "was not addressed to any person or group in particular" and "his tone, although loud, was no louder than that of the other people in the area. [At] best, [the] statement could be taken as counsel for present moderation; at worst, it amounted to nothing more than advocacy of illegal action at some indefinite future time." This was insufficient, under *Brandenburg*, to punish appellant's words, as the State had, on the ground that they had a "tendency to produce violence." It could not be said that appellant "was advocating, in the normal

sense, any action" and there was "no evidence" that "his words were intended to produce, and likely to produce, *imminent* disorder."

REHNQUIST, J., joined by Burger, C.J., and Blackmun, J., dissented: "The simple explanation for the result in this case is that the majority has interpreted the evidence differently from the courts below." The dissenters quarrelled with the Court's conclusion that appellant's advocacy "was not directed towards inciting imminent action. [T]here are surely possible constructions of the statement which would encompass more or less immediate and continuing action against the police. They should not be rejected out of hand because of an unexplained preference for other acceptable alternatives."[a]

5. Does *Yates* survive *Brandenburg*'s emphasis on *imminent* lawless action? Is light shed on the question by *Communist Party of Indiana v. Whitcomb*, 414 U.S. 441, 94 S.Ct. 656, 38 L.Ed.2d 635 (1974), invalidating an Indiana statute denying a political party or its candidates access to the ballot unless the party files an affidavit that it "does not advocate the overthrow of local, state or national government by force or violence"? The Court, per Brennan J., maintained that the required oath (which had been interpreted to include advocacy of abstract doctrine) violated the principle of *Brandenburg* and stated that the principle applied not only to attempted denials of public employment, bar licensing, and tax exemption, but also to ballot access denials. The flaw with the state's position was that it furnished access to the ballot "not because the Party urges others 'to *do* something now *or in the future* [but] merely to believe in something,' [*Yates*]" (Second emphasis added).

What happened to the "imminent lawless action" requirement? Does the *Whitcomb* language clarify *Brandenburg*? Modify it? Is the Court simply confused?

6. Does *Brandenburg* apply to the advocacy of trivial crimes? Suppose the advocacy of trespass across a lawn? What result under *Brandenburg*? What result under *Dennis*? Is *Dennis* potentially more speech protective than *Brandenburg*?

7. Does *Brandenburg* apply to solicitation of crime in private or non-ideological contexts? Consider Shiffrin, note 3 supra, at 950: "How different it might be if the factual context were to involve advocacy of murder in a non-socio-political context. One suspects that little rhetoric about the marketplace of ideas or other first amendment values would be employed and that the serious and explicit advocacy of murder in a concrete way would suffice to divorce the speech from first amendment protection even in the absence of a specific showing of likelihood." Would it matter if it were not explicit or not concrete? For trenchant analysis of the issues raised by the shift in context from public to

a. See also *NAACP v. Claiborne Hardware Co.*, 458 U.S. 886, 102 S.Ct. 3409, 73 L.Ed.2d 1215 (1982). The Court stated that the remarks of Charles Evers "might have been understood" as inviting violence, but stated that when "such appeals do not incite lawless action, they must be regarded as protected speech." If violent action had followed his remarks, a "substantial question" of liability would have been raised. The Court also observed, however, that the defendant might be held criminally liable for the acts of others if the speeches could be taken as evidence that the defendant gave "other specific instructions to carry out violent acts or threats." Compare *Watts v. United States*, 394 U.S. 705, 89 S.Ct. 1399, 22 L.Ed.2d 664 (1969) (statute prohibiting knowing and wilful threat of bodily harm upon the President is constitutional on its face) (dictum). For commentary on threats and the first amendment, compare Justice Linde's opinion in *State v. Robertson*, 293 Or. 402, 649 P.2d 569 (1982) with Greenawalt, *Criminal Coercion and Freedom of Speech*, 78 Nw.U.L.Rev. 1081 (1984).

private or in subject matter from ideological to non-ideological, see Greenawalt, *Speech and Crime,* 1980 Am.B.Found.Res.J. 645.

8. Should the line of cases from *Schenck* to *Brandenburg* fuel cynicism about the binding force of legal doctrine and about the willingness or capacity of the judiciary to protect dissent? [b] To what extent does the focus on Supreme Court cases exaggerate the frailty of legal doctrine? [c]

II. REPUTATION AND PRIVACY

In an important article, Harry Kalven coined the phrase "two level theory." Kalven, *The Metaphysics of the Law of Obscenity,* 1960 Sup.Ct.Rev. 1, 11. As he described it, *Beauharnais,* infra, and other cases employed a first amendment methodology that classified speech at two levels. Some speech—libel, obscenity, "fighting words"—was thought to be so bereft of social utility as to be beneath first amendment protection. At the second level, speech of constitutional value was thought to be protected unless it presented a clear and present danger of a substantive evil.

In considering libel and privacy, we will witness the collapse of "two level theory." The purpose is not a detailed examination of libel and privacy law. Our interests include the initial exclusion of defamation from first amendment protection, the themes and methods contributing to the erosion of that exclusion, and the articulation of basic first amendment values having implications and applications beyond defamation and the right to privacy.

A. GROUP LIBEL

BEAUHARNAIS v. ILLINOIS, 343 U.S. 250, 72 S.Ct. 725, 96 L.Ed. 919 (1952), per FRANKFURTER, J., sustained a statute prohibiting exhibition in any public place of any publication portraying "depravity, criminality, unchastity, or lack of virtue of a class of citizens, of any race, color, creed or religion [which exposes such citizens] to contempt, derision or obloquy or which is productive of breach of the peace or riots." The Court affirmed a conviction for organizing the distribution of a leaflet which petitioned the Mayor and City Council of Chicago "to halt the further encroachment, harassment and invasion of white people, their property, neighborhoods and persons by the Negro"; called for "one million self respecting white people in Chicago to unite"; and warned that if "the need to prevent the white race from becoming mongrelized by the Negro will not unite us, then the [aggressions], rapes, robberies, knives, guns, and marijuana of the Negro, surely will.":

"Today every American jurisdiction [punishes] libels directed at individuals. '[There] are certain well-defined and narrowly limited classes of speech, the prevention and punishment of which have never been thought to raise any constitutional problem. These include the lewd and obscene, the profane, the libelous, and the insulting or "fighting" words—those which by their very

b. In fashioning first amendment doctrine, should the overriding objective be at "all times [to] equip the first amendment to do maximum service in those historical periods when intolerance of unorthodox ideas is most prevalent and when governments are most able and most likely to stifle dissent systematically"? Should the first amendment "be targeted for the worst of times"? What impact would such a perspective have on the general development of first amendment doctrine? See Blasi, *The Pathological Perspective and the First Amendment,* 85 Colum.L.Rev. 449 (1985).

c. For a comprehensive review and critical analysis of the problems and policies raised by advocacy of illegal action, see Greenawalt, note 7 supra.

utterance inflict injury or tend to incite to an immediate breach of the peace. It has been well observed that such utterances are no essential part of any exposition of ideas, and are of such slight social value as a step to truth that any benefit that may be derived from them is clearly outweighed by the social interest in order and morality. "Resort to epithets or personal abuse is not in any proper sense communication of information or opinion safeguarded by the Constitution, and its punishment as a criminal act would raise no question under that instrument." *Cantwell v. Connecticut,* [p. 842 infra].' Such were the views of a unanimous Court in *Chaplinsky v. New Hampshire,* 315 U.S. 568, 62 S.Ct. 766, 86 L.Ed. 1031 (1942).[6]

"No one will gainsay that it is libelous falsely to charge another with being a rapist, robber, carrier of knives and guns, and user of marijuana. The [question is whether the fourteenth amendment] prevents a State from punishing such libels—as criminal libel has been defined, limited and constitutionally recognized time out of mind—directed at designated collectivities and flagrantly disseminated. [I]f an utterance directed at an individual may be the object of criminal sanctions, we cannot deny to a State power to punish the same utterance directed at a defined group, unless we can say that this is a wilful and purposeless restriction unrelated to the peace and well-being of the State.

"Illinois did not have to look beyond her own borders to await the tragic experience of the last three decades to conclude that wilful purveyors of falsehood concerning racial and religious groups promote strife and tend powerfully to obstruct the manifold adjustments required for free, orderly life in a metropolitan, polyglot community. From the murder of the abolitionist Lovejoy in 1837 to the Cicero riots of 1951, Illinois has been the scene of exacerbated tension between races, often flaring into violence and destruction. In many of these outbreaks, utterances of the character here in question, so the Illinois legislature could conclude, played a significant [part.]

"In the face of this history and its frequent obligato of extreme racial and religious propaganda, we would deny experience to say that the Illinois legislature was without reason in seeking ways to curb false or malicious defamation of racial and religious groups, made in public places and by means calculated to have a powerful emotional impact on those to whom it was presented. [I]t would be out of bounds for the judiciary to deny the legislature a choice of policy, provided it is not unrelated to the problem and not forbidden by some explicit limitation on the State's power. That the legislative remedy might not in practice mitigate the evil, or might itself raise new problems, would only manifest once more the paradox of reform. It is the price to be paid for the trial-and-error inherent in legislative efforts to deal with obstinate social issues.

"[It would] be arrant dogmatism, quite outside the scope of our authority [for] us to deny that the Illinois Legislature may warrantably believe that a man's job and his educational opportunities and the dignity accorded him may depend as much on the reputation of the racial and religious group to which he willynilly belongs, as on his own merits. This being so, we are precluded from saying that speech concededly punishable when immediately directed at individuals cannot be outlawed if directed at groups with whose position and esteem in society the affiliated individual may be inextricably involved. * * *[18]

---

6. In all but five States, the constitutional guarantee of free speech to every person is explicitly qualified by holding him "responsible for the abuse of that right." * * *

18. [If] a statute sought to outlaw libels of political parties, quite different problems not now before us would be raised. For one thing, the whole doctrine of fair comment as indis-

"As to the defense of truth, Illinois in common with many States requires a showing not only that the utterance state the facts, but also that the publication be made 'with good motives and for justifiable ends'. Both elements are necessary if the defense is to prevail. [The] teaching of a century and a half of criminal libel prosecutions in this country would go by the board if we were to hold that Illinois was not within her rights in making this combined requirement. Assuming that defendant's offer of proof directed to a part of the defense was adequate, it did not satisfy the entire requirement which Illinois could exact."

The Court ruled that the trial court properly declined to require the jury to find a "clear and present danger": "Libelous utterances not being within the area of constitutionally protected speech, it is unnecessary, either for us or for the State courts, to consider the issues behind the phrase 'clear and present danger.' Certainly no one would contend that obscene speech, for example, may be punished only upon a showing of such circumstances. Libel, as we have seen, is in the same class."

BLACK, J., joined by Douglas, J., dissented: "[The Court] acts on the bland assumption that the First Amendment is wholly irrelevant. [Today's] case degrades First Amendment freedoms to the 'rational basis' level. [We] are cautioned that state legislatures must be left free to 'experiment' and to make legislative judgments. [State] experimentation in curbing freedom of expression is startling and frightening doctrine in a country dedicated to self-government by its people.

"[As] 'constitutionally recognized,' [criminal libel] has provided for punishment of false, malicious, scurrilous charges against individuals, not against huge groups. This limited scope of the law of criminal libel is of no small importance. It has confined state punishment of speech and expression to the narrowest of areas involving nothing more than private feuds. Every expansion of the law of criminal libel so as to punish discussion of matters of public concern means a corresponding invasion of the area dedicated to free expression by the First Amendment.

"[Whether] the words used in their context here are 'fighting words' in the same sense [as *Chaplinsky*] is doubtful, but whether so or not they are not addressed to or about *individuals*. Moreover, the leaflet used here was also the means adopted by an assembled group to enlist interest in their efforts to have legislation enacted. And the 'fighting' words were but a part of arguments on questions of wide public interest and importance. Freedom of petition, assembly, speech and press could be greatly abridged by a practice of meticulously scrutinizing every editorial, speech, sermon or other printed matter to extract two or three naughty words on which to hang charges of 'group libel.'

"[If] there be minority groups who hail this holding as their victory, they might consider the possible relevancy of this ancient remark: 'Another such victory and I am undone.' "

REED, J., joined by Douglas, J., dissenting, argued that the statute was unconstitutionally vague: "These words—'virtue,' 'derision,' and 'obloquy'—have neither general nor special meanings well enough known to apprise those within their reach as to limitations on speech. Philosophers and poets, thinkers of high and low degree from every age and race have sought to expound the meaning of

pensable to the democratic political process
would come into play. Political parties, like
public men, are, as it were, public property.

virtue. * * * Are the tests of the Puritan or the Cavalier to be applied, those of the city or the farm, the Christian or non-Christian, the old or the young?"

DOUGLAS, J., dissented: "Hitler and his Nazis showed how evil a conspiracy could be which was aimed at destroying a race by exposing it to contempt, derision, and obloquy. I would be willing to concede that such conduct directed at a race or group in this country could be made an indictable offense. For such a project would be more than the exercise of free speech. [It] would be free speech plus.

"I would also be willing to concede that even without the element of conspiracy there might be times and occasions when the legislative or executive branch might call a halt to inflammatory talk, such as the shouting of 'fire' in a school or a theatre.

"My view is that if in any case other public interests are to override the plain command of the First Amendment, the peril of speech must be clear and present, leaving no room for argument, raising no doubts as to the necessity of curbing speech in order to prevent disaster."

JACKSON, J., dissenting, argued that the fourteenth amendment does not incorporate the first, as such, but permits the states more latitude than the Congress. He concluded, however, that due process required the trier of fact to evaluate the evidence as to the truth and good faith of the speaker and the clarity and presence of the danger. He was unwilling to assume danger from the tendency of the words and felt that the trial court had precluded the defendant's efforts to show truth and good motives.

Notes and Questions

1. *The right to petition.* Should it make a difference that the leaflet was in the form of a petition to the mayor and city council? Does the right of the people "to petition the Government for a redress of grievances" add anything of substance to Beauharnais' other first amendment arguments? Consider Kalven, *The Negro and the First Amendment* 40 (1965): "If it would make a difference whether the petition was genuine and not just a trick of form, can the Court penetrate the form and appraise the true motivation or must it, as it does with congressional committees accept the official motivation?" [a]

2. *Equality and freedom of speech.* Consider the following hypothetical commentary: "Group libel statutes pose uniquely difficult issues for they involve a clash between two constitutional commitments: the principle of equality and the principle of free speech. They force us to decide what we want to express as a nation: Do we want a powerful symbol of our belief in uninhibited debate or do we want to be the kind of nation that will not tolerate the public calumny of religious, ethnic, and racial groups?" Compare Beth, *Group Libel and Free Speech,* 39 Minn.L.Rev. 167, 180–81 (1955).

3. *Tolerance and freedom of speech.* Should the first amendment be a means of institutionalizing a national commitment to the value of tolerance? By tolerating the intolerable, would we carve out one area of social interaction for extraordinary self-restraint and thereby develop [b] and demonstrate a vital social capacity? See generally Bollinger, *The Tolerant Society: Freedom of Speech and*

---

a. See *McDonald v. Smith,* __ U.S. __, 105 S.Ct. 2787, 86 L.Ed.2d 384 (1985) (denying any special first amendment status for the Petition Clause).

b. For skepticism about the capacity of courts to achieve any substantial impact in promoting tolerance, see Nagel, *How Useful Is Judicial Review in Free Speech Cases?,* 69 Corn.L.Rev. 302 (1984).

Extremist Speech in America (1986); Bollinger, *Free Speech and Intellectual Values*, 92 Yale L.J. 438 (1983); Bollinger, *Book Review*, 80 Mich.L.Rev. 617 (1982).

4. *Civility and freedom of speech.* By allowing prosecutions for group libel in the most "odious cases" or cases "so public and offensive that they cannot be avoided" would we "encourage confidence in the discipline of judging itself" and "encourage others to make judgments as well, not simply on group defamation, but on other matters that raise questions about propriety and decency and the obligations that individuals may have to one another"? See Arkes, *Civility and the Restriction of Speech: Rediscovering the Defamation of Groups,* 1974 Sup.Ct. Rev. 281, 331.

5. *Libel, group libel, and seditious libel.* Consider Kalven, supra, at 15, 16 and 50–51: Seditious libel "is the doctrine that criticism of government officials and policy may be viewed as defamation of government and may be punished as a serious crime. [On] my view, the absence of seditious libel as a crime is the true pragmatic test of freedom of speech. This I would argue is what freedom of speech is about. [The] most revealing aspect of the opinions, and particularly that of Justice Frankfurter, is the absence of any sense of the proximity of the case before them to seditious libel. The case presents almost a perfect instance of that competition among analogies which Edward Levi has emphasized as the essential circumstance of legal reasoning. In the middle we have group libel and Justice Frankfurter's urging its many resemblances to individual libel. [If] the Court's speech theory had been more grounded, as it seems to me it should be, on the relevance of the concept of seditious libel and less on the analogy to the law of attempts found in the slogan 'clear and present danger,' it is difficult to believe that either the debate or the result in *Beauharnais* would have been the same."

B. PUBLIC OFFICIALS AND SEDITIOUS LIBEL

NEW YORK TIMES CO. v. SULLIVAN

376 U.S. 255, 84 S.Ct. 710, 11 L.Ed.2d 686 (1964).

MR. JUSTICE BRENNAN delivered the opinion of the Court.

[Sullivan, the Montgomery, Ala. police commissioner, sued the New York Times and four black Alabama clergymen for alleged libelous statements in a paid, full-page fund-raising advertisement signed by a "Committee to defend Martin Luther King and the struggle for freedom in the South." The advertisement stated that "truckloads of police armed with shotguns and tear-gas ringed Alabama State College Campus" in Montgomery, and that "the Southern violators [have] bombed [Dr. King's] home, assaulted his person [and] arrested him seven times." In several respects the statements were untrue. Several witnesses testified that they understood the statements to refer to Sullivan because he supervised Montgomery police. Sullivan proved he did not participate in the events described. He offered no proof of pecuniary loss.[3] Pursuant to Alabama law, the trial court submitted the libel issue to the jury, giving general and punitive damages instructions. It returned a $500,000 verdict for Sullivan against all of the defendants.] We hold that the rule of law applied by the Alabama courts is constitutionally deficient for failure to provide the safeguards

---

3. Approximately 394 copies of the edition of the Times containing the advertisement were circulated in Alabama. Of these, about 35 copies were distributed in Montgomery County. The total circulation of the Times for that day was approximately 650,000 copies.

for freedom of speech and of the press that are required by the First and Fourteenth Amendments in a libel action brought by a public official against critics of his official conduct.[4] We further hold that under the proper safeguards the evidence presented in this case is constitutionally insufficient to support the judgment for respondent.

I. [The] publication here [communicated] information, expressed opinion, recited grievances, protested claimed abuses, and sought financial support on behalf of a movement whose existence and objectives are matters of the highest public interest and concern. That the Times was paid for publishing the advertisement is as immaterial in this connection as is the fact that newspapers and books are sold. *Smith v. California* [p. 515 infra]. Any other conclusion would discourage newspapers from carrying "editorial advertisements" of this type, and so might shut off an important outlet for the promulgation of information and ideas by persons who do not themselves have access to publishing facilities.

II. Under Alabama law [once] "libel per se" has been established, the defendant has no defense as to stated facts unless he can persuade the jury that they were true in all their particulars. [His] privilege of "fair comment" for expressions of opinion depends on the truth of the facts upon which the comment is based. [Unless] he can discharge the burden of proving truth, general damages are presumed, and may be awarded without proof of pecuniary injury.

[Respondent] relies heavily, as did the Alabama courts, on statements of this Court to the effect that the Constitution does not protect libelous publications. Those statements do not foreclose our inquiry here. None of the cases sustained the use of libel laws to impose sanctions upon expression critical of the official conduct of public officials. [L]ibel can claim no talismanic immunity from constitutional limitations. It must be measured by standards that satisfy the First Amendment.

The First Amendment, said Judge Learned Hand, "presupposes that right conclusions are more likely to be gathered out of a multitude of tongues, than through any kind of authoritative selection. To many this is, and always will be, folly; but we have staked upon it our all." [Thus] we consider this case against the background of a profound national commitment to the principle that debate on public issues should be uninhibited, robust, and wide-open, and that it may well include vehement, caustic, and sometimes unpleasantly sharp attacks on government and public officials. The present advertisement, as an expression of grievance and protest on one of the major public issues of our time, would seem clearly to qualify for the constitutional protection. The question is whether it forfeits that protection by the falsity of some of its factual statements and by its alleged defamation of respondent.

---

4. [The] Times contends that the assumption of jurisdiction over its corporate person by the Alabama courts overreaches the territorial limits of the Due Process Clause. The latter claim is foreclosed from our review by the ruling of the Alabama courts that the Times entered a general appearance in the action and thus waived its jurisdictional objection. * * *

[Since *New York Times* the Court has upheld expansive personal jurisdiction against media defendants. *Calder v. Jones*, 465 U.S.

783, 104 S.Ct. 1482, 79 L.Ed.2d 804 (1984); *Keeton v. Hustler*, 465 U.S. 770, 104 S.Ct. 1473, 79 L.Ed.2d 790 (1984). *Calder* rejected the suggestion that first amendment concerns enter into jurisdictional analysis. It feared complicating the inquiry and argued that because first amendment concerns are taken into account in limiting the substantive law of defamation, "to reintroduce those concerns at the jurisdictional stage would be a form of double counting."]

Authoritative interpretations of the First Amendment guarantees have consistently refused to recognize an exception for any test of truth—whether administered by judges, juries, or administrative officials—and especially not one that puts the burden of proving truth on the speaker. [E]rroneous statement is inevitable in free debate, and [it] must be protected if the freedoms of expression are to have the "breathing space" that they "need [to] survive."

[Injury] to official reputation affords no more warrant for repressing speech that would otherwise be free than does factual error. Where judicial officers are involved, this Court has held that concern for the dignity and reputation of the courts does not justify the punishment as criminal contempt of criticism of the judge or his decision. This is true even though the utterance contains "half-truths" and "misinformation." Such repression can be justified, if at all, only by a clear and present danger of the obstruction of justice. If judges are to be treated as "men of fortitude, able to thrive in a hardy climate," surely the same must be true of other government officials, such as elected city commissioners. Criticism of their official conduct does not lose its constitutional protection merely because it is effective criticism and hence diminishes their official reputations.

If neither factual error nor defamatory content suffices to remove the constitutional shield from criticism of official conduct, the combination of the two elements is no less inadequate. This is the lesson to be drawn from the great controversy over the Sedition Act of 1798, 1 Stat. 596, which first crystallized a national awareness of the central meaning of the First Amendment. [Although] the Sedition Act was never tested in this Court, the attack upon its validity has carried the day in the court of history. Fines levied in its prosecution were repaid by Act of Congress on the ground that it was unconstitutional. * * * Jefferson, as President, pardoned those who had been convicted and sentenced under the Act and remitted their fines. [Its] invalidity [has] also been assumed by Justices of this Court. [These] views reflect a broad consensus that the Act, because of the restraint it imposed upon criticism of government and public officials, was inconsistent with the First Amendment. * * *

What a State may not constitutionally bring about by means of a criminal statute is likewise beyond the reach of its civil law of libel. The fear of damage awards under a rule such as that invoked by the Alabama courts here may be markedly more inhibiting than the fear of prosecution under a criminal statute. [The] judgment awarded in this case—without the need for any proof of actual pecuniary loss—was one thousand times greater than the maximum fine provided by the Alabama criminal [libel law], and one hundred times greater than that provided by the Sedition Act. And since there is no double-jeopardy limitation applicable to civil lawsuits, this is not the only judgment that may be awarded against petitioners for the same publication.[18] Whether or not a newspaper can survive a succession of such judgments, the pall of fear and timidity imposed upon those who would give voice to public criticism is an atmosphere in which the First Amendment freedoms cannot [survive].

The state rule of law is not saved by its allowance of the defense of truth. A defense for erroneous statements honestly made is no less essential here than was the requirement of proof of guilty knowledge which, in *Smith v. California,*

---

18. The Times states that four other libel suits based on the advertisement have been filed against it by [others]; that another $500,000 verdict has been awarded in [one]; and that the damages sought in the other three total $2,000,000.

we held indispensable to a valid conviction of a bookseller for possessing obscene writings for [sale].

A rule compelling the critic of official conduct to guarantee the truth of all his factual assertions—and to do so on pain of libel judgments virtually unlimited in amount—leads to a comparable "self-censorship." Allowance of the defense of truth, with the burden of proving it on the defendant, does not mean that only false speech will be deterred.[19] [Under] such a rule, would-be critics of official conduct may be deterred from voicing their criticism, even though it is believed to be true and even though it is in fact true, because of doubt whether it can be proved in court or fear of the expense of having to do so. They tend to make only statements which "steer far wider of the unlawful zone." The rule thus dampens the vigor and limits the variety of public [debate].

The constitutional guarantees require, we think, a federal rule that prohibits a public official from recovering damages for a defamatory falsehood relating to his official conduct unless he proves that the statement was made with "actual malice"—that is, with knowledge that it was false or with reckless disregard of whether it was false or [not].

Such a privilege for criticism of official conduct is appropriately analogous to the protection accorded a public official when *he* is sued for libel by a private citizen. In *Barr v. Matteo*, 360 U.S. 564, 575, 79 S.Ct. 1335, 1341, 3 L.Ed.2d 1434 (1959), this Court held the utterance of a federal official to be absolutely privileged if made "within the outer perimeter" of his duties. The States accord the same immunity to statements of their highest officers, although some differentiate their lesser officials and qualify the privilege they enjoy. But all hold that all officials are protected unless actual malice can be proved. The reason for the official privilege is said to be that the threat of damage suits would otherwise "inhibit the fearless, vigorous, and effective administration of policies of government" and "dampen the ardor of all but the most resolute, or the most irresponsible, in the unflinching discharge of their duties." *Barr*. Analogous considerations support the privilege for the citizen-critic of government. It is as much his duty to criticize as it is the official's duty to administer. [It] would give public servants an unjustified preference over the public they serve, if critics of official conduct did not have a fair equivalent of the immunity granted to the officials themselves. We conclude that such a privilege is required by the First and Fourteenth Amendments.[23]

III. [W]e consider that the proof presented to show actual malice lacks the convincing clarity [a] which the constitutional standard demands, and hence that it would not constitutionally sustain the judgment for respondent under the proper rule of law. [T]here is evidence that the Times published the advertisement without checking its accuracy against the news stories in the Times' own

---

19. Even a false statement may be deemed to make a valuable contribution to the public debate, since it brings about "the clearer perception and livelier impression of truth, produced by its collision with error." Mill, *On Liberty* 15 (1947).

23. We have no occasion here to determine how far down into the lower ranks of government employees the "public official" designation would extend for purposes of this rule, or otherwise to specify categories of persons who would or would not be included. [Nor] need we here determine the boundaries of the "official conduct" concept. ＊ ＊ ＊

a. Compare *Bose Corp. v. Consumers Union*, 466 U.S. 485, 104 S.Ct. 1949, 80 L.Ed. 2d 502 (1984) (appellate courts "must exercise independent judgment and determine whether the record establishes actual malice with convincing clarity."). Should independent appellate judgment be required in all first amendment cases? All constitutional cases? For broadranging commentary, see Monaghan, *Constitutional Fact Review*, 85 Colum.L.Rev. 229 (1985).

files. The mere presence of the stories in the files does [not] establish that the Times "knew" the advertisement was false, since the state of mind required for actual malice would have to be brought home to the persons in the Times' organization having responsibility for the publication of the advertisement. With respect to the failure of those persons to make the check, the record shows that they relied upon their knowledge of the good reputation of many [whose] names were listed as sponsors of the advertisement, and upon the letter from A. Philip Randolph, known to them as a responsible individual, certifying that the use of the names was authorized. There was testimony that the persons handling the advertisement saw nothing in it that would render it unacceptable under the Times' policy of rejecting advertisements containing "attacks of a personal character"; their failure to reject it on this ground was not unreasonable. We think the evidence against the Times supports at most a finding of negligence in failing to discover the misstatements, and is constitutionally insufficient to show the recklessness that is required for a finding of actual malice.

[T]he evidence was constitutionally defective in another respect: it was incapable of supporting the jury's finding that the allegedly libelous statements were made "of and concerning" respondent. [On this point, the Supreme Court of Alabama] based its ruling on the proposition that: "[The] average person knows that municipal agents, such as police and firemen, and others, are under the control and direction of the city governing body, and more particularly under the direction and control of a single commissioner. In measuring the performance or deficiencies of such groups, praise or criticism is usually attached to the official in complete control of the body."

This proposition has disquieting implications for criticism of governmental conduct. [It would transmute] criticism of government, however impersonal it may seem on its face, into personal criticism, and hence potential libel, of the officials of whom the government is composed. [Raising] as it does the possibility that a good-faith critic of government will be penalized for his criticism, the proposition relied on by the Alabama courts strikes at the very center of the constitutionally protected area of free expression. We hold that such a proposition may not constitutionally be utilized to establish that an otherwise impersonal attack on governmental operations was a libel of an official responsible for those operations. Since it was relied on exclusively here, and there was no other evidence to connect the statements with respondent, the evidence was constitutionally insufficient to support a finding that the statements referred to respondent. * * * [b]

MR. JUSTICE BLACK, with whom MR. JUSTICE DOUGLAS joins (concurring).

* * * "Malice," even as defined by the Court, is an elusive, abstract concept, hard to prove and hard to disprove. The requirement that malice be proved provides at best an evanescent protection for the right critically to discuss public affairs and certainly does not measure up to the sturdy safeguard embodied in the First Amendment. Unlike the Court, therefore, I vote to reverse exclusively on the ground that the Times and the individual defendants had an absolute, unconditional constitutional right to publish in the Times advertisement their criticisms of the Montgomery agencies and [officials].

b. For a similar ruling that impersonal criticism of a government operation cannot be the basis for defamation "of and concerning" the supervisor of the operation, see *Rosenblatt* *v. Baer*, 383 U.S. 75, 86 S.Ct. 669, 15 L.Ed.2d 597 (1966): "[T]antamount to a demand for recovery based on libel of government."

The half-million-dollar verdict [gives] dramatic proof [that] state libel laws threaten the very existence of an American press virile enough to publish unpopular views on public affairs and bold enough to criticize the conduct of public officials. [B]riefs before us show that in Alabama there are now pending eleven libel suits by local and state officials against the Times seeking $5,600,000, and five such suits against the Columbia Broadcasting System seeking $1,700,000. Moreover, this technique for harassing and punishing a free press—now that it has been shown to be possible—is by no means limited to cases with racial overtones; it can be used in other fields where public feelings may make local as well as out-of-state newspapers easy prey for libel verdict seekers.

In my opinion the Federal Constitution has dealt with this deadly danger to the press in the only way possible without leaving the press open to destruction—by granting the press an absolute immunity for criticism of the way public officials do their public duty.

[This] Nation, I suspect, can live in peace without libel suits based on public discussions of public affairs and public officials. But I doubt that a country can live in freedom where its people can be made to suffer physically or financially for criticizing their government, its actions, or its officials. * * *[c]

Professor Kalven observed that the Court in *New York Times* was moving toward "the theory of free speech that Alexander Meiklejohn has been offering us for some fifteen years now." Kalven, *The New York Times Case: A Note On "The Central Meaning of the First Amendment,"* 1964 Sup.Ct.Rev. 191, 221. Indeed Kalven reported Meiklejohn's view that the case was " 'an occasion for dancing in the streets.' " Id. at 221 n. 125. Consider the following excerpts from Meiklejohn's most significant work and Zechariah Chafee's pointed response.

ALEXANDER MEIKLEJOHN—FREE SPEECH AND ITS RELATION TO SELF–GOVERNMENT

3, 26–27, 93–94, 89–91 (1948), reprinted in Meiklejohn, *Political Freedom* 9, 27–28, 79–80, 75–77 (1960).
Reprinted with permission of the publisher; copyright © 1948, 1960 by Harper & Brothers.

We Americans think of ourselves as politically free. We believe in self-government. If men are to be governed, we say, then that governing must be done, not by others, but by themselves. So far, therefore, as our own affairs are concerned, we refuse to submit to alien control. That refusal, if need be, we will carry to the point of rebellion, of revolution. And if other men, within the jurisdiction of our laws, are denied their right to political freedom, we will, in the same spirit, rise to their defense. Governments, we insist, derive their just powers from the consent of the governed. If that consent be lacking, governments have no just powers.

[The] principle of the freedom of speech springs from the necessities of the program of self-government. It is not a Law of Nature or of Reason in the abstract. It is a deduction from the basic American agreement that public issues shall be decided by universal suffrage.

---

c. Goldberg, J., joined by Douglas, J., concurring, also asserted for "the citizen and [the] press an absolute unconditional privilege to criticize official conduct," but maintained that the imposition of liability for "[p]urely private defamation" did not abridge the first amendment because it had "little to do with the political ends of a self-governing society."

If, then, on any occasion in the United States it is allowable to say that the Constitution is a good document it is equally allowable, in that situation, to say that the Constitution is a bad document. If a public building may be used in which to say, in time of war, that the war is justified, then the same building may be used in which to say that it is not justified. If it be publicly argued that conscription for armed service is moral and necessary, it may likewise be publicly argued that it is immoral and unnecessary. If it may be said that American political institutions are superior to those of England or Russia or Germany, it may, with equal freedom, be said that those of England or Russia or Germany are superior to ours. These conflicting views may be expressed, must be expressed, not because they are valid, but because they are relevant. If they are responsibly entertained by anyone, we, the voters, need to hear them. When a question of policy is "before the house," free men choose to meet it not with their eyes shut, but with their eyes open. To be afraid of ideas, any idea, is to be unfit for self-government. Any such suppression of ideas about the common good, the First Amendment condemns with its absolute disapproval. The freedom of ideas shall not be abridged. * * *

If, however, as our argument has tried to show, the principle of the freedom of speech is derived, not from some supposed "Natural Right," but from the necessities of self-government by universal suffrage, there follows at once a very large limitation of the scope of the principle. The guarantee given by the First Amendment is not, then, assured to all speaking. It is assured only to speech which bears, directly or indirectly, upon issues with which voters have to deal—only, therefore, to the consideration of matters of public interest. Private speech, or private interest in speech, on the other hand, has no claim whatever to the protection of the First Amendment. If men are engaged, as we so commonly are, in argument, or inquiry, or advocacy, or incitement which is directed toward our private interests, private privileges, private possessions, we are, of course, entitled to "due process" protection of those activities. But the First Amendment has no concern over such protection. * * *

Here, then, are the charges which I would bring against the "clear and present danger" theory. They are all, it is clear, differing forms of the basic accusation that the compact of self-government has been ignored or repudiated.

First, the theory denies or obscures the fact that free citizens have two distinct sets of civil liberties. As the makers of the laws, they have duties and responsibilities which require an absolute freedom. As the subjects of the laws, they have possessions and rights, to which belongs a relative freedom.

Second, the theory fails to keep clear the distinction between the constitutional status of discussions of public policy and the corresponding status of discussions of private policy.

Third, the theory fails to recognize that, under the Constitution, the freedom of advocacy or incitement to action *by the government* may never be abridged. It is only advocacy or incitement to action by individuals or nonpolitical groups which is open to regulation.

Fourth, the theory regards the freedom of speech as a mere device which is to be abandoned when dangers threaten the public welfare. On the contrary, it is the very presence of those dangers which makes it imperative that, in the midst of our fears, we remember and observe a principle upon whose integrity rests the entire structure of government by consent of the governed.

Fifth, the Supreme Court, by adopting a theory which annuls the First Amendment, has struck a disastrous blow at our national education. It has denied the belief that men can, by processes of free public discussion, govern themselves. * * *

The unabridged freedom of public discussion is the rock on which our government stands. With that foundation beneath us, we shall not flinch in the face of any clear and present—or, even, terrific—danger.

ZECHARIAH CHAFEE, JR.—BOOK REVIEW

62 Harv.L.Rev. 891, 894–901 (1949).
Reprinted with permission of the publisher; copyright © 1949, by the
Harvard Law Review Association.

[M]y main objection to Mr. Meiklejohn's book [is that he] places virtually all his argument against current proposals for suppression on a constitutional position which is extremely dubious. Whereas the supporters of these measures are genuinely worried by the dangers of Communism, he refuses to argue that these dangers are actually small. Instead, his constitutional position obliges him to argue that these dangers are irrelevant. No matter how terrible and immediate the dangers may be, he keeps saying, the First Amendment will not let Congress or anybody else in the Government try to deal with Communists who have not yet committed unlawful [acts.]

Mr. Meiklejohn's basic proposition is that there are two distinct kinds of freedom of speech, protected by quite different clauses of the Constitution. Freedom of speech on matters affecting self-government is protected by the First Amendment and is not open to restrictions by the Government. [By] contrast, private discussion is open to restrictions because it is protected by [fifth amendment due process].

The truth is, I think, that the framers had no very clear idea as to what they meant by "the freedom of speech or of the press," but we can say three things with reasonable assurance. First, these politicians, lawyers, scholars, churchgoers and philosophers, scientists, agriculturalists, and wide readers used the phrase to embrace the whole realm of thought. Second, they intended the First Amendment to give all the protection they desired, and had no idea of supplementing it by the Fifth Amendment. Finally, the freedom which Congress was forbidden to abridge was not, for them, some absolute concept which had never existed on earth. It was the freedom which they believed they already had— what they had wanted before the Revolution and had acquired through independence. In thinking about it, they took for granted the limitations which had been customarily applied in the day-to-day work of colonial courts. Now, they were setting up a new federal government of great potential strength, and (as in the rest of Bill of Rights) they were determined to make sure that it would not take away the freedoms which they then enjoyed in their thirteen sovereign states.

Still, the First Amendment has the power of growing to meet new needs. As Marshall said, it is a *Constitution* which we are interpreting. Although in 1791 the Amendment did not mean what Mr. Meiklejohn says, perhaps it ought to mean that now. But the Supreme Court is unlikely to think so in any foreseeable future. The author condemns the clear and present danger test as "a peculiarly inept and unsuccessful attempt to formulate an exception" to the constitutional protection of public discussion, but he does not realize how unworkable his own views would prove when applied in litigation.

In the first place, although it may be possible to draw a fairly bright line between speech which is completely immune and action which may be punished, some speech on public questions is so hateful that the Court would be very reluctant to protect it from statutory penalties. We are not dealing with a philosopher who can write what he pleases, but with at least five men who are asked to block legislators and prosecutors. The history of the Court Plan in 1937 shows how sure judges have to be of their ground to do that. Take a few examples. A newspaper charges the mayor with taking bribes. Ezra Pound broadcasts from an Italian radio station that our participation in the war is an abominable mistake. A speaker during a very bad food shortage tells a hungry mass of voters that the rationing board is so incompetent and corrupt that the best way to avoid starvation is to demand the immediate death of its members, unless they are ready to resign. Plainly few judges can grant constitutional protection to such speeches.

Even the author begins to hedge. Although his main insistence is on immunity for all speech connected with self-government, as my examples surely are, occasionally he concedes that "repressive action by the government is imperative for the sake of the general welfare," e.g., against libelous assertions, slander, words inciting men to crime, sedition, and treason by words. Here he is diving into very deep water. Once you push punishment beyond action into the realm of language, then you have to say pretty plainly how far back the law should go. You must enable future judges and jurymen to know where to stop. That is just what Holmes did when he drew his line at clear and present danger and the author gives us no substitute test for distinguishing between good public speech and bad public speech. He never faces the problem of Mark Anthony's Oration—discussion which is calculated to produce unlawful acts without ever mentioning them.

At times he hints that the line depends on the falsity of the assertions or the bad motives of the speakers. In the mayor's case, it is no answer to say that false charges are outside the Constitution; the issue is whether a jury shall be permitted to find them false even if they are in fact true. Moreover, in such charges a good deal of truth which might be useful to the voters is frequently mixed with some falsehood, so that the possibility of a damage action often keeps genuine information away from voters. And the low character of speakers and writers does not necessarily prevent them from uttering wholesome truths about politics. Witness the Essays of Francis Bacon. Mr. Meiklejohn has a special dislike for paid "lobbyists for special interests." But if discussing public questions with money in sight is outside the First Amendment, how about speeches by aspirants to a $75,000 job in Washington or editorials in newspapers or books on Free Speech? Dr. Johnson declared that any man who writes except for money is a fool. In short, the trouble with the bad-motive test is that courts and juries would apply it only to the exponents of unpopular views. If what is said happens to be our way, the speaker is as welcome as an ex-revolutionist to the Un-American Committee.

The most serious weakness in Mr. Meiklejohn's argument is that it rests on his supposed boundary between public speech and private speech. That line is extremely blurred. Take the novel *Strange Fruit*, which was lately suppressed in Massachusetts. It did not discuss any question then before the voters, but it dealt thoughtfully with many problems of the relations between whites and Negroes, a matter of great national concern. Was this under the First Amendment or the Fifth? [The] truth is that there are public aspects to practically every subject. [The] author recognizes this when he says that the First Amendment is directed against "mutilation of the thinking process of the community." [This] attitude, however, offers such a wide area for the First Amendment that very little is left for his private speech under the Fifth Amendment. For example, if books and plays are public speech, how can they be penalized for gross obscenity or libels?

On the other hand, if private speech does include scholarship (as the author suggests) and also art and literature, it is shocking to deprive these vital matters of the protection of the inspiring words of the First Amendment. The individual interest in freedom of speech, which Socrates voiced when he said that he would rather die than stop talking, is too precious to be left altogether to the vague words of the due process clause. Valuable as self-government is, it is in itself only a small part of our lives. That a philosopher should subordinate all other activities to it is indeed surprising.

[Even] if Holmes had agreed with Mr. Meiklejohn's view of the First Amendment, his insistence on such absolutism would not have persuaded a single colleague, and scores of men would have gone to prison who have been speaking freely for three decades. After all, a judge who is trying to establish a doctrine which the Supreme Court will promulgate as law cannot write like a solitary philosopher. He has to convince at least four men in a specific group and convince them very soon. The true alternative to Holmes' view of the First Amendment was not at all the perfect immunity for public discussion which Mr. Meiklejohn desires. It was no immunity at all in the face of legislation. Any danger, any tendency in speech to produce bad acts, no matter how remote, would suffice to validate a repressive statute, and the only hope for speakers and writers would lie in being tried by liberal jurymen. * * * Holmes worked out a formula which would invalidate a great deal of suppression, and won for it the solid authority of a unanimous Court. Afterwards, again and again, when his test was misapplied by the majority, Holmes restated his position in ringing words which, with the help of Brandeis and Hughes, eventually inspired the whole Court.[a]

Notes and Questions

1. To what extent does *New York Times* incorporate Meiklejohn's perspective?[b] What is the "central meaning" of the first amendment?

a. Compare Berns, *Freedom, Virtue and the First Amendment* 50–56 (Gateway ed. 1965): "The first thing to be remembered [about the clear and present danger test] is that Schenck was sent to jail with it. The second is that Abrams and Gitlow, with Holmes dissenting in ringing clear and present danger language, were jailed despite it. The third is that [the communists in *Dennis*] were sent to jail with it. [Only *Taylor v. Mississippi*, 319 U.S. 583, 63 S.Ct. 1200, 87 L.Ed. 1600 (1943), reversing the conviction of Jehovah's Witnesses, prosecuted under a wartime state sedition law for publicly urging people not to support the war and for advocating and teaching refusal to salute the flag], can illustrate the use of the [Holmes] doctrine to cause the triumph of free speech over national [security]. Thus, [in] the area in which the rule was first enunciated, the clear and present danger test has been of assistance only to a Jehovah's Witness—not to a Socialist like Debs or a Communist like Gitlow or Dennis, or to anyone else whose opinions are both hated *and* feared. [The test] actually becomes a rationale for avoiding the impossible prohibitions of the First Amendment and for convicting persons for speech that the government has forbidden."

b. For elaboration and modification of Meiklejohn's views, see Meiklejohn, *The First Amendment Is an Absolute*, 1961 Sup.Ct.Rev. 245. For commentary, see Bollinger, *Free Speech and Intellectual Values*, 92 Yale L.J. 438 (1983); Kalven, p. 684 supra. For work proceeding from a politically based interpretation of the first amendment, see Anastaplo, *The Constitutionalist* (1971); BeVier, *The First Amendment and Political Speech: An Inquiry Into the Substance and Limits of Principle*, 30 Stan.L.Rev. 299 (1978); Bloustein, *The First Amendment and Privacy: The Supreme Court Justice and the Philosopher*, 28 Rutg.L.Rev. 41 (1974); Bork, *Neutral Principles and Some First Amendment Problems*, 47 Ind.L.J. 1 (1971). See also Brennan, *The Supreme Court and the Meiklejohn Interpretation*

2. *New York Times, definitional balancing, and the two-level theory of the first amendment.* By holding that some libel was within the protection of the first amendment, did the Court dismantle its two-level theory? See Kalven, supra, at 217–218. Or did the Court merely rearrange its conception of what was protected and what was not?

Does *Garrison v. Louisiana,* 379 U.S. 64, 85 S.Ct. 209, 13 L.Ed.2d 125 (1964) shed light on the question? The Court stated: "Calculated falsehood falls into that class of utterances '[of] such slight social value as a step to truth that any benefit that may be derived from them is clearly outweighed by the social interest in order and morality.' *Chaplinsky.*"

Could the judicial process here fairly be called *definitional* classification— defining which categories of libel are to be viewed as "speech" within the first amendment, and which are not? Consider Nimmer, *The Right to Speak from Times to Time, First Amendment Theory Applied to Libel and Misapplied to Privacy,* 56 Calif.L.Rev. 935, 942–43 (1968): "[*New York Times*] points the way to the employment of the balancing process on the definitional rather than the litigation or ad hoc level, [that is,] balancing not for the purpose of determining which litigant deserves to prevail in the particular case, but only for the purpose of defining which forms of speech are to be regarded as 'speech' within the meaning of the first amendment. [By] in effect holding that knowingly and recklessly false speech was not 'speech' within the meaning of the first amendment, the Court must have implicitly (since no explicit explanation was offered) referred to certain competing policy considerations. This is surely a kind of balancing, but it is just as surely not ad hoc balancing." [c]

3. *The scope of New York Times.* Professor Kalven argued that given the Court's conception of freedom of speech, its holding could not be confined: "the invitation to follow a dialectic progression from public official to government policy to public policy to matters in the public domain, like art, seems * * * overwhelming." Kalven, supra, at 221.

(a) *Public officials. New York Times,* fn. 23 left open "how far down into the lower ranks of governmental employees" the rule would extend, but later applied the rule in *Rosenblatt v. Baer,* 383 U.S. 75, 86 S.Ct. 669, 15 L.Ed.2d 597 (1966) to the supervisor of a publicly owned ski resort, saying it applies to those who "appear to the public to [have] substantial responsibility for or control over the conduct of government affairs." Should criticism of the official conduct of

---

of the First Amendment, 79 Harv.L.Rev. 1 (1965).

c. The literature about balancing is voluminous. Compare, e.g., Frantz, *The First Amendment in the Balance,* 71 Yale L.J. 1424 (1962); Frantz, *Is the First Amendment Law? —A Reply to Professor Mendelson,* 51 Calif.L. Rev. 729 (1963) with Mendelson, *On the Meaning of the First Amendment: Absolutes in the Balance,* 50 Calif.L.Rev. 821 (1962); Mendelson, *The First Amendment and the Judicial Process: A Reply to Mr. Frantz,* 17 Vand.L. Rev. 479 (1984). For a philosophical attack on cost benefit analysis, see Tribe, *Policy Science: Analysis or Ideology?,* 2 Phil. & Pub.Aff. 66 (1972); Tribe, *Technology Assessment and the Fourth Discontinuity: The Limits of Instrumental Rationality,* 46 So.Cal.L.Rev. 617 (1973). For philosophical defenses of balancing, see Schlag, *An Attack on Categorical Ap-*

proaches to Freedom of Speech, 30 U.C.L.A.L. Rev. 671 (1983); Shiffrin, *Liberalism, Radicalism, and Legal Scholarship,* 30 U.C.L.A.L.Rev. 1103 (1983) (both resisting any necessary connection between balancing and instrumentalism or cost-benefit analysis). For more doctrinally focused analysis, compare, e.g., Emerson, *First Amendment Doctrine and the Burger Court,* 68 Calif.L.Rev. 422 (1980); Tribe, *Constitutional Calculus: Equal Justice or Economic Efficiency?,* 98 Harv.L.Rev. 592 (1985) with Schauer, *Categories and the First Amendment: A Play in Three Acts,* 34 Vand.L.Rev. 265 (1981); Shiffrin, *The First Amendment and Economic Regulation: Away From a General Theory of the First Amendment,* 78 Nw. U.L.Rev. 1212 (1983); Van Alstyne, *A Graphic Review of the Free Speech Clause,* 70 Calif.L. Rev. 107 (1982).

very high ranking government officials (e.g., the President, the Secretary of State, a general commanding troops in war) be given greater protection than that afforded in *New York Times?*

(b) *Private conduct of public officials and candidates. Garrison,* extended *New York Times* to "anything which might touch on an official's fitness for office," even if the defamation did not concern official conduct in office. Invoking that standard, *Monitor Patriot Co. v. Roy,* 401 U.S. 265, 91 S.Ct. 621, 28 L.Ed. 2d 35 (1971) applied *New York Times* to a news column describing a candidate for public office as a "former small-time bootlegger."

(c) *Public figures.* In CURTIS PUB. CO. v. BUTTS and ASSOCIATED PRESS v. WALKER, 388 U.S. 130, 87 S.Ct. 1975, 18 L.Ed.2d 1094 (1967), HARLAN, J., contended that because public figures were not subject to the restraints of the political process, any criticism of them was not akin to seditious libel and was, therefore, a step removed from the central meaning of the first amendment. Nonetheless, he argued that public figure actions should not be left entirely to the vagaries of state defamation law and would have required that public figures show "highly unreasonable conduct constituting an extreme departure from the standards of investigation and reporting ordinarily adhered to by responsible publishers" as a prerequisite to recovery. In response, WARREN, C.J., argued that the inapplicability of the restraints of the political process to public figures underscored the importance for uninhibited debate about their activities since "public opinion may be the only instrument by which society can attempt to influence their conduct." He observed that increasingly "the distinctions between governmental and private sectors are blurred," that public figures, like public officials, "often play an influential role in ordering society," and as a class have a ready access to the mass media "both to influence policy and to counter criticism of their views and activities." He accordingly concluded that the *New York Times* rule should be extended to public figures. Four other justices in *Butts* and *Walker* were willing to go at least as far as Warren, C.J., and subsequent cases have settled on the position that public figures must meet the *New York Times* requirements in order to recover in a defamation action. The critical issues are how to define the concept of public figure and how to apply it in practice. See *Gertz,* infra.

(d) *Private plaintiffs and public issues.* Without deciding whether any first amendment protection should extend to matters not of general or public interest, a plurality led by BRENNAN, J., joined by Burger, C.J., and Blackmun, J., argued in ROSENBLOOM v. METROMEDIA, INC., 403 U.S. 29, 91 S.Ct. 1811, 29 L.Ed. 2d 296 (1971), that the *New York Times* rule should be extended to defamatory statements involving matters of public or general interest "without regard to whether the persons involved are famous or anonymous." BLACK, J., would have gone further, opining that the first amendment "does not permit the recovery of libel judgments against the news media even when statements are broadcast with knowledge they are false," and Douglas, J., shared Black, J.'s approach (at least with respect to matters of public interest, although he did not participate in *Rosenbloom.*) WHITE, J., felt that the *New York Times* rule should apply to reporting on the official actions of public servants and to reporting on those involved in or affected by their official action. That principle was broad enough to cover Rosenbloom, a distributor of nudist magazines who had been arrested by the Philadelphia police for distributing obscene materials. The defamatory broadcast wrongly assumed his guilt. Dissenting, Harlan, Stewart and Marshall, JJ., counselled an approach similar to that taken in *Gertz,* infra.

After *Rosenbloom* the lower courts rather uniformly followed the approach taken by the plurality. By 1974, however, the composition of the Court had changed and so had the minds of some of the justices.

C. PRIVATE INDIVIDUALS AND PUBLIC FIGURES

GERTZ v. ROBERT WELCH, INC.

418 U.S. 323, 94 S.Ct. 2997, 41 L.Ed.2d 789 (1974).

MR. JUSTICE POWELL delivered the opinion of the Court.

[Respondent published *American Opinion,* a monthly outlet for the John Birch Society. It published an article falsely stating that Gertz, a lawyer, was the "architect" in a "communist frameup" of a policeman convicted of murdering a youth whose family Gertz represented in resultant civil proceedings, and that Gertz had a "criminal record" and had been an officer in a named "Communist-fronter" organization that advocated violent seizure of our government. In Gertz' libel action there was evidence that *Opinion* 's managing editor did not know the statements were false and had relied on the reputation of the article's author and prior experience with the accuracy of his articles. After a $50,000 verdict for Gertz, the trial court entered judgment n.o.v., concluding that the *New York Times* rule applied to any discussion of a "public issue." The court of appeals affirmed, ruling that the publisher did not have the requisite "awareness of probable falsity." The Court held that *New York Times* did not apply to defamation of private individuals, but remanded for a new trial "because the jury was allowed to impose liability without fault [and] to presume damages without proof of injury."]

II. The principal issue in this case is whether a newspaper or broadcaster that publishes defamatory falsehoods about an individual who is neither a public official nor a public figure may claim a constitutional privilege against liability for the injury inflicted by those statements. * * *

In his opinion for the plurality in *Rosenbloom,* Mr. Justice Brennan took the *Times* privilege one step further [than *Butts* and *Walker*]. He concluded that its protection should extend to defamatory falsehoods relating to private persons if the statements concerned matters of general or public interest. He abjured the suggested distinction between public officials and public figures on the one hand and private individuals on the other. He focused instead on society's interest in learning about certain issues: "If a matter is a subject of public or general interest, it cannot suddenly become less so merely because a private individual is involved or because in some sense the individual did not choose to become involved." Thus, under the plurality opinion, a private citizen involuntarily associated with a matter of general interest has no recourse for injury to his reputation unless he can satisfy the demanding requirements of the *Times* [test].

III. [Under] the First Amendment there is no such thing as a false idea. However pernicious an opinion may seem, we depend for its correction not on the conscience of the judges and juries but on the competition of other ideas. But there is no constitutional value in false statements of fact. Neither the intentional lie nor the careless error materially advances society's interest in "uninhibited, robust, and wide-open" debate on public issues. * * *

Although the erroneous statement of fact is not worthy of constitutional protection, it is nevertheless inevitable in free debate. [P]unishment of error runs the risk of inducing a cautious and restrictive exercise of the constitutionally guaranteed freedoms of speech and press. [The] First Amendment requires that we protect some falsehood in order to protect speech that matters.

The need to avoid self-censorship by the news media is, however, not the only societal value at issue. [The] legitimate state interest underlying the law of libel is the compensation of individuals for the harm inflicted on them by defamatory falsehoods. We would not lightly require the State to abandon this purpose, for, as Mr. Justice Stewart has reminded us, the individual's right to the protection of his own good name "reflects no more than our basic concept of the essential dignity and worth of every human being—a concept at the root of any decent system of ordered liberty. * * *" *Rosenblatt.*

Some tension necessarily exists between the need for a vigorous and uninhibited press and the legitimate interest in redressing wrongful injury. [In] our continuing effort to define the proper accommodation between these competing concerns, we have been especially anxious to assure to the freedoms of speech and press that "breathing space" essential to their fruitful exercise. To that end this Court has extended a measure of strategic protection to defamatory falsehood.

The *New York Times* standard defines the level of constitutional protection appropriate to the context of defamation of [public figures and those who hold governmental office]. Plainly many deserving plaintiffs, including some intentionally subjected to injury, will be unable to surmount the barrier of the *New York Times* test. [For] the reasons stated below, we conclude that the state interest in compensating injury to the reputation of private individuals requires that a different rule should obtain with respect to them.

[W]e have no difficulty in distinguishing among defamation plaintiffs. The first remedy of any victim of defamation is self-help—using available opportunities to contradict the lie or correct the error and thereby to minimize its adverse impact on reputation. Public officials and public figures usually enjoy significantly greater access to the channels of effective communication and hence have a more realistic opportunity to counteract false statements than private individuals normally enjoy.[9] Private individuals are therefore more vulnerable to injury, and the state interest in protecting them is correspondingly greater.

More important than the likelihood that private individuals will lack effective opportunities for rebuttal, there is a compelling normative consideration underlying the distinction between public and private defamation plaintiffs. An individual who decides to seek governmental office must accept certain necessary consequences of that involvement in public affairs. He runs the risk of closer public scrutiny than might otherwise be the case. [Those] classed as public figures stand in a similar [position.]

Even if the foregoing generalities do not obtain in every instance, the communications media are entitled to act on the assumption that public officials

---

9. Of course, an opportunity for rebuttal seldom suffices to undo harm of defamatory falsehood. Indeed, the law of defamation is rooted in our experience that the truth rarely catches up with a lie. But the fact that the self-help remedy of rebuttal, standing alone, is inadequate to its task does not mean that it is irrelevant to our inquiry. [Consider Shiffrin, *Defamatory Non-Media Speech and First Amendment Methodology,* 25 U.C.L.A.L.Rev. 915, 952–53 (1978): "[F]ootnote nine, has seemingly left the first amendment in a peculiar spot. *Gertz* holds that the first amendment offers some protection for defamatory utterances presumably so that our Constitution can continue 'to preserve an uninhibited marketplace of ideas in which truth will ultimately prevail. * * *' And yet the Court recognizes that 'an opportunity for rebuttal seldom suffices to undo [the] harm of defamatory falsehood,' i.e., truth does not emerge in the marketplace of ideas. Is the Court trapped in an obvious contradiction?"]

and public figures have voluntarily exposed themselves to increased risk of injury from defamatory falsehoods concerning them. No such assumption is justified with respect to a private individual. He has not accepted public office nor assumed an "influential role in ordering society." *Butts*. He has relinquished no part of his interest in the protection of his own good name, and consequently he has a more compelling call on the courts for redress of injury inflicted by defamatory falsehood. Thus, private individuals are not only more vulnerable to injury than public officials and public figures; they are also more deserving of recovery.

For these reasons we conclude that the States should retain substantial latitude in their efforts to enforce a legal remedy for defamatory falsehood injurious to the reputation of a private individual. The extension of the *Times* test proposed by the *Rosenbloom* plurality would abridge this legitimate state interest to a degree that we find unacceptable. And it would occasion the additional difficulty of forcing state and federal judges to decide on an ad hoc basis which publications address issues of "general or public interest" and which do not—to determine, in the words of Mr. Justice Marshall, "what information is relevant to self-government." *Rosenbloom.* We doubt the wisdom of committing this task to the conscience of judges. [The] "public or general interest" test for determining the applicability of the *Times* standard to private defamation actions inadequately serves both of the competing values at stake. On the one hand, a private individual whose reputation is injured by defamatory falsehood that does concern an issue of public or general interest has no recourse unless he can meet the rigorous requirements of *Times*. This is true despite the factors that distinguish the state interest in compensating private individuals from the analogous interest involved in the context of public persons. On the other hand, a publisher or broadcaster of a defamatory error which a court deems unrelated to an issue of public or general interest may be held liable in damages even if it took every reasonable precaution to ensure the accuracy of its assertions. And liability may far exceed compensation for any actual injury to the plaintiff, for the jury may be permitted to presume damages without proof of loss and even to award punitive damages.

We hold that, so long as they do not impose liability without fault, the States may define for themselves the appropriate standard of liability for a publisher or broadcaster of defamatory falsehood injurious to a private individual. This approach provides a more equitable boundary between the competing concerns involved here. It recognizes the strength of the legitimate state interest in compensating private individuals for wrongful injury to reputation, yet shields the press and broadcast media from the rigors of strict liability for defamation. At least this conclusion obtains where, as here, the substance of the defamatory statement "makes substantial danger to reputation apparent." *Butts*. This phrase places in perspective the conclusion we announce today. Our inquiry would involve considerations somewhat different from those discussed above if a State purported to condition civil liability on a factual misstatement whose content did not warn a reasonably prudent editor or broadcaster of its defamatory potential. Cf. *Time, Inc. v. Hill* [Part D infra]. Such a case is not now before us, and we intimate no view as to its proper resolution.

IV. [T]he strong and legitimate state interest in compensating private individuals for injury to reputation [extends] no further than compensation for actual injury. For the reasons stated below, we hold that the States may not permit recovery of presumed or punitive damages, at least when liability is not based on a showing of knowledge of falsity or reckless disregard for the truth.

The common law of defamation is an oddity of tort [law]. Juries may award substantial sums as compensation for supposed damage to reputation without any proof that such harm actually occurred. [This] unnecessarily compounds the potential of any system of liability for defamatory falsehood to inhibit the vigorous exercise of First Amendment freedoms [and] invites juries to punish unpopular opinion rather than to compensate individuals for injury sustained by the publication of a false fact. More to the point, the States have no substantial interest in securing for plaintiffs such as this petitioner gratuitous awards of money damages far in excess of any actual injury.

We would not, of course, invalidate state law simply because we doubt its wisdom, but here we are attempting to reconcile state law with a competing interest grounded in the constitutional command of the First Amendment. It is therefore appropriate to require that state remedies for defamatory falsehood reach no farther than is necessary to protect the legitimate interest involved. It is necessary to restrict defamation plaintiffs who do not prove knowledge of falsity or reckless disregard for the truth to compensation for actual injury. We need not define "actual injury," as trial courts have wide experience in framing appropriate jury instructions in tort action. Suffice it to say that actual injury is not limited to out-of-pocket loss. Indeed, the more customary types of actual harm inflicted by defamatory falsehood include impairment of reputation and standing in the community, personal humiliation, and mental anguish and suffering. Of course, juries must be limited by appropriate instructions, and all awards must be supported by competent evidence concerning the injury, although there need be no evidence which assigns an actual dollar value to the injury.

We also find no justification for allowing awards of punitive damages against publishers and broadcasters held liable under state-defined standards of liability for defamation. In most jurisdictions jury discretion over the amounts awarded is limited only by the gentle rule that they not be excessive. Consequently, juries assess punitive damages in wholly unpredictable amounts bearing no necessary relation to the actual harm caused. And they remain free to use their discretion selectively to punish expressions of unpopular views. [J]ury discretion to award punitive damages unnecessarily exacerbates the danger of media self-censorship; [punitive] damages are wholly irrelevant to the state interest that justifies a negligence standard for private defamation actions. They are not compensation for injury. Instead, they are private fines levied by civil juries to punish reprehensible conduct and to deter its future occurrence. In short, the private defamation plaintiff who establishes liability under a less demanding standard than that stated by *Times* may recover only such damages as are sufficient to compensate him for actual injury.[a]

V. Notwithstanding our refusal to extend the *New York Times* privilege to defamation of private individuals, respondent contends that we should affirm the judgment below on the ground that petitioner is [a] public figure. [That] designation may rest on either of two alternative bases. In some instances an individual may achieve such pervasive fame or notoriety that he becomes a public figure for all purposes and in all contexts. More commonly, an individual voluntarily injects himself or is drawn into a particular public controversy and thereby becomes a public figure for a limited range of issues. In either case such persons assume special prominence in the resolution of public questions.

a. On remand, Gertz was awarded $100,000 in compensatory damages and $300,000 in punitive damages. In the prior trial, he had been awarded only $50,000 in damages.

Petitioner has long been active in community and professional affairs. He has served as an officer of local civic groups and of various professional organizations, and he has published several books and articles on legal subjects. Although petitioner was consequently well known in some circles, he had achieved no general fame or notoriety in the community. None of the prospective jurors called at the trial had ever heard of petitioner prior to this litigation, and respondent offered no proof that this response was atypical of the local population. We would not lightly assume that a citizen's participation in community and professional affairs rendered him a public figure for all purposes. Absent clear evidence of general fame or notoriety in the community, and pervasive involvement in the affairs of society, an individual should not be deemed a public personality for all aspects of his life. It is preferable to reduce the public-figure question to a more meaningful context by looking to the nature and extent of an individual's participation in the particular controversy giving rise to the defamation.

In this context it is plain that petitioner was not a public figure. He played a minimal role at the coroner's inquest, and his participation related solely to his representation of a private client. He took no part in the criminal prosecution of Officer Nuccio. Moreover, he never discussed either the criminal or civil litigation with the press and was never quoted as having done so. He plainly did not thrust himself into the vortex of this public issue, nor did he engage the public's attention in an attempt to influence its outcome. We are persuaded that the trial court did not err in refusing to characterize petitioner as a public figure for the purpose of this litigation.

We therefore conclude that the *New York Times* standard is inapplicable to this case and that the trial court erred in entering judgment for respondent. Because the jury was allowed to impose liability without fault and was permitted to presume damages without proof of injury, a new trial is necessary.[b]

MR. JUSTICE BRENNAN, dissenting.

[I] adhere to my view expressed in *Rosenbloom* that we strike the proper accommodation between avoidance of media self-censorship and protection of individual reputations only when we require States to apply the *New York Times* knowing-or-reckless-falsity standard in civil libel actions concerning media reports of the involvement of private individuals in events of public or general interest. [Although] acknowledging that First Amendment values are of no less significance when media reports concern private persons' involvement in matters of public concern, the Court refuses to provide, in such cases, the same level of constitutional protection that has been afforded the media in the context of defamation of public [persons].

---

b. Blackmun, J., concurred: "[Although I joined Brennan, J.'s plurality opinion in *Rosenbloom,* from which the Court's opinion in the present case departs, I join] the Court's opinion and its judgment for two reasons:

"1. By removing the spectres of presumed and punitive damages in the absence of *Times* malice, the Court eliminates significant and powerful motives for self-censorship that otherwise are present in the traditional libel action. By so doing, the Court leaves what should prove to be sufficient and adequate breathing space for a vigorous press. What the Court has done, I believe, will have little,

if any, practical effect on the functioning of responsible journalism.

"2. The Court was sadly fractionated in *Rosenbloom.* A result of that kind inevitably leads to uncertainty. I feel that it is of profound importance for the Court to come to rest in the defamation area and to have a clearly defined majority position that eliminates the unsureness engendered by *Rosenbloom's* diversity. If my vote were not needed to create a majority, I would adhere to my prior view. A definitive ruling, however, is paramount."

While [the Court's] arguments are forcefully and eloquently presented, I cannot accept them for the reasons I stated in *Rosenbloom:* "The *New York Times* standard was applied to libel of a public official or public figure to give effect to the Amendment's function to encourage ventilation of public issues, not because the public official has any less interest in protecting his reputation than an individual in private life. [In] the vast majority of libels involving public officials or public figures, the ability to respond through the media will depend on the same complex factor on which the ability of a private individual depends: the unpredictable event of the media's continuing interest in the story. Thus the unproved, and highly improbable, generalization that an as yet [not fully defined] class of 'public figures' involved in matters of public concern will be better able to respond through the media than private individuals also involved in such matters seems too insubstantial a reed on which to rest a constitutional distinction."

[Adoption], by many States, of a reasonable care standard in cases where private individuals are involved in matters of public interest—the probable result of today's decision—[will] lead to self-censorship since publishers will be required carefully to weigh a myriad of uncertain factors before publication. The reasonable care standard is "elusive," *Time, Inc. v. Hill;* it saddles the press with "the intolerable burden of guessing how a jury might assess the reasonableness of steps taken by it to verify the accuracy of every reference to a name, picture or portrait." Ibid. Under a reasonable care regime, publishers and broadcasters will have to make pre-publication judgments about juror assessment of such diverse considerations as the size, operating procedures, and financial condition of the newsgathering system, as well as the relative costs and benefits of instituting less frequent and more costly reporting at a higher level of accuracy. See 85 Harv.L.Rev. 228 (1971). [And] most hazardous, the flexibility which inheres in the reasonable care standard will create the danger that a jury will convert it into "an instrument for the suppression of those 'vehement, caustic, and sometimes unpleasantly sharp attacks,' [which] must be protected if the guarantees of the First and Fourteenth Amendments are to prevail." *Monitor Patriot Co.*

[A] jury's latitude to impose liability for want of due care poses a far greater threat of suppressing unpopular views than does a possible recovery of presumed or punitive damages. Moreover, the Court's broad-ranging examples of "actual injury" [allow] a jury bent on punishing expression of unpopular views a formidable weapon for doing so. [E]ven a limitation of recovery to "actual injury"—however much it reduces the size or frequency of recoveries—will not provide the necessary elbow room for First Amendment expression. "[The] very possibility of having to engage in litigation, an expensive and protracted process, is threat enough to cause discussion and debate to 'steer far wider of the unlawful zone' thereby keeping protected discussion from public cognizance. * * *" *Rosenbloom.*

[I] reject the argument that my *Rosenbloom* view improperly commits to judges the task of determining what is and what is not an issue of "general or public interest." [3] I noted in *Rosenbloom* that performance of this task would

---

3. The Court, taking a novel step, would not limit application of First Amendment protection to private libels involving issues of general or public interest, but would forbid the States from imposing liability without fault in any case where the substance of the defamatory statement made substantial danger to reputation apparent. As in *Rosenbloom,* I would leave open the question of what constitutional standard, if any, applies when defamatory falsehoods are published or broadcast concerning either a private or pub-

not always be easy. But surely the courts, the ultimate arbiters of all disputes concerning clashes of constitutional values, would only be performing one of their traditional functions in undertaking this duty. [The] public interest is necessarily broad; any residual self-censorship that may result from the uncertain contours of the "general or public interest" concept should be of far less concern to publishers and broadcasters than that occasioned by state laws imposing liability for negligent falsehood. * * * [c]

MR. JUSTICE WHITE, dissenting.

[T]he Court, in a few printed pages, has federalized major aspects of libel law by declaring unconstitutional in important respects the prevailing defamation law in all or most of the 50 States. * * *

I. [These] radical changes in the law and severe invasions of the prerogatives of the States [should] at least be shown to be required by the First Amendment or necessitated by our present circumstances. Neither has been [demonstrated.]

The central meaning of *New York Times,* and for me the First Amendment as it relates to libel laws, is that seditious libel—criticism of government and public officials—falls beyond the police power of the State. In a democratic society such as ours, the citizen has the privilege of criticizing his government and its officials. But neither *New York Times* nor its progeny suggest that the First Amendment intended in all circumstances to deprive the private citizen of his historic recourse to redress published falsehoods damaging to reputation or that, contrary to history and precedent, the amendment should now be so interpreted. Simply put, the First Amendment did not confer a "license to defame the citizen." Douglas, *The Right of the People* 38 (1958).

[T]he law has heretofore put the risk of falsehood on the publisher where the victim is a private citizen and no grounds of special privilege are invoked. The Court would now shift this risk to the victim, even though he has done nothing to invite the calumny, is wholly innocent of fault, and is helpless to avoid his injury. I doubt that jurisprudential resistance to liability without fault is sufficient ground for employing the First Amendment to revolutionize the law of libel, and in my view, that body of legal rules poses no realistic threat to the

---

lic person's activities not within the scope of the general or public interest.

Parenthetically, my Brother White argues that the Court's view and mine will prevent a plaintiff—unable to demonstrate some degree of fault—from vindicating his reputation by securing a judgment that the publication was false. This argument overlooks the possible enactment of statutes, not requiring proof of fault, which provide for an action for retraction or for publication of a court's determination of falsity if the plaintiff is able to demonstrate that false statements have been published concerning his activities. Cf. Note, *Vindication of the Reputation of a Public Official,* 80 Harv.L.Rev. 1730, 1739–1747 (1967). Although it may be that questions could be raised concerning the constitutionality of such statutes, certainly nothing I have said today (and, as I read the Court's opinion, nothing said there) should be read to imply that a private plaintiff, unable to prove fault, must inevitably be denied the opportunity to secure

a judgment upon the truth or falsity of statements published about him.

c. Douglas, J., dissented, objecting to "continued recognition of the possibility of state libel suits for public discussion of public issues" as diluting first amendment protection. He added: "Since this case involves a discussion of public affairs, I need not decide at this point whether the First Amendment prohibits all libel actions. 'An unconditional right to say what one pleases about public affairs is what I consider to be *the minimum guarantee* of the First Amendment.' *New York Times* (Black, J., concurring) (emphasis added). But 'public affairs' includes a great deal more than merely political affairs. Matters of science, economics, business, art, literature, etc., are all matters of interest to the general public. Indeed, any matter of sufficient general interest to prompt media coverage may be said to be a public affair. Certainly police killings, 'Communist conspiracies,' and the like qualify."

press and its service to the public. The press today is vigorous and robust. To me, it is quite incredible to suggest that threats of libel suits from private citizens are causing the press to refrain from publishing the truth. I know of no hard facts to support that proposition, and the Court furnishes none.

[I]f the Court's principal concern is to protect the communications industry from large libel judgments, it would appear that its new requirements with respect to general and punitive damages would be ample protection. Why it also feels compelled to escalate the threshold standard of liability I cannot fathom, particularly when this will eliminate in many instances the plaintiff's possibility of securing a judicial determination that the damaging publication was indeed false, whether or not he is entitled to recover money damages. [I] find it unacceptable to distribute the risk in this manner and force the wholly innocent victim to bear the injury; for, as between the two, the defamer is the only culpable party. It is he who circulated a falsehood that he was not required to publish. * * *[d]

V. [I] fail to see how the quality or quantity of public debate will be promoted by further emasculation of state libel laws for the benefit of the news media.[41] If anything, this trend may provoke a new and radical imbalance in the communications process. Cf. Barron, *Access to the Press—A New First Amendment Right,* 80 Harv.L.Rev. 1641, 1657 (1967). It is not at all inconceivable that virtually unrestrained defamatory remarks about private citizens will discourage them from speaking out and concerning themselves with social problems. This would turn the First Amendment on its head. Note, *The Scope of First Amendment Protection for Good-Faith Defamatory Error,* 75 Yale L.J. 642, 649 (1966). * * *[e]

Notes and Questions

1. *Gertz and Meiklejohn.* By affording some constitutional protection to all media defamatory speech whether or not it relates to public issues, does the Court squarely reject the Meiklejohn theory of the first amendment?[f] Consider Shiffrin, *Defamatory Non-Media Speech and First Amendment Methodology,* 25 U.C.L.A.L.Rev. 915, 929 (1978): "It may be that the Court has refused to adopt the Meiklejohn 'public issues' test not because it believes that private speech (i.e., speech unrelated to public issues) is as important as public speech but rather because it doubts its ability to distinguish unerringly between the two.

d. White, J., also argued strongly against the Court's rulings on actual and punitive damages.

41. Cf. Pedrick, *Freedom of the Press and the Law of Libel: The Modern Revised Translation,* 49 Cornell L.Q. 581, 601–02 (1964): "A great many forces in our society operate to determine the extent to which men are free in fact to express their ideas. Whether there is a privilege for good faith defamatory misstatements on matters of public concern or whether there is strict liability for such statements may not greatly affect the course of public discussion. How different has life been in those states which heretofore followed the majority rule imposing strict liability for misstatements of fact defaming public figures from life in the minority states where the good faith privilege held sway?" See also Emerson, *The System of Freedom of Expres-*

sion 519 (1970): "[O]n the whole the role of libel law in the system of freedom of expression has been relatively minor and essentially erratic."

e. Burger, C.J., also dissented: "I am frank to say I do not know the parameters of a 'negligence' doctrine as applied to the news media. [I] would prefer to allow this area of law to continue to evolve as it has up to now with respect to private citizens rather then embark on a new doctrinal theory which has no jurisprudential ancestry. [I would remand] for reinstatement of the verdict of the jury and the entry of an appropriate judgment on that verdict."

f. For consideration of the distinction between public and private speech and of the media non–media distinction, see *Greenmoss,* p. 576 infra.

[B]y placing all defamatory media speech within the scope of the first amendment, the Court may believe it has protected relatively little non-public speech. On the other hand, [putting aside comments about public officials and public figures], the Court may fear that if *Gertz* were extended to non-media speech, the result would be to protect much speech having nothing to do with public issues, while safeguarding relatively little that does." [g]

2. *Public figures.* TIME, INC. v. FIRESTONE, 424 U.S. 448, 96 S.Ct. 958, 47 L.Ed.2d 154 (1976), per REHNQUIST, J., declared that persons who have not assumed a role of especial prominence in the affairs of society are not public figures unless they have " 'thrust themselves to the forefront of particular public controversies in order to influence the resolution of the issues involved.' " It held that a divorce proceeding involving one of America's wealthiest industrial families and containing testimony concerning the extramarital sexual activities of the parties did not involve a "public controversy," "even though the marital difficulties of extremely wealthy individuals may be of interest to some portion of the reading public." Nor was the filing of a divorce suit, or the holding of press conferences ("to satisfy inquiring reporters") thought to be freely publicizing the issues in order to influence their outcome. Recall *Gertz* doubted the wisdom of forcing judges to determine on an ad hoc basis what is and is not of "general or public interest." Is there a basis for distinguishing a public figure test requiring judges to determine on an ad hoc basis what is or is not a "public controversy"?

What does it mean to assume a role of especial prominence in the affairs of society? If Elmer Gertz, a prominent Illinois attorney, does not qualify, does Johnny Carson? Julia Child? Mr. Rogers? If so, is the slide from public officials to television chefs and personalities too precipitous because the latter "have little, if any effect, on questions of politics, public policy, or the organization and determination of societal affairs"? See Schauer, *Public Figures,* 25 Wm. & Mary L.Rev. 905 (1984). For replies, see Ashdown, *Of Public Figures and Public Interest—The Libel Law Conundrum,* Id. at 937; Daniels, *Public Figures Revisited,* Id. at 957. Does a narrow definition of public figures discriminate in favor of orthodox media and discourage attempts "to illuminate previously unexposed aspects of society." Does the negligence concept itself threaten to discriminate "against media or outlets whose philosophies and methods deviate from those of the mainstream"? See generally Anderson, *Libel and Press Self-Censorship,* 53 Tex.L.Rev. 422, 453, 455 (1975).

3. *"There is no constitutional value in false statements of fact."* Consider Shiffrin, supra at 954: "This is dangerous doctrine. It begins with the presumption that false speech is unprotected and looks to determine if other factors are present which necessitate protection nonetheless. This begs the basic first amendment question: When can government perceptions of truth or falsity be imposed upon the individual? Moreover, it demeans the interests of self-

g. For the claim that speech on private matters deserves as much protection as speech on public matters, see id. at 938–42. For discussion of the different meanings of public and private speech, see Schauer, *"Private" Speech and the "Private" Forum: Givhan v. Western Line School District,* 1979 Sup.Ct.Rev. 217. For additional commentary on the question of whether *Gertz* should extend to nonmedia defendants see, e.g., Hill, *Defamation and Privacy Under the First Amendment,* 76 Colum.L.Rev. 1205 (1976); Lange, *The Speech and Press Clauses,* 23 U.C.L.A.L.Rev. 77 (1975); Nimmer, *Is Freedom of the Press a Redundancy: What Does It Add to Freedom of Speech?,* 26 Hast.L.J. 639 (1975); Van Alstyne, Comment: *The Hazards to the Press of Claiming a "Preferred Position,"* 28 Hast.L.J. 761 (1977); Note, *Mediaocracy and Mistrust: Extending New York Times Defamation Protection to Nonmedia Defendants,* 95 Harv.L.Rev. 1876 (1982).

expression and cathartic release. In the final analysis, however, the *Gertz* formulation may make no difference. By recognizing that some false speech must be protected in order to prevent true speech from being driven out of the marketplace, *Gertz* arrives at the same results which would be reached if it were assumed that speech is protected whether true or false unless other important interests predominate. Nonetheless, starting points can influence [decisions]." See also Schauer, *Categories and the First Amendment: A Play in Three Acts,* 34 Vand.L.Rev. 265, 280–81 (1981).

4. *"Under The First Amendment there is no such thing as a false idea."* *Gertz* has been widely interpreted to protect defamatory "opinions." For commentary on the sagacity of such a reading and on the utility and meaning of the fact/opinion distinction, see Christie, *Defamatory Opinions and the Restatement (Second) of Torts,* 75 Mich.L.Rev. 1621 (1977); Hill, supra; Franklin & Bussel, *The Plaintiff's Burden in Defamation: Awareness and Falsity,* 25 Wm. & Mary L.Rev. 825 (1984); Schauer, *Language, Truth and the First Amendment: An Essay in Memory of Harry Canter,* 64 Va.L.Rev. 263 (1978); Comment, *The Fact-Opinion Distinction in First Amendment Libel Law: The Need For a Bright-Line Rule,* 72 Geo.L.J. 1817 (1984).

5. *The Law in Practice and Pleas for Reform.* For valuable material on how the *Gertz* rules work in practice, see Franklin, *Suing Media for Libel: A Litigation Study,* 1981 Am.B.Found.Res.J. 795; Franklin, *Winners and Losers and Why: A Study of Defamation Litigation,* 1980 Am.B.Found.Res.J. 455. For commentary suggesting reforms, see Lewis, *New York Times v. Sullivan Reconsidered: Time to Return to "The Central Meaning of the First Amendment,"* 83 Colum.L.Rev. 603 (1983); Franklin, *Good Names and Bad Law: A Critique of Libel Law and a Proposal,* 18 U.S.F.L.Rev. 1 (1983); Ingber, *Defamation: A Conflict Between Reason and Decency,* 65 Va.L.Rev. 785 (1979); Smolla, *Let the Author Beware: The Rejuvenation of the American Law of Libel,* 132 U.Pa.L. Rev. 1 (1983).

D. PRIVACY

TIME, INC. v. HILL, 385 U.S. 374, 87 S.Ct. 534, 17 L.Ed.2d 456 (1967), applied the *New York Times* knowing and reckless falsity standard to a right of privacy action for publishing an erroneous but not defamatory report about private individuals involved in an incident of public interest. In 1952 the Hill family was the subject of national news coverage when held hostage in its home for 19 hours by three escaped convicts who treated the family courteously with no violence. This incident formed part of the basis for a novel, later made into a play, which involved violence against the hostage family. In 1955 *Life* published a picture story that showed the play's cast reenacting scenes from the play in the former Hill home. According to *Life,* the play "inspired by the [Hill] family's experience" "is a heartstopping account of how a family arose to heroism in a crisis." Hill secured a $30,000 judgment for compensatory damages against the publisher under the New York Right to Privacy statute, which, as interpreted, made truth a complete defense to actions based on "newsworthy people or events" but gave a right of action to one whose name or picture was the subject of an article containing "material and substantial falsification." The Court, per BRENNAN, J., reversed, holding that "the constitutional protections for speech and press preclude the application of the New York statute to redress false reports of matters of public interest in the absence of proof that the defendant published the report with knowledge of its falsity or in reckless disregard of the truth," and that the instructions did not adequately advise the jury that a verdict for Hill required a finding of knowing or reckless falsity:

"The guarantees for speech and press are not the preserve of political expression or comment upon public affairs, essential as those are to healthy government. One need only pick up any newspaper or magazine to comprehend the vast range of published matter which exposes persons to public view, both private citizens and public officials. Exposure of the self to others in varying degrees is a concomitant of life in a civilized community. The risk of this exposure is an essential incident of life in a society which places a primary value on freedom of speech and press. [We] have no doubt that the subject of the *Life* article, the opening of a new play linked to an actual incident, is a matter of public interest. 'The line between the informing and the entertaining is too elusive for the protection of [freedom of the press.]' Erroneous statement is no less inevitable in such case than in the case of comment upon public affairs, and in both, if innocent or merely negligent, '[it] must be protected if the freedoms of expression are to have the "breathing space" that they "need [to] survive".' [*New York Times*.] We create a grave risk of serious impairment of the indispensable service of a free press in a free society if we saddle the press with the impossible burden of verifying to a certainty the facts associated in news articles with a person's name, picture or portrait, particularly as related to non-defamatory matter. Even negligence would be a most elusive standard, especially when the content of the speech itself affords no warning of prospective harm to another through falsity. A negligence test would place on the press the intolerable burden of guessing how a jury might assess the reasonableness of steps taken by it to verify the accuracy of every reference to a name, picture or [portrait].

"We find applicable here the standard of knowing or reckless falsehood not through blind application of *New York Times*, relating solely to libel actions by public officials, but only upon consideration of the factors which arise in the particular context of the application of the New York statute in cases involving private individuals."

BLACK, J., joined by Douglas, J., concurred in reversal on the grounds stated in the Brennan opinion "in order for the Court to be able at this time to agree on an opinion in this important case based on the prevailing constitutional doctrine expressed in *New York Times*," but reaffirmed their belief that the "malicious," "reckless disregard of the truth" and "knowing and reckless falsity" exceptions were impermissible "abridgments" of freedom of expression. DOUGLAS, J., also filed a separate concurrence, deeming it "irrelevant to talk of any right of privacy in this context. Here a private person is catapulted into the news by events over which he had no control. He and his activities are then in the public domain as fully as the matters at issue in *New York Times*. Such privacy as a person normally has ceases when his life has ceased to be private."

HARLAN, J., concurring in part and dissenting in part, would have made the test of liability negligence, rather than the *New York Times* "reckless falsity": "It would be unreasonable to assume that Mr. Hill could find a forum for making a successful refutation of the *Life* material or that the public's interest in it would be sufficient for the truth to win out by comparison as it might in that area of discussion central to a free society. Thus the state interest in encouraging careful checking and preparation of published material is far stronger than in *Times*. The dangers of unchallengeable untruth are far too well documented to be summarily dismissed.

"Second, there is a vast difference in the state interest in protecting individuals like Mr. Hill from irresponsibly prepared publicity and the state interest in similar protection for a public official. In *Times* we acknowledged public officials to be a breed from whom hardiness to exposure to charges, innuendos, and criticisms might be demanded and who voluntarily assumed the risk of such things by entry into the public arena. But Mr. Hill came to public attention through an unfortunate circumstance not of his making rather than his voluntary actions and he can in no sense be considered to have 'waived' any protection the State might justifiably afford him from irresponsible publicity. Not being inured to the vicissitudes of journalistic scrutiny such an individual is more easily injured and his means of self-defense are more limited. The public is less likely to view with normal skepticism what is written about him because it is not accustomed to seeing his name in the press and expects only a disinterested report.

"The coincidence of these factors in this situation leads me to the view that a State should be free to hold the press to a duty of making a reasonable investigation of the underlying facts and limiting itself to 'fair comment' on the materials so gathered. Theoretically, of course, such a rule might slightly limit press discussion of matters touching individuals like Mr. Hill. But, from a pragmatic standpoint, until now the press, at least in New York, labored under the more exacting handicap of the existing New York privacy law and has certainly remained robust. Other professional activity of great social value is carried on under a duty of reasonable care and there is no reason to suspect the press would be less hardy than medical practitioners or attorneys." [a]

Notes and Questions

1. Does *Hill* survive *Gertz*? Consider the following statement: "In *Hill* and *Gertz* the same class of plaintiffs have to meet different constitutional standards in order to recover. Only the name of the tort has changed. This makes no sense." Is the state interest significantly different in *Gertz* than in *Hill*? Should it matter whether the statement at issue would appear innocuous to a reasonable editor? Offensive? What if a post-*Gertz* plaintiff sues for negligent infliction of emotional distress? Does *Hill* bar recovery without a showing of knowing or reckless falsehood? For commentary on the "quite startling" possibilities for plaintiffs, see Van Alstyne, *First Amendment Limitations on Recovery From the Press—An Extended Comment on "The Anderson Solution,"* 25 Wm. & Mary L.Rev. 793 (1984).

2. *False news.* Is injury to any particular person a prerequisite to state regulation of false publications? Consider *Keeton v. Hustler Magazine, Inc.*, 465 U.S. 770, 104 S.Ct. 1473, 79 L.Ed.2d 790 (1984): "False statements of fact harm both the subject of the falsehood *and* the readers of the statement. New Hampshire may rightly employ its libel laws to discourage the deception of its citizens." Could New Hampshire make it a criminal offense to publish false statements with knowledge of their falsity without any requirement of injury to any particular person?

3. *Truth and privacy.* Should privacy or defamation recoveries depend upon a showing of falsity? Suppose a disgruntled ex-lover posts true notices about the sex life of a person all over a small town? Should it make a difference if embarrassing private facts are published without malice? Compare *Briscoe v.*

---

a. Fortas, J., joined by Warren, C.J., and Clark, J., dissented, because "the jury instruc-   tions, although [not] a textbook model, satisfied [the *New York Times*] standard."

Reader's Digest, 4 Cal.3d 529, 93 Cal.Rptr. 866, 483 P.2d 34 (1971) (truthful reports about suspects of recent crimes protected by first amendment, but otherwise non-newsworthy plaintiff states cause of action for violation of privacy against truthful publication that he had committed and been convicted of a hijacking eleven years previously) with *Cox Broadcasting Corp. v. Cohn,* 420 U.S. 469, 95 S.Ct. 1029, 43 L.Ed.2d 328 (1975) (state cannot impose right of privacy liability for dissemination of the name of a rape victim derived from public court documents; "[A]t the very least, the First and Fourteenth Amendments will not allow exposing the press to liability for truthfully publishing information released to the public in [official records].")[b]

III. OBSCENITY

A. EVOLUTION TOWARD A STANDARD

Roth v. United States, infra, contains the Court's first extended discussion of the constitutionality of obscenity laws. The Court's opinion was framed by briefs that proceeded from sharply different visions of first amendment law. Roth argued that no speech including obscenity could be prohibited without meeting the clear and present danger test, that a danger of lustful thoughts was not the type of evil with which a legislature could be legitimately concerned, and that no danger of anti-social conduct had been shown. On the other hand, the government urged the Court to adopt a balancing test that prominently featured a consideration of the value of the speech involved. The government tendered an illustrative hierarchy of nineteen speech categories with political, religious, economic, and scientific speech at the top; entertainment, music, and humor in the middle; and libel, obscenity, profanity, and commercial pornography at the bottom.

ROTH v. UNITED STATES

ALBERTS v. CALIFORNIA

354 U.S. 476, 77 S.Ct. 1304, 1 L.Ed.2d 1498 (1957).

MR. JUSTICE BRENNAN delivered the opinion of the Court. [Roth and Alberts were convicted of violating the federal and California obscenity laws respectively. The issues raised were whether the statutes, "*on their faces and in a vacuum,* violated the freedom of expression and definiteness requirements of the Constitution."[a]]

The dispositive question is whether obscenity is utterance within the area of protected speech and press.[8] Although this is the first time the question has been squarely presented to this Court [expressions] found in numerous opinions indicate that this Court has always assumed that obscenity is not protected by the freedoms of speech and press.

---

b. For a sampling of the abundant commentary, see Zimmerman, *Requiem for a Heavyweight: A Farewell to Warren and Brandeis's Privacy Tort,* 68 Corn.L.Rev. 291 (1983); Emerson, *The Right of Privacy and Freedom of the Press,* 14 Harv.C.R.–C.L.L.Rev. 329 (1979); Hill, *Defamation and Privacy Under the First Amendment,* 76 Colum.L.Rev. 1205 (1976); Nimmer, *The Right to Speak from Times to Time: First Amendment Theory*

Applied to Libel and Misapplied to Privacy, 56 Calif.L.Rev. 935 (1968); Kalven, *Privacy in Tort Law—Were Warren and Brandeis Wrong?,* 31 Law & Contemp.Prob. 326 (1966).

a. See Lockhart & McClure, *Censorship of Obscenity: The Developing Constitutional Standards,* 45 Minn.L.Rev. 5, 13 (1960).

8. No issue is presented in either case concerning the obscenity of the material involved.

The guaranties of freedom of expression in effect in 10 of the 14 States which by 1792 had ratified the Constitution, gave no absolute protection for every utterance. Thirteen of the 14 States provided for the prosecution of libel, and all of those States made either blasphemy or profanity, or both, statutory crimes. As early as 1712, Massachusetts made it criminal to publish "any filthy, obscene, or profane song, pamphlet, libel or mock sermon" in imitation or mimicking of religious services. * * *

In light of this history, it is apparent that the unconditional phrasing of the First Amendment was not intended to protect every utterance. This phrasing did not prevent this Court from concluding that libelous utterances are not within the area of constitutionally protected speech. *Beauharnais*. At the time of the adoption of the First Amendment, obscenity law was not as fully developed as libel law, but there is sufficiently contemporaneous evidence to show that obscenity, too, was outside the protection intended for speech and press.[b]

The protection given speech and press was fashioned to assure unfettered interchange of ideas for the bringing about of political and social changes desired by the people. [All] ideas having even the slightest redeeming social importance—unorthodox ideas, controversial ideas, even ideas hateful to the prevailing climate of opinion—have the full protection of the guaranties, unless excludable because they encroach upon the limited area of more important interests. But implicit in the history of the First Amendment is the rejection of obscenity as utterly without redeeming social importance. This rejection for that reason is mirrored in the universal judgment that obscenity should be restrained, reflected in the international agreement of over 50 nations, in the obscenity laws of all of the 48 States, and in the 20 obscenity laws enacted by the Congress from 1842 to 1956. This is the same judgment expressed by this Court in *Chaplinsky* [p. 519 infra]: "There are certain well-defined and narrowly limited classes of speech, the prevention and punishment of which have never been thought to raise any Constitutional problem. *These include the lewd and obscene. [It] has been well observed that such utterances are no essential part of any exposition of ideas, and are of such slight social value as a step to truth that any benefit that may be derived from them is clearly outweighed by the social interest in order and morality.*" (Emphasis added [by Court].)

We hold that obscenity is not within the area of constitutionally protected speech or press.

It is strenuously urged that these obscenity statutes offend the constitutional guaranties because they punish incitation to impure sexual *thoughts*, not shown to be related to any overt antisocial conduct which is or may be incited in the persons stimulated to such *thoughts*. [It] is insisted that the constitutional guaranties are violated because convictions may be had without proof either that

b. The Court here cited three state court decisions (1808 to 1821) recognizing as a common law offense the distribution or display of obscene or indecent materials, and four state statutes aimed at similar conduct (1800 to 1842). For the contention that obscenity is not "speech" within the meaning of the first amendment (let alone, not *protected* speech), see Schauer, *Free Speech: A Philosophical Enquiry* 181–84 (1982) (a sex aid, not speech). See generally Schauer, *Speech and "Speech"— Obscenity and "Obscenity": An Exercise in the Interpretation of Constitutional Language*, 67 Geo.L.J. 899 (1979). But see Alexander & Horton, *The Impossibility of a Free Speech Principle*, 78 Nw.U.L.Rev. 1319, 1331–34 (1984). Compare Greenawalt, *Criminal Coercion and Freedom of Speech*, 78 Nw.U.L.Rev. 1081 (1983) (discussing the question of whether all ordinary language should be included within the scope of the first amendment, even if much is ultimately unprotected, and contending that some ordinary language should be wholly outside the scope of the first amendment). But see Haiman, *Comments on Kent Greenawalt's Criminal Coercion and Freedom of Speech*, id. at 1125.

obscene material will perceptibly create a clear and present danger of antisocial conduct, or will probably induce its recipients to such conduct. But, in light of our holding that obscenity is not protected speech, the complete answer to this argument is in the holding of this Court in *Beauharnais:* "Libelous utterances not being within the area of constitutionally protected speech, it is unnecessary, either for us or for the State courts, to consider the issues behind the phrase 'clear and present danger.' Certainly no one would contend that obscene speech, for example, may be punished only upon a showing of such circumstances. * * *"

However, sex and obscenity are not synonymous. Obscene material is material which deals with sex in a manner appealing to prurient interest.[20] The portrayal of sex, e.g., in art, literature and scientific works, is not itself sufficient reason to deny material the constitutional protection of freedom of speech and press. Sex, a great and mysterious motive force in human life, has indisputably been a subject of absorbing interest to mankind through the ages; it is one of the vital problems of human interest and public [concern].

The fundamental freedoms of speech and press have contributed greatly to the development and well-being of our free society and are indispensable to its continued growth. [It] is therefore vital that the standards for judging obscenity safeguard the protection of freedom of speech and press for material which does not treat sex in a manner appealing to prurient interest.

The early leading standard of obscenity allowed material to be judged merely by the effect of an isolated excerpt upon particularly susceptible persons. *Regina v. Hicklin,* [1868] L.R. 3 Q.B. 360. Some American courts adopted this standard but later decisions have rejected it and substituted this test: whether to the average person, applying contemporary community standards, the dominant theme of the material taken as a whole appeals to prurient interest. The *Hicklin* test, judging obscenity by the effect of isolated passages upon the most susceptible persons, might well encompass material legitimately treating with sex, and so it must be rejected as unconstitutionally restrictive of the freedoms of speech and press. On the other hand, the substituted standard provides safeguards adequate to withstand the charge of constitutional infirmity. Both trial courts below sufficiently followed the proper standard. Both courts used the proper definition of obscenity.[c]

20. I.e., material having a tendency to excite lustful thoughts. *Webster's New International Dictionary* (Unabridged, 2d ed., 1949) defines *prurient,* in pertinent part, as follows:

"Itching; longing; uneasy with desire or longing; of persons, having itching, morbid, or lascivious longings; of desire, curiosity, or propensity, lewd * * *."

We perceive no significant difference between the meaning of obscenity developed in the case law and the definition of the A.L.I., *Model Penal Code,* § 207.10(2) (Tent. Draft No. 6, 1957), viz.: "[A] thing is obscene if, considered as a whole, its predominant appeal is to prurient interest, i.e. a shameful or morbid interest in nudity, sex, or excretion, and if it goes substantially beyond customary limits of candor in description or representation of such [matters]." See Comment, id. at 10, and the discussion at page 29 et seq.

c. The opinion quoted with apparent approval from the trial court's instruction in *Roth:* "[The] test is not whether it would arouse sexual desires or sexual impure thoughts in those comprising a particular segment of the community, the young, the immature or the highly prudish or would leave another segment, the scientific or highly educated or the so-called worldly-wise and sophisticated indifferent and unmoved. [The] test in each case is the effect of the book, picture or publication considered as a whole, not upon any particular class, but upon all those whom it is likely to reach. In other words, you determine its impact upon the average person in the community. The books, pictures and circulars must be judged as a whole, in their entire context, and you are not to consider detached or separate portions in reaching a conclusion. You judge the circulars, pictures and publications which have been put in evi-

[It] is argued that the statutes do not provide reasonably ascertainable standards of guilt and therefore violate the constitutional requirements of due process. *Winters v. New York*, 333 U.S. 507, 68 S.Ct. 665, 92 L.Ed. 840 (1948). The federal obscenity statute makes punishable the mailing of material that is "obscene, lewd, lascivious, or filthy [or] other publication of an indecent character." The California statute makes punishable, inter alia, the keeping for sale or advertising material that is "obscene or indecent." The thrust of the argument is that these words are not sufficiently precise because they do not mean the same thing to all people, all the time, everywhere. Many decisions have recognized that these terms of obscenity statutes are not precise. This Court, however, has consistently held that lack of precision is not itself offensive to the requirements of due process. "[T]he Constitution does not require impossible standards"; all that is required is that the language "conveys sufficiently definite warning as to the proscribed conduct when measured by common understanding and [practices.]" * * *

In summary, then, we hold that these statutes, applied according to the proper standard for judging obscenity, do not offend constitutional safeguards against convictions based upon protected material, or fail to give men in acting adequate notice of what is prohibited. * * *

Affirmed.

MR. CHIEF JUSTICE WARREN, concurring in the result.

[It] is not the book that is on trial; it is a person. The conduct of the defendant is the central issue, not the obscenity of a book or picture. The nature of the materials is, of course, relevant as an attribute of the defendant's conduct. [The] defendants in both these cases were engaged in the business of purveying textual or graphic matter openly advertised to appeal to the erotic interest of their customers. They were plainly engaged in the commercial exploitation of the morbid and shameful craving for materials with prurient effect. * * *

MR. JUSTICE HARLAN, concurring in the result in [*Alberts*], and dissenting in [*Roth*].

I. [The] Court seems to assume that "obscenity" is a peculiar genus of "speech and press," which is as distinct, recognizable, and classifiable as poison ivy is among other plants. On this basis the *constitutional* question before us simply becomes, as the Court says, whether "obscenity," as an abstraction, is protected by the First and Fourteenth Amendments, and the question whether a *particular* book may be suppressed becomes a mere matter of classification, of "fact," to be entrusted to a fact-finder and insulated from independent constitutional judgment. But surely the problem cannot be solved in such a generalized fashion. Every communication has an individuality and "value" of its own. The suppression of a particular writing or other tangible form of expression is, therefore, an *individual* matter, and in the nature of things every such suppression raises an individual constitutional problem, in which a reviewing court must determine for *itself* whether the attacked expression is suppressable within constitutional [standards].

I do not think that reviewing courts can escape this responsibility by saying that the trier of the facts, be it a jury or a judge, has labeled the questioned matter as "obscene," for, if "obscenity" is to be suppressed, the question whether a particular work is of that character involves not really an issue of fact but a question of constitutional *judgment* of the most sensitive and delicate kind.

dence by present-day standards of the community. You may ask yourselves does it offend the common conscience of the community by present-day standards."

Many juries might find that Joyce's "Ulysses" or Bocaccio's "Decameron" was obscene, and yet the conviction of a defendant for selling either book would raise, for me, the gravest constitutional problems, for no such verdict could convince me, without more, that these books are "utterly without redeeming social importance." [I] am very much afraid that the broad manner in which the Court has decided these cases will tend to obscure the peculiar responsibilities resting on state and federal courts in this field and encourage them to rely on easy labeling and jury verdicts as a substitute for facing up to the tough individual problems of constitutional judgment involved in every obscenity case.

[In] California the book must have a "tendency to deprave or corrupt its readers"; under the federal statute it must tend "to stir sexual impulses and lead to sexually impure thoughts." [T]he Court compounds confusion when it superimposes on these two statutory definitions a third, drawn from the American Law Institute's *Model Penal Code,* Tentative Draft No. 6: "A thing is obscene if, considered as a whole, its predominant appeal is to prurient interest." The bland assurance that this definition is the same as the ones with which we deal flies in the face of the authors' express rejection of the "deprave and corrupt" and "sexual thoughts" tests.[d] [T]he Court merely assimilates the various tests into one indiscriminate potpourri. * * *

II. I concur in [*Alberts*]. [T]he [California] legislature has made the judgment that printed words *can* "deprave or corrupt" the reader—that words can incite to anti-social or immoral action. [It] is well known, of course, that the validity of this assumption is a matter of dispute among critics, sociologists, psychiatrists, and penologists. [I]t is not our function to decide this question. That function belongs to the state legislature. [I]t is not irrational, in our present state of knowledge, to consider that pornography can induce a type of sexual conduct which a State may deem obnoxious to the moral fabric of [society].

Furthermore, even assuming that pornography cannot be deemed ever to cause, in an immediate sense, criminal sexual conduct, other interests within the proper cognizance of the States may be protected by the prohibition placed on such materials. The State can reasonably draw the inference that over a long period of time the indiscriminate dissemination of materials, the essential character of which is to degrade sex, will have an eroding effect on moral standards. And the State has a legitimate interest in protecting the privacy of the home against invasion of unsolicited obscenity.

[I] concur in the judgment because, upon an independent perusal of the material involved, and in light of the considerations discussed above, I cannot say that its suppression would so interfere with the communication of "ideas" in any proper sense of that term that it would offend the Due Process Clause.[e]

d. The opinion quoted the explanation in the Tentative Draft: "Obscenity [in the Tentative Draft] is defined in terms of material which appeals predominantly to prurient interest in sexual matters and which goes beyond customary freedom of expression in these matters. We reject the prevailing test of tendency to arouse lustful thoughts or desires because it is unrealistically broad for a society that plainly tolerates a great deal of erotic interest in literature, advertising, and art, and because regulation of thought or desire, unconnected with overt misbehavior, raises the most acute constitutional as well as practical difficulties. We likewise reject the common definition of obscene as that which 'tends to corrupt or debase.' If this means anything different from tendency to arouse lustful thought and desire, it suggests that change of character or actual misbehavior follows from contact with obscenity. Evidence of such consequences is lacking. [On] the other hand, 'appeal to prurient interest' refers to qualities of the material itself: the capacity to attract individuals eager for a forbidden look."

e. Harlan, J., dissented in *Roth*. He would have limited federal power to reach only

MR. JUSTICE DOUGLAS, with whom MR. JUSTICE BLACK concurs, dissenting.

When we sustain these convictions, we make the legality of a publication turn on the purity of thought which a book or tract instills in the mind of the reader. I do not think we can approve that standard and be faithful to the command of the First Amendment * * *.

The tests by which these convictions were obtained require only the arousing of sexual thoughts. Yet the arousing of sexual thoughts and desires happens every day in normal life in dozens of ways. Nearly 30 years ago a questionnaire sent to college and normal school women graduates asked what things were most stimulating sexually. Of 409 replies, 9 said "music"; 18 said "pictures"; 29 said "dancing"; 40 said "drama"; 95 said "books"; and 218 said "man." Alpert, *Judicial Censorship of Obscene Literature*, 52 Harv.L.Rev. 40, 73 (1938).

The test of obscenity the Court endorses today gives the censor free range over a vast domain. To allow the State to step in and punish mere speech or publication that the judge or the jury thinks has an *undesirable* impact on thoughts but that is not shown to be a part of unlawful action is drastically to curtail the First Amendment. As recently stated by two of our outstanding authorities on obscenity, "The danger of influencing a change in the current moral standards of the community, or of shocking or offending readers, or of stimulating sex thoughts or desires apart from objective conduct, can never justify the losses to society that result from interference with literary freedom." Lockhart & McClure, *Literature, The Law of Obscenity, and the Constitution*, 38 Minn.L.Rev. 295, 387 (1954).

If we were certain that impurity of sexual thoughts impelled to action, we would be on less dangerous ground in punishing the distributors of this sex literature. But it is by no means clear that obscene literature, as so defined, is a significant factor in influencing substantial deviations from the community standards. [The] absence of dependable information on the effect of obscene literature on human conduct should make us wary. It should put us on the side of protecting society's interest in literature, except and unless it can be said that the particular publication has an impact on action that the government can [control.]

Any test that turns on what is offensive to the community's standards is too loose, too capricious, too destructive of freedom of expression to be squared with the First Amendment. Under that test, juries can censor, suppress, and punish what they don't like, provided the matter relates to "sexual impurity" or has a tendency "to excite lustful thoughts." This is community censorship in one of its worst forms. It creates a regime where in the battle between the literati and the Philistines, the Philistines are certain to win. If experience in this teaches anything, it is that "censorship of obscenity has almost always been both irrational and indiscriminate." Lockhart & McClure at 371.

[The Court today defines] obscene material as that "which deals with sex in a manner appealing to prurient interest." [T]hat standard does not require any nexus between the literature which is prohibited and action which the legislature can regulate or [prohibit].

I do not think that the problem can be resolved by the Court's statement that "obscenity is not expression protected by the First Amendment." With the exception of *Beauharnais* none of our cases has resolved problems of free speech

"what the Government has termed as 'hard-core' pornography." He stressed both the absence of federal "power over sexual morality" and the danger to free expression of a "blanket ban over the Nation" on such books as *Lady Chatterley's Lover.*

and free press by placing any form of expression beyond the pale of the absolute prohibition of the First Amendment. Unlike the law of libel, wrongfully relied on in *Beauharnais*, there is no special historical evidence that literature dealing with sex was intended to be treated in a special manner by those who drafted the First Amendment. [I] reject too the implication that problems of freedom of speech and of the press are to be resolved by weighing against the values of free expression, the judgment of the Court that a particular form of that expression has "no redeeming social importance." * * *

I would give the broad sweep of the First Amendment full support. I have the same confidence in the ability of our people to reject noxious literature as I have in their capacity to sort out the true from the false in theology, economics, politics, or any other field.

Notes and Questions

1. *Non-obscene advocacy of "sexual immorality."* Two years after *Roth*, KINGSLEY INT'L PICTURES CORP. v. REGENTS, 360 U.S. 684, 79 S.Ct. 1362, 3 L.Ed.2d 1512 (1959), per STEWART, J., underlined the distinction between obscenity and non-obscene "portrayal of sex" in art and literature. *Kingsley* held invalid New York's denial of a license to exhibit the film *Lady Chatterley's Lover* pursuant to a statute requiring such denial when a film "portrays acts of sexual immorality [as] desirable, acceptable or proper patterns of behavior":

"The Court of Appeals unanimously and explicitly rejected any notion that the film is obscene [but] found that the picture as a whole 'alluringly portrays adultery as proper behavior.' [What] New York has done, [is] to prevent the exhibition of a motion picture because that picture advocates an idea—that adultery under certain circumstances may be proper behavior. Yet the First Amendment's basic guarantee is of freedom to advocate ideas. The State, quite simply, has thus struck at the very heart of constitutionally protected liberty.

"[T]he guarantee is not confined to the expression of ideas that are conventional or shared by a majority. It protects advocacy of the opinion that adultery may sometimes be proper, no less than advocacy of socialism or the single tax. And in the realm of ideas it protects expression which is eloquent no less than that which is unconvincing. Advocacy of conduct proscribed by law is not, as Mr. Justice Brandeis long ago pointed out, 'a justification for denying free speech where the advocacy falls short of incitement and there is nothing to indicate that the advocacy would be immediately acted on.' *Whitney*." [f]

2. *Ideas and the first amendment.* Consider Kalven, *The Metaphysics of the Law of Obscenity,* 1960 Sup.Ct.Rev. 1, 15–16: "The classic defense of John Stuart Mill and the modern defense of Alexander Meiklejohn do not help much when the question is why the novel, the poem, the painting, the drama, or the piece of sculpture falls within the protection of the First Amendment. Nor do the famous opinions of Hand, Holmes, and Brandeis. [The] people do not need novels or dramas or paintings or poems because they will be called upon to vote. Art and belles-lettres do not deal in such ideas—at least not good art or belles-

f. While joining the opinion, Black and Douglas, JJ., also stated that prior censorship of motion pictures violates the first amendment. See discussion of this issue in Sec. 2, II infra. Harlan, J., joined by Frankfurter and Whittaker, JJ., concurred in the result. While "granting that abstract public discussion [of] adultery, unaccompanied by obscene portrayal or actual incitement [may] not constitutionally be proscribed," they concluded that the New York Court of Appeals had found the film obscene, but on viewing the film they concluded it was not obscene. Clark, J., concurred in the result because the statutory standard was too vague.

lettres—and it makes little sense here to talk [of] whether there is still time for counter-speech.

[B]eauty has constitutional status too, [and] the life of the imagination is as important to the human adult as the life of the intellect. I do not think that the Court would find it difficult to protect Shakespeare, even though it is hard to enumerate the important ideas in the plays and poems. I am only suggesting that Mr. Justice Brennan might not have found it so easy to dismiss obscenity because it lacked socially useful ideas if he had recognized that as to this point, at least, obscenity is in the same position as all art and literature."

3. *The moral rationale for prohibition.* Consider Clor, *Obscenity and Public Morality* 41–43 (1969): *Roth* "rejected the government's formula for the decision of obscenity cases, a formula which would have involved it in judgments concerning the importance of public morality and the role of government, as well as judgments concerning the effects of obscenity and the relative value of different forms of speech. The Court preferred to decide the case on the narrow and negative grounds that obscenity is without redeeming social importance. [W]hile the idea of redeeming social importance can be valuable as a definition of what should be protected, it cannot serve as a defense of regulation. Justices Harlan and Douglas can be answered only by a course of reasoning which provides some grounds for government activity in the area of morality, showing that the ends are legitimate and important, which provides some justification for the claims of community conscience, and which explores, more thoroughly than does the Court, the character of the 'thoughts' with which the law is here concerned."

The Court does assert that any value of obscenity as a step to truth is "outweighed by the social interest in order and morality.'" But consider Richards, *Free Speech and Obscenity Law: Toward A Moral Theory of the First Amendment*, 123 U.Pa.L.Rev. 45, 81 (1974): "[P]ornography can be seen as the unique medium of a vision of sexuality * * * a view of sensual delight in the erotic celebration of the body, a concept of easy freedom without consequences, a fantasy of timelessly repetitive indulgence. In opposition to the Victorian view that narrowly defines proper sexual function in a rigid way that is analogous to ideas of excremental regularity and moderation, pornography builds a model of plastic variety and joyful excess in sexuality. In opposition to the sorrowing Catholic dismissal of sexuality as an unfortunate and spiritually superficial concomitant of propagation, pornography affords the alternative idea of the independent status of sexuality as a profound and shattering ecstasy."

Even if these characterizations were somewhat overwrought with respect to Roth's publications (e.g., *Wild Passion* and *Wanton By Night*) what of the view that individuals should be able to decide what they want to read and make moral decisions for themselves? Consider John Stuart Mill's statement of the harm principle in *On Liberty:* "[T]he only purpose for which power can be rightfully exercised over any member of a civilized community, against his will is to prevent harm to others."

Does the liberal view overestimate human rational capacity and underestimate the importance of the state in promoting a virtuous citizenry? See generally Clor, supra. Do liberals fail to appreciate the morally corrosive effects of obscenity? Consider the following observation: "Obscenity emphasizes the base animality of our nature, reduces the spirituality of humanity to mere bodily functions, and debases civilization by transforming the private into the public." Consider Kristol, *Reflections of a Neoconservative* 45, 47 (1983): "Bearbaiting and cockfighting are prohibited only in part out of compassion for the suffering animals; the main reason they were abolished was because it was felt that they debased and brutalized the citizenry who flocked to witness such spectacles. And the question we face with regard to pornography and obscenity is whether [they] can or will brutalize and debase our citizenry. We are, after all, not dealing with one passing incident—one book, or one play, or one movie. We are dealing with a general tendency that is suffusing our entire culture. [W]hen men and women make love, as we say, they prefer to be alone—because it is only when you are alone that you can make love, as distinct from merely copulating in an animal and casual way. And that, too, is why those who are voyeurs, if they are not irredeemably sick, also feel ashamed at what they are witnessing. When sex is a public spectacle, a human relationship has been debased into a mere animal connection." See also Clor, supra; Berns, *Pornography vs. Democracy: The Case for Censorship,* 22 Pub.Int. 13 (1971).

4. *Feminism and pornography.* Does the Court's cryptic recitation of the interests in order and morality obscure the implications of pornography for women in a male-dominated culture? Consider Brownmiller, *Against Our Will: Men, Women & Rape* 442–43, 444 (1976): Pornography is a "systematized commercially successful propaganda machine" encouraging males to get a "sense of power from viewing females as anonymous, panting playthings, adult toys, dehumanized objects to be used, abused, broken and discarded." See also MacKinnon, *Not a Moral Issue,* 2 Yale L. & Pol.Rev. 321, 327 (1984): "[T]he liberal defense of pornography as human sexual liberation, as de-repression— whether by feminists, lawyers, or neo-Freudians—is a defense not only of force and sexual terrorism, but of the subordination of women. Sexual liberation in the liberal sense frees male sexual aggression in the feminist sense. What in the liberal view looks like love and romance looks a lot like hatred and torture to the feminist. Pleasure and eroticism become violation. Desire appears as lust for dominance and submission."

5. *The impact of obscenity on anti-social conduct.* After citing the conclusion of the U.S. Commission on Obscenity and Pornography that " 'empirical research has found no evidence to date that exposure to explicit sexual materials plays a significant role in the causation of delinquent or criminal behaviour among youth or adults,' " the British Committee on Obscenity and Film Censorship concluded: "It is still possible to say [that] there does not appear to be any strong evidence that exposure to sexually explicit material triggers off anti-social sexual behaviour. [T]his is consistent with what we learned from the clinical experience of those experienced medical witnesses we consulted." Williams, Chair, *Report of the Committee on Obscenity and Film Censorship* § 6.16, at 66 (1979). More recent studies claim to strongly "link exposure to pornographic material among men to an increase in the acceptance of violence against women." Malamuth & Billings, *Why Pornography? Models of Functions and Effects,* 34 J. of Comm. 117, 129 (1984). For an analysis of much of the recent research (some of it contending that the changes in attitudes and arousal are directly related to aggression against women), see *Pornography & Sexual Aggression* (Malamuth & Donnerstein eds. 1984).

———

After a majority of the Court agreed on the *Roth* standard for obscenity in 1957 without applying it to particular materials, it was not until *Miller* in 1973 that a majority could again reach agreement upon the key issue—the standard for determining what material is outside the first amendment because "obscene." But during that era a majority of the justices, voting on the basis of differing views as to the appropriate method of dealing with obscenity, produced informal coalitions that reached consistent results. *Memoirs* reflects the divisions within the Court on that key issue during this era.

MEMOIRS v. MASSACHUSETTS, 383 U.S. 413, 86 S.Ct. 975, 16 L.Ed.2d 1 (1966), reversed a ruling that Clelland's *Memoirs of a Woman of Pleasure ("Fanny Hill")* was obscene under Massachusetts law and not entitled to first amendment protection. BRENNAN, J., joined by Warren, C.J., and Fortas, J., delivered the plurality opinion: "[T]he sole question before the state courts was whether *Memoirs* satisfies the test of obscenity established in *Roth* [under whose definition of obscenity], as elaborated in subsequent cases, three elements must coalesce: it must be established that (a) the dominant theme of the material taken as a whole appeals to a prurient interest in sex; (b) the material is patently offensive because it affronts contemporary community standards relating to the description or representation of sexual matters;[a] and (c) the material is utterly without redeeming social value.[b]

"[R]eversal is required because the [Supreme Judicial Court] misinterpreted the social value criterion [thus]: 'It remains to consider whether the book can be said to be "utterly without social importance." We are mindful that there was expert testimony, much of which was strained, [that] *Memoirs* is a structural novel with literary merit; that the book displays a skill in characterization and a gift for comedy; that it plays a part in the history of the development of the English novel; and that it contains a moral, namely, that sex with love is superior to sex in a brothel. But the fact that the testimony may indicate this book has some minimal literary value does not mean it is of any social importance. We do not interpret the "social importance" test as requiring that a book which appeals to prurient interest and is patently offensive must be unqualifiedly worthless before it can be deemed obscene.'

"The Supreme Judicial Court erred in holding that a book need not be 'unqualifiedly worthless before it can be deemed obscene.' A book can not be proscribed unless it is found to be *utterly* without redeeming social value. This is so even though the book is found to possess the requisite prurient appeal and to be patently offensive. Each of the three federal constitutional criteria is to be applied independently; the social value of the book can neither be weighed against nor canceled by its prurient appeal or patent offensiveness. Hence, even on the view of the court below that *Memoirs* possessed only a modicum of social value, its judgment must be reversed as being founded on an erroneous interpretation of a federal constitutional standard.

"It does not necessarily follow from this reversal that a determination that *Memoirs* is obscene in the constitutional sense would be improper under all circumstances. On the premise, which we have no occasion to assess, that

---

a. This element crept into the standard for obscenity in an opinion by Harlan, J., joined only by Stewart, J., in *Manual Enterprises, Inc. v. Day,* 370 U.S. 478, 82 S.Ct. 1432, 8 L.Ed. 2d 639 (1962). They concluded that photographs of nude males were not obscene because not "so offensive on their face as to affront community standards of decency." In their view, obscenity required "patent offensiveness" as well as "appeal to the prurient interest." The other justices concurred in the result on grounds that did not reach the obscenity issue.

b. While absence of "social value" was not expressly stated in the standard for obscenity in *Roth,* the opinion gave its absence as a reason for not protecting obscenity. Brennan, J., joined only by Goldberg, J., expressly stated the "utterly without social importance" requirement for the first time in *Jacobellis v. Ohio,* 378 U.S. 184, 84 S.Ct. 1676, 12 L.Ed.2d 793 (1964), where none of the other justices expressed views on that factor.

Memoirs has the requisite prurient appeal and is patently offensive, but has only a minimum of social value, the circumstances of production, sale, and publicity are relevant in determining whether or not the publication or distribution of the book is constitutionally protected. Evidence that the book was commercially exploited for the sake of prurient appeal, to the exclusion of all other values, might justify the conclusion that the book was utterly without redeeming social importance. It is not that in such a setting the social value test is relaxed so as to dispense with the requirement that a book be *utterly* devoid of social value, but rather that [where] the purveyor's sole emphasis is on the sexually provocative aspects of his publications, a court could accept his evaluation at its face value."

Black and Douglas, JJ., each independently concurred in the reversal, restating their views that the first amendment afforded protection for obscene materials. BLACK, J.'s criticism of the social value test maintained that "Whether a particular treatment of a particular subject is with or without social value in this evolving, dynamic society of ours is a question upon which no uniform agreement could possibly be reached among politicians, statesmen, professors, philosophers, scientists, religious groups or any other type of group."

STEWART, J., separately concurred, citing his dissent in *Ginzburg v. United States*, 383 U.S. 463, 86 S.Ct. 942, 16 L.Ed.2d 31 (1966) that only hard core pornography could be constitutionally suppressed. Having said in a prior case that "I cannot define it, but I know it when I see it," he elaborated in *Ginzburg:* "In order to prevent any possible misunderstanding, I have set out in the margin description, borrowed from the Solicitor General's brief, of the kind of thing to which I have reference.[3] See also Lockhart and McClure, [1960] 63–64."

HARLAN, J.'s separate dissent limited the federal government to the regulation of hard core pornography that he would describe "substantially" as does Stewart, J. For state governments, he would require only that it "apply criteria rationally related to the accepted notion of obscenity and that it reach results not wholly out of step with current American standards."

CLARK and WHITE, JJ., each separately dissenting, rejected social value as a "separate and distinct" or "independent test of obscenity" but viewed it as "relevant." Clark, J., would consider evidence of "social importance [together] with evidence that the material [appeals] to prurient interest and is patently offensive." White, J., viewed "social importance" as "relevant only to determining the predominant prurient interest of the material [based] on the material itself and all the [evidence], expert or otherwise." Each would have upheld the obscenity finding in *Memoirs* and rejected the possibility that "beautiful prose" or "literary style" could protect well-written obscenity.

Notes and Questions

1. *Utterly without redeeming social value.* Should material dealing with sex be entitled to full immunity if it has slight social value, regardless of its

---

3. "[Such] materials include photographs, both still and motion picture, with no pretense of artistic value, graphically depicting acts of sexual intercourse, including various acts of sodomy and sadism, and sometimes involving several participants in scenes of orgy-like character. They also include strips of drawings in comic-book format grossly depicting similar activities in an exaggerated fashion. There are, in addition, pamphlets and book-lets, sometimes with photographic illustrations, verbally describing such activities in a bizarre manner with no attempt whatsoever to afford portrayals of character or situation and with no pretense to literary value. All of this material [cannot] conceivably be characterized as embodying communication of ideas or artistic values inviolate under the First Amendment."

prurience and offensiveness? Should courts require *redeeming* social value?
Consider Clor, supra, at 78: "Justice Brennan's opinion constitutes a rejection
[of] judicial effort to attach some meaning to the first two words in the
expression 'redeeming social importance.' Since opposing factors may not be
weighed, judges may not consider whether the values ascribed to a work are
indeed 'redemptive.' And it would seem that they are also forbidden to consider
whether the importance ascribed to a work is really 'social' importance. [Evi-
dently] a work is to be protected though its 'dominant theme, taken as a whole'
be both prurient and patently offensive. In this manner the Court goes to the
verge of an explicit rejection of the *Roth* rule, while continuing to affirm that
that rule governs obscenity cases."

See also Frank, *Obscenity: Some Problems of Values and the Use of Experts,*
41 Wash.L.Rev. 631, 665 (1966): "The practical difference between the Brennan
approach and the Clark-White approach is illustrated in *Fanny Hill.* The book
is as totally dedicated to the appeal to prurience as anything can be—it has lived
for this purpose alone for two hundred years. Certainly no one would choose it
very seriously for the sake of the story or for the skill of its expression or as a
serious description of 18th century London; * * * Justice Clark makes absolute hash out of its literary pretensions. Yet it is not totally without literary
skill in the sense that a dirty postcard might be; it is at least passable writing.
If no more is required, then under the Brennan test the book clears; while if the
exceedingly low level of literary accomplishment is balanced against other
factors, then the book fails."

2. *Variable obscenity.* The plurality's suggestion that the same book may
be obscene in some contexts but not in others has been endorsed in several
different contexts. *Butler v. Michigan,* 352 U.S. 380, 77 S.Ct. 524, 1 L.Ed.2d 412
(1957) held that the state could not ban sales to the general public of material
unsuitable for children: "The State insists that [by] quarantining the general
reading public against books not too rugged for grown men and women in order
to shield juvenile innocence, it is exercising its power to promote the general
welfare. Surely, this is to burn the house to roast the pig. [The] incidence of
this enactment is to reduce the adult population of Michigan to reading only
what is fit for children." *Ginsberg v. New York,* 390 U.S. 629, 88 S.Ct. 1274, 20
L.Ed.2d 195 (1968), however, held that the state could bar the distribution to
children of books that were suitable for adults, the Court recognizing it was
adopting a "variable" concept of obscenity.[c]

The approach had previously been advocated and elaborated by Lockhart
and McClure, *Censorship of Obscenity: The Developing Constitutional Standards,*
45 Minn.L.Rev. 5, 77 (1960): "Under variable obscenity, material is judged by its
appeal to and effect upon the audience to which the material is primarily
directed. In this view, material is never inherently obscene; instead, its obscenity varies with the circumstances of its dissemination. Material may be obscene
when directed to one class of persons but not when directed to [another].
Variable obscenity also makes it possible to reach, under obscenity statutes, the
panderer who advertises and pushes non-pornographic material as if it were

---

c. See also *Ginzburg v. United States,* supra ("pandering" method of marketing supports obscenity conviction even though the
materials might not otherwise have been considered obscene); *Mishkin v. New York,* 383
U.S. 502, 86 S.Ct. 958, 16 L.Ed.2d 56 (1966)
(material designed for and primarily disseminated to deviant sexual group can meet prurient appeal requirement even if the material
lacks appeal to an average member of the
general public; appeal is to be tested with
reference to the sexual interests of the intended and probable recipient group).

hard-core pornography, seeking out an audience of the sexually immature who bring their 'pornographic intent to something which is not itself pornographic.' "

See also Krislov, *From Ginzburg to Ginsberg: The Unhurried Children's Hour in Obscenity Litigation*, 1968 Sup.Ct.Rev. 153, 196: " 'Variable obscenity' provides an oven to roast the pig—and a precisely fitted one at that. There is no longer need to burn the barn." Compare Schauer, *The Law of Obscenity*, 95 (1976): "[W]hat the idea of variable obscenity adds in terms of realities and flexibility, it may subtract in terms of the best possible notice or warning of what is prohibited. As with any statutory or regulatory scheme, maximum predictability often provides less than optimum 'fairness,' and the converse is equally true."

3. *The law in action.* The Court's failure in *Memoirs* to arrive at a definition of obscenity did not prevent it from reversing obscenity findings in 31 cases between 1967 and 1971,[d] usually by reference to REDRUP v. NEW YORK, 386 U.S. 767, 87 S.Ct. 1414, 18 L.Ed.2d 515 (1967), an opinion which was crafted to transcend the Court's differences. The key language in *Redrup* stated that: "Two members of the Court have consistently adhered to the view that a State is utterly without power to suppress, control, or punish the distribution of any writings or pictures upon the ground of their 'obscenity.' A third has held to the opinion that a State's power in this area is narrowly limited to a distinct and clearly identifiable class of material. Others have subscribed to a not dissimilar standard [quoting the three-factor formula in Brennan, J.'s *Memoirs* opinion.] Another justice has not viewed the 'social value' element as an independent factor in the judgment of obscenity. Whichever of these constitutional views is brought to bear upon the cases before us, it is clear that the judgments cannot stand."

B. THE SEARCH FOR A RATIONALE

STANLEY v. GEORGIA, 394 U.S. 557, 89 S.Ct. 1243, 22 L.Ed.2d 542 (1969), per MARSHALL, J., reversed a conviction for knowing "possession of obscene matter," based on three reels of obscene films found in Stanley's home when police entered under a search warrant for other purposes: "[*Roth*] and the cases following it discerned [an] 'important interest' in the regulation of commercial distribution of obscene material. That holding cannot foreclose an examination of the constitutional implications of a statute forbidding mere private possession of such material. [The constitutional] right to receive information and ideas, regardless of their social worth [*Winters*] is fundamental to our free society. Moreover, in the context of this case—a prosecution for mere possession of printed or filmed matter in the privacy of a person's own home—that right takes on an added dimension. For also fundamental is the right to be free, except in very limited circumstances, from unwanted governmental intrusions into one's privacy.

" 'The makers of our Constitution undertook to secure conditions favorable to the pursuit of happiness. They recognized the significance of man's spiritual

---

d. In *Huffman v. United States*, 470 F.2d 386, 395–402 (D.C.Cir.1971), Leventhal, J., classified and described the materials involved in each such case. Where the material was textual, all obscenity findings were reversed, including books featuring monotonously repeated explicit descriptions of varieties of sexual episodes. Where the materials were picto-rial, still or in motion, obscenity findings were reversed where only nudity was shown, including those that focused on male and female genitalia, and where sexual activity was only suggested. But where pictures explicitly depicted sexual activity, the obscenity findings were allowed to stand.

nature, of his feelings and of his intellect. [They] sought to protect Americans in their beliefs, their thoughts, their emotions and their sensations. They conferred, as against the government, the right to be let alone—the most comprehensive of rights and the right most valued by civilized man.' *Olmstead v. United States,* 277 U.S. 438, 48 S.Ct. 564, 72 L.Ed. 944 (1928) (Brandeis, J., dissenting). * * *

"These are the rights that appellant is asserting in the case before us. He is asserting the right to read or observe what he pleases—the right to satisfy his intellectual and emotional needs in the privacy of his own home. He is asserting the right to be free from state inquiry into the contents of his library. Georgia contends that appellant does not have these rights, that there are certain types of materials that the individual may not read or even possess. [W]e think that mere categorization of these films as 'obscene' is insufficient justification for such a drastic invasion of personal liberties guaranteed by the First and Fourteenth Amendments. Whatever may be the justifications for other statutes regulating obscenity, we do not think they reach into the privacy of one's own home. If the First Amendment means anything, it means that a State has no business telling a man, sitting alone in his own house, what books he may read or what films he may watch. Our whole constitutional heritage rebels at the thought of giving government the power to control men's minds.

"[I]n the face of these traditional notions of individual liberty, Georgia asserts the right to protect the individual's mind from the effects of obscenity. We are not certain that this argument amounts to anything more than the assertion that the State has the right to control the moral content of a person's thoughts.[8] To some, this may be a noble purpose, but it is wholly inconsistent with the philosophy of the First Amendment. [*Kingsley Pictures.*] Nor is it relevant that obscenity in general, or the particular films before the Court, are arguably devoid of any ideological content. The line between the transmission of ideas and mere entertainment is much too elusive for this Court to draw, if indeed such a line can be drawn at all. [*Winters*]. Whatever the power of the state to control public dissemination of ideas inimical to the public morality, it cannot constitutionally premise legislation on the desirability of controlling a person's private thoughts.

"[Georgia] asserts that exposure to obscenity may lead to deviant sexual behavior or crimes of sexual violence. There appears to be little empirical basis for that assertion. But more importantly, if the State is only concerned about literature inducing antisocial conduct, we believe that in the context of private consumption of ideas and information we should adhere to the view that '[a]mong free men, the deterrents ordinarily to be applied to prevent crime are education and punishment for violations of the [law].' *Whitney* (Brandeis, J., concurring). See Emerson, *Toward a General Theory of the First Amendment,* 72 Yale L.J. 877, 938 (1963). Given the present state of knowledge, the State may no more prohibit mere possession of obscenity on the ground that it may lead to antisocial conduct than it may prohibit possession of chemistry books on the ground that they may lead to the manufacture of homemade spirits.

---

8. "Communities believe, and act on the belief, that obscenity is immoral, is wrong for the individual, and has no place in a decent society. They believe, too, that adults as well as children are corruptible in morals and character, and that obscenity is a source of corruption that should be eliminated. Obscenity is not suppressed primarily for the protection of others. Much of it is suppressed for the purity of the community and for the salvation and welfare of the 'consumer.' Obscenity, at bottom, is not crime. Obscenity is sin." Henkin, *Morals and the Constitution: The Sin of Obscenity,* 63 Col.L.Rev. 391, 395 (1963).

"It is true that in *Roth* this Court rejected the necessity of proving that exposure to obscene material would create a clear and present danger of antisocial conduct or would probably induce its recipients to such conduct. But that case dealt with public distribution of obscene materials and such distribution is subject to different objections. For example, there is always the danger that obscene material might fall into the hands of children, see *Ginsberg*, or that it might intrude upon the sensibilities or privacy of the general public. No such dangers are present in this [case.]

"We hold that the First and Fourteenth Amendments prohibit making mere private possession of obscene material a crime. *Roth* and the cases following that decision are not impaired by today's holding. As we have said, the States retain broad power to regulate obscenity; that power simply does not extend to mere possession by the individual in the privacy of his own home." [a]

Notes and Questions

1. *Obscenity and the first amendment.* Is *Stanley* consistent with the constitutional theory of *Roth?* Can the first amendment rationally be viewed as applicable to *private use* but not to *public distribution* of obscenity? Cf. Katz, *Privacy and Pornography,* 1969 Sup.Ct.Rev. 203, 210–11. Might the definitional two-level approach reconcile *Stanley* with *Roth?*

2. *Implications of Stanley.* Could *Stanley's* recognition of a first amendment right to "receive" and use obscene matter in the home fairly be viewed as implying a right to purchase it from commercial suppliers, or to import it for personal use, or to view it in a theater limited to consenting adults?

PARIS ADULT THEATRE v. SLATON
413 U.S. 49, 93 S.Ct. 2628, 37 L.Ed.2d 446 (1973).

[The entrance to Paris Adult Theatres I & II was conventional and inoffensive without any pictures. Signs read: "Adult Theatre—You must be 21 and able to prove it. If viewing the nude body offends you, Please Do Not Enter." The District Attorney, nonetheless, had brought an action to enjoin the showing of two films that the Georgia Supreme Court described as "hard core pornography" leaving "little to the imagination." The Georgia Supreme Court assumed that the adult theaters in question barred minors and gave a full warning to the general public of the nature of the films involved, but held that the showing of the films was not constitutionally protected.]

Mr. Chief Justice Burger delivered the opinion of the Court. * * *

[We] categorically disapprove the theory [that] obscene, pornographic films acquire constitutional immunity from state regulation simply because they are exhibited for consenting adults only. [Although we have] recognized the high importance of the state interest in regulating the exposure of obscene materials to juveniles and unconsenting adults, this Court has never declared these to be the only legitimate state interests permitting regulation of obscene material. * * *

[W]e hold that there are legitimate state interests at stake in stemming the tide of commercialized obscenity, even assuming it is feasible to enforce effective

---

a. Black, J., concurred separately. Stewart, J., joined by Brennan and White, JJ.,   concurred in the result on search and seizure grounds.

safeguards against exposure to juveniles and to the passerby.[7] [These] include the interest of the public in the quality of life and the total community environment, the tone of commerce in the great city centers, and, possibly, the public safety itself. The Hill-Link Minority Report of the Commission on Obscenity and Pornography indicates that there is at least an arguable correlation between obscene material and crime. Quite apart from sex crimes, however, there remains one problem of large proportions aptly described by Professor Bickel: "It concerns the tone of the society, the mode, or to use terms that have perhaps greater currency, the style and quality of life, now and in the future. A man may be entitled to read an obscene book in his room, or expose himself indecently there. [We] should protect his privacy. But if he demands a right to obtain the books and pictures he wants in the market, and to foregather in public places—discreet, if you will, but accessible to all—with others who share his tastes, *then to grant him his right is to affect the world about the rest of us, and to impinge on other privacies.* Even supposing that each of us can, if he wishes, effectively avert the eye and stop the ear (which, in truth, we cannot), what is commonly read and seen and heard and done intrudes upon us all, want it or not." 22 *The Public Interest* 25, 25–26 (Winter, 1971). (Emphasis supplied.) [T]here is a "right of the Nation and of the States to maintain a decent [society]," *Jacobellis* (Warren, C.J., dissenting).

But, it is argued, there is no scientific data which conclusively demonstrates that exposure to obscene materials adversely affects men and women or their society. It is urged [that], absent such a demonstration, any kind of state regulation is "impermissible." We reject this argument. It is not for us to resolve empirical uncertainties underlying state legislation, save in the exceptional case where that legislation plainly impinges upon rights protected by the Constitution itself. [Although] there is no conclusive proof of a connection between antisocial behavior and obscene material, the legislature of Georgia could quite reasonably determine that such a connection does or might exist. In deciding *Roth,* this Court implicitly accepted that a legislature could legitimately act on such a conclusion to protect "*the social interest in order and morality.*"

From the beginning of civilized societies, legislators and judges have acted on various unprovable assumptions. Such assumptions underlie much lawful state regulation of commercial and business affairs. See *Ferguson v. Skrupa; Lincoln Fed. Labor Union v. Northwestern Iron & Metal Co.* [p. 263 supra]. The same is true of the federal securities, antitrust laws and a host of other federal regulations. [Likewise], when legislatures and administrators act to protect the physical environment from pollution and to preserve our resources of forests, streams and parks, they must act on such imponderables as the impact of a new highway near or through an existing park or wilderness area. [The] fact that a congressional directive reflects unprovable assumptions about what is good for the people, including imponderable aesthetic assumptions, is not a sufficient reason to find that statute unconstitutional.

7. It is conceivable that an "adult" theatre can—if it really insists—prevent the exposure of its obscene wares to juveniles. An "adult" bookstore, dealing in obscene books, magazines, and pictures, cannot realistically make this claim. The Hill-Link Minority Report of the Commission on Obscenity and Pornography emphasizes evidence (the Abelson National Survey of Youth and Adults) that, although most pornography may be bought by elders, "the heavy users and most highly exposed people to pornography are adolescent females (among women) and adolescent and young males (among men)." *The Report of the Commission on Obscenity 401* (1970). The legitimate interest in preventing exposure of juveniles to obscene materials cannot be fully served by simply barring juveniles from the immediate physical premises of "adult" bookstores, when there is a flourishing "outside business" in these materials.

If we accept the unprovable assumption that a complete education requires certain books, and the well nigh universal belief that good books, plays, and art lift the spirit, improve the mind, enrich the human personality and develop character, can we then say that a state legislature may not act on the corollary assumption that commerce in obscene books,[a] or public exhibitions focused on obscene conduct, have a tendency to exert a corrupting and debasing impact leading to antisocial behavior? [The] sum of experience, including that of the past two decades, affords an ample basis for legislatures to conclude that a sensitive, key relationship of human existence, central to family life, community welfare, and the development of human personality, can be debased and distorted by crass commercial exploitation of sex. Nothing in the Constitution prohibits a State from reaching such a conclusion and acting on it legislatively simply because there is no conclusive evidence or empirical data.

[Nothing] in this Court's decisions intimates that there is any "fundamental" privacy right "implicit in the concept of ordered liberty" to watch obscene movies in places of public accommodation. [W]e have declined to equate the privacy of the home relied on in *Stanley* with a "zone" of "privacy" that follows a distributor or a consumer of obscene materials wherever he goes.[b]

[W]e reject the claim that Georgia is here attempting to control the minds or thoughts of those who patronize theatres. Preventing unlimited display or distribution of obscene material, which by definition lacks any serious literary, artistic, political, or scientific value as communication, is distinct from a control of reason and the intellect. Cf. Finnis, *"Reason and Passion": The Constitutional Dialectic of Free Speech and Obscenity,* 116 U.Pa.L.Rev. 222, 229–230, 241–243 (1967).

[Finally], petitioners argue that conduct which directly involves "consenting adults" only has, for that sole reason, a special claim to constitutional protection. Our Constitution establishes a broad range of conditions on the exercise of power by the States, but for us to say that our Constitution incorporates the proposition that conduct involving consenting adults only is always beyond state regulation,[14] is a step we are unable to take.[15] [The] issue in this context goes beyond

---

a. The only case after *Roth* in which the Court upheld a conviction based upon books was in *Mishkin* and most, if not all, of those books were illustrated. *Kaplan v. California,* 413 U.S. 115, 93 S.Ct. 2680, 37 L.Ed.2d 492 (1973) held that books without pictures can be legally obscene "in the sense of being unprotected by the First Amendment." It observed that books are "passed hand to hand, and we can take note of the tendency of widely circulated books of this category to reach the impressionable young and have a continuing impact. A State could reasonably regard the 'hard core' conduct described by *Suite 69* as capable of encouraging or causing antisocial behavior, especially in its impact on young people." Is *Kaplan's* explanation in tension with *Butler v. Michigan?* Why should the obscenity standard focus on the average adult if the underlying worry is that books will fall in the hands of children?

b. In a series of cases, the Court limited *Stanley* to its facts. It held that *Stanley* did not protect the mailing of obscene material to consenting adults, *United States v. Reidel,* 402

U.S. 351, 91 S.Ct. 1410, 28 L.Ed.2d 813 (1971) or the transporting or importing of obscene materials for private use, *United States v. Orito,* 413 U.S. 139, 93 S.Ct. 2674, 37 L.Ed.2d 513 (1973) (transporting); *United States v. 12 200 Ft. Reels,* 413 U.S. 123, 93 S.Ct. 2665, 37 L.Ed.2d 500 (1973) (importing). Dissenting in *Reels,* Douglas, J., argued that *Stanley* rights could legally be realized "only if one wrote or designed a tract in his attic and printed or processed it in his basement, so as to be able to read it in his study." Do these decisions take the first amendment out of *Stanley?* Are they justified by the rationale in *Paris Adult Theatre?* For example, does importation for personal use intrude "upon us all"? Affect the total community environment?

14. Cf. Mill, *On Liberty* 13 (1955).

15. The state statute books are replete with constitutionally unchallenged laws against prostitution, suicide, voluntary self-mutilation, brutalizing "bare fist" prize fights, and duels, although these crimes may only directly involve "consenting adults." Statutes

whether someone, or even the majority, considers the conduct depicted as "wrong" or "sinful." The States have the power to make a morally neutral judgment that public exhibition of obscene material, or commerce in such material, has a tendency to injure the community as a whole, to endanger the public safety, or to jeopardize, in Mr. Chief Justice Warren's words, the States' "right [to] maintain a decent society." *Jacobellis* (dissenting). * * *

MR. JUSTICE BRENNAN, with whom MR. JUSTICE STEWART and MR. JUSTICE MARSHALL join, dissenting.

[I] am convinced that the approach initiated 15 years ago in *Roth* and culminating in the Court's decision today, cannot bring stability to this area of the law without jeopardizing fundamental First Amendment values, and I have concluded that the time has come to make a significant departure from that [approach.]

[The] decision of the Georgia Supreme Court rested squarely on its conclusion that the State could constitutionally suppress these films even if they were displayed only to persons over the age of 21 who were aware of the nature of their contents and who had consented to viewing them. [I] am convinced of the invalidity of that conclusion [and] would therefore vacate the [judgment]. I have no occasion to consider the extent of State power to regulate the distribution of sexually oriented materials to juveniles or to unconsenting [adults.] [*Stanley*] reflected our emerging view that the state interests in protecting children and in protecting unconsenting adults may stand on a different footing from the other asserted state interests. It may well be, as one commentator has argued, that "exposure to [erotic material] is for some persons an intense emotional experience. A communication of this nature, imposed upon a person contrary to his wishes, has all the characteristics of a physical assault * * *. [And it] constitutes an invasion of his [privacy]."[24] [But] whatever the strength of the state interests in protecting juveniles and unconsenting adults from exposure to sexually oriented materials, those interests cannot be asserted in defense of the holding of the Georgia Supreme Court, [which] assumed for the purposes of its decision that the films in issue were exhibited only to persons over the age of 21 who viewed them willingly and with prior knowledge of the nature of their contents. [The] justification for the suppression must be found, therefore, in some independent interest in regulating the reading and viewing habits of consenting [adults].

In *Stanley* we pointed out that "[t]here appears to be little empirical basis for" the assertion that "exposure to obscene materials may lead to deviant sexual behavior or crimes of sexual violence." In any event, we added that "if the State is only concerned about printed or filmed materials inducing antisocial conduct, we believe that in the context of private consumption of ideas and information we should adhere to the view that '[a]mong free men, the deterrents ordinarily to be applied to prevent crime are education and punishment for violations of the [law].'"

Moreover, in *Stanley* we rejected as "wholly inconsistent with the philosophy of the First Amendment," the notion that there is a legitimate state concern in the "control [of] the moral content of a person's thoughts." [The] traditional description of state police power does embrace the regulation of morals as well as

making bigamy a crime surely cut into an individual's freedom to associate, but few today seriously claim such statutes violate the First Amendment or any other constitutional provision.

24. Emerson, *The System of Freedom of Expression* 496 (1970).

the health, safety, and general welfare of the citizenry. [But] the State's interest in regulating morality by suppressing obscenity, while often asserted, remains essentially unfocused and ill-defined. And, since the attempt to curtail unprotected speech necessarily spills over into the area of protected speech, the effort to serve this speculative interest through the suppression of obscene material must tread heavily on rights protected by the First Amendment. * * *[27]

In short, while I cannot say that the interests of the State—apart from the question of juveniles and unconsenting adults—are trivial or nonexistent, I am compelled to conclude that these interests cannot justify the substantial damage to constitutional rights and to this Nation's judicial machinery that inevitably results from state efforts to bar the distribution even of unprotected material to consenting adults.[c]

MR. JUSTICE DOUGLAS, dissenting. * * *

"Obscenity" at most is the expression of offensive ideas. There are regimes in the world where ideas "offensive" to the majority (or at least to those who control the majority) are suppressed. There life proceeds at a monotonous pace. Most of us would find that world offensive. One of the most offensive experiences in my life was a visit to a nation where bookstalls were filled only with books on mathematics and books on religion.

I am sure I would find offensive most of the books and movies charged with being obscene. But in a life that has not been short, I have yet to be trapped into seeing or reading something that would offend me. I never read or see the materials coming to the Court under charges of "obscenity," because I have thought the First Amendment made it unconstitutional for me to act as a censor.

* * *

When man was first in the jungle he took care of himself. When he entered a societal group, controls were necessarily imposed. But our society—unlike most in the world—presupposes that freedom and liberty are in a frame of reference that makes the individual, not government, the keeper of his tastes, beliefs, and ideas. That is the philosophy of the First Amendment; and it is the article of faith that sets us apart from most nations in the world.

C. A REVISED STANDARD

MILLER v. CALIFORNIA

413 U.S. 15, 93 S.Ct. 2607, 37 L.Ed.2d 419 (1973).

MR. CHIEF JUSTICE BURGER delivered the opinion of the Court. [The Court remanded, "for proceedings not inconsistent" with the opinion's obscenity standard, Miller's conviction under California's obscenity law for mass mailing of unsolicited pictorial advertising brochures depicting men and women in a variety of group sexual activities.]

This is one of a group of "obscenity-pornography" cases being reviewed by the Court in a re-examination of standards enunciated in earlier cases involving what Mr. Justice Harlan called "the intractable obscenity problem." [I]n this context[a] [we] are called on to define the standards which must be used to identify obscene material that a State may [regulate].

---

27. See Henkin, *Morals and the Constitution: The Sin of Obscenity,* 63 Col.L.Rev. 391, 395 (1963).

c. For the portion of Brennan, J.'s dissent addressing the difficulties of formulating an

acceptable constitutional standard, see *Miller v. California,* infra.

a. The "context" was that in *Miller* "sexually explicit materials have been thrust by aggressive sales action upon unwilling recipi-

[E]ven as they repeated the words of *Roth,* the *Memoirs* plurality produced a drastically altered test that called on the prosecution to prove a negative, i.e., that the material was "*utterly* without redeeming social value"—a burden virtually impossible to discharge under our criminal standards of proof. [Apart] from the initial formulation in *Roth,* no majority of the Court has at any given time been able to agree on a standard to determine what constitutes obscene, pornographic material subject to regulation under the States' police power. See, e.g., *Redrup.* [3] This is not remarkable, for in the area of freedom of speech and press the courts must always remain sensitive to any infringement on genuinely serious literary, artistic, political, or scientific expression. * * *

II. This much has been categorically settled by the Court, that obscene material is unprotected by the First Amendment. [We] acknowledge, however, the inherent dangers of undertaking to regulate any form of expression. State statutes designed to regulate obscene materials must be carefully limited. As a result, we now confine the permissible scope of such regulation to works which depict or describe sexual conduct. That conduct must be specifically defined by the applicable state law, as written or authoritatively construed.[6] A state offense must also be limited to works which, taken as a whole, appeal to the prurient interest in sex, which portray sexual conduct in a patently offensive way, and which, taken as a whole, do not have serious literary, artistic, political, or scientific value.

The basic guidelines for the trier of fact must be: (a) whether "the average person, applying contemporary community standards" would find that the work, taken as a whole, appeals to the prurient interest, (b) whether the work depicts or describes, in a patently offensive way, sexual conduct specifically defined by the applicable state law, and (c) whether the work, taken as a whole, lacks serious literary, artistic, political, or scientific value. We do not adopt as a constitutional standard the "*utterly* without redeeming social value" test of *Memoirs;* that concept has never commanded the adherence of more than three Justices at one time.[7] If a state law that regulates obscene material is thus limited, as written or construed, the First Amendment values applicable to the

---

ents." But nothing in *Miller* limited the revised standard to that context, and the companion case, *Paris Adult Theatre,* applied the same standard to dissemination limited to consenting adults.

[3]. In the absence of a majority view, this Court was compelled to embark on the practice of summarily reversing convictions for the dissemination of materials that at least five members of the Court, applying their separate tests, found to be protected by the First Amendment. *Redrup.* [Beyond] the necessity of circumstances, however, no justification has ever been offered in support of the *Redrup* "policy." The *Redrup* procedure has cast us in the role of an unreviewable board of censorship for the 50 States, subjectively judging each piece of material brought before us.

6. See, e.g., Oregon Laws 1971, c. 743, Art. 29, §§ 255–262, and Hawaii Penal Code, Tit. 37, §§ 1210–1216, 1972 Hawaii Session Laws, pp. 126–129, Act 9, Pt. II, as examples of state laws directed at depiction of defined physical conduct, as opposed to expression. [We] do not hold, as Mr. Justice Brennan intimates,

that all States other than Oregon must now enact new obscenity statutes. Other existing state statutes, as construed heretofore or hereafter, may well be adequate.

7. "[We] also reject, as a constitutional standard, the ambiguous concept of 'social importance'." [*Hamling v. United States,* 418 U.S. 87, 94 S.Ct. 2887, 41 L.Ed.2d 590 (1974) upheld a conviction in which the jury had been instructed to find that the material was "utterly without redeeming social value." Defendant argued that the latter phrase was unconstitutionally vague and cited *Miller.* The Court rejected the vagueness challenge: "[O]ur opinion in *Miller* plainly indicates that we rejected the '[social] value' formulation, not because it was so vague as to deprive criminal defendants of adequate notice, but instead because it represented a departure from [*Roth*], and because in calling on the prosecution to 'prove a negative,' it imposed a '[prosecutorial] burden virtually impossible to discharge' and which was not constitutionally required."]

States [are] adequately protected by the ultimate power of appellate courts to conduct an independent review of constitutional claims when necessary.

We emphasize that it is not our function to propose regulatory schemes for the States. [It] is possible, however, to give a few plain examples of what a state statute could define for regulation under the second part (b) of the standard announced in this opinion, supra:

(a) Patently offensive representations or descriptions of ultimate sexual acts, normal or perverted, actual or simulated.

(b) Patently offensive representations or descriptions of masturbation, excretory functions, and lewd exhibition of the genitals.[b]

Sex and nudity may not be exploited without limit by films or pictures exhibited or sold in places of public accommodation any more than live sex and nudity can be exhibited or sold without limit in such public places.[8] At a minimum, prurient,[c] patently offensive depiction or description of sexual conduct must have serious literary, artistic, political, or scientific value to merit First Amendment protection. For example, medical books for the education of physicians and related personnel necessarily use graphic illustrations and descriptions of human anatomy. In resolving the inevitably sensitive questions of fact and law, we must continue to rely on the jury system, accompanied by the safeguards that judges, rules of evidence, presumption of innocence and other protective features [provide].

Mr. Justice Brennan [has] abandoned his former positions and now maintains that no formulation of this Court, the Congress, or the States can adequately distinguish obscene material unprotected by the First Amendment from protected expression, *Paris Adult Theatre v. Slaton* (Brennan, J., dissenting). Paradoxically, Mr. Justice Brennan indicates that suppression of unprotected obscene material is permissible to avoid exposure to unconsenting adults, as in this case, and to juveniles, although he gives no indication of how the division between protected and nonprotected materials may be drawn with greater precision for these purposes than for regulation of commercial exposure to

---

b. *Jenkins v. Georgia*, 418 U.S. 153, 94 S.Ct. 2750, 41 L.Ed.2d 642 (1974) held the film *Carnal Knowledge* not obscene because it did not " 'depict or describe patently offensive "hard core" sexual conduct' " as required by *Miller*: "[While there] are scenes in which sexual conduct including 'ultimate sexual acts' is to be understood to be taking place, the camera does not focus on the bodies of the actors at such times. There is no exhibition whatever of the actors' genitals, lewd or otherwise, during these scenes. There are occasional scenes of nudity, but nudity alone is not enough to make material legally obscene under the *Miller* standards." *Ward v. Illinois*, 431 U.S. 767, 97 S.Ct. 2085, 52 L.Ed.2d 738 (1977) held that it was not necessary for the legislature or the courts to provide an "exhaustive list of the sexual conduct [the] description of which may be held obscene." It is enough that a state adopt *Miller*'s explanatory examples. Stevens, J., joined by Brennan, Stewart and Marshall, JJ., dissented: "[I]f the statute need only describe the 'kinds' of proscribed sexual conduct, it adds no protection to what the Constitution itself creates.

[The] specificity requirement as described in *Miller* held out the promise of a principled effort to respond to [the vagueness] argument. By abandoning that effort today, the Court withdraws the cornerstone of the *Miller* [structure]."

8. Although we are not presented here with the problem of regulating lewd public conduct itself, the States have greater power to regulate nonverbal, physical conduct than to suppress depictions or descriptions of the same behavior. ⋆ ⋆ ⋆

c. *Brockett v. Spokane Arcades, Inc.*, ___ U.S. ___, 105 S.Ct. 2794, 86 L.Ed.2d 394 (1985) held that appeals to prurient interest could not be taken to include appeals to "normal" interests in sex. Only appeals to a "shameful or morbid interest in sex" are prurient. Although the Court was resolute in its position that appeals to "good, old fashioned, healthy" interests in sex were constitutionally protected, it did not further specify how "normal" sex was to be distinguished from the "shameful" or "morbid."

consenting adults only. Nor does he indicate where in the Constitution he finds the authority to distinguish between a willing "adult" one month past the state law age of majority and a willing "juvenile" one month younger.

Under the holdings announced today, no one will be subject to prosecution for the sale or exposure of obscene materials unless these materials depict or describe patently offensive "hard core" sexual conduct specifically defined by the regulating state law, as written or construed. We are satisfied that these specific prerequisites will provide fair notice to a dealer in such materials that his public and commercial activities may bring prosecution. If the inability to define regulated materials with ultimate, god-like precision altogether removes the power of the States or the Congress to regulate, then "hard core" pornography may be exposed without limit to the juvenile, the passerby, and the consenting adult alike, as indeed, Mr. Justice Douglas contends.

[N]o amount of "fatigue" should lead us to adopt a convenient "institutional" rationale—an absolutist, "anything goes" view of the First Amendment—because it will lighten our burdens. [Nor] should we remedy "tension between state and federal courts" by arbitrarily depriving the States of a power reserved to them under the Constitution, a power which they have enjoyed and exercised continuously from before the adoption of the First Amendment to this day. See *Roth*. "Our duty admits of no 'substitute for facing up to the tough individual problems of constitutional judgment involved in every obscenity case.'" *Jacobellis* (opinion of Brennan, J.).

III. Under a national Constitution, fundamental First Amendment limitations on the powers of the States do not vary from community to community, but this does not mean that there are, or should or can be, fixed, uniform national standards of precisely what appeals to the "prurient interest" or is "patently offensive." These are essentially questions of fact, and our nation is simply too big and too diverse for this Court to reasonably expect that such standards could be articulated for all 50 States in a single formulation, even assuming the prerequisite consensus exists. When triers of fact are asked to decide whether "the average person, applying contemporary community standards" would consider certain materials "prurient," it would be unrealistic to require that the answer be based on some abstract formulation. The adversary system, with lay jurors as the usual ultimate factfinders in criminal prosecutions, has historically permitted triers-of-fact to draw on the standards of their community, guided always by limiting instructions on the law. To require a State to structure obscenity proceedings around evidence of a *national* "community standard" would be an exercise in [futility].

We conclude that neither the State's alleged failure to offer evidence of "national standards," nor the trial court's charge that the jury consider state community standards, were constitutional errors. Nothing in the First Amendment requires that a jury must consider hypothetical and unascertainable "national standards" when attempting to determine whether certain materials are obscene as a matter of [fact].

It is neither realistic nor constitutionally sound to read the First Amendment as requiring that the people of Maine or Mississippi accept public depiction of conduct found tolerable in Las Vegas, or New York City. People in different States vary in their tastes and attitudes, and this diversity is not to be strangled by the absolutism of imposed uniformity. As the Court made clear in *Mishkin*, the primary concern with requiring a jury to apply the standard of "the average person, applying contemporary community standards" is to be certain that, so far as material is not aimed at a deviant group, it will be judged by its impact on an average person, rather than a particularly susceptible or sensitive person—or indeed a totally insensitive one.[d] [We] hold the requirement that the jury evaluate the materials with reference to "contemporary standards of the State of California" serves this protective purpose and is constitutionally adequate.[e]

* * *

In sum we (a) reaffirm the *Roth* holding that obscene material is not protected by the First Amendment, (b) hold that such material can be regulated by the States, subject to the specific safeguards enunciated above, without a showing that the material is "*utterly* without redeeming social value," and (c) hold that obscenity is to be determined by applying "contemporary community standards," not "national standards." * * *

MR. JUSTICE DOUGLAS, dissenting. * * *

My contention is that until a civil proceeding has placed a tract beyond the pale, no criminal prosecution should be sustained. For no more vivid illustration of vague and uncertain laws could be designed than those we have fashioned. [If] a specific book [or] motion picture has in a civil proceeding been condemned as obscene and review of that finding has been completed, and thereafter a person publishes [or] displays that particular book or film, then a vague law has been made specific. There would remain the underlying question whether the First Amendment allows an implied exception in the case of obscenity. I do not think it does and my views on the issue have been stated over and again. But at least a criminal prosecution brought at that juncture would not violate the time-honored void-for-vagueness test.[8]

No such protective procedure has been designed by California in this case. Obscenity—which even we cannot define with precision—is a hodge-podge. To send men to jail for violating standards they cannot understand, construe, and apply is a monstrous thing to do in a Nation dedicated to fair trials and due process. * * *

MR. JUSTICE BRENNAN, with whom MR. JUSTICE STEWART and MR. JUSTICE MARSHALL join, dissenting.

In my dissent in *Paris Adult Theatre,* decided this date, I noted that I had no occasion to consider the extent of state power to regulate the distribution of

---

d. *Pinkus v. United States,* 436 U.S. 293, 98 S.Ct. 1808, 56 L.Ed.2d 293 (1978) upheld a jury instruction stating "you are to judge these materials by the standard of the hypothetical average person in the community, but in determining this average standard you must include the *sensitive and the insensitive,* in other words, [everyone] in the community." On the other hand, in the absence of evidence that "children were the intended recipients" or that defendant "had reason to know children were likely to receive the materials," it was considered erroneous to instruct the jury that children were part of the relevant community. *Butler.* When the evidence would support such a charge, the Court stated that prurient appeal to deviant sexual groups could be substituted for appeal to the average person; moreover, the jury was entitled to take pandering into account. *Ginzburg.*

e. *Jenkins,* fn. b supra, stated that a judge may instruct a jury to apply "contemporary community standards" without any further specification. Alternatively, the state may choose "to define the standards in more precise geographic terms, as was done by California in *Miller.*" *Hamling v. United States,* fn. 7 supra, interpreted a federal obscenity statute to make the relevant community the one from which the jury was drawn. The judge's instruction to consider the "community standards of the 'nation as a whole' delineated a wider geographical area than would be warranted by [*Miller*]" or the Court's construction of the statute, but the error was regarded as harmless under the circumstances. After these decisions, what advice should lawyers give to publishers who distribute in national markets?

8. The Commission on Obscenity and Pornography has advocated such a procedure. [See] *Report of the Commission on Obscenity and Pornography* 70–71 (1970).

sexually oriented material to juveniles or the offensive exposure of such material to unconsenting adults. [I] need not now decide whether a statute might be drawn to impose, within the requirements of the First Amendment, criminal penalties for the precise conduct at issue here. For it is clear that under my dissent in *Paris Adult Theatre,* the statute under which the prosecution was brought is unconstitutionally overbroad, and therefore invalid on its face.

* * *

[In his *Paris Adult Theatre* dissent, Justice Brennan, joined by Stewart and Marshall, JJ., argued that the state interests in regulating obscenity were not strong enough to justify the degree of vagueness. He criticized not only the Court's standard in *Miller,* but also a range of alternatives:]

II.   [The] essence of our problem [is] that we have been unable to provide "sensitive tools" to separate obscenity from other sexually oriented but constitutionally protected speech, so that efforts to suppress the former do not spill over into the suppression of the latter. [The dissent traced the Court's experience with *Roth* and its progeny.]

III.   Our experience with the *Roth* approach has certainly taught us that the outright suppression of obscenity cannot be reconciled with the fundamental principles of the First and Fourteenth Amendments. For we have failed to formulate a standard that sharply distinguishes protected from unprotected speech, and out of necessity, we have resorted to the *Redrup* approach, which resolves cases as between the parties, but offers only the most obscure guidance to legislation, adjudication by other courts, and primary conduct. [T]he vagueness problem would be largely of our own creation if it stemmed primarily from our failure to reach a consensus on any one standard. But after 15 years of experimentation and debate I am reluctantly forced to the conclusion that none of the available formulas, including the one announced today, can reduce the vagueness to a tolerable level while at the same time striking an acceptable balance between the protections of the First and Fourteenth Amendments, on the one hand, and on the other the asserted state interest in regulating the dissemination of certain sexually oriented materials. Any effort to draw a constitutionally acceptable boundary on state power must resort to such indefinite concepts as "prurient interest," "patent offensiveness," "serious literary value," and the like. The meaning of these concepts necessarily varies with the experience, outlook, and even idiosyncracies of the person defining them. Although we have assumed that obscenity does exist and that we "know it when [we] see it," *Jacobellis* (Stewart, J., concurring), we are manifestly unable to describe it in advance except by reference to concepts so elusive that they fail to distinguish clearly between protected and unprotected speech.

[Added to the inherent vagueness of standards] is the further complication that the obscenity of any particular item may depend upon nuances of presentation and the context of its dissemination. See *Ginzburg.* [N]o one definition, no matter how precisely or narrowly drawn, can possibly suffice for all situations, or carve out fully suppressable expression from all media without also creating a substantial risk of encroachment upon the guarantees of the Due Process Clause and the First Amendment.

[The] resulting level of uncertainty is utterly intolerable, not alone because it makes "[b]ookselling [a] hazardous profession," *Ginsberg* (Fortas, J., dissenting), but as well because it invites arbitrary and erratic enforcement of the law. [We] have indicated that "stricter standards of permissible statutory vagueness may be applied to a statute having a potentially inhibiting effect on speech; a man may the less be required to act at his peril here, because the free dissemination of ideas may be the loser." * * *

The problems of fair notice and chilling protected speech are very grave standing alone. But [a] vague statute in this area creates a third [set] of problems. These [concern] the institutional stress that inevitably results where the line separating protected from unprotected speech is excessively vague. [Almost] every obscenity case presents a constitutional question of exceptional difficulty. [As] a result of our failure to define standards with predictable application to any given piece of material, there is no probability of regularity in obscenity decisions by state and lower federal courts. [O]ne cannot say with certainty that material is obscene until at least five members of this Court, applying inevitably obscure standards, have pronounced it [so].

We have managed the burden of deciding scores of obscenity cases by relying on per curiam reversals or denials of certiorari—a practice which conceals the rationale of decision and gives at least the appearance of arbitrary action by this Court. More important, [the] practice effectively censors protected expression by leaving lower court determinations of obscenity intact even though the status of the allegedly obscene material is entirely unsettled until final review here. In addition, the uncertainty of the standards creates a continuing source of tension between state and federal [courts].

The severe problems arising from the lack of fair notice, from the chill on protected expression, and from the stress imposed on the state and federal judicial machinery persuade me that a significant change in direction is urgently required. I turn, therefore, to the alternatives that are now open.

IV. 1. The approach requiring the smallest deviation from our present course would be to draw a new line between protected and unprotected speech, still permitting the States to suppress all material on the unprotected side of the line. In my view, clarity cannot be obtained pursuant to this approach except by drawing a line that resolves all doubts in favor of state power and against the guarantees of the First Amendment. We could hold, for example, that any depiction or description of human sexual organs, irrespective of the manner or purpose of the portrayal, is outside the protection of the First Amendment and therefore open to suppression by the States. That formula would, no doubt, offer much fairer notice [and] give rise to a substantial probability of regularity in most judicial determinations under the standard. But such a standard would be appallingly overbroad, permitting the suppression of a vast range of literary, scientific, and artistic masterpieces. Neither the First Amendment nor any free community could possibly tolerate such a standard.

2. [T]he Court today recognizes that a prohibition against any depiction or description of human sexual organs could not be reconciled with the guarantees of the First Amendment. But the Court [adopts] a restatement of the *Roth-Memoirs* definition of obscenity [that] permits suppression if the government can prove that the materials lack "*serious* literary, artistic, political or scientific value." [In] *Roth* we held that certain expression is obscene, and thus outside the protection of the First Amendment, precisely *because* it lacks even the slightest redeeming social value. [The] Court's approach necessarily assumes that some works will be deemed obscene—even though they clearly have *some* social value—because the State was able to prove that the value, measured by some unspecified standard, was not sufficiently "serious" to warrant constitutional protection. That result [is] nothing less than a rejection of the fundamental First Amendment premises and rationale of the *Roth* opinion and an

invitation to widespread suppression of sexually oriented speech. Before today, the protections of the First Amendment have never been thought limited to expressions of *serious* literary or political value. *Gooding v. Wilson; Cohen v. California; Terminiello v. Chicago* [Part IV infra].

[T]he Court's approach [can] have no ameliorative impact on the cluster of problems that grow out of the vagueness of our current standards. Indeed, even the Court makes no argument that the reformulation will provide fairer notice to booksellers, theatre owners, and the reading and viewing public. Nor does the Court contend that the approach will provide clearer guidance to law enforcement officials or reduce the chill on protected expression [or] mitigate [the] institutional [problems].

Of course, the Court's restated *Roth* test does limit the definition of obscenity to depictions of physical conduct and explicit sexual acts. And that limitation may seem, at first glance, a welcome and clarifying addition to the *Roth-Memoirs* formula. But just as the agreement in *Roth* on an abstract definition of obscenity gave little hint of the extreme difficulty that was to follow in attempting to apply that definition to specific material, the mere formulation of a "physical conduct" test is no assurance that it can be applied with any greater facility. [The] Court surely demonstrates little sensitivity to our own institutional problems, much less the other vagueness-related difficulties, in establishing a system that requires us to consider whether a description of human genitals is sufficiently "lewd" to deprive it of constitutional protection; whether a sexual act is "ultimate"; whether the conduct depicted in materials before us fits within one of the categories of conduct whose depiction the state or federal governments have attempted to suppress; and a host of equally pointless inquiries. * * *

If the application of the "physical conduct" test to pictorial material is fraught with difficulty, its application to textual material carries the potential for extraordinary abuse. Surely we have passed the point where the mere written description of sexual conduct is deprived of First Amendment protection. Yet the test offers no guidance to us, or anyone else, in determining which written descriptions of sexual conduct are protected, and which are not.

Ultimately, the reformulation must fail because it still leaves in this Court the responsibility of determining in each case whether the materials are protected by the First Amendment. * * *

3. I have also considered the possibility of reducing our own role, and the role of appellate courts generally, in determining whether particular matter is obscene. Thus, [we] might adopt the position that where a lower federal or state court has conscientiously applied the constitutional standard, its finding of obscenity will be no more vulnerable to reversal by this Court than any finding of fact. [E]ven if the Constitution would permit us to refrain from judging for ourselves the alleged obscenity of particular materials, that approach would solve at best only a small part of our problem. For while it would mitigate the institutional stress, [it] would neither offer nor produce any cure for the other vices of vagueness. Far from providing a clearer guide to permissible primary conduct, the approach would inevitably lead to even greater uncertainty and the consequent due process problems of fair notice. And the approach would expose much protected, sexually oriented expression to the vagaries of jury determinations. Plainly, the institutional gain would be more than offset by the unprecedented infringement of First Amendment rights.

4. Finally, I have considered the view, urged so forcefully since 1957 by our Brothers Black and Douglas, that the First Amendment bars the suppression of any sexually oriented expression. That position would effect a sharp reduction, although perhaps not a total elimination, of the uncertainty that surrounds our current approach. Nevertheless, I am convinced that it would achieve that desirable goal only by stripping the States of power to an extent that cannot be justified by the commands of the Constitution, at least so long as there is available an alternative approach that strikes a better balance between the guarantee of free expression and the States' legitimate interests.

[I] f would hold, therefore, that at least in the absence of distribution to juveniles or obtrusive exposure to unconsenting adults, the First and Fourteenth Amendments prohibit the state and federal governments from attempting wholly to suppress sexually oriented materials on the basis of their allegedly "obscene" contents. Nothing in this approach precludes those governments from taking action to serve what may be strong and legitimate interests through regulation of the manner of distribution of sexually oriented material.

VI. [I] do not pretend to have found a complete and infallible [answer]. Difficult questions must still be faced, notably in the areas of distribution to juveniles and offensive exposure to unconsenting adults. Whatever the extent of state power to regulate in those areas,[29] it should be clear that the view I espouse today would introduce a large measure of clarity to this troubled area, would reduce the institutional pressure on this Court and the rest of the State and Federal judiciary, and would guarantee fuller freedom of expression while leaving room for the protection of legitimate governmental interests. * * *

Notes and Questions

1. *Serious value.* Consider Clor, *Obscenity and the First Amendment: Round Three,* 7 Loy.L.A.L.Rev. 207, 210, 218 (1974): "The *Miller* decision abandons the requirement that a censorable work must be '*utterly* without redeeming social value' and substitutes the rule of 'serious value'—literary, artistic, political, or scientific. This is the most important innovation in the law of obscenity introduced by these decisions. [Serious] literature is to be protected regardless of majority opinions about prurience and offensiveness. *This* is the national principle which is not subject to variation from community to community. If it is to perform this function, the rule will have to be elaborated and the meaning of 'serious value' articulated in some measure. This is the most important item on the legal agenda."

(a) *An independent factor?* Under *Miller* would material found to have "serious artistic value" be entitled to first amendment protection regardless how offensive or prurient? Must each factor in the *Miller* guidelines be independently satisfied, as in *Memoirs? Should* that be so? Would or should that preclude the degree of offensiveness or prurient appeal from affecting the conclusion on the value factor?

(b) *"Serious."* Do you find any guidance for determining when a first amendment value in material depicting sexual conduct is sufficiently "serious" to preclude finding it obscene? Can the "serious" value requisite be reconciled

---

f. For the portion of Brennan, J.'s dissent addressing the strength and legitimacy of the state interests, see *Paris Adult Theatre,* supra.

29. The Court erroneously states, *Miller,* that the author of this opinion "indicates that suppression of unprotected obscene material is permissible to avoid exposure to unconsenting adults [and] to juveniles * * *." I defer expression of my views as to the scope of state power in these areas until cases squarely presenting these questions are before the Court.

with the first amendment? May material fairly be viewed as having "serious value" whenever the "intent is to convey a literary, artistic, political or scientific idea or message, or to impart information, or advocate a position" rather than "to 'dress up' or try to 'redeem' otherwise obscene matter?" Cf. Schauer, supra, at 140.

(c) *Scope of protected values.* Could the Court consistent with the first amendment exclude serious educational value from those that preclude a finding of obscenity? Serious entertainment value? Could the guidelines be interpreted to include such values? What might explain their omission?

(d) *Based on "community" standards?* Under *Miller* is the presence of "serious value" to be determined under "contemporary community standards" like the offensiveness and pruriency factors? Would this be consistent with the first amendment? With *Miller's* stress on the Court's duty to face up to "the tough individual problems of constitutional judgment in every obscenity case"? Cf. 87 Harv.L.Rev. 169 (1973).

2. *Vagueness and scienter.* Is the *Miller* test intolerably vague? Are there any alternatives that could mitigate the problem? Consider Lockhart, *Escape from the Chill of Uncertainty: Explicit Sex and the First Amendment*, 9 Ga.L. Rev. 533, 563 (1975): "[E]ither legislative action, or constitutional adjudication, could establish as a defense to a criminal obscenity prosecution that the defendant *reasonably believed* that the material involved was not obscene, that is, was constitutionally protected. [Material] that would support such a court or jury finding is not the kind that requires or justifies quick action by the police and prosecutor. The public interest in preventing distribution of borderline material that can reasonably be believed not obscene is not so pressing as to require immediate criminal sanctions and can adequately be protected by a declaratory judgment or injunction action to establish the obscenity of the material."

Smith v. California, 361 U.S. 147, 80 S.Ct. 215, 4 L.Ed.2d 205 (1959) invalidated an ordinance that dispensed with any requirement that a seller of an obscene book have knowledge of its contents, but did not decide what sort of mental element was needed to prosecute. *Hamling v. United States,* supra, stated that it was constitutionally sufficient to show that a distributor of an advertising collage of pictures of sexual acts "had knowledge of the contents of the materials [and] that he knew the character and nature of the materials." Would it be consistent with *Hamling* to afford constitutional protection to a distributor who reasonably believed the material disseminated was not obscene? See Lockhart, supra, at 568.

D. VAGUENESS AND OVERBREADTH: AN OVERVIEW

In *Paris Adult Theatre,* Brennan, J., dissents on the ground that the obscenity statute is unconstitutionally vague. He envisions the possibility that an obscenity statute might overcome his vagueness objection if it were tailored to combat distribution to unconsenting adults or to children. In *Miller,* the materials were in fact distributed to unconsenting adults. There Brennan, J., does not reach the vagueness question but objects on the ground that the statute is overbroad,—i.e., it is not confined to the protection of unconsenting adults and children, but also prohibits distribution of obscene materials to consenting adults. In Brennan, J.'s view, even if the particular conduct at issue in *Miller* might be constitutionally prohibited by a narrower statute, it cannot be reached under a statute that sweeps so much protected speech within its terms.

The doctrines of "vagueness" and "overbreadth" referred to in Brennan, J.'s dissents are deeply embedded in first amendment jurisprudence. At first glance, the doctrines appear discrete. A statute that prohibits the use of the words "kill" and "President" in the same sentence may not be vague, but it is certainly overbroad even though some sentences using those words may be unprotected. Conversely, a vague statute may not be overbroad; it may not pertain to first amendment freedoms at all, or it may clearly be intended to exclude all protected speech from its prohibition but use vague language to accomplish that purpose.

Ordinarily, however, the problems of "vagueness" and "overbreadth" are closely related; indeed the two concepts often merge. Consider, for example, an actual and a hypothetical "red flag" ban. A statute prohibiting anyone from "publicly display[ing] a red flag [or] device of any color or form whatever [as] a sign, symbol or emblem of opposition to organized government" was held fatally vague in *Stromberg v. California*, 283 U.S. 359, 51 S.Ct. 532, 75 L.Ed. 1117 (1931). The statute purported to be less than a total ban, but how much less was ambiguous and uncertain. The "opposition to organized government" language was vague because it might (or might not) be read as banning constitutionally protected red flag displays, e.g., those flown as an expression of peaceful and orderly opposition to the political party currently in power by members of another political party. But a hypothetical "absolute ban" on red flag displays, for any reason or under any circumstances, although *superficially* clear, would presumably also be struck down—for "overbreadth." The same may be said for a hypothetical statute "absolutely banning" picketing or parades—or the sale of literature containing any description of human sexual organs, regardless of the manner or purpose of the portrayal, the dominant theme of the material, the primary audience to which it is sold, or the social, literary, scientific or artistic value of the work.

The *language* of these hypothetical bans may not be vague, but if the language literally covers a variety of constitutionally protected activities, it *cannot be read literally*. Thus, the clarity of the language "is delusive, since it will have to be recast in order to separate the constitutional from the unconstitutional applications. If it is read as applicable only where constitutionally so, the reading uncovers the vagueness that is latent in its terms" and the problem of an "overbroad" law can emerge as "a special case of the problem of vagueness." See Freund, *The Supreme Court of the United States* 67–68 (1961). In other words, one may regard the aforementioned "overbroad" hypothetical statutes as no less vague and indefinite than laws whose very language forbids the public display of a red flag "except where one is constitutionally entitled to display it" or bans picketing "unless, under the circumstances, such conduct is constitutionally protected" or bars literature containing descriptions of human sexual organs "except where such descriptions do not constitute sufficient cause to deny the material the constitutional protection of freedom of speech and press."

Of course, statutes may be interpreted in ways that will avoid vagueness or overbreadth difficulties. See, e.g., *Scales v. United States*, p. 450 supra. It is established doctrine, for example, that an attack based either upon vagueness or overbreadth will be unsuccessful in federal court if the statute in question is "readily subject to a narrowing construction by the state courts." *Young v. American Mini-Theatres, Inc.; Erznoznik v. Jacksonville*, Part VI, A infra.

Moreover, "[f]or the purpose of determining whether a state statute is too vague and indefinite to constitute valid legislation [the Court takes] 'the statute as though it read precisely as the highest court of the State has interpreted it.'" *Wainwright v. Stone,* 414 U.S. 21, 94 S.Ct. 190, 38 L.Ed.2d 179 (1973). Under this policy, a litigant can be prosecuted successfully for violating a statute that by its terms appears vague or overbroad but is interpreted by the state court in the same prosecution to mean something clearer or narrower than its literal language would dictate. *Cox v. New Hampshire,* p. 642 infra. The harshness of this doctrine is mitigated somewhat by the fact that "unexpected" or "unforeseeable" judicial constructions in such contexts violate due process. See *Marks v. United States,* 430 U.S. 188, 97 S.Ct. 990, 51 L.Ed.2d 260 (1977).

Somewhat more complicated is the issue of when general attacks on a statute are permitted. Plainly litigants may argue that statutes are vague as to their own conduct or that their own speech is protected. In other words, litigants are always free to argue that a statute is invalid "as applied" to their own conduct. The dispute concerns when litigants can attack a statute without reference to their own conduct, an attack sometimes called "on its face."

A separate question is: when should such attacks result in partial or total invalidation of a statute? The terminology here has become as confused as the issues. In the past, the Court has frequently referred to facial attacks on statutes in a way that embraces attempts at either partial or total invalidation. In some recent opinions, however, including those quoted below, it uses the term "facial attack" or "on its face" to refer only to arguments seeking total invalidation of a statute.

Terminology aside, one of the recurrent questions has been the extent to which litigants may argue that a statute is unconstitutionally overbroad even though their own conduct would not otherwise be constitutionally protected. This is often characterized as a standing issue. Ordinarily litigants do not have standing to raise the rights of others. See Ch. 13, Sec. 1, II, B. But, it has been argued that "[u]nder 'conventional' standing principles, a litigant has always had the right to be judged in accordance with a constitutionally valid rule of law." Monaghan, *Overbreadth,* 1981 S.Ct.Rev. 1, 3. On this view, if a statute is unconstitutionally overbroad, it is not a valid rule of law, and any defendant prosecuted under the statute has standing to raise the overbreadth issue.[a] However the issue may be characterized, White, J., has contended for many years that a litigant whose own conduct is unprotected should not prevail on an overbreadth challenge without a showing that the statute's overbreadth is "real and substantial." After much litigation, White, J., has finally prevailed. The "substantial" overbreadth doctrine now burdens all litigants who argue that a statute should be declared overbroad when their own conduct is unprotected.[b] *Brockett v. Spokane Arcades, Inc.; New York v. Ferber,* p. 537 infra.

Less clear are the circumstances in which a litigant whose conduct *is* protected can go beyond a claim that the statute is unconstitutional "as applied." Again, litigants are always free to argue that their own conduct is protected. Moreover, the Court has stated that "[t]here is no reason to limit challenges to

a. For more recent elaboration, see Monaghan, *Third Party Standing,* 84 Colum.L. Rev. 277 (1984). See also Sedler, *The Assertion of Constitutional Jus Tertii: A Substantive Approach,* 70 Calif.L.Rev. 1308, 1327 (1982) ("It may be the potential chilling effect upon others' expression that makes the statute invalid, but the litigant has his own right

not to be subject to the operation of an invalid statute.").

b. For commentary on the concept of "substantial" overbreadth, see Redish, *The Warren Court, The Burger Court and the First Amendment Overbreadth Doctrine,* 78 Nw.U.L.Rev. 1031, 1056–69 (1983).

case-by-case 'as applied' challenges when the statute [in] all its applications falls short of constitutional demands." [c] *Maryland v. Joseph H. Munson Co.,* 467 U.S. 947, 104 S.Ct. 2839, 81 L.Ed.2d 786 (1984). How far beyond this the Court will go is unclear. In *Brockett v. Spokane Arcades, Inc.,* p. 508 supra, it referred to the "normal rule that partial, rather than facial invalidation" of statutes is to be preferred and observed that: "[A]n individual whose own speech or expressive conduct may validly be prohibited or sanctioned is permitted to challenge a statute on its face because it also threatens others not before the court—those who desire to engage in legally protected expression but who may refrain from doing so rather than risk prosecution or undertake to have the law declared partially invalid. If the overbreadth is 'substantial,' the law may not be enforced against anyone, including the party before the court, until it is narrowed to reach only unprotected activity, whether by legislative action or by judicial construction or partial invalidation.

"It is otherwise where the parties challenging the statute are those who desire to engage in protected speech that the overbroad statute purports to punish, or who seek to publish both protected and unprotected material. There is then no want of a proper party to challenge the statute, no concern that an attack on the statute will be unduly delayed or protected speech discouraged. The statute may forthwith be declared invalid to the extent that it reaches too far, but otherwise left intact." [d]

Brockett takes the view that it must give standing to the otherwise unprotected to raise an overbreadth challenge, in order to secure the rights of those whose speech should be protected. But it sees no purpose in giving standing to the protected in order to secure rights for those whose speech should not be protected. This position is not without its ironies. In some circumstances, a litigant whose speech is unprotected will be in a better position than one whose speech is protected, at least if the litigant's goal is completely to stop enforcement of a statute. Viewed from a standing perspective, those whose speech is protected have no standing to invoke the substantial overbreadth doctrine. Viewed as a substantive rule of law, the substantial overbreadth challenge is selectively available.

The issues with respect to vagueness challenges are similar. It remains possible, however, that the Court will resolve them in ways different from the approaches it has fashioned in the law of overbreadth. White, J., clearly would pursue a different course. He has suggested that vagueness challenges should be confined to "as applied" attacks unless a statute is vague in all of its applications. Accordingly, if a statute clearly proscribes the conduct of a particular defendant, to allow that defendant to challenge a statute for vagueness is in his view "to confound vagueness and overbreadth." *Kolender v. Lawson,* 461 U.S. 352, 103 S.Ct. 1855, 75 L.Ed.2d 903 (1983) (White, J., dissenting). In response,

c. There is a terminological dispute here. Compare *Los Angeles City Council v. Taxpayers For Vincent,* p. 690 infra (such challenges are not overbreadth challenges) with *Munson,* supra (such challenges are properly called overbreadth challenges).

d. After the Court has declared that the statute is invalid to the extent it reaches too far, the remaining portion of the statute will be examined to determine whether that portion is severable. That is, it could well be the intent of the legislature that the statute

stands or falls as a single package. To invalidate a part, then, could be to invalidate the whole. Alternatively, the legislature may have intended to salvage whatever it might. The question of severability is regarded as one of legislative intent, but, at least with respect to federal legislation, courts will presume that severability was intended. See, e.g., *Regan v. Time, Inc.,* ___ U.S. ___, 104 S.Ct. 3262, 82 L.Ed.2d 487 (1984). The question of whether a provision of a state statute is severable is one of state law.

the Court has stated that a facial attack upon a statute need not depend upon a showing of vagueness in all of a statute's applications: "[W]e permit a facial challenge if a law reaches 'a substantial amount of constitutionally protected conduct,'" *Kolender,* supra. Moreover, the Court has previously allowed litigants to raise the vagueness issue "even though there is no uncertainty about the impact of the ordinances on their own rights." *Young.* But see, e.g., *Broadrick v. Oklahoma,* p. 535 infra, in which White, J., writing for the Court suggests that standing to raise the vagueness argument should not be permitted in this situation.

Much less clear are the circumstances in which litigants whose conduct is *not* clearly covered by a statute can go beyond an "as applied" attack.[e] One approach would be to apply the same rule to all litigants, e.g., allowing total invalidation of statutes upon a showing of a "substantial" vagueness. In *Kolender,* the Court made no determination whether the statute involved was vague as to the defendant's own conduct; arguably, the opinion implied that it made no difference. Another approach would analogize to the approach suggested in *Brockett* for overbreadth challenges. Thus, a court might refrain from total invalidation of a statute and confine itself to striking the vague part insofar as the vague part seems to cover protected speech, leaving the balance of the statute intact. *Kolender* itself recites that the Court has "traditionally regarded vagueness and overbreadth as logically related and similar doctrines," but the Court's attitudes toward vagueness remain unclear. The questions of what standards should govern challenges to statutes that go beyond the facts before the Court, who should be able to raise the challenges, and under what circumstances continue to divide the Court.[f]

IV. "FIGHTING WORDS," OFFENSIVE WORDS AND HOSTILE AUDIENCES

A. FIGHTING WORDS

CHAPLINSKY v. NEW HAMPSHIRE, 315 U.S. 568, 62 S.Ct. 766, 86 L.Ed. 1031 (1942): In the course of proselytizing on the streets, appellant, a Jehovah's Witness, denounced organized religion. Despite the city marshal's warning to "go slow" because his listeners were upset with his attacks on religion, appellant continued and a disturbance occurred. At this point, a police officer led appellant toward the police station, without arresting him. While enroute, appellant again encountered the city marshal who had previously admonished him. Appellant then said to the marshal (he claimed, but the marshal denied, in response to the marshal's cursing him): "You are a God damned racketeer" and "a damned Fascist and the whole government of Rochester are Fascists or agents of Fascists." He was convicted of violating a state statute forbidding anyone to address "any offensive, derisive or annoying word to any other person who is

e. Conceivably, it could make a difference whether the litigants in this class of those "not clearly covered" have engaged in protected or unprotected conduct.

f. For commentary on vagueness and overbreadth, see, e.g., *Nimmer on Freedom of Speech,* 4–147—4–162 (1984); Alexander, *Is There an Overbreadth Doctrine?,* 22 San Diego L.Rev. 541 (1985); Amsterdam, *The Void-For-Vagueness Doctrine in the Supreme Court,* 109 U.Pa.L.Rev. 67 (1960); Bogen, *First Amendment Ancillary Doctrines,* 37 Md.L.Rev. 679, 705–26 (1978); Monaghan, supra; Redish, supra; Note, *The First Amendment Overbreadth Doctrine,* 83 Harv.L.Rev. 844 (1970). On the relationship between the overbreadth doctrine and the less drastic means test, see fn. b in *Central Hudson Gas & Elec. Corp. v. Public Serv. Comm'n,* p. 565 infra.

lawfully in any [public place] [or] call[ing] him by any offensive or derisive name." The Court, per MURPHY, J., upheld the conviction:

"There are certain well-defined and narrowly limited classes of speech, the prevention and punishment of which have never been thought to raise any Constitutional problem.[a] These include the lewd and obscene, the profane, the libelous, and the insulting or 'fighting' words—those which by their very utterance inflict injury or tend to incite an immediate breach of the peace. [S]uch utterances are no essential part of any exposition of ideas, and are of such slight social value as a step to truth that any benefit that may be derived from them is clearly outweighed by the social interest in order and morality. * * *

"On the authority of its earlier decisions, the state court declared that the statute's purpose was to preserve the public peace, no words being 'forbidden except such as have a direct tendency to cause acts of violence by the person to whom, individually, the remark is addressed'. It was further said: 'The word "offensive" is not to be defined in terms of what a particular addressee thinks. [The] test is what men of common intelligence would understand would be words likely to cause an average addressee to fight. [The] English language has a number of words and expressions which by general consent are "fighting words" when said without a disarming smile. [Such] words, as ordinary men know, are likely to cause a fight. So are threatening, profane or obscene revilings. Derisive and annoying words can be taken as coming within the purview of the statute as heretofore interpreted only when they have this characteristic of plainly tending to excite the addressee to a breach of the peace. [The] statute, as construed, does no more than prohibit the face-to-face words plainly likely to cause a breach of the peace by the addressee, words whose speaking constitute a breach of the peace by the speaker—including "classical fighting words", words in current use less "classical" but equally likely to cause violence, and other disorderly words, including profanity, obscenity and threats.'

"[A] statute punishing verbal acts, carefully drawn so as not unduly to impair liberty of expression, is not too vague for a criminal law. * * *[8]

"Nor can we say that the application of the statute to the facts disclosed by the record substantially or unreasonably impinges upon the privilege of free speech. Argument is unnecessary to demonstrate that the appellations 'damn

---

a. See Haiman, *How Much of Our Speech is Free?*, The Civ.Lib.Rev., Winter, 1975, pp. 111, 123: "[T]his discrimination between two classes of speech made its first U.S. Supreme Court appearance in *Cantwell v. Connecticut* (1940) [p. 842 infra]." Jehovah's Witnesses had been convicted of religious solicitation without a permit and of breach of the peace. The Court set aside both convictions. It invalidated the permit system for "religious" solicitation, because it permitted the licensing official to determine what causes were "religious," thus allowing a "censorship of religion." In setting aside the breach of peace conviction, because the offense covered much protected conduct and left "too wide a discretion in its application," the Court, per Roberts, J., noted: "One may, however, be guilty of [breach of the peace] if he commits acts or makes statements likely to provoke violence and disturbance of good order. [I]n practically all [such decisions to this effect], the provoc-

ative language [held to constitute] a breach of the peace consisted of profane, indecent or abusive remarks directed to the person of the hearer. *Resort to epithets or personal abuse is not in any proper sense communication of information or opinion safeguarded by the Constitution,* and its punishment as a criminal act [under a narrowly drawn statute] would raise no question under that instrument." (Emphasis added).

8. [Even] if the interpretative gloss placed on the statute by the court below be disregarded, the statute had been previously construed as intended to preserve the public peace by punishing conduct, the direct tendency of which was to provoke the person against whom it was directed to acts of violence.

Appellant need not therefore have been a prophet to understand what the statute condemned.

racketeer' and 'damn Fascist' are epithets likely to provoke the average person to retaliation, and thereby cause a breach of the peace.

"The refusal of the state court to admit evidence of provocation and evidence bearing on the truth or falsity of the utterances is open to no Constitutional objection. Whether the facts sought to be proved by such evidence constitute a defense to the charge or may be shown in mitigation are questions for the state court to determine. Our function is fulfilled by a determination that the challenged statute, on its face and as applied, does not contravene the Fourteenth Amendment."

Notes and Questions

1. *Fighting words and free speech values.* (a) *Self realization.* Does speech have to step toward truth to be of first amendment value? Consider Redish, *The Value of Free Speech,* 130 U.Pa.L.Rev. 591, 626 (1982): "Why not view Chaplinsky's comments as a personal catharsis, as a means to vent his frustration at a system he deemed—whether rightly or wrongly—to be oppressive? Is it not a mark of individuality to be able to cry out at a society viewed as crushing the individual? Under this analysis, so-called 'fighting words' represent a significant means of self-realization, whether or not they can be considered a means of attaining some elusive 'truth.'"

(b) *Fighting words and truth.* Are fighting words always false? Should truth be a defense? Always?

(c) *Fighting words and self-government.* Was Chaplinsky's statement *something other than* the expression of an idea? Did he wish to inform the marshal of his opinion of him and did he do so "in a way which was not only unquestionably clear, [but] all too clear"? Loewy, *Punishing Flag Desecrators,* 49 N.C.L.Rev. 48, 82 (1970). How significant is it that Chaplinsky's remarks were not made in the context of a public debate or discussion of political or social issues? Taking into account the events preceding Chaplinsky's remarks, and that the addressee was "an important representative of the Rochester city government," may Chaplinsky's epithets be viewed as "a sharply-expressed form of political protest against indifferent or biased police services in the enforcement of his right to free speech"? Rutzick, *Offensive Language and the Evolution of First Amendment Protection,* 9 Harv.Civ.Rts.—Civ.Lib.L.Rev. 1 (1974). If the speech is directed at a police officer or other official in his representative capacity, is "the real target the government"? Is even the most outrageous abuse in this context "an expression of some opinion concerning governmental policies or practices"? See id.

2. *The social interest in order and morality.* What was the social interest in this case? (a) *The likelihood and immediacy of violent retaliation?* Should the Court have considered whether a *law enforcement officer* so reviled would have been provoked to retaliate? Whatever is assumed about the reaction of an average citizen to offensive words, may it be assumed that police are "trained to remain calm in the face of citizen anger such as that expressed by Chaplinsky"? Rutzick, supra, at 10. See also Powell, J., concurring in *Lewis v. New Orleans,* p. 531 infra; Note, 53 B.U.L.Rev. 834, 847 (1973).

(b) *The highly personal nature of the insult, delivered face to face?* Was the marshal "verbally slapped in the face"? May the *Chaplinsky* statute be viewed as "a special type of assault statute"? See Loewy, supra, at 83–84. See also Emerson, *The System of Freedom of Expression* 337–38 (1970). To what extent should the tort of intentional infliction of emotional distress raise constitutional problems? Compare Haiman, *Speech and Law in a Free Society* 148–56 (1981) with Downs, *Skokie Revisited: Hate Group Speech and the First Amendment,* 60 Not.D.Law. 629, 673–85 (1985).

B. HOSTILE AUDIENCES

TERMINIELLO v. CHICAGO, 337 U.S. 1, 69 S.Ct. 894, 93 L.Ed. 1131 (1949): Petitioner "vigorously, if not viciously" criticized various political and racial groups and condemned "a surging, howling mob" gathered in protest outside the auditorium in which he spoke. He called his adversaries "slimy scum," "snakes," "bedbugs," and the like. Those inside the hall could hear those on the outside yell, "Fascists, Hitlers!" The crowd outside tried to tear the clothes off those whose entered. About 28 windows were broken; stink bombs were thrown. But in charging the jury, the trial court defined "breach of the peace" to include speech which "stirs the public to anger, *invites dispute,* [or] brings about a condition of unrest (emphasis added)." A 5–4 majority, per DOUGLAS, J., struck down the breach of peace ordinance as thus construed: "[A] function of free speech under our system of government is to invite dispute. It may indeed best serve its high purpose when it induces a condition of unrest, creates dissatisfaction with conditions as they are, or even stirs people to anger. [That] is why freedom of speech, though not absolute, *Chaplinsky,* is nevertheless protected against censorship or punishment, unless shown likely to produce a clear and present danger of a serious substantive evil that rises far above public inconvenience, annoyance, or unrest."

FEINER v. NEW YORK, 340 U.S. 315, 71 S.Ct. 303, 95 L.Ed. 295 (1951): Petitioner made a speech on a street corner in a predominantly black residential section of Syracuse, N.Y. A crowd of 75 to 80 persons, black and white, gathered around him, and several pedestrians had to go into the highway in order to pass by. A few minutes after he started, two police officers arrived and observed the rest of the meeting. In the course of his speech, publicizing a meeting of the Young Progressives of America to be held that evening in a local hotel and protesting the revocation of a permit to hold the meeting in a public school auditorium, petitioner referred to the President as a "bum," to the American Legion as "a Nazi Gestapo," and to the Mayor of Syracuse as a "champagne-sipping bum" who "does not speak for the Negro people." He also indicated in an excited manner: "The Negroes don't have equal rights; they should rise up in arms and fight for them."

These statements "stirred up a little excitement." One man indicated that if the police did not get that "S . . . O . . . B . . . " off the stand, he would do so himself. There was not yet a disturbance, but according to police testimony "angry muttering and pushing." In the words of the arresting officer whose testimony was accepted by the trial judge, he "stepped in to prevent it from resulting in a fight." After disregarding two requests to stop speaking, petitioner was arrested and convicted for disorderly conduct. The Court, per VINSON, C.J., affirmed: "The language of *Cantwell* is appropriate here. '[Nobody would] suggest that the principle of freedom of speech sanctions incitement to riot or that religious liberty connotes the privilege to exhort others to physical attack upon those belonging to another sect. When clear and present danger of riot, disorder, interference with traffic upon the public street or other immediate threat to public safety, peace, or order, appears, the power of the State to prevent or punish is obvious.'

"[It] is one thing to say that the police cannot be used as an instrument for the suppression of unpopular views, and another to say that, when as here the speaker passes the bounds of argument or persuasion and undertakes incitement to riot, they are powerless to prevent a breach of the peace. Nor in this case can we condemn the considered judgment of three New York courts approving the means which the police, faced with a crisis, used in the exercise of their power and duty to preserve peace and order."

BLACK, J., dissented: "The Court's opinion apparently rests on this reasoning: The policeman, under the circumstances detailed, could reasonably conclude that serious fighting or even riot was imminent; therefore he could stop petitioner's speech to prevent a breach of peace; accordingly, it was 'disorderly conduct' for petitioner to continue speaking in disobedience of the officer's request. As to the existence of a dangerous situation on the street corner, it seems far-fetched to suggest that the 'facts' show any imminent threat of riot or uncontrollable disorder. It is neither unusual nor unexpected that some people at public street meetings mutter, mill about, push, shove, or disagree, even violently, with the speaker. Indeed, it is rare where controversial topics are discussed that an outdoor crowd does not do some or all of these things. Nor does one isolated threat to assault the speaker forebode disorder. Especially should the danger be discounted where, as here, the person threatening was a man whose wife and two small children accompanied him and who, so far as the record shows, was never close enough to petitioner to carry out the threat.

"Moreover, assuming that the 'facts' did indicate a critical situation, I reject the implication of the Court's opinion that the police had no obligation to protect petitioner's constitutional right to talk. The police of course have power to prevent breaches of the peace. But if, in the name of preserving order, they ever can interfere with a lawful public speaker, they first must make all reasonable efforts to protect him. Here the policemen did not even pretend to try to protect petitioner. According to the officers' testimony, the crowd was restless but there is no showing of any attempt to quiet it; pedestrians were forced to walk into the street, but there was no effort to clear a path on the sidewalk; one person threatened to assault petitioner but the officers did nothing to discourage this when even a word might have sufficed. Their duty was to protect petitioner's right to talk, even to the extent of arresting the man who threatened to interfere. Instead, they shirked that duty and acted only to suppress the right to speak.

"Finally, I cannot agree with the Court's statement that petitioner's disregard of the policeman's unexplained request amounted to such 'deliberate defiance' as would justify an arrest or conviction for disorderly conduct. On the contrary, I think that the policeman's action was a 'deliberate defiance' of ordinary official duty as well as of the constitutional right of free speech. For at least where time allows, courtesy and explanation of commands are basic elements of good official conduct in a democratic society. Here petitioner was 'asked' then 'told' then 'commanded' to stop speaking, but a man making a lawful address is certainly not required to be silent merely because an officer directs it. Petitioner was entitled to know why he should cease doing a lawful act. Not once was he told."

DOUGLAS, J., joined by Minton, J., dissented: "A speaker may not, of course, incite a riot any more than he may incite a breach of the peace by the use of 'fighting words'. But this record shows no such extremes. It shows an unsympathetic audience and the threat of one man to haul the speaker from the stage.

It is against that kind of threat that speakers need police protection. If they do not receive it and instead the police throw their weight on the side of those who would break up the meetings, the police become the new censors of speech. Police censorship has all the vices of the censorship from city halls which we have repeatedly struck down."

Notes and Questions

1. What was the subject of disagreement in *Feiner*? (1) The standard for police interruption of a speech when danger of violence exists and the speaker intends to create disorder rather than to communicate ideas? (2) The standard when such danger exists, but the speaker only desires to communicate ideas? (3) Whether the danger of disorder and violence *was* plain and imminent? (4) Whether the speaker *did* intend to create disorder and violence?

May *Feiner* be limited to the proposition that when a speaker "incites to riot"—but only then—police may stop him without bothering to keep his audience in check? Cf. *Sellers v. Johnson,* 163 F.2d 877 (8th Cir.1947), cert. denied, 332 U.S. 851 (1948). See Stewart, *Public Speech and Public Order in Britain and the United States,* 13 Vand.L.Rev. 625, 632–33 (1960).

Should the speech *always* be prohibitable when the speaker intends to create disorder, rather than communicate ideas? Should the speech be prohibitable *only* under these circumstances? Should a speech *ever* be prohibitable because listeners arrive or will arrive, as they would have in *Sellers,* with a preconceived intent to create disturbance? Is the only really difficult problem in this area posed when *neither* the speaker *nor* the audience which gathers intends to create disorder, but the audience becomes *genuinely* aroused, honestly—whether or not justifiably—enraged? Here, should the police protect the speechmaking to the fullest extent possible? If they are firmly told they must before they can arrest the speaker, what is the likelihood that adequate preventive steps will be taken? See Gellhorn, *American Rights* 55–62 (1960); Note, 49 Colum.L.Rev. 1118, 1123–24 (1949).

Granted that it is undesirable for the continuation of a demonstration to turn on a police judgment whether a crowd is uncontrollable and that frequently, at least, the police will be able to handle the crowd if they are determined to do so, will occasions arise when crowd hostility *is* uncontrollable? May the demonstrators argue that "they have an interest in the publicity value of their own bloodshed or in any event that they have a right to determine their own risks"? See Note, 80 Harv.L.Rev. 1773, 1775 (1967). In such a case, does the ensuing violence pose a danger to innocent bystanders and the police as well as the demonstrators themselves? See id. If and when, despite their best efforts, law enforcement officers simply cannot "quell the mob," must they be allowed to "quell the speaker"?

2. *Edwards v. South Carolina,* 372 U.S. 229, 83 S.Ct. 680, 9 L.Ed.2d 697 (1963) reversed a breach of the peace conviction of civil rights demonstrators who refused to disperse within 15 minutes of a police command. The Court maintained that the 200 to 300 onlookers did not threaten violence and that the police protection was ample. It described the situation as a "far cry from [*Feiner*]." Clark, J., dissenting, pointed to the racially charged atmosphere ("200 youthful Negro demonstrators were being aroused to a 'fever pitch' before a crowd of some 300 people who undoubtedly were hostile.") and concluded that city officials in good faith believed that disorder and violence were imminent. Did *Edwards* miss a golden opportunity to clarify *Feiner*? What if the crowd had been

pushing, shoving and pressing more closely around the demonstrators in *Edwards*? Would the case still be a "far cry" from *Feiner* because the demonstrators had not "passed the bounds of argument or persuasion and undertaken incitement to riot"?

3. In the advocacy of illegal action context, the fear of violence arises from audience cooperation with the speaker. In the hostile audience context, the fear of violence arises from audience conflict with the speaker. How do the elements set out in *Brandenburg* relate to those implied in *Feiner*? How should they relate? Should the standard for "fighting words" cases be different from the "hostile audience" cases?

4. Should police be able to prosecute or silence disruptive audiences? Heckling audiences? In what contexts? See generally *In re Kay*, 1 Cal.3d 930, 83 Cal.Rptr. 686, 464 P.2d 142 (1970).

C. OFFENSIVE WORDS

COHEN v. CALIFORNIA

403 U.S. 15, 91 S.Ct. 1780, 29 L.Ed.2d 284 (1971).

MR. JUSTICE HARLAN delivered the opinion of the Court.

[Defendant was convicted of violating that part of a general California disturbing-the-peace statute which prohibits "maliciously and willfully disturb[ing] the peace or quiet of any neighborhood or person" by "offensive conduct." He had worn a jacket bearing the plainly visible words "Fuck the Draft" in a Los Angeles courthouse corridor, where women and children were present. He testified that he did so as a means of informing the public of the depth of his feelings against the Vietnam War and the draft. He did not engage in, nor threaten, any violence, nor was anyone who saw him violently aroused. Nor was there any evidence that he uttered any sound prior to his arrest. In affirming, the California Court of Appeal construed "offensive conduct" to mean "behavior which has a tendency to provoke *others* to acts of violence or to in turn disturb the peace" and held that the state had proved this element because it was "reasonably foreseeable" that defendant's conduct "might cause others to rise up to commit a violent act against [him] or attempt to forceably remove his jacket."]

In order to lay hands on the precise issue which this case involves, it is useful first to canvass various matters which this record does *not* present.

The conviction quite clearly rests upon the asserted offensiveness of the *words* Cohen used to convey his message to the public. The only "conduct" which the State sought to punish is the fact of communication. Thus, we deal here with a conviction resting solely upon "speech," not upon any separately identifiable conduct which allegedly was intended by Cohen to be perceived by others as expressive of particular views but which, on its face, does not necessarily convey any message and hence arguably could be regulated without effectively repressing Cohen's ability to express himself. Cf. *United States v. O'Brien* [p. 621 infra]. Further, the State certainly lacks power to punish Cohen for the underlying content of the message the inscription conveyed. At least so long as there is no showing of an intent to incite disobedience to or disruption of the draft, Cohen could not, consistently with the First and Fourteenth Amendments, be punished for asserting the evident position on the inutility or immorality of the draft his jacket reflected. *Yates.*

Appellant's conviction, then, rests squarely upon his exercise [of] "freedom of speech" [and] can be justified, if at all, only as a valid regulation of the manner in which he exercised that freedom, not as a permissible prohibition on the substantive message it conveys. This does not end the inquiry, of course, for the First and Fourteenth Amendments have never been thought to give absolute protection to every individual to speak whenever or wherever he pleases, or to use any form of address in any circumstances that he chooses. In this vein, too, however, we think it important to note that several issues typically associated with such problems are not presented here.

In the first place, Cohen was tried under a statute applicable throughout the entire State. Any attempt to support this conviction on the ground that the statute seeks to preserve an appropriately decorous atmosphere in the court-house where Cohen was arrested must fail in the absence of any language in the statute that would have put appellant on notice that certain kinds of otherwise permissible speech or conduct would nevertheless, under California law, not be tolerated in certain places. No fair reading of the phrase "offensive conduct" can be said sufficiently to inform the ordinary person that distinctions between certain locations are thereby created.[3]

In the second place, as it comes to us, this case cannot be said to fall within those relatively few categories of instances where prior decisions have established the power of government to deal more comprehensively with certain forms of individual expression simply upon a showing that such a form was employed. This is not, for example, an obscenity case. Whatever else may be necessary to give rise to the States' broader power to prohibit obscene expression, such expression must be, in some significant way, erotic. *Roth.* It cannot plausibly be maintained that this vulgar allusion to the Selective Service System would conjure up such psychic stimulation in anyone likely to be confronted with Cohen's crudely defaced jacket.

This Court has also held that the States are free to ban the simple use, without a demonstration of additional justifying circumstances, of so-called "fighting words," those personally abusive epithets which, when addressed to the ordinary citizen, are, as a matter of common knowledge, inherently likely to provoke violent reaction. *Chaplinsky.* While the four-letter word displayed by Cohen in relation to the draft is not uncommonly employed in a personally provocative fashion, in this instance it was clearly not "directed to the person of the hearer." No individual actually or likely to be present could reasonably have regarded the words on appellant's jacket as a direct personal insult. Nor do we have here an instance of the exercise of the State's police power to prevent a speaker from intentionally provoking a given group to hostile reaction. Cf. *Feiner; Terminiello.* There is, as noted above, no showing that anyone who saw Cohen was in fact violently aroused or that appellant intended such a result.

[T]he mere presumed presence of unwitting listeners or viewers does not serve automatically to justify curtailing all speech capable of giving offense. While this Court has recognized that government may properly act in many situations to prohibit intrusion into the privacy of the home of unwelcome views and ideas which cannot be totally banned from the public dialogue, we have at the same time consistently stressed that "we are often 'captives' outside the

---

3. It is illuminating to note what transpired when Cohen entered a courtroom in the building. He removed his jacket and stood with it folded over his arm. Meanwhile, a policeman sent the presiding judge a note suggesting that Cohen be held in contempt of court. The judge declined to do so and Cohen was arrested by the officer only after he emerged from the courtroom.

sanctuary of the home and subject to objectionable speech." The ability of government, consonant with the Constitution, to shut off discourse solely to protect others from hearing it is, in other words, dependent upon a showing that substantial privacy interests are being invaded in an essentially intolerable manner. Any broader view of this authority would effectively empower a majority to silence dissidents simply as a matter of personal predilections.

[Given] the subtlety and complexity of the factors involved if Cohen's "speech" was otherwise entitled to constitutional protection, we do not think the fact that some unwilling "listeners" in a public building may have been briefly exposed to it can serve to justify this breach of the peace conviction where, as here, there was no evidence that persons powerless to avoid appellant's conduct did in fact object to it, and where [unlike another portion of the same statute barring the use of "vulgar, profane or indecent language within [the] hearing of women or children, in a loud and boisterous manner"], the [challenged statutory provision] evinces no concern [with] the special plight of the captive auditor, but, instead, indiscriminately sweeps within its prohibitions all "offensive conduct" that disturbs "any neighborhood or person."

Against this background, the issue flushed by this case stands out in bold relief. It is whether California can excise, as "offensive conduct," one particular scurrilous epithet from the public discourse, either upon the theory of the court below that its use is inherently likely to cause violent reaction or upon a more general assertion that the States, acting as guardians of public morality, may properly remove this offensive word from the public vocabulary.

The rationale of the California court is plainly untenable. At most it reflects an "undifferentiated fear or apprehension of disturbance [which] is not enough to overcome the right to freedom of expression." *Tinker* [p. 629 infra]. We have been shown no evidence that substantial numbers of citizens are standing ready to strike out physically at whoever may assault their sensibilities with execrations like that uttered by Cohen. There may be some persons about with such lawless and violent proclivities, but that is an insufficient base upon which to erect, consistently with constitutional values, a governmental power to force persons who wish to ventilate their dissident views into avoiding particular forms of expression. The argument amounts to little more than the self-defeating proposition that to avoid physical censorship of one who has not sought to provoke such a response by a hypothetical coterie of the violent and lawless, the States may more appropriately effectuate that censorship themselves.

Admittedly, it is not so obvious that the First and Fourteenth Amendments must be taken to disable the States from punishing public utterance of this unseemly expletive in order to maintain what they regard as a suitable level of discourse within the body politic. We think, however, that examination and reflection will reveal the shortcomings of a contrary viewpoint.

[The] constitutional right of free expression is powerful medicine in a society as diverse and populous as ours. It is designed and intended to remove governmental restraints from the arena of public discussion, putting the decision as to what views shall be voiced largely into the hands of each of us, in the hope that use of such freedom will ultimately produce a more capable citizenry and more perfect polity and in the belief that no other approach would comport with the premise of individual dignity and choice upon which our political system rests.

To many, the immediate consequence of this freedom may often appear to be only verbal tumult, discord, and even offensive utterance. These are, however, within established limits, in truth necessary side effects of the broader enduring values which the process of open debate permits us to achieve. That the air may at times seem filled with verbal cacophony is, in this sense not a sign of weakness but of strength. We cannot lose sight of the fact that, in what otherwise might seem a trifling and annoying instance of individual distasteful abuse of a privilege, these fundamental societal values are truly implicated.

* * *

Against this perception of the constitutional policies involved, we discern certain more particularized considerations that peculiarly call for reversal of this conviction. First, the principle contended for by the State seems inherently boundless. How is one to distinguish this from any other offensive word? Surely the State has no right to cleanse public debate to the point where it is grammatically palatable to the most squeamish among us. Yet no readily ascertainable general principle exists for stopping short of that result were we to affirm the judgment below. For, while the particular four-letter word being litigated here is perhaps more distasteful than most others of its genre, it is nevertheless often true that one man's vulgarity is another's lyric. Indeed, we think it is largely because governmental officials cannot make principled distinctions in this area that the Constitution leaves matters of taste and style so largely to the individual.

Additionally, we cannot overlook the fact, because it is well illustrated by the episode involved here, that much linguistic expression serves a dual communicative function: it conveys not only ideas capable of relatively precise, detached explication, but otherwise inexpressible emotions as well. In fact, words are often chosen as much for their emotive as their cognitive force. We cannot sanction the view that the Constitution, while solicitous of the cognitive content of individual speech, has little or no regard for that emotive function which, practically speaking, may often be the more important element of the overall message sought to be communicated. * * *

Finally, and in the same vein, we cannot indulge the facile assumption that one can forbid particular words without also running a substantial risk of suppressing ideas in the process. Indeed, governments might soon seize upon the censorship of particular words as a convenient guise for banning the expression of unpopular views. We have been able [to] discern little social benefit that might result from running the risk of opening the door to such grave results.

It is, in sum, our judgment that, absent a more particularized and compelling reason for its actions, the State may not, consistently with the First and Fourteenth Amendments, make the simple public display here involved of this single four-letter expletive a criminal offense. Because that is the only arguably sustainable rationale for the conviction here at issue, the judgment below must be

Reversed.

[BLACKMUN, J., joined by Burger, C.J., and Black, J., dissented for two reasons: (1) "Cohen's absurd and immature antic [was] mainly conduct and little speech" and the case falls "well within the sphere of *Chaplinsky*"; (2) although it declined to review the state court of appeals' decision in *Cohen*, the California Supreme Court subsequently narrowly construed the breach-of-the-peace statute in another case and *Cohen* should be remanded to the California Court of Appeal in the light of this subsequent construction. White, J., concurred with the dissent on the latter ground.]

Notes and Questions

1.   For criticism of *Cohen,* see Bickel, *The Morality of Consent* 72 (1975) (Cohen's speech "constitutes an assault" and this sort of speech "may create [an] environment [in which] actions that were not possible before become possible"); Cox, *The Role of the Supreme Court in American Government* 47–48 (1976) (state has interest in "level at which public discourse is conducted"; state should not have to "allow exhibitionists and [others] trading upon our lower prurient interests to inflict themselves upon the public consciousness and dull its sensibilities").   For a defense (but what not a few would consider a narrow reading) of *Cohen,* see Farber, *Civilizing Public Discourse: An Essay on Professor Bickel, Justice Harlan, and the Enduring Significance of Cohen v. California,* 1980 Duke L.J. 283.   See also Ely, *Democracy and Distrust* 114 (1980); Tribe, *American Constitutional Law* 578, 618–19, 666, 680–81 (1978).   For an overview of Harlan, J.'s approach to the first amendment, see Farber & Nowak, *Justice Harlan and the First Amendment,* 2 Const.Comm. 425 (1985).

2.   To what extent, if at all, and in what ways, if any, does *Cohen* restrict the "fighting words" doctrine?   Consider Arkes, *Civility and the Restriction of Speech: Rediscovering the Defamation of Groups,* 1974 Sup.Ct.Rev. 281, 316: *Cohen* turned "the presumptions in *Chaplinsky* around: instead of presuming that profane or defamatory speech was beneath constitutional protection, he presumed that the speech was protected and that the burden of proof lay with those who would restrict it."   If "one man's vulgarity is another's lyric," how are discriminations to be made in the "fighting words" area?   See Rutzick, p. 521 supra, at 20; Note, 53 B.U.L.Rev. 834, 842 (1973).

3.   Was the flaw in the *Chaplinsky* formulation that "[i]ts paradigm was a debating society, a sedate assembly of speakers who calmly discussed the issues of the day and became ultimately persuaded by the logic of one of the competing positions"?   That it viewed "emotion" as never entering the debate, "for emotion had nothing to do with 'truth' "?   See Rutzick 18.   Once it is conceded that "the offensiveness of language used in a political protest often measures the intensity of interest in the outcome of a governmental decision," does "protection for the use of offensive language [become] not a luxury but a necessity in a democratic society"?   See id. at 19.

4.   By characterizing the proclivities of those who might react violently as "lawless," did the *Cohen* Court give "new vigor to the proposition advanced by Justice Black [in his *Feiner* dissent] that the proper method to prevent such a violent response to controversial speech [is] to apply the criminal sanction directly to the reactive conduct rather than [to] the initial speech"?   See Rutzick 21.

D.   OFFENSIVE LANGUAGE: A STATE CONSTITUTIONAL PERSPECTIVE

STATE v. HARRINGTON

67 Or.App. 608, 680 P.2d 666 (1984).

GILLETTE, PRESIDING JUDGE.

The state appeals a trial court order sustaining defendant's demurrer to a complaint charging racial intimidation.   The intimidation statute enhances the penalty [for] harassment when such crimes are motivated by the race, color, religion or national origin of the victim.   * * *

The complaint charges: "The defendant [by] reason of race and color and with intent to harass, annoy and alarm John Thomas Ritchey, [did] unlawfully publicly insult John Thomas Ritchey by abusive words in a manner likely to provoke a violent and disorderly response, by repeatedly calling John Thomas Ritchey a 'fucking nigger.'"

ORS 166.065(1)(b) provides, in pertinent part: "A person commits the crime of harassment if, with intent to harass, annoy or alarm another person, the actor: * * * Publicly insults another by abusive or obscene words or gestures in a manner likely to provoke a violent or disorderly [response]."

Article I, section 8, of the Oregon Constitution provides: "No law shall be passed restraining the free expression of opinion, or restricting [the] right to speak, write, or print freely on any subject whatever; but every person shall be responsible for the abuse of this right."

In *State v. Robertson,* 293 Or. 402, 649 P.2d 569 (1982), the Oregon Supreme Court held that "Article I, section 8, [forecloses] the enactment of any law written in terms directed to the substance of any 'opinion' or any 'subject' of communication, unless the scope of the restraint is wholly confined within some historical exception that was well established when the first American guarantees of freedom of expression were adopted and that the guarantees then or in 1859 demonstrably were not intended to [reach]." [*Robertson*] requires answering two questions. The first is whether ORS 166.065(1)(b) is "directed to the substance of any opinion or any subject of communication." *Robertson* explains the constitutionally significant distinction between legislation directed against the pursuit of a forbidden effect and a provision directed against speech itself: "[A]rticle I, section 8, prohibits lawmakers from enacting restrictions that focus on the content of speech or writing, either because that content itself is deemed socially undesirable or offensive, or because it is thought to have adverse consequences. [L]aws must focus on proscribing the pursuit or accomplishment of forbidden results rather than on the suppression of speech or writing either as an end in itself or as a means to some other legislative end."

The state argues that ORS 166.065(1)(b) is directed against an "effect," namely, prevention of violence. Both the language of the statute itself and the legislative commentary indicate otherwise.[3] [The] statute indicates that the statute was intended to *protect the listener* from exposure to abusive or obscene language rather than to protect anyone from physical violence. [We] hold that ORS 166.065(1)(b) is directed at communication.

The second question under *Robertson* is whether the statute falls within some historical exception to Article I, section 8. The state argues that the language "likely to provoke a violent or disorderly response" limits the type of language that may be punished to so-called "fighting words" and that punishment of fighting words is an historical exception to Article I, section 8. The basis of this argument is *Chaplinsky* [where] the Supreme Court stated: "[There] are certain well-defined narrowly limited classes of speech, the prevention and punishment of which have never been thought to raise any Constitutional problem. These include the lewd and obscene, profane, the libelous, and the insulting, or 'fighting words'—those which by their very utterances inflict injury or intend to incite an immediate breach of the peace." On the other hand, more recent Supreme Court opinions have struck down statutes proscribing offensive

3. If the legislature's aim is to prevent fights, the legislature could make it a crime to provoke a fight. *See* Linde, *"Clear and Pres-* *ent Danger" Reexamined: Dissonance in the Brandenburg Concerto,* 22 Stan.L.Rev. 1163, 1179–82 (1970).

language as overbroad under the First Amendment. See *Gooding v. Wilson*, 405 U.S. 518, 92 S.Ct. 1103, 31 L.Ed.2d 408 (1972); see also *Lewis v. New Orleans,* 415 U.S. 130, 94 S.Ct. 970, 39 L.Ed.2d 214 (1974).[5] Thus, *Chaplinsky* is not necessarily in point.

Even if we were to determine that ORS 166.065(1)(b) codifies the *Chaplinsky* fighting words exception to the First Amendment, however, that would not end our inquiry. *Chaplinsky* stands for the proposition that the United States Supreme Court may determine that some forms of communication are unprotected because "any benefit that may be derived from them is clearly outweighed by the social interest in order and morality." In other words, the court used a balancing test to determine that some forms of expression are unworthy of constitutional protection.

Article I, section 8, by contrast, forbids legislation "restricting the right to speak freely on *any subject whatever.*" (Emphasis supplied). Article I, section 8, precludes the state legislature or the courts from balancing away the right to free expression. The legislature may only proscribe expression when the scope of the restraint is wholly within an historical exception to Article I, section 8.[6] Examples of such historical exceptions are "perjury, solicitation or verbal assistance in crime, some forms of theft, forgery and fraud and their contemporary variants." *Robertson.* As "examples" we do not consider this list to be—or to have been intended to be—exclusive. [L]egislation directed against obscene or abusive speech was not enacted until sometime after the adoption of the Oregon Constitution in 1859. We therefore determine that obscene or abusive language spoken with intent to annoy or alarm is not an "historical exception that was well established when the first American guarantees of freedom of expression were adopted and that the guarantees then or in 1859 demonstrably were not intended to [reach]." *Robertson.* It follows that the trial court's ruling was correct: the statutory scheme offends Article I, section 8, of the Oregon Constitution.

Affirmed.

Notes and Questions

1. Is the interpretive approach applied by the Oregon court to its constitution superior to that used by the United States Supreme Court in interpreting the first amendment? Would the results have been better for the country if the Oregon approach had been applied to the first amendment? [a]

5. The problems in drafting a constitutional statute have been summarized as follows: "[C]lassifying particularly offensive expressions is difficult. Forms of expression vary so much in their contexts and inflections that one cannot specify particular words or phrases as being always 'fighting.' What is gross insult in one setting is crude humor in another. And what is offensive shifts over time." Greenawalt, *Speech and Crime,* 1980 Am.B. Found.Res.J. 645, 770.

6. Article I, section 8, does not preclude a civil action for abuse of the right to speak freely. See also Comment, *Defamation and State Constitutions: The Search for a State Law Based Standard After Gertz,* 19 Will.L. Rev. 665 (1983). For example, the victim might bring a tort action for intentional infliction of emotional distress. Cf. *Contreras v.*

Crown Zellerbach, 88 Wash.2d 735, 565 P.2d 1173 (1977) (abusive racial slurs may constitute "outrageous" conduct within the meaning of *Restatement (Second) Torts* (1965)); see also *Hall v. The May Dept. Stores,* 292 Or. 131, 637 P.2d 126 (1981) (damages recoverable for intentional infliction of emotional distress).

a. For assembling of and commentary upon state freedom of speech and press provisions, see Collins, *Bills and Declarations of Rights Digest* in *The American Bench* 2483, 2485, 2502–05 (3d ed. 1985) ("[S]tate free speech and press provisions have more in common with each other than they do with the First Amendment."). For commentary on the relationship between state constitutions and the federal constitution, see Linde, *E Pluribus—Constitutional Theory and State Courts,* 18 Ga.L.Rev. 165 (1984); Collins, *Reli-*

2. Should (does) the first amendment bar an action for intentional infliction of emotional distress under the facts of this case? Is it enough that the words in question inflict injury or must the victim show that the words were likely to promote a fight? Suppose a crowd of whites gathers to taunt a young black child on the way to a previously all white school? Suppose short of using violence, they do everything they can to harm the child? Is it the case that "no government that would call itself a decent government would fail to intervene [and] disperse the crowd" and that "the rights of the crowd [cannot] really stand on the same plane" as the child on the way to school? See Arkes, *Civility and the Restriction of Speech: Rediscovering the Defamation of Groups,* 1979 Sup.Ct. Rev. 281, 310–11. Should the first amendment bar state criminal or civil actions precisely tailored to punish racial insults? Insults directed against the handicapped? For the case in favor of a tort action against racial insults, see Delgado, *Words That Wound: A Tort Action for Racial Insults, Epithets, and Name-Calling,* 17 Harv.Civ.Rts.-Civ.Lib.L.Rev. 133 (1982). For a spirited exchange, see Heins, *Banning Words: A Comment on "Words that Wound,"* 18 Har.Civ.Rts.-Civ.Lib.L.Rev. 585 (1983) and *Professor Delgado Replies,* Id. at 593.

3. A series of cases in the early 1970s reversed convictions involving abusive language. *Gooding v. Wilson* invalidated a Georgia ordinance primarily because it had been previously applied to "utterances where there was no likelihood that the person addressed would make an immediate violent utterance." *Lewis v. New Orleans* ruled that vulgar or offensive speech was protected under the first amendment. Because the statute punished "opprobrious language," it was deemed by the Court to embrace words that do not " 'by their very utterance inflict injury or tend to invite an immediate breach of the peace.' "

Although *Gooding* seemed to require a danger of immediate violence, *Lewis* recited that infliction of injury was sufficient. Dissenting in both cases, Burger, C.J., and Blackmun and Rehnquist, JJ., complained that the majority invoked vagueness and overbreadth analysis "indiscriminately without regard to the nature of the speech in question, the possible effect the statute or ordinance has upon such speech, the importance of the speech in relation to the exposition of ideas, or the purported or asserted community interest in preventing that speech." The dissenters focused upon the facts of the cases (e.g., Gooding to a police officer: "White son of a bitch, I'll kill you," "You son of a bitch, I'll choke you to death," and "You son of a bitch, if you ever put your hands on me again, I'll cut you to pieces."). They complained that the majority had relegated the facts to "footnote status, conveniently distant and in less disturbing focus." In *Gooding, Lewis,* and the other cases, Powell, J., insisted upon the importance of context in decisionmaking. Dissenting in *Rosenfeld v. New Jersey,* 408 U.S. 901, 92 S.Ct. 2479, 33 L.Ed.2d 321 (1972), he suggested that *Chaplinsky* be extended to the "wilful use of scurrilous language calculated to offend the sensibilities of an unwilling audience"; concurring in *Lewis,* he maintained that allowing prosecutions for offensive language directed at police officers invited law enforcement abuse. Finally, he suggested in *Rosenfeld* that whatever the scope of the "fighting words" doctrine, overbreadth analysis was inappropriate in such cases. He doubted that such statutes deter others from exercising first amendment rights.[b]

ance on State Constitutions: The Montana Disaster, 63 Tex.L.Rev. 1095 (1985); Simon, *Independent But Inadequate: State Constitutions and Protection of Freedom of Expression,* 33 U.Kan.L.Rev. 305 (1985).

b. For commentary on Powell, J.'s approach, see Gunther, *In Search of Judicial Quality on a Changing Court: The Case of Justice Powell,* 24 Stan.L.Rev. 1001, 1029–35 (1972).

V. NEW CATEGORIES

Suppose a legislature were to outlaw speech whose dominant theme appeals to a morbid interest in violence, that is patently offensive to contemporary community standards, and that lacks serious literary, artistic, political or scientific value. Constitutional? One approach would be to contend that speech is protected unless it falls into already established categorical exceptions to first amendment protection. Another would be to argue by analogy, e.g., if obscenity is beneath first amendment protection, this speech should (or should not) be beneath such protection. Similarly, one could argue that exceptions to first amendment protection has been fashioned by resort to a balancing methodology and that balancing the relevant interests is the right approach. Alternatively, one could proceed from a particular substantive vision of the first amendment, such as the Meiklejohn view. Which approach has been applied by the Court? [a]

New York v. Ferber, infra, is interesting because it involves a new category.

A. HARM TO CHILDREN AND THE OVERBREADTH DOCTRINE

NEW YORK v. FERBER, 458 U.S. 747, 102 S.Ct. 3348, 73 L.Ed.2d 1113 (1982), per WHITE, J., upheld conviction of a seller of films depicting young boys masturbating, under N.Y.Penal Law § 263.15, for "promoting [a] a sexual performance," defined as "any performance [which] includes sexual conduct [b] by a child" under 16. The Court addressed the "single question": " 'To prevent the abuse of children who are made to engage in sexual conduct for commercial purposes, could the New York State Legislature, consistent with the First Amendment, prohibit the dissemination of material which shows children engaged in sexual conduct, regardless of whether such material is obscene?' [c] * * *

"The *Miller* standard, like its predecessors, was an accommodation between the state's interests in protecting the 'sensibilities of unwilling recipients' from exposure to pornographic material and the dangers of censorship inherent in unabashedly content-based laws. Like obscenity statutes, laws directed at the dissemination of child pornography run the risk of suppressing protected expression by allowing the hand of the censor to become unduly heavy. For the following reasons, however, we are persuaded that the States are entitled to greater leeway in the regulation of pornographic depictions of children.

a. For commentary on the Court's methodology, see Redish, *Freedom of Expression: A Critical Analysis* (1984); Van Alstyne, *Interpretations of the First Amendment* (1984); Van Alstyne, *A Graphic Review of the Free Speech Clause,* 70 Calif.L.Rev. 107 (1982); Farber, *Content Regulation and the First Amendment: A Revisionist View,* 68 Geo.L.J. 727 (1980); Schauer, *Categories and the First Amendment: A Play in Three Acts,* 34 Vand.L. Rev. 265 (1981); Schlag, *Rules and Standards,* 33 U.C.L.A.L.Rev. 379 (1985); Shiffrin, *Defamatory Non-Media Speech and First Amendment Methodology,* 25 U.C.L.A.L.Rev. 915 (1978).

a. "Promote" was defined to include all aspects of production, distribution, exhibition and sale.

b. Sec. 263.3 defined "sexual conduct" as "actual or simulated sexual intercourse, devi-

ate sexual intercourse, sexual bestiality, masturbation, sado-masochistic abuse, or lewd exhibition of the genitals."

c. The opinion gave the background for such legislation: "In recent years, the exploitive use of children in the production of pornography has become a serious national problem. The federal government and forty-seven States have sought to combat the problem with statutes specifically directed at the production of child pornography. At least half of such statutes do not require that the materials produced be legally obscene. Thirty-five States and the United States Congress have also passed legislation prohibiting the distribution of such materials; twenty States prohibit the distribution of material depicting children engaged in sexual conduct without requiring that the material be legally obscene. New York is one of the twenty."

"First. [The] prevention of sexual exploitation and abuse of children constitutes a government objective of surpassing importance. The legislative findings accompanying passage of the New York laws reflect this concern. * * *

"We shall not second-guess this legislative judgment. Respondent has not intimated that we do so. Suffice it to say that virtually all of the States and the United States have passed legislation proscribing the production of or otherwise combatting 'child pornography.' The legislative judgment, as well as the judgment found in the relevant literature, is that the use of children as subjects of pornographic materials is harmful to the physiological, emotional, and mental health of the child. That judgment, we think, easily passes muster under the First Amendment.

"Second. The distribution of photographs and films depicting sexual activity by juveniles is intrinsically related to the sexual abuse of children in at least two ways. First, the materials produced are a permanent record of the children's participation and the harm to the child is exacerbated by their circulation. Second, the distribution network for child pornography must be closed if the production of material which requires the sexual exploitation of children is to be effectively controlled. Indeed, there is no serious contention that the legislature was unjustified in believing that it is difficult, if not impossible, to halt the exploitation of children by pursuing only those who produce the photographs and movies. While the production of pornographic materials is a low-profile, clandestine industry, the need to market the resulting products requires a visible apparatus of distribution. The most expeditious if not the only practical method of law enforcement may be to dry up the market for this material by imposing severe criminal penalties on persons selling, advertising, or otherwise promoting the product. Thirty-five States and Congress have concluded that restraints on the distribution of pornographic materials are required in order to effectively combat the problem, and there is a body of literature and testimony to support these legislative conclusions.

"[The] *Miller* standard, like all general definitions of what may be banned as obscene, does not reflect the State's particular and more compelling interest in prosecuting those who promote the sexual exploitation of children. Thus, the question under the *Miller* test of whether a work, taken as a whole, appeals to the prurient interest of the average person bears no connection to the issue of whether a child has been physically or psychologically harmed in the production of the work. Similarly, a sexual explicit depiction need not be 'patently offensive' in order to have required the sexual exploitation of a child for its production. In addition, a work which, taken on the whole, contains serious literary, artistic, political, or scientific value may nevertheless embody the hardest core of child pornography. 'It is irrelevant to the child [who has been abused] whether or not the material [has] a literary, artistic, political, or social value.' We therefore cannot conclude that the *Miller* standard is a satisfactory solution to the child pornography problem.

"Third. The advertising and selling of child pornography provides an economic motive for and is thus an integral part of the production of such materials, an activity illegal throughout the nation. 'It rarely has been suggested that the constitutional freedom for speech and press extends its immunity to speech or writing used as an integral part of conduct in violation of a valid criminal statute.' * * *

"Fourth. The value of permitting live performances and photographic reproductions of children engaged in lewd sexual conduct is exceedingly modest, if not de minimis. We consider it unlikely that visual depictions of children performing sexual acts or lewdly exhibiting their genitals would often constitute an important and necessary part of a literary performance or scientific or educational work. As the trial court in this case observed, if it were necessary for literary or artistic value, a person over the statutory age who perhaps looked younger could be utilized. ⁕ ⁕ ⁕

"Fifth. Recognizing and classifying child pornography as a category of material outside the protection of the First Amendment is not incompatible with our earlier decisions. 'The question whether speech is, or is not protected by the First Amendment often depends on the content of the speech.' *Young v. American Mini Theatres, Inc.* [p. 547 infra]. '[I]t is the content of an utterance that determines whether it is a protected epithet or [an] unprotected "fighting comment"'. Leaving aside the special considerations when public officials are the target, *New York Times Co. v. Sullivan,* a libelous publication is not protected by the Constitution. *Beauharnais.* [It] is not rare that a content-based classification of speech has been accepted because it may be appropriately generalized that within the confines of the given classification, the evil to be restricted so overwhelmingly outweighs the expressive interests, if any, at stake, that no process of case-by-case adjudication is required. When a definable class of material, such as that covered by § 263.15, bears so heavily and pervasively on the welfare of children engaged in its production, we think the balance of competing interests is clearly struck and that it is permissible to consider these materials as without the protection of the First Amendment.

"There are, of course, limits on the category of child pornography which, like obscenity, is unprotected by the First Amendment. As with all legislation in this sensitive area, the conduct to be prohibited must be adequately defined by the applicable state law, as written or authoritatively construed. Here the nature of the harm to be combatted requires that the state offense be limited to works that *visually* depict sexual conduct by children below a specified age. The category of 'sexual conduct' proscribed must also be suitably limited and described.

"The test for child pornography is separate from the obscenity standard enunciated in *Miller,* but may be compared to it for purpose of clarity. The *Miller* formulation is adjusted in the following respects: A trier of fact need not find that the material appeals to the prurient interest of the average person; it is not required that sexual conduct portrayed be done so in a patently offensive manner; and the material at issue need not be considered as a whole. We note that the distribution of descriptions or other depictions of sexual conduct, not otherwise obscene, which do not involve live performance or photographic or other visual reproduction of live performances, retains First Amendment protection. As with obscenity laws, criminal responsibility may not be imposed without some element of scienter on the part of the defendant. ⁕ ⁕ ⁕

"It remains to address the claim that the New York statute is unconstitutionally overbroad because it would forbid the distribution of material with serious literary, scientific, or educational value or material which does not threaten the harms sought to be combated by the State. ⁕ ⁕ ⁕

"The traditional rule is that a person to whom a statute may constitutionally be applied may not challenge that statute on the ground that it may conceivably be applied unconstitutionally to others in situations not before the Court. *Broadrick v. Oklahoma,* 413 U.S. 601, 93 S.Ct. 2908, 37 L.Ed.2d 830 (1973). In *Broadrick,* we recognized that this rule reflects two cardinal principles of our constitutional order: the personal nature of constitutional rights and prudential limitations on constitutional adjudication.[20]   [By] focusing on the factual situation before us, and similar cases necessary for development of a constitutional rule,[21] we face 'flesh-and-blood' legal problems with data 'relevant and adequate to an informed judgment.' This practice also fulfills a valuable institutional purpose: it allows state courts the opportunity to construe a law to avoid constitutional infirmities.

"What has come to be known as the First Amendment overbreadth doctrine is one of the few exceptions to this principle and must be justified by weighty countervailing policies. The doctrine is predicated on the sensitive nature of protected expression: persons whose expression is constitutionally protected may well refrain from exercising their rights for fear of criminal sanctions by a statute susceptible of application to protected expression. * * *

"In *Broadrick,* we explained [that]: '[T]he plain import of our cases is, at the very least, that facial overbreadth adjudication is an exception to our traditional rules of practice and that its function, a limited one at the outset, attenuates as the otherwise unprotected behavior that it forbids the State to sanction moves from "pure speech" toward conduct and that conduct—even if expressive—falls within the scope of otherwise valid criminal laws that reflect legitimate state interests in maintaining comprehensive controls over harmful, constitutionally unprotected conduct. * * *'

"[*Broadrick*] examined a regulation involving restrictions on political campaign activity, an area not considered 'pure speech,' and thus it was unnecessary to consider the proper overbreadth test when a law arguably reaches traditional forms of expression such as books and films. As we intimated in *Broadrick,* the requirement of substantial overbreadth extended 'at the very least' to cases involving conduct plus speech. This case, which poses the question squarely, convinces us that the rationale of *Broadrick* is sound and should be applied in the present context involving the harmful employment of children to make sexually explicit materials for distribution.

"The premise that a law should not be invalidated for overbreadth unless it reaches a substantial number of impermissible applications is hardly novel. On most occasions involving facial invalidation, the Court has stressed the embracing sweep of the statute over protected expression.[26]   Indeed, Justice Brennan observed in his dissenting opinion in *Broadrick* : 'We have never held that a statute should be held invalid on its face merely because it is possible to conceive of a single impermissible application, and in that sense a requirement of substantial overbreadth is already implicit in the doctrine.'

"The requirement of substantial overbreadth is directly derived from the purpose and nature of the doctrine. While a sweeping statute, or one incapable of limitation, has the potential to repeatedly chill the exercise of expressive activity by many individuals, the extent of deterrence of protected speech can be expected to decrease with the declining reach of the regulation. This observa-

20. In addition to prudential restraints, the traditional rule is grounded in Art. III limits on the jurisdiction of federal courts to actual cases and controversies. * * *

21. Overbreadth challenges are only one type of facial attack. A person whose activity may be constitutionally regulated nevertheless may argue that the statute under which he is convicted or regulated is invalid on its face. See, e.g., *Terminiello.* See generally Monaghan, *Overbreadth,* 1981 S.Ct.Rev. 1, 10–14.

26. In *Gooding v. Wilson,* the Court's invalidation of a Georgia statute making it a misdemeanor to use " 'opprobrious words or abusive language, tending to cause a breach of the peace' " followed from state judicial decisions indicating that "merely to speak words offensive to some who hear them" could constitute a "breach of the peace." * * *

tion appears equally applicable to the publication of books and films as it is to activities, such as picketing or participation in election campaigns, which have previously been categorized as involving conduct plus speech. We see no appreciable difference between the position of a publisher or bookseller in doubt as to the reach of New York's child pornography law and the situation faced by the Oklahoma state employees with respect to the State's restriction on partisan political activity.[d] * * *

"Applying these principles, we hold that § 263.15 is not substantially overbroad. We consider this the paradigmatic case of a state statute whose legitimate reach dwarfs its arguably impermissible applications. [While] the reach of the statute is directed at the hard core of child pornography, the Court of Appeals was understandably concerned that some protected expression, ranging from medical textbooks to pictorials in the National Geographic would fall prey to the statute. How often, if ever, it may be necessary to employ children to engage in conduct clearly within the reach of § 263.15 in order to produce educational, medical, or artistic works cannot be known with certainty. Yet we seriously doubt, and it has not been suggested, that these arguably impermissible applications of the statute amount to more than a tiny fraction of the materials within the statute's reach."[e]

Notes and Questions

1. Consider Schauer, *Codifying the First Amendment: New York v. Ferber*, 1982 Sup.Ct.Rev. 285, 295: The new category created in *Ferber* "bears little resemblance to the category of obscenity delineated by *Miller*. The Court in

d. *Brockett v. Spokane Arcades, Inc.*, p. 508 supra, stated: "The Court of Appeals erred in holding that the *Broadrick* substantial overbreadth requirement is inapplicable where pure speech rather than conduct is at issue. *Ferber* specifically held to the contrary." For commentary on the overbreadth discussion in *Broadrick* and *Ferber*, see Redish, *The Warren Court, The Burger Court and the First Amendment Overbreadth Doctrine*, 78 Nw.U.L.Rev. 1031, 1056–69 (1983).

e. Brennan, J., joined by Marshall, J., agreed "with much of what is said in the Court's opinion. [This] special and compelling interest (in protecting the well-being of the State's youth), and the particular vulnerability of children, afford the State the leeway to regulate pornographic material, the promotion of which is harmful to children, even though the State does not have such leeway when it seeks only to protect consenting adults from exposure to such materials. * * * I also agree with the Court that the 'tiny fraction' of material of serious artistic, scientific or educational value that could conceivably fall within the reach of the statute is insufficient to justify striking the statute on grounds of overbreadth." But the concurrence stated that application of the statute to such materials as "do have serious artistic, scientific or medical value would violate the First Amendment."

On that issue O'Connor, J., wrote a short concurrence: "Although I join the Court's opinion, I write separately to stress that the Court does not hold that New York must except 'material with serious literary, scientific or educational value' from its statute. The Court merely holds that, even if the First Amendment shelters such material, New York's current statute is not sufficiently overbroad to support respondent's facial attack. The compelling interests identified in today's opinion suggest that the Constitution might in fact permit New York to ban knowing distribution of works depicting minors engaged in explicit sexual conduct, regardless of the social value of the depictions. For example, a 12-year-old child photographed while masturbating surely suffers the same psychological harm whether the community labels the photograph 'edifying' or 'tasteless.' The audience's appreciation of the depiction is simply irrelevant to New York's asserted interest in protecting children from psychological, emotional, and mental harm."

Stevens, J., also concurred in the judgment in a short opinion that noted his conclusion that the films in the case were not entitled to first amendment protection, and his view that overbreadth analysis should be avoided by waiting until the hypothetical case actually arises.

Blackmun, J., concurred in the result without opinion.

Ferber explicitly held that child pornography need not appeal to the prurient interest, need not be patently offensive, and need not be based on a consideration of the material as a whole. This last aspect is most important, because it means that the presence of some serious literary, artistic, political, or scientific matter will not constitutionally redeem material containing depictions of sexual conduct by children. The Court referred to the foregoing factors in terms of having 'adjusted' the *Miller* test, but that is like saying a butterfly is an adjusted camel." What precisely is the new category created in *Ferber*?

2. What test or standard of review did the Court use to determine whether the speech should be protected? For general discussion, see Schauer, supra. Did it apply a different test or a standard of review when it formulated its rules in *Gertz*? Are tests or standards of review needed in these contexts? Desirable? Consider Shiffrin, *The First Amendment and Economic Regulation: Away From a General Theory of the First Amendment,* 78 Nw.U.L.Rev. 1212, 1268 (1983): "The complex set of rules produced in *Gertz,* right or wrong, resulted from an appreciation that the protection of truth was important but that the protection of reputation also was important. The Court wisely avoided discussion of levels of scrutiny because any resort to such abstractions would have constitutionalized reductionism." Is "constitutionalized reductionism" desirable because it protects speech and provides guidance to the lower courts?

B. HARM TO WOMEN: FEMINISM AND PORNOGRAPHY

Catharine MacKinnon and Andrea Dworkin have drafted an anti-pornography ordinance that is being considered by a number of jurisdictions. A modified and less comprehensive version was passed by Indianapolis.

PROPOSED LOS ANGELES COUNTY ANTI–PORNOGRAPHY CIVIL RIGHTS LAW

Section 1. Statement of Policy

Pornography is sex discrimination. It exists in the County of Los Angeles, posing a substantial threat to the health, safety, welfare and equality of citizens in the community. Existing state and federal laws are inadequate to solve these problems in the County of Los Angeles.

Section 2. Findings

Pornography is a systematic practice of exploitation and subordination based on sex which differentially harms women. The harm of pornography includes dehumanization, sexual exploitation, forced sex, forced prostitution, physical injury, and social and sexual terrorism and inferiority presented as entertainment. The bigotry and contempt pornography promotes, with the acts of aggression it fosters, diminish opportunities for equality of rights in employment, education, property, public accommodations and public services; create public and private harassment, persecution and denigration; promote injury and degradation such as rape, battery, child sexual abuse, and prostitution and inhibit just enforcement of laws against these acts; contribute significantly to restricting women in particular from full exercise of citizenship and participation in public life, including in neighborhoods; damage relations between the sexes; and undermine women's equal exercise of rights to speech and action guaranteed to all citizens under the Constitutions and laws of the United States, the State of California and the County of Los Angeles.

Section 3. Definitions

1. *Pornography* is the graphic sexually explicit subordination of women through pictures and/or words that also includes one or more of the following: (i) women are presented dehumanized as sexual objects, things or commodities; or (ii) women are presented as sexual objects who enjoy pain or humiliation; or (iii) women are presented as sexual objects who experience sexual pleasure in being raped; or (iv) women are presented as sexual objects tied up or cut up or mutilated or bruised or physically hurt; or (v) women are presented in postures of sexual submission, servility, or display; or (vi) women's body parts—including but not limited to vaginas, breasts, or buttocks—are exhibited such that women are reduced to those parts; or (vii) women are presented as whores by nature; or (viii) women are presented as being penetrated by objects or animals; or (ix) women are presented in scenarios of degradation, injury, torture, shown as filthy or inferior, bleeding, bruised or hurt in a context that makes these conditions sexual.

2. The use of men, children, or transsexuals in the place of women in (1) above is also pornography for purposes of this law.

Section 4. Unlawful Practices

1. *Coercion into pornography*: It shall be sex discrimination to coerce, intimidate, or fraudulently induce (hereafter, "coerce") any person, including transsexual, into performing for pornography, which injury may date from any appearance or sale of any product(s) of such performance(s). The maker(s), seller(s), exhibitor(s) and/or distributor(s) of said pornography may be sued, including for an injunction to eliminate the product(s) of the performance(s) from the public view.

Proof of one or more of the following facts or conditions shall not, without more, negate a finding of coercion:

(i) that the person is a woman; or

(ii) that the person is or has been a prostitute; or

(iii) that the person has attained the age of majority; or

(iv) that the person is connected by blood or marriage to anyone involved in or related to the making of the pornography; or

(v) that the person has previously had, or been thought to have had, sexual relations with anyone, including anyone involved in or related to the making of the pornography; or

(vi) that the person has previously posed for sexually explicit pictures with or for anyone, including anyone involved in or related to the making of the pornography at issue; or

(vii) that anyone else, including a spouse or other relative, has given permission on the person's behalf; or

(viii) that the person actually consented to a use of the performance that is changed into pornography; or

(ix) that the person knew that the purpose of the acts or events in question was to make pornography; or

(x) that the person showed no resistance or appeared to cooperate actively in the photographic sessions or in the events that produced the pornography; or

(xi) that the person signed a contract, or made statements affirming a willingness to cooperate in the production of pornography; or

(xii) that no physical force, threats, or weapons were used in the making of the pornography; or

(xiii) that the person was paid or otherwise compensated.

2. *Trafficking in pornography:* It shall be sex discrimination to produce, sell, exhibit, or distribute pornography, including through private clubs.

(i) City, state, and federally funded public libraries or private and public university and college libraries in which pornography is available for study, including on open shelves but excluding special display presentations, shall not be construed to be trafficking in pornography.

(ii) Isolated passages or isolated parts shall not be actionable under this section.

(iii) Any woman has a claim hereunder as a woman acting against the subordination of women. Any man, child, or transsexual who alleges injury by pornography in the way women are injured by it also has a claim.

3. *Forcing pornography on a person:* It shall be sex discrimination to force pornography on a person, including child or transsexual, in any place of employment, education, home, or public place. Only the perpetrator of the force and/or institution responsible for the force may be sued.

4. *Assault or physical attack due to pornography:* It shall be sex discrimination to assault, physically attack or injure any person, including child or transsexual, in a way that is directly caused by specific pornography. The perpetrator of the assault or attack may be sued. The maker(s), distributor(s), seller(s), and/or exhibitor(s) may also be sued, including for an injunction against the specific pornography's further exhibition, distribution or sale.

Section 5. Defenses

1. It shall not be a defense that the defendant in an action under this law did not know or intend that the materials were pornography or sex discrimination.

2. No damages or compensation for losses shall be recoverable under Sec. 4(2) or other than against the perpetrator of the assault or attack in Sec. 4(4) unless the defendant knew or had reason to know that the materials were pornography.

3. In actions under Sec. 4(2) or other than against the perpetrator of the assault or attack in Sec. 4(4), no damages or compensation for losses shall be recoverable against maker(s) for pornography made, against distributor(s) for pornography distributed, against seller(s) for pornography sold, or against exhibitor(s) for pornography exhibited, prior to the effective date of this law.

Section 6. Enforcement

a. Civil Action: Any person, or their estate, aggrieved by violations of this law may enforce its provisions by means of a civil action. No criminal penalties shall attach for any violation of the provisions of this law. Relief for violations of this law, except as expressly restricted or precluded herein, may include compensatory and punitive damages and reasonable attorney's fees, costs and disbursements.

b. Injunction: Any person who violates this law may be enjoined except that:

(i) In actions under Sec. 4(2), and other than against the perpetrator of the assault or attack under Sec. 4(4), no temporary or permanent injunction shall issue prior to a final judicial determination that the challenged activities constitute a violation of this law.

(ii) No temporary or permanent injunction shall extend beyond such material(s) that, having been described with reasonable specificity by the injunction, have been determined to be validly proscribed under this law.

Section 7. Severability

Should any part(s) of this law be found legally invalid, the remaining part(s) remain valid. A judicial declaration that any part(s) of this law cannot be applied validly in a particular manner or to a particular case or category of cases shall not affect the validity of that part(s) as otherwise applied, unless such other application would clearly frustrate the intent of the Board of Supervisors in adopting this law.

Section 8. Limitation of Action

Actions under this law must be filed within one year of the alleged discriminatory acts.

Notes and Questions

1. *Relationship between obscenity and pornography.* Consider Andrea Dworkin, *Against the Male Flood: Censorship, Pornography, and Equality,* 8 Harv. Women's L.J. 1, 8–9 (1985): "What is at stake in obscenity law is always erection: under what conditions, in what circumstances, how, by whom, by what materials men want it produced in themselves. Men have made this public policy. Why they want to regulate their own erections through law is a question of endless interest and importance to feminists. * * *

"The insult pornography offers, invariably, to sex is accomplished in the active subordination of women: the creation of a sexual dynamic in which the putting-down of women, the suppression of women, and ultimately the brutalization of women, *is* what sex is taken to be. Obscenity in law, and in what it does socially, is erection. Law recognizes the act in this. Pornography, however, is a broader, more comprehensive act, because it crushes a whole class of people through violence and subjugation: and sex is the vehicle that does the crushing. The penis is not the test, as it is in obscenity. Instead, the status of women is the issue. Erection is implicated in the subordinating, but who it reaches and how are the pressing legal and social questions. Pornography, unlike obscenity, is a discrete, identifiable system of sexual exploitation that hurts women as a class by creating inequality and abuse."

Consider MacKinnon, *Pornography, Civil Rights, and Speech,* 20 Harv.Civ. Rts.-Civ.Lib.L.Rev. 1, 50–52 & 16–17 (1985): "To reach the magnitude of this problem on the scale it exists, our law makes trafficking in pornography— production, sale, exhibition, or distribution—actionable. Under the obscenity rubric, much legal and psychological scholarship has centered on a search for the elusive link between pornography defined as obscenity and harm. They have looked high and low—in the mind of the male consumer, in society or in its 'moral fabric,' in correlations between variations in levels of anti-social acts and liberalization of obscenity laws. The only harm they have found has been one they have attributed to 'the social interests in order and morality.' Until recently, no one looked very persistently for harm to women, particularly harm to women through men. The rather obvious fact that the sexes *relate* has been overlooked in the inquiry into the male consumer and his mind. The pornography doesn't just drop out of the sky, go into his head and stop there. Specifically, men rape, batter, prostitute, molest, and sexually harass women. Under conditions of inequality, they also hire, fire, promote, and grade women, decide how much or whether or not we are worth paying and for what, define and approve and disapprove of women in ways that count, that determine our lives.

"In pornography, there it is, in one place, all of the abuses that women had to struggle so long even to begin to articulate, all the *unspeakable* abuse: the rape, the battery, the sexual harassment, the prostitution, and the sexual abuse of children. Only in the pornography it is called something else: sex, sex, sex, sex, and sex, respectively. Pornography sexualizes rape, battery, sexual harassment, prostitution, and child sexual abuse; it thereby celebrates, promotes, authorizes, and legitimizes them. More generally, it eroticizes the dominance and submission that is the dynamic common to them all. It makes hierarchy sexy and calls that 'the truth about sex' or just a mirror of reality." See generally Dworkin, *Pornography: Men Possessing Women* (1981). For a review of the social science evidence relating to pornography and aggression against women, see *Pornography and Sexual Aggression* (Malamuth & Donnerstein, eds. 1984).

2. *The trafficking section.* Is the trafficking section constitutional under *Miller?* Consider the following hypothetical commentary: "The Dworkin-MacKinnon proposal focuses on a narrower class of material than *Miller* because it excludes erotic materials that do not involve subordination. That class of material upon which it does focus appeals to prurient interest because it is graphic and sexually explicit. Moreover, the eroticization of dominance in the ways specified in the ordinance is so patently offensive to community standards that it can be said as a matter of law that this class of materials lacks *serious* literary, artistic, political, or scientific value as a matter of law." Do you agree?

Is there a good analogy to *Beauharnais?* To *Ferber?* Did more or less harm exist in *Gertz? Miller? Ferber?* Was there more or less of a threat to first amendment values in *Gertz? Miller? Ferber?* Should this be accepted as a new category? Consider, Kaminer, *Pornography and the First Amendment: Prior Restraints and Private Action,* 239, 245 in *Take Back the Night: Women on Pornography* (Lederer ed. 1980): "The Women's Movement is a civil rights movement, and we should appreciate the importance of individual freedom of choice and the danger of turning popular sentiment into law in areas affecting individual privacy.

"Legislative or judicial control of pornography is simply not possible without breaking down the legal principles and procedures that are essential to our own right to speak and, ultimately, our freedom to control our own lives. We must continue to organize against pornography and the degradation and abuse of women, but we must not ask the government to take up our struggle for us. The power it will assume to do so will be far more dangerous to us all than the 'power' of pornography." [a]

---

a. Compare Hunter & Law, *Brief Amici Curiae of Feminist Anti-Censorship Taskforce* (on appeal in *Hudnut,* below) 14 & 43–44 (1985): The ordinance conceivably "would require the judiciary to impose its views of correct sexuality on a diverse community. The inevitable result would be to disapprove those images that are least conventional and privilege those that are closest to majoritarian beliefs about proper sexuality. [Moreover] [b]y defining sexually explicit images of women as subordinating and degrading to them, the ordinance reinforces the stereotypical view that 'good' women do not seek and enjoy sex. [Finally], the ordinance perpetuates a stereotype of women as helpless victims, incapable of consent, and in need of protection."

3. *The pornography definition.* Is the proposed definition too vague? Is it more or less vague than the terminology employed in *Miller?* Is there a core of clear meaning? How would you revise it to clarify its meaning? Is the definition overbroad? What revisions, if any, would you suggest to narrow its scope?

Consider Emerson, *Pornography and the First Amendment: A Reply to Professor MacKinnon,* 3 Yale L. & Pol. Rev. 130, 131–32 (1985): "The sweep of the Indianapolis Ordinance is breathtaking. It would subject to governmental ban virtually all depictions of rape, verbal or pictorial, and a substantial proportion of other presentations of sexual encounters. More specifically, it would outlaw such works of literature as the *Arabian Nights,* John Cleland's *Fanny Hill,* Henry Miller's *Tropic of Cancer,* William Faulkner's *Sanctuary,* and Norman Mailer's *Ancient Evenings,* to name but a few. The ban would extend from Greek mythology and Shakespeare to the millions of copies of 'romance novels' now being sold in the supermarkets. It would embrace much of the world's art, from ancient carvings to Picasso, well-known films too numerous to mention, and a large amount of commercial advertising.

"The scope of the Indianapolis Ordinance is not accidental. Nor could it be limited by more precise drafting without defeating the purpose of its authors. As Professor MacKinnon emphasizes, male domination has deep, pervasive and ancient roots in our society, so it is not surprising that our literature, art, entertainment and commerical practices are permeated by attitudes and behavior that create and reflect the inferior status of women. If the answer to the problem, as Professor MacKinnon describes it, is government suppression of sexual expression that contributes to female subordination, then the net of restraint has to be cast on a nearly limitless scale. Even narrowing the proscribed area to depictions of sexual activities involving violence would outlaw a large segment of the world's literature and art."

Is the proposed ordinance susceptible to a narrower construction than that offered by Professor Emerson?

4. *The coercion into pornography section.* Is this part of the proposed ordinance a straightforward application of *Ferber?* Is the conception of coercion constitutional? What was the conception in *Ferber?* If modifications are needed, what should they be?

5. *The assault provision.* Should the maker of a pornographic work be responsible for assaults prompted by the work? Should the maker of non-pornographic works be responsible for imitative assaults. In *Olivia N. v. NBC,* 126 Cal.App.3d 488, 178 Cal.Rptr. 888 (1981), the victim of a sexual assault allegedly imitating a sexual assault in NBC's "Born Innocent" sued the network. Olivia N. claimed that NBC negligently exposed her to serious risk because it knew or should have known that someone would imitate the act portrayed in the movie. Suppose Olivia N. could show that NBC had been advised that such an assault was likely if the movie were shown? Should a court analogize to cases

For a variety of feminist perspectives, see *Take Back the Night,* supra. See also Snitow, Stansell & Thompson, etc., *Powers of Desire* 419–67 (1983). For general discussion of the legal issues, see Bryden, *Between Two Constitutions: Feminism and Pornography,* 2 Const. Comm. 147 (1985); Gershel, *Evaluating a Proposed Civil Rights Approach to Pornography: Legal Analyses as if Women Mattered,* 11 Wm. Mitchell L.Rev. 41 (1985); Hoffman, *Feminism, Pornography, and Law,* 133 U.Pa.L.Rev. 497 (1985); Tigue, *Civil Rights and Censorship—Incompatible Bedfellows,* 11 Wm.Mitchell L.Rev. 81 (1985); Note, *Anti-Pornography Laws and First Amendment Values,* 98 Harv. L.Rev. 460 (1984). See also *American Booksellers Ass'n v. Hudnut,* 771 F.2d 323 (7th Cir.1985) (declaring Indianapolis ordinance unconstitutional).

like *Gertz?* The California court ruled that Olivia N. could not prevail unless she met the *Brandenburg* standard.

C. RACIST SPEECH REVISITED: THE NAZIS

"What do you want to sell in the marketplace? What idea? The idea of murder?"

Erna Gans, a concentration camp survivor and active leader in the Skokie B'nai B'rith.[a]

COLLIN v. SMITH, 578 F.2d 1197 (7th Cir.), cert. denied, 439 U.S. 916, 99 S.Ct. 291, 58 L.Ed.2d 264 (1978), per PELL, J., struck down a Village of Skokie *"Racial Slur" Ordinance,* making it a misdemeanor to disseminate any material (defined to include "public display of markings and clothing of symbolic significance") promoting and inciting racial or religious hatred. The Village would apparently apply this ordinance to the display of swastikas and military uniforms by the NSPA, a "Nazi organization" which planned to peacefully demonstrate for some 20–30 minutes in front of the Skokie Village Hall.

Although there was some evidence that some individuals "might have difficulty restraining their reactions to the Nazi demonstration," the Village "does not rely on a fear of responsive violence to justify the ordinance, and does not even suggest that there will be any physical violence if the march is held. This confession takes the case out of the scope of *Brandenburg* and *Feiner.* [It] also eliminates any argument based on the fighting words doctrine of *Chaplinsky,* [which] applied only to words with a direct tendency to cause violence by the persons to whom, individually, the words were addressed."

The court rejected, inter alia, the argument that the Nazi march, with its display of swastikas and uniforms, "will create a substantive evil that it has a right to prohibit: the infliction of psychic trauma on resident holocaust survivors [some 5,000] and other Jewish residents. [The] problem with engrafting an exception on the First Amendment for such situations is that they are indistinguishable in principle from speech that 'invite[s] dispute [or] induces a condition of unrest [or] even stirs people to anger,' *Terminiello.* Yet these are among the 'high purposes' of the First Amendment. [Where,] as here, a crime is made of a silent march, attended only by symbols and not by extrinsic conduct offensive in itself, we think the words of *Street v. New York* [p. 636 infra] are very much on point: '[A]ny shock effect [must] be attributed to the content of the ideas expressed. [P]ublic expression of ideas may not be prohibited merely because the ideas are themselves offensive to some of their hearers.' "

Nor was the court impressed with the argument that the proposed march was "not speech, [but] rather an invasion, intensely menacing no matter how peacefully conducted" (most of Skokie's residents are Jewish): "There *need be* no captive audience, as Village residents may, if they wish, simply avoid the Village Hall for thirty minutes on a Sunday afternoon, which no doubt would be their normal course of conduct on a day when the Village Hall was not open in the regular course of business. Absent such intrusion or captivity, there is no justifiable substantial privacy interest to save [the ordinance], when it attempts, by fiat, to declare the entire Village, at all times, a privacy zone that may be sanitized from the offensiveness of Nazi ideology and symbols." [b]

a. Quoted in Friendly & Elliot, *The Constitution: That Delicate Balance* 83 (1984).

b. See also *Skokie v. National Socialist Party,* 69 Ill.2d 605, 14 Ill.Dec. 890, 373 N.E.2d 21 (1978). For commentary relating the Skokie issue to regulation of pornography, and of commercial speech, for the purpose of asking whether there are general principles of free-

Notes and Questions

1. Is *Beauharnais,* p. 460 supra, still "good law"?

2. *Justifying the result.* Consider Bollinger, *Book Review,* 80 Mich.L.Rev. 617, 631 (1982) (reviewing Neier, *Defending My Enemy: American Nazis, The Skokie Case, and the Risks of Freedom* (1979)): "The value of any act is dependent upon the reasons behind it, and in free speech, as in any other area, getting the reasons straight is of first importance. One can understand [a] choice to protect the free speech activities of Nazis, but not because people should value their message in the slightest or believe it should be seriously entertained, not because a commitment to self-government or rationality logically demands that such ideas be presented for consideration, not because of a simple hope *qua* conviction that anti-Nazi sentiment will win in the end, not because the anti-Nazi belief will be stimulated by open confrontation and argument with the Nazi belief, not because a line could not be drawn that would exclude this ideology without inevitably encroaching on ideas that one likes—not for any of these reasons nor others related to them that are a part of the traditional baggage of the free speech argumentation; but rather because the danger of intolerance toward ideas is so pervasive an issue in our social lives, the process of mastering a capacity for tolerance so difficult, that it makes sense somewhere in the system to attempt to confront that problem and exercise more self-restraint than may be otherwise required. We should be, in short, more concerned with addressing through the act of tolerance the potential problems of intolerance than with valuing the act of speech itself.

"On this basis, then, tolerance becomes not merely a futile attempt at shoring up the legal barricades, a response devoid of intrinsic value and meaning, but instead a symbolic act indicating an awareness of the risks and dangers of intolerance and a commitment to developing a certain attitude toward the ideas and beliefs of others. At least a part of this attitude is a willingness to recognize the existence of ideas within society that we might otherwise prefer to ignore, and to see the risks involved in succumbing to the wish to refuse to acknowledge their existence. Self-knowledge may be the best defense available against the ideas that we hate."

For rich elaboration of this perspective, see Bollinger, *The Tolerant Society: Freedom of Speech and Extremist Speech in America* (1986).

VI. IS SOME PROTECTED SPEECH LESS EQUAL THAN OTHER PROTECTED SPEECH?

A. NEAR OBSCENE SPEECH

ERZNOZNIK v. JACKSONVILLE, 422 U.S. 205, 95 S.Ct. 2268, 45 L.Ed.2d 125 (1975), per POWELL, J., held invalid on its face an ordinance that prohibited drive-in theaters from showing films containing nudity ("bare buttocks, * * * female bare breasts, or human bare pubic areas") when visible from a public street or public place: "Appellee concedes that its ordinance sweeps far beyond the permissible restraints on obscenity, and thus applies to films that are

dom of expression and whether freedom of expression should be category-dependent, see Scanlon, *Freedom of Expression and Categories of Expression,* 40 U.Pitt.L.Rev. 519 (1979). For assessment of the complicated connection between Skokie and equality values especially in light of the rest of first amendment law, see Tribe, *Constitutional Choices* 219–20 (1985). Compare Downs, *Skokie Revisited: Hate Group Speech and the First Amendment,* 60 Not.D.Law. 629 (1985).

protected by the First Amendment. [Its] primary argument is that it may protect its citizens against unwilling exposure to materials that may be offensive. Jacksonville's ordinance, however, does not protect citizens from all movies that might offend; rather it singles out films containing nudity, presumably because the lawmakers considered them especially offensive to passersby. * * *

"The plain, if at times disquieting, truth is that in our pluralistic society, constantly proliferating new and ingenious forms of expression, 'we are inescapably captive audiences for many purposes.' Much that we encounter offends our esthetic, if not our political and moral, sensibilities. Nevertheless, the Constitution does not permit the government to decide which types of otherwise protected speech are sufficiently offensive to require protection for the unwilling listener or viewer. Rather,[6] the burden normally falls upon the viewer to 'avoid further bombardment of [his] sensibilities simply by averting [his] eyes.' *Cohen v. California.* The Jacksonville ordinance discriminates among movies solely on the basis of content.[7] Its effect is to deter drive-in theaters from showing movies containing any nudity, however innocent or even educational.[8] This discrimination cannot be justified as a means of preventing significant intrusions on privacy. The ordinance seeks only to keep these films from being seen from public streets and places where the offended viewer readily can avert his eyes. In short, the screen of a drive-in theater is not 'so obtrusive as to make it impossible for an unwilling individual to avoid exposure to it.' *Redrup.* Thus, we conclude that the limited privacy interest of persons on the public streets cannot justify this censorship of otherwise protected speech on the basis of its [content].

6. It has also been suggested that government may proscribe, by a properly framed law, "the willful use of scurrilous language calculated to offend the sensibilities of an unwilling audience." *Rosenfeld* (Powell, J., dissenting). [In] the present case, however, appellant is not trying to reach, much less shock, unwilling viewers. Appellant manages a commercial enterprise which depends for its success on *paying* customers, not on freeloading passersby. Presumably, where economically feasible, the screen of a drive-in theater will be shielded from those who do not pay.

7. Scenes of nudity in a movie, like pictures of nude persons in a book, must be considered as a part of the whole work. In this respect such nudity is distinguishable from the kind of public nudity traditionally subject to indecent exposure laws.

The Chief Justice's dissent, in response to this point, states that "[u]nlike persons reading books, passersby cannot consider fragments of drive-in movies as a part of the 'whole work' for the simple reason that they see but do not *hear* the [performance]." (emphasis in original). At issue here, however, is not the viewing rights of unwilling viewers but rather the rights of those who operate drive-in theatres and the public that attends these establishments. The effect of the Jacksonville ordinance is to increase the cost of showing films containing nudity. See n. 8, infra. In certain circumstances theatres will avoid showing these movies rather than incur

the additional costs. As a result persons who want to see such films at drive-ins will be unable to do so. It is in this regard that a motion picture must be considered as a whole, and not as isolated fragments or scenes of nudity.

[The Chief Justice's response to fn. 7 also stated: "[T]hose persons who legitimately desire to consider the 'work as a whole' are not foreclosed from doing so. The record shows that the film from which appellant's prosecution arose was exhibited in several indoor theaters in the Jacksonville area. And the owner of a drive-in movie theater is not prevented from exhibiting nonobscene films involving nudity so long as he effectively shields the screen from public view. Thus, regardless of whether the ordinance involved here can be loosely described as regulating the content of a certain type of display, it is not a restriction of any 'message.' The First Amendment interests involved in this case are trivial at best."]

8. Such a deterrent, although it might not result in total suppression of these movies, is a restraint on free expression. The record does not indicate how much it would cost to block public view of appellant's theater. Such costs generally will vary with circumstances. In one case the expense was estimated at approximately a quarter million dollars. See *Olympic Drive-In Theatre, Inc. v. Pagedale,* 441 S.W.2d 5, 8 (Mo.1969).

"In this case, assuming the ordinance is aimed at prohibiting youths from viewing the films, the restriction is broader than permissible. The ordinance is not directed against sexually explicit nudity, nor is it otherwise limited. Rather, [it] would bar a film containing a picture of a baby's buttocks, the nude body of a war victim, or scenes from a culture in which nudity is indigenous. The ordinance also might prohibit newsreel scenes of the opening of an art exhibit as well as shots of bathers on a beach. Clearly all nudity cannot be deemed obscene even as to minors. See *Ginsberg*. Nor can such a broad restriction be justified by any other governmental interest pertaining to minors. Speech that is neither obscene as to youths nor subject to some other legitimate proscription cannot be suppressed solely to protect the young from ideas or images that a legislative body thinks unsuitable for them." [a]

BURGER, C.J., joined by Rehnquist, J., dissented: "[T]he conclusion that only a limited interest of persons on the public streets is at stake here can be supported only if one completely ignores the unique visual medium to which the Jacksonville ordinance is directed. Whatever validity the notion that passersby may protect their sensibilities by averting their eyes may have when applied to words printed on an individual's jacket, see *Cohen*, [it] distorts reality to apply that notion to the outsize screen of a drive-in movie [theater].

"[The] screen of a drive-in movie theater is a unique type of eye-catching display that can be highly intrusive and distracting. Public authorities have a legitimate interest in regulating such displays under the police power; for example, even though traffic safety may not have been the only target of the ordinance in issue here, I think it not unreasonable for lawmakers to believe that public nudity on a giant screen, visible at night to hundreds of drivers of automobiles, may have a tendency to divert attention from their task and cause accidents." [b]

YOUNG v. AMERICAN MINI THEATRES, INC.

427 U.S. 50, 96 S.Ct. 2440, 49 L.Ed.2d 310 (1976).

MR. JUSTICE STEVENS delivered the opinion of the Court.*

[Detroit "Anti-Skid Row" ordinances prohibited "adult motion picture theaters" and "adult book stores" within 1,000 feet of any two other "regulated uses," which included such theaters and book stores, liquor stores, pool halls, pawnshops, and the like. The ordinances defined "adult motion picture theater" as one "presenting material distinguished or characterized by an emphasis on matter depicting, describing or relating to 'Specified Sexual Activities' [a] or

---

a. The Court also rejected the argument that the ordinance was aimed at traffic regulation: "[The] ordinance applies to movie screens visible from public places as well as public streets, thus indicating that it is not a traffic regulation. But even if this were the purpose [it] would be invalid" because "strikingly underinclusive" in "singling out [even] the most fleeting and innocent glimpses of nudity," which violated both the equal protection clause and the first amendment by discriminating on the basis of content without justification, since "other scenes in the customary screen diet, ranging from soap opera to violence, would be [no] less distracting to the passing motorist."

b. White, J., also dissented. Douglas, J., concurred.

* Part III of this opinion is joined only by The Chief Justice, Mr. Justice White, and Mr. Justice Rehnquist.

a. "Specified Sexual Activities" were defined thus:

"1. Human Genitals in a state of sexual stimulation or arousal;

"2. Acts of human masturbation, sexual intercourse or sodomy;

"3. Fondling or other erotic touching of human genitals, public region, buttock or female breast."

'Specified Anatomical Areas' " [b] and "adult book store" in substantially the same terms. The Court upheld the ordinances, reversing a decision in a federal declaratory judgment action by two theater owners wishing regularly to exhibit "adult" motion pictures.]

I. [R]espondents claim that the ordinances are too vague [because] they cannot determine how much of the ["specified"] activity may be permissible before the exhibition is "characterized by an emphasis" on such matter. [We] find it unnecessary to consider the validity of [this argument. Both] theaters propose to offer adult fare on a regular basis. [Therefore], the element of vagueness in these ordinances has not affected these respondents. * * *

Because the ordinances affect communication protected by the First Amendment, respondents argue that they may raise the vagueness issue even though there is no uncertainty about the impact of the ordinances on their own rights. On several occasions we have determined that a defendant whose own speech was unprotected had standing to challenge the constitutionality of a statute which purported to prohibit protected speech, or even speech arguably protected. *Broadrick*. The exception is justified by the overriding importance of maintaining a free and open market for the interchange of ideas. Nevertheless, if the statute's deterrent effect of legitimate expression is not "both real and substantial" and if the statute is "readily subject to a narrowing construction by the state courts" the litigant is not permitted to assert the rights of third parties.

We are not persuaded that the Detroit Zoning Ordinances will have a significant deterrent effect on the exhibition of films protected by the First Amendment. [T]he only vagueness in the ordinances relates to the amount of sexually explicit activity that may be portrayed before the material can be said to be "characterized by an emphasis" on such matter. For most films the question will be readily answerable; to the extent that an area of doubt exists, we see no reason why the statute is not "readily subject to a narrowing construction by the state courts." Since there is surely a less vital interest in the uninhibited exhibition of material that is on the border line between pornography and artistic expression than in the free dissemination of ideas of social and political significance,[c] and since the limited amount of uncertainty in the statute is easily susceptible of a narrowing construction, we think this is an inappropriate case in which to adjudicate the hypothetical claims of persons not before the Court. * * *

II. [T]he ordinances prohibit theaters which are not licensed as "adult motion picture theaters" from exhibiting films which are protected by the First Amendment. Respondents argue that the ordinances are therefore invalid as prior restraints on free speech. The ordinances are not challenged on the

---

b. "Specified Anatomical Areas" were defined thus:

"1. Less than completely and opaquely covered: (a) human genitals, pubic region, (b) buttock, and (c) female breast below a point immediately above the top of the areola, and

"2. Human male genitals in a discernibly turgid state, even if completely and opaquely covered."

c. But see Hunter & Law, p. 542 supra, at 28–29: "[S]exual speech is political. One core insight of modern feminism is that the personal is political. The question of who does the

dishes and rocks the cradle affects both the nature of the home and the composition of the legislature. The dynamics of intimate relations are likewise political, both to the individuals involved and by their multiplied effects to the wider society. To argue [that] sexually explicit speech is less important than other categories of discourse reinforces the conceptual structures that have identified women's concerns with relationships and intimacy as less significant and valuable precisely because those concerns are falsely regarded as having no bearing on the structure of social and political life."

ground that they impose a limit on the total number of adult theaters which may operate in the city of Detroit. There is no claim that distributors or exhibitors of adult films are denied access to the market or conversely, that the viewing public is unable to satisfy its appetite for sexually explicit fare. Viewed as an entity, the market for this commodity is essentially unrestrained.

It is true, however, that adult films may only be exhibited commercially in licensed theaters. But that is also true of all motion pictures. The city's general zoning laws require all motion picture theaters to satisfy certain locational as well as other requirements; we have no doubt that the municipality may control the location of theaters as well as the location of other commercial establishments, either by confining them to certain specified commercial zones or by requiring that they be dispersed throughout the city. The mere fact that the commercial exploitation of material protected by the First Amendment is subject to zoning and other licensing requirements is not a sufficient reason for invalidating these ordinances.

Putting to one side for the moment the fact that adult motion picture theaters must satisfy a locational restriction not applicable to other theaters, we are also persuaded that the 1,000-foot restriction does not, in itself, create an impermissible restraint on protected communication. The city's interest in planning and regulating the use of property for commercial purposes is clearly adequate to support that kind of restriction applicable to all theaters within the city limits. In short, apart from the fact that the ordinances treat adult theaters differently from other theaters and the fact that the classification is predicated on the content of material shown in the respective theaters, the regulation of the place where such films may be exhibited does not offend the First Amendment. We turn, therefore, to the question whether the classification is consistent with the Equal Protection Clause.

III. [T]he use of streets and parks for the free expression of views on national affairs may not be conditioned upon the sovereign's agreement with what a speaker may intend to say. [If] picketing in the vicinity of a school is to be allowed to express the point of view of labor, that means of expression in that place must be allowed for other points of view as well. As we said in [*Chicago Police Dep't v. Mosley,* p. 643 infra], "The central problem with Chicago's ordinance is that it describes permissible picketing in terms of its subject matter. [A]bove all else, the First Amendment means that government has no power to restrict expression because of its message, its ideas, its subject matter, or its content. [Any] restriction on expressive activity because of its content would completely undercut the 'profound national commitment to the principle that debate on public issues should be uninhibited, robust, and wide-open.' [*New York Times*]. Selective exclusions from a public forum may not be based on content alone, and may not be justified by reference to content alone."

This statement, and others to the same effect, read literally and without regard for the facts of the case in which it was made, would absolutely preclude any regulation of expressive activity predicated in whole or in part on the content of the communication. But we learned long ago that broad statements of principle, no matter how correct in the context in which they are made, are sometimes qualified by contrary decisions before the absolute limit of the stated principle is reached. When we review this Court's actual adjudications in the First Amendment area, we find this to have been the case with the stated principle that there may be no restriction whatever on expressive activity because of its content. * * *

The question whether speech is, or is not, protected by the First Amendment often depends on the content of the speech. Thus, the line between permissible advocacy and impermissible incitement to crime or violence depends, not merely on the setting in which the speech occurs, but also on exactly what the speaker had to say. Similarly, it is the content of the utterance that determines whether it is a protected epithet or an unprotected "fighting comment." And in time of war "the publication of the sailing dates of transports or the number and location of troops" may unquestionably be restrained, see *Near v. Minnesota* [p. 584 infra].

Even within the area of protected speech, a difference in content may require a different governmental response. [*New York Times*] held that a public official may not recover damages from a critic of his official conduct without proof of "malice" as specially defined in that opinion. Implicit in the opinion is the assumption that if the content of the newspaper article had been different— that is, if its subject matter had not been a public official—a lesser standard of proof would have been adequate. [We] have recently held that the First Amendment affords some protection to commercial speech. [The] measure of [protection] to commercial speech will surely be governed largely by the content of the communication.[32]   *   *   *

More directly in point are opinions dealing with the question whether the First Amendment prohibits the state and federal governments from wholly suppressing sexually oriented materials on the basis of their "obscene character." In *Ginsberg*, the Court upheld a conviction for selling to a minor magazines which were concededly not "obscene" if shown to adults. Indeed, the Members of the Court who would accord the greatest protection to such materials have repeatedly indicated that the State could prohibit the distribution or exhibition of such materials to juveniles and consenting adults. Surely the First Amendment does not foreclose such a prohibition; yet it is equally clear that any such prohibition must rest squarely on an appraisal of the content of material otherwise within a constitutionally protected area.

Such a line may be drawn on the basis of content without violating the Government's paramount obligation of neutrality in its regulation of protected communication. For the regulation of the places where sexually explicit films may be exhibited is unaffected by whatever social, political, or philosophical message the film may be intended to communicate; whether the motion picture ridicules or characterizes one point of view or another, the effect of the ordinances is exactly the same.

Moreover, even though we recognize that the First Amendment will not tolerate the total suppression of erotic materials that have some arguably artistic value, it is manifest that society's interest in protecting this type of expression is of a wholly different, and lesser, magnitude than the interest in untrammeled political debate that inspired Voltaire's immortal comment.[d] Whether political oratory or philosophical discussion moves us to applaud or to despise what is said, every school-child can understand why our duty to defend the right to speak remains the same. But few of us would march our sons and daughters off to war to preserve the citizen's right to see "Specified Sexual Activities" exhibited in the theaters of our choice. Even though the First

---

32. As Mr. Justice Stewart pointed out in *Virginia Pharmacy,* [p. 554 infra], the "differences between commercial price and product advertising [and] ideological communication" permits regulation of the former that the First Amendment would not tolerate with respect to the latter (concurring opinion).

d. The opinion had earlier quoted Voltaire: "I disapprove of what you say, but I will defend to the death your right to say it."

Amendment protects communication in this area from total suppression, we hold that the State may legitimately use the content of these materials as the basis for placing them in a different classification from other motion pictures.

The remaining question is whether the line drawn by these ordinances is justified by the city's interest in preserving the character of its neighborhoods. [The] record discloses a factual basis for the Common Council's conclusion that this kind of restriction will have the desired effect.[34] It is not our function to appraise the wisdom of its decision to require adult theaters to be separated rather than concentrated in the same areas. In either event, the city's interest in attempting to preserve the quality of urban life is one that must be accorded high respect. Moreover, the city must be allowed a reasonable opportunity to experiment with solutions to admittedly serious problems.

Since what is ultimately at stake is nothing more than a limitation on the place where adult films may be exhibited,[35] even though the determination of whether a particular film fits that characterization turns on the nature of its content, we conclude that the city's interest in the present and future character of its neighborhoods adequately supports its classification of motion pictures.

* * *

MR. JUSTICE POWELL, concurring in the judgment and portions of the opinion.

Although I agree with much of what is said in the plurality opinion, and concur in Parts I and II, my approach to the resolution of this case is sufficiently different to prompt me to write separately.[1] I view the case as presenting an example of innovative land-use regulation, implicating First Amendment concerns only incidentally and to a limited extent. * * *

In this case, there is no indication that the application of the Anti-Skid Row Ordinance to adult theaters has the effect of suppressing production of or, to any significant degree, restricting access to adult movies. Nortown concededly will not be able to exhibit adult movies at its present location, and the ordinance limits the potential location of the proposed Pussy Cat. The constraints of the ordinance with respect to location may indeed create economic loss for some who are engaged in this business. But in this respect they are affected no differently than any other commercial enterprise that suffers economic detriment as a result of land-use regulation. The cases are legion that sustained zoning against claims of serious economic damage.

The inquiry for First Amendment purposes is not concerned with economic impact; rather, it looks only to the effect of this ordinance upon freedom of expression. This prompts essentially two inquiries: (i) does the ordinance impose any content limitation on the creators of adult movies or their ability to

---

34. The City Council's determination was that a concentration of "adult" movie theaters causes the area to deteriorate and become a focus of crime, effects which are not attributable to theaters showing other types of films. It is this secondary effect which this zoning ordinance attempts to avoid, not the dissemination of "offensive" speech. In contrast, in *Erznoznik*, the justifications offered by the city rested primarily on the city's interest in protecting its citizens from exposure to unwanted, "offensive" speech. * * *

35. The situation would be quite different if the ordinance had the effect of suppressing, or greatly restricting access to, lawful speech. Here, however, the District Court specifically found that "[t]he Ordinances do not affect the operation of existing establishments but only the location of new ones. There are myriad locations in the City of Detroit which must be over 1000 feet from existing regulated establishments. This burden on First Amendment rights is slight." * * *

1. I do not think we need reach, nor am I inclined to agree with, the holding in Part III (and supporting discussion) that nonobscene, erotic materials may be treated differently under First Amendment principles from other forms of protected expression. I do not consider the conclusions in Part I of the opinion to depend on distinctions between protected speech.

make them available to whom they desire, and (ii) does it restrict in any significant way the viewing of these movies by those who desire to see them? On the record in this case, these inquiries must be answered in the negative. At most the impact of the ordinance on these interests is incidental and minimal.[2] Detroit has silenced no message, has invoked no censorship, and has imposed no limitation upon those who wish to view them. The ordinance is addressed only to the places at which this type of expression may be presented, a restriction that does not interfere with content. Nor is there any significant overall curtailment of adult movie presentations, or the opportunity for a message to reach an audience. On the basis of the District Court's finding, it appears that if a sufficient market exists to support them the number of adult movie theaters in Detroit will remain approximately the same, free to purvey the same message. To be sure some prospective patrons may be inconvenienced by this dispersal. But other patrons, depending upon where they live or work, may find it more convenient to view an adult movie when adult theaters are not concentrated in a particular section of the city.

In these circumstances, it is appropriate to analyze the permissibility of Detroit's action under the four-part test of *United States v. O'Brien* [p. 621 infra].[e] Under that test, a governmental regulation is sufficiently justified, despite its incidental impact upon First Amendment interests, "if it is within the constitutional power of the Government; if it furthers an important government interest; if the government interest is unrelated to the suppression of free expression; and if the incidental restriction [on] First Amendment freedoms is no greater than is essential to the furtherance of that interest." [Powell, J., concluded that the Detroit ordinance satisfied the *O'Brien* test.]

MR. JUSTICE STEWART, with whom MR. JUSTICE BRENNAN, MR. JUSTICE MARSHALL and MR. JUSTICE BLACKMUN join, dissenting.

[This case involves] the constitutional permissibility of selective interference with protected speech whose content is thought to produce distasteful effects. It is elementary that a prime function of the First Amendment is to guard against just such interference. By refusing to invalidate Detroit's ordinance the Court rides roughshod over cardinal principles of First Amendment law, which require that time, place and manner regulations that affect protected expression be content-neutral except in the limited context of a captive or juvenile audience. In place of these principles the Court invokes a concept wholly alien to the First Amendment. Since "few of us would march our sons and daughters off to war to preserve the citizen's right to see 'Specified Sexual Activities' exhibited in the theaters of our choice," the Court implies that these films are not entitled to the full protection of the Constitution. This stands "Voltaire's immortal comment," on its head. For if the guarantees of the First Amendment were reserved for expression that more than a "few of us" would take up arms to defend, then the right of free expression would be defined and circumscribed by current popular opinion. The guarantees of the Bill of Rights were designed to protect against precisely such majoritarian limitations on individual liberty.

The fact that the "offensive" speech here may not address "important" topics—"ideas of social and political significance," in the Court's terminology—

---

2. The communication involved here is not a kind in which the content or effectiveness of the message depends in some measure upon where or how it is conveyed. * * *

e. The *O'Brien* test was announced in a case where a course of conduct (publicly burn-

ing a selective service card) combined unprotected nonspeech elements (destroying the card) with protected speech elements (expressing antiwar views).

does not mean that it is less worthy of constitutional protection. "Wholly neutral futilities [come] under the protection of free speech as fully as do Keats' poems or Donne's sermons." *Winters* (Frankfurter, J., dissenting), accord, *Cohen v. California.* Moreover, in the absence of a judicial determination of obscenity, it is by no means clear that the speech is not "important" even on the Court's terms [*Roth; Kingsley Pictures*].

I can only interpret today's decision as an aberration. The Court is undoubtedly sympathetic, as am I, to the well-intentioned efforts of Detroit to "clean up" its streets and prevent the proliferation of "skid rows." But it is in those instances where protected speech grates most unpleasantly against the sensibilities that judicial vigilance must be at its [height].

The factual parallels between [*Erznoznik* and this case] are striking. There, as here, the ordinance did not forbid altogether the "distasteful" expression but merely required an alteration in the physical setting of the forum. There, as here, the city's principal asserted interest was in minimizing the "undesirable" effects of speech having a particular content. [And] the particular content of the restricted speech at issue in *Erznoznik* precisely parallels the content restricted in [Detroit's] definition of "Specified Anatomical Areas." * * *

The Court must never forget that the consequences of rigorously enforcing the guarantees of the First Amendment are frequently unpleasant. Much speech that seems to be of little or no value will enter the marketplace of ideas, threatening the quality of our social discourse and, more generally, the serenity of our lives. But that is the price to be paid for constitutional freedom. * * * [f]

Notes and Questions

1. *A hierarchy of protected speech.* Stevens, J., contends that as a matter of law some "protected" speech is less worthy than other protected speech. The dissenters and Powell, J., reject that view. Which approach is more likely to preserve first amendment values? Would treating all protected speech equally invite a dilution of the force of the first amendment with respect to the speech that "really" matters? Is the process of allowing judges to pick and choose between types of protected speech too dangerous? Would it be dangerous to protect political speech more than sexually explicit speech? Is sexually explicit speech non-political? If the plaintiff's approach were accepted, would the Court ultimately "rank speech in all its myriad forms, in order of its perceived importance," with new rankings being "created and old ones rejected depending on the Court's view of the worthiness of the speech at issue"? Goldman, *A Doctrine of Worthier Speech: Young v. American Mini Theatres, Inc.,* 21 St. Louis U.L.J. 281, 300–01 (1977).

2. *The exhibitor's free expression.* Did Powell, J., assume that the "first amendment rights [involved] in *Young* were primarily vested in creator and audience"? Note, 42 Mo.L.Rev. 461, 468 (1977); Note, 28 Case W.Res.L.Rev. 456, 482 (1978). Does the plurality opinion and its fn. 35 reflect similar lack of

f. Blackmun, J., joined by the other three dissenters, also filed a dissent that protested the rejection of the vagueness argument, concluding on this issue: "As to the third reason, that 'adult' material is simply entitled to less protection, it certainly explains the lapse in applying settled vagueness principles, as in- deed it explains this whole case. In joining Mr. Justice Stewart I have joined his forth- right rejection of the notion that First Amend- ment protection is diminished for 'erotic materials' that only a 'few of us' see the need to protect."

concern for exhibitor's interests? How would a record be built to distinguish *Young* from a similar ordinance in another city?

3. *Exclusionary zoning.* *Schad v. Mt. Ephraim,* 452 U.S. 61, 101 S.Ct. 2176, 68 L.Ed.2d 671 (1981) invalidated a Borough ordinance that permitted adult theaters and bookstores, but excluded live entertainment from its commercial zone. Even as applied to nude dancing, the Court found that the ordinance was not narrowly drawn to serve a sufficiently substantial state interest. The Court observed that there was no evidence to show that the entertainment at issue was available in reasonably nearby areas. What if it were? Suppose the Borough banned adult theaters and bookstores, but could show they were available nearby?

4. *Public display of "adult" material.* Suppose a city allows the sale of adult material only in establishments that announce their nature, but does not allow their contents to be seen from the outside. Consider Williams, Chair, *Report of the Committee on Obscenity and Film Censorship* 97 (1979): "The basic point that pornography involves by its nature some violation of lines between public and private is compounded when the pornography not only exists for private consumption, but is publicly displayed. The original violation is then forced on the attention of those who have not even volunteered to be voyeurs." Should cities be able to restrict public display of materials they could not otherwise ban? Should a feminist perspective yield different conclusions than those suggested by the Williams report? Is it sufficient to say that people can avoid bombardment by averting their eyes? Should the government be able to "zone" vulgar words on the airwaves to the late hours of the evening? See *FCC v. Pacifica Foundation,* p. 712 infra. For Ronald Dworkin's commentary on the Williams Report, see *A Matter of Principle* 335–72 (1985).

B. COMMERCIAL SPEECH

VIRGINIA STATE BOARD OF PHARMACY v. VIRGINIA CITIZENS CONSUMER COUNCIL

425 U.S. 748, 96 S.Ct. 1817, 48 L.Ed.2d 346 (1976).

MR. JUSTICE BLACKMUN delivered the opinion of the Court.

[The Court held invalid a Virginia statute that made advertising the prices of prescription drugs "unprofessional conduct," subjecting pharmacists to license suspension or revocation. Prescription drug prices strikingly varied within the same locality, in Virginia and nationally, sometimes by several hundred percent. Such drugs were dispensed exclusively by licensed pharmacists but 95% were prepared by manufacturers, not compounded by the pharmacists.]

[Appellants] contend that the advertisement of prescription drug prices is outside the protection of the First Amendment because it is "commercial speech." There can be no question that in past decisions the Court has given some indication that commercial speech is unprotected.[a]

Last Term, in *Bigelow v. Virginia,* 421 U.S. 809, 95 S.Ct. 2222, 44 L.Ed.2d 600 (1975), the notion of unprotected "commercial speech" all but passed from the scene. We reversed a conviction for violation of a Virginia statute that

---

a. Starting with *Valentine v. Chrestensen,* 316 U.S. 52, 62 S.Ct. 920, 86 L.Ed. 1262 (1942), the opinion summarized the decisions and dicta that gave such "indication." Long after *Chrestensen,* strong arguments against a first amendment exception for commercial speech had appeared. See Redish, *The First Amendment in the Market Place,* 39 Geo.Wash.L.Rev. 420 (1971); Note, 50 Ore.L.Rev. 177 (1971); cf. Note, 78 Harv.L.Rev. 1191 (1965).

made the circulation of any publication to encourage or promote the processing of an abortion in Virginia a misdemeanor. The defendant had published in his newspaper the availability of abortions in New York. The advertisement in question, in addition to announcing that abortions were legal in New York, offered the services of a referral agency in that State. [We] concluded that "the Virginia courts erred in their assumptions that advertising, as such, was entitled to no First Amendment protection," and we observed that the "relationship of speech to the marketplace of products or of services does not make it valueless in the marketplace of ideas."

Some fragment of hope for the continuing validity of a "commercial speech" exception arguably might have persisted because of the subject matter of the advertisement in *Bigelow*. We noted that in announcing the availability of legal abortions in New York, the advertisement "did more than simply propose a commercial transaction. It contained factual material of clear 'public interest.' " And, of course, the advertisement related to activity with which, at least in some respects, the State could not interfere. See *Roe v. Wade* [p. 328 infra]. Indeed, we observed: "We need not decide in this case the precise extent to which the First Amendment permits regulation of advertising that is related to activities the State may legitimately regulate or even prohibit." [b]

Here, [the] question whether there is a First Amendment exception for "commercial speech" is squarely before us. Our pharmacist does not wish to editorialize on any subject, cultural, philosophical, or political. He does not wish to report any particularly newsworthy fact, or to make generalized observations even about commercial matters. The "idea" he wishes to communicate is simply this: "I will sell you the X prescription drug at the Y price." Our question, then, is whether this communication is wholly outside the protection of the First Amendment.

V. [Speech] does not lose its First Amendment protection because money is spent to project it, as in a paid advertisement of one form or another. *New York Times Co. v. Sullivan*. Speech likewise is protected even though it is carried in a form that is "sold" for profit. *Smith v. California*. [Our] question is whether speech which does "no more than propose a commercial transaction," is so removed from any "exposition of ideas," and from "truth, science, morality, and arts in general, in its diffusion of liberal sentiments on the administration of Government", *Roth*, that it lacks all protection. Our answer is that it is not.

Focusing first on the individual parties to the transaction that is proposed in the commercial advertisement, we may assume that the advertiser's interest is a purely economic one. That hardly disqualifies him for protection under the First Amendment. The interests of the contestants in a labor dispute are primarily economic, but it has long been settled that both the employee and the employer are protected by the First Amendment when they express themselves on the merits of the dispute in order to influence its outcome. * * *[17]

---

b. *Bigelow* continued: "Regardless of the particular label asserted by the State—whether it calls speech 'commercial' or 'commercial advertising' or 'solicitation'—a court may not escape the task of assessing the First Amendment interest at stake and weighing it against the public interest allegedly served by the regulation."

17. The speech of labor disputants, of course, is subject to a number of restrictions. The Court stated in *NLRB v. Gissel Packing*

Co., 395 U.S., at 618, 89 S.Ct., at 1942, 23 L.Ed. 2d, at 581 (1969), for example, that an employer's threats of retaliation for the labor actions of his employees are "without the protection of the First Amendment." The constitutionality of restrictions upon speech in the special context of labor disputes is not before us here. We express no views on that complex subject, and advert to cases in the labor field only to note that in some circumstances speech of an

As to the particular consumer's interest in the free flow of commercial information, that interest may be as keen, if not keener by far, than his interest in the day's most urgent political debate. Appellees' case in this respect is a convincing one. Those whom the suppression of prescription drug price information hits the hardest are the poor, the sick, and particularly the aged. A disproportionate amount of their income tends to be spent on prescription drugs; yet they are the least able to learn, by shopping from pharmacist to pharmacist, where their scarce dollars are best spent. When drug prices vary as strikingly as they do, information as to who is charging what becomes more than a convenience. It could mean the alleviation of physical pain or the enjoyment of basic necessities.

Generalizing, society also may have a strong interest in the free flow of commercial information. Even an individual advertisement, though entirely "commercial," may be of general public interest. The facts of decided cases furnish illustrations: advertisements stating that referral services for legal abortions are available, *Bigelow;* that a manufacturer of artificial furs promotes his product as an alternative to the extinction by his competitors of fur-bearing mammals, see *Fur Information & Fashion Council, Inc. v. E.F. Timme & Son,* 364 F.Supp. 16 (SDNY 1973); and that a domestic producer advertises his product as an alternative to imports that tend to deprive American residents of their jobs, cf. *Chicago Joint Board v. Chicago Tribune Co.,* 435 F.2d 470 (CA7 1970), cert. denied, 402 U.S. 973 (1971). Obviously, not all commercial messages contain the same or even a very great public interest element. There are few to which such an element, however, could not be added. Our pharmacist, for example, could cast himself as a commentator on store-to-store disparities in drug prices, giving his own and those of a competitor as proof. We see little point in requiring him to do so, and little difference if he does not.

Moreover, there is another consideration that suggests that no line between publicly "interesting" or "important" commercial advertising and the opposite kind could ever be drawn. Advertising, however tasteless and excessive it sometimes may seem, is nonetheless dissemination of information as to who is producing and selling what product, for what reason, and at what price. So long as we preserve a predominantly free enterprise economy, the allocation of our resources in large measure will be made through numerous private economic decisions. It is a matter of public interest that those decisions, in the aggregate, be intelligent and well informed. To this end, the free flow of commercial information is indispensable. And if it is indispensable to the proper allocation of resources in a free enterprise system, it is also indispensable to the formation of intelligent opinions as to how that system ought to be regulated or altered. Therefore, even if the First Amendment were thought to be primarily an instrument to enlighten public decisionmaking in a democracy, we could not say that the free flow of information does not serve that goal.

Arrayed against these substantial individual and societal interests are a number of justifications for the advertising ban. These have to do principally with maintaining a high degree of professionalism on the part of licensed pharmacists. [Price] advertising, it is argued, will place in jeopardy the pharmacist's expertise and, with it, the customer's health. It is claimed that the aggressive price competition that will result from unlimited advertising will

entirely private and economic character enjoys the protection of the First Amendment.

[For the contention that labor speech receives less protection than commercial speech,

see Pope, *The Three-Systems Ladder of First Amendment Values: Two Rungs and a Black Hole,* 11 Hast.Con.L.Q. 189 (1984)].

make it impossible for the pharmacist to supply professional services in the compounding, handling, and dispensing of prescription drugs. Such services are time-consuming and expensive; if competitors who economize by eliminating them are permitted to advertise their resulting lower prices, the more painstaking and conscientious pharmacist will be forced either to follow suit or to go out of business. [It] is further claimed that advertising will lead people to shop for their prescription drugs among the various pharmacists who offer the lowest prices, and the loss of stable pharmacist-customer relationships will make individual [attention] impossible. Finally, it is argued that damage will be done to the professional image of the pharmacist. This image, that of a skilled and specialized craftsman, attracts talent to the profession and reinforces the better habits of those who are in [it].

The strength of these proffered justifications is greatly undermined by the fact that high professional standards, to a substantial extent, are guaranteed by the close regulation to which pharmacists in Virginia are subject. [At] the same time, we cannot discount the Board's justifications entirely. The Court regarded justifications of this type sufficient to sustain the advertising bans challenged on due process and equal protection [grounds].[c]

The challenge now made, however, is based on the First Amendment. This casts the Board's justifications in a different light, for on close inspection it is seen that the State's protectiveness of its citizens rests in large measure on the advantages of their being kept in ignorance. The advertising ban does not directly affect professional standards one way or the other. It affects them only through the reactions it is assumed people will have to the free flow of drug price information. There is no claim that the advertising ban in any way prevents the cutting of corners by the pharmacist who is so inclined. That pharmacist is likely to cut corners in any event. The only effect the advertising ban has on him is to insulate him from price competition and to open the way for him to make a substantial, and perhaps even excessive, profit in addition to providing an inferior service. The more painstaking pharmacist is also protected but, again, it is a protection based in large part on public ignorance.

It appears to be feared that if the pharmacist who wishes to provide low cost, and assertedly low quality, services is permitted to advertise, he will be taken up on his offer by too many unwitting customers. They will choose the low-cost, low-quality service and drive the "professional" pharmacist out of business. [They] will go from one pharmacist to another, following the discount, and destroy the pharmacist-customer relationship. They will lose respect for the profession because it advertises. All this is not in their best interests, and all this can be avoided if they are not permitted to know who is charging what.

[A]n alternative to this highly paternalistic approach [is] to assume that this information is not in itself harmful, that people will perceive their own best interests if only they are well enough informed, and that the best means to that end is to open the channels of communication rather than to close them. If they are truly open, nothing prevents the "professional" pharmacist from marketing his own assertedly superior product, and contrasting it with that of the low-cost, high-volume prescription drug retailer. But the choice among these alternative approaches is not ours to make or the Virginia General Assembly's. It is precisely this kind of choice, between the dangers of suppressing information,

---

c. The Court referred here to cases upholding bans on advertising prices for eyeglass frames and optometrist and dental services.

and the dangers of its misuse if it is freely available, that the First Amendment makes for [us].

VI. In concluding that commercial speech, like other varieties, is protected, we of course do not hold that it can never be regulated in any way. Some forms of commercial speech regulation are surely permissible. We mention a few. [There] is no claim, for example, that the prohibition on prescription drug price advertising is a mere time, place, and manner restriction. We have often approved restrictions of that kind provided that they are justified without reference to the content of the regulated speech, that they serve a significant governmental interest, and that in so doing they leave open ample alternative channels for communication of the information. Whatever may be the proper bounds of time, place, and manner restrictions on commercial speech, they are plainly exceeded by this Virginia statute, which singles out speech of a particular content and seeks to prevent its dissemination completely.

Nor is there any claim that prescription drug price advertisements are forbidden because they are false or misleading in any way. Untruthful speech, commercial or otherwise, has never been protected for its own sake. *Gertz.* Obviously much commercial speech is not provably false, or even wholly false, but only deceptive or misleading. We foresee no obstacle to a State's dealing effectively with this problem.[24] The First Amendment, as we construe it today, does not prohibit the State from insuring that the stream of commercial information flows cleanly as well as freely.

Also, there is no claim that the transactions proposed in the forbidden advertisements are themselves illegal in any way. Finally, the special problems of the electronic broadcast media are likewise not in this case.

What is at issue is whether a State may completely suppress the dissemination of concededly truthful information about entirely lawful activity, fearful of that information's effect upon its disseminators and its recipients. Reserving other questions,[25] we conclude that the answer to this one is in the negative.

*   *   *

---

24. [C]ommonsense differences between speech that does "no more than propose a commercial transaction," *Pittsburgh Press* [p. 594 infra,] and other varieties [suggest] that a different degree of protection is necessary to insure that the flow of truthful and legitimate commercial information is unimpaired. The truth of commercial speech, for example, may be more easily verifiable by its disseminator than, let us say, news reporting or political commentary, in that ordinarily the advertiser seeks to disseminate information about a specific product or service that he himself provides and presumably knows more about than anyone else. Also, commercial speech may be more durable than other kinds. Since advertising is the sine qua non of commercial profits, there is little likelihood of its being chilled by proper regulation and foregone entirely.

Attributes such as these, the greater objectivity and hardiness of commercial speech, may make it less necessary to tolerate inaccurate statements for fear of silencing the speaker. They may also make it appropriate to require that a commercial message appear in such a form, or include such additional information, warnings and disclaimers, as are necessary to prevent its being deceptive. They may also make inapplicable the prohibition on prior restraints. Compare *New York Times v. United States* [p. 595 infra] with *Donaldson v. Read Magazine*, 333 U.S. 178, 68 S.Ct. 591, 92 L.Ed. 628 (1948).

25. We stress that we have considered in this case the regulation of commercial advertising by pharmacists. Although we express no opinion as to other professions, the distinctions, historical and functional, between professions, may require consideration of quite different factors. Physicians and lawyers, for example, do not dispense standardized products; they render professional *services* of almost infinite variety and nature, with the consequent enhanced possibility for confusion and deception if they were to undertake certain kinds of advertising.

MR. JUSTICE STEWART, concurring.[d]

[I] write separately to explain why I think today's decision does not preclude [governmental regulation of false or deceptive advertising]. The Court has on several occasions addressed the problems posed by false statements of fact in libel cases. [Factual] errors are inevitable in free debate, and the imposition of liability for [such errors] can "dampe[n] the vigor and limi[t] the variety of public debate" by inducing "self-censorship." [In] contrast to the press, which must often attempt to assemble the true facts from sketchy and sometimes conflicting sources under the pressure of publication deadlines, the commercial advertiser generally knows the product or service he seeks to sell and is in a position to verify the accuracy of his factual representations before he disseminates them. The advertiser's access to the truth about his product and its price substantially eliminates any danger that governmental regulation of false or misleading price or product advertising will chill accurate and nondeceptive commercial [expression].

Since the factual claims contained in commercial price or product advertisements relate to tangible goods or services, they may be tested empirically and corrected to reflect the truth without in any manner jeopardizing the free dissemination of thought. Indeed, the elimination of false and deceptive claims serves to promote the one facet of commercial price and product advertising that warrants First Amendment protection—its contribution to the flow of accurate and reliable information relevant to public and private decisionmaking.

MR. JUSTICE REHNQUIST, dissenting.

[Under] the Court's opinion the way will be open not only for dissemination of price information but for active promotion of prescription drugs, liquor, cigarettes and other products the use of which it has previously been thought desirable to discourage. Now, however, such promotion is protected by the First Amendment so long as it is not misleading or does not promote an illegal product or [enterprise].

The Court speaks of the consumer's interest in the free flow of commercial information. [This] should presumptively be the concern of the Virginia Legislature, which sits to balance [this] and other claims in the process of making laws such as the one here under attack. The Court speaks of the importance in a "predominantly free enterprise economy" of intelligent and well-informed decisions as to allocation of resources. While there is again much to be said for the Court's observation as a matter of desirable public policy, there is certainly nothing in the United States Constitution which requires the Virginia Legislature to hew to the teachings of Adam Smith in its legislative decisions regulating the pharmacy profession. E.g., *Nebbia v. New York; Olsen v. Nebraska* [Ch. 6, Sec. 3].

[There] are undoubted difficulties with an effort to draw a bright line between "commercial speech" on the one hand and "protected speech" on the other, and the Court does better to face up to these difficulties than to attempt to hide them under labels. In this case, however, the Court has unfortunately substituted for the wavering line previously thought to exist between commercial speech and protected speech a no more satisfactory line of its own—that between "truthful" commercial speech, on the one hand, and that which is "false and misleading" on the other. The difficulty with this line is not that it wavers, but on the contrary that it is simply too Procrustean to take into account the

d. Burger, C.J., separately concurring, stressed the reservation in fn. 25 of the opinion with respect to advertising by attorneys and physicians. Stevens, J., took no part.

congeries of factors which I believe could, quite consistently with the First and Fourteenth Amendments, properly influence a legislative decision with respect to commercial advertising.

[S]uch a line simply makes no allowance whatever for what appears to have been a considered legislative judgment in most States that while prescription drugs are a necessary and vital part of medical care and treatment, there are sufficient dangers attending their widespread use that they simply may not be promoted in the same manner as hair creams, deodorants, and toothpaste. The very real dangers that general advertising for such drugs might create in terms of encouraging, even though not sanctioning, illicit use of them by individuals for whom they have not been prescribed, or by generating patient pressure upon physicians to prescribe them are simply not dealt with in the Court's opinion.

* * *

Notes and Questions

1. As compared to political decisionmaking, is commercial advertising "neither more nor less significant than a host of other market activities that legislatures concededly may regulate."? Is there an "absence of any principled distinction between commercial soliciting and other aspects of economic activity"? Has economic due process been "resurrected, clothed in the ill-fitting garb of the first amendment"? See Jackson & Jeffries, *Commercial Speech: Economic Due Process and the First Amendment,* 65 Va.L.Rev. 1, 18 and 30 (1979). Why may government "be paternalistic regarding the purchase of goods but may not be paternalistic regarding information about those goods"? Alexander, *Speech in the Local Marketplace: Implications of Virginia State Board of Pharmacy v. Virginia Citizens Consumer Council, Inc. for Local Regulatory Power,* 14 San Diego L.Rev. 357, 376 (1977).

2. Footnote 24 suggests that *deceptive* commercial speech may be regulated in ways that would be barred if the speech were political. Sound distinction?

(a) *"Commonsense" differences between commercial speech and other speech.* (1) *Verifiability.* Consider Farber, *Commercial Speech and First Amendment Theory,* 74 Nw.U.L.Rev. 372, 385–86 (1979): "[C]ommercial speech is not necessarily more verifiable than other speech. There may well be uncertainty about some quality of a product, such as the health effect of eggs * * *. On the other hand, political speech is often quite verifiable by the speaker. A political candidate knows the truth about his own past and his present intentions, yet misrepresentations on these subjects are immune from state regulation." (2) *Durability.* Consider Redish, *The Value of Free Speech,* 130 U.Pa.L.Rev. 591, 633 (1982): "[I]t is also incorrect to distinguish commercial from political expression on the ground that the former is somehow hardier because of the inherent profit motive. It could just as easily be said that we need not fear that commercial magazines and newspapers will cease publication for fear of governmental regulation, because they are in business for profit. Of course, the proper response to this contention is that our concern is not *whether* they will publish, but *what* they will publish: fear of regulation might deter them from dealing with controversial subjects."

(b) *Commercial speech and self-expression.* Is commercial speech distinguishable from political speech because it is unrelated to self-expression? Consider Baker, *Commercial Speech: A Problem in the Theory of Freedom,* 62 Iowa L.Rev. 1, 17 (1976): In commercial speech, the dissemination of the profit motive "breaks the connection between speech and any vision, or attitude, or value of the individual or group engaged in advocacy. Thus the content and form of commercial speech cannot be attributed to individual value allegiances." For criticism, see, e.g., Schlag, *An Attack on Categorical Approaches to Freedom of Speech,* 30 U.C.L.A.L.Rev. 671, 710–21 (1983); Shiffrin, *The First Amendment and Economic Regulation: Away From A General Theory of the First Amendment,* 78 Nw.U.L.Rev. 1212 (1983).

(c) *Contract approach to commercial speech.* Is commercial advertising distinguishable from other forms of speech because of the state interest in regulating contracts? Consider Farber, supra, at 389: "[C]ommercial speech is [more] akin to conduct than are other forms of speech. The unique aspect of commercial speech is that it is a prelude to, and therefore becomes integrated into, a contract, the essence of which is the presence of a promise. Because a promise is an undertaking to ensure that a certain state of affairs takes place, promises obviously have a closer connection with conduct than with self-expression. Second, this approach focuses on the distinctive and powerful state interests implicated by the process of contract formation. In a fundamentally market economy, the government understandably is given particular deference in its enforcement of contractual expectations. Indeed, the Constitution itself gives special protection to contractual expectations in the contract clause. Finally, this approach connects a rather nebulous area of first amendment law with the commonplaces of contract law of which every lawyer has knowledge. Obviously, the technicalities of contract law, with its doctrines of privity, consideration, and the like, should not be blindly translated into first amendment jurisprudence. The basic doctrines of contract law, however, provide a helpful guide in considering commercial speech problems." For discussion, see Alexander & Farber, *Commercial Speech and First Amendment Theory: A Critical Exchange,* 75 Nw.U.L.Rev. 307 (1980).

3. *Limits on regulation of deceptive advertising. Bates v. State Bar,* 433 U.S. 350, 97 S.Ct. 2691, 53 L.Ed.2d 810 (1977), struck down an Arizona Supreme Court rule against a lawyer "publicizing himself" through advertising. It rejected the claim that attorney price advertising was inherently misleading, but left open the "peculiar problems" associated with advertising claims regarding the quality of legal services.[e] Could a lawyer truthfully advertise that he or she has (1) tried twice as many personal injury cases as any other lawyer in the country? (2) averaged $10,000 more in recoveries per case than any other lawyer in the county? (3) graduated from Harvard Law School in the upper 10% of the class? (4) received "the best legal education this country offers"? Should an advertisement be protected if it is "sufficiently factual to be subject to verification" even if "implications of quality might be drawn from it"? See Canby and Gellhorn, *Physician Advertising: The First Amendment and the Sherman Act,* 1978 Duke L.J. 543, 560–62. Should the Court have deferred to the judgment of the State Bar of Arizona? If not, should it defer to the SEC

---

e. *Zauderer v. Office of Disciplinary Counsel,* p. 731 infra, held that a state may not discipline attorneys who solicit legal business through newspaper advertisements containing "truthful and nondeceptive information and advice regarding the legal rights of potential clients" or for the advertising use of "accurate and nondeceptive" illustrations. Zauderer had placed illustrated ads in 36 Ohio newspapers publicizing his availability to represent women who had suffered injuries from use of a contraceptive device known as the Dalkon

Shield Intrauterine Device. In the ad Zauderer stated that he had represented other women in Dalkon Shield litigation. The Court observed that accurate statements of fact cannot be proscribed "merely because it is possible that some readers will infer that he has some expertise in those areas." But it continued to "leave open the possibility that States may prevent attorneys from making non-verifiable claims regarding the quality of their services. *Bates.*"

when it regulates the advertising of securities? The FTC when it regulates automobile advertising? The Virginia Board of Pharmacy when it regulates quality advertising by pharmacists? For deferential treatment of a state ban on the use of tradenames by optometrists, see *Friedman v. Rogers*, 440 U.S. 1, 99 S.Ct. 887, 59 L.Ed.2d 100 (1979).

4. *Truth and commercial advertising.* Should Mercedes Benz be able to truthfully advertise that Frank Sinatra drives its car without getting Sinatra's permission? See Liebeler, *A Property Rights Approach to Judicial Decision Making,* 4 Cato J. 783, 802–03 (1985); Shiffrin, supra note 2, at 1257–58 n. 275; Treece, *Commercial Exploitation of Names, Likenesses, and Personal Histories,* 51 Tex.L.Rev. 637 (1973). Should the state be able to prevent homeowners from posting "for sale" signs in order to prevent panic selling in order to maintain an integrated neighborhood? See *Linmark Associates, Inc., v. Willingboro,* 431 U.S. 85, 97 S.Ct. 1614, 52 L.Ed.2d 155 (1977). May a state regulate the content of contraceptive advertising in order to minimize its offensive character? Cf. *Carey v. Population Services Int'l.* (1977), p. 326 supra (total ban on contraceptive advertising unconstitutional).

———

OHRALIK v. OHIO STATE BAR ASS'N, 436 U.S. 447, 98 S.Ct. 1912, 56 L.Ed.2d 444 (1978) upheld the indefinite suspension of an attorney for violating the anti-solicitation provisions of the Ohio Code of Professional Responsibility. Those provisions generally do not allow lawyers to recommend themselves to anyone who has not sought "their advice regarding employment of a lawyer." Albert Ohralik had approached two young accident victims to solicit employment—Carol McClintock in a hospital room where she lay in traction and Wanda Lou Holbert on the day she came home from the hospital. He employed a concealed tape recorder with Holbert, apparently to insure he would have evidence of her assent to his representation. The next day, when Holbert's mother informed Ohralik that she and her daughter did not want to have appellant represent them, he insisted that the daughter had entered into a binding agreement. McClintock also discharged Ohralik, and Ohralik sued her for breach of contract. The Court ruled, per POWELL, J., that a state may forbid in-person solicitation of clients by lawyers for pecuniary gain:

"Expression concerning purely commercial transactions has come within the ambit of the Amendment's protection only recently. In rejecting the notion that such speech is wholly outside the protection of the First Amendment, *Virginia Pharmacy,* we were careful not to hold that it is wholly undifferentiable from other forms of speech.

"We have not discarded the common sense distinction between speech proposing a commercial transaction, which occurs in an area traditionally subject to government regulation, and other varieties of speech. To require a parity of constitutional protection for commercial and noncommercial speech alike could invite dilution, simply by a leveling process, of the force of the Amendment's guarantee with respect to the latter kind of speech. Rather than subject the First Amendment to such a devitalization, we instead have afforded commercial speech a limited measure of protection, commensurate with its subordinate position in the scale of First Amendment values, while allowing modes of regulation that might be impermissible in the realm of noncommercial expression.

"Moreover, 'it has never been deemed an abridgment of freedom of speech or press to make a course of conduct illegal merely because the conduct was in part initiated, evidenced, or carried out by means of language, either spoken, written, or printed.' *Giboney v. Empire Storage & Ice Co.*, 336 U.S. 490, 502, 69 S.Ct. 684, 691, 93 L.Ed. 834 (1949). Numerous examples could be cited of communications that are regulated without offending the First Amendment, such as the exchange of information about securities, *SEC v. Texas Gulf Sulphur Co.*, 401 F.2d 833 (CA2 1968), cert. denied, 394 U.S. 976, 89 S.Ct. 1454, 22 L.Ed.2d 756 (1969), corporate proxy statements, *Mills v. Electric Auto-Lite Co.*, 396 U.S. 375, 90 S.Ct. 616, 24 L.Ed.2d 593 (1970), the exchange of price and production information among competitors, *American Column & Lumber Co. v. United States*, 257 U.S. 377, 42 S.Ct. 114, 66 L.Ed. 284 (1921), and employers' threats of retaliation for the labor activities of employees, *NLRB v. Gissel Packing Co.*, 395 U.S. 575, 618, 89 S.Ct. 1918, 1942, 23 L.Ed.2d 547 (1969). Each of these examples illustrates that the State does not lose its power to regulate commercial activity deemed harmful to the public whenever speech is a component of that activity. Neither *Virginia Pharmacy* nor *Bates* purported to cast doubt on the permissibility of these kinds of commercial regulation.

"In-person solicitation by a lawyer of remunerative employment is a business transaction in which speech is an essential but subordinate component. While this does not remove the speech from the protection of the First Amendment, as was held in *Bates* and *Virginia Pharmacy*, it lowers the level of appropriate judicial scrutiny. [A] lawyer's procurement of remunerative employment is a subject only marginally affected with First Amendment concerns. It falls within the State's proper sphere of economic and professional regulation. While entitled to some constitutional protection, appellant's conduct is subject to regulation in furtherance of important state [interests].

" 'The interest of the States in regulating lawyers is especially great since lawyers are essential to the primary function of administering justice and have historically been officers of the courts' [and] act 'as trusted agents of their clients and as assistants to the court in search of a just solution to disputes.'

"[The] substantive evils of solicitation have been stated over the years in sweeping terms: stirring up litigation, assertion of fraudulent claims, debasing the legal profession, and potential harm to the solicited client in the form of overreaching, overcharging, underrepresentation, and misrepresentation." In providing information about the availability and terms of proposed legal services "in-person solicitation serves much the same function as the advertisement at issue in *Bates*. But there are significant differences as well. Unlike a public advertisement, which simply provides information and leaves the recipient free to act upon it or not, in-person solicitation may exert pressure and often demands an immediate response, without providing an opportunity for comparison or reflection. The aim and effect of in-person solicitation may be to provide a one-sided presentation and to encourage speedy and perhaps uninformed decisionmaking; there is no opportunity for intervention or counter-education by agencies of the Bar, supervisory authorities, or persons close to the solicited individual. The admonition that 'the fitting remedy for evil counsels is good ones' is of little value when the circumstances provide no opportunity for any remedy at all. In-person solicitation is as likely as not to discourage persons needing counsel from engaging in a critical comparison of the 'availability, nature, and prices' of legal services; it actually may disserve the individual and societal interest, identified in *Bates,* in facilitating 'informed and reliable decisionmaking.'

"[Appellant's argument that none of the evils of solicitation were found in his case] misconceives the nature of the State's interest. The rules prohibiting solicitation are prophylactic measures whose objective is the prevention of harm before it occurs. The rules were applied in this case to discipline a lawyer for soliciting employment for pecuniary gain under circumstances likely to result in the adverse consequences the State seeks to avert. In such a situation, which is inherently conducive to overreaching and other forms of misconduct, the State has a strong interest in adopting and enforcing rules of conduct designed to protect the public from harmful solicitation by lawyers whom it has [licensed].

"The efficacy of the State's effort to prevent such harm to prospective clients would be substantially diminished if, having proved a solicitation in circumstances like those of this case, the State were required in addition to prove actual injury. Unlike the advertising in *Bates,* in-person solicitation is not visible or otherwise open to public scrutiny. Often there is no witness other than the lawyer and the lay person whom he has solicited, rendering it difficult or impossible to obtain reliable proof of what actually took place. This would be especially true if the lay person were so distressed at the time of the solicitation that he or she could not recall specific details at a later date. If appellant's view were sustained, in-person solicitation would be virtually immune to effective oversight and regulation by the State or by the legal profession, in contravention of the State's strong interest in regulating members of the Bar in an effective, objective, and self-enforcing manner. It therefore is not unreasonable, or violative of the Constitution, for a State to respond with what in effect is a prophylactic rule." [a]

Notes and Questions

1. *Companion case.* IN RE PRIMUS, 436 U.S. 412, 98 S.Ct. 1893, 56 L.Ed. 2d 417 (1978), per POWELL, J., held that a state could not constitutionally discipline an ACLU "cooperating lawyer" who, after advising a gathering of allegedly illegally sterilized women of their rights, initiated further contact with one of the women by writing her a letter informing her of the ACLU's willingness to provide free legal representation for women in her situation and of the organization's desire to file a lawsuit on her behalf. "South Carolina's action in punishing appellant for soliciting a prospective litigant by mail, on behalf of ACLU, must withstand the 'exacting scrutiny applicable to limitations on core First Amendment rights.' [Where] political expression or association is at issue, this Court has not tolerated the degree of imprecision that often characterizes government regulation of the conduct of commercial affairs. The approach we adopt today in *Ohralik* that the State may proscribe in-person solicitation for pecuniary gain under circumstances likely to result in adverse consequences, cannot be applied to appellant's activity on behalf of the ACLU. Although a showing of potential danger may suffice in the former context, appellant may not be disciplined unless her activity in fact involved the type of misconduct at which South Carolina's broad prohibition is said to be directed. The record does not support appellee's contention that undue influence, overreaching, misrepresentation, or invasion of privacy actually occurred in this case."

2. *A hierarchy of protected speech.* Consider Shiffrin, supra, at 1218 & 1220–21 (1983). In *Virginia Pharmacy,* "the Court never admitted that commer-

---

a. Marshall and Rehnquist, JJ., each separately concurred in the judgment. Brennan, J., did not participate.

cial speech was less valuable than political speech. The 'commonsense differences' had nothing to do with value. [Although] Justice Blackmun labored to defend the asserted equal relationship between commercial speech and political speech for the *Virginia Pharmacy* majority, Justice Powell in *Ohralik* was content to lead the Court to an opposite position without explanation. In so doing, Justice Powell steered the Court to accept a hierarchy of protected speech for the first time, despite his own stated opposition [in *Young*] to creating any such hierarchy." Does the concern that the protection of non-commercial speech would be subject to dilution if it were placed on a par with commercial speech presuppose an unexplained difference between the two types of speech? See id. at 1221 n. 59.

CENTRAL HUDSON GAS & ELEC. CORP. v. PUBLIC SERVICE COMM'N, 447 U.S. 557, 100 S.Ct. 2343, 65 L.Ed.2d 341 (1980), per POWELL, J., invalidated a Commission regulation that, in an effort to conserve power, prohibited promotional advertising by an electric utility except for encouraging shifts of consumption from peak demand times: "The Commission's order restricts only commercial speech, that is, expression related solely to the economic interests of the speaker and its audience. [In] commercial speech cases, [a] four-part analysis has developed. At the outset, we must determine whether the expression is protected by the First Amendment. For commercial speech to come within that provision, it at least must concern lawful activity [a] and not be misleading. Next, we ask whether the asserted governmental interest is substantial. If both inquiries yield positive answers, we must determine whether the regulation directly advances the governmental interest asserted, and whether it is not more extensive than is necessary to serve that interest.[b]

"[T]he State's interest in energy conservation is directly advanced by the Commission order at issue here. There is an immediate connection between advertising and the demand for electricity. [Thus], we find a direct link between the state interest in conservation and the Commission's order.

"[T]he critical inquiry [is] whether the Commission's complete suppression of speech ordinarily protected by the First Amendment is no more extensive than necessary to further the State's interest in energy conservation. The Commission's order reaches all promotional advertising, regardless of the impact of the touted service on overall energy use. But the energy conservation rationale, as important as it is, cannot justify suppressing information about electric devices or services that would cause no net increase in total energy use. In addition, no showing has been made that a more limited restriction on the content of promotional advertising would not serve adequately the State's interests.

a. *Pittsburgh Press Co. v. Human Relations Comm'n,* p. 594 infra, upheld an order forbidding publication of sex-designated help-wanted columns as a forbidden "aid" to prohibited sex discrimination in employment: "Discrimination in employment is *illegal* commercial activity under the ordinance. We have no doubt that a newspaper constitutionally could be forbidden to publish a want-ad proposing a sale of narcotics or soliciting prostitutes."

b. In an earlier footnote, the Court emphasized that this requirement was "not an application of the 'overbreadth' doctrine. The lat-

ter theory permits the invalidation of regulations on First Amendment grounds even when the litigant challenging the regulation has engaged in no constitutionally protected activity. [In] this case, the Commission's prohibition acts directly against the promotional activities of Central Hudson, and to the extent the limitations are unnecessary to serve the state's interest, they are invalid." For a different perspective on the overbreadth doctrine, see Redish, *The Warren Court, The Burger Court and the First Amendment Overbreadth Doctrine,* 78 Nw.U.L.Rev. 1031 (1983).

"Appellant insists that but for the ban, it would advertise products and services that use energy efficiently. These include the 'heat pump,' which both parties acknowledge to be a major improvement in electric heating, and the use of electric heat as a 'back-up' to solar and other heat sources. Although the Commission has questioned the efficiency of electric heating before this Court, neither the Commission's Policy Statement nor its order denying rehearing made findings on this issue. In the absence of authoritative findings to the contrary, we must credit as within the realm of possibility the claim that electric heat can be an efficient alternative in some circumstances.

"The Commission's order prevents appellant from promoting electric services that would reduce energy use by diverting demand from less efficient sources, or that would consume roughly the same amount of energy as do alternative sources. In neither situation would the utility's advertising endanger conservation or mislead the public. To the extent that the Commission's order suppresses speech that in no way impairs the State's interest in energy conservation, the Commission's order violates the First and Fourteenth Amendments and must be invalidated.

"The Commission also has not demonstrated that its interest in conservation cannot be protected adequately by more limited regulation of appellant's commercial expression. To further its policy of conservation, the Commission could attempt to restrict the format and content of Central Hudson's advertising. It might, for example, require that the advertisements include information about the relative efficiency and expense of the offered service, both under current conditions and for the foreseeable future.[13] In the absence of a showing that more limited speech regulation would be ineffective, we cannot approve the complete suppression of Central Hudson's advertising."

BLACKMUN, J., joined by Brennan, J., concurring in the judgment, saw in the Court's "four-part analysis" approval of "an intermediate level of scrutiny" whenever a restraint on commercial speech " 'directly advance[s]' a 'substantial' governmental interest and is 'not more extensive than is necessary to serve that interest.' I agree with the Court that this level of intermediate scrutiny is appropriate for a restraint on commercial speech designed to protect consumers from misleading or coercive speech, or a regulation related to the time, place, or manner of commercial speech. I do not agree, however, that the Court's four-part test is the proper one to be applied when a State seeks to suppress information about a product in order to manipulate a private economic decision that the State cannot or has not regulated or outlawed directly.

"Since the Court, without citing empirical data or other authority, finds a 'direct link' between advertising and energy consumption, it leaves open the possibility that the State may suppress advertising of electricity in order to lessen demand for electricity. I, of course, agree with the Court that, in today's world, energy conservation is a goal of paramount national and local importance. I disagree with the Court, however, when it says that suppression of speech may be a permissible means to achieve that goal. * * *

---

13. The Commission also might consider a system of previewing advertising campaigns to insure that they will not defeat conservation policy. It has instituted such a program for approving "informational" advertising under the Policy Statement challenged in this case. We have observed that commercial speech is such a sturdy brand of expression that traditional prior restraint doctrine may not apply to it. *Virginia Pharmacy.* And in other areas of speech regulation, such as obscenity, we have recognized that a prescreening arrangement can pass constitutional muster if it includes adequate procedural safeguards.

"The Court recognizes that we have never held that commercial speech may be suppressed in order to further the State's interest in discouraging purchases of the underlying product that is advertised. Permissible restraints on commercial speech have been limited to measures designed to protect consumers from fraudulent, misleading, or coercive sales techniques. Those designed to deprive consumers of information about products or services that are legally offered for sale consistently have been invalidated.

"I seriously doubt whether suppression of information concerning the availability and price of a legally offered product is ever a permissible way for the State to 'dampen' demand for or use of the product. Even though 'commercial' speech is involved, such a regulatory measure strikes at the heart of the First Amendment. This is because it is a covert attempt by the State to manipulate the choices of its citizens, not by persuasion or direct regulation, but by depriving the public of the information needed to make a free choice. As the Court recognizes, the State's policy choices are insulated from the visibility and scrutiny that direct regulation would entail and the conduct of citizens is molded by the information that government chooses to give [them].

"If the First Amendment guarantee means anything, it means that, absent clear and present danger, government has no power to restrict expression because of the effect its message is likely to have on the public. See generally Comment, *First Amendment Protection for Commercial Advertising: The New Constitutional Doctrine*, 44 U.Chi.L.Rev. 205, 243–51 (1976). Our cases indicate that this guarantee applies even to commercial speech."

The opinion quoted from *Virginia Pharmacy, Linmark*, and *Carey*, noting that "*Linmark* resolved beyond all doubt that a strict standard of review applies to suppression of commercial information, where the purpose of the restraint is to influence behavior by depriving citizens of information," and that *Carey* "also applied to content-based restraints on commercial speech the same standard of review we have applied to other varieties of speech. * * *

"Our prior references to the 'commonsense differences' between commercial speech and other speech 'suggest that a different degree of protection is necessary to insure that the flow of truthful and legitimate commercial information is unimpaired.' *Linmark*. We have not suggested that the 'commonsense differences' between commercial speech and other speech justify relaxed scrutiny of restraints that suppress truthful, nondeceptive, noncoercive commercial [speech].

"It appears that the Court would permit the State to ban all direct advertising of air conditioning, assuming that a more limited restriction on such advertising would not effectively deter the public from cooling its homes. In my view, our cases do not support this type of suppression. If a governmental unit believes that use or over-use of air conditioning is a serious problem, it must attack that problem directly, by prohibiting air conditioning or regulating thermostat levels."

STEVENS, J., joined by Brennan, J., also concurred: "Because 'commercial speech' is afforded less constitutional protection than other forms of speech, it is important that the commercial speech concept not be defined too broadly lest speech deserving of greater constitutional protection be inadvertently suppressed. The issue in this case is whether New York's prohibition on the promotion of the use of electricity through advertising is a ban on nothing but commercial [speech].

"This case involves a governmental regulation that completely bans promotional advertising by an electric utility. This ban encompasses a great deal more than mere proposals to engage in certain kinds of commercial transactions. It prohibits all advocacy of the immediate or future use of electricity. It curtails expression by an informed and interested group of persons of their point of view on questions relating to the production and consumption of electrical energy— questions frequently discussed and debated by our political leaders. For example, an electric company's advocacy of the use of electric heat for environmental reasons, as opposed to wood-burning stoves, would seem to fall squarely within New York's promotional advertising ban and also within the bounds of maximum First Amendment protection. The breadth of the ban thus exceeds the boundaries of the commercial speech concept, however that concept may be defined.

"The justification for the regulation is nothing more than the expressed fear that the audience may find the utility's message persuasive. Without the aid of any coercion, deception, or misinformation, truthful communication may persuade some citizens to consume more electricity than they otherwise would. I assume that such a consequence would be undesirable and that government may therefore prohibit and punish the unnecessary or excessive use of electricity. But if the perceived harm associated with greater electrical usage is not sufficiently serious to justify direct regulation, surely it does not constitute the kind of clear and present danger that can justify the suppression of speech.

* * *

"In sum, I concur in the result because I do not consider this to be a 'commercial speech' case. Accordingly, I see no need to decide whether the Court's four-part analysis adequately protects commercial speech—as properly defined—in the face of a blanket ban of the sort involved in this case."

REHNQUIST, J., dissented in a long opinion, summarized in his introduction: "The Court's analysis in my view is wrong in several respects. Initially, I disagree with the Court's conclusion that the speech of a state-created monopoly, which is the subject of a comprehensive regulatory scheme, is entitled to protection under the First Amendment. I also think that the Court errs here in failing to recognize that the state law is most accurately viewed as an economic regulation and that the speech involved (if it falls within the scope of the First Amendment at all) occupies a significantly more subordinate position in the hierarchy of First Amendment values than the Court gives it today. Finally, the Court in reaching its decision improperly substitutes its own judgment for that of the State in deciding how a proper ban on promotional advertising should be drafted. With regard to this latter point, the Court adopts as its final part of a four-part test a 'no more extensive than necessary' analysis that will unduly impair a state legislature's ability to adopt legislation reasonably designed to promote interests that have always been rightly thought to be of great importance to the State."

In commenting on the Court's four part test, Rehnquist, J., stated: "The [test] elevates the protection accorded commercial speech that falls within the scope of the First Amendment to a level that is virtually indistinguishable from that of noncommercial speech. I think the Court in so doing has effectively accomplished the 'devitalization' of the First Amendment that it counseled against in *Ohralik*. I think it has also by labeling economic regulation of business conduct as a restraint on 'free speech' gone far to resurrect the discredited doctrine of cases such as *Lochner*. New York's order here is in my view more akin to an economic regulation to which virtually complete deference should be accorded by this Court.

"I doubt there would be any question as to the constitutionality of New York's conservation effort if the Public Service Commission had chosen to raise the price of electricity, to condition its sale on specified terms, or to restrict its production. In terms of constitutional values, I think that such controls are virtually indistinguishable from the State's ban on promotional advertising."

Notes and Questions

1. *The four part test.* Is Rehnquist, J., correct in stating that the Court's test "elevates the protection of commercial speech to a level that is virtually indistinguishable from that of noncommercial speech"? Is it possible to state "the" test that has been applied to noncommercial speech?

2. *Paternalism and Central Hudson.* Consider Blasi, *The Pathological Perspective and the First Amendment,* 85 Colum.L.Rev. 449, 487 (1985): "[T]he claim of the regulators in the drug and lawyer advertising cases was that consumers would be influenced by the advertising to act against their own self-interest; in the promotional advertising case, the fear was that consumers would act against the public interest in pursuit of their own short range self-interest. The rationale in the first type of case is more paternalistic because it necessarily assumes that listeners cannot evaluate the message even when they have every incentive to try to do so. The rationale in the promotional advertising case is consistent with respect for the message-screening capacities of listeners; what the rationale doubts is the capacity of listeners to behave as public-spirited citizens when prompted to act selfishly by sophisticated advertising techniques."

3. *Defining commercial speech.* In what sense was the speech in *Central Hudson* solely in the economic interests of speaker and audience? [c] Should the Court decide on an ad hoc basis which advertisements have political impact and which do not? In addressing this question, *Central Hudson,* noted that any product could be tied to public concerns and that since companies are otherwise free to speak about public issues,[d] "there is no reason for providing similar protection when such statements are made only in the context of commercial transactions." Compare *Bolger v. Youngs Drug Products Corp.,* 463 U.S. 60, 103 S.Ct. 2875, 77 L.Ed.2d 469 (1983) ("advertisers should not be permitted to immunize false or misleading product information from government regulation simply by including references to public issues"). If a cigarette company buys space in the *New York Times* to print a deceptive message about health and cigarettes, under what circumstances would the communication be properly characterized as commercial speech? Consider Tribe, *Constitutional Choices* 218 (1985): "The distinction between commercial and noncommercial speech [exemplifies] a propensity for pigeonholing as a method for deciding First Amendment questions. Such a method masks the essentially political nature of the underlying issues by pretending to cabin judicial discretion within the limits established by the category itself." Does this sort of pigeonholing "pars[e] First Amendment doctrine too fine"? Does it "endange[r] the pigeon?" See id.

C. PRIVATE SPEECH

When District Attorney Connick proposed to transfer Assistant D.A. Myers to a different section of the criminal court, she strongly opposed it. Shortly

---

c. Is this category intended to be larger than the category of proposing a commercial transaction? Consider the question in connection with *Greenmoss,* p. 576 infra.

d. See Sec. 10 infra.

thereafter, Myers prepared and distributed to the other assistants a question-naire concerning office transfer policy, office morale, the need for a grievance committee and two questions Connick particularly objected to—the level of confidence in various supervisors and whether employees felt pressured to work in political campaigns. Connick then told Myers that she was being terminated for refusal to accept the transfer and that he considered distribution of the questionnaire an act of insubordination. Myers filed suit under 42 U.S.C. § 1983, contending that she was wrongfully discharged because she had exer-cised her right of free speech. The district court agreed. It found that the questionnaire was the real reason for Myers' termination, and that the state had not "clearly demonstrated" that the survey "substantially interfered" with the operation of the District Attorney's office. The Fifth Circuit affirmed. But CONNICK v. MYERS, 461 U.S. 138, 103 S.Ct. 1684, 75 L.Ed.2d 708 (1983), per WHITE, J., held that respondent's discharge did not offend the first amendment:

"For most of this century, the unchallenged dogma was that a public employee had no right to object to conditions placed upon the terms of employ-ment—including those which restricted the exercise of constitutional rights. The classic formulation of this position was Justice Holmes', who, when sitting on the Supreme Judicial Court of Massachusetts, observed: 'A policeman may have a constitutional right to talk politics, but he has no constitutional right to be a policeman.' *McAuliffe v. Mayor,* 155 Mass. 216, 220, 29 N.E. 517, 517 (1892). For many years, Holmes' epigram expressed this Court's law. *Adler v. Bd. of Educ.,* 342 U.S. 485, 72 S.Ct. 380, 96 L.Ed. 517 (1952); *Garner v. Bd. of Pub. Works,* 341 U.S. 716, 71 S.Ct. 909, 95 L.Ed. 1317 (1951)."

The Court proceeded, however, to recount a series of cases in which it had subsequently repudiated Holmes' epigram.[a] Indeed, for some two decades it had become wholly impermissible to deny freedom of expression "by the denial of or placing of conditions upon a benefit or a privilege." As the Court characterized the public employee cases, they were all rooted in the rights of public employees to participate in public affairs.[b] In particular, the Court focused upon *Pickering v. Bd. of Educ.,* 391 U.S. 563, 88 S.Ct. 1731, 20 L.Ed.2d 811 (1968): "In *Pickering,* we stated that a public employee does not relinquish First Amendment rights to comment on matters of public interest by virtue of government employment. [The] repeated emphasis in *Pickering* on the right of a public employee 'as a citizen, in commenting upon matters of public concern,' was not accidental. This language, reiterated in all of *Pickering's* progeny, reflects both the historical evolvement of the rights of public employees, and the common sense realization that government offices could not function if every employment decision became a constitutional matter.[5] * * *

"*Pickering* [held] impermissible under the First Amendment the dismissal of a high school teacher for openly criticizing the Board of Education on its allocation of school funds between athletics and education and its methods of informing taxpayers about the need for additional revenue. *Pickering's* subject was a matter of legitimate public concern upon which free and open debate is vital to informed decision-making by the electorate. [Most] recently, in *Givhan*

---

a. Most of the cases involved the right of public employees to associate. See Sec. 9, II infra.

b. But see *Letter Carriers,* p. 734 infra.

5. The question of whether expression is of a kind that is of legitimate concern to the public is also the standard in determining

whether a common-law action for invasion of privacy is present. See Restatement (Second) of Torts, § 652D. See also *Cox Broadcasting Co. v. Cohn* (action for invasion of privacy cannot be maintained when the subject-mat-ter of the publicity is matter of public record); *Time, Inc. v. Hill.*

v. Western Line Cons. School Dist., 439 U.S. 410, 99 S.Ct. 693, 58 L.Ed.2d 619 (1979), we held that First Amendment protection applies when a public employee arranges to communicate privately with his employer rather than to express his views publicly. Although the subject-matter of Mrs. Givhan's statements were not the issue before the Court, it is clear that her statements concerning the school district's allegedly racially discriminatory policies involved a matter of public concern.

"Pickering, its antecedents and progeny, lead us to conclude that if Myers' questionnaire cannot be fairly characterized as constituting speech on a matter of public concern, it is unnecessary for us to scrutinize the reasons for her discharge. When employee expression cannot be fairly considered as relating to any matter of political, social, or other concern to the community, government officials should enjoy wide latitude in managing their offices, without intrusive oversight by the judiciary in the name of the First Amendment. ＊ ＊ ＊ We do not suggest, however, that Myers' speech, even if not touching upon a matter of public concern, is totally beyond the protection of the First Amendment. ＊ ＊ ＊ [We] in no sense suggest that speech on private matters falls into one of the narrow and well-defined classes of expression which carries so little social value, such as obscenity, that the state can prohibit and punish such expression by all persons in its jurisdiction. See *Chaplinsky; Roth; Ferber.* For example, an employee's false criticism of his employer on grounds not of public concern may be cause for his discharge but would be entitled to the same protection in a libel action accorded an identical statement made by a man on the street. We hold only that when a public employee speaks not as a citizen upon matters of public concern, but instead as an employee upon matters only of personal interest, absent the most unusual circumstances, a federal court is not the appropriate forum in which to review the wisdom of a personnel decision taken by a public agency allegedly in reaction to the employee's behavior. Our responsibility is to ensure that citizens are not deprived of fundamental rights by virtue of working for the government; this does not require a grant of immunity for employee grievances not afforded by the First Amendment to those who do not work for the state.

"Whether an employee's speech addresses a matter of public concern must be determined by the content, form, and context of a given statement, as revealed by the whole record. In this case, with but one exception, the questions posed by Myers to her coworkers do not fall under the rubric of matters of 'public concern.' We view the questions pertaining to the confidence and trust that Myers' coworkers possess in various supervisors, the level of office morale, and the need for a grievance committee as mere extensions of Myers' dispute over her transfer to another section of the criminal court. ＊ ＊ ＊ Indeed, the questionnaire, if released to the public, would convey no information at all other than the fact that a single employee is upset with the status quo. [T]he focus of Myers' questions is not to evaluate the performance of the office but rather to gather ammunition for another round of controversy with her superiors. These questions reflect one employee's dissatisfaction with a transfer and an attempt to turn that displeasure into a cause celèbre.[8] ＊ ＊ ＊

8. This is not a case like *Givhan,* where an employee speaks out as a citizen on a matter of general concern, not tied to a personal employment dispute, but arranges to do so privately. Mrs. Givhan's right to protest racial discrimination—a matter inherently of public concern—is not forfeited by her choice of a private forum. Here, however, a questionnaire not otherwise of public concern does not attain that status because its subject matter could, in different circumstances, have been the topic of a communication to the public that might be of general interest. The dissent's analysis of whether discussions of

"One question in Myers' questionnaire, however, does touch upon a matter of public concern. Question 11 inquires if assistant district attorneys 'ever feel pressured to work in political campaigns on behalf of office supported candidates.' [This issue] is a matter of interest to the community upon which it is essential that public employees be able to speak out freely without fear of retaliatory dismissal.

"Because one of the questions in Myers' survey touched upon a matter of public concern, and contributed to her discharge we must determine whether Connick was justified in discharging Myers. Here the District Court again erred in imposing an unduly onerous burden on the state to justify Myers' discharge. The District Court viewed the issue of whether Myers' speech was upon a matter of 'public concern' as a threshold inquiry, after which it became the government's burden to 'clearly demonstrate' that the speech involved 'substantially interfered' with official responsibilities. Yet *Pickering* unmistakably states, and respondent agrees, that the state's burden in justifying a particular discharge varies depending upon the nature of the employee's expression. Although such particularized balancing is difficult, the courts must reach the most appropriate possible balance of the competing interests.   *   *   *

"We agree with the District Court that there is no demonstration here that the questionnaire impeded Myers' ability to perform her responsibilities. The District Court was also correct to recognize that 'it is important to the efficient and successful operation of the District Attorney's office for Assistants to maintain close working relationships with their superiors.' Connick's judgment, and apparently also that of his first assistant [who] characterized Myers' actions as causing a 'mini-insurrection', was that Myers' questionnaire was an act of insubordination which interfered with working relationships. When close working relationships are essential to fulfilling public responsibilities, a wide degree of deference to the employer's judgment is appropriate. Furthermore, we do not see the necessity for an employer to allow events to unfold to the extent that the disruption of the office and the destruction of working relationships is manifest before taking action. We caution that a stronger showing may be necessary if the employee's speech more substantially involved matters of public concern.   *   *   *

"Also relevant is the manner, time, and place in which the questionnaire was distributed. '[When] a government employee personally confronts his immediate superior, the employing agency's institutional efficiency may be threatened not only by the content of the employee's message but also by the manner, time, and place in which it is delivered.' Here the questionnaire was prepared, and distributed at the office; the manner of distribution required not only Myers to leave her work but for others to do the same in order that the questionnaire be completed.[13] Although some latitude in when official work is performed is to be allowed when professional employees are involved, and Myers did not violate announced office policy, the fact that Myers, unlike Pickering, exercised her rights to speech at the office supports Connick's fears that the functioning of his office was endangered.

office morale and discipline could be matters of public concern is beside the point—it does not answer whether *this* questionnaire is such speech.

13. The record indicates that some, though not all, of the questionnaires were distributed during lunch. Employee speech which transpires entirely on the employee's own time, and in non-work areas of the office, bring different factors into the *Pickering* calculus, and might lead to a different conclusion.

"Finally, the context in which the dispute arose is also significant. This is not a case where an employee, out of purely academic interest, circulated a questionnaire so as to obtain useful research. Myers acknowledges that it is no coincidence that the questionnaire followed upon the heels of the transfer notice. When employee speech concerning office policy arises from an employment dispute concerning the very application of that policy to the speaker, additional weight must be given to the supervisor's view that the employee has threatened the authority of the employer to run the office. Although we accept the District Court's factual finding that Myers' reluctance to accede to the transfer order was not a sufficient cause in itself for her dismissal, [this] does not render irrelevant the fact that the questionnaire emerged after a persistent dispute between Myers and Connick and his deputies over office transfer policy.

"Myers' questionnaire touched upon matters of public concern in only a most limited sense; her survey, in our view, is most accurately characterized as an employee grievance concerning internal office policy. The limited First Amendment interest involved here does not require that Connick tolerate action which he reasonably believed would disrupt the office, undermine his authority, and destroy close working relationships. Myers' discharge therefore did not offend the First Amendment. * * *

"Our holding today is grounded in our long-standing recognition that the First Amendment's primary aim is the full protection of speech upon issues of public concern, as well as the practical realities involved in the administration of a government office. Although today the balance is struck for the government, this is no defeat for the First Amendment. For it would indeed be a Pyrrhic victory for the great principles of free expression if the Amendment's safeguarding of a public employee's right, as a citizen, to participate in discussions concerning public affairs were confused with the attempt to constitutionalize the employee grievance that we see presented here."

BRENNAN, J., joined by Marshall, Blackmun and Stevens, JJ., dissented: "It is hornbook law [that] speech about 'the manner in which government is operated or should be operated' is an essential part of the communications necessary for self-governance the protection of which was a central purpose of the First Amendment. Because the questionnaire addressed such matters and its distribution did not adversely affect the operations of the District Attorney's Office or interfere with Myers' working relationship with her fellow employees, I dissent. * * *

"The balancing test articulated in *Pickering* comes into play only when a public employee's speech implicates the government's interests as an employer. When public employees engage in expression unrelated to their employment while away from the work place, their First Amendment rights are, of course, no different from those of the general public. Thus, whether a public employee's speech addresses a matter of public concern is relevant to the constitutional inquiry only when the statements at issue—by virtue of their content or the context in which they were made—may have an adverse impact on the government's ability to perform its duties efficiently.

"The Court's decision today is flawed in three respects. First, the Court distorts the balancing analysis required under *Pickering* by suggesting that one factor, the context in which a statement is made, is to be weighed *twice*—first in determining whether an employee's speech addresses a matter of public concern and then in deciding whether the statement adversely affected the government's interest as an employer. Second, in concluding that the effect of respondent's personnel policies on employee morale and the work performance of the District Attorney's Office is not a matter of public concern, the Court impermissibly narrows the class of subjects on which public employees may speak out without fear of retaliatory dismissal. Third, the Court misapplies the *Pickering* balancing test in holding that Myers could constitutionally be dismissed for circulating a questionnaire addressed to at least one subject that *was* 'a matter of interest to the community,' in the absence of evidence that her conduct disrupted the efficient functioning of the District Attorney's Office.

"[Based] on its own narrow conception of which matters are of public concern, the Court implicitly determines that information concerning employee morale at an important government office will not inform public debate. To the contrary, the First Amendment protects the dissemination of such information so that the people, not the courts may evaluate its usefulness. The proper means to ensure that the courts are not swamped with routine employee grievances mischaracterized as First Amendment cases is not to restrict artificially the concept of 'public concern,' but to require that adequate weight be given to the public's important interests in the efficient performance of governmental functions and in preserving employee discipline and harmony sufficient to achieve that end.

"The District Court weighed all of the relevant factors identified by our cases. It found that petitioner failed to establish that Myers violated either a duty of confidentiality or an office policy. Noting that most of the questionnaires were distributed during lunch, it rejected the contention that the distribution of the questionnaire impeded Myers' performance of her duties, and it concluded that 'Connick has not shown *any* evidence to indicate that the plaintiff's work performance was adversely affected by her expression.' (emphasis supplied).

"The Court accepts all of these findings. It concludes, however, that the District Court failed to give adequate weight to the context in which the questionnaires were distributed and to the need to maintain close working relationships in the District Attorney's Office. In particular, the Court suggests the District Court failed to give sufficient weight to the disruptive potential of Question 10, which asked whether the Assistants had confidence in the word of five named supervisors. The District Court, however, explicitly recognized that this was petitioner's 'most forceful argument'; but after hearing the testimony of four of the five supervisors named in the question, it found that the question had no adverse effect on Myers' relationship with her superiors.

"To this the Court responds that an employer need not wait until the destruction of working relationships is manifest before taking action. In the face of the District Court's finding that the circulation of the questionnaire had no disruptive effect, the Court holds that respondent may be dismissed because petitioner 'reasonably believed [the action] would disrupt the office, undermine his authority and destroy close working relationships.' Even though the District Court found that the distribution of the questionnaire did not impair Myers' working relationship with her supervisors, the Court bows to petitioner's judgment because '[w]hen close working relationships are essential to fulfilling public responsibilities, a wide degree of deference to the employer's judgment is appropriate.'

"Such extreme deference to the employer's judgment is not appropriate when public employees voice critical views concerning the operations of the agency for which they work. Although an employer's determination that an employee's statements have undermined essential working relationships must be carefully weighed in the *Pickering* balance, we must bear in mind that 'the threat of dismissal from public employment is [a] potent means of inhibiting speech.' If the employer's judgment is to be controlling, public employees will not speak out when what they have to say is critical of their supervisors. In order to protect public employees' First Amendment right to voice critical views on issues of public importance, the courts must make their own appraisal of the effects of the speech in question.

"[T]he District Court found that 'it cannot be said that the defendant's interest in promoting the efficiency of the public services performed through his employees was either adversely affected or substantially impeded by plaintiff's distribution of the questionnaire.' Based on these findings the District Court concluded that the circulation of the questionnaire was protected by the First Amendment. The District Court applied the proper legal standard and reached an acceptable accommodation between the competing interests. * * *

"The Court's decision today inevitably will deter public employees from making critical statements about the manner in which government agencies are operated for fear that doing so will provoke their dismissal. As a result, the public will be deprived of valuable information with which to evaluate the performance of elected officials. Because protecting the dissemination of such information is an essential function of the First Amendment, I dissent."

Notes and Questions

1. *Holmes' epigram.* Does the Court reject Holmes' epigram with one hand and embrace it with the other? Does it to some extent hold that because there is no right to hold a government job, its retention is a revocable privilege? Consider Tribe, *Constitutional Choices* 208 (1985): "*Connick* resurrects the right-privilege doctrine for 'private' speech by government employees. By hinging protection on the distinction between public and private speech, the Court has embarked on a difficult definitional course. The stated test, which includes the 'content, form, and context' of the expression, provides little guidance. As Justice Brennan pointed out in dissent, the Court significantly narrowed the concept of a public issue in holding that criticism of governmental officials is not necessarily of public concern, but provided no clear alternative formulation. The mere fact that expression constitutes an employee grievance surely cannot be decisive, since the Court found that pressure upon employees to work on political campaigns was of public concern. Nor can the absence of partisan political concerns be determinative, since an employee grievance criticizing hiring and personnel management policies is of public concern if based upon a claim of racial discrimination. What is clear is that, at least until the precise reach of *Connick* is determined, public employees, who often possess unique information, will be discouraged from adding their voices to the debate on government performance." [c]

2. Is *Connick* inconsistent with *Gertz* because it distinguishes public speech from private on an ad hoc basis? Inconsistent with the position of the five justices in *Young* who rejected a hierarchy of "protected" speech? Is *Connick* a public employees case or does it suggest something more general about first

---

c. Much of the literature relevant to the "right-privilege" distinction is cited in Ch. 7, Sec. 4. For recent commentary with substantial attention to first amendment issues, see Kreimer, *Allocational Sanctions: The Problem of Negative Rights in a Positive State,* 132 U.Pa.L.Rev. 1293 (1984).

amendment theory? For relevant pre-*Connick* commentary, see Schauer, *"Private" Speech and the "Private" Forum: Givhan v. Western Line School District,* 1981 Sup.Ct.Rev. 217.

———

Before studying *Dun & Bradstreet,* below, review *Gertz,* p. 476 supra, and the materials on commercial speech.

Dun & Bradstreet, Inc., a credit reporting agency, falsely and negligently reported to five of its subscribers that Greenmoss Builders, Inc. had filed a petition for bankruptcy and also negligently misrepresented Greenmoss' assets and liabilities. In the ensuing defamation action, Greenmoss recovered $50,000 in compensatory damages and $300,000 in punitive damages. Dun & Bradstreet argued that, under *Gertz,* its first amendment rights had been violated because presumed and punitive damages had been imposed without instructions requiring a showing of *New York Times* malice. Greenmoss argued that the *Gertz* protections did not extend to non-media defendants and, in any event, did not extend to commercial speech. DUN & BRADSTREET, INC. v. GREENMOSS BUILDERS, INC., __ U.S. __, 105 S.Ct. 2939, 86 L.Ed.2d 593 (1985), rejected Dun & Bradstreet's contention, but there was no opinion of the Court. The common theme of the five justices siding with Greenmoss was that the first amendment places less value on "private" speech than upon "public" speech.

POWELL, J., joined by Rehnquist and O'Connor, JJ., noted that the Vermont Supreme Court below had held "as a matter of federal constitutional law" that "the media protections outlined in *Gertz* are inapplicable to nonmedia defamation actions." In affirming, Powell, J., stated that his reasons were "different from those relied upon by the Vermont Supreme Court": "Like every other case in which this Court has found constitutional limits to state defamation laws, *Gertz* involved expression on a matter of undoubted public concern. * * *

"We have never considered whether the *Gertz* balance obtains when the defamatory statements involve no issue of public concern. To make this determination, we must employ the approach approved in *Gertz* and balance the State's interest in compensating private individuals for injury to their reputation against the First Amendment interest in protecting this type of expression. This state interest is identical to the one weighed in *Gertz.* * * *

"The First Amendment interest, on the other hand, is less important than the one weighed in *Gertz.* We have long recognized that not all speech is of equal First Amendment importance.[5] It is speech on 'matters of public concern'

5. This Court on many occasions has recognized that certain kinds of speech are less central to the interests of the First Amendment than others. Obscene speech and "fighting words" long have been accorded no protection. *Roth; Chaplinsky.* In the area of protected speech, the most prominent example of reduced protection for certain kinds of speech concerns commercial speech. Such speech, we have noted, occupies a "subordinate position in the scale of First Amendment values." *Ohralik.* * * *

Other areas of the law provide further examples. In *Ohralik* we noted that there are "[n]umerous examples [of] communications that are regulated without offending the First Amendment, such as the exchange of information about securities, * * * corporate proxy statements, [the] exchange of price and production information among competitors, [and] employers' threats of retaliation for the labor activities of employees." Yet similar regulation of political speech is subject to the most rigorous scrutiny. Likewise, while the power of the State to license lawyers, psychiatrists, and public school teachers—all of whom speak for a living—is unquestioned, this Court has held that a law requiring licensing of union organizers is unconstitutional under the First Amendment. *Thomas v. Collins,* [p. 584 infra]; see also *Rosenbloom v. Metromedia* (opinion of Brennan, J.) ("the determinant whether the First Amendment applies to state libel actions is whether the utterance involved concerns an issue of public or general concern").

that is 'at the heart of the First Amendment's protection.' [In] contrast, speech on matters of purely private concern is of less First Amendment concern. As a number of state courts, including the court below, have recognized, the role of the Constitution in regulating state libel law is far more limited when the concerns that activated *New York Times* and *Gertz* are absent.[6] In such a case, '[t]here is no threat to the free and robust debate of public issues; there is no potential interference with a meaningful dialogue of ideas concerning self-government; and there is no threat of liability causing a reaction of self-censorship by the press. The facts of the present case are wholly without the First Amendment concerns with which the Supreme Court of the United States has been struggling.' *Harley-Davidson Motorsports, Inc. v. Markley*, 279 Or. 361, 366, 568 P.2d 1359, 1363 (1977).

"While such speech is not totally unprotected by the First Amendment, see *Connick*, its protections are less stringent. [In] light of the reduced constitutional value of speech involving no matters of public concern, we hold that the state interest adequately supports awards of presumed and punitive damages—even absent a showing of 'actual malice.'[7]

"The only remaining issue is whether petitioner's credit report involved a matter of public concern. In a related context, we have held that '[w]hether [speech] addresses a matter of public concern must be determined by [the expression's] content, form, and context [as] revealed by the whole record.' *Connick*. These factors indicate that petitioner's credit report concerns no public issue.[8] It was speech solely in the individual interest of the speaker and its specific business audience. Cf. *Central Hudson*. This particular interest warrants no special protection when—as in this case—the speech is wholly false and clearly damaging to the victim's business reputation. Moreover, since the credit report was made available to only five subscribers, who, under the terms of the subscription agreement, could not disseminate it further, it cannot be said that the report involves any 'strong interest in the free flow of commercial information.' *Virginia Pharmacy*. There is simply no credible argument that this type of credit reporting requires special protection to ensure that 'debate on public issues [will] be uninhibited, robust, and wide-open.' *New York Times*.

6. As one commentator has remarked with respect to "the case of a commercial supplier of credit information that defames a person applying for credit"—the case before us today—"If the first amendment requirements outlined in *Gertz* apply, there is something clearly wrong with the first amendment or with *Gertz*." Shiffrin, *The First Amendment and Economic Regulation: Away From a General Theory of the First Amendment*, 78 Nw.L. Rev. 1212, 1268 (1983).

7. The dissent, purporting to apply the same balancing test that we do today, concludes that even speech on purely private matters is entitled to the protections of *Gertz*.

* * *

The dissent's "balance" [would] lead to the protection of all libels—no matter how attenuated their constitutional interest. If the dissent were the law, a woman of impeccable character who was branded a "whore" by a jealous neighbor would have no effective recourse unless she could prove "actual malice" by clear and convincing evidence. This is not malice in the ordinary sense, but in the more demanding sense of *New York Times*. The dissent would, in effect, constitutionalize the entire common law of libel.

8. The dissent suggests that our holding today leaves all credit reporting subject to reduced First Amendment protection. This is incorrect. The protection to be accorded a particular credit report depends on whether the report's "content, form, and context" indicate that it concerns a public matter. We also do not hold, as the dissent suggests we do, that the report is subject to reduced constitutional protection because it constitutes economic or commercial speech. We discuss such speech, along with advertising, only to show how many of the same concerns that argue in favor of reduced constitutional protection in those areas apply here as well.

"In addition, the speech here, like advertising, is hardy and unlikely to be deterred by incidental state regulation. See *Virginia Pharmacy*. It is solely motivated by the desire for profit, which, we have noted, is a force less likely to be deterred than others. Arguably, the reporting here was also more objectively verifiable than speech deserving of greater protection. In any case, the market provides a powerful incentive to a credit reporting agency to be accurate, since false credit reporting is of no use to creditors. Thus, any incremental 'chilling' effect of libel suits would be of decreased significance.

"We conclude that permitting recovery of presumed and punitive damages in defamation cases absent a showing of 'actual malice' does not violate the First Amendment when the defamatory statements do not involve matters of public concern."

Although expressing the view that *Gertz* should be overruled and that the *New York Times* malice definition should be reconsidered, BURGER, C.J., concurring, stated that: "The single question before the Court today is whether *Gertz* applies to this case. The plurality opinion holds that *Gertz* does not apply because, unlike the challenged expression in *Gertz,* the alleged defamatory expression in this case does not relate to a matter of public concern. I agree that *Gertz* is limited to circumstances in which the alleged defamatory expression concerns a matter of general public importance, and that the expression in question here relates to a matter of essentially private concern. I therefore agree with the plurality opinion to the extent that it holds that *Gertz* is inapplicable in this case for the two reasons indicated. No more is needed to dispose of the present case."

WHITE, J., who had dissented in *Gertz,* was prepared to overrule that case or to limit it, but he disagreed with Powell, J.'s, suggestion that the plurality's resolution of the case was faithful to *Gertz:*

"It is interesting that Justice Powell declines to follow the *Gertz* approach in this case. I had thought that the decision in *Gertz* was intended to reach cases that involve any false statements of fact injurious to reputation, whether the statement is made privately or publicly and whether or not it implicates a matter of public importance. Justice Powell, however, distinguishes *Gertz* as a case that involved a matter of public concern, an element absent here. Wisely, in my view, Justice Powell does not rest his application of a different rule here on a distinction drawn between media and non-media defendants. On that issue, I agree with Justice Brennan that the First Amendment gives no more protection to the press in defamation suits than it does to others exercising their freedom of speech. None of our cases affords such a distinction; to the contrary, the Court has rejected it at every turn. It should be rejected again, particularly in this context, since it makes no sense to give the most protection to those publishers who reach the most readers and therefore pollute the channels of communication with the most misinformation and do the most damage to private reputation. If *Gertz* is to be distinguished from this case, on the ground that it applies only where the allegedly false publication deals with a matter of general or public importance, then where the false publication does not deal with such a matter, the common-law rules would apply whether the defendant is a member of the media or other public disseminator or a non-media individual publishing privately. Although Justice Powell speaks only of the inapplicability of the *Gertz* rule with respect to presumed and punitive damages, it must be that the *Gertz* requirement of some kind of fault on the part of the defendant is also inapplicable in cases such as this. * * *

"The question before us is whether *Gertz* is to be applied in this case. For either of two reasons, I believe that it should not. First, I am unreconciled to the *Gertz* holding and believe that it should be overruled. Second, as Justice Powell indicates, the defamatory publication in this case does not deal with a matter of public importance."

BRENNAN, J., joined by Marshall, Blackmun and Stevens, JJ., dissented:

"This case involves a difficult question of the proper application of *Gertz* to credit reporting—a type of speech at some remove from that which first gave rise to explicit First Amendment restrictions on state defamation law—and has produced a diversity of considered opinions, none of which speaks for the Court. Justice Powell's plurality opinion affirming the judgment below would not apply the *Gertz* limitations on presumed and punitive damages [because] the speech involved a subject of purely private concern and was circulated to an extremely limited audience. * * * Justice White also would affirm; he would not apply *Gertz* to this case on the ground that the subject matter of the publication does not deal with a matter of general or public importance. The Chief Justice apparently agrees with Justice White. The four who join this opinion would reverse the judgment of the Vermont Supreme Court. We believe that, although protection of the type of expression at issue is admittedly not the 'central meaning of the First Amendment,' *Gertz* makes clear that the First Amendment nonetheless requires restraints on presumed and punitive damage awards for this expression. * * *

"[Respondent urged that *Gertz* be restricted] to cases in which the defendant is a 'media' entity. Such a distinction is irreconcilable with the fundamental First Amendment principle that '[t]he inherent worth [of] speech in terms of its capacity for informing the public does not depend upon the identity of its source, whether corporation, association, union, or individual.' *First National Bank v. Bellotti* [p. 783 infra]. First Amendment difficulties lurk in the definitional questions such an approach would generate. And the distinction would likely be born an anachronism.[7] Perhaps most importantly, the argument that *Gertz* should be limited to the media misapprehends our cases. We protect the press to ensure the vitality of First Amendment guarantees. This solicitude implies no endorsement of the principle that speakers other than the press deserve lesser First Amendment protection. * * *

"The free speech guarantee gives each citizen an equal right to self-expression and to participation in self-government. [Accordingly,] at least six Members of this Court (the four who join this opinion and Justice White and The Chief Justice) agree today that, in the context of defamation law, the rights of the institutional media are no greater and no less than those enjoyed by other individuals or organizations engaged in the same activities.[10] * * *

"Purporting to 'employ the approach approved in *Gertz*,' Justice Powell balances the state interest in protecting private reputation against the First Amendment interest in protecting expression on matters not of public concern.[11]

7. Owing to transformations in the technological and economic structure of the communications industry, there has been an increasing convergence of what might be labeled "media" and "nonmedia."

10. Justice Powell's opinion does not expressly reject the media/nonmedia distinction,

but does expressly decline to apply that distinction to resolve this case.

11. One searches *Gertz* in vain for a single word to support the proposition that limits on presumed and punitive damages obtained only when speech involved matters of public concern. *Gertz* could not have been grounded in

"The five Members of the Court voting to affirm the damage award in this case have provided almost no guidance as to what constitutes a protected 'matter of public concern.' Justice White offers nothing at all, but his opinion does indicate that the distinction turns on solely the subject matter of the expression and not on the extent or conditions of dissemination of that expression. Justice Powell adumbrates a rationale that would appear to focus primarily on subject matter.[12] The opinion relies on the fact that the speech at issue was 'solely in the individual interest of the speaker and its *business* audience.' Analogizing explicitly to advertising, the opinion also states that credit reporting is 'hardy' and 'solely motivated by the desire for profit.' These two strains of analysis suggest that Justice Powell is excluding the subject matter of credit reports from 'matters of public concern' because the speech is predominantly in the realm of matters of economic concern."

Brennan, J., pointed to precedents (particularly labor cases) protecting speech on economic matters and argued that, "the breadth of this protection evinces recognition that freedom of expression is not only essential to check tyranny and foster self-government but also intrinsic to individual liberty and dignity and instrumental in society's search for truth."

Moreover, he emphasized the importance of credit reporting: "The credit reporting of Dun & Bradstreet falls within any reasonable definition of 'public concern' consistent with our precedents. Justice Powell's reliance on the fact that Dun & Bradstreet publishes credit reports 'for profit' is wholly unwarranted. Time and again we have made clear that speech loses none of its constitutional protection 'even though it is carried in a form that is "sold" for profit.' *Virginia Pharmacy.* More importantly, an announcement of the bankruptcy of a local company is information of potentially great concern to residents of the community where the company is [located]. And knowledge about solvency and the effect and prevalence of bankruptcy certainly would inform citizen opinions about questions of economic regulation. It is difficult to suggest that a bankruptcy is not a subject matter of public concern when federal law requires invocation of judicial mechanisms to effectuate it and makes the fact of the bankruptcy a matter of public record. * * *

"Even if the subject matter of credit reporting were properly considered—in the terms of Justice White and Justice Powell—as purely a matter of private discourse, this speech would fall well within the range of valuable expression for which the First Amendment demands protection. Much expression that does not directly involve public issues receives significant protection. Our cases do permit some diminution in the degree of protection afforded one category of

such a premise. Distrust of placing in the courts the power to decide what speech was of public concern was precisely the rationale *Gertz* offered for rejecting the *Rosenbloom* plurality approach. * * *

12. Justice Powell also appears to rely in part on the fact that communication was limited and confidential. Given that his analysis also relies on the subject matter of the credit report, it is difficult to decipher exactly what role the nature and extent of dissemination plays in Justice Powell's analysis. But because the subject matter of the expression at issue is properly understood as a matter of public concern, it may well be that this element of confidentiality is crucial to the outcome as far as

Justice Powell's opinion is concerned. In other words, it may be that Justice Powell thinks this particular expression could not contribute to public welfare because the public generally does not receive it. This factor does not suffice to save the analysis. See n. 18 infra.

[In fn. 18, Brennan, J., indicated that, "Dun & Bradstreet doubtless provides thousands of credit reports to thousands of subscribers who receive the information pursuant to the same strictures imposed on the recipients in this case. As a systemic matter, therefore, today's decision diminishes the free flow of information because Dun & Bradstreet will generally be made more reticent in providing information to all its subscribers."]

speech about economic or commercial matters. 'Commercial speech'—defined as advertisements that 'do no more than propose a commercial transaction'—may be more closely regulated than other types of speech. [Credit] reporting is not 'commercial speech' as this Court has defined the term.

"[In] *every* case in which we have permitted more extensive state regulation on the basis of a commercial speech rationale—the speech being regulated was pure advertising—an offer to buy or sell goods and services or encouraging such buying and selling. Credit reports are not commercial advertisements for a good or service or a proposal to buy or sell such a product. We have been extremely chary about extending the 'commercial speech' doctrine beyond this narrowly circumscribed category of advertising because often vitally important speech will be uttered to advance economic interests and because the profit motive making such speech hardy dissipates rapidly when the speech is not advertising." [a]

Finally, Brennan, J., argued that even if credit reports were characterized as commercial speech, "unrestrained" presumed and punitive damages would violate the commercial speech requirement that "the regulatory means chosen be narrowly tailored so as to avoid any unnecessary chilling of protected expression. [Accordingly,] Greenmoss Builders should be permitted to recover for any actual damage it can show resulted from Dun & Bradstreet's negligently false credit report, but should be required to show actual malice to receive presumed or punitive damages."

Notes and Questions

1. Which of the following are "private" according to the opinions of Powell, J., Burger, C.J., and White, J.? (a) a report in the *Wall Street Journal* that Greenmoss has gone bankrupt; (b) a confidential report by Dun & Bradstreet to a bank that a famous politician has poor credit. Would the answer be different if the subject of the report were an actor? (c) a statement in the campus newspaper or by one student to another that a law professor is an alcoholic. Would it make a difference if the law professor was being considered for a Supreme Court appointment?

Consider the relationship between the public/private focus of the *Greenmoss* decision and the "public controversy" aspect of the public figure definition. If the speech does not relate to a "public" controversy, can it be "public" within the terms of *Greenmoss*? Reconsider *Time, Inc. v. Firestone*, p. 484 supra. [b]

Finally, does it matter why the D & B subscribers received the information about Greenmoss? Suppose, for investment or insurance purposes, the subscribers had asked for reports on all aspects of the construction industry in Vermont?

2. Should the focus of the decision have been commercial speech instead of private speech? Would an expansion of the commercial speech definition have been preferable to the promotion of ad hoc decisionmaking about the nature of

a. Brennan, J., cited *Consolidated Edison*, p. 784 infra, which invalidated a regulation that prohibited a utility company from inserting its views on "controversial issues of public policy" into its monthly electrical bill mailings. The mailing that prompted the regulation advocated nuclear power.

b. For discussion of the different meanings of public and private speech, see Schauer, *"Private" Speech and the "Private" Forum: Givhan v. Western Line School District*, 1979

Sup.Ct.Rev. 217. Compare Perry, *Freedom of Expression: An Essay on Theory and Doctrine*, 78 Nw.U.L.Rev. 1137 (1983) (denying any meaningful distinction between personal and political decisions). See generally Symposium, *The Public/Private Distinction*, 130 U.Pa. L.Rev. 1289 (1982). For commentary on the question of whether Gertz should extend to non-media defendants see e.g. sources cited in note 1 after *Gertz*, p. 483 supra.

"private" speech? Consider Shiffrin, *The First Amendment and Economic Regulation: Away From A General Theory of the First Amendment,* 78 Nw.U.L.Rev. 1212, 1269 n. 327 (1983): "[D]rawing lines based on underlying first amendment values is a far cry from sending out the judiciary on a general ad hoc expedition to separate matters of general public interest from matters that are not. A commitment to segregate certain commercial speech from *Gertz* protection is not a commitment to general ad hoc determinations."

3. According to Powell, J., in fn. 5, are the *Ohralik* examples, i.e., exchange of information about securities, corporate proxy statements and the like, examples of protected speech subject to regulation? In what sense, are those examples of communication protected? What is the significance of Powell, J.'s suggestion that they are something other than commercial speech? Where do those examples fit into Brennan, J.'s view of the first amendment? For general discussion, see Shiffrin, note 2 supra.

SECTION 2. PRIOR RESTRAINTS

Prior restraint is a technical term in first amendment law. A criminal statute prohibiting all advocacy of violent action would *restrain* speech and would have been enacted *prior* to any restrained communication. The statute would be overbroad, but it would not be a prior restraint. A prior restraint refers only to closely related, distinctive methods of regulating expression that are said to have in common their own peculiar set of evils and problems, in addition to those that accompany most any governmental interference with free expression. "The issue is not whether the government may impose a particular restriction of substance in an area of public expression, such as forbidding obscenity in newspapers, but whether it may do so by a particular method, such as advance screening of newspaper copy. In other words, restrictions which could be validly imposed when enforced by subsequent punishment are, nevertheless, forbidden if attempted by prior restraint." Emerson, *The Doctrine of Prior Restraint,* 20 Law and Contemp.Prob. 648 (1955).

The classic prior restraints were the English licensing laws which required a license in advance to print any material or to import or to sell any book. One of the questions raised in this chapter concerns the types of government conduct beyond the classic licensing laws that should be characterized as prior restraints. Another concerns the question of when government licensing of speech, press, or assembly should be countenanced. Perhaps, most important, the Section explores the circumstances in which otherwise protected speech may be restrained on an ad hoc basis.

I. FOUNDATION CASES

A. LICENSING

LOVELL v. GRIFFIN, 303 U.S. 444, 58 S.Ct. 666, 82 L.Ed. 949 (1938), per HUGHES, C.J., invalidated an ordinance prohibiting the distribution of handbooks, advertising or literature within the city of Griffin, Georgia without obtaining written permission of the City Manager: "[T]he ordinance is invalid on its face. Whatever the motive which induced its adoption, its character is such that it strikes at the very foundation of the freedom of the press by subjecting it to license and censorship. The struggle for the freedom of the press was primarily directed against the power of the licensor. It was against that power that John Milton directed his assault by his 'Appeal for the Liberty of Unlicensed Printing.' And the liberty of the press became initially a right to publish '*without* a license what formerly could be published only *with* one.'[1] While this freedom from previous restraint upon publication cannot be regarded as exhausting the guaranty of liberty, the prevention of that restraint was a leading purpose in the adoption of the constitutional provision. Legislation of the type of the ordinance in question would restore the system of license and censorship in its baldest form.

"The liberty of the press is not confined to newspapers and periodicals. It necessarily embraces pamphlets and leaflets. These indeed have been historic weapons in the defense of liberty, as the pamphlets of Thomas Paine and others in our own history abundantly attest. The press in its historic connotation comprehends every sort of publication which affords a vehicle of information and opinion. * * *

"The ordinance cannot be saved because it relates to distribution and not to publication. 'Liberty of circulating is as essential to that freedom as liberty of publishing; indeed, without the circulation, the publication would be of little value.' *Ex parte Jackson,* 96 U.S. (6 Otto) 727, 733, 24 L.Ed. 877 (1877).

"[As] the ordinance is void on its face, it was not necessary for appellant to seek a permit under it. She was entitled to contest its validity in answer to the charge against her.

"[Reversed and] remanded."[a]

Notes and Questions

1. *First amendment procedure.* Notice that Lovell would get the benefit of the prior restraint doctrine even if the material she distributed was obscene or otherwise unprotected. In that respect, the prior restraint doctrine is similar to the doctrines of overbreadth and vagueness. For particular concerns that underlie the prior restraint doctrine, consider Emerson, *The System of Freedom of Expression* 506 (1970):

"A system of prior restraint is in many ways more inhibiting than a system of subsequent punishment: It is likely to bring under government scrutiny a far wider range of expression; it shuts off communication before it takes place; suppression by a stroke of the pen is more likely to be applied than suppression through a criminal process; the procedures do not require attention to the safeguards of the criminal process; the system allows less opportunity for public appraisal and criticism; the dynamics of the system drive toward excesses, as the history of all censorship shows."

2. *Scope and character of the doctrine.* What is the vice of the licensing scheme in *Lovell*? Is the concern that like vague statutes it affords undue discretion and potential for abuse? Is the real concern the uncontrolled power of the licensor to deny licenses? Suppose licenses were automatically issued to anyone who applied?

To what extent should the prior restraint doctrine apply to non-press activities? To a licensing ordinance that otherwise forbids soliciting membership in organizations that exact fees of their members? See *Staub v. Baxley,* 355 U.S. 313, 78 S.Ct. 277, 2 L.Ed.2d 302 (1958) (yes). To a licensing ordinance that otherwise prohibits attempts to secure contributions for charitable or religious

1. See Wickwar, "The Struggle for the Freedom of the Press," p. 15.　　　a. Cardozo, J., took no part.

causes? See *Cantwell v. Connecticut*, 310 U.S. 296, 60 S.Ct. 900, 84 L.Ed. 1213 (1940) (yes).

Suppose, in the above cases, that the authority of the licensor were confined by narrow, objective, and definite standards or that licenses were automatically issued to anyone who applied. *Hynes v. Mayor*, 425 U.S. 610, 96 S.Ct. 1755, 48 L.Ed.2d 243 (1976), per Burger, C.J., stated in dictum that a municipality could regulate house to house soliciting by requiring advance notice to the police department in order to protect its citizens from crime and undue annoyance: "A narrowly drawn ordinance, that does not vest in municipal officials the undefined power to determine what messages residents will hear, may serve these important interests without running afoul of the First Amendment." But cf. *Thomas v. Collins*, 323 U.S. 516, 65 S.Ct. 315, 89 L.Ed. 430 (1945) (registration requirement for paid union organizers invalid prior restraint); *Talley v. California*, 362 U.S. 60, 80 S.Ct. 536, 4 L.Ed.2d 559 (1960) (ban on anonymous handbills "void on its face," noting that the "obnoxious press licensing law of England, which was also enforced on the Colonies was due in part to the knowledge that exposure of the names of printers, writers and distributors would lessen the circulation of literature critical of the government").

B. INJUNCTIONS

NEAR v. MINNESOTA

283 U.S. 697, 51 S.Ct. 625, 75 L.Ed. 1357 (1931).

Mr. Chief Justice Hughes delivered the opinion of the Court.

[The *Saturday Press* published articles charging that through graft and incompetence named public officials failed to expose and punish gangsters responsible for gambling, bootlegging, and racketeering in Minneapolis. It demanded a special grand jury and special prosecutor to deal with the situation and to investigate an alleged attempt to assassinate one of its publishers. Under a statute that authorized abatement of a "malicious, scandalous and defamatory newspaper" the state secured, and its supreme court affirmed, a court order that "abated" the Press and perpetually enjoined the defendants from publishing or circulating "any publication whatsoever which is a malicious, scandalous or defamatory newspaper." The order did not restrain the defendants from operating a newspaper "in harmony with the general welfare."]

The object of the statute is not punishment, in the ordinary sense, but suppression of the offending newspaper. [In] the case of public officers, it is the reiteration of charges of official misconduct, and the fact that the newspaper [is] principally devoted to that purpose, that exposes it to suppression. [T]he operation and effect of the statute [is] that public authorities may bring the owner or publisher of a newspaper or periodical before a judge upon a charge of conducting a business of publishing scandalous and defamatory matter—in particular that the matter consists of charges against public officers of official dereliction—and, unless the owner or publisher is able and disposed to bring competent evidence to satisfy the judge that the charges are true and are published with good motives and for justifiable ends, his newspaper or periodical is suppressed and further publication is made punishable as a contempt. This is of the essence of censorship.

The question is whether a statute authorizing such proceedings [is] consistent with the conception of the liberty of the press as historically conceived and guaranteed. [I]t has been generally, if not universally, considered that it is the chief purpose of the guaranty to prevent previous restraints upon publication. The struggle in England, directed against the legislative power of the licenser, resulted in renunciation of the censorship of the press. The liberty deemed to be established was thus described by Blackstone: "The liberty of the press is indeed essential to the nature of a free state; but this consists in laying no *previous* restraints upon publications, and not in freedom from censure for criminal matter when published. Every freeman has an undoubted right to lay what sentiments he pleases before the public; to forbid this, is to destroy the freedom of the press; but if he publishes what is improper, mischievous or illegal, he must take the consequence of his own temerity." [The] criticism upon Blackstone's statement has not been because immunity from previous restraint upon publication has not been regarded as deserving of special emphasis, but chiefly because that immunity cannot be deemed to exhaust the conception of the liberty guaranteed by State and Federal Constitutions.

[T]he protection even as to previous restraint is not absolutely unlimited. But the limitation has been recognized only in exceptional cases. [N]o one would question but that a government might prevent actual obstruction to its recruiting service or the publication of the sailing dates of transports or the number and location of troops. On similar grounds, the primary requirements of decency may be enforced against obscene publications. The security of the community life may be protected against incitements to acts of violence and the overthrow by force of orderly [government].[a]

The exceptional nature of its limitations places in a strong light the general conception that liberty of the press, historically considered and taken up by the Federal Constitution, has meant, principally although not exclusively, immunity from previous restraints or censorship. The conception of liberty of the press in this country had broadened with the exigencies of the colonial period and with the efforts to secure freedom from oppressive administration. That liberty was especially cherished for the immunity it afforded from previous restraint of the publication of censure of public officers and charges of official [misconduct].

The fact that for approximately one hundred and fifty years there has been almost an entire absence of attempts to impose previous restraints upon publications relating to the malfeasance of public officers is significant of the deep-seated conviction that such restraints would violate constitutional right. Public officers, whose character and conduct remain open to debate and free discussion in the press, find their remedies for false accusations in actions under libel laws providing for redress and punishment, and not in proceedings to restrain the publication of newspapers and periodicals. [The] fact that the liberty of the press may be abused by miscreant purveyors of scandal does not make any the less necessary the immunity of the press from previous restraint in dealing with official misconduct. Subsequent punishment for such abuses as may exist is the appropriate remedy, consistent with constitutional [privilege].

The statute in question cannot be justified by reason of the fact that the publisher is permitted to show, before injunction issues, that the matter published is true and is published with good motives and for justifiable ends. If such a statute, authorizing suppression and injunction on such a basis, is constitutionally valid, it would be equally permissible for the Legislature to provide that at any time the publisher of any newspaper could be brought before a court, or

---

a. For critical commentary on the concessions in *Near*, see Linde, *Courts and Censorship*, 66 Minn.L.Rev. 171 (1981).

even an administrative officer (as the constitutional protection may not be regarded as resting on mere procedural details), and required to produce proof of the truth of his publication, or of what he intended to publish and of his motives, or stand enjoined. If this can be done, the Legislature may provide machinery for determining in the complete exercise of its discretion what are justifiable ends and restrain publication accordingly. And it would be but a step to a complete system of censorship.

[For] these reasons we hold the statute, so far as it authorized the proceedings in this action, [to] be an infringement of the liberty of the press guaranteed by the Fourteenth Amendment. * * *

MR. JUSTICE BUTLER (dissenting).

[T]he *previous restraints* referred to by [Blackstone] subjected the press to the arbitrary will of an administrative officer. [The] Minnesota statute does not operate as a *previous* restraint on publication within the proper meaning of that phrase. It does not authorize administrative control in advance such as was formerly exercised by the licensers and censors, but prescribes a remedy to be enforced by a suit in equity. In this case [t]he business and publications unquestionably constitute an abuse of the right of free press. [A]s stated by the state Supreme Court [they] threaten morals, peace, and good order. [The] restraint authorized is only in respect of continuing to do what has been duly adjudged to constitute a nuisance. [It] is fanciful to suggest similarity between the granting or enforcement of the decree authorized by this statute to prevent *further* publication of malicious, scandalous, and defamatory articles and the *previous restraint* upon the press by licensers as referred to by Blackstone and described in the history of the times to which he alludes. * * *

It is well known, as found by the state supreme court, that existing libel laws are inadequate effectively to suppress evils resulting from the kind of business and publications that are shown in this case. The doctrine [of this decision] exposes the peace and good order of every community and the business and private affairs of every individual to the constant and protracted false and malicious assaults of any insolvent publisher who may have purpose and sufficient capacity to contrive and put into effect a scheme or program for oppression, blackmail or extortion. * * *

MR. JUSTICE VAN DEVANTER, MR. JUSTICE MCREYNOLDS, and MR. JUSTICE SUTHERLAND concur in this opinion.[b]

Notes and Questions

1. *Near and seditious libel: a misuse of prior restraint?* *Near* was decided three decades before *New York Times v. Sullivan,* p. 464 supra. Should the Court have looked to the substance of the regulation rather than its form? Consider Jeffries, *Rethinking Prior Restraint,* 92 Yale L.J. 409, 416–17 (1983): "In truth, *Near* involved nothing more or less than a repackaged version of the law of seditious libel, and this the majority rightly refused to countenance. Hence, there was pressure, so typical of this doctrine, to cram the law into the disfavored category of prior restraint, even though it in fact functioned very differently from a scheme of official licensing. Here there was no license and no censor, no ex parte determination of what was prohibited, and no suppression of publication based on speculation about what somebody might say. Here the

b. For background on the *Near* case, see Friendly, *Minnesota Rag* (1981); Murphy, *Near v. Minnesota in the Context of Historical*   *Developments,* 66 Minn.L.Rev. 95, 133–60 (1981).

decision to suppress was made by a judge (not a bureaucrat), after adversarial (not ex parte) proceedings, to determine the legal character of what had been (and not what might be) published. The only aspect of prior restraint was the incidental fact that the defendants were commanded not to repeat that which they were proved to have done.

"[I]f *Near* reached the right result, does it really matter that it gave the wrong reason? The answer, I think, is that it does matter, at least that it has come to matter as *Near* has become a prominent feature of the First Amendment landscape—a landmark, as the case is so often called, from which we chart our course to future decisions. [T]he Court has yet to explain (at least in terms that I understand) what it is about an injunction that justifies this independent rule of constitutional disfavor."

Should a court be able to enjoin the continued distribution of material it has finally adjudicated to be unprotected defamation under existing law? Suppose it enjoins the publication of any material that does not comply with the mandates of *New York Times* and *Gertz*?

2. *The collateral bar rule.* Does the collateral bar rule shed light on the relationship between prior restraints and injunctions? That rule insists "that a court order must be obeyed until it is set aside, and that persons subject to the order who disobey it may not defend against the ensuing charge of criminal contempt on the ground that the order was erroneous or even unconstitutional." Barnett, *The Puzzle of Prior Restraint*, 29 Stan.L.Rev. 539, 552 (1977). WALKER v. BIRMINGHAM, 388 U.S. 307, 87 S.Ct. 1824, 18 L.Ed.2d 1210 (1967) upheld the rule against a first amendment challenge in affirming the contempt conviction of defendants for violating an ex parte injunction issued by an Alabama court enjoining them from engaging in street parades without a municipal permit issued pursuant to the city's parade ordinance. The Court, per STEWART, J., (Warren, C.J., Brennan, Douglas, and Fortas, JJ., dissenting) held that because the petitioners neither moved to dissolve the injunction nor sought to comply with the city's parade ordinance, their claim that the injunction and ordinance were unconstitutional[c] did not need to be considered: "This Court cannot hold that the petitioners were constitutionally free to ignore all the procedures of the law and carry their battle to the streets. [R]espect for judicial process is a small price to pay for the civilizing hand of law, which alone can give abiding meaning to constitutional freedom." Although *Walker* suggested that its holding might be different if the court issuing the injunction lacked jurisdiction or if the injunction were "transparently invalid or had only a frivolous pretense to validity," it held that Alabama's invocation of the collateral bar rule was not itself unconstitutional.

Cf. *Poulos v. New Hampshire*, 345 U.S. 395, 73 S.Ct. 760, 97 L.Ed. 1105 (1953) (claim of arbitrary refusal to issue license for open air meeting need not be entertained when a licensing statute is considered to be valid on its face in circumstance where speaker fails to seek direct judicial relief and proceeds without a license).[d] Does *Poulos* pose considerable danger to first amendment interests because the low visibility of the administrative decision permits easy abridgement of free expression? See Monaghan, *First Amendment "Due Process,"* 83 Harv.L.Rev. 518, 543 (1970). Do *Lovell, Walker,* and *Poulos* fit easily

c. Indeed, the ordinance in question was declared unconstitutional two years later. *Shuttlesworth v. Birmingham*, 394 U.S. 147, 89 S.Ct. 935, 22 L.Ed.2d 162 (1969) (ordinance conferring unbridled discretion to prohibit any parade or demonstration is unconstitutional prior restraint).

d. For consideration of when licensing statutes for assemblies are valid, see *Cox v. New Hampshire*, p. 642 infra.

together? Consider Blasi, *Prior Restraints on Demonstrations,* 68 Mich.L.Rev. 1482, 1555 (1970): "A refuses to apply for a permit; he undertakes a march that could have been prohibited in the first place; he is prosecuted for parading without a permit under a statute that is defective for overbreadth. B applies for a permit; he is rudely rebuffed by a city official in clear violation of the state permit statute (which is not invalid on its face); he marches anyway in a manner that would be protected by the first amendment, he is prosecuted for parading without a permit. C applies for a permit; he is rudely rebuffed; he notifies city officials that he will march anyway; the officials obtain an injunction against the march; the injunction is overbroad and is also based on a state statute that is overbroad; C marches in a manner ordinarily within his constitutional rights; he is prosecuted for contempt. Under the law as it now stands, A wins, but B and C lose!"

3. *The commentators, injunctions, and prior restraint.* Should the link between prior restraint doctrine and injunctions depend upon the collateral bar rule? Does the analogy between licensing systems and injunctions hold only in that event? See Fiss, *The Civil Rights Injunction* 30, 69–74 (1978); Barnett, note 2 supra, at 553–54. Should the prior restraint doctrine be wholly inapplicable to injunctions so long as "expedited appellate review allows an immediate opportunity to test the validity of an injunction against speech and only so long as that opportunity is genuinely effective to allow timely publication should the injunction ultimately be adjudged invalid"? Jeffries, note 1 supra, at 433.[e] Indeed should the whole concept of prior restraint be abandoned? Consider id. at 433–34: "In the context of administrative preclearance, talking of prior restraint is unhelpful, though not inapt. A more informative frame of reference would be overbreadth, the doctrine that explicitly identifies why preclearance is specially objectionable. In the context of injunctions, however, the traditional doctrine of prior restraint is not merely unhelpful, but positively misleading. It focuses on a constitutionally inconsequential consideration of form and diverts attention away from the critical substantive issues of First Amendment coverage. The result is a two-pronged danger. On the one hand, vindication of First Amendment freedoms in the name of prior restraint may exaggerate the legitimate reach of official competence to suppress by subsequent punishment. On the other hand, insistence on special disfavor for prior restraints outside the realm of substantive protection under the First Amendment may deny to the government an appropriate choice of means to vindicate legitimate interests. In my view, neither risk is justified by any compelling reason to continue prior restraint as a doctrinally independent category of contemporary First Amendment analysis."

For a nuanced argument that the prior restraint doctrine should apply to injunctions even in those jurisdictions that reject the applicability of the collateral bar rule to first amendment arguments, see Blasi, *Toward a Theory of Prior Restraint: The Central Linkage,* 66 Minn.L.Rev. 11 (1981). Except in particular contexts, Professor Blasi does not claim that the chilling effect of injunctions on speech is more severe than those associated with criminal laws and civil liability rules. He does argue that unlike criminal laws and civil liability rules, regula-

e. For the argument that regulation by injunction is generally more speech protective than regulation via subsequent punishment, see Mayton, *Toward A Theory of First Amendment Process: Injunctions of Speech, Subsequent Punishment, and the Costs of the Prior Restraint Doctrine,* 67 Corn.L.Rev. 245 (1982). For the contention that this should count in favor of subsequent punishment in many contexts, see Redish, *The Proper Role of the Prior Restraint Doctrine in First Amendment Theory,* 70 Va.L.Rev. 53, 92–93 (1984).

tion of speech by licensing and injunctions requires abstract and unduly speculative adjudication, stimulates overuse by regulatory agents, can to some extent distort the way in which audiences perceive the message at issue, and unreasonably implies that the activity of disseminating controversial communications is "a threat to, rather than an integral feature of, the social order." Id. at 85. He argues that many of these factors are aggravated if the collateral bar rule applies and that other undesirable features are added. For example, speakers are forced to reveal planned details about their communication. He concludes that the "concept of prior restraint is coherent at the core." Id. at 93.[f]

II. PRIOR RESTRAINTS, OBSCENITY, AND COMMERCIAL SPEECH

KINGSLEY BOOKS, INC. v. BROWN, 354 U.S. 436, 77 S.Ct. 1325, 1 L.Ed.2d 1469 (1957), per FRANKFURTER, J., upheld a state court decree, issued pursuant to a New York statute, enjoining the publisher from further distribution of 14 booklets the state court found obscene. On appeal to the Supreme Court the publisher challenged only the prior restraint, not the obscenity finding:

"The phrase 'prior restraint' is not a self-wielding sword. Nor can it serve as a talismatic test. The duty of closer analysis and critical judgment in applying the thought behind the phrase has thus been authoritatively put by one who brings weighty learning to his support of constitutionally protected liberties: 'What is needed,' writes Professor Paul A. Freund, 'is a pragmatic assessment of its operation in the particular circumstances. The generalization that prior restraint is particularly obnoxious in civil liberties cases must yield to more particularistic analysis.' The Supreme Court and Civil Liberties, 4 Vand.L.Rev. 533, 539.

"Wherein does § 22–a differ in its effective operation from the type of statute upheld in Alberts, [p. 488 supra]. One would be bold to assert that the in terrorem effect of [criminal] statutes less restrains booksellers in the period before the law strikes than does § 22–a. Instead of requiring the bookseller to dread that the offer for sale of a book may, without prior warning, subject him to a criminal prosecution with the hazard of imprisonment, the civil procedure assures him that such consequences cannot follow unless he ignores a court order specifically directed to him for a prompt and carefully circumscribed determination of the issue of obscenity. Until then, he may keep the book for sale and sell it on his own judgment rather than steer 'nervously among the treacherous shoals.'[a]

"Criminal enforcement and the proceeding under § 22–a interfere with a book's solicitation of the public precisely at the same stage. In each situation the law moves after publication; the book need not in either case have yet passed into the hands of the public. [H]ere as a matter of fact copies of the booklets whose distribution was enjoined had been on sale for several weeks when process was served. In each case the bookseller is put on notice by the complaint that sale of the publication charged with obscenity in the period before trial may subject him to penal consequences. In the one case he may suffer fine and imprisonment for violation of the criminal statute, in the other,

---

f. For detailed criticism of Blasi's position, all in defense of a different core, see Redish, fn. e, at 59–75.

a. In fact, § 22–a did not require a civil adjudication before criminal prosecution, as intimated by the opinion. The feasibility of such a requirement is considered in Lockhart, *Escape from the Chill of Uncertainty*, 9 Ga.L. Rev. 533, 569–86 (1975).

for disobedience of the temporary injunction. The bookseller may of course stand his ground and confidently believe that in any judicial proceeding the book could not be condemned as obscene, but both modes of procedure provide an effective deterrent against distribution prior to adjudication of the book's content—the threat of subsequent penalization.[2]"

The Court pointed out that in both criminal misdemeanor prosecutions and injunction proceedings a jury could be called as a matter of discretion, but that defendant did not request a jury trial and did not attack the statute for its failure to require a jury.

"Nor are the consequences of a judicial condemnation for obscenity under § 22–a more restrictive of freedom of expression than the result of conviction for a misdemeanor. In *Alberts,* the defendant was fined $500, sentenced to sixty days in prison, and put on probation for two years on condition that he not violate the obscenity statute. Not only was he completely separated from society for two months but he was also seriously restrained from trafficking in all obscene publications for a considerable time. Appellants, on the other hand, were enjoined from displaying for sale or distributing only the particular booklets theretofore published and adjudged to be obscene. Thus, the restraint upon appellants as merchants in obscenity was narrower than that imposed on *Alberts.*

"Section 22–a's provision for the seizure and destruction of the instruments of ascertained wrongdoing expresses resort to a legal remedy sanctioned by the long history of Anglo-American law. See Holmes, *The Common Law,* 24–26.

"[It] only remains to say that the difference between *Near* and this case is glaring in fact. The two cases are no less glaringly different when judged by the appropriate criteria of constitutional law. Minnesota empowered its courts to enjoin the dissemination of future issues of a publication because its past issues had been found offensive. In the language of Mr. Chief Justice Hughes, 'This is of the essence of censorship.' As such, it was enough to condemn the statute wholly apart from the fact that the proceeding in *Near* involved not obscenity but matters deemed to be derogatory to a public officer. Unlike *Near,* § 22–a is concerned solely with obscenity and, as authoritatively construed, it studiously withholds restraint upon matters not already published and not yet found to be offensive."[b]

TIMES FILM CORP. v. CHICAGO

365 U.S. 43, 81 S.Ct. 391, 5 L.Ed.2d 403 (1961).

MR. JUSTICE CLARK delivered the opinion of the Court.

Petitioner challenges on constitutional grounds the validity on its face of that portion of § 155–4 [1] of the Municipal Code of the City of Chicago which

2. This comparison of remedies takes note of the fact that we do not have before us a case where, although the issue of obscenity is ultimately decided in favor of the bookseller, the State nevertheless attempts to punish him for disobedience of the interim injunction. For all we know, New York may impliedly condition the temporary injunction so as not to subject the bookseller to a charge of contempt if he prevails on the issue of obscenity.

b. Warren, C.J., dissented, objecting that the New York law "places the book on trial" without any consideration of its "manner of use." Black and Douglas, JJ., dissented, objecting to a state-wide decree depriving the publisher of separate trials in different communities, and to substituting "punishment by contempt for punishment by jury trial." Brennan, J., dissenting, contended that a jury trial is required to apply properly the *Roth* standard for obscenity.

1. The portion of the section here under attack is as follows: "Such permit shall be granted only after the motion picture film for which said permit is requested has been produced at the office of the commissioner of

requires submission of all motion pictures for examination prior to their public exhibition. Petitioner is a New York corporation owning the exclusive right to publicly exhibit in Chicago the film known as "Don Juan." It applied for a permit, as Chicago's ordinance required, and tendered the license fee but refused to submit the film for examination. The appropriate city official refused to issue the permit and his order was made final on appeal to the Mayor. The sole ground for denial was petitioner's refusal to submit the film for examination as required. Petitioner then brought this suit seeking injunctive relief ordering the issuance of the permit without submission of the [film] * * *. Its sole ground is that the provision of the ordinance requiring submission of the film constitutes, on its face, a prior restraint [2] * * * [Admittedly,] the challenged section of the ordinance imposes a previous restraint, and the broad justiciable issue is therefore present as to whether the ambit of constitutional protection includes complete and absolute freedom to exhibit, at least once, any and every kind of motion picture. It is that question alone which we decide.

[T]here is not a word in the record as to the nature and content of "Don Juan." We are left entirely in the dark in this regard, as were the city officials and the other reviewing courts. Petitioner claims that the nature of the film is irrelevant, and that even if this film contains the basest type of pornography, or incitement to riot, or forceful overthrow of orderly government, it may nonetheless be shown without prior submission for examination. The challenge here is to the censor's basic authority; it does not go to any statutory standards employed by the censor or procedural requirements as to the submission of the film. * * *

Petitioner would have us hold that the public exhibition of motion pictures must be allowed under any circumstances. The State's sole remedy, it says, is the invocation of criminal process under the Illinois pornography statute and then only after a transgression. But this position [is] founded upon the claim of absolute privilege against prior restraint under the First Amendment—a claim without sanction in our cases. To illustrate its fallacy, we need only point to one of the "exceptional cases" which Chief Justice Hughes enumerated in *Near*, namely, "the primary requirements of decency [that] may be enforced against obscene publications." Moreover, we later held specifically "that obscenity is not within the area of constitutionally protected speech or press." *Roth*. Chicago emphasizes here its duty to protect its people against the dangers of obscenity in the public exhibition of motion pictures. To this argument petitioner's only answer is that regardless of the capacity for, or extent of, such an evil, previous restraint cannot be justified. With this we cannot agree. We recognized in [*Joseph Burstyn, Inc. v. Wilson*, 343 U.S. 495, 72 S.Ct. 777, 96 L.Ed. 1098 (1952)] that "capacity for evil [may] be relevant in determining the permissible scope of community control," and that motion pictures were not "necessarily subject to the precise rules governing any other particular method of expression.

police for examination or censorship. * * *"

2. That portion of § 155–4 of the Code providing standards is as follows: "If a picture or series of pictures, for the showing or exhibition of which an application for a permit is made, is immoral or obscene, or portrays, depravity, criminality, or lack of virtue of a class of citizens of any race, color, creed, or religion and exposes them to contempt, derision, or obloquy, or tends to produce a breach of the peace or riots, or purports to represent any hanging, lynching, or burning of a human being, it shall be the duty of the commissioner of police to refuse such permit; otherwise it shall be his duty to grant such permit.

"In case the commissioner of police shall refuse to grant a permit as hereinbefore provided, the applicant for the same may appeal to the mayor. Such appeal shall be presented in the same manner as the original application to the commissioner of police. The action of the mayor on any application for a permit shall be final." * * *

Each method," we said, "tends to present its own peculiar problems." [It] is not for this Court to limit the State in its selection of the remedy it deems most effective to cope with such a problem, absent, of course, a showing of unreasonable strictures on individual liberty resulting from its application in particular circumstances. * * *

As to what may be decided when a concrete case involving a specific standard provided by this ordinance is presented, we intimate no opinion. [At] this time we say no more than this—that we are dealing only with motion pictures and, even as to them, only in the context of the broadside attack presented on this record.

Affirmed.

MR. CHIEF JUSTICE WARREN, with whom MR. JUSTICE BLACK, MR. JUSTICE DOUGLAS and MR. JUSTICE BRENNAN join, dissenting.

I cannot agree either with the conclusion reached by the Court or with the reasons advanced for its support. To me, this case clearly presents the question of our approval of unlimited censorship of motion pictures before exhibition through a system of administrative licensing. Moreover, the decision presents a real danger of eventual censorship for every form of communication, be it newspapers, journals, books, magazines, television, radio or public speeches. The Court purports to leave these questions for another day, but I am aware of no constitutional principle which permits us to hold that the communication of ideas through one medium may be censored while other media are immune. Of course each medium presents its own peculiar problems, but they are not of the kind which would authorize the censorship of one form of communication and not others. * * *

I hesitate to disagree with the Court's formulation of the issue before us, but, with all deference, I must insist that the question presented in this case is *not* whether a motion picture exhibitor has a constitutionally protected, "complete and absolute freedom to exhibit, at least once, any and every kind of motion picture." [The] question here presented is whether the City of Chicago—or, for that matter, any city, any State or the Federal Government—may require all motion picture exhibitors to submit all films to a police chief, mayor or other administrative official, for licensing and censorship prior to public exhibition within the jurisdiction.

[In *Near*,] the Court recognized that the First Amendment's rejection of prior censorship through licensing and previous restraint is an inherent and basic principle of freedom of speech and press. Now, the Court strays from that principle; it strikes down that tenet without requiring any demonstration that this is an "exceptional case," whatever that might be, and without any indication that Chicago has sustained the "heavy burden" which was supposed to have been placed upon it. Clearly, this is neither an exceptional case nor has Chicago sustained *any* burden. * * *

The booklets enjoined from distribution in *Kingsley* were concededly obscene. There is no indication that this is true of the moving picture here. This was treated as a particularly crucial distinction. Thus, the Court has suggested that, in times of national emergency, the Government might impose a prior restraint upon "the publication of the sailing dates of transports or the number and location of troops." *Near.* But, surely this is not to suggest that the Government might require that all newspapers be submitted to a censor in order to assist it in preventing such information from reaching print. Yet in this case the Court gives its blessing to the censorship of all motion pictures in order to prevent the exhibition of those it feels to be constitutionally unprotected.

[E]ven if the impact of the motion picture is greater than that of some other media, that fact constitutes no basis for the argument that motion pictures should be subject to greater suppression. This is the traditional argument made in the censor's behalf; this is the argument advanced against newspapers at the time of the invention of the printing press. The argument was ultimately rejected in England, and has consistently been held to be contrary to our Constitution.[a] No compelling reason has been predicated for accepting the contention now. * * *[b]

Notes and Questions

1. Should the producers of *Bambi* be forced to submit their film to show it in a particular city? Should they be forced to pay a license fee? Suppose hundreds of cities adopted the Chicago system? If films must be submitted before exhibition, can a city constitutionally require that books be submitted before distribution? What are the "peculiar problems" associated with films?

2. *Procedural safeguards.* FREEDMAN v. MARYLAND, 380 U.S. 51, 85 S.Ct. 734, 13 L.Ed.2d 649 (1965), per BRENNAN, J., set out procedural safeguards designed to reduce the dangers associated with prior restraints of films. It required that the procedure must "assure a prompt final judicial decision, to minimize the deterrent effect of an interim and possibly erroneous denial of a license," that the censor must promptly institute the proceedings, that the burden of proof to show that the speech in question is unprotected must rest on the censor, and that the proceedings be adversarial. The *Freedman* standards have been applied in other contexts. *Blount v. Rizzi,* 400 U.S. 410, 91 S.Ct. 423, 27 L.Ed.2d 498 (1971) (postal stop orders of obscene materials); *United States v. Thirty-Seven Photographs,* 402 U.S. 363, 91 S.Ct. 1400, 28 L.Ed.2d 822 (1971) (customs seizure of obscene materials); *Southeastern Promotions Ltd. v. Conrad,* 420 U.S. 546, 95 S.Ct. 1239, 43 L.Ed.2d 448 (1975) (denial of permit to use municipal theater for the musical, Hair); *Carroll v. President and Commissioners,* 393 U.S. 175, 89 S.Ct. 347, 21 L.Ed.2d 325 (1968) (10 day restraining order against particular rallies or meetings invalid because *ex parte*). Should the collateral bar rule apply to *Carroll* ? Do the *Freedman* standards make the *Times Film* decision palatable?[c] For thorough discussion of the procedural issues, see Monaghan, *First Amendment "Due Process,"* 83 Harv.L.Rev. 518 (1970).

3. *Enjoining habitual use of premises to exhibit obscene films.* Could a state authorize state courts to "abate" the "nuisance" of "habitual use [of premises for] commercial exhibition of obscene" films by enjoining future exhibition of any obscene films at the theater, once a finding of such habitual use is made, based on two or more convictions under the obscenity laws? Cf. *Vance v. Universal Amusement Co.,* 445 U.S. 308, 100 S.Ct. 1156, 63 L.Ed.2d 413 (1980). Would this be consistent with *Freedman?* If such an injunction incorporated the

---

a. For the contention that the argument has in fact received a warm reception in the twentieth century, see Lively, *Fear and the Media: A First Amendment Horror Show,* 69 Minn.L.Rev. 1071 (1985).

b. Douglas, J., joined by Warren, C.J., and Black, J., dissenting, elaborated on the evils connected with systems of censorship.

c. For the contention that *Freedman* procedures fail to address the main concern of the prior restraint doctrine, see Redish, *The Proper Role of the Prior Restraint Doctrine in First Amendment Theory,* 70 Va.L.Rev. 53, 75–89 (1984).

Miller obscenity standard, would it intrude on first amendment values any more than a criminal statute forbidding exhibition of obscenity? Cf. *Vance*, White, J., dissenting.

4. *Comparing obscenity and commercial speech.* To combat deception, could commercial advertising be constitutionally subjected to a *Times Film* regime? Would such a scheme be permissible for advertising via some media, but not others? Reconsider fn. 24 in *Virginia Pharmacy*, p. 558 supra. Should the prohibition on prior restraints be inapplicable to injunctions against commercial advertising? Should *Freedman* standards be required? Should injunctions be permitted against a newspaper that carries unprotected advertising in addition to the advertiser? PITTSBURGH PRESS CO. v. HUMAN RELATIONS COMM'N, 413 U.S. 376, 93 S.Ct. 2553, 37 L.Ed.2d 669 (1973), per POWELL, J., upheld an order forbidding Pittsburgh Press to carry sex-designated "help wanted" ads, except for exempt jobs: "As described by Blackstone, the protection against prior restraint at common law barred only a system of administrative censorship. [While] the Court boldly stepped beyond this narrow doctrine in *Near* [it] has never held that all injunctions are impermissible. See *Lorain Journal Co. v. United States*, 342 U.S. 143, 72 S.Ct. 181, 96 L.Ed. 162 (1951).[d] The special vice of a prior restraint is that communication will be suppressed, either directly or by inducing excessive caution in the speaker, before an adequate determination that it is unprotected by the First Amendment.

"The present order does not endanger arguably protected speech. Because the order is based on a continuing course of repetitive conduct, this is not a case in which the Court is asked to speculate as to the effect of publication. Moreover, the order is clear and sweeps no more broadly than necessary. And because no interim relief was granted, the order will not have gone into effect until it was finally determined that the actions of Pittsburgh Press were unprotected."

STEWART, J., joined by Douglas, J., dissented: Putting to one side "the question of governmental power to prevent publication of information that would clearly imperil the military defense of our Nation," "no government agency can tell a newspaper in advance what it can print and what it cannot."[e]

Does *Pittsburgh Press* indicate the Court will not limit permissible prior restraints to the *Near* "exceptional" areas? Does it mean that when a "continuing course of repetitive conduct" enables a court to make an "adequate determination that [a publication] is unprotected by the First Amendment" the policy against prior restraints does not apply when the restraint will not go "into effect until it [is] finally determined [judicially] that the actions [were] unprotected"? If so, what are the implications for the future of the prior restraint doctrine? Or can *Pittsburgh Press* be narrowly limited as applicable only to repetitive conduct in commercial advertising?

5. *Informal prior restraints.* BANTAM BOOKS, INC. v. SULLIVAN, 372 U.S. 58, 83 S.Ct. 631, 9 L.Ed.2d 584 (1963), per BRENNAN, J., (Harlan, J. dissenting) held unconstitutional the activities of a government commission that would identify "objectionable" books (some admittedly not obscene), notify the distributor in writing, inform the distributor of the Commission's duty to recommend obscenity prosecutions to the Attorney General and that the Com-

---

d. *Lorain* upheld a Sherman Act injunction restraining a newspaper from seeking to monopolize commerce by refusing to carry advertising from merchants who advertised through a competing radio station.

e. Blackmun, J., dissented "for substantially the reasons stated by" Stewart, J. Burger, C.J., dissenting, argued that the majority had mischaracterized the character and interim effect of the Commission's order.

mission's list of objectionable books was distributed to local police departments. The Commission thanked distributors in advance for their "cooperation," and a police officer usually visited the distributor to learn what action had been taken. In characterizing these practices as a system of prior administrative restraints, rather than mere legal advice, the Court observed that it did not mean to foreclose private consultation between law enforcement officers and distributors so long as such consultations were "genuinely undertaken with the purpose of aiding the distributor to comply" with the laws and avoid prosecution. What if the Commission circulated its list to distributors, police and prosecutors without mentioning prosecution? What if the prosecutor circulates a list of sixty books he or she regards as obscene and subject to prosecution?

III. PRIOR RESTRAINTS AND NATIONAL SECURITY

NEW YORK TIMES CO. v. UNITED STATES [THE PENTAGON PAPERS CASE]

403 U.S. 713, 91 S.Ct. 2140, 29 L.Ed.2d 822 (1971).

PER CURIAM.

We granted certiorari in these cases in which the United States seeks to enjoin the *New York Times* and the *Washington Post* from publishing the contents of a classified study entitled "History of U.S. Decision-Making Process on Viet Nam Policy." [a]

"Any system of prior restraints of expression comes to this Court bearing a heavy presumption against its constitutional validity." *Bantam Books;* see also *Near.* The Government "thus carries a heavy burden of showing justification for the enforcement of such a restraint." [The district court in the *Times* case and both lower federal courts] in the *Post* case held that the Government had not met that burden. We agree. [T]he stays entered [by this Court five days previously] are vacated. * * *

MR. JUSTICE BLACK, with whom MR. JUSTICE DOUGLAS joins, concurring.

I adhere to the view that the Government's case against the *Post* should have been dismissed and that the injunction against the *Times* should have been vacated without oral argument when the cases were first presented to this Court. I believe that every moment's continuance of the injunctions against these newspapers amounts to a flagrant, indefensible, and continuing violation of the First Amendment. Furthermore, after oral arguments, I agree [with] the reasons stated by my Brothers Douglas and Brennan. In my view it is unfortunate that some of my Brethren are apparently willing to hold that the publication of news may sometimes be enjoined. Such a holding would make a shambles of the First Amendment.

[F]or the first time in the 182 years since the founding of the Republic, the federal courts are asked to hold that the First Amendment does not mean what it says, but rather means that the Government can halt the publication of current news of vital importance to the people of this country.

a. On June 12–14, 1971 the *New York Times* and on June 18 the *Washington Post* published portions of this "top secret" Pentagon study. Government actions seeking temporary restraining orders and injunctions progressed through two district courts and two courts of appeals between June 15–23. After a June 26 argument, ten Supreme Court opinions were issued on June 30, 1971.

[Both] the history and language of the First Amendment support the view that the press must be left free to publish news, whatever the source, without censorship, injunctions, or prior restraints.

In the First Amendment the Founding Fathers gave the free press the protection it must have to fulfill its essential role in our democracy. The press was to serve the governed, not the governors. The Government's power to censor the press was abolished so that the press would remain forever free to censure the Government. The press was protected so that it could bare the secrets of government and inform the people. Only a free and unrestrained press can effectively expose deception in government. * * *

The Government does not even attempt to rely on any act of Congress. Instead it makes the bold and dangerously far-reaching contention that the courts should take it upon themselves to "make" a law abridging freedom of the press in the name of equity, presidential power and national security, even when the representatives of the people in Congress have adhered to the command of the First Amendment and refused to make such a law. To find that the President has "inherent power" to halt the publication of news by resort to the courts would wipe out the First Amendment and destroy the fundamental liberty and security of the very people the Government hopes to make "secure." [The] word "security" is a broad, vague generality whose contours should not be invoked to abrogate the fundamental law embodied in the First Amendment. * * *

MR. JUSTICE DOUGLAS, with whom MR. JUSTICE BLACK joins, concurring.

While I join the opinion of the Court I believe it necessary to express my views more fully.

[The First Amendment leaves] no room for governmental restraint on the press.

There is, moreover, no statute barring the publication by the press of the material which the *Times* and *Post* seek to use. * * *

These disclosures may have a serious impact. But that is no basis for sanctioning a previous restraint on the press * * *.

The dominant purpose of the First Amendment was to prohibit the widespread practice of governmental suppression of embarrassing information. [A] debate of large proportions goes on in the Nation over our posture in Vietnam. That debate antedated the disclosure of the contents of the present documents. The latter are highly relevant to the debate in progress.

Secrecy in government is fundamentally anti-democratic, perpetuating bureaucratic errors. Open debate and discussion of public issues are vital to our national health. * * *

The stays in these cases that have been in effect for more than a week constitute a flouting of the principles of the First Amendment as interpreted in *Near*.

MR. JUSTICE BRENNAN, concurring.

I write separately [to] emphasize what should be apparent: that our judgment in the present cases may not be taken to indicate the propriety, in the future, of issuing temporary stays and restraining orders to block the publication of material sought to be suppressed by the Government. So far as I can determine, never before has the United States sought to enjoin a newspaper from publishing information in its possession. * * *

The entire thrust of the Government's claim throughout these cases has been that publication of the material sought to be enjoined "could," or "might," or "may" prejudice the national interest in various ways. But the First Amendment tolerates absolutely no prior judicial restraints of the press predicated upon surmise or conjecture that untoward consequences may result.* Our cases, it is true, have indicated that there is a single, extremely narrow class of cases in which the First Amendment's ban on prior judicial restraint may be overriden. Our cases have thus far indicated that such cases may arise only when the Nation "is at war," [*Schenck*]. Even if the present world situation were assumed to be tantamount to a time of war, or if the power of presently available armaments would justify even in peacetime the suppression of information that would set in motion a nuclear holocaust, in neither of these actions has the Government presented or even alleged that publication of items from or based upon the material at issue would cause the happening of an event of that nature. [Thus,] only governmental allegation and proof that publication must inevitably, directly and immediately cause the occurrence of an event kindred to imperiling the safety of a transport already at sea can support even the issuance of an interim restraining order. In no event may mere conclusions be sufficient: for if the Executive Branch seeks judicial aid in preventing publication, it must inevitably submit the basis upon which that aid is sought to scrutiny by the judiciary. And therefore, every restraint issued in this case, whatever its form, has violated the First Amendment—and not less so because that restraint was justified as necessary to afford the courts an opportunity to examine the claim more thoroughly. Unless and until the Government has clearly made out its case, the First Amendment commands that no injunction may issue.

MR. JUSTICE STEWART, with whom MR. JUSTICE WHITE joins, concurring.

[I]n the cases before us we are asked neither to construe specific regulations nor to apply specific laws. We are asked, instead, to perform a function that the Constitution gave to the Executive, not the Judiciary. We are asked, quite simply, to prevent the publication by two newspapers of material that the Executive Branch insists should not, in the national interest, be published. I am convinced that the Executive is correct with respect to some of the documents involved. But I cannot say that disclosure of any of them will surely result in direct, immediate, and irreparable damage to our Nation or its people. That being so, there can under the First Amendment be but one judicial resolution of the issues before us. I join the judgments of the Court.

MR. JUSTICE WHITE, with whom MR. JUSTICE STEWART joins, concurring.

I concur in today's judgments, but only because of the concededly extraordinary protection against prior restraints enjoyed by the press under our constitutional system. I do not say that in no circumstances would the First Amendment permit an injunction against publishing information about government plans or operations. Nor, after examining the materials the Government characterizes as the most sensitive and destructive, can I deny that revelation of these documents will do substantial damage to public interests. Indeed, I am confident that their disclosure will have that result. But I nevertheless agree that the United States has not satisfied the very heavy burden which it must

---

* *Freedman* and similar cases regarding temporary restraints of allegedly obscene materials are not in point. For those cases rest upon the proposition that "obscenity is not protected by the freedoms of speech and press." *Roth*. Here there is no question but that the material sought to be suppressed is within the protection of the First Amendment; the only question is whether, notwithstanding that fact, its publication may be enjoined for a time because of the presence of an overwhelming national interest. * * *

meet to warrant an injunction against publication in these cases, at least in the absence of express and appropriately limited congressional authorization for prior restraints in circumstances such as these.

The Government's position is simply stated: The responsibility of the Executive for the conduct of the foreign affairs and for the security of the Nation is so basic that the President is entitled to an injunction against publication of a newspaper story whenever he can convince a court that the information to be revealed threatens "grave and irreparable" injury to the public interest; and the injunction should issue whether or not the material to be published is classified, whether or not publication would be lawful under relevant criminal statutes enacted by Congress and regardless of the circumstances by which the newspaper came into possession of the information.

At least in the absence of legislation by Congress, based on its own investigations and findings, I am quite unable to agree that the inherent powers of the Executive and the courts reach so far as to authorize remedies having such sweeping potential for inhibiting publications by the press. [To] sustain the Government in these cases would start the courts down a long and hazardous road that I am not willing to travel at least without congressional guidance and direction.

* * * Prior restraints require an unusually heavy justification under the First Amendment; but failure by the Government to justify prior restraints does not measure its constitutional entitlement to a conviction for criminal publication. That the Government mistakenly chose to proceed by injunction does not mean that it could not successfully proceed in another way.

* * * Congress has addressed itself to the problems of protecting the security of the country and the national defense from unauthorized disclosure of potentially damaging information. Cf. [*Steel Seizure Case,* p. 148 supra]. It has not, however, authorized the injunctive remedy against threatened publication. It has apparently been satisfied to rely on criminal sanctions and their deterrent effect on the responsible as well as the irresponsible press. * * *

MR. JUSTICE HARLAN, with whom THE CHIEF JUSTICE and MR. JUSTICE BLACKMUN join, dissenting. * * *

With all respect, I consider that the Court has been almost irresponsibly feverish in dealing with these cases.

Both [the] Second Circuit and [the] District of Columbia Circuit rendered judgment on June 23. [This] Court's order setting a hearing before us on June 26 at 11 a.m., a course which I joined only to avoid the possibility of even more peremptory action by the Court, was issued less than 24 hours before. The record in the *Post* case was filed with the Clerk shortly before 1 p.m. on June 25; the record in the *Times* case did not arrive until 7 or 8 o'clock that same night. The briefs of the parties were received less than two hours before argument on June 26.

This frenzied train of events took place in the name of the presumption against prior restraints created by the First Amendment. Due regard for the extraordinarily important and difficult questions involved in these litigations should have led the Court to shun such a precipitate timetable. In order to decide the merits of these cases properly, some or all of the following questions should have been faced: * * *

2. Whether the First Amendment permits the federal courts to enjoin publication of stories which would present a serious threat to national security. See *Near* (dictum). * * *

4. Whether the unauthorized disclosure of any of these particular documents would seriously impair the national security.

5. What weight should be given to the opinion of high officers in the Executive Branch of the Government with respect to questions 3 and 4. * * *

7. Whether the threatened harm to the national security or the Government's possessory interest in the documents justifies the issuance of an injunction against publication in light of—

a. The strong First Amendment policy against prior restraints on publication; b. The doctrine against enjoining conduct in violation of criminal statutes; and c. The extent to which the materials at issue have apparently already been otherwise disseminated.

These are difficult questions of fact, of law, and of judgment; the potential consequences of erroneous decision are enormous. The time which has been available to us, to the lower courts, and to the parties has been wholly inadequate for giving these cases the kind of consideration they deserve. It is a reflection on the stability of the judicial process that these great issues—as important as any that have arisen during my time on the Court—should have been decided under the pressures engendered by the torrent of publicity that has attended these litigations from their inception.

Forced as I am to reach the merits of these cases, I dissent from the opinion and judgments of the Court. Within the severe limitations imposed by the time constraints under which I have been required to operate, I can only state my reasons in telescoped form, even though in different circumstances I would have felt constrained to deal with the cases in the fuller sweep indicated above.

[It] is plain to me that the scope of the judicial function in passing upon the activities of the Executive Branch of the Government in the field of foreign affairs is very narrowly restricted. This view is, I think, dictated by the concept of separation of powers upon which our constitutional system [rests.] I agree that, in performance of its duty to protect the values of the First Amendment against political pressures, the judiciary must review the initial Executive determination to the point of satisfying itself that the subject matter of the dispute does lie within the proper compass of the President's foreign relations power. Constitutional considerations forbid "a complete abandonment of judicial control." Moreover, the judiciary may properly insist that the determination that disclosure of the subject matter would irreparably impair the national security be made by the head of the Executive Department concerned—here the Secretary of State or the Secretary of Defense—after actual personal consideration by that officer. This safeguard is required in the analogous area of executive claims of privilege for secrets of state.

But in my judgment the judiciary may not properly go beyond these two inquiries and redetermine for itself the probable impact of disclosure on the national security. "[T]he very nature of executive decisions as to foreign policy is political, not judicial. Such decisions are wholly confided by our Constitution to the political departments of the government, Executive and Legislative. They are delicate, complex, and involve large elements of prophecy. They are and should be undertaken only by those directly responsible to the people whose welfare they advance or imperil. They are decisions of a kind for which the judiciary has neither aptitude, facilities nor responsibility and which has long been held to belong in the domain of political power not subject to judicial intrusion or inquiry." *Chicago & S. Air Lines v. Waterman S.S. Corp.* (Jackson, J.), 333 U.S. 103, 68 S.Ct. 431, 92 L.Ed. 568 (1948).

Even if there is some room for the judiciary to override the executive determination, it is plain that the scope of review must be exceedingly narrow. I can see no indication in the opinions of either the District Court or the Court of Appeals in the *Post* litigation that the conclusions of the Executive were given even the deference owing to an administrative agency, much less that owing to a co-equal branch of the Government operating within the field of its constitutional prerogative. ＊ ＊ ＊

Pending further hearings in each case conducted under the appropriate ground rules, I would continue the restraints on publication. I cannot believe that the doctrine prohibiting prior restraints reaches to the point of preventing courts from maintaining the status quo long enough to act responsibly in matters of such national importance as those involved here.

MR. JUSTICE BLACKMUN, dissenting.

[The First Amendment] is only one part of an entire Constitution. Article II of the great document vests in the Executive Branch primary power over the conduct of foreign affairs and places in that branch the responsibility for the Nation's safety. Each provision of the Constitution is important, and I cannot subscribe to a doctrine of unlimited absolutism for the First Amendment at the cost of downgrading other provisions. First Amendment absolutism has never commanded a majority of this Court. What is needed here is a weighing, upon properly developed standards, of the broad right of the press to print and of the very narrow right of the Government to prevent. Such standards are not yet developed. The parties here are in disagreement as to what those standards should be. But even the newspapers concede that there are situations where restraint is in order and is constitutional. Mr. Justice Holmes gave us a suggestion when he said in *Schenck*, "It is a question of proximity and degree. When a nation is at war many things that might be said in time of peace are such a hindrance to its effort that their utterance will not be endured so long as men fight and that no Court could regard them as protected by any constitutional right."

I therefore would remand these cases to be developed expeditiously, of course, but on a schedule permitting the orderly presentation of evidence from both sides [and] with the preparation of briefs, oral argument and court opinions of a quality better than has been seen to this point. [T]hese cases and the issues involved and the courts, including this one, deserve better than has been produced thus far. ＊ ＊ ＊[b]

Notes and Questions

1. *What did the case decide?* Do you agree that "the case [did] not make any law at all, good or bad"? That on the question "whether injunctions against the press are permissible, it is clear that [the case] can supply no precedent?" See Junger, *Down Memory Lane: The Case of the Pentagon Papers*, 23 Case

---

b. Marshall, J., concurring, did not deal with first amendment issues but only with separation of powers—the government's attempt to secure through the Court injunctive relief that Congress had refused to authorize.

Burger, C.J., dissenting, complained that because of "unseemly haste," "we do not know the facts of this case. [W]e literally do not know what we are acting on." He expressed no views on the merits, apart from his joinder in Harlan, J.'s opinion, and a statement that he would have continued the temporary restraints in effect while returning the cases to the lower courts for more thorough exploration of the facts and issues: "I cannot believe that the doctrine prohibiting prior restraints reaches to the point of preventing courts from maintaining the status quo long enough to act responsibly in matters of such national importance as those involved here."

W.Res.L.Rev. 3, 4–5 (1971). Or do you find in several concurring opinions a discernible standard that must be satisfied before a majority of the Court would permit an injunction against the press on national security grounds? Cf. 85 Harv.L.Rev. 199, 205–06 (1971). Do you find guidance as to the outcome if Congress were to authorize an injunction in narrow terms to protect national security? Cf. id. at 204–05. Might it fairly be said that this is a separation of powers decision, like the *Steel Seizure* case, as well as a first amendment decision? See Junger, supra, at 19.

2. *Injunctions against publishing specific material.* Is the special policy against prior restraints, as distinct from use of criminal sanctions, appropriately applied to a specific injunction against publishing identified material? Or should the policy against prior restraints, when applied to court injunctions after a hearing, be limited to broad orders against forbidden types of publications, as in *Near*? To what extent are the evils that underlie the general policy against prior restraints applicable to the specific injunction sought in *Pentagon Papers*? Cf. 85 Harv.L.Rev. at 207–08 (1971).

3. *"De facto" prior restraint.* One difficulty with viewing the prior restraint doctrine as "simply creat[ing] a 'presumption' against the validity of the restraint" (Emerson's characterization of the current approach) rather than as "a prohibition on all restraints subject to certain categorical exceptions," observes Emerson, *First Amendment Doctrine and the Burger Court*, 68 Calif.L.Rev. 422, 457–58 (1980), is that "the requirement of ad hoc scrutiny of prior restraints is itself likely to result in a 'de facto' prior restraint." Pointing to Brennan, J.'s comment in *Pentagon Papers* that "every restraint issued in this case [has] violated the First Amendment—and not less so because that restraint was justified as necessary to afford the courts an opportunity to examine the claim more thoroughly," Emerson notes that "[t]his is exactly what happened when the government sought to enjoin *The Progressive* magazine from publishing an article on the manufacture of the hydrogen bomb. The Supreme Court refused to order an expedited appeal from the [federal district court] injunction against publication [and, although the case was ultimately dismissed by the Seventh Circuit,] *The Progressive* remained under effective prior restraint for nearly seven months."

Compare *Near* and *Pentagon Papers* with UNITED STATES v. PROGRESSIVE, INC., 467 F.Supp. 990 (W.D.Wis.1979) (preliminary injunction issued Mar. 28, 1979), request for writ of mandamus den. sub nom. *Morland v. Sprecher*, 443 U.S. 709, 99 S.Ct. 3086, 61 L.Ed.2d 860 (1979), case dismissed, Nos. 79–1428, 79–1664 (7th Cir. Oct. 1, 1979).[c] *The Progressive* planned to publish an article entitled, "The H-Bomb Secret—How We Got It, Why We're Telling It," maintaining that the article would contribute to informed opinion about nuclear weapons and demonstrate the inadequacies of a system of secrecy and classification. Although the government conceded that at least some of the information contained in the article was "in the public domain" or had been "declassified," it argued that "national security" permitted it to censor information originating in the public domain "if when drawn together, synthesized and collated, such information acquires the character of presenting immediate, direct and irreparable harm to the interests of the United States." The Secretary of State stated that publication would increase thermonuclear proliferation and that this would "irreparably impair the national security of the United States." The Secretary

---

c. The government's action against *The Progressive* was abandoned after information similar to that it sought to enjoin was published elsewhere.

of Defense maintained that dissemination of the Morland article would lead to a substantial increase in the risk of thermonuclear proliferation and to use or threats that would "adversely affect the national security of the United States."

Although recognizing that this constituted "the first instance of prior restraint against a publication in this fashion in the [nation's history]," the district court enjoined defendants, pending final resolution of the litigation, from publishing or otherwise disclosing any information designated by the government as "restricted data" within the meaning of The Atomic Energy Act of 1954: "What is involved here is information dealing with the most destructive weapon in the history of mankind, information of sufficient destructive potential to nullify the right to free speech and to endanger the right to life itself. [Faced] with a stark choice between upholding the right to continued life and the right to freedom of the press, most jurists would have no difficulty in opting for the chance to continue to breathe and function as they work to achieve perfect freedom of expression.

"[A] mistake in ruling against *The Progressive* will seriously infringe cherished First Amendment rights. [A] mistake in ruling against the United States could pave the way for thermonuclear annihilation for us all. In that event, our right to life is extinguished and the right to publish becomes moot.

"[W]ar by foot soldiers has been replaced in large part by machines and bombs. No longer need there be any advance warning or any preparation time before a nuclear war could be commenced. [In light of these factors] publication of the technical information on the hydrogen bomb contained in the article is analogous to publication of troop movements or locations in time of war and falls within the extremely narrow exception to the rule against prior restraint [recognized in *Near*].[d]

"The government has met its burden under § 2274 of The Atomic Energy Act [which authorizes injunctive relief against one who would communicate or disclose restricted data 'with reason to believe such data will be utilized to injure the United States or to secure an advantage to any foreign nation.'] [I]t has also met the test enunciated by two Justices in *Pentagon Papers,* namely grave, direct, immediate and irreparable harm to the United States."

The court distinguished *Pentagon Papers* as follows: "[T]he study involved [there] contained historical data relating to events some three to twenty years previously. Secondly, the Supreme Court agreed with the lower court that no cogent reasons were advanced by the government as to why the article affected national security except that publication might cause some embarrassment to the United States. A final and most vital difference between these two cases is the fact that a specific statute is involved here [§ 2274 of The Atomic Energy Act]."

4. *CIA secrecy agreement.* The Central Intelligence Agency requires employees to sign a "secrecy agreement" as a condition of employment, an agreement committing the employee not to reveal classified information nor to publish any information obtained during the course of employment without prior approval of the Agency. In SNEPP v. UNITED STATES, 444 U.S. 507, 100 S.Ct. 763, 62 L.Ed.2d 704 (1980), Snepp had published a book called *Decent Interval*

d. One of the reasons the court gave for finding that the objected-to technical portions of the article fell within the *Near* exception was that it was "unconvinced that suppression of [these portions] would in any plausible fashion impede the defendants in their laudable crusade to stimulate public knowledge of nuclear armament and bring about enlightened debate on national policy questions." Should this have been a factor in the decision to issue the preliminary injunction?

about certain CIA activities in South Vietnam based on his experiences as an agency employee without seeking prepublication review. At least for purposes of the litigation, the government conceded that Snepp's book divulged no confidential information. The Court, per curiam (Stevens, J., joined by Brennan and Marshall, JJ., dissenting) held that Snepp's failure to submit the book was a breach of trust and the government was entitled to a constructive trust on the proceeds of the book: "[E]ven in the absence of an express agreement, the CIA could have acted to protect substantial government interests by imposing reasonable restrictions on employee activities that in other contexts might be protected by the First Amendment. The Government has a compelling interest in protecting both the secrecy of information important to our national security and the appearance of confidentiality so essential to the effective operation of our foreign intelligence service." [e] When employees or past employees do submit publications for clearance, should *Freedman* standards apply? Can former CIA employees be required to submit all public speeches relating to their former employment for clearance? Are extemporaneous remarks permitted? To what extent can secrecy agreements be required of public employees outside the national security area? [f]

SECTION 3. FAIR ADMINISTRATION OF JUSTICE AND THE FIRST AMENDMENT AS SWORD

This section poses two connected problems. The first implicates familiar themes, albeit in a different context. The government seeks to deter or punish speech it regards as threatening to the fair administration of justice, but the speech at issue falls into no recognized category of unprotected speech. Thus, the courts must consider whether absolute protection is called for, or, alternatively, whether new categories or ad hoc determinations are appropriate, and whether prior restraints are permissible.

A second problem is unique. Government seeks not to punish speech, but to administer justice in private. It refuses to let the public or press witness its handling of prisoners, or its conduct of trial or pre-trial proceedings. The question is whether the first amendment can serve as a sword allowing citizen-critics to gather information. Assuming it can, what are its limits within the justice system? Does a right of access reach beyond the justice system?

Finally, a recurring issue concerns the role of the press. If the press cannot be prevented from speaking about trials, can prosecutors, defense attorneys, litigants and potential witnesses be prevented from speaking to the press? Is this one problem or many problems? Does the first amendment require that the press be granted access not afforded the public? Does the first amendment permit differential access? If so, what are the limits on how government defines the press?

e. Compare *Haig v. Agee,* 453 U.S. 280, 101 S.Ct. 2766, 69 L.Ed.2d 640 (1981), stating that "repeated disclosures of intelligence operations and names of intelligence personnel" for the "purpose of obstructing intelligence operations and the recruiting of intelligence personnel" are "clearly not protected by the Constitution." What if the publisher of the information merely has "reason to believe that such activities would impair or impede the foreign intelligence activities of the United States"? See 50 U.S.C. § 421.

f. For criticism of *Snepp,* see Cheh, *Judicial Supervision of Executive Secrecy,* 69 Cornell L.Rev. 690 (1984); Koffler & Gershman, *The New Seditious Libel,* 69 Corn.L.Rev. 816 (1984); Medow, *The First Amendment and the Secrecy State: Snepp v. United States,* 130 U.Pa.L.Rev. 775 (1982).

I. JUSTICE AND THE FIRST AMENDMENT AS SHIELD

In a number of cases, defendants have asserted that their rights to a fair trial have been abridged by newspaper publicity. SHEPPARD v. MAXWELL, 384 U.S. 333, 86 S.Ct. 1507, 16 L.Ed.2d 600 (1966) is probably the most notorious "trial by newspaper" case. The Court, per CLARK, J., (Black, J. dissenting) agreed with the "finding" of the Ohio Supreme Court that the atmosphere of defendant's murder trial was that of a " 'Roman holiday' for the news media." The courtroom was jammed with reporters. And in the corridors outside the courtroom, "a host of photographers and television personnel" photographed witnesses, counsel and jurors as they entered and left the courtroom. Throughout the trial, there was a deluge of publicity, much of which contained information never presented at trial, yet the jurors were not sequestered until the trial was over and they had begun their deliberations.

The Court placed the primary blame on the trial judge. He could "easily" have prevented "the carnival atmosphere of the trial" since "the courtroom and courthouse premises" were subject to his control. For example, he should have provided privacy for the jury, insulated witnesses from the media, instead of allowing them to be interviewed at will, and "made some effort to control the release of leads, information, and gossip to the press by police officers, witnesses, and the counsel for both sides." No one "coming under the jurisdiction of the court should be permitted to frustrate its function."

The Court recognized that "there is nothing that proscribes the press from reporting events that transpire in the courtroom. But where there is a reasonable likelihood that prejudicial news prior to trial will prevent a fair trial, the judge should continue the case until the threat abates, or transfer it to another county not so permeated with publicity. In addition, sequestration of the jury was something the judge should have raised sua sponte with counsel. If publicity during the proceedings threatens the fairness of the trial, a new trial should be ordered. But we must remember that reversals are but palliatives; the cure lies in those remedial measures that will prevent the prejudice at its inception."

The Court, however, reiterated its extreme reluctance "to place any direct limitations on the freedom traditionally exercised by the news media for '[w]hat transpires in the courtroom is public property.' " The press "does not simply publish information about trials but guards against the miscarriage of justice by subjecting the police, prosecutors, and judicial processes to extensive public scrutiny and criticism."

In anticipation of the trial of Simants for a mass murder which had attracted widespread news coverage, the county court prohibited everyone in attendance from, inter alia, releasing or authorizing for publication "any testimony given or evidence adduced." Simants' preliminary hearing (open to the public) was held the same day, subject to the restrictive order. Simants was bound over for trial. Respondent Nebraska state trial judge then entered an order which, as modified by the state supreme court, restrained the press and broadcasting media from reporting any confessions or incriminating statements made by Simants to law enforcement officers or third parties, except members of the press, and from reporting other facts "strongly implicative" of the defendant. The order expired when the jury was impaneled. NEBRASKA PRESS ASS'N v.

STUART, 427 U.S. 539, 96 S.Ct. 2791, 49 L.Ed.2d 683 (1976), per BURGER, C.J., struck down the state court order:

"To the extent that the order prohibited the reporting of evidence adduced at the open preliminary hearing, it plainly violated settled principles: 'There is nothing that proscribes the press from reporting events that transpire in the courtroom.' *Sheppard*." [a] To the extent that the order prohibited publication "based on information gained from other sources, [the] heavy burden imposed as a condition to securing a prior restraint was not met." The portion of the order regarding "implicative" information was also "too vague and too broad" to survive scrutiny of restraints on first amendment rights.

"[P]retrial publicity—even pervasive, adverse publicity—does not inevitably lead to an unfair trial. The capacity of the jury eventually impaneled to decide the case fairly is influenced by the tone and extent of the publicity, which is in part, and often in large part, shaped by what attorneys, police and other officials do to precipitate news coverage. [T]he measures a judge takes or fails to take to mitigate the effects of pretrial publicity—the measures described in *Sheppard*—may well determine whether the defendant receives a trial consistent [with] due process.

"[The] Court has interpreted [first amendment] guarantees to afford special protection against orders that prohibit the publication or broadcast of particular information or commentary—orders that impose [a] 'prior' restraint on speech. None of our decided cases on prior restraint involved restrictive orders entered to protect a defendant's right to a fair and impartial jury, but [they] have a common thread relevant to this case. * * *

"The thread running through [*Near* and *Pentagon Papers*], is that prior restraints on speech and publication are the most serious and the least tolerable infringement on First Amendment rights. A criminal penalty or a judgment in a defamation case is subject to the whole panoply of protections afforded by deferring the impact of the judgment until all avenues of appellate review have been exhausted. [But] a prior restraint [has] an immediate and irreversible sanction. If it can be said that a threat of criminal or civil sanctions after publication 'chills' speech, prior restraint 'freezes' it at least for the time.

"[I]f the authors of [the first and sixth amendments], fully aware of the potential conflicts between them, were unwilling or unable to resolve the issue by assigning to one priority over the other, it is not for us to rewrite the Constitution by undertaking what they declined. [Yet] it is nonetheless clear that the barriers to prior restraint remain high unless we are to abandon what the Court has said for nearly a quarter of our national existence and implied throughout all of [it.]

"We turn now to the record in this case to determine whether, as Learned Hand put it, 'the gravity of the "evil," discounted by its improbability, justifies such invasion of free speech as is necessary to avoid the danger,' *Dennis* [2d Cir.], aff'd. To do so, we must examine the evidence before the trial judge when the order was entered to determine (a) the nature and extent of pretrial news coverage; (b) whether other measures would be likely to mitigate the effects of unrestrained pretrial publicity; (c) how effectively a restraining order would operate to prevent the threatened danger. The precise terms of the restraining order are also important. We must then consider whether the record supports

a. The Court added, however, that the county court "could not know that closure of the preliminary hearing was an alternative open to it until the Nebraska Supreme Court so construed state law."

the entry of a prior restraint on publication, one of the most extraordinary remedies known to our jurisprudence."

As to (a), although the trial judge was justified in concluding there would be extensive pretrial publicity concerning this case, he "found only 'a clear and present danger that pretrial publicity *could* impinge upon the defendant's right to a fair trial.' [Emphasis added by the Court]. His conclusion as to the impact of such publicity on prospective jurors was of necessity speculative, dealing as he was with factors unknown and unknowable."

As to (b), "there is no finding that alternative means [e.g., change of venue, postponement of trial to allow public attention to subside, searching questions of prospective jurors] would not have protected Simants' rights, and the Nebraska Supreme Court did no more than imply that such measures might not be adequate. Moreover, the record is lacking in evidence to support such a finding."

As to (c), in view of such practical problems as the limited territorial jurisdiction of the trial court issuing the order, the difficulties of predicting what information "will in fact undermine the impartiality of jurors," the problem of drafting an order that will "effectively keep prejudicial information from prospective jurors," and that the events "took place in a community of only 850 people"—throughout which, "it is reasonable to assume," rumors that "could well be more damaging than reasonably accurate news accounts" would "travel swiftly by word of mouth"—"it is far from clear that prior restraint on publication would have protected Simants' rights."

"[It] is significant that when this Court has reversed a state conviction because of prejudicial publicity, it has carefully noted that some course of action short of prior restraint would have made a critical difference. However difficult it may be, we need not rule out the possibility of showing the kind of threat to fair trial rights that would possess the requisite degree of certainty to justify restraint. [We] reaffirm that the guarantees of freedom of expression are not an absolute prohibition under all circumstances, but the barriers to prior restraint remain high and the presumption against its use continues intact. We hold that, with respect to the order entered in this case [the] heavy burden imposed as a condition to securing a prior restraint was not [met]."

BRENNAN, J., joined by Stewart and Marshall, JJ., concurring, would hold that "resort to prior restraints on the freedom of the press is a constitutionally impermissible method for enforcing [the right to a fair trial by a jury]; judges have at their disposal a broad spectrum of devices for ensuring that fundamental fairness is accorded the accused without necessitating so drastic an incursion on the equally fundamental and salutary constitutional mandate that discussion of public affairs in a free society cannot depend on the preliminary grace of judicial censors": "Commentary and reporting on the criminal justice system is at the core of First Amendment values, for the operation and integrity of that system is of crucial import to citizens concerned with the administration of Government. Secrecy of judicial action can only breed ignorance and distrust of courts and suspicion concerning the competence and impartiality of judges; free and robust reporting, criticism, and debate can contribute to public understanding of the rule of law and to comprehension of the functioning of the entire criminal justice system, as well as improve the quality of that system by subjecting it to the cleansing effects of exposure and public accountability.

"[In] effect, we are now told by respondents that the [first and sixth amendments] can no longer coexist when the press possesses and seeks to publish 'confessions and admissions against interest' and other information 'strongly implicative' of a criminal defendant as the perpetrator of a crime, and that one or the other right must therefore be subordinated. I disagree. Settled case law concerning the impropriety and constitutional invalidity of prior restraints on the press compels the conclusion that there can be no prohibition on the publication by the press of any information pertaining to pending judicial proceedings or the operation of the criminal justice system, no matter how shabby the means by which the information is obtained.[15] This does not imply, however, any subordination of Sixth Amendment rights, for an accused's right to a fair trial may be adequately assured through methods that do not infringe First Amendment values.

"[The narrow national security exception mentioned in *Near* and *Pentagon Papers*] does not mean, as the Nebraska Supreme Court assumed, that prior restraints can be justified on an ad hoc balancing approach that concludes that the 'presumption' must be overcome in light of some perceived 'justification.' Rather, this language refers to the fact that, as a matter of procedural safeguards and burden of proof, prior restraints even within a recognized exception to the rule against prior restraints will be extremely difficult to justify; but as an initial matter, the purpose for which a prior restraint is sought to be imposed 'must fit within one of the narrowly defined exceptions to the prohibition against prior restraints.' Indeed, two Justices in [*Pentagon Papers*] apparently controverted the existence of even a limited 'military security' exception to the rule against prior restraints on the publication of otherwise protected material. (Black, J., concurring); (Douglas, J., concurring). And a majority of the other Justices who expressed their views on the merits made it clear that they would take cognizance only of a 'single, extremely narrow class of cases in which the First Amendment's ban on prior judicial restraint may be overridden.' (Brennan, J., concurring). * * *

"The only exception that has thus far been recognized even in dictum to the blanket prohibition against prior restraints against publication of material which would otherwise be constitutionally shielded was the 'military security' situation addressed in [*Pentagon Papers*]. But unlike the virtually certain, direct, and immediate harm required for such a restraint [the] harm to a fair trial that might otherwise eventuate from publications which are suppressed pursuant to orders such as that under review must inherently remain speculative.

"[O]nce the jury is impaneled, the techniques of sequestration of jurors and control over the courtroom and conduct of trial should prevent prejudicial publicity from infecting the fairness of judicial proceedings. Similarly, judges may stem much of the flow of prejudicial publicity at its source, before it is obtained by representatives of the press. But even if the press nevertheless obtains potentially prejudicial information and decides to publish that information, the Sixth Amendment rights of the accused may still be adequately protected. In particular, the trial judge should employ the voir dire to probe fully into the effect of publicity. [We] have indicated that even in a case involving outrageous publicity and a 'carnival atmosphere' in the courtroom, 'these procedures would have been sufficient to guarantee [the defendant] a fair trial.' [For] this reason, the one thing *Sheppard* did not approve were 'any direct

---

15. Of course, even if the press cannot be enjoined from reporting certain information, that does not necessarily immunize it from civil liability for libel or invasion of privacy or from criminal liability for transgressions of general criminal laws during the course of obtaining that information.

limitations on the freedom traditionally exercised by the news media.' Indeed, the traditional techniques approved in *Sheppard* for ensuring fair trials would have been adequate in every case in which we have found that a new trial was required due to lack of fundamental fairness to the accused. ＊ ＊ ＊

"There are additional, practical reasons for not starting down the path urged by respondents. The ['military security' exception] involves no judicial weighing of the countervailing public interest in receiving the suppressed information; the direct, immediate, and irreparable harm that would result from disclosure is simply deemed to outweigh the public's interest in knowing, for example, the specific details of troop movements during wartime. [H]owever, any attempt to impose a prior restraint on the reporting of information concerning the operation of the criminal justice system will inevitably involve the courts in an ad hoc evaluation of the need for the public to receive particular information that might nevertheless implicate the accused as the perpetrator of a crime. [T]he press may be arrogant, tyrannical, abusive, and sensationalist, just as it may be incisive, probing, and informative. But at least in the context of prior restraints on publication, the decision of what, when, and how to publish is for editors, not judges. Every restrictive order imposed on the press in this case was accordingly an unconstitutional prior restraint ＊ ＊ ＊."

Although they joined the Court's opinion, White and Powell, JJ., also filed brief concurrences. WHITE, J., expressed "grave doubts" that these types of restrictive orders "would ever be justifiable." POWELL, J., "emphasize[d] the unique burden" resting upon one who "undertakes to show the necessity for prior restraint on pretrial publicity." In his judgment, a prior restraint "requires a showing that (i) there is a clear threat to the fairness of trial, (ii) such a threat is posed by the actual publicity to be restrained, and (iii) no less restrictive alternatives are available. Notwithstanding such a showing, a restraint may not issue unless it also is shown that previous publicity or publicity from unrestrained sources will not render the restraint inefficacious. [A]ny restraint must comply with the standards of specificity always required in the First Amendment context."

STEVENS, J., concurred in the judgment. For the reasons articulated by Brennan, J., he "agree[d] that the judiciary is capable of protecting the defendant's right to a fair trial without enjoining the press from publishing information in the public domain, and that it may not do so." But he reserved judgment, until further argument, on "[w]hether the same absolute protection would apply no matter how shabby or illegal the means by which the information is obtained, no matter how serious an intrusion on privacy might be involved, no matter how demonstrably false the information might be, no matter how prejudicial it might be to the interests of innocent persons, and no matter how perverse the motivation for publishing it." He indicated that "if ever required to face the issue squarely" he "may well accept [Brennan, J.'s] ultimate conclusion." [b]

Notes and Questions

1. *Why the prior restraint reliance?* Does "the reasoning used by all of the justices premised solely on the traditional aversion to prior restraints, insufficiently" protect the press? Sack, *Principle and Nebraska Press Association v.*

b. For background on *Nebraska Press,* see Friendly & Elliot, *The Constitution: That Delicate Balance* 148–58 (1984).

Stuart, 29 Stan.L.Rev. 411, 411 (1977). Would the *Nebraska Press* order have been "equally objectionable" if "framed as a statutory sanction punishing publication after it had occurred"? Id. at 415. See also Barnett, *The Puzzle of Prior Restraint*, 29 Stan.L.Rev. 539, 542–44, 560 (1977).

2. *Why the Dennis citation?* Consider Schmidt, *Nebraska Press Association: An Expansion of Freedom and Contraction of Theory*, 29 Stan.L.Rev. 431, 459–60 (1977): Burger, C.J.'s reliance on *Dennis* "is remarkable, almost unbelievable, because that test is both an exceedingly odd means of determining the validity of a prior restraint and a controversial and recently neglected technique of first amendment adjudication. [If] the [*Dennis*] test is the right one for prior restraints, what tests should govern a subsequent punishment case resting on legislation?" See also Barnett, note 1 supra, at 542–44. Burger, C.J.'s citation to *Dennis* should be read in conjunction with dictum in his majority opinion in *Landmark Communications, Inc. v. Virginia*, note 6 infra. There he questioned reliance upon the clear and present danger standard but observed: "Properly applied, the test requires a court to make its own inquiry into the imminence and magnitude of the danger said to flow from the particular utterance and then to balance the character of the evil, as well as its likelihood, against the need for free and unfettered expression. The possibility that other measures will serve the State's interests should also be weighed."

3. *Future press restraints.* Was *Nebraska Press* a strong case for restraint? Is it "difficult to believe that any other case will provide an exception to the rule against prior restraints in fair trial/free press cases"? Goodale, *The Press Ungagged: The Practical Effect on Gag Order Litigation of Nebraska Press Association v. Stuart*, 29 Stan.L.Rev. 497, 504 (1977). If so, does the dispute between the justices over the right standard make a difference? Does the collateral bar rule shed light on that question? See id. at 511–12; Barnett, note 1 supra, at 553–58. Should the collateral bar rule apply in this situation?

4. *Application to non-press defendants.* Should *Nebraska Press* standards apply to court orders preventing prosecutors, witnesses, potential witnesses, jurors, defendants, or defense attorneys from talking to the press about the case? Should different standards apply to each category—e.g., do defendants and defense attorneys deserve as much protection as the press? See Freedman & Starwood, *Prior Restraints on Freedom of Expression by Defendants and Defense Attorneys: Ratio Decidendi v. Obiter Dictum*, 29 Stan.L.Rev. 607 (1977).

5. *Obstructing justice.* A series of cases have held that the first amendment greatly restricts contempt sanctions against persons whose comments on pending cases were alleged to have created a danger of obstruction of the judicial process. "Such repression can be justified, if at all, only by a clear and present danger of the obstruction of justice." *New York Times Co. v. Sullivan*, p. 464 supra. In *Bridges v. California*, 314 U.S. 252, 62 S.Ct. 190, 86 L.Ed. 192 (1941), union leader Bridges had caused publication or acquiesced in publication of a telegram threatening a strike if an "outrageous" California state decision involving Bridges' dock workers were enforced. The Court reversed Bridges' contempt citation. Consider Tribe, *American Constitutional Law* 624 (1978): "If Bridges' threat to cripple the economy of the entire West Coast did not present danger enough, the lesson of the case must be that almost nothing said outside the courtroom is punishable as contempt." [c]

c. Compare Rieger, *Lawyers' Criticism of Judges: Is Freedom of Speech A Figure of Speech?*, 2 Const.Comm. 69 (1985).

Would it make a difference if a petit jury were impaneled? Suppose Bridges published an open letter to petit jurors? What if copies were sent by Bridges to each juror? Cf. *Wood v. Georgia,* 370 U.S. 375, 82 S.Ct. 1364, 8 L.Ed.2d 569 (1962) (open letter to press and grand jury—contempt citation reversed). But cf. *Cox v. Louisiana,* p. 647 infra (statute forbidding parades near courthouse with intent to interfere with administration of justice upheld): ("[W]e deal not with the contempt power [but] a statute narrowly drawn to punish" not a pure form of speech but expression mixed with conduct "that infringes a substantial state interest in protecting the judicial process.").

6. *Confidentiality and privacy.* A series of cases has rebuffed state efforts to protect confidentiality or privacy by prohibiting publication. *Cox Broadcasting Corp. v. Cohn,* p. 488 supra (state could not impose liability for public dissemination of the name of rape victim derived from public court documents); *Oklahoma Pub. Co. v. District Court,* 430 U.S. 308, 97 S.Ct. 1045, 51 L.Ed.2d 355 (1977) (pretrial order enjoining press from publishing name or picture of 11-year-old boy accused of murder invalid when reporters had been lawfully present at a prior public hearing and had photographed him en route from the courthouse); *Landmark Communications, Inc. v. Virginia,* 435 U.S. 829, 98 S.Ct. 1535, 56 L.Ed.2d 1 (1978) (statute making it a crime to publish information about particular confidential proceedings invalid as applied to non-participant in the proceedings, at least when the information had been lawfully acquired); *Smith v. Daily Mail Pub. Co.,* 443 U.S. 97, 99 S.Ct. 2667, 61 L.Ed.2d 399 (1979) (statute making it a crime for newspapers (but not broadcasters) to publish the name of any youth charged as a juvenile offender invalid as applied to information lawfully acquired from private sources). But cf. *Seattle Times Co. v. Rhinehart,* 467 U.S. 20, 104 S.Ct. 2199, 81 L.Ed.2d 17 (1984) (order enjoining newspaper from disseminating information acquired as a litigant in pretrial discovery valid so long as order is entered on a showing of good cause and does not restrict the dissemination of the information if gained from other sources).

II. JUSTICE AND THE FIRST AMENDMENT AS SWORD

By 1978, no Supreme Court holding contradicted Burger, C.J.'s contention for a plurality in *Houchins v. KQED,* 438 U.S. 1, 98 S.Ct. 2588, 57 L.Ed.2d 553 (1978) that, "neither the First Amendment nor the Fourteenth Amendment mandates a right of access to government information or sources of information within the government's control." Or as Stewart, J., put it in an often-quoted statement, "The Constitution itself is neither a Freedom of Information Act nor an Official Secrets Act." *"Or of the Press,"* 26 Hast.L.J. 631, 636 (1975). *Richmond Newspapers,* infra, constitutes the Court's first break with its past denials of first amendment rights to information within governmental control.

RICHMOND NEWSPAPERS, INC. v. VIRGINIA
448 U.S. 555, 100 S.Ct. 2814, 65 L.Ed.2d 973 (1980).

[At the commencement of his fourth trial on a murder charge (his first conviction having been reversed and two subsequent retrials having ended in mistrials), defendant moved, without objection by the prosecutor or two reporters present, that the trial be closed to the public—defense counsel stating that he did not "want any information being shuffled back and forth when we have a recess as [to] who testified to what." The trial judge granted the motion, stating that "the statute gives me that power specifically." He presumably referred to Virginia Code § 19.2–266, providing that in all criminal trials "the court may, in its discretion, exclude [any] persons whose presence would impair the conduct of a fair trial, provided that the [defendant's right] to a public trial shall not be violated." Later the same day the trial court granted appellants' request for a hearing on a motion to vacate the closure order. At the closed hearing, appellants observed that prior to the entry of its closure order the court had failed to make any evidentiary findings or to consider any other, less drastic measures to ensure a fair trial. Defendant stated that he "didn't want information to leak out," be published by the media, perhaps inaccurately, and then be seen by the jurors. Noting inter alia that "having people in the Courtroom is distracting to the jury" and that if "the rights of the defendant are infringed in any way [and if his closure motion] doesn't completely override all rights of everyone else, then I'm inclined to go along with" the defendant, the court denied the motion to vacate the closure order. Defendant was subsequently found not guilty.]

MR. CHIEF JUSTICE BURGER announced the judgment of the Court and delivered an opinion in which MR. JUSTICE WHITE and MR. JUSTICE STEVENS joined.

[T]he precise issue presented here has not previously been before this Court for decision. [*Gannett Co. v. DePasquale*, 443 U.S. 368, 99 S.Ct. 2898, 61 L.Ed.2d 608 (1979)] was not required to decide whether a right of access to *trials*, as distinguished from hearings on *pre*trial motions, was constitutionally guaranteed. The Court held that the Sixth Amendment's guarantee to the accused of a public trial gave neither the public nor the press an enforceable right of access to a *pre*trial suppression hearing. One concurring opinion specifically emphasized that "a hearing on a motion before trial to suppress evidence is not a *trial*." (Burger, C.J., concurring). Moreover, the Court did not decide whether the First and Fourteenth Amendments guarantee a right of the public to attend trials; nor did the dissenting opinion reach this issue. [H]ere for the first time the Court is asked to decide whether a criminal trial itself may be closed to the public upon the unopposed request of a defendant, without any demonstration that closure is required to protect the defendant's superior right to a fair trial, or that some other overriding consideration requires closure.

[T]he historical evidence demonstrates conclusively that at the time when our organic laws were adopted, criminal trials both here and in England had long been presumptively open [, thus giving] assurance that the proceedings were conducted fairly to all concerned, [and] discourag[ing] perjury, the misconduct of participants, and decisions based on secret bias or partiality. [Moreover, the] early history of open trials in part reflects the widespread acknowledgment [that] public trials had significant therapeutic value. [When] a shocking crime occurs, a community reaction of outrage and public protest often follows. Thereafter the open processes of justice serve an important prophylactic purpose, providing an outlet for community concern, hostility, and emotion.

[The] crucial prophylactic aspects of the administration of justice cannot function in the dark; no community catharsis can occur if justice is "done in a corner [or] in any covert manner." [To] work effectively, it is important that society's criminal process "satisfy the appearance of justice," and the appearance of justice can best be provided by allowing people to observe it.

[From] this unbroken, uncontradicted history, supported by reasons as valid today as in centuries past, we are bound to conclude that a presumption of openness inheres in the very nature of a criminal trial under our system of criminal justice. [Nevertheless,] the State presses its contention that neither the Constitution nor the Bill of Rights contains any provision which by its terms guarantees to the public the right to attend criminal trials. Standing alone, this is correct, but there remains the question whether, absent an explicit provision, the Constitution affords protection against exclusion of the public from criminal trials.

[The] expressly guaranteed [first amendment] freedoms share a common core purpose of assuring freedom of communication on matters relating to the functioning of government. Plainly it would be difficult to single out any aspect of government of higher concern and importance to the people than the manner in which criminal trials are conducted * * *.

The Bill of Rights was enacted against the backdrop of the long history of trials being presumptively open. [In] guaranteeing freedoms such as those of speech and press, the First Amendment can be read as protecting the right of everyone to attend trials so as to give meaning to those explicit guarantees. * * * Free speech carries with it some freedom to listen. "In a variety of contexts this Court has referred to a First Amendment right to 'receive information and ideas.'" *Kleindienst v. Mandel*, 408 U.S. 753, 762, 92 S.Ct. 2576, 2581, 33 L.Ed.2d 683 (1972).[a] What this means in the context of trials is that the First Amendment guarantees of speech and press, standing alone, prohibit government from summarily closing courtroom doors which had long been open to the public at the time that amendment was adopted.

[It] is not crucial whether we describe this right to attend criminal trials to hear, see, and communicate observations concerning them as a "right of access," cf. *Gannett* (Powell, J., concurring); *Saxbe v. Washington Post Co.*, 417 U.S. 843, 94 S.Ct. 2811, 41 L.Ed.2d 514 (1974); *Pell v. Procunier*, 417 U.S. 817, 94 S.Ct. 2800, 41 L.Ed.2d 495 (1974),[11] or a "right to gather information," for we have recognized that "without some protection for seeking out the news, freedom of the press could be eviscerated." *Branzburg v. Hayes*, [p. 758 supra]. The explicit, guaranteed rights to speak and to publish concerning what takes place at a trial would lose much meaning if access to observe the trial could, as it was here, be foreclosed arbitrarily.

The right of access to places traditionally open to the public, as criminal trials have long been, may be seen as assured by the amalgam of the First Amendment guarantees of speech and press; and their affinity to the right of assembly is not without relevance. From the outset, the right of assembly was regarded not only as an independent right but also as a catalyst to augment the free exercise of the other First Amendment rights with which it was deliberately linked by the draftsmen. * * * Subject to the traditional time, place, and manner restrictions, streets, sidewalks, and parks are places traditionally open, where First Amendment rights may be exercised [see generally Sec. 5 infra]; a trial courtroom also is a public place where the people generally—and representatives of the media—have a right to be present, and where their presence historically has been thought to enhance the integrity and quality of what takes place.

a. *Mandel* held that the Executive had plenary power to exclude a Belgium journalist from the country, at least so long as it operated on the basis of a facially legitimate and bona fide reason for exclusion. Although the Court decided ultimately not to balance the government's particular justification against the first amendment interest, it recognized that those who sought personal communication with the excluded alien did have a first amendment interest at stake. The Court apparently assumed that the excluded speaker had no rights at stake, and none were asserted on his behalf.

11. *Procunier* and *Saxbe* are distinguishable in the sense that they were concerned with penal institutions which, by definition, are not "open" or public places. * * * See also *Greer v. Spock* (military bases) [p. 648 infra].

* * * Notwithstanding the appropriate caution against reading into the Constitution rights not explicitly defined, the Court has acknowledged that certain unarticulated rights are implicit in enumerated guarantees [referring, inter alia, to the rights of association and of privacy. See generally Ch. 7, Sec. 2]. [T]hese important but unarticulated rights [have] been found to share constitutional protection in common with explicit guarantees. The concerns expressed by Madison and others have thus been [resolved].[b]

We hold that the right to attend criminal trials [17] is implicit in the guarantees of the First Amendment; without the freedom to attend such trials, which people have exercised for centuries, important aspects of freedom of speech and "of the press could be eviscerated." *Branzburg.*

[In the present case,] the trial court made no findings to support closure; no inquiry was made as to whether alternative solutions would have met the need to ensure fairness; there was no recognition of any right under the Constitution for the public or press to attend the trial. In contrast to the pretrial proceeding dealt with in *Gannett,* there exist in the context of the trial itself various tested alternatives to satisfy the constitutional demands of fairness. [For example, there was nothing] to indicate that sequestration of the jurors would not have guarded against their being subjected to any improper information.[c] * * * Absent an overriding interest articulated in findings, the trial of a criminal case must be open to the public. * * *

Reversed.[d]

MR. JUSTICE BRENNAN, with whom MR. JUSTICE MARSHALL joins, concurring in the judgment.

[*Gannett*] held that the Sixth Amendment right to a public trial was personal to the accused, conferring no right of access to pretrial proceedings that is separately enforceable by the public or the press. [This case] raises the question whether the First Amendment, of its own force and as applied to the States through the Fourteenth Amendment, secures the public an independent right of access to trial proceedings. Because I believe that [it does secure] such a public right of access, I agree [that], without more, agreement of the trial judge and the parties cannot constitutionally close a trial to the public.[1]

While freedom of expression is made inviolate by the First Amendment, and with only rare and stringent exceptions, may not be suppressed, the First Amendment has not been viewed by the Court in all settings as providing an equally categorical assurance of the correlative freedom of access to informa-

b. The Chief Justice noted "the perceived need" of the Constitution's draftsmen "for some sort of constitutional 'saving clause' [which] would serve to foreclose application to the Bill of Rights of the maxim that the affirmation of particular rights implies a negation of those not expressly defined. Madison's efforts, culminating in the Ninth Amendment, served to allay the fears of those who were concerned that expressing certain guarantees could be read as excluding others."

17. Whether the public has a right to attend [civil trials is] not raised by this case, but we note that historically both civil and criminal trials have been presumptively open.

c. Once the jurors are selected, when, if ever, will their sequestration *not* be a satisfactory alternative to closure?

d. Powell, J., took no part. In *Gannett,* he took the position that a first amendment right of access applied to courtroom proceedings, albeit subject to overriding when justice so demanded or when confidentiality was necessary.

1. Of course, the Sixth Amendment remains the source of the *accused's* own right to insist upon public judicial proceedings. *Gannett.*

That the Sixth Amendment explicitly establishes a public trial right does not impliedly foreclose the derivation of such a right from other provisions of the Constitution. The Constitution was not framed as a work of carpentry, in which all joints must fit snugly without overlapping. * * *

tion.[2] Yet the Court has not ruled out a public access component to the First Amendment in every circumstance. Read with care and in context, our decisions must therefore be understood as holding only that any privilege of access to governmental information is subject to a degree of restraint dictated by the nature of the information and countervailing interests in security or confidentiality. [Cases such as *Houchins, Saxbe* and *Pell*] neither comprehensively nor absolutely deny that public access to information may at times be implied by the First Amendment and the principles which animate it.

The Court's approach in right of access cases simply reflects the special nature of a claim of First Amendment right to gather information. Customarily, First Amendment guarantees are interposed to protect communication between speaker and listener. When so employed against prior restraints, free speech protections are almost insurmountable. See generally Brennan, *Address,* 32 Rutg.L.Rev. 173, 176 (1979). But the First Amendment embodies more than a commitment to free expression and communicative interchange for their own sakes; it has a *structural* role to play in securing and fostering our republican system of self-government. Implicit in this structural role is not only "the principle that debate on public issues should be uninhibited, robust, and wide-open," but the antecedent assumption that valuable public debate—as well as other civic behavior—must be informed. The structural model links the First Amendment to that process of communication necessary for a democracy to survive, and thus entails solicitude not only for communication itself, but for the indispensable conditions of meaningful communication.

[A]n assertion of the prerogative to gather information must [be] assayed by considering the information sought and the opposing interests invaded. This judicial task is as much a matter of sensitivity to practical necessities as it is of abstract reasoning. But at least two helpful principles may be sketched. First, the case for a right of access has special force when drawn from an enduring and vital tradition of public entree to particular proceedings or information. Such a tradition commands respect in part because the Constitution carries the gloss of history. More importantly, a tradition of accessibility implies the favorable judgment of experience. Second, the value of access must be measured in specifics. Analysis is not advanced by rhetorical statements that all information bears upon public issues; what is crucial in individual cases is whether access to a particular government process is important in terms of that very process.

[This Court has] persistently defended the public character of the trial process. *In re Oliver,* 333 U.S. 257, 68 S.Ct. 499, 92 L.Ed. 682 (1948), established that [fourteenth amendment due process] forbids closed criminal trials [and] acknowledged that open trials are indispensable to First Amendment political and religious freedoms.

By the same token, a special solicitude for the public character of judicial proceedings is evident in the Court's rulings upholding the right to report about the administration of justice. While these decisions are impelled by the classic protections afforded by the First Amendment to pure communication, they are also bottomed upon a keen appreciation of the structural interest served in

---

2. A conceptually separate, yet related, question is whether the media should enjoy greater access rights than the general public. But no such contention is at stake here. Since the media's right of access is at least equal to that of the general public, this case is resolved by a decision that the state statute unconstitutionally restricts public access to trials. As a practical matter, however, the institutional press is the likely, and fitting, chief beneficiary of a right of access because it serves as the "agent" of interested citizens, and funnels information about trials to a large number of individuals.

opening the judicial system to public inspection. So, in upholding a privilege for reporting truthful information about judicial misconduct proceedings, *Landmark* emphasized that public scrutiny of the operation of a judicial disciplinary body implicates a major purpose of the First Amendment—"discussion of governmental affairs." Again, *Nebraska Press* noted that the traditional guarantee against prior restraint "should have particular force as applied to reporting of criminal proceedings." And *Cox Broadcasting* instructed that "[w]ith respect to judicial proceedings in particular, the function of the press serves to guarantee the fairness of trials and to bring to bear the beneficial effects of public scrutiny upon the administration of justice."

* * * Open trials play a fundamental role in furthering the efforts of our judicial system to assure the criminal defendant a fair and accurate adjudication of guilt or innocence. But, as a feature of our governing system of justice, the trial process serves other, broadly political, interests, and public access advances these objectives as well. To that extent, trial access possesses specific structural significance.

[For] a civilization founded upon principles of ordered liberty to survive and flourish, its members must share the conviction that they are governed equitably. That necessity * * * mandates a system of justice that demonstrates the fairness of the law to our citizens. One major function of the trial is to make that demonstration.

Secrecy is profoundly inimical to this demonstrative [purpose]. Public access is essential, therefore, if trial adjudication is to achieve the objective of maintaining public confidence in the administration of justice. But the trial [also] plays a pivotal role in the entire judicial process, and, by extension, in our form of government. Under our system, judges are not mere umpires, but, in their own sphere, lawmakers—a coordinate branch of *government*. [Thus], so far as the trial is the mechanism for judicial factfinding, as well as the initial forum for legal decisionmaking, it is a genuine governmental proceeding.

[More] importantly, public access to trials acts as an important check, akin in purpose to the other checks and balances that infuse our system of government. "The knowledge that every criminal trial is subject to contemporaneous review in the forum of public opinion is an effective restraint on possible abuse of judicial power," *Oliver*—an abuse that, in many cases, would have ramifications beyond the impact upon the parties before the court. * * *

Popular attendance at trials, in sum, substantially furthers the particular public purposes of that critical judicial proceeding.[22] In that sense, public access is an indispensable element of the trial process itself. Trial access, therefore, assumes structural importance in our "government of laws."

As previously noted, resolution of First Amendment public access claims in individual cases must be strongly influenced by the weight of historical practice and by an assessment of the specific structural value of public access in the circumstances. With regard to the case at hand, our ingrained tradition of public trials and the importance of public access to the broader purposes of the trial process, tip the balance strongly toward the rule that trials be open.[23]

22. In advancing these purposes, the availability of a trial transcript is no substitute for a public presence at the trial itself. As any experienced appellate judge can attest, the "cold" record is a very imperfect reproduction of events that transpire in the courtroom. * * *

23. The presumption of public trials is, of course, not at all incompatible with reasonable restrictions imposed upon courtroom behavior in the interests of decorum. Thus, when engaging in interchanges at the bench, the trial judge is not required to allow public or press intrusion upon the huddle. Nor does

What countervailing interests might be sufficiently compelling to reverse this presumption of openness need not concern us now,[24] for the statute at stake here authorizes trial closures at the unfettered discretion of the judge and parties.[25] [Thus it] violates the First and Fourteenth Amendments * * *.

MR. JUSTICE STEWART, concurring in the judgment.

Whatever the ultimate answer [may] be with respect to pretrial suppression hearings in criminal cases, the First and Fourteenth Amendments clearly give the press and the public a right of access to trials themselves, civil as well as criminal.[2] * * *

In conspicuous contrast to a military base, *Greer v. Spock*; a jail, *Adderley v. Florida* [p. 648 infra]; or a prison, *Pell,* a trial courtroom is a public place. Even more than city streets, sidewalks, and parks as areas of traditional First Amendment activity, a trial courtroom is a place where representatives of the press and of the public are not only free to be, but where their presence serves to assure the integrity of what goes on.

But this does not mean that the First Amendment right of members of the public and representatives of the press to attend civil and criminal trials is absolute. Just as a legislature may impose reasonable time, place and manner restrictions upon the exercise of First Amendment freedoms, so may a trial judge impose reasonable limitations upon the unrestricted occupation of a courtroom by representatives of the press and members of the public. Moreover, [there] may be occasions when not all who wish to attend a trial may do so.[3] And while there exist many alternative ways to satisfy the constitutional demands of a fair trial, those demands may also sometimes justify limitations upon the unrestricted presence of spectators in the courtroom.[5]

Since in the present case the trial judge appears to have given no recognition to the right [of] the press and [the] public to be present at [the] murder trial over which he was presiding, the judgment under review must be reversed.

* * *

MR. JUSTICE WHITE, concurring.

This case would have been unnecessary had *Gannett* construed the Sixth Amendment to forbid excluding the public from criminal proceedings except in narrowly defined circumstances. But the Court there rejected the submission of four of us to this effect, thus requiring that the First Amendment issue involved here be addressed. On this issue, I concur in the opinion of the Chief Justice.

---

this opinion intimate that judges are restricted in their ability to conduct conferences in chambers, inasmuch as such conferences are distinct from trial proceedings.

24. For example, national security concerns about confidentiality may sometimes warrant closures during sensitive portions of trial proceedings, such as testimony about state secrets.

25. Significantly, closing a trial lacks even the justification for barring the door to pretrial hearings: the necessity of preventing dissemination of suppressible prejudicial evidence to the public before the jury pool has become, in a practical sense, finite and subject to sequestration.

2. [The] right to speak implies a freedom to listen, *Kleindienst v. Mandel.* The right to

publish implies a freedom to gather information, *Branzburg.* See concurring opinion of Justice Brennan, supra.

3. In such situations, representatives of the press must be assured access, *Houchins* (concurring opinion).

5. This is not to say that only constitutional considerations can justify such restrictions. The preservation of trade secrets, for example, might justify the exclusion of the public from at least some segments of a civil trial. And the sensibilities of a youthful prosecution witness, for example, might justify similar exclusion in a criminal trial for rape, so long as the defendant's Sixth Amendment right to a public trial were not impaired.

Mr. Justice Blackmun, concurring in the judgment.

My opinion and vote in partial dissent [in] *Gannett* compels my vote to reverse the judgment. [It] is gratifying [to] see the Court now looking to and relying upon legal history in determining the fundamental public character of the criminal trial. * * *

The Court's ultimate ruling in *Gannett,* with such clarification as is provided by the opinions in this case today, apparently is now to the effect that there is no *Sixth* Amendment right on the part of the public—or the press—to an open hearing on a motion to suppress. I, of course, continue to believe that *Gannett* was in error, both in its interpretation of the Sixth Amendment generally, and in its application to the suppression hearing, for I remain convinced that the right to a public trial is to be found where the Constitution explicitly placed it— in the Sixth Amendment.

[But] with the Sixth Amendment set to one side in this case, I am driven to conclude, as a secondary position, that the First Amendment must provide some measure of protection for public access to the trial. The opinion in partial dissent in *Gannett* explained that the public has an intense need and a deserved right to know about the administration of justice in general; about the prosecution of local crimes in particular; about the conduct of the judge, the prosecutor, defense counsel, police officers, other public servants, and all the actors in the judicial arena; and about the trial itself. It is clear and obvious to me, on the approach the Court has chosen to take, that, by closing this criminal trial, the trial judge abridged these First Amendment interests of the public. * * *

Mr. Justice Stevens, concurring.

This is a watershed case. Until today the Court has accorded virtually absolute protection to the dissemination of information or ideas, but never before has it squarely held that the acquisition of newsworthy matter is entitled to any constitutional protection whatsoever. An additional word of emphasis is therefore appropriate.

Twice before, the Court has implied that any governmental restriction on access to information, no matter how severe and no matter how unjustified, would be constitutionally acceptable so long as it did not single out the press for special disabilities not applicable to the public at large. In a dissent joined by [Brennan and Marshall, JJ.] in *Saxbe,* Justice Powell unequivocally rejected [that conclusion.] And in *Houchins,* I explained at length why [Brennan, Powell, JJ.] and I were convinced that "[a]n official prison policy of concealing * * * knowledge from the public by arbitrarily cutting off the flow of information at its source abridges [first amendment freedoms]." Since [Marshall and Blackmun, JJ.] were unable to participate in that case, a majority of the Court neither accepted nor rejected that conclusion or the contrary conclusion expressed in the prevailing opinions. Today, however, for the first time, the Court unequivocally holds that an arbitrary interference with access to important information is an abridgment of the freedoms of speech and of the press protected by the First Amendment.

It is somewhat ironic that the Court should find more reason to recognize a right of access today than it did in *Houchins.* For *Houchins* involved the plight of a segment of society least able to protect itself, an attack on a longstanding policy of concealment, and an absence of any legitimate justification for abridging public access to information about how government operates. In this case we are protecting the interests of the most powerful voices in the community, we are concerned with an almost unique exception to an established tradition of openness in the conduct of criminal trials, and it is likely that the closure order was motivated by the judge's desire to protect the individual defendant from the burden of a fourth criminal trial.[2]

In any event, for the reasons stated [in] my *Houchins* opinion, as well as those stated by the Chief Justice today, I agree that the First Amendment protects the public and the press from abridgment of their rights of access to information about the operation of their government, including the Judicial Branch; given the total absence of any record justification for the closure order entered in this case, that order violated the First Amendment * * *.

MR. JUSTICE REHNQUIST, dissenting.

[For] the reasons stated in my separate concurrence in *Gannett*, I do not believe that [anything in the Constitution] require[s] that a State's reasons for denying public access to a trial, where both [the prosecution and defense] have consented to [a court-approved closure order], are subject to any additional constitutional review at our hands.

[The] issue here is not whether the "right" to freedom of the press * * * overrides the defendant's "right" to a fair trial, [but] whether any provision in the Constitution may fairly be read to prohibit what the [trial court] did in this case. Being unable to find any such prohibition in the First, Sixth, Ninth, or any other Amendments to [the] Constitution, or in the Constitution itself, I dissent.

Notes and Questions

1. *Beyond the justice system.* May (should) "public access to information about how government operates" (to use Stevens, J.'s phrase) be denied, as the Chief Justice suggests, simply on the ground that the place at issue has not been *traditionally* open to the public (recall how the Chief Justice distinguishes penal institutions from criminal trials) or should the government also have to advance, as Stevens, J., suggests, "legitimate justification" for "abridging" public access? Compare the controversy over whether "the right to a public forum" should turn on whether the place at issue has *historically* been dedicated to the exercise of first amendment rights or on whether the manner of expression is *basically incompatible* with the normal activity of the place at a particular time. See generally the materials on "Off Limits" Public Property, Sec. 5, II infra. See also Note, *The First Amendment Right to Gather State-Held Information*, 89 Yale L.J. 923, 933–39 (1979). Consider, too, Blasi, *The Checking Value in First Amendment Theory*, 1977 Am.B.Found.Res.J. 521, 609–10:

"[S]ince, under the checking value [the value that first amendment freedoms can serve in checking the abuse of power by public officials], the dissemination of information about the behavior of government officials is the paradigm First Amendment activity, policies and practices that reduce the amount and quality of information disseminated to the public should not be upheld simply because they serve the convenience, or embody traditional prerogatives, of the government. At a minimum, restrictions on press coverage of official activities should be upheld only if it can be shown that the restrictions substantially promote an

2. Neither that likely motivation nor facts showing the risk that a fifth trial would have been necessary without closure of the fourth are disclosed in this record, however. The absence of any articulated reason for the closure order is a sufficient basis for distinguishing this case from *Gannett*. The decision to-day is in no way inconsistent with the perfectly unambiguous holding in *Gannett* that the rights guaranteed by the Sixth Amendment are rights that may be asserted by the accused rather than members of the general public. * * *

important governmental objective that cannot be promoted sufficiently by alternative policies having a less restrictive impact on what interested outsiders can learn about official conduct. For example, under this standard all journalists could not be excluded from a police inspection of the scene of a recent crime if a single pool reporter and/or photographer could be admitted without disrupting the investigation.

"Second, under the checking value, the interest of the press (and ultimately the public) in learning certain information relevant to the abuse of official power would sometimes take precedence over perfectly legitimate and substantial government interests such as efficiency and confidentiality. Thus, the First Amendment may require that journalists have access as a general matter to some records, such as certain financial documents, which anyone investigating common abuses of the public trust would routinely want to inspect, even though the granting of such access would undoubtedly entail some costs and risks. Also, the balance might be tilted even more in the direction of access if a journalist could demonstrate that there are reasonable grounds to believe that certain records contain evidence of misconduct by public officials."

But cf. Kamisar, *Right of Access to Information Generated or Controlled by the Government: Richmond Newspapers Examined and Gannett Revisited* in Choper, Kamisar & Tribe, The Supreme Court: Trends and Developments, 1979–80 145, 166 (1981): "I am sure I am not alone when I say that these law review commentaries go quite far. But *someday* the views they advance may be the law of the land. In the meantime, however, many more battles will have to be fought. *Someday* we may look back on *Richmond Newspapers* as the '*Powell v. Alabama*' of the right of access to government-controlled information—but it was a long, hard road from *Powell* to *Gideon*." [e]

2. *Within the justice system.* How far does (should) *Richmond Newspapers* extend within the justice system? To criminal pre-trial proceedings? How is a trial defined? Should it extend to conferences in chambers or at the bench? To grand jury hearings? To civil trials? To depositions? To records of any or all of the above? Should it apply outside judicial proceedings? Should wardens be permitted to completely preclude access by the public and press to prisons? To executions? What if the prisoner wants to close the execution? For wide-ranging discussion of these and related questions, see Choper, Kamisar, and Tribe, note 1 supra, at 145–206 (Professor Tribe was winning counsel in *Richmond Newspapers*). See also Fenner & Koley, *Access to Judicial Proceedings: To Richmond Newspapers and Beyond,* 16 Harv.Civ.Rts-Civ.Lib.L.Rev. 415 (1981).

3. *Closing trials.* After *Richmond Newspapers,* what showing should suffice to justify closure of a criminal trial? See *Globe Newspaper Co. v. Superior Court,* 457 U.S. 596, 102 S.Ct. 2613, 73 L.Ed.2d 248 (1982) (routine exclusion of press and public during testimony of minor victim of sex offense unconstitutional); *Press-Enterprise Co. v. Superior Court,* 464 U.S. 501, 104 S.Ct. 819, 78 L.Ed.2d 629 (1984) (extending *Richmond Newspapers* to voir dire examination of jurors). To overcome either the first amendment or the sixth amendment right to a public trial, the Court has required that the party seeking to close the proceedings "must advance an overriding interest that is likely to be prejudiced, the

---

e. For endorsements of generous access, see Haiman, *Speech and Law in a Free Society* 108–14, 368–97 (1981); Yudof, *When Government Speaks* 246–55 (1983); Emerson, *Legal Foundations of the Right to Know,* 1976 Wash. U.L.Q. 1, 14–17; Lewis, *A Public Right to Know about Public Institutions: The First Amendment as Sword,* 1980 Sup.Ct.Rev. 1. But see BeVier, *An Informed Public, an Informing Press: The Search for a Constitutional Principle,* 68 Calif.L.Rev. 482 (1980).

closure must be no broader than necessary to protect that interest, the trial court must consider reasonable alternatives to closing the proceeding, and it must make findings adequate to support the closure." *Waller v. Georgia,* 467 U.S. 39, 104 S.Ct. 2210, 81 L.Ed.2d 31 (1984).

4. *Special access rights for the press.* Is a press section in public trials required when the seating capacity would be exhausted by the public? Is a press section permitted? What limits attach to government determinations of who shall get press passes? See, e.g., *Sherrill v. Knight,* 569 F.2d 124 (D.C.Cir.1977) (denial of White House press pass infringes upon first amendment guarantees in the absence of adequate process); *Borreca v. Fasi,* 369 F.Supp. 906 (D.Haw.1974) (preliminary injunction against denial of access of a reporter to Mayor's press conferences justified when basis for exclusion is allegedly "inaccurate" and "irresponsible" reporting); *Los Angeles Free Press, Inc. v. Los Angeles,* 9 Cal.App. 3d 448, 88 Cal.Rptr. 605 (1970) (exclusion of weekly newspaper from scenes of disaster and police press conferences upheld when newspaper did not report policy and fire events "with some regularity"). When access is required, may the press be prevented from taking notes? Is the right to bring tape recorders into public trials protected under *Richmond Newspapers?* What about "unobtrusive" television cameras? Consider Ares, *Chandler v. Florida: Television, Criminal Trials, and Due Process,* 1981 Sup.Ct.Rev. 157, 174: "Television in the courtroom expands public access to public institutions both qualitatively, because of its immediacy, and quantitatively, because of its reach. It is reported that a majority of Americans acquire their news primarily from television rather than from newspapers. To exclude the most important source of information about the working of courts without some compelling reason cannot be squared with the First Amendment." Cf. *Chandler v. Florida,* 449 U.S. 560, 101 S.Ct. 802, 66 L.Ed.2d 740 (1981) (subject to certain safeguards a state may *permit* electronic media and still photography coverage of public criminal proceedings over the objection of the accused).

Does *Chandler's* holding demean the interest in fair trials? Consider Griswold, *The Standards of the Legal Profession: Canon 35 Should Not Be Surrendered,* 48 A.B.A.J. 615, 617 (1962): "The presence of cameras and television [has] an inhibiting effect on some people, and an exhilarating effect on others. In either event, there would be distortion, and an inevitable interference with the administration of justice. With all the improved techniques in the world, the introduction of radio and television to the courtroom will surely and naturally convert it into a stage for those who can act, and into a place of additional burden for those who cannot." Do these objections apply with the same force to appellate proceedings?[f] Consider Kamisar, *Chandler v. Florida: What Can Be Said for a "Right of Access" to Televise Judicial Proceedings?* in Choper, Kamisar, & Tribe, The Supreme Court: Trends and Developments 1980–81, at 149, 168 (1982): "At the present time, no federal court allows TV coverage. *The place to begin* may well be the place that is likely to be the last holdout—the United States Supreme Court."

SECTION 4. UNCONVENTIONAL FORMS OF COMMUNICATION

Special first amendment questions are often said to arise by regulation of the time, place, and manner of speech as opposed to regulation of its content. But the two types of regulation are not mutually exclusive. It is possible to

---

f. See Ares, supra, at 189–90.

regulate time, place, manner, and content in the same regulation. For example, in *Linmark,* p. 562 supra, the township outlawed signs (but not leaflets) advertising a house for sale (but not other advertisements or other messages) on front lawns (but not other places).

Further, the terms, manner and content are strongly contested concepts. Indeed, an issue recurring in this section is whether the regulations in question are of manner or content. To the extent this section is about manner regulation, it is not exhaustive—much comes later. This section is confined to unconventional forms of expression. Speakers claim protection for burning draft cards, wearing armbands, mutilating flags, nude dancing, wearing long hair. Fact patterns such as these fix renewed attention on the question of how "speech" should be defined. It may be a nice question as to whether obscenity is not speech within the first amendment lexicon, whether it is such speech but has been balanced into an unprotected state, or whether it is not *freedom* of speech or *the* freedom of speech.[a] But assassinating a public figure, even to send a message, raises no first amendment problem. Robbing a bank does not raise a free speech issue. What does? How do we decide?

The fact patterns in this section also invite scrutiny of other issues that appear in succeeding sections. Should it make a difference if the state's interest in regulating speech is unrelated to what is being said? Suppose the state's concern arises from the non-communicative impact of the speech act—from its manner. Should that distinction make a constitutional difference, and, if so, how much? These questions become more complicated because in context it is often difficult to determine what the state interest is and sometimes difficult to determine whether there is a meaningful distinction between what is said and how it is said.

Finally, in this and succeeding sections the question arises of the extent to which freedom of speech should require special sensitivity to the methods and communications needs of the less powerful.

UNITED STATES v. O'BRIEN

391 U.S. 367, 88 S.Ct. 1673, 20 L.Ed.2d 672 (1968).

MR. CHIEF JUSTICE WARREN delivered the opinion of the Court.

On the morning of March 31, 1966, David Paul O'Brien and three companions burned their Selective Service registration certificates on the steps of the South Boston Courthouse. A sizable crowd, including several [FBI agents] witnessed the event. Immediately after the burning, members of the crowd began attacking O'Brien [and he was ushered to safety by an FBI agent.] O'Brien stated to FBI agents that he had burned his registration certificate because of his beliefs, knowing that he was violating federal law.

[For this act, O'Brien was convicted in federal court.] He [told] the jury that he burned the certificate publicly to influence others to adopt his antiwar beliefs, as he put it, "so that other people would reevaluate their positions with Selective Service, with the armed forces, and reevaluate their place in the culture of today, to hopefully consider my position."

The indictment upon which he was tried charged that he "wilfully and knowingly did mutilate, destroy, and change by burning [his] Registration Certificate; in violation of [§ 462(b)(3) of the Universal Military Training and Service Act of 1948], amended by Congress in 1965 (adding the words italicized

a. See fn. b in *Roth,* p. 489 supra.

below), so that at the time O'Brien burned his certificate an offense was committed by any person, "who forges, alters, *knowingly destroys, knowingly mutilates,* or in any manner changes any such certificate ∗ ∗ ∗." (Italics supplied.)

[On appeal, the] First Circuit held the 1965 Amendment unconstitutional as a law abridging freedom of speech. At the time the Amendment was enacted, a regulation of the Selective Service System required registrants to keep their registration certificates in their "personal possession at all times." Wilful violations of regulations promulgated pursuant to the Universal Military Training and Service Act were made criminal by statute. The Court of Appeals, therefore, was of the opinion that conduct punishable under the 1965 Amendment was already punishable under the nonpossession regulation, and consequently that the Amendment served no valid purpose; further, that in light of the prior regulation, the Amendment must have been "directed at public as distinguished from private destruction." On this basis, the Court concluded that the 1965 Amendment ran afoul of the First Amendment by singling out persons engaged in protests for special treatment. ∗ ∗ ∗

When a male reaches the age of 18, he is required by the Universal Military Training and Service Act to register with a local draft board. He is assigned a Selective Service number, and within five days he is issued a registration certificate. Subsequently, and based on a questionnaire completed by the registrant, he is assigned a classification denoting his eligibility for induction, and "[a]s soon as practicable" thereafter he is issued a Notice of Classification.
∗ ∗ ∗

Both the registration and classification certificates bear notices that the registrant must notify his local board in writing of every change in address, physical condition, and occupational, marital, family, dependency, and military status, and of any other fact which might change his classification. Both also contain a notice that the registrant's Selective Service number should appear on all communications to his local board.

[The 1965] Amendment does not distinguish between public and private destruction, and it does not punish only destruction engaged in for the purpose of expressing views.[a] A law prohibiting destruction of Selective Service certificates no more abridges free speech on its face than a motor vehicle law prohibiting the destruction of drivers' licenses, or a tax law prohibiting the destruction of books and records.

O'Brien nonetheless argues [first] that the 1965 Amendment is unconstitutional [as] applied to him because his act of burning his registration certificate was protected "symbolic speech" within the First Amendment. [He claims that] the First Amendment guarantees include all modes of "communication of ideas by conduct," and that his conduct is within this definition because he did it in "demonstration against the war and against the draft."

We cannot accept the view that an apparently limitless variety of conduct can be labelled "speech" whenever the person engaging in the conduct intends thereby to express an idea. However, even on the assumption that the alleged communicative element in O'Brien's conduct is sufficient to bring into play the First Amendment, it does not necessarily follow that the destruction of a

---

a. But compare Chief Judge Aldrich below, 376 F.2d at 541: "We would be closing our eyes in the light of the prior law if we did not see on the face of the amendment that it was precisely directed at public as distinguished from private destruction. [In] singling out persons engaging in protest for special treatment the amendment strikes at the very core of what the First Amendment protects."

registration certificate is constitutionally protected activity. This Court has held that when "speech" and "nonspeech" elements are combined in the same course of conduct, a sufficiently important governmental interest in regulating the nonspeech element can justify incidental limitations on First Amendment freedoms. To characterize the quality of the governmental interest which must appear, the Court has employed a variety of descriptive terms: compelling; substantial; subordinating; paramount; cogent; strong. [W]e think it clear that a government regulation is sufficiently justified if it is within the constitutional power of the government; if it furthers an important or substantial governmental interest; if the governmental interest is unrelated to the suppression of free expression; [b] and if the incidental restriction on alleged First Amendment freedom is no greater than is essential to the furtherance of that interest. We find that the 1965 Amendment meets all of these requirements, and consequently that O'Brien can be constitutionally convicted for violating it. [Pursuant to its power to classify and conscript manpower for military service], Congress may establish a system of registration for individuals liable for training and service, and may require such individuals within reason to cooperate in the registration system. The issuance of certificates indicating the registration and eligibility classification of individuals is a legitimate and substantial administrative aid in the functioning of this system. And legislation to insure the continuing availability of issued certificates serves a legitimate and substantial purpose in the system's administration.

[O'Brien] essentially adopts the position that [Selective Service] certificates are so many pieces of paper designed to notify registrants of their registration or classification, to be retained or tossed in the wastebasket according to the convenience or taste of the registrant. Once the registrant has received notification, according to this view, there is no reason for him to retain the certificates. [However, the registration and classification certificates serve] purposes in addition to initial notification. Many of these purposes would be defeated by the certificates' destruction or mutilation. Among these are [simplifying verification of the registration and classification of suspected delinquents, evidence of availability for induction in the event of emergency, ease of communication between registrants and local boards, continually reminding registrants of the need to notify local boards of changes in status].

The many functions performed by Selective Service certificates establish beyond doubt that Congress has a legitimate and substantial interest in preventing their wanton and unrestrained destruction and assuring their continuing availability by punishing people who knowingly and wilfully destroy or mutilate them. And we are unpersuaded that the pre-existence of the nonpossession regulations in any way negates this interest.

In the absence of a question as to multiple punishment, it has never been suggested that there is anything improper in Congress providing alternative statutory avenues of prosecution to assure the effective protection of one and the same interest. Here, the pre-existing avenue of prosecution was not even statutory. Regulations may be modified or revoked from time to time by

---

b. For the contention that the many tests formulated by the Court are best regarded as prophylactic rules designed to assure that the forbidden purpose of suppressing ideas does not underlie government acts, see Bogen, *Balancing Freedom of Speech*, 38 Md.L.Rev. 387 (1979); Bogen, *The Supreme Court's Interpretation of the Guarantee of Freedom of Speech*, 35 Md.L.Rev. 555 (1976). See generally Bogen, *Bulwark of Liberty: The Court and the First Amendment* (1984).

administrative discretion. Certainly, the Congress may change or supplement a regulation.

[The] gravamen of the offense defined by the statute is the deliberate rendering of certificates unavailable for the various purposes which they may serve. Whether registrants keep their certificates in their personal possession at all times, as required by the regulations, is of no particular concern under the 1965 Amendment, as long as they do not mutilate or destroy the certificates so as to render them unavailable. [The 1965 amendment] is concerned with abuses involving *any* issued Selective Service certificates, not only with the registrant's own certificates. The knowing destruction or mutilation of someone else's certificates would therefore violate the statute but not the nonpossession regulations.

We think it apparent that the continuing availability to each registrant of his Selective Service certificates substantially furthers the smooth and proper functioning of the system that Congress has established to raise armies. * * *

It is equally clear that the 1965 Amendment specifically protects this substantial governmental interest. We perceive no alternative means that would more precisely and narrowly assure the continuing availability of issued Selective Service certificates than a law which prohibits their wilful mutilation or destruction. The 1965 Amendment prohibits such conduct and does nothing more. [The] governmental interest and the scope of the 1965 Amendment are limited to preventing a harm to the smooth and efficient functioning of the Selective Service System. When O'Brien deliberately rendered unavailable his registration certificate, he wilfully frustrated this governmental interest. For this noncommunicative impact of his conduct, and for nothing else, he was convicted.

The case at bar is therefore unlike one where the alleged governmental interest in regulating conduct arises in some measure because the communication allegedly integral to the conduct is itself thought to be harmful [distinguishing *Stromberg*, p. 516 supra].

[B]ecause of the Government's substantial interest in assuring the continuing availability of issued Selective Service certificates, because amended § 462(b) is an appropriately narrow means of protecting this interest and condemns only the independent noncommunicative impact of conduct within its reach, and because the noncommunicative impact of O'Brien's act of burning his registration certificate frustrated the Government's interest, a sufficient governmental interest has been shown to justify O'Brien's conviction.

O'Brien finally argues that the 1965 Amendment is unconstitutional as enacted because what he calls the "purpose" of Congress was "to suppress freedom of speech." We reject this argument because under settled principles the purpose of Congress, as O'Brien uses that term, is not a basis for declaring this legislation unconstitutional.

It is a familiar principle of constitutional law that this Court will not strike down an otherwise constitutional statute on the basis of an alleged illicit legislative motive.[c]

[I]f we were to examine legislative purpose in the instant case, we would be obliged to consider not only [the statements of the three members of Congress who addressed themselves to the amendment, all viewing draft-card burning as a brazen display of unpatriotism] but also the more authoritative reports of the

---

c. See generally Ch. 10, Sec. 2, III.

Senate and House Armed Services Committees. [B]oth reports make clear a concern with the "defiant" destruction of so-called "draft cards" and with "open" encouragement to others to destroy their cards, [but they] also indicate that this concern stemmed from an apprehension that unrestrained destruction of cards would disrupt the smooth functioning of the Selective Service System. * * *

Reversed.[d]

MR. JUSTICE HARLAN concurring. * * *

I wish to make explicit my understanding that [the Court's analysis] does not foreclose consideration of First Amendment claims in those rare instances when an "incidental" restriction upon expression, imposed by a regulation which furthers an "important or substantial" governmental interest and satisfies the Court's other criteria, in practice has the effect of entirely preventing a "speaker" from reaching a significant audience with whom he could not otherwise lawfully communicate. This is not such a case, since O'Brien manifestly could have conveyed his message in many ways other than by burning his draft card.

MR. JUSTICE DOUGLAS, dissenting.

[Douglas, J., thought that "the underlying and basic problem in this case" was the constitutionality of a draft "in the absence of a declaration of war" and that the case should be put down for reargument on this question. The following Term, concurring in *Brandenburg,* p. 455 supra, he criticized *O'Brien* on the merits. After recalling that the Court had rejected O'Brien's first amendment argument on the ground that "legislation to insure the continuing availability of issued certificates serves a legitimate and substantial purpose in the [selective service] system's administration," he commented: "But O'Brien was not prosecuted for not having his draft card available when asked for by a federal agent. He was indicted, tried, and convicted for burning the card. And this Court's affirmance [was not] consistent with the First Amendment." He observed, more generally in *Brandenburg:*

["Action is often a method of expression and within the protection of the First Amendment. Suppose one tears up his own copy of the Constitution in eloquent protest to a decision of this Court. May he be indicted? Suppose one rips his own Bible to shreds to celebrate his departure from one 'faith' and his embrace of atheism. May he be indicted? * * *

["The act of praying often involves body posture and movement as well as utterances. It is nonetheless protected by the Free Exercise Clause. Picketing [is] 'free speech plus.' [Therefore], it can be regulated when it comes to the 'plus' or 'action' side of the protest. It can be regulated as to the number of pickets and the place and hours, because traffic and other community problems would otherwise suffer. But none of these considerations are implicated in the symbolic protest of the Vietnam war in the burning of a draft card."]

Notes and Questions

1. *Expression v. action.* What of the Court's rejection of the idea that conduct is speech "whenever the person engaging in the conduct intends thereby to express an idea." Was it right to question whether O'Brien's conduct was speech? What was it about O'Brien's conduct that made the Court doubt that it was speech? What if O'Brien had burned a copy of the Constitution? Consider Emerson, *The System of Freedom of Expression* 80 & 84 (1970): "To some extent expression and action are always mingled; most conduct includes elements of

---

d. Marshall, J., took no part.

both. Even the clearest manifestations of expression involve some action, as in the case of holding a meeting, publishing a newspaper, or merely talking. At the other extreme, a political assassination includes a substantial mixture of expression. The guiding principle must be to determine which element is predominant in the conduct under consideration. Is expression the major element and the action only secondary? Or is the action the essence and the expression incidental? The answer, to a great extent, must be based on a common-sense reaction, made in light of the functions and operations of a system of freedom of expression. * * *

"The burning of a draft card is, of course, conduct that involves both communication and physical acts. Yet it seems quite clear that the predominant element in such conduct is expression (opposition to the draft) rather than action (destruction of a piece of cardboard). The registrant is not concerned with secret or inadvertent burning of his draft card, involving no communication with other persons. The main feature, for him, is the public nature of the burning, through which he expresses to the community his ideas and feelings about the war and the draft."

Compare Ely, *Flag Desecration: A Case Study in the Roles of Categorization and Balancing in First Amendment Analysis,* 88 Harv.L.Rev. 1482, 1495 (1975): "[B]urning a draft card to express opposition to the draft is an undifferentiated whole, 100% action and 100% expression. It involves no conduct that is not at the same time communication, and no communication that does not result from conduct. Attempts to determine which element 'predominates' will therefore inevitably degenerate into question-begging judgments about whether the activity should be protected.

"The *O'Brien* Court thus quite wisely dropped the 'speech-conduct' distinction as quickly as it had picked it up." [e]

Consider, too, Baker, *Scope of the First Amendment Freedom of Speech,* 25 U.C.L.A.L.Rev. 964, 1010–12 (1978): "[S]ince both verbal and nonverbal conduct advances first amendment values, the purpose of the [expression-action] distinction is unclear. Moreover, only an extremely crabbed reading of other clauses of the first amendment will be consistent with implementing an expression-action dichotomy. If religion plays a significant role in one's life, its *free exercise* normally will require doing or abstaining from certain conduct. And people typically assemble and associate to multiply their power in order to do something. Nevertheless, even if his 'expression-action' dichotomy is not very helpful, Emerson consistently makes very perceptive analyses of concrete situations; and these analyses frequently appear to make a different distinction: whether or not the conduct is, or is intended to be, coercive or physically injurious to another. All Emerson's examples of unprotected conduct, 'action,' involve coercion or injury to or physical interference with another or damage to physical property. * * *

"Expressive political protests sometimes involve acts of physical obstruction like lying down in front of troop trains, blocking traffic in a city, or pouring blood over files. Emerson argues that these must be considered 'action,' [but] [n]either the physical activity nor the motives of the actor distinguish these

---

e. But, as Dean Ely recognizes, the Court picked it up again in *Cohen,* p. 525 supra: "[W]e deal here with a conviction resting solely upon 'speech', cf. *Stromberg,* not upon any separately identifiable conduct which allegedly was intended by Cohen to be perceived by others as expressive of particular views but which, on its face, does not necessarily convey any message and hence arguably could be regulated without effectively repressing Cohen's ability to express himself. Cf. *O'Brien.*"

'action' cases from draft card burning, which Emerson characterizes as expression. Rather, Emerson classifies the first examples of civil disobedience 'action' because the '[c]ivil disobedience attempts to achieve results through a kind of *coercion or pressure * * *.*' However, [draft-card burning], unlike failing to carry a draft card [which presumably 'interferes' or 'obstructs' the working of the selective service system], does not involve coercing or directly injuring or physically obstructing any person or government activity. This fact apparently explains why Emerson concludes that the expression element clearly predominates in draft card burning." [f]

2. *Nature of the state interest and first amendment methodology.* Melville Nimmer, *The Meaning of Symbolic Speech under the First Amendment,* 21 U.C. L.A.L.Rev. 29 (1973), followed by John Hart Ely, note 1 supra, and Laurence Tribe, infra, has proposed that the crucial starting point for first amendment methodology is and should be the nature of the state interest.[g] As Ely puts it, at 1497: "The critical question would therefore seem to be whether the harm that the state is seeking to avert is one that grows out of the fact that the defendant is communicating, and more particularly out of the way people can be expected to react to his message, or rather would arise even if the defendant's conduct had no communicative significance whatever."

For one view of the difference that the distinction makes, see Tribe, *American Constitutional Law* § 12–2, at 582 (1978): "The Supreme Court has evolved two distinct approaches to the resolution of first amendment claims; the two correspond to the two ways in which government may 'abridge' speech. If a government regulation is aimed at the communicative impact of an act, analysis should proceed along what we will call *track one.* On that track, a regulation is unconstitutional unless government shows that the message being suppressed poses a 'clear and present danger,' constitutes a defamatory falsehood, or otherwise falls on the unprotected side of one of the lines the Court has drawn to distinguish those expressive acts privileged by the first amendment from those open to government regulation with only minimal due process scrutiny. If a government regulation is aimed at the noncommunicative impact of an act, its analysis proceeds on what we will call *track two.* On that track, a regulation is constitutional, even as applied to expressive conduct, so long as it does not unduly constrict the flow of information and ideas. On track two, the 'balance' between the values of freedom of expression and the government's regulatory interests is struck on a case-by-case basis, guided by whatever unifying principles may be found in past decisions."

Professor Nimmer, in distinguishing between anti-speech interests (track one) and non-speech interests (track two), would apply definitional balancing (with a presumption in favor of speech) to the former and the *O'Brien* test to the latter. Dean Ely would prevent all regulations on track one except for speech that falls "within a few clearly and narrowly defined catagories." Ely, *Democracy and Distrust* 110 (1980) (emphasis deleted). On track two, Ely insists that balancing is desirable and unavoidable. Ely, note 1 supra, at 1496–1502.

(a) *Normative value of the distinction.* Is balancing unavoidable on either track? How does one decide what the categories should be without balancing? Does the metaphor of balancing wrongly imply that all values are reduced to a

f. For discussion of Professor Baker's approach and refinement of the expression-action dichotomy, see Emerson, *First Amendment Doctrine and the Burger Court,* 68 Calif. L.Rev. 422, 474–80 (1980).

g. The distinction is a major organizing principle in *Nimmer on Freedom of Speech* (1984).

single measure and imply non-existent quantitative capacities? Is the distinction between the tracks important enough to require rules on track one, even if ad hoc procedures are allowable on track two? Would this mean that *Pentagon Papers,* p. 595 supra is wrong in suggesting that meeting a "heavy burden" could in some circumstances justify a prior restraint to protect national security? On the other hand, if the *Pentagon Papers* presumption is a "rule," what isn't?

Is the distinction between the two tracks at least strong enough to justify a rebuttable presumption that regulation on track one is invalid, but regulation on track two is not? Consider a regulation governing express warranties in commercial advertising. Is much of contract law on track one? Consider "a nationwide ban on *all* posters (intended to conserve paper)." Isn't that on track two? Do these examples suggest that too much emphasis is being placed on a single factor? See Farber, *Content Regulation and the First Amendment: A Revisionist View,* 68 Geo.U.L.Rev. 727, 746–47 (1980).[h]

(b) *Application to O'Brien.* Consider Ely, note 1 supra, at 1498–99: "The interests upon which the government relied were interests, having mainly to do with the preservation of selective service records, that would have been equally threatened had O'Brien's destruction of his draft card totally lacked communicative significance—had he, for example, used it to start a campfire for a solitary cookout or dropped it in his garbage disposal for a lark. (The law prohibited all knowing destructions, public or private)."

Compare Nimmer, note 2 supra, at 41—contending that the *O'Brien* statute was "overnarrow": "[An overnarrow statute] may be said to create a conclusive presumption that in fact the state interest which the statute serves is an anti- rather than a non-speech interest. If the state interest asserted in *O'Brien* were truly the non-speech interest of assuring availability of draft cards, why did Congress choose not to prohibit any knowing conduct which leads to unavailability, rather than limiting the scope of the statute to those instances in which the proscribed conduct carries with it a speech component hostile to governmental policy? The obvious inference to be drawn is that in fact the Congress was completely indifferent to the 'availability' objective, and was concerned only with an interest which the *O'Brien* opinion states is impermissible—an interest in the suppression of free expression." [i]

(c) *Descriptive value of the distinction.* Does the distinction between the two tracks fully explain the Court's approach in *O'Brien*? Suppose again that an assassin truthfully claims that his or her killing was intended to and did communicate an idea? The assassin's first amendment claim would not prevail, but would it fail because the *O'Brien* test was not met or because no first amendment problem was implicated at all? Is a speech/conduct distinction a necessary prerequisite to the application of the *O'Brien* test? [j]

How different is the *O'Brien* test from the methods used to make decisions on track one? Is the *O'Brien* test as phrased potentially more speech protective than its application in the principal case would suggest? More speech protective than tests sometimes used on track one?

h. See generally Redish, *The Content Distinction in First Amendment Analysis,* 34 Stan.L.Rev. 113 (1981). See notes after *Chicago Police Dept. v. Mosley,* p. 643 infra.

i. For consideration of whether the Court's considerations of motive or purpose in *O'Brien* is consistent with its treatment of that issue in freedom of religion, regulation of commerce, and equal protection, see Eisenberg, *Disproportionate Impact and Illicit Motive: Theories of Constitutional Adjudication,* 52 N.Y.U.L.Rev. 36 (1977).

j. For commentary on the difficulties in defining speech, see Alexander & Horton, *The Impossibility of a Free Speech Principle,* 78 Nw.U.L.Rev. 1319 (1984).

3. *Scope of O'Brien.* Is the *O'Brien* test confined to unconventional forms of communication? Would a distinction of this type be defensible? See Ely, note 1 supra, at 1489: "The distinction is its own objection." See also Alfange, *Free Speech and Symbolic Conduct: The Draft-Card Burning Case,* 1968 Sup.Ct.Rev. 1, 23–24; Velvel, *Freedom of Speech and the Draft Card Burning Cases,* 16 U.Kan. L.Rev. 149, 153 (1968); Henkin, *On Drawing Lines,* 82 Harv.L.Rev. 63, 79 (1968).

TINKER v. DES MOINES SCHOOL DISTRICT

393 U.S. 503, 89 S.Ct. 733, 21 L.Ed.2d 731 (1969).

MR. JUSTICE FORTAS delivered the opinion of the Court.

[Petitioners, two high school students and one junior high student, wore black armbands to school to publicize their objections to the Vietnam conflict and their advocacy of a truce. They refused to remove the armbands when asked to do so. In accordance with a ban on armbands which the city's school principals had adopted two days before in anticipation of such a protest, petitioners were sent home and suspended from school until they would return without the armbands. They sought a federal injunction restraining school officials from disciplining them, but the lower federal courts upheld the constitutionality of the school authorities' action on the ground that it was reasonable in order to prevent a disturbance which might result from the wearing of the armbands.]

[T]he wearing of armbands in the circumstances of this case was entirely divorced from actually or potentially disruptive conduct by those participating in it. It was closely akin to "pure speech" which, we have repeatedly held, is entitled to comprehensive protection under the First Amendment. * * *

First Amendment rights, applied in light of the special characteristics of the school environment, are available to teachers and students. It can hardly be argued that either students or teachers shed their constitutional rights to freedom of speech or expression at the schoolhouse gate. This has been the unmistakable holding of this Court for almost 50 years. In *Meyer v. Nebraska* [1923] [discussed in *Griswold v. Connecticut,* p. 312 supra], this Court [held that fourteenth amendment due process] prevents States from forbidding the teaching of a foreign language to young students. Statutes to this effect, the Court held, unconstitutionally interfere with the liberty of teacher, student, and parent. * * *

The problem presented by the present case does not relate to regulation of the length of skirts or the type of clothing, to hair style or deportment. [It] does not concern aggressive, disruptive action or even group demonstrations. Our problem involves direct, primary First Amendment rights akin to "pure speech."

The school officials banned and sought to punish petitioners for a silent, passive, expression of opinion, unaccompanied by any disorder or disturbance on the part of petitioners. There is here no evidence whatever of petitioners' interference, actual or nascent, with the school's work or of collision with the rights of other students to be secure and to be let alone. Accordingly, this case does not concern speech or action that intrudes upon the work of the school or the rights of other students.

Only a few of the 18,000 students in the school system wore the black armbands. Only five students were suspended for wearing them. There is no indication that the work of the school or any class was disrupted. Outside the classrooms, a few students made hostile remarks to the children wearing armbands, but there were no threats or acts of violence on school premises.

[I]n our system, undifferentiated fear or apprehension of disturbance [the District Court's basis for sustaining the school authorities' action] is not enough to overcome the right to freedom of expression. Any departure from absolute regimentation may cause trouble. Any variation from the majority's opinion may inspire fear. Any words spoken, in class, in the lunchroom or on the campus, that deviates from the views of another person, may start an argument or cause a disturbance. But our Constitution says we must take this risk [and] our history says that it is this sort of hazardous freedom—this kind of openness—that is the basis of our national strength and of the independence and vigor of Americans who grow up and live in this relatively permissive, often disputatious society.

In order for the State in the person of school officials to justify prohibition of a particular expression of opinion, it must be able to show that its action was caused by something more than a mere desire to avoid the discomfort and unpleasantness that always accompany an unpopular viewpoint. Certainly where there is no finding and no showing that the exercise of the forbidden right would "materially and substantially interfere with the requirements of appropriate discipline in the operation of the school," the prohibition cannot be sustained. *Burnside v. Byars.*[a]

In the present case, the District Court made no such finding, and our independent examination of the record fails to yield evidence that the school authorities had reason to anticipate that the wearing of the armbands would substantially interfere with the work of the school or impinge upon the rights of other students. Even an official memorandum prepared after the suspension that listed the reasons for the ban on wearing the armbands made no reference to the anticipation of such disruption.[3]

On the contrary, the action of the school authorities appears to have been based upon an urgent wish to avoid the controversy which might result from the expression, even by the silent symbol of armbands, of opposition to this Nation's part in the conflagration in Vietnam. * * *

---

a. In *Burnside,* 363 F.2d 744 (1966), the Fifth Circuit ordered that high school authorities be enjoined from enforcing a regulation forbidding students to wear "freedom buttons." The Supreme Court deemed it "instructive" [fn. 1] that "in *Blackwell v. Issaquena County Board of Education,* 363 F.2d 749 (1966), the same panel on the same day reached the opposite result on different facts. It declined to enjoin enforcement of such a regulation in another high school where the students wearing freedom buttons harassed students who did not wear them and created much disturbance."

Query: why, in *Issaquena,* didn't the school authorities discipline the small number of button-wearers creating the disturbance rather than strike at the idea of wearing the buttons itself? See *Ferrell v. Dallas Ind. School Dist.,* 392 F.2d 697, 705 & n. 1 (5th Cir.1968) (Tuttle, J., dissenting); Wright, *The Constitution on the Campus,* 22 Vand.L.Rev. 1027, 1054 (1969).

3. The only suggestions of fear of disorder in the report are these: "A former student of one of our high schools was killed in Viet Nam. Some of his friends are still in school and it was felt that if any kind of a demonstration existed, it might evolve into something which would be difficult to control.

"Students at one of the high schools were heard to say they would wear arm bands of other colors if the black bands prevailed."

Moreover, the testimony of school authorities at trial indicates that it was not fear of disruption that motivated the regulation prohibiting the armbands; the regulation was directed against "the principle of the demonstration" itself. School authorities simply felt that "the schools are no place for demonstrations," and if the students "didn't like the way our elected officials were handling things, it should be handled with the ballot box and not in the halls of our public schools."

It is also relevant that the school authorities did not purport to prohibit the wearing of all symbols of political or controversial significance. The record shows that students in some of the schools wore buttons relating to national political campaigns, and some even wore the Iron Cross, traditionally a symbol of nazism. The order prohibiting the wearing of armbands did not extend to these. Instead, a particular symbol—black armbands worn to exhibit opposition to this Nation's involvement in Vietnam—was singled out for prohibition. Clearly, the prohibition of expression of one particular opinion, at least without evidence that it is necessary to avoid material and substantial interference with school work or discipline, is not constitutionally permissible.[b]

In our system, state-operated schools may not be enclaves of totalitarianism. School officials do not possess absolute authority over their students. Students in school as well as out of school are "persons" under our Constitution. They are possessed of fundamental rights which the State must respect, just as they themselves must respect their obligations to the State. In our system, students may not be regarded as closed-circuit recipients of only that which the State chooses to communicate. They may not be confined to the expression of those sentiments that are officially approved. In the absence of a specific showing of constitutionally valid reasons to regulate their speech, students are entitled to freedom of expression of their views.

[The principle of prior cases underscoring the importance of diversity and exchange of ideas in the schools,] is not confined to the supervised and ordained discussion which takes place in the classroom. The principal use to which the schools are dedicated is to accommodate students during prescribed hours for the purpose of certain types of activities. Among those activities is personal inter-communication among the students.[6] This is not only an inevitable part of the process of attending school. It is also an important part of the educational process.

A student's rights therefore, do not embrace merely the classroom hours. When he is in the cafeteria, or on the playing field, or on the campus during the authorized hours, he may express his opinions, even on controversial subjects like the conflict in Vietnam, if he does so "[without] materially and substantially interfering [with] appropriate discipline in the operation of the school" and without colliding with the rights of others. *Burnside.* But conduct by the

b. Cf. *Guzick v. Drebus*, 305 F.Supp. 473 (N.D.Ohio 1969), upholding "a long-standing and consistently-applied rule prohibiting the wearing of buttons and other insignia on school grounds during school hours unless these are related to a school-sponsored activity" as "reasonably related to the prevention of the distractions and disruptive and violent conduct" at a racially tense high school; although the button in the instant case did not convey an inflammatory message, the blanket prohibition avoids a situation "in which inflammatory and often insulting buttons would be worn"; a policy permitting certain buttons and excluding others would be "unworkable" in the context of the particular school and "would very likely lead to disruption itself"; a selective policy could not "practically be enforced, for it would require the school authorities to patrol the halls and classes in search of offending buttons"; moreover, such a policy would "necessarily involve the school adminis-tration in the controversies" at the school, destroy its "image of complete neutrality," "undermine the structure of discipline" and "materially and substantially affect the educational process"; and any attempt to enforce such a selective policy "would likely entangle the school authorities in the First Amendment prohibition against prior restraints on free speech."

6. In *Hammond v. South Carolina State College*, 272 F.Supp. 947 (D.C.D.S.C.1967). District Judge Hemphill had before him a case involving a meeting on campus of 300 students to express their views on school practices. He pointed out that a school is not like a hospital or a jail enclosure. It is a public place and its dedication to specific uses does not imply that the constitutional rights of persons entitled to be there are to be gauged as if the premises were purely private property.

student, in class or out of it, which for any reason—whether it stems from time, place, or type of behavior—materially disrupts classwork or involves substantial disorder or invasion of the rights of others is, of course, not immunized by the [first amendment].

We properly read [the first amendment] to permit reasonable regulation of speech-connected activities in carefully restricted circumstances. But we do not confine the permissible exercise of First Amendment rights to a telephone booth or the four corners of a pamphlet, or to supervised and ordained discussion in a school classroom.[c] * * *

Reversed and remanded.

MR. JUSTICE STEWART, concurring.

Although I agree with much of what is said in the Court's opinion, and with its judgment in this case, I cannot share the Court's uncritical assumption that, school discipline aside, the First Amendment rights of children are co-extensive with those of adults. Indeed, I had thought the Court decided otherwise just last Term in *Ginsberg v. New York* [p. 499 supra.] I continue to hold the view I expressed in that case: "[A] State may permissibly determine that, at least in some precisely delineated areas, a child—like someone in a captive audience—is not possessed of that full capacity for individual choice which is the presupposition of First Amendment guarantees." (concurring opinion).

MR. JUSTICE WHITE, concurring.

While I join the Court's opinion, I deem it appropriate to note, first, that the Court continues to recognize a distinction between communicating by words and communicating by acts or conduct which sufficiently impinge on some valid state interest; and, second, that I do not subscribe to everything the Court of Appeals said about free speech in its opinion in *Burnside,* a case relied upon by the Court in the matter now before us.

MR. JUSTICE BLACK, dissenting. * * *

Assuming that the Court is correct in holding that the conduct of wearing armbands for the purpose of conveying political ideas is protected by the First Amendment [the] crucial remaining questions are whether students and teachers may use the schools at their whim as a platform for the exercise of free speech— "symbolic" or "pure"—and whether the Courts will allocate to themselves the function of deciding how the pupils' school day will be spent. * * *

While the record does not show that any of these armband students shouted, used profane language, or were violent in any manner, detailed testimony by some of them shows their armbands caused comments, warnings by other students, the poking of fun at them, and a warning by an older football player that other, nonprotesting students had better let them alone. There is also evidence that the professor of mathematics had his lesson period practically "wrecked" chiefly by disputes with Beth Tinker, who wore her armband for her "demonstration." Even a casual reading of the record shows that this armband did divert students' minds from their regular lessons, and that talk, comments, etc., made John Tinker "self-conscious" in attending school with his armband. While the absence of obscene or boisterous and loud disorder perhaps justifies the Court's statement that the few armband students did not actually "disrupt" the classwork, I think the record overwhelmingly shows that the armbands did exactly what the elected school officials and principals foresaw it would, that is,

c. See also Yudof, *When Governments Speak: Toward a Theory of Government Ex-* *pression and the First Amendment,* 57 Tex.L. Rev. 863, 884–85 (1979).

took the students' minds off their classwork and diverted them to thoughts about the highly emotional subject of the Vietnam war.

[E]ven if the record were silent as to protests against the Vietnam war distracting students from their assigned class work, members of this Court, like all other citizens, know, without being told, that the disputes over the wisdom of the Vietnam war have disrupted and divided this country as few other issues ever have.   Of course students, like other people, cannot concentrate on lesser issues when black armbands are being ostentatiously displayed in their presence to call attention to the wounded and dead of the war, some of the wounded and the dead being their friends and neighbors.   It was, of course, to distract the attention of other students that some students insisted up to the very point of their own suspension from school that they were determined to sit in school with their symbolic armbands.   *   *   *

MR. JUSTICE HARLAN, dissenting.

I certainly agree that state public school authorities in the discharge of their responsibilities are not wholly exempt from the requirements of the Fourteenth Amendment respecting the freedoms of expression and association.   At the same time I am reluctant to believe that there is any disagreement between the majority and myself on the proposition that school officials should be accorded the widest authority in maintaining discipline and good order in their institutions.   To translate that proposition into a workable constitutional rule, I would, in cases like this, cast upon those complaining the burden of showing that a particular school measure was motivated by other than legitimate school concerns—for example, a desire to prohibit the expression of an unpopular point of view, while permitting expression of the dominant opinion.

Finding nothing in this record which impugns the good faith of respondents in promulgating the arm band regulation, I would affirm the judgment below.

Notes and Questions

1.   By equating the wearing of armbands with "pure speech," did the Court avoid the difficult problem of establishing criteria for determining which varieties of symbolic conduct should be viewed as "speech"?   See Denno, *Mary Beth Tinker Takes the Constitution to School,* 38 Ford.L.Rev. 35, 43–44 (1968).   Which of the following are "pure speech"?   Which are not speech, pure or otherwise?   Which should trigger the *O'Brien* test?

(a) *Hair.* See *Freeman v. Flake,* 448 F.2d 258, 260 (10th Cir.1971) (long hair not protected under *Tinker:* "The wearing of long hair is not akin to pure speech.   At the most it is symbolic speech indicative of expressions of individuality rather than a contribution to the storehouse of ideas.")

New Rider v. Board of Educ., 414 U.S. 1097, 94 S.Ct. 733, 38 L.Ed.2d 556 (1974), declined to review a tenth circuit decision upholding the indefinite suspension from school of male Pawnee Indians who sought to wear their hair in long braids in violation of an Oklahoma school hair-length regulation forbidding hair reaching the shirt collar or ears.   Douglas, J., joined by Marshall, J., dissented from the denial of certiorari: "Petitioners [were] attempting to broadcast a clear and specific message to their fellow students and others—their pride in being Indian.   This [should] clearly bring this case within the ambit of *Tinker.* [School officials opined] that allowing petitioners to wear their hair in an Indian manner while restricting the hair length of white students would somehow be 'disruptive' in that an 'integrated school system cannot countenance *different groups* and remain *one* organization.'   But as we noted in *Tinker,* this Court long ago recognized that our constitutional system repudiates the idea that a State may conduct its schools 'to foster a homogeneous people.' "

Should hair grown in a particular manner in order to convey a given political or cultural "message" be distinguished from other hair styles? Is the wearing of any given hair style done, at least in part (although perhaps not always consciously) for its "meaning effect"? Compare Note, 84 Harv.L.Rev. 1702, 1707–10 (1971) with Nimmer, note 2 supra, 59–60.

Should school authorities be able to ban an "Afro" or Indian braid, or even "long hair," without a showing that such hair styles are likely to cause substantial disruption of, or material interference with, school activities? Would a non-speech interest such as cleanliness suffice? Would an across-the-board restriction on "long hair" per se be defectively overbroad? See Nimmer, supra.

Does the question of hair, and dress, and appearance of school children generally, involve a significantly less crucial form of expression than "political protest"? Compare Professor Chafee's criticism of the supposed "public"-"private" speech boundary, Sec. 1, II, B supra. Do these questions raise a first amendment question at all or a "right to privacy" issue? See *Kelley v. Johnson,* p. 370 supra, and accompanying discussion. See also the materials on gender discrimination, Ch. 10, Sec. 3, IV infra.

(b) *Nude dancing.* Should nude dancing be excluded from first amendment protection because it is not intended to communicate ideas? Should protection for paintings depend upon whether "ideas" are expressed? See *Schad v. Mt. Ephraim,* p. 554 supra: "[N]ude dancing is not without its First Amendment protections from official regulation." Are hair styles distinguishable from nude dancing on the ground that the latter is a form of expressive entertainment? If so, should video games be afforded first amendment protection? See Note, *The First Amendment Side Effects of Curing Pac-Man Fever,* 84 Colum.L.Rev. 744 (1984). But see Schauer, *Book Review,* 84 Colum.L.Rev. 558, 565 (1984) ("Maybe there is something I am missing, but the first amendment importance of the messages from an automatic teller to the bank's central computer completely escapes me, as does the first amendment importance of the mutual exchange of electronic and visual symbols between me and the Pac-Man machine.")

(c) *Sleeping in the park. Clark v. Community for Creative Non-Violence,* 468 U.S. 288, 104 S.Ct. 3065, 82 L.Ed.2d 221 (1984) assumed but did not decide that overnight sleeping in a public park in connection with a demonstration to call attention to the plight of the homeless "is expressive conduct protected to some extent by the First Amendment." The Court found that a ban against sleeping in the park was a reasonable time, place, and manner restriction and sustainable under the *O'Brien* test. In determining whether conduct ordinarily perceived as non-communicative is communicative in a particular instance, should the courts consider whether there is a nexus between the act and the message? Does such a nexus increase "the likelihood that the act was intended to be communicative, and will be understood to be so"? See Note, *First Amendment Protection of Ambiguous Conduct,* 84 Colum.L.Rev. 467, 493 (1984).

2. Would the school authorities' action have been sustained if they had permitted the wearing of armbands on school property, generally, e.g., in the cafeteria and on the playing fields, and merely required their removal while attending class? Fortas, J., points out that school authorities could not forbid discussion of the Vietnam conflict "anywhere on school property except as part of a prescribed classroom exercise." Is the more relevant inquiry whether discussion of the Vietnam conflict could be *permitted* everywhere on school

property *except in prescribed classes*? May a student be prohibited from voicing his opinion of the Vietnam War in the middle of a math class? If so, why can't he be prevented from expressing his views on the same issue in the same class by means of "symbolic speech"? Cf. Nahmod, *Beyond Tinker: The High School as an Educational Public Forum*, 5 Harv.Civ.Rts. & Civ.Lib.L.Rev. 278 (1970).

3. Would the *Tinker* regulation have been sustained if many students, rather than a few, made hostile remarks to the children wearing armbands? If the wearing of armbands had generated acts of violence on school premises? Or the school authorities could reasonably forecast that they would? If so, is such "justification" much more likely to exist when the message is unpopular, or at least controversial? Why should the question whether the wearing of armbands or other forms of protest is to be constitutionally protected turn on whether such protest produces, or is likely to produce, violent reaction by those who would deprive the protestors of the very rights they seek to assert? See generally Sec. 1, V supra.

4. Could school authorities adopt a regulation forbidding *teachers* to wear black armbands in the classroom? Or prohibiting teachers from wearing *all* symbols of political or controversial significance in the classroom or anywhere on school property? Are students a "captive" group? Do the views of a teacher occupying a position of authority carry much more influence with a student than would those of students inter sese? Consider *James v. Bd. of Educ.*, 461 F.2d 566 (2d Cir.1972), holding that school officials violated a high school teacher's constitutional rights by discharging him because he had worn a black armband in class in symbolic protest of the Vietnam War. But the court stressed that "the armband did not disrupt classroom activities [nor] have any influence on any students and did not engender protest from any student, teacher or parent." What if it had? By implication, did the court confirm the potency of the "heckler's veto"? See Note, 39 Brook.L.Rev. 918 (1973). Same result if appellant had been a 3rd grade teacher rather than an 11th grade teacher? See Shiffrin, *Government Speech*, 27 U.C.L.A.L.Rev. 565, 647–53 (1980).

SPENCE v. WASHINGTON, 418 U.S. 405, 94 S.Ct. 2727, 41 L.Ed.2d 842 (1974): On May 10, 1970, a few days after the invasion of Cambodia and the killings at Kent State University, appellant, a college student, hung his United States flag upside down from the window of his apartment, attaching to the front and back a peace symbol (a circle enclosing a trident) made of removable black tape. The flag measured about three by five feet and was plainly visible to passersby. The peace symbol occupied roughly half the surface of the flag. Appellant was charged with violating a statute regulating the ways to display or exhibit the American flag. The statute prohibits any person from placing "any word, figure, mark, picture, design, drawing or advertisement of any nature upon any [United States] flag" or "expos[ing] to public view any such [decorated] flag." It was uncontroverted that appellant's actions were a protest to the invasion of Cambodia and the killings at Kent State and that his purpose was to associate the American flag with peace instead of war and violence: "[I] felt that the flag stood for America and I wanted people to know that I thought America stood for peace." The Court held, per curiam, that his conviction violated the first amendment. Among the factors the Court deemed "important" were that the flag was privately-owned, displayed on private property, involved no risk of breach of the peace—"there is no evidence that anyone other than the three [arresting] officers observed the flag"—and, as the State conceded, the display of the flag and its superimposed peace symbol was "a form of communication." The state's concession "is inevitable on this record." Because "appellant did not choose to articulate his views through printed or spoken words," it was "necessary to determine whether his activity was sufficiently imbued with elements of communication to fall within the scope of the [first amendment]. But the nature of appellant's activity, combined with the factual context and environment in which it was undertaken, lead to the conclusion that he engaged in a form of protected expression."

"Moreover, the context in which a symbol is used for purposes of expression is important, for the context may give meaning to the symbol. See *Tinker.* [A]ppellant's activity was roughly simultaneous with and concededly triggered by the Cambodian incursion and the Kent State tragedy, [like the Vietnam hostilities protested in *Tinker*] issues of great public moment. A flag bearing a peace symbol and displayed upside down by a student might be interpreted as nothing more than bizarre behavior, but it would have been difficult for the great majority of citizens to miss the drift of appellant's point at the time that he made it. [Furthermore], this was not an act of mindless nihilism. Rather, it was a pointed expression of anguish by appellant about the then-current domestic and foreign affairs of his government. An intent to convey a particularized message was present, and in the surrounding circumstances the likelihood was great that the message would be understood by those who viewed it.

"[The] first interest at issue is prevention of breach of the peace. [It] is totally without support in the record.

"We are also unable to affirm the judgment below on the ground that the State may have desired to protect the sensibilities of passersby. 'It is firmly settled that under our Constitution the public expression of ideas may not be prohibited merely because the ideas are themselves offensive to some of their hearers.' *Street v. New York,* [394 U.S. 576, 592, 89 S.Ct. 1354, 1366, 22 L.Ed.2d 572 (1969).] Moreover, appellant did not impose his ideas upon a captive audience. Anyone who might have been offended could easily have avoided the display. See *Cohen.* Nor may appellant be punished for failing to show proper respect for our national emblem.[a]

"We are brought then to the state court's thesis that Washington has an interest in preserving the national flag as an unalloyed symbol of our country. The [state] court did not define this interest; it simply asserted it. The dissenting opinion today adopts essentially the same approach. Presumably, this interest might be seen as an effort to prevent the appropriation of a revered national symbol [where] there was a risk that association of the symbol with a particular product or viewpoint might be taken erroneously as evidence of governmental endorsement.[7] Alternatively, it might be argued that the interest asserted is based on the uniquely universal character of the national flag as a symbol. [If the flag] may be destroyed or permanently disfigured, it could be

a. *Street* stated that: "We have no doubt that the constitutionally guaranteed 'freedom to be intellectually * * * diverse or even contrary,' and the 'right to differ as to things that touch the heart of the existing order,' encompass the freedom to express publicly one's opinions about our flag, including those opinions which are defiant or contemptuous."

7. Undoubtedly such a concern underlies that portion of the improper use statute forbidding the utilization of representations of

the flag in a commercial context. [There] is no occasion in this case to address the application of the challenged statute to commercial behavior. Cf. *Halter v. Nebraska,* 205 U.S. 34, 27 S.Ct. 419, 51 L.Ed. 696 (1907). The dissent places major reliance on *Halter,* despite the fact [it] was decided nearly 20 years before the Court concluded that the First Amendment applies to the States by virtue of the Fourteenth Amendment.

argued that it will lose its capability of mirroring the sentiments of all who view it.

"But we need not decide in this case whether the interest advanced by the court below is valid.[8] We assume arguendo that it is. The statute is nonetheless unconstitutional as applied to appellant's activity. There was no risk that appellant's acts would mislead viewers into assuming that the Government endorsed his viewpoint. To the contrary, he was plainly and peacefully [10] protesting the fact that it was not. Appellant was not charged under the desecration statute, nor did he permanently disfigure the flag or destroy it. He displayed it as a flag of his country in a way closely analogous to the manner in which flags have always been used to convey ideas. Moreover, his message was direct, likely to be understood, and within the contours of the First Amendment. Given the protected character of his expression and in light of the fact that no interest the State may have in preserving the physical integrity of a privately-owned flag was significantly impaired on these facts, the conviction must be invalidated." [b]

REHNQUIST, J., joined by Burger, C.J., and White, J., dissented: "The statute under which petitioner was convicted is no stranger to this Court, a virtually identical statute having been before the Court in *Halter* [which] held that the State of Nebraska could enforce its statute to prevent use of a flag representation on beer bottles, stating flatly that 'a State will be wanting in care for the well-being of its people if it ignores the fact that they regard the flag as a symbol of their country's power and prestige. [Such] a use tends to degrade and cheapen the flag in the estimation of the people, as well as to defeat the object of maintaining it as an emblem of National power and National honor.'

"The Court today finds *Halter* irrelevant to the present case, pointing out that it was decided almost 20 years before the First Amendment was applied to the States and further noting that it involved 'commercial behavior,' a form of expression the Court presumably will consider another day. Insofar as *Halter* assesses the State's interest, of course, the Court's argument is simply beside the point. [Yet] if the Court is suggesting that *Halter* would now be decided differently, and that the State's interest in the flag falls before any speech which is 'direct, likely to be understood, and within the contours of the First Amendment,' that view would mean the flag could be auctioned as a background to anyone willing and able to buy or copy one. I find it hard to believe the Court intends to presage that result.

"Turning to the question of the State's interest in the flag, it seems to me that the Court's treatment lacks all substance. The suggestion that the State's interest somehow diminishes when the flag is decorated with *removable* tape

---

8. If this interest is valid, we note that it is directly related to expression in the context of activity like that undertaken by appellant. For that reason and because no other governmental interest unrelated to expression has been advanced or can be supported on this record, the four-step analysis of *O'Brien* is inapplicable.

10. Appellant's activity occurred at a time of national turmoil over the introduction of United States forces into Cambodia and the deaths at Kent State University. It is difficult now, more than four years later, to recall vividly the depth of emotion that pervaded most colleges and universities at the time, and

that was widely shared by young Americans everywhere. A spontaneous outpouring of feeling resulted in widespread action, not all of it rational when viewed in retrospect. This included the closing down of some schools, as well as other disruptions of many centers of education. It was against this highly inflamed background that appellant chose to express his own views in a manner that can fairly be described as gentle and restrained as compared to the actions undertaken by a number of his peers.

b. Douglas, J., wrote a brief concurrence; Blackmun, J., concurred without opinion.

trivializes something which is not trivial. [Surely] the Court does not mean to imply that petitioner *could* be prosecuted if he subsequently tore the flag in the process of trying to take the tape off. Unlike flag desecration statutes [the instant statute] seeks to prevent personal *use* of the flag, not simply particular forms of *abuse*. The [state] has chosen to set the flag apart for a special purpose, and has directed that it not be turned into a common background for an endless variety of superimposed messages. The physical condition of the flag itself is irrelevant to that purpose.

"The true nature of the State's interest in this case is not only one of preserving 'the physical integrity of the flag,' but also one of preserving the flag as 'an important symbol of nationhood and unity.' [White, J., concurring in *Smith v. Goguen*, 415 U.S. 566, 94 S.Ct. 1242, 39 L.Ed.2d 605 (1974)] Although the Court treats this important interest with a studied inattention, it is hardly one of recent invention and has previously been accorded considerable respect by this Court. * * *

"There was no question in *Halter* of physical impairment of a flag, since no actual flag was even involved. And it certainly would have made no difference to the Court's discussion of the State's interest if the petitioner in that case had chosen to advertise his product by decorating the flag with beer bottles fashioned from some removable substance. It is the character, not the cloth, of the flag which the State seeks to protect.

"The value of this interest has been emphasized in recent as well as distant times. Mr. Justice Fortas, for example, noted in *Street* that 'the flag is a special kind of personalty,' a form of property 'burdened with peculiar obligations and restrictions.' Mr. Justice White has observed that 'the flag is a national property, and the Nation may regulate those who would make, imitate, sell, possess, or use it.' *Goguen* (concurring opinion).[c] I agree. What petitioner here seeks is simply license to use the flag however he pleases, so long as the activity can be tied to a concept of speech, regardless of any state interest in having the flag used only for more limited purposes. I find no reasoning in the Court's opinion which convinces me that the Constitution requires such license to be given.

"The fact that the State has a valid interest in preserving the character of the flag does not mean, of course, that it can employ all conceivable means to enforce it. It certainly could not require all citizens to own the flag or compel citizens to salute one. *Barnette*. It presumably cannot punish criticism of the flag, or the principles for which it stands, any more than it could punish criticism of this country's policies or ideas. But the [instant statute] demands no such allegiance. Its operation does not depend upon whether a particular message is deemed commercial or political; upon whether the use of the flag is respectful or contemptuous; or upon whether any particular segment of the State's citizenry might applaud or oppose the intended message.[7] It simply

c. In *Goguen*, White, J., thought it clear that Congress could protect the "physical integrity" or "physical character" of the national flag, just as it could forbid "the mutilation of the Lincoln Memorial [or] prevent overlaying it with words or other objects. The flag is itself a monument, subject to similar protection."

7. It is quite apparent that the Court does have considerable sympathy for at least the *form* of petitioner's message [noting that "ap-

pellant chose to express his own views in a manner that can fairly be described as gentle and restrained as compared to the actions undertaken by a number of his peers." One would hope that this last observation does not introduce a doctrine of "comparative" expression, which gives more leeway to certain forms of expression when more destructive methods of expression are being employed by others.

withdraws a unique national symbol from the roster of materials that may be used as a background for communications." d

Notes and Questions

1. *Especially protected speech*? Consider Blasi, *The Checking Value in First Amendment Theory*, 1977 Am.B.Found.Res.J. 521, 640: "[A] proponent of the checking value should be particularly solicitous of conduct that attacks the government's own symbols—for example, the burning or defacing of the American flag—because historically the manipulation of patriotic symbols has been one important way by which tyrannical and abusive governments have overwhelmed their critics."

2. What is the significance of *Spence's* observations that "it would have been difficult for the great majority of citizens to miss the drift of appellant's point"; this "was not an act of mindless nihilism [but] a pointed expression of anguish"; "an intent to convey a particularized message was present"; the message "was direct [and] likely to be understood"? Does the Court mean that flag misuse with less obvious communicative purpose, such as that in *Goguen*, would not be protected under a properly-drawn statute? That in order for symbolic conduct to fall "within the contours of the First Amendment," it must be sufficiently "pointed", "direct" or "likely to be understood"? If so, why? Has any court ever held that the incoherence or obscurity of a *spoken* or *written* message strips it of first amendment protection? See Note, 50 Wash.L.Rev. 169, 183, 187 & n. 104 (1974).

Compare *People v. Cowgill*, 274 Cal.App.2d Supp. 923, 78 Cal.Rptr. 853 (1969), dismissed, 396 U.S. 371, 90 S.Ct. 613, 24 L.Ed.2d 590 (1970) (person who cut up and sewed flag into vest and wore the vest on public streets convicted for violating law making it a misdemeanor to publicly mutilate, deface or defile the American flag). For a first amendment claim to be made, is it necessary that viewers of the vest perceived a message *and* that the wearer of the vest communicated a message? Should the focus instead be on the reasons why the state wanted to punish the actor's conduct? For commentary by Cowgill's counsel, see Nimmer, supra, at 57. Compare Note, *Symbolic Conduct*, 68 Colum. L.Rev. 1091, 1109–17 (1968).

3. *Hypothetical national anthem "misuse" or "desecration" statute.* Does the government have a valid interest in preserving the character of the national anthem as an important symbol of nationhood and unity? Could this symbol be withdrawn from the roster of material that may be used as a background for communication? Could Congress prohibit impairment of the "integrity" of the national anthem by those who would ridicule, degrade, cheapen or cast contempt upon it by punishing all public parodying of the anthem? Could one who expressed opposition to or resentment of national attitudes or governmental policies (e.g., alleged failure to accord blacks or females equal treatment) by changing the words of the Star-Spangled Banner (e.g., "land of the female slaves," "home of the white hypocrites") be successfully prosecuted under such a statute? What would Burger, C.J., Rehnquist, J., and White, J., say?

4. Is the state's interest in preserving the "integrity" of the flag "non-speech" or "anti-speech"? Is a symbol qua symbol essentially a component of speech? Is protection of the flag's "physical integrity" in actuality protection of

---

d. Burger, C.J., also wrote a brief dissent, maintaining "it should be left to each state and ultimately the common sense of its people to decide how the flag, as a symbol of national unity, should be protected."

its *meaning*? Is a flag desecration statute, in effect, "a governmental command that one idea (embodied in the flag symbol) is not to be countered by another idea (embodied in the act of flag desecration)"? When the American flag is the medium of expression, as opposed to parades and demonstrations, is the situation in reality always one of "pure communication"? See Nimmer, supra, at 56–57; 50 Wash.L.Rev., note 2 supra, at 186, 189.

5. How significant is it that the federal government "permits, indeed encourages, people to fly [the flag] as a sign of support for the government"? See Loewy, *Punishing Flag Desecrators: The Ultimate in Flag Desecration,* 49 N.C.L. Rev. 48, 64 (1970), pointing out that 36 U.S.C. § 174(d) urges the flag to be displayed "on all days when the weather permits, especially on," e.g., Inauguration Day, Washington's Birthday, Lincoln's Birthday, Mother's Day, Memorial Day, Independence Day, Navy Day, Veteran's Day, Christmas Day. If the government permits the flag to be used "to credit the country," must it also permit it to be used "to discredit the country"? See Loewy, supra. Cf. *Schacht v. United States,* 398 U.S. 58, 90 S.Ct. 1555, 26 L.Ed.2d 44 (1970) (statute authorizing wearing of U.S. military uniform if the portrayal does not tend to discredit the military violates first amendment).

In considering whether flag burning statutes are "neutral as to content" and whether flag burning is "inherently offensive," how significant is it that 36 U.S.C. § 176(j) provides that "when it is in such condition that it is no longer a fitting emblem for display," the flag "should be destroyed in a dignified way, *preferably by burning*" (emphasis added)? See Loewy, supra, at 79–80.

SECTION 5. GOVERNMENT PROPERTY AND THE PUBLIC FORUM [a]

The case law treating the question of when persons can speak on public property has come to be known as public forum doctrine. But "[t]he public forum saga began, and very nearly ended," Stone, *Fora Americana: Speech in Public Places,* 1974 Sup.Ct.Rev. 233, 236, with an effort by Holmes, J., then on the Supreme Judicial Court of Massachusetts, "to solve a difficult first amendment problem by simplistic resort to a common-law concept," Blasi, *Prior Restraints on Demonstrations,* 68 Mich.L.Rev. 1482, 1484 (1970). For holding religious meetings on the Boston Common, a preacher was convicted under an ordinance prohibiting "any public address" upon publicly-owned property without a permit from the mayor. In upholding the permit ordinance Holmes, J., observed: "For the legislature absolutely or conditionally to forbid public speaking in a highway or public park is no more an infringement of rights of a member of the public than for the owner of a private house to forbid it in the house." *Davis v. Massachusetts,* 162 Mass. 510, 511 (1895). On appeal, a unanimous Supreme Court adopted the Holmes position, 167 U.S. 43, 17 S.Ct. 731, 42 L.Ed. 71 (1897): "[T]he right to absolutely exclude all right to use [public property], necessarily includes the authority to determine under what circumstances such use may be availed of, as the greater power contains the lesser."

This view survived until *Hague v. CIO,* 307 U.S. 496, 59 S.Ct. 954, 83 L.Ed. 1423 (1939), which rejected Jersey City's claim that its ordinance requiring a permit for an open air meeting was justified by the "plenary power" rationale of

---

a. For treatment of the related question whether, and if so under what circumstances, there is a first amendment right of access to privately-owned facilities, such as shopping centers, see *Marsh v. Alabama,* p. 1095 infra; *Hudgens v. NLRB,* p. 1120 infra; *Pruneyard Shopping Center v. Robins,* p. 729 infra.

Davis. In rejecting the implications of the *Davis* dictum, Roberts, J., in a plurality opinion, uttered a famous "counter dictum," which has played a central role in the evolution of public forum theory: "Wherever the title of streets and parks may rest, they have immemorially been held in trust for the use of the public and, time out of mind, have been used for purposes of assembly, communicating thoughts between citizens, and discussing public questions. Such use of the streets and public places has, from ancient times, been a part of the privileges, immunities, rights, and liberties of citizens. [This privilege of a citizen] is not absolute, but relative, and must be exercised in subordination to the general comfort and convenience, and in consonance with peace and good order; but it must not, in the guise of regulation, be abridged or denied." Eight months later, the *Hague* dictum was given impressive content by Roberts, J., for the Court, in *Schneider* infra.

I. FOUNDATION CASES

A. MANDATORY ACCESS

SCHNEIDER v. IRVINGTON, 308 U.S. 147, 60 S.Ct. 146, 84 L.Ed. 155 (1939), per ROBERTS, J., invalidated several ordinances prohibiting leafleting on public streets or other public places: "Municipal authorities, as trustees for the public, have the duty to keep their communities' streets open and available for movement of people and property, the primary purpose to which the streets are dedicated. So long as legislation to this end does not abridge the constitutional liberty of one rightfully upon the street to impart information through speech or the distribution of literature, it may lawfully regulate the conduct of those using the streets. For example, a person could not exercise this liberty by taking his stand in the middle of a crowded street, contrary to traffic regulations, and maintain his position to the stoppage of all traffic; a group of distributors could not insist upon a constitutional right to form a cordon across the street and to allow no pedestrian to pass who did not accept a tendered leaflet; nor does the guarantee of freedom of speech or of the press deprive a municipality of power to enact regulations against throwing literature broadcast in the streets. Prohibition of such conduct would not abridge the constitutional liberty since such activity bears no necessary relationship to the freedom to speak, write, print or distribute information or opinion. * * *

"In *Lovell* [p. 804 supra] this court held void an ordinance which forbade the distribution by hand or otherwise of literature of any kind without written permission from the city manager. [Similarly] in *Hague v. C.I.O.*, an ordinance was held void on its face because it provided for previous administrative censorship of the exercise of the right of speech and assembly in appropriate public places.

"The [ordinances] under review do not purport to license distribution but all of them absolutely prohibit it in the streets and, one of them, in other public places as well.

"The motive of the legislation under attack in Numbers 13, 18 and 29 is held by the courts below to be the prevention of littering of the streets and, although the alleged offenders were not charged with themselves scattering paper in the streets, their convictions were sustained upon the theory that distribution by them encouraged or resulted in such littering. We are of opinion that the purpose to keep the streets clean and of good appearance is insufficient to justify an ordinance which prohibits a person rightfully on a public street from handing literature to one willing to receive it. Any burden imposed upon the city authorities in cleaning and caring for the streets as an indirect consequence of such distribution results from the constitutional protection of the freedom of speech and press. This constitutional protection does not deprive a city of all power to prevent street littering. There are obvious methods of preventing littering. Amongst these is the punishment of those who actually throw papers on the streets.

"It is suggested that [the] ordinances are valid because their operation is limited to streets and alleys and leaves persons free to distribute printed matter in other public places. But, as we have said, the streets are natural and proper places for the dissemination of information and opinion; and one is not to have the exercise of his liberty of expression in appropriate places abridged on the plea that it may be exercised in some other place."

McREYNOLDS, J., "is of opinion that the judgment in each case should be affirmed."

Notes and Questions

1. *Leaflets and the streets as public forum.* Consider Kalven, *The Concept of the Public Forum: Cox v. Louisiana,* 1965 S.Ct.Rev. 1, 18 & 21: "Leaflet distribution in public places in a city is a method of communication that carries as an inextricable and expected consequence substantial littering of the streets, which the city has an obligation to keep clean. It is also a method of communication of some annoyance to a majority of people so addressed; that its impact on its audience is very high is doubtful. Yet the constitutional balance in *Schneider* was struck emphatically in favor of keeping the public forum open for this mode of communication.

"[The] operative theory of the Court, at least for the leaflet situation, is that, although it is a method of communication that interferes with the public use of the streets, the right to the streets as a public forum is such that leaflet distribution cannot be prohibited and can be regulated only for weighty reasons."

2. *Litter prevention as a substantial interest.* Does the interest in distributing leaflets always outweigh the interest in preventing littering? Suppose helicopters regularly dropped tons of leaflets on the town of Irvington?

3. *Beyond leaflets.* COX v. NEW HAMPSHIRE, 312 U.S. 569, 61 S.Ct. 762, 85 L.Ed. 1049 (1941), per HUGHES, C.J., upheld convictions of sixty-eight Jehovah's Witnesses for parading without a permit. They had marched in four or five groups (with perhaps twenty others) along the sidewalk in single file carrying signs and handing out leaflets: "[T]he state court considered and defined the duty of the licensing authority and the rights of the appellants to a license for their parade, with regard only to consideration of time, place and manner so as to conserve the public convenience." The licensing procedure was said to "afford opportunity for proper policing" and " 'to prevent confusion by overlapping parades, [to] secure convenient use of the streets by other travelers, and to minimize the risk of disorder.' " A municipality "undoubtedly" has "authority to control the use of its public streets for parades or processions." But see Baker, *Unreasoned Reasonableness: Mandatory Parade Permits and Time, Place, and Manner Regulations,* 78 Nw.U.L.Rev. 937, 992 (1984): Approximately 26,000 people walked on the same sidewalks during the same hour the defendants in *Cox* "marched." "This single difference in what [the defendants] did—'marching in formation,' which they did for expressive purposes and which presumably is an 'assembly' that the first amendment protects—turned out to

have crucial significance. This sole difference, engaging in first amendment protected conduct, made them guilty of a criminal offense. [Surely] something is wrong with this result."

4. *Charging for use of public forum.* *Cox* said there was nothing "contrary to the Constitution" in the exaction of a fee " 'incident to the administration of the [licensing] Act and to the maintenance of public order in the matter licensed.' " Could leafleters be charged for the costs of cleaning up litter? Controversial speakers for the expense of police protection? See generally Goldberger, *A Reconsideration of Cox v. New Hampshire: Can Demonstrators Be Required to Pay the Costs of Using America's Public Forums?*, 62 Tex.L.Rev. 403 (1983); Blasi, *Demonstrations*, supra at 1527–32.

5. *Reasonable time, place, and manner regulations.* As *Cox* reveals, a right of access to a public forum does not guarantee immunity from reasonable time, place, and manner regulations. In *Heffron v. International Soc. For Krishna Consciousness*, 452 U.S. 640, 101 S.Ct. 2559, 69 L.Ed.2d 298 (1981), for example, the Court, per White, J., upheld a state fair rule prohibiting the distribution of printed material or the solicitation of funds except from a duly licensed booth on the fairgrounds. The Court noted that consideration of a forum's special attributes is relevant to the determination of reasonableness, and the test of reasonableness is whether the restrictions "are justified without reference to the content of the regulated speech, that they serve a significant governmental interest, and that in doing so they leave open ample alternative channels for communication of the information"[a] Is there any difference between the *O'Brien* test and the approach used in *Schneider*? Should there be a difference?

B. EQUAL ACCESS

CHICAGO POLICE DEP'T v. MOSLEY, 408 U.S. 92, 92 S.Ct. 2286, 33 L.Ed. 2d 212 (1972), invalidated an ordinance banning all picketing within 150 feet of a school building while the school is in session and one half-hour before and afterwards, except "the peaceful picketing of any school involved in a labor dispute."

The suit was brought by a federal postal employee who, for seven months prior to enactment of the ordinance, had frequently picketed a high school in Chicago. "During school hours and usually by himself, Mosley would walk the public sidewalk adjoining the school, carrying a sign that read: 'Jones High School practices black discrimination. Jones High School has a black quota.' His lonely crusade was always peaceful, orderly, and [quiet]." The Court, per MARSHALL, J., viewed the ordinance as drawing "an impermissible distinction between labor picketing and other peaceful picketing": "The central problem with Chicago's ordinance is that it describes permissible picketing in terms of its subject matter. Peaceful picketing on the subject of a school's labor-management dispute is permitted, but all other peaceful picketing is prohibited. The operative distinction is the message on a picket sign. But, above all else, the First Amendment means that government has no power to restrict expression because of its message, its ideas, its subject matter, or its content.

"[U]nder the Equal Protection Clause, not to mention the First Amendment itself,[a] government may not grant the use of a forum to people whose views it

---

a. Brennan, J., joined by Marshall and Stevens, JJ., dissented in part as did Blackmun, J., in a separate opinion. Their dispute was not with the Court's test, but its application.

a. *Consolidated Edison Co. v. Public Service Comm'n*, p. 784 infra, abandoned equal protection and cited *Mosley* as a first amendment case: "The First Amendment's hostility

finds acceptable, but deny use to those wishing to express less favored or more controversial views. And it may not select which issues are worth discussing or debating in public facilities. There is an 'equality of status in the field of ideas,' and government must afford all points of view an equal opportunity to be heard. Once a forum is opened up to assembly or speaking by some groups, government may not prohibit others from assembling or speaking on the basis of what they intend to say. Selective exclusions from a public forum may not be based on content alone, and may not be justified by reference to content alone.

"[Not] all picketing must always be allowed. We have continually recognized that reasonable 'time, place and manner' regulations of picketing may be necessary to further significant governmental interests. Similarly, under an equal protection analysis, there may be sufficient regulatory interests justifying selective exclusions or distinctions among picketers. [But] [b]ecause picketing plainly involves expressive conduct within the protection of the First Amendment, discriminations among picketers must be tailored to serve a substantial governmental interest. In this case, the ordinance itself describes impermissible picketing not in terms of time, place and manner, but in terms of subject matter. The regulation 'thus slip[s] from the neutrality of time, place and circumstance into a concern about content.' This is never permitted. * * *

"Although preventing school disruption is a city's legitimate concern, Chicago itself has determined that peaceful labor picketing during school hours is not an undue interference with school. Therefore, under the Equal Protection clause, Chicago may not maintain that other picketing disrupts the school unless that picketing is clearly more disruptive than the picketing Chicago already permits. If peaceful labor picketing is permitted, there is no justification for prohibiting all nonlabor picketing, both peaceful and nonpeaceful. 'Peaceful' labor picketing, however the term 'peaceful' is defined, is obviously no less disruptive than 'peaceful' nonlabor picketing. But Chicago's ordinance permits the former and prohibits the latter.

"[We also] reject the city's argument that, although it permits peaceful labor picketing, it may prohibit all nonlabor picketing because, as a class, nonlabor picketing is more prone to produce violence than labor picketing. Predictions about imminent disruption from picketing involve judgments appropriately made on an individualized basis, not by means of broad classifications, especially those based on subject matter. Freedom of expression, and its intersection with the guarantee of equal protection, would rest on a soft foundation indeed if government could distinguish among picketers on such a wholesale and categorical basis. '[I]n our system, undifferentiated fear or apprehension of disturbance is not enough to overcome the right to freedom of expression.' *Tinker.* Some labor picketing is peaceful, some disorderly; the same is true for picketing on other themes. No labor picketing could be more peaceful or less prone to violence than Mosley's solitary vigil. In seeking to restrict nonlabor picketing which is clearly more disruptive than peaceful labor picketing, Chicago may not prohibit all nonlabor picketing at the school forum." [b]

to content-based regulation extends not only to restrictions on particular viewpoints, but also to prohibition of public discussion of an entire topic." But see, e.g., *Minnesota State Board v. Knight,* 465 U.S. 271, 104 S.Ct. 1058,

79 L.Ed.2d 299 (1984) (stating that *Mosley* is an equal protection case).

b. Burger, C.J., joined the Court's opinion, but also concurred. Blackmun and Rehnquist, JJ., concurred in the result.

Notes and Questions

1. Consider Karst, *Equality as a Central Principle in the First Amendment*, 43 U.Chi.L.Rev. 20, 28 (1975): "*Mosley* is a landmark first amendment decision. It makes two principal points: (1) the essence of the first amendment is its denial to government of the power to determine which messages shall be heard and which suppressed * * *. (2) Any 'time, place and manner' restriction that selectively excludes speakers from a public forum must survive careful judicial scrutiny to ensure that the exclusion is the minimum necessary to further a significant government interest. Taken together, these statements declare a principle of major importance. The Court has explicitly adopted the principle of equal liberty of expression. [The] principle requires courts to start from the assumption that all speakers and all points of view are entitled to a hearing, and permits deviation from this basic assumption only upon a showing of substantial necessity."

2. What if the *Mosley* ordinance had not excepted labor picketing, but had banned *all* picketing within 150 feet of a school during school hours? Consider Karst 37–38: "The burden of this restriction would fall most heavily on those who have something to communicate to the school [population]. Student picketers presenting a grievance against a principal, or striking custodians with a message growing out of a labor dispute, would be affected more seriously by this ostensibly content-neutral ordinance than would, say the proponents of a candidate for Governor [who could just as effectively carry their message elsewhere]. This differential impact amounts to de facto content discrimination, presumptively invalid under the first amendment equality principle.

"[The city faces] an apparent dilemma. [If it] bars all picketing within a certain area, it will effectively discriminate against those groups that can communicate to their audience only by picketing within that area. But if the city adjusts its ordinance to this differential impact, as by providing a student-picketing or labor-picketing exemption, [it runs] afoul of *Mosley* itself. The city can avoid the dilemma by amending the ordinance to ban not all picketing but only noisy picketing." [c]

3. Does equality fully explain the special concern with content regulation? Consider Stone, *Content Regulation and the First Amendment*, 25 Wm. & Mary L.Rev. 189, 207 (1983): "The problem, quite simply, is that restrictions on expression are rife with 'inequalities,' many of which have nothing whatever to do with content. The ordinance at issue in *Mosley*, for example, restricted picketing near schools, but left unrestricted picketing near hospitals, libraries, courthouses, and private homes. The ordinance at issue in *Erznoznik* restricted drive-in theaters that are visible from a public street, but did not restrict billboards. [Whatever] the effect of these content-neutral inequalities on first amendment analysis, they are not scrutinized in the same way as content-based inequalities. Not all inequalities, in other words, are equal. And although the concern with equality may support the content-based/content-neutral distinction, it does not in itself have much explanatory power."

Is the concern with content discrimination explainable because of concerns about communicative impact, distortion of public debate, or government motivation? See generally Stone, supra. See also sources cited in notes 1 & 2 after

---

c. As Professor Karst notes, such an ordinance was upheld in *Grayned v. Rockford*, Part II infra, the companion case to *Mosley*.

O'Brien, Sec. 4 supra and Cass, *First Amendment Access to Government Facilities,* 65 Va.L.Rev. 1287, 1323–25 (1979); Stephan, *The First Amendment and Content Discrimination,* 68 Va.L.Rev. 203 (1982); Stone, *Restrictions of Speech Because of its Content: The Peculiar Case of Subject-Matter Restrictions,* 46 U.Chi.L.Rev. 81 (1978).

4. An Illinois statute prohibited picketing residences or dwellings—except when the dwelling is "used as a place of business," or is "a place of employment involved in a labor dispute or the place of holding a meeting [on] premises commonly used to discuss subjects of general public interest," or when a "person is picketing his own [dwelling]. Can a conviction for picketing the Mayor of Chicago's home be upheld? Is *Mosley* distinguishable? See *Carey v. Brown,* 447 U.S. 455, 100 S.Ct. 2286, 65 L.Ed.2d 263 (1980). What if all residential picketing were proscribed?

II. NEW FORUMS

Are first amendment rights on government property confined to streets and parks? "[W]hat about other publicly owned property, ranging from the grounds surrounding a public building, to the inside of a welfare office, publicly run bus, or library, to a legislative gallery?" Stone, *Fora Americana,* supra, at 245. Compare the approaches in *Grayned* and *Greer* infra.

GRAYNED v. ROCKFORD, 408 U.S. 104, 92 S.Ct. 2294, 33 L.Ed.2d 222 (1972): Appellant and some 200 others participated in a demonstration about 100 feet from a high school building, protesting the principal's failure to act on black students' grievances. They were convicted, inter alia, of violating an "anti-noise" ordinance providing: "[N]o person, while on public or private grounds adjacent to any [school] building in which [a class] is in session, shall willfully make or assist in the making of any noise or diversion which disturbs or tends to disturb the peace or good order of such school session." An 8–1 majority, per MARSHALL, J., upheld the ordinance against vagueness and overbreadth objections.

As for the vagueness claim, it was clear to the Court that "the ordinance as a whole" prohibits "deliberately noisy or diversionary activity which disrupts or is about to disrupt normal school activities." In light of Illinois cases construing similar ordinances, "only actual or imminent interference with the 'peace or good order' of the school" is prohibited. At issue is not "a vague, general 'breach of the peace' ordinance, but a specific statute for the school context, where the prohibited disturbances are easily measured by their impact on the normal activities of the school. Given this 'particular context,' the ordinance gives 'fair notice to whom it is directed.' [Rockford's] anti-noise ordinance does not permit punishment for the expression of an unpopular point of view, and it contains no broad invitation to subjective or discriminatory enforcement."

As for the overbreadth claim: "[G]overnment has no power to restrict [expressive] activity because of its message [but] reasonable 'time, place and manner' regulations may be necessary to further significant governmental interests, and are permitted. For example, two parades cannot march on the same street simultaneously, and government may allow only one. *Cox v. New Hampshire.* A demonstration or parade on a large street during rush hour might put an intolerable burden on the essential flow of traffic, and for that reason could be prohibited. If overamplified loudspeakers assault the citizenry, government may turn them down.

"The nature of a place, 'the pattern of its normal activities, dictates the kinds of regulations of time, place, and manner that are reasonable.' Although a silent vigil may not unduly interfere with a public library, *Brown v. Louisiana,* 383 U.S. 131, 86 S.Ct. 719, 15 L.Ed.2d 637 (1966) [a] making a speech in the reading room almost certainly would. That same speech should be perfectly appropriate in a park. The crucial question is whether the manner of expression is basically incompatible with the normal activity of a particular place at a particular time. Our cases make clear that in assessing the reasonableness of regulation, we must weigh heavily the fact that communication is involved; the regulation must be narrowly tailored to further the State's legitimate interest. 'Access to [the streets, sidewalks, parks, and other similar public places] for the purpose of exercising [First Amendment rights] cannot constitutionally be denied broadly * * *.' Free expression 'must not, in the guise of regulation, be abridged or denied.'

"In light of these general principles, we do not think that Rockford's ordinance is an unconstitutional regulation of activity around a school. [Just] as *Tinker* made clear that school property may not be declared off-limits for expressive activity by students, we think it clear that the public sidewalk adjacent to school grounds may not be declared off-limits for expressive activity by members of the public. But in each case, expressive activity may be prohibited if it 'materially disrupts classwork or involves substantial disorder or invasion of the rights of others.' * * *

"Rockford's anti-noise ordinance goes no further than *Tinker* says a municipality may go to prevent interference with its schools. It is narrowly tailored to further Rockford's compelling interest in having an undisrupted school session conducive to the students' learning, and does not unnecessarily interfere with First Amendment rights. Far from having an impermissibly broad prophylactic ordinance, Rockford punishes only conduct which disrupts or is about to disrupt normal school activities. That decision is made, as it should be, on an individualized basis, given the particular fact situation. Peaceful picketing which does not interfere with the ordinary functioning of the school is permitted. And the ordinance gives no license to punish anyone because of what he is saying.

"We recognize that the ordinance prohibits some picketing which is neither violent nor physically obstructive. Noisy demonstrations which disrupt or are incompatible with normal school activities are obviously within the ordinance's reach. Such expressive conduct may be constitutionally protected at other places or other times, but next to a school, while classes are in session, it may be prohibited. The anti-noise ordinance imposes no such restriction on expressive activity before or after the school session, while the student/faculty 'audience' enters and leaves the school.

"In *Cox v. Louisiana,* 379 U.S. 559, 85 S.Ct. 476, 13 L.Ed.2d 487 (1965), this Court indicated that, because of the special nature of the place, persons could be constitutionally prohibited from picketing 'in or near' a courthouse 'with the intent of interfering with, obstructing, or impeding the administration of jus-

---

a. In *Brown,* only three justices (Fortas, J., joined by Warren and Douglas, JJ.) held there was a constitutional right to conduct a silent demonstration in the library. Brennan, J., found the statute involved to be overbroad and thus found it unnecessary to decide whether the actual conduct was constitutionally protected. White, J., concluded that the demonstrators had been unconstitutionally punished because of their race. Black, J., dissenting joined by Clark, Harlan, and Stewart, JJ., insisted that the first amendment "does not guarantee to any person the right to use someone else's property, even that owned by government and dedicated to other purposes, as a stage to express dissident ideas."

tice.'[b] [Similarly], Rockford's modest restriction on some peaceful picketing represents a considered and specific legislative judgment that some kinds of expressive activity should be restricted at a particular time and place, here in order to protect the schools. Such a reasonable regulation is not inconsistent with the First and Fourteenth Amendments.[49] The anti-noise ordinance is not invalid on its face."[c]

GREER v. SPOCK, 424 U.S. 828, 96 S.Ct. 1211, 47 L.Ed.2d 505 (1976), per STEWART, J., upheld two regulations of the Fort Dix, N.J., Military Reservation, one banning demonstrations, picketing, protest marches, political speeches and similar activities on the post; the other prohibiting the distribution or posting of any publication without prior written approval of post headquarters:[a] "The Court of Appeals was mistaken, in thinking that * * * [whenever] members of the public are permitted freely to visit a place owned or operated by the Government, then that place becomes a 'public forum' for purposes of the First Amendment.[b] Such a principle of constitutional law has never existed, and does not exist now. The guarantees of the First Amendment have never meant 'that people who want to propagandize protests or views have a constitutional right to do so whenever and however and wherever they please.' *Adderley.* 'The State, no less than a private owner of property, has power to preserve the property under its control for the use to which it is lawfully dedicated.' Id. * * *

"One of the very purposes for which the Constitution was ordained and established was to 'provide for the common defence,' and this Court over the years has on countless occasions recognized the special constitutional function of the military in our national life, a function both explicit and indispensable. In short, it is 'the primary business of armies and navies to fight or be ready to fight wars should the occasion arise.' And it is consequently the business of a military installation like Fort Dix to train soldiers, not to provide a public forum. [The] notion that federal military reservations, like municipal streets and parks,

---

b. But cf. *United States v. Grace,* 461 U.S. 171, 103 S.Ct. 1702, 75 L.Ed.2d 736 (1983) (invalidating statute prohibiting all leafleting and picketing on sidewalk adjoining Supreme Court).

49. Cf. *Adderley v. Florida,* 385 U.S. 39, 87 S.Ct. 242, 17 L.Ed.2d 149 (1966). In *Adderley* the Court held that demonstrators could be barred from jailhouse grounds not ordinarily open to the public, at least where the demonstration obstructed the jail driveway and interfered with the functioning of the jail. In *Tinker,* we noted that "a school is not like a hospital or a jail enclosure."

[In *Adderley,* Black J. (over the dissent of Douglas, J., joined by Warren, C.J., Brennan, and Fortas, JJ.), had observed broadly that the state no less than a private property owner had power "to control the use of its own property for its own lawful nondiscriminatory purpose." He opposed the premise that "people who want to propagandize protests or views have a constitutional right to do so whenever and however and wherever they please."]

c. Blackmun, J., concurred in the result. Douglas, J., dissented, maintaining that there was no violence, or boisterous conduct. "[T]he disruptive force loosened at this school was an issue dealing with race—an issue that is pre-eminently one for solution by First Amendment means. That is all that was done here; and the entire picketing [was] done in the best First Amendment tradition."

a. Those challenging the Regulations included People's Party and Socialist Workers Party candidates for national political office, who had been denied permission to enter the base for the purpose of distributing campaign literature and discussing election issues with service personnel, and others who had been evicted on several occasions for distributing literature not previously approved and who had been barred from re-entering the post.

b. See also *United States v. Albertini,* ___ U.S. ___, 105 S.Ct. 2897, 86 L.Ed.2d 536 (1985) (50,000 people come to military base for open house; suggestion of temporary public forum characterized as "dubious").

have traditionally served as a place for free public assembly and communication of thoughts by private citizens is thus historically and constitutionally false.[c]

"The respondents, therefore, had no generalized constitutional right to make political speeches or distribute leaflets at Fort Dix, and it follows that [the challenged Regulations] are not constitutionally invalid on their face. These regulations, moreover, were not unconstitutionally applied in the circumstances disclosed by the record in the present case.[10]

"What the record shows [is] a considered Fort Dix policy, objectively and evenhandedly applied, of keeping official military activities there wholly free of entanglement with partisan political campaigns of any kind. Under such a policy members of the Armed Forces stationed at Fort Dix are wholly free as individuals to attend political rallies, out of uniform and off base. But the military as such is insulated from both the reality and the appearance of acting as a handmaiden for partisan political causes or candidates.

"Such a policy is wholly consistent with the American constitutional tradition of a politically neutral military establishment under civilian control. [And] it is a policy that the military authorities at Fort Dix were constitutionally free to pursue." [d]

Burger, C.J., and Powell, J., joined the Court's opinion, but also wrote concurrences. POWELL, J., stated that: "An approach analogous to that which must be employed in this case was described in *Grayned*. The Court is to inquire 'whether the manner of expression is basically incompatible with the normal activity of a particular place at a particular time.' As *Tinker* demonstrates, it is not sufficient that the area in which the right of expression is sought to be exercised be dedicated to some purpose other than use as a 'public forum,' or even that the primary business to be carried on in the area may be disturbed by the unpopular viewpoint expressed. [Some] basic incompatibility must be discerned between the communication and the primary activity of an area. Fort Dix is not only an area of property owned by the Government and dedicated to a public purpose. It is also the enclave of a system that stands apart from and outside of many of the rules that govern ordinary civilian life in our country. [In] this context our inquiry is not limited to claims that the exercise of First Amendment rights is disruptive of base activity. We also must consider their

---

c. Is there an unbroken tradition of exclusion? *Flower v. United States,* 407 U.S. 197, 92 S.Ct. 1842, 32 L.Ed.2d 653 (1972) summarily reversed a conviction for distributing peace leaflets on a "public street" at a point within a military post after petitioner had been removed therefrom and ordered not to re-enter. "Whatever power [he] may have to restrict general access to a military facility, here the Fort Commander chose not to exclude the public from the street where petitioner was arrested." Under the circumstances, e.g., no guard stationed at either entrance or along the route and a constant flow of civilian vehicular and pedestrian traffic through the post on this street, "the military has abandoned any claim that it has special interests in who walks, talks, or leaflets on the avenue." The Court in *Greer* distinguished *Flower* saying that no abandonment had occurred at Fort Dix.

Brennan, J., dissenting, argued that the purported lack of abandonment in *Greer* was difficult to reconcile with a prior "history of unimpeded civilian access" to the military post.

10. The fact that other civilian speakers and entertainers had sometimes been invited to appear at Fort Dix did not of itself serve to convert Fort Dix into a public forum or to confer upon political candidates a First or Fifth Amendment right to conduct their campaigns there. The decision of the military authorities that a civilian lecture on drug abuse, a religious service by a visiting preacher at the base chapel, or a rock musical concert would be supportive of the military mission of Fort Dix surely did not leave the authorities powerless thereafter to prevent any civilian from entering Fort Dix to speak on any subject whatever.

d. Stevens, J., did not participate.

functional and symbolic incompatibility with the 'specialized society separate from civilian society,' that has its home on the base."

Powell, J., concluded that "the public interest in insuring the political neutrality of the military justifies the limited infringement on First Amendments rights imposed by [Fort Dix's ban on political rallies and similar activities within the environs of the base]": "Our national policy has been to preserve a distinction between the role of the soldier and that of the citizen. A reasonable place to draw the line is between political activities on military bases and elsewhere. The military enclave is kept free of partisan influences, but individual servicemen are not isolated from participation as citizens in our democratic process."

Burger, C.J., concurring, argued that "keeping the military separate from political affairs" is a "200-year tradition" that is a "constitutional corollary to the express provision for civilian control of the military in Art. II, § 2, of the Constitution." He observed that "the hard question for me is whether the Constitution requires a ban on [the distribution on base of all political leaflets]." He concluded though that the decision whether to permit distribution is "one properly committed to the judgment of the military authorities."

Brennan, J., joined by Marshall, J., dissented: "The Court's opinion speaks in absolutes, exalting the need for military preparedness and admitting of no careful and solicitous accommodation of First Amendment interests to the competing concerns that all concede are substantial. It parades general propositions useless to precise resolution of the problem at hand. According to the Court, [it is the] 'business of a military installation like Fort Dix to train soldiers, not to provide a public forum.' But the training of soldiers does not as a practical matter require exclusion of those who would publicly express their views from streets and theater parking lots open to the general public. Nor does readiness to fight require such exclusion, unless, of course, the battlefields are the streets and parking lots, or the war is one of ideologies and not men. * * *[6]

"[Respondents] carefully and appropriately distinguish between a military base considered as a whole and those portions of a military base open to the public. And not only do respondents not go so far as to contend that open places constitute a 'public forum,' but also they need not go so far. [T]he determination that a locale is a "public forum" has never been erected as an absolute prerequisite to all forms of demonstrative First Amendment activity. [In] *Brown,* for example, the First Amendment protected the use of a public library as a site for a silent and peaceful protest by five young black men against discrimination. There was no finding by the Court that the library was a public forum. Similarly, in *Edwards v. South Carolina,* the First Amendment protect-

---

6. The concurring opinion of my Brother Powell properly recognizes at least the need for careful inquiry in such cases. But I completely disagree with his characterization of the need to secure the Government's interest in a politically neutral military as an interest protected by prohibiting conduct of "symbolic incompatibility" with a military base. I gather that by this notion of "symbolic incompatibility," my Brother Powell means only to accord recognition to the interest in neutrality, an interest qualitatively different from the more immediate functional interest in training recruits. I, of course, have no quarrel with recognition of the interest. But that recognition as articulated by my Brother Powell is so devoid of limiting principle as to contravene fundamentals of First Amendment jurisprudence. This Court many times has held protected by the First Amendment conduct which was "symbolically incompatible" with the activity upon which it impacted. *See Spence; West Virginia State Bd. of Educ. v. Barnette* [p. 843 infra]. Indeed, the very symbolisms of many of our institutions have been the subject of criticisms held to be unassailably protected by the First Amendment.

ed a demonstration on the grounds of a state capitol building. Again, the Court never expressly determined that those grounds constituted a public forum. And in *Tinker,* the First Amendment shielded students' schoolroom antiwar protest, consisting of the wearing of black armbands. Moreover, none of the opinions that have expressly characterized locales as public forums has really gone that far, for a careful reading of those opinions reveals that their characterizations were always qualified, indicating that not every conceivable form of public expression would be protected. *Mosley, Cox v. New Hampshire.*

"Those cases permitting public expression without characterizing the locale involved as a public forum, together with those cases recognizing the existence of a public forum, albeit qualifiedly, evidence the desirability of a flexible approach to determining when public expression should be protected. Realizing that the permissibility of a certain form of public expression at a given locale may differ depending on whether it is asked if the locale is a public forum or if the form of expression is compatible with the activities occurring at the locale, it becomes apparent that there is need for a flexible approach. Otherwise, with the rigid characterization of a given locale as not a public forum, there is the danger that certain forms of public speech at the locale may be suppressed, even though they are basically compatible with the activities otherwise occurring at the locale.

"The Court's final retreat in justifying the prohibitions upheld today is the principle of military neutrality. [I] could not agree more that the military should not become a political faction in this country. [But] it borders on casuistry to contend that by evenhandedly permitting public expression to occur in unrestricted portions of a military installation, the military will be viewed as sanctioning the causes there espoused. If there is any risk of partisan involvement, real or apparent, it derives from the exercise of a choice, in this case, the Fort commander's choice to exclude respondents, while, for example, inviting speakers in furtherance of the Fort's religious program. * * *

"More fundamentally, however, the specter of partiality does not vanish with the severing of all partisan contact. It is naive to believe that any organization, including the military, is value neutral. More than this, where the interests and purpose of an organization are peculiarly affected by national affairs, it becomes highly susceptible of politicization. For this reason, it is precisely the nature of a military organization to tend toward that end.[16] That tendency is only facilitated by action that serves to isolate the organization's members from the opportunity for exposure to the moderating influence of other ideas, particularly where, as with the military, the organization's activities pervade the lives of its members. For this reason, any unnecessary isolation only erodes neutrality and invites the danger that neutrality seeks to avoid." [e]

---

16. The testimony in the District Court of the officer representing the commanding officer of Fort Dix is exemplary:

"Q I see. Well, doesn't the war with Vietnam deal with your mission?

"A Oh, yes.

"Q Well, what I guess I am trying to get at is isn't it true that the content of what a proposed visitor intends to say is the basis for whether he is allowed to come on or not? If, for instance, he says 'I intend to urge the soldiers not to use drugs,' that, from what you have said, would be something that the Base might favorably look on. If he is going to

inform them of some management principle that they are not aware of—

"A That would further our mission, yes.

"Q But if they are to speak against the war in Vietnam—

"A That certainly wouldn't forward our mission, would it?

"Q So the content of what they are to say, that is the basis of whether or not they are approved?

"A Yes, to a great extent." * * *

e. For support for this view, see Blasi, *The Checking Value in First Amendment Theory,*

Notes and Questions

1. *The right test.* Should one test be applied to all cases including access to government property? *Grayned's* incompatibility test? *Greer's* public forum test? The *O'Brien* test? [f]

2. Why does *Greer* fail to cite *Grayned?* Is *Greer* a military case rather than a case enunciating public forum doctrine? Was *Grayned* silently repudiated?

3. Is *Greer* inconsistent with *Mosley?* Is it content discrimination to permit speakers on drug abuse to address the troops but not presidential candidates? Is the suggestion that discriminating among speakers in terms of subject matter in certain forms is acceptable so long as there is no discrimination in terms of viewpoint? See Tribe, *American Constitutional Law* 691 n.21. Would the military be obligated to afford access to a speaker with a different point of view on drug abuse? Is the point that in non-public forum contexts the government has a free hand in drawing lines according to content? See Stone, *Restrictions of Speech Because of its Content: The Peculiar Case of Subject-Matter Restrictions,* 46 U.Chi.L.Rev. 81, 95–96 (1978). That government's latitude for content discrimination increases when government has an intent to communicate? Is the *Mosley* language "ill-suited for application to schools, to libraries, [and] to military training classrooms"? See Shiffrin, *Government Speech,* 27 U.C.L.A.L. Rev. 565, 579 (1980). See generally Yudof, *When Government Speaks: Politics, Law, and Government Expression in America* (1983); Yudof, *When Governments Speak: Toward a Theory of Government Expression and the First Amendment,* 57 Tex.L.Rev. 863 (1979).

III. LIMITED PUBLIC FORUMS AND NONPUBLIC FORUMS

A collective bargaining agreement between the board of education and Perry Education Association (PEA), the duly elected exclusive bargaining representative of the school district's teachers, granted PEA access to the interschool mail system and teacher mailboxes in the district, access rights not available to any rival union such as Perry Local Educators' Association (PLEA). (Prior to the 1978 collective bargaining agreement, PLEA had had equal access to the school mailboxes and delivery system). PLEA maintained that PEA's exclusive access to these facilities violated the first amendment and equal protection. PERRY EDUC. ASS'N v. PERRY LOCAL EDUCATORS' ASS'N, 460 U.S. 37, 103 S.Ct. 948, 74 L.Ed.2d 794 (1983), per WHITE, J., rejected both contentions: "The existence of a right of access to public property and the standard by which limitations upon such a right must be evaluated differ depending on the character of the property at issue.

"In places which by long tradition or by government fiat have been devoted to assembly and debate, the rights of the state to limit expressive activity are

1977 Am.B.Found.Res.J. 521, 643–44; Yudof, *When Governments Speak: Toward a Theory of Government Expression and the First Amendment,* 57 Tex.L.Rev. 863, 887 (1979).

f. For advocacy of an "openness" test, see Zillman & Imwinkelried, *The Legacy of Greer v. Spock: The Public Forum Doctrine and the Principle of the Military's Political Neutrality,* 65 Geo.L.J. 773 (1977). For criticism of the "public forum" test, see *Nimmer on Freedom of Speech* 4–67 to 4–81 (1984); Tribe, *American Constitutional Law* 688–93 (1978); Karst, *Public Enterprise and the Public Forum: A Comment on Southeastern Promotions, Ltd. v. Conrad,* 37 Ohio St.L.J. 247 (1976); Stone, *Fora Americana,* supra; Note, *The Public Forum: Minimum Access, Equal Access, and the First Amendment,* 28 Stan.L.Rev. 117, 132–48 (1975). See also note 1 after *Perry* infra.

sharply circumscribed. At one end of the spectrum are streets and parks which 'have immemorially been held in trust for the use of the public, and, time out of mind, have been used for purposes of assembly, communicating thoughts between citizens, and discussing public questions.' *Hague.* In these quintessential public forums, the government may not prohibit all communicative activity. For the state to enforce a content-based exclusion it must show that its regulation is necessary to serve a compelling state interest and that it is narrowly drawn to achieve that end. The state may also enforce regulations of the time, place, and manner of expression which are content-neutral, are narrowly tailored to serve a significant government interest, and leave open ample alternative channels of communication. *Grayned; Schneider.*

"A second category consists of public property which the state has opened for use by the public as a place for expressive activity. The Constitution forbids a state to enforce certain exclusions from a forum generally open to the public even if it was not required to create the forum in the first place. * * *[7] Although a state is not required to indefinitely retain the open character of the facility, as long as it does so it is bound by the same standards as apply in a traditional public forum. Reasonable time, place and manner regulations are permissible, and a content-based prohibition must be narrowly drawn to effectuate a compelling state interest.

"Public property which is not by tradition or designation a forum for public communication is governed by different standards. [In] addition to time, place, and manner regulations, the state may reserve the forum for its intended purposes, communicative or otherwise, as long as the regulation on speech is reasonable and not an effort to suppress expression merely because public officials oppose the speaker's view.[a]

"The school mail facilities at issue here fall within this third category. [But PLEA contends] that the school mail facilities have become a 'limited public forum' from which it may not be excluded because of the periodic use of the system by private non-school connected groups, and PLEA's own unrestricted access to the system prior to PEA's certification as exclusive representative.

"Neither of these arguments is persuasive. The use of the internal school mail by groups not affiliated with the schools is no doubt a relevant consideration. If by policy or by practice the Perry School District has opened its mail system for indiscriminate use by the general public, then PLEA could justifiably argue a public forum has been created. This, however, is not the case. As the case comes before us, there is no indication in the record that the school mailboxes and interschool delivery system are open for use by the general public. Permission to use the system to communicate with teachers must be secured from the individual building principal. There is [no evidence] that this permission has been granted as a matter of course to all who seek to distribute material. We can only conclude that the schools do allow some outside organizations such as the YMCA, Cub Scouts, and other civic and church organizations to use the facilities. This type of selective access does not transform government property into a public forum. In *Greer,* the fact that other civilian speaker and

---

7. A public forum may be created for a limited purpose such as use by certain groups, e.g., *Widmar v. Vincent* [p. 815 infra] (student groups), or for the discussion of certain subjects, e.g., *City of Madison Joint School District v. Wisconsin Pub. Employ. Relat.*

Comm'n, 429 U.S. 167, 97 S.Ct. 421, 50 L.Ed.2d 376 (1976) (school board business).

a. Can speakers be excluded from the Oval Room of the White House "merely because public officials oppose the speaker's view"?

entertainers had sometimes been invited to appear at Fort Dix did not convert the military base into a public forum. * * *

"Moreover, even if we assume that by granting access to the Cub Scouts, YMCAs, and parochial schools, the school district has created a 'limited' public forum, the constitutional right of access would in any event extend only to other entities of similar character. * * *

"[According to the Court of Appeals], the access policy adopted by the Perry schools favors a particular viewpoint, that of the PEA, on labor relations, and consequently must be strictly scrutinized regardless of whether a public forum is involved. There is, however, no indication that the school board intended to discourage one viewpoint and advance another. We believe it is more accurate to characterize the access policy as based on the *status* of the respective unions rather than their views. Implicit in the concept of the nonpublic forum is the right to make distinctions in access on the basis of subject matter and speaker identity. These distinctions may be impermissible in a public forum but are inherent and inescapable in the process of limiting a nonpublic forum to activities compatible with the intended purpose of the property. The touchstone for evaluating these distinctions is whether they are reasonable in light of the purpose which the forum at issue serves.

"The differential access provided PEA and PLEA is reasonable because it is wholly consistent with the district's legitimate interest in 'preserv[ing] the property [for] the use to which it is lawfully dedicated.' Use of school mail facilities enables PEA to perform effectively its obligations as exclusive representative of *all* Perry Township teachers. Conversely, PLEA does not have any official responsibility in connection with the school district and need not be entitled to the same rights of access to school mailboxes. [W]hen government property is not dedicated to open communication the government may—without further justification—restrict use to those who participate in the forum's official business. * * *

"Finally, the reasonableness of the limitations on PLEA's access to the school mail system is also supported by the substantial alternative channels that remain open for union-teacher communication to take place. These means range from bulletin boards to meeting facilities to the United States mail. During election periods, PLEA is assured of equal access to all modes of communication. There is no showing here that PLEA's ability to communicate with teachers is seriously impinged by the restricted access to the internal mail system. The variety and type of alternative modes of access present here compare favorably with those in other nonpublic forum cases where we have upheld restrictions on access. See, e.g. *Greer* (servicemen free to attend political rallies off-base).

"The Court of Appeals also held that the differential access provided the rival unions constituted impermissible content discrimination in violation of the Equal Protection Clause of the Fourteenth Amendment. We have rejected this contention when cast as a First Amendment argument, and it fares no better in equal protection garb. [Because] PLEA did not have a First Amendment or other right of access to the interschool mail system [the] decision to grant such privileges to the PEA need not be tested by the strict scrutiny applied when government action impinges upon a fundamental right protected by the Constitution. The school district's policy need only rationally further a legitimate state purpose. That purpose is clearly found in the special responsibilities of an exclusive bargaining representative.

"[PLEA's reliance on *Mosley* and *Carey* is misplaced. [The] key to those decisions [was] the presence of a public forum. In a public forum, by definition, all parties have a constitutional right of access and the state must demonstrate compelling reasons for restricting access to a single class of speakers, a single viewpoint, or a single subject.

"When speakers and subjects are similarly situated, the state may not pick and choose. Conversely on government property that has not been made a public forum, not all speech is equally situated, and the state may draw distinctions which relate to the special purpose for which the property is used. As we have explained above, for a school mail facility, the difference in status between the exclusive bargaining representative and its rival is such a distinction."

BRENNAN, J., joined by Marshall, Powell, and Stevens, JJ., dissented: "Based on a finding that the interschool mail system is not a 'public forum,' the Court states that the respondents have no right of access to the system, and that the school board is free 'to make distinctions in access on the basis of subject matter and speaker identity,' if the distinctions are 'reasonable in light of the purpose which the forum at issue serves.'

"[The] Court fundamentally misperceives the essence of [PLEA's claims]. This case does not involve an 'absolute access' claim. It involves an 'equal access' claim. As such it does not turn on whether the internal school mail system is a 'public forum.' In focusing on the public forum issue, the Court disregards the First Amendment's central proscription against censorship, in the form of viewpoint discrimination, in any forum, public or nonpublic. [Generally], the concept of content neutrality prohibits the government from choosing the subjects that are appropriate for public discussion. The content neutrality cases frequently refer to the prohibition against viewpoint discrimination and both concepts have their roots in the First Amendment's bar against censorship. But unlike the viewpoint discrimination concept, which is used to strike down government restrictions on speech by particular speakers, the content neutrality principle is invoked when the government has imposed restrictions on speech related to an entire subject area. The content neutrality principle can be seen as an outgrowth of the core First Amendment prohibition against viewpoint discrimination. See generally, Stone, *Restrictions of Speech Because of its Content: The Peculiar Case of Subject-Matter Restrictions,* 46 U.Chi.L.Rev. 81 (1978). * * *

"Once the government permits discussion of certain subject matter, it may not impose restrictions that discriminate among viewpoints on those subjects whether a nonpublic forum is involved or not.[5] This prohibition is implicit in the *Mosley* line of cases, in *Tinker,* and in those cases in which we have approved content-based restrictions on access to government property that is not a public forum.[b]

"[The] Court responds to the allegation of viewpoint discrimination by suggesting that there is no indication that the board intended to discriminate

---

5. This is not to suggest that a government may not close a nonpublic forum altogether or limit access to the forum to those involved in the "official business" of the agency. Restrictions of this type are consistent with the government's right "to preserve the property under its control for the use to which it is lawfully dedicated."

b. Brennan, J., characterized *Greer* as involving an unusual nonpublic forum where the speech had been determined to be incompatible with the forum. He concluded that *Greer* and other cases authorized the exclusion of some subjects from such forums, but argued that the exclusions had been viewpoint neutral.

and that the exclusive access policy is based on the parties' status rather than on their views. In this case, for the reasons discussed below, the intent to discriminate can be inferred from the effect of the policy, which is to deny an effective channel of communication to the respondents, and from other facts in the case. In addition, the petitioner's status has nothing to do with whether viewpoint discrimination in fact has occurred. If anything, the petitioner's status is relevant to the question of whether the exclusive access policy can be justified, not to whether the board has discriminated among viewpoints.

"Addressing the question of viewpoint discrimination directly, free of the Court's irrelevant public forum analysis, it is clear that the exclusive access policy discriminates on the basis of viewpoint. The Court of Appeals found that 'the access policy * * * favors a particular viewpoint on labor relations in the Perry schools * * *: the teachers inevitably will receive from [the petitioner] self-laudatory descriptions of its activities on their behalf and will be denied the critical perspective offered by [the respondents].' This assessment of the effect of the policy is eminently reasonable. Moreover, certain other factors strongly suggest that the policy discriminates among viewpoints.

"On a practical level, the only reason for the petitioner to seek an exclusive access policy is to deny its rivals access to an effective channel of communication. No other group is explicitly denied access to the mail system. In fact, as the Court points out, many other groups have been granted access to the system. Apparently, access is denied to the respondents because of the likelihood of their expressing points of view different from the petitioner's on a range of subjects. The very argument the petitioner advances in support of the policy, the need to preserve labor peace, also indicates that the access policy is not viewpoint-neutral. * * *

"The petitioner attempts to justify the exclusive access provision based on its status as the exclusive bargaining representative for the teachers and on the state's interest in efficient communication between collective bargaining representatives and the members of the unit. The petitioner's status and the state's interest in efficient communication are important considerations. They are not sufficient, however, to sustain the exclusive access policy.

"[But] the exclusive access policy is both 'overinclusive and underinclusive' as a means of serving the state's interest in the efficient discharge of the petitioner's legal duties to the teachers. The policy is overinclusive because it does not strictly limit the petitioner's use of the mail system to performance of its special legal duties and underinclusive because the board permits outside organizations with no special duties to the teachers, or to the students, to use the system. The Court of Appeals also suggested that even if the board had attempted to tailor the policy more carefully by denying outside groups access to the system and by expressly limiting the petitioner's use of the system to messages relating to its official duties, 'the fit would still be questionable, for it might be difficult—both in practice and in principle—effectively to separate "necessary" communications from propaganda.' * * *

"Putting aside the difficulties with the fit between this policy and the asserted interests, the Court of Appeals properly pointed out that the policy is invalid 'because it furthers no discernible state interest.' While the board may have a legitimate interest in granting the petitioner access to the system, it has no legitimate interest in making that access exclusive by denying access to the respondents. * * *

"Although the state's interest in preserving labor peace in the schools in order to prevent disruption is unquestionably substantial, merely articulating the interest is not enough to sustain the exclusive access policy in this case. There must be some showing that the asserted interest is advanced by the policy. In the absence of such a showing, the exclusive access policy must fall.[13]"

Notes and Questions

1. *The first amendment and geography.* Consider Farber & Nowak, *The Misleading Nature of Public Forum Analysis: Content and Context in First Amendment Adjudication,* 70 Va.L.Rev. 1219, 1234–35 (1984): "Classification of public places as various types of forums has only confused judicial opinions by diverting attention from the real first amendment issues involved in the cases. Like the fourth amendment, the first amendment protects people, not places. Constitutional protection should depend not on labeling the speaker's physical location but on the first amendment values and governmental interests involved in the case. Of course, governmental interests are often tied to the nature of the place. [To] this extent, the public forum doctrine is a useful heuristic [device]. But when the heuristic device becomes the exclusive method of analysis, only confusion and mistakes can result."

2. *Footnote 7 forums.* What is the relationship between the Court's second category of property and fn. 7? Is the discretion to create forums limited? Is it necessary to show that restrictions on such forums are necessary to achieve a compelling state interest? If a restriction (to certain speakers or subjects) is challenged, can the restrictions be used to show that that the property is not a public forum of the second category? Is this inadmissible circularity? See Tribe, *Equality as a First Amendment Theme: The "Government—as—Private Actor" Exception* in Choper, Kamisar & Tribe, The Supreme Court: Trends and Developments 1982–1983, at 221, 226 (1984).[c] In any event, does fn. 7 create a fourth category of property without setting guiding standards? Are the *Perry* mailboxes fn. 7 forums?

13. The Court also cites the availability of alternative channels of communication in support of the "reasonableness" of the exclusive access policy. In a detailed discussion, the Court of Appeals properly concluded that the other channels of communication available to the respondents were "not nearly as effective as the internal mail system." In addition, the Court apparently disregards the principle that "one is not to have the exercise of his liberty of expression in appropriate places abridged on the plea that it may be exercised in some other place." *Schneider.* In this case, the existence of inferior alternative channels of communication does not affect the conclusion that the petitioner has failed to justify the viewpoint-discriminatory exclusive access policy.

c. Compare Blackmun, J., dissenting in *Cornelius v. NAACP Legal Defense and Educational Fund, Inc.,* __ U.S. __, 105 S.Ct. 3439, 87 L.Ed.2d 567 (1985): "If the Government does not create a limited public forum unless it intends to provide an 'open forum' for expressive activity, and if the exclusion of some speakers is evidence that the Government did not intend to create such a forum, no speaker challenging denial of access will ever be able to prove that the forum is a limited public forum. The very fact that the Government denied access to the speaker indicates that the Government did not intend to provide an open forum for expressive activity, and [that] fact alone would demonstrate that the forum is not a limited public forum." In *Cornelius,* a 4–3 majority, per O'Connor, J., determined that "government does not create a public forum by inaction or by permitting limited discourse, but only by intentionally opening a non-traditional forum for public discourse." Observing that the Court will look to the policy and practice of the government, the nature of the property and its compatibility with expressive activity in discerning intent, O'Connor, J., insisted that "we will not find that a public forum has been created in the face of clear evidence of a contrary intent, nor will we infer that the Government intended to create a public forum when the nature of the property is inconsistent with expressive activity."

3. *Alternative channels.* Does consideration of alternative channels of communication violate *Schneider's* observation that "one is not to have the exercise of his liberty of expression in appropriate places abridged on the plea that it may be exercised in some other place?" For discussion emphasizing the importance of considering alternative channels of communications and the methods for doing so, see generally Cass, *First Amendment Access to Government Facilities,* 65 Va.L.Rev. 1287 (1979).

4. For commentary on speaker-based restrictions, see Stone, *Content Regulation and the First Amendment,* 25 Wm. & Mary L.Rev. 189, 244–51 (1983).

SECTION 6. GOVERNMENT SUPPORT OF SPEECH

Public forum doctrine recognizes that government is obligated to permit some of its property to be used for communicative purposes without content discrimination, but public forum doctrine also allows other government property to be restricted to some speakers or for talk about selected subjects. See *Greer; Perry.* In short, in some circumstances government can provide resources for some speech while denying support for other speech. Indeed, government is a significant actor in the marketplace of ideas. Sometimes the government speaks as government; sometimes it subsidizes speech without purporting to claim that the resulting message is its own. It supports speech in many ways: official government messages; statements of public officials at publicly subsidized press conferences; artistic, scientific, or political subsidies, even the classroom communications of public school teachers.

If content distinctions are suspect when government acts as censor, they are the norm when government speaks or otherwise subsidizes speech. Government makes editorial judgments; it decides that some content is appropriate for the occasion and other content is not. The public museum curator makes content decisions in selecting exhibits; the librarian in selecting books; the public board in selecting recipients for research grants; the public official in composing press releases.

The line between support for speech and censorship of speech is not always bright, however. In any event, the Constitution limits the choices government may make in supporting speech. For example, government support of religious speech is limited under the establishment clause. See Ch. 9. This section explores the extent to which the speech clause or constitutional conceptions of equality should limit government discretion in supporting speech.

I. SUBSIDIES AND TAX EXPENDITURES

REGAN v. TAXATION WITH REPRESENTATION OF WASHINGTON

461 U.S. 540, 103 S.Ct. 1997, 76 L.Ed.2d 129 (1983).

JUSTICE REHNQUIST delivered the opinion of the Court.

[Section 501(c) of the Internal Revenue Code affords tax exempt status to various nonprofit organizations. Section 501(c)(19) affords a tax exemption to veterans' organizations. Moreover, contributions to veterans' organizations are treated by the IRS as deductible (up to 20% of adjusted gross income) even if the veterans organizations engage in substantial lobbying activity at state or federal levels. Section 501(c)(3) grants exempt status to various groups commonly called "charitable" organizations that are "organized and operated exclusively for religious, charitable, scientific [or] educational purposes * * * no substantial part of the activities of which is carrying on propaganda, or otherwise attempting to influence legislation [and] which does not participate in, or intervene in (including the publishing or distributing of statements), any political campaign on behalf of any candidate for public office." Section 501(c)(4) grants exempt status to groups organized for the purposes identified in 501(c)(3) (and for some other purposes) regardless of the amount of lobbying or political activity. Contributions made to groups meeting 501(c)(3) standards are deductible (up to 50% of adjusted gross income); contributions to 501(c)(4) groups are not deductible.

[Taxpayers for Representation of Washington ("TWR"), a group organized to represent the taxpayer's public interest in Washington was denied 501(c)(3) status because of its lobbying activities. It argued that affording tax deductible contributions to the substantial lobbying activities of veterans while denying such benefits to charitable organizations involved in similar activities was unconstitutional discrimination.[a] The District of Columbia Court of Appeals agreed with TWR:[b] "If veterans' organizations and organizations such as Taxation lobby on different sides of the same questions, Congress has chosen to favor one lobbyist on a particular issue over another. If veterans' organizations and [charitable] organizations lobby on entirely distinct matters, Congress has ensured that greater attention will be devoted to some causes than others."

[It concluded that, "[A] First Amendment concern must inform the equal protection analysis in this case. Courts must scrutinize with special care any act of Congress that facilitates the speech of one speaker over another, even when legislation is enacted in the dry, classification-ridden context of the Internal Revenue Code. By subsidizing the lobbying activities of veterans' organizations while failing to subsidize the lobbying of [TWR] and other charitable groups, Congress has violated the equal protection guarantees of the Constitution. * * *

["The First Amendment occupies a preferred place in our scheme of government. This does not mean, however, that its application in a legal dispute is always simple. The lines will seem clearer when Congress directly prohibits a particular group from speaking in a particular place, and more confused when Congress subsidizes First Amendment expression unevenly through the intricacies of the Internal Revenue Code. Nevertheless, the principle remains the same."

[The Supreme Court reversed:] * * *

Both tax exemptions and tax-deductibility are a form of subsidy[c] that is administered through the tax system. A tax exemption has much the same effect as a cash grant to the organization of the amount of tax it would have to

---

a. TWR also argued that although the government had no obligation to grant tax advantages to charities, it could not condition receipt of tax advantages on a surrender of the first amendment right to lobby. The Court denied that the tax code called for any such surrender. It suggested that TWR could separately incorporate a lobbying organization under § 501(c)(4) and a non-lobbying organization under § 501(c)(3) so long as it kept records adequate to show that tax deductible contributions were not used for lobbying.

b. *Taxation With Representation of Washington v. Regan,* 676 F.2d 715, (D.C.Cir.1982).

c. The IRS accepted "the analogy between tax exemptions and direct government subsidies" for purposes of the case (676 F.2d at 725 n. 19), but the question of what should be characterized as a subsidy is much debated in tax circles. Compare e.g., Bittker & Kaufman, *Taxes and Civil Rights: "Constitutionalizing" the Internal Revenue Code,* 82 Yale L.J. 51, 63–68 (1972) with Surrey & McDaniel, *The Tax Expenditure Concept and the Budget Re-*

pay on its income. Deductible contributions are similar to cash grants of the amount of a portion of the individual's contributions.[5] The system Congress has enacted provides this kind of subsidy to non profit civic welfare organizations generally, and an additional subsidy to those charitable organizations that do not engage in substantial lobbying. In short, Congress chose not to subsidize lobbying as extensively as it chose to subsidize other activities that non profit organizations undertake to promote the public welfare.

[Congress] has not violated TWR's First Amendment rights by declining to subsidize its First Amendment activities. The case would be different if Congress were to discriminate invidiously in its subsidies in such a way as to " 'aim[ ] at the suppression of dangerous ideas.' " But the veterans' organizations that qualify under § 501(c)(19) are entitled to receive tax-deductible contributions regardless of the content of any speech they may use, including lobbying. We find no indication that the statute was intended to suppress any ideas or any demonstration that it has had that effect. The sections of the Internal Revenue Code here at issue do not employ any suspect classification. The distinction between veterans' organizations and other charitable organizations is not at all like distinctions based on race or national origin.

The Court of Appeals nonetheless held that "strict scrutiny" is required because the statute "*affect[s]* First Amendment rights on a discriminatory basis." Its opinion suggests that strict scrutiny applies whenever Congress subsidizes some speech, but not all speech. This is not the law. Congress could, for example, grant funds to an organization dedicated to combatting teenage drug abuse, but condition the grant by providing that none of the money received from Congress should be used to lobby state legislatures. [S]uch a statute would be valid. Congress might also enact a statute providing public money for an organization dedicated to combatting teenage alcohol abuse, and impose no condition against using funds obtained from Congress for lobbying. The existence of the second statute would not make the first statute subject to strict scrutiny. * * *

These are scarcely novel principles. We have held [that] a legislature's decision not to subsidize the exercise of a fundamental right does not infringe the right, and thus is not subject to strict scrutiny. *Buckley v. Valeo,* [p. 772 infra] upheld a statute that provides federal funds for candidates for public office who enter primary campaigns, but does not provide funds for candidates who do not run in party primaries. We rejected First Amendment and equal protection challenges to this provision without applying strict scrutiny.[d]

The reasoning [is] simple: "although government may not place obstacles in the path of a [person's] exercise [of] freedom of [speech], it need not remove those not of its own creation." * * * Congress—not TWR or this Court—has the

---

form Act of 1974, 17 B.C. Indust. & Comm.L. Rev. 679 (1976).

5. In stating that exemptions and deductions, on one hand, are like cash subsidies, on the other, we of course do not mean to assert that they are in all respects identical. See, e.g., *Walz v. Tax Commission* [p. 810 infra].

d. In *Buckley,* Rehnquist, J., dissenting, complained that the scheme for public funding of Presidential candidates "enshrined the Republican and Democratic Parties in a permanently preferred position, and has established requirements for funding minor-party

and independent candidates to which the two major parties are not subject. [B]ecause of the First Amendment overtones of the appellants' Fifth Amendment equal protection claim, something more than a merely rational basis for the difference in treatment must be shown, as the Court apparently recognizes." *Buckley* found the funding scheme to be "in furtherance of *sufficiently important* government interests and has not unfairly or unnecessarily burdened the political opportunity of any party or candidate." (Emphasis added).

authority to determine whether the advantage the public would receive from additional lobbying by charities is worth the money the public would pay to subsidize that lobbying, and other disadvantages that might accompany that lobbying. It appears that Congress was concerned that exempt organizations might use tax-deductible contributions to lobby to promote the private interests of their members.[e] It is not irrational for Congress to decide that tax exempt charities such as TWR should not further benefit at the expense of taxpayers at large by obtaining a further subsidy for lobbying.

It is also not irrational for Congress to decide that, even though it will not subsidize substantial lobbying by charities generally, it will subsidize lobbying by veterans' organizations. Veterans have "been obliged to drop their own affairs and take up the burdens of the nation," "subjecting themselves to the mental and physical hazards as well as the economic and family detriments which are peculiar to military service and which do not exist in normal civil life." Our country has a long standing policy of compensating veterans for their past contributions by providing them with numerous advantages.[f] This policy has "always been deemed to be legitimate."[g]   *   *   *

Notes and Questions

1. The Court observes that veterans' organizations receive tax benefits "regardless of the content of any speech they may use." Is this disingenuous because the content of veterans' organizations' speech is predictable? Could the Congress give money to Republican party organizations "regardless of the content of any speech they may use." What if Congress said it was benefiting veterans' organizations in part because Congress thought such organizations were delivering a message that deserved to be heard? Does it matter that favorable tax treatment assists veterans' lobbying at local, state, and federal levels? Could Congress withdraw favorable tax treatment from some veterans' organizations on the ground that their lobbying was not "worth the money"? Could Congress benefit charitable organizations, but not the veterans? Some charitable organizations, but not others? Could Congress give favorable tax treatment to lobbying of the Moral Majority, but no other group?[h]

2. Was TWR the wrong plaintiff? Was its claim weak because it failed to show viewpoint discrimination? Should a group whose primary purpose conflicts with that of veterans' groups be granted relief? See Note, *The Tax Code's Differential Treatment of Lobbying Under Section 501(c)(3): A Proposed First Amendment Analysis*, 66 Va.L.Rev. 1513 (1980).

3. If TWR had prevailed, what would have been the appropriate remedy? Denial of the veterans' benefit? Extension of the veterans' benefit to all charitable organizations?

e. Does this concern apply equally to veterans' organizations? See Note, *Charitable Lobbying Restraints and Tax Exempt Organizations: Old Problems, New Directions?*, 1984 Utah L.Rev. 337, 357–59 (1984).

f. Is it a sufficient response to note that veterans can be rewarded in many ways that do not tread on first amendment equality values?

g. Blackmun, J., joined by Brennan and Marshall, JJ., joined the opinion, but concurred to emphasize the importance of the tax code being administered in a manner that did not discourage lobbying by TWR or other groups.

h. For general criticism of the tax code's treatment of charitable organizations, see Clark, *The Limitation on Political Activities: A Discordant Note in the Law of Charities*, 46 Va.L.Rev. 439 (1960); Garrett, *Federal Tax Limitations on Political Activities of Public Interest and Educational Organizations*, 59 Geo.L.J. 561 (1971); Troyer, *Charities, Law-Making, and the Constitution: The Validity of the Restrictions on Influencing Legislation*, 31 N.Y.U.Inst. on Fed. Tax'n 1415 (1973).

4.   Treasury regulations provide that a charitable organization whose primary purpose is education may retain its § 501(c)(3) status even if it advocates a particular position or viewpoint "so long as it presents a sufficiently full and fair exposition of the pertinent facts as to permit an individual or the public to form an independent opinion or conclusion." Treas.Reg. § 1.501(c)(3)–1(d)(3)(i) (1959). Should tax benefits depend upon IRS determinations of "fairness" and its identification of "pertinent" facts? Compare *Big Mama Rag, Inc. v. United States,* 631 F.2d 1030 (D.C.Cir.1980) with *National Alliance v. United States,* 710 F.2d 868 (D.C.Cir.1983).

5.   Suppose that nothing in the tax law bars veterans' organizations from using tax deductible contributions for participation in political campaigns on behalf of candidates for public office.   Is this more troublesome than the lobbying benefits?   Suppose instead of supporting the political speech of others, government itself enters the political fray.   Should a city government be able to buy media time to speak on behalf of candidates?   To influence the outcome of initiative campaigns? [i]

II. GOVERNMENT AS EDUCATOR AND EDITOR

BOARD OF EDUCATION v. PICO, 457 U.S. 853, 102 S.Ct. 2799, 73 L.Ed.2d 435 (1982): Several members of the Island Trees Board of Education attended a conference sponsored by Parents of New York United (PONYU), a politically conservative organization.   At the conference these board members obtained lists of books they described as "objectionable" and "improper fare for school students."   On ascertaining that its school libraries contained eleven of the books,[a] the Board informally directed, over the objection of the school superintendent, that the books be delivered to the Board's offices so that Board members could read them.   The Board justified its action by characterizing the listed books as "anti-American, anti-Christian, anti-Semitic, and just plain filthy" and concluding that it had a "duty" and a "moral obligation" "to protect the children in our school from this moral danger as surely as from physical and medical dangers."   The Board then appointed a parent-teacher "Book Review Committee" to recommend to the board which books should be retained.   The Committee recommended that only two books be removed and a third be available to students only with parental approval.   But the Board, without giving any reasons, decided that nine books should be removed and that another should be

---

i. For a variety of views, see Yudof, *When Government Speaks: Politics, Law, and Government Expression in America* (1983); Emerson, *The Affirmative Side of the First Amendment,* 15 Ga.L.Rev. 795 (1981); Kamenshine, *The First Amendment's Implied Political Establishment Clause,* 67 Calif.L.Rev. 1104 (1979); Shiffrin; *Government Speech,* 27 U.C. L.A.L.Rev. 565 (1980); Schauer, *Book Review,* 35 Stan.L.Rev. 373 (1983); Yudof, *When Governments Speak: Toward A Theory of Government Expression and the First Amendment,* 57 Tex.L.Rev. 863 (1979); Ziegler, *Government Speech and the Constitution: The Limits of Official Partisanship,* 21 B.C.L.Rev. 578 (1980); Note, *The Constitutionality of Municipal Advocacy in Statewide Referendum Campaigns,* 93 Harv.L.Rev. 535 (1980).

a.   As the plurality opinion noted: "The nine [listed] books in the High School library

were: *Slaughter House Five,* by Kurt Vonnegut, Jr.; *The Naked Ape,* by Desmond Morris; *Down These Mean Streets,* by Piri Thomas; *Best Short Stories of Negro Writers,* edited by Langston Hughes; *Go Ask Alice,* of anonymous authorship; *Laughing Boy,* by Oliver LaFarge; *Black Boy,* by Richard Wright; *A Hero Ain't Nothin' But A Sandwich,* by Alice Childress; and *Soul On Ice,* by Eldridge Cleaver.   The [listed] book in the Junior High School library was *A Reader for Writers,* edited by Jerome Archer.   Still another listed book, *The Fixer,* by Bernard Malamud, was found to be included in the curriculum of a twelfth grade literature course."

The Board subsequently decided that only *Laughing Boy* should be returned to the library without restriction, and that *Black Boy* should be made available subject to parental approval.

made available subject to parental approval. Respondent students then brought an action for declaratory and injunctive relief under 42 U.S.C. § 1983, contending that the Board's actions had violated their first amendment rights. The district court granted summary judgment for the Board, stating that the Board had "restricted access only to certain books which [it] believed to be, in essence, vulgar." A 2–1 majority of the Second Circuit reversed. One member of the majority concluded that at least at the summary judgment stage, the Board had not offered sufficient justification for its action. A second member of the majority "viewed the case as turning on the contested factual issue of whether [the Board's] removal decision was motivated by a justifiable desire to remove books containing vulgarities and sexual explicitness, or rather by an impermissible desire to suppress ideas." The Supreme Court (5–4) upheld reversal of the summary dismissal of the suit, but there was no opinion of the Court. BRENNAN, J., announced the judgment of the Court in an opinion joined by Marshall and Stevens, JJ., and in part by Blackmun, J.:

"The principal question presented is whether the First Amendment imposes limitations upon the exercise by a local school board of its discretion to remove library books from high school and junior high school libraries.

"[P]ublic schools are vitally important 'in the preparation of individuals for participation as citizens,' and as vehicles for 'inculcating fundamental values necessary to the maintenance of a democratic political system.' We are therefore in full agreement with petitioners that local school boards must be permitted 'to establish and apply their curriculum in such a way as to transmit community values,' and that 'there is a legitimate and substantial community interest in promoting respect for authority and traditional values be they social, moral, or political.'

"At the same time, however, we have necessarily recognized that the discretion of the States and local school boards in matters of education must be exercised in a manner that comports with the transcendent imperatives of the First Amendment. In *West Virginia v. Barnette* [p. 843 infra] we held that under the First Amendment a student in a public school could not be compelled to salute the flag. We reasoned that 'Boards of Education * * * have, of course, important, delicate, and highly discretionary functions, but none that they may not perform within the limits of the Bill of Rights. That they are educating the young for citizenship is reason for scrupulous protection of Constitutional freedoms of the individual, if we are not to strangle the free mind at its source and teach youth to discount important principles of our government as mere platitudes.' * * * [I]n sum, students do not 'shed their rights to freedom of speech or expression at the schoolhouse gate,' * * * *Tinker.*

"[We] think that the First Amendment rights of students may be directly and sharply implicated by the removal of books from the shelves of a school library. * * * [W]e have held that in a variety of contexts 'the Constitution protects the right to receive information and ideas.' *Stanley v. Georgia.* [First,] the right to receive ideas follows ineluctably from the *sender's* First Amendment right to send them * * *.

"More importantly, the right to receive ideas is a necessary predicate to the *recipient's* meaningful exercise of his own rights of speech, press, and political freedom. [Of] course all First Amendment rights accorded to students must be construed 'in light of the special characteristics of the school environment.' *Tinker.* But the special characteristics of the school *library* make that environment especially appropriate for the recognition of the First Amendment rights of students.

"A school library, no less than any other public library, is 'a place dedicated to quiet, to knowledge, and to beauty.' *Brown. Keyishian v. Board of Regents* [p. 733 infra] observed that 'students must always remain free to inquire, to study and to evaluate, to gain new maturity and understanding.' The school library is the principal locus of such freedom. [Petitioners] emphasize the inculcative function of secondary education, and argue that they must be allowed *unfettered* discretion to 'transmit community values' through the Island Trees schools. But that sweeping claim overlooks the unique role of the school library. It appears from the record that use of the Island Trees school libraries is completely voluntary on the part of students. Their selection of books from these libraries is entirely a matter of free choice; the libraries afford them an opportunity at self-education and individual enrichment that is wholly optional. Petitioners might well defend their claim of absolute discretion in matters of *curriculum* by reliance upon their duty to inculcate community values. But we think that petitioners' reliance upon that duty is misplaced where, as here, they attempt to extend their claim of absolute discretion beyond the compulsory environment of the classroom, into the school library and the regime of voluntary inquiry that there holds sway.

"In rejecting petitioners' claim of absolute discretion to remove books from their school libraries, we do not deny that local school boards have a substantial legitimate role to play in the determination of school library content. [But] that discretion may not be exercised in a narrowly partisan or political manner. If a Democratic school board, motivated by party affiliation, ordered the removal of all books written by or in favor of Republicans, few would doubt that the order violated the constitutional rights of the students denied access to those books. The same conclusion would surely apply if an all-white school board, motivated by racial animus, decided to remove all books authored by blacks or advocating racial equality and integration. Our Constitution does not permit the official suppression of *ideas*. Thus whether petitioners' removal of books from their school libraries denied respondents their First Amendment rights depends upon the motivation behind petitioners' actions. If petitioners *intended* by their removal decision to deny respondents access to ideas with which petitioners disagreed, and if this intent was the decisive factor in petitioners' decision,[22] then petitioners have exercised their discretion in violation of the Constitution. To permit such intentions to control official actions would be to encourage the precise sort of officially prescribed orthodoxy unequivocally condemned in *Barnette*. On the other hand, respondents implicitly concede that an unconstitutional motivation would *not* be demonstrated if it were shown that petitioners had decided to remove the books at issue because those books were pervasively vulgar. And again, respondents concede that if it were demonstrated that the removal decision was based solely upon the 'educational suitability' of the books in question, then their removal would be 'perfectly permissible.' In other words, in respondents' view such motivations if decisive of petitioners' actions, would not carry the danger of an official suppression of ideas, and thus would not violate respondents' First Amendment rights.

"[N]othing in our decision today affects in any way the discretion of a local school board to choose books to *add* to the libraries of their schools. Because we

---

22. By "decisive factor" we mean a "substantial factor" in the absence of which the opposite decision would have been reached.

are concerned in this case with the suppression of ideas, our holding today affects only the discretion to *remove* books. In brief, we hold that local school boards may not remove books from school library shelves simply because they dislike the ideas contained in those books and seek by their removal to 'prescribe what shall be orthodox in politics, nationalism, religion, or other matters of opinion.' *Barnette.* Such purposes stand inescapably condemned by our precedents.

"We now turn to the remaining question presented by this case: Do the evidentiary materials that were before the District Court, when construed most favorably to respondents, raise a genuine issue of material fact whether petitioners exceeded constitutional limitations in exercising their discretion to remove the books from the school libraries? We conclude that the materials do raise such a question, which forecloses summary judgment in favor of petitioners.

"Before the District Court, respondents claimed that petitioners' decision to remove the books 'was based upon [their] personal values, morals and tastes.' Respondents also claimed that petitioners objected to the books in part because excerpts from them were 'anti-American.' The accuracy of these claims was partially conceded by petitioners,[23] and petitioners' own affidavits lent further support to respondents' claims. In addition, the record developed in the District Court shows that when petitioners offered their first public explanation for the removal of the books, they relied in part on the assertion that the removed books were 'anti-American,' and 'offensive [to] Americans in general.' Furthermore, while the Book Review Committee appointed by petitioners was instructed to make its recommendations based upon criteria that appear on their face to be permissible—the books' 'educational suitability,' 'good taste,' 'relevance,' and 'appropriateness to age and grade level'—the Committee's recommendations that five of the books be retained and that only two be removed were essentially rejected by petitioners, without any statement of reasons for doing so. Finally, while petitioners originally defended their removal decision with the explanation that 'these books contain obscenities, blasphemies, and perversion beyond description,' one of the books, *A Reader for Writers,* was removed even though it contained no such language.

"Standing alone, this evidence respecting the substantive motivations behind petitioners' removal decision would not be decisive. This would be a very different case if the record demonstrated that petitioners had employed established, regular, and facially unbiased procedures for the review of controversial materials. But the actual record in the case before us suggests the exact opposite. Petitioners' removal procedures were vigorously challenged below by respondents, and the evidence on this issue sheds further light on the issue of petitioners' motivations. Respondents alleged that in making their removal decision petitioners ignored 'the advice of literary experts,' the views of 'librarians and teachers within the Island Trees School system,' the advice of the superintendent of schools, and the guidance of 'publications that rate books for junior and senior high school students.' Respondents also claimed that petitioners' decision was based solely on the fact that the books were named on the PONYU list [and] that petitioners 'did not undertake an independent review of other books in the [school] libraries.' Evidence before the District Court lends support to these claims. [In] sum, respondents' allegations and some of the

23. Petitioners acknowledged that their "evaluation of the suitability of the books was based on [their] personal values, morals, tastes and concepts of educational suitability." But they did not accept, and thus apparently denied, respondents' assertion that some excerpts were objected to as "anti-American."

evidentiary materials presented below do not rule out the possibility that petitioners' removal procedures were highly irregular and ad hoc—the antithesis of those procedures that might tend to allay suspicions regarding petitioners' motivations.

"Construing these claims, affidavit statements, and other evidentiary materials in a manner favorable to respondents, we cannot conclude that petitioners were 'entitled to a judgment as a matter of law.' The evidence plainly does not foreclose the possibility that petitioners' decision to remove the books rested decisively upon disagreement with constitutionally protected ideas in those books, or upon a desire on petitioners' part to impose upon the students of the Island Trees High School and Junior High School a political orthodoxy to which petitioners and their constituents adhered."

In the view of BLACKMUN, J., concurring, "the principle involved here is both narrower and more basic than 'the right to receive information' identified by the plurality. I do not suggest that the State has any affirmative obligation to provide students with information or ideas, something that may well be associated with a 'right to receive.' And I do not believe, as the plurality suggests, that the right at issue here is somehow associated with the peculiar nature of the school library; if schools may be used to inculcate ideas, surely libraries may play a role in that process.[1] Instead, I suggest that certain forms of state discrimination *between* ideas are improper. In particular, our precedents command the conclusion that the State may not act to deny access to an idea simply because state officials disapprove of that idea for partisan or political reasons.[2]

* * *

"As I view it, this is a narrow principle. School officials must be able to choose one book over another, without outside interference, when the first book is deemed more relevant to the curriculum, or better written, or when one of a host of other politically neutral reasons is present. These decisions obviously will not implicate First Amendment values. And even absent space or financial limitations, First Amendment principles would allow a school board to refuse to make a book available to students because it contains offensive language, cf. *FCC v. Pacifica Foundation* [p. 712 infra] (Powell, J., concurring), or because it is psychologically or intellectually inappropriate for the age group, or even, perhaps, because the ideas it advances are 'manifestly inimical to the public

---

1. As a practical matter, however, it is difficult to see the First Amendment right that I believe is at work here playing a role in a school's choice of curriculum. The school's finite resources—as well as the limited number of hours in the day—require that education officials make sensitive choices between subjects to be offered and competing areas of academic emphasis; subjects generally are excluded simply because school officials have chosen to devote their resources to one rather than to another subject. [In] any event, the Court has recognized that students' First Amendment rights in most cases must give way if they interfere "with the schools' work or [with] the rights of other students to be secure and to be let alone," *Tinker,* and such interference will rise to intolerable levels if public participation in the management of the curriculum becomes commonplace. In contrast, library books on a shelf intrude not at all on the daily operation of a school.

I also have some doubt that there is a theoretical distinction between removal of a book and failure to acquire a book. But as Judge Newman observed, there is a profound practical and evidentiary distinction between the two actions: "removal, more than failure to acquire, is likely to suggest that an impermissible political motivation may be present. There are many reasons why a book is not acquired, the most obvious being limited resources, but there are few legitimate reasons why a book, once acquired, should be removed from a library not filled to capacity."

2. In effect, my view presents the obverse of the plurality's analysis: while the plurality focuses on the failure to provide information, I find crucial the State's decision to single out an idea for disapproval and then deny access to it.

welfare.' And, of course, school officials may choose one book over another because they believe that one subject is more important, or is more deserving of emphasis.

"[I] believe that tying the First Amendment right to the *purposeful* suppression of ideas makes the concept more manageable than Justice Rehnquist acknowledges. Most people would recognize that refusing to allow discussion of current events in Latin class is a policy designed to 'inculcate' Latin, not to suppress ideas. Similarly, removing a learned treatise criticizing American foreign policy from an elementary school library because the students would not understand it is an action unrelated to the *purpose* of suppressing ideas. In my view, however, removing the same treatise because it is 'anti-American' raises a far more difficult issue.

"It is not a sufficient answer to this problem that a State operates a school in its role as 'educator,' rather than its role as 'sovereign,' (Rehnquist, J., dissenting), for the First Amendment has application to all the State's activities. While the State may act as 'property owner' when it prevents certain types of expressive activity from taking place on public lands, for example, few would suggest that the State may base such restrictions on the content of the speaker's message, or may take its action for the purpose of suppressing access to the ideas involved. *Mosley*. And while it is not clear to me from Justice Rehnquist's discussion whether a State operates its public libraries in its 'role as sovereign,' surely difficult constitutional problems would arise if a State chose to exclude 'anti-Amnerican' books from its public libraries—even if those books remained available at local bookstores.

"[S]chool officials may seek to instill certain values 'by persuasion and example,' or by choice of emphasis. That sort of positive educational action, however, is the converse of an intentional attempt to shield students from certain ideas that officials find politically distasteful. Arguing that the majority in the community rejects the ideas involved, does not refute this principle: 'The very purpose of a Bill of Rights was to withdraw certain subjects from the vicissitudes of political controversy, to place them beyond the reach of majorities and officials * * *.' *Barnette*."

WHITE, J., who concurred in the judgment, noted that although the District Court found that the books were removed because the school board believed them "to be, in essence, vulgar," both Court of Appeals judges in the majority concluded that there was a material issue of fact that precluded summary judgment for petitioners. As White, J., understood it, "[t]he unresolved factual issue [is] the reason or reasons underlying the school board's removal of the books" and he was "not inclined to disagree with the Court of Appeals on such a fact-bound issue. [The] Court seems compelled to go further and issue a dissertation on the extent to which the First Amendment limits the discretion of the school board to remove books from the school library. I see no necessity for doing so at this point. When findings of fact and conclusions of law are made by the District Court, that may end the case."

BURGER, C.J., joined by Powell, Rehnquist, and O'Connor, JJ., dissented: "The First Amendment, as with other parts of the Constitution, must deal with new problems in a changing world. In an attempt to deal with a problem in an area traditionally left to the states, a plurality of the Court, in a lavish expansion going beyond any prior holding under the First Amendment, expresses its view that a school board's decision concerning what books are to be in the school library is subject to federal court review. Were this to become the law, this Court would come perilously close to becoming a 'super censor' of school board library decisions. Stripped to its essentials, the issue comes down to two important propositions: first, whether local schools are to be administered by elected school boards, or by federal judges and teenage pupils; and second, whether the values of morality, good taste, and relevance to education are valid reasons for school board decisions concerning the contents of a school library. In an attempt to place this case within the protection of the First Amendment, the plurality suggests a new 'right' that, when shorn of the plurality's rhetoric, allows this Court to impose its own views about what books must be made available to students. * * *

"It is true that where there is a willing distributor of materials, the government may not impose unreasonable obstacles to dissemination by the third party. And where the speaker desires to express certain ideas, the government may not impose unreasonable restraints. It does not follow, however, that a school board must affirmatively aid the speaker in its communication with the recipient. In short the plurality suggests today that if a writer has something to say, the government through its schools must be the courier. None of the cases cited by the plurality establish this broad-based proposition.

"[The] plurality concludes that under the Constitution school boards cannot choose to retain or dispense with books if their discretion is exercised in a 'narrowly partisan or political manner.' The plurality concedes that permissible factors are whether the books are 'pervasively vulgar' or educationally unsuitable. 'Educational suitability,' however, is a standardless phrase. This conclusion will undoubtedly be drawn in many—if not most—instances because of the decisionmaker's content-based judgment that the ideas contained in the book or the idea expressed from the author's method of communication are inappropriate for teenage pupils. * * *

"Further, there is no guidance whatsoever as to what constitutes 'political' factors. [V]irtually all educational decisions necessarily involve 'political' determinations.

"What the plurality views as valid reasons for removing a book at their core involve partisan judgments. Ultimately the federal courts will be the judge of whether the motivation for book removal was 'valid' or 'reasonable.' Undoubtedly the validity of many book removals will ultimately turn on a judge's evaluation of the books. Discretion must be used, and the appropriate body to exercise that discretion is the local elected school board, not judges. * * *

"No amount of 'limiting' language could rein in the sweeping 'right' the plurality would create. The plurality distinguishes library books from textbooks because library books 'by their nature are optional rather than required reading.' It is not clear, however, why this distinction requires *greater* scrutiny before 'optional' reading materials may be removed. It would appear that required reading and textbooks have a greater likelihood of imposing a 'pall of orthodoxy' over the educational process than do optional reading. In essence, the plurality's view transforms the availability of this 'optional' reading into a 'right' to have this 'optional' reading maintained at the demand of teenagers.

"The plurality also limits the new right by finding it applicable only to the *removal* of books once acquired. Yet if the First Amendment commands that certain books cannot be *removed,* does it not equally require that the same books be *acquired?* Why does the coincidence of timing become the basis of a constitutional holding? According to the plurality, the evil to be avoided is the 'official suppression of ideas.' It does not follow that the decision to *remove* a book is less 'official suppression' than the decision not to acquire a book desired by someone.[8] Similarly, a decision to eliminate certain material from the curriculum, history for example, would carry an equal—probably greater—prospect of 'official suppression.' Would the decision be subject to our review?"

POWELL, J., also dissented: "The plurality's reasoning is marked by contradiction. It purports to acknowledge the traditional role of school boards and parents [in] 'inculcating fundamental values necessary to the maintenance of a democratic political system.' * * * Yet when a school board, as in this case, takes its responsibilities seriously and seeks to decide what the fundamental values are that should be imparted, the plurality finds a constitutional violation.

"[A] school board's attempt to instill in its students the ideas and values on which a democratic system depends is viewed as an impermissible suppression of other ideas and values on which other systems of government and other societies thrive. Books may not be removed because they are indecent; extoll violence, intolerance and racism; or degrade the dignity of the individual. Human history, not the least of the twentieth century, records the power and political life of these very ideas. But they are not our ideas or values. Although I would leave this educational decision to the duly constituted board, I certainly would not *require* a school board to promote ideas and values repugnant to a democratic society or to teach such values to *children*.

"In different contexts and in different times, the destruction of written materials has been the symbol of despotism and intolerance. But the removal of nine vulgar or racist books from a high school library by a concerned local school board does not raise this specter. For me, today's decision symbolizes a debilitating encroachment upon the institutions of a free people." [b]

REHNQUIST, J., joined by Burger, C.J., and Powell, J., "disagree[d] with Justice Brennan's opinion because it is largely hypothetical in character, failing to take account of the facts as admitted by the parties [and] because it is analytically unsound and internally inconsistent":

"Considering only the respondents' description of the factual aspects of petitioners' motivation, Justice Brennan's apparent concern that the Board's action may have been a sinister political plot 'to suppress ideas' may be laid to rest. The members of the Board, in deciding to remove these books, were undoubtedly influenced by their own 'personal values, morals, and tastes,' just as any member of a school board is apt to be so influenced in making decisions as to whether a book is educationally suitable. Respondents essentially conceded that some excerpts of the removed books 'contained profanities, some were sexually explicit, some were ungrammatical, some were anti-American, and some were offensive to racial, religious, or ethnic groups.'

"Respondents also agreed that, '[a]lthough the books themselves were excluded from use in the schools in any way, [petitioners] have not precluded discussion about the themes of the books or the books themselves.' Justice Brennan's concern with the 'suppression of ideas' thus seems entirely unwar-

---

8. The formless nature of the "right" found by the plurality in this case is exemplified by this purported distinction. Presumably a school district could, for any reason, choose not to purchase a book for its library. Once it purchases that book, however, it is "locked in" to retaining it on the school shelf until it can justify a reason for its removal. This anomolous result of "book tenure" was pointed out by the District Court in this case.

Under the plurality view, if a school board wants to be assured that it maintains control over the education of its students, every page of every book sought to be acquired must be read before a purchase decision is made.

b. Powell, J., appended a summary of excerpts from the books at issue collected in the opinion of Judge Mansfield dissenting below.

ranted on this state of the record, and his creation of constitutional rules to cover such eventualities is entirely gratuitous. [Although] I entirely disagree with Justice Brennan's treatment of the constitutional issue, I also disagree with his opinion for the entirely separate reason that it is not remotely tailored to the facts presented by this [case.]

"I can cheerfully concede [that a Democratic school board could not, for political reasons, remove all books by or in favor of Republicans, and that an all-white school board, motivated by racial animus, could not remove all books authored by blacks or advocating racial equality], but as in so many other cases the extreme examples are seldom the ones that arise in the real world of constitutional litigation. In *this case* the facts taken most favorably to respondents suggest that nothing of this sort happened. The nine books removed undoubtedly did contain 'ideas,' but in the light of the excerpts from them found in the dissenting opinion [in the court below], it is apparent that eight of them contained demonstrable amounts of vulgarity and profanity and the ninth contained nothing that could be considered partisan or political. [R]espondents admitted as much. Petitioners did not, for the reasons stated hereafter, run afoul of the First and Fourteenth Amendments by removing these particular books from the library in the manner in which they did. I would save for another day—feeling quite confident that that day will not arrive—the extreme examples posed in Justice Brennan's opinion.

"Considerable light is shed on the correct resolution of the constitutional question in this case by examining the role played by petitioners. Had petitioners been the members of a town council, I suppose all would agree that, absent a good deal more than is present in this record, they could not have prohibited the sale of these books by private booksellers within the municipality. But we have also recognized that the government may act in other capacities than as sovereign, and when it does the First Amendment may speak with a different voice * * *. By the same token, expressive conduct which may not be prohibited by the State as sovereign may be proscribed by the State as property owner [quoting from *Adderley*, p. 648 supra].

"With these differentiated roles of government in mind, it is helpful to assess the role of government as educator, as compared with the role of government as sovereign. When it acts as an educator, at least at the elementary and secondary school level, the government is engaged in inculcating social values and knowledge in relatively impressionable young people. Obviously there are innumerable decisions to be made as to what courses should be taught, what books should be purchased, or what teachers should be employed. In every one of these areas the members of a school board will act on the basis of their own personal or moral values, will attempt to mirror those of the community, or will abdicate the making of such decisions to so-called 'experts.' [5] [In] the very course of administering the many-faceted operations of a school district, the mere decision to purchase some books will necessarily preclude the possibility of purchasing others. The decision to teach a particular subject may preclude the possibility of teaching another subject. A decision to replace a teacher because of ineffectiveness may by implication be seen as a disparagement of the subject matter taught. In each of these instances, however, the book or the exposure to

5. There are intimations in Justice Brennan's opinion that if petitioners had only consulted literary experts, librarians, and teachers their decision might better withstand First Amendment attack. These observations seem to me wholly fatuous; surely ideas are no more accessible or no less suppressed if the school board merely ratifies the opinion of some other group rather than following its own opinion.

the subject matter may be acquired elsewhere. The managers of the school district are not proscribing it as to the citizenry in general, but are simply determining that it will not be included in the curriculum or school library. In short, actions by the government as educator do not raise the same First Amendment concerns as actions by the government as sovereign.

"Justice Brennan would hold that the First Amendment gives high school and junior high school students a 'right to receive ideas' in the school. This right is a curious entitlement. It exists only in the library of the school, and only if the idea previously has been acquired by the school in book form. It provides no protection against a school board's decision not to acquire a particular book, even though that decision denies access to ideas as fully as removal of the book from the library, and it prohibits removal of previously acquired books only if the remover 'dislike[s] the ideas contained in those books,' even though removal for any other reason also denies the students access to the books.

"But it is not the limitations which Justice Brennan places on the right with which I disagree; they simply demonstrate his discomfort with the new doctrine which he fashions out of whole cloth. It is the very existence of a right to receive information in the junior high school and high school setting, which I find wholly unsupported by our past decisions and inconsistent with the necessarily selective process of elementary and secondary education. * * *

"There are even greater reasons for rejecting Justice Brennan's analysis [than] the significant fact that we have never adopted it in the past. [The] idea that [public school] students have a right of access, *in the school,* to information other than that thought by their educators to be necessary is contrary to the very nature of an inculcative education.

"Education consists of the selective presentation and explanation of ideas. The effective acquisition of knowledge depends upon an orderly exposure to relevant information. Nowhere is this more true than in elementary and secondary schools, where, unlike the broad-ranging inquiry available to university students, the courses taught are those thought most relevant to the young students' individual development. Of necessity, elementary and secondary educators must separate the relevant from the irrelevant, the appropriate from the inappropriate. Determining what information *not* to present to the students is often as important as identifying relevant material. This winnowing process necessarily leaves much information to be discovered by students at another time or in another place, and is fundamentally inconsistent with any constitutionally required eclecticism in public education.

"[Unlike] university or public libraries, elementary and secondary school libraries are not designed for free-wheeling inquiry; they are tailored, as the public school curriculum is tailored, to the teaching of basic skills and ideas. Thus, Justice Brennan cannot rely upon the nature of school libraries to escape the fact that the First Amendment right to receive information simply has no application to the one public institution which, by its very nature, is a place for the selective conveyance of ideas.

"After all else is said, however, the most obvious reason that petitioners' removal of the books did not violate respondents' right to receive information is the ready availability of the books elsewhere. Students are not denied books by their removal from a school library. The books may be borrowed from a public library, read at a university library, purchased at a bookstore, or loaned by a friend. The government as educator does not seek to reach beyond the confines of the school. Indeed, following the removal from the school library of the books at issue in this case, the local public library put all nine books on display for public inspection. Their contents were fully accessible to any inquisitive student.

"[If] Justice Brennan truly has found a 'right to receive ideas,' [his] distinction between acquisition and removal makes little sense. The failure of a library to acquire a book denies access to its contents just as effectively as does the removal of the book from the library's shelf. As a result of either action the book cannot be found in the 'principal locus' of freedom discovered by Justice Brennan. * * *

"The final limitation placed by Justice Brennan upon his newly discovered right is a motive requirement: the First Amendment is violated only '[i]f petitioners *intended* by their removal decision to deny respondents access to ideas with which petitioners disagreed.' (Emphasis in original). But bad motives and good motives alike deny access to the books removed. If Justice Brennan truly recognizes a constitutional right to receive information, it is difficult to see why the reason for the denial makes any difference. Of course Justice Brennan's view is that intent matters because the First Amendment does not tolerate an officially prescribed orthodoxy. But this reasoning mixes First Amendment apples and oranges. The right to receive information differs from the right to be free from an officially prescribed orthodoxy. Not every educational denial of access to information casts a pall of orthodoxy over the classroom.

"It is difficult to tell from Justice Brennan's opinion just what motives he would consider constitutionally impermissible. I had thought that the First Amendment proscribes content-based restrictions on the marketplace of ideas. Justice Brennan concludes, however, that a removal decision based solely upon the 'educational suitability' of a book or upon its perceived vulgarity is 'perfectly permissible.' But such determinations are based as much on the content of the book as determinations that the book espouses pernicious political views.

"Moreover, Justice Brennan's motive test is difficult to square with his distinction between acquisition and removal. If a school board's removal of books might be motivated by a desire to promote favored political or religious views, there is no reason that its acquisition policy might not also be so motivated. And yet the 'pall of orthodoxy' cast by a carefully executed book-acquisition program apparently would not violate the First Amendment under Justice Brennan's view."

"Intertwined as a basis for Justice Brennan's opinion, along with the 'right to receive information,' is the statement that 'our Constitution does not permit the official suppression of *ideas*.' (Emphasis in original). There would be few champions, I suppose, of the idea that our Constitution *does* permit the official suppression of ideas; my difficulty is not with the admittedly appealing catchiness of the phrase, but with my doubt that it is really a useful analytical tool in solving difficult First Amendment problems.

"[In] the case before us the petitioners may in one sense be said to have 'suppressed' the 'ideas' of vulgarity and profanity, but that is hardly an apt description of what was done. They ordered the removal of books containing vulgarity and profanity, but they did not attempt to preclude discussion about the themes of the books or the books themselves. Such a decision, on respondents' version of the facts in this case, is sufficiently related to 'educational suitability' to pass muster under the First Amendment. * * *

"Accepting as true respondents' assertion that petitioners acted on the basis of their own 'personal values, morals, and tastes,' I find the actions taken in this case hard to distinguish from the myriad choices made by school boards in the routine supervision of elementary and secondary schools. 'Courts do not and cannot intervene in the resolution of conflicts which arise in the daily operation of school systems and which do not directly and sharply implicate basic constitutional values.' In this case respondents' rights of free speech and expression were not infringed, and by respondents' own admission no ideas were 'suppressed.' I would leave to another day the harder cases."

In a brief separate dissent, O'CONNOR, J., observed: "If the school board can set the curriculum, select teachers, and determine initially what books to purchase for the school library, it surely can decide which books to discontinue or remove from the school library so long as it does not also interfere with the right of students to read the material and to discuss it. As Justice Rehnquist persuasively argues, the plurality's analysis overlooks the fact that in this case the government is acting in its special role as educator.

"I do not personally agree with the board's action with respect to some of the books in question here, but it is not the function of the courts to make the decisions that have been properly relegated to the elected members of school boards. It is the school board that must determine educational suitability, and it has done so in this case. I therefore join the Chief Justice's dissent."

Notes & Question

1. Consider Yudof, *Library Book Selection and Public Schools: The Quest for the Archimedean Point,* 59 Ind.L.J. 527, 530 (1984): The critical questions in *Pico* are "who will control socialization of the young, what are the values to which they will be socialized, and how will cultural grounding and critical reflection be accommodated." On the latter point, see Mendelson, *The Habermas-Gadamer Debate,* New German Critique 18 (1979). See also Unger, *Knowledge and Politics* (1975); Cornell, *Toward a Modern/Postmodern Reconstruction of Ethics,* 133 U.Pa.L.Rev. 291 (1985).[c]

2. Should librarians have a first amendment right to select and retain books against the objections of a school board? Against a city council in a non-school context? See O'Neil, *Libraries, Librarians and First Amendment Freedoms,* 4 Hum.Rts. 295 (1975); O'Neil, *Libraries, Liberties and the First Amendment,* 42 U.Cin.L.Rev. 209 (1973). Should elementary school teachers have a first amendment right to resist interference with their teaching by "politically" motivated administrators or school boards? At secondary levels? Should student newspapers have a first amendment right to resist ad hoc intervention by administrators? See Canby, *The First Amendment and the State as Editor:*

c. For a range of views on the scope and propriety of government promotion of particular values, see sources collected in fn. i after *Regan* supra. See also Dworkin, *A Matter of Principle* 181–204, 221–33 (1985); Tussman, *Government and the Mind* (1977); Diamond, *The First Amendment and Public Schools: The Case Against Judicial Intervention,* 59 Tex.L.Rev. 477 (1981); Garvey, *Children and the First Amendment,* 57 Tex.L.Rev. 321 (1979); Goldstein, *The Asserted Constitutional Right of Public School Teachers to Determine What They Teach,* 124 U.Pa.L.Rev. 1293

(1976); Moskowitz, *The Making of the Moral Child: Legal Implications of Values Education,* 6 Pepp.L.Rev. 105 (1978); Nahmod, *Controversy in the Classroom: The High School Teacher and Freedom of Expression,* 39 Geo. Wash.L.Rev. 1032 (1971); van Geel, *The Search for Constitutional Limits on Governmental Authority to Inculcate Youth,* 62 Tex. L.Rev. 197 (1983); Note, *State Indoctrination and the Protection of Non-State Voices in the Schools: Justifying a Prohibition of School Library Censorship,* 35 Stan.L.Rev. 497 (1983).

Implications for Public Broadcasting, 52 Tex.L.Rev. 1123 (1974). What of an approach that allows (requires?) administrators to set policies and procedures but prohibits ad hoc intervention?

3. Every Justice recognizes that some content discrimination is permitted in selecting books and making curricular decisions. The line between a public forum and a facility subject to the government's editorial discretion, however, may be hard to draw. SOUTHEASTERN PROMOTIONS, LTD. v. CONRAD, 420 U.S. 546, 95 S.Ct. 1239, 43 L.Ed.2d 448 (1975), reacting to reports that the musical *Hair* included nudity and was obscene, a publicly-appointed board denied *Hair's* producers a permit to use a theater dedicated for "cultural advancement and for clean, healthful, entertainment which will make for the upbuilding of a better citizenship." The Court, per BLACKMUN, J., held that the theater was a public forum "designed for and dedicated to expressive activities" and that the board's procedures amounted to a prior restraint in violation of *Freedman* requirements, p. 593 supra. One of the dissenters, REHNQUIST, J., asked: "May a municipal theater devote an entire season to Shakespeare, or is it required to book any potential producer on a first come, first served basis? [T]he Court's opinion [seems] to give no constitutionally permissible role in the way of selection to the municipal authorities." For commentary, see Karst, *Public Enterprise and the Public Forum: A Comment on Southeastern Promotions, Ltd. v. Conrad,* 37 Ohio St.L.J. 247 (1976); Shiffrin, fn. i after *Regan,* supra, at 581–88; Comment, *Access to State-Owned Communications Media—The Public Forum Doctrine,* 26 U.C.L.A.L.Rev. 1410, 1440–44 (1979).

III. GOVERNMENT INVOLVEMENT WITH SPEECH AND THE CAPTIVE AUDIENCE

PUBLIC UTILITIES COMM'N v. POLLAK, 343 U.S. 451, 72 S.Ct. 813, 96 L.Ed. 1068 (1952): A District of Columbia transit company installed FM receivers in its buses and streetcars. An FM station broadcast special programs—in this case 90% music, 5% news and 5% commercial advertising—to which the bus and streetcar radios were fixed-tuned. Advertisers paid "a dollar a thousand people" and were assured, "If they can hear—they can hear your commercial." The station described itself to the trade as "delivering a guaranteed audience." [a]

After a hearing, the PUC concluded that the radio programs were not inconsistent with public convenience, comfort and safety and "tends to improve the conditions under which the public ride." Two protesting passengers appealed. The court of appeals ruled that at least the broadcasting of "commercials" and "announcements" infringed constitutional rights. But the Court per BURTON, J., reversed. [b] Assuming that the action of the federally regulated transit company "amounts to sufficient Federal Government action to make the First and Fifth Amendments applicable," neither amendment was violated:

"Pollak and Martin contend that the radio programs interfere with their freedom of conversation and that of other passengers by making it necessary for them to compete against the programs in order to be heard. The Commission, however, did not find, and the testimony does not compel a finding, that the programs interfered substantially with the conversation of passengers or with

---

a. See Black, *He Cannot Choose But Hear: The Plight of the Captive Auditor,* 53 Colum.L. Rev. 960, 961 (1953) (the author was counsel for Pollak).

b. Frankfurter, J., recused himself because "my feelings are so strongly engaged as a victim of the [challenged] practice."

rights of communication constitutionally protected in public places. It is suggested also that the First Amendment guarantees a freedom to listen only to such points of view as the listener wishes to hear. There is no substantial claim that the programs have been used for objectionable propaganda. There is no issue of that kind before us.[9] The inclusion in the programs of a few announcements explanatory and commendatory of Capital Transit's own services does not sustain such an objection.

"[The protesting passengers] claim is that no matter how much the [transit company] may wish to use [the radios] as part of its service to its passengers and as a source of income, no matter how much the great majority of its passengers may desire [such radios],[c] and however [favorable the Commission's findings on such use], if one passenger objects to the programs as an invasion of his constitutional right of privacy, the use of radio must be discontinued. This position wrongly assumes that the Fifth Amendment secures to each passenger on a [federally regulated public vehicle] a right of privacy substantially equal to the privacy to which he is entitled in his own home. [But the right of privacy] is substantially limited by the rights of other when its possessor [rides] in a public conveyance."

BLACK, J., concurred "in the Court's holding that this record shows no violation of the Due Process Clause of the Fifth Amendment. I also agree that Capital Transit's musical programs have not violated the First Amendment. I am of the opinion, however, that subjecting Capital Transit's passengers to the broadcasting of news, public speeches, views, or propaganda of any kind and by any means would violate the First Amendment. To the extent, if any, that the Court holds the contrary, I dissent."

DOUGLAS, J., dissenting, dwelt on "the right to be let alone"—"the beginning of all freedom": "The present case involves a form of coercion to make people listen. The listeners are of course in a public place. [But] in a practical sense they are forced to ride, since this mode of transportation is today essential for many thousands. Compulsion which comes from circumstances can be as real as compulsion which comes from a command. [T]he man on the streetcar has no choice but to sit and listen, or perhaps to sit and try *not* to listen. When we force people to listen to another's ideas, we give the propagandist a powerful weapon. [Once] a man is forced to submit to one type of radio program, he can be forced to submit to another. It may be but a short step from a cultural program to a political program."

Notes and Questions

1. Consider Emerson, *The System of Freedom of Expression* 711 (1970): "It should be noted that the *Pollak* case did not present a clear-cut issue of government expression. "State action" was involved, to some degree, because the Public Utilities Commission had power to permit or prohibit the communication. But the government of the District of Columbia was not actually doing the broadcasting. [Had] the Capital Transit Company been a governmentally operated enterprise, however, surely broadcasts to the captive audience would have

---

9. The Communications Act of 1934, 48 Stat. 1064 et seq., as amended, 47 U.S.C. § 151 et seq., 47 U.S.C.A. § 151 et seq., has been interpreted by the Federal Communications Commission as imposing upon each licensee the duty of fair presentation of news and controversial issues.

c. A poll considered by the PUC revealed that 76% favored buscasting; 17% didn't know or care; only 6.6% disapproved, of whom about half were firmly opposed.

violated the First Amendment. Government communication of that kind, at least on any substantial scale, would quickly destroy freedom of expression. The resulting system would be closer to that depicted in George Orwell's *1984* than to any envisaged by the First Amendment. It has fortunately not been necessary to define the exact contours of the principle that the government may not engage in expression directed at a captive audience, or otherwise force its citizens to listen. There can be no doubt, however, that the principle is central to any system of freedom of expression."

2. Is it a weakness of the *Pollak* case, as presented by the complainants, that they did not pursue the point that the "captive audience" *was being* "propagandized"? The record shows that after the date had been set for the Commission hearing, but prior to the hearing itself, "buscasts" defending "bus-casting" were made. The record also discloses that there were "news" broadcasts. Does not this imply the transmission of "views," absolute impartiality being impossible? See Note, 1 J.Pub.L. 507, 512–13 (1952). Moreover, the transit company "buscast" political advertising limited in length to thirty seconds and clearly identified as paid advertising as well as "capsules" of the Republican and Democratic National Conventions. Id.

3. Do captive audiences of government speech have a first amendment right not to be propagandized? Do children educated in public schools have such a right? If ad hoc methods of separating education from propaganda are unreliable, are any institutional structures or processes required? Should this be a constitutional right without a remedy? Consider also captive audiences of prisoners, soldiers, or workers in public institutions. On government speech and the captive audience, see Yudof, *When Government Speaks,* p. 662 supra, at 169–70, 213–18, 231–33, 296–99.

LEHMAN v. SHAKER HEIGHTS
418 U.S. 298, 94 S.Ct. 2714, 41 L.Ed.2d 770 (1974).

MR. JUSTICE BLACKMUN announced the judgment of the Court and an opinion, in which THE CHIEF JUSTICE, MR. JUSTICE WHITE, and MR. JUSTICE REHNQUIST, join.

[A city operating a public transit system sold commercial and public service advertising space for car cards on its vehicles, but permitted no "political" or "public issue" advertising. When petitioner, a candidate for the office of State Representative to the Ohio General Assembly, failed in his effort to have advertising promoting his candidacy accepted, he unsuccessfully sought declaratory and injunctive relief in the state courts.]

It is urged that the car cards here constitute a public forum protected by the First Amendment, and that there is a guarantee of nondiscriminatory access to such publicly owned and controlled areas of communication "regardless of the primary purpose for which the area is dedicated." We disagree.

* * * "[T]he truth is that open spaces and public places differ very much in their character, and before you could say whether a certain thing could be done in a public place you would have to know the history of the particular place." Although American constitutional jurisprudence, in the light of the First Amendment, has been jealous to preserve access to public places for purposes of free speech, the nature of the forum and the conflicting interests involved have remained important in determining the degree of protection afforded by the Amendment to the speech in question.

Here, we have no open spaces, no meeting hall, park, street corner, or other public thoroughfare. Instead, the city is engaged in commerce. [The] car card space, although incidental to the provision of public transportation, is a part of the commercial venture. In much the same way that a newspaper or periodical, or even a radio or television station, need not accept every proffer of advertising from the general public, a city transit system has discretion to develop and make reasonable choices concerning the type of advertising that may be displayed in its vehicles. * * *

Because state action exists, however, the policies and practices governing access to the transit system's advertising space must not be arbitrary, capricious, or invidious. Here, the city has decided that "[p]urveyors of goods and services saleable in commerce may purchase advertising space on an equal basis, whether they be house builders or butchers." * * * Revenue earned from long-term commercial advertising could be jeopardized by a requirement that short-term candidacy or issue-oriented advertisements be displayed on car cards. Users would be subjected to the blare of political propaganda. There could be lurking doubts about favoritism, and sticky administrative problems might arise in parceling out limited space to eager politicians. In these circumstances, the managerial decision to limit car card space to innocuous and less controversial commercial and service oriented advertising does not rise to the dignity of a First Amendment violation. [Otherwise], display cases in public hospitals, libraries, office buildings, military compounds, and other public facilities would become Hyde Parks open to every would-be pamphleteer and politician. This the Constitution does not require.

No First Amendment forum is here to be found. The city consciously has limited access to its transit system advertising space in order to minimize chances of abuse, the appearance of favoritism, and the risk of imposing upon a captive audience. These are reasonable legislative objectives advanced by the city in a proprietary capacity.

[A]ffirmed.

MR. JUSTICE DOUGLAS, concurring in the judgment. * * *

If the streetcar or bus were a forum for communication akin to that of streets or public parks, considerable problems would be presented. [But] a streetcar or bus is plainly not a park or sidewalk or other meeting place for discussion any more than is a highway. It is only a way to get to work or back home. The fact that it is owned and operated by the city does not without more make it a forum.

Bus and streetcar placards are in the category of highway billboards, [a] form of communication [that] has been significantly curtailed by state regulation adopted pursuant to the Highway Beautification Act of 1965. [T]he fact that land on which a billboard rests is municipal land does not curtail or enhance such regulatory schemes.

If a bus is a forum it is more akin to a newspaper than to a park. Yet, [as we hold today in *Miami Herald Publishing Co. v. Tornillo,* p. 696 infra] the [newspaper] owner cannot be forced to include in his offerings news or other items which outsiders may desire but which the owner abhors. [And] if we are to turn a bus or streetcar into either a newspaper or a park, we take great liberties with people who because of necessity become commuters and at the same time captive viewers or listeners. [T]he right of the commuters to be free from forced intrusions on their privacy precludes the city from transforming its [public vehicles] into forums for the dissemination of ideas upon this captive audience.

Buses are not recreational vehicles [as a public park might be used on holidays]; they are a practical necessity for millions in our urban centers. I have already stated this view in my [*Pollak*] dissent: "[One] who hears disquieting or unpleasant programs in public places [can] get up and leave. But the man on the streetcar has no choice but to sit and listen, or perhaps to sit and to try *not* to listen." There is no difference when the message is visual, not auricular. In each the viewer or listener is captive. * * *

I do not view the content of the message as relevant either to petitioner's right to express it or to the commuters' right to be free from it. Commercial advertisements may be as offensive and intrusive to captive audiences as any political message. But the validity of the commercial advertising program is not before us since we are not faced with one complaining of an invasion of privacy through forced exposure to commercial ads. Since I do not believe that petitioner has any constitutional right to spread his message before this captive audience, I concur in the Court's judgment.

MR. JUSTICE BRENNAN, with whom MR. JUSTICE STEWART, MR. JUSTICE MARSHALL, and MR. JUSTICE POWELL, join, dissenting.

[T]he city created a forum for the dissemination of information and expression of ideas when it accepted and displayed commercial and public service advertisements on its rapid transit vehicles. Having opened a forum for communication, the city is barred by the First and Fourteenth Amendments from discriminating among forum users solely on the basis of message content.

[The city] attempts to justify its ban against political advertising by arguing that the interior advertising space is an inappropriate forum for political expression and debate. To be sure, there are some public places which are so clearly committed to other purposes that their use as public forums for communication is anomalous. [The] determination of whether a particular type of public property or facility constitutes a "public forum" requires the Court to strike a balance between the competing interests of the government, on the one hand, and the speaker and his audience, on the other. Thus, the Court must assess the importance of the primary use to which the public property or facility is committed and the extent to which that use will be disrupted if access for free expression is permitted. [Compare *Edwards* (state capitol grounds) with *Adderley* (jailhouse curtilage)]. In the circumstances of this case, however, we need not decide whether public transit cars *must* be made available as forums for the exercise of First Amendment rights. By accepting commercial and public service advertising, the city effectively waived any argument that advertising in its transit cars is incompatible with the rapid transit system's primary function of providing transportation. A forum for communication was voluntarily established * * *.

[W]hile it is possible that commercial advertising may be accorded *less* First Amendment protection than [political speech], it is "speech" nonetheless, often communicating information and ideas found by many persons to be controversial. [Once] such messages have been accepted and displayed, the existence of a forum for communication cannot be gainsaid. To hold otherwise, and thus sanction the bland commercialism and noncontroversial public service messages over "uninhibited, robust and wide-open" debate on public issues, would reverse the traditional priorities of the First Amendment.

Once a public forum for communication has been established, both free speech and equal protection principles prohibit discrimination based *solely* upon subject matter or content. *Mosley.* [That] the discrimination is among entire classes of ideas, rather than among points of view within a particular class, does not render it any less odious. Subject matter or content censorship in any form is forbidden.[9]

[Few] examples are required to illustrate the scope of the city's policy and practice. For instance, a commercial advertisement peddling snowmobiles would be accepted, while a counter-advertisement calling upon the public to support legislation controlling the environmental destruction and noise pollution caused by snowmobiles would be rejected. [This,] and other examples,[10] make perfectly clear that the selective exclusion of political advertising is not the product of even-handed application of neutral "time, place, and manner" regulations. Rather, the operative—and constitutionally impermissible—distinction is the message of the sign. That conclusion is not dispelled by any of the city's asserted justifications for selectively excluding political advertising.

[The city's solicitous regard for "captive riders"] has a hollow ring in the present case, where [it] has voluntarily opened its rapid transit system as a forum for communication. In that circumstance, the occasional appearance of provocative speech should be expected. * * *

The line between ideological and nonideological speech is impossible to draw with accuracy. By accepting commercial and public service advertisements, the city opened the door to "sometimes controversial or unsettling speech" and determined that such speech does not unduly interfere with the rapid transit system's primary purpose of transporting passengers. In the eyes of many passengers, certain commercial or public service messages [referring, e.g., to church advertising] are as profoundly disturbing as some political advertisements might be to other passengers. There is certainly no evidence in the record of this case indicating that political advertisements, as a class, are so disturbing when displayed that they are more likely than commercial or public service advertisements to impair the rapid transit system's primary function of transportation. In the absence of such evidence, the city's selective exclusion of political advertising constitutes an invidious discrimination on the basis of subject matter, in violation of the First and Fourteenth Amendments.

9. The existence of other public forums for the dissemination of political messages is, of course, irrelevant [quoting from *Schneider*].

10. In declaring unconstitutional an advertising policy remarkably similar to the city's policy in the present case, the California Supreme Court detailed "the paradoxical scope of the [transit] district's policy [banning political advertising]" in the following manner: "A cigarette company is permitted to advertise the desirability of smoking its brand, but a cancer society is not entitled to caution by advertisements that cigarette smoking is injurious to health. A theater may advertise a motion picture that portrays sex and violence, but the Legion for Decency has no right to post a message calling for clean films. A lumber company may advertise its wood products, but a conservation group cannot implore citizens to write to the President or Governor about protecting our natural resources. An oil refinery may advertise its products, but a citizens' organization cannot demand enforcement of existing air pollution statutes. An insurance company may announce its available policies, but a senior citizens' club cannot plead for legislation to improve our social security program. The district would accept an advertisement from a television station that is commercially inspired, but would refuse a paid nonsolicitation message from a strictly educational television station. Advertisements for travel, foods, clothing, toiletries, automobiles, legal drugs—all these are acceptable, but the American Legion would not have the right to place a paid advertisement reading, 'Support Our Boys in Viet Nam. Send Holiday Packages,' " 68 Cal.2d at 57, 434 P.2d at 986.

Moreover, even if it were possible to draw a manageable line between controversial and noncontroversial messages, the city's practice of censorship for the benefit of "captive audiences" still would not be justified. [The accepted advertisements] are not broadcast over loudspeakers in the transit cars. The privacy of the passengers is not, therefore, dependent upon their ability "to sit and try *not* to listen." *Pollak* (Douglas, J., dissenting). Should passengers chance to glance at advertisements they find offensive, they can "effectively avoid further bombardment of their sensibilities simply by averting their eyes." *Cohen.* Surely that minor inconvenience is a small price to pay for the continued preservation of so precious a liberty as free speech.

[E]qually unpersuasive [is the city's argument that acceptance of political advertising would suggest political favoritism or city support of the candidate advertised]. Clearly, such ephemeral concerns do not provide the city with carte blanche authority to exclude an entire category of speech from a public forum. [Moreover,] neutral regulations [can] be narrowly tailored to allay the city's fears. The impression of city endorsement can be dispelled by requiring disclaimers to appear prominently on the face of every advertisement. And [the] appearance of favoritism can be avoided by the even-handed regulation of time, place and manner for all advertising, irrespective of subject matter. * * *

Notes and Questions

1. *Turning freedom of expression "upside down."* Does Blackmun, J.'s view that "the managerial decision to limit car card space to innocuous and less controversial commercial and service oriented advertising does not rise to the dignity of a First Amendment violation" turn freedom of expression "upside down"? How, or why, can "speech of sufficient importance to merit the 'dignity' of First Amendment protection [be] excluded from display on the city's trains, while less important speech is allowed"? See Haiman, *How Much of Our Speech Is Free?*, The Civ.Lib.Rev., Winter 1975, pp. 111, 129–30.

Does either the plurality or Douglas, J., explain why political advertising is more controversial or offensive than public service messages for religious organizations or commercial advertising for certain personal products? See Karst, *Equality as a Central Principle in the First Amendment*, 43 U.Chi.L.Rev. 20, 35 (1976). In any event, can greater restraints on "controversial" speech be reconciled with "the familiar first amendment principle that the value of free speech comprehends unsettling or provocative ideas"? See 88 Harv.L.Rev. 154 (1974). Reconsider *Cohen* and *Terminiello*, Sec. 1, V supra.

2. *Lehman and Mosley.* Consider Karst, note 1 supra, at 36: "What made *Mosley* and *Lehman* easy cases—the outrage of *Lehman* being that it was an easy case, wrongly decided—was that in restricting the use of picketing and bus advertising the cities did not merely regulate the time, place or manner of speech, but imposed discriminatory controls over the content of speech." Does *Perry* lend any conceptual support for *Lehman*? Where would the car cards fit into *Perry's* classification scheme?

3. Is Blackmun, J.'s point that since all those seeking to purchase advertising space for commercial purposes are treated alike, "whether they be house builders or butchers," and all those seeking public issue or political advertising are also treated alike, the equal protection issue disappears? Does it? Were all labor picketers treated alike, and all non-labor picketers treated alike, in *Mosley*? Is the key equal protection question whether all those *within* the

defined classes are treated equally *or* whether the classification *itself* is permissible? See Stone, *Fora Americana,* at 276.

4. Suppose the city decided that it did not want to promote health problems and refused space for cigarette advertisements? Suppose it wanted to avoid offense and refused space for advertisements of X rated films? Must the city treat all advertisers alike?

5. Would access to the card spaces have turned every government bulletin board into a Hyde park? Consider Shiffrin, *Government Speech,* at 579–80: "If the bus space in *Lehman* had been used for messages about the operation of the bus service, an analogy could have properly been made to display cases in other public facilities. [But] the public facilities in *Lehman* were not being used to convey a government message. By letting out the space to private groups for their own messages, the government had admitted that the space was not needed for government purposes. To grant access for political messages would have reaffirmed *Mosley's* equality principle without implying any right of access to every government bulletin board."

6. *"Captivity."* Does "captivity," in the sense of unavoidable *initial* exposure to communication, exist with respect to virtually all forms of communication? While browsing through a newspaper, may an individual unwittingly come across an offensive article or photograph? While switching on his TV or radio, may he suddenly be confronted with distasteful views? Does the "true measure" of an individual's privacy from unwanted communications consist "not in his total protection from *initial* exposure to unwelcome ideas, but rather in his ability to avoid *continued* exposure to those ideas once he has rejected them"? See Stone, *Fora Americana,* at 267. (Emphasis added.) Does exposure to car cards displayed on the interior of a public vehicle "in any sense directly interfere with the ability of passengers to read, converse, meditate, work or even catch a short nap"? See id. at 270. Do passengers exposed to such car cards constitute a captive audience under the *Cohen* formulation—"the ability of government [to] shut off discourse solely to protect others from hearing it [is] dependent upon a showing that substantial privacy interests are being invaded in an essentially intolerable manner"?

7. *The "fifth vote" in Lehman.* Is the "greatest irony" of *Lehman* that "the fifth vote which made it possible for Justices Burger, Blackmun, Rehnquist, and White to prevail came not from Justice Powell but from Justice Douglas"? See Haiman, note 1 supra, at 131. Is Douglas, J.'s failure to deal with Lehman's equal protection claim anomalous? If a transit system accepted commercial advertising, but refused to provide space on an equal basis to blacks, would Douglas, J., hold that the passengers' constitutional right of privacy, without more, defeated the blacks' constitutional claims? See 88 Harv.L.Rev., note 1 supra, at 150 n. 15.

SECTION 7. CLOSING PARTICULAR CHANNELS OF COMMUNICATION

This section treats cases in which many themes of prior sections coalesce. Prior sections, confronted everything from the banning of black arm bands to the banning of leaflet distribution on public streets. In this section, many of the Justices focus on the banning of a particular channel of communication as a first amendment category.

Sec. 6, III considered the interest in preventing audiences from being captives of speech supported by the government. A theme which runs through many of the cases in this section is an interest in protecting potential "captive" audiences not necessarily from "propaganda," but from the intrusiveness of noise and visual pollution by communication. What importance to attach to the interest in preventing captivity may depend not only on the source (a government or a private speaker) and the place of captivity (for example, at home or in a public forum), but also upon the content of the communication. *Metromedia,* infra, for example, concerns a billboard ban discriminating in part against commercial speech, thus causing reconsideration of the place of commercial speech among first amendment values and the relationship between content discrimination and discrimination against a particular point of view. Finally, *Vincent,* infra, involves the relationship between public forum doctrine and the more general time, place, and manner doctrine.

METROMEDIA, INC. v. SAN DIEGO, 453 U.S. 490, 101 S.Ct. 2882, 69 L.Ed. 2d 800 (1981): An ordinance banning the use of billboards provided for two types of exceptions. First, it allowed "on-site" signs defined to include those "designating the name of the owner or occupant of the premises upon which such signs are placed, or identifying such premises; or signs advertising goods manufactured or produced or services rendered on the premises upon which such signs are placed."

Second, it provided for special categories of exceptions including government signs; signs at bus stops; commemorative plaques of recognized historical societies and organizations; religious symbols; indoor signs not visible from any point on the boundary of the premises; for sale signs; public service signs limited to the depiction of time, temperature or news; signs of buses and taxicabs; and temporary political campaign signs.

The ordinance was challenged by companies engaged in the "outdoor advertising business," i.e., they owned signs and sold space on them. The parties stipulated that "[v]aluable commercial, political and social information is communicated" via the signs, that alternative forms of communication are "insufficient, inappropriate and prohibitively expensive," and that the ordinance would "eliminate the outdoor advertising business" in San Diego. The California Supreme Court upheld the ordinance. WHITE, J., joined by Stewart, Marshall, and Powell, JJ., announcing the judgment of the Court, reversing and remanding, criticized the ordinance's treatment of non-commercial speech: "The California courts may sustain the ordinance by limiting its reach to commercial speech, assuming the ordinance is susceptible to this treatment." On the latter point, Stevens, J., otherwise dissenting, announced that he joined the commercial speech sections of the plurality opinion.

Preliminarily, White, J., observed: "Each method of communicating ideas is 'a law unto itself' and that law must reflect the 'differing natures, values, abuses and dangers' of each method. We deal here with the law of billboards.

"Billboards are a well-established medium of communication, used to convey a broad range of different kinds of messages. [But] whatever its communicative function, the billboard remains a 'large, immobile, and permanent structure which like other structures is subject [to] regulation.' Moreover, because it is designed to stand out and apart from its surroundings, the billboard creates a unique set of problems for land-use planning and development."

Directing his attention first to the ban on off-site commercial billboards, White, J., concluded that the *Central Hudson* test [p. 565 supra] was satisfied.

There can be no "substantial doubt" that "traffic safety and the appearance of the city" are "substantial governmental goals." The only serious question was whether those interests were directly advanced. Despite a "meager record," White, J., found nothing to suggest that the "legislative judgment that billboards are traffic hazards" was "unreasonable." As for aesthetic interests, he found no "impermissible purpose": "It is nevertheless argued that the city denigrates its interest in traffic safety and beauty and defeats its own case by permitting on-site advertising and other specified signs. * * *

"In the first place, whether on-site advertising is permitted or not, the prohibition of off-site advertising is directly related to the stated objectives of traffic safety and esthetics. This is not altered by the fact that the ordinance is underinclusive because it permits on-site advertising. Second, the city may believe that off-site advertising, with its periodically changing content, presents a more acute problem than does on-site advertising. Third, San Diego has obviously chosen to value one kind of commercial speech—on-site advertising—more than another kind of commercial speech—off-site advertising. The ordinance reflects a decision by the city that the former interest, but not the latter, is stronger than the city's interests in traffic safety and esthetics. [We] do not reject that judgment. As we see it, the city could reasonably conclude that a commercial enterprise—as well as the interested public—has a stronger interest in identifying its place of business and advertising the products or services available there than it has in using or leasing its available space for the purpose of advertising commercial enterprises located elsewhere. * * *

"It does not follow, however, that San Diego's general ban on signs carrying noncommercial advertising is also valid under the First and Fourteenth Amendments. [O]ur recent commercial speech cases have consistently accorded noncommercial speech a greater degree of protection than commercial speech. San Diego effectively inverts this judgment, by affording a greater degree of protection to commercial than to noncommercial speech. There is a broad exception for on-site commercial advertisements, but there is no similar exception for noncommercial speech. [The] city does not explain how or why noncommercial billboards located in places where commercial billboards are permitted would be more threatening to safe driving or would detract more from the beauty of the city. Insofar as the city tolerates billboards at all, [it] may not conclude that the communication of commercial information concerning goods and services connected with a particular site is of greater value than the communication of noncommercial messages.

"Furthermore, the ordinance contains exceptions that permit various kinds of noncommercial signs, whether on property where goods and services are offered or not, that would otherwise be within the general ban. A fixed sign may be used to identify any piece of property and its owner. Any piece of property may carry or display religious symbols, commemorative plaques of recognized historical societies and organizations, signs carrying news items or telling the time or temperature, signs erected in discharge of any governmental function, or temporary political campaign signs.[19] No other noncommercial or ideological signs meeting the structural definition are permitted, regardless of their effect on traffic safety or esthetics.

---

19. In this sense, this case presents the opposite situation from that in *Lehman*. In both of those cases a government agency had chosen to prohibit from a certain forum speech relating to political campaigns, while other kinds of speech were permitted. In both cases this Court upheld the prohibition, but both cases turned on unique fact situations involving government-created forums and have no application here.

"Although the city may distinguish between the relative value of different categories of commercial speech, the city does not have the same range of choice in the area of noncommercial speech to evaluate the strength of, or distinguish between, various communicative interests. *Carey; Mosley.* [Because] some noncommercial messages may be conveyed on billboards throughout the commercial and industrial zones, San Diego must similarly allow billboards conveying other noncommercial messages throughout those zones.[20] * * *

"Because the San Diego ordinance reaches too far into the realm of protected speech, we conclude that it is unconstitutional on its face."

BRENNAN, J., joined by Blackmun, J., concurring, maintained that the practical effect of the ordinance was a total ban on outdoor advertising that would be permissible only if the city could show a sufficiently substantial government interest directly furthered by the ban, and "that any more narrowly drawn restriction, i.e., anything less than a total ban, would promote less well the achievement of that goal." He found a lack of evidence to support a connection between the ordinance and traffic safety. Moreover, he thought the city had failed to show a substantial interest in aesthetics in the commercial and industrial areas of San Diego: "A billboard is not *necessarily* inconsistent with oil storage tanks, blighted areas, or strip development." He expressed confidence that billboard bans could be defended in a "historical community" such as Williamsburg, Virginia or in an environment like Yellowstone National Park. But he expressed no view whether San Diego or other large cities would ever be able to make the required showing.

In addressing the commercial speech issue, "I cannot agree with the plurality's view that an ordinance totally banning commercial billboards but allowing noncommercial billboards would be constitutional.[13] [Of] course the plurality is correct when it observes that 'our cases have consistently distinguished between the constitutional protection afforded commercial as opposed to noncommercial speech,' but it errs in assuming that a *governmental unit* may be put in the position in the first instance of deciding whether the proposed speech is commercial or noncommercial. In individual cases, this distinction is anything but clear. Because making such determinations would entail a substantial exercise of discretion by city's officials, it presents a real danger of curtailing noncommercial speech in the guise of regulating commercial speech.

"[I] would be unhappy to see city officials dealing with the following series of billboards and deciding which ones to permit: the first billboard contains the message 'Visit Joe's Ice Cream Shoppe'; the second, 'Joe's Ice Cream Shoppe uses only the highest quality dairy products'; the third, 'Because Joe thinks that dairy products are good for you, please shop at Joe's Shoppe'; and the fourth, 'Joe says to support dairy price supports; they mean lower prices for you at his Shoppe.' Or how about some San Diego Padres baseball fans—with no connection to the team—who together rent a billboard and communicate the message

20. Because a total prohibition of outdoor advertising is not before us, we do not indicate whether such a ban would be consistent with the First Amendment. But see *Schad* [p. 554 supra] on the constitutional problems created by a total prohibition of a particular expressive forum, live entertainment in that case. Despite Justice Stevens' insistence to the contrary, we do not imply that the ordinance is unconstitutional because it "does not abridge enough speech." * * *

13. Of course, as a matter of marketplace economics, such an ordinance may prove the undoing of *all* billboard advertising, both commercial and noncommercial. It may well be that no company would be able to make a profit maintaining billboards used solely for noncommercial messages. [Therefore,] the plurality's prescription may represent a *de facto* ban on both commercial and noncommercial billboards. This is another reason to analyze this case as a "total ban" case.

'Support the San Diego Padres, a great baseball team.' May the city decide that a United Automobile Workers billboard with the message 'Be a patriot—do not buy Japanese-manufactured cars' is 'commercial' and therefore forbid it? What if the same sign is placed by Chrysler? [14]

"[I] have no doubt that those who seek to convey commercial messages will engage in the most imaginative of exercises to place themselves within the safe haven of noncommercial speech, while at the same time conveying their commercial message. Encouraging such behavior can only make the job of city officials—who already are inclined to ban billboards—that much more difficult and potentially intrusive upon legitimate noncommercial expression."

STEVENS, J., dissenting, saw the issue as whether the city "may entirely ban one medium of communication." His affirmative answer was not affected by what he described as the "content neutral" exceptions contained in the ordinance. He did not think, however, that plaintiffs should have standing to assert the interests of a hypothetical "public spirited or eccentric businessman" wanting "to use a permanent sign on his commercial property to display a noncommercial message."

On the ban question, Stevens, J., thought the case was unique: "Our cases upholding regulation of the time, place, or manner of communication have been decided on the implicit assumption that the net effect of the regulation on free expression would not be adverse. In this case, however, [t]he parties have stipulated, correctly in my view, that the net effect of the city's ban on billboards will be a reduction in the total quantity of communication in San Diego. If the ban is enforced, some present users of billboards will not be able to communicate in the future as effectively as they do now. This ordinance cannot, therefore, be sustained on the assumption that the remaining channels of communication will be just as effective for all persons as a communications marketplace which includes a thousand or more large billboards available for hire.

"The unequivocal language of the First Amendment prohibits any law 'abridging the freedom of speech.' That language could surely be read to foreclose any law reducing the quantity of communication within a jurisdiction. I am convinced, however, that such a reading would be incorrect. [For example, archeologists] use the term 'graffiti' to describe informal inscriptions on tombs and ancient monuments. The graffito was familiar in the culture of Egypt and Greece, in the Italian decorative art of the 15th-century, and it survives today in some subways and on the walls of public buildings. It is an inexpensive means of communicating political, commercial, and frivolous messages to large numbers of people; some creators of graffiti have no effective alternate means of publicly expressing themselves. Nevertheless, I believe a community has the right to decide that its interests in protecting property from damaging trespasses and in securing beautiful surroundings outweigh the countervailing interest in uninhibited expression by means of words and pictures in public places. If the First Amendment categorically protected the marketplace of ideas from any quantitative restraint, a municipality could not outlaw graffiti.

"Our prior decisions are not inconsistent with this proposition. Whether one interprets the Court's decision in *Kovacs v. Cooper,* 336 U.S. 77, 69 S.Ct. 448, 93 L.Ed. 513 (1949), as upholding a total ban on the use of sound trucks, or

---

14. These are not mere hypotheticals that can never occur. The Oil, Chemical and Atomic Workers Int'l Union, AFL–CIO actually placed a billboard advertisement stating: "Support America's First Environment Strike. Don't Buy Shell!" What if Exxon had placed the advertisement? Could Shell respond in kind?

merely a ban on the 'loud and raucous' use of amplifiers, the case at least stands for the proposition that a municipality may enforce a rule that curtails the effectiveness of a particular means of communication. [*Kovacs,*] I believe, forecloses any claim that a prohibition of billboards must fall simply because it has some limiting effect on the communications market.[23]

"[It] seems to be accepted by all that a zoning regulation excluding billboards from residential neighborhoods is justified by the interest in maintaining pleasant surroundings and enhancing property values. The same interests are at work in commercial and industrial zones. Reasonable men may assign different weights to the conflicting interests, but in constitutional terms I believe the essential inquiry is the same throughout the city. * * *

"If one is persuaded, as I am, that a wholly impartial total ban on billboards would be permissible, it is difficult to understand why the exceptions in San Diego's ordinance present any additional threat to the interests protected by the First Amendment. The plurality suggests that, because the exceptions are based in part on the subject matter of noncommercial speech, the city somehow is choosing the permissible subjects for public debate. While this suggestion is consistent with some of the broad dictum in *Consolidated Edison Co. v. Public Service Commission* [p. 784 infra] it does not withstand analysis in this case.

"The essential concern embodied in the First Amendment is that government not impose its viewpoint on the public or select the topics on which public debate is permissible. The San Diego ordinance simply does not implicate this concern. Although *Consolidated Edison* broadly identified regulations based on the subject matter of speech as impermissible content-based regulations, essential First Amendment concerns were implicated in that case because the government was attempting to limit discussion of controversial topics, and thus was shaping the agenda for public debate. [But except] * * * for the provision allowing signs to be used for political campaign purposes for limited periods, none of the exceptions even arguably relates to any controversial subject matter. As a whole they allow a greater dissemination of information than could occur under a total plan. Moreover, it was surely reasonable for the city to conclude that exceptions for clocks, thermometers, historic plaques, and the like, would have a lesser impact on the appearance of the city than the typical large billboards.

"The exception for political campaign signs presents a different question. For I must assume that these signs may be just as unsightly and hazardous as other off-site billboards. Nevertheless, the fact that the community places a special value on allowing additional communication to occur during political campaigns is surely consistent with the interests the First Amendment was designed to protect. Of course, if there were reason to believe that billboards were especially useful to one political party or candidate, this exception would be suspect. But nothing of that sort is suggested by this record. In the aggregate, therefore, it seems to me that the exceptions in this ordinance cause it to have a less serious effect on the communications market than would a total ban."

BURGER, C.J., dissented: "Today the Court takes an extraordinary—even a bizarre—step by severely limiting the power of a city to act on risks it perceives to traffic safety and the environment posed by large, permanent billboards.

23. Our decisions invalidating ordinances prohibiting or regulating door-to-door solicitation and leafletting are not to the contrary. In those cases, the state interests the ordinances purported to serve—for instance, the prevention of littering or fraud—were only indirectly furthered by the regulation of communicative activity. See, e.g., *Schneider; Martin v. Struthers,* 319 U.S. 141, 147–148, 63 S.Ct. 862, 865, 87 L.Ed. 1313 (1943). * * *

Those joining the plurality opinion invalidate a city's effort to minimize these traffic hazards and eyesores simply because, in exercising rational legislative judgment, it has chosen to permit a narrow class of signs that serve special needs.

"Relying on simplistic platitudes about content, subject matter, and the dearth of other means to communicate, the billboard industry attempts to escape the real and growing problems every municipality faces in protecting safety and preserving the environment in an urban area. The Court's disposition of the serious issues involved exhibits insensitivity to the impact of these billboards on those who must live with them and the delicacy of the legislative judgments involved in regulating them. American cities desiring to mitigate the dangers mentioned must, as a matter of *federal constitutional law,* elect between two unsatisfactory options: (a) allowing all 'noncommercial' signs, no matter how many, how dangerous, or how damaging to the environment; or (b) forbidding signs altogether. Indeed, lurking in the recesses of today's opinions is a not-so-veiled threat that the second option, too, may soon be withdrawn. This is the long arm and voracious appetite of federal power—this time judicial power—with a vengeance, reaching and absorbing traditional concepts of local authority."

The Chief Justice argued that it made no difference whether the regulation was "viewed as a regulation regarding time, place, and manner, or as a total prohibition on a medium with some exceptions defined, in part, by content": "Although we must ensure that any regulation of speech 'further[s] a sufficiently substantial government interest,' *Schad,* given a reasonable approach to a perceived problem, this Court's duty is not to make the primary policy decisions but instead is to determine whether the legislative approach is essentially neutral to the messages conveyed and leaves open other adequate means of conveying those messages. This is the essence of both democracy and federalism, and we gravely damage both when we undertake to throttle legislative discretion and judgment at the 'grass roots' of our system." [a]

In his view, the ordinance did not discriminate "among ideas or topics": "The city has not undertaken to determine paternalistically, 'what information is relevant to self-government.'" *Gertz.* "[Where] the ordinance does differentiate among topics, it simply allows such noncontroversial things as conventional signs identifying a business enterprise, time-and-temperature signs, historical markers, and for-sale signs. It borders—if not trespasses—on the frivolous to suggest that, by allowing such signs but forbidding noncommercial billboards, the city has infringed freedom of speech. This ignores what we recognized in *Mosley,* that 'there may be sufficient regulatory interests justifying selective exclusions or [distinctions].' For each exception, the city is either acknowledging the unique connection between the medium and the message conveyed, or promoting a legitimate public interest in information. Similarly, in each in-

a. In response, the plurality complained that the test employed by Burger, C.J., was drawn almost exclusively from cases involving time, place, and manner restrictions: "[T]his Court has never held that the less strict standard of review applied to time, place, and manner restrictions is appropriately used in every First Amendment case, or that it is the most that the First Amendment requires of government legislation which infringes on protected speech. If this were the case, there would be no need for the detailed inquiry this Court consistently pursues in order to answer the question of whether a challenged restriction is in fact a time, place, and manner restriction—the same standard of review would apply regardless of the outcome of that inquiry. [T]he San Diego ordinance is not such a restriction and there is, therefore, no excuse for applying a lower standard of First Amendment review to that ordinance."

stance, the city reasonably could conclude that the balance between safety and aesthetic concerns on the one hand and the need to communicate on the other has tipped the opposite way. More important, in no instance is the exempted topic controversial; there can be no rational debate over, for example, the time, the temperature, the existence of an offer of sale, or the identity of a business establishment. The danger of San Diego setting the agenda of public discussion is not simply de minimis; it is nonexistent. * * *[7]

"The fatal flaw in the plurality's logic comes when it concludes that San Diego, by exempting on-site commercial signs, thereby has 'afford[ed] a greater degree of protection to commercial than to noncommercial speech.' The 'greater degree of protection' our cases have given noncommercial speech establishes a narrow range of constitutionally permissible regulation. To say noncommercial speech receives a greater degree of *constitutional* protection, however, does not mean that a legislature is forbidden to afford differing degrees of *statutory* protection when the restrictions on each form of speech—commercial and non-commercial—otherwise pass constitutional muster under the standards respectively applicable.

"[By] allowing communication of certain commercial ideas via billboards, but forbidding noncommercial signs altogether, a city does not necessarily place a greater 'value' on commercial speech.[8] In these situations, the city is simply recognizing that it has greater latitude to distinguish among various forms of commercial communication when the same distinctions would be impermissible if undertaken with regard to noncommercial speech. Indeed, when adequate alternative channels of communication are readily available so that the message may be freely conveyed through other means, a city arguably is more faithful to the Constitution by treating all noncommercial speech the same than by attempting to impose the same classifications in noncommercial as it has in commercial areas. To undertake the same kind of balancing and content judgment with noncommercial speech that is permitted with commercial speech is far more likely to run afoul of the First Amendment.[9]

"Thus, we may, consistent with the First Amendment, hold that a city may—and perhaps must—take an all-or-nothing approach with noncommercial speech yet remain free to adopt selective exceptions for commercial speech, as long as the latter advance legitimate governmental interests."

REHNQUIST, J., dissenting, expressed substantial agreement with the views of Burger, C.J., and Stevens, J.: "Nothing in my experience on the bench has led me to believe that a judge is in any better position than a city or county commission to make decisions in an area such as aesthetics. Therefore, little can be gained in the area of constitutional law, and much lost in the process of democratic decisionmaking, by allowing individual judges in city after city to

7. As Justice Brennan recognizes, the plurality's treatment of the ordinance may well create this very danger, for the plurality appears willing to allow municipal officials to determine what is and is not noncommercial speech.

8. Indeed, in *Lehman* we upheld a municipal policy allowing commercial but not political advertising on city buses. I cannot agree with the plurality that *Lehman* "ha[s] no application here." Although *Lehman* dealt with limited space leased by the city and this case deals with municipal regulation of privately leased space, the constitutional principle is the same: a city may forgo the "lurking doubts about favoritism" in granting space to some, but necessarily not all, political advertisers. The same constitutional dangers do not arise in allocating space among commercial advertisers.

9. See n. 8, supra. If a city were to permit onsite noncommercial billboards, one can imagine a challenge based on the argument that this favors the views of persons who can afford to own property in commercial districts. I intimate no view on whether I would accept such an argument should that case ever arise.

second-guess such legislative or administrative determinations. [In] a case where city planning commissions and zoning boards must regularly confront constitutional claims of this sort, it is a genuine misfortune to have the Court's treatment of the subject be a virtual Tower of Babel, from which no definitive principles can be clearly [drawn]."

Notes and Questions

1. Is a total ban on billboards realistically possible under the plurality opinion? Would a city really prevent a grocery store from putting up a sign saying "grocery store"? How would a business area operate without such signs? If a city allows a grocery store to identify itself, does it follow that it must permit political signs? Could a city function without government signs? Is the plurality suggesting that if a city allows stop signs, it must allow all other non-commercial signs? If not, what is the plurality saying? How may an ordinance be drafted that would satisfy the plurality?

2. *"We deal here with the law of billboards."* Is that all?

(a) In *Martin v. Struthers*, 319 U.S. 141, 63 S.Ct. 862, 87 L.Ed. 1313 (1943), a city forbade knocking on the door or ringing the doorbell of a resident in order to deliver handbills (in an industrial community where many worked night shifts and slept during the day). In striking down the ordinance, the Court, per Black, J., pointed out that the city's objectives could be achieved by means of a law making it an offense for any person to ring the doorbell of a householder who has "appropriately indicated that he is unwilling to be disturbed. This or any similar regulation leaves the decision as to whether distributors of literature may lawfully call at a home where it belongs—with the homeowner himself." [b] By contrast, *Breard v. Alexandria*, 341 U.S. 622, 71 S.Ct. 920, 95 L.Ed. 1233 (1951) upheld an ordinance forbidding the practice of going door to door to solicit orders for the sale of goods. The commercial element was said to distinguish *Martin*. Does *Breard* survive *Virginia Pharmacy*? (p. 554 supra). Does (should) *Metromedia* settle the issue? What if, as in *Breard*, the solicitor is selling subscriptions for magazines?

(b) Compare *Schneider*, p. 641 supra (prohibition against leaflet distribution on streets unconstitutional) with *Valentine*, p. 554 supra (prohibition against distribution of commercial leaflets upheld). Does (should) the *holding* of *Valentine* survive *Virginia Pharmacy*? Does *Metromedia* settle the issue? [c]

---

b. Compare *Lamont v. Postmaster General*, 381 U.S. 301, 85 S.Ct. 1493, 14 L.Ed.2d 398 (1965) (invalidating a federal statute permitting delivery of "communist political propaganda" only if the addressee specifically requested in writing that it be delivered because of the chilling effect on willing recipients) and *Rowan v. Post Office*, 397 U.S. 728, 90 S.Ct. 1484, 25 L.Ed.2d 736 (1970) (upholding statute authorizing Postmaster General to issue enforceable orders directing senders to refrain from future mailings to addressees who have notified Post Office that they believe mailings to be erotically arousing or sexually provocative) ("the mailer's right to communicate is circumscribed only by an affirmative act of the addressee giving notice that he wishes no further mailings from that mailer"). Is *Rowan* problematic because addressees must not only give notice that they want no further

mailings, but also that they deem the material to be erotic? Does this implicate impermissible content discrimination? See Stone, *Restrictions of Speech Because of its Content: The Peculiar Case of Subject-Matter Restrictions*, 46 U.Chi.L.Rev. 81, 84–85 (1978).

c. For relevant commentary on the normative issues, see Baker, *Commercial Speech: A Problem in the Theory of Freedom*, 62 Iowa L.Rev. 1 (1976); Redish, *The First Amendment in the Marketplace: Commercial Speech and the Values of Free Expression*, 39 Geo.Wash.L. Rev. 429 (1971); Redish, *The Value of Free Speech*, 130 U.Pa.L.Rev. 591 (1982); Shiffrin, *The First Amendment and Economic Regulation: Away From a General Theory of the First Amendment*, 78 Nw.U.L.Rev. 1212, 1220, 1276–82 (1983).

3. What test should apply when the use of a particular medium of communication is foreclosed?[d] See Schauer, *Codifying the First Amendment: New York v. Ferber*, 1982 S.Ct.Rev. 285, 301–02; Stone, *Content Regulation and the First Amendment*, 25 Wm. & M.L.Rev. 189, 234–36 (1983). Does the test not matter because however phrased we will end up with the law of sound trucks, of billboards, of leaflets, etc.?

Los Angeles prohibits posting signs on public property (e.g., sidewalks, crosswalks, street lamp posts, hydrants, or traffic signs). A group ("Taxpayers") contracted with a company to post cardboard campaign signs ("Roland Vincent— City Council") on the cross-arms supporting utility poles. Taxpayers argued that the ordinance was unconstitutional at least as applied to the placing of signs on the cross-arms of utility poles.[a] LOS ANGELES CITY COUNCIL v. TAXPAYERS FOR VINCENT, 466 U.S. 789, 104 S.Ct. 2118, 80 L.Ed.2d 772 (1984), per Stevens, J., upheld the ordinance: "[T]he First Amendment forbids the government from regulating speech in ways that favor some viewpoints or ideas at the expense of others. That general rule has no application to this case. For there is not even a hint of bias or censorship in [this] ordinance.

"In *O'Brien*, the Court set forth the appropriate framework for reviewing a viewpoint neutral regulation of this kind:[b] '[A] government regulation is sufficiently justified if it is within the constitutional power of the Government; if it furthers an important or substantial governmental interest; if the governmental interest is unrelated to the suppression of free expression; and if the incidental restriction on alleged First Amendment freedoms is no greater than is essential to the furtherance of that interest.'

"In this case, [Taxpayers does] not dispute that it is within the constitutional power of the City to attempt to improve its appearance, or that this interest is basically unrelated to the suppression of ideas. Therefore the critical inquiries are whether that interest is sufficiently substantial to justify the effect of the ordinance on appellees' expression, and whether that effect is no greater than necessary to accomplish the City's purpose.[c]

"In *Kovacs v. Cooper*, the Court rejected the notion that a city is powerless to protect its citizens from unwanted exposure to certain methods of expression which may legitimately be deemed a public nuisance. In upholding an ordinance that prohibited loud and raucous sound trucks, the Court held that the

---

d. Consider Anastaplo, *Self-Government and the Mass Media: A Practical Man's Guide* in The Mass Media and Modern Democracy 161, 223–24 (Clor ed. 1974): "I see in the abolition of television no serious First Amendment problem. Rather than abridge the 'freedom of speech' [, the] abolition of television (and hence a radical reform of the mass media) would enlarge freedom of speech among us. Television interferes, I have argued, with serious general education in a country such as ours: it affects the ability to read, and hence the ability to think and the very status of thought among us, playing up as it does to the passions. Thus abolition of television would probably contribute *among us* to the preservation of self-government and hence genuine freedom."

a. Taxpayers also argued that the ordinance was overbroad and should be declared invalid on its face. The Court concluded that Taxpayers had failed to demonstrate "a realistic danger that the ordinance [would] significantly compromise recognized First Amendment protections of individuals not before the Court." It, therefore, refused to entertain an overbreadth challenge.

b. Is the Court suggesting that the *O'Brien* test is the appropriate framework for all viewpoint neutral regulations or just for regulations "of this kind"? What "kind" of ordinance is this? How is it different from other kinds of viewpoint neutral regulations?

c. Is this the same as the *O'Brien* test?

state had a substantial interest in protecting its citizens from unwelcome noise.[24]

*   *   *

"*Metromedia* considered the city's interest in avoiding visual clutter, and seven Justices explicitly concluded that this interest was sufficient to justify a prohibition of billboards.[d] [The] problem addressed by this ordinance—the visual assault on the citizens of Los Angeles presented by an accumulation of signs posted on public property—constitutes a significant substantive evil within the City's power to prohibit. *   *   *

"We turn to the question whether the scope of the restriction on appellees' expressive activity is substantially broader than necessary to protect the City's interest in eliminating visual clutter.[e] The incidental restriction on expression which results from the City's attempt to accomplish such a purpose is considered justified as a reasonable regulation of the time, place, or manner of expression if it is narrowly tailored to serve that interest. [By] banning these signs, the City did no more than eliminate the exact source of the evil it sought to remedy. [The] ordinance curtails no more speech than is necessary to accomplish its purpose.[f]

"The Court of Appeals accepted the argument that a prohibition against the use of unattractive signs cannot be justified on esthetic grounds if it fails to apply to all equally unattractive signs wherever they might be located. A comparable argument was categorically rejected in *Metromedia*. In that case it was argued that the city could not simultaneously permit billboards to be used for on-site advertising and also justify the prohibition against offsite advertising on esthetic grounds, since both types of advertising were equally unattractive. The Court held, however, that the city could reasonably conclude that the esthetic interest was outweighed by the countervailing interest in one kind of advertising even though it was not outweighed by the other. So here, the validity of the esthetic interest in the elimination of signs on public property is not compromised by failing to extend the ban to private property. The private citizen's interest in controlling the use of his own property justifies the disparate treatment. Moreover, by not extending the ban to all locations, a significant opportunity to communicate by means of temporary signs is preserved, and private property owners' esthetic concerns will keep the posting of signs on their property within reasonable bounds. Even if some visual blight remains, a partial, content-neutral ban may nevertheless enhance the City's appearance.

"Furthermore, there is no finding that in any area where appellees seek to place signs, there are already so many signs posted on adjacent private property that the elimination of appellees' signs would have an inconsequential effect on the esthetic values with which the City is concerned. There is simply no predicate in the findings of the District Court for the conclusion that the

---

24. Justice Reed wrote: "The unwilling listener is not like the passer-by who may be offered a pamphlet in the street but may not be made to take it. In his home or on the street he is practically helpless to escape this interference with his privacy by loud speakers except through the protection of the municipality." *   *   *

d. Compare fn. 20 of the plurality opinion in *Metromedia* supra.

e. Does this depart from the *O'Brien* test?

f. The Court distinguished *Schneider*, p. 641 supra by observing that an anti-littering

statute would have been a less restrictive alternative in that case. Does this trivialize *Schneider*? Consider Stone, *O.T. 1983 and the Era of Aggressive Majoritarianism: A Court in Transition*, 19 Ga.L.Rev. 15, 21 (1984): "The Court understood in *Schneider* that not everyone can afford a newspaper or television campaign. In *Vincent*, the Court gave short shrift to this central first amendment insight." See generally Tribe, *Constitutional Calculus: Equal Justice or Economic Efficiency?*, 98 Harv.L.Rev. 592, 601–03 (1985).

prohibition against the posting of appellees' signs fails to advance the City's esthetic interest.[g]

"While the First Amendment does not guarantee the right to employ every conceivable method of communication at all times and in all places, a restriction on expressive activity may be invalid if the remaining modes of communication are inadequate.[h] * * * [Notwithstanding] appellees' general assertions in their brief concerning the utility of political posters, nothing in the findings indicates that the posting of political posters on public property is a uniquely valuable or important mode of communication, or that appellees' ability to communicate effectively is threatened by ever-increasing restrictions on expression.[30]

"Appellees suggest that the public property covered by the ordinance is either itself a 'public forum' for First Amendment purposes, or at least should be treated in the same respect as the 'public forum' in which the property is located. [But they] fail to demonstrate the existence of a traditional right of access respecting such items as utility poles for purposes of their communication comparable to that recognized for public streets and parks. * * *

"Lampposts can of course be used as signposts, but the mere fact that government property can be used as a vehicle for communication does not mean that the Constitution requires such uses to be permitted. Public property which is not by tradition or designation a forum for public communication may be reserved by the state 'for its intended purposes, communicative or otherwise, as long as the regulation on speech is reasonable and not an effort to suppress expression merely because public officials oppose the speaker's view.' *Perry*. Given our analysis of the legitimate interest served by the ordinance, its viewpoint neutrality, and the availability of alternative channels of communication, the ordinance is certainly constitutional as applied to appellees under this standard.[32]

"[We] hold that on this record [the city] interests are sufficiently substantial to justify this content neutral, impartially administered prohibition against the posting of appellees' temporary signs on public property and that such an application of the ordinance does not create an unacceptable threat to the 'profound national commitment to the principle that debate on public issues

g. How much advancement is required under the *O'Brien* test?

h. Does this modify the *O'Brien* test?

30. Although the Court has shown special solicitude for forms of expression that are much less expensive than feasible alternatives and hence may be important to a large segment of the citizenry, see, e.g., *Martin v. Struthers* ("Door to door distribution of circulars is essential to the poorly financed causes of little people."), this solicitude has practical boundaries, see, e.g., *Kovacs v. Cooper* ("That more people may be more easily and cheaply reached by sound trucks [is] not enough to call forth constitutional protection for what those charged with public welfare reasonably think is a nuisance when easy means of publicity are open."). * * *

32. Just as it is not dispositive to label the posting of signs on public property as a discrete medium of expression, it is also of limited utility in the context of this case to focus on whether the tangible property itself should be deemed a public forum. Generally an analysis of whether property is a public forum provides a workable analytical tool. However, "the analytical line between a regulation of the 'time, place, and manner' in which First Amendment rights may be exercised in a traditional public forum, and the question of whether a particular piece of personal or real property owned or controlled by the government is in fact a 'public forum' may blur at the edges," *United States Postal Service v. Greenburgh Civic Ass'n*, 453 U.S. 114, 132, 101 S.Ct. 2676, 2686, 69 L.Ed.2d 517 (1981), and this is particularly true in cases falling between the paradigms of government property interests essentially mirroring analogous private interests and those clearly held in trust, either by tradition or recent convention, for the use of citizens at large.

should be uninhibited, robust, and wide-open.' *New York Times Co. v. Sullivan.* "

BRENNAN, J., joined by Marshall and Blackmun, JJ., dissented because that "Los Angeles' total ban sweeps so broadly and trenches so completely on appellees' use of an important medium of political expression" and because "the Court's lenient approach towards the restriction of speech for reasons of aesthetics threatens seriously to undermine the protections of the First Amendment":

"The Court finds that the City's 'interest is sufficiently substantial to justify the restrictive effect of the ordinance on appellees' expression' and that the effect of the ordinance on speech is 'no greater than necessary to accomplish the City's purpose.' These are the right questions [but] Los Angeles has not shown that its interest in eliminating 'visual clutter' justifies its restriction of appellees' ability to communicate with the local electorate. * * *

"In deciding [the] First Amendment question, the critical importance of the posting of signs as a means of communication must not be overlooked. Use of this medium of communication is particularly valuable in part because it entails a relatively small expense in reaching a wide audience, allows flexibility in accommodating various formats, typographies, and graphics, and conveys its message in a manner that is easily read and understood by its reader or viewer. There may be alternative channels of communication, but the prevalence of a large number of signs in Los Angeles is a strong indication that, for many speakers, those alternatives are far less satisfactory.

"Nevertheless, the City of Los Angeles asserts that ample alternative avenues of communication are available. The City notes that, although the posting of signs on public property is prohibited, the posting of signs on private property and the distribution of handbills are not. But there is no showing that either of these alternatives would serve appellees' needs nearly as well as would the posting of signs on public property. First, there is no proof that a sufficient number of private parties would allow the posting of signs on their property. Indeed, common sense suggests the contrary at least in some instances. * * *

"Similarly, the adequacy of distributing handbills is dubious, despite certain advantages of handbills over signs. Particularly when the message to be carried is best expressed by a few words or a graphic image, a message on a sign will typically reach far more people than one on a handbill. The message on a posted sign remains to be seen by passersby as long as it is posted, while a handbill is typically read by a single reader and discarded. Thus, not only must handbills be printed in large quantity, but many hours must be spent distributing them. The average cost of communicating by handbill is therefore likely to be far higher than the average cost of communicating by poster. For that reason, signs posted on public property are doubtless 'essential to the poorly financed causes of little people,' and their prohibition constitutes a total ban on an important medium of communication. Cf. Stone, *Fora Americana: Speech in Public Places*, 1974 Sup.Ct.Rev. 233, 257. Because the City has completely banned the use of this particular medium of communication, and because, given the circumstances, there are no equivalent alternative media that provide an adequate substitute, the Court must examine with particular care the justifications that the City proffers for its ban. * * *

"The fundamental problem in this kind of case [is] the unavoidable subjectivity of aesthetic judgments—the fact that 'beauty is in the eye of the beholder.' As a consequence of this subjectivity, laws defended on aesthetic grounds raise problems for judicial review that are not presented by laws defended on more objective grounds—such as national security, public health, or public safety. In practice, therefore, the inherent subjectivity of aesthetic judgments makes it all too easy for the government to fashion its justification for a law in a manner that impairs the ability of a reviewing court meaningfully to make the required inquiries.

"Initially, a reviewing court faces substantial difficulties [because the] asserted interest in aesthetics may be only a facade for content-based suppression. [A] governmental interest in aesthetics cannot be regarded as sufficiently compelling to justify a restriction of speech based on an assertion that the content of the speech is, in itself, aesthetically displeasing. *Cohen v. California.* Because aesthetic judgments are so subjective, however, it is too easy for government to enact restrictions on speech for just such illegitimate reasons and to evade effective judicial review by asserting that the restriction is aimed at some displeasing aspect of the speech that is not solely communicative—for example, its sound, its appearance, or its location. An objective standard for evaluating claimed aesthetic judgments is therefore essential * * *.

"For example, in evaluating the ordinance before us in this case, the City might be pursuing either of two objectives, motivated by two very different judgments. One objective might be the elimination of 'visual clutter.' [A] second objective might simply be the elimination of the messages typically carried by the signs.[5] In that case, the aesthetic judgment would be that the signs' messages are themselves displeasing. The first objective is lawful, of course, but the second is not. Yet the City might easily mask the second objective by asserting the first and declaring that signs constitute visual clutter. In short, we must avoid unquestioned acceptance of the City's bare declaration of an aesthetic objective lest we fail in our duty to prevent unlawful trespasses upon First Amendment protections.

"A total ban on an important medium of communication may be upheld only if the government proves that the ban (1) furthers a substantial government objective, and (2) constitutes the least speech-restrictive means of achieving that objective. Here too, however, meaningful judicial application of these standards is seriously frustrated.

"[The] possibility of interdependence between means and ends in the development of policies to promote aesthetics poses a major obstacle to judicial review of the availability of alternative means that are less restrictive of speech. Indeed, when a court reviews a restriction of speech imposed in order to promote an aesthetic objective, there is a significant possibility that the court will be able to do little more than pay lip service to the First Amendment inquiry into the availability of less restrictive alternatives. The means may fit the ends only because the ends were defined with the means in mind. In this case, for example, the City has expressed an aesthetic judgment that signs on public property constitute visual clutter throughout the City and that its objective is to eliminate visual clutter. We are then asked to determine whether that objective could have been achieved with less restriction of speech. But to ask the question is to highlight the circularity of the inquiry. Since the goal, at least as currently expressed, is essentially to eliminate all signs, the only available means of achieving that goal is to eliminate all signs.

5. The fact that a ban on temporary signs applies to all signs does not necessarily imply content-neutrality. Because particular media are often used disproportionately for certain types of messages, a restriction that is content-neutral on its face may, in fact, be content-hostile. Cf. Stone, supra.

"The ease with which means can be equated with aesthetic ends only confirms the importance of close judicial scrutiny of the substantiality of such ends. In this case, for example, it is essential that the Court assess the City's ban on signs by evaluating whether the City has a substantial interest in eliminating the visual clutter caused by *all* posted signs *throughout* the City—as distinguished from an interest in banning signs in some areas or in preventing densely packed signs. If, in fact, either of the latter two objectives constitute the substantial interest underlying this ordinance, they could be achieved by means far less restrictive of speech than a total ban on signs, and the ban, therefore, would be invalid.

"Regrettably, the Court's analysis is seriously inadequate. Because the Court has failed to develop a reliable means of gauging the nature or depth of the City's commitment to pursuing the goal of eradicating 'visual clutter,' it simply approves the ordinance with only the most cursory degree of judicial oversight. [W]here a total ban is imposed on a particularly valuable method of communication, a court should require the government to provide tangible proof of the legitimacy and substantiality of its aesthetic objective. Justifications for such restrictions articulated by the government should be critically examined to determine whether the government has committed itself to addressing the identified aesthetic problem. * * *

"This does not mean that a government must address all aesthetic problems at one time or that a government should hesitate to pursue aesthetic objectives. What it does mean, however, is that when such an objective is pursued, it may not be pursued solely at the expense of First Amendment freedoms, nor may it be pursued by arbitrarily discriminating against a form of speech that has the same aesthetic characteristics as other forms of speech that are also present in the community.

"Accordingly, in order for Los Angeles to succeed in defending its total ban on the posting of signs, the City would have to demonstrate that it is pursuing its goal of eliminating visual clutter in a serious and comprehensive manner. Most importantly, the City would have to show that it is pursuing its goal through programs other than its ban on signs, that at least some of those programs address the visual clutter problem through means that do not entail the restriction of speech, and that the programs parallel the ban in their stringency, geographical scope, and aesthetic focus. In this case, however, [there] is no indication that the City has addressed its visual clutter problem in any way other than by prohibiting the posting of signs—throughout the City and without regard to the density of their presence."

Notes and Questions

1. Why does the Court turn to the *O'Brien* test rather than the public forum line of cases?[i] Does *Vincent* suggest that *O'Brien* should replace the *Perry* standards? Complement them? To what extent does *Vincent* suggest that the *O'Brien* test should apply to all viewpoint neutral regulations? Is there a general point to be drawn from *Vincent*? Or do we deal here with the law of cross-arms supporting utility poles?

2. The Court states that *O'Brien* supplies the appropriate framework, yet seems to deviate from its literal terms at various points in the opinion. Are those constructive modifications of the *O'Brien* test?

i. For commentary on the relationship between the *O'Brien* test and the tests employed in the public forum line of cases, see *Nimmer on Freedom of Speech* 4–67 to 4–81 (1984).

3. In reciting the facts, the Court observes that "among the 1,207 signs removed from public property during that week, 48 were identified as 'Roland Vincent' signs. Most of the other signs identified in that report were apparently commercial in character." Should the Court take the predominance of commercial signs into account? The insubstantial development of the messages involved? Do these factors minimize the force of Professor Stone's suggestion, fn. f, that *Vincent* is insensitive to the equality values at stake? In any event, does *Vincent's* appreciation of aesthetic values outstrip the facts? Is a utility pole more beautiful without a sign? Does it make aesthetic sense to allow signs everywhere on business property except on the utility poles?

SECTION 8. BROADCAST REGULATION AND ACCESS TO THE MASS MEDIA

The mass media are not invariably the most effective means of communication. For example, the right to place messages on utility poles concerning a lost dog may be more important than access to a radio or a television station. In some circumstances, picketing outside a school or placing leaflets in teachers' mailboxes may be the most effective communications medium. Nonetheless, the law regulating access to the mass media is of vital societal importance. This section considers first cases in which government seeks to force newspapers and broadcasters to grant access; second, in *CBS v. DNC*, infra, a claim that the first amendment requires government to afford access for excluded groups to the broadcast media; third, cases in which government commands broadcasters not to carry particular programming at particular times or not to editorialize. A persistent theme is that broadcasting is "special," but whether it is, why it is, and what difference it should make are matters of considerable debate. Beyond this, attitudes about the most effective channel of communication raise questions about our commitment to and understanding of first amendment principles. If the assumption that broadcasting is special is a masquerade, why the masquerade?

I. ACCESS TO THE MASS MEDIA

A. ACCESS BY STATUTE: THE FIRST AMENDMENT AS SHIELD

MIAMI HERALD PUB. CO. v. TORNILLO, 418 U.S. 241, 94 S.Ct. 2831, 41 L.Ed.2d 730 (1974), per BURGER, C.J., unanimously struck down a Florida "right of reply" statute, which required any newspaper that "assails" the personal character or official record of a candidate in any election to print, on demand, free of cost, any reply the candidate may make to the charges, in as conspicuous a place and the same kind of type, provided the reply takes up no more space than the charges. The opinion carefully explained the aim of the statute to "ensure that a wide variety of views reach the public" even though "chains of newspapers, national newspapers, national wire and news services, and one-newspaper towns, are the dominant features of a press that has become noncompetitive and enormously powerful and influential in its capacity to manipulate popular opinion and change the course of events," placing "in a few hands the power to inform the American people and shape public opinion."[a] Nonetheless,

---

a. The opinion developed these views at greater length, citing "generally" Barron, *Access to the Press—A New First Amendment* *Right,* 80 Harv.L.Rev. 1641 (1967); Lange, *The Role of the Access Doctrine in the Regulation*

the Court concluded that to require the printing of a reply violated the first amendment:

"Compelling editors or publishers to publish that which ' "reason" tells them should not be published' is what is at issue in this case. The Florida statute operates as a command in the same sense as a statute or regulation forbidding appellant from publishing specified matter. [The] Florida statute exacts a penalty on the basis of the content of a newspaper. The first phase of the penalty resulting from the compelled printing of a reply is exacted in terms of the cost in printing and composing time and materials and in taking up space that could be devoted to other material the newspaper may have preferred to print. It is correct, as appellee contends, that a newspaper is not subject to the finite technological limitations of time that confront a broadcaster but it is not correct to say that, as an economic reality, a newspaper can proceed to infinite expansion of its column space to accommodate the replies that a government agency determines or a statute commands the readers should have available.

"Faced with the penalties that would accrue to any newspaper that published news or commentary arguably within the reach of the right of access statute, editors might well conclude that the safe course is to avoid controversy and that, under the operation of the Florida statute, political and electoral coverage would be blunted or reduced. Government enforced right of access inescapably 'dampens the vigor and limits the variety of public debate,' *New York Times.*

"Even if a newspaper would face no additional costs to comply with a compulsory access law and would not be forced to forego publication of news or opinion by the inclusion of a reply, the Florida statute fails to clear the barriers of the First Amendment because of its intrusion into the function of editors. A newspaper is more than a passive receptacle or conduit for news, comment, and advertising. The choice of material to go into a newspaper, and the decisions made as to limitations on the size of the paper, and content, and treatment of public issues and public officials—whether fair or unfair—constitutes the exercise of editorial control and judgment. It has yet to be demonstrated how governmental regulation of this crucial process can be exercised consistent with First Amendment guarantees of a free press as they have evolved to this time." [b]

The Federal Communications Commission has long imposed on radio and television broadcasters the "fairness doctrine"—requiring that stations (1) devote

of the Mass Media: A Critical Review and Assessment, 52 N.C.L.Rev. 1, 8–9 (1973).

b. Brennan, J., joined by Rehnquist, J., joined the Court's opinion in a short statement to express the understanding that the opinion "implies no view upon the constitutionality of 'retraction' statutes affording plaintiffs able to prove defamatory falsehoods a statutory action to require publication of a retraction. See generally Note, *Vindication of the Reputation of a Public Official,* 80 Harv.L.Rev. 1730, 1739–1747 (1967)."

White, J., concurred. After agreeing that "prior compulsion by government in matters going to the very nerve center of a newspaper—the decision as to what copy will or will not be included in any given edition—collides with the First Amendment," he returned to

his attack on *Gertz,* decided the same day: "Reaffirming the rule that the press cannot be forced to print an answer to a personal attack made by it [throws] into stark relief the consequences of the new balance forged by the Court in the companion case also announced today. *Gertz* goes far toward eviscerating the effectiveness of the ordinary libel action, which has long been the only potent response available to the private citizen libeled by the press. [To] me it is a near absurdity to so deprecate individual dignity, as the Court does in *Gertz,* and to leave the people at the complete mercy of the press, at least in this stage of our history when the press, as the majority in this case so well documents, is steadily becoming more powerful and much less likely to be deterred by threats of libel suits."

a reasonable percentage of broadcast time to discussion of public issues and (2) assure fair coverage for each side.[c] At issue in RED LION BROADCASTING CO. v. FCC, 395 U.S. 367, 89 S.Ct. 1794, 23 L.Ed.2d 371 (1969), were the application of the fairness doctrine to a particular broadcast [d] and two specific access regulations promulgated under the doctrine: (1) the "political editorial" rule, requiring that when a broadcaster, in an editorial, "endorses or opposes" a political candidate, it must notify the candidate opposed, or the rivals of the candidate supported, and afford them a "reasonable opportunity" to respond; (2) the "personal attack" rule, requiring that "when, during the presentation of views on a controversial issue of public importance, an attack is made on the honesty, character [or] integrity [of] an identified person or group," the person or group attacked must be given notice, a transcript of the attack, and an opportunity to respond.[e] "[I]n view of [the] scarcity of broadcast frequencies, the Government's role in allocating those frequencies, and the legitimate claims of those unable without government assistance to gain access to those frequencies for expression of their views," a 7–0 majority, per WHITE, J., upheld both access regulations:[f]

"[The broadcasters] contention is that the First Amendment protects their desire to use their allotted frequencies continuously to broadcast whatever they choose, and to exclude whomever they choose from ever using that frequency. No man may be prevented from saying or publishing what he thinks, or from refusing in his speech or other utterances to give equal weight to the views of his opponents. This right, they say, applies equally to broadcasters.

"Although broadcasting is clearly a medium affected by a First Amendment interest, differences in the characteristics of new media justify differences in the First Amendment standards applied to [them]. Just as the Government may limit the use of sound-amplifying equipment potentially so noisy that it drowns out civilized private speech, so may the Government limit the use of broadcast equipment. The right of free speech of a broadcaster, the user of a sound truck, or any other individual does not embrace a right to snuff out the free speech of [others].

"Where there are substantially more individuals who want to broadcast than there are frequencies to allocate, it is idle to posit an unabridgeable First Amendment right to broadcast comparable to the right of every individual to speak, write, or publish. [It] would be strange if the First Amendment, aimed at protecting and furthering communications, prevented the Government from making radio communication possible by requiring licenses to broadcast and by limiting the number of licenses so as not to overcrowd the spectrum. * * *

c. For helpful background on the origins, justification and administration of the fairness doctrine, see Barrow, *The Fairness Doctrine: A Double Standard for Electronic and Print Media,* 26 Hast.L.J. 659 (1975); Schmidt, *Freedom of the Press vs. Public Access* 157–98 (1976).

d. *Red Lion* grew out of a series of radio broadcasts by fundamentalist preacher Billy James Hargis, who had attacked Fred J. Cook, author of an article attacking Hargis and "hate clubs of the air." When Cook heard about the broadcast, he demanded that the station give him an opportunity to reply. Cook refused to pay for his "reply time" and the FCC ordered the station to give Cook the opportunity to reply whether or not he would pay for it. The Supreme Court upheld the order of free reply time. See Schmidt, fn. c supra, at 161–63.

e. Excepted were "personal attacks [by] legally qualified candidates [on] other such candidates" and "bona fide newscasts, bona fide news interviews, and on-the-spot coverage of a bona fide news event."

f. Surprisingly, none of the justices joining White, J.'s opinion felt the need to make additional remarks, but Douglas, J., who did not participate in *Red Lion,* expressed his disagreement with it in the *CBS* case, infra.

"By the same token, as far as the First Amendment is concerned those who are licensed stand no better than those to whom licenses are refused. A license permits broadcasting, but the licensee has no constitutional right [to] monopolize a radio frequency to the exclusion of his fellow citizens. There is nothing in the First Amendment which prevents the Government from requiring a licensee to share his frequency with others and to conduct himself as a proxy or fiduciary with obligations to present those views and voices which are representative of his community and which would otherwise, by necessity, be barred from the air-waves.

"[The] people as a whole retain their interest in free speech by radio and their collective right to have the medium function consistently with the ends and purposes of the First Amendment. It is the right of the viewers and listeners, not the right of the broadcasters, which is paramount. [It] is the purpose of the First Amendment to preserve an uninhibited marketplace of ideas in which truth will ultimately prevail, rather than to countenance monopolization of that market, whether it be by the Government itself or a private licensee. [It] is the right of the public to receive suitable access to social, political, esthetic, moral, and other ideas and experiences which is crucial [here.]

"In terms of constitutional principle, and as enforced sharing of a scarce resource, the personal attack and political editorial rules are indistinguishable from the equal-time provision of § 315 [of the Communications Act], a specific enactment of Congress requiring [that stations allot equal time to qualified candidates for public office] and to which the fairness doctrine and these constituent regulations are important complements. [Nor] can we say that it is inconsistent with the First Amendment goal of producing an informed public capable of conducting its own affairs to require a broadcaster to permit answers to personal attacks occurring in the course of discussing controversial issues, or to require that the political opponents of those endorsed by the station be given a chance to communicate with the public. Otherwise, station owners and a few networks would have unfettered power to make time available only to the highest bidders, to communicate only their own views on public issues, people and candidates, and to permit on the air only those with whom they agreed. There is no sanctuary in the First Amendment for unlimited private censorship operating in a medium not open to all.

"[It is contended] that if political editorials or personal attacks will trigger an obligation in broadcasters to afford the opportunity for expression to speakers who need not pay for time and whose views are unpalatable to the licensees, then broadcasters will be irresistibly forced to self-censorship and their coverage of controversial public issues will be eliminated or at least rendered wholly ineffective. Such a result would indeed be a serious matter, [but] that possibility is at best speculative. [If these doctrines turn out to have this effect], there will be time enough to reconsider the constitutional implications. The fairness doctrine in the past has had no such overall effect. That this will occur now seems unlikely, however, since if present licensees should suddenly prove timorous, the Commission is not powerless to insist that they give adequate and fair attention to public issues. It does not violate the First Amendment to treat licensees given the privilege of using scarce radio frequencies as proxies for the entire community, obligated to give suitable time and attention to matters of great public concern. To condition the granting or renewal of licenses on a willingness to present representative community views on controversial issues is consistent with the ends and purposes of those constitutional provisions forbidding the abridgment of freedom of speech and freedom of the press." [g]

Notes and Questions

1. *Tension between Miami Herald and Red Lion.* Consider Bollinger, *Freedom of the Press and Public Access: Toward a Theory of Partial Regulation of the Mass Media,* 75 Mich.L.Rev. 1, 4–6, 10–12 (1976): "What seems so remarkable about the unanimous *Miami Herald* opinion is the complete absence of any reference to the Court's unanimous decision five years earlier in *Red Lion* [, upholding] the so-called personal attack rule, [which] is almost identical in substance to the Florida statute declared unconstitutional in *Miami Herald.* That omission, however, is no more surprising than the absence of any discussion in *Red Lion* of the cases in which the Court expressed great concern about the risks attending government regulation of the print media.

"[The] scarcity rationale [articulated in *Red Lion* does not] explain why what appears to be a similar phenomenon of natural monopolization within the newspaper industry does not constitute an equally appropriate occasion for access regulation. A difference in the cause of concentration—the exhaustion of a physical element necessary for communication in broadcasting as contrasted with the economic constraints on the number of possible competitors in the print media—would seem far less relevant from a first amendment standpoint than the fact of concentration itself.

"[Instead] of exploring the relevance for the print media of the new principle developed in broadcasting, the Court merely reiterated the opposing, more traditional, principle that the government cannot tell editors what to publish. It thus created a paradox, leaving the new principle unscathed while preserving tradition."

2. *The absence of balancing in Miami Herald.* Did *Miami Herald* present a confrontation between the rights of speech and press? "Nowhere does [*Miami Herald*] explicitly acknowledge [such a confrontation], but implicit recognition of the speech interest," observes Nimmer, *Is Freedom of the Press a Redundancy? What Does it Add to Freedom of Speech?,* 26 Hast.L.J. 639, 645, 657 (1975), "may be found in the Court's reference to the access advocates' argument that, given the present semimonopolistic posture of the press, speech can be effective and therefore free only if enhanced by devices such as a right of reply statute. The Court in accepting the press clause argument in effect necessarily found it to be superior to any competing speech clause claims. [But] the issue cannot be resolved merely by noting, as did [*Miami Herald*], that a right of reply statute 'constitutes the [state] exercise of editorial control and judgment.' This is but one half of the equation. [*Miami Herald*] ignored the strong conflicting claims

g. The Court noted that it "need not deal with the argument that even if there is no longer a technological scarcity of frequencies limiting the number of broadcasters, there nevertheless is an economic scarcity in the sense that the Commission could or does limit entry to the broadcasting market on economic grounds and license no more stations than the market will support. Hence, it is said, the fairness doctrine or its equivalent is essential to satisfy the claims of those excluded and of the public generally. A related argument, which we also put side, is that quite apart from scarcity of frequencies, technological or economic, Congress does not abridge freedom of speech or press by legislation directly or indirectly multiplying the voices and views presented to the public through time sharing, fairness doctrines, or other devices which limit or dissipate the power of those who sit astride the channels of communication with the general public." For background and discussion of *Red Lion,* see Friendly, *The Good Guys, The Bad Guys and the First Amendment* (1975).

of 'speech.' Perhaps on balance the press should still prevail, but those who doubt the efficacy of such a result are hardly persuaded by an approach that apparently fails to recognize that any balancing of speech and press rights is required." [h]

3. *Scope of Miami Herald.* Consider Schmidt, supra, note c, at 233–35: "From the perspective of First Amendment law generally, *Miami Herald* would be a stark and unexplained deviation if one were to read the decision as creating absolute prohibitions on access obligations.[i] [The] fact the Court offers no discussion as to why First Amendment rules respecting access should be absolute, while all other rules emanating from that Amendment are relative, suggests that the principle of *Miami Herald* probably is destined for uncharted qualifications and exceptions." Would a statute requiring nondiscriminatory access to the classified ads section of a newspaper pass muster under *Miami Herald?* A requirement that legal notices be published?

4. *Absolute editorial autonomy—some of the time.* Is it ironic that *Gertz,* p. 476 supra was decided the same day as *Miami Herald?* Which poses a greater threat to editorial autonomy—a negligence standard in defamation cases or the guaranteed access contemplated by the Florida statute? Whose autonomy is important—the editors or the owners? May government protect editors from ad hoc intervention by corporate owners? See generally Baker, *Press Rights and Government Power to Structure the Press,* 34 U.Miami L.Rev. 819 (1980).

5. *Why was the Court so averse to a limited right of access to the print media?* "One possible explanation," suggests Blasi, 1977 Am.B.Found.Res.J. 521, 621–22, and one "consistent with the checking value," is that even "such a narrow right of reply could have the effect of shifting newspaper coverage away from topics that are central to the checking function—discussions of the fitness of candidates, particularly those with records in office—and toward less valued subjects for which the reply right would be inapplicable. A more likely reason is that the Justices perceived the print media as having historically enjoyed an adversary relationship with government which could only be compromised, symbolically as well as materially, if officials could dictate, for whatever reason, what the content of a particular publication must be. It is significant in this respect that the only Justice who elaborated on the concept of journalistic discretion as it relates to newspapers, [concurring] Justice White, stressed the role of the press as a watchdog over government. It is even possible that the Court responded more favorably to the print journalists' claim to be free from access legislation than to the similar claim of broadcast journalists precisely because the Justices viewed the electronic media as fulfilling, historically as well as currently, a somewhat different and less significant role in the checking process. The Court may well have been influenced by the fact that the networks have never really had an I.F. Stone or a Seymour Hersh or a Woodward and Bernstein."

---

h. Does *Miami Herald* demonstrate, as Professor Nimmer believes, at 644–46, that free speech and press can be distinct, even conflicting interests? Lewis, *A Preferred Position for Journalism?,* 7 Hof.L.Rev. 595, 603 (1979), thinks not: "[T]he vice of the [Florida right of reply] law lay in the compulsion to publish; and I think the result would be no different if the case involved a compulsion to speak. If a state statute required any candidate who spoke falsely about another to make a corrective speech, would it survive challenge under the first amendment?"

i. "Even in the area of 'the central freedom of the First Amendment,' which is criticism of the governmental acts of public officials," recalls Professor Schmidt, fn. c supra, at 232, "there is no absolute protection for expression."

6. *The threat to editorial autonomy in Red Lion.* Consider Schmidt, fn. c supra, at 166: *Red Lion* "left broadcaster autonomy almost entirely at the mercy of the FCC." See also Van Alstyne, *The Möbius Strip of the First Amendment: Perspectives on Red Lion,* 29 S.C.L.Rev. 539, 571 (1978): "Indeed, if one continues to be troubled by *Red Lion,* I think it is not because one takes lightly the difficulty of forum allocation in a society of scarce resources. Rather, it is because one believes that the technique of the fairness doctrine in particular may represent a very trivial egalitarian gain and a major first amendment loss; that a twist has been given to the equal protection idea by a device the principal effect of which is merely to level down the most vivid and versatile forum we have, to flatten it out and to render it a mere commercial mirror of each community. What may have been lost is a willingness to risk the partisanship of licensees as catalysts and as active advocates with a freedom to exhort, a freedom that dares to exclaim 'Fuck the draft,' and not be made to yield by government at once to add, 'but on the other hand there is also the view, held by many.'"

Is the right of reply portion of the fairness doctrine less threatening than general fairness requirements? Consider Blasi, note 5 supra, at 627: "I do not believe that loss of editorial control requested by [narrowly] defined rights of reply is likely to undercut journalistic autonomy to such a degree as to dissipate the ethos that makes news organizations view themselves as guardians of the public welfare. And if one's conception of journalistic autonomy derives from the checking value, the preservation of this ethos is the appropriate measure, not some notion of total control analogous to that which an individual must enjoy within a certain sphere if he is to be truly autonomous." But see Karst, *Equality as a Central Principle in the First Amendment,* 43 U.Chi.L.Rev. 20, 49 (1975): "Even though the right-of-reply portion of the fairness doctrine upheld in *Red Lion* is less threatening than the doctrine's more general insistence on fair coverage of issues, a right of reply will give added encouragement to an editorial blandness already promoted by the broadcasters' commercial advertisers; broadcasters will simply minimize the number of newscasts to which a fairness doctrine obligation will attach." Did similar reasoning lead *Miami Herald* to invalidate the state right-of-reply statute directed at newspapers?

7. *The best of both worlds.* "[T]he critical difference between what the Court was asked to do in *Red Lion* and what it was asked to do in *Miami Herald,*" maintains Professor Bollinger note 1 supra, at 27, "involved choosing between a partial regulatory system and a universal one. Viewed from that perspective, the Court reached the correct result in both cases." Continues Bollinger at 27, 32–33, 36–37: "[T]here are good first amendment reasons for being both receptive to and wary of access regulation. This dual nature of access legislation suggests the need to limit carefully the intrusiveness of the regulation in order safely to enjoy its remedial benefits. Thus, a proper judicial response is one that will permit the legislature to provide the public with access *somewhere* within the mass media, but not throughout the press. The Court should not, and need not, be forced into an all-or-nothing position on this matter; there is nothing in the first amendment that forbids having the best of both worlds."

8. *Cable television.* Can government require cable operators to grant an access channel for the public, for the government, and for educational institutions? Which is the better analogy: *Red Lion* or *Miami Herald?* See, e.g., Pool, *Technologies of Freedom* 151–88 (1983); Price, *Taming Red Lion: The First Amendment and Structural Approaches to Media Regulation,* 31 Fed.Comm.L.J. 215 (1979); Comment, *Access to Cable Television: A Critique of the Affirmative*

Duty Theory of the First Amendment, 70 Calif.L.Rev. 1393 (1982). For discussion of other technologies, see Special Issue, *Videotex,* 36 Fed.Comm.L.J. 119 (1984).

B. ACCESS BY CONSTITUTIONAL RIGHT: THE FIRST AMENDMENT AS SWORD

"Like many equal protection issues," observes Karst, note 6 supra, at 45, "the media-access problem should be approached from two separate constitutional directions. First, what does the Constitution *compel* government to do in the way of equalizing? Second, what does the Constitution *permit* government to do in equalizing by statute?" *Red Lion* and *Miami Herald* presented the second question; the first is raised by COLUMBIA BROADCASTING SYSTEM, INC. v. DEMOCRATIC NAT'L COMMITTEE, 412 U.S. 94, 93 S.Ct. 2080, 36 L.Ed.2d 772 (1973) (*CBS*): The FCC rejected the claims of Business Executives' Move for Vietnam Peace (BEM) and the Democratic National Committee (DNC) that "responsible" individuals and groups are entitled to purchase advertising time to comment on public issues, even though the broadcaster has complied with the fairness doctrine. The District of Columbia Circuit held that "a flat ban on paid public issue announcements" violates the first amendment "at least when other sorts of paid announcements are accepted," [a] and remanded to the FCC to develop "reasonable procedures and regulations determining which and how many 'editorial advertisements' will be put on the air." The Supreme Court, per Burger, C.J., reversed, holding that neither the "public interest" standard of the Communications Act (which draws heavily from the first amendment) nor the first amendment itself—assuming that refusal to accept such advertising constituted "governmental action" for first amendment purposes[b]—requires broadcasters to accept paid editorial announcements. As pointed out in Blasi, note 5 supra, at 613–14, although the Chief Justice "built to some extent" on *Red Lion,* his opinion "evinced a most important change of emphasis. For whereas Justice White based his argument in *Red Lion* on the premise that broadcasters are mere 'proxies' or 'fiduciaries' for the general public, the Chief Justice's opinion [in *CBS*] invoked a concept of 'journalistic independence' or 'journalistic discretion,' the essence of which is that broadcasters do indeed have special First Amendment interests which have to be considered in the constitutional calculus."

Observed the Chief Justice: "[From various provisions of the Communications Act of 1934] it seems clear that Congress intended to permit private broadcasting to develop with the widest journalistic freedom consistent with its public obligations. Only when the interests of the public are found to outweigh the private journalistic interests of the broadcasters will government power be asserted within the framework of the Act. License renewal proceedings, in which the listening public can be heard, are a principal means of such regulation.

a. Compare the access claim advanced in the city bus advertising context in *Lehman v. Shaker Heights,* p. 676 supra.

b. Burger, C.J., joined by Stewart and Rehnquist, JJ., concluded that a broadcast licensee's refusal to accept an advertisement was not "governmental action" for first amendment purposes. Although White, Blackmun and Powell, JJ., concurred in other parts of the Chief Justice's opinion, they did not decide this question for, *assuming* governmental action, they found that the challenged ban did not violate the first amendment. Douglas, J., who concurred in the result, assumed *no* governmental action. Dissenting, Brennan, J., joined by Marshall, J., found that the challenged ban did constitute "governmental action." See p. 1124 infra.

"[W]ith the advent of radio a half century ago, Congress was faced with a fundamental choice between total Government ownership and control of the new medium—the choice of most other countries—or some other alternative. Long before the impact and potential of the medium was realized, Congress opted for a system of private broadcasters licensed and regulated by Government. The legislative history suggests that this choice was influenced not only by traditional attitudes toward private enterprise, but by a desire to maintain for licensees, so far as consistent with necessary regulation, a traditional journalistic [role.]

"The regulatory scheme evolved slowly, but very early the licensee's role developed in terms of a 'public trustee' charged with the duty of fairly and impartially informing the public audience. In this structure the Commission acts in essence as an 'overseer,' but the initial and primary responsibility for fairness, balance, and objectivity rests with the licensee. This role of the Government as an overseer and ultimate arbiter and guardian of the public interest and the role of the licensee as a journalistic 'free agent' call for a delicate balancing of competing interests. The maintenance of this balance for more than 40 years has called on both the regulators and the licensees to walk a 'tightrope' to preserve the First Amendment values written into the Radio Act and its successor, the Communications Act.

"The tensions inherent in such a regulatory structure emerge more clearly when we compare a private newspaper with a broadcast licensee. The power of a privately owned newspaper to advance its own political, social, and economic views is bounded by only two factors: first, the acceptance of a sufficient number of readers—and hence advertisers—to assure financial success; and, second, the journalistic integrity of its editors and publishers. A broadcast licensee has a large measure of journalistic freedom but not as large as that exercised by a newspaper. A licensee must balance what it might prefer to do as a private entrepreneur with what it is required to do as a 'public trustee.' To perform its statutory duties, the Commission must oversee without censoring. This suggests something of the difficulty and delicacy of administering the Communications Act—a function calling for flexibility and the capacity to adjust and readjust the regulatory mechanism to meet changing problems and needs.

"The licensee policy challenged in this case is intimately related to the journalistic role of a licensee for which it has been given initial and primary responsibility by Congress. The licensee's policy against accepting editorial advertising cannot be examined as an abstract proposition, but must be viewed in the context of its journalistic role. It does not help to press on us the idea that editorial ads are 'like' commercial ads, for the licensee's policy against editorial spot ads is expressly based on a journalistic judgment that 10- to 60-second spot announcements are ill-suited to intelligible and intelligent treatment of public issues; the broadcaster has chosen to provide a balanced treatment of controversial questions in a more comprehensive form. Obviously, the licensee's evaluation is based on its own journalistic judgment of priorities and newsworthiness.

"Moreover, the Commission has not fostered the licensee policy challenged here; it has simply declined to command particular action because it fell within the area of journalistic discretion. [The] Commission's reasoning, consistent with nearly 40 years of precedent, is that so long as a licensee meets its 'public trustee' obligation to provide balanced coverage of issues and events, it has broad discretion to decide how that obligation will be met. We do not reach the question whether the First Amendment or the Act can be read to preclude the

Commission from determining that in some situations the public interest requires licensees to re-examine their policies with respect to editorial advertisements.[c] The Commission has not yet made such a determination; it has, for the present at least, found the policy to be within the sphere of journalistic discretion which Congress has left with the licensee.

"[I]t must constantly be kept in mind that the interest of the public is our foremost concern. With broadcasting, where the available means of communication are limited in both space and time, [Meiklejohn's admonition] that '[w]hat is essential is not that everyone shall speak, but that everything worth saying shall be said' is peculiarly appropriate.

"[Congress] has time and again rejected various legislative attempts that would have mandated a variety of forms of individual access. [It] has chosen to leave such questions with the Commission, to which it has given the flexibility to experiment with new ideas as changing conditions require. In this case, the Commission has decided that on balance the undesirable effects of the right of access urged by respondents would outweigh the asserted [benefits.]

"The Commission was justified in concluding that the public interest in providing access to the marketplace of 'ideas and experiences' would scarcely be served by a system so heavily weighted in favor of the financially affluent, or those with access to wealth. Even under a first-come-first-served system [the] views of the affluent could well prevail over those of others, since they would have it within their power to purchase time more frequently. Moreover, there is the substantial danger [that] the time allotted for editorial advertising could be monopolized by those of one political persuasion.

"These problems would not necessarily be solved by applying the Fairness Doctrine, including the *Cullman* doctrine [requiring broadcasters to provide free time for the presentation of opposing views if a paid sponsor is unavailable], to editorial advertising. If broadcasters were required to provide time, free when necessary, for the discussion of the various shades of opinion on the issue discussed in the advertisement, the affluent could still determine in large part the issues to be discussed. Thus, the very premise of the Court of Appeals' holding—that a right of access is necessary to allow individuals and groups the opportunity for self-initiated speech—would have little meaning to those who could not afford to purchase time in the first instance.

"If the Fairness Doctrine were applied to editorial advertising, there is also the substantial danger that the effective operation of that doctrine would be jeopardized. To minimize financial hardship and to comply fully with its public responsibilities a broadcaster might well be forced to make regular programming time available to those holding a view different from that expressed in an editorial advertisement. [The] result would be a further erosion of the journalistic discretion of broadcasters in the coverage of public issues, and a transfer of control over the treatment of public issues from the licensees who are accountable for broadcast performance to private individuals who are not. The public interest would no longer be 'paramount' but rather subordinate to private whim

c. *Columbia Broadcasting System, Inc. v. FCC,* 453 U.S. 367, 101 S.Ct. 2813, 69 L.Ed.2d 706 (1981) upheld FCC administration of a statutory provision guaranteeing "reasonable" access to the airwaves for federal election candidates. The Court, per Burger, C.J., observed that "the Court has never approved a *general* right of access to the media. *Miami Herald; CBS v. DNC.* Nor do we do so to-day." But it found that the limited right of access "properly balances the First Amendment rights of federal candidates, the public, and broadcasters." White, J., joined by Rehnquist and Stevens, JJ., dissented on statutory grounds. For criticism on constitutional grounds, see Polsby, *Candidate Access to the Air: The Uncertain Future of Broadcaster Discretion,* 1981 Sup.Ct.Rev. 223.

especially since, under the Court of Appeals' decision, a broadcaster would be largely precluded from rejecting editorial advertisements that dealt with matters trivial or insignificant or already fairly covered by the broadcaster. If the Fairness Doctrine and the *Cullman* doctrine were suspended to alleviate these problems, as respondents suggest might be appropriate, the question arises whether we would have abandoned more than we have gained. Under such a regime the congressional objective of balanced coverage of public issues would be seriously threatened.

"Nor can we accept the Court of Appeals' view that every potential speaker is 'the best judge' of what the listening public ought to hear or indeed the best judge of the merits of his or her views. All journalistic tradition and experience is to the contrary. For better or worse, editing is what editors are for; and editing is selection and choice of material. That editors—newspaper or broadcast—can and do abuse this power is beyond doubt, but that is not reason to deny the discretion Congress provided. Calculated risks of abuse are taken in order to preserve higher values. The presence of these risks is nothing new; the authors of the Bill of Rights accepted the reality that these risks were evils for which there was no acceptable remedy other than a spirit of moderation and a sense of responsibility—and civility—on the part of those who exercise the guaranteed freedoms of expression.

"It was reasonable for Congress to conclude that the public interest in being informed requires periodic accountability on the part of those who are entrusted with the use of broadcast frequencies, scarce as they are. In the delicate balancing historically followed in the regulation of broadcasting Congress and the Commission could appropriately conclude that the allocation of journalistic priorities should be concentrated in the licensee rather than diffused among many. This policy gives the public some assurance that the broadcaster will be answerable if he fails to meet their legitimate needs. No such accountability attaches to the private individual, whose only qualifications for using the broadcast facility may be abundant funds and a point of view. To agree that debate on public issues should be 'robust, and wide-open' does not mean that we should exchange 'public trustee' broadcasting, with all its limitations, for a system of self-appointed editorial commentators.

"[T]he risk of an enlargement of Government control over the content of broadcast discussion of public issues [is] inherent in the Court of Appeals' remand requiring regulations and procedures to sort out requests to be heard—a process involving the very editing that licensees now perform as to regular programming. [Under] a constitutionally commanded and government supervised right-of-access system urged by respondents and mandated by the Court of Appeals, the Commission would be required to oversee far more of the day-to-day operations of broadcasters' conduct, deciding such questions as whether a particular individual or group has had sufficient opportunity to present its viewpoint and whether a particular viewpoint has already been sufficiently aired. Regimenting broadcasters is too radical a therapy for the ailment respondents complain of.

"Under the Fairness Doctrine the Commission's responsibility is to judge whether a licensee's overall performance indicates a sustained good faith effort to meet the public interest in being fully and fairly informed. The Commission's responsibilities under a right-of-access system would tend to draw it into a continuing case-by-case determination of who should be heard and when. Indeed, the likelihood of Government involvement is so great that it has been suggested that the accepted constitutional principles against control of speech content would need to be relaxed with respect to editorial advertisements. To sacrifice First Amendment protections for so speculative a gain is not warranted, and it was well within the Commission's discretion to construe the Act so as to avoid such a result.

"The Commission is also entitled to take into account the reality that in a very real sense listeners and viewers constitute a 'captive audience.' [It] is no answer to say that because we tolerate pervasive commercial advertisement [we] can also live with its political counterparts.

"The rationale for the Court of Appeals' decision imposing a constitutional right of access on the broadcast media was that the licensee impermissibly discriminates by accepting commercial advertisements while refusing editorial advertisements. The court relied on [lower court cases] holding that state-supported school newspapers and public transit companies were forbidden by the First Amendment from excluding controversial editorial advertisements in favor of commercial advertisements.[d] The court also attempted to analogize this case to some of our decisions holding that States may not constitutionally ban certain protected speech while at the same time permitting other speech in public areas [citing e.g., *Grayned* and *Mosley*, Sec. 5 supra].

"These decisions provide little guidance, however, in resolving the question whether the First Amendment required the Commission to mandate a private right of access to the broadcast media. In none of those cases did the forum sought for expression have an affirmative and independent statutory obligation to provide full and fair coverage of public issues, such as Congress has imposed on all broadcast licensees. In short, there is no 'discrimination' against controversial speech present in this case. The question here is not whether there is to be discussion of controversial issues of public importance on the broadcast media, but rather who shall determine what issues are to be discussed by whom, and when."

DOUGLAS, J., concurred in the result, but "for quite different reasons." Because the Court did not decide whether a broadcast licensee is "a federal agency within the context of this case," he assumed that it was not. He "fail[ed] to see," then "how constitutionally we can treat TV and the radio differently than we treat newspapers"[e]:

"I did not participate in [*Red Lion* and] would not support it. The Fairness Doctrine has no place in our First Amendment regime. It puts the head of the camel inside the tent and enables administration after administration to toy with TV or radio in order to serve its sordid or its benevolent ends. [The uniqueness of radio and TV] is due to engineering and technical problems. But the press in a realistic sense is likewise not available to all. [T]he daily newspapers now established are unique in the sense that it would be virtually impossible for a competitor to enter the field due to the financial exigencies of this era. The result is that in practical terms the newspapers and magazines, like the TV and radio, are available only to a select few. [That] may argue for a redefinition of the responsibilities of the press in First Amendment terms. But I do not think it gives us carte blanche to design systems of supervision and control nor empower [the government to] make 'some' laws 'abridging' freedom of the press.

d. But see *Lehman v. Shaker Heights.*

e. Cf. *Miami Herald;* Barrow, p. 698 supra, at 683–91.

"[O]ne hard and fast principle which [the First Amendment] announces is that government shall keep its hands off the press. [That means] that TV and radio, as well as the more conventional methods for disseminating news, are all included in the concept of 'press' as used in the First Amendment and therefore are entitled to live under the laissez faire regime which the First Amendment [sanctions].

"Licenses are, of course, restricted in time and while, in my view, Congress has the power to make each license limited to a fixed term and nonreviewable, there is no power to deny renewals for editorial or ideological reasons [for] the First Amendment gives no preference to one school of thought over the others.

"The Court in today's decision by endorsing the Fairness Doctrine sanctions a federal saddle on broadcast licensees that is agreeable to the traditions of nations that never have known freedom of press and that is tolerable in countries that do not have a written constitution containing prohibitions as absolute as those in the First Amendment." [f]

BRENNAN, J., joined by Marshall, J., dissented, viewing "the *absolute* ban on the sale of air time for the discussion of controversial issues" as "governmental action" [g] violating the first amendment: "As a practical matter, the Court's reliance on the Fairness Doctrine as an 'adequate' alternative to editorial advertising seriously overestimates the ability—or willingness—of broadcasters to expose the public to the 'widest possible dissemination of information from diverse and antagonistic sources.' [Indeed,] in light of the strong interest of broadcasters in maximizing their audience, and therefore their profits, it seems almost naive to expect the majority of broadcasters to produce the variety and controversiality of material necessary to reflect a full spectrum of viewpoints. Stated simply, angry customers are not good customers and, in the commercial world of mass communications, it is simply 'bad business' to espouse—or even to allow others to espouse—the heterodox or the controversial. As a result, even under the Fairness Doctrine, broadcasters generally tend to permit only established—or at least moderated—views to enter the broadcast world's 'marketplace of ideas.' [24]

"Moreover, the Court's reliance on the Fairness Doctrine as the *sole* means of informing the public seriously misconceives and underestimates the public's interest in receiving ideas and information directly from the advocates of those ideas without the interposition of journalistic middlemen. Under the Fairness Doctrine, broadcasters decide what issues are 'important,' how 'fully' to cover them, and what format, time and style of coverage are 'appropriate.' The retention of such *absolute* control in the hands of a few government licensees is inimical to the First Amendment, for vigorous, free debate can be attained only when members of the public have at least *some* opportunity to take the initiative and editorial control into their own hands.

"[S]tanding alone, [the Fairness Doctrine] simply cannot eliminate the need for a further, complementary airing of controversial views through the limited availability of editorial advertising. Indeed, the availability of at least *some* opportunity for editorial advertising is imperative if we are ever to attain the 'free and general discussion of public matters [that] seems absolutely essential to prepare the people for an intelligent exercise of their rights as citizens.'

f. Noting that his views "closely approach those expressed by Mr. Justice Douglas," Stewart, J., also concurred.

24. [Citing many secondary sources to support this statement.]

g. See fn. b supra and p. 1128 infra.

"Moreover, a proper balancing of the competing First Amendment interests at stake in this controversy must consider, not only the interests of broadcasters and of the listening and viewing public, but also the independent First Amendment interest of groups and individuals in effective self-expression. [I]n a time of apparently growing anonymity of the individual in our society, it is imperative that we take special care to preserve the vital First Amendment interest in assuring 'self-fulfillment [of expression] for each individual.' For our citizens may now find greater than ever the need to express their own views directly to the public, rather than through a governmentally appointed surrogate, if they are to feel that they can achieve at least some measure of control over their own destinies.

"[F]reedom of speech does not exist in the abstract. [It] can flourish only if it is allowed to operate in an effective forum—whether it be a public park, a schoolroom, a town meeting hall, a soapbox, or a radio and television frequency. For in the absence of an effective means of communication, the right to speak would ring hollow indeed. And, in recognition of these principles, we have consistently held that the First Amendment embodies not only the abstract right to be free from censorship, but also the right of an individual to utilize an appropriate and effective medium for the expression of his views.

"[W]ith the assistance of the Federal Government, the broadcast industry has become what is potentially the most efficient and effective 'marketplace of ideas' ever devised. [Thus], although 'full and free discussion' of ideas may have been a reality in the heyday of political pamphleteering, modern technological developments in the field of communications have made the soapbox orator and the leafleteer virtually obsolete. And, in light of the current dominance of the electronic media as the most effective means of reaching the public, any policy that *absolutely* denies citizens access to the airwaves necessarily renders even the concept of 'full and free discussion' practically meaningless.

"[T]he challenged ban can be upheld only if it is determined that such editorial advertising would unjustifiably impair the broadcaster's assertedly overriding interest in exercising *absolute* control over 'his' frequency. Such an analysis, however, hardly reflects the delicate balancing of interests that this sensitive question demands. Indeed, this 'absolutist' approach wholly disregards the competing First Amendment rights of all 'nonbroadcaster' citizens, ignores the teachings of our recent decision in *Red Lion*, and is not supported by the historical purposes underlying broadcast regulation in this Nation. [T]here is simply no overriding First Amendment interest of broadcasters that can justify the *absolute* exclusion of virtually all of our citizens from the most effective 'marketplace of ideas' ever devised.

"[T]his case deals *only* with the allocation of *advertising* time—airtime that broadcasters regularly relinquish to others without the retention of significant editorial control. Thus, we are concerned here not with the speech of broadcasters themselves but, rather, with their 'right' to decide which *other* individuals will be given an opportunity to speak in a forum that has already been opened to the public.

"Viewed in this context, the *absolute* ban on editorial advertising seems particularly offensive because, although broadcasters refuse to sell any airtime whatever to groups or individuals wishing to speak out on controversial issues of public importance, they make such airtime readily available to those 'commercial' advertisers who seek to peddle their goods and services to the public. [Yet an] individual seeking to discuss war, peace, pollution, or the suffering of the poor is denied this right to speak. Instead, he is compelled to rely on the beneficence of a corporate 'trustee' appointed by the Government to argue his case for him.

"It has been long recognized, however, that although access to public forums may be subjected to reasonable 'time, place, and manner' regulations, '[s]elective exclusions from a public forum, may not be based on *content* alone.' *Mosley* (emphasis added). Here, of course, the differential treatment accorded 'commercial' and 'controversial' speech clearly violates that principle. Moreover, and not without some irony, the favored treatment given 'commercial' speech under the existing scheme clearly reverses traditional First Amendment priorities. For it has generally been understood that 'commercial' speech enjoys *less* First Amendment protection than speech directed at the discussion of controversial issues of public importance." [h]

Notes and Questions

1. *"Elitism" and the CBS case?* Consider Bollinger, *Elitism, The Masses and the Idea of Self-Government,* in Constitutional Government in America 99, 104–05 (Collins ed. 1980): "[*CBS*] seemed to rely on the problems of administration and the need for journalistic discretion as the primary reasons for its result. It was this latter theory of the case that caused the decision to be hailed by the press [as] representing a substantial shift in the Court's thinking from that found in *Red Lion.* [But], the opinion is deceptive on that score; for the emphasis on journalistic discretion did not arise from a pure belief in the wisdom of journalists but rather from a perceived need to maintain control of the content of broadcasting in the hands of those who live under the aegis of government scrutiny.

"[The] difficulty with the claim of BEM and DNC was that it opened the broadcast doors to people who were not made 'responsible' through the subtle processes of government selection and oversight. And the possibilities of exploitation of mass public opinion on such vital matters as the war effort, through techniques of distortion and emotional appeals, was a more pressing danger than any commercial speech * * *.

"All of this is to suggest that [an] elitist view colored the thinking of the Court in *CBS,* as it has in other areas of broadcast regulation. The phenomenon cannot be explained away as simply the reactionary stance of conservative justices to anti-war speech. Whatever one thinks of the outcome of the *CBS* case, the fear of manipulation as a motivating factor in our thinking is not a distinctive characteristic of any particular ideological group. It also supports the position, advocated by many liberals, that something ought to be done to remove or lessen the amount of violence on television."

2. *Confronting scarcity.* Consider Tribe, *American Constitutional Law* 699 (1978): "*CBS* took a step away from *Red Lion* by its treatment of broadcasters as part of the 'press' with an important editorial function to perform rather than as analogous to the postal or telephone systems, but *CBS* was firmly in the *Red Lion* tradition when it refused to consider the possibility that either the technologically scarce radio and television channels, or the finite time available on such channels, might be allocated much as economically scarce newspaper opportunities are allocated: by a combination of market mechanisms and chance rather than by government design coupled with broadcaster autonomy."

h. Cf. Brennan, J.'s dissent in *Lehman v. Shaker Heights.*

Suppose the government sold the airwaves to the highest bidder and allowed subsequent exchange according to property and contract law. Consider Note, *Reconciling Red Lion and Tornillo: A Consistent Theory of Media Regulation,* 28 Stan.L.Rev. 563, 583 (1976): "This regulatory strategy would remove the government from direct determination of the particular individuals who are allowed to broadcast, leaving this decision to market forces, and would avoid the need for specific behavioral commands and sanctions now necessary to secure compliance by broadcasters with the various obligations imposed by the public interest standard. [Under] strict scrutiny, then, the existence of this clearly identifiable less restrictive alternative indicates that the Communications Act is unconstitutional."

But see Van Alstyne, p. 702 supra, at 563: "Congress may indeed be free to 'sell off' the airwaves, and it may be wholly feasible to allocate most currently established broadcast signals by competitive bidding that, when done, may well produce private licensees operating truly without subsidy. But only a singularly insensitive observer would believe that this choice is not implicitly also a highly speech-restrictive choice by Congress. It is fully as speech-restrictive as though, in the case of land, government were to withdraw from *all* ownership and all subsidized maintenance of all land, including parks, auditoriums, and streets and to remain in the field exclusively as a policeman to enforce the proprietary decisions of all private landowners."

3. *The "fairness" doctrine.* The Court's assumption that the fairness doctrine works tolerably well has been roasted by the commentators. See, e.g., Rowan, *Broadcast Fairness: Doctrine, Practice, Prospects* (1984); Simmons, *The Fairness Doctrine and the Media* (1978); Johnson & Dystel, *A Day in the Life: The Federal Communications Commission,* 82 Yale L.J. 1575 (1973). Consider Krattenmaker & Powe, *The Fairness Doctrine Today: A Constitutional Curiosity and an Impossible Dream,* 1985 Duke L.J. 151, 175: "If the doctrine is to be taken seriously then suspected violations lurk everywhere and the FCC should undertake continuous oversight of the industry. If the FCC will not—or cannot—do that, then the doctrine must be toothless except for the randomly-selected few who are surprised to feel its bite after the fact." For a vigorous defense of the fairness doctrine, see Ferris & Kirkland, *Fairness—The Broadcaster's Hippocratic Oath,* 34 Cath.U.L.Rev. 605 (1985).

4. *The worst of both worlds.* Evaluate the following hypothetical commentary: "*CBS v. DNC* allows government to grant virtually exclusive control over American's most valuable communication medium to corporations who regard it as their mission to 'deliver' audiences to advertisers. The system gives us the worst of both worlds: the world of profit-seeking—without a free market; the world of regulation—without planning." For discussion of alternatives, see Cass, *Revolution in the Wasteland* (1981); Owen, *Economics and Freedom of Expression: Media Structure and the First Amendment* (1975); Firestone & Jacklin, *Deregulation and the Pursuit of Fairness* in Telecommunications Policy and the Citizen 107 (Haight ed. 1979); Owen, *Structural Approaches to the Problem of Television Network Economic Dominance,* 1979 Duke L.J. 191.

5. *First amendment consequences of finding "governmental action."* Although Stewart, J., found no "governmental action" in *CBS,* he observed: "Were the Government really operating the electronic press, it would, as my Brother Douglas points out, be *prevented* by the First Amendment from selection of broadcast content and the exercise of editorial judgment." In articulating his reasons for refusing to find governmental action, Burger, C.J., suggested a

similar position: "Journalistic discretion would in many ways be lost to the rigid limitations that the First Amendment imposes on government."[i] Do these characterizations misconceive the role of the government as editor? See, e.g., Canby, *The First Amendment and the State as Editor,* 52 Tex.L.Rev. 1123, 1124–25 (1974). See also Sec. 6 supra.

II. BROADCASTING AND CONTENT REGULATION: BEYOND THE FAIRNESS DOCTRINE

FCC v. PACIFICA FOUNDATION
438 U.S. 726, 98 S.Ct. 3026, 57 L.Ed.2d 1073 (1978).

[MR. JUSTICE STEVENS delivered the opinion of the Court (Parts I, II, III, and IV–C) and an opinion in which CHIEF JUSTICE BURGER and MR. JUSTICE REHNQUIST joined (Parts IV–A and IV–B).

[In an early afternoon weekday broadcast in October 1973, respondent's New York radio station aired a 12-minute selection called "Filthy Words," from a comedy album by a satiric humorist, George Carlin. The monologue, which had evoked frequent laughter from a live theater audience before whom it had originally been delivered, began by referring to Carlin's thought about the seven words you can't say on the public airwaves, "the ones you definitely wouldn't say ever." He then listed the words ("shit," "piss," "fuck," "motherfucker," "cocksucker," "cunt," and "tits"), "the ones that will curve your spine, grow hair on your hands and (laughter) maybe, even bring us, God help us, peace without honor (laughter) um, and a bourbon (laughter)," and repeated them over and over in a variety of colloquialisms. The monologue was played as part of the station's regular program, which was devoted that day to contemporary attitudes toward the use of language. Immediately prior to the broadcast of the Carlin monologue, listeners were advised that it included sensitive language which some might regard as offensive. Those who might be offended were advised to change the station and return in fifteen minutes.

[The FCC received a complaint from a man in New York stating that while driving in his car with his young son he had heard the broadcast of the Carlin monologue. In response, the FCC issued a Declaratory Order granting the complaint and holding that Pacifica "could have been the subject of administrative sanctions," but that this order would only be "associated with the station's license file, and in the event that subsequent complaints are received, the Commission will then decide whether it should utilize any of the available sanctions it has been granted by Congress."]

The Commission characterized the language used in the Carlin monologue as "patently offensive," though not necessarily obscene, and expressed the opinion that it should be regulated by principles analogous to those found in the law of nuisance where the "law generally speaks to *channeling* behavior more

---

i. Perhaps the most notable "access to state-owned print media" case is *Avins v. Rutgers,* 385 F.2d 151 (3d Cir.1967). In the course of upholding the refusal of the *Rutgers Law Review* to publish an article by a well-known legal commentator, the Third Circuit observed: "[One] does not have the right [to] commandeer the press and columns of [a state university publication] for the publication of his article, at the expense of [the] subscribers and [state] taxpayers, to the exclusion of other articles deemed by the editors to be more suitable for publication. [T]he acceptance or rejection of articles [by a] law review necessarily involves the exercise of editorial judgment and this is in no wise lessened by the fact that the law review is supported [by] the State." But *Avins* may be read narrowly, for "the medium involved, a law review, is one that traditionally has been selective in accepting articles for publication." Schmidt, *Freedom of the Press vs. Public Access* 106 (1976).

than actually prohibiting it. [T]he concept of 'indecent' is intimately connected with the exposure of children to language that describes, in terms patently offensive as measured by contemporary community standards for the broadcast medium, sexual or excretory activities and organs, at times of the day when there is a reasonable risk that children may be in the audience."[5]

Applying these considerations to the language used in the monologue as broadcast by respondent, the Commission concluded that certain words depicted sexual and excretory activities in a patently offensive manner, noted that they "were broadcast at a time when children were undoubtedly in the audience (i.e., in the early afternoon)," and that the prerecorded language, with these offensive words "repeated over and over," was "deliberately broadcast." In summary, the Commission stated: "We therefore hold that the language as broadcast was indecent and prohibited by 18 U.S.C. 1464 [forbidding the use of "any obscene, indecent or profane language" by means of radio communications.]"[6] [The Commission subsequently clarified its opinion, pointing out] that it "never intended to place an absolute prohibition on the broadcast of this type of language, but rather sought to channel it to times of day when children most likely would not be exposed to it." * * *

I. The general statements in the Commission's memorandum opinion do not change the character of its order. Its action was an adjudication under 5 U.S.C. § 554(e); it did not purport to engage in formal rulemaking or in the promulgation of any regulations. The order "was issued in a special factual context"; questions concerning possible action in other contexts were expressly reserved for the future. The specific holding was carefully confined to the monologue "as broadcast." * * *

II. The relevant statutory questions are whether the Commission's action is forbidden "censorship" within the meaning of 47 U.S.C. § 326 and whether speech that concededly is not obscene may be restricted as "indecent" under the authority of 18 U.S.C. § 1464. [The] prohibition against censorship unequivocally denies the Commission any power to edit proposed broadcasts in advance [but] has never been construed to deny the Commission the power to review the content of completed broadcasts in the performance of its regulatory duties. * * *

III. The only other statutory question presented by this case is whether the afternoon broadcast of the "Filthy Words" monologue was indecent within the meaning of § 1464.[13] Even that question is narrowly confined by the arguments of the parties.

---

5. Thus, the Commission suggested, if an offensive broadcast had literary, artistic, political or scientific value, and were preceded by warnings, it might not be indecent in the late evening, but would be so during the day, when children are in the audience.

6. Chairman Wiley concurred in the result without joining the opinion. Commissioners Reid and Quello filed separate statements expressing the opinion that the language was inappropriate for broadcast at any time. Commissioner Robinson, joined by Commissioner Hooks filed a concurring statement expressing the opinion that "we can regulate offensive speech to the extent it constitutes a public nuisance. [The] governing idea is that

'indecency' is not an inherent attribute of words themselves; it is rather a matter of context and conduct. [If] I were called on to do so, I would find that Carlin's monologue, if it were broadcast at an appropriate hour and accompanied by suitable warning, was distinguished by sufficient literary value to avoid being 'indecent' within the meaning of the statute."

13. [The] statutes authorizing civil penalties incorporate § 1464, a criminal statute. But the validity of the civil sanctions is not linked to the validity of the criminal penalty. [Thus,] we need not consider any question relating to the possible application of § 1464 as a criminal statute.

* * * Pacifica's claim that the broadcast was not indecent within the meaning of the statute rests entirely on the absence of prurient appeal.

The plain language of the statute does not support Pacifica's argument. The words "obscene, indecent, or profane" are written in the disjunctive, implying that each has a separate meaning. Prurient appeal is an element of the obscene, but the normal definition of "indecent" merely refers to nonconformance with accepted standards of morality.

Pacifica argues, however, that this Court has construed the term "indecent" in related statutes to mean "obscene," as that term was defined in *Miller* [p. 506 supra]. Pacifica relies most heavily on the construction this Court gave to 18 U.S.C. § 1461 [prohibiting the mailing of "obscene, lewd, lascivious, indecent, filthy or vile" material] in *Hamling v. United States* [p. 507 supra].

Because neither our prior decisions nor the language or history of § 1464 supports the conclusion that prurient appeal is an essential component of indecent language, we reject Pacifica's construction of the statute. When that construction is put to one side, there is no basis for disagreeing with the Commission's conclusion that indecent language was used in this broadcast.

IV. Pacifica makes two constitutional attacks on the Commission's order. First, it argues that the Commission's construction of the statutory language broadly encompasses so much constitutionally protected speech that reversal is required even if Pacifica's broadcast of the "Filthy Words" monologue is not itself protected by the First Amendment. Second, Pacifica argues that inasmuch as the recording is not obscene, the Constitution forbids any abridgment of the right to broadcast it on the radio.

A. The first argument fails because our review is limited to the question whether the Commission has the authority to proscribe this particular broadcast. As the Commission itself emphasized, its order was "issued in a specific factual context." That approach is appropriate for courts as well as the Commission when regulation of indecency is at stake, for indecency is largely a function of context—it cannot be adequately judged in the abstract.

The approach is also consistent with *Red Lion*. In that case the Court rejected an argument that the Commission's regulations defining the fairness doctrine were so vague that they would inevitably abridge the broadcasters' freedom of speech. * * *

It is true that the Commission's order may lead some broadcasters to censor themselves. At most, however, the Commission's definition of indecency will deter only the broadcasting of patently offensive references to excretory and sexual organs and activities.[18] While some of these references may be protected, they surely lie at the periphery of First Amendment concern. The danger dismissed so summarily in *Red Lion,* in contrast, was that broadcasters would respond to the vagueness of the regulations by refusing to present programs dealing with important social and political controversies. Invalidating any rule on the basis of its hypothetical application to situations not before the Court is "strong medicine" to be applied "sparingly and only as a last resort." *Broadrick* [p. 535 supra]. We decline to administer that medicine to preserve the vigor of patently offensive sexual and excretory speech.

B. When the issue is narrowed to the facts of this case, the question is whether the First Amendment denies government any power to restrict the

---

18. A requirement that indecent language be avoided will have its primary effect on the form, rather than the content, of serious communication. There are few, if any, thoughts that cannot be expressed by the use of less offensive language.

public broadcast of indecent language in any circumstances. For if the government has any such power, this was an appropriate occasion for its exercise.

The words of the Carlin monologue are unquestionably "speech" within the meaning of the First Amendment. It is equally clear that the Commission's objections to the broadcast were based in part on its content. The order must therefore fall if, as Pacifica argues, the First Amendment prohibits all governmental regulation that depends on the content of speech. Our past cases demonstrate, however, that no such absolute rule is mandated * * *.

The question in this case is whether a broadcast of patently offensive words dealing with sex and excretion may be regulated because of its content.[20] Obscene materials have been denied the protection of the First Amendment because their content is so offensive to contemporary moral standards. *Roth*. But the fact that society may find speech offensive is not a sufficient reason for suppressing it. Indeed, if it is the speaker's opinion that gives offense, that consequence is a reason for according it constitutional protection. For it is a central tenet of the First Amendment that the government must remain neutral in the marketplace of ideas. If there were any reason to believe that the Commission's characterization of the Carlin monologue as offensive could be traced to its political content—or even to the fact that it satirized contemporary attitudes about four letter words [22]—First Amendment protection might be required. But that is simply not this case. These words offend for the same reasons that obscenity offends. Their place in the hierarchy of First Amendment values was aptly sketched by Mr. Justice Murphy when he said, "such utterances are no essential part of any exposition of ideas, and are of such slight social value as a step to truth that any benefit that may be derived from them is clearly outweighed by the social interest in order and morality." *Chaplinsky*.

Although these words ordinarily lack literary, political, or scientific value, they are not entirely outside the protection of the First Amendment. Some uses of even the most offensive words are unquestionably protected. Indeed, we may assume, arguendo, that this monologue would be protected in other contexts. Nonetheless, the constitutional protection accorded to a communication containing such patently offensive sexual and excretory language need not be the same in every context. It is a characteristic of speech such as this that both its capacity to offend and its "social value," to use Mr. Justice Murphy's term, vary with the circumstances. Words that are commonplace in one setting are shocking in another. To paraphrase Mr. Justice Harlan, one occasion's lyric is another's vulgarity. Cf. *Cohen v. California*.[25]

20. Although neither Justice Powell nor Justice Brennan directly confronts this question, both have answered it affirmatively, the latter explicitly, at fn. 3, infra, and the former implicitly by concurring in a judgment that could not otherwise stand.

22. The monologue does present a point of view; it attempts to show that the words it uses are "harmless" and that our attitudes toward them are "essentially silly." The Commission objects, not to this point of view, but to the way in which it is expressed. The belief that these words are harmless does not necessarily confer a First Amendment privilege to use them while proselytizing just as the conviction that obscenity is harmless does not license one to communicate that convic-

tion by the indiscriminate distribution of an obscene leaflet.

25. The importance of context is illustrated by the *Cohen* case. [So] far as the evidence showed no one in the courthouse was offended by [Cohen's jacket.]

In holding that criminal sanctions could not be imposed on Cohen for his political statement in a public place, the Court rejected the argument that his speech would offend unwilling viewers; it noted that "there was no evidence that persons powerless to avoid [his] conduct did in fact object to it." In contrast, in this case the Commission was responding to a listener's strenuous complaint, and Pacifica does not question its determination that this afternoon broadcast was likely to offend lis-

In this case it is undisputed that the content of Pacifica's broadcast was "vulgar," "offensive," and "shocking." Because content of that character is not entitled to absolute constitutional protection under all circumstances, we must consider its context in order to determine whether the Commission's action was constitutionally permissible.

C. We have long recognized that each medium of expression presents special First Amendment problems. And of all forms of communication, it is broadcasting that has received the most limited First Amendment [protection.]

The reasons for these distinctions are complex, but two have relevance to the present case. First, the broadcast media have established a uniquely pervasive presence in the lives of all Americans. Patently offensive, indecent material presented over the airwaves confronts the citizen, not only in public, but also in the privacy of the home, where the individual's right to be let alone plainly outweighs the First Amendment rights of an intruder. *Rowan.* Because the broadcast audience is constantly tuning in and out, prior warnings cannot completely protect the listener or viewer from unexpected program content. To say that one may avoid further offense by turning off the radio when he hears indecent language is like saying that the remedy for an assault is to run away after the first blow. One may hang up on an indecent phone call, but that option does not give the caller a constitutional immunity or avoid a harm that has already taken place.[27]

Second, broadcasting is uniquely accessible to children, even those too young to read. Although Cohen's written message might have been incomprehensible to a first grader, Pacifica's broadcast could have enlarged a child's vocabulary in an instant. Other forms of offensive expression may be withheld from the young without restricting the expression at its source. Bookstores and motion picture theaters, for example, may be prohibited from making indecent material available to children. We held in *Ginsberg* [p. 720 supra] that the government's interest in the "well being of its youth" and in supporting "parents' claim to authority in their own household" justified the regulation of otherwise protected expression.[28] The ease with which children may obtain access to broadcast material, coupled with the concerns recognized in *Ginsberg,* amply justify special treatment of indecent broadcasting.

It is appropriate, in conclusion, to emphasize the narrowness of our holding. This case does not involve a two-way radio conversation between a cab driver and a dispatcher, or a telecast of an Elizabethan comedy. We have not decided that an occasional expletive in either setting would justify any sanction or, indeed, that this broadcast would justify a criminal prosecution. The Commission's decision rested entirely on a nuisance rationale under which context is all-important. The concept requires consideration of a host of variables. The time

teners. It should be noted that the Commission imposed a far more moderate penalty on Pacifica than the state court imposed on Cohen. Even the strongest civil penalty at the Commission's command does not include criminal prosecution.

27. Outside the home, the balance between the offensive speaker and the unwilling audience may sometimes tip in favor of the speaker, requiring the offended listener to turn away. See *Erznoznik.* * * *

28. The Commission's action does not by any means reduce adults to hearing only what

is fit for children. Cf. *Butler v. Michigan* [p. 720 supra]. Adults who feel the need may purchase tapes and records or go to theatres and nightclubs to hear these words. In fact, the Commission has not unequivocally closed even broadcasting to speech of this sort; whether broadcast audiences in the late evening contain so few children that playing this monologue would be permissible is an issue neither the Commission nor this Court has decided.

of day was emphasized by the Commission. The content of the program in which the language is used will also affect the composition of the audience, and differences between radio, television, and perhaps closed-circuit transmissions, may also be relevant. As Mr. Justice Sutherland wrote, a "nuisance may be merely a right thing in the wrong place—like a pig in the parlor instead of the barnyard." We simply hold that when the Commission finds that a pig has entered the parlor, the exercise of its regulatory power does not depend on proof that the pig is obscene.

[R]eversed.

MR. JUSTICE POWELL, with whom MR. JUSTICE BLACKMUN joins, concurring.

I join Parts I, II, III, and IV(C) of Justice Stevens' opinion. The Court today reviews only the Commission's holding that Carlin's monologue was indecent "as broadcast" at two o'clock in the afternoon, and not the broad sweep of the Commission's opinion. In addition to being consistent with our settled practice of not deciding constitutional issues unnecessarily, this narrow focus also is conducive to the orderly development of this relatively new and difficult area of law, in the first instance by the Commission, and then by the reviewing courts.

I also agree with much that is said in Part IV of Justice Stevens' opinion, and with its conclusion that the Commission's holding in this case does not violate the First Amendment. Because I do not subscribe to all that is said in Part IV, however, I state my views separately.

[T]he language employed is, to most people, vulgar and offensive. It was chosen specifically for this quality, and it was repeated over and over as a sort of verbal shock treatment. The Commission did not err in characterizing the narrow category of language used here as "patently offensive" to most people regardless of age.

The issue, however, is whether the Commission may impose civil sanctions on a licensee radio station for broadcasting the monologue at two o'clock in the afternoon. The Commission's primary concern was to prevent the broadcast from reaching the ears of unsupervised children who were likely to be in the audience at that hour. In essence, the Commission sought to "channel" the monologue to hours when the fewest unsupervised children would be exposed to it. In my view, this consideration provides strong support for the Commission's holding.

[The] Commission properly held that the speech from which society may attempt to shield its children is not limited to that which appeals to the youthful prurient interest. The language involved in this case is as potentially degrading and harmful to children as representations of many erotic acts.

In most instances, the dissemination of this kind of speech to children may be limited without also limiting willing adults' access to it. Sellers of printed and recorded matter and exhibitors of motion pictures and live performances may be required to shut their doors to children, but such a requirement has no effect on adults' access. See *Ginsberg*. The difficulty is that such a physical separation of the audience cannot be accomplished in the broadcast media. During most of the broadcast hours, both adults and unsupervised children are likely to be in the broadcast audience, and the broadcaster cannot reach willing adults without also reaching children. This, as the Court emphasizes, is one of the distinctions between the broadcast and other media to which we often have adverted as justifying a different treatment of the broadcast media for First Amendment purposes. In my view, the Commission was entitled to give substantial weight to this difference in reaching its decision in this case.

[Another difference] is that broadcasting—unlike most other forms of communication—comes directly into the home, the one place where people ordinarily have the right not to be assaulted by uninvited and offensive sights and sounds. *Erznoznik; Cohen; Rowan.* Although the First Amendment may require unwilling adults to absorb the first blow of offensive but protected speech when they are in public before they turn away, see, e.g., *Erznoznik,* but cf. *Rosenfeld* (Powell, J., dissenting), a different order of values obtains in the home. "That we are often 'captives' outside the sanctuary of the home and subject to objectionable speech and other sound does not mean we must be captives everywhere." *Rowan.* The Commission also was entitled to give this factor appropriate weight in the circumstances of the instant case. This is not to say, however, that the Commission has an unrestricted license to decide what speech, protected in other media, may be banned from the airwaves in order to protect unwilling adults from momentary exposure to it in their homes.[2] * * *

The Commission's holding does not prevent willing adults from purchasing Carlin's record, from attending his performances, or, indeed, from reading the transcript reprinted as an appendix to the Court's opinion. On its face, it does not prevent respondent from broadcasting the monologue during late evening hours when fewer children are likely to be in the audience, nor from broadcasting discussions of the contemporary use of language at any time during the day. The Commission's holding, and certainly the Court's holding today, does not speak to cases involving the isolated use of a potentially offensive word in the course of a radio broadcast, as distinguished from the verbal shock treatment administered by respondent here. In short, I agree that on the facts of this case, the Commission's order did not violate respondent's First Amendment rights.

As the foregoing demonstrates, my views are generally in accord with what is said in Part IV(C) of opinion. I therefore join that portion of his opinion. I do not join Part IV(B), however, because I do not subscribe to the theory that the Justices of this Court are free generally to decide on the basis of its content which speech protected by the First Amendment is most "valuable" and hence deserving of the most protection, and which is less "valuable" and hence deserving of less protection.[3] In my view, the result in this case does not turn on whether Carlin's monologue, viewed as a whole, or the words that comprise it, have more or less "value" than a candidate's campaign speech. This is a judgment for each person to make, not one for the judges to impose upon him.[4]

The result turns instead on the unique characteristics of the broadcast media, combined with society's right to protect its children from speech general-

---

2. It is true that the radio listener quickly may tune out speech that is offensive to him. In addition, broadcasters may preface potentially offensive programs with warnings. But such warnings do not help the unsuspecting listener who tunes in at the middle of a program. In this respect, too, broadcasting appears to differ from books and records, which may carry warnings on their faces, and from motion pictures and live performances, which may carry warnings on their marquees.

3. The Court has, however, created a limited exception to this rule in order to bring commercial speech within the protection of the First Amendment. See *Ohralik* [p. 562 supra].

4. For much the same reason, I also do not join Part IV(A). I had not thought that the application vel non of overbreadth analysis should depend on the Court's judgment as to the value of the protected speech that might be deterred. Except in the context of commercial speech, see *Bates* [p. 561 supra], it has not in the past. See, e.g., *Lewis v. New Orleans; Gooding.*

As Justice Stevens points out, however, the Commission's order was limited to the facts of this case; "it did not purport to engage in formal rulemaking or in the promulgation of any regulations." In addition, since the Commission may be expected to proceed cautiously, as it has in the past, I do not foresee an undue "chilling" effect on broadcasters' exercise of their rights. I agree, therefore, that respondent's overbreadth challenge is meritless.

ly agreed to be inappropriate for their years, and with the interest of unwilling adults in not being assaulted by such offensive speech in their homes. Moreover, I doubt whether today's decision will prevent any adult who wishes to receive Carlin's message in Carlin's own words from doing so, and from making for himself a value judgment as to the merit of the message and words. These are the grounds upon which I join the judgment of the Court as to Part IV.

MR. JUSTICE BRENNAN, with whom MR. JUSTICE MARSHALL joins, dissenting.

I agree with Justice Stewart that, under *Hamling,* the word "indecent" in 18 U.S.C. § 1464 must be construed to prohibit only obscene speech. I would, therefore, normally refrain from expressing my views on any constitutional issues implicated in this case. However, I find the Court's misapplication of fundamental First Amendment principles so patent, and its attempt to impose *its* notions of propriety on the whole of the American people so misguided, that I am unable to remain silent.

For the second time in two years, see *Young v. American Mini Theatres* [p. 547], the Court refuses to embrace the notion, completely antithetical to basic First Amendment values, that the degree of protection the First Amendment affords protected speech varies with the social value ascribed to that speech by five Members of this Court. See opinion of Justice Powell. Moreover, [all] Members of the Court agree that [the monologue] does not fall within one of the categories of speech, such as "fighting words," or obscenity, that is totally without First Amendment protection. [Yet] despite the Court's refusal to create a sliding scale of First Amendment protection calibrated to this Court's perception of the worth of a communication's content, and despite our unanimous agreement that the Carlin monologue is protected speech, a majority of the Court [1] nevertheless finds that, on the facts of this case, the FCC is not constitutionally barred from imposing sanctions on Pacifica for its airing of the Carlin monologue. This majority apparently believes that the FCC's disapproval of Pacifica's afternoon broadcast of Carlin's "Dirty Words" recording is a permissible time, place, and manner regulation. [The opinions of both Stevens and Powell, JJ.,] rely principally on two factors in reaching this conclusion: (1) the capacity of a radio broadcast to intrude into the unwilling listener's home, and (2) the presence of children in the listening audience. Dispassionate analysis, removed from individual notions as to what is proper and what is not, starkly reveals that these justifications, whether individually or together, simply do not support even the professedly moderate degree of governmental homogenization of radio communications—if, indeed, such homogenization can ever be moderate given the pre-eminent status of the right of free speech in our constitutional scheme—that the Court today permits.

[In] finding [the privacy interests of an individual in his home] sufficient to justify the content regulation of protected speech, [the] Court commits two errors. First, it misconceives the nature of the privacy interests involved where an individual voluntarily chooses to admit radio communications into his home. Second, it ignores the constitutionally protected interests of both those who wish to transmit and those who desire to receive broadcasts that many—including the FCC and this Court—might find offensive.

[A]n individual's actions in switching on and listening to communications transmitted over the public airways and directed to the public at-large do not

---

1. Where I refer without differentiation to the actions of "the Court," my reference is to this majority, which consists of my Brothers Powell and Stevens and those Members of the Court joining their separate opinions.

implicate fundamental privacy interests, even when engaged in within the home. Instead, because the radio is undeniably a public medium, these actions are more properly viewed as a decision to take part, if only as a listener, in an ongoing public discourse. Although an individual's decision to allow public radio communications into his home undoubtedly does not abrogate all of his privacy interests, the residual privacy interests he retains vis-à-vis the communication he voluntarily admits into his home are surely no greater than those of the people present in the corridor of the Los Angeles courthouse in *Cohen* who bore witness to the words "Fuck the Draft" emblazoned across Cohen's jacket. Their privacy interests were held insufficient to justify punishing Cohen for his offensive communication.

Even if an individual who voluntarily opens his home to radio communications retains privacy interests of sufficient moment to justify a ban on protected speech if those interests are "invaded in an essentially intolerable manner," *Cohen,* the very fact that those interests are threatened only by a radio broadcast precludes any intolerable invasion of privacy; for unlike other intrusive modes of communication, such as sound trucks, "[t]he radio can be turned off"—and with a minimum of effort. As Judge Bazelon aptly observed below, "having elected to receive public airwaves, the scanner who stumbles onto an offensive program is in the same position as the unsuspected passers-by in *Cohen* and *Erznoznik;* he can avert his attention by changing channels or turning off the set." Whatever the minimal discomfort suffered by a listener who inadvertently tunes into a program he finds offensive during the brief interval before he can simply extend his arm and switch stations or flick the "off" button, it is surely worth the candle to preserve the broadcaster's right to send, and the right of those interested to receive, a message entitled to full First Amendment protection. To reach a contrary balance, as does the Court, is clearly, to follow Justice Stevens' reliance on animal metaphors, "to burn the house to roast the pig."

The Court's balance, of necessity, fails to accord proper weight to the interests of listeners who wish to hear broadcasts the FCC deems offensive. It permits majoritarian tastes completely to preclude a protected message from entering the homes of a receptive, unoffended minority. No decision of this Court supports such a result. Where the individuals comprising the offended majority may freely choose to reject the material being offered, we have never found their privacy interests of such moment to warrant the suppression of speech on privacy grounds. [In] *Rowan,* the court upheld a statute, permitting householders to require that mail advertisers stop sending them lewd or offensive materials and remove their names from mailing lists. Unlike the situation here, householders who wished to receive the sender's communications were not prevented from doing so. Equally important, the determination of offensiveness vel non under the statute involved in *Rowan* was completely within the hands of the individual householder; no governmental evaluation of the worth of the mail's content stood between the mailer and the householder. In contrast, the visage of the censor is all too discernable here.

[Although] the government unquestionably has a special interest in the well-being of children and consequently "can adopt more stringent controls on communicative materials available to youths than on those available to adults," *Erznoznik,* the Court has accounted for this societal interest by adopting a "variable obscenity" standard that permits the prurient appeal of material available to children to be assessed in terms of the sexual interests of minors. *Ginsberg.* [But] we have made it abundantly clear that "under any test of obscenity as to minors [to] be obscene 'such expression must be, in some significant way, erotic.' "

Because the Carlin monologue is obviously not an erotic appeal to the prurient interests of children, the Court, for the first time, allows the government to prevent minors from gaining access to materials that are not obscene, and are therefore protected, as to them.[2] It thus ignores our recent admonition that "[s]peech that is neither obscene as to youths nor subject to some other legitimate proscription cannot be suppressed solely to protect the young from ideas or images that a legislative body thinks unsuitable for them." *Erznoznik*.[3] The Court's refusal to follow its own pronouncements is especially lamentable since it has the anomalous subsidiary effect, at least in the radio context at issue here, of making completely unavailable to adults material which may not constitutionally be kept even from children. This result violates in spades the principle of *Butler v. Michigan.* [Powell, J.'s opinion] acknowledges that there lurks in today's decision a potential for " 'reduc[ing] the adult population [to] [hearing] only what is fit for children,' " but expresses faith that the FCC will vigilantly prevent this potential from ever becoming a reality. I am far less certain than [he] that such faith in the Commission is warranted; and even if I shared it, I could not so easily shirk the responsibility assumed by each Member of this Court jealously to guard against encroachments on First Amendment freedoms.

[T]he opinions of Justices Powell and Stevens both stress the time-honored right of a parent to raise his child as he sees fit—a right this Court has consistently been vigilant to protect. Yet this principle supports a result directly contrary to that reached by the Court. *Yoder* and *Pierce,* [Ch. 9, Sec. 2, I], hold that parents, *not* the government, have the right to make certain decisions regarding the upbringing of their children. As surprising as it may be to individual Members of this Court, some parents may actually find Mr. Carlin's unabashed attitude towards the seven "dirty words" healthy, and deem it desirable to expose their children to the manner in which Mr. Carlin defuses the taboo surrounding the words. Such parents may constitute a minority of the American public, but the absence of great numbers willing to exercise the right to raise their children in this fashion does not alter the right's nature or its existence. Only the Court's regrettable decision does that.[4]

As demonstrated above, neither of the factors relied on by both [Justices Powell and Stevens]—the intrusive nature of radio and the presence of children in the listening audience—can, when taken on its own terms, support the FCC's

2. Even if the monologue appealed to the prurient interest of minors, it would not be obscene as to them unless, as to them, "the work, taken as a whole, lacks serious literary, artistic, political, or scientific value." *Miller.*

3. It may be that a narrowly drawn regulation prohibiting the use of offensive language on broadcasts directed specifically at younger children constitutes one of the "other legitimate proscription[s]" alluded to in *Erznoznik.* This is so both because of the difficulties inherent in adapting the *Miller* formulation to communications received by young children, and because such children are "not possessed of that full capacity for individual choice which is the presupposition of the First Amendment guarantees." *Ginsberg.* (Stewart, J., concurring). I doubt, as my Brother

Stevens suggests, that such a limited regulation amounts to a regulation of speech based on its content, since, by hypothesis, the only persons at whom the regulated communication is directed are incapable of evaluating its content. To the extent that such a regulation is viewed as a regulation based on content, it marks the outermost limits to which content regulation is permissible.

4. The opinions of my Brothers Powell and Stevens rightly refrain from relying on the notion of "spectrum scarcity" to support their result. As Chief Judge Bazelon noted below, "although scarcity has justified *increasing* the diversity of speakers and speech, it has never been held to justify censorship." See *Red Lion.*

disapproval of the Carlin monologue. These two asserted justifications are further plagued by a common failing: the lack of principled limits on their use as a basis for FCC censorship. No such limits come readily to mind, and neither of the opinions comprising the Court serve to clarify the extent to which the FCC may assert the privacy and children-in-the-audience rationales as justification for expunging from the airways protected communications the Commission finds offensive. Taken to their logical extreme, these rationales would support the cleansing of public radio of any "four-letter words" whatsoever, regardless of their context. The rationales could justify the banning from radio of a myriad of literary works, novels, poems, and plays by the likes of Shakespeare, Joyce, Hemingway, Ben Jonson, Henry Fielding, Robert Burns, and Chaucer; they could support the suppression of a good deal of political speech, such as the Nixon tapes; and they could even provide the basis for imposing sanctions for the broadcast of certain portions of the Bible.

In order to dispel the spectre of the possibility of so unpalatable a degree of censorship, and to defuse Pacifica's overbreadth challenge, the FCC insists that it desires only the authority to reprimand a broadcaster on facts analogous to those present in this case. [Justices Powell and Stevens] take the FCC at its word, and consequently do no more than permit the Commission to censor the afternoon broadcast of the "sort of verbal shock treatment," opinion of Justice Powell, involved here. To insure that the FCC's regulation of protected speech does not exceed these bounds, my Brother Powell is content to rely upon the judgment of the Commission while my Brother Stevens deems it prudent to rely on this Court's ability accurately to assess the worth of various kinds of speech.[6] For my own part, even accepting that this case is limited to its facts,[7] I would place the responsibility and the right to weed worthless and offensive communications from the public airways where it belongs and where, until today, it resided: in a public free to choose those communications worthy of its attention from a marketplace unsullied by the censor's hand.

The absence of any hesitancy in the opinions of my Brothers Powell and Stevens to approve the FCC's censorship of the Carlin monologue on the basis of two demonstrably inadequate grounds is a function of their perception that the decision will result in little, if any, curtailment of communicative exchanges protected by the First Amendment. Although the extent to which the Court stands ready to countenance FCC censorship of protected speech is unclear from today's decision, I find the reasoning by which my Brethren conclude that the FCC censorship they approve will not significantly infringe on First Amendment values both disingenuous as to reality and wrong as a matter of law.

6. Although ultimately dependent upon the outcome of review in this Court, the approach taken by my Brother Stevens would not appear to tolerate the FCC's suppression of any speech, such as political speech, falling within the core area of First Amendment concern. The same, however, cannot be said of the approach taken by my Brother Powell, which, on its face, permits the Commission to censor even political speech if it is sufficiently offensive to community standards. A result more contrary to rudimentary First Amendment principles is difficult to imagine.

7. Having insisted that it seeks to impose sanctions on radio communications only in the limited circumstances present here, I believe that the FCC is estopped from using either

this decision or its own orders in this case, as a basis for imposing sanctions on any public radio broadcast other than one aired during the daytime or early evening and containing the relentless repetition, for longer than a brief interval, of "language that describes, in terms patently offensive as measured by contemporary community standards for the broadcast medium, sexual or excretory activities and organs." For surely broadcasters are not now on notice that the Commission desires to regulate any offensive broadcast other than the type of "verbal shock treatment" condemned here, or even this "shock treatment" type of offensive broadcast during the late evening.

My Brother Stevens, in reaching a result apologetically described as narrow, takes comfort in his observation that "[a] requirement that indecent language be avoided will have its primary effect on the form, rather than the content, of serious communication," and finds solace in his conviction that "[t]here are few, if any, thoughts that cannot be expressed by the use of less offensive language." The idea that the content of a message and its potential impact on any who might receive it can be divorced from the words that are the vehicle for its expression is transparently fallacious. A given word may have a unique capacity to capsule an idea, evoke an emotion, or conjure up an image. Indeed, for those of us who place an appropriately high value on our cherished First Amendment rights, the word "censor" is such a word. Mr. Justice Harlan, speaking for the Court, recognized the truism that a speaker's choice of words cannot surgically be separated from the ideas he desires to express when he warned that "we cannot indulge the facile assumption that one can forbid particular words without also running a substantial risk of suppressing ideas in the process." *Cohen.* Moreover, even if an alternative phrasing may communicate a speaker's abstract ideas as effectively as those words he is forbidden to use, it is doubtful that the sterilized message will convey the emotion that is an essential part of so many communications. This, too, was apparent to Mr. Justice Harlan and the Court in *Cohen.*

[Stevens, J.] also finds relevant to his First Amendment analysis the fact that "[a]dults who feel the need may purchase tapes and records or go to theatres and nightclubs to hear [the tabooed] words." [Powell, J.,] agrees. [The] opinions of my Brethren display both a sad insensitivity to the fact that these alternatives involve the expenditure of money, time, and effort that many of those wishing to hear Mr. Carlin's message may not be able to afford, and a naive innocence of the reality that in many cases, the medium may well be the message.

The Court apparently believes that the FCC's actions here can be analogized to the zoning ordinances upheld in *American Mini Theatres.* For two reasons, it is wrong. First, the zoning ordinances found to pass constitutional muster [had] valid goals other than the channeling of protected speech. No such goals are present here. Second, and crucial to the opinions of my Brothers Powell and Stevens in *American Mini Theatres*—opinions, which, as they do in this case, supply the bare five-person majority of the Court—the ordinances did not restrict the access of distributors or exhibitors to the market or impair the viewing public's access to the regulated material. Again, this is not the situation [here.]

It is quite evident that I find the Court's attempt to unstitch the warp and woof of First Amendment law in an effort to reshape its fabric to cover the patently wrong result the Court reaches in this case dangerous as well as lamentable. Yet there runs throughout the opinions of my Brothers Powell and Stevens another vein I find equally disturbing: a depressing inability to appreciate that in our land of cultural pluralism, there are many who think, act, and talk differently from the Members of this Court, and who do not share their fragile sensibilities. It is only an acute ethnocentric myopia that enables the Court to approve the censorship of communications solely because of the words they [contain.]

Today's decision will thus have its greatest impact on broadcasters desiring to reach, and listening audiences comprised of, persons who do not share the Court's view as to which words or expressions are acceptable and who, for a variety of reasons, including a conscious desire to flout majoritarian conventions, express themselves using words that may be regarded as offensive by those from different socio-economic backgrounds.[8] In this context, the Court's decision may be seen for what, in the broader perspective, it really is: another of the dominant culture's inevitable efforts to force those groups who do not share its mores to conform to its way of thinking, acting, and speaking.

Pacifica, in response to an FCC inquiry about its broadcast of Carlin's satire on "the words you couldn't say on the public airwaves," explained that "Carlin is not mouthing obscenities, he is merely using words to satirize as harmless and essentially silly our attitudes towards those words." In confirming Carlin's prescience as a social commentator by the result it reaches today, the Court evinces an attitude towards the "seven dirty words" that many others besides Mr. Carlin and Pacifica might describe as "silly." Whether today's decision will similarly prove "harmless" remains to be seen. One can only hope that it will.

Mr. Justice Stewart, with whom Mr. Justice Brennan, Mr. Justice White, and Mr. Justice Marshall join, dissenting.

[The Court today] disregards [the] need to construe an Act of Congress so as to avoid, if possible, passing upon its constitutionality. It is apparent that the constitutional questions raised by the order of the Commission in this case are substantial. Before deciding them, we should be certain that it is necessary to do so.

[T]he clear holding of *Hamling* is that "indecent" as used in 18 U.S.C. § 1461 [prohibiting the mailing of "obscene, lewd, lascivious, indecent, filthy or vile article[s]"] has the same meaning as "obscene" as that term was defined in the *Miller* case.

Nothing requires the conclusion that the word "indecent" has any meaning in § 1464 other than that ascribed to the same word in § 1461. Indeed, although the legislative history is largely silent, such indications as there are support the view that §§ 1461 and 1464 should be construed similarly. * * *

I would hold, therefore, that Congress intended by using the word "indecent" in § 1464, to prohibit nothing more than obscene speech. Under that reading of the statute, the Commission's order in this case was not authorized, and on that basis I would affirm the judgment [below].

Notes and Questions

1. *Implications for broadcasting.* Consider Krattenmaker & Powe, *Televised Violence: First Amendment Principles and Social Science Theory,* 64 Va.L. Rev. 1123, 1228 (1978): *Pacifica* "marks the first time any theory other than scarcity has received the official imprimatur of the Court. [S]carcity could not have authorized the result in *Pacifica* because regardless of whether one thinks the incredible abundance of radio stations in the United States (and especially in New York City) is insufficient, scarcity supports adding voices not banning them." What is the significance of the Court's comment that "the broadcast media have established a uniquely pervasive presence in the lives of all Americans"? Consider Brenner, *Censoring the Airwaves: The Supreme Court's Pacifica Decision* in Free But Regulated: Conflicting Traditions in Media Law 175, 177

---

8. Under the approach taken by my Brother Powell, the availability of broadcasts *about* groups whose members comprise such audiences might also be affected. Both news broadcasts about activities involving these groups and public affairs broadcasts about their concerns are apt to contain interviews, statements, or remarks by group leaders and members which may contain offensive language to an extent my Brother Powell finds unacceptable.

& 79 (1982): "[N]ewspapers, drive-in movies, direct mail advertisements and imprinted T-shirts are media that have also 'established a uniquely pervasive presence' in our lives, in and out of [home]. Offhand comments about broadcasting enjoying 'the most limited' First Amendment protection—What of comic books? Playing cards? Chinese cookie fortunes?—are not simply harmless baffle; they constitute Delphic pronouncements made at a watershed period in the development of electronic media."

Is the Court suggesting that the broadcast media are uniquely powerful? If so, should that factor cut for or against government regulation? See Powe, "*Or of the [Broadcast] Press,*" 55 Tex.L.Rev. 39, 58–62 (1976). Does the *Pacifica* rationale support regulation of sex and violence on television, of "offensive" commercials, of advertising directed toward children? Does it have implications for the regulation of cable?

2. *Cohen and Pacifica.* Consider Tribe, *American Constitutional Law* 66 n. 51 (1979 Supp.): "In order to make *Cohen* illustrate his theme that context is everything, Justice Stevens reinterprets *Cohen,* casting it in the mold of a 'fighting words' case [referring to fn. 25]. [But in] *Cohen* what was clear to Harlan was that California did not arrest [petitioner] to preserve the peace [but] to cleanse public debate of offensive language, something Harlan was certain the state could not safely be entrusted to do. Justice Stevens cannot reasonably claim that his opinion has been misread if one concludes that his position is essentially California's claim against Cohen, albeit limited to the airwaves."

But Farber, *Civilizing Public Disclosure: An Essay on Professor Bickel, Justice Harlan, and the Enduring Significance of Cohen v. California,* 1980 Duke L.J. 283, 294, maintains that *Cohen* has "little relevance" to *Pacifica*: The FCC's justifications for regulating speech in *Pacifica* "turned on the context of the midafternoon broadcast, whereas Justice Harlan found that none of the possible context-related justifications were properly presented in *Cohen.* Instead, the issue [Harlan] did find to be properly presented—and therefore the only issue he decided—was whether the state, acting as a paternalistic guardian of public morality, could ban the use of certain words in *all* contexts. Because *Pacifica* dealt with context and *Cohen* dealt only with content, *Cohen* contributes little to the issue presented in *Pacifica.*"

3. "Offensive speech," observes 92 Harv.L.Rev. 156 (1978), "is a method of precisely communicating the strength of feeling with which an idea is held. In *Pacifica,* for example, Justice Powell was particularly disturbed that indecent words were used in steady repetition to achieve a verbal shock treatment. Yet, precisely that sort of treatment could be seen as a necessary part of Carlin's attempt to satirize society's attitudes toward essentially harmless words."

4. "The strangest thing about the Court's decision in *Pacifica,*" comments Tribe, supra, at 64–65, "was that no one could suppose that children were listening to WBAI [the radio station that broadcast the Carlin monologue] that October afternoon in 1973. WBAI is a listener-supported station that carries no ads, does not play 'top forty' records, and directs its programming at a distinctly adult, left-to-radical, upper-middle class audience. [S]tudies show that virtually no children listen to any radio station whatsoever at that hour on a weekday for the reason that most children are then in school. That left at risk the two-, three-, and four-year olds who weren't busy watching Sesame Street or playing with their toys.

"[T]he record showed that only one person complained—an unidentified citizen who, while driving in his car with his son, tuned into WBAI, heard Carlin's monologue, and apparently chose not to turn the dial further."

SECTION 9. THE RIGHT NOT TO SPEAK, THE RIGHT TO ASSOCIATE, AND THE RIGHT NOT TO ASSOCIATE

NAACP v. Alabama ex rel Patterson, 357 U.S. 449, 78 S.Ct. 1163, 2 L.Ed.2d 1488 (1958), per Harlan, J., held that the first amendment barred Alabama from compelling production of NAACP membership lists. The opinion used the phrase freedom of association repeatedly, "elevat[ing] freedom of association to an independent right, possessing an equal status with the other rights specifically enumerated in the first amendment." Emerson, *Freedom of Association and Freedom of Expression,* 74 Yale L.J. 1, 2 (1964).

From the materials on advocacy of illegal action (Sec. 1, I supra) onward, it has been evident that individuals have rights to join with others for expressive purposes. This section explores other aspects of the freedom to associate and its corollary, the freedom not to associate. First, we explore cases which the Court bases on a right not to speak, but might better be understood as establishing a right not to be associated with particular ideas. Second, we explore aspects of free association in the employment context—in particular the claims of employees not to be associated with a political party, or a union or its policies. Those claims are to some extent derived from the cases establishing a right not to be associated with particular ideas. Third, instead of persons resisting forced membership in a group, we confront a group resisting members.

Finally, freedom of association is used to resist government mandated disclosure. There is no general right not to speak. Every day witnesses are subpoenaed to testify against their will. But the first amendment affords a particularized right not to speak when forced disclosure would jeopardize important associational rights. One of the questions of the final part is whether press relationships with confidential sources are uniquely protected associations. That issue carries beyond the subject of the section and back to the question of whether the Constitution contemplates a special role for the institutional press.

I. THE RIGHT NOT TO BE ASSOCIATED WITH PARTICULAR IDEAS

"If there is any fixed star in our constitutional constellation, it is that no official, high or petty, can prescribe what shall be orthodox in politics, nationalism, religion, or other matter of opinion or force citizens to confess by word or act their faith therein."

West Virginia State Bd. of Educ. v. Barnette, p. 843 infra (Jackson, J.) (upholding right of public school students to refuse to salute flag).

———

New Hampshire required that noncommercial vehicles bear license plates embossed with the state motto, "Live Free or Die." "Refus[ing] to be coerced by the State into advertising a slogan which I find morally, ethically, religiously and politically abhorrent," appellee, a Jehovah's Witness, covered up the motto on his license plate, a misdemeanor under state law. After being convicted several times of violating the misdemeanor statute, appellee sought federal injunctive and declaratory relief. WOOLEY v. MAYNARD, 430 U.S. 705, 97 S.Ct. 1428, 51 L.Ed.2d 752 (1977), per BURGER, C.J., held that requiring appellee to display the motto on his license plates violated his first amendment right to "refrain from speaking":

"[T]he freedom of thought protected by the First Amendment [includes] both the right to speak freely and the right to refrain from speaking at all. See *Barnette.* The right to speak and the right to refrain from speaking are complementary components of the broader concept of 'individual freedom of mind.' This is illustrated [by] *Miami Herald Publishing Co. v. Tornillo* [p. 696 infra], where we held unconstitutional a Florida statute placing an affirmative duty upon newspapers to publish the replies of political candidates whom they had criticized.

" * * * Compelling the affirmative act of a flag salute [the situation in *Barnette*] involved a more serious infringement upon personal liberties than the passive act of carrying the state motto on a license plate, but the difference is essentially one of degree. Here, as in *Barnette,* we are faced with a state measure which forces an individual as part of his daily life—indeed constantly while his automobile is in public view—to be an instrument for fostering public adherence to an ideological point of view he finds unacceptable. In doing so, the State 'invades the sphere of intellect and spirit which it is the purpose of the First Amendment [to] reserve from all official control.' *Barnette.*

"New Hampshire's statute in effect requires that appellees use their private property as a 'mobile billboard' for the State's ideological message—or suffer a penalty, as Maynard already has. [The] fact that most individuals agree with the thrust of [the] motto is not the test; most Americans also find the flag salute acceptable. The First Amendment protects the right of individuals to hold a point of view different from the majority and to refuse to foster, in the way New Hampshire commands, an idea they find morally objectionable."

The Court next considered whether "the State's countervailing interest" was "sufficiently compelling" to justify appellees to display the motto on their license plates. The two interests claimed by the state were (1) facilitating the identification of state license plates from those of similar colors of other states and (2) promoting "appreciation of history, state pride, [and] individualism." As to (1), the record revealed that these state license plates were readily distinguishable from others without reference to the state motto and, in any event, the state's purpose could be achieved by "less drastic means," i.e., by alternative methods less restrictive of first amendment freedoms. As to (2), where the State's interest is to communicate an "official view" as to history and state pride or to disseminate any other "ideology," "such interest cannot outweigh an individual's First Amendment right to avoid becoming the courier for such message."

REHNQUIST, J., joined by Blackmun, J., dissented, not only agreeing with what he called "the Court's implicit recognition that there is no protected 'symbolic speech' in this case," but maintaining that "that conclusion goes far to undermine the Court's ultimate holding that there is an element of protected expression here. The State has not forced appellees to 'say' anything; and it has not forced them to communicate ideas with nonverbal actions reasonably likened to 'speech,' such as wearing a lapel button promoting a political candidate or waving a flag as a symbolic gesture.[a] The State has simply required that *all*

---

a. Does *compelled* expression have to be understood by others to be "speech" or does it suffice that the Maynards *subjectively believed* that they were being forced to make an expression? See note 1 following this case.

noncommercial automobiles bear license tags with the state motto. [Appellees] have not been forced to affirm or reject that motto; they are simply required by the State [to] carry a state auto license tag for identification and registration purposes. [The] issue, unconfronted by the Court, is whether appellees, in displaying, as they are required to do, state license tags, the format of which is known to all as having been prescribed by the State, would be considered to be advocating political or ideological views.

"[H]aving recognized the rather obvious differences between [*Barnette* and this case], the Court does not explain why the same result should obtain. The Court suggests that the test is whether the individual is forced 'to be an instrument for fostering public adherence to an ideological point of view he finds unacceptable,' [but] these are merely conclusory words. [For] example, were New Hampshire to erect a multitude of billboards, each proclaiming 'Live Free or Die,' and tax all citizens for the cost of erection and maintenance, clearly the message would be 'fostered' by the individual citizen-taxpayers and just as clearly those individuals would be 'instruments' in that communication. Certainly, however, that case would not fall within the ambit of *Barnette*. In that case, as in this case, there is no *affirmation* of belief. For First Amendment principles to be implicated, the State must place the citizen in the position of either appearing to, or actually, 'asserting as true' the message. This was the focus of *Barnette,* and clearly distinguishes this case from that one." [b]

Notes and Questions

1. *Compelled expression vs. symbolic speech.* In *Wooley,* the lower court had held that by covering up the state motto on their automobile license plate, appellees were engaging in "symbolic speech," inferring the requisite intent to communicate from the use of reflective red tape to mask the motto—which not only called attention to the obscuring of the motto, but also conveyed disagreement with it. But the Supreme Court found it unnecessary to pass judgment on this issue, finding "more appropriate grounds" to affirm the judgment. It did, however, note that the symbolic speech claim was "substantially undermined" by a request for plates without the motto. Were appellees engaged in symbolic speech? If they were not, was *Wooley* correctly decided? Does the answer turn on whether *the state* was engaging in "speech"? Consider Note, 1977 Utah L.Rev. 797, 805–07: "While an objective approach is perhaps useful in finding 'symbolic speech,' [it] becomes suspect when applied to finding 'compelled expression.' [Utilizing] an objective test to find compelled expression defeats [one of the goals of the first amendment], for it forces an individual to express a view not his own. This situation clearly invades 'the sphere [which] it is the purpose of the First Amendment [to] reserve from all official control.' *Barnette.*

"Care must be exercised, however, to distinguish compelled symbolic expression from compelled acts which have no expressive conduct [e.g., compelling one to place a license plate on his car or number on his house]. To make this distinction, an objective test is correctly applied first to ascertain if the [government] intended to communicate [a] message. If it did, then a subjective test is properly applied to determine if the individual citizen was compelled to communicate that message. '[E]xpression' is a prerequisite of 'compelled expression,' and 'expression,' if symbolic in nature, is properly found by using an objective

---

b. White, J., joined by Blackmun and Rehnquist, JJ., dissented on procedural grounds.

test. Expression that is compelled, however, must be found subjectively if the guarantees of the first amendment are to have any real significance. In [*Wooley*], there can be little doubt that the state intended to communicate a message. [Thus], the majority properly applied a subjective test to find that such expression had been compelled in violation of the Maynards' first amendment rights."

2. *Compelling citizens through taxes.* The *Wooley* majority, notes Tribe, *American Constitutional Law* 590 n. 8 (1978), "silently accepted Justice Rehnquist's assertion that citizens of New Hampshire could be compelled through their taxes to pay for the cost of erecting and maintaining billboards proclaiming 'Live Free or Die.'" Should the majority have done so? Consider Tribe, supra: "Any notion that the very relation of taxpayer to government makes the refund argument inherently inapt seems refuted by positing a hypothetical instance in which, say, half the state budget [is spent] broadcasting 'Live Free or Die' across the countryside. In such a case, even assuming that this allocation of public resources does not itself violate the first and fourteenth amendments, the Supreme Court should probably conclude that the broadcast cannot constitutionally be financed with the involuntary contributions of persons who disagree with the message."

3. *Use of private property as a forum for the speech of others.* Appellees sought to enjoin a shopping center from denying them access to the center's central courtyard in order to solicit signatures from passersby for petitions opposing a U.N. resolution. The California Supreme Court held they were entitled to conduct their activity at the center, construing the state constitution to protect "speech and petitioning, reasonably exercised, in shopping centers, even [when] privately owned." PRUNEYARD SHOPPING CENTER v. ROBINS, 447 U.S. 74, 100 S.Ct. 2035, 64 L.Ed.2d 741 (1980) per REHNQUIST, J., affirmed, rejecting, inter alia, the argument, based on *Wooley,* that "a State may not constitutionally require an individual to participate in the dissemination of an ideological message by displaying it on his private property [so] that it be observed and read by the public":

"[In *Wooley*] the government itself prescribed the message, required it to be displayed openly on appellee's personal property that was used 'as part of his daily life,' and refused to permit him [to] cover up the motto even though the Court found that the display of the motto served no important state interest. Here, by contrast, there are a number of distinguishing factors. Most important, [the center] is not limited to the personal use of appellants, [but is] a business establishment that is open to the public to come and go as they please. The views expressed by members of the public in passing out pamphlets or seeking signatures for a petition thus will not likely be identified with those of the owner. Second, no specific message is dictated by the State to be displayed on appellants' property. There consequently is no danger of government discrimination for or against a particular message. Finally, [it appears] appellants can expressly disavow any connection with the message by simply posting signs in the area where the speakers or handbillers stand."

The Court also found appellants' reliance on *Barnette* and *Tornillo* misplaced: Unlike *Barnette,* appellants "are not [being] compelled to affirm their belief in any governmentally prescribed position or view, and they are free to publicly dissociate themselves from the views of the speakers or handbillers. [*Tornillo*] rests on the principle that the State cannot tell a newspaper what it must print. [There was also a danger in *Tornillo* that the invalidated statute requiring a newspaper to publish a political candidate's reply to previously published criticism would deter] editors from publishing controversial political [statements]. Thus, the statute was found to be an 'intrusion into the function of editors.' These concerns obviously are not present here."

POWELL, J., joined by White, J., concurring in part and in the judgment, agreed that "the owner of this shopping center has failed to establish a cognizable First Amendment claim," but maintained that "state action that transforms privately owned property into a forum for the expression of the public's views could raise serious First Amendment questions": "I do not believe that the result in *Wooley* would have changed had [the state] directed its citizens to place the slogan 'Live Free or Die' in their shop windows rather than on their automobiles. [The *Wooley* principle] on its face protects a person who refuses to allow use of his property as a market place for the ideas of others. [One] who has merely invited the public onto his property for commercial purposes cannot fairly be said to have relinquished his right 'to decline to be an instrument for fostering public adherence to an ideological point of view he finds unacceptable.' *Wooley*.

"[E]ven when [as here] no particular message is mandated by the State, First Amendment interests are affected by state action that forces a property owner to admit third-party speakers. [A] right of access [may be] no less intrusive than speech compelled by the State itself. For example, a law requiring that a newspaper permit others to use its columns imposes an unacceptable burden upon the newspaper's First Amendment right to select material for publication. *Tornillo*.

"[If] a state law mandated public access to the bulletin board of a freestanding store [or] small shopping center [or allowed soliciting or pamphleteering in the entrance area of a store] customers might well conclude that the messages reflect the view of the proprietor. [He] either could permit his customers to receive a mistaken impression [or] disavow the messages. Should he take the first course, he effectively has been compelled to affirm someone else's belief. Should he choose the second, he has been forced to speak when he would prefer to remain silent. In short, he has lost control over his freedom to speak or not to speak on certain issues. The mere fact that he is free to dissociate himself from the views expressed on his property cannot restore his 'right to refrain from speaking at all.' *Wooley*.

"A property owner may also be faced with speakers who wish to use his premises as a platform for views that he finds morally repugnant [, for example, a] minority-owned business confronted with leafleteers from the American Nazi Party or the Ku Klux Klan, [or] a church-operated enterprise asked to host demonstrations in favor of abortion. [The] strong emotions evoked by speech in such situations may virtually compel the proprietor to respond.

"The pressure to respond is particularly apparent [in the above cases, but] an owner who strongly objects to some of the causes to which the state-imposed right of access would extend may oppose ideological activities 'of *any* sort' that are not related to the purposes for which he has invited the public onto his property. See *Abood*. To require the owner to specify the particular ideas he finds objectionable enough to compel a response would force him to relinquish his 'freedom to maintain his own beliefs without public disclosure.' *Abood*. Thus, the right to control one's own speech may be burdened impermissibly even when listeners will not assume that the messages expressed on private property are those of the owner.

"[On this record] I cannot say that customers of this vast center [occupying several city blocks and containing more than 65 shops] would be likely to assume that appellees' limited speech activity expressed the views of [the center]. [Moreover, appellants] have not alleged that they object to [appellees' views, nor asserted] that some groups who reasonably might be expected to speak at [the center] will express views that are so objectionable as to require a response even when listeners will not mistake their source. [Thus,] I join the judgment of the Court, [but] I do not interpret our decision today as a blanket approval for state efforts to transform privately owned commercial property into public forums." [c]

4. *Economic pressure to engage in political activity.* NAACP v. CLAIBORNE HARDWARE CO., 458 U.S. 886, 102 S.Ct. 3409, 73 L.Ed.2d 1215 (1982): The NAACP had organized a consumer boycott whose principal objective was, according to the lower court, "to force the white merchants [to] bring pressure upon [the government] to grant defendants' demands or, in the alternative, to suffer economic ruin." Mississippi characterized the boycott as a tortious and malicious interference with the plaintiffs' businesses. The Court, per STEVENS, J., held that the NAACP boycott was immune from state prohibition: Although labor boycotts organized for economic ends had long been subject to prohibition, "speech to protest racial discrimination" was "essential political speech lying at the core of the First Amendment" and was therefore distinguishable. Is the boycott protected association? Are there association rights on the other side? Does the state have a legitimate interest in protecting merchants from being forced to support political change they would otherwise oppose? Cf. *NLRB v. Retail Store Employees Union,* 447 U.S. 607, 100 S.Ct. 2372, 65 L.Ed.2d 377 (1980) (ban on labor picketing encouraging consumer boycott of neutral employer upheld). Are the white merchants neutral? [d] For commentary, compare Harper, *The Consumer's Emerging Right to Boycott: NAACP v. Claiborne Hardware and Its Implications for American Labor Law,* 93 Yale L.J. 409 (1984) with Schwarzschild & Alexander, *Consumer Boycotts and Freedom of Association: Comment on a Recently Proposed Theory,* 22 San Diego L.Rev. 555 (1985).

5. *Orthodoxy and commercial advertising.* ZAUDERER v. OFFICE OF DISCIPLINARY COUNSEL, __ U.S. __, 105 S.Ct. 2265, 85 L.Ed.2d 652 (1985), per WHITE, J., upheld an Ohio requirement that an attorney advertising availability on a contingency basis must disclose in the ad that the clients would have to pay costs if their lawsuits should prove unsuccessful whenever that is the proposed financial arrangement: "[T]he interests at stake in this case are not of the same order as those discussed in *Wooley, Tornillo,* and *Barnette.* Ohio has not attempted to 'prescribe what shall be orthodox in politics, nationalism, religion, or other matters of opinion or force citizens to confess by word or act their faith therein.' The State has attempted only to prescribe what shall be orthodox in commercial advertising, and its prescription has taken the form of a requirement that appellant include in his advertising purely factual and uncontroversial [e] information about the terms under which his services will be available. Because the extension of First Amendment protection to commercial speech is justified principally by the value to consumers of the information such speech

c. For commentary, see Levinson, *Freedom of Speech and the Right of Access to Private Property Under State Constitutional Law* in Developments in State Constitutional Law 51 (McGraw ed. 1985).

d. Stevens, J., also argued in *Claiborne* that the boycott was protected as a right to petition the government. Are the white merchants the government?

e. What if the requested disclosures are controverted? Do cigarette companies have first amendment grounds to resist forced disclosures?

provides, *Virginia Pharmacy,* appellant's constitutionally protected interest in *not* providing any particular factual information in his advertising is minimal.

* * * *

"We do not suggest that disclosure requirements do not implicate the advertiser's First Amendment rights at all. We recognize that unjustified or unduly burdensome disclosure requirements might offend the First Amendment by chilling protected commercial speech. But we hold that an advertiser's rights are adequately protected as long as disclosure requirements are reasonably related to the State's interest in preventing deception of consumers."

The Court stated that the first amendment interests "implicated by disclosure requirements are substantially weaker than those at stake when speech is actually suppressed." Accordingly it rejected any requirement that the advertisement in question be shown to be deceptive absent the disclosure or that the state meet a "least restrictive means" analysis.

BRENNAN, J., joined by Marshall, J., dissenting on this issue, conceded that the distinction between disclosure and suppression "supports some differences in analysis," but thought the Court had exaggerated the importance of the distinction: "We have noted in traditional First Amendment cases that an affirmative publication requirement 'operates as a command in the same sense as a statute or regulation forbidding [someone] to publish specified matter,' and that a compulsion to publish that which 'reason tells [one] should not be published' therefore raises substantial first amendment concerns. *Tornillo.*" Accordingly, he would have required a demonstration that the advertising was inherently likely to deceive or record evidence that the advertising was in fact deceptive, or a showing that another substantial interest was directly advanced by state action extending only as far as the interest served. Applying this standard, Brennan, J., agreed with the Court that a state may require an advertising attorney to include a costs disclaimer, but concluded that the state had provided Zauderer with inadequate notice of what he was required to include in the advertisement.

II. FREEDOM OF ASSOCIATION AND EMPLOYMENT

ELROD v. BURNS, 427 U.S. 347, 96 S.Ct. 2673, 49 L.Ed.2d 547 (1976), (Stevens, J., not participating) declared unconstitutional the dismissal of nonpolicymaking and nonconfidential state and local government employees solely on the ground that they were not affiliated with or sponsored by a particular political party. (The newly elected Democratic Sheriff of Cook County, Illinois, had sought to replace noncivil-service employees in his office, all Republicans, with members of his own party. The employees who brought suit were process servers and a juvenile court bailiff). BRENNAN, J., announced the judgment and an opinion joined by White and Marshall, JJ.: "The cost of the practice of patronage is the restraint it places on freedoms of belief and association. [The] free functioning of the electoral process also suffers. Conditioning political employment on partisan support prevents support of competing public interests. [As] government employment, state or federal, becomes more pervasive, the greater the dependence on it becomes, and therefore the greater becomes the power to starve political [opposition]. Patronage thus tips the electoral process in favor of the incumbent party.

"[P]olitical belief and association constitute the core of those activities protected by the First Amendment. Regardless of the nature of the inducement, whether it be by the denial of public employment or, as in *Barnette,* by the influence of a teacher over students, '[no government official] can prescribe what shall be orthodox in politics [or] other matters of opinion or force citizens to confess by word or act their faith therein.' Ibid. And, though freedom of belief is central, '[t]he First Amendment protects political association as well as political expression.' *Buckley v. Valeo* [p. 772 infra]. * * *

"The Court recognized in *United Public Workers v. Mitchell,* 330 U.S. 75, 100, 67 S.Ct. 556, 569, 91 L.Ed. 754 (1947), that 'Congress may not "enact a regulation providing that no Republican, Jew or Negro shall be appointed to federal office." ' This principle was reaffirmed in *Wieman v. Updegraff,* 344 U.S. 183, 73 S.Ct. 215, 97 L.Ed. 216 (1952), which held that a State could not require its employees to establish their loyalty by extracting an oath denying past affiliation with Communists. And in *Cafeteria Workers v. McElroy,* 367 U.S. 886, 898, 81 S.Ct. 1743, 1750, 6 L.Ed.2d 1230 (1961), the Court recognized again that the government could not deny employment because of previous membership in a particular party.[11]

"Particularly pertinent to the constitutionality of the practice of patronage dismissals are *Keyishian v. Board of Regents,* 385 U.S. 589, 87 S.Ct. 675, 17 L.Ed. 2d 629 (1967), and *Perry v. Sindermann,* 408 U.S. 593, 92 S.Ct. 2694, 33 L.Ed.2d 570 (1972). In *Keyishian,* the Court invalidated New York statutes barring employment merely on the basis of membership in 'subversive' organizations. *Keyishian* squarely held that political association alone could not, consistently with the First Amendment, constitute an adequate ground for denying public employment.[12] In *Perry,* the Court broadly rejected the validity of limitations on First Amendment rights as a condition to the receipt of a governmental benefit, stating that the government 'may not deny a benefit to a person on a basis that infringes his constitutionally protected interests—especially, his interest in freedom of speech. For if the government could deny a benefit to a person because of his constitutionally protected speech or associations, his exercise of those freedoms would in effect be penalized and inhibited. This would allow the government to "produce a result which [it] could not command directly." *Speiser v. Randall.* Such interference with constitutional rights is impermissible.' * * *[13]"

---

11. Protection of First Amendment interests has not been limited to invalidation of conditions on government employment requiring allegiance to a particular political party. This Court's decisions have prohibited conditions on public benefits, in the form of jobs or otherwise, which dampen the exercise generally of First Amendment rights, however slight the inducement to the individual to forsake those rights.

[T]he First Amendment prohibits limiting the grant of a tax exemption to only those who affirm their loyalty to the State granting the exemption. *Speiser v. Randall,* 357 U.S. 513, 78 S.Ct. 1332, 2 L.Ed.2d 1460 (1958).

12. Thereafter, *United States v. Robel,* 389 U.S. 258, 88 S.Ct. 419, 19 L.Ed.2d 508 (1967), similarly held that mere membership in the Communist Party could not bar a person from employment in private defense establishments important to national security.

13. The increasingly pervasive nature of public employment provides officials with substantial power through conditioning jobs on partisan support, particularly in this time of high unemployment. Since the government however, may not seek to achieve an unlawful end either directly or indirectly, the inducement afforded by placing conditions on a benefit need not be particularly great in order to find that rights have been violated. Rights are infringed both where the government fines a person a penny for being a Republican and where it withholds the grant of a penny for the same reason.

Petitioners contend that even though the government may not provide that public employees may retain their jobs only if they become affiliated with or provide support for the in-party, respondents here have waived any objection to such requirements. The difficulty with this argument is that it completely swallows the rule. Since the qualification may not be constitutionally imposed absent an appropriate justification, to accept the waiver argument is to say that the government may do what it may not do. A finding of waiver in this case, therefore, would be contrary to our

If the practice is to survive constitutional challenge, "it must further some vital government end by a means that is least restrictive of freedom of belief and association in achieving that end, and the benefit gained must outweigh the loss of constitutionally protected rights." The plurality then considered and rejected three interests offered in justification of patronage—(1) "the need to insure effective government"; (2) "the need for political loyalty of employees" to assure implementation of the new administration's policies; and (3) "the preservation of the democratic process" and the continued vitality of "party politics":

As to (1), the argument fails, inter alia, "because it is doubtful that the mere difference of political persuasion motivates poor performance; nor do we think it legitimately may be used for imputing such behavior. [At] all events, less drastic means for insuring [this interest] are available"—discharge for good cause, "such as insubordination or poor job performance, when those bases exist."

"[Moreover] the lack of any justification for patronage dismissals as a means of furthering government effectiveness and efficiency distinguishes this case from *CSC v. Letter Carriers*, 413 U.S. 548, 93 S.Ct. 2880, 37 L.Ed.2d 796 (1973), and *Mitchell*. In both of those cases, legislative restraints on political management and campaigning by public employees were upheld despite their encroachment on First Amendment rights because, inter alia, they did serve in a necessary manner to foster and protect efficient and effective government. Interestingly, the activities that were restrained by the legislation involved in those cases are characteristic of patronage practices. As the Court observed in *Mitchell*, 'The conviction that an actively partisan governmental personnel threatens good administration has deepened since [1882]. Congress recognizes danger to the service in that political rather than official effort may earn advancement and to the public in that governmental favor may be channeled through political connections.' "

As for the second interest, the need for political loyalty and implementation of new policies "may be adequately met" by limiting patronage dismissals to "policymaking positions." As for the third interest—one "premised on the centrality of partisan politics in the democratic process"—"we are not persuaded [that] the interdiction of patronage dismissals [will cause] the demise of party politics." Political parties existed prior to active patronage and "they have survived substantial reduction in their patronage power through the establishment of the merit system.

"Patronage dismissals thus are not the least restrictive alternative to achieving the contributions they may make to the democratic process. The process functions as well without the practice, perhaps even better, for patronage dismissals clearly also retard that practice. [U]nlike the gain to representative government provided by the Hatch Act in *Letter Carriers* and *Mitchell*, the gain to representative government provided by [the practice], if any, would be insufficient to justify its sacrifice of First Amendment rights.

"To be sure, *Letter Carriers* and *Mitchell* upheld Hatch Act restraints sacrificing political campaigning and management, activities themselves protected by the First Amendment. But in those cases it was the Court's judgment that congressional subordination of those activities was permissible to safeguard the core interests of individual belief and association. Subordination of some First Amendment activity was permissible to protect other such activity. Today, we

view that a partisan job qualification abridges the First Amendment.

hold that subordination of other First Amendment activity, that is, patronage dismissals, not only is permissible, but also is mandated by the First Amendment. And since patronage dismissals fall within the category of political campaigning and management, this conclusion irresistibly flows from *Mitchell* and *Letter Carriers*. For if the First Amendment did not place individual belief and association above political campaigning and management, at least in the setting of public employment, the restraints on those latter activities could not have been judged permissible in *Mitchell* and *Letter Carriers*."

STEWART, J., joined by Blackmun, J., concurred: "This case does not require us to consider the broad contours of the so-called patronage system, with all its variations and permutations. In particular, it does not require us to consider the constitutional validity of a system that confines the hiring of some governmental employees to those of a particular political party, and I would intimate no views whatever on that question.

"The single substantive question involved in this case is whether a nonpolicymaking, nonconfidential government employee can be discharged or threatened with discharge from a job that he is satisfactorily performing upon the sole ground of his political beliefs. I agree with the plurality that he cannot. See *Perry v. Sindermann*."

POWELL, J., joined by Burger, C.J., and Rehnquist, J., dissented: "[Here, we have] complaining employees who apparently accepted patronage jobs knowingly and willingly, while fully familiar with the 'tenure' practices long prevailing in the Sheriff's Office. Such employees have *benefited* from their political beliefs and activities; they have not been penalized for them. In these circumstances, I am inclined to [the view that they] may not be heard to challenge [the patronage system] when it comes their turn to be replaced."

Beyond waiver, he complained that the Court "unnecessarily constitutionalizes another element of American life—an element not without its faults but one which generations have accepted on balance as having merit." Powell, J., stressed the importance of political parties and their dependency upon patronage. "History and long prevailing practice across the country support the view that patronage hiring practices make a sufficiently substantial contribution to the practical functioning of our democratic system to support their relatively modest intrusion on First Amendment interests. * * *

"It is difficult to disagree with the view, as an abstract proposition, that government employment ordinarily should not be conditioned upon one's political beliefs or activities. But we deal here with a highly practical and rather fundamental element of our political system, not the theoretical abstraction of a political science seminar. [T]he plurality seriously underestimates the strength of the government interest—especially at the local level—in allowing some patronage hiring practices, and it exaggerates the perceived burden on First Amendment rights. * * *

"It is naive to think that [local political activity supporting parties is] motivated [by] some academic interest in 'democracy' or other public service impulse. For the most part, the hope of some reward generates a major portion of [such activity]. It is difficult to overestimate the contributions to our system by the major political parties, fortunately limited in number compared to the fractionalization that has made the continued existence of democratic government doubtful in some other countries. * * *

"It is against decades of experience to the contrary, then, that the plurality opinion concludes that patronage hiring practices interfere with the 'free functioning of the electoral process.' This *ad hoc* judicial judgment runs counter to the judgments of the representatives of the people in state and local governments, representatives who have chosen, in most instances, to retain some patronage practices in combination with a merit-oriented civil service. One would think that elected representatives of the people are better equipped than we to weigh the need for some continuation of patronage practices in light of the interests above identified,[9] and particularly in view of local conditions. *Letter Carriers; Mitchell.*"[a]

Notes and Questions

1. BRANTI v. FINKEL, 445 U.S. 507, 100 S.Ct. 1287, 63 L.Ed.2d 574 (1980), per STEVENS, J., applied *Elrod* to "protect an assistant public defender who is satisfactorily performing his job from discharge solely because of his political beliefs."[b] The Court rejected the argument that even if party sponsorship is an unconstitutional condition for retaining low-level public employees it is a permissible requirement for an assistant public defender: "[P]arty affiliation is not necessarily relevant to every policymaking or confidential position. The coach of a state university's football team formulates policy, but no one could seriously claim that Republicans make better coaches than Democrats, or vice versa, no matter which party is in control of the state government. On the other hand, it is equally clear that the governor of a state may appropriately believe that the official duties of various assistants who help him write speeches, explain his views to the press, or communicate with the legislature cannot be performed effectively unless those persons share his political beliefs and party commitments. In sum, the ultimate inquiry is not whether the label 'policymaker' or 'confidential' fits a particular position; rather, the question is whether the hiring authority can demonstrate that party affiliation is an appropriate requirement for the effective performance of the public office involved."

The Court concluded that neither the policymaking of an assistant public defender nor the access of client's confidential information had any bearing on partisan political considerations.

2. Might Communists be treated differently from Republican or Democrats for some confidential employment? Consider White, J., dissenting in *Robel* (cited in Brennan, J.'s opinion fn. 12): "[D]enying the opportunity to be employed

---

9. The plurality might be taken to concede some promotion of the democratic process by patronage hiring practices but to conclude that in net effect such practices will reduce political debate impermissibly by affecting some employees or potential employees and thereby depriving society of the 'unfettered judgment of each citizen on matters of political concern.' In the past the Court has upheld congressional actions designed to increase the overall level of political discourse but affecting adversely the First Amendment interests of some individuals. In *Letter Carriers* we indicated specifically that the First Amendment freedoms of federal employees could be limited in an effort to further the functioning of the democratic process. I do not believe that local legislative judgments as to what will further the democratic process in

light of local conditions should receive less weight than these congressional judgments. Surely that should be the case until we have a record, if one could be created, showing the fears of the plurality to be justified.

a. Burger, C.J., dissented, contending that the decision "represents a significant intrusion into the area of legislative and policy concerns."

b. The Court noted that in *Elrod,* as in the instant case, "the only practice at issue was the *dismissal* of public employees for partisan reasons" and thus there was "no occasion to address petitioner's argument that there is a compelling governmental interest in maintaining a political sponsorship system for *filling vacancies* in the public defender's office." (Emphasis added.)

in some defense plants in a much smaller deterrent to the exercise of associational rights that [a] criminal penalty attached solely to membership, and the Government's interest in keeping potential spies and saboteurs from defense plants is much greater than its interest [in] committing all Party members to prison." Compare Israel, *Elfbrandt v. Russell: The Demise of the Oath?*, 1966 Sup.Ct.Rev. 193, 201–07 and O'Neil, *Unconstitutional Conditions,* 54 Calif.L.Rev. 443 (1966) with Van Alstyne, *The Constitutional Rights of Employees,* 16 U.C. L.A.L.Rev. 751 (1969).

COLE v. RICHARDSON, 405 U.S. 676, 92 S.Ct. 1332, 31 L.Ed.2d 593 (1972), per BURGER, C.J. (over the dissents of Douglas, J., and Marshall, J., joined by Brennan, J.), upheld the dismissal of Richardson's employment at a state hospital for refusing to sign a loyalty oath calling in part for an affirmation that "I will oppose the overthrow of the government [by] force, violence, or by any illegal or unconstitutional method": "Since there is no constitutionally protected right to overthrow a government by force, violence, or illegal or unconstitutional means, no constitutional right is infringed by an oath to abide by the constitutional system in the future." [c] Should the first amendment permit requiring public employees to oppose that which they have a right to advocate? Is *Cole* consistent with the cases cited in the plurality opinion? With *Robel*? With *Wooley*?

3. The plurality argues that its conclusion flows irresistibly from *Mitchell* and *Letter Carriers*? Were these cases rightly decided? Is a ban on active participation in political campaigns by government employees necessary (as the Court thought in *Letter Carriers*) to avoid the impression that the government practices "political justice" or to prevent the government work force from becoming a "peaceful, invincible, and perhaps corrupt political machine"? Would prohibitions against coercion (such as those commanded by *Elrod*) be sufficient? If not, is the concern about coercion relevant only to participation on behalf of incumbents? See Blasi, *The Checking Value in First Amendment Theory,* 1977 Am.B.Found.Res.J. 521, 634–35. Is it of major import that the restrictions are "not aimed at particular parties, groups or points of [view]"? *Letter Carriers.* Does an emphasis on this factor, denigrate the liberty and associational interests of government employees? See Redish, *The Content Distinction in First Amendment Analysis,* 34 Stan.L.Rev. 113 (1981). Consider the tension between *Letter Carriers* and the *Pickering-Connick* [Sec. 1, VII, C supra] line of cases. Consider also the relationship between *Pickering, Connick,* and *Elrod.* Suppose a deputy sheriff is discharged for meeting with a political opponent of the incumbent sheriff. Does *Elrod* apply or *Pickering-Connick?* What is the difference? For discussion, see Note, *Politics and the Non-Civil Service Public Employee: A Categorical Approach to First Amendment Protection,* 85 Colum.L.Rev. 558 (1985).

In ABOOD v. DETROIT BD. OF EDUC., 431 U.S. 209, 97 S.Ct. 1782, 52 L.Ed. 2d 261 (1977), a Michigan statute permitted an "agency shop" arrangement, whereby all local governmental employees represented by a union, even though not themselves union members, must, as a condition of employment, pay to the union "service charges" equal in amount to union dues. Alleging that they were unwilling to pay union dues, that (1) they opposed public sector collective bargaining and that (2) the union was engaged in non-collective bargaining political-ideological activities which they disapproved, public school teachers

c. Powell and Rehnquist, JJ., took no part.

challenged the validity of the agency-shop clause in a collective bargaining agreement between the Board of Education and the union. The Court, per STEWART, J., rejected plaintiffs' first contention, but sustained the second—the union's expenditure of a part of such "service charges" "to contribute to political candidates and to express political views unrelated to its duties as exclusive bargaining representative" violates the first amendment rights of non-union employees who oppose such causes.

"To compel employees financially to support their collective-bargaining representative has an impact upon their First Amendment interests. An employee may very well have ideological objections to a wide variety of activities undertaken by the union in its role as exclusive representative. His moral or religious views about the desirability of abortion may not square with the union's policy in negotiating a medical benefits plan. One individual might disagree with a union policy of negotiating limits on the right to strike, believing that to be the road to serfdom for the working class, while another might have economic or political objections to unionism itself. An employee might object to the union's wage policy because it violates guidelines designed to limit inflation, or might object to the union's seeking a clause in the collective-bargaining agreement proscribing racial discrimination. The examples could be multiplied. To be required to help finance the union as a collective-bargaining agent might well be thought, therefore, to interfere in some way with an employee's freedom to associate for the advancement of ideas, or to refrain from doing so, as he sees fit. But the judgment clearly made in [*Railway Employees' Dep't v. Hanson*, 351 U.S. 225, 76 S.Ct. 714, 100 L.Ed. 1112 (1956), upholding against first amendment challenge a union-shop clause, authorized by the Railway Labor Act (RLA), requiring financial support of the union by every member of the bargaining unit, and *International Ass'n of Machinists v. Street*, 367 U.S. 740, 81 S.Ct. 1784, 6 L.Ed.2d 1141 (1961), avoiding serious constitutional issues by construing RLA to prohibit the use of compulsory union dues for political purposes] is that such interference as exists is constitutionally justified by the legislative assessment of the important contribution of the union shop to the system of labor relations established by the Congress. '[As long as the union leadership acts] to promote the cause which justified bringing the group together, the individual cannot withdraw his financial support merely because he disagrees with the group's strategy.' *Street* (Douglas, J., concurring).

"[The] desirability of labor peace is no less important in the public sector, nor is the risk of 'free riders' any smaller. [Thus], insofar as the service charge is used to finance expenditures by the union for the purposes of collective bargaining, contract administration, and grievance adjustment, [*Hanson* and *Street*] appear to require validation of the agency-shop agreement before us."

In agreeing with plaintiffs' contention that they fall within the protection of *Elrod* and other cases guaranteeing the freedom to associate for the purpose of advancing ideas and forbidding the government to require one to relinquish first amendment rights as a condition of public employment "because they have been prohibited not from actively associating, but rather from refusing to associate," and in ruling that plaintiffs could constitutionally prevent the union's spending a part of their required service fees for political and ideological purposes unrelated to collective bargaining, the Court pointed out: "The fact that [plaintiffs] are compelled to make, rather than prohibited from making, contributions for political purposes works no less an infringement of their constitutional rights. For at the heart of the First Amendment is the notion that an individual should be free to believe as he will, and that in a free society one's beliefs should be shaped by his mind and his conscience rather than coerced by the State. See [*Elrod.*]

"These principles prohibit a State from compelling an individual [to] associate with a political party, *Elrod,* as a condition of employment. They are no less applicable to the case at bar, and they thus prohibit the [union] from requiring any [plaintiff] to contribute to the support of an ideological cause he may oppose as a condition of holding a job as a public school teacher.

"We do not hold that a union cannot constitutionally spend funds for the expression of political views, on behalf of political candidates, or towards the advancement of other ideological causes not germane to its duties as collective bargaining representative. Rather, the Constitution requires only that expenditures be financed from [charges] paid by employees who do not object to advancing those ideas and who are not coerced into doing so against their will by the threat of loss of government employment."

The Court remanded to devise an appropriate "way of preventing subsidization of ideological activity by employees who object thereto without restricting the union's ability to require every employee to contribute to the cost of collective-bargaining activities."

POWELL, J., joined by Burger, C.J., and Blackmun, J., agreed that a state cannot constitutionally compel public employees to contribute to union political activities which they oppose and thus joined the Court's judgment remanding the case for further proceedings, but balked at the Court's apparent ruling "that public employees can be compelled by the State to pay full union dues to a union with which they disagree, subject only to a possible rebate or deduction if they are willing to step forward, declare their opposition to the union, and initiate a proceeding to establish that some portion of their dues has been spent on 'ideological activities unrelated to collective bargaining.' Such a sweeping limitation of First Amendment rights by the Court is not only unnecessary on this record; it [is] unsupported by either precedent or reason. * * *

"The Court's extensive reliance on *Hanson* and *Street* requires it to rule that there is no constitutional distinction between what the Government can require of its own employees and what it can permit private employees to do. To me the distinction is fundamental. Under the First Amendment the Government may authorize private parties to enter into voluntary agreements whose terms it could not adopt as its own.

"[The] collective-bargaining agreement to which a public agency is a party is not merely analogous to legislation; it has all of the attributes of legislation for the subjects [e.g., residency requirements for state employees] with which it deals. [The] State in this case has not merely authorized union-shop agreements between willing parties; it has negotiated and adopted such an agreement itself. [It] has undertaken to compel employees to pay full dues [to] a union as a condition of employment. Accordingly, the [Board of Education's] collective-bargaining agreement, like any other enactment of state law, is fully subject to the constraints that the Constitution imposes on coercive governmental regulation.

"[I] would make it more explicit [than has the majority] that compelling a government employee to give financial support to a union in the public sector—regardless of the use to which the union puts the contribution—impinges seriously upon interests in free speech and association protected by the First Amendment.

"In *Buckley* [we held that] limitations on political contributions 'impinge on protected associational freedoms.' [That] *Buckley* dealt with a contribution limitation requirement does not alter its importance for this case. An individual can no more be required to affiliate with a candidate by making a contribution than he can be prohibited from such affiliation. The only question after *Buckley* is whether a union in the public sector is sufficiently distinguishable from a political candidate or committee to remove the withholding of financial contributions from First Amendment protection. In my view no principled distinction exists.

"The ultimate objective of a union in the public sector, like that of a political party, is to influence public decisionmaking in accordance with the views and perceived interests of the membership. [In this sense], the public sector union is indistinguishable from the traditional political party in this country.

"[It] is possible that paramount governmental interests may be found—at least with respect to certain narrowly defined subjects of bargaining—that would support this restriction on First Amendment rights. But 'the burden is on the government to show the existence of such an interest.' *Elrod.* Because this appeal reaches this Court on a motion to dismiss, the record is barren of any demonstration by the State that excluding minority views from the processes by which governmental policy is made is necessary to serve overriding governmental objectives. * * *

"Before today it had been well established that when state law intrudes upon protected speech, the State itself must shoulder the burden of proving that its action is justified by overriding state interests. See *Elrod; Speiser v. Randall.* The Court, for the first time in a First Amendment case, simply reverses this principle. Under today's decision, a nonunion employee who would vindicate his First Amendment rights apparently must initiate a proceeding to prove that the union has allocated some portion of its budget to 'ideological activities unrelated to collective bargaining.' I would adhere to established First Amendment principles and require the State to come forward and demonstrate, as to each union expenditure for which it would exact support from minority employees, that the compelled contribution is necessary to serve overriding governmental objectives."

REHNQUIST, J., concurring, noted that had he joined the *Elrod* plurality, he "would find it virtually impossible to join the Court's opinion in this case." He did not "read the Court's opinion as leaving intact the 'unfettered judgment of each citizen on matters of political concern' [*Elrod*] when it holds that Michigan [may] require an objecting member of a public employees' union to contribute to the funds necessary for the union to carry out its bargaining activities. Nor does the Court's opinion leave such a member free 'to believe as he will and to act and associate according to his beliefs' [*Elrod*]." He was "unable to see a constitutional distinction between a governmentally imposed requirement that a public employee be a Democrat or Republican or else lose his job, and a similar requirement that a public employee contribute to the collective-bargaining expenses of a labor union." [a]

---

a. Stevens, J., also filed a brief concurrence: "The Court's opinion does not foreclose the argument that the Union should not be permitted to exact a service fee from nonmembers without first establishing a procedure which will avoid the risk that their funds will be used, even temporarily, to finance ideological activities unrelated to collective bargaining."

Notes and Questions

1.   Reading *Elrod* and *Abood* together, Powell, J., and Burger, C.J., main-tain that public employees may be forced to support a political party, but not the union which represents them in collective bargaining.   Brennan, J., takes exactly the opposite position, except for support of the non-collective bargaining ideological activities of the union.   Blackmun, J., votes against forced support across the board.   Rehnquist, J., sees no difference between forced support of political parties and union collective bargaining expenses (he permits both), but apparently sees a difference between forced support of the ideological activities of political parties (he would permit it) and forced support of the non-collective bargaining ideological activities of unions (by joining the majority, he would not permit it).   Which, if any, of the above positions is defensible?

2.   Does *Abood* exaggerate the first amendment interests?   If Michigan subsidized unions directly, would dissenting taxpayers have a first amendment claim?   Suppose Michigan taxed those most likely to benefit from union activity, i.e., the employees?   Are compelled contributions different from government taxation?   See Shiffrin, *Government Speech,* 27 U.C.L.A.L.Rev. 565, 594 (1980). Suppose the union contract provided for a direct payment from the employer and that union dues were not required of employees?   Would this arrangement affect the rules set out in *Abood* ?

3.   How should the *Abood* rules apply to forced employee payments for union conventions, union newsletters, union social activities or union organiz-ing?   See *Ellis v. Brotherhood of Railway, Airline & Steamship Clerks,* 466 U.S. 435, 104 S.Ct. 1883, 80 L.Ed.2d 428 (1984).   For exploration of the issues raised by *Abood,* see Cantor, *Forced Payments to Service Institutions and Constitutional Interests in Ideological Non-Association,* 36 Rut.L.Rev. 3 (1984).

III.   INTIMATE ASSOCIATION AND EXPRESSIVE ASSOCIATION: THE RIGHT TO EXCLUDE MEMBERS

ROBERTS v. UNITED STATES JAYCEES, __ U.S. __, 104 S.Ct. 3244, 82 L.Ed.2d 462 (1984): Appellee U.S. Jaycees, a nonprofit national membership corporation whose objective is to pursue educational and charitable purposes that promote the growth and development of young men's civic organizations, limits regular membership to young men between the ages of 18 and 35. Associate membership is available to women and older men.   An associate member may not vote or hold local or national office.   Two local chapters in Minnesota violated appellee's bylaws by admitting women as regular members. When they learned that revocation of their charters was to be considered, members of both chapters filed discrimination charges with the Minnesota Department of Human Rights, alleging that the exclusion of women from full membership violated the Minnesota Human Rights Act (Act), which makes it an "unfair discriminatory practice" to deny anyone "the full and equal enjoyment of goods, services, facilities, privileges, advantages, and accommodations of a place of accommodation" because, inter alia, of sex.

Before a hearing on the state charge took place, appellee brought federal suit, alleging that requiring it to accept women as regular members would violate the male members' constitutional "freedom of association."   A state hearing officer decided against appellee and the federal district court certified to the Minnesota Supreme Court the question whether appellee is "a place of public accommodation" within the meaning of the Act. With the record of the administrative hearing before it, the state supreme court answered that question in the affirmative. The U.S. Court of Appeals held that application of the Act to appellee's membership policies would violate its freedom of association.[a]

In rejecting appellee's claims,[b] the Court, per BRENNAN, J., pointed out that the Constitution protects " 'freedom of association' in two distinct senses," what might be called "freedom of intimate association" and "freedom of expressive association": "In one line of decisions, the Court has concluded that choices to enter into and maintain certain intimate human relationships must be secured against undue intrusion by the State because of the role of such relationships in safeguarding the individual freedom that is central to our constitutional scheme. In this respect, freedom of association receives protection as a fundamental element of personal liberty. In another set of decisions, the Court has recognized a right to associate for the purpose of engaging in those activities protected by the First Amendment—speech, assembly, petition for the redress of grievances, and the exercise of religion. The Constitution guarantees freedom of association of this kind as an indispensable means of preserving other individual liberties."

The freedom of intimate association was deemed important because, "certain kinds of personal bonds have played a critical role in the culture and traditions of the Nation by cultivating and transmitting shared ideals and beliefs; they thereby foster diversity and act as critical buffers between the individual and the power of the State.[c] Moreover, the constitutional shelter afforded such relationships reflects the realization that individuals draw much of their emotional enrichment from close ties with others. Protecting these relationships from unwarranted state interference therefore safeguards the ability independently to define one's identity that is central to any concept of liberty.

"The personal affiliations that exemplify these considerations [are] distinguished by such attributes as relative smallness, a high degree of selectivity in decisions to begin and maintain the affiliation, and seclusion from others in critical aspects of the relationship. As a general matter, only relationships with these sorts of qualities are likely to reflect the considerations that have led to an understanding of freedom of association as an intrinsic element of personal liberty. Conversely, an association lacking these qualities—such as a large business enterprise—seems remote from the concerns giving rise to this constitutional protection. * * *

"Between these poles, of course, lies a broad range of human relationships that may make greater or lesser claims to constitutional protection from particular incursions by the State. [We] need not mark the potentially significant points on this terrain with any precision. We note only that factors that may be relevant include size, purpose, policies, selectivity, congeniality, and other char-

a. When the state supreme court held that appellee was "a place of public accommodation" within the meaning of the Act, it suggested that, unlike appellee, the Kiwanis Club might be sufficiently "private" to be outside the scope of the Act. Appellee then amended its complaint to allege that the state court's interpretation of the Act rendered it unconstitutionally vague. The Eighth Circuit so held, but the Supreme Court reversed.

b. There was no dissent. Rehnquist, J., concurred in the judgment. O'Connor, J.,

joined part of the Court's opinion and concurred in the judgment. See infra. Burger, C.J., and Blackmun, J., took no part.

c. For commentary on this aspect of association from a variety of perspectives, see Nisbet, *The Quest For Community* (1969); McIntyre, *After Virtue* (1981); Unger, *Knowledge and Politics* (1975); Frug, *The City as a Legal Concept*, 93 Harv.L.Rev. 1057 (1980); Karst, *Equality and Community: Lessons From the Civil Rights Era*, 56 Not.D.Law. 183 (1980).

acteristics that in a particular case may be pertinent. In this case, however, several features of the Jaycees clearly place the organization outside of the category of relationships worthy of this kind of constitutional protection.

"The undisputed facts reveal that the local chapters of the Jaycees are large and basically unselective groups. * * * Apart from age and sex, neither the national organization nor the local chapters employs any criteria for judging applicants for membership, and new members are routinely recruited and admitted with no inquiry into their backgrounds. In fact, a local officer testified that he could recall no instance in which an applicant had been denied membership on any basis other than age or sex. Furthermore, despite their inability to vote, hold office, or receive certain awards, women affiliated with the Jaycees attend various meetings, participate in selected projects, and engage in many of the organization's social functions. Indeed, numerous non-members of both genders regularly participate in a substantial portion of activities central to the decision of many members to associate with one another, including many of the organization's various community programs, awards ceremonies, and recruitment meetings.

"[Thus], we conclude that the Jaycees chapters lack the distinctive characteristics that might afford constitutional protection to the decision of its members to exclude women. We turn therefore to consider the extent to which application of the Minnesota statute to compel the Jaycees to accept women infringes the group's freedom of expressive association. * * *

"Government actions that may unconstitutionally infringe upon [freedom of expressive association] can take a number of forms. Among other things, government may seek to impose penalties or withhold benefits from individuals because of their membership in a disfavored group; it may attempt to require disclosure of the fact of membership in a group seeking anonymity; and it may try to interfere with the internal organization or affairs of the group. By requiring the Jaycees to admit women as full voting members, the Minnesota Act works an infringement of the last type. There can be no clearer example of an intrusion into the internal structure or affairs of an association than a regulation that forces the group to accept members it does not desire. Such a regulation may impair the ability of the original members to express only those views that brought them together. Freedom of association therefore plainly presupposes a freedom not to associate. See *Abood.*

"The right to associate for expressive purposes is not, however, absolute. Infringements on that right may be justified by regulations adopted to serve compelling state interests, unrelated to the suppression of ideas, that cannot be achieved through means significantly less restrictive of associational freedoms. We are persuaded that Minnesota's compelling interest in eradicating discrimination against its female citizens justifies the impact that application of the statute to the Jaycees may have on the male members' associational freedoms.

"[I]n upholding Title II of the Civil Rights Act of 1964, which forbids race discrimination in public accommodations, we emphasized that its 'fundamental object [was] to vindicate "the deprivation of personal dignity that surely accompanies denials of equal access to public establishments." ' *Heart of Atlanta Motel.* That stigmatizing injury, and the denial of equal opportunities that accompanies it, is surely felt as strongly by persons suffering discrimination on the basis of their sex as by those treated differently because of their race.

"Nor is the state interest in assuring equal access limited to the provision of purely tangible goods and services. A State enjoys broad authority to create rights of public access on behalf of its citizens. *Pruneyard.* Like many States and municipalities, Minnesota has adopted a functional definition of public accommodations that reaches various forms of public, quasi-commercial conduct. This expansive definition reflects a recognition of the changing nature of the American economy and of the importance, both to the individual and to society, of removing the barriers to economic advancement and political and social integration that have historically plagued certain disadvantaged groups, including women. * * *

"In applying the Act to the Jaycees, the State has advanced those interests through the least restrictive means of achieving its ends. Indeed, the Jaycees have failed to demonstrate that the Act imposes any serious burdens on the male members' freedom of expressive association. See *Hishon v. King & Spalding,* 467 U.S. 69, 104 S.Ct. 2229, 81 L.Ed.2d 59 (1984) (law firm 'has not shown how its ability to fulfill [protected] function[s] would be inhibited by a requirement that it consider [a woman lawyer] for partnership on her merits'). To be sure, a 'not insubstantial part' of the Jaycees' activities constitutes protected expression on political, economic, cultural, and social affairs. [There] is, however, no basis in the record for concluding that admission of women as full voting members will impede the organization's ability to engage in these protected activities or to disseminate its preferred views. The Act requires no change in the Jaycees' creed of promoting the interests of young men, and it imposes no restrictions on the organization's ability to exclude individuals with ideologies or philosophies different from those of its existing members. Moreover, the Jaycees already invite women to share the group's views and philosophy and to participate in much of its training and community activities. Accordingly, any claim that admission of women as full voting members will impair a symbolic message conveyed by the very fact that women are not permitted to vote is attenuated at best.

"[In] claiming that women might have a different attitude about such issues as the federal budget, school prayer, voting rights, and foreign relations, or that the organization's public positions would have a different effect if the group were not 'a purely young men's association,' the Jaycees rely solely on unsupported generalizations about the relative interests and perspectives of men and women. Although such generalizations may or may not have a statistical basis in fact with respect to particular positions adopted by the Jaycees, we have repeatedly condemned legal decisionmaking that relies uncritically on such assumptions. In the absence of a showing far more substantial than that attempted by the Jaycees, we decline to indulge in the sexual stereotyping that underlies appellee's contention that, by allowing women to vote, application of the Minnesota Act will change the content or impact of the organization's speech.

"In any event, even if enforcement of the Act causes some incidental abridgement of the Jaycees' protected speech, that effect is no greater than is necessary to accomplish the State's legitimate purposes. [A]cts of invidious discrimination in the distribution of publicly available goods, services, and other advantages cause unique evils that government has a compelling interest to prevent—wholly apart from the point of view such conduct may transmit. Accordingly, like violence or other types of potentially expressive activities that produce special harms distinct from their communicative impact, such practices are entitled to no constitutional protection."

O'CONNOR, J., concurring, joined the Court's opinion except for its analysis of freedom of expressive association. She maintained that "the Court has adopted a test that unadvisedly casts doubt on the power of States to pursue the profoundly important goal of ensuring nondiscriminatory access to commercial opportunities" yet "accords insufficient protection to expressive associations and places inappropriate burdens on groups claiming the protection of the First Amendment":

"The Court analyzes Minnesota's attempt to regulate the Jaycees' membership using a test that I find both over-protective of activities undeserving of constitutional shelter and under-protective of important First Amendment concerns. The Court declares that the Jaycees' right of association depends on the organization's making a 'substantial' showing that the admission of unwelcome members 'will change the message communicated by the group's speech.' I am not sure what showing the Court thinks would satisfy its requirement of proof of a membership-message connection, but whatever it means, the focus on such a connection is objectionable.

"Imposing such a requirement, especially in the context of the balancing-of-interests test articulated by the Court, raises the possibility that certain commercial associations, by engaging occasionally in certain kinds of expressive activities, might improperly gain protection for discrimination. The Court's focus raises other problems as well. [W]ould the Court's analysis of this case be different if, for example, the Jaycees membership had a steady history of opposing public issues thought (by the Court) to be favored by women? It might seem easy to conclude, in the latter case, that the admission of women to the Jaycees' ranks would affect the content of the organization's message, but I do not believe that should change the outcome of this case. Whether an association is or is not constitutionally protected in the selection of its membership should not depend on what the association says or why its members say it.

"The Court's readiness to inquire into the connection between membership and message reveals a more fundamental flaw in its analysis. The Court pursues this inquiry as part of its mechanical application of a 'compelling interest' test, under which the Court weighs the interests of the State of Minnesota in ending gender discrimination against the Jaycees' First Amendment right of association. The Court entirely neglects to establish at the threshold that the Jaycees is an association whose activities or purposes should engage the strong protections that the First Amendment extends to expressive associations.

"On the one hand, an association engaged exclusively in protected expression enjoys First Amendment protection of both the content of its message and the choice of its members. Protection of the message itself is judged by the same standards as protection of speech by an individual. Protection of the association's right to define its membership derives from the recognition that the formation of an expressive association is the creation of a voice, and the selection of members is the definition of that voice. [A] ban on specific group voices on public affairs violates the most basic guarantee of the First Amendment—that citizens, not the government, control the content of public discussion.

"On the other hand, there is only minimal constitutional protection of the freedom of *commercial* association. There are, of course, some constitutional protections of commercial speech—speech intended and used to promote a commercial transaction with the speaker. But the State is free to impose any rational regulation on the commercial transaction itself. The Constitution does not guarantee a right to choose employees, customers, suppliers, or those with whom one engages in simple commercial transactions, without restraint from the State. A shopkeeper has no constitutional right to deal only with persons of one sex.

"[A]n association should be characterized as commercial, and therefore subject to rationally related state regulation of its membership and other associational activities, when, and only when, the association's activities are not predominantly of the type protected by the First Amendment. It is only when the association is predominantly engaged in protected expression that state regulation of its membership will necessarily affect, change, dilute, or silence one collective voice that would otherwise be heard. An association must choose its market. Once it enters the marketplace of commerce in any substantial degree it loses the complete control over its membership that it would otherwise enjoy if it confined its affairs to the marketplace of ideas.

"[N]otwithstanding its protected expressive activities, [appellee] is, first and foremost, an organization that, at both the national and local levels, promotes and practices the art of solicitation and management. The organization claims that the training it offers its members gives them an advantage in business, and business firms do indeed sometimes pay the dues of individual memberships for their employees. Jaycees members hone their solicitation and management skills, under the direction and supervision of the organization, primarily through their active recruitment of new members. * * *

"Recruitment and selling are commercial activities, even when conducted for training rather than for profit. The 'not insubstantial' volume of protected Jaycees activity found by the Court of Appeals is simply not enough to preclude state regulation of the Jaycees' commercial activities. The State of Minnesota has a legitimate interest in ensuring nondiscriminatory access to the commercial opportunity presented by membership in the Jaycees. The members of the Jaycees may not claim constitutional immunity from Minnesota's anti-discrimination law by seeking to exercise their First Amendment rights through this commercial organization."

Notes and Questions

1. *Freedom of intimate association.* The reference to the freedom of intimate association is the first in the Court's history, but the notion that the concept should serve as an organizing principle is found in Karst, *Freedom of Intimate Association*, 89 Yale L.J. 624 (1980). To what extent should freedom of intimate association itself be regarded as a first amendment right? Compare Karst with Baker, *Scope of the First Amendment Freedom of Speech*, 25 U.C. L.A.L.Rev. 964 (1978) and Raggi, *An Independent Right to Freedom of Association*, 12 Harv.Civ.Rts.-Civ.Lib.L.Rev. 1 (1977).

Although the freedom of intimate association has limited relevance for the 295,000 member Jaycees, the concept "has important implications for other private associations with discriminatory membership policies." Linder, *Freedom of Association After Roberts v. United States Jaycees*, 82 Mich.L.Rev. 1878, 1885 (1984). What are (should be) the implications for golf and country clubs, fraternal societies, athletic clubs and downtown or city clubs? Consider Comment, *Discrimination in Private Social Clubs: Freedom of Association and Right to Privacy*, 1970 Duke L.J. 1181, 1222: "Whether this society is capable of free evolution to social equality seems irrelevant in light of the influence of the social club in perpetuating general racial and religious economic and social inferiority and in light of the urgent need for reversal of racial polarization. Many private social clubs have become so affected with the public interest that some regulation of their membership practices is not only a proper but also a necessary exercise of legislative power." See generally Burns, *The Exclusion of Women From Influential Men's Clubs: The Inner Sanctum and the Myth of Full Equality,* 18 Harv.Civ.Rts.-Civ.Lib.L.Rev. 321 (1983). How do O'Connor and Brennan, JJ., differ on such questions. For appreciation of O'Connor, J.'s perspective, see Linder, supra. For defense of Brennan, J.'s perspective, see Note, 98 Harv.L.Rev. 195 (1984).

2. *A feminist perspective.* From a feminist perspective, is *Roberts* a victory or a defeat? Note that what *Roberts* guarantees is the right of women to join an organization dedicated to promoting the interests of young men. What if a state attacked the goal of the organization as itself violative of civil rights? Could the Ku Klux Klan or the Nazis be outlawed by a civil rights statute? Reconsider *Beauharnais,* Sec. 1, II, A supra. Is the distinction between race and sex of any importance in this context? Should a distinction be made between organizations designed to promote the interests of advantaged groups and those designed to promote the interests of disadvantaged groups? Compare Ch. 10, Sec. 2, V and Ch. 10, Sec. 3, IV.

IV. GOVERNMENT MANDATED DISCLOSURES AND FREEDOM OF ASSOCIATION

A. BACKGROUND CASES: THE SCOPE OF LEGISLATIVE POWER

KILBOURN v. THOMPSON, 103 U.S. 168, 26 L.Ed. 377 (1881): In 1876, after Jay Cooke's banking firm, a depository of federal funds, had failed, the House of Representatives authorized a committee to investigate financial dealings between Cooke and a "real estate pool," managed by Kilbourn. For refusing to answer certain questions put to him as a witness concerning the pool and to produce certain documents in relation thereto, Kilbourn was, by an order of the House, imprisoned for 45 days in the common jail of the District of Columbia. The Court, per MILLER, J., vindicated Kilbourn, who sued for false imprisonment: "[The Constitution vests no judicial power] in the Congress or either branch of it, save in the cases specifically enumerated [e.g., determining the qualification of its own members and punishing them for disorderly conduct]. If the [Committee's investigation] was judicial in its character, [and] if it related to a matter wherein relief or redress could be had only by a judicial proceeding, [it is clear] that the power attempted to be exercised was one confided by the Constitution to the judicial and not to the legislative department of the government. * * *

"In all the argument of the case no suggestion has been made of what [Congress] could have done in the way of remedying the wrong or securing the creditors of Jay Cooke & Co., or even the United States. Was it to be simply a fruitless investigation into the personal affairs of individuals? If so, the House of Representatives had no power or authority in the matter more than any other equal number of gentlemen interested for the government of their country. By 'fruitless' we mean that it could result in no valid legislation on the subject to which the inquiry referred.

"What was this committee charged to do? To inquire into the nature and history of the real-estate pool. How indefinite! What was the real-estate pool? Is it charged with any crime of offence? If so, the courts alone can punish the members of it. Is it charged with a fraud against the government? Here, again, [only the courts] can afford a remedy. [If the legal rights involved cannot be determined by a committee report or a congressional act], what authority has the House to enter upon this investigation into the private affairs of individuals who hold no office under the government."

Consider the commentary on *Kilbourn* in Fairman, *Mr. Justice Miller and the Supreme Court* 333 (1939): "His sharp differentiation of judicial from legislative power seems doctrinaire and unrealistic. He shows himself zealous to resolve any doubts against the good faith of the House."

––––––––

McGRAIN v. DAUGHERTY, 273 U.S. 135, 47 S.Ct. 319, 71 L.Ed. 580 (1927): As a result of various charges of misfeasance and nonfeasance in the Department of Justice, the Senate adopted a resolution authorizing a committee to investigate the alleged failure of Attorney General Daugherty to prosecute various violations of law. Mally S. Daugherty, a bank president and brother of the Attorney General, twice failed to answer a subpoena issued by the committee. In a habeas corpus proceeding stemming from his seizure by the Sergeant at Arms, pursuant to a Senate resolution to bring him before the bar of the Senate, a unanimous Court, per VAN DEVANTER, J., upheld the Senate, narrowly construing *Kilbourn:* "[T]he [*Kilbourn*] resolution contained no suggestion of contemplated legislation; [the] matter was one in respect to which no valid legislation could be had; [the matters] were still pending in the bankruptcy court; and [all] creditors were free to press their claims in that proceeding.
* * *

"We are of opinion that the power of inquiry—with process to enforce it—is an essential and appropriate auxiliary to the legislative function. [Lawmakers] cannot legislate wisely or effectively in the absence of information respecting the conditions which the legislation is intended to affect or change; and where the legislative body does not itself possess the requisite information—which not infrequently is true—recourse must be had to others who do possess it. [M]ere requests for such information which is volunteered is not always accurate or complete; so some means of compulsion are essential to obtain what is needed."

––––––––

SINCLAIR v. UNITED STATES, 279 U.S. 263, 49 S.Ct. 268, 73 L.Ed. 692 (1929): Doubts having arisen about the legality and wisdom of government oil and gas land leases, the Senate directed one of its standing committees to investigate the entire subject of such leases and to "ascertain what, if any, other or additional legislation may be advisable." After suit had begun against his company, and while criminal action was impending against himself, appellant was subpoenaed. He refused to disclose certain information for the reasons that it related to his private affairs and, in any event, pertained to matters cognizable only in the courts wherein they were pending. A unanimous Court, per BUTLER, J., sustained the Senate's power to adjudge appellant in contempt: "[The authority of Congress] to require pertinent disclosures in aid of its own constitutional power is not abridged because the information sought to be elicited may also be of use in such suits. [It] is plain that investigation of the matters involved in suits brought or to be commenced under [the resolution directing litigation] might directly aid in respect of legislative action."

––––––––

UNITED STATES v. RUMELY, 345 U.S. 41, 73 S.Ct. 543, 97 L.Ed. 770 (1953): In 1949, the House established the House Select Committee on Lobbying Activities, authorizing it to study and investigate, inter alia, "all lobbying activities, intended to influence, encourage, promote, or retard legislation." Respondent, secretary of an organization whose activities included the sale of books of a polical nature, refused to disclose the names of those who made bulk purchases of these books for further distribution and to identify a Toledo woman who made a bulk purchase of a specified book. He was adjudged guilty of contempt. Avoiding constitutional questions, the Court, per FRANKFURTER, J., set aside the contempt conviction on the ground that the information the committee had sought from respondent was beyond the scope of the House's authorizing resolution. But DOUGLAS, J., joined by Black, J., concurring, maintained that the authorizing resolution could not be so narrowly construed, and consequently reached the constitutional questions:

"Once the government can demand of a publisher the names of the purchasers of his publicatons, the free press as we know it disappears. Then the spectre of a government agent will look over the shoulder of everyone who reads. The purchase of a book or pamphlet today may result in a subpoena tomorrow. [If] the lady from Toledo can be required to disclose what she read yesterday and what she will read tomorrow, fear will take the place of freedom in the libraries, book stores, and homes of the land. Through the harassment of hearings, investigations, reports, and subpoenas government will hold a club over speech and over the press. Congress could not do this by law. The power of investigation is also limited. Inquiry into personal and private affairs is precluded. [S]o is any matter in respect to which no valid legislation could be had. [Since] Congress could not by law require of respondent what the House demanded, it may not take the first step in an inquiry ending in fine or imprisonment."

WATKINS v. UNITED STATES, 354 U.S. 178, 77 S.Ct. 1173, 1 L.Ed.2d 1273 (1957): Petitioner, a labor organizer and former union officer, was subpoenaed by a Subcommittee of the House Committee on Un-American Activities. His testimony was complete and candid at many points, e.g., he admitted that in the past he had "cooperated with the Communist Party." He was willing to "answer questions about those persons whom I knew to be members of the Communist Party and whom I believe still are," but balked at testifying about those who may have been Communists "but who to the best of my knowledge and belief have long since removed themselves from the Communist movement." His refusal to testify was not based on self-incrimination grounds but on the belief that the committee had no "right to undertake the public exposure of persons because of their past activities." The Court, per WARREN, C.J., reversed a federal conviction for "contempt of Congress," for refusing to answer questions "pertinent to [the] inquiry":[a]

"Clearly, an investigation is subject to the command that the Congress shall make no law abridging freedom of speech or press or assembly. [A]n investigation is part of lawmaking. It is justified solely as an adjunct to the legislative process. The First Amendment may be invoked against infringement of the protected freedoms by law or by lawmaking. [The] critical element [in accommodating Congress' need for information with the individual interest in privacy] is

a. Frankfurter, J., concurred; Clark, J., dissented; Burton and Whittaker, JJ., did not participate.

the existence of, and the weight to be ascribed to, the interest of the Congress in demanding disclosures from an unwilling witness. [But to simply assume] that every congressional investigation is justified by a public need that overbalances any private rights [involved] would be to abdicate the [judiciary's constitutional responsibility] to insure that the Congress does not unjustifiably encroach upon an individual's right to privacy nor abridge his liberty of speech, press, religion or assembly.

"[T]here is no congressional power to expose for the sake of exposure. The public is, of course, entitled to be informed concerning the workings of its government. That cannot be inflated into a general power to expose where the predominant result can only be an invasion of the private rights of individuals. [But the motives of the committee members] alone would not vitiate an investigation which had been instituted by a House of Congress if that assembly's legislative purpose is being served.

"[It] is the responsibility of the Congress, in the first instance, to insure that compulsory process is used only in furtherance of a legislative purpose. That requires that the instructions to an investigating committee spell out that group's jurisdiction and purpose with sufficient particularity. Those instructions are embodied in the authorizing resolution. That document is the committee's charter. [The] more vague [it] is, the greater becomes the possibility that the committee's specific actions are not in conformity with the will of the parent House of Congress.

"The authorizing resolution of the Un-American Activities Committee [defines] the Committee's authority as follows: 'The Committee [is] authorized to [investigate] (i) the extent, character, and objects of un-American propaganda activities in the United States, (ii) the diffusion within the United States of subversive and un-American propaganda [attacking] the principle of the form of government as guaranteed by our Constitution, and (iii) all other questions in relation thereto that would aid Congress in any necessary remedial legislation.' It would be difficult to imagine a less explicit authorizing resolution. Who can define the meaning of 'un-American'? What is that single, solitary 'principle of the form of government as guaranteed by our Constitution'? There is no need to dwell upon the language, however, [for] events that have transpired in the fifteen years before the interrogation of petitioner [now] make such a construction impossible.

"[U]nder [the contempt] statute, the courts must accord to the defendants every [criminal procedural safeguard, including] the right to have available, through a sufficiently precise statute, information revealing the standard of criminality before the commission of the alleged offense. Applied to persons prosecuted under [the statute] this raises a special problem in that the statute defines the crime as refusal to answer 'any question pertinent to the question under inquiry.' [Petitioner] is charged with refusing to tell the Subcommittee whether or not he knew that certain named persons had been members of the Communist Party in the past. The Subcommittee's counsel read the list from the testimony of a previous witness who had identified them as Communists. Although this former witness was identified with labor, he had not stated that the persons he named were involved in union affairs. Of the thirty names propounded to petitioner, seven were completely unconnected with organized labor. [Under these circumstances], the inference becomes strong that the subject before the Subcommittee was not defined in terms of Communism in labor. The final source of evidence as to the 'question under inquiry' is the

Chairman's response when petitioner objected to the questions on the grounds of lack of pertinency. The Chairman then announced that the Subcommittee was investigating 'subversion and subversive propaganda.' This is a subject at least as broad and indefinite as the authorizing resolution of the Committee, if not more so.

"Having exhausted the several possible indicia of the 'question under inquiry', we remain unenlightened as to the subject to which the questions asked petitioner were pertinent. Certainly, if the point is that obscure after trial and appeal, it was not adquately revealed to petitioner when he had to decide at his peril whether or not to answer."

————

SWEEZY v. NEW HAMPSHIRE, 354 U.S. 234, 77 S.Ct. 1203, 1 L.E.2d 1311 (1957): The state's Subversive Activities Act of 1951 imposed various disabilities on "subversive" persons and organizations. Pursuant to a 1953 legislative resolution making him a one-person legislative committee to investigate violations of the 1951 act, the attorney general summoned petitioner, who considered himself a "classical Marxist" and a "socialist." The witness was generally cooperative, but he refused to answer questions about lectures he had recently delivered at the state university, and about his knowledge of the Progressive Party and its adherents, maintaining that these questions were not pertinent to the matter under inquiry and that they infringed first amendment freedoms. At the request of the Attorney General, a state court then put the questions to petitioner. When he again refused to answer, he was jailed for contempt.

The Court reversed (6–2), Frankfurter and Harlan, JJ., concurring in the result, Clark and Burton, JJ., dissenting. Although Warren, C.J., who wrote the principal opinion, found it unnecessary to decide whether a countervailing state interest justified the imposition of a sanction on petitioner's exercise of free expression (on the ground that the delegation to the attorney general had been so broad that the legislature could not have ascertained a need for the information sought), the concurring justices did reach this question and concluded that the state supreme court's determination that the state's need for self-protection outweighed petitioner's "right to political privacy" had no factual basis.

WARREN, C.J., reasoned: "There was nothing to connect the questioning of petitioner with [the state's interest in preventing forcible overthrow of the government]. Petitioner had been interrogated by a one-man legislative committee, not by the legislature itself. The relationship of the committee to the full assembly is vital, therefore, as revealing the relationship of the questioning to the state interest. [The] Attorney General has been given such a sweeping and uncertain mandate that it is his decision which picks out the subjects that will be pursued, what witnesses will be summoned and what questions will be asked. In this circumstance, it cannot be stated authoritatively that the legislature asked the Attorney General to gather the kind of facts comprised in the subjects upon which petitioner was interrogated.

"[I]f the Attorney General's interrogation of petitioner were in fact wholly unrelated to the object of the legislature in authorizing the inquiry, the Due Process Clause would preclude the endangering of constitutional liberties. We believe that an equivalent situation is presented in this case. The lack of any indications that the legislature wanted the information the Attorney General attempted to elicit from petitioner must be treated as the absence of authority. It follows that the use of the contempt power [violated] due process requirements.

"[Our conclusion] is not grounded upon the doctrine of separation of powers [but] upon a separation of the power of a state legislature to conduct investigations from the responsibility to direct the use of that power insofar as that separation causes a deprivation of the constitutional rights of individuals and a denial of due process of law."

FRANKFURTER, J., joined by Harlan, J., concurred: "The case must be judged as though the whole body of the legislature had demanded the information of petitioner. It would make the deepest inroads upon our federal system for this Court now to hold that it can determine the appropriate distribution of powers and their delegation within the forty-eight states. * * *

"When weighed against the grave harm resulting from governmental intrusion into the intellectual life of a university, [the] justification for compelling a witness to discuss the contents of his lecture appears grossly inadequate. Particularly is this so where the witness has sworn that neither in the lecture nor at any other time did he ever advocate overthrowing the Government by force and violence.

"[Whatever may] be the justification for not regarding the Communist Party as a conventional political party, no such justification has been afforded in regard to the Progressive Party. A foundation in fact and reason would have to be established far weightier than the intimations that appear in the record to warrant such a view of the Progressive Party. This precludes the questioning that petitioner resisted in regard to that Party."

B. POLITICAL ASSOCIATION

BARENBLATT v. UNITED STATES
360 U.S. 109, 79 S.Ct. 1081, 3 L.Ed.2d 1115 (1959).

MR. JUSTICE HARLAN delivered the opinion of the Court. * * *

Broad as it is, the [congressional power of inquiry] is not, however, without limitations. Since Congress may only investigate into those areas in which it may potentially legislate or appropriate, it cannot inquire into matters which are within the exclusive province of one or the other branch of the Government. [And] the Congress, in common with all branches of the Government, must exercise its powers subject to the limitations placed by the Constitution on governmental action, more particularly in the context of this case the relevant limitations of the Bill of Rights.

[In] the present case congressional efforts to learn the extent of a nationwide, indeed world-wide, problem have brought one of its investigating committees into the field of education. Of course, broadly viewed, inquiries cannot be made into the teaching that is pursued in any of our educational institutions. When academic teaching-freedom and its corollary learning-freedom, so essential to the well-being of the Nation, are claimed, this Court will always be on the alert against intrusion by Congress into this constitutionally protected domain. But this does not mean that the Congress is precluded from interrogating a witness merely because he is a teacher. An educational institution is not a constitutional sanctuary from inquiry into matters that may otherwise be within the constitutional legislative domain merely for the reason that inquiry is made of someone within its walls. * * *

We here review petitioner's conviction under 2 U.S.C. § 192 for contempt of Congress, arising from his refusal to answer certain questions put to him by a Subcommittee of the House Committee on Un-American Activities during the course of an inquiry concerning alleged Communist infiltration into the field of education. * * *

Pursuant to a subpoena, and accompanied by counsel, petitioner on June 28, 1954, appeared as a witness before this congressional Subcommittee. After answering a few preliminary questions and testifying that he had been a graduate student and teaching fellow at the University of Michigan from 1947 to 1950 and an instructor in psychology at Vassar College from 1950 to shortly before his appearance before the Subcommittee, petitioner objected generally to the right of the Subcommittee to inquire into his "political" and "religious" beliefs or any "other personal and private affairs" or "associational activities," upon grounds set forth in a previously prepared memorandum which he was allowed to file with the Subcommittee.[2] Thereafter petitioner specifically declined to answer [the following questions]:

"Are you now a member of the Communist Party? (Count One.)

"Have you ever been a member of the Communist Party? (Count Two.)

* * *

"Were you ever a member of the Haldane Club of the Communist Party while at the University of Michigan? (Count Four.) * * *"

In each instance the grounds of refusal were those set forth in the prepared statement. Petitioner expressly disclaimed reliance upon "the Fifth Amendment." [Upon conviction under all counts in a federal court, petitioner was sentenced to 6 months imprisonment.]

Undeniably, the First Amendment in some circumstances protects an individual from being compelled to disclose his associational relationships. However, the protections of the First Amendment, unlike a proper claim of the privilege against self-incrimination under the Fifth Amendment, do not afford a witness the right to resist inquiry in all circumstances. Where First Amendment rights are asserted to bar governmental interrogation resolution of the issue always involves a balancing by the courts of the competing private and public interests at stake in the particular circumstances shown. * * *

The first question is whether this investigation was related to a valid legislative purpose, for Congress may not constitutionally require an individual to disclose his political relationships or other private affairs except in relation to such a purpose.

That Congress has wide power to legislate in the field of Communist activity in this Country, and to conduct appropriate investigations in aid thereof, is hardly debatable. The existence of such power has never been questioned by this Court, and it is sufficient to say, without particularization, that Congress has enacted or considered in this field a wide range of legislative measures, not a few of which have stemmed from recommendations of the very Committee whose actions have been drawn in question here. In the last analysis this power rests on the right of self-preservation, "the ultimate value of any society," *Dennis*. Justification for its exercise in turn rests on the long and widely accepted view that the tenets of the Communist Party include the ultimate overthrow of the Government of the United States by force and violence, a view which has been given formal expression by the Congress.

2. In the words of the panel of the Court of Appeals which first heard the case this memorandum "can best be described as a lengthy legal brief attacking the jurisdiction of the committee to ask appellant any questions or to conduct any inquiry at all, based on the First, Ninth and Tenth Amendments, the prohibition against bills of attainder, and the doctrine of separation of powers."

We think that investigatory power in this domain is not to be denied Congress solely because the field of education is involved. [Indeed] we do not understand petitioner here to suggest that Congress in no circumstances may inquire into Communist activity in the field of education. Rather, his position is in effect that this particular investigation was aimed not at the revolutionary aspects but at the theoretical classroom discussion of communism.

In our opinion this position rests on a too constricted view of the nature of the investigatory process, and is not supported by a fair assessment of the record before us. An investigation of advocacy of or preparation for overthrow certainly embraces the right to identify a witness as a member of the Communist Party and to inquire into the various manifestations of the Party's tenets. The strict requirements of a prosecution under the Smith Act are not the measure of the permissible scope of a congressional investigation into "overthrow," for of necessity the investigatory process must proceed step by step. Nor can it fairly be concluded that this investigation was directed at controlling what is being taught at our universities rather than at overthrow. The statement of the Subcommittee Chairman at the opening of the investigation evinces no such intention,[31] and so far as this record reveals nothing thereafter transpired which would justify our holding that the thrust of the investigation later changed. [C]ertainly the conclusion would not be justified that the questioning of petitioner would have exceeded permissible bounds had he not shut off the Subcommittee at the threshold.

Nor can we accept the further contention that this investigation should not be deemed to have been in furtherance of a legislative purpose because the true objective of the Committee and of the Congress was purely "exposure." So long as Congress acts in pursuance of its constitutional power, the judiciary lacks authority to intervene on the basis of the motives which spurred the exercise of that power. [Having] scrutinized this record we cannot say that the unanimous panel of the Court of Appeals which first considered this case was wrong in concluding that "the primary purposes of the inquiry were in aid of legislative processes." * * *

Finally, the record is barren of other factors which in themselves might sometimes lead to the conclusion that the individual interests at stake were not subordinate to those of the state. There is no indication in this record that the Subcommittee was attempting to pillory witnesses. Nor did petitioner's appearance as a witness follow from indiscriminate dragnet procedures, lacking in probable cause for belief that he possessed information which might be helpful to the Subcommittee. And the relevancy of the questions put to him by the Subcommittee is not open to doubt.

---

31. The following are excerpts from that statement: "[In] opening this hearing, it is well to make clear to you and others just what the nature of this investigation is.

"From time to time, the committee has investigated Communists and Communist activities within the entertainment, newspaper, and labor fields, and also within the professions and the Government. In no instance has the work of the committee taken on the character of an investigation of entertainment organizations, newspapers, labor unions, the professions, or the Government, as such, and it is not now the purpose of this committee to investigate education or educational institutions, as [such.]

"The Committee is equally concerned with the opportunities that the Communist Party has to wield its influence upon members of the teaching profession and students through Communists who are members of the teaching profession. Therefore, the objective of this investigation is to ascertain the character, extent and objects of Communist Party activities when such activities are carried on by members of the teaching profession who are subject to the directives and discipline of the Communist Party." * * *

We conclude that the balance between the individual and the governmental interests here at stake must be struck in favor of the latter, and that therefore the provisions of the First Amendment have not been offended. * * *

Affirmed.

MR. JUSTICE BLACK, with whom THE CHIEF JUSTICE, and MR. JUSTICE DOUGLAS concur, dissenting. * * *

I do not agree that laws directly abridging First Amendment freedoms can be justified by a congressional or judicial balancing process. There are, of course, cases [such as those involving the right of a city to control its streets] suggesting that a law which primarily regulates conduct but which might also indirectly affect speech can be upheld if the effect on speech is minor in relation to the need for control of the conduct. With these cases I agree. [But they do not] even remotely suggest that a law directly aimed at curtailing speech and political persuasion could be saved through a balancing process. * * *

But even assuming what I cannot assume, that some balancing is proper in this case, I feel that the Court after stating the test ignores it completely. At most it balances the right of the Government to preserve itself, against Barenblatt's right to refrain from revealing Communist affiliations. Such a balance, however, mistakes the factors to be weighed. In the first place, it completely leaves out the real interest in Barenblatt's silence, the interest of the people as a whole in being able to join organizations, advocate causes and make political "mistakes" without later being subjected to governmental penalties for having dared to think for themselves. It is this right, the right to err politically, which keeps us strong as a Nation. [It] is these interests of society, rather than Barenblatt's own right to silence, which I think the Court should put on the balance against the demands of the Government, if any balancing process is to be tolerated. Instead they are not mentioned, while on the other side the demands of the Government are vastly overstated and called "self preservation." [Such an approach] reduces "balancing" to a mere play on words and is completely inconsistent with the rules this Court has previously given for applying a "balancing test," where it is proper. * * *

Finally, I think Barenblatt's conviction violates the Constitution because the chief aim, purpose and practice of the House Un-American Activities Committee, as disclosed by its many reports, is to try witnesses and punish them because they are or have been Communists or because they refuse to admit or deny Communist affiliations. The punishment imposed is generally punishment by humiliation and public shame. [T]he proof that the Un-American Activities Committee is here undertaking a purely judicial function is [overwhelming].

It is the protection from arbitrary punishments through the right to a judicial trial with all these safeguards which over the years has distinguished America from lands where drum-head courts and other similar "tribunals" deprive the weak and the unorthodox of life, liberty and property without due process of law. It is this same right which is denied to Barenblatt, because the Court today fails to see what is here for all to see—that exposure and punishment is the aim of this Committee and the reason for its existence. To deny this aim is to ignore the Committee's own claims and the reports it has issued ever since it was established. * * *

Ultimately all the questions in this case really boil down to one—whether we as a people will try fearfully and futilely to preserve democracy by adopting totalitarian methods, or whether in accordance with our traditions and our Constitution we will have the confidence and courage to be free.

[Brennan, J., dissenting, expressed his "complete agreement with my Brother Black that no purpose for the investigation of Barenblatt is revealed by the record except exposure purely for the sake of exposure. This is not a purpose to which Barenblatt's rights under the First Amendment can validly be subordinated."]

Notes and Questions

1. *Compelling testimony vs. investigating.* Is the power of Congress to *compel testimony* in aid of legislation as broad as its power to *investigate* for this purpose. *Ought* it be? When Congress calls a hostile witness, is it concerned with this person's appraisal of the general problem or his advice? What does it contribute to legislative insight, how does it aid the consideration of general legislation, to call a witness who wishes to *conceal* some thing about his individual case or that of his friends? To "inventory the Communists in the United States one at a time"? Kalven, *Mr. Alexander Meiklejohn and the Barenblatt Opinion,* 27 U.Chi.L.Rev. 315, 327 (1960).

2. *"Balancing".* (a) In "balancing the interests," did *Barenblatt* adequately consider and weigh the *alternative methods* for achieving the investigative purpose? Did it consider the necessity of gathering the information sought by the Subcommittee in the particular way it attempted to obtain it from Barenblatt: by forcing him to disclose or deny Communist affiliation at a *public* hearing? See Kauper, *Civil Liberties and the Constitution* 121 (1962).

(b) What *are* the "interests" on either side that the Court must "balance"? Whatever they are, on what basis can a judge compare them qualitatively without some independent standard to which they can be referred? Does the "balancing process" make it more—or less—difficult for judges to rest on their predispositions? See Frantz, *The First Amendment in the Balance,* 71 Yale L.J. 1424 (1962).

3. *Fifth vs. first amendments.* *Barenblatt* points out that "the protections of the First Amendment, unlike a proper claim of the privilege against self-incrimination [do] not afford a witness the right to resist inquiry in all circumstances. Where First Amendment rights are asserted [the] issue *always* involves a balancing by the courts of the competing private and public interests at stake." (Emphasis added.) Why, when confronted by the same national danger must the fifth amendment always prevail over the care for national security, but the first amendment give way to it? Should the interest of a citizen, and of the nation, in freedom of speech and association be entitled to less weight than the interest of a private individual in his safety from self-incrimination? See Meiklejohn, *The Balancing of Self-Preservation Against Political Freedom,* 49 Calif.L.Rev. 4, 6–7 (1961).

4. *The "Equality Principle."* Although disclosure cases do not follow a uniform course, the Court has manifested more concern about the impact of disclosure on private associations than is exhibited in *Barenblatt.* It has been especially protective of the NAACP. Consider Karst, *Equality as a Central Principle in the First Amendment,* 43 U.Chi.L.Rev. 20, 42–43 (1975): "In the late 1950s, when the civil rights movement was gathering momentum in the South, public disclosure of one's membership in the NAACP typically was followed by annoyances [and] often by more tangible reprisals like being fired. In a series of

cases, the Court held that [government] could not constitutionally insist on such disclosure, either by the NAACP itself [a] or by individual members.[b]

"The governments' demands for information in these cases usually were presented for ostensibly neutral purposes. [The] Court, solemnly going along with the gag, took these asserted justifications at face value but concluded nonetheless that the required disclosures unconstitutionally invaded first amendment rights of political association.

"[The] Court's concern in these cases grows out of the first amendment's equality principle. If all the school teachers in Arkansas were to disclose their respective memberships in organizations, it is a safe bet that most Rotarians and Job's Daughters would not be greeted with heavy breathing when they answered the phone at night. The private harassment that concerned the Court was reserved for those associated with an unpopular challenge to the local orthodoxy. The point here is not simply that first amendment liberties normally matter most to underdogs; it is also that these decisions parallel one type of solution to the 'state action' problem that historically has plagued efforts to use the equal protection clause to protect individuals against private racial discrimination. In the disclosure cases, the state is seen as 'encouraging' private discrimination against those who espouse ideas with a particular content, even though the encouragement is embodied in a formally neutral law."

5. *Election disclosure requirements.* BROWN v. SOCIALIST WORKERS, 459 U.S. 87, 103 S.Ct. 416, 74 L.Ed.2d 250 (1982), per MARSHALL, J., held that an Ohio statute requiring every political party to report the names and addresses of campaign contributors and recipients of campaign disbursements could not be applied to the Socialist Workers Party. Citing *Buckley v. Valeo,* p. 772 infra, the Court held that the " 'evidence offered [by a minor party] need show only a reasonable probability that the compelled disclosure [of] names will subject them to threats, harassment, or reprisals from either Government officials or private parties.' " Consider Stone & Marshall, *Brown v. Socialist Workers: Inequality As A Command of the First Amendment,* 1983 Sup.Ct.Rev. 583, 592: "[I]n *Brown* the Court expressly exempted particular political parties from an otherwise content-neutral regulation for reasons directly related to the content of their expression. [The] constitutionally compelled exemption substitutes a content-based law for one that is content neutral. It stands the presumption in favor of

a. GIBSON v. FLORIDA LEG. INVESTIG. COMM., 372 U.S. 539, 83 S.Ct. 889, 9 L.Ed.2d 929 (1963), per GOLDBERG, J., reversed a Florida Supreme Court holding that the custodian of NAACP records could be compelled to bring membership lists to legislative hearings so that he could be forced to refer to them in determining whether individuals suspected as being communists were NAACP members. This could not be required said the Court without a substantial relation between the NAACP and "conduct in which the State may have a compelling regulatory concern." Because no substantial relation was shown, compelling the NAACP to disclose its membership presented "a question wholly different from compelling the Communist Party to disclose its own membership." HARLAN, J., joined by Clark, Stewart, and White, JJ., dissenting, complained that the Court had required "an investigating agency to prove in advance the very things it is trying to find out."

b. *Shelton v. Tucker,* 364 U.S. 479, 81 S.Ct. 247, 5 L.Ed.2d 231 (1960) held that teachers could not be required as a condition of employment to list all of the organizations they had belonged to or contributed to during the preceding five years. Professor Karst suggests that Barenblatt should have received the same hospitality. But what standard should govern? Should the Court endorse a general right not to speak? A right not to speak about political associations? Suppose, after a wave of racially motivated bombings, the leader of a white racist organization is called before a grand jury and asked to reveal the group's membership. What standard should govern?

'content neutrality' on its head." Is the decision, nonetheless, consistent with first amendment values? See Stone & Marshall, supra.

C. REPORTER'S PRIVILEGE

BRANZBURG v. HAYES

40 U.S. 665, 92 S.Ct. 2646, 33 L.Ed.2d 626 (1972).

MR. JUSTICE WHITE delivered the opinion of the Court.

[Branzburg, a Kentucky reporter, wrote articles describing his observations of local hashish-making and other drug violations. He refused to testify before a grand jury regarding his information. The state courts rejected his claim of a first amendment privilege.

[Pappas, a Massachusetts TV newsman-photographer, was allowed to enter and remain inside a Black Panther headquarters on condition he disclose nothing. When an anticipated police raid did not occur, he wrote no story. Summoned before a local grand jury, he refused to answer any questions about what had occurred inside the Panther headquarters or to identify those he had observed. The state courts denied his claim of a first amendment privilege.

[Caldwell, a N.Y. Times reporter covering the Black Panthers, was summoned to appear before a federal grand jury investigating Panther activities. A federal court issued a protective order providing that although he had to divulge information given him "for publication," he could withhold "confidential" information "developed or maintained by him as a professional journalist." Maintaining that absent a specific need for his testimony he should be excused from attending the grand jury altogether, Caldwell disregarded the order and was held in contempt. The Ninth Circuit reversed, holding that absent "compelling reasons" Caldwell could refuse even to attend the grand jury, because of the potential impact of such an appearance on the flow of news to the public.]

[Petitioners' first amendment claims] may be simply put: that to gather news it is often necessary to agree either not to identify [sources] or to publish only part of the facts revealed, or both; that if the reporter is nevertheless forced to reveal these confidences to a grand jury, the source so identified and other confidential sources of other reporters will be measurably deterred from furnishing publishable information, all to the detriment of the free flow of information protected by the First Amendment. Although petitioners do not claim an absolute privilege [they] assert that the reporter should not be forced either to appear or to testify before a grand jury or at trial until and unless sufficient grounds are shown for believing that the reporter possesses information relevant to a crime the grand jury is investigating, that the information the reporter has is unavailable from other sources, and that the need for the information is sufficiently compelling to override the claimed invasion of First Amendment interests occasioned by the disclosure. [The] heart of the claim is that the burden on news gathering resulting from compelling reporters to disclose confidential information outweighs any public interest in obtaining the information.

[We agree] that news gathering [qualifies] for First Amendment protection; without some protection for seeking out the news, freedom of the press could be eviscerated. But this case involves no intrusions upon speech [and no] command that the press publish what it prefers to withhold. [N]o penalty, civil or criminal, related to the content of published material is at issue here. The use of confidential sources by the press is not forbidden or restricted; reporters remain free to seek news from any source by means within the law. No attempt is made to require the press to publish its sources of information or indiscriminately to disclose them on request.

The sole issue before us is the obligation of reporters to respond to grand jury subpoenas as other citizens do and to answer questions relevant to an investigation into the commission of crime. The claim is, [that] reporters are exempt from [the average citizen's] obligations because if forced to respond to subpoenas and identify their sources or disclose other confidences, their informants will refuse or be reluctant to furnish newsworthy information in the future.

[T]he First Amendment does not guarantee the press a constitutional right of special access to information not available to the public generally. [Although] news gathering may be hampered, the press is regularly excluded from grand jury proceedings, our own conferences, the meetings of other official bodies gathered in executive session, and the meetings of private organizations. Newsmen have no constitutional right of access to the scenes of crime or disaster when the general public is excluded, and they may be prohibited from attending or publishing information about trials if such restrictions are necessary to assure a defendant a fair trial before an impartial tribunal. [It] is thus not surprising that the great weight of authority is that newsmen are not exempt from the normal duty of appearing before a grand jury and answering questions relevant to a criminal investigation.

[Because] its task is to inquire into the existence of possible criminal conduct and to return only well-founded indictments, [the grand jury's] investigative powers are necessarily broad. [T]he long standing principle that "the public has a right to every man's evidence," except for those persons protected by a constitutional, common law, or statutory privilege, is particularly applicable to grand jury proceedings.

A [minority] of States have provided newsmen a statutory privilege of varying breadth, [but] none has been provided by federal statute. [We decline to create one] by interpreting the First Amendment to grant newsmen a testimonial privilege that other citizens do not enjoy. [On] the records now before us, we perceive no basis for holding that the public interest in law enforcement and in ensuring effective grand jury proceedings is insufficient to override the consequential, but uncertain, burden on news gathering which is said to result from insisting that reporters, like other citizens, respond to relevant questions put to them in the course of a valid grand jury investigation or criminal trial.

This conclusion [does not] threaten the vast bulk of confidential relationships between reporters and their sources. Grand juries address themselves to the issues of whether crimes have been committed and who committed them. Only where news sources themselves are implicated in crime or possess information relevant to the grand jury's task need they or the reporter be concerned about grand jury subpoenas. Nothing before us indicates that a large number or percentage of *all* confidential news sources fall into either category and would in any way be deterred by [our holding].

It would be frivolous to assert—and no one does in these cases—that the First Amendment, in the interest of securing news or otherwise, confers a license on either the reporter or his news sources to violate otherwise valid criminal laws. [W]e cannot seriously entertain the notion that the First Amendment protects a newsman's agreement to conceal the criminal conduct of his source, or evidence thereof, on the theory that it is better to write about crime than to do something about [it.]

There remain those situations where a source is not engaged in criminal conduct but has information suggesting illegal conduct by others. [But] we remain unclear how often and to what extent informers are actually deterred from furnishing information when newsmen are forced to testify before a grand jury. The available data indicates that some newsmen rely a great deal on confidential sources and that some informants are particularly sensitive to the threat of exposure and may be silenced if it is held by this Court that, ordinarily, newsmen must testify pursuant to subpoenas, but the evidence fails to demonstrate that [our holding would cause] a significant constriction of the flow of news to the public * * *. Estimates of the inhibiting effect of such subpoenas on the willingness of informants to make disclosures to newsmen are widely divergent and to a great extent speculative. It would be difficult to canvass the views of the informants themselves; surveys of reporters on this topic are chiefly opinions of predicted informant behavior and must be viewed in the light of the professional self-interest of the interviewees.[33] Reliance by the press on confidential informants does not mean that all such sources will in fact dry up because of the later possible appearance of the newsman before a grand jury. The reporter may never be called and if he objects to testifying, the prosecution may not insist. Also, the relationship of many informants to the press is a symbiotic one which is unlikely to be greatly inhibited by the threat of subpoena: quite often, such informants are members of a minority political or cultural group which relies heavily on the media to propagate its views, publicize its aims, and magnify its exposure to the public. * * *

Accepting the fact, however, that an undetermined number of informants not themselves implicated in crime will nevertheless, for whatever reason, refuse to talk to newsmen if they fear identification by a reporter in an official investigation, we cannot accept the argument that the public interest in possible future news about crime from undisclosed, unverified sources must take precedence over the public interest in pursuing and prosecuting those crimes reported to the press by informants and in thus deterring the commission of such crimes in the future.

[C]oncealment of crime and agreements to do so are not looked upon with favor. Such conduct deserves no encomium, and we decline now to afford it First Amendment [protection].

We are admonished that refusal to provide a First Amendment reporter's privilege will undermine the freedom of the press to collect and disseminate news. But this is not the lesson history teaches us. [T]he common law recognized no such privilege, and the constitutional argument was not even asserted until 1958. From the beginning of our country the press has operated without constitutional protection for press informants, and the press has [flourished.]

The argument for [a] constitutional privilege rests heavily on those cases holding that the infringement of protected First Amendment rights must be no broader than necessary to achieve a permissible governmental purpose. We do not deal, however, with a governmental institution that has abused its proper

---

33. In his *Press Subpoenas: An Empirical and Legal Analysis* 6–12 (1971), Prof. Blasi discusses these methodological problems. [His] survey found that slightly more than half of the 975 reporters questioned said that they relied on regular confidential sources for at least 10% of their stories. Of this group of reporters, only 8% were able to say with some certainty that their professional functioning had been adversely affected by the threat of subpoena; another 11% were not certain whether or not they had been adversely affected. [See also Blasi, *The Newsman's Privilege: An Empirical Study,* 70 Mich.L.Rev. 229 (1971).]

function, as a legislative committee does when it "expose[s] for the sake of exposure." [Nor is there any] attempt here by the grand juries to invade protected First Amendment rights by forcing wholesale disclosure of names and organizational affiliations for a purpose which is not germane to the determination of whether crime has been committed, and the characteristic secrecy of grand jury proceedings is a further protection against the undue invasion of such rights. * * *

[The] requirements of those cases which hold that a State's interest must be "compelling" or "paramount" to justify even an indirect burden on First Amendment rights, are also met here. [If] the test is that the Government "convincingly show a substantial relation between the information sought and a subject of overriding and compelling state interest," *Gibson,* it is quite apparent (1) that the State has the necessary interest in extirpating the traffic in illegal drugs, in forestalling assassination attempts on the President, and in preventing the community from being disrupted by violent disorders endangering both persons and property; and (2) that, based on the stories Branzburg and Caldwell wrote and Pappas' admitted conduct, the grand jury called these reporters as they would others—because it was likely that they could supply information to help the Government determine whether illegal conduct had occurred and, if it had, whether there was sufficient evidence to return an indictment.

Similar considerations dispose of the reporters' claims that preliminary to requiring their grand jury appearance, the State must show that a crime has been committed and that they possess relevant information not available from other sources, for only the grand jury itself can make this determination. [A] grand jury investigation "is not fully carried out until every available clue has been run down and all witnesses examined in every proper way to find if a crime has been committed." * * *

[The] privilege claimed here is conditional, not absolute; given the suggested preliminary showings and compelling need, the reporter would be required to testify. [If] newsmen's confidential sources are as sensitive as they are claimed to be, the prospect of being unmasked whenever a judge determines the situation justifies it is hardly a satisfactory solution to the problem. For them, it would appear that only an absolute privilege would suffice.

We are unwilling to embark the judiciary on a long and difficult journey to such an uncertain destination. The administration of a constitutional newsman's privilege would present practical and conceptual difficulties of a high order. Sooner or later, it would be necessary to define those categories of newsmen who qualified for the privilege, a questionable procedure in light of the traditional doctrine that liberty of the press is the right of the lonely pamphleteer who uses carbon paper or a mimeograph just as much as of the large metropolitan publisher who utilizes the latest photocomposition methods. [The] informative function asserted by representatives of the organized press in the present cases is also performed by lecturers, political pollsters, novelists, academic researchers, and dramatists. Almost any author may quite accurately assert that he is contributing to the flow of information to the public, that he relies on confidential sources of information, and that these sources will be silenced if he is forced to make disclosures before a grand jury.

In each instance where a reporter is subpoenaed to testify, the courts would also be embroiled in preliminary factual and legal determinations with respect to whether the proper predicate had been laid for the reporters' appearance. [I]n the end, by considering whether enforcement of a particular law served a "compelling" governmental interest, the courts would be inextricably involved in distinguishing between the value of enforcing different criminal laws. By requiring testimony from a reporter in investigations involving some crimes but not in others, they would be making a value judgment which a legislature had declined to [make.]

At the federal level, Congress has freedom to determine whether a statutory newsman's privilege is necessary and desirable and to fashion standards and rules as narrow or broad as deemed necessary [and], equally important, to re-fashion those rules as experience from time to time may dictate. There is also merit in leaving state legislatures free, within First Amendment limits, to fashion their own standards in light of the conditions and problems with respect to the relations between law enforcement officials and press in their own areas.

* * *

In addition, there is much force in the pragmatic view that the press has at its disposal powerful mechanisms of communication and is far from helpless to protect itself from harassment or substantial harm. Furthermore, if what the newsmen urged in these cases is true—that law enforcement cannot hope to gain and may suffer from subpoenaing newsmen before grand juries—prosecutors will be loath to risk so much for so little. Thus, at the federal level the Attorney General has already fashioned a set of rules for federal officials in connection with subpoenaing members of the press to testify before grand juries or at criminal trials.[a] These rules are a major step in the direction petitioners desire to move. They may prove wholly sufficient to resolve the bulk of disagreements and controversies between press and federal officials.

[G]rand jury investigations if instituted or conducted other than in good faith, would pose wholly different issues for resolution under the First Amendment. Official harassment of the press undertaken not for purposes of law enforcement but to disrupt a reporter's relationship with his news sources would have no justification. Grand juries are subject to judicial control and subpoenas to motions to quash. We do not expect courts will forget that grand juries must operate within the limits of the First Amendment as well as the Fifth.

We turn, therefore, to the disposition of the cases before us. [*Caldwell*] must be reversed. If there is no First Amendment privilege to refuse to answer the relevant and material questions asked during a good-faith grand jury investigation, then it is a fortiori true that there is no privilege to refuse to appear before such a grand jury until the Government demonstrates some "compelling need" for a newsman's testimony. [*Branzburg*] must be affirmed. Here, petitioner refused to answer questions that directly related to criminal conduct which he had observed and written about. [If] what petitioner wrote was true, he had direct information to provide the grand jury concerning the commission of serious crimes. [In *Pappas*, we] affirm [and] hold that petitioner must appear before the grand jury to answer the questions put to him, subject, of course, to the supervision of the presiding judge as to "the propriety, purposes, and scope of the grand jury inquiry and the pertinence of the probable testimony."

MR. JUSTICE POWELL, concurring in the opinion of the Court.

---

a. The "Guidelines for Subpoenas to the News Media," noted the Court, recognize that "compulsory process in some circumstances may have a limiting effect on the exercise of First Amendment rights" and provide, inter alia, that that factor "must [be] weight[ed]" in every case against the public interest to be served in administering justice.

I add this brief statement to emphasize what seems to me to be the limited nature of the Court's holding. The Court does not hold that newsmen, subpoenaed to testify before a grand jury, are without constitutional rights with respect to the gathering of news or in safeguarding their sources. [As] indicated in the concluding portion of the opinion, the Court states that no harassment of newsmen will be tolerated. If a newsman believes that the grand jury investigation is not being conducted in good faith he is not without remedy. Indeed, if the newsman is called upon to give information bearing only a remote and tenuous relationship to the subject of the investigation, or if he has some other reason to believe that his testimony implicates confidential source relationships without a legitimate need of law enforcement, he will have access to the Court on a motion to quash and an appropriate protective order may be entered. The asserted claim to privilege should be judged on its facts by the striking of a proper balance between freedom of the press and the obligation of all citizens to give relevant testimony with respect to criminal conduct. The balance of these vital constitutional and societal interests on a case-by-case basis accords with the tried and traditional way of adjudicating such questions.*

In short, the courts will be available to newsmen under circumstances where legitimate First Amendment interests require protection.

MR. JUSTICE DOUGLAS, dissenting. * * *

It is my view that there is no "compelling need" that can be shown [by the Government] which qualifies the reporter's immunity from appearing or testifying before a grand jury, unless the reporter himself is implicated in a crime. His immunity in my view is therefore quite complete, for absent his involvement in a crime, the First Amendment protects him against an appearance before a grand jury and if he is involved in a crime, the Fifth Amendment stands as a barrier. Since in my view there is no area of inquiry not protected by a privilege, the reporter need not appear for the futile purpose of invoking one to each [question.]

Two principles which follow from [Alexander Meiklejohn's] understanding of the First Amendment are at stake here. One is that the people, the ultimate governors, must have absolute freedom of and therefore privacy of their individual opinions and beliefs regardless of how suspect or strange they may appear to others. Ancillary to that principle is the conclusion that an individual must also have absolute privacy over whatever information he may generate in the course of testing his opinions and beliefs. In this regard, Caldwell's status as a reporter is less relevant than is his status as a student who affirmatively pursued empirical research to enlarge his own intellectual viewpoint. The second principle is that effective self-government cannot succeed unless the people are immersed in a steady, robust, unimpeded, and uncensored flow of opinion and reporting which are continuously subjected to critique, rebuttal, and re-examina-

---

* It is to be remembered that Caldwell asserts a constitutional privilege not even to appear before the grand jury unless a court decides that the government has made a showing that meets the three preconditions specified in [Stewart, J.'s dissent]. To be sure, this would require a "balancing" of interests by the Court, but under circumstances and constraints significantly different from the balancing that will be appropriate under the Court's decision. The newsman witness, like all other witnesses, will have to appear; he will not be in a position to litigate at the threshold the State's very authority to subpoena him. Moreover, absent the constitutional preconditions that [the dissent] would impose as heavy burdens of proof to be carried by the State, the court—when called upon to protect a newsman from improper or prejudicial questioning—would be free to balance the competing interests on their merits in the particular case. The new constitutional rule endorsed by [the dissent] would, as a practical matter, defeat such a fair balancing and the essential societal interest in the detection and prosecution of crime would be heavily subordinated.

tion. In this respect, Caldwell's status as a newsgatherer and an integral part of that process becomes critical. * * *

Sooner or later any test which provides less than blanket protection to beliefs and associations will be twisted and relaxed so as to provide virtually no protection at all. [A] compelling interest test may prove as pliable as did the clear and present danger test. Perceptions of the worth of state objectives will change with the composition of the Court and with the intensity of the politics of the [times.]

Today's decision will impede the wide open and robust dissemination of ideas and counterthought which a free press both fosters and protects and which is essential to the success of intelligent self-government. Forcing a reporter before a grand jury [will lead] dissidents to communicate less openly to trusted reporters [and] cause editors and critics to write with more restrained pens. * * *

MR. JUSTICE STEWART, with whom MR. JUSTICE BRENNAN and MR. JUSTICE MARSHALL join, dissenting.

The Court's crabbed view of the First Amendment reflects a disturbing insensitivity to the critical role of an independent press in our society. [While] Mr. Justice Powell's enigmatic concurring opinion gives some hope of a more flexible view in the future, the Court in these cases holds that a newsman has no First Amendment right to protect his sources when called before a grand jury. The Court thus invites state and federal authorities to undermine the historic independence of the press by attempting to annex the journalistic profession as an investigative arm of government. Not only will this decision impair performance of the press' constitutionally protected functions, but it will, I am convinced, in the long run, harm rather than help the administration of justice.

[As] private and public aggregations of power burgeon in size and the pressures for conformity necessarily mount, there is obviously a continuing need for an independent press to disseminate a robust variety of information and opinion through reportage, investigation and criticism, if we are to preserve our constitutional tradition of maximizing freedom of choice by encouraging diversity of expression. * * *

A corollary of the right to publish must be the right to gather news. [This right] implies, in turn, a right to a confidential relationship between a reporter and his source. This proposition follows as a matter of simple logic once three factual predicates are recognized: (1) newsmen require informants to gather news; (2) confidentiality—the promise or understanding that names or certain aspects of communications will be kept off-the-record—is essential to the creation and maintenance of a news-gathering relationship with informants; and (3) the existence of an unbridled subpoena power—the absence of a constitutional right protecting, in *any* way, a confidential relationship from compulsory process—will either deter sources from divulging information or deter reporters from gathering and publishing information. * * *

After today's decision, the potential informant can never be sure that his identity or off-the-record communications will not subsequently be revealed through the compelled testimony of a newsman. A public spirited person inside government, who is not implicated in any crime, will now be fearful of revealing corruption or other governmental wrong-doing, because he will now know he can subsequently be identified by use of compulsory process. The potential source must, therefore, choose between risking exposure by giving information or avoiding the risk by remaining silent.

The reporter must speculate about whether contact with a controversial source or publication of controversial material will lead to a subpoena. In the event of a subpoena, under today's decision, the newsman will know that he must choose between being punished for contempt if he refuses to testify, or violating his profession's ethics [10] and impairing his resourcefulness as a reporter if he discloses confidential information. ＊ ＊ ＊

The impairment of the flow of news cannot, of course, be proven with scientific precision, as the Court seems to demand. [But] we have never before demanded that First Amendment rights rest on elaborate empirical studies demonstrating beyond any conceivable doubt that deterrent effects exist; we have never before required proof of the exact number of people potentially affected by governmental action, who would actually be dissuaded from engaging in First Amendment activity.

Rather, on the basis of common sense and available information, we have asked, often implicitly, (1) whether there was a rational connection between the cause (the governmental action) and the effect (the deterrence or impairment of First Amendment activity) and (2) whether the effect would occur with some regularity, i.e., would not be de minimus. And, in making this determination, we have shown a special solicitude towards the "indispensable liberties" protected by the First Amendment, *NAACP v. Alabama,* for "freedoms such as these are protected not only against heavy-handed frontal attack, but also from being stifled by more subtle government interference." Once this threshold inquiry has been satisfied, we have then examined the competing interests in determining whether there is an unconstitutional infringement of First Amendment freedoms. ＊ ＊ ＊

Surely the analogous claim of deterrence here is as securely grounded in evidence and common sense as the claims in [such cases as *NAACP v. Alabama*], although the Court calls the claim "speculative." [To] require any greater burden of proof is to shirk our duty to protect values securely embedded in the Constitution. We cannot await an unequivocal—and therefore unattainable— imprimatur from empirical studies. We can and must accept the evidence developed in the record, and elsewhere, that overwhelmingly supports the premise that deterrence will occur with regularity in important types of news-gathering relationships. Thus, we cannot escape the conclusion that when neither the reporter nor his source can rely on the shield of confidentiality against unrestrained use of the grand jury's subpoena power, valuable information will not be published and the public dialogue will inevitably be impoverished.

[A]ny exemption from the duty to testify before the grand jury "presupposes a very real interest to be protected." Such an interest must surely be the First Amendment protection of a confidential relationship. [This protection] functions to insure nothing less than democratic decisionmaking through the free flow of information to the public, and it serves, thereby, to honor the "profound national commitment to the principle that debate on public issues should be uninhibited, robust and wideopen." *New York Times v. Sullivan.*

[W]hen an investigation impinges on First Amendment rights, the government must not only show that the inquiry is of "compelling and overriding importance" but it must also "convincingly" demonstrate that the investigation

---

10. The American Newspaper Guild has adopted the following rule as part of the newsman's code of ethics: "Newspaper men shall refuse to reveal confidences or disclose sources of confidential information in court or before other judicial or investigative bodies."

is "substantially related" to the information sought. Governmental officials must, therefore, demonstrate that the information sought is *clearly* relevant to a *precisely* defined subject of governmental inquiry. They must demonstrate that it is reasonable to think the witness in question has that information. And they must show that there is not any means of obtaining the information less destructive of First Amendment liberties. * * *

I believe the safeguards developed in our decisions involving governmental investigations must apply to the grand jury inquiries in these cases. Surely the function of the grand jury to aid in the enforcement of the law is no more important than the function of the legislature, and its committees, to make the law. [T]he vices of vagueness and overbreadth which legislative investigations may manifest are also exhibited by grand jury inquiries, since grand jury investigations are not limited in scope to specific criminal acts.

[Thus,] when a reporter is asked to appear before a grand jury and reveal confidences, I would hold that the government must (1) show that there is probable cause to believe that the newsman has information which is clearly relevant to a specific probable violation of law; (2) demonstrate that the information sought cannot be obtained by alternative means less destructive of First Amendment rights; and (3) demonstrate a compelling and overriding interest in the information. * * *

The crux of the Court's rejection of any newsman's privilege is its observation that only "where news sources themselves are implicated in crime or possess information *relevant* to the grand jury's task need they or the reporter be concerned about grand jury subpoenas." (emphasis supplied). But this is a most misleading construct. [G]iven the grand jury's extraordinarily broad investigative powers and the weak standards of relevance and materiality that apply during such inquiries, reporters, if they have no testimonial privilege, will be called to give information about informants who have neither committed crimes nor have information about crime. It is to avoid deterrence of such sources and thus to prevent needless injury to First Amendment values that I think the government must be required to show probable cause that the newsman has information which is clearly relevant to a specific probable violation of criminal law. * * *

Both the "probable cause" and "alternative means" requirements [would] serve the vital function of mediating between the public interest in the administration of justice and the constitutional protection of the full flow of information. These requirements would avoid a direct conflict between these competing concerns, and they would generally provide adequate protection for newsmen.[35] No doubt the courts would be required to make some delicate judgments in working out this accommodation. But that, after all, is the function of courts of law. Better such judgments, however difficult, than the simplistic and stultifying absolutism adopted by the Court in denying any force to the First Amendment in these cases.[36]

[I]n the name of advancing the administration of justice, the Court's decision, I think, will only impair the achievement of that goal. People entrusted

35. We need not, therefore, reach the question of whether government's interest in these cases is "overriding and compelling." I do not, however, believe, as the Court does, that *all* grand jury investigations automatically would override the newsman's testimonial privilege.

36. The disclaimers in Mr. Justice Powell's concurring opinion leave room for the hope that in some future case the Court may take a less absolute position in this area.

with law enforcement responsibility, no less than private citizens, need general information relating to controversial social problems. [W]hen a grand jury may exercise an unbridled subpoena power, and sources involved in sensitive matters become fearful of disclosing information, the newsman will not only cease to be a useful grand jury witness; he will cease to investigate and publish information about issues of public import.

[In Stewart, J.'s view, the Ninth Circuit correctly ruled that in the circumstances of the case, Caldwell need not divulge confidential information and, moreover, that in this case Caldwell had established that "his very appearance [before] the grand jury would jeopardize his relationship with his sources, leading to a severance of the news gathering relationship and impairment of the flow of news to the public." But because "only in very rare circumstances would a confidential relationship between a reporter and his source be so sensitive [as to preclude] his mere appearance before the grand jury," Stewart, J., would confine "*this* aspect of the *Caldwell* judgment [to] its own facts." Thus, he would affirm in *Caldwell* and remand the other cases for further proceedings not inconsistent with his views.]

Notes and Questions

1. *The role of the press.* Consider Blasi, *The Checking Value in First Amendment Theory,* 1977 Am.B.Found.Res.J. 521, 593: The White, J., opinion "characterized the press as a private-interest group rather than an institution with a central function to perform in the constitutional system of checks and balances [and] labeled the source relationships that the reporters sought to maintain 'a private system of informers operated by the press to report on criminal conduct' [cautioning] that this system would be 'unaccountable to the public' were a reporter's privilege to be recognized." In contrast to White, J.'s perspective, consider the remarks of Stewart, J., in a much-discussed address, *"Or of the Press,"* 26 Hast.L.J. 631, 634 (1975): "In setting up the three branches of the Federal Government, the Founders deliberately created an internally competitive [b] system. [The] primary purpose [c] of [the Free Press Clause] was a similar one: to create a fourth institution outside the Government as an additional check on the three official branches." [d] Proceeding from variations of this fourth estate view of the press, most commentators endorse a reporter's privilege. See, e.g.,[e] Baker, *Press Rights and Government Power to Structure the*

b. For commentary on how the "cozy connections" between press and government demonstrate that the relationship is often more cooperative than adversarial, see Soifer, *Freedom of the Press in the United States* in Press Law in Modern Democracies 79, 108–110 (Lahav, ed., 1985).

c. For spirited debate about the historical evidence, compare Anderson, *The Origins of the Press Clause,* 30 U.C.L.A.L.Rev. 455 (1983) with Levy, *On the Origins of the Free Press Clause,* 32 U.C.L.A.L.Rev. 177 (1984). See generally Levy, *Emergence of a Free Press* (1985).

d. For Brennan, J.'s views, see *Address,* 32 Rutg.L.Rev. 173 (1979).

e. For criticism of the notion of an independent press clause, see Lange, *The Speech and Press Clauses,* 23 U.C.L.A.L.Rev. 77 (1975); Lewis, *A Preferred Position for Jour-*

nalism?, 7 Hof.L.Rev. 595 (1979); Van Alstyne, *The First Amendment and the Free Press: A Comment on Some New Trends and Some Old Theories,* 9 Hof.L.Rev. 1 (1980); Van Alstyne, *The Hazards to the Press of Claiming a "Preferred Position",* 28 Hast.L.J. 761 (1977). But see Abrams, *The Press is Different: Reflections on Justice Stewart and the Autonomous Press,* 7 Hof.L.Rev. 563 (1979). For an effort to transcend the issues involved, see generally Sack, *Reflections on the Wrong Question: Special Constitutional Privilege for the Institutional Press,* 7 Hof.L.Rev. 629 (1979). Finally, for commentary on the "tension between journalism as the political, sometimes partisan fourth estate and journalism as a profession" purporting to operate as a "neutral and objective medium," see Lahav, *An Outline for a General Theory of Press Law in Democracy* in Press Law in Modern Democra-

Press, 34 U.Miami L.Rev. 819, 858 (1980) (absolute protection). But see Bezanson, *The New Free Press Guarantee,* 63 Va.L.Rev. 731, 759–62 (1977) (press clause prevents special governmental assistance for press). Claims for an independent press-clause, however, need not interpret the press clause along fourth estate lines, see *Nimmer on Freedom of Speech* 2–104—2–129 (1984).

2. Whatever role is assigned to the press, are press relationships with confidential sources not entitled to at least the same protections afforded to civil rights groups and minority parties? Does *Branzburg* exhibit insensitivity to free speech values? Consider Blasi, note 1 supra, at 593: Two of the journalists before the Court "were covering the Black Panther Party, [which] claimed to be the victim of an official nationwide policy of persecution and extermination. Yet the White opinion made no reference to the speech value of news about possible official misbehavior obtained from persons against whom abuses of power may have been directed. Instead, Justice White spoke only of the criminal activities of the sources themselves and their peers, and denigrated the speech value at stake as that in 'possible future news about crime from undisclosed, unverified sources.' "

3. *Evaluating Powell, J.'s concurrence.* Did five justices—or only four—hold that grand juries may pursue their goals by any means short of bad faith? May one conclude that the information sought bears "only a remote and tenuous relationship to the subject of investigation" on grounds falling short of demonstrating "bad faith"? Does Powell, J.'s suggested test—the privilege claim "should be judged on its facts by [balancing the] vital constitutional and societal interests on a case-by-case basis"—resemble Stewart, J.'s dissenting approach more than White, J.'s? Extrajudicially, Stewart, J., has referred to *Branzburg* as a case which rejected claims for a journalist's privilege "by a vote of 5–4, or, considering Mr. Justice Powell's concurring opinion, perhaps by a vote of 4½–4½." Stewart, *"Or of the Press,"* 26 Hast.L.J. 631, 635 (1975). The majority of courts applying *Branzburg* have concluded that Powell, J.'s opinion read together with the dissents affords the basis for a qualified privilege. Among the issues litigated are whether the privilege should be confined to journalists (or extended e.g. to academics) and the related question of how to define journalists and whether the privilege belongs to the source, the reporter, or both. For an exhaustive survey, see Goodale, Moodhe & Imes, *Reporter's Privilege Cases* in Communications Law 1984, at 339 (1984).

4. *Other contexts.* Does *Branzburg's* emphasis on the grand jury's special role in the American criminal justice system warrant different treatment of the journalist's privilege when a prosecutor seeks disclosure? See Murasky, *The Journalist's Privilege: Branzburg and Its Aftermath,* 52 Tex.L.Rev. 829, 885 (1974). Are the interests of civil litigants in compelling disclosure of a journalist's confidences significantly weaker than those of criminal litigants? Should there be an absolute journalist's privilege in civil discovery proceedings? See id. at 898–903. What if the journalist is a party to the litigation?

5. *State "shield laws" and a criminal defendant's right to compulsory process.* As of 1984, 26 states had enacted "shield" laws. Some protect only journalists' sources; some (including New Jersey) protect undisclosed informa-

cies 339, 352–54 (Lahav ed. 1985). See also Bollinger, *The Press and the Public Interest: An Essay on the Relationship Between Social Behavior and the Language of First Amendment Theory,* 82 Mich.L.Rev. 1447, 1457 (1984) (commenting generally on the pitfalls connect-

ed with justifying a free press by arguing that it serves the public interest: "More than most groups (compare lawyers, for example) the press is in conflict over its relationship to the world on which it regularly reports.").

tion obtained in the course of a journalist's professional activities as well as sources. See Goodale, Moodhe & Imes, note 3 supra.

In re Farber, 78 N.J. 259, 394 A.2d 330 (1978), cert. denied, 439 U.S. 997, 99 S.Ct. 598, 58 L.Ed.2d 670 (1978): *New York Times* investigative reporter Myron Farber wrote a series of articles claiming that an unidentified "Doctor X" had caused the death of several patients by poisoning. This led to the indictment and eventual prosecution of Dr. Jascalevich for murder. (He was ultimately acquitted.) In response to the defendant's request, the trial court demanded the disclosure of Farber's sources and the production of his interview notes and other information for his in camera inspection. Relying on the first amendment and the state shield law, Farber refused to comply with the subpoenas. After White, J., and then Marshall, J., had denied stays, each deeming it unlikely that four justices would grant certiorari at this stage of the case, Farber was jailed for civil contempt and the *Times* heavily fined.

The state supreme court (5–2) upheld civil and criminal convictions of the *Times* and Farber. Under the circumstances, it ruled, the first amendment did not protect Farber against disclosure. Nor did the New Jersey shield law, for Farber's statutory rights had to yield to Dr. Jascalevich's sixth amendment right "to have compulsory process for obtaining witnesses in his favor." [e]

ZURCHER v. STANFORD DAILY, 436 U.S. 547, 98 S.Ct. 1970, 56 L.Ed.2d 525 (1978), again declined to afford the press special protection—dividing very much as in *Branzburg.*[a] A student newspaper that had published articles and photographs of a clash between demonstrators and police brought this federal action, claiming that a search of its offices for film and pictures showing events at the scene of the police-demonstrators clash (the newspaper was not involved in the unlawful acts) had violated its first and fourth amendment rights. A 5–3 majority, per WHITE, J., held that the fourth amendment does not prevent the government from issuing a search warrant (based on reasonable cause to believe that the "things" to be searched for are located on the property) simply because the owner or possessor of the place to be searched is not reasonably suspected of criminal involvement. The Court also rejected the argument that "whatever may be true of third-party searches generally, where the third party is a newspaper, there are additional [first amendment factors justifying] a nearly per se rule forbidding the search warrant and permitting only the subpoena duces tecum. The general submission is that searches of newspaper offices for evidence of crime reasonably believed to be on the premises will seriously threaten the ability of the press to gather, analyze, and disseminate news.

"[Although] [a]ware of the long struggle between Crown and press and desiring to curb unjustified official intrusions, [the Framers] did not forbid warrants where the press was involved, did not require special showing that subpoenas would be impractical, and did not insist that the owner of the place to

---

e. For an exhaustive analysis of the case, see Note, 32 Rutg.L.Rev. 545 (1979). The case is also discussed at length by *New York Times* columnist Anthony Lewis, *A Preferred Position for Journalism?*, 7 Hof.L.Rev. 595, 610–18 (1979). See also Nowak, Rotunda & Young, *Constitutional Law* 912–13 (2d ed. 1983); Tribe, *American Constitutional Law* 73–74 n. 88 (1979 Supp.)

a. In both cases, White, J., joined by Burger, C.J., Blackmun, Powell and Rehnquist,

JJ., delivered the opinion of the Court and in both cases the "fifth vote"—Powell, J.,—also wrote a separate opinion which seemed to meet the concerns of the dissent part way. In both cases Stewart, J., dissented, maintaining that the Court's holding would seriously impair "newsgathering." Stevens, J., who had replaced Douglas, J., also dissented in *Zurcher,* as had Douglas in *Branzburg.* Brennan, J., who had joined Stewart, J.'s dissent in *Branzburg,* did not participate in *Zurcher.*

be searched, if connected with the press, must be shown to be implicated in the offense being investigated. Further, the prior cases do no more than insist that the courts apply the warrant requirements with particular exactitude when First Amendment interests would be endangered by the search. [N]o more than this is required where the warrant requested is for the seizure of criminal evidence reasonably believed to be on the premises occupied by a newspaper. Properly administered, the preconditions for a warrant—probable cause, specificity [as to] place [and] things to be seized and overall reasonableness—should afford [the press] sufficient protection * * *.

"[R]espondents and amici have pointed to only a very few instances [since] 1971 involving [newspaper office searches]. This reality hardly suggests abuse, and if abuse occurs, there will be time enough to deal with it. Furthermore, the press [is] not easily intimidated—nor should it be."

POWELL, J., concurring, rejected Stewart, J.'s dissenting view that the press is entitled to "a special procedure, not available to others," when the government requires evidence in its possession, but added: "This is not to say [that a warrant] sufficient to support the search of an apartment or an automobile would be reasonable in supporting the search of a newspaper office. [While] there is no justification for the establishment of a separate Fourth Amendment procedure for the press, a magistrate asked to issue a warrant for the search of press offices can and should take cognizance of the independent values protected by the First Amendment—such as those highlighted by [Stewart, J., dissenting]—when he weighs such factors." [b]

STEWART, joined by Marshall, J., dissented: "A search warrant allows police officers to ransack the files of a newspaper, reading each and every document until they have found the one named in the warrant, while a subpoena would permit the newspaper itself to produce only the specific documents requested. A search, unlike a subpoena, will therefore lead to the needless exposure of confidential information completely unrelated to the purpose of the investigation. The knowledge that police officers can make an unannounced raid on a newsroom is thus bound to have a deterrent effect on the availability of confidential news sources. [The result] will be a diminishing flow of potentially important information to the public.

"[Here, unlike Branzburg, the newspaper does] not claim that any of the evidence sought was privileged [, but] only that a subpoena would have served equally well to produce that evidence. Thus, we are not concerned with the principle, central to Branzburg, that ' "the public [has] a right to everyman's evidence," ' but only with whether any significant social interest would be impaired if the police were generally required to obtain evidence from the press by means of a subpoena rather than a search. * * *

"Perhaps as a matter of abstract policy a newspaper office should receive no more protection from unannounced police searches than, say, the office of a doctor or the office of a bank. But we are here to uphold a Constitution. And our Constitution does not explicitly protect the practice of medicine or the business of banking from all abridgement by government. It does explicitly protect the freedom of the press." [c]

b. Powell, J., noted that his Branzburg concurrence may "properly be read as supporting the view expressed in the text above, and in the Court's [Zurcher] opinion," that under the warrant requirement "the magistrate should consider the values of a free press

as well as the societal interest in enforcing the criminal laws."

c. Stevens, J., dissented on the general fourth amendment issue.

Notes and Questions

1. The distinctions between search and subpoena are underscored in Tribe, *American Constitutional Law* 73–75 (1979 Supp.): "When a subpoena is served on the media, it has the opportunity to assert whatever constitutional and statutory rights [such as 'shield laws,' enacted in many states, protecting reporters from divulging information given them in confidence] the press may invoke to keep confidential the information it has gathered. Such protection is circumvented when officials can proceed *ex parte,* by search warrant. And the risk of abuse may be greatest exactly when the press plays its most vital and creative role in our political system, the role of watchdog on official corruption and abuse. Officials who find themselves the targets [of] media investigation may use *Zurcher* as an excuse for conducting searches aimed at finding out precisely what various journalists have discovered, to retaliate against [those] who have unearthed and reported official wrongdoing."

2. The difficulty in identifying suspects at the early stages of a criminal investigation, relied on by the *Zurcher* majority, does not, maintains Note, 92 Harv.L.Rev. 206–07 (1978), "require that the court refuse to adopt a special rule for those *classes* of witnesses who are so unlikely to destroy evidence as to deserve special protection from third party searches. [One reasonable approach] would be a narrow rule favoring the use of the subpoena only when the material is sought from neutral observers who possess evidence specifically because of the nature of their work, such as journalists, doctors, lawyers and accountants. Such parties are relatively easy to identify and are extremely unlikely to be either culpable or sympathetic to those who are culpable."

Is the clear message of both *Branzburg* and *Zurcher,* however, that the Court "perceives as peculiarly within the competence of legislative bodies the task of revising ordinary [criminal procedures] to account for communicative values"? See Tribe, supra, at 75.[d]

SECTION 10. WEALTH AND THE POLITICAL PROCESS: CONCERNS FOR EQUALITY

The idea of equality has loomed large throughout this chapter. Some feel it should be a central concern of the first amendment. See Tribe, *Constitutional Choices* 188–220 (1985); Karst, *Equality as a Central Principle in the First Amendment,* 43 U.Chi.L.Rev. 20 (1975). Equality has been championed by those who seek access to government property and to media facilities. It has been invoked in support of content regulation and against it. This section considers government efforts to prevent the domination of the political process by wealthy individuals and business corporations. In the end, it would be appropriate to reconsider the arguments for and against a marketplace conception of the first amendment, to ask whether the Court's interpretations overall (e.g., taking the public forum materials, the media materials, and the election materials together) have adequately considered the interest in equality, and to inquire generally about the relationship between liberty and equality in the constitutional scheme.

---

d. For discussion of executive and legislative response to *Zurcher,* see Goodale, Moodhe, and Imes, note 3 supra after *Branzburg,* at 375–77. In particular, see The Privacy Protection Act of 1980, 42 U.S.C. §§ 2000aa–2000aa–12 (limiting the impact of *Zurcher* on the media).

BUCKLEY v. VALEO

424 U.S. 1, 96 S.Ct. 612, 46 L.Ed.2d 659 (1976).

PER CURIAM.

[In this portion of a lengthy opinion dealing with the validity of the Federal Election Campaign Act of 1971, as amended in 1974, the Court considers those parts of the Act limiting *contributions* to a candidate for federal office (all sustained), and those parts limiting *expenditures* in support of such candidacy (all held invalid).[a]]

A. *General Principles.* The Act's contribution and expenditure limitations operate in an area of the most fundamental First Amendment activities. Discussion of public issues and debate on the qualifications of candidates are integral to the operation of the system of government established by our Constitution.

[Appellees] contend that what the Act regulates is conduct, and that its effect on speech and association is incidental at most. Appellants respond that contributions and expenditures are at the very core of political speech, and that the Act's limitations thus constitute restraints on First Amendment liberty that are both gross and [direct.]

We cannot share the view [that] the present Act's contribution and expenditure limitations are comparable to the restrictions on conduct upheld in *O'Brien* [p. 621 supra]. The expenditure of money simply cannot be equated with such conduct as destruction of a draft card. Some forms of communication made possible by the giving and spending of money involve speech alone, some involve conduct primarily, and some involve a combination of the two. Yet this Court has never suggested that the dependence of a communication on the expenditure of money operates itself to introduce a non-speech element or to reduce the exacting scrutiny required by the First Amendment. * * *

Even if the categorization of the expenditure of money as conduct were accepted, the limitations challenged here would not meet the *O'Brien* test because the governmental interests advanced in support of the Act involve "suppressing communication." The interests served by the Act include restricting the voices of people and interest groups who have money to spend and reducing the overall scope of federal election campaigns. [Unlike] *O'Brien*, where [the] interest in the preservation of draft cards was wholly unrelated to their use as a means of communication, it is beyond dispute that the interest in regulating the alleged "conduct" of giving or spending money "arises in some measure because the communication allegedly integral to the conduct is itself thought to be harmful."

Nor can the Act's contribution and expenditure limitations be sustained, as some of the parties suggest, by reference to the constitutional principles reflected in such decisions as *Cox v. Louisiana, Adderley,* and *Kovacs,* [Secs. 6, II and 8 supra]. [The] critical difference between this case and those time, place and manner cases is that the present Act's contribution and expenditure limitations impose direct quantity restrictions on political communication and association by persons, groups, candidates and political parties in addition to any reasonable time, place, and manner regulations otherwise imposed.

---

a. Other aspects of *Buckley* are briefly considered in Sec. 6, I supra (public funding); Sec. 9, IV supra (disclosure).

A restriction on the amount of money a person or group can spend on political communication during a campaign necessarily reduces the quantity of expression by restricting the number of issues discussed, the depth of their exploration, and the size of the audience reached. This is because virtually every means of communicating ideas in today's mass society requires the expenditure of [money].

The expenditure limitations contained in the Act represent substantial rather than merely theoretical restraints on the quantity and diversity of political speech. The $1,000 ceiling on spending "relative to a clearly identified candidate," 18 U.S.C. § 608(e)(1), would appear to exclude all citizens and groups except candidates, political parties and the institutional press from any significant use of the most effective modes of communication.[20] * * *

By contrast with a limitation upon expenditures for political expression, a limitation [on] the amount of money a person may give to a candidate or campaign organization [involves] little direct restraint on his political communication, for it permits the symbolic expression of support evidenced by a contribution but does not in any way infringe the contributor's freedom to discuss candidates and issues. While contributions may result in political expression if spent by a candidate or an association to present views to the voters, the transformation of contributions into political debate involves speech by someone other than the contributor.

[There] is no indication [that] the contribution limitations imposed by the Act would have any dramatic adverse effect on the funding of campaigns and political associations.[23] The overall effect of the Act's contribution ceilings is merely to require candidates and political committees to raise funds from a greater number of persons and to compel people who would otherwise contribute amounts greater than the statutory limits to expend such funds on direct political expression, rather than to reduce the total amount of money potentially available to promote political expression. * * *

In sum, although the Act's contribution and expenditure limitations both implicate fundamental First Amendment interests, its expenditure ceilings impose significantly more severe restrictions on protected freedoms of political expression and association than do its limitations on financial contributions.

B. *Contribution Limitations.* [Section] 608(b) provides, with certain limited exceptions, that "no person shall make contributions to any candidate with respect to any election for Federal office which, in the aggregate, exceeds $1,000." [b] * * *

---

20. The record indicates that, as of January 1, 1975, one full-page advertisement in a daily edition of a certain metropolitan newspaper costs $6,971.04—almost seven times the annual limit on expenditures "relative to" a particular candidate imposed on the vast majority of individual citizens and associations by § 608(e)(1).

23. Statistical findings agreed to by the parties reveal that approximately 5.1% of the $73,483,613 raised by the 1161 candidates for Congress in 1974 was obtained in amounts in excess of $1,000. In 1974, two major-party senatorial candidates, Ramsey Clark and Senator Charles Mathias, Jr., operated large-scale campaigns on contributions raised under a voluntarily imposed $100 contribution limitation.

b. As defined, "person" includes "an individual, partnership, committee, association, corporation or any other organization or group." The limitation applies to: (1) anything of value, such as gifts, loans, advances, and promises to give, (2) contributions made direct to the candidate or to an intermediary, or a committee authorized by the candidate, (3) the aggregate amounts contributed to the candidate for each election, treating primaries, run-off elections and general elections separately and all Presidential primaries within a single calendar year as one election.

Appellants contend that the $1,000 contribution ceiling unjustifiably burdens First Amendment freedoms, employs overbroad dollar limits, and discriminates against candidates opposing incumbent officeholders and against minor-party candidates in violation of the Fifth Amendment.

[In] view of the fundamental nature of the right to associate, governmental "action which may have the effect of curtailing the freedom to associate is subject to the closest scrutiny." Yet, it is clear that "[n]either the right to associate nor the right to participate in political activities is absolute." *Letter Carriers* [p. 734 supra]. Even a " 'significant interference' with protected rights of political association" may be sustained if the State demonstrates a sufficiently important interest and employs means closely drawn to avoid unnecessary abridgment of associational freedoms. * * *

It is unnecessary to look beyond the Act's primary purpose—to limit the actuality and appearance of corruption resulting from large individual financial contributions—in order to find a constitutionally sufficient justification for the $1,000 contribution limitation. [The] increasing importance of the communications media and sophisticated mass mailing and polling operations to effective campaigning make the raising of large sums of money an ever more essential ingredient of an effective candidacy. To the extent that large contributions are given to secure political quid pro quos from current and potential office holders, the integrity of our system of representative democracy is undermined. Although the scope of such pernicious practices can never be reliably ascertained, the deeply disturbing examples surfacing after the 1972 election demonstrate that the problem is not an illusory one.

Of almost equal concern as the danger of actual quid pro quo arrangements is the impact of the appearance of corruption stemming from public awareness of the opportunities for abuse inherent in a regime of large individual financial contributions. In *Letter Carriers,* the Court found that the danger to "fair and effective government" posed by partisan political conduct on the part of federal employees charged with administering the law was a sufficiently important concern to justify broad restrictions on the employees' right of partisan political association. Here, as there, Congress could legitimately conclude that the avoidance of the appearance of improper influence "is also critical [if] confidence in the system of representative Government is not to be eroded to a disastrous extent." [29]

Appellants contend that the contribution limitations must be invalidated because bribery laws and narrowly-drawn disclosure requirements constitute a less restrictive means of dealing with "proven and suspected quid pro quo arrangements." But laws [against] bribes deal with only the most blatant and specific attempts of those with money to influence governmental action. [And] Congress was surely entitled to conclude that disclosure was only a partial measure, and that contribution ceilings were a necessary legislative concomitant to deal with the reality or appearance of corruption inherent in a system permitting unlimited financial contributions, even when the identities of the contributors and the amounts of their contributions are fully disclosed.

The Act's $1,000 contribution limitation focuses precisely on the problem of large campaign contributions—the narrow aspect of political association where

---

29. Although the Court in *Letter Carriers* found that this interest was constitutionally sufficient to justify legislation prohibiting federal employees from engaging in certain partisan political activities, it was careful to emphasize that the limitations did not restrict an employee's right to express his views on political issues and candidates.

the actuality and potential for corruption have been identified—while leaving persons free to engage in independent political expression, to associate actively through volunteering their services. [The] Act's contribution limitations [do] not undermine to any material degree the potential for robust and effective discussion of candidates and campaign [issues].

We find that, under the rigorous standard of review established by our prior decisions, the weighty interests served by restricting the size of financial contributions to political candidates are sufficient to justify the limited effect upon First Amendment freedoms caused by the $1,000 contribution ceiling.[c]

C. *Expenditure Limitations.* [1.] Section 608(e)(1) provides that "[n]o person may make any expenditure [relative] to a clearly identified candidate during a calendar year which, when added to all other expenditures made by such person during the year advocating the election or defeat of such candidate, exceeds $1,000." [Its] plain effect [is] to prohibit all individuals, who are neither candidates nor owners of institutional press facilities, and all groups, except political parties and campaign organizations, from voicing their views "relative to a clearly identified candidate" through means that entail aggregate expenditures of more than $1,000 during a calendar year. The provision, for example, would make it a federal criminal offense for a person or association to place a single one-quarter page advertisement "relative to a clearly identified candidate" in a major metropolitan newspaper.

[Although] "expenditure," "clearly identified," and "candidate" are defined in the Act, there is no definition clarifying what expenditures are "relative to" a candidate. [But the "when" clause in § 608(e)(1)] clearly permits, if indeed it does not require, the phrase "relative to" a candidate to be read to mean "advocating the election or defeat of" a candidate.

But while such a construction of § 608(e)(1) refocuses the vagueness question, [it hardly] eliminates the problem of unconstitutional vagueness altogether. For the distinction between discussion of issues and candidates and advocacy of election or defeat of candidates may often dissolve in practical application. Candidates, especially incumbents, are intimately tied to public issues involving legislative proposals and governmental actions. Not only do candidates campaign on the basis of their positions on various public issues, but campaigns themselves generate issues of public interest.

[Constitutionally deficient uncertainty which "compels the speaker to hedge and trim"] can be avoided only by reading § 608(e)(1) as limited to communications that include explicit words of advocacy of election or defeat of a candidate,

c. The Court rejected the challenges that the $1,000 limit was overbroad because (1) most large contributors do not seek improper influence over a candidate, and (2) much more than $1,000 would still not be enough to influence improperly a candidate or office holder. With respect to (1), "Congress was justified in concluding that the interest in safeguarding against the appearance of impropriety requires that the opportunity for abuse inherent in the process of raising large monetary contributions be eliminated." With respect to (2), "As the Court of Appeals observed, '[a] court has no scalpel to probe, whether, say, a $2,000 ceiling might not serve as well as $1,000.' Such distinctions in degree become significant only when they can be said to amount to differences in kind."

The Court also rejected as without support in the record the claims that the contribution limitations worked invidious discrimination between incumbents and challengers to whom the same limitations applied.

The Court then upheld (1) exclusion from the $1,000 limit of the value of unpaid volunteer services and of certain expenses paid by the volunteer up to a maximum of $500; (2) the higher limit of $5,000 for contributions to a candidate by established, registered political committees with at least 50 contributing supporters and fielding at least five candidates for federal office; and (3) the $25,000 limit on total contributions to all candidates by one person in one calendar year.

much as the definition of "clearly identified" in § 608(e)(2) requires that an explicit and unambiguous reference to the candidate appear as part of the communication. This is the reading of the provision suggested by the non-governmental appellees in arguing that "[f]unds spent to propagate one's views on issues without expressly calling for a candidate's election or defeat are thus not covered." We agree that in order to preserve the provision against invalidation on vagueness grounds, § 608(e)(1) must be construed to apply only to expenditures for communications that in express terms advocate the election or defeat of a clearly identified candidate for federal office.

We turn then to the basic First Amendment question—whether § 608(e)(1), even as thus narrowly and explicitly construed, impermissibly burdens the constitutional right of free expression. * * *

We find that the governmental interest in preventing corruption and the appearance of corruption is inadequate to justify § 608(e)(1)'s ceiling on independent expenditures. First, assuming arguendo that large independent expenditures pose the same dangers of actual or apparent quid pro quo arrangements as do large contributions, § 608(e)(1) does not provide an answer that sufficiently relates to the elimination of those dangers. Unlike the contribution limitations' total ban on the giving of large amounts of money to candidates, § 608(e)(1) prevents only some large expenditures. So long as persons and groups eschew expenditures that in express terms advocate the election or defeat of a clearly identified candidate, they are free to spend as much as they want to promote the candidate and his views. The exacting interpretation of the statutory language necessary to avoid unconstitutional vagueness thus undermines the limitation's effectiveness as a loophole-closing provision by facilitating circumvention by those seeking to exert improper influence upon a candidate or office-holder. It would naively underestimate the ingenuity and resourcefulness of persons and groups desiring to buy influence to believe that they would have much difficulty devising expenditures that skirted the restriction on express advocacy of election or defeat but nevertheless benefited the candidate's campaign. * * *

Second, [the] independent advocacy restricted by the provision does not presently appear to pose dangers of real or apparent corruption comparable to those identified with large campaign contributions. The parties defending § 608(e)(1) contend that it is necessary to prevent would-be contributors from avoiding the contribution limitations by the simple expedient of paying directly for media advertisements or for other portions of the candidate's campaign activities. [Section] 608(b)'s contribution ceilings rather than § 608(e)(1)'s independent expenditure limitation prevent attempts to circumvent the Act through prearranged or coordinated expenditures amounting to disguised contributions.[53] By contrast, § 608(e)(1) limits expenditures for express advocacy of candidates made totally independently of the candidate and his campaign. [The] absence of prearrangement and coordination of an expenditure with the candidate or his agent not only undermines the value of the expenditure to the candidate, but also alleviates the danger that expenditures will be given as a

---

53. Section 608(e)(1) does not apply to expenditures "on behalf of a candidate within the meaning of" § 608(2)(B). That section provides that expenditures "authorized or requested by the candidate, an authorized committee of the candidate, or an agent of the candidate" are to be treated as expenditures of the candidate and contributions by the person or group making the expenditure. [In] view of [the] legislative history and the purposes of the Act, we find that the "authorized or requested" standard of the Act operates to treat all expenditures placed in cooperation with or with the consent of a candidate, his agents, or an authorized committee of the candidate as contributions subject to the limitations set forth in § 608(b).

quid pro quo for improper commitments from the candidate. Rather than preventing circumvention of the contribution limitations, § 608(e)(1) severely restricts all independent advocacy despite its substantially diminished potential for abuse.

While the independent expenditure ceiling thus fails to serve any substantial governmental interest in stemming the reality or appearance of corruption in the electoral process, it heavily burdens core First Amendment expression. [Advocacy] of the election or defeat of candidates for federal office is no less entitled to protection under the First Amendment than the discussion of political policy generally or advocacy of the passage or defeat of legislation.

It is argued, however, that the ancillary governmental interest in equalizing the relative ability of individuals and groups to influence the outcome of elections serves to justify the limitation on express advocacy of the election or defeat of candidates imposed by § 608(e)(1)'s expenditure ceiling. But the concept that government may restrict the speech of some elements of our society in order to enhance the relative voice of others [d] is wholly foreign to the First Amendment, which was designed "to secure 'the widest possible dissemination of information from diverse and antagonistic sources,'" and " 'to assure unfettered interchange of ideas for the bringing about of political and social changes desired by the people.'" *New York Times Co. v. Sullivan.* The First Amendment's protection against governmental abridgement of free expression cannot properly be made to depend on a person's financial ability to engage in public discussion.[55]

* * * *Mills v. Alabama,* 384 U.S. 214, 86 S.Ct. 1434, 16 L.Ed.2d 484 (1966), held that legislative restrictions on advocacy of the election or defeat of political candidates are wholly at odds with the guarantees of the First Amendment. [Yet] the prohibition on election day editorials invalidated in *Mills* is clearly a lesser intrusion on constitutional freedom than a $1,000 limitation on the amount of money any person or association can spend *during an entire election year* in advocating the election or defeat of a candidate for public office.

For the reasons stated, we conclude that § 608(e)(1)'s independent expenditure limitation is unconstitutional under the First Amendment.

2. [The] Act also sets limits on expenditures by a candidate "from his personal funds, or the personal funds of his immediate family, in connection with his campaigns during any calendar year." § 608(a)(1).[e]

The ceiling on personal expenditures by candidates on their own behalf [imposes] a substantial restraint on the ability of persons to engage in protected First Amendment expression. The candidate, no less than any other person, has a First Amendment right to engage in the discussion of public issues and vigorously and tirelessly to advocate his own election and the election of other candidates. Indeed, it is of particular importance that candidates have the unfettered opportunity to make their views known so that the electorate may intelligently evaluate the candidates' personal qualities and their positions on

---

d. The lower court characterized the issue somewhat differently. Can "the wealthy few [claim] a constitutional guarantee to a stronger political voice than the unwealthy many because they are able to give and spend more money, and because the amounts they give and spend cannot be limited"? 519 F.2d 821, 841 (D.C.Cir.1975).

55. Neither the voting rights cases [Ch. 10, Sec. 4, I, B] nor the Court's decision upholding the FCC's fairness doctrine [p. 698 supra]

lends support to appellees' position that the First Amendment permits Congress to abridge the rights of some persons to engage in political expression in order to enhance the relative voice of other segments of our society. * * *

e. $50,000 for Presidential or Vice Presidential candidates; $35,000 for Senate candidates; $25,000 for most candidates for the House of Representatives.

vital public issues before choosing among them on election day. [Section] 608(a)'s ceiling on personal expenditures by a candidate in furtherance of his own candidacy thus clearly and directly interferes with constitutionally protected freedoms.

The primary governmental interest served by the Act—the prevention of actual and apparent corruption of the political process—does not support the limitation on the candidate's expenditure of his own personal funds. [Indeed], the use of personal funds reduces the candidate's dependence on outside contributions and thereby counteracts the coercive pressures and attendant risks of abuse to which the Act's contribution limitations are directed.

The ancillary interest in equalizing the relative financial resources of candidates competing for elective office, therefore, provides the sole relevant rationale for Section 608(a)'s expenditure ceiling. That interest is clearly not sufficient to justify the provision's infringement of fundamental First Amendment rights. First, the limitation may fail to promote financial equality among candidates. [Indeed], a candidate's personal wealth may impede his [fundraising efforts]. Second, and more fundamentally, the First Amendment simply cannot tolerate § 608(a)'s restriction upon the freedom of a candidate to speak without legislative limit on behalf of his own candidacy. We therefore hold that § 608(a)'s restrictions on a candidate's personal expenditures is unconstitutional.

3. [Section] 608(c) of the Act places limitations on overall campaign expenditures by candidates [seeking] election to federal office. [For Presidential candidates the ceiling is $10,000,000 in seeking nomination and $20,000,000 in the general election campaign; for House of Representatives candidates it is $70,000 for each campaign—primary and general; for candidates for Senator the ceiling depends on the size of the voting age population.]

No governmental interest that has been suggested is sufficient to justify [these restrictions] on the quantity of political expression. [The] interest in alleviating the corrupting influence of large contributions is served by the Act's contribution limitations and disclosure provisions rather than by § 608(c)'s campaign expenditure ceilings. [There] is no indication that the substantial criminal penalties for violating the contribution ceilings combined with the political repercussion of such violations will be insufficient to police the contribution provisions. Extensive reporting, auditing, and disclosure requirements applicable to both contributions and expenditures by political campaigns are designed to facilitate the detection of illegal contributions. * * *

The interest in equalizing the financial resources of candidates competing for federal office is no more convincing a justification for restricting the scope of federal election campaigns. Given the limitation on the size of outside contributions, the financial resources available to a candidate's campaign, like the number of volunteers recruited, will normally vary with the size and intensity of the candidate's support. There is nothing invidious, improper, or unhealthy in permitting such funds to be spent to carry the candidate's message to the electorate. Moreover, the equalization of permissible campaign expenditures might serve not to equalize the opportunities of all candidates but to handicap a candidate who lacked substantial name recognition or exposure of his views before the start of the campaign.

The campaign expenditure ceilings appear to be designed primarily to serve the governmental interests in reducing the allegedly skyrocketing costs of political campaigns. [But the] First Amendment denies government the power to determine that spending to promote one's political views is wasteful, excessive, or unwise. In the free society ordained by our Constitution it is not the government but the people individually as citizens and candidates and collectively as associations and political committees who must retain control over the quantity and range of debate on public issues in a political campaign.

For these reasons we hold that § 608(c) is constitutionally invalid. * * *

MR. CHIEF JUSTICE BURGER, concurring in part and dissenting in part.

[I] agree fully with that part of the Court's opinion that holds unconstitutional the limitations the Act puts on campaign expenditures. [Yet] when it approves similarly stringent limitations on contributions, the Court ignores the reasons it finds so persuasive in the context of expenditures. For me contributions and expenditures are two sides of the same First Amendment coin.

[Limiting] contributions, as a practical matter, will limit expenditures and will put an effective ceiling on the amount of political activity and debate that the Government will permit to take place.[5]

The Court attempts to separate the two communicative aspects of political contributions—the "moral" support that the gift itself conveys, which the Court suggests is the same whether the gift is of $10 or $10,000,[6] and the fact that money translates into communication. The Court dismisses the effect of the limitations on the second aspect of contributions: "[T]he transformation of contributions into political debate involves speech by someone other than the contributor." On this premise—that contribution limitations restrict only the speech of "someone other than the contributor"—rests the Court's justification for treating contributions differently from expenditures. The premise is demonstrably flawed; the contribution limitations will, in specific instances, limit exactly the same political activity that the expenditure ceilings limit, and at least one of the "expenditure" limitations the Court finds objectionable operates precisely like the "contribution" limitations.[8]

The Court's attempt to distinguish the communication inherent in political *contributions* from the speech aspects of political *expenditures* simply will not wash. We do little but engage in word games unless we recognize that people—candidates and contributors—spend money on political activity because they wish to communicate ideas, and their constitutional interest in doing so is precisely the same whether they or someone else utter the words.

[T]he restrictions are hardly incidental in their effect upon particular campaigns. Judges are ill-equipped to gauge the precise impact of legislation, but a law that impinges upon First Amendment rights requires us to make the attempt. It is not simply speculation to think that the limitations on contribu-

---

5. The Court notes that 94.9% of the funds raised by congressional candidates in 1974 came in contributions of less than $1,000, n. 27, and suggests that the effect of the contribution limitations will be minimal. This logic ignores the disproportionate influence large contributions may have when they are made early in a campaign; "seed money" can be essential, and the inability to obtain it may effectively end some candidacies before they begin. Appellants have excerpted from the record data on nine campaigns to which large, initial contributions were critical. Campaigns such as these will be much harder, and perhaps impossible, to mount under the Act.

6. Whatever the effect of the limitation, it is clearly arbitrary—Congress has imposed

the same ceiling on contributions to a New York or California senatorial campaign that it has put on House races in Alaska or Wyoming. Both the strength of support conveyed by the gift of $1,000 *and* the gift's potential for corruptly influencing the recipient will vary enormously from place to place. * * *

8. The Court treats the Act's provisions limiting a candidate's spending from his *personal resources* as *expenditure* limits, as indeed the Act characterizes them, and holds them unconstitutional. As Mr. Justice Marshall points out, infra, by the Court's logic these provisions could as easily be treated as limits on *contributions,* since they limit what the candidate can give to his own campaign.

tions will foreclose some candidacies.[9] The limitations will also alter the nature of some electoral contests drastically.[10]

[In] striking down the limitations on campaign expenditures, the Court relies in part on its conclusion that other means—namely, disclosure and contribution ceilings—will adequately serve the statute's aim. It is not clear why the same analysis is not also appropriate in weighing the need for contribution ceilings in addition to disclosure requirements. Congress may well be entitled to conclude that disclosure was a "partial measure," but I had not thought until today that Congress could enact its conclusions in the First Amendment area into laws immune from the most searching review by this Court. * * *[f]

MR. JUSTICE WHITE, concurring in part and dissenting in part. * * *

I [agree] with the Court's judgment upholding the limitations on contributions. I dissent [from] the Court's view that the expenditure limitations [violate] the First Amendment. [This] case depends on whether the nonspeech interests of the Federal Government in regulating the use of money in political campaigns are sufficiently urgent to justify the incidental effects that the limitations visit upon the First Amendment interests of candidates and their supporters.

[The Court] accepts the congressional judgment that the evils of unlimited contributions are sufficiently threatening to warrant restriction regardless of the impact of the limits on the contributor's opportunity for effective speech and in turn on the total volume of the candidate's political communications by reason of his inability to accept large sums from those willing to give.

The congressional judgment, which I would also accept, was that other steps must be taken to counter the corrosive effects of money in federal election campaigns. One of these steps is § 608(e), which [limits] what a contributor may independently spend in support or denigration of one running for federal office. Congress was plainly of the view that these expenditures also have corruptive potential; but the Court strikes down the provision, strangely enough claiming more insight as to what may improperly influence candidates than is possessed by the majority of Congress that passed this Bill and the President who signed it. Those supporting the Bill undeniably included many seasoned professionals who have been deeply involved in elective processes and who have viewed them at close range over many years.

It would make little sense to me, and apparently made none to Congress, to limit the amounts an individual may give to a candidate or spend with his approval but fail to limit the amounts that could be spent on his behalf. Yet the Court permits the former while striking down the latter limitation. [I] would take the word of those who know—that limiting independent expenditures is essential to prevent transparent and widespread evasion of the contribution limits. * * *

---

9. Candidates who must raise large initial contributions in order to appeal for more funds to a broader audience will be handicapped. See n. 5, supra. It is not enough to say that the contribution ceilings "merely require candidates [to] raise funds from a greater number of persons," where the limitations will effectively prevent candidates without substantial personal resources from doing just that.

10. Under the Court's holding, candidates with personal fortunes will be free to contribute to their own campaigns as much as they like, since the Court chooses to view the Act's provisions in this regard as unconstitutional "expenditure" limitations rather than "contribution" limitations. See n. 8, supra.

f. Blackmun, J., also dissented separately from that part of the Court's opinion upholding the Act's restrictions on campaign contributions, unpersuaded that "a principled constitutional distinction" could be made between the contribution and expenditure limitations involved.

The Court also rejects Congress' judgment manifested in § 608(c) that the federal interest in limiting total campaign expenditures by individual candidates justifies the incidental effect on their opportunity for effective political speech. I disagree both with the Court's assessment of the impact on speech and with its narrow view of the values the limitations will serve.

[M]oney is not always equivalent to or used for speech, even in the context of political campaigns. [There are] many expensive campaign activities that are not themselves communicative or remotely related to speech. Furthermore, campaigns differ among themselves. Some seem to spend much less money than others and yet communicate as much or more than those supported by enormous bureaucracies with unlimited financing. The record before us no more supports the conclusion that the communicative efforts of congressional and Presidential candidates will be crippled by the expenditure limitations than it supports the contrary. The judgment of Congress was that reasonably effective campaigns could be conducted within the limits established by the Act and that the communicative efforts of these campaigns would not seriously suffer. In this posture of the case, there is no sound basis for invalidating the expenditure limitations, so long as the purposes they serve are legitimate and sufficiently substantial, which in my view they are.

[E]xpenditure ceilings reinforce the contribution limits and help eradicate the hazard of corruption. [Without] limits on total expenditures, campaign costs will inevitably and endlessly escalate. Pressure to raise funds will constantly build and with it the temptation to resort in "emergencies" to those sources of large sums, who, history shows, are sufficiently confident of not being caught to risk flouting contribution [limits.]

The ceiling on candidate expenditures represents the considered judgment of Congress that elections are to be decided among candidates none of whom has overpowering advantage by reason of a huge campaign war chest. At least so long as the ceiling placed upon the candidates is not plainly too low, elections are not to turn on the difference in the amounts of money that candidates have to spend. This seems an acceptable purpose and the means chosen a common sense way to achieve [it.]

I also disagree with the Court's judgment that § 608(a), which limits the amount of money that a candidate or his family may spend on his campaign, violates the Constitution. Although it is true that this provision does not promote any interest in preventing the corruption of candidates, the provision does, nevertheless, serve salutary purposes related to the integrity of federal campaigns. By limiting the importance of personal wealth, § 608(a) helps to assure that only individuals with a modicum of support from others will be viable candidates. This in turn would tend to discourage any notion that the outcome of elections is primarily a function of money. Similarly, § 608(a) tends to equalize access to the political arena, encouraging the less wealthy, unable to bankroll their own campaigns, to run for political office.[g]

g. Marshall, J., dissented from that part of the Court's opinion invalidating the limitation on the amount a candidate or his family may spend on his campaign. He considered "the interest in promoting the reality and appearance of equal access to the political arena" sufficient to justify the limitation: "[T]he wealthy candidate's immediate access to a substantial personal fortune may give him an initial advantage that his less wealthy opponent can never overcome. [With the option of large contributions removed by § 608(b)], the less wealthy candidate is without the means to match the large initial expenditures of money of which the wealthy candidate is capable. In short, the limitations on contributions put a premium on a candidate's personal wealth. "[Section 608(a) then] emerges not simply as a device to reduce the natural advantage of the wealthy candidate, but as a

Notes and Questions

1. *Expenditure limitations.* Is it "foreign" to the first amendment to curb the spending of the wealthy in an effort to preserve the integrity of the elections process? Would it have been "foreign" to first amendment doctrine to engage in some type of balancing? Does the Court's expenditure ruling denigrate the interest in equality? See, e.g., Tribe, *Constitutional Choices* 193–94 (1985); Nicholson, *Buckley v. Valeo: The Constitutionality of the Federal Election Campaign Act Amendments of 1974,* 1977 Wis.L.Rev. 323, 336; Wright, *Money and the Pollution of Politics: Is the First Amendment an Obstacle to Political Equality?,* 82 Colum.L.Rev. 609 (1982). Even if the concept of political equity is a "legitimizing myth," is *Buckley* flawed because it underestimates the necessity of promoting political leadership that is autonomous and independent of pluralistic forces? Is state autonomy necessary for minimally adequate state regulation of the economy? See Blum, *The Divisible First Amendment: A Critical Functionalist Approach to Freedom of Speech and Electoral Campaign Spending,* 58 N.Y. U.L.Rev. 1273, 1369–78 (1983). Alternatively, would it be better to solve the wealth problem by redistribution (and control of corporate power), while holding fast to a strong liberty principle? See Baker, *Realizing Self-Realization: Corporate Political Expenditures and Redish's The Value of Free Speech,* 130 U.Pa.L. Rev. 646, 652 (1982); Baker, *Scope of the First Amendment Freedom of Speech,* 25 U.C.L.A.L.Rev. 964, 983–90 (1978).

2. *Varying scrutiny.* (a) Did *Buckley* apply less exacting scrutiny to impairment of associational freedoms by contribution limits than to impairment of free expression by expenditure limits? Cf. 90 Harv.L.Rev. 178–79 (1976). "Granted that freedom of association is merely ancillary to speech, a means of amplifying and effectuating communication but logically secondary to speech," is this also "true of expenditures of money in aid of speech"? See Polsby, *Buckley v. Valeo: The Special Nature of Political Speech,* 1976 Sup.Ct.Rev. 1, 22. Can a lesser degree of scrutiny be justified for contributions? Or were the differing results based on the Court's perceiving a greater threat to first amendment interests in the expenditure limits and less risk of corruption and undue influence in unlimited independent expenditures? Cf. Nicholson, note 1 supra, at 340–45. Does the opinion indicate why greater deference was paid to congressional judgment on review of the contribution limits than on review of the expenditure limits? Cf. Note, 76 Colum.L.Rev. 852, 862 (1976). For a defense of strict scrutiny across the board, see BeVier, *Money and Politics: A Perspective on the First Amendment and Campaign Finance Reform,* 73 Calif.L. Rev. 1045 (1985).

(b) *The O'Brien analogy.* May the Court's rejection of the less-exacting *O'Brien* standard on the ground that the expenditure of money did not introduce a non-speech element fairly be criticized for asking the wrong question: whether "*pure speech* can be regulated where there is some incidental effect on *money,*" rather than whether "the use of *money* can be regulated, by analogy to such conduct as draft-card burning, where there is an undoubted incidental effect on *speech*"? See Wright, *Politics and the Constitution: Is Money Speech?,* 85 Yale L.J. 1001, 1007 (1976).

provision providing some symmetry to a regulatory scheme that otherwise enhances the natural advantage of the wealthy."

For background on the *Buckley* case, see Friendly & Elliot, *The Constitution: That Delicate Balance* 91–107 (1984).

3. *Federal funding and expenditure limitations.* A separate section of the *Buckley* opinion seemed to approve expenditure limitations imposed upon candidates who accept federal funding: "[A]cceptance of federal funding entails voluntary acceptance of an expenditure ceiling." The existence of federal funding for a candidate has not, however, served to justify limitations on expenditures by groups who work on behalf of, but independently of, the candidate. FEC v. NATIONAL CONSERVATIVE POLITICAL ACTION COMM., __ U.S. __, 105 S.Ct. 1459, 84 L.Ed.2d 455 (1985), per REHNQUIST, J., invalidated a provision making it a political offense for such groups to expend more than $1000 to further the nomination or election of a candidate receiving federal financing. The Court argued that *Buckley* protected the freedom of association of "large numbers of individuals of modest means" to join together and amplify their voices.[h] The Court stressed that the case involved expenditures, not contributions within the meaning of *Buckley;* that the provision was not directed to the size of the contributions the organizations received, and was not confined to corporations.

In dissent, White, J., noted his continuing objection to the distinction between contributions and expenditures, and Marshall, J., a new convert to that position, separately dissented on the same ground. Even assuming *Buckley* was correctly decided, White, J., argued that contributors to political committees were not engaging in speech to any greater extent than those who contribute directly to political campaigns: only the donee had changed. Moreover, he worried, as had Congress, that candidates would "go around hat in hand, begging for money from Washington-based special interest groups, political action committees whose sole purpose for existing is to seek a quid pro quo. [The] candidate may be forced to please the spenders rather than the voters, and the two groups are not identical."

FIRST NAT'L BANK v. BELLOTTI, 435 U.S. 765, 98 S.Ct. 1407, 55 L.Ed.2d 707 (1978), per POWELL, J., held invalid under the first and fourteenth amendments a Massachusetts criminal statute prohibiting banks or business corporations from making contributions or expenditures to influence "the vote on any question submitted to the voters, other than one materially affecting any of the property, business or assets of the corporation," defined to exclude from the exception questions "concerning the taxation of the income, property or transactions of individuals":

"The speech proposed by appellants is at the heart of the First Amendment's protection. [If] the speakers here were not corporations, no one would suggest that the state could silence their proposed speech. It is the type of speech indispensable to decisionmaking in a democracy, and this is no less true because the speech comes from a corporation rather than an individual. The inherent worth of the speech in terms of its capacity for informing the public does not depend upon the identity of its source, whether corporation, association, union or individual.

"The court below nevertheless held that corporate speech is protected by the First Amendment only when it pertains directly to the corporation's business interests. In deciding whether this novel and restrictive gloss on the First Amendment comports with the Constitution and the precedents of this Court, we need not survey the outer boundaries of the Amendment's protection of corpo-

---

h. One defendant had received an average of $75 from 101,000 people during 1979–80; another, an average of $25 from approximately 100,000 people.

rate speech, or address the abstract question whether corporations have the full measure of rights that individuals enjoy under the First Amendment.[13] The question in this case, simply put, is whether the corporate identity of the speaker deprives this proposed speech of what otherwise would be its clear entitlement to protection. We turn now to that question.

"[A]ppellee suggests that First Amendment rights generally have been afforded only to corporations engaged in the communications business or through which individuals express themselves. [But] the Court's decisions involving corporations in the business of communication or entertainment are based not only on the role of the First Amendment in fostering individual self-expression but also on its role in affording the public access to discussion, debate, and the dissemination of information and ideas. See *Red Lion,* [p. 698 supra]; *Stanley v. Georgia,* [p. 500 supra]; *Time, Inc. v. Hill,* [p. 485 supra].

"[We] find no support in the First or Fourteenth Amendments, or in the decisions of this Court, for the proposition that speech that otherwise would be within the protection of the First Amendment loses that protection simply because its source is a corporation that cannot prove, to the satisfaction of a court, a material effect on its business or property. The 'materially affecting' requirement is not an identification of the boundaries of corporate speech etched by the Constitution itself. Rather, it amounts to an impermissible legislative prohibition of speech based on the identity of the interests that spokesmen may represent in public debate over controversial issues and a requirement that the speaker have a sufficiently great interest in the subject to justify communication.

"[In] the realm of protected speech, the legislature is constitutionally disqualified from dictating the subjects about which persons may speak and the speakers who may address a public issue. *Chicago Police Dep't v. Mosley,* [p. 643 supra]. If a legislature may direct business corporations to 'stick to business,' it also may limit other corporations—religious, charitable, or civic—to their respective 'business' when addressing the public. Such power in government to channel the expression of views is unacceptable under the First Amendment. Especially where, as here, the legislature's suppression of speech suggests an attempt to give one side of a debatable public question an advantage in expressing its views to the people, the First Amendment is plainly offended. * * *

"The constitutionality of § 8's prohibition of the 'exposition of ideas' by corporations turns on whether it can survive the exacting scrutiny necessitated by a state-imposed restriction of freedom of speech. Especially where, as here, a prohibition is directed at speech itself,[23] and the speech is intimately related to the process of governing, 'the State may prevail only upon showing a subordinat-

---

13. Nor is there any occasion to consider in this case whether, under different circumstances, a justification for a restriction on speech that would be inadequate as applied to individuals might suffice to sustain the same restriction as applied to corporations, unions, or like entities.

[*Consolidated Edison Co. v. Public Serv. Comm'n,* 447 U.S. 530, 100 S.Ct. 2326, 65 L.Ed. 2d 319 (1980) held that neither Consolidated Edison's corporate status, nor its status as a government regulated monopoly precluded it from asserting a first amendment right to insert controversial messages in its billing en-

velopes. Citing *Bellotti,* the Court stressed that the worth of speech does not depend upon its source.]

23. It is too late to suggest "that the dependence of a communication on the expenditure of money operates itself to introduce a nonspeech element or to reduce the exacting scrutiny required by the First Amendment." *Buckley.* Furthermore, § 8 is an "attempt directly to control speech [rather than] to protect, from an evil shown to be grave, some interest clearly within the sphere of governmental concern." *Speiser* [p. 733 supra]. Compare *O'Brien.*

ing interest which is compelling.' *Bates v. Little Rock,* 361 U.S. 516, 80 S.Ct. 412, 4 L.Ed.2d 480 (1960).

"Preserving the integrity of the electoral process, preventing corruption, and 'sustain[ing] the active, alert responsibility of the individual citizen in a democracy for the wise conduct of government' are interests of the highest importance. *Buckley.* Preservation of the individual citizen's confidence in government is equally important.

"[Appellee's arguments] that these interests are endangered by corporate participation in discussion of a referendum [issue] hinge upon the assumption that such participation would exert an undue influence on the outcome of a referendum vote, and—in the end—destroy the confidence of the people in the democratic process and the integrity of government. According to appellee, corporations are wealthy and powerful and their views may drown out other points of view. If appellee's arguments were supported by record or legislative findings that corporate advocacy threatened imminently to undermine democratic processes, thereby denigrating rather than serving First Amendment interests,[a] these arguments would merit our consideration.[b] Cf. *Red Lion.* But there has been no showing that the relative voice of corporations has been overwhelming or even significant in influencing referenda in Massachusetts, or that there has been any threat to the confidence of the citizenry in government.

"[Referenda] are held on issues, not candidates for public office. The risk of corruption perceived in cases involving candidate elections simply is not present [c] in a popular vote on a public issue.[26] To be sure, corporate advertising may

a. Legislatures wishing to support such findings need not look far. See, e.g., Lowenstein, *Campaign Spending and Ballot Propositions: Recent Experience, Public Choice Theory and the First Amendment,* 29 U.C.L.A. L.Rev. 505 (1982); Schockley, *Direct Democracy, Campaign Finance, and the Courts: Can Corruption, Undue Influence, and Declining Voter Confidence Be Found?,* 39 U.Miami L.Rev. 377 (1985). For additional information and commentary, see Cox, *Constitutional Issues in the Regulation of the Financing of Election Campaigns,* 31 Clev.St.L.Rev. 395 (1982); Symposium, *Political Action Committees and Campaign Finance,* 22 Ariz.L.Rev. 351 (1981); Symposium, *Campaign Finance Reform,* 10 Hast.Con.L.Q. 463 (1983).

b. "[I]f *Tornillo* and *Buckley* slammed the door on excessive power arguments, [*Bellotti*] opened a window. [The] Court did not pause, however, to explain why factors found in *Buckley* and *Tornillo* would have to be foreign to the first amendment would have 'merited consideration' in *Bellotti.*" Shiffrin, *Government Speech,* 27 U.C.L.A. L.Rev. 565, 598–99 (1980).

c. *Citizens Against Rent Control v. Berkeley,* 454 U.S. 290, 102 S.Ct. 434, 70 L.Ed.2d 492 (1981) (White, J., dissenting) struck down a city ordinance placing a $250 limitation on contributions to committees formed to support or oppose ballot measures submitted to popular vote. The Court, per Burger, C.J., observed that the case did not involve an ordinance confined to contributions by corporations and that the case involved ballot

measures, not candidate elections. Rehnquist, J., concurring noted the presence of a corporate petitioner, but emphasized that the ordinance was not aimed only at corporations. In separate concurrences Marshall, J., and Blackmun, J., joined by O'Connor, J., noted that the record did not contain the kind of evidence that would warrant consideration under *Bellotti.* For commentary, see Tribe, *Constitutional Choices* 195–97 (1985); Lowenstein, fn. a supra, at 584–602; Nicholson, *The Constitutionality of Contribution Limitations in Ballot Measure Elections,* 9 Ecol.L.Q. 683 (1981).

26. [Appellants] do not challenge the constitutionality of laws prohibiting or limiting corporate contributions to political candidates or committees, or other means of influencing candidate elections. About half of these laws, including the Federal Corrupt Practices Act, by their terms do not apply to referendum votes. [The] overriding concern behind the enactment of statutes such as the Federal Corrupt Practices Act was the problem of corruption of elected representatives through the creation of political debts. [The] case before us presents no comparable problem, and our consideration of a corporation's right to speak on issues of general public interest implies no comparable right in the quite different context of participation in a political campaign for election to public office. Congress might well be able to demonstrate the existence of a danger of real or apparent corruption in inde-

influence the outcome of the vote; this would be its purpose. But the fact that advocacy may persuade the electorate is hardly a reason to suppress [it.] We noted only recently that 'the concept that government may restrict the speech of some elements of our society in order to enhance the relative voice of others is wholly foreign to the First Amendment.' *Buckley.* Moreover, the people in our democracy are entrusted with the responsibility for judging and evaluating the relative merits of conflicting arguments.[31] They may consider, in making their judgment, the source and credibility of the advocate. But if there be any danger that the people cannot evaluate the information and arguments advanced by appellants, it is a danger contemplated by the Framers of the First Amendment."

The Court rejected the argument that § 8 was justified by the interest in preventing use of corporate resources to advance views with which some shareholders disagreed. In this respect the statute was under-inclusive in not forbidding "the expenditure of corporate funds on any public issue until it becomes the subject of a referendum, though the displeasure of disapproving shareholders is unlikely to be any less. The fact that a particular kind of ballot question has been singled out for special treatment undermines the likelihood of a genuine state interest in protecting shareholders. It suggests instead that the legislature may have been concerned with silencing corporations on a particular subject. Indeed, appellee has conceded that 'the legislative and judicial history of the statute indicates [that] the second crime was "tailor-made" to prohibit corporate campaign contributions to oppose a graduated income tax amendment.'

"[The] over-inclusiveness of the statute is demonstrated by the fact that § 8 would prohibit a corporation from supporting or opposing a referendum proposal even if its shareholders unanimously authorized the contribution or expenditure. Ultimately shareholders may decide, through the procedures of corporate democracy, whether their corporation should engage in debate on public issues.[34]"

pendent expenditures by corporations to influence candidate elections. Cf. *Buckley.*

31. Government is forbidden to assume the task of ultimate judgment, lest the people lose their ability to govern themselves. The First Amendment rejects the "highly paternalistic" approach of statutes like § 8 which restrict what the people may hear. *Virginia Pharmacy* [p. 554 supra].

34. [White, J.'s] repeatedly expressed concern for corporate shareholders who may be "coerced" into supporting "causes with which they disagree" apparently is not shared by appellants' shareholders. Not a single shareholder has joined appellee in defending the Massachusetts statute, or so far as the record shows, has interposed any objection to the right asserted by the corporations to make the proscribed expenditures.

The dissent of Mr. Justice White relies heavily on *Abood v. Detroit Bd. of Educ.* and *International Assn. of Machinists v. Street,* [Sec. 9, II supra]. These decisions involved the First Amendment rights of employees in closed or agency shops not to be compelled, as a condition of employment, to support with financial contributions the political activities of other union members with which the dissenters disagreed.

Street and *Abood* are irrelevant to the question presented in this case. In those cases employees were required, either by state law or by agreement between the employer and the union, to pay dues or a "service fee" to the exclusive bargaining representative. To the extent that these funds were used by the union in furtherance of political goals, unrelated to collective bargaining, they were held to be unconstitutional because they compelled the dissenting union member "to furnish contributions of money for the propagation of opinions which he disbelieves."

The critical distinction here is that no shareholder has been "compelled" to contribute anything. Apart from the fact, noted by the dissent, that compulsion by the State is wholly absent, the [shareholder] invests in a corporation of his own volition and is [free to withdraw his investment at any time and for any reason.] A more relevant analogy, therefore, is to the situation where an employee voluntarily joins a union, or an individual voluntarily joins an association, and later finds himself in disagreement with its stance on a political issue. * * *

BURGER, C.J., who joined the Court's opinion, concurred: "A disquieting aspect of Massachusetts' position is that it may carry the risk of impinging on the First Amendment rights of those who employ the corporate form—as most do—to carry on the business of mass communications, particularly the large media conglomerates. This is so because of the difficulty, and perhaps impossibility, of distinguishing, either as a matter of fact or constitutional law, media corporations from corporations such as appellants.

"Making traditional use of the corporate form, some media enterprises have amassed vast wealth and power and conduct many activities, some directly related—and some not—to their publishing and broadcasting activities. See *Miami Herald.* Today, a corporation might own the dominant newspaper in one or more large metropolitan centers, television and radio stations in those same centers and others, a newspaper chain, news magazines with nationwide circulation, national or worldwide wire news services, and substantial interests in book publishing and distribution enterprises. Corporate ownership may extend, vertically, to pulp mills and pulp timberlands to insure an adequate, continuing supply of newsprint and to trucking and steamship lines for the purpose of transporting the newsprint to the presses. Such activities would be logical economic auxiliaries to a publishing conglomerate. Ownership also may extend beyond to business activities unrelated to the task of publishing newspapers and magazines or broadcasting radio and television programs. Obviously, such far-reaching ownership would not be possible without the state-provided corporate form and its 'special rules relating to such matters as limited liability, perpetual life, and the accumulation, distribution, and taxation of assets'. (White, J., dissenting).

"In terms of 'unfair advantage in the political process' and 'corporate domination of the electoral process,' it could be argued that such media conglomerates as I describe pose a much more realistic threat to valid interests than do appellants and similar entities not regularly concerned with shaping popular opinion on public issues. See *Miami Herald.*

"In terms of Massachusetts' other concern, the interests of minority shareholders, I perceive no basis for saying that the managers and directors of the media conglomerates are more or less sensitive to the views and desires of minority shareholders than are corporate officers generally. Nor can it be said, even if relevant to First Amendment analysis—which it is not—that the former are more virtuous, wise, or restrained in the exercise of corporate power than are the latter. Thus, no factual distinction has been identified as yet that would justify government restraints on the right of appellants to express their views without, at the same time, opening the door to similar restraints on media conglomerates with their vastly greater influence."

WHITE, J., joined by Brennan and Marshall, JJ., dissented, stressing two arguments: (1) The statute was designed to protect first amendment rights by "preventing institutions which have been permitted to amass wealth as a result of special advantages extended by the State for certain economic purposes from using that wealth to acquire an unfair advantage in the political process, especially where, as here, the issue involved has no material connection with the business of the corporation. The State need not permit its own creation to consume it. Massachusetts could permissibly conclude that not to impose limits upon the political activities of corporations would have placed it in a position of departing from neutrality and indirectly assisting the propagation of corporate views because of the advantages its laws give to the corporate acquisition of funds to finance such activities. Such expenditures may be viewed as seriously threatening the role of the First Amendment as a guarantor of a free marketplace of ideas.

"[This] Nation has for many years recognized the need for measures designed to prevent corporate domination of the political process. The Corrupt Practices Act, first enacted in 1907, has consistently barred corporate contributions in connection with federal elections. This Court has repeatedly recognized that one of the principal purposes of this prohibition is 'to avoid the deleterious influences on federal elections resulting from the use of money by those who exercise control over large aggregations of capital.' *United States v. United Auto. Workers,* 352 U.S. 567, 585, 77 S.Ct. 529, 538, 1 L.Ed.2d 563 (1957). Although this Court has never adjudicated the constitutionality of the Act, there is no suggestion in its cases construing it that this purpose is in any sense illegitimate or deserving of other than the utmost respect; indeed, the thrust of its opinions, until today, has been to the contrary."

(2) The Massachusetts law advances the "overriding interest [of] assuring that shareholders are not compelled to support and financially further beliefs with which they disagree, where [the issue] does not materially affect the business, property, or other affairs of the corporation.[12] [The law] protects the very freedoms that this Court has held to be guaranteed by the First Amendment. [Last Term, in *Abood,* we] held that, a State may not, even indirectly, require an individual to contribute to the support of an ideological cause he may oppose as a condition of [employment].

"Presumably, unlike [*Street* and *Abood,*] the use of funds invested by shareholders with opposing views by Massachusetts corporations in connection with referenda or elections would not constitute state action and, consequently, not violate the First Amendment. Until now, however, the States have always been free to adopt measures designed to further rights protected by the Constitution even when not compelled to do so."

REHNQUIST, J., dissenting, argued that "the Fourteenth Amendment does not require a State to endow a business corporation with the power of political speech": "A State grants to a business corporation the blessings of potentially perpetual life and limited liability to enhance its efficiency as an economic entity. It might reasonably be concluded that those properties, so beneficial in the economic sphere, pose special dangers in the political sphere. [T]he States might reasonably fear that the corporation would use its economic power to obtain further benefits beyond those already bestowed. I would think that any particular form of organization upon which the State confers special privileges or immunities different from those of natural persons would be subject to like regulation, whether the organization is a labor union, a partnership, a trade association, or a corporation." [d]

Notes and Questions

1. *Protecting the privileged.* Consider Tushnet, *An Essay on Rights,* 62 Tex.L.Rev. 1363, 1387 (1984): "The first amendment has replaced the due

---

12. This, of course, is an interest that was not present in *Buckley,* and would not justify limitations upon the activities of associations, corporate or otherwise, formed for the express purpose of advancing a political or social cause.

d. Rehnquist, J., suggested that when the state creates a corporation such as a newspa-

per, "it necessarily assumes that the corporation is entitled to the liberty of the press essential to the conduct of its business." But a newspaper has "no greater right than any other corporation" to contribute money to political campaigns although its right to endorse a candidate in its editorial columns would be fully protected.

process clause as the primary guarantor of the privileged. Indeed, it protects the privileged more perniciously than the due process clause ever did. Even in its heyday the due process clause stood in the way only of specific legislation designed to reduce the benefits of privilege. Today, in contrast, the first amendment stands as a general obstruction to all progressive legislative efforts. To protect their positions of privilege, the wealthy can make prudent investments either in political action or, more conventionally, in factories or stocks. But since the demise of substantive due process, their investments in factories and stocks can be regulated by legislatures. Under *Buckley* and *Bellotti*, however, their investments in politics—or politicians—cannot be regulated significantly. Needless to say, careful investment in politics may prevent effective regulation of traditional investments." See also Tushnet, *Corporations and Free Speech* in The Politics of Law 253 (Kairys ed. 1982).[e]

Compare Levinson, *Book Review*, 83 Mich.L.Rev. 939, 945 (1985): "Overtly, justifying restriction of campaign spending by reference to the idea of fair access to the public forum may seem content neutral. However, it is worth considering to what extent we in fact support such restrictions because of tacit assumptions about the contents of the views held by the rich, who would obviously feel most of the burden of the restrictions. If both political views and the propensity to spend money on politics were distributed randomly among the entire populace, it is hard to see why anyone would be very excited about the whole issue of campaign finance."

2. *Distinguishing media corporations.* Consider Nicholson, *The Constitutionality of the Federal Restrictions on Corporate and Union Campaign Contributions and Expenditures*, 65 Corn.L.Rev. 945, 959 (1980): "A solution may be to focus on the distinction between media activities and other activities. A diversified corporation, partially involved in the media, would be entitled to full first amendment protection for its media-related operations. Under this approach, a newspaper would not lose its first amendment rights because it purchased a pulp mill, but it could not extend these rights to its pulp mill operations. An oil company that purchased a newspaper would not gain first amendment rights for its oil operations, but it would be able to assert these first amendment rights in the operation of its newspaper. The problem is not, to paraphrase Chief Justice Burger, the impracticability of making a distinction, but rather the difficulty of finding a theory that will justify a distinction."

Can self-expression serve as a distinguishing factor? See id. at 959–60. Is there more freedom "to choose and create the content of the delivered speech in the communications industry than in other industries"? Does the communication industry "display less allegiance to the profit motive than other industries"? Does it matter that the communications industry's product is speech? Can a fourth estate theory distinguish the press? On that premise, is there no reason to expand the definition of the press to include business corporations? See generally Baker, *Commercial Speech: A Problem in the Theory of Freedom*, 62 Iowa L.Rev. 1, 25–40 (1976); Baker, *Press Rights and Government Power to Structure the Press*, 34 U.Miami L.Rev. 819, 822–36 (1980).

3. *Protecting shareholders.* After *Bellotti*, could government "authorize management to make some kinds of corporate speech, such as commercial speech, but not others, such as political or noncommercial speech, without the approval or express consent of stockholders"? See generally Brudney, *Business*

e. For discussion on a broad range of issues concerning the relationship between speech values and property values in Burger Court decisions, see Dorsen & Gara, *Free Speech, Property, and the Burger Court: Old Values, New Balances*, 1982 Sup.Ct.Rev. 195.

Corporations and Stockholders' Rights Under the First Amendment, 91 Yale L.J. 235 (1981).

4. *Protecting associational rights.* Should the Court have considered the possibly "stronger argument: corporate political expression should be protected as the speech and associational activity of the individual owners"? Cf. Note, 92 Harv.L.Rev. 163, 165–66 (1978). Does this argument slight the extent to which the state has altered political influence by creating corporations and conferring advantages upon them? See Patton & Bartlett, *Corporate "Persons" and Freedom of Speech: The Political Impact of Legal Mythology,* 1981 Wis.L.Rev. 494. Does the association argument also assume too much about the connection between the owners' views and the corporation's speech? See Baker, *Commercial Speech,* note 2 supra and Brudney note 3 supra.

5. *Protecting listeners.* Is *Bellotti* justifiable because of listeners' rights? See Redish, *Self-Realization, Democracy, and Freedom of Expression: A Reply to Professor Baker,* 130 U.Pa.L.Rev. 678–79 (1982). But see Note, *Statutory Limitations on Corporate Spending in Ballot Measure Campaigns: The Case for Constitutionality,* 36 Hast.L.J. 433 (1985) (legal and market limitations on corporate speech inherently negate its value for listeners). Reconsider the arguments for and against the marketplace of ideas argument, Sec. 1, I supra.

6. *Aftermath of fn. 26.* 2 U.S.C. § 441(b) prohibits corporations or unions from making contributions or expenditures in connection with federal elections, but allows corporations and unions to establish and pay the expenses of segregated funds to be used for political purposes during federal elections. It prohibits corporations from soliciting contributions from persons other than its "stockholders and their families and its executive or administrative personnel and their families." In lieu of shareholders, corporations without capital stock are permitted to solicit contributions for such a fund from their "members." FEC v. NATIONAL RIGHT TO WORK COMM., 459 U.S. 197, 103 S.Ct. 552, 74 L.Ed.2d 364 (1982), per Rehnquist, J., characterized these provisions as sufficiently tailored to prevent corruption or its appearance and to protect corporate contributors as to negate any judgment that restriction on associational interests was "undue." The National Right to Work Committee is an advocacy group organized as a nonprofit corporation without capital stock. It conceded that it was required to set up a segregated fund under § 441(b) but argued that it was entitled to solicit contributions from anyone that had previously responded to any of its prior mass mailings. The Court unanimously held that this conception of membership would render the statutory corporation "meaningless." Without requiring any evidentiary showing, the Court stated that the interest in avoiding corruption or its appearance justified "treating unions, corporations, and similar organizations differently from individuals."

FEC v. National Conservative Political Action Comm., p. 783 supra, per Rehnquist, J., characterized *National Right to Work Committee* as proceeding from the premise that "in return for the special advantages that the State confers on the corporate form, individuals acting jointly through corporations forgo some of the rights they have as individuals." But, citing *Bellotti's* fn. 26, he suggested that the question of whether a corporation could constitutionally be restricted in making independent expenditures to influence elections for public office was still open. Should advocacy groups organized in corporate form be treated like business corporations?

Chapter 9

FREEDOM OF RELIGION

This chapter concerns the "religion clauses" of the first amendment, commonly known as the "establishment clause" (forbidding laws "respecting an establishment of religion") and the "free exercise clause" (forbidding laws "prohibiting the free exercise thereof"). It is difficult to explore either clause in isolation from the other. The extent to which the clauses interact may be illustrated by the matter of public financial aid to parochial schools, the subject of a number of cases that follow: On the one hand, does such aid violate the establishment clause? On the other hand, does a state's failure to provide such aid violate the free exercise clause? Another example of the potential conflict between the clauses—also considered in the materials below—is whether, on the one hand, a state's exemption of church buildings from property taxes contravenes the establishment clause or whether, on the other hand, a state's taxing these buildings contravenes the free exercise clause.

Despite this interrelationship of the two clauses, Sec. 1 deals almost exclusively with the establishment clause. Sec. 2, I then considers conventional problems under the free exercise clause. Sec. 2, II examines the complex issues of defining "religion" for purposes of the first amendment and determining the bona fides of an asserted "religious" belief—both matters usually presumed in the cases decided by the Supreme Court and the former never specifically addressed by a majority of the justices. Finally, issues under each clause having been explored in some detail, Sec. 3 discusses problems presented by government action that attempts to accommodate the seemingly opposing demands of the two religion clauses.

SECTION 1. ESTABLISHMENT CLAUSE

Prior to 1947, only two decisions concerning the establishment clause produced any significant consideration by the Court. Since 1947, however, a substantial number of cases have dealt with the meaning of the establishment clause. The major areas of controversy have concerned public financial assistance to church-related institutions (mainly parochial schools) and religious practices in the public schools. Other decisions have involved regulatory laws that "aid" religion and, most recently, government action that publicly acknowledges religion.[a]

---

a. For discussion of the various "articulated justifications for the special constitutional place of religion" since 1937 by members of the Supreme Court, see Smith, *The Special*

EVERSON v. BOARD OF EDUC., 330 U.S. 1, 67 S.Ct. 504, 91 L.Ed. 711 (1947): A New Jersey township reimbursed parents for the cost of sending their children "on regular buses operated by the public transportation system," to and from schools, including nonprofit private and parochial schools. The Court, per BLACK, J., rejected a municipal taxpayer's contention that payment for Catholic parochial school students violated the establishment clause, observing that the religion clauses of the first amendment, "as made applicable to the states by the Fourteenth," "reflected in the minds of early Americans a vivid mental picture of conditions and practices which they fervently wished to stamp out in order to preserve liberty for themselves and for their posterity."

The Court detailed the history of religious persecution in Europe "before and contemporaneous with the colonization of America" and the "repetition of many of the old world practices" in the colonies—emphasizing the compulsion "to pay tithes and taxes to support government-sponsored churches whose ministers preached inflammatory sermons designed to strengthen and consolidate the established faith by generating a burning hatred against dissenters." The abhorrence of these practices "reached its dramatic climax in Virginia in 1785–86" when "Madison wrote his great Memorial and Remonstrance" against renewal of "Virginia's tax levy for support of the established church" and the Virginia Assembly "enacted the famous 'Virginia Bill for Religious Liberty' originally written by Thomas Jefferson. [This] Court has previously recognized that the provisions of the First Amendment, in the drafting and adoption of which Madison and Jefferson played such leading roles, had the same objective and were intended to provide the same protection against governmental intrusion on religious liberty as the Virginia statute. [The] interrelationship of these complementary clauses was well summarized [in] *Watson v. Jones,* 13 Wall. 679, 730, 20 L.Ed. 666: 'The structure of our government has, for the preservation of civil liberty, rescued the temporal institutions from religious interference. On the other hand, it has secured religious liberty from the invasions of the civil authority.'

"The 'establishment of religion' clause of the First Amendment means at least this: Neither a state nor the Federal Government can set up a church. Neither can pass laws which aid one religion, aid all religions, or prefer one religion over another. Neither can force nor influence a person to go to or to remain away from church against his will or force him to profess a belief or disbelief in any religion. No person can be punished for entertaining or professing religious beliefs or disbeliefs, for church attendance or non-attendance. No tax in any amount, large or small can be levied to support any religious activities or institutions, whatever they may be called, or whatever form they may adopt to teach or practice religion. Neither a state nor the Federal Government can, openly or secretly, participate in the affairs of any religious organizations or groups and vice versa. In the words of Jefferson, the clause against establishment of religion by law was intended to erect 'a wall of separation between Church and State.'

"We must [not invalidate the New Jersey statute] if it is within the state's constitutional power even though it approaches the verge of that power. New Jersey cannot consistently with the 'establishment of religion' clause of the First Amendment contribute tax-raised funds to the support of an institution which teaches the tenets and faith of any church. On the other hand, other language of the amendment commands that New Jersey cannot hamper its citizens in the free exercise of their own religion. Consequently, it cannot exclude individual Catholics, Lutherans, Mohammedans, Baptists, Jews, Methodists, Non-believers, Presbyterians, or the members of any other faith, *because of their faith, or lack of it,* from receiving the benefits of public welfare legislation. While we do not mean to intimate that a state could not provide transportation only to children attending public schools, we must be careful, in protecting the citizens of New Jersey against state-established churches, to be sure that we do not inadvertently prohibit New Jersey from extending its general State law benefits to all its citizens without regard to their religious belief."

Noting that "the New Jersey legislature has decided that a public purpose will be served" by having children "ride in public buses to and from schools rather than run the risk of traffic and other hazards incident to walking or 'hitchhiking,'" the Court conceded "that children are helped to get to church schools. There is even a possibility that some of the children might not be sent to the church schools if the parents were compelled to pay their children's bus fares out of their own pockets when transportation to a public school would have been paid for by the State. [But] state-paid policemen, detailed to protect children going to and from church schools from the very real hazards of traffic, would serve much the same [purpose]. Similarly, parents might be reluctant to permit their children to attend schools which the state had cut off from such general government services as ordinary police and fire protection, connections for sewage disposal, public highways and sidewalks. Of course, cutting off church schools from these services, so separate and so indisputably marked off from the religious function, would make it far more difficult for the schools to operate. But such is obviously not the purpose of the First Amendment. That Amendment requires the state to be a neutral in its relations with groups of religious believers and non-believers; it does not require the state to be their adversary. State power is no more to be used so as to handicap religions, than it is to favor them.

"This Court had said that parents may, in the discharge of their duty under state compulsory education laws, send their children to a religious rather than a public school if the school meets the secular educational requirements which the state has power to impose. See *Pierce v. Society of Sisters,* [p. 313 supra]. It appears that these parochial schools meet New Jersey's requirements. The State contributes no money to the schools. It does not support them. Its legislation, as applied, does no more than provide a general program to help parents get their children, regardless of their religion, safely and expeditiously to and from accredited schools.

"The First Amendment has erected a wall between church and state. That wall must be kept high and impregnable. We could not approve the slightest breach. New Jersey has not breached it here."

RUTLEDGE, J., joined by Frankfurter, Jackson and Burton, JJ., filed the principal dissent, arguing that the statute aided children "in a substantial way to get the very thing which they are sent to the particular school to secure, namely, religious training and teaching. * * * Commingling the religious with the secular teaching does not divest the whole of its religious permeation and emphasis or make them of minor part, if proportion were material. Indeed, on any other view, the constitutional prohibition always could be brought to naught by adding a modicum of the secular. [Transportation] cost is as much a part of the total expense, except at times in amount, as the cost of textbooks, of school lunches, of athletic equipment, of writing and other [materials]. Payment of transportation is [no] less essential to education, whether religious or secular, than payment for tuitions, for teachers' salaries, for buildings, equipment and necessary materials. [No] rational line can be drawn between payment for such larger, but not more necessary, items and payment for transportation. [Now], as in Madison's time, not the amount but the principle of assessment is wrong.

* * *

"But we are told that the New Jersey statute is valid [because] the appropriation is for a public, not a private purpose, namely, the promotion of education, and the majority accept this idea in the conclusion that all we have here is 'public welfare legislation.' If that is true and the Amendment's force can be thus destroyed, what has been said becomes all the more pertinent. For then there could be no possible objection to more extensive support of religious education by New Jersey.

"* * * Public money devoted to payment of religious costs, educational or other, brings the quest for more. It brings too the struggle of sect against sect for the larger share or for any. Here one by numbers alone will benefit most, there another. That is precisely the history of societies which have had an established religion and dissident groups. It is the very thing Jefferson and Madison experienced and sought to guard against, whether in its blunt or in its more screened forms. The end of such strife cannot be other than to destroy the cherished liberty. The dominating group will achieve the dominant benefit; or all will embroil the state in their dissensions. * * *

"No one conscious of religious values can be unsympathetic toward the burden which our constitutional separation puts on parents who desire religious instruction mixed with secular for their children. They pay taxes for others' children's education, at the same time the added cost of instruction for their own. [But] discrimination in the legal sense does not exist. The child attending the religious school has the same right as any other to attend the public school. But he forgoes exercising it because the same guaranty which assures his freedom forbids the public school or any agency of the state to give or aid him in securing the religious instruction he seeks. * * *

"Nor is the case comparable to one of furnishing fire or police protection, or access to public highways. These things are matters of common right, part of the general need for safety. Certainly the fire department must not stand idly by while the church burns."

The Court did not again confront the subject of aid to parochial schools until 1968. These decisions are considered in Part III infra. During the intervening two decades, however, the Court was presented with other problems that enabled it to further develop the establishment clause rationale begun in *Everson*.

I. RELIGION AND PUBLIC SCHOOLS

McCOLLUM v. BOARD OF EDUC., 333 U.S. 203, 68 S.Ct. 461, 92 L.Ed. 649 (1948), per BLACK, J., held that a Champaign, Illinois public school released time program violated the establishment clause. Privately employed religious teachers held weekly classes, on public school premises, in their respective religions, for students whose parents signed request cards, while non-attending students pursued secular studies in other parts of the building. "Here not only are the state's tax-supported public school buildings used for the dissemination of religious doctrines. The State also affords sectarian groups an invaluable aid in that it helps to provide pupils for their religious classes through use of the state's compulsory public school machinery."

FRANKFURTER, J., joined by Jackson, Rutledge, and Burton, JJ., concurred: "Designed to serve as perhaps the most powerful agency for promoting cohesion among the heterogeneous democratic people, the public school must keep scrupulously free from entanglement in the strife of sects." In answer to the defense that the program was voluntary, he maintained, "That a child is offered an alternative may reduce the constraint; it does not eliminate the operation of influence by the school in matters sacred to conscience and outside the school's domain. The law of imitation operates, and nonconformity is not an outstanding characteristic of children. The result is an obvious pressure upon children to attend." Jackson, concurred in the result. Reed, J., dissented.

ZORACH v. CLAUSON, 343 U.S. 306, 72 S.Ct. 679, 96 L.Ed. 954 (1952), per DOUGLAS, J., upheld a New York City released time program in which the religious classes were held in church buildings: "[This] program involves neither religious instruction in public school classrooms nor the expenditure of public funds. All costs, including the application blanks, are paid by the religious organizations. The case is therefore unlike *McCollum*."

First, "it takes obtuse reasoning to inject any issue of the 'free exercise' of religion into the present case" because "there is no evidence [that] the system involves the use of coercion to get public school students into religious classrooms. [If] it were established that any one or more teachers were using their office to persuade or force students to take the religious instruction, a wholly different case would be presented.'"

As to the establishment clause: "[T]he First Amendment reflects the philosophy that Church and State should be separated [and] within the scope of its coverage permits no exception; the prohibition is absolute. The First Amendment, however, does not say that in every and all respects there shall be a separation of Church and State. Rather, it studiously defines the manner, the specific ways, in which there shall be no concert or union or dependency one on the other. That is the common sense of the matter. Otherwise the state and religion would be aliens to each other—hostile, suspicious, and even unfriendly. Churches could not be required to pay even property taxes. Municipalities would not be permitted to render police or fire protection to religious groups. Policemen who helped parishioners into their places of worship would violate the Constitution. Prayers in our legislative halls; the appeals to the Almighty in the messages of the Chief Executive; the proclamations making Thanksgiving Day a holiday; 'so help me God' in our courtroom oaths—these and all other references to the Almighty that run through our laws, our public rituals, our ceremonies would be flouting the First Amendment. A fastidious atheist or agnostic could even object to the supplication with which the Court opens each session: 'God save the United States and this Honorable Court.'

"[The] nullification of this law would have wide and profound effects. A Catholic student applies to his teacher for permission to leave the school during hours on a Holy Day of Obligation to attend a mass. A Jewish student asks his teacher for permission to be excused for Yom Kippur. A Protestant wants the

---

7. [The] only allegation in the complaint that bears on the issue is that the operation of the program "has resulted and inevitably results in the exercise of pressure and coercion upon parents and children to secure attendance by the children for religious instruction." But this charge does not even implicate the school authorities. * * *

afternoon off for a family baptismal ceremony. In each case the teacher requires parental consent in writing. In each case the teacher, in order to make sure the student is not a truant, goes further and requires a report from the priest, the rabbi, or the minister. The teacher in other words cooperates in a religious program to the extent of making it possible for her students to participate in it. Whether she does it occasionally for a few students, regularly for one, or pursuant to a systematized program designed to further the religious needs of all the students does not alter the character of the act.

"We are a religious people whose institutions presuppose a Supreme Being. We guarantee the freedom to worship as one chooses. * * * We sponsor an attitude on the part of government that shows no partiality to any one group and that lets each flourish according to the zeal of its adherents and the appeal of its dogma. When the state encourages religious instruction or cooperates with religious authorities by adjusting the schedule of public events to sectarian needs, it follows the best of our traditions. For it then respects the religious nature of our people and accommodates the public service to their spiritual needs. To hold that it may not would be to find in the Constitution a requirement that the government show a callous indifference to religious groups. That would be preferring those who believe in no religion over those who do believe. [The] problem, like many problems in constitutional law, is one of degree."

JACKSON, J., dissented: "If public education were taking so much of the pupils' time as to injure the public or the students' welfare by encroaching upon their religious opportunity, simply shortening everyone's school day would facilitate voluntary and optional attendance at Church classes. But that suggestion is rejected upon the ground that if they are made free many students will not go to the Church. Hence, they must be deprived of freedom for this period, with Church attendance put to them as one of the two permissible ways of using it.

"The greater effectiveness of this system over voluntary attendance after school hours is due to the truant officer who, if the youngster fails to go to the Church school, dogs him back to the public schoolroom. Here schooling is more or less suspended during the 'released time' so the nonreligious attendants will not forge ahead of the churchgoing absentees. But it serves as a temporary jail for a pupil who will not go to Church. It takes more subtlety of mind than I possess to deny that this is governmental constraint in support of religion." As to "the Court's suggestion that opposition to this plan can only be antireligious, atheistic, or agnostic," "my evangelistic brethren confuse an objection to compulsion with an objection to religion. It is possible to hold a faith with enough confidence to believe that what should be rendered to God does not need to be decided and collected by Caesar. * * *

"[The] distinction attempted between [this case and *McCollum*] is trivial * * *. The wall which the Court was professing to erect between Church and State has become even more warped and twisted than I expected. Today's judgment will be more interesting to students of psychology and of the judicial process than to students of constitutional law." [a]

a. Frankfurter, J., who agreed with Jackson, J.'s opinion, also filed a separate dissent. Black, J., also dissented.

For a description of the interaction of the justices in fashioning the *Everson, McCollum* and *Zorach* opinions, see Note, *The "Released Time" Cases Revisited: A Study of Group Decisionmaking by the Supreme Court,* 83 Yale L.J. 1202 (1974).

Notes and Questions

1. *Cost.* Can *Zorach* be reconciled with *McCollum* on the ground that the *McCollum* plan involved a significantly greater cost to the public? Brennan, J., has distinguished the cases "not [because] of the difference in public expenditures involved. True, the *McCollum* program involved the regular use of school facilities, classrooms, heat and light and time from the regular school day—even though the actual incremental cost may have been negligible. [But the] deeper difference was that the *McCollum* program placed the religious instructor in the public school classroom in precisely the position of authority held by the regular teachers of secular subjects, while the *Zorach* program did not. The *McCollum* program, in lending to the support of sectarian instruction all the authority of the governmentally operated public school system, brought government and religion into that proximity which the Establishment Clause forbids." *School Dist. v. Schempp,* infra (concurring opinion).

2. *Coercion.* (a) Do you agree that *Zorach* did not involve "the use of coercion to get public school students into religious classrooms"? Would the *Zorach* plan be inherently coercive, and therefore unconstitutional, if it were shown that most children found religious instruction more appealing than remaining in the public schools? Even if the alternative for those remaining was secular instruction with academic credit? See generally Regan, *The Dilemma of Religious Instruction and the Public Schools,* 10 Catholic Law. 42 (1964). If so, would it be permissible to excuse children from classes to enable them to attend special religious services of their faith? Would the first amendment forbid attendance at parochial schools, as an alternative to public schools, on the ground that this was simply one hundred per cent released time?

Under this analysis, would a program of "dismissed time" (all children released early permitting those who so wish to attend religious schools) be unconstitutional? Would "dismissed time" be nonetheless invalid if it could be shown that the purpose for the early school closing was to facilitate religious education? Or is this merely an accommodation "adjusting the schedule of public events to sectarian needs"?

(b) What of the argument that the *Zorach* program is inherently coercive, and therefore unconstitutional, because "the law of imitation operates" placing "an obvious pressure upon children to attend" religious classes? Under this analysis, what result in the case of excusing students to attend a religious service? In the case of parochial schools? In the case of "dismissed time"? Do you agree with Jackson, J.'s assertion in *McCollum* that "it may be doubted whether the Constitution [protects] one from the embarrassment that always attends nonconformity, whether in religion, politics, behavior or dress"?

SCHOOL DISTRICT v. SCHEMPP

374 U.S. 203, 83 S.Ct. 1560, 10 L.Ed.2d 844 (1963).

MR. JUSTICE CLARK delivered the opinion of the Court.

[These cases were brought by parents and their children in public schools— *Schempp,* by Unitarians in Abington Township, Pa.; *Murray* by "professed atheists" in Baltimore, Md.—challenging reading of the Bible (without comment) and recitation of the Lord's Prayer as part of daily opening exercises in the schools. In *Schempp,* various students read passages they selected from any version of the Bible. Mr. Schempp testified that "specific religious doctrines purveyed by a literal reading of the Bible" were contrary to the family's religious beliefs; one expert testified that "portions of the New Testament were offensive to Jewish tradition" and, if "read without explanation, they could [be] psychologically harmful to the child and had caused a divisive force within the social media of the school"; a defense expert testified "that the Bible [was] nonsectarian within the Christian faiths." Mr. Schempp had decided against having his children excused from the exercise (as they could be) because he believed "that the children's relationships with their teachers and classmates would be adversely affected." In *Murray,* the child was excused on request of the parent.]

The wholesome "neutrality" [toward religion] of which this Court's cases speak [stems] from a recognition of the teachings of history that powerful sects or groups might bring about a fusion of governmental and religious functions or a concert or dependency of one upon the other to the end that official support of the State or Federal Government would be placed behind the tenets of one or of all orthodoxies. This the Establishment Clause prohibits. And a further reason for neutrality is found in the Free Exercise Clause, which recognizes the value of religious training, teaching and observance and, more particularly, the right of every person to freely choose his own course with reference thereto, free of any compulsion from the state. This the Free Exercise Clause guarantees. Thus, as we have seen, the two clauses may overlap. [The] test may be stated as follows: what are the purpose and the primary effect of the enactment? If either is the advancement or inhibition of religion then the enactment exceeds the scope of legislative power as circumscribed by the Constitution. That is to say that to withstand the strictures of the Establishment Clause there must be a secular legislative purpose and a primary effect that neither advances nor inhibits religion. *Everson; McGowan v. Maryland,* [Part II infra]. The Free Exercise Clause['s] purpose is to secure religious liberty in the individual by prohibiting any invasions thereof by civil authority. Hence it is necessary in a free exercise case for one to show the coercive effect of the enactment as it operates against him in the practice of his religion. The distinction between the two clauses is apparent—a violation of the Free Exercise Clause is predicated on coercion while the Establishment Clause violation need not be so attended.

Applying the Establishment Clause principles to the cases at bar we find that the States are requiring [these exercises] as part of the curricular activities of students who are required by law to attend school. They are held in the school buildings under the supervision and with the participation of teachers employed in those schools. None of these factors, other than compulsory school attendance, was present in the program upheld in *Zorach.* The trial court in [*Schempp*] has found that such an opening exercise is a religious ceremony and was intended by the State to be so. [But the states contend] that the program is an effort to extend its benefits to all public school children without regard to their religious belief. Included within its secular purposes, it says, are the promotion of moral values, the contradiction to the materialistic trends of our times, the perpetuation of our institutions and the teaching of literature. [But] even if its purpose is not strictly religious, it is sought to be accomplished through readings, without comment, from the Bible. Surely the place of the Bible as an instrument of religion cannot be gainsaid, and the State's recognition of the pervading religious character of the ceremony is evident from the rule's specific permission of the alternative use of the Catholic Douay version as well as the recent amendment permitting nonattendance at the exercises. None of these factors is consistent with the contention that the Bible is here used either as an instrument for nonreligious moral inspiration or as a reference for the teaching of secular subjects.

The conclusion follows that in both cases the laws require religious exercises and such exercises are being conducted in direct violation of the rights of the appellees and petitioners.   Nor are these required exercises mitigated by the fact that individual students may absent themselves upon parental request, for that fact furnishes no defense to a claim of unconstitutionality under the Establishment Clause.   See *Engel*.[a]   Further, it is no defense to urge that the religious practices here may be relatively minor encroachments on the First Amendment.   The breach of neutrality that is today a trickling stream may all too soon become a raging torrent * * *.

It is insisted that unless these religious exercises are permitted a "religion of secularism" is established in the schools.   * * * We do not agree, however, that this decision in any sense has that effect.   In addition, it might well be said that one's education is not complete without a study of comparative religion or the history of religion and its relationship to the advancement of civilization.   It certainly may be said that the Bible is worthy of study for its literary and historic qualities.   Nothing we have said here indicates that such study of the Bible or of religion, when presented objectively as part of a secular program of education, may not be effected * * *.

Finally, we cannot accept that the concept of neutrality, which does not permit a State to require a religious exercise even with the consent of the majority of those affected, collides with the majority's right to free exercise of religion.[10]   While the Free Exercise Clause clearly prohibits the use of state action to deny the rights of free exercise to *anyone*, it has never meant that a majority could use the machinery of the State to practice its beliefs.   * * *

MR. JUSTICE BRENNAN, concurring.   * * *

I join fully in the opinion and the judgment of the Court.   * * *

A too literal quest for the advice of the Founding Fathers upon the issues of these cases seems to me futile and misdirected for several reasons: First, on our precise problem the historical record is at best ambiguous * * *.

a.   *Engel v. Vitale*, 370 U.S. 421, 82 S.Ct. 1261, 8 L.Ed. 601 (1962), per Black, J., held that daily class recitation of a prayer composed by the New York Board of Regents violated the establishment clause.   Neither the fact "that the Regents' prayer was 'nondenominational' " nor that students who so wished might "remain silent or be excused from the room" could save it.   The Court distinguished "the fact that school children and others are officially encouraged to express love for our country by reciting historical documents such as the Declaration of Independence which contain references to the Deity or by singing officially espoused anthems which include the composer's professions of faith in a Supreme Being, or with the fact that there are many manifestations in our public life of belief in God.   Such patriotic or ceremonial occasions bear no true resemblance to the unquestioned religious exercise that New York has sponsored in this instance." Douglas, J., concurred.

Stewart, J., dissented: Neither the daily invocation to God in the Supreme Court, prayers in Congress, invocations of God by all of our presidents, the third stanza of The Star-Spangled Banner (which has religious lan-

guage), the pledge of allegiance (which contains the words "under God"), the congressionally directed National Day of Prayer, the words "In God We Trust" on our coins, the Declaration of Independence (which relies on "Divine Providence"), nor the Regents' prayer established an "official religion."   Frankfurter and White, JJ., did not participate.

For commentary, see Griswold, *Absolute is in the Dark—A Discussion of the Approach of the Supreme Court to Constitutional Questions,* 8 Utah L.Rev. 167 (1963); Kauper, *Prayer, Public Schools and the Supreme Court,* 61 Mich.L.Rev. 1031 (1963); Kurland, *The Regents' Prayer Case: "Full of Sound and Fury, Signifying * * *,"* 1962 Sup.Ct.Rev. 1; Pollak, *Public Prayers in Public Schools,* 77 Harv. L.Rev. 62 (1963); Sutherland, *Establishment According to Engel,* 76 Harv.L.Rev. 25 (1962).

10.   We [do] not pass upon a situation such as military service, where the Government regulates the temporal and geographic environment of individuals to a point that, unless it permits voluntary religious services to be conducted with the use of government facilities, military personnel would be unable to engage in the practice of their faiths.

Second, the structure of American education has greatly changed since the First Amendment was adopted. * * *

Third, [t]oday the Nation is far more heterogeneous religiously, including as it does substantial minorities not only of Catholics and Jews but as well of those who worship according to no version of the Bible and those who worship no God at all. In the face of such profound changes, practices which may have been objectionable to no one in the time of Jefferson and Madison may today be highly offensive to many persons, the deeply devout and the non-believers alike. [Thus], our use of the history of their time must limit itself to broad purposes, not specific practices. * * *

First, it is argued that however clearly religious may have been the origins and early nature of daily prayer and Bible reading, these practices today serve so clearly secular educational purposes that their religious attributes may be overlooked. [These purposes] fall into two categories—those which depend upon an immediately religious experience shared by the participating children; and those which appear sufficiently divorced from the religious content of the devotional material that they can be served equally by nonreligious materials. With respect to the first objective, much has been written about the moral and spiritual values of infusing some religious influence or instruction into the public school classroom. To the extent that only *religious* materials will serve this purpose, it seems to me that the purpose as well as the means is so plainly religious that the exercise is necessarily forbidden by the Establishment Clause. The fact that purely secular benefits may eventually result [could] no doubt have been claimed for the released time program invalidated in *McCollum.*

The second justification assumes that religious exercises at the start of the school day may directly serve solely secular ends—for example, by fostering harmony and tolerance among the pupils, enhancing the authority of the teacher, and inspiring better discipline. To the extent that such benefits result not from the content of the readings and recitation, but simply from the holding of such a solemn exercise at the opening assembly or the first class of the day, it would seem that less sensitive materials might equally well serve the same purpose. * * *

Second, it is argued that the particular practices involved in the two cases before us are unobjectionable because they prefer no particular sect or sects at the expense of others. [But] any version of the Bible is inherently sectarian * * *.

The more difficult question, however, is whether the availability of excusal for the dissenting child serves to refute challenges to these practices under the Free Exercise Clause. [The] answer is [that] by requiring what is tantamount in the eyes of teachers and schoolmates to a profession of disbelief, or at least of nonconformity, the procedure may well deter those children who do not wish to participate for any reason based upon the dictates of conscience from exercising an indisputably constitutional right to be excused. * * *

[What] the Framers meant to foreclose, and what our decisions under the Establishment Clause have forbidden, are those involvements of religious with secular institutions which (a) serve the essentially religious activities of religious institutions; (b) employ the organs of government for essentially religious purposes; or (c) use essentially religious means to serve governmental ends, where secular means would suffice. When the secular and religious institutions become involved in such a manner, there inhere in the relationship precisely those dangers—as much to church as to state—which the Framers feared would subvert religious liberty and the strength of a system of secular government. On the other hand, there may be myriad forms of involvements of government with religion which do not import such dangers * * *. I think a brief survey of certain of these forms of accommodation will reveal that the First Amendment commands not official hostility toward religion, but only a strict neutrality * * *.

A. The Conflict Between Establishment and Free Exercise.—There are certain practices, conceivably violative of the Establishment Clause, the striking down of which might seriously interfere with certain religious liberties also protected by the First Amendment. Provisions for churches and chaplains at military establishments for those in the armed services may afford one such example. The like provision by state and federal governments for chaplains in penal institutions may afford another * * *.

Such activities and practices seem distinguishable from the sponsorship of daily Bible reading and prayer recital. For one thing, there is no element of coercion present * * *; the soldier or convict who declines the opportunities for worship would not ordinarily subject himself to the suspicion or obloquy of his peers. Of special significance to this distinction is the fact that we are here usually dealing with adults, not with impressionable children as in the public schools. Moreover, [the] student's compelled presence in school for five days a week in no way renders the regular religious facilities of the community less accessible to him than they are to [others.] I do not say that government *must* provide chaplains * * *.

MR. JUSTICE GOLDBERG, with whom MR. JUSTICE HARLAN joins, concurring.

[I] join the opinion and judgment of the Court. [But] untutored devotion to the concept of neutrality can lead to invocation or approval of results which partake not simply of that noninterference and noninvolvement with the religious which the Constitution commands, but of a brooding and pervasive devotion to the secular and a passive, or even active, hostility to the religious. Such results are not only not compelled by the Constitution, but, it seems to me, are prohibited by [it.] The pervasive religiosity and direct governmental involvement inhering in the prescription of prayer and Bible reading in the public schools, during and as part of the curricular day, involving young impressionable children whose school attendance is statutorily compelled, and utilizing the prestige, power, and influence of school administration, staff, and authority, cannot realistically be termed simply accommodation, and must fall within the interdiction of the First Amendment. I find nothing in the opinion of the Court which says more than this. [The] First Amendment does not prohibit practices which by any realistic measure create none of the dangers which it is designed to prevent and which do not so directly or substantially involve the state in religious exercises or in the favoring of religion as to have meaningful and practical impact. It is of course true that great consequences can grow from small beginnings, but the measure of constitutional adjudication is the ability and willingness to distinguish between real threat and mere shadow.

MR. JUSTICE STEWART, dissenting. * * *

That the central value embodied in the First Amendment—and, more particularly, in the guarantee of "liberty" contained in the Fourteenth—is the safeguarding of an individual's right to free exercise of his religion has been consistently recognized [and] there is involved in these cases a substantial free exercise claim on the part of those who affirmatively desire to have their children's school day open with the reading of passages from the Bible.

[It] might be argued here that parents who wanted their children to be exposed to religious influences in school could, under *Pierce v. Society of Sisters* send their children to private or parochial schools. [But] "Freedom of speech, freedom of the press, freedom of religion are available to all, not merely to those who can pay their own way." *Murdock v. Pennsylvania*, [Sec. 2, I infra].

It might also be argued that parents who want their children exposed to religious influences can adequately fulfill that wish off school property and outside school time. [But] a compulsory state educational system so structures a child's life that if religious exercises are held to be an impermissible activity in schools, religion is placed at an artificial and state-created disadvantage. [A] refusal to permit religious exercises thus is seen, not as the realization of state neutrality, but rather as the establishment of a religion of secularism, or at the least, as government support of the beliefs of those who think that religious exercises should be conducted only in private. * * *

The dangers both to government and to religion inherent in official support of instruction in the tenets of various religious sects are absent in the present cases, which involve only a reading from the Bible unaccompanied by comments which might otherwise constitute instruction. [In] the absence of coercion upon those who do not wish to participate—because they hold less strong beliefs, other beliefs, or no beliefs at all—such provisions cannot, in my view, be held to represent the type of support of religion barred by the Establishment Clause. For the only support which such rules provide for religion is the withholding of state hostility—a simple acknowledgment on the part of secular authorities that the Constitution does not require extirpation of all expression of religious belief.

I have said that these provisions authorizing religious exercises are properly to be regarded as measures making possible the free exercise of religion. But it is important to stress that [the] question presented is not whether exercises such as those at issue here are constitutionally compelled, but rather whether they are constitutionally invalid. And that issue, in my view, turns on the question of coercion. [I]t seems to me clear that certain types of exercises would present situations in which no possibility of coercion on the part of secular officials could be claimed to exist. Thus, if such exercises were held either before or after the official school day, or if the school schedule were such that participation were merely one among a number of desirable alternatives, it could hardly be contended that the exercises did anything more than to provide an opportunity for the voluntary expression of religious belief. On the other hand, a law which provided for religious exercises during the school day and which contained no excusal provision would obviously be unconstitutionally coercive upon those who did not wish to participate. And even under a law containing an excusal provision, if the exercises were held during the school day, and no equally desirable alternative were provided by the school authorities, the likelihood that children might be under at least some psychological compulsion to participate would be great. In a case such as the latter, however, I think we would err if we *assumed* such coercion in the absence of any evidence. [No] evidence at all was adduced in the *Murray* case, because it was decided upon a demurrer. [In] the *Schempp* case the record shows no more than a subjective prophecy by a parent of what he thought would happen if a request were made to be excused from participation in the exercises under the amended statute. [It] is conceivable that these school boards, or even all school boards, might eventually find it impossible to administer a system of religious exercises during school hours in such a way as to meet this constitutional standard—in such a way as completely to free from any kind of official coercion those who do not affirmatively want to participate.[8] But I think we must not assume that school boards so lack the qualities of inventiveness and good will as to make impossible the achievement of that goal.

I would remand both cases for further hearings.[a]

Notes and Questions

1. *The Court's test.* Is the Court's "purpose and primary effect" test consistent with prior decisions? Do the factors by which the Court distinguishes *Zorach* relate to "purpose and primary effect"? What was the *primary* effect of the plan in *Everson*? Is this concept meaningful? What result in the examples of Stewart, J., in *Engel*? Consider Johnson, *Concepts and Compromise in First Amendment Religious Doctrine,* 72 Calif.L.Rev. 817, 827 (1984): "[There is great difficulty] making sense out of the crucial distinction between *religious* purpose or effect and *secular* purpose or effect. Governments usually act out of secular motives, even when they are directly aiding a particular religious sect. An atheistic ruler might well create an established church because he thinks it a useful way of raising money, or of ensuring that the clergy do not preach seditious doctrines. In democratic societies, elected officials have an excellent secular reason to accommodate (or at least to avoid offending) groups and individuals who are religious, as well as groups and individuals who are not. They wish to be re-elected, and they do not want important groups to feel that the community does not honor their values."

2. *Coercion.* (a) What significance do the opinions in *Schempp* attribute to the "coercive effect" of religious exercises in public schools? Consider Kauper, *Religion and the Constitution* 72 (1964): "[Clark, J.] did not find it enough to say that here the government was sanctioning a practice directed to religious ends, but went on to emphasize the elements of compulsion in this case. He noted that the prayer was approved by state authorities, was prescribed for daily use in a public school for children required to attend under the compulsory education laws, and was supervised by [a] public school teacher. If strict neutrality were the criterion, then it should have been unnecessary for the court to discuss the elements of compulsion." See generally Schumb, *Church, State and the Public Schools,* 4 Santa Clara Law. 54 (1963).

(b) Consider Choper, *Religion in the Public Schools: A Proposed Constitutional Standard,* 47 Minn.L.Rev. 329, 330 (1963): "The [standard is that] the establishment clause [is] violated when the state engages in what may be fairly characterized as *solely religious activity* that is likely to result in (1) *compromising* the student's religious or conscientious beliefs or (2) *influencing* the student's freedom of religious or conscientious choice."

Does this test differ from Stewart, J.'s? What evidence of coercion does he require? That the objectors first ask to be excused from participation and then show that social pressures were brought to bear on them? Would this force an objector to surrender his rights in order to vindicate them?

3. *Other public school practices.* (a) STONE v. GRAHAM, 449 U.S. 39, 101 S.Ct. 192, 66 L.Ed.2d 199 (1980), per curiam, held that a Kentucky statute— requiring "the posting of a copy of the Ten Commandments, purchased with

---

8. For example, if the record in [*Schempp*] contained proof (rather than mere prophecy) that the timing of morning announcements by the school was such as to handicap children who did not want to listen to the Bible reading, or that the excusal provision was so ad-

ministered as to carry any overtones of social inferiority, then impermissible coercion would clearly exist.

a. The concurring opinion of Douglas, J., who joined the Court's opinion, is omitted.

private contributions, on the wall of each public classroom in the State," with the notation at the bottom that "The secular application of the Ten Commandments is clearly seen in its adoption as the fundamental legal code of Western Civilization and the Common Law of the United States"—had "no secular legislative purpose": "The Ten Commandments is undeniably a sacred text in the Jewish and Christian faiths, and no legislative recitation of a supposed secular purpose can blind us to that [fact]. Posting of religious texts on the wall serves [no] educational function. If the posted copies of the Ten Commandments are to have any effect at all, it will be to induce the school children to read, meditate upon, perhaps to venerate and obey, the Commandments. However desirable this might be as a matter of private devotion, it is not a permissible state objective under the Establishment Clause."

REHNQUIST, J., dissented: "The Court's summary rejection of a secular purpose articulated by the legislature and confirmed by the state court is without precedent in Establishment Clause jurisprudence. [This] Court has recognized that 'religion has been closely identified with our history and government,' *Schempp*, and that 'the history of man is inseparable from the history of religion,' *Engel*. Kentucky has decided to make students aware of this fact by demonstrating the secular impact of the Ten Commandments." [b]

(b) In 1978, Alabama enacted § 16–1–20 authorizing a one-minute period of silence in all public schools "for meditation"; in 1981, it enacted § 16–1–20.1 authorizing a period of silence "for meditation or voluntary prayer." WALLACE v. JAFFREE, __ U.S. __, 105 S.Ct. 2479, 86 L.Ed.2d 29 (1985), per STEVENS, J., held that the 1981 law violated the establishment clause, relying, inter alia, on its sponsor's statements that the law's only purpose was an "effort to return voluntary prayer to our public schools," and the fact that "the State did not present evidence of *any* secular purpose": "[E]ven though a statute that is motivated in part by a religious purpose may satisfy the ["secular legislative purpose" requirement], the First Amendment requires that a statute must be invalidated if it is entirely motivated by a purpose to advance religion. * * *

"The legislative intent to return prayer to public schools is, of course, quite different from merely protecting every student's right to engage in voluntary prayer during an appropriate moment of silence during the school day. The 1978 statute already protected that right, containing nothing that prevented any student from engaging in voluntary prayer during a silent minute of meditation. [The] Legislature enacted § 16–1–20.1 despite the existence of § 16–1–20 for the sole purpose of expressing the State's endorsement of prayer activities. [The] addition of 'or voluntary prayer' indicates that the State intended to characterize prayer as a favored practice. Such an endorsement is not consistent with the established principle that the Government must pursue a course of complete neutrality toward religion."

O'CONNOR, J., concurred in the judgment: "A state sponsored moment of silence in the public schools is different from state sponsored vocal prayer or Bible reading. First, a moment of silence is not inherently religious. Silence, unlike prayer or Bible reading, need not be associated with a religious exercise. Second, a pupil who participates in a moment of silence need not compromise his or her beliefs. During a moment of silence, a student who objects to prayer is left to his or her own thoughts, and is not compelled to listen to the prayers or

b. Stewart, J., also dissented. Burger, C.J., and Blackmun, J., dissented from not giving the case plenary consideration.

thoughts of others. [It] is difficult to discern a serious threat to religious liberty from a room of silent, thoughtful schoolchildren.

"[Even] if a statute specifies that a student may choose to pray silently during a quiet moment, the State has not thereby encouraged prayer over other specified alternatives. Nonetheless, it is also possible that a moment of silence statute, either as drafted or as actually implemented, could effectively favor the child who prays over the child who does not. For example, the message of endorsement would seem inescapable if the teacher exhorts children to use the designated time to pray. Similarly, the face of the statute or its legislative history may clearly establish that it seeks to encourage or promote voluntary prayer over other alternatives, rather than merely provide a quiet moment that may be dedicated to prayer by those so inclined. The crucial question is whether the State has conveyed or attempted to convey the message that children should use the moment of silence for prayer. This question cannot be answered in the abstract, but instead requires courts to examine the history, language, and administration of a particular statute to determine whether it operates as an endorsement of religion.

"Some general observations on the proper scope of the inquiry are in order. First, the inquiry into the purpose of the legislature in enacting a moment of silence law should be deferential and limited. In determining whether the government intends a moment of silence statute to convey a message of endorsement or disapproval of religion, a court has no license to psychoanalyze the legislators. If a legislature expresses a plausible secular purpose for a moment of silence statute in either the text or the legislative history, or if the statute disclaims an intent to encourage prayer over alternatives during a moment of silence, then courts should generally defer to that stated intent. [Even] if the text and official history of a statute express no secular purpose, the statute should be held to have an improper purpose only if it is beyond purview that endorsement of religion or a religious belief 'was and is the law's reason for existence.' Since there is arguably a secular pedagogical value to a moment of silence in public schools, courts should find an improper purpose behind such a statute only if the statute on its face, in its official legislative history, or in its interpretation by a responsible administrative agency suggests it has the primary purpose of endorsing prayer.

"Justice Rehnquist suggests that this sort of deferential inquiry into legislative purpose 'means little,' because 'it only requires the legislature to express any secular purpose and omit all sectarian references.' It is not a trivial matter, however, to require that the legislature manifest a secular purpose and omit all sectarian endorsements from its laws. That requirement is precisely tailored to the Establishment Clause's purpose of assuring that Government not intentionally endorse religion or a religious practice. It is of course possible that a legislature will enunciate a sham secular purpose for a statute. I have little doubt that our courts are capable of distinguishing a sham secular purpose from a sincere one, or [that] inquiry into the effect of an enactment would help decide those close cases where the validity of an expressed secular purpose is in doubt. [A] moment of silence law that is clearly drafted and implemented so as to permit prayer, meditation, and reflection within the prescribed period, without endorsing one alternative over the others, should pass this test.

"The analysis above suggests that moment of silence laws in many States should pass Establishment Clause scrutiny because they do not favor the child who chooses to pray during a moment of silence over the child who chooses to meditate or reflect. Alabama Code § 16–1–20.1 does not stand on the same footing. However deferentially one examines its text and legislative history, however objectively one views the message attempted to be conveyed to the public, the conclusion is unavoidable that the purpose of the statute is to endorse prayer in public schools. [Given] this legislative history, it is not surprising that the State of Alabama conceded in the courts below that the purpose of the statute was to make prayer part of daily classroom activity, and that both the District Court and the Court of Appeals concluded that the law's purpose was to encourage religious activity. In light of the legislative history and the findings of the courts below, I agree with the Court that the State intended § 16–1–20.1 to convey a message that prayer was the endorsed activity during the state-prescribed moment of silence.[5]" [c]

BURGER, C.J., dissented: "The statute does not remotely threaten religious liberty; it affirmatively furthers the values of religious freedom and tolerance that the Establishment Clause was designed to protect. Without pressuring those who do not wish to pray, the statute simply creates an opportunity to think, to plan, or to pray if one wishes—as Congress does by providing chaplains and chapels. [The] statute also provides a meaningful opportunity for schoolchildren to appreciate the absolute constitutional right of each individual to worship and believe as the individual wishes. The statute 'endorses' only the view that the religious observances of others should be tolerated and, where possible, accommodated. If the government may not accommodate religious needs when it does so in a wholly neutral and noncoercive manner, the 'benevolent neutrality' that we have long considered the correct constitutional standard will quickly translate into the 'callous indifference' that the Court has consistently held the Establishment Clause does not require. * * *

"The several preceding opinions conclude that the principal difference between § 16–1–20.1 and its predecessor statute proves that the sole purpose behind the inclusion of the phrase 'or voluntary prayer' in § 16–1–20.1 was to endorse and promote prayer. * * * Congress amended the statutory Pledge of Allegiance 31 years ago to add the words 'under God.' Do the several opinions in support of the judgment today render the Pledge unconstitutional?[3] [T]he inclusion of the words 'or voluntary prayer' in § 16–1–20.1 is wholly consistent with the clearly permissible purpose of clarifying that silent, voluntary prayer is not *forbidden* in the public school building."

REHNQUIST, J., dissented, examining the history of the religion clauses at some length—including the debates in the First Congress (where "Madison was

---

5. The Chief Justice suggests that one consequence of the Court's emphasis on the difference between § 16–1–20.1 and its predecessor statute might be to render the Pledge of Allegiance unconstitutional because Congress amended it in 1954 to add the words "under God". I disagree. In my view, the words "under God" in the Pledge serve as an acknowledgement of religion with "the legitimate secular purposes of solemnizing public occasions, [and] expressing confidence in the future."

c. Powell, J., who was the fifth justice to join the Court's opinion, concurred, agreeing "fully with Justice O'Connor's assertion that some moment-of-silence statutes may be constitutional, a suggestion set forth in the Court's opinion as well. * * * I would vote

to uphold the Alabama statute if it also had a clear secular purpose. See *Mueller v. Allen*, [Part III infra] (the Court is 'reluctan[t] to attribute unconstitutional motives to the state, particularly when a plausible secular purpose may be discerned from the face of the statute')."

3. The House Report on the legislation amending the Pledge states that the purpose of the amendment was to affirm the principle that "our people and our Government [are dependent] upon the moral directions of the Creator." If this is simply "acknowledgement," not "endorsement," of religion, (O'Connor, J., concurring in the judgment), the distinction is far too infinitesimal for me to grasp.

undoubtedly the most important architect among the members of the House of the amendments which became the Bill of Rights"), the Thanksgiving proclamations issued by Presidents Washington, Adams and Madison, and 19th century congressional appropriations "in support of sectarian Indian education carried on by religious organizations": "The Framers intended the Establishment Clause to prohibit the designation of any church as a 'national' one. The Clause was also designed to stop the Federal Government from asserting a preference for one religious denomination or sect over others. Given the 'incorporation' of the Establishment Clause as against the States via the Fourteenth Amendment in *Everson*, States are prohibited as well from establishing a religion or discriminating between sects. As its history abundantly shows, however, nothing in the Establishment Clause requires government to be strictly neutral between religion and irreligion, nor does that Clause prohibit Congress or the States from pursuing legitimate secular ends through nondiscriminatory sectarian means.

"[There] is simply no historical foundation for the proposition that the Framers intended to build the 'wall of separation' that was constitutionalized in *Everson*. [In] the 38 years since *Everson* our Establishment Clause cases have been neither principled nor unified. [The "purpose" and "effect" tests] have the same historical deficiencies as the wall concept itself: they are in no way based on either the language or intent of the drafters. * * *

"If a constitutional theory has no basis in the history of the amendment it seeks to interpret, is difficult to apply and yields unprincipled results, I see little use in it. [It] would come as much of a shock to those who drafted the Bill of Rights as it will to a large number of thoughtful Americans today to learn that the Constitution, as construed by the majority, prohibits the Alabama Legislature from 'endorsing' prayer."[d]

4. *Public school secularism.* Consider Manning, *The Douglas Concept of God in Government*, 39 Wash.L.Rev. 47, 63 (1964): "[I]f we forbid the teaching of recognized religions in our public schools and forbid a prayer which simply acknowledges the existence of God and at the same time permit—as, indeed, we must—the teaching of some code of ethical conduct, some system of value norms, does not the system which the school then sponsors become the system of Secular Humanism or simply secular humanism? Do we not then prefer, in public education, one religion, Secular Humanism, over other religions which are founded upon a belief in the existence of God?" Compare Kauper, *Schempp and Sherbert: Studies in Neutrality and Accommodation*, 1963 Relig. & Pub.Or. 3, 23: "[I]n the interest of neutrality as between theistic and humanistic religions, the public schools must carefully avoid any program of indoctrination in ultimate values." May it be argued in response that, simply because the religion of Secular Humanism "adopts" as its own a moral or ideological tenet that is also a publicly accepted behavioral standard, this does not make it a "religious" tenet under the establishment clause for the purpose of its being taught in the public schools? See note 4, Sec. 2, II infra. May public schools teach the theory of evolution to the exclusion of other theories of human origin? See Note, *Freedom of Religion and Science Instruction in Public Schools*, 87 Yale L.J. 515 (1978). If government requires that public employees be of "good moral character," is this a "religious test" for public office? See Freund, *Public Aid to Parochial Schools*, 82 Harv.L.Rev. 1680, 1690 (1969). Compare *McGowan v. Maryland*, Sec. II infra.

---

d. White, J., also dissented, "for the most part agreeing with the opinion of the Chief Justice," and, noting that in light of Rehnquist, J.'s "explication of the history of the religion clauses, [it] would be quite understandable if we undertook to reassess our cases dealing with these clauses, particularly [the] Establishment Clause."

See generally Note, *Humanistic Values In The Public School Curriculum: Problems In Defining An Appropriate "Wall Of Separation,"* 61 Nw.U.L.Rev. 795 (1966).

5. *"Political" perspective.* Should the Court have avoided decision on the prayer issue altogether? Consider McCloskey, *Principles, Powers, and Values: The Establishment Clause and the Supreme Court,* 1964 Relig. & Pub.Or. 3, 28: "On the basis of power and value considerations taken together, a strong case could be made for judicial avoidance * * *. The subject seems peculiarly well calculated to generate resistance and backlash and peculiarly ill calculated to enlist adequate countervailing support. Congressmen feel that defending prayer is like defending motherhood: it wins them some votes and costs them almost none. If the evil aimed at by the Court was a great one, this expenditure of judicial power might not be excessive. But the evil in its present manifestations is fairly moderate. Even so, judicial correction of it might be warranted, if there were not other, graver wrongs simultaneously pressing for judicial attention and also taxing the power capacities of the Court. [It] would be unfortunate if the Court, in its zeal to wipe out public pieties, impaired its ability to cope with race discrimination, injustice to accused persons, and inhibitions on free expression, not to speak of other massive self-assigned tasks such as control of legislative apportionment, or of further threats to just government that might appear tomorrow or the next day." Are these "legitimate" considerations for the Court in the exercise of its discretion to decide cases?

II. REGULATION IN AID OF RELIGION

McGOWAN v. MARYLAND, 366 U.S. 420, 81 S.Ct. 1101, 6 L.Ed.2d 393 (1961), per WARREN, C.J., held that the "present purpose and effect" of Maryland's Sunday Closing Laws were not religious and did not violate the establishment clause. Although "the original laws which dealt with Sunday labor were motivated by religious forces," the Court showed that secular emphases in language and interpretation have come about, that recent "legislation was supported by labor groups and trade associations," and that "secular justifications have been advanced for making Sunday a day of rest, a day when people may recover from the labors of the week just passed and may physically and mentally prepare for the week's work to come."

"[T]he 'Establishment' Clause does not ban federal or state regulation of conduct whose reason or effect merely happens to coincide or harmonize with the tenets of some or all religions. In many instances, the Congress or state legislatures conclude that the general welfare of society, wholly apart from any religious considerations, demands such regulation." The Court rejected the contention, "however relevant this argument may be," "that the State has other means at its disposal to accomplish its secular purpose, other courses that would not remotely or incidentally give state aid to religion." A "one-day-in-seven" statute might not serve the purpose of setting "one day apart from all others as a day of rest, repose, recreation, [a] day which all members of the family and community have the opportunity to spend and enjoy together * * *. It would seem unrealistic for enforcement purposes and perhaps detrimental to the general welfare to require a State to choose a common day of rest other than that which most persons would select of their own accord."

"Finally, we [do] not hold that Sunday legislation may not be a violation of the 'Establishment' Clause if it can be demonstrated that its purpose—evidenced either on the face of the legislation, in conjunction with its legislative history, or in its operative effect—is to use the State's coercive power to aid religion."

FRANKFURTER, J., joined by Harlan, J., filed a separate opinion that followed substantially the same lines. It applied also to *Braunfeld v. Brown,* Sec. 2, I infra: "If the primary end achieved by a form of regulation is the affirmation or promotion of religious doctrine—primary, in the sense that all secular ends which it purportedly serves are derivative from, not wholly independent of, the advancement of religion—the regulation is beyond the power of the state. This was the case in *McCollum.* Or if a statute furthers both secular and religious ends by means unnecessary to the effectuation of the secular ends alone—where the same secular ends could equally be attained by means which do not have consequences for promotion of religion—the statute cannot stand."

DOUGLAS, J., dissented, his opinion, applying also to *Braunfeld:* "No matter how much is written, no matter what is said," Sunday is a Christian holiday. "There is an 'establishment' of religion in the constitutional sense if any practice of any religious group has the sanction of law behind it."

EPPERSON v. ARKANSAS, 393 U.S. 97, 89 S.Ct. 266, 21 L.Ed.2d 228 (1968), per FORTAS, J., held that an "anti-evolution" statute, forbidding teachers in public schools "to teach the theory or doctrine that mankind ascended or descended from a lower order of animals," violated "the First Amendment's prohibition of laws respecting an establishment of religion or prohibiting the free exercise thereof." "It is of no moment whether the law is deemed to prohibit mention of Darwin's theory, or to forbid any or all of the infinite varieties of communication embraced within the term 'teaching,'" because "Arkansas' law selects from the body of knowledge a particular segment which it proscribes for the sole reason that it is deemed to conflict with a particular religious doctrine." Government may not "promote one religion or religious theory against another or even against the militant opposite."

Citing newspaper advertisements and letters supporting adoption of the statute in 1928, the Court found it "clear that fundamentalist sectarian conviction was and is the law's reason for existence. Its antecedent, Tennessee's 'monkey law,' candidly stated" a religious purpose. "Perhaps the sensational publicity attendant upon the *Scopes* trial induced Arkansas to adopt less explicit language [but] there is no doubt that the motivation for the law was the same * * *. Arkansas' law cannot be defended as an act of religious neutrality. Arkansas did not seek to excise from the curricula of its schools and universities all discussion of the origin of man." [b]

Notes and Questions

The Court's test. If the "purpose" of the *Epperson* statute, or of some Sunday Closing Law, is found to be "religious," should that alone be enough to invalidate it under the establishment clause? Would these laws "create the dangers the establishment clause was designed to prevent" (Goldberg, J., in *Schempp*)? Would they "subvert religious liberty" (Brennan, J., in *Schempp*)? Some other kind of "liberty"? Are they distinguishable from a public school "dismissed time" program implemented to facilitate religious education? What result, under *Epperson,* for a law requiring that the Biblical version be taught

---

b. Harlan, J., concurred in the Court's "establishment of religion" rationale. Black and Stewart, JJ., concurred on the ground of vagueness.

along with other theories of creation? For discussion of the view that "courts carefully consider the legislative history of a law in order to evaluate claims that religion played an impermissibly central role in the law's passage," see Note, *The Establishment Clause and Religious Influences on Legislation,* 75 Nw.U.L. Rev. 944 (1980). Compare Choper, *The Religion Clauses of the First Amendment: Reconciling the Conflict,* 41 U.Pitt.L.Rev. 673, 686–87 (1980): "[I]t is only when religious purpose is coupled with threatened impairment of religious freedom that government action should be held to violate the Establishment Clause. [Conceding] that the [*Epperson*] statute had a solely religious purpose, [there] was no evidence that religious beliefs were either coerced, compromised or influenced. That is, it was not shown, nor do I believe that it could be persuasively argued, that the anti-evolution law either (1) induced children of fundamentalist religions to accept the biblical theory of creation, or (2) conditioned other children for conversion to fundamentalism. [Thus,] the accommodation for religion in [*Epperson*] should have survived the Establishment Clause challenge."

III. FINANCIAL AID TO RELIGION

The issue of aid to parochial schools first arose again after *Everson* in BOARD OF EDUC. v. ALLEN, 392 U.S. 236, 88 S.Ct. 1923, 20 L.Ed.2d 1060 (1968). The Court, per WHITE, J., held that New York's lending state-approved secular textbooks to all secondary school children did not violate the establishment clause. Applying the *Schempp* "test," the New York law, like that in *Everson,* had "a secular legislative purpose and a primary effect that neither advances nor inhibits religion." Its purpose "was stated by the New York Legislature to be furtherance of the educational opportunities available to the young. [T]he financial benefit is to parents and children, not to schools.[6] Perhaps free books make it more likely that some children choose to attend a sectarian school, but that was true of the state-paid bus fares in *Everson* * * *. Absent evidence we cannot assume that school authorities [are] unable to distinguish between secular and religious books or that they will not honestly discharge their duties under the law. [On] the meager record before us in this case, we cannot agree [that] all teaching in a sectarian school is religious or that the processes of secular and religious training are so intertwined that secular textbooks furnished to students by the public are in fact instrumental in the teaching of religion." [a]

The problem of aid to parochial schools received extensive consideration in 1971. In the interim, however, the following opinion greatly influenced the Court's subsequent decisions.

WALZ v. TAX COMM'N, 397 U.S. 664, 90 S.Ct. 1409, 25 L.Ed.2d 697 (1970), per BURGER, C.J., upheld a state tax exemption for "real or personal property used exclusively for religious, educational or charitable purposes": "The legislative purpose of a property tax exemption is neither the advancement nor the inhibition of religion; it is neither sponsorship nor hostility. New York, in common with the other States, has determined that certain entities that exist in a harmonious relationship to the community at large, and that foster its 'moral

---

6. [T]he record contains no evidence that any of the private schools in appellants' districts previously provided textbooks for their students. * * *

a. Black, Douglas and Fortas, JJ., dissented. See also Note, *Sectarian Books, The Supreme Court and the Establishment Clause,* 79 Yale L.J. 111 (1969).

or mental improvement,' should not be inhibited in their activities by property taxation or the hazard of loss of those properties for nonpayment of taxes. It [has] granted exemption to all houses of religious worship within a broad class of property owned by nonprofit, quasi-public corporations which include hospitals, libraries, playgrounds, scientific, professional, historical and patriotic groups.

* * *

"We find it unnecessary to justify the tax exemption on the social welfare services or 'good works' that some churches perform for parishioners and others—family counselling, aid to the elderly and the infirm, and to children. [To] give emphasis to so variable an aspect of the work of religious bodies would introduce an element of governmental evaluation and standards as to the worth of particular social welfare programs, thus producing a kind of continuing day-to-day relationship which the policy of neutrality seeks to minimize. * * *

" * * * We must also be sure that the end result—the effect—is not an excessive government entanglement with religion. The test is inescapably one of degree. * * * Elimination of exemption would tend to expand the involvement of government by giving rise to tax valuation of church property, tax liens, tax foreclosures, and the direct confrontations and conflicts that follow in the train of those legal processes.

"Granting tax exemptions to churches necessarily operates to afford an indirect economic benefit and also gives rise to some, but yet a lesser, involvement than taxing [them]. Obviously a direct money subsidy would be a relationship pregnant with involvement and, as with most governmental grant programs, could encompass sustained and detailed administrative relationships for enforcement of statutory or administrative standards, but that is not this case.

* * *

"It is obviously correct that no one acquires a vested or protected right in violation of the Constitution by long [use]. Yet an unbroken practice of according the exemption to churches [is] not something to be lightly cast aside."

BRENNAN, J., concurred, finding "two basic secular purposes" for the exemption: "First, these organizations are exempted because they, among a range of other private, nonprofit organizations contribute to the well-being of the community in a variety of nonreligious ways, and thereby bear burdens that would otherwise either have to be met by general taxation, or be left undone * * *.

"Second, government [may] properly include religious institutions among the variety of private, nonprofit groups which receive tax exemptions, for each group contribute to the diversity of association, viewpoint and enterprise essential to a vigorous, pluralistic society. * * *

"Tax exemptions and general subsidies [both] provide economic assistance, [but a] subsidy involves the direct transfer of public monies to the subsidized enterprise and uses resources exacted from taxpayers as a whole. An exemption, on the other hand, involves no such transfer.[a] It assists the exempted enterprise only passively, by relieving a privately funded venture of the burden of paying taxes." [b]

DOUGLAS, J., dissented: "If history be our guide, then tax exemption of church property in this country is indeed highly suspect, as it arose in the early days when the church was an agency of the state. [The] financial support

a. What of the fact that exemption for churches augments the tax bills of others? See generally Bittker, *Churches, Taxes and The Constitution,* 78 Yale L.J. 1285 (1969).

b. Harlan, J., also concurred.

rendered here is to the church, the place of worship. A tax exemption is a subsidy."

Notes and Questions

1. *Secular purpose.* (a) Does *Walz* abandon the "secular purpose" prerequisite of the "test" developed in *Schempp* and relied on in *Allen?* Consider Duval, *The Constitutionality of State Aid to Nonpublic Elementary and Secondary Schools,* 1970 U.Ill.L.F. 342, 349: "The emphasis in *Walz* is not on whether legislation is intended to promote and in fact does promote purely secular ends. Rather the question is whether either the purpose or effect is to advance or inhibit religion. Thus under *Walz* but not *Allen* if neither the purpose nor effect is to advance or inhibit religion, it is immaterial whether the legislation serves a secular objective." Thus viewed, is *Walz* a direct descendant of *Zorach?*

(b) Do either (or both) of Brennan, J.'s "two basic secular purposes" satisfy the *Schempp-Allen* test? Does the first justify tax exemption for *all* churches? Does it justify direct subsidies to *some* churches? Does the second justify general subsidies to *all* churches—at least so long as other groups that "contribute to the diversity essential to a vigorous, pluralistic society" are included?

2. *Direct subsidies vs. tax exemption.* Apart from the issue of the economic equivalence of subsidies and exemptions, consider Davidow, *Governmental Aid to Church-Affiliated Colleges,* 43 N.D.L.Rev. 659, 687 (1967): "[B]ecause such aid is less 'direct' than that involved in the granting of funds, the degree of governmental approbation of specific religious practices is less; hence, it is not as likely that those not aided will feel pressures to conform—i.e., to affiliate with some groups which are aided through tax exemption." Would small grants to all religions for religious symbols in houses of worship generate "pressures to conform"?

Consider Van Alstyne, *Constitutional Separation of Church and State: The Quest for a Coherent Position,* 57 Am.Pol.Sci.Rev. 865, 881 (1963): "To finance expanding government services, [taxes] may gradually divert an increasing fraction of total personal income, necessarily leaving proportionately less money in the private sector to each person to spend according to his individual choice, in support of religion or other undertakings. To the extent that the tax revenues thus collected may not be spent by government to support religious enterprises, but must be used exclusively for secular purposes, the net effect, arguably, is to reduce the relative supply of funds available to religion." Does this warrant tax exemption for "religion"? Does it "warrant the judicial junking of the establishment clause"? Id. Is it "equally arguable that government fiscal activity, far from reducing disposable personal income, actually increases it"? Id. See also Schwartz, *The Nonestablishment Principle: A Reply to Professor Giannella,* 81 Harv.L.Rev. 1465, 1469–70 (1968).

3. *"Excessive government entanglement."* To what extent does *Walz* turn on this element? Precisely what does this notion encompass? Consider Warren, Krattenmaker & Snyder, *Property Tax Exemptions for Charitable, Educational, Religious and Governmental Institutions in Connecticut,* 4 Conn.L.Rev. 181, 209 (1971): "The argument that evaluation of property owned by churches may give rise to secular-sectarian clashes seems farfetched. Alternative use market values would surely serve as a suitable, ideologically neutral touchstone."

LEMON v. KURTZMAN, 403 U.S. 602, 91 S.Ct. 2105, 29 L.Ed.2d 745 (1971), involved states paying all or part of the salaries of teachers of secular subjects in nonpublic schools. Various restrictions sought to assure that state funds would not be used to teach religion in any form. The Court, per BURGER, C.J., articulated a three-part test for judging establishment clause challenges: "First, the statute must have a secular legislative purpose; second, its principal or primary effect must be one that neither advances nor inhibits religion, *Allen*; finally the statute must not foster 'an excessive government entanglement with religion.' *Walz.*"

Although the Court found that the state programs had a secular purpose, they were held to violate the establishment clause: "We [do] not assume that teachers in parochial schools will be guilty of bad faith [but] simply recognize that a dedicated religious person, teaching in a school affiliated with his or her faith and operated to inculcate its tenets, will inevitably [find] it hard to make a total separation between secular teaching and religious doctrine. [A] comprehensive, discriminating, and continuing state surveillance will inevitably be required to ensure [against a "principal or primary effect" that advances religion]. These prophylactic contacts will involve excessive and enduring entanglement between state and church. * * *

"A broader base of entanglement of yet a different character is presented by the divisive political potential of these state programs [because] it can be assumed that state assistance will entail considerable political activity. [B]ut political division along religious lines was one of the principal evils against which the First Amendment was intended to protect. Freund, *Public Aid to Parochial Schools*, 82 Harv.L.Rev. 1680, 1692 (1969)." [a]

Only WHITE, J., dissented: "The Court * * * creates an insoluble paradox for the State and the parochial schools. The State cannot finance secular instruction if it permits religion to be taught in the same classroom; but if it exacts a promise that religion not be so taught—a promise the school and its teachers are quite willing and on this record able to give—and enforces it, it is then entangled in the 'no entanglement' aspect of the Court's Establishment Clause jurisprudence."

---

a. Compare Schwartz, *No Imposition of Religion: The Establishment Clause Value*, 77 Yale L.J. 692, 711 (1968): "If avoidance of strife were an independent [establishment clause] value, no legislation could be adopted on any subject which aroused strong and divided [religious] feelings." See Choper, *The Establishment Clause and Aid to Parochial Schools*, 56 Calif.L.Rev. 260, 273 (1968): "Nor would a denial of aid to parochial schools largely diminish the extent of religious political activity. In fact, it 'might lead to greater political ruptures caused by the alienation of segments of the religious community.' Those who send their children to parochial schools might intensify opposition to increased governmental aid to public education." See also Nowak, Rotunda & Young, *Constitutional Law* 867–68 (1978). Contrast Valente & Stanmeyer, *Public Aid to Parochial Schools—A Reply to Professor Freund*, 59 Geo.L.J. 59, 70

n. 46 (1970): "[O]ne's assessment of the accuracy of the views of Professors Freund Schwartz, and Choper as to likely political repercussions is itself a political judgment and not judicial, and [the] weighing of political reactions is a function of legislatures and not of courts." See also Ripple, *The Entanglement Test of the Religion Clauses—A Ten Year Assessment*, 27 U.C.L.A.L.Rev. 1195 (1980). For the view that the historical evidence shows "that it is misguided to interpret the first amendment as prohibiting legislative consideration of an issue affecting religion on the ground that the very act of consideration will spawn impermissible religious division," see Schotten, *The Establishment Clause and Excessive Governmental-Religious Entanglement: The Constitutional Status of Aid to Nonpublic Elementary and Secondary Schools*, 15 Wake For.L.Rev. 207, 225 (1979).

TILTON v. RICHARDSON, 403 U.S. 672, 91 S.Ct. 2091, 29 L.Ed.2d 790 (1971), upheld federal construction grants for college and university buildings and facilities that were subject to statutory conditions for 20 years, enforced primarily by on-site inspections, to assure use "exclusively for secular educational purposes."[b] BURGER, C.J., joined by Harlan, Stewart and Blackmun, JJ., rejected appellants' attempt to construct a "composite profile" of the "typical sectarian" institution of higher education: "[A]ppellants' position depends on the validity of the proposition that religion so permeates the secular education provided by church-related colleges and universities that their religious and secular educational functions are in fact inseparable. The [record] provides no basis for any such assumption here. * * *

"There are generally significant differences between the religious aspects of church-related institutions of higher learning and parochial elementary and secondary schools. The 'affirmative, if not dominant, policy' of the instruction in pre-college church-schools is 'to assure future adherents to a particular faith by having control of their total education at an early age.' There is substance to the contention that college students are less impressionable and less susceptible to religious indoctrination. [Further], by their very nature, college and postgraduate courses tend to limit the opportunities for sectarian influence by virtue of their own internal disciplines. Many church-related colleges and universities are characterized by a high degree of academic freedom and seek to evoke free and critical responses from their students. [Thus,] the necessity for intensive government surveillance is diminished and the resulting entanglements between government and religion lessened."[c]

Decisions since *Tilton* have continued to uphold aid to higher education. See e.g., *Roemer v. Board of Pub. Works*, 426 U.S. 736, 96 S.Ct. 2337, 49 L.Ed.2d 179 (1976) (annual grants, of 15% of student cost in state college system, to colleges that promise not to use funds "for sectarian purposes" and who file annual report "describing and itemizing the use of the funds").[f]

However, as discussed in *Grand Rapids School Dist. v. Ball* and *Aguilar v. Felton*, below, the decisions since *Lemon* on aid to elementary and secondary schools have been more complicated than those concerning colleges. Most such forms of aid were held invalid on the *Lemon* analysis that, despite the existence of a "secular legislative purpose," there is "a primary effect that advances religion" and/or "excessive government entanglement with religion." But some programs were sustained. Indeed, *Committee for Pub. Educ. v. Regan*, 444 U.S. 646, 100 S.Ct. 840, 63 L.Ed.2d 94 (1980), per White, J., observed that the "decisions have tended to avoid categorical imperatives and absolutist approaches at either end of the range of possible outcomes. This course sacrifices clarity and predictability for flexibility * * *." For the view "that application of the Court's three-prong test has generated ad hoc judgments which are incapable of

---

b. Without dissent, however, the 20 year provision was held invalid: "It cannot be assumed that a substantial structure has no value after that period and hence the unrestricted use of a valuable property is in effect a contribution of some value to a religious body."

c. White, J., concurred in the result; Black, Douglas, Brennan and Marshall, JJ.,

dissented; all were unable to distinguish *Lemon*.

f. Brennan, Marshall, Stevens and Stewart, JJ., dissented, the last finding *Tilton* distinguishable because "here [the] compulsory theology courses may be 'devoted to deepening religious experiences in the particular faith * * *.'"

being reconciled on any principled basis," see Choper, note after *Epperson*, Part II supra, at 680–81.

The following decision, although not involving financial assistance to elementary and secondary education, played a significant role in *Mueller v. Allen*, below—one the Court's most recent pronouncements on aid to parochial schools.

WIDMAR v. VINCENT, 454 U.S. 263, 102 S.Ct. 269, 70 L.Ed.2d 440 (1981), per POWELL, J., held that through its policy of routinely providing university facilities for the meetings of student organizations, the University of Missouri at Kansas City (UMKC) had "created a forum generally open for use by student groups. Having done so, the University has assumed an obligation to justify the discriminations and exclusions under applicable constitutional norms." Thus UMKC's exclusion of a registered student group that wished to use university facilities for "religious worship and discussion" constituted "a content-based discrimination" which could only be justified if "necessary to serve a compelling state interest" and "narrowly drawn to achieve that end."

UMKC argued that "it cannot offer its facilities to religious groups and speakers on the terms available to other groups without violating the Establishment Clause." The Court responded "that an open-forum policy, including nondiscrimination against religious speech, would have a secular purpose [10] and would avoid entanglement with religion.[11]" As for "primary effect," "it is possible—perhaps even foreseeable—that religious groups will benefit from access to University facilities. But this Court has explained that a religious organization's enjoyment of merely 'incidental' benefits does not violate the prohibition against 'primary advancement' of religion. *McGowan*. [First], an open forum in a public university does not confer any imprimatur of State approval on religious sects or practices. [Second], the forum is available [to] over 100 recognized student groups at UMKC. The provision of benefits to so broad a spectrum of groups is an important index of secular effect. [At] least in the absence of empirical evidence that religious groups will dominate UMKC's open forum, [the] advancement of religion would not be the forum's 'primary effect.' " [a]

10. It is the avowed purpose of UMKC to provide a forum in which students can exchange ideas. The University argues that use of the forum for religious speech would undermine this secular aim. But by creating a forum the University does not thereby endorse or promote any of the particular ideas aired there. Undoubtedly many views are advocated in the forum with which the University desires no association.

Because this case involves a forum already made generally available to student groups, it differs from those cases in which this Court has invalidated statutes permitting school facilities to be used for instruction by religious groups, but *not* by others. See, e.g., *McCollum*. In those cases the school may appear to sponsor the views of the speaker.

[May high schools that permit student groups to use their facilities also permit student-initiated voluntary prayer sessions held before or after the curricular day? See generally Comment, *Widmar v. Vincent and the*

Public Forum Doctrine: Time to Reconsider Public School Prayer, 1984 Wis.L.Rev. 147.]

11. [T]he University would risk greater "entanglement" by attempting to enforce its exclusion of "religious worship and religious speech." Initially, the University would need to determine which words and activities fall within "religious worship and religious teaching." This alone could prove "an impossible task in an age where many and various beliefs meet the constitutional definition of religion." There would also be a continuing need to monitor group meetings to ensure compliance with the rule.

a. Stevens, J., concurred in the judgment.

After *Widmar*, may elementary or secondary schools permit their facilities to be used for instruction by religious groups if they also permit instruction by outside teachers of art, music, crafts, dance, etc. (cf. *McCollum*)? May they post the Ten Commandments if they also post the symbols of other civic or charitable groups (cf. *Stone*)?

WHITE, J., dissented, arguing that the case involved only the question of whether UMKC must permit use of its facilities for "religious worship"—as distinguished from "communication of religious views to a non-religious, public audience" as in cases like *Heffron,* p. 643 supra: "I know of no precedent holding that simply because a public forum is open to all kinds of speech—including speech about religion—it must be open to regular religious worship services as well."

He thought "plainly wrong" the view that "because religious worship uses speech, it is protected by the Free Speech Clause": "Were it right, 'the Religion Clauses would be emptied of any independent meaning in circumstances in which religious practice took the form of speech.' *Stone v. Graham,* "necessarily presumed that the state could not ignore the religious content of the written message, nor was it permitted to treat that content as it would, or must treat, other—secular—messages under the First Amendment's protection of speech. Similarly, the Court's decisions prohibiting prayer in the public schools rest on a content-based distinction between varieties of speech: as a speech act, apart from its content, a prayer is indistinguishable from a biology lesson. Operation of the Free Exercise Clause is equally dependent, in certain circumstances, on recognition of a content-based distinction between religious and secular speech. Thus, in *Torcaso v. Watkins,* [Sec. 2, II infra], the Court struck down, as violative of the Free Exercise Clause, a state requirement that made a declaration of belief in God a condition of state employment. A declaration is again a speech act, but it was the content of the speech that brought the case within the scope of the Free Exercise Clause." [b]

MUELLER v. ALLEN

463 U.S. 388, 103 S.Ct. 3062, 77 L.Ed.2d 721 (1983).

JUSTICE REHNQUIST delivered the opinion of the Court.

Minnesota allows taxpayers, in computing their state income tax, to deduct certain expenses incurred in providing for the education of their children.[1] The

---

b. The Court found "at least three difficulties with this distinction."

"First, the dissent fails to establish that the distinction has intelligible content. There is no indication when 'singing hymns, reading scripture, and teaching biblical principles' cease to [be] 'speech,' despite their religious subject matter—and become unprotected 'worship.'

"Second, even if the distinction drew an arguably principled line, it is highly doubtful that it would lie within the judicial competence to administer. Merely to draw the distinction would require [courts] to inquire into the significance of words and practices to different religious faiths, and in varying circumstances by the same faith. Such inquiries would tend inevitably to entangle the State with religion in a manner forbidden by our cases. E.g., *Walz.*

"Finally, the dissent [gives] no reason why the Establishment Clause [would] require different treatment for religious speech designed to win religious converts, see *Heffron,* than for religious worship by persons already convert-

ed. It is far from clear that the State gives greater support in the latter case than in the former."

1. Minn.Stat. § 290.09(22) (1982) permits a taxpayer to deduct from his or her computation of gross income the following: "[The] amount he has paid to others, not to exceed $500 for each dependent in grades K to 6 and $700 for each dependent in grades 7 to 12, for tuition, textbooks and transportation of each dependent in attending an elementary or secondary school [wherein] a resident of this state may legally fulfill the state's compulsory attendance laws, which is not operated for profit, and which adheres to the provisions of the Civil Rights Act of 1964 ∗ ∗ ∗. As used in this subdivision, 'textbooks' shall mean and include books and other instructional materials and equipment used in elementary and secondary schools in teaching only those subjects legally and commonly taught in public elementary and secondary schools in this state and shall not include instructional books and materials used in the teaching of religious tenets, doctrines or worship ∗ ∗ ∗."

United States Court of Appeals for the Eighth Circuit held that the Establishment Clause of the First and Fourteenth Amendments was not offended by this arrangement. [A]bout 820,000 students attended [Minnesota's public] school system in the most recent school year. During the same year, approximately 91,000 elementary and secondary students attended some 500 privately supported schools located in Minnesota, and about 95% of these students attended schools considering themselves to be sectarian. * * *

Today's case is no exception to our oft-repeated statement that the Establishment Clause presents especially difficult questions of interpretation and application. [It] is not at all easy [to] apply this Court's various decisions construing the Clause to governmental programs of financial assistance to sectarian schools and the parents of children attending those schools. Indeed, in many of these decisions "we have expressly or implicitly acknowledged that 'we can only dimly perceive the lines of demarcation in this extraordinarily sensitive area of constitutional law.' " *Lemon.*

One fixed principle in this field is our consistent rejection of the argument that "any program which in some manner aids an institution with a religious affiliation" violates the Establishment Clause. * * *

Notwithstanding the repeated approval given programs such as those in *Allen* and *Everson,* our decisions also have struck down arrangements resembling, in many respects, these forms of assistance. See, e.g., [*Lemon.*] Petitioners place particular reliance on our decision in *Committee for Pub. Educ. v. Nyquist,* 413 U.S. 756, 93 S.Ct. 2955, 37 L.Ed.2d 948 (1973), where we held invalid a New York [statute] granting thinly disguised "tax benefits," actually amounting to tuition grants, to the parents of children attending private schools. As explained below, we conclude that § 290.09(22) bears less resemblance to the arrangement struck down in *Nyquist* than it does to assistance programs upheld in our prior [decisions].

Little time need be spent on the question of whether the Minnesota tax deduction has a secular purpose. Under our prior decisions, governmental assistance programs have consistently survived this inquiry even when they have run afoul of other aspects of the *Lemon* framework. This reflects, at least in part, our reluctance to attribute unconstitutional motives to the states, particularly when a plausible secular purpose for the state's program may be discerned from the face of the statute.

A state's decision to defray the cost of educational expenses incurred by parents—regardless of the type of schools their children attend—evidences a purpose that is both secular and understandable. An educated populace is essential to the political and economic health of any community, and a state's efforts to assist parents in meeting the rising cost of educational expenses plainly serves this secular purpose of ensuring that the state's citizenry is well-educated. Similarly, Minnesota, like other states, could conclude that there is a strong public interest in assuring the continued financial health of private schools, both sectarian and non-sectarian. By educating a substantial number of students such schools relieve public schools of a correspondingly great burden—to the benefit of all taxpayers. In addition, private schools may serve as a benchmark for public schools * * *.

We turn therefore to the more difficult but related question whether the Minnesota statute has "the primary effect of advancing the sectarian aims of the non-public schools." In concluding that it does not, we find several features of the Minnesota tax deduction particularly significant. First, an essential feature of Minnesota's arrangement is the fact that § 290.09(22) is only one among many deductions—such as those for medical expenses and charitable contributions [a]— available under the Minnesota tax laws.[5] Our decisions consistently have recognized that [the] legislature's judgment that a deduction for educational expenses fairly equalizes the tax burden of its citizens and encourages desirable expenditures for educational purposes is entitled to substantial deference.[6]

Other characteristics of § 290.09(22) argue equally strongly for the provision's constitutionality. Most importantly, the deduction is available for educational expenses incurred by *all* parents, including those whose children attend public schools and those whose children attend non-sectarian private schools or sectarian private schools. Just as in *Widmar*, [so] here: "the provision of benefits to so broad a spectrum of groups is an important index of secular effect."

In this respect, as well as others, this case is vitally different from the scheme struck down in *Nyquist*. There, public assistance amounting to tuition grants, was provided only to parents of children in *nonpublic* schools. This fact had considerable bearing on our decision striking down the New York statute at issue; we explicitly distinguished both *Allen* and *Everson* on the grounds that "In both cases the class of beneficiaries included *all* schoolchildren, those in public as well as those in private schools." Moreover, we intimated that "public assistance (e.g., scholarships) made available generally without regard to the sectarian-nonsectarian or public-nonpublic nature of the institution benefited," might not offend the Establishment Clause. We think the tax deduction adopted by Minnesota is more similar to this latter type of program than it is to the arrangement struck down in *Nyquist*. Unlike the assistance at issue in *Nyquist*, § 290.09(22) permits *all* parents—whether their children attend public school or private—to deduct their children's educational expenses. As *Widmar* and our other decisions indicate, a program, like § 290.09(22), that neutrally provides

a. Compare Choper, *Public Financial Assistance to Church-Related Schools*, in Choper, Kamisar & Tribe, *The Supreme Court: Trends and Developments 1982–83*, 48 (1984): "[This is] like saying that an appropriation to build a new church for the First Presbyterian congregation in Washington, D.C. is only one of many appropriations. The reasoning is that since Congress appropriates money for the University of the District of Columbia and for all kinds of other things, this appropriation to build a church should be treated just like one of many appropriations."

5. Deductions for charitable contributions, allowed by Minnesota law, include contributions to religious institutions, and exemptions from property tax for property used for charitable purposes under Minnesota law include property used for wholly religious purposes. In each case, it may be that religious institutions benefit very substantially from the allowance of such deductions. The Court's holding in *Walz* indicates, however, that this does not require the conclusion that such provisions of a state's tax law violate the Establishment Clause.

6. Our decision in *Nyquist* is not to the contrary on this point. We expressed considerable doubt there that the "tax benefits" provided by New York law properly could be regarded as parts of a genuine system of tax laws. Plainly, the outright grants to low-income parents ["of $50 to $100 per child (but no more than 50% of tuition actually paid)"] did not take the form of ordinary tax benefits. As to the benefits provided to middle-income parents, the Court said: "The amount of the deduction is unrelated to the amount of money actually expended by any parent on tuition, but is calculated on the basis of a formula contained in the statute. The formula is apparently the product of a legislative attempt to assure that each family would receive a carefully estimated net benefit, and that the tax benefit would be comparable to, and compatible with, the tuition grant for lower income families." Indeed, the question whether a program having the elements of a "genuine tax deduction" would be constitutionally acceptable was expressly reserved in *Nyquist*. While the economic consequences of the program in *Nyquist* and that in this case may be difficult to distinguish, we have recognized on other occasions that "the form of the [state's assistance to parochial schools must be examined] for the light that it casts on the substance." The fact that the Minnesota plan embodies a "genuine tax deduction" is thus of some relevance, especially given the traditional rule of deference accorded legislative classifications in tax statutes.

state assistance to a broad spectrum of citizens is not readily subject to challenge under the Establishment Clause.

We also agree with the Court of Appeals that, by channeling whatever assistance it may provide to parochial schools through individual parents, Minnesota has reduced the Establishment Clause objections to which its action is subject. It is true, of course, that financial assistance provided to parents ultimately has an economic effect comparable to that of aid given directly to the schools attended by their children. It is also true, however, that under Minnesota's arrangement public funds become available only as a result of numerous, private choices of individual parents of school-age children. [It] is noteworthy that all but one of our recent cases invalidating state aid to parochial schools have involved the direct transmission of assistance from the state to the schools themselves. The exception, of course, was *Nyquist,* which, as discussed previously is distinguishable from this case on other grounds. Where, as here, aid to parochial schools is available only as a result of decisions of individual parents no "imprimatur of State approval," *Widmar,* can be deemed to have been conferred on any particular religion, or on religion generally.

[The] Establishment Clause of course extends beyond prohibition of a state church or payment of state funds to one or more churches. We do not think, however, that its prohibition extends to the type of tax deduction established by Minnesota. The historic purposes of the clause simply do not encompass the sort of attenuated financial benefit, ultimately controlled by the private choices of individual parents, that eventually flows to parochial schools from the neutrally available tax benefit at issue in this case.

Petitioners argue that, notwithstanding the facial neutrality of § 290.09(22), [most] parents of public school children incur no tuition expenses, and that other expenses deductible under § 290.09(22) are negligible in value; moreover, they claim that 96% of the children in private schools in 1978–1979 attended religiously-affiliated institutions. Because of all this, they reason, the bulk of deductions taken under § 290.09(22) will be claimed by parents of children in sectarian schools. Respondents reply that petitioners have failed to consider the impact of deductions for items such as transportation, summer school tuition, tuition paid by parents whose children attended schools outside the school districts in which they resided, rental or purchase costs for a variety of equipment, and tuition for certain types of instruction not ordinarily provided in public schools.

We need not consider these contentions in detail. We would be loath to adopt a rule grounding the constitutionality of a facially neutral law on annual reports reciting the extent to which various classes of private citizens claimed benefits under the law. Such an approach would scarcely provide the certainty that this field stands in need of, nor can we perceive principled standards by which such statistical evidence might be evaluated. Moreover, the fact that private persons fail in a particular year to claim the tax relief to which they are entitled—under a facially neutral statute—should be of little importance in determining the constitutionality of the statute permitting such relief.

Finally, [if] parents of children in private schools choose to take especial advantage of the relief provided by § 290.09(22), it is no doubt due to the fact that they bear a particularly great financial burden in educating their children. More fundamentally, whatever unequal effect may be attributed to the statutory classification can fairly be regarded as a rough return for the benefits, discussed above, provided to the state and all taxpayers by parents sending their children to parochial schools. In the light of all this, we believe it wiser to decline to engage in the type of empirical inquiry into those persons benefited by state law which petitioners urge. * * *

Turning to the third part of the *Lemon* inquiry, we have no difficulty in concluding that the Minnesota statute does not "excessively entangle" the state in religion. [T]hat state officials must determine whether particular textbooks qualify for a deduction [does] not differ substantially from making the types of decisions approved in [*Allen*].[11]

Affirmed.

JUSTICE MARSHALL, with whom JUSTICE BRENNAN, JUSTICE BLACKMUN and JUSTICE STEVENS join, dissenting.

[The] Minnesota tax statute violates the Establishment Clause for precisely the same reason as the statute struck down in *Nyquist:* it has a direct and immediate effect of advancing religion. [Although it] allows a deduction for the tuition expenses of children attending public schools, Minnesota public schools [may] assess tuition charges only for students accepted from outside the district. In the 1978–1979 school year, only 79 public school students fell into this category. * * *

As we recognized in *Nyquist,* direct government subsidization of parochial school tuition is impermissible because "the effect of the aid is unmistakably to provide desired financial support for nonpublic, sectarian institutions." "[A]id to the educational function of [parochial schools] necessarily results in aid to the sectarian enterprise as a whole" because "[t]he very purpose of those schools is to provide an integrated secular and religious education." * * *

Indirect assistance in the form of financial aid to parents for tuition payments is similarly impermissible because it is not "subject [to] restrictions" which "guarantee the separation between secular and religious educational functions [and] ensure that State financial aid supports only the former." *Lemon.* [As] was true of the law struck down in *Nyquist,* "it is precisely the function of [Minnesota's] law to provide assistance to private schools, the great majority of which are sectarian. By reimbursing parents for a portion of their tuition bill, the State seeks to relieve their financial burdens sufficiently to assure that they continue to have the option to send their children to religion-oriented schools. And while the other purposes for that aid—to perpetuate a pluralistic educational environment and to protect the fiscal integrity of overburdened public schools—are certainly unexceptional, the effect of the aid is unmistakably to provide desired financial support for nonpublic, sectarian institutions."

---

11. No party to this litigation has urged that the Minnesota plan is invalid because it runs afoul of the rather elusive inquiry, subsumed under the third part of the *Lemon* test, whether the Minnesota statute partakes of the "divisive political potential" condemned in *Lemon.* [Since] this aspect of the "entanglement" inquiry originated with *Lemon,* and the Court's opinion there took pains to distinguish both *Everson* and *Allen,* the Court in *Lemon* must have been referring to a phenomenon which, although present in that case, would have been absent in the two cases it distinguished.

The Court's language in *Lemon* respecting political divisiveness was made in the context of Pennsylvania and Rhode Island statutes which provided for either direct payments of, or reimbursement of, a proportion of teachers' salaries in parochial schools. We think, in the light of the treatment of the point in later cases discussed above, the language must be regarded as confined to cases where direct financial subsidies are paid to parochial schools or to teachers in parochial schools.

That parents receive a reduction of their tax liability, rather than a direct reimbursement, is of no greater significance here than it was in *Nyquist.* "[F]or purposes of determining whether such aid has the effect of advancing religion," it makes no difference whether the qualifying "parent receives an actual cash payment [or] is allowed to reduce [the] sum he would otherwise be obliged to pay over to the State." It is equally irrelevant whether a reduction in taxes takes the form of a tax "credit," a tax "modification," or a tax "deduction." What is of controlling significance is not the form but the "substantive impact" of the financial aid. * * *

The majority first attempts to distinguish *Nyquist* on the ground that Minnesota makes all parents eligible to deduct up to $500 or $700 for each dependent, whereas the New York law allowed a deduction only for parents whose children attended nonpublic schools. Although Minnesota taxpayers who send their children to local public schools may not deduct tuition expenses because they incur none, they may deduct other expenses, such as the cost of gym clothes, pencils, and notebooks, which are shared by all parents of school-age children. * * *

That the Minnesota statute makes some small benefit available to all parents cannot alter the fact that the most substantial benefit provided by the statute is available only to those parents who send their children to schools that charge tuition.[2] Of the total number of taxpayers who are eligible for the tuition deduction, approximately 96% send their children to religious schools. [In] *Nyquist* we unequivocally rejected any suggestion that, in determining the effect of a tax statute, this Court should look exclusively to what the statute on its face purports to do and ignore the actual operation of the challenged provision. In determining the effect of the New York statute, we emphasized [that] "tax reductions authorized by this law flow primarily to the parents of children attending sectarian, nonpublic schools." Similarly, in *Sloan v. Lemon,* 413 U.S. 825, 93 S.Ct. 2982, 37 L.Ed.2d 939 (1973), we considered important to our "consider[ation of] the new law's effect [that] 'more than 90% of the children attending nonpublic schools in the Commonwealth of Pennsylvania are enrolled in schools that are controlled by religious institutions or that have the purpose of propagating and promoting religious faith.'" * * *

The majority also asserts that the Minnesota statute is distinguishable from the statute struck down in *Nyquist* in another respect: [Under] the New York law, the amount of deduction was not dependent upon the amount actually paid for tuition but was a predetermined amount which depended on the tax bracket of each taxpayer. The deduction was designed to yield roughly the same amount of tax "forgiveness" for each taxpayer.

This is a distinction without a difference. [As the majority] concedes, the "economic consequence" of these programs is the same, n. 6, for in each case the "financial assistance provided to parents ultimately has an economic effect comparable to that of aid given directly to the schools." It was precisely the substantive impact of the financial support, and not its particular form, that rendered the programs in *Nyquist* and *Sloan* unconstitutional.

2. Even if the Minnesota statute allowed parents of public school students to deduct expenses that were likely to be equivalent to the tuition expenses of private school students, it would still be unconstitutional. Insofar as the Minnesota statute provides a deduction for parochial school tuition, it provides a benefit to parochial schools that furthers the religious mission of those schools. *Nyquist* makes clear that the State may not provide any financial assistance to parochial schools unless that assistance is limited to secular uses.

* * * Financial assistance for tuition payments has a consequence that "is quite unlike the sort of 'indirect' and 'incidental' benefits that flowed to sectarian schools from programs aiding *all* parents by supplying bus transportation and secular textbooks for their children. *Such benefits were carefully restricted to the purely secular side of church-affiliated institutions* and provided no special aid for those who had chosen to support religious schools. Yet such aid approached the 'verge' of the constitutionally impermissible." *Sloan* (emphasis added in part). As previously noted, the Minnesota tuition tax deduction is not available to *all* parents, but only to parents whose children attend schools that charge tuition, which are comprised almost entirely of sectarian schools. More importantly, the assistance that flows to parochial schools as a result of the tax benefit is not restricted, and cannot be restricted, to the secular functions of those schools.

In my view, Minnesota's tax deduction for the cost of textbooks and other instructional materials is also constitutionally infirm. * * *

The instructional materials which are subsidized by the Minnesota tax deduction plainly may be used to inculcate religious values and belief. In *Meek v. Pittenger,* 421 U.S. 349, 95 S.Ct. 1753, 44 L.Ed.2d 217 (1975), we held that even the use of "wholly neutral, secular instructional material and equipment" by church-related schools contributes to religious instruction because " '[t]he secular education those schools provide goes hand in hand with the religious mission that is the only reason for the schools' existence.' " In *Wolman v. Walter,* 433 U.S. 229, 97 S.Ct. 2593, 53 L.Ed.2d 714 (1977), we concluded that precisely the same impermissible effect results when the instructional materials are loaned to the pupil or his parent, rather than directly to the schools. We stated that "it would exalt form over substance if this distinction were found to justify a result different from that in *Meek.*" It follows that a tax deduction to offset the cost of purchasing instructional materials for use in sectarian schools, like a loan of such materials to parents, "necessarily results in aid to the sectarian school enterprise as a whole" and is therefore a "substantial advancement of religious activity" that "constitutes an impermissible establishment of religion."

There is no reason to treat Minnesota's tax deduction for textbooks any differently. Secular textbooks, like other secular instructional materials, contribute to the religious mission of the parochial schools that use those books. [D]istinguishing secular instructional materials and secular textbooks is simply untenable, and is inconsistent with many of our more recent decisions concerning state aid to parochial schools. * * * [6]

[For] the first time, the Court has upheld financial support for religious schools without any reason at all to assume that the support will be restricted to the secular functions of those schools and will not be used to support religious instruction. This result is flatly at odds with the fundamental principle that [the] Court stated in *Everson* and has often repeated, see, e.g., *Meek; Nyquist,* "No tax in any amount, large or small, can be levied to support any religious activities or institutions, whatever they may be called, or whatever form they may adopt to teach or practice religion."

---

6. For similar reasons, I would hold that the deduction for transportation expenses is constitutional only insofar as it relates to the costs of traveling between home and school. See *Wolman* (reimbursement of nonpublic schools for field trip transportation impermissibly fosters religion because the nonpublic schools control the timing, frequency, and destination of the trips, which, for sectarian schools, are an integral part of the sectarian education). * * *

GRAND RAPIDS SCHOOL DIST. v. BALL

__ U.S. __, 105 S.Ct. 3216, 87 L.Ed.2d 267 (1985).

JUSTICE BRENNAN delivered the opinion of the Court.

[In 1976, the school district adopted two publicly financed programs held on parochial school premises. Under the Shared Time Program, "remedial" and "enrichment" courses in mathematics and reading, and courses in art, music and physical education were taught during the regular school day by public school teachers; supplies, material and equipment were provided at public expense. Under the Community Education Program, classes for children and adults—in subjects such as "Arts and Crafts, Home Economics, Spanish, Gymnastics, Yearbook Production, Christmas Arts and Crafts, Drama, Newspaper, Humanities, Chess, Model Building, and Nature Appreciation"—were taught at the end of the regular school day. Both programs were conducted in parochial school classrooms which were "leased" by the school district and which had to be free of any religious symbols; during the programs, a posted sign stated that it was a "public school classroom." No attempt was made in either program "to monitor [the] courses for religious content."]

Since *Everson,* [we] have often grappled with the problem of state aid to nonpublic, religious schools. In all of these cases, our goal has been to give meaning to the sparse language and broad purposes of the [Establishment] Clause, while not unduly infringing on the ability of the States to provide for [the] education of schoolchildren [which] is surely a praiseworthy purpose. But our cases have consistently recognized that even such a praiseworthy, secular purpose cannot validate government aid to parochial schools when the aid has the effect of promoting a single religion or religion generally or when the aid unduly entangles the government in matters religious. [T]he three-part test first articulated in [*Lemon*] "must not be viewed as setting the precise limits to the necessary constitutional inquiry, but serve[s] only as guidelines with which to identify instances in which the objectives of the Establishment Clause have been impaired." We have particularly relied on *Lemon* in every case involving the sensitive relationship between government and religion in the education of our children. * * *

As has often been true in school aid cases, there is no dispute [that] the purpose of the Community Education and Shared Time programs was "manifestly secular." We [go] on to consider whether the primary or principal effect of the challenged programs is to advance or inhibit religion.

Our inquiry must begin with a consideration of the nature of the institutions in which the programs operate. Of the 41 private schools where these "part-time public schools" have operated, 40 are identifiably religious schools. It is true that each school may not share all of the characteristics of religious schools as articulated, for example, in the complaint in *Lemon.* The District Court found, however, "[that] the religious institutions receiving instructional services from the public schools are sectarian in the sense that a substantial portion of their functions are subsumed in the religious mission." [6] [Thus, the programs] may impermissibly advance religion in three different ways. * * *

---

6. [Many] of the schools in this case include prayer and attendance at religious services as a part of their curriculum, are run by churches or other organizations whose members must subscribe to particular religious tenets, have faculties and student bodies composed largely of adherents of the particular denomination, and give preference in attendance to children belonging to the denomination.

(1) [In] *Meek,* the Court invalidated a statute providing for the loan of state-paid professional staff—including teachers—to nonpublic schools to provide remedial and accelerated instruction, guidance counseling and testing, and other services on the premises of the nonpublic schools. Such a program, if not subjected to a "comprehensive, discriminating, and continuing state surveillance," *Lemon,* would entail an unacceptable risk that the the state-sponsored instructional personnel would "advance the religious mission of the church-related schools in which they serve." Even though the teachers were paid by the State, "[t]he potential for impermissible fostering of religion under these circumstances, although somewhat reduced, is nonetheless present." * * *

The programs before us today share the defect that we identified in *Meek.* With respect to the Community Education Program, the District Court found that "virtually every Community Education course conducted on facilities leased from nonpublic schools has an instructor otherwise employed full time by the same nonpublic school." These instructors, many of whom no doubt teach in the religious schools precisely because they are adherents of the controlling denomination and want to serve their religious community zealously, are expected during the regular school day to inculcate their students with the tenets and beliefs of their particular religious faiths. Yet the premise of the program is that those instructors can put aside their religious convictions and engage in entirely secular Community Education instruction as soon as the school day is over. [T]here is a substantial risk that, overtly or subtly, the religious message they are expected to convey during the regular school day will infuse the supposedly secular classes they teach after school. The danger arises "not because the public employee [is] likely deliberately to subvert his task to the service of religion, but rather because the pressures of the environment might alter his behavior from its normal course." *Wolman.* * * *

The Shared Time program [poses] a substantial risk of state-sponsored indoctrination. The most important difference between the programs is that most of the instructors in the Shared Time program are full-time teachers hired by the public schools [although] "[a] significant portion" of the Shared Time instructors previously worked in the religious schools.[7] [They] are teaching academic subjects in religious schools in courses virtually indistinguishable from the other courses offered during the regular religious-school day [and] may well subtly (or overtly) conform their instruction to the environment in which they teach, while students will perceive the instruction provided in the context of the dominantly religious message of the institution, thus reinforcing the indoctrinating effect. [Unlike] types of aid that the Court has upheld, such as state-created standardized tests, *Regan,* or diagnostic services, *Wolman,* there is a "substantial risk" that programs operating in this environment would "be used for religious educational purposes."

[T]hat respondents adduced no evidence of specific incidents of religious indoctrination in this case [is] not dispositive. When conducting a supposedly secular class in the pervasively sectarian environment of a religious school, a teacher may knowingly or unwillingly tailor the content of the course to fit the school's announced goals. If so, there is no reason to believe that this kind of ideological influence would be detected or [reported]. After spending the balance of their school day in classes heavily influenced by a religious perspective, [the students] would have little motivation or ability to discern improper ideological

---

7. Approximately 10 percent of the Shared Time instructors were previously employed by the religious schools, and many of these were reassigned back to the school at which they had previously taught.

content that may creep into a Shared Time or Community Education course. Neither their parents nor the parochial schools would have cause to complain if the effect of the publicly-supported instruction were to advance the schools' sectarian mission. And the public school system itself has no incentive to detect or report any specific incidents of improper state-sponsored indoctrination. * * *

(2) Our cases have recognized that the Establishment Clause guards against more than direct, state-funded efforts to indoctrinate youngsters in specific religious beliefs. [A]n important concern of the effects test is whether the symbolic union of church and state effected by the challenged governmental action is sufficiently likely to be perceived by adherents of the controlling denominations as an endorsement, and by the nonadherents as a disapproval, of their individual religious choices. The [symbolism] of a union between church and state is most likely to influence children of tender years, whose experience is limited and whose beliefs consequently are the function of environment as much as of free and voluntary choice.[10] Consequently, even the student who notices the "public school" sign temporarily posted would have before him a powerful symbol of state endorsement and encouragement of the religious beliefs taught in the same class at some other time during the day. * * *

(3) [With] but one exception, our [cases] have struck down attempts by States to make payments out of public tax dollars directly to primary or secondary religious educational institutions. See, e.g., *Nyquist* (reimbursement for maintenance and repair expenses); *Levitt v. Committee for Pub. Educ.*, 413 U.S. 472, 93 S.Ct. 2814, 37 L.Ed.2d 736 (1973) (reimbursement for teacher-prepared tests); *Lemon.* But see *Regan* (permitting public subsidy for certain routinized recordkeeping and testing services performed by nonpublic schools but required by state law).

Aside from cash payments, the Court has distinguished between two categories of programs in which public funds are used to finance secular activities that religious schools would otherwise fund from their own resources. In the first category, the Court has noted ["that] not every law that confers an 'indirect,' 'remote,' or 'incidental' benefit upon religious institutions is, for that reason alone, constitutionally invalid." In such "indirect" aid cases, the government has used primarily secular means to accomplish a primarily secular end, and no "primary effect" of advancing religion has thus been found. On this rationale, the Court has upheld programs providing for loans of secular textbooks to nonpublic school students, *Allen;* see also *Wolman; Meek,* and programs providing bus transportation for nonpublic school children, *Everson.*

In the second category of cases, the Court has relied on the Establishment Clause prohibition of forms of aid that provide "direct and substantial advancement of the sectarian enterprise." In such "direct aid" cases, the government, although acting for a secular purpose, has done so by directly supporting a religious institution. Under this rationale, the Court has struck down state schemes providing for tuition grants and tax benefits for parents whose children attend religious school, see *Sloan; Nyquist,* and programs providing for "loan" of instructional materials to be used in religious schools, see *Wolman; Meek.* In *Sloan* and *Nyquist,* the aid was formally given to parents and not directly to the religious schools, while in *Wolman* and *Meek,* the aid was in-kind assistance

10. Compare *Meek* (invalidating program providing for state-funded remedial services on religious-school premises) with *Wolman* (upholding program providing for similar services at neutral sites off the premises of the religious school).

rather than the direct contribution of public funds. Nonetheless, these differences in form were insufficient to save programs whose effect was indistinguishable from that of a direct subsidy to the religious school.

Thus, the Court has never accepted the mere possibility of subsidization, as the above cases demonstrate, as sufficient to invalidate an aid program. On the other hand, this effect is not wholly unimportant for Establishment Clause purposes. If it were, the public schools could gradually take on themselves the entire responsibility for teaching secular subjects on religious school premises. The question in each case must be whether the effect of the proffered aid is "direct and substantial," or indirect and incidental. "The problem, like many problems in constitutional law, is one of degree." *Zorach.* Cf. *Wolman* (upholding provision of diagnostic services, which were "general welfare services for children that may be provided by the State regardless of the incidental benefit that accrues to church-related schools.") * * *

Petitioners claim that the aid here, like the textbooks in *Allen*, flows primarily to the students, not to the religious schools.[13] Of course, all aid to religious schools ultimately "flows to" the students, and petitioners' argument if accepted would validate all forms of nonideological aid to religious schools, including those explicitly rejected in our prior cases. Yet in *Meek*, we held unconstitutional the loan of instructional materials to religious schools and in *Wolman*, we rejected the fiction that a similar program could be saved by masking it as aid to individual students. It follows a fortiori that the aid here, which includes not only instructional materials but also the provision of instructional services by teachers in the parochial school building, "inescapably [has] the primary effect of providing a direct and substantial advancement of the sectarian enterprise." * * *

Petitioners also argue that this "subsidy" effect is not significant in this case, because the Community Education and Shared Time programs supplemented the curriculum with courses not previously offered in the religious schools and not required by school rule or state regulation. [But first,] there is no way of knowing whether the religious schools would have offered some or all of these courses if the public school system had not offered them first. The distinction between courses that "supplement" and those that "supplant" the regular curriculum is therefore not nearly as clear as petitioners allege. Second, although the precise courses offered in these programs may have been new to the participating religious schools, their general subject matter—reading, math, etc.—was surely a part of the curriculum in the past, and the concerns of the Establishment Clause may thus be triggered despite the "supplemental" nature of the courses. Third, and most important, petitioners' argument would permit the public schools gradually to take over the entire secular curriculum of the religious school, for the latter could surely discontinue existing courses so that they might be replaced a year or two later by a Community Education or Shared Time course with the same content. The average religious school student, for instance, now spends 10 percent of the school day in Shared Time classes. But there is no principled basis on which this Court can impose a limit on the percentage of the religious-school day that can be subsidized by the public school. To let the genie out of the bottle in this case would be to permit ever larger segments of the religious school curriculum to be turned over to the public school

---

13. [Unlike] *Mueller*, the aid provided here is unmediated by the tax code and the "nu- merous, private choices of individual parents of school-age children."

system, thus violating the cardinal principle that the State may not in effect become the prime supporter of the religious school system. * * *

[AGUILAR v. FELTON, ___ U.S. ___, 105 S.Ct. 3232, 87 L.Ed.2d 290 (1985), a companion case, involved Title I of a federal plan—for "educationally deprived children from low-income families"—similar to the *Grand Rapids* Shared Time Program. Since 1966, New York City paid federal funds to public employees (teachers, guidance counselors, psychologists and social workers) for "remedial" courses and "guidance" services provided in parochial school classrooms (the "vast majority" of which were Catholic) [8] which had to be "clear [of] all religious symbols." Unlike Grand Rapids, New York "adopted a system for monitoring the religious content" of the classes. The Court, per BRENNAN, J., relying on the "administrative surveillance" aspect of *Lemon,* held that "the supervisory system * * * inevitably results in the excessive entanglement of church and state, an Establishment Clause concern distinct from that addressed by the effects doctrine."]

JUSTICE POWELL concurring [in] the Court's opinions * * *.

I agree with the Court that [the] Establishment Clause is violated because there is too great a risk of government entanglement in the administration of the religious schools [and] is compounded by the additional risk of political divisiveness stemming from the aid to religion at issue here. I do not suggest that at this point in our history [the] plans could result in the establishment of a state religion. There likewise is small chance that these programs would result in significant religious or denominational control over our democratic processes. Nonetheless, there remains a considerable risk of continuing political strife over the propriety of direct aid to religious schools and the proper allocation of limited governmental resources. * * *

I recognize the difficult dilemma in which governments are placed by the interaction of the "effects" and entanglement prongs of the *Lemon* test. Our decisions require governments extending aid to parochial schools to tread an extremely narrow line between being certain that the "principal or primary effect" of the aid is not to advance religion, and avoiding excessive entanglement. Nonetheless, the Court has never foreclosed the possibility that some types of aid to parochial schools could be valid under the Establishment Clause [citing *Mueller, Allen* and *Everson,* where] the assistance programs made funds available equally to public and nonpublic schools without entanglement. [If,] for example, Congress could fashion a program of evenhanded financial assistance to both public and private schools that could be administered, without governmental supervision in the private schools, so as to prevent the diversion of the aid from secular purposes, we would be presented with a different question. * * *

CHIEF JUSTICE BURGER, concurring [and] dissenting in part [in *Grand Rapids* and] dissenting [in *Aguilar*].

I agree with the Court that, [under] *Lemon,* the Grand Rapids Community Education Program violates the Establishment Clause. As to the Shared Time

---

8. Appellants suggest that the degree of sectarianism differs from school to school. This has little bearing on our analysis. As Judge Friendly, writing for the court below, noted: "It may well be that the degree of sectarianism in Catholic schools in, for example, black neighborhoods, with considerable proportions of non-Catholic pupils and teachers, is relatively low; by the same token, in other schools it may be relatively high. [Yet] enforcement of the Establishment Clause does not rest on means or medians. [It] would be simply incredible [that] all, or almost all, New York City's parochial schools receiving Title I aid [have] abandoned 'the religious mission that is the only reason for the schools' existence."

Program, I dissent for the reasons stated [hereafter in my dissent in *Aguilar*]. The Court today fails to demonstrate how that interaction occasioned by the program at issue presents any threat to the values underlying the Establishment Clause.

I cannot join in striking down a program that, in the words of the Court of Appeals, "has done so much good and little, if any, detectable harm." The notion that denying these ["desperately needed remedial teaching] services to students in religious schools is a neutral act to protect us from an Established Church has no support in logic, experience, or history. Rather than showing the neutrality the Court boasts of, it exhibits nothing less than hostility toward religion and the children who attend church-sponsored schools.

JUSTICE O'CONNOR, concurring [and] dissenting in part [in *Grand Rapids* and], with whom JUSTICE REHNQUIST joins as to Parts II and III, dissenting [in *Aguilar*].

For the reasons stated [in respect to New York's program, below,] I dissent from the Court's holding that the Grand Rapids Shared Time Program impermissibly advances religion. [But] Community Education courses in the parochial schools are overwhelmingly taught by instructors who are current full-time employees of the parochial school. [In] addition, the supervisors of the Community Education program in the parochial schools are by and large the principals of the very schools where the classes are offered. When full-time parochial school teachers receive public funds to teach secular courses to their parochial school students under parochial school supervision, I agree that the program has the perceived and actual effect of advancing the religious aims of the church-related schools. * * *

I. [By contrast, in New York], in 19 years there has never been a single incident in which a Title I instructor "subtly or overtly" attempted to "indoctrinate the students in particular religious tenets at public expense."

Common sense suggests a plausible explanation for this unblemished record. New York City's public Title I instructors are professional educators who can and do follow instructions not to inculcate religion in their classes. They are unlikely to be influenced by the sectarian nature of the parochial schools where they teach, not only because they are carefully supervised by public officials, but also because the vast majority of them visit several different schools each week and are not of the same religion as their parochial students. In light of the ample record, an objective observer of the implementation of the Title I program in New York would hardly view it as endorsing the tenets of the participating parochial schools. * * *

The only type of impermissible effect that arguably could carry over from the *Grand Rapids* decision to this litigation, then, is the effect of subsidizing "the religious functions of the parochial schools by taking over a substantial portion of their responsibility for teaching secular subjects." That effect is tenuous, however, in light of the statutory directive that Title I funds may be used only to provide services that otherwise would not be available to the participating students. * * *

Even if we were to assume that Title I remedial classes in New York may have duplicated to some extent instruction parochial schools would have offered in the absence of Title I, the Court's delineation of this third type of effect proscribed by the Establishment Clause would be seriously flawed. Our Establishment Clause decisions have not barred remedial assistance to parochial school children, but rather remedial assistance *on the premises of the parochial* *school.* Under *Wolman,* the New York City classes prohibited by the Court today would have survived Establishment Clause scrutiny if they had been offered in a neutral setting off the property of the private school. Yet it is difficult to understand why a remedial reading class offered on parochial school premises is any more likely to supplant the secular course offerings of the parochial school than the same class offered in a portable classroom next door to the school. * * *

II. Recognizing the weakness of any claim of an improper purpose or effect, the Court today relies entirely on the entanglement prong of *Lemon* to invalidate the New York City Title I program [which] I acknowledge, finds support in some of this Court's precedents. * * *

I would accord these decisions the appropriate deference commanded by the doctrine of stare decisis if I could discern logical support for their analysis. But experience has demonstrated that the analysis [is] flawed. [It] is not intuitively obvious that a dedicated public school teacher will tend to disobey instructions and commence proselytizing students at public expense merely because the classroom is within a parochial school. [Given] that not a single incident of religious indoctrination has been identified as occurring in the thousands of classes offered in Grand Rapids and New York over the past two decades, it is time to acknowledge that the risk [is] greatly exaggerated.

Just as the risk that public schoolteachers in parochial classrooms will inculcate religion has been exaggerated, so has the degree of supervision required to manage that risk. In [New York, public] officials have prepared careful instructions warning public schoolteachers of their exclusively secular mission, and have required Title I teachers to study and observe them. Under the rules, Title I teachers are not accountable to parochial or private school officials; they have sole responsibility for selecting the students who participate in their class, must administer their own tests for determining eligibility, cannot engage in team teaching or cooperative activities with parochial school teachers, must make sure that all materials and equipment they use are not otherwise used by the parochial school, and must not participate in religious activities in the schools or introduce any religious matter into their teaching. To ensure compliance with the rules, a field supervisor and a program coordinator, who are full-time public school employees, make unannounced visits to each teacher's classroom at least once a month. [This] does not differ significantly from the supervision any public schoolteacher receives, regardless of the location of the classroom. Justice Powell suggests that the required supervision is extensive because the State must be *certain* that public schoolteachers do not inculcate religion. That reasoning would require us to close our public schools, for there is always some chance that a public schoolteacher will bring religion into the classroom, regardless of its location. Even if I remained confident of the usefulness of entanglement as an Establishment Clause test, I would conclude that New York's efforts [have] been adequate and have not caused excessive institutional entanglement of church and state.

The Court's reliance on the potential for political divisiveness as evidence of undue entanglement is also unpersuasive. There is little record support for the proposition that New York's admirable Title I program has ignited any controversy other than this litigation. [M]any of the inconsistencies in our Establishment Clause decisions can be ascribed to our insistence that parochial aid programs with a valid purpose and effect may still be invalid by virtue of undue entanglement. For example, we permit a State to pay for bus transportation to a parochial school, *Everson,* but preclude States from providing buses for parochial school field trips, on the theory such trips involve excessive state supervision of the parochial officials who lead them. *Wolman.* To a great extent, the anomalous results in our Establishment Clause cases are "attributable to [the] 'entanglement' prong." Choper, *The Religion Clauses of the First Amendment: Reconciling the Conflict,* 41 U.Pitt.L.Rev. 673, 681 (1980).

[S]tate efforts to ensure that public resources are used only for nonsectarian ends should not in themselves serve to invalidate an otherwise valid statute. The State requires sectarian organizations to cooperate on a whole range of matters without thereby advancing religion or giving the impression that the government endorses religion. *Wallace v. Jaffree* (dissenting opinion of Rehnquist, J.) (noting that State educational agencies impose myriad curriculum, attendance, certificate, fire, and safety regulations on sectarian schools). If a statute lacks a purpose or effect of advancing or endorsing religion, I would not invalidate it merely because it requires some ongoing cooperation between church and state or some state supervision to ensure that state funds do not advance religion.

III. Today's ruling does not spell the end of the Title I program of remedial education for disadvantaged children. [The] only disadvantaged children who lose under the Court's holding are those in cities where it is not economically and logistically feasible to provide public facilities for remedial education adjacent to the parochial school. But [this] includes more than 20,000 New York City schoolchildren and uncounted others elsewhere in the country.

For these children, the Court's decision is tragic. The Court deprives them of a program that offers a meaningful chance at success in life, and it does so on the untenable theory that public schoolteachers (most of whom are of different faiths than their students) are likely to start teaching religion merely because they have walked across the threshold of a parochial school. * * * [a]

Notes and Questions

1. *Primary effect.* If "religion pervades" parochial schools, which "operate on one budget" and "money not spent for one purpose becomes available for other purposes," does bus transportation or secular textbooks for parochial school students "have a primary effect that advances religion"? If so, would this forbid stationing traffic police near parochial schools? Having the fire department put out fires in them? Furnishing sidewalks in front of them? If the public did not provide parochial schools with sidewalks and police and fire protection, would the schools have to include these items in their budgets? If so, does the public's supplying them "release" funds? May a public library lend books to parochial school students in which readings have been assigned by their teacher? Suppose it were shown that these books were "in fact instrumental in the teaching of religion"?

Consider Tribe, *American Constitutional Law* 844 (1978): "[T]he provision of such secular services is not offensive because no one perceives police or fire protection as part of the educational enterprise. Such aid goes to institutions not as schools but as parts of the general public. Similarly, aid for secular programs in all colleges, including those with church affiliation, is generally perceived as assistance to non-religious activities. But the moment aid is sent to

---

a. The opinions of White, J., dissenting in *Grand Rapids* and *Aguilar* on the basis of his views in *Lemon,* and of Rehnquist, J., dissent-ing on the basis of his dissent in *Wallace v. Jaffree,* Part I supra, are omitted.

a parochial school as such, it is widely seen as aid to religion. The number of dollars released for religious purposes may be identical; the symbolism, and hence the constitutional result, is not."

2. *Broad spectrum of beneficiary groups.* (a) After *Mueller,* would an "education voucher" plan pass muster if the vouchers were given to *all* parents for use in *any* school? Consider Sugarman, *Family Choice: The Next Step in the Quest for Equal Educational Opportunity?* 38 Law & Contemp.Probs. 513, 527–28 (1974): "Perhaps we are left [with] a sliding scale which depends upon both the nature and specificity of the program itself and the identity of the beneficiaries. Hence, if the government builds structures for voluntary membership associations, it may not build halls of worship for church groups simply because it builds most of its buildings for non-church groups. This is so because the item which the government provides itself is religious. On the other hand, the state would be able to build a hospital for a church group as part of a general program of building hospitals, even though this means that the church could now afford to build a chapel, and even though undeniably religious activities occur in the hospital along with health care. Since hospitals do in the main serve secular functions, and since the program in fact includes a substantial number of beneficiaries which are not religion-associated, further judicial scrutiny into whether the state is in fact getting full secular value for money may not be needed to protect the concerns underlying the establishment clause. * * * Viewing the voucher plan scenario under this approach to the 'primary effect' test, the argument would be that while the plan does assist religious schools, since the beneficiaries are only in part religious school users, and since schooling is in the main secular, the assistance to religious schools [is] only incidental." See also Nowak, *The Supreme Court, The Religion Clauses and the Nationalization of Education,* 70 Nw.U.L.Rev. 883 (1976).

Compare Choper, fn. a in *Mueller,* at 53–55: "[*Mueller*] opens up a whole new ball game for aid to parochial schools [which] has now become just a matter of form. For example, what New York should have done in *Nyquist* [is] take the statute that had been struck down and amend it to also give the tax credit to parents who send their children to public schools. It would cost New York virtually nothing because there will be virtually no deductions by such parents. [However, in] *Mueller,* the Court said there's a difference between giving tax deductions and giving actual grants. [T]he real practical difference is [if] you can only rely on a tax deduction for the tuition that you pay to a parochial school, the only way you can get the benefit of it is if you have sufficient income to be subject to a tax liability. But if you're a low income person, you are not going to be able to get the benefit of this unless the state can give you an outright grant. [I]f the Court is serious about a tax deduction being different from a grant, then the vouchers may still be invalid."

In light of the position of each justice in *Grand Rapids* and *Aguilar,* would a voucher plan be constitutional?

(b) *Political divisiveness.* To what extent does a "broad spectrum" of beneficiary groups affect this criterion? Consider Note, *The Constitutionality of Tax Relief for Parents of Children Attending Public and Nonpublic Schools,* 67 Minn.L.Rev. 793, 820–21 (1983): "Legislation that primarily aids sectarian education disrupts political equality and promotes rivalry among religious sects by favoring those groups that emphasize private primary and secondary education. [In] contrast, aid which broadly benefits secular as well as sectarian groups is less likely to generate interfaith rivalries or imbalances of power. Even if only some sects receive aid directly, members of other faiths will probably benefit as members of the broader legislative class. Because particular religious groups will not be perceived as the primary beneficiaries of state aid, competition among sects for government funds will also be reduced." For further consideration of "political divisiveness," see *Lynch v. Donnelly,* Part IV infra.

3. *Delegation of government power.* LARKIN v. GRENDEL'S DEN, INC., 454 U.S. 116, 103 S.Ct. 505, 74 L.Ed.2d 297 (1982), per Burger, C.J., held that a Massachusetts law (§ 16C), giving churches and schools the power "to veto applications for liquor licenses within a five hundred foot radius of the church or school, violates the Establishment Clause": "[T]here can be little doubt about the power of a state to regulate the environment in the vicinity of schools, churches, hospitals and the like by exercise of reasonable zoning laws. [But] § 16C is not simply a legislative exercise of zoning power [because it] delegates * * * discretionary governmental powers [to] religious bodies.[b]

"[The] valid secular objectives [of protecting] spiritual, cultural, and educational centers from the 'hurly-burly' associated with liquor outlets [can] be readily accomplished by other means—either through an absolute legislative ban on liquor outlets within reasonable prescribed distances from churches, schools, hospitals and like institutions, or by ensuring a hearing for the views of affected institutions at licensing proceedings * * *. [But the] churches' power under the statute is standardless [and] may therefore be used by churches [for] explicitly religious goals, for example, favoring liquor licenses for members of that congregation or adherents of that faith. [In] addition, the mere appearance of a joint exercise of legislative authority by Church and State provides a significant symbolic benefit to religion in the minds of some by reason of the power conferred. It does not strain our prior holdings to say that the statute can be seen as having a 'primary' and 'principal' effect of advancing religion. [Finally, § 16C] enmeshes churches in the processes of government and creates the danger of 'political fragmentation and divisiveness along religious lines.' "

Rehnquist, J., dissented: A "flat ban [on] the grant of an alcoholic beverages license to any establishment located within 500 feet of a church or a [school], which the majority concedes is valid, is more protective of churches and more restrictive of liquor sales than the present § 16C. * * * Nothing in the Court's opinion persuades me why the more rigid prohibition would be constitutional, but the more flexible not. [It] does not sponsor or subsidize any religious group or activity. It does not encourage, much less compel, anyone to participate in religious activities or to support religious institutions. To say that it 'advances' religion is to strain at the meaning of the word. [If] a church were to seek to advance the interests of its members [by favoring them for licenses], there would be an occasion to determine whether it had violated any right of an unsuccessful applicant for a liquor license. But our ability to discern a risk of such abuse does not render § 16C violative of the Establishment Clause."

4. *Other approaches.* Many commentators have proposed various "tests" to measure the validity of public aid to church-related schools. In evaluating those that follow, what results would they produce in the decided cases?

(a) Consider Gordon, *The Unconstitutionality of Public Aid to Parochial Schools,* in The Wall Between Church and State 73, 92 (Oaks ed. 1963): "The [test] is whether it is the church (or church institution) or the state that performs or controls the performance of the services paid for by the state. [It] is reasonable to assume that services performed or controlled by a religious

---

b. Does the "delegation" to church-related schools of the authority to satisfy state requirements for elementary and secondary education violate the establishment clause?

institution could and would be used to further the religious objectives of that institution, whereas services performed or controlled by a public body would be secular in purpose and form." What result in *Everson* if the buses were rented by the parochial school? What about lunches preceded by prayers in the parochial school cafeteria?

(b) Consider Choper, fn. a in *Lemon*, at 265–66: "[G]overnmental financial aid may be extended directly or indirectly to support parochial schools [so] long as such aid does not exceed the value of the secular educational service rendered by the school." [c] Would such aid have "a secular legislative purpose and a primary effect that neither advances nor inhibits religion"? Compare Hammett, *The Homogenized Wall*, 53 A.B.A.J. 929, 932–33 (1967): "[T]he enactment must contain a state secular purpose paramount over any religious purpose which the church attaches to the conduct regulated or promoted by the state. Labeling the religious purpose 'incidental' could be misleading; the purpose, though incidentally religious from the secular state's viewpoint, may have overwhelming religious significance from the church's viewpoint. [If] the net effect of the financial aid is to increase proportionally the influence of both the church and the state, so that their influence relative to each other remains at the same original ratio, the 'primary' effect on religion has been neutral." Contrast Sugarman, *New Perspectives on "Aid" to Private School Users*, in Nonpublic School Aid 64, 66 (West ed. 1976): "Even if the [effect] principle were limited to cases in which there was (or the legislature knew there would be) a *large* beneficial impact on religion, it would intolerably inhibit secular government action. For example, perhaps building roads and running public transportation on Sunday may be shown to have large beneficial impacts on religion. [For] me the concerns underlying the Establishment clause could be satisfied with an affirmative answer to this hypothetical question: Would the legislature have acted as it did were there no interdependency with religion involved? If so, then I think it would be fair to say that there is no subsidy of religion, that the religious benefits are constitutionally permitted side effects." [d]

IV.   OFFICIAL ACKNOWLEDGMENT OF RELIGION

MARSH v. CHAMBERS, 463 U.S. 783, 103 S.Ct. 3330, 77 L.Ed.2d 1019 (1983), per BURGER, C.J., upheld the practice of opening each day of the Nebraska legislature with a prayer by a chaplain (since 1965, a Presbyterian minister) paid by the state ($319.75 per month when the legislature is in session) as being "deeply embedded in the history and tradition of this country." The Court pointed, inter alia, to the practice in the colonies (including Virginia after adopting its Declaration of Rights which has been "considered the precursor of both the Free Exercise and Establishment Clauses"), to the opening invocations in federal courts (including the Supreme Court), and to the Continental Congress and First Congress: "Clearly the men who wrote the First Amendment Religion Clause did not view paid legislative chaplains and opening prayers as a violation of that Amendment, for the practice of opening sessions with prayer has continued without interruption ever since that early session of Congress. It has also been followed consistently in most of the states." Although "standing alone, historical patterns cannot justify contemporary violations of constitutional guarantees, [i]n this context, historical evidence sheds light not only on what the

---

c. See also West, *An Economic Analysis of the Law and Politics of Nonpublic School "Aid"*, in Nonpublic School Aid 1 (West ed. 1976).

d. Problems under the free exercise clause raised by the exclusion of parochial schools from public aid programs are considered in note 4 after *Sherbert v. Verner*, Sec. 2, I infra.

draftsmen intended the Establishment Clause to mean, but also on how they thought that Clause applied to the practice authorized by the First Congress— their actions reveal their intent." [a]

The Court noted that "here, the individual claiming injury by the practice is an adult, presumably not readily susceptible to 'religious indoctrination,' see *Tilton,* or peer pressure, compare *Schempp* (Brennan, J., concurring). In light of the unambiguous and unbroken history of more than 200 years, there can be no doubt that the practice of opening legislative sessions with prayer has become part of the fabric of our society. To invoke Divine guidance on a public body entrusted with making the laws [is] simply a tolerable acknowledgment of beliefs widely held among the people of this country. As Justice Douglas observed, 'we are a religious people whose institutions presuppose a Supreme Being.' *Zorach.*"

BRENNAN, J., joined by Marshall, J.—noting that "the Court makes no pretense of subjecting Nebraska's practice of legislative prayer to any of the formal 'tests' that have traditionally structured our inquiry under the Establishment Clause"—dissented: "I have no doubt that, if any group of law students were asked to apply the principles of *Lemon* to the question of legislative prayer, they would nearly unanimously find the practice to be unconstitutional. * * *

"Legislative prayer clearly violates [the] fundamental message of *Engel* and *Schempp.* It intrudes on the right to conscience by forcing some legislators either to participate in a 'prayer opportunity,' with which they are in basic disagreement, or to make their disagreement a matter of public comment by declining to participate. It forces all residents of the State to support a religious exercise that may be contrary to their own beliefs. It requires the State to commit itself on fundamental theological issues. It has the potential for degrading religion by allowing a religious call to worship to be intermeshed with a secular call to order. [This is not] a case in which a State is accommodating individual religious interests. "[S]pecific historical practice should not in this case override [the] clear constitutional imperative.[30] [M]ost importantly, the argument tendered by the Court is misguided because the Constitution is not a static document whose meaning on every detail is fixed for all time by the life experience of the Framers."

STEVENS, J., also filed a brief dissent: "[D]esignation of a member of one religious faith to serve as the sole official chaplain of a state legislature for a period of 16 years constitutes the preference of one faith over another in violation of the Establishment Clause."

LYNCH v. DONNELLY
465 U.S. 668, 104 S.Ct. 1355, 79 L.Ed.2d 604 (1984).

THE CHIEF JUSTICE delivered the opinion of the Court. * * *

Each year, [the] City of Pawtucket, Rhode Island, erects a Christmas display as part of its observance of the Christmas holiday season. The display [includes]

---

a. Of what relevance is it that, subsequently, "Madison acknowledged that he had been quite mistaken in approving—as a member of the House, in 1789—bills for the payment of congressional chaplains"? Van Alstyne, *Trends in the Supreme Court: Mr. Jefferson's Crumbling Wall,* 1984 Duke L.J. 770, 776.

30. Indeed, the sort of historical argument made by the Court should be advanced with some hesitation in light of certain other skeletons in the congressional closet. See, e.g., An Act for the Punishment of certain Crimes against the United States (1790) (enacted by the First Congress and requiring that persons convicted of certain theft offenses "be publicly whipped, not exceeding thirty-nine stripes"); Act of July 23, 1866 (reaffirming the racial segregation of the public schools in the District of Columbia; enacted exactly one week after Congress proposed Fourteenth Amendment to the States).

a Santa Claus house, reindeer pulling Santa's sleigh, candy-striped poles, a Christmas tree, carolers, cutout figures representing such characters as a clown, an elephant, and a teddy bear, hundreds of colored lights, a large banner that reads "SEASONS GREETINGS," and the crèche at issue here [which] consists of the traditional figures, including the Infant Jesus, Mary and Joseph, angels, shepherds, kings, and animals, all ranging in height from 5" to 5'. In 1973, when the present crèche was acquired, it cost the City $1365; it now is valued at $200. The erection and dismantling of the crèche costs the City about $20 per year; nominal expenses are incurred in lighting the crèche. No money has been expended on its maintenance for the past 10 years. [The] District Court held that the City's inclusion of the crèche in the display violates the Establishment Clause [and] the Court of Appeals for the First Circuit affirmed. * * *

There is an unbroken history of official acknowledgment by all three branches of government of the role of religion in American life from at least 1789. [L]ong before Independence, a day of Thanksgiving was celebrated at a religious holiday to give thanks for the bounties of Nature as gifts from God. President Washington and his successors proclaimed Thanksgiving, with all its religious overtones, a day of national celebration and Congress made it a National Holiday more than a century ago. That holiday has not lost its theme of expressing thanks for Divine aid any more than has Christmas lost its religious significance.

Executive Orders and other official announcements of Presidents and of the Congress have proclaimed both Christmas and Thanksgiving National Holidays in religious terms [and] it has long been the practice that federal employees are released from duties on these National Holidays, while being paid from the same public revenues that provide the compensation of the Chaplains of the Senate and the House and the military services. Thus, it is clear that Government has long recognized—indeed it has subsidized—holidays with religious significance.

Other examples of reference to our religious heritage are found in the statutorily prescribed national motto "In God We Trust," [and] in the language "One nation under God," as part of the Pledge of Allegiance * * *.

Art galleries supported by public revenues display religious paintings of the 15th and 16th centuries, predominantly inspired by one religious faith. The National Gallery in Washington, maintained with Government support, for example, has long exhibited masterpieces with religious messages, notably the Last Supper, and paintings depicting the Birth of Christ, the Crucifixion, and the Resurrection, among many others with explicit Christian themes and messages. The very chamber in which oral arguments on this case were heard is decorated with a notable and permanent—not seasonal—symbol of religion: Moses with Ten Commandments. Congress has long provided chapels in the Capitol for religious worship and meditation [and] has directed the President to proclaim a National Day of Prayer each [year]. Presidential Proclamations and messages have also issued to commemorate Jewish Heritage Week and the Jewish High Holy Days. One cannot look at even this brief resume without finding that our history is pervaded by expressions of religious beliefs * * *.

This history may help explain why the Court consistently has declined to take a rigid, absolutist view of the Establishment Clause. [In] the line-drawing process we have often found it useful to inquire whether the challenged law or conduct has a secular purpose, whether its principal or primary effect is to advance or inhibit religion, and whether it creates an excessive entanglement of government with religion. But, we have repeatedly emphasized our unwillingness to be confined to any single test or criterion in this sensitive area. * * * We did not, for example, consider that analysis relevant in *Marsh.* * * *

In this case, the focus of our inquiry must be on the crèche in the context of the Christmas season. [F]or example, [*Schempp*] specifically noted that nothing in the Court's holding was intended to "indicat[e] that such study of the Bible or of religion, when presented objectively as part of a secular program of education, may not be effected consistently with the First Amendment." Focus exclusively on the religious component of any activity would inevitably lead to its invalidation under the Establishment Clause.

The Court has invalidated legislation or governmental action on the ground that a secular purpose was lacking, but only when it has concluded there was no question that the statute or activity was motivated wholly by religious considerations. See, e.g., *Stone; Epperson; Schempp; Engel.* Even where the benefits to religion were substantial, as in *Everson; Allen; Walz; Tilton,* we saw a secular purpose and no conflict with the Establishment Clause.

[When] viewed in the proper context of the Christmas Holiday season, it is apparent that, on this record, there is insufficient evidence to establish that the inclusion of the crèche is a purposeful or surreptitious effort to express some kind of subtle governmental advocacy of a particular religious message. In a pluralistic society a variety of motives and purposes are implicated. The City, like the Congresses and Presidents, however, has principally taken note of a significant historical religious event long celebrated in the Western World. The crèche in the display depicts the historical origins of this traditional event long recognized as a National Holiday. [These] are legitimate secular purposes.[6] The District Court's inference, drawn from the religious nature of the crèche, that the City has no secular purpose was, on this record, clearly erroneous.[7]

The District Court found that the primary effect of including the crèche is to confer a substantial and impermissible benefit on religion in general and on the Christian faith in particular. Comparisons of the relative benefits to religion of different forms of governmental support are elusive and difficult to make. But to conclude that the primary effect of including the crèche is to advance religion in violation of the Establishment Clause would require that we view it as more beneficial to and more an endorsement of religion, for example, than [that upheld in *Allen; Everson; Tilton; Roemer; Walz; McGowan; Zorach;* and *Marsh*]. What was said about the legislative prayers in *Marsh,* and implied about the Sunday Closing Laws in *McGowan* is true of the City's inclusion of the crèche: its "reason or effect merely happens to coincide or harmonize with the tenets of [some] religions." [W]hatever benefit to one faith or religion or to all religions, is indirect, remote and incidental; display of the crèche is no more an advancement or endorsement of religion that the Congressional and Executive recognition of the origins of the Holiday itself as "Christ's Mass," or the exhibition of literally hundreds of religious paintings in governmentally supported museums. * * *

6. The City contends that the purposes of the display are "exclusively secular." We hold only that Pawtucket has a secular purpose for its display, which is all that *Lemon* requires. Were the test that the government must have "exclusively secular" objectives, much of the conduct and legislation this Court has approved in the past would have been invalidated.

7. Justice Brennan argues that the City's objectives could have been achieved without including the crèche in the display. True or not, that is irrelevant. The question is whether the display of the crèche violates the Establishment Clause.

Entanglement is a question of kind and degree. In this case, however, there is no reason to disturb the District Court's finding on the absence of administrative entanglement. There is no evidence of contact with church authorities concerning the content or design of the exhibit prior to or since Pawtucket's purchase of the crèche. No expenditures for maintenance of the crèche have been necessary; and since the City owns the crèche, now valued at $200, the tangible material it contributes is de minimis. In many respects the display requires far less ongoing, day-to-day interaction between church and state than religious paintings in public galleries. * * *

The Court of Appeals correctly observed that this Court has not held that political divisiveness alone can serve to invalidate otherwise permissible conduct. And we decline to so hold today. This case does not involve a direct subsidy to church-sponsored schools or colleges, or other religious institutions, and hence no inquiry into potential political divisiveness is even called for, *Mueller,* n. 11. In any event, apart from this litigation there is no evidence of political friction or divisiveness over the crèche in the 40-year history of Pawtucket's Christmas celebration. [A] litigant cannot, by the very act of commencing a lawsuit, however, create the appearance of divisiveness and then exploit it as evidence of entanglement. * * *

Of course the crèche is identified with one religious faith but no more so than the examples we have set out from prior cases in which we found no conflict with the Establishment Clause. See, e.g., *McGowan; Marsh.* It would be ironic, however, if the inclusion of a single symbol of a particular historic religious event, as part of a celebration acknowledged in the Western World for 20 centuries, and in this country by the people, by the Executive Branch, by the Congress, and the courts for two centuries, would so "taint" the City's exhibit as to render it violative of the Establishment Clause. To forbid the use of this one passive symbol—the crèche—at the very time people are taking note of the season with Christmas hymns and carols in public schools and other public places, and while the Congress and Legislatures open sessions with prayers by paid chaplains would be a stilted over-reaction contrary to our history and to our holdings. If the presence of the crèche in this display violates the Establishment Clause, a host of other forms of taking official note of Christmas, and of our religious heritage, are equally offensive to the Constitution.

The Court has acknowledged that the "fears and political problems" that gave rise to the Religion Clauses in the 18th century are of far less concern today. We are unable to perceive the Archbishop of Canterbury, the Vicar of Rome, or other powerful religious leaders behind every public acknowledgment of the religious heritage long officially recognized by the three constitutional branches of government. Any notion that these symbols pose a real danger of establishment of a state church is far-fetched indeed.

[R]eversed.

JUSTICE O'CONNOR, concurring.

I concur in the opinion of the Court. I write separately to suggest a clarification of our Establishment Clause doctrine. * * *

The Establishment Clause prohibits government from making adherence to a religion relevant in any way to a person's standing in the political community. Government can run afoul of that prohibition in two principal ways. One is excessive entanglement with religious institutions, which may interfere with the independence of the institutions, give the institutions access to government or governmental powers not fully shared by nonadherents of the religion, and foster the creation of political constituencies defined along religious lines. E.g., *Grendel's Den.* The second and more direct infringement is government endorsement or disapproval of religion. Endorsement sends a message to nonadherents that they are outsiders, not full members of the political community, and an accompanying message to adherents that they are insiders, favored members of the political community. Disapproval sends the opposite message. See generally *Schempp.*

In this case, as even the District Court found, there is no institutional entanglement. [In] my view, political divisiveness along religious lines should not be an independent test of constitutionality. * * *

The central issue in this case is whether Pawtucket has endorsed Christianity by its display of the crèche. [The] purpose prong of the *Lemon* test asks whether government's actual purpose is to endorse or disapprove of religion. The effect prong asks whether, irrespective of government's actual purpose, the practice under review in fact conveys a message of endorsement or disapproval. An affirmative answer to either question should render the challenged practice invalid.

* * * I would find that Pawtucket did not intend to convey any message of endorsement of Christianity or disapproval of nonChristian religions. The evident purpose of including the crèche in the larger display [was] celebration of the public holiday through its traditional symbols. [This] is a legitimate secular purpose. * * *

Pawtucket's display of its crèche, I believe, does not communicate a message that the government intends to endorse the Christian beliefs represented by the crèche. [T]he overall holiday setting changes what viewers may fairly understand to be the purpose of the display—as a typical museum setting, though not neutralizing the religious content of a religious painting, negates any message of endorsement of that content. The display celebrates a public holiday [with] very strong secular components and traditions. Government celebration of the holiday, which is extremely common, generally is not understood to endorse the religious content of the holiday, just as government celebration of Thanksgiving is not so understood. The crèche is a traditional symbol of the holiday that is very commonly displayed along with purely secular symbols, as it was in Pawtucket.

These features combine to make the government's display of the crèche in this particular physical setting no more an endorsement of religion than such governmental "acknowledgments" of religion as legislative prayers of the type approved in *Marsh,* government declaration of Thanksgiving as a public holiday, printing of "In God We Trust" on coins, and opening court sessions with "God save the United States and this honorable court." Those government acknowledgments of religion serve, in the only ways reasonably possible in our culture, the legitimate secular purposes of solemnizing public occasions, expressing confidence in the future, and encouraging the recognition of what is worthy of appreciation in society. For that reason, and because of their history and ubiquity, those practices are not understood as conveying government approval of particular religious beliefs. * * *

Justice Brennan, with whom Justice Marshall, Justice Blackmun and Justice Stevens join, dissenting.

[The] Court's decision implicitly leaves open questions concerning the constitutionality of the public display on public property of a crèche standing alone, or the public display of other distinctively religious symbols such as a cross.

Despite the narrow contours of the Court's opinion, [n]othing in the history of such practices or the setting in which the City's crèche is presented obscures or diminishes the plain fact that Pawtucket's action amounts to an impermissible governmental endorsement of a particular faith.

[T]he City claims that its purposes were exclusively secular [—] to participate in the celebration of a national holiday and to attract people to the downtown area in order to promote pre-Christmas retail sales and to help engender the spirit of goodwill and neighborliness commonly associated with the Christmas season. [But] all of Pawtucket's "valid secular objectives can be readily accomplished by other means." Plainly, the City's interest in celebrating the holiday and in promoting both retail sales and goodwill are fully served by the elaborate display of Santa Claus, reindeer, and wishing wells that are already a part of Pawtucket's annual Christmas display. More importantly, the nativity scene, unlike every other element of the Hodgson Park display, reflects a sectarian exclusivity that the avowed purposes of celebrating the holiday season and promoting retail commerce simply do not encompass. [Plainly,] the City and its leaders understood that the inclusion of the crèche in its display would serve the wholly religious purpose of "keep[ing] 'Christ in Christmas.'" From this record, therefore, it is impossible to say with the kind of confidence that was possible in *McGowan* that a wholly secular goal predominates.

The "primary effect" [is] to place the government's imprimatur of approval on the particular religious beliefs exemplified by the crèche. Those who believe in the message of the nativity receive the unique and exclusive benefit of public recognition and approval of their views. [The] effect on minority religious groups, as well as on those who may reject all religion, is to convey the message that their views are not similarly worthy of public recognition nor entitled to public support. * * *

Finally, it is evident that [the] display does pose a significant threat of fostering "excessive entanglement." [A]fter today's decision, administrative entanglements may well develop. Jews and other non-Christian groups, prompted perhaps by the Mayor's remark that he will include a Menorah in future displays, can be expected to press government for inclusion of their symbols, and faced with such requests, government will have to become involved in accommodating the various demands. More importantly, although no political divisiveness was apparent in Pawtucket prior to the filing of respondents' lawsuit, [that] does not immediately suggest the absence of any division on the point [for] the quiescence of those opposed to the crèche may have reflected nothing more than their sense of futility in opposing the majority.[9]

[The] Court apparently believes that once it finds that the designation of Christmas as a public holiday is constitutionally acceptable, it is then free to conclude that virtually every form of governmental association with the celebra-

---

9. The suggestion in *Mueller,* n. 11, relied upon by the Court today, that inquiry into potential political divisiveness is unnecessary absent direct subsidies to church-sponsored schools or colleges, derives from a distorted reading of our prior cases. Simply because the Court in *Lemon*—a case involving such subsidies—inquired into potential divisiveness while distinguishing *Everson* and *Allen*—cases not involving such subsidies—does not provide any authority for the proposition that the Court in *Lemon* meant to confine the divisive-

ness inquiry only to cases factually identical to *Lemon* itself. Indeed, in *Walz,* the Court considered the question of divisiveness in the context of state tax exemptions to all religious institutions. I agree, however, with Justice O'Connor's helpful suggestion that while political divisiveness is "an evil addressed by the Establishment Clause," the ultimate inquiry must always focus on "the character of the government activity that might cause such divisiveness."

tion of the holiday is also constitutional. The vice of this dangerously superficial argument is that it overlooks the fact that the Christmas holiday in our national culture contains both secular and sectarian elements. To say that government may recognize the holiday's traditional, secular elements of giftgiving, public festivities and community spirit, does not mean that government may indiscriminately embrace the distinctively sectarian aspects of the holiday. Indeed, in its eagerness to approve the crèche, the Court has advanced a rationale so simplistic that it would appear to allow the Mayor of Pawtucket to participate in the celebration of a Christmas mass, since this would be just another unobjectionable way for the City to "celebrate the holiday."   * * *

When government decides to recognize Christmas day as a public holiday, it does no more than accommodate the calendar of public activities to the plain fact that many Americans will expect on that day to spend time visiting with their families, attending religious services, and perhaps enjoying some respite from preholiday activities. The Free Exercise Clause, of course, does not necessarily compel the government to provide this accommodation, but neither is the Establishment Clause offended by such a step. Cf. *Zorach*. [If] public officials go further and participate in the *secular* celebration of Christmas—by, for example, decorating public places with such secular images as wreaths, garlands or Santa Claus figures—they move closer to the limits of their constitutional power but nevertheless remain within the boundaries set by the Establishment Clause. But when those officials participate in or appear to endorse the distinctively religious elements of this otherwise secular event, they encroach upon First Amendment freedoms. For it is at that point that the government brings to the forefront the theological content of the holiday, and places the prestige, power and financial support of a civil authority in the service of a particular faith.

[T]he crèche is far from a mere representation of a "particular historic religious event." It is, instead, best understood as a mystical re-creation of an event that lies at the heart of Christian faith. To suggest, as the Court does, that such a symbol is merely "traditional" and therefore no different from Santa's house or reindeer is not only offensive to those for whom the crèche has profound significance, but insulting to those who insist for religious or personal reasons that the story of Christ is in no sense a part of "history" nor an unavoidable element of our national "heritage."

[The] Court seems to assume that forbidding Pawtucket from displaying a crèche would be tantamount to forbidding a state college from including the Bible or Milton's Paradise Lost in a course on English literature. But in those cases the religiously-inspired materials are being considered solely as literature. The purpose is plainly not to single out the particular religious beliefs that may have inspired the authors, but to see in these writings the outlines of a larger imaginative universe shared with other forms of literary expression. The same may be said of a course devoted to the study of art; when the course turns to Gothic architecture, the emphasis is not on the religious beliefs which the cathedrals exalt, but rather upon the "aesthetic consequences of [such religious] thought."

In this case, by contrast, the crèche plays no comparable secular role. Unlike the poetry of Paradise Lost which students in a literature course will seek to appreciate primarily for aesthetic or historical reasons, the angels, shepherds, Magi and infant of Pawtucket's nativity scene can only be viewed as symbols of a particular set of religious beliefs. It would be another matter if the crèche were displayed in a museum setting, in the company of other religiously-inspired artifacts, as an example, among many, of the symbolic representation of religious myths. In that setting, we would have objective guarantees that the crèche could not suggest that a particular faith had been singled out for public favor and recognition. The effect of Pawtucket's crèche, however, is not confined by any of these limiting attributes. In the absence of any other religious symbols or of any neutral disclaimer, the inescapable effect of the crèche will be to remind the average observer of the religious roots of the celebration he is witnessing and to call to mind the scriptural message that the nativity symbolizes. The fact that Pawtucket has gone to the trouble of making such an elaborate public celebration and of including a crèche in that otherwise secular setting inevitably serves to reinforce the sense that the City means to express solidarity with the Christian message of the crèche and to dismiss other faiths as unworthy of similar attention and support. * * *

Intuition tells us that some official "acknowledgment" is inevitable in a religious society if government is not to adopt a stilted indifference to the religious life of the people. It is equally true, however, that if government is to remain scrupulously neutral in matters of religious conscience, as our Constitution requires, then it must avoid those overly broad acknowledgments of religious practices that may imply governmental favoritism toward one set of religious beliefs. * * *

[T]he Court has never comprehensively addressed the extent to which government may acknowledge religion by, for example, incorporating religious references into public ceremonies and proclamations, and I do not presume to offer a comprehensive approach. Nevertheless, it appears from our prior decisions that at least three principles [may] be identified. First, although the government may not be compelled to do so by the Free Exercise Clause, it may, consistently with the Establishment Clause, act to accommodate to some extent the opportunities of individuals to practice their religion. See [Zorach. This] would justify government's decision to declare December 25th a public holiday.

Second, our cases recognize that while a particular governmental practice may have derived from religious motivations and retain certain religious connotations, it is nonetheless permissible for the government to pursue the practice when it is continued today solely for secular reasons. [McGowan.] Thanksgiving Day, in my view, fits easily within this principle, for despite its religious antecedents, the current practice of celebrating Thanksgiving is unquestionably secular and patriotic. We all may gather with our families on that day to give thanks both for personal and national good fortune, but we are free, given the secular character of the holiday, to address that gratitude either to a divine beneficence or to such mundane sources as good luck or the country's abundant natural wealth.

Finally, we have noted that government cannot be completely prohibited from recognizing in its public actions the religious beliefs and practices of the American people as an aspect of our national history and culture. See Engel, n. 21. While I remain uncertain about these questions, I would suggest that such practices as the designation of "In God We Trust" as our national motto, or the references to God contained in the Pledge of Allegiance can best be understood [as] a form of "ceremonial deism," protected from Establishment Clause scrutiny chiefly because they have lost through rote repetition any significant religious content. Moreover, these references are uniquely suited to serve such wholly secular purposes as solemnizing public occasions, or inspiring commitment to meet some national challenge in a manner that simply could not be fully served in our culture if government were limited to purely non-religious phrases. The practices by which the government has long acknowledged religion are therefore probably necessary to serve certain secular functions, and that necessity, coupled with their long history, gives those practices an essentially secular meaning.

The crèche fits none of these categories. Inclusion of the crèche is not necessary to accommodate individual religious expression. [Nor] is the inclusion of the crèche necessary to serve wholly secular goals; it is clear that the City's secular purposes of celebrating the Christmas holiday and promoting retail commerce can be fully served without the crèche. And the crèche, because of its unique association with Christianity, is clearly more sectarian than those references to God that we accept in ceremonial phrases or in other contexts that assure neutrality. * * *

The American historical experience concerning the public celebration of Christmas, if carefully examined, provides no support for the Court's decision. [T]here is no evidence whatsoever that the Framers would have expressly approved a Federal celebration of the Christmas holiday including public displays of a nativity scene; accordingly, the Court's repeated invocation of the decision in *Marsh*, is not only baffling, it is utterly irrelevant. Nor is there any suggestion that publicly financed and supported displays of Christmas crèche are supported by a record of widespread, undeviating acceptance that extends throughout our history. Therefore, our prior decisions which relied upon concrete, specific historical evidence to support a particular practice simply have no bearing on the question presented in this case. Contrary to today's careless decision, those prior cases have all recognized that the "illumination" provided by history must always be focused on the particular practice at issue in a given case. Without that guiding principle and the intellectual discipline it imposes, the Court is at sea, free to select random elements of America's varied history solely to suit the views of five Members of this Court. * * * [a]

SECTION 2.   FREE EXERCISE CLAUSE AND RELATED PROBLEMS

I. CONFLICT WITH STATE REGULATION

The most common problem respecting free exercise of religion arises when a government regulation, whose purpose is nonreligious, either makes illegal (or otherwise burdens) conduct that is dictated by some religious belief, or requires (or otherwise encourages) conduct that is forbidden by some religious belief. Thus, REYNOLDS v. UNITED STATES, 98 U.S. 145, 25 L.Ed. 244 (1879), the first major decision on the free exercise clause, upheld application of a federal law making polygamy illegal to a Mormon whose religious duty was to practice polygamy: "Congress was deprived of all legislative power over mere opinion, but was left free to reach actions which were in violation of social duties or subversive of good order."   CANTWELL v. CONNECTICUT, 310 U.S. 296, 60 S.Ct. 900, 84 L.Ed. 1213 (1940), reemphasized this distinction between religious

a. The brief dissenting opinion of Blackmun, J., joined by Stevens, J., is omitted.

After *Lynch* and *Widmar v. Vincent*, may a city that permits use of its park for a wide variety of displays and activities—including religious services and singing Christmas carols—deny its use for a privately financed nativity scene during the Christmas season? See *McCreary v. Stone*, 739 F.2d 716 (2d Cir. 1984) (denial invalid), affirmed by an equally divided Court, ___ U.S. ___, 105 S.Ct. 1859, 85 L.Ed.2d 63 (1985) (Powell, J., not participating).

opinion or belief, on the one hand, and action taken because of religion, on the other, although the Court spoke somewhat more solicitously about the latter: "The [Constitution] forestalls compulsion by law of the acceptance of any creed or the practice of any form of worship. Freedom of conscience and freedom to adhere to such religious organization or form of worship as the individual may choose cannot be restricted by law. [Free exercise] embraces two concepts,— freedom to believe and freedom to act. The first is absolute but, in the nature of things, the second cannot be. [The] freedom to act must have appropriate definition to preserve the enforcement of that protection [although] the power to regulate must be so exercised as not, in attaining a permissible end, unduly to infringe the protected freedom."

Even before *Cantwell*—which first held that the fourteenth amendment made the free exercise guarantee applicable to the states—several decisions invalidating state laws as unreasonably interfering with the "liberty" secured by the fourteenth amendment due process clause (see, e.g., *Pierce v. Society of Sisters,* Sec. 1 supra), carried significant overtones for religious freedom. By contrast, *Hamilton v. Regents,* 293 U.S. 245, 55 S.Ct. 197, 79 L.Ed. 343 (1934), held that a state statute—requiring all male students at the state university to take a course in military training—was not a deprivation of "liberty" without due process of members of the Methodist Episcopal Church whose conscientious beliefs forbade military training.

Beginning with *Cantwell*, a number of cases invalidated application of state laws to conduct undertaken pursuant to religious beliefs. Like *Cantwell*, these decisions, set forth in Ch. 8,[a] rested in whole or in part on the freedom of expression provisions of the first and fourteenth amendments. Similarly, WEST VIRGINIA STATE BD. OF EDUC. v. BARNETTE, 319 U.S. 624, 63 S.Ct. 1178, 87 L.Ed. 1628 (1943),[b] held that compelling a flag salute by public school children whose religious scruples forbade it violated the first amendment: "The test of legislation which collides with the Fourteenth Amendment, because it also collides with the principles of the First, is much more definite than the test when only the Fourteenth is involved. [The] right of a state to regulate, for example, a public utility may well include, so far as the due process test is concerned, power to impose all of the restrictions which a legislature may have a 'rational basis' for adopting. But freedoms of speech and of press, of assembly, and of worship may not be infringed on such slender grounds. They are susceptible of restriction only to prevent grave and immediate danger to interests which the state may lawfully protect. [If] there is any fixed star in our constitutional constellation, it is that no official, high or petty, can prescribe what shall be orthodox in politics, nationalism or other matters of opinion or force citizens to confess by word or act their faith therein."

Other decisions dealt exclusively with the free exercise clause. PRINCE v. MASSACHUSETTS, 321 U.S. 158, 64 S.Ct. 438, 88 L.Ed. 645 (1944), upheld a state law making it a crime for children to sell merchandise in public places as applied to a child who was distributing religious literature with her guardian, emphasizing the state's interest in "the healthy, well-rounded growth of young people" and "the crippling effects of child employment, more especially in public

---

a. E.g., *Schneider v. Irvington,* p. 641 supra; *Lovell v. Griffin,* p. 582 supra; *Martin v. Struthers,* p. 689 supra; compare *Cox v. New Hampshire,* p. 642 supra; *Poulos v. New Hampshire,* p. 587 supra. See also *Marsh v. Alabama,* p. 1095 infra.

b. Overruling *Minersville School Dist. v. Gobitis,* 310 U.S. 586, 60 S.Ct. 1010, 84 L.Ed. 1375 (1940).

places, and the possible harms arising from other activities subject to all the diverse influences of the street."

BRAUNFELD v. BROWN, 366 U.S. 599, 81 S.Ct. 1144, 6 L.Ed.2d 563 (1961), upheld application of Pennsylvania's Sunday Closing Law (whose nonreligious purpose was sustained in a companion case, *McGowan v. Maryland,* Sec. 1, II supra), to Orthodox Jews whose ability "to earn a livelihood" would be impaired by Sunday closing because their religion forbade work on Saturday. The plurality opinion was by WARREN, C.J., joined by Black, Clark and Whittaker, JJ.: "[L]egislative power over mere opinion is forbidden but it may reach people's actions when they are found to be in violation of important social duties or subversive of good order, even when the actions are demanded by one's religion. [*Barnette*] was careful to point out that 'The freedom asserted by these appellees does not bring them into collision with rights asserted by any other individual. It is such conflicts which most frequently require intervention of the State to determine where the rights of one end and those of another begin. [T]he compulsory flag salute and pledge requires *affirmation of a belief* and an *attitude of mind.*'

"[In *Reynolds* and *Prince*], the religious practices themselves conflicted with the public interest. In such cases, to make accommodation between the religious action and an exercise of state authority is a particularly delicate task because resolution in favor of the State results in the choice to the individual of either abandoning his religious principle or facing criminal prosecution.

"[But] the statute at bar does not make unlawful any religious practices of appellants; the Sunday law simply regulates a secular activity and, as applied to appellants, operates so as to make the practice of their religious beliefs more expensive. [R]ecognizing that the alternatives open to appellants and others similarly situated—retaining their present occupations and incurring economic disadvantage or engaging in some other commercial activity which does not call for either Saturday or Sunday labor—may well result in some financial sacrifice in order to observe their religious beliefs, still the option is wholly different than when the legislation attempts to make a religious practice itself unlawful.

"To strike down, without the most critical scrutiny, legislation which imposes only an indirect burden on the exercise of religion, i.e., legislation which does not make unlawful the religious practice itself, would radically restrict the operating latitude of the legislature. Statutes which tax income and limit the amount which may be deducted for religious contributions impose an indirect economic burden on the observance of the religion of the citizen whose religion requires him to donate a greater amount to his church; statutes which require the courts to be closed on Saturday and Sunday impose a similar indirect burden on the observance of the religion of the trial lawyer whose religion requires him to rest on a weekday. The list of legislation of this nature is nearly limitless. * * *

"Of course, to hold unassailable all legislation regulating conduct which imposes solely an indirect burden on the observance of religion would be a gross oversimplification. If the purpose or effect of a law is to impede the observance of one or all religions or is to discriminate invidiously between religions, that law is constitutionally invalid even though the burden may be characterized as being only indirect. But if the State regulates conduct by enacting a general law within its power, the purpose and effect of which is to advance the State's secular goals, the statute is valid despite its indirect burden on religious observance unless the State may accomplish its purpose by means which do not impose such a burden. See *Cantwell.*[4]

"As we pointed out in *McGowan,* we cannot find a State without power to provide a weekly respite from all labor and, at the same time, to set one day of the week apart from the others as a day of rest, repose, recreation and tranquility * * *. [To permit an exemption for Sabbatarians] might well undermine the State's goal of providing a day that, as best possible, eliminates the atmosphere of commercial noise and activity. Although not dispositive of the issue, enforcement problems would be more difficult since there would be two or more days to police rather than one and it would be more difficult to observe whether violations were occurring."[c]

BRENNAN, J., dissented because the law's "effect is that appellants may not simultaneously practice their religion and their trade, without being hampered by a substantial competitive disadvantage." He relied on *Barnette* for the "appropriate standard of constitutional adjudication in cases in which a statute is assertedly in conflict with the First Amendment":

"What, then, is the compelling state interest which impels Pennsylvania to impede appellants' freedom of worship? What overbalancing need is so weighty in the constitutional scale that it justifies this substantial, though indirect, limitation of appellants' freedom? It is not the desire to stamp out a practice deeply abhorred by society, such as polygamy, as in *Reynolds* [nor] is it the State's traditional protection of children, as in *Prince* * * *. It is not even the interest in seeing that everyone rests one day a week, for appellants' religion requires that they take such a rest. It is the mere convenience of having everyone rest on the same day. * * *

"It is true, I suppose, that [granting an exemption for Sabbatarians] would make Sundays a little noisier, and the task of police and prosecutor a little more difficult. It is also true that a majority [of] States which have general Sunday regulations have exemptions of this kind. We are not told that those States are significantly noisier or that their police are significantly more burdened, than Pennsylvania's."

STEWART, J., also dissented: "Pennsylvania has passed a law which compels an Orthodox Jew to choose between his religious faith and his economic survival. That is a cruel choice [and] is not something that can be swept under the rug and forgotten in the interest of enforced Sunday togetherness."

In SHERBERT v. VERNER, 374 U.S. 398, 83 S.Ct. 1790, 10 L.Ed.2d 965 (1963), a Seventh-day Adventist, discharged by her employer "because she would not work on Saturday, the Sabbath Day of her faith," was denied unemployment compensation by South Carolina on the ground that she refused to accept "suitable work" due to her religious restriction on Saturday labor. The Court, per BRENNAN, J., held that the "burden on the free exercise of appellant's

---

4. Thus in cases like *Murdock v. Pennsylvania,* 319 U.S. 105, 63 S.Ct. 870, 87 L.Ed. 1292 (1943), and *Follett v. McCormick,* 321 U.S. 573, 64 S.Ct. 717, 88 L.Ed. 938 (1944) [overruling *Jones v. Opelika,* 316 U.S. 584, 62 S.Ct. 1231, 86 L.Ed. 1691 (1942)], this Court struck down municipal ordinances which, in application, required religious colporteurs [Jehovah's Witnesses] to pay a license tax as a condition to the pursuit of their activities [of spreading religious doctrine by distributing religious pamphlets] because the State's interest, the obtaining of revenue, could be easily satisfied by imposing this tax on nonreligious sources.

c. Frankfurter and Harlan, JJ., rejected the free exercise claim in a separate opinion. Douglas, J., dissented. For extracts from both opinions, see *McGowan,* Sec. 1, II supra.

religion" must be justified by a "compelling state interest": "[T]he consequences of such a disqualification to religious principles and practices may be only an indirect result of welfare legislation within the State's general competence to enact; it is true that no criminal sanctions directly compel appellant to work a six-day week. But this is only the beginning, not the end of our inquiry. [T]o condition the availability of benefits upon this appellant's willingness to violate a cardinal principle of her religious faith effectively penalizes the free exercise of her constitutional liberties.

"Significantly South Carolina expressly saves the Sunday worshipper from having to make the kind of choice which we here hold infringes the Sabbatarian's religious liberty. When in times of 'national emergency' the textile plants are authorized by the State Commissioner of Labor to operate on Sunday, 'if any employee should refuse to work on Sunday on account of [conscience] he or she shall not jeopardize his or her seniority by such refusal or be discriminated against in any other manner.' S.C.Code, § 64–4. [The] unconstitutionality of the disqualification of the Sabbatarian is thus compounded by the religious discrimination which South Carolina's general statutory scheme necessarily effects.

"[A]ppellees suggest no more than a possibility that the filing of fraudulent claims by unscrupulous claimants feigning religious objections to Saturday work [might] dilute the unemployment compensation fund [but] there is no proof whatever to warrant such fears of malingering or deceit [and] it is highly doubtful whether such evidence would be sufficient to warrant a substantial infringement of religious liberties. For [it] would plainly be incumbent upon the appellees to demonstrate that no alternative forms of regulation would combat such abuses without infringing First Amendment rights.

"[T]he state interest asserted in the present case is wholly dissimilar to the interests which were found to justify the less direct burden upon religious practices in *Braunfeld*. [T]he statute [was] saved by a countervailing factor which finds no equivalent in the instant case—a strong state interest in providing one uniform day of rest for all workers. That secular objective could be achieved, the Court found, only by declaring Sunday to be that day of rest. Requiring exemptions for Sabbatarians, while theoretically possible, appeared to present an administrative problem of such magnitude, or afford the exempted class so great a competitive advantage that such a requirement would have rendered the entire statutory scheme unworkable. In the present case no such justifications underlie the determination of the [state].

"In holding as we do, plainly we are not fostering the 'establishment' of the Seventh-day Adventist religion in South Carolina, for the extension of unemployment benefits to Sabbatarians in common with Sunday worshippers reflects nothing more than the governmental obligation of neutrality in the face of religious differences, and does not represent that involvement of religious with secular institutions which it is the object of the Establishment Clause to forestall. [Nor] do we, by our decision today, declare the existence of a constitutional right to unemployment benefits on the part of all persons whose religious convictions are the cause of their unemployment. This is not a case in which an employee's religious convictions serve to make him a nonproductive member of society." Douglas, J., filed a separate concurrence.

STEWART, J., concurred in the result but, pointing particularly to the school prayer decisions in *Engel* and *Schempp*, argued that the result in *Sherbert* is "clearly to require the State to violate the Establishment Clause as construed by this Court. This poses no problem for me, because I think the Court's mechanistic concept of the Establishment Clause is historically unsound and constitutionally wrong." d

Further, "I cannot agree that today's decision can stand consistently with *Braunfeld.* [The] impact upon the appellant's religious freedom in the present case is considerably less onerous. [Even] upon the unlikely assumption that the appellant could not find suitable non-Saturday employment, the appellant at the worst would be denied a maximum of 22 weeks compensation payments" whereas the "undisputed effect" of the criminal statute in *Braunfeld,* "as pointed out by Mr. Justice Brennan in his dissenting opinion in that case, was that 'Plaintiff [will] be unable to continue in his business if he may not stay open on Sunday and he will thereby lose his capital investment.' "

HARLAN, J., joined by White, J., dissented, also maintaining that "the decision necessarily overrules *Braunfeld.*" Further, "in no proper sense can it be said that the State discriminated against the appellant on the basis of her religious beliefs or that she was denied benefits *because* she was a Seventh-day Adventist. She was denied benefits just as any other claimant would be denied benefits who was not 'available for work' for personal reasons. [Thus, the] meaning of today's holding [is] that the [state] must *single out* for financial assistance those whose behavior is religiously motivated, even though it denied such assistance to others whose identical behavior (in this case, inability to work on Saturdays) is not religiously motivated.[2]

"It has been suggested that such singling out of religious conduct for special treatment may violate the constitutional limitations on state action. See Kurland, *Of Church and State and The Supreme Court,* 29 U. of Chi.L.Rev. 1. My own view, however, is that at least under the circumstances of this case it would be a permissible accommodation of religion for the State, if it *chose* to do so, to create an exception to its eligibility requirements for persons like the appellant. [Those] situations in which the Constitution may require special treatment on account of religion are, in my view, few and far between * * *. Such compulsion in the present case is particularly inappropriate in light of the indirect, remote, and insubstantial effect of the decision below on the exercise of appellant's religion and in light of the direct financial assistance to religion that today's decision requires." e

Notes and Questions

1. *Braunfeld and Sherbert.* Consider Note, *A Braunfeld v. Brown Test for Indirect Burdens on the Free Exercise of Religion,* 48 Minn.L.Rev. 1165, 1177–78 (1964): "The state's goals of providing subsistence to the state's unemployed would not be advanced by denying relief to the appellant unless allowing religious claims would so burden the state's program as to necessitate abandon-

---

d. The conflict between the establishment and free exercise clauses is considered in note 4, Sec. 3 infra.

2. The Court does suggest, in a rather startling disclaimer, that its holding is limited in applicability to those whose religious convictions do not make them "non-productive" members of society [but it cannot] be suggesting that it will make a value judgment in each case as to whether a particular individual's religious convictions prevent him from being "productive." I can think of no more inappropriate function for this Court to perform.

e. In *Thomas v. Review Bd.* (1981), Part II infra, petitioner, a Jehovah's Witness, quit his job when he was transferred to weapons production because this was contrary "to his religious convictions." The Court, per Burger, C.J., relying on *Sherbert,* held that Indiana's denial of employment compensation, on the ground that petitioner did not quit for "good cause in connection with the work," violated free exercise.

ment of all unemployment relief. The state made no showing that such a burden existed. Further, any slight burden of establishing the validity of religious claims would be offset by the more successful satisfaction of the state's goal of providing relief in all appropriate cases of hardship. [In] *Braunfeld* a significant part of the secular goal was to provide a uniform day of rest, which could be accomplished only by allowing no exceptions; on the other hand, in *Sherbert* the goal of relieving the onus of unemployment is more successful when the benefits are not denied." Under this analysis, may a state deny worker's compensation to the widow of an employee who, after being injured at work, died because of his refusal on religious grounds to accept a blood transfusion?

2. *Hamilton and Barnette.* Is *Hamilton v. Regents,* supra, consistent with *Braunfeld* in that it "simply made the practice of religious beliefs more expensive"? Is it consistent with *Sherbert?* What state purpose would be frustrated by exempting these students? Of what significance is it that these students were exempt from the draft because of their religious belief? May the state's purpose be satisfied by alternative means? See Note, 48 Minn.L.Rev. at 1174–75.

Did the law in *Barnette* impose a direct or indirect burden? Is *Barnette* distinguishable from *Hamilton* because college attendance is voluntary, while if the children refused to salute the flag, they would be expelled from school and their parents prosecuted for causing delinquency? If the children could attend a private school where the flag salute was not required, would the case be distinguishable from *Hamilton?* Suppose the children could not afford to attend a private school? Or is *Hamilton* distinguishable because the state has a greater interest in compelling military training than it does in compelling a flag salute?

3. *Aid to parochial schools.* (a) Is the Court's conclusion, that denial of financial benefits to parochial schools does not infringe the free exercise rights of attending children, consistent with *Sherbert?* After *Everson,* could a student bus transportation program exclude children who attend parochial schools? See *Luetkemeyer v. Kaufmann,* 419 U.S. 888, 95 S.Ct. 167, 42 L.Ed.2d 134 (1974). If some religions impose a duty on parents to send children to religious schools, may these parents argue that, since they must pay public school taxes, the state's failure to support parochial as well as public schools and thus defray their parochial school tuition costs imposes a serious financial burden on their exercise of religion? That "if the state gives financial assistance only to the school where education is deliberately divorced from religion [this is] preferential treatment of irreligion"? See Drinan, *The Constitutionality of Public Aid to Parochial Schools,* in The Wall Between Church and State 55, 68 (Oaks ed. 1963). That, under *Sherbert,* "conditioning the availability of benefits upon their willingness to violate a cardinal principle of their religious faith effectively penalizes the free exercise of their constitutional liberties"; that there is no "compelling state interest to justify the substantial infringement of their First Amendment rights"? May these parents further argue that their position is stronger than *Sherbert* because the purpose of granting an exemption in that case was *solely* to aid religion whereas there is a wholly nonreligious purpose in giving aid to all nonpublic schools—improving the quality of the secular education?

Consider Kauper, *Religion and the Constitution* 36–37 (1964): "If the public policy of the state is to limit the use of educational funds to schools under public control, this involves no discrimination except the distinction between schools under public and those under private control—a distinction well recognized in our law. But if public funds are made available for all educational institutions whether public or private except those that are under the control of a religious body, it is indeed hard to avoid the conclusion that the religious factor is being used as a ground for disqualification from public benefits." Compare 25 U.Pitt. L.Rev. 713 (1964): "If the state in *Sherbert could not deny* compensation to one refusing work for religious reasons how could the state in *Everson* deny transportation reimbursement to students who choose for religious reasons to attend a parochial rather than public school? Suppose that the statute in *Everson* had dictated that all those attending nonpublic schools should not obtain free transportation, except that those students who attended religious schools because of the dictates of their religion also should qualify for fare reimbursement. It is submitted that under the rationale of *Sherbert* such a statute would be constitutional." But see the dictum in *Sloan v. Lemon*, p. 821 supra: "[V]alid aid to nonpublic, nonsectarian schools would provide no lever for aid to their sectarian counterparts."

(b) If a state fluoridates drinking water, must it supply nonfluoridated water to persons whose religion forbids such "medicinal aids"? If a state gives financial support to various voluntary and eleemosynary institutions, does *Sherbert* require it to give such support to churches?

WISCONSIN v. YODER
406 U.S. 205, 92 S.Ct. 1526, 32 L.Ed.2d 15 (1972).

MR. CHIEF JUSTICE BURGER delivered the opinion of the Court.

[Respondents, members of the Amish Church who declined to send their children to public school after completing the eighth grade, were convicted for violating a law compelling attendance to age 16 and fined $5 each.] They believed that by sending their children to high school, they [would] endanger their own salvation and that of their children. The State stipulated that respondents' religious beliefs were sincere.

* * * Amish beliefs require members of the community to make their living by farming or closely related activities. [They object to] higher education generally because [it] tends to emphasize intellectual and scientific accomplishments, self-distinction, competitiveness, worldly success, and social life with other students. Amish society emphasizes informal learning-through-doing, a life of "goodness," rather than a life of intellect, wisdom, rather than technical knowledge, community welfare rather than competition, and separation, rather than integration with contemporary worldly society. * * *

The Amish do not object to elementary education [because] they agree that their children must have basic skills in the "three R's" in order to read the Bible, to be good farmers and citizens and to be able to deal with non-Amish people [and] because it does not significantly expose their children to worldly values or interfere with their development in the Amish community during the crucial adolescent period. [An "expert on Amish society"] testified that compulsory high school attendance could not only result in great psychological harm to Amish children, because of the conflicts it would produce, but would, in his opinion, ultimately result in the destruction of the Old Order Amish church community * * *.

[Under *Pierce v. Society of Sisters*], a State's interest in universal education, however highly we rank it, is not totally free from a balancing process when it impinges on other fundamental rights and interests, such as those specifically protected by the Free Exercise Clause [and] the traditional interest of parents with respect to the religious upbringing of their children so long as they, in the words of *Pierce,* "prepare [them] for additional obligations." [O]nly those interests of the highest order and those not otherwise served can overbalance legitimate claims to the free exercise of religion. ＊ ＊ ＊

We come then to the quality of the claims of [respondents]. A way of life, however virtuous and admirable, may not be interposed as a barrier to reasonable state regulation of education if it is based on purely secular considerations; to have the protection of the Religion Clauses, the claims must be rooted in religious belief. Although a determination of what is a "religious" belief or practice entitled to constitutional protection may present a most delicate question, the very concept of ordered liberty precludes allowing every person to make his own standards on matters of conduct in which society as a whole has important interests. Thus, if the Amish asserted their claims because of their subjective evaluation and rejection of the contemporary secular values accepted by the majority, much as Thoreau rejected the social values of his time and isolated himself at Walden Pond, their claim would not rest on a religious basis. Thoreau's choice was philosophical and personal rather than religious, and such belief does not rise to the demands of the Religion Clauses.

Giving no weight to such secular considerations, however, we see that the record in this case abundantly supports the claim that the traditional way of life of the Amish is not merely a matter of personal preference, but one of deep religious conviction, shared by an organized group, and intimately related to daily living. [This] is shown by the fact that it is in response to their literal interpretation of the Biblical injunction from the Epistle of Paul to the Romans, "Be not conformed to this world ＊ ＊ ＊." This command is fundamental to the Amish faith. Moreover, for the Old Order Amish, religion is not simply a matter of theocratic belief. As the expert witnesses explained, the Old Order Amish religion pervades and determines virtually their entire way of life, regulating it with the detail of the Talmudic diet through the strictly enforced rules of the church community. ＊ ＊ ＊

The impact of the compulsory attendance law on respondents' practice of the Amish religion is not only severe, but inescapable, for the Wisconsin law affirmatively compels them, under threat of criminal sanction, to perform acts undeniably at odds with fundamental tenets of their religious beliefs. See *Braunfeld.* [It poses] a very real threat of undermining the Amish community and religious practice as it exists today; they must either abandon belief and be assimilated into society at large, or be forced to migrate to some other and more tolerant region.[9] ＊ ＊ ＊

[The] Court must not ignore the danger that an exception from a general obligation of citizenship on religious grounds may run afoul of the Establishment Clause, but that danger cannot be allowed to prevent any exception no matter how vital it may be to the protection of values promoted by the right of free exercise. ＊ ＊ ＊

The State [argues] that some degree of education is necessary to prepare citizens to participate effectively and intelligently in our open political system [and] to be self-reliant and self-sufficient participants in society. ＊ ＊ ＊

---

9. Some States have developed working arrangements with the Amish regarding high school attendance. However, the danger to the continued existence of an ancient religious faith cannot be ignored simply because of the assumption that its adherents will continue to be able, at considerable sacrifice, to relocate in some more tolerant State or country or work out accommodations under threat of criminal prosecution. Forced migration of religious minorities was an evil which lay at the heart of the Religion Clauses.

However, the evidence adduced by the Amish in this case is persuasively to the effect that an additional one or two years of formal high school for Amish children in place of their long established program of informal vocational education would do little to serve those interests. [It] is one thing to say that compulsory education for a year or two beyond the eighth grade may be necessary when its goal is the preparation of the child for life in modern society as the majority live, but it is quite another if the goal of education be viewed as the preparation of the child for life in the separated agrarian community that is the keystone of the Amish faith.

The State attacks respondents' position as one fostering "ignorance" from which the child must be protected by the State. [But] this record strongly shows that the Amish community has been a highly successful social unit within our society even if apart from the conventional "mainstream." Its members are productive and very law-abiding members of society; they reject public welfare in any of its usual modern forms. The Congress itself recognized their self-sufficiency by authorizing exemption of such groups as the Amish from the obligation to pay social security taxes.

It is neither fair nor correct to suggest that the Amish are opposed to education beyond the eighth grade level. ["An expert witness on education"] testified that their system of learning-by-doing was an "ideal system" of education in terms of preparing Amish children for life as adults in the Amish community * * *. A way of life that is odd or even erratic but interferes with no rights or interests of others is not to be condemned because it is different.

The State, however, supports its interest [because] of the possibility that some such children will choose to leave the Amish community, and that if this occurs they will be ill-equipped for life. [But there] is no specific evidence of the loss of Amish adherents by attrition, nor is there any showing that upon leaving the Amish community Amish children, with their practical agricultural training and habits of industry and self-reliance, would become burdens on society because of educational shortcomings. [The] independence and successful social functioning of the Amish community for a period approaching almost three centuries [is] strong evidence that there is at best a speculative gain, in terms of meeting the duties of citizenship, from an additional one or two years of compulsory formal education. Against this background it would require a more particularized showing from the State on this point to justify the severe interference with religious freedom * * *.

We should also note [that there] is no intimation that the Amish employment of their children on family farms is in any way deleterious to their health or that Amish parents exploit children at tender years. * * *

Finally, the State, on authority of *Prince v. Massachusetts,* argues that a decision exempting Amish children from the State's requirement fails to recognize the substantive right of the Amish child to a secondary education * * *. The State has at no point tried this case on the theory that respondents were preventing their children from attending school against their expressed desires, and indeed the record is to the contrary.[21] * * *

The State's argument [appears] to rest on the potential that exemption of Amish parents [might] allow some parents to act contrary to the best interests of

---

21. The only relevant testimony in the record is to the effect that the wishes of the one child who testified corresponded with those of her parents. * * *

[Stewart and Brennan, JJ., who joined the Court's opinion, filed a short concurrence emphasizing this point.]

their children by foreclosing their opportunity to make an intelligent choice between the Amish way of life and that of the outside world. The same argument could, of course, be made with respect to all church schools short of college. There is nothing in the record or in the ordinary course of human experience to suggest that non-Amish parents generally consult with children up to ages 14–16 if they are placed in a church school of the parents' faith.

Indeed it seems clear that if the State is empowered, as parens patriae, to "save" a child from himself or his Amish parents by requiring an additional two years of compulsory formal high school education, the State will in large measure influence, if not determine, the religious future of the child. [But] *Pierce* stands as a charter of the rights of parents to direct the religious upbringing of their children. And, when the interests of parenthood are combined with a free exercise claim of the nature revealed by this record, more than merely a "reasonable relation to some purpose within the competency of the state" is required to sustain the validity of the State's requirement under the First Amendment. To be sure, the power of the parent, even when linked to a free exercise claim, may be subject to limitation under *Prince* if it appears that parental decisions will jeopardize the health or safety of the child, or have a potential for significant social burdens. But in this case, the Amish have introduced persuasive evidence undermining the arguments the State has advanced to support its claims in terms of the welfare of the child and society as a whole. * * * [22] [C]ourts must move with great circumspection in performing the sensitive and delicate task of weighing a State's legitimate social concern when faced with religious claims for exemption from generally applicable educational requirements. It cannot be overemphasized that we are not dealing with a way of life and mode of education by a group claiming to have recently discovered some "progressive" or more enlightened process for rearing children for modern life.

[Respondents have carried the] difficult burden of demonstrating the adequacy of their alternative mode of continuing informal vocational education in terms of precisely those overall interests that the State advances in support of its program of compulsory high school education. In light of this convincing showing, one which probably few other religious groups or sects could make, and weighing the minimal difference between what the State would require and what the Amish already accept, it was incumbent on the State to show with more particularity how its admittedly strong interest in compulsory education would be adversely affected by granting an exemption to the Amish. *Sherbert.* * * * [23]

Affirmed.

---

22. What we have said should meet the suggestion that [an exemption for respondents constitutes] an impermissible establishment of religion. * * * Accommodating the religious beliefs of the Amish can hardly be characterized as sponsorship or active involvement. The purpose and effect of such an exemption are not to support, favor, advance, or assist the Amish, but to allow their centuries-old religious society, here long before the advent of any compulsory education, to survive free from the heavy impediment compliance with the Wisconsin compulsory education law would impose. * * *

23. Several States have now adopted plans to accommodate Amish religious beliefs through the establishment of an "Amish vocational school." These are not schools in the traditional sense of the word. [There] is no basis to assume that Wisconsin will be unable to reach a satisfactory accommodation with the Amish in light of what we now hold, so as to serve its interests without impinging on respondents' protected free exercise of their religion.

MR. JUSTICE POWELL and MR. JUSTICE REHNQUIST took no part in the consideration or decision of this case.

MR. JUSTICE WHITE, with whom MR. JUSTICE BRENNAN and MR. JUSTICE STEWART join, concurring. * * *

Decision in cases such as [this] will inevitably involve the kind of close and perhaps repeated scrutiny of religious practices, as exemplified in today's opinion, which the Court has heretofore been anxious to avoid. But such entanglement does not create a forbidden establishment of religion where it is essential to implement free exercise values threatened by an otherwise neutral program instituted to foster some permissible, nonreligious state objective. I join the Court because the sincerity of the Amish religious policy here is uncontested, because the potential adverse impact of the state requirement is great and because the State's valid interest in education has already been largely satisfied by the eight years the children have already spent in school.

MR. JUSTICE DOUGLAS, dissenting in part. * * *

I think the emphasis of the Court on the "law and order" record of this Amish group of people is quite irrelevant. A religion is a religion irrespective of what the misdemeanor or felony records of its members might be. I am not at all sure how the Catholics, Episcopalians, the Baptists, Jehovah's Witnesses, the Unitarians, and my own Presbyterians would make out if we were subjected to such a test. It is, of course, true that if a group or society was organized to perpetuate crime and if that is its motif, we would have rather startling problems akin to those that were raised when some years back a particular sect was challenged here as operating on a fraudulent basis. *United States v. Ballard.* But no such factors are present here, and the Amish, whether with a high or low criminal record, certainly qualify by all historic standards as a religion within the meaning of the First Amendment. * * *

In another way, however, the Court retreats when in reference to Henry Thoreau it says his "choice was philosophical and personal rather than religious, and such belief does not rise to the demands of the Religion Clause." That is contrary to what we held in *United States v. Seeger* [b] * * *.

UNITED STATES v. LEE, 455 U.S. 252, 102 S.Ct. 1051, 71 L.Ed.2d 127 (1982), per BURGER, C.J., held that the free exercise clause does not require an exemption for members of the Old Order Amish from payment of social security taxes even though the Court accepted their contention "that both payment and receipt of social security benefits is forbidden by the Amish faith": "The state may justify a limitation on religious liberty by showing that it is essential to accomplish an overriding governmental interest [and] mandatory participation is indispensable to the fiscal vitality of the social security system. [To] maintain an organized society that guarantees religious freedom to a great variety of faiths requires that some religious practices yield to the common good. [The] tax system could not function if denominations were allowed to challenge the tax system because tax payments were spent in a manner that violates their religious belief. * * * [12]"

b. The *Ballard* and *Seeger* cases and the question of what constitutes "religion" are discussed in Part II infra.

12. We note that here the statute compels contributions to the system by way of taxes; it does not compel anyone to accept benefits.

Indeed, it would be possible for an Amish member, upon qualifying for social security benefits, to receive and pass them along to an Amish fund having parallel objectives. It is not for us to speculate whether this would

STEVENS, J., concurred in the judgment: "In my opinion, it is the objector who must shoulder the burden of demonstrating that there is a unique reason for allowing him a special exemption from a valid law of general applicability. [As] a matter of fiscal policy, an enlarged exemption probably would benefit the social security system because the nonpayment of these taxes by the Amish would be more than offset by the elimination of their right to collect benefits.[c] * * * Nonetheless, I agree with the Court's conclusion that the difficulties associated with processing other claims to tax exemption on religious grounds justify a rejection of this claim.[2] "

GILLETTE v. UNITED STATES, 401 U.S. 437, 91 S.Ct. 828, 28 L.Ed.2d 168 (1971), per MARSHALL, J., held that the free exercise clause does not forbid Congress from "conscripting persons who oppose a particular war on grounds of conscience and religion. * * * [23] ": "The conscription laws [are] not designed to interfere with any religious ritual or practice, and do not work a penalty against any theological position. The incidental burdens felt by persons in petitioners' position are strictly justified by substantial governmental interests that relate directly to the very impacts questioned. And more broadly, of course, there is the Government's interest in procuring the manpower necessary for military purposes * * *."

DOUGLAS, J., dissented: "The question, can a conscientious objector, whether his objection be rooted in 'religion' or in moral values, be required to kill? has never been answered by the court.

"[M]y choice is the dicta of Chief Justice Hughes who, dissenting in *Macintosh,* spoke for Holmes, Brandeis, and Stone: '[Among] the most eminent statesmen here and abroad have been those who condemned the action of their country in entering into wars they thought to be unjustified. [If] the mere holding of religious or conscientious scruples against all wars should not disqualify a citizen from holding office in this country, or an applicant otherwise qualified from being admitted to citizenship, there would seem to be no reason why a reservation of religious or conscientious objection to participation in wars believed to be unjust should constitute such a disqualification.'

"[It] is true that the First Amendment speaks of the free exercise of religion not of the free exercise of conscience or belief. Yet conscience and belief are [the] bedrock of free speech as well as religion. The implied First Amendment right of 'conscience' is certainly as high as the 'right of association' * * *."[d]

---

ease or mitigate the perceived sin of participation.

   c. Stevens, J., found the distinction between this case and *Yoder* "unconvincing because precisely the same religious interest is implicated in both cases and Wisconsin's interest in requiring its children to attend school until they reach the age of 16 is surely not inferior to the federal interest in collecting these social security taxes."

   2. In my opinion, the principal reason for adopting a strong presumption against such claims is not a matter of administrative convenience. It is the overriding interest in keeping the government—whether it be the legislature or the courts—out of the business of evaluating the relative merits of differing reli-

gious claims. The risk that governmental approval of some and disapproval of others will be perceived as favoring one religion over another is an important risk the Establishment Clause was designed to preclude.

   23. We are not faced with the question whether the Free Exercise Clause itself would require exemption of any class other than objectors to particular wars. * * * We note that the Court has previously suggested that relief for conscientious objectors is not mandated by the Constitution. See *Hamilton v. Regents; United States v. Macintosh,* 283 U.S. at 623–24, 51 S.Ct. at 574–75, 75 L.Ed. 1302 (1931).

   d. Did *Gillette* discard the "alternative means" approach of *Sherbert* and *Yoder.* Con-

BOB JONES UNIV. v. UNITED STATES, 461 U.S. 574, 103 S.Ct. 2017, 76 L.Ed.2d 157 (1983), per BURGER, C.J., held that IRS denial of tax exempt status to private schools that practice racial discrimination on the basis of sincerely held religious beliefs does not violate the free exercise clause: "[T]he Government has a fundamental, overriding interest in eradicating racial discrimination in education [which] substantially' outweighs whatever burden denial of tax benefits places on petitioners' exercise of their religious beliefs. The interests asserted by petitioners cannot be accommodated with that compelling governmental interest, see *Lee*; and no 'less restrictive means' are available to achieve the governmental interest." [e] Rehnquist, J., agreeing with the Court's free exercise analysis, dissented on the ground that Congress had not authorized the IRS denial of tax exemption.

In JOHNSON v. ROBISON, 415 U.S. 361, 94 S.Ct. 1160, 39 L.Ed.2d 391 (1974), a federal statute granted educational benefits for veterans who served on active duty but disqualified conscientious objectors who performed alternate civilian service. The Court, per BRENNAN, J., found a "rational basis" for the classification and thus no violation of equal protection: The "disruption caused by military service is quantitatively greater" because "the military veteran remains subject to [a Reserve] obligation after release from active duty" whereas a conscientious objector is only "obligated to work for two years." The disruptions are also "qualitatively different. Military veterans suffer a far greater loss of personal freedom during their service careers." The "classification also bears a rational relationship" to the objective of "enhancing and making more attractive" military service.

Further, the statute "involves only an incidental burden upon appellee's free exercise of religion—if, indeed, any burden exists at all.[19] [T]he Government's substantial interest in raising and supporting armies is of 'a kind and weight' clearly sufficient to sustain the challenged legislation, for the burden upon appellee's free exercise [is] not nearly of the same order or magnitude as" in *Gillette.*

sider 85 Harv.L.Rev. 184–85 (1971): "Even though the option of a volunteer army might have seemed too expensive a departure to force on Congress or even inconsistent with conscription's purpose of spreading the burden of military service throughout the society, the Court might have considered alternatives such as an extended conscientious objector term—for example, four years instead of the present two." Or is such "evaluation of alternatives" a task that "inevitably involves judgments about costs and policy objectives that are customarily left to legislatures"? Id.

See generally Macgill, *Selective Conscientious Objection: Divine Will and Legislative Grace,* 54 Va.L.Rev. 1355 (1968); Hochstadt, *The Right to Exemption from Military Service of a Conscientious Objector to a Particular War,* 3 Harv.Civ.Rts.-Civ.Lib.L.Rev. 1 (1967).

e. For a contrary view, see Laycock, *Tax Exemptions for Racially Discriminatory Religious Schools,* 60 Tex.L.Rev. 259 (1982); Freed & Polsby, *Race, Religion, and Public Policy: Bob Jones University v. United States,* 1983 Sup.Ct.Rev. 1, 20–30.

Most recently, four justices rejected the claim, that Nebraska's denial of a driver's license to a person whose sincerely held religious beliefs—pursuant to the Second Commandment prohibition of "graven images"—forbade her to be photographed, violated the free exercise clause. *Quaring v. Peterson,* 728 F.2d 1121 (8th Cir.1984) (free exercise violation), affirmed by an equally divided Court, ___ U.S. ___, 105 S.Ct. 3492, 86 L.Ed.2d 383 (1985) (Powell, J., not participating.)

19. * * * Congress has bestowed relative benefits upon conscientious objectors by permitting them to perform their alternate service obligation as civilians. Thus, Congress' decision to grant educational benefits to military servicemen might arguably be viewed as an attempt to equalize the burdens of military service and civilian alternate service, rather than an effort [to] place a relative burden upon a conscientious objector's free exercise of religion.

DOUGLAS, J., dissented: "Full benefits are available to occupants of safe desk jobs and the thousands of veterans who performed civilian type duties at home and for whom the 'rigors' of the war were far from 'totally disruptive' * * *. Where Government places a price on the Free Exercise of one's religious scruples it crosses the forbidden line." Unlike *Gillette,* this classification is not "religiously neutral" but "excludes only those [with] religious-based objections to war"—and "the only government interest here is the financial one of denying these appellees educational benefits."

———

McDANIEL v. PATY, 435 U.S. 618, 98 S.Ct. 1322, 55 L.Ed.2d 593 (1978)—an unusual case because it involved a law that singled out religion [f]—invalidated Tennessee provisions disqualifying clergy from being legislators. BURGER, C. J., joined by Powell, Rehnquist and Stevens, JJ., characterized the disqualification as "directed primarily at status, acts and conduct" rather than at "belief." Thus, "the Free Exercise Clause's absolute prohibition of infringements on the 'freedom to believe' is inapposite here." Rather, relying on the "delicate balancing" required by *Sherbert* and *Yoder,* they found the restriction violative of free exercise: "The essence of the rationale underlying the Tennessee restriction on ministers is that if elected to public office they will necessarily exercise their powers and influence to promote the interests of one sect or thwart the interests of another thus pitting one against the others, contrary to the antiestablishment principle with its command of neutrality. [But] American experience provides no persuasive support for the fear that clergymen in public office will be less careful of antiestablishment interests or less faithful to their oaths of civil office than their unordained counterparts." [g]

BRENNAN, J., joined by Marshall, J., concurred: "The characterization of the exclusion as one burdening appellant's 'career or calling' and not religious belief cannot withstand analysis. [T]o bar from political office persons regarded as deeply committed to religious participation because of that participation— participation itself not regarded as harmful by the State and which therefore must be conceded to be protected"—is "absolutely prohibited" by the free exercise clause. [h]

Further, "the State's goal of preventing sectarian bickering and strife may not be accomplished by regulating religious speech and political association." The "exclusion manifests patent hostility toward, not nonneutrality in respect of, religion, forces or influences a minister or priest to abandon his ministry as the price of public office, and in sum, has a primary effect which inhibits religion." Thus, it also violates the establishment clause. [i]

f. See also *Torcaso v. Watkins,* Part II infra.

g. Compare Marty, *Of Darters and Schools and Clergymen: The Religion Clauses Worse Confounded,* 1978 Sup.Ct.Rev. 171, 183: "[I]n issues having to do with everything from homosexuality to the Equal Rights Amendment to abortion to pornography, lay and especially clerical leadership in many denominations has been more aggressive, always with an eye to having one's own sect prevail in the legislative and judicial arenas."

h. Stewart, J., concurred separately, essentially on this ground.

i. White, J., concurred, on equal protection grounds, pointing to cases (Ch. 10, Sec. 4, I, C infra) requiring "States to provide substantial justification for any requirement that prevents a class of citizens from gaining ballot access." Blackmun, J., did not participate.

For general reviews of the cases and refined "balancing" approaches, see Dodge, *The Free Exercise of Religion: A Sociological Approach,* 67 Mich.L.Rev. 679 (1969); Giannella, *Religious Liberty, Nonestablishment, and Doctrinal Development—Part I. The Religious Liberty Guarantee,* 80 Harv.L.Rev. 1381–1423 (1967); Rodes, *Sub Deo et Lege: A Study of*

II. UNUSUAL RELIGIOUS BELIEFS AND PRACTICES

1. In UNITED STATES v. BALLARD, 322 U.S. 78, 64 S.Ct. 882, 88 L.Ed. 1148 (1944), defendant was indicted for mail fraud. He had solicited funds for the "I Am" movement, asserting, inter alia, that he had been selected as a divine messenger, had the divine power of healing incurable diseases, and had talked with Jesus and would transmit these conversations to mankind. The Court, per DOUGLAS, J., held that the first amendment barred submitting to the jury the question of whether these religious beliefs were true: "Men may believe what they cannot prove. * * * Religious experiences which are as real as life to some may be incomprehensible to others. [The] miracles of the New Testament, the Divinity of Christ, life after death, the power of prayer are deep in the religious convictions of many. If one could be sent to jail because a jury in a hostile environment found those teachings false, little indeed would be left of religious freedom."

(a) Should the prosecution be permitted to prove that, irrespective of whether the incidents described by defendant happened, he did not honestly believe that they had? If so, may the prosecution introduce evidence that the incidents did not in fact happen and that therefore defendant could not honestly believe that they did? Should this line of proof be permitted in the prosecution of an official of the Catholic church for soliciting funds to construct a shrine commemorating the Miracle of Fatima in 1930?

(b) Could Ballard be convicted on the ground that fraudulent procurement of money, just like polygamy, is conduct which may be constitutionally prohibited even if done in the name of religion?

2. *What is "religion."* May the Court determine that asserted religious beliefs and practices do not constitute a valid religion? Consider Weiss, *Privilege, Posture and Protection—"Religion" in the Law,* 73 Yale L.J. 593, 604 (1964): "[T]o define the limits of religious expression may be impossible if philosophically desirable. Moreover, any definition of religion would seem to violate religious freedom in that it would dictate to religions, present and future, what they must [be]. Furthermore, an attempt to define religion, even for purposes of increasing freedom for religions, would run afoul of the 'establishment' clause as excluding some religions, or even as establishing a notion respecting religion."

Is it relevant that the beliefs of a group do not include the existence of God? TORCASO v. WATKINS, per BLACK, J., 367 U.S. 488, 81 S.Ct. 1680, 6 L.Ed.2d 982 (1961), invalidating a Maryland provision requiring a declaration of belief in the existence of God as a test for public office, stated: "Neither [a state nor the federal government can] impose requirements which aid all religions as against nonbelievers, and neither can aid those religions based on a belief in the existence of God as against those religions founded on different beliefs." The Court noted that "among religions in this country which do not teach what would generally be considered a belief in the existence of God are Buddhism, Taoism, Ethical Culture, Secular Humanism and others."

What if the Communist Party claimed religious status? Consider Kauper, *Religion and the Constitution* 31 (1964): "What makes secular humanism a

Free Exercise, 4 Relig. & Pub.Or. 3 (1968); Clark, *Guidelines for the Free Exercise Clause,* 83 Harv.L.Rev. 327 (1969); Marcus, *The Forum of Conscience: Applying Standards Under the Free Exercise Clause,* 1973 Duke L.J. 1217.

For the conflict between free exercise and the exigencies of prison discipline, see *Cruz v. Beto,* 405 U.S. 319, 92 S.Ct. 1079, 31 L.Ed.2d 263 (1972); Note, *The Religious Rights of the Incarcerated,* 125 U.Pa.L.Rev. 812 (1977).

religion? Is it because it is an ideology or system of belief that attempts to furnish a rationale of life? But if any ideology, creed, or philosophy respecting man and society is a religion, then must not democracy, fascism, and communism also qualify as religions? It is not uncommon to refer to these as secular or quasi religions, for some find in these systems an adequate explanation of the meaning and purpose of life and the source of values that command faith and devotion. Certainly in the case of communism, with its discipline, its cultus, its sense of community, and its obligation to duties owing to the system, the resemblance to religion in the conventional sense is [clear]."

May a single person establish his own religion? Consider Konvitz, *Religious Liberty and Conscience* 84 (1968): "[Many religions] had their origin in a 'private and personal' religious experience. Mohammed did not take over an on-going, established religion; the history of Islam records the names of his first three converts. John Wesley is given credit as the founder of Methodism. Mrs. Mary Baker Eddy was the founder of the Christian Science church. Menno Simons organized a division of Anabaptists that in due course became the sect known as the Mennonites. Jacob Ammon broke away from the Mennonites and founded the sect known as the Amish."

How important is it that the group has regular weekly services? Designated leaders who conduct these services? Ceremonies for naming, marrying and burying members? Are any of these factors dispositive? Does the first amendment extend only to those groups that conform to the "conventional" concept of religion? Consider Cox (Harvard Divinity School), N.Y.Times 25 (Feb. 16, 1977): "[C]ourts [often] turn to some vague 'man-in-the-street' idea of what 'religion' should be. [But] a man-in-the-street approach would surely have ruled out early Christianity, which seemed both subversive and atheistic to the religious Romans of the day. The truth is that one man's 'bizarre cult' is another's true path to salvation, and the Bill of Rights was designed to safeguard minorities from the man-on-the-street's uncertain capacity for tolerance. The new challenge to our pluralism often comes from Oriental religious movements, because their views of religion differ so fundamentally from ours." To what extent should a group's "brainwashing," mental coercion techniques affect its constitutional status as a "religion"? Compare Delgado, *Religious Totalism: Gentle and Ungentle Persuasion Under the First Amendment,* 51 So.Cal.L.Rev. 1 (1977) with Note, *Conservatorship and Religious Cults: Divining A Theory of Free Exercise,* 53 N.Y.U.L.Rev. 1247 (1978).

UNITED STATES v. SEEGER, 380 U.S. 163, 85 S.Ct. 850, 13 L.Ed.2d 733 (1965), interpreted § 6(j) of the Universal Military Training and Service Act, which exempted from combat any person "who, by reason of religious training and belief, is conscientiously opposed to participation in war in any form. Religious training and belief in this connection means an individual's belief in a relation to a Supreme Being involving duties superior to those arising from any human relation, but does not include essentially political, sociological or philosophical views or a merely personal moral code." [a] The Court, per CLARK, J., avoided constitutional questions and upheld the claims for exemption of three conscientious objectors. Seeger declared "that he preferred to leave the question as to his belief in a Supreme Being open, [and] that his was a 'belief in and devotion to goodness and virtue for their own sakes, and a religious faith in a purely ethical creed.'" Jakobson "believed in a 'Supreme Being' [and] that his

---

a. The statute was subsequently amended to omit the "belief in a Supreme Being" element.

religious and social thinking had developed after much meditation and thought. He had concluded that man must be 'partly spiritual' [and] that his 'most important religious law' was that 'no man ought ever to wilfully sacrifice another man's life as a means to any other end.'" Peter said "that he felt it a violation of his moral code to take human life and that he considered this belief superior to his obligation to the state. As to whether his conviction was religious, he quoted with approval Reverend John Haynes Holmes' definition of religion as 'the consciousness of some power manifest in nature which helps man in the ordering of his life in harmony with its demands * * *; it is man thinking his highest, feeling his deepest, and living his best.' The source of his conviction he attributed to reading and meditation 'in our democratic American culture, with its values derived from the western religious and philosophical tradition.' As to his belief in a Supreme Being, Peter stated that he supposed 'you could call that a belief in the Supreme Being or God. These just do not happen to be the words I use.'"

The Court "concluded that Congress, in using the expression 'Supreme Being' rather than the designation 'God,' was merely clarifying the meaning of religious training and belief so as to embrace all religions and to exclude essentially political, sociological, or philosophical views [and that] the test of belief 'in a relation to a Supreme Being' is whether a given belief that is sincere and meaningful occupies a place in the life of its possessor parallel to that filled by the orthodox belief in God of one who clearly qualifies for the exemption.[b] [No] party claims to be an atheist * * *. We do not deal with or intimate any decision on that situation in these cases. [The] use by Congress of the words 'merely personal' seems to us to restrict the exception to a moral code which is not only personal but which is the sole basis for the registrant's belief and is in no way related to a Supreme Being. [Congress did] not distinguish between externally and internally derived beliefs. Such a determination [would] prove impossible as a practical matter."

In WELSH v. UNITED STATES, 398 U.S. 333, 90 S.Ct. 1792, 26 L.Ed.2d 308 (1970), petitioner, in his application for exemption, "struck the word 'religious' entirely and later characterized his beliefs as having been formed 'by reading in the fields of history and sociology.'" BLACK, J., joined by Douglas, Brennan and Marshall, JJ., held that, under *Seeger,* "if an individual deeply and sincerely holds beliefs which are purely ethical or moral in source and content but that nevertheless impose upon him a duty of conscience to refrain from participating in any war at any time, those beliefs certainly occupy in the life of that individual 'a place parallel to that filled [by] God' in traditionally religious persons." "Although [Welsh] originally characterized his beliefs as nonreligious, he later upon reflection wrote a long and thoughtful letter to his Appeal Board in which he declared that his beliefs were 'certainly religious in the ethical sense of that word.' * * * § 6(j)'s exclusion of those persons with 'essentially political, sociological, or philosophical views or a merely personal moral code' should [not] be read to exclude those who hold strong beliefs about our domestic and foreign affairs or even those whose conscientious objection to participation in all wars is founded to a substantial extent upon considerations of public policy. The two groups of registrants which obviously do fall within these

b. Consider Note, *Toward a Constitutional Definition of Religion*, 91 Harv.L.Rev. 1056, 1065 n. 37 (1978): "[*Seeger*] left several important questions unanswered: What does it mean to say that a principle occupies a place parallel to that of a traditional deity? Must that principle explain the existence of the cosmos, of humankind? Need it be the source of moral precepts, punishing infractions in this life or the next?"

exclusions from the exemption are those whose beliefs are not deeply held and those whose objection to war does not rest at all upon moral, ethical, or religious principle but instead rests solely upon considerations of policy, pragmatism, or expediency." [c]

3. *What is "religious belief"?* (a) Of what significance is it that the practice is an "age-old form" of religious conduct (see *Murdock*)? Is a "cardinal principle" of the asserted religious faith (see *Sherbert*)? Consider Laycock, *Towards a General Theory of the Religion Clauses*, 81 Colum.L.Rev. 1373, 1390–91 (1981): "Many activities that obviously are exercises of religion are not required by conscience or doctrine. Singing in the church choir and saying the Roman Catholic rosary are two common examples. Any activity engaged in by a church as a body is an exercise of religion. [Indeed,] many would say that an emphasis on rules and obligations misconceives the essential nature of some religions." Compare Giannella, fn. i, Sec. I supra, at 1427–28: "[Use of hallucinogenics] should be denied the status of religious claims [because] denial [does] not create problems for the individual's conscience similar to those created by traditionally religious claims to freedom of worship. Personal alienation from one's Maker, frustration of one's ultimate mission in life, and violation of the religious person's integrity are all at stake when the right to worship is threatened. Although the seeker of new psychological worlds may feel equally frustrated when deprived of his gropings for a higher reality, there is not the same sense of acute loss—the loss of the Be-all and End-all of life. [A] different problem presents itself when an individual who does not believe in a supernatural or personal God asserts conscientious objection to certain conduct because of its injurious effects on his fellow man. [T]his ethical belief may be held with such a degree of intensity that its violation occasions the same interior revulsion and anguish as does violation of the law of God to the pious." Under this approach, on what evidence should these factual questions be determined? Suppose a drug-use defendant claims "that its use was essential to attain a unique level of spiritual consciousness [and] compared the effect of depriving him of marihuana with that of forbidding a Catholic to celebrate the Mass"? Finer, *Psychedelics and Religious Freedom*, 19 Hastings L.J. 667, 692 (1968).

For the view that "belief [in] 'extratemporal consequences'—whether the effects of actions taken pursuant or contrary to the dictates of a person's beliefs extend in some meaningful way beyond his lifetime—is a sensible and desirable criterion (albeit plainly far short of ideal) for determining when the free exercise clause should trigger judicial consideration of whether an exemption from general government regulations of conduct is constitutionally required," see Choper, *Defining "Religion" in the First Amendment*, 1982 U.Ill.L.Rev. 579, 599, 603–04: [d] "It may be persuasively argued that *all* beliefs that invoke a transcendent reality—and especially those that provide their adherents with glimpses of meaning and truth that make them so important and so uncompromisable—

---

c. In separate opinions, Harlan, J., and White, J., (joined by Burger, C. J., and Stewart, J.) dissented on the issue of statutory construction. For their views on the constitutional issue, see note 4(b), Sec. 3 infra.

See generally Note, *Defining Religion*, 32 U.Chi.L.Rev. 533 (1965); Boyan, *Defining Religion in Operational and Institutional Terms*, 116 U.Pa.L.Rev. 479 (1968); Hollingsworth, *Constitutional Religious Protection: Antiquated Oddity or Vital Reality?* 34 Ohio St.L.J. 15

(1973); Note, *The Sacred and the Profane: A First Amendment Definition of Religion*, 61 Tex.L.Rev. 139 (1982). For criticism of "sincerity," see Comment, *The Legal Relationship of Conscience to Religion: Refusals to Bear Arms*, 38 U.Chi.L.Rev. 583 (1971).

d. For criticism of this view, see Note, *Religion and Morality Legislation: A Reexamination of Establishment Clause Analysis*, 59 N.Y.U.L.Rev. 301, 346–52 (1984).

should be encompassed by the special constitutional protection granted 'religion' by the free exercise clause. [In] many ways, however, transcendental explanations of worldly realities are essentially no different [than] conventional exegeses for temporal outcomes that are based on such 'rational' disciplines as economics, political science, sociology, or psychology, or even such 'hard' sciences [as] physics. When justifying competing government policies on such varied matters as social welfare, the economy, and military and foreign affairs, there is at bedrock only a gossamer line between 'rational' and 'supernatural' causation— the former really being little more capable of 'scientific proof' than the latter. [Therefore, government's] plenary authority to regulate the worldly affairs of society [should] not be restricted because of the nature of the causes, which are all basically unverifiable, that different groups believe will produce consequences that the state seeks to achieve."

For the view that this approach "does not promise to yield sound results for many free exercise cases," see Greenawalt, *Religion as a Concept in Constitutional Law,* 72 Calif.L.Rev. 753, 763, 815 (1984): "No specification of essential conditions will capture all and only the beliefs, practices, and organizations that are regarded as religious in modern culture and should be treated as such under the Constitution. [Rather, determining] whether questionable beliefs, practices, and organizations are religious by seeing how closely they resemble what is undeniably religious is a method that has been implicitly used by courts in difficult borderline cases [and] is consonant with Supreme Court decisions." See also Freeman, *The Misguided Search for the Constitutional Definition of "Religion,"* 71 Geo.L.J. 1519 (1983).

(b) *Judicial role.* In THOMAS v. REVIEW BD., fn. e in *Sherbert,* petitioner testified that, although his religious convictions forebade him to manufacture weapons, "he could, in good conscience, engage indirectly in the production of materials that might be used ultimately to fabricate arms—for example, as an employee of a raw material supplier or of a roll foundry." The Indiana Supreme Court, viewing petitioner's positions as inconsistent, ruled that "Thomas had made a merely 'personal philosophical choice rather than a religious choice.'"

The Court, per BURGER, C.J. reversed: "The determination of what is a 'religious' belief or practice is more often than not a difficult and delicate task, as the division in the Indiana Supreme Court attests. However, the resolution of that question is not to turn upon a judicial perception of the particular belief or practice in question; religious beliefs need not be acceptable, logical, consistent, or comprehensible to others in order to merit First Amendment protection.

" * * * Thomas' statements reveal no more than that he found work in the roll foundry sufficiently insulated from producing weapons of war. We see, therefore, that Thomas drew a line and it is not for us to say that the line he drew was an unreasonable one. Courts should not undertake to dissect religious beliefs because the believer admits that he is 'struggling' with his position or because his beliefs are not articulated with the clarity and precision that a more sophisticated person might employ.

"The Indiana court also appears to have given significant weight to the fact that another Jehovah's Witness had no scruples about working on tank turrets; for that other Witness, at least, such work was 'scripturally' acceptable. Intrafaith differences of that kind are not uncommon among followers of a particular creed, and the judicial process is singularly ill equipped to resolve such differences in relation to the Religion Clauses. One can, of course, imagine an asserted claim so bizarre, so clearly nonreligious in motivation, as not to be entitled to protection under the Free Exercise Clause; but that is not the case here, and the guarantee of free exercise is not limited to beliefs which are shared by all of the members of a religious sect. Particularly in this sensitive area, it is not within the judicial function and judicial competence to inquire whether the petitioner or his fellow worker more correctly perceived the commands of their common faith. Courts are not arbiters of scriptural interpretation.

"The narrow function of a reviewing court in this context is to determine whether there was an appropriate finding that petitioner terminated his work because of an honest conviction that such work was forbidden by his religion."

4. *Variable definition.* May "religion" be defined differently for purposes of the establishment clause than the free exercise clause? Consider Galanter, *Religious Freedom in the United States: A Turning Point?* 1966 Wis.L.Rev. 217, 266–67: "[For purposes of the establishment clause, the] effect and purpose of government action are not to be assessed by the religious sensibilities of the person who is complaining of the alleged establishment. It must be essentially religious in some widely shared public understanding. [But, for the free exercise clause, the] claimants' view of religion controls the characterization of their objection as a religious one." See also Tribe, supra, at 827–28. Does this analysis solve the dilemma of Manning, note 5, after *Schempp,* supra, at 66: "If religion need not be predicated on a belief in God or even in a god and if it may not be tested by the common consensus of what reasonable men would reasonably call religion, if it is so private that—so long as it does not inflict injury on society—it is immured from governmental interference and from judicial inquiry, [might] not a group of gymnasts proclaiming on their trampolines that physical culture is their religion be engaged in a religious exercise? And if Congress, in a particular Olympic year, appropriated funds to subsidize their calisthenics would this not [be] an establishment of religion?" See generally Note, *Transcendental Meditation and the Meaning of Religion Under the Establishment Clause,* 62 Minn.L.Rev. 887 (1978).

SECTION 3. PREFERENCE FOR AND AMONG RELIGIONS

LARSON v. VALENTE, 456 U.S. 228, 102 S.Ct. 1673, 72 L.Ed.2d 33 (1982), involved a challenge by the Unification Church ("Moonies") to "a Minnesota statute, imposing certain registration and reporting requirements upon only those religious organizations that solicit more than fifty per cent of their funds from nonmembers." The Court, per BRENNAN, J., noting that the "constitutional prohibition of denominational preferences is inextricably connected with the continuing vitality of the Free Exercise Clause," held that the statute violated the establishment clause because it did not survive "strict scrutiny." [a] The

a. The Court rejected the argument that the statute was merely "a law based upon secular criteria which may not identically affect all religious organizations." This "is not simply a facially neutral statute, the provisions of which happen to have a 'disparate impact' upon different religious organizations. On the contrary [it] makes explicit and deliberate distinctions between different religious organizations [and] effectively distinguishes between 'well-established churches' that have 'achieved strong but not total financial support from their members,' on the one hand,

and 'churches which are new and lacking in a constituency, or, which, as a matter of policy, may favor public solicitation over general reliance on financial support from members,' on the other hand."

The Court found *Gillette v. United States,* Sec. 2, I supra, "readily distinguishable": "In that case, we rejected an Establishment Clause attack upon § 6(j) of the Military Selective Service Act of 1967, which afforded 'conscientious objector' status to any person who, 'by reason of religious training and be-

Court assumed that the state's "interest in protecting its citizens from abusive practices in the solicitation of funds for charity" was "compelling," but concluded that the state "failed to demonstrate that the fifty per cent rule [is] 'closely fitted' " to furthering that interest. Moreover, the statute failed the third *Lemon* "test": "The fifty per cent [rule] effects the *selective* legislative imposition of burdens and advantages upon particular denominations. The 'risk of politicizing religion' that inheres in such legislation is obvious, and indeed is confirmed by the provision's legislative history [which] demonstrates that the provision was drafted with the explicit intention of including particular religious denominations and excluding others."

WHITE, J., joined by Rehnquist, J., dissented,[b] disagreeing with the Court's view "that the rule on its face represents an explicit and deliberate preference for some religious beliefs over others": "The rule [names] no churches or denominations that are entitled to or denied the exemption. [Some] religions will qualify and some will not, but this depends on the source of their contributions, not on their brand of religion. [The Court's assertion] that the limitation might burden the less well-organized denominations [is contrary to the state's claim] that both categories include not only well-established, but also not so well-established organizations. The Court appears to concede that the Minnesota law at issue does not constitute an establishment of religion merely because it has a disparate impact. An intentional preference must be expressed. To find that intention on the face of the provision at issue here seems to me to be patently wrong." [c]

Further, "I cannot join the Court's easy rejection of the state's submission that a valid secular purpose justifies basing the exemption on the percentage of external funding." Finally, there is arguably "a more evident secular reason for exempting religious organizations who rely on their members to a great extent than there is to exempt all religious organizations, [which] could be said to prefer religious organizations over non-religious organizations and hence amount to an establishment of religion."

Notes and Questions

1. *The Gillette rationale.* (a) Should the existence of a "neutral, secular justification" suffice to permit government preference—de jure or de facto— among religions? Consider Greenawalt, *All or Nothing at All: The Defeat of Selective Conscientious Objection*, 1971 Sup.Ct.Rev. 31, 71: "If a sociological survey indicated that Protestants generally work harder than Catholics, the government might simplify its hiring problems by interviewing only Protestants. If the doctors of Catholic hospitals were determined to be on the average more qualified than those at Lutheran hospitals, aid might be limited to the Catholic hospitals. It is, of course, inconceivable that such legislation would be passed

lief,' was 'conscientiously opposed to participation in war in any form * * *.' Section 6(j) 'focused on individual conscientious belief, not on sectarian affiliation.' Under § 6(j), conscientious objector status was available on an equal basis to both the Quaker and the Roman Catholic, despite the distinction drawn by the latter's church between 'just' and 'unjust' wars. As we noted in *Gillette*, the 'critical weakness of petitioners' establishment claim' arose 'from the fact that § 6(j), on its face, simply [did] not discriminate on the basis of

religious affiliation.' In contrast, the statute challenged in the case before us focuses precisely and solely upon religious organizations."

b. Rehnquist, J., joined by Burger, C.J. and White and O'Connor, JJ., also dissented on the ground that appellee Unification Church had no standing.

c. *Gillette* held that there was no religious "gerrymander" if there was "a neutral, secular basis for the lines government has drawn."

and its unconstitutionality is [apparent]." How significant was the Court's observation that the *Gillette* law "attempts to accommodate free exercise values"?

(b) Was the Draft Act of 1917, which exempted only conscientious objectors affiliated with some "well-recognized religious sect" whose principles forbade participation in war, also valid under the *Gillette* rationale? Consider 48 Minn. L.Rev. 776–77 (1964): "Since pacifism often arises from religious beliefs, a workable method for ascertaining sincerity may have to be couched in terms of those beliefs. Such a test should be permissible, even though it may theoretically 'prefer' some sincere conscientious objectors over others, if it reasonably advances the [statute's] purpose by aiding local draft boards in administering the act. For example, since membership in an organized pacifist sect may be better evidence of sincerity than the mere assertion of pacificist beliefs, a requirement to that effect should be permissible." See also Comment, 64 Colum.L.Rev. 938 (1964).

2. *The Larson rationale.* Consider Choper, *The Free Exercise Clause*, in Choper, Kamisar & Tribe, *The Supreme Court: Trends and Developments 1982–83*, 79–84 (1984): "*Larson* is really a free exercise clause decision parading in an establishment clause disguise. [The Court's holding] that discrimination among religions must survive strict scrutiny [is] classic free exercise clause analysis. [The] major disagreement between the majority and the dissent was over whether this law discriminated among religions or was simply a neutral law with a disparate impact on different religious groups. [But] even if the Minnesota statute does not explicitly distinguish among religious sects or churches, nonetheless, isn't it bad enough that it expressly deals with the subject of religion and ends up favoring some and disfavoring others? Shouldn't it be as vulnerable as a general, neutral law that says nothing about religion but that happens to have an adverse impact on some religions—like the Wisconsin compulsory education to age 16 law? [The] problem is that when the Court has used the establishment clause, it has applied a much more lenient test for laws that expressly deal with religion and subject some religions to discriminatory treatment, than it has applied under the free exercise clause for general, neutral laws that come into conflict with religious beliefs. [*Gillette*] ruled that under the establishment clause, as long as there is some secular basis for the law, that is enough to validate it. [If] all that was required in [*Larson*] was *some* secular basis, there'd be no problem at all in sustaining the statute. [In] reality, I believe that the federal statute in *Gillette* survived strict scrutiny [because of the] strong government interest in raising an army and the difficulties in administering a draft exemption based on 'just war' beliefs. [I] think the *Gillette* doctrine has now effectively been abandoned, and I suggest rightly so. I think discrimination among religions—a preference of one religion over another—[should] be treated under the free exercise clause. I think *Larson*, although it certainly doesn't say it's using the free exercise clause, explicitly has a rationale that leads to that conclusion."

3. *Preference for "religious" objectors.* Is Congress' limitation of draft exemption to "religious" conscientious objectors valid? Consider Mansfield, *Conscientious Objection—1964 Term*, 1965 Relig. & Pub.Or. 3, 76: "[T]here are really no convincing reasons why the religious objector should be exempt and not the non-religious conscientious objector. [T]he religious objector's opposition rests on somewhat more fundamental grounds [and] makes reference to realities that can more easily be described as spiritual. But the non-religious conscientious objector's opposition does rest on basic propositions about the nature of

reality and the significance of human existence; this is what distinguishes it from objection that is not even conscientious. Even if the non-religious conscientious objector does not subscribe to the answers nor perceive the vision of the religious objector, he does at least address himself to questions that are nearly as fundamental, and it is in respect to the dialogue within this general area of fundamental issues that government should take care not to prefer one answer over another." See Cohen & Greenspan, *Conscientious Objection, Democratic Theory, and the Constitution,* 29 U.Pitt.L.Rev. 389, 403 (1968): "Nothing is more repugnant to a sense of fairness than the rejection of the claim of a conscientious objector because he does not believe in a transcendent reality. If his belief were coupled with a belief that the sun controlled man's destiny, communicating it through sun-spots, his exemption would be immediately granted. This places a premium upon madness and is a celebration of cranks and utopians. The concerned citizen, whose belief is intelligible and commends itself more to our understanding is turned away because he did not indulge in fantastic flights of imagination." Does the "religious" exemption result in more or less government "entanglement" with religion than an exemption for *all* conscientious objectors?

4. *The establishment-free exercise "dilemma."* (a) Do the decisions in *Sherbert* and *Yoder* violate the establishment clause because if "government must sanction otherwise prohibited conduct merely because of its religious orientation and if the same activity is forbidden to nonreligionists, is this not a preferential establishment"? Donnici, *Governmental Encouragement of Religious Ideology: A Study of the Current Conscientious Objector Exemption from Military Service,* 13 J.Pub.L. 16, 43 (1964). Consider Kurland, *Religion and the Law* 112 (1962): "The [free exercise and establishment] clauses should be read as stating a single precept: that government cannot utilize religion as a standard for action or inaction because these clauses, read together as they should be, prohibit classification in terms of religion either to confer a benefit or to impose a burden." [a] Similarly, for the view that the free exercise clause should generally only guarantee "equality of treatment for those who act out of sincere religious belief" and should afford special protection only for acts of "worship," as defined, see Fernandez, *The Free Exercise of Religion,* 36 So.Calif.L.Rev. 546 (1963). For the view that free exercise claims should be treated "no differently than free expression claims," see Marshall, *Solving the Free Exercise Dilemma: Free Exercise as Expression,* 67 Minn.L.Rev. 545 (1983).

Do these approaches falter because they fail to recognize "that both clauses are designed to maximize religious freedoms and that in particular the uniquely American establishment clause is largely designed to implement the free exercise clause"; thus, that "at least some governmental accommodations to religion which are designed to protect the free exercise of religion should be permissible under the establishment clause"? Moore, *The Supreme Court and the Relationship Between the "Establishment" and "Free Exercise" Clauses,* 42 Tex.L.Rev. 142, 196 (1963).

(b) Did the statute in *Gillette,* exempting only "religious" conscientious objectors, impermissibly prefer religion over nonreligion? In WELSH v. UNITED STATES, Sec. 2, II supra, four justices addressed the issue. WHITE, J., joined by Burger, C. J., and Stewart, J., found it valid: "First, § 6(j) may represent a

---

a. For thoughtful comment, see Kauper, *Book Review,* 41 Texas L.Rev. 467 (1963); Pfeffer, *Religion-Blind Government,* 15 Stan.L. Rev. 389 (1963); Mansfield, *Book Review,* 52 Calif.L.Rev. 212 (1964). See generally Note, *The Conscientious Objector and the First Amendment,* 34 U.Chi.L.Rev. 79 (1966); Kauper, *Government and Religion: The Search for Absolutes,* 11 Mich.Q.Rev., No. 3 (1972).

purely practical judgment that religious objectors, however admirable, would be of no more use in combat than many others unqualified for military service. [On] this basis, the exemption has neither the primary purpose nor the effect of furthering religion. * * *

"Second, Congress may have [believed that] to deny the exemption would violate the Free Exercise Clause or at least raise grave problems in this respect. True, this Court has more than once stated its unwillingness to construe the First Amendment, standing alone, as requiring draft exemptions for religious believers. [But] just as in *Katzenbach v. Morgan,* [p. 1149 infra], where we accepted the judgment of Congress as to what legislation was appropriate to enforce the Equal Protection Clause of the Fourteenth Amendment, here we should respect congressional judgment accommodating the Free Exercise Clause and the power to raise armies. This involves no surrender of the Court's function as ultimate arbiter in disputes over interpretation of the Constitution. But it was enough in *Katzenbach* 'to perceive a basis upon which the Congress might resolve the conflict as it did' * * *.

"[If] it is 'favoritism' and not 'neutrality' to exempt religious believers from the draft, is it 'neutrality' and not 'inhibition' of religion to compel religious believers to fight * * *? It cannot be ignored that the First Amendment itself contains a religious classification [and the free exercise clause] protects conduct as well as religious belief and speech. [It] was not suggested [in *Braunfeld*] that the Sunday closing laws in 21 States exempting Sabbatarians and others violated the Establishment Clause because no provision was made for others who claimed nonreligious reasons for not working on some particular day of the week. Nor was it intimated in *Zorach* that the no-establishment holding might be infirm because only those pursuing religious studies for designated periods were released from the public school routine; neither was it hinted that a public school's refusal to institute a released time program would violate the Free Exercise Clause. The Court in *Sherbert* construed the Free Exercise Clause to require special treatment for Sabbatarians under the State's unemployment compensation law. But the State could deal specially with Sabbatarians whether the Free Exercise Clause required it or not * * *.

"The Establishment Clause [is] not wholly auxiliary to the Free Exercise Clause. It bans some involvements of the State with religion which otherwise might be consistent with the Free Exercise Clause. But when in the rationally based judgment of Congress free exercise of religion calls for shielding religious objectors from compulsory combat duty, I am reluctant to frustrate the legislative will by striking down the statutory exemption because it does not also reach those to whom the Free Exercise Clause offers no protection whatsoever."

HARLAN, J., disagreed, believing that Congress could "eliminate *all* exemptions for conscientious objectors. Such a course would be wholly 'neutral' * * *. However, having chosen to exempt, it cannot draw the line between theistic or nontheistic religious beliefs on the one hand and secular beliefs on the other. [I]t must encompass the class of individuals it purports to exclude, those whose beliefs emanate from a purely moral, ethical, or philosophical source.[9] The common denominator must be the intensity of moral conviction with which a belief is [held]. *Everson,* the *Sunday Closing Law Cases* and *Allen,* all

---

9. * * * I suggested [in *Sherbert*] that a State could constitutionally create exceptions to its program to accommodate religious scruples. [But] any such exception in order to satisfy the Establishment Clause [would] have to be sufficiently broad so as to be religiously neutral. This would require creating an exception for anyone who, as a matter of conscience, could not comply with the statute. * * *

sustained legislation on the premise that it was neutral in its application and thus did not constitute an establishment, notwithstanding the fact that it may have assisted religious groups by giving them the same benefits accorded to nonreligious groups.[12]   To the extent that *Zorach* and *Sherbert* stand for the proposition that the Government may (*Zorach*), or must (*Sherbert*), shape its secular programs to accommodate the beliefs and tenets of religious groups, I think these cases unsound.[13] "

(c) In THOMAS v. REVIEW BD., fn. e in *Sherbert*, REHNQUIST, J., dissented, finding the result "inconsistent with many of our prior Establishment Clause cases"[2]: "If Indiana were to legislate what the Court today requires—an unemployment compensation law which permitted benefits to be granted to those persons who quit their jobs for religious reasons—the statute would 'plainly' violate the Establishment Clause as interpreted in such cases as *Lemon* and *Nyquist*.   First, [the] proviso would clearly serve only a religious purpose.   It would grant financial benefits for the sole purpose of accommodating religious beliefs.   Second, there can be little doubt that the primary effect of the proviso would be to 'advance' religion by facilitating the exercise of religious belief. Third, any statute including such a proviso would surely 'entangle' the State in religion far more than the mere grant of tax exemptions, as in *Walz*, or the award of tuition grants and tax credits, as in *Nyquist*.   By granting financial benefits to persons solely on the basis of their religious beliefs, the State must necessarily inquire whether the claimant's belief is 'religious' and whether it is sincerely held.   [Just] as I think that Justice Harlan in *Sherbert* correctly stated the proper approach to free exercise questions, I believe that Justice Stewart, dissenting in *Schempp*, accurately stated the reach of the Establishment Clause. He explained that the Establishment Clause is limited to 'government support of proselytizing activities of religious sects by throwing the weight of secular authorities behind the dissemination of religious tenets.'   See *McCollum* (Reed, J., dissenting) (impermissible aid is only 'purposeful assistance directly to the church itself or to some religious [group] performing ecclesiastical functions'). Conversely, governmental assistance which does not have the effect of 'inducing' religious belief, but instead merely 'accommodates' or implements an indepen-

12. [I] fail to see how [§ 6(j)] has "any substantial legislative purpose" apart from honoring the conscience of individuals who oppose war on only religious grounds.

* * *

13. [At] the very least the Constitution requires that the State not excuse students early for the purpose of receiving religious instruction when it does not offer to nonreligious students the opportunity to use school hours for spiritual or ethical instruction of a nonreligious nature.   Moreover, whether a released-time program cast in terms of improving "conscience" to the exclusion of artistic or cultural pursuits, would be "neutral" and consistent with the requirement of "voluntarism," is by no means an easy question.   * * *

2. To the extent *Sherbert* was correctly decided, it might be argued that cases such as *McCollum, Engel, Schempp, Lemon,* and *Nyquist* were wrongly decided.   The "aid" rendered to religion in these latter cases may not be significantly different, in kind or degree, than the "aid" afforded Mrs. Sherbert or

Thomas.   For example, if the State in *Sherbert* could not deny compensation to one refusing work for religious reasons, it might be argued that a State may not deny reimbursement to students who choose for religious reasons to attend parochial schools.   The argument would be that although a State need not allocate any funds to education, once it has done so, it may not require any person to sacrifice his religious beliefs in order to obtain an equal education.   There can be little doubt that to the extent secular education provides answers to important moral questions without reference to religion or teaches that there are no answers, a person in one sense sacrifices his religious belief by attending secular schools.   And even if such "aid" were not constitutionally compelled by the Free Exercise Clause, Justice Harlan may well be right in *Sherbert* when he finds sufficient flexibility in the Establishment Clause to permit the States to voluntarily choose to grant such benefits to individuals.

dent religious choice does not impermissibly involve the government in religious choices and therefore does not violate the Establishment [Clause]. I would think that in this case, as in *Sherbert,* had the state voluntarily chosen to pay unemployment compensation benefits to persons who left their jobs for religious reasons, such aid would be constitutionally permissible because it redounds directly to the benefit of the individual."

See also Schwartz, *No Imposition of Religion: The Establishment Clause Value,* 77 Yale L.J. 692, 693, 723, 728 (1968): "[T]he dilemma results from an unnecessarily broad reading of the establishment clause; that clause should be read to prohibit only aid which has as its motive or substantial effect the imposition of religious belief or practice * * *. Conversely, aid which does not have the effect of inducing religious belief, but merely accommodates or implements an individual religious choice, does not increase the danger of religion and [does] not violate the no-imposition standard. * * * Exemption of Mrs. Sherbert [represents] a judgment that the exercise of Seventh-day Adventism is more worthy than bowling on Saturdays, but the exemption has no significant effect and arguably no effect at all upon whether someone becomes a Seventh-day Adventist. Similarly, the Sabbatarian exemption from Sunday closing laws does not induce one to become a Jew; draft exemption to conscientious objectors does not normally induce one to become a Quaker; closing the public schools on all religious holidays or on every Wednesday at 2 P.M. does not induce the adoption of religion; and compulsory Sunday closing, while implementing an independent desire to attend church services, has no substantial effect upon the creation of such desire. The availability of preferential aid to religious exercise may, to be sure, induce false claims of religious belief, but the establishment clause is not concerned with false claims of belief, only with induced belief." Does this distinguish *Engel* from *Sherbert?* Do you agree with all of the *factual* assumptions made? Under this analysis, what result in *Epperson?* What of a small governmental payment to all persons who would lose salary because they have to be absent from their jobs in order to attend religious services?

Compare Choper, note after *Epperson* supra, at 691, 697–700: "My proposal for resolving the conflict between the two Religion Clauses seeks to implement their historically and contemporarily acknowledged common goal: to safeguard religious liberty. [I]t is only when an accommodation would jeopardize religious liberty—when it would coerce, compromise, or influence religious choice—that it would fail. [For example, in *Yoder,* unless] it could be shown that relieving the Amish [would] tend to coerce, compromise, or influence religious choice—and it is extremely doubtful that it could—the exemption was permissible under the Establishment Clause. In contrast, in *Sherbert,* [the] exemption results in impairment of religious liberty because compulsorily raised tax funds must be used to subsidize Mrs. Sherbert's exercise of religion. [In the draft exemption cases], professing a personal 'religion' (as opposed to 'essentially political, sociological or philosophical considerations') was enough to gain the enormous advantage of avoiding combat duty. [D]raftees seeking exemption would have to formulate a statement of personal doctrine that would pass muster. This endeavor would involve deep and careful thought, and perhaps reading in philosophy and religion. Some undoubtedly would be persuaded by what they read. Moreover, the theory of 'cognitive dissonance'—which posits that to avoid madness we tend to become what we hold ourselves to be and what others believe us to be—also suggests that some initially fraudulent claims of belief in a personal religion would develop into true belief. Thus, a draft exemption for religious objectors threatens values of religious freedom by encouraging the adoption of religious beliefs by those who seek to qualify for the benefit."

(d) Was the "aid" rendered religion by the programs in *McCollum, Engel* and *Schempp* any different, in kind or degree, than the "aid" afforded religion by statutory exemptions from Sunday Closing Laws for Sabbatarians, by draft exemptions for religious conscientious objectors, by government provision of military chaplains? May it be said of any of these that its purpose is "secular" or "nonreligious"? Consider Katz, *Note on the Constitutionality of Shared Time*, 1964 Relig. & Pub.Or. 85, 88: "It is no violation of neutrality for the government to express its concern for religious freedom by measures which merely neutralize what would otherwise be restrictive effects of government action. Provision for voluntary worship in the armed forces is constitutional, not because government policy may properly favor religion, but because the government is not required to exercise its military powers in a manner restrictive of religious freedom. Affirmative government action to maintain religious freedom in these instances serves the secular purpose of promoting a constitutional right, the free exercise of religion."

(e) THORNTON v. CALDOR, INC., ___ U.S. ___, 105 S.Ct. 2914, 86 L.Ed.2d 557 (1985), per BURGER, C.J., held that a Connecticut law—which provided "that those who observe a Sabbath any day of the week as a matter of religious conviction must be relieved of the duty to work on that day, no matter what burden or inconvenience this imposes on the employer or fellow workers"—"has a primary effect that impermissibly advances a particular religious practice" and thus violates the establishment clause: "The statute arms Sabbath observers with an absolute and unqualified right not to work on whatever day they designate as their Sabbath [and thus] goes beyond having an incidental or remote effect of advancing religion." [b]

O'CONNOR, J., joined by Marshall, J., concurred, distinguishing "the religious accommodation provisions of Title VII of the Civil Rights Act [which] require private employers to reasonably accommodate the religious practices of employees unless to do so would cause undue hardship to the employer's business": "In my view, a statute outlawing employment discrimination based on race, color, religion, sex or national origin has the valid secular purpose of assuring employment opportunity to all groups in our pluralistic society. Since Title VII calls for reasonable rather than absolute accommodation and extends that requirement to all religious beliefs and practices rather than protecting only the Sabbath observance, I believe an objective observer would perceive it as an anti-discrimination law rather than an endorsement of religion or a particular religious practice." [c]

Was the purpose or effect of the *Thornton* statute any different than that of the Court's decisions in *Sherbert, Thomas* and *Yoder?* For purposes of the establishment clause, of what significance, if any, is the fact that the *Thornton* statute grants "an absolute and unqualified right not to work" rather than a Title VII-like exemption? Consider Moore, supra, at 196–97: "[L]aws which protect the *free exercise* of religion should be distinguished from those which merely promote the *exercise* of a particular religion or religious belief. Almost any law favoring religion would fall into this latter [category]. For example, in *Engel* the use of the officially written Regent's prayer in the public schools promotes the exercise of a particular religious belief. The use of the prayer,

---

b. Rehnquist, J., dissented without opinion.

c. See also O'Connor, J.'s concurrence in *Wallace v. Jaffree*, below.

though, does not protect the free exercise of religion. In fact, strong arguments can be made that such use indirectly threatens free exercise. Because of this distinction, admittedly one of degree, the *Engel* decision under the establishment clause is in no way in conflict with the free exercise clause." If the Regents' prayer "does not protect the *free exercise* of religion," does exempting Mrs. Sherbert do so? Does the state's failure to "favor religion" in each case simply "make the practice of religious beliefs more expensive"?

Does the *Thornton* statute "promote" and "endorse" a particular "religion" or "religious belief" or "religious practice" any moreso than the Court's decisions in *Sherbert, Thomas* and *Yoder,* or than the statutory exemptions from the draft or Sunday Closing Laws? Do all these exemptions simply "accommodate" religion? See Choper, supra.

Consider also O'Connor, J., concurring in *Wallace v. Jaffree,* Sec. 1, I supra, "[A] rigid application of the *Lemon* test would invalidate legislation exempting religious observers from generally applicable government obligations. By definition, such legislation has a religious purpose and effect in promoting the free exercise of religion. On the other hand, judicial deference to all legislation that purports to facilitate the free exercise of religion would completely vitiate the Establishment Clause. Any statute pertaining to religion can be viewed as an 'accommodation' of free exercise rights. Indeed, the statute at issue in *Lemon* [can] be viewed as an accommodation of the religious beliefs of parents who choose to send their children to religious schools.

"It [is] difficult to square any notion of 'complete neutrality' with the mandate of the Free Exercise Clause that government must sometimes exempt a religious observer from an otherwise generally applicable obligation. A government that confers a benefit on an explicitly religious basis is not neutral toward religion. See *Welsh* (White, J., dissenting).

"The solution to the conflict between the religion clauses lies not in 'neutrality,' but rather in identifying workable limits to the Government's license to promote the free exercise of religion. [O]ne can plausibly assert that government pursues free exercise clause values when it lifts a government-imposed burden on the free exercise of religion. If a statute falls within this category, then the standard Establishment Clause test should be modified accordingly. [T]he Court should simply acknowledge that the religious purpose of such a statute is legitimated by the Free Exercise Clause. I would also go further. In assessing the effect of such a statute—that is, in determining whether the statute conveys the message of endorsement of religion or a particular religious belief—courts should assume that the 'objective observer,' is acquainted with the Free Exercise Clause and the values it promotes. Thus individual perceptions, or resentment that a religious observer is exempted from a particular government requirement, would be entitled to little weight if the Free Exercise Clause strongly supported the exemption.

"While this 'accommodation' analysis would help reconcile our Free Exercise and Establishment Clause standards, it would not save Alabama's moment of silence law. If we assume that the religious activity that Alabama seeks to protect is silent prayer, then it is difficult to discern any state-imposed burden on that activity that is lifted by Alabama Code § 16-1-20.1. No law prevents a student who is so inclined from praying silently in public schools. [Of] course, the State might argue that § 16-1-20.1 protects not silent prayer, but rather group silent prayer under State sponsorship. Phrased in these terms, the burden lifted by the statute is not one imposed by the State of Alabama, but by the Establishment Clause as interpreted in *Engel* and *Schempp*. In my view, it is beyond the authority of the State of Alabama to remove burdens imposed by the Constitution itself."

Assuming the validity of the distinction between *McCollum, Engel,* and *Schempp,* on the one hand, and the programs such as exemption from the draft etc. on the other, are the above approaches nonetheless undesirable because they result not merely in protection of free exercise (or neutrality or accommodation) but in relieving persons with certain religious beliefs of significant burdens from which many other persons strongly desire to be exempted? That, in this sense, there is "preference" for minority religions and "discrimination" against the other persons because of their religion or lack of it? Should free exercise exemptions "be allowed only if the petitioner agrees to the imposition of some alternative duty or burden"? Note, 91 Harv.L.Rev. at 1082. Consider Galanter, note 4, Sec. 2, II supra, at 290–91: "[In *Sherbert*] it was clear that the state was already solicitous of the scruples of Sunday worshippers, though not of Saturday ones. In such a case, it is easy to appreciate that the exception [required by the decision] is restorative or equalizing. It puts the minority in the same position that the majority enjoys. [But] can it be said that the kind of disparity found in *Sherbert* between the treatment of majority and minority is a unique or unusual thing? Whatever seriously interferes with majority religious beliefs and practices is unlikely to become a legal requirement—for example, work on Sunday or Christmas. And whatever the majority considers necessary for its religious practice is quite unlikely to be prohibited by law. And whatever the majority finds religiously objectionable is unlikely to become a legal requirement—for example, medical practices which substantial groups find abhorrent, like contraception, sterilization, euthanasia, or abortion. Exceptions then, give to minorities what majorities have by virtue of suffrage and representative government. The question is not whether the state may prefer these minorities, but whether it may counterbalance the natural advantages of majorities."

Chapter 10

EQUAL PROTECTION

Virtually no legislation applies universally and treats all persons equally; all laws classify (or "discriminate") by imposing special burdens (or granting exemptions from such burdens) or by conferring special benefits on some people and not others. Under what circumstances do such laws violate the fourteenth amendment's command that no state shall "deny to any person within its jurisdiction the equal protection of the laws"? [a]

Despite the fact that the language of the equal protection clause is not confined to racial discrimination, the *Slaughter-House Cases,* p. 250 supra (the first decision interpreting the Civil War amendments), "doubt[ed] very much whether any action of a state not directed by way of discrimination against the negroes as a class, or on account of their race, will ever be held to come within the purview of this provision." Sec. 2 will concern the "strict scrutiny" given to racial (and ethnic) classifications which the Court has deemed to be "suspect." Sec. 3 will consider the extension of a nondeferential standard of review to government action that disadvantages several other discrete groups. At least as early as 1897, however, the Court invoked the equal protection clause to invalidate a commonplace economic regulation that obligated railroad defendants (but not others) to pay the attorneys' fees of successful plaintiffs. The Court acknowledged that "as a general proposition, [it] is undeniably true [that] it is not within the scope of the Fourteenth Amendment to withhold from States the power of classification." But "it must appear" that a classification is "based upon some reasonable ground—some difference which bears a just and proper

---

a. By its terms, the equal protection clause does not apply to the federal government. A series of decisions, however, has held that the fifth amendment's due process clause—although not containing the language of equal protection—forbids "unjustifiable" discrimination (*Bolling v. Sharpe,* Sec. 2, II infra) and that—except under special circumstances (see Sec. 3, II infra: "Alienage")—the "approach to Fifth Amendment equal protection claims has always been precisely the same as to equal protection claims under the Fourteenth Amendment" (*Weinberger v. Wiesenfeld,* Sec. 3, IV infra).

In 1976, *Hampton v. Wong,* Sec. 3, II infra, advanced a different approach. It stated that "when a federal rule is applicable to only a limited territory, such as the District of Columbia, or an insular possession, and when there is no special national interest involved, the Due Process Clause has been construed as having the same significance as the Equal Protection Clause," but suggested a different standard for "a federal rule having a nationwide impact." Subsequent decisions, however, have continued to treat equal protection claims against the federal government under the fifth amendment in the same way as equal protection claims against the states under the fourteenth amendment, even though the challenged federal rule had "nationwide impact." See generally Karst, *The Fifth Amendment's Guarantee of Equal Protection,* 55 N.C.L.Rev. 541 (1977).

relation to the attempted classification—and is not a mere arbitrary selection." *Gulf, C. & S. F. Ry. v. Ellis,* 165 U.S. 150, 17 S.Ct. 255, 41 L.Ed. 666 (1897).

Sec. 1 deals with this "traditional approach" under the equal protection clause to general economic and social welfare regulations, as distinguished from either "suspect" or "quasi-suspect" classifications (Secs. 2–3) or laws that affect what have come to be known as "fundamental rights" (Sec. 4).

SECTION 1. TRADITIONAL APPROACH

As observed in Ch. 6, Sec. 2, the due process clause was the usual provision used by the Court in the first third of this century to overturn a great many economic and social welfare regulations. But despite Holmes, J.'s reference during this period to the equal protection clause as "the usual last resort of constitutional arguments," [a] the Court held that approximately twenty such state and local laws violated equal protection. In doing so, the Court employed the deferential standard of judicial review called for by the "traditional approach" which granted a state "a broad discretion in classification in the exercise of its power of regulation" and interposed the "constitutional guaranty of equal protection" only "against discriminations that are entirely arbitrary." [c]

But fuller articulations of the standard of review often appeared to vary significantly. For example, LINDSLEY v. NATURAL CARBONIC GAS CO., 220 U.S. 61, 31 S.Ct. 337, 55 L.Ed. 369 (1911), illustrates an extremely deferential formulation: "1. The equal protection clause [does] not take from the state the power to classify in the adoption of police laws, but admits of the exercise of a wide scope of discretion in that regard, and avoids what is done only when it is without any reasonable basis and therefore is purely arbitrary. 2. A classification having some reasonable basis does not offend against that clause merely because it is not made with mathematical nicety, or because in practice it results in some inequality. 3. When the classification in such a law is called in question, if any state of facts reasonably can be conceived that would sustain it, the existence of that state of facts at the time the law was enacted must be assumed. 4. One who assails the classification in such a law must carry the burden of showing that it does not rest upon any reasonable basis, but is essentially arbitrary." [d] In contrast, ROYSTER GUANO CO. v. VIRGINIA, 253 U.S. 412, 40 S.Ct. 560, 64 L.Ed. 989 (1920), suggests a more active judicial role: "[T]he classification must be reasonable, not arbitrary, and must rest upon some ground of difference having a fair and substantial relation to the object of the legislation, so that all persons similarly circumstanced shall be treated alike."

The materials that follow concern the Court's use of the "traditional approach" under equal protection to economic and social welfare regulations since the late 1930s when it abandoned active substantive due process review of such legislation.

---

a. *Buck v. Bell,* 274 U.S. 200, 47 S.Ct. 584, 71 L.Ed. 1000 (1927).

c. *Smith v. Cahoon,* 283 U.S. 553, 51 S.Ct. 582, 75 L.Ed. 1264 (1931).

d. For more recent reliance on this language, see *McGowan v. Maryland,* 366 U.S.

420, 81 S.Ct. 1101, 6 L.Ed.2d 393 (1961), per Warren, C.J., unanimously rejecting an equal protection challenge to state laws requiring stores to be closed on Sunday but containing numerous exemptions.

RAILWAY EXPRESS AGENCY v. NEW YORK

336 U.S. 106, 69 S.Ct. 463, 93 L.Ed. 533 (1949).

MR. JUSTICE DOUGLAS delivered the opinion of the Court.

[T]he Traffic Regulations of the City of New York [provide]: "No person shall operate [on] any street an advertising vehicle; [except for] business notices upon business delivery vehicles, so long as such vehicles are engaged in the usual business [of] the owner and not used merely or mainly for advertising."

Appellant [operates] about 1,900 trucks in New York City and sells the space on the exterior sides of these trucks for advertising [for] the most part unconnected with its own business. It was convicted * * *.

The court [below] concluded that advertising on [vehicles] constitutes a distraction to vehicle drivers and to pedestrians alike and therefore affects the safety of the public in the use of the streets. We do not sit to weigh evidence on the due process issue in order to determine whether the regulation is sound or appropriate; nor is it our function to pass judgment on its wisdom. See *Olsen v. Nebraska* [p. 262 supra]. * * *

The question of equal protection of the laws is pressed more strenuously on us. [It] is said, for example, that one of appellant's trucks carrying the advertisement of a commercial house would not cause any greater distraction of pedestrians and vehicle drivers than if the commercial house carried the same advertisement on its own truck. Yet the regulation allows the latter to do what the former is forbidden from doing. It is therefore contended that the classification which the regulation makes has no relation to the traffic problem since a violation turns not on what kind of advertisements are carried on trucks but on whose trucks they are carried.

That, however, is a superficial way of analyzing the [problem]. The local authorities may well have concluded that those who advertised their own wares on their trucks do not present the same traffic problem in view of the nature or extent of the advertising which they use. * * *

We cannot say that that judgment is not an allowable one. Yet if it is, the classification has relation to the purpose for which it is made and does not contain the kind of discrimination against which the Equal Protection Clause affords protection. It is by such practical considerations based on experience rather than by theoretical inconsistencies that the question of equal protection is to be answered. And the fact that New York City sees fit to eliminate from traffic this kind of distraction but does not touch what may be even greater ones in a different category, such as the vivid displays on Times Square, is immaterial. It is no requirement of equal protection that all evils of the same genus be eradicated or none at all. * * *

Affirmed.

MR. JUSTICE RUTLEDGE acquiesces in the Court's opinion and judgment, dubitante on the question of equal protection of the laws.

MR. JUSTICE JACKSON, concurring. * * *

The burden should rest heavily upon one who would persuade us to use the due process clause to strike down a substantive [law]. Even its provident use against municipal regulations frequently disables all government—state, municipal and federal—from dealing with the conduct in question because the requirement of due process is also applicable to State and Federal Governments.
* * *

Invocation of the equal protection clause, on the other hand, does not disable any governmental body from dealing with the subject at hand. It merely means that the prohibition or regulation must have a broader impact. I regard it as a salutary doctrine that cities, states and the Federal Government must exercise their powers so as not to discriminate between their inhabitants except upon some reasonable differentiation fairly related to the object of regulation. [T]here is no more effective practical guaranty against arbitrary and unreasonable government than to require that the principles of law which officials would impose upon a minority must be imposed generally. Conversely, nothing opens the door to arbitrary action so effectively as to allow those officials to pick and choose only a few to whom they will apply legislation and thus to escape the political retribution that might be visited upon them if larger numbers were affected. Courts can take no better measure to assure that laws will be just than to require that laws be equal in operation. * * *

[The] courts of New York have declared that the sole nature and purpose of the regulation before us is to reduce traffic hazards. There is not even a pretense here that the traffic hazard created by the advertising which is forbidden is in any manner or degree more hazardous than that which is permitted. * * *

* * * I do not think differences of treatment under law should be approved on classification because of differences unrelated to the legislative purpose. The equal protection clause ceases to assure either equality or protection if it is avoided by any conceivable difference that can be pointed out between those bound and those left free. This Court has often announced the principle that the differentiation must have an appropriate relation to the object of the [legislation].

The question in my mind comes to this. Where individuals contribute to an evil or danger in the same way and to the same degree, may those who do so for hire be prohibited, while those who do so for their own commercial ends but not for hire be allowed to continue? I think the answer has to be that the hireling may be put in a class by himself and may be dealt with differently than those who act on their own. But this is not merely because such a discrimination will enable the lawmaker to diminish the evil. That might be done by many classifications, which I should think wholly unsustainable. It is rather because there is a real difference between doing in self-interest and doing for hire, so that it is one thing to tolerate action from those who act on their own and it is another thing to permit the same action to be promoted for a price. * * *

NEW ORLEANS v. DUKES
427 U.S. 297, 96 S.Ct. 2513, 49 L.Ed.2d 511 (1976).

PER CURIAM.

[A 1972 New Orleans ordinance banned all pushcart food vendors in the French Quarter ("Vieux Carre") except those who had continuously operated there for eight or more years. Two vendors had done so for twenty or more years and qualified under the "grandfather clause." Appellee, who had operated a pushcart for only two years, attacked the ordinance.]

* * * Stating expressly [that] *Morey v. Doud,* 354 U.S. 457, 77 S.Ct. 1344, 1 L.Ed.2d 1485 (1957),[a] was "our chief guide in resolving this case," the Court of

---

a. *Morey* held that an Illinois statute that comprehensively regulated companies that sold money orders, but exempted American Express Co. by name, violated equal protection.

Appeals focused on the "exclusionary character" of the ordinance and its concomitant "creation of a protected monopoly for the favored class member." [Thus,] the ordinance was declared violative of [equal protection].

When local economic regulation is challenged solely as violating the Equal Protection Clause, this Court consistently defers to legislative determinations as to the desirability of particular statutory discriminations. Unless a classification trammels fundamental personal rights or is drawn upon inherently suspect distinctions such as race, religion, or alienage, our decisions presume the constitutionality of the statutory discriminations and require only that the classification challenged be rationally related to a legitimate state interest. States are accorded wide latitude in the regulation of their local economies under their police powers, and rational distinctions may be made with substantially less than mathematical exactitude. Legislatures may implement their program step by step in such economic areas, adopting regulations that only partially ameliorate a perceived evil and deferring complete elimination of the evil to future regulations. See, e.g., *Williamson v. Lee Optical Co.*[b] In short, the judiciary may not sit as a superlegislature to judge the wisdom or desirability of legislative policy determinations made in areas that neither affect fundamental rights nor proceed along suspect lines; in the local economic sphere, it is only the invidious discrimination, the wholly arbitrary act, which cannot stand consistently with the Fourteenth Amendment. See, e.g., *Ferguson v. Skrupa.*[5]

[New Orleans'] classification rationally furthers the purpose which [the] city had identified as its objective in enacting the provision, that is, as a means "to preserve the appearance and custom valued by the Quarter's residents and attractive to tourists." The legitimacy of that objective is obvious. The City Council plainly could further that objective by making the reasoned judgment that street peddlers and hawkers tend to interfere with the charm and beauty of an historic area [and] that to ensure the economic vitality of that area, such businesses should be substantially curtailed in the Vieux Carre, if not totally banned.

It is suggested that the "grandfather provision" [was] a totally arbitrary and irrational method of achieving the city's purpose. But rather than proceeding by the immediate and absolute abolition of all pushcart food vendors, the city could rationally [decide] that newer businesses were less likely to have built up substantial reliance interests in continued operation in the Vieux Carre and that the two vendors who qualified under the "grandfather clause" [had] themselves become part of the distinctive character and charm that distinguishes the Vieux Carre. We cannot say that these judgments so lack rationality that they constitute a constitutionally impermissible denial of equal protection.

Nevertheless, [the] Court of Appeals held that even though the exemption of the two vendors was rationally related to legitimate city interests on the basis of

---

b. In *Lee Optical*, p. 263 supra, the statute generally prohibiting the fitting of eyeglasses without a prescription exempted businesses that sold ready-to-wear glasses. The Court found no violation of equal protection: "Evils in the same field may be of different dimensions and proportions, requiring different remedies. Or so the legislature may think. Or the reform may take one step at a time, addressing itself to the phase of the problem which seems most acute to the legislative mind. The legislature may select one phase of one field and apply a remedy there, neglecting the others. [For] all this record shows, the ready-to-wear branch of this business may not loom large in Oklahoma or may present problems of regulation distinct from the other branch."

5. *Ferguson* [p. 263 supra] presented an analogous situation. There, a Kansas statute excepted lawyers from the prohibition of a statute making it a misdemeanor for any person to engage in the business of debt adjusting. We held that the exception of lawyers was not a denial of [equal protection].

facts extant when the ordinance was amended, the "grandfather clause" still could not stand because "the hypothesis that a present eight year veteran of the pushcart hot dog market in the Vieux Carre will continue to operate in a manner more consistent with the traditions of the Quarter than would any other operator is without foundation." Actually, the reliance on the statute's potential irrationality in *Morey*, as the dissenters in that case correctly pointed out, (Frankfurter, J., joined by Harlan, J., dissenting), was a needlessly intrusive judicial infringement on the State's legislative powers, and we have concluded that the equal protection analysis employed in that opinion should no longer be followed. *Morey* was the only case in the last half century to invalidate a wholly economic regulation solely on equal protection grounds, and we are now satisfied that the decision was erroneous. * * *

Reversed.

Mr. Justice Marshall concurs in the judgment.

Mr. Justice Stevens took no part in [the] case.

Notes and Questions

1. *Legislative purpose.* Of what relevance in *Railway Express* was it that the state courts "declared that the sole purpose" of the law "is to reduce traffic hazards"? Would it be more accurate (and realistic) to describe the purpose as being "to promote public safety slightly by reducing the number of distractions on the sides of moving vehicles to the extent this is feasible without jeopardizing the economic well-being of those merchants who advertise on their own trucks," Note, *Legislative Purpose, Rationality and Equal Protection*, 82 Yale L.J. 123, 144 (1972)—a purpose to which the classification unquestionably was "rationally related"? Is it not true that many government programs "involve goals that reflect an accommodation of various purposes which are determined by subtle or blatant policy trade-offs"? Id. That often "the legislature is simply a 'market-like arena' in which individuals and special interest groups trade with each other through representatives to further their own private ends"? Bice, *Rationality Analysis in Constitutional Law*, 65 Minn.L.Rev. 1, 19 (1980).

Are such legislative purposes (or goals) "legitimate"? "Constitutionally permissible"? Consider Tussman & tenBroek, *The Equal Protection of the Laws*, 37 Calif.L.Rev. 341, 350 (1949): "[T]he requirement that laws be equal rests upon a theory of legislation quite distinct from that of pressure groups—a theory which puts forward some conception of a 'general good' as the 'legitimate public purpose' at which legislation must aim, and according to which the triumph of private or group pressure marks the corruption of the legislative process." Compare Posner, *The DeFunis Case and the Constitutionality of Preferential Treatment of Racial Minorities*, 1974 Sup.Ct.Rev. 1, 27: "[A] vast part of the output of the governmental process would be seen to consist of discrimination, in the sense of an effort to redistribute wealth (in one form or another) from one group in the community to another, founded on the superior ability of one group to manipulate the political process rather than on any principle of justice or efficiency. Yet it would be odd, indeed, to condemn as unconstitutional the most characteristic product of a democratic (perhaps of any) political system."

The legislative history of state and local legislation is often unrecorded and not readily available. Should the Court "assess the rationality of the [classification] in terms of the *state's* purposes, rather than hypothesizing conceivable justifications on its own initiative"? Gunther, *In Search of Evolving Doctrine on a Changing Court: A Model for a Newer Equal Protection*, 86 Harv.L.Rev. 1, 46

(1972). Consider id. at 44–46: "If the Court were to require an articulation of purpose from an authoritative state source"—"a state court's or attorney general's office description of purpose should be acceptable"—"rather than hypothesizing one on its own, there would at least be indirect pressure on the legislature to state its own reasons for selecting particular means and classifications [and thus] improve the quality of the political process [by] encouraging a fuller airing in the political arena of the grounds for legislative action." Is such improvement of the political process a proper function of the judiciary?

2. *Underinclusion.* (a) Does the "step by step" approach, which permits "underinclusive" legislation [b]—allowing "officials to pick and choose only a few to whom they will apply legislation and thus to escape the political retribution that might be visited upon them if larger numbers were affected"—promote "arbitrary and unreasonable government"? Is it inconsistent with the *Carolene Products* concern, Ch. 1, Sec. 1, for "prejudice against discrete and insular minorities"? See REHNQUIST, J., dissenting in *Sugarman v. Dougall* and *In re Griffiths*, Sec. 3, II infra, which held state discriminations against aliens subject to "strict scrutiny": "Our society, consisting of over 200 million individuals of multitudinous origins, customs, tongues, beliefs, and cultures is, to say the least, diverse. It would hardly take extraordinary ingenuity for a lawyer to find 'insular and discrete' minorities at every turn of the road. Yet, unless the Court can precisely define and constitutionally justify both the terms and analysis it uses, [the] Court can choose a 'minority' it 'feels' deserves 'solicitude' and thereafter prohibit the States from classifying that 'minority' differently from the 'majority.' I cannot find [any] constitutional authority for such a 'ward of the Court' approach to equal protection."

The post 1930s cases considered to this point almost all invoke the extremely deferential "minimum rationality" standard of review. This approach has been used often in recent years in rejecting equal protection challenges to economic and social welfare legislation. Several such decisions, in which the challengers unsuccessfully sought to have the classifications characterized as being "suspect" or involving "fundamental rights" (and thus subject to "strict scrutiny"), are considered in Sec. 4 infra. In some situations, however, although employing the traditional "rational basis" standard, the Court has held laws violative of equal protection.[e]

Furthermore, the Court has periodically articulated the "traditional" standard in a way that suggests a more active judicial examination of the challenged classification. For example, JOHNSON v. ROBISON, p. 855 supra, per BRENNAN, J., upheld a federal statute granting educational benefits to military veterans but not to conscientious objectors who performed alternate civilian service under the "rational basis" standard, but stated the *Royster Guano* formulation that the classification "must rest upon some ground of difference having a fair and substantial relation to the object of the legislation," and then devoted several pages to considering the justification.[f]

b. For the classic discussion of various types of legislative classifications, see Tussman & tenBroek, note 1 supra.

e. See, e.g., *Eisenstadt v. Baird* (1972), p. 324 supra; *United States Dep't of Agriculture v. Moreno* (1973), Sec. 4, IV infra; *Baxtrom v. Herold*, 383 U.S. 107, 86 S.Ct. 760, 15 L.Ed.2d 620 (1966) (extensive procedural rights prior to civil commitment except for persons who are ending a prison term); *Logan v. Zimmerman Brush Co.,* infra.

f. See also *Reed v. Reed* (1971), Sec. 3, IV infra, per Burger, C.J., using this formulation in holding a law that discriminated against women violative of equal protection.

NEW YORK CITY TRANSIT AUTH. v. BEAZER, 440 U.S. 568, 99 S.Ct. 1355, 59 L.Ed.2d 587 (1979), per STEVENS, J., upheld the exclusion of all methadone users from any Transit Authority (TA) employment. It reversed the federal district court's conclusion that, because about 75% of "patients who have been on methadone maintenance for at least a year are free from illicit drug use" and because the exclusion applied to non-safety sensitive jobs, it had "no rational relation to the demands of the job to be performed": "[A]ny special rule short of total exclusion that TA might adopt is likely to be less precise—and will assuredly be more costly—than the one that it currently enforces. If eligibility is marked at any intermediate point—whether after one year of treatment or later—the classification will inevitably discriminate between employees or applicants equally or almost equally apt to achieve full recovery. [By] contrast, the 'no drugs' policy now enforced by TA is supported by the legitimate inference that as long as a treatment program (or other drug use) continues, a degree of uncertainty persists. Accordingly, [the TA policy] is rational. It is neither unprincipled nor invidious in the sense that it implies disrespect for the excluded subclass." [a]

POWELL, J., concurred in the Court's opinion as "to employees or applicants who are currently on methadone" but interpreted TA's policy as also excluding "persons currently free of methadone use but who had been on the drug within the previous five years": "[T]here is no rational basis for an absolute bar against the employment of persons who have completed successfully a methadone maintenance program."

WHITE, J., joined by Marshall, J., dissented: Both courts below "found that those who have been maintained on methadone for at least a year and who are free from the use of illicit drugs and alcohol can easily be identified through normal personnel procedures and, for a great many jobs, are as employable as and present no more risk than applicants from the general population. [On] the facts as found [one] can reach the Court's result only if [equal protection] imposes no real constraint at all in this situation.

[T]he rule's classification of successfully maintained persons as dispositively different from the general population is left without any justification and, with its irrationality and invidiousness thus uncovered, must fall before the Equal Protection Clause.[15]" [b]

---

a. See also *Vance v. Bradley* (1979), Sec. 3, I infra, per White, J., (sustaining mandatory retirement at age 60 for federal Foreign Service personnel), conceding that the classification was "to some extent both under-and over-inclusive" but holding that "perfection is by no means required. [In] an equal protection case of this type, [those] challenging the legislative judgment must convince the court that the legislative facts on which the classification is apparently based could not reasonably be conceived to be true by the governmental decisionmaker."

Minnesota v. Clover Leaf Creamery Co. (1981), p. 289 supra, per Brennan, J., relied on this language in unanimously rejecting an equal protection challenge to economic legislation.

15. I have difficulty also with the Court's easy conclusion that the challenged rule was "[q]uite plainly" not motivated "by any special animus against a specific group of persons." Heroin addiction is a special problem of the poor, and the addict population is composed largely of racial minorities that the Court has previously recognized as politically powerless and historical subjects of majoritarian neglect. Persons on methadone maintenance have few interests in common with members of the majority, and thus are unlikely to have their interests protected, or even considered, in governmental decisionmaking. [On] the other hand, the afflictions to which petitioners are more sympathetic, such as alcoholism and mental illness, are shared by both white and black, rich and poor.

Some weight should also be given to the history of the rule. Petitioners admit that it was not the result of a reasoned policy decision and stipulated that they had never studied the ability of those on methadone maintenance to perform petitioners' jobs.

UNITED STATES R.R. RETIREMENT BD. v. FRITZ

449 U.S. 166, 101 S.Ct. 453, 66 L.Ed.2d 368 (1980).

JUSTICE REHNQUIST delivered the opinion of the Court.

The United States District Court [held violative of the "equal protection component of the Fifth Amendment" § 231b(h)] of the Railroad Retirement Act of 1974. [Under the] Act's predecessor statute, a person who worked for both railroad and nonrailroad employers and who qualified for railroad retirement benefits and social security benefits received retirement benefits under both systems and an accompanying "windfall" benefit. [Congress] determined to place the system on a "sound financial basis" by eliminating future accruals of those benefits. Congress also enacted various transitional provisions [which] expressly preserved windfall benefits for some classes of employees.

* * * First, those employees who lacked the requisite 10 years of railroad employment to qualify for railroad retirement benefits as of January 1, 1975, the changeover date, would have their retirement benefits computed under the new system and would not receive any windfall benefit. Second, those individuals already retired and already receiving dual benefits [would] continue to receive a windfall benefit. Third, those employees who had qualified for both railroad and social security benefits as of the changeover date, but who had not yet retired as of that date (and thus were not yet receiving dual benefits), were entitled to windfall benefits if they had (1) performed some railroad service in 1974 or (2) had a "current connection" with the railroad industry as of December 31, 1974,[6] or (3) completed 25 years of railroad service as of December 31, 1974. * * *

Thus, an individual who, as of the changeover date, was unretired and had 11 years of railroad employment and sufficient nonrailroad employment to qualify for social security benefits is eligible for the full windfall amount if he worked for the railroad in 1974 or had a current connection with the railroad as of December 31, 1974, or his later retirement date. But an unretired individual with 24 years of railroad service and sufficient nonrailroad service to qualify for social security benefits is not eligible for a full windfall amount unless he worked for the railroad in 1974, or had a current connection with the railroad as of December 31, 1974 or his later retirement date. * * *

The District Court agreed with appellees that a differentiation based solely on whether an employee was "active" in the railroad business as of 1974 was not "rationally related" to the congressional purposes of insuring the solvency of the railroad retirement system and protecting vested benefits. We disagree and reverse.

The initial issue [is] the appropriate standard of judicial review to be applied when social and economic legislation enacted by Congress is challenged as being violative of the Fifth Amendment. [B]ecause the distinctions drawn in § 231b(h) do not burden fundamental constitutional rights or create "suspect" classifica-

---

Petitioners are not directly accountable to the public, are not the type of official body that normally makes legislative judgments of fact such as those relied upon by the majority today, and are by nature more concerned with business efficiency than with other public policies for which they have no direct responsibility. Both the State and City of New York, which do exhibit those democratic characteristics, hire persons in methadone programs in similar jobs.

These factors together strongly point to a conclusion of invidious discrimination. * * *

b. White, J., joined by Brennan, J., also dissented on statutory grounds.

6. The term "current connection" is defined [to] mean, in general, employment in the railroad industry in 12 of the preceding 30 calendar months.

tions, such as race or national origin, we may put cases involving judicial review of such claims to one side.

Despite the narrowness of the issue, this Court in earlier cases has not been altogether consistent in its pronouncements in this area [contrasting the language in *National Carbonic* and *Royster Guano,* set forth supra].

In more recent years, however, the Court in cases involving social and economic benefits has consistently refused to invalidate on equal protection grounds legislation which it simply deemed unwise or unartfully drawn [discussing *Dandridge v. Williams,* Sec. 4, IV infra, *Vance v. Bradley* and *New Orleans v. Dukes.*]

Applying those principles to this case, the plain language of § 231b(h) marks the beginning and end of our inquiry.[10] There Congress determined that some of those who in the past received full windfall benefits would not continue to do so. Because Congress could have eliminated windfall benefits for all classes of employees, it is not constitutionally impermissible for Congress to have drawn lines between groups of employees for the purpose of phasing out those benefits. *Dukes.*

The only remaining question is whether Congress achieved its purpose in a patently arbitrary or irrational way. [Congress] could properly conclude that persons who had actually acquired statutory entitlement to windfall benefits while still employed in the railroad industry had a greater equitable claim to those benefits than the members of appellees' class who were no longer in railroad employment when they became eligible for dual benefits. Furthermore, the "current connection" test is not a patently arbitrary means for determining which employees are "career railroaders" * * *. Congress could assume that those who had a current connection with the railroad industry when the Act was passed in 1974, or who returned to the industry before their retirement, were more likely than those who had left the industry prior to 1974 and who never returned, to be among the class of persons who pursue careers in the railroad industry, the class for whom the Railroad Retirement Act was designed.

Where, as here, there are plausible reasons for Congress' action, our inquiry is at an end. It is, of course, "constitutionally irrelevant whether this reasoning in fact underlay the legislative decision," because this Court has never insisted that a legislative body articulate its reasons for enacting a statute. This is particularly true where the legislature must necessarily engage in a process of line drawing. The "task of classifying persons for [benefits] inevitably requires that some persons who have an almost equally strong claim to favorite treatment be placed on different sides of the line," *Mathews v. Diaz,* [Sec. 3, II infra], and the fact the line might have been drawn differently at some points is a matter for legislative, rather than judicial consideration.

---

10. This opinion and Justice Brennan's dissent cite a number of equal protection [cases]. The most arrogant legal scholar would not claim that all of these cases applied a uniform or consistent test under the Equal Protection Clause. And realistically speaking, we can be no more certain that this opinion will remain undisturbed than were those who joined the opinion in *National Carbonic Gas, Royster Guano,* or any of the other cases referred to in this opinion and in the dissenting opinion. But like our predecessors and our successors, we are obliged to apply the equal protection component of the Fifth Amendment as we believe the Constitution requires and in so doing we have no hesitation in asserting, contrary to the dissent, that where social or economic regulations are involved *Dandridge* [and] this case, state the proper application of the test. The comments in the dissenting opinion about the proper cases for which to look for the correct statement of the equal protection rational basis standard, and about which cases limit earlier cases, are just that: comments in a dissenting opinion.

Finally, we disagree with the District Court's conclusion that Congress was unaware of what it accomplished or that it was misled by the groups that appeared before it. If this test were applied literally to every member of any legislature that ever voted on a law, there would be very few laws which would survive it. The language of the statute is clear, and we have historically assumed that Congress intended what it enacted. To be sure, appellees lost a political battle in which they had a strong interest, but this is neither the first nor the last time that such a result will occur in the legislative forum. * * *

JUSTICE STEVENS, concurring in the judgment.

In my opinion Justice Brennan's criticism of the Court's approach to this case merits a more thoughtful response than that contained in footnote 10. [When] Congress deprives a small class of persons of vested [rights,] I believe the Constitution requires something more than merely a "conceivable" or a "plausible" explanation for the unequal treatment.

I do not, however, share Justice Brennan's conclusion that every statutory classification must further an objective that can be confidently identified as the "actual purpose" of the legislature. Actual purpose is sometimes unknown. Moreover, undue emphasis on actual motivation may result in identically worded statutes being held valid in one State and invalid in a neighboring State. I therefore believe that we must discover a correlation between the classification and either the actual purpose of the statute or a legitimate purpose that we may reasonably presume to have motivated an impartial legislature. If the adverse impact on the disfavored class is an apparent aim of the legislature, its impartiality would be suspect. If, however, the adverse impact may reasonably be viewed as an acceptable cost of achieving a larger goal, an impartial lawmaker could rationally decide that that cost should be incurred.

In this case, however, we need not look beyond the actual purpose of the legislature. As is often true, this legislation is the product of multiple and somewhat inconsistent purposes that led to certain compromises. One purpose was to eliminate in the future the benefit that is described by the Court as a "windfall benefit" and by Justice Brennan as an "earned dual benefit." That aim was incident to the broader objective of protecting the solvency of the entire railroad retirement program. Two purposes that conflicted somewhat with this broad objective were the purposes of preserving those benefits that had already vested and of increasing the level of payments to beneficiaries whose rights were not otherwise to be changed. As Justice Brennan emphasizes, Congress originally intended to protect *all* vested benefits, but it ultimately sacrificed some benefits in the interest of achieving other objectives.

Given these conflicting purposes, I believe the decisive questions are (1) whether Congress can rationally reduce the vested benefits of some employees to improve the solvency of the entire program while simultaneously increasing the benefits of others; and (2) whether, in deciding which vested benefits to reduce, Congress may favor annuitants whose railroad service was more recent than that of disfavored annuitants who had an equal or greater quantum of employment.

My answer to both questions is in the affirmative. The congressional purpose to eliminate dual benefits is unquestionably legitimate; that legitimacy is not undermined by the adjustment in the level of remaining benefits in response to inflation in the economy. As for the second question, some hardship—in the form of frustrated long-term expectations—must inevitably result from any reduction in vested benefits. Arguably, therefore, Congress had a duty—and surely it had the right to decide—to eliminate no more vested benefits than necessary to achieve its fiscal purpose. Having made that decision, any distinction it chose within the class of vested beneficiaries would involve a difference of degree rather than a difference in entitlement. I am satisfied that a distinction based upon currency of railroad employment represents an impartial method of identifying that sort of difference. Because retirement plans frequently provide greater benefits for recent retirees than for those who retired years ago—and thus give a greater reward for recent service than for past service of equal duration—the basis for the statutory discrimination is supported by relevant precedent. It follows, in my judgment, that the timing of the employees' railroad service is a "reasonable basis" for the classification as that term is used in *National Carbonic Gas* and *Dandridge,* as well as a "ground of difference having a fair and substantial relation to the object of the legislation," as those words are used in *Royster Guano.* * * *

JUSTICE BRENNAN, with whom JUSTICE MARSHALL joins, dissenting.

[T]he legal standard applicable to this case is the "rational basis" test. [The] Court today purports to apply this standard, but [fails] to scrutinize the challenged classification in the manner established by our governing precedents. I suggest that the mode of analysis employed by the Court in this case virtually immunizes social and economic legislative classifications from judicial review.

[Perhaps] the clearest statement of this Court's present approach to "rational basis" scrutiny may be found in *Johnson v. Robison,* [where] eight Members of this Court agreed [to the *Royster Guano* formulation]. The enactments of Congress are entitled to a presumption of constitutionality, and the burden rests on those challenging a legislative classification to demonstrate that it does not bear the "fair and substantial relation to the object of the legislation" required under the Constitution.

Nonetheless, the rational basis standard "is not a toothless one," *Mathews v. Lucas,* [Sec. 3, III infra], and will not be satisfied by flimsy or implausible justifications for the legislative classification, proffered after the fact by Government attorneys. See, e.g., *U.S. Dept. of Agriculture v. Moreno.* When faced with a challenge to a legislative classification under the rational basis test, the court should ask, first, what the purposes of the statute are, and second, whether the classification is rationally related to achievement of those purposes.

The purposes of the Railroad Retirement Act of 1974 are clear, because Congress has commendably stated them in the House and Senate reports accompanying the Act. A section of the reports is entitled "Principal Purpose of the Bill." It notes generally that "[t]he bill provides for a complete restructuring of the Railroad Retirement Act of 1937, and will place it on a sound financial basis," and then states: "Persons who already have vested rights under both the Railroad Retirement and the Social Security systems will in the future be permitted to receive benefits computed under both systems just as is true under existing law." [3] Moreover, Congress explained that this purpose was based on considerations of fairness and the legitimate expectations of the retirees * * *.

Thus, a "principal purpose" [was] to preserve the vested earned benefits of retirees who had already qualified for them. The classification at issue here,

---

3. Several pages later, the reports again make clear that persons with vested rights to earned dual benefits would retain [them].

Only in technical discussions and in the section-by-section analyses do the reports re-

flect the actual consequences of the Act on the appellee class. * * *

which deprives some retirees of vested dual benefits that they had earned prior to 1974, directly conflicts with Congress' stated purpose. As such, the classification is not only rationally unrelated to the congressional purpose; it is inimical to it.

The Court today avoids the conclusion that § 231b(h) must be invalidated by deviating in three ways from traditional rational basis analysis. * * *

A. The Court states that "the plain language of § 231b(h) marks the beginning and end of our inquiry." [Since] § 231b(h) of the Act deprives appellees of their vested earned dual benefits, the Court apparently assumes that Congress must have *intended* that result. But by presuming purpose from result, the Court reduces analysis to tautology. It may always be said that Congress intended to do what it in fact did. If that were the extent of our analysis, we would find every statute, no matter how arbitrary or irrational, perfectly tailored to achieve its purpose. But equal protection scrutiny under the rational basis test requires the courts first to deduce the independent objectives of the statute, usually from statements of purpose and other evidence in the statute and legislative history, and second to analyze whether the challenged classification rationally furthers achievement of those objectives. The Court's tautological approach will not suffice.

B. The Court analyzes the rationality of § 231b(h) in terms of a justification suggested by Government attorneys, but never adopted by Congress. [But] this Court has frequently recognized that the actual purposes of Congress, rather than the post hoc justifications offered by Government attorneys, must be the primary basis for analysis under the rational basis test. [For example], in *San Antonio Independent School District v. Rodriguez* [Sec. 4, IV infra], this Court stated that a challenged classification will pass muster under "rational basis" scrutiny only if it "rationally furthers some legitimate, *articulated* state purpose," (emphasis added), and in *Massachusetts Board of Retirement v. Murgia* [Sec. 3, I infra], we stated that such a classification will be sustained only if it "rationally furthers the purpose *identified by the State.*" (Emphasis added.) * * *

The Court argues that Congress chose to discriminate against appellees for reasons of equity, [but, as] I have shown, Congress expressed the view that it would be inequitable to deprive any retirees of any portion of the benefits they had been promised and that they had earned under prior law. The Court is unable to cite even one statement in the legislative history by a Representative or Senator that makes the equitable judgment it imputes to Congress. In the entire legislative history of the Act, the only persons to state that the equities justified eliminating appellees' earned dual benefits were representatives of railroad management and labor, whose self-serving interest in bringing about this result destroys any basis for attaching weight to their statements. [They] were not appointed by public officials, nor did they represent the interests of the appellee class, who were no longer active railroaders or union members.

[L]abor representatives demanded that benefits be increased for their current members, the cost to be offset by divesting the appellee class of a portion of the benefits they had earned under prior law. [In] fact, the [management and labor representatives] and Railroad Retirement Board members who testified at congressional hearings perpetuated the inaccurate impression that all retirees with earned vested dual benefits under prior law would retain their benefits unchanged. * * *

Of course, a misstatement or several misstatements by witnesses before Congress would not ordinarily lead us to conclude that Congress misapprehended what it was doing. In this instance, however, where complex legislation was drafted by outside parties and Congress relied on them to explain it, where the misstatements are frequent and unrebutted, and where no Member of Congress can be found to have stated the effect of the classification correctly, we are entitled to suspect that Congress may have been misled. As the District Court found: "At no time during the hearings did Congress even give a hint that it understood that the bill by its language eliminated an earned benefit of plaintiff's class."

Therefore, I do not think that this classification was rationally related to an *actual* governmental purpose.

C. The third way in which the Court has deviated from the principles of rational basis scrutiny is its failure to analyze whether the challenged classification is genuinely related to the purpose identified by the Court. Having suggested that "equitable considerations" underlay the challenged classification—in direct contradiction to Congress' evaluation of those considerations, and in the face of evidence that the classification was the product of private negotiation by interested parties, inadequately examined and understood by Congress—the Court proceeds to accept that suggestion without further analysis.

An unadorned claim of "equitable" considerations is, of course, difficult to assess. It seems to me that before a court may accept a litigant's assertion of "equity," it must inquire what principles of equity or fairness might genuinely support such a judgment. * * *

In my view, the following considerations are of greatest relevance to the equities of this case: (1) contribution to the system; (2) reasonable expectation and reliance; (3) need; and (4) character of service to the railroad industry. With respect to each of these considerations, I would conclude that appellees have as great an equitable claim to their earned dual benefits as do their more favored coworkers, who remain entitled to their earned dual benefits under § 231b(h).

[Because] the Court is willing to accept a tautological analysis of congressional purpose, an assertion of "equitable" considerations contrary to the expressed judgment of Congress, and a classification patently unrelated to achievement of the identified purpose, it succeeds in effectuating neither equity nor congressional intent. * * *

Notes and Questions

1. *"Actual purpose."* Does *Fritz* put to rest—at least for a majority of the Court—the issue of "actual" vs. "hypothetically conceivable" legislative purpose? Within three months after *Fritz*, SCHWEIKER v. WILSON, 450 U.S. 221, 101 S.Ct. 1074, 67 L.Ed.2d 186 (1981), per BLACKMUN, J., upheld Congress' denial of SSI "comfort allowances" to needy aged, blind and disabled persons confined in public institutions unless the institutions received federal Medicaid funds: "[T]he pertinent inquiry is whether the [classification] advances legitimate legislative goals in a rational fashion. The Court has said that, although this rational basis standard is 'not a toothless one,' *Mathews v. Lucas*, it does not allow us to substitute our personal notions of good public [policy].[a] We believe

---

a. See also *Schweiker v. Hogan*, 457 U.S. 569, 102 S.Ct. 2597, 73 L.Ed.2d 227 (1982) (unanimous opinion, per Stevens, J., applying "rationality" test to Medicaid benefits discrimination despite the fact that it "may be inequitable or unwise").

that the decision to incorporate the Medicaid eligibility standards into the SSI scheme must be considered Congress' deliberate, considered choice." It "is rationally related to the legitimate legislative desire to avoid spending federal resources on behalf of individuals whose care and treatment are being fully provided for by state and local government units" and "may be said to implement a congressional policy choice to provide supplemental financial assistance for only those residents of public institutions who already receive significant federal support in the form of Medicaid coverage."

POWELL, J., joined by Brennan, Marshall and Stevens, JJ., dissented: "In my view, the Court should receive with some skepticism post hoc hypotheses about legislative purpose, unsupported by the legislative history. When no indication of legislative purpose appears other than the current position of the Secretary, the Court should require that the classification bear a 'fair and substantial relation' to the asserted purpose. See *Royster Guano*. This marginally more demanding scrutiny indirectly would test the plausibility of the tendered purpose, and preserve equal protection review as something more than 'a mere tautological recognition of the fact that Congress did what it intended to do.' *Fritz* (Stevens, J., concurring). * * * I conclude that Congress had no rational reason for refusing to pay a comfort allowance to appellee, while paying it to numerous otherwise identically situated disabled indigents. This unexplained difference in treatment must have been a legislative oversight."

2. *"Means/end fit."* To what extent should the Court employ a "strengthened 'rational' scrutiny" by requiring "that legislative means must substantially further legislative ends"? Gunther, note 1 after *Dukes*, supra. Consider id.: "Examination of means in light of asserted state purposes would directly promote public consideration of the benefits assertedly sought by the proposed legislation; indirectly, it would stimulate fuller political examination, in relation to those benefits, of the costs that would be incurred if the proposed means were adopted."

Compare REHNQUIST, J., dissenting in *Trimble v. Gordon*, Sec. 3, III infra, which held that an Illinois statute, forbidding illegitimate children to inherit from their fathers by intestate succession, violated equal protection: "[Judicial review of means/end fit] requires a conscious second-guessing of legislative judgment in an area where this Court has no special expertise whatever. [In] most cases, [the] 'fit' will involve a greater or lesser degree of imperfection. Then the Court asks itself how much 'imperfection' between means and ends is permissible? In making this judgment it must throw into the judicial hopper the whole range of factors which were first thrown into the legislative hopper. What alternatives were reasonably available? What reasons are there for the legislature to accomplish this 'purpose' in the way it did? What obstacles stood in the way of other solutions?

"[Without] any antecedent constitutional mandate, we have created on the premises of the Equal Protection Clause a school for legislators, whereby opinions of this Court are written to instruct them in a better understanding of how to accomplish their ordinary legislative tasks. [Since] Illinois' distinction is not mindless and patently irrational, I would [affirm]."

For recent expressions of the Court on this issue, see fn. a in *Beazer*, supra.

3. *"Irrationality."* In LOGAN v. ZIMMERMAN BRUSH CO. (1982), p. 407 supra, for the first time in 25 years, a majority of the justices employed "the lowest level of permissible equal protection scrutiny" and found a violation of equal protection. Appellant filed an employment discrimination complaint

before an Illinois Commission which inadvertently scheduled the hearing at a date after the statutory time period expired. The state court held that this deprived the Commission of jurisdiction and terminated appellant's claim. BLACKMUN, J., joined by Brennan, Marshall and O'Connor, JJ., found this "patently irrational in light of [the law's] stated purpose": "I cannot agree that terminating a claim that the State itself has misscheduled is a rational way of expediting the resolution of disputes. [The] state's rationale must be something more than the exercise of a strained imagination; while the connection between means and ends need not be precise, it, at the least, must have some objective basis. That is not so here."

POWELL, J., joined by Rehnquist, J., concurred as to "this unusual classification": "As appellants possessed no power to convene hearings, it is unfair and irrational to punish them for the Commission's failure to do so." [d]

SECTION 2. RACE AND ETHNIC ANCESTRY

I. DISCRIMINATION AGAINST RACIAL AND ETHNIC MINORITIES

The "evil to be remedied" by the equal protection clause, declared the *Slaughter-House Cases,* was "the existence of laws in the States where the newly emancipated negroes resided, which discriminated with gross injustice and hardship against them as a class." STRAUDER v. WEST VIRGINIA, 100 U.S. 303, 25 L.Ed. 664 (1880)—the first post-Civil War racial discrimination case to reach the Court—per STRONG, J., invalidating the state murder conviction of a black on the ground that state law forbade blacks from serving on grand or petit juries, observed that "the true spirit and meaning" of the Civil War amendments was "securing to a race recently emancipated [the] enjoyment of all the civil rights that under the law are enjoyed by [whites]. What is [equal protection but] that all persons, whether colored or white, shall stand equal before the laws of the States, and, in regard to the colored race, for whose protection the amendment was primarily designed, that no discrimination shall be made against them by law because of their color? The words of the amendment [contain] a positive immunity or right, most valuable to the colored race,—the right to exemption from unfriendly legislation against them distinctively as colored,—exemption from legal discriminations, implying inferiority in civil society, lessening the security of their enjoyment of the rights which others enjoy, and discriminations which are steps towards reducing them to the condition of a subject race.

"That the West Virginia statute respecting juries [is] such a discrimination ought not to be doubted. [And if] in those States where the colored people constitute a majority of the entire population a law should be enacted excluding all white men from jury service, [we] apprehend no one would be heard to claim that it would not be a denial to white men of the equal protection of the laws.[b] Nor if a law should be passed excluding all naturalized Celtic Irishmen, would there be any doubt of its inconsistency with the spirit of the amendment.

* * *

"We do not say that within the limits from which it is not excluded by the amendment a State may not prescribe the qualifications of its jurors, and in so

---

d. See also *G.D. Searle & Co. v. Cohn,* 455 U.S. 404, 102 S.Ct. 1137, 71 L.Ed.2d 250 (1982), for a dissent by Stevens, J., finding no "rational basis" for a statutory classification.

b. The issue of discrimination against the majority race—that of "favorable," "reverse," or "benign" discrimination—is considered in Part V infra.

doing make discriminations. It may confine the selection to males, to freeholders, to citizens, to persons within certain ages, or to persons having educational qualifications. We do not believe the Fourteenth Amendment was ever intended to prohibit this. Looking at its history, it is clear it had no such purpose. Its aim was against discrimination because of race or color."

Thus, as stated in *Brown v. Board of Education,* Part II infra, "in the first cases in this Court construing the Fourteenth Amendment, decided shortly after its adoption, the Court interpreted it as proscribing all state-imposed discriminations against the Negro race." Subsequent decisions extended this proscription to state discrimination against persons because of their national origin, such as those of Chinese or Mexican ancestry.[c]

KOREMATSU v. UNITED STATES, 323 U.S. 214, 65 S.Ct. 193, 89 L.Ed. 194 (1944), per BLACK, J., upheld a 1942 military order (promulgated pursuant to Executive Order 9066) excluding all persons of Japanese ancestry from the West Coast war area, as applied to petitioner, an American citizen whose loyalty to the U. S. was not questioned: "[L]egal restrictions which curtail the civil rights of a single racial group are immediately suspect. [C]ourts must subject them to the most rigid scrutiny. Pressing public necessity may sometimes justify the existence of such restrictions; racial antagonism never can."

The Court, emphasizing that it was passing only on the exclusion order and not on petitioner's subsequent detention in a relocation center, relied on *Hirabayashi v. United States*, 320 U.S. 81, 63 S.Ct. 1375, 87 L.Ed. 1774 (1943), which sustained a conviction for violating a military curfew order for all persons of Japanese ancestry in the West Coast area. "Nothing short of apprehension by the proper military authorities of the gravest imminent danger to the public safety can constitutionally justify either [order]. But exclusion from a threatened area, no less than curfew, has a definite and close relationship to the prevention of espionage and sabotage, * * *

"Here, as in *Hirabayashi,* 'we cannot reject as unfounded the judgment of the military authorities and of Congress that there were disloyal members of that population, whose number and strength could not be precisely and quickly ascertained. We cannot say that the war-making branches of the Government did not have ground for believing that in a critical hour such persons could not readily be isolated and separately dealt with, and constituted a menace to the national defense and safety, which demanded that prompt and adequate measures be taken to guard against it.' [That] there were members of the group who retained loyalties to Japan has been confirmed by investigations made subsequent to the exclusion. Approximately five thousand American citizens of Japanese ancestry refused to swear unqualified allegiance to the United States and to renounce allegiance to the Japanese Emperor, and several thousand evacuees requested repatriation to Japan.

"[H]ardships are part of war, and war is an aggregation of hardships. [E]xclusion of large groups of citizens from their homes, except under circumstances of direst emergency and peril, is inconsistent with our basic governmental institutions. But when under conditions of modern warfare our shores are threatened by hostile forces, the power to protect must be commensurate with the threatened danger. [To] cast this case into outlines of racial prejudice,

c. *Yick Wo v. Hopkins* (1886), Sec. III infra; *Hernandez v. Texas,* 347 U.S. 475, 74 S.Ct. 667, 98 L.Ed. 866 (1954).

without reference to the real military dangers which were presented, merely confuses the issue."

MURPHY, J., dissented: "This exclusion [falls] into the ugly abyss of racism. [The] main reasons relied upon by those responsible for the forced evacuation [do] not prove a reasonable relation between the group characteristics of Japanese Americans and the dangers of invasion, sabotage and espionage. The reasons appear, instead, to be largely an accumulation of much of the misinformation, half-truths and insinuations that for years have been directed against Japanese Americans by people with racial and economic prejudices—the same people who have been among the foremost advocates of the evacuation. [Nor] is there any denial of that fact that not one person of Japanese ancestry was accused or convicted of espionage or sabotage after Pearl Harbor while they were still free, a fact which is some evidence of the loyalty of the vast majority of these individuals and of the effectiveness of the established methods of combatting these evils. It seems incredible that under these circumstances it would have been impossible to hold loyalty hearings for the mere 112,000 persons involved—or at least for the 70,000 American citizens—especially when a large part of this number represented children and elderly men and women."

JACKSON, J., dissented: "It would be impracticable and dangerous idealism to expect or insist that each specific military command in an area of probable operations will conform to conventional tests of constitutionality. When an area is so beset that it must be put under military control at all, the paramount consideration is that its measures be successful, rather than legal. * * *

"The limitation under which courts always will labor in examining the necessity for a military order are illustrated by this case. How does the Court know that these orders have a reasonable basis in necessity? No evidence whatever on that subject has been taken by this or any other court. There is sharp controversy as to the credibility of the DeWitt report. So the Court, having no real evidence before it, has no choice but to accept General DeWitt's own unsworn, self-serving statement, untested by any cross-examination, that what he did was reasonable.

"[A] military order, however unconstitutional, is not apt to last longer than the military emergency. [But] once a judicial opinion rationalizes such an order to show that it conforms to the Constitution, or rather rationalizes the Constitution to show that the Constitution sanctions such an order, the Court for all time has validated the principle of racial discrimination in criminal procedure and of transplanting American citizens. The principle then lies about like a loaded weapon ready for the hand of any authority that can bring forward a plausible claim of an urgent [need]. I do not suggest that the courts should have attempted to interfere with the Army in carrying out its task. But I do not think they may be asked to execute a military expedient that has no place in law under the Constitution."

ROBERTS, J., also dissented.

Notes and Questions

1. *Standard of review.* *Hirabayashi* and *Korematsu* have been the last instances in which the Court has failed to invalidate intentional (or "de jure") government discrimination against a racial or ethnic minority.[d] In 1967, the

d. On the same day as *Korematsu, Ex parte Endo,* 323 U.S. 283, 65 S.Ct. 208, 89 L.Ed. 243 (1944), per Douglas, J., held that Executive Order 9066 did not authorize the continued detention of concededly loyal persons of Japanese ancestry: "This Court [has] favored

Court observed that laws imposing "invidious racial discriminations" bear a "very heavy burden of justification" and "if they are ever to be upheld, they must be shown to be necessary to the accomplishment of some permissible state objective"; they are unlike statutes "involving no racial discrimination" where "the Court has merely asked whether there is any rational foundation for the discriminations, and has deferred to the wisdom of the state legislatures." [e]

2. *"Rigid scrutiny" and "special traits."* Should state discrimination against a racial minority ever be upheld? May a state require that all blacks undergo a blood test for sickle cell anemia? Suppose that "studies have indicated that seven to nine percent of the American Black population carries the sickle cell trait, while 0.3 percent suffer from the disease" and that "the incidence of sickle cell anemia in the White population is negligible"? Note, *Constitutional and Practical Considerations in Mandatory Sickle Cell Anemia Testing,* 7 U.C. D.L.Rev. 509, 519 (1974). Should it make a difference if the state, rather than the individual, pays for the blood test? May "overinclusive" racial laws be distinguished on the basis of the severity of the burden imposed? Compare *Hirabayashi, Korematsu* and *Endo.*

II. SEGREGATION AND OTHER CLASSIFICATIONS

Sec. I involved laws that imposed burdens on racial and ethnic minorities. This section concerns laws that segregate or otherwise classify on a racial basis but, at least in a literal sense, treat all races identically. The principal question is whether (and, if so, why) such laws should be subject to the same "rigid" standard of review.

PLESSY v. FERGUSON

163 U.S. 537, 16 S.Ct. 1138, 41 L.Ed. 256 (1896).

MR. JUSTICE BROWN delivered the opinion of the Court.

[An 1890 Louisiana law required that railway passenger cars have "equal but separate accommodations for the white, and colored races." Plessy, alleging that he "was seven-eights Caucasian and one-eighth African blood; that the mixture of colored blood was not discernible in him; and that he was entitled to every right [of] the white race," was arrested for refusing to vacate a seat in a coach for whites.]

That it does not conflict with the thirteenth amendment [is] too clear for argument. Slavery implies involuntary servitude,—a state of bondage * * *. This amendment [was] regarded by the statesmen of that day as insufficient to protect the colored race from certain laws [imposing] onerous disabilities and burdens, and curtailing their rights in the pursuit of life, liberty, and property to such an extent that their freedom was of little value; [and] the fourteenth amendment was devised to meet this exigency. * * *

The object of the amendment was undoubtedly to enforce the absolute equality of the two races before the law, but, in the nature of things, it could not have been intended to abolish distinctions based upon color, or to enforce social, as distinguished from political, equality, or a commingling of the two races upon terms unsatisfactory to either. [Laws] requiring their separation, in places where they are liable to be brought into contact [have] been generally, if not

that interpretation of legislation which gives it the greater chance of surviving the test of constitutionality."

e. *Loving v. Virginia,* Part II infra. For discussion of "refinements" of the "test," see note 1 after *Loving.*

universally, recognized as within the competency of the state legislatures in the exercise of their police power. The most common instance of this is connected with the establishment of separate schools for white and colored children, which have been [upheld] even by courts of states where the political rights of the colored race have been longest and most earnestly enforced [citing cases from Mass., Ohio, Mo., Cal., La., N.Y., Ind. and Ky.].

Laws forbidding the intermarriage of the two races may be said in a technical sense to interfere with the freedom of contract, and yet have been universally recognized as within the police power of the state. [S]tatutes for the separation of the two races upon public conveyances were held to be constitutional in [federal decisions and cases from Pa., Mich., Ill., Tenn. and N.Y. It is suggested] that the same argument that will justify the state legislature in requiring railways to provide separate accommodations for the two races will also authorize them to require separate cars to be provided for people whose hair is of a certain color, or who are aliens, or who belong to certain nationalities, or to enact laws requiring colored people to walk upon one side of the street, and white people upon the other, or requiring white men's houses to be painted white, and colored men's black, or their vehicles or business signs to be of different colors, upon the theory that one side of the street is as good as the other, or that a house or vehicle of one color is as good as one of another color. The reply to all this is that every exercise of the police power must be reasonable, and extend only to such laws as are enacted in good faith for the promotion of the public good, and not for the annoyance or oppression of a particular class. [In] determining the question of reasonableness, [the state] is at liberty to act with reference to the established usages, customs, and traditions of the people, and with a view to the promotion of their comfort, and the preservation of the public peace and good order. Gauged by this standard, we cannot say [this law] is unreasonable, or more obnoxious to the fourteenth amendment than the [acts] requiring separate schools for colored children in the District of Columbia, the constitutionality of which does not seem to have been questioned or the corresponding acts of state legislatures.

We consider the underlying fallacy of the plaintiff's argument to consist in the assumption that the enforced separation of the two races stamps the colored race with a badge of inferiority. If this be so, it is not by reason of anything found in the act, but solely because the colored race chooses to put that construction upon it. [The] argument also assumes that social prejudices may be overcome by legislation, and that equal rights cannot be secured to the negro except by an enforced commingling of the two races. We cannot accept this proposition. If the two races are to meet upon terms of social equality, it must be the result [of] voluntary consent of individuals. * * * Legislation is powerless to eradicate racial instincts, or to abolish distinctions based upon physical differences, and the attempt to do so can only result in accentuating the difficulties of the present situation. * * *

Affirmed.

MR. JUSTICE BREWER did [not] participate in the decision of this case.

MR. JUSTICE HARLAN dissenting.

[No] legislative body or judicial tribunal may have regard to the race of citizens when the civil rights of those citizens are involved. * * *

It was said in argument that the statute of Louisiana does not discriminate against either race, but prescribes a rule applicable alike to white and colored citizens. But [e]very one knows that [it] had its origin in the purpose, not so much to exclude white persons from railroad cars occupied by blacks, as to exclude colored people from coaches occupied by or assigned to white persons. [The] fundamental objection, therefore, to the statute, is that it interferes with the personal freedom of citizens. * * *

The white race deems itself to be the dominant race in this country. And so it is, in prestige, in achievements, in education, in wealth, and in power. So, I doubt not, it will continue to be for all time, if it remains true to its great heritage, and holds fast to the principles of constitutional liberty. But in view of the constitution, in the eye of the law, there is in this country no superior, dominant, ruling class of citizens. There is no caste here. Our constitution is color-blind * * *.

In my opinion, the judgment this day rendered will, in time, prove to be quite as pernicious as the decision made by this tribunal in the *Dred Scott Case* [that] the descendants of Africans who were imported into this country, and sold as slaves, were not included nor intended to be included under the word "citizens" in the constitution; [that,] at the time of the adoption of the constitution, they were "considered as a subordinate and inferior class of beings, who had been subjugated by the dominant race, and, whether emancipated or not, yet remained subject to their authority, and had no rights or privileges but such as those who held the power and the government might choose to grant them." 19 How. 393, 404. The recent amendments of the constitution, it was supposed, had eradicated these principles from our institutions. [What] can more certainly arouse race hate, what more certainly create and perpetuate a feeling of distrust between these races, than state enactments which, in fact, proceed on the ground that colored citizens are so inferior and degraded that they cannot be allowed to sit in public coaches occupied by white citizens? [The] thin disguise of "equal" accommodations for passengers in railroad coaches will not mislead any one, nor atone for the wrong this day done. * * *

I do not deem it necessary to review the decisions of state courts to which reference was made in argument. Some [are] inapplicable, because rendered prior to the adoption of the last amendments of the [constitution]. Others were made at a time [when] race prejudice was, practically, the supreme law of the land. Those decisions cannot be guides in the era introduced by the recent amendments of the supreme law, which established universal civil freedom * * *.

BROWN v. BOARD OF EDUCATION
347 U.S. 483, 74 S.Ct. 686, 98 L.Ed. 873 (1954).

MR. CHIEF JUSTICE WARREN delivered the opinion of the Court.

These cases come to us from the States of Kansas, South Carolina, Virginia, and Delaware. * * *

In each of the cases, minors of the Negro race [seek] the aid of the courts in obtaining admission to the public schools of their community on a nonsegregated basis. [In] each of the cases other than the Delaware case, a three-judge federal district court denied relief to the plaintiffs on the so-called "separate but equal" doctrine announced by this Court in [*Plessy*]. In the Delaware case, the Supreme Court of Delaware adhered to that doctrine, but ordered that the plaintiffs be admitted to the white schools because of their superiority to the Negro schools.

* * * Argument was heard in the 1952 Term, and reargument was heard this Term on certain questions propounded by the Court.

Reargument was largely devoted to the circumstances surrounding the adoption of the Fourteenth Amendment in 1868. It covered exhaustively consideration of the Amendment in Congress, ratification by the states, then existing practices in racial segregation, and the views of proponents and opponents of the Amendment. This discussion and our own investigation convince us that, although these sources cast some light, it is not enough to resolve the problem with which we are faced. At best, they are inconclusive. The most avid proponents of the post-War Amendments undoubtedly intended them to remove all legal distinctions among "all persons born or naturalized in the United States." Their opponents, just as certainly, were antagonistic to both the letter and the spirit of the Amendments and wished them to have the most limited effect. What others in Congress and the state legislatures had in mind cannot be determined with any degree of certainty.

An additional reason for the inconclusive nature of the Amendment's history, with respect to segregated schools, is the status of public education at that time. In the South, the movement toward free common schools, supported by general taxation, had not yet taken hold. Education of white children was largely in the hands of private groups. Education of Negroes was almost nonexistent, and practically all of the race were illiterate. In fact, any education of Negroes was forbidden by law in some states. Today, in contrast, many Negroes have achieved outstanding success in the arts and sciences as well as in the business and professional world. It is true that public school education at the time of the Amendment had advanced further in the North, but the effect of the Amendment on Northern States was generally ignored in the congressional debates. Even in the North, the conditions of public education did not approximate those existing today. The curriculum was usually rudimentary; ungraded schools were common in rural areas; the school term was but three months a year in many states; and compulsory school attendance was virtually unknown. As a consequence, it is not surprising that there should be so little in the history of the Fourteenth Amendment relating to its intended effect on public education.

In the first cases in this Court construing the Fourteenth Amendment, decided shortly after its adoption, the Court interpreted it as proscribing all state-imposed discriminations against the Negro race.[5] The doctrine of "separate but equal" did not make its appearance in this Court until 1896 in *Plessy*, involving not education but transportation. [In] this Court, there have been six cases involving the "separate but equal" doctrine in the field of public education. In *Cumming v. Board of Education*, 175 U.S. 528, 20 S.Ct. 197, 44 L.Ed. 262, and *Gong Lum v. Rice*, 275 U.S. 78, 48 S.Ct. 91, 72 L.Ed. 172, the validity of the doctrine itself was not challenged.[8] In more recent cases, all on the graduate school level, inequality was found in that specific benefits enjoyed by white students were denied to Negro students of the same educational qualifications.

---

5. *Slaughter-House Cases; Strauder* * * *. See also *Virginia v. Rives*, 1879, 100 U.S. 313, 318, 25 L.Ed. 667; *Ex parte Virginia*, 1879, 100 U.S. 339, 344–345, 25 L.Ed. 676. [See generally Brief for the Committee of Law Teachers Against Segregation in Legal Education, *Segregation and the Equal Protection Clause*, 34 Minn.L.Rev. 289 (1950).]

8. In *Cumming*, Negro taxpayers sought an injunction requiring the defendant school board to discontinue the operation of a high school for white children until the board resumed operation of a high school for Negro children. Similarly, in *Gong Lum*, the plaintiff, a child of Chinese descent, contended only that state authorities had misapplied the doctrine by classifying him with Negro children and requiring him to attend a Negro school.

Missouri ex rel. Gaines v. Canada, 305 U.S. 337, 59 S.Ct. 232, 83 L.Ed. 208 [a]; *Sipuel v. Oklahoma,* 332 U.S. 631, 68 S.Ct. 299, 92 L.Ed. 247; *Sweatt v. Painter,* 339 U.S. 629, 70 S.Ct. 848, 94 L.Ed. 1114 [b]; *McLaurin v. Oklahoma State Regents,* 339 U.S. 637, 70 S.Ct. 851, 94 L.Ed. 1149.[c] In none of these cases was it necessary to re-examine the doctrine to grant relief to the Negro plaintiff. And in *Sweatt,* the Court expressly reserved decision on the question whether *Plessy* should be held inapplicable to public education.

In the instant cases, that question is directly presented. [T]here are findings below that the Negro and white schools involved have been equalized, or are being equalized, with respect to buildings, curricula, qualifications and salaries of teachers, and other "tangible" factors. Our decision, therefore, cannot turn on merely a comparison of these tangible factors in the Negro and white schools involved in each of the cases. We must look instead to the effect of segregation itself on public education.

In approaching this problem, we cannot turn the clock back to 1868 when the Amendment was adopted, or even to 1896 when *Plessy* was written. We must consider public education in the light of its full development and its present place in American life throughout the Nation. Only in this way can it be determined if segregation in public schools deprives these plaintiffs of the equal protection of the laws.

Today, education is perhaps the most important function of state and local governments. Compulsory school attendance laws and the great expenditures for education both demonstrate our recognition of the importance of education to our democratic society. It is required in the performance of our most basic public responsibilities, even service in the armed forces. It is the very foundation of good citizenship. Today it is a principal instrument in awakening the child to cultural values, in preparing him for later professional training, and in helping him to adjust normally to his environment. In these days, it is doubtful that any child may reasonably be expected to succeed in life if he is denied the opportunity of an education. Such an opportunity, where the state has undertaken to provide it, is a right which must be made available to all on equal terms.

a. *Gaines,* in 1938, invalidated the refusal to admit blacks to the University of Missouri School of Law, despite the state's offer to pay petitioner's tuition at an out-of-state law school pending establishment of a state law school for blacks.

b. *Sweatt,* in 1950, required admission of blacks to the University of Texas Law School despite the recent establishment of a state law school for blacks: "In terms of number of the faculty, variety of courses and opportunity for specialization, size of the student body, scope of the library, availability of law review and similar activities, the University of Texas Law School is superior. What is more important, the University of Texas Law School possesses to a far greater degree those qualities which are incapable of objective measurement but which make for greatness in a law school. Such qualities, to name but a few, include reputation of the faculty, experience of the administration, position and influence of the alumni, standing in the community, traditions and prestige. [Moreover, the law school] cannot be effective in isolation from the individuals and institutions with which the law interacts. Few students and no one who has practiced law would choose to study in an academic vacuum, removed from the interplay of ideas and the exchange of views with which the law is concerned. The law school to which Texas is willing to admit petitioner excludes from its student body members of the racial groups which number 85% of the population of the State and include most of the lawyers, witnesses, jurors, judges and other officials with whom petitioner will inevitably be dealing when he becomes a member of the Texas Bar."

c. *McLaurin,* in 1950, held violative of equal protection requirements that black graduate students at the University of Oklahoma sit at separate desks adjoining the classrooms and separate tables outside the library reading room, and eat at separate times in the school cafeteria.

We come then to the question presented: Does segregation of children in public schools solely on the basis of race, even though the physical facilities and other "tangible" factors may be equal, deprive the children of the minority group of equal educational opportunities? We believe that it does.

In *Sweatt,* in finding that a segregated law school for Negroes could not provide them equal educational opportunities, this Court relied in large part on "those qualities which are incapable of objective measurement but which make for greatness in a law school." In *McLaurin,* the Court, in requiring that a Negro admitted to a white graduate school be treated like all other students, again resorted to intangible considerations: "[his] ability to study, to engage in discussions and exchange views with other students, and in general, to learn his profession." Such considerations apply with added force to children in grade and high schools. To separate them from others of similar age and qualifications solely because of their race generates a feeling of inferiority as to their status in the community that may affect their hearts and minds in a way unlikely ever to be undone. The effect of this separation on their educational opportunities was well stated by a finding in the Kansas case by a court which nevertheless felt compelled to rule against the Negro plaintiffs: "Segregation of white and colored children in public schools has a detrimental effect upon the colored children. The impact is greater when it has the sanction of the law; for the policy of separating the races is usually interpreted as denoting the inferiority of the Negro group. A sense of inferiority affects the motivation of a child to learn. Segregation with the sanction of law, therefore, has a tendency to [retard] the educational and mental development of Negro children and to deprive them of some of the benefits they would receive in a racial[ly] integrated school system." [10] Whatever may have been the extent of psychological knowledge at the time of *Plessy,* this finding is amply supported by modern authority.[11] Any language in *Plessy* contrary to this finding is rejected.

We conclude that in the field of public education the doctrine of "separate but equal" has no place. Separate educational facilities are inherently unequal. Therefore, we hold that the plaintiffs and others similarly situated for whom the actions have been brought are, by reason of the segregation complained of, deprived of [equal protection].

Because these are class actions, because of the wide applicability of this decision, and because of the great variety of local conditions, the formulation of decrees in these cases presents problems of considerable complexity. On reargument, the consideration of appropriate relief was necessarily subordinated to the primary question—the constitutionality of segregation in public education. We have now announced that such segregation is a denial of the equal protection of the laws. In order that we may have the full assistance of the parties in formulating decrees, the cases will be restored to the docket, and the parties are

10. A similar finding was made in the Delaware case: "I conclude from the testimony that in our Delaware society, State-imposed segregation in education itself results in the Negro children, as a class, receiving educational opportunities which are substantially inferior to those available to white children otherwise similarly situated."

11. Clark, *Effect of Prejudice and Discrimination on Personality Development* (Midcentury White House Conference on Children and Youth, 1950); Witmer and Kotinsky, *Personal-* *ity in the Making* (1952), c. VI; Deutscher and Chein, *The Psychological Effects of Enforced Segregation: A Survey of Social Science Opinion,* 26 J.Psychol. 259 (1948); Chein, *What are the Psychological Effects of Segregation Under Conditions of Equal Facilities?,* 3 Int.J. Opinion and Attitude Res. 229 (1949); Brameld, *Educational Costs in Discrimination and National Welfare* (MacIver, ed., 1949), 44–48; Frazier, *The Negro in the United States* (1949), 674–681. And, see generally Myrdal, *An American Dilemma* (1944).

requested to present further argument on Questions 4 and 5 previously propounded by the Court for the reargument this Term.[13] The Attorney General of the United States is again invited to participate. The Attorney General of the states requiring or permitting segregation in public education will also be permitted to appear * * *.

Notes and Questions

1. *The Court's rationale.* What was the specific basis for the decision?

(a) *Social science materials.* At trial in several of the cases, psychiatrists and social scientists testified as to the harmful effects of state-imposed segregation on black children. On appeal, appellants filed a statement to this effect by 32 sociologists, anthropologists, psychologists, and psychiatrists who worked in the area of American race relations—reprinted in 37 Minn.L.Rev. 427 (1953).

Was the decision based on this information? Is this desirable? Should *Brown* be modified or overruled if new social science data reaches different conclusions?

(b) Does *Brown* rest on a finding that "in terms of the most familiar and universally accepted standards of right and wrong [racial] segregation under government auspices inevitably inflicts humiliation, [and] official humiliation of innocent, law-abiding citizens is psychologically injurious and morally evil"? Cahn, *Jurisprudence*, 30 N.Y.U.L. Rev. 150, 159 (1955). If so, where are such "universally accepted standards" found? See Dworkin, *Social Sciences and Constitutional Rights—The Consequences of Uncertainty,* 6 J.L. & Ed. 3 (1977).

(c) *Historical considerations.* (i) Would it have been better for the Court to rely upon the original purpose of the fourteenth amendment as stated in *Strauder:* to grant blacks "the right to exemption from unfriendly legislation against them as distinctively colored"? If so, how should *Plessy* have been treated? Was the *Brown* Court in 1954 a better judge of fourteenth amendment intent than the *Plessy* Court in 1896? Than the *Strauder* Court in 1879?

(ii) Apart from the specific intentions of the framers and ratifiers of the fourteenth amendment in respect to school segregation, of what significance is the fact that "every one of the twenty-six states that had any substantial racial differences among its people either approved the operation of segregated schools already in existence or subsequently established such schools by action of the same law-making body which considered the Fourteenth Amendment"? *Declaration of Constitutional Principles Issued by 19 Senators and 77 Representatives*

---

13. "4. Assuming it is decided that segregation in public schools violates the Fourteenth Amendment

"(a) would a decree necessarily follow providing that, within the limits set by normal geographic school districting, Negro children should forthwith be admitted to schools of their choice, or

"(b) may this Court, in the exercise of its equity powers, permit an effective gradual adjustment to be brought about from existing segregated systems to a system not based on color distinctions?

"5. On the assumption on which questions 4(a) and (b) are based, and assuming further that this Court will exercise its equity powers to the end described in question 4(b),

"(a) should this Court formulate detailed decrees in these cases;

"(b) if so, what specific issues should the decrees reach;

"(c) should this Court appoint a special master to hear evidence with a view to recommending specific terms for such decrees;

"(d) should this Court remand to the courts of first instance with directions to frame decrees in these cases, and if so what general directions should the decrees of this Court include and what procedures should the courts of first instance follow in arriving at the specific terms of more detailed decrees?"

of the Congress, N.Y. Times, p. 19, col. 2, March 12, 1956. What justified the Court's consideration of "public education in the light of its full development and its present place in American life throughout the Nation"? Consider Bickel, *The Original Understanding and the Segregation Decision*, 69 Harv.L.Rev. 1, 59 (1955): "If the fourteenth amendment were a statute, a court might very well hold [that] it was foreclosed from applying it to segregation in public schools. [But] we are dealing with a constitutional amendment, not a statute. The tradition of a broadly worded organic law not frequently or lightly amended was well-established by 1866, and [it] cannot be assumed that [anyone] expected or wished the future role of the Constitution in the scheme of American government to differ from the past. Should not the search for congressional purpose therefore, properly be twofold? One inquiry should be directed at the congressional understanding of the immediate effect of the enactment on conditions then present. Another should aim to discover what if any thought was given to the long-range effect, under future circumstances, of provisions necessarily intended for permanence."

2. *"Neutral principles."* Consider Wechsler, *Toward Neutral Principles of Constitutional Law*, 73 Harv.L.Rev. 1, 34 (1959): "[A]ssuming equal facilities, the question posed by state-enforced segregation is not one of discrimination at all. Its human and its constitutional dimensions lie [in] the denial by the state of freedom to associate, a denial that impinges in the same way on any groups or races that may be involved. [But] if the freedom of association is denied by segregation, integration forces an association upon those for whom it is unpleasant or repugnant. [W]here the state must practically choose between denying the association to those individuals who wish it or imposing it on those who would avoid it, is there a basis in neutral principles for holding that the Constitution demands that the claims for association should prevail?"

In reply, consider the following from a "draft opinion" of *Brown* by Pollak, *Racial Discrimination and Judicial Integrity: A Reply to Professor Wechsler*, 108 U.Pa.L.Rev. 1, 27, 29–30 (1959): "[W]e start from the base point that in the United States 'all legal restrictions which curtail the civil rights of a single racial group are immediately suspect.' *Korematsu.* [T]here is special need for 'a searching judicial inquiry into the legislative judgment in situations where prejudice against discrete and insular minorities may tend to curtail the operation of those political processes ordinarily to be relied on to protect minorities.' See *United States v. Carolene Products*, n. 4 [p. 23 supra]. We could not, therefore, sustain the reasonableness of these racial distinctions and the absence of harm said to flow from them, unless we were prepared to say that no factual case can be made the other way. [To] the extent that implementation of this decision forces racial mingling on school children against their will, [this] consequence follows because the community through its political processes has [chosen] compulsory education. [The resulting] coerced association [cannot] be said to emanate from this Court or from the Constitution. In any event, parents sufficiently disturbed at the prospect of having their children educated in democratic fashion in company with their peers are presumably entitled to fulfill their educational responsibilities in other ways."

See also Black, *The Lawfulness of the Segregation Decisions*, 69 Yale L.J. 421, 429 (1960): "The fourteenth amendment [forbids] disadvantaging the Negro race by law. It was surely anticipated that the following of this directive would entail some disagreeableness for some white southerners. [When] the directive of equality cannot be followed without displeasing the white, then something that can be called a 'freedom' of the white must be impaired. If the fourteenth amendment commands equality, and if segregation violates equality, then the status of the reciprocal 'freedom' is automatically settled." [f]

3. *Extent of the decision.* (a) Did *Brown* bar all forms of state-imposed racial segregation? Or did it apply only to public schools?

(b) After *Brown,* the Court, by means of rather summary per curiam decisions, citing *Brown,* consistently held invalid state imposed racial segregation in other public facilities.

4. *Segregation by the federal government.* BOLLING v. SHARPE, 347 U.S. 497, 74 S.Ct. 693, 98 L.Ed. 884 (1954), per WARREN, C.J., held—on the same day as *Brown*—that public school segregation in the District of Columbia "constitutes an arbitrary deprivation [of] liberty in violation of the Due Process Clause" of the fifth amendment: "The Fifth Amendment [does] not contain an equal protection clause as does the Fourteenth Amendment which applies only to the states. But the concepts of equal protection and due process, both stemming from our American ideal of fairness, are not mutually exclusive. The 'equal protection of the laws' is a more explicit safeguard of prohibited unfairness than 'due process of law,' and, therefore, we do not imply that the two are always interchangeable phrases. But, as this Court has recognized, discrimination may be so unjustifiable as to be violative of due process.

"Classifications based solely upon race must be scrutinized with particular care, since they are contrary to our traditions and hence constitutionally suspect. ["Liberty"] extends to the full range of conduct which the individual is free to pursue, and it cannot be restricted except for a proper governmental objective. Segregation in public education is not reasonably related to any proper governmental objective * * *.

"In view of our decision that the Constitution prohibits the states from maintaining racially segregated public schools, it would be unthinkable that the same Constitution would impose a lesser duty on the Federal Government." [h]

BROWN v. BOARD OF EDUCATION
349 U.S. 294, 75 S.Ct. 753, 99 L.Ed. 1083 (1955).

MR. CHIEF JUSTICE WARREN delivered the opinion of the Court.

These cases were decided on May 17, 1954. [There] remains for consideration the manner in which relief is to be accorded. * * *

Full implementation of these constitutional principles may require solution of varied local school problems. School authorities have the primary responsibility for elucidating, assessing, and solving [them]; courts will have to consider whether the action of school authorities constitutes good faith implementation of the governing constitutional principles. Because of their proximity to local conditions and the possible need for further hearings, the courts which originally heard these cases can best perform this judicial appraisal. Accordingly, we believe it appropriate to remand the cases to those courts.

In fashioning and effectuating the decrees, the courts will be guided by equitable principles. Traditionally, equity has been characterized by a practical flexibility in shaping its remedies and by a facility for adjusting and reconciling

---

f. For the view that "the decision in *Brown* to break with the Court's long-held position on [segregation] cannot be understood without some consideration of the decision's value to whites [in] policymaking positions able to see the economic and political advances at home and abroad that would follow abandonment of segregation," see Bell, *Brown v. Board of Education and the Interest-Convergence Dilemma,* 93 Harv.L.Rev. 518 (1980).

h. See fn. a, p. 872 supra.

public and private needs. [A]t stake is the personal interest of the plaintiffs in admission to public schools as soon as practicable on a nondiscriminatory basis. To effectuate this interest may call for elimination of a variety of obstacles in making the transition to school systems operated in accordance with the constitutional principles set forth in our May 17, 1954, decision. Courts of equity may properly take into account the public interest in the elimination of such obstacles in a systematic and effective manner. But it should go without saying that the vitality of these constitutional principles cannot be allowed to yield simply because of disagreement with them.

While giving weight to these public and private considerations, the courts will require that the defendants make a prompt and reasonable start toward full compliance with our May 17, 1954, ruling. Once such a start has been made, the courts may find that additional time is necessary to carry out the ruling in an effective manner. The burden rests upon the defendants to establish that such time is necessary in the public interest and is consistent with good faith compliance at the earliest practicable date. To that end, the courts may consider problems related to administration, arising from the physical condition of the school plant, the school transportation system, personnel, revision of school districts and attendance areas into compact units to achieve a system of determining admission to the public schools on a nonracial basis, and revision of local laws and regulations which may be necessary in solving the foregoing problems. They will also consider the adequacy of any plans the defendants may propose to meet these problems and to effectuate a transition to a racially nondiscriminatory school system. During this period of transition, the courts will retain jurisdiction of these cases.

The [cases are remanded] to take such proceedings and enter such orders and decrees consistent with this opinion as are necessary and proper to admit to public schools on a racially nondiscriminatory basis with all deliberate speed the parties to these cases. * * *

Notes and Questions

1. *"Individual" vs. "race" rights.* Was the decree consistent with *Brown I?* Since plaintiffs had only a limited number of years of school remaining, did postponement of relief partially or totally destroy the very rights the decree was intended to enforce? Does the "deliberate speed" formula assume that "Negroes (unlike whites) possess rights as a race rather than as individuals, so that a particular Negro can rightly be delayed in the enjoyment of his established rights if progress is being made in improving the legal status of Negroes generally"? Lusky, *The Stereotype: Hard Core of Racism,* 13 Buf.L.Rev. 450, 457 (1963). See also Carter, *The Warren Court and Desegregation,* 67 Mich.L.Rev. 237, 243 (1968). To what extent may the "deliberate speed" decree "have served the interests of blacks even while it accommodated the opposition of whites"? Gewirtz, *Remedies and Resistance,* 92 Yale L.J. 585, 609–28 (1983).

2. *"Deliberate speed" and the slow pace of desegregation.* What of Black, J.'s view that this formula "delayed the process of outlawing segregation" and that it would have been preferable to treat *Brown* "as an ordinary law suit and force that judgment on the counties it affected that minute"? Transcript, *Justice Black and the Bill of Rights,* CBS News Special, Dec. 3, 1968. Should the Court have relied on social science data that "prompt, decisive action on the part of recognized authorities usually results in less anxiety and less resistance in cases where the public is opposed to the action than does a more hesitant and

gradual procedure"? Clark, *Introduction to Argument: The Complete Oral Argument in Brown, 1952–55,* xxxiii (Friedman ed. 1969). Compare Graglia, *The Brown Cases Revisited: Where Are They Now?,* 1 Benchmark 23, 27 (Mar.–Apr. 1984): "There can be little doubt that if the Court had ordered the end of segregation in 1954 or 1955 the result would have been the closing of public schools in much of the South, about which the Court could have done nothing. The principal impact would have been on poor blacks, and *Brown* could have come to be seen as a blunder and symbol of judicial impotence." [b]

LOVING v. VIRGINIA, 388 U.S. 1, 87 S.Ct. 1817, 18 L.Ed.2d 1010 (1967), invalidated the state antimiscegenation statute prohibiting "interracial marriages involving white persons." The Court, per WARREN, C.J., rejected the contention—allegedly supported by legislative debate at the time of the fourteenth amendment's adoption—that equal protection requires "only that state penal laws containing an interracial element as part of the definition of the offense must equally apply to whites and Negroes in the sense that members of each race are punished to the same degree." That factor "does not immunize the statute from the very heavy burden of justification which the Fourteenth Amendment has traditionally required of state statutes drawn according to race."

Pace v. Alabama, 106 U.S. 583, 1 S.Ct. 637, 27 L.Ed. 207 (1883), upholding imposition of special penalties on interracial adultery or fornication, had been repudiated in *McLaughlin v. Florida,* 379 U.S. 184, 85 S.Ct. 283, 13 L.Ed.2d 222 (1964), invalidating a law making interracial cohabitation a special offense. "At the very least, the Equal Protection Clause demands that racial classifications, especially suspect in criminal statutes be subjected to the 'most rigid scrutiny,' and, if they are ever to be upheld they must be shown to be necessary to the accomplishment of some permissible state objective, independent of the racial discrimination which it was the object of the Fourteenth Amendment to eliminate." [c] The Virginia statute was "obviously an endorsement of White Supremacy," and "even assuming an even-handed state purpose to protect the 'integrity' of all races," "there is patently no legitimate overriding purpose independent of invidious racial discrimination which justifies this classification."

Finally, to deny the "fundamental freedom" of marriage "on so unsupportable a basis as the racial classifications embodied in these statutes" deprives "all the State's citizens of liberty without due process."

STEWART, J., concurred on the basis of his view in *McLaughlin* (there joined by Douglas, J.) that "it is simply not possible for a state law to be valid under our Constitution which makes the criminality of an act depend upon the race of the actor."

Notes and Questions

1. *Standard of review.* Is the constitutional test for laws that *classify* by race or ethnicity different from that for laws that *discriminate* against racial or

---

b. The developments in implementing *Brown* are considered in Part IV, A infra.

c. *McLaughlin* also stated that racial classifications were " 'in most circumstances irrelevant' to any constitutionally acceptable legislative purpose." Harlan, J., concurring, added that "necessity, not mere reasonable relationship, is the proper test"; this "test which developed to protect free speech against state infringement should be equally applicable in a case involving state racial discrimination—prohibition of which lies at the very heart of the Fourteenth Amendment."

ethnic minorities? Does *Loving* require only that the state purpose be "permissible" in contrast to *Korematsu's* requirement of "pressing public necessity"? Is *Loving's* seemingly more deferential test attributable to the fact that the antimiscegenation law "punished members of each race to the same degree"? See 2 Dorsen, Bender, Neuborne & Law, *Political and Civil Rights in the United States* 82–85 (Law School ed., 4th ed. 1979). Compare *In re Griffiths,* Sec. 3, II infra: "In order to justify the use of a suspect classification, a State must show that its purpose or interest is both constitutionally permissible [8] and substantial,[9] and that its use of the classification is 'necessary to the accomplishment' of its purpose or the safeguarding of its interest."

2. *Racial information.* ANDERSON v. MARTIN, 375 U.S. 399, 84 S.Ct. 454, 11 L.Ed.2d 430 (1964), held violative of equal protection a statute requiring that the race of candidates for elective office be on the ballot: "The vice lies [in] the placing of the power of the State behind a racial classification that induces racial prejudice at the polls." Should the result turn on whether a black candidate is likely to receive more or less votes because of race being designated? On whether the statute contributes to a more informed electorate? See Comments, 15 Stan.L.Rev. 339 (1963); 111 U.Pa.L.Rev. 827 (1963). May a state collect racial statistics within school districts to effectuate a policy of integration? May a national census include racial information? May a state, for statistical purposes, require designation of the parties' race on every divorce decree? See *Tancil v. Woolls,* 379 U.S. 19, 85 S.Ct. 157, 13 L.Ed.2d 91 (1964).

3. *Family issues.* PALMORE v. SIDOTI, 466 U.S. 429, 104 S.Ct. 1879, 80 L.Ed.2d 421 (1984), per BURGER, C.J., held that Florida's denial of child custody to a white mother because her new husband was black violated equal protection: "There is a risk that a child living with a step-parent of a different race may be subject to a variety of pressures and stresses not present if the child were living with parents of the same racial or ethnic origin. [But the] effects of racial prejudice, however real, cannot justify a racial classification removing an infant child from the custody of its natural mother found to be an appropriate person to have such custody."

4. *Law enforcement issues.* May a police department assign all black officers to black residential areas and all white officers to white residential areas? May it *ever* consider race in determining assignment? May prison officials take racial tensions among prisoners into account in maintaining security, discipline, or good order? Cf. *Lee v. Washington,* 390 U.S. 333, 88 S.Ct. 994, 19 L.Ed.2d 1212 (1968).

III. DE JURE VS. DE FACTO DISCRIMINATION

Part I involved laws that explicitly discriminated against racial and ethnic minorities. But intentional (or "de jure") discrimination may exist even though the law in question is racially "neutral" on its face: the law may be deliberately administered in a discriminatory way; or a law, although neutral in its language and applied in accordance with its terms, may have been enacted with a purpose (or motive) to disadvantage a "suspect" class. This section concerns these additional types of "de jure" discrimination as well as government action that is

---

8. Discrimination or segregation for its own sake is not, of course, a constitutionally permissible purpose.

9. The state interest required has been characterized as "overriding," *Loving,* "compelling," *Graham v. Richardson* [Sec. 3, II infra], "important," *Dunn v. Blumstein,* [Sec. 4, II infra], or "substantial," ibid. We attribute no particular significance to these variations in diction.

racially neutral in its terms, administration, and purpose but which has a discriminatory effect or impact ("de facto" discrimination).

YICK WO v. HOPKINS, 118 U.S. 356, 6 S.Ct. 1064, 30 L.Ed. 220 (1886): A San Francisco ordinance made it unlawful to operate a laundry without the consent of the board of supervisors except in a brick or stone building. Yick Wo, a Chinese alien who had operated a laundry for 22 years, had certificates from the health and fire authorities, but was refused consent by the board. For violating the ordinance, he was fined $10 and jailed for nonpayment. It was admitted that "there were about 320 laundries in the city [and] about 240 were owned [by] subjects of China, and of the whole number, viz., 320, about 310 were constructed of wood"; that "petitioner, and more than 150 of his countrymen, have been arrested" for violating the ordinance "while those who are not subjects of China, and who are conducting 80 odd laundries under similar conditions, are left unmolested."

A unanimous Court reversed: "Though the law itself be fair on its face, [if] it is applied and administered by public authority with an evil eye and an unequal hand, [the] denial of equal justice is still within the prohibition of the constitution. [The] fact of this discrimination is admitted. No reason for it is shown, and the conclusion cannot be resisted that no reason for it exists except hostility to [Yick Wo's] race and nationality."

Notes and Questions

Proving intentional discrimination. (a) *Jury selection.* In CASTANEDA v. PARTIDA, 430 U.S. 482, 97 S.Ct. 1272, 51 L.Ed.2d 498 (1977), respondent challenged the grand jury that indicted him in 1972. He showed that, although 79% of the county's population had Spanish surnames, the average percentage of Spanish-surnamed grand jurors between 1962–72 was 39%. In 1972, 52.5% of persons on the grand jury list had Spanish surnames as did 50% of those on respondent's grand jury list. The Court, per BLACKMUN, J., held that respondent had established a prima facie case of discrimination against Mexican-Americans: [a]

"While the earlier cases involved absolute exclusion of an identifiable group, later cases established the principle that substantial underrepresentation of the group constitutes a constitutional violation as well, if it results from purposeful discrimination. [T]he degree of underrepresentation must be proved, by comparing the proportion of the group in the total population to the proportion called to serve as grand jurors, over a significant period of time.[13] [A] selection procedure that is susceptible of abuse or is not racially neutral supports the presumption of discrimination raised by the statistical showing.[b] Once the defendant has shown substantial underrepresentation of his group, he has made out a prima facie case

---

a. Burger, C.J., and Stewart, Powell and Rehnquist, JJ., dissented.

13. [If] a disparity is sufficiently large, then it is unlikely that it is due solely to chance or accident, and, in the absence of evidence to the contrary, one must conclude that racial or other class-related factors entered into the selection process.

b. The Court observed that, "as in *Alexander v. Louisiana,* 405 U.S. 625, 92 S.Ct. 1221,

31 L.Ed.2d 536 (1972), the selection procedure [here] is not racially neutral with respect to Mexican-Americans; Spanish surnames are just as easily identifiable as race was from the questionnaires in *Alexander* or the notations and card colors in *Whitus v. Georgia,* 385 U.S. 545, 87 S.Ct. 643, 17 L.Ed.2d 599 (1967)."

of discriminatory purpose, and the burden then shifts to the State to rebut that case."

Should the state's proof that a majority of the jury commissioners were Mexican-American rebut the prima facie case? A majority of elected officials in the county? See *Castaneda.*

(b) *Executive appointments.* In MAYOR OF PHILA. v. EDUCATIONAL EQUALITY LEAGUE, 415 U.S. 605, 94 S.Ct. 1323, 39 L.Ed.2d 630 (1974), respondents contended that in 1971 the mayor had racially discriminated in appointments to the city's Nominating Panel which nominated school board members. Under the city charter, the Panel had thirteen persons—four appointed from the citizenry at large and the others being the highest-ranking officers of nine city-wide organizations (e.g., labor union council, commerce group, parent-teacher association, etc.). Approximately "34% of the population of Philadelphia and approximately 60% of the students attending the city's various schools were Negroes" but "the 1971 Panel had 11 whites and two Negroes."

The Court, per POWELL, J., held the proof "too fragmentary and speculative" to establish "a prima facie case of racial discrimination." The statistics were "simplistic percentage comparisons [in] the context of this case"; because of the designated qualifications for Panel members, it could not "be assumed that all citizens are fungible for purposes of determining whether members of a particular class have been unlawfully excluded." [d]

WASHINGTON v. DAVIS
426 U.S. 229, 96 S.Ct. 2040, 48 L.Ed.2d 597 (1976).

MR. JUSTICE WHITE delivered the opinion of the Court.

This case involves the validity of a qualifying test administered to applicants for positions as police officers in the District of Columbia. [T]he police recruit was required to satisfy certain physical and character standards, to be a high school graduate or its equivalent and to receive a grade of at least 40 out of 80 on "Test 21," which is "an examination that is used generally throughout the federal service," which "was developed by the Civil Service Commission, not the Police Department," and which was "designed to test verbal ability, vocabulary, reading and comprehension."

[Respondents'] evidence, the District Court said, warranted three conclusions: "(a) The number of black police officers, while substantial, is not proportionate to the population mix of the city. (b) A higher percentage of blacks fail the Test than whites. (c) The Test has not been validated to establish its reliability for measuring subsequent job performance." This showing was deemed sufficient to shift the burden of proof to the defendants [but] the court nevertheless concluded that on the undisputed facts [plaintiffs] were not entitled to relief. The District Court relied on several factors. Since August 1969, 44% of new police force recruits had been black; that figure also represented the proportion of blacks on the total force and was roughly equivalent to 20–29-year-old blacks in the 50-mile radius in which the recruiting efforts of the Police Department had been concentrated. It was undisputed that the Department had systematically and affirmatively sought to enroll black officers many of whom passed the test but failed to report for duty. The District Court rejected the

---

d. White, J., joined by Douglas, Brennan and Marshall, JJ., dissented.

assertion that Test 21 was culturally slanted to favor whites and was "satisfied that the undisputable facts prove the test to be reasonably and directly related to the requirements of the police recruit training program and that it is neither so designed nor operates to discriminate against otherwise qualified blacks." [The Court of Appeals held] that lack of discriminatory intent in designing and administering Test 21 was irrelevant; the critical fact was rather [that] four times as many [blacks] failed the test than did whites. This disproportionate impact [was] held sufficient to establish a constitutional violation, absent proof by petitioners that the test was an adequate measure of job performance in addition to being an indicator of probable success in the training program, a burden which the court ruled petitioners had failed to discharge. * * *

The central purpose of the Equal Protection Clause [is] the prevention of official conduct discriminating on the basis of race. [But] our cases have not embraced the proposition that a law or other official act, without regard to whether it reflects a racially discriminatory purpose, is unconstitutional *solely* because it has a racially disproportionate impact.

Almost 100 years ago, *Strauder* established that the exclusion of Negroes from grand and petit juries in criminal proceedings violated the Equal Protection Clause, but the fact that a particular jury or a series of juries does not statistically reflect the racial composition of the community does not in itself make out an invidious discrimination forbidden by the Clause. "A purpose to discriminate must be present which may be proven by systematic exclusion of eligible jurymen of the prescribed race or by an unequal application of the law to such an extent as to show intentional discrimination." * * *

The school desegregation cases have also adhered to the basic equal protection principle that the invidious quality of a law claimed to be racially discriminatory must ultimately be traced to a racially discriminatory purpose. That there are both predominantly black and predominantly white schools in a community is not alone violative of the Equal Protection Clause. The essential element ["differentiating] between de jure segregation and so-called de facto segregation [is] *purpose* or *intent* to segregate." *Keyes v. School Dist.,* [Part IV infra]. The Court has also recently rejected allegations of racial discrimination based solely on the statistically disproportionate racial impact of various provisions of the Social Security Act because "[t]he acceptance of appellants' constitutional theory would render suspect each difference in treatment among the grant classes, however lacking in racial motivation and however otherwise rational the treatment might be." *Jefferson v. Hackney,* 406 U.S. 535, 548, 92 S.Ct. 1724, 1732, 32 L.Ed.2d 285, 297 (1972).[a]

This is not to say that the necessary discriminatory racial purpose must be express or appear on the face of the statute, or that a law's disproportionate impact is irrelevant. [A] statute, otherwise neutral on its face, must not be applied so as invidiously to discriminate on the basis of race. *Yick Wo.* It is also clear from the cases dealing with racial discrimination in the selection of juries that [a] prima facie case of discriminatory purpose may be proved [by] the absence of Negroes on a particular jury combined with the failure of the jury commissioners to be informed of eligible Negro jurors in a community, or with racially non-neutral selection procedures. With a prima facie case made out,

---

a. *Jefferson* rejected the contention that Texas' system—of granting a lower percentage of need to AFDC welfare recipients than to other groups of welfare recipients—violated "equal protection because the proportion of AFDC recipients who are Black or Mexican-American is higher than the proportion of the aged, blind or disabled welfare recipients who fall within these minority groups."

"the burden of proof shifts to the State to rebut the presumption of unconstitutional action by showing that permissible racially neutral selection criteria and procedures have produced the monochromatic result."

Necessarily, an invidious discriminatory purpose may often be inferred from the totality of the relevant facts, including [that] the law bears more heavily on one race than another. It is also not infrequently true that the discriminatory impact—in the jury cases for example, the total or seriously disproportionate exclusion of Negroes from jury venires—may for all practical purposes demonstrate unconstitutionality because in various circumstances the discrimination is very difficult to explain on nonracial grounds. Nevertheless, we have not held that a law, neutral on its face and serving ends otherwise within the power of government to pursue, is invalid under the Equal Protection Clause simply because it may affect a greater proportion of one race than of another. Disproportionate impact [s]tanding alone [does] not trigger the rule that racial classifications are to be subjected to the strictest scrutiny and are justifiable only by the weightiest of considerations.

There are some indications to the contrary in our cases. In *Palmer v. Thompson*, 403 U.S. 217, 91 S.Ct. 1940, 29 L.Ed.2d 438 (1971), the city of Jackson, Miss., following a court decree to this effect, desegregated all of its public facilities save five swimming pools which [were] closed by ordinance pursuant to a determination by the city council that closure was necessary to preserve peace and order and that integrated pools could not be economically operated. [T]his Court rejected the argument that [the] otherwise seemingly permissible ends served by the ordinance could be impeached by demonstrating that racially invidious motivations had prompted the city council's action. [The] opinion warned against grounding decision on legislative purpose or motivation, thereby lending support for the proposition that the operative effect of the law rather than its purpose is the paramount factor. But [w]hatever dicta the opinion may contain, the decision did not involve, much less invalidate, a statute or ordinance having neutral purposes but disproportionate racial consequences.[11]

[Test 21] seeks to ascertain whether those who take it have acquired a particular level of verbal skill; and it is untenable that the Constitution prevents the government from seeking modestly to upgrade the communicative abilities of its employees rather than to be satisfied with some lower level of competence, particularly where the job requires special ability to communicate orally and in writing. Respondents, as Negroes, could no more successfully claim that the test denied them equal protection than could white applicants who also failed. The conclusion would not be different in the face of proof that more Negroes than whites had been disqualified by Test 21. * * *

Nor on the facts of the case before us would the disproportionate impact of Test 21 warrant the conclusion that it is a purposeful device to discriminate against Negroes * * *. [T]he test is neutral on its face and rationally may be said to serve a purpose the government is constitutionally empowered to pursue. Even agreeing with the District Court that the differential racial effect of Test 21 called for further inquiry, we think the District Court correctly held that the affirmative efforts of the Metropolitan Police Department to recruit black

---

11. To the extent that *Palmer* suggests a generally applicable proposition that legislative purpose is irrelevant in constitutional adjudication, our prior cases—as indicated in the text—are to the contrary; and very shortly after *Palmer*, all Members of the Court majority in that case [joined] *Lemon v. Kurtzman*, [p. 813 supra], [that] the validity of public aid to church-related schools includes close inquiry into the purpose of the challenged statute.

officers, the changing racial composition of the recruit classes and of the force in general, and the relationship of the test to the training program negated any inference that the Department discriminated on the basis of race * * *.

Under Title VII [of the Civil Rights Act of 1964], Congress provided that when hiring and promotion practices disqualifying substantially disproportionate numbers of blacks are challenged, discriminatory purpose need not be proved, and that it is an insufficient response to demonstrate some rational basis for the challenged practices. It is necessary, in addition, that they be "validated" in terms of job performance * * *. However this process proceeds, it involves a more probing judicial review of, and less deference to, the seemingly reasonable acts of administrators and executives than is appropriate under the Constitution where special racial impact, without discriminatory purpose, is claimed. We are not disposed to adopt this more rigorous standard for the purposes of applying the Fifth and the Fourteenth Amendments in cases such as this.

A rule that a statute designed to serve neutral ends is nevertheless invalid, absent compelling justification, if in practice it benefits or burdens one race more than another would be far-reaching and would raise serious questions about, and perhaps invalidate, a whole range of tax, welfare, public service, regulatory, and licensing statutes that may be more burdensome to the poor and to the average black than to the more affluent white.[14]

Given that rule, such consequences would perhaps be likely to follow. However, in our view, extension of the rule beyond those areas where it is already applicable by reason of statute, such as in the field of public employment, should await legislative prescription. * * *[c]

Mr. Justice Stevens [who joined the Court's opinion] concurring. * * *

Frequently the most probative evidence of intent will be objective evidence of what actually happened rather than evidence describing the subjective state of mind of the actor. For normally the actor is presumed to have intended the natural consequences of his deeds. This is particularly true in the case of governmental action which is frequently the product of compromise, of collective decisionmaking, and of mixed motivation. It is unrealistic, on the one hand, to require the victim of alleged discrimination to uncover the actual subjective intent of the decisionmaker or conversely, to invalidate otherwise legitimate action simply because an improper motive affected the deliberation of a participant in the decisional process. A law conscripting clerics should not be invalidated because an atheist voted for it.

My point [is] to suggest that the line between discriminatory purpose and discriminatory impact is not nearly as bright, and perhaps not quite as critical, as the reader of the Court's opinion might assume. I agree [that] a constitutional issue does not arise every time some disproportionate impact is shown. On the other hand, when the disproportion is as dramatic as in *Gomillion v.*

---

14. Goodman, *De Facto School Segregation: A Constitutional and Empirical Analysis,* 60 Calif.L.Rev. 275, 300 (1972), suggests that disproportionate-impact analysis might invalidate "tests and qualifications for voting, draft deferment, public employment, jury service, and other government-conferred [benefits]; [s]ales taxes, bail schedules, utility rates, bridge tolls, license fees, and other state-imposed charges." It has also been argued that minimum wage and usury laws as well as professional licensing requirements would require major modifications in light of the unequal-impact rule. Silverman, *Equal Protection, Economic Legislation, and Racial Discrimination,* 25 Vand.L.Rev. 1183 (1972). * * *

c. Brennan, J., joined by Marshall, J., did not address the constitutional questions but dissented on statutory grounds.

Lightfoot, 364 U.S. 339, 81 S.Ct. 125, 5 L.Ed.2d 110 (1960) [d] or *Yick Wo,* it really does not matter whether the standard is phrased in terms of purpose or effect. Therefore, although I accept the statement of the general rule in the Court's opinion, I am not yet prepared to indicate how that standard should be applied in the many cases which have formulated the governing standard in different language. * * *

ARLINGTON HEIGHTS v. METROPOLITAN HOUSING DEV. CORP., 429 U.S. 252, 97 S.Ct. 555, 50 L.Ed.2d 450 (1977), per POWELL, J.—holding that petitioner Village's refusal to rezone land from single-family (R–3) to multiple-family (R–5), so as to permit respondent MHDC's construction of racially integrated housing, did not violate equal protection—amplified *Davis:*

"Determining whether invidious discriminatory purpose was a motivating factor demands a sensitive inquiry into such circumstantial and direct evidence of intent as may be available.[12] The impact of the official action [may] provide an important starting point. Sometimes a clear pattern, unexplainable on grounds other than race, emerges from the effect of the state action even when the governing legislation appears neutral on its face. *Yick Wo; Guinn v. United States,* 238 U.S. 347, 35 S.Ct. 926, 59 L.Ed. 1340 (1915); *Lane v. Wilson,* 307 U.S. 268, 59 S.Ct. 872, 83 L.Ed. 1281 (1939); [a] *Gomillion.* The evidentiary inquiry is then relatively easy.[13] But such cases are rare. Absent a pattern as stark as that in *Gomillion* or *Yick Wo,* impact alone is not determinative,[14] and the Court must look to other evidence.[15]

"The historical background of the decision is one evidentiary source, particularly if it reveals a series of official actions taken for invidious purposes. See *Lane.* The specific sequence of events leading up to the challenged decision also may shed some light on the decision-maker's purposes. *Reitman v. Mulkey,* [p. 1113 infra]. For example, if the property involved here always had been zoned

---

d. In *Gomillion,* an Alabama statute changed the Tuskegee city boundaries from a square to a 28 sided figure, allegedly removing "all save only four or five of its 400 Negro voters while not removing a single white voter or resident." The Court held that the complaint "amply alleges a claim of racial discrimination" in violation of the fifteenth amendment. "If these allegations upon a trial remained uncontradicted or unqualified, the conclusion would be irresistible, tantamount for all practical purposes to a mathematical demonstration, that the legislation is solely concerned with segregating white and colored voters by fencing Negro citizens out of town so as to deprive them of their pre-existing municipal vote."

12. For a scholarly discussion of legislative motivation, see Brest, *Palmer v. Thompson: An Approach to The Problem of Unconstitutional Motive,* 1971 Sup.Ct. 95, 116–118. [Compare Ely, *Legislative and Administrative Motivation in Constitutional Law,* 79 Yale L.J. 1205 (1970).]

a. *Guinn* held that Oklahoma's literacy test for voting violated the fifteenth amendment because its "grandfather clause" effectively exempted whites. Oklahoma then im-

mediately enacted a new law providing that all persons who previously voted were qualified for life but that all others must register within a twelve day period or be permanently disenfranchised. *Lane* held that this new law violated the fifteenth amendment.

13. Several of our jury selection cases fall into this category. Because of the nature of the jury selection task, however, we have permitted a finding of constitutional violation even when the statistical pattern does not approach the extremes of *Yick Wo* or *Gomillion.*

14. This is not to say that a consistent pattern of official racial discrimination is a necessary predicate to a violation of [equal protection]. A single invidiously discriminatory governmental act—in the exercise of the zoning power as elsewhere—would not necessarily be immunized by the absence of such discrimination in the making of other comparable decisions.

15. In many instances, to recognize the limited probative value of disproportionate impact is merely to acknowledge the "heterogeneity" of the nation's population.

R–5 but suddenly was changed to R–3 when the town learned of MHDC's plans to erect integrated housing, we would have a far different case. Departures from the normal procedural sequence also might afford evidence that improper purposes are playing a role. Substantive departures too may be relevant, particularly if the factors usually considered important by the decisionmaker strongly favor a decision contrary to the one reached.

"The legislative or administrative history may be highly relevant, especially where there are contemporary statements by members of the decisionmaking body, minutes of its meetings, or reports. In some extraordinary instances the members might be called to the stand at trial to testify concerning the purpose of the official action, although even then such testimony frequently will be barred by privilege. See *Tenney v. Brandhove*, 341 U.S. 367, 71 S.Ct. 783, 95 L.Ed. 1019 (1951); *United States v. Nixon*, (p. 175 supra).[18]

"[This] summary identifies, without purporting to be exhaustive, subjects of proper inquiry in determining whether racially discriminatory intent existed."

Both courts below found that the rezoning denial was not racially motivated.

"We also have reviewed the evidence. The impact of the Village's decision does arguably bear more heavily on racial minorities. [But] there is little about the sequence of events leading up to the decision that would spark suspicion. The area [has] been zoned R–3 since 1959, the year when Arlington Heights first adopted a zoning map. Single-family homes surround the 80-acre site, and the Village is undeniably committed to single-family homes as its dominant residential land use. The rezoning request progressed according to the usual procedures. * * *

"The statements by the Plan Commission and Village Board members, as reflected in the official minutes, focused almost exclusively on the zoning aspects of the MHDC petition, and the zoning factors on which they relied are not novel criteria in the Village's rezoning decisions. There is no reason to doubt that there has been reliance by some neighboring property owners on the maintenance of single-family zoning in the vicinity. The Village originally adopted its buffer policy long before MHDC entered the picture and has applied the policy too consistently for us to infer discriminatory purpose from its application in this case. Finally, MHDC called one member of the Village Board to the stand at trial. Nothing in her testimony supports an inference of invidious purpose.

"In sum, [r]espondents simply failed to carry their burden of proving that discriminatory purpose was a motivating factor in the Village's decision.[21] This conclusion ends the constitutional inquiry."

PERSONNEL ADMINISTRATOR v. FEENEY, 442 U.S. 256, 99 S.Ct. 2282, 60 L.Ed.2d 870 (1979), per STEWART, J.,—relying on *Davis* and *Arlington Heights*—upheld Massachusetts' "absolute lifetime preference to veterans" for state civil service positions, even though "the preference operates overwhelming-

---

18. This Court has recognized, ever since *Fletcher v. Peck* [p. 247 supra], that judicial inquiries into legislative or executive motivation represent a substantial intrusion into the workings of other branches of government. Placing a decisionmaker on the stand is therefore "usually to be avoided."

21. Proof that the decision by the Village was motivated in part by a racially discriminatory purpose would not necessarily have required invalidation of the challenged decision. Such proof would, however, have shifted to the Village the burden of establishing that the same decision would have resulted even had the impermissible purpose not been considered. If this were established, the complaining party in a case of this kind no longer fairly could attribute the injury complained of to improper consideration of a discriminatory purpose.

ly to the advantage of males" [a] : "When a statute gender-neutral on its face is challenged on the ground that its effects upon women are disproportionably adverse, a two-fold inquiry [is] appropriate. The first question is whether the statutory classification is indeed neutral * * *. If the classification itself, covert or overt, is not based upon gender, the second question is whether the adverse effect reflects invidious gender-based discrimination. In this second inquiry, impact provides an 'important starting point,' *Arlington Heights,* but purposeful discrimination is 'the condition that offends the Constitution.' "

As to the first question, "The District Court [found] first, that ch. 31 serves legitimate and worthy purposes; second, that the absolute preference was not established for the purpose of discriminating against women. [Thus,] the distinction between veterans and nonveterans drawn by ch. 31 is not a pretext for gender discrimination. * * *

"If the impact of this statute could not be plausibly explained on a neutral ground, impact itself would signal that the real classification made by the law was in fact not neutral. But there can be but one answer to the question whether this veteran preference excludes significant numbers of women from preferred state jobs because they are women or because they are nonveterans. [T]his is not a law that can plausibly be explained only as a gender-based classification. Indeed, it is not a law that can rationally be explained on that ground. Veteran status is not uniquely male. Although few women benefit from the preference, the nonveteran class is not substantially all-female. To the contrary, significant numbers of nonveterans are men, and all nonveterans— male as well as female—are placed at a disadvantage. Too many men are affected by ch. 31 to permit the inference that the statute is but a pretext for preferring men over women. * * *

"The dispositive question, then, is whether the appellee has shown that a gender-based discriminatory purpose has, at least in some measure, shaped [ch. 31. Her] contention that this veterans' preference is 'inherently non-neutral' or 'gender-biased' presumes that the State, by favoring veterans, intentionally incorporated into its public employment policies the panoply of sex-based and assertedly discriminatory federal laws that have prevented all but a handful of women from becoming veterans. There are two serious difficulties with this argument. First, it is wholly at odds with the District Court's central finding that Massachusetts has not offered a preference to veterans for the purpose of discriminating against women. Second, it cannot be reconciled with the assumption made by both the appellee and the District Court that a more limited hiring preference for veterans could be sustained. Taken together, these difficulties are fatal.

"[D]iscrimination does not become less so because the discrimination accomplished is of a lesser magnitude.[23] Discriminatory intent is simply not amenable to calibration. It either is a factor that has influenced the legislative choice or it is not. The District Court's conclusion that the absolute veterans' preference was not originally enacted or subsequently reaffirmed for the purpose of giving an advantage to males as such necessarily compels the conclusion that the State

---

a. Sex discrimination is considered in Sec. 3, IV infra. Although such discrimination has not been held to be "suspect," it has been held to be subject to special judicial scrutiny and the Court's approach to the "purpose" vs. "impact" issue has been similar to cases involving discrimination against racial or ethnic minorities.

23. This is not to say that the degree of impact is irrelevant to the question of intent. But it is to say that a more modest preference, while it might well lessen impact and, as the State argues, might lessen the effectiveness of the statute in helping veterans, would not be any more or less "neutral" in the constitutional sense.

intended nothing more than to prefer 'veterans.' Given this finding, simple logic suggests that an intent to exclude women from significant public jobs was not at work in this law. [The] enlistment policies of the armed services may well have discriminated on the basis of sex. But the history of discrimination against women in the military is not on trial in this case.

"The appellee's ultimate argument rests upon the presumption, common to the criminal and civil law, that a person intends the natural and foreseeable consequences of his voluntary actions. * * *

" 'Discriminatory purpose,' however, implies more than intent as volition or intent as awareness of consequences. It implies that the decisionmaker, in this case a state legislature, selected or reaffirmed a particular course of action at least in part 'because of,' not merely 'in spite of,' its adverse effects upon an identifiable group.[25] Yet nothing in the record demonstrates that this preference for veterans was originally devised or subsequently re-enacted because it would accomplish the collateral goal of keeping women in a stereotypic and predefined place in the Massachusetts Civil Service."

STEVENS, J., joined by White, J., concurred in the Court's opinion, adding: "If a classification is not overtly based on gender, I am inclined to believe the question whether it is covertly gender-based is the same as the question whether its adverse effects reflect invidious gender-based discrimination. However the question is phrased, for me the answer is largely provided by the fact that the number of males disadvantaged by Massachusetts' Veterans Preference (1,867,000) is sufficiently large—and sufficiently close to the number of disadvantaged females (2,954,000)—to refute the claim that the rule was intended to benefit males as a class over females as a class."

MARSHALL, J., joined by Brennan, J., dissented: "In my judgment, [ch. 31] evinces purposeful gender-based discrimination. * * *

"[T]he impact of the Massachusetts statute on women is undisputed. Any veteran with a passing grade on the civil service exam must be placed ahead of a nonveteran, regardless of their respective scores. [Because] less than 2% of the women in Massachusetts are veterans, the absolute preference formula has rendered desirable state civil service employment an almost exclusively male prerogative. [Where] the foreseeable impact of a facially neutral policy is so disproportionate, the burden should rest on the State to establish that sex-based considerations played no part in the choice of the particular legislative scheme.

"Clearly, that burden was not sustained here. The legislative history of the statute reflects the Commonwealth's patent appreciation of the impact the preference system would have on women, and an equally evident desire to mitigate that impact only with respect to certain traditionally female occupations. Until 1971, the statute [and] regulations exempted from operation of the preference any job requisitions 'especially calling for women.' In practice, this exemption, coupled with the absolute preference for veterans, has created a gender-based civil service hierarchy, with women occupying low grade clerical

---

25. This is not to say that the inevitability or foreseeability of consequences of a neutral rule has no bearing upon the existence of discriminatory intent. Certainly, when the adverse consequences of a law upon an identifiable group are as inevitable as the gender-based consequences of ch. 31, a strong inference that the adverse effects were desired can reasonably be drawn. But in this inquiry— made as it is under the Constitution—an inference is a working tool, not a synonym for proof. When as here, the impact is essentially an unavoidable consequence of a legislative policy that has in itself always been deemed to be legitimate, and when, as here, the statutory history and all of the available evidence affirmatively demonstrate the opposite, the inference simply fails to ripen into proof.

and secretarial jobs and men holding more responsible and remunerative positions.

"[Such] a statutory scheme both reflects and perpetuates precisely the kind of archaic assumptions about women's roles which we have previously held invalid [citing cases in Sec. 3, IV infra]. Particularly when viewed against the range of less discriminatory alternatives available to assist veterans,[2] Massachusetts's choice of a formula that so severely restricts public employment opportunities for women cannot reasonably be thought gender-neutral. The Court's conclusion to the contrary—that 'nothing in the record' evinces a 'collateral goal of keeping women in a stereotypic and predefined place in the Massachusetts Civil Service'—displays a singularly myopic view of the facts established below.[3]"

MOBILE v. BOLDEN, Sec. 4, I, A infra, involved the question of whether a fifteenth amendment violation requires "discriminatory purpose." STEWART, J., joined by Burger, C.J., and Powell and Rehnquist, JJ., relying on *Guinn, Lane* and *Gomillion,* found that it did. WHITE, J., appeared to avoid explicitly addressing the question, finding that the election scheme at issue had a discriminatory purpose. BLACKMUN, J., "assuming that proof of intent is a prerequisite," agreed with White, J.'s finding. STEVENS, J., did not directly address the question, but disagreed with Stewart, J.'s "reach[ing] out to decide [it]."

MARSHALL, J., dissented: "*Davis* required a showing of discriminatory purpose to support racial discrimination claims largely because it feared that a standard based solely on disproportionate impact would unduly interfere with the far-ranging governmental distribution of constitutional gratuities [citing *Davis'* text at fn. 14]. Underlying the Court's decision was a determination that, since the Constitution does not entitle any person to such governmental benefits, courts should accord discretion to those officials who decide how the government shall allocate its scarce resources. If the plaintiff proved only that governmental distribution of constitutional gratuities had a disproportionate effect on a racial minority, the Court was willing to presume that the officials who approved the allocation scheme either had made an honest error or had foreseen that the decision would have a discriminatory impact and had found persuasive, legitimate reasons for imposing it nonetheless. * * *

"Such judicial deference to official decisionmaking has no place under the Fifteenth Amendment. [The] right to vote is of such fundamental importance in the constitutional scheme that the Fifteenth Amendment's command that it shall not be 'abridged' on account of race must be interpreted as providing that the votes of citizens of all races shall be of substantially equal weight. Furthermore, a disproportionate-impact test under the Fifteenth Amendment would not lead to constant judicial intrusion into the process of official decisionmaking. Rather, the standard would reach only those decisions having a discriminatory effect upon the minority's vote. The Fifteenth Amendment cannot tolerate that kind of decision, even if made in good faith, because the Amendment grants

---

2. Only four States afford a preference comparable in [scope]. Other States and the Federal Government grant point or tie-breaking preferences that do not foreclose opportunities for women.

3. Although it is relevant that the preference statute also disadvantages a substantial group of men, it is equally pertinent that 47% of Massachusetts men over 18 are veterans, as compared to 0.8% of Massachusetts women. Given this disparity, and the indicia of intent noted supra, the absolute number of men denied preference cannot be dispositive, especially since they have not faced the barriers to achieving veteran status confronted by women.

racial minorities the full enjoyment of the right to vote, not simply protection against the unfairness of intentional vote dilution along racial lines.[32]

"In addition, it is beyond dispute that a standard based solely upon the motives of official decisionmakers creates significant problems of proof [and] creates the risk that officials will be able to adopt policies that are the products of discriminatory intent so long as they sufficiently mask their motives through the use of subtlety and illusion. [That] risk becomes intolerable [when] the precious right to vote protected by the Fifteenth Amendment is concerned."

In a brief opinion, BRENNAN, J., agreed with Marshall, J.'s conclusion.[a]

In MEMPHIS v. GREENE, 451 U.S. 100, 101 S.Ct. 1584, 67 L.Ed.2d 769 (1981), the city—at the behest of citizens of Hein Park, a white residential community within Memphis—closed a street, West Drive, that traversed Hein Park and was used mainly by blacks who lived in an adjacent area. The Court, per STEVENS, J., agreeing that "the adverse impact on blacks was greater than on whites," found no violation of 42 U.S.C. § 1982 [p. 1135 infra] or the thirteenth amendment: "[T]he critical facts established by the record are these: The city's decision to close West Drive was motivated by its interest in protecting the safety and tranquility of a residential neighborhood. The procedures followed in making the decision were fair and were not affected by any racial or other impermissible factors. The city has conferred a benefit on certain white property owners but there is no reason to believe that it would refuse to confer a comparable benefit on black property owners. The closing has not affected the value of property owned by black citizens, but it has caused some slight inconvenience to black motorists."

As for the thirteenth amendment, the Court "left open the question of whether § 1 of the Amendment by its own terms did anything more than abolish slavery [because] the record discloses no racially discriminatory motive on the part of the City Council [and] a review of the justification for the official action challenged in this case demonstrates that its disparate impact on black citizens could not [be] fairly characterized as a badge or incident of slavery.

"[To] decide the narrow constitutional question presented by this record we need not speculate about the sort of impact on a racial group that might be prohibited by the Amendment itself. We merely hold that the impact of the closing of West Drive on nonresidents of Hein Park [does] not reflect a violation of the Thirteenth Amendment."

MARSHALL, J., joined by Brennan and Blackmun, JJ., dissented on the ground that "a proper reading of the record demonstrates" (1) "that respondents produced at trial precisely the kind of evidence of intent that we deemed probative in *Arlington Heights,*" and (2) "substantial harm to respondent's property rights":

"I [do] not mean to imply that all municipal decisions that affect Negroes adversely and benefit whites are prohibited by the Thirteenth Amendment. I

---

32. Even if a municipal policy is shown to dilute the right to vote, however, the policy will not be struck down if the city shows that it serves highly important local interests and is closely tailored to effectuate only those interests.

a. For an opinion of the Court per White, J.—joined by Burger, C.J., and Brennan, Mar-

shall, Blackmun and O'Connor, JJ.—even more strongly suggesting that a fifteenth amendment violation requires a "discriminatory purpose," see *Rogers v. Lodge,* Sec. 4, I, A infra.

would, however, insist that the government carry a heavy burden of justification before I would sustain against Thirteenth Amendment challenge conduct as egregious as erection of a barrier to prevent predominantly-Negro traffic from entering a historically all-white neighborhood. [I] do not believe that the city has discharged that burden in this case, and for that reason I would hold that the erection of the barrier at the end of West Drive amounts to a badge or incident of slavery forbidden by the Thirteenth Amendment."

Notes and Questions

1. *The "discriminatory purpose" requirement.* (a) Should "racially disproportionate impact" alone trigger special judicial scrutiny? Consider Note, 81 Harv.L.Rev. 1511, 1522 (1968): "The close scrutiny traditionally accorded to statutes which single out individuals for differential treatment on the basis of race [can] be attributed to a judicial suspicion that such statutes are the product of a legislature which is not pursuing permissible ends at all, but acting from a desire to make a discriminatory classification for its own sake. [G]overnment action which adversely affects [blacks] may well stem from decisions [which,] although not racially prejudiced, are nevertheless unresponsive to [their needs. Thus,] judges should not be reluctant to intervene." Compare Bennett, *"Mere" Rationality in Constitutional Law: Judicial Review and Democratic Theory,* 67 Calif.L.Rev. 1049, 1076 (1979): "If members of racial minorities statistically obtain benefits and suffer detriments as one or another piece of legislation is passed without attention to its racial impact, they are obtaining, not being deprived of, equal protection of the laws. To forbid all legislation that disadvantages them would give them the gains from political bargaining without the losses. This would be so regardless of the degree of the racially disproportionate impact or the importance of the interest affected."

Contrast Perry, *The Disproportionate Impact Theory of Racial Discrimination,* 125 U.Pa.L.Rev. 540, 559–60 (1977): "Laws employing a racial criterion of selection are inherently more dangerous than laws involving no racial criterion. The former, unlike the latter, directly encourage racialism [and] are usually difficult if not impossible to justify on legitimate grounds. By contrast, laws having a disproportionate racial impact are quite easy to explain on legitimate grounds because such laws serve a legitimate function in addition to the function of racial selection. Accordingly, the standard of review [should be] more rigorous than that required by the rational relationship test but less rigorous than that required by the strict scrutiny test. [In] determining whether a disproportionate disadvantage is justified, a court would weigh several factors: (1) the degree of disproportion in the impact; (2) the private interest disadvantaged; (3) the efficiency of the challenged law in achieving its objective and the availability of alternative means having a less disproportionate impact; and (4) the government objective sought to be advanced." [a]

Is there a "discriminatory purpose" if it is determined that the challenged law would not have been passed "if its racial impact had been reversed, i.e., if the disparate impact had been on whites rather than on blacks"? Schnapper, *Two Categories of Discriminatory Intent,* 17 Harv.Civ.Rts.—Civ.Lib.L.Rev. 31, 51 (1982). Consider id. at 55–56: "The central issue [in *Feeney*] is whether Massachusetts would have adopted in 1896 a veterans' preference [that would have

---

a. For the view that "serious scrutiny is preferable to ad hoc balancing," see Binion, *Intent and Equal Protection: A Reconsideration,* 1983 Sup.Ct.Rev. 397—comprehensively

criticizing the "discriminatory purpose" requirement as developed and applied in the cases.

excluded 98% of all male applicants] or would have amended its statutes successively in 1919, 1943, 1949, and 1968 to assure such preferential treatment for new generations of predominantly female veterans. The all too familiar history of discrimination on the basis of sex in this country renders implausible the suggestion * * *."

(b) *First amendment freedoms.* In cases holding "neutral" laws that had an adverse impact on speech, association or religion to violate the first amendment—such as *In re Primus* (p. 564 supra) and *Wisconsin v. Yoder* (p. 849 supra)—in which the Court required a "compelling state interest" or "more than merely a 'reasonable relation to some purpose within the competency of the state,'" did the Court find that the challenged state programs had a "discriminatory purpose"? If not, how is the disproportionate racial impact situation distinguishable? Consider Perry, supra, at 556: "The first amendment protects values and interests believed indispensable to the democratic functioning of the political process. Government is charged with the duty, under the first amendment, of safeguarding those values and interests [by] acting solicitously toward them as well as by refraining from deliberately abridging them. The equal protection clause serves principally as a brake on the lamentable tendency of the majority race wilfully to oppress or exploit racial minorities, and in this regard it prohibits, absent compelling justification, the use of race as a criterion of selection. Traditionally, however, it has not been thought wrong—unfortunate, perhaps, but not wrong—that an individual or group is incidentally burdened by a law serving the public good. [Thus], with respect to racial discrimination equal protection doctrine has focused almost exclusively on *wilful* oppression or exploitation of minorities by the majority. This focus is especially understandable in light of what historically has been this society's severest moral affliction, racial animus." Compare Eisenberg, fn. a supra, at 165–66: "In comparing the relative need for an impact test in race and religion cases, it is unquestionable that those suffering adverse impact because of race lack the modification or abandonment options that are at least physically possible for those suffering because of religious belief. Second, the establishment clause imposes a limitation on official concessions to religious belief that has no direct parallel in the race [area.] Third, consider the relative historical treatment of race and religion. [I] doubt that any religious group could make out a plausible case that it has been subjected in this country to the same degree of mistreatment. In short, the Court's failure to search for an alternative to motive in race cases borders on the irrational when contrasted with its willingness to use impact in religious belief cases." [b]

2. *Prior state discrimination.* Should there be special judicial scrutiny if the disproportionate racial impact of a law, whose purpose is racially neutral, is produced (influenced) by prior intentional state discrimination? See *Lane v. Wilson,* fn. a in *Arlington Heights.* Suppose a state requires that all applicants furnish recommendations from alumni and that there are no black alumni because the university admitted no blacks in the past? Suppose a state hires teachers wholly on the basis of merit and racial segregation in schools has rendered the quality of education of black teachers inferior to that of whites? Would (should) there have been special judicial scrutiny in *Feeney* if the disproportionate impact had been produced (influenced) by prior intentional discrimination by Massachusetts rather than military personnel practices of the federal

b. As to whether "discriminatory purpose" is required in respect to laws that allegedly violate equal protection because they affect "fundamental rights," see *Mobile v. Bolden,* Sec. 4, I, A infra.

government? If so, why should Massachusetts' "incorporation" of intentional discrimination by another government agency make a "constitutional difference"?

3. *Consequences of "discriminatory purpose."* If it is found that a law "was motivated by a racially discriminatory purpose," should the state be permitted to prove "that the same decision would have resulted had the impermissible purpose not been considered"? *Arlington Heights,* fn. 21. Or should the Court invalidate the law and "remand to the legislature for a reconsideration [on] the basis of purely legitimate factors"? Schwemm, fn. a supra, at 1020. Would the latter course be futile "because the legislature could immediately pass an identical statute for valid reasons"? Eisenberg, supra, at 116. Consider id.: "[I]t is absurd to assume that all legislators would completely ignore a court holding that the legislature used constitutionally impermissible criteria in initially passing a statute. Some legislators, after being informed that they initially acted unconstitutionally, may refuse to vote for reenactment. Furthermore, if a statute is invalidated on judicial review, the legislature often will decline or fail to consider a new law. In many situations, therefore, judicial action on the basis of motive results in an effective, not a futile, invalidation." If there is a remand and the law is reenacted, should there be a presumption "that the decisionmaker continues to entertain the motives that led to the original decision (and to its invalidation)"? Brest, fn. 12 in *Arlington Heights,* at 125–26.

IV. REMEDYING SEGREGATION

Although there was prompt compliance with *Brown* in the District of Columbia and some of the border states, the initial response in the deep south was one of "massive resistance"—exemplified by the Governor's use of the Arkansas national guard in 1957 to prevent desegregation in Little Rock and Virginia's 1956 legislation closing any racially mixed public schools. See generally McKay, *"With All Deliberate Speed": Legislative Reaction and Judicial Development 1956–1957,* 43 Va.L.Rev. 1205 (1957).

———

COOPER v. AARON, 358 U.S. 1, 78 S.Ct. 1401, 3 L.Ed.2d 5 (1958), the first decision to follow the remands in *Brown,* involved the Little Rock school board's request to stay an integration plan that had been in operation at Central High School during the 1957–58 school year, but only after federal troops had been sent by the President to protect black students from "extreme public hostility" engendered largely by the Governor's and Legislature's opposition. The opinion, unprecedented in that it was signed by all nine justices (including those appointed since *Brown*), "unanimously reaffirmed" *Brown.* The Court agreed that "the educational progress of all the students [will] continue to suffer if the conditions which prevailed last year are permitted to continue," but denied the request for delay: "The constitutional rights of [black children] are not to be sacrificed or yielded to the violence and disorder which have followed upon the actions of the Governor and Legislature." The difficulties, created by state action, "can also be brought under control by state action." *Brown* "can neither be nullified openly and directly by state legislators or state executive or judicial officers, nor nullified indirectly by them through evasive schemes."

———

GRIFFIN v. COUNTY SCHOOL BD., 377 U.S. 218, 84 S.Ct. 1226, 12 L.Ed.2d 256 (1964): In 1959, Prince Edward County, Va. closed its public schools rather than comply with a desegregation order. Private schools, supported by state and local tuition grants and tax credits, were operated for white children. The Court, per BLACK, J., held the closing to deny blacks equal protection: States have "wide discretion in deciding whether laws shall operate statewide or shall operate only in certain counties [but] Prince Edward's public schools were closed and private schools operated in their place with state and county assistance, for one reason [only]. Whatever nonracial grounds might support a State's allowing a county to abandon public schools, the object must be a constitutional one, and grounds of race and opposition to desegregation do not qualify as constitutional." [b]

In the late 1950s, some states sought to comply with *Brown* by simply permitting students to apply for transfer to another school. Procedures were complex and time-consuming; standards were vague, making it difficult to show that denials were due to race. See Note, *The Federal Courts and Integration of Southern Schools: Troubled Status of the Pupil Placement Act,* 62 Colum.L.Rev. 1448 (1962). By the early 1960s, most federal courts refused to accept these "tokenism" plans. See Bickel, *The Decade of School Desegregation: Progress and Prospects,* 64 Colum.L.Rev. 193 (1964). *Rogers v. Paul,* 382 U.S. 198, 86 S.Ct. 358, 15 L.Ed.2d 265 (1965), ordered "immediate transfer" of petitioning students who still attended segregated schools because, under the grade-a-year plan, their grade had not been covered. Finally, *Alexander v. Holmes Cty. Bd. of Educ.,* 396 U.S. 19, 90 S.Ct. 29, 24 L.Ed.2d 19 (1969), ordered denial of "all motions for additional time" and made clear that "the obligation of every school district is to terminate dual school systems at once and to operate now and hereafter only unitary schools."

GREEN v. COUNTY SCHOOL BD., 391 U.S. 430, 88 S.Ct. 1689, 20 L.Ed.2d 716 (1968): The population of New Kent County in rural Virginia was about half black. Although there was no residential segregation, its two combined elementary and high schools, previously segregated by law, remained wholly segregated in fact until 1964. In 1965, the board adopted a "freedom-of-choice" plan to remain eligible for federal financial aid under federal guidelines.[c] After three years, no white child chose to go to the black school which 85% of the black children continued to attend. School buses traveled "overlapping routes throughout the county to transport pupils to and from the two schools."

b. The Court affirmed the district court's order enjoining public financial aid to the private schools and held (Clark and Harlan, JJ. disagreeing) that "the District Court [may] require the Supervisors to exercise the power that is theirs to levy taxes to raise funds adequate to reopen, operate, and maintain without racial discrimination a public school system [like] that operated in other counties in Virginia."

c. The Civil Rights Act of 1964 bars federal financial assistance for any program administered in a racially discriminatory manner. Pursuant thereto, the Dep't of Health, Education and Welfare conditioned eligibility for federal aid to local school districts either on

compliance with existing court desegregation orders or, in the absence of such an order, on submission of a desegregation plan consistent with HEW "guidelines."

In the 1964–65 school year, before implementation of the guidelines, only 2.14% of black students in the eleven "southern states" attended schools in which they were not the racial majority. In 1968, the figure was reported at 20.3%. By the 1972–73 school year, it was 46.3%. Statistical Abstract of the United States 124 (1974). The comparable figure for 1972–73 in the six "border states and the District of Columbia" was 31.8%; for the 32 "northern and western states" it was 28.3%. Id.

A unanimous Court, per BRENNAN, J., held "it is against this background that 13 years after *Brown II* commanded the abolition of dual systems we must measure the effectiveness of [respondent's] 'freedom-of-choice' plan to achieve that end. The School Board contends that it has fully discharged its obligation by adopting a plan by which every student, regardless of race, may 'freely' choose the school he will attend [and which] may be faulted only by reading the Fourteenth Amendment as universally requiring 'compulsory integration.' [But] what is involved here is the question whether the Board has achieved the 'racially nondiscriminatory school system' *Brown II* held must be [effectuated]. School boards [then] operating state-compelled dual systems [were] clearly charged with the affirmative duty to take whatever steps might be necessary to convert to a unitary system in which racial discrimination would be eliminated root and branch. [It] is incumbent upon the school board to establish that its proposed plan promises meaningful and immediate progress toward disestablishing state-imposed segregation. [Where] more promising courses of action are open to the board, that may indicate a lack of good faith; and at the least it places a heavy burden upon the board to explain its preference for an apparently less effective method. [The instant] plan has operated simply to burden children and their parents with a responsibility which *Brown II* placed squarely on the School Board. The Board must be required to formulate a new plan and, in light of other courses which appear open to the Board, such as zoning, [or consolidating the two schools, one serving grades 1–7, the other, grades 8–12,] fashion steps which promise realistically to convert promptly to a system without a 'white' school and a 'Negro' school, but just schools."

SWANN v. CHARLOTTE–MECKLENBURG BD. OF EDUC.

402 U.S. 1, 91 S.Ct. 1267, 28 L.Ed.2d 554 (1971).

MR. CHIEF JUSTICE BURGER delivered the opinion of the Court.

[This case concerned desegregation of the Charlotte, N.C. metropolitan area school district, which had had a statutorily mandated dual system.[a] The history included the district court's rejection in 1969 of three plans submitted by respondent board of education; its acceptance of a plan prepared at its request by "an expert in education administration"; modification of the district court decree by the court of appeals; and the district court's subsequent rejection of a plan prepared by HEW and its conclusion that either the education expert's plan or a new plan submitted by a minority of the school board was "reasonable and acceptable."]

The problems encountered by the [lower federal courts] make plain that we should now try to amplify guidelines, however incomplete and imperfect, for the assistance of school authorities and courts. [Elimination of dual school systems] has been rendered more difficult by changes since 1954 in the structure and patterns of communities, the growth of student population, movement of families, and other changes, some of which had marked impact on school planning, sometimes neutralizing or negating remedial action before it was fully implemented. Rural areas accustomed for half a century to the consolidated school systems implemented by bus transportation could make adjustments more readily than metropolitan areas with dense and shifting population, numerous schools, congested and complex traffic patterns. * * *

---

a. A companion case involved Mobile, Ala.

If school authorities fail in their affirmative obligations ["to eliminate from the public schools all vestiges of state-imposed segregation"] judicial authority may be invoked. Once a right and a violation have been shown, the scope of a district court's equitable powers to remedy past wrongs is broad, for breadth and flexibility are inherent in equitable remedies. [The] task is to correct, by a balancing of the individual and collective interests, the condition that offends the Constitution. [But] it is important to remember that judicial powers may be exercised only on the basis of a constitutional violation. * * *

School authorities are traditionally charged with broad power to formulate and implement educational policy and might well conclude, for example, that in order to prepare students to live in a pluralistic society each school should have a prescribed ratio of Negro to white students reflecting the proportion for the district as a whole. To do this as an educational policy is within the broad discretionary powers of school authorities; absent a finding of a constitutional violation, however, that would not be within the authority of a federal court. * * *

The school authorities argue that the equity powers of federal district courts have been limited by Title IV of the Civil Rights Act of 1964, 42 U.S.C.A. [§ 2000c(b) which states]: " 'Desegregation' means the assignment of students to public schools and within such schools without regard to their race, color, religion, or national origin, but 'desegregation' shall not mean the assignment of students to public schools in order to overcome racial imbalance."

Section 2000c–6, authorizing the Attorney General to institute federal suits, contains the following proviso: "nothing herein shall empower any official or court of the United States to issue any order seeking to achieve a racial balance in any school by requiring the transportation of pupils [or] otherwise enlarge the existing power of the court to insure compliance with constitutional standards."

* * * § 2000c–6 is in terms designed to foreclose any interpretation of the Act as expanding the *existing* powers of federal courts to enforce the Equal Protection Clause. There is no suggestion of an intention to restrict those powers or withdraw from courts their historic equitable remedial powers. The legislative history of Title IV indicates that Congress was concerned that the Act might be read as creating a right of action under the Fourteenth Amendment in the situation of so-called "de facto segregation," where racial imbalance exists in the schools but with no showing that this was brought about by discriminatory action of state authorities. In short, there is nothing in the Act which provides us material assistance in answering the question of remedy for state-imposed segregation in violation of *Brown I.* * * *

* * * Independent of student assignment, where it is possible to identify a "white school" or a "Negro school" simply by reference to the racial composition of teachers and staff, the quality of school buildings and equipment, or the organization of sports activities, a prima facie case of violation of substantive constitutional rights under the Equal Protection Clause is shown.

When a system has been dual in these respects, the first remedial responsibility of school authorities is to eliminate invidious racial distinctions. With respect to such matters as transportation, supporting personnel, and extracurricular activities, no more than this may be necessary. Similar corrective action must be taken with regard to the maintenance of buildings and the distribution of equipment. In these areas, normal administrative practice should produce schools of like quality, facilities, and staffs. Something more must be said, however, as to faculty assignment and new school construction.

In the companion *Mobile* case, the Mobile school board has argued that the Constitution requires that teachers be assigned on a "color blind" basis. It also argues that the Constitution prohibits district courts from using their equity power to order assignment of teachers to achieve a particular degree of faculty desegregation. We reject that contention. * * *

The construction of new schools and the closing of old [ones,] when combined with one technique or another of student assignment, will determine the racial composition of the student body in each school in the [system.] People gravitate toward school facilities, just as schools are located in response to the needs of people. The location of schools may thus influence the patterns of residential development of a metropolitan area and have important impact on composition of inner city neighborhoods. [In] devising remedies where legally imposed segregation has been established, it is the responsibility of local authorities and district courts to see to it that future school construction and abandonment is not used and does not serve to perpetuate or re-establish the dual system.

* * *

The central issue in this case is that of student assignment, and there are essentially four problem areas: * * *

(1) *Racial Balances or Racial Quotas.* [I]t is urged that the District Court has imposed a racial balance requirement of 71%–29% on individual schools, [reflecting] the pupil constituency of the system. If we were to read the holding of the District Court to require, as a matter of substantive constitutional right, any particular degree of racial balance or mixing, that approach would be disapproved [for the] constitutional command to desegregate schools does not mean that every school in every community must always reflect the racial composition of the school system as a whole.

[But] the use made of mathematical ratios was no more than a starting point in the process of shaping a [remedy]. As we said in *Green,* a school authority's remedial plan or a district court's remedial decree is to be judged by its effectiveness. Awareness of the racial composition of the whole school system is likely to be a useful starting point in shaping a remedy to correct past constitutional violations. In sum, the very limited use made of mathematical ratios was within the equitable remedial discretion of the District Court.[d]

(2) *One-Race Schools.* The record in this case reveals the familiar phenomenon that in metropolitan areas minority groups are often found concentrated in one part of the city. In some circumstances certain schools may remain all or largely of one race until new schools can be provided or neighborhood patterns change. [T]he existence of some small number of one-race, or virtually one-race schools within a district is not in and of itself the mark of a system which still practices segregation by law. [But] the burden upon the school authorities will be to satisfy the court that their racial composition is not the result of present or past discriminatory action on their part.

An optional majority-to-minority transfer provision [is] an indispensable remedy for those students willing to transfer to other schools in order to lessen the impact on them of the state-imposed stigma of segregation. [S]uch a transfer arrangement must grant the transferring student free transportation and space must be made available in the school to which he desires to move. * * *

d. Cf. Rehnquist, J., joined by Burger, C.J., and Powell, J., dissenting from denial of certiorari in *Cleveland Bd. of Educ. v. Reed,* 445 U.S. 935, 100 S.Ct. 1329, 63 L.Ed.2d 770 (1980), in which the district court's remedy required that "every grade in every school [have] a ratio of black and white students in approximate proportion to the systemwide ratio."

(3) *Remedial Altering of Attendance Zones.* [O]ne of the principal tools employed by school planners and by courts to break up the dual school system has been a frank—and sometimes drastic—gerrymandering of school districts and attendance zones. An additional step was pairing, "clustering," or "grouping" of schools with attendance assignments made deliberately to accomplish the transfer of Negro students out of formerly segregated Negro schools and transfer of white students to formerly all-Negro schools. More often than not, these zones are neither compact nor contiguous; indeed they may be on opposite ends of the city. As an interim corrective measure, this cannot be said to be beyond the broad remedial powers of a court.

Absent a constitutional violation there would be no basis for judicially ordering assignment of students on a racial basis. All things being equal, with no history of discrimination, it might well be desirable to assign pupils to schools nearest their homes. But all things are not equal in a system that has been deliberately constructed and maintained to enforce racial segregation. The remedy for such segregation may be administratively awkward, inconvenient and even bizarre in some situations and may impose burdens on some; but [this] cannot be avoided in the interim period when remedial adjustments are being made to eliminate the dual school systems.

No fixed or even substantially fixed guidelines can be established as to how far a court can go, but it must be recognized that there are limits. The objective is to dismantle the dual school system. "Racially neutral" assignment plans [may] fail to counteract the continuing effects of past school segregation resulting from discriminatory location of school sites or distortion of school size in order to achieve or maintain an artificial racial separation. When school authorities present a district court with a "loaded game board," affirmative action in the form of remedial altering of attendance zones is proper to achieve truly non-discriminatory assignments. [W]e must of necessity rely to a large extent, as this Court has for more than 16 years, on the informed judgment of the district courts in the first instance and on courts of appeals. * * *

(4) *Transportation of Students.* [No] rigid guidelines as to student transportation can be given for application to the infinite variety of problems presented in thousands of situations. Bus transportation has been an integral part of the public education system for [years]. Eighteen million of the nation's public school children, approximately 39%, were transported to their schools by bus in 1969–1970 in all parts of the country. * * *

The decree provided that [trips] for elementary school pupils average about seven miles and the District Court found that they would take "not over 35 minutes at the most." [12] This system compares favorably with the transportation plan previously operated in Charlotte under which each day 23,600 students on all grade levels were transported an average of 15 miles one way for an average trip requiring over an hour. In these circumstances, we find no basis for holding that the local school authorities may not be required to employ bus transportation as one tool of school desegregation. Desegregation plans cannot be limited to the walk-in school.

An objection to transportation of students may have validity when the time or distance of travel is so great as to risk either the health of the children or

12. The District Court found that the school system would have to employ 138 more buses than it had previously operated. But 105 of those buses were already available and the others could easily be obtained. Addition-ally, it should be noted that North Carolina requires provision of transportation for all students who are assigned to schools more than one and one-half miles from their homes.

significantly impinge on the educational process. District courts must weigh the soundness of any transportation plan in light of what is said in subdivisions (1), (2), and (3) above. [L]imits on time of travel will vary with many factors, but probably with none more than the age of the students. The reconciliation of competing values in a desegregation case is, of course, a difficult task with many sensitive facets but fundamentally no more so than remedial measures courts of equity have traditionally employed. * * *

At some point, these school authorities and others like them should have achieved full compliance with this Court's decision in *Brown I.* * * *

It does not follow that the communities served by such systems will remain demographically stable, for in a growing, mobile society, few will do so. Neither school authorities nor district courts are constitutionally required to make year-by-year adjustments of the racial composition of student bodies once the affirmative duty to desegregate has been accomplished and racial discrimination through official action is eliminated from the system. This does not mean that federal courts are without power to deal with future problems; but in the absence of a showing that either the school authorities or some other agency of the State has deliberately attempted to fix or alter demographic patterns to affect the racial composition of the schools, further intervention by a district court should not be necessary. * * *[e]

Notes and Questions

1. *Scope of duty.* (a) May a school district that had a statutorily mandated dual system be relieved of its remedial duty if it proves that continued racial imbalance in its schools is not attributable to its earlier school segregation law? Or do *Green* and *Swann* effectively create an "irrebuttable presumption" that "yesterday's intentionally segregative laws [have] influenced family residential choices and contributed to the formation of today's one-race neighborhoods [and] today's one-race neighborhood schools"? Goodman, *The Desegregation Dilemma: A Vote for Voluntarism,* 1979 Wash.U.L.Q. 407, 409. See generally Fiss, *School Desegregation: The Uncertain Path of the Law,* 4 Phil. & Pub.Afrs. 3, 18–21 (1974). Compare Yudof, *Equal Educational Opportunity and the Courts,* 51 Tex. L.Rev. 411, 452 (1973): "There is no evidence that segregated schools materially influenced racial isolation by neighborhood in Southern communities. Where the whole structure of society reflects the inferior status assigned to blacks, it is difficult to say that any particular practice or institution caused segregated neighborhoods. [S]egregated housing is far more prevalent in the North where officially sanctioned school segregation was relatively rare."

(b) Do *Green* and *Swann* require school boards that had de jure segregated systems to take "*whatever* steps might be necessary" for "meaningful and immediate progress toward disestablishing state-imposed segregation" (*Green*)? Or need they only adopt plans that are "reasonable, *feasible* and workable" (*Swann*)? Who determines what is "feasible"?

2. *Legislation.* In response to *Swann,* legislation to drastically limit busing was introduced in Congress. The result was the Education Amendments Act of 1972, see fn. b supra. The Education Amendments Act of 1974, however,

---

e. In a companion case, *North Carolina State Bd. of Educ. v. Swann,* 402 U.S. 43, 91 S.Ct. 1284, 28 L.Ed.2d 586 (1971), the Court held that an Anti-Busing Law, enacted during the instant litigation—barring (1) pupil as- signment on the basis of race or to create a racial balance or ratio in the schools, and (2) busing for such purposes—contravened the doctrine "that all reasonable methods be available to formulate an effective remedy."

requires (§ 214) that federal courts and agencies give priority to nonbusing remedies and provides (§ 215) that "no court, department or agency of the United States shall" (a) "order the implementation of a plan that would require the transportation of any student to a school other than the school closest or next closest to his place of residence which provides the appropriate grade level and type of education for such student," or (b) "require directly or indirectly the transportation of any student if such transportation poses a risk to the health of such student or constitutes a significant impingement on the educational process with respect to such student." But this is prefaced by § 203(b)'s statement "that the provisions of this title are not intended to modify or diminish the authority of the courts of the United States to enforce fully the fifth and fourteenth amendments." Since then, several annual appropriations acts in the 1970s have prohibited the use of federal funds to require busing "to a school other than the school which is nearest the students' home, and which offers the courses of study pursued by such student" in order to comply with the desegregation provisions of the Civil Rights Act of 1964.[f]

3. *Resegregation.* In PASADENA BD. OF EDUC. v. SPANGLER, 427 U.S. 424, 96 S.Ct. 2697, 49 L.Ed.2d 599 (1976), a court ordered plan to remedy de jure segregation resulted in no racially imbalanced schools in 1970. But this lasted only one year; by 1974, five of the district's 32 schools were over half black. The Court, per REHNQUIST, J., reversed the district judge's order "to require annual readjustment of attendance zones so that there would not be a majority of any minority in any Pasadena public school": "[The] quite normal pattern of human migration resulted in some changes in the demographics of Pasadena's residential patterns, with resultant shifts in the racial makeup of some of the schools. [But] these shifts were not attributed to any segregative actions on the part of the defendants. [H]aving once implemented a racially neutral attendance pattern in order to remedy the perceived constitutional violations on the part of the defendants, the District Court had fully performed its function of providing the appropriate remedy for previous racially discriminatory attendance patterns."[g]

KEYES v. SCHOOL DIST., 413 U.S. 189, 93 S.Ct. 2686, 37 L.Ed.2d 548 (1973), was the first case of segregation that had never been statutorily mandated. The district court found that the Denver school board—by school construction, gerrymandering attendance zones, and excessive use of mobile classroom units—"had engaged over almost a decade after 1960 in an unconstitutional policy of deliberate racial segregation with respect to the Park Hill schools," and ordered their desegregation. However, although the "core city schools" were also segregated in fact, the district court found that the school board had no segregative policy as to them and declined to order their desegregation.

The Court, per BRENNAN, J., reversed, first holding that since, in the southwest, Negroes and Hispanos "suffer identical discrimination in treatment when compared with the treatment afforded Anglo[s,] schools with a combined predominance of Negroes and Hispanos [should be] included in the category of 'segregated' schools." It then held that "where plaintiffs prove that the school

---

f. For consideration of the constitutionality of such legislation, see note 6(e) p. 1157 infra (§ 5 of the fourteenth amendment).

g. The Court thought "it important to note [that] this case does not involve [a] plan embodying specific revisions of the attendance zones for particular schools, as well as provisions for later appraisal of whether such discrete individual modifications had achieved the 'unitary system' required by *Brown I*."

Marshall, J., joined by Brennan, J., dissented on the ground that a "unitary system" had not been established. Stevens, J., did not participate.

authorities have carried out a systematic program of segregation affecting a substantial portion of the students, schools, teachers and facilities [it] is only common sense to conclude that there exists a predicate for a finding of the existence of a dual school system" because "racially inspired school board actions have an impact beyond the particular schools that are the subjects of those actions. This is not to say, of course, that there can never be a case in which the geographical structure of or the natural boundaries within a school district may have the effect of dividing the district into separate, identifiable and unrelated units. Such a determination is essentially a question of fact to be resolved by the trial court [but] such cases must be rare."

Finally, emphasizing "that the differentiating factor between de jure segregation and so-called de facto segregation [is] *purpose* or *intent* to segregate," it held "that a finding of intentionally segregative school board actions in a meaningful portion of a school system [creates] a prima facie case of unlawful segregative design on the part of school authorities, and shifts to those authorities the burden of proving that other segregated schools within the system are not also the result of intentionally segregative actions. This is true even if it is determined that different areas of the school district should be viewed independently of each [other].[a] In discharging that burden, it is not enough, of course, that the school authorities rely upon some allegedly logical, racially neutral explanation for their actions. Their burden is to adduce proof sufficient to support a finding that segregative intent was not among the factors that motivated their actions." Further, "if the actions of school authorities were to any degree motivated by segregative intent and the segregation resulting from those actions continues to exist, the fact of remoteness in time certainly does not make those actions any less 'intentional.'

"This is not to say, however, that the prima facie case may not be met by evidence supporting a finding that a lesser degree of segregated schooling in the core city area would not have resulted even if the Board had not acted as it [did]. Intentional school segregation in the past may have been a factor in creating a natural environment for the growth of further segregation. Thus, if respondent School Board cannot disprove segregative intent, it can rebut the prima facie case only by showing that its past segregative acts did not create or contribute to the current segregated condition of the core city schools."

Respondent invoked "its 'neighborhood school policy' as explaining racial and ethnic concentrations within the core city schools. [But] the mere assertion of such a policy is not dispositive where, as in this case, the school authorities have been found to have practiced de jure segregation * * *."[b]

POWELL, J., filed a lengthy separate opinion, believing that "the facts deemed necessary to establish de jure discrimination present problems of subjective intent which the courts cannot fairly resolve." "In my view we should abandon [the de jure-de facto distinction] and formulate constitutional principles of

---

a. What constitutes a "substantial" or "meaningful portion" of a school system? Consider Comment, *Unlocking the Northern Schoolhouse Doors,* 9 Harv.Civ.Rts.—Civ.Lib. L.Rev. 124, 150 (1974): "Park Hill is a neighborhood of eight schools educating less than thirty-eight percent of Denver's black students and less than ten percent of all pupils in the district. [Thus], a decree compelling extensive desegregation will almost invariably flow from a finding of localized de jure practices." Does

"a finding of intentionally segregative school board actions" for all elementary schools "create a prima facie case of unlawful segregative design" for all secondary schools?

b. Burger, C.J., concurred in the result. Douglas, J., joined the Court's opinion but stated "that there [is] no difference between de facto and de jure segregation." White, J., did not participate.

national rather than merely regional application. [In] imposing on metropolitan southern school districts an affirmative duty, entailing large-scale transportation of pupils, to eliminate segregation in the schools, the Court required these districts to alleviate conditions which in large part did *not* result from historic, state-imposed de jure segregation. Rather, the familiar root cause of segregated schools in *all* the biracial metropolitan areas of our country is essentially the same: one of segregated residential and migratory patterns the impact of which on the racial composition of the schools was often perpetuated and rarely ameliorated by action of public school authorities. This is a national, not a southern phenomenon. And it is largely unrelated to whether a particular State had or did not have segregative school laws. * * * [c]

"I would hold [that] where segregated public schools exist within a school district to a substantial degree, there is a prima facie case that the duly constituted public authorities [are] sufficiently responsible to impose upon them a nationally applicable burden to demonstrate they nevertheless are operating a genuinely integrated school system. [A] system would be integrated in accord with constitutional standards if the responsible authorities had taken appropriate steps to (i) integrate faculties and administration; (ii) scrupulously assure equality of facilities, instruction and curricula opportunities throughout the district; (iii) utilize their authority to draw attendance zones to promote integration; and (iv) locate new schools, close old ones, and determine the size and grade categories with this same objective in mind. Where school authorities decide to undertake the transportation of students, this also must be with integrative opportunities in mind. [An] integrated school system does not mean—and indeed could not mean in view of the residential patterns of most of our major metropolitan areas—that *every school* must in fact be an integrated unit."

REHNQUIST, J., dissented: "[I]t would be a quite unprecedented application of principles of equitable relief to determine that if the gerrymandering of one attendance zone were proven, particular racial mixtures could be required by a federal district court for every school in the district. [U]nless the Equal Protection Clause [be] held to embody a principle of 'taint,' [such] a result can only be described as the product of judicial fiat. * * *

"The drastic extension of *Brown* which *Green* represented was barely, if at all, explicated in the latter opinion. To require that a genuinely 'dual' system be disestablished, in the sense that the assignment to a child of a particular school

c. Powell, J., quoted from Goodman, *De Facto School Segregation: A Constitutional and Empirical Analysis,* 60 Calif.L.Rev. 275, 297 (1972): "Ohio discarded [legally mandated segregation] in 1887, Indiana in 1949, [New York in 1938, New Mexico and Wyoming in 1954 (85 Harv.L.Rev. 85 n. 72 (1971))]. [T]here is no reason to suppose that 1954 is a universally appropriate dividing line between de jure segregation that may safely be assumed to have spent itself and that which may not. For many remedial purposes, adoption of an arbitrary but easily administrable cutoff point might not be objectionable. But in a situation such as school desegregation, where both the rights asserted and the remedial burdens imposed are of such magnitude, and where the resulting sectional discrimination is passionately resented, it is surely questionable whether such arbitrariness is either politically or morally acceptable."

Consider also Karst, *Not One Law at Rome and Another at Athens: The Fourteenth Amendment in Nationwide Application,* 1972 Wash.U.L.Q. 383, 388–89: "If the decisions of a southern school board concerning school location and school sizes can be said to have contributed to racial segregation among residential areas, then with far greater force it can be argued that official state action in northern and western cities has produced residential segregation. Until 1948, racially restrictive covenants in deeds were regularly enforced by state courts; governmental action has often located public housing [as] to intensify residential segregation; and, in a variety of ways, the federal government's programs of subsidy and loan guarantees have explicitly encouraged racial segregation in private housing."

is not made to depend on his race, is one thing. To require that school boards affirmatively undertake to achieve racial mixing in schools where such mixing is not achieved in sufficient degree by neutrally drawn boundary lines is quite obviously something else. [Whatever] may be the soundness of that decision in the context of a genuinely 'dual' school system, where segregation [had] once been mandated by law, I can see no constitutional justification for it in a situation such as that which the record shows to have obtained in Denver."

COLUMBUS BOARD OF EDUC. v. PENICK
443 U.S. 449, 99 S.Ct. 2941, 61 L.Ed.2d 666 (1979).

MR. JUSTICE WHITE delivered the opinion of the Court.

The public schools of Columbus, Ohio, are highly segregated by race. In 1976, over 32% of the 96,000 students in the system were black. About 70% of all students attended schools that were at least 80% black or 80% white. Half of the 172 schools were 90% black or 90% white. * * *

We have discovered no reason [to] disturb the judgment of the Court of Appeals, based on the findings and conclusions of the District Court, that the Board's conduct at the time of trial [in 1975] and before not only was animated by an unconstitutional, segregative purpose, but also had current, segregative impact that was sufficiently systemwide to warrant the [systemwide] remedy ordered by the District Court. * * *

First, [t]he Board insists that, since segregated schooling was not command-ed by state law ["at least since 1888,"] and since not all schools were wholly black or wholly white in 1954, the District Court was not warranted in finding a dual system. But the District Court found that the "Columbus Public Schools were *officially* segregated by race in 1954";[6] and in any event, there is no reason to question the finding that as the "direct result of cognitive acts or omissions" the Board maintained "an enclave of separate, black schools on the near east side of Columbus." Proof of purposeful and effective maintenance of a body of separate black schools in a substantial part of the system itself is prima facie proof of a dual school system and supports a finding to this effect absent sufficient contrary proof by the Board, which was not forthcoming in this case. *Keyes.*

Second, both courts below declared that since the decision in *Brown II,* the Columbus Board has been under a continuous constitutional obligation to dises-tablish its dual school system. [Each] failure or refusal to fulfill this affirmative duty continues the violation of the Fourteenth Amendment. *Wright v. Emporia,* 407 U.S. 451, 460, 92 S.Ct. 2196, 2202, 33 L.Ed.2d 51 (1972);[a] *United States v. Scotland Neck Bd. of Educ.,* 407 U.S. 484, 92 S.Ct. 2214, 33 L.Ed.2d 75 (1972)

---

6. The dissenters [claim] a better grasp of the historical and ultimate facts than the two courts below had. But on the issue of wheth-er there was a dual school system [in] 1954, on the record before us we are much more im-pressed by the views of the judges who have lived with the case over the years. Also, our dissenting Brothers' suggestion that this Court should play a special oversight role in reviewing the factual determinations of the lower courts in school desegregation cases, asserts an omnipotence and omniscience that we do not have and should not claim.

a. *Emporia,* per Stewart, J., upheld a dis-trict court injunction against "carving out a new school district from an existing district that has not yet completed the process of dismantling" its dual system because the "ef-fect"—wholly apart from the "purpose or mo-tivation"—"hinders [the] process of school de-segregation." Burger, C.J., joined by Blackmun, Powell and Rehnquist, JJ., dissent-ed.

(creation of a new school district in a city that had operated a dual school system but was not yet the subject of court-ordered desegregation).[b] * * *

The Board [has] pointed to nothing in the record persuading us that at the time of trial the dual school system and its effects had been disestablished. The Board does not appear to challenge the finding [that] at the time of trial most blacks were still going to black schools and most whites to white schools. Whatever the Board's current purpose with respect to racially separate education might be, it knowingly continued its failure to eliminate the consequences of its past intentionally segregative policies. * * *

Third, the District Court [also] found that in the intervening years there had been a series of Board actions and practices that could not "reasonably be explained without reference to racial concerns," and that "intentionally aggravated, rather than alleviated," racial separation in the schools. These matters included the general practice of assigning black teachers only to those schools with substantial black student populations, a practice that was terminated only in 1974[;] the intentionally segregative use of optional attendance zones,[8] discontiguous attendance areas,[9] and boundary changes;[10] and the selection of sites for new school construction that had the foreseeable and anticipated effect of maintaining the racial separation of the schools.[11] The court generally noted that "[s]ince the 1954 *Brown* decision, the Columbus defendants or their predecessors were adequately put on notice of the fact that action was required to correct and to prevent the increase in" segregation, yet failed to heed their duty to alleviate racial separation in the schools.[12]

[It] is urged that the courts below failed to heed the requirements of *Keyes, Washington v. Davis,* and *Arlington Heights,* that a plaintiff seeking to make out an equal protection violation on the basis of racial discrimination must show purpose. [But] the District Court correctly noted that actions having foreseeable and anticipated disparate impact are relevant evidence to prove the ultimate fact, forbidden purpose. Those cases do not forbid "the foreseeable effects

b. In *Scotland Neck,* the school officials defended their action as "necessary to avoid 'white flight' [but this cannot] be accepted as a reason for achieving anything less than complete uprooting" of the dual system. For critical analysis, see Note, *White Flight as a Factor in Desegregation Analysis: A Judicial Recognition of Reality,* 66 Va.L.Rev. 961 (1980). For the view that the Court's "rejection of the white flight argument should not be understood as an absolute principle," see Gewirtz, *Remedies and Resistance,* 92 Yale L.J. 585, 628–65 (1983).

8. Despite petitioners' avowedly strong preference for neighborhood schools, in times of residential racial transition the Board created optional attendance zones to allow white students to avoid predominantly black schools, which were often closer to the homes of the white pupils. * * *

9. This technique was applied when neighborhood schools would have tended to desegregate the involved schools. In the 1960s, a group of white students were bused past their neighborhood school to a "whiter" school. The District Court could "discern no other explanation than a racial one for the existence of the Moler discontiguous attendance

area for the period 1963 through 1969." * * *

10. Gerrymandering of boundary lines also continued after 1954. * * *

11. The District Court found that, of the 103 schools built by the Board between 1950 and 1975, 87 opened with racially identifiable student bodies and 71 remained that way at the time of trial. This result was reasonably foreseeable under the circumstances in light of the sites selected, and the Board was often specifically warned that it was, without apparent justification, choosing sites that would maintain or further segregation. * * *

12. [F]or example, the University Commission in 1968 made certain recommendations that it thought not only would assist desegregation of the schools but would encourage integrated residential patterns. The Board['s] response was "minimal." Additionally, the Board refused to create a site selection advisory group to assist in avoiding sites with a segregative effect, refused to ask state education officials to present plans for desegregating the Columbus public schools, and refused to apply for federal desegregation-assistance funds. * * *

standard from being utilized as one of the several kinds of proofs from which an inference of segregative intent may be properly drawn." * * *

It is also urged that the District Court and the Court of Appeals failed to observe the requirements [of] *Dayton Bd. of Educ. v. Brinkman (Dayton I)*, 433 U.S. 406, 97 S.Ct. 2766, 53 L.Ed.2d 851 (1977), which reiterated the accepted rule that the remedy imposed by a court of equity should be commensurate with the violation ascertained, and held that the remedy for the violations that had then been established in that case should be aimed at rectifying the "incremental segregative effect" of the discriminatory acts identified.[13] In *Dayton I*, only a few apparently isolated discriminatory practices had been found; yet a systemwide remedy had been imposed without proof of a systemwide impact.[c] Here, however, the District Court [and the Court of Appeals] repeatedly emphasized that it had found purposefully segregative practices with current, systemwide impact.[15] * * *

Affirmed.[d]

MR. JUSTICE REHNQUIST, with whom MR. JUSTICE POWELL joins, dissenting.

The school desegregation remedy imposed [is] as complete and dramatic a displacement of local authority by the federal judiciary as is possible in our federal system [—] 42,000 of the system's 96,000 students are reassigned to new schools. There are like reassignment of teachers, staff, and administrators, reorganization of the grade structure of virtually every elementary school in the system, the closing of 33 schools, and the additional transportation of 37,000 students. * * *

Today the Court affirms [this case] and *Dayton II* in opinions so Delphic that lower courts will be hard pressed to fathom their implications for school desegregation litigation. I can only offer two suggestions. The first is that the Court, possibly chastened by the complexity and emotion that accompanies school desegregation cases, wishes to relegate the determination of a violation of [equal protection] in any plan of pupil assignment, and the formulation of a remedy for its violation, to the judgment of a single District Judge. That judgment should be subject to review under the "clearly erroneous" standard by the appropriate Court of Appeals, in much the same way that actions for an accounting between private partners in a retail shoe business [are] handled.

---

13. Petitioners have indicated that a few of the recent violations specifically discussed by the District Court involved so few students and lasted for such a short time that they are unlikely to have any current impact. But that contention says little or nothing about the incremental impact of systemwide practices extending over many years. Petitioners also argue that because many of the involved schools were in areas that had become predominantly black residential areas by the time of trial the racial separation in the schools would have occurred even without the unlawful conduct of petitioners. But, as the District Court found, petitioners' evidence in this respect was insufficient to counter respondents' proof. And the phenomenon described by petitioners seems only to confirm, not disprove, the evidence accepted by the District Court that school segregation is a contributing cause of housing segregation. See *Keyes; Swann.*

c. *Dayton I*, per Rehnquist, J., also observed: "The finding [that many Dayton] schools are either predominantly white or predominantly black"—"standing by itself, is not a violation of the Fourteenth Amendment in the absence of a showing that this condition resulted from intentionally segregative actions on the part of the Board. *Davis.*"

15. Mr. Justice Rehnquist's dissent erroneously states that we have "reliev[ed] school desegregation plaintiffs from any showing of a causal nexus between intentional segregative actions and the conditions they seek to remedy." [But both courts below] found that the Board's purposefully discriminatory conduct and policies had current, systemwide impact— an essential predicate, as both courts recognized, for a systemwide remedy. * * *

d. The concurring opinions of Burger, C.J., and Stewart, J., and the dissenting opinion of Powell, J., appear after *Dayton II*, infra.

"Discriminatory purpose" and "systemwide violation" are to be treated as talismanic phrases which once invoked, warrant only the most superficial scrutiny by appellate courts.

Such an [approach] disparages both this Court's oft-expressed concern for the important role of local autonomy in educational matters and the significance of the constitutional rights involved. It also holds out the disturbing prospect of very different remedies being imposed on similar school systems because of the predilections of individual judges and their good faith but incongruent efforts to make sense of this Court's confused pronouncements today. * * *

[Alternatively, the] Court suggests a radical new approach to desegregation cases in systems without a history of statutorily mandated separation of the races: if a district court concludes—employing what in honesty must be characterized as an irrebuttable presumption—that there was a "dual" school system at the time of *Brown I,* it must find post-1954 constitutional violations in a school board's failure to take every affirmative step to integrate the system. Put differently, *racial imbalance* at the time the complaint is filed is sufficient to support a systemwide, racial balance school busing remedy if the district court can find *some* evidence of discriminatory purpose prior to 1954, without any inquiry into the causal relationship between those pre-1954 violations and current segregation in the school system.

[As] a matter of history, case law, or logic, there is nothing to support the novel proposition that the primary inquiry in school desegregation cases involving systems without a history of statutorily mandated racial assignment is what happened in those systems before 1954. As a matter of history, 1954 makes no more sense as a benchmark—indeed it makes *less* sense—than 1968, 1971 or 1973. Perhaps the latter year has the most to commend it, if one insists on a benchmark, because in *Keyes* this Court first confronted the problem of school segregation in the context of systems without a history of statutorily mandated separation of the races.

As a matter of logic, the majority's decision to turn the year 1954 into a constitutional Rubicon also fails. [It] is sophistry to suggest that a school board in Columbus in 1954 could have read *Brown* and gleaned from it a constitutional duty "to diffuse black students throughout the system" or take whatever other action the Court today thinks it should have taken. And not only was the school board to anticipate the state of the law 20 years hence, but also to have a full appreciation for discrete acts or omissions of school boards 20 to 50 years earlier.[9] * * *

Causality plays a central role in *Keyes* [which] held that before the burden of production shifts to the school board, the plaintiffs must prove "that the school authorities have carried out a systematic program of segregation *affecting a substantial portion of the students, schools, teachers and facilities within the school system."* The Court recognized that a trial court might find "that [at] some point in time the relationship between past segregative acts and present segregation may become so attenuated as to be incapable of supporting a finding of de jure segregation warranting judicial intervention." The relevance of past acts of the school board was to depend on whether "segregation resulting from those actions continues to exist." That inquiry is not central under the approach approved by the Court today. Henceforth, the question is apparently whether pre-1954 acts contributed in some unspecified manner to segregated

9. [I]ncidents relied on by the District Court occurred anywhere from 1909 to 1943.

conditions that existed in 1954. If the answer is yes, then the only question is whether the school board has exploited all integrative opportunities that presented themselves in the subsequent 25 years. If not, a systemwide remedy is in order, despite the plaintiff's failure to demonstrate a link between those past acts and current racial imbalance.

The Court's use of the term "affirmative duty" implies that integration be the pre-eminent—indeed, the controlling—educational consideration in school board decisionmaking. It takes precedence over other legitimate educational objectives subject to some vague feasibility limitation. That implication is dramatically demonstrated in this case. Both lower courts necessarily gave special significance to the Columbus School Board's post-1954 school construction and siting policies as supporting the systemwide remedy in this case. [The opinion then reviews the record in detail.]

Once a showing is made that the District Court believes satisfies the *Keyes* requirement of purposeful discrimination in a substantial part of the school system, the school board will almost invariably rely on its neighborhood school policy and residential segregation to show that it is not responsible for the existence of certain predominantly black and white schools in other parts of the school system. Under the District Court's reasoning, [not] only is that evidence not probative on the Board's lack of responsibility, it itself supports an inference of a constitutional violation. In addition, the District Court relied on a general proposition that "there is often a substantial reciprocal effect between the color of the school and the color of the neighborhood it serves" to block any inquiry into whether racially identifiable schools were the product of racially identifiable neighborhoods or whether past discriminatory acts bore a "but for" relationship to current segregative conditions. [But] as the District Court recognized, other factors play an important role in determining segregated residential patterns. [Yet] today the School Board is called to task for all the forces beyond their control that shaped residential segregation in Columbus. There is thus no room for *Keyes* or *Swann* rebuttal either with respect to the school system today or that of 30 years ago. * * *

DAYTON BOARD OF EDUC. v. BRINKMAN
(DAYTON II)
443 U.S. 526, 99 S.Ct. 2971, 61 L.Ed.2d 720 (1979).

MR. JUSTICE WHITE delivered the opinion of the Court.

[The] public schools of Dayton are highly segregated. [In 1972, when] the complaint was filed, 43% of the students in the Dayton system were black, but 51 of the 69 schools in the system were virtually all-white or all-black. * * *

The District Court's judgment that the Board had violated the Fourteenth Amendment was affirmed by the Court of Appeals * * *.

We reversed [in *Dayton I*, and the District Court then dismissed] the complaint [because] plaintiffs had failed to prove that acts of intentional segregation over 20 years old had any current incremental segregative effects [and that] plaintiffs had failed to show either discriminatory purpose or segregative effect, or both, with respect to the challenged practices and policies of the [Board].

The Court of Appeals reversed [and] held that, "at the time of *Brown I*, defendants were intentionally operating a dual school [system]" and that the "finding of the District Court to the contrary is clearly erroneous." On the record before us, we perceive no basis for petitioners' challenge to this holding of the Court of Appeals.[8]

Concededly, in the early 1950's, "77.6 percent of all students attended schools in which one race accounted for 90 percent or more of the students and 54.3 percent of the black students were assigned to four schools that were 100 percent black." One of these schools was Dunbar High School, which [had] been established as a districtwide black high school [and] remained so at the time of *Brown I* and up until 1962. The District Court also found that "among" the early and relatively undisputed acts of purposeful segregation was the establishment of Garfield as a black elementary school. The Court of Appeals found that two other elementary schools were, through a similar process of optional attendance zones and the creation and maintenance of all-black faculties, intentionally designated and operated as all-black schools in the 1930's [and] at the time of *Brown I*. Additionally, the District Court had specifically found that in 1950 the faculty at 100% black schools was 100% black and that the faculty at all other schools was 100% white.

These facts, the Court of Appeals held, made clear that the Board was purposefully operating segregated schools in a substantial part of the district [at the time of *Brown I*], which warranted an inference and a finding that segregation in other parts of the system was also purposeful absent evidence [as required by *Keyes*.[9]] Based on its review of the entire record, the Court of Appeals concluded that the Board had not responded with sufficient evidence to counter the inference that a dual system was in existence in Dayton in 1954.

* * *

Given intentionally segregated schools in 1954, [the] Court of Appeals was quite right in holding that the Board was thereafter under a continuing duty to eradicate the effects of that system, and that the systemwide nature of the violation furnished prima facie proof that current segregation in the Dayton schools was caused at least in part by prior intentionally segregative official acts. Thus, judgment for the plaintiffs was authorized and required absent sufficient countervailing evidence by the defendant school officials. *Keyes*. At the time of trial, Dunbar High School and the three black elementary schools, or the schools that succeeded them, remained black schools; and most of the schools in Dayton

---

8. We have no quarrel with our Brother Stewart's general conclusion that there is great value in appellate courts showing deference to the fact-finding of local trial judges. The clearly erroneous standard serves that purpose well. [The] Court of Appeals performed its unavoidable duty in this case and concluded that the District Court had erred. [W]e see no reason on the record before us to upset the judgment of the Court of Appeals in this respect.

9. We do not deprecate the relevance of segregated faculty assignments as one of the factors in proving the existence of a school system that is dual for teachers *and* students; but to the extent that the Court of Appeals understood *Swann* as holding that faculty segregation makes out a prima facie case [of] purposeful racial assignment of students, this is an overreading of *Swann*.

The Court of Appeals also held that the District Court had not given proper weight to

Oliver v. Michigan Bd. of Educ., 508 F.2d 178, 182 (CA6 1974), cert. denied, 421 U.S. 963 (1975), where the Court of Appeals had held that "[a] presumption of segregative purpose arises when plaintiffs establish that the natural, probable, and foreseeable result of public officials' action or inaction was an increase or perpetuation of public school segregation" * * *. We have never held that as a general proposition the foreseeability of segregative consequences makes out a prima facie case of purposeful racial discrimination and shifts the burden of producing evidence to the defendants * * *. Of course, as we hold in *Columbus* today, proof of foreseeable consequences is one type of quite relevant evidence of racially discriminatory purpose, and it may itself show a failure to fulfill the duty to eradicate the consequences of prior purposefully discriminatory conduct.

were virtually one-race schools, as were 80% of the classrooms. [Against] this background, the Court of Appeals held [that] defendants had failed to come forward with evidence to deny "that the current racial composition of the school population reflects the systemwide impact" of the Board's prior discriminatory conduct.

Part of the affirmative duty imposed by our cases [is] the obligation not to take any action that would impede the process of disestablishing the dual system and its effects. [T]he measure of the post-*Brown* conduct of a school board under an unsatisfied duty to liquidate a dual system is the effectiveness, not the purpose, of the actions in decreasing or increasing the segregation caused by the dual system. *Emporia.* As was clearly established in *Keyes* and *Swann,* the Board had to do more than abandon its prior discriminatory purpose. The Board has had an affirmative responsibility to see that pupil assignment policies and school construction and abandonment practices "are not used and do not serve to perpetuate or re-establish the dual school system," *Columbus,* and the Board has a " 'heavy burden' " of showing that actions that increased or continued the effects of the dual system serve important and legitimate ends.

[Though] the Board was often put on notice of the effects of its acts or omissions, the District Court found that "with one [counterproductive] exception [no] attempt was made to alter the racial characteristics of any of the schools." The Court of Appeals held that far from performing its constitutional duty, the Board had engaged in "post-1954 actions which actually have exacerbated the racial separation existing at the time of *Brown I.*" [We] see no reason to disturb these factual determinations, which conclusively show the breach of duty found by the Court of Appeals.

[The] Court of Appeals was also quite justified in utilizing the Board's total failure to fulfill its affirmative duty—and indeed its conduct resulting in increased segregation—to trace the current, systemwide segregation back to the purposefully dual system of the 1950's and to the subsequent acts of intentional discrimination. * * *

Affirmed.

MR. JUSTICE STEWART, with whom THE CHIEF JUSTICE joins, concurring in the result in [*Columbus*] and dissenting in [*Dayton II*]. * * *

Whether actions that produce racial separation are intentional [present] very difficult and subtle factual questions. Similarly intricate may be factual inquiries into the breadth of any constitutional violation, and hence of any permissible remedy. [I] suspect that it is impossible for a reviewing court factually to know a case from a 6,600 page printed record as well as the trial judge knew it. [T]herefore, I think appellate courts should accept even more readily than in most cases the factual findings of the courts of first instance.

[W]hen the factual issues are as elusive as these, who bears the burden of proof can easily determine who prevails in the litigation. [The] prejudices of the school boards of 1954 (and earlier) cannot realistically be assumed to haunt the school boards of today. [It] is unrealistic to assume that the hand of 1954 plays any major part in shaping the current school systems in [Columbus or Dayton]. For these reasons, I simply cannot accept the shift in the litigative burden of proof adopted by the Court. [Just] as I would defer to the findings of fact made by the District Court in the *Dayton* case, I would accept the trial court's findings in [the *Columbus* case].

MR. JUSTICE REHNQUIST, with whom MR. JUSTICE POWELL joins, dissenting [in *Dayton II*].

* * * Little would be gained by another "blow-by-blow" recitation in dissent of how the Court's cascade of presumptions in this case sweeps away the distinction between de facto and de jure segregation.

[The] District Judge in *Dayton* did not employ a post-1954 "affirmative duty" test. Violations he did identify were found not to have any causal relationship to existing conditions of segregation in the Dayton school system. He did not employ a foreseeability test for intent, hold the school system responsible for residential segregation, or impugn the neighborhood school policy, as an explanation for some existing one race schools. In short, the Dayton and Columbus district judges had completely different ideas of what the law required. [And] I have no doubt that the Court of Appeals' heavy-handed approach in this case is to some degree explained by the perceived inequity of imposing a systemwide racial-balance remedy on Columbus while finding no violation in Dayton. The simple meting out of equal remedies, however, is [not] "equal justice under law."

MR. JUSTICE POWELL, dissenting in [*Columbus*] and [*Dayton II*]. * * *

Holding the school boards of these two cities responsible for *all* of the segregation in the Dayton and Columbus systems and prescribing fixed racial ratios in every school as the constitutionally required remedy necessarily implies a belief that the same school boards—under court supervision—will be capable of bringing about and maintaining the desired racial balance in each of these schools. The experience in city after city demonstrates that this is an illusion. The process of resegregation, stimulated by resentment against judicial coercion and concern as to the effect of court supervision of education, will follow today's decisions as surely as it has in other cities subjected to similar sweeping decrees.

* * *

MR. CHIEF JUSTICE BURGER, concurring in the judgment [in *Columbus*].

* * * I agree [with] Mr. Justice Rehnquist's opinion that criticizes the Court's reliance on the finding that both Columbus and Dayton operated "dual school systems" at the time of *Brown I* as a basis for holding that these school boards have labored under an unknown and unforeseeable affirmative duty to desegregate their schools for the past 25 years. Nothing in reason or our previous decisions provides foundation for this novel legal standard.

I also agree with many of the concerns expressed by Mr. Justice Powell [whether] massive public transportation really accomplishes the desirable objectives sought. Nonetheless our prior decisions have sanctioned its use when a constitutional violation of sufficient magnitude has been found. We cannot retry these sensitive and difficult issues in this Court; we can only set the general legal standards and, within the limits of appellate review, see that they are followed.

Notes and Questions

1. *"De facto" school segregation.* (a) Contrary to *Dayton I,* in the absence of any "intentionally segregative actions" on the part of any state agency, *should* the fact that many schools in a district "are either predominantly white or predominantly black" "standing by itself" violate equal protection? For an early view, see Fiss, *Racial Imbalance in the Public Schools: The Constitutional Concepts,* 78 Harv.L.Rev. 564 (1965).

(b) *Effect on students.* Consider Note, *Racial Imbalance in the Public Schools: Constitutional Dimensions and Judicial Response,* 18 Vand.L.Rev. 1290, 1295–96 (1965): "Fiss points out 'that students in such schools are also deprived of the intellectual stimulation that comes from the exchange of ideas and the development of personal relationships in a racially and socially heterogeneous context.' [Because *Brown*] found that 'to separate [blacks] from others of similar age and qualifications solely because of their race generates a feeling of inferiority,' proponents of racial balance in the schools argue analogously that racial imbalance also breeds inferiority. [A] more damaging aspect of racial imbalance relates to [a] corollary goal of education [which is] 'to induct the young person systematically into the culture and society to which he is an heir and in which he should be a partner.' The Supreme Court recognized [this] in *Brown*. [It] seems clear that regardless of the cause of the separation of the races the isolation of a minority race will prevent the achievement of this educational goal." Compare Yudof, note 1(a) after *Swann,* at 436: "One study of the psychological impact of segregation on black children has found that the black child's self-concept is inversely related to the proportion of white students in the school; the whiter his school the lower the black child rated himself. Other studies have reached the opposite conclusion. Studies of the relationship between personality development and segregation are similarly conflicting. [Moreover,] available studies are inconclusive as to whether integration in fact accelerates academic achievement. Further complicating the evidence are the many additional variables that may alter the effect of integration or segregation: the degree of interracial hostility, the percentage of black students in relation to the school population, the socio-economic makeup of the student body, the existence of ability grouping, and the attitudes of parents, teachers, and administrators."

(c) *Constitutional "values" and judicial interpretation.* Consider Goodman, *Racial Imbalance in the Oakland Schools* 21–23 (1966): "[T]here is a *moral* difference of the first importance between a law which discriminates against citizens solely on the ground of race and one which, though based on racially neutral criteria, operates to the detriment of a minority group.[g] [A] second important difference between legislation requiring, and legislation merely resulting in, racial segregation is the absence in the former case of any legitimate State interest which might countervail the harm inflicted on Negro children. [The] only rationale for segregation which has even a semblance of plausibility is that it helps to avoid needless friction between the races and thus preserves tranquility both in the classroom and in the larger society. In the long run, however, by creating barriers to normal intergroup relations and arousing the resentment and frustration of the minority group, segregation probably does more to defeat than to promote racial peace. And even were this not so, it still could not be said that segregation is a necessary means to that end, for there are many other ways of dealing with the problem of racial conflict. [This] is not the case with de facto segregation. Here the psychological injury suffered by Negro children results from the use of otherwise legitimate means (geographical districting criteria) to accomplish an otherwise legitimate end (the neighborhood school) which could not be accomplished in any other way."

Even if de jure and de facto segregation are distinguishable, is "the cause of racial integration entitled to a 'preferred position' in the hierarchy of constitu-

---

g. Compare Goodman, fn. c in *Keyes,* at 319: "Is there really a decisive moral difference between the state of mind that produces de facto segregation and that which produced de jure segregation? Those who advocate the neighborhood school may not want segregation, but they well know their policy begets it; either they see no harm or they deem the harm an acceptable cost. On the other hand, if de facto segregation is rarely inadvertent, de jure segregation is not always malevolent. Many an avowed segregationist genuinely believes his policy benefits all, black and white alike, offering them a classroom free from racial friction."

tional values"? Dorsen, *Northern School Segregation,* 10 How.L.J. 127, 129 (1964).

Does *Washington v. Davis* plainly reject the view that "other values" should be disregarded in "the cause of racial integration"? Consider Goodman, note b supra, at 306: "[If] it is true that de facto, like de jure segregation, generates feelings of racial inferiority in black school children, the injury is one they incur distinctively as blacks, solely on account of their race. A white child similarly situated would not be similarly affected. In that sense, the neighborhood school policy can be said to inflict a 'racially specific' harm, a harm differing in kind from that inflicted by [the] examples of state action [in fn. 14 of *Davis*] that hurt more blacks than whites, but hurt the individual black no more than his white counterpart."

3. *Interdistrict remedies.* (a) *Schools.* In MILLIKEN v. BRADLEY, 418 U.S. 717, 94 S.Ct. 3112, 41 L.Ed.2d 1069 (1974), the district court found that various actions of the Detroit Board of Education, the State Board of Education and the Michigan legislature (e.g., barring use of state funds for busing), produced de jure segregation in Detroit; that, because of the city's racial composition, desegregation plans limited to Detroit "would accentuate the racial identifiability of the district as a Black school system, and would not accomplish desegregation." Thus, the district judge ordered a plan encompassing 53 neighboring suburban school districts (in Oakland and Macomb counties). The Court, per BURGER, C.J.,—emphasizing that, apart from one "isolated instance affecting two of the school districts," the record "contains evidence of de jure segregated conditions only in" Detroit—reversed, stating the issue as "whether a federal court may impose a multidistrict [remedy] absent any finding that the other included school districts have failed to operate unitary school systems within their districts, [that] the boundary lines of any affected school district were established with the purpose of fostering racial segregation [, that] the included districts committed acts which effected segregation within the other districts, and absent a meaningful opportunity for the included neighboring school districts to [be] heard on the propriety of a multidistrict remedy or on the question of constitutional violations by those neighboring districts":

"The controlling principle [is] that the scope of the remedy is determined by the nature and extent of the constitutional violation. *Swann.* [Before] imposing a cross-district remedy, it must first be shown that there has been a constitutional violation within one district that produces a significant segregative effect in [another] [a]. The constitutional right of the Negro respondents residing in Detroit is to attend a unitary school system in that district. Unless petitioners drew the district lines in a discriminatory fashion, or arranged for White students residing in the Detroit district to attend schools in Oakland and Macomb Counties, they were under no constitutional duty to make provisions for Negro students to do [so.]"

The courts below assumed "that the Detroit schools could not be truly desegregated—in their view of what constituted desegregation—unless the racial composition of the student body of each school substantially reflected the racial

---

a. Is this allocation of the burden of proof consistent with *Keyes?* Are there reasons for a presumption of segregative intent or effect in a *Keyes*-type situation but not in a *Milliken*-type one?

For a listing of subsequent cases imposing interdistrict remedies, see Note, *Interdistrict Remedies for Segregated Schools,* 79 Colum.L. Rev. 1168 n. 5 (1979).

composition of the population of the metropolitan area as a whole. [But this is contrary to] the clear import of" *Swann*.[c]

"No single tradition in public education is more deeply rooted than local [control. Here,] consolidation would give rise to an array [of] problems [such as]: What would be the status and authority of the present popularly elected school boards? [What] board or boards would levy taxes for school operations in these 54 districts constituting the consolidated metropolitan area? [Would] the validity of long-term bonds be jeopardized unless approved by all of the component districts as well as the State? [Who] would establish attendance zones, purchase school equipment, locate and construct new schools, and indeed attend to all the myriad day-to-day decisions that are necessary to school [operations]? [A]bsent a complete restructuring of the laws of Michigan relating to school districts the District Court will become first, a de facto 'legislative authority' to resolve these complex questions, and then the 'school superintendent' for the entire area. This [would] deprive the people of control of schools through their elected representatives." [d]

WHITE, J., joined by Douglas, Brennan and Marshall, JJ., dissented: "[The] most promising [proposed "Detroit-only" remedy] would 'leave many of its schools 75 to 90 per cent Black.' Transportation on a 'vast scale' would be required [and] the plan 'would change a school system which is now Black and White to one that would be perceived as Black, thereby increasing the flight of [Whites].' [In] proceeding to design its [interdistrict plan, the district] court's express finding was [that] 'desegregation within the area described is physically easier and more practicable and feasible, than desegregation efforts limited [to] Detroit.' The Court of Appeals [concluded] that an interdistrict remedy 'is supported by the status of school districts under Michigan law and by the historical control exercised over local school districts by the legislature of Michigan and by State agencies and officials.' Obviously, whatever difficulties there might be, they are surmountable; for the Court itself concedes that had there been sufficient evidence of an interdistrict violation, the District Court could have fashioned a single remedy for the districts implicated * * *.

"I am even more mystified how the Court can ignore the legal reality that the constitutional violations, even if occurring locally, were committed by gov-

---

c. Cf. Rehnquist, J., joined by Stewart and Powell, JJ., dissenting from denial of certiorari in *Delaware State Bd. of Educ. v. Evans*, 446 U.S. 923, 100 S.Ct. 1862, 64 L.Ed.2d 278 (1980), in which the district court found an interdistrict violation and ordered that (1) the county's eleven school boards be replaced by a single board to be court-appointed for five years, and (2) all pupils be reassigned to accomplish a racial balance reflecting the racial composition of the total area involved. The district court acknowledged that the remedy was "formulated without exacting consideration of whether [it] returned [the] county schools to the precise position they would have assumed 'but for' the found constitutional violations."

Burger, C.J. would have granted certiorari if a full Court had been available to consider the case. Stevens, J., did not participate. See also fn. d in *Swann*.

d. Stewart, J., who joined the Court's opinion, concurred "in view of some of the extravagant language of the [dissents.] [S]egregative acts within the city alone cannot be presumed to have produced [an] increase in the number of Negro students *in the city as a whole*. It is this essential fact of a predominantly Negro school population in Detroit—caused by unknown and perhaps unknowable factors such as in-migration, birth rates, economic changes, or cumulative acts of private racial fears— that accounts for the 'growing core of Negro schools,' a 'core' that has grown to include virtually the entire city. The Constitution simply does not allow federal courts to attempt to change that situation unless [it] is shown that the State, or its political subdivisions, have contributed to cause the situation to exist[—e.g., "by purposeful racially discriminatory use of state housing or zoning laws."]"

ernmental entities for which the State is responsible and that it is the State that must respond to the command of the Fourteenth Amendment. * * *

"[The] majority's suggestion that judges should not attempt to grapple with the administrative problems attendant on a reorganization of school attendance patterns is wholly without foundation. It is precisely this sort of task which the district courts have been properly exercising to vindicate the constitutional rights of Negro students since [*Brown I*]."

MARSHALL, J., joined by Douglas, Brennan, and White, JJ., dissented: "Ironically purporting to base its result on the principle that the scope of the remedy [should] be determined by the nature and the extent of the constitutional violation, the Court's answer is to provide no remedy at [all].

"The State's creation, through de jure acts of segregation, of a growing core of all-Negro schools inevitably acted as a magnet to attract Negroes to the areas served by such schools [and] helped drive whites to other areas of the city or to the suburbs. [Having] created a system where whites and Negroes were intentionally kept apart so that they could not become accustomed to learning together, the State is responsible for the fact that many whites will react to the dismantling of that segregated system by attempting to flee to the suburbs.

"The State's duty should be no different here than in cases where it is shown that certain of a State's voting districts are malapportioned in violation of the Fourteenth Amendment. See *Reynolds v. Sims,* [Sec. 4, I, A infra]. Overrepresented electoral districts are required to participate in reapportionment, although their only 'participation' in the violation was to do nothing about it. Similarly, electoral districts which themselves meet representation standards must frequently be redrawn as part of a remedy for other over- and under-inclusive districts. No finding of fault on the part of each electoral district and no finding of a discriminatory effect on each district is a prerequisite to its involvement in the constitutionally required remedy." [f]

(b) *Housing.* In HILLS v. GAUTREAUX, 425 U.S. 284, 96 S.Ct. 1538, 47 L.Ed.2d 792 (1976), the district court found that the federal Dep't of Housing (HUD) and the Chicago Housing Authority (CHA) had racially segregated public housing projects in Chicago. The Court, per STEWART, J., held that "nothing in [*Milliken*] suggests a per se rule that federal courts lack authority to order parties found to have violated the Constitution to undertake remedial efforts beyond the municipal boundaries of the city where the violation occurred. [The] proposed remedy in *Milliken* was impermissible because of the limits on the federal judicial power to interfere with the operation of state political entities that were not implicated in unconstitutional conduct. Here, [a] judicial order directing relief beyond the boundary lines of Chicago will not necessarily entail coercion of uninvolved governmental units, because [both] CHA and HUD have the authority to operate outside the Chicago city limits.[14]

"[In] contrast to the desegregation order in [*Milliken*], a metropolitan relief order directed to HUD would not consolidate or in any way restructure local governmental units. The remedial decree would neither force suburban governments to submit public housing proposals to HUD nor displace the rights and powers accorded local government entities under federal or state housing statutes or existing land use laws. The order would have the same effect on the

f. Douglas, J., also filed a brief dissent.

14. [Although] the state officials in *Milliken* had the authority to operate across school district lines, the exercise of that authority [would] have eliminated numerous independent school districts or at least have displaced important powers granted those uninvolved governmental entities under state law.

suburban governments as a discretionary decision by HUD to use its statutory powers to provide the respondents with alternatives to the racially segregated Chicago public housing system created by CHA and HUD." [a]

(c) *Other remedies.* In MILLIKEN v. BRADLEY (MILLIKEN II), 433 U.S. 267, 97 S.Ct. 2749, 53 L.Ed.2d 745 (1977), the district court, on remand, fashioned a new decree which required (in addition to a pupil assignment plan for the Detroit school system) a number of "educational components"—including remedial reading and revised testing and counseling programs for pupils, and a training program for teachers. The state, which was ordered to pay for part of these programs, appealed. The Court, per BURGER, C.J., affirmed: "[T]he District Court found that [the] educational components [were] necessary to restore the victims of discriminatory conduct to the position they would have enjoyed in terms of education had these four components been provided in a nondiscriminatory manner in a school system free from pervasive de jure racial segregation. [D]iscriminatory student assignment policies can themselves manifest and breed other inequalities built into a dual system founded on racial discrimination."

V. AFFIRMATIVE ACTION AND "BENIGN" DISCRIMINATION

Swann ruled that state officials may—and, in some circumstances, seemingly must—use racial criteria to remedy unconstitutional segregation. This section concerns voluntary government action that employs racial/ethnic criteria or favors members of racial/ethnic minorities in order to remedy (a) unlawful discrimination other than segregation, or (b) racial/ethnic inequality that occurs in the absence of a judicial finding of illegal discrimination.

———

UNITED JEWISH ORGANIZATIONS v. CAREY, 430 U.S. 144, 97 S.Ct. 996, 51 L.Ed.2d 229 (1977): Three New York City counties became subject to § 5 of the Voting Rights Act (p. 1140 infra) because in 1968 they had used a literacy test for voting and less than 50% of the eligible residents had voted. To comply with the Act's requirement that the Attorney General conclude that any new reapportionment have neither "the purpose [nor] the effect [of] abridging the right to vote on account of race or color," the New York legislature produced a plan that "deliberately increased the nonwhite majorities in certain districts in order to enhance the opportunity for election of nonwhite representatives from those districts." Petitioners sued on behalf of an Hasidic Jewish community which had been in one district with a white majority but was now split into two districts with nonwhite majorities. Although there was no opinion for the Court, it upheld the plan.

WHITE, J., joined by Brennan, Blackmun and Stevens, JJ., held that "the permissible use of racial criteria is not confined to eliminating the effects of past discriminatory districting or apportionment."

WHITE, J., joined by Rehnquist and Stevens, JJ., also upheld the plan wholly apart from the requirements of the Voting Rights Act. Although the plan "deliberately used race," it "represented no racial slur or stigma with respect to whites or any other race [and] did not minimize or unfairly cancel out white voting strength. [It] left white majorities in approximately 70% of the [districts] which had a county-wide population that was 65% white. Thus, even if voting in the county occurred strictly according to race, whites would not be under-represented relative to their share of the population." [b]

BURGER, C.J., dissented: "While petitioners certainly have no constitutional right to remain unified within a single political district, they do have, in my view, the constitutional right not to be carved up so as to create a voting bloc composed of some other ethnic or racial group through the kind of racial gerrymandering the Court condemned in *Gomillion v. Lightfoot.*"

REGENTS OF UNIV. OF CALIFORNIA v. BAKKE

438 U.S. 265, 98 S.Ct. 2733, 57 L.Ed.2d 750 (1978).

MR. JUSTICE POWELL announced the judgment of the Court.

This case presents a challenge to the special admissions program of the petitioner, the Medical School of the University of California at Davis * * *.

For the reasons stated in the following opinion, I believe that so much of the judgment of the California court as holds petitioner's special admissions program unlawful and directs that respondent be admitted to the Medical School must be affirmed. For the reasons expressed in a separate opinion, my Brothers The Chief Justice, Mr. Justice Stewart, Mr. Justice Rehnquist, and Mr. Justice Stevens concur in this judgment.

I also conclude [that] the portion of the court's judgment enjoining petitioner from according any consideration to race in its admissions process must be reversed. For reasons expressed in separate opinions, my Brothers Mr. Justice Brennan, Mr. Justice White, Mr. Justice Marshall, and Mr. Justice Blackmun concur in this judgment. * * *

I.[†] [Under] the regular admissions procedure, [c]andidates whose overall undergraduate grade point averages fell below 2.5 on a scale of 4.0 were summarily rejected. About one out of six applicants was invited for a personal interview [and] each candidate was rated on a scale of 1 to 100 * * *. The rating embraced the interviewers' summaries, the candidate's overall grade point average, grade point average in science courses, and scores on the Medical College Admissions Test (MCAT), letters of recommendation, extracurricular activities, and other biographical data. The ratings were added together to arrive at each candidate's "benchmark" score. Since five committee members rated each candidate in 1973, a perfect score was 500; in 1974, six members rated each candidate, so that a perfect score was 600. The full committee then reviewed the file and scores of each applicant and made offers of [admission]. The chairman was responsible for placing names on the waiting list. They were not placed in strict numerical order; instead, the chairman had discretion to include persons with "special skills."

The special admissions program operated with a separate committee, a majority of whom were members of minority groups. On the 1973 application

---

b. Stewart, J., joined by Powell, J., concurred, finding no "invidious purpose." Brennan, J., concurred exclusively on the basis of the Voting Rights Act. Marshall, J., did not participate.

† Mr. Justice Brennan, Mr. Justice White, Mr. Justice Marshall, and Mr. Justice Blackmun join Parts I and V–C of this opinion. Mr. Justice White also joins Part III–A of this opinion.

form, candidates were asked to indicate whether they wished to be considered as "economically and/or educationally disadvantaged" applicants; on the 1974 form the question was whether they wished to be considered as members of a "minority group," which the medical school apparently viewed as "Blacks," "Chicanos," "Asians," and "American Indians." [No] formal definition of "disadvantage" was ever produced, but the chairman of the special committee screened each application to see whether it reflected economic or educational deprivation. [T]he applications then were rated by the special committee in a fashion similar to that used by the general admissions committee, except that special candidates did not have to meet the 2.5 grade point average [cut-off]. About one-fifth of the total number of special applicants were invited for interviews in 1973 and 1974 [and] the special committee assigned each [a] benchmark score [and] presented its top choices to the general admissions committee. The latter did not rate or compare the special candidates against the general applicants, but could reject recommended special candidates for failure to meet course requirements or other specific deficiencies. The special committee continued to recommend special applicants until a number prescribed by faculty vote were admitted. [I]n 1973 and 1974, when the class size had doubled to 100, the prescribed number of special admissions also doubled, to 16. [Although] disadvantaged whites applied to the special program in large numbers, none received an offer of admission through that process. Indeed, in 1974, at least, the special committee explicitly considered only "disadvantaged" special applicants who were members of one of the designated minority groups.

Allan Bakke is a white male who applied [in] 1973 and 1974. In [1973, despite] a strong benchmark score of 468 out of 500, Bakke was rejected. [In 1974, his] faculty interviewer [was] Dr. Lowrey to whom he had written in protest of the special admissions program. Dr. Lowrey found Bakke "rather limited in his approach" to the problems of the medical profession and found disturbing Bakke's "very definite opinions which were based more on his personal viewpoints than upon a study of the total problem." Dr. Lowrey gave Bakke the lowest of his six ratings, an 86; his total was 549 out of 600. Again, Bakke's application was rejected. In neither year did the chairman of the admissions committee, Dr. Lowrey, exercise his discretion to place Bakke on the waiting list. In both years, applicants were admitted under the special program with grade point averages, MCAT scores, and benchmark scores significantly lower than Bakke's. * * *

II. [Powell, J., found that Title VI of the Civil Rights Act of 1964—which provides that "No person in the United States shall, on the ground of race, color, or national origin, be excluded from participation in, be denied the benefits of, or be subjected to, discrimination under any program or activity receiving Federal financial assistance"—proscribes "only those racial classifications that would violate the Equal Protection Clause or the Fifth Amendment."]

III. A. [T]he parties fight a sharp preliminary action over the proper characterization of the special admissions program. Petitioner prefers to view it as establishing a "goal" of minority representation in the medical school. Respondent, echoing the courts below, labels it a racial quota.

This semantic distinction is beside the [point]. To the extent that there existed a pool of at least minimally qualified minority applicants to fill the 16 special admissions seats, white applicants could compete only for 84 seats in the entering class, rather than the 100 open to minority applicants. Whether this limitation is described as a quota or a goal, it is a line drawn on the basis of race and ethnic status.

[P]etitioner argues that the court below erred in applying strict scrutiny to the special admissions programs because white males, such as respondent, are not a "discrete and insular minority" requiring extraordinary protection from the majoritarian political process. *Carolene Products Co.*, n. 4, [p. 27 supra. These] characteristics may be relevant in deciding whether or not to add new types of classifications to the list of "suspect" categories or whether a particular classification survives close examination. Racial and ethnic classifications, however, are subject to stringent examination without regard to these additional characteristics. [*Hirabayashi; Korematsu*]

B. This perception of racial and ethnic distinctions is rooted in our Nation's constitutional and demographic history. The Court's initial view of the Fourteenth Amendment was that its "one pervading purpose" was "the freedom of the slave race * * *." *Slaughter-House Cases.* [During] the dormancy of the Equal Protection Clause, the United States had become a nation of minorities. Each had to struggle—and to some extent struggles still—to overcome the prejudices not of a monolithic majority, but of a "majority" composed of various minority groups of whom it was said—perhaps unfairly in many cases—that a shared characteristic was a willingness to disadvantage other groups. As the Nation filled with the stock of many lands, the reach of the Clause was gradually extended to all ethnic groups seeking protection from official discrimination. * * *

Over the past 30 years, this Court has embarked upon the crucial mission of interpreting the Equal Protection Clause with the view of assuring to all persons "the protection of equal laws" in a Nation confronting a legacy of slavery and racial discrimination. * * *

Petitioner urges us to adopt for the first time a more restrictive view [and] hold that discrimination against members of the white "majority" cannot be suspect if its purpose can be characterized as "benign." [34] [But it] is far too late to argue that the guarantee of equal protection to *all* persons permits the recognition of special wards entitled to a degree of protection greater than that accorded others. * * *

Once the artificial line of a "two-class theory" of the Fourteenth Amendment is put aside, the difficulties entailed in varying the level of judicial review according to a perceived "preferred" status of a particular racial or ethnic minority are intractable. The concepts of "majority" and "minority" necessarily

34. In the view of Mr. Justice Brennan, Mr. Justice White, Mr. Justice Marshall, and Mr. Justice Blackmun, the pliable notion of "stigma" is the crucial element in analyzing racial classifications. The Equal Protection Clause is not framed in terms of "stigma." Certainly the word has no clearly defined constitutional meaning. It reflects a subjective judgment that is standardless. *All* state-imposed classifications that rearrange burdens and benefits on the basis of race are likely to be viewed with deep resentment by the individuals burdened. The denial to innocent persons of equal rights and opportunities may outrage those so deprived and therefore may be perceived as invidious. These individuals are likely to find little comfort in the notion that the deprivation they are asked to endure is merely the price of membership in the dominant majority and that its imposition is inspired by the supposedly benign purpose of aiding others. One should not lightly dismiss the inherent unfairness of, and the perception of mistreatment that accompanies, a system of allocating benefits and privileges on the basis of skin color and ethnic origin. Moreover, Mr. Justice Brennan, Mr. Justice White, Mr. Justice Marshall, and Mr. Justice Blackmun offer no principle for deciding whether preferential classifications reflect a benign remedial purpose or a malevolent stigmatic classification, since they are willing in this case to accept mere post hoc declarations by an isolated state entity—a medical school faculty—unadorned by particularized findings of past discrimination, to establish such a remedial purpose.

reflect temporary arrangements and political judgments. As observed above, the white "majority" itself is composed of various minority groups, most of which can lay claim to a history of prior discrimination at the hands of the state and private individuals. Not all of these groups can receive preferential treatment and corresponding judicial tolerance of distinctions drawn in terms of race and nationality, for then the only "majority" left would be a new minority of White Anglo-Saxon Protestants. There is no principled basis for deciding which groups would merit "heightened judicial solicitude" and which would not.[36] Courts would be asked to evaluate the extent of the prejudice and consequent harm suffered by various minority groups. Those whose societal injury is thought to exceed some arbitrary level of tolerability then would be entitled to preferential classifications at the expense of individuals belonging to other groups. Those classifications would be free from exacting judicial scrutiny. As these preferences began to have their desired effect, and the consequences of past discrimination were undone, new judicial rankings would be necessary. The kind of variable sociological and political analysis necessary to produce such rankings simply does not lie within the judicial competence—even if they otherwise were politically feasible and socially desirable.[37]

Moreover, there are serious problems of justice connected with the idea of preference itself. First, it may not always be clear that a so-called preference is in fact benign. Courts may be asked to validate burdens imposed upon individual members of particular groups in order to advance the group's general interest. Nothing in the Constitution supports the notion that individuals may be asked to suffer otherwise impermissible burdens in order to enhance the societal standing of their ethnic groups. Second, preferential programs may only reinforce common stereotypes holding that certain groups are unable to achieve success without special protection based on a factor having no relationship to individual

36. [M]y Brothers Brennan, White, Marshall, and Blackmun [would] require as a justification for a program such as petitioner's, only two findings: (i) that there has been some form of discrimination against the preferred minority groups "by society at large" (it being conceded that petitioner had no history of discrimination), and (ii) that "there is reason to believe" that the disparate impact sought to be rectified by the program is the "product" of such discrimination * * *.

The breadth of this hypothesis is unprecedented in our constitutional system. The first step is easily taken. No one denies the regrettable fact that there has been societal discrimination in this country against various racial and ethnic groups. The second step, however, involves a speculative leap: but for this discrimination by society at large, Bakke "would have failed to qualify for admission" because Negro applicants—nothing is said about Asians—would have made better scores. Not one word in the record supports this conclusion, and the plurality offers no standard for courts to use in applying such a presumption of causation to other racial or ethnic classifications. This failure is a grave one, since if it may be concluded *on this record* that each of the minority groups preferred by the petitioner's special program is entitled to the benefit of the presumption, it would seem difficult to

determine that any of the dozens of minority groups that have suffered "societal discrimination" cannot also claim it, in any area of social intercourse. See Part IV-B, infra.

37. Mr. Justice Douglas has noted the problems associated with such inquiries [in] *DeFunis v. Odegaard,* 416 U.S. 312, 94 S.Ct. 1704, 40 L.Ed.2d 164 (1974) [involving the University of Washington Law School's special admissions program for Blacks, Chicanos, American Indians and Filipinos. The Court held the case moot—see p. 1178 infra. Only Douglas, J., addressed the merits: "[T]hat the state school employed a racial classification in selecting its students subjects it to the strictest scrutiny [and] is in my view 'invidious.' [The] key to the problem is the consideration of each application *in a racially neutral way.*" This may include "cultural backgrounds, [an] applicant's prior achievements in light of the barriers that he had to overcome [and] the likelihood that a particular candidate will more likely employ his legal skills to serve communities that are not now adequately represented than will competing candidates." "Such a policy would not be limited to Blacks, or Chicanos or Filipinos or American Indians, although undoubtedly groups such as they may in practice be the principal beneficiaries of it."]

worth. Third, there is a measure of inequity in forcing innocent persons in respondent's position to bear the burdens of redressing grievances not of their making.

By hitching the meaning of the Equal Protection Clause to these transitory considerations, we would be holding [that] judicial scrutiny of classifications touching on racial and ethnic background may vary with the ebb and flow of political forces. Disparate constitutional tolerance of such classifications well may serve to exacerbate racial and ethnic antagonisms. [Also,] the mutability of a constitutional principle, based upon shifting political and social judgments, undermines the chances for consistent application of the Constitution from one generation to the next, a critical feature of its coherent interpretation. * * *

If it is the individual who is entitled to judicial protection against classifications based upon his racial or ethnic background because such distinctions impinge upon personal rights, rather than the individual only because of his membership in a particular group, then constitutional standards may be applied consistently. Political judgments regarding the necessity for the particular classification may be weighed in the constitutional balance, *Korematsu*, but the standard of justification will remain constant. This is as it should be, since those political judgments are the product of rough compromise struck by contending groups within the democratic process. When they touch upon an individual's race or ethnic background, he is entitled to a judicial determination that the burden he is asked to bear on that basis is precisely tailored to serve a compelling governmental interest. * * *

C. Petitioner contends that on several occasions this Court has approved preferential classifications without applying the most exacting scrutiny. * * *

The school desegregation cases are inapposite. Each involved remedies for clearly determined constitutional violations.[39] [Here,] there was no judicial determination of constitutional violation as a predicate for [a] remedial classification.

The employment discrimination cases also do not advance petitioner's cause. For example, in *Franks v. Bowman Transportation Co.*, 424 U.S. 747, 96 S.Ct. 1251, 47 L.Ed.2d 444 (1975), we approved a retroactive award of seniority to a class of Negro truck drivers who had been the victims of discrimination—not just by society at large, but by the respondent in that case. While this relief imposed some burdens on other employees, it was held necessary " 'to make [the victims] whole for injuries suffered on account of unlawful employment discrimination.' " [But] we have never approved preferential classifications in the absence of proven constitutional or statutory violations.[41]

39. [In] *Offermann v. Nitkowski*, 378 F.2d 22 (CA2 1967) [and] *Springfield School Committee v. Barksdale*, 348 F.2d 261 (CA1 1965) [courts] did approve voluntary districting designed to eliminate discriminatory attendance patterns. In neither, however, was there any showing that the school board planned extensive pupil transportation that might threaten liberty or privacy interests. Nor were white students deprived of an equal opportunity for education.

Respondent's position is wholly dissimilar to that of a pupil bused from his neighborhood school to a comparable school in another neighborhood in compliance with a desegregation decree. Petitioner did not arrange for

respondent to attend a different medical school in order to desegregate Davis Medical School; instead, it denied him admission and may have deprived him altogether of a medical education.

41. This case does not call into question congressionally authorized administrative actions, such as consent decrees under Title VII or approval of reapportionment plans under § 5 of the Voting Rights Act of 1965. In such cases, there has been detailed legislative consideration of the various indicia of previous constitutional or statutory violations, e.g., *South Carolina v. Katzenbach*, [p. 1139 infra], and particular administrative bodies have been charged with monitoring various activi-

Nor is petitioner's view as to the applicable standard supported by the fact that gender-based classifications are not subjected to this level of scrutiny [citing cases in Sec. 3, IV infra]. [With] respect to gender there are only two possible classifications. The incidence of the burdens imposed by preferential classifications is clear. There are no rival groups who can claim that they, too, are entitled to preferential treatment. Classwide questions as to the group suffering previous injury and groups which fairly can be burdened are relatively manageable for reviewing courts. * * * More importantly, the perception of racial classifications as inherently odious stems from a lengthy and tragic history that gender-based classifications do not share. In sum, the Court has never viewed such classification as inherently suspect or as comparable to racial or ethnic classifications for the purpose of equal-protection analysis.

[P]etitioner contends that our recent decision in *United Jewish Orgs.* [approves] racial classifications designed to benefit certain minorities, without denominating the classifications as "suspect." [*UJO*] properly is viewed as a case in which the remedy for an administrative finding of discrimination encompassed measures to improve the previously disadvantaged group's ability to participate, without excluding individuals belonging to any other group from enjoyment of the relevant opportunity—meaningful participation in the electoral process.

In this case, [there] has been no determination by the legislature or a responsible administrative agency that the University engaged in a discriminatory practice requiring remedial efforts. Moreover, the operation of petitioner's special admissions [program] prefers the designated minority groups at the expense of other individuals who are totally foreclosed from competition for the 16 special admissions seats in every medical school class. [When] a classification denies an individual opportunities or benefits enjoyed by others solely because of his race or ethnic background, it must be regarded as suspect.

IV. [The] special admissions program purports to serve the purposes of: (i) "reducing the historic deficit of traditionally disfavored minorities in medical schools and the medical profession," (ii) countering the effects of societal discrimination;[43] (iii) increasing the number of physicians who will practice in commu-

ties in order to detect such violations and formulate appropriate remedies.

Furthermore, we are not here presented with an occasion to review legislation by Congress pursuant to its powers under § 2 of the Thirteenth Amendment and § 5 of the Fourteenth Amendment to remedy the effects of prior discrimination. *Katzenbach v. Morgan; Jones v. Alfred H. Mayer Co.,* [p. 1169 infra].

43. A number of distinct sub-goals have been advanced as falling under the rubric of "compensation for past discrimination." For example, it is said that preferences for Negro applicants [serve] as a form of reparation by the "majority" to a victimized group as a whole. Bittker, *The Case for Black Reparations* (1973). That justification for racial or ethnic preference has been subjected to much criticism. Finally, it has been argued that ethnic preferences "compensate" the group by providing examples of success whom other members of the group will emulate, thereby advancing the group's interest and society's interest in encouraging new generations to overcome the barriers and frustrations of the past. Redish, *Preferential Law School Admissions and the Equal Protection Clause: An Analysis of the Competing Arguments,* 22 U.C. L.A.L.Rev. 343, 391 (1974). For purposes of analysis these sub-goals need not be considered separately.

Racial classifications in admissions conceivably could serve a fifth purpose, one which petitioner does not articulate: fair appraisal of each individual's academic promise in the light of some cultural bias in grading or testing procedures. To the extent that race and ethnic background were considered only to [cure] established inaccuracies in predicting academic performance, it might be argued that there is no "preference" at all. Nothing in this record, however, suggests either that any of the quantitative factors considered by the Medical School were culturally biased or that petitioner's special admissions program was formulated to correct for any such biases. Furthermore, if race or ethnic background were used solely to arrive at an unbiased

nities currently underserved; and (iv) obtaining the educational benefits that flow from an ethnically diverse student body. It is necessary to decide which, if any, of these purposes is substantial enough to support the use of a suspect classification.

A. If petitioner's purpose is to assure within its student body some specified percentage of a particular group merely because of its race or ethnic origin, such a preferential purpose must be rejected not as insubstantial but as facially invalid. Preferring members of any one group for no reason other than race or ethnic origin is discrimination for its own sake. This the Constitution forbids. E.g., *Loving*.

B. The State certainly has a legitimate and substantial interest in ameliorating, or eliminating where feasible, the disabling effects of identified discrimination. [That] goal [is] far more focused than the remedying of the effects of "societal discrimination," an amorphous concept of injury that may be ageless in its reach into the past.

We have never approved a classification that aids persons perceived as members of relatively victimized groups at the expense of other innocent individuals in the absence of judicial, legislative, or administrative findings of constitutional or statutory violations. After such findings[,] the governmental interest in preferring members of the injured groups at the expense of others is substantial, since the legal rights of the victims must be vindicated. In such a case, the extent of the injury and the consequent remedy will have been judicially, legislatively, or administratively defined. Also, the remedial action usually remains subject to continuing oversight to assure that it will work the least harm possible to other innocent persons competing for the benefit. Without such findings of constitutional or statutory violations,[44] it cannot be said that the government has any greater interest in helping one individual than in refraining from harming another. Thus, the government has no compelling justification for inflicting such harm.

Petitioner does not purport to have made, and is in no position to make, such findings. Its broad mission is education, not the formulation of any

---

prediction of academic success, the reservation of fixed numbers of seats would be inexplicable.

44. Mr. Justice Brennan, Mr. Justice White, Mr. Justice Marshall, and Mr. Justice Blackmun misconceive the scope of this Court's holdings under Title VII when they suggest that "disparate impact" alone is sufficient to establish a violation of that statute and, by analogy, other civil rights measures. [This] was made quite clear in the seminal decision in this area, *Griggs v. Duke Power Co.*, 401 U.S. 424, 91 S.Ct. 849, 28 L.Ed.2d 158 (1971): "*Discriminatory preference* for any group, minority or majority, is precisely and only what Congress has proscribed. What is required by Congress is the removal of *artificial, arbitrary, and unnecessary barriers* to employment when the barriers operate invidiously to discriminate on the basis of racial or other impermissible classification." Thus, disparate impact is a basis for relief under Title VII only if the practice in question is not founded on "business necessity," or lacks "a manifest relationship to the employment in

question." Nothing *in this record*—as opposed to some of the general literature cited by Mr. Justice Brennan, Mr. Justice White, Mr. Justice Marshall, and Mr. Justice Blackmun—even remotely suggests that the disparate impact of the general admissions program at Davis Medical School, resulting primarily from the sort of disparate test scores and grades set forth in footnote 7, supra, is without educational justification.

Moreover, the presumption in *Griggs*—that disparate impact without any showing of business justification established the existence of discrimination in violation of the statute—was based on legislative determinations, wholly absent here, that past discrimination had handicapped various minority groups to such an extent that disparate impact could be traced to identifiable instances of past discrimination * * *. Thus, Title VII principles support the proposition that findings of identified discrimination must precede the fashioning of remedial measures embodying racial classifications.

legislative policy or the adjudication of particular claims of illegality. For reasons similar to those stated in Part III of this opinion, isolated segments of our vast governmental structures are not competent to make those decisions, at least in the absence of legislative mandates and legislatively determined criteria.[45] Cf. *Hampton v. Wong* [Sec. 3, II infra]. Compare n. 41, supra. Before relying upon these sorts of findings in establishing a racial classification, a governmental body must have the authority and capability to establish, in the record, that the classification is responsive to identified discrimination. See, e.g., *Califano v. Webster; Califano v. Goldfarb* [Sec. 3, IV infra]. Lacking this capability, petitioner has not carried its burden of justification on this issue.

Hence, the purpose of helping certain groups whom the faculty of the Davis Medical School perceived as victims of "societal discrimination" does not justify a classification that imposes disadvantages upon persons like respondent, who bear no responsibility for whatever harm the beneficiaries of the special admissions program are thought to have suffered. To hold otherwise would be to convert a remedy heretofore reserved for violations of legal rights into a privilege that all institutions throughout the Nation could grant at their pleasure to whatever groups are perceived as victims of societal discrimination. That is a step we have never approved. Cf. *Pasadena Bd. of Ed. v. Spangler.*

C. Petitioner identifies, as another purpose of its program, improving the delivery of health care services to communities currently underserved. It may be assumed that in some situations a State's interest in facilitating the health care of its citizens is sufficiently compelling to support the use of a suspect classification. But there is virtually no evidence in the record indicating that petitioner's special admissions program is either needed or geared to promote that goal. The court below addressed this failure of proof: "The University concedes it cannot assure that minority doctors who entered under the program, all of whom express an 'interest' in participating in a disadvantaged community, will actually do so. It may be correct to assume that some of them will carry out this intention, and that it is more likely they will practice in minority communities than the average white doctor. Nevertheless, there are more precise and reliable [ways]. An applicant of whatever race who has demonstrated his concern for disadvantaged minorities in the past and who declares that practice in such a community is his primary professional goal would be more likely to contribute to alleviation of the medical shortage than one who is chosen entirely on the basis of race and disadvantage. * * * *"[a] * * *

45. For example, the University is unable to explain its selection of only the four favored groups—Negroes, Mexican-Americans, American Indians, and Asians—for [preference]. The inclusion of the last group is especially curious in light of the substantial numbers of Asians admitted through the regular admissions process.

a. Consider Graglia, *Racially Discriminatory Admission to Public Institutions of Higher Education,* in Constitutional Government in America 255, 259–60 (Collins ed. 1980): "It [is] said that some members of non-white groups would prefer to be served by professionals of the same group. [This is a preference] that we can accept in the interest of honoring individual choice, even the choice to racially discriminate, but not one that we should encourage or take extraordinary steps

to satisfy. [T]he law should take the position that the individual's race is irrelevant, in the hope that the educative effect of law will help make this so even where it is not so already. [If] we are concerned [with] increasing the availability of professional services to the poor, that concern can be met simply, directly, and appropriately by subsidizing such services by payments to the poor or to those who serve them." Compare Sandalow, *Minority Preferences in Law School Admissions,* in id. 277, 282: "The ability to 'speak the language' of the client, to understand his perception of his problem, and to deal with others in the community on his behalf are qualities essential to being a 'good lawyer.' These qualifications are more likely to be found among lawyers who share the client's racial or ethnic identity, at least to the extent that the client's life is

D. The fourth goal asserted by petitioner is the attainment of a diverse student body. * * * Academic freedom, though not a specifically enumerated constitutional right, long has been viewed as a special concern of the First Amendment. [Thus,] in arguing that its universities must be accorded the right to select those students who will contribute the most to the "robust exchange of ideas," petitioner invokes a countervailing constitutional interest, [and] must be viewed as seeking to achieve a goal that is of paramount importance in the fulfillment of its mission. * * *

Ethnic diversity, however, is only one element in a range of factors a university properly may consider in attaining the goal of a heterogeneous student body. Although a university must have wide discretion in making the sensitive judgments as to who should be admitted, constitutional limitations protecting individual rights may not be disregarded. [As] the interest of diversity is compelling in the context of a university's admissions program,[b] the question remains whether the program's racial classification is necessary to promote this interest.

V. A. [P]etitioner's argument that this is the only effective means of serving the interest of diversity is seriously flawed. [The] diversity that furthers a compelling state interest encompasses a far broader array of qualifications and characteristics of which racial or ethnic origin is but a single though important element. Petitioner's special admissions program, focused *solely* on ethnic diversity, would hinder rather than further attainment of genuine diversity.

Nor would the state interest in genuine diversity be served by expanding petitioner's two-track system into a multitrack program with a prescribed number of seats set aside for each identifiable category of applicants. Indeed, it is inconceivable that a university would thus pursue the logic of petitioner's two-track program to the illogical end of insulating each category of applicants with certain desired qualifications from competition with all other applicants.

The experience of other university admissions programs, which take race into account in achieving the educational diversity valued by the First Amendment, demonstrates that the assignment of a fixed number of places to a minority group is not a necessary means toward that end. An illuminating example is found in the Harvard College program:

"In recent years Harvard College has expanded the concept of diversity to include students from disadvantaged economic, racial and ethnic groups. [When] the Committee on Admissions reviews the large middle group of applicants who are 'admissible' and deemed capable of doing good work in their

bound up in a community defined in these terms."

b. Consider McCormack, *Race and Politics in the Supreme Court: Bakke to Basics,* 1979 Utah L.Rev. 491, 530: "Most educators would agree that some element of diversity in a student body is healthy, but few would assert that this factor is the primary motivation behind minority preferences. [Thus], one problem with this approach is that it is simply not the most honest statement of the objective of the programs. [Further,] it is hard to believe that racial classifications disfavoring racial or ethnic minorities could be justified by a school's claim of academic freedom. This justification would be considered ludicrous if advanced as a basis for preferring members of

the white majority. These considerations rob the principle of the very neutrality that Justice Powell was seeking elsewhere in the opinion and suggest the instability of the rationale."

Does Powell, J.'s point lead to the further conclusion "that there is a strong societal interest in [the] equal participation of blacks [whenever] a 'black [can] bring something that a white person cannot offer,'" and that this extends to *all* "institutions of government, the 'power professions' [such] as law and medicine, [and] the economic system"? Sedler, *Racial Preference and the Constitution: The Societal Interest in the Equal Participation Objective,* 26 Wayne L.Rev. 1227 (1980).

courses, the race of an applicant may tip the balance in his favor just as geographic origin or a life spent on a farm may tip the balance in other candidates' cases. * * *

"In Harvard College admissions the Committee has not set target-quotas for the number of blacks, or of musicians, football players, physicists or Californians to be admitted in a given year [c] [but that awareness of the necessity of including more than a token number of black students means] that in choosing among thousands of applicants who are not only 'admissible' academically but have other strong qualities, the Committee, with a number of criteria in mind, pays some attention to distribution among many types and categories of students." Brief for Columbia University, Harvard University, Stanford University, and the University of Pennsylvania, as amici curiae.

In such an admissions program, race or ethnic background may be deemed a "plus" in a particular applicant's file,[d] yet it does not insulate the individual from comparison with all [others]. The file of a particular black applicant may be examined for his potential contribution to diversity without the factor of race being decisive when compared, for example, with that of an applicant identified as an Italian-American if the latter is thought to exhibit qualities more likely to promote beneficial educational pluralism. Such qualities could include exceptional personal talents, unique work or service experience, leadership potential, maturity, demonstrated compassion, a history of overcoming disadvantage, ability to communicate with the poor, or other qualifications deemed important.

* * *

This kind of program treats each applicant as an individual in the admissions process. The applicant who loses out [to] another candidate receiving a "plus" on the basis of ethnic background will not have been foreclosed from all consideration [simply] because he was not the right color or had the wrong surname. It would mean only that his combined qualifications, which may have

---

c. The portion of this paragraph of the Harvard program—omitted by Powell, J., in his opinion but reprinted in full in an appendix to the opinion—is as follows: "At the same time the Committee is aware that if Harvard College is to provide a truly heterogeneous environment that reflects the rich diversity of the United States, it cannot be provided without some attention to numbers. It would not make sense, for example, to have 10 or 20 students out of 1,100 whose homes are west of the Mississippi. Comparably, 10 or 20 black students could not begin to bring to their classmates and to each other the variety of points of view, backgrounds and experiences of blacks in the United States. Their small numbers might also create a sense of isolation [and] thus make it more difficult for them to develop and achieve their potential. Consequently, when making its decisions, the Committee on Admissions is aware that there is some relationship between numbers and achieving the benefits to be derived from a diverse student body, and between numbers and providing a reasonable environment for those students admitted."

d. See Posner, *The De Funis Case and the Constitutionality of Preferential Treatment of Racial Minorities,* 1974 Sup.Ct.Rev. 1, 12–13:

"The applicant cannot be relied upon to classify himself correctly. [Thus] admissions officials confront the problem both of determining what constitutes membership in a racial group and of requiring appropriate evidence that an applicant belongs to it. In the case of blacks, it is necessary to determine what percentage of Negro ancestry should be required. [If] the president of Mexico marries an American woman and they have a child who is brought up in the United States, is the child a Chicano? Or is the term meant to imply some connection with life in a barrio? [T]he possession (or lack) of a Spanish surname is not decisive evidence since Puerto Ricans, Spaniards, and Latin Americans other than Mexicans also have Spanish surnames, and since a Chicano might be the product of the union of a Chicano woman and a non-Chicano man. [Many] people have some Indian blood without being recognizable as Indian or having a characteristically Indian name. This problem could be avoided by limiting preferential treatment to Indians on reservations, but such a limitation would be difficult to justify to Indians who have recently (or not so recently) left the reservation and may have encountered substantial difficulties in adjusting to life on the outside."

included similar nonobjective factors, did not outweigh those of the other applicant. His qualifications would have been weighed fairly and competitively, and he would have no basis to complain of unequal treatment under the Fourteenth Amendment.

It has been suggested that an admissions program which considers race only as one factor is simply a subtle and more sophisticated—but no less effective—means of according racial preference than the Davis program. A facial intent to discriminate, however, is evident [in] this case. No such facial infirmity exists in an admissions program where race or ethnic background is simply one element—to be weighed fairly against other elements—in the selection process. "A boundary line," as Mr. Justice Frankfurter remarked in another connection, "is none the worse for being narrow." And a Court would not assume that a university, professing to employ a facially nondiscriminatory admissions policy, would operate it as a cover for the functional equivalent of a quota system. In short, good faith would be presumed in the absence of a showing to the contrary in the manner permitted by our cases. See, e.g., *Arlington Heights; Washington v. Davis.*[53]

B. [W]hen a State's distribution of benefits or imposition of burdens hinges on the color of a person's skin or ancestry, that individual is entitled to a demonstration that the challenged classification is necessary to promote a substantial state interest. Petitioner has failed to carry this burden. For this reason, that portion of the California court's judgment holding petitioner's special admissions program invalid under the Fourteenth Amendment must be affirmed.

C. In enjoining petitioner from ever considering the race of any applicant, however, the courts below failed to recognize that the State has a substantial interest that legitimately may be served by a properly devised admissions program involving the competitive consideration of race and ethnic origin. For this reason, so much of the California court's judgment as enjoins petitioner from any consideration of the race of any applicant must be reversed.

VI. With respect to respondent's entitlement to an injunction directing his admission to the Medical School, petitioner has conceded that it could not carry its burden of proving that, but for the existence of its unlawful special admissions program, respondent still would not have been admitted. Hence, respondent is entitled to the injunction, and that portion of the judgment must be affirmed.

Opinion of MR. JUSTICE BRENNAN, MR. JUSTICE WHITE, MR. JUSTICE MARSHALL, and MR. JUSTICE BLACKMUN, concurring in the judgment in part and dissenting.

[The] difficulty of this issue [has] resulted in many opinions, no single one speaking for the Court. But [this] must not mask the central meaning of today's opinions: Government may take race into account when it acts not to demean or insult any racial group, but to remedy disadvantages cast on minorities by past racial prejudice, at least when appropriate findings have been made by judicial, legislative, or administrative bodies with competence to act in this area. ✶ ✶ ✶

---

53. [There] also are strong policy reasons that correspond to the constitutional distinction between petitioner's preference program and one that assures a measure of competition among all applicants. Petitioner's program will be viewed as inherently unfair by the public generally as well as by [applicants]. Fairness in individual competition for oppor-tunities, especially those provided by the State, is a widely cherished American ethic. Indeed, in a broader sense, an underlying assumption of the rule of law is the worthiness of a system of justice based on fairness to the individual. As Mr. Justice Frankfurter declared in another connection, "[j]ustice must satisfy the appearance of justice."

We agree with Mr. Justice Powell that, as applied to the case before us, Title VI goes no further in prohibiting the use of race than the Equal Protection [Clause].[e] Since we conclude that the [Davis program] is constitutional, we would reverse the judgment below in all respects. Mr. Justice Powell agrees that some uses of race in university admissions are permissible and, therefore, he joins with us to make five votes reversing the judgment below insofar as it prohibits the University from establishing race-conscious programs in the future.[1]

I. [E]ven today officially sanctioned discrimination is not a thing of the past. Against this background, claims that law must be "color-blind" or that the datum of race is no longer relevant to public policy must be seen as aspiration rather than as description of reality. This is not to denigrate aspiration; for reality rebukes us that race has too often been used by those who would stigmatize and oppress minorities. Yet we cannot [let] color blindness become myopia which masks the reality that many "created equal" have been treated within our lifetimes as inferior both by the law and by their fellow citizens.

* * *

III. A. [Our] cases have always implied that an "overriding statutory purpose," *McLaughlin v. Florida,* could be found that would justify racial classifications. See, e.g., *Loving; Korematsu.* [W]e turn [to] articulating what our role should be in reviewing state action that expressly classifies by race.

B. [A] government practice or statute which restricts "fundamental rights" or which contains "suspect classifications" is to be subjected to "strict scrutiny" * * *. But no fundamental right is involved here. See *San Antonio Ind. School Dist. v. Rodriguez,* [Sec. 4, IV infra]. Nor do whites as a class have any of the "traditional indicia of suspectness: the class is not saddled with such disabilities, or subjected to such a history of purposeful unequal treatment, or relegated to such a position of political powerlessness as to command extraordinary protection from the majoritarian political process." Id.

Moreover, [this] is not a case where racial classifications are "irrelevant and therefore prohibited." *Hirabayashi.* Nor has anyone suggested that the University's purposes contravene the cardinal principle that racial classifications that stigmatize—because they are drawn on the presumption that one race is inferior to another or because they put the weight of government behind racial hatred and separatism—are invalid without more. See *Yick Wo.* * * *

On the other hand, the fact that this case does not fit neatly into our prior analytic framework for race cases does not mean that it should be analyzed by applying the very loose rational-basis [standard]. "[T]he mere recitation of a benign, compensatory purpose is not an automatic shield which protects against any inquiry into the actual purposes underlying a statutory scheme." *Califano v. Webster.* Instead, a number of considerations—developed in gender discrimination cases but which carry even more force when applied to racial classifications—lead us to conclude that racial classifications designed to further remedial purposes "must serve important governmental objectives and must be substantially related to achievement of those objectives." *Craig v. Boren,* [Sec. 3, IV infra].[35]

---

e. The separate opinion of White, J.—that Title VI does not provide for a private cause of action—is omitted.

1. We also agree [that] a plan like the "Harvard" plan is constitutional [at] least so long as the use of race to achieve an integrat-ed student body is necessitated by the lingering effects of past discrimination.

35. We disagree with our Brother Powell's suggestion, that the presence of "rival groups who can claim that they, too, are entitled to preferential treatment," distinguishes the gen-

First, race, like, "gender-based classifications too often [has] been inexcusably utilized to stereotype and stigmatize politically powerless segments of society." While a carefully tailored statute designed to remedy past discrimination could avoid these vices, see *Califano v. Webster,* we nonetheless have recognized that the line between honest and thoughtful appraisal of the effects of past discrimination and paternalistic stereotyping is not so clear and that a statute based on the latter is patently capable of stigmatizing all women with a badge of inferiority. State programs designed ostensibly to ameliorate the effects of past racial discrimination obviously create the same hazard of stigma, since they may promote racial separatism and reinforce the views of those who believe that members of racial minorities are inherently incapable of succeeding on their own.

Second, race, like gender and illegitimacy, is an immutable characteristic which its possessors are powerless to escape or set aside. While a classification is not per se invalid because [of this], it is nevertheless true that such divisions are contrary to our deep belief that "legal burdens should bear some relationship to individual responsibility or wrongdoing," and that advancement sanctioned, sponsored, or approved by the State should ideally be based on individual merit or achievement, or at the least on factors within the control of an individual.[f]

der cases or is relevant to the question of scope of judicial review of race classifications.

[W]ere we asked to decide whether any given rival group—German-Americans for example—must constitutionally be accorded preferential treatment, we do have a "principled basis" for deciding this question, one that is well-established in our cases: The Davis program expressly sets out four classes which receive preferred status. The program clearly distinguishes whites, but one cannot reason from this to a conclusion that German-Americans, as a national group, are singled out for invidious treatment. And even if the Davis program had a differential impact on German-Americans, they would have no constitutional claim unless they could prove that Davis intended invidiously to discriminate against German-Americans. See *Arlington Heights; Davis.* If this could not be shown, then [the] only question is whether it was rational for Davis to conclude that the groups it preferred had a greater claim to compensation than the groups it excluded. *Rodriguez* (applying *Katzenbach v. Morgan* test to state action intended to remove discrimination in educational opportunity). Thus, claims of rival groups, although they may create thorny political problems, create relatively simple problems for the courts.

[Consider Greenawalt, *Judicial Scrutiny of "Benign" Racial Preference in Law School Admissions,* 75 Colum.L.Rev. 559, 597 (1975): "Under the rational basis standard, a law school would be left free to divide much of the 'pie' of places in the student body by preferences for a multiplicity of minority groups. In many parts of the country, a number of minorities make up the majority of the population. If each minority group were assured 'proportional representation,' the result would be much closer to a maximum quota for presently overrepresented groups than any existing preferential policies. The rational basis approach would leave an applicant from an overrepresented group almost defenseless against this result." Would Brennan, J., permit "proportional representation" for minority groups? See his Part IV–C, infra. Would Powell, J.'s "diversity" justification permit it?]

f. Consider Karst & Horowitz, *Affirmative Action and Equal Protection,* 60 Va.L.Rev. 955, 962 (1974): "Whether 'merit' be defined in terms of demonstrated [or] potential achievement, it includes a large and hard-to-isolate ingredient of native talents. These talents resemble race in that they are beyond the control of the individual whose 'merit' is being evaluated. If racial classifications are 'suspect' partly for this reason, then it may be appropriate to insist that public rewards for native talents be justified by a showing of compelling necessity." See also Nagel, *Equal Treatment and Compensatory Discrimination,* 2 Phil. & Pub.Afrs. 348, 357 (1973): "The greatest injustice in this society [is] neither racial nor sexual but intellectual. [Society] provides on the average much larger rewards for tasks that require superior intelligence than for those that do not. This is simply the way things work out in a technologically advanced society with a market economy. It does not reflect a social judgment that smart people *deserve* the opportunity to make more [money]. They may deserve richer educational opportunity, but they do not therefore deserve the material wealth that goes with it. Similar things could be said about society's differential reward of achievements facilitated by other talents or gifts, like beauty, athletic ability, musicality, etc. But intelligence and

Because this principle is so deeply rooted it might be supposed that it would be considered in the legislative process and weighed against the benefits of programs preferring individuals because of their race. But [t]he "natural consequence of our governing processes [may well be] that the most 'discrete and insular' of whites [will] be called upon to bear the immediate, direct costs of benign discrimination." *UJO* (concurring opinion). [Thus] our review under the Fourteenth Amendment should be strict—not " 'strict' in theory and fatal in fact," because it is stigma that causes fatality—but strict and searching nonetheless.

IV. Davis' articulated purpose of remedying the effects of past societal discrimination is, under our cases, sufficiently important to justify the use of race-conscious admissions programs where there is a sound basis for concluding that minority underrepresentation is substantial and chronic, and that the handicap of past discrimination is impeding access of minorities to the medical school.

A. At least since *Green v. County School Bd.,* [a] public body which has itself been adjudged to have engaged in racial discrimination cannot bring itself into compliance with the Equal Protection Clause simply by ending its unlawful acts and adopting a neutral stance. Three years later, *Swann* [held] that courts could enter desegregation orders which assigned students and faculty by reference to race, and that local school boards could *voluntarily* adopt desegregation plans which made express reference to race if this was necessary to remedy the effects of past discrimination. Moreover, we stated that school boards, even in the absence of a judicial finding of past discrimination, could voluntarily adopt plans which assigned students with the end of creating racial pluralism by establishing fixed ratios of black and white students in each school. *Swann.*

* * *

Finally, the conclusion that state educational institutions may constitutionally adopt admissions programs designed to avoid exclusion of historically disadvantaged minorities, even when such programs explicitly take race into account, finds direct support in our cases construing congressional legislation designed to overcome the present effects of past discrimination. Congress can and has outlawed actions which have a disproportionately adverse and unjustified impact upon members of racial minorities and has required or authorized race-conscious action to put individuals disadvantaged by such impact in the position they otherwise might have enjoyed. See *Franks v. Bowman; Teamsters v. United States,* 431 U.S. 324, 97 S.Ct. 1843, 52 L.Ed.2d 396 (1977). Such relief does not require as a predicate proof that recipients of preferential advancement have been individually discriminated against; it is enough that each recipient is within a general class of persons likely to have been the victims of discrimination. See id. Nor is it an objection to such relief that preference for minorities will upset the settled expectations of nonminorities. See *Franks.* In addition, we have held that Congress, to remove barriers to equal opportunity, can and has required employers to use test criteria that fairly reflect the qualifications of minority applicants vis-à-vis nonminority applicants, even if this means interpreting the qualifications of an applicant in light of his race. See *Albemarle v. Moody,* 422 U.S. 405, 435, 95 S.Ct. 2362, 45 L.Ed.2d 280 (1975).[37]

its development by education provide a particularly significant and pervasive example."

37. In *Albemarle,* we approved "differential validation" of employment tests. That procedure requires that an employer must en-

sure that a test score of, for example, 50 for a minority job applicant means the same thing as a score of 50 for a nonminority applicant. By implication, were it determined that [a] 50 for a minority corresponded in "potential for

These cases cannot be distinguished [on] the ground that the entity using explicit racial classifications had itself violated § 1 of the Fourteenth Amendment or an antidiscrimination regulation, for again race-conscious remedies have been approved where this is not the case. See *UJO* (opinion of White, Blackmun, Rehnquist, and Stevens, JJ.); id. (opinion of White, Rehnquist, and Stevens, JJ.). Moreover, [the] claims of those burdened by the race-conscious actions of a university or employer who has never been adjudged in violation of an antidiscrimination law are not any more or less entitled to deference than the claims of the burdened nonminority workers in *Franks,* in which the employer had violated Title VII, for in each case the employees are innocent of past discrimination. And, although it might be argued that, where an employer has violated an antidiscrimination law, the expectations of nonminority workers are themselves products of discrimination and hence "tainted," and therefore more easily upset, the same argument can be made with respect to respondent. If it was reasonable to conclude—as we hold that it was—that the failure of minorities to qualify for admission at Davis under regular procedures was due principally to the effects of past discrimination, then there is a reasonable likelihood that, but for pervasive racial discrimination, respondent would have failed to qualify for admission even in the absence of Davis' special admissions program.[41]

Thus, our cases under Title VII [have] held that, in order to achieve minority participation in previously segregated areas of public life, Congress may require or authorize preferential treatment for those likely disadvantaged by societal racial discrimination. Such legislation has been sustained even without a requirement of findings of intentional racial discrimination by those required or authorized to accord preferential treatment, or a case-by-case determination that those to be benefited suffered from racial discrimination. These decisions compel the conclusion that States also may adopt race-conscious programs designed to overcome substantial, chronic minority underrepresentation where there is reason to believe that the evil addressed is a product of past racial discrimination.[42]

employment" to a 60 for whites, the test could not be used consistent with Title VII unless the employer hired minorities with scores of 50 even though he might not hire nonminority applicants with scores above 50 but below 60. Thus, it is clear that employers, to ensure equal opportunity, may have to adopt race-conscious hiring practices.

[Are racial preferences more justifiable in some contexts than others? Consider Neuborne, *Observations on Weber,* 54 N.Y.U.L. Rev. 546, 547 (1979): "In most settings, [we] do not allocate goods on the basis of an open-ended search for excellence. Rather, we seek a guarantee of a respectable level of competence, and, once that guarantee is present, we use criteria unrelated to competence—such as seniority, first-come first-served, personality, appearance, acquaintanceship, or hunch—to break ties. [But] where desirable positions are allocated on the basis of an open-ended search for excellence, race should never be permitted to effect the substitution of a less qualified candidate for the most qualified candidate. Such a substitution [would] frustrate legitimate expectations which are generally the result of strenuous individual preparation.

Moreover, the societal loss [would] be substantial." Under this rationale, what result in *Bakke?*]

41. Our cases cannot be distinguished by suggesting, as our Brother Powell does, that in none of them was anyone deprived of "the relevant benefit." Our school cases have deprived whites of the neighborhood school of their choice; our Title VII cases have deprived nondiscriminating employees of their settled seniority expectations; and *UJO* deprived the Hassidim of bloc voting strength. Each of these injuries was constitutionally cognizable as is respondent's here.

42. We do not understand Mr. Justice Powell to disagree that providing a remedy for past racial prejudice can constitute a compelling purpose sufficient to meet strict scrutiny. Yet, because petitioner is a university, he would not allow it to exercise such power in the absence of "judicial, legislative, or administrative findings of constitutional or statutory violations." While we agree that reversal in this case would follow a fortiori had Davis been guilty of invidious racial discrimination or if a federal statute mandated that universi-

Title VII was enacted pursuant to Congress' power under the Commerce Clause and § 5 of the Fourteenth Amendment. To the extent that Congress acted under the Commerce Clause power, it was restricted in the use of race in governmental decisionmaking by the equal protection component of the Due Process Clause of the Fifth Amendment precisely to the same extent as are the States by § 1 of the Fourteenth Amendment. Therefore, to the extent that Title VII rests on the Commerce Clause power, our decisions such as *Franks* and *Teamsters* implicitly recognize that the affirmative use of race is consistent with the equal protection component of the Fifth Amendment and therefore of the Fourteenth Amendment. To the extent that Congress acted pursuant to § 5 of the Fourteenth Amendment, those cases impliedly recognize that Congress was empowered under that provision to accord preferential treatment to victims of past discrimination in order to overcome the effects of segregation, and we see no reason to conclude that the States cannot voluntarily accomplish under § 1 of the Fourteenth Amendment what Congress under § 5 of the Fourteenth Amendment validly may authorize or compel either the States or private persons to do.

* * *

B. * * * Davis had a sound basis for believing that the problem of underrepresentation of minorities was substantial and chronic and that the problem was attributable to handicaps imposed on minority applicants by past and present racial discrimination. Until at least 1973, the practice of medicine in this country [was] largely the prerogative of whites. * * *

Moreover, Davis had very good reason to believe that the national pattern of underrepresentation of minorities in medicine would be perpetuated if it retained a single admissions standard. For example, the entering classes in 1968 and 1969, [when] such a standard was used, included only one Chicano and two Negroes out of 100 admittees. Nor is there any relief from this pattern of underrepresentation in the statistics for the regular admissions program in later years.

Davis clearly could conclude that the serious and persistent underrepresentation [is] the result of handicaps under which minority applicants labor as a consequence of a background of deliberate, purposeful discrimination against minorities in education and in society generally, as well as in the medical profession. From the inception of our national life, Negroes have been subjected to unique legal [disabilities]. The generation of minority students applying to Davis Medical School since it opened in 1968—most of whom were born before or about the time *Brown I* was decided—clearly have been victims of

ties refrain from applying any admissions policy that had a disparate and unjustified racial impact, we do not think it of constitutional significance that Davis has not been so adjudged.

Generally, the manner in which a State chooses to delegate governmental functions is for it to decide. California, by constitutional provision, has chosen to place authority over the operation of the University of California in the Board of Regents [who] have been vested with full legislative (including policymaking), administrative, and adjudicative powers. [W]e, unlike our Brother Powell, find nothing in the Equal Protection Clause that requires us to depart from established principle by limiting the scope of power the Regents may exercise more narrowly than the powers that may constitutionally be wielded by the Assembly.

Because the Regents can exercise plenary legislative and administrative power, it elevates form over substance to insist that Davis could not use race-conscious remedial programs until it had been adjudged in violation of the Constitution or an antidiscrimination statute. For, if the Equal Protection Clause required such a violation as a predicate, the Regents could simply have promulgated a regulation prohibiting disparate treatment not justified by the need to admit only qualified students, and could have declared Davis to have been in violation of such a regulation on the basis of the exclusionary effect of the admissions policy applied during the first two years of its operation.

this discrimination. Judicial decrees recognizing discrimination in public education in California testify to the fact of widespread discrimination suffered by California-born minority applicants; many minority group members living in California, moreover, were born and reared in school districts in southern States segregated by law. [T]he conclusion is inescapable that applicants to medical school must be few indeed who endured the effects of de jure segregation, the resistance to *Brown I,* or the equally debilitating pervasive private discrimination fostered by our long history of official discrimination, cf. *Reitman v. Mulkey,* [p. 1113 infra], and yet come to the starting line with an education equal to whites.

Moreover, [HEW], the expert agency charged by Congress [with] enforcing Title VI, [has concluded] that race may be taken into account in situations where a failure to do so would limit participation by minorities in federally funded programs, and regulations promulgated by the Department expressly contemplate that appropriate race-conscious programs may be adopted by universities to remedy unequal access to university programs caused by their own or by past societal discrimination. [A]lthough an amendment to an appropriations bill was introduced just last year [to prevent HEW] from mandating race-conscious programs in university admissions, proponents of this measure, significantly, did not question the validity of voluntary implementation of race-conscious admissions criteria. In these circumstances, the conclusion implicit in the regulations—that the lingering effects of past discrimination continue to make race-conscious remedial programs appropriate means for ensuring equal educational opportunity in universities—deserves considerable judicial deference. See, e.g., *Katzenbach v. Morgan.*

C. The second prong of our test—whether the Davis program stigmatizes any discrete group or individual and whether race is reasonably used in light of the program's objectives—is clearly satisfied by the Davis program.

It is not even claimed that Davis' program in any way operates to stigmatize or single out any discrete and insular, or even any identifiable, nonminority group. Nor will harm comparable to that imposed upon racial minorities by exclusion or separation on grounds of race be the likely result of the program. It does not, for example, establish an exclusive preserve for minority [students]. Rather, its purpose is to overcome the effects of segregation by bringing the races together. True, whites are excluded from participation in the special admissions program, but this fact only operates to reduce the number of whites to be admitted in the regular admissions program in order to permit admission of a reasonable percentage—less than their proportion of the California population [57]—of otherwise underrepresented qualified minority applicants.[58]

57. Negroes and Chicanos alone [comprise] 22% of California's population.

58. The constitutionality of [the] program is buttressed by its restriction to only 16% of the positions in the Medical School, a percentage less than that of the minority population in California, and to those minority applicants deemed qualified for admission and deemed likely to contribute to the medical school and the medical profession. This is consistent with the goal of putting minority applicants in the position they would have been in if not for the evil of racial discrimination. Accordingly, this case does not raise the question whether even a remedial use of race would be unconstitutional if it admitted unqualified minority applicants in preference to qualified applicants or admitted, as a result of preferential consideration, racial minorities in numbers significantly in excess of their proportional representation in the relevant population. Such programs might well be inadequately justified by the legitimate remedial objectives. Our allusion to the proportional percentage of minorities in the population of the State administering the program is not intended to establish either that figure or that population universe as a constitutional benchmark.
* * *

Nor was Bakke in any sense stamped as inferior by [rejection]. Indeed, it is conceded by all that he satisfied those criteria regarded by the School as generally relevant to academic performance better than most of the minority members who were admitted. Moreover, there is absolutely no basis for concluding that Bakke's rejection as a result of Davis' use of racial preference will affect him throughout his life in the same way as the segregation of the Negro school children in [*Brown I*]. Unlike discrimination against racial minorities, the use of racial preferences for remedial purposes does not inflict a pervasive injury upon individual whites in the sense that wherever they go or whatever they do there is a significant likelihood that they will be treated as second-class citizens because of their color. This distinction does not mean that the exclusion of a white resulting from the preferential use of race is not sufficiently serious to require justification; but it does mean that the injury inflicted by such a policy is not distinguishable from disadvantages caused by a wide range of government actions, none of which has ever been thought impermissible for that reason alone.

In addition, there is simply no evidence that the Davis program discriminates intentionally or unintentionally against any minority group which it purports to benefit. The program does not establish a quota in the invidious sense of a ceiling on the number of minority applicants to be admitted. Nor can the program reasonably be regarded as stigmatizing the program's beneficiaries or their race as inferior. The Davis program does not simply advance less qualified applicants; rather, it compensates applicants, whom it is uncontested are fully qualified to study medicine, for educational disadvantage which it was reasonable to conclude was a product of state-fostered discrimination. Once admitted, these students must satisfy the same degree [requirements]; they are taught by the same faculty in the same classes; and their performance is evaluated by the same standards by which regularly admitted students are judged. Under these circumstances, their performance and degrees must be regarded equally with the regularly admitted students with whom they compete for standing. Since minority graduates cannot justifiably be regarded as less well qualified than nonminority graduates by virtue of the special admissions program, there is no reasonable basis to conclude that [they] would be stigmatized as inferior by the existence of such programs.[h]

D. We disagree with the lower courts' conclusion that the Davis program's use of race was unreasonable in light of its objectives. First, as petitioner argues, there are no practical means by which it could achieve its ends in the foreseeable future without the use of race-conscious measures. With respect to any factor (such as poverty or family educational background) that may be used as a substitute for race as an indicator of past discrimination, whites greatly outnumber racial minorities simply because whites make up a far larger percent-

---

h. But see Nagel, fn. f supra, at 362: "Not only does [a racially preferential policy] inevitably produce resentment in the better qualified who are passed over [but] it also allows those in the discriminated-against group who would in fact have failed to gain a desired position in any case on the basis of their qualifications to feel that they may have lost out to someone less [qualified]. Similarly, such a practice cannot do much for the self-esteem of those who know they have benefited from it, and it may threaten the self-esteem of those in the favored group who would in fact have gained their positions even in the absence of the discriminatory policy, but who cannot be sure that they are not among its beneficiaries." Compare O'Neil, *Racial Preference and Higher Education: The Larger Context*, 60 Va.L.Rev. 925, 941 (1974): [I]t would be perverse if a court were to strike down on this ground a program which had been sought and extensively utilized by minority applicants themselves. Such a judgment would imply a dangerously gratuitous concern about the welfare of minority groups."

age of the total population and therefore far outnumber minorities in absolute terms at every socio-economic level. For example, of a class of recent medical school applicants from families with less than $10,000 income, at least 71% were white. Of all 1970 families headed by a person *not* a high school graduate which included related children under 18, 80% were white and 20% were racial minorities. Moreover, while race is positively correlated with differences in GPA and MCAT scores, economic disadvantage is not. Thus, it appears that economically disadvantaged whites do not score less well than economically advantaged whites, while economically advantaged blacks score less well than do disadvantaged whites. * * *

Second, [the] program does not simply equate minority status with disadvantage. Rather, Davis considers [each] applicant's personal history to determine whether he or she has likely been disadvantaged by racial discrimination. The record makes clear that only minority applicants likely to have been isolated from the mainstream of American life are considered in the special [program]. True, the procedure by which disadvantage is detected is informal, but we have never insisted that educators conduct their affairs through adjudicatory [proceedings]. A case-by-case inquiry into the extent to which each individual applicant has been affected, either directly or indirectly, by racial discrimination, would seem to be, as a practical matter, virtually impossible, despite the fact that there are excellent reasons for concluding that such effects generally exist. When individual measurement is impossible or extremely impractical, there is nothing to prevent a State from using categorical means to achieve its ends, at least where the category is closely related to the goal. Cf. *Katzenbach v. Morgan*. And it is clear from our cases that specific proof that a person has been victimized by discrimination is not a necessary predicate to offering him relief where the probability of victimization is great. See *Teamsters*.

E. Finally, Davis' special admissions program cannot be said to violate the Constitution simply because it has set aside a predetermined number of places for qualified minority applicants rather than using minority status as a positive factor to be considered in evaluating the applications of disadvantaged minority applicants. For purposes of constitutional adjudication, there is no difference between the two approaches. In any admissions program which accords special consideration to disadvantaged racial minorities, a determination of the degree of preference to be given is unavoidable, and any given preference that results in the exclusion of a white candidate is no more or less constitutionally acceptable than a program such as that at Davis. Furthermore, the extent of the preference inevitably depends on how many minority applicants the particular school is seeking to admit in any particular year so long as the number of qualified minority applicants exceeds that number. There is no sensible, and certainly no constitutional, distinction between, for example, adding a set number of points to the admissions rating of disadvantaged minority applicants as an expression of the preference with the expectation that this will result in the admission of an approximately determined number of qualified minority applicants and setting a fixed number of places for such applicants as was done here.[63]

[That] the Harvard approach does not also make public the extent of the preference and the precise workings of the system while the Davis program employs a specific, openly stated number, does not condemn the [latter]. It may be that the Harvard plan is more acceptable to the public than is the Davis

---

63. The excluded white applicant, despite Mr. Justice Powell's contention to the contrary, receives no more or less "individualized consideration" under our approach than under his.

"quota." If it is, any State [is] free to adopt it in preference to a less acceptable alternative, just as it is generally free [to] abjure granting any racial preferences in its admissions program. But there is no basis for preferring a particular preference program simply because in achieving the same goals that [Davis] is pursuing, it proceeds in a manner that is not immediately apparent to the public.[j] * * *

MR. JUSTICE MARSHALL.

[I]t must be remembered that, during most of the past 200 years, the Constitution as interpreted by this Court did not prohibit the most ingenious and pervasive forms of discrimination against the Negro. Now, when a State acts to remedy the effects of that legacy of discrimination, I cannot believe that this same Constitution stands as a barrier. * * *

The position of the Negro today in America is the tragic but inevitable consequence of centuries of unequal treatment. Measured by any benchmark of comfort or achievement, meaningful equality remains a distant dream for the Negro [—comparing Negro and white statistics on life expectancy, infant mortality, median income, poverty, unemployment, and percentages in professions].

In light of the sorry history of discrimination and its devastating impact on the lives of Negroes, bringing the Negro into the mainstream of American life should be a state interest of the highest order. To fail to do so is to ensure that America will forever remain a divided society. * * *

Since the Congress that considered and rejected the objections to the 1866 Freedmen's Bureau Act concerning special relief to Negroes also proposed the Fourteenth Amendment, it is inconceivable that the Fourteenth Amendment was intended to prohibit all race-conscious relief measures.[k] [T]o hold that it barred state action to remedy the effects [of] discrimination [would] pervert the

---

j. Consider Perry, *Modern Equal Protection: A Conceptualization and Appraisal,* 79 Colum.L.Rev. 1023, 1048 (1979): "One reason for subjecting any preferential program disadvantaging white persons [to] a heavier burden of justification is that such a program inevitably foments racial resentment and thereby strains the effort to gain wider acceptance for the principle of the moral equality of the races. Therefore, it makes sense to insist, as Powell did, that any preferential program be designed to accomplish its objective in a manner that causes as little resentment as possible." See also Mishkin, *The Uses of Ambivalence: Reflections on the Supreme Court and the Constitutionality of Affirmative Action,* 131 U.Pa.L.Rev. 907, 928 (1983): "The description of race as simply 'another factor' among a lot of others considered in seeking diversity tends to minimize the sense that minority students are separate and different and the recipients of special dispensations. [These] perceptions [can] facilitate or hamper the development of relationships among individuals and groups; they can advance or retard the educational process for all—including, particularly, minority students whose self-image is most crucially involved." Compare Blasi, *Bakke as Precedent: Does Mr. Justice Powell Have a Theory?* 67 Calif.L.Rev. 21, 60 (1979): "[I]t is almost always a bad thing

for constitutional standards to be based on the purported perceptions of the populace regarding what is fair or rational rather than on well-considered and explicitly defended arguments respecting fairness and rationality. It is too easy to manufacture a 'general belief' or a 'widespread feeling.' [Second], if admissions programs are to be evaluated not on the basis of what they really entail but instead in terms of how they are generally perceived, educational institutions can only regard the constitutional standard as a legitimation of subterfuge and hypocrisy."

k. Consider Pollak, "*Mr. Chief Justice; May It Please the Court:*", in Constitutional Government in America 247, 252 (Collins ed. 1980): "[T]he Freedmen's Bureau [authorized] a large remedial apparatus for the education and economic advancement [of] the freedmen. What could more clearly show that the fourteenth amendment, far from precluding remedial programs particularly designed to assist those groups battered by American history, was expected to be implemented in just such ways?" Compare Graglia, fn. a supra, at 263: "[T]his argument proves too much. It is equally clear that the fourteenth amendment was not intended to prohibit school segregation either."

intent of the framers by substituting abstract equality for the genuine equality the amendment was intended to achieve. * * *

While I applaud the judgment of the Court that a university may consider race in its admissions process, it is more than a little ironic that, after several hundred years of class-based discrimination against Negroes, the Court is unwilling to hold that a class-based remedy for that discrimination is permissible. [It] is unnecessary in 20th century America to have individual Negroes demonstrate that they have been victims of racial discrimination; the racism of our society has been so pervasive that none, regardless of wealth or position, has managed to escape its impact. The experience of Negroes in America has been different in kind, not just in degree, from that of other ethnic groups. It is not merely the history of slavery alone but also that a whole people were marked as inferior by the law. And that mark has endured. The dream of America as the great melting pot has not been realized for the Negro; because of his skin color he never even made it into the pot.[1]

[H]ad the Court [held in *Plessy*] that the Equal Protection Clause forbids differences in treatment based on race, we would not be faced with this dilemma in 1978. We must remember, however, that the principle that the "Constitution is color-blind" appeared only in the opinion of the lone dissenter. [F]or the next 60 years, from *Plessy* to *Brown,* ours was a Nation where, *by law,* an individual could be given "special" treatment based on the color of his skin.

It is because of a legacy of unequal treatment that we now must permit the institutions of this society to give consideration to race in making decisions about who will hold the positions of influence, affluence and prestige in America. * * *

I fear that we have come full circle. After the Civil War our government started several "affirmative action" programs. This Court in the *Civil Rights Cases,* [p. 1090 infra], and *Plessy* destroyed the movement toward complete equality. For almost a century no action was taken, and this nonaction was with the tacit approval of the courts. Then we had *Brown* and the Civil Rights Acts of Congress, followed by numerous affirmative action programs. *Now,* we have this Court again stepping in, this time to stop affirmative action programs of the type used by the University of California.

Mr. Justice Blackmun. * * *

I yield to no one in my earnest hope that the time will come when an "affirmative action" program is unnecessary and is, in truth, only a relic of the past. I would hope that we could reach this stage within a decade at the most. But the story of *Brown,* decided almost a quarter of a century ago, suggests that that hope is a slim one. At some time, however, beyond any period of what some would claim is only transitional inequality, the United States must and will reach a stage of maturity where action along this line is no longer necessary. Then persons will be regarded as persons, and discrimination of the type we address today will be an ugly feature of history that is instructive but that is behind us. * * *

It is somewhat ironic to have us so deeply disturbed over a program where race is an element of consciousness, and yet to be aware of the fact, as we are,

---

1. Consider Calabresi, *Bakke as Pseudo-Tragedy,* 28 Cath.U.L.Rev. 427, 432 (1979): "[I]f benign quotas are limited to blacks and perhaps to American Indians, so long as those groups—however society chooses to define them—remain sufficiently disadvantaged *as groups* so that membership in them can by itself constitute disadvantage without more, no major rejection of the basic universalist, meritocratic ideal would be entailed."

that institutions of higher learning, albeit more on the undergraduate than the graduate level, have given conceded preferences up to a point to those possessed of athletic skills, to the children of alumni, to the affluent who may bestow their largess on the institutions, and to those having connections with celebrities, the famous, and the powerful. * * *

[That] the Fourteenth Amendment has expanded beyond its original 1868 conception [does] not mean for me, however, that the Fourteenth Amendment has broken away from its moorings and its original intended purposes. Those original aims persist. And that, in a distinct sense, is what "affirmative action," in the face of proper facts, is all about. If this conflicts with idealistic equality, that tension is original Fourteenth Amendment tension [and] it is part of the Amendment's very nature until complete equality is achieved in the area. In this sense, constitutional equal protection is a shield. * * *

I suspect that it would be impossible to arrange an affirmative action program in a racially neutral way and have it successful. To ask that this be so is to demand the impossible. In order to get beyond racism, we must first take account of race. There is no other way. And in order to treat some persons equally, we must treat them differently. We cannot—we dare not—let the Equal Protection Clause perpetrate racial supremacy.

* * * Today, again, we are expounding a *Constitution.* The same principles that governed McCulloch's case in 1819 govern Bakke's case in 1978. There can be no other answer.

MR. JUSTICE STEVENS, with whom THE CHIEF JUSTICE, MR. JUSTICE STEWART, and MR. JUSTICE REHNQUIST join, concurring in the judgment in part and dissenting in part.[1]

[Bakke] challenged petitioner's special admissions program [and the] California Supreme Court upheld his challenge and ordered him admitted. If the state court was correct in its view that the University's special program was illegal, and that Bakke was therefore unlawfully excluded from the medical school because of his race, we should affirm its judgment, regardless of our views about the legality of admissions programs that are not now before the Court.

[Stevens, J., then construed the state court opinion as containing no "outstanding injunction forbidding any consideration of racial criteria in processing applications."] It is therefore perfectly clear that the question whether race can ever be used as a factor in an admissions decision is not an issue in this case, and that discussion of that issue is inappropriate.

[Stevens, J., then interpreted Title VI as prohibiting "the exclusion of *any* individual from a federally funded program 'on the ground of race.' "] It is therefore our duty to affirm the judgment ordering Bakke admitted * * *.

Notes and Questions

1. *Composition of decisionmaking body.* (a) Of what relevance should it be that those disadvantaged by a racially preferential program are not a "discrete and insular minority requiring extraordinary protection from the majoritarian political process"? Consider Ely, *The Constitutionality of Reverse Racial Discrimination,* 41 U.Chi.L.Rev. 723, 735 (1974): "[T]he reasons for being unusually suspicious, and, consequently, employing a stringent brand of review, are lack-

1. Four Members of the Court have undertaken to announce the legal and constitutional effect of this Court's judgment. See opinion of Justices Brennan, White, Marshall, and Blackmun. [But] only a majority can speak for the Court or determine what is the "central meaning" of any judgment of the Court.

ing. A White majority is unlikely to disadvantage itself for reasons of racial prejudice; nor is it likely to be tempted either to underestimate the needs and deserts of Whites relative to those of others, or to overestimate the costs of devising an alternative classification that would extend to certain Whites the advantages generally extended to Blacks." Under this rationale, may a city with a black majority enact an affirmative action program in hiring for public jobs? May a city with a white majority provide that every qualified black voter shall have two votes for all city officers?

(b) Consider Sandalow, *Racial Preferences in Higher Education: Political Responsibility and the Judicial Role,* 42 U.Chi.L.Rev. 653, 694–99 (1975): "Ely's analysis [is] troublesome on several grounds. First, in American politics majorities [typically] are coalitions of minorities which have varying [interests]. Resolution of the dispute depends upon which of the minorities is more successful in forging an alliance with those groups which are less immediately affected. The issue whether state schools ought to adopt preferential admissions policies is no exception. The immediate beneficiaries of these policies are the minorities which receive preferential treatment. But there is no reason to suppose that the costs of such policies are borne equally by sub-groups within the white population. To the extent that they are not, the discrimination—though nominally against a majority—is in reality against those sub-groups. * * * Universities have adopted preferential admissions policies without legislative sanction. The precise issue [is] not whether such policies are valid when adopted by a broadly representative, politically responsible legislature, but whether they are valid when adopted by a university [and] whether in determining the validity of state action that trenches upon constitutional values, the courts ought to consider whether the judgment under review is that of the legislature or of an agency that is less representative of the public and lacking direct political responsibility. [O]nly by ignoring all that we know about legislative behavior could it be supposed that a legislature's failure to limit the power of such bodies is equivalent to affirmative legislative approval of their decisions." See also Greenawalt, fn. 35 in *Bakke,* at 573–74: "We may safely suppose that the faculty of most state law schools is almost entirely white, but we may not assume that most faculty members will identify more with marginal white applicants than with black applicants. As most law teachers have done very well academically [they] may have trouble identifying themselves with marginal applicants. [M]any intellectuals may actually find it easier to identify with the plight of the 'oppressed' than the problems of the 'Philistine' middle and lower middle classes, from whom many marginal white applicants may come. Furthermore, two things that are in the obvious and immediate interest of faculty members and administrators are campus peace and a minimum of administrative burdens. Without doubt, some university programs for blacks [have] been adopted after considerable pressure that threatened or actually resulted in disruption. And a straight preferential policy applicable to all members of a minority group is likely to demand much less faculty or administrative time than careful examination of individual applications. Thus, it would be a mistake for judges to suppose that since most law school teachers and educational administrators are white they will not employ preferential policies ill-advisedly."

2. *Remedying constitutional and statutory violations.* Is it clear that at least five justices—Brennan, White, Marshall, Blackmun *and* Powell, JJ.,— would have upheld the Davis plan against constitutional challenge if there had been "judicial, legislative, or administrative findings of constitutional or statutory violations [by] a government body [with] the authority and capability to

establish, in the record, that the classification is responsive to identified discrimination" (Powell, J.)? Is it clear that these criteria would be satisfied by findings of Congress? [a] The California legislature? The Board of Regents—at least if it had a "legislative mandate and legislatively determined criteria" (Powell, J.)? Compare Van Alstyne, fn. b supra, at 289–90; O'Neil, *Bakke in Balance: Some Preliminary Thoughts,* 67 Calif.L.Rev. 143, 153–58 (1979), with Choper, *The Constitutionality of Affirmative Action: Views From the Supreme Court,* 70 Ky. L.J. 1, 9–12 (1981–82); Posner, *The Bakke Case and the Future of "Affirmative Action,"* 67 Calif.L.Rev. 171, 178–80 (1979). Would at least five justices have upheld the Davis plan against constitutional challenge if the California legislature—or the Regents—had found "that the disparate impact of Davis' general admissions program resulted primarily from test scores and grades which were without educational justification" (Powell, J., fn. 44)?

Must the legislatively/administratively identified constitutional or statutory violations have been by the Davis Medical School? Or is it enough that the findings trace the illegality to some other government unit? See Powell, J., at fn. 40; Sedler, *Beyond Bakke: The Constitution and Redressing the Social History of Racism,* 14 Harv.Civ.Rights—Civ.Lib.L.Rev. 133, 151–55 (1979). Could the Davis plan be "responsive" to "identified past discrimination" by public elementary, secondary and undergraduate schools—both in and out of California? See Brennan, J.'s Part IV–B. Consider Greenawalt, *The Unresolved Problems of Reverse Discrimination,* 67 Calif.L.Rev. 87, 127 (1979): "[G]iven the lingering effects of discrimination against earlier generations, given people's inevitable advancement through stages of life, and given the tremendous geographic mobility in the United States, people whose opportunities are unequal because of earlier discrimination will typically not have been affected by any discrimination by the organization from which they now seek a job or other benefit. It is not sensible to demand as a matter of constitutional law that that organization itself have discriminated before racial preferences are permissible."

Could a Davis-like plan—in education, employment, or otherwise—be "responsive" to legislatively/administratively "identified" *private* discrimination that is illegal under statutes such as Title VII (which do not require that the discrimination be intentional)—or that would have been illegal if such statutes had been in effect at the time the private discrimination occurred? If so, will any racial preference plan promulgated by a "competent" legislative/administrative body ever be held to violate equal protection?

3. *"Burdens" on "innocent individuals."* (a) Are any justices in *Bakke* of the view that the nature of the burden imposed on innocent persons to remedy constitutional or statutory violations is of no consequence? Of what relevance is the availability of remedial measures that spread the burden more widely (equitably)? Compare *Fullilove v. Klutznick,* infra. Consider McCormack, fn. b in *Bakke,* at 536: "Traditional tort theories assume that as between two innocent persons, a loss should stay where it has fallen unless there is some reason to shift its burden to another. In employment contexts, compensation can be made by requiring the employer to pay both innocents, but education operates with limited resources—seats in a class—and often results in a zero sum game." See also Comment, *Beyond Strict Scrutiny: The Limits of Congressional Power to Use Racial Classifications,* 74 Nw.U.L.Rev. 617, 633 (1979): "[In *Milliken II,*] the court-ordered expenditure of public funds to assist black students in overcoming the effects of past discrimination clearly had the effect of

---

a. See *Fullilove v. Klutznick,* infra.

reducing the funds available for general educational purposes. Therefore, white students, who were not themselves responsible for the historic discrimination, were saddled with the burden of the program, since there was a reduction in funds available for general use."

(b) UNITED STEEL WORKERS v. WEBER, 443 U.S. 193, 99 S.Ct. 2721, 61 L.Ed.2d 480 (1979), per BRENNAN, J., held that "an affirmative action plan— collectively bargained by an employer and a union—that reserves for black employees 50% of the openings in an inplant craft training program until the percentage of black craft workers in the plant is commensurate with the percentage of blacks in the local labor force," did not violate Title VII of the Civil Rights Act of 1964—which, inter alia, makes it "unlawful [for] any employer, labor organization, or joint labor-management committee [to] discriminate against any individual because of his race, color, religion, sex, or national origin in admission [to] any program established to provide apprenticeship or other training." [b] "We need not today define in detail the line of demarcation between permissible and impermissible affirmative action plans. It suffices to hold that the challenged [plan] falls on the permissible side of the line. The purposes [were] designed to break down old patterns of racial segregation and hierarchy. [At] the same time the plan does not unnecessarily trammel the interests of the white employees. The plan does not require the discharge of white workers and their replacement with new black hires. Cf. *McDonald v. Santa Fe Trail Trans. Co.,* 427 U.S. 273, 96 S.Ct. 2574, 49 L.Ed.2d 493 (1976).[c] Nor does the plan create an absolute bar to the advancement of white employees; half of those trained in the program will be white. Moreover, the plan is a temporary measure; it is not intended to maintain racial balance, but simply to eliminate a manifest racial imbalance. Preferential selection of craft trainees at the Gramercy plant will end as soon as the percentage of black skilled craft workers in the Gramercy plant approximates the percentage of blacks in the local labor force." [d]

(c) In FIREFIGHTERS v. STOTTS, 467 U.S. 561, 104 S.Ct. 2576, 81 L.Ed.2d 483 (1984), blacks in the Memphis fire department had entered into a consent decree with the city (which did not admit past intentional discrimination) to increase black employment. A budget shortage subsequently required reduction of personnel. Although the city's layoff proposal "was not adopted with [the] intent to discriminate," it had an adverse proportionate impact on blacks. The Court, per WHITE, J., held that Title VII precludes a federal district court from modifying the consent decree so as to displace "a non-minority employee with seniority under the contractually established seniority system absent either a finding that the seniority system was adopted with discriminatory intent or a determination that such a remedy was necessary to make whole a proven victim of discrimination": "Title VII protects bona fide seniority systems, and it is inappropriate to deny an innocent employee the benefits of his seniority in order to provide a remedy in [a] suit such as this." Stevens, J., concurred on narrower grounds. Blackmun, J., joined by Brennan and Marshall, JJ., dissented.

4. *Remedying de facto segregation.* In addition to *Swann's* dictum—that "school authorities might well conclude that in order to prepare students to live

---

b. The Court emphasized that since the plan "does not involve state action, this case does not present an alleged violation of the Equal Protection Clause."

c. *McDonald,* emphasizing that it was not considering an affirmative action program, held that an employer violated Title VII (and 42 U.S.C.A. § 1981—pp. 1135, 1172 infra) by discharging white, but not black, employees for theft of company property.

d. Rehnquist, J., joined by Burger, C. J., dissented. Powell and Stevens, JJ., did not participate.

in a pluralistic society each school should have a prescribed ratio of Negro to white students reflecting the proportion for the district as a whole"—do Powell, J.'s fn. 39 and Brennan, J.'s fn. 41 settle the issue that school officials may voluntarily act on a racial basis to alleviate de facto school segregation?

5. *Repealing remedies for de facto segregation.* (a) In WASHINGTON v. SEATTLE SCHOOL DIST., 458 U.S. 457, 102 S.Ct. 3187, 73 L.Ed.2d 896 (1982), shortly after appellee implemented a mandatory busing plan to reduce de facto school segregation, the Washington electorate adopted Initiative 350, providing— with a number of broad exceptions—that "no school board [shall] directly or indirectly require any student to attend a school other than the school which is geographically nearest or next nearest the student's place of residence." The Court, per BLACKMUN, J.—relying on *Hunter v. Erickson,* 393 U.S. 385, 89 S.Ct. 557, 21 L.Ed.2d 616 (1969) [a]—held this violated equal protection: "[T]he political majority may generally restructure the political process to place obstacles in the path of everyone seeking to secure the benefits of governmental action. But a different analysis is required when the State allocates governmental power non-neutrally, by explicitly using the *racial* nature of a decision to determine the decisionmaking process. State action of this kind, [*Hunter*] said, 'places *special* burdens on racial minorities within the governmental process,' (emphasis added), thereby 'making it *more* difficult for certain racial and religious minorities [than for other members of the community] to achieve legislation that is in their interest.' (emphasis added) (Harlan, J., concurring). * * *

"[D]espite its facial neutrality there is little doubt that the initiative was effectively drawn for racial purposes. [T]he District Court found that the text [was] carefully tailored to interfere only with desegregative busing.[b] [It] in fact allows school districts to bus their students 'for most, if not all,' of the non-integrative purposes required by their educational policies. [It] is true [that] the proponents of mandatory integration cannot be classified by race. [But] desegregation of the public schools [at] bottom inures primarily to the benefit of the minority, and is designed for that purpose. [Given] the racial focus of Initiative 350, this suffices to trigger application of the *Hunter* doctrine.

"We are also satisfied that the practical effect of Initiative 350 is to work a reallocation of power of the kind condemned in *Hunter.* [Those] favoring the elimination of de facto school segregation now must seek relief from the state legislature, or from the statewide electorate. Yet authority over all other student assignment decisions, as well as over most other areas of educational policy, remains vested in the local school board. [As] in *Hunter,* then, the community's political mechanisms are modified to place effective decisionmaking authority over a racial issue at a different level of government.[23]

a. In *Hunter,* after the Akron, Ohio city council enacted a fair housing ordinance, the voters amended the city charter to prevent "any ordinance dealing with racial, religious, or ancestral discrimination without the approval of a majority of the voters." The Court, per White, J., held this "explicitly racial classification" whose "impact falls on the minority" violative of equal protection. Black, J., dissented.

b. "The initiative envisioned busing for racial purposes in only one circumstance: it did not purport to 'prevent any court of competent jurisdiction from adjudicating constitutional issues relating to the public schools.'"

23. [W]hat we find objectionable about Initiative 350 is the comparative burden it imposes on minority participation in the political process—that is, the racial nature of the way in which it structures the *process* of decisionmaking. It is evident, then, that the horribles paraded by the dissent, n. 14—which have nothing to do with the ability of minorities to participate in the process of self-government— are entirely unrelated to this case. It is equally clear [that] the State remains free to vest all decisionmaking power in state officials, or to remove authority from local school boards in a race-neutral manner.

"To be sure, 'the simple repeal or modification of desegregation or anti-discrimination laws, without more, never has been viewed as embodying a presumptively invalid racial classification.' *Crawford v. Los Angeles Bd. of Educ.* [infra].

"Initiative 350, however, works something more than the 'mere repeal' of a desegregation law by the political entity that created it. It burdens all future attempts to integrate Washington schools [by] lodging decisionmaking authority over the question at a new and remote level of government. Indeed, the initiative, like the charter amendment at issue in *Hunter,* has its most pernicious effect on integration programs that do '*not* arouse extraordinary controversy.' In such situations the initiative makes the enactment of racially beneficial legislation difficult, though the particular program involved might not have inspired opposition had it been promulgated through the usual legislative processes used for comparable legislation. [And] when the State's allocation of power places unusual burdens on the ability of racial groups to enact legislation specifically designed to overcome the 'special condition' of prejudice, the governmental action seriously 'curtail[s] the operation of those political processes ordinarily to be relied upon to protect minorities.' *Carolene Products,* n. 4."

POWELL, J., joined by Burger, C.J., and Rehnquist and O'Connor, JJ., dissented: "[I]n the absence of a prior constitutional violation, the States are under no constitutional duty to adopt integration programs in their schools, and certainly [not] to establish a regime of mandatory busing.[6] It is not questioned that the [School] District itself [could have] cancelled its integration program without violating the Federal Constitution. Yet this Court holds that neither the legislature nor the people [of] Washington could alter what the District had decided. [It] is a strange notion [that] local governmental bodies can forever preempt the ability of a State—the sovereign power—to address a matter of compelling concern to the State. * * *

"This is certainly not a case where a State [has] established a racially discriminatory requirement. Initiative 350 [is] neutral on its face, and racially neutral as public policy. Children of all races benefit from neighborhood [schools].[9] * * *

"Nothing in *Hunter* supports the Court's extraordinary invasion into the State's distribution of authority. [Initiative 350] simply does not place unique political obstacles in the way of racial minorities. In this case, unlike in *Hunter,*

---

6. [Indeed], in the absence of a finding of segregation by the School District, mandatory busing on the basis of race raises constitutional difficulties of its own. Extensive pupil transportation may threaten liberty or privacy interests. See *Bakke* (opinion of Powell, J.) * * *.

9. [The] people of the State legitimately could decide that unlimited mandatory busing places too great a burden on the liberty and privacy interests of families and students of all races. It might decide that the reassignment of students to distant schools, on the basis of race, was too great a departure from the ideal of racial neutrality in State action. And, in light of the experience with mandatory busing in other cities, the State might conclude that such a program ultimately would lead to greater racial imbalance in the schools.

[See also Sunstein, *Public Values, Private Interests, and the Equal Protection Clause,* 1982 Sup.Ct.Rev. 127, 149, 157–58: "A classification [that] singles out a racial problem for special and disadvantageous treatment is peculiarly likely to be supported by invidious justifications. Like the heightened scrutiny applied to facial racial classifications, heightened scrutiny in *Hunter* is justified by a suspicion that improper justifications are at work. [A]rguments against busing are less likely to be animated by racial bias than are arguments against legislation preventing discrimination in housing. *Seattle* might therefore have been treated differently from *Hunter* on the ground that invidious motives may well not have been at work."]

the political system has *not* been redrawn or altered. The authority of the State over the public school system, acting through Initiative or the legislature, is plenary. Thus, the State's political system is not altered when it adopts for the first time a policy, concededly within the area of its authority, for the regulation of local school districts. And certainly racial minorities are not uniquely or comparatively burdened by the State's adoption of a policy that would be lawful if adopted by any School District in the State. * * *[14]."

(b) In CRAWFORD v. LOS ANGELES BD. OF EDUC., 458 U.S. 527, 102 S.Ct. 3211, 73 L.Ed.2d 948 (1982), after the state courts had ordered substantial busing to remedy de facto school segregation which the state courts had found violative of the state constitution, the California electorate amended the state constitution by adopting Proposition I, providing that "state courts shall not order mandatory pupil assignment or transportation unless a federal court would do so to remedy a violation of the Equal Protection Clause." The Court, per POWELL, J., found no violation of equal protection, "rejecting the contention that once a State chooses to do 'more' than the Fourteenth Amendment requires, it may never recede. [E]ven after Proposition I, the California Constitution still imposes a greater duty of desegregation than does the Federal Constitution. The state courts of California continue to have an obligation under state law to order segregated school districts to use voluntary desegregation techniques, whether or not there has been a finding of intentional segregation. The school districts themselves retain a state law obligation to take reasonably feasible steps to desegregate, and they remain free to adopt reassignment and busing plans to effectuate desegregation.[12]

"* * * Proposition I does not embody a racial classification. It neither says nor implies that persons are to be treated differently on account of their race. [The] benefit it seeks to confer—neighborhood schooling—is made available regardless of race in the discretion of school boards. Indeed, even if Proposition I had a racially discriminatory effect, in view of the demographic mix of the District it is not clear which race or races would be affected the most or in what way.[16] * * *[18] * * *

14. The Court's decision intrudes deeply into normal State decisionmaking. Under its holding the people [apparently] are forever barred from developing a different policy on mandatory busing where a School District previously has adopted one of its own. This principle would not seem limited to the question of mandatory busing. Thus, if the admissions committee of a State law school developed an affirmative action plan that came under fire, the Court apparently would find it unconstitutional for any higher authority to intervene unless that authority traditionally dictated admissions policies. As a constitutional matter, the Dean of the Law School, the faculty of the University as a whole, the University President, the Chancellor of the University System, and the Board of Regents might be powerless to intervene despite their greater authority under State law.

After today's decision it is unclear whether the State may set policy in any area of race relations where a local governmental body arguably has done "more" than the Fourteenth Amendment requires. If local employment or benefits are distributed on a racial

basis to the benefit of racial minorities, the State apparently may not thereafter ever intervene. Indeed, under the Court's theory one must wonder whether [even] the Federal Government could assert its superior authority to regulate in these areas.

12. In this respect this case differs from the situation presented in *Seattle.*

16. In the Los Angeles school district, white students are now the racial minority. [I]n Los Angeles County, racial minorities, including those of Spanish origin, constitute the majority of the population.

18. Proposition I is not limited to busing for the purpose of racial desegregation. It applies neutrally to "pupil school assignment or pupil transportation" in general. [For a possibly different interpretation of Proposition I, see Choper, *The Repeal of Remedies for De Facto School Segregation,* in Choper, Kamisar & Tribe, *The Supreme Court: Trends and Developments 1981–82* 43–44 (1983).] Even so, it is clear that court ordered busing in *excess* of that required by the Fourteenth Amendment, as one means of desegregating schools,

"Were we to hold that the mere repeal of race related legislation is unconstitutional, we would limit seriously the authority of States to deal with the problems of our heterogeneous population. States would be committed irrevocably to legislation that has proven unsuccessful or even harmful in practice. And certainly the purposes of the Fourteenth Amendment would not be advanced by an interpretation that discouraged the States from providing greater protection to racial minorities. * * *

"*Hunter* involved more than a 'mere repeal' of the fair housing ordinance: persons seeking anti-discrimination housing laws—presumptively racial minorities—were 'singled out for mandatory referendums while no other [group] face[d] that obstacle.' By contrast, [Proposition I] is less than a 'repeal' of the California Equal Protection Clause. As noted above, after Proposition I, the State Constitution still places upon school boards a greater duty to desegregate than does the Fourteenth Amendment.

"Nor can it be said that Proposition I distorts the political process for racial reasons or that it allocates governmental or judicial power on the basis of a discriminatory principle. [The] remedies available for violation of the antitrust laws, for example, are different than those available for violation of the Civil Rights Acts. Yet a 'dual court system'—one for the racial majority and one for the racial minority—is not established simply because civil rights remedies are different from those available in other areas. [H]aving gone beyond the requirements of the Federal Constitution, the State was free to return in part to the standard prevailing generally throughout the United States. * * *

"The California Court of Appeal also rejected petitioners' claim that Proposition I, if facially valid, was nonetheless unconstitutional because enacted with a discriminatory purpose. The court reasoned that the purposes of the Proposition were well stated in the Proposition itself. Voters may have been motivated by any of these purposes, chief among them the educational benefits of neighborhood schooling. [It] characterized petitioners' claim of discriminatory intent on the part of millions of voters as but 'pure speculation.' [Here, as in *Reitman v. Mulkey,*] involving the circumstances of passage and the potential impact of a Proposition adopted at a state-wide election, we see no reason to differ with the conclusions of the state appellate court."

BLACKMUN, J., joined by Brennan, J., although joining the Court's opinion, concurred "to address [the] critical distinctions between this case [and] *Seattle*": "State courts do not create the rights they enforce; those rights originate elsewhere—in the state legislature, in the State's political subdivisions, or in the state constitution itself. When one of those rights is repealed, and therefore is rendered unenforceable in the courts, that action hardly can be said to restructure the State's decisionmaking mechanism. While the California electorate may have made it more difficult to achieve desegregation when it enacted Proposition I, [it] did so not by working a structural change in the political *process* so much as by simply repealing the right to invoke a judicial busing remedy. Indeed, ruling for petitioners on a *Hunter* theory seemingly would mean that statutory affirmative action or antidiscrimination programs never could be repealed, for a repeal of the enactment would mean that enforcement authority previously lodged in the state courts was being removed by another political entity.

prompted the initiation and probably the
adoption of Proposition I.

"In short, the people of California—the same 'entity' that put in place the state constitution, and created the enforceable obligation to desegregate—have made the desegregation obligation judicially unenforceable. The 'political process or the decisionmaking mechanism used to *address* racially conscious legislation' has not been 'singled out for peculiar and disadvantageous treatment,' *Seattle,* for those political mechanisms that create and repeal the rights ultimately enforced by the courts were left entirely unaffected by Proposition I."

MARSHALL, J., dissented: "I fail to see how a fundamental redefinition of the governmental decisionmaking structure with respect to the same racial issue can be unconstitutional when the state seeks to remove the authority from local school boards, yet constitutional when the state attempts to achieve the same result by limiting the power of its [courts]. Despite Proposition I's apparent neutrality, it is 'beyond reasonable dispute,' *Seattle,* and the majority today concedes, that 'court ordered busing in *excess* of that required by [equal protection] prompted the initiation and probably the adoption of Proposition I.'

* * *

"Nor can there be any doubt that Proposition I works a substantial reallocation of state power. [After its adoption], the only method of enforcing against a recalcitrant school board the state constitutional duty to eliminate racial isolation is to petition either the state legislature or the electorate as a whole. [It] is equally clear [that] Proposition I is not a 'mere repeal.' [I]n *Seattle, Hunter,* and *Reitman,* the three times that this Court has explicitly rejected the argument that a proposed change constituted a 'mere repeal' of an existing policy, the alleged rescission was accomplished by a governmental entity other than the entity that had taken the initial action, and resulted in a drastic alteration of the substantive effect of existing policy. This case falls squarely within this latter category.

" [Certainly], *Hunter* and *Seattle* cannot be distinguished on the ground that they concerned the reallocation of legislative power, whereas Proposition I redistributes the inherent power of a court to tailor the remedy to the violation. [Indeed], Proposition I, by denying full access to the only branch of government that has been willing to address this issue meaningfully, is far worse for those seeking to vindicate the plainly unpopular cause of racial integration in the public schools than a simple reallocation of an often unavailable and unresponsive legislative process."

6.   *"Benign quotas."* May a state limit blacks in a public housing project to that percentage—say 35%—which, if exceeded, would likely cause white persons to leave, thus frustrating integration? Is this valid because its purpose is to *avoid* segregation? Of what significance is the fact that some blacks—those denied entrance because the quota is already filled—are being "discriminated" against because of their race?

FULLILOVE v. KLUTZNICK, 448 U.S. 448, 100 S.Ct. 2758, 65 L.Ed.2d 902 (1980), rejected "a facial constitutional challenge" to the Public Works Employment Act of 1977 (appropriating $4 billion to state and local governments for public works projects). Section 103(f)(2), the "minority business enterprise" or "MBE" provision, required that: "Except to the extent that the Secretary determines otherwise, no grant shall be made under this Act for any local public works project unless the applicant gives satisfactory assurance to the Secretary that at least 10 per centum of the amount of each grant shall be expended for minority business enterprises. [T]he term 'minority business enterprise' means a business at least 50 per centum of which is owned by minority group members or, in case of a publicly owned business, at least 51 per centum of the stock of which is owned by minority group members. For the purposes of the preceding sentence, minority group members are citizens of the United States who are Negroes, Spanish-speaking, Orientals, Indians, Eskimos, and Aleuts."

BURGER, C.J., announced the judgment and an opinion joined by White and Powell, JJ.: "The origin of the provision was an amendment [on] the floor of the House [which was changed to make clear] that the federal administrator would have discretion to waive the 10% requirement where its application was not feasible. [The] device of a 10% MBE participation requirement, subject to administrative waiver, was thought to be required to assure minority business participation; otherwise it was thought that repetition of the prior experience could be expected, with participation by minority business accounting for an inordinately small percentage of government contracting. The causes of this disparity were perceived as involving the longstanding existence and maintenance of barriers impairing access by minority enterprises to public contracting opportunities, or sometimes as involving more direct discrimination, but not relating to lack ['of] capable and qualified minority [enterprises.']

"The legislative objectives of the MBE provision must be considered against the background of ongoing efforts directed toward deliverance of the century-old promise of equality of economic opportunity. [As] Congress began consideration of the Public Works Employment Act of 1977, the House Committee on Small Business issued a lengthy report [which] summarized a 1975 committee report [prepared] by the House Subcommittee on SBA Oversight and Minority Enterprise [which] took 'full notice [as] evidence for its consideration' of reports submitted to the Congress by the General Accounting Office and by the U.S. Commission on Civil Rights. [The] Civil Rights Commission report discussed at some length the barriers encountered by minority businesses in gaining access to government contracting opportunities at the federal, state and local levels. Among the major difficulties [were] deficiencies in working capital, inability to meet bonding requirements, disabilities caused by an inadequate 'track record,' lack of awareness of bidding opportunities, unfamiliarity with bidding procedures, preselection before the formal advertising process, and the exercise of discretion by government procurement officers to disfavor minority businesses.

* * *

"Against this backdrop, [it] is inconceivable that Members of both Houses were not fully aware of the objectives of the MBE [provision].

"[T]he Secretary of Commerce promulgated regulations [and the Economic Development Administration (EDA) published guidelines that make] clear the administrative understanding that a waiver or partial waiver is justified (and will be granted) to avoid subcontracting with a minority business enterprise at an 'unreasonable' price, i.e., a price above competitive levels which cannot be attributed to the minority firm's attempt to cover costs inflated by the present effects of disadvantage or discrimination.

"This administrative approach is consistent with the legislative intention. [I]n the report of the House Subcommittee on SBA Oversight and Minority Enterprise the subcommittee took special care to note that when using the term 'minority' it intended to include 'only such minority individuals as [are] economically or socially disadvantaged.' The subcommittee also was cognizant of existing administrative regulations designed to ensure that firms maintained on the lists of bona fide minority business enterprises be those whose competitive position is impaired by the effects of disadvantage and discrimination. [The] sponsors of the MBE provision, in their reliance on prior administrative practice, intended that the term 'minority business enterprise' would be given that same limited application; this even found expression in the legislative [debates].

"The EDA technical bulletin * * * clarifies the definition of 'minority group members.'[a] It [also] outlines a procedure for the processing of complaints of 'unjust participation by an enterprise or individuals in the MBE program,' or of improper administration of the MBE requirement.[b]

"[The] program was designed to ensure [that] grantees who elect to participate would not employ procurement practices that Congress had decided might result in perpetuation of the effects of prior discrimination which had impaired or foreclosed access by minority businesses to public contracting opportunities. The MBE program does not mandate the allocation of federal funds according to inflexible percentages solely based on race or ethnicity.

"Our analysis proceeds in two steps. At the outset, we must inquire whether the *objectives* of this legislation are within the power of Congress. * * *

"A. In enacting the MBE provision, it is clear that Congress employed an amalgam of its specifically delegated powers. The [Act,] by its very nature, is primarily an exercise of the Spending Power [whose reach] is at least as broad as the regulatory powers of Congress. If, pursuant to its regulatory powers, Congress could have achieved the objectives of the MBE program, then it may do so under the Spending Power. [The] legislative history of the MBE provision shows that there was a rational basis for Congress to conclude that the subcontracting practices of prime contractors could perpetuate the prevailing impaired access by minority businesses to public contracting opportunities, and that this inequity has an effect on interstate commerce. [Insofar] as the MBE program pertains to the actions of private prime contractors, the Congress could have achieved its objectives under the Commerce Clause. We conclude that in this respect the objectives of the MBE provision are within the scope of the Spending Power.

a. The definitions, set out in an Appendix to Burger, C.J.'s opinion, are:

"a) Negro—An individual of the black race of African origin.

"b) Spanish-speaking—An individual of a Spanish-speaking culture and origin or parentage.

"c) Oriental—An individual of a culture, origin or parentage traceable to the areas south of the Soviet Union, East of Iran, inclusive of islands adjacent thereto, and out to the Pacific including but not limited to Indonesia, Indochina, Malaysia, Hawaii and the Philippines.

"d) Indian—An individual having origins in any of the original people of North America and who is recognized as an Indian by either a tribe, tribal organization or a suitable authority in the community. (A suitable authority in the community may be: educational institutions, religious organizations, or state agencies.)

"e) Eskimo—An individual having origins in any of the original peoples of Alaska.

"f) Aleut—An individual having origins in any of the original peoples of the Aleutian Islands."

b. The procedure, set out in the Appendix, is:

"Any person [with] information indicating unjust participation by an enterprise or individuals in the MBE program or who believes that the MBE participation requirement is being improperly applied should contact the appropriate EDA [grantee].

"Upon receipt of a complaint, the grantee should attempt to resolve the issues in dispute. [If] the grantee requires assistance in reaching a determination, the grantee should contact the Civil Rights Specialist in the appropriate Regional Office.

"If the complainant believes that the grantee has not satisfactorily resolved the issues raised in his complaint, he may personally contact the EDA Regional Office."

[W]e look to § 5 of the Fourteenth Amendment for the power to regulate the procurement practices of state and local [government] grantees of federal funds. [I]n *Oregon v. Mitchell,* [p. 1159 infra], we upheld [a] nationwide prohibition on the use of various voter-qualification tests and devices in federal, state and local elections. The Court was unanimous [in] concluding [that] Congress could reasonably determine that its legislation was an appropriate method of attacking the perpetuation of prior purposeful discrimination, even though the use of these tests or devices might have discriminatory effects only. See *Rome v. United States,* [p. 1167 infra]. Our cases reviewing the parallel power of Congress to enforce the provisions of the Fifteenth Amendment confirm that congressional authority extends beyond the prohibition of purposeful discrimination to encompass state action that has discriminatory impact perpetuating the effects of past discrimination. *South Carolina v. Katzenbach.*

"With respect to the MBE provision, Congress had abundant evidence from which it could conclude that minority businesses have been denied effective participation in public contracting opportunities by procurement practices that perpetuated the effects of prior discrimination. Congress, of course, may legislate without compiling the kind of 'record' appropriate with respect to judicial or administrative proceedings. Congress had before it, among other data, evidence of a long history of marked disparity in the percentage of public contracts awarded to minority business enterprises. This disparity was considered to result not from any lack of capable and qualified minority businesses, but from the existence and maintenance of barriers to competitive access which had their roots in racial and ethnic discrimination, and which continue today, even absent any intentional discrimination or other unlawful conduct. Although much of this history related to the experience of minority businesses in the area of federal procurement, there was direct evidence before the Congress that this pattern of disadvantage and discrimination existed with respect to state and local construction contracting as well. In relation to the MBE provision, Congress acted within its competence to determine that the problem was national in scope.

"Although the Act recites no preambulary 'findings' on the subject, we are satisfied that Congress had abundant historical basis from which it could conclude that traditional procurement practices, when applied to minority businesses, could perpetuate the effects of prior discrimination. Accordingly, Congress reasonably determined that the prospective elimination of these barriers to minority firm access to public contracting opportunities generated by the 1977 Act was appropriate to ensure that those businesses were not denied equal opportunity to participate in federal grants to state and local governments, which is one aspect of the equal protection of the laws. Insofar as the MBE program pertains to the actions of state and local grantees, Congress could have achieved its objectives by use of its power under § 5 of the Fourteenth Amendment. We conclude that in this respect the objectives of the MBE provision are within the scope of the Spending Power. * * *

"B. We now turn to the question whether, as a *means* to accomplish these plainly constitutional objectives, Congress may use racial and ethnic criteria, in this limited [way. We] are not dealing with a remedial decree of a court but with the legislative authority of Congress. Furthermore, petitioners have challenged the constitutionality of the MBE provision on its face; they have not sought damages or other specific relief for injury allegedly flowing from specific applications of the program; nor have they attempted to show that as applied in identified situations the MBE provision violated the constitutional or statutory rights of any party to this case.[71] * * *

"Our review of the regulations and guidelines [reveals] that Congress enacted the program as a strictly remedial measure; moreover, it is a remedy that functions prospectively, in the manner of an injunctive decree. * * *

"As a threshold matter, we reject the contention that in the remedial context the Congress must act in a wholly 'color-blind' fashion. [*Swann.* In the] school desegregation cases we dealt with the authority of a federal court to formulate a remedy for unconstitutional racial discrimination. However, the authority of a court to incorporate racial criteria into a remedial decree also extends to statutory [violations.] *Franks v. Bowman;* see *Teamsters v. United States; Albemarle v. Moody.* In another setting, we have held that a state may employ racial criteria that are reasonably necessary to assure compliance with federal voting rights legislation, even though the state action does not entail the remedy of a constitutional violation. *UJO.* * * *

"Here we deal [not] with the limited remedial powers of a federal court, [but] with the broad remedial powers of Congress. It is fundamental that in no organ of government, state or federal, does there repose a more comprehensive remedial power than in the Congress, expressly charged by the Constitution with competence and authority to enforce equal protection guarantees. Congress not only may induce voluntary action to assure compliance with existing federal statutory or constitutional antidiscrimination provisions, but also, where Congress has authority to declare certain conduct unlawful, it may, as here, authorize and induce state action to avoid such conduct. * * *

"It is not a constitutional defect in this program that it may disappoint the expectations of nonminority firms. When effectuating a limited and properly tailored remedy to cure the effects of prior discrimination, such 'a sharing of the burden' by innocent parties is not impermissible. *Franks;* see *Albemarle.* The actual 'burden' shouldered by nonminority firms is relatively light in this connection when we consider the scope of this public works program as compared with overall construction contracting opportunities.[72] Moreover, although we may assume that the complaining parties are innocent of any discriminatory conduct, it was within congressional power to act on the assumption that in the past some nonminority businesses may have reaped competitive benefit over the years from the virtual exclusion of minority firms from these contracting opportunities.

"Another challenge to the validity of the MBE program is the assertion that it is underinclusive—that it limits its benefit to specified minority groups rather than extending its remedial objectives to all businesses whose access to government contracting is impaired by the effects of disadvantage or discrimination. [But there] has been no showing in this case that Congress has inadvertently effected an invidious discrimination by excluding from coverage an identifiable

71. In their complaint, in order to establish standing to challenge the validity of the program, petitioners alleged as "[s]pecific examples" of economic injury three instances where one of their number assertedly would have been awarded a public works contract but for enforcement of the MBE provision. Petitioners requested only declaratory and injunctive relief against continued enforcement of the MBE provision; they did not seek any remedy for these specific instances * * *.

72. The Court of Appeals [found] that the $4.2 billion in federal grants conditioned upon compliance with the MBE provision amounted to about 2.5% of the total of nearly $170 billion spent on construction in the United States during 1977. Thus, the 10% minimum minority business participation contemplated by this program would account for only 0.25% of the annual expenditure for construction work in the United States.

minority group that has been the victim of a degree of disadvantage and discrimination equal to or greater than that suffered by the groups encompassed by the MBE program. It is not inconceivable that on very special facts a case might be made to challenge the congressional decision to limit MBE eligibility to the particular minority groups identified in the Act. * * *

"It is also contended that the MBE program is overinclusive—that it bestows a benefit on businesses identified by racial or ethnic criteria which cannot be justified on the basis of competitive criteria or as a remedy for the present effects of identified prior discrimination. It is conceivable that a particular application of the program may have this effect; however, the peculiarities of specific applications are not before [us. But even] in the context of a facial challenge such as is presented in this case, the MBE provision cannot pass muster unless, with due account for its administrative program, it provides a reasonable assurance that application of racial or ethnic criteria will be limited to accomplishing the remedial objectives of Congress and that misapplications of the program will be promptly and adequately remedied administratively. * * *

"The administrative program contains measures to effectuate the congressional objective of assuring legitimate participation by disadvantaged MBE's. Administrative definition has tightened some less definite aspects of the statutory identification of the minority groups encompassed by the program.[73] There is administrative scrutiny to identify and eliminate from participation in the program MBE's who are not 'bona-fide' [;] for example, spurious minority-front entities can be exposed. A significant aspect of this surveillance is the complaint procedure available for reporting 'unjust participation by an enterprise or individuals in the MBE program.' And even as to specific contract awards, waiver is available to avoid dealing with an MBE who is attempting to exploit the remedial aspects of the program by charging an unreasonable price, i.e., a price not attributable to the present effects of past discrimination. We must assume that Congress intended close scrutiny of false claims and prompt action on them.

"Grantees are given the opportunity to demonstrate that their best efforts will not succeed or have not succeeded in achieving the statutory 10% target for minority firm [participation]. In these circumstances a waiver or partial waiver is available once compliance has been demonstrated. * * *

"That the use of racial and ethnic criteria is premised on assumptions rebuttable in the administrative process gives reasonable assurance that application of the MBE program will be limited to accomplishing the remedial objectives contemplated by Congress and that misapplications of the racial and ethnic criteria can be remedied. In dealing with this facial challenge to the statute, doubts must be resolved in support of the congressional judgment that this limited program is a necessary step to effectuate the constitutional mandate for equality of economic opportunity. The MBE provision may be viewed as a pilot

---

73. * * * Minority group members are defined as "citizens of the United States who are Negroes, Spanish-speaking, Orientals, Indians, Eskimos and Aleuts." The administrative definitions are set out in [fn. a]. These categories also are classified as minorities in the regulations implementing the nondiscrimination requirements of the Railroad Revitalization and Regulatory Reform Act of 1976, on which Congress relied as precedent for the MBE provision. The House Subcommittee on SBA Oversight and Minority Enterprise [also] recognized that these categories were included within the Federal Government's definition of "minority business enterprise." The specific inclusion of these groups in the MBE provision demonstrates that Congress concluded they were victims of discrimination. Petitioners did not press any challenge to Congress' classification categories in the Court of Appeals; there is no reason for this Court to pass upon the issue at this time.

project, appropriately limited in extent and duration, and subject to reassessment [by] Congress prior to any extension or re-enactment. Miscarriages of administration could have only a transitory economic impact on businesses not encompassed by the program, and would not be irremediable. * * *

"Any preference based on racial or ethnic criteria must necessarily receive a most searching examination. [This] opinion does not adopt, either expressly or implicitly, the formulas of analysis articulated in such cases as *Bakke.* However, our analysis demonstrates that the MBE provision would survive judicial review under either 'test' articulated in the several *Bakke* opinions."

POWELL, J., concurring "separately to apply the analysis set forth in my opinion in *Bakke,*" found that § 103(f)(2) "serves the compelling government interest in eradicating the continuing effects of past discrimination identified by Congress": "Because the distinction between permissible remedial action and impermissible racial preference rests on the existence of a constitutional or statutory violation, [a] race-conscious remedy is not compelling unless an appropriate governmental authority has found that such a violation has occurred.

"[Unlike] the Regents of the University of California, Congress properly may—and indeed must—address directly the problems of discrimination in our society [relying, inter alia, on *Katzenbach v. Morgan, South Carolina v. Katzenbach* and *Oregon v. Mitchell.*] It is beyond question [that] Congress has the authority to identify unlawful discriminatory practices, to prohibit those practices, and to prescribe remedies to eradicate their continuing effects. The next inquiry is whether Congress has made findings adequate to support its determination that minority contractors have suffered extensive discrimination.

"The petitioners contend that [this] Court should treat the debates on § 103(f)(2) as the complete 'record' of congressional decisionmaking. [But] creation of national rules for the governance of our society simply does not entail the same concept of record-making that is appropriate to a judicial or administrative proceeding. Congress['s] special attribute as a legislative body lies in its broader mission to investigate and consider all facts and opinions that may be [relevant]. One appropriate source is the information and expertise that Congress acquires in the consideration and enactment of earlier legislation. * * *

"In my view, the legislative [history] demonstrates that Congress reasonably concluded that private and governmental discrimination had contributed to the negligible percentage of public contracts awarded minority contractors.[4] [I] believe that a court must accept [the] conclusion that purposeful discrimination contributed significantly to the small percentage of federal contracting funds that minority business enterprises have received. Refusals to subcontract work to minority contractors may, depending upon the identity of the discriminating party, violate Title VI of the Civil Rights Act of 1964 or the Fourteenth Amendment. Although the discriminatory activities were not identified with the exactitude expected in judicial or administrative adjudication, it must be

---

4. I cannot accept the suggestion [that] § 103(f)(2) must be viewed as serving a compelling state interest if the reviewing court can "perceive a basis" for legislative action, quoting *Katzenbach v. Morgan.* The "perceive a basis" standard refers to congressional authority to act, not to the distinct question whether that action violates the Due Process Clause of the Fifth Amendment.

In my view, a court should uphold a reasonable congressional finding of discrimination.

A more stringent standard of review would impinge upon Congress' ability to address problems of discrimination; a standard requiring a court to "perceive a basis" is essentially meaningless in this context. Such a test might allow a court to justify legislative action even in the absence of affirmative evidence of congressional findings.

remembered that 'Congress may paint with a much broader brush than may this Court.' *Oregon v. Mitchell* (Stewart, J., concurring and dissenting in part).

"[This conclusion] leads to the inquiry whether use of a 10% set-aside is a constitutionally appropriate means. [We] have recognized that the choice of remedies to redress racial discrimination is a 'balancing process left, within appropriate constitutional or statutory limits, to the sound discretion of the trial court.' *Franks v. Bowman* (Powell, J., concurring and dissenting in part). I believe that the enforcement clauses of the Thirteenth and Fourteenth Amendments give Congress a similar measure of discretion. [But the] Judicial Branch has the special responsibility to make a searching inquiry into the justification for employing a race-conscious remedy. Courts must be sensitive to the possibility that less intrusive means might serve the compelling state interest equally as well. I believe that Congress' choice of a remedy should be upheld, however, if the means selected are equitable and reasonably necessary to the redress of identified discrimination. Such a test allows the Congress to exercise necessary discretion but preserves the essential safeguard of judicial review of racial classifications. * * *

"[The] set-aside is not a permanent part of federal contracting requirements. As soon as the PWEA program concludes, this set-aside program ends. The temporary nature of this remedy ensures that a race-conscious program will not last longer than the discriminatory effects it is designed to eliminate. * * *

"The percentage chosen for the set-aside is within the scope of congressional discretion. [10%] falls roughly halfway between the present percentage of minority contractors and the percentage of minority group members in the Nation.

"Although the set-aside is pegged at a reasonable figure, its effect might be unfair if it were applied rigidly in areas of the country where minority group members constitute a small percentage of the population. To meet this concern, Congress enacted a waiver [provision]. The factors governing issuance of a waiver include the availability of qualified minority contractors in a particular geographic area, the size of the locale's minority population, and the efforts made to find minority contractors. We have been told that 1261 waivers had been granted by September 9, 1979. * * *

"Consideration of these factors [and others discussed by Burger, C.J.,] persuades me that the set-aside is a reasonably necessary means of furthering the compelling governmental interest in redressing the discrimination. [As my *Bakke*] opinion made clear, I believe that the use of racial classifications [cannot] be imposed simply to serve transient social or political goals, however worthy they may be. [But] Congress has been given a unique constitutional role in the enforcement of the post-Civil War Amendments."

MARSHALL, J., joined by Brennan and Blackmun, JJ., concurred in the judgment: "[T]he racial classifications employed [are] substantially related to the achievement of the important and congressionally articulated goal of remedying the present effects of past racial discrimination. The provision, therefore, passes muster under the equal protection standard I adopted in *Bakke*."

STEWART, J., joined by Rehnquist, J., dissented: "[T]oday's decision is wrong for the same reason that *Plessy* was wrong. [O]ur cases have made clear that the Constitution is wholly neutral in [forbidding] racial discrimination, whatever the race may be of those who are its victims [discussing *Anderson v. Martin, Loving* and *McLaughlin*].[3]

"This history contains one clear lesson. Under our Constitution, the government may never act to the detriment of a person solely because of that person's race.[4] The color of a person's skin and the country of his origin are immutable facts that bear no relation to ability, disadvantage, moral culpability, or any other characteristics of constitutionally permissible interest to government. [From] the perspective of a person detrimentally affected by a racially discriminatory law, the arbitrariness and unfairness is entirely the same, whatever his skin color and whatever the law's purpose, be it purportedly 'for the promotion of the public good' or otherwise. [If] a law is unconstitutional, it is no less unconstitutional just because it is a product of the Congress * * *.

"The Court's attempt to characterize the law as a proper remedial measure [is] remarkably unconvincing. The Legislative Branch of government is not a court of equity. It has neither the dispassionate objectivity nor the flexibility that are needed to mold a race-conscious remedy around the single objective of eliminating the effects of past or present discrimination.

"But even assuming that Congress has the power, under § 5 of the Fourteenth Amendment or some other constitutional provision, to remedy previous illegal racial discrimination, there is no evidence that Congress has in the past engaged in racial discrimination in its disbursement of federal contracting funds. The MBE provision thus pushes the limits of any such justification far beyond the equal protection standard of the Constitution. Certainly, nothing in the Constitution gives Congress any greater authority to impose detriments on the basis of race than is afforded the Judicial Branch. And a judicial decree that imposes burdens on the basis of race can be upheld only where its sole purpose is to eradicate the actual effects of illegal race discrimination. See *Pasadena Bd. of Educ. v. Spangler.*

"The provision at issue here does not satisfy this condition. Its legislative history suggests that it had at least two other objectives in addition to that of counteracting the effects of past or present racial discrimination in the public works construction industry. One such purpose appears to have been to assure to minority contractors a certain percentage of federally funded public works contracts. But, [since] equal protection immunizes from capricious governmental treatment 'persons'—not 'races,' it can never countenance laws that seek racial balance as a goal in [itself.] Second, there are indications that the MBE provision may have been enacted to compensate for the effects of social, educational, and economic 'disadvantage.' No race, however, has a monopoly on

---

3. *Bakke* and *UJO* do not suggest a different rule. The Court in *Bakke* invalidated the racially preferential [program]. In *UJO*, [no person] was deprived of his electoral franchise.

[D]uring the Second World War, this Court did find constitutional a governmental program imposing injury on the basis of race. See *Korematsu; Hirabayashi.* Significantly, those cases were decided not only in time of war, but in an era before the Court had held that the Due Process Clause of the Fifth Amendment imposes the same equal protection standard upon the Federal Government

that the Fourteenth Amendment imposes upon the States.

4. A court of equity may, of course, take race into account in devising a remedial decree to undo a violation of a law prohibiting discrimination on the basis of race. See *Teamsters; Franks; Swann.* But such a judicial decree, following litigation in which a violation of law has been determined, is wholly different from generalized legislation that awards benefits and imposes detriments dependent upon the race of the recipients. See text infra.

social, educational, or economic disadvantage,[11] and any law that indulges in such a presumption clearly violates the constitutional guarantee of equal protection.[12]

"[Because] of the Court's decision today, our statute books will once again have to contain laws that reflect the odious practice of delineating the qualities that make one person a Negro and make another white. Moreover, racial discrimination, even 'good faith' racial discrimination, is inevitably a two-edged sword. '[P]referential programs may only reinforce common stereotypes holding that certain groups are unable to achieve success without special protection based on a factor having no relationship to individual worth.' *Bakke* (opinion of Powell, J.). Most importantly, by making race a relevant criterion once again in its own affairs, the Government implicitly teaches the public that the apportionment of rewards and penalties can legitimately be made according to race— rather than according to merit or ability—and that people can, and perhaps should, view themselves and others in terms of their racial characteristics. Notions of 'racial entitlement' will be fostered, and private discrimination will necessarily be encouraged. See Van Alstyne, *Rites of Passage: Race, the Supreme Court, and the Constitution*, 46 U.Chi.L.Rev. 775 (1979)." [d]

STEVENS, J., dissented: "Because racial characteristics so seldom provide a relevant basis for disparate treatment, and because classifications based on race are potentially so harmful to the entire body politic,[5] it is especially important that the reasons for any such classification be clearly identified and unquestionably legitimate.

---

11. For instance, in 1978, 83.4% of persons over the age of 25 who had not completed high school were "white," and in 1977, 79.0% of households with annual incomes of less than $5,000 were "white."

12. Moreover, [even] assuming that the MBE provision was intended solely as a remedy for past and present racial discrimination, it sweeps far too broadly. [No] waiver is provided for any governmental entity that can prove a history free of racial discrimination. Nor is any exemption permitted for nonminority contractors that are able to demonstrate that they have not engaged in racially discriminatory behavior. Finally, the statute makes no attempt to direct the aid it provides solely toward those minority contracting firms that arguably still suffer from the effects of past or present discrimination.

These are not the characteristics of [a] decree that is closely tailored to the evil to be corrected. In today's society, it constitutes far too gross an oversimplification to assume that every single Negro, Spanish-speaking citizen, Oriental, Indian, Eskimo, and Aleut potentially interested in construction contracting currently suffers from the effects of past or present racial discrimination. Since the MBE set-aside must be viewed as resting upon such an assumption, it necessarily paints with too broad a brush. Except to make whole the identified victims of racial discrimination, the guarantee of equal protection prohibits the government from taking detrimental action against innocent people on the basis of the sins of others of their own race.

d. See also *Minnick v. California Dep't of Corrections*, 452 U.S. 105, 101 S.Ct. 2211, 68 L.Ed.2d 706 (1981), involving a challenge to respondent's affirmative action program for hiring and promoting minorities and women. The Court dismissed for want of a "final judgment," but Stewart, J., reached the merits, relying on his views in *Fullilove* and adding: "[I]t is wholly irrelevant whether the State gives a 'plus' or 'minus' value to a person's race, whether the discrimination occurs in a decision to hire or fire or promote, or whether the discrimination is called 'affirmative action' or by some less euphemistic term. * * * California's policy of racial discrimination was sought to be justified as an antidote for previous discrimination in favor of white people. But, even in this context, two wrongs do not make a right. Two wrongs simply make two wrongs." Rehnquist, J., agreed with the Court that there was no "final judgment," but would otherwise "join the dissenting opinion of Justice Stewart."

5. Indeed, the very attempt to define with precision a beneficiary's qualifying racial characteristics is repugnant to our constitutional ideals. The so-called guidelines [fn. a], are so general as to be fairly innocuous; as a consequence they are too vague to be useful. [If] the National Government is to make a serious effort to define racial classes by criteria that can be administered objectively, it must study precedents such as the First Regulation to the Reichs Citizenship Law of November 14, 1935 [defining "Jews."]

"The statutory definition of the preferred class includes 'citizens of the United States who are Negroes, Spanish-speaking, Orientals, Indians, Eskimos, and Aleuts.' All aliens and all nonmembers of the racial class are excluded. No economic, social, geographical or historical criteria are relevant for exclusion or inclusion. There is not one word in the remainder of the Act or in the legislative history that explains why any Congressman or Senator favored this particular definition over any other or that identifies the common characteristics that every member of the preferred class was believed to share.[6] Nor does the Act or its history explain why 10% of the total appropriation was the proper amount to set aside for investors in each of the six racial subclasses.[7]

"Four different, though somewhat interrelated, justifications for the racial classification in this Act have been advanced: first, that the 10% set aside is a form of reparation for past injuries to the entire membership of the class; second, that it is an appropriate remedy for past discrimination against minority business enterprises that have been denied access to public contracts; third, that the members of the favored class have a special entitlement to 'a piece of the action' when government is distributing benefits; and, fourth, that the program is an appropriate method of fostering greater minority participation in a competitive economy. * * *

"I. [In] his eloquent separate opinion in *Bakke*, Mr. Justice Marshall recounted the tragic class-based discrimination against Negroes that is an indelible part of America's history. I assume that the wrong committed against the Negro class is both so serious and so pervasive that it would constitutionally justify an appropriate classwide recovery measured by a sum certain for every member of the injured class. [But] the history of discrimination against black citizens in America cannot justify a grant of privileges to Eskimos or Indians.

"Even if we assume that each of the six racial subclasses has suffered its own special injury at some time in our history, surely it does not necessarily follow that each of those subclasses suffered harm of identical magnitude. Although 'the Negro was dragged to this country in chains to be sold in slavery,' the 'Spanish-speaking' subclass came voluntarily, frequently without invitation, and the Indians, the Eskimos and the Aleuts had an opportunity to exploit America's resources before most American citizens arrived. * * *

"At best, the statutory preference is a somewhat perverse form of reparation for the members of the injured classes. For those who are the most disadvantaged within each class are the least likely to receive any benefit from the

---

6. In 1968, almost 10 years before the Act was passed, the Small Business Administration had developed a program to assist small business concerns owned or controlled by "socially or economically disadvantaged persons." The Agency's description of persons eligible [stated] that such "persons include, but are not limited to, black Americans, American Indians, Spanish-Americans, oriental Americans, Eskimos and Aleuts." [But] the SBA's class of socially or economically disadvantaged persons neither included all persons in the racial class nor excluded all nonmembers of the racial class. Race was used as no more than a factor in identifying the class of the disadvantaged. The difference between the statutory quota involved in this case and the

SBA's 1968 description [is] thus at least as great as the difference between the University of California's racial quota and the Harvard admissions system that Mr. Justice Powell regarded as critical in *Bakke*.

7. [The] 10% figure bears no special relationship to the relative size of the entire racial class, to any of the six subclasses, or to the population of the subclasses in the areas where they primarily reside. The Aleuts and the Eskimos, for example, respectively represent less than 1% and 7% of the population of Alaska, while Spanish-speaking or Negro citizens represent a majority or almost a majority in a large number of urban areas.

special privilege even though they are the persons most likely still to be suffering the consequences of the past wrong. * * *

"[We] can never either erase or ignore the history that Mr. Justice Marshall has recounted. But if that history can justify such a random distribution of benefits on racial lines, [it] will serve [as] a permanent source of justification for grants of special privileges. For if there is no duty to attempt either to measure the recovery by the wrong or to distribute that recovery within the injured class in an evenhanded way, our history will adequately support a legislative preference for almost any ethnic, religious, or racial group with the political strength to negotiate 'a piece of the action' for its members. * * *

"II. [T]he statute grants the special preference to a class that includes (1) those minority owned firms that have successfully obtained business in the past on a free competitive basis and undoubtedly are capable of doing so in the future as well; (2) firms that have never attempted to obtain any public business in the past; (3) firms that were initially formed after the Act was passed, including those that may have been organized simply to take advantage of its provisions; (4) firms that have tried to obtain public business but were unsuccessful for reasons that are unrelated to the racial characteristics of their stockholders; and (5) those firms that have been victimized by racial discrimination.

"Since there is no reason to believe that any of the firms in the first four categories had been wrongfully excluded from the market for public contracts, the statutory preference for those firms cannot be justified as a remedial measure. And since a judicial remedy was already available [under Title VI] for the firms in the fifth category, it seems inappropriate to regard the preference as a remedy designed to redress any specific wrongs.[13] In any event, since it is highly unlikely that the composition of the fifth category is at all representative of the entire class of firms to which the statute grants a valuable preference, it is ill-fitting to characterize this as a 'narrowly tailored' remedial measure.

"III. [In] the short run our political processes might benefit from [the] ability of representatives of minority groups to disseminate patronage to their political backers. [But this] is, in my opinion, a plainly impermissible justification for this racial classification.

"IV. The interest in [facilitating] minority business enterprises in the economy is unquestionably legitimate. [This] statute, however, is not designed to remove any barriers to entry. Nor does its sparse legislative history detail any insuperable or even significant obstacles to entry into the competitive market. * * *

"It [is] true that irrational racial prejudice [continues] to obstruct minority participation in a variety of economic pursuits, presumably including the construction industry. But there are two reasons why this legislation will not [even] tend to eliminate such prejudice. First, prejudice is less likely to be a significant factor in the public sector of the economy than in the private sector because both federal and state laws have prohibited discrimination in the award of public contracts for many years. Second, and of greater importance, an absolute

---

13. I recognize that the EDA has issued a technical bulletin, relied on heavily by The Chief Justice, which distinguishes between higher bids quoted by minority subcontractors which are attributable to the effects of disadvantage or discrimination and those which are not. [But] even assuming that the technical bulletin accurately reflects Congress' intent in enacting the set-aside, it is not easy to envision how one could realistically demonstrate with any degree of precision, if at all, the extent to which a bid has been inflated by the effects of disadvantage or past discrimination. Consequently, while The Chief Justice describes the set-aside as a remedial measure, it plainly operates as a flat quota.

preference that is unrelated to a minority firm's ability to perform a contract inevitably will engender resentment on the part of competitors excluded from the market for a purely racial reason and skepticism on the part of customers and suppliers aware of the statutory classification. * * *

"The argument that our history of discrimination has left the entire membership of each of the six racial classes identified in the Act less able to compete in a free market [is] more easily stated than proved. The reduction in prejudice that has occurred during the last generation has accomplished much less than was anticipated; it nevertheless remains true that increased opportunities have produced an ever increasing number of demonstrations that members of disadvantaged races are entirely capable not merely of competing on an equal basis, but also of excelling in the most demanding professions. But, even though it is not the actual predicate for this legislation, a statute of this kind inevitably is perceived by many as resting on an assumption that those who are granted this special preference are less [qualified]. Because that perception—especially when fostered by [Congress]—can only exacerbate rather than reduce racial prejudice, it will delay the time when race will become a truly irrelevant, or at least insignificant, factor. Unless Congress clearly articulates the need and basis for a racial classification, and also tailors the classification to its justification, the Court should not uphold this kind of statute. * * *

"The ultimate goal must be to eliminate entirely from governmental decisionmaking such irrelevant factors as a human being's race. The removal of barriers to access to political and economic processes serves that goal. But the creation of new barriers can only frustrate true progress.

"[I] am not convinced that the [Due Process] Clause contains an absolute prohibition against any statutory classification based on race. I am nonetheless persuaded that it does impose a special obligation to scrutinize any governmental decisionmaking process that draws nationwide distinctions between citizens on the basis of their race and incidentally also discriminates against noncitizens in the preferred racial classes. [T]hat Congress for the first time in the Nation's history has created a broad legislative classification for entitlement to benefits based solely on racial characteristics identifies a dramatic difference between this Act and the thousands of statutes that preceded it. This dramatic point of departure is not even mentioned in the statement of purpose of the Act or in the reports of either the House or the Senate Committee that processed the legislation,[25] and was not the subject of any testimony or inquiry. * * *

"Whenever Congress creates a classification that would be subject to strict scrutiny under the Equal Protection Clause [if] it had been fashioned by a state legislature, it seems to me that judicial review should include a consideration of the procedural character of the decisionmaking process. A holding that the classification was not adequately preceded by a consideration of less drastic

---

25. [The] Court quotes three paragraphs from a lengthy report issued by the House Committee on small business in 1977, implying that the contents of that report were considered by Congress when it enacted the 10% minority set aside. But that report was not mentioned by anyone during the very brief discussion of the set-aside amendment. When one considers the vast quantity of written material turned out by the dozens of congressional committees and subcommittees these days, it is unrealistic to assume that a significant number of legislators read, or even were aware of, that report. Even if they did, the report does not contain an explanation of this 10% set-aside for six racial subclasses.

Indeed, the broad racial classification in this Act is totally unexplained. Although the legislative history discussed by The Chief Justice and by Mr. Justice Powell explains why Negro citizens are included within the preferred class, there is absolutely no discussion of why Spanish-speaking, Orientals, Indians, Eskimos, and Aleuts were also included. See n. 6, supra.

alternatives or adequately explained by a statement of legislative purpose would be far less intrusive than a final determination that the substance of the decision is not 'narrowly tailored to the achievement of that goal.' [It] is up to Congress to demonstrate that its unique statutory preference is justified by a relevant characteristic that is shared by the members of the preferred class. In my opinion, because it has failed to make that demonstration, it has also failed to discharge its duty to govern impartially embodied in the Fifth [Amendment]."

SECTION 3. SPECIAL SCRUTINY FOR OTHER CLASSIFICATIONS

I. IN GENERAL

In view of the history and announced purposes of the equal protection clause (see *Slaughter-House Cases,* Sec. 1 supra and *Strauder,* Sec. 2, I supra), are there any classes other than racial and ethnic minorities against whom discrimination should be held "suspect"—or at least subject to judicial scrutiny greater than the "minimum rationality" requirement of the "traditional approach"? Consider Bickel, *The Original Understanding and the Segregation Decision,* 69 Harv.L. Rev. 1, 60 (1955): "[T]he fourteenth amendment, on its face, deals not only with racial discrimination * * *. This cannot have been accidental, since the alternative considered [did] apply only to racial discrimination. Everyone's immediate preoccupation in the 39th Congress [was], of course, with hardships being visited on the colored race. Yet the fact that the proposed constitutional amendment was couched in more general terms could not have escaped those who voted for it."

If there are other classifications that should be subject to special scrutiny, by what criteria should they be identified?

1. *"Unalterable traits."* (a) How significant should it be that legislation discriminates on the basis of "congenital and unalterable traits over which an individual has no control and for which he should receive neither blame nor reward"? Note, *Equal Protection,* 82 Harv.L.Rev. 1065, 1126–27 (1969).

Consider Ely, *The Constitutionality of Reverse Racial Discrimination,* 41 U.Chi.L.Rev. 723, 730 n. 36 (1974): "[M]any characteristics that are theoretically changeable are not practically so; distinctions of constitutional magnitude should not partake of the pretense that any poor working man can significantly change his lot in life, or that any optician can become an optometrist, if he will only shape up. Most important, proponents of this view make no attempt [to] build a logical bridge from the immutability of the classifying characteristic to the conclusion that we should be suspicious of the classification." Must a trait be "congenital" in order to be "unalterable"? If not, is discrimination against a person because of a trait over which he "has no control" especially "invidious"?

Or is the "touch-stone" in respect to unalterable traits the fact that such classifications "will usually be perceived as a stigma of inferiority and a badge of opprobrium"? Note, 82 Harv.L.Rev. at 1127. That many (most) such classifications "bear no relation to one's ability to perform or contribute to society"? Id. at 1173. That often (usually) they involve "a traditionally disfavored class in our society [which] is more likely to be used without pausing to consider its justification"; that "habit, rather than analysis, makes it seem acceptable and natural [b]ut that sort of stereotyped reaction may have no rational relationship—other than pure prejudicial discrimination—to the stated purpose for which the classification is made"? Stevens, J., joined by Brennan and Marshall, JJ., dissenting in *Mathews v. Lucas,* Part III infra (concerning discrimination against illegitimate children). Of what significance is it that the unalterable trait, like race, is one of "high visibility"? [a]

(b) *Age.* MASSACHUSETTS BD. OF RETIREMENT v. MURGIA, 427 U.S. 307, 96 S.Ct. 2562, 49 L.Ed.2d 520 (1976), per curiam, upheld—"under the rational basis standard"—a law requiring uniformed state police officers to retire at age 50. After first rejecting the contention "that a right of governmental employment per se is fundamental" so as to make the legislative classification subject to "strict scrutiny" (see Sec. 4, IV infra), the Court continued: "While the treatment of the aged in this Nation has not been wholly free of discrimination, such persons, unlike, say, those who have been discriminated against on the basis of race or national origin, have not experienced a 'history of purposeful unequal treatment' or been subjected to unique disabilities on the basis of stereotyped characteristics not truly indicative of their abilities. The [Massachusetts statute] cannot be said to discriminate only against the elderly. Rather, it draws the line at a certain age in middle life. But even old age does not define a 'discrete and insular' group, *Carolene Products Co.,* n. 4, in need of 'extraordinary protection from the majoritarian political process.' Instead, it marks a stage that each of us will reach if we live out our normal span. Even if the statute could be said to impose a penalty upon a class defined as the aged, it would not impose a distinction sufficiently akin to those classifications that we have found suspect to call for strict judicial scrutiny." [b]

MARSHALL, J., dissented from "the rigid two-tier model [that] still holds sway as the Court's articulated description of the equal protection test," urging the "flexible equal protection standard" developed in his earlier opinions in *Dandridge v. Williams* and *San Antonio Ind. School Dist. v. Rodriguez,* Sec. 4, IV infra—which would focus "upon the character of the classification in question, the relative importance to individuals in the class discriminated against of the governmental benefits that they do not receive, and the state interests asserted in the support of the classification": "[T]he Court is quite right in suggesting that distinctions exist between the elderly and traditional suspect classes such as [blacks]. The elderly are protected not only by certain antidiscrimination legislation, but by legislation that provides them with positive benefits not enjoyed by the public at large. Moreover, the elderly are not isolated in society, and discrimination against them is not pervasive but is centered primarily in employment. The advantage of a flexible equal protection standard, however, is that it can readily accommodate such variables. The elderly are undoubtedly discriminated against, and when legislation denies them an important benefit— employment—I conclude that to sustain the legislation the Commonwealth must show a reasonably substantial interest and a scheme reasonably closely tailored to achieving that interest."

2. *"Political impotence."* (a) How significant should it be that legislation discriminates against a "discrete and insular" minority? How are such groups to be identified? See note 3(a) after *New Orleans v. Dukes,* Sec. 1 supra.

---

a. For the view that "the doctrine of suspect classifications is a roundabout way of uncovering official attempts to inflict inequality for its own sake—to treat a group worse not in the service of some overriding social goal but largely for the sake of simply disadvantaging its members," see Ely, *Democracy and Distrust* 145–57 (1980). See also Loewy, *A* *Different and More Viable Theory of Equal Protection,* 57 N.C.L.Rev. 1 (1978).

b. See also *Vance v. Bradley,* 440 U.S. 93, 99 S.Ct. 939, 59 L.Ed.2d 171 (1979), upholding mandatory retirement at age 60 for federal Foreign Service personnel.

Consider Goodman, *De Facto School Segregation: A Constitutional and Empirical Analysis,* 60 Cal.L.Rev. 275, 313 (1972): "[If] there are groups that have no voice or visibility [it] is by no means clear that the urban black is among them. Numerically, blacks approach a majority in many large cities and are an increasingly formidable voting bloc in most. Numbers aside, they speak with a voice ever more audible [through] civil rights organizations and ad hoc community [groups]. Seldom have their demands been totally ignored."

(b) Consider Ely, note 1(a) supra, at 732–33: "Racial classifications that disadvantage minorities are rooted in 'we-they' generalizations and balances as opposed to 'they-they' generalizations and balances. Few legislators are opticians; but few are optometrists either.[e] Thus, although a decision to distinguish opticians from optometrists incorporates a stereotypical comparison of two classes of people, it is a comparison of two 'they' stereotypes, viz., *'They* [opticians] generally differ from *them* [optometrists] in certain respects that we find sufficient on balance to justify the decision to classify on this basis.' Legislators, however, have traditionally not only not been Black; they have been White. A decision to distinguish Blacks from Whites therefore has its roots in a comparison between a 'we' stereotype and a 'they' stereotype * * *.

"The choice between classifying on the basis of a comparative generalization and attempting to come up with a more discriminating formula always involves balancing the increase in fairness that greater individualization will produce against the added costs it will entail. But in we-they situations two dangers inherent in this balancing process are significantly intensified. The first is that legislators will overestimate the costs of bringing 'them' into a position of equality with 'us.' [The second is] an undervaluation of the countervailing interest in fairness. [By] seizing upon the positive myths about our own class and the negative myths about theirs, or for that matter the realities respecting some or most members of the two classes, legislators may too readily assume that not many of 'them' will be unfairly deprived, nor many of 'us' unfairly benefitted, by the proposed classification.[43] "[f]

Compare Sandalow, *The Distrust of Politics,* 56 N.Y.U.L.Rev. 446, 464 (1981): "[T]he wealthy—of if you prefer the very wealthy—are surely a minority in our legislatures and are the victims of widespread prejudice that denies them the empathetic understanding of legislators. How many legislators appreciate the costs imposed upon the wealthy by progressive income and estate taxation? Significantly, our statute books contain far more legislation that discriminates on the basis of wealth and income than legislation that employs racial classifications. Why, then, are blacks but not the wealthy entitled to the benefit of special judicial protection?" See also Posner, *The De Funis Case and the Constitutionality of Preferential Treatment of Racial Minorities,* 1974 Sup.Ct.

---

e. The reference is to *Williamson v. Lee Optical Co.,* fn. b in *New Orleans v. Dukes,* Sec. 1 supra.

43. The analysis suggested in the text probably should be limited to situations where most of the "we"s have always been, and expect to remain "we"s, and will therefore have difficulty being objective about precisely what the difference entails. Classifications based on youth or age should therefore be excluded from the suspicious category. * * *

f. Might the optician-optometrist case be characterized as a "we" (consumers)—"they"

(optical suppliers) generalization? Is this particularly true when *all* sellers of a particular product are subjected to legislative regulation? Is a legislatively (judicially) promulgated lawyer-client privilege "suspect" because most legislators (judges) are lawyers? Cf. *Ferguson v. Skrupa,* fn. 5 in *New Orleans v. Dukes,* Sec. 1 supra. A salary raise for legislators? What about discriminations against "conscientious objectors"? See *Johnson v. Robison,* 415 U.S. 361, 375 n. 14, 94 S.Ct. 1160, 39 L.Ed.2d 301 (1974).

Rev. 1, 21: "Ely accepts the legitimacy of comparing the costs of discriminating against the members of a racial or ethnic minority with the benefits from thereby avoiding the need to make individual distinctions. He only wants assurance that the balance will be accurately struck. [His] suspicion only warrants that the reviewing court satisfy itself that the legislature has in fact assessed the costs and benefits of the discrimination accurately. Suppose the Post Office were able to demonstrate convincingly that blacks had, on average, inferior aptitudes to whites for supervisory positions, that the costs to the postal system of inadequate supervisors were very great, and that the costs of conducting the inquiries necessary to ascertain whether an individual black had the requisite aptitudes were also great in relation to the probability of discovering qualified blacks. It would seem to follow from Ely's analysis that the Post Office could adopt a rule barring blacks from supervisory positions. By condemning only inefficient discriminations, Ely reduces the scope of the Equal Protection Clause to triviality * * *."

3. *Poverty.* (a) Although the Warren Court had *stated* on several occasions that "lines drawn on the basis of wealth or property" "render a classification highly suspect," [a] the Burger Court observed in 1973 that the Court had "never held that wealth discrimination alone provides an adequate basis for invoking strict scrutiny," [b] and, in 1980, *Harris v. McRae,* p. 352 supra, said that "this Court has held repeatedly that poverty, standing alone, is not a suspect classification. See, e.g. *James v. Valtierra* [infra]." In fact, explicit (or "de jure") government discriminations against poor people are rare. The more common problems concerning poverty and equal protection (considered in Sec. 4, III infra) arise from "de facto" discriminations—e.g., when the state requires payment for certain privileges or benefits (such as a poll tax for voting or a charge for a trial transcript needed to appeal a criminal conviction).[c]

(b) JAMES v. VALTIERRA, 402 U.S. 137, 91 S.Ct. 1331, 28 L.Ed.2d 678 (1971), per BLACK, J., upheld Art. 34 of the California constitution that no low-income public housing project could be developed unless approved by referendum in the locality: "Provisions for referendums demonstrate devotion to democracy, not to bias, discrimination, or prejudice." "California law reveals that persons advocating low-income housing have not been singled out for mandatory referendums [which] are required for approval of state constitutional amendments, for the issuance of general obligation long-term bonds by local governments, and for certain municipal territorial annexations." [d]

MARSHALL, J., joined by Brennan and Blackmun, JJ., dissented,[e] noting that under California law, "publicly assisted housing developments designed to accommodate the aged, veterans, state employees, persons of moderate income, or any class of citizens other than the poor, need not be approved by prior referenda. [Art. 34 is] an explicit classification on the basis of poverty—a suspect classification which demands exacting judicial scrutiny."

(c) Should explicit discriminations against poor people be held "suspect"? Consider Michelman, *On Protecting the Poor Through the Fourteenth Amend-*

a. *Harper v. Virginia Bd. of Elections* and *McDonald v. Board of Elec. Comm'rs,* Sec. 4, I, B infra.

b. *San Antonio Ind. School Dist. v. Rodriguez,* Sec. 4, IV infra.

c. Such requirements do not automatically exclude poor people (as would a de jure provision that no poor person may vote or appeal a conviction) but their effect seriously disadvantages people with limited funds.

d. If a statute forbade all minors, teachers, lawyers and blacks from serving on juries, would the statute explicitly discriminate against blacks and thus be "suspect"? See *Hunter v. Erickson,* Sec. 2, V supra.

e. Douglas, J., did not participate.

ment, 83 Harv.L.Rev. 7, 21 (1969): "[I]f money is power, then a class deliberately defined so as to include everyone who has less wealth or income than any person outside it may certainly be deemed [to] be especially susceptible to abuse by majoritarian process; and classification of 'the poor' as such, may, like classification of racial minorities as such, be popularly understood as a badge of inferiority. Especially is this so in light of the extreme difficulty of imagining proper governmental objectives which require for their achievement the explicit carving out, for relatively disadvantageous treatment, of a class defined by relative paucity of wealth or income." [f] Compare Winter, *Poverty, Economic Equality, and the Equal Protection Clause,* 1972 Sup.Ct.Rev. 41, 97–98: "Race is [the] basis of a stereotype which served as a systematic vehicle of governmental discrimination. Moreover, it is not a stereotype with a pretense at being related to individual merit, even though it [is] unalterable by the individual. [But] poverty is not absolutely unalterable for all those afflicted by it. The history of this nation is a history of virtually all of its people bettering themselves [economically].[g] Beyond that, [t]here simply has not been any legislation invoking a poverty classification even remotely resembling the widespread, official, racial segregation of schools and other facilities. To the contrary, there is an enormous amount of legislation [to] help the poor. [Finally], to the extent low income is related to low productivity—and it is to a large extent—poverty is not entirely unrelated to individual merit. One need not adopt productivity as the sole criterion of merit to say that poverty resulting from low productivity is far different from legal exclusion from public facilities because of one's race."

II. ALIENAGE

Up to the late 1940s, the Court found a "special public interest" [a] in rejecting almost all challenges to state discriminations against aliens respecting such activities as land ownership, *Terrace v. Thompson,* 263 U.S. 197, 44 S.Ct. 15, 68 L.Ed. 255 (1923); killing wild game, *Patsone v. Pennsylvania,* 232 U.S. 138, 34 S.Ct. 281, 58 L.Ed. 539 (1914); operating poolhalls, *Clarke v. Deckebach,* 274 U.S. 392, 47 S.Ct. 630, 71 L.Ed. 1115 (1927); and working on public construction projects, *Crane v. New York,* 239 U.S. 195, 36 S.Ct. 85, 60 L.Ed. 218 (1915).[b] But *Takahashi v. Fish & Game Comm'n,* 334 U.S. 410, 68 S.Ct. 1138, 92 L.Ed. 1478 (1948), relying on both Congress' "broad constitutional powers in determining what aliens shall be admitted to the United States" and the fourteenth amendment's "general policy" of "equality," invalidated California's denial of licenses

f. What result if the state were to make it a crime for a person without visible means of support to refuse employment? Bar welfare recipients from public housing because of the risk of rental nonpayment? May the state require welfare recipients to accept "suitable employment"? Job training? To disclose certain intimate personal details?

g. See also 85 Harv.L.Rev. 129 (1972): "The poor seem to be a less cohesive and less readily identifiable group than are racial minorities. Because the class of 'poor' is constantly in flux, the reinforced sense of stigma which characterizes de jure racial classifications is probably mitigated even where explicit wealth classifications are concerned."

Compare Clune, *The Supreme Court's Treatment of Wealth Discriminations Under the Fourteenth Amendment,* 1975 Sup.Ct.Rev. 289,

329–30: "[Poverty] is one of the most startlingly stable social phenomena (the strata of personal income have remained in uncannily stable ratios to each other for decades); it seems totally immune to political attack or even war; the disabilities and abilities associated with wealth are pervasive and among the most highly important on our scale of values. [Whether] or not some individuals escape is insignificant compared to those who do not. If the non-escapees are vulnerable and weak economically, socially, and politically, their situation is identical to another class whose individual members are less able to escape."

a. *Truax v. Raich,* 239 U.S. 33, 36 S.Ct. 7, 60 L.Ed. 131 (1915).

b. *Truax,* however, invalidated Arizona's forbidding employers of five or more persons from hiring over 20% aliens.

for commercial fishing in coastal waters to aliens lawfully residing in the state.[c] Finally, *Graham v. Richardson,* 403 U.S. 365, 91 S.Ct. 1848, 29 L.Ed.2d 534 (1971), reasoning that "aliens as a class are a prime example of a 'discrete and insular minority'" and ruling that "classifications based on alienage [are] inherently suspect and subject to close judicial scrutiny," held that state laws denying welfare benefits to aliens violate equal protection.

BERNAL v. FAINTER
467 U.S. 216, 104 S.Ct. 2312, 81 L.Ed.2d 175 (1984).

JUSTICE MARSHALL delivered the opinion of the Court. * * *

Petitioner, a native of Mexico, is a resident alien who has lived in the United States since 1961. He works as a paralegal for Texas Rural Legal Aid, Inc., helping migrant farm workers on employment and civil rights matters. In order to administer oaths to these workers and to notarize their statements for use in civil litigation, petitioner applied in 1978 to become a notary public. [The] Texas Secretary of State denied petitioner's application because he failed to satisfy the statutory requirement that a notary public be a citizen of the United States. Tex.Civ.Stat.Ann., Art. 5949(2). * * *

As a general matter, a State law that discriminates on the basis of alienage [must] advance a compelling State interest by the least restrictive means available. Applying this principle, we have invalidated an array of State statutes that denied aliens the right to pursue various occupations. In *Sugarman v. Dougall,* 413 U.S. 634, 93 S.Ct. 2842, 37 L.Ed.2d 853 (1973), we struck down a State statute barring aliens from employment in permanent positions in the competitive class of the State civil service. In *In re Griffiths,* 413 U.S. 717, 93 S.Ct. 2851, 37 L.Ed.2d 910 (1973), we nullified a State law excluding aliens from eligibility for membership in the State bar. And in *Examining Bd. v. de Otero,* 426 U.S. 572, 96 S.Ct. 2264, 49 L.Ed.2d 65 (1976), we voided a State law that excluded aliens from the practice of civil engineering.[a]

We have, however, developed a narrow exception to the rule that discrimination based on alienage triggers strict scrutiny. This exception has been labelled the "political function" exception and applies [the "rational basis" standard] to laws that exclude aliens from positions intimately related to the process of democratic self-government. [In] *Foley v. Connelie,* 435 U.S. 291, 98 S.Ct. 1067, 55 L.Ed.2d 287 (1978), we held that a State may require police to be citizens because, in performing a fundamental obligation of government, police "are clothed with authority to exercise an almost infinite variety of discretionary powers" often involving the most sensitive areas of daily life.[b] In *Ambach v. Norwick,* 441 U.S. 68, 99 S.Ct. 1589, 60 L.Ed.2d 49 (1979), we held that a State may bar aliens who have not declared their intent to become citizens from

---

c. See also *Oyama v. California,* 332 U.S. 633, 68 S.Ct. 269, 92 L.Ed. 249 (1948) (statutory presumption—that land conveyed to citizen, but paid for by alien ineligible to own land, was held for the benefit of the alien—violates equal protection).

a. *Nyquist v. Mauclet,* 432 U.S. 1, 97 S.Ct. 2120, 53 L.Ed.2d 63 (1977), invalidated a state law that denied aliens state financial aid for higher education. Burger, C.J., one of the four dissenters (see note 1 infra), argued that "the prior cases [invalidated] statutes which prohibited aliens from engaging in certain oc-

cupations or professions, thereby impairing their ability to earn a livelihood. [The] only other case striking down a classification on the basis of alienage, *Graham,* involved the denial of *welfare* benefits essential to sustain [life. In] my view, [w]here a fundamental personal interest is not at stake—and higher education is hardly that—the State must be free to exercise its largesse in any reasonable manner."

b. Marshall, J., joined by Brennan and Stevens, JJ., dissented.

teaching in the public schools because teachers, like police, possess a high degree of responsibility and discretion in the fulfillment of a basic governmental obligation. They have direct, day-to-day contact with students, exercise un-supervised discretion over them, act as role models and influence their students about the government and the political process.[c] Finally, in *Cabell v. Chavez-Salido,* 454 U.S. 432, 102 S.Ct. 735, 70 L.Ed.2d 677 (1982), we held that a State may bar aliens from positions as probation officers because they, like police and teachers, routinely exercise discretionary power, involving a basic governmental function, that places them in a position of direct authority over other individuals.[d]

The rationale behind the political function exception is that within broad boundaries a State may establish its own form of government and limit the right to govern to those who are full-fledged members of the political community.[e]

* * *

To determine whether a restriction based on alienage fits within the narrow political function exception, we devised in *Cabell* a two-part test. "First, [a] classification that is substantially overinclusive or underinclusive tends to un-dercut the governmental claim that the classification serves legitimate political [ends.] Second, even if the classification is sufficiently tailored, it may be applied in the particular case only to 'persons holding state elective or important nonelective executive, legislative, and judicial positions,' those officers who 'participate directly in the formulation, execution, or review of broad public policy' and hence 'perform functions that go right to the heart of representative government.'"[7] [Unlike] the statute invalidated in *Sugarman,* Article 5949(2) does not indiscriminately sweep within its ambit a wide range of offices and [occupations]. Less clear is whether Article 5942(2) is fatally underinclusive. Texas does not require court reporters to be United States citizens even though they perform some of the same services as notaries. Nor does Texas require that its Secretary of State be a citizen, even though he holds the highest appointive position in the State and performs many important functions, including supervision of the licensing of all notaries public. We need not decide this issue, however, because of our decision with respect to the second prong of the *Cabell* test. * * *

The State maintains that [the] duties of Texas notaries entail the performance of functions sufficiently consequential to be deemed "political." The Court of Appeals ably articulated this argument: "With the power to acknowledge instruments such as wills and deeds and leases and mortgages; to take out-of-court depositions; to administer oaths; and the discretion to refuse to perform any of the foregoing acts, notaries public in Texas are involved in countless matters of importance to the day-to-day functioning of state government. [Land]

---

c. Blackmun, J., joined by Brennan, Mar-shall and Stevens, JJ., dissented. They found it "impossible to differentiate" *Griffiths;* and pointed out that both litigants (from England and Finland) had been in the United States more than twelve years, graduated from American colleges, were married to U.S. citi-zens, and were willing to swear to support the U.S. and state constitutions.

d. Blackmun, J., joined by Brennan, Mar-shall and Stevens, JJ., dissented.

e. See also *Skafte v. Rorex,* 191 Colo. 399, 553 P.2d 830 (1976), appeal dismissed 430 U.S.

961, 97 S.Ct. 1638, 52 L.Ed.2d 352 (1977) (deni-al of vote to aliens); *Perkins v. Smith,* 370 F.Supp. 134 (D.Md.1974), affirmed 426 U.S. 913, 96 S.Ct. 2616, 49 L.Ed.2d 368 (1976) (ex-clusion of aliens from juries).

7. We emphasize, as we have in the past, that the political-function exception must be narrowly construed; otherwise the exception will swallow the rule and depreciate the sig-nificance that should attach to the designation of a group as a "discrete and insular" minori-ty for whom heightened judicial solicitude is appropriate.

titles and property succession depend upon the care and integrity of the notary public, as well as the familiarity of the notary with the community, to verify the authenticity of the execution of the documents." [But] a notary's duties, important as they are, hardly implicate responsibilities that go to the heart of representative government. Rather, these duties are essentially clerical and ministerial. [To] be sure, considerable damage could result from the negligent or dishonest performance of a notary's duties. But the same could be said for the duties performed by cashiers, building inspectors, the janitors who clean up the offices of public officials, and numerous other categories of personnel upon whom we depend for careful, honest service. What distinguishes such personnel from those to which the political function exception is properly applied is that the latter are either invested with policy-making responsibility or broad discretion in the execution of public policy that requires the routine exercise of authority over individuals. Neither of these characteristics pertain to the functions performed by Texas notaries.

[If] it is improper to apply the political function exception to a citizenship requirement governing eligibility for membership in a State bar, [*Griffiths,*] it would be anomalous to apply the exception to the citizenship requirement that governs eligibility to become a Texas notary. We conclude, then, that the "political function" exception is inapplicable to Article 5949(2) and that the statute is therefore subject to strict judicial scrutiny [and violates equal protection].

JUSTICE REHNQUIST, dissenting.

I dissent for the reasons stated in my dissenting opinion in *Sugarman* [see note 1 infra].

Notes and Questions

1. *Alienage as a "suspect" classification.* Compare REHNQUIST, J., dissenting in *Sugarman* and *Griffiths:* "[T]here is no language [in the fourteenth amendment] nor any historical evidence as to the intent of the Framers, which would suggest to the slightest degree that it was intended to render alienage a 'suspect' classification, that it was designed in any way to protect 'discrete and insular minorities' other than racial minorities * * *.[f]

"Not only do the numerous classifications on the basis of citizenship that are set forth in the Constitution curb against [these] cases; the very Amendment which the Court reads to prohibit classifications based on citizenship establishes [in § 1] the very distinction which the Court now condemns as 'suspect.' [Decisions] holding that an alien is a 'person' within the meaning of the Equal Protection Clause [are] irrelevant to the question of whether [the] Amendment prohibits legislative classifications based upon this particular status. Since that Amendment by its own terms first defined those who had the status as a lesser included class of all 'persons,' the Court's failure to articulate why such classifications under the same Amendment are now forbidden serves only to illuminate the absence of any constitutional foundation for [these] decisions."

In *Mauclet,* the statute (as in *Ambach*) applied only to aliens who declined to affirm their intent to apply for citizenship when eligible. REHNQUIST, J., joined by Burger, C.J., dissented: "[I]t is no doubt true that all aliens are, at some time, members of a discrete and insular minority in that they are

f. See also Rehnquist, J.'s views re "discrete and insular minorities" in note 3(a) after *New Orleans v. Dukes,* Sec. 1 supra.

identified by a status which they are powerless to change until eligible to become citizens of this country. [Since the statute] does *not* create a discrete and insular minority by placing an inevitable disability based on status, the Court's heightened judicial scrutiny is unwarranted." [g] The Court, per BLACKMUN, J., responded: "By the logic of the dissenting opinion, the suspect class for alienage would be defined to include at most only those who have resided in this country for less than five years, since after that time, if not before, resident aliens are generally eligible to become citizens. 8 U.S.C. § 1427(a). The Court has never suggested, however, that the suspect class is to be defined so narrowly."

2. *The role of the supremacy clause. Graham* also held that "an additional reason why the state statutes [in] these cases do not withstand constitutional scrutiny emerges from the area of federal-state relations. [State] laws that restrict the eligibility of aliens for [welfare] conflict [with] overriding national policies in an area constitutionally entrusted to the Federal Government. [In] *Takahashi* it was said that the States 'can neither add to nor take from the conditions lawfully imposed by Congress upon admission, naturalization and residence of aliens in the United States or the several states.'"

TOLL v. MORENO, 458 U.S. 1, 102 S.Ct. 2977, 73 L.Ed.2d 563 (1982), per BRENNAN, J., held that a University of Maryland rule—flatly denying "in-state" tuition to nonimmigrant aliens with G–4 visas (issued to employees of certain international organizations and their immediate families)—violates the supremacy clause. The Court observed that "commentators have noted [that] many of the Court's decisions concerning alienage classifications, such as *Takahashi,* are better explained in preemption than equal protection terms. See, e.g., Perry, *Modern Equal Protection: A Conceptualization and Appraisal,* 79 Colum.L.Rev. 1023, 1060–65 (1979). [Read] together, *Takahashi* and *Graham* stand for the broad principle [17] that 'state regulation not congressionally sanctioned that discriminates against aliens lawfully admitted to the country is impermissible if it imposes additional burdens not contemplated by Congress.' To be sure, when Congress has done nothing more than permit a class of aliens to enter the country temporarily, the proper application of the principle is likely to be a matter of some dispute. But [in] light of Congress' explicit decision not to bar G–4 aliens from acquiring domicile, [the Maryland rule] surely amounts to an ancillary 'burden not contemplated by Congress.' [Further, as] a result of an array of treaties, international agreements, and federal statutes, G–4 visa holders employed by [various international organizations] are relieved of federal, and in many instances, state and local taxes, on the salaries paid by the organizations. [The Maryland rule] frustrates these federal policies." [h]

REHNQUIST, J., joined by Burger, C.J., dissented: "[T]hat a state statute can be said to discriminate against aliens does not, standing alone, demonstrate that the statute is preempted. [A] state law is invalid only if there is 'such actual conflict between the two schemes of regulation that both cannot stand in the same area,' or if Congress has in some other way unambiguously declared its intention to foreclose the state law in question. [The] Court offers no evidence

---

g. Powell, J., joined by Burger, C.J., and Stewart, J., also dissented, "for the reasons set forth in Mr. Justice Rehnquist's dissent, that New York's scheme of financial assistance in higher education does not discriminate against a suspect class."

17. Our cases do recognize, however, that a State, in the course of defining its political community, may, in appropriate circum-

stances, limit the participation of noncitizens in the States' political and governmental functions. See, e.g., *Cabell; Ambach; Foley; Sugarman.*

h. Blackmun, J., who joined the Court's opinion, concurred, vehemently denying the suggestion in Rehnquist, J.'s dissent that "decisions holding resident aliens to be a 'suspect class' no longer are good law."

that Congress' intent in permitting respondents to establish 'domicile in the United States' has any bearing at all on the tuition available to them at state universities." As for tax relief, "First, the Federal Government has not barred the States from collecting taxes from many, if not most, G–4 visa holders. Second, as to those G–4 nonimmigrants who *are* immune from state income taxes by treaty, Maryland's tuition policy cannot fairly be said to conflict with those treaties in a manner requiring its preemption."[i]

3. *Federal discrimination.* (a) It has long been held that the national government has power "to exclude aliens altogether from the United States, or to prescribe the terms and conditions upon which they may come to this country." *Sing v. United States,* 158 U.S. 538, 15 S.Ct. 967, 39 L.Ed. 1082 (1895). Thus, MATHEWS v. DIAZ, 426 U.S. 67, 96 S.Ct. 1883, 48 L.Ed.2d 478 (1976), per STEVENS, J., upheld a federal statute denying Medicare benefits to aliens unless they have (1) been admitted for permanent residence and (2) resided for at least five years in the United States: Although "aliens and citizens alike, are protected by the Due Process Clause, [i]n the exercise of its broad power over naturalization and immigration, Congress regularly makes rules that would be unacceptable if applied to citizens. * * *

"Since it is obvious that Congress has no constitutional duty to provide *all aliens* with the welfare benefits provided to citizens, the party challenging the constitutionality of the particular line Congress has drawn"—"allowing benefits to some aliens but not to others"—"has the burden of advancing principled reasoning that will at once invalidate that line and yet tolerate a different line separating some aliens from others. [Since neither of the two requirements] is wholly irrational, this case essentially involves nothing more than a claim that it would have been more reasonable for Congress to select somewhat different requirements of the same kind. [But] it remains true that some line is essential, that any line must produce some harsh and apparently arbitrary consequences, and, of greatest importance, that those who qualify under the test Congress has chosen may reasonably be presumed to have a greater affinity to the United States than those who do not."

(b) HAMPTON v. WONG, 426 U.S. 88, 96 S.Ct. 1895, 48 L.Ed.2d 495 (1976), per STEVENS, J., held that a federal Civil Service Commission regulation, generally barring resident aliens from civil service employment, denied "liberty without due process of law": "[T]he federal power over aliens is [not] so plenary that any agent of the National Government may arbitrarily subject all resident aliens to different substantive rules than those applied to citizens. * * *

"The rule [has] its impact on an identifiable class of persons who [are] already subject to disadvantages not shared by the remainder of the community. [The] added disadvantage resulting [from] ineligibility for employment in a major sector of the economy [is] of sufficient significance to be characterized as a deprivation of an interest in liberty. [It] follows that some judicial scrutiny of the deprivation is mandated by the Constitution. * * *

i. O'Connor, J., concurred in part and dissented in part: "I conclude that the Supremacy Clause does not prohibit the University from charging out-of-state tuition to those G–4 aliens who are exempted by federal law from federal taxes only." See Choper, *Discrimination Against Aliens,* in Choper, Kamisar & Tribe, *The Supreme Court: Trends and Developments 1981–82* 14–21 (1983) for the view that (1) *Toll*'s use of the supremacy clause was a "salutory development," but that (2) "the Court's major difficulty resulted from its going beyond its 'broad principle' and getting into the gory details of whether the Maryland regulation actually came into some direct conflict with congressional policy"; "Rehnquist, J.'s argument was fairly strong once you accept *his* premise" of what is required for preemption.

"When the Federal Government asserts an overriding national interest as justification for a discriminatory rule which would violate the Equal Protection Clause if adopted by a State, due process requires that there be a legitimate basis for presuming that the rule was actually intended to serve that interest.[a] If the agency which promulgates the rule has direct responsibility for fostering or protecting that interest, it may reasonably be presumed that the asserted interest was the actual predicate for the rule. [Or], if the rule were expressly mandated by the Congress or the President, we might presume that any interest which might rationally be served by the rule did in fact give rise to its adoption.

"[We] may assume [that] if the Congress or the President had expressly imposed the citizenship requirement, it would be justified by the national interest in providing an incentive for aliens to become naturalized, or possibly even as providing the President with an expendable token for treaty negotiating purposes; but we are not willing to presume that the Chairman of [CSC] was deliberately fostering an interest so far removed from his normal responsibilities."

The Court reviewed the history of the regulation dating to 1884, concluding that it "cannot fairly be construed to evidence either congressional [or presidential] approval or disapproval of the [rule].   [Thus,] our inquiry is whether the national interests which the Government identifies as justifications for the Commission rule are interests on which that agency may properly rely in making a decision implicating the constitutional and social values at stake in this litigation. ＊ ＊ ＊

"The only concern of [the] Commission is the promotion of an efficient federal service. In general it is fair to assume that its goal would be best served by removing unnecessary restrictions on the eligibility of qualified applicants for employment. With only one exception, the interests [put] forth as supporting the Commission regulation at issue in this case are not matters which are properly the business of the Commission. That one exception is the administrative desirability of having one simple rule excluding all noncitizens when it is manifest that citizenship is an appropriate and legitimate requirement for some important and sensitive positions. Arguably, therefore, administrative convenience may provide a rational basis for the general rule.

"[But there] is nothing [to] indicate that the Commission actually made any considered evaluation of the relative desirability of a simple exclusionary rule on the one hand, or the value to the service of enlarging the pool of eligible employees on the other. [Of] greater significance, however, is the quality of the interest at stake. Any fair balancing of the public interest in avoiding the wholesale deprivation of employment opportunities caused by the Commission's indiscriminate policy, as opposed to what may be nothing more than a hypothetical justification, requires rejection of the argument of administrative convenience in this case."[b]

REHNQUIST, J., joined by Burger, C.J., and White and Blackmun, JJ., dissented: "The Court's opinion enunciates a novel conception of the procedural due

---

a. See fn. a, p. 872 supra.

b. Brennan, J., joined by Marshall, J., joined the Court's opinion "understanding that there are reserved the equal protection questions that would be raised by congressional or Presidential enactment of a bar on employment of aliens by the Federal Government."

President Ford subsequently issued such an executive order. Valid? See *Vergara v. Hampton,* 581 F.2d 1281 (7th Cir.1978), cert. denied, 441 U.S. 905 (1979); *Jalil v. Campbell,* 590 F.2d 1120 (D.C.Cir.1978).

process guaranteed by the Fifth Amendment, and from this concept proceeds to evolve a doctrine of delegation of legislative authority which seems to me to be quite contrary to the doctrine established by a long [line of] decisions. * * *

"[T]he exclusive power of Congress to prescribe the terms and conditions of entry includes the power to regulate aliens in various ways once they are here. [This] broad congressional power is in some respects subject to procedural limitations imposed by the Due Process Clause of the Fifth Amendment. If an alien * * * lawfully obtains tenured government employment, and is thereby protected against discharge except for cause, he is entitled to a hearing before being discharged. *Arnett v. Kennedy,* [p. 595 supra]. But neither an alien nor a citizen has any protected liberty interests in obtaining federal employment.

"[U]nder the traditional standards governing the delegation of authority the CSC was fully empowered to act in the manner in which it did in this case. [Once] it is determined that [CSC] was properly delegated the power by Congress to make decisions regarding citizenship of prospective civil servants, then the reasons for which that power was exercised are as foreclosed from judicial scrutiny as if Congress had made the decision itself. The fact that Congress has delegated a power does not provide a back door through which to attack a policy which would otherwise have been immune from attack."

III. ILLEGITIMACY

MATHEWS v. LUCAS

427 U.S. 495, 96 S.Ct. 2755, 49 L.Ed.2d 651 (1976).

MR. JUSTICE BLACKMUN delivered the opinion of the Court.

[The Social Security Act provides survivor's benefits to children who are "dependent" on the deceased parent at time of death; legitimate children and some classes of illegitimate children are statutorily presumed to be dependent; other illegitimate children must prove "that the deceased wage earner was the claimant child's parent and at the time of his death, was living with the child or was contributing to his support." Appellees, illegitimate children, proved that the deceased was their father but "failed to demonstrate their dependency."

[T]he District Court concluded [that] legislation treating legitimate and illegitimate offspring differently is constitutionally suspect * * *. We disagree.

It is true, of course, that the legal status of illegitimacy, however defined, is, like race or national origin, a characteristic determined by causes not within the control of the illegitimate individual, and it bears no relation to the individual's ability to participate in and contribute to society. The Court recognized in *Weber v. Aetna Casualty & Surety Co.,* 406 U.S. 164, 92 S.Ct. 1400, 31 L.Ed.2d 768 (1972), that visiting condemnation upon the child in order to express society's disapproval of the parents' liaisons "is illogical and unjust. Moreover, imposing disabilities on the illegitimate child is contrary to the basic concept of our system that legal burdens should bear some relationship to individual responsibility or wrongdoing. Obviously, no child is responsible for his birth and penalizing the illegitimate child is an ineffectual—as well as an unjust—way of deterring the parent." But where the law is arbitrary in such a way, we have had no difficulty in finding the discrimination impermissible on less demanding standards than those advocated here. *Levy v. Louisiana,* 391 U.S. 68, 88 S.Ct. 1509,

20 L.Ed.2d 436 (1968).[a] And such irrationality in some classifications does not in itself demonstrate that other, possibly rational, distinctions made in part on the basis of legitimacy are inherently untenable. Moreover, while the law has long placed the illegitimate child in an inferior position relative to the legitimate in certain circumstances, particularly in regard to obligations of support or other aspects of family law, see generally, e.g., Krause, *Illegitimacy: Law and Social Policy* 21–42 (1971); Gray & Rudovsky, *The Court Acknowledges the Illegitimate*, 118 U.Pa.L.Rev. 1, 19–38 (1969), perhaps in part because the roots of the discrimination rest in the conduct of the parents rather than the child, and perhaps in part because illegitimacy does not carry an obvious badge, as race or sex do, this discrimination against illegitimates has never approached the severity or pervasiveness of the historic legal and political discrimination against women and Negroes.

We therefore adhere to our earlier view, see *Labine v. Vincent*, 401 U.S. 532, 91 S.Ct. 1017, 28 L.Ed.2d 288 (1971),[b] that the Act's discrimination between individuals on the basis of their legitimacy does not "command extraordinary protection from the majoritarian political process," which our most exacting scrutiny would entail.

Relying on *Weber*,[c] the Court, in *Gomez v. Perez*, 409 U.S. 535, 538, 93 S.Ct. 872, 875, 35 L.Ed.2d 56 (1973), held that "once a State posits a judicially enforceable right on behalf of children to needed support from their natural fathers there is no constitutionally sufficient justification for denying such an essential right to a child simply because its natural father has not married its mother." [d] The same principle, which we adhere to now, applies when the judicially enforceable right to needed support lies against the Government rather than a natural father. See *New Jersey Welfare Rights Org. v. Cahill*, 411 U.S. 619, 93 S.Ct. 1700, 36 L.Ed.2d 543 (1973).[e] * * *

Congress' purpose in adopting [the] presumptions of dependency was obviously to serve administrative convenience. While Congress was unwilling to assume that every child of a deceased insured was dependent at the time of death, by presuming dependency on the basis of relatively readily documented facts, such as legitimate birth, or existence of a support order or paternity decree, which could be relied upon to indicate the likelihood of continued actual dependency, Congress was able to avoid the burden and expense of specific case-by-case determination in the large number of cases where dependency is objec-

---

a. *Levy*, per Douglas, J., involved a statute denying illegitimate children the right to recover for the wrongful death of their mother: "[The test] is whether the line drawn is a rational one [but] we have been extremely sensitive when it comes to basic civil rights and have not hesitated to strike down an invidious classification even though it had history and tradition on its side." Harlan, joined by Black and Stewart, JJ., dissented.

b. *Labine*, per Black, J., upheld a law denying an illegitimate child the same rights as a legitimate child in inheriting from its father who dies intestate even though the father had publicly acknowledged the illegitimate child. Brennan, J., joined by Douglas, White and Marshall, JJ., dissented, finding "no rational basis" for the law.

c. *Weber*, per Powell, J., invalidated a law denying dependent, unacknowledged, illegiti-

mate children recovery of workmen's compensation for the death of their father—finding the discrimination "justified by no legitimate state interest, compelling or otherwise." Blackmun, J., concurred on the ground that, unlike *Labine*, the decedent in *Weber* was unable, under state law, to qualify the child for benefits. Rehnquist, J., dissented on the ground that equal protection "requires neither that state enactments be 'logical' [nor] 'just' in the common meaning of those terms. It requires only that there be some conceivable set of facts which may justify the classification."

d. Stewart and Rehnquist, JJ., dissented on procedural grounds.

e. *Cahill* invalidated a law denying welfare to households with illegitimate children. Rehnquist, J., dissented.

tively probable. Such presumptions in aid of administrative functions, though they may approximate, rather than precisely mirror, the results that case-by-case adjudication would show, are permissible under the Fifth Amendment, so long as that lack of precise equivalence does not exceed the bounds of substantiality tolerated by the applicable level of scrutiny.

In cases of strictest scrutiny, such approximations must be supported at least by a showing that the Government's dollar "lost" to overincluded benefit recipients is returned by a dollar "saved" in administrative expense avoided. Under the standard of review appropriate here, however, the materiality of the relation between the statutory classifications and the likelihood of dependency they assertedly reflect need not be "scientifically substantiated." Nor, in any case, do we believe that Congress is required in this realm of less than strictest scrutiny to weigh the burdens of administrative inquiry solely in terms of dollars ultimately "spent," ignoring the relative amounts devoted to administrative rather than welfare uses. Finally, while the scrutiny by which their showing is to be judged is not a toothless one, the burden remains upon the appellees to demonstrate the insubstantiality of that relation.

Applying these principles, we think that the statutory classifications challenged here are justified as reasonable empirical judgments that are consistent with a design to qualify entitlement to benefits upon a child's dependency at the time of the parent's death. [It] could not have been fairly argued, with respect to any of the statutes struck down in [*Cahill, Gomez, Weber* and *Levy*], that the legitimacy of the child was simply taken as an indication of dependency, or of some other valid ground of qualification. Under all but one of the statutes, not only was the legitimate child automatically entitled to benefits, but an illegitimate child was denied benefits solely and finally on the basis of illegitimacy, and regardless of any demonstration of dependency or other legitimate factor. [Here], the statute does not broadly discriminate between legitimates and illegitimates without more, but is carefully tuned to alternative considerations. The presumption of dependency is withheld only in the absence of any significant indication of the likelihood of actual dependency. * * *

To be sure, none of [the] statutory criteria compels the extension of a presumption of dependency. But the constitutional question is not whether such a presumption is required, but whether it is permitted. [These] matters of practical judgment and empirical calculation are for Congress. [Our] role is simply to determine whether Congress' assumptions are so inconsistent or insubstantial as not to be reasonably supportive of its conclusions that individualized factual inquiry [is] unwarranted as an administrative exercise. [We] cannot say that these exceptions are unfounded, or so indiscriminate as to render the statute's classifications baseless. * * *

Reversed.

Mr. Justice Stevens, with whom Mr. Justice Brennan and Mr. Justice Marshall join, dissenting.

* * * I believe an admittedly illogical and unjust result should not be accepted without both a better explanation and also something more than a "possibly rational" basis. * * *

In this statute, one or another of the criteria giving rise to a "presumption of dependency" exists to make almost all children of deceased wage earners eligible. If a child is legitimate, he qualifies. If the child is illegitimate only because of a nonobvious defect in his parents' marriage, he qualifies. If a court has declared his father to be in fact his father, or has issued an order of support against his father, or if the father has acknowledged the child in writing, he qualifies. Apart from any of these qualifications, if the child is lucky enough to live in a State which allows him to inherit from his intestate father on a par with other children, he also qualifies. And in none of these situations need he allege, much less prove, actual dependency. Indeed, if the contrary fact is undisputed, he is nevertheless qualified. [The presumptions] make eligible many children who are no more likely to be "dependent" than are the children in appellees' situation. Yet in the name of "administrative convenience" the Court allows these survivors' benefits to be allocated on grounds which have only the most tenuous connection to the supposedly controlling factor—the child's dependency on his father.

I am persuaded that the classification [is] more probably the product of a tradition of thinking of illegitimates as less deserving persons than legitimates.[g] The sovereign should firmly reject that tradition. The fact that illegitimacy is not as apparent to the observer as sex or race does not make this governmental classification any less odious. It cannot be denied that it is a source of social opprobrium, even if wholly unmerited, or that it is a circumstance for which the individual has no responsibility whatsoever. * * *

LALLI v. LALLI, 439 U.S. 259, 99 S.Ct. 518, 58 L.Ed.2d 503 (1978), upheld a law forbidding illegitimate children to inherit from their fathers by intestate succession—even though there is "convincing proof of paternity"—unless there was a judicial finding of paternity during the father's lifetime. POWELL, J., joined by Burger, C.J., and Stewart, J., found that the law was "substantially related to the important state interests" of providing "for the just and orderly disposition of property at death" in light of "the peculiar problems of proof implicated in paternal inheritance by illegitimate children": "We do not question that there will be some illegitimate children who would be able to establish their relationship to their deceased fathers without serious disruption of the administration of estates and that, as applied to such individuals, § 4–1.2 appears to operate unfairly. But [our inquiry] does not focus on the abstract 'fairness' of a state law, but on whether the statute's relation to the state interests it is intended to promote is so tenuous that it lacks the rationality contemplated by the Fourteenth Amendment. The Illinois statute in *Trimble v. Gordon,* 430 U.S. 762, 97 S.Ct. 1459, 52 L.Ed.2d 31 (1977), was constitutionally unacceptable because it effected a total statutory disinheritance of children born out of wedlock who were not legitimated by the subsequent marriage of their parents. The reach of the statute was far in excess of its justifiable purposes.[a] Section 4–1.2 does not share this defect."

Rehnquist, J., concurred in the judgment "for the reasons stated in his dissent in *Trimble.*"[b] Blackmun, J., concurred in the judgment, but was

---

g. See Stevens, J.'s amplification of this idea in note 1(a), Part I supra.

a. *Trimble,* per Powell, J., applying *Lucas'* "not-toothless-scrutiny" approach, observed that "difficulties of proving paternity in some situations do not justify the total statutory disinheritance of illegitimate children whose fathers die intestate. The facts of this case"—in which the deceased had been earlier found to be the father in a state court paternity action—"graphically illustrate the constitutional defect." Although *Labine* was not spe-

cifically overruled, "it is difficult to place in the pattern of this Court's equal protection decisions, and subsequent cases [such as *Weber*] have limited its force as a precedent." Burger, C.J., and Stewart, Blackmun and Rehnquist, JJ., dissented.

b. In the course of his long *Trimble* dissent (see note 1 after *N.Y.C. Transit Auth. v. Beazer,* Sec. 1 supra), Rehnquist, J., argued: "The essential problem of the Equal Protection Clause [is] determining where the courts are to look for guidance in defining ["equal"].

unconvinced by "the plurality's valiant struggle to distinguish, rather than overrule, *Trimble*," which he would.

BRENNAN, J., joined by White, Marshall and Stevens, JJ., dissented: "New York has available less drastic means of screening out fraudulent claims of paternity. "[I] see no reason to retreat [from] *Trimble*. The New York [statute] discriminates against illegitimates through means not substantially related to the legitimate interests that the statute purports to promote." [c]

Notes and Questions

Federal immigration power. FIALLO v. BELL, 430 U.S. 787, 97 S.Ct. 1473, 52 L.Ed.2d 50 (1977), per POWELL, J., upheld a federal law granting immigration preference to "children" and "parents" of citizens—except to (1) an illegitimate child of a citizen who is its natural father and (2) the natural father of a citizen who is his illegitimate child. The Court, emphasizing that Congress' "power over aliens is of a political character and therefore subject only to narrow judicial review," rejected the claim for "more searching judicial scrutiny." [d]

Since the Amendment grew out of the Civil War [the] core prohibition was early held to be aimed at the protection of blacks. If race was an invalid sorting tool where blacks were concerned, it followed logically that it should not be valid where other races were concerned either. A logical, though not inexorable, next step, was the extension of the protection to prohibit classifications resting on national origin.

"[W]hen the Court has been required to adjudicate equal protection claims not based on race or national origin, it has faced a much more difficult task. In cases involving alienage, for example, it has concluded that such classifications are 'suspect' because, though not necessarily involving race or national origin, they are enough like the latter to warrant similar treatment. While there may be individual disagreement as to how such classes are to be singled out and as to whether specific classes are sufficiently close to the core area of race and national origin to warrant such treatment, one cannot say that the inquiry is not germane to the meaning of the Clause.

"Illegitimacy [has] never been held by the Court to be a 'suspect classification.' Nonetheless, in several opinions of the Court, statements are found which suggest [that], laws which treat them differently from those born in wedlock will receive a more far-reaching scrutiny under the Equal Protection Clause than will other laws regulating economic and social conditions. The Court's opinion today contains language to that effect [which] is a source of confusion, since the unanswered question remains as to the precise sort of scrutiny to which classifications based on illegitimacy will be subject."

Compare *Mills v. Habluetzel,* 456 U.S. 91, 102 S.Ct. 1549, 71 L.Ed.2d 770 (1982), per Rehnquist, J., holding that a Texas statute—

which then provided that, in order to obtain support, a paternity suit must be brought before the child is one year old—violated equal protection: "[I]n support suits by illegitimate children, more than in support suits by legitimate children, the State has an interest in preventing the prosecution of stale or fraudulent claims, and may impose greater restrictions on the former than it imposes on the latter. Such restrictions will survive equal protection scrutiny to the extent they are substantially related to a legitimate state interest. [First], the period for obtaining support granted by Texas to illegitimate children must be sufficiently long in duration to present a reasonable opportunity for those with an interest in such children to assert claims on their behalf. Second, any time limitation placed on that opportunity must be substantially related to the State's interest in avoiding the litigation of stale or fraudulent claims." O'Connor, J., joined by Burger, C.J., and Brennan and Blackmun, JJ.,—and by Powell, J., in his own brief opinion—wrote "separately because I fear that the [Court's] opinion may be misinterpreted as approving the four-year statute of limitations now used in Texas."

A unanimous Court reached the same result for Tennessee's two-year statute of limitations. *Pickett v. Brown,* 462 U.S. 1, 103 S.Ct. 2199, 76 L.Ed.2d 372 (1983).

c. See generally Maltz, *Illegitimacy and Equal Protection,* 1980 Ariz.St.L.J. 831, contending that "the case law from *Levy* to *Lalli* yields no obvious unifying principles," and analyzing the decisions "to determine whether the challenged classification appears to be based upon prejudice against illegitimates or upon some extrinsic justification."

d. Marshall, J., joined by Brennan J.—and "substantially" by White J.—dissented.

IV. GENDER

Prior to 1971, the Court used the deferential "traditional approach" (see Sec. 1 supra) for classifications based on gender. The earliest case, *Bradwell v. Illinois,* 83 U.S. 130, 21 L.Ed. 442 (1873), upheld a law denying women the right to practice law—Bradley, J., concurring with Swayne and Field, JJ., explained that "the natural and proper timidity and delicacy which belongs to the female sex evidently unfits it for many of the occupations of civil life. [The] paramount destiny and mission of woman are to fulfill the noble and benign offices of wife and mother. This is the law of the Creator." *Muller v. Oregon,* 208 U.S. 412, 28 S.Ct. 324, 52 L.Ed. 551 (1908), per Brewer, J., upheld a law barring factory work by women for more than ten hours a day, reasoning that "as healthy mothers are essential to vigorous offspring, the physical well-being of a woman becomes an object of public interest and care." *Goesaert v. Cleary,* 335 U.S. 464, 69 S.Ct. 198, 93 L.Ed. 163 (1948), per Frankfurter, J., upheld a law denying bartender's licenses to most women, reasoning that "the fact that women may now have achieved the virtues that men have long claimed as their prerogatives and now indulge in vices that men have long practiced, does not preclude the States from drawing a sharp line between the sexes, certainly in such matters as the regulation of the liquor traffic." Finally, *Hoyt v. Florida,* 368 U.S. 57, 82 S.Ct. 159, 7 L.Ed.2d 118 (1961), per Harlan, J., sustained a law placing women on the jury list only if they made special request, stating that "woman is still regarded as the center of home and family life."

The first decision holding sex discrimination violative of equal protection, REED v. REED, 404 U.S. 71, 92 S.Ct. 251, 30 L.Ed.2d 225 (1971), per BURGER, C.J., involved a law preferring males to females when two persons were otherwise equally entitled to be the administrator of an estate: "A classification 'must be reasonable, not arbitrary, and must rest upon some ground of difference having a fair and substantial relation to the object of the [law].' *Royster Guano,* [Sec. 1 supra]. The question" is whether the classification "bears a rational relationship to a state objective that is sought to be advanced by the [law]." It was contended that the law had the reasonable "objective of reducing the workload on probate courts by eliminating one class of contests" and that the legislature might reasonably have "concluded that in general men are better qualified to act as an administrator than are women." But "to give a mandatory preference to members of either sex over members of the other, merely to accomplish the elimination of hearings on the merits, is to make the very kind of arbitrary legislative choice forbidden by [equal protection]."

This was followed by FRONTIERO v. RICHARDSON, 411 U.S. 677, 93 S.Ct. 1764, 36 L.Ed.2d 583 (1973), which held violative of equal protection a federal statute permitting males in the armed services an automatic dependency allowance for their wives but requiring servicewomen to prove that their husbands were dependent. BRENNAN, J., joined by Douglas, White and Marshall, JJ., argued that "classifications based upon sex [are] inherently suspect and must therefore be subjected to close judicial scrutiny," finding "at least implicit support for such an approach in [*Reed's*] departure from 'traditional' rational basis analysis": [c] "[O]ur Nation has had a long and unfortunate history of sex discrimination. Traditionally, such discrimination was rationalized by an attitude of 'romantic paternalism' which, in practical effect, put women not on a pedestal, but in a cage. * * *

"As a result of notions such as these, [statutes] became laden with gross, stereotypical distinctions between the sexes and, indeed, throughout much of the 19th century the position of women in our society was, in many respects, comparable to that of blacks under the pre-Civil War slave codes. Neither slaves nor women could hold office, serve on juries, or bring suit in their own names, and married women traditionally were denied the legal capacity to hold or convey property or to serve as legal guardians of their own children.[d] And although blacks were guaranteed the right to vote in 1870, women were denied even [that] until adoption of the Nineteenth Amendment half a century later.

"It is true, of course, that the position of women in America has improved markedly in recent decades. [But] in part because of the high visibility of the sex characteristic, women still face pervasive, although at times more subtle, discrimination in our educational institutions, on the job market and, perhaps most conspicuously, in the political arena.[17]

c. For discussion of *Reed's* use of "a disguised balancing test," see Note, *Legislative Purpose, Rationality, and Equal Protection*, 82 Yale L.J. 123, 150–51 (1972).

d. See Note, *Sex Discrimination and Equal Protection: Do We Need a Constitutional Amendment?* 84 Harv.L.Rev. 1499, 1507 (1971): "Arguments justifying different treatment for the sexes on the grounds of female inferiority, need for male protection, and happiness in their assigned roles bear a striking resemblance to the half-truths surrounding the myth of the 'happy slave.'" For discussion of the dissimilarities between race and gender for these purposes, see Wasserstrom, *Racism, Sexism, and Preferential Treatment: An Approach to the Topics*, 24 U.C.L.A.L.Rev. 581 (1977); Rutherglen, *Sexual Equality in Fringe-Benefit Plans*, 65 Va.L.Rev. 199, 205–12 (1979).

17. It is true [that] when viewed in the abstract, women do not constitute a small and powerless minority. Nevertheless, in part because of past discrimination, women are vastly underrepresented in this Nation's decision-making councils. * * *

[See also Note, 84 Harv.L.Rev. at 1505 n. 48: "Political power is a difficult concept [to] define. Furthermore, many [women] are not aware of or do not care about the inequalities based on sex in the legal structure. Others may have decided that, on balance, they are benefited rather than burdened by current laws distinguishing the sexes, and thus they may oppose the principle that no such distinctions should be allowed. These considerations weaken the argument that women can protect their interests through their political power, however defined. Even if women could use their political power to protect their interests, but do not choose to do so, the minority who

feel they are discriminated against still should have a right to constitutional protection."

[Compare Ely, *Democracy and Distrust* 166–69 (1980): "[I]n assessing suspiciousness it cannot be enough simply to note that a group does not function as a political bloc. [We must] see if there are systemic bars [to] access. On that score it seems important that today discussion about the appropriate 'place' of women is common among both women and men, and between the sexes as well. The very stereotypes that gave rise to laws 'protecting' women by barring them from various activities are under daily and publicized attack, and are the subject of equally spirited defense. [Given] such open discussion [the] claim that the numerical majority is being 'dominated' [is] one it has become impossible to maintain except at the most inflated rhetorical level. It also renders the broader argument self-contradictory, since to make such a claim in the context of the current debate one must at least implicitly grant the validity of the stereotype, that women are in effect mental infants who will believe anything men tell them to believe. [But] most laws classifying by sex [probably] pre-date woman suffrage]: they should be invalidated. [To] put on the group affected the burden of using its recently unblocked access to get the offending laws repealed would be to place in their path an additional hurdle that the rest of us do not have to contend with in order to protect ourselves—hardly an appropriate response to the realization that they have been unfairly blocked in the past. In fact I may be wrong in supposing that because women now are in a position to protect themselves they will, that we are thus unlikely to see in the future the sort of official gender discrimination that has marked our past. But if women don't protect

"Moreover, since sex, like race and national origin, is an immutable characteristic [the] imposition of special disabilities [would] seem to violate 'the basic concept of our system that legal burdens should bear some relationship to individual responsibility.' *Weber.* And what differentiates sex from such non-suspect statuses as intelligence or physical disability [is] that the sex characteristic frequently bears no relation to ability to perform or contribute to society. As a result, statutory distinctions between the sexes often have the effect of invidiously relegating the entire class of females to inferior legal status without regard to the actual capabilities of its individual members.

"[The] Government [maintains] that, as an empirical matter, wives in our society frequently are dependent upon their husbands, while husbands rarely are dependent upon their wives. Thus, the Government argues that Congress might reasonably have concluded that it would be both cheaper and easier simply conclusively to presume that wives of male members are financially dependent upon their husbands, while burdening female members with the task of establishing dependency in fact.

"The Government offers no concrete evidence, however, tending to support its view that such differential treatment in fact saves the Government any money. [And any] statutory scheme which draws a sharp line between the sexes, *solely* [for] administrative convenience [violates equal protection]."

POWELL, J., joined by Burger, C.J., and Blackmun, J., concurring, would rely "on the authority of *Reed* and reserve for the future any expansion of its rationale" because of the "Equal Rights Amendment, which if adopted will resolve [the] question." Stewart, J., concurred, "agreeing that the [statutes] work an invidious discrimination [*Reed.*]" Rehnquist, J., dissented.[e]

Two decisions during this period upheld gender classifications. KAHN v. SHEVIN, 416 U.S. 351, 94 S.Ct. 1734, 40 L.Ed.2d 189 (1974), per DOUGLAS, J., involved a property tax exemption for widows (but not widowers). Unlike *Reed,* the law is "reasonably designed to further the state policy of cushioning the financial impact of spousal loss upon the sex for whom that loss imposes a disproportionately heavy burden." Unlike *Frontiero,* the classification here is not "*solely* for administrative convenience," nor were the statutes there "in any sense designed to rectify the effects of past discrimination against women."[f]

SCHLESINGER v. BALLARD, 419 U.S. 498, 95 S.Ct. 572, 42 L.Ed.2d 610 (1975), per STEWART, J., upheld a federal statute providing for the discharge of naval "line" officers who had not been promoted for nine years (males) or

themselves from sex discrimination in the future, it [will be] because for one reason or another—substantive disagreement or more likely the assignment of a low priority to the issue—they don't choose to."]

   e. See also *Stanton v. Stanton,* 421 U.S. 7, 95 S.Ct. 1373, 43 L.Ed.2d 688 (1975), per Blackmun, J., relying on *Reed,* holding that a statute requiring child support for males to age 21 but for females only to age 18 violated equal protection: To distinguish "the boy in order to assure him parental support while he attains his education and training, [is] to be self-serving: if the female is not to be supported so long as the male, she hardly can be expected to attend school as long as he does,

and bringing her education to an end earlier coincides with the role-typing society has long imposed." Rehnquist, J., dissented on procedural grounds.

   f. Brennan, J., joined by Marshall, J., dissented: "[I]n providing special benefits for a needy segment of society long the victim of purposeful discrimination and neglect, the statute serves the compelling state interest of achieving equality for such groups." But it "is plainly overinclusive [because] the State could readily narrow the class of beneficiaries to those widows for whom the effects of past economic discrimination against women have been a practical reality." White, J., also dissented along similar lines.

thirteen years (females): In "*Reed* and *Frontiero* the challenged classifications [were] premised on overbroad generalizations" and were sought to be justified solely on "administrative convenience." Here, because of navy restrictions on combat and sea duty for women, "Congress [may] quite rationally have believed that women line officers had less opportunity for promotion than did their male counterparts, and that a longer period of tenure for women officers would, therefore, be consistent with the goal to provide women officers with 'fair and equitable career advancement programs.' Cf. *Kahn*." [g]

WEINBERGER v. WIESENFELD, 420 U.S. 636, 95 S.Ct. 1225, 43 L.Ed.2d 514 (1975), per BRENNAN, J., held that Social Security Act § 402(g)'s payment of benefits to the wife—but not to the husband—of a deceased wage earner with minor children violated equal protection because it "unjustifiably discriminated against women wage-earners": As in *Frontiero,* an " 'archaic and overbroad' generalization [underlies] the distinction drawn by § 402(g), namely, that male [but not female] workers' earnings are vital to the support of their families." Unlike *Kahn,* "it is apparent both from the statutory scheme itself and from the legislative history of § 402(g) that Congress' purpose [was] not to provide an income to women who were, because of economic discrimination, unable to provide for themselves. Rather, § 402(g), linked as it is directly to responsibility for minor children, was intended to permit women to elect not to work and to devote themselves to the care of children. Since this purpose in no way is premised upon any special disadvantages of women, [the] gender-based distinction of § 402(g) is entirely irrational." [i]

CALIFANO v. GOLDFARB, 430 U.S. 199, 97 S.Ct. 1021, 51 L.Ed.2d 270 (1977), held that Social Security Act § 402(f)'s payment of benefits to a widow of a covered employee, but not to a widower unless he proves dependency on his deceased wife-employee, violated equal protection. BRENNAN, J., joined by White, Marshall and Powell, JJ., found *Wiesenfeld* "dispositive."

STEVENS, J., concurred, noting his agreement with the dissent's contentions that "the relevant discrimination in this case is against surviving male spouses, rather than against deceased female wage earners" and that "a classification which treats certain aged widows more favorably than their male counterparts is not 'invidious.' " Nonetheless, since "the history of the statute is entirely consistent with the view that Congress simply assumed that all widows should be regarded as 'dependents' in some general sense," he was "persuaded that this discrimination against a group of males is merely the accidental by-product of a traditional way of thinking about females." [j]

REHNQUIST, J., joined by Burger, C.J., and Stewart and Blackmun, JJ., dissented: "[F]avoring aged widows "is scarcely an invidious discrimination. [It] in no way perpetuates the economic discrimination which has been the basis for heightened scrutiny of gender-based classifications, and is, in fact, explainable as

---

g. Brennan, J., joined by Douglas and Marshall, JJ.—and "for the most part" by White, J.—dissented.

i. Powell, J., joined by Burger, C.J., "concur[red] generally in the opinion of the Court." Rehnquist, J., disclaiming reliance on

Frontiero, concurred in the result because § 402(g) "does not rationally serve any valid legislative purpose, including that for which § 402(g) was obviously designed."

j. Stevens, J., also strongly suggested that he disagreed with *Kahn.*

a measure to ameliorate the characteristically depressed condition of aged widows. *Kahn.*" [1]

CRAIG v. BOREN, 429 U.S. 190, 97 S.Ct. 451, 50 L.Ed.2d 397 (1976), per BRENNAN, J., involving a law forbidding sale of 3.2% beer to males under age 21 and to females under 18, was the first decision (a) to hold an unambiguous discrimination against males violative of equal protection, and (b) to articulate a formal standard of review: "[P]revious cases establish that classifications by gender must serve important governmental objectives and must be substantially related to achievement of those objectives. * * * Decisions following *Reed* [have] rejected administrative ease and convenience as sufficiently important objectives to justify gender-based classifications. * * *

"*Reed* has also provided the underpinning for decisions that have invalidated statutes employing gender as an inaccurate proxy for other, more germane bases of classification. Hence, 'archaic and overbroad' generalizations concerning the financial position of servicewomen, *Frontiero*, and working women, *Wiesenfeld*, could not justify use of a gender line in determining eligibility for certain governmental entitlements. Similarly increasingly outdated misconceptions concerning the role of females in the home rather than in the 'marketplace and world of ideas' were rejected as loose-fitting characterizations incapable of supporting state statutory schemes that were premised upon their accuracy. *Stanton.* In light of the weak congruence between gender and the characteristic or trait that gender purported to represent, it was necessary that the legislatures choose either to realign their substantive laws in a gender-neutral fashion, or to adopt procedures for identifying those instances where the sex-centered generalization actually comported to fact."

The Court reviewed in detail the state's "statistical evidence" concerning "age-sex differentials" in respect to "drinking and driving" and found that it "cannot support the conclusion that the gender-based distinction closely serves to achieve" the "important" objective of "enhancement of traffic safety [23]": [m]

POWELL, J., joined the Court's opinion, but with "reservations as to some of the discussion concerning the appropriate standard for equal protection analysis.*" Relying on *Reed*, he found that "this gender-based classification does not bear a fair and substantial relation to the object of the legislation."

STEVENS, J., who joined the Court's opinion, concurred: "I am inclined to believe that what has become known as the two-tiered analysis of equal protection claims [is] a method the Court has employed to explain decisions that actually apply a single standard in a reasonably consistent fashion. * * *

"In this case, the classification [is] objectionable because it is based on an accident of birth, because it is a mere remnant of the now almost universally

---

1. *Wengler v. Druggists Mut. Ins. Co.*, 446 U.S. 142, 100 S.Ct. 1540, 64 L.Ed.2d 107 (1980), per White, J., held that a virtually identical state workers' compensation law discriminated against women (relying on *Goldfarb*, *Wiesenfeld* and *Frontiero*)—and against men (relying on Stevens, J.'s concurrence in *Goldfarb*)—and thus violated equal protection. Stevens, J., concurred on the basis of his *Goldfarb* concurrence. Only Rehnquist, J., dissented.

23. Insofar as *Goesaert v. Cleary* may be inconsistent, that decision is disapproved. * * *

m. Stewart, J., concurred, relying on *Reed*.

* [As] has been true of *Reed* and its progeny, our decision today will be viewed by some as a "middle-tier" approach. While I would not endorse that characterization[,] candor compels the recognition that the relatively deferential "rational basis" standard of review normally applied takes on a sharper focus when we address a gender-based classification. * * *

rejected tradition of discriminating against males in this age bracket, and because, to the extent it reflects any physical difference between males and females, it is actually perverse.[4] * * *

"The classification is not totally irrational. For the evidence does indicate that there are more males than females in this age bracket who drive and also more who drink. Nevertheless, [i]t is difficult to believe that the statute was actually intended to cope with the problem of traffic safety, since it has only a minimal effect on access to a not-very-intoxicating beverage and does not prohibit its consumption. Moreover, [the] legislation imposes a restraint on one hundred percent of the males in the class allegedly because about 2% of them have probably violated one or more laws relating to the consumption of alcoholic beverages."

REHNQUIST, J.—with whom Burger, C.J., was "in general agreement"—dissented: The Court's "elevated or 'intermediate' level scrutiny, like that invoked in cases dealing with discrimination against females, raises the question of why the statute here should be treated any differently than countless legislative classifications unrelated to sex which have been upheld under a minimum rationality standard. [There] is no suggestion [that] males in this age group are in any way peculiarly disadvantaged, subject to systematic discriminatory treatment, or otherwise in need of special solicitude from the courts. [T]here being no plausible argument that this is a discrimination against females,[2] the Court's reliance on our previous sex-discrimination cases is ill-founded. * * *

"The Court's [standard of review] comes out of thin air. * * * I would think we have had enough difficulty with the two standards of review which our cases have recognized—the norm of 'rational basis,' and the 'compelling state interest' required where a 'suspect classification' is involved—so as to counsel weightily against the insertion of still another 'standard' between those two. How is this Court to divine what objectives are important? How is it to determine whether a particular law is 'substantially' related to the achievement of such objective, rather than related in some other way to its achievement? Both of the phrases used are so diaphanous and elastic as to invite subjective judicial preferences or prejudices relating to particular types of legislation, masquerading as judgments whether such legislation is directed at 'important' objectives or, whether the relationship to those objectives is 'substantial' enough."

CALIFANO v. WEBSTER

430 U.S. 313, 97 S.Ct. 1192, 51 L.Ed.2d 360 (1977).

PER CURIAM.

[Social Security Act § 215(b)(3)'s formula—which has since been amended—afforded the chance of higher old-age benefits to female wage earners than to similarly situated males.]

4. Because males are generally heavier than females, they have a greater capacity to consume alcohol without impairing their driving ability than do females.

2. I am not unaware of the argument [that] all discriminations between the sexes ultimately redound to the detriment of females, because they tend to reinforce "old notions" restricting the roles and opportunities of women. As a general proposition applying equally to all sex categorizations, I believe that this argument was implicitly found to carry little weight in our decisions upholding gender-based differences. See *Ballard; Kahn.* Seeing no assertion that it has special applicability [here], I believe it can be dismissed as an insubstantial consideration.

[See generally Sherry, *Selective Judicial Activism in the Equal Protection Context,* 73 Geo. L.J. 89 (1984).]

To withstand scrutiny under [equal protection], "classifications by gender must serve important governmental objectives and must be substantially related to achievement of those objectives." *Craig*. Reduction of the disparity in economic condition between men and women caused by the long history of discrimination against women has been recognized as such an important governmental objective. *Ballard; Kahn*. But "the mere recitation of a benign, compensatory purpose is not an automatic shield which protects against any inquiry into the actual purposes underlying a statutory scheme." *Wiesenfeld*. Accordingly, we have rejected attempts to justify gender classifications as compensation for past discrimination against women when the classifications in fact penalized women wage earners, *Goldfarb; Wiesenfeld*, or when the statutory structure and its legislative history revealed that the classification was not enacted as compensation for past discrimination. *Goldfarb; Wiesenfeld*.

[This statute] is more analogous to those upheld in *Kahn* and *Ballard* than to those struck down in *Wiesenfeld* and *Goldfarb*. The more favorable treatment of the female wage earner enacted here was not a result of "archaic and overbroad generalizations" about women, or of "the role-typing society has long imposed" upon women such as casual assumptions that women are "the weaker sex" or are more likely to be child-rearers or dependents. Rather, "the only discernible purpose of [§ 215's more favorable treatment is] the permissible one of redressing our society's longstanding disparate treatment of women." *Goldfarb*.

The challenged statute operated directly to compensate women for past economic discrimination. Retirement benefits [are] based on past earnings. But as we have recognized, "[w]hether from overt discrimination or from the socialization process of a male-dominated culture, the job market is inhospitable to the woman seeking any but the lowest paid jobs." *Kahn*. Thus, allowing women, who as such have been unfairly hindered from earning as much as men, to eliminate additional low-earning years from the calculation of their retirement benefits works directly to remedy some part of the effect of past discrimination. * * *

Reversed.

MR. CHIEF JUSTICE BURGER, with whom MR. JUSTICE STEWART, MR. JUSTICE BLACKMUN, and MR. JUSTICE REHNQUIST join, concurring in the judgment.

* * * I find it somewhat difficult to distinguish [*Goldfarb*]. I question whether certainty in the law is promoted by hinging the validity of important statutory schemes on whether five Justices view them to be more akin to the "offensive" provisions struck down in *Wiesenfeld* and *Frontiero*, or more like the "benign" provisions upheld in *Ballard* and *Kahn*. I therefore concur in the judgment [for] reasons stated by Mr. Justice Rehnquist in his dissenting opinion in *Goldfarb*, in which Mr. Justice Stewart, Mr. Justice Blackmun, and I joined.

Notes and Questions

Sex-specific traits. GEDULDIG v. AIELLO, 417 U.S. 484, 94 S.Ct. 2485, 41 L.Ed.2d 256 (1974), per STEWART, J., held that exclusion of "disability that accompanies normal pregnancy and childbirth" from California's disability insurance system "does not exclude [anyone] because of gender * * *. While it is true that only women can become pregnant, it does not follow that every legislative classification concerning pregnancy is [sex-based]. Absent a showing that distinctions involving pregnancy are mere pretexts designed to effect an invidious discrimination against the members of one sex or the other, lawmakers are constitutionally free to include or exclude pregnancy from the coverage of legislation such as this on any reasonable basis, just as with respect to any other physical condition. [The] program divides potential recipients into two groups— pregnant women and nonpregnant persons. While the first group is exclusively female, the second includes members of both sexes. The fiscal and actuarial benefits of the program thus accrue to members of both sexes.[a] [There] is no risk from which men are protected and women are not. Likewise, there is no risk from which women are protected and men are not.[21] "[b]

BRENNAN, J., joined by Douglas and Marshall, JJ., dissented, finding "sex discrimination" in the state's "singling out for less favorable treatment a gender-linked disability peculiar to women [while] men receive full compensation for all disabilities suffered, including those that affect only or primarily their sex, such as prostatectomies, circumcision, hemophilia and gout." [c]

MISSISSIPPI UNIV. FOR WOMEN v. HOGAN
458 U.S. 718, 102 S.Ct. 3331, 73 L.Ed.2d 1090 (1982).

JUSTICE O'CONNOR delivered the opinion of the Court.

[MUW, "the oldest state-supported all-female college in the United States," denied Hogan admission to its School of Nursing solely because of his sex.[a]]

* * * That this statute discriminates against males rather than against females does not exempt it from scrutiny or reduce the standard of review.[8] Our

a. Query: Consider the following description of a law that forbids blacks from unaccredited law schools from becoming lawyers: "The law divides all persons who wish to become lawyers into two groups—blacks from unaccredited schools and all others. While the first group is exclusively black, the second includes members of both races."

What result under *Geduldig* if the disability program excluded only sickle-cell anemia?

How does the rule of *Washington v. Davis* bear on these questions?

21. Indeed, the [data indicated] that both the annual claim rate and the annual claim cost are greater for women than for [men.]

b. *General Electric Co. v. Gilbert*, 429 U.S. 125, 97 S.Ct. 401, 50 L.Ed.2d 343 (1976), held that Title VII's prohibition of sex discrimination did not prevent companies from excluding pregnancy from their disability plans. (But see *Nashville Gas Co. v. Satty*, 434 U.S. 136, 98 S.Ct. 347, 54 L.Ed.2d 356 (1977) (denial of accumulated seniority to persons who take mandatory pregnancy leave violates Title VII).) In response, Congress enacted the Pregnancy Discrimination Act, 42 U.S.C. § 2000e(k) (1978), which defined sex discrimination to include pregnancy discrimination. Some states have given maternity leave rights that go beyond that afforded to non-pregnant employees who are unable to work. Is this sex discrimination? Does a doctrine that ignores the biological differences between men and women regarding abortion, reproduction, and creation of another human being mean that "women can claim equality only insofar as they are like men"? Law, *Rethinking Sex*

and the Constitution, 132 U.Pa.L.Rev. 955, 1007 (1984). See also Kay, *Models of Equality*, 1985 U.Ill.L.Rev. 39; Kay, *Equality and Difference: The Case of Pregnancy*, 1 Berkeley Women's L.J. 1 (1985). More generally, should a law be considered discriminatory whenever it "participates in the systematic social deprivation of one sex because of sex"? Are steps that empower a group "whose depowering is the problem" the antithesis of sex discrimination? See generally MacKinnon, *Sexual Harassment of Working Women*, 101–41 (1979). Alternatively, is an approach based upon "special treatment" for women a "double-edged sword"? Williams, *The Equality Crisis: Some Reflections on Culture, Courts and Feminism*, 7 Women's Rts.L.Rptr. 175, 196 (1982) ("if we can't have it both ways, we need to think carefully about which way we want to have it"). Does the phrase "special treatment" presuppose a male perspective?

c. For invalidation of a disability for pregnant women, on constitutional grounds other than equal protection, see *Cleveland State Bd. of Educ. v. La Fleur*, Sec. 5 infra.

a. The Court declined "to address the question of whether MUW's admissions policy, as applied to males seeking admission to schools other than the School of Nursing, violates the Fourteenth Amendment."

8. Without question, MUW's admissions policy worked to Hogan's disadvantage. [Hogan] could have attended [one] of Mississippi's state-supported coeducational nursing programs [only] by driving a considerable distance from his home. * * *

decisions also establish that the party seeking to uphold a statute that classifies individuals on the basis of their gender must carry the burden of showing an "exceedingly persuasive justification" for the classification. *Kirchberg v. Feenstra*, 450 U.S. 455, 461, 101 S.Ct. 1195, 1199, 67 L.Ed.2d 428 (1981).[b] The burden is met only by showing at least that the classification serves "important governmental objectives and that the discriminatory means employed" are "substantially related to the achievement of those objectives." [9]

Although the test [is] straightforward, it must be applied free of fixed notions concerning the roles and abilities of males and females. [Thus,] if the statutory objective is to exclude or "protect" members of one gender because they are presumed to suffer from an inherent handicap or to be innately inferior, the objective itself is illegitimate. See *Frontiero*.

If the State's objective is legitimate and important, we next determine whether the requisite direct, substantial relationship between objective and means is present. The purpose of requiring that close relationship is to assure that the validity of a classification is determined through reasoned analysis rather than through the mechanical application of traditional, often inaccurate, assumptions about the proper roles of men and women. The need for the requirement is amply revealed by reference to the broad range of statutes already invalidated by this Court, statutes that relied upon the simplistic, outdated assumption that gender could be used as a "proxy for other, more germane bases of classification," *Craig*, to establish a link between objective and classification. * * *

The State's primary justification for maintaining the single-sex admissions policy of MUW's School of Nursing is that it compensates for discrimination against women and, therefore, constitutes educational affirmative action. [A] state can evoke a compensatory purpose to justify an otherwise discriminatory classification only if members of the gender benefited by the classification actually suffer a disadvantage related to the classification. We considered such a situation in *Webster* [and *Ballard*].

In sharp contrast, Mississippi has made no showing that women lacked opportunities to obtain training in the field of nursing or to attain positions of leadership in that field when the MUW School of Nursing opened its door or that women currently are deprived of such opportunities. In fact, in 1970, the year before the School of Nursing's first class enrolled, women earned 94 percent of the nursing baccalaureate degrees conferred in Mississippi and 98.6 percent of the degrees earned nationwide.[14]

Rather than compensate for discriminatory barriers faced by women, MUW's [policy] tends to perpetuate the stereotyped view of nursing as an exclusively woman's job.[15] By assuring that Mississippi allots more openings in

---

b. *Kirchberg* per Marshall, J., held that a Louisiana statute giving a husband exclusive control over disposition of community property was not "substantially related to the achievement of an important governmental objective." Stewart, J., joined by Rehnquist, J., concurred in the result "since men and women were similarly situated for all relevant purposes with respect to the management and disposition of community property."

9. [Because] we conclude that the challenged statutory classification is not substantially related to an important objective, we

need not decide whether classifications based upon gender are inherently suspect.

14. Relatively little change has taken place during the past 10 years. In 1980, women received more than 94 percent of the baccalaureate degrees conferred nationwide and constituted 96.5 percent of the registered nurses in the labor force.

15. Officials of the American Nurses Association have suggested that excluding men from the field has depressed nurses' wages. To the extent the exclusion of men has that effect, MUW's admissions policy actually pe-

its state-supported nursing schools to women than it does to men, MUW's admissions policy lends credibility to the old view that women, not men, should become nurses, and makes the assumption that nursing is a field for women a self-fulfilling prophecy. Thus, we conclude that, although the State recited a "benign, compensatory purpose," it failed to establish that the alleged objective is the actual purpose underlying the discriminatory classification.[16]

The policy is invalid also because [the] State has made no showing that the gender-based classification is substantially and directly related to its proposed compensatory objective. To the contrary, MUW's policy of permitting men to attend classes as auditors fatally undermines its claim that women, at least those in the School of Nursing, are adversely affected by the presence of men.[17]

Affirmed [c]

CHIEF JUSTICE BURGER, dissenting.

I agree generally with Justice Powell's dissenting opinion. I write separately, however, to emphasize that [s]ince the Court's opinion relies heavily on its finding that women have traditionally dominated the nursing profession, it suggests that a State might well be justified in maintaining, for example, the option of an all-women's business school or liberal arts program.

JUSTICE POWELL, with whom JUSTICE REHNQUIST joins, dissenting.

The Court's opinion bows deeply to conformity. Left without honor—indeed, held unconstitutional—is an element of diversity that has characterized much of American education and enriched much of American life. The Court in effect holds today that no State now may provide even a single institution of higher learning open only to women students. [The] only groups with any personal acquaintance with MUW to file amicus briefs are female students and alumnae of MUW. And they have emphatically rejected respondent's arguments. [T]he Court errs seriously by assuming [that] the equal protection standard generally applicable to sex discrimination is appropriate here. That standard was designed to free women from "archaic and overbroad generalizations." *Ballard.* In no previous case have we applied it to invalidate state efforts to *expand* women's choices. Nor are there prior sex discrimination decisions by this Court in which a male plaintiff, as in this case, had the choice of an equal benefit. * * *

By applying heightened equal protection analysis to this case,[9] the Court frustrates the liberating spirit of the Equal Protection Clause. It forbids the

nalizes the very class the State purports to benefit. Cf. *Wiesenfeld.*

16. Even were we to assume that discrimination against women affects their opportunity to obtain an education or to obtain leadership roles in nursing, the challenged policy nonetheless would be invalid, for the State has failed to establish that the legislature intended the single-sex policy to compensate for any perceived discrimination. * * *

17. Justice Powell's dissent suggests that a second objective is served by the gender-based classification in that Mississippi has elected to provide women a choice of educational environments. Since any gender-based classification provides one class a benefit or choice not available to the other class, however, that argument begs the question. The issue is not whether the benefited class profits from the classification, but whether the State's decision

to confer a benefit only upon one class by means of a discriminatory classification is substantially related to achieving a legitimate and substantial goal.

c. The state's contention that Congress had authorized the MUW policy is considered at p. 1157 infra.

9. Even the Court does not argue that the appropriate standard here is "strict scrutiny"—a standard that none of our "sex discrimination" cases ever has adopted. Sexual segregation in education differs from the tradition [of] "separate but equal" *racial* segregation. It was characteristic of racial segregation that segregated facilities were offered, not as alternatives to increase the choices available to blacks, but as the *sole* alternative. MUW stands in sharp contrast. Of Mississippi's eight public universities and 16 public junior colleges, only MUW considers sex as a

States from providing women with an opportunity to choose the type of university they prefer. And yet it is these women whom the Court regards as the *victims* of an illegal, stereotyped perception of the role of women in our society. The Court reasons this way in a case in which no woman has complained, and the only complainant is a man who advances no claims on behalf of anyone else. His claim [is] not that he is being denied a substantive educational opportunity, or even the right to attend an all-male or a coeducational college. It is *only* that the colleges open to him are located at inconvenient distances.

* * * I would sustain Mississippi's right to continue MUW on a rational basis analysis. But I need not apply this "lowest tier" of scrutiny. [More] than 2,000 women presently evidence their preference for MUW by having enrolled [there.] Generations of our finest minds, both among educators and students, have believed that single-sex, college-level institutions afford distinctive benefits. There are many persons, of course, who have different views. But simply because there are these differences is no reason—certainly none of constitutional dimension—to conclude that no substantial state interest is served when such a choice is made available.[17]d

Notes and Questions

1. *Segregation.* In *Hogan,* the Court stated that it was "not faced with the question of whether States can provide 'separate but equal' undergraduate institutions for males and females. Cf. *Vorchheimer v. School Dist. of Philadelphia,* 532 F.2d 880 (3d Cir.1976), aff'd by an equally divided Court, 430 U.S. 703 (1977) (Rehnquist, J., not participating; upholding "separate but equal" public schools for boys and girls"). May public schools have separate athletic programs for boys and girls? In all sports? See Stroud, *Sex Discrimination in High School Athletics,* 6 Ind.L.Rev. 661 (1973). May state prisons be sexually segregated? See Note, *The Sexual Segregation of American Prisons,* 82 Yale L.J. 1229 (1973). May state buildings have separate bathrooms for men and women? Of what significance is the constitutional "right of privacy"? See Ch. 7, Sec. 2. Are there reasons to distinguish between race and sex segregation in the above situations? In some, but not all? See generally Wasserstrom, fn. d supra.

2. *The poverty of means-end scrutiny.* Consider Freedman, *Sex Equality, Sex Differences, and the Supreme Court,* 92 Yale L.J. 913, 952–53 (1983): "[When] means-end rationality becomes the dominant element in the opinions, [the] most powerful message the opinions convey is that sex discrimination is irrational as a means to promote the legislature's own goals. [The emphasis] on means-ends rationality runs into difficulty [in] what Professor Wendy Williams has appropriately termed the 'hard' sex discrimination cases [including *Hogan, Michael M.* and *Rostker,* infra]: those in which the Court, and society more generally, is seriously split over whether perceived sex differences are indeed based on 'outmoded' sex stereotypes, or whether the stereotypes are accurate and desirable." See also Karst, *Woman's Constitution,* 1984 Duke L.J. 447, 449: "Any search for the 'true' nature of women will be hindered by the imprint of the

criterion for admission. Women consequently are free to select a coeducational education environment for themselves if they so desire; their attendance of MUW is not a matter of coercion.

17. [It] is understandable that MUW might believe that it could allow men to audit courses without materially affecting its environment. MUW charges tuition but gives no

academic credit for auditing. The University evidently is correct in believing that few men will choose to audit under such circumstances. This deviation from a perfect relationship between means and ends is insubstantial.

d. Blackmun, J.'s brief dissenting opinion—agreeing essentially with Powell, J.—is omitted.

stereotype of woman on the mind of the person who is searching, whether that person be male or female. The prevailing construct of woman is largely a male product, for it is men who have held the power to define roles and institutions in our society. And the male stereotype of woman is crucially influenced by men's need to define woman in order to define themselves as men." See generally MacKinnon, *Feminism, Marxism, Method, and the State: Toward Feminist Jurisprudence,* 8 Signs 635, at 635 (1983) ("male and female are created through the erotization of dominance and submission. The man/woman difference and the dominance/submission dynamic define each other").

3. *Other discriminations against men.* (a) *Alimony.* ORR v. ORR, 440 U.S. 268, 99 S.Ct. 1102, 59 L.Ed.2d 306 (1979), considered "two legislative objectives" for an Alabama statute providing that only husbands may be required to pay alimony—(1) to "provide help for needy spouses, using sex as a proxy for need," and (2) to "compensate women for past discrimination during marriage, which assertedly has left them unprepared to fend for themselves." The Court, per BRENNAN, J., held this failed the *Craig* standard: "Under the statute, individualized hearings at which the parties' relative financial circumstances are considered *already* occur. There is no reason, therefore, to use sex as a proxy for need. Needy males could be helped along with needy females with little if any additional burden on the [state.] Similarly, since individualized hearings can determine which women were in fact discriminated against vis à vis their husbands, as well as which family units defied the stereotype and left the husband dependent on the wife, Alabama's alleged compensatory purpose may be effectuated without placing burdens solely on husbands." [e]

(b) *Adoption.* CABAN v. MOHAMMED, 441 U.S. 380, 99 S.Ct. 1760, 60 L.Ed.2d 297 (1979), per POWELL, J., held violative of equal protection a New York statute granting the mother (but not the father) of an illegitimate child the right to veto the child's adoption: "Even if the special difficulties attendant upon locating and identifying unwed fathers at birth would justify a legislative distinction between mothers and fathers of newborns, these difficulties need not persist past infancy. When the adoption of an older child is sought, the State's interest in proceeding with adoption cases can be protected by means that do not draw such an inflexible gender-based distinction as that made in § 111. In those cases where the father never has come forward to participate in the rearing of his child, nothing in the Equal Protection Clause precludes the State from withholding from him the privilege of vetoing the adoption of that child. [But] in cases such as this, where the father has established a substantial relationship with the child and admitted his paternity, a State should have no difficulty in identifying [him.] Section 111 both excludes some loving fathers from full participation in the decision whether their children will be adopted and, at the same time, enables some alienated mothers arbitrarily to cut off the paternal rights of fathers. We conclude that this undifferentiated distinction [does] not bear a substantial relationship to the State's asserted interests."

STEVENS, J., joined by Burger, C.J., and Rehnquist, J., dissented: "[I]n the more common adoption situations, the mother [of an illegitimate child] will be the more, and often the only, responsible parent, and [a] paternal consent requirement will constitute a hindrance to the adoption process. Because this general rule is amply justified in its normal application, I would therefore require the party challenging its constitutionality to make some demonstration

---

e. Blackmun, J., concurred. Burger, C.J., and Powell and Rehnquist, JJ., dissented on procedural grounds to which Stevens, J.'s concurrence responded.

of unfairness in a significant number of situations before concluding that it violates [equal protection]. That the Court has found a violation without requiring such a showing can only be attributed to its own 'stereotyped reaction' to what is unquestionably, but in this case justifiably, a gender-based distinction." [f]

(c) *Wrongful death.* PARHAM v. HUGHES, 441 U.S. 347, 99 S.Ct. 1742, 60 L.Ed.2d 269 (1979), upheld a law denying the father (but not the mother) of an illegitimate child the right to sue for the child's wrongful death unless he had legitimated the child. STEWART, J., joined by Burger, C.J., and Rehnquist and Stevens, JJ., found it "clear that the Georgia statute does not invidiously discriminate against the appellant simply because he is of the male sex. The fact is that mothers and fathers of illegitimate children are not similarly situated. Under Georgia law, only a father can by voluntary unilateral action make an illegitimate child legitimate. Unlike the mother of an illegitimate [child,] the identity of the father will frequently be unknown. *Lalli.* [Georgia] has chosen to deal with this problem by allowing only fathers who have established their paternity by legitimating their children to sue for wrongful death, and we cannot say that this solution is an irrational one. [Thus] it is constitutionally irrelevant that the appellant may be able to prove paternity in another manner.

"[Since] fathers who do legitimate their children can sue for wrongful death in precisely the same circumstances as married fathers whose children were legitimate ab initio, the statutory classification does not discriminate against fathers as a class but instead distinguishes between fathers who have legitimated their children and those who have not.[9] Such a classification is quite unlike those condemned in the *Reed, Frontiero,* and *Stanton* cases which were premised upon overbroad generalizations and excluded all members of one sex even though they were similarly situated with members of the other sex."

POWELL, J., concurred because "the gender-based distinction [is] substantially related to achievement of the important state objective of avoiding difficult problems in proving paternity after the death of an illegitimate child."

WHITE, J., joined by Brennan, Marshall and Blackmun, JJ., dissented, finding a "startling circularity" in the plurality's argument: "The issue [is] whether Georgia may require unmarried fathers, but not unmarried mothers, to have pursued the statutory legitimization [procedure]. Seemingly, it is irrelevant that as a matter of state law mothers may not legitimate their children, for they are not required to do so in order to maintain a wrongful death action. That only fathers *may* resort to the legitimization process cannot dissolve the sex discrimination in *requiring* them to.[2] Under the plurality's bootstrap rationale,

---

f. For other decisions dealing with paternal rights in respect to adoption and custody of illegitimate children, see *Stanley v. Illinois,* Sec. 5 infra, and *Quilloin v. Walcott,* p. 534 supra.

9. The ability of a father to make his child legitimate under Georgia law distinguishes this case from *Caban* [where] the father could neither change his children's status nor his own for purposes of the New York adoption statute.

2. The plurality not only fails to examine whether required resort by fathers to the legitimization procedure bears more than a rational relationship to any state interest, but also fails even to address the constitutionality of the sex discrimination in allowing fathers but not mothers to legitimate their children. It is anomalous, at least, to assert that sex discrimination in one statute is constitutionally invisible because it is tied to sex discrimination in another statute, without subjecting *either* [to] an appropriate level of scrutiny.

a State could require that women, but not men, pass a course in order to receive a taxi license, simply by limiting admission to the course to women.[3] "

(d) *Statutory rape.* MICHAEL M. v. SUPERIOR COURT, 450 U.S. 464, 101 S.Ct. 1200, 67 L.Ed.2d 437 (1981), upheld a "statutory rape" law which punished the male, but not the female, party to intercourse when the female was under 18 and not the male's wife. REHNQUIST, J., joined by Burger, C.J., and Stewart and Powell, JJ., observed "that the traditional minimum rationality test takes on a somewhat 'sharper focus' when gender-based classifications are challenged. See *Craig* (Powell, J., concurring). [But] this court has consistently upheld statutes where the gender classification is not invidious, but rather realistically reflects the fact that the sexes are not similarly situated in certain circumstances. *Parham; Webster; Ballard; Kahn.* As the Court has stated, a legislature may 'provide for the special problems of women.' *Wiesenfeld.* ∗ ∗ ∗

"We are satisfied not only that the prevention of illegitimate [teenage] pregnancy is at least one of the 'purposes' of the statute, but that the State has a strong interest in preventing such pregnancy.[7]

"Because virtually all of the significant harmful and inescapably identifiable consequences of teenage pregnancy fall on the young female, a legislature acts well within its authority when it elects to punish only the participant who, by nature, suffers few of the consequences of his conduct. It is hardly unreasonable for a legislature acting to protect minor females to exclude them from punishment. Moreover, the risk of pregnancy itself constitutes a substantial deterrence to young females. [A] criminal sanction imposed solely on males thus serves to roughly 'equalize' the deterrents on the sexes.

"[The] State persuasively contends that a gender-neutral statute would frustrate its interest in effective enforcement. Its view is that a female is surely less likely to report violations of the statute if she herself would be subject to criminal prosecution. In an area already fraught with prosecutorial difficulties, we decline to hold that the Equal Protection Clause requires a legislature to enact a statute so broad that it may well be incapable of enforcement.

"[Finally], the statute places a burden on males [not] shared by females. But we find nothing to suggest that men, because of past discrimination or peculiar disadvantages, are in need of the special solicitude of the courts.[g] Nor is this a case where the gender classification is made 'solely [for] administrative convenience,' as in *Frontiero,* or rests on 'the baggage of sexual stereotypes' as in *Orr.*" [h]

---

3. Men and women would therefore not be "similarly situated." Yet requiring a course for women but not for men is quite obviously a classification on the basis of sex.

7. Although petitioner concedes that the State has a "compelling" interest in preventing teenage pregnancy, he contends that the "true" purpose [is] to protect the virtue and chastity of young women. As such, the statute is unjustifiable because it rests on archaic stereotypes. [Even] if the preservation of female chastity were one of the motives of the statute, and even if that motive be impermissible, petitioner's argument must fail because "[this] court will not strike down an otherwise constitutional statute on the basis of an alleged illicit legislative motive." *United States v. O'Brien,* [p. 621 supra].

g. Does the statute also discriminate against females? Consider Law, *Rethinking Sex and the Constitution,* 132 U.Pa.L.Rev. 955, 1001 (1984): "[U]nder the California law a young man is free to be sexual as long as he chooses a partner who is older than eighteen, while a young woman may not legally have sex with anyone, except her husband if she is married. [The decision] accepts and reinforces the sex-based stereotype that young men may legitimately engage in sexual activity and young women may not."

h. Blackmun, J., concurred in the judgment on the test "exemplified by" *Reed* and *Craig* "and by *Ballard, Wiesenfeld,* and *Kahn.*"

Stewart, J., concurred, noting "that the statutory discrimination, when viewed as part of

BRENNAN, J., joined by White and Marshall, JJ., dissented: "None of the three opinions upholding the California statute fairly applies the equal protection analysis this Court has so carefully developed since *Craig*. [The] plurality assumes that a gender-neutral statute would be less effective [in] deterring sexual activity because a gender-neutral statute would create significant enforcement problems. [But] a State's bare assertion [is] not enough to meet its burden of proof under *Craig*. Rather, the State must produce evidence that will persuade the Court that its assertion is true [and the] State has [not].

"The second flaw in the State's assertion is that even assuming that a gender-neutral statute would be more difficult to enforce, the State has still not shown that those enforcement problems would make such a statute less effective than a gender-based statute in deterring minor females from engaging in sexual intercourse. Common sense, however, suggests that a gender-neutral statutory rape law is potentially a *greater* deterrent of sexual activity than a gender-based law, for the simple reason that a gender-neutral law subjects both men and women to criminal sanctions and thus arguably has a deterrent effect on twice as many potential violators. Even if fewer persons were prosecuted under the gender-neutral law, as the State suggests, it would still be true that twice as many persons would be *subject* to arrest."

STEVENS, J., also dissented: "[T]hat a female confronts a greater risk of harm than a male is a reason for applying the prohibition to her—not a reason for granting her a license to use her own judgment on whether or not to assume the risk. Surely, if we examine the problem from the point of view of society's interest in preventing the risk-creating conduct from occurring at all, it is irrational to exempt 50% of the potential violators. * * *

"Finally, even if my logic is faulty and there actually is some speculative basis for treating equally guilty males and females differently, I still believe that any such speculative justification would be outweighed by the paramount interest in even-handed enforcement of the law. A rule that authorizes punishment of only one of two equally guilty wrongdoers violates the essence of the constitutional requirement that the sovereign must govern impartially." [i]

(e) *Draft registration.* ROSTKER v. GOLDBERG, 453 U.S. 57, 101 S.Ct. 2646, 69 L.Ed.2d 478 (1981), per REHNQUIST, J., upheld a Military Selective Service Act (MSSA) provision "authorizing the President to require the registration of males and not females": "The case arises in the context of Congress' authority over national defense and military affairs, and perhaps in no other area has the Court accorded Congress greater deference. * * *

the wider scheme of California law, is not as clearcut as might at first appear. Females are not freed from criminal liability in California for engaging in sexual activity that may be harmful. It is unlawful, for example, for any person, of either sex, [to] contribute to the delinquency of anyone under 18 years of age. All persons are prohibited [from] consensual intercourse with a child under 14. [Finally,] females may be brought within the proscription of § 261.5 itself, since a female may be charged with aiding and abetting its violation. [A]pproximately 14% of the juveniles arrested for participation in acts made unlawful by § 261.5 between 1975 and 1979 were females. Moreover, an underage female who is as cul-

pable as her male partner, or more culpable, may be prosecuted as a juvenile delinquent."

i. Consider Olsen, *Statutory Rape: A Feminist Critique of Rights Analysis,* 63 Tex.L.Rev. 391, ___ (1984): "[The statute] protects minor females from exploitative intercourse with anyone, but does not protect minor males from exploitative intercourse with females who are above the age of consent. [In the dissenters' view,] 'neutrality' would be achieved by placing blame and criminal liability on the woman, not by treating young men as equally in need of state protection or as equally vulnerable to sexual objectification by the state."

"Not only is the scope of Congress' constitutional power in this area broad, but the lack of competence on the part of the courts is marked. * * *

"None of this is to say that Congress is free to disregard the Constitution when it acts in the area of military affairs. [B]ut the tests and limitations to be applied may differ because of the military context. We of course do not abdicate our ultimate responsibility to decide the constitutional question, but simply recognize that the Constitution itself requires such deference to congressional choice. In deciding the question before us we must be particularly careful not to substitute our judgment of what is desirable for that of Congress, or our own evaluation of evidence for a reasonable evaluation by [Congress].

"No one could deny that under the test of *Craig,* the Government's interest in raising and supporting armies is an 'important governmental interest.' Congress and its committees carefully considered and debated two alternative means of furthering that interest: the first was to register only males for potential conscription, and the other was to register both sexes. Congress chose the former alternative. When that decision is challenged on equal protection grounds, the question a court must decide is not which alternative it would have chosen, [but] whether that chosen by Congress denies equal protection of the laws. * * *

"This case is quite different from several of the gender-based discrimination cases we have considered in [that] Congress did not act 'unthinkingly' or 'reflexively and not for any considered reason.' The question of registering women for the draft not only received considerable national attention and was the subject of wide-ranging public debate, but also was extensively considered by Congress in hearings, floor debate, and in committee. [This] clearly establishes that the decision to exempt women from registration was not the 'accidental byproduct of a traditional way of thinking about women.' *Webster.* * * *

"Congress determined that any future draft, which would be facilitated by the registration scheme, would be characterized by a need for combat troops. [Since] women are [statutorily] excluded from combat, Congress concluded that they would not be needed in the event of a draft, and therefore decided not to register them. [The] exemption of women from registration is not only sufficiently but closely related to Congress' purpose in authorizing registration. See *Michael M.; Craig; Reed.* [As] was the case in *Ballard,* 'the gender classification is not invidious, but rather realistically reflects the fact that the sexes are not similarly situated' in this case. *Michael M.* The Constitution requires that Congress treat similarly situated persons similarly, not that it engage in gestures of superficial equality.

"In holding the MSSA constitutionally invalid the District Court relied heavily on the President's decision to seek authority to register women and the testimony of members of the Executive Branch and the military in support of that decision. As stated by the Administration's witnesses before Congress, however, the President's 'decision to ask for authority to register women is based on equity.' * * * Congress was certainly entitled, in the exercise of its constitutional powers to raise and regulate armies and navies, to focus on the question of military need rather than 'equity.' * * *

"Although the military experts who testified in favor of registering women uniformly opposed the actual drafting of women, there was testimony that in the event of a draft of 650,000 the military could absorb some 80,000 female inductees [to] fill noncombat positions, freeing men to go to the front. In relying on this testimony, [the] District Court palpably exceeded its authority when it ignored Congress' considered response to this line of reasoning.

"In the first place, assuming that a small number of women could be drafted for noncombat roles, Congress simply did not consider it worth the added burdens of including women in draft and registration plans. * * *

"Congress also concluded that whatever the need for women for noncombat roles during mobilization, [it] could be met by volunteers.

"Most significantly, Congress determined that staffing noncombat positions with women during a mobilization would be positively detrimental to the important goal of military flexibility. [The] District Court was quite wrong in undertaking an independent evaluation of this evidence, rather than adopting an appropriately deferential examination of *Congress'* evaluation of that evidence."

WHITE, J., joined by Brennan, J., dissented: "I assume what has not been challenged in this case—that excluding women from combat positions does not offend the Constitution. Granting that, it is self evident that if during mobilization for war, all noncombat military positions must be filled by combat-qualified personnel available to be moved into combat positions, there would be no occasion whatsoever to have any women in the Army, whether as volunteers or inductees. The Court appears to say that Congress concluded as much and that we should accept that judgment even though the serious view of the Executive Branch, including the responsible military services, is to the contrary. * * * I perceive little, if any, indication that Congress itself concluded that every position in the military, no matter how far removed from combat, must be filled with combat-ready men. Common sense and experience in recent wars, where women volunteers were employed in substantial numbers, belie this view of reality. * * *

"I would also have little difficulty agreeing to a reversal if all the women who could serve in wartime without adversely affecting combat readiness could predictably be obtained through volunteers. In that event, [equal protection] would not require the United States to go through, and a large segment of the population to be burdened with, the expensive and essentially useless procedure of registering women. But again I cannot agree with the Court that Congress concluded or that the legislative record indicates that each of the services could rely on women volunteers to fill all the positions for which they might be eligible in the event of mobilization. On the contrary, the [record] supports the District Court's finding that the services would have to conscript at least 80,000 persons to fill positions for which combat-ready men would not be required. * * *

"The Court also submits that because the primary purpose of registration and conscription is to supply combat troops and because the great majority of noncombat positions must be filled by combat-trained men ready to be rotated into combat, the absolute number of positions for which women would be eligible is so small as to be de minimis and of no moment for equal protection purposes, especially in light of the administrative burdens involved in registering all women of suitable age. There is some sense to this; but at least on the record before us, the number of women who could be used in the military without sacrificing combat-readiness is not at all small or insubstantial, and administrative convenience has not been sufficient justification for the kind of outright gender-based discrimination involved [here]."

MARSHALL, J., joined by Brennan, J., dissented: "The Court today places its imprimatur on one of the most potent remaining public expressions of 'ancient canards about the proper role of women.' [W]e are not called upon to decide whether either men or women can be drafted at all, whether they must be drafted in equal numbers, in what order they should be drafted, or once inducted, how they are to be trained for their respective functions. In addition, this case does not involve a challenge to the statutes or policies that prohibit female members of the Armed Forces from serving in combat. It is with this understanding that I turn to the task at hand. [In] my judgment, there simply is no basis for concluding in this case that excluding women from registration is substantially related to the achievement of a concededly important governmental interest in maintaining an effective defense. * * *

"The Government does not defend the exclusion of women from registration on the ground that preventing women from serving in the military is substantially related to the effectiveness of the Armed Forces. Indeed, the successful experience of women serving in all branches of the Armed Services would belie any such claim. * * *

"The most authoritative discussion of Congress' reasons [is] contained in the report prepared by the Senate Armed Services Committee on the Fiscal Year 1981 Defense Authorization Bill. S.Rep. No. 96–826. * * *

"According to the Senate Report, '[t]he policy precluding the use of women in combat is [the] most important reason for not including women in a registration system.' [T]he Report declared: 'Registering women for assignment to combat [would] leave the actual performance of sexually mixed units as an experiment to be conducted in war with unknown risk—a risk that the committee finds militarily unwarranted and dangerous. Moreover, the committee feels that any attempt to assign women to combat positions could affect the national resolve at the time of mobilization, a time of great strain on all aspects of the Nation's resources.' [The] Court then reasons that since women are not eligible for assignment to combat, Congress' decision to exclude them from registration is not unconstitutional discrimination inasmuch as '[m]en and women, because of the combat restrictions on women, are simply not similarly situated for purposes of a draft or registration for a draft.' There is a certain logic to this reasoning, but the Court's approach is fundamentally flawed.

"In the first place, although the Court purports to apply the *Craig* test, the 'similarly situated' analysis the Court employs is in fact significantly different from the *Craig* approach. Compare *Kirchberg* (employing *Craig* test) with id. (Stewart, J., concurring) (employing 'similarly situated' analysis). The Court essentially reasons that the gender classification employed by the MSSA is constitutionally permissible because nondiscrimination is not necessary to achieve the purpose of registration to prepare for a draft of combat troops. In other words, the majority concludes that women may be excluded from registration because they will not be needed in the event of a draft.

"This analysis, however, focuses on the wrong question. The relevant inquiry under the *Craig* test is not whether a *gender-neutral* classification would substantially advance important governmental interests. Rather, the question is whether the gender-based classification is itself substantially related to the achievement of the asserted governmental interest. Thus, the Government's task in this case is to demonstrate that excluding women from registration substantially furthers the goal of preparing for a draft of combat troops. Or to put it another way, the Government must show that registering women would substantially impede its efforts to prepare for such a draft. Under our precedents, the Government cannot meet this burden without showing that a gender neutral statute would be a less effective means of attaining this end. [In] this case, the Government makes no claim that preparing for a draft of combat troops cannot be accomplished just as effectively by *registering* both men and women but *drafting* only men if only men turn out to be needed.[11] Nor can the Government argue that this alternative entails the additional cost and administrative inconvenience of registering women. This Court has repeatedly stated that [administrative convenience] is not an adequate constitutional justification under the *Craig* test.

"The fact that registering women in no way obstructs the governmental interest in preparing for a draft of combat troops points up a second flaw in the Court's analysis. The Court essentially reduces the question of the constitutionality of male-only *registration* to the validity of a hypothetical program for *conscripting* only men. [If] it could indeed be guaranteed in advance that conscription would be reimposed by Congress only in circumstances where, and in a form under which, all conscripts would have to be trained for and assigned to combat or combat rotation positions from which women are categorically excluded, then it could be argued that registration of women would be pointless.

"But of course, no such guarantee is possible. Certainly, nothing about the MSSA limits Congress to reinstituting the draft only in such circumstances. For example, Congress may decide that the All-Volunteer Armed Forces are inadequate to meet the Nation's defense needs even in times of peace and reinstitute peacetime conscription. In that event, the hypothetical draft the Court relied [on] would presumably be of little relevance * * *. The fact that registration is a first step in the conscription process does not mean that a registration law expressly discriminating between men and women may be justified by a valid conscription program which would, in retrospect, make the current discrimination appear functionally related to the program that emerged.

"But even addressing the Court's reasoning on its own terms, its analysis is flawed because the entire argument rests on a premise that is demonstrably false. As noted, the majority simply assumes that registration prepares for a draft in which *every* draftee must be available for assignment to combat. But [this] finds no support in either the testimony before Congress, or more importantly, in the findings of the Senate Report. * * * Testimony about personnel requirements in the event of a draft established that women could fill at least 80,000 of the 650,000 positions for which conscripts would be inducted. Thus, [the] statutes and policies barring women from combat do not provide a reason for distinguishing between male and female potential conscripts; the two groups are, in the majority's parlance, 'similarly situated.' As such, the combat restrictions cannot by themselves supply the constitutionally required justification for the MSSA's gender-based classification. [T]he Court asserts that 'Congress determined that staffing noncombat positions with women during a mobilization would be positively detrimental to the important goal of military flexibility.' [But] to justify the exclusion of women from registration and the draft on this ground, there must be a further showing that staffing even a limited number of noncombat positions with women would impede military flexibility. I find nothing in the Senate Report to provide any basis for the Court's representation that Congress believed this to be the case.

---

11. Alternatively, the Government could employ a classification that is related to the statutory objective but is not based on gender, for example, combat eligibility. Under the current scheme, large subgroups of the male population who are ineligible for combat because of physical handicaps or conscientious objector status are nonetheless required to register.

"The Senate Report concluded [that] drafting *'very large numbers* of women' would hinder military flexibility. [But the] testimony on this issue at the congressional hearings was that drafting a limited number of women is quite compatible with the military's need for flexibility. In concluding that the Armed Services could usefully employ at least 80,000 women conscripts out of a total of 650,000 draftees that would be needed in the event of a major European war, the Defense Department took into account both the need for rotation of combat personnel and the possibility that some support personnel might have to be sent into combat. [The] combat restrictions that would prevent a female draftee from serving in a combat or combat rotation position also apply to the 150,000–250,000 women volunteers in the Armed Services. If the presence of increasing but controlled numbers of female volunteers has not unacceptably 'divide[d] the military into two groups,' it is difficult to see how the induction of a similarly limited additional number of women could accomplish this result. [T]he Senate Report establishes that induction of a large number of men but only a limited number of women [would] be substantially related to important governmental interests. But the discussion and findings in the Senate Report do not enable the Government to carry its burden of demonstrating that *completely* excluding women from the draft by excluding them from registration substantially furthers important governmental objectives." [j]

4. *Equal Rights Amendment.* This proposed amendment—that "equality of rights under the law shall not be denied or abridged by the United States or by an State on account of sex"—was approved by 35 states (three less than required for ratification) at its expiration in 1982. How would this affect the issues considered in this section?

V. MENTAL RETARDATION

CLEBURNE v. CLEBURNE LIVING CENTER, INC.

__ U.S. __, 105 S.Ct. 3249, 87 L.Ed.2d 313 (1985).

JUSTICE WHITE delivered the opinion of the Court.

A Texas city denied a special permit for the operation of [the Featherston] group home for the mentally retarded. [The] general rule [under the Equal Protection Clause] is that legislation is presumed to be valid and will be sustained if the classification drawn by the statute is rationally related to a

---

j. Consider Williams, fn. b, p. 1003 supra, at 189–90: "As for *Rostker,* the conflicts among feminists were overtly expressed. Some of us felt it essential that we support the notion that a single-sex draft was unconstitutional; others felt that feminists should not take such a position. These latter groups explicitly contrasted the female ethic of nurturance and life-giving with a male ethic of aggression and militarism and asserted that if we argued to the Court that single-sex registration is unconstitutional we would be betraying ourselves and supporting what we find least acceptable about the male world.

"To me, this latter argument quite overtly taps qualities that the culture has ascribed to woman-as-childrearer and converts them to a normative value statement, one with which it is easy for us to sympathize. This is one of the circumstances in which the feeling that 'I want what he's got but I don't want to be what he's had to be in order to get it' comes quickly to the surface. But I also believe that the reflexive response based on these deeper cultural senses leads us to untenable positions. [To] me, *Rostker* never posed the question of whether women should be forced as men now are to fight wars, but whether we, like them, must take the responsibility for deciding whether or not to fight, whether or not to bear the cost of risking our lives, on the one hand, or resisting in the name of peace, on the other. And do we not, by insisting upon our differences at these crucial junctures, promote and reinforce the us-them dichotomy that permits the Rehnquists and the Stewarts to resolve matters of great importance and complexity by the simplistic, reflexive assertion that men and women 'are simply not similarly situated?' "

legitimate state interest. *Schweiker v. Wilson; United States R.R. Retirement Bd. v. Fritz; Vance v. Bradley; New Orleans v. Dukes,* [Sec. 1 supra]. * * *

The general rule gives way, however, when a statute classifies by race, alienage or national origin. These factors are so seldom relevant to the achievement of any legitimate state interest that laws grounded in such considerations are deemed to reflect prejudice and antipathy—a view that those in the burdened class are not as worthy or deserving as others. For these reasons and because such discrimination is unlikely to be soon rectified by legislative means, these laws are subjected to strict scrutiny * * *.

Legislative classifications based on gender also call for a heightened standard of review. [Rather] than resting on meaningful considerations, statutes distributing benefits and burdens between the sexes in different ways very likely reflect outmoded notions of the relative capabilities of men and women. A gender classification fails unless it is substantially related to a sufficiently important governmental interest. Because illegitimacy is beyond the individual's control and bears "no relation to the individual's ability to participate in and contribute to society," official discriminations resting on that characteristic are also subject to somewhat heightened review. Those restrictions "will survive equal protection scrutiny to the extent they are substantially related to a legitimate state interest." *Mills v. Habluetzel,* [Part III supra].

We have declined, however, to extend heightened review to differential treatment based on [age]. The lesson of *Murgia,* [Part I supra], is that where individuals in the group affected by a law have distinguishing characteristics relevant to interests the state has the authority to implement, the courts have been very reluctant, as they should be in our federal system and with our respect for the separation of powers, to closely scrutinize legislative choices as to whether, how and to what extent those interests should be pursued. In such cases, the Equal Protection Clause requires only a rational means to serve a legitimate end.

Against this background, we conclude [that] the Court of Appeals erred in holding mental retardation a quasi-suspect classification. [First, those] who are mentally retarded have a reduced ability to cope with and function in the everyday world. [How] this large and diversified group is to be treated under the law is a difficult and often a technical matter, very much a task for legislators guided by qualified professionals and not by the perhaps ill-informed opinions of the judiciary. Heightened scrutiny inevitably involves substantive judgments about legislative decisions, and we doubt that the predicate for such judicial oversight is present where the classification deals with mental retardation.

Second, the distinctive legislative response, both national and state, to the plight of those who are mentally retarded demonstrates not only that they have unique problems, but also that the lawmakers have been addressing their difficulties in a manner that belies a continuing antipathy or prejudice and a corresponding need for more intrusive oversight by the judiciary. Thus, the federal government has not only outlawed discrimination against the mentally retarded in federally funded programs, see § 504 of the Rehabilitation Act of 1973, 29 U.S.C. § 794, but it has also provided the retarded with the right to receive "appropriate treatment, services, and habilitation" in a setting that is "least restrictive of [their] personal liberty." Developmental Disabilities Assistance and Bill of Rights Act, 42 U.S.C. §§ 6010(1), (2). * * * Texas has similarly enacted legislation that acknowledges the special status of the mentally retarded by conferring certain rights upon them, such as "the right to live in the least restrictive setting appropriate to [their] individual needs and abilities," * * *. [It] may be, as CLC contends, that legislation designed to benefit, rather than disadvantage, the retarded would generally withstand examination under a test of heightened scrutiny. The relevant inquiry, however, is whether heightened scrutiny is constitutionally mandated in the first instance. Even assuming that many of these laws could be shown to be substantially related to an important governmental purpose, merely requiring the legislature to justify its efforts in these terms may lead it to refrain from acting at all. Much recent legislation intended to benefit the retarded also assumes the need for measures that might be perceived to disadvantage them. The Education of the Handicapped Act, for example, requires an "appropriate" education, not one that is equal in all respects to the education of non-retarded children; clearly, admission to a class that exceeded the abilities of a retarded child would not be appropriate. Similarly, the Developmental Disabilities Assistance Act and the Texas act give the retarded the right to live only in the "least restrictive setting" appropriate to their abilities, implicitly assuming the need for at least some restrictions that would not be imposed on others. Especially given the wide variation in the abilities and needs of the retarded themselves, governmental bodies must have a certain amount of flexibility and freedom from judicial oversight in shaping and limiting their remedial efforts.

Third, the legislative response, which could hardly have occurred and survived without public support, negates any claim that the mentally retarded are politically powerless in the sense that they have no ability to attract the attention of the lawmakers. Any minority can be said to be powerless to assert direct control over the legislature, but if that were a criterion for higher level scrutiny by the courts, much economic and social legislation would now be suspect.

Fourth, if the large and amorphous class of the mentally retarded were deemed quasi-suspect, [it] would be difficult to find a principled way to distinguish a variety of other groups who have perhaps immutable disabilities setting them off from others, who cannot themselves mandate the desired legislative responses, and who can claim some degree of prejudice from at least part of the public at large. One need mention in this respect only the aging, the disabled, the mentally ill, and the infirm. We are reluctant to set out on that course, and we decline to do so.

Doubtless, there have been and there will continue to be instances of discrimination against the retarded that are in fact invidious, and that are properly subject to judicial correction under constitutional norms. But the appropriate method of reaching such instances is [to] look to the likelihood that governmental action premised on a particular classification is valid as a general matter, not merely to the specifics of the case before us. * * *

Our refusal to recognize the retarded as a quasi-suspect class does not leave them entirely unprotected from invidious discrimination. To withstand equal protection review, legislation that distinguishes between the mentally retarded and others must be rationally related to a legitimate governmental purpose. This standard, we believe, affords government the latitude necessary both to pursue policies designed to assist the retarded in realizing their full potential, and to freely and efficiently engage in activities that burden the retarded in what is essentially an incidental manner. The State may not rely on a classification whose relationship to an asserted goal is so attenuated as to render

the distinction arbitrary or irrational. See *Zobel v. Williams,* [Sec. 4, II infra];
U.S. Dep't of Agriculture v. Moreno, [Sec. 4, II infra]. Furthermore, some
objectives—such as "a bare * * * desire to harm a politically unpopular
group," *Moreno* —are not legitimate state interests. Beyond that, the mentally
retarded, like others, have and retain their substantive constitutional rights in
addition to the right to be treated equally by the law. * * *

The constitutional issue is clearly posed. The City does not require a special
use permit in an R–3 zone for apartment houses, multiple dwellings, boarding
and lodging houses, fraternity or sorority houses, dormitories, apartment hotels,
hospitals, sanitariums, nursing homes for convalescents or the aged (other than
for the insane or feeble-minded or alcoholics or drug addicts), private clubs or
fraternal orders, and other specified uses. [I]n our view the record does not
reveal any rational basis for believing that the Featherston home would pose any
special threat to the city's legitimate interests * * *.

The District Court found that the City Council's insistence on the permit
rested on several factors. First, the Council was concerned with the negative
attitude of the majority of property owners located within 200 feet of the
Featherston facility, as well as with the fears of elderly residents of the
neighborhood. But mere negative attitudes, or fear, unsubstantiated by factors
which are properly cognizable in a zoning proceeding, are not permissible bases
for treating a home for the mentally retarded differently from apartment houses,
multiple dwellings, and the like. * * *

Second, the Council [was] concerned that the facility was across the street
from a junior high school, and it feared that the students might harass the
occupants of the Featherston home. But the school itself is attended by about 30
mentally retarded students, and denying a permit based on such vague, undifferentiated fears is again permitting some portion of the community to validate
what would otherwise be an equal protection violation. * * *

In the courts below the city also urged that the ordinance is aimed at
avoiding concentration of population and at lessening congestion of the streets.
These concerns obviously fail to explain why apartment houses, fraternity and
sorority houses, hospitals and the like, may freely locate in the area without a
permit. So, too, the expressed worry about fire hazards, the serenity of the
neighborhood, and the avoidance of danger to other residents fail rationally to
justify singling out a home such as 201 Featherston for the special use permit,
yet imposing no such restrictions on the many other uses freely permitted in the
neighborhood.

The short of it is that requiring the permit in this case appears to us to rest
on an irrational prejudice against the mentally retarded. [Thus, the] judgment
of the Court of Appeals is affirmed insofar as it invalidates the zoning ordinance
as applied to the Featherston home. * * *

JUSTICE STEVENS, with whom THE CHIEF JUSTICE joins, concurring.

[O]ur cases reflect a continuum of judgmental responses to differing classifications which have been explained in opinions by terms ranging from "strict
scrutiny" at one extreme to "rational basis" at the other. I have never been
persuaded that these so called "standards" adequately explain the decisional
process. * * *

In every equal protection case, we have to ask certain basic questions. What
class is harmed by the legislation, and has it been subjected to a "tradition of
disfavor" by our laws? What is the public purpose that is being served by the
law? What is the characteristic of the disadvantaged class that justifies the

disparate treatment? In most cases the answer to these questions will tell us whether the statute has a "rational basis." The answers will result in the virtually automatic invalidation of racial classifications and in the validation of most economic classifications, but they will provide differing results in cases involving classifications based on alienage, gender, or illegitimacy. But that is not because we apply an "intermediate standard of review" in these cases; rather it is because the characteristics of these groups are sometimes relevant and sometimes irrelevant to a valid public purpose, or, more specifically, to the purpose that the challenged laws purportedly intended to serve.

Every law that places the mentally retarded in a special class is not presumptively irrational. [But] through ignorance and prejudice the mentally retarded "have been subjected to a history of unfair and often grotesque mistreatment." The [record in this case] convinces me that this permit was required because of the irrational fears of neighboring property owners, rather than for the protection of the mentally retarded persons who would reside in respondent's home. * * *

Accordingly, I join the opinion of the Court.

JUSTICE MARSHALL, with whom JUSTICE BRENNAN and JUSTICE BLACKMUN join, concurring in the judgment in part and dissenting in part.

* * * Cleburne's ordinance surely would be valid under the traditional rational basis test applicable to economic and commercial regulation. In my view, it is important to articulate, as the Court does not, the facts and principles that justify subjecting this zoning ordinance to the searching review—the heightened scrutiny—that actually leads to its invalidation. * * *

The Court, for example, concludes that legitimate concerns for fire hazards or the serenity of the neighborhood do not justify singling out respondents to bear the burdens of these concerns, for analogous permitted uses appear to pose similar threats. Yet under the traditional and most minimal version of the rational basis test, "reform may take one step at a time, addressing itself to the phase of the problem which seems most acute to the legislative mind." The "record" is said not to support the ordinance's classifications, but under the traditional standard we do not sift through the record to determine whether policy decisions are squarely supported by a firm factual foundation. [The] same imprecision in a similar ordinance that required opticians but not optometrists to be licensed to practice, see *Williamson v. Lee Optical Co.,* [Sec. 1 supra], or that excluded new but not old businesses from parts of a community, see *Dukes,* [Sec. 1 supra], would hardly be fatal to the statutory scheme.

The refusal to acknowledge that something more than minimum rationality review is at work here is, in my view, unfortunate in at least two respects.[4] The suggestion that the traditional rational basis test allows this sort of searching inquiry creates precedent for this Court and lower courts to subject economic and commercial classifications to similar and searching "ordinary" rational basis review—a small and regrettable step back toward the days of *Lochner v. New York* [Ch. 6, Sec. 1, V]. Moreover, by failing to articulate the factors that justify today's "second order" rational basis review, the Court provides no principled

---

4. The two cases the Court cites in its rational basis discussion, *Zobel* and *Moreno,* expose the special nature of the rational basis test employed today. As two of only a handful of modern equal protection cases striking down legislation under what purports to be a rational basis standard, these cases must be and generally have been viewed as intermediate review decisions masquerading in rational basis language. See, e.g., Tribe, *American Constitutional Law* 1090, n. 10 (1978). (discussing *Moreno);* see also *Moreno* (Douglas, J., concurring); *Zobel* (Brennan, J., concurring).

foundation for determining when more searching inquiry is to be invoked. Lower courts are thus left in the dark on this important question, and this Court remains unaccountable for its decisions employing, or refusing to employ, particularly searching scrutiny. * * *

I have long believed the level of scrutiny employed in an equal protection case should vary with "the constitutional and societal importance of the interest adversely affected and the recognized invidiousness of the basis upon which the particular classification is drawn." *Rodriguez* (Marshall, J., dissenting). See also *Dandridge* (Marshall, J., dissenting). When a zoning ordinance works to exclude the retarded from all residential districts in a community, these two considerations require that the ordinance be convincingly justified as substantially furthering legitimate and important purposes.

First, the interest [in] establishing group homes is substantial, [for] as deinstitutionalization has progressed, group homes have become the primary means by which retarded adults can enter life in the community. * * *

Second, the mentally retarded have been subject to a "lengthy and tragic history" of segregation and discrimination that can only be called grotesque. [The] searching scrutiny I would give to restrictions on the ability of the retarded to establish community group homes leads me to conclude that Cleburne's vague generalizations [are] not substantial or important enough to overcome the suspicion that the ordinance rests on impermissible assumptions or outmoded and perhaps invidious stereotypes. * * *

The Court downplays the lengthy "history of purposeful unequal treatment" of the retarded by pointing to recent legislative action that is said to "beli[e] a continuing antipathy or prejudice." [But it] is natural that evolving standards of equality come to be embodied in legislation. When that occurs, courts should look to the fact of such change as a source of guidance on evolving principles of equality * * *.

Moreover, even when judicial action *has* catalyzed legislative change, that change certainly does not eviscerate the underlying constitutional principle. The Court, for example, has never suggested that race-based classifications became any less suspect once extensive legislation had been enacted on the subject.

For the retarded, just as for Negroes and women, much has changed in recent years, but much remains the same; outdated statutes are still on the books, and irrational fears or ignorance, traceable to the prolonged social and cultural isolation of the retarded, continue to stymie recognition of the dignity and individuality of retarded people. * * *

The Court also offers a more general view of heightened [scrutiny]. First, heightened scrutiny is said to be inapplicable where *individuals* in a group have distinguishing characteristics that legislatures properly may take into account in some circumstances. Heightened scrutiny is also purportedly inappropriate when many legislative classifications affecting the *group* are likely to be [valid.]

If the Court's first principle were sound, heightened scrutiny would have to await a day when people could be cut from a cookie mold. Women are hardly alike in all their characteristics, but heightened scrutiny applies to them because legislatures can rarely use gender itself as a proxy for these other characteristics. [Similarly,] that some retarded people have reduced capacities in some areas does not justify using retardation as a proxy for reduced capacity in areas where relevant individual variations in capacity do exist.

The Court's second assertion—that the standard of review must be fixed with reference to the number of classifications to which a characteristic would validly be relevant—is similarly flawed. * * * Heightened but not strict scrutiny is considered appropriate in areas such as gender, illegitimacy, or alienage because the Court views the trait as relevant under some circumstances but not others. * * *

Potentially discriminatory classifications exist only where some constitutional basis can be found for presuming that equal rights are required. [With] regard to economic and commercial matters, no basis for such a conclusion exists, for [t]he structure of economic and commercial life is a matter of political compromise, not constitutional principle, and no norm of equality requires that there be as many opticians as optometrists, see *Lee Optical,* or new businesses as old, see *Dukes.* * * *[24] * * *

SECTION 4. "FUNDAMENTAL RIGHTS"

I. DISCRIMINATION IN RESPECT TO VOTING

A. "DILUTION" OF THE RIGHT: APPORTIONMENT

The Court's initial hesitancy to consider malapportioned legislatures—largely the product of districts drawn when the nation's rural/urban population ratio was vastly different than in mid 20th century—and its subsequent assertion of jurisdiction are presented in BAKER v. CARR, p. 30 supra.

The first full post-*Baker* opinion on the problem was GRAY v. SANDERS, 372 U.S. 368, 83 S.Ct. 801, 9 L.Ed.2d 821 (1963), invalidating the "county unit system" employed in Georgia primaries for statewide officers. The candidate receiving the highest number of votes in each county obtained "two votes for each representative to which the county is entitled in the lower House of the General Assembly," and the winner was determined on the basis of the county unit vote. Because counties were not represented in the state legislature in

---

24. No single talisman can define those groups likely to be the target of classifications offensive to the Fourteenth Amendment and therefore warranting heightened or strict scrutiny; experience, not abstract logic, must be the primary guide. The "political powerlessness" of a group may be relevant, but that factor is neither necessary, as the gender cases demonstrate, nor sufficient, as the example of minors illustrates. [Similarly,] immutability of the trait at issue may be relevant, but many immutable characteristics, such as height or blindness, are valid bases of governmental action and classifications under a variety of circumstances.

The political powerlessness of a group and the immutability of its defining trait are relevant insofar as they point to a social and cultural isolation that gives the majority little reason to respect or be concerned with that group's interests and needs. Statutes discriminating against the young have not been common nor need be feared because those who do vote and legislate were once themselves young, typically have children of their own, and certainly interact regularly with minors. Their social integration means that minors, unlike discrete and insular minorities, tend to be treated in legislative arenas with full concern and respect, despite their formal and complete exclusion from the electoral process.

The discreteness and insularity warranting a "more searching judicial inquiry" must therefore be viewed from a social and cultural perspective as well as a political one. To this task judges are well suited, for the lessons of history and experience are surely the best guide as to when, and with respect to what interests, society is likely to stigmatize individuals as members of an inferior caste or view them as not belonging to the community. Because prejudice spawns prejudice, and stereotypes produce limitations that confirm the stereotype on which they are based, a history of unequal treatment requires sensitivity to the prospect that its vestiges endure. In separating those groups that are discrete and insular from those that are not, as in many important legal distinctions, "a page of history is worth a volume of logic."

accordance with their population, "combination of the units from the counties having the smallest population gives counties having population of one-third of the total in the state a clear majority of county units." The Court, per DOUGLAS, J., emphasizing that the case did not involve legislative districting, held that equal protection requires that "once the geographical unit for which a representative is to be chosen is designated, all who participate in the election are to have an equal vote." HARLAN, J., dissented.

WESBERRY v. SANDERS, 376 U.S. 1, 84 S.Ct. 526, 11 L.Ed.2d 481 (1964), per BLACK, J., struck down the Georgia congressional districting statute which accorded some districts more than twice the population of others: "[T]he command of Art. I, § 2, that Representatives be chosen 'by the People of the several States' means that as nearly as is practicable one man's vote in a congressional election is to be worth as much as another's." [b]

REYNOLDS v. SIMS
377 U.S. 533, 84 S.Ct. 1362, 12 L.Ed.2d 506 (1964).

MR. CHIEF JUSTICE WARREN delivered the opinion of the Court.

[Although the Alabama constitution required the legislature to reapportion decennially on the basis of population, none had taken place since 1901. The federal district court held the existing malapportionment violative of equal protection. Under] 1960 census figures, only 25.1% of the State's total population resided in districts represented by a majority of the members of the Senate, and only 25.7% lived in counties which could elect a majority of the members of the House of Representatives. Population-variance ratios of up to about 41-to-1 existed in the Senate, and up to about 16-to-1 in the House. * * *

Gray and *Wesberry* are of course not dispositive [of] these cases involving state legislative [apportionment]. But neither are they wholly inapposite. [*Gray*] established the basic principle of equality among voters within a State, [and] *Wesberry* clearly established that the fundamental principle of representative government in this country is one of equal representation for equal numbers of people, without regard to race, sex, economic status, or place of residence within a State. Our problem, then, is to ascertain [whether] there are any constitutionally cognizable principles which would justify departures from the basic standard of equality among voters in the apportionment of seats in state legislatures.

A predominant consideration in determining whether a State's legislative apportionment scheme constitutes an invidious discrimination [is] that the rights allegedly impaired are individual and personal in nature. [Since] the right of suffrage is a fundamental matter in a free and democratic society [and] is preservative of other basic civil and political rights, any alleged infringement [must] be carefully and meticulously scrutinized. * * *

Legislators represent people, not trees or acres. Legislators are elected by voters, not farms or cities or economic interests. As long as ours is a representative form of government, [the] right to elect legislators in a free and unimpaired fashion is a bedrock of our political system. [It] is inconceivable that a state law to the effect that, in counting votes for legislators, the votes of citizens in one

---

b. Harlan, J., would have adhered to *Colegrove* and, on the merits (joined by Stewart, J.,) dissented.

part of the State would be multiplied by two, five, or 10, while the votes of persons in another area would be counted only at face value, could be [constitutional]. Of course, the effect of state legislative districting schemes which give the same number of representatives to unequal numbers of constituents is identical. * * *

Logically, in a society ostensibly grounded on representative government, it would seem reasonable that a majority of the people of a State could elect a majority of that State's legislators. [T]o sanction minority control of state legislative bodies would appear to deny majority rights in a way that far surpasses any possible denial of minority rights that might otherwise be thought to result. [T]he concept of equal protection has been traditionally viewed as requiring the uniform treatment of persons standing in the same relation to the governmental action questioned or challenged. With respect to the allocation of legislative representation, all voters, as citizens of a State, stand in the same relation regardless of where they live. Any suggested criteria for the differentiation of citizens are insufficient to justify any discrimination, as to the weight of their votes, unless relevant to the permissible purposes of legislative apportionment. Since the achieving of fair and effective representation for all citizens is concededly the basic aim of legislative apportionment, we conclude that the Equal Protection Clause guarantees the opportunity for equal participation by all voters in the election of state legislators. Diluting the weight of votes because of place of residence impairs basic constitutional rights under the Fourteenth Amendment just as much as invidious discriminations based upon factors such as race, or economic status. Our constitutional system amply provides for the protection of minorities by means other than giving them majority control of state legislatures. * * *

We are told that the matter of apportioning representation in a state legislature is a complex and many-faceted one. We are advised that States can rationally consider factors other than [population]. We are admonished not to restrict the power of the States to impose differing views as to political philosophy on their citizens. We are cautioned about the dangers of entering into political thickets and mathematical quagmires. Our answer is this: a denial of constitutionally protected rights demands judicial protection; our oath and our office require no less of us. [To] the extent that a citizen's right to vote is debased, he is that much less a citizen. * * * Population is, of necessity, [the] controlling criterion for judgment in legislative [apportionment]. This is the clear and strong command of our Constitution's Equal Protection Clause. This is an essential part of the concept of a government of laws and not men. This is at the heart of Lincoln's vision of "government of the people, by the people, [and] for the people." * * *

We hold that, as a basic constitutional standard, the Equal Protection Clause requires that the seats in both houses of a bicameral state legislature must be apportioned on a population basis. [We] find the federal analogy inapposite and irrelevant to state legislative districting schemes. [T]he Founding Fathers clearly had no intention of establishing a pattern or model for the apportionment of seats in state legislatures when the system of representation in the Federal Congress was adopted. Demonstrative of this is the fact that the Northwest Ordinance, adopted in the same year, 1787, as the Federal Constitution, provided for the apportionment of seats in territorial legislatures solely on the basis of population.

The system of representation in the two Houses of the Federal Congress [is] based on the consideration that in establishing our type of federalism a group of formerly independent States bound themselves together under one national government. [A] compromise between the larger and smaller States on this matter averted a deadlock in the constitutional convention * * *.

Political subdivisions of States [never] have been considered as sovereign entities. Rather, they have been traditionally regarded as subordinate governmental instrumentalities created by the State. * * *

[The] right of a citizen to equal representation and to have his vote weighted equally with those of all other citizens in the election of members of one house of a bicameral state legislature would amount to little if States could effectively submerge the equal-population principle in the apportionment of seats in the other house. * * * Deadlock between the two bodies might result in compromise and concession on some issues. But in all too many cases the more probable result would be frustration of the majority will through minority veto in the house not apportioned on a population [basis].

We do not believe that the concept of bicameralism is rendered anachronistic and meaningless when the predominant basis of representation in the two state legislative bodies is required to be the same—population. A prime reason for bicameralism, modernly considered, is to insure mature and deliberate consideration of, and to prevent precipitate action on, proposed legislative measures. Simply because the controlling criterion for apportioning representation is required to be the same in both houses does not mean that there will be no differences in the composition and complexion of the two bodies. [The] numerical size of the two bodies could be made to differ, even significantly, and the geographical size of districts from which legislators are elected could also be made to differ. [T]he Equal Protection Clause requires that a State make an honest and good faith effort to construct districts, in both houses of its legislature, as nearly of equal population as is practicable. We realize that it is a practical impossibility to arrange legislative districts so that each one has an identical number of residents, or citizens, or voters. Mathematical exactness or precision is hardly a workable constitutional requirement.

[So] long as the divergences from a strict population standard are based on legitimate considerations incident to the effectuation of a rational state policy, some deviations from the equal-population principle are constitutionally permissible, [b]ut neither history alone, nor economic or other sorts of group interests, are permissible factors in attempting to justify disparities from population-based representation. Citizens, not history or economic interests, cast votes. Considerations of area alone provide an insufficient justification for deviations from the equal-population principle. Again, people, not land or trees or pastures, vote. Modern developments and improvements in transportation and communications make rather hollow, in the mid-1960's, most claims [for] allowing such deviations in order to insure effective representation for sparsely settled areas and to prevent legislative districts from becoming so large that the availability of access of citizens to their representatives is impaired. * * *

A consideration that appears to be of more substance [is] according political subdivisions some independent representation in at least one body of the state legislature, as long as the basic standard of equality of population among districts is maintained. [In] many States much of the legislature's activity involves the enactment of so-called local legislation, directed only to the concerns of particular political subdivisions. And a State may legitimately desire to construct districts along political subdivision lines to deter the possibilities of gerrymandering. However, permitting deviations from population-based representation does not mean that each local governmental unit or political subdivision can be given separate representation, regardless of [population].

* * * Decennial reapportionment appears to be a rational approach to readjustment of legislative representation in order to take into account population shifts and growth [and] if reapportionment were accomplished with less frequency, it would assuredly be constitutionally suspect. * * *

[T]he court below acted with proper judicial restraint, after the Alabama Legislature had failed to act effectively in remedying the constitutional deficiencies in the State's legislative apportionment scheme, in ordering its own temporary reapportionment plan into effect, at a time sufficiently early to permit the holding of elections pursuant to that plan without great difficulty, and in prescribing a plan admittedly provisional in purpose so as not to usurp the primary responsibility for reapportionment which rests with the legislature.[a]

LUCAS v. FORTY–FOURTH GEN. ASSEMBLY, 377 U.S. 713, 84 S.Ct. 1459, 12 L.Ed.2d 632 (1964): In a 1962 referendum, "the Colorado electorate adopted proposed Amendment No. 7 by a vote of 305,700 to 172,725, and defeated proposed Amendment No. 8 by a vote of 311,749 to 149,822." No. 8 provided that "both houses of [the] Legislature would [be] apportioned on a population basis." No. 7, approved by a majority of the voters in every county, "provided for the apportionment of the House of Representatives on the basis of population, but essentially maintained the existing apportionment in the Senate, which was based on a combination of population and various other factors." A three-judge federal court upheld No. 7. The Court, per WARREN, C.J., reversed. Although "the initiative device provides a practicable political remedy to obtain relief against alleged legislative malapportionment," "an individual's constitutionally protected right to cast an equally weighted vote cannot be denied even by a vote of a majority of a State's electorate, if the apportionment scheme adopted by the voters fails to measure up to the requirements of the Equal Protection Clause. [A] citizen's constitutional rights can hardly be infringed simply because a majority of the people choose that it be."

STEWART, J., joined by Clark, J., dissented in *Lucas* and *WMCA, Inc. v. Lomenzo*, 377 U.S. 633, 84 S.Ct. 1418, 12 L.Ed.2d 568 (1964), which invalidated New York's apportionment: "First, says the Court, it is 'established that the fundamental principle of representative government in this country is one of equal representation for equal numbers of [people].' [But] this 'was not the

a. Clark and Stewart, JJ., each concurred in the result. Harlan, J., dissented from all the 1964 apportionment decisions. His opinion appears at the end of the summaries of the other cases, infra. Further on remedies, *Scott v. Germano*, 381 U.S. 407, 85 S.Ct. 1525, 14 L.Ed.2d 477 (1965), held that federal courts should stay reapportionment proceedings if the state courts are actively concerned with the problem. *Travia v. Lomenzo*, 381 U.S. 431, 85 S.Ct. 1582, 14 L.Ed.2d 480 (1965), refused to stay a district court's order that New York hold a special legislative election—thus shortening the terms of legislators elected under an invalid apportionment—under a reapportionment plan enacted by the legislature but held invalid by the state court because it provided for more legislators than permitted under the state constitution.

May a court order that a convention be called to amend the state constitution apportionment provisions? Require that all plans be submitted to it for approval? Cf. *Burns v. Richardson*, 384 U.S. 73, 86 S.Ct. 1286, 16 L.Ed.2d 376 (1966). Require changing the size of the legislature? See *67th Minnesota State Senate v. Beens*, 406 U.S. 187, 92 S.Ct. 1477, 32 L.Ed.2d 1 (1972). Order that a malapportioned legislature meet only for limited purposes? See *Fortson v. Toombs*, 379 U.S. 621, 85 S.Ct. 598, 13 L.Ed.2d 527 (1965).

colonial system, it was not the system chosen for the national government by the Constitution, it was not the system exclusively or even predominantly practiced by the States at the time of adoption of the Fourteenth Amendment, it is not predominantly practiced by the States today.' Secondly, says the Court, unless legislative districts are equal in population, voters in the more populous districts will suffer a 'debasement' amounting to a constitutional injury. [I] find it impossible to understand how or why a voter in California, for instance, either feels or is less a citizen than a voter in Nevada, simply because, despite their population disparities, each of those States is represented by two United States Senators.

"[My] own understanding of the various theories of representative government is that no one theory has ever commanded unanimous [assent]. But even if it were thought that the rule announced today by the Court is, as a matter of political theory, the most desirable, [I] could not join in the fabrication of a constitutional mandate which imports and forever freezes one theory of political thought into our Constitution, and forever denies to every State any opportunity for enlightened and progressive innovation * * *.

"Representative government is a process of accommodating group interests through democratic institutional arrangements. * * * Appropriate legislative apportionment, therefore, should ideally be designed to insure effective representation in the State's legislature, in cooperation with other organs of political power, of the various groups and interests making up the electorate. In practice, of course, this ideal is approximated in the particular apportionment system of any State by a realistic accommodation of the diverse and often conflicting political forces operating within the State.

"[The] fact of geographic districting, the constitutional validity of which the Court does not question, carries with it an acceptance of the idea of legislative representation of regional needs and interests. Yet if geographical residence is irrelevant, as the Court suggests, and the goal is solely that of equally 'weighted' votes, I do not understand why the Court's constitutional rule does not require the abolition of districts and the holding of all elections at large.[12]

"The fact is, of course, that population factors must often to some degree be subordinated in devising a legislative apportionment plan which is to achieve the important goal of ensuring a fair, effective, and balanced representation of the regional, social, and economic interests within a State. And the further fact is that throughout our history the apportionments of State Legislatures have reflected the strongly felt American tradition that the public interest is com-

---

12. Even with legislative districts of exactly equal voter population, 26% of the electorate (a bare majority of the voters in a bare majority of the districts) can, [by] the kind of theoretical mathematics embraced by the Court, elect a majority of the legislature under our simple majority electoral system. Thus, the Court's constitutional rule permits minority rule.

Students of the mechanics of voting systems tell us that if all that matters is that votes count equally, the best vote-counting electoral system is proportional representation in statewide elections. [B]ecause electoral systems are intended to serve functions other than satisfying mathematical theories, [however,] proportional representation has not been widely adopted.

[Compare Auerbach, *The Reapportionment Cases: One Person, One Vote—One Vote, One Value,* 1964 Sup.Ct.Rev. 1, 31–34 who demonstrates, historically and statistically, that "the theoretical possibility of minority rule to which Justice Stewart alludes [is] not very real," and concludes: "The Court's figures emphasize the point that territorial constituencies of unequal population enhance the likelihood that the existing system of election and representation will not be consistent with majority rule. For with constituencies of unequal population, the theoretical minimum percentage electing a majority can be considerably less than 26%."]

posed of many diverse interests, and that in the long run it can better be expressed by a medley of component voices than by the majority's monolithic command. [I] think the cases should be decided by application of accepted principles of constitutional adjudication under the Equal Protection Clause [and that] demands but two basic attributes of any plan of state legislative apportionment. First, it demands that, in the light of the State's own characteristics and needs, the plan must be a rational one. Secondly, it demands that the plan must be such as not to permit the systematic frustration of the will of a majority of the electorate of the State. * * *

"*Colorado.* [In] the Colorado House, the majority unquestionably [rules]. It is true that, as a matter of theoretical arithmetic, a minority of 36% of the voters could elect a majority of the Senate, but this percentage has no real meaning in terms of the legislative process. [N]o possible combination of Colorado senators from rural districts, even assuming arguendo that they would vote as a bloc, could control the Senate. To arrive at the 36% figure, one must include [a] substantial number of urban [districts].

"[T]he people living in each of [the state's] four regions have interests unifying themselves and differentiating them from those in other regions. Given these underlying facts, certainly it was not irrational to conclude [that] planned departures from a strict per capita standard of representation were a desirable way of assuring [that] districts should be small enough in area, in a mountainous State like Colorado, where accessibility is affected by configuration as well as compactness of districts, to enable each senator to have firsthand knowledge of his entire district and to maintain close contact with his constituents * * *.

"[I]f per capita representation were the rule in both houses of the Colorado Legislature, counties having small populations would have to be merged with larger counties having totally dissimilar interests. Their representatives would not only be unfamiliar with the problems of the smaller county, but the interests of the smaller counties might well be totally submerged to the interests of the larger counties with which they are joined. * * *[d]

d. Under *Reynolds,* could Colorado still give such counties "effective representation" by permitting them each to have a representative in the legislature, but granting that legislator only a fractional vote determined on a population basis (or granting him a full vote but giving legislators from larger counties a more heavily weighted vote)? Consider Dixon, *Reapportionment Perspectives: What is Fair Representation?*, 51 A.B.A.J. 319, 322 (1965): "[W]eighted voting may be nullified for several reasons. One of the most important reasons would be the consideration that one man casting nineteen votes is not as effective in terms of representation as nineteen separate voices (or lobbyists). Another would be that nineteen men separately elected would provide more opportunity for expression of divergent views. [B]oth of these arguments involve going beyond the simple mathematical tenor of the Supreme Court's 'one-man, one-vote' decisions. They involve putting reapportionment in the context of the actual complexities of representation—and the difficulties in de-termining what is fair and effective representation." Does this objection go similarly to fractional voting?

What about a system of cumulative voting? Consider Note, *Apportionment Problems in Local Government,* 49 Not.D.Law. 671, 683–84 (1974): "[E]ach elector has as many votes as there are representatives to be elected from the area at large, and he may cast his votes in any combination for the candidates on the slate. If there are three candidates to be elected, the voter may cast all three votes for one candidate, or give one candidate two votes and give another candidate one vote, or give one vote to each of three candidates. The three candidates with the highest number of votes are the winners. [Where] there are several positions to be filled minority groups can easily achieve a voice by running only a few candidates (or only one) and then voting in blocs. In this manner cumulative voting becomes very much like proportional representation."

"The present apportionment, adopted overwhelmingly by the people [is] entirely rational, [and] the majority has consciously chosen to protect the minority's interests, and under the liberal initiative provisions of the Colorado Constitution, it retains the power to reverse its decision to do so. Therefore, there can be no question of frustration of the basic principle of majority rule.

"*New York.* [The] apportionment [is] rational, it is applied systematically, and it is kept reasonably current. The formula [provides] that each county shall have at least one representative in the Assembly, that the smaller counties shall have somewhat greater representation in the legislature than representation based solely on numbers would accord, and that some limits be placed on the representation of the largest counties in order to prevent one megalopolis from completely dominating ＊ ＊ ＊. The rationality of individual county representation becomes particularly apparent in States where legislative action applicable only to one or more particular counties is the permissible tradition.

"[T]he 10 most populous counties in the State control both houses of the legislature under the existing apportionment system. Each of these counties is heavily urban; each is in a metropolitan area. [Thus], the existing system of apportionment clearly guarantees effective majority representation and [control].

"But this is not the whole story. New York City, with [a] budget larger than that of the State, has, by virtue of its concentration of population, homogeneity of interest,[e] and political cohesiveness, acquired [influence] of its own hardly measurable simply by counting the number of its representatives in the legislature. [Surely] it is not irrational for the State [to] be justifiably concerned about balancing such a concentration of political [power]. What the State has done is to adopt a [plan] designed in a rational way to ensure that minority voices may be heard, but that the will of the majority shall prevail." [f]

e. Do all New York City's people have "homogeneity of interest"? Who represents the "interest" of the following New York City resident: a white Republican, whose annual income is $50,000, derived half from his salary as a labor organizer and half from interest and dividends on $300,000 inherited securities, etc., etc.? Must a Negro of Puerto Rican origin be content with the fact that "nonwhites" are represented despite his contention that his interests are distinct from those of other blacks? Must an Irish-Catholic be content with representation by an Italian-Catholic? See *United Jewish Orgs. v. Carey,* Sec. 2, V supra.

f. Consider Irwin, *Representation and Election: The Reapportionment Cases in Retrospect,* 67 Mich.L.Rev. 729, 748–49 (1969): "For the Court to have made any attempt whatever to insure the accommodation of any interest— geographical, economic, ethnic, partisan, or 'historical'—in the legislative process would have catapulted [it] into the continuing political questions, not simply of whether, but also of *which* groups are to receive political advantages in the legislative process. Such [questions] entice the Court into the very political morass which virtually everyone agreed in principle that it should avoid." See also Ely, *Democracy and Distrust* 124–25 (1980): "Everyone without a strong personal stake in the status quo granted that [refusal by the Court

to enter the area] was no more compatible with the underlying theory of our Constitution than taking away some people's votes altogether. So the Court entered, and *precisely because of considerations of administrability,* soon found itself with no perceived alternative but to move to a one person, one vote standard. Actually this move was characteristic of the Warren Court, which on several occasions adopted what seemed on the surface the more intrusive rule on the theory that it would be less intrusive in practice. Part of the theory behind *Gideon v. Wainwright,* requiring appointed counsel in all felony cases, was that the previously prevailing 'special circumstances rule,' though requiring counsel on fewer occasions, in fact had repeatedly resulted [in] friction-generating factual inquiries into every case. [Sometimes] more is less." Compare Dixon, *Democratic Representation: Reapportionment in Law and Politics* 19–20 (1968): "All apportionment being fully political, any order made by a court has a significant political impact. Therefore the only relevant question is whether the concededly 'political' judicial order is good or bad, fair or unfair, equitable or inequitable. Such ascertainment is not advanced by putting on blinders and excluding certain kinds of relevant evidence, or even certain kinds of relevant, albeit politically embarrassing questions, on

MR. JUSTICE HARLAN, dissenting [in all the cases decided that day.][g]

The Court's constitutional discussion [is] remarkable [for] its failure to address itself at all to the Fourteenth Amendment as a whole or to the legislative history of the Amendment pertinent to the matter at hand. [I] am unable to understand the Court's utter disregard of [§ 2 of the fourteenth amendment], which expressly recognizes the States' power to deny "or in any way" abridge the right of their inhabitants to vote for "the members of the [State] Legislature," and its express provision of a remedy for such denial or abridgement. The comprehensive scope of the second section and its particular reference to the state legislatures precludes the suggestion that the first section was intended to have the result reached by the [Court].

The history of the adoption of the Fourteenth Amendment provides conclusive evidence that neither those who proposed nor those who ratified the Amendment believed that the Equal Protection Clause limited the power of the States to apportion their legislatures as they saw fit. Moreover, the history demonstrates that the intention to leave this power undisturbed was deliberate and was widely believed to be essential to the adoption of the Amendment.[h] [N]ote should [also] be taken of the Fifteenth and Nineteenth Amendments. [If] constitutional amendment was the only means by which all men and, later, women, could be guaranteed the right to vote at all, even for *federal* officers, how can it be that the far less obvious right to a particular kind of apportionment of *state* legislatures—a right to which is opposed a far more plausible conflicting interest of the State than the interest which opposes the general right to vote— can be conferred by judicial construction of the Fourteenth Amendment?

[The] consequence of today's decision is that in all but the handful of States which may already satisfy the new requirements the [courts] are given blanket authority and the constitutional duty to supervise apportionment of the State Legislatures. It is difficult to imagine a more intolerable and inappropriate interference by the judiciary with the independent legislatures of the States. [No] set of standards can guide a court which has to decide how many legislative districts a State shall have, or what the shape of the districts shall be, [or] whether a State should have single-member districts or multi-member districts or some combination of both. No such standard can control the balance between keeping up with population shifts and having stable districts. In all these respects, the courts will be called upon to make particular decisions with respect to which a principle of equally populated districts will be of no assistance whatsoever.[i]   *   *   *

the ground that to consider [them] would be to 'wallow' in the political thicket."

g. In addition to *Reynolds, Lucas,* and *WMCA,* the Court invalidated apportionments in Maryland, *Maryland Comm. for Fair Rep. v. Tawes,* 377 U.S. 656, 84 S.Ct. 1442, 12 L.Ed. 2d 595; Virginia, *Davis v. Mann,* 377 U.S. 678, 84 S.Ct. 1453, 12 L.Ed.2d 609; Delaware, *Roman v. Sincock,* 377 U.S. 695, 84 S.Ct. 1462, 12 L.Ed.2d 620.

h. For refutation of Harlan, J.'s lengthy historical argument, see Van Alstyne, *The Fourteenth Amendment, The "Right" to Vote, and the Understanding of the Thirty-Ninth Congress,* 1965 Sup.Ct.Rev. 33; Goldberg, *Mr. Justice Harlan, The Uses of History, and the Congressional Globe,* 15 J.Pub.L. 181 (1966).

i. See also Dixon, *Apportionment Standards and Judicial Power,* 38 Notre Dame Law. 367, 387 (1963): "[I]nteresting possibilities exist in the process of apportionment even when existing county lines are used. [A]ssume that County A has 25,000 voters and one seat in the legislature, which Party Y captures because it has a 20,000 to 5,000 edge over Party X in that county. Let us assume that County B has 100,000 voters and also has one seat in the legislature, which Party X captures because it has a 55,000 to 45,000 edge over Party Y in that county. As between the two counties, the 100,000 voters in County B seem underrepresented by a four to one ratio because they have only one seat and County A's 25,000 voters also have one seat. But looking at the political parties in this two-

Although the Court—necessarily, as I believe—provides only generalities in elaboration of its main thesis, its opinion nevertheless fully demonstrates how far removed these problems are from fields of judicial competence. Recognizing that "indiscriminate districting" is an invitation to "partisan gerrymandering," the Court nevertheless excludes virtually every basis for the formation of electoral districts other than "indiscriminate districting." In one or another of today's opinions, the Court declares it unconstitutional for a State to give effective consideration to any of the following in establishing legislative districts: (1) history; (2) "economic or other sorts of group interests"; (3) area; (4) geographical considerations; (5) a desire "to insure effective representation for sparsely settled areas"; (6) "availability of access of citizens to their representatives"; (7) theories of bicameralism (except those approved by the Court); (8) occupation; (9) "an attempt to balance urban and rural power"; (10) the preference of a majority of voters in the State. So far as presently appears, the *only* factor which a State may consider, apart from numbers, is political subdivisions. But even "a clearly rational state policy" recognizing this factor is unconstitutional if "population is submerged as the controlling consideration * * *."

I know of no principle of logic or practical or theoretical politics, still less any constitutional principle, which establishes all or any of these exclusions. [L]egislators can represent their electors only by speaking for their interests—economic, social, political—many of which do reflect the place where the electors live. The Court does not establish, or indeed even attempt to make a case for the proposition that conflicting interests within a State can only be adjusted by disregarding them when voters are grouped for purposes of representation.

* * *

[The] Constitution is not a panacea for every blot upon the public welfare, nor [does] this Court [serve] its high purpose when it exceeds its authority, even to satisfy justified impatience with the slow workings of the political [process.]j

Notes and Questions

1. *Results.* By mid-1968, "congressional district lines were redrawn in thirty-seven states"; "only nine states had any district with a population deviation in excess of ten per cent from the state average, while twenty-four states had no deviation as large as five per cent from the state norm"; every state legislature "had made some adjustment, and it seemed probable that more

county area we see substantial equality. Party X has a combined total of 60,000 votes in the two counties and gets one seat; Party Y a combined total of 65,000 votes and one seat. If we now reapportion [by] raising County B to four seats we achieve exact numerical equality. But the resultant impact on political party representation will be that Party X with 60,000 votes in this two-county area now has four seats, and Party Y with 65,000 votes has only one seat."

And see Dixon, *The Court, The People, and "One Man, One Vote,"* in Reapportionment in the 1970's 7, 13 (Polsby ed. 1971): "[U]sing new single-member districts, the Democrats in California in 1966 elected majorities of 21–19 and 42–38 in the state senate and house, respectively, even though they polled fewer statewide legislative votes than the Republicans. In the same election the Democrats gained a 21–17 edge in congressional seats, again with a minority of the statewide congressional vote. In New Jersey in 1966 the Democrats gained a 9–6 edge in congressional seats, despite a Republican plurality in the popular vote. By contrast, for the state legislature in New Jersey, using a mixture of new single- and multi-member districts, a comfortable but not overwhelming Republican plurality in popular votes in 1967 produced a sweep of two-thirds of the seats in each house."

j. A week later, the Court invalidated apportionments in nine additional states. The opinions begin at 378 U.S. 553, 84 S.Ct. 1904, 12 L.Ed.2d 1033.

than thirty of the state legislatures satisfied any reasonable interpretation of the equal-population principle." McKay, *Reapportionment: Success Story of the Warren Court,* 67 Mich.L.Rev. 223, 229 (1968).

2. *High vote requirements.* (a) GORDON v. LANCE, 403 U.S. 1, 91 S.Ct. 1889, 29 L.Ed.2d 273 (1971), per BURGER, C.J., upheld a West Virginia rule that forbade political subdivisions from incurring bonded indebtedness or increasing tax rates beyond designated limits without 60% approval in a referendum: "The defect [in *Gray v. Sanders* and *Cipriano v. Houma,* Part B infra] lay in the denial or dilution of voting power because of group characteristics—geographic location and property ownership—that bore no valid relation to the interest of those groups in the subject matter of the [election]. In contrast we can discern no independently identifiable group or category that favors bonded indebtedness over other forms of financing. Consequently no sector of the population may be said to be 'fenced out' from the franchise because of the way they will vote. [T]here is nothing in the language of the Constitution, our history or our cases that requires that a majority always prevail on every issue. [The] Constitution itself provides that a simple majority vote is insufficient on some issues [and] the Bill of Rights removes entire areas of legislation from the concept of majoritarian supremacy. * * *[6]"[a]

(b) LOCKPORT v. CITIZENS FOR COMMUNITY ACTION, 430 U.S. 259, 97 S.Ct. 1047, 51 L.Ed.2d 313 (1977), per STEWART, J., upheld New York laws "that a new county charter will go into effect only if [approved] by separate majorities of the voters who live in the cities [and] outside the cities": "The equal protection principles applicable in gauging the fairness of an election involving the choice of legislative representatives are of limited relevance [in] analyzing the propriety of recognizing distinctive voter interests in a 'single-shot' referendum. [I]nstead of sending legislators off to the state capitol to vote on a multitude of issues, the referendum puts one discrete issue to the voters. That issue is capable [of] being analyzed to determine whether [it] will have a disproportionate impact on an identifiable group of voters. [If the] question were posed in the context of annexation proceedings, the fact that the residents of the annexing city and the residents of the area to be annexed formed sufficiently different constituencies with sufficiently different interests could be readily perceived. [T]he structural decision to annex or consolidate is similar in impact to the decision to restructure county government in New York. In each case, separate voter approval requirements are based on the perception that the real and long-term impact of a restructuring of local government is felt quite differently by the different county constituent [units]." Burger, C.J. concurred in the judgment.

(c) Are *Lance* and *Lockport* compatible with *Reynolds?* Consider Israel, *Nonpopulation Factors Relevant to an Acceptable Standard of Apportionment,* 38 Not.D.Law. 499, 512 (1963): "[I]f a state can reasonably demand that some legislative action be based on a broader consensus than a bare majority, why could it not insist upon a broader consensus for all legislative action? [If] so, then why not achieve the same minority security by allocating approximately one-half of the legislative seats to regional minority groups which represent one-third of the population?" Compare Auerbach, fn. 12 supra, at 48: "The analogy between the rules for choosing legislative representatives and the rules for deciding issues in legislative assemblies [ignores] the difference between the

---

6. We intimate no view on the constitutionality of a provision requiring unanimity or giving a veto power to a very small group. Nor do we decide whether a State [may] require extraordinary majorities for the election of public officers.

a. Harlan, J., concurred in the result. Brennan and Marshall, JJ., dissented.

power to take action and the power to block it. Even those who deny that 'effective minority rule' exists simply because a qualified majority is required to take action agree that it exists if a simple majority is required to block action proposed by a minority. [But] this is precisely the consequence of malapportionment. Let us take an [example]—40 per cent of the population lives in legislative (single-member) districts which, theoretically, could elect 67 members of a legislative body of 100 members and 60 per cent live in districts which, theoretically, could elect 33 members. If the legislative body were required to take action by a two-thirds vote, but the 100 districts contained equal numbers of people, members representing 60 per cent of the people could not take any action without the concurrence of at least 7 of the members representing the minority of the population. But then, neither could the 40 members representing the minority take any action unless they obtained the concurrence of at least 27 members of the majority. In the example given, however, members representing 60 per cent of the people are unable to take any action, even under a simple majority rule, while members representing 40 per cent of the people have the power to take any action they please, even under a two-thirds rule. Effective minority rule, theoretically, exists." How clear is the distinction, in respect to "effective minority rule," between "the power to take action and the power to block it"?

3. *"Popularly" mandated malapportionment.* Do you agree that malapportionment violates equal protection even if adopted "by a vote of a majority of a State's electorate" (*Lucas*)? What would such a "majority" likely consist of? A combination of (1) almost all those that would be overrepresented plus (2) a minority of those that would be underrepresented? Should such a "majority" mandated malapportionment be insulated from the constitutional challenge of the "minority" that is underrepresented?

Suppose that the "majority" included a majority of those that would be underrepresented? Would this nonetheless be invalid because "a citizen's constitutional rights can hardly be infringed simply because a majority of the people choose that it be"? Would a plan for racially segregated education, supported in a referendum by a majority of both racial groups, be immune from attack under equal protection? Is the "right to cast an equally weighted vote" an "individual" right in the same sense as the right to be free of state imposed racial segregation? Does the relief sought in the segregation situation demand more than that the individual plaintiffs be accorded their constitutional rights? In the apportionment situation? See generally Neal, *Baker v. Carr, Politics in Search of Law,* 1962 Sup.Ct.Rev. 252, 271–74; Choper, *On the Warren Court and Judicial Review,* 17 Cath.U.L.Rev. 20, 31–32 (1967).

4. *Permissible population deviation.* (a) MAHAN v. HOWELL, 410 U.S. 315, 93 S.Ct. 979, 35 L.Ed.2d 320 (1973), per REHNQUIST, J., upheld Virginia's state legislative apportionment, which had a maximum percentage deviation from the ideal of "16.4%—[one] district being overrepresented by 6.8% and [another] being underrepresented by 9.6%. [T]he minimum population necessary to elect a majority of the House of Delegates was 49.29%":

"In *Kirkpatrick v. Preisler,* 394 U.S. 526, 89 S.Ct. 1225, 22 L.Ed.2d 519 (1969) and *Wells v. Rockefeller,* 394 U.S. 542, 89 S.Ct. 1234, 22 L.Ed.2d 535 (1969), this Court invalidated state reapportionment statutes for federal congressional districts having maximum percentage deviations of 5.97% and 13.1% respectively. [I]t was concluded that [*Wesberry's*] command 'permits only the limited population variances which are unavoidable despite a good-faith effort to achieve absolute equality, or for which justification is shown.'

"[*Reynolds* suggested] more flexibility was constitutionally permissible with respect to state legislative reapportionment than in congressional redistricting. Consideration was given to the fact [that] there is a significantly larger number of seats in state legislative bodies to be distributed within a State than Congressional seats, and that therefore it may be feasible for a State to use political subdivision lines to a greater [extent]. [But] *Wesberry* recognized no excuse [other] than the practical impossibility of drawing equal districts with mathematical precision. * * * [b]

"[Under] Virginia's Constitution, the General Assembly is given extensive power to enact special legislation [regarding] counties, cities, towns and other political subdivisions. The statute redistricting the House of Delegates consistently sought to avoid the fragmentation of such subdivisions, assertedly to afford them a voice in Richmond to seek such local legislation. * * *

"We are not prepared to say that [this] is irrational. [But] a State's policy urged in justification of disparity in district population, however, rational, cannot constitutionally be permitted to emasculate the goal of substantial equality. * * *

"Neither courts nor legislatures are furnished any specialized calipers which enable them to extract from the general language of the Equal Protection Clause [the] mathematical formula which establishes what range of percentage deviations are permissible, and what are not. [While] this percentage may well approach tolerable limits, we do not believe it exceeds them."

BRENNAN, J., joined by Marshall and Douglas, JJ., dissented: "While the State may have a broader range of interests to which it can point in attempting to justify a failure to achieve precise equality in the context of legislative apportionment [than in the context of congressional districting], it by no means follows that the State is subject to a lighter burden of proof or that the controlling constitutional standard is in any sense distinguishable. [*Swann v. Adams,* 385 U.S. 440, 87 S.Ct. 569, 17 L.Ed.2d 501 (1967)] decisively refutes any suggestion that unequal representation will be upheld so long as some rational basis for the discrimination can be found. A showing of necessity, not rationality is [what] *Swann* requires. * * *

"[I]n asserting its interest in preserving the integrity of county boundaries, the Commonwealth offers [only] vague references to 'local legislation,' without describing such legislation with precision, without indicating whether such legislation amounts to a significant proportion of the legislature's business, and

---

b. *Kirkpatrick,* per Brennan, J., rejected a "de minimis approach" because there was "no nonarbitrary way to pick a cutoff point" and it "would encourage legislators to strive for that range" rather than for "precise mathematical equality." Even minimizing "opportunities for partisan gerrymandering" could not constitute a satisfactory justification. Opportunities "for gerrymandering are greatest when there is freedom to construct unequally populated districts." Harlan, Stewart and White, JJ., dissented.

See 83 Harv.L.Rev. 103 (1969): "Political subdivision boundaries, natural or historical

demarcations, and the goal of district geographical compactness give a political body some sort of guidelines for the task of districting. To require that such guidelines not be used is to take away one of the tools that citizens and members of legislatures use to measure the fairness of districting plans. [When] fragmentation of political subdivisions and bizarrely shaped districts can be explained by politicians as necessary to comply with the 'as nearly as practicable' standard, critics of such districting must launch their attack deprived of any popularly accepted test for the existence of gerrymandering."

without demonstrating that the District Court's plan would materially affect the treatment of such legislation."   Powell, J., did not participate.

(b) *"Per se" rule for state legislative districts.* GAFFNEY v. CUMMINGS, 412 U.S. 735, 93 S.Ct. 2321, 37 L.Ed.2d 298 (1973), per WHITE, J., held that a Connecticut apportionment, with a maximum deviation from the ideal totaling 7.83%, "failed to make out a prima facie violation" of equal protection "whether those deviations are considered alone or in combination with the additional fact that another plan could be conceived with lower deviations."   The "insignificant population variations" required no "justification by the State."   "The 'population' of a legislative district is just not that knowable to be used for such refined judgments" because "district populations are constantly changing, often at different rates, up or down" and "if it is the weight of a person's vote that matters, total population—even if stable and accurately taken—may not actually reflect that body of voters whose votes must be counted and weighed for the purposes of reapportionment, because 'census persons' are not voters."   Brennan, J., joined by Douglas and Marshall, JJ., dissented.[e]

(c) *Congressional districts.*   KARCHER v. DAGGETT, 462 U.S. 725, 103 S.Ct. 2653, 77 L.Ed.2d 133 (1983), per BRENNAN, J., reaffirmed *Kirkpatrick's* "population equality as nearly as is practicable" standard—rejecting a maximum percentage deviation of only .7%: "Any number of consistently applied legislative policies might justify some ['minor population deviations'], including, for instance, making districts compact, respecting municipal boundaries, preserving the cores of prior districts, [preserving voting strength of racial minorities], and avoiding contests between incumbent Representatives.[f] [The] State must, however, show with some specificity that a particular objective required the specific deviations in its plan, rather than simply relying on general assertions [as here.]"[g]

---

e. *White v. Regester,* 412 U.S. 755, 93 S.Ct. 2332, 37 L.Ed.2d 314 (1973) (similarly divided), used the same analysis to uphold a Texas apportionment in which "the total variation between largest and smallest district" was 9.9%—although "very likely larger differences would not be tolerable without qualification."

Most recently, *Brown v. Thompson,* 462 U.S. 835, 103 S.Ct. 2690, 77 L.Ed.2d 214 (1983), per Powell, J., upheld Wyoming's allocation of one seat in its House of Representatives to its least populous county, resulting in a maximum deviation of 89%.   The Court emphasized that "appellants deliberately have limited their challenge to the alleged dilution of their voting power resulting from the one representative given to Niobrara County" rather than "the state apportionment plan as a whole."

O'Connor, J., joined by Stevens, J., expressed "the gravest doubts that a statewide legislative plan with an 85% maximum deviation would survive constitutional scrutiny despite the presence of the State's strong interest in preserving county boundaries.   I join the Court's opinion on the understanding that nothing in it suggests that this Court would uphold such a scheme."

Brennan, J., joined by White, Marshall and Blackmun, JJ.,—although "stressing how extraordinarily narrow [the decision] is, and how empty of likely precedential value"—dissented.

f. *White v. Weiser,* 412 U.S. 783, 93 S.Ct. 2348, 37 L.Ed.2d 335 (1973), per White, J., *suggested* the validity of a state "policy frankly aimed at maintaining existing relationships between incumbent congressmen and their constituents and preserving the seniority members of the State's delegation have achieved in [the] House of Representatives."

But see Casper, *Apportionment and the Right to Vote: Standards of Judicial Scrutiny,* 1973 Sup.Ct.Rev. 1, 12: "[A] 'state policy' favoring incumbents often is no more than an euphemism [for] perpetuating themselves as a power elite unaccountable to the voters because of skewed districting.   Put differently, 'rotten' legislators can render the right to vote quite as ineffective as 'rotten' boroughs."

g. Stevens, J., who joined the Court's opinion, concurred, relying on the equal protection clause (rather than Art. I, § 2), and contending that it should be held to bar apportionments that egregiously curtail the strength of any defined political group (see his opinion in *Mobile v. Bolden,* infra). Powell, J., dissented,

WHITE, J., joined by Burger, C.J., and Powell and Rehnquist, JJ., dissented "from the Court's unreasonable insistence on an unattainable perfection. * * * I would not entertain judicial challenges, absent extraordinary circumstances, where the maximum deviation is less than 5%. Somewhat greater deviations, if rationally related to an important state interest may also be permissible."

FORTSON v. MORRIS, 385 U.S. 231, 87 S.Ct. 446, 17 L.Ed.2d 330 (1966): In the 1966 Georgia gubernatorial election, no candidate received a majority of the popular vote. Georgia provided that in such case the Georgia legislature shall elect the governor from the two candidates receiving the highest popular vote. The Court, per BLACK, J., upheld the election: There is no federal constitutional provision "which either expressly or impliedly dictates the method a State must use to select its Governor. A method which would be valid if initially employed is equally valid when employed as an alternative."

DOUGLAS, J., joined by Warren, C.J., and Brennan and Fortas, JJ., dissented, viewing "the legislative choice" as "only a part of the popular election machinery. [A] candidate who received a minority of the popular vote might receive a clear majority of the votes cast in the legislature," thus "contrary to the principle of 'one person, one vote.'"

Scope of the decision. May a state provide that a popularly elected governor shall appoint the entire legislature? Appoint the legislator from any district in which no candidate received a majority (²/₃) (³/₄) of the popular vote? That all local officials shall be appointed by the legislature or some part thereof? What provision(s) of the Constitution are most germane in considering these issues? See generally Ely, *Democracy and Distrust* 116–25 (1980); Levinson, *Judicial Review and the Problem of the Comprehensible Constitution*, 59 Tex.L.Rev. 395, 413–15 (1981).[i]

LOCAL GOVERNMENT UNITS

AVERY v. MIDLAND COUNTY, 390 U.S. 474, 88 S.Ct. 1114, 20 L.Ed.2d 45 (1968): The Midland County (Tex.) Commissioners Court was elected from single-member districts of unequal population—414; 828; 852; and 67,906 (the city of Midland, the county's only urban center). The Court, per WHITE, J., finding that the Commissioners Court had "general responsibility and power for local affairs," held that when a state "delegates lawmaking power to local government and provides for the election of local officials from districts [those] qualified to vote [must] have the right to an equally effective voice in the election process.[6]

"Were the Commissioners Court a special purpose unit of government assigned the performance of functions affecting definable groups of constituents more than other constituents, we would have to confront the question whether

but essentially agreed with Stevens, J., in respect to "partisan gerrymandering."

   i. *Rodriguez v. Popular Democratic Party,* 457 U.S. 1, 102 S.Ct. 2194, 72 L.Ed.2d 628 (1982), per Burger, C.J., relied on *Fortson* to uphold a Puerto Rico statute providing that vacancies in the Puerto Rico legislature caused by death, resignation or removal may be filled—until the next regularly scheduled election—by the political party with which the

previous incumbent was affiliated: Puerto Rico "could reasonably conclude that [this] would more fairly reflect the will of the voters than appointment by the Governor or some other elected official."

   6. Inequitable apportionment of local governing bodies offends the Constitution even if adopted by a properly apportioned legislature [*Lucas*].

such bodies may be apportioned in ways which give greater influence to the citizens most affected by the organization's functions."

Sailors v. Board of Educ., 387 U.S. 105, 87 S.Ct. 1549, 18 L.Ed.2d 650 (1967) [a] and *Dusch v. Davis*, 387 U.S. 112, 87 S.Ct. 1554, 18 L.Ed.2d 656 (1967) [b] "demonstrate that the Constitution and this Court are not roadblocks in the path of innovation, experiment, and development among units of local government."

HARLAN, J., dissented: "[L]ocal governments [are] often specialized in function. Application of the *Reynolds* rule to such local governments [may] result in a denial of equal treatment to those upon whom the exercise of the special powers has unequal impact."[c]

HADLEY v. JUNIOR COLLEGE DIST., 397 U.S. 50, 90 S.Ct. 791, 25 L.Ed.2d 45 (1970): Pursuant to Missouri law, a consolidated junior college district was created by referendum in eight school districts. The Kansas City School District, containing about 60% of the consolidated "school population," was apportioned only three of the six trustees who were empowered to tax, issue bonds, condemn property, and generally manage the junior college.

The Court, per BLACK, J., found "that these powers, while not [as] broad [as] the Midland County Commissioners," "show that the trustees perform important governmental functions": "[A]s a general rule, whenever a state or local government decides to select persons by popular election to perform governmental functions," equal protection requires that if these persons "are chosen from separate districts, each district must be established on [an equal population basis]." To distinguish "between elections for 'legislative' officials and those for 'administrative' officers" would be "unmanageable." Because of available techniques such as those upheld in *Sailors* and *Dusch*, "we do not feel that the States will be inhibited in finding ways to insure that legitimate political goals of representation are achieved." Harlan, J., joined by Burger, C.J., and Stewart, J., dissented.

Notes and Questions

1. *Appointment vs. election.* Under *Sailors,* could the members of the *Avery* Commissioners Court be appointed by the state legislature rather than elected? If so, could the legislature provide for (or follow the practice of) appointing one member of the Commissioners Court from each of the four previously existing districts? If so, suppose state law provided that the members of the Commissioners Court be appointed by four officials, elected one each from the four previously existing districts?

a. *Sailors,* noted 81 Harv.L.Rev. 151 (1967), "upheld a procedure for choosing a school board that placed the selection with school boards of component districts even though the component boards had equal votes and served unequal populations." The Court could "find no constitutional reason why state or local officers of the non-legislative character involved here may not be chosen by the governor, by the legislature, or by some other appointive means." "We need not decide [whether] a State may constitute a local legislative body through the appointive rather than the elective process."

b. *Dusch* permitted a city "to choose its legislative body by a scheme that included at-large voting for candidates, some of whom had to be residents of particular districts, even though [the] districts varied widely in population." The scheme followed a city-county consolidation and reflected "a detente between urban and rural communities."

c. Stewart and Fortas, JJ., each dissented stressing this point. Marshall, J., did not participate.

2. *Residence requirements.* (a) Under *Dusch,* could the members of the Commissioners Court be elected at-large in Midland County, but one member required to be a resident of each of the previously existing districts? Does such a plan comport with *Avery's* (and *Hadley's*) mandate that "those qualified to vote have the right to an equally effective voice in the elective process"? See *Dallas Cty. v. Reese,* 421 U.S. 477, 95 S.Ct. 1706, 44 L.Ed.2d 312 (1975).

(b) MOORE v. OGILVIE, 394 U.S. 814, 89 S.Ct. 1493, 23 L.Ed.2d 1 (1969), per DOUGLAS, J., invalidated a statute requiring that a petition to nominate independent candidates for a state-wide election be signed by at least 25,000 voters, including 200 from each of at least 50 of the state's 102 counties: "Under this Illinois law the electorate in 49 of the counties which contain 93.4% of the registered voters may not form a new political party and place its candidates on the ballot. Yet 25,000 of the remaining 6.6% of registered voters properly distributed among the 53 remaining counties [may]. This law thus discriminates against the residents of the populous counties [in] favor of rural sections." [g]

MOBILE v. BOLDEN

446 U.S. 55, 100 S.Ct. 1490, 64 L.Ed.2d 47 (1980).

MR. JUSTICE STEWART announced the judgment of the Court and delivered an opinion in which THE CHIEF JUSTICE, MR. JUSTICE POWELL, and MR. JUSTICE REHNQUIST join.

The City of Mobile, Ala., has since 1911 been governed by a City Commission consisting of three members elected by the voters of the city at-large. [This] is the same basic electoral system that is followed by literally thousands of municipalities and other local governmental units throughout the Nation.

*   *   *

[The] constitutional objection to multimember districts is not and cannot be that, as such, they depart from apportionment on a population basis in violation of *Reynolds* and its progeny. Rather the focus in such cases has been on the lack of representation multimember districts afford various elements of the voting population in a system of representative legislative democracy. "Criticism [of multimember districts] is rooted in their winner-take-all aspects, their tendency to submerge minorities, [a] general preference for legislatures reflecting community interests as closely as possible and disenchantment with political parties and elections as devices to settle policy differences between contending interests." *Whitcomb v. Chavis,* 403 U.S. 124, 91 S.Ct. 1858, 29 L.Ed.2d 363 (1971).

Despite repeated constitutional attacks upon multimember legislative districts, the Court has consistently held that they are not unconstitutional per se, e.g., *White v. Regester; Whitcomb; Burns v. Richardson; Fortson v. Dorsey,* 379 U.S. 433, 85 S.Ct. 498, 13 L.Ed.2d 401 (1965). We have recognized, however, that such legislative apportionments could violate the Fourteenth Amendment if their purpose were invidiously to minimize or cancel out the voting potential of racial or ethnic minorities. To prove such a purpose it is not enough to show that the group allegedly discriminated against has not elected representatives in proportion to its numbers. A plaintiff must prove that the disputed plan was "conceived or operated as [a] purposeful device[ ] to further racial discrimination." *Whitcomb.*

g. Stewart, J., joined by Harlan, J., dissented, relying on *Dusch.*

This burden of proof is simply one aspect of the basic principle that only if there is purposeful discrimination can there be a violation of [equal protection]. See *Washington v. Davis; Arlington Heights; Personnel Adm'r v. Feeney,* [Sec. 2, III supra].

In only one case has the Court sustained a claim that multimember legislative districts unconstitutionally diluted the voting strength of a discrete group. [*Regester*] upheld a constitutional challenge by Negroes and Mexican-Americans to parts of a legislative reapportionment plan adopted by the State of Texas. [T]he Court held that the plaintiffs had been able to "produce evidence to support the finding that the political processes leading to nomination and election were not equally open to participation by the group[s] in question." In so holding, the Court relied upon evidence in the record that included a long history of official discrimination against minorities as well as indifference to their needs and interests on the part of white elected officials. [I]t is clear that the evidence in the present case fell far short of showing that the appellants "conceived or operated [a] purposeful device[ ] to further racial discrimination." *Whitcomb.*

[T]he District Court [affirmed by the Court of Appeals] based its conclusion of unconstitutionality primarily on the fact that no Negro had ever been elected to the City Commission, apparently because of the pervasiveness of racially polarized voting in Mobile. The trial court also found that city officials had not been as responsive to the interests of Negroes as to those of white persons. On the basis of these findings, the court concluded that the political processes in Mobile were not equally open to Negroes, despite its seemingly inconsistent findings that there were no inhibitions against Negroes becoming candidates, and that in fact Negroes had registered and voted without hindrance. * * *

First, [i]t may be that Negro candidates have been defeated, but that fact alone does not work a constitutional deprivation.

Second, [evidence] of discrimination by white officials in Mobile is relevant only as the most tenuous and circumstantial evidence of the constitutional invalidity of the electoral system under which they attained their offices.

Third, the District Court and the Court of Appeals supported their conclusion by drawing upon the substantial history of official racial discrimination in Alabama. But past discrimination cannot, in the manner of original sin, condemn governmental action that is not itself unlawful. The ultimate question remains whether a discriminatory intent has been proved in a given [case].

Finally, the District Court and the Court of Appeals pointed to the mechanics of the at-large electoral system itself as proof that the votes of Negroes were being invidiously canceled out. But those features of that electoral system, such as the majority vote requirement, tend naturally to disadvantage any voting minority [and] are far from proof that the at-large electoral scheme represents purposeful discrimination against Negro voters.

We turn finally [to] Justice Marshall's dissenting opinion. The theory [appears] to be that every "political group," or at least every such group that is in the minority, has a federal constitutional right to elect candidates in proportion to its numbers.[22] Moreover, a political group's "right" to have its candi-

---

22. The dissenting opinion seeks to disclaim this description of its theory by suggesting that a claim of vote dilution may require, in addition to proof of electoral defeat, some evidence of "historical and social factors" indicating that the group in question is without political influence. Putting to the side the evident fact that these gauzy sociological considerations have no constitutional basis, it remains far from certain that they could, in any principled manner, exclude the claims of any discrete political group that

dates elected is said to be a "fundamental interest," the infringement of which may be established without proof that a State has acted with the purpose of impairing anybody's access to the political process. This dissenting opinion finds the "right" infringed [because] no Negro has been elected to the Mobile City Commission.

Whatever appeal the dissenting opinion's view may have as a matter of political theory, it is not the law. The Equal Protection Clause [does] not require proportional representation as an imperative of political organization. * * *

It is of course true that a law that impinges upon a fundamental right explicitly or implicitly secured by the Constitution is presumptively unconstitutional. See *Shapiro v. Thompson,* [Part II infra]. See also *San Antonio Ind. School Dist. v. Rodriguez,* [Part IV infra]. But plainly "[i]t is not the province of this Court to create substantive constitutional rights in the name of guaranteeing equal protection of the laws," id. [In] *Whitcomb,* the trial court had found that a multimember state legislative district had invidiously deprived Negroes and poor persons of rights guaranteed them by the Constitution, notwithstanding the absence of any evidence whatever of discrimination against them. Reversing the trial court, this Court said: "The District Court's holding, although on the facts of this case limited to guaranteeing one racial group representation, is not easily contained. It is expressive of the more general proposition that any group with distinctive interests must be represented in legislative halls if it is numerous enough to command at least one seat and represents a majority living in an area sufficiently compact to constitute a single-member district. This approach would make it difficult to reject claims of Democrats, Republicans, or members of any political [organization]. There are also union oriented workers, the university community, religious or ethnic groups occupying identifiable areas of our heterogeneous cities and urban areas. Indeed, it would be difficult for a great many, if not most, multi-member districts to survive analysis under the District Court's view unless combined with some voting arrangement such as proportional representation or cumulative voting aimed at providing representation for minority parties or interests. At the very least, affirmance [would] spawn endless litigation concerning the multi-member district systems now widely employed in this country." * * *

MR. JUSTICE BLACKMUN, concurring in the result.

Assuming that proof of intent is a prerequisite to appellees' prevailing on their constitutional claim of vote dilution, I am inclined to agree with Mr. Justice White that, in this case, "the findings of the District Court amply support an inference of purposeful discrimination." I concur in the Court's judgment of reversal, however, because I believe that the relief afforded appellees by the District Court [ordering a new form of government "of a Mayor and a City Council with members elected from single-member districts"] was not commensurate with the sound exercise of judicial discretion. * * *

MR. JUSTICE STEVENS, concurring in the judgment.

[T]his case draws into question a political structure that treats all individuals as equals but adversely affects the political strength of a racially identifiable group. Although I am satisfied that such a structure may be challenged under the Fifteenth Amendment as well as under the Equal Protection Clause of the

happens, for whatever reason, to elect fewer of its candidates than arithmetic indicates it might. Indeed, the putative limits are bound to prove illusory if the express purpose in-forming their application would be, as the dissent assumes, to redress the "inequitable distribution of political influence."

Fourteenth Amendment, I believe that under either provision it must be judged by a standard that allows the political process to function effectively. * * *

[No] case decided by this Court establishes a constitutional right to proportional representation for racial minorities. What *Gomillion* [Sec. 2, III supra] holds is that a sufficiently "uncouth" or irrational racial gerrymander violates the Fifteenth Amendment. [The] fact that the "gerrymander" condemned in *Gomillion* was equally vulnerable under both Amendments indicates that the essential holding of that case is applicable, not merely to gerrymanders directed against racial minorities, but to those aimed at religious, ethnic, economic and political groups as well.[7]

In my view, the proper standard is suggested by three characteristics of the gerrymander condemned in *Gomillion:* (1) the 28-sided configuration [was] manifestly not the product of a routine or a traditional political decision; (2) it had a significant adverse impact on a minority group; and (3) it was unsupported by any neutral justification and thus was either totally irrational or entirely motivated by a desire to curtail the political strength of the minority. These characteristics suggest that a proper test should focus on the objective effects of the political decision rather than the subjective motivation of the decisionmaker. In this case, if the commission form of government in Mobile were extraordinary, or if it were nothing more than a vestige of history, with no greater justification than the grotesque figure in *Gomillion*, it would surely violate the Constitution. That conclusion would follow simply from its adverse impact on black voters plus the absence of any legitimate justification for the system, without reference to the subjective intent of the political body that has refused to alter it.

Conversely, I am also persuaded that a political decision that affects group voting rights may be valid even if it can be proved that irrational or invidious factors have played some part in its enactment or retention. The standard for testing the acceptability of such a decision must take into account the fact that the responsibility for drawing political boundaries is generally committed to the legislative process and that the process inevitably involves a series of compromises among different group interests. If the process is to work, it must reflect an awareness of group interests and it must tolerate some attempts to advantage or to disadvantage particular segments of the voting populace. [Accordingly], a political decision that is supported by valid and articulable justifications cannot be invalid simply because some participants in the decisionmaking process were motivated by a purpose to disadvantage a minority group.

The decision to retain the commission form of government in Mobile, Ala., is such a decision. [The] fact that these at-large systems characteristically place one or more minority groups at a significant disadvantage in the struggle for political power cannot invalidate all such systems. See *Whitcomb.* Nor can it be the law that such systems are valid when there is no evidence that they were instituted or maintained for discriminatory reasons, but that they may be selectively condemned on the basis of the subjective motivation of some of their supporters. A contrary view "would spawn endless litigation concerning the multimember districts now widely employed in this Country," and would entangle the judiciary in a voracious political thicket.

MR. JUSTICE BRENNAN, dissenting.

---

7. [See], e.g., *Whitcomb* (districts that are "conceived or operated as purposeful devices to further racial *or economic* discrimination" are prohibited by the Fourteenth Amendment) (emphasis supplied); *Dorsey* (an apportionment scheme would be invalid [if] it "operate[d] to minimize or cancel out the voting strength of racial *or political* elements of the voting population") (emphasis supplied).

I dissent because I agree with Mr. Justice Marshall that proof of discriminatory impact is sufficient in these cases. I also dissent because, even accepting the plurality's premise that discriminatory purpose must be shown, I agree with [Marshall and White, JJ.,] that the appellees have clearly met that burden.

MR. JUSTICE WHITE, dissenting.

[Both] the District Court and the Court of Appeals properly found that an invidious discriminatory purpose could be inferred from the totality of facts in this case. The Court's cryptic rejection of their conclusions ignores the principles that an invidious discriminatory purpose can be inferred from objective factors of the kind relied on in *Regester* and that the trial courts are in a special position to make such intensely local appraisals.

[T]he plurality today rejects the inference of purposeful discrimination apparently because each of the factors relied upon by the courts below is alone insufficient to support the inference. [By] viewing each of the factors relied upon below in isolation, and ignoring the fact that racial bloc voting at the polls makes it impossible to elect a black commissioner under the at-large system, the plurality rejects the "totality of the circumstances" approach we endorsed in *Regester, Davis,* and *Arlington Heights* * * *.

MR. JUSTICE MARSHALL, dissenting.

[Under our prior] line of cases, an electoral districting plan is invalid if it has the effect of affording an electoral minority "less opportunity [than] other residents in the district to participate in the political processes and to elect legislators of their choice," *Regester.* It is also apparent that the Court in *Regester* considered equal access to the political process as meaning more than merely allowing the minority the opportunity to vote. *Regester* stands for the proposition that an electoral system may not relegate an electoral minority to political impotence by diminishing the importance of its [vote].

The plurality fails to apply the discriminatory effect standard of *Regester* because that approach conflicts with what the plurality takes to be an elementary principle of law. "[O]nly if there is purposeful discrimination," announces the plurality, "can there be a violation of [equal protection]." That proposition [fails] to distinguish between two distinct lines of equal protection decisions: those involving suspect classifications, and those involving fundamental rights. * * *

Under the Equal Protection Clause, if a classification "impinges upon a fundamental right explicitly or implicitly protected by the [Constitution], strict judicial scrutiny" is required, *Rodriguez,* regardless of whether the infringement was intentional. As I will explain, our cases recognize a fundamental right to equal electoral participation that encompasses protection against vote dilution. Proof of discriminatory purpose is, therefore, not required to support a claim of vote dilution. The plurality's erroneous conclusion to the contrary is the result of a failure to recognize the central distinction between *Regester* and *Davis:* the former involved an infringement of a constitutionally protected right, while the latter dealt with a claim of racially discriminatory distribution of an interest to which no citizen has a constitutional entitlement. * * *

Reynolds and its progeny focused solely on the discriminatory *effects* of malapportionment. [In] the present cases, the alleged vote dilution, though caused by the combined effects of the electoral structure and social and historical factors rather than by unequal population distribution, is analytically the same concept: the unjustified abridgement of a fundamental right. It follows, then, that a showing of discriminatory intent is just as unnecessary under the vote-dilution approach adopted in *Dorsey* and applied in *Regester,* as it is under our reapportionment cases. * * *

The plurality's response is that my approach amounts to nothing less than a constitutional requirement of proportional representation for groups. That assertion amounts to nothing more than a red herring. [Appellees] proved that no Negro had ever been elected to the Mobile City Commission, despite the fact that Negroes constitute about one-third of the electorate, and that the persistence of severe racial bloc voting made it highly unlikely that any Negro could be elected at-large in the foreseeable future. Contrary to the plurality's contention, however, I do not find unconstitutional vote dilution in this case simply because of that showing. The plaintiffs convinced the District Court that Mobile Negroes were unable to use alternative avenues of political influence. They showed that Mobile Negroes still suffered pervasive present effects of massive historical official and private discrimination, and that the city commission had been quite unresponsive to the needs of the minority community. Mobile has been guilty of such pervasive racial discrimination in hiring employees that extensive intervention by the Federal District Court has been required. Negroes are grossly underrepresented on city boards and committees. The city's distribution of public services is racially discriminatory. City officials and police were largely unmoved by Negro complaints about police brutality and "mock lynchings." The District Court concluded that "[t]his sluggish and timid response is another manifestation of the low priority given to the needs of the black citizens and of the [commissioners'] political fear of a white backlash vote when black citizens' needs are at stake."

[T]he protection against vote dilution recognized by our prior cases serves as a minimally intrusive guarantee of political survival for a discrete political minority that is effectively locked out of governmental decisionmaking processes. So understood, the doctrine hardly " 'create[s] substantive constitutional rights in the name of guaranteeing equal protection of the laws,' " [but] is a simple reflection of the basic principle that the Equal Protection Clause protects "[t]he right of a citizen to equal representation and to have his vote weighted equally with those of all other citizens." *Reynolds.*

[The] plurality's requirement of proof of *intentional discrimination* [may] represent an attempt to bury the legitimate concerns of the minority beneath the soil of a doctrine almost as impermeable as it is specious. If so, the superficial tranquility created by such measures can be but short-lived. If this Court refuses to honor our long-recognized principle that the Constitution "nullifies sophisticated as well as simple-minded modes of discrimination," it cannot expect the victims of discrimination to respect political channels of seeking redress. I dissent.

ROGERS v. LODGE, 458 U.S. 613, 102 S.Ct. 3272, 73 L.Ed.2d 1012 (1982), per WHITE, J., affirmed a decision that the at-large election system for a Georgia county Board of Commissioners violated equal protection: "The District Court [demonstrated] its understanding of the controlling standard by observing that a determination of discriminatory intent is 'a requisite to a finding of unconstitutional vote dilution' [and] concluded that the [system] 'although racially neutral when adopted, is being *maintained* for invidious purposes.' [For] the most part, the District Court dealt with the evidence in terms of the factors [that had been used by the district court in *Mobile*], but as the Court of Appeals stated: 'Judge Alaimo [did] not treat [those factors] as absolute, but rather considered them only to the extent that they were relevant to the question of discriminatory intent.' Although a tenable argument can be made to the contrary, we are not inclined to disagree with the Court of Appeals' conclusion that the District Court applied the proper legal standard. * * *

"The Court of Appeals [stated that the] District Court correctly anticipated *Mobile* and required appellees to prove that the at-large voting system was maintained for a discriminatory purpose. The Court of Appeals also held that the District Court's findings not only were not clearly erroneous, but its conclusion that the at-large system was maintained for invidious purposes was 'virtually mandated by the overwhelming proof.' [This Court has] noted that issues of intent are commonly treated as factual matters [and] has frequently noted its reluctance to disturb findings of fact concurred in by two lower courts."

POWELL, J., joined by Rehnquist, J., dissented: "[T]he Court's opinion cannot be reconciled persuasively with [*Mobile*]. There are some variances in the largely sociological evidence presented in the two cases. But *Mobile* held that this *kind* of evidence was not enough. * * *

"The Court's decision today relies heavily on the capacity of the federal district courts—essentially free from any standards prepounded by this Court— to determine whether at-large voting systems are 'being maintained for the invidious purpose of diluting the voting strength of the black population.' Federal courts thus are invited to engage in deeply subjective inquiries into the motivations of local officials in structuring local governments. Inquiries of this kind not only can be 'unseemly,' they intrude the federal courts—with only the vaguest constitutional direction—into an area of intensely local and political concern.

"Emphasizing these considerations, Justice Stevens argues forcefully [that] subjective intent is irrelevant to the establishment of a case of racial vote [dilution].[a] I agree with much of what he says [but] would not accept this view. 'The central purpose of the Equal Protection Clause [is] the prevention of official conduct discriminating on the basis of race.' *Davis*. Because I am unwilling to abandon this central principle in cases of this kind, I cannot join Justice Stevens's opinion. [But] in the absence of proof of discrimination by reliance on the kind of objective factors identified by Justice Stevens, I would hold that the factors cited by the Court of Appeals are too attenuated as a matter of law to support an inference of discriminatory intent."[b]

Notes and Questions

Gerrymandering.[a] (a) Has the Court made clear that equal protection bars apportionment gerrymanders that deny "full and effective participation in the political processes"? For alleged racial gerrymanders, see *Connor v. Johnson,* 265 F.Supp. 492 (S.D.Miss.1966), aff'd 386 U.S. 483 (1967); *Ferrell v. Hall,* 339 F.Supp. 73 (W.D.Okl.), aff'd 406 U.S. 939 (1972); compare *United Jewish Orgs. v.*

a. Stevens, J.'s long dissent expanded his views expressed in *Mobile.*

b. For subsequent congressional action relevant to the problem, p. 1169 infra.

a. See Tyler, *Court Versus Legislature,* 27 Law & Contemp.Prob. 390, 400–01 (1962): "[A]n urban majority is converted into a legislative minority by the time-polished techniques of 'cracking [and] stacking' districts. The 'cracked' district is the huge metropolitan center, torn apart into separate pieces, each of which is attached to and outvoted by a surrounding rural hinterland. [The] 'stacked' district is the child of the gerrymander, a delicately carved creature, resembling nothing more than the partisan and rapacious soul of his political creator." For a broader definition of gerrymander to include any intentional manipulation of districts for partisan advantage, see Baker, fn. b in *Mahan,* supra.

Carey, Sec. 2, V supra. For alleged political gerrymanders, see *Gaffney v. Cummings,* infra. Consider Auerbach, fn. 12 in *Reynolds,* at 65: "[I]t would not be desirable for the Court to attack the partisan gerrymander as a constitutional problem. The 'One Vote, One Value' principle will make gerrymandering more difficult and even more obvious. Inequities in apportionment should not be justified simply because inequities in districting cannot be eliminated at the same time. The great mobility of the American people, the accelerating pace of socioeconomic change and the increasing uncertainties in the futures of both major parties, may be expected to combine with constitutional apportionment to make partisan districting an increasingly risky enterprise." Do you agree? Even if "there are computer techniques for districting which preclude gerrymandering and produce contiguous, compact districts nearly equal in population without breaking up population centers"? Id.

(b) How are gerrymanders to be identified? If districting departs substantially from natural geographic or political boundaries, should a "rational" state policy insulate it from a charge of gerrymandering? Consider Note, *Apportionment and the Courts—A Synopsis and Prognosis: Herein of Gerrymanders and Other Dragons,* 59 Nw.U.L.Rev. 500, 531 (1964): "A legislature might reasonably conclude [that] a minority interest bloc should be concentrated so as to assure that at least one representative will be dedicated to protecting the bloc from submergence. On the other hand, a legislature might reasonably conclude that the election of representatives committed to the general welfare is best accomplished by forming districts that proportionately reflect the composition of the state as a whole." Is gerrymandering on the basis of political party, economic status, or social position "rational"? Constitutional?

(c) Apart from racial groups or political parties, what other groups (or "interests") may be the object of a gerrymander? How are they to be identified? What about "independent voters"? In GAFFNEY v. CUMMINGS, note 4(b) after *Reynolds,* supra, the Court noted "the reality [that] districting inevitably [is] intended to have substantial political consequences." Thus, the fact "that virtually every Senate and House district line was drawn with the conscious intent to create a districting plan that would achieve a rough approximation of the statewide political strengths of the Democratic and Republican Parties, the only two parties in the State large enough to elect legislators from discernible geographic areas," did not invalidate the plan.

B. DENIAL OR QUALIFICATION OF THE RIGHT

HARPER v. VIRGINIA BD. OF ELEC., 383 U.S. 663, 86 S.Ct. 1079, 16 L.Ed. 2d 169 (1966), per Douglas, J., overruling *Breedlove v. Suttles,* 302 U.S. 277, 58 S.Ct. 205, 82 L.Ed. 252 (1937), held that Virginia's $1.50 poll tax as "a prerequisite of voting" was "an 'invidious' discrimination": "[T]he right to vote in state elections is nowhere expressly mentioned" in the Constitution, but "once the franchise is [granted] lines may not be drawn which [violate equal protection]."

"Long ago in *Yick Wo,* [Sec. 2, III supra], the Court referred to 'the political franchise of voting' as a 'fundamental political right, because preservative of all rights.' * * * Wealth, like race, creed, or color, is not germane to one's ability to participate intelligently in the electoral process. Lines drawn on the basis of wealth or property, like those of race, are traditionally disfavored. See *Edwards v. California,* [p. 220 supra] (Jackson, J., concurring); *Griffin v. Illinois; Douglas v. California,* [Part III infra]. To introduce wealth or payment of a fee as a measure of a voter's qualifications is to introduce a capricious or irrelevant factor. * * *

"In determining what lines are unconstitutionally discriminatory, we have never been confined to historic notions of equality" and "notions of what constitutes equal treatment for purposes of the Equal Protection Clause *do* change [citing *Plessy* and *Brown*, Sec. 2, II supra]. Our conclusion, like that in *Reynolds*, is founded not on what we think governmental policy should be, but on what the Equal Protection Clause requires.

"We have long been mindful that where fundamental rights and liberties are asserted under the Equal Protection Clause, classifications which might invade or restrain them must be closely scrutinized and carefully confined. See, e.g., *Reynolds; Carrington v. Rash.*"[a]

BLACK, J., dissented: "[U]nder a proper interpretation of the Equal Protection Clause States are to have the broadest kind of leeway in areas where they have a general constitutional competence to act. [P]oll tax legislation can 'reasonably,' 'rationally' and without an 'invidious' or evil purpose to injure anyone be found to rest on a number of state policies including (1) the State's desire to collect its revenue, and (2) its belief that voters who pay a poll tax will be interested in furthering the State's welfare when they vote. [And] history is on the side of 'rationality' of the State's poll tax policy. Property qualifications existed in the Colonies and were continued by many States after the Constitution was adopted. [The Court] seems to be using the old 'natural-law-due-process formula' to justify striking down state laws as violations of [equal protection]."

HARLAN, J., joined by Stewart, J., dissented: "The [equal protection] test evolved by this Court [is whether] a classification can be deemed to be founded on some rational and otherwise constitutionally permissible state [policy].[3] *Reynolds* [also] marked a departure from these traditional and wise principles. [I]t was probably accepted as sound political theory by a large percentage of Americans through most of our history, that people with some property have a deeper stake in community affairs, and are consequently more responsible, more educated, more knowledgeable, more worthy of [confidence. It] is all wrong, in my view, for the Court to adopt the political doctrines popularly accepted at a particular moment of our history and to declare all others to be irrational and invidious * * *."

LUBIN v. PANISH, 415 U.S. 709, 94 S.Ct. 1315, 39 L.Ed.2d 702 (1974), per BURGER, C.J., held that California's requirement of a filing fee to get on a primary election ballot or to be a write-in candidate—in this case, 2% of the annual salary for the state office sought ($701.60)—as applied to indigents, violated "equal protection [and] rights of expression and association." The Court "recognized that the State's interest in keeping its ballots within manageable, understandable limits is of the highest order [but it] must be achieved by a means that does not unfairly or unnecessarily burden either a minority party's or an individual candidate's equally important interest in the continued availa-

---

a. *Carrington*, 380 U.S. 89, 85 S.Ct. 775, 13 L.Ed.2d 675 (1965), per Stewart, J., held a Texas provision, barring military personnel who moved to Texas from voting in state elections so long as they remained in the military, "an invidious discrimination"—the classification was not "reasonable in light of its purpose."

3. I think the somewhat different application of the Equal Protection Clause to racial discrimination cases finds justification in the fact that insofar as that clause may embody a particular value in addition to rationality, the historical origins of the Civil War Amendments might attribute to racial equality this special status. * * *

bility of political opportunity. [V]oters can assert their preferences only through candidates or parties or both and it is this broad interest that must be weighed in the balance. [A] voter hopes to find on the ballot a candidate who comes near to reflecting his policy preferences on contemporary issues. This does not mean every voter can be assured that a candidate to his liking will be on the ballot, but the process of qualifying candidates [may] not constitutionally be measured solely in dollars."

[The Court relied on *Bullock v. Carter*, 405 U.S. 134, 92 S.Ct. 849, 31 L.Ed.2d 92 (1972), per Burger, C.J., invalidating a Texas statute requiring candidates to pay $50 plus their pro rata share of the costs of the election in order to get on the primary ballot, resulting in fees as high as $8,900: "Because the Texas [scheme] has a real and appreciable impact on the exercise of the franchise, and because this impact is related to the resources of the voters supporting a particular candidate, we conclude, as in *Harper*, that the laws must be 'closely scrutinized' and found reasonably necessary to the accomplishment of legitimate state [objectives]."] [d]

"[A] wealthy candidate with not the remotest chance of election may secure a place on the ballot by writing a check [but, due to filing fees, impecunious but serious candidates may be prevented from running. [W]e hold that in the absence of reasonable alternative means of ballot access, a State may [not] require from an indigent candidate filing fees he cannot pay." [f]

KRAMER v. UNION FREE SCHOOL DISTRICT
395 U.S. 621, 89 S.Ct. 1886, 23 L.Ed.2d 583 (1969).

Mr. Chief Justice Warren delivered the opinion of the Court.

[§ 2012 of the New York Education Law] provides that in certain New York school districts residents [may] vote in the school district election only if they [or their spouse] (1) own (or lease) taxable real property within the district, or (2) are parents (or have custody of) children enrolled in the local public schools. Appellant, a bachelor who neither owns nor leases taxable real property, [claimed] § 2012 denied him equal protection * * *.

[I]t is important to note what is *not* at issue in this case. The requirements of § 2012 that school district voters must (1) be citizens of the United States, (2) be bona fide residents of the school district, and (3) be at least 21 years of age are not challenged. * * *

[S]tatutes distributing the franchise constitute the foundation of our representative society. Any unjustified discrimination in determining who may participate in political affairs or in the selection of public officials undermines

---

d. In *Bullock*, the Court rejected "the theory that since the candidates are availing themselves of the primary machinery, it is appropriate that they pay that share of the cost which they have occasioned. [A] primary system designed to give the voters some influence at the nominating stage should spread the cost among all of the voters in an attempt to distribute the influence without regard to wealth. Viewing the myriad governmental functions supported from general revenues, it is difficult to single out any of a higher order than the conduct of elections at all levels to bring forth those persons desired by their fellow citizens to govern. Without making light

of the State's interest in husbanding its revenues, we fail to see such an element of necessity in the State's present means of financing primaries as to justify the resulting incursion on the prerogatives of voters."

f. Douglas, J., joined the Court's opinion adding: "Since classifications based on wealth are 'traditionally disfavored,' *Harper*, the State's inability to show a compelling interest in conditioning the right to run for office on payment of fees cannot stand."

Blackmun, J., joined by Rehnquist, J., concurred in part.

the legitimacy of representative government. [Therefore,] if a [statute] grants the right to vote to some bona fide residents of requisite age and citizenship and denies the franchise to others, the Court must determine whether the exclusions are necessary to promote a compelling state interest. See *Carrington.*

[The] presumption of constitutionality and the approval given "rational" classifications in other types of enactments are based on an assumption that the institutions of state government are structured so as to represent fairly all the people. However, when the challenge to the statute is in effect a challenge of this basic assumption, the assumption can no longer serve as the basis for presuming constitutionality. And, the assumption is no less under attack because the legislature which decides who may participate at the various levels of political choice is fairly elected. * * * [10]

The need for exacting judicial scrutiny of statutes distributing the franchise is undiminished simply because, under a different statutory scheme, the offices subject to election might have been filled through appointment [11] [since] "once the franchise is granted to the electorate, lines may not be drawn which are inconsistent with [equal protection]." *Harper.*

Nor is the need for close judicial examination affected because the district [and] the school board do not have "general" legislative powers. Our exacting examination is necessitated not by the subject of the election [but] because some resident citizens are permitted to participate and some are not. * * *

Besides appellant and others who similarly live in their parents' homes, the statute also disenfranchises the following persons (unless they are parents or guardians of children enrolled in the district public school): senior citizens and others living with children or relatives; clergy, military personnel and others who live on tax-exempt property; boarders and lodgers; parents who neither own nor lease qualifying property and whose children are too young to attend school [or] attend private schools.

[A]ppellees argue that the State has a legitimate interest in limiting the franchise in school district elections [to] those "primarily interested in such elections" [and] that the State may reasonably and permissibly conclude that "property taxpayers" (including lessees of taxable property who share the tax burden through rent payments) and parents of the children enrolled in the district's schools are those "primarily interested" in school affairs. * * *

[A]ssuming, arguendo, that New York legitimately might limit the franchise in these school district elections to those "primarily interested in school affairs," close scrutiny of the § 2012 classifications demonstrates that they do not accomplish this purpose with sufficient precision to justify denying appellant the franchise.

[T]he classifications must be tailored so that the exclusion of appellant and members of his class is necessary to achieve the articulated state goal.[14] Section 2012 does not meet the exacting standard of precision [because it permits] inclusion of many persons who have, at best, a remote and indirect interest in

---

10. [See] *Avery v. Midland County.*

11. Similarly, no less a showing of a compelling justification for disenfranchising residents is required merely because the questions scheduled for the election need not have been submitted to the voters.

14. Of course, if the exclusions are necessary to promote the articulated state interest, we must then determine whether the interest promoted by limiting the franchise constitutes a compelling state interest. We do not reach that issue in this case.

school affairs and on the other hand, exclude[s] others who have a distinct and direct interest in the school meeting decisions.[15] * * *

MR. JUSTICE STEWART, with whom MR. JUSTICE BLACK and MR. JUSTICE HARLAN join, dissenting. * * *

Clearly a State may reasonably assume that its residents have a greater stake in the outcome of elections held within its boundaries than do other persons [and] that residents, being generally better informed regarding state affairs than are nonresidents, will be more likely [to] vote responsibly. And the same may be said of legislative assumptions regarding the electoral competence of adults and literate persons on the one hand, and of minors and illiterates on the other. It is clear, of course, that lines thus drawn cannot infallibly perform their intended legislative function. Just as "[i]lliterate people may be intelligent voters," nonresidents or minors might also in some instances be interested, informed, and intelligent participants in the electoral process. Persons who commute across a state line to work may well have a great stake in the affairs of the State in which they are employed; some college students under 21 may be both better informed and more passionately interested in political affairs than many adults. But such discrepancies are the inevitable concomitant of the line-drawing that is essential to lawmaking. So long as the classification is rationally related to a permissible legislative end, therefore—as are residence, literacy, and age requirements imposed with respect to voting—there is no denial of equal protection.

Thus judged, the statutory classification involved here seems to me clearly to be valid [and] the Court does not really argue the contrary. Instead, it [asserts] that the traditional equal protection standard is [inapt]. But the asserted justification for applying [a stricter] standard cannot withstand analysis. [The] voting qualifications at issue have been promulgated not by Union Free School District, but by the New York State Legislature, and the appellant is of course fully able to participate in the election of representatives in that body. There is simply no claim whatever here that the state government is not "structured so as to represent fairly all the people," including the appellant.

[§ 2012] does not involve racial classifications [and] is not one that impinges upon a constitutionally protected right, and that consequently can be justified only by a "compelling" state interest. For "the Constitution of the United States does not confer the right of suffrage upon any one."

In any event, it seems to me that under *any* equal protection standard, short of a doctrinaire insistence that universal suffrage is somehow mandated by the Constitution, the appellant's claim must be rejected. * * *

PHOENIX v. KOLODZIEJSKI, 399 U.S. 204, 90 S.Ct. 1990, 26 L.Ed.2d 523 (1970), per WHITE, J., relying on *Kramer* and *Cipriano v. Houma*, 395 U.S. 701, 89 S.Ct. 1897, 23 L.Ed.2d 647 (1969),[b] held violative of equal protection a statute

---

15. For example, appellant resides with his parents in the school district, pays state and federal taxes and is interested in and affected by school board decisions [but] an uninterested unemployed young man who pays no state or federal taxes, but who rents an apartment in the district, can [vote].

b. *Cipriano* held violative of equal protection a statute giving "only 'property taxpayers' the right to vote in elections [for] issuance

of revenue bonds by a municipal utility," pointing out that "the benefits and burdens of the bond issue fall indiscriminately on property owner and nonproperty owner alike." Black and Stewart, JJ., concurred in the result, finding the classification " 'wholly irrelevant to achievement' of the State's objective." Harlan, J., feeling bound by prior decisions, concurred in the result.

permitting only real property taxpayers to vote on "general obligation bonds," issued to finance various municipal improvements, and to be serviced partly by property taxes: "[P]roperty owners and nonproperty owners alike, have a substantial interest in the public facilities and the services available in the city and will be substantially affected by the ultimate outcome of the bond election." Even if *only* property tax revenues were used to service the bonds, "the justification would be insufficient. Property taxes may be paid initially by property owners, but a significant part of the ultimate burden of each year's tax on rental property will very likely be borne by the [tenant]. Moreover, property taxes on commercial property [will] normally be reflected in the prices of goods and services [purchased]." [c]

Notes and Questions

1. *Other laws "distributing the franchise."* (a) After *Kramer,* what of the validity of age, residency and literacy requirements for voting? Consider 83 Harv.L.Rev. 81 (1969): "[T]he danger of an impermissible selection is much less when the goal of a voting test is to select competent voters than when interest differences are involved. The Court refused to assume that some voters have no interest whatsoever, but it must acknowledge that some citizens, like two-year olds and the insane, are not competent. Since such cases of permissible exclusion can be conceived of, a competency classification cannot be termed impermissible in its general purpose." Does this "interest-competency" distinction adequately respond to Stewart, J.'s objections? If *all* 2-year-olds are incompetent, are *all* 17-year-olds? If not, would an 18-year-old voting qualification "meet the exacting standard of precision required of statutes which selectively distribute the franchise"? See *Oregon v. Mitchell,* p. 1159 infra.

(b) *Felons.* RICHARDSON v. RAMIREZ, 418 U.S. 24, 94 S.Ct. 2655, 41 L.Ed. 2d 551 (1974), per REHNQUIST, J.,—relying on § 2 of the fourteenth amendment— held California's disenfranchising felons not violative of equal protection: "[T]he express language of § 2 [and] the historical and judicial interpretation of the Amendment's applicability to state laws disenfranchising felons, is of controlling significance in distinguishing such laws from those other state limitations on the franchise which have been held [invalid. We] rest on the demonstrably sound proposition that § 1, in dealing with voting rights as it does, could not have been meant to bar outright a form of disenfranchisement which was expressly exempted from the less drastic sanction of reduced representation which § 2 imposed for other forms of disenfranchisement." [a]

(c) *Special purpose units.* (i) SALYER LAND CO. v. TULARE LAKE BASIN WATER STORAGE DIST., 410 U.S. 719, 93 S.Ct. 1224, 35 L.Ed.2d 659 (1973), per REHNQUIST, J., upheld California statutes permitting only landowners to vote in "water storage districts" elections and apportioning votes according to the assessed valuation of the land within the districts. These districts planned projects for water acquisition, conservation and distribution; they were empow-

---

c. Stewart, J., joined by Burger, C.J., and Harlan, J., dissented: Since "the weight of repaying [general obligation] bonds will legally fall" on real property owners, this is "an entirely rational public policy."

a. Marshall, J., joined by Brennan, J., dissented, arguing that "§ 2 was not intended [to] be a limitation on the other sections of the Fourteenth Amendment" and that, under the "compelling state interest test," "the blanket

disenfranchisement of ex-felons cannot stand." Douglas, J., dissented on procedural grounds.

Consider Tribe, *American Constitutional Law* 771 (1978): "[§ 2] provides no warrant for circumscribing the reach of the equal protection clause [which] is not bound to the political theories of a particular era but draws much of its substance from changing social norms and evolving conceptions of equality."

ered to fix charges for use of water in proportion to services rendered; project costs were assessed against land in accordance with benefits accruing to each tract. Appellee district had a population of 77 (including 18 children), most employed by one of four corporations that farmed 85% of the land; there were also about 200 other small landowners; one of the corporations (Boswell Co.) held a majority of the votes.

"[Appellee], although vested with some typical governmental powers, has relatively limited authority." Apart from water,[8] "it [does] not exercise what might be thought of as 'normal governmental' authority, [and] its actions disproportionately affect landowners" because of the method of allocating project costs and service charges. Thus, the franchise restriction is valid unless " 'wholly irrelevant to achievement of the regulation's objectives.' No doubt residents within the district may be affected by its activities. But [California] could quite reasonably have concluded that the number of landowners and owners of sufficient amounts of acreage whose consent was necessary to organize the district would not have subjected their land to the lien of its possibly very substantial assessments unless they had a dominant voice in its control."

DOUGLAS, J., joined by Brennan and Marshall, JJ., dissented: In the past, floods were averted by storing water in Buena Vista Lake. "But that was not done in the great 1969 flood" because the board—"dominated [by] Boswell Co.—voted 6–4 to table the motion" because it had an "agricultural lease in the Buena Vista Lake Basin and flooding it would have interfered" with its crops. As a result, the residence of one of the non-landowner appellants "was 15½ feet below the water level of the crest of the flood." "Measured by the *Hadley* test," the district "surely performs 'important governmental functions' which 'have sufficient impact throughout the district' to justify the application of the *Avery* principle. [The] result [here] is a corporate political kingdom undreamed of [by] our Constitution."

(ii) BALL v. JAMES, 451 U.S. 355, 101 S.Ct. 1811, 68 L.Ed.2d 150 (1981), per STEWART, J., applied *Salyer* to an Arizona water district which limited voting to landowners on a "one acre, one vote" basis. Although the district was formed for "storage, delivery, and conservation of water," it had become "a major generator and supplier of hydroelectric power in the State, [and] roughly 40% of the water it delivers goes to urban areas for nonagricultural uses." Although "the District has $290 million of general obligation bonds outstanding that are secured by a lien on lands owned by the voting members, [the] bonds have so far been serviced out of the District's electricity revenues, [and] all capital improvements have been financed by revenue bonds": "[N]o matter how great the number of nonvoting residents buying electricity from the District, the relationship between them and the District's power operations is essentially that between consumers and a business enterprise from which they buy. [The] voting landowners are the only residents [subject] to the acreage-based taxing power of the District, [and] the only residents who have ever committed capital to the District through stock assessments charged by the Association.[20]"

---

8. Appellants strongly urge that districts [engage] in flood control activities [but these] are incident to the exercise of the district's primary functions of water storage and distribution.

20. The appellees, of course, are qualified voters in Arizona and so remain equal participants in the election of the state legislators who created and have the power to change the District.

[Powell, J., who joined the Court's opinion, emphasized "the importance [of] the Arizona Legislature's control over voting requirements for the [District. It] is large enough and the resources it manages are basic enough that the people will act through their elected legis-

WHITE, J., joined by Brennan, Marshall and Blackmun, JJ., dissented: The "landowners could not themselves afford to finance their own project and turned to a public agency [which] now subsidizes the storage and delivery of irrigation water for agricultural purposes by selling electricity to the public at prices that neither the voters nor any representative public agency has any right to control. Unlike the situation in *Salyer,* the financial burden of supplying irrigation water has been shifted from the landowners to the consumers of electricity. * * *[11]" d

(d) *Nonresidents.* HOLT CIVIC CLUB v. TUSCALOOSA, 439 U.S. 60, 99 S.Ct. 383, 58 L.Ed.2d 292 (1978), per REHNQUIST, J., upheld the Alabama "police jurisdiction" statute, which extended a city's police and sanitary regulations and its business-licensing powers (at ½ the fees for city businesses) to residents of adjacent unincorporated communities, but did not permit them to vote in city elections: "[O]ur cases have uniformly recognized that a government unit may legitimately restrict the right to participate in its political processes to those who reside within its borders. See, e.g., *Dunn v. Blumstein,* [Part II infra]; *Kramer; Carrington.* [A] city's decisions inescapably affect individuals living immediately outside its borders. The granting of building permits for highrise apartments, industrial plants, and the like on the city's fringe unavoidably contributes to problems of traffic congestion, school districting, and law enforcement immediately outside the city. A rate change in the city's sales or ad valorem tax could well have a significant impact on retailers and property values in areas bordering the city. The condemnation of real property on the city's edge for construction of a municipal [dump] would have obvious implications for neighboring nonresidents. [Yet] no one would suggest that nonresidents likely to be affected [have] a constitutional right to participate in the political processes bringing it about. * * *

"Thus stripped of its voting rights attire, the equal protection issue [is] whether the Alabama statutes [bear] some rational relationship to a legitimate state [purpose]."

STEVENS, J., who joined the Court's opinion, added: "The powers of extraterritorial jurisdiction granted by the challenged statutes are limited. [Nor] is there any claim [that] residents of the police jurisdictions have been charged unreasonable costs for the services they receive."

BRENNAN, J., joined by White and Marshall, JJ., dissented: "The residents of Tuscaloosa's police jurisdiction are vastly more affected by Tuscaloosa's decision-making processes than were the plaintiffs in either *Kramer* or *Cipriano* affected by the decisionmaking processes from which they had been unconstitutionally excluded. * * *

"[There] is a crystal distinction between those who reside in Tuscaloosa's police jurisdiction, and who are therefore subject to that city's police and

lature when further changes in the governance of the District are warranted. [For] this Court to dictate how the Board of the District must be elected would detract from the democratic process we profess to protect."]

11. [In] most situations involving a state agency or even a city, the state legislature and ultimately the people could exercise control since any municipal corporation is a creature of the State. The Fourteenth Amendment requires a far more direct sense of democratic participation in elective schemes which is not satisfied by the indirect and imprecise voter control suggested by the Court [in fn. 20] and by Justice Powell.

d. For a careful analysis distinguishing *Ball* from *Salyer* on the ground that the system in *Salyer* (but not in *Ball*) distributed benefits and burdens in a way comporting with the way in which the vote was distributed, see Durchslag, *Salyer, Ball and Holt: Reappraising the Right to Vote in Terms of Political "Interest" and Vote Dilution,* 33 Case W.Res.L.Rev. 1 (1982).

sanitary ordinances, licensing fees, and the jurisdiction of its recorders' courts, and those who reside in neither the city nor its police jurisdiction, and who are thus merely affected by the indirect impact of the city's decisions. This distinction [is] consistent with, if not mandated by, the very conception of a political community underlying constitutional recognition of bona fide residency requirements."

(e) *Absentee ballots.* (i) McDONALD v. BOARD OF ELEC., 394 U.S. 802, 89 S.Ct. 1404, 22 L.Ed.2d 739 (1969), per WARREN, C.J., upheld an Illinois statute granting absentee ballots to designated classes but not to "unsentenced inmates awaiting trial." The Court applied "the more traditional standards [for] equal protection claims [because it is] not the right to vote that is at stake here but a claimed right to receive absentee ballots."[6] "Indeed, appellants' challenge seems to disclose not an arbitrary scheme or plan but [a] consistent and laudable state policy of adding, over a 50-year period, groups to the absentee [coverage]. That Illinois has not gone still further [should] not render void its remedial legislation, which need [not] 'strike at all evils at the same time.' "

(ii) O'BRIEN v. SKINNER, 414 U.S. 524, 94 S.Ct. 740, 38 L.Ed.2d 702 (1974), per BURGER, C.J., held "wholly arbitrary" and thus violative of equal protection New York's denial of absentee ballots to persons being held for trial and to convicted misdemeanants. Since state law permitted absentee ballots to persons absent from their home county, those held in jail in a county other than their residence could vote, "yet persons confined for the same reason in the county of their residence are completely denied the ballot." BLACKMUN, J., joined by Rehnquist, J., dissented, relying on *McDonald:* Since the state "need not have provided for *any* absentee registration or absentee voting," the "legislature traditionally has been allowed to take reform 'one step at a [time].' "

2. *"Remedial" or "reform" legislation "extending" the franchise.* (a) In KATZENBACH v. MORGAN, p. 1149 infra, Congress suspended state English literacy tests for voting for citizens "educated in American-flag schools (schools located within United States jurisdiction)." The Court held this was not "an invidious discrimination" against other foreign-language citizens. Because the statute "does not restrict or deny the franchise but in effect extends" it, "the principle that calls for the closest scrutiny of distinctions in laws *denying* fundamental rights is inapplicable; for the distinction challenged [is] presented only as a limitation on a reform measure aimed at eliminating an existing barrier to the exercise of the franchise. Rather, in deciding the constitutional propriety of the limitations in such a reform measure we are guided by the familiar principles that a 'statute is not invalid under the Constitution because it might have gone further than it did,' [and] that 'reform may take one step at a time, addressing itself to the phase of the problem which seems most acute to the legislative mind.' "[d]

(b) Does this add any perspective to *McDonald*? By what test does (should) the Court determine whether legislation "distributing the franchise" "restricts or denies" it rather than "extends" it? Is it that if the group given the vote had been excluded by the state, the exclusion would be held "necessary to promote a

---

6. [T]he record is barren of any indication that the State might not, for instance, possibly furnish the jails with special polling booths or facilities on election day, or provide guarded transportation to the polls themselves for certain inmates, or entertain motions for temporary reductions in bail to allow some inmates to get to the polls on their own.

d. Douglas, J., reserved judgment on the question.

See also *Schilb v. Kuebel*, 404 U.S. 357, 92 S.Ct. 479, 30 L.Ed.2d 502 (1971) (bail reform law).

compelling state interest"? Or is the matter more complex? Did the *Morgan* statute "grant the right to vote to some bona fide residents of requisite age and citizenship and deny the franchise to others"?

Does "extension" of the right to vote "dilute" the voting rights of others? If so, should extensions be justified only by a "compelling state interest"? May a city extend the vote in local elections to all nonresidents who own property in the city? If so, under what standard should its refusal to extend it also to nonresidents who work in the city be judged? Should the "traditional" equal protection standard be applicable because use of the "stricter" standard would invalidate most classifications and the state might well then eliminate extensions altogether? Was such a choice realistically (constitutionally) available to the state after *Reynolds*? *Avery*? *Carrington*? *Harper*? *Kramer* and *Phoenix*? *Salyer*? *Holt*? In some of these, but not all?

II. DISCRIMINATION IN RESPECT TO TRAVEL

SHAPIRO v. THOMPSON

394 U.S. 618, 89 S.Ct. 1322, 22 L.Ed.2d 600 (1969).

MR. JUSTICE BRENNAN delivered the opinion of the Court.

These three appeals [are from federal courts] holding unconstitutional [Conn., Pa. and D.C. statutes denying welfare] to residents [who] have not resided within their jurisdictions for at least one [year].

There is no dispute that the effect of the waiting-period requirement [is] to create two classes of needy resident families indistinguishable from each other except that one is composed of residents who have resided a year or more, and the second of residents who have resided less than a year, in the jurisdiction. [T]he second class is denied welfare aid upon which may depend the ability of the families to obtain the very means to subsist—food, shelter, and other necessities of life. [We] agree [that the statutes deny equal protection]. The interests which appellants assert are promoted by the classification either may not constitutionally be promoted by government or are not compelling governmental interests.

Primarily, appellants justify the waiting-period requirement as a protective device to preserve the fiscal integrity of state public assistance programs. It is asserted that people who require welfare assistance during their first year of residence in a State are likely to become continuing burdens on state welfare programs. Therefore, the argument runs, if such people can be deterred from entering the jurisdiction by denying them welfare benefits during the first year, state programs to assist long-time residents will not be impaired. [But] the purpose of inhibiting migration by needy persons into the State is constitutionally impermissible.

This Court long ago recognized that the nature of our Federal Union and our constitutional concepts of personal liberty unite to require that all citizens be free to travel throughout the length and breadth of our land uninhibited by statutes, rules, or regulations which unreasonably burden or restrict this movement. [See *United States v. Guest,* p. 1142 infra.

Alternatively, appellants argue that even if it is impermissible for a State to attempt to deter the entry of all indigents, the challenged classification may be justified as a permissible state attempt to discourage those indigents who would enter the State solely to obtain larger benefits. [But] a State may no more try to fence out those indigents who seek higher welfare benefits than it may try to fence out indigents generally. [W]e do not perceive why a mother who is seeking to make a new life for herself and her children should be regarded as less deserving because she considers, among other factors, the level of a State's public assistance. Surely such a mother is no less deserving than a mother who moves into a particular State in order to take advantage of its better educational facilities.

Appellants argue further that the challenged classification may be sustained as an attempt to distinguish between new and old residents on the basis of the contribution they have made to the community through the payment of taxes. [But this] would logically permit the State to bar new residents from schools, parks, and libraries or deprive them of police and fire protection. Indeed it would permit the State to apportion all benefits and services according to the past tax contributions of its citizens. The Equal Protection Clause prohibits such an apportionment of state services.[10]

We recognize that a State [may] legitimately attempt to limit its expenditures, whether for public assistance, public education, or any other program. But a State may not accomplish such a purpose by invidious distinctions between classes of its citizens. It could not, for example, reduce expenditures for education by barring indigent children from its schools. [Thus], appellants must do more than show that denying welfare benefits to new residents saves [money.]

Appellants next advance as justification [four] administrative and related governmental objectives allegedly served by the waiting-period requirement.

* * *

At the outset, we reject appellants' argument that a mere showing of a rational relationship between the waiting period and these four admittedly permissible state objectives will suffice, [for] in moving from State to State or to the District of Columbia appellees were exercising a constitutional right, and any classification which serves to penalize the exercise of that right, unless shown to be necessary to promote a *compelling* governmental interest, is unconstitutional. Cf. *Skinner v. Oklahoma*, [p. 311 supra]; *Korematsu*, [Sec. 2, I supra]; *Sherbert v. Verner*, [p. 845 supra].

The argument that the waiting-period requirement facilitates budget predictability is wholly unfounded. The records in all three cases are utterly devoid of evidence [of use of] the one-year requirement as a means to predict the number of people who will require assistance in the budget year. * * *

The argument that the waiting period serves as an administratively efficient rule of thumb for determining residency similarly will not withstand scrutiny. [Before] granting an application, the welfare authorities investigate the applicant [and] in the course of the inquiry necessarily learn the facts upon which to determine whether the applicant is a resident.

Similarly, there is no need for a State to use the one-year waiting period as a safeguard against fraudulent receipt of benefits; for less drastic means are available, and are employed * * *.

Pennsylvania suggests that the one-year waiting period is justified as a means of encouraging new residents to join the labor force promptly. But this logic would also require a similar waiting period for long-term [residents.]

We conclude therefore that appellants [have] no need to use the one-year requirement for the governmental purposes suggested. Thus, even under tradi-

---

10. We are not dealing here with state insurance programs which may legitimately tie the amount of benefits to the individual's contributions.

tional equal protection tests [the classification] would seem irrational and unconstitutional. But [s]ince the classification here touches on the fundamental right of interstate movement, its constitutionality must be judged by the stricter standard of whether it promotes a *compelling* state interest. Under this standard, the waiting period requirement clearly violates the Equal Protection Clause.[21]

[The Court rejected the contention that Social Security Act § 402(b) approved imposition of one-year residence requirements. But] even if it could be argued that the constitutionality of § 402(b) is [in issue,] Congress may not authorize the States to violate the Equal Protection Clause. * * *

Affirmed.[a]

MR. CHIEF JUSTICE WARREN with whom MR. JUSTICE BLACK joins, dissenting.

[§ 402(b)] intended to authorize state residence requirements of up to one [year.] Congress, pursuant to its commerce power, has enacted a variety of restrictions upon interstate travel. It has taxed air and rail fares and [gasoline]. Many of the federal safety regulations of common carriers which cross state lines burden the right to travel. And Congress has prohibited by criminal statute interstate travel for certain purposes. * * *

The Court's right-to-travel cases lend little support to the view that congressional action is invalid merely because it burdens the right to travel. [Here], travel itself is not prohibited. Any burden inheres solely in the fact that a potential welfare recipient might take into consideration the loss of welfare benefits for a limited period of time if he changes his residence. Not only is this burden of uncertain degree,[5] but appellees themselves assert there is evidence that few welfare recipients have in fact been deterred by residence requirements.

The insubstantiality of the restriction imposed by residence requirements must then be evaluated in light of the possible congressional reasons for such requirements. [Given] the apprehensions of many States that an increase in benefits without minimal residence requirements would result in an inability to provide an adequate welfare system, Congress deliberately adopted the intermediate course of a cooperative program. [Our] cases require only that Congress have a rational basis for finding that a chosen regulatory scheme is necessary to the furtherance of interstate commerce. * * *

MR. JUSTICE HARLAN, dissenting. * * *

In upholding the equal protection argument, the Court has applied an equal protection doctrine of relatively recent vintage [—the] "compelling interest" doctrine [which constitutes] an increasingly significant exception to the long-established rule that a statute does not deny equal protection if it is rationally related to a legitimate governmental objective. The "compelling interest" doctrine has two branches. [The] "suspect" criteria [branch today] apparently has been further enlarged to include classifications based upon recent interstate movement, and perhaps those based upon the exercise of *any* constitutional [right].

---

21. We imply no view of the validity of waiting period *or* residence requirements determining eligibility to vote, [for] tuition-free education, to obtain a license to practice a profession, to hunt or fish, [etc. These] may promote compelling state interests on the one hand, or, on the other, may not be penalties upon the exercise of the constitutional right of interstate travel.

a. Stewart, J., joined the Court's opinion, emphasizing that "the Court simply recognizes" that the statutes impinge upon "the constitutional right of interstate travel."

5. [I]ndigents who are disqualified from categorical assistance by residence requirements are not left wholly without assistance. Each of the appellees in these cases found alternative sources of assistance * * *.

I think that this branch of the "compelling interest" doctrine is sound when applied to racial classifications, for historically the Equal Protection Clause was largely a product of the desire to eradicate legal distinctions founded upon race. However, I believe that the more recent extensions have been unwise. [When] a classification is based upon the exercise of rights guaranteed against state infringement by the federal Constitution, then there is no need for any resort to the Equal Protection Clause; in such instances, this Court may properly and straightforwardly invalidate any undue burden upon those rights under the Fourteenth Amendment's Due Process Clause.

The second branch of the "compelling interest" principle is even more troublesome. For it has been held that a statutory classification is subject to the "compelling interest" test if the result of the classification may be to affect a "fundamental right," regardless of the basis of the classification. This rule was foreshadowed in *Skinner* [and] re-emerged in *Reynolds v. Sims,* [again] in *Carrington v. Rash* [and] was also an alternate ground in *Harper* and apparently was a basis of the holding in *Williams v. Rhodes.* It has reappeared today in the Court's cryptic suggestion that the "compelling interest" test is applicable merely because the result of the classification may be to deny the appellees "food, shelter, and other necessities of life," as well as in the Court's statement that "[s]ince the classification here touches on the fundamental right of inter-state movement, its constitutionality must be judged by the stricter standard of whether it promotes a *compelling* state interest."

I think this branch [is] unfortunate because it creates an exception which threatens to swallow the standard equal protection rule. Virtually every state statute affects important rights. This Court has repeatedly held, for example, that the traditional equal protection standard is applicable to statutory classifi-cations affecting such fundamental matters as the right to pursue a particular occupation, the right to receive greater or smaller wages or to work more or less hours, and the right to inherit property. Rights such as these are in principle indistinguishable from those involved here, and to extend the "compelling interest" rule to all cases in which such rights are affected would go far toward making this Court a "super-legislature." This branch of the doctrine is also unnecessary. When the right affected is one assured by the federal Constitution, any infringement can be dealt with under the Due Process Clause. But when a statute affects only matters not mentioned in the federal Constitution and is not arbitrary or irrational, I must reiterate that I know of nothing which entitles this Court to pick out particular human activities, characterize them as "funda-mental," and give them added protection under an unusually stringent equal protection test. * * *

For reasons hereafter set forth, a legislature might rationally find that the imposition of a welfare residence requirement would aid in the accomplishment of at least four valid governmental objectives. It might also find that residence requirements have advantages not shared by other methods of achieving the same goals. [Thus], it cannot be said that the requirements are "arbitrary" or "lacking in rational justification." Hence, I can find no objection to these residence requirements under [equal protection].

The next issue [is] whether a one-year welfare residence requirement amounts to an undue burden upon the right of interstate travel [which I conclude] is a "fundamental" right [that] should be regarded as having its source in the Due Process Clause of the Fifth Amendment.

The next question is the decisive one: whether the governmental interests served by residence requirements outweigh the burden imposed upon the right to travel. In my view, [they do].

Notes and Questions

1. *Equal protection vs. due process.* If a state simply eliminated welfare, or granted lower payments than other states, would this "touch on the fundamental right of interstate movement" just as harshly as the programs in *Shapiro?* "Fence out indigents" at least as much? Would it be invalid under *Shapiro* "unless shown to be necessary to promote a *compelling* governmental interest"? See generally Harvith, *The Constitutionality of Residence Tests for General and Categorical Assistance Programs,* 54 Calif.L.Rev. 567, 593–95 (1966). Or does *Shapiro* deal only with "invidious distinctions between classes of citizens"? Does Harlan, J.'s contention—that "when the right affected is one assured by the Constitution, any infringement can be dealt with under the Due Process Clause"—render the *Shapiro* approach superfluous? Or does *Shapiro's* equal protection analysis add another dimension to the problem by distinguishing between the state interest needed to justify (a) reducing expenditures generally, and (b) reducing expenditures by denying benefits to recent travellers? See *Chicago Police Dep't. v. Mosley,* p. 643 supra. See generally Reinstein, *The Welfare Cases: Fundamental Rights, The Poor, and the Burden of Proof in Constitutional Litigation,* 44 Temp.L.Q. 1, 36–40 (1970); Choper, Kamisar & Tribe, *The Supreme Court: Trends and Developments 1978–1979,* 263–64, 311–12 (1979).

2. *Residence requirements.* (a) After *Shapiro,* may a state deny welfare assistance to transients who have no intention of remaining permanently in the state? Did *Shapiro* not really involve "the interest in freedom of travel" but rather "only the narrower interest in freedom of interstate migration"—i.e., to "resettle, find a new job, and start a new life"? See *Memorial Hosp. v. Maricopa Cty.,* note 3(b) infra.

(b) DOE v. BOLTON, p. 336 supra, invalidated the residency requirement of the Georgia abortion law: "Just as the Privileges and Immunities Clause, Art. IV, § 2, protects persons who enter other States to ply their trade, so must it protect persons who enter Georgia seeking the medical services that are available there. A contrary holding would mean that a State could limit to its own residents the general medical care available within its borders." Is *Doe* consistent with the analysis in note (a) supra? Compare *Carrington v. Rash,* Part I, B supra. On Art. IV, § 2, see generally Ch. 4, Sec. 1, VII.

(c) What of a residency requirement that affects both freedom of travel and freedom of interstate migration? McCARTHY v. PHILADELPHIA CIVIL SERVICE COMM'N, 424 U.S. 645, 96 S.Ct. 1154, 47 L.Ed.2d 366 (1976), per curiam—involving a Philadelphia fireman who was terminated when he moved to New Jersey—held that "a municipal regulation requiring employees of the city [to] be residents of the city" did not impair the "right to travel interstate as defined in *Shapiro,*" which questioned neither "the validity of a condition placed upon municipal employment that a person be a resident *at the time* of his application," [6] nor "the validity of appropriately defined and uniformly applied bona fide residence requirements." [b] Is *McCarthy* consistent with *Shapiro* and *Doe?*

(d) MARTINEZ v. BYNUM, 461 U.S. 321, 103 S.Ct. 1838, 75 L.Ed.2d 879 (1983), per POWELL, J., upheld Texas' denial of free public education to children who, apart from their parents or guardians, reside in the school district "for the

---

6. Nor did [it] involve a public agency's relationship with its own employees which, of course, may justify greater control than over the citizenry at large. Cf. *Pickering v. Board* of *Educ.* [p. 570 supra]; *Broadrick v. Oklahoma,* [p. 535 supra].

b. Burger, C.J., and Brennan and Blackmun, JJ., would set the case for argument.

sole purpose of attending" the public schools: "A bona fide residence requirement [with] respect to attendance in public free schools does not violate the Equal Protection Clause [7] [nor does it] burden or penalize the constitutional right of interstate travel, for any person is free to move to a State and to establish residence there. [A]t the very least, a school district generally would be justified in requiring school-age children or their parents to satisfy the traditional, basic residence criteria—i.e., to live in the district with a bona fide intention of remaining there—before it treated them as residents." Marshall, J., dissented, mainly on the ground that an "intention of remaining" is not a proper criterion for a bona fide residence requirement. Is *Martinez* consistent with *Shapiro* and *Doe?*

(e) May a state deny welfare to a person who has permanently left the state but who cannot obtain welfare elsewhere? CALIFANO v. TORRES, 435 U.S. 1, 98 S.Ct. 906, 55 L.Ed.2d 65 (1978), per curiam, upheld Social Security Act provisions, which made benefits available in the fifty states but not in Puerto Rico, as applied to U.S. residents who lost benefits when they moved to Puerto Rico. The lower court had "held that the Constitution requires that a person who travels to Puerto Rico must be given benefits superior to those enjoyed by other residents of Puerto Rico if the newcomer enjoyed those benefits in the State from which he came. This Court has never held that the constitutional right to travel embraces any such doctrine [which] would bid fair to destroy the independent power of each State [to] enact laws uniformly applicable to all of its residents." [c]

3. *Other waiting-period requirements.* (a) *Voting.* DUNN v. BLUMSTEIN, 405 U.S. 331, 92 S.Ct. 995, 31 L.Ed.2d 274 (1972), per MARSHALL, J., held that Tennessee's voting registration requirements—of residence in the state for one year and in the county for three months—violate equal protection. Although "States have the power to require that voters be bona fide residents of the relevant political subdivision," it is the "additional *durational* residence requirement which appellee challenges. [Here], whether we look to the benefit withheld by the classification (the opportunity to vote) or the basis for the classification (recent interstate travel)," the classification must be "*necessary* to promote a *compelling* governmental interest." [a]

(b) *Medical care.* MEMORIAL HOSPITAL v. MARICOPA COUNTY, 415 U.S. 250, 94 S.Ct. 1076, 39 L.Ed.2d 306 (1974), per MARSHALL, J., held an Arizona statute—requiring one year's residence in the county for indigents to receive nonemergency hospitalization or medical care at county expense—violative of equal protection: "Although any durational residence requirement impinges to some extent on the right to travel," *Shapiro* "did not declare such requirements to be per se unconstitutional." It is only a state classification that "operates to *penalize* [indigents] for exercising their right to migrate to and settle in that state" which "must be justified by a compelling state interest. [*Dunn*] found that the denial of the franchise, 'a fundamental political right,' was a penalty [and *Shapiro*] found denial of the basic 'necessities of life' to be a penalty.

---

7. A bona fide residence requirement implicates no "suspect" classification, and therefore is not subject to strict scrutiny. Indeed, there is nothing invidiously discriminatory about a bona fide residence requirement if it is uniformly applied. Thus the question is simply whether there is a rational basis for it.

This view assumes, of course, that the "service" that the State would deny to nonresidents is not a fundamental right protected by the Constitution. * * *

c. Brennan, J., dissented. Marshall, J., would have set the case for full argument.

a. Blackmun, J., concurred in the result. Powell and Rehnquist, JJ., did not participate. Burger, C.J., dissented.

Nonetheless, the Court has declined to strike down state statutes requiring one year of residence as a condition to lower tuition at state institutions of higher education.[12] Whatever the ultimate parameters of the *Shapiro* penalty analysis, it is at least clear that medical care is as much 'a basic necessity of life' to an indigent as welfare assistance." For reasons similar to those in *Shapiro*, the state has not met its "heavy burden of justification." [c]

REHNQUIST, J., dissented: "[F]ees for use of transportation facilities such as taxes on airport users,[12] have been upheld [against] attacks based upon the right to travel. [T]he line to be derived from our prior cases is that some financial impositions on interstate travelers have such indirect or inconsequential impact on travel that they simply do not constitute the type of direct purposeful barriers struck down" in *Shapiro*. "The solicitude which the Court has shown in cases involving the right to vote, and the virtual denial of entry inherent in denial of welfare benefits—'the very means by which to live'—ought not be so casually extended to the alleged deprivation here."

(c) *Divorce.* SOSNA v. IOWA, 419 U.S. 393, 95 S.Ct. 553, 42 L.Ed.2d 532 (1975), per REHNQUIST, J., upheld a one-year residency requirement to file for divorce: The laws in *Shapiro* and *Maricopa* "were justified on the basis of budgetary or record-keeping considerations which were held insufficient to outweigh the constitutional claims of the individuals. But Iowa's divorce residency requirement is of a different stripe. [A] decree of divorce [will] affect [both spouses'] marital status and very likely their property rights. Where a married couple has minor children, a decree of divorce would usually include provisions for their custody and support. With consequences of such moment riding on a divorce decree issued by its courts, Iowa may insist that one seeking to initiate such a proceeding have the modicum of attachment to the State required here." [d]

MARSHALL, J., joined by Brennan, J., dissented, relying on *Boddie v. Connecticut*, Part III infra: The right to divorce "is of such fundamental importance" that the law "penalizes interstate travel within the meaning of *Shapiro, Dunn*, and *Maricopa*. [The] Court has not only declined to apply the 'compelling interest' test to this case, it has conjured up possible justifications for the State's restriction in a manner much more akin to the lenient standard" of equal protection review. A "simple requirement of domicile—physical presence plus intent to remain—[would] remove the rigid one-year barrier while permitting the State to restrict the availability of its divorce process to citizens who are genuinely its own." [e]

(d) *The decisions' rationale.* Do the cases explain how the Court determines whether a "waiting-period" requirement "operates to *penalize*" the right to travel? In both *Dunn* and *Maricopa* the Court conceded "that there is no evidence in the record before us that anyone was actually deterred from traveling by the challenged restriction [but] *Shapiro* did not rest upon a finding that denial of welfare actually deterred travel. Nor have other 'right to travel' [cases] always relied on the presence of actual deterrence." Consider 88 Harv.L.

---

12. See *Vlandis v. Kline* [Sec. 5 infra].

c. Burger, C.J., and Blackmun, J., concurred in the result. Douglas, J., filed a separate opinion: "So far as interstate travel per se is considered, I share the doubts of my Brother Rehnquist. [Here,] invidious discrimination against the poor [is] the critical issue."

12. See *Evansville-Vanderburgh Airport Auth. Dist. v. Delta Airlines*, 405 U.S. 707, 92 S.Ct. 1349, 31 L.Ed.2d 620 (1972).

d. White, J., dissented on procedural grounds.

e. For the view that "durational residency requirements for state benefits and services are permissible only to the extent they respond to a reasonable concern for proof of domiciliary intent," see Cohen, *Equal Treatment for Newcomers: The Core Meaning of National and State Citizenship*, 1 Const.Comment. 9 (1984).

Rev. 117–18 (1974): "[T]he Court should consider the deterrent effect [rather] than attempt, as does Justice Marshall's 'penalty' analysis, to assess the importance of various state benefits to immigrants. Insofar as the validity of a given requirement depends upon the latter, what is being protected is not the right to travel, but the right to the withheld benefit."

4. *Length of residence requirements.* ZOBEL v. WILLIAMS, 457 U.S. 55, 102 S.Ct. 2309, 72 L.Ed.2d 672 (1982), per BURGER, C.J., held that Alaska's scheme of distributing its revenue from state-owned oil reserves to its citizens "in varying amounts, based on the length of each citizen's residence, violates the equal protection rights of newer state citizens." The Court held that two of Alaska's stated objectives—"creating a financial incentive for individuals to establish and maintain Alaska residence, and assuring prudent management of the [oil revenues] and the State's natural and mineral resources"—were "not rationally related to the distinctions Alaska seeks to draw." And, under *Shapiro,* the objective of rewarding "contributions of various kinds, both tangible and intangible, which residents have made during their years of residence," was "not a legitimate state purpose. [Such] reasoning could open the door to state apportionment of other rights, benefits and services according to length of residency. It would permit the states to divide citizens into expanding numbers of permanent classes. Such a result would be clearly impermissible."

BRENNAN, J., joined by Marshall, Blackmun and Powell, JJ., joined the Court's opinion, adding that "the Citizenship Clause of the Fourteenth Amendment [bars] degrees of citizenship based on length of residence. And the Equal Protection Clause would not tolerate such distinctions. In short, as much as the right to travel, equality of citizenship is of the essence in our republic. [Thus], discrimination on the basis of residence must be supported by a valid state interest independent of the discrimination itself. [L]ength of residence may, for example, be used to test the bona fides of citizenship—and allegiance and attachment may bear some rational relationship to a very limited number of legitimate state purposes. Cf. *Chimento v. Stark,* 353 F.Supp. 1211 (D.N.H.), affirmed, 414 U.S. 802, 94 S.Ct. 125, 38 L.Ed.2d 39 (1973) (seven year citizenship requirement to run for governor); U.S. Const., art. I, § 2, cl. 2, § 3, cl. 3; art. II, § 1, cl. 4. But those instances in which length of residence could provide a legitimate basis for distinguishing one citizen from another are rare."

O'CONNOR, J., concurred: "A desire to compensate citizens for their prior contributions is neither inherently invidious nor irrational. Under some circumstances, the objective may be wholly reasonable.[1] Even a generalized desire to reward citizens for past endurance, particularly in a State where years of hardship only recently have produced prosperity, is not innately improper. The difficulty is that plans enacted to further this objective necessarily treat new residents of a State less favorably than the longer-term residents who have past contributions to 'reward.' * * * Stripped to its essentials, the plan denies non-

---

1. A State, for example, might choose to divide its largesse among all persons who previously have contributed their time to volunteer community organizations. If the State graded its dividends according to the number of years devoted to prior community service, it could be said that the State intended "to reward citizens for past contributions." Alternatively, a State might enact a tax credit for citizens who contribute to the State's ecology by building alternative fuel sources or estab-lishing recycling plants. If the State made this credit retroactive, to benefit those citizens who launched these improvements before they became fashionable, the State once again would be rewarding past contributions. The Court's opinion would dismiss these objectives as wholly illegitimate. I would recognize them as valid goals and inquire only whether their implementation infringed any constitutionally protected interest.

Alaskans settling in the State the same privileges afforded longer-term residents. The Privileges and Immunities Clause of Article IV [addresses] just this type of discrimination.

" * * * I believe [that] application of the Privileges and Immunities Clause to controversies involving the 'right to travel' would at least begin the task of reuniting this elusive right with the constitutional principles it embodies. [I] conclude that Alaska's disbursement scheme violates [the] Privileges and Immunities Clause" because there is nothing "to indicate that noncitizens constitute a peculiar source of the evil at which the statute is aimed" and no " 'substantial relationship' between the evil and the discrimination practiced against the noncitizens. *Hicklin v. Orbeck,* [p. 235 supra]."

REHNQUIST, J., dissented: "[T]he illegitimacy of a State's recognizing past contributions of its citizens has been established by the Court only in certain cases considering an infringement of the right to travel, and the majority itself rightly declines to apply the strict scrutiny analysis of those right-to-travel cases. The distribution scheme at issue in this case impedes no person's right to travel to and settle in Alaska; if anything, the prospect of receiving annual cash dividends would encourage immigration to Alaska." [g]

III. DISCRIMINATORY IMPACT ON THE POOR IN THE LITIGATION PROCESS

Several Warren Court decisions (in addition to *Harper v. Virginia Bd. of Elec.,* Part I, B supra) held that state laws or practices that operated to the disadvantage of poor people—in contrast to "de jure" discrimination against the poor (Sec. 3, 1 supra)—violated equal protection (and/or due process). Most of these rulings, as well as those of the Burger Court following this path, concern the question of whether states must waive fees (or provide certain services without charge) to poor people who could not otherwise effectively participate in criminal or civil litigation. These decisions are the subject of this section. Other kinds of laws that have a disproportionate impact on the poor are considered in the section that follows.

GRIFFIN v. ILLINOIS, 351 U.S. 12, 76 S.Ct. 585, 100 L.Ed. 891 (1956), held that a state must furnish an indigent criminal defendant with a free trial transcript (or its equivalent) if it were necessary for "adequate and effective appellate review" of the conviction. BLACK, J., joined by Warren, C.J., and Douglas and Clark, JJ., found that "both equal protection and due process emphasize [that in] criminal trials a State can no more discriminate on account of poverty than on account of religion, race, or color. Plainly the ability to pay costs in advance bears no rational relationship to a defendant's guilt or innocence and could not be used as an excuse to deprive a defendant of a fair trial. [It] is true that a State is not required by the federal constitution to provide

---

g. See also *Hooper v. Bernalillo County Assessor,* ___ U.S. ___, 105 S.Ct. 2862, 86 L.Ed. 2d 487 (1985), per Burger, C.J., holding that a New Mexico property tax exemption for only those Vietnam veterans who were state residents before May 1976 "is not rationally related to the State's asserted legislative goal[s]," and thus "suffers the same constitutional flaw [as] *Zobel* ": "[T]he Equal Protection Clause [forbids] the State to prefer established resi-

dent veterans over newcomers in [the] apportionment of an economic benefit."

Stevens, J., joined by Rehnquist and O'Connor, JJ., dissented: The classification "rationally furthers a legitimate state purpose. [The] need to budget for the future is itself a valid reason for [a limit] on the size of potential beneficiaries."

appellate [review]. See, e.g., *McKane v. Durston,* 153 U.S. 684, 687–88, 14 S.Ct. 913, 914–15, 38 L.Ed. 687 (1894). But that is not to say that a State that does grant appellate review can do so in a way that discriminates against some convicted defendants on account of their poverty." [a]

———

DOUGLAS v. CALIFORNIA, 372 U.S. 353, 83 S.Ct. 814, 9 L.Ed.2d 811 (1963), per DOUGLAS, J., relying on *Griffin,* held that a state must appoint counsel for an indigent for "the first appeal, granted as a matter of [statutory right] from a criminal conviction." It disapproved California's system of appointing counsel only when the appellate court made "an independent investigation of the record and determine[d] it would be of advantage to the defendant or helpful to [the] court": "[A] state can, consistently with the Fourteenth Amendment, provide for differences so long as the result does not amount to a denial of due process or an 'invidious discrimination.' Absolute equality is not [required]. But where the merits of the one and only appeal an indigent has as of right are decided without benefit of counsel, we think an unconstitutional line has been drawn between rich and poor."

HARLAN, J., joined by Stewart, J., dissented from the Court's reliance, as in *Griffin,* "on a blend of the Equal Protection and Due Process Clauses," believing that "this case should be judged solely under the Due Process Clause": "States, of course, are prohibited by the Equal Protection Clause from discriminating between 'rich' and 'poor' *as such* in the formulation and application of their laws. But it is a far different thing to suggest that this provision prevents the State from adopting a law of general applicability that may affect the poor more harshly than it does the rich, or, on the other hand, from making some effort to redress economic imbalances while not eliminating them entirely.

"Every financial exaction which the State imposes on a uniform basis is more easily satisfied by the well-to-do than by the indigent. Yet I take it that no one would dispute the constitutional power of the State to levy a uniform sales tax, to charge tuition at a state university, to fix rates for the purchase of water from a municipal corporation, to impose a standard fine for criminal violations, or to establish minimum bail for various categories of offenses. Nor could it be contended that the State may not classify as crimes acts which the poor are more likely to commit than are the rich. And surely, there would be no basis for attacking a state law which provided benefits for the needy simply because those benefits fell short of the goods or services that others could purchase for themselves.

"Laws such as these do not deny equal protection to the less fortunate for one essential reason: the Equal Protection Clause does not impose on the States 'an affirmative duty to lift the handicaps flowing from differences in economic circumstances.' To so construe it would be to read into the Constitution a philosophy of leveling that would be foreign to many of our basic concepts of the proper relations between government and society. [N]o matter how far the state rule might go in providing counsel for indigents, it could never be expected to satisfy an affirmative duty—if one existed—to place the poor on the same level as those who can afford the best legal talent available."

As for due process, "we have today held [that] there is an absolute right to the services of counsel at trial. *Gideon v. Wainwright,* [p. 303 supra]. But

---

a. Frankfurter, J., concurred in the result. Burton, Minton, Reed and Harlan, JJ., dissented.

[a]ppellate review is in itself not required by the Fourteenth Amendment, [and] thus the question presented is the narrow one whether the State's rules with respect to the appointment of counsel are so arbitrary or unreasonable, *in the context of the particular appellate procedure that it has established,* as to require their invalidation." Clark, J., also dissented.

ROSS v. MOFFIT, 417 U.S. 600, 94 S.Ct. 2437, 41 L.Ed.2d 341 (1974), per REHNQUIST, J., held that *Douglas* does not require counsel for discretionary state appeals or for applications for review in the Supreme Court: As for due process, "it is clear that the State need not provide any appeal at all. The fact that an appeal *has* been provided does not automatically mean that a State then acts unfairly by refusing to provide counsel to indigent defendants at every stage of the way. Unfairness results only if indigents are singled out by the State and denied meaningful access to that system because of their poverty. That question is more profitably considered under an equal protection analysis [which] 'does not require absolute equality or precisely equal advantages,' [but] does require that the state appellate system be 'free of unreasoned distinctions' and that indigents have an adequate opportunity to present their claims fairly within the adversarial system.

"[P]rior to his seeking discretionary review in the State Supreme Court, [respondent's] claims 'had once been presented by a lawyer and passed upon by an [intermediate] appellate court.' *Douglas.* We do not believe that it can be said, therefore, that [respondent] is denied meaningful access to the North Carolina Supreme Court simply because the State does not appoint counsel to aid him in seeking review in that court. At that stage he will have, at the very least, [a record] of trial proceedings, a brief on his behalf in the Court of Appeals setting forth his claims of error, and in many cases an opinion by the Court of Appeals disposing of his case. These materials, supplemented by whatever submission respondent may make pro se, would appear to provide the Supreme Court of North Carolina with an adequate basis on which to base its [decision]." Douglas, J., joined by Brennan and Marshall, JJ., dissented.[c]

TATE v. SHORT, 401 U.S. 395, 91 S.Ct. 668, 28 L.Ed.2d 130 (1971): An indigent accumulated $425 in fines for traffic offenses. Texas law provided only for fines but required that those unable to pay be incarcerated to satisfy their fines at the rate of $5 per day. The Court, per BRENNAN, J., reversed: Equal protection " 'requires that the statutory ceiling placed on imprisonment for any substantive offense be the same for all defendants irrespective of their economic status.' *Williams v. Illinois,* 399 U.S. 235, 90 S.Ct. 2018, 26 L.Ed.2d 586 (1970). [Thus, Texas cannot] limit the punishment to payment of the fine if one is able to pay it, yet convert the fine into a prison term for an [indigent]. Imprisonment in such a case is not imposed to further any penal objective of the State. * * *

"There are, however, other alternatives [such as procedures for paying fines in installments] to which the State may constitutionally resort to serve its concededly valid interest in enforcing payment of fines. [O]ur decision [should not] be understood as precluding imprisonment as an enforcement method when alternative means are unsuccessful despite the defendant's reasonable efforts to

---

c. See also *Lassiter v. Department of Social Servs.,* 452 U.S. 18, 101 S.Ct. 2153, 68 L.Ed.2d 640 (1981) (due process does not *always* require appointment of counsel for indigent parents in state suit to terminate parental status).

satisfy the fines by those means; the determination of the constitutionality of [that] must await the presentation of a concrete case." Black, J., concurred in the result.[a]

BEARDEN v. GEORGIA, 461 U.S. 660, 103 S.Ct. 2064, 76 L.Ed.2d 221 (1983), per O'CONNOR, J.,—noting that "due process and equal protection principles converge in these cases"—held that "it is fundamentally unfair" to "revoke a defendant's probation for failure to pay the imposed fine and restitution, absent evidence and findings that the defendant was somehow responsible for the failure or that alternative forms of punishment were inadequate": Probation "reflects a determination by the sentencing court that the State's penological interests do not require imprisonment. A probationer's failure to make reasonable efforts to repay his debt to society may indicate that this original determination needs reevaluation, [but 'only if alternate measures' such as 'extend[ing] the time for making payments, or reduc[ing] the fine, or direct[ing] that the probationer perform some form of labor or public service in lieu of the fine'] are not adequate to meet the State's interests in punishment and deterrence may the court imprison a probationer who has made sufficient bona fide efforts to pay."[b]

BODDIE v. CONNECTICUT, 401 U.S. 371, 91 S.Ct. 780, 28 L.Ed.2d 113 (1971), per HARLAN, J., sustained indigents' challenge to the state's requiring court fees and costs (averaging $60) in order to sue for divorce: "[M]arriage involves interests of basic importance in our society. [Without] a prior judicial imprimatur, individuals may freely enter into and rescind commercial contracts, for example, but we are unaware of any jurisdiction where private citizens may covenant for or dissolve marriages without state approval. [Thus], although they assert here due process rights as would-be plaintiffs, we think appellants' plight [is] akin to that of defendants faced with exclusion from the only forum effectively empowered to settle their disputes. [D]ue process requires, at a minimum, that absent a countervailing state interest of overriding significance, persons forced to settle their claims of right and duty through the judicial process must be given a meaningful opportunity to be heard."[d]

UNITED STATES v. KRAS, 409 U.S. 434, 93 S.Ct. 631, 34 L.Ed.2d 626 (1973), per BLACKMUN, J., held that the Bankruptcy Act's conditioning the right to discharge on payment of $50 fees does not violate fifth amendment due process, including "equal protection": "[A] debtor, in theory, and often in actuality, may adjust his debts by negotiated agreement with his creditors. [Thus,] *Boddie's* emphasis on [judicial] exclusivity finds no counterpart in the bankrupt's situation." Moreover, unlike free speech or marriage, bankruptcy is not a "fundamental" right demanding "the lofty requirement of a compelling governmental interest before [it] may be significantly regulated." Bankruptcy

a. Harlan, J., concurred on the basis of his concurrence in *Williams* where he "dissociated" himself from the Court's "equal protection rationale" which, if "fully realized," "would require that the consequence of punishment be the same for all individuals."

b. White, J., joined by Burger, C.J., and Powell and Rehnquist, JJ., concurred on the ground that the sentencing judge had "auto-

matically" imposed a "long prison term" rather than making "a good-faith effort to impose a jail sentence that in terms of the state's sentencing objectives will be roughly equivalent to the fine and restitution that the defendant failed to pay."

d. Douglas, J., and Brennan, J., concurred, but relied on the equal protection rationale of *Griffin*. Black, J., dissented.

legislation "is in the area of economics and social welfare. See *Dandridge v. Williams* [Part IV infra]." Thus, the standard is "rational justification"—and "the rational basis for the fee requirement is readily apparent": Congress' desire "to make the system self-sustaining and paid for by those who use [it]."

STEWART, J., joined by Douglas, Brennan and Marshall, JJ., dissented: "The bankrupt is bankrupt precisely for the reason that the State stands ready to exact all of his debts through garnishment, attachment, and the panoply of other creditor remedies. [I]n the unique situation of the indigent bankrupt the government provides the only effective means of his ever being free of these government imposed obligations. [While] the creditors of a bankrupt with assets might well desire to reach a compromise settlement, that possibility is foreclosed to the truly indigent bankrupt. [The] Court today holds that Congress may say that some of the poor are too poor even to go bankrupt." [e]

LITTLE v. STREATER, 452 U.S. 1, 101 S.Ct. 2202, 68 L.Ed.2d 627 (1981), per BURGER, C.J., held violative of due process Connecticut's refusal to pay the cost of blood grouping tests for indigent defendants in paternity actions. The Court stressed "the unique quality of blood grouping tests as a source of exculpatory evidence, the State's prominent role in the litigation,"—since the child was receiving welfare state law required the mother to institute the paternity action—"the 'quasi-criminal' overtones" of paternity proceedings, and the fact that state law made the defendant's testimony alone "insufficient to overcome the plaintiff's prima facie case": "Because appellant has no choice of an alternative forum and his interests, as well as those of the child, are constitutionally significant, this case is comparable to *Boddie* rather than to *Kras* and *Ortwein*."

IV. CONFINEMENT OF "FUNDAMENTAL RIGHTS"

DANDRIDGE v. WILLIAMS, 397 U.S. 471, 90 S.Ct. 1153, 25 L.Ed.2d 491 (1970): Maryland's Aid to Families with Dependent Children program gave most eligible families their computed "standard of need," but imposed a "maximum limitation" on the total amount any family could receive. The Court, per STEWART, J., held this did not violate equal protection: "[H]ere we deal with state regulation in the social and economic field, not affecting freedoms guaranteed by the Bill of Rights, and claimed to violate the Fourteenth Amendment only because the regulation results in some disparity in grants of welfare payments to the largest AFDC families.[16] In [this area] a State does not violate [equal protection] merely because the classifications made by its laws are imperfect." "It is enough that the State's action be rationally based and free from invidious discrimination. [T]he intractable economic, social, and even philosophical problems presented by public welfare assistance programs are not the business of this Court."

MARSHALL, J., joined by Brennan, J., dissented: [a] "[T]he only distinction between those children with respect to whom assistance is granted and those

---

e. Douglas, J., joined by Brennan, J., as well as Marshall, J., also dissented.

See also *Ortwein v. Schwab*, 410 U.S. 656, 93 S.Ct. 1172, 35 L.Ed.2d 572 (1973), upholding a requirement that indigents appealing an adverse decision in a welfare hearing pay a $25 state appellate court filing fee.

16. Cf. *Shapiro*, where, by contrast, the Court found state interference with the constitutionally protected freedom of interstate travel.

a. Douglas, J., dissented on the ground (agreed to also by Marshall and Brennan, JJ.)

[denied] is the size of the family into which the child permits himself to be born. [This] is grossly underinclusive in terms of the class which the AFDC program was designed to assist, namely *all* needy dependent children, [and requires] a persuasive justification * * *.

"The Court never undertakes to inquire for such a justification; rather it avoids the task by focusing upon the abstract dichotomy between two different approaches to equal protection problems which have been utilized by this Court.

"[The] cases relied on by the Court, in which a 'mere rationality' test was actually used, e.g., *Williamson v. Lee Optical Co.* [Sec. 1 supra], [involve] regulation of business interests. The extremes to which the Court has gone in dreaming up rational bases for state regulation in that area may in many instances be ascribed to a healthy revulsion from the Court's earlier excesses in using the Constitution to protect interests which have more than enough power to protect themselves in the legislative halls.[b] This case, involving the literally vital interests of a powerless minority—poor families without breadwinners—is far removed from the area of business regulation, as the Court concedes.[c]

* * *

"In my view, equal protection analysis of this case is not appreciably advanced by the a priori definition of a 'right,' fundamental [and thus invoking the "compelling" test] or otherwise. Rather, concentration must be placed upon the character of the classification in question, the relative importance to individuals in the class discriminated against of the governmental benefits which they do not receive, and the asserted state interests in support of the classification.

* * *

"It is the individual interests here [that] most clearly distinguish this case from the 'business regulation' [cases]. AFDC support to needy dependent children provides the stuff which sustains those children's lives: food, clothing, shelter. [G]overnmental discrimination between children on the basis of a factor over which they have no control [bears] some resemblance to the classification between legitimate and illegitimate children which we condemned [in Sec. 3, III supra]."

---

that the Maryland law was inconsistent with the Social Security Act.

b. Compare Wilkinson, *The Supreme Court, the Equal Protection Clause, and the Three Faces of Constitutional Equality,* 61 Va. L.Rev. 945, 1008–09 (1975): "*Lochner* and cases like it arose precisely because business was not getting its way, because what were then thought traditional employer prerogatives were succumbing to a rising tide of social and regulatory legislation. Conversely, [the] legislative trend ever since the New Deal has been running more and more toward social welfare programs, [whose] stated purpose is to help the poor and less well off. Indiscriminate application of [Marshall, J.'s] position, therefore, would invite the thought that the major change since *Lochner* is that the Court has switched political sides."

c. Compare Winter, *Poverty, Economic Equality, and the Equal Protection Clause,*

1972 Sup.Ct.Rev. 41, 100–01: "All economic regulation involves the allocation of scarce resources and the distribution of income. One may prefer one kind [over] another kind, but the judgment must be based on personal [values. In] constitutional principle the issues are indivisible. Consider a state minimum wage law. Invalidation of such a law by the Court would surely be considered an illegitimate exercise of substantive due process because what is involved is labeled the '[r]egulation of business or industry.' Many believe such laws help the poor. Most economists [disagree]. Spelling out a 'suspect classification'/'fundamental interest' argument to invalidate such a law would be child's play to a judge whose policy preferences impel him in that direction."

On examination, the asserted state interests were either "arbitrary," impermissible, of "minimum rationality," "drastically overinclusive," or "grossly underinclusive."

LINDSEY v. NORMET, 405 U.S. 56, 92 S.Ct. 862, 31 L.Ed.2d 36 (1972), per WHITE, J., employing the "traditional" equal protection standard, upheld an Oregon statute permitting a landlord to bring an expedited action for possession under certain circumstances. The Court rejected the contention "that the 'need for decent shelter' and the 'right to retain peaceful possession of one's home' are fundamental interests which are particularly important to the poor and which may be trenched upon only after the State demonstrates some superior interest": "We do not denigrate the importance of decent, safe and sanitary housing. But the Constitution does not provide judicial remedies for every social and economic ill. We are unable to perceive in that document any constitutional guarantee of access to dwellings of a particular quality or any recognition of the right of a tenant to occupy the real property of his landlord beyond the term of his [lease]. Absent constitutional mandate, the assurance of adequate housing and the definition of landlord-tenant relationships are legislative not judicial functions." Douglas, J., dissented on due process grounds; Brennan, J., dissented on procedural grounds; Powell and Rehnquist, JJ., did not participate.

SAN ANTONIO IND. SCHOOL DIST. v. RODRIGUEZ

411 U.S. 1, 93 S.Ct. 1278, 36 L.Ed.2d 16 (1973).

MR. JUSTICE POWELL delivered the opinion of the Court.

This suit attacking the Texas system of financing public education was initiated by Mexican-American parents [as] a class action on behalf of school children throughout the State who are members of minority groups or who are poor and reside in school districts having a low property tax base. * * *

Recognizing the need for increased state funding to help offset disparities in local spending [because of sizable differences in the value of assessable property between local school districts,] the state legislature [established the] Minimum Foundation School Program [which] accounts for approximately half of the total educational expenditures in Texas. [It] calls for state and local contributions to a fund earmarked specifically for teacher salaries, operating expenses, and transportation costs. The State [finances] approximately [80%]. The districts' share, known as the Local Fund Assignment, is apportioned among the school districts under a formula designed to reflect each district's relative taxpaying ability. * * *

The school district in which appellees reside, [Edgewood,] has been compared throughout this litigation with the Alamo Heights [District. Edgewood] is situated in the core-city sector of San Antonio in a residential neighborhood that has little commercial or industrial property. [A]pproximately 90% of the student population is Mexican-American and over 6% is Negro. The average assessed property value per pupil is $5,960—the lowest in the metropolitan area—and the median family income ($4,686) is also the lowest. At an equalized tax rate of $1.05 per $100 of assessed property—the highest in the metropolitan area—the district contributed $26 to the education of each child for the 1967–1968 school year above its Local Fund Assignment for the Minimum Foundation Program. The Foundation Program contributed $222 per pupil for a state-local total of $248. Federal funds added another $108 for a total of $356 per pupil.

Alamo Heights is the most affluent school district in San Antonio. [Its] school population [has] only 18% Mexican-Americans and less than 1% Negroes. The assessed property value per pupil exceeds $49,000 and the median family income is $8,001. In 1967–1968 the local tax rate of $.85 per $100 of valuation yielded $333 per pupil over and above its contribution to the Foundation Program. Coupled with the $225 provided from that Program, the district was able to supply $558 per student. Supplemented by a $36 per pupil grant from federal sources, Alamo Heights spent $594 per pupil.

[M]ore recent partial statistics indicate that [the] trend of increasing state aid has been significant. For the 1970–1971 school year, the Foundation School Program allotment for Edgewood was $356 per [pupil and] Alamo Heights [received] $491 per [pupil].[35] These recent figures also reveal the extent to which these two districts' allotments were funded from their own required contributions to the Local Fund Assignment. Alamo Heights, because of its relative wealth, was required to contribute out of its local property tax collections approximately $100 per pupil, or about 20% of its Foundation grant. Edgewood, on the other hand, paid only $8.46 per pupil, which is about 2.4% of its [grant.]

II. [The] wealth discrimination discovered [is] quite unlike any of the forms of wealth discrimination heretofore reviewed by this Court. [The] individuals who constituted the class discriminated against in our prior cases shared two distinguishing characteristics: because of their impecunity they were completely unable to pay for some desired benefit, and as a consequence, they sustained an absolute deprivation of a meaningful opportunity to enjoy that benefit [discussing *Griffin v. Illinois* and *Bullock v. Carter*]. *Douglas v. California* [provides] no relief for those on whom the burdens of paying for a criminal defense are, relatively speaking, great but not insurmountable. Nor does it deal with relative differences in the quality of counsel acquired by the less wealthy. [And] *Williams* and *Tate* [do] not touch on the question whether equal protection is denied to persons with relatively less money on whom designated fines impose heavier burdens. * * *

[Even] a cursory examination however, demonstrates that neither of the two distinguishing characteristics of wealth classifications can be found here. First, [there] is reason to believe that the poorest families are not necessarily clustered in the poorest property districts. A [recent] Connecticut study found, not surprisingly, that the poor were clustered around commercial and industrial areas—those same areas that provide the most attractive sources of property tax income for school districts. Whether a similar pattern would be discovered in Texas is not known, but there is no basis on the record [for] assuming [otherwise].

Second, [lack] of personal resources has not occasioned an absolute deprivation of the desired benefit. The argument here is not that the children [are]

---

35. [I]t is apparent that Alamo Heights has enjoyed a larger gain [due] to the emphasis in the State's allocation formula on the guaranteed minimum salaries for teachers. Higher salaries are guaranteed to teachers having more years of experience and possessing more advanced degrees. Therefore, Alamo Heights, which has a greater percentage of experienced personnel with advanced degrees, receives more State support. * * * Because more dollars have been given to districts that al-ready spend more per pupil, such Foundation formulas have been described as "anti-equalizing." The formula, however, is anti-equalizing only if viewed in absolute terms. The percentage disparity between the two Texas districts is diminished substantially by State aid. Alamo Heights derived in 1967–1968 almost 13 times as much money from local taxes as Edgewood did. The State aid grants to each district in 1970–1971 lowered the ratio to approximately two to [one].

receiving no public education; rather, it is that they are receiving a poorer quality education [than] children in districts having more assessable wealth. [A] sufficient answer to appellees' argument is that at least where wealth is involved the Equal Protection Clause does not require absolute equality or precisely equal advantages. Nor indeed, in view of the infinite variables affecting the educational process, can any system assure equal quality of education except in the most relative sense. Texas asserts that the Minimum Foundation Program provides an "adequate" education for all children in the State. [No] proof was offered at trial persuasively discrediting or refuting the State's assertion.[60]

This brings us [to] the third way in which the classification scheme might be defined—*district* wealth discrimination. Since the only correlation indicated by the evidence is between district property wealth and expenditures, it may be argued that discrimination might be found without regard to the individual income characteristics of district residents. * * *

However described, it is clear that appellees' suit asks this Court to extend its most exacting scrutiny to review a system that allegedly discriminates against a large, diverse, and amorphous class, unified only by the common factor of residence in districts that happen to have less taxable wealth than other districts. The system of alleged discrimination and the class it defines have none of the traditional indicia of suspectness: the class is not saddled with such disabilities, or subjected to such a history of purposeful unequal treatment, or relegated to such a position of political powerlessness as to command extraordinary protection from the majoritarian political process.

We thus conclude that the Texas system does not operate to the peculiar disadvantage of any suspect class. But [recognizing] that this Court has never heretofore held that wealth discrimination alone provides an adequate basis for invoking strict scrutiny, appellees [also] assert that the State's system impermissibly interferes with the exercise of a "fundamental" right [requiring] the strict standard of judicial review. * * *

Nothing this Court holds today in any way detracts from our historic dedication to public education. [But] the importance of a service performed by the State does not determine whether it must be regarded as fundamental for purposes of examination under the Equal Protection Clause. [In *Shapiro,* the] right to interstate travel had long been recognized as a right of constitutional significance, and the Court's decision therefore did not require an ad hoc determination as to the social or economic importance of that right. *Lindsey* [as well as *Dandridge*] firmly reiterates that social importance is not the critical determinant for subjecting state legislation to strict scrutiny. * * *

The lesson of these cases [is that it] is not the province of this Court to create substantive constitutional rights in the name of guaranteeing equal protection of the laws. Thus the key to discovering whether education is "fundamental" is not to be found in comparisons of the relative societal significance of education as opposed to subsistence or housing [or] by weighing whether education is as important as the right to travel. Rather, the answer lies in assessing whether

---

60. [If] elementary and secondary education were made available by the State only to those able to pay a tuition assessed against each pupil, there would be a clearly defined class of "poor" people—definable in terms of their inability to pay the prescribed sum—who would be absolutely precluded from receiving an education. That case would present a far more compelling set of circumstances for judicial assistance than [this one].

there is a right to education explicitly or implicitly guaranteed by the Constitution. *Dunn;*[74] *Skinner.*[76]

Education, of course, is not among the rights afforded explicit protection under [the] Constitution. Nor do we find any basis for saying it is implicitly so protected.[a] [But] appellees [contend] that education is distinguishable from other services and benefits provided by the State because it bears a peculiarly close relationship to other rights and liberties accorded protection under the Constitution [in that] it is essential to the effective exercise of First Amendment freedoms and to intelligent utilization of the right to vote. In asserting a nexus between speech and education, appellees urge that the right to speak is meaningless unless the speaker is capable of articulating his thoughts intelligently and persuasively. [A] similar line of reasoning is pursued with respect to the right to [vote]: a voter cannot cast his ballot intelligently unless his reading skills and thought processes have been adequately developed.

We need not dispute any of these propositions. [Yet] we have never presumed to possess either the ability or the authority to guarantee to the citizenry the most *effective* speech or the most *informed* electoral choice. That these may be desirable goals [is] not to be doubted. [But] they are not values to be implemented by judicial intrusion into otherwise legitimate state activities.

Even if it were conceded that some identifiable quantum of education is a constitutionally protected prerequisite to the meaningful exercise of either right, we have no indication that the [present] system fails to provide each child with an opportunity to acquire the basic minimal skills [necessary]. Furthermore, the logical limitations on appellees' nexus theory are difficult * * *. Empirical examination might well buttress an assumption that the ill-fed, ill-clothed, and ill-housed are among the most ineffective participants in the political process and that they derive the least enjoyment from the benefits of the First Amendment. * * *

[The] present case, in another basic sense, is significantly different from any of the cases in which the Court has applied strict scrutiny [to] legislation touching upon constitutionally protected rights. [These] involved legislation which "deprived," "infringed," or "interfered" with the free exercise of some such fundamental personal right or liberty. [Every] step leading to the establishment of the system Texas utilizes today [was] implemented in an effort to *extend* public education and to improve its quality. Of course, every reform that benefits some more than others may be criticized for what it fails to accomplish. But we think it plain that, in substance, the thrust of the Texas system is

---

74. *Dunn* fully canvasses this Court's voting rights cases and explains that "this Court has made clear that a citizen has a *constitutionally protected right* to participate in elections on an equal basis with other citizens in the jurisdiction." (emphasis supplied) The constitutional underpinnings of [this right] can no longer be doubted even though, as the Court noted in *Harper,* "the right to vote in state elections is nowhere expressly mentioned."

76. *Skinner* applied the standard of close scrutiny to a state law permitting forced sterilization of "habitual criminals." Implicit in the Court's opinion is the recognition that the right of procreation is among the rights of personal privacy protected under the Constitution. See *Roe v. Wade.*

a. For the view that education *is* "fundamental," see Coons, Clune & Sugarman, *Educational Opportunity: A Workable Constitutional Test for State Financial Structures,* 57 Calif.L.Rev. 305 (1969). As to housing, see Sager, *Tight Little Islands: Exclusionary Zoning, Equal Protection, and the Indigent,* 21 Stan.L.Rev. 767 (1969). As to various municipal services, see Ratner, *Inter-Neighborhood Denials of Equal Protection in the Provision of Municipal Services,* 4 Harv.Civ.Rts.—Civ.Lib. L.Rev. 1 (1968); Abascal, *Municipal Services and Equal Protection: Variations on a Theme by Griffin v. Illinois,* 20 Hast.L.J. 1367 (1969).

Massachusetts Bd. of Retirement v. Murgia (1976), Sec. 3, I supra, held that a "right of governmental employment" is *not* fundamental.

affirmative and reformatory and, therefore, should be scrutinized under judicial principles sensitive to the nature of the State's efforts and to the rights reserved to the States under the Constitution.

[A] century of Supreme Court adjudication under the Equal Protection Clause affirmatively supports the application of the traditional standard of review, which requires only that the State's system be shown to bear some rational relationship to legitimate state purposes. This case represents [a] direct attack on the way in which Texas has chosen to raise and disburse state and local tax revenues. [This] Court has often admonished against such interferences with the State's fiscal policies under the Equal Protection Clause [and] we continue to acknowledge that the Justices of this Court lack both the expertise and the familiarity with local problems so necessary to the making of wise decisions with respect to the raising and disposition of public revenues. Yet we are urged to direct the States either to alter drastically the present system or to throw out the property tax altogether in favor of some other form of taxation. No scheme of taxation [has] yet been devised which is free of all discriminatory impact. In such a complex arena in which no perfect alternatives exist, the Court does well not to impose too rigorous a standard of scrutiny lest all local fiscal schemes become subjects of criticism under the Equal Protection Clause.

[T]his case also involves the most persistent and difficult questions of educational policy, another area in which this Court's lack of specialized knowledge and experience counsels against premature interference with the informed judgments made at the state and local levels. [On] even the most basic questions in this area the scholars and educational experts are divided. Indeed, one of the hottest sources of controversy concerns the extent to which there is a demonstrable correlation between educational expenditures and the quality of education—an assumed correlation underlying virtually every legal conclusion drawn by the District [Court].

It must be remembered also that every claim arising under the Equal Protection Clause has implications for the relationship between national and state power under our federal system. [I]t would be difficult to imagine a case having a greater potential impact on our federal system than the one now before us, in which we are urged to abrogate systems of financing public education presently in existence in virtually every State. * * *

III. [The] State's contribution, under the Minimum Foundation Program, was designed to provide an adequate minimum educational offering in every school in the State. [T]o fulfill its local Fund Assignment, every district must impose an ad valorem tax on property located within its borders. The Fund Assignment was designed to remain sufficiently low to assure that each district would have some ability to provide a more enriched educational program. [In] large measure, these additional local revenues are devoted to paying higher salaries to more teachers. Therefore, the primary distinguishing attributes of schools in property-affluent districts are lower pupil-teacher ratios and higher salary schedules.[101] [In] part, local control [means] freedom to devote more money to the education of one's children. Equally important, however, is the opportunity it offers for participation in the decision-making process that determines how those local tax dollars will be spent. [No] area of social concern

---

101. [As] previously noted, the extent to which the quality of education varies with expenditure per pupil is debated inconclusively by the most thoughtful students of public education. While all would agree that there is a correlation up to the point of providing the recognized essentials, [the] issues of greatest disagreement include the effect on the quality of education of pupil-teacher ratios and of higher teacher [salaries].

stands to profit more from a multiplicity of viewpoints and from a diversity of approaches than does public education.

[While] it is no doubt true that reliance on local property taxation for school revenues provides less freedom of choice with respect to expenditures for some districts than for others,[107] the existence of "some inequality" in the manner in which the State's rationale is achieved is not alone a sufficient basis for striking down the entire system. [Nor] must the financing system fail because, as appellees suggest, other methods of satisfying the State's interest, which occasion "less drastic" disparities in expenditures, might be conceived. Only where state action impinges on the exercise of fundamental constitutional rights or liberties must it be found to have chosen the least restrictive alternative. It is also well to remember that even those districts that have reduced ability to make free decisions with respect to how much they spend on education still retain under the present system a large measure of authority as to how available funds will be allocated. They further enjoy the power to make numerous other decisions with respect to the operation of the schools.[108] The people of Texas may be justified in believing [that] along with increased control of the purse strings at the state level will go increased control over local policies.

[A]ny scheme of local taxation—indeed the very existence of identifiable local governmental units—requires the establishment of jurisdictional boundaries that are inevitably arbitrary. It is equally inevitable that some localities are going to be blessed with more taxable assets than others. Nor is local wealth a static quantity. Changes [may] result from any number of events, some of which local residents can and do influence. For instance, commercial and industrial enterprises may be encouraged to locate within a district by various actions—public and private.

Moreover, if local taxation for local expenditure is an unconstitutional method of providing for education then it may be an equally impermissible means of providing other necessary services customarily financed largely from local property taxes, including local police and fire protection, public health and hospitals, and public utility facilities of various kinds. [It has] never been within the constitutional prerogative of this Court to nullify statewide measures for financing public services merely because the burdens or benefits thereof fall unevenly depending upon the relative wealth of the political subdivisions in which citizens live.

[In] its essential characteristics the Texas plan for financing public education reflects what many educators for a half century have thought was an

---

107. Mr. Justice White suggests in his dissent that the Texas system violates [equal protection] because the means it has selected to effectuate its interest in local autonomy fail to guarantee complete freedom of choice to every district. He places special emphasis on the statutory provision that establishes a maximum rate of $1.50 per $100 valuation at which a local school district may tax for school maintenance. The maintenance rate in Edgewood when this case was litigated [was] $.55 per $100, barely one-third of the allowable rate. (The tax rate of $1.05 per $100 is the equalized rate for maintenance and for the retirement of bonds.) Appellees do not claim that the ceiling presently bars desired tax increases in Edgewood or in any

other Texas district. Therefore, the constitutionality of that statutory provision is not before [us].

108. Mr. Justice Marshall['s] assertion, that genuine local control does not exist in Texas, simply cannot be supported. It is abundantly refuted by the elaborate statutory division of responsibilities set out in the Texas Education Code. Although policy decision-making and supervision in certain areas are reserved to the State, the day-to-day authority over the "management and control" of all public elementary and secondary schools is squarely placed on the local school boards [listing a number of their specific powers].

enlightened approach to a problem for which there is no perfect solution. We are unwilling to assume for ourselves a level of wisdom superior to that of legislators, scholars, and educational authorities in 49 States, especially where the alternatives proposed are only recently conceived and nowhere yet tested.

* * *

IV. [T]his Court's action today is not to be viewed as placing its judicial imprimatur on the status quo. The need is apparent for reform in tax systems which may well have relied too long and too heavily on the local property tax. And certainly innovative new thinking as to public education, its methods and its funding, is necessary to assure both a higher level of quality and greater uniformity of opportunity. These matters merit the continued attention of the scholars who already have contributed much by their challenges. But the ultimate solutions must come from the lawmakers and from the democratic pressures of those who elect them.

Reversed.[b]

MR. JUSTICE BRENNAN, dissenting.

Although I agree with my Brother White that the Texas statutory scheme is devoid of any rational basis, [I] also record my disagreement with the Court's rather distressing assertion that a right may be deemed "fundamental" for the purposes of equal protection analysis only if it is "explicitly or implicitly guaranteed by the Constitution." As my Brother Marshall convincingly demonstrates our prior cases stand for the proposition that "fundamentality" is, in large measure, a function of the right's importance in terms of the effectuation of those rights which are in fact constitutionally guaranteed. * * *

MR. JUSTICE WHITE, with whom MR. JUSTICE DOUGLAS and MR. JUSTICE BRENNAN join, dissenting.

[T]his case would be quite different if it were true that the Texas system, while insuring minimum educational expenditures in every district through state funding, extends a meaningful option to all local districts to increase their per-pupil [expenditures. But for] districts with a low per-pupil real estate tax base [the] Texas system utterly fails to extend a realistic choice to parents, because the property tax, which is the only revenue-raising mechanism extended to school districts, is practically and legally unavailable. * * *

In order to equal the highest yield in any other Bexar County district, Alamo Heights would be required to tax at the rate of 68¢ per $100 of assessed valuation. Edgewood would be required to tax at the prohibitive rate of $5.76 per $100. But state law places a $1.50 per $100 ceiling on the maintenance tax [rate]. Requiring the State to establish only that unequal treatment is in furtherance of a permissible goal, without also requiring the State to show that the means chosen to effectuate that goal are rationally related to its achievement, makes equal protection analysis no more than an empty gesture. * * *

MR. JUSTICE MARSHALL, with whom MR. JUSTICE DOUGLAS, concurs, dissenting.

[T]he majority's holding can only be seen as a retreat from our historic commitment to equality of educational opportunity. [The issue] is not whether Texas is doing its best to ameliorate the worst features of a discriminatory scheme, but rather whether the scheme itself is in fact unconstitutionally discriminatory.[35] Authorities concerned with educational quality no doubt

---

b. The concurring opinion of Stewart, J., who joined the Court's opinion, is omitted.

35. * * * Texas' financing scheme is hardly remedial legislation of the type for which we have previously shown substantial tolerance. Such legislation may in fact extend the vote to "persons who otherwise would be denied it by state law," *Katzenbach v. Mor-*

disagree as to the significance of variations in per pupil spending. [But it] is an inescapable fact that if one district has more funds available per pupil than another district, the former will have greater choice in educational [planning].

At the very least, in view of the substantial interdistrict disparities in funding, [the] burden of proving that these disparities do not in fact affect the quality of children's education must fall upon the appellants. Yet [they] have argued no more than that the relationship is ambiguous. * * *

Nor can I accept the appellants' apparent suggestion [that equal protection] cannot be offended by substantially unequal state treatment of persons who are similarly situated so long as the State provides everyone with some unspecified amount of education which evidently is "enough." [The] Equal Protection Clause is not addressed to the minimal sufficiency but rather to the unjustifiable inequalities of state action. [Even] if the Equal Protection Clause encompassed some theory of constitutional adequacy, discrimination in the provision of educational opportunity would certainly seem to be a poor candidate for its application. Neither the majority nor appellants informs us how judicially manageable standards are to be derived for determining how much education is "enough" to excuse constitutional discrimination. [In] light of the data introduced before the District Court, the conclusion that the school children of property poor districts constitute a sufficient class for our purposes seems indisputable to me. [Whether] this discrimination, against [them] is violative of the Equal Protection Clause is the question to which we must now turn.

[The] Court apparently seeks to establish [that] equal protection cases fall into one of two neat categories which dictate the appropriate standard of review—strict scrutiny or mere rationality. But [a] principled reading of what this Court has done reveals that it has applied a spectrum of standards [which] clearly comprehends variations in the degree of care with which the Court will scrutinize particular classifications, depending [on] the constitutional and societal importance of the interest adversely affected and the recognized invidiousness of the basis upon which the particular classification is drawn.[c] * * *

I therefore cannot accept the majority's labored efforts to demonstrate that fundamental interests, which call for strict scrutiny of the challenged classification, encompass only established rights which we are somehow bound to recognize from the text of the Constitution itself. * * *[59]

I would like to know where the Constitution guarantees the right to procreate, *Skinner,* or the right to vote in state elections, e.g., *Reynolds v. Sims,*[60] or the right to an appeal from a criminal conviction, e.g., *Griffin.*[61]

---

gan, or it may eliminate the evils of the private bail bondsman, *Schilb v. Kuebel* [Part I, B supra]. But those are instances in which a legislative body has sought to remedy problems for which it cannot be said to have been directly responsible. By contrast, [it] is the State's own scheme which has caused the funding problem, and, thus viewed, that scheme can hardly be deemed remedial.

c. In *Vlandis v. Kline,* Sec. 5 infra,—decided after *Rodriquez*—White, J., stated that he, too, agreed that this has been the Court's approach in applying the equal protection clause. See also the dissent of Marshall, J., joined by Brennan and Blackmun, JJ., in *Cleburne v. Cleburne Living Center, Inc.,* Sec. 3, V supra.

59. Indeed, the Court's theory would render the established concept of fundamental interests in the context of equal protection analysis superfluous, for the substantive constitutional right itself requires that this Court strictly scrutinize any asserted state interest for restricting or denying access to any particular guaranteed right.

60. It is interesting that in its effort to reconcile the state voting rights cases with its theory of fundamentality the majority can muster nothing more than the contention that "[t]he constitutional underpinnings of the *right to equal treatment in the voting process* can no longer be doubted." If, by this, the

61. See note 61 on page 1075.

These are instances in which, due to the importance of the interests at stake, the Court has displayed a strong concern with the existence of discriminatory state treatment. But the Court has [never] indicated that these are interests which independently enjoy full-blown constitutional protection. * * *

The majority is, of course, correct when it suggests that the process of determining which interests are fundamental is a difficult one. But I do not think the problem is insurmountable. [The task] should be to determine the extent to which constitutionally guaranteed rights are dependent on interests not mentioned in the Constitution. As the nexus between the specific constitutional guarantee and the nonconstitutional interest draws closer, the nonconstitutional interest becomes more fundamental and the degree of judicial scrutiny applied when the interest is infringed on a discriminatory basis must be adjusted accordingly. * * * Procreation is now understood to be important because of its interaction with the established constitutional right of privacy. The exercise of the state franchise is closely tied to basic civil and political rights inherent in the First Amendment. And access to criminal appellate processes enhances the integrity of the range of rights implicit in the Fourteenth Amendment guarantee of due process of law. Only if we closely protect the related interests from state discrimination do we ultimately ensure the integrity of the constitutional guarantee itself. This is the real lesson that must be taken from our previous decisions involving interests deemed to be fundamental.

The effect of the interaction of individual interests with established constitutional guarantees upon the degree of care exercised by this Court in reviewing state discrimination affecting such interests is amply illustrated [by] *Eisenstadt v. Baird,* [p. 324 supra]. [The] Court purported to test the statute under its traditional standard [but] clearly did not adhere to these highly tolerant standards of traditional rational review. [Yet] I think the Court's action was entirely appropriate for access to and use of contraceptives bears a close relationship to the individual's constitutional right of privacy.

A similar process of analysis with respect to the invidiousness of the basis on which a particular classification is drawn has also influenced the Court as to the appropriate degree of scrutiny to be accorded any particular case. [It] may be that all of [the] considerations, which make for particular judicial solicitude in the face of discrimination on the basis of race, nationality, or alienage, do not coalesce—or at least not to the same degree—in other forms of discrimination. Nevertheless, these considerations have undoubtedly influenced the care with which the Court has scrutinized other forms of discrimination. [Thus], in *Reed v. Reed,* [Sec. 3, IV supra], the Court [resorted] to a more stringent standard of equal protection review than that employed in cases involving commercial matters. [T]he particularly invidious character of the classification caused the Court to pause and scrutinize with more than traditional care the rationality of state discrimination. Discrimination on the basis [of] sex posed for the Court the spectre of forms of discrimination which it implicitly recognized to have deep social and legal roots without necessarily having any basis in actual differences.

Court intends to recognize a substantive constitutional "right to equal treatment in the voting process" independent of the Equal Protection Clause, the source of such a right is certainly a mystery to me.

61. It is true that *Griffin* and *Douglas* also involved discrimination against [indigents]. But, as the majority points out, the Court has never deemed wealth discrimination alone to be sufficient to require strict judicial scrutiny; rather, such review of wealth classifications has been applied only where the discrimination affects an important individual interest, see, e.g., *Harper.* Thus, I believe *Griffin* and *Douglas* can only be understood as premised on a recognition of the fundamental importance of the criminal appellate process.

Still, the Court's sensitivity to the invidiousness of the basis for discrimination is perhaps most apparent in its decisions protecting the interests of children born out of wedlock from discriminatory state action. [Sec. 3, III supra].

[In] the context of economic interests, we find that discriminatory state action is almost always sustained for such interests are generally far removed from constitutional guarantees. [But] the situation differs markedly when discrimination against important individual interests with constitutional implications and against particularly disadvantaged or powerless classes is involved.[d] The majority suggests, however, that a variable standard of review would give this Court the appearance of a "superlegislature." I cannot agree. Such an approach seems to me a part of the guarantees of our Constitution and of the historic experiences with oppression of and discrimination against discrete, powerless minorities which underlie that Document. In truth, the Court itself will be open to the criticism raised by the majority so long as it continues on its present course of effectively selecting in private which cases will be afforded special consideration without acknowledging the true basis of its action. [Such] obfuscated action may be appropriate to a political body such as a legislature, but it is not appropriate to this Court. Open debate of the bases for the Court's action is essential to the rationality and consistency of our decisionmaking process. * * *

[It] is true that this Court has never deemed the provision of free public education to be required by the Constitution. [But] the fundamental importance of education is amply indicated by the prior decisions of this Court, by the unique status accorded public education by our society, and by the close relationship between education and some of our most basic constitutional [values].

[I]t has frequently been suggested that education is the dominant factor affecting political consciousness and participation.[72] * * * [74] [T]he issue is neither provision of the most *effective* speech nor of the most *informed* vote. Appellees do not now seek the best education Texas might provide [but] an end to state [discrimination].[75]

---

d. In *Massachusetts Bd. of Retirement v. Murgia*, Marshall, J., further explained his approach: "[T]here remain rights, not now classified as 'fundamental,' that remain vital to the flourishing of a free society, and classes, not now classified as 'suspect,' that are unfairly burdened by invidious discrimination unrelated to the individual worth of their members. Whatever we call these rights and classes, we simply cannot forgo all judicial protection against discriminatory legislation bearing upon them, but for the rare instances when the legislative choice can be termed 'wholly irrelevant' to the legislative goal."

72. [I]t should be obvious that the political process, like most other aspects of social intercourse, is to some degree competitive. It is thus of little benefit to an individual from a property poor district to have "enough" education if those around him have more than "enough."

74. [Whatever] the severity of the impact of insufficient food or inadequate housing on a person's life, they have never been considered to bear the same direct and immediate relationship to constitutional concerns for free speech and for our political processes as education has long been recognized to bear. Perhaps, the best evidence of this fact is the unique status which has been accorded public education as the single public service nearly unanimously guaranteed in the constitutions of our States. Education, in terms of constitutional values, is much more analogous in my judgment, to the right to vote in state elections than to public welfare or public housing. [Indeed,] we have long recognized education as an essential step in providing the disadvantaged with the tools necessary to achieve economic self-sufficiency.

75. The majority's reliance on this Court's traditional deference to legislative bodies in matters of taxation falls wide of the mark [for] in this case we are presented with a claim [that] the revenue producing mechanism directly discriminates against the interests of some of the intended beneficiaries; and in contrast to the taxpayer suits, the interest adversely affected is of substantial constitutional and societal importance. * * *

[We] are told that in every prior case involving a wealth classification, the members of the disadvantaged class have "shared two distinguishing characteristics: because of their impecunity they were completely unable to pay for some desired benefit, and as a consequence, they sustained an absolute deprivation of a meaningful opportunity to enjoy that benefit." I cannot agree. * * *

In *Harper,* the Court struck down [a] poll tax in toto; it did not order merely that those too poor to pay the tax be exempted; complete impecunity clearly was not determinative. [In] *Griffin* and *Douglas* [t]he right of appeal itself was not absolutely denied to those too poor to pay; but because of the cost of a transcript and of counsel, the appeal was a substantially less meaningful right for the poor than for the rich. [This] clearly encompassed degrees of discrimination on the basis of wealth which do not amount to outright denial of the affected right or interest.[77]

[That] wealth classifications alone have not necessarily been considered to bear the same high degree of suspectness as have classifications based on, for instance, race or alienage may be explainable on a number of grounds. The "poor" may not be seen as politically powerless as certain discrete and insular minority groups. Personal poverty may entail much the same social stigma as historically attached to certain racial or ethnic groups [but it] is not a permanent disability; its shackles may be escaped. Perhaps, most importantly, though, personal wealth may not necessarily share the general irrelevance as a basis for legislative action that race or nationality is recognized to have. While the "poor" have frequently been a legally disadvantaged group, it cannot be ignored that social legislation must frequently take cognizance of the economic status of our citizens. Thus, we have generally gauged the invidiousness of wealth classifications with an awareness of the importance of the interests being affected and the relevance of personal wealth to those interests.

When evaluated with these considerations in mind, it seems to me that discrimination on the basis of group wealth in this case likewise calls for careful judicial scrutiny. First, [it] bears no relationship whatsoever to the interest of Texas school children in the educational opportunity afforded them [by] Texas. Given the importance of that interest, we must be particularly sensitive to the invidious characteristics of any form of discrimination that is not clearly intended to serve it, as opposed to some other distinct state interest. Discrimination on the basis of group wealth may not, to be sure, reflect the social stigma frequently attached to personal poverty. Nevertheless, insofar as group wealth discrimination involves wealth over which the disadvantaged individual has no significant control,[83] it represents in fact a more serious basis of discrimination than does personal wealth. For such discrimination is no reflection of the individual's characteristics or his abilities. And thus—particularly in the context of a disadvantaged class composed of children—we have previously treated discrimi-

---

77. Even putting aside its misreading of *Griffin* and *Douglas*, the Court fails to offer any reasoned constitutional basis for restricting cases involving wealth discrimination to instances in which there is an absolute deprivation of the interest affected. [Equal protection] guarantees equality of treatment of those persons who are similarly situated; it does not merely bar some form of excessive discrimination between such persons. Outside the context of wealth discrimination, the Court's re-

apportionment decisions clearly indicate that relative discrimination is within the purview of the Equal Protection Clause. * * *

83. True, a family may move to escape a property poor school district, assuming it has the means to do so. But such a view would itself raise a serious constitutional question concerning an impermissible burdening of the right to travel, or, more precisely, the concomitant right to remain where one is.

nation on a basis which the individual cannot control as constitutionally disfavored. Cf. *Weber; Levy,* [Sec. 3, III supra].

The disability of the disadvantaged class in this case extends as well into the political processes upon which we ordinarily rely as adequate for the protection and promotion of all interests. Here legislative reallocation of the State's property wealth must be sought in the face of inevitable opposition from significantly advantaged districts that have a strong vested interest in the preservation of the status [quo]. *Griffin, Douglas, Williams, Tate,* and our other prior cases have dealt with discrimination on the basis of indigency which was attributable to the operation of the private sector. But we have no such simple de facto wealth discrimination here. The means for financing public education in Texas are selected and specified by the State. [At] the same time, governmentally imposed land use controls have undoubtedly encouraged and rigidified natural trends in the allocation of particular areas for residential or commercial use, and thus determined each district's amount of taxable property wealth. In short, this case, in contrast to the Court's previous wealth discrimination decisions, can only be seen as "unusual in the extent to which governmental action *is* the cause of the wealth classifications."

[Here] both the nature of the interest and the classification dictate close judicial [scrutiny. I] do not question that local control of public education, as an abstract matter, constitutes a very substantial state interest. [But] on this record, it is apparent that the State's purported concern with local control is offered primarily as an excuse rather than as a justification for interdistrict inequality.

In Texas statewide laws regulate [the] most minute details of local public education. For example, the State prescribes required courses. All textbooks must be submitted for state [approval]. The State has established the qualifications necessary for teaching in Texas public schools and the procedures for obtaining certification. The State has even legislated on the length of the school [day.]

Moreover, even if we accept Texas' general dedication to local control in educational matters, [i]f Texas had a system truly dedicated to local fiscal control one would expect the quality of the educational opportunity provided in each district to vary with the decision of the voters in that district as to the level of sacrifice they wish to make for public education. [But local] districts cannot choose to have the best education [by] imposing the highest tax rate. Instead, the quality of the educational opportunity offered by any particular district is largely determined by the amount of taxable property located in the district—a factor over which local voters can exercise no control.

The study introduced in the District Court showed a direct inverse relationship between equalized taxable district property wealth and district tax effort with the result that the property poor districts making the highest tax effort obtained the lowest per pupil yield. * * *

In my judgment, any substantial degree of scrutiny of the operation of the Texas financing scheme reveals that the State has selected means wholly inappropriate to secure its purported interest in assuring its school districts local fiscal control.[96] At the same time, appellees have pointed out a variety of

---

96. [Although] my Brother White purports to reach this result by application of that lenient standard of mere rationality, [it] seems to be that the care with which he scrutinizes the practical effectiveness of the present local property tax as a device for affording local fiscal control reflects the application of a more stringent standard of [review].

alternative financing schemes which may serve the State's purported interest in local control as well as, if not better than, the present scheme without the current impairment of the educational opportunity of vast numbers of Texas schoolchildren. * * *

Notes and Questions

1. *Wealth classifications.* (a) Does *Rodriguez* hold that de facto discriminations against poor people are subject to "strict scrutiny" only if the classification involves a right "explicitly or implicitly guaranteed by the Constitution"? May *all* the prior "wealth discrimination" cases be explained on this basis? Or does the Court's fn. 60 suggest that a state payment requirement resulting in "an absolute deprivation" of an "important" (albeit not "fundamental") right requires "strict scrutiny"? If so, what are other "important" rights?

(b) *Affirmative obligation.* Suppose a state simply shut its public schools and left the task to private entrepreneurs? In what way is this different than the situation posited in fn. 60? Suppose a state simply shut off all relief and welfare assistance? Is this state action subject to "strict scrutiny" under equal protection? Or does this beg the "state action" issue?

May a state bar impoverished citizens from public housing? If not, may it charge rentals for all public housing that the impoverished can't afford? If not, may it simply not construct public housing, leaving the impoverished to fend for themselves? Or does government have the affirmative obligation to afford at least "minimum protection" (if not "equal protection") to all citizens in respect to those services that are "of such fundamental importance" that "severe deprivation" would otherwise result? See generally Michelman, *On Protecting the Poor Through the Fourteenth Amendment,* 83 Harv.L.Rev. 7 (1969). For the view that it is improper for the judiciary to decide issues of economic allocation, see Wilkinson, fn. b in *Dandridge;* Winter, fn. c in *Dandridge.* Compare generally Rawls, *A Theory of Justice* (1971) with Nozick, *Anarchy, State and Utopia* (1974).

(c) *Discrimination against fundamental rights.* MAHER v. ROE, p. 350 supra, per POWELL, J., held that Connecticut's refusal to give medicaid for nontherapeutic abortions, even though it gives medicaid for childbirth, does not violate equal protection: "The Constitution imposes no obligation on the States to pay the pregnancy-related medical expenses of indigent women, or indeed to pay any of the medical expenses of indigents.[5] But when a State decides to alleviate some of the hardships of poverty by providing medical care, the manner in which it dispenses benefits is subject to constitutional limitations. * * *

"This case involves no discrimination against a suspect class. An indigent woman desiring an abortion does not come within the limited category of disadvantaged classes so recognized by our cases. Nor does the fact that the impact of the regulation falls upon those who cannot pay lead to a different conclusion. In a sense, every denial of welfare to an indigent creates a wealth classification as compared to nonindigents who are able to pay for the desired goods or services. But this Court has never held that financial need alone identifies a suspect [class]. See *Rodriguez; Dandridge.*[6] Accordingly, the cen-

---

5. [Because] Connecticut has made no attempt to monopolize the means for terminating pregnancies through abortion the present case is easily distinguished from *Boddie.* [Does this similarly distinguish *Harper* and *Lubin v. Panish?*]

6. [*Griffin* and *Douglas*] are grounded in the criminal justice system, a governmental monopoly in which participation is compelled. Cf. n. 5, supra. Our subsequent decisions have made it clear that the principles under-

tral question in this case is whether the regulation 'impinges upon a fundamental right explicitly or implicitly protected by the Constitution.'"

In reasoning that "the Connecticut regulation places no obstacles—absolute or otherwise—in the pregnant woman's path to an abortion" the Court also found that "appellees' reliance on the penalty analysis of *Shapiro* and *Maricopa* is misplaced.[8]"

In rejecting the Court's distinction between a state's direct interference with a fundamental right and encouraging an alternative activity, BRENNAN, J., joined by Marshall and Blackmun, JJ., dissenting, added that "First Amendment decisions have consistently held [that] the compelling state interest test is applicable not only to outright denials but also to restraints that make exercise of those rights more difficult. See, e.g., *Sherbert*. [The] compelling state interest test has been applied in voting cases, even where only relatively small infringements upon voting power, such as dilution of voting strength caused by malapportionment, have been involved. [The] Connecticut scheme cannot be distinguished from other grants and withholdings of financial benefits that we have held unconstitutionally burdened a fundamental right.[a] [The] governing principle is the same [as in *Sherbert*], for Connecticut grants and withholds financial benefits in a manner that discourages significantly the exercise of a fundamental constitutional right. Indeed, the case for application of the principle actually is stronger than in *Sherbert* since appellees are all indigents and therefore even

lying *Griffin* and *Douglas* do not extend to legislative classifications generally.

[For incisive comparison of *Maher* with *Griffin* and *Douglas* —and with *Shapiro* (see fn. 8 infra)—see Brudno, *Wealth Discrimination in the Supreme Court: Equal Protection for the Poor from Griffin to Maher,* in Constitutional Government in America 229 (Collins ed. 1980).]

8. * * * Penalties are most familiar to the criminal law, where criminal sanctions are imposed as a consequence of proscribed conduct. *Shapiro* and *Maricopa* recognized that denial of welfare to one who had recently exercised the right to travel across state lines was sufficiently analogous to a criminal fine to justify strict judicial scrutiny.

If Connecticut denied general welfare benefits to all women who had obtained abortions and who were otherwise entitled to the benefits, we would have a close analogy to the facts in *Shapiro,* and strict scrutiny might be [appropriate]. But the claim here is that the State "penalizes" the woman's decision to have an abortion by refusing to pay for it. *Shapiro* and *Maricopa* did not hold that States would penalize the right to travel interstate by refusing to pay the bus fares of the indigent travelers. We find no support in the right to travel cases for the view that Connecticut must show a compelling interest for its decision not to fund elective abortions.

Sherbert v. Verner, [p. 845 supra], similarly is inapplicable here. In addition, that case was decided in the significantly different context of a constitutionally imposed "governmental obligation of neutrality" originating in

[the] Religion Clauses of the First Amendment.

a. Does the Connecticut regulation "discriminate against," rather than simply "burden," a fundamental right? Is there a constitutional difference? See note 1 after *Shapiro,* Part II supra. Consider 91 Harv.L.Rev. 144 (1977): "It can hardly be [that] the state could provide a free forum for indigents' speech only on the condition that no unpopular views be espoused, even though this policy would deny only the specific costs of exercising disfavored speech rights. Similarly, it is difficult to imagine that the Court would uphold a policy of providing free justices of the peace for intraracial but not racially mixed marriages, thereby declining to pay the specific costs of a disfavored but constitutionally protected union, notwithstanding that the state has merely made intraracial marriage a more attractive alternative without creating an obstacle to private marriage opportunities."

See also Brennan, J., dissenting in *Harris v. McRae* (1980), p. 352 supra (which relied on *Maher* to sustain denial of medicaid even for "medically necessary" abortions): "Whether the State withholds only the special costs of a disfavored option or penalizes the individual more broadly for the manner in which she exercises her choice, it cannot interfere with a constitutionally protected decision through the coercive use of governmental largess."

Did *Dandridge* uphold a policy of providing welfare to indigent parents only for sustaining four children and no more? If so, is the law in *Maher* distinguishable?

more vulnerable to the financial pressures imposed by the Connecticut regulations."

MARSHALL, J., dissented: "[*Rodriguez*] stated a test for analyzing discrimination on the basis of wealth that would, if fairly applied here, strike down the regulations. The Court there held that a wealth discrimination claim is made out by persons ['who] because of their impecunity [are] completely unable to pay for some desired benefit, and as a consequence [sustain] an absolute deprivation of a meaningful opportunity to enjoy that benefit.' Medicaid recipients are, almost by definition, 'completely unable to pay for' abortions, and are thereby completely denied 'a meaningful opportunity' to obtain them.[6]"

(d) Whatever the scope of "strict scrutiny" for de facto discriminations against (or among) poor people, does *Rodriguez* restrict the analysis to state action that imposes "payment requirements"? See *Jefferson v. Hackney* (1972), fn. a in *Washington v. Davis,* Sec. 2, III supra.

2. PLYLER v. DOE, 457 U.S. 202, 102 S.Ct. 2382, 72 L.Ed.2d 786 (1982), per BRENNAN, J., held that a Texas statute (§ 21.031) denying free public education to illegal alien children violated equal protection: "Persuasive arguments support the view that a State may withhold its beneficience from those whose very presence within the United States is the product of their own unlawful conduct. [But the children] in these cases 'can affect neither their parents' conduct nor their own status.' *Trimble v. Gordon,* [Sec. 3, III supra]. Even if the State found it expedient to control the conduct of adults by acting against their children, legislation directing the onus of a parent's misconduct against his children does not comport with fundamental conceptions of justice. * * * *Weber v. Aetna Casualty & Surety Co.* [Sec. 3, III supra].

"We reject the claim that 'illegal aliens' are a 'suspect class.' [U]ndocumented status is not irrelevant to any proper legislative goal. Nor is [it] an absolutely immutable characteristic since it is the product of conscious, indeed unlawful, action. But § 21.031 [imposes] its discriminatory burden on the basis of a legal characteristic over which children can have little control. It is thus difficult to conceive of a rational justification for penalizing these children for their presence within the United States. * * *

"Public education is not a 'right' granted to individuals by the Constitution. *Rodriguez.* But neither is it merely some governmental 'benefit' indistinguishable from other forms of social welfare legislation. Both the importance of education in maintaining our basic institutions, and the lasting impact of its deprivation on the life of the child, mark the distinction. [We] cannot ignore the

---

6. Application of the flexible equal protection standard [urged in Marshall, J.'s *Rodriguez* dissent] would allow the Court to strike down the regulations in these cases without calling into question laws funding public education or English language teaching in public schools. [See the majority's discussion of this point at p. 350 supra.] By permitting a court to weigh all relevant factors, the flexible standard does not logically require acceptance of any equal protection claim that is "identical in principle" under the traditional approach to those advanced here.

[Is there any way other than use of a "flexible equal protection standard" to distinguish *Maher* from the problems raised by the majority in respect to *Meyer* and *Pierce*? Consider

Perry, *The Abortion Funding Cases: A Comment on the Supreme Court's Role in American Government,* 66 Geo.L.J. 1191, 1199–1200 (1978): "One need not disapprove of private schools to acknowledge the wisdom of providing free, public education. [But the state's decision in *Maher*] is recognizable solely as a disapproval of and an effort to discourage abortion." See also Perry, *Why the Supreme Court Was Plainly Wrong in the Hyde Amendment Case: A Brief Comment on Harris v. McRae,* 32 Stan.L.Rev. 1113 (1980). Tribe, *American Constitutional Law* 933 n. 77 (1978). Compare Fahy, *The Abortion Funding Cases: A Response to Professor Perry,* 67 Geo.L.J. 1205 (1979).]

significant social costs borne by our Nation when select groups are denied the means to absorb the values and skills upon which our social order rests.[20] [Thus], the discrimination contained in § 21.031 can hardly be considered rational unless it furthers some substantial goal of the State.

" * * * Faced with an equal protection challenge respecting the treatment of aliens, we agree that the courts must be attentive to congressional policy; the exercise of congressional power might well affect the State's prerogatives to afford differential treatment to a particular class of aliens. [But] there is no indication that the disability imposed by § 21.031 corresponds to any identifiable congressional policy. The State does not claim that the conservation of state educational resources was ever a congressional concern in restricting immigration. More importantly, the classification reflected in § 21.031 does not operate harmoniously within the federal program. [In] light of the discretionary federal power to grant relief from deportation, a State cannot realistically determine that any particular undocumented child will in fact be deported until after deportation proceedings have been completed. It would of course be most difficult for the State to justify a denial of education to a child enjoying an inchoate federal permission to remain.

"We are reluctant to impute to Congress the intention to withhold from these children, for so long as they are present in this country through no fault of their own, access to a basic education. In other contexts, undocumented status, coupled with some articulable federal policy, might enhance State authority with respect to the treatment of undocumented aliens. But in the area of special constitutional sensitivity presented by this case, and in the absence of any contrary indication fairly discernible in the present legislative record, we perceive no national policy that supports the State in denying these children an elementary education.[a] [We] therefore turn to the state objectives that are said to support § 21.031. * * *

"First, appellants appear to suggest that the State may seek to protect the State from an influx of illegal immigrants. While a State might have an interest in mitigating the potentially harsh economic effects of sudden shifts in population, [t]here is no evidence in the record suggesting that illegal entrants impose any significant burden on the State's economy. To the contrary, the available evidence suggests that illegal aliens underutilize public services, while contributing their labor to the local economy and tax money to the State fisc. The dominant incentive for illegal entry [into] Texas is the availability of employment; few if any illegal immigrants come to this country [to] avail themselves of a free education. * * *

"Second, [appellants] suggest that undocumented children are appropriately singled out for exclusion because of the special burdens they impose on the State's ability to provide high quality public education. But the record in no way supports the claim [and], even if improvement in the quality of education were a likely result of barring some *number* of children from the schools of the State, the State must support its selection of *this* group as the appropriate target

---

20. * * * Whatever the current status of these children, the courts below concluded that many will remain here permanently and that some indeterminate number will eventually become citizens. * * *

a. For the view that "the Court should have followed the lead of *Toll v. Moreno*, [Sec. 3, II supra], and used the Supremacy Clause"

to hold the *Plyler* statute invalid because it was neither "sanctioned nor contemplated by Congress," see Choper, fn. i, Sec. 3, II supra, at 21–32. See also 96 Harv.L.Rev. 130 (1982). Compare Gerety, *Children in the Labyrinth: The Complexities of Plyler v. Doe*, 44 U.Pitt.L. Rev. 379, 380–87 (1983).

for exclusion. In terms of educational cost and need, however, undocumented children are 'basically indistinguishable' from legally resident alien children.

"Finally, appellants suggest that undocumented children are appropriately singled out because their unlawful presence within the United States renders them less likely than other children to remain within the boundaries of the State, and to put their education to productive social or political use within the State. Even assuming that such an interest is legitimate, it is an interest that is most difficult to quantify. The State has no assurance that any child, citizen or not, will employ the education provided by the State within the confines of the State's borders. In any event, the record is clear that many of the undocumented children disabled by this classification will remain in this country indefinitely, and that some will become lawful residents or citizens of the United States. It is difficult to understand precisely what the State hopes to achieve by promoting the creation and perpetuation of a subclass of illiterates within our boundaries, surely adding to the problems and costs of unemployment, welfare, and crime. It is thus clear that whatever savings might be achieved [are] wholly insubstantial in light of the costs involved to these children, the State, and the Nation."[b]

BLACKMUN, J., who joined the Court's opinion, concurred: "I joined [the] Court in *Rodriguez*, and I continue to believe that it provides the appropriate model for resolving most equal protection disputes. [But] I believe the Court's experience has demonstrated that the *Rodriguez* formulation does not settle every issue of 'fundamental rights' arising under the Equal Protection Clause. Only a pedant would insist that there are *no* meaningful distinctions among the multitude of social and political interests regulated by the States * * *. Children denied an education are placed at a permanent and insurmountable competitive [disadvantage]. And when those children are members of an identifiable group, that group—through the State's action—will have been converted into a discrete underclass. Other benefits provided by the State, such as housing and public assistance, are of course important: to an individual in immediate need, they may be more desirable than the right to be educated. But classifications involving the complete denial of education are in a sense unique, for they strike at the heart of equal protection values by involving the State in the creation of permanent class distinctions. Cf. *Rodriguez* (Marshall, J., dissenting). In a sense, then, denial of an education is the analogue of denial of the right to vote: the former relegates the individual to second-class social status; the latter places him at a permanent political disadvantage.

"This conclusion is fully consistent with *Rodriguez*. The Court there reserved judgment on the constitutionality of a state system that 'occasioned an absolute denial of educational opportunities to any of its children,' noting that 'no charge fairly could be made that the system [at issue in *Rodriguez*] fails to provide each child with an opportunity to acquire * * * basic minimal skills.' [In] such circumstances, the voting decisions suggest that the State must offer something more than a rational basis for its classification."

POWELL, J., who joined the Court's opinion, concurred "to emphasize the unique character of the case": "Although the analogy is not perfect, our holding today does find support in decisions of this Court with respect to the status of illegitimates. [Thus,] review in a case such as this is properly heightened.

---

b. Marshall, J., joined the Court's opinion but emphasized "that the facts of these cases demonstrate the wisdom of rejecting a rigidi-fied approach to equal protection analysis, and of employing" his suggested approach in *Dandridge* and *Rodriguez*.

[These children] have been singled out for a lifelong penalty and stigma. A legislative classification that threatens the creation of an underclass of future citizens and residents cannot be reconciled with one of the fundamental purposes of the Fourteenth Amendment. In these unique circumstances, the Court properly may require that the State's interests be substantial and that the means bear a 'fair and substantial relation' to these interests.[3]"

BURGER, C.J., joined by White, Rehnquist and O'Connor, JJ., dissented: "[B]y patching together bits and pieces of what might be termed quasi-suspect-class and quasi-fundamental-rights analysis, the Court spins out a theory custom-tailored to the facts [and its] opinion rests on such a unique confluence of theories and rationales that it will likely stand for little beyond the results in these particular [cases].[c]

"[I]n some circumstances persons generally, and children in particular, may have little control over or responsibility for such things as their ill health, need for public assistance, or place of residence. Yet a state legislature is not barred from considering, for example, relevant differences between the mentally-healthy and the mentally-ill, or between the residents of different counties,[5] simply because these may be factors unrelated to individual choice or to any 'wrongdoing.' The Equal Protection Clause protects against arbitrary and irrational classifications, and against invidious discrimination stemming from prejudice and hostility; it is not an all-encompassing 'equalizer' designed to eradicate every distinction for which persons are not 'responsible.' * * *[d]

"The Court's analogy to cases involving discrimination against illegitimate children is grossly misleading. The State has not thrust any disabilities upon appellees due to their 'status of birth.' Cf. *Weber.* Rather, appellees' status is predicated upon the circumstances of their concededly illegal presence in this [country].

"The central question in these cases, as in every equal protection case not involving truly fundamental rights 'explicitly or implicitly guaranteed by the Constitution,' *Rodriguez,* is whether there is some legitimate basis for a legislative distinction between different classes of persons. The fact that the distinction is drawn in legislation affecting access to public education—as opposed to legislation allocating other important governmental benefits, such as public assistance, health care, or housing—cannot make a difference in the level of scrutiny applied.

---

3. [I]n *Rodriguez* no group of children was singled out by the State and then penalized because of their parents' status. [Nor] was any group of children totally deprived of all education as in this case. If the resident children of illegal aliens were denied welfare assistance, made available by government to all other children who qualify, this also—in my opinion—would be an impermissible penalizing of children because of their parents' status.

c. See generally Hutchinson, *More Substantive Equal Protection? A Note on Plyler v. Doe,* 1982 Sup.Ct.Rev. 167.

5. Appellees "lack control" over their illegal residence in this country in the same sense as lawfully resident children lack control over the school district in which their parents reside. Yet in *Rodriguez,* [t]here was no suggestion [that] a child's "lack of responsibility" for his residence in a particular school district had any relevance to the proper standard of review of his [claims.]

d. Compare Choper, supra, at 29: "Although it is true that the children in *Rodriguez* had no effective choice as to where they lived, the statute in *Plyler* [is] much more stigmatizing. It [says] to a class of children that they are no good; that even though what is wrong with them is something over which they have no control, the state is going to penalize them nonetheless. I think [this] provided an effective doctrinal hook on which the Court could have more explicitly hung its decision."

"Once it is conceded—as the Court does—that illegal aliens are not a suspect class, and that education is not a fundamental right, our inquiry should focus on and be limited to whether the legislative classification at issue bears a rational relationship to a legitimate state purpose. [I]t simply is not 'irrational' for a State to conclude that it does not have the same responsibility to provide benefits for persons whose very presence in the State and this country is illegal as it does to provide for persons lawfully present. * * *

"It is significant that the federal government has seen fit to exclude illegal aliens from numerous social welfare [programs]. Although these exclusions do not conclusively demonstrate the constitutionality of the State's use of the same classification for comparable purposes, at the very least they tend to support the rationality of excluding illegal alien residents of a State from such programs so as to preserve the State's finite revenues for the benefit of lawful residents. * * *

"Denying a free education to illegal alien children is not a choice I would make were I a legislator. Apart from compassionate considerations, the long-range costs of excluding any children from the public schools may well outweigh the costs of educating them. But [the] fact that there are sound *policy* arguments against the Texas legislature's choice does not render that choice an unconstitutional one. [While] the 'specter of a permanent caste' of illegal Mexican residents of the United States is indeed a disturbing one, it is but one segment of a larger problem, which is for the political branches to solve."

3. *Standards of equal protection review.* (a) Do *Plyler* and Marshall, J.'s *Rodriguez* dissent demonstrate that the Court "has applied a spectrum of standards" as to "the degree of care with which it will scrutinize particular classifications"? See also fns. e and f following *New Orleans v. Dukes,* Sec. 1 supra; *Cleburne,* Sec. 3, V supra.[a]

(b) UNITED STATES DEP'T OF AGRICULTURE v. MORENO, 413 U.S. 528, 93 S.Ct. 2821, 37 L.Ed.2d 782 (1973), per BRENNAN, J., applying " 'traditional' equal protection analysis," held that a provision of the Food Stamp Act—excluding "any household containing an individual who is unrelated to any other member of the household"—was "wholly without any rational basis": It "is clearly irrelevant to the stated purposes of the Act [which are to] raise levels of nutrition among low-income households. [Thus], the challenged classification must rationally further some legitimate governmental interest other than those specifically stated in the congressional 'declaration of policy.'

"[The] little legislative history [that] does exist" indicates that the provision "was intended to [prevent] 'hippie communes' from participating in the food stamp program. [But equal protection] at the very least mean[s] that a bare congressional desire to harm a politically unpopular group cannot constitute a *legitimate* governmental interest." Nor does the classification "operate so as

---

a. For analysis urging that the Court use three levels of equal protection review and "should validate a statute [that "limits the exercise of a fundamental right by a class of persons"] only if the means used bear a factually demonstrable relationship to a state interest capable of withstanding analysis," see Nowak, *Realigning the Standard of Review Under the Equal Protection Guarantee—Prohibited, Neutral, and Permissive Classifications,* 62 Geo.L.J. 1071 (1974): "The Court will scrutinize the factual support for the legisla-

tion to determine whether its ends are capable of withstanding analysis and whether its means are rationally related to that end."

For analysis urging that the Court weigh the *"nature* of the affected interest" and the *"magnitude* of disadvantage" against the *"nature* of the state's interest" and the "relationship between *means and ends,"* see Simson, *A Method for Analyzing Discriminatory Effects Under the Equal Protection Clause,* 29 Stan.L. Rev. 663 (1977).

rationally to further the prevention of fraud" because, under the Act, "two *unrelated* persons living together" may "avoid the 'unrelated person' exclusion simply by altering their living arrangements so as [to] create two separate 'households,' both of which are eligible for assistance. [Thus], in practical operation, the [provision] excludes from participation [not] those persons who are 'likely to abuse the program' but, rather, only those persons who are so desperately in need of aid that they cannot even afford to alter their living arrangements so as to retain their eligibility."

DOUGLAS, J., concurred: "I could not say that [this] provision has no 'rational' relation to control of fraud. We deal here, however, with the right of association, protected by the First Amendment." Thus, the classification "can be sustained only on a showing of a 'compelling' governmental interest."

REHNQUIST, J., joined by Burger, C.J., dissented: "Congress attacked the problem with a rather blunt instrument, [b]ut I do not think it is unreasonable for Congress to conclude that the basic unit which it was willing to support [with] food stamps is some variation on the family as we know it—a household consisting of related individuals. This unit provides a guarantee which is not provided by households containing unrelated individuals that the household exists for some purpose other than to collect federal food stamps.

"Admittedly, [the] limitation will make ineligible many households which have not been formed for the purpose of collecting federal food stamps, and will [not] wholly deny food stamps to those households which may have been formed in large part to take advantage of the program. But, as the Court concedes, 'traditional' equal protection analysis does not require that every classification be drawn with precise mathematical nicety." [b]

(c) MATHEWS v. de CASTRO, 429 U.S. 181, 97 S.Ct. 431, 50 L.Ed.2d 389 (1976), per STEWART, J., relying on *Dandridge*, upheld a provision of the Social Security Act, granting benefits for a minor or dependent child in her care, to the wife (but not to the divorced former wife) of a man who is retired or disabled: "To be sure, the standard by which legislation ["providing for governmental payments of monetary benefits"] must be judged 'is not a toothless one,' *Mathews v. Lucas*, [Sec. 3, III supra]. But the challenged statute is entitled to a strong presumption of constitutionality. * * * Congress could have rationally assumed that divorced husbands and wives depend less on each other for financial and other support than do couples who stay married." Marshall, J., concurred in the judgment.

SECTION 5.   IRREBUTTABLE PRESUMPTIONS

A series of decisions in the early 1970s held that "permanent irrebuttable presumptions," which "have long been disfavored under the Due Process Clause," violated "procedural due process," *Vlandis*, infra. But, as the materials indicate, since the analysis of these cases is strikingly similar to the "fundamental rights" branch of equal protection, they are usefully studied here.

———

VLANDIS v. KLINE, 412 U.S. 441, 93 S.Ct. 2230, 37 L.Ed.2d 63 (1973): Connecticut imposed higher state university tuition on nonresidents. The Court, per STEWART, J., invalidated the statutory conclusive presumption that because the legal address of a student, if married, was outside the state at the time of

---

b. For invalidation of another Food Stamp Act provision, but on a different constitutional theory, see *United States Dep't of Agriculture v. Murry*, Sec. 5 infra.

application or, if unmarried, was outside the state at any point during the preceding year, he remains a nonresident for this purpose during the entire period of attendance at the university:

"*Bell v. Burson*, 402 U.S. 535, 91 S.Ct. 1586, 29 L.Ed.2d 90 (1971), involved a Georgia statute which provided that if an uninsured motorist was involved in an accident and could not post security for the amount of damages claimed, his driver's license must be suspended * * *. The Court held that since the State purported to be concerned with fault in suspending a driver's license, it could not, consistent with procedural due process, conclusively presume fault from the fact that the uninsured motorist was involved in an accident, and could not, therefore, suspend his driver's license without a hearing on that crucial factor.

"Likewise, in *Stanley v. Illinois*, 405 U.S. 645, 92 S.Ct. 1208, 31 L.Ed.2d 551 (1972), the Court [struck] Illinois' irrebuttable statutory presumption that all unmarried fathers are unqualified to raise their children. [T]he statute required the State, upon the death of the mother, to take custody of all such illegitimate [children]. It may be, the Court said, 'that most unmarried fathers are unsuitable and neglectful parents. [But] all unmarried fathers are not in this category; some are wholly suited to have custody of their children.' Hence, [the state] was required by the Due Process Clause to provide a hearing on that [issue].

"The same considerations obtain here. [S]ince Connecticut purports to be concerned with residency [it] is forbidden by the Due Process Clause to deny an individual the resident rates on the basis of a permanent and irrebuttable presumption of nonresidence, when that presumption is not necessarily or universally true in [fact]. Rather, standards of due process require that the State allow such an individual the opportunity to present evidence showing that he is a bona fide resident entitled to the in-state rates." [a]

BURGER, C.J., joined by Rehnquist, J., dissented: "[T]he Court applies 'strict scrutiny' [without] explaining why the statute impairs a genuine constitutional interest. [A]t least [*Stanley*] essayed to explain that the rights of fatherhood and family were regarded as 'essential' and 'basic civil rights of man.' [*Burson*] noted that revocation of a driver's license might impair the pursuit of a livelihood, thereby infringing 'important interests of the licensees.' [L]iterally thousands of state statutes create classifications permanent in duration, which are less than perfect, as all legislative classifications are, and might be improved on by individualized determinations so as to avoid the untoward results produced here due to the very unusual facts of this case. [F]or example, a State provides that a person may not be licensed to practice medicine or law unless he or she is a graduate of an accredited professional graduate school; a perfectly capable practitioner may as a consequence be barred 'permanently and irrebuttably' from pursuing his calling, without ever having an opportunity to prove his personal skills." [b]

UNITED STATES DEP'T OF AGRICULTURE v. MURRY, 413 U.S. 508, 93 S.Ct. 2832, 37 L.Ed.2d 767 (1974), per DOUGLAS, J., invalidated a federal statute

---

a. White, J., concurred in the judgment on equal protection grounds. As "the weight and value of the individual interest escalates, the less likely it is that mere administrative convenience" will suffice.

b. Compare Burger, C.J.'s opinion for the Court in *Jimenez v. Weinberger* —discussed in

Mathews v. Lucas, Sec. 3, III supra—using an irrebuttable presumption-like rationale to hold a discrimination against some classes of illegitimate children violative of equal protection. Rehnquist, J., dissented.

that "any household which includes a member who has reached his eighteenth birthday and who is claimed as a dependent child for federal income tax purposes by a taxpayer who is not a member of an eligible household, shall be ineligible to participate in any food stamp program [during] the tax period such dependency is claimed and for a period of one year after the expiration of such tax period." The provision created "an irrebuttable presumption often contrary to fact." [c]

CLEVELAND BD. OF EDUC. v. LaFLEUR, 414 U.S. 632, 94 S.Ct. 791, 39 L.Ed.2d 52 (1974), per STEWART, J., invalidated school board rules requiring pregnant teachers to take leave without pay at least five months before the expected date of birth: "This Court has long recognized that freedom of personal choice in matters of marriage and family life is one of the liberties protected by [due process. The] provisions amount to a conclusive presumption that every pregnant teacher who reaches the fifth or sixth month of pregnancy is physically incapable of continuing." [d]

Notes and Questions

"Type" of due process. (a) Is the "irrebuttable presumption" doctrine grounded in *procedural* or *substantive* due process? Consider Note, *The Conclusive Presumption Doctrine: Equal Process or Due Protection?*, 72 Mich.L.Rev. 800, 824 (1974): "The [cases] appear to be purely substantive in nature. First, the appellees admitted that the relevant statutory provisions had been properly applied [and], in effect, challenged the legislative fact-finding and demanded that new issues be made relevant. In essence, the Court required that the states extend benefits to those in the appellees' class; in procedural cases the Court does not expand the class of people entitled to receive the benefit but only deals with what procedures are necessary when affecting that interest."

(b) Are the "irrebuttable presumption" cases limited to securing rights that are "explicitly or implicitly guaranteed by the Constitution" (*Rodriguez* Sec. 4, IV supra)—e.g., travel (*Vlandis*), procreation (*Stanley, LaFleur*), association (*Murry*)? See Bezanson, *Some Thoughts on the Emerging Irrebuttable Presumption Doctrine*, 7 Ind.L.Rev. 644, 652 (1974).

WEINBERGER v. SALFI, 422 U.S. 749, 95 S.Ct. 2457, 45 L.Ed.2d 522 (1975), per REHNQUIST, J., —distinguishing *Stanley* and *La Fleur* as involving claims with a "constitutionally protected status"—upheld "duration of relationship requirements of [the Social Security Act which] exclude surviving wives and stepchildren who had their respective relationships to a deceased wage earner for less than nine months prior to his death":

"We think [that] extension of the holdings of *Stanley, Vlandis* and *LaFleur* to the eligibility requirement in issue here would turn the doctrine of those cases into a virtual engine of destruction for countless legislative judgments which have heretofore been thought wholly consistent with [due process]. This would

---

c. Stewart and Marshall, JJ., joined the Court's opinion, but also concurred separately. Rehnquist, J., joined by Burger, C.J., and Powell, J., dissented; Blackmun, J., also dissented.

d. Powell, J., concurred in the result because "these regulations are invalid under

rational basis standards of equal protection review." Douglas, J., concurred in the result. Rehnquist, J., joined by Burger, C.J., dissented.

represent a degree of judicial involvement in the legislative function which we have eschewed except in the most unusual circumstances * * *.

"[The] question is whether Congress, its concern having been reasonably aroused by the possibility of an abuse, [could] rationally have concluded both that a particular limitation or qualification would protect against its occurrence, and that the expense and other difficulties of individual determinations justified the inherent imprecision of a prophylactic rule. We conclude that the duration-of-relationship test meets this constitutional standard.

"The danger of persons entering a marriage relationship not to enjoy its traditional benefits, but instead to enable one spouse to claim benefits upon the anticipated early death of the wage earner, has been recognized from the very beginning of the Social Security program. [The statute] undoubtedly excludes some surviving wives who married with no anticipation of shortly becoming widows, and it may be that appellee Salfi is among them. It likewise may be true that the requirement does not filter out every such claimant, if a wage earner lingers longer than anticipated, or in the case of illnesses which can be recognized as terminal more than nine months prior to death. But neither of these facts necessarily renders the statutory scheme unconstitutional."

BRENNAN, J., joined by MARSHALL, J., —arguing that the Court "attempts to wish away" *Vlandis, Murry,* and *Jimenez*—dissented: "[Not] *all* statutory provisions based on assumptions about underlying facts are per se unconstitutional unless individual hearings are provided. But in this case, as in the others in which we have stricken down conclusive presumptions, it *is* possible to specify those factors which, if proven in a hearing, would disprove a rebuttable presumption. See, e.g., *Vlandis.* For example, persuasive evidence of good health at the time of marriage would be sufficient, I should think, to disprove that the marriage was collusive." Douglas, J., also dissented.

Does the doctrine survive *Salfi?*

Chapter 11

THE CONCEPT OF STATE ACTION

SECTION 1. INTRODUCTION

The "state action" doctrine has long established that, due to their language or history, most provisions of the Constitution that protect individual liberty— including those set forth in Art. 1, §§ 9 and 10, the Bill of Rights, and the fourteenth and fifteenth amendments—impose restrictions or obligations only on government. The subject received its first extensive treatment in the CIVIL RIGHTS CASES, 109 U.S. 3, 3 S.Ct. 18, 27 L.Ed. 835 (1883), which held, per BRADLEY, J., that neither the thirteenth nor fourteenth amendments empowered Congress to pass the Civil Rights Act of 1875, making racial discrimination unlawful in public accommodations (inns, public conveyances, places of public amusement, etc.)—"and no other ground of authority for its passage being suggested, it must necessarily be declared void." Although the issue presented did not simply concern the authority granted the *Court* under § 1 of the thirteenth and fourteenth amendments, but rather involved the scope of *Congress'* power under the final sections of these amendments to enforce their substantive provisions "by appropriate legislation" (a topic to be considered in detail in Ch. 12), the Court's discussion of "state action" remains the classic exposition of the doctrine.

The Court held that, under the fourteenth amendment, "it is state action of a particular character that is prohibited. Individual invasion of individual rights is not the subject-matter of the amendment. [It] nullifies and makes void all state legislation, and state action of every kind, which impairs the privileges and immunities of citizens of the United States, or which injures them in life, liberty, or property without due process of law, or which denies to any of them the equal protection of the laws. [T]he last section of the amendment invests congress with power [to] adopt appropriate legislation for correcting the effects of such prohibited state law and state acts, and thus to render them effectually null, void, and innocuous. [It] does not authorize congress to create a code of municipal law for the regulation of private rights; but to provide modes of redress against the operation of state laws, and the action of state officers, executive or judicial, when these are subversive of the fundamental rights specified in the amendment. * * *

"An inspection of the law shows that [it] proceeds ex directo to declare that certain acts committed by individuals shall be deemed offenses, and shall be prosecuted [by] the United States. It does not profess to be corrective of any constitutional wrong committed by the states; [it] applies equally to cases arising

1090

in states which have the justest laws respecting the personal rights of citizens, and whose authorities are ever ready to enforce such laws as to those which arise in states that may have violated the prohibition of the amendment. In other words, it steps into the domain of local jurisprudence, and lays down rules for the conduct of individuals in society towards each other * * *. [C]ivil rights, such as are guarantied by the constitution against state aggression, cannot be impaired by the wrongful acts of individuals, unsupported by state authority in the shape of laws, customs, or judicial or executive proceedings. The wrongful act of an individual, unsupported by any such authority, is simply a private wrong, or a crime of that individual * * *. An individual cannot deprive a man of his right to vote, to hold property, to buy and to sell, to sue in the courts, or to be a witness or a juror; he may, by force or fraud, interfere with the enjoyment of the right in a particular case; [but] unless protected in these wrongful acts by some shield of state law or state authority, he cannot destroy or injure the right; he will only render himself amenable to satisfaction or punishment; and amenable therefor to the laws of the state where the wrongful acts are committed. [The] abrogation and denial of rights, for which the states alone were or could be responsible, was the great seminal and fundamental wrong which was intended to be remedied."

The Court recognized that the thirteenth amendment "is not a mere prohibition of state laws establishing or upholding slavery, but an absolute declaration that slavery or involuntary servitude shall not exist in any part of the United States [and] that the power vested in congress to enforce the article by appropriate legislation, clothes congress with power to pass all laws necessary and proper for abolishing all badges and incidents of slavery, in the United States * * *. [T]he civil rights bill of 1866, passed in view of the thirteenth amendment, before the fourteenth was adopted, undertook to wipe out these burdens and disabilities, * * * namely, the same right to make and enforce contracts, to sue, be parties, give evidence, and to inherit, purchase, lease, sell, and convey property, as is enjoyed by white citizens. Whether this legislation was fully authorized by the thirteenth amendment alone, without the support which it afterwards received from the fourteenth amendment, after the adoption of which it was re-enacted with some additions, it is not necessary to inquire. It is referred to for the purpose of showing that at that time (in 1866) congress did not assume, under the authority given by the thirteenth amendment, to adjust what may be called the social rights of men and races in the community; but only to declare and vindicate those fundamental rights which appertain to the essence of citizenship, and the enjoyment or deprivation of which constitutes the essential distinction between freedom and slavery.

"[It] would be running the slavery argument into the ground to make it apply to every act of discrimination which a person may see fit to make as to the guests he will entertain, or as to the people he will take into his coach or cab or car, or admit to his concert or theater, or deal with in other matters of intercourse or business. Innkeepers and public carriers, by the laws of all the states, so far as we are aware, are bound, to the extent of their facilities, to furnish proper accommodation to all unobjectionable persons who in good faith apply for them. If the laws themselves make any unjust discrimination, amenable to the prohibitions of the fourteenth amendment, congress has full power to afford a remedy under that amendment and in accordance with it." [a]

a. In *Bell v. Maryland*, 378 U.S. 226, 84 S.Ct. 1814, 12 L.Ed.2d 822 (1964), Goldberg, J., joined by Warren, C.J., and Douglas, J., examining the "historical evidence" in detail, concluded that the *Civil Rights Cases* were based on the assumption of the framers of the four-

HARLAN, J., dissented: "Was it the purpose of the nation [by the thirteenth amendment] simply to destroy the institution [of slavery], and remit the race, theretofore held in bondage, to the several states for such protection, in their civil rights, necessarily growing out of freedom, as those states, in their discretion, choose to provide? [S]ince slavery [was] the moving or principal cause of the adoption of that amendment, and since that institution rested wholly upon the inferiority, as a race, of those held in bondage, their freedom necessarily involved immunity from, and protection against, all discrimination against them, because of their race, in respect of such civil rights as belong to freemen of other races. Congress, therefore, under its express power to enforce that amendment, by appropriate legislation, may enact laws of a direct and primary character, operating upon states, their officers and agents, and also upon, at least, such individuals and corporations as exercise public functions and wield power and authority under the state. * * *

"It remains now to inquire what are the legal rights of colored persons in respect of the accommodations * * *.

"1. As to public conveyances on land and water. [In] *Olcott v. Sup'rs*, 16 Wall. 694, it was ruled that railroads [are] none the less public highways because controlled and owned by private corporations; that it is a part of the function of government to make and maintain highways for the conveyance of the public; that no matter who is the agent, and what is the agency, the function performed is *that of the state* * * *.

"Such being the relations these corporations hold to the public, it would seem that the right of a colored person to use an improved public highway, upon the terms accorded to freemen of other races, is as fundamental in the state of freedom, established in this country, as are any of the rights which my brethren concede to be so far fundamental as to be deemed the essence of civil freedom.

"2. As to inns. [The] authorities are sufficient to show that a keeper of an inn is in the exercise of a quasi public employment. The law gives him special privileges, and he is charged with certain duties and responsibilities to the public. The public nature of his employment forbids him from discriminating against any person asking admission as a guest on account of the race or color of that person.

"3. As to places of public amusement. [W]ithin the meaning of the act of 1875, [they] are such as are established and maintained under direct license of the law. [The] local government granting the license represents [the colored race] as well as all other races within its jurisdiction. A license from the public to establish a place of public amusement, imports, in law, equality of right, at such places, among all the members of that public.[b]"

teenth amendment that "under state law, when the Negro's disability as a citizen was removed, he would be assured the same public civil rights that the law had guaranteed white persons," and that "the duties of the proprietors of places of public accommodation would remain as they had long been and that the States would now be affirmatively obligated to insure that these rights ran to Negro as well as white citizens." Black, J., joined by Harlan and White, JJ., disagreed. Cf. Tribe, *American Constitutional Law* 1152 n. 14 (1978). See generally Frank & Munro, *The Original Understanding of "Equal Protection of the Laws,"* 1972 Wash.U.L.Q. 421, 468–72.

b. The position that such businesses cannot constitutionally discriminate has found modern support with Douglas, J., concurring in *Garner v. Louisiana*, 368 U.S. 157, 183–85, 82 S.Ct. 248, 261–63, 7 L.Ed.2d 207, 225–26 (1961) and *Lombard v. Louisiana*, 373 U.S. 267, 281–83, 83 S.Ct. 1122, 1129–30, 10 L.Ed.2d 338, 347–48 (1963). Compare *Moose Lodge v. Irvis*, Sec. 4 infra.

For general support of Harlan, J.'s thirteenth amendment view, see Kinoy, *The Constitutional Right of Negro Freedom*, 21 Rutg.L. Rev. 387 (1967). Although the Court has since ruled that the thirteenth amendment grants broad enforcement power to *Congress* (see p.

Turning to the fourteenth amendment, "the first clause of the first section— 'all persons born or naturalized in the United States, and subject to the jurisdiction thereof, are citizens of the United States, and of the state wherein they reside'—is of a distinctly affirmative character. In its application to the colored race, previously liberated, it created and granted, as well citizenship of the United States, as citizenship of the state in which they respectively resided. [Further], they were brought, by this supreme act of the nation, within the direct operation of that provision of the constitution which declares that 'the citizens of each state shall be entitled to all privileges and immunities of citizens in the several states.' Article IV, § 2.

"The citizenship thus acquired [may be protected] by congressional legislation of a primary direct character; this, because the power of congress is not restricted to the enforcement of prohibitions upon state laws or state action. It is, in terms distinct and positive, to enforce 'the *provisions of this article*' of amendment * * * *all* of the provisions,—affirmative and prohibitive * * *.

"But what was secured to colored citizens of the United States—as between them and their respective states—by the grant to them of state citizenship? With what rights, privileges, or immunities did this grant from the nation invest them? There is one, if there be no others—exemption from race discrimination in respect of any civil right belonging to citizens of the white race in the same state [by] the state, or its officers, or by individuals, or corporations exercising public functions or authority * * *. It was perfectly well known that the great danger to the equal enjoyment by citizens of their rights, as citizens, was to be apprehended, not altogether from unfriendly state legislation, but from the hostile action of corporations and individuals in the states. * * *

"But if it were conceded that the power of congress could not be brought into activity until the rights specified in the act of 1875 had been abridged or denied by some state law or state action, I maintain that the decision of the court is erroneous. [In] every material sense applicable to the practical enforcement of the fourteenth amendment, railroad corporations, keepers of inns, and managers of places of public amusement are agents of the state, because amenable, in respect of their public duties and functions, to public regulation. * * * I agree that if one citizen chooses not to hold social intercourse with another, he is not and cannot be made amenable to the law for his conduct in that regard; for no legal right of a citizen is violated by the refusal of others to maintain merely social relations with him, even upon grounds of race. [The] rights which congress, by the act of 1875, endeavored to secure and protect are legal, not social, rights. The right, for instance, of a colored citizen to use the accommodations of a public highway upon the same terms as are permitted to white citizens is no more a social right than his right, under the law, to use the public streets of a city, or a town, or a turnpike road, or a public market, or a post-office, or his right to sit in a public building with others, of whatever race, for the purpose of hearing the political questions of the day discussed."

The basic doctrine of the *Civil Rights Cases*—that it is "state action" that is prohibited by the fourteenth amendment—has remained undisturbed. But the

1169 infra), the Court has confined its use of the amendment, absent congressional legislation, to holding state peonage laws invalid. See *Memphis v. Greene*, p. 912 supra. For discussion of cases on what constitutes "slav- ery," "involuntary servitude," or "peonage" under the thirteenth amendment and federal enforcement statutes, see Shapiro, *Involuntary Servitude*, 19 Rutg.L.Rev. 65 (1964).

question of what constitutes "state action" has generated significant controversy. It is settled that the term comprehends statutes enacted by national, state and local legislative bodies and the official actions of all government officers. The more difficult problems arise when the conduct of private individuals or groups is challenged as being unconstitutional. Although—as will be pointed out in the materials that follow (see, e.g., note 7 after *Shelley v. Kraemer,* Sec. 3 infra)—it has often been argued that the inquiries are misperceived, the questions that the Court has asked are whether the private actor (a) is performing a "government function," or (b) is sufficiently "involved with" or "encouraged by" the state so as to be held to the state's constitutional obligations. These subjects will be developed in the next two sections of this chapter.

Until quite recently, most of the cases have involved racial discrimination (or, occasionally, denial of free speech). But, as will be detailed in Ch. 12, the enactment and strengthening of federal (and state) civil rights statutes in the past two decades has largely mooted the problem of private racial discrimination. Further, with the growth under the equal protection clause of the number of "suspect" and "quasi-suspect" classifications (see Ch. 10, Sec. 3) and the expansion under the due process clause of the procedural rights that the state must afford persons before depriving them of liberty or property (see Ch. 7, Sec. 5), an increasing number of cases (as will be seen in the final section of this chapter) have involved attempts to require "private" adherence to these constitutional responsibilities.

SECTION 2. "GOVERNMENT FUNCTION"

SMITH v. ALLWRIGHT, 321 U.S. 649, 64 S.Ct. 757, 88 L.Ed. 987 (1944), held the fifteenth amendment forebade exclusion of blacks from primary elections conducted by the Democratic Party of Texas, pursuant to party resolution. The Court, per REED, J., relied heavily on a case from Louisiana, *United States v. Classic* (1941), p. 1475 infra, which "makes clear that state delegation to a party of the power to fix the qualifications of primary elections is delegation of a state function that may make the party's action the action of the state." The Court concluded that the "right to participate in the choice of elected officials without restriction by any state because of race [is] not to be nullified by a state through casting its electoral process in a form which permits a private organization to practice racial discrimination in the election." Frankfurter, J., concurred in the result. Roberts, J., dissented.

TERRY v. ADAMS, 345 U.S. 461, 73 S.Ct. 809, 97 L.Ed. 1152 (1953), involved the exclusion of blacks from the "pre-primary" elections of the Jaybird Democratic Association, an organization of all the white voters in a Texas county that was run like a regular political party and whose candidates since 1889 had nearly always run unopposed and won in the regular Democratic primary and the general election. The record showed "complete absence of any compliance with the state law or practice, or cooperation by or with the State." Although there was no majority opinion, the Court held the election subject to the fifteenth amendment.

BLACK, J., joined by Douglas and Burton, JJ., found that "the admitted party purpose" was "to escape the Fifteenth Amendment's command." The "Amendment excludes social or business clubs" but "no election machinery could be sustained if its purpose or effect was to deny Negroes on account of their race an effective voice in the governmental affairs." "The only election that has counted in this Texas county for more than fifty years has been that held by the Jaybirds." "For a state to permit such a duplication of its election processes is to permit a flagrant abuse [of] the Fifteenth Amendment."

CLARK, J., joined by Vinson, C.J., and Reed and Jackson, JJ., described the Jaybirds as not merely a "private club" "organized to influence public candidacies or political action," but rather a "part and parcel of the Democratic Party, an organization existing under the auspices of Texas law. [W]hen a state structures its electoral apparatus in a form which devolves upon a political organization the uncontested choice of public officials, that organization itself, in whatever disguise, takes on those attributes of government which draw the Constitution's safeguards into play." Frankfurter, J., also concurred.

Only MINTON, J., dissented: The Jaybird's activity "seems to differ very little from situations common in many other places [where] a candidate must obtain the approval of a religious group. [It] must be recognized that elections and other public business are influenced by all sorts of pressures from carefully organized groups. [Far] from the activities of these groups being properly labeled as state action, [they] are to be considered as attempts to influence or obtain state action."

———

MARSH v. ALABAMA, 326 U.S. 501, 66 S.Ct. 276, 90 L.Ed. 265 (1946), held that "a State, consistently with the First and Fourteenth Amendments," cannot "impose criminal punishment on a person who undertakes to distribute religious literature on the premises of a company-owned town contrary to the wishes of the town's management." The town, owned by a shipbuilding company, had "all the characteristics of any other American town." Appellant, a Jehovah's Witness, was warned that she could not distribute the literature and when she refused to leave the sidewalk of the town's "business block," a deputy sheriff, who was paid by the company to serve as the town's policeman, arrested her and she was convicted of trespass.

The Court, per BLACK, J., reversed: Under *Lovell v. Griffin,* p. 582 supra, an ordinary municipality could not have barred appellant's activities, and the fact that "a single company had legal title to all the town" may not result in impairing "channels of communication" of its inhabitants or those persons passing through. "Ownership does not always mean absolute dominion. The more an owner, for his advantage, opens up his property for use by the public in general, the more do his rights become circumscribed by the statutory and constitutional rights of those who use it. Thus, the owners of privately held bridges, ferries, turnpikes and railroads may not operate them as freely as a farmer does his farm. Since these facilities are built and operated primarily to benefit the public and since their operation is essentially a public function, it is subject to state regulation." In balancing property rights against freedom of press and religion, "the latter occupy a preferred position" and the former do not "justify the State's permitting a corporation to govern a community of citizens so as to restrict their fundamental liberties and the enforcement of such restraint by the application of a State statute."

Frankfurter, J., concurred and Jackson, J., did not participate. REED, J., joined by Vinson, C.J., and Burton, J., dissented, noting that "there was [no] objection to appellant's use of the nearby public highway and under our decisions she could rightfully have continued her activities [thirty feet parallel] from the spot she insisted upon using." [b]

EVANS v. NEWTON, 382 U.S. 296, 86 S.Ct. 486, 15 L.Ed.2d 373 (1966): In 1911, Senator A.O. Bacon devised land to Macon, Ga., to be used as a park for whites only. After *Pennsylvania v. Board of Trusts,* 353 U.S. 230, 77 S.Ct. 806, 1 L.Ed.2d 792 (1957)—holding that there is "state action" when public officials act as trustees under a private will requiring racial discrimination—the city permitted blacks to use the park. When Bacon's heirs sued to remove the city as trustee, the Georgia courts accepted the city's resignation and appointed private individuals as trustees so that the trust's purpose would not fail.

The Court, per DOUGLAS, J., reversed, first relying on the fact that "so far as this record shows, there has been no change in municipal maintenance and concern over this facility. [If] the municipality remains entwined in the management or control of the park, it remains subject to the restraints of the Fourteenth Amendment."

Second, the Court noted that "the range of government activities is broad and varied, and the fact that government has engaged in a particular activity does not necessarily mean that an individual entrepreneur or manager of the same kind of undertaking suffers the same constitutional inhibitions. While a State may not segregate public schools so as to exclude one or more religious groups, those sects may maintain their own parochial educational systems. *Pierce v. Society of Sisters,* [p. 313 supra]." But "the service rendered even by a private park of this character is municipal in nature," "more like a fire department or police department" than like "golf clubs, social centers, luncheon clubs, schools such as Tuskegee was at least in origin, and other like organizations in the private sector." "Mass recreation through the use of parks is plainly in the public domain and state courts that aid private parties to perform that public function on a segregated basis implicate the State in conduct proscribed by the Fourteenth Amendment. Like the streets of the company town in *Marsh,* the elective process of *Terry v. Adams,* and the transit system of *Public Utilities Comm'n v. Pollak,* [c] the predominant character and purpose of this park are municipal."

HARLAN, J., joined by Stewart, J., dissented: The failing of the majority's theory "can be shown by comparing [the] 'public function' of privately established schools with that of privately owned parks. Like parks, the purpose schools serve is important to the public. Like parks, private control exists, but there is also a very strong tradition of public control in this field. Like parks, schools may be available to almost anyone of one race or religion but to no others. Like parks, there are normally alternatives for those shut out but there may also be inconveniences and disadvantages caused by the restriction. Like parks, the extent of school intimacy varies greatly depending on the size and character of the institution." [f]

---

b. The *Marsh* rationale was extended to a privately owned shopping center in *Food Employees v. Logan Valley Plaza* (1968). *Logan Valley* was subsequently limited in *Lloyd Corp. v. Tanner* (1972) and then overruled in *Hudgens v. NLRB* (1976), set forth in Sec. 4 infra.

c. In *Pollak,* 343 U.S. 451, 72 S.Ct. 813, 96 L.Ed. 1068 (1952), a city transit company subject to public regulation was considered in "sufficiently close relation" with the government as to cause the Court to determine whether the company's playing of radio programs on buses violated due process.

f. For further consideration of "private schools," see note 4 after *Burton v. Wilmington Parking Auth.,* Sec. 3 infra.

"While this process of analogy might be spun out to reach privately owned orphanages, libraries, garbage collection companies, detective agencies, and a host of other functions commonly regarded as nongovernmental though paralleling fields of governmental activity, the example of schools is, I think, sufficient to indicate the pervasive potentialities of this 'public function' theory of state action. It substitutes for the comparatively clear and concrete tests of state action a catch-phrase approach as vague and amorphous as it is far-reaching. [And] it carries the seeds of transferring to federal authority vast areas of concerns whose regulation has wisely been left by the Constitution to the States." [g]

Notes and Questions

1. *Scope of the decisions.* (a) How "pervasive" are the "potentialities of this 'public function' theory of state action"? Do the decisions logically extend to *all* private activities for which there is "parallel government activity"? Or is their reach limited to those activities—such as conducting elections for public office or operating a town—that are traditionally performed only (almost only) by government?

(b) *Parks.* Into which of the above categories do parks fall? Is there a "strong tradition" of private as well as public operation of parks in cities? Is it likely that, if Senator Bacon had not provided the park in *Evans,* the city would have provided its own? Is this approach too "vague and amorphous" to serve as a constitutional standard?

(c) In *Marsh,* could the shipbuilding company discriminate against blacks in hiring production workers? In hiring peace officers or street cleaners for the town? In *Smith v. Allwright,* could the Democratic Party refuse to hire Jewish secretaries? In *Terry,* could the Jaybirds refuse to hire black secretaries? May "private organizations" that perform "government functions" be subject to some constitutional limitations but not others?

(d) The "government function" issue is considered further in Sec. 4 infra.

2. *"Private" function.* (a) If the activities of private persons or groups may rise to the performance of a "government function," may certain official activities of government ever be considered the performance of a "private function"? Such as acting as trustee under a private will? Is the nature of the trust property relevant? In any case, does the state's official "entwinement" end the matter?

(b) If a privately owned amusement park contracts with a state deputy sheriff, who is regularly employed by the park, to enforce its racial segregation policy, may the state convict blacks, whom the deputy arrests when they refuse to leave the premises, for trespass? See *Griffin v. Maryland,* 378 U.S. 130, 84 S.Ct. 1770, 12 L.Ed.2d 754 (1964).

(c) *State university scholarship funds.* May a state university constitutionally award scholarships which the donor has designated for whites only? For persons of a particular religion only? If the donor personally selects the scholarship recipients each year and racially discriminates, may the university constitutionally admit those selected? Is there a "difference of substance" between these two situations? May a state university constitutionally solicit

---

g. White, J., concurred on a separate ground. Black, J., dissented on procedural grounds.

For subsequent litigation in respect to this park, see *Evans v. Abney,* Sec. 3 infra.

scholarships to be awarded on racial bases? See generally Note, *Constitutionality of Restricted Scholarships,* 33 N.Y.U.L.Rev. 604 (1958).

SECTION 3. STATE "INVOLVEMENT" OR "ENCOURAGEMENT"

BURTON v. WILMINGTON PARKING AUTHORITY
365 U.S. 715, 81 S.Ct. 856, 6 L.Ed.2d 45 (1961).

MR. JUSTICE CLARK delivered the opinion of the Court.

In this action for declaratory and injunctive relief it is admitted that the Eagle Coffee Shoppe, Inc., a restaurant located within an off-street automobile parking building in Wilmington, Delaware, has refused to serve appellant food or drink solely because he is a Negro. The parking building is owned and operated by the Wilmington Parking Authority, an agency of the State of Delaware, and the restaurant is the Authority's lessee. [The] Supreme Court of Delaware has held that Eagle was acting in "a purely private capacity" under its lease; that its action was not that of the Authority and was not, therefore, state action * * *. It also held that under 24 Del.Code § 1501,[1] Eagle was a restaurant, not an inn, and that as such it "is not required [under Delaware law] to serve any and all persons entering its place of business." * * *

The Authority['s] statutory purpose is to provide adequate parking facilities for the convenience of the public and [the] first project undertaken by the Authority was the erection of a parking facility * * *. [T]he Authority was advised by its retained experts that the anticipated revenue from the parking of cars and proceeds from sale of its bonds would not be sufficient to finance the construction costs of the facility. [To] secure additional capital [the] Authority decided it was necessary to enter long-term leases with responsible tenants for commercial use of some of the space available in the projected "garage building." The public was invited to bid for these leases.

In April 1957 such a private lease, for 20 years [was] made with Eagle Coffee Shoppe, Inc., for use as a "restaurant, dining room, banquet hall, cocktail lounge and bar * * *." [The] lease, however, contains no requirement that its restaurant services be made available to the general public on a nondiscriminatory basis, in spite of the fact that the Authority has power to adopt rules and regulations respecting the use of its facilities * * *.

Other portions of the structure were leased to other tenants, including a bookstore, a retail jeweler, and a food store. Upon completion of the building, the Authority located at appropriate places thereon official signs indicating the public character of the building, and flew from mastheads on the roof both the state and national flags.

[It] is clear, as it always has been since the *Civil Rights Cases,* [that] private conduct abridging individual rights does no violence to the Equal Protection Clause unless to some significant extent the State in any of its manifestations has been found to have become involved in it. Because the virtue of the right to equal protection of the laws could lie only in the breadth of its application, its constitutional assurance was reserved in terms whose imprecision was necessary

---

1. The statute provides that: "No keeper of an inn, tavern, hotel, or restaurant, or other place of public entertainment or refreshment of travelers, guests, or customers shall be obliged, by law, to furnish entertainment or refreshment to persons whose reception or entertainment by him would be offensive to the major part of his customers, and would injure his business. * * *"

if the right were to be enjoyed in the variety of individual-state relationships which the Amendment was designed to embrace. For the same reason, to fashion and apply a precise formula for recognition of state responsibility under the Equal Protection Clause is an "impossible task" which "This Court has never attempted." Only by sifting facts and weighing circumstances can the nonobvious involvement of the State in private conduct be attributed its true significance.

[T]he Delaware Supreme Court seems to have placed controlling emphasis on its conclusion, as to the accuracy of which there is doubt, that only some 15% of the total cost of the facility was "advanced" from public funds; that the cost of the entire facility was allocated three-fifths to the space for commercial leasing and two-fifths to parking space; that anticipated revenue from parking was only some 30.5% of the total income, the balance of which was expected to be earned by the leasing; that the Authority had no original intent to place a restaurant in the building, it being only a happenstance resulting from the bidding; that Eagle expended considerable moneys on furnishings; that the restaurant's main and marked public entrance is on Ninth Street without any public entrance direct from the parking area; and that "the only connection Eagle has with the public facility [is] the furnishing [of] rent which is used by the Authority to defray a portion of the operating expense of an otherwise unprofitable enterprise." While these factual considerations are indeed validly accountable aspects[,] we cannot say that they lead inescapably to the conclusion that state action is not present. Their persuasiveness is diminished when evaluated in the context of other factors which must be acknowledged.

The land and building were publicly owned. As an entity, the building was dedicated to "public uses" in performance of the Authority's "essential governmental functions." The costs of land acquisition, construction, and maintenance are defrayed entirely from donations by the City of Wilmington, from loans and revenue bonds and from the proceeds of rentals and parking services out of which the loans and bonds were payable. Assuming that the distinction would be significant, cf. *Derrington v. Plummer,* 5 Cir., 240 F.2d 922, 925, the commercially leased areas were not surplus state property, but constituted a physically and financially integral and, indeed, indispensable part of the State's plan to operate its project as a self-sustaining unit. Upkeep and maintenance of the building, including necessary repairs, were responsibilities of the Authority and were payable out of public funds. * * * Guests of the restaurant are afforded a convenient place to park their automobiles, even if they cannot enter the restaurant directly from the parking area. Similarly, its convenience for diners may well provide additional demand for the Authority's parking facilities. Should any improvements effected in the leasehold by Eagle become part of the realty, there is no possibility of increased taxes being passed on to it since the fee is held by a tax-exempt government agency. Neither can it be ignored, especially in view of Eagle's affirmative allegation that for it to serve Negroes would injure its business, that profits earned by discrimination not only contribute to, but also are indispensable elements in, the financial success of a governmental agency.

Addition of all these activities, obligations and responsibilities of the Authority, the benefits mutually conferred, together with the obvious fact that the restaurant is operated as an integral part of a public building devoted to a public parking service, indicates that degree of state participation and involvement in discriminatory action which it was the design of the Fourteenth Amendment to condemn. It is irony amounting to grave injustice that in one part of a single building, erected and maintained with public funds by an agency of the State to serve a public purpose, all persons have equal rights, while in another portion, also serving the public, a Negro is a second-class citizen [but] at the same time fully enjoys equal access to nearby restaurants in wholly privately owned buildings. [I]n its lease with Eagle the Authority could have affirmatively required Eagle to discharge the responsibilities under the Fourteenth Amendment imposed upon the private enterprise as a consequence of state participation. But no State may effectively abdicate its responsibilities by either ignoring them or by merely failing to discharge them whatever the motive may be. It is of no consolation to an individual denied the equal protection of the laws that it was done in good faith. [By] its inaction, the Authority, and through it the State, has not only made itself a party to the refusal of service, but has elected to place its power, property and prestige behind the admitted discrimination. The State has so far insinuated itself into a position of interdependence with Eagle that it must be recognized as a joint participant in the challenged activity, which, on that account, cannot be considered to have been so "purely private" as to fall without the scope of the Fourteenth Amendment.

Because readily applicable formulae may not be fashioned, the conclusions drawn from the facts and circumstances of this record are by no means declared as universal truths on the basis of which every state leasing agreement is to be tested. Owing to the very "largeness" of government, a multitude of relationships might appear to some to fall within the Amendment's embrace, but that, it must be remembered, can be determined only in the framework of the peculiar facts or circumstances present. * * * Specifically defining the limits of our inquiry, what we hold today is that when a State leases public property in the manner and for the purpose shown to have been the case here, the proscriptions of the Fourteenth Amendment must be complied with by the lessee * * *.

Reversed and remanded.

[STEWART, J., concurred, believing that, by relying on § 1501, the Delaware court "construed this legislative enactment as authorizing discriminatory classification based exclusively on color. Such a law seems to me clearly violative of the Fourteenth Amendment."

[HARLAN, J., joined by Whittaker, J., dissented: "The Court's opinion, by a process of first undiscriminatingly throwing together various factual bits and pieces and then undermining the resulting structure by an equally vague disclaimer, seems to me to leave completely at sea just what it is in this record that satisfies the requirement of 'state action.'" Rather than pass on that question, "the case should first be sent back to the state court for clarification" in respect to how it construed § 1501.[a] If Stewart, J., was correct, Harlan, J., would agree with his conclusion, but the state court could have "meant no more than that under the statute, as at common law, Eagle was free to serve only those whom it pleased."[b]]

Notes and Questions

1. *The basis for the decision.* Was there any single factor which persuaded, or should have persuaded, the Court to find state action? See generally Lewis,

a. Frankfurter, J., agreeing with this point, also dissented.

b. What result if "a state passed a statute which provided that individuals shall have the legal right to engage in racial discrimination in their own homes"? Williams, *The Twilight of State Action*, 41 Texas L.Rev. 347, 384 (1963). See note 2 after *Reitman v. Mulkey,* infra.

Burton v. Wilmington Parking Authority—A Case Without Precedent, 61 Colum. L.Rev. 1458 (1961).

(a) *Publicly owned property.* What is the significance of the fact that "the land and building were publicly owned"? If the space had been leased to a law firm, could it constitutionally discriminate among its clients?

(i) *"Public function."* In *Derrington v. Plummer,* 240 F.2d 922 (5th Cir.1956), cert. denied, 353 U.S. 924 (1957), a cafeteria in a courthouse was leased to a private party who refused to serve blacks. The conduct of the lessee was held to be state action. The lessee was found to be performing a public function because "the express purpose of the lease was to furnish cafeteria service for the benefit of persons having occasion to be in the County Courthouse."

May Eagle be found to be performing a "public function" because it "constituted a financially integral and indispensable part of the State's plan to operate its project"? If so, may the other tenants racially discriminate? If Wilmington, instead of including rental space in the parking building, had relied on rental income from other of its properties located throughout the city to help finance the parking facility, could lessees of these properties refuse to do business with blacks?

(ii) *The "motive" test.* Would *Burton* have been an easier case if "the real purpose of the lease" was to permit Eagle to exclude blacks. Is this a logical or desirable point to draw the line? Is either the state's involvement or the effect of discrimination any less if the state's purpose is not discriminatory?

(b) What is the significance of the fact that the location of the restaurant in the parking facility "confers mutual benefits"? Suppose Eagle were located in a private building immediately adjacent to the public parking building?

(c) What is the significance of the fact that the city is "profiting from the discrimination" because if it forbade it, Eagle would not pay as high a rental? If the state sells surplus property without requiring its nondiscriminatory use because such a requirement would bring the city a lower price, may the purchaser constitutionally discriminate? If such a requirement were financially irrelevant but the state neglected to include it, may the buyer discriminate?

(d) What is the significance of the facts that the Authority was responsible for "maintenance of the building" and that the property was tax-exempt? Are these factors simply paid for by Eagle in higher rental?

(e) What is the significance of the fact that the Authority "insinuated itself into a position of [financial] interdependence with Eagle"? Consider 75 Harv.L. Rev. 146 (1961): "Thus analyzed, the decision might justify the application of the equal protection clause to the private contractor who built the garage, or to the businessmen who trade extensively with a government agency."

(f) What is the significance of the fact that discrimination exists because of the Authority's "inaction"? Does *Burton* stand for the proposition that anytime the state could prevent discrimination, failure to do so is state action?

2. *Extent of the decision.* May Eagle racially discriminate in hiring employees? In buying from suppliers? May Eagle refuse to rent its banquet room to one political party if it rents it to others. May its conduct constitute state action for purposes of the equal protection clause but not for the first amendment?

3. *Sales of public property.* Would the result in *Burton* have been different if Eagle had been sold a fee in the property? Suppose a city sells its swimming

pool on condition that the buyer continue to so operate it; if not, reverter to the city. What result if the buyer racially segregates?

4. *Private schools.* (a) NORWOOD v. HARRISON, 413 U.S. 455, 93 S.Ct. 2804, 37 L.Ed.2d 723 (1973), per BURGER, C.J., enjoined Mississippi's lending of textbooks to all students in public and private schools as applied to racially segregated private schools: "[T]hat the Constitution may compel toleration of private discrimination in some circumstances does not mean that it requires state support for such discrimination. * * *

"We do not suggest that a State violates its constitutional duty merely because it has provided *any* form of state service that benefits private schools said to be racially discriminatory. Textbooks are a basic educational tool and, like tuition grants, they are provided only in connection with schools; they are to be distinguished from generalized services government might provide to schools in common with others. Moreover, the textbooks provided to private school students by the State in this case are a form of assistance readily available from sources entirely independent of the State—unlike, for example, 'such necessities of life as electricity, water, and police and fire protection.'"

Under *Board of Educ. v. Allen*, [p. 810 supra], states *may* lend textbooks to students in parochial schools "because assistance properly confined to the secular functions of sectarian schools does not substantially promote the readily identifiable religious mission of those schools [but] in the context of this case the legitimate educational function cannot be isolated from discriminatory practices. [In contrast to *Allen*], although the Constitution does not proscribe private bias, it places no value on discrimination as it does on the values inherent in the Free Exercise Clause." Douglas and Brennan, JJ., concurred in the result.

(b) In GILMORE v. MONTGOMERY, 417 U.S. 556, 94 S.Ct. 2416, 41 L.Ed.2d 304 (1974), a federal court enjoined the city's "permitting the use of public park recreational facilities by private segregated school groups and by other non-school groups that racially discriminate in their membership." The Court, per BLACKMUN, J., modified the decree in part: It "was wholly proper for the city to be enjoined from permitting *exclusive* access to public recreational facilities by segregated private schools" (emphasis added), which had been "formed in reaction against" the federal court's school desegregation order. "[T]his assistance significantly tended to undermine the federal court order mandating [a] unitary school system in Montgomery."

But, "upon this record, we are unable to draw a conclusion as to whether the use of zoos, museums, parks, and other recreational facilities by private school groups *in common with others,* and by private nonschool organizations, involves government so directly in the actions of those users as to warrant" intervention (emphasis added). "It is possible that certain uses of city facilities will be judged to be in contravention of the parks [or school] desegregation order, [or] in some way to constitute impermissible 'state action' ascribing to the city the discriminatory actions of the groups."

The latter issue concerns "whether there is significant state involvement in the private discrimination alleged. * * * Traditional state monopolies, such as electricity, water, and police and fire protection—all generalized governmental services—do not by their mere provision constitute a showing of state involvement in invidious discrimination. *Norwood.* The same is true of a broad spectrum of municipal recreational facilities * * *.

"If, however, the city or other governmental entity rations otherwise freely accessible recreational facilities, the case for state action will naturally be stronger than if the facilities are simply available to all comers without condition or reservation. Here, for example, petitioners allege that the city engages in scheduling softball games for an all-white church league and provides balls, equipment, fields, and lighting. The city's role in that situation would be dangerously close to what was found to exist in *Burton* * * *." [a]

WHITE, J., joined by Douglas, J., concurred: "[T]he question is not whether there is state action, but whether the conceded action by the city, and hence by the State, is such that the State must be deemed to have denied the equal protection of the laws. In other words, by permitting a segregated school or group to use city-owned facilities, has the State furnished such aid to the group's segregated policies or become so involved in them that the State itself may fairly be said to have denied equal protection? Under *Burton,* it is perfectly clear that to violate the Equal Protection Clause the State itself need not make, advise, or authorize the private decision to discriminate that involves the State in the practice of segregation or would appear to do so in the minds of ordinary citizens." [b]

(c) *Significance of remedy.* In contrast to *Burton* (where plaintiff sought an injunction against Eagle Coffee Shoppe), since the only remedy sought in *Norwood* and *Gilmore* was against the state or city itself, did these cases really present any "state action" issue at all? Consider Brown, *State Action Analysis of Tax Expenditures,* 11 Harv.Civ.Rts.-Civ.Lib.L. 97, 115–19 (1976): "[T]wo kinds of 'state action' cases should [be] distinguished: only in suits in which relief is sought against a private actor should the private actor's interests be taken into account. [Thus,] it is quite possible that a plaintiff proceeding under a state action theory might prevail in enjoining the government's action but fail in his efforts to enjoin the private activity." Compare McCoy, *Current State Action Theories, the Jackson Nexus Requirement, and Employee Discharges by Semi-Public and State-Aided Institutions,* 31 Vand.L.Rev. 785, 802 (1978): "Although this theoretical distinction has considerable superficial appeal, primarily because it is formulated in terms of balancing competing constitutional interests, closer inspection reveals no significant difference between the cases. [E]ither kind of suit presents the private actor with precisely the same basic option—either modify the private action to conform to fourteenth amendment standards or do without the state aid. In other words, the two kinds of suits are indistinguishable in terms of the private interest interfered with, and therefore they should not present significantly different standards for the level of state aid required." Contrast Brown, supra, at 119 n. 102: "It is of course true that the removal of the government aid will have a coercive effect on the private actor. In some cases the pressure to conform private behavior to constitutional standards generated by the loss of assistance will be as coercive as an injunction. In such a case, however, the fact that withdrawing the aid had a strong influence on private behavior would imply a high level of significance of government involvement with the private actor. In that case it would be appropriate to impose relief on the private actor as well as on the government, so the remedy distinction would not apply."

In any event, since the practices in *Norwood* and *Gilmore* were not shown to be "motivated" to perpetuate racial discrimination, can these decisions be

a. Brennan, J., concurred in part but would enjoin *any* "school-sponsored or directed uses of the city recreational facilities that enable private segregated schools to duplicate public school operations at public expense."

b. Marshall, J., generally agreed with White, J.

squared with *Washington v. Davis,* p. 903 supra? Given the doctrines that (1) public financial aid to parochial schools violates the establishment clause if either the *purpose or effect* advances religion (Ch. 9, Sec. 1, III), whereas (2) a racially discriminatory *purpose* must exist for violation of the equal protection clause (Ch. 10, Sec. 2, III), can *Norwood* be squared with *Board of Educ. v. Allen?* See Choper, *Thoughts on State Action: The "Government Function" and "Power Theory" Approaches,* 1979 Wash.U.L.Q. 757, 765–69.

(d) What results in *Norwood* and *Gilmore* if the remedy sought had been to compel the private schools to desegregate? Should some or all private schools be held to the requirements of the equal protection clause? [c]

5. *Tax exempt organizations.* May government give tax exemptions (or permit tax deductions for donations) to private schools, fraternal groups and charitable foundations that fail to adhere to fourteenth amendment requirements? See generally Bittker & Kaufman, *Taxes and Civil Rights: "Constitutionalizing" the Internal Revenue Code,* 82 Yale L.J. 51 (1972). Consider Note, *State Action and the United States Junior Chamber of Commerce,* 43 Geo.Wash. L.Rev. 1407, 1423–24 (1975): "As the legislative history indicates, the Internal Revenue Code's tax exemptions for charitable organizations are based upon the theory that the Government is compensated for the loss of revenue by being relieved of the financial burden that would otherwise have to be met by appropriations of government funds. [Where] the private entity is thus acting as a surrogate for the government, any discrimination connected with the performance of public services, even if not affirmatively approved by the government, subjects the victims to discrimination that would not have occurred had the government performed the services directly. The government cannot avoid these constitutional limitations by delegating its functions to private entities, even if the delegation is well-intentioned." See also Parker, *Evans v. Newton and the Racially Restricted Charitable Trust,* 13 How.L.J. 223 (1967). Reconsider note 4(c) supra.

SHELLEY v. KRAEMER

334 U.S. 1, 68 S.Ct. 836, 92 L.Ed. 1161 (1948).

MR. CHIEF JUSTICE VINSON delivered the opinion of the Court.

[In two cases from Missouri and Michigan, petitioners were blacks who had purchased houses from whites despite the fact that the properties were subject to restrictive covenants, signed by most property owners in the block, providing that for a specified time (in one case fifty years from 1911) the property would be sold only to Caucasians. Respondents, owners of other property subject to the covenants, sued to enjoin the blacks from taking possession and to divest them of title. The state courts granted the relief.]

Whether the equal protection clause * * * inhibits judicial enforcement by state courts of restrictive covenants based on race or color is a question which this Court has not heretofore been called upon to consider. * * *

---

c. See *Runyon v. McCrary,* p. 1517 infra, holding that a federal statute prohibits private schools from refusing to accept black students. See generally Note, *The Wall of Racial Separation: The Role of Private and Parochial Schools in Racial Integration,* 43 N.Y.U.L.Rev. 514 (1968); Note, *Segregation* *Academies and State Action,* 82 Yale L.J. 1436 (1973); O'Neil, *Private Universities and Public Law,* 19 Buf.L.Rev. 155 (1970).

For further consideration of this issue, see note 2(b) after *Flagg Bros. v. Brooks,* Sec. 4 infra.

It cannot be doubted that among the civil rights intended to be protected from discriminatory state action by the Fourteenth Amendment are the rights to acquire, enjoy, own and dispose of property. Equality in the enjoyment of property rights was regarded by the framers of that Amendment as an essential pre-condition to the realization of other basic civil rights and liberties which the Amendment was intended to guarantee.[7] Thus, § 1978 of the Revised Statutes, derived from § 1 of the Civil Rights Act of 1866 which was enacted by Congress while the Fourteenth Amendment was also under consideration, provides:

"All citizens of the United States shall have the same right, in every State and Territory, as is enjoyed by white citizens thereof to inherit, purchase, lease, sell, hold, and convey real and personal property." * * *

It is likewise clear that restrictions on the right of occupancy of the sort sought to be created by the private agreements in these cases could not be squared with the requirements of the Fourteenth Amendment if imposed by state statute or local ordinance. * * *

But the present cases [do] not involve action by state legislatures or city councils. Here the particular patterns of discrimination and the areas in which the restrictions are to operate, are determined, in the first instance, by the terms of agreements among private individuals. Participation of the State consists in the enforcement of the restrictions so defined. * * *

Since the decision of this Court in the *Civil Rights Cases,* the principle has become firmly embedded in our constitutional law that the action inhibited by the first section of the Fourteenth Amendment is only such action as may fairly be said to be that of the States. That Amendment erects no shield against merely private conduct, however discriminatory or wrongful.

We conclude, therefore, that the restrictive agreements standing alone cannot be regarded as a violation of any rights guaranteed to petitioners by the Fourteenth Amendment. So long as the purposes of those agreements are effectuated by voluntary adherence to their terms, it would appear clear that there has been no action by the State and the provisions of the Amendment have not been violated.

But here there was more. These are cases in which the purposes of the agreements were secured only by judicial enforcement by state courts of the restrictive terms of the agreements. The respondents urge that judicial enforcement of private agreements does not amount to state action; or, in any event, the participation of the State is so attenuated in character as not to amount to state action within the meaning of the Fourteenth Amendment. Finally, it is suggested, even if the States in these cases may be deemed to have acted in the constitutional sense, their action did not deprive petitioners of rights guaranteed by the Fourteenth Amendment. * * *

That the action of state courts and of judicial officers in their official capacities is to be regarded as action of the State within the meaning of the Fourteenth Amendment, is a proposition which has long been established * * *. Thus, in *Virginia v. Rives,* 1880, 100 U.S. 313, 318, 25 L.Ed. 667, this Court stated: "It is doubtless true that a State may act through different agencies,—either by its legislative, its executive, or its judicial authorities; and the prohibitions of the amendment extend to all action of the State denying equal protection of the laws, whether it be action by one of these agencies or by

7. *Slaughter-House Cases* [p. 250 supra].
See Flack, *The Adoption of the Fourteenth Amendment.*

another." [In] the *Civil Rights Cases,* this Court pointed out that the Amendment makes void "state action of every kind" which is inconsistent with the guaranties therein contained, and extends to manifestations of "state authority in the shape of laws, customs, or judicial or executive proceedings." * * *

One of the earliest applications of the prohibitions contained in the Fourteenth Amendment to action of state judicial officials occurred in cases in which Negroes had been excluded from jury service * * *. These cases demonstrate, also, the early recognition by this Court that state action in violation of the Amendment's provisions is equally repugnant to the constitutional commands whether directed by state statute or taken by a judicial official in the absence of statute. * * *

The action of state courts in imposing penalties or depriving parties of other substantive rights without providing adequate notice and opportunity to defend, has, of course, long been regarded as a denial of the due process of law guaranteed by the Fourteenth Amendment.

In numerous cases, this Court has reversed criminal convictions in state courts for failure of those courts to provide the essential ingredients of a fair hearing. Thus it has been held that convictions obtained in state courts under the domination of a mob are void. Convictions obtained by coerced confessions, by the use of perjured testimony known by the prosecution to be such, or without the effective assistance of counsel, have also been held to be exertions of state authority in conflict with the fundamental rights protected by the Fourteenth Amendment.

But the examples of state judicial action which have been held by this Court to violate the Amendment's commands are not restricted to situations in which the judicial proceedings were found in some manner to be procedurally unfair. It has been recognized that the action of state courts in enforcing a substantive common-law rule formulated by those courts, may result in the denial of rights guaranteed by the Fourteenth Amendment * * *. Thus, in *AFL v. Swing,* 1941, 312 U.S. 321, 61 S.Ct. 568, 85 L.Ed. 855, enforcement by state courts of the common-law policy of the State, which resulted in the restraining of peaceful picketing, was held to be state action of the sort prohibited by the Amendment's guaranties of freedom of discussion. In *Cantwell v. Connecticut,* 1940, 310 U.S. 296, 60 S.Ct. 900, 84 L.Ed. 1213, a conviction in a state court of the common-law crime of breach of the peace was, under the circumstances of the case, found to be a violation of the Amendment's commands relating to freedom of religion. In *Bridges v. California,* 1941, 314 U.S. 252, 62 S.Ct. 190, 86 L.Ed. 192, enforcement of the state's common-law rule relating to contempts by publication was held to be state action inconsistent with the prohibitions of the Fourteenth Amendment. * * *

We have no doubt that there has been state action in these cases in the full and complete sense of the phrase. The undisputed facts disclose that petitioners were willing purchasers of properties upon which they desired to establish homes. The owners of the properties were willing sellers; and contracts of sale were accordingly consummated. It is clear that but for the active intervention of the state courts, supported by the full panoply of state power, petitioners would have been free to occupy the properties in question without restraint.

These are not cases, as has been suggested, in which the States have merely abstained from action, leaving private individuals free to impose such discriminations as they see fit. Rather, these are cases in which the States have made available to such individuals the full coercive power of government to deny to petitioners, on the grounds of race or color, the enjoyment of property rights in premises which petitioners are willing and financially able to acquire and which the grantors are willing to sell. ＊ ＊ ＊

The enforcement of the restrictive agreements by the state courts in these cases was directed pursuant to the common-law policy of the States as formulated by those courts in earlier decisions. [The] judicial action in each case bears the clear and unmistakable imprimatur of the State. We have noted that previous decisions of this Court have established the proposition that judicial action is not immunized from the operation of the Fourteenth Amendment simply because it is taken pursuant to the state's common-law policy. Nor is the Amendment ineffective simply because the particular pattern of discrimination, which the State has enforced, was defined initially by the terms of a private agreement. State action, as that phrase is understood for the purposes of the Fourteenth Amendment, refers to exertions of state power in all forms. ＊ ＊ ＊ We have noted that freedom from discrimination by the States in the enjoyment of property rights was among the basic objectives sought to be effectuated by the framers of the Fourteenth Amendment. That such discrimination has occurred in these cases is clear. ＊ ＊ ＊

Respondents urge, however, that since the state courts stand ready to enforce restrictive covenants excluding white persons[,] enforcement of covenants excluding colored persons may not be deemed a denial of equal protection of the laws to the colored persons who are thereby affected. This contention does not bear scrutiny. [The] rights created by the first section of the Fourteenth Amendment are, by its terms, guaranteed to the individual. The rights established are personal rights. It is, therefore, no answer to these petitioners to say that the courts may also be induced to deny white persons rights of ownership and occupancy on grounds of race or color. Equal protection of the laws is not achieved through indiscriminate imposition of inequalities. ＊ ＊ ＊

Reversed.

Mr. Justice Reed, Mr. Justice Jackson, and Mr. Justice Rutledge took no part in the consideration or decision of these cases.[a]

Notes and Questions

1. *Authority of prior decisions.* Do the cases holding that "judicial action is state action" call for the result in *Shelley*? Consider Comment, *The Impact of Shelley v. Kraemer on the State Action Concept*, 44 Calif.L.Rev. 718, 724 (1956): "In the cases exemplifying 'orthodox' judicial violation the prohibited activity [e.g., barring blacks from juries] was practiced by the judge himself. [But in *Shelley*] the discrimination originated with private persons." May this be said about "convictions obtained under the domination of a mob"?

As to those cases (*Swing, Cantwell, Bridges*) involving "the action of state courts in enforcing a substantive common-law rule," consider Comment, 45 Mich. L.Rev. 733, 742–43 (1947): "The difficulty of attributing the discrimination effected by the covenants to the enforcing tribunal is not to be escaped by pretending that it forms an element of the common law from which the right to enforcement is derived. The common law is simply the policy of the state in certain of its aspects, [and] that policy as seen in respect to these facts looks no further than to the protection of property and contract rights." Did the state policy in *Cantwell* look any further than to the protection of public tranquility?

a. For a history of the battle against re-   *in the Covenant Cases,* 6 W.Res.L.Rev. 101 strictive covenants, see Vose, *NAACP Strategy*   (1955).

Did it, in *Bridges,* look any further than to the protection of the integrity of the court? For careful analysis, see Van Alstyne, *Mr. Justice Black, Constitutional Review, and the Talisman of State Action,* 1965 Duke L.J. 219.

Are the considerations in *Shelley* different from all of these cases because it involves equal protection rather than due process? Because these other cases involve the right of free speech? Should there be a distinction between civil suits and criminal prosecutions? Consider Comment, 45 Mich.L.Rev. 733, 746 (1947): "The theory of civil remedies is that the interest of the state in the protection of property and contract rights is ordinarily secondary to that of the individual citizen, that the extent to which the protection of the law is obtained for them is largely discretionary with him. [A] criminal statute is an expression of state policy of a much higher order. In theory, the state pursues purposes of its own in criminal legislation."

2. Is *Shelley* supportable because "so long as it is unconstitutional for a state to require racial segregation by zoning statutes [it] is equally unconstitutional for the state to bring it about by any other form of state action"? McGovney, *Racial Residential Segregation by State Court Enforcement of Restrictive Agreements, Covenants or Conditions in Deeds is Unconstitutional,* 33 Calif. L.Rev. 5, 30 (1945). Is the source of the discrimination the same in both instances? Or is this a variation of the "government function" approach? Consider Groner & Helfeld, *Race Discrimination in Housing,* 57 Yale L.J. 426, 454 (1948): "Where covenants do not presently cover entire areas, experience shows that, if encouraged by court enforcement, covenants do in time cover all of the area available for desirable residences." See also Ming, *Racial Restrictions and the Fourteenth Amendment: The Restrictive Covenant Cases,* 16 U.Chi.L.Rev. 203 (1949).

3. BARROWS v. JACKSON, 346 U.S. 249, 73 S.Ct. 1031, 97 L.Ed. 1586 (1953), held that an action by a co-covenantor to recover damages from a property owner who sold to a black was barred by equal protection. Would this suit, like the one in *Shelley,* involve "the full coercive power of government to deny [on] grounds of race [the] enjoyment of property rights"? Would the suit in *Barrows* have the same effect as a suit to enjoin a white property owner from breaching the covenant? See *Hurd v. Hodge,* 334 U.S. 24, 68 S.Ct. 847, 92 L.Ed. 1187 (1948).

4. *The limits of Shelley.* (a) Consider Comment, 44 Calif.L.Rev. 718, 733 (1956): "If obtaining court aid to carry out 'private' activity 'converts' such private action into 'state' action, then there could never be any private action in any practical sense. So entwined are our lives with the law that the logical result would be that almost *all* action, to be effective, must result in state action. Thus all private activity would be required to 'conform' with the standards of conduct imposed on the states by the fourteenth amendment."

(b) "Professor Louis Pollak [*Racial Discrimination and Judicial Integrity,* 108 U.Pa.L.Rev. 1, 13 (1959)] would apply *Shelley* to prevent the state from enforcing a discrimination by one who does not wish to discriminate; [b] but he would allow the state to give its support to willing discrimination * * *. [H]is proposal requires important limitation of *Shelley,* and raises a number of possible objections. One may argue, for instance, that while the fourteenth amendment may perhaps protect an individual's 'liberty' to refuse to discrimi-

---

b. See *Moose Lodge v. Irvis,* Sec. 4 infra, for this application of *Shelley*—in the only opinion of the Court (apart from *Barrows v.* *Jackson*) that has relied on *Shelley* to find state action. Cf. also fn. 10 in *Flagg Bros. v. Brooks,* Sec. 4 infra, and note 1 thereafter.

nate as it may protect another's liberty to discriminate, that hardly seems to be the focus of the equal protection clause. That clause seems to be designed to protect the victim against discrimination, not to protect an unwilling 'actor' against being compelled to discriminate. It would seem also an eccentric constitutional provision which protected the aggrieved against involuntary discrimination by private persons but not against voluntary private discrimination. Moreover, the distinction is offered as a definition of 'state action.' But whether the judgment of a court enforces a voluntary discrimination or compels a no-longer-voluntary discrimination, the discrimination is private in origin; in both cases it requires a court judgment to make the discrimination effective. * * * Finally, in *Shelley* itself, is it acceptable to think of the case as one in which the state was compelling discrimination by a grantor of property who no longer wished to discriminate? In essence, the state was enforcing discrimination by the other parties to the covenant." Henkin, *Shelley v. Kraemer: Notes for a Revised Opinion,* 110 U.Pa.L.Rev. 473, 477–78 & n. 10 (1962).

Compare Horowitz, *The Misleading Search for "State Action" Under the Fourteenth Amendment,* 30 So.Cal.L.Rev. 208, 213 (1957): "There is involved here a question of the degree of effect of different forms of state action on a prospective Negro buyer's opportunity to purchase and use land * * *. The state does not substantially deny the Negro that opportunity by *permitting* a private person to refuse to deal with him because of his race. This would be the situation where there was 'voluntary adherence' to the restrictive covenant by the landowner. But the state does to a far greater degree deny the Negro the opportunity to acquire land, because of his race, if it *compels* a landowner not to deal with the Negro. This is the situation where the state enforces the restrictive covenant after a landowner has decided not to adhere to it."

Since restraints on alienation of property are presumptively void, being valid generally only if the court finds the restraint a reasonable one and consistent with public policy, Restatement, *Property* § 406 (1944), was there state action in *Shelley* because the court placed its imprimatur on a racially discriminatory restraint? Might it be argued that, due to this, the source of discrimination was public rather than private? See Choper, *Thoughts on State Action,* 1979 Wash.U.L.Q. 757, 769–71.

(c) Consider Comment, 44 Calif.L.Rev. 718, 735 (1956): "It is submitted that the doctrine of judicial enforcement as interpreted by *Shelley* is applicable only when the court action abets private discrimination which in the absence of such judicial aid would be ineffective. * * * Where the private activity, admitted in *Shelley* to be valid in itself, is already effective, it is not to be said that the court, recognizing or failing to abolish the activity, is itself an arm of the discrimination; the situation has remained the same, court action or no. It is only where the proponents of discrimination, unable to further their ends privately, seek court aid is the state itself causing discrimination under *Shelley.*"

(i) Suppose plaintiff is denied relief in a breach of contract suit against a cemetery for refusing to bury a black because the burial lot purchase contract was restricted to Caucasians? Compare *Rice v. Sioux City Mem'l Park Cem.,* 349 U.S. 70, 75 S.Ct. 614, 99 L.Ed. 897 (1955) with *Spencer v. Flint Mem'l Park Ass'n,* 4 Mich.App. 157, 144 N.W.2d 622 (1966). What result under *Shelley?* Under the above theory? Would denial of plaintiff's cause of action make the discrimination "effective"? If the body had already been interred, could the cemetery obtain the court's aid in removing it?

(ii) Suppose a landlord seeks the court's aid to evict a tenant whose defense is that the eviction is solely on the grounds of race (or religion, or speech)?

Suppose the tenant seeks to restrain the landlord from recovering possession of the leased premises? If the tenant refuses to give up possession and is forcibly evicted by the landlord, what result in the tenant's suit for assault? Would a desirable rule produce different results in the above situations?

(iii) At common law, no person who offered his property for sale could be enjoined from arbitrarily refusing to sell to another. Suppose an owner refuses to sell solely because of the buyer's race. Consider Huber, *Revolution in Private Law?* 6 S.C.L.Q. 8, 26 (1953): "It would seem, under *Shelley,* that he could bring suit alleging denial of equal protection of the laws. Even if the court wished to dismiss the suit as not stating a cause of action [it] would seem that the court could not do so without supporting the discrimination."

5. On remand, after *Evans v. Newton,* the Georgia courts interpreted Senator Bacon's will and held that "because the park's segregated, whites-only character was an essential and inseparable part of the testator's plan," the "cy pres doctrine to amend the terms of the will by striking the racial restrictions" was inapplicable; that, therefore, the trust failed and the trust property "by operation of law reverted to the heirs of Senator Bacon." EVANS v. ABNEY, 396 U.S. 435, 90 S.Ct. 628, 24 L.Ed.2d 634 (1970), per BLACK, J., affirmed, finding that "the Georgia court had no alternative under its relevant trust laws, which are long standing and neutral with regard to race, but to end the Baconsfield trust": "[T]he Constitution imposes no requirement upon the Georgia court to approach Bacon's will any differently than it would approach any will creating any charitable trust of any kind. [T]here is not the slightest indication that any of the Georgia judges involved were motivated by racial animus or discriminatory intent of any sort in construing and enforcing Senator Bacon's will. Nor is there any indication that Senator Bacon in drawing up his will was persuaded or induced to include racial restrictions by the fact that such restrictions were permitted by the Georgia trust statutes." *Shelley* was "easily distinguishable" because here "the termination of the park was a loss shared equally by the white and Negro citizens of Macon."

BRENNAN, J., dissented: "For almost half a century Baconsfield has been a public park." When "a public facility would remain open but for the constitutional command that it be operated on a nonsegregated basis, the closing of that facility conveys an unambiguous message of community involvement in racial discrimination. [But] the Court finds that in this case it is not the State or city but 'a private party which is injecting the racially discriminatory motivation.'" Nonetheless, "this discriminatory closing is permeated with state action": "First, there is state action whenever a State enters into an arrangement which creates a private right to compel or enforce the reversion of a public facility" and, here, "in accepting title to the park," city officials agreed to that "if the city should ever incur a constitutional obligation to desegregate the park. [The] decision whether or not a public facility shall be operated in compliance with the Constitution is an essential *governmental* decision." Second, "nothing in the record suggests that after our decision in *Evans v. Newton* the City of Macon retracted its previous willingness to manage Baconsfield on a nonsegregated basis, or that the white beneficiaries of Senator Bacon's generosity were unwilling to share it with Negroes, rather than have the park revert to his heirs." Thus, contrary to *Shelley,* "this is a case of a state court's enforcement of a racial restriction to prevent willing parties from dealing with one another." [d]

d. Brennan, J., also pointed to White, J.'s opinion in *Evans v. Newton,* contending that the will's racial restriction was so "en-   couraged" by the 1905 Georgia statute as to make the state "significantly involved" in the discrimination—citing *Burton* and *Reitman v.*

DOUGLAS, J., dissented: "Bacon's will did not leave any remainder or reversion in 'Baconsfield' to his heirs." Thus, giving them the property does "as much violence to Bacon's purpose as would conversion of an 'all-white' park into an 'all-Negro' park. [The] purpose of the will was to dedicate the land for some municipal use. * * * Letting both races share the facility is closer to a realization of Bacon's desire than a complete destruction of the will." Marshall, J., did not participate.

6. *The balancing approach.* Is the ultimate solution in *Shelley,* and other cases, a balancing of *all* of the particular interests involved? Consider Van Alstyne & Karst, *State Action,* 14 Stan.L.Rev. 3, 44–45 (1961): "[There has been] an attempt to discover or invent the *kind* of state connection which will satisfy the state action requirement. It is suggested, for example, that the state acts in the sense of the amendment when it coerces private discrimination, but not when it simply lends its aid to such racial discrimination as private individuals may choose to practice. [This analysis] perpetuates the untenable distinction between the state action requirement on the one hand and the balance of 'substantive' constitutional interests on the other. This way of looking at the problem [is] even more dangerous than the suggestion's other unfortunate aspect: its assumption that every private discrimination is invalid once the right formal state connection has been found." See also Williams, *Mulkey v. Reitman and State Action,* 14 U.C.L.A.L.Rev. 26 (1966).

Compare Henkin, note 4(b) supra at 496: "Generally, the equal protection clause precludes state enforcement of private discrimination. There is, however, a small area of liberty favored by the Constitution even over claims to equality. Rights of liberty and property, of privacy and voluntary association, must be balanced, in close cases, against the right not to have the state enforce discrimination against the victim. In the few instances in which the right to discriminate is protected or preferred by the Constitution, the state may enforce it." [e] Is it the contention that the inquiry is not whether state action is present but whether the state policy preference, expressed through its laws, between conflicting claims of individuals, denies equal protection?

See Horowitz, *Fourteenth Amendment Aspects of Racial Discrimination in "Private" Housing,* 52 Calif.L.Rev. 1, 12–20 (1964): "The determination of the constitutionality under the fourteenth amendment of state law permitting a private person to discriminate, on racial grounds, against another private person in a specific fact situation requires consideration of various interdependent factors: the nature and degree of injury to the person discriminated against, the interest of the discriminator in being permitted to discriminate, and the interest of the discriminatee in having opportunity of access equal to that of other persons to the benefits of governmental assistance to the discriminator * * *. If there is extensive state participation and involvement related to the activities of the discriminator, it is more likely that those activities will be public in nature, with consequent public indignity and humiliation suffered by the person discriminated against, and more likely that denial of access to those activities will be of some significance to the discriminatee. [When] there is governmental assistance to the discriminator in carrying on his activities, and the assistance is being provided to further the purposes of a governmental program designed to

Mulkey, infra. See note 2 after *Reitman,* infra.

e. For support, see Douglas, J., concurring in *Lombard v. Louisiana,* fn. b, p. 1092 supra. See also Black, *"State Action," Equal Protec-* *tion, and California's Proposition 14,* 81 Harv. L.Rev. 69, 83–109 (1967); Sengstock & Sengstock, *Discrimination: A Constitutional Dilemma,* 9 Wm. & M.L.Rev. 59 (1967).

provide benefits for the public or a permissible segment of the public, the effect of the discrimination is to deny to the discriminatee the opportunity to have equal opportunity of access to the benefits of the governmental program." [f]

Compare Choper, *Thoughts on State Action*, 1979 Wash.U.L.Q. 757, 762: "[The balancing approaches] contradict a central feature of the fourteenth amendment. Although its major purpose was to augment the authority of the national government to secure certain constitutional rights, its primary thrust was to accomplish this goal by outlawing deprivations of these rights by state governments and their legal structures rather than by the impact of private choice. By effectively obliterating the distinction between state action and private action, these theories eviscerate the fourteenth amendment's restriction on the authority of the national government vis-à-vis the states regarding the regulation of the myriad relationships that occur between one individual and another. [A]t the initiative of any litigant who is offended by another person's behavior, these theories would subject to the scrutiny of federal judges, under substantive constitutional standards customarily developed for measuring the actions of government, all sorts of private conduct that because of political constraints and collective good sense would probably never be mandated by law. Further, by permitting private actors to violate constitutional norms when they have a constitutionally protected liberty interest to do so, these theories would delegate to federal judges the power to implement the vague mandate of the due process clause in speaking the final word about the validity of virtually all transactions between individuals. In doing so, the national judiciary would be required to determine whether private conduct was constitutionally immune from government control even though, because of general political sensitivity to individual autonomy, such private conduct probably would never be regulated by the state." See also Lewis, *The Role of Law in Regulating Discrimination in Places of Public Accommodation*, 13 Buf.L.Rev. 402, 416–18 (1964).

Consider also Haber, *Notes on the Limits of Shelley v. Kraemer*, 18 Rutgers L.Rev. 811, 813, 824–25 (1964): "[I]t is dangerous to let any constitutional guarantee rest on an ad hoc balancing test. [I]t is extremely difficult to weigh liberty against equality; the outcome depends entirely on the views of the particular judges. While to some extent this must always be true in constitutional adjudications, it is nevertheless incumbent upon lawyers to develop a principle that will put some restraint even on the membership of the Supreme Court.   *   *   *

"[T]he state can prohibit all racial discrimination. There is no liberty to discriminate. Whatever other incidents of property may be protected by the due process clause, the property and liberty protected by it occurring in the same amendment which guarantees the equal protection of the laws, does not include the right to treat people differently on the basis of their race and color."

Professor Haber would limit *Shelley* as follows: "the principle of state action as applied to judicial and police aid to private discrimination permits such aid only in the following instances: (1) Where the suit is by the victim and he seeks a new remedy based entirely on the discrimination, the state may deny the remedy. (2) Though this is doubtful, conceivably [the] state may also deny the

---

f. For other discussions of a balancing approach, see Glennon & Nowak, *A Functional Analysis of the Fourteenth Amendment "State Action" Requirement*, 1976 Sup.Ct.Rev. 221; Quinn, *State Action: A Pathology and a Proposed Cure*, 64 Calif.L.Rev. 146 (1976); Thomp- son, *Piercing the Veil of State Action: The Revisionist Theory and a Mythical Application to Self-Help Repossession*. 1977 Wis.L.Rev. 1; Morris & Powe, *Constitutional & Statutory Rights to Open Housing*, 44 Wash.L.Rev. 1–56 (1968).

remedy based on a contract voluntarily entered into with the discriminator by the victim of the discrimination or his privy, where the discriminator defends on the basis of a discriminatory provision in the contract. (3) The state may protect all property and personal rights of the discriminator other than the act of discrimination. (4) The state may even protect the act of discrimination provided it has offered the victim an adequate alternative remedy."

REITMAN v. MULKEY
387 U.S. 369, 87 S.Ct. 1627, 18 L.Ed.2d 830 (1967).

MR. JUSTICE WHITE delivered the opinion of the Court.

[Section 26 of the California constitution], an initiated measure submitted to the people [in] a statewide ballot in 1964, provides in part as follows: "Neither the State nor any subdivision or agency thereof shall deny, limit or abridge, directly or indirectly, the right of any person, who is willing or desires to sell, lease or rent any part or all of his real property, to decline to sell, lease or rent such property to such person or persons as he, in his absolute discretion, chooses." The real property covered by § 26 is limited to residential property and contains an exception for state-owned real estate.

[Respondents] sued under § 51 and § 52 of the California Civil Code [forbidding racial discrimination "in all business establishments"] alleging that petitioners had refused to rent them an apartment solely on account of their race. An injunction and damages were demanded. Petitioners moved for summary judgment on the ground that §§ 51 and 52, insofar as they were the basis for the Mulkeys' action, had been rendered null and void by the adoption of [§ 26] after the filing of the complaint. The trial court granted the motion [but the California Supreme Court held that § 26] was invalid as denying [equal protection].

We affirm the judgment [which] quite properly undertook to examine the constitutionality of § 26 in terms of its "immediate objective," its "ultimate impact" and its "historical context and the conditions existing prior to its enactment." Judgments such as these we have frequently undertaken ourselves. *Yick Wo v. Hopkins; Lombard v. Louisiana; Anderson v. Martin.* But here the California Supreme Court has addressed itself to these matters and we should give careful consideration to its views because they concern the purpose, scope, and operative effect of a provision of the California Constitution.

First, the court considered whether § 26 was concerned at all with private discriminations in residential housing. This involved a review of past efforts by the California Legislature to regulate such discriminations. The Unruh Act, on which respondents based their cases, was passed in 1959. [I]n 1963, came the Rumford Fair Housing Act * * * prohibiting racial discriminations in the sale or rental of any private dwelling containing more than four units. * * *

It was against this background that [§ 26] was enacted. Its immediate design and intent, the California court said, was "to overturn state laws that bore on the right of private sellers and lessors to discriminate," the Unruh and Rumford Acts, and "to forestall future state action that might circumscribe this right." * * *

Second, the court conceded that the State was permitted a neutral position with respect to private racial discriminations and that the State was not bound by the Federal Constitution to forbid them. But [the] court deemed it necessary to determine whether [§ 26] invalidly involved the State in racial discriminations in the housing market. Its conclusion was that it did.

To reach this result, the state court examined certain prior decisions in this Court in which discriminatory state action was identified. Based on these cases, it concluded that a prohibited state involvement could be found "even where the state can be charged with only encouraging," rather than commanding discrimination. Also of particular interest to the court was Mr. Justice Stewart's concurrence in *Burton*, where it was said that the Delaware courts had construed an existing Delaware statute as "authorizing" racial discrimination in restaurants and that the statute was therefore invalid. To the California court "[t]he instant case presents an undeniably analogous situation" wherein the State had taken affirmative action designed to make private discriminations legally possible. Section 26 was said to have changed the situation from one in which discriminatory practices were restricted "to one wherein it is encouraged, within the meaning of the cited decisions"; § 26 was legislative action "which authorized private discrimination" and made the State "at least a partner in the instant act of discrimination ∗ ∗ ∗." The court could "conceive of no other purpose for an application of section 26 aside from authorizing the perpetration of a purported private discrimination ∗ ∗ ∗." ∗ ∗ ∗

There is no sound reason for rejecting this judgment. [It] did not read either our cases or the Fourteenth Amendment as establishing an automatic constitutional barrier to the repeal of an existing law prohibiting racial discriminations in housing; nor did the court rule that a State may never put in statutory form an existing policy of neutrality with respect to private discriminations. [It] dealt with § 26 as though it expressly authorized and constitutionalized the private right to discriminate [and] the court assessed the ultimate impact of § 26 in the California environment and concluded that the section would encourage and significantly involve the State in private racial discrimination contrary to the Fourteenth Amendment.

The California court could very reasonably conclude that § 26 would and did have wider impact than a mere repeal of existing statutes. ∗ ∗ ∗ Private discriminations in housing were now not only free from Rumford and Unruh but they also enjoyed a far different status than was true before the passage of those statutes. The right to discriminate, including the right to discriminate on racial grounds, was now embodied in the State's basic charter, immune from legislative, executive, or judicial regulation at any level of the state government. Those practicing racial discriminations need no longer rely solely on their personal choice. They could now invoke express constitutional authority, free from censure or interference of any kind from official sources. ∗ ∗ ∗

This Court has never attempted the "impossible task" of formulating an infallible test for determining whether the State "in any of its manifestations" has become significantly involved in private discriminations. [Here] the California court, armed as it was with the knowledge of the facts and circumstances concerning the passage and potential impact of § 26, and familiar with the milieu in which that provision would operate, has determined that the provision would involve the State in private racial discriminations to an unconstitutional degree. We accept this holding of the California court. [Section 26] was intended to authorize, and does authorize, racial discrimination in the housing market. The right to discriminate is now one of the basic policies of the State. The California Supreme Court believes that the section will significantly encourage and involve the State in private discriminations. We have been presented with no persuasive considerations indicating that this judgment should be overturned.

Affirmed.[a]

MR. JUSTICE HARLAN, whom MR. JUSTICE BLACK, MR. JUSTICE CLARK, and MR. JUSTICE STEWART join, dissenting.

[California] has decided to remain "neutral" in the realm of private discrimination affecting the sale or rental of private residential property * * *. In short, all that has happened is that California has effected a pro tanto repeal of its prior statutes forbidding private discrimination. This runs no more afoul of the Fourteenth Amendment than would have California's failure to pass any such antidiscrimination statutes in the first instance. The fact that such repeal was also accompanied by a constitutional prohibition against future enactment of such laws by the California Legislature cannot well be thought to affect, from a federal constitutional standpoint, the validity of what California has done.

* * *

The Court attempts to fit § 26 within the coverage of the Equal Protection Clause by characterizing it as in effect an affirmative call to residents of California to discriminate. [But § 26] is neutral on its face, and it is only by in effect asserting that this requirement of passive official neutrality is camouflage that the Court is able to reach its conclusion. In depicting the provision as tantamount to active state encouragement of discrimination the Court essentially relies on the fact that the California Supreme Court so concluded. * * * I agree, of course, that *findings of fact* by a state court should be given great weight, but this familiar proposition hardly aids the Court's holding in this case.

There is no disagreement whatever but that § 26 was meant to nullify California's fair-housing legislation and thus to remove from private residential property transactions the state-created impediment upon freedom of choice. There were no disputed issues of fact at all * * *. There was no finding, for example, that the defendants' actions were anything but the product of their own private choice. [There] were no findings as to the general effect of § 26. The Court declares that the California court "held the purpose and intent of § 26 was to authorize private racial discriminations in the housing market," but there is no supporting fact in the record for this characterization. * * *

A state enactment, particularly one that is simply permissive of private decision-making rather than coercive[,] should not be struck down [without] persuasive evidence of an invidious purpose or effect. [Section 26 is] a neutral provision restoring to the sphere of free choice, left untouched by the Fourteenth Amendment, private behavior within a limited area of the racial problem. The denial of equal protection emerges only from the conclusion reached by the Court that the implementation of a new policy of governmental neutrality [has] the effect of lending encouragement to those who wish to discriminate. In the context of the actual facts of the case, this conclusion appears to me to state only a truism: people who want to discriminate but were previously forbidden to do so by state law are now left free because the State has chosen to have no law on the subject at all. Obviously whenever there is a change in the law it will have resulted from the concerted activity of those who desire the change, and its enactment will allow those supporting the legislation to pursue their private goals.

a. The concurring opinion of Douglas, J., is omitted.

A moment of thought will reveal the far-reaching possibilities of the Court's new doctrine, which I am sure the Court does not intend. Every act of private discrimination is either forbidden by state law or permitted by it. There can be little doubt that such permissiveness—whether by express constitutional or statutory provision, or implicit in the common law—to some extent "encourages" those who wish to discriminate to do so. Under this theory "state action" in the form of laws that do nothing more than passively permit private discrimination could be said to tinge *all* private discrimination with the taint of unconstitutional state encouragement. * * *

I think that this decision is not only constitutionally unsound, but in its practical potentialities short-sighted. Opponents of state antidiscrimination statutes are now in a position to argue that such legislation should be defeated because, if enacted, it may be unrepealable. More fundamentally, the doctrine underlying this decision may hamper, if not preclude, attempts to deal with the delicate and troublesome problems of race relations through the legislative process. * * *

Notes and Questions

1. *Court's rationale.* (a) What was the specific basis for § 26's invalidity? Was it that it "constitutionalized the private right to discriminate" in housing, making it "immune from legislative, executive, or judicial regulation at any level of state government"—thus making it much more difficult for minorities to get governmental antidiscrimination help? Would this call for the same result even if California had never enacted the Unruh or Rumford Acts? Suppose a state provides that *all* legislation requires approval by ⅔ of the voters? All legislation having *anything* to do with the sale and purchase of real and personal property? Was § 26 a less "neutral provision"? Sufficiently "nonneutral"? Was *this* the thrust of the opinion? If so, does *Reitman* hold that racial discrimination in housing by private individuals in California is "state action"?

(b) Or did the Court rest on the finding (whose finding?) that § 26, given "the milieu in which that provision would operate," "would involve the State in private racial discriminations to an unconstitutional degree"? If so, could "mere repeal of existing statutes" so operate? Failure to enact a proposed antidiscrimination law? The mere absence of an antidiscrimination law? Consider Cox, *The Warren Court* 45 (1968): "The truth would seem to be that the absence of legal restraints gives encouragement of a sort to anyone minded to engage in discrimination, and any defeat of proposed restraints after strong public debate will give moral support to some persons who might not otherwise have been ready to discriminate. The degree of support that is given seems likely to depend upon a congeries of factors far more diffuse and subtle than the differences between repeal of a statute and amendment of a constitution." Compare 42 Wash.L.Rev. 285 (1966). See generally Black, *"State Action," Equal Protection, and California's Proposition 14*, 81 Harv.L.Rev. 69 (1967); Kurland, *Egalitarianism and the Warren Court*, 68 Mich. 629, 668–70 (1970).

Suppose a school board rescinds a resolution of its predecessor that recognized the boards' responsibility for segregation and called for—but did not enact—any remedial action? See *Dayton Bd. of Educ. v. Brinkman*, 433 U.S. 406, 413–14, 97 S.Ct. 2766, 2772, 53 L.Ed.2d 851, 859 (1977).

(c) Did the Court simply "nod in the direction of federalism" and "permit a state court to make the ultimate determinations," with the result "that one state law, impartial on its face but which, in the context of California politics, authorized and encouraged racial discrimination, was held contrary to the fourteenth amendment"—thus leaving open all questions raised above? Horan, *Law and Social Change: The Dynamics of the "State Action" Doctrine,* 17 J.Pub. L. 258, 281 (1968). Consider Karst & Horowitz, *Reitman v. Mulkey: A Telophase of Substantive Equal Protection,* 1967 Sup.Ct.Rev. 39, 48–49: "The Constitution is both a body of national law and a symbol of national unity. The Supreme Court's final responsibility for the law and for the symbol cannot lightly be passed to other bodies. [When] the critical issue decided by the state court depends on the way in which the Supreme Court's own precedents should be interpreted, deference to a purported local assessment of the constitutional balance is both circular in logic and empty of the ingredients of factfinding and value preference that should be indispensable to the making of constitutional law."

2. *State "encouragement" or "authorization."* (a) To what extent does *Reitman* establish the principle that state law which *encourages* (or *authorizes*) private conduct results in "state action"?[b] Is this the basis for Stewart, J.'s concurrence in *Burton?* Consider Burke & Reber, fn. c after *Shelley,* at 1105–09 (1973): "[The] basic principle limiting the scope of the fourteenth amendment would be destroyed by equating state action with action authorized or encouraged by state law. [California] statutory law authorizes [the] use of force in self-defense; the disposition of real and personal property; [the] creation of a contractual relationship; [the] execution of a will; the formation of a corporation [etc.]. If state authority or encouragement is a valid state action test, then all of the above forms of private conduct would present fourteenth amendment equal protection and due process problems. [The] fallacy in the thesis [is] most readily apparent when one considers the impact of judicial law. It is almost impossible to consider any form of activity that is not somehow authorized by state decisional law. [As] long as the law is permissive in nature and leaves the initial decision to take the action entirely within the realm of private choice, neither the state nor the individual should be held constitutionally responsible under the fourteenth amendment. [Further], constitutional significance should not attach to such extraneous considerations as whether the law restates a long-standing law, clarifies an existing law, changes the law, creates entirely new law or repeals existing law. [First], the effect of a statute as a form of state law authorizing private conduct is precisely the same regardless of the statute's longevity * * *. Second, untoward consequences would follow from a holding that the statute is unconstitutional because of its newness or because it repeals an existing law considered more socially desirable by the Court. Such a holding would constitutionally freeze into state law every form of social legislation or decisional or administrative law deemed constitutionally proper by the Court and would thereby discourage states from experimenting in this regard. It would also produce anomalous and illogical results since the identical private conduct authorized and encouraged by the identical statutory or judicial law

b. In *Lombard v. Louisiana* and *Peterson v. Greenville,* reversing "sit-in" convictions for trespass at segregated restaurants, the Court held that where a city ordinance (or other "official command"—i.e., statements by city officials) requires racial segregation, "a conviction under the State's criminal processes employed in a way which enforces the discrimination mandated by that ordinance cannot stand." This was held to be so even if the private discriminator "would have acted as he did independently of the existence of the ordinance." Harlan J., dissented from this position. 373 U.S. 244, 267, 83 S.Ct. 1119, 1122, 10 L.Ed.2d 323, 338 (1963). See also fn. a following *Burton v. Wilmington Parking Auth.,* Sec. 3 infra.

would be valid in some states under the fourteenth amendment but invalid in others solely because of the age of the state law in each jurisdiction."

(b) The "state 'encouragement' or 'authorization'" issue is considered further in *Flagg Bros. v. Brooks*, Sec. 4 infra.

3. *Repeal of discriminatory legislation.* Recall *Lombard and Peterson.* Suppose all official pronouncements *requiring* discrimination are repealed or retracted? Is subsequent "private" discrimination in respect to matters previously covered by official pronouncements "state action"? Is the state "significantly involved" because its repeals have now made "private discriminations legally possible"? Have they "authorized" and "encouraged" discrimination? Or is this "mere repeal of existing statutes"? Is discrimination more "authorized and encouraged" by repeal of laws requiring discrimination or by repeal of laws forbidding it?

SECTION 4. RECENT DEVELOPMENTS

MOOSE LODGE v. IRVIS, 407 U.S. 163, 92 S.Ct. 1965, 32 L.Ed.2d 627 (1972), per REHNQUIST, J., held that Lodge's ban, contained in its constitution and by-laws, on blacks as members or guests was not "state action" despite its possession of a state liquor license: "The Court has never held [that] discrimination by an otherwise private entity would be violative of the Equal Protection Clause if the private entity receives any sort of benefit or service at all from the State, or if it is subject to state regulation in any degree whatever. Since state-furnished services include such necessities of life as electricity, water, and police and fire protection, such a holding would utterly emasculate the distinction between private as distinguished from State conduct. [With] one exception, [there] is no suggestion in this record that the Pennsylvania statutes and regulations are intended either overtly or covertly to encourage discrimination.[a] * * *

"Here there is nothing approaching the symbiotic relationship between lessor and lessee that was present in *Burton* * * *. Far from apparently holding itself out as a place of public accommodation Moose Lodge quite ostentatiously proclaims the fact that it is not open to the public at large. Nor is it located and operated in such surroundings that although private in name, it discharges a function or performs a service that would otherwise in all likelihood be performed by the State. In short, while Eagle was a public restaurant in a public building, Moose Lodge is a private social club in a private building."

DOUGLAS, J., joined by Marshall, J., dissented: "My view of the First Amendment and the related guarantees of the Bill of Rights is that they create a zone of privacy which precludes government from interfering with private clubs or groups. [And] the fact that a private club gets some kind of permit from the [State] does not make it ipso facto a public enterprise or undertaking, any more than the grant to a householder of a permit to operate an incinerator puts the householder in the public domain. [But, in this case, there] is a complex quota system [for liquor licenses which makes it very difficult for] a group desiring to form a nondiscriminatory club. [Thus, the state] is putting the weight of its liquor license, concededly a valued and important adjunct to a private club, behind racial discrimination."

a. A Liquor Control Board regulation required that "every club licensee shall adhere to all provisions of its constitution and by-laws." Even though this regulation was "neutral in its terms," the Court unanimously held that *Shelley v. Kraemer* forbade the state to invoke its sanctions "to enforce a concededly discriminatory private rule."

BRENNAN, J., joined by Marshall, J., dissented on the ground that "Pennsylvania became an active participant in the operation of the Lodge bar" because "Liquor licensing laws [are] primarily pervasive regulatory schemes under which the State dictates and continually supervises virtually every detail of the operation of the licensee's business." [b]

Notes and Questions

1. *Issue before the Court.* Was the issue in *Moose Lodge* whether the club's refusal to serve Irvis constituted "state action"? Or was it whether Pennsylvania could grant a liquor license to a club that practiced racial discrimination? Are these constitutional issues the same? See note 4(c) after *Burton.*

2. *Court's rationale.* Does *Moose Lodge* rest ultimately on a "balancing approach"? See Note, *State Action and the Burger Court,* 60 Va.L.Rev. 840 (1974). If so, consider Note, *Developing Legal Vistas for the Discouragement of Private Club Discrimination,* 58 Ia.L.Rev. 108, 139 (1972): "[In cases of] large, nationwide fraternal orders which are segregated pursuant to national constitutions, [there] is evidence that these clubs serve substantially economic interests. Furthermore, a glance at the membership requirement and size of these clubs indicates they are not closely knit clubs involving a high quotient of intimacy. They are certainly not primarily religious or political in nature. Hence, under the balancing approach, the associational rights asserted by these clubs would not seem strong."

3. *The "Moral Exemplar Model."* Consider Stone, *Corporate Vices and Corporate Virtues: Do Public/Private Distinctions Matter?,* 130 U.Pa.L.Rev. 1441, 1449–1501 (1982): "[W]e should be readier to deem an actor 'public' when [it is 'symbolically public' and] when the preponderant costs of doing so will be imposed on the benefitting public at-large. * * * There are several ways to interpret the contrasting results in *Burton* and *Moose Lodge.* One way is to contrast the symbolic elements of the situation: after all, the parking authority building flew, quite literally, the flags of government. [Second,] in *Burton,* the government stood to capture essentially all the economic benefits of the discrimination, assuming perfect competition among bidders for the lease. Hence, the Court's decision prohibiting the arrangement eliminated from public revenues essentially the full measure of the ill-gotten gains. [T]he preponderant costs of setting a morally correct example will be borne by the public, which is exactly where they ought to lie. Note that the same consequence, the apportionment of essentially all 'fairness' costs on general revenues, would not result from a plaintiff's victory when the government is insuring mortgages, or guaranteeing loans, or is a regulatory licensor, as in *Moose Lodge.* [In] those situations, extending state action would concentrate costs on a distinct sub-group, a result that courts have been reluctant to decree."

SHOPPING CENTER CASES

AMALGAMATED FOOD EMPLOYEES UNION v. LOGAN VALLEY PLAZA, 391 U.S. 308, 88 S.Ct. 1601, 20 L.Ed.2d 603 (1968), per MARSHALL, J.,— reasoning that a large privately owned shopping center was the "functional equivalent of the business district [involved] in *Marsh*"—held that it could not

---

b. Irvis also complained to the Pennsylvania Human Rights Commission. *Commonwealth v. Loyal Order of Moose,* 448 Pa. 451, 294 A.2d 594, appeal dismissed, 409 U.S. 1052 (1972), upheld the Commission's ruling that the Harrisburg Moose Lodge was a "public accommodation" under state law and could not bar guests on the basis of race.

enjoin peaceful union picketing on its property against a store located in the shopping center. Black and White, JJ., dissented; Harlan, J., did not reach the merits.

Four years later, LLOYD CORP. v. TANNER, 407 U.S. 551, 92 S.Ct. 2219, 33 L.Ed.2d 131 (1972), per POWELL, J., held that a shopping center's refusal to permit antiwar handbilling on its premises was not state action violative of the first and fourteenth amendments. *Logan Valley* was distinguished on the grounds that the picketing there had been specifically directed to a store in the shopping center and the pickets had no other reasonable opportunity to reach their intended audience. *Marsh* was said to have "involved the assumption by a private enterprise of semi-official municipal functions as a delegate of the State. In effect, the owner of the company town was performing the full spectrum of municipal powers and stood in the shoes of the State. In the instant case there is no comparable assumption or exercise of municipal functions or power." [a] Marshall, J., joined by Douglas, Brennan and Stewart, JJ., dissented, finding "no valid distinction" from *Logan Valley*.

Finally, HUDGENS v. NLRB, 424 U.S. 507, 96 S.Ct. 1029, 47 L.Ed.2d 196 (1976), per STEWART, J.,—involving picketing of a store in a shopping center by a union with a grievance against the store's warehouse (located elsewhere)— overruled *Logan Valley* on the ground that *"Lloyd* amounted to [its] total rejection."[b]

MARSHALL, J., joined by Brennan, J., dissented: "*Logan Valley* [recognized] that the owner of the modern shopping center complex, by dedicating his property to public use as a business district, to some extent displaces the 'State' from control of historical First Amendment forums, and may acquire a virtual monopoly of places suitable for effective communication. The roadways, parking lots, and walkways of the modern shopping center may be as essential for effective speech as the streets and sidewalks in the municipal or company-owned town. [No] one would seriously question the legitimacy of the values of privacy and individual autonomy traditionally associated with privately owned property. [But] when a property owner opens his property to public use the force of those values diminishes."

---

a. *Lloyd* also stated: "Although accommodations between the values protected by [the first amendment, the due process clause, and the fifth amendment just compensation clause] are sometimes necessary, and the courts properly have shown a special solicitude for the guarantees of the First Amendment, this Court has never held that a trespasser or an uninvited guest may exercise general rights of free speech on property privately owned and used nondiscriminatorily for private purposes only. Even where public property is involved, the Court has recognized that it is not necessarily available for speaking, picketing, or other communicative activities [*Adderley v. Florida*, p. 874 supra]." "It is true that facilities at the Center are used for certain meetings and for various promotional activities. The obvious purpose [is] to bring potential shoppers to the Center, to create a favorable impression, and to generate goodwill. There is no open-ended invitation to the public to use the Center for any and all purposes, however incompatible with the interests of both the stores and the shoppers whom they serve."

b. White, J., concurred in the result, finding that *Logan Valley* "does not cover the facts of this case. The pickets of the Butler Shoe Co. store [were] not purporting to convey information about the 'manner in which that particular [store] was being operated' but rather about the operation of a warehouse not located on the center's premises. The picketing was thus not 'directly related in its purpose to the use to which the shopping center property was being put.'" Powell, J., joined by Burger, C.J., agreed that "the present case can be distinguished narrowly from *Logan Valley*." Nevertheless, they joined the Court's opinion, agreeing with Black, J.'s dissent in *Logan Valley* that that case and *Marsh* "cannot be harmonized in a principled way." Stevens, J., did not participate.

JACKSON v. METROPOLITAN EDISON CO., 419 U.S. 345, 95 S.Ct. 449, 42 L.Ed.2d 477 (1974): Respondent, "a heavily regulated private utility" with a state certificate of public convenience to sell electricity, terminated service to petitioner for nonpayment pursuant to a provision of its general tariff that had been filed with the Pennsylvania Public Utilities Commission. Petitioner claimed that termination "without adequate notice and a hearing before an impartial body" deprived her of property without due process of law. The Court, per REHNQUIST, J., held "that the termination did not constitute state action": "It may well be that acts of a heavily regulated utility with at least something of a governmentally protected monopoly will more readily be found to be 'state' [acts]. But the inquiry must be whether there is a sufficiently close nexus between the State and the challenged action of the regulated entity so that the action of the latter may be fairly treated as that of the State itself."

Even assuming that the state had granted Metropolitan a monopoly, "this fact is not determinative." As to the contention that respondent performs a "public function," "if we were dealing with the exercise by Metropolitan of some power delegated to it by the State which is traditionally associated with sovereignty, such as eminent domain, our case would be [different]. But while the Pennsylvania statute imposes an obligation to furnish service on regulated utilities," unlike the situation in *Terry, Marsh* and *Evans v. Newton*, "the supplying of utility service is not traditionally the exclusive prerogative of the State." Further, although Metropolitan may have been a regulated business "providing arguably essential goods and services, 'affected with a public interest,'" so too are "doctors, optometrists, lawyers" and many others. "We do not believe that such a status converts their every action, absent more, into that of the State." Finally, *Pollak* was distinguishable because there the government agency had its "imprimatur placed on the practice" complained of. Here, the termination provision "has appeared in Metropolitan's previously filed tariffs for many years and has never been the subject of a hearing or other scrutiny by the commission."

DOUGLAS, J., dissented: Metropolitan "is the only public utility furnishing electric power to the town. When power is denied a householder, the home, under modern conditions, is likely to become unlivable." Further, "Pennsylvania has undertaken to regulate numerous aspects of respondent's operations [and] the State would presumably lend its weight and authority to facilitate the enforcement of respondent's published procedures. Cf. *Reitman; Shelley.*" Finally, under *Burton*, "it is not enough to examine seriatim each of the factors upon which a claimant relies and to dismiss each individually as being insufficient to support a finding of state action. It is the aggregate that is controlling."

MARSHALL, J., also dissented: "[W]here the State has so thoroughly insinuated itself into the operations of the enterprise, it should not be fatal if the State has not affirmatively sanctioned the particular practice in question." That the termination provision "was not seriously questioned before approval [suggests], that the commission was satisfied to permit the company to proceed in the termination area as it had done in the past." Under the majority's rationale, "authorization and approval would require the kind of hearing that was held in *Pollak*, where the Public Utilities Commission expressly stated that the bus company's installation of radios in buses and streetcars was not inconsistent with the public convenience, safety and necessity. I am afraid that the majority has in effect restricted *Pollak* to its [facts]."

The Court "reads the 'public function' argument too narrowly. [W]hen the activity in question is of such public importance that the State invariably either provides the service itself or permits private companies to act as state surrogates in providing it, much more is involved than just a matter of public interest. In those cases, the State has determined that if private companies wish to enter the field, they will have to surrender many of the prerogatives normally associated with private enterprise and behave in may ways like a governmental body. And when the State's regulatory scheme has gone that far, it seems entirely consistent to impose on the public utility the constitutional burdens normally reserved for the State.

"Private parties performing functions affecting the public interest can often make a persuasive claim to be free of the constitutional requirements applicable to governmental institutions because of the value of preserving a private sector in which the opportunity for individual choice is maximized. Maintaining the private status of parochial schools [advances] just this value. In the due process area, a similar value of diversity may often be furthered by allowing various private institutions the flexibility to select procedures that fit their particular needs. But [t]he values of pluralism and diversity are simply not relevant when the private company is the only electric company in town.

"[The] Court has not adopted the notion, accepted elsewhere, that different standards should apply to state action analysis when different constitutional claims are presented.[c] Thus, the majority's analysis would seemingly apply as well to a company that refused to extend service to Negroes, welfare recipients, or any other group that the company preferred, for its own reasons, not to serve. I cannot believe that this Court would hold that the State's involvement with the utility company was not sufficient to impose upon the company an obligation to meet the constitutional mandate of nondiscrimination."

BRENNAN, J., dissented on procedural grounds.

Notes and Questions

1. *The "power" theory.* (a) Of what significance should it be that Metropolitan was "the only public utility furnishing electricity to the city"? Might it be argued that the "power" held by certain organizations today was conceived by the framers of the fourteenth amendment to be only within the possession of government? That, under a "living Constitution," such "power" creates such a threat to individual freedom that it should fall within the purview of state action? See Note, *State Action: Theories for Applying Constitutional Restrictions to Private Activity,* 74 Colum.L.Rev. 656 (1974).

Does this approach help explain other state action decisions? Consider Nerkin, *A New Deal for the Protection of Fourteenth Amendment Rights: Challenging the Doctrinal Bases of the Civil Rights Cases and State Action Theory,* 12 Harv.Civ.Rts.-Civ.Lib.L.Rev. 297, 364–65 (1977): "For example, the seller in *Shelley* who was being bound to a rule that he could not sell to blacks was not simply a property owner, but rather an owner who had involved his property in a network of power relations through covenants. Thus the Court's concern in *Shelley* was not simply in the two contracting parties before the court [but] the larger social organism which the covenantors represented. Similarly, [we] might end the futile discussion of whether or not shopping malls are a 'public function' by recognizing that, because malls have become centers of commercial activity,

c. See note 2 after *Burton*; note 1(c) after *Evans v. Newton.*

the mall which seeks to expel a political protester has the power to guarantee that a large part of the community will have no other opportunity to benefit from such exercise of rights."

Is the "power theory" approach beyond the permissible bounds of constitutional interpretation? Does it extend to holding the only ice skating rink in town to the state's constitutional responsibilities? Or is it limited to an activity that "is of such public importance that the State invariably either provides the service itself or permits private companies to act as state surrogates in providing it"? Does this invoke the "public function"—or "government function"—approach (to be considered further in note 2 after *Flagg Bros. v. Brooks,* infra)? In any event, does *Jackson* preclude this line of analysis?

(b) Does (should) the "power theory" depend on state participation in conferring the status? Suppose a large powerful union, without statutory authority or assistance, becomes the exclusive bargaining agent in a particular industry. May it constitutionally discriminate against blacks? See generally Wellington, *The Constitution, The Labor Union, and "Governmental Action,"* 70 Yale L.J. 345, 346–50 (1961). If not, must such a union afford a member "due process" before expelling him? May such a union refuse to hire black secretaries?

(c) Does the "power theory" aid in analyzing the last series of questions? Might it be argued, for example, that a particular industrial labor union has sufficient "power" in respect to job opportunities in the industry as to be constitutionally forbidden from racially discriminating among its members but insufficient power over general job opportunities as to be constitutionally barred from using a religious test for its office employees? That the "state's duty to take preventive action [or the "state action" issue] varies with the magnitude of the discrimination and the consequent problem it creates"? Friendly, *The Dartmouth College Case and the Public-Private Penumbra* 22 (1969). See generally Choper, *Thoughts on State Action,* 1979 Wash.U.L.Q. 757; compare Leedes, *State Action Limitations on Courts and Congressional Power,* 60 N.C.L.Rev. 747, 757–61 (1981).

2. *Constitutional rights of "power holders."* (a) In COLUMBIA BROADCASTING SYSTEM v. DEMOCRATIC NAT'L COMM., p. 703 supra—in which the FCC had ruled that a broadcaster is not required to accept editorial advertisements—some justices addressed the question of whether the action of the broadcast licensee was "governmental action" for purposes of the first amendment. BURGER, C.J., joined by Stewart and Rehnquist, JJ., concluded that it was not: "The historic aversion to censorship led Congress [to] explicitly [prohibit] the Commission from interfering with the exercise of free speech over the broadcast frequencies * * *. [T]he Commission acts in essence as an 'overseer,' but the initial and primary responsibility for fairness, balance and objectivity rests with the licensee. * * * Moreover, the Commission has not fostered the licensee policy challenged here; it has simply declined to command particular action because it fell within the area of journalistic discretion. * * *

"Thus, it cannot be said that the government is a 'partner' to the action of the broadcast licensee complained of here, nor is it engaged in a 'symbiotic relationship' with the licensee, profiting from the invidious discrimination of its proxy. [In *Pollak*], Congress had expressly authorized the agency to undertake plenary intervention into the affairs of the carrier and it was pursuant to that authorization that the agency investigated the challenged policy and approved it * * *. A more basic distinction, [is] that *Pollak* was concerned with a transportation utility that itself derives no protection from the First Amendment.

"Were we to read the First Amendment to spell out governmental action in the circumstances presented here, few licensee decisions on the content of broadcasts or the processes of editorial evaluation would escape constitutional scrutiny. In this sensitive area so sweeping a concept of governmental action would go far in practical effect to undermine nearly a half century of unmistakable congressional purpose to maintain—no matter how difficult the task— essentially private broadcast journalism held only broadly accountable to public interest standards."

BRENNAN, J., joined by Marshall, J., disagreed: "[T]he public nature of the airwaves, the governmentally created preferred status of broadcast licensees, the pervasive federal regulation of broadcast programming, and the Commission's specific approval of the challenged broadcaster policy combine in this case to bring the promulgation and enforcement of that policy within the orbit of constitutional imperatives. [Here], as in *Pollak,* the broadcast licensees operate 'under the regulatory supervision of [an] agency authorized by Congress.' And, again as in *Pollak,* that agency received 'protests' against the challenged policy and, after formal consideration, 'dismissed' the complaints on the ground that the 'public interest, convenience, and necessity' were not 'impaired' by that policy. Indeed, the argument for finding 'governmental action' here is even stronger than in *Pollak,* for this case concerns not an incidental activity of a bus company but, rather, the primary activity of the regulated entities—communication. * * *[12]"

(b) *Newspapers.* Is the conduct of the only newspaper in a metropolitan area "state action"? May it offer free "society news" space to whites only? May it refuse to hire black employees? After the *CBS* case, may a licensed broadcaster engage in such actions?

RENDELL–BAKER v. KOHN
457 U.S. 830, 102 S.Ct. 2764, 73 L.Ed.2d 418 (1982).

CHIEF JUSTICE BURGER delivered the opinion of the Court.

[New Perspectives is a private school that] specializes in dealing with students who have experienced difficulty completing public high [schools]. In recent years, nearly all of the students at the school have been referred to it by the Brookline or Boston school committees, or by the Drug Rehabilitation Division of the Massachusetts Department of Mental Health. The school issues high school diplomas certified by the Brookline School Committee. In recent years, public funds have accounted for at least 90%, and in one year 99%, of respondent's operating budget. * * *

---

12. In his separate concurring opinion, my Brother Stewart suggests [that] a finding of governmental involvement in this case "would simply strip broadcasters of their own First Amendment rights." [W]here, as here, the Government has implicated itself in the actions of an otherwise private individual, that individual must exercise his own rights with due regard for the First Amendment rights of others. In other words, an accommodation of competing rights is required, and "balancing," not the "absolutist" approach suggested by my Brother Stewart, is the result. * * *

I might also note that, contrary to the suggestion of my Brother Stewart, a finding of governmental involvement in this case does not in any sense command a similar conclusion with respect to newspapers. [The] decision as to who shall operate newspapers is made in the free market, not by Government fiat. The newspaper industry is not extensively regulated and, indeed, in light of the differences between the electronic and printed media, such regulation would violate the First Amendment with respect to newspapers. * * *

To be eligible for tuition funding under Chapter 766, the school must comply with a variety [of] detailed regulations concerning matters ranging from record-keeping to student-teacher ratios. Concerning personnel policies, [the] regulations require the school to maintain written job descriptions [and] statements describing personnel standards and procedures, but they impose few specific requirements. * * *

[Petitioners were discharged by the school for, inter alia, supporting student criticisms against various school policies and sued under 42 U.S.C. § 1983.]

While five of the six petitioners were teachers at the school, petitioner Rendell-Baker was a vocational counselor hired under a grant from the federal Law Enforcement Assistance Administration, whose funds are distributed in Massachusetts through the State Committee on Criminal Justice. * * *

Rendell-Baker * * * demanded reinstatement or a hearing. The school agreed to apply a new policy, calling for appointment of a grievance committee, to consider her claims. Rendell-Baker also complained to the State Committee on Criminal Justice, which asked the school to provide a written explanation for her discharge. [The] Committee told Rendell-Baker that it had no authority to order a hearing, although it would refuse to approve the hiring of another counselor if the school disregarded its agreement to apply its new grievance procedure in her case. [The] core issue presented [is] not whether petitioners were discharged because of their speech or without adequate procedural protections, but whether the school's action in discharging them can fairly be seen as state action. * * *

In *Blum v. Yaretsky,* 457 U.S. 991, 102 S.Ct. 2777, 43 L.Ed.2d 534 (1982), [t]he Court considered whether certain nursing homes were state actors for the purpose of determining whether decisions regarding transfers of patients could be fairly attributed to the state, and hence be subjected to Fourteenth Amendment due process requirements. The challenged transfers primarily involved decisions, made by physicians and nursing home administrators, to move patients from "skilled nursing facilities" to less expensive "health related facilities." Like the New Perspectives School, the nursing homes were privately owned and operated. [T]he Court held that, "[A] State normally can be held responsible for a private decision only when it has exercised coercive power or has provided such significant encouragement, either overt or covert, that the choice must in law be deemed to be that of the State." In determining that the transfer decisions were not actions of the state, the Court considered each of the factors alleged by petitioners here to make the discharge decisions of the New Perspective School fairly attributable to the state.

First, the nursing homes, like the school, depended on the State for funds; the State subsidized the operating and capital costs of the nursing homes, and paid the medical expenses of more than 90% of the patients. * * *

The school, like the nursing homes, is not fundamentally different from many private corporations whose business depends primarily on contracts to build roads, bridges, dams, ships, or submarines for the government. Acts of such private contractors do not become acts of the government by reason of their significant or even total engagement in performing public contracts. * * *

A second factor considered in *Blum* was the extensive regulation of the nursing homes by the State. There the State was indirectly involved in the transfer decisions challenged in that case because a primary goal of the State in regulating nursing homes was to keep costs down by transferring patients from intensive treatment centers to less expensive facilities when possible.ᵃ Both state and federal regulations encouraged the nursing homes to transfer patients to less expensive facilities when appropriate. The nursing homes were extensively regulated in many other ways as well. The Court relied on *Jackson,* where we held that state regulation, even if "extensive and detailed," did not make a utility's actions state action.

Here the decisions to discharge the petitioners were not compelled or even influenced by any state regulation. ＊ ＊ ＊

The third factor asserted to show that the school is a state actor is that it performs a "public function." However, our holdings have made clear that the relevant question [is] whether the function performed has been "traditionally the *exclusive* prerogative of the State." [Until] recently the State had not undertaken to provide education for students who could not be served by traditional public schools. That a private entity performs a function which serves the public does not make its acts state action.⁷

Fourth, petitioners argue that there is a "symbiotic relationship" [as] in *Burton.* Such a claim was rejected in *Blum,* and we reject it here. In *Burton,* [i]n response to the argument that the restaurant's profits, and hence the State's financial position, would suffer if it did not discriminate, the Court concluded that this showed that the State profited from the restaurant's discriminatory conduct. [Here] the school's fiscal relationship with the State is not different from that of many contractors performing services for the government.ᵇ ＊ ＊ ＊

Affirmed.ᶜ

JUSTICE MARSHALL, with whom JUSTICE BRENNAN joins, dissenting.

[I]t is difficult to imagine a closer relationship between a government and a private enterprise. [The] school's very survival depends on the State. If the State chooses, it may exercise complete control over the school's operations simply by threatening to withdraw financial support if the school takes action that it considers objectionable. [Almost] every decision the school makes is substantially affected in some way by the State's regulations.¹

The fact that the school is providing a substitute for public education is also an important indicium of state action. [The] State should not be permitted to avoid constitutional requirements simply by delegating its statutory duty to a private entity. ＊ ＊ ＊

a. Brennan, J., joined by Marshall, J., dissented in *Blum:* "[A]n accurate and realistic appraisal of the procedures actually employed in the State of New York leaves no doubt that not only has the State established the system of treatment levels and utilization review in order to further its own fiscal goals, but that the State prescribes with as much precision as is possible the standards by which individual determinations are to be made. [The] Court thus fails to perceive the decisive involvement of the State in the private conduct challenged by the respondents."

7. There is no evidence that the State has attempted to avoid its constitutional duties by a sham arrangement which attempts to disguise provision of public services as acts of private parties. Cf. *Evans v. Newton.*

[Compare Brennan, J., joined by Marshall, J., dissenting in *Blum:* "For many, the totali-

ty of their social network is the nursing home community. Within that environment, the nursing home operator is the immediate authority, the provider of food, clothing, shelter, and health care, and, in every significant respect, the functional equivalent of a State. Cf. *Marsh.*"]

b. Does this adopt the "moral exemplar model" in note 3 after *Moose Lodge?*

c. White, J., concurred in the judgment (and in *Blum*): "For me, the critical factor is the absence of any allegation that the employment decision was itself based upon some rule of conduct or policy put forth by the State."

1. [By] analyzing the various indicia of state action separately, without considering their cumulative impact, the majority commits a fundamental error.

The majority repeatedly compares the school to a private contractor ＊ ＊ ＊. Although shipbuilders and dambuilders, like the school, may be dependent on government funds, they are not so closely supervised by the government. And unlike most private contractors, the school is performing a statutory duty of the State. ＊ ＊ ＊

FLAGG BROS., INC. v. BROOKS
436 U.S. 149, 98 S.Ct. 1729, 56 L.Ed.2d 185 (1978).

MR. JUSTICE REHNQUIST delivered the opinion of the Court.

The question presented [is] whether a warehouseman's proposed sale of goods entrusted to him for storage, as permitted by New York Uniform Commercial Code § 7–210, is an action properly attributable to the State ＊ ＊ ＊.

[R]espondent Shirley Brooks and her family were evicted from their apartment in Mount Vernon, N.Y., on June 13, 1973. The city marshal arranged for Brooks' possessions to be stored by petitioner Flagg Brothers, Inc., in its warehouse. Brooks was informed of the cost of moving and storage, and she instructed the workmen to proceed, although she found the price too high. On August 25, 1973, after a series of disputes over the validity of the charges being claimed by petitioner Flagg Brothers, Brooks received a letter demanding that her account be brought up to date within 10 days "or your furniture will be sold." A series of subsequent letters from respondent and her attorneys produced no satisfaction.

Brooks thereupon initiated this class action in the District Court under 42 U.S.C. § 1983, seeking damages, an injunction against the threatened sale of her belongings, and the declaration that such a sale pursuant to § 7–210 would violate [due process]. She was later joined in her action by [Jones,] whose goods had been stored by Flagg Brothers following her eviction. [T]he District Court ＊ ＊ ＊ dismissed the complaint [and] the Court of Appeals reversed. ＊ ＊ ＊

It must be noted that respondents have named no public officials as defendants in this action. The city marshal, who supervised their evictions, was dismissed from the case by the consent of all the parties. This total absence of overt official involvement plainly distinguishes this case from earlier decisions imposing procedural restrictions on creditors' remedies such as *North Georgia Finishing, Inc., v. Di-Chem, Inc.,* 419 U.S. 601, 95 S.Ct. 719, 42 L.Ed.2d 751 (1975); *Fuentes v. Shevin,* 407 U.S. 67, 92 S.Ct. 1983, 32 L.Ed.2d 556 (1972); *Sniadach v. Family Finance Corp.,* 395 U.S. 337, 89 S.Ct. 1820, 23 L.Ed.2d 349 (1969).[a]

a. *Sniadach* held that a statute—authorizing a creditor to get a summons from a court clerk and thereby obtain prejudgment garnishment of a debtor's wages—violated due process because the statute did not provide the debtor with prior notice and opportunity for a hearing.

Fuentes held that a statute—authorizing a seller of goods under a conditional sales contract to get a writ from a court clerk and thereby obtain prejudgment repossession with the sheriff's help—violated due process because the statute did not provide the buyer with prior notice and opportunity for a hearing.

North Georgia Finishing held violative of due process a statute authorizing a creditor to obtain prejudgment garnishment of a debtor's assets by filing an affidavit with a court clerk stating reasons to fear that the property would otherwise be lost. The Court distinguished *Mitchell v. W.T. Grant Co.,* 416 U.S. 600, 94 S.Ct. 1895, 40 L.Ed.2d 406 (1974), which had upheld a statute that, without requiring prior notice to a buyer-debtor, permitted a seller-creditor holding a vendor's lien to secure a writ of sequestration and, having filed a bond, to cause the sheriff to take possession of the property at issue. *North Georgia Finishing* emphasized that under the sequestration statute in *Mitchell,* unlike the garnishment statute at bar, the writ "was issuable only by a judge upon the filing of an affidavit going beyond mere conclusory allegations and clearly setting out the facts entitling the creditor to sequestration" and that the

[While] as a factual matter any person with sufficient physical power may deprive a person of his property, only a State or a private person whose action "may be fairly treated as that of the State itself," *Jackson,* may deprive him of "an interest encompassed within the Fourteenth Amendment's protection," *Fuentes* * * *.

Respondents' primary contention is that New York has delegated to Flagg Brothers a power "traditionally exclusively reserved to the State." *Jackson.* They argue that the resolution of private disputes is a traditional function of civil government, and that the State in § 7–210 has delegated this function to Flagg Brothers. Respondents, however, have read too much into the language of our previous cases. While many functions have been traditionally performed by governments, very few have been "exclusively reserved to the State."

One such area has been elections. * * * *Terry v. Adams; Smith v. Allwright.* Although the rationale of these cases may be subject to some dispute, their scope is carefully defined. The doctrine does not reach to all forms of private political activity, but encompasses only state-regulated elections or elections conducted by organizations which in practice produce "the uncontested choice of public officials." *Terry* (Clark, J., concurring). * * *

A second line of cases under the public-function doctrine originated with *Marsh.* Just as the Texas Democratic Party in *Smith* and the Jaybird Democratic Association in *Terry* effectively performed the entire public function of selecting public officials, so too the Gulf Shipbuilding Corp. performed all the necessary municipal functions in the town of Chickasaw, Ala., which it owned. * * *

These two branches of the public-function doctrine have in common the feature of exclusivity.[8] Although the elections held by the Democratic Party and its affiliates were the only meaningful elections in Texas, and the streets owned by the Gulf Shipbuilding Corp. were the only streets in Chickasaw, the proposed sale by Flagg Brothers under § 7–210 is not the only means of resolving this purely private dispute. Respondent Brooks has never alleged that state law barred her from seeking a waiver of Flagg Brothers' right to sell her goods at the time she authorized their storage. Presumably, respondent Jones, who alleges that she never authorized the storage of her goods, could have sought to replevy her goods at any time under state law. The challenged statute itself provides a damages remedy against the warehouseman for violations of its provisions. This system of rights and remedies, recognizing the traditional place of private arrangements in ordering relationships in the commercial world,[9] can hardly be

---

Mitchell statute "expressly entitled the debtor to an immediate hearing after seizure and to dissolution of the writ absent proof by the creditor of the grounds on which the writ was issued."

For general discussion of these cases, see Scott, *Constitutional Regulation of Provisional Creditor Remedies: The Cost of Procedural Due Process,* 61 Va.L.Rev. 807 (1975); Silberman, *Shaffer v. Heitner: The End of an Era,* 53 N.Y.U.L.Rev. 33, 53–62 (1978).

8. Respondents also contend that *Evans v. Newton* establishes that the operation of a park for recreational purposes is an exclusively public function. We doubt that *Newton* intended to establish any such broad doctrine in the teeth of the experience of several Amer-

ican entrepreneurs who amassed great fortunes by operating parks for recreational purposes. We think *Newton* rests on a finding of ordinary state action under extraordinary circumstances. The Court's opinion emphasizes that the record showed "no change in the municipal maintenance and concern over this facility" after the transfer of title to private trustees. That transfer had not been shown to have eliminated the actual involvement of the city in the daily maintenance and care of the park.

9. Unlike the parade of horribles suggested by our Brother Stevens in dissent, this case does not involve state authorization of private breach of the peace.

said to have delegated to Flagg Brothers an exclusive prerogative of the sovereign.[10]

Whatever the particular remedies available under New York law, we do not consider a more detailed description of them necessary to our conclusion that the settlement of disputes between debtors and creditors is not traditionally an exclusive public function.[11] Creditors and debtors have had available to them historically a far wider number of choices than has one who would be an elected public official, or a member of Jehovah's Witnesses who wished to distribute literature in Chickasaw, Ala. * * *[12] This is true whether these commercial rights and remedies are created by statute or decisional law. To rely upon the historical antecedents of a particular practice would result in the constitutional condemnation in one State of a remedy found perfectly permissible in another.

[W]e would be remiss if we did not note that there are a number of state and municipal functions not covered by our election cases or governed by the reasoning of *Marsh* which have been administered with a greater degree of exclusivity by States and municipalities than has the function of so-called

---

10. [It] would intolerably broaden, beyond the scope of any of our previous cases, the notion of state action [to] hold that the mere existence of a body of property law in a State, whether decisional or statutory, itself amounted to "state action" even though no state process or state officials were ever involved in enforcing that body of law.

This situation is clearly distinguishable from cases such as *North Georgia Finishing; Fuentes;* and *Sniadach.* In each of those cases a government official participated in the physical deprivation of what had concededly been the constitutional plaintiff's property under state law before the deprivation occurred. The constitutional protection attaches not because, as in *North Georgia Finishing,* a clerk issued a ministerial writ out of the court, but because as a result of that writ the property of the debtor was seized and impounded by the affirmative command of the law of Georgia. The creditor in *North Georgia Finishing* had not simply sought to pursue the collection of his debt by private means permissible under Georgia law; he had invoked the authority of the Georgia court, which in turn had ordered the garnishee not to pay over money which previously had been the property of the debtor. See *Virginia v. Rives; Shelley v. Kraemer.*

* * *

11. It may well be, as my Brother Stevens' dissent contends, that "[t]he power to order legally binding surrenders of property and the constitutional restrictions on that power are necessary correlatives in our system." But here New York, unlike Florida in *Fuentes,* Georgia in *North Georgia Finishing,* and Wisconsin in *Sniadach,* has not ordered respondents to surrender any property whatever. It has merely enacted a statute which provides that a warehouseman conforming to the provisions of the statute may convert his traditional lien into good title. There is no reason whatever to believe that either Flagg Brothers or respondents could not, if they wished, seek

resort to the New York courts in order to either compel or prevent the "surrenders of property" to which that dissent refers, and that the compliance of Flagg Brothers with applicable New York property law would be reviewed after customary notice and hearing in such a proceeding.

The fact that such a judicial review of a self-help remedy is seldom encountered bears witness to the important part that such remedies have played in our system of property rights. This is particularly true of the warehouseman's lien, which is the source of this provision in the Uniform Commercial Code which is the law in 49 States and the District of Columbia. The lien in this case, particularly because it is burdened by procedural constraints and provides for a compensatory remedy and judicial relief against abuse, is not atypical of creditors' liens historically, whether created by statute or legislatively enacted. The conduct of private actors in relying on the rights established under these liens to resort to self-help remedies does not permit their conduct to be ascribed to the State.

12. This is not to say that dispute resolution between creditors and debtors involves a category of human affairs that is never subject to constitutional constraints. We merely address the public-function doctrine as respondents would apply it to this case.

Self-help of the type involved in this case is not significantly different from creditor remedies generally, whether created by common law or enacted by legislatures. New York's statute has done nothing more than authorize (and indeed limit)—without participation by any public official—what Flagg Brothers would tend to do, even in the absence of such authorization, i.e., dispose of respondents' property in order to free up its valuable storage space. The proposed sale pursuant to the lien in this case is not a significant departure from traditional private arrangements.

"dispute resolution." Among these are such functions as education, fire and police protection, and tax collection. We express no view as to the extent, if any, to which a city or State might be free to delegate to private parties the performance of such functions and thereby avoid the strictures of the Fourteenth Amendment. * * *

Respondents further urge that Flagg Brothers' proposed action is properly attributable to the State because the State has authorized and encouraged it in enacting § 7–210. Our cases state "that a State is responsible for [the] act of a private party when the State, by its law, has compelled the act." This Court, however, has never held that a State's mere acquiescence in a private action converts that action into that of the State. The Court rejected a similar argument in *Jackson* * * *. The clearest demonstration of this distinction appears in *Moose Lodge*, which held that the Commonwealth of Pennsylvania, although not responsible for racial discrimination voluntarily practiced by a private club, could not by law require the club to comply with its own discriminatory rules. These cases clearly rejected the notion that our prior cases permitted the imposition of Fourteenth Amendment restraints on private action by the simple device of characterizing the State's inaction as "authorization" or "encouragement."

It is quite immaterial that the State has embodied its decision not to act in statutory form. If New York had no commercial statutes at all, its courts would still be faced with the decision whether to prohibit or to permit the sort of sale threatened here the first time an aggrieved bailor came before them for relief. A judicial decision to deny relief would be no less an "authorization" or "encouragement" of that sale than the legislature's decision embodied in this statute. [If] the mere denial of judicial relief is considered sufficient encouragement to make the State responsible for those private acts, all private deprivations of property would be converted into public acts whenever the State, for whatever reason, denies relief sought by the putative property owner. * * *

Here, the State of New York has not compelled the sale of a bailor's goods, but has merely announced the circumstances under which its courts will not interfere with a private sale. Indeed, the crux of respondents' complaint is not that the State *has* acted, but that it has *refused* to act. This statutory refusal to act is no different in principle from an ordinary statute of limitations whereby the State declines to provide a remedy for private deprivations of property after the passage of a given period of time. * * *

Reversed.

MR. JUSTICE STEVENS, with whom MR. JUSTICE WHITE and MR. JUSTICE MARSHALL join, dissenting.

[The] question is whether a state statute which authorizes a private party to deprive a person of his property without his consent must meet the requirements of the Due Process Clause of the Fourteenth Amendment. This question must be answered in the affirmative unless the State has virtually unlimited power to transfer interests in private property without any procedural protections.

[Under the Court's] approach a State could enact laws authorizing private citizens to use self-help in countless situations without any possibility of federal challenge. A state statute could authorize the warehouseman to retain all proceeds of the lien sale, even if they far exceeded the amount of the alleged debt; it could authorize finance companies to enter private homes to repossess merchandise; or indeed, it could authorize "any person with sufficient physical power" to acquire and sell the property of his weaker neighbor. An attempt to challenge the validity of any such outrageous statute would be defeated by the reasoning the Court uses today: The Court's rationale would characterize action pursuant to such a statute as purely private action, which the State permits but does not compel, in an area not exclusively reserved to the State.

As these examples suggest, the distinctions between "permission" and "compulsion" on the one hand, and "exclusive" and "non-exclusive," on the other, cannot be determinative factors in state-action analysis. There is no great chasm between "permission" and "compulsion" requiring particular state action to fall within one or the other definitional camp. Even *Moose Lodge,* * * * recognizes that there are many intervening levels of state involvement in private conduct that may support a finding of state action. In this case, the State of New York, by enacting § 7–210 of the Uniform Commercial Code, has acted in the most effective and unambiguous way a State can act. This section specifically authorizes petitioner Flagg Brothers to sell respondents' possessions; it details the procedures that petitioner must follow; and it grants petitioner the power to convey good title to goods that are now owned by respondents to a third party.

While Members of this Court have suggested that statutory authorization alone may be sufficient to establish state action,[6] it is not necessary to rely on those suggestions in this case because New York has authorized the warehouseman to perform what is clearly a state function. [P]etitioners have attempted to argue that the nonconsensual transfer of property rights is not a traditional function of the sovereign. The overwhelming historical evidence is to the contrary, however,[7] and the Court wisely does not adopt this position. Instead, the Court reasons that state action cannot be found because the State has not delegated to the warehouseman an *exclusive* sovereign function.[8] This distinction, however, is not consistent with our prior decisions on state action; is not even adhered to by the Court in this case;[10] and, most importantly, is inconsistent with the line of cases beginning with *Sniadach.*

---

6. See, e.g., *Burton* (Stewart, J., concurring); (Frankfurter, J., dissenting); and (Harlan, J., dissenting).

7. The New York State courts have recognized that the execution of a lien is a traditional function of the State. See also 3 W. Blackstone, *Commentaries* §§ 7–11, pp. * 3–6, which notes that the right of self-help at common law was severely limited.

I fully agree with the Court that the decision of whether or not a statute is subject to due process scrutiny should not depend on " 'whether a particular class of creditor did or did not enjoy the same freedom to act in Elizabethan or Georgian England.' " Nonetheless some reference to history and well-settled practice is necessary to determine whether a particular action is a "traditional state function." * * *

8. As I understand the Court's notion of "exclusivity," the sovereign function here is not exclusive because there may be other state remedies, under different statutes or common-law theories, available to respondents. Even if I were to accept the notion that sovereign functions must be "exclusive," the Court's description of exclusivity is incomprehensible. The question is whether a particular action is a uniquely sovereign function, not whether

state law forecloses any possibility of recovering for damages for such activity. For instance, it is clear that the maintenance of a police force is a unique sovereign function, and the delegation of police power to a private party will entail state action. Under the Court's analysis, however, there would be no state action if the State provided a remedy, such as an action for wrongful imprisonment, for the individual injured by the "private" policeman. This analysis is not based on "exclusivity," but on some vague, and highly inappropriate, notion that respondents should not complain about this state statute if the State offers them a glimmer of hope of redeeming their possessions, or at least the value of the goods, through some other state action. Of course, the availability of other state remedies may be relevant in determining whether the statute provides sufficient procedural protections under the Due Process Clause, but it is not relevant to the state-action issue.

10. As the Court is forced to recognize, its notion of exclusivity simply cannot be squared with the wide range of functions that are typically considered sovereign functions, such as "education, fire and police protection, and tax collection."

Since *Sniadach* this Court has scrutinized various state statutes regulating the debtor-creditor relationship for compliance with the Due Process Clause. In each of these cases a finding of state action was a prerequisite to the Court's decision. The Court today seeks to explain these findings on the ground that in each case there was some element of "overt official involvement." [But] until today, this Court had never held that purely ministerial acts of "minor governmental functionaries" were sufficient to establish state action. The suggestion that this was the basis for due process review in *Sniadach, Fuentes,* and *North Georgia Finishing* marks a major and, in my judgment, unwise expansion of the state-action doctrine. The number of private actions in which a governmental functionary plays some ministerial role is legion; [12] to base due process review on the fortuity of such governmental intervention would demean the majestic purposes of the Due Process Clause.

Instead, cases such as *North Georgia Finishing* must be viewed as reflecting this Court's recognition of the significance of the State's role in defining *and controlling* the debtor-creditor relationship. [In *Fuentes*, the] statutes placed the state power to repossess property in the hands of an interested private party, just as the state statute in this case places the state power to conduct judicially binding sales in satisfaction of a lien in the hands of the warehouseman. "Private parties, serving their own private advantage, may unilaterally invoke state power to replevy goods from another. No state official participates in the decision to seek a writ; no state official reviews the basis for the claim to repossession; and no state official evaluates the need for immediate seizure. There is not even a requirement that the plaintiff provide any information to the court on these matters." Ibid. [Yet] the very defect that made the statutes in *Fuentes* and *North Georgia Finishing* unconstitutional—lack of state control—is, under today's decision, the factor that precludes constitutional review of the state statute. The Due Process Clause cannot command such incongruous results. If it is unconstitutional for a State to allow a private party to exercise a traditional state power because the state supervision of that power is purely mechanical, the State surely cannot immunize its actions from constitutional *scrutiny* by removing even the mechanical supervision. * * *

Whether termed "traditional," "exclusive," or "significant," the state power to order binding, nonconsensual resolution of a conflict between debtor and creditor is exactly the sort of power with which the Due Process Clause is concerned. And the State's delegation of that power to a private party is, accordingly, subject to due process scrutiny. This, at the very least, is the teaching of *Sniadach, Fuentes,* and *North Georgia Finishing*.

It is important to emphasize that, contrary to the Court's apparent fears, this conclusion does not even remotely suggest that "all private deprivations of property [will] be converted into public acts whenever the State, for whatever reason, denies relief sought by the putative property owner." The focus is not on the private deprivation but on the state authorization. [The] State's conduct in this case takes the concrete form of a statutory enactment, and it is that statute that may be challenged.

[It] is only what the State itself has enacted that [respondents] may ask the federal court to review in a § 1983 case. If there should be a deviation from the state statute—such as a failure to give the notice required by the state law—the

---

12. For instance, state officials often perform ministerial acts in the transferring of ownership in motor vehicles or real estate. It is difficult to believe that the Court would hold that all car sales are invested with state action.

defect could be remedied by a state court and there would be no occasion for § 1983 relief. [Under] this approach, the federal courts do not have jurisdiction to review every foreclosure proceeding in which the debtor claims that there has been a procedural defect constituting a denial of due process of law. Rather, the federal district court's jurisdiction under § 1983 is limited to challenges to the constitutionality of the state procedure itself * * *.

Finally, it is obviously true that the overwhelming majority of disputes in our society are resolved in the private sphere. But it is no longer possible, if it ever was, to believe that a sharp line can be drawn between private and public actions. The Court['s] description of what is state action does not even attempt to reflect the concerns of the Due Process Clause, for the state-action doctrine is, after all, merely one aspect of this broad constitutional protection.

In the broadest sense, we expect government "to provide a reasonable and fair framework of rules which facilitate commercial transactions." This "framework of rules" is premised on the assumption that the State will control nonconsensual deprivations of property and that the State's control will, in turn, be subject to the restrictions of the Due Process Clause. * * *[b]

Notes and Questions

1. *Authority of prior decisions.* (a) Does the Court's use of *Shelley v. Kraemer* (in fn. 10) refute the dissent's objection that the Court's handling of the prior debtor-creditor decisions establishes the principle that "purely ministerial acts of minor governmental functionaries" constitute state action? If so, then would the Court have found state action in *Flagg Bros.* if the state courts had to be used to enforce the warehouseman's lien? Would this read *Shelley* for all it is worth? Does fn. 10 so read *Shelley*? In any event, is the dissent correct in complaining that "the very defect that made the statutes in *Fuentes* and *North Georgia Finishing* unconstitutional—lack of state control—is, under *Flagg Bros.*, the factor that precludes constitutional review of the state statute"?

(b) LUGAR v. EDMONDSON OIL CO., 457 U.S. 922, 102 S.Ct. 2744, 73 L.Ed. 2d 482 (1982), per WHITE, J.,—involving a statute that authorized a creditor to file a petition with a court clerk and thus obtain a prejudgment attachment of a debtor's property which was executed by the sheriff—relied on all the debtor-creditor decisions as establishing the doctrine "that a private party's joint participation with state officials in the seizure of disputed property is sufficient to characterize that party as a 'state actor' for purposes of the Fourteenth Amendment." POWELL, J., joined by REHNQUIST and O'CONNOR, JJ., dissented: "It is unclear why a private party engages in state action when filing papers seeking an attachment of property, but not [when] summoning police to investigate a suspected crime." BURGER, C.J., also dissented.

2. *"Governmental function."* (a) *Dispute resolution.* Do you agree that the authority exercised by the warehouseman under the New York statute was not a "governmental function"? Consider 92 Harv.L.Rev. 128 (1978): "The exclusivity of the function's exercise may shed some light on this inquiry, but it does not give a final answer to the basic question. Regardless of the fact that there are many ways to go about resolving a private dispute, the ability to conclude unresolved disputes by making authoritative determinations of rights in property is central to our conception of government's role in society. If a state chose to assign part of its judicial function to private tribunals, giving them all the

---

b. The separate dissent of Marshall, J., is omitted. Brennan, J., did not participate.

authority of trial courts, there would be little doubt that a vital attribute of sovereignty was involved."

What result in *Flagg Bros.* if the warehouseman's lien had not been "burdened by procedural constraints" and had not provided "for a compensatory remedy and judicial relief against abuse"?

(b) *Education.* Would (should) the Court hold that private schools perform a "government function"? If so, under what circumstances? Consider Choper, *Thoughts on State Action,* 1979 Wash.U.L.Q. 757, 778: "[I]t is clear that the operation of elementary and secondary schools is not an enterprise that is 'traditionally *exclusively* reserved to the State.' But a comprehensive survey of school districts in the United States would surely show that virtually all maintained at least one public elementary and secondary school unless, because of some peculiar development, the educational needs of the community's children were historically always met by a privately funded school. Such a school—or at least one of such schools if there are several in the hypothetical community (and which one is *the* one may present a nice question)—is, in effect, serving as a substitute for the conventional public school that the school district would otherwise provide. In this sense, it is performing a function 'traditionally *exclusively* reserved to the State.' "

3. *The limits (or lack of limits) of the state action concept.* Do you agree that "an ordinary statute of limitations whereby the State declines to provide a remedy for private deprivations of property after the passage of a given period of time" is *not* state action? If it *is* state action, then is New York's rule—that "its courts will not interfere with a private sale" pursuant to a warehouseman's lien—also state action? If so, is it not true that "all private deprivations of property would be converted into public acts whenever the State, for whatever reason, denies relief sought by the putative property owner"? Of what relevance is it that "the State's conduct in *Flagg Bros.* takes the concrete form of a statutory enactment"? May a "state procedure" providing a "framework of rules which facilitate commercial transactions" be promulgated by common law as well as by statute? See generally Brest, *State Action and Liberal Theory: A Casenote on Flagg Brothers v. Brooks,* 130 U.Pa.L.Rev. 1296 (1982).

Chapter 12

CONGRESSIONAL ENFORCEMENT
OF CIVIL RIGHTS

The exercise of congressional authority under the commerce and spending powers to protect civil rights was examined in detail in Ch. 2, Secs. 2, V and 3. But the potentially most pervasive sources of federal legislative power to enforce personal liberty are found in the final sections of the thirteenth, fourteenth, and fifteenth amendments which grant Congress power to enforce the substantive provisions of these amendments "by appropriate legislation." Some exertions of this power have already been referred to, see, e.g., pp. 918, 970 supra. Here, detailed consideration is undertaken.

SECTION 1. HISTORICAL FRAMEWORK

I. LEGISLATION

The Civil Rights Act of 1866, enacted pursuant to the thirteenth amendment, was the first Reconstruction Act seeking "to protect all persons in the United States in their civil rights." (See "Historical Background," p. 250 supra.) Its current provisions are:

42 U.S.C. § 1981. "*Equal rights under the law.* All persons within the jurisdiction of the United States shall have the same right in every State and Territory to make and enforce contracts, to sue, be parties, give evidence, and to the full and equal benefit of all laws and proceedings for the security of persons and property as is enjoyed by white citizens, and shall be subject to like punishment, pains, penalties, taxes, licenses, and exactions of every kind, and to no other."

42 U.S.C. § 1982. "*Property rights of citizens.* All citizens of the United States shall have the same right, in every State and Territory, as is enjoyed by white citizens thereof to inherit, purchase, lease, sell, hold, and convey real and personal property."

The 1866 Act then provided criminal penalties against any person denying such rights under color of law. With certain changes (the most important being addition of the word "willfully" in 1909, 35 Stat. 1092, and the substantial increase of penalties in 1968, 82 Stat. 75), this has survived as a significant federal criminal statute enforcing civil rights:

18 U.S.C. § 242. *"Deprivation of rights under color of law.* Whoever, under color of any law, statute, ordinance, regulation, or custom, willfully subjects any inhabitant of any State, Territory, or District to the deprivation of any rights, privileges, or immunities secured or protected by the Constitution or laws of the United States, or to different punishments, pains or penalties, on account of such inhabitant being an alien, or by reason of his color, or race, than are prescribed for the punishment of citizens, shall be fined not more than $1,000 or imprisoned not more than one year, or both; and if death results shall be subject to imprisonment for any term of years or for life."

Doubt as to the adequacy of the thirteenth amendment to support the 1866 Act was a significant force leading to adoption of the fourteenth amendment. After ratification of the fifteenth amendment, Congress passed the Act of May 31, 1870, 16 Stat. 140. One section, barring private conspiracies, evolved as an important existing protection:

18 U.S.C. § 241. *"Conspiracy against rights of citizens.* If two or more persons conspire to injure, oppress, threaten, or intimidate any citizen in the free exercise or enjoyment of any right or privilege secured to him by the Constitution or laws of the United States, or because of his having exercised the same; or

"If two or more persons go on the highway, or on the premises of another, with intent to prevent or hinder his free exercise or enjoyment of any right or privilege so secured—

"They shall be fined not more than $10,000 or imprisoned not more than ten years, or both; and if death results, they shall be subject to imprisonment for any term of years or for life."

Next came the Ku Klux Klan Act of 1871, 17 Stat. 13, which made criminal private conspiracies against the operations of government officials or courts, or to deprive persons of equal protection of the laws.[b] The Act also established civil liabilities that have evolved to be important existing provisions. One is the civil counterpart of 18 U.S.C. § 242:

42 U.S.C. § 1983. *"Civil action for deprivation of rights.* Every person who, under color of any statute, ordinance, regulation, custom, or usage, of any State or Territory, subjects, or causes to be subjected, any citizen of the United States or other persons within the jurisdiction thereof to the deprivation of any rights, privileges or immunities secured by the Constitution and laws, shall be liable to the person injured in an action of law, suit in equity, or other proper proceedings for redress." [d]

No significant congressional action to enforce civil rights took place between 1875 and the Civil Rights Act of 1957. The principal thrust of the 1957 Act and of the Civil Rights Act of 1960 was against racial discrimination in voting. The

b. The latter proviso was held unconstitutional, as not supported by the fourteenth amendment, in *United States v. Harris,* 106 U.S. 629, 1 S.Ct. 601, 27 L.Ed. 290 (1882), because "directed exclusively against the action of private persons, without reference to the laws of the State or their administration by her officers." The entire part was repealed in 1909, 35 Stat. 1153–54.

d. For general discussion and evolution of the Reconstruction civil rights legislation, see Gressman, *The Unhappy History of Civil Rights Legislation,* 50 Mich.L.Rev. 1323 (1952); Maslow & Robison, *Civil Rights Legislation and the Fight for Equality, 1862–1952,* 20 U.Chi.L.Rev. 363 (1953); U.S. Comm'n on Civil Rights, *Enforcement* 103–40 (1965).

Civil Rights Act of 1964, although principally concerned with matters already considered, also dealt with voting. But the most comprehensive federal legislation in aid of the franchise is the Voting Rights Act of 1965, 42 U.S.C. § 1973 (examined in detail in *South Carolina v. Katzenbach* and *Katzenbach v. Morgan*, Sec. 2 infra) and its 1970 Amendments (discussed in *Oregon v. Mitchell*, Sec. 2 infra). Finally, the Civil Rights Act of 1968 provides protection against interference with designated "federally protected activities," 18 U.S.C. § 245, and against discrimination in housing, 42 U.S.C. §§ 3601–31—both considered at several points infra.

II. JUDICIAL DECISIONS

1. *Necessity of "state action" for violation of constitutional rights.* (a) *In general.* Shortly after enactment of the Reconstruction civil rights laws, the Court, in a series of decisions culminating in the *Civil Rights Cases* in 1883 significantly limited their impact by interpreting the fourteenth (and fifteenth) amendments as barring only "state action," thus precluding congressional legislation against "private individuals" for violating rights of persons created by these amendments.

(b) *Sec. 241 exceptions.* But the Court has long recognized that there is a limited category of constitutional rights, protected by § 241, that, as stated in UNITED STATES v. WILLIAMS, 341 U.S. 70, 71 S.Ct. 581, 95 L.Ed. 758 (1951), "Congress can beyond doubt constitutionally secure against interference by private individuals. [T]his category includes rights which arise from the relationship of the individual and the Federal Government. The right of citizens to vote in congressional elections, for instance, may obviously be protected by Congress from individual as well as from State interference. *Ex parte Yarbrough*, 110 U.S. 651, 4 S.Ct. 152, 28 L.Ed. 274." [b] The Court has also included, as "attributes of national citizenship," "the right of the people peaceably to assemble for the purpose of petitioning Congress for a redress of grievances" [c] and the "constitutional right to travel from one State to another." [d]

2. *Sec. 242.* SCREWS v. UNITED STATES, 325 U.S. 91, 65 S.Ct. 1031, 89 L.Ed. 1495 (1945): Defendants were Georgia police who, after arresting a black, knocked him unconscious when he allegedly reached for a gun and beat him to death. There was evidence that defendant Screws held a personal grudge against him. Defendants were convicted under § 242 for violating the prisoner's right to due process which gave one charged with a crime "the right to be tried by a jury and sentenced by a court."

(a) *Color of law.* First, defendants argued that they had not acted "under color of any law" per § 242 because their action was in violation of state law. Six justices rejected the contention. DOUGLAS, J., joined by Stone, C.J., and Black and Reed, JJ., said: " 'Misuse of power, possessed by virtue of state law and made possible only because the wrongdoer is clothed with the authority of state

---

b. *United States v. Classic*, 313 U.S. 299, 61 S.Ct. 1031, 85 L.Ed. 1368 (1941), included within this category the right to vote in the Louisiana congressional primary: "Interference with [this right is] an interference with the effective choice of the voters at the only stage of the election procedure when their choice is of significance, since it is at the only stage when such interference could have any practical effect on the ultimate result * * *."

c. *United States v. Cruikshank*, 92 U.S. 542, 23 L.Ed. 588 (1875) (dictum). For potential expansion, see Feuerstein, *Civil Rights Crimes and the Federal Power to Punish Private Individuals for Interference With Federally Secured Rights*, 19 Vand.L.Rev. 641, 654–59 (1966).

d. *United States v. Guest*, Sec. 2 infra.

law, is action taken "under color of" state law.' " Rutledge and Murphy, JJ., agreed in separate opinions. Roberts, J., joined by Frankfurter and Jackson, JJ., dissented.

(b) *Vagueness.* Second, defendants argued that "there is no ascertainable standard of guilt" because the Court has given "broad and fluid definitions of due process." The DOUGLAS opinion construed "willfully" in § 242 "as connoting a purpose to deprive a person of a specific constitutional right. [W]here the punishment imposed is only for an act knowingly done with the purpose of doing that which the statute prohibits, the accused cannot be said to suffer from lack of warning or knowledge that the act which he does is a violation of law. [Take] the case of a local officer who persists in enforcing a type of ordinance which the Court has held invalid as violative of the guarantees of free speech or freedom of worship. Or a local official continues to select juries in a manner which flies in the teeth of decisions of the Court. If those acts are done willfully, how can the officer possibly claim that he had no fair warning that his acts were prohibited by the statute? He violates the statute not merely because he has a bad purpose but because he acts in defiance of announced rules of law. * * *

"The difficulty here is that this question of intent was not submitted to the jury with the proper instructions." [g]

Dissenting, the ROBERTS opinion contended that "to base federal prosecutions on the shifting and indeterminate decisions of courts is to sanction prosecutions for crimes based on definitions made by courts. This is tantamount to creating a new body of federal criminal common law." [h]

3. *Sec. 1983.* (a) *Damages.* MONROE v. PAPE, 365 U.S. 167, 81 S.Ct. 473, 5 L.Ed.2d 492 (1961), was an action for damages under § 1983 against Chicago police officers for unlawful invasion of plaintiff's home and illegal search, seizure, and detention. The Court, per DOUGLAS, J., relying on *Screws,* held that the complaint alleged a deprivation of a "right secured by the Constitution" (the fourth amendment's guarantee against unreasonable searches and seizures made applicable to the states by the fourteenth amendment) by persons acting "under color of" state law. Further, since § 1983, unlike § 242, establishes a *civil* remedy and does not contain the word "willfully," plaintiff need not prove the "specific intent" required in *Screws*: § 1983 "should be read against the background of tort liability that makes a man responsible for the natural consequences of his actions." [i]

g. Rutledge, J., concurred in reversing and remanding for further proceedings so that five justices might make similar disposition of the cause. But he agreed with Murphy, J., that there was no real issue of vagueness in this case, the jury instructions were adequate, and the conviction should be affirmed.

h. On retrial, defendants in *Screws* were acquitted. Proof of the elements of the offense required by *Screws* "is a difficult burden to satisfy and permits the defense attorney to make the persuasive argument to the jury that only a constitutional lawyer would know enough to be able to harbor the requisite intent." Heyman, *Federal Remedies for Voteless Negroes,* 48 Calif.L.Rev. 190, 200 (1960). See generally 5 U.S. Comm'n on Civil Rights, *Justice* 45–52 (1961).

i. As to the measure of damages under § 1983, see *Carey v. Piphus,* 435 U.S. 247, 98

S.Ct. 1042, 55 L.Ed.2d 252 (1978), holding that common-law tort rules of damages should be adapted to provide "fair compensation for injuries caused by the deprivation of a constitutional right," and that damages should not be *presumed* to flow from every deprivation. See generally Love, *Damages: A Remedy for the Violation of Constitutional Rights,* 67 Calif.L. Rev. 1242 (1979).

Although no federal statute expressly provides civil remedies for a *federal* officer's violation of a person's constitutional rights, *Bivins v. Six Unknown Agents,* 403 U.S. 388, 91 S.Ct. 1999, 29 L.Ed.2d 619 (1971), held that the federal courts could award money damages ("where federally protected rights have been invaded, it has been the rule from the beginning that courts will be alert to adjust their remedies so as to grant the necessary

(b) *Specificity of constitutional right.* PAUL v. DAVIS, p. 405 per REHN-QUIST, J., held that § 1983 did not afford respondent a cause of action for his having been defamed by government officials: Unlike *Monroe,* "respondent [has] pointed to no specific constitutional guarantee safeguarding the interest he asserts has been invaded. [If] respondent's view is to prevail, [it] would seem almost necessarily to result in every legally cognizable injury which may have been inflicted by a state official acting under 'color of law' establishing a violation of the Fourteenth Amendment. [S]uch a reading would make of the Fourteenth Amendment a font of tort law to be superimposed upon whatever systems may already be administered by the States." [j]

(c) *"Custom or usage."* ADICKES v. S.H. KRESS & CO., 398 U.S. 144, 90 S.Ct. 1598, 26 L.Ed.2d 142 (1970), involved a damages action against a restaurant for having deprived plaintiff of equal protection—alleging that defendant acted "under color [of] custom, or usage, of any State." The Court (Douglas and Brennan, JJ., dissenting; Marshall, J., not participating) held "that a 'custom or usage' for purposes of § 1983 requires state involvement and is not simply a practice which reflects long-standing social habits, generally observed by the people in a locality"; it "must have the force of law by virtue of the persistent practices of state officials." [k]

SECTION 2. MODERN DEVELOPMENTS

SOUTH CAROLINA v. KATZENBACH, 383 U.S. 301, 86 S.Ct. 803, 15 L.Ed. 2d 769 (1966): South Carolina challenged the Voting Rights Act of 1965 (enacted pursuant to § 2 of the fifteenth amendment)—"the heart of [which] is a complex scheme of stringent remedies aimed at areas where voting discrimination has been most flagrant." The Court, per WARREN, C.J., referred to "the voluminous legislative history" that showed, inter alia, "unremitting and ingenious defiance of the Constitution," the enactment of literacy tests in Alabama, Georgia, Louisiana, Mississippi, North Carolina, South Carolina, and Virginia, still in use, which, because of their various qualifications, "were specifically designed to prevent Negroes from voting." It pointed out that "discriminatory application of voting tests" "pursuant to a widespread 'pattern or practice'" "is now the principal method used to bar Negroes from the polls," and gave a number of illustrations; that "case-by-case litigation against voting discrimination" under federal statutes of 1957, 1960 and 1964 has "done little to cure the problem."

"As against the reserved powers of the States, Congress may use any rational means to effectuate the constitutional prohibition of racial discrimination in voting. * * *

"The basic test to be applied in a case involving § 2 of the Fifteenth Amendment is the same as in all cases concerning the express powers of Congress with relation to the reserved powers of the [states.] 'Let the end be legitimate, let it be within the scope of the constitution, and all means which are appropriate, which are plainly adapted to that end, which are not prohibited, but

---

relief"). See further *Nixon v. Fitzgerald* and *Harlow v. Fitzgerald,* pp. 183, 187 supra.

j. For the dissenting views of Brennan, White and Marshall, JJ., see p. 406 supra.

k. For general analysis and discussion of litigation under § 1983 and its predecessors, and of immunities for states (but not municipalities) and various government officials that have been established by statutory interpretation, see McCormack, *Federalism and Section 1983: Limitations on Judicial Enforcement of Constitutional Protections,* 60 Va.L.Rev. 1, 250 (1974); Whitman, *Constitutional Torts,* 79 Mich.L.Rev. 5 (1980); Note, *Section 1983 and Federalism,* 90 Harv.L.Rev. 1133 (1977).

consist with the letter and spirit of the constitution, are constitutional.' *McCulloch v. Maryland* [p. 60 supra].

"We therefore reject South Carolina's argument that Congress may appropriately do no more than to forbid violations of the Fifteenth Amendment in general terms—that the task of fashioning specific remedies or of applying them to particular localities must necessarily be left entirely to the courts. [In] the oft-repeated words of Chief Justice Marshall, referring to another specific legislative authorization in the Constitution, 'This power, like all others vested in Congress, is complete in itself, may be exercised to its utmost extent, and acknowledges no limitations, other than are prescribed in the constitution.' *Gibbons v. Ogden* [p. 68 supra]."

The Court first held that the prescription of "remedies for voting discrimination which go into effect without any need for prior adjudication" "was clearly a legitimate response to the problem."

The "coverage formula" of the Act applied "to any State, or to any separate political subdivision [for] which two findings have been made: (1) the Attorney General has determined that on November 1, 1964, it maintained a 'test or device,' and (2) the Director of the Census has determined that less than 50% of its voting-age residents were registered on November 1, 1964, or voted in the presidential election of November 1964. These findings are not reviewable * * *. § 4(b). [T]he phrase 'test or device' means any requirement that a registrant or voter must '(1) demonstrate the ability to read, write, understand, or interpret any matter, (2) demonstrate any educational achievement or his knowledge of any particular subject, (3) possess good moral character, or (4) prove his qualifications by the voucher of registered voters or members of any other class.' § 4(c)." Statutory coverage was terminated by a so-called "bail out" provision—if the area obtained a judgment from a three-judge federal court in the District of Columbia "that tests and devices have not been used during the preceding five years to abridge the franchise on racial grounds." "In acceptable legislative fashion, Congress chose to limit its attention to the geographic areas where immediate action seemed necessary."

The areas covered, "for which there was evidence of actual voting discrimination,"—Alabama, Louisiana, Mississippi, Georgia, South Carolina and much of North Carolina—shared the "two characteristics incorporated by Congress into the coverage formula." "It was therefore permissible to impose the new remedies on the few remaining States and political subdivisions covered by the formula, at least in the absence of proof that they have been free of substantial voting discrimination in recent years." That there are excluded areas "for which there is evidence of voting discrimination by other means" is irrelevant: "Congress strengthened existing remedies for voting discrimination in other areas of the country. Legislation need not deal with all phases of a problem in the same way, so long as the distinctions drawn have some basis in political experience." "There are no States or political subdivisions exempted from coverage under § 4(b) in which the record reveals recent racial discrimination involving tests and devices. This fact confirms the rationality of the formula." The findings "which trigger application of the coverage formula" "consist of objective statistical determinations" and the termination procedure "serves as a partial substitute for direct judicial review."

In areas covered, § 4(a) suspended "literacy tests and similar voting qualifications for a period of five years from the last occurrence of substantial voting discrimination," and § 5 suspended "all new voting regulations pending review by [the Attorney General or a three-judge court in the District of Columbia] to determine whether their use would perpetuate voting discrimination." [a] Both were upheld as a "legitimate response to the problem," the Court recounting the evidence Congress had before it of prior discriminatory administration of old tests and use of new tests to evade court decrees. "Congress knew that continuance of the tests and devices in use at the present time, no matter how fairly administered in the future, would freeze the effect of past discrimination in favor of unqualified white registrants. Congress permissibly rejected the alternatives of requiring a complete re-registration of all voters, believing that this would be too harsh on many whites who had enjoyed the franchise for their entire adult lives."

Finally, §§ 6(b), 7, 9, and 13(a) provided that "the Civil Service Commission shall appoint voting examiners whenever the Attorney General certifies either of the following facts: (1) that he has received meritorious written complaints from at least 20 residents alleging that they have been disenfranchised under color of law because of their race, or (2) that the appointment of examiners is otherwise necessary to effectuate the guarantees of the Fifteenth Amendment." These examiners were empowered to list as "eligible voters" "any person who meets the voting requirements of state law." Termination was provided for "(1) if the Attorney General informs the Civil Service Commission that all persons listed by examiners have been placed on the official voting rolls, and that there is no longer reasonable cause to fear abridgement of the franchise on racial grounds, or (2) if the political subdivision has obtained a declaratory judgment from the District Court for the District of Columbia, ascertaining the same facts which govern termination by the Attorney General, and the Director of the Census has determined that more than 50% of the non-white residents of voting age are registered to vote." This, too, was upheld: "In many of the political subdivisions covered by § 4(b) of the Act, voting officials have persistently employed a variety of procedural tactics to deny Negroes the franchise, often in direct defiance or evasion of federal court decrees. Congress realized that merely to suspend voting rules which have been misused or are subject to misuse might leave this localized evil undisturbed." [b]

ROME v. UNITED STATES, 446 U.S. 156, 100 S.Ct. 1548, 64 L.Ed.2d 119 (1980), per MARSHALL, J., held that for states within the "coverage formula," the Act's "bail out" procedure—satisfaction of which would avoid preclearance of new voting regulations by the Attorney General or the three-judge federal court—could only be used by the state itself and not by separate political units within the state. POWELL, J., dissented: "The Court's interpretation [renders the Act] unconstitutional as applied to the city of Rome. The preclearance require-

a. For examples of the Court's subsequent broad interpretation of "voting regulations" that are subject to the suspension provision of section 5, see *United Jewish Orgs. v. Carey*, p. 937 supra (new or revised reapportionment plan); *Rome v. United States*, infra (election of officials "at large" rather than by district; annexation of adjacent area thus increasing number of eligible voters).

b. Black, J., agreed "with substantially all of the Court's opinion" but dissented in respect to § 5: "[I]f all the provisions of our Constitution which limit the power of the Fed-

eral Government and reserve other power to the States are to mean anything, they mean at least that the States have power to pass laws [without] first sending their officials hundreds of miles away to beg federal authorities to approve them."

See also Powell, J.'s "reservations as to the constitutionality of the Act['s] selective coverage of certain States only and to the intrusive preclearance procedure," *United States v. Board of Comm'rs*, 435 U.S. 110, 98 S.Ct. 965, 55 L.Ed.2d 148 (1978) (concurring opinion).

ment both intrudes on the prerogatives of state and local governments and abridges the voting rights of all citizens in States covered under the Act. [In] view of the District Court finding that Rome has not denied or abridged the voting rights of blacks, the Fifteenth Amendment provides no authority for continuing those deprivations until the entire State of Georgia satisfies the bailout standards." Rehnquist, J., joined by Stewart, J., dissented on broader grounds—see note 4 after *Oregon v. Mitchell,* infra.

UNITED STATES v. GUEST

383 U.S. 745, 86 S.Ct. 1170, 16 L.Ed.2d 239 (1966).

MR. JUSTICE STEWART delivered the opinion of the Court.

[Defendants were indicted] for criminal conspiracy in violation of § 241 [to] deprive Negro citizens of the free exercise and enjoyment of several specified rights secured by the Constitution and laws of the United States. The defendants [successfully] moved to dismiss the indictment on the ground that it did not charge an offense under the laws of the United States. [As] in *Price,* decided today, we deal here with issues of statutory construction, not with issues of constitutional power. * * *[a]

II. The second numbered paragraph of the indictment alleged that the defendants conspired to injure, oppress, threaten, and intimidate Negro citizens of the United States in the free exercise of enjoyment of: "The right to the equal utilization, without discrimination upon the basis of race, of public facilities in the vicinity of Athens, Georgia, owned, operated, or managed by [the State]."

Correctly characterizing this paragraph as embracing rights protected by the Equal Protection Clause [the] District Court held as a matter of statutory construction that § 241 does not encompass any Fourteenth Amendment [rights. This] was in error, as [*Price*] makes abundantly clear. * * *

Moreover, inclusion of Fourteenth Amendment rights within the compass of § 241 does not render the statute unconstitutionally vague. Since the gravamen of the offense is conspiracy, the requirement that the offender must act with a specific intent to interfere with the federal rights in question is satisfied. *Screws.* * * *

Unlike the indictment in *Price,* however, the indictment in the present case names no person alleged to have acted in any way under the color of state law. [The] Equal Protection Clause speaks to the State or to those acting under the color of its authority.

In this connection, we emphasize that § 241 by its clear language incorporates no more than the Equal Protection Clause itself; the statute does not purport to give substantive, as opposed to remedial, implementation to any rights secured by that Clause. Since we therefore deal here only with the bare terms of the Equal Protection Clause itself, nothing said in this opinion goes to the question of what kinds of other and broader legislation Congress might constitutionally enact under § 5 of the Fourteenth Amendment to implement that Clause or any other provision of the Amendment.

It is a commonplace that rights under the Equal Protection Clause itself arise only where there has been involvement of the State or of one acting under the color of its authority. * * *

a. *United States v. Price,* 383 U.S. 787, 86 S.Ct. 1152, 16 L.Ed.2d 267 (1966), unanimously held that "private persons, jointly engaged with state officers in the prohibited action, are acting 'under color' of law for the purposes of" 18 U.S.C.A. § 242.

This is not to say, however, that the involvement of the State need be either exclusive or direct. In a variety of situations the Court has found state action of a nature sufficient to create rights under the Equal Protection Clause even though the participation of the State was peripheral, or its action was only one of several cooperative [forces].

This case, however, requires no determination of the threshold level that state action must attain in order to create rights under the Equal Protection Clause [because] the indictment in fact contains an express allegation of state involvement sufficient at least to require the denial of a motion to dismiss. One of the means of accomplishing the object of the conspiracy, according to the indictment, was "By causing the arrest of Negroes by means of false reports that such Negroes had committed criminal acts." [The] allegation of the extent of official involvement in the present case is not clear. [But it] is broad enough to cover a charge of active connivance by agents of the State in the making of the "false reports," or other conduct amounting to official discrimination clearly sufficient to constitute denial of rights protected by the Equal Protection Clause. Although it is possible [that] the proof if the case goes trial, would disclose no cooperative action of that kind by officials of the State, the allegation is enough to prevent dismissal of this branch of the indictment.

III. The fourth numbered paragraph of the indictment alleged that the defendants conspired to injure, oppress, threaten, and intimidate Negro citizens of the United States in the free exercise and enjoyment of: "The right to travel freely to and from the State of [Georgia]."

The District Court was in error in dismissing the indictment as to this paragraph. The constitutional right to travel from one State to another, and necessarily to use the highways and other instrumentalities of interstate commerce in doing so, occupies a position fundamental to the concept of our Federal Union. [See the Court's discussion, Ch. 7, Sec. 3.]

This does not mean, of course, that every criminal conspiracy affecting an individual's right of free interstate passage is within the sanction of § 241. A specific intent to interfere with the federal right must be [proved]. Thus, for example, a conspiracy to rob an interstate traveler would not, of itself, violate § 241. But if the predominant purpose of the conspiracy is to impede or prevent the exercise of the right of interstate travel, or to oppress a person because of his exercise of that right, then, whether or not motivated by racial discrimination, the conspiracy becomes a proper object of the federal law under which the indictment in this case was brought. * * *

Reversed and remanded.

MR. JUSTICE CLARK, with whom MR. JUSTICE BLACK and MR. JUSTICE FORTAS join, concurring.

I join the opinion of the Court in this case but believe it worthwhile to comment on [Part II]. The Court's interpretation of the indictment clearly avoids the question whether Congress, by appropriate legislation, has the power to punish private conspiracies that interfere with Fourteenth Amendment rights, such as the right to utilize public facilities. My Brother Brennan, however, [suggests] that the Court indicates sub silentio that Congress does not have the power to outlaw such conspiracies. Although the Court specifically rejects any such connotation, it is, I believe, both appropriate and necessary under the circumstances here to say that there now can be no doubt that the specific language of § 5 empowers the Congress to enact laws punishing all conspiracies—with or without state action—that interfere with Fourteenth Amendment rights.

MR. JUSTICE HARLAN, concurring in part and dissenting in part.

I join [Part] II of the Court's opinion, but I cannot subscribe to Part III in its full sweep. To the extent that it is there held that § 241 reaches conspiracies, embracing only the action of private persons, [to] interfere with the right of citizens freely to engage in interstate travel, I am constrained to dissent. On the other hand, I agree that § 241 does embrace state interference with such interstate travel, and I therefore consider that this aspect of the indictment is sustainable on the reasoning of Part II of the Court's opinion.

This right to travel must be found in the Constitution itself. This is so because [no] "right to travel" can be found in § 241 or in any other law of the United States. [While] past cases do indeed establish that there is a constitutional "right to travel" between States free from unreasonable *governmental* interference, today's decision is the first to hold that such movement is also protected against *private* interference * * *.

[Harlan, J., first reviewed the cases stating "that the right is a privilege and immunity of national citizenship" and concluded] that those cases all dealt with the right of travel simply as affected by oppressive *state* action. * * *

A second possible constitutional basis for the right [is] the Commerce Clause. [Yet] this approach to the right to travel, like that found in the privileges and immunities cases, is concerned with the interrelation of state and federal power, not [with] private interference. * * *

One other possible source for the right to travel should be mentioned [—due process, which] would clearly make it inapplicable to the present case, for due process speaks only to governmental action. * * *

As a general proposition it seems to me very dubious that the Constitution was intended to create certain rights of private individuals as against other private individuals. The Constitutional Convention was called to establish a nation, not to reform the common law. Even the Bill of Rights, designed to protect personal liberties, was directed at rights against governmental authority, not other individuals. It is true that there are a very narrow range of rights against individuals which have been read into the Constitution [referring to cases discussed in note 1(b), Sec. 1, II supra, but these] are narrow, and are essentially concerned with the vindication of important relationships with the Federal Government—voting in federal elections, involvement in federal law enforcement, communicating with the Federal Government. The present case stands on a considerably different footing.

It is arguable that the same considerations which led the Court on numerous occasions to find a right of free movement against oppressive state action now justifies a similar result with respect to private impediments. *Crandall v. Nevada* spoke of the need to travel to the capital, to serve and consult with the offices of government. A basic reason for the formation of this Nation was to facilitate commercial intercourse; intellectual, cultural, scientific, social, and political interests are likewise served by free movement. Surely these interests can be impeded by private vigilantes as well as by state action. Although this argument is not without force, [t]here is a difference in power between States and private groups so great that analogies between the two tend to be misleading. If the State obstructs free intercourse of goods, people, or ideas, the bonds of the union are threatened; if a private group effectively stops such communication, there is at most a temporary breakdown of law and order, to be remedied by the exercise of state authority or by appropriate federal legislation.

[As] to interstate commerce [b]ecause Congress has wide authority to legislate in this area, it seems unnecessary [to] strain to find a dubious constitutional right.[a]

[T]he immunities and commerce provisions of the Constitution leave the way open for the finding of this "private" constitutional right, since they do not speak solely in terms of governmental action. [But to] do so subjects § 241 to serious challenge on the score of vagueness and serves in effect to place this Court in the position of making criminal law under the name of constitutional interpretation. * * *

MR. JUSTICE BRENNAN, with whom THE CHIEF JUSTICE and MR. JUSTICE DOUGLAS join, concurring in part and dissenting in part.

I [reach] the same result as the Court on that branch of the indictment discussed in Part III of its opinion but for other reasons. See footnote 3, infra. And I agree with so much of Part II as construes § 241 to encompass conspiracies to injure, oppress, threaten or intimidate citizens in the free exercise or enjoyment of Fourteenth Amendment rights and holds that, as so construed, § 241 is not void for indefiniteness. I do not agree, however, with the remainder of Part II, which holds, as I read the opinion, that a conspiracy to interfere with the exercise of the right to equal utilization of state facilities is not within the meaning of § 241 [unless] discriminatory conduct by state officers is involved in the alleged conspiracy.

* * * I believe that § 241 reaches such a private conspiracy, not because the Fourteenth Amendment of its own force prohibits such a conspiracy, but because § 241, as an exercise of congressional power under § 5 of that Amendment, prohibits *all* conspiracies to interfere with the exercise of a "right * * * secured [by] the Constitution" and because the right to equal utilization of state facilities is a "right * * * secured [by] the Constitution" within the meaning of that phrase as used in § 241.[3]

My difference with the Court stems from its construction of the term "secured" as used in § 241 * * *. The Court tacitly construes the term "secured" so as to restrict the coverage of § 241 to those rights that are "fully protected" by the Constitution or another federal law. Unless private interferences with the exercise of the right in question are prohibited by the Constitution itself or another federal law, the right cannot, in the Court's view, be deemed "secured [by] the Constitution or laws of the United States" so as to make § 241 applicable to a private conspiracy to interfere with the exercise of that right. The Court then premises that neither the Fourteenth Amendment nor any other federal law prohibits private interferences with the exercise of the right to equal utilization of state facilities.

In my view, however, a right can be deemed "secured [by] the Constitution or laws of the United States," within the meaning of § 241, even though only

a. The Civil Rights Act of 1968, 18 U.S.C.A. § 245(b), penalizes all persons who interfere etc. (see fn. e, Sec. 1, II supra) with "(2) any person because of his race, color, religion or national origin and because he is or has been * * * (E) traveling in or using any facility of interstate commerce, or using any vehicle, terminal, or facility of any common carrier by motor, rail, water, or air."

3. Similarly, I believe that § 241 reaches a private conspiracy to interfere with the right to travel from State to State. I therefore need not reach the question whether the Constitution of its own force prohibits private interferences with that right; for I construe § 241 to prohibit such interferences, and as so construed I am of the opinion that § 241 is a valid exercise of congressional power.

governmental interferences with the exercise of the right are prohibited by the Constitution itself (or another federal law). The term "secured" means "created by, arising under, or dependent upon," rather than "fully protected." A right is "secured [by] the Constitution" within the meaning of § 241 if it emanates from the Constitution, if it finds its source in the Constitution. Section 241 must thus be viewed, in this context, as an exercise of congressional power to amplify prohibitions of the Constitution addressed, as is invariably the case, to government officers; contrary to the view of the Court, I think we are dealing here with a statute that seeks to implement the Constitution, not with the "bare terms" of the Constitution. * * *

For me, the right to use state facilities without discrimination on the basis of race is, within the meaning of § 241, a right created by, arising under and dependent upon the Fourteenth Amendment and hence is a right "secured" by that Amendment. It finds its source in that Amendment. [The] Fourteenth Amendment commands the State to provide the members of all races with equal access to the public facilities it owns or manages, and the right of a citizen to use those facilities without discrimination on the basis of race is a basic corollary of this command. Whatever may be the status of the right to equal utilization of *privately owned facilities,* it must be emphasized that we are here concerned with the right to equal utilization of *public facilities owned or operated by or on behalf of the State.* * * *

In reversing the District Court's dismissal of the second numbered paragraph, I would therefore hold that proof at the trial of the conspiracy charged to the defendants in that paragraph will establish a violation of § 241 without regard to whether there is also proof that state law enforcement officers actively connived in causing the arrests of Negroes by means of false reports.

My view as to the scope of § 241 requires that I reach the question [of] whether § 241 or legislation indubitably designed to punish entirely private conspiracies to interfere with the exercise of Fourteenth Amendment rights constitutes a permissible exercise of the power granted to Congress by § 5 * * *.

A majority of the members of the Court[6] express the view today that § 5 empowers Congress to enact laws punishing *all* conspiracies to interfere with the exercise of Fourteenth Amendment rights, whether or not state officers or others acting under the color of state law are implicated in the conspiracy. * * * § 5 authorizes Congress to make laws that it concludes are reasonably necessary to protect a right created by and arising under that Amendment; and Congress is thus fully empowered to determine that punishment of private conspiracies interfering with the exercise of such a right is necessary to its full protection. * * *

I acknowledge that some of the decisions of this Court, most notably an aspect of the *Civil Rights Cases,* have declared that Congress' power under § 5 is confined to the adoption of "appropriate legislation for correcting the effects [of] prohibited state law and state [acts]." I do not accept—and a majority of the Court today rejects—this interpretation of § 5. It reduces the legislative power to enforce the provisions of the Amendment to that of the judiciary;[7] and it

6. The majority consists of the Justices joining my Brother Clark's opinion and the Justices joining this opinion. * * *

7. Congress, not the judiciary, was viewed as the more likely agency to implement fully the guarantees of equality, and thus it could

be presumed the primary purpose of the Amendments was to augment the power of Congress, not the judiciary. See James, *The Framing of the Fourteenth Amendment,* 184 (1956); Harris, *The Quest for Equality,* 53–54 (1960); Frantz, *Congressional Power to Enforce*

attributes a far too limited objective to the Amendment's sponsors.[8] [For amplification, see Brennan, J.'s opinion for the Court in *Katzenbach v. Morgan,* infra.]

Viewed in its proper perspective, § 5 appears as a positive grant of legislative power, authorizing Congress to exercise its discretion in fashioning remedies to achieve civil and political equality for all citizens. No one would deny [that] Congress has the power to punish state officers who, in excess of their authority and in violation of state law, conspire to threaten, harass and murder Negroes for attempting to use [state] facilities. And I can find no principle of federalism nor word of the Constitution that denies Congress power to determine that in order adequately to protect the right to equal utilization of state facilities, it is also appropriate to punish other individuals—neither state officers nor acting in concert with state officers—who engage in the same brutal conduct for the same misguided purpose.

Section 241 is certainly not model legislation for punishing private conspiracies to interfere with the exercise of the right of equal utilization of state facilities. It deals in only general language [which] brings § 241 close to the danger line of being void for vagueness.

But, as the Court holds, a stringent scienter requirement saves § 241 from condemnation * * *.

Notes and Questions

1. *Interference with fourteenth (and fifteenth) amendment rights.* Are private persons, who intimidate state officials in an attempt to thwart their racial integration of schools, subject to prosecution under § 241? Private persons who intimidate black school children or their parents in an attempt to stop them from going to integrated schools? Who lynch a prisoner, thus preventing his fair trial by the state? Who intimidate blacks in an effort to prevent them from voting? Cf. note after *South Carolina v. Katzenbach.* Who detain a judge in an effort to prevent him from setting bail?

2. *Scope of congressional power under § 5.* (a) Do you agree with "a majority of the members of the Court" in *Guest* that "§ 5 empowers Congress to enact laws punishing *all* conspiracies to interfere with the exercise of Fourteenth Amendment rights, whether or not state officers or others acting under color of state law are implicated in the conspiracy"? Consider Feuerstein, fn. c, Sec. 1, II supra, at 674–75: "[They] start with the proposition that there is a right to use state facilities without discrimination based upon race, when actually they are saying that there is a right to use state facilities without racial discrimination from any quarter—state or private. The traditional view of the equal protection clause is that it creates a right to be free of discrimination by the state. So defined, the right can only be infringed by state action, and legislation under § 5 must be directed at that infringement. Unfortunately,

the Fourteenth Amendment Against Private Acts, 73 Yale L.J. 1353, 1356 (1964).

8. As the first Mr. Justice Harlan said in dissent in the *Civil Rights Cases:* "It was perfectly well known that the great danger to equal enjoyment by citizens of their rights, as citizens, was to be apprehended, not altogether from unfriendly state legislation, but from the hostile action of corporations and individuals in the states. And it is to be presumed that it was intended, by [§ 5], to clothe congress with power and authority to meet that danger."

[For the view that the fourteenth amendment's "Privileges or Immunities Clause (coupled with the § 5 Enforcement Clause)" was intended "as an authorization of Federal legislation to prohibit private racial discrimination if the states did not," see Lusky, *By What Right?* 181–203 (1975). See also Frantz, fn. 7 supra.]

neither the Brennan nor the Clark opinion directly confronts this traditional approach." [b] Is the majority's rationale limited to "conspiracies" or is Congress empowered, beyond § 241, to penalize individual private acts? Does Brennan, J.'s rationale extend to "the right to equal utilization of *privately owned facilities*"?

(b) *Civil Rights Act of 1968.* 18 U.S.C.A. § 245(b): "Whoever, whether or not acting under color of law, by force or threat of force willfully injures, intimidates or interferes with, or attempts to injure, intimidate or interfere with—* * *

"(2) any person because of his race, color, religion or national origin and because he is or has been—

"(A) enrolling in or attending any public school or public college;

"(B) participating in or enjoying any benefit, service, privilege, program, facility or activity provided or administered by any State or subdivision thereof;

"(C) applying for or enjoying employment, or any perquisite thereof, by any private employer or any agency of any State or subdivision thereof, or joining or using the services or advantages of any labor organization, hiring hall, or employment agency;

"(D) serving, or attending upon any court of any State in connection with possible service, as a grand or petit juror; * * *

"(F) enjoying the goods, services, facilities, privileges, advantages, or accommodations of any inn, hotel, motel, or other establishment which provides lodging to transient guests, or of any restaurant, cafeteria, lunchroom, lunch counter, soda fountain, or other facility which serves the public and which is principally engaged in selling food or beverages for consumption on the premises, or of any gasoline station, or of any motion picture house, theater, concert hall, sports arena, stadium, or any other place of exhibition or entertainment which serves the public, or of any other establishment which serves the public and (i) which is located within the premises of any of the aforesaid establishments or within the premises of which is physically located any of the aforesaid establishments, and (ii) which holds itself out as serving patrons of such establishments; or * * *

"(5) any citizen because he is or has been, or in order to intimidate such citizen or any other citizen from lawfully aiding or encouraging other persons to participate, without discrimination on account of race, color, religion or national origin, in any of the benefits or activities described [or] participating lawfully in speech or peaceful assembly opposing any denial of the opportunity to so participate—

"shall be fined not more than $1,000, or imprisoned not more than one year, or both; and if bodily injury results shall be fined not more than $10,000, or imprisoned not more than ten years, or both; and if death results shall be subject to imprisonment for any term of years or for life. * * * Nothing in subparagraph (2)(F) * * * of this subsection shall apply to the proprietor of

b. Compare Stevens, J., concurring in *Great American Fed. S. & L. Ass'n v. Novotny,* 442 U.S. 366, 99 S.Ct. 2345, 60 L.Ed.2d 957 (1979): "[I]f private persons take conspiratorial action that prevents or hinders the constituted authorities of any State from giving or securing equal treatment, the private persons would cause those authorities to violate the Fourteenth Amendment; [but if] private persons engage in purely private acts of discrimination, [they] do not violate the Equal Protection Clause of the Fourteenth Amendment. The rights secured by the Equal Protection and Due Process Clauses of the Fourteenth Amendment are rights to protection against unequal or unfair treatment by the State, not by private parties."

any establishment which provides lodging to transient guests, or to any employee acting on behalf of such proprietor, with respect to the enjoyment of the goods, services, facilities, privileges, advantages, or accommodations of such establishment if such establishment is located within a building which contains not more than five rooms for rent or hire and which is actually occupied by the proprietor as his residence."

(c) Suppose a private individual murders a black. It is clear that the *effect* (irrespective of the murderer's *intent*) is to prevent the victim's equal use of state facilities; that it prevents his right to vote, etc. These facts would be equally true if the victim were white. May the murderer be punished under § 241? Under a more narrowly drawn federal criminal statute? Consider Cox, *Constitutional Adjudication and the Promotion of Human Rights,* 80 Harv.L.Rev. 91, 116 (1966): "It seems unlikely that much constitutional significance will attach to distinctions in terms of intent. The differences between purpose, awareness that a consequence must follow, conscious indifference, and responsibility for the natural and probable consequences of an act are far too elusive to measure the scope of congressional power. Furthermore, if violence and intimidation are actually interfering with the right to vote or to enjoy state facilities, there is scant practical relevance in the wrongdoers' motivation. The suggestion was once made that the power of Congress to regulate local activities under the commerce clause depended upon the intent with which the activities were conducted, but the idea was shortly abandoned in favor of legislative or administrative determination of the practical effects on commerce."

Does congressional power fail in the above instance because "its authority is confined to instances in which there is a special relationship between the person injured and the state"? Because there is "an utter lack of proportion between the federal punishment [and] the federal interest in safeguarding enjoyment of the constitutional right"? Or is "the responsibility for the federal system" left to Congress: "possession of congressional power should not be confused with its exercise"? Id. at 116–17, 119.

KATZENBACH v. MORGAN

384 U.S. 641, 86 S.Ct. 1717, 16 L.Ed.2d 828 (1966).

MR. JUSTICE BRENNAN delivered the opinion of the Court.

[Section] 4(e) of the Voting Rights Act of 1965 [provides] that no person who has successfully completed the sixth primary grade in a [school] accredited by the Commonwealth of Puerto Rico in which the language of instruction was other than English shall be denied the right to vote in any election because of his inability to read or write English. Appellees, registered voters in New York City, brought this suit to challenge the constitutionality of § 4(e) insofar as it pro tanto prohibits the enforcement of the election laws of New York requiring an ability to read and write English * * *.

Under the distribution of powers effected by the Constitution, [the] qualifications established by the States for voting for members of the most numerous branch of the state legislature also determine who may vote for United States Representatives and Senators, Art. I, § 2; Seventeenth Amendment. But, of course, the States have no power to grant or withhold the franchise on conditions that are forbidden by the Fourteenth Amendment * * *.

The Attorney General of New York argues that an exercise of congressional power under § 5 of the Fourteenth Amendment that prohibits the enforcement of a state [law] cannot be sustained as appropriate legislation to enforce the

Equal Protection Clause unless the judiciary decides—even with the guidance of a congressional judgment—that the application of the English literacy requirement prohibited by § 4(e) is forbidden by the Equal Protection Clause itself. We disagree. Neither the language nor history of § 5 supports such a construction.[7] [A] construction of § 5 that would require a judicial determination that the enforcement of the state law precluded by Congress violated the Amendment, as a condition of sustaining the congressional enactment [would] confine the legislative power in this context to the insignificant role of abrogating only those state laws that the judicial branch was prepared to adjudge unconstitutional, or of merely informing the judgment of the judiciary by particularizing the "majestic generalities" of [§ 1]. Accordingly, our decision in *Lassiter v. Northampton Cty. Bd. of Elec.*, 360 U.S. 45, 79 S.Ct. 985, 3 L.Ed.2d 1072 (1959), sustaining the North Carolina English literacy requirement as not in all circumstances prohibited by the first sections of the Fourteenth and Fifteenth Amendments, [did] not present the question before us here: Without regard to whether the judiciary would find that the Equal Protection Clause itself nullifies New York's English literacy requirement as so applied, could Congress prohibit the enforcement of the state law by legislating under § 5? In answering this question, our task is limited to determining whether such legislation is, as required by § 5, appropriate legislation to enforce the Equal Protection Clause.

By including § 5 the draftsmen sought to grant to Congress [the] same broad powers expressed in the Necessary and Proper Clause.[9] The classic formulation of the reach of those powers was established by Chief Justice Marshall in *McCulloch v. Maryland* * * *. *Ex parte Virginia*, decided 12 years after the adoption of the Fourteenth Amendment, held that congressional power under § 5 had this same broad scope * * *. Section 2 of the Fifteenth Amendment grants Congress a similar power [and] we recently held in *South Carolina v. Katzenbach* that [the test was] the one formulated in *McCulloch*. * * * Correctly viewed, § 5 is a positive grant of legislative power authorizing Congress to exercise its discretion in determining whether and what legislation is needed to secure the guarantees of the Fourteenth Amendment. * * *[10]

There can be no doubt that § 4(e) may be regarded as an enactment to enforce the Equal Protection Clause. [S]pecifically, § 4(e) may be viewed as a measure to secure for the Puerto Rican community residing in New York nondiscriminatory treatment by government—both in the imposition of voting

7. For the historical evidence suggesting that the sponsors and supporters of the Amendment were primarily interested in augmenting the power of Congress, rather than the judiciary, see generally tenBroek, *The Antislavery Origins of the Fourteenth Amendment* 187–217 (1951). [But see Burt, *Miranda and Title II: A Morganatic Marriage,* 1969 Sup.Ct.Rev. 81–100.]

9. In fact, earlier drafts of the proposed Amendment employed the "necessary and proper" terminology to describe the scope of congressional power under the Amendment. The substitution of the "appropriate legislation" formula was never thought to have the effect of diminishing the scope of this congressional power. See, e.g., Cong. Globe, 42d Cong., 1st Sess., App. 83 * * *. [But see Note, *Theories of Federalism and Civil Rights,* 75 Yale L.J. 1007, 1046 n. 200 (1966). Com-

pare discussion in *Argument: The Oral Argument Before the Supreme Court in Brown v. Board of Education of Topeka,* 1952–55, 93–94 (Friedman ed. 1969).]

10. Contrary to the suggestion of the dissent, § 5 does not grant Congress power to exercise discretion in the other direction and to enact "statutes so as in effect to dilute equal protection and due process decisions of this Court." We emphasize that Congress' power under § 5 is limited to adopting measures to enforce the guarantees of the Amendment; § 5 grants Congress no power to restrict, abrogate, or dilute these guarantees. Thus, for example, an enactment authorizing the States to establish racially segregated systems of education would not be—as required by § 5—a measure "to enforce" the Equal Protection Clause since that clause of its own force prohibits such state laws.

qualifications and the provision or administration of governmental services, such as public schools, public housing and law enforcement.

Section 4(e) may be readily seen as "plainly adapted" to furthering these aims of the Equal Protection Clause. The practical effect of § 4(e) is to prohibit New York from denying the right to vote to large segments of its Puerto Rican community [—the] right that is "preservative of all rights." This enhanced political power will be helpful in gaining nondiscriminatory treatment in public services for the entire Puerto Rican community.[11] Section 4(e) thereby enables the Puerto Rican minority better to obtain "perfect equality of civil rights and equal protection of the laws." [It] was for Congress, as the branch that made this judgment, to assess and weigh the various conflicting considerations—the risk or pervasiveness of the discrimination in governmental services, the effectiveness of eliminating the state restriction on the right to vote as a means of dealing with the evil, the adequacy or availability of alternative remedies, and the nature and significance of the state interests that would be affected by the nullification of the English literacy requirement * * *. It is not for us to review the congressional resolution of these factors. It is enough that we be able to perceive a basis upon which the Congress might resolve the conflict as it did. There plainly was such a [basis]. Any contrary conclusion would require us to be blind to the realities familiar to the legislators.[12]

The result is no different if we confine our inquiry to the question whether § 4(e) was merely legislation aimed at the elimination of an invidious discrimination in establishing voter qualifications. We are told that New York's English literacy requirement originated in the desire to provide an incentive for non-English speaking immigrants to learn the English language and in order to assure the intelligent exercise of the franchise. Yet Congress might well have questioned, in light of the many exemptions provided,[13] and some evidence suggesting that prejudice played a prominent role in the enactment of the requirement,[14] whether these were actually the interests being served. Congress might have also questioned whether denial of a right deemed so precious and fundamental in our society was a necessary or appropriate means of encouraging persons to learn English, or of furthering the goal of an intelligent exercise of the franchise. Finally, Congress might well have concluded that as a means of furthering the intelligent exercise of the franchise, an ability to read or understand Spanish is as effective as ability to read English for those to whom Spanish-language newspapers and Spanish-language radio and television programs are available to inform them of election issues and governmental affairs.[16]

---

11. Cf. * * * United States v. Darby [p. 90 supra], that the power of Congress to regulate interstate commerce "extends to those activities intrastate which so affect interstate commerce or the exercise of the power of Congress over it as to make regulation of them appropriate means to the attainment of a legitimate end * * *."

12. See, e.g., 111 Cong.Rec. 10676, 10680 (May 20, 1965), 15671 (July 9, 1965); Literacy Tests and Voter Requirements in Federal and State Elections, Senate Hearings 507–508.

13. The principal exemption complained of is that for persons who had been eligible to vote before January 1, 1922.

14. This evidence consists in part of statements made in the Constitutional Convention first considering the English literacy requirement * * *. Congress was aware of this evidence. See, e.g., Literacy Tests and Voter Requirements in Federal and State Elections, Senate Hearings 507–513; Voting Rights, House Hearings 508–513.

16. See, e.g., 111 Cong.Rec. 10675 (May 20, 1965), 15102 (July 6, 1965), 15666 (July 9, 1965). The record in this case includes affidavits describing the nature of New York's two major Spanish-language newspapers [and] its three full-time Spanish-language radio stations and affidavits from those who have campaigned in Spanish speaking areas.

Since Congress undertook to legislate so as to preclude the enforcement of the state law, and did so in the context of a general appraisal of literacy requirements for voting, see *South Carolina v. Katzenbach,* to which it brought a specially informed legislative competence,[17] it was Congress' prerogative to weigh these competing considerations. Here again, it is enough that we perceive a basis upon which Congress might predicate a judgment that the application of New York's English literacy requirement * * * constituted an invidious discrimination in violation of the Equal Protection Clause.

[The Court rejected the contention that the "American-flag schools" limitation itself violates "the letter and spirit of the Constitution," see p. 1052 supra].

Reversed.

MR. JUSTICE HARLAN, whom MR. JUSTICE STEWART joins, dissenting.

[Harlan, J., first argued that the New York law was not forbidden by the equal protection clause itself.] I believe the Court has confused the issue of how much enforcement power Congress possesses under § 5 with the distinct issue of what questions are appropriate for congressional determination and what questions are essentially judicial in nature.

When recognized state violations of federal constitutional standards have occurred, Congress is of course empowered by § 5 to take appropriate remedial [measures]. But it is a judicial question whether the condition with which Congress has thus sought to deal is in truth an infringement of the Constitution, something that is the necessary prerequisite to bringing the § 5 power into play at all. Thus, in *Ex parte Virginia,* involving a federal statute making it a federal crime to disqualify anyone from jury service because of race, the Court first held as a matter of constitutional law that "the Fourteenth Amendment secures [an] impartial jury trial, by jurors indifferently selected or chosen without discrimination against such jurors because of their color." Only then did the Court hold that to enforce this prohibition upon state discrimination, Congress could enact a criminal statute of the type under consideration. [In] *South Carolina v. Katzenbach,* [we] reviewed first the "voluminous legislative history" as well as judicial precedents supporting the basic congressional finding that the clear commands of the Fifteenth Amendment had been infringed by various state subterfuges. Given the existence of the evil, we held the remedial steps taken by the legislature under the Enforcement Clause of the Fifteenth Amendment to be a justifiable exercise of congressional initiative.

[The] question here is not whether the statute is appropriate remedial legislation to cure an established violation of a constitutional command, but whether there has in fact been an infringement of that constitutional command, that is, whether a particular state practice or, as here, a statute is so arbitrary or irrational as to offend the command of [equal protection]. That question is one for the judicial branch ultimately to determine. [In] view of [*Lassiter*], I do not think it is open to Congress to limit the effect of that decision as it has undertaken to do by § 4(e). In effect the Court reads § 5 of the Fourteenth Amendment as giving Congress the power to define the *substantive* scope of the Amendment. If that indeed be the true reach of § 5, then I do not see why Congress should not be able as well to exercise its § 5 "discretion" by enacting statutes so as in effect to dilute equal protection and due process decisions of this Court. In all such cases there is room for reasonable men to differ as to whether

17. See, e.g., 111 Cong.Rec. 10676 (Senator Long of Louisiana and Senator Young), 10678 (Senator Holland) (May 20, 1965), drawing on their experience with voters literate in a language other than English. * * *

or not a denial of equal protection or due process has occurred, and the final decision is one of judgment. Until today this judgment has always been one for the judiciary to resolve.

I do not mean to suggest in what has been said that a legislative judgment of the type incorporated in § 4(e) is without any force whatsoever. Decisions on questions of equal protection and due process are based not on abstract logic, but on empirical foundations. To the extent "legislative facts" are relevant to a judicial determination, Congress is well equipped to investigate them, and such determinations are of course entitled to due respect.[a] In *South Carolina v. Katzenbach,* such legislative findings were made to show that racial discrimination in voting was actually occurring. Similarly, in *Heart of Atlanta Motel, Inc. v. United States,* and *Katzenbach v. McClung,* [pp. 103, 105 supra], the congressional determination that racial discrimination in a clearly defined group of public accommodations did effectively impede interstate commerce was based on "voluminous testimony" which had been put before the Congress and in the context of which it passed remedial legislation.

But no such factual data provide a legislative record supporting § 4(e)[9] by way of showing that Spanish-speaking citizens are fully as capable of making informed decisions in a New York election as are English-speaking citizens. Nor was there any showing whatever to support the Court's alternative argument that § 4(e) should be viewed as but a remedial measure designed to cure or assure against unconstitutional discrimination of other varieties, e.g., in "public schools, public housing and law enforcement" * * *.

Thus, we have [here] what can at most be called a legislative announcement that Congress believes a state law to entail an unconstitutional deprivation of equal protection. Although this kind of declaration is of course entitled to the most respectful consideration, coming as it does from a concurrent branch and one that is knowledgeable in matters of popular political participation, I do not believe it lessens our responsibility to decide the fundamental issue of whether in fact the state enactment violates federal constitutional rights.

In assessing the deference we should give to this kind of congressional expression of policy, it is relevant that the judiciary has always given to congressional enactments a presumption of validity. However, it is also a canon of judicial review that state statutes are given a similar presumption, [and] although it has been suggested that this Court should give somewhat more deference to Congress than to a State Legislature,[10] such a simple weighing of presumptions is hardly a satisfying way of resolving a matter that touches the distribution of state and federal power in an area so sensitive as that of the regulation of the franchise. Rather it should be recognized that while the Fourteenth Amendment is a "brooding omnipresence" over all state legislation, the substantive matters which it touches are all within the primary legislative competence of the States. Federal authority, legislative no less than judicial, does not intrude unless there has been a denial by state action of Fourteenth Amendment [limitations]. At least in the area of primary state concern a state

---

a. For the view that "Congress cannot alter the *normative component* of a judicial decision" but that "the *empirical component* [is] the province of Congress," see Gordon, *The Nature and Uses of Congressional Power Under Section Five of the Fourteenth Amendment to Overcome Decisions of the Supreme Court,* 72 Nw.U.L.Rev. 656 (1977). See note 6(b) infra.

9. There were no committee hearings or reports referring to this section, which was introduced from the floor during debate on the full Voting Rights Act.

10. See Thayer, *The Origin and Scope of the American Doctrine of Constitutional Law,* 7 Harv.L.Rev. 129, 154–155 (1893).

statute that passes constitutional muster under the judicial standard of rationality should not be permitted to be set at naught by a mere contrary congressional pronouncement unsupported by a legislative record justifying that conclusion.

[To] hold, on this record, that § 4(e) overrides the New York literacy requirement seems to me tantamount to allowing the Fourteenth Amendment to swallow the State's constitutionally ordained primary authority in this field. For if Congress by what, as here, amounts to mere ipse dixit can set that otherwise permissible requirement partially at naught I see no reason why it could not also substitute its judgment for that of the States in other fields of their exclusive primary competence as well. * * *

Notes and Questions

1. *Congress and equal protection.* After *Morgan,* may Congress enact legislation prohibiting *all* state discrimination on the basis of alienage, illegitimacy and gender? Cf. Ch. 10, Sec. 3. Forbidding state discrimination against pushcart food vendors, opticians, debt adjustors and methadone users? Cf. Ch. 10, Sec. 1. For the view that, since the Court "underenforces" the provisions of § 1 of the fourteenth amendment because of "institutional" reasons "based upon questions of propriety or capacity," Congress has "the authority to enact legislation which fills in that body's conception" of those provisions, see Sager, *Fair Measure: The Legal Status of Underenforced Constitutional Norms,* 91 Harv.L. Rev. 1212 (1978).

After *Morgan,* may Congress outlaw *all* age and residence requirements for voting? Consider Bickel, *The Voting Rights Cases,* 1966 Sup.Ct.Rev. 79, 100: "[S]uppose Congress decided that aliens or eighteen-year-olds or residents of New Jersey are being discriminated against in New York. The decision would be as plausible as the one concerning Spanish-speaking Puerto Ricans. Could Congress give these groups the vote? If Congress may freely bestow the vote as a means of curing other discriminations, which it fears may be practiced against groups deprived of the vote, essentially because of this deprivation and on the basis of no other evidence, then there is nothing left of state autonomy in setting qualifications for voting."

2. *Analogy to commerce power.* On the scope of Congress' power under the commerce clause (Ch. 2, Sec. 1), is Congress' discretion limited to determining what are "appropriate means" for regulating intrastate commerce that affects commerce in more than one state, or does it extend to determining *whether* intrastate commerce affects commerce in more than one state? See Comment, 20 Rutg.L.Rev. 826 (1966). Is the *Morgan* standard of judicial review of Congress' power under § 5 the same as the standard for reviewing Congress' power under the commerce clause? Consider Cox note 2(c) after *Guest* at 104: "Conclusory but qualifying phrases like 'reasonable relation' and 'rational' are notably absent from the opinion, in contrast to the public accommodations and voting rights cases where [the opinions] were limited by the need to use terms acceptable to a unanimous bench. It is sufficient that the law 'may be viewed' as a measure for securing equal protection and that the Court can 'perceive a basis' upon which Congress might predicate its judgment. The choice of words cannot have been casual. Evidently, the Court intends to validate any legislation under section 5—at least any legislation dealing with state action—without judging the substantiality of its relation to a permissible federal objective."

3. *Need for a "legislative record."* What of Harlan, J.'s suggestion that other broad exertions of congressional power have been sustained only on the

basis of "factual data" or "voluminous testimony"? Consider Cox, supra, at 105: "[His view] is at odds with the presumption of constitutionality and with a long line of precedents holding that a statute must be judged constitutional if any set of facts which can reasonably be conceived would sustain it. No case has ever held that a record is constitutionally required. The majority's view is also supported by the cases upholding congressional legislation under the commerce clause prior to the 1930s, much of which apparently rested upon factual conclusions for which no legislative record could be cited. The principle is not merely one of deference to Congress or the states. It rests upon appreciation of the fact that the fundamental basis for legislative action is the knowledge, experience, and judgment of the people's representatives only a small part, or even none, of which may come from the hearings and reports of committees or debates upon the floor."

4. *Congress and due process.* After *Morgan,* may Congress impose the federal rules of civil and criminal procedure on the states on the ground that the fourteenth amendment requires that due process be accorded all litigants and that in "its discretion" the federal rules are "needed to secure the guarantees of the Fourteenth Amendment"? Apart from "specific" constitutional prohibitions, under *Morgan,* what are the limits of congressional power? See generally Note, *Congressional Power to Enforce Due Process Rights,* 80 Colum.L.Rev. 1265 (1980).

5. *Congress and state action.* If *Morgan* gives Congress "the power to define the *substantive* scope" of equal protection (and due process), does it similarly permit Congress to determine the question of what constitutes "state action"? For example, might Congress, in "exercise of its discretion," determine that any judicial enforcement of racial discrimination shall be prohibited? That racial discrimination in the sale and rental of housing exists because of the failure of the states to make such discrimination illegal, and that this state "inaction" is state action under the fourteenth amendment that should "appropriately" be "remedied" by federal fair housing legislation? See fn. 8 in Brennan, J.'s opinion in *Guest.*

(a) For another post-*Morgan* approach re federal housing legislation, consider Cox, supra, at 120: "So long as Negroes are confined to racial ghettos, there will be actual or dangerously potential state discrimination in the quantity or quality of public services. First, the isolation of unpopular minorities in poverty-stricken, socially and economically isolated neighborhoods, lacking political influence, invites a lower quality of state services just as withholding the vote from many citizens in Puerto Rican neighborhoods made it less likely that they would receive equal services. Second, the very existence of the ghetto renders it more difficult [for] a state to provide equal services. Children in black ghettos, with an inferior cultural and economic background, lack the environment and associations essential to truly equal educational opportunity. [*Morgan* held that] Congress might legislate to remove an obstacle to the state's performance of its constitutional duty not to discriminate in providing public services, even though the immediate subject matter of the legislation—there the requirement of English literacy—was not itself a violation of the fourteenth amendment. It follows that Congress may likewise legislate to eliminate racial ghettos as obstacles to the states' performance of that same constitutional duty, even though the immediate subject matter of this legislation—the practices that result in ghettos—do not themselves involve violations of the fourteenth amendment. The only important difference is that in *Morgan* the obstacle was itself a state law whereas discrimination in housing has a private origin. [But] that difference in the source of the threat to performance of the state's obligation is irrelevant." [b]

(b) *Civil Rights Act of 1968, Title VIII: Fair Housing.* After declaring "the policy of the United States to provide, within constitutional limitations, for fair housing throughout the United States" (42 U.S.C.A. § 3601), the Act makes unlawful various discriminations "because of race, color, religion, or national origin" (§ 3604) "in the sale or rental of housing" that is "owned or operated by the Federal Government," or financed or supported by various federal programs (§ 3603(a)). It is also applicable "to all other dwellings" *except* "any single family house" when its owner then "does not own" nor have "any interest in" "more than three such," *and* the private owner does not use a real estate broker, or advertising that states a discriminatory preference (§ 3603(b)(1)). § 3603(b)(2) further exempts "rooms or units in dwellings containing living quarters occupied or intended to be occupied by no more than four families living independently of each other, if the owner actually maintains and occupies one of such living quarters as his residence." § 3607 permits certain sales and rentals by "religious" groups to be limited "to persons of the same religion" "unless membership in such religion is restricted on account of race, color, or national origin" and permits "a private club" that "provides lodgings" to limit them "to its members." Constitutional?

6. *Congressional dilution of fourteenth amendment rights.* (a) After *Morgan,* does Congress have power "to dilute equal protection and due process decisions" of the Court? Consider Cox, supra, at 106 n. 86: "According to the conventional theory [enunciated in fn. 10 of *Morgan*], the Court has invalidated state statutes under the due process and equal protection clauses only when no state of facts which can reasonably be conceived would sustain them. Where that is true, a congressional effort to withdraw the protection granted by the clause would lack the foundation of a reasonably conceivable set of facts and would therefore be just as invalid as the state legislation. But while that is true in the realm of economic regulation, the Court has often substituted its own evaluation of actual conditions in reviewing legislation dealing with 'preferred rights.' It is hard to see how the Court can consistently give weight to the congressional judgment in expanding the definition of equal protection in the area of human rights but refuse to give it weight in narrowing the definition where the definition depends upon appraisal of the facts." Does the "answer" lie in a theory that justifies judicial review principally on the need to afford protection to certain minority "rights" from the majority will? Consider Cohen, *Congressional Power to Interpret Due Process and Equal Protection,* 27 Stan.L. Rev. 603, 614 (1975): "[A] theory that distinguishes between congressional competence to make 'liberty' and 'federalism' judgments resolves the dilemma. A congressional judgment rejecting a judicial interpretation of the due process or equal protection clauses—an interpretation that had given the individual procedural or substantive protection from state and federal government alike—is entitled to no more deference than the identical decision of a state legislature. [c] Congress is no more immune to momentary passions of the majority than are the

b. See also Notes, *Toward Limits on Congressional Enforcement Power Under the Civil War Amendments,* 34 Stan.L.Rev. 453 (1982); *Congressional Power Under Section Five of the Fourteenth Amendment,* 25 Stan.L.Rev. 885 (1973).

c. For the view that equal protection challenges to congressional action should be

judged by a more lenient (but not "toothless") standard of review than state action, see Bohrer, *Bakke, Weber and Fullilove: Benign Discrimination and Congressional Power to Enforce the Fourteenth Amendment,* 56 Ind. L.J. 473 (1981).

state legislatures. But a congressional judgment resolving at the national level an issue that could—without constitutional objection—be decided in the same way at the state level, ought normally to be binding on the courts, since Congress presumably reflects a balance between both national and state interests and hence is better able to adjust such conflicts." See also Choper, *Judicial Review and the National Political Process* 198–200 (1980).

In MISSISSIPPI UNIV. FOR WOMEN v. HOGAN, p. 1005 supra, "the State contended that Congress, in enacting [the] Education Amendments of 1972, expressly had authorized MUW to continue its single-sex admissions policy by exempting public undergraduate institutions that traditionally have used single-sex admissions policies from the gender discrimination prohibition of Title IX. Through that provision, the State argued, Congress limited the reach of the Fourteenth Amendment by exercising its power under § 5 of the Amendment." The Court, relying on fn. 10 of *Morgan,* responded: "Although we give deference to congressional decisions and classifications, neither Congress nor a State can validate a law that denies the rights guaranteed by the Fourteenth Amendment." The four dissenting justices did not address the issue.

(b) *Competence as to "facts."* Does *Miranda v. Arizona,* 384 U.S. 436, 86 S.Ct. 1602, 16 L.Ed.2d 694 (1966), rest on the *factual* assumption that there is "compulsion inherent in custodial surroundings" and thus "no statement obtained from the defendant can truly be the product of his free choice"? Does *Mapp v. Ohio,* p. 304 supra, rest on the *factual* assumption that the exclusionary rule is a "deterrent safeguard without insistence upon which the Fourth Amendment would have been reduced to 'a form of words' "? Does *Gideon v. Wainwright,* 372 U.S. 335, 83 S.Ct. 792, 9 L.Ed.2d 799 (1963), rest on the *factual* assumption that a person "who is too poor to hire a lawyer, cannot be assured a fair trial unless counsel is provided for him"? Does *Brown v. Board of Education,* p. 892 supra, rest on the *factual* assumption that racially "separate educational facilities are inherently unequal"? If so, may Congress, pursuant to § 5, find the *facts* to be otherwise and legislate a contrary rule? See S.Rep. No. 1097, 90th Cong., 2d Sess. 59–63 (1968).

(c) *Line-drawing.* What deference is owed congressional action, pursuant to § 5, that precisely defines (i) how long a delay constitutes denial of the "right to a speedy trial," see *Barker v. Wingo,* 407 U.S. 514, 92 S.Ct. 2182, 33 L.Ed.2d 101 (1972); (ii) how great a deviation from absolute population equality among legislative districts constitutes a violation of the "one person-one vote" requirement, see Ch. 10, Sec. 4, I, A?

(d) *Conflicting constitutional provisions.* May de facto racial segregation in the schools arguably violate equal protection; may use of racial criteria to alleviate de facto segregation arguably violate equal protection (see Ch. 10, Secs. 2, IV–V)? May failure to exempt persons with certain religious beliefs from the burden of some government regulations arguably violate the free exercise clause; may exemption of these persons arguably violate the establishment clause (see Ch. 9, Sec. 2, III)? If so, what deference is owed congressional action, pursuant to § 5, dealing with these matters? See opinion of White, J., in *Welsh v. United States,* p. 865 supra.

(e) *Rights vs. remedies.* May Congress, pursuant to § 5, withdraw (or replace) the "exclusionary rule" of *Mapp v. Ohio* on the ground that this does not "dilute" any substantive constitutional right but merely modifies a remedy for its violation? See fn. g, p. 304 supra. On similar analysis, may Congress forbid busing (or substitute alternatives) to remedy school segregation? See note 2, p.

921 supra. Consider Note, *The Nixon Busing Bills and Constitutional Power,* 81 Yale L.J. 1542, 1570–71 (1972): "Because busing is one remedy among many, Bork [*Constitutionality of the President's Busing Proposals* 21–22 (1972)] argues [that the anti-busing bill] leaves intact the duty *Brown* imposed upon formerly segregated school districts. Such an argument creates an artificial distinction between rights and remedies; the right which cannot be vindicated is not a right at all, and the most that can be said for the distinction is that it may be useful where a right can be vindicated in several ways. [If] busing is in some cases—as it was in *Swann*—the only remedy that would produce desegregation in any real sense, then Bork's argument falls. The real question about the constitutionality of the busing bills is the question that Bork hesitates to answer directly: to what extent does the Equal Protection Clause require that once segregated schools achieve a racial balance? *Swann,* of course, had a simple and direct answer: to the greatest extent possible." See also Rotunda, *Congressional Power to Restrict the Jurisdiction of the Lower Federal Courts and the Problem of School Busing,* 64 Geo.L.J. 839 (1976).

For the view that many judicial decisions implementing constitutional rights are not "true constitutional interpretations" but rather only "constitutional common law" rules that may be modified by Congress, see Monaghan, *Constitutional Common Law,* 89 Harv.L.Rev. 1 (1975). Compare Schrock & Welsh, *Reconsidering the Constitutional Common Law,* 91 Harv.L.Rev. 1117 (1978).

(f) *Definition of "dilution."* If Congress believed that more wrongdoers would be convicted and crime deterred by changing the *Miranda* rule, would such legislation "dilute" the due process rights of the accused, or "secure" the rights of the public generally not to be denied life or property without due process of law? Who should *ultimately* determine these issues?

(g) *"Human Life Bill."* What of the constitutionality of the following proposed statute, S. 158 and H.R. 900, 97th Cong., 1st Sess. (1981):

"Sec. 1. The Congress finds that present day scientific evidence indicates a significant likelihood that actual human life exists from conception.

"The Congress further finds that the fourteenth amendment to the Constitution of the United States was intended to protect all human beings.

"Upon the basis of these findings, and in the exercise of the powers of the Congress, including its power under section 5 of the fourteenth amendment to the Constitution of the United States, the Congress hereby declares that for the purpose of enforcing the obligation of the States under the fourteenth amendment not to deprive persons of life without due process of law, human life shall be deemed to exist from conception, without regard to race, sex, age, health, defect, or condition of dependency; and for this purpose 'person' shall include all human life as defined herein. * * *" [d]

(i) *Questions of "fact."* Do the issues of when "human life" begins and what is a "person" involve questions of fact? Consider Tribe, *Prepared Statement,* Hearings on S. 158 at 251: "Such questions [call] at bottom for normative judgments no less profound than those involved in defining 'liberty' or 'equality.' [They] entail 'question[s] to which science can provide no answer,' as the National Academy of Sciences itself acknowledged * * *. Congress cannot

---

d. For argument in favor of its validity, see Galebach, *A Human Life Statute,* 7 Human Life Rev. 3 (1981), reprinted in Hearings on S. 158, before the Subcomm. on Separation of Powers of the Senate Comm. on the Judiciary, 97th Cong., 1st Sess. 205 (1981);

Nagel, *Prepared Statement,* id. 321. For exhaustive consideration, see Estreicher, *Congressional Power and Constitutional Rights: Reflections on Proposed "Human Life" Legislation,* 68 Va.L.Rev. 333 (1982).

transform an issue of religion, morality, and law into one of fact by waving the magic wand of Section 5 [which] no more authorizes Congress to transmute a matter of values into a matter of scientific observation than it authorizes Congress to announce a mathematical formula for human freedom." See also Cox, *Prepared Statement,* id. at 340–41.

(ii) *"Dilution" vs. "expansion."* Does the Bill dilute the right to an abortion? Consider Noonan, *Prepared Statement,* id. at 266–67: "In recognizing the unborn as persons, [the] Act treats no one unequally but gives equal protection to one class of humanity now unequally treated. * * * Necessarily, the expression of the rights of one class of human beings has an impact on the rights of others. The elimination of literacy tests in this way 'diluted' the voting rights of the literate. It is inescapable that congressional expression of the right to life will have an impact on the abortion right; but in the eyes of Congress, [there] will be a net gain for Fourteenth Amendment rights by the expansion and the attendant diminution."

OREGON v. MITCHELL

400 U.S. 112, 91 S.Ct. 260, 27 L.Ed.2d 272 (1970).

[In original jurisdiction suits, brought by Oregon and Texas against the Attorney General and by the United States against Arizona and Idaho, the states challenged Congress' power to enact Titles II and III of the Voting Rights Act Amendments of 1970. (1) Section 302 forbade states to deny any citizen, otherwise qualified to vote, the right to vote in any federal, state or local election "on account of age if such citizen is eighteen years of age or older." Black, Douglas, Brennan, White and Marshall, JJ., voted to uphold this provision as to federal elections; Burger, C.J., and Black, Harlan, Stewart and Blackmun, JJ., voted to hold it unconstitutional as to state and local elections. (2) Section 201 extended the Voting Rights Act of 1965 for an additional five years (to 1975) and also extended nationwide § 4(a)'s prohibition of "any test or device" (including literacy tests) "as a prerequisite for voting or registration." This was upheld unanimously.[a] (3) Sec. 202 abolished any state "durational residency requirement as a precondition to voting for President and Vice President"; it required the registration "of all duly qualified residents of such State who apply, not later than thirty days immediately prior to any presidential election," and the provision of "absentee ballots" to those "who may be absent [on] the day such election is held and who have applied therefor not later than seven days immediately prior to such election"; an "otherwise qualified" voter who changes state residency within thirty days of such election must be permitted to vote either "in person" or "by absentee ballot" "in the State or political subdivision in which he resided immediately prior to his removal." Only Harlan, J., voted to hold this provision invalid.]

MR. JUSTICE BLACK, announcing the judgments of the Court in an opinion expressing his own view of the cases.

---

a. In 1975, the Act was amended to extend for an additional seven years, to make § 4(a)'s suspension of "any test or device" indefinite, and to greatly expand the geographic coverage (including, inter alia, areas with at least 5% language minorities) of the requirement that new voting regulations be reviewed by the Attorney General or a federal court. See generally Hunter, *The 1975 Voting Rights Act and Language Minorities,* 25 Cath.U.L.Rev. 250 (1976). The seven year extension was upheld in *Rome v. United States,* note 4 infra. In 1982, the Act's preclearance mechanism was extended for 25 years.

[T]he responsibility of the States for setting the qualifications of voters in congressional elections [in Art. I, § 2] was made subject to the power of Congress to make or alter such regulations [in Art. I, § 4].

Moreover, the power of Congress to make election regulations in national elections is augmented by the Necessary and Proper Clause.[b] [Similarly], it is the prerogative of Congress to oversee the conduct of presidential and vice presidential elections and to set the qualifications for voters for electors for those offices. * * *

On the other hand, [n]o function is more essential to the separate and independent existence of the States [than] the power to determine within the limits of the Constitution the qualifications of their own voters for state, county, and municipal [offices].

Of course, we have upheld congressional legislation under the Enforcement Clauses in some cases where Congress has interfered with state regulation of the local electoral process [*Morgan; South Carolina v. Katzenbach*]. But division of power between state and national governments, like every provision of the Constitution, was expressly qualified by the Civil War Amendments' ban on racial discrimination. * * *

In enacting the 18-year-old vote provisions of the Act now before the Court, Congress made no legislative findings that 21-year-old vote requirements were used by the States to disenfranchise voters on account of race. I seriously doubt that such a finding, if made, could be supported by substantial evidence. [On] the other hand, [i]n enacting the literacy test ban of Title II Congress had before it a long history of the discriminatory use of literacy tests to disfranchise voters on account of their race. [A]s to the Nation as a whole, Congress had before it statistics which demonstrate that voter registration and voter participation are consistently greater in States without literacy tests. [Finally in enacting the residency and absentee voting] regulations for national elections Congress was attempting to insure a fully effective voice to all citizens in national elections. What I said [about Congress' power to regulate federal elections] applies with equal force here. * * *

MR. JUSTICE BRENNAN, MR. JUSTICE WHITE, and MR. JUSTICE MARSHALL dissent from the judgment insofar as it declares § 302 unconstitutional as applied to state and local elections * * *.

[Literacy: Arizona] urges that to the extent that any citizens of Arizona have been denied the right to vote because of illiteracy resulting from discriminatory governmental practices, the unlawful discrimination has been by governments other than [Arizona. But] congressional power to remedy the evils resulting from state-sponsored racial discrimination does not end when the subject of that discrimination removes himself from the jurisdiction in which the injury occurred. * * *

[Residency: A] durational residence requirement operates to penalize those persons, and only those persons, who have exercised their constitutional right of interstate migration. [I]n such a case, governmental action may withstand constitutional scrutiny only upon a clear showing that the burden imposed is necessary to protect a compelling and substantial governmental interest. *Shapiro v. Thompson* [p. 1361 supra]. [W]e find ample justification ["in § 5 of the Fourteenth Amendment"] for the congressional conclusion that § 202 is a

---

b. Could the substance of the 24th amendment, barring payment of a poll tax as a condition to vote in federal elections, have been enacted simply by a federal statute?

reasonable means for eliminating an unnecessary burden on the right of interstate migration. *Guest.*

[Age:] We believe there is serious question whether a statute [denying] the franchise to citizens [between] the ages of 18 and 21 could, in any event, withstand present scrutiny under the Equal Protection Clause. Regardless of the answer to this question, however, it is clear to us that proper regard for the special function of Congress in making determinations of legislative fact compels this Court to respect those determinations unless they are contradicted by evidence far stronger than anything that has been adduced in these cases.

* * *

A. [W]hen exclusions from the franchise are challenged as violating [equal protection] "the Court must determine whether the exclusions are necessary to promote a compelling state interest."

In the present cases, the States justify exclusion of 18- to 21-year-olds from the voting rolls solely on the basis of the States' interests in promoting intelligent and responsible exercise of the franchise. [But no state] requires attendance at school beyond the age of 18. [T]hat 18-year-olds as a class may be less educated than some of their elders cannot justify restriction of the franchise for the States themselves have determined that this incremental education is irrelevant to voting qualifications. * * *

[No] State seeking to uphold its denial of the franchise to 18-year-olds has adduced anything beyond the mere difference in age. [But] perhaps more important is the uniform experience of those States—Georgia since 1943, and Kentucky since 1955—that have permitted 18-year-olds to vote. [E]very person who spoke to the issue in either the House or Senate was agreed that 18-year-olds in both States were at least as interested, able, and responsible in voting as were their [elders].

B. [When] a state legislative classification is subjected to judicial challenge as violating the Equal Protection Clause, it comes before the courts cloaked by the presumption that the legislature has, as it should, acted within constitutional limitations. [But] this limitation on judicial review of state legislative classifications is a limitation stemming not from the Fourteenth Amendment itself, but from the nature of [the] judicial process [which] makes it an inappropriate forum for the determination of complex factual questions of the kind so often involved in constitutional adjudication. [Should Congress, however, pursuant to § 5] undertake an investigation in order to determine whether the factual basis necessary to support a state legislative discrimination actually exists, it need not stop once it determines that some reasonable men could believe the factual basis exists. Section 5 empowers Congress to make its own determination on the matter. See *Morgan.* It should hardly be necessary to add that if the asserted factual basis necessary to support a given state discrimination does not exist, § 5 of the Fourteenth Amendment vests Congress with power to remove the discrimination by appropriate means.

The scope of our review in such matters has been established by a long line of consistent decisions. * * * "[W]here we find that the legislators, in light of the facts and testimony before them, have a rational basis for finding a chosen regulatory scheme necessary [our] investigation is at an end." *Katzenbach v. McClung; Morgan.*[32]

32. As we emphasized in *Morgan,* "§ 5 does not grant Congress power [to] enact 'statutes so as in effect to dilute equal protection and due process decisions of this Court.'" As indicated above, a decision of this Court striking down a state statute expresses, among

[The] core of dispute [here] is a conflict between state and federal legislative determinations of the factual issues upon which depends decision of a federal constitutional question—the legitimacy, under [equal protection], of state discrimination against persons between the ages of 18 and 21. Our cases have repeatedly emphasized that, when state and federal claims come into conflict, the primacy of federal power requires that the federal finding of fact control. The Supremacy Clause requires an identical result when the conflict is one of legislative, not judicial, findings.

Finally, it is no answer to say that Title III intrudes upon a domain reserved to the States—the power to set qualifications for voting. It is no longer open to question that the Fourteenth Amendment applies to this, as to all other, exercises of state power. * * *

C. [T]he language of the Fourteenth Amendment [applies] on its face to all assertions of state power, however made. More than 40 years ago, this Court faced for the first time the question whether a State could deny Negroes the right to vote in primary elections. Writing for a unanimous Court, Mr. Justice Holmes observed tartly that "[w]e find it unnecessary to consider the Fifteenth Amendment, because it seems to us hard to imagine a more direct and obvious infringement of the Fourteenth." *Nixon v. Herndon*, 273 U.S. 536, 540–541, 47 S.Ct. 446, 71 L.Ed. 759 (1927). * * *

In any event, it seems to us, the historical record will not bear the weight our Brother Harlan has placed upon it. [Our] reading of the historical background [results] in a somewhat imperfect picture of an era of constitutional confusion, confusion which the Amendment did little to resolve. [The opinion examines in some detail the historical setting, the "politics of the day," the changes in language of the proposed Amendment made in the Joint Congressional Committee on Reconstruction, and the "obscure" and sometimes "incongruous" statements made in congressional debates, campaign speeches and the press. It] suggests an alternative hypothesis: that the Amendment was framed by men who possessed differing views on the great question of the suffrage and [who] papered over their differences with the broad, elastic language of § 1 and left to future interpreters of their Amendment the task of resolving in accordance with future vision and future needs the issues which they left unresolved.

* * *

In sum, Congress had ample evidence upon which it could have based the conclusion [under § 5] that exclusion of citizens 18 to 21 years of age from the franchise is wholly unnecessary to promote any legitimate interest the States may have in assuring intelligent and responsible voting. * * *

MR. JUSTICE HARLAN, concurring in part and dissenting in part.

[Similar to his dissent in *Reynolds v. Sims*, [p. 1029 supra], Harlan, J., argued at length "that the history of the Fourteenth Amendment makes it clear beyond any reasonable doubt" that § 1 was never intended to "reach discriminatory voting qualifications," again emphasizing § 2—providing for reduced congressional representation for states denying 21-year old male citizens the right to vote.[c] That] constitutional amendments were deemed necessary to bring about

other things, our conclusion that the legislative findings upon which the statute is based are so far wrong as to be unreasonable. Unless Congress were to unearth new evidence in its investigation, its identical findings on the identical issue would be no more reasonable than those of the state legislature.

c. "To be sure, one might argue that § 2 is simply a rhetorical flourish, and that the qualifications listed there are merely the ones which the Framers deemed to be consistent with the alleged prohibition of § 1. This argument is not only unreasonable on its face and untenable in light of the historical record;

federal abolition of state restrictions on voting by reason of race (Amend. XV), sex (Amend. XIX), and, even with respect to federal elections, the failure to pay state poll taxes (Amend. XXIV), is itself forceful evidence of the common understanding in 1869, 1919, and 1962, respectively, that the Fourteenth Amendment did not empower Congress to legislate in these respects. * * *

[Although] Congress' expression of the view that it does have power to alter state suffrage qualifications is entitled to the most respectful consideration by the judiciary, [this] cannot displace the duty of this Court to make an independent determination whether Congress has exceeded its powers. The reason for this goes beyond Marshall's assertion that "It is emphatically the province and duty of the judicial department to say what the law is." *Marbury*.[86] It inheres in the structure of the constitutional system itself. Congress is subject to none of the institutional restraints imposed on judicial decisionmaking; it is controlled only by the political process. In Article V, the Framers expressed the view that the political restraints on Congress alone were an insufficient control over the process of constitution-making. The concurrence of two-thirds of each House and of three-fourths of the States was needed for the political check to be adequate. [Nor] is that structure adequately protected by a requirement that the judiciary be able to perceive a basis for the congressional interpretation, the only restriction laid down in *Morgan*.

It is suggested that the proper basis for the doctrine enunciated in *Morgan* lies in the relative fact-finding competence of Court, Congress, and state legislatures. * * *

When my Brothers refer to "complex factual questions," they call to mind disputes about primary, objective facts dealing with such issues as the number of persons between the ages of 18 and 21, the extent of their education, and so forth. [But the] disagreement in these cases revolves around the evaluation [of] largely uncontested factual material. On the assumption that maturity and experience are relevant to intelligent and responsible exercise of the elective franchise, are the immaturity and inexperience of the average 18-, 19-, or 20-year-old sufficiently serious to justify denying such a person a direct voice in decisions affecting his or her life? Whether or not this judgment is characterized as "factual," it calls for striking a balance between incommensurate interests. Where the balance is to be struck depends ultimately on the values and the perspective of the decisionmaker. It is a matter as to which men of good will can and do reasonably differ.

I fully agree that judgments of the sort involved here are beyond the institutional competence and constitutional authority of the judiciary. [But judicial] deference is based, not on relative fact-finding competence, but on due regard for the decision of the body constitutionally appointed to decide. Establishment of voting qualifications is a matter for state legislatures. Assuming any authority at all, only when the Court can say with some confidence that the legislature has demonstrably erred in adjusting the competing interests is it justified in striking down the legislative judgment. * * *

it is fatal to the validity of the reduction of the voting age [before] us.

"The only sensible explanation of § 2, therefore, is that the racial voter qualifications it was designed to penalize were understood to be permitted by § 1 * * *."

86. In fact, however, I do not understand how the doctrine of deference to rational con-

stitutional interpretation by Congress, espoused by the majority in *Morgan*, is consistent with this statement of Chief Justice Marshall or with our reaffirmation of it in *Cooper v. Aaron* [p. 12 supra] * * *.

The same considerations apply, and with almost equal force, to Congress' displacement of state decisions with its own ideas of wise policy. The sole distinction between Congress and the Court in this regard is that Congress, being an elective body, presumptively has popular authority for the value judgment it makes. But since the state legislature has a like authority, this distinction between Congress and the judiciary falls short of justifying a congressional veto on the state judgment. The perspectives and values of national legislators on the issue of voting qualifications are likely to differ from those of state legislators, but I see no reason a priori to prefer those of the national figures, whose collective decision, applying nationwide, is necessarily less able to take account of peculiar local conditions. Whether one agrees with this judgment or not, it is the one expressed by the Framers in leaving voter qualifications to the States. The Supremacy Clause does not, as my colleagues seem to argue, represent a judgment that federal decisions are superior to those of the States whenever the two may differ.

To be sure, my colleagues do not expressly say that Congress or this Court is empowered by the Constitution to substitute its own judgment for those of the States. However, before sustaining a state judgment they require a "clear showing that the burden imposed is necessary to protect a compelling and substantial governmental interest." [88] I should think that [if] my colleagues or a majority of Congress deem a given voting qualification undesirable as a matter of policy, they must consider that the state interests involved are not "compelling" or "substantial" or that they can be adequately protected in other ways. It follows that my colleagues must be prepared to hold invalid as a matter of federal constitutional law all state voting qualifications which they deem unwise, as well as all such qualifications which Congress reasonably deems unwise. For this reason, I find their argument subject to the same objection as if it explicitly acknowledged such a conclusion.

It seems to me that the notion of deference to congressional interpretation of the Constitution, which the Court promulgated in *Morgan,* is directly related to this higher standard of constitutionality which the Court [brought] to fruition in *Kramer v. Union Free School Dist.,* p. 1046 supra. When the scope of federal review of state determinations became so broad as to be judicially unmanageable, it was natural for the Court to seek assistance from the national legislature. [In] this area, to rely on Congress would make that body a judge in its own cause. The role of final arbiter belongs to this Court. * * *

MR. JUSTICE STEWART, with whom THE CHIEF JUSTICE and MR. JUSTICE BLACKMUN join, concurring in part and dissenting in part. * * *

[Literacy:] Because the justification for extending the ban on literacy tests to the entire Nation need not turn on whether literacy tests unfairly discriminate against Negroes in every State in the Union, Congress was not required to make state-by-state findings * * *. In the interests of uniformity, Congress may paint with a much broader brush than may this Court, which must confine itself to the judicial function of deciding individual cases and controversies upon individual records. * * * Experience gained under the 1965 Act has now led Congress to conclude that it should go the whole distance. This approach to the

---

88. It might well be asked why this standard is not equally applicable to the congressional expansion of the franchise before us. Lowering of voter qualifications dilutes the voting power of those who could meet the higher standard, and it has been held that "the right of suffrage can be denied by a debasement or dilution of the weight of a citizen's vote just as effectively as by wholly prohibiting the free exercise of the franchise." *Reynolds v. Sims.* * * *

problem is a rational one; consequently it is within [the] power of Congress under § 2 of the Fifteenth Amendment.

[Residency:] Freedom to travel from State to State [is] a privilege of United States citizenship [which Congress may protect under] the Necessary and Proper Clause. ＊ ＊ ＊

But even though general constitutional power clearly exists, Congress may not overstep the letter or spirit of any constitutional restriction in the exercise of that power. For example, Congress clearly has power to regulate interstate commerce, but it may not, in the exercise of that power, impinge upon the guarantees of the Bill of Rights. ＊ ＊ ＊

The Constitution withholds from Congress any general authority to change by legislation the qualifications for voters in federal elections. ＊ ＊ ＊ Article I, § 2, and the Seventeenth Amendment prescribe [as] the federal standard the standard which each State has chosen for itself. ＊ ＊ ＊

Contrary to the submission of my Brother Black, Article I, § 4 does not create in the federal legislature the power to alter the constitutionally established qualifications to vote in congressional elections. [The] "manner" of holding elections can hardly be read to mean the *qualifications* for voters ＊ ＊ ＊.

[I] am persuaded that the constitutional provisions discussed above are not sufficient to prevent Congress from protecting a person who exercises his constitutional right to enter and abide in any State in the Union from losing his opportunity to vote, when Congress may protect the right of interstate travel from other less fundamental disabilities. The power [which] Congress has exercised in enacting § 202 [is] confined to federal action against a particular problem clearly within the purview of congressional authority. ＊ ＊ ＊

[Age:] Mr. Justice Black is surely correct when he writes, "[T]he whole Constitution reserves to the States the power to set voter qualifications in state and local elections, except to the limited extent that the people through constitutional amendments have specifically narrowed the powers of the States." [I]t is equally plain to me that the Constitution just as completely withholds from Congress the power to alter by legislation qualifications for voters in federal elections, in view of the explicit provisions of Article I, Article II, and the Seventeenth Amendment.

To be sure, recent decisions have established that state action regulating suffrage is not immune from the impact of the Equal Protection Clause. But we have been careful in those decisions to note the undoubted power of a State to establish a qualification for voting based on age. See, e.g., *Kramer*. Indeed, none of the opinions filed today suggest that the States have anything but a constitutionally unimpeachable interest in establishing some age qualification as such. Yet to test the power to establish an age qualification by the "compelling interest" standard is really to deny a State any choice at all, because no State could demonstrate a "compelling interest" in drawing the line with respect to age at one point rather than another. ＊ ＊ ＊ [14]

Morgan does not hold that Congress has the power to determine what are and what are not "compelling state interests" for equal protection purposes. [*Morgan*] upheld the statute on two grounds: that Congress could conclude that enhancing the political power of the Puerto Rican community by conferring the

---

14. [S]o long as a State does not set the voting age higher than 21, the reasonableness of its choice is confirmed by the very Four-teenth Amendment upon which the Government relies [see § 2].

right to vote was an appropriate means of remedying discriminatory treatment in public services; and that Congress could conclude that the New York statute was tainted by the impermissible purpose of denying the right to vote to Puerto Ricans, an undoubted invidious discrimination under the Equal Protection Clause. Both of these decisional grounds were far-reaching. The Court's opinion made clear that Congress could impose on the States a remedy for the denial of equal protection which elaborated upon the direct command of the Constitution, and that it could override state laws on the ground that they were in fact used as instruments of invidious discrimination even though a court in an individual lawsuit might not have reached that factual conclusion.

But it is necessary to go much further to sustain § 302. The state laws which it invalidates do not invidiously discriminate against any discrete and insular minority. Unlike the statute considered in *Morgan,* § 302 is valid only if Congress has the power not only to provide the means of eradicating situations which amount to a violation of the Equal Protection Clause, but also to determine as a matter of substantive constitutional law what situations fall within the ambit of the clause, and what state interests are "compelling."　＊　＊　＊[d]

Notes and Questions

1. *Mitchell's "interpretation" of Morgan.* (a) To what extent do the opinions in *Mitchell* clarify (or cloud) the scope of Congress' power delineated in *Morgan?* Do either Brennan or Harlan, JJ., do more in *Mitchell* than restate their *Morgan* analyses? Do Black and Stewart, JJ., accurately "read" *Morgan?* Consider Cox, *The Role of Congress in Constitutional Determinations,* 40 U.Cin.L. Rev. 199, 237 (1971): "Justice Stewart's summary of *Morgan* [is] historically inaccurate: the New York literacy statute antedates by decades the arrival of numerous Puerto Ricans. Second, [the] *Morgan* opinion barely hints that Congress was concerned to ascribe a racist purpose to the New York lawmakers. [Finally], even by Justice Stewart's own account, the *Morgan* case sustained a congressional finding of substantive unconstitutionality and thus belies his later assertion that Congress lacks power to make a substantive determination of constitutional law." Do you agree? If Congress believed that "prejudice played a prominent role in the enactment" of the state literacy law in *Morgan,* is it important against which minority group the prejudice was directed? If this was the basis of Congress' "constitutional determination" in *Morgan,* is it the same kind of "substantive determination of constitutional law" by Congress that Brennan, J. sought to uphold in *Mitchell?*

(b) In any event, does Stewart, J.'s "reading" of *Morgan*—that Congress may "override state laws on the ground that they were in fact used as instruments of invidious discrimination"—mean that Congress may outlaw all "de facto" discriminations against "any discrete and insular minority"? Consider 85 Harv.L. Rev. 162–63 (1971): "Congress might be able to revamp a host of state benefit programs that impose particular disabilities on the poor on the rational basis that, in fact, a large fraction of the poor were blacks or members of ethnic minorities. [T]he literacy test analogy seems instructive: the class of citizens to whom the device was a serious obstacle was surely wider than merely blacks, yet Congress' conclusion that a large number of blacks were seriously disadvantaged [was] sufficient to uphold abolishing the practice under Congress' enforcement powers. [On] the other hand, Justice Stewart did not expressly indicate that

---

d. Douglas, J.'s separate opinion, upholding all provisions, is omitted.

congressional power to protect such minorities could be stretched this far, since at no point did he indicate what fraction of a group burdened by a given state classification must be blacks or other 'discrete and insular minorities' to justify section five intervention. If Justice Stewart, Justice Blackmun, and Chief Justice Burger are unwilling to review legislative findings carefully, however, it would appear that Congress, as long as it purported to aid blacks or ethnic minorities, could restructure a wide range of state programs it felt treated the poor unfairly. Congress could do this even though the Court itself might refuse to take similar steps on its own for want of the overwhelming proof usually demanded that the programs operate with the effect of invidious discrimination." Do you agree? Or does Stewart, J.'s "reading" of *Morgan* only comprehend congressional power over state laws it finds "tainted by [an] impermissible purpose"? See note 4 infra. See generally Choper, *Congressional Power to Expand Judicial Definitions of the Substantive Terms of the Civil War Amendments,* 67 Minn.L.Rev. 299, 328–34 (1982).

2. *Present status of Morgan.* Between *Morgan* and *Mitchell,* three members of the seven-justice majority in *Morgan* left the Court (Warren, C.J., and Clark and Fortas, JJ.); they were replaced by Burger, C.J., and Marshall and Blackmun, JJ. Since *Mitchell,* Black, Harlan, Douglas and Stewart, JJ., have been succeeded by Powell, Rehnquist, Stevens and O'Connor, JJ. Of what significance is the fact that Burger, C.J. (and Stewart, J.) joined the opinion of White, J., in *Welsh v. United States,* p. 865 supra, which invoked *Morgan?* That Blackmun and Powell, JJ., joined the opinion of White, J., in *Trafficante v. Metropolitan Life Ins. Co.,* p. 1188 infra, which invoked both *Morgan and* the opinion of *Brennan, J.,* in *Mitchell?*

In EEOC v. WYOMING, p. 134 supra, BURGER, C.J., joined by Powell, Rehnquist and O'Connor, JJ., dissenting—after pointing out that the Court had rejected equal protection challenges to mandatory retirement schemes (p. 981 supra)—denied that Congress had power under § 5 to apply the Age Discrimination in Employment Act to state hiring: "Allowing Congress [to] define rights wholly independently of our case law * * * fundamentally alters our scheme of government. Although the *South Carolina v. Katzenbach* line of cases may be read to allow Congress a degree of flexibility in deciding what the Fourteenth Amendment safeguards, I have always read *Mitchell* as finally imposing a limitation on the extent to which Congress may substitute its own judgment for that of the states and assume this Court's 'role of final arbiter,' (Harlan, J., dissenting)." [d]

3. *De facto discrimination.* (a) ROME v. UNITED STATES (1980), supra, involved the Attorney General's refusal to approve, under § 5 of the Voting Rights Act, various changes in the city's electoral system and a number of city annexations. A federal court found that the city had not employed any discriminatory barriers to black voting or black candidacy in the past 17 years and that the city had proved that the electoral changes and annexations were not discriminatorily motivated, but that they were prohibited by the Act because they had a discriminatory effect. The Court, per MARSHALL, J., affirmed: "[T]he Act's ban on electoral changes that are discriminatory in effect is an appropriate method of promoting the purposes of the Fifteenth Amendment, even if it is assumed that § 1 of the Amendment prohibits only intentional discrimination in voting. [See *Mobile v. Bolden,* p. 911 supra.] Congress could rationally have

---

d. For the view that "the scope of the definitional power" granted Congress in *Morgan,* "although by no means insignificant, may nonetheless be quite limited," see Choper, note 1(b) supra.

concluded that, because electoral changes by jurisdictions with a demonstrable history of intentional racial discrimination in voting create the risk of purposeful discrimination, it was proper to prohibit changes that have a discriminatory impact. See *South Carolina v. Katzenbach.*" [f]

REHNQUIST, J., joined by Stewart, J., dissented: "[Prior] decisions indicate that congressional prohibition of some conduct which may not itself violate the Constitution is 'appropriate' legislation 'to enforce' the Civil War Amendments if that prohibition is necessary to remedy prior constitutional violations by the governmental unit, or if necessary to effectively prevent purposeful discrimination by a governmental unit. [The] Court today identifies the constitutional wrong which was the object of this congressional exercise of power as purposeful discrimination by local governments in structuring their political processes in an effort to reduce black voting strength. [What] the Court explicitly ignores is that in this case the city has proven that these changes are not discriminatory in purpose. * * *

"Congress had before it evidence that various governments were enacting electoral changes and annexing territory to prevent the participation of blacks in local government by measures other than outright denial of the franchise. [G]iven the difficulties of proving that an electoral change or annexation has been undertaken for the purpose of discriminating against blacks, Congress could properly conclude that as a remedial matter it was necessary to place the burden of proving lack of discriminatory purpose on the localities. See *South Carolina v. Katzenbach.* But all of this does not support the conclusion that Congress is acting remedially when it continues the presumption of purposeful discrimination even after the locality has disproved that presumption. Absent other circumstances, it would be a topsy-turvy judicial system which held that electoral changes which have been affirmatively proven to be permissible under the Constitution nonetheless violate the Constitution. [Thus,] the result of the Court's holding is that Congress effectively has the power to determine for itself that this conduct violates the Constitution. This result violates previously well-established distinctions between the Judicial Branch and the Legislative or Executive Branches of the Federal Government." Powell, J., dissented on narrower grounds, see this Sec., supra.

(b) Do you agree that *Rome* empowers Congress "to determine for itself [what] conduct violates the Constitution"? Consider Choper, note 1(b) supra, at 331–32: "[*Rome's*] rationale permits Congress to create a 'conclusive presumption' of racial motivation with respect to specified state or local practices that Congress finds have been widely or consistently employed for the purpose of disadvantaging racial minorities—and thus effectively authorizes a congressional conclusion that such practices violate the substance of the fourteenth amendment. But this is a much narrower license than empowering Congress to declare that all state or local rules with a racially disproportionate impact violate equal protection for that reason alone. [A] variety of factors make it extremely difficult for plaintiffs to prove that a state legislative or administrative body has acted with discriminatory intent and make it much more appropriate for Congress than for the judiciary to combat the problem of illicit motivation. Thus, there are powerful reasons for Congress to choose not to rely upon district judges for the highly sensitive task of ascertaining racially discriminatory intent on a case by case basis in respect to state of local schemes whose real purpose

f. On congressional power to prohibit action that has only a discriminatory impact but which perpetuates the effects of past pur-poseful discrimination, see *Fullilove v. Klutznick,* p. 968 supra (opinion of Burger, C.J.).

Congress has grounds to suspect. [*Rome*] did no more than recognize this reality when is [used] what is principally a remedial or prophylactic rationale."

(c) At the time of *Mobile* and *Rogers v. Lodge,* pp. 1037, 1042 supra, § 2 of the Voting Rights Act simply provided that "no voting qualification or prerequisite to voting or standard, practice, or procedure shall be imposed or applied by any State or political subdivision *to deny or abridge* the right of any citizen of the United States to vote on account of race or color." [Emphasis added.] *Mobile* interpreted § 2 as "intended to have an effect no different from that of the Fifteenth Amendment itself." In 1982, Congress substituted the words "in a manner which results in a denial or abridgement of" for those words in § 2 italicized above. The Voting Rights Act Amendment of 1982 added: "The extent to which members of a protected class have been elected to office in the State or political subdivision is one circumstance which may be considered: Provided, That nothing in this section establishes a right to have members of a protected class elected in numbers equal to their proportion in the population."

JONES v. ALFRED H. MAYER CO.

392 U.S. 409, 88 S.Ct. 2186, 20 L.Ed.2d 1189 (1968).

MR. JUSTICE STEWART delivered the opinion of the Court.

In this case we are called upon to determine the scope and the constitutionality [of] 42 U.S.C. § 1982 [Sec. 1, I supra].

[P]etitioners filed a complaint [that] respondents had refused to sell them a home [for] the sole reason that petitioner [is] a Negro. Relying in part upon § 1982, the petitioners sought injunctive and other relief.[1] The [courts below] sustained the respondents' motion to dismiss [concluding] that § 1982 applies only to state action * * *.[5]

[It] is true that a dictum in [*Hurd v. Hodge,* 334 U.S. 24, 68 S.Ct. 847, 92 L.Ed. 1187 (1948)] said that § 1982 was directed only toward "governmental action," but neither *Hurd* nor any other case before or since has presented that precise issue for adjudication in this Court.[25] * * *

On its [face] § 1982 appears to prohibit *all* discrimination against Negroes in the sale or rental of property—discrimination by private owners as well as discrimination by public authorities. * * * Stressing what they consider to be the revolutionary implications of so literal a reading of § 1982, the respondents argue that Congress cannot possibly have intended any such result. Our examination of the relevant history, however, persuades us that Congress meant exactly what it said.

In its original form, § 1982 was part [of] the Civil Rights Act of 1866. [The Court then extensively examined antecedent statutes and studies and debate in the Congress, contemporaneous with the proposal and ratification of the thirteenth amendment, in support of its conclusion respecting § 1982.]

---

1. To vindicate their rights under § 1982, the petitioners invoked the jurisdiction of the District Court to award "damages [or] equitable or other relief under any Act of Congress providing for the protection of civil rights * * *." 28 U.S.C. § 1343(4). * * *

5. Because we have concluded that the discrimination alleged in the petitioners' complaint violated a federal statute that Congress had the power to enact under the Thirteenth Amendment, we find it unnecessary to decide whether that discrimination also violated [equal protection].

25. Two of this Court's early opinions contain dicta to the general effect that § 1982 is limited to state action. *Virginia v. Rives,* 100 U.S. 313, 317–318, 25 L.Ed. 667; *Civil Rights Cases.* * * *

Nor was the scope of the 1866 Act altered when it was re-enacted in 1870, some two years after the ratification of the Fourteenth Amendment. It is quite true that some members of Congress supported the Fourteenth Amendment "in order to eliminate doubt as to the constitutional validity of the Civil Rights Act as applied to the States." *Hurd.* But it certainly does not follow that the adoption of the Fourteenth Amendment or the subsequent readoption of the Civil Rights Act were meant somehow to *limit* its application to state action. The legislative history furnishes not the slightest factual basis for any such speculation, and the conditions prevailing in 1870 make it highly implausible.

*   *   *

The remaining question is whether Congress has power under the Constitution to do what § 1982 purports to [do]. Our starting point is the Thirteenth Amendment, for it was pursuant to that constitutional provision that Congress originally enacted what is now § 1982. [It] has never been [doubted] "that the power vested in Congress to enforce the article by appropriate legislation," [*Civil Rights Cases,*] includes the power to enact laws "direct and primary, operating upon the acts of individuals, whether sanctioned by State legislation or not." Id.

[The] constitutional question in this case, therefore, comes to this: Does the authority of Congress to enforce the Thirteenth Amendment "by appropriate legislation" include the power to eliminate all racial barriers to the acquisition of real and personal property? We think the answer to that question is plainly yes.

"By its own unaided force and effect," the Thirteenth Amendment "abolished slavery, and established universal freedom." *Civil Rights Cases.* Whether or not the Amendment *itself* did any more than that—a question not involved in this case—it is at least clear that the Enabling Clause of that Amendment empowered Congress to do much more.[a] For that clause clothed "Congress with power to pass *all laws necessary and proper for abolishing all badges and incidents of slavery in the United States."* Ibid. (Emphasis added.)

Those who opposed passage of the Civil Rights Act of 1866 argued in effect that the Thirteenth Amendment merely authorized Congress to dissolve the legal bond by which the Negro slave was held to his master. Yet [the] majority leaders in Congress—who were, after all, the authors of the Thirteenth Amendment—had no doubt that its Enabling Clause contemplated the sort of positive legislation that was embodied in the 1866 Civil Rights Act. Their chief spokesman, Senator Trumbull of Illinois, the Chairman of the Judiciary Committee, [argued] that, if the narrower construction of the Enabling Clause were correct, then "the trumpet of freedom that we have been blowing throughout the land has given an 'uncertain sound,' and the promised freedom is a delusion. [I] have no doubt that under this provision [we] may destroy all these discriminations in civil rights against [blacks]. Who is to decide what that appropriate legislation is to be? The Congress * * *."

Surely Senator Trumbull was right. Surely Congress has the power under the Thirteenth Amendment rationally to determine what are the badges and the incidents of slavery, and the authority to translate that determination into effective legislation. Nor can we say that the determination Congress has made is an irrational one. For this Court recognized long ago that, whatever else they may have encompassed, the badges and incidents of slavery—its "burdens and

---

a. For discussion of the use of judicial power under § 1 of the amendment, see fn. b, p. 1092 supra.

disabilities"—included restraints upon "those fundamental rights which are the essence of civil freedom, namely the same right [to] inherit, purchase, lease, sell and convey property, as is enjoyed by white citizens." *Civil Rights Cases.* Just as the Black Codes, enacted after the Civil War to restrict the free exercise of those rights, were substitutes for the slave system, so the exclusion of Negroes from white communities became a substitute for the Black Codes. And when racial discrimination herds men into ghettos and makes their ability to buy property turn on the color of their skin, then it too is a relic of slavery.

[At] the very least, the freedom that Congress is empowered to secure under the Thirteenth Amendment includes the freedom to buy whatever a white man can buy, the right to live wherever a white man can live. If Congress cannot say that being a free man means at least this much, then the Thirteenth Amendment made a promise the Nation cannot keep. * * *

Reversed.

MR. JUSTICE HARLAN, whom MR. JUSTICE WHITE joins, dissenting.

[I] believe that the Court's construction of § 1982 as applying to purely private action is almost surely wrong, and at the least is open to serious doubt. The issue of the constitutionality of § 1982, as construed by the Court, and of liability under the Fourteenth Amendment alone, also present formidable difficulties. Moreover, the political processes of our own era [have] given birth to a civil rights statute embodying "fair housing" provisions which would at the end of this year make available to others [the] type of relief which the petitioners now seek. It seems to me that this latter factor so diminishes the public importance of this case that by far the wisest course would be [to] dismiss the writ as improvidently granted.

[In a lengthy opinion, Harlan, J., relied on statements in prior Supreme Court opinions, the use of the word "right" in § 1982, the legislative history and debates of the Civil Rights Act of 1866 and of companion legislation, and on the ethics of the times to demonstrate that the Court's construction of § 1982 was "open to the most serious doubt" if not "wholly untenable."][b]

SULLIVAN v. LITTLE HUNTING PARK, INC., 396 U.S. 229, 90 S.Ct. 400, 24 L.Ed.2d 386 (1969), involved a "nonstock corporation organized to operate a community park [for] the benefit of residents in an area" of Virginia. Sullivan, owner of a membership share, rented his home and assigned his share to Freeman. The corporation board "refused to approve the assignment because Freeman was a Negro." When Sullivan protested, he was expelled. Sullivan and Freeman sued in state court under § 1982 for injunctions and damages. Relief was denied. The Court, per DOUGLAS, J., reversed, stating that Little Hunting Park was not a "private social club," being "open to every white person within the geographic area." The "effective equitable remedy" that *Mayer* found could be fashioned by a federal court is "available in the state court, if that court is empowered to grant injunctive relief generally, as is the Virginia court." As to damages, the Court pointed to 28 U.S.C.A. § 1343(4), fn. 1 in *Mayer*: "The existence of a statutory right implies the existence of all necessary and appropriate remedies."

b. The concurring opinion of Douglas, J., is omitted. For conflicting views as to § 1982's legislative history, compare Fairman, *Reconstruction and Reunion: 1864–1888, Part One* (1971) with Levinson, *Book Review,* 26 Stan.L. Rev. 461 (1974); Kohl, *The Civil Rights Act of 1866, Its Hour Come Round at Last,* 55 Va.L. Rev. 272 (1969) with Casper, *Jones v. Mayer: Clio, Bemused and Confused Muse,* 1968 Sup. Ct.Rev. 89.

Harlan, J., joined by Burger, C.J., and White, J., "would dismiss the writ [as] improvidently granted," for reasons stated in *Mayer* and to avoid "the complexities involved in (1) giving Sullivan relief and (2) engrafting a damage remedy onto § 1982 in a case arising from a state court."

RUNYON v. McCRARY, 427 U.S. 160, 96 S.Ct. 2586, 49 L.Ed.2d 415 (1976), per STEWART, J., relying on *Mayer's* interpretation of § 1982, held that § 1981 Sec. 1, I supra, prohibits private schools—that were operated commercially and open to the public in that they engaged in general advertising to attract students—from refusing to accept blacks. POWELL, J., joined the opinion, but added that "choices, including those involved in entering into a contract, that are 'private' in the sense that they are not part of a commercial relationship offered generally or widely, and that reflect the selectivity exercised by an individual entering into a personal relationship, certainly were never intended to be restricted by" § 1981. Stevens, J., joined the Court's opinion, feeling bound by, but disagreeing with, the statutory interpretation in *Mayer*. White, J., joined by Rehnquist, J., dissented on grounds of statutory interpretation.

Notes and Questions

1. *Scope of §§ 1982 and 1981.* (a) What other discriminations against blacks are presently prohibited by these provisions? Consider Henkin, *On Drawing Lines,* 82 Harv.L.Rev. 63, 85–86 (1968): "Will no bequest stand up which includes a racial discrimination since that would deprive Negroes of 'the same right [to] inherit'? Has there been an easier answer to [Senator Bacon's] will all this time while the Court struggled with theories of state action to find escape from his discrimination [see *Evans v. Newton* and *Evans v. Abney,* pp. 1096, 1110 supra.]? Indeed, does not the Court's reading render superfluous the Civil Rights Act of 1964? Title II of that Act provides that certain places of public accommodations may not discriminate on the basis of race in selling goods and services; the Court's construction of § 1982, when applied to personal property, renders the title (and its limitations) superfluous. Moreover, by the Court's technique of construction, the right 'to make and enforce contracts' guaranteed by [§ 1981] should prevent a restaurant or hotel management from refusing on grounds of race to 'make a contract' for service with a Negro. Indeed, that construction should prevent any employer from refusing 'to make a contract' of employment with a Negro; and the fair employment provisions of the 1964 Act likewise become superfluous, as does the entire struggle, since the days of the New Deal, to enact adequate fair employment legislation."

See also Larson, *The New Law of Race Relations,* 1969 Wis.L.Rev. 470, 502–03: "[Sec. 1981] could properly be applied to any [private] club or association when it can be said that the essence of the arrangement is that the club or association supplies certain services or facilities in exchange for the payment of dues. * * * Tested by the standards suggested, a country club falls within the category of organizations supplying valuable services, such as the availability of a golf course, dining rooms, and club rooms, for the payment of a sum of money." c

(b) *Constitutionality.* Are the above racial discriminations "badges and incidents of slavery"? What of the practice by sellers of certain goods or services

---

c. Does § 1981 make the result in *Moose Lodge v. Irvis,* p. 1118 supra, incorrect? Or do   other constitutional provisions (values) justify the decision?

of charging blacks higher prices? See Note, *Discriminatory Housing Markets, Racial Unconscionability, and Section 1988,* 80 Yale L.J. 516 (1971). Is the initial question inaccurately stated? Do these instances "run the slavery argument into the ground" (*Civil Rights Cases*)?

Does the thirteenth amendment empower Congress to prohibit action that has a racially disproportionate impact, regardless of its purpose? Do §§ 1981–82 do so? See Note, *Section 1981: Discriminatory Purpose or Disproportionate Impact?* 80 Colum.L.Rev. 137 (1980); *Memphis v. Greene,* p. 912 supra.[d]

3. *Beyond racial discrimination.* May Congress "rationally determine" that discriminations against groups other than blacks are "badges and incidents of slavery"? See *McDonald v. Santa Fe Trail Trans. Co.* (1976), fn. c. in *United Steelworkers v. Weber,* p. 962 supra ("Congress is authorized under [§ 2] to legislate in regard to 'every race and individual' "). Consider Note, *Jones v. Mayer: The Thirteenth Amendment and the Federal Anti-Discrimination Laws,* 69 Colum.L.Rev. 1019, 1025–26 (1969): "[T]he Court's conclusion that housing discrimination *today* is a badge or incident of slavery is itself a recognition that the 'slavery' referred to in the thirteenth amendment now encompasses the second class citizenship imposed on members of disparate minority groups. By doing so, the Court has implicitly interpreted 'slavery' as the word has come to mean. [A] victim's people need not have been enslaved in order to invoke its protection. He need only be suffering today under conditions that could reasonably be called symptoms of a slave society, inability to raise a family with dignity caused by unemployment, poor schools and housing, and lack of a place in the body politic. By removing the time element from badges and incidents of slavery, an aggrieved party need not show a continuous link between his plight and actual slavery in order to benefit from the guarantees of the thirteenth amendment." [e] Compare Note, *The "New" Thirteenth Amendment: A Preliminary Analysis,* 82 Harv.L.Rev. 1294 (1969). Consider Choper, note 1(b) after *Mitchell* at 313–14: "*Jones* need not be interpreted as conferring any *definitional* authority on Congress. Rather, it can be persuasively argued on either of two theories that the Court upheld the Civil Rights Act of 1866 as only a *remedial* exercise of Congress's enforcement power under the thirteenth amendment. First, 'slavery' may be regarded as a status to be defined by the Court, [and] the 'badges and incidents of slavery' may be regarded, not as elements of that definition, but as stigmas and disabilities related to slavery. [Thus] to say that Congress may rationally determine the badges and incidents of slavery is nothing more than to say that Congress may prohibit certain practices, although those practices themselves do not constitute slavery, when Congress rationally finds that their prohibition will help to *prevent* slavery.[83] Alternatively, since Congress's power under *Morgan's* remedial branch encompasses eradicating the *effects* of constitutional violations as well as preventing future ones, the congressional prohibition in *Jones* may be readily sustained as an effort to eliminate the persistent legacies of the past condition of slavery."

d. For further discussion of Congress' power to enforce the thirteenth amendment against "racially discriminatory private action aimed at depriving [black citizens] of the basic rights that the law secures to all free men," see *Griffin v. Breckenridge,* 403 U.S. 88, 91 S.Ct. 1790, 29 L.Ed.2d 338 (1971).

e. For the view that *McDonald* strongly supports this approach, see Calhoun, *The Thirteenth and Fourteenth Amendments: Con-*

stitutional Authority for Federal Legislation Against Private Sex Discrimination, 61 Minn. L.Rev. 313 (1977). For criticism of *McDonald,* see Note, *The Thirteenth Amendment and Private Affirmative Action,* 89 Yale L.J. 399 (1979).

83. Engdahl, *Constitutional Power: Federal and State in a Nutshell* 247–48 (1974) (emphasis added).

4. *Self-executing force of thirteenth amendment.* Apart from federal legislation pursuant to § 2, are any (all) of the discriminations referred to above made unconstitutional by § 1 of "the Amendment *itself*"? If so, by what means should (can) the Court enforce § 1?

Chapter 13

LIMITATIONS ON JUDICIAL POWER AND REVIEW

SECTION 1. CASE OR CONTROVERSY

I. ADVISORY OPINIONS

MUSKRAT v. UNITED STATES, 219 U.S. 346, 31 S.Ct. 250, 55 L.Ed. 246 (1911): In 1902, Congress made a "final" allotment of lands to certain Cherokee Indians. Subsequent legislation increased the number of allottees. Congress then enacted a statute authorizing four named allottees under the 1902 act to bring suits against the United States in the court of claims with appeal to the Supreme Court, "on their own behalf and on behalf of all other Cherokee citizens" who were allottees under the 1902 act, "to determine the validity of any acts of Congress passed since the said act." For "the speedy disposition of the questions involved" such suits were to be given preference by the courts, and attorneys' fees were to be paid out of tribal funds held by the government if the subsequent legislation were held invalid. Suits were instituted and the court of claims sustained the validity of the subsequent legislation.

The Court, per DAY, J., held that "the jurisdiction conferred" was not "within the power of Congress, having in view the limitations of the judicial power, as established by the Constitution" because "the judicial power is limited to 'cases' and 'controversies.' " Art. III "does not extend the judicial power to every violation of the Constitution which may possibly take place." "By cases and controversies are intended the claims of litigants brought before the courts for determination by such regular proceedings as are established by law or custom for the protection or enforcement of rights, or the prevention, redress, or punishment of wrongs. [The] term implies the existence of present or possible adverse parties, whose contentions are submitted to the court for adjudication."

The Court pointed out that "as early as 1792, an act of Congress" authorized federal courts to decide certain pension claims against the government, subject to revision by the Secretary of War. *Hayburn's Case*, 2 Dall. 409, held that such duties were beyond the judicial power; "by the Constitution, neither the Secretary at War, nor any other executive officer, nor even the legislature, are authorized to sit as a court of errors on the judicial acts or opinions of this court." [a] In 1793, the Court, in response to a request by President Washington

---

a. Consider Currie, *Federal Courts* 9 (3d ed. 1982): "[Such cases are] most easily under- stood in terms of the independence of the courts. The Constitution protects the judges

and Secretary of State Jefferson, declined to offer its advice on "the construction of treaties, laws of nations and laws of the land, which the Secretary said were often presented under circumstances which *'do not give a cognizance of them to the tribunals of the country.'*"

The act in *Muskrat* was found to be nothing more "than an attempt to provide for a judicial determination, final in this court, of the constitutional validity of an act of Congress. [It] is true the United States is made a defendant to this action, but it has no interest adverse to the claimants. The object is not to assert a property right as against the government, or to demand compensation for alleged wrongs because of action upon its part. [The] judgment will not conclude private parties, when actual litigation brings to the court the question of the constitutionality of such legislation. In a legal sense the judgment [amounts] to no more than an expression of opinion upon the validity of the" 1902 act. "If such actions as are here attempted [are] sustained, the result will be that this court, instead of keeping within the limits of judicial power, and deciding cases or controversies arising between opposing parties, [will] be required to give opinions in the nature of advice concerning legislative action,—a function never conferred upon it by the Constitution."

Notes and Questions

1. *Pro's and con's of advisory opinions.* (a) Do you agree with the established principle that bars the Court from advising Congress on the constitutionality of legislation? Consider Note, *Advisory Opinions on the Constitutionality of Statutes,* 69 Harv.L.Rev. 1302, 1305 (1956): "Before it is successfully challenged, an unconstitutional statute may discourage legitimate activity; or, conversely, it may encourage reliance which, when the statute is invalidated, will [cause] injury to those who have based action upon it. Further [there] is frequently an unnecessary expenditure of time and money when the state enacts a statute, invalidates it in lengthy judicial proceedings, and subsequently must enact new legislation; this waste would seem particularly great when the government sets up elaborate machinery to implement a statute later held unconstitutional." See also Note, *The Case for an Advisory Function in the Federal Judiciary,* 50 Geo.L.J. 785, 799 (1962).

(b) Consider Comment, *The Advisory Opinion and the United States Supreme Court,* 5 Ford.L.Rev. 94, 108 (1936): "The advisory opinion, it is said [by Frankfurter, *A Note on Advisory Opinions,* 37 Harv.L.Rev. 1002 (1924)], would distort the entire focus of the judicial function in that it would require the Court to express its judgment on abortive issues without the benefit of all the relevant facts which, in crucial constitutional questions, are the very heart of the case. In addition, the operation of the device would debilitate the creative responsibility of the legislature in that it would tend to induce reliance upon the judiciary, depriving the former of submitting its convictions to the test of trial and error

from indirect pressures on their decisions by guaranteeing them tenure during good behavior at an irreducible salary; to subject their decisions to executive review is a much more direct interference." But, "how far should this principle be carried? Congress, after all, can defeat any money judgment against the United States by failing to vote money to pay it; should the courts therefore refuse to entertain money actions against the Government? Since the President can refuse to enforce judgments against state officers or private litigants, should the courts decline to act at all?" Id. Should the Court refuse to interpret acts of Congress because the Court's decision may be negated by congressional revision? Decline to enforce the terms of executive regulations against executive officers because they may choose to amend or revoke the regulations? See *United States v. Nixon,* p. 175 supra.

and of accumulating new facts for the vindication of its judgment which, a priori, may run counter to settled legal principles."

(i) As to the "facts" argument, might this be cured by having Congress present the Court with a specific set of facts, real or assumed? Or by having the Court confine its opinion to the statute's application to what it considers the most common set of facts intended to be covered?

(ii) As to the "responsibility of the legislature" argument, might this be cured by limiting the advisory opinion to statutes fully considered and already passed by Congress?[d] Is there *any* answer to the point that the cumulative experience of a statute's operation may shed great light on its constitutionality? If not, is this sufficient to sustain the present advisory opinion practice?

(c) Is the opposition to advisory opinions justified by the necessity for "actual antagonistic assertion of rights by one individual against another"? Consider Note, 69 Harv.L.Rev. 1302, 1309–10 (1956): "Argument in advisory proceedings might in some situations provide more assistance to the court than would argument in a normal adversary proceeding. Representation of diversified interests might provide the justices with a more realistic perspective on the statute than representation of only two parties; and, unlike ordinary litigation where the prosecutor or plaintiff [may] be able to select an opponent with little interest in the proceeding or one who is peculiarly culpable, the parties seeking to appear will generally be strong antagonists."

(d) Consider Note, *Judicial Determinations in Nonadversary Proceedings*, 72 Harv.L.Rev. 723, 724 (1959): "The requirement that a specific injury have been suffered or that the danger of such injury be substantial [probably] has its basis, at least partially, in the belief that the respect in which the courts are held varies with the restraint exercised in deciding only the most critical questions." Is this "belief" founded on the premise that the Court's ability to preserve constitutional values is limited and should be reserved for situations in which it is absolutely necessary? If so, may occasions for some advisory opinions present such a necessity? Or should the enactments of popularly elected representatives be invalidated by a Court of lifetime appointees only when injury is imminent? Even when the popularly elected representatives request the Court's advice? Even when they believe that the withholding of such advice may produce very grave injuries?

2. *Mootness.* (a) Is the principle that "moot cases [are] beyond the judicial power" simply an application of the bar against advisory opinions? That "there is no case or controversy once the matter has been resolved"? Wright, *Federal Courts* 55 (4th ed. 1983). Or is the doctrine merely a judicially created rule for judicial economy? Of what significance is the point in litigation at which a case becomes moot? Consider Note, *Cases Moot on Appeal: A Limit on the Judicial Power,* 103 U.Pa.L.Rev. 772, 774 (1955): "[M]oot cases do not present all the dangers of advisory opinions. The 'impact of actuality' may well be lacking if [the] decrees cannot affect the rights of the parties. But there is a record to which the court may look for facts; there is probably as much experience under the statute as might be had in a case which is not moot; and there are advocates before the court who are prepared to argue the issues."

d. The Voting Rights Act Amendments of 1970, some of which were not to take effect until elections held in 1971, became law on June 22, 1970. Motions for leave to file suits within the Court's original jurisdiction, involving four states challenging the act's constitutionality, were granted on Oct. 6, 1970. The cases were argued on Oct. 19 and decided on Dec. 21, 1970. See *Oregon v. Mitchell,* p. 1159 supra.

(b) In DE FUNIS v. ODEGAARD, p. 941 supra, petitioner was admitted to the University of Washington Law School after a state trial court had sustained his claim that the school's special admissions policy violated equal protection. The Washington supreme court reversed but its judgment was stayed. By the time the case was argued in the Supreme Court, petitioner had registered for the final term of his third year. Although the school stated that if its admissions policy were upheld, petitioner would be subject to it if he had to register for any additional terms, his present registration "would not be cancelled [regardless] of the outcome of this litigation." The Court, per curiam, held the case moot: "There is a line of decisions in this Court standing for the proposition that the 'voluntary cessation of allegedly illegal conduct does not deprive the tribunal of power to hear and determine the case, i.e., does not make the case moot,'" because "otherwise, 'the defendant is free to return to his old ways' * * *. But mootness in the present case depends not at all upon a 'voluntary cessation' of the admissions practices that were the subject of this litigation. It depends, instead, upon the simple fact that DeFunis is now in the final quarter of the final year of his course of study, and the settled and unchallenged policy of the Law School to permit him to complete the term for which he is now enrolled."

BRENNAN, J., joined by Douglas, White and Marshall, JJ., dissented: "Any number of unexpected events—illness, economic necessity, even academic failure—might prevent his graduation at the end of the term. Were that misfortune to befall, and were petitioner required to register for yet another term, the prospect that he would again face the hurdle of the admissions policy is real * * *.[e] Few constitutional questions in recent history have stirred as much debate, and they will not disappear. [Because] avoidance of repetitious litigation serves the public interest, that inevitability counsels against mootness determinations, as here, not compelled by the record."[f]

3. *Collusiveness.* The Court "will not hear collusive cases.[15] Though the rule is not in terms so confined, it is principally applied in constitutional cases, on the notion that 'it never was the thought that by means of a friendly suit, a party beaten in the legislature could transfer to the courts an inquiry as to the constitutionality of the legislative act.'[16] Even here application of the rule has not always been rigid—some of the most famous constitutional decisions have come in what now seem to have been collusive cases.[17]" Wright, supra, at 56.

II. STANDING AND RIPENESS

INTRODUCTORY NOTE

The doctrines of "standing" and "ripeness" both go to determining whether there is a dispute capable of and suitable for judicial resolution. These two

---

e. In response to this point, the Court said: "But such speculative contingencies afford no basis for our passing on the substantive issues" in the absence of "evidence that this is a prospect of 'immediacy and reality.'"

f. "In rare instances the power to refrain from deciding moot cases has been used by the Court to avoid decision of an otherwise difficult matter. In [*Atherton Mills v. Johnston,* 259 U.S. 13, 42 S.Ct. 422, 66 L.Ed. 814 (1922), a law was challenged] regulating the labor of youths between the ages of 14 and 16. The Court held the case for two and a half years after argument, and then decided that since

the plaintiff was by that time over 16, and no longer affected by the statute, the case was moot." Wright, *Federal Courts* 36 (2d ed. 1970).

15. *Lord v. Veazie,* 1850, 8 How. 251, 12 L.Ed. 1067.

16. *Chicago & G.T. Ry. Co. v. Wellman.* See also *U.S. v. Johnson,* 1943, 63 S.Ct. 1075, 319 U.S. 302, 87 L.Ed. 1413.

17. E.g., *Fletcher v. Peck,* [p. 247 supra]; *Dred Scott v. Sandford,* [discussed in *Plessy v. Ferguson,* p. 892 supra.

issues frequently overlap, but may roughly be described as concerning (1) *who* may assert certain contentions (the claimant or someone else)—"standing," and (2) *when* (if ever) may these claims be asserted (now or at some subsequent time after other events have occurred)—"ripeness."

Both doctrines relate to whether there is a "case or controversy" under Art. III. But they also implicate "prudential" principles of "judicial self-restraint," some perspective on which may be found in the following statement of the Court, per RUTLEDGE, J., in RESCUE ARMY v. MUNICIPAL COURT, 331 U.S. 549, 67 S.Ct. 1409, 91 L.Ed. 1666 (1947):

"[T]his Court has followed a policy of strict necessity in disposing of constitutional issues [which] has not been limited to jurisdictional determinations. For, in addition, 'the Court [has] developed, for its own governance in the cases confessedly within its jurisdiction, a series of rules under which it has avoided passing upon a large part of all the constitutional questions pressed upon it for decision.'[31] [Thus], constitutional issues affecting legislation will not be determined in friendly, non-adversary proceedings; in advance of the necessity of deciding them; in broader terms than are required by the precise facts to which the ruling is to be applied; if the record presents some other ground upon which the case may be disposed of; at the instance of one who fails to show that he is injured by the statute's operation, or who has availed himself of its benefits * * *.[a]

"[E]very application has been an instance of reluctance, indeed of refusal, to undertake the most important and the most delicate of the Court's [functions].

"Indeed in origin and in practical effects, though not in technical function, it is a corollary offshoot of the case and controversy rule. And often the line between applying the policy or the rule is very thin.[37] * * *

"The policy's ultimate foundations, some if not all of which also sustain the jurisdictional limitation, [are] found in the delicacy of that function, particularly in view of possible consequences for others stemming also from constitutional roots; the comparative finality of those consequences; the consideration due to the judgment of other repositories of constitutional power concerning the scope of their authority; the necessity, if government is to function constitutionally, for each to keep within its power, including the courts; the inherent limitations of the judicial process, arising especially from its largely negative character and limited resources of enforcement; withal in the paramount importance of constitutional adjudication in our system.

"[Its] execution has involved a continuous choice between the obvious advantages it produces [and] the very real disadvantages, for the assurance of rights, which deferring decision very often entails.[b] On the other hand it is not

31. Brandeis, J., with whom Stone, Roberts and Cardozo, JJ., concurred in *Ashwander v. TVA*, 297 U.S. 288, concurring opinion at 346, 56 S.Ct. 466, 482, 80 L.Ed. 688.

a. One of the rules set forth by Brandeis, J., in *Ashwander* was that "when the validity of an act of the Congress is drawn in question, and even if a serious doubt of constitutionality is raised, it is a cardinal principle that this Court will first ascertain whether a construction of the statute is fairly possible by which the question may be avoided." For illustrations of this technique, see *Yates v. United States*, p. 447 supra; *Jones v. Alfred H. Mayer Co.*, p. 1169 supra. But compare *Marbury v.*

Madison, p. 1 supra; *United States v. Robel*, p. 733 supra.

37. Indeed more than once the policy has been applied in order to avoid the necessity of deciding the "case or controversy" jurisdictional question, when constitutional issues were at stake on the merits * * *.

b. "Whether 'justiciability' exists, therefore, has most often turned on evaluating both the appropriateness of the issues for decision by courts and the hardship of denying judicial relief." Frankfurter, J., concurring in *Joint Anti-Fascist Refugee Comm. v. McGrath*, 341 U.S. 123, 71 S.Ct. 624, 95 L.Ed. 817 (1951).

altogether speculative that a contrary policy of accelerated decision, might do equal or greater harm for the security of private rights ＊ ＊ ＊. For premature and relatively abstract decision, which such a policy would be most likely to promote, have their part too in rendering rights uncertain and insecure.

" ＊ ＊ ＊ Time and experience [have] verified for both that the choice was wisely made. Any other indeed might have put an end to or seriously impaired the distinctively American institution of judicial review.[38] "

A. INJURY REQUIRED FOR STANDING: SUITS BY TAXPAYERS AND CITIZENS

MASSACHUSETTS v. MELLON and FROTHINGHAM v. MELLON, 262 U.S. 447, 43 S.Ct. 597, 67 L.Ed. 1078 (1923), involved a challenge to a federal statute providing funds to states undertaking programs to reduce maternal and infant mortality. The Court, per SUTHERLAND, J., dismissed both cases "for want of jurisdiction."

Massachusetts contended that the act invaded "the power of local self-government, reserved to the states" by the tenth amendment; that a state had an "unconstitutional option either to yield to the federal government a part of their reserved rights or lose their share of the moneys." The Court reasoned that the "powers of the state are not invaded, since the statute imposes no obligation but simply extends an option which the state is free to accept or reject. But we do not rest here." The Court's power under Art. III extends only to proceedings "of a justiciable character ＊ ＊ ＊. In the last analysis, the complaint of the plaintiff state is brought to the naked contention that Congress has usurped the reserved powers of the several states by the mere enactment of the statute, though nothing has been done and nothing is to be done without their consent; and it is plain that that question, as it is thus presented, is political, and not judicial in character, and therefore is not a matter which admits of the exercise of the judicial power. [W]e are called upon to adjudicate, not rights of person or property, not rights of dominion over physical domain, not quasi sovereign rights actually invaded or threatened, but abstract questions of political power, of sovereignty, of government."

Because "citizens of Massachusetts are also citizens of the United States," neither could the state sue as parens patriae "as the representative of its citizens" "to protect citizens of the United States from the operation of the statutes thereof. [I]t is the United States, and not the state which represents them as parens patriae [and] to the former, and not to the latter, they must look for such protective measures as flow from that status."

Frothingham, a federal taxpayer, also contended that the Maternity Act exceeded Congress' power and "that the effect of the appropriations complained of will be to increase the burden of future taxation and thereby take her property without due process of law." The Court distinguished suits by munici-pal taxpayers: "The interest of a taxpayer of a municipality in the application of its moneys is direct and immediate and the remedy by injunction to prevent their misuse is not inappropriate." But a federal taxpayer's "interest in the moneys of the treasury [is] shared with millions of others, is comparatively minute and indeterminable, and the effect upon future taxation, of any payment

---

38. It is not without significance for the policy's validity that the periods when the power has been exercised most readily and broadly have been the ones in which this Court and the institution of judicial review have had their stormiest experiences. See e.g., Brant, *Storm Over the Constitution* (1936).

out of the funds, so remote, fluctuating and uncertain, that no basis is afforded for an appeal to the preventive powers of a court of equity." To permit such suits might result in attacks on "every other appropriation act and statute whose administration requires the outlay of public money * * *. The bare suggestion of such a result, with its attendant inconveniences, goes far to sustain the conclusion which we have reached, that a suit of this character cannot be maintained." A person asking the Court to hold a federal act unconstitutional "must be able to show, not only that the statute is invalid, but that he has sustained or is immediately in danger of sustaining some direct injury as the result of its enforcement, and not merely that he suffers in some indefinite way in common with people generally." Here, the complaint "is merely that [federal officials] will execute an act of Congress asserted to be unconstitutional; and this we are asked to prevent. To do so would be, not to decide a judicial controversy, but to assume a position of authority over the governmental acts of another and coequal department, an authority which plainly we do not possess."

In DOREMUS v. BOARD OF EDUC., 342 U.S. 429, 72 S.Ct. 394, 96 L.Ed. 475 (1952), a state court had held that Bible-reading in public schools was not an establishment of religion. Appellants had sued as "citizens" and "taxpayers"; one had a child in the schools who had graduated by the time the case came to the Supreme Court. The Court, per JACKSON, J., dismissed the appeal: As to the graduated student, the matter was held to be moot. Although municipal taxpayers have standing to enjoin "a measurable appropriation or disbursement of [municipal] funds occasioned solely by the activities complained of," there "is no allegation that this activity is supported by any separate tax or paid for from any particular appropriation or that it adds any sum whatever to the cost of conducting the school." Although state courts may render advisory opinions on federal constitutional questions, "because our own jurisdiction is cast in terms of 'case or controversy,' we cannot * * *. The taxpayer's action can meet this test, but only when it is a good-faith pocketbook action." [c]

DOUGLAS, J., joined by Reed and Burton, JJ. dissented: "There is no group more interested in [the] public schools than the taxpayers who support them and the parents whose children attend them. [W]here the clash of interests is as real and as strong as it is here, it is odd indeed to hold there is no case or controversy within the meaning of art. III."

c. Consider Freund in *Supreme Court & Supreme Law* 35 (Cahn ed. 1954): "I think it is a needed change to make standing to raise a federal constitutional question, itself a federal question, so that it will be decided uniformly throughout the country. I disagree with *Doremus* in so far as it lets the state judgment stand and merely declines review. [T]he Court should have [held that] the petition should stand dismissed in the state court and the decree vacated so that it would not be a precedent even in the state court." Does *Doremus* "let the state judgment stand and merely decline review"? What action would the Court have taken if the New Jersey court had found the statute violative of the first amendment? See Tribe, *American Constitutional Law* 15 n. 56 (Supp.1979). What action should the Court take if a state court refuses to entertain a taxpayer's suit, involving "pocketbook" injury, challenging the constitutionality of a state statute?

See generally Murphy, *Supreme Court Review of Abstract State Court Decisions on Federal Law: A Justiciability Analysis*, 25 St.L.U. L.J. 473 (1981).

FLAST v. COHEN
392 U.S. 83, 88 S.Ct. 1942, 20 L.Ed.2d 947 (1968).

MR. CHIEF JUSTICE WARREN delivered the opinion of the Court.

[As federal taxpayers, appellants sought to enjoin federal expenditures for parochial schools, alleging violation of the religion clauses of the first amendment. A three-judge federal court held that under *Frothingham* appellants lacked standing.]

The jurisdiction of federal courts is defined and limited by [Art. III]. Embodied in the words "cases" and "controversies" are two complementary but somewhat different limitations. In part those words limit the business of federal courts to questions presented in an adversary context and in a form historically viewed as capable of resolution through the judicial process. And in part those words define the role assigned to the judiciary in a tripartite allocation of power to assure that the federal courts will not intrude into areas committed to the other branches of government. Justiciability is the term of art employed to give expression to this dual limitation * * *.

[T]he Government's position is that the constitutional scheme of separation of powers, and the deference owed by the federal judiciary to the other two branches of government within that scheme, presents an absolute bar to taxpayer suits challenging the validity of federal spending programs.[17]

Standing is an aspect of justiciability [and] there are at work in the standing doctrine the many subtle pressures which tend to cause policy considerations to blend into constitutional limitations. [The] fundamental aspect of standing is that it focuses on the party seeking to get his complaint before a federal court and not on the issues he wishes to have adjudicated. The "gist of the question of standing" is whether the party seeking relief has "alleged such a personal stake in the outcome of the controversy as to assure that concrete adverseness which sharpens the presentation of issues upon which the court so largely depends for illumination of difficult constitutional questions." *Baker v. Carr,* [p. 30 supra]. In other words, when standing is placed in issue in a case, the question is whether the person whose standing is challenged is a proper party to request an adjudication of a particular issue and not whether the issue itself is justiciable. Thus, a party may have standing in a particular case, but the federal court may nevertheless decline to pass on the merits of the case because, for example, it presents a political question. [The] question whether a particular person is a proper party to maintain the action does not, by its own force, raise separation of powers problems related to improper judicial interference in areas committed to other branches of the Federal Government. Such problems arise, if at all, only from the substantive issues the individual seeks to have adjudicated. Thus, in terms of Article III limitations on federal court jurisdiction, the question of standing is related only to whether the dispute sought to be adjudicated will be presented in an adversary context and in a form historically viewed as capable of

17. The logic of the Government's argument would compel it to concede that a taxpayer would lack standing even if Congress engaged in such palpably unconstitutional conduct as providing funds for the construction of churches for particular sects. The Government [contends] there might be individuals in society other than taxpayers who could invoke federal judicial power to challenge such unconstitutional appropriations. However, if as we conclude there are circumstances under which a taxpayer will be a proper and appropriate party to seek judicial review of federal statutes, the taxpayer's access to federal courts should not be barred because there might be at large in society a hypothetical plaintiff who might possibly bring such a suit.

judicial resolution. [A] taxpayer may or may not have the requisite personal stake in the outcome, depending upon the circumstances of the particular case. [I]n ruling on standing, it is both appropriate and necessary to look to the substantive issues [to] determine whether there is a logical nexus between the status asserted and the claim sought to be adjudicated [to] assure that [the litigant] is a proper and appropriate party to invoke federal judicial power [so as] to satisfy Article III requirements.

The nexus demanded of federal taxpayers has two aspects to it. First, the taxpayer must establish a logical link between that status and the type of legislative enactment attacked. Thus, a taxpayer will be a proper party to allege the unconstitutionality only of exercises of congressional power under the taxing and spending clause of Art. I, § 8, of the Constitution. It will not be sufficient to allege an incidental expenditure of tax funds in the administration of an essentially regulatory statute. This requirement is consistent with the limitation imposed upon state taxpayer standing in federal courts in *Doremus*. Secondly, the taxpayer must establish a nexus between that status and the precise nature of the constitutional infringement alleged. Under this requirement, the taxpayer must show that the challenged enactment exceeds specific constitutional limitations imposed upon the exercise of the congressional taxing and spending power and not simply that the enactment is generally beyond the powers delegated to Congress by Art. I, § 8. * * *

The taxpayer-appellants in this case have satisfied both nexuses * * *. Their constitutional challenge is made to an exercise by Congress of its power under Art. I, § 8, to spend for the general welfare, and the challenged program involves a substantial expenditure of federal tax funds. In addition, appellants have alleged that the challenged expenditures violate the Establishment and Free Exercise Clauses of the First Amendment. Our history vividly illustrates that one of the specific evils feared by those who drafted the Establishment Clause [was] that the taxing and spending power would be used to favor one religion over another or to support religion in general [and] that religious liberty ultimately would be the victim * * *. [T]hat clause of the First Amendment operates as a specific constitutional limitation upon the exercise by Congress of the taxing and spending power conferred by Art. I, § 8.

[The] taxpayer in *Frothingham* attacked a federal spending program and she, therefore, established the first nexus required. However, [she] alleged essentially that Congress, by enacting the challenged statute, had exceeded the general powers delegated to it by Art. I, § 8, and that Congress had thereby invaded the legislative province reserved to the States by the Tenth Amendment. To be sure, Mrs. Frothingham made the additional allegation that her tax liability would be increased as a result of the allegedly unconstitutional enactment, and she framed that allegation in terms of a deprivation of property without due process of law. However, the Due Process Clause of the Fifth Amendment does not protect taxpayers against increases in tax liability * * *. In essence, Mrs. Frothingham was attempting to assert the States' interest in their legislative prerogatives and not a federal taxpayer's interest in being free of taxing and spending in contravention of specific constitutional limitations imposed upon Congress' taxing and spending power.

We have noted that the Establishment Clause of the First Amendment does specifically limit the taxing and spending power conferred by Art. I, § 8. Whether the Constitution contains other specific limitations can be determined only in the context of future cases. [Under] such circumstances, we feel confident that the questions will be framed with the necessary specificity, that the issues will be contested with the necessary adverseness and that the litigation will be pursued with the necessary vigor to assure that the constitutional challenge will be made in a form traditionally thought to be capable of judicial resolution. We lack that confidence in cases such as *Frothingham* where a taxpayer seeks to employ a federal court as a forum in which to air his generalized grievances about the conduct of government or the allocation of power in the Federal System. * * *

Reversed.

MR. JUSTICE DOUGLAS [who joined the Court's opinion], concurring. * * *

There has long been a school of thought here that the less the judiciary does, the better. It is often said that judicial intrusion should be infrequent [but the] judiciary is an indispensable part of the operation of our federal system. With the growing complexities of government it is often the one and only place where effective relief can be obtained [and] where wrongs to individuals are done by violation of specific guarantees, it is abdication for courts to close their [doors].

MR. JUSTICE STEWART [who joined the Court's opinion], concurring.

[Because the Establishment Clause plainly prohibits taxing and spending in aid of religion, every taxpayer can claim a personal constitutional right not to be taxed for the support of a religious institution. The present case is thus readily distinguishable from *Frothingham* * * *.[a]

MR. JUSTICE HARLAN, dissenting.

[F]ederal taxpayers may, as taxpayers, contest the constitutionality of tax obligations imposed severally upon them by federal statute. Such a challenge may be made by way of defense to an action by the United States to recover the amount of a challenged tax debt, or to a prosecution for willful failure to pay [the tax].

The lawsuits here and in *Frothingham* are fundamentally different. They present the question whether federal taxpayers qua taxpayers may, in suits in which they do not contest the validity of their previous or existing tax obligations, challenge the constitutionality of the uses for which Congress has authorized the expenditure of public funds. [An] action brought to contest the validity of tax liabilities assessed to the plaintiff is designed to vindicate interests that are personal and proprietary * * *. The relief [here] consists entirely of the vindication of rights held in common by all citizens. * * *

Surely it is plain that the rights and interests of taxpayers who contest the constitutionality of public expenditures are markedly different from those of "Hohfeldian" plaintiffs,[5] including those taxpayer-plaintiffs who challenge the validity of their own tax liabilities. We must recognize that these non-Hohfeldian plaintiffs complain [not] as taxpayers, but as "private attorneys-general." [These are] "public actions" brought to vindicate public rights.[7]

It does not, however, follow that suits brought by non-Hohfeldian plaintiffs are excluded by the "case or controversy" clause of [Art. III]. This and other federal courts have repeatedly held that individual litigants, acting as private

---

a. The concurring opinion of Fortas, J., is omitted.

5. The phrase is Professor Jaffe's, adopted, of course, from W. Hohfeld, *Fundamental Legal Conceptions* (1923). I have here employed the phrases "Hohfeldian" and "non-Hohfeldian" plaintiffs to mark the distinction between the personal and proprietary interests of the traditional plaintiff, and the representative and public interests of the plaintiff in a public action. * * *

7. Jaffe, *Judicial Control of Administrative Action* 483 (1965).

attorneys-general, may have standing as "representatives of the public interest." *Scripps-Howard Radio v. FCC*, 316 U.S. 4, 15, 62 S.Ct. 875, 882, 86 L.Ed. 1229. See also *Associated Industries v. Ickes*, 134 F.2d 694 * * *.[b]

The Court's analysis consists principally of the observation that the requirements of standing are met if a taxpayer has the "requisite personal stake in the outcome" of his suit. [The] Court implements this standard with the declaration that taxpayers will be "deemed" to have the necessary personal interest if their suits satisfy two [criteria]. The difficulties with these criteria [are] that they are not in any sense a measurement of any plaintiff's interest in the outcome of any [suit.]

It is surely clear that a plaintiff's interest in the outcome of a suit in which he challenges the constitutionality of a federal expenditure is not made greater or smaller by the unconnected fact that the expenditure is, or is not, "incidental" to an "essentially regulatory program." * * * Presumably the Court does not believe that regulatory programs are necessarily less destructive of First Amendment rights, or that regulatory programs are necessarily less prodigal of public funds than are grants-in-aid, for both these general propositions are demonstrably false. * * *

The Court's second criterion is similarly unrelated to its standard for the determination of standing. The intensity of a plaintiff's interest in a suit is not measured, even obliquely, by the fact that the constitutional provision under which he claims is, or is not, a "specific limitation" upon Congress' spending powers. * * *

Although the Court does not altogether explain its position, the essence of its reasoning is evidently that a taxpayer's claim under the Establishment Clause is "not merely one of ultra vires," but instead asserts "an abridgment of individual religious liberty" * * *. Choper, *The Establishment Clause and Aid to Parochial Schools*, 56 Calif.L.Rev. 260, 276. [But] the Court has not adduced, historical evidence that properly permits the Court to distinguish, as it has here, among the Establishment Clause, the Tenth Amendment and the Due Process Clause of the Fifth Amendment as limitations upon Congress' taxing and spending powers. * * *[18]

b. *Scripps-Howard* held that the Communications Act conferred standing on a radio station, as a "person aggrieved," to contest the FCC's grant of a license to an additional station: "The purpose of the Act was to protect the public interest in communications. [T]hese private litigants have standing [as] representatives of the public interest." Consider Jaffe, *Standing to Secure Judicial Review: Public Actions*, 74 Harv.L.Rev. 1265, 1314 (1961): "It might be argued that whatever the purported rationale [of] *Scripps-Howard*, a decision upholding the justiciability of a suit brought by a person of a very limited class which is in fact adversely affected is not a precedent for permitting actions by the unlimited class of citizen or taxpayer. But in *Associated Industries*, Judge Frank, following what he believed to be the rationale of [*Scripps-Howard*], did apply it to a consumer, a member of a class which is coterminous with the entire human population [and] characterized the appellant as a 'private Attorney General.'" Nonetheless, argues Davis, *Standing:*

Taxpayers and Others, 35 U.Chi.L.Rev. 601, 616 (1968), "I think it entirely clear that the Court has always required 'economic and other personal interests' as the basis for standing, without exception." See his discussion of the cases, id. at 613–17. For the view that "the notion that the constitution demands injury to a personal interest as a prerequisite to attacks on allegedly unconstitutional action is historically unfounded," see Berger, *Standing to Sue in the Public Actions: Is it a Constitutional Requirement?* 78 Yale L.J. 816 (1969).

The issue of congressionally authorized standing is considered in this Part infra.

18. I have equal difficulty with the argument that the religious clauses of the First Amendment create a "personal constitutional right," held by all *citizens*, such that any *citizen* may, under those clauses, contest the constitutionality of federal expenditures. The essence of the argument would presumably be that freedom from establishment is a right that inheres in every citizen * * *. The

[This] Court has previously held that individual litigants have standing to represent the public interest, despite their lack of economic or other personal interests, if Congress has appropriately authorized such suits.[c] I would adhere to that principle. Any hazards to the proper allocation of authority among the three branches of the Government would be substantially diminished if public actions had been pertinently authorized by Congress and the President. * * *

Notes and Questions

1. *The first nexus.* (a) After *Flast,* may a federal taxpayer challenge the issuance of a "commemorative Christmas postage stamp" as violating the establishment clause? Assuming the issuance "involves a substantial expenditure of federal tax funds," does it concern an "exercise of congressional power under the taxing and spending clause" or is it merely an "incidental expenditure of tax funds in the administration of an essentially regulatory" program? *Should* this question be relevant to the taxpayer's standing? Consider 82 Harv.L.Rev. 230 (1968): "If a governmental regulation does violate the establishment clause, a taxpayer would sustain a special injury to conscience by the expenditure of any revenues under the regulatory scheme. Therefore, taxpayers could be designated as properly adverse article III parties to sue to vindicate the public interest. But governmental regulatory action will usually encroach on the legally protected interests of a significant portion of the citizenry as well. Thus there is no justification for concluding that the establishment clause itself should be said to designate a special injury class of litigants as proper parties to challenge this category of governmental conduct." See also Hennigan, *The Essence of Standing: The Basis of a Constitutional Right to be Heard,* 10 Ariz.L.Rev. 438 (1968). Is this analysis consistent with *Flast's* fn. 17?

(b) *The "pocketbook" injury requirement.* On the likely assumption that if this particular stamp is not issued some other one will be, does this activity—like that in *Doremus*—not "add any sum whatever to the cost of conducting" the postal system? If so, is the establishment clause evil nonetheless present because the stamp issuance "involves a substantial expenditure of tax funds" allegedly "to favor one religion over another"? If the school authorities in *Doremus* had annually expended $100 ($10) for the purchase of Bibles, would "appellants [have] established the requisite special injury necessary to a taxpayer's case or controversy"? See Davis, *Standing: Taxpayers and Others,* 35 U.Chi. L.Rev. 601 (1968). Or may it be said that the Bible-reading resulted in the public school being "used to favor one religion over another or to support religion in general" and thus the "substantial expenditure of tax funds" for general operation of the schools was allegedly violative of the establishment clause? See Stuart, *Standing to Contest Federal Appropriations,* 22 Sw.L.J. 612 (1968). Should there be taxpayer standing in both cases? Do the above queries lead to the conclusion that in all these cases taxpayers are "non-Hohfeldian plaintiffs [suing] to vindicate public rights"?

2. *The second nexus.* Does *Flast* find *Frothingham* distinguishable because the different "substantive issues" involved make Mrs. Flast but not Mrs. Frothingham an "appropriate party [as a taxpayer] to invoke federal judicial power,"

Establishment Clause is, after all, only one of many provisions of the Constitution that might be characterized in this fashion. [I]t might even be urged that the Ninth and Tenth Amendments, since they are largely confirmatory of rights created elsewhere in the Constitution, were intended to declare the standing of individual citizens to contest the validity of governmental activities. * * *

c. See fn. b supra.

i.e., "Mrs. Frothingham was attempting to assert the States' interest in their legislative prerogatives" whereas (as phrased by Stewart, J.) Mrs. Flast was asserting "a personal constitutional right not to be taxed for the support of a religious institution"? That Mrs. Flast did—but Mrs. Frothingham did *not*—allegedly suffer a constitutionally prohibited injury?

Does Harlan, J., effectively refute the position that federal taxpayers hold a "personal constitutional right" under the establishment clause? If this "right" is *not to have money collected from the individual by taxation expended for religion by government,* is its existence denied by the fact that a suit to enjoin expenditures does not allege "that the contested expenditures will in any fashion affect the amount of the taxpayers' own existing or foreseeable tax obligations"?

Do all of these analyses speak to the merits rather than standing?

CONGRESSIONAL POWER TO CREATE STANDING

SIERRA CLUB v. MORTON, 405 U.S. 727, 92 S.Ct. 1361, 31 L.Ed.2d 636 (1972): A membership corporation with "a special interest in the conservation and sound maintenance of the national parks," relied on Administrative Procedure Act § 10 (authorizing judicial review by persons "suffering legal wrong" or "adversely affected or aggrieved") as permitting it, as a "representative of the public," to challenge construction of a recreation area in a national forest as violative of federal statutes for preservation of national parks, etc. The Court, per STEWART, J., denied standing: "[Where] Congress has authorized public officials to perform certain functions according to law, and has provided by statute for judicial review of those actions under certain circumstances, the inquiry as to standing must begin with a determination of whether the statute in question authorizes review at the behest of the plaintiff.[3] * * *

"The trend of cases arising under the APA and other statutes authorizing judicial review of federal agency action has been towards recognizing that injuries other than economic harm are sufficient to bring a person within the meaning of the statutory language, and towards discarding the notion that an injury that is widely shared is ipso facto not an injury sufficient to provide the basis for judicial review. We noted this development with approval in [*Association of Data Processing Service Organizations, Inc. v. Camp,* 397 U.S. 150, 90 S.Ct. 827, 25 L.Ed.2d 184 (1970)] in saying that the interest alleged to have been injured 'may reflect "aesthetic, conservational, and recreational" as well as economic values.' But broadening the categories of injury that may be alleged in support of standing is a different matter from abandoning the requirement that the party seeking review must have himself suffered an injury." Here, "the Sierra Club failed to allege that it or its members [use the site in the national forest] for any purpose, much less that they use it in any way that would be significantly affected by the proposed" construction.[a]

---

3. [W]here a dispute is otherwise justiciable, the question whether the litigant is a "proper party to request an adjudication of a particular issue," is one within the power of Congress to determine.

a. Douglas, J., dissented, contending for standing "in the name of the inanimate object about to be despoiled, defaced or invaded by roads and bulldozers and where injury is the subject of public outrage." (See Stone, *Should Trees Have Standing?—Toward Legal Rights*

for Natural Objects, 45 So.Cal.L.Rev. 450 (1972)). Blackmun, J. dissented, calling (with Brennan, J.) for "an imaginative expansion of our traditional concepts of standing in order to enable an organization such as the Sierra Club, possessed, as it is, of pertinent, bona-fide and well-recognized attributes and purposes in the area of environment, to litigate environmental issues." (See Sedler, *Standing, Justiciability and All That: A Behavioral Analy-*

TRAFFICANTE v. METROPOLITAN LIFE INS. CO., 409 U.S. 205, 93 S.Ct. 364, 34 L.Ed.2d 415 (1972), per DOUGLAS, J., held that tenants of an apartment complex had standing to complain that the owner racially discriminated in renting in violation of the Civil Rights Act of 1968. The Act gave "persons aggrieved" the right to sue—defined as "any person who claims to have been injured by a discriminatory housing practice." The tenants "claimed they had been injured in that (1) they had lost the social benefits of living in an integrated community; (2) they had missed business and professional advantages which would have accrued if they had lived with members of minority groups; (3) they had suffered embarrassment and economic damage in social, business, and professional activities from being 'stigmatized' as residents of a 'white ghetto.'"

Observing that "the role of 'private attorneys general' is not uncommon in modern legislative programs," the Court found that "the language of the Act is broad and inclusive" and "concluded that the words used showed 'a congressional intention to define standing as broadly as is permitted by [Art. III].' Individual injury or injury in fact to petitioners, the ingredient found missing in *Sierra Club*, is alleged here." [b]

UNITED STATES v. SCRAP, 412 U.S. 669, 93 S.Ct. 2405, 37 L.Ed.2d 254 (1973), per STEWART, J., held that appellee environmental groups, who challenged the ICC's failure to suspend a surcharge on railroad freight rates as violative of the ICC's statutory duties, had standing as persons "adversely affected or aggrieved" under the APA. Appellees alleged "that their members used the forests, streams, mountains, and other resources in the Washington metropolitan area for camping, hiking, fishing, and sightseeing." The Court was willing to follow an "attenuated line of causation to the eventual injury of which the appellees complained—a general rate increase would allegedly cause increased use of nonrecyclable commodities as compared to recyclable goods, thus resulting in the need to use more natural resources to produce such goods, some of which resources might be taken from the Washington area, and resulting in more refuse that might be discarded in national parks in the Washington area." [c]

WHITE, J., joined by Burger, C.J. and Rehnquist, J., dissented: "The allegations here do not satisfy the threshold requirement of injury in fact [for] a justiciable case or controversy. [T]he alleged injuries are so remote, speculative, and insubstantial" as to "no more qualify these appellees to litigate than allegations of a taxpayer that governmental expenditures will increase his taxes and have an impact on his pocketbook, or allegations that governmental decisions are offensive to reason or morals. [If] they are sufficient here, we are well on our way to permitting citizens at large to litigate any decisions of the Government which fall in an area of interest to them and with which they disagree."

---

sis, 25 Vand.L.Rev. 479 (1973)). Powell and Rehnquist, JJ., did not participate.

The Sierra Club subsequently amended its complaint and obtained standing by alleging its members' use of the national forest.

b. White, J., joined by Blackmun and Powell, JJ., concurred: "Absent the Civil Rights Act of 1968, I would have great difficulty in concluding that petitioners' complaint in this case presented a case or controversy [under]

Art. III. But [cf.] *Katzenbach v. Morgan; Oregon v. Mitchell* [opinion of Brennan, J.]"—Ch. 12, Sec. 2.

See also *Gladstone Realtors v. Bellwood*, 441 U.S. 91, 99 S.Ct. 1601, 60 L.Ed.2d 66 (1979) (standing under Fair Housing Act).

c. Blackmun, J., joined by Brennan, J. (and with whom Douglas, J., agreed) concurred, following their view in *Sierra Club* that "injury in fact" need not be required.

Notes and Questions

1. *The cases' rationale.* Do *Sierra Club, Trafficante* and *SCRAP* establish that a litigant must have suffered "injury in fact" to satisfy the case-or-controversy requirement? Or does the Court's definition of "individual injury" in these cases in reality permit "citizens at large to litigate"? Consider Albert, *Standing to Challenge Administrative Action: An Inadequate Surrogate Claim for Relief,* 83 Yale L.J. 425, 489 (1974): "The interests of consumers and environmentalists, while held in common with many, are plainly not equivalent to a citizen's interest in good government. To the contrary, such interests, going to matters that affect the quality of life, leisure, and health, are as tangible and palpable as the typical fare for adjudication. People are injured in real and recognizable ways when action despoiling parks and woodlands is authorized, when a licensee with a poor or discriminatory broadcasting record is renewed, or when an agency fails to act upon unsafe regulated products. [If] litigants presenting these claims, as in *Sierra Club,* do not show injury to themselves from government action, Article III is a barrier. But there is nothing inherent in the nature of the interests or their shared character that raises problems under Article III."

2. *Congressional power and Art. III.* After *Frothingham,* could Congress authorize suit by *any* taxpayer to test the constitutionality of the Maternity Act? *Any* citizen?[d] What was the view of Harlan, J., in *Flast*? Would "such individuals demonstrate the necessary stake in the outcome to satisfy Article III requirements"? How could they if *Frothingham* did not present a "judicial controversy"? Do they suffer greater "injury in fact" than a federal officer who brings a criminal prosecution, or a civil action to enforce regulatory prohibitions, against a private individual? See Sedler, *Standing and the Burger Court: An Analysis and Some Proposals for Legislative Reform,* 30 Rutg.L.Rev. 863, 881–85 (1977). Consider Jaffe, *The Citizen as Litigant in Public Actions: The Non-Hohfeldian or Ideological Plaintiff,* 116 U.Pa.L.Rev. 1033, 1037–38 (1968): "[T]he very fact of [an "ideological plaintiff"] investing money in a lawsuit from which one is to acquire no further monetary profit argues, to my mind, a quite exceptional kind of interest, and one peculiarly indicative of a desire to say all that can be said in the support of one's contention. From this I would conclude that, insofar as the argument for a traditional plaintiff runs in terms of the need for effective advocacy, the argument is not persuasive." See also Tushnet, *The Sociology of Article III,* 93 Harv.L.Rev. 1698, 1711 (1980): "In a legal system based on precedent, a successful litigant benefits from those in the future who can invoke the earlier decision, [yet] the present litigant cannot capture those potential benefits. Thus, as a general proposition, it seems that rational Hohfeldian litigants should underinvest in their litigation. [On the other hand, studies] from the perspective of economics [and] sociology have demonstrated that ["ideological"] litigants who have a continuing interest in the substantive outcomes of litigation, and who have a continuing interest in the development of legal rules favorable to their position, are more likely to invest adequate resources and therefore to succeed in their litigation."

If the "ideological plaintiff" satisfies the case-or-controversy requirement, is there any lawsuit in which plaintiff is not "a proper party to request an adjudication of a particular issue"? Does restriction of standing to "traditional

---

d. The Endangered Species Act, 16 U.S.C. § 1540(g), authorizes "any person" to enjoin violations. See *TVA v. Hill,* 437 U.S. 153, 98 S.Ct. 2279, 57 L.Ed.2d 117 (1978).

plaintiffs" serve other significant constitutional ends? Should there be standing for "public actions" irrespective of congressional authorization? See note 2 after *Allen v. Wright*, infra.

UNITED STATES v. RICHARDSON, 418 U.S. 166, 94 S.Ct. 2940, 41 L.Ed.2d 678 (1974), per BURGER, C.J., held that a federal taxpayer had no standing to contend that the Central Intelligence Agency Act, which provides that CIA appropriations and expenditures not be made public, violates Art. I, § 9, cl. 7— "a regular Statement of Account of the Receipts and Expenditures of all public money shall be published from time to time": Respondent "makes no claim that appropriated funds are being spent in violation of a 'specific constitutional limitation upon [the] taxing and spending power * * *.' Rather, he asks the courts to compel the Government to give him information on precisely how the CIA spends its funds [without which] he cannot intelligently follow the actions of Congress or the Executive, nor can he properly fulfill his obligations as a member of the electorate in voting for candidates seeking national office.

"This is surely the kind of a generalized grievance described in both *Frothingham* and *Flast* since the impact on him is plainly undifferentiated and 'common to all members of the public.' *Ex parte Levitt*, 302 U.S. 633, 58 S.Ct. 1, 82 L.Ed. 493 (1983).[a] While we can hardly dispute that this respondent has a genuine interest in the use of funds and that his interest may be prompted by his status as a taxpayer, he has not alleged that, as a taxpayer, he is in danger of suffering any particular concrete injury as a result of the operation of this statute. * * *[11]

"[T]he absence of any particular individual or class to litigate these claims gives support to the argument that the subject matter is committed to the surveillance of Congress, and ultimately to the political process. [T]hat the Constitution does not afford a judicial remedy does not, of course, completely disable the citizen * * *. Slow, cumbersome and unresponsive though the traditional electoral process may be thought at times, our system provides for changing members of the political branches when dissatisfied citizens convince a sufficient number of their fellow electors that elected representatives are delinquent in performing duties committed to them."

POWELL, J., who joined the Court's opinion, concurred: "[T]here can be little doubt about respondent's fervor in pursuing his case [and the] intensity of his interest appears to bear no relationship to the fact that, literally speaking, he is not challenging directly a congressional exercise of the taxing and spending power. On the other hand, [it] requires no great leap in reasoning to conclude that the Statement and Account Clause [is] inextricably linked to that power. And that clause might well be seen as a 'specific' limitation on congressional spending. Indeed, it could be viewed as the most democratic of limitations.

---

a. *Levitt* held that a private individual had no standing to challenge the appointment of a Supreme Court justice as violative of Art. I, § 6, cl. 2.

11. Although we need not reach or decide precisely what is meant by "a regular Statement of Account," it [is] open to serious question whether the Framers of the Constitution ever imagined that general directives to the Congress or the Executive would be subject to enforcement by an individual citizen.

[H]istorical analysis of the genesis of cl. 7 suggests that it was intended to permit some degree of secrecy of governmental operations. The ultimate weapon of enforcement available to the Congress would, of course, be the "power of the purse." Independent of the statute here challenged by respondent, Congress could grant standing to taxpayers or citizens, or both, limited, of course, by the "Cases" and "Controversies" provisions of Art. III. * * *

Thus, although the Court's application of *Flast* to the instant case is probably literally correct, adherence to the *Flast* test in this instance suggests, as does *Flast* itself, that the test is not a sound or logical limitation on standing. [D]espite the diminution of standing requirements in the last decade, the Court has not broken with the traditional requirement that, in the absence of a specific statutory grant of the right of review, a plaintiff must allege some particularized injury that sets him apart from the man on the street. * * *[17]"

STEWART, J., joined by Marshall, J., dissented: "[Respondent] contends that the Statement and Account Clause gives him a right to receive the information and burdens the Government with a correlative duty to supply it. [When] a party is seeking a judicial determination that a defendant owes him an affirmative duty, it seems clear to me that he has standing to litigate the issue of the existence vel non of this duty once he shows that the defendant has declined to honor his claim. [Thus,] there is no necessity to resort to any extended analysis, such as the *Flast* nexus tests [which "were no more than a response to the problem of taxpayer standing to challenge federal legislation enacted in the exercise of the taxing and spending power."] Certainly, after *SCRAP*, it does not matter that those to whom the duty is owed may be many."

BRENNAN, J., dissented, relying on his dissent in *Reservists*, this Sec. infra: "Richardson plainly alleged injury in fact [in] respect of his right as a citizen to know how Congress was spending the public fisc [and] as a voter to receive information to aid his decision how and for whom to vote. These claims may ultimately fail on the merits, but Richardson has 'standing' to assert them." [b]

SCHLESINGER v. RESERVISTS COMM. TO STOP THE WAR, 418 U.S. 208, 94 S.Ct. 2925, 41 L.Ed.2d 706 (1974), per BURGER, C.J., held that respondents lacked standing as citizens to contend that the Secretary of Defense's permitting Members of Congress to be in the Armed Forces Reserve violated the Incompatibility Clause of Art. I, § 6, cl. 2—"No person holding any office under the United States shall be a Member of either House during his continuance in office." Respondents alleged injury because "nonobservance of [the] Clause deprives citizens of the faithful discharge of the legislative duties of Reservist members of Congress" since they would "be subject to the possibility of undue influence by the Executive Branch [and] possible inconsistent obligations." The Court responded:

"[T]hat claimed nonobservance, standing alone, would adversely affect only the generalized interest of all citizens in constitutional governance, and that is an abstract injury. [T]he requirement of concrete injury [serves] the function of insuring that [constitutional] adjudication does not take place unnecessarily. [T]he discrete factual context within which the concrete injury occurred or is threatened insures the framing of relief no more broad than required by the precise facts to which the court's ruling would be applied. This is especially important when the relief sought produces a confrontation with one of the coordinate branches of the government. [T]he fact that the adverse parties sharply conflicted in their interests and views and were supported by able briefs and arguments [is] not a substitute for the actual injury needed [to] focus

---

17. *Baker v. Carr* may have a special claim to sui generis status. It was perhaps a necessary response to the manifest distortion of democratic principles practiced by malapportioned legislatures * * *. *Flast* may also have been a reaction to what appeared at the

time as an immutable political logjam that included unsuccessful efforts to confer specific statutory grants of standing.

b. Douglas, J., also dissented.

litigation efforts and judicial decision-making. Moreover, [a] logical corollary to this approach would be the manifestly untenable view that the inadequacy of the presentation on the merits would be an appropriate basis for denying standing.[a] [Our] system of government leaves many crucial decisions to the political processes. The assumption that if respondents have no standing to sue, no one would have standing, is not a reason to find standing. See *Richardson*." [b]

STEWART, J., who joined the Court's opinion, concurred: "[U]nlike *Richardson*, the respondents do not allege that the petitioners have refused to perform an affirmative duty imposed upon them by the Constitution. ＊ ＊ ＊ Standing is not today found wanting because an injury has been suffered by many, but rather because *none* of the respondents has alleged the sort of direct, palpable injury required for standing under [Art. III]."

MARSHALL, J., dissented: Respondents' "specific interest"—"to have the Congress take all the steps necessary to terminate American involvement in Vietnam"—"is certainly not a 'general interest common to all members of the public.' [It] is a sad commentary on our priorities that a litigant who contends that a violation of a federal stature has interfered with his aesthetic appreciation of natural resources can have a claim heard by a federal court, see *SCRAP*, while one who contends that a violation of a specific provision of [the] Constitution has interfered with the effectiveness of expression protected by the First Amendment is turned away." Douglas, J., also dissented.

Notes and Questions

Nature of constitutional provision. (a) Did the claimants in *Reservists* and *Richardson* allege "concrete injury" or only "the generalized interest of all citizens in constitutional governance"? Consider Albert, *Justiciability and Theories of Judicial Review: A Remote Relationship*, 50 So.Cal.L.Rev. 1139, 1153 (1977): "[*Reservists* and *Richardson*] illustrate that the article III concept of 'injury in fact' [involves] a subtle judicial judgment founded upon a construction of the substantive constitutional mandate in issue. [In the Court's view, the Incompatibility Clause and the Statement and Account Clause] gave rise to no definable legal interest, and therefore there was no immediacy or actuality to the alleged harms. But there is no objective calculus for saying that these harms are less immediate or real than injury to schoolchildren from unequal educational financing or to voters from unequal districting. What differs is the source of the judgment, the law on which the claim is founded. Hence, it was a choice between competing views of the unconstrued constitutional provisions in *Richardson* and *Reservists* that determined whether there was 'injury in fact.' "

a. See Davis, *Administrative Law Text* 427–28 (3d ed. 1972): "Standing should not depend upon the probable manner in which a party will present a case; it should depend only upon the question whether the plaintiff should be entitled to judicial assistance in order that justice may be done. Two simple illustrations, one at each pole, should suffice to show this: (1) The best law firm in the country, no matter how skillful its presentation to the court may be, *obviously* lacks standing to get an adjudication of an abstract question of law when neither it nor its client has any interest at stake. (2) An illiterate pauper who refuses legal assistance *obviously* has standing to challenge a $10 fine imposed on him, no matter how badly he may present his case."

b. The Court also denied respondents standing as taxpayers because they "did not challenge an enactment under Art. I, § 8, but rather the action of the Executive Branch." Douglas, J., dissented on this point because "Acts of Congress make various appropriations for the services of reservists" and the Incompatibility Clause " 'was designed as a specific bulwark against such potential abuses [and] operates as a specific constitutional limitation upon' such expenditures." Brennan, J., dissenting, also "would find the injury-in-fact requirement met by the respondents' taxpayer allegation."

(b) Were *Reservists* and *Richardson* based on the judgment that enforcement of the Incompatibility Clause and the Statement and Account Clause should be left "to the political process"? That—as with the states' rights issue in *Frothingham* and unlike the establishment clause issue in *Flast*—no one has "standing to sue"? Consider Davis, *Administrative Law of the Seventies* 522–23 (1976): "The way to protect against too much government by judges is to limit *what* the judges decide, not to limit *who* can raise a question for a court to decide. [The Court] can better accomplish [its] purpose if [it] focuses on the *what*, not on the *who*. [The] law of 'political question' is a much better judicial tool than the law of standing for deciding *what* the courts should decide." Compare Bogen, *Standing Up for Flast: Taxpayer and Citizen Standing to Raise Constitutional Issues*, 67 Ky.L.J. 147, 162 (1978–79): "If the constitutional provision in question is intended to protect a particular right from the majoritarian political process, the Court should not remand the plaintiff to those same processes. The critical question should center on the nature of the constitutional provision in question and whether the particular provision would be more effective if enforced by citizen suits. This issue has not been addressed by the Court."

VALLEY FORGE CHRISTIAN COLLEGE v. AMERICANS UNITED FOR SEPARATION OF CHURCH AND STATE, INC., 454 U.S. 464, 102 S.Ct. 752, 70 L.Ed.2d 700 (1982), per REHNQUIST, J., held that respondents lacked standing as taxpayers or citizens to challenge, as violative of the establishment clause, the giving of surplus federal property to a church college that trained students "for Christian services as either ministers or laymen": "While the [power of judicial review] is a formidable means of vindicating individual rights, when employed unwisely or unnecessarily it is also the ultimate threat to the continued effectiveness of the federal courts in performing that role. '[R]epeated and essentially head-on confrontations between the life-tenured branch and the representative branches of government will not, in the long run, be beneficial to either. The public confidence essential to the former and the vitality critical to the latter may well erode if we do not exercise self-restraint in the utilization of our power to negative the actions of the other branches.' *Richardson* (Powell, J., concurring).[a] Proper regard for the complex nature of our constitutional structure requires neither that the judicial branch shrink from a confrontation with the other two coequal branches of the federal government, nor that it hospitably accept for adjudication claims of constitutional violation by other branches of government where the claimant has not suffered cognizable injury. * * * Art. III, which is every bit as important in its circumscription of the judicial power of the United States as in its granting of that power, is not merely a troublesome hurdle to be overcome if possible so as to reach the 'merits' of a lawsuit * * *.

"[R]espondents fail the first prong of the [*Flast*] test for taxpayer standing [in] two respects. First, the source of their complaint is not a congressional action, but a decision by HEW to transfer a parcel of federal property. *Flast* limited taxpayer standing to challenges directed 'only [at] exercises of congressional power.' Second, [the] property transfer [was] not an exercise of authority conferred by the taxing and spending clause of Art. I, § 8. The authorizing legislation [was] an evident exercise of Congress' power under the Property Clause, Art. IV, § 3, cl. 2.

a. See generally Brilmayer, *The Jurisprudence of Article III: Perspectives on the "Case or Controversy" Requirement*, 93 Harv.L.Rev. 297 (1979).

"[The Court of Appeals] decided that respondents' claim differed from those in *Reservists* and *Richardson* [because] 'it is at the very least arguable that the Establishment Clause creates in each citizen a "personal constitutional right" to a government that does not establish religion.' [These cases cannot] be distinguished on the ground that the Incompatibility and Accounts Clauses are in some way less 'fundamental' than the Establishment Clause. Each establishes a norm of conduct which the federal government is bound to honor—to no greater or lesser extent than any other inscribed in the Constitution. To the extent the Court of Appeals relied on a view of standing under which the Art. III burdens diminish as the 'importance' of the claim on the merits increases, we reject that notion. The requirement of standing 'focuses on the party seeking to get his complaint before a federal court and not on the issues he wishes to have adjudicated.' *Flast.* Moreover, we know of no principled basis on which to create a hierarchy of constitutional values or a complementary 'sliding scale' of standing which might permit respondents to invoke the judicial power of the United States. 'The proposition that all constitutional provisions are enforceable by any citizen simply because citizens are the ultimate beneficiaries of those provisions has no boundaries.' *Reservists.*

"The complaint in this case shares a common deficiency with those in *Reservists* and *Richardson.* Although they claim that the Constitution has been violated, [they] fail to identify any personal injury suffered by the plaintiffs *as a consequence* of the alleged constitutional error, other than the psychological consequence presumably produced by observation of conduct with which one disagrees. That is not an injury sufficient to confer standing under Art. III, even though the disagreement is phrased in constitutional terms. It is evident that respondents are firmly committed to the constitutional principle of separation of church and State, but standing is not measured by the intensity of the litigant's interest or the fervor of his advocacy. * * *

"In reaching this conclusion, we do not retreat from our earlier holdings that standing may be predicated on noneconomic injury. See, e.g., *SCRAP, Data Processing Service.* We simply cannot see that respondents have alleged an *injury* of *any* kind, economic or otherwise, sufficient to confer standing.[22] [Their] claim that the government has violated the Establishment Clause does not provide a special license to roam the country in search of governmental wrongdoing and to reveal their discoveries in federal court. [Their] claim of standing implicitly rests on the presumption that violations of the Establishment Clause typically will not cause injury sufficient to confer standing under the 'traditional' view of Art. III. But '[t]he assumption that if respondents have no standing to sue, no one would have standing, is not a reason to find standing.' *Reservists.* This view would convert standing into a requirement that must be observed only when satisfied. Moreover, we are unwilling to assume that injured parties are nonexistent simply because they have not joined respondents in their suit. The law of averages is not a substitute for standing.

---

22. [The] plaintiffs in *Schempp* [p. 797 supra] had standing, not because their complaint rested on the Establishment Clause—for as *Doremus* demonstrated, that is insufficient—but because impressionable schoolchildren were subjected to unwelcome religious exercises or were forced to assume special burdens to avoid them. Respondents have alleged no comparable injury. [See generally Black, *Re-* *ligion, "Standing," and the Supreme Court's Role,* 13 J.Pub.L. 459 (1964); Brown, *Quis Custodiet Ipsos Custodes?—The School Prayer Cases,* 1963 Sup.Ct.Rev. 1; Choper, *Religion in the Public Schools: A Proposed Constitutional Standard,* 47 Minn.L.Rev. 329, 366–67 (1963); Dixon, *Religion, Schools, and the Open Society: A Socio-Constitutional Issue,* 13 J.Pub.L. 267 (1964).]

"Were we to accept respondents' claim of standing in this case, there would be no principled basis for confining our exception to litigants relying on the Establishment Clause. Ultimately, that exception derives from the idea that the judicial power requires nothing more for its invocation than important issues and able litigants.[26] [W]e are unwilling to countenance such a departure from the limits on judicial power contained in Art. III * * *."

BRENNAN, J., joined by Marshall and Blackmun, JJ.,[b] dissented: "The Court makes a fundamental mistake when it determines that a plaintiff has failed to satisfy [the] 'injury-in-fact' test, or indeed any other test of 'standing,' without first determining whether the Constitution [defines] injury, and creates a cause of action for redress of that injury, in precisely the circumstance presented to the Court.[5] [One] of the primary purposes of the Establishment Clause was to prevent the use of tax monies for religious purposes. *The taxpayer was the direct and intended beneficiary of the prohibition on financial aid to religion.* [It] may be that Congress can tax for *almost* any reason, or for no reason at all. There is, so far as I have been able to discern, but one constitutionally imposed limit on that authority. Congress cannot use tax money to support a church, or to encourage religion. [T]he history of the Establishment Clause [makes] this clear. History also makes it clear that the federal taxpayer is a singularly 'proper and appropriate party to invoke a federal court's jurisdiction' to challenge a federal bestowal of largesse as a violation of the Establishment Clause. Each, and indeed every, federal taxpayer suffers precisely the injury that the Establishment Clause guards against when the Federal Government directs that funds be taken from the pocketbooks of the citizenry and placed into the coffers of the ministry. * * *

"Blind to history, the Court attempts to distinguish this case from *Flast* by wrenching snippets of language from our opinions, and by perfunctorily applying that language under color of the first prong of *Flast's* two-part nexus test." As for the fact that HEW transferred the property, "to be sure, the First Amendment is phrased as a restriction on Congress' legislative authority; this is only natural since the Constitution assigns the authority to legislate and appropriate only to the Congress. But it is difficult to conceive of an expenditure for which the last governmental actor, either implementing directly the legislative will, or acting within the scope of legislatively delegated authority, is not an Executive Branch official. The First Amendment binds the Government as a whole, regardless of which branch is at work in a particular instance.

"The Court's second purported distinction between this case and *Flast* is equally unavailing. [It] can make no constitutional difference [whether] the donation to the defendant here was in the form of a cash grant to build a facility, see *Tilton v. Richardson,* [p. 814 supra], or in the nature of a gift of property

---

26. Were we to recognize standing premised on an "injury" consisting solely of an alleged violation of a " 'personal constitutional right' to a government that does not establish religion," a principled consistency would dictate recognition of respondents' standing to challenge execution of every capital sentence on the basis of a personal right to a government that does not impose cruel and unusual punishment, or standing to challenge every affirmative action program on the basis of a personal right to a government that does not deny equal protection of the laws, to choose but two among as many possible examples as there are commands in the Constitution.

b. Stevens, J., dissented separately, agreeing with Brennan, J.

5. When the Constitution makes it clear that a particular person is to be protected from a particular form of government action, then that person has a "right" to be free of that action; when that right is infringed, then there is injury, and a personal stake, within the meaning of Article III.

including a facility already [built.] [19] Whether undertaken pursuant to the Property Clause or the Spending Clause, the breach of the Establishment Clause, and the relationship of the taxpayer to that breach, is precisely the same."

Notes and Questions

1. *Other "injured parties."* After *Valley Forge,* would a neighboring college, that alleges competitive disadvantage because of the federal grant of property to Valley Forge Christian, have "an injury sufficient to confer standing"? If Mrs. Frothingham had refused to pay part of her federal income taxes and was prosecuted for income tax evasion, could she defend on the ground that the Maternity Act expenditures were beyond congressional power?

2. *Other constitutional provisions.* Apart from the establishment clause, are there any other "specific limitations on the taxing and spending power" that *taxpayers* have standing to enforce? Suppose Congress appropriated funds for racially segregated facilities? See McCoy & Nevins, *Standing and Adverseness in Challenges of Tax Exemptions for Discriminatory Private Schools,* 52 Ford.L. Rev. 441, 453–56 (1984). For polygraphs to be used on all criminal defendants? For a federal censorship office? For subsidies to some newspapers? For the administration of general loyalty oaths to all public employees? Assuming that all of these activities are unconstitutional, whose "rights" do they violate? Taxpayers' "rights"? How about an appropriation of "$50 to every member of the Republican Party"?

3. *State suits.* Are the Court's strictures on federal taxpayer and citizen standing also applicable to Supreme Court review of state taxpayer and citizen suits? Consider Scharpf, *Judicial Review and the Political Question: A Functional Analysis,* 75 Yale L.J. 517, 521 n. 12 (1966): "In *Frothingham,* the Court based its narrow interpretation of [the 'case and controversy'] requirement upon an understanding of the *federal* allocation of functions to the three departments of government: the Court's only legitimate function *within that framework* is to decide 'normal' cases and controversies, and any expansion of that concept would change this balance. [However, the] Constitution would seem to leave the states free to divide their functions of government differently, and to define the 'judicial power' of their own courts somewhat more broadly than [Art. III]. Thus, if a state permits its own courts to decide taxpayers' suits, and if a federal question should be determined by a state court in such a suit, it seems that the 'separation-of-powers' rationale should carry little or no weight for the Supreme Court's definition of what is a proper 'case and controversy' for purposes of appellate jurisdiction. In this situation 'case and controversy' might well have a more permissive content, protecting only the functional requisites for the correctness of the Court's constitutional decision: a well developed case, litigated by the best possible parties."

WARTH v. SELDIN
422 U.S. 490, 95 S.Ct. 2197, 45 L.Ed.2d 343 (1975).

MR. JUSTICE POWELL delivered the opinion of the Court.

Petitioners, various organizations and individuals resident in the Rochester, New York, metropolitan area, brought this action [against] the Town of Penfield,

---

19. [By] failing to require any payment from the defendant college, the Secretary apparently determined that the benefit to the United States exceeded the fair market value. But it is entirely clear from *Tilton* that if the facility is and was used for sectarian purposes, the government was required to obtain full market value at the time such use commences.

an incorporated municipality adjacent to Rochester, and against members of Penfield's Zoning, Planning, and Town Boards. Petitioners claimed that the town's zoning [ordinance] effectively excluded persons of low and moderate income from living in the town, in contravention of petitioners' First, Ninth, and Fourteenth Amendment rights and in violation of 42 U.S.C. §§ 1981, 1982, and 1983. The [federal courts below held] that none of the plaintiffs [had standing].

In its constitutional dimension, standing imports justiciability: whether the plaintiff has made out a "case or controversy" between himself and the defendant within the meaning of Art. III. * * *

Apart from this minimum constitutional mandate, this Court has recognized other ["prudential"] limits on the class of persons who may invoke the courts' decisional and remedial powers. First, the Court has held that when the asserted harm is a "generalized grievance" shared in substantially equal measure by all or a large class of citizens, that harm alone normally does not warrant exercise of jurisdiction. E.g., *Reservists*. Second, even when the plaintiff has alleged injury sufficient to meet the "case or controversy" requirement, this Court has held that the plaintiff generally must assert his own legal rights and interests, and cannot rest his claim to relief on the legal rights or interests of third parties.[a] Without such limitations—closely related to Art. III concerns but essentially matters of judicial self-governance—the courts would be called upon to decide abstract questions of wide public significance even though other governmental institutions may be more competent to address the questions and even though judicial intervention may be unnecessary to protect individual rights.

Although standing in no way depends on the merits of the plaintiff's contention that particular conduct is illegal, e.g., *Flast*, it often turns on the nature and source of the claim asserted. The actual or threatened injury required by Art. III may exist solely by virtue of "statutes creating legal rights, the invasion of which creates standing * * *." See *Sierra Club*. Moreover, the source of the plaintiff's claim to relief assumes critical importance with respect to the prudential rules of standing * * *. Essentially, the standing question in such cases is whether the constitutional or statutory provision on which the claim rests properly can be understood as granting persons in the plaintiff's position a right to judicial relief.[12] In some circumstances, countervailing considerations may outweigh the concerns underlying the usual reluctance to exert judicial power when the plaintiff's claim to relief rests on the legal rights of third parties. In such instances, the Court has found, in effect, that the constitutional or statutory provision in question implies a right of action in the plaintiff. Moreover, Congress may grant an express right of action to persons who otherwise would be barred by prudential standing rules. Of course, Art. III's requirement remains: the plaintiff still must allege a distinct and palpable injury to himself, even if it is an injury shared by a large class of other possible litigants. E.g., *SCRAP*. But so long as this requirement is satisfied, persons to whom Congress has granted a right of action, either expressly or by clear implication, may have standing to seek relief on the basis of the legal rights and

---

a. This topic is considered in Part B infra.

12. A similar standing issue arises when the litigant asserts the rights of third parties defensively, as a bar to judgment against him. E.g., *Barrows v. Jackson; McGowan v. Maryland* [Part B infra]. In such circumstances, there is no Art. III standing problem; but the prudential question is governed by considerations closely related to the question whether a person in the litigant's position would have a right of action on the claim.

interests of others, and, indeed, may invoke the general public interest in support of their claim. E.g., *Sierra Club.* ∗ ∗ ∗

III. With these general considerations in mind, we turn first to the claims of petitioners Ortiz, Reyes, Sinkler, and Broadnax, each of whom asserts standing as a person of low or moderate income and, coincidentally, as a member of a minority racial or ethnic group. We must assume, taking the allegations of the complaint as true, that Penfield's zoning ordinance and the pattern of enforcement [have] the purpose and effect of excluding [such persons]. We also assume, for purposes here, that such intentional exclusionary practices, if proved in a proper case, would be adjudged violative of the constitutional and statutory rights of the persons excluded.

But the fact that these petitioners share attributes common to persons who may have been excluded from residence in the town is an insufficient predicate for the conclusion that petitioners themselves have been excluded, or that the respondents' assertedly illegal actions have violated their rights. Petitioners must allege and show that they personally have been injured ∗ ∗ ∗.

In their complaint, petitioners Ortiz, Reyes, Sinkler, and Broadnax alleged in conclusory terms that they are among the persons excluded by respondents' actions. None of them has ever resided in Penfield; each claims at least implicitly that he desires, or has desired, to do so. Each asserts, moreover, that he made some effort, at some time, to locate housing in Penfield that was at once within his means and adequate for his family's needs. Each claims that his efforts proved fruitless. We may assume, as petitioners alleged, that respondents' actions have contributed, perhaps substantially, to the cost of housing in Penfield. But there remains the question whether petitioners' inability to locate suitable housing in Penfield reasonably can be said to have resulted, in any concretely demonstrable way, from respondents' alleged constitutional and statutory infractions. Petitioners must allege facts from which it reasonably could be inferred that, absent the respondents' restrictive zoning practices, there is a substantial probability that they would have been able to purchase or lease in Penfield and that, if the court affords the relief requested, the asserted inability of petitioners will be removed.

We find the record devoid of the necessary allegations. [N]one of these petitioners has a present interest in any Penfield property; none is himself subject to the ordinance's strictures; and none has ever been denied a variance or permit by respondent officials. Instead, petitioners claim that respondents' enforcement of the ordinance against third parties—developers, builders, and the like—has had the consequence of precluding the construction of housing suitable to their needs at prices they might be able to afford. The fact that the harm to petitioners may have resulted indirectly does not in itself preclude standing. When a governmental prohibition or restriction imposed on one party causes specific harm to a third party, harm that a constitutional provision or statute was intended to prevent, the indirectness of the injury does not necessarily deprive the person harmed of standing to vindicate his rights. But it may make it substantially more difficult to meet the minimum requirement of Art. III: to establish that, in fact, the asserted injury was the consequence of the defendants' actions, or that prospective relief will remove the harm.

Here, by their own admission, realization of petitioners' desire to live in Penfield always has depended on the efforts and willingness of third parties to build low- and moderate-cost housing. The record specifically refers to only two such efforts: that of Penfield Better Homes Corporation, in late 1969, to obtain the rezoning of certain land in Penfield to allow the construction of subsidized cooperative townhouses that could be purchased by persons of moderate income; and a similar effort by O'Brien Homes, Inc., in late 1971.[15] But the record is devoid of any indication that these projects or other like projects, would have satisfied petitioners needs at prices they could afford, or that, were the court to remove the obstructions attributable to respondents, such relief would benefit petitioners. Indeed, petitioners' descriptions of their individual financial situations and housing needs suggest precisely the contrary—that their inability to reside in Penfield is the consequence of the economics of the area housing market, rather than of respondents' assertedly illegal acts.[16] In short, the facts alleged fail to support an actionable causal relationship between Penfield's zoning practices and petitioners' asserted injury.[18] * * *

V. We turn next to the standing problems presented by the petitioner associations * * *.

A. Petitioner Metro-Act [claims] that, as a result of the persistent pattern of exclusionary zoning [its] members who are Penfield residents are deprived of the benefits of living in a racially and ethnically integrated community. * * *

15. Penfield Better Homes contemplated a series of one to three bedroom units and hoped to sell them—at that time—to persons who earned from $5,000 to $8,000 per year. * * * O'Brien Homes, Inc., projected 51 buildings, each containing four family units, designed for single people and small families, and capable of being purchased by persons "of low income and accumulated funds" * * *.

16. Ortiz states in his affidavit that he [is] concerned with finding a house or apartment large enough for himself, his wife and seven children, but states that he can afford to spend a maximum of $120 per month for housing. Broadnax seeks a four-bedroom house or apartment for herself and six children, and can spend a maximum of about $120 per month for housing. Sinkler also states that she can spend $120 per month for housing for herself and two children. Thus, at least in the cases of Ortiz and Broadnax, it is doubtful that their stated needs could have been satisfied by the small housing units contemplated in the only moderate cost projects specifically described in the record. Moreover, there is no indication that any of the plaintiffs had the resources necessary to acquire the housing available in the projects. The matter is left entirely obscure. The income and housing budget figures supplied in petitioners' affidavits are presumably for the year 1972. The vague description of the proposed O'Brien development strongly suggests that the units, even if adequate to their needs, would have been beyond the means at least of Sinkler and Broadnax. See n. 15, supra. The Penfield Better Homes projected price figures were for 1969, and must be assumed—even if subsidies might still be available—to have increased substantially by 1972, when the complaint was filed. Petitioner Reyes presents a special case: she states that her family has an income of over $14,000 per year, that she can

afford $231 per month for housing, and that, in the past and apparently now, she wants to purchase a residence. [T]he term "low and moderate income" is nowhere defined in the complaint; but Penfield Better Homes defined the term as between $5,000 and $8,000 per year. See n. 15, supra. Since that project was to be subsidized, presumably petitioner Reyes would have been ineligible. There is no indication that in nonsubsidized projects, removal of the challenged zoning restrictions—in 1972—would have reduced the price on new single-family residences to a level that petitioner Reyes thought she could afford.

18. [We] also note that zoning laws and their provisions, long considered essential to effective urban planning, are peculiarly within the province of state and local legislative authorities. They are, of course, subject to judicial review in a proper case. But citizens dissatisfied with provisions of such laws need not overlook the availability of the normal democratic process.

[For a case in which a potential home buyer demonstrated a "substantial probability" that he would have been able to purchase if rezoning were granted and thus "adequately averred an 'actionable causal relationship' between the zoning practice and his asserted injury," see *Arlington Heights v. Metropolitan Housing Dev. Corp.*, 429 U.S. 252, 97 S.Ct. 555, 50 L.Ed.2d 450 (1977). See also *Duke Power Co. v. Carolina Environmental Study Group, Inc.*, Part C infra, finding a "substantial likelihood" of "a 'but for' causal connection" between the injuries alleged and the challenged government action. For a lenient application of this doctrine, upholding standing to raise a nonconstitutional claim, see *Bryant v. Yellen*, 447 U.S. 352, 100 S.Ct. 2232, 65 L.Ed.2d 184 (1980)].

Metro-Act does not assert on behalf of its members any right of action under the 1968 Civil Rights [Act]. In this, we think, lies the critical distinction between *Trafficante* and the situation here. ＊ ＊ ＊

B. Petitioner Home Builders [asserted] standing to represent its member firms engaged in the development and construction of residential housing in the Rochester area, including Penfield. Home Builders alleged that the Penfield zoning restrictions [had] deprived some of its members of "substantial business opportunities and profits." ＊ ＊ ＊

Home Builders [can] have standing as the representative of its members only if it has alleged facts sufficient to make out a case or controversy had the members themselves brought suit. No such allegations were made. The complaint refers to no specific project of any of its members that is currently precluded either by the ordinance or by respondents' action in enforcing it. ＊ ＊ ＊

A like problem is presented with respect to petitioner Housing Council [which] includes in its membership "at least seventeen" groups that have been, are, or will be involved in the development of low- and moderate-cost housing. But, with one exception, the complaint does not suggest that any of these groups has focused its efforts on Penfield or has any specific plan to do so. [The] exception is the Penfield Better Homes Corporation. As we have observed above, it applied to respondents in late 1969 for a zoning variance to allow construction of a housing project designed for persons of moderate income. [It] is therefore possible that in 1969, or within a reasonable time thereafter, Better Homes itself and possibly Housing Council as its representative would have had standing to seek review of respondents' action. The complaint, however, does not allege that the Penfield Better Homes project remained viable in 1972 when this complaint was filed, or that respondents' actions continued to block a then current construction project.[23] In short, neither the complaint nor the record supplies any basis from which to infer that the controversy between respondents and Better Homes, however vigorous it may once have been, remained a live, concrete dispute when this complaint was filed. ＊ ＊ ＊

Affirmed.

MR. JUSTICE BRENNAN, with whom MR. JUSTICE WHITE and MR. JUSTICE MARSHALL join, dissenting.

[T]he opinion, which tosses out of court almost every conceivable kind of plaintiff who could be injured by the activity claimed to be unconstitutional, can be explained only by an indefensible hostility to the claim on the merits. [I]t is quite clear, when the record is viewed with dispassion, that at least three of the groups of plaintiffs have made allegations, and supported them with affidavits and documentary evidence, sufficient to survive a motion to dismiss for lack of standing.

[O]ne glaring defect of the Court's opinion is that it views each set of plaintiffs as if it were prosecuting a separate lawsuit, refusing to recognize that the interests are intertwined ＊ ＊ ＊. For example, the Court says that the low-income-minority plaintiffs have not alleged facts sufficient to show that but for the exclusionary practices claimed, they would be able to reside in Penfield. The Court then intimates that such a causal relationship could be shown only if "the

---

23. If it had been averred that the zoning ordinance or respondents were unlawfully blocking a pending construction project, there would be a further question as to whether Penfield Better Homes had employed available administrative remedies, and whether it should be required to do so before a federal court can intervene.

initial focus [is] on a particular project." Later, the Court objects to the ability of the Housing Council to prosecute the suit on behalf of its member, Penfield Better Homes Corporation, *despite* the fact that Better Homes *had* displayed an interest in a particular project, because that project was no longer live. Thus, we must suppose that even if the low-income plaintiffs had alleged a desire to live in the Better Homes project, that allegation would be insufficient because it appears that particular project might never be built. The rights of low-income-minority plaintiffs who desire to live in a locality, then, seem to turn on the willingness of a third party to litigate the legality of preclusion of a particular project, despite the fact that the third party may have no economic incentive to incur the costs of litigation with regard to one project, and despite the fact that the low-income-minority plaintiff's interest is *not* to live in a particular project but to live somewhere in the town in a dwelling they can afford.

[In] effect, the Court tells the low-income-minority and building company plaintiffs they will not be permitted to prove what they have alleged—that they could and would build and live in the town if changes were made in the zoning ordinance and its application—because they have not succeeded in breaching, before the suit was filed, the very barriers which are the subject of the suit.[c]

Low-Income and Minority Plaintiffs. [P]laintiffs Ortiz, Broadnax, Reyes, and Sinkler alleged that "as a result" of respondents' exclusionary practices, they were unable, despite attempts, to find the housing they desired in Penfield, and consequently have incurred high commuting expenses, received poorer municipal services, and, in some instances, been relegated to live in substandard [housing.]

Here, the very fact that, as the Court stresses, these petitioners' claim rests in part upon proving the intentions and capabilities of third parties to build in Penfield suitable housing which they can afford, coupled with the exclusionary character of the claim on the merits, makes it particularly inappropriate to assume that these petitioners' lack of specificity reflects a fatal weakness in their theory of causation.[7] Obviously they cannot be expected, prior to discovery and trial, to know the future plans of building companies, the precise details of

---

c. See also Tribe, *American Constitutional Law* 95 (1978): "[The] Court has not generally required identification of the specific transaction or project that would proceed unhindered but for a challenged rule or practice. Any contrary rule would confront excluded groups with a kind of Catch 22: the more severely and successfully exclusionary a challenged scheme is, the more difficult it would be to find insiders or developers willing to incur the inconvenience and expense of joining outsiders in designing a project or transaction that could meet any judicial test of specific identification."

7. The Court, glancing at the projects mentioned in the record which might have been built but for the exclusionary practices alleged, concludes that petitioners Ortiz and Broadnax earned too little to afford suitable housing in them, and that petitioner Reyes earned too much. As the Court implicitly acknowledges, petitioner Sinkler at least may well have been able to live in the Better Homes Project. Further, there appears in the record as it stands a Report of the Penfield

Housing Task Force [which] defines "moderate income families as families having incomes between $5,500 and $11,000 per year, depending on the size of the family," and moderate-income housing as housing "priced below $20,000 or [carrying] a retail price of less than $150 a month." [The] petitioners here under discussion fell within the Board's own definition of moderate-income families, except for petitioner Reyes * * *. And the Task Force Report *does* set out changes in the zoning ordinance and its application which could result in housing which moderate-income people could afford, even to the extent of setting out a budget provided by a builder for a house costing $18,900. The causation theory which the Court finds improbable, then, was adopted by a Task Force of the Town Board itself. Of course, we do not know at this stage whether the particular named plaintiffs would *certainly* have benefited from the changes recommended by the Task Force, but at least there is a good chance that, after discovery and trial, they could show they would.

the housing market in Penfield, or everything which has transpired in 15 years of application of the Penfield zoning ordinance, including every housing plan suggested and refused. To require them to allege such facts is to require them to prove their case on paper in order to get into court at all, reverting to the form of fact-pleading long abjured in the federal courts. ∗ ∗ ∗[d]

SIMON v. EASTERN KY. WELFARE RIGHTS ORG., 426 U.S. 26, 96 S.Ct. 1917, 48 L.Ed.2d 450 (1976), per POWELL, J., held that respondents—including persons who had been denied hospital services because of their indigency—had no standing to sue the Secretary of the Treasury under APA § 10 on the ground that a new Revenue Ruling, which granted favorable tax treatment to hospitals despite their refusal to give full service to indigents, was contrary to the Internal Revenue Code: "[T]he constitutional standing requirement under [APA § 10 requires] allegations which, if true, would establish that the plaintiff had been injured in fact by the action he sought to have reviewed. [The] necessity that the plaintiff who seeks to invoke judicial power stand to profit in some personal interest remains an Art. III requirement." Relying on *Warth*, the Court reasoned that "Art. III still requires that a federal court act only to redress injury that fairly can be traced to the challenged action of the defendant, and not injury that results from the independent action of some third party not before the court.[b]

"The complaint here alleged only that petitioners, by the adoption of Revenue Ruling 69–545, had 'encouraged' hospitals to deny service to indigents. The implicit corollary of this allegation is that a grant of respondents' requested relief, resulting in a requirement that all hospitals serve indigents as a condition to favorable tax treatment, would 'discourage' hospitals from denying their services to respondents. But it [is] purely speculative whether the denials of service specified in the complaint fairly can be traced to petitioners' 'encouragement' or instead result from decisions made by the hospitals without regard to the tax implications.

"It is equally speculative whether the desired exercise of the court's remedial powers in this suit would result in the availability to respondents of such services. So far as the complaint sheds light, it is just as plausible that the hospitals to which respondents may apply for service would elect to forego favorable tax treatment to avoid the undetermined financial drain of an increase in the level of uncompensated services." Accordingly, the complaint should be dismissed.[c]

---

d. The dissenting opinion of Douglas, J., is omitted.

b. The Court recognized "Congress' power to create new interests the invasion of which will confer standing. See *Trafficante*. [But when] Congress has so acted, the requirements of Art. III remain: 'the plaintiff still must allege a distinct and palpable injury to himself, even if it is an injury shared by a large class of other possible litigants.' *Warth*. See also *SCRAP*; cf. *Sierra Club*."

Must the "distinct and palpable injury" alleged by plaintiff at the time suit is filed continue throughout the litigation? See *United States Parole Comm'n v. Geraghty*, fn. g, Part I, supra.

c. Stewart, J., joined the Court's opinion, adding "that I cannot now imagine a case, at least outside the First Amendment area, where a person whose own tax liability was not affected ever could have standing to litigate the federal tax liability of someone else."

See also *Los Angeles v. Lyons*, 461 U.S. 95, 103 S.Ct. 1660, 75 L.Ed.2d 675 (1983) (although person who was subject to allegedly unconstitutional "chokehold" by police after being stopped for traffic violation has standing to sue for damages, that does not constitute sufficiently real and immediate threat of future injury to justify federal injunctive relief). Marshall, J., joined by Brennan, Blackmun and Stevens, JJ., dissented. For criticism of

BRENNAN, J., joined by Marshall, J., dissented from the Court's reasoning: "Any prudential, nonconstitutional considerations that underlay the Court's disposition of the injury in fact standing requirement in cases such as *Linda R.S.* and *Warth* are simply inapposite when review is sought under a congressionally enacted statute conferring standing and providing for judicial review. In such a case considerations respecting 'the allocation of power at the national level [and] a shift away from a democratic form of government,' *Richardson* (Powell, J., concurring), are largely ameliorated. * * *

"Our previous decisions concerning standing to sue under the Administrative Procedure Act conclusively show that the injury in fact demanded is the constitutional minimum identified in *Baker v. Carr*—the allegation of such a 'personal stake in the outcome of the controversy as to ensure' concrete adverseness. *Sierra Club.* True, the Court has required that the person seeking review allege that he personally has suffered or will suffer the injury sought to be avoided, *Sierra Club.* But there can be no doubt that respondents here, by demonstrating a connection between the disputed ruling and the hospitals affecting them, could have adequately served the policy implicated by the pleading requirement of *Sierra Club*—putting 'the decision as to whether review will be sought in the hands of those who have a direct stake in the outcome.' In such a case respondents would not be attempting merely to 'vindicate their own value preferences through the judicial process.' * * *

"Furthermore, our decisions regarding standing to sue in actions brought under the Administrative Procedure Act make plain that standing is not to be denied merely because [the] administrative action ultimately affects the complaining party only through responses to incentives by third parties * * *. *SCRAP.* And the ultimate harm to respondents threatened here is obviously much more 'direct and perceptible' and the 'line of causation' less 'attenuated' than that found sufficient for standing in *SCRAP.* * * *

"Of course the most disturbing aspect of today's opinion is the Court's insistence on resting its decision regarding standing squarely on the irreducible Art. III minimum of injury in fact, thereby effectively placing its holding beyond congressional power to rectify. Thus, any time Congress chooses to legislate in favor of certain interests by setting up a scheme of incentives for third parties, judicial review of administrative action that allegedly frustrates the congressionally intended objective will be denied, because any complainant will be required to make an almost impossible showing."

In ALLEN v. WRIGHT, 468 U.S. 737, 104 S.Ct. 3315, 82 L.Ed.2d 556 (1984), parents of black public school children in districts in the process of desegregating brought a "nationwide class action" seeking (1) a declaratory judgment that IRS guidelines and procedures were inadequate "to fulfill its obligation to deny tax-exempt status to racially discriminatory private schools," and (2) an injunction requiring the IRS to deny tax exemptions to a greater number of private schools. The Court, per O'CONNOR, J., held that respondents had no standing.

First, as for their "claim of stigmatic injury, or denigration, suffered by all members of a racial group when the Government discriminates on the basis of race," respondents "do not allege a stigmatic injury suffered as a direct result of having personally been denied equal treatment. [If] the abstract stigmatic

Lyons, see Fallon, Of Justiciability, Remedies, and Public Law Litigation: Notes on the Ju- *risprudence of Lyons,* 59 N.Y.U.L.Rev. 1 (1984); Tribe, *Constitutional Choices* 99 (1985).

injury were cognizable, standing would extend nationwide to all members of the particular racial groups against which the Government was alleged to be discriminating by its grant of tax exemption to a racially discriminatory school, regardless of the location of that school. * * * Constitutional limits on the role of federal courts preclude [this]."

Second, as for their claim "that the federal tax exemptions to racially discriminatory private schools in their communities impair their ability to have their public schools desegregated," under *Eastern Ky.*, the "injury alleged is not fairly traceable to the Government conduct respondents challenge": "The diminished ability of respondent's children to receive a desegregated education would be fairly traceable to unlawful IRS grants of tax exemptions only if there were enough racially discriminatory private schools receiving tax exemptions in respondents' communities for withdrawal of those exemptions to make an appreciable difference in public-school integration. Respondents have made no such allegation. It is, first, uncertain how many racially discriminatory private schools are in fact receiving tax exemptions. Moreover, it is entirely speculative [whether] withdrawal of a tax exemption from any particular school would lead the school to change its policies. It is just as speculative whether any given parent of a child attending such a private school would decide to transfer the child to public school as a result of any changes in educational or financial policy made by the private school once it was threatened with loss of tax-exempt status. It is also pure speculation whether, in a particular community, a large enough number of the numerous relevant school officials and parents would reach decisions that collectively would have a significant impact on the racial composition of the public schools.

"[R]espondents' complaint, which aims at nationwide relief and does not challenge particular identified unlawful IRS actions, alleges no connection between the asserted desegregation injury and the challenged IRS conduct direct enough to overcome the substantial separation-of-powers barriers to a suit seeking an injunction to reform administrative procedures."

BRENNAN, J., dissented: "Viewed in light of the injuries they claim, the respondents have alleged a direct causal relationship between the government action they challenge and the injury they suffer: their inability to receive an education in a racially integrated school is directly and adversely affected by the tax-exempt status granted by the IRS to racially discriminatory schools in their respective school districts. Commonsense alone would recognize that the elimination of tax-exempt status for racially discriminatory private schools would serve to lessen the impact that those institutions have in defeating efforts to desegregate the public schools. [With] all due respect, the Court has either misread the complaint or is improperly requiring the respondents to prove their case on the merits in order to defeat a motion to dismiss. For example, the respondents specifically refer by name to at least 32 private schools that discriminate on the basis of race and yet continue to benefit illegally from tax-exempt status. Eighteen of those schools [are] located in [Memphis] which has been the subject of several court orders to desegregate. * * * [6]

"[By] interposing its own version of pleading formalities between the respondents and the federal courts, the Court not only has denied access to litigants who properly seek vindication of their constitutional rights, but has also ignored

---

6. Even if the Court were correct in its conclusion that there is an insufficient factual basis alleged in the complaint, the proper dis- position would be to remand in order to afford the respondents an opportunity to amend their complaint.

the important historical role that the courts have played in the Nation's efforts to eliminate racial discrimination from our schools."

STEVENS, J., joined by Blackmun, J., agreeing with Brennan, J.'s general analysis, also dissented: "If racially discriminatory private schools lose the 'cash grants' that flow from the operation of the statutes, the education they provide will become more expensive and hence less of their services will be purchased [, thus] reducing their competitiveness for parents seeking 'a racially segregated alternative' to public schools, which is what respondents have alleged many white parents in desegregating school districts seek. [Thus], the laws of economics * * * compel the conclusion that the injury respondents have alleged—the increased segregation of their children's schools because of the ready availability of private schools that admit whites only—will be redressed if these schools' operations are inhibited through the denial of preferential tax treatment.[6]"[a]

Marshall, J., did not participate.

Notes and Questions

1. *"Causation."* How broad are the consequences for the law of standing of the "causation" requirement imposed by *Warth, Eastern Ky.* and *Allen?* Consider 90 Harv.L.Rev. 210 (1976): "As a practical matter, the [requirement] will be largely insignificant in most cases in which private parties seek review of government actions. Where the plaintiff sues the government for an injury inflicted directly by an agency, it is axiomatic that any causation requirement is satisfied and that a court order to the government will affect the alleged harm. Indeed, only in those cases in which a plaintiff sues the government to complain of an injury suffered as a result of the impact of government action on third parties not before the court will the causation/relief issue arise."

2. *Congressional power and Art. III.* (a) Given *Trafficante* and *SCRAP,* to what extent does *Eastern Ky.* limit congressional power to grant standing? For example, suppose Congress authorized "any citizen" to challenge the constitutionality of armed forces reserve status for members of Congress (*Reservists*), or the constitutionality of the secrecy provisions of the CIA Act (*Richardson*)? Any citizen who alleges that such policies diminish his "ability to persuade a member of Congress to vote in a particular way"? Would such litigants allege "concrete harm" (*Reservists*)? A "distinct and palpable injury" (*Eastern Ky.,* fn. b)? What is the significance of *Warth's* categorizing the "generalized grievance" obstacle to standing as "prudential" rather than "constitutional"? See Bice, *Congress' Power to Confer Standing in the Federal Courts,* in Constitutional Government in America 291 (Collins ed. 1980); Nichol, *Standing on the Constitution: The Supreme Court and Valley Forge,* 61 N.C.L.Rev. 798 (1983).

---

6. [W]hile here the source of the causal nexus is the price that white parents must pay to obtain a segregated education, which is inextricably intertwined with the school's tax status, in *Eastern Ky.* the plaintiffs were seeking free care, which hospitals could decide not to provide for any number of reasons unrelated to their tax status. Moreover, in *Eastern Ky.,* the hospitals had to spend money in order to obtain charitable status. Therefore, they had an economic incentive to forego preferential treatment. [Here] the financial incentives run in only one direction.

a. Stevens, J. "doubt[ed] that a nationwide class would be appropriate, but at this stage respondents' allegations of injury must be taken as true, and hence we must assume that respondents can prove the existence of a nationwide policy and its alleged effects."

Is such proof provided by "commonsense alone" (Brennan, J.) or by "the laws of economics" (Stevens, J.)?

(b) What result in *Eastern Ky.* if respondents had sued under a statute specifically conferring standing on such persons instead of under APA § 10 which authorizes judicial review only for persons "adversely affected or aggrieved by agency action"? What result after *Allen* if Congress authorizes "any member of a minority racial group" to challenge "any government discrimination against that group"? If Congress believes that the case-or-controversy requirement is satisfied, should (must) the Court defer (at least to some degree) to the legislative determination? See fn. b in *Trafficante;* cf. *Marbury v. Madison.* Even if the Court agrees that a congressionally authorized suit satisfies Art. III, must the Court decide it despite its own reservations based on "prudential" principles of "self-restraint"? See Monaghan, *Constitutional Adjudication: The Who and When,* 82 Yale L.J. 1363 (1973).

(c) Of what significance is the fact that the question presented—with or without congressional authorization—is constitutional (as in *Richardson* and *Reservists*) rather than one only of statutory interpretation (as in *Trafficante* and *SCRAP*)? That the Court "is asked to undertake constitutional adjudication, the most important and delicate of its responsibilities" (*Reservists*)? That the Court "has followed a policy of strict necessity in disposing of constitutional issues" (*Ashwander*)? Compare Scott, *Standing in the Supreme Court—A Functional Analysis,* 86 Harv.L.Rev. 645 (1973) with Broderick, *The Warth Optional Standing Doctrine: Return to Judicial Supremacy?* 25 Cath.U.L.Rev. 467 (1976). See note 4 after *Poe v. Ullman,* Part C infra.

B. ASSERTION OF THIRD PARTY RIGHTS

BARROWS v. JACKSON, 346 U.S. 249, 73 S.Ct. 1031, 97 L.Ed. 1586 (1953): A homeowner who had agreed with other homeowners in the neighborhood, by signing a restrictive covenant, not to sell her home to a Negro, broke the covenant and was sued for damages for breach by a co-covenantor. Earlier, *Shelley v. Kraemer*, Ch. 12, Sec. 3, had held "that racial restrictive covenants could not be enforced [by injunction] against Negro purchasers because such enforcement would constitute state action denying equal protection of the laws to the Negroes."

The Court, per MINTON, J., first held that "if a state court awards damages for breach of a restrictive covenant, a prospective seller of restricted land will either refuse to sell to non-Caucasians or else will require non-Caucasions to pay a higher price," thus violating the equal protection rights of non-Caucasions. But "no non-Caucasion is before the Court," only the Caucasian signatories to the covenant.

"Ordinarily, one may not claim standing in this Court to vindicate the constitutional rights of some third party [even] though [the person before the Court] will suffer a direct substantial injury." "But in the instant case, we are faced with a unique situation in which it is the action of the state *court* which might result in a denial of constitutional rights and in which it would be difficult if not impossible for the persons whose rights are asserted to present their grievance before any court. Under the peculiar circumstances of this case, we believe the reasons which underlie our rule denying standing to raise another's rights, which is only a rule of practice, are outweighed by the need to protect the fundamental rights which would be denied by permitting the damages action to be maintained."

The Court observed that restrictive covenants are "widely condemned by the courts" and that the selling homeowner "is the only effective adversary of the unworthy covenant in its last stand."[a]

GRISWOLD v. CONNECTICUT, p. 312 supra, held that birth control clinic officials convicted of abetting married persons in violating the same statute barring use of contraceptives, had standing to assert the constitutional rights of the married persons: "Certainly the accessory should have standing to assert that the offense which he is charged with assisting is not, or cannot constitutionally be a crime. [The] rights of husband and wife, pressed here, are likely to be diluted or adversely affected unless those rights are considered in a suit involving those who have this kind of confidential relation to them."

EISENSTADT v. BAIRD, p. 324 supra, held that a person, convicted for violating a statute forbidding distribution of contraceptive materials to unmarried persons, had standing to assert the constitutional rights of the unmarried persons: "Enforcement of the Massachusetts statute will materially impair the ability of single persons to obtain contraceptives."

Consider Hart & Wechsler's *The Federal Courts and the Federal System* 190 (2d ed. 1973): "Isn't the real question whether the constitutional right of unmarried persons to have contraceptives—if it exists—substantively implies constitutional protection against conviction for supplying contraceptives to such persons? [I]f the state cannot constitutionally prohibit unmarried persons from possessing and using contraceptives, the question whether it can nevertheless prohibit distribution to them depends, does it not, on the substantive scope and purpose of the constitutional policy involved? And doesn't the formulation of the issue in terms of whether a defendant has standing to raise the rights of recipients obscure the true nature of the issue?"

In SINGLETON v. WULFF, 428 U.S. 106, 96 S.Ct. 2868, 49 L.Ed.2d 826 (1976), BLACKMUN, J., joined by Brennan, White and Marshall, JJ., ruled that doctors—who alleged that they "provided, and anticipate providing abortions to welfare patients who are eligible for Medicaid"—had standing to challenge a statute denying Medicaid benefits for abortions:

"A. [The] physicians suffer concrete injury from the operation of the challenged statute. [The] relationship between the parties is classically adverse, and there clearly exists [a] case or controversy in the constitutional sense.

"B. [T]he Court of Appeals also accorded the doctors standing to assert [the] rights of their patients. * * *

"[T]he Court has looked primarily to two factual elements to determine whether the [general rule against assertion of third party rights] should apply in a particular case. The first is the relationship of the litigant to the person whose right he seeks to assert. If the enjoyment of the right is inextricably bound up with the activity the litigant wishes to pursue, the court at least can be sure that its construction of the right is not unnecessary in the sense that the right's enjoyment will be unaffected by the outcome of the suit. Furthermore, the relationship between the litigant and the third party may be such that the former is fully, or very nearly, as effective a proponent of the right as the latter. [See *Griswold; Eisenstadt; Barrows.*][a]

---

a. Vinson, C.J., dissented. Reed and Jackson, JJ., did not participate.

a. For cases upholding the standing of sellers, in actions in which they were plaintiffs

"The other factual element to which the Court has looked is the ability of the third party to assert his own right. Even where the relationship is close, the reasons for requiring persons to assert their own rights will generally still apply. If there is some genuine obstacle to such assertion, however, the third party's absence from court loses its tendency to suggest that his right is not truly at stake, or truly important to him, and the party who is in court becomes by the default the right's best available proponent. [See *Eisenstadt; Barrows.*] [6]

"Application of these principles to the present case quickly yields its proper result. The closeness of the relationship is patent. [A] woman cannot safely secure an abortion without the aid of a physician, and an impecunious woman cannot easily secure an abortion without the physician's being paid by the State.

* * *

"As to the woman's assertion of her own rights, there are several obstacles. For one thing she may be chilled from such assertion by a desire to protect the very privacy of her decision from the publicity of a court suit. A second obstacle is [that in only] a few months, at the most, after the maturing of the decision to undergo an abortion, her right thereto will have been irrevocably lost, assuming, as it seems fair to assume, that unless the impecunious woman can establish Medicaid eligibility she must forgo abortion. It is true that these obstacles are not insurmountable. Suit may be brought under a pseudonym, as so frequently has been done. A woman who is no longer pregnant may nonetheless retain the right to litigate the point because it is 'capable of repetition yet evading review.' *Roe v. Wade.* And it may be that a class could be assembled, whose fluid membership always included some women with live claims. But if the assertion of the right is to be 'representative' to such an extent anyway, there seems little loss in terms of effective advocacy from allowing its assertion by a physician." [b]

POWELL, J., joined by Burger, C.J., and Stewart and Rehnquist, JJ., agreed with Part A but dissented as to Part B because "of whether it is prudent to proceed to decision on particular issues even at the instance of a party whose Art. III standing is clear. * * * [T]he litigation of third-party rights cannot be justified in this case. [T]he 'obstacles' identified by the plurality as justifying departure from the general rule simply are not significant."

---

seeking declaratory and injunctive relief, see *Craig v. Boren,* p. 1000 supra (seller of beer has standing to assert males' equal protection claim against law prohibiting sale of beer to males under age 21 and females under age 18) and *Carey v. Population Services Int'l,* p. 326 supra (seller of contraceptives has standing to assert potential purchasers' right of privacy claims against law regulating distribution of contraceptives). These cases reasoned that if the sellers could not challenge the laws they would be deterred from selling the products and that this "would result indirectly in the violation of third parties' rights."

6. Mr. Justice Powell objects [that] our prior cases allow assertion of third party rights only when such assertion by the third parties themselves would be "in all practicable terms impossible." Carefully analyzed, our cases do not go that far. The Negro real-estate pur-

chaser in *Barrows,* if he could prove that the racial covenant alone stood in the way of his purchase (as presumably he could easily have done, given the amicable posture of the seller in that case), could surely have sought a declaration of its invalidity or an injunction against its enforcement. [The] recipients of contraceptives in *Eisenstadt* (or their counterparts in *Griswold* and *Doe,* for that matter) could have sought similar relief as necessary to the enjoyment of their constitutional rights. The point is not that these were easy alternatives, but that they differed only in the degree of difficulty, if they differed at all, from the alternative in this case of the women themselves seeking a declaration or injunction that would force the State to pay the doctors for their abortions.

b. Stevens, J., concurred in the result but not all of the reasoning in Part B.

C. TIMING OF ADJUDICATION

UNITED PUBLIC WORKERS v. MITCHELL, 330 U.S. 75, 67 S.Ct. 556, 91 L.Ed.2d 754 (1947): Appellants, federal civil service employees, sought a federal declaratory judgment that the Hatch Act's prohibition against taking "any active part in political management or in political campaigns" violated their first amendment rights. They also requested injunctive relief. Only one appellant (Poole) had actually violated the Act. The others alleged that they desired to do so by, inter alia, serving as party officials, writing articles and circulating petitions to support candidates, acting as poll watchers, transporting voters to the polls.[a] The Court, per REED, J., held that "these appellants seem clearly to seek advisory opinions" and that "the facts of their personal interest in their civil rights, of the general threat of possible interference with those rights by the Civil Service Commission under its rules, if specified things are done by appellants, does not make a justiciable case or controversy. * * * We can only speculate as to the kinds of political activity the appellants desire to engage in or as to the contents of their proposed public statements or the circumstances of their publication. [Such] generality of objection is really an attack on the political expediency of the Hatch Act, not the presentation of legal issues. It is beyond the competence of courts to render such a decision. [No] threat of interference by the Commission with rights of these appellants appears beyond that implied by the existence of the law and the regulations [and a] hypothetical threat is not enough."

Poole, however, "has been charged by the Commission with political activity and a proposed order for his removal from his position adopted subject to his right under Commission procedure to reply * * *. Since Poole admits that he violated the rule against political activity and that removal from office is therefore mandatory under the [act], we see no reason why a declaratory judgment action, even though constitutional issues are involved, does not lie." The Court then rejected Poole's challenge on the merits.

DOUGLAS, J., filed the principal dissent: "What these appellants propose to do is plain enough. If they do what they propose to do, it is clear that they will be discharged * * *. The threat against them is real not fanciful, immediate not remote. The case is therefore an actual not a hypothetical one. [T]o require these employees first to suffer the hardship of a discharge is not only to make them incur a penalty; it makes inadequate, if not wholly illusory, any legal remedy which they may have. Men who must sacrifice their means of livelihood in order to test their rights to their jobs must either pursue prolonged and expensive litigation as unemployed persons or pull up their roots, change their life careers, and seek employment in other fields. At least to the average person in the lower income groups the burden of taking that course is irreparable injury[4] * * *."[b]

---

a. One did allege that, at the last congressional election, he wanted to be a poll watcher but was informed by a Civil Service Commission official "that if I used my watcher's certificate, the Civil Service Commission would see that I was dismissed from my job." This matter, the Court found, "had long been moot when this complaint was filed."

4. If the prayer for declaratory relief be considered separately from the prayer for an injunction, as it may be, allegations of irreparable injury threatened are not required.

b. Black, J., agreed with Douglas, J. "that all the petitioners' complaints state a case or controversy" and further that "the challenged provision is unconstitutional on its face." Rutledge, J., agreed with Black, J., as to Poole; as to the others, however, the controversy "is not yet appropriate for the discretionary exercise of declaratory judgment jurisdiction."

Notes and Questions

1. *The Court's rationale.* Specifically, what more could appellants have done? Does the majority accept the proposition that "what these appellants propose to do is plain enough [and] if they do what they propose to do, it is clear that they will be discharged"? If not, should appellants have written their proposed speeches and letters and submitted them to the Court? Or should they have first submitted them to the Commission? Suppose the Commission took the position that it would not give "advisory opinions"? Or is the Court's requirement that all cases must be as "ripe" as Poole's in order to be adjudicated?

2. ADLER v. BOARD OF EDUC., (1952), p. 570 supra, upheld a state law disqualifying from employment in public schools any persons who advocate overthrow of the government by force, or who belong to an organization which so advocates, or who utter any treasonable or seditious words, or do any treasonable or seditious acts. Appellants seeking a declaratory judgment in state court were taxpayers, parents of attending school children, and teachers. The Court discussed only the merits despite FRANKFURTER, J.'s dissent that the case should be dismissed for want of "standing of the parties and ripeness of the constitutional question." In addition to arguing that both the scope of the statutory provisions and the definition of key terms were unclear, he stated: "The allegations in the present action fall short of those found insufficient in [*Mitchell*]. These teachers do not allege that they have engaged in proscribed conduct or that they have any intention to do so. They do not suggest that they have been, or are, deterred from supporting causes or from joining organizations for fear of the [statute's] interdict, except to say generally that the system complained of will have this effect on teachers as a group. They do not assert that they are threatened with action under the law, or that steps are imminent whereby they would incur the hazard of punishment for conduct innocent at the time."

Was *Mitchell* "overruled"?[c] Consider Scharpf, *Judicial Review and the Political Question: A Functional Analysis,* 75 Yale L.J. 517, 528–32 (1966): "[T]he public interest in responsible and realistic constitutional decision is much too serious to be left unprotected against the accidents of ordinary litigation. If this protection cannot be afforded by an enlargement of the Court's jurisdiction to permit the most competent parties to sue, or by an enlargement of the Court's procedural powers to conduct an independent investigation of facts and issues, then it seems reasonable to expect that this protection will be provided by restrictive techniques which will permit the Court to screen the cases in order to select those which provide an adequate basis for the responsible performance of the reviewing function. In order to qualify for the exercise of judicial review, the factual situation of the case would have to illuminate in a concrete fashion the practical implications of the constitutional issue, and the litigants themselves would have to be vitally and antagonistically interested, not only in the outcome of their lawsuit, but in the determination of the constitutional issue as such. I submit that it is this screening function which is being served by the Court's use of the nonconstitutional rules of standing, ripeness and adversariness. [In *Mitchell*] the Court may well have regarded the constitutional balance

Frankfurter, J., concurred in the Court's opinion. Murphy and Jackson, JJ., took no part.

c. Note the 1973 description of *Mitchell* in *United States Civil Service Comm'n v. National Ass'n of Letter Carriers,* p. 734 supra (again upholding the Hatch Act): "[*Mitchell*] determined that with respect to all but one of the plaintiffs there was no case or controversy present within the meaning of Art. III."

between the political rights of civil servants and the legitimate public interest in a neutral civil service as an extremely close one, depending very much upon the actual scope of enforcement and upon the concrete nature of the activities against which sanctions were to be applied. In [*Adler*], the *Mitchell* rule should have applied a fortiori. [But, for the Court majority,] the statute was clearly constitutional * * *. Justices Black and Douglas, dissenting, also saw no reason to worry about standing or ripeness. For them the statute was clearly unconstitutional * * *.[d] The conclusion seems inevitable that Justice Frankfurter alone advocated avoidance because he alone defined the substantive issues in terms of a close balance between the equally legitimate interests of society in its self-preservation and of the teachers in their freedom of thought, inquiry and expression. Thus, in order to strike this balance in the particular case, Frankfurter would have had to know much more about the actual practices of enforcement and the degree of surveillance to which the teachers would be subjected than the bare text of an unenforced statute permitted him to know." See also Albert, note 1 after *Reservists,* at 1158–60.

  3. *The discretionary exercise of declaratory judgment jurisdiction.* Should this be influenced by the fact that a constitutional question is involved? See Goldberg-Ambrose, *Access to the Federal Courts in Constitutional Cases,* in Constitutional Government in America 311 (Collins ed. 1980). That the case arises in a state court (*Adler*) rather than a federal court (*Mitchell*)? That the case concerns a state statute rather than a federal statute? Is the *difficulty* of the constitutional question a relevant inquiry? The matter of how *many* people, other than the litigants, will be affected by decision? See *Golden v. Zwickler,* 394 U.S. 103, 89 S.Ct. 956, 22 L.Ed.2d 113 (1969). The nature of the asserted constitutional right? The fact that Congress wishes a determination of constitutionality as quickly as possible? See *Buckley v. Valeo,* 424 U.S. 1, 113–18, 96 S.Ct. 612, 680–82, 46 L.Ed.2d 659 (1976). Whether the Court is inclined to hold the statute valid or invalid? Do some (all) of these questions go beyond the "principled" discretion of the Court? See note 4 after *Poe v. Ullman,* infra. See generally Varat, supra.

LAIRD v. TATUM

408 U.S. 1, 92 S.Ct. 2318, 33 L.Ed.2d 154 (1972).

  Mr. Chief Justice Burger delivered the opinion of the Court.

  Respondents brought this class action in the District Court seeking declaratory and injunctive relief on their claim that their rights were being invaded by the Army's alleged "surveillance of lawful civilian political activity." * * *

  The system put into operation as a result of the Army's 1967 experience [with civil disorders] consisted essentially of the collection of information about public activities that were thought to have at least some potential for civil disorder, the reporting of that information to Army Intelligence headquarters at Fort Holabird, Maryland, the dissemination of these reports from headquarters to major Army posts around the country, and the storage of the reported information in a computer data bank located at Fort Holabird. [T]he principal sources of information were the news media and publications in general circulation. Some of the information came from Army Intelligence agents who attended meetings that were open to the public and who wrote field reports describing the meetings, giving such data as the name of the sponsoring organization, the

  d. For detailed consideration of the question of whether laws allegedly violative of the first amendment should be held "void on their face," see p. 515 supra.

identity of speakers, the approximate number of persons in attendance, and an indication of whether any disorder occurred. And still other information was provided to the Army by civilian law enforcement agencies. * * *

By early 1970 [the] Army, in the course of a review of the system, ordered a significant reduction in its scope[:] "[R]eports [will] be limited [to] outbreaks of violence or incidents with a high potential for violence beyond the capability of state and local police and the National Guard to control. These reports [will] not be placed in a computer [and] are destroyed 60 days after publication or 60 days after the end of the disturbance. This limited reporting system will ensure that the Army is prepared to respond to whatever directions the President may issue in civil disturbance situations and without watching lawful activities of civilians." * * *[5]

In reversing, the Court of Appeals noted that [respondents] "freely admit that they complain of no specific action of the Army against them. [There] is no evidence of illegal or unlawful surveillance activities. [So] far as is yet shown, the information gathered is nothing more than a good newspaper reporter would be able to gather by attendance at public meetings and the clipping of articles from publications available on any newsstand."

[T]he Court of Appeals [also] had this to say: "[While respondents] do indeed argue that in the future it is possible that information relating to matters far beyond the responsibilities of the military may be misused by the military to the detriment of these [respondents], yet [respondents] do not attempt to establish this as a definitely foreseeable event, or to base their complaint on this ground. Rather, [respondents] contend that the *present existence of this system* of gathering and distributing information, allegedly far beyond the mission requirements of the Army, constitutes an impermissible burden on [respondents] and other persons similarly situated which exercises a *present inhibiting effect* on their full expression and utilization of their First Amendment rights." * * *

In recent years this Court has found in a number of cases that constitutional violations may arise from the deterrent, or "chilling," effect of governmental regulations that fall short of a direct prohibition against the exercise of First Amendment rights. E.g., *Keyishian v. Board of Regents*, [p. 733 supra]. In none of these cases, however, did the chilling effect arise merely from the individual's knowledge that a governmental agency was engaged in certain activities or from the individual's concomitant fear that, armed with the fruits of those activities, the agency might in the future take some *other* and additional action detrimental to that individual. Rather, in each of these cases, the challenged exercise of governmental power was regulatory, proscriptive, or compulsory in nature, and the complainant was either presently or prospectively subject to the regulations, proscriptions, or compulsions * * *.

[T]hese decisions have in no way eroded the "established principle that to entitle a private individual to invoke the judicial power to determine the validity of executive or legislative action he must show that he has sustained or is immediately in danger of sustaining a direct injury as the result of that action."

---

5. In the course of the oral argument, the District Judge [asked] what exactly it was in the Army's activities that tended to chill respondents and others in the exercise of their constitutional rights. Counsel responded that it was "precisely the threat in this case that *in some future civil disorder* of some kind, the Army is going to come in with its list of trouble-makers [and] go rounding up people and putting them in military prisons somewhere." (Emphasis added.) To this the court responded that "we still sit here with the writ of habeas corpus." At another point, counsel for respondents took a somewhat different approach in arguing that "*we're not quite sure exactly what they have in mind* and that is precisely what causes [the] chilling effect." (Emphasis added.)

The respondents do not meet this test; [their] alleged "chilling" effect may perhaps be seen as arising from respondents' very perception of the system as inappropriate to the Army's role under our form of government, or as arising from respondents' beliefs that it is inherently dangerous for the military to be concerned with activities in the civilian sector, or as arising from respondents' less generalized yet speculative apprehensiveness that the Army may at some future date misuse the information in some way that would cause direct harm to respondents.[7] Allegations of a subjective "chill" are not an adequate substitute for a claim of specific present objective harm or a threat of specific future harm; "the federal courts established pursuant to Article III of the Constitution do not render advisory opinions." *Mitchell.*

Stripped to its essentials, what respondents appear to be seeking is a broad scale investigation, conducted by themselves as private parties armed with the subpoena power of a federal district court and the power of cross-examination, to probe into the Army's intelligence-gathering activities, with the district court determining at the conclusion of that investigation the extent to which those activities may or may not be appropriate to the Army's mission. * * *

Carried to its logical end, this approach would have the federal courts as virtually continuing monitors of the wisdom and soundness of Executive action; such a role is appropriate for the Congress [not for] the judiciary, absent actual present or immediately threatened injury resulting from unlawful governmental action.

[O]n this record the respondents have not presented a case for resolution by the courts. * * *

Reversed.

MR. JUSTICE DOUGLAS, with whom MR. JUSTICE MARSHALL concurs, dissenting.

[When] refusal of the Court to pass on the constitutionality of an Act under the normal consideration of forbearance "would itself have an inhibitory effect on freedom of speech" then the Court will act. * * *

One need not wait to sue until he loses his job or until his reputation is defamed. To withhold standing to sue until that time arrives would in practical effect immunize from judicial scrutiny all surveillance activities regardless of their misuse and their deterrent effect. * * *

The present controversy is not a remote, imaginary conflict. Respondents were targets of the Army's surveillance. First, the surveillance was not casual but massive and comprehensive. Second, the intelligence reports were regularly and widely circulated and were exchanged with reports of the FBI, state and municipal police departments, and the CIA. Third, the Army's surveillance was not collecting material in public records but staking-out teams of agents, infiltrating undercover agents, creating command posts inside meetings, posing as

---

7. Not only have respondents left somewhat unclear the precise connection between the mere existence of the challenged system and their own alleged chill, but they have also cast considerable doubt on whether they themselves are in fact suffering from any such chill. [At] the oral argument before the District Court, counsel for respondents admitted that his clients were "not people, obviously, who are cowed and chilled"; indeed, they were quite willing "to open themselves up to public investigation and public scrutiny."

But, counsel argued, these respondents must "represent millions of Americans not nearly as forward [and] courageous" as themselves. [Even] assuming a justiciable controversy, if respondents themselves are not chilled, but seek only to represent those "millions" whom they believe are so chilled, respondents clearly lack that "personal stake in the outcome of the controversy" essential to standing. [A] litigant "has standing to seek redress for injuries done to him, but may not seek redress for injuries done to others."

press photographers and newsmen, posing as TV newsmen, posing as students, shadowing public figures.

Finally, [reports] of the Army have been "taken from the Intelligence Command's highly inaccurate civil disturbance teletype and filed in Army dossiers on persons who have held, or were being considered for, security clearances, thus contaminating what are supposed to be investigative reports with unverified gossip and rumor. This practice directly jeopardized the employment and employment opportunities of persons seeking sensitive positions with the federal government or defense industry."

[The] fact that since this litigation started the Army's surveillance may have been cut back is not an end of the matter. Whether there has been an actual cutback or whether the announcements are merely a ruse can be determined only after a hearing in the District Court. * * *[a]

Notes and Questions

1. *Consistency with prior decisions.* Does *Tatum* confirm the continued vitality of *Mitchell*? Could it be argued in *Tatum* (as Douglas, J., argued in *Mitchell*) that what respondents "propose to do is plain enough" and if they do so "it is clear that they will be discharged from their positions"? Consider 86 Harv.L.Rev. 134 (1972): "Granted, misuse in the *Tatum* situation is conjectural even after the protected activity is pursued, whereas injury for violation of a regulatory or prohibitive statute is clear and immediate. But the temptation to avoid the protected activity which risks unfavorable consequences may be no less when those consequences are undefined; indeed, it will be all the greater if the lack of definition implies the absence of an upward limit on injury."

To what extent did *Tatum* turn on the fact that respondents sought to speak not simply for themselves but for "millions of Americans not nearly as courageous"? Consider id. at 135: "Any decision on the merits would have required a court to weigh in some fashion the first amendment injury against the sufficiency of the Government's interest in military surveillance. Such an undertaking would have necessitated a determination of the relevance of the information gathered to the alleged governmental interest in the suppression of domestic insurrection without the application of blind force. Since the plaintiffs were bringing a class action seeking an injunction of all military surveillance activity and the destruction of all files unrelated to the Army's legitimate mission, this determination would have required consideration of an enormous bulk of information." Is this factor relevant to the discretionary exercise of declaratory judgment jurisdiction? Does it distinguish *Tatum* from *Mitchell*? From *Alder*? Or does this factor go to the substance of the first amendment's scope? Reconsider Scharpf, note 2 after *Mitchell*.

2. *Remote or hypothetical threat of injury.* (a) In O'SHEA v. LITTLETON, 414 U.S. 488, 94 S.Ct. 669, 38 L.Ed.2d 674 (1974), black and white residents who had protested racial discrimination in Cairo, Illinois obtained a federal injunction against state judicial officers, alleging a deliberate pattern of illegal bail, sentencing and jury fee practices against them due to their race and exercise of first amendment rights. Although some respondents "had actually been defendants in proceedings before petitioners and had suffered from the alleged unconstitutional practices," the Court, per WHITE, J., reversed: "Of course, past wrongs are evidence bearing on whether there is a real and immediate threat of

---

a. Brennan, J., joined by Stewart and Marshall, JJ., also dissented, agreeing with the Court of Appeals that the case was justiciable and respondents had standing.

repeated injury. [But] respondents here have not pointed to any imminent prosecutions contemplated against any of their number and they naturally do not suggest that any one of them expects to violate valid criminal laws. [Thus], the threat of injury from the alleged course of conduct they attack is simply too remote to satisfy the 'case or controversy' requirement and permit adjudication by a federal court." [b]

Even if there were "an existing case or controversy," however, "a proper balance in the concurrent operation of federal and state courts" precludes federal equitable relief. The decision below "would contemplate interruption of state proceedings to adjudicate assertions of noncompliance by petitioners. This seems to us nothing less than an ongoing federal audit of state criminal proceedings [that] is antipathetic to established principles of comity.[c] [Respondents] have failed, moreover, to establish the basic requisites of the issuance of equitable relief in these circumstances—the likelihood of substantial and immediate irreparable injury, and the inadequacy of remedies at law. [I]f any of the respondents are ever prosecuted and face trial, or if they are illegally sentenced, there are available state and federal procedures which could provide relief from the wrongful conduct alleged"—e.g., direct review, collateral relief, and federal criminal prosecution of petitioners.[d]

(b) In DOE v. BOLTON, p. 336 supra, physicians with pregnant patients sought a federal declaratory judgment that a state criminal abortion statute deterred them from practicing their profession in violation of their constitutional rights. The Court, per BLACKMUN, J., held that they "present a justiciable controversy and do have standing despite the fact that the record does not disclose that any one of them has been prosecuted, or threatened with prosecution * * *. The physician is the one against whom these criminal statutes directly operate in the event he procures an abortion that does not meet the statutory exceptions and conditions. [They], therefore, assert a sufficiently direct threat of personal detriment. They should not be required to await and undergo a criminal prosecution as the sole means of seeking relief."

Is *Doe* consistent with *Tatum? O'Shea?*

POE v. ULLMAN

367 U.S. 497, 81 S.Ct. 1752, 6 L.Ed.2d 989 (1961).

MR. JUSTICE FRANKFURTER announced the judgment of the Court and an opinion in which THE CHIEF JUSTICE, MR. JUSTICE CLARK and MR. JUSTICE WHITTAKER join.

These appeals challenge the constitutionality [of] Connecticut statutes [which] prohibit the use of contraceptive devices and the giving of medical advice in the use of such devices. In proceedings seeking declarations of law [brought by married couples and their doctor, the state] court has ruled that these statutes would be applicable in the case of married couples and even under claim

---

b. For similar analysis, see *Rizzo v. Goode,* 423 U.S. 362, 96 S.Ct. 598, 46 L.Ed.2d 561 (1976).

c. Compare *Allee v. Medrano,* 416 U.S. 802, 94 S.Ct. 2191, 40 L.Ed.2d 566 (1974), upholding a federal injunction against state police disruption of unionization efforts. For fuller consideration of the delicacy of federal interference with state criminal proceedings, see Sec. 2, II infra. See also *Rizzo v. Goode,* fn. b,

discussed at 90 Harv.L.Rev. 238 (1976), holding that "principles of equity, comity, and federalism" also restrict federal court supervision of state executive or administrative agencies—in this case, the disciplinary practices of a city police department.

d. Blackmun, J., concurred in the first part of the Court's opinion. Douglas, J., joined by Brennan and Marshall, JJ., dissented.

that conception would constitute a serious threat to the health or life of the female spouse. * * *

Appellants' complaints [do] not clearly, and certainly do not in terms, allege that appellee Ullman threatens to prosecute [them]. The allegations are merely that, in the course of his public duty, he intends to prosecute any offenses against Connecticut law, and that he claims that use of and advice concerning contraceptives would constitute offenses. The lack of immediacy of the threat described by these allegations might alone raise serious questions of non-justiciability of appellants' claims. See *Mitchell*. But even were we to read the allegations to convey a clear threat of imminent prosecutions, we are not bound to accept as true all that is alleged on the face of the complaint and admitted, technically, by demurrer, any more than the Court is bound by stipulation of the parties. Formal agreement between parties that collides with plausibility is too fragile a foundation for indulging in constitutional adjudication.

The Connecticut law prohibiting the use of contraceptives has been on the State's books since 1879. During the more than three-quarters of a century since its enactment, a prosecution for its violation seems never to have been initiated, save in *State v. Nelson,* 126 Conn. 412, 11 A.2d 856. The circumstances of that case, decided in 1940, only prove the abstract character of what is before us. There, a test case was brought to determine the constitutionality of the Act as applied against two doctors and a nurse who had allegedly disseminated contraceptive information. After the Supreme Court of Errors sustained the legislation on appeal from a demurrer to the information, the State moved to dismiss the information. * * * We were advised by counsel for appellants that contraceptives are commonly and notoriously sold in Connecticut drug stores. Yet no prosecutions are recorded; and certainly such ubiquitous, open, public sales would more quickly invite the attention of enforcement officials than the conduct in which the present appellants wish to engage—the giving of private medical advice by a doctor to his individual patients, and their private use of the devices prescribed. The undeviating policy of nullification by Connecticut of its anticontraceptive laws throughout all the long years that they have been on the statute books bespeaks more than prosecutorial paralysis. What was said in another context is relevant here. "Deeply embedded traditional ways of carrying out state policy * * *"—or not carrying it out—"are often tougher and truer law than the dead words of the written text."

The restriction of our jurisdiction to cases and controversies within the meaning of Article III of the Constitution is not the sole limitation on the exercise of our appellate powers, especially in cases raising constitutional questions. The policy reflected in numerous cases and over a long period was thus summarized in the oft-quoted statement of Mr. Justice Brandeis: "The Court [has] developed, for its own governance in the cases confessedly within its jurisdiction, a series of rules under which it has avoided passing upon a large part of all the constitutional questions pressed upon it for decision." In part the rules summarized in the *Ashwander* opinion have derived from the historically defined, limited nature and function of courts and from the recognition that, within the framework of our adversary system, the adjudicatory process is most securely founded when it is exercised under the impact of a lively conflict between antagonistic demands, actively pressed, which make resolution of the controverted issue a practical necessity. * * *

These considerations press with special urgency in cases challenging legislative action or state judicial action as repugnant to the Constitution. [The] various doctrines of "standing," "ripeness," and "mootness," [are] but several manifestations—each having its own "varied application"—of the primary conception that federal judicial power is to be exercised to strike down legislation, whether state or federal, only at the instance of one who is himself immediately harmed, or immediately threatened with harm, by the challenged action. [It] was with respect to a state-originating declaratory judgment proceeding that we said [that] "the discretionary element characteristic of declaratory jurisdiction [offers] a convenient instrument for making * * * effective" the policy against premature constitutional decision. *Rescue Army v. Municipal Court,* [Part II supra, "Introductory Note"].

[If] the prosecutor expressly agrees not to prosecute, a suit against him for declaratory and injunctive relief is not such an adversary case as will be reviewed here. Eighty years of Connecticut history demonstrate a similar, albeit tacit agreement.

[W]e cannot accept, as the basis of constitutional adjudication, other than as chimerical the fear of enforcement of provisions that have during so many years gone uniformly and without exception unenforced.

Justiciability is of course not a legal concept with a fixed content or susceptible of scientific verification. Its utilization is the resultant of many subtle pressures, including the appropriateness of the issues for decision by this Court and the actual hardship to the litigants of denying them the relief sought. Both these factors justify withholding adjudication of the constitutional issue raised under the circumstances and in the manner in which they are now before the Court.

Dismissed.

MR. JUSTICE BLACK dissents because he believes that the constitutional questions should be reached and decided.

MR. JUSTICE BRENNAN, concurring in the judgment.

[The] true controversy in this case is over the opening of birth-control clinics on a large scale; it is that which the State has prevented in the [past]. It will be time enough to decide the constitutional questions urged upon us when, if ever, that real controversy flares up again. * * *

MR. JUSTICE DOUGLAS, dissenting.

[The] Court [goes] outside the record to conclude that there exists a "tacit agreement" that these statutes will not be enforced. No lawyer, I think, would advise his clients to rely on that "tacit agreement." No police official, I think, would feel himself bound by that "tacit agreement." After our national experience during the prohibition era, it would be absurd to pretend that all criminal statutes are adequately enforced. But that does not mean that bootlegging was the less a crime. * * *

When the Court goes outside the record to determine that Connecticut has adopted "The undeviating policy of nullification [of] its anti-contraceptive laws," it selects a particularly poor case in which to exercise such a novel power. This is not a law which is a dead letter. Twice since 1940, Connecticut has reenacted these laws as part of general statutory revisions. Consistently, bills to remove the statutes from the books have been rejected by the legislature. In short, the statutes—far from being the accidental left-overs of another era—are the center of a continuing controversy * * *.

[O]n oral argument, counsel for the appellee stated on his own knowledge that several proprietors had been prosecuted in the "minor police courts of

Connecticut" after they had been "picked up" for selling contraceptives. The enforcement of criminal laws in minor courts has just as much impact as in those cases where appellate courts are resorted to. ⁎ ⁎ ⁎

What are these people—doctor and patients—to do? Flout the law and go to prison? Violate the law surreptitiously and hope they will not get caught? By today's decision we leave them no other alternatives. It is not the choice they need have under the regime of the declaratory judgment ⁎ ⁎ ⁎.

[On the merits, Douglas J., and Harlan, J., in his opinion that follows, argued that the statute was unconstitutional.]

MR. JUSTICE HARLAN, dissenting.

[There] is no lack of "ripeness" [since] appellants have stated in their pleadings fully and unequivocally what it is that they intend to do; no clarifying or resolving contingency stands in their way before they may embark on that conduct. Thus there is no circumstance besides that of detection or prosecution to make remote the particular controversy. And it is clear beyond cavil that the mere fact that a controversy such as this is rendered still more unavoidable by an actual prosecution, is not *alone* sufficient to make the case too remote ⁎ ⁎ ⁎.

[This] is not a feigned, hypothetical, friendly or colorable suit such as discloses "a want of a truly adversary contest." ⁎ ⁎ ⁎ I think both the plurality and concurring opinions confuse [the] predictive likelihood that, had [appellants] not brought themselves to appellee's attention, he would not enforce the statute against them, with some entirely suppositious "tacit agreement" not to prosecute, thereby ignoring the prosecutor's claim, asserted in these very proceedings, of a right, at his unbounded prosecutorial discretion, to enforce the statute. ⁎ ⁎ ⁎

We are brought, then, to the precise failing in these proceedings which is said to justify refusal to exercise our mandatory appellate jurisdiction: that there has been but one recorded Connecticut case dealing with a *prosecution* under the statute. ⁎ ⁎ ⁎ I think it is pure conjecture, and indeed conjecture which to me seems contrary to realities, that an open violation of the statute by a doctor (or more obviously still by a birth-control clinic) would not result in a substantial threat of prosecution. Crucial to the opposite conclusion is the description of the 1940 prosecution instituted in *State v. Nelson* as a "test case" ⁎ ⁎ ⁎. [T]he respect in which *Nelson* was a test case is only that it was brought for the purpose of making entirely clear the State's power and willingness to enforce against "*any* person, whether a physician or layman" (emphasis supplied), the statute and to eliminate from future cases the very doubt about the existence of these elements which had resulted in eight open birth-control clinics, and which would have made unfair the conviction of Nelson.

⁎ ⁎ ⁎ I fear that the Court has indulged in a bit of sleight of hand to be rid of this case. It has treated the significance of the absence of prosecutions during the twenty years since *Nelson* as identical with that of the absence of prosecutions during the years before *Nelson*. It has ignored the fact that the very purpose of the *Nelson* prosecution was to change defiance into compliance. It has ignored the very possibility that this purpose may have been successful. ⁎ ⁎ ⁎

The Court's disposition assumes that to decide the case now, in the absence of any consummated prosecutions, is unwise because it forces a difficult decision in advance of any exigent necessity therefor. [D]espite speculation as to a "tacit agreement" that this law will not be enforced, there is, of course, no suggestion of an estoppel against the State if it should attempt to prosecute appellants. Neither the plurality nor the concurring opinion suggests that appellants have some legally cognizable right not to be prosecuted if the statute is Constitutional. What is meant is simply that the appellants are more or less free to act without fear of prosecution because the prosecuting authorities of the State, in their discretion and at their whim, are, as a matter of prediction, unlikely to decide to prosecute.

Here is the core of my disagreement with the present disposition. [T]he most substantial claim which these married persons press is their right to enjoy the privacy of their marital relations free of the enquiry of the criminal law, whether it be in a prosecution of them or of a doctor whom they have consulted. And I cannot agree that their enjoyment of this privacy is not substantially impinged upon, when they are told that if they use contraceptives, indeed whether they do so or not, the only thing which stands between them and being forced to render criminal account of their marital privacy is the whim of the prosecutor. [Indeed] it appears that whereas appellants would surely have been entitled to review were this a new statute [the] State here is enabled to maintain at least some substantial measure of compliance with this statute and still obviate any review in this Court, by the device of purely discretionary prosecutorial inactivity. It seems to me to destroy the whole purpose of anticipatory relief to consider the prosecutor's discretion, once all legal and administrative channels have been cleared, as in any way analogous to those other contingencies which make remote a controversy presenting Constitutional claims. * * *

MR. JUSTICE STEWART, dissenting.

For the reasons so convincingly advanced by both Mr. Justice Douglas and Mr. Justice Harlan, I join them in dissenting from the dismissal of these appeals.

* * * *[a]

Notes and Questions

1. *The Court's rationale.* (a) Does *Poe* undermine the idea that law—good or bad—is to be obeyed? Or does it take the position that the Connecticut statutes were not really "*law*"? Does *Poe* ignore the fact that some (many?) people wish to (will?) obey the law simply because it is "the law," whether or not it will ever be enforced?

(b) Was the law not "a dead letter [because] consistently, bills to remove the statutes from the books have been rejected by the legislature"? Consider Bickel, *The Passive Virtues,* 75 Harv.L.Rev. 40, 63 (1961): "[G]reater strength must be mobilized to repeal a statute than to resist its enactment. When the law is consistently not enforced, the chance of mustering opposition sufficient to move the legislature is reduced to the vanishing point. For consistent failure to enforce is itself a political concession to the opposition, and will satisfy at least some portions of it. [The] unenforced statute is not, in the normal way, a continuing reflection of the balance of political pressures."

2. Is *Poe* distinguishable from *Epperson v. Arkansas,* p. 809 supra, where there was no record of enforcement of a forty year old statute making the teaching of evolution unlawful and, after her school adopted a textbook teaching evolution, a biology teacher sought a declaration that the statute was unconstitutional and an injunction against her dismissal?

a. For a further constitutional test, see *Griswold v. Connecticut,* p. 312 supra.

3. *"Discretionary" dismissal of appeals.* Was the disposition in *Poe* inconsistent with the fact that the case came to the Court on appeal, thus within the "obligatory jurisdiction" (Ch. 1, Sec. 4)? Consider Comment, *Threat of Enforcement—Prerequisite of a Judicial Controversy,* 62 Colum.L.Rev. 106, 126 (1962): "When an appeal is taken from a federal court decision, the Supreme Court, as the ultimate interpreter of federal law may derive its discretionary authority to deny adjudication from the nature of the injunction and declaratory judgment remedies. [B]ut it would seem that state construction of state remedies should be conclusively binding on the Supreme Court in the absence of article III objections. To justify discretion as an inherent power of the Court is equally unsatisfactory in view of the obligatory character of the appeal jurisdiction." Does this distinguish *Mitchell* from *Adler?*

Was the Court's refusal to decide *Poe* justified as commendable restraint in avoiding possibly unnecessary constitutional decision? Consider Note, *The Discretionary Power of the Supreme Court to Dismiss Appeals from State Courts,* 63 Colum.L.Rev. 688, 707 (1963): "[T]he assertion of discretion to refuse the jurisdiction that is given [by Congress] is inimical to fundamental postulates of principled judicial restraint; the declaration by the Court of such discretion itself violates the separation of powers philosophy upon which the Court has consistently relied. For by asserting power to make exceptions to its jurisdiction, the Court has assumed a power expressly delegated by the Constitution to Congress." See generally Gunther, *The Subtle Vices of the "Passive Virtues"—A Comment on Principle and Expediency in Judicial Review,* 64 Colum.L.Rev. 1 (1964). Does this argument draw an unrealistic dichotomy between (1) what Congress intended in conferring appeal jurisdiction and (2) the Court's rules of "self-limitation" from decision on the merits? See *Molinaro v. New Jersey,* 396 U.S. 365, 90 S.Ct. 498, 24 L.Ed.2d 586 (1970) (appeal dismissed because appellant was fugitive from justice); cf. *Ohio v. Wyandotte Chemicals Corp.,* 401 U.S. 493, 91 S.Ct. 1005, 28 L.Ed.2d 256 (1971) (declining to exercise statutorily granted original jurisdiction). Does it make an unwarranted assumption as to the clarity of the Constitution's allocation of power?

Consider Choper, *Judicial Review and the National Political Process* 406–09, 414 (1980): "[T]he Court should be hesitant to attribute an intention to the political branches that requires [it] to engage in the delicate process of constitutional adjudication despite the Justices' belief that it would be inappropriate or wasteful for the Court to do so. [This] suggested ground for nondecision would, of course, be unavailable if a clearly articulated legislative intent forbade a limiting construction of the jurisdictional statute. [In these circumstances, to] justify its deliberate refusal to decide some constitutional questions [the Court] should hold that political edicts to the contrary infringe 'the judicial Power of the United States.' Like all other constitutionally enumerated powers [this] clause implies those accessory powers necessary to its effective discharge, and final interpretation of its meaning belongs to the Supreme Court. [I]t is highly important to recognize the peculiar quality of the judicial assumption of power at issue. Viewed realistically, it is a judicial authority not to enhance the Court's power but rather to confine it, a course not of self-arrogation but rather one of self-denial—a capacity of the judiciary to refrain from exerting influence not wholly dissimilar (though the analogy is far from perfect) to whatever discretion the executive has to decline to enforce laws * * *."

SECTION 2. ELEVENTH AMENDMENT

CHARLES ALAN WRIGHT—FEDERAL COURTS

287–92 (4th ed. 1983).

[In EX PARTE YOUNG, 209 U.S. 123, 28 S.Ct. 441, 52 L.Ed. 714 (1908), railroads sued in federal court to enjoin Young, the Attorney General of Minnesota, from enforcing a state law reducing railroad rates. The railroads alleged that the rates were confiscatory, depriving them of their property without due process. Relief] was given over Young's objection that the suit was in fact a suit against the state, to which the state had not consented, and thus barred by the Eleventh Amendment. * * *

The Supreme Court did not write on a clean slate in deciding Young's case. In 1793, in the unpopular decision of *Chisholm v. Georgia*,[4] it had held that the Constitution permitted a citizen of one state to sue another state in federal court, though the state had not consented to such suit. The Eleventh Amendment was ratified five years later to take away the judicial power of the federal courts in such cases, and though in terms it does not so provide, it was construed as barring suits against a state without its consent even where, as in Young's case, the suit was brought by a citizen of the state and the basis of the jurisdiction was a claim under federal law.[6] [T]he Court held that the injunction against Young was proper. Justice PECKHAM, for the Court, announced the rule which has since been repeatedly followed: "The [use] of the name of the state to enforce an unconstitutional act to the injury of the complainants is a proceeding without the authority of, and one which does not affect, the state in its sovereign or governmental capacity. It is simply an illegal act upon the part of a state official * * *. If the act which the state Attorney General seeks to enforce be a violation of the federal Constitution, the officer in proceeding under such enactment comes into conflict with the superior authority of that Constitution, and he is in that case stripped of his official or representative character and is subject in his person to the consequences of his individual conduct."

Only the first Justice HARLAN dissented [:] "The suit was, as to the defendant Young, one against him as, and only because he was, Attorney General of Minnesota. No relief was sought against him individually but only in his capacity as Attorney General. And the manifest—indeed, the avowed and admitted—object of seeking such relief was to tie the hands of the [state]. It would therefore seem clear that within the true meaning of the Eleventh Amendment suit brought in the federal court was one, in legal effect, against the state."

There is no doubt that the reality is as Justice Harlan stated [it]. The fiction has its own illogic. The Fourteenth Amendment runs only to the states;

---

4. 1793, 2 Dall. 419, 1 L.Ed. 440. [See generally Goebel, *Antecedents and Beginnings to 1801*, 726–41 (1971).]

6. *Hans v. Louisiana*, 1890, 10 S.Ct. 504, 134 U.S. 1, 33 L.Ed. 842. [Compare *Parden v. Terminal Ry.*, 377 U.S. 184, 84 S.Ct. 1207, 12 L.Ed.2d 233 (1964) (state, that began operation of interstate railroad after enactment of Federal Employers' Liability Act, "necessarily consented" to federal court suits provided by the Act) with *Employees of Dep't of Public Health v. Dep't of Public Health*, 411 U.S. 279, 93 S.Ct. 1614, 36 L.Ed.2d 251 (1973) (congressional extension of Fair Labor Standards Act to state hospitals and schools did not intend to authorize federal court suits for enforcement by employees). See generally Cullison, *Interpretation of the Eleventh Amendment*, 5 Hous. L.Rev. 1 (1967).

[But neither the eleventh amendment, nor any other provision of the Constitution, affords a state immunity from being sued in the courts of another state. *Nevada v. Hall*, 440 U.S. 410, 99 S.Ct. 1182, 59 L.Ed.2d 416 (1979).]

in order to have a right to relief under the amendment the plaintiff must be able to show that state action is involved in the denial of his rights. [The Court] created the anomaly that enforcement of the Minnesota statute is state action for purposes of the Fourteenth Amendment but merely the individual wrong of Edward T. Young for purposes of the Eleventh Amendment.

What if the action of the state officer is beyond his authority as a matter of state law? [I]t was settled five years after *Young* that action by a state officer claiming to act under authority of the state can be enjoined, even if the state has not authorized such action.[20]

The effect of *Young* is to bring within the scope of federal judicial review actions that might otherwise escape such review * * *. If *Young* had been decided the other way, there would have been no practicable means for the railroads to obtain a court determination of the new rates Minnesota wanted them to charge. The state could, of course, consent to suit, either in its own courts or in federal court, simply as a matter of grace, but even today most states have not done so. The railroads could have refused to obey the new law, and asserted its unconstitutionality as a defense to an action against them for its enforcement, but the state might have chosen to enforce the law by the criminal sanctions it supplied, and these were so severe that the railroads could not risk the possibility that they might lose and have to pay crushing fines. In some situations, as where a state has failed to desegregate its schools, affirmative action is required of the state to fulfill its constitutional obligations, and there would not be even the possibility of raising the constitutional issue defensively.

* * *

The decision [was] greeted with harsh criticism [for] years thereafter. For half a century Congress and the Court have vied in placing restrictions on the doctrine there announced.[a]

Notes and Questions

Scope of congressional power. (a) In EDELMAN v. JORDAN, 415 U.S. 651, 94 S.Ct. 1347, 39 L.Ed.2d 662 (1974), the federal courts below found that Illinois had violated federal regulations under the federal-state funded Aid to the Aged, Blind and Disabled program, and ordered retroactive payment by state officials of the benefits wrongfully withheld. The Court, per REHNQUIST, J., reversed: "[A] suit by private parties seeking to impose a liability which must be paid from public funds in the state treasury is barred by the Eleventh Amendment.[11]

---

20. *Home Tel. & Tel. Co. v. Los Angeles,* 1913, 33 S.Ct. 312, 227 U.S. 278, 57 L.Ed. 510. [But *Cory v. White,* 457 U.S. 85, 102 S.Ct. 2325, 72 L.Ed.2d 694 (1982), reaffirmed that the eleventh amendment *does* bar federal suits against state officers who are not alleged either "to be acting contrary to federal law or against the authority of state law." And *Pennhurst State Sch. & Hosp. v. Halderman,* 465 U.S. 89, 104 S.Ct. 900, 79 L.Ed.2d 67 (1984), held (5–4) that the eleventh amendment also bars federal suits against state officers for alleged violations of *state* law, reasoning that, unlike the situation in *Young,* federal jurisdiction is not needed "to promote the supremacy of federal law."]

a. Various restrictions—including the congressional provision in 1910 (virtually eliminated in 1976) that no federal injunction re-

straining a state officer from enforcing a state law on grounds of unconstitutionality shall be issued except by a court of three judges (with direct appeal to the Supreme Court)—are discussed in Wright, supra, at 292–302.

11. It may be true, as stated by our Brother Douglas in dissent, that "[m]ost welfare decisions by the federal courts have a financial impact on the States." But we cannot agree [with him] that "[w]hether the decree is prospective only or requires payments for the weeks or months wrongfully skipped over by state officials, the nature of the impact on the state treasury is precisely the same." This argument neglects the fact that where the State has a definable allocation to be used in the payment of public aid benefits, and pursues a certain course of action such as the processing of applications within certain time

"As in most areas of the law, the difference between the type of relief barred by the Eleventh Amendment and that permitted under *Young* will not in many instances be that between day and night. The injunction issued in *Young* was not totally without effect on the State's revenues, since the state law which the Attorney General was enjoined from enforcing provided substantial monetary penalties against railroads which did not conform to its provisions. Later cases from this Court have authorized equitable relief which has probably had greater impact on state treasuries than did that awarded in *Young.* In *Graham v. Richardson,* [p. 985 supra] Arizona and Pennsylvania welfare officials were prohibited from denying welfare benefits to otherwise qualified recipients who were aliens. [But] the fiscal consequences to state treasuries in these cases were the necessary result of compliance with decrees which by their terms were prospective in nature.[b] While the Court of Appeals described this retroactive award of monetary relief as a form of 'equitable restitution,' it is in practical effect indistinguishable in many aspects from an award of damages against the State. It will to a virtual certainty be paid from state funds, and not from the pocket of the individual state official who was the defendant in the action [—and thus is contrary to *Ford Motor Co. v. Department of Treas.,* 323 U.S. 459, 65 S.Ct. 347, 89 L.Ed. 389 (1945)]. There a taxpayer, who had, under protest, paid taxes to the State of Indiana, sought a refund of those taxes from the Indiana state officials who were charged with their collection. The taxpayer claimed that the tax had been imposed in violation of the United States Constitution. [Yet] this Court had no hesitation in holding that the taxpayer's action was a suit against the State, and barred by the Eleventh Amendment. * * *

"The Court of Appeals held in the alternative that even if the Eleventh Amendment be deemed a bar to the retroactive [relief,] Illinois had waived [its] immunity and consented to the bringing of such a suit by participating in the federal AABD program.[c] [But] we will find waiver only where stated 'by the most express language or [by] other overwhelming implications from the [text],' " a condition satisfied here neither by the relevant federal welfare statutes nor by 42 U.S.C.A. § 1983,[d] nor by any action on the part of the state.

(b) FITZPATRICK v. BITZER, 427 U.S. 445, 96 S.Ct. 2666, 49 L.Ed.2d 614 (1976), per REHNQUIST, J., held that the eleventh amendment did not prevent a federal court from awarding retroactive money damages against the state treasury, for the state's having discriminated against plaintiff-employees on the basis of sex in violation of the Title VII of the Civil Rights Act of 1964 (enacted by Congress under § 5 of the fourteenth amendment): "[T]he Eleventh Amendment, and the principle of state sovereignty which it embodies, are necessarily limited by the enforcement provisions of § 5 of the Fourteenth Amendment. [When] Congress acts pursuant to § 5, [it] is exercising that authority under one section of a constitutional Amendment whose other sections by their own terms

---

periods as did Illinois here, the subsequent ordering by a federal court of retroactive payments to correct delays in such processing will invariably mean there is less money available for payments for the continuing obligations of the public aid system. * * *

b. For the view that "the history of the eleventh amendment supports the Court's distinction between retroactive and prospective relief," see 88 Harv.L.Rev. 243 (1974).

For further reliance on this distinction in awarding relief with "substantial impact on

the state treasury," see *Milliken v. Bradley,* 433 U.S. 267, 97 S.Ct. 2749, 53 L.Ed.2d 745 (1977), discussed in Frug, *The Judicial Power of the Purse,* 126 U.Pa.L.Rev. 715, 750–57 (1978).

c. Douglas, J.—and Marshall, J., joined by Blackmun, J.—dissented on this theory. Brennan, J., also dissented.

d. The conclusion as to § 1983 was reaffirmed in *Quern v. Jordan,* 440 U.S. 332, 99 S.Ct. 1139, 59 L.Ed.2d 358 (1979).

embody limitations on state authority. We think that Congress may, in determining what is 'appropriate legislation' for the purpose of enforcing the provisions of the Fourteenth Amendment, provide for private suits against States or state officials which are constitutionally impermissible in other contexts.[11] See *Edelman; Ford Motor.*" [e]

---

11. Apart from their claim that the Eleventh Amendment bars enforcement of the remedy established by Title VII in this case, respondents do not contend that the substantive provisions of Title VII as applied here are not a proper exercise of congressional authority under § 5 of the Fourteenth Amendment.

e. Brennan and Stevens, JJ., concurred in the result.

For the view that Congress has authority, pursuant to any of its delegated powers, to authorize federal court suits for damages against the states, see Nowak, *The Scope of Congressional Power to Create Causes of Action Against State Governments and the History of the Eleventh and Fourteenth Amendments,* 75 Colum.L.Rev. 1413 (1975); Tribe, *Intergovernmental Immunities in Litigation, Taxation, and Regulation: Separation of Powers Issues in Controversies About Federalism,* 89 Harv.L.Rev. 682–99 (1976).

For the view that the eleventh amendment does not bar suits against states when another jurisdictional basis—such as federal question or admiralty—exists, see Fletcher, *A Historical Interpretation of the Eleventh Amendment: A Narrow Construction of an Affirmative Grant of Jurisdiction Rather than a Prohibition Against Jurisdiction,* 35 Stan.L.Rev. 1033 (1983); Gibbons, *The Eleventh Amendment and State Sovereign Immunity: A Reinterpretation,* 83 Colum.L.Rev. 1889 (1983). This position has been adopted by Brennan, J., joined by Marshall, Blackmun and Stevens, JJ., dissenting in *Atascadero State Hosp. v. Scanlon,* ___ U.S. ___, 105 S.Ct. 3142, 87 L.Ed.2d 171 (1985).

For the view that state sovereign immunity from suit is only a "common law requirement" and "has no constitutional sanction," see Field, *The Eleventh Amendment and Other Sovereign Immunity Doctrines: Part One,* 126 U.Pa.L.Rev. 515 (1977).

Appendix A

THE JUSTICES OF THE SUPREME COURT

Prepared by JOHN J. COUND

Professor of Law, University of Minnesota

The data which follow, summarizing the prior public careers of the ninety-eight individuals who have served upon the Supreme Court of the United States, are not presented with any notion that they did presage or now explain their judicial performance or constitutional philosophy. The experience which the justices have at any one time brought to bear upon the issues before the Court, however, seem worthy of interest, and may serve as a consideration in assessing charges that the Court has in particular cases rendered "ivory tower" decisions, unaware or heedless of "the realities."

Two conclusions are manifest. First, the diversity of distinguished experience which the bench of the Court has at all times reflected, always among its members and frequently in a single justice, is startling. William Howard Taft is unique, but surely few Americans have lived lives of diversified public service so rich as John Jay, Levi Woodbury, Lucius Q.C. Lamar, Charles Evans Hughes and Fred M. Vinson. Second, a broad background in public service has not assured prominence upon the Court, nor has its absence precluded it. Gabriel Duvall, with prior executive, legislative and judicial experience, was forgotten in the first edition of the *Dictionary of American Biography.* Samuel F. Miller and Joseph P. Bradley, with no prior public offices, surely stand among the front rank of the justices. (The interested student will find stimulation in Frankfurter, *The Supreme Court in the Mirror of Justice,* 105 U.Pa.L.Rev. 781 (1957), which treats particularly of the relevance of prior judicial office).

In the data, the first dates in parentheses are those of birth and death; these are followed by the name of the appointing President, and the dates of service on the Court. The state in which the justice was residing when appointed and his political affiliation at that time are then given. In detailing prior careers, I have followed chronological order, with two exceptions: I have listed first that a justice was a signer of the Declaration of Independence or the Federal Constitution, and I have indicated state legislative experience only once for each justice. I have not distinguished between different bodies in the state legislature, and I have omitted service in the Continental Congresses. Private practice, except where deemed especially signficant, and law teaching have been omitted, except where the justice was primarily engaged therein upon his appointment. (Black-

1225

mun, Burger, Douglas, Fortas, Holmes, Hughes, L.Q.C. Lamar, Lurton, McReynolds, Murphy, Roberts, W. Rutledge, Stevens, Stone and Van Devanter in addition to Taft and Frankfurter, had all taught before going on the Court; Story, Strong and Wilson taught while on the court or after leaving it). The activity in which a justice was engaged upon appointment has been italicized. Figures in parentheses indicate years of service in the position. In only a few cases, a justice's extra-Court or post-Court activity has been indicated, or some other note made. An asterisk designates the Chief Justices.

For detailed information on the individuals who have served as members of the Supreme Court, see L. Friedman & F. Israel, eds., *The Justices of the United States Supreme Court 1789–1969: Their Lives and Major Opinions* (Chelsea House, 1969), and the bibliographical references collected therein.

The accompanying Table of Justices on pages [3] and [4] has been planned so that the composition of the Court at any time can be readily ascertained.

(This material has been compiled from a great number of sources, but special acknowledgment must be made to the *Dictionary of American Biography* (Charles Scribner's Sons), the A.N. Marquis Company works, and Ewing, *The Judges of the Supreme Court, 1789–1937* (University of Minnesota Press, 1938).)

BALDWIN, HENRY (1780–1844; Jackson 1830–1844). Pa.Dem.—U.S., House of Representatives (5). *Private practice.*

BARBOUR, PHILIP P. (1783–1841; Jackson, 1836–1841). Va.Dem.—Va., Legislature (2). U.S., House of Representatives (14). Va., Judge, General Court (2); President, State Constitutional Convention, 1829–30, *U.S., Judge, District Court (5).*

BLACK, HUGO L. (1886–1971; F.D. Roosevelt, 1937–1971). Ala.Dem.— Captain, Field Artillery, World War I. Ala., Judge, Police Court (1); County Solicitor (2). *U.S., Senate (10).*

BLACKMUN, HARRY A. (1908–____; Nixon, 1970–____). Minn.Rep.—Resident Counsel, Mayo Clinic, (10). *U.S., Judge, Court of Appeals (11).*

BLAIR, JOHN (1732–1800; Washington, 1789–1796). Va.Fed.—Signer, U.S. Constitution, 1787. Va., Legislature (9); Judge and Chief Justice, General Court (2), *Court of Appeals (9).* His opinion in *Commonwealth v. Caton,* 4 Call 5, 20 (Va.1782), is one of the earliest expressions of the doctrine of judicial review.

BLATCHFORD, SAMUEL (1820–1893; Arthur, 1882–1893). N.Y.Rep.— U.S., Judge, District Court (5); *Circuit Court (10).*

BRADLEY, JOSEPH P. (1803–1892; Grant, 1870–1892). N.J.Rep.—Actuary. *Private practice.*

BRANDEIS, LOUIS D. (1856–1941; Wilson, 1916–1939). Mass.Dem.—*Private practice.* Counsel, variously for the government, for industry, and "for the people", in numerous administrative and judicial proceedings, both state and federal.

BRENNAN, WILLIAM J. (1906–____; Eisenhower, 1956–____). N.J.Dem.— U.S. Army, World War II. N.J., Judge, Superior Court (1); Appellate Division (2); *Supreme Court (4).*

BREWER, DAVID J. (1837–1910; B. Harrison, 1889–1910). Kans.Rep.— Kans., Judge, County Criminal and Probate Court (1), District Court (4); County Attorney (1); Judge, Supreme Court (14), *U.S., Judge, Circuit Court (5).*

BROWN, HENRY, B. (1836–1913; B. Harrison, 1890–1906). Mich.Rep.— U.S., Assistant U.S. Attorney (5). Mich., Judge, Circuit Court (1). *U.S., Judge, District Court (15).*

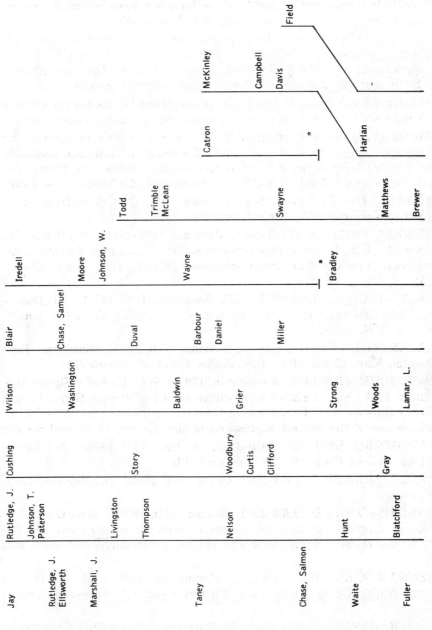

Years (columns): 1890, 1892, 1893, 1894, 1895, 1898, 1902, 1903, 1906, 1909, 1910, 1912, 1914, 1916, 1921, 1922, 1923, 1925, 1930, 1932, 1937, 1938, 1939, 1940, 1941, 1943, 1945, 1946, 1949, 1953, 1955, 1956, 1957, 1958, 1962, 1965, 1966, 1967, 1968, 1969, 1970, 1972, **1975**, 1981

Seat 1: McKenna — Stone — Jackson, R. (**) — Rehnquist

Seat 2: Pitney — Sanford — Roberts — Burton — Stewart — O'Connor

Seat 3: Hughes — Clarke — Sutherland — Reed — Whittaker — White, B.

Seat 4: Shiras — Day — Butler — Murphy — Clark — Marshall, T.

Seat 5: Brown — Moody — Lamar, J. — Brandeis — Douglas — **Stevens**

Seat 6: Jackson, H. — Peckham — Lurton — McReynolds — Byrnes — Rutledge — Minton — Brennan

Seat 7: Holmes — Cardozo — Frankfurter — Goldberg — Fortas — Blackmun

Seat 8: White, E. — Van Devanter (**) — Black — Powell

Chief Justices: White, E. — Taft — Hughes — Stone — Vinson — Warren — Burger

** Fuller died in 1910, and White was named Chief Justice. Hughes resigned in 1941, and Stone was named Chief Justice.

*BURGER, WARREN E. (1907-____; Nixon, 1969-). Va.Rep.—U.S., Assistant Attorney General, Civil Division (3), *Judge, Court of Appeals (13)*.

BURTON, HAROLD H. (1888–1964; Truman, 1945–1958). Ohio Rep.—Capt., U.S.A., World War I. Ohio, Legislature (2). Mayor, Cleveland, O. (5). *U.S., Senate (4)*.

BUTLER, PIERCE (1866–1939; Harding, 1922–1939). Minn.Dem.—Minn., County Attorney (4). *Private practice*.

BYRNES, JAMES F. (1879–1972; F.D. Roosevelt, 1941–1942). S.C.Dem.—S.C., Solicitor, Circuit Court (2). U.S., House of Representatives (14); *Senate (12)*. Resigned from the Court to become U.S. Director of Economic Stabilization.

CAMPBELL, JOHN A. (1811–1889; Pierce, 1853–1861). Ala.Dem.—*Private practice*. After his resignation, he became Assistant Secretary of War, C.S.A.

CARDOZO, BENJAMIN N. (1870–1938; Hoover, 1932–1938). N.Y.Dem.—N.Y., Judge, Supreme Court (6 weeks); Associate Judge and *Chief Judge, Court of Appeals (18)*.

CATRON, JOHN (1778–1865; Van Buren, 1837–1865). Tenn.Dem.—Tenn., Judge and Chief Justice, Supreme Court of Errors and Appeals (10). *Private practice*.

*CHASE, SALMON P. (1808–1873; Lincoln 1864–1873). Ohio Rep.—U.S., Senate (6). Ohio, Governor (4). *U.S., Secretary of the Treasury (3)*.

CHASE, SAMUEL (1741–1811; Washington, 1796–1811). Md.Fed.—Signer, U.S., Declaration of Independence, 1776. Md., Legislature (20); Chief Judge, Court of Oyer and Terminer (2), *General Court (5)*. Impeached and acquitted, 1804–05.

CLARK, TOM C. (1899–1977; Truman, 1949–1967). Tex.Dem.—U.S. Army, World War I. Tex., Civil District Attorney (5). U.S., Assistant Attorney General (2), *Attorney General (4)*.

CLARKE, JOHN H. (1857–1945; Wilson, 1916–1922). Ohio Dem.—*U.S. Judge, District Court (2)*.

CLIFFORD, NATHAN (1803–1881; Buchanan, 1858–1881). Me.Dem.—Me., Legislature (4); Attorney General (4). U.S., House of Representatives (4); Attorney General (2); Minister Plenipotentiary to Mexico, 1848. *Private practice*.

CURTIS, BENJAMIN R. (1809–1874; Fillmore, 1851–1857). Mass.Whig.—Mass., Legislature (1). *Private practice*.

CUSHING, WILLIAM (1732–1810; Washington, 1789–1810). Mass.Fed.—Mass., Judge, Superior Court (3); Justice and *Chief Justice, Supreme Judicial Court (14)*.

DANIEL, PETER V. (1784–1860; Van Buren, 1841–1860). Va.Dem.—Va., Legislature (3); Member, Privy Council (23). *U.S., Judge, District Court (5)*.

DAVIS, DAVID (1815–1886; Lincoln, 1862–1877). Ill.Rep.—Ill., Legislature (2); *Judge, Circuit Court (14)*. His resignation to become U.S. Senator upset the agreed-upon composition of the Hayes-Tilden Electoral Commission.

DAY, WILLIAM R. (1849–1923; T. Roosevelt, 1903–1922). Ohio Rep.—Ohio, Judge, Court of Common Pleas (4). U.S., Assistant Secretary of State (1), Secretary of State (½); Chairman, U.S. Peace Commissioners, 1898; *Judge, Circuit Court of Appeals (4)*.

DOUGLAS, WILLIAM O. (1898–1980; F.D. Roosevelt, 1939–1975). Conn. Dem.—Pvt., U.S. Army, World War I. *U.S., Chairman, Securities and Exchange Commission (3)*.

DUVAL(L), GABRIEL (1752–1844; Madison, 1811–1935). Md.Rep.—Declined to serve as delegate, U.S. Constitutional Convention, 1787. Md., State Council (3). U.S., House of Representatives (2). Md., Judge, General Court (6). *U.S., Comptroller of the Treasury (9).*

*ELLSWORTH, OLIVER (1745–1807; Washington, 1796–1800). Conn. Fed.—Delegate, U.S. Constitutional Convention, 1787. Conn., Legislature (2); Member, Governor's Council (4); Judge, Superior Court (5). *U.S., Senate (7).*

FIELD, STEPHEN J. (1816–1899; Lincoln, 1863–1897). Calif.Dem.—*Calif., Justice, and Chief Justice, Supreme Court (6).* His was the longest tenure in the history of the Court.

FORTAS, ABE (1910–1982; L.B. Johnson, 1965–1969). Tenn.Dem.—U.S. Government attorney and consultant (A.A.A., S.E.C., P.W.A., Dep't of Interior (9); Undersecretary of Interior (4). *Private practice in Washington, D.C.* Nominated as Chief Justice; nomination withdrawn, 1968. Resigned.

FRANKFURTER, FELIX (1882–1965; F.D. Roosevelt, 1939–1962). Mass. Independent.—U.S., Assistant U.S. Attorney (4); Law Officer, War Department, Bureau of Insular Affairs (3); Assistant to Secretary of War (1). *Professor of Law (25).*

*FULLER, MELVILLE W. (1833–1910; Cleveland, 1888–1910). Ill.Dem.—Ill., Legislature (2). *Private practice.*

GOLDBERG, ARTHUR J. (1908–___; Kennedy, 1962–1965). Ill.Dem.—Major, U.S.A., World War II. General Counsel, USW–AFL–CIO (13). *U.S., Secretary of Labor (1).* Resigned to become Ambassador to U.N.

GRAY, HORACE (1828–1902; Arthur, 1881–1902). Mass.Rep.—*Mass.,* Associate Justice and *Chief Justice, Supreme Judicial Court (18).*

GRIER, ROBERT O. (1794–1870; Polk, 1846–1870). Pa.Dem.—*Pa., Presiding Judge, District Court (13).*

HARLAN, JOHN M. (1833–1911; Hayes, 1877–1911). Ky.Rep.—Ky., Judge, County Court (1). Col., Union Army, 1861–63. Ky., Attorney General (4). U.S., Member, President's Louisiana Commission, 1877. *Private practice.* Grandfather of:

HARLAN, JOHN M. (1899–1971; Eisenhower, 1955–1971). N.Y.Rep.—Col., U.S.A.A.F., World War II. N.Y. Chief Counsel, State Crime Commission (2). *U.S., Judge, Court of Appeals (1).*

HOLMES, OLIVER W., JR. (1841–1935; T. Roosevelt, 1902–1932). Mass. Rep.—Lt. Col., Mass. Volunteers, Civil War. *Mass.,* Associate Justice, and *Chief Justice, Supreme Judicial Court (20).*

*HUGHES, CHARLES E. (1862–1948; Taft, 1910–1916, and Hoover, 1930–1941). N.Y.Rep.—N.Y., Counsel, legislative committees investigating gas and insurance industries, 1905–06. U.S., Special Assistant to Attorney General for Coal Investigation, 1906. *N.Y., Governor (3).* [Between appointments to the Supreme Court: Presidential Nominee, Republican Party, 1916. U.S., Secretary of State (4). *Member, Permanent Court of Arbitration, The Hague (4). Judge, Permanent Court of International Justice (2).*] Chief Justice on second appointment.

HUNT, WARD (1810–1886; Grant, 1872–1882). N.Y.Rep.—N.Y., Legislature (2). Mayor of Utica, N.Y. (1). N.Y. Associate Judge, and Chief Judge, Court of Appeals (4); *Commissioner of Appeals (4).* He did not sit from 1879 to his retirement in 1882.

IREDELL, JAMES (1750–1799; Washington, 1790–1799). N.C.Fed.—Comptroller of Customs (6), Collector of Port (2), Edenton, N.C., N.C., Judge, Superior Court (½); Attorney General (2); Member, Council of State, 1787; *Reviser of Statutes (3).*

JACKSON, HOWELL E. (1832–1895; B. Harrison, 1893–1895). Tenn. Dem.—Tenn., Judge, Court of Arbitration (4); Legislature (1). U.S. Senate (5); *Judge, Circuit Court of Appeals (7).*

JACKSON, ROBERT H. (1892–1954; F.D. Roosevelt, 1941–1954). N.Y. Dem.—U.S., General Counsel, Bureau of Internal Revenue (2); Assistant Attorney General (2); Solicitor General (2); *Attorney General (1).*

*JAY, JOHN (1745–1829; Washington, 1789–1795). N.Y.Fed.—N.Y., Chief Justice, Supreme Court (2). U.S., Envoy to Spain (2); Commissioner, Treaty of Paris, 1782–83; Secretary for Foreign Affairs (6). Co-author, The Federalist.

JOHNSON, THOMAS (1732–1819; Washington, 1791–1793). Md.Fed.—Md., Brigadier-General, Militia (1); Legislature (5); Governor (2); *Chief Judge, General Court (1).*

JOHNSON, WILLIAM (1771–1834; Jefferson, 1804–1834). S.C.Rep.—S.C., Legislature (4); *Judge, Court of Common Pleas (6).*

LAMAR, JOSEPH R. (1857–1916; Taft, 1910–1916). Ga.Dem.—Ga., Legislature (3); Commissioner to Codify Laws (3); Associate Justice, Supreme Court (4). *Private practice.*

LAMAR, LUCIUS Q.C. (1825–1893; Cleveland, 1888–1893). Miss.Dem.—Ga., Legislature (2). U.S., House of Representatives (4). Draftsman, Mississippi Ordinance of Secession, 1861. C.S.A., Lt. Col. (1); Commissioner to Russia (1); Judge-Advocate, III Corps. Army of No. Va. (1). U.S., House of Representatives (4); Senate (8); *Secretary of the Interior (3).*

LIVINGSTON, (HENRY) BROCKHOLST (1757–1823; Jefferson, 1806–1823). N.Y.Rep.—Lt. Col., Continental Army. *N.Y., Judge, Supreme Court (4).*

LURTON, HORACE H. (1844–1914; Taft, 1909–1914). Tenn.Dem.—Sgt. Major, C.S.A. Tenn., Chancellor (3); Associate Justice and Chief Justice, Supreme Court (7). *U.S., Judge, Circuit Court of Appeals (16).*

McKENNA, JOSEPH (1843–1926; McKinley, 1898–1925). Calif.Rep.—Calif., District Attorney (2); Legislature (2). U.S., House of Representatives (7); *Judge, Circuit Court of Appeals (5); Attorney General (1).*

McKINLEY, JOHN (1780–1852; Van Buren, 1837–1852). Ala.Dem.—Legislature (4). U.S., Senate (5); House of Representatives (2); *re-elected to Senate, but appointed to Court before taking seat.*

McLEAN, JOHN (1785–1861; Jackson, 1829–1861). Ohio Dem.—U.S., House of Representatives (4). Ohio, Judge, Supreme Court (6). U.S., Commissioner, General Land Office (1); *Postmaster-General (6).*

McREYNOLDS, JAMES C. (1862–1946; Wilson, 1914–1941). Tenn.Dem.— U.S., Assistant Attorney General (4); *Attorney General (1).*

*MARSHALL, JOHN (1755–1835; J. Adams, 1801–1835). Va.Fed.—Va., Legislature (7); U.S., Envoy to France (1); House of Representatives (1); *Secretary of State (1).*

MARSHALL, THURGOOD (1908–____; L.B. Johnson, 1967–____). N.Y. Dem.—Counsel, Legal Defense and Educational Fund, NAACP (21). U.S., Judge, Court of Appeals (4); *Solicitor General (2).*

MATTHEWS, STANLEY (1824–1889; Garfield, 1881–1889). Ohio Rep.—Ohio, Judge, Court of Common Pleas (2); Legislature (3). U.S., District Attorney (3). Col., Ohio Volunteers. Ohio, Judge, Superior Court (2). Counsel before Hayes-Tilden Electoral Commission, 1877. U.S., Senate (2). *Private practice.* His first appointment to the Court by Hayes in 1881 was not acted upon by the Senate.

MILLER, SAMUEL F. (1816–1890; Lincoln, 1862–1890). Iowa Rep.—Physician. *Private practice.*

MINTON, SHERMAN (1890–1965; Truman, 1949–1956). Ind.Dem.—Capt., Inf., World War I. U.S., Senate (6); *Judge, Court of Appeals (8).*

MOODY, WILLIAM H. (1853–1917; T. Roosevelt, 1906–1910). Mass.Rep.—U.S., District Attorney (5), House of Representatives (7); Secretary of the Navy (2); *Attorney General (2).*

MOORE, ALFRED (1755–1810; J. Adams, 1799–1804). N.C.Fed.—N.C., Col. of Militia; Legislature (2); Attorney General (9). U.S. Commissioner, Treaty with Cherokee Nation (1); *N.C., Judge, Superior Court (1).*

MURPHY, FRANK (1893–1949; F.D. Roosevelt, 1940–1949). Mich.Dem.—Capt., Inf., World War I. U.S., Assistant U.S. Attorney (1). Mich., Judge, Recorder's Court (7). Mayor, Detroit, Mich. (3). U.S., Governor-General, and High Commissioner, P.I. (3). Mich., Governor (2). *U.S., Attorney General (1).*

NELSON, SAMUEL (1792–1873; Tyler, 1845–1872). N.Y.Dem.—N.Y., Judge, Circuit Court (8); Associate Justice, and *Chief Justice, Supreme Court (14).*

O'CONNOR, SANDRA DAY (1930–____; Reagan, 1981–____. Ariz.Rep.—Ariz., Assistant Attorney General (4); Legislature (6). Ariz., Judge, Superior Court (4); *Court of Appeals (2).*

PATERSON, WILLIAM (1745–1806; Washington, 1793–1806). N.J.Fed.—Signer, U.S. Constitution, 1787. N.J., Legislature (2); Attorney General (7). U.S., Senate (1). *N.J., Governor (3).* Reviser of English Pre-Revolutionary Statutes in Force in N.J.

PECKHAM, RUFUS W. (1838–1909; Cleveland, 1895–1909). N.Y.Dem.—N.Y., District Attorney (1); Justice, Supreme Court (3); *Associate Judge, Court of Appeals (9).*

PITNEY, MAHLON (1858–1924; Taft, 1912–1922). N.J.Rep.—U.S., House of Representatives (4). N.J., Legislature (2); Associate Justice, Supreme Court (7); Chancellor (4).

POWELL, LEWIS F. (1907–____; Nixon, 1972–____). Va.Dem.—Col., U.S. A.A.F., World War II. *Private practice.*

REED, STANLEY F. (1884–1980; F.D. Roosevelt, 1938–1957). Ky.Dem.—Ky., Legislature (4). 1st Lt., U.S.A., World War I. U.S., General Counsel, Federal Farm Board (3); General Counsel, Reconstruction Finance Corporation (3); *Solicitor General (3).*

REHNQUIST, WILLIAM H. (1924–____; Nixon, 1972–____). Ariz.Rep.—U.S.A.F., World War II. Law Clerk, Justice Jackson, 1952–53. *U.S., Assistant Attorney General (3).*

ROBERTS, OWEN J. (1875–1955; Hoover, 1930–1945). Pa.Rep.—Pa., Assistant District Attorney (3). U.S., Special Deputy Attorney General in Espionage Act Cases, World War I; Special Prosecutor, Oil Cases, 1924. *Private practice.*

*RUTLEDGE, JOHN (1739–1800; Washington, 1789–1791, and Washington, 1795). S.C.Fed.—Signer, U.S. Constitution, 1787. S.C., Legislature (18); Attorney General (1); President and Governor (6); *Chancellor (7).* [Between appointments to the Supreme Court: *S.C., Chief Justice, Court of Common Pleas and Sessions (4).*] He did not sit under his first appointment; he sat with a recess appointment as Chief Justice, but his regular appointment was rejected by the Senate.

RUTLEDGE, WILEY B. (1894–1949; F.D. Roosevelt, 1943–1949). Iowa Dem.—Mo., then Iowa, Member, National Conference of Commissioners on Uniform State Laws (10). *U.S., Judge, Court of Appeals (4).*

SANFORD, EDWARD T. (1865–1930; Harding, 1923–1930). Tenn.Rep.— U.S., Assistant Attorney General (1); *Judge, District Court (15).*

SHIRAS, GEORGE (1832–1924; B. Harrison, 1892–1903). Pa.Rep. *Private practice.*

STEVENS, JOHN PAUL (1920–____; Ford, 1975–____). Ill.Independent.— U.S.N.R., World War II. Law Clerk, Justice Wiley Rutledge, 1947–48. *Judge, Court of Appeals (5).*

STEWART, POTTER (1915–1985; Eisenhower, 1958–1981). Ohio Rep.—Lt., U.S.N.R., World War II. *U.S., Judge, Court of Appeals (4).*

*STONE, HARLAN F. (1872–1946; Coolidge, later F.D. Roosevelt, 1925–1946). N.Y.Rep.—*U.S., Attorney General (1).* Chief Justice, 1941–1946.

STORY, JOSEPH (1779–1845; Madison, 1811–1845). Mass.Rep.—Mass., Legislature (5). U.S., House of Representatives (2). *Private practice.*

STRONG, WILLIAM (1808–1895; Grant, 1870–1880). Pa.Rep.—U.S., House of Representatives (4). Pa., Justice, Supreme Court (11). *Private practice.*

SUTHERLAND, GEORGE (1862–1942; Harding, 1922–1938). Utah Rep.— Utah, Legislature (4). U.S., House of Representatives (2); Senate (12). *Private practice.*

SWAYNE, NOAH H. (1804–1884; Lincoln, 1862–1881). Ohio Rep.—Ohio, County Attorney (4); Legislature (2). U.S., District Attorney (9). *Private practice.*

*TAFT, WILLIAM H. (1857–1930; Harding, 1921–1930). Conn.Rep.—U.S., Collector of Internal Revenue (1). Ohio, Judge, Superior Court (3). U.S., Solicitor General (2); Judge, Circuit Court of Appeals (8); Governor-General, P.I. (3); Secretary of War (4); President (4). *Professor of Law.*

*TANEY, ROGER B. (1777–1864; Jackson, 1836–1864). Md.Dem.—Md., Legislature (7); Attorney General (2). U.S., Attorney General (2), Secretary of the Treasury (³/₄; rejected by the Senate). *Private practice.*

THOMPSON, SMITH (1768–1843; Monroe, 1823–1843). N.Y.Rep.—N.Y., Legislature (2); Associate Justice, and Chief Justice, Supreme Court (16). *U.S., Secretary of the Navy (4).*

TODD, THOMAS (1765–1826; Jefferson, 1807–1826). Ky.Rep.—*Ky., Judge, and Chief Justice, Court of Appeals (6).*

TRIMBLE, ROBERT (1777–1828; J.Q. Adams, 1826–1828). Ky.Rep.—Ky., Legislature (2). Judge, Court of Appeals (2). U.S., District Attorney (4); *Judge, District Court (9).*

VAN DEVANTER, WILLIS (1859–1941; Taft, 1910–1937). Wyo.Rep.—Wyo., Legislature (2); Chief Justice, Supreme Court (1). U.S., Assistant Attorney General (Interior Department) (6); *Judge, Circuit Court of Appeals (7).*

*VINSON, FRED M. (1890–1953; Truman, 1946–1953). Ky.Dem.—Ky., Commonwealth Attorney (3). U.S., House of Representatives (14); Judge, Court of Appeals (5); Director, Office of Economic Stabilization (2); Federal Loan

Administrator (1 mo.); Director, Office of War Mobilization and Reconversion (3 mo.); *Secretary of the Treasury (1).*

*WAITE, MORRISON R. (1816–1888; Grant, 1874–1888). Ohio Rep.—Ohio, Legislature (2). Counsel for United States, U.S.—Gr. Brit. Arbitration ("Alabama" Claims), 1871–72. *Private practice.*

*WARREN, EARL (1891–1974; Eisenhower, 1953–1969). Calif.Rep.—1st Lt., Inf., World War I. Deputy City Attorney (1); Deputy District Attorney (5); District Attorney (14); Attorney General (4); *Governor (10).*

WASHINGTON, BUSHROD (1762–1829; J. Adams, 1798–1829). Pa.Fed.—Va., Legislature (1). *Private practice.*

WAYNE, JAMES M. (1790–1867; Jackson, 1835–1867). Ga.Dem.—Ga., Officer, Hussars, War of 1812; Legislature (2). Mayor of Savannah, Ga. (2). Ga., Judge, Superior Court (5). *U.S., House of Representatives (6).*

WHITE, BYRON R. (1917–____; Kennedy, 1962–____). Colo.Dem.—U.S. N.R., World War II. Law Clerk, Chief Justice Vinson, 1946–47. *U.S., Deputy Attorney General (1).*

*WHITE, EDWARD D. (1845–1921; Cleveland, later Taft, 1894–1921). La. Dem.—La., Legislature (4); Justice, Supreme Court (2). *U.S., Senate (3).* Chief Justice, 1910–1921.

WHITTAKER, CHARLES E. (1901–1973; Eisenhower, 1957–1962). Mo. Rep.—U.S., Judge, District Court (2); *Court of Appeals (1).*

WILSON, JAMES (1724–1798; Washington, 1789–1798). Pa.Fed.—Signer, U.S. Declaration of Independence, 1776, and U.S. Constitution, 1787. Although he was strongly interested in western-land development companies for several years prior to his appointment, his primary activity in the period immediately preceding his appointment was in obtaining ratification of the Federal and Pennsylvania Constitutions.

WOODBURY, LEVI (1789–1851; Polk, 1845–1851). N.H. Dem.—N.H., Associate Justice, Superior Court (6); Governor (2); Legislature (1). U.S., Senate (6); Secretary of the Navy (3); Secretary of the Treasury (7); *Senate (4).*

WOODS, WILLIAM B. (1824–1887; Hayes, 1880–1887). Ga.Rep.—Mayor, Newark, O. (1). Ohio, Legislature (4). Brevet Major General, U.S. Vol., Civil War. Ala., Chancellor (1). *U.S., Judge, Circuit Court (11).*

Appendix B

THE CONSTITUTION OF THE UNITED STATES

PREAMBLE

We the People of the United States, in Order to form a more perfect Union, establish Justice, insure domestic Tranquility, provide for the common defence, promote the general Welfare, and secure the Blessings of Liberty to ourselves and our Posterity, do ordain and establish this Constitution for the United States of America.

ARTICLE I

Section 1. All legislative Powers herein granted shall be vested in a Congress of the United States, which shall consist of a Senate and House of Representatives.

Section 2. [1] The House of Representatives shall be composed of Members chosen every second Year by the People of the several States, and the Electors in each State shall have the Qualifications requisite for Electors of the most numerous Branch of the State Legislature.

[2] No Person shall be a Representative who shall not have attained to the Age of twenty five Years, and been seven Years a Citizen of the United States, and who shall not, when elected, be an Inhabitant of that State in which he shall be chosen.

[3] Representatives and direct Taxes shall be apportioned among the several States which may be included within this Union, according to their respective Numbers, which shall be determined by adding to the whole Number of free Persons, including those bound to Service for a Term of Years, and excluding Indians not taxed, three fifths of all other Persons. The actual Enumeration shall be made within three Years after the first Meeting of the Congress of the United States, and within every subsequent Term of ten Years, in such Manner as they shall by Law direct. The Number of Representatives shall not exceed one for every thirty Thousand, but each State shall have at Least one Representative; and until such enumeration shall be made, the State of New Hampshire shall be entitled to chuse three, Massachusetts eight, Rhode Island and Providence Plantations one, Connecticut five, New York six, New Jersey four, Pennsylvania eight, Delaware one, Maryland six, Virginia ten, North Carolina five, South Carolina five, and Georgia three.

[4] When vacancies happen in the Representation from any State, the Executive Authority thereof shall issue Writs of Election to fill such Vacancies.

[5] The House of Representatives shall chuse their Speaker and other Officers; and shall have the sole Power of Impeachment.

Section 3. [1] The Senate of the United States shall be composed of two Senators from each State, chosen by the Legislature thereof, for six Years; and each Senator shall have one Vote.

[2] Immediately after they shall be assembled in Consequence of the first Election, they shall be divided as equally as may be into three Classes. The Seats of the Senators of the first Class shall be vacated at the Expiration of the Second Year, of the second Class at the Expiration of the fourth Year, and of the third Class at the Expiration of the sixth Year, so that one third may be chosen every second Year; and if Vacancies happen by Resignation, or otherwise, during the Recess of the Legislature of any State, the Executive thereof may make temporary Appointments until the next Meeting of the Legislature, which shall then fill such Vacancies.

[3] No Person shall be a Senator who shall not have attained to the Age of thirty Years, and been nine Years a Citizen of the United States, and who shall not, when elected, by an Inhabitant of that State for which he shall be chosen.

[4] The Vice President of the United States shall be President of the Senate, but shall have no Vote, unless they be equally divided.

[5] The Senate shall chuse their other Officers, and also a President pro tempore, in the Absence of the Vice President, or when he shall exercise the Office of President of the United States.

[6] The Senate shall have the sole Power to try all Impeachments. When sitting for that Purpose, they shall be on Oath or Affirmation. When the President of the United States is tried, the Chief Justice shall preside: And no Person shall be convicted without the Concurrence of two thirds of the Members present.

[7] Judgment in Cases of Impeachment shall not extend further than to removal from Office, and disqualification to hold and enjoy any Office of honor, Trust, or Profit under the United States: but the Party convicted shall nevertheless be liable and subject to Indictment, Trial, Judgment, and Punishment, according to Law.

Section 4. [1] The Times, Places and Manner of holding Elections for Senators and Representatives, shall be prescribed in each State by the Legislature thereof; but the Congress may at any time by Law make or alter such Regulations, except as to the Places of chusing Senators.

[2] The Congress shall assemble at least once in every Year, and such Meeting shall be on the first Monday in December, unless they shall by Law appoint a different Day.

Section 5. [1] Each House shall be the Judge of the Elections, Returns, and Qualifications of its own Members, and a Majority of each shall constitute a Quorum to do Business; but a smaller Number may adjourn from day to day, and may be authorized to compel the Attendance of absent Members, in such Manner, and under such Penalties as each House may provide.

[2] Each House may determine the Rules of its Proceedings, punish its Members for disorderly Behavior, and, with the Concurrence of two thirds, expel a Member.

[3] Each House shall keep a Journal of its Proceedings, and from time to time publish the same, excepting such Parts as may in their Judgment require Secrecy; and the Yeas and Nays of the Members of either House on any question shall, at the Desire of one fifth of those Present, be entered on the Journal.

[4] Neither House, during the Session of Congress, shall without the Consent of the other, adjourn for more than three days, nor to any other Place than that in which the two Houses shall be sitting.

Section 6.   [1] The Senators and Representatives shall receive a Compensation for their Services, to be ascertained by Law, and paid out of the Treasury of the United States. They shall in all Cases, except Treason, Felony and Breach of the Peace, be privileged from Arrest during their Attendance at the Session of their respective Houses, and in going to and returning from the same; and for any Speech or Debate in either House, they shall not be questioned in any other Place.

[2] No Senator or Representative shall, during the Time for which he was elected, be appointed to any civil Office under the Authority of the United States, which shall have been created, or the Emoluments whereof shall have been increased during such time; and no Person holding any Office under the United States, shall be a Member of either House during his Continuance in Office.

Section 7.   [1] All Bills for raising Revenue shall originate in the House of Representatives; but the Senate may propose or concur with Amendments as on other Bills.

[2] Every Bill which shall have passed the House of Representatives and the Senate, shall, before it become a Law, be presented to the President of the United States; If he approve he shall sign it, but if not he shall return it, with his Objections to the House in which it shall have originated, who shall enter the Objections at large on their Journal, and proceed to reconsider it. If after such Reconsideration two thirds of that House shall agree to pass the Bill, it shall be sent together with the Objections, to the other House, by which it shall likewise be reconsidered, and if approved by two thirds of that House, it shall become a Law. But in all such Cases the Votes of both Houses shall be determined by yeas and Nays, and the Names of the Persons voting for and against the Bill shall be entered on the Journal of each House respectively. If any Bill shall not be returned by the President within ten Days (Sundays excepted) after it shall have been presented to him, the Same shall be a Law, in like Manner as if he had signed it, unless the Congress by their Adjournment prevent its Return in which Case it shall not be a Law.

[3] Every Order, Resolution, or Vote, to Which the Concurrence of the Senate and House of Representatives may be necessary (except on a question of Adjournment) shall be presented to the President of the United States; and before the Same shall take Effect, shall be approved by him, or being disapproved by him, shall be repassed by two thirds of the Senate and House of Representatives, according to the Rules and Limitations prescribed in the Case of a Bill.

Section 8.   [1] The Congress shall have Power To lay and collect Taxes, Duties, Imposts and Excises, to pay the Debts and provide for the common Defence and general Welfare of the United States; but all Duties, Imposts and Excises shall be uniform throughout the United States;

[2] To borrow money on the credit of the United States;

[3] To regulate Commerce with foreign Nations, and among the several States, and with the Indian Tribes;

[4] To establish an uniform Rule of Naturalization, and uniform Laws on the subject of Bankruptcies throughout the United States;

[5] To coin Money, regulate the Value thereof, and of foreign Coin, and fix the Standard of Weights and Measures;

[6] To provide for the Punishment of counterfeiting the Securities and current Coin of the United States;

[7] To Establish Post Offices and Post Roads;

[8] To promote the Progress of Science and useful Arts, by securing for limited Times to Authors and Inventors the exclusive Right to their respective Writings and Discoveries;

[9] To constitute Tribunals inferior to the supreme Court;

[10] To define and punish Piracies and Felonies committed on the high Seas, and Offenses against the Law of Nations;

[11] To declare War, grant Letters of Marque and Reprisal, and make Rules concerning Captures on Land and Water;

[12] To raise and support Armies, but no Appropriation of Money to that Use shall be for a longer Term than two Years;

[13] To provide and maintain a Navy;

[14] To make Rules for the Government and Regulation of the land and naval Forces;

[15] To provide for calling forth the Militia to execute the Laws of the Union, suppress Insurrections and repel Invasions;

[16] To provide for organizing, arming, and disciplining, the Militia, and for governing such Part of them as may be employed in the Service of the United States, reserving to the States respectively, the Appointment of the Officers, and the Authority of training the Militia according to the discipline prescribed by Congress;

[17] To exercise exclusive Legislation in all Cases whatsoever, over such District (not exceeding ten Miles square) as may, by Cession of particular States, and the Acceptance of Congress, become the Seat of the Government of the United States, and to exercise like Authority over all Places purchased by the Consent of the Legislature of the State in which the Same shall be, for the Erection of Forts, Magazines, Arsenals, dock-Yards, and other needful Buildings;—And

[18] To make all Laws which shall be necessary and proper for carrying into Execution the foregoing Powers, and all other Powers vested by this Constitution in the Government of the United States, or in any Department or Officer thereof.

Section 9. [1] The Migration or Importation of Such Persons as any of the States now existing shall think proper to admit, shall not be prohibited by the Congress prior to the Year one thousand eight hundred and eight, but a Tax or duty may be imposed on such Importation, not exceeding ten dollars for each Person.

[2] The privilege of the Writ of Habeas Corpus shall not be suspended, unless when in Cases of Rebellion or Invasion the public Safety may require it.

[3] No Bill of Attainder or ex post facto Law shall be passed.

[4] No Capitation, or other direct, Tax shall be laid, unless in Proportion to the Census or Enumeration herein before directed to be taken.

[5] No Tax or Duty shall be laid on Articles exported from any State.

[6] No Preference shall be given by any Regulation of Commerce or Revenue to the Ports of one State over those of another: nor shall Vessels bound to, or from, one State be obliged to enter, clear, or pay Duties in another.

[7] No money shall be drawn from the Treasury, but in Consequence of Appropriations made by Law; and a regular Statement and Account of the Receipts and Expenditures of all public Money shall be published from time to time.

[8] No Title of Nobility shall be granted by the United States: And no Person holding any Office of Profit or Trust under them, shall, without the Consent of the Congress, accept of any present, Emolument, Office, or Title, of any kind whatever, from any King, Prince, or foreign State.

Section 10. [1] No State shall enter into any Treaty, Alliance, or Confederation; grant Letters of Marque and Reprisal; coin Money; emit Bills of Credit; make any Thing but gold and silver Coin a Tender in Payment of Debts; pass any Bill of Attainder, ex post facto Law, or Law impairing the Obligation of Contracts, or grant any Title of Nobility.

[2] No State shall, without the Consent of the Congress, lay any Imposts or Duties on Imports or Exports, except what may be absolutely necessary for executing it's inspection Laws: and the net Produce of all Duties and Imposts, laid by any State on Imports or Exports, shall be for the Use of the Treasury of the United States; and all such Laws shall be subject to the Revision and Controul of the Congress.

[3] No State shall, without the Consent of Congress, lay any Duty of Tonnage, keep Troops, or Ships of War in time of Peace, enter into any Agreement or Compact with another State, or with a foreign Power, or engage in War, unless actually invaded, or in such imminent Danger as will not admit of delay.

ARTICLE II

Section 1. [1] The executive Power shall be vested in a President of the United States of America. He shall hold his Office during the Term of four Years, and, together with the Vice President, chosen for the same Term, be elected, as follows:

[2] Each State shall appoint, in such Manner as the Legislature thereof may direct, a Number of Electors, equal to the whole Number of Senators and Representatives to which the State may be entitled in the Congress; but no Senator or Representative, or Person holding an Office of Trust or Profit under the United States, shall be appointed an Elector.

[3] The Electors shall meet in their respective States, and vote by Ballot for two Persons, of whom one at least shall not be an Inhabitant of the same State with themselves. And they shall make a List of all the Persons voted for, and of the Number of Votes for each; which List they shall sign and certify, and transmit sealed to the Seat of the Government of the United States, directed to the President of the Senate. The President of the Senate shall, in the Presence of the Senate and House of Representatives, open all the Certificates, and the Votes shall then be counted. The Person having the greatest Number of Votes shall be the President, if such Number be a Majority of the whole Number of

Electors appointed; and if there be more than one who have such Majority, and have an equal Number of Votes, then the House of Representatives shall immediately chuse by Ballot one of them for President; and if no Person have a Majority, then from the five highest on the List the said House shall in like Manner chuse the President. But in chusing the President, the Votes shall be taken by States the Representation from each State having one Vote; A quorum for this Purpose shall consist of a Member or Members from two thirds of the States, and a Majority of all the States shall be necessary to a Choice. In every Case, after the Choice of the President, the Person having the greater Number of Votes of the Electors shall be the Vice President. But if there should remain two or more who have equal Votes, the Senate shall chuse from them by Ballot the Vice President.

[4] The Congress may determine the Time of chusing the Electors, and the Day on which they shall give their Votes; which Day shall be the same throughout the United States.

[5] No person except a natural born Citizen, or a Citizen of the United States, at the time of the Adoption of this Constitution, shall be eligible to the Office of President; neither shall any Person be eligible to that Office who shall not have attained to the Age of thirty five Years, and been fourteen Years a Resident within the United States.

[6] In case of the removal of the President from Office, or of his Death, Resignation or Inability to discharge the Powers and Duties of the said Office, the Same shall devolve on the Vice President, and the Congress may by Law provide for the Case of Removal, Death, Resignation or Inability, both of the President and Vice President, declaring what Officer shall then act as President, and such Officer shall act accordingly, until the Disability be removed, or a President shall be elected.

[7] The President shall, at stated Times, receive for his Services, a Compensation, which shall neither be increased nor diminished during the Period for which he shall have been elected, and he shall not receive within that Period any other Emolument from the United States, or any of them.

[8] Before he enter on the Execution of his Office, he shall take the following Oath or Affirmation: "I do solemnly swear (or affirm) that I will faithfully execute the Office of President of the United States, and will to the best of my Ability, preserve, protect and defend the Constitution of the United States."

Section 2. [1] The President shall be Commander in Chief of the Army and Navy of the United States, and of the militia of the several States, when called into the actual Service of the United States; he may require the Opinion, in writing, of the principal Officer in each of the Executive Departments, upon any Subject relating to the Duties of their respective Offices, and he shall have Power to grant Reprieves and Pardons for Offenses against the United States, except in Cases of Impeachment.

[2] He shall have Power, by and with the Advice and Consent of the Senate to make Treaties, provided two thirds of the Senators present concur; and he shall nominate, and by and with the Advice and Consent of the Senate, shall appoint Ambassadors, other public Ministers and Consuls, Judges of the supreme Court, and all other Officers of the United States, whose Appointments are not herein otherwise provided for, and which shall be established by Law; but the Congress may by Law vest the Appointment of such inferior Officers, as they

think proper, in the President alone, in the Courts of Law, or in the Heads of Departments.

[3] The President shall have Power to fill up all Vacancies that may happen during the Recess of the Senate, by granting Commissions which shall expire at the End of their next Session.

Section 3.   He shall from time to time give to the Congress Information of the State of the Union, and recommend to their Consideration such Measures as he shall judge necessary and expedient; he may, on extraordinary Occasions, convene both Houses, or either of them, and in Case of Disagreement between them, with Respect to the Time of Adjournment, he may adjourn them to such Time as he shall think proper; he shall receive Ambassadors and other public Ministers; he shall take Care that the Laws be faithfully executed, and shall Commission all the Officers of the United States.

Section 4.   The President, Vice President and all civil Officers of the United States, shall be removed from Office on Impeachment for, and Conviction of, Treason, Bribery, or other high Crimes and Misdemeanors.

ARTICLE III

Section 1.   The judicial Power of the United States, shall be vested in one supreme Court, and in such inferior Courts as the Congress may from time to time ordain and establish.   The Judges, both of the supreme and inferior Courts, shall hold their Offices during good Behaviour, and shall, at stated Times, receive for their Services a Compensation, which shall not be diminished during their Continuance in Office.

Section 2.   [1] The judicial Power shall extend to all Cases, in Law and Equity, arising under this Constitution, the Laws of the United States, and Treaties made, or which shall be made, under their Authority;—to all Cases affecting Ambassadors, other public Ministers and Consuls;—to all Cases of admiralty and maritime Jurisdiction;—to Controversies to which the United States shall be a Party;—to Controversies between two or more States;—between a State and Citizens of another State;—between Citizens of different States;—between Citizens of the same State claiming Lands under the Grants of different States, and between a State, or the Citizens thereof, and foreign States, Citizens or Subjects.

[2]   In all Cases affecting Ambassadors, other public Ministers and Consuls, and those in which a State shall be a Party, the supreme Court shall have original Jurisdiction.   In all the other Cases before mentioned, the supreme Court shall have appellate Jurisdiction, both as to Law and Fact, with such Exceptions, and under such Regulations as the Congress shall make.

[3]   The trial of all Crimes, except in Cases of Impeachment, shall be by Jury; and such Trial shall be held in the State where the said Crimes shall have been committed; but when not committed within any State, the Trial shall be at such Place or Places as the Congress may by Law have directed.

Section 3.   [1] Treason against the United States, shall consist only in levying War against them, or, in adhering to their Enemies, giving them Aid and Comfort.   No Person shall be convicted of Treason unless on the Testimony of two Witnesses to the same overt Act, or on Confession in open Court.

[2]   The Congress shall have Power to declare the Punishment of Treason, but no Attainder of Treason shall work Corruption of Blood, or Forfeiture except during the Life of the Person attainted.

ARTICLE IV

Section 1. Full Faith and Credit shall be given in each State to the public Acts, Records, and judicial Proceedings of every other State. And the Congress may by general Laws prescribe the Manner in which such Acts, Records and Proceedings shall be proved, and the Effect thereof.

Section 2. [1] The Citizens of each State shall be entitled to all Privileges and Immunities of Citizens in the several States.

[2] A Person charged in any State with Treason, Felony, or other Crime, who shall flee from Justice, and be found in another State, shall on demand of the executive Authority of the State from which he fled, be delivered up, to be removed to the State having Jurisdiction of the Crime.

[3] No Person held to Service or Labour in one State, under the Laws thereof, escaping into another, shall, in Consequence of any Law or Regulation therein, be discharged from such Service or Labour, but shall be delivered up on Claim of the Party to whom such Service or Labour may be due.

Section 3. [1] New States may be admitted by the Congress into this Union; but no new State shall be formed or erected within the Jurisdiction of any other State; nor any State be formed by the Junction of two or more States, or Parts of States, without the Consent of the Legislatures of the States concerned as well as of the Congress.

[2] The Congress shall have Power to dispose of and make all needful Rules and Regulations respecting the Territory or other Property belonging to the United States; and nothing in this Constitution shall be so construed as to Prejudice any Claims of the United States, or of any particular State.

Section 4. The United States shall guarantee to every State in this Union a Republican Form of Government, and shall protect each of them against Invasion; and on Application of the Legislature, or of the Executive (when the Legislature cannot be convened) against domestic Violence.

ARTICLE V

The Congress, whenever two thirds of both Houses shall deem it necessary, shall propose Amendments to this Constitution, or, on the Application of the Legislatures of two thirds of the several States, shall call a Convention for proposing Amendments, which, in either Case, shall be valid to all Intents and Purposes, as part of this Constitution, when ratified by the Legislatures of three fourths of the several States, or by Conventions in three fourths thereof, as the one or the other Mode of Ratification may be proposed by the Congress; Provided that no Amendment which may be made prior to the Year One thousand eight hundred and eight shall in any Manner affect the first and fourth Clauses in the Ninth Section of the first Article; and that no State, without its Consent, shall be deprived of its equal Suffrage in the Senate.

ARTICLE VI

[1] All Debts contracted and Engagements entered into, before the Adoption of this Constitution shall be as valid against the United States under this Constitution, as under the Confederation.

[2] This Constitution, and the Laws of the United States which shall be made in Pursuance thereof; and all Treaties made, or which shall be made, under the Authority of the United States, shall be the supreme Law of the Land;

and the Judges in every State shall be bound thereby, any Thing in the Constitution or Laws of any State to the Contrary notwithstanding.

[3] The Senators and Representatives before mentioned, and the Members of the several State Legislatures, and all executive and judicial Officers, both of the United States and of the several States, shall be bound by Oath or Affirmation, to support this Constitution; but no religious Test shall ever be required as a Qualification to any Office or public Trust under the United States.

ARTICLE VII

The Ratification of the Conventions of nine States shall be sufficient for the Establishment of this Constitution between the States so ratifying the Same.

ARTICLES IN ADDITION TO, AND AMENDMENT OF, THE CONSTITUTION OF THE UNITED STATES OF AMERICA, PROPOSED BY CONGRESS, AND RATIFIED BY THE LEGISLATURES OF THE SEVERAL STATES PURSUANT TO THE FIFTH ARTICLE OF THE ORIGINAL CONSTITUTION.

AMENDMENT I [1791]

Congress shall make no law respecting an establishment of religion, or prohibiting the free exercise thereof; or abridging the freedom of speech, or of the press; or the right of the people peaceably to assemble, and to petition the Government for a redress of grievances.

AMENDMENT II [1791]

A well regulated Militia, being necessary to the security of a free State, the right of the people to keep and bear Arms, shall not be infringed.

AMENDMENT III [1791]

No Soldier shall, in time of peace be quartered in any house, without the consent of the Owner, nor in time of war, but in a manner to be prescribed by law.

AMENDMENT IV [1791]

The right of the people to be secure in their persons, houses, papers, and effects, against unreasonable searches and seizures, shall not be violated, and no Warrants shall issue, but upon probable cause, supported by Oath or affirmation and particularly describing the place to be searched, and the persons or things to be seized.

AMENDMENT V [1791]

No person shall be held to answer for a capital, or otherwise infamous crime, unless on a presentment or indictment of a Grand Jury, except in cases arising in the land or naval forces, or in the Militia, when in actual service in time of War or public danger; nor shall any person be subject for the same offence to be twice put in jeopardy of life or limb; nor shall be compelled in any criminal case to be a witness against himself, nor be deprived of life, liberty, or property, without due process of law; nor shall private property be taken for public use, without just compensation.

AMENDMENT VI [1791]

In all criminal prosecutions, the accused shall enjoy the right to a speedy and public trial, by an impartial jury of the State and district wherein the crime shall have been committed, which district shall have been previously ascertained by law, and to be informed of the nature and cause of the accusation; to be confronted with the witnesses against him; to have compulsory process for obtaining witnesses in his favor, and to have the Assistance of Counsel for his defence.

AMENDMENT VII [1791]

In Suits at common law, where the value in controversy shall exceed twenty dollars, the right of trial by jury shall be preserved, and no fact tried by jury, shall be otherwise re-examined in any Court of the United States, than according to the rules of the common law.

AMENDMENT VIII [1791]

Excessive bail shall not be required, nor excessive fines imposed, nor cruel and unusual punishments inflicted.

AMENDMENT IX [1791]

The enumeration in the Constitution, of certain rights, shall not be construed to deny or disparage others retained by the people.

AMENDMENT X [1791]

The powers not delegated to the United States by the Constitution, nor prohibited by it to the States, are reserved to the States respectively, or to the people.

AMENDMENT XI [1798]

The Judicial power of the United States shall not be construed to extend to any suit in law or equity, commenced or prosecuted against one of the United States by Citizens of another State, or by Citizens or Subjects of any Foreign State.

AMENDMENT XII [1804]

The Electors shall meet in their respective states and vote by ballot for President and Vice-President, one of whom, at least, shall not be an inhabitant of the same state with themselves; they shall name in their ballots the person voted for as President, and in distinct ballots the person voted for as Vice-President, and they shall make distinct lists of all persons voted for as President, and of all persons voted for as Vice-President, and of the number of votes for each, which lists they shall sign and certify, and transmit sealed to the seat of the government of the United States, directed to the President of the Senate;— The President of the Senate shall, in the presence of the Senate and House of Representatives, open all the certificates and the votes shall then be counted;— The person having the greatest number of votes for President, shall be the President, if such number be a majority of the whole number of Electors appointed; and if no person have such majority, then from the persons having the highest numbers not exceeding three on the list of those voted for as

President, the House of Representatives shall choose immediately, by ballot, the President. But in choosing the President, the votes shall be taken by states, the representation from each state having one vote; a quorum for this purpose shall consist of a member or members from two-thirds of the states, and a majority of all the states shall be necessary to a choice. And if the House of Representatives shall not choose a President whenever the right of choice shall devolve upon them before the fourth day of March next following, then the Vice-President shall act as President, as in the case of the death or other constitutional disability of the President.—The person having the greatest number of votes as Vice-President, shall be the Vice-President, if such number be a majority of the whole number of Electors appointed, and if no person have a majority, then from the two highest numbers on the list, the Senate shall choose the Vice-President; a quorum for the purpose shall consist of two-thirds of the whole number of Senators, and a majority of the whole number shall be necessary to a choice. But no person constitutionally ineligible to the office of President shall be eligible to that of Vice-President of the United States.

AMENDMENT XIII [1865]

Section 1. Neither slavery nor involuntary servitude, except as a punishment for crime whereof the party shall have been duly convicted, shall exist within the United States, or any place subject to their jurisdiction.

Section 2. Congress shall have power to enforce this article by appropriate legislation.

AMENDMENT XIV [1868]

Section 1. All persons born or naturalized in the United States, and subject to the jurisdiction thereof, are citizens of the United States and of the State wherein they reside. No State shall make or enforce any law which shall abridge the privileges or immunities of citizens of the United States; nor shall any State deprive any person of life, liberty, or property, without due process of law; nor deny to any person within its jurisdiction the equal protection of the laws.

Section 2. Representatives shall be apportioned among the several States according to their respective numbers, counting the whole number of persons in each State, excluding Indians not taxed. But when the right to vote at any election for the choice of electors for President and Vice President of the United States, Representatives in Congress, the Executive and Judicial officers of a State, or the members of the Legislature thereof, is denied to any of the male inhabitants of such State, being twenty-one years of age, and citizens of the United States, or in any way abridged, except for participation in rebellion, or other crime, the basis of representation therein shall be reduced in the proportion which the number of such male citizens shall bear to the whole number of male citizens twenty-one years of age in such State.

Section 3. No person shall be a Senator or Representative in Congress, or elector of President and Vice President, or hold any office, civil or military, under the United States, or under any State, who having previously taken an oath, as a member of Congress, or as an officer of the United States, or as a member of any State legislature, or as an executive or judicial officer of any State, to support the Constitution of the United States, shall have engaged in insurrection or rebellion against the same, or given aid or comfort to the enemies thereof. But Congress may by a vote of two-thirds of each House, remove such disability.

Section 4. The validity of the public debt of the United States, authorized by law, including debts incurred for payment of pensions and bounties for services in suppressing insurrection or rebellion, shall not be questioned. But neither the United States nor any State shall assume or pay any debt or obligation incurred in aid of insurrection or rebellion against the United States, or any claim for the loss or emancipation of any slave; but all such debts, obligations and claims shall be held illegal and void.

Section 5. The Congress shall have power to enforce, by appropriate legislation, the provisions of this article.

AMENDMENT XV [1870]

Section 1. The right of citizens of the United States to vote shall not be denied or abridged by the United States or by any State on account of race, color, or previous condition of servitude.

Section 2. The Congress shall have power to enforce this article by appropriate legislation.

AMENDMENT XVI [1913]

The Congress shall have power to lay and collect taxes on incomes, from whatever source derived, without apportionment among the several States, and without regard to any census or enumeration.

AMENDMENT XVII [1913]

[1] The Senate of the United States shall be composed of two Senators from each State, elected by the people thereof, for six years; and each Senator shall have one vote. The electors in each State shall have the qualifications requisite for electors of the most numerous branch of the State legislatures.

[2] When vacancies happen in the representation of any State in the Senate, the executive authority of such State shall issue writs of election to fill such vacancies: *Provided,* That the legislature of any State may empower the executive thereof to make temporary appointments until the people fill the vacancies by election as the legislature may direct.

[3] This amendment shall not be so construed as to affect the election or term of any Senator chosen before it becomes valid as part of the Constitution.

AMENDMENT XVIII [1919]

Section 1. After one year from the ratification of this article the manufacture, sale, or transportation of intoxicating liquors within, the importation thereof into, or the exportation thereof from the United States and all territory subject to the jurisdiction thereof for beverage purposes is hereby prohibited.

Section 2. The Congress and the several States shall have concurrent power to enforce this article by appropriate legislation.

Section 3. This article shall be inoperative unless it shall have been ratified as an amendment to the Constitution by the legislatures of the several States, as provided in the Constitution, within seven years from the date of the submission hereof to the States by the Congress.

AMENDMENT XIX [1920]

[1] The right of citizens of the United States to vote shall not be denied or abridged by the United States or by any State on account of sex.

[2] Congress shall have power to enforce this article by appropriate legislation.

AMENDMENT XX [1933]

Section 1. The terms of the President and Vice President shall end at noon on the 20th day of January, and the terms of Senators and Representatives at noon on the 3d day of January, of the years in which such terms would have ended if this article had not been ratified; and the terms of their successors shall then begin.

Section 2. The Congress shall assemble at least once in every year, and such meeting shall begin at noon on the 3d day of January, unless they shall by law appoint a different day.

Section 3. If, at the time fixed for the beginning of the term of the President, the President elect shall have died, the Vice President elect shall become President. If the President shall not have been chosen before the time fixed for the beginning of his term, or if the President elect shall have failed to qualify, then the Vice President elect shall act as President until a President shall have qualified; and the Congress may by law provide for the case wherein neither a President elect nor a Vice President elect shall have qualified, declaring who shall then act as President, or the manner in which one who is to act shall be selected, and such person shall act accordingly until a President or Vice President shall have qualified.

Section 4. The Congress may by law provide for the case of the death of any of the persons from whom the House of Representatives may choose a President whenever the right of choice shall have devolved upon them, and for the case of the death of any of the persons from whom the Senate may choose a Vice President whenever the right of choice shall have devolved upon them.

Section 5. Sections 1 and 2 shall take effect on the 15th day of October following the ratification of this article.

Section 6. This article shall be inoperative unless it shall have been ratified as an amendment to the Constitution by the legislatures of three-fourths of the several States within seven years from the date of its submission.

AMENDMENT XXI [1933]

Section 1. The eighteenth article of amendment to the Constitution of the United States is hereby repealed.

Section 2. The transportation or importation into any State, Territory, or possession of the United States for delivery or use therein of intoxicating liquors, in violation of the laws thereof, is hereby prohibited.

Section 3. This article shall be inoperative unless it shall have been ratified as an amendment to the Constitution by conventions in the several States, as provided in the Constitution, within seven years from the date of the submission hereof to the States by the Congress.

AMENDMENT XXII [1951]

Section 1. No person shall be elected to the office of the President more than twice, and no person who has held the office of President, or acted as President, for more than two years of a term to which some other person was elected President shall be elected to the office of President more than once. But this Article shall not apply to any person holding the office of President when this Article was proposed by the Congress, and shall not prevent any person who may be holding the office of President, or acting as President, during the term within which this Article becomes operative from holding the office of President or acting as President during the remainder of such term.

Section 2. This article shall be inoperative unless it shall have been ratified as an amendment to the Constitution by the legislatures of three-fourths of the several States within seven years from the date of its submission to the States by the Congress.

AMENDMENT XXIII [1961]

Section 1. The District constituting the seat of Government of the United States shall appoint in such manner as the Congress may direct:

A number of electors of President and Vice President equal to the whole number of Senators and Representatives in Congress to which the District would be entitled if it were a State, but in no event more than the least populous state; they shall be in addition to those appointed by the states, but they shall be considered, for the purposes of the election of President and Vice President, to be electors appointed by a state; and they shall meet in the District and perform such duties as provided by the twelfth article of amendment.

Section 2. The Congress shall have power to enforce this article by appropriate legislation.

AMENDMENT XXIV [1964]

Section 1. The right of citizens of the United States to vote in any primary or other election for President or Vice President, for electors for President or Vice President, or for Senator or Representative in Congress, shall not be denied or abridged by the United States or any State by reason of failure to pay any poll tax or other tax.

Section 2. The Congress shall have power to enforce this article by appropriate legislation.

AMENDMENT XXV [1967]

Section 1. In case of the removal of the President from office or of his death or resignation, the Vice President shall become President.

Section 2. Whenever there is a vacancy in the office of the Vice President, the President shall nominate a Vice President who shall take office upon confirmation by a majority vote of both Houses of Congress.

Section 3. Whenever the President transmits to the President pro tempore of the Senate and the Speaker of the House of Representatives his written declaration that he is unable to discharge the powers and duties of his office, and until he transmits to them a written declaration to the contrary, such powers and duties shall be discharged by the Vice President as Acting President.

Section 4. Whenever the Vice President and a majority of either the principal officers of the executive departments or of such other body as Congress may by law provide, transmit to the President pro tempore of the Senate and the Speaker of the House of Representatives their written declaration that the President is unable to discharge the powers and duties of his office, the Vice President shall immediately assume the powers and duties of the office as Acting President.

Thereafter, when the President transmits to the President pro tempore of the Senate and the Speaker of the House of Representatives his written declaration that no inability exists, he shall resume the powers and duties of his office unless the Vice President and a majority of either the principal officers of the executive department or of such other body as Congress may by law provide, transmit within four days to the President pro tempore of the Senate and the Speaker of the House of Representatives their written declaration that the President is unable to discharge the powers and duties of his office. Thereupon Congress shall decide the issue, assembling within forty-eight hours for that purpose if not in session. If the Congress, within twenty-one days after receipt of the latter written declaration, or, if Congress is not in session, within twenty-one days after Congress is required to assemble, determines by two-thirds vote of both Houses that the President is unable to discharge the powers and duties of his office, the Vice President shall continue to discharge the same as Acting President; otherwise, the President shall resume the powers and duties of his office.

AMENDMENT XXVI [1971]

Section 1. The right of citizens of the United States, who are eighteen years of age or older, to vote shall not be denied or abridged by the United States or by any State on account of age.

Section 2. The Congress shall have power to enforce this article by appropriate legislation.

*

Index

References are to Pages

†